WH   CISE

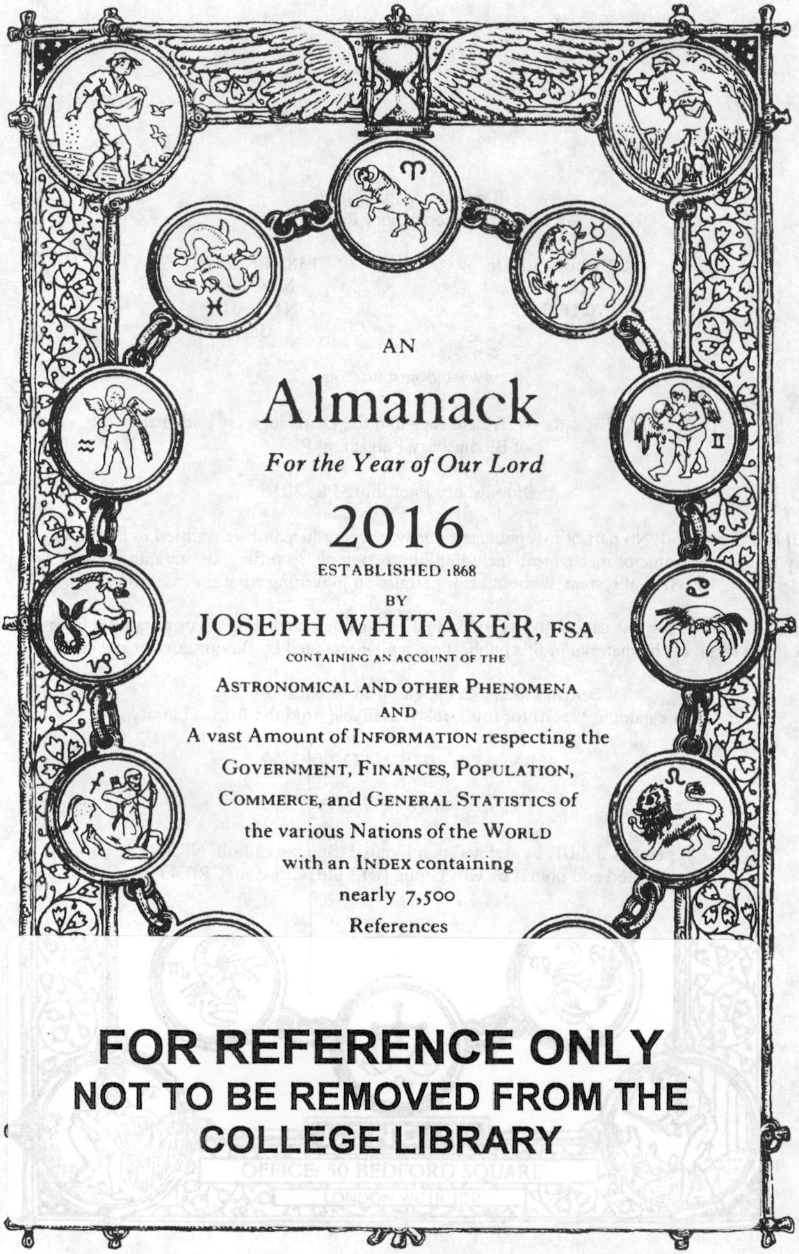

AN

Almanack

For the Year of Our Lord

2016

ESTABLISHED 1868

BY

JOSEPH WHITAKER, FSA

CONTAINING AN ACCOUNT OF THE

ASTRONOMICAL AND OTHER PHENOMENA

AND

A vast Amount of INFORMATION respecting the

GOVERNMENT, FINANCES, POPULATION,

COMMERCE, and GENERAL STATISTICS of

the various Nations of the WORLD

with an INDEX containing

nearly 7,500

References

The traditional design of the title page for Whitaker's Almanack which has appeared in each edition since 1868

BLOOMSBURY

LONDON · OXFORD · NEW YORK · NEW DELHI · SYDNEY

Bloomsbury Publishing
An imprint of Bloomsbury Publishing Plc

50 Bedford Square
London
WC1B 3DP
UK

1385 Broadway
New York
NY 10018
USA

www.bloomsbury.com

WHITAKER's, the W Trident logo and the Diana logo are trademarks
of Bloomsbury Publishing Plc

British Library Cataloguing-in-Publication Data
A catalogue record for this book is available from the British Library.

ISBN: PB: 978-1-4729-0932-9

2 4 6 8 10 9 7 5 3 1

Typeset in the UK by RefineCatch Limited, Bungay, Suffolk NR35 1EF
Printed and bound by CPI Group (UK) Ltd, Croydon, CR0 4YY

FSC
www.fsc.org
MIX
Paper from
responsible sources
FSC® C013604

To find out more about our authors and books visit www.bloomsbury.com. Here you will find
extracts, author interviews, details of forthcoming events and the option to sign up for our
newsletters.

CONTENTS

How fitting to have the 800th anniversary of the sealing of the Magna Carta and a General Election in the same year. When King John sealed the Magna Carta in June 1215, he was presented with at least 13 copies of the manuscript, to be dispatched across his kingdom. Of these originals, only four are known to have survived to the present day and, as part of the celebrations to mark the anniversary of the charter's issue, the manuscripts were brought together at the British Library for the first time since their initial dispersal.

At the start of the election year it seemed a foregone conclusion that we would have another coalition government of some description following the General Election on 7 May. Against all media predictions, and mainly down to the dramatic effect of the Scottish National Party's gains from Labour across Scotland, it was a clear win for the Conservatives, who have a working majority of 16 in the new parliament. Complete election results for every constituency, the current list of MPs and manifesto commitments made by the main parties are all fully detailed in this edition.

Internationally it has been a tumultuous year: the Nepal earthquake in April had devastating effects, the Greek financial crisis and subsequent bailouts and financial restructuring of the country will have a knock-on effect for years to come, and the continuing terrorism of IS in the Middle East and the civil war in Syria has resulted in an unforeseen and unplanned for influx of refugees into Europe. This turmoil in Europe is particularly poignant as 2015 was the 70th anniversary of Victory in Europe Day, which fell on the day after the General Election and was marked by events across the country. A Service of Remembrance at the Cenotaph was attended by the re-elected Prime Minister David Cameron and the now ex-leaders of the main parties who had fallen on their swords following defeat at the polls on the previous day.

Sport provided a welcome relief with the England team beating Germany to finish in third place at the 2015 FIFA Women's World Cup, the best performance by an England team since 1966. This was swiftly followed by England's win in The Ashes and, at the time of writing, the Rugby World Cup 2015 has got off to a great start: the first time the Cup has been hosted solely in England.

As always I would like to thank our numerous contributors. I would also like to take the opportunity to let our readers know of our new subscription website which will be arriving in Spring 2016. If you would like to be kept informed of developments regarding this, or provide any feedback or comments on this edition, please do email us: whitakersalmanackteam@bloomsbury.com

Ruth Northey
Executive Editor

JACKET PHOTOGRAPHS

Main image: A general view of the Houses of Parliament in Central London © PA

Top, from left to right:
1. Seal of King John © Getty Images
2. National banks open for one day to allow Greek pensioners to collect rationed payouts © Getty Images
3. VE Day 70th Anniversary © Getty Images
4. George Ford, England v France – RBS Six Nations © Getty Images

SOURCES

Whitaker's was compiled with the assistance of HM Revenue and Customs; Keesing's Worldwide; The Met Office; Oxford Cartographers; Press Association; UK Hydrographic Office; WM/Reuters; and The World Bank. Crown copyright material is reproduced with the permission of the Controller of Her Majesty's Stationery Office.

EDITORIAL STAFF

Executive Editor: Ruth Northey
Senior Project Editor/Infographic Design: Oli Lurie
Assistant Editor: James McCall
Editorial Assistants: Claire Constable; Lucy Thoms
Head of Yearbooks: Katy McAdam

Thanks to Omer Ali, Lucy Beevor, John Bromham, John Flannery, Rob Hardy, Stephen Kershaw, Elizabeth Kingston, Hilary Marsden

CONTRIBUTORS (where not listed)

Sheridan Williams (Astronomy); Anthea Lipsett, Caroline Macready (Education); Clive Longhurst (Insurance); Richard McMeeken, Chris Priestley (Legal Notes); and Jill Papworth (Taxation)

Terrestrial Magnestism data supplied by Dr Susan Macmillan of the British Geological Survey

THE YEAR 2016

CHRONOLOGICAL CYCLES AND ERAS

Dominical Letter	CB
Epact	21
Golden Number (Lunar Cycle)	III
Julian Period	6729
Roman Indiction	9
Solar Cycle	9

	Beginning
*Muslim year AH 1437	14 Oct 2015
Japanese year Heisei 28	1 Jan
Roman year 2769 AUC	14 Jan
Regnal year 65	6 Feb
Chinese year of the Monkey	8 Feb
Sikh new year	14 Mar
Indian (Saka) year 1938	21 Mar
Hindu new year (Chaitra)	8 Apr
*Jewish year AM 5777	3 Oct

* Year begins at sunset on the previous day

RELIGIOUS CALENDARS

CHRISTIAN

Epiphany	6 Jan
Presentation of Christ in the Temple	2 Feb
Ash Wednesday	10 Feb
The Annunciation	25 Mar
Palm Sunday	20 Mar
Maundy Thursday	24 Mar
Good Friday	25 Mar
Easter Day (western churches)	27 Mar
Easter Day (Eastern Orthodox)	1 May
Rogation Sunday	1 May
Ascension Day	5 May
Pentecost (Whit Sunday)	15 May
Trinity Sunday	22 May
Corpus Christi	26 May
All Saints' Day	1 Nov
Advent Sunday	27 Nov
Christmas Day	25 Dec

HINDU

Makar Sankranti	14 Jan
Vasant Panchami (Sarasvati Puja)	12 Feb
Shivaratri	8 Mar
Holi	23 Mar
Chaitra (Spring new year)	8 Apr
Ram Navami	15 Apr
Raksha-bandhan	18 Aug
Krishna Janmashtami	25 Aug
Ganesh Chaturthi, first day	5 Sep
Navaratri festival (Durga Puja), first day	1 Oct
Dussehra	11 Oct
Diwali (New Year festival of lights), first day	30 Oct

JEWISH

Purim	24 Mar
Pesach (Passover), first day	23 Apr
Shavuot (Feast of Weeks), first day	12 June
Rosh Hashanah (Jewish new year)	3 Oct
Yom Kippur (Day of Atonement)	12 Oct
Succot (Feast of Tabernacles), first day	17 Oct
Hanukkah, first day	25 Dec

MUSLIM†

Al-Hijra (Muslim new year)	14 Oct 2015
Ashura	23 Oct 2015
Ramadan, first day	6 Jun
Eid-ul-Fitr	6 Jul
Hajj, first day	9 Sep
Eid-ul-Adha	11 Sep

† The Islamic calendar is lunar so religious dates may vary by one or two days locally and according to when the new Moon is first seen

SIKH

Birthday of Guru Gobind Singh Ji	5 Jan
1 Chet (Sikh new year)	14 Mar
‡Hola Mohalla	24 Mar
Baisakhi	14 Apr
Martyrdom of Guru Arjan Dev Ji	16 Jun
‡Birthday of Guru Nanak Dev Ji	14 Nov
Martyrdom of Guru Tegh Bahadur Ji	24 Nov

‡ Currently celebrated according to the lunar, rather than Nanakshahi, calendar, so the date varies annually

CIVIL CALENDAR

Duchess of Cambridge's birthday	9 Jan
Countess of Wessex's birthday	20 Jan
Accession of the Queen	6 Feb
Duke of York's birthday	19 Feb
St David's Day	1 Mar
Earl of Wessex's birthday	10 Mar
Commonwealth Day	14 Mar
St Patrick's Day	17 Mar
Birthday of the Queen	21 Apr
St George's Day	23 Apr
Europe Day	9 May
Coronation Day	2 Jun
Duke of Edinburgh's birthday	10 Jun
The Queen's Official Birthday	11 Jun
Duke of Cambridge's birthday	21 Jun
Duchess of Cornwall's birthday	17 Jul
Princess Royal's birthday	15 Aug
Lord Mayor's Day	12 Nov
Remembrance Sunday	13 Nov
Prince of Wales' birthday	14 Nov
Wedding Day of the Queen	20 Nov
St Andrew's Day	30 Nov

LEGAL CALENDAR

LAW TERMS

Hilary Term	11 Jan to 23 Mar
Easter Term	5 Apr to 27 May
Trinity Term	7 Jun to 29 Jul
Michaelmas Term	3 Oct to 21 Dec

QUARTER DAYS	TERM DAYS
England, Wales and Northern Ireland	*Scotland*
Lady – 25 Mar	Candlemas – 28 Feb
Midsummer – 24 Jun	Whitsunday – 28 May
Michaelmas – 29 Sep	Lammas – 28 Aug
Christmas – 25 Dec	Martinmas – 28 Nov

2016

JANUARY

Sunday		3	10	17	24	31
Monday		4	11	18	25
Tuesday		5	12	19	26
Wednesday		6	13	20	27
Thursday		7	14	21	28
Friday	1	8	15	22	29
Saturday	2	9	16	23	30

FEBRUARY

Sunday			7	14	21	28
Monday	1	8	15	22	29
Tuesday	2	9	16	23
Wednesday	3	10	17	24
Thursday	4	11	18	25
Friday	5	12	19	26
Saturday	6	13	20	27

MARCH

Sunday		6	13	20	27
Monday		7	14	21	28
Tuesday	1	8	15	22	29
Wednesday	2	9	16	23	30
Thursday	3	10	17	24	31
Friday	4	11	18	25
Saturday	5	12	19	26

APRIL

Sunday		3	10	17	24
Monday		4	11	18	25
Tuesday		5	12	19	26
Wednesday		6	13	20	27
Thursday		7	14	21	28
Friday	1	8	15	22	29
Saturday	2	9	16	23	30

MAY

Sunday	1	8	15	22	29
Monday	2	9	16	23	30
Tuesday	3	10	17	24	31
Wednesday	4	11	18	25
Thursday	5	12	19	26
Friday	6	13	20	27
Saturday	7	14	21	28

JUNE

Sunday		5	12	19	26
Monday		6	13	20	27
Tuesday		7	14	21	28
Wednesday	1	8	15	22	29
Thursday	2	9	16	23	30
Friday	3	10	17	24
Saturday	4	11	18	25

JULY

Sunday		3	10	17	24	31
Monday		4	11	18	25
Tuesday		5	12	19	26
Wednesday		6	13	20	27
Thursday		7	14	21	28
Friday	1	8	15	22	29
Saturday	2	9	16	23	30

AUGUST

Sunday			7	14	21	28
Monday	1	8	15	22	29
Tuesday	2	9	16	23	30
Wednesday	3	10	17	24	31
Thursday	4	11	18	25
Friday	5	12	19	26
Saturday	6	13	20	27

SEPTEMBER

Sunday		4	11	18	25
Monday		5	12	19	26
Tuesday		6	13	20	27
Wednesday		7	14	21	28
Thursday	1	8	15	22	29
Friday	2	9	16	23	30
Saturday	3	10	17	24

OCTOBER

Sunday		2	9	16	23	30
Monday		3	10	17	24	31
Tuesday		4	11	18	25
Wednesday		5	12	19	26
Thursday		6	13	20	27
Friday		7	14	21	28
Saturday	1	8	15	22	29

NOVEMBER

Sunday		6	13	20	27
Monday		7	14	21	28
Tuesday	1	8	15	22	29
Wednesday	2	9	16	23	30
Thursday	3	10	17	24
Friday	4	11	18	25
Saturday	5	12	19	26

DECEMBER

Sunday		4	11	18	25
Monday		5	12	19	26
Tuesday		6	13	20	27
Wednesday		7	14	21	28
Thursday	1	8	15	22	29
Friday	2	9	16	23	30
Saturday	3	10	17	24	31

PUBLIC HOLIDAYS	England and Wales	Scotland	Northern Ireland
New Year	1 January†	1, 4† January	1 January†
St Patrick's Day	—	—	17 March
*Good Friday	25 March	25 March	25 March
Easter Monday	28 March	—	28 March
Early May	2 May†	2 May	2 May†
Spring	30 May	30 May†	30 May
Battle of the Boyne	—	—	12 July‡
Summer	29 August	1 August	29 August
St Andrew's Day	—	30 November§	—
*Christmas	26, 27 December	26†, 27 December	26, 27 December

* In England, Wales and Northern Ireland, Christmas Day and Good Friday are common law holidays

† Subject to royal proclamation

‡ Subject to proclamation by the Secretary of State for Northern Ireland

§ The St Andrew's Day Holiday (Scotland) Bill was approved by parliament on 29 November 2006; it does not oblige employers to change their existing pattern of holidays but provides the legal framework in which the St Andrew's Day bank holiday could be substituted for an existing local holiday from another date in the year

Note: In the Channel Islands, Liberation Day is a bank and public holiday

2017

JANUARY					
Sunday	1	8	15	22	29
Monday	2	9	16	23	30
Tuesday	3	10	17	24	31
Wednesday	4	11	18	25	
Thursday	5	12	19	26	
Friday	6	13	20	27	
Saturday	7	14	21	28	

FEBRUARY					
Sunday		5	12	19	26
Monday		6	13	20	27
Tuesday		7	14	21	28
Wednesday	1	8	15	22	
Thursday	2	9	16	23	
Friday	3	10	17	24	
Saturday	4	11	18	25	

MARCH					
Sunday		5	12	19	26
Monday		6	13	20	27
Tuesday		7	14	21	28
Wednesday	1	8	15	22	29
Thursday	2	9	16	23	30
Friday	3	10	17	24	31
Saturday	4	11	18	25	

APRIL					
Sunday		2	9	16	23	30
Monday		3	10	17	24	
Tuesday		4	11	18	25	
Wednesday		5	12	19	26	
Thursday		6	13	20	27	
Friday		7	14	21	28	
Saturday	1	8	15	22	29	

MAY					
Sunday		7	14	21	28
Monday	1	8	15	22	29
Tuesday	2	9	16	23	30
Wednesday	3	10	17	24	31
Thursday	4	11	18	25	
Friday	5	12	19	26	
Saturday	6	13	20	27	

JUNE					
Sunday		4	11	18	25
Monday		5	12	19	26
Tuesday		6	13	20	27
Wednesday		7	14	21	28
Thursday	1	8	15	22	29
Friday	2	9	16	23	30
Saturday	3	10	17	24	

JULY					
Sunday		2	9	16	23	30
Monday		3	10	17	24	31
Tuesday		4	11	18	25	
Wednesday		5	12	19	26	
Thursday		6	13	20	27	
Friday		7	14	21	28	
Saturday	1	8	15	22	29	

AUGUST					
Sunday		6	13	20	27
Monday		7	14	21	28
Tuesday	1	8	15	22	29
Wednesday	2	9	16	23	30
Thursday	3	10	17	24	31
Friday	4	11	18	25	
Saturday	5	12	19	26	

SEPTEMBER					
Sunday		3	10	17	24
Monday		4	11	18	25
Tuesday		5	12	19	26
Wednesday		6	13	20	27
Thursday		7	14	21	28
Friday	1	8	15	22	29
Saturday	2	9	16	23	30

OCTOBER					
Sunday	1	8	15	22	29
Monday	2	9	16	23	30
Tuesday	3	10	17	24	31
Wednesday	4	11	18	25	
Thursday	5	12	19	26	
Friday	6	13	20	27	
Saturday	7	14	21	28	

NOVEMBER					
Sunday		5	12	19	26
Monday		6	13	20	27
Tuesday		7	14	21	28
Wednesday	1	8	15	22	29
Thursday	2	9	16	23	30
Friday	3	10	17	24	
Saturday	4	11	18	25	

DECEMBER					
Sunday		3	10	17	24	31
Monday		4	11	18	25	
Tuesday		5	12	19	26	
Wednesday		6	13	20	27	
Thursday		7	14	21	28	
Friday	1	8	15	22	29	
Saturday	2	9	16	23	30	

PUBLIC HOLIDAYS

	England and Wales	Scotland	Northern Ireland
New Year	2 January†	2, 3† January	2 January†
St Patrick's Day	—	—	17 March
*Good Friday	14 April	14 April	14 April
Easter Monday	17 April	—	17 April
Early May	1 May†	1 May	1 May†
Spring	29 May	29 May†	29 May
Battle of the Boyne	—	—	13 July‡
Summer	28 August	7 August	28 August
St Andrew's Day	—	30 November§	—
*Christmas	25, 26 December	25†, 26 December	25, 26 December

* In England, Wales and Northern Ireland, Christmas Day and Good Friday are common law holidays

† Subject to royal proclamation

‡ Subject to proclamation by the Secretary of State for Northern Ireland

§ The St Andrew's Day Holiday (Scotland) Bill was approved by parliament on 29 November 2006; it does not oblige employers to change their existing pattern of holidays but provides the legal framework in which the St Andrew's Day bank holiday could be substituted for an existing local holiday from another date in the year

Note: In the Channel Islands, Liberation Day is a bank and public holiday

FORTHCOMING EVENTS

* Provisional dates

JANUARY 2016
8–17 London Boat Show, Excel, London Docklands
8–17 London Short Film Festival
14–31 Celtic Connections Music Festival, Glasgow
19–21 UK Open Dance Championships, Bournemouth
20–24 London Art Fair, Business Design Centre

FEBRUARY
3–21 Leicester Comedy Festival
14 British Academy Film Awards, Royal Opera House, London
26–6 Mar Bath Literature Festival

MARCH
3 World Book Day
8 International Women's Day
*8–15 Belfast Children's Festival
9–15 BADA Antiques and Fine Art Fair, Duke of York Square, London
10–13 Crufts Dog Show, NEC, Birmingham
17 St Patrick's Day Parade, Piccadilly, London
18–3 Apr Ideal Home Show, Olympia, London
21 World Poetry Day

APRIL
2–10 Oxford Literary Festival
12–14 London Book Fair, Olympia, London
22 Earth Day
*24–1 May 9th Stratford-upon-Avon Literary Festival

MAY
11–14 Museums at Night, London
21–28 82nd Glyndebourne Festival
24–28 RHS Chelsea Flower Show, Royal Hospital, London
*25 Belfast Titanic Maritime Festival
26–5 June 29th Hay Festival of Literature and the Arts, Hay-on-Wye

JUNE
4 Strawberry Fair, Cambridge
9–12 Isle of Wight Festival
11 Trooping the Colour, Horse Guards Parade, London
22–26 Glastonbury Festival of Contemporary Performing Arts, Somerset
23–26 175th Royal Highland Show, Edinburgh

JULY
5–10 RHS Hampton Court Palace Flower Show, Surrey
6–17 Cheltenham Music Festival
*15–10 Sep BBC Promenade Concerts, Royal Albert Hall, London
20–24 RHS Flower Show, Tatton Park, Cheshire
Mid-Jul The Welsh Proms, St David's Hall, Cardiff
*21–24 WOMAD Festival, Charlton Park, Wiltshire
25–1 Aug Three Choirs Festival, Gloucester
*28–31 Cambridge Folk Festival
29–6 Aug National Eisteddfod of Wales, Monmouthshire

AUGUST
5–27 Edinburgh Military Tattoo, Edinburgh Castle
5–29 Edinburgh International Festival
7 Brecon Jazz Festival
21–28 International Beatles Week, Liverpool
*27–28 Notting Hill Carnival, London

SEPTEMBER
*1 Brighton Pride, Brighton and Hove
2–6 Nov Blackpool Illuminations, Blackpool Promenade
3 Braemar Royal Highland Gathering, Aberdeenshire
8 International Literacy Day
Mid-Sep TUC Annual Congress
21–26 Liberal Democrat Party Conference, Brighton
Sep–Oct Labour Party Conference, Liverpool
Sep–Oct Conservative Party Conference, Birmingham

OCTOBER
4–8 Frieze Art Fair, Regent's Park, London
Early-Oct Booker Prize Awards
Mid-Oct BFI London Film Festival

NOVEMBER
12 Nov Lord Mayor's Procession and Show, City of London
Mid-Nov CBI Annual Conference

SPORTS EVENTS

JANUARY 2016
10–17   Snooker: Masters, Alexandra Palace, London

18–31   Tennis: Australian Open, Melbourne, Australia

FEBRUARY
6–19 Mar   Rugby Union: Six Nations Championship, Europe

7   American Football: Super Bowl 50, Santa Clara, USA

8–14   Squash: British National Championships, Manchester

28   Football: League Cup Final, Wembley Stadium, London

MARCH
2–6   Cycling: World Track Championships, London

11–3 Apr   Cricket: ICC World Twenty20, India

17–20   Athletics: World Indoor Championships, Portland, USA

APRIL
7–9   Horse Racing: Grand National, Aintree, Liverpool

7–10   Golf: Masters, Augusta, Georgia, USA

16–2 May   Snooker: World Championship, Crucible Theatre, Sheffield

24   Athletics: London Marathon

27   Rowing: The Boat Race, Putney to Mortlake, London

MAY
4–8   Equestrian: Badminton Horse Trials, Badminton

7   Horse Racing: Kentucky Derby, Louisville, Kentucky

Early May   Horse Racing: Guineas Festival, Newmarket

11–15   Equestrian: Royal Windsor Horse Show, Home Park, Windsor

14   Rugby Union: The European Rugby Champions Cup, Lyon, France

18   Football: UEFA Europa League Final, Basel, Switzerland

22–5 Jun   Tennis: French Open, Paris

21   Football: FA Cup Final, Wembley Stadium, London

21   Football: Scottish Cup Final, Hampden Park, Glasgow

28   Football: UEFA Champions League Final, Milan, Italy

28–10 Jun   Motorcycling: TT Races, Isle of Man

JUNE
3–26   Football: Copa America Centenario, USA

4   Horse Racing: The Derby, Epsom Downs

10   Football: 2016 UEFA European Championship, France

13–18   Golf: British Amateur Golf Championship, Royal Porthcawl, South Glamorgan

14–18   Horse Racing: Royal Ascot

16–19   Golf: US Open, Oakmont Country Club, Pennsylvania

27–10 Jul   Tennis: Wimbledon Championship, All England Lawn Tennis Club, London

29–3 Jul   Rowing: Henley Royal Regatta, Henley-on-Thames

JULY
2–24   Cycling: Tour de France

6–10   Athletics: European Athletics Championships, Amsterdam, the Netherlands

8   Horse Racing: Cambridgeshire Meeting, Newmarket

14–17   Golf: Open Championship, Royal Troon Golf Club, Ayrshire

23   Horse Racing: King George VI and Queen Elizabeth Diamond Stakes, Ascot

25–31   Golf: PGA Championship, Baltusrol Golf Club, New Jersey, USA

28–31   Golf: Women's British Open, Woburn Golf and Country Club

AUGUST
5–21   XXXI Summer Olympic Games, Rio de Janeiro, Brazil

6–13   Sailing: Cowes Week, Isle of Wight

21–28   Rowing: World Rowing Championships, Rotterdam

29   Rugby League: Challenge Cup Final, Wembley Stadium, London

29–11 Sep   Tennis: US Open, New York

SEPTEMBER
1–4   Equestrian: Burghley Horse Trials, Stamford, Lincolnshire

7–10   Horse Racing: St Leger, Doncaster

7–18   Summer Paralympic Games, Rio de Janeiro, Brazil

17–1 Oct   Ice Hockey: World Cup of Hockey, Canada

30–2 Oct   Golf: Ryder Cup, Hazeltine National Golf Club, Minnesota, USA

Late Sep–Early Oct   Athletics: Great North Run, Newcastle

OCTOBER
Early Oct   Equestrian: Horse of the Year Show, NEC, Birmingham

Early–Mid-Oct   Rugby League: Super League Final, Old Trafford, Manchester

Mid-Oct   Horse Racing: Champions Meeting, Newmarket

Oct–Nov   Rugby League: Rugby League Four Nations, England

NOVEMBER
7–11   Tennis: ATP World Tour Finals, O2 Arena, London

CENTENARIES

2016

1716
20 Jan	King Charles III of Spain, born
5 Aug	Silahdar Damat Ali Pasha, Grand Vizier of the Ottoman Empire (1713–16), died

1816
20 Mar	Queen Maria I of Portugal, died.
21 Apr	Charlotte Brontë, novelist and poet, born
5 Jun	Giovanni Paisiello, Italian composer, died
30 Jun	Richard Lindon, inventor of the rugby ball, born
9 Jul	Argentina declared independence from Spain
13 Dec	Ernst Werner von Siemens, German inventor and industrialist, born

1916
6 Feb	Rubén Darío, Nicaraguan writer, died
21 Feb	Battle of Verdun began
28 Feb	Henry James, writer, died
6 Mar	German car manufacturer BMW, founded
11 Mar	Harold Wilson, prime minister 1974–6, born
5 Apr	Gregory Peck, American actor, born
22 April	Yehudi Menuhin, violinist, born
24 April	Easter Rising began in Ireland
31 May	Battle of Jutland began
4 Jun	The Brusilov Offensive began
5 Jun	Lord Kitchener (1st Earl Kitchener), Secretary of State for War (1914–16), died
8 Jun	Francis Crick, molecular biologist and co-discoverer of the structure of DNA, born
1 Jul	Battle of the Somme began
23 Jul	Sir William Ramsay, Scottish chemist, born
13 Sep	Roald Dahl, children's author, born
11 Oct	King Otto of Bavaria, died
21 Oct	Karl von Stürgkh, Austrian prime minister, assassinated
26 Oct	François Mitterand, President of France 1981–95, born
21 Nov	Emperor Franz Joseph I of Austria, died
22 Nov	Jack London, American author, died
9 Dec	Kirk Douglas, American actor, born
17 Dec	Grigori Rasputin, Russian mystic and private adviser to the Romanovs, murdered

2017

1517
17 Jan	Henry Grey, 1st Duke of Suffolk and father of Lady Jane Grey, born
31 Oct	Martin Luther posted his Ninety-Five Theses on a church door in Wittenberg
21 Nov	Sikandar Lodi, Sultan of Delhi, died

1617
21 Mar	Pocahontas, Native American noblewoman, died
4 Apr	John Napier, mathematician who discovered logarithms, died

1717
19 Feb	David Garrick, actor and manager of the Drury Lane Theatre, born
13 May	Maria Theresa, Austrian Holy Roman Empress, born
24 Jun	The first Masonic Grand Lodge was founded in St. Paul's Churchyard
5 Sep	King George I issued the Act of Grace, pardoning all pirates
24 Sep	Horace Walpole, gothic novelist and son of Robert Walpole, born

1817
19 Jan	Argentine general José de San Martin lead an army across the Andes into Chile
25 Jan	*The Scotsman* was published for the first time in Edinburgh
8 Mar	The New York Stock Exchange was founded
12 Jul	Henry David Thoreau, American author and naturalist, born
17 Jul	Premier of Handel's *Water Music* in London
18 Jul	Jane Austen, novelist, died
5 Nov	The British East India Company defeated the Maratha Empire at the battle of Khadki
22 Nov	The Roman emerald mines at Sikait, Egypt were discovered
7 Dec	William Bligh, captain of the HMS *Bounty*, died

1917
10 Jan	William Frederick Cody, American frontiersman known as Buffalo Bill, died
12 Jan	Maharishi Mahesh Yogi, guru and spiritual leader, born
2 Feb	Bread rationing was introduced in the UK
8 Mar	Ferdinand von Zeppelin, German airship inventor, died
20 Mar	Vera Lynn, actor and singer, born
9 Apr	The First World War Battle of Vimy Ridge began in France
25 Apr	Ella Fitzgerald, American jazz singer, born
29 May	John F. Kennedy, 35th president of the USA, born
7 Jun	Dean Martin, American singer and member of the 'Rat Pack', born
10 June	Eric Hobsbawm, historian, born
17 Jul	The British Royal Family adopted the surname Windsor
31 Jul	Battle of Passchendaele (Third Battle of Ypres) began in Flanders, Belgium
28 Aug	Jack Kirby, American comic book artist, born
8 Nov	Colin Blythe, cricketer, died
16 Dec	Arthur C. Clarke, science fiction author, born

THE UNITED KINGDOM

THE UK IN FIGURES

The United Kingdom comprises Great Britain (England, Wales and Scotland) and Northern Ireland. The Isle of Man and the Channel Islands are Crown dependencies with their own legislative systems and are not part of the UK.

ABBREVIATIONS
ONS   Office for National Statistics
NISRA   Northern Ireland Statistics and
                     Research Agency
All data is for the UK unless otherwise stated.

AREA OF THE UNITED KINGDOM

	Sq. km	Sq. miles
United Kingdom	243,122	93,870
England	130,280	50,301
Wales	20,733	8,005
Scotland	77,958	30,100
Northern Ireland	14,150	5,463

Source: ONS (Crown copyright)

POPULATION

The first official census of population in England, Wales and Scotland was taken in 1801 and a census has been taken every ten years since, except in 1941 when there was no census because of the Second World War. The last official census in the UK was taken on 27 March 2011.

The first official census of population in Ireland was taken in 1841. However, all figures given below refer only to the area which is now Northern Ireland. Figures for Northern Ireland in 1921 and 1931 are estimates based on the censuses taken in 1926 and 1937 respectively.

Estimates of the population of England before 1801, calculated from the number of baptisms, burials and marriages, are:

1570	4,160,221	1670	5,773,646
1600	4,811,718	1700	6,045,008
1630	5,600,517	1750	6,517,035

Further details are available on the ONS website (W www.ons.gov.uk).

CENSUS RESULTS *Thousands*

	United Kingdom			England and Wales			Scotland			Northern Ireland		
	Total	Male	Female	Total	Male	Female	Total	Male	Female	Total	Male	Female
1801	—	—	—	8,893	4,255	4,638	1,608	739	869	—	—	—
1811	13,368	6,368	7,000	10,165	4,874	5,291	1,806	826	980	—	—	—
1821	15,472	7,498	7,974	12,000	5,850	6,150	2,092	983	1,109	—	—	—
1831	17,835	8,647	9,188	13,897	6,771	7,126	2,364	1,114	1,250	—	—	—
1841	20,183	9,819	10,364	15,914	7,778	8,137	2,620	1,242	1,378	1,649	800	849
1851	22,259	10,855	11,404	17,928	8,781	9,146	2,889	1,376	1,513	1,443	698	745
1861	24,525	11,894	12,631	20,066	9,776	10,290	3,062	1,450	1,612	1,396	668	728
1871	27,431	13,309	14,122	22,712	11,059	11,653	3,360	1,603	1,757	1,359	647	712
1881	31,015	15,060	15,955	25,974	12,640	13,335	3,736	1,799	1,936	1,305	621	684
1891	34,264	16,593	17,671	29,003	14,060	14,942	4,026	1,943	2,083	1,236	590	646
1901	38,237	18,492	19,745	32,528	15,729	16,799	4,472	2,174	2,298	1,237	590	647
1911	42,082	20,357	21,725	36,070	17,446	18,625	4,761	2,309	2,452	1,251	603	648
1921	44,027	21,033	22,994	37,887	18,075	19,811	4,882	2,348	2,535	1,258	610	648
1931	46,038	22,060	23,978	39,952	19,133	20,819	4,843	2,326	2,517	1,243	601	642
1951	50,225	24,118	26,107	43,758	21,016	22,742	5,096	2,434	2,662	1,371	668	703
1961	52,709	25,481	27,228	46,105	22,304	23,801	5,179	2,483	2,697	1,425	694	731
1971	55,515	26,952	28,562	48,750	23,683	25,067	5,229	2,515	2,714	1,536	755	781
1981	55,848	27,104	28,742	49,155	23,873	25,281	5,131	2,466	2,664	1,533*	750	783
1991	56,467	27,344	29,123	49,890	24,182	25,707	4,999	2,392	2,607	1,578	769	809
2001	58,789	28,581	30,208	52,042	25,327	26,715	5,062	2,432	2,630	1,685	821	864
2011	63,182	31,028	32,153	56,076	27,574	28,502	5,295	2,567	2,728	1,810	887	923

* Figure includes 44,500 non-enumerated persons

ISLANDS

	Isle of Man			Jersey			Guernsey		
	Total	Male	Female	Total	Male	Female	Total	Male	Female
1901	54,752	25,496	29,256	52,576	23,940	28,636	40,446	19,652	20,794
1921	60,284	27,329	32,955	49,701	22,438	27,263	38,315	18,246	20,069
1951	55,123	25,749	29,464	57,296	27,282	30,014	43,652	21,221	22,431
1971	56,289	26,461	29,828	72,532	35,423	37,109	51,458	24,792	26,666
1991	69,788	33,693	36,095	84,082	40,862	43,220	58,867	28,297	30,570
2001	76,315	37,372	38,943	87,186	42,485	44,701	59,807	29,138	30,669
2006	80,058	39,523	40,535	—	—	—	—	—	—
2011	84,497	41,971	42,526	97,857	48,296	49,561	62,915	31,025	31,890

Source: Guernsey Annual Publication Bulletin, Isle of Man Government, States of Jersey Statistics Unit

RESIDENT POPULATION

ACTUAL AND PROJECTED BY COUNTRY
people, thousands

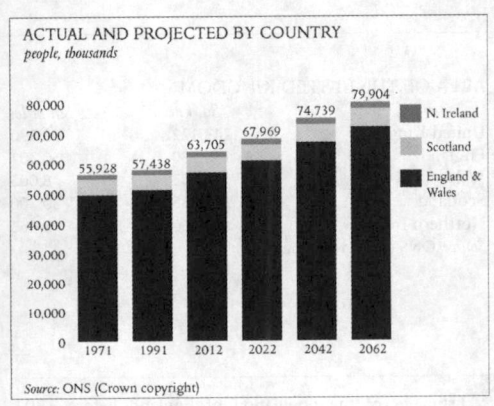

Source: ONS (Crown copyright)

ACTUAL AND PROJECTED BY AGE
by age, thousands

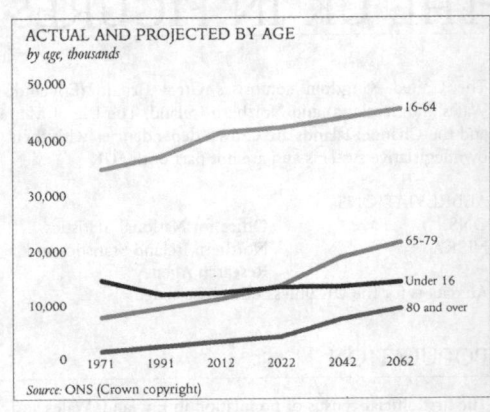

Source: ONS (Crown copyright)

NON-UK BORN RESIDENTS BY COUNTRY OF BIRTH
thousands

	2001	2013
India	468	760
Poland	61	688
Pakistan	321	516
Republic of Ireland	534	378
Germany	266	297
Bangladesh	154	228
South Africa	141	221
USA	158	197
China	53	191
Nigeria	88	185

Source: ONS (Crown Copyright)

BY AGE AND SEX (UK), 2014
people, thousands

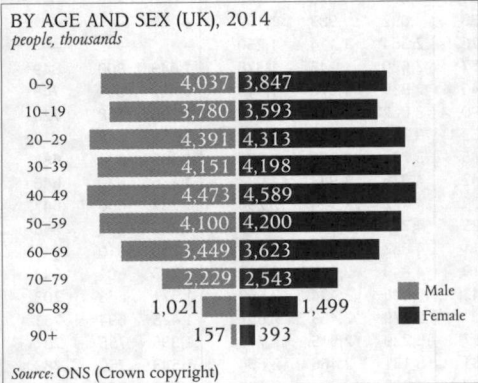

Source: ONS (Crown copyright)

ASYLUM

NATIONALITIES APPLYING FOR UK ASYLUM
year ending in March

Top 5 Nationalities	2014	2015
Eritrea	1,578	3,552
Pakistan	3,294	2,421
Syria	1,709	2,222
Iran	2,234	2,000
Sudan	776	1,603

Source: Home Office, Immigration Statistics

BIRTHS

	Live births	Birth rate*
	2014	2014
United Kingdom	776,352	12
England and Wales	695,233	12.1
Scotland	56,725	10.6
†Northern Ireland	24,394	13.3

* Live births per 1,000 population
Source: General Register Office for Scotland, NISRA, ONS (Crown copyright)

FERTILITY RATES
Total fertility rate is the average number of children which would be born to a woman if she experienced the age-specific fertility rates of the period in question throughout her child-bearing life span. The figures for the years 1960–2 are estimates.

	1960–2	2000	2014
United Kingdom	3.07	1.62	1.30
England and Wales	2.77	1.65	1.83
Scotland	2.98	1.48	1.62
Northern Ireland	3.47	1.75	1.97

Source: General Register Office for Scotland, NISRA, ONS (Crown copyright)

MATERNITY RATES FOR ENGLAND AND WALES 2013

	All maternities*	Singleton	All multiple†	Twins	Triplets
All ages	690,820	680,037	10,783	10,593	187
<20	29,126	28,948	178	176	2
20–24	119,208	118,144	1,064	1,052	12
25–29	195,032	192,550	2,482	2,446	35
30–34	209,515	205,884	3,631	3,574	57
35–39	109,546	107,037	2,509	2,451	56
40–44	26,551	25,807	744	728	16
45+	1,842	1,667	175	166	9

* Includes stillbirths
† Total includes rates for twins, triplets, quads and above
Source: ONS (Crown copyright)

TOP TEN BABY NAMES (ENGLAND AND WALES)

	1984		2014	
	Girls	Boys	Girls	Boys
1	Sarah	Christopher	Amelia	Oliver
2	Laura	James	Olivia	Jack
3	Gemma	David	Isla	Harry
4	Emma	Daniel	Emily	Jacob
5	Rebecca	Michael	Poppy	Charlie
6	Clare	Matthew	Ava	Thomas
7	Victoria	Andrew	Isabella	George
8	Samantha	Richard	Jessica	Oscar
9	Rachel	Paul	Lily	James
10	Amy	Mark	Sophie	William

Source: ONS (Crown copyright)

LIVE BIRTHS (ENGLAND AND WALES)
by age of mother and registration type

Outside marriage/civil partnership

Year	under 20	20–29	30–39	40+	All ages
1943	6,385	25,423	10,357	1,544	43,709
1963	15,603	30,505	11,197	1,799	59,104
1983	30,423	54,599	13,391	838	99,211
2003	39,898	133,972	77,003	6,352	257,225
2013	27,864	188,512	103,384	11,134	330,894

Within marriage/civil partnership

Year	under 20	20–29	30–39	40+	All ages
1943	17,877	346,601	247,001	27,122	640,625
1963	56,037	500,295	216,900	21,719	794,951
1983	23,636	351,371	148,882	6,034	529,923
2003	4,338	139,581	207,597	12,728	364,244
2013	1,272	127,900	220,422	18,024	367,618

Source: ONS (Crown copyright)

MARRIAGE AND DIVORCE

	Marriages 2014	Divorces 2014
United Kingdom	*299,414	*130,162
England and Wales	*262,240	*118,140
Scotland	29,048	9,619
Northern Ireland	8,126	2,403

* Figures for England and Wales are for 2012
Source: NISRA, ONS (Crown copyright), Scottish Government

LEGAL ABORTIONS

	2003	2014
England and Wales	181,582	184,571
Scotland	12,308	11,475

Source: Department of Health, NHS Scotland

DEATHS

INFANT MORTALITY RATE 2013*

United Kingdom	3.9
England and Wales	3.8
Scotland	3.3
Northern Ireland	4.6

* Deaths of infants under one year of age per 1,000 live births
Source: NISRA, ONS (Crown copyright), Scottish Government

DEATHS IN THE UK
people

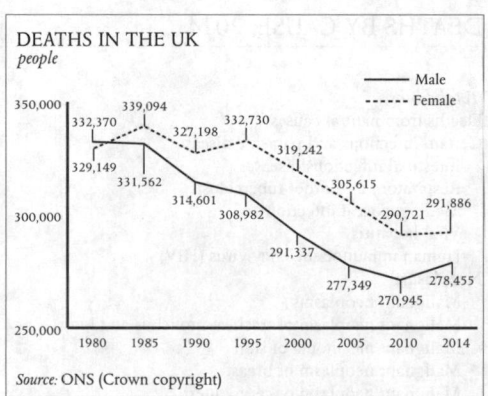

Source: ONS (Crown copyright)

EMPLOYMENT

MEDIAN FULL-TIME GROSS ANNUAL EARNINGS BY REGION (£)

Region	2004	2014
UK	22,056	27,195
England	22,418	27,487
North East	19,247	24,876
North West	20,717	25,229
Yorkshire and the Humber	20,433	24,999
East Midlands	20,691	25,027
West Midlands	20,765	24,920
East	22,242	26,830
London	28,750	35,069
South East	23,748	28,629
South West	20,694	25,571
Wales	20,085	24,384
Scotland	20,598	27,045
Northern Ireland	19,622	24,020

Source: ONS (Crown Copyright)

HOUSE PRICES

Average Price

Year	£	Year	£
1930	1,000	2000	102,000
1950	2,000	2005	191,000
1960	3,000	2010	251,000
1970	5,000	2011	245,000
1980	24,000	2012	246,000
1990	60,000	2013	251,000
1995	66,000	2014	267,000

Source: ONS (Crown Copyright)

UK RESIDENTS' VISITS ABROAD

Year	Visits (thousands)	Spending (£m)
1980	17,507	2,738
1985	21,610	4,871
1990	31,150	9,886
1995	41,345	15,386
2000	56,837	24,251
2005	66,441	32,154
2010	55,562	31,820
2011	56,836	31,701
2012	56,538	32,450
2013	57,792	34,510
2014	60,082	35,537

DEATHS BY CAUSE, 2014

	England and Wales	Scotland	N. Ireland
Total deaths	501,424	54,239	14,673
Deaths from natural causes	481,564	51,678	13,977
Certain infectious and parasitic diseases	5,182	716	154
Intestinal infectious diseases	1,272	132	46
Respiratory and other tuberculosis	289	28	6
Meningococcal infection	44	2	0
Viral hepatitis	262	22	3
Human immunodeficiency virus (HIV)	159	14	5
Neoplasms	147,000	16,167	4,415
Malignant neoplasms	143,638	15,840	4,323
Malignant neoplasm of trachea, bronchus and lung	30,868	4,117	978
Malignant melanoma of skin	2,237	176	53
Malignant neoplasm of breast	10,158	976	323
Malignant neoplasm of cervix uteri	780	88	25
Malignant neoplasm of prostate	10,153	906	242
Leukaemia	4,118	364	—
Diseases of the blood and blood-forming organs and certain disorders involving the immune mechanism	960	86	29
Endocrine, nutritional and metabolic diseases	7,176	1,017	284
Diabetes mellitus	5,314	800	199
Mental and behavioural disorders	41,113	3,952	1,137
Vascular and unspecified dementia	40,200	3,576	—
Diseases of the nervous system	24,432	2,593	801
Meningitis (excluding meningococcal)	150	13	3
Alzheimer's disease	11,298	1,339	406
Diseases of the circulatory system	135,904	15,016	3,719
Ischaemic heart diseases	60,509	6,872	1,782
Cerebrovascular diseases	34,157	4,123	1,002
Diseases of the respiratory system	66,572	6,706	2,004
Influenza	86	23	4
Pneumonia	25,336	1,719	739
Bronchitis, emphysema and other chronic obstructive pulmonary diseases	26,267	3,116	728
Asthma	1,114	64	30
Diseases of the digestive system	24,219	2,952	696
Gastric and duodenal ulcer	1,870	128	31
Diseases of the liver	7,655	981	177
Diseases of the skin and subcutaneous tissue	1,753	163	30
Diseases of the musculo-skeletal system and connective tissue	3,844	327	94
Osteoporosis	1,025	48	11
Diseases of the genitourinary system	8,811	1,169	319
Complications of pregnancy, childbirth and the puerperium	46	5	1
Certain conditions originating in the perinatal period*	195	105	64
Congenital malformations, deformations and chromosomal abnormalities*	1,369	150	85
Symptoms, signs and abnormal findings not classified elsewhere	11,091	549	145
Senility	7,701	286	104
Sudden infant death syndrome	129	14	5
Deaths from external causes	19,860	2,561	701
Suicide and intentional self-harm	4,047	549	191
Assault	†293	52	16

* Excludes neonatal deaths (those at age under 28 days): for England and Wales neonatal deaths are included in the total number of deaths but excluded from the cause figures

† This will not be a true figure as registration of homicide and assault deaths in England and Wales is often delayed by adjourned inquests

Source: General Register Office for Scotland, NISRA, ONS (Crown copyright)

THE NATIONAL FLAG

The national flag of the United Kingdom is the Union Flag, generally known as the Union Jack.

The Union Flag is a combination of the cross of St George, patron saint of England, the cross of St Andrew, patron saint of Scotland and the cross of St Patrick, patron saint of Ireland.

Cross of St George: cross Gules in a field Argent (red cross on a white ground)

Cross of St Andrew: saltire Argent in a field Azure (white diagonal cross on a blue ground)

Cross of St Patrick: saltire Gules in a field Argent (red diagonal cross on a white ground)

A flag combining the cross of St George and the cross of St Andrew was first introduced by royal decree in 1606 following the conjoining of the English and Scottish crowns in 1603. In 1707 this flag became the flag of Great Britain after the parliaments of the two kingdoms were united. The cross of St Patrick was added in 1801 after the union of Great Britain and Ireland.

See also Flags of the World colour plates.

FLYING THE UNION FLAG

The correct orientation of the Union Flag when flying is with the broader diagonal band of white uppermost in the hoist (ie near the pole) and the narrower diagonal band of white uppermost in the fly (ie furthest from the pole).

The flying of the Union Flag on government buildings is decided by the Department for Culture, Media and Sport (DCMS) at the Queen's command. There is no formal definition of a government building but it is generally accepted to mean a building owned or used by the Crown and/or predominantly occupied or used by civil servants or the Armed Forces.

The Scottish or Welsh governments are responsible for drawing up their own flag-flying guidance for their buildings. In Northern Ireland, the flying of flags is constrained by The Flags Regulations (Northern Ireland) 2000 and the Police Emblems and Flag Regulations (Northern Ireland) 2002. Individuals, local authorities and other organisations may fly the Union Flag whenever they wish, subject to compliance with any local planning requirement.

FLAGS AT HALF-MAST

Flags are flown at half-mast (ie two-thirds up between the top and bottom of the flagstaff) on the following occasions:
- from the announcement of the death of the sovereign until the funeral
- the death or funeral of a member of the royal family*
- the funerals of foreign rulers*
- the funerals of prime ministers and ex-prime ministers of the UK*
- the funerals of first ministers and ex-first ministers of Scotland, Wales and Northern Ireland (unless otherwise commanded by the sovereign, this only applies to flags in their respective countries)*
- other occasions by special command from the Queen

* By special command from the Queen in each case

DAYS FOR FLYING FLAGS

On 25 March 2008 the DCMS announced that UK government departments in England, Scotland and Wales may fly the Union Flag on their buildings whenever they choose and not just on the designated days listed below. In addition, on the patron saints' days of Scotland and Wales, the appropriate national flag may be flown alongside the Union Flag on UK government buildings in the wider Whitehall area. When flying on designated days flags are hoisted from 8am to sunset.

Duchess of Cambridge's birthday	9 Jan
Countess of Wessex's birthday	20 Jan
Accession of the Queen	6 Feb
Duke of York's birthday	19 Feb
St David's Day (in Wales only)*	1 Mar
Earl of Wessex's birthday	10 Mar
Commonwealth Day (2016)	14 Mar
St Patrick's Day (in Northern Ireland only)†	17 Mar
The Queen's birthday	21 Apr
St George's Day (in England only)*	23 Apr
Europe Day†	9 May
Coronation Day	2 Jun
Duke of Edinburgh's birthday	10 Jun
The Queen's official birthday (2016)	11 Jun
Duke of Cambridge's birthday	21 Jun
Duchess of Cornwall's birthday	17 Jul
Princess Royal's birthday	15 Aug
Remembrance Day (2016)	13 Nov
Prince of Wales' birthday	14 Nov
Wedding Day of the Queen	20 Nov
St Andrew's Day (in Scotland only)*	30 Nov
Opening of parliament by the Queen‡	
Prorogation of parliament by the Queen‡	

* The appropriate national flag, or the European flag, may be flown in addition to the Union Flag (where there are two or more flagpoles), but not in a superior position

† Only the Union Flag should be flown

‡ Only in the Greater London area, whether or not the Queen performs the ceremony in person

THE ROYAL STANDARD

The Royal Standard comprises four quarterings – two for England (three lions passant), one for Scotland* (a lion rampant) and one for Ireland (a harp).

The Royal Standard is flown when the Queen is in residence at a royal palace, on transport being used by the Queen for official journeys and from Victoria Tower when the Queen attends parliament. It may also be flown on any building (excluding ecclesiastical buildings) during a visit by the Queen. If the Queen is to be present in a building, advice on flag flying can be obtained from the DCMS.

The Royal Standard is never flown at half-mast, even after the death of the sovereign, as the new monarch immediately succeeds to the throne.

* In Scotland a version with two Scottish quarterings is used

THE ROYAL FAMILY

THE SOVEREIGN

ELIZABETH II, by the Grace of God, of the United Kingdom of Great Britain and Northern Ireland and of her other Realms and Territories Queen, Head of the Commonwealth, Defender of the Faith
Her Majesty Elizabeth Alexandra Mary of Windsor, elder daughter of King George VI and of HM Queen Elizabeth the Queen Mother
Born 21 April 1926, at 17 Bruton Street, London W1
Ascended the throne 6 February 1952
Crowned 2 June 1953, at Westminster Abbey
Married 20 November 1947, in Westminster Abbey, HRH the Prince Philip, Duke of Edinburgh
Official residences Buckingham Palace, London SW1A 1AA; Windsor Castle, Berks; Palace of Holyroodhouse, Edinburgh
Private residences Sandringham, Norfolk; Balmoral Castle, Aberdeenshire

HUSBAND OF THE QUEEN

HRH THE PRINCE PHILIP, DUKE OF EDINBURGH, KG, KT, OM, GBE, Royal Victorian Chain, AC, QSO, PC, Ranger of Windsor Park
Born 10 June 1921, son of Prince and Princess Andrew of Greece and Denmark, naturalised a British subject 1947, created Duke of Edinburgh, Earl of Merioneth and Baron Greenwich 1947

CHILDREN OF THE QUEEN

HRH THE PRINCE OF WALES (Prince Charles Philip Arthur George), KG, KT, GCB, OM and Great Master of the Order of the Bath, AK, QSO, PC, ADC(P)
Born 14 November 1948, created Prince of Wales and Earl of Chester 1958, succeeded as Duke of Cornwall, Duke of Rothesay, Earl of Carrick and Baron Renfrew, Lord of the Isles and Great Steward of Scotland 1952
Married (1) 29 July 1981 Lady Diana Frances Spencer (Diana, Princess of Wales (1961–97), youngest daughter of the 8th Earl Spencer and the Hon. Mrs Shand Kydd), marriage dissolved 1996; (2) 9 April 2005 Mrs Camilla Rosemary Parker Bowles, now HRH the Duchess of Cornwall, GCVO (*born* 17 July 1947, daughter of Major Bruce Shand and the Hon. Mrs Rosalind Shand)
Residences Clarence House, London SW1A 1BA; Highgrove, Doughton, Tetbury, Glos GL8 8TN; Birkhall, Ballater, Aberdeenshire
Issue
1. HRH Duke of Cambridge (Prince William Arthur Philip Louis), KG, KT *born* 21 June 1982, *created* Duke of Cambridge, Earl of Strathearn and Baron Carrickfergus 2011 *married* 29 April 2011 Catherine Elizabeth Middleton, now HRH the Duchess of Cambridge (*born* 9 January 1982, elder daughter of Michael and Carole Middleton), and has issue, HRH Prince George of Cambridge (Prince George Alexander Louis), *born* 22 July 2013; HRH Princess Charlotte of Cambridge (Princess Charlotte Elizabeth Diana), *born* 2 May 2015
Residence Kensington Palace, London W8 4PU; Anmer Hall, Norfolk PE31 6RW
2. HRH Prince Henry of Wales (Prince Henry Charles Albert David), KCVO *born* 15 September 1984
Residence Nottingham Cottage, Kensington Palace, London W8 4PU

HRH THE PRINCESS ROYAL (Princess Anne Elizabeth Alice Louise), KG, KT, GCVO
Born 15 August 1950, declared the Princess Royal 1987
Married (1) 14 November 1973 Captain Mark Anthony Peter Phillips, CVO (*born* 22 September 1948); marriage dissolved 1992; (2) 12 December 1992 Vice-Adm. Sir Timothy James Hamilton Laurence, KCVO, CB, ADC (P) (*born* 1 March 1955)
Residence Gatcombe Park, Minchinhampton, Glos GL6 9AT
Issue
1. Peter Mark Andrew Phillips, *born* 15 November 1977, *married* 17 May 2008 Autumn Patricia Kelly, and has issue, Savannah Phillips, *born* 29 December 2010; Isla Elizabeth Phillips, *born* 29 March 2012
2. Zara Anne Elizabeth Tindall, MBE, *born* 15 May 1981, *married* 30 July 2011 Michael James Tindall, MBE, and has issue, Mia Grace Tindall, *born* 17 January 2014

HRH THE DUKE OF YORK (Prince Andrew Albert Christian Edward), KG, GCVO, ADC(P)
Born 19 February 1960, created Duke of York, Earl of Inverness and Baron Killyleagh 1986
Married 23 July 1986 Sarah Margaret Ferguson, now Sarah, Duchess of York (*born* 15 October 1959, younger daughter of Major Ronald Ferguson and Mrs Hector Barrantes), marriage dissolved 1996
Residence Royal Lodge, Windsor Great Park, Berks
Issue
1. HRH Princess Beatrice of York (Princess Beatrice Elizabeth Mary), *born* 8 August 1988
2. HRH Princess Eugenie of York (Princess Eugenie Victoria Helena), *born* 23 March 1990

HRH THE EARL OF WESSEX (Prince Edward Antony Richard Louis), KG, GCVO, ADC(P)
Born 10 March 1964, created Earl of Wessex, Viscount Severn 1999
Married 19 June 1999 Sophie Helen Rhys-Jones, now HRH the Countess of Wessex, GCVO (*born* 20 January 1965, daughter of Mr and Mrs Christopher Rhys-Jones)
Residence Bagshot Park, Bagshot, Surrey GU19 5HS
Issue
1. Lady Louise Mountbatten-Windsor (Louise Alice Elizabeth Mary Mountbatten-Windsor), *born* 8 November 2003
2. Viscount Severn (James Alexander Philip Theo Mountbatten-Windsor), *born* 17 December 2007

NEPHEW AND NIECE OF THE QUEEN

Children of HRH the Princess Margaret, Countess of Snowdon and the Earl of Snowdon (*see* House of Windsor):

DAVID ALBERT CHARLES ARMSTRONG-JONES, VISCOUNT LINLEY, *born* 3 November 1961, *married* 8 October 1993 Hon. Serena Alleyne Stanhope, and has issue, Hon. Charles Patrick Inigo Armstrong-Jones, *born* 1 July 1999; Hon. Margarita Elizabeth Alleyne Armstrong-Jones, *born* 14 May 2002

LADY SARAH CHATTO (Sarah Frances Elizabeth), *born* 1 May 1964, *married* 14 July 1994 Daniel Chatto, and has issue, Samuel David Benedict Chatto, *born* 28 July 1996; Arthur Robert Nathaniel Chatto, *born* 5 February 1999

COUSINS OF THE QUEEN

Child of HRH the Duke of Gloucester and HRH Princess Alice, Duchess of Gloucester (*see* House of Windsor):
HRH THE DUKE OF GLOUCESTER (Prince Richard Alexander Walter George), KG, GCVO, Grand Prior of the Order of St John of Jerusalem
Born 26 August 1944
Married 8 July 1972 Birgitte Eva van Deurs, now HRH the Duchess of Gloucester, GCVO (*born* 20 June 1946, daughter of Asger Henriksen and Vivian van Deurs)
Residence Kensington Palace, London W8 4PU
Issue
1. Earl of Ulster (Alexander Patrick Gregers Richard), *born* 24 October 1974 *married* 22 June 2002 Dr Claire Alexandra Booth, and has issue, Lord Culloden (Xan Richard Anders), *born* 12 March 2007; Lady Cosima Windsor (Cosima Rose Alexandra), *born* 20 May 2010
2. Lady Davina Lewis (Davina Elizabeth Alice Benedikte), *born* 19 November 1977 *married* 31 July 2004 Gary Christie Lewis, and has issue, Senna Kowhai Lewis, *born* 22 June 2010; Tane Mahuta Lewis, *born* 25 May 2012
3. Lady Rose Gilman (Rose Victoria Birgitte Louise), *born* 1 March 1980 *married* 19 July 2008 George Edward Gilman, and has issue, Lyla Beatrix Christabel Gilman, *born* 30 May 2010; Rufus Gilman, *born* 2 November 2012

Children of HRH the Duke of Kent and Princess Marina, Duchess of Kent (*see* House of Windsor):

HRH THE DUKE OF KENT (Prince Edward George Nicholas Paul Patrick), KG, GCMG, GCVO, ADC(P)
Born 9 October 1935
Married 8 June 1961 Katharine Lucy Mary Worsley, now HRH the Duchess of Kent, GCVO (*born* 22 February 1933, daughter of Sir William Worsley, Bt.)
Residence Wren House, Palace Green, London W8 4PY
Issue
1. Earl of St Andrews (George Philip Nicholas), *born* 26 June 1962, *married* 9 January 1988 Sylvana Tomaselli, and has issue, Lord Downpatrick (Edward Edmund Maximilian George), *born* 2 December 1988; Lady Marina-Charlotte Windsor (Marina-Charlotte Alexandra Katharine Helen), *born* 30 September 1992; Lady Amelia Windsor (Amelia Sophia Theodora Mary Margaret), *born* 24 August 1995

2. Lady Helen Taylor (Helen Marina Lucy), *born* 28 April 1964, *married* 18 July 1992 Timothy Verner Taylor, and has issue, Columbus George Donald Taylor, *born* 6 August 1994; Cassius Edward Taylor, *born* 26 December 1996; Eloise Olivia Katharine Taylor, *born* 3 March 2003; Estella Olga Elizabeth Taylor, *born* 21 December 2004
3. Lord Nicholas Windsor (Nicholas Charles Edward Jonathan), *born* 25 July 1970, *married* 4 November 2006 Princess Paola Doimi de Lupis Frankopan Subic Zrinski, and has issue, Albert Louis Philip Edward Windsor, *born* 22 September 2007; Leopold Ernest Augustus Guelph Windsor, *born* 8 September 2009; Louis Arthur Nicholas Felix Windsor, *born* 27 May 2014

HRH PRINCESS ALEXANDRA, THE HON. LADY OGILVY (Princess Alexandra Helen Elizabeth Olga Christabel), KG, GCVO
Born 25 December 1936
Married 24 April 1963 the Rt. Hon. Sir Angus Ogilvy, KCVO (1928–2004), second son of 12th Earl of Airlie
Residence Thatched House Lodge, Richmond Park, Surrey TW10 5HP
Issue
1. James Robert Bruce Ogilvy, *born* 29 February 1964, *married* 30 July 1988 Julia Rawlinson, and has issue, Flora Alexandra Ogilvy, *born* 15 December 1994; Alexander Charles Ogilvy, *born* 12 November 1996
2. Marina Victoria Alexandra Ogilvy, *born* 31 July 1966, *married* 2 February 1990 Paul Julian Mowatt (marriage dissolved 1997), and has issue, Zenouska May Mowatt, *born* 26 May 1990; Christian Alexander Mowatt, *born* 4 June 1993

HRH PRINCE MICHAEL OF KENT (Prince Michael George Charles Franklin), GCVO
Born 4 July 1942
Married 30 June 1978 Baroness Marie-Christine Agnes Hedwig Ida von Reibnitz, now HRH Princess Michael of Kent (*born* 15 January 1945, daughter of Baron Gunther von Reibnitz)
Residence Kensington Palace, London W8 4PU
Issue
1. Lord Frederick Windsor (Frederick Michael George David Louis), *born* 6 April 1979, *married* 12 September 2009 Sophie Winkleman, and has issue, Maud Elizabeth Daphne Marina, *born* 15 August 2013
2. Lady Gabriella Windsor (Gabriella Marina Alexandra Ophelia), *born* 23 April 1981

ORDER OF SUCCESSION

The Succession to the Crown Act 2013, received royal assent on 25 April 2013 and makes provision for the order of succession to the Crown not to be dependent on gender and for those members of the royal family married to a Roman Catholic to retain the right of succession to the throne. The provisions of the Act came into force on 26 March 2015, following its ratification by all 15 Realms of the Commonwealth.

On the Act's commencement HRH Prince Michael of Kent and the Earl of St Andrews were restored to the succession. In addition, all male members of the royal family born after 28 October 2011 no longer precede any elder female siblings; and their place in the order of succession changed accordingly.

The following list includes all living descendants of the sons of King George V eligible to succeed to the Crown under the current legislation. Lord Nicholas Windsor, Lord Downpatrick and Lady Marina-Charlotte Windsor renounced their rights to the throne on converting to Roman Catholicism in 2001, 2003 and 2008 respectively. Their children remain in succession provided that they are in communion with the Church of England.

1	HRH the Prince of Wales	29	Senna Lewis
2	HRH the Duke of Cambridge	30	Tane Lewis
3	HRH Prince George of Cambridge	31	Lady Rose Gilman
4	HRH Princess Charlotte of Cambridge	32	Lyla Gilman
5	HRH Prince Henry of Wales	33	Rufus Gilman
6	HRH the Duke of York	34	HRH the Duke of Kent
7	HRH Princess Beatrice of York	35	Earl of St Andrews
8	HRH Princess Eugenie of York	36	Lady Amelia Windsor
9	HRH the Earl of Wessex	37	Albert Windsor
10	Viscount Severn	38	Leopold Windsor
11	Lady Louise Mountbatten-Windsor	39	Louis Windsor
12	HRH the Princess Royal	40	Lady Helen Taylor
13	Peter Phillips	41	Columbus Taylor
14	Savannah Phillips	42	Cassius Taylor
15	Isla Phillips	43	Eloise Taylor
16	Zara Tindall	44	Estella Taylor
17	Mia Tindall	45	HRH Prince Michael of Kent
18	Viscount Linley	46	Lord Frederick Windsor
19	Hon. Charles Armstrong-Jones	47	Maud Windsor
20	Hon. Margarita Armstrong-Jones	48	Lady Gabriella Windsor
21	Lady Sarah Chatto	49	HRH Princess Alexandra, the Hon. Lady Ogilvy
22	Samuel Chatto	50	James Ogilvy
23	Arthur Chatto	51	Alexander Ogilvy
24	HRH the Duke of Gloucester	52	Flora Ogilvy
25	Earl of Ulster	53	Marina Ogilvy
26	Lord Culloden	54	Christian Mowatt
27	Lady Cosima Windsor	55	Zenouska Mowatt
28	Lady Davina Lewis		

ROYAL HOUSEHOLD

The PRIVATE SECRETARY is responsible for:

• informing and advising the Queen on constitutional, governmental and political matters in the UK, her other Realms and the wider Commonwealth, including communications with the prime minister and government departments
• organising the Queen's domestic and overseas official programme
• the Queen's speeches, messages, patronage, photographs, portraits and official presents
• communications in connection with the role of the royal family
• dealing with correspondence to the Queen from members of the public
• royal travel policy
• coordinating and initiating research to support engagements by members of the royal family

The DIRECTOR OF ROYAL COMMUNICATIONS is in charge of Buckingham Palace's communications office and reports to the Private Secretary. The director is responsible for:

• developing communications strategies to enhance the public understanding of the role of the monarchy
• briefing the British and international media on the role and duties of the Queen and issues relating to the royal family
• responding to media enquiries
• arranging media facilities in the UK and overseas to support royal functions and engagements
• the management of the royal website

The Private Secretary is keeper of the royal archives and is responsible for the care of the records of the sovereign and the royal household from previous reigns, preserved in the royal archives at Windsor. As keeper, it is the Private Secretary's responsibility to ensure the proper management of the records of the present reign with a view to their transfer to the archives as and when appropriate. The Private Secretary is an *ex officio* trustee of the Royal Collection Trust.

The KEEPER OF THE PRIVY PURSE AND TREASURER TO THE QUEEN is responsible for:

• the Sovereign Grant, which is the money paid from the government's Consolidated Fund to meet official expenditure relating to the Queen's duties as Head of State and Head of the Commonwealth and is provided by the government in return for the net surplus from the Crown Estate and other hereditary revenues (*see also* Royal Finances)
• through the Director of Human Resources, the planning and management of personnel policy across the royal household, the allocation of employee and pensioner housing and the administration of all its pension schemes and private estates employees
• information systems and telecommunications
• property services at occupied royal palaces in England, comprising Buckingham Palace, St James's Palace, Clarence House, Marlborough House Mews, the residential and office areas of Kensington Palace, Windsor Castle and buildings in the Home and Great Parks of Windsor and Hampton Court Mews and Paddocks
• audit services
• health and safety; insurance matters
• the privy purse, which is mainly financed by the net income of the Duchy of Lancaster, and meets both official and private expenditure incurred by the Queen

• liaison with other members of the royal family and their households on financial matters
• the Queen's private estates at Sandringham and Balmoral, the Queen's Racing Establishment and the Royal Studs and liaison with the Ascot Authority
• the Home Park at Windsor and liaison with the Crown Estate Commissioners concerning the Home Park and the Great Park at Windsor
• the Royal Philatelic Collection
• administrative aspects of the Military Knights of Windsor
• administration of the Royal Victorian Order, of which the Keeper of the Privy Purse is secretary, Long and Faithful Service Medals, and the Queen's cups, medals and prizes, and policy on commemorative medals

The Keeper of the Privy Purse is one of three royal trustees (in respect of his responsibilities for the Sovereign Grant) and is Receiver-General of the Duchy of Lancaster and a member of the Duchy's Council.

The Keeper of the Privy Purse is an *ex officio* trustee of the Royal Collection Trust and the Historic Royal Palaces Trust.

The DIRECTOR OF THE PROPERTY SECTION has day-to-day responsibility for the royal household's property section:

• fire and health and safety
• repairs and refurbishment of buildings and new building work
• utilities and telecommunications
• putting up stages, tents and other work in connection with ceremonial occasions, garden parties and other official functions

The property section is also responsible, on a sub-contract basis from the DCMS, for the maintenance of Marlborough House (which is occupied by the Commonwealth Secretariat).

The MASTER OF THE HOUSEHOLD is responsible for:

• delivering the majority of the official and private entertaining in the Queen's annual programme across all the occupied palaces and residences in the UK when required
• periodic support for entertaining by all other members of the royal family
• furnishings and internal decorative refurbishment of all the occupied palaces in the UK in conjunction with the Director, Royal Collection Trust
• all operational, domestic and kitchen staff in the royal household

The COMPTROLLER, LORD CHAMBERLAIN'S OFFICE is responsible for:

• the organisation of all ceremonial engagements, including state visits to the Queen in the UK, royal weddings and funerals, the state opening of parliament, Guards of Honour at Buckingham Palace, investitures, and the Garter and Thistle ceremonies
• garden parties at Buckingham Palace and the Palace of Holyroodhouse
• the Crown Jewels, which are part of the Royal Collection, when they are in use on state occasions
• coordination of the arrangements for the Queen to be represented at funerals and memorial services and at the arrival and departure of visiting heads of state
• delivery of all official and approved travel operations

- advising on matters of precedence, style and titles, dress, flying of flags, gun salutes, mourning and other ceremonial issues
- supervising the applications for Royal Warrants of Appointment
- advising on the commercial use of royal emblems and contemporary royal photographs
- the ecclesiastical household, the medical household, the bodyguards and certain ceremonial appointments such as Gentlemen Ushers and Pages of Honour
- the Lords in Waiting, who represent the Queen on various occasions and escort visiting heads of state during incoming state visits
- the Queen's bargemaster and watermen and the Queen's swans
- the Royal Almonry and Royal Maundy Service

The Comptroller is also responsible for the Royal Mews, assisted by the CROWN EQUERRY, who has day-to-day responsibility for:

- the provision of carriage processions for the state opening of parliament, state visits, Trooping of the Colour, Royal Ascot, the Garter Ceremony, the Thistle Service, the presentation of credentials to the Queen by incoming foreign ambassadors and high commissioners, and other state and ceremonial occasions
- the provision of chauffeur-driven cars
- coordinating travel arrangements by road in respect of the royal household
- supervision and administration of the Royal Mews at Buckingham Palace, Windsor Castle, Hampton Court and the Palace of Holyroodhouse

The comptroller also has overall responsibility for the MARSHAL OF THE DIPLOMATIC CORPS, who is responsible for the relationship between the royal household and the Diplomatic Heads of Mission in London; and the SECRETARY OF THE CENTRAL CHANCERY OF THE ORDERS OF KNIGHTHOOD, who administers the Orders of Chivalry, makes arrangements for investitures and the distribution of insignia, and ensures the proper public notification of awards through *The London Gazette;* and the DIRECTOR OF OPERATIONS, ROYAL TRAVEL, who is responsible for the provision of travel arrangements by air and rail.

The DIRECTOR, ROYAL COLLECTION TRUST is responsible for:

- the administration and custodial control of the Royal Collection in all royal residences
- the care, display, conservation and restoration of items in the collection
- initiating and assisting research into the collection and publishing catalogues and books on the collection
- making the collection accessible to the public and educating and informing the public about the collection

The Royal Collection, which contains a large number of works of art, is held by the Queen as sovereign in trust for her successors and the nation and is not owned by her as an individual. The administration, conservation and presentation of the Royal Collection are funded by the Royal Collection Trust solely from income from visitors to Windsor Castle, Buckingham Palace and the Palace of Holyroodhouse. The Royal Collection Trust is chaired by the Prince of Wales. The Lord Chamberlain, the Private Secretary and the Keeper of the Privy Purse are *ex officio* trustees and there are three external trustees appointed by the Queen.

The Director, Royal Collection Trust is also at present the SURVEYOR OF THE QUEEN'S WORKS OF ART,

responsible for paintings, miniatures and works of art on paper, including the watercolours, prints and drawings in the Print Room at Windsor Castle, and for the books, manuscripts, coins, medals and insignia in the Royal Library.

Royal Collection Enterprises Limited is the trading subsidiary of the Royal Collection Trust. The company, whose chair is the Keeper of the Privy Purse, is responsible for:

- managing access by the public to Windsor Castle (including Frogmore House), Buckingham Palace (including the Royal Mews and the Queen's Gallery) and the Palace of Holyroodhouse (including the Queen's Gallery)
- running shops at each location
- managing the images and intellectual property rights of the Royal Collection

The Director, Royal Collection Trust is also an *ex officio* trustee of Historic Royal Palaces.

PRIVATE SECRETARIES

THE QUEEN
Office: Buckingham Palace, London SW1A 1AA T 020-7930 4832
Private Secretary to the Queen, Rt. Hon. Sir Christopher Geidt, KCB, KCVO, OBE

PRINCE PHILIP, THE DUKE OF EDINBURGH
Office: Buckingham Palace, London SW1A 1AA T 020-7930 4832
Private Secretary, Brig. Archie Miller-Bakewell

THE PRINCE OF WALES AND THE DUCHESS OF CORNWALL
Office: Clarence House, London SW1A 1BA T 020-7930 4832
Principal Private Secretary, Clive Alderton, LVO

THE DUKE AND DUCHESS OF CAMBRIDGE
Office: Kensington Palace, Palace Green, London W8 4PU
T 020-7930 4832
Private Secretary to the Duke of Cambridge, Miguel Head
Private Secretary to the Duchess of Cambridge, Rebecca Deacon

PRINCE HENRY OF WALES
Office: Kensington Palace, Palace Green, London W8 4PU
T 020-7930 4832
Private Secretary, Ed Lane-Fox

THE DUKE OF YORK
Office: Buckingham Palace, London SW1A 1AA T 020-7024 4227
Private Secretary, Amanda Thirsk, LVO

THE EARL AND COUNTESS OF WESSEX
Office: Bagshot Park, Surrey GU19 5PL T 01276-707040
Private Secretary, Tim Roberts

THE PRINCESS ROYAL
Office: Buckingham Palace, London SW1A 1AA T 020-7024 4199
Private Secretary, Capt. N. P. Wright, CVO, RN

THE DUKE AND DUCHESS OF GLOUCESTER
Office: Kensington Palace, London W8 4PU T 020-7368 1000
Private Secretary, Lt.-Col. Alastair Todd

THE DUKE OF KENT
Office: York House, St James's Palace, London SW1A 1BQ
T 020-7930 4872
Private Secretary, Nicholas Marden

THE DUCHESS OF KENT
Office: York House, St James's Palace, London SW1A 1BQ
T 020-7024 5790
Personal Secretary, Serena Brown

PRINCE AND PRINCESS MICHAEL OF KENT
Office: Kensington Palace, London W8 4PU
W www.princemichael.org.uk
Private Secretary, Nicholas Chance, CVO

PRINCESS ALEXANDRA, THE HON. LADY OGILVY
Office: Buckingham Palace, London SW1A 1AA
T 020-7024 4270
Private Secretary, Diane Duke, LVO

SENIOR MANAGEMENT OF THE ROYAL HOUSEHOLD

Lord Chamberlain, Earl Peel, GCVO, PC
HEADS OF DEPARTMENT
Private Secretary to The Queen, Rt. Hon. Sir Christopher Geidt, KCB, KCVO, OBE
Keeper of the Privy Purse, Sir Alan Reid, GCVO
Master of the Household, Vice-Adm. Tony Johnstone-Burt, CB, OBE
Comptroller, Lord Chamberlain's Office, Lt.-Col. Sir Andrew Ford, KCVO
Director of the Royal Collection, Jonathan Marsden, CVO
NON-EXECUTIVE MEMBERS
Private Secretary to the Duke of Edinburgh, Brig. Archie Miller-Bakewell
Principal Private Secretary to the Prince of Wales and the Duchess of Cornwall, Clive Alderton, LVO

ASTRONOMER ROYAL

The post of Astronomer Royal dates back to 1675, when astronomy had many practical applications in navigation. Today the post is largely honorary, although the Astronomer Royal is expected to be available for consultation on scientific matters for as long as the holder remains a professional astronomer. The Astronomer Royal receives a stipend of £100 a year and is a member of the royal household.

Astronomer Royal, Lord Rees of Ludlow, OM, *apptd* 1995

MASTER OF THE QUEEN'S MUSIC

The office of Master of the Queen's Music is an honour conferred on a musician of great distinction. The office was first created in 1626, when the master was responsible for the court musicians. Since the reign of King George V, the position has had no fixed duties, although the Master may choose to produce compositions to mark royal or state occasions. The Master of the Queen's Music is paid an annual stipend of £15,000. In 2004 the length of appointment was changed from life tenure to a ten-year term.

Master of the Queen's Music, Judith Weir, CBE, *apptd* 2014

POET LAUREATE

The post of Poet Laureate was officially established when John Dryden was appointed by royal warrant as Poet Laureate and Historiographer Royal in 1668. The post is attached to the royal household and was originally conferred on the holder for life; in 1999 the length of appointment was changed to a ten-year term. It is customary for the Poet Laureate to write verse to mark events of national importance. The postholder currently receives an honorarium of £5,750 a year.

The Poet Laureate, Dame Carol Ann Duffy, DBE, *apptd* 2009

ROYAL FINANCES

Dating back to the late 17th century the Civil List was originally used by the sovereign to supplement hereditary revenues for paying the salaries of judges, ambassadors and other government officers as well as the expenses of the royal household. In 1760, on the accession of George III, it was decided that the Civil List would be provided by parliament to cover all relevant expenditure in return for the king surrendering the hereditary revenues of the Crown. At that time parliament undertook to pay the salaries of judges, ambassadors etc. In 1831 parliament agreed also to meet the costs of the royal palaces in return for a reduction in the Civil List.

Until 1 April 2012 the Civil List met the central staff costs and running expenses of the Queen's official household. Annual grants-in-aid provided for the maintenance of the occupied royal palaces (see Royal Household for a list of occupied palaces) and royal travel.

THE SOVEREIGN GRANT

Under the Sovereign Grant Act 2011, which came into force on 1 April 2012, the funding previously provided by the Civil List and the grants-in-aid was consolidated in the Sovereign Grant, which was set at £37.9m for 2014–15. It is provided by HM Treasury from public funds in exchange for the surrender by the Queen of the revenue of the Crown Estate.

Official expenditure met by the Sovereign Grant in 2014–15 amounted to £35.7m. Royal travel accounted for £5.1m of the expenditure and property maintenance for £11.7m. The excess of Sovereign Grant over expenditure of £2.2m was transferred to the Sovereign Grant reserve. The Sovereign Grant is calculated based on 15 per cent of the income account net surplus of the Crown Estate for the two financial years previous. The Crown Estate surplus for the financial year 2012–13 amounted to £252.6m, providing for a Sovereign Grant of £37.9m for 2014–15.

The legislative requirement is for Sovereign Grant accounts to be audited by the Comptroller and Auditor-General, scrutinised by the National Audit Office, and submitted to parliament annually. They are then subjected to the same audit scrutiny as for any other government department. The annual report for the year to 31 March 2015, was published in June 2015.

	2013–14	2014–15
Sovereign Grant	£36,100,000	£37,900,000
Draw-down from		
(transfer to) the reserve	(£400,000)	(£2,200,000)
Net Funding Receipts	£35,700,000	£35,700,000
Net Expenditure	(£35,700,000)	(£35,700,000)

PARLIAMENTARY ANNUITIES

The Civil List acts provided for other members of the royal family to receive parliamentary annuities from government funds to meet the expenses of carrying out their official duties. Since 1993 these annuities have been a statutory anomaly as the Queen reimbursed HM Treasury for all of them except those paid to the late Queen Elizabeth the Queen Mother and the Duke of Edinburgh. The Sovereign Grant Act 2011 repealed all the parliamentary annuities paid to the royal family, with the exception of the Duke of Edinburgh. The Duke of Edinburgh's annuity (£359,000) is now paid directly from the Consolidated Fund.

THE PRIVY PURSE

The funds received by the privy purse pay for official expenses incurred by the Queen as head of state and for some of the Queen's private expenditure. The revenues of the Duchy of Lancaster are the principal source of income for the privy purse. The revenues of the Duchy were retained by George III in 1760 when the hereditary revenues were surrendered. The Duchy Council reports to the Chancellor of the Duchy of Lancaster, who is accountable directly to the sovereign rather than to parliament. However the chancellor does answer parliamentary questions on matters relating to the Duchy's responsibilities.

THE DUCHY OF LANCASTER, 1 Lancaster Place, London WC2E 7ED
Chancellor of the Duchy of Lancaster, Rt. Hon. Oliver Letwin, MP, *apptd* 2014
Chair of the Council, Mark Hudson
Chief Executive and Clerk, Nathan Thompson
Receiver-General, Sir Alan Reid, GCVO
Attorney-General, Robert Miles, QC

PERSONAL INCOME

The Queen's personal income derives mostly from investments, and is used to meet private expenditure.

PRINCE OF WALES' FUNDING

The Duchy Estate was created in 1337 by Edward III for his son and heir Prince Edward (the Black Prince) who became the Duke of Cornwall. The Duchy's primary function is to provide an income from its assets for the Prince of Wales. Under a 1337 charter, confirmed by subsequent legislation, the Prince of Wales is not entitled to the proceeds or profit on the sale of Duchy assets but only to the annual income which is generated. The Duchy is responsible for the sustainable and commercial management of its properties, investment portfolio and 53,400.3 hectares of land, based mostly in the south-west of England. The Prince of Wales has chosen to use a proportion of his income to meet the cost of his public and charitable work. The Duchy also funds the public, charitable and private activities of the Duchess of Cornwall, the Duke and Duchess of Cambridge and Prince Henry of Wales.

THE DUCHY OF CORNWALL, 10 Buckingham Gate, London SW1E 6LA T 020-7834 7346 W www.duchyofcornwall.org
Lord Warden of the Stannaries, Sir Nicholas Bacon, Bt., OBE
Receiver-General, Hon. James Leigh-Pemberton, CVO
Attorney-General, Jonathan Crow, QC
Secretary and Keeper of the Records, Alastair Martin

TAXATION

The sovereign is not legally liable to pay income tax or capital gains tax. In 1992 the Queen offered to pay income and capital gains tax on a voluntary basis from 6 April 1993, and the Prince of Wales offered to pay tax on a voluntary basis on his income from the Duchy of Cornwall (he was already taxed in all other respects).

The main provisions for the Queen and the Prince of Wales to pay tax, set out in a Memorandum of Understanding on Royal Taxation presented to parliament on 11 February 1993, are that the Queen will pay income tax and capital gains tax in respect of her private income and assets, and on the proportion of the income and capital gains of the Privy Purse used for private purposes. Inheritance tax will be paid on the Queen's assets, except for those which pass to the next sovereign, whether automatically or by gift or bequest. The Prince of Wales will pay income tax on income from the Duchy of Cornwall used for private purposes.

ROYAL SALUTES

ENGLAND

The basic royal salute is 21 rounds with an extra 20 rounds fired at Hyde Park because it is a royal park. At the Tower of London 62 rounds are fired on royal anniversaries (21 plus a further 20 because the Tower is a royal palace and a further 21 'for the City of London') and 41 on other occasions. When the Queen's official birthday coincides with the Duke of Edinburgh's birthday, 124 rounds are fired from the Tower (62 rounds for each birthday). Gun salutes occur on the following royal anniversaries:

• Accession Day
• The Queen's birthday
• Coronation Day
• Duke of Edinburgh's birthday
• The Queen's Official Birthday
• The Prince of Wales' birthday
• State opening of parliament

Gun salutes also occur when parliament is prorogued by the sovereign, on royal births and when a visiting head of state meets the sovereign in London, Windsor or Edinburgh.

In London, salutes are fired at Hyde Park and the Tower of London although on some occasions (state visits, state opening of parliament and the Queen's birthday parade) Green Park is used instead of Hyde Park. Other military saluting stations in England are at Colchester, Dover, Plymouth, Woolwich and York.

Constable of the Royal Palace and Fortress of London, Gen. Lord Dannatt, GCB, CBE, MC
Lieutenant of the Tower of London, Lt. Gen. Sir Simon Mayall, KBE, CB
Master Gunner of St James's Park, Gen. Sir Timothy Granville-Chapman, GBE, KCB, ADC
Resident Governor and Keeper of the Jewel House, Col. Richard Harrold, OBE
Master Gunner within the Tower, HRH Prince Michael of Kent, GCVO

SCOTLAND

Royal salutes are authorised at Edinburgh Castle and Stirling Castle. A salute of 21 guns is fired on the following occasions:

• the anniversaries of the birth, accession and coronation of the sovereign
• the anniversary of the birth of the Duke of Edinburgh

A salute of 21 guns is fired in Edinburgh on the occasion of the opening of the general assembly of the Church of Scotland. A salute of 21 guns may also be fired in Edinburgh on the arrival of HM The Queen or a member of the royal family who is a Royal Highness on an official visit.

Military saluting stations are also situated at Cardiff Castle in Wales, Hillsborough Castle in Northern Ireland and in Gibraltar.

MILITARY RANKS AND TITLES

THE QUEEN
ARMY
Colonel-in-Chief
The Life Guards; The Blues and Royals (Royal Horse Guards and 1st Dragoons); The Royal Scots Dragoon Guards (Carabiniers and Greys); The Royal Lancers; Royal Tank Regiment; Corps of Royal Engineers; Grenadier Guards; Coldstream Guards; Scots Guards; Irish Guards; Welsh Guards; The Royal Regiment of Scotland; The Duke of Lancaster's Regiment (King's, Lancashire and Border); The Royal Welsh; Adjutant General's Corps; The Governor General's Horse Guards (of Canada); The King's Own Calgary Regiment (Royal Canadian Armoured Corps); Canadian Forces Military Engineering Branch; Le Royal 22e Regiment (of Canada); The Governor General's Foot Guards (of Canada); The Canadian Grenadier Guards; The Stormont, Dundas and Glengarry Highlanders; Le Régiment de la Chaudière (of Canada); The Royal New Brunswick Regiment; The North Shore (New Brunswick) Regiment; 48th Highlanders of Canada; The Argyll and Sutherland Highlanders of Canada (Princess Louise's); The Calgary Highlanders; Royal Australian Engineers; Royal Australian Infantry Corps; Royal Australian Army Ordnance Corps; Royal Australian Army Nursing Corps; The Corps of Royal New Zealand Engineers; Royal New Zealand Infantry Regiment; Malawi Rifles
Affiliated Colonel-in-Chief
The Queen's Gurkha Engineers
Captain-General
Royal Regiment of Artillery; The Honourable Artillery Company; Combined Cadet Force; Royal Regiment of Canadian Artillery; Royal Regiment of Australian Artillery; Royal Regiment of New Zealand Artillery; Royal New Zealand Armoured Corps
Royal Colonel
Balaklava Company, 5th Battalion The Royal Regiment of Scotland
Patron
Royal Army Chaplains' Department
ROYAL AIR FORCE
Air Commodore-in-Chief
Royal Auxiliary Air Force; Royal Air Force Regiment; Air Reserve (of Canada); Royal Australian Air Force Reserve; Territorial Air Force (of New Zealand)
Commandant-in-Chief
RAF College, Cranwell
Royal Honorary Air Commodore
RAF Marham; 603 (City of Edinburgh) Squadron Royal Auxiliary Air Force
TRI-SERVICE
Colonel-in-Chief
The Canadian Armed Forces Legal Branch

PRINCE PHILIP, DUKE OF EDINBURGH
ROYAL NAVY
Lord High Admiral of the United Kingdom
Admiral of the Fleet
Admiral of the Fleet, Royal Australian Navy
Admiral of the Fleet, Royal New Zealand Navy
Admiral, Royal Canadian Navy
Admiral, Royal Canadian Sea Cadets
ROYAL MARINES
Captain-General
ARMY
Field Marshal

Field Marshal, Australian Military Forces
Field Marshal, New Zealand Army
General, Royal Canadian Army
Colonel-in-Chief
The Queen's Royal Hussars (Queen's Own and Royal Irish); The Rifles; Corps of Royal Electrical and Mechanical Engineers; Intelligence Corps; Army Cadet Force Association; The Royal Canadian Regiment; The Royal Hamilton Light Infantry (Wentworth Regiment of Canada); The Cameron Highlanders of Ottawa; The Queen's Own Cameron Highlanders of Canada; The Seaforth Highlanders of Canada; The Royal Canadian Army Cadets; The Royal Australian Corps of Electrical and Mechanical Engineers; The Australian Army Cadet Corps
Colonel
Grenadier Guards
Royal Colonel
The Highlanders, 4th Battalion The Royal Regiment of Scotland
Honorary Colonel
City of Edinburgh University Officers' Training Corps; The Trinidad and Tobago Regiment
Member
Honourable Artillery Company
ROYAL AIR FORCE
Marshal of the Royal Air Force
Marshal of the Royal Australian Air Force
Marshal of the Royal New Zealand Air Force
General, Royal Canadian Air Force
Air Commodore-in-Chief
Air Training Corps; Royal Canadian Air Cadets
Honorary Air Commodore
RAF Northolt

THE PRINCE OF WALES
ROYAL NAVY
Admiral of the Fleet
Commodore-in-Chief
Royal Naval Command Plymouth; Fleet Atlantic, Royal Canadian Navy
ARMY
Field Marshal
Colonel-in-Chief
The Royal Dragoon Guards; The Parachute Regiment; The Royal Gurkha Rifles; Army Air Corps; The Royal Canadian Dragoons; Lord Strathcona's Horse (Royal Canadians); The Royal Regiment of Canada; Royal Winnipeg Rifles; Royal Australian Armoured Corps; The Royal Pacific Islands Regiment; 1st The Queen's Dragoon Guards; The Black Watch (Royal Highland Regiment) of Canada; The Toronto Scottish Regiment (Queen Elizabeth The Queen Mother's Own); The Mercian Regiment; 2nd Battalion The Irish Regiment of Canada
Royal Colonel
The Black Watch, 3rd Battalion The Royal Regiment of Scotland; 51st Highland, 7th Battalion The Royal Regiment of Scotland (Territorial Army)
Colonel
The Welsh Guards
Royal Honorary Colonel
The Queen's Own Yeomanry
ROYAL AIR FORCE
Marshal of the RAF
Honorary Air Commodore
RAF Valley

Air Commodore-in-Chief
Royal New Zealand Air Force
Colonel-in-Chief
Air Reserve Canada

THE DUCHESS OF CORNWALL
ROYAL NAVY
Commodore-in-Chief
Royal Naval Medical Services; Naval Chaplaincy Services
ARMY
Colonel-in-Chief
Queen's Own Rifles of Canada; Royal Australian Corps of Military Police
Royal Colonel
4th Battalion The Rifles
ROYAL AIR FORCE
Honorary Air Commodore
RAF Halton; RAF Leeming

THE DUKE OF CAMBRIDGE
ROYAL NAVY
Lieutenant
Commodore-in-Chief
Scotland Command; Submarines Command
ARMY
Colonel
Irish Guards
Captain
The Blues and Royals (Royal Horse Guards and 1st Dragoons)
ROYAL AIR FORCE
Flight Lieutenant
Honorary Air Commandant
RAF Coningsby

PRINCE HENRY OF WALES
ROYAL NAVY
Commodore-in-Chief
Small Ships and Diving Command
ARMY
Captain
The Blues and Royals (Royal Horse Guards and 1st Dragoons)
ROYAL AIR FORCE
Honorary Air Commandant
RAF Honington

THE DUKE OF YORK
ROYAL NAVY
Vice-Admiral
Commodore-in-Chief
Fleet Air Arm
Admiral of the Marine Society and Sea Cadets
ARMY
Colonel-in-Chief
The Royal Irish Regiment (27th (Inniskilling), 83rd, 87th and The Ulster Defence Regiment); The Yorkshire Regiment (14th/15th, 19th and 33rd/76th Foot); Small Arms School Corps; The Queen's York Rangers (First Americans); Royal New Zealand Army Logistics Regiment; The Royal Highland Fusiliers of Canada; The Princess Louise Fusiliers (Canada)
Deputy Colonel-in-Chief
The Royal Lancers
Royal Colonel
The Royal Highland Fusiliers, 2nd Battalion The Royal Regiment of Scotland
ROYAL AIR FORCE
Honorary Air Commodore
RAF Lossiemouth

THE EARL OF WESSEX
ROYAL NAVY
Commodore-in-Chief
Royal Fleet Auxiliary
Patron
Royal Fleet Auxiliary Association
ARMY
Colonel-in-Chief
Hastings and Prince Edward Regiment; Saskatchewan Dragoons; Prince Edward Island Regiment
Royal Colonel
2nd Battalion, The Rifles
Royal Honorary Colonel
Royal Wessex Yeomanry; The London Regiment
ROYAL AIR FORCE
Honorary Air Commodore
RAF Waddington

THE COUNTESS OF WESSEX
ARMY
Colonel-in-Chief
Corps of Army Music; Queen Alexandra's Royal Army Nursing Corps; The Lincoln and Welland Regiment; South Alberta Light Horse Regiment
Royal Colonel
5th Battalion, The Rifles
Patron
Queen Alexandra's Royal Army Nursing Corps Association
ROYAL AIR FORCE
Honorary Air Commodore
RAF Wittering
ROYAL NAVY
Sponsor
HMS *Daring*

THE PRINCESS ROYAL
ROYAL NAVY
Admiral (Chief Commandant for Women in the Royal Navy)
Commodore-in-Chief
HM Naval Base Portsmouth; Fleet Pacific, Royal Canadian Navy
ARMY
Colonel-in-Chief
The King's Royal Hussars; Royal Corps of Signals; Royal Logistic Corps; The Royal Army Veterinary Corps; 8th Canadian Hussars (Princess Louise's); Royal Newfoundland Regiment; Canadian Forces Communications and Electronics Branch; The Grey and Simcoe Foresters; The Royal Regina Rifles; Canadian Forces Medical Branch; Royal Canadian Hussars; Royal Australian Corps of Signals; Royal Australian Corps of Transport; Royal New Zealand Corps of Signals; Royal New Zealand Nursing Corps
Affiliated Colonel-in-Chief
The Queen's Gurkha Signals; The Queen's Own Gurkha Transport Regiment
Royal Colonel
The Royal Scots Borderers, 1st Battalion The Royal Regiment of Scotland; 52nd Lowland, 6th Battalion The Royal Regiment of Scotland
Colonel
The Blues and Royals (Royal Horse Guards and 1st Dragoons)
Honorary Colonel
University of London Officers' Training Corps
Commandant-in-Chief
First Aid Nursing Yeomanry (Princess Royal's Volunteer Corps)

ROYAL AIR FORCE
Honorary Air Commodore
   RAF Brize Norton; University of London Air Squadron

THE DUKE OF GLOUCESTER
ARMY
Colonel-in-Chief
   The Royal Anglian Regiment; Royal Army Medical Corps;
   Royal New Zealand Army Medical Corps
Deputy Colonel-in-Chief
   The Royal Logistic Corps
Royal Colonel
   6th Battalion, The Rifles
Royal Honorary Colonel
   Royal Monmouthshire Royal Engineers (Militia)
ROYAL AIR FORCE
Honorary Air Marshal
Honorary Air Commodore
   RAF Odiham; No. 501 (County of Gloucester) Logistic
   Support Squadron

THE DUCHESS OF GLOUCESTER
ARMY
Colonel-in-Chief
   Royal Army Dental Corps; Royal Australian Army
   Educational Corps; Royal New Zealand Army Educational
   Corps; Royal Canadian Dental Corps; The Bermuda
   Regiment
Deputy Colonel-in-Chief
   Adjutant General's Corps
Royal Colonel
   7th Battalion, The Rifles
Vice-Patron
   Adjutant General's Corps Regimental Association
Patron
   Royal Army Educational Corps Association; Army
   Families Federation

THE DUKE OF KENT
ARMY
Field Marshal
Colonel-in-Chief
   The Royal Regiment of Fusiliers; Lorne Scots (Peel,
   Dufferin and Hamilton Regiment)
Deputy Colonel-in-Chief
   The Royal Scots Dragoon Guards (Carabiniers and Greys)

Royal Colonel
   1st Battalion The Rifles
Colonel
   Scots Guards
ROYAL AIR FORCE
Honorary Air Chief Marshal

THE DUCHESS OF KENT
ARMY
Honorary Major-General
Deputy Colonel-in-Chief
   The Royal Dragoon Guards; Adjutant General's Corps;
   The Royal Logistic Corps

PRINCE MICHAEL OF KENT
ROYAL NAVY
Honorary Vice-Admiral of the Royal Naval Reserves
Commodore-in-Chief of the Maritime Reserves
ARMY
Colonel-in-Chief
   Essex and Kent Scottish Regiment (Ontario)
Royal Honorary Colonel
   Honourable Artillery Company
Senior Colonel
   King's Royal Hussars
ROYAL AIR FORCE
Honorary Air Marshal
   RAF Benson

PRINCESS ALEXANDRA, THE HON. LADY OGILVY
ROYAL NAVY
Patron
   Queen Alexandra's Royal Naval Nursing Service
ARMY
Colonel-in-Chief
   The Canadian Scottish Regiment (Princess Mary's)
Deputy Colonel-in-Chief
   The Royal Lancers
Royal Colonel
   3rd Battalion The Rifles
Royal Honorary Colonel
   The Royal Yeomanry
ROYAL AIR FORCE
Patron and Air Chief Commandant
   Princess Mary's RAF Nursing Service

KINGS AND QUEENS

ENGLISH KINGS AND QUEENS 927 TO 1603

HOUSES OF CERDIC AND DENMARK

Reign

927–939 **ÆTHELSTAN** Son of Edward the Elder, by Ecgwynn, and grandson of Alfred *acceded* to Wessex and Mercia *c.*924, established direct rule over Northumbria 927, effectively creating the Kingdom of England *reigned* 15 years

939–946 **EDMUND I** *born* 921, son of Edward the Elder, by Eadgifu *married* (1) Ælfgifu (2) Æthelflæd *killed* aged 25 *reigned* 6 years

946–955 **EADRED** Son of Edward the Elder, by Eadgifu *reigned* 9 years

955–959 **EADWIG** *born* before 943, son of Edmund and Ælfgifu *married* Ælfgifu *reigned* 3 years

959–975 **EDGAR I** *born* 943, son of Edmund and Ælfgifu *married* (1) Æthelflæd (2) Wulfthryth (3) Ælfthryth *died* aged 32 *reigned* 15 years

975–978 **EDWARD I (the Martyr)** *born c.*962, son of Edgar and Æthelflæd *assassinated* aged *c.*16 *reigned* 2 years

978–1016 **ÆTHELRED (the Unready)** *born* 968/9, son of Edgar and Ælfthryth *married* (1) Ælfgifu (2) Emma, daughter of Richard I, Count of Normandy, 1013–14 dispossessed of kingdom by Swegn Forkbeard (King of Denmark 987–1014) *died* aged *c.*47, *reigned* 38 years

1016 **EDMUND II (Ironside)** *born* before 993, **(Apr–Nov)** son of Æthelred and Ælfgifu *married* Ealdgyth died aged over 23 *reigned* 7 months

1016–1035 **CNUT (Canute)** *born c.*995, son of Swegn Forkbeard, King of Denmark, and Gunhild *married* (1) Ælfgifu (2) Emma, widow of Æthelred the Unready. Gained submission of West Saxons 1015, Northumbrians 1016, Mercia 1016, King of all England after Edmund's death, King of Denmark 1019–35, King of Norway 1028–35 *died* aged *c.*40 *reigned* 19 years

1035–1040 **HAROLD I (Harefoot)** *born* 1016/17, son of Cnut and Ælfgifu *married* Ælfgifu 1035 recognised as regent for himself and his brother Harthacnut; 1037 recognised as king *died* aged *c.*23 *reigned* 4 years

1040–1042 **HARTHACNUT (Harthacanute)** *born c.*1018, son of Cnut and Emma. Titular king of Denmark from 1028, acknowledged King of England 1035–7 with Harold I as regent; effective king after Harold's death *died* aged *c.*24 *reigned* 2 years

1042–1066 **EDWARD II (the Confessor)** *born* between 1002 and 1005, son of Æthelred the Unready and Emma *married* Eadgyth, daughter of Godwine, Earl of Wessex *died* aged over 60 *reigned* 23 years

1066 **HAROLD II (Godwinesson)** *born c.*1020, **(Jan–Oct)** son of Godwine, Earl of Wessex, and Gytha *married* (1) Eadgyth (2) Ealdgyth *killed* in battle aged *c.*46 *reigned* 10 months

THE HOUSE OF NORMANDY

1066–1087 **WILLIAM I (the Conqueror)** *born* 1027/8, son of Robert I, Duke of Normandy; obtained the Crown by conquest *married* Matilda, daughter of Baldwin, Count of Flanders *died* aged *c.*60, *reigned* 20 years

1087–1100 **WILLIAM II (Rufus)** *born* between 1056 and 1060, third son of William I; succeeded his father in England only *killed* aged *c.*40 *reigned* 12 years

1100–1135 **HENRY I (Beauclerk)** *born* 1068, fourth son of William I *married* (1) Edith or Matilda, daughter of Malcolm III of Scotland (2) Adela, daughter of Godfrey, Count of Louvain *died* aged 67 *reigned* 35 years

1135–1154 **STEPHEN** *born* not later than 1100, third son of Adela, daughter of William I, and Stephen, Count of Blois *married* Matilda, daughter of Eustace, Count of Boulogne. Feb–Nov 1141 held captive by adherents of Matilda, daughter of Henry I, who contested the Crown until 1153 *died* aged over 53 *reigned* 18 years

THE HOUSE OF ANJOU (PLANTAGENETS)

1154–1189 **HENRY II (Curtmantle)** *born* 1133, son of Matilda, daughter of Henry I, and Geoffrey, Count of Anjou *married* Eleanor, daughter of William, Duke of Aquitaine, and divorced queen of Louis VII of France *died* aged 56 *reigned* 34 years

1189–1199 **RICHARD I (Coeur de Lion)** *born* 1157, third son of Henry II *married* Berengaria, daughter of Sancho VI, King of Navarre *died* aged 42 *reigned* 9 years

1199–1216 **JOHN (Lackland)** *born* 1167, fifth son of Henry II *married* (1) Isabella or Avisa, daughter of William, Earl of Gloucester (divorced) (2) Isabella, daughter of Aymer, Count of Angoulême *died* aged 48 *reigned* 17 years

1216–1272 **HENRY III** *born* 1207, son of John and Isabella of Angoulême *married* Eleanor, daughter of Raymond, Count of Provence *died* aged 65 *reigned* 56 years

1272–1307 **EDWARD I (Longshanks)** *born* 1239, eldest son of Henry III *married* (1) Eleanor, daughter of Ferdinand III, King of Castile (2) Margaret, daughter of Philip III of France *died* aged 68 *reigned* 34 years

1307–1327 **EDWARD II** *born* 1284, eldest surviving son of Edward I and Eleanor *married* Isabella, daughter of Philip IV of France *deposed* Jan 1327 *killed* Sep 1327 aged 43 *reigned* 19 years

1327–1377 **EDWARD III** *born* 1312, eldest son of Edward II *married* Philippa, daughter of William, Count of Hainault *died* aged 64 *reigned* 50 years

1377–1399 **RICHARD II** *born* 1367, son of Edward (the Black Prince), eldest son of Edward III *married* (1) Anne, daughter of Emperor Charles IV (2) Isabelle, daughter of Charles VI of France *deposed* Sep 1399 *killed* Feb 1400 aged 33 *reigned* 22 years

THE HOUSE OF LANCASTER

1399–1413 **HENRY IV**   *born* 1366, son of John of Gaunt, fourth son of Edward III, and Blanche, daughter of Henry, Duke of Lancaster *married* (1) Mary, daughter of Humphrey, Earl of Hereford (2) Joan, daughter of Charles, King of Navarre, and widow of John, Duke of Brittany *died* aged *c.*47 *reigned* 13 years

1413–1422 **HENRY V**   *born* 1387, eldest surviving son of Henry IV and Mary *married* Catherine, daughter of Charles VI of France *died* aged 34 *reigned* 9 years

1422–1471 **HENRY VI**   *born* 1421, son of Henry V *married* Margaret, daughter of René, Duke of Anjou and Count of Provence *deposed* Mar 1461 *restored* Oct 1470 *deposed* Apr 1471 *killed* May 1471 aged 49 *reigned* 39 years

THE HOUSE OF YORK

1461–1483 **EDWARD IV**   *born* 1442, eldest son of Richard of York (grandson of Edmund, fifth son of Edward III; and son of Anne, great-granddaughter of Lionel, third son of Edward III) *married* Elizabeth Woodville, daughter of Richard, Lord Rivers, and widow of Sir John Grey *acceded* Mar 1461 *deposed* Oct 1470 *restored* Apr 1471 *died* aged 40 *reigned* 21 years

1483 **EDWARD V**   *born* 1470, eldest son of
(Apr–Jun) Edward IV *deposed* Jun 1483, *died* probably Jul–Sep 1483, aged 12 *reigned* 2 months

1483–1485 **RICHARD III**   *born* 1452, fourth son of Richard of York *married* Anne Neville, daughter of Richard, Earl of Warwick, and widow of Edward, Prince of Wales, son of Henry VI *killed* in battle aged 32 *reigned* 2 years

THE HOUSE OF TUDOR

1485–1509 **HENRY VII**   *born* 1457, son of Margaret Beaufort (great-granddaughter of John of Gaunt, fourth son of Edward III) and Edmund Tudor, Earl of Richmond *married* Elizabeth, daughter of Edward IV *died* aged 52 *reigned* 23 years

1509–1547 **HENRY VIII**   *born* 1491, second son of Henry VII *married* (1) Catherine, daughter of Ferdinand II, King of Aragon, and widow of his elder brother Arthur (divorced) (2) Anne, daughter of Sir Thomas Boleyn (executed) (3) Jane, daughter of Sir John Seymour (died in childbirth) (4) Anne, daughter of John, Duke of Cleves (divorced) (5) Catherine Howard, niece of the Duke of Norfolk (executed) (6) Catherine, daughter of Sir Thomas Parr and widow of Lord Latimer *died* aged 55 *reigned* 37 years

1547–1553 **EDWARD VI**   *born* 1537, son of Henry VIII and Jane Seymour *died* aged 15 *reigned* 6 years

1553 **JANE**   *born* 1537, daughter of Frances
*(6/10– (daughter of Mary Tudor, the younger
19 Jul) daughter of Henry VII) and Henry Grey, Duke of Suffolk *married* Lord Guildford Dudley, son of the Duke of Northumberland *deposed*

Jul 1553 *executed* Feb 1554 aged 16 *reigned* 13/9 days

1553–1558 **MARY I**   *born* 1516, daughter of Henry VIII and Catherine of Aragon *married* Philip II of Spain *died* aged 42 *reigned* 5 years

1558–1603 **ELIZABETH I**   *born* 1533, daughter of Henry VIII and Anne Boleyn *died* aged 69 *reigned* 44 years

BRITISH KINGS AND QUEENS SINCE 1603

THE HOUSE OF STUART
Reign

1603–1625 **JAMES I (VI OF SCOTLAND)**   *born* 1566, son of Mary, Queen of Scots (granddaughter of Margaret Tudor, elder daughter of Henry VII), and Henry Stewart, Lord Darnley *married* Anne, daughter of Frederick II of Denmark *died* aged 58 *reigned* 22 years

1625–1649 **CHARLES I**   *born* 1600, second son of James I *married* Henrietta Maria, daughter of Henry IV of France *executed* 1649 aged 48 *reigned* 23 years

INTERREGNUM 1649–1660

1649–1653 Government by a council of state
1653–1658 Oliver Cromwell, Lord Protector
1658–1659 Richard Cromwell, Lord Protector

Reign

1660–1685 **CHARLES II**   *born* 1630, eldest son of Charles I *married* Catherine, daughter of John IV of Portugal *died* aged 54 *reigned* 24 years

1685–1688 **JAMES II (VII OF SCOTLAND)**   *born* 1633, second son of Charles I *married* (1) Lady Anne Hyde, daughter of Edward, Earl of Clarendon (2) Mary, daughter of Alphonso, Duke of Modena reign ended with flight from kingdom Dec 1688 *died* 1701 aged 67 *reigned* 3 years

INTERREGNUM
11 Dec 1688 to 12 Feb 1689

Reign

1689–1702 **WILLIAM III**   *born* 1650, son of William II, Prince of Orange, and Mary Stuart, daughter of Charles I *married* Mary, elder daughter of James II *died* aged 51 *reigned* 13 years

and

1689–1694 **MARY II**   *born* 1662, elder daughter of James II and Anne *died* aged 32 *reigned* 5 years

1702–1714 **ANNE**   *born* 1665, younger daughter of James II and Anne *married* Prince George of Denmark, son of Frederick III of Denmark *died* aged 49 *reigned* 12 years

THE HOUSE OF HANOVER

1714–1727 **GEORGE I (Elector of Hanover)**   *born* 1660, son of Sophia (daughter of Frederick, Elector Palatine, and Elizabeth Stuart, daughter of James I) and Ernest Augustus, Elector of Hanover *married* Sophia Dorothea, daughter of George William, Duke of Lüneburg-Celle *died* aged 67 *reigned* 12 years

1727–1760 **GEORGE II**   *born* 1683, son of George I *married* Caroline, daughter of John Frederick, Margrave of Brandenburg-Anspach *died* aged 76 *reigned* 33 years

* Depending on whether the date of her predecessor's death (6 July) or that of her official proclamation as Queen (10 July) is taken as the beginning of her reign

1760–1820 **GEORGE III** *born* 1738, son of Frederick, eldest son of George II *married* Charlotte, daughter of Charles Louis, Duke of Mecklenburg-Strelitz *died* aged 81 *reigned* 59 years

REGENCY 1811–1820
Prince of Wales regent owing to the insanity of George III

Reign
1820–1830 **GEORGE IV** *born* 1762, eldest son of George III *married* Caroline, daughter of Charles, Duke of Brunswick-Wolfenbüttel *died* aged 67 *reigned* 10 years

1830–1837 **WILLIAM IV** *born* 1765, third son of George III *married* Adelaide, daughter of George, Duke of Saxe-Meiningen *died* aged 71 *reigned* 7 years

1837–1901 **VICTORIA** *born* 1819, daughter of Edward, fourth son of George III *married* Prince Albert of Saxe-Coburg and Gotha *died* aged 81 *reigned* 63 years

THE HOUSE OF SAXE-COBURG AND GOTHA
1901–1910 **EDWARD VII** *born* 1841, eldest son of Victoria and Albert *married* Alexandra, daughter of Christian IX of Denmark *died* aged 68 *reigned* 9 years

THE HOUSE OF WINDSOR
1910–1936 **GEORGE V** *born* 1865, second son of Edward VII *married* Victoria Mary, daughter of Francis, Duke of Teck *died* aged 70 *reigned* 25 years

1936 **EDWARD VIII** *born* 1894, eldest son of
(20 Jan– George V *married* (1937) Mrs Wallis Simpson
11 Dec) *abdicated* 1936 *died* 1972 aged 77 *reigned* 10 months

1936–1952 **GEORGE VI** *born* 1895, second son of George V *married* Lady Elizabeth Bowes-Lyon, daughter of 14th Earl of Strathmore and Kinghorne *died* aged 56 *reigned* 15 years

1952– **ELIZABETH II** *born* 1926, elder daughter of George VI *married* Philip, son of Prince Andrew of Greece

KINGS AND QUEENS OF SCOTS 1016 TO 1603

Reign
1016–1034 **MALCOLM II** *born* c.954, son of Kenneth II *acceded* to Alba 1005, secured Lothian c.1016, obtained Strathclyde for his grandson Duncan c.1016, thus reigning over an area approximately the same as that governed by later rulers of Scotland *died* aged c.80 *reigned* 18 years

THE HOUSE OF ATHOLL
1034–1040 **DUNCAN I** son of Bethoc, daughter of Malcolm II, and Crinan, Mormaer of Atholl *married* a cousin of Siward, Earl of Northumbria *reigned* 5 years

1040–1057 **MACBETH** *born* c.1005, son of a daughter of Malcolm II and Finlaec, Mormaer of Moray *married* Gruoch, granddaughter of Kenneth III *killed* aged c.52 *reigned* 17 years

1057–1058 **LULACH** *born* c.1032, son of Gillacomgan,
(Aug–Mar) Mormaer of Moray, and Gruoch (and stepson of Macbeth) *died* aged c.26 *reigned* 7 months

1058–1093 **MALCOLM III (Canmore)** *born* c.1031, elder son of Duncan I *married* (1) Ingibiorg (2) Margaret (St Margaret), granddaughter of Edmund II of England *killed* in battle aged c.62 *reigned* 35 years

1093–1097 **DONALD III BÁN** *born* c.1033, second son of Duncan I *deposed* May 1094 *restored* Nov 1094 *deposed* Oct 1097 *reigned* 3 years

1094 **DUNCAN II** *born* c.1060, elder son of
(May–Nov) Malcolm III and Ingibiorg *married* Octreda of Dunbar *killed* aged c.34 *reigned* 6 months

1097–1107 **EDGAR** *born* c.1074, second son of Malcolm III and Margaret *died* aged c.32 *reigned* 9 years

1107–1124 **ALEXANDER I (the Fierce)** *born* c.1077, fifth son of Malcolm III and Margaret *married* Sybilla, illegitimate daughter of Henry I of England *died* aged c.47 *reigned* 17 years

1124–1153 **DAVID I (the Saint)** *born* c.1085, sixth son of Malcolm III and Margaret *married* Matilda, daughter of Waltheof, Earl of Huntingdon *died* aged c.68 *reigned* 29 years

1153–1165 **MALCOLM IV (the Maiden)** *born* c.1141, son of Henry, Earl of Huntingdon, second son of David I *died* aged c.24 *reigned* 12 years

1165–1214 **WILLIAM I (the Lion)** *born* c.1142, brother of Malcolm IV *married* Ermengarde, daughter of Richard, Viscount of Beaumont *died* aged c.72 *reigned* 49 years

1214–1249 **ALEXANDER II** *born* 1198, son of William I *married* (1) Joan, daughter of John, King of England (2) Marie, daughter of Ingelram de Coucy *died* aged 50 *reigned* 34 years

1249–1286 **ALEXANDER III** *born* 1241, son of Alexander II and Marie *married* (1) Margaret, daughter of Henry III of England (2) Yolande, daughter of the Count of Dreux *killed* accidentally aged 44 *reigned* 36 years

1286–1290 **MARGARET (the Maid of Norway)** *born* 1283, daughter of Margaret (daughter of Alexander III) and Eric II of Norway *died* aged 7 *reigned* 4 years

FIRST INTERREGNUM 1290–1292
Throne disputed by 13 competitors. Crown awarded to John Balliol by adjudication of Edward I of England

THE HOUSE OF BALLIOL
Reign
1292–1296 **JOHN (Balliol)** *born* c.1250, son of Dervorguilla, great-great-granddaughter of David I, and John de Balliol *married* Isabella, daughter of John, Earl of Surrey *abdicated* 1296 *died* 1313 aged c.63 *reigned* 3 years

SECOND INTERREGNUM 1296–1306
Edward I of England declared John Balliol to have forfeited the throne for contumacy in 1296 and took the government of Scotland into his own hands

THE HOUSE OF BRUCE
Reign
1306–1329 **ROBERT I (Bruce)** *born* 1274, son of Robert Bruce and Marjorie, Countess of Carrick, and great-grandson of the second daughter of David, Earl of Huntingdon,

brother of William I *married* (1) Isabella,
daughter of Donald, Earl of Mar (2) Elizabeth,
daughter of Richard, Earl of Ulster *died* aged
54 *reigned* 23 years

1329–1371   **DAVID II**   *born* 1324, son of Robert I and
Elizabeth *married* (1) Joanna, daughter of
Edward II of England (2) Margaret
Drummond, widow of Sir John Logie
(divorced) *died* aged 46 *reigned* 41 years
1332 (Sep–Dec) Edward Balliol, son of John
Balliol
1333–1336 Edward Balliol

THE HOUSE OF STEWART

1371–1390   **ROBERT II (Stewart)**   *born* 1316, son of
Marjorie (daughter of Robert I) and Walter,
High Steward of Scotland *married*
(1) Elizabeth, daughter of Sir Robert Mure of
Rowallan (2) Euphemia, daughter of Hugh,
Earl of Ross *died* aged 74 *reigned* 19 years

1390–1406   **ROBERT III**   *born* c.1337, son of Robert II
and Elizabeth *married* Annabella, daughter of
Sir John Drummond of Stobhall *died* aged c.69
reigned 16 years

1406–1437   **JAMES I**   *born* 1394, son of Robert III *married*
Joan Beaufort, daughter of John, Earl of
Somerset *assassinated* aged 42 *reigned* 30 years

1437–1460   **JAMES II**   *born* 1430, son of James I *married*
Mary, daughter of Arnold, Duke of Gueldres
killed accidentally aged 29 *reigned* 23 years

1460–1488   **JAMES III**   *born* 1452, son of James II
married Margaret, daughter of Christian I of
Denmark *assassinated* aged 36 *reigned* 27 years

1488–1513   **JAMES IV**   *born* 1473, son of James III *married*
Margaret Tudor, daughter of Henry VII of
England *killed* in battle aged 40 *reigned* 25 years

1513–1542   **JAMES V**   *born* 1512, son of James IV *married*
(1) Madeleine, daughter of Francis I of France
(2) Mary of Lorraine, daughter of the Duc de
Guise *died* aged 30 *reigned* 29 years

1542–1567   **MARY**   *born* 1542, daughter of James V and
Mary *married* (1) the Dauphin, afterwards
Francis II of France (2) Henry Stewart, Lord
Darnley (3) James Hepburn, Earl of Bothwell
abdicated 1567, prisoner in England from
1568, *executed* 1587 *reigned* 24 years

1567–1625   **JAMES VI (and I of England)**   *born* 1566,
son of Mary, Queen of Scots, and Henry, Lord
Darnley *acceded* 1567 to the Scottish throne
reigned 58 years *succeeded* 1603 to the English
throne, so joining the English and Scottish
crowns in one person. The two kingdoms
remained distinct until 1707 when the
parliaments of the kingdoms became conjoined

WELSH SOVEREIGNS AND PRINCES

Wales was ruled by sovereign princes from the earliest times
until the death of Llywelyn in 1282. The first English Prince
of Wales was the son of Edward I, who was born in
Caernarvon town on 25 April 1284. According to a
discredited legend, he was presented to the Welsh chieftains
as their prince, in fulfilment of a promise that they should
have a prince who 'could not speak a word of English' and
should be native born. This son, who afterwards became
Edward II, was created 'Prince of Wales and Earl of Chester'
at the Lincoln Parliament on 7 February 1301.

The title Prince of Wales is borne after individual
conferment and is not inherited at birth, though some

Princes have been declared and styled Prince of Wales but
never formally so created (*s*.). The title was conferred on
Prince Charles by the Queen on 26 July 1958. He was
invested at Caernarvon on 1 July 1969.

INDEPENDENT PRINCES AD 844 TO 1282

844–878	Rhodri the Great
878–916	Anarawd, son of Rhodri
916–950	Hywel Dda, the Good
950–979	Iago ab Idwal (or Ieuaf)
979–985	Hywel ab Ieuaf, the Bad
985–986	Cadwallon, his brother
986–999	Maredudd ab Owain ap Hywel Dda
999–1005	Cynan ap Hywel ab Ieuaf
1005–1018	Aeddan ap Blegywryd
1018–1023	Llywelyn ap Seisyll
1023–1039	Iago ab Idwal ap Meurig
1039–1063	Gruffydd ap Llywelyn ap Seisyll
1063–1075	Bleddyn ap Cynfyn
1075–1081	Trahaern ap Caradog
1081–1137	Gruffydd ap Cynan ab Iago
1137–1170	Owain Gwynedd
1170–1194	Dafydd ab Owain Gwynedd
1194–1240	Llywelyn Fawr, the Great
1240–1246	Dafydd ap Llywelyn
1246–1282	Llywelyn ap Gruffydd ap Llywelyn

ENGLISH PRINCES SINCE 1301

1301	Edward (Edward II)
1343	Edward the Black Prince, son of Edward III
1376	Richard (Richard II), son of the Black Prince
1399	Henry of Monmouth (Henry V)
1454	Edward of Westminster, son of Henry VI
1471	Edward of Westminster (Edward V)
1483	Edward, son of Richard III (*d.* 1484)
1489	Arthur Tudor, son of Henry VII
1504	Henry Tudor (Henry VIII)
1610	Henry Stuart, son of James I (*d.* 1612)
1616	Charles Stuart (Charles I)
c.1638 (*s.*)	Charles Stuart (Charles II)
1688 (*s.*)	James Francis Edward Stuart (The Old Pretender), son of James II (*d.* 1766)
1714	George Augustus (George II)
1729	Frederick Lewis, son of George II (*d.* 1751)
1751	George William Frederick (George III)
1762	George Augustus Frederick (George IV)
1841	Albert Edward (Edward VII)
1901	George (George V)
1910	Edward (Edward VIII)
1958	Charles, son of Elizabeth II

PRINCESSES ROYAL

The style Princess Royal is conferred at the sovereign's
discretion on his or her eldest daughter. It is an honorary
title, held for life, and cannot be inherited or passed on. It
was first conferred on Princess Mary, daughter of Charles I,
in approximately 1642.

c.1642	Princess Mary (1631–60), daughter of Charles I
1727	Princess Anne (1709–59), daughter of George II
1766	Princess Charlotte (1766–1828), daughter of George III
1840	Princess Victoria (1840–1901), daughter of Victoria
1905	Princess Louise (1867–1931), daughter of Edward VII
1932	Princess Mary (1897–1965), daughter of George V
1987	Princess Anne (*b.* 1950), daughter of Elizabeth II

THE HOUSE OF WINDSOR

King George V assumed by royal proclamation (17 July 1917) for his House and family, as well as for all descendants in the male line of Queen Victoria who are subjects of these realms, the name of Windsor.

KING GEORGE V

(George Frederick Ernest Albert), second son of King Edward VII *born* 3 June 1865 *married* 6 July 1893 HSH Princess Victoria Mary Augusta Louise Olga Pauline Claudine Agnes of Teck (Queen Mary *born* 26 May 1867 *died* 24 March 1953) *succeeded* to the throne 6 May 1910 *died* 20 January 1936. *Issue*

1. HRH PRINCE EDWARD Albert Christian George Andrew Patrick David *born* 23 June 1894 *succeeded* to the throne as King Edward VIII, 20 January 1936 *abdicated* 11 December 1936 *created* Duke of Windsor 1937 *married* 3 June 1937 Mrs Wallis Simpson (Her Grace The Duchess of Windsor *born* 19 June 1896 *died* 24 April 1986) *died* 28 May 1972

2. HRH PRINCE ALBERT Frederick Arthur George *born* 14 December 1895 *created* Duke of York 1920 *married* 26 April 1923 Lady Elizabeth Bowes-Lyon, youngest daughter of the 14th Earl of Strathmore and Kinghorne (HM Queen Elizabeth the Queen Mother *born* 4 August 1900 *died* 30 March 2002) *succeeded* to the throne as King George VI, 11 December 1936 *died* 6 February 1952. *Issue*
   (1) HRH Princess Elizabeth Alexandra Mary *succeeded* to the throne as Queen Elizabeth II, 6 February 1952 (*see* Royal Family)
   (2) HRH Princess Margaret Rose (later HRH The Princess Margaret, Countess of Snowdon) *born* 21 August 1930 *married* 6 May 1960 Anthony Charles Robert Armstrong-Jones, GCVO *created* Earl of Snowdon 1961 (marriage dissolved 1978) *died* 9 February 2002, having had issue (*see* Royal Family)

3. HRH PRINCESS (Victoria Alexandra Alice) MARY *born* 25 April 1897 *created* Princess Royal 1932 *married* 28 February 1922 Viscount Lascelles, later the 6th Earl of Harewood (1882–1947) *died* 28 March 1965. *Issue*

(1) George Henry Hubert Lascelles, 7th Earl of Harewood, KBE *born* 7 February 1923 *died* 11 July 2011 *married* (1) 1949 Maria (Marion) Stein (marriage dissolved 1967) *issue (a)* David Henry George, 8th Earl of Harewood *born* 1950 *(b)* James Edward *born* 1953 *(c)* (Robert) Jeremy Hugh *born* 1955 (2) 1967 Patricia Tuckwell *issue (d)* Mark Hubert *born* 1964
(2) Gerald David Lascelles *born* 21 August 1924 *died* 27 February 1998 *married* (1) 1952 Angela Dowding (marriage dissolved 1978) *issue (a)* Henry Ulick *born* 1953 (2) 1978 Elizabeth Collingwood (Elizabeth Colvin) *issue (b)* Martin David *born* 1962

4. HRH PRINCE HENRY William Frederick Albert *born* 31 March 1900 *created* Duke of Gloucester, Earl of Ulster and Baron Culloden 1928 *married* 6 November 1935 Lady Alice Christabel Montagu-Douglas-Scott, daughter of the 7th Duke of Buccleuch and Queensberry (HRH Princess Alice, Duchess of Gloucester *born* 25 December 1901 *died* 29 October 2004) *died* 10 June 1974. *Issue*
   (1) HRH Prince William Henry Andrew Frederick *born* 18 December 1941 accidentally *killed* 28 August 1972
   (2) HRH Prince Richard Alexander Walter George (HRH The Duke of Gloucester, *see* Royal Family)

5. HRH PRINCE GEORGE Edward Alexander Edmund *born* 20 December 1902 *created* Duke of Kent, Earl of St Andrews and Baron Downpatrick 1934 *married* 29 November 1934 HRH Princess Marina of Greece and Denmark (*born* 30 November 1906 *died* 27 August 1968) *killed* on active service 25 August 1942. *Issue*
   (1) HRH Prince Edward George Nicholas Paul Patrick (HRH The Duke of Kent, *see* Royal Family)
   (2) HRH Princess Alexandra Helen Elizabeth Olga Christabel (HRH Princess Alexandra, the Hon. Lady Ogilvy, *see* Royal Family)
   (3) HRH Prince Michael George Charles Franklin (HRH Prince Michael of Kent, *see* Royal Family)

6. HRH PRINCE JOHN Charles Francis *born* 12 July 1905 *died* 18 January 1919

DESCENDANTS OF QUEEN VICTORIA

I. HRH Princess Victoria Adelaide Mary Louisa, Princess Royal (1840–1901) *m* Friedrich III (1831–88), later German Emperor

II. HRH Prince Albert Edward (HM KING EDWARD VII) (1841–1910) *succeeded* 22 Jan 1901 *m* HRH Princess Alexandra of Denmark (1844–1925)

III. HRH Princess Alice Maud Mary (1843–78) *m* Prince Ludwig (1837–92), later Grand Duke of Hesse

IV. HRH Prince Alfred Ernest Albert, Duke of Edinburgh (1844–1900) *succeeded* as Duke of Saxe-Coburg and Gotha 1893 *m* Grand Duchess Marie Alexandrovna of Russia (1853–1920)

Column I

1. HIM Wilhelm II (1859–1941), later German Emperor *m* (1) Princess Augusta Victoria of Schleswig-Holstein-Sonderburg-Augustenburg (1858–1921) (2) Princess Hermine of Reuss (1887–1947). *Issue* Wilhelm (1882–1951); Eitel-Friedrich (1883–1942); Adalbert (1884–1948); August Wilhelm (1887–1949); Oskar (1888–1958); Joachim (1890–1920); Viktoria Luise (1892–1980)

2. Charlotte (1860–1919) *m* Bernhard, Duke of Saxe-Meiningen (1851–1928). *Issue* Feodora (1879–1945)

3. Heinrich (1862–1929) *m* Princess Irene of Hesse (*see* III.3). *Issue* Waldemar (1889–1945); Sigismund (1896–1978); Heinrich (1900–4)

Column II

1. Albert Victor, Duke of Clarence and Avondale (1864–92)

2. George (HM KING GEORGE V) (1865–1936) (*see* House of Windsor)

3. Louise (1867–1931), later Princess Royal *m* 1st Duke of Fife (1849–1912). *Issue* Alexandra (1891–1959); Maud (1893–1945)

4. Victoria (1868–1935)

5. Maud (1869–1938) *m* Prince Carl of Denmark (1872–1957), later King Haakon VII of Norway. *Issue* Olav V (1903–91)

6. Alexander (6–7 Apr 1871)

Column III

1. Victoria (1863–1950) *m* Prince Louis of Battenberg (1854–1921), later 1st Marquess of Milford Haven. *Issue* Alice (1885–1969); Louise (1889–1965); George (1892–1938); Louis (1900–79)

2. Elizabeth (1864–1918) *m* Grand Duke Sergius of Russia (1857–1905)

3. Irene (1866–1953) *m* Prince Heinrich of Prussia (*see* I.3)

4. Ernst Ludwig (1868–1937), Grand Duke of Hesse, *m* (1) Princess Victoria Melita of Saxe-Coburg (see IV.3) (2) Princess Eleonore of Solms-Hohensolms-Lich (1871–1937). *Issue* Elizabeth (1895–1903); George (1906–37); Ludwig (1908–68)

5. Frederick William (1870–3)

6. Alix (Tsaritsa of Russia) (1872–1918) *m* Nicholas II, Tsar of All the Russias (1868–1918). *Issue* Olga (1895–1918); Tatiana (1897–1918); Marie (1899–1918); Anastasia (1901–18); Alexis (1904–18)

7. Marie (1874–8)

---

4. Sigismund (1864–6)

5. Victoria (1866–1929) *m* (1) Prince Adolf of Schaumburg-Lippe (1859–1916) (2) Alexander Zubkov (1900–36)

6. Waldemar (1868–79)

7. Sophie (1870–1932) *m* Constantine I (1868–1923), later King of the Hellenes. *Issue* George II (1890–1947); Alexander I (1893–1920); Helena (1896–1982); Paul I (1901–64); Irene (1904–74); Katherine (1913–2007)

8. Margarethe (1872–1954) *m* Prince Friedrich Karl of Hesse (1868–1940). *Issue* Friedrich Wilhelm (1893–1916); Maximilian (1894–1914); Philipp (1896–1980); Wolfgang (1896–1989); Richard (1901–69); Christoph (1901–43)

QUEEN VICTORIA (Alexandrina Victoria) (1819–1901) *succeeded* 20 Jun 1837 *m* (Francis) Albert Augustus Charles Emmanuel, Duke of Saxony, Prince of Saxe-Coburg and Gotha (HRH Albert, Prince Consort) (1819–61)

| VI. HRH Princess Louise Caroline Alberta (1848–1939) *m* Marquess of Lorne (1845–1914), later 9th Duke of Argyll | VII. HRH Prince Arthur William Patrick Albert, Duke of Connaught (1850–1942) *m* Princess Louisa of Prussia (1860–1917) | VIII. HRH Prince Leopold George Duncan Albert, Duke of Albany (1853–84) *m* Princess Helena of Waldeck (1861–1922) | IX. HRH Princess Beatrice Mary Victoria Feodore (1857–1944) *m* Prince Henry of Battenberg (1858–96) |

VI.

1. Alfred, Prince of Saxe-Coburg (1874–99)

2. Marie (1875–1938) *m* Ferdinand (1865–1927), later King of Roumania. *Issue* Carol II (1893–1953); Elisabeth (1894–1956); Marie (1900–61); Nicolas (1903–78); Ileana (1909–91); Mircea (1913–16)

3. Victoria Melita (1876–1936) *m* (1) Grand Duke Ernst Ludwig of Hesse (*see* III.4) (2) Grand Duke Kirill of Russia (1876–1938). *Issue* Marie (1907–51); Kira (1909–67); Vladimir (1917–92)

4. Alexandra (1878–1942) *m* Ernst, Prince of Hohenlohe Langenburg (1863–1950). *Issue* Gottfried (1897–1960); Maria (1899–1967); Alexandra (1901–63); Irma (1902–86)

5. Beatrice (1884–1966) *m* Alfonso of Orleans, Infante of Spain (1886–1975). *Issue* Alvaro (1910–97); Alonso (1912–36); Ataulfo (1913–74)

VII.

1. Margaret (1882–1920) *m* Crown Prince Gustaf Adolf (1882–1973), later King of Sweden. *Issue* Gustaf Adolf (1906–47); Sigvard (1907–2002); Ingrid (1910–2000); Bertil (1912–97); Count Carl Bernadotte (1916–2012)

2. Arthur (1883–1938) *m* HH Duchess of Fife (1891–1959). *Issue* Alastair Arthur (1914–43)

3. (Victoria) Patricia (1886–1974) *m* Adm. Hon. Sir Alexander Ramsay (1881–1972). *Issue* Alexander (1919–2000)

VIII.

1. Alice (1883–1981) *m* Prince Alexander of Teck (1874–1957), later 1st Earl of Athlone. *Issue* May (1906–94); Rupert (1907–28); Maurice (Mar–Sep 1910)

2. Charles Edward (1884–1954), Duke of Albany until title suspended 1917, Duke of Saxe-Coburg-Gotha *m* Princess Victoria Adelheid of Schleswig-Holstein-Sonderburg-Glücksburg (1885–1970). *Issue* Johann Leopold (1906–72); Sibylla (1908–72); Dietmar Hubertus (1909–43); Caroline (1912–83); Friedrich Josias (1918–98)

IX.

1. Alexander, 1st Marquess of Carisbrooke (1886–1960) *m* Lady Irene Denison (1890–1956). *Issue* Iris (1920–82)

2. Victoria Eugénie (1887–1969) *m* Alfonso XIII, King of Spain (1886–1941). *Issue* Alfonso (1907–38); Jaime (1908–75); Beatriz (1909–2002); Maria (1911–96); Juan (1913–93); Gonzalo (1914–34)

3. Maj. Lord Leopold Mountbatten (1889–1922)

4. Maurice (1891–1914)

V. HRH Princess Helena Augusta Victoria (1846–1923) *m* Prince Christian of Schleswig-Holstein-Sonderburg-Augustenburg (1831–1917)	
1. Christian Victor (1867–1900)	4. Marie Louise (1872–1956), *m* Prince Aribert of Anhalt (1864–1933)
2. Albert (1869–1931), later Duke of Schleswig-Holstein	
3. Helena (1870–1948)	5. Harold (12–20 May 1876)

PRECEDENCE

ENGLAND AND WALES

The Sovereign
The Prince Philip, Duke of Edinburgh
The Prince of Wales
The Sovereign's younger sons
The Sovereign's grandsons
The Sovereign's cousins
Archbishop of Canterbury
Lord High Chancellor
Archbishop of York
The Prime Minister
Lord President of the Council
Speaker of the House of Commons
Speaker of the House of Lords
President of the Supreme Court
Lord Chief Justice of England and
  Wales
Lord Privy Seal
Ambassadors and High Commissioners
Lord Great Chamberlain
Earl Marshal
Lord Steward of the Household
Lord Chamberlain of the Household
Master of the Horse
Dukes, according to their patent of
  creation:
  1. of England
  2. of Scotland
  3. of Great Britain
  4. of Ireland
  5. those created since the Union
Eldest sons of Dukes of the Blood
  Royal
Ministers, Envoys, and other important
  overseas visitors
Marquesses, according to their patent
  of creation:
  1. of England
  2. of Scotland
  3. of Great Britain
  4. of Ireland
  5. those created since the Union
Dukes' eldest sons
Earls, according to their patent of
  creation:
  1. of England
  2. of Scotland
  3. of Great Britain
  4. of Ireland
  5. those created since the Union
Younger sons of Dukes of Blood Royal
Marquesses' eldest sons

Dukes' younger sons
Viscounts, according to their patent of
  creation:
  1. of England
  2. of Scotland
  3. of Great Britain
  4. of Ireland
  5. those created since the Union
Earls' eldest sons
Marquesses' younger sons
Bishop of London
Bishop of Durham
Bishop of Winchester
Other English Diocesan Bishops,
  according to seniority of
  consecration
Retired Church of England Diocesan
  Bishops, according to seniority of
  consecration
Suffragan Bishops, according to
  seniority of consecration
Secretaries of State, if of the degree of a
  Baron
Barons, according to their patent of
  creation:
  1. of England
  2. of Scotland (Lords of Parliament)
  3. of Great Britain
  4. of Ireland
  5. those created since the Union,
    including Life Barons
Master of the Rolls
Deputy President of the Supreme
  Court
Justices of the Supreme Court,
  according to seniority of
  appointment
Treasurer of the Household
Comptroller of the Household
Vice-Chamberlain of the Household
Secretaries of State under the degree of
  Baron
Viscounts' eldest sons
Earls' younger sons
Barons' eldest sons
Knights of the Garter
Privy Counsellors
Chancellor of the Order of the Garter
Chancellor of the Exchequer
Chancellor of the Duchy of Lancaster
President of the Queen's Bench
  Division
President of the Family Division

Chancellor of the High Court
Lord Justices of Appeal, according to
  seniority of appointment
Judges of the High Court, according to
  seniority of appointment
Viscounts' younger sons
Barons' younger sons
Sons of Life Peers
Baronets, according to date of patent
Knights of the Thistle
Knights Grand Cross of the Bath
Knights Grand Cross of St Michael and
  St George
Knights Grand Cross of the Royal
  Victorian Order
Knights Grand Cross of the British
  Empire
Knights Commanders of the Bath
Knights Commanders of St Michael
  and St George
Knights Commanders of the Royal
  Victorian Order
Knights Commanders of the British
  Empire
Knights Bachelor
Circuit Judges, according to priority
  and order of their respective
  appointments
Master of the Court of Protection
Companions of the Bath
Companions of St Michael and St
  George
Commanders of the Royal Victorian
  Order
Commanders of the British Empire
Companions of the Distinguished
  Service Order
Lieutenants of the Royal Victorian
  Order
Officers of the British Empire
Companions of the Imperial Service
  Order
Eldest sons of younger sons of peers
Baronets' eldest sons
Eldest sons of knights, in the same
  order as their fathers
Members of the Royal Victorian Order
Members of the British Empire
Baronets' younger sons
Knights' younger sons, in the same
  order as their fathers
Esquires
Gentlemen

WOMEN

Women take the same rank as their husbands or as their brothers; but the daughter of a peer marrying a commoner retains her title as Lady or Honourable. Daughters of peers rank next immediately after the wives of their elder brothers, and before their younger brothers' wives. Daughters of peers marrying peers of a lower degree take the same order of precedence as that of their husbands; thus the daughter of a

Duke marrying a Baron becomes of the rank of Baroness only, while her sisters married to commoners retain their rank and take precedence over the Baroness. Merely official rank on the husband's part does not give any similar precedence to the wife.

Peeresses in their own right take the same precedence as peers of the same rank, ie from their date of creation.

SCOTLAND

The Sovereign
The Prince Philip, Duke of Edinburgh
The Lord High Commissioner to the General Assembly of the Church of Scotland (while that assembly is sitting)
The Duke of Rothesay (eldest son of the Sovereign)
The Sovereign's younger sons
The Sovereign's grandsons
The Sovereign's nephews
Lord-Lieutenants
Lord Provosts, during their term of office*
Sheriffs Principal, during their term of office and within the bounds of their respective sheriffdoms
Lord Chancellor of Great Britain
Moderator of the General Assembly of the Church of Scotland
Keeper of the Great Seal of Scotland (the First Minister)
Presiding Officer
The Secretary of State for Scotland
Hereditary High Constable of Scotland
Hereditary Master of the Household in Scotland
Dukes, as in England
Eldest sons of Dukes of the Blood Royal

Marquesses, as in England
Dukes' eldest sons
Earls, as in England
Younger sons of Dukes of Blood Royal
Marquesses' eldest sons
Dukes' younger sons
Lord Justice General
Lord Clerk Register
Lord Advocate
The Advocate General
Lord Justice Clerk
Viscounts, as in England
Earls' eldest sons
Marquesses' younger sons
Lords of Parliament or Barons, as in England
Eldest sons of Viscounts
Earls' younger sons
Eldest sons of Lords of Parliament or Barons
Knights and Ladies of the Garter
Knights and Ladies of the Thistle
Privy Counsellors
Senators of the College of Justice (Lords of Session)
Viscounts' younger sons
Younger sons of Lords of Parliament or Barons
Baronets
Knights and Dames Grand Cross of orders, as in England

Knights and Dames Commanders of orders, as in England
Solicitor-General for Scotland
Lord Lyon King of Arms
Sheriffs Principal, when not within own county
Knights Bachelor
Sheriffs
Companions of Orders, as in England
Commanders of the Royal Victorian Order
Commanders of the British Empire
Lieutenants of the Royal Victorian Order
Companions of the Distinguished Service Order
Officers of the British Empire
Companions of the Imperial Service Order
Eldest sons of younger sons of peers
Eldest sons of baronets
Eldest sons of knights, as in England
Members of the Royal Victorian Order
Members of the British Empire
Baronets' younger sons
Knights' younger sons
Queen's Counsel
Esquires
Gentlemen

* The Lord Provosts of Aberdeen, Dundee, Edinburgh and Glasgow are Lord-Lieutenants for these cities *ex officio* and take precedence as such

THE PEERAGE

ABBREVIATIONS AND SYMBOLS

S.	Scottish title	*c.p.*	civil partnership
I.	Irish title	*w.*	widower or widow
**	hereditary peer remaining in the House of Lords	M.	minor
°	there is no 'of' in the title	†	heir not ascertained at time of going to press
b.	born	F_	represents forename
s.	succeeded	S_	represents surname
m.	married	cr.	created
§	life peer disqualified from sitting in the House of Lords as a member of the judiciary	¶	life peer who has resigned permanently from the House of Lords

The rules which govern the creation and succession of peerages are extremely complicated. There are, technically, five separate peerages, the Peerage of England, of Scotland, of Ireland, of Great Britain, and of the United Kingdom. The Peerage of Great Britain dates from 1707 when an Act of Union combined the two kingdoms of England and Scotland and separate peerages were discontinued. The Peerage of the United Kingdom dates from 1801 when Great Britain and Ireland were combined under an Act of Union. Some Scottish peers have received additional peerages of Great Britain or of the UK since 1707, and some Irish peers additional peerages of the UK since 1801.

The Peerage of Ireland was not entirely discontinued from 1801 but holders of Irish peerages, whether pre-dating or created subsequent to the Union of 1801, were not entitled to sit in the House of Lords if they had no additional English, Scottish, Great Britain or UK peerage. However, they are eligible for election to the House of Commons and to vote in parliamentary elections. An Irish peer holding a peerage of a lower grade which enabled him to sit in the House of Lords was introduced there by the title which enabled him to sit, though for all other purposes he was known by his higher title.

In the Peerage of Scotland there is no rank of Baron; the equivalent rank is Lord of Parliament, abbreviated to 'Lord' (the female equivalent is 'Lady').

All peers of England, Scotland, Great Britain or the UK who are 21 years or over, and of British, Irish or Commonwealth nationality were entitled to sit in the House of Lords until the House of Lords Act 1999, when hereditary peers lost the right to sit. However, section two of the act provided an exception for 90 hereditary peers plus the holders of the office of Earl Marshal and Lord Great Chamberlain to remain as members of the House of Lords for their lifetime or pending further reform. Of the 90 hereditary peers, 75 were elected by the hereditary peers in their political party, or Crossbench grouping, and the remaining 15 by the whole house. Until 7 November 2002 any vacancy arising due to the death of one of the 90 excepted hereditary peers was filled by the runner-up to the original election. From 7 November 2002 any vacancy due to a death has been filled by holding a by-election. By-elections are conducted in accordance with arrangements made by the Clerk of the Parliaments and have to take place within three months of a vacancy occurring. If the vacancy is among the 75, only the excepted hereditary peers in the relevant party or Crossbench grouping are entitled to vote. If the vacancy is among the other 15, the whole house is entitled to vote.

In the list below, peers currently holding one of the 92 hereditary places in the House of Lords are indicated by **.

HEREDITARY WOMEN PEERS

Most hereditary peerages pass on death to the nearest male heir, but there are exceptions, and several are held by women.

A woman peer in her own right retains her title after marriage, and if her husband's rank is the superior she is designated by the two titles jointly, the inferior one second. Her hereditary claim still holds good in spite of any marriage whether higher or lower. No rank held by a woman can confer any title or even precedence upon her husband but the rank of a hereditary woman peer in her own right is inherited by her eldest son (or in some cases daughter).

After the Peerage Act 1963, hereditary women peers in their own right were entitled to sit in the House of Lords, subject to the same qualifications as men, until the House of Lords Act 1999.

LIFE PEERS

From 1876 to 2009 non-hereditary or life peerages were conferred on certain eminent judges to enable the judicial functions of the House of Lords to be carried out. These lords were known as Lords of Appeal in Ordinary or law lords. The judicial role of the House of Lords as the highest appeal court in the UK ended on 30 July 2009 and since 1 October 2009, under the Constitutional Reform Act 2005, any peer who holds a senior judicial office is disqualified from sitting in the House of Lords until they retire from that office. In the list of life peerages which follows, members of the judiciary who are currently disqualified from sitting and voting in the House of Lords until retirement, are marked by a '§'.

Under the Constitutional Reform and Governance Act 2010, five peers permanently resigned from the House of Lords.

Since 1958 life peerages have been conferred upon distinguished men and women from all walks of life, giving them seats in the House of Lords in the degree of Baron or Baroness. They are addressed in the same way as hereditary lords and barons, and their children have similar courtesy titles.

HOUSE OF LORDS REFORM ACT 2014

The House of Lords Reform Act 2014 makes provision for a member of the House of Lords who is a peer to retire or resign by giving notice in writing to the Clerk of Parliaments. Resignations may not be rescinded. A number of life peers and elected hereditary peers have already retired permanently under this provision. The Act also makes provision for the expulsion of peers who do not attend the

House of Lords for an entire parliamentary session which is longer than six months. Peers on leave of absence or subject to a suspension or disqualification which results in absenteeism for an entire session will not be expelled. The House can also resolve that a peer should not be expelled by reason of special circumstances.

All life peers who have resigned permanently from the House of Lords are indicated by a '¶' in the following list

PEERAGES EXTINCT SINCE THE LAST EDITION
BARONIES: Birdwood (cr. 1938); Strang (cr. 1954)

LIFE PEERAGES: Barnett (cr. 1983); Brittan of Spennithorne (cr. 2000); Gavron (cr. 1999); Griffiths (cr. 1985); James of Holland Park (cr. 1991); Knights (cr. 1987); Mackie of Benshie (cr. 1974); Mason of Barnsley (cr. 1987); Molyneaux of Killead (cr. 1997); Moser (cr. 2001); Mustill (cr. 1992); Platt of Writtle (cr. 1981); Rendell of Babergh (cr. 1997); Sheppard of Didgemere (cr. 1994); Williamson of Horton (cr. 1999)

DISCLAIMER OF PEERAGES
The Peerage Act 1963 enables peers to disclaim their peerages for life. Peers alive in 1963 could disclaim within twelve months after the passing of the act (31 July 1963); a person subsequently succeeding to a peerage may disclaim within 12 months (one month if an MP) after the date of succession, or of reaching 21, if later. The disclaimer is irrevocable but does not affect the descent of the peerage after the disclaimant's death, and children of a disclaimed peer may, if they wish, retain their precedence and any courtesy titles and styles borne as children of a peer. The disclaimer permitted the disclaimant to sit in the House of Commons if elected as an MP. As the House of Lords Act 1999 removed hereditary peers from the House of Lords, they are now entitled to sit in the House of Commons without having to disclaim their titles.

The following peerages are currently disclaimed:
EARLDOM: Selkirk (1994)
BARONIES: Reith (1972); Sanderson of Ayot (1971); Silkin (2002)
PEERS WHO ARE MINORS (ie under 21 years of age)
    BARONS: Hawke (b. 1995); Rodney (b. 1999)

FORMS OF ADDRESS
Forms of address are given under the style for each individual rank of the peerage. Both formal and social forms of address are given where usage differs; nowadays, the social form is generally preferred to the formal, which increasingly is used only for official documents and on very formal occasions.

ROLL OF THE PEERAGE
Crown Office, House of Lords, London SW1A 0PW

The Roll of the Peerage is kept at the Crown Office and maintained by the Registrar and Assistant Registrar of the Peerage in accordance with the terms of a 2004 royal warrant. The roll records the names of all living life peers and hereditary peers who have proved their succession to the satisfaction of the Lord Chancellor. The Roll of the Peerage is maintained in addition to the Clerk of the Parliaments' register of hereditary peers eligible to stand for election in House of Lords' by-elections.

A person whose name is not entered on the Roll of the Peerage can not be addressed or mentioned by the title of a peer in any official document.
Registrar, Ian Denyer, MVO
Assistant Registrar, Grant Bavister

HEREDITARY PEERS

as at 31 August 2015

PEERS OF THE BLOOD ROYAL

Style, His Royal Highness the Duke of __/His Royal Highness the Earl of__/His Royal Highness the Lord__
Style of address (formal) May it please your Royal Highness; *(informal)* Sir

Created	Title, order of succession, name, etc	Heir
	Dukes	
1947	*Edinburgh (1st),* HRH the Prince Philip, Duke of Edinburgh	The Prince of Wales *
1337	*Cornwall,* HRH the Prince of Wales, s. 1952	‡
1398 S.	*Rothesay,* HRH the Prince of Wales, s. 1952	‡
2011	*Cambridge (1st),* HRH Prince William of Wales	HRH Prince George of Cambridge
1986	*York (1st),* Prince Andrew, HRH the Duke of York	None
1928	*Gloucester (2nd),* Prince Richard, HRH the Duke of Gloucester, s. 1974	Earl of Ulster
1934	*Kent (2nd),* Prince Edward, HRH the Duke of Kent, s. 1942	Earl of St Andrews
	Earl	
1999	*Wessex (1st),* Prince Edward, HRH the Earl of Wesex	Viscount Severn

* In June 1999 Buckingham Palace announced that the current Earl of Wessex will be granted the Dukedom of Edinburgh when the title reverts to the Crown. The title will only revert to the Crown on both the death of the current Duke of Edinburgh and the Prince of Wales' succession as king

‡ The title is held by the sovereign's eldest son from the moment of his birth or the sovereign's accession

DUKES

Coronet, Eight strawberry leaves

Style, His Grace the Duke of _
   Envelope (formal), His Grace the Duke of _; *(social),* The Duke of _. *Letter (formal),* My Lord Duke; *(social),* Dear Duke.
Spoken (formal), Your Grace; *(social),* Duke
Wife's style, Her Grace the Duchess of _
   Envelope (formal), Her Grace the Duchess of _; *(social),* The Duchess of _. *Letter (formal),* Dear Madam; *(social),* Dear
Duchess. *Spoken,* Duchess
Eldest son's style, Takes his father's second title as a courtesy title (*see* Courtesy Titles)
Younger sons' style, 'Lord' before forename (F_) and surname (S_)
   Envelope, Lord F_ S_. *Letter (formal),* My Lord; *(social),* Dear Lord F_. *Spoken (formal),* My Lord; *(social),* Lord F_
Daughters' style, 'Lady' before forename (F_) and surname (S_)
   Envelope, Lady F_ S_. *Letter (formal),* Dear Madam; *(social),* Dear Lady F_. *Spoken,* Lady F_

Created	Title, order of succession, name, etc	Heir
1868 I.	*Abercorn (5th),* James Hamilton, KG, *b.* 1934, *s.* 1979, *m.*	Marquess of Hamilton, *b.* 1969
1701 S.	*Argyll (13th),* Torquhil Ian Campbell, *b.* 1968, *s.* 2001, *m.*	Marquess of Lorne, *b.* 2004
1703 S.	*Atholl (12th),* Bruce George Ronald Murray, *b.* 1960, *s.* 2012, *m.*	Marquis of Tullibardine, *b.* 1985
1682	*Beaufort (11th),* David Robert Somerset, *b.* 1928, *s.* 1984, *m.*	Marquess of Worcester, *b.* 1952
1694	*Bedford (15th),* Andrew Ian Henry Russell, *b.* 1962, *s.* 2003, *m.*	Marquess of Tavistock, *b.* 2005
1663 S.	*Buccleuch (10th) and Queensberry (12th) (S. 1684),* Richard Walter John Montagu Douglas Scott, KBE, *b.* 1954, *s.* 2007, *m.*	Earl of Dalkeith, *b.* 1984
1694	*Devonshire (12th),* Peregrine Andrew Morny Cavendish, KCVO, CBE, *b.* 1944, *s.* 2004, *m.*	Earl of Burlington, *b.* 1969
1900	*Fife (4th),* David Charles Carnegie, *b.* 1961, *s.* 2015, *m.*	Earl of Southesk, *b.* 1989
1675	*Grafton (12th),* Henry Oliver Charles FitzRoy, *b.* 1978, *s.* 2011, *m.*	Earl of Euston, *b.* 2012
1643 S.	*Hamilton (16th) and Brandon (13th) (1711),* Alexander Douglas Douglas-Hamilton, *b.* 1978, *s.* 2010, *m. Premier Peer of Scotland*	Marquess of Douglas and Clydesdale, *b.* 2012
1766 I.	*Leinster (9th),* Maurice FitzGerald, *b.* 1948, *s.* 2004, *m. Premier Duke, Marquess and Earl of Ireland*	Edward F., *b.* 1988
1719	*Manchester (13th),* Alexander Charles David Drogo Montagu, *b.* 1962, *s.* 2002, *m.*	Lord Kimble W. D. M., *b.* 1964
1702	*Marlborough (12th),* Charles James Spencer-Churchill, *b.* 1955, *s.* 2014, *m.*	Marquess of Blandford, *b.* 1992
1707 S.	** *Montrose (8th),* James Graham, *b.* 1935, *s.* 1992, *w.*	Marquis of Graham, *b.* 1973
1483	** *Norfolk (18th),* Edward William Fitzalan-Howard, *b.* 1956, *s.* 2002, *m. Premier Duke and Earl Marshal*	Earl of Arundel and Surrey, *b.* 1987
1766	*Northumberland (12th),* Ralph George Algernon Percy, *b.* 1956, *s.* 1995, *m.*	Earl Percy, *b.* 1984
1675	*Richmond (10th) and Gordon (5th) (1876),* Charles Henry Gordon Lennox, *b.* 1929, *s.* 1989, *m.*	Earl of March and Kinrara, *b.* 1955
1707 S.	*Roxburghe (10th),* Guy David Innes-Ker, *b.* 1954, *s.* 1974, *m. Premier Baronet of Scotland*	Marquis of Bowmont and Cessford, *b.* 1981
1703	*Rutland (11th),* David Charles Robert Manners, *b.* 1959, *s.* 1999, *m.*	Marquess of Granby, *b.* 1999
1684	*St Albans (14th),* Murray de Vere Beauclerk, *b.* 1939, *s.* 1988, *m.*	Earl of Burford, *b.* 1965
1547	** *Somerset (19th),* John Michael Edward Seymour, *b.* 1952, *s.* 1984, *m.*	Lord Seymour, *b.* 1982
1833	*Sutherland (7th),* Francis Ronald Egerton, *b.* 1940, *s.* 2000, *m.*	Marquess of Stafford, *b.* 1975
1814	** *Wellington (9th),* Arthur Charles Valerian Wellesley, OBE, *b.* 1945, *s.* 2014, *m.*	Marquess of Douro, *b.* 1978
1874	*Westminster (6th),* Gerald Cavendish Grosvenor, KG, CB, CVO, OBE, TD, *b.* 1951, *s.* 1979, *m.*	Earl Grosvenor, *b.* 1991

MARQUESSES

Coronet, Four strawberry leaves alternating with four silver balls

Style, The Most Hon. the Marquess (of) _ . In Scotland the spelling 'Marquis' is preferred for pre-Union creations
    Envelope (formal), The Most Hon. the Marquess of _; *(social),* The Marquess of _. *Letter (formal),* My Lord; *(social),* Dear Lord _. *Spoken (formal),* My Lord; *(social),* Lord _
Wife's style, The Most Hon. the Marchioness (of) _
    Envelope (formal), The Most Hon. the Marchioness of _; *(social),* The Marchioness of _. *Letter (formal),* Madam; *(social),* Dear Lady _. *Spoken,* Lady _
Eldest son's style, Takes his father's second title as a courtesy title (*see* Courtesy Titles)
Younger sons' style, 'Lord' before forename and surname, as for Duke's younger sons
Daughters' style, 'Lady' before forename and surname, as for Duke's daughter

Created	Title, order of succession, name, etc	Heir
1915	*Aberdeen and Temair (7th),* Alexander George Gordon, *b.* 1955, *s.* 2002, *m.*	Earl of Haddo, *b.* 1983
1876	*Abergavenny (6th) and 10th Earl of Abergavenny (1784),* Christopher George Charles Nevill, *b.* 1955, *s.* 2000, *m.*	To Earldom only, David M. R. N., *b.* 1941
1821	*Ailesbury (8th),* Michael Sidney Cedric Brudenell-Bruce, *b.* 1926, *s.* 1974	Earl of Cardigan, *b.* 1952
1831	*Ailsa (9th),* David Thomas Kennedy, *b.* 1958, *s.* 2015, *m.*	Earl of Cassilis, *b.* 1995
1815	*Anglesey (8th),* Charles Alexander Vaughan Paget, *b.* 1950, *s.* 2013, *m.*	Earl of Uxbridge, *b.* 1986
1789	*Bath (7th),* Alexander George Thynn, *b.* 1932, *s.* 1992, *m.*	Viscount Weymouth, *b.* 1974
1826	*Bristol (8th),* Frederick William Augustus Hervey, *b.* 1979, *s.* 1999	Timothy H. H., *b.* 1960
1796	*Bute (7th),* John Colum Crichton-Stuart, *b.* 1958, *s.* 1993, *m.*	Earl of Dumfries, *b.* 1989
1812	° *Camden (6th),* David George Edward Henry Pratt, *b.* 1930, *s.* 1983	Earl of Brecknock, *b.* 1965
1815	** *Cholmondeley (7th),* David George Philip Cholmondeley, KCVO, *b.* 1960, *s.* 1990, *m. Lord Great Chamberlain*	Earl of Rocksavage, *b.* 2010
1816 I.	° *Conyngham (8th),* Henry Vivian Pierpoint Conyngham, *b.* 1951, *s.* 2009, *m.*	Earl of Mount Charles, *b.* 1975
1791 I.	*Donegall (8th),* Arthur Patrick Chichester, *b.* 1952, *s.* 2007, *m.*	Earl of Belfast, *b.* 1990
1789 I.	*Downshire (9th),* (Arthur Francis) Nicholas Wills Hill, *b.* 1959, *s.* 2003, *m.*	Earl of Hillsborough, *b.* 1996
1801 I.	*Ely (9th),* Charles John Tottenham, *b.* 1943, *s.* 2006, *m.*	Lord Timothy C. T., *b.* 1948
1801	*Exeter (8th),* (William) Michael Anthony Cecil, *b.* 1935, *s.* 1988, *m.*	Lord Burghley, *b.* 1970
1800 I.	*Headfort (7th),* Thomas Michael Ronald Christopher Taylour, *b.* 1959, *s.* 2005, *m.*	Earl of Bective, *b.* 1989
1793	*Hertford (9th),* Henry Jocelyn Seymour, *b.* 1958, *s.* 1997, *m.*	Earl of Yarmouth, *b.* 1993
1599 S.	*Huntly (13th),* Granville Charles Gomer Gordon, *b.* 1944, *s.* 1987, *m. Premier Marquess of Scotland*	Earl of Aboyne, *b.* 1973
1784	*Lansdowne (9th),* Charles Maurice Mercer Nairne Petty-Fitzmaurice, LVO *b.* 1941, *s.* 1999, *m.*	Earl of Kerry, *b.* 1970
1902	*Linlithgow (4th),* Adrian John Charles Hope, *b.* 1946, *s.* 1987, *m.*	Earl of Hopetoun, *b.* 1969
1816 I.	*Londonderry (10th),* Frederick Aubrey Vane-Tempest-Stewart, *b.* 1972, *s.* 2012	Lord Reginald A. V-T-S, *b.* 1977
1701 S.	*Lothian (13th) and Baron Kerr of Monteviot (life peerage, 2010),* Michael Andrew Foster Jude Kerr (Michael Ancram), PC, QC, *b.* 1945, *s.* 2004, *m.*	Lord Ralph W. F. J. K., *b.* 1957
1917	*Milford Haven (4th),* George Ivar Louis Mountbatten, *b.* 1961, *s.* 1970, *m.*	Earl of Medina, *b.* 1991
1838	*Normanby (5th),* Constantine Edmund Walter Phipps, *b.* 1954, *s.* 1994, *m.*	Earl of Mulgrave, *b.* 1994
1812	*Northampton (7th),* Spencer Douglas David Compton, *b.* 1946, *s.* 1978, *m.*	Earl Compton, *b.* 1973
1682 S.	*Queensberry (12th),* David Harrington Angus Douglas, *b.* 1929, *s.* 1954, *m.*	Viscount Drumlanrig, *b.* 1967
1926	*Reading (4th),* Simon Charles Henry Rufus Isaacs, *b.* 1942, *s.* 1980, *m.*	Viscount Erleigh, *b.* 1986
1789	*Salisbury (7th) and Baron Gascoyne-Cecil (life peerage, 1999),* Robert Michael James Gascoyne-Cecil, KCVO, PC, *b.* 1946, *s.* 2003, *m.*	Viscount Cranborne, *b.* 1970
1800 I.	*Sligo (12th),* Sebastian Ulick Browne, *b.* 1964, *s.* 2014, *m.*	Earl of Altamont, *b.* 1988
1787	° *Townshend (8th),* Charles George Townshend, *b.* 1945, *s.* 2010, *m.*	Viscount Raynham, *b.* 1977
1694 S.	*Tweeddale (14th),* Charles David Montagu Hay, *b.* 1947, *s.* 2005	(Lord) Alistair J. M. H., *b.* 1955
1789 I.	*Waterford (9th),* Henry Nicholas de la Poer Beresford, *b.* 1958, *s.* 2015, *m.*	Earl of Tyrone, *b.* 1987
1551	*Winchester (18th),* Nigel George Paulet, *b.* 1941, *s.* 1968, *m. Premier Marquess of England*	Earl of Wiltshire, *b.* 1969
1892	*Zetland (4th),* Lawrence Mark Dundas, *b.* 1937, *s.* 1989, *m.*	Earl of Ronaldshay, *b.* 1965

EARLS

Coronet, Eight silver balls on stalks alternating with eight gold strawberry leaves

Style, The Rt. Hon. the Earl (of) _
  Envelope (formal), The Rt. Hon. the Earl (of) _; *(social),* The Earl (of) _. *Letter (formal),* My Lord; *(social),* Dear Lord _. *Spoken (formal),* My Lord; *(social),* Lord _.
Wife's style, The Rt. Hon. the Countess (of) _
  Envelope (formal), The Rt. Hon. the Countess (of) _; *(social),* The Countess (of) _. *Letter (formal),* Madam; *(social),* Lady _. *Spoken (formal),* Madam; *(social),* Lady _.
Eldest son's style, Takes his father's second title as a courtesy title (*see* Courtesy Titles)
Younger sons' style, 'The Hon.' before forename and surname, as for Baron's children
Daughters' style, 'Lady' before forename and surname, as for Duke's daughter

Created	Title, order of succession, name, etc	Heir
1639 S.	*Airlie (13th),* David George Coke Patrick Ogilvy, KT, GCVO, PC, Royal Victorian Chain, b. 1926, s. 1968, m.	Lord Ogilvy, b. 1958
1696	*Albemarle (10th),* Rufus Arnold Alexis Keppel, b. 1965, s. 1979, m.	Viscount Bury, b. 2003
1952	° *Alexander of Tunis (2nd),* Shane William Desmond Alexander, b. 1935, s. 1969, m.	Hon. Brian J. A., CMG, b. 1939
1662 S.	*Annandale and Hartfell (11th),* Patrick Andrew Wentworth Hope Johnstone, b. 1941, s. 1983, m. claim established 1985	Lord Johnstone, b. 1971
1789 I.	° *Annesley (12th),* Michael Robert Annesley, b. 1933, s. 2011, m.	Viscount Glerawly, b. 1957
1785 I.	*Antrim (9th),* Alexander Randal Mark McDonnell, b. 1935, s. 1977, m.	Viscount Dunluce, b. 1967
1762 I.	** *Arran (9th) and 5th UK Baron Sudley (1884),* Arthur Desmond Colquhoun Gore, b. 1938, s. 1983, m.	William H. G., b. 1950 (to the Earldom)
1955	° ** *Attlee (3rd),* John Richard Attlee, b. 1956, s. 1991, m.	None
1714	*Aylesford (12th),* Charles Heneage Finch-Knightley, b. 1947, s. 2008, m.	Lord Guernsey, b. 1985
1937	** *Baldwin of Bewdley (4th),* Edward Alfred Alexander Baldwin, b. 1938, s. 1976, w.	Viscount Corvedale, b. 1973
1922	*Balfour (5th),* Roderick Francis Arthur Balfour, b. 1948, s. 2003, m.	Charles G. Y. B., b. 1951
1772	° *Bathurst (9th),* Allen Christopher Bertram Bathurst, b. 1961, s. 2011, m.	Lord Apsley, b. 1990
1919	° *Beatty (3rd),* David Beatty, b. 1946, s. 1972, m.	Viscount Borodale, b. 1973
1797 I.	° *Belmore (8th),* John Armar Lowry-Corry, b. 1951, s. 1960, m.	Viscount Corry, b. 1985
1739 I.	*Bessborough (12th),* Myles Fitzhugh Longfield Ponsonby, b. 1941, s. 2002, m.	Viscount Duncannon, b. 1974
1815	*Bradford (7th),* Richard Thomas Orlando Bridgeman, b. 1947, s. 1981, m.	Viscount Newport, b. 1980
1469 S.	*Buchan (17th),* Malcolm Harry Erskine, b. 1930, s. 1984, m.	Lord Cardross, b. 1960
1746	*Buckinghamshire (10th),* (George) Miles Hobart-Hampden, b. 1944, s. 1983, m.	Sir John V. Hobart, Bt., b. 1945
1800	° *Cadogan (8th),* Charles Gerald John Cadogan, KBE, b. 1937, s. 1997, m.	Viscount Chelsea, b. 1966
1878	° *Cairns (6th),* Simon Dallas Cairns, CVO, CBE, b. 1939, s. 1989, m.	Viscount Garmoyle, b. 1965
1455 S.	** *Caithness (20th),* Malcolm Ian Sinclair, PC, b. 1948, s. 1965, w.	Lord Berriedale, b. 1981
1800 I.	*Caledon (7th),* Nicholas James Alexander, KCVO, b. 1955, s. 1980, m.	Viscount Alexander, b. 1990
1661	*Carlisle (13th),* George William Beaumont Howard, b. 1949, s. 1994	Hon. Philip C. W. H., b. 1963
1793	*Carnarvon (8th),* George Reginald Oliver Molyneux Herbert, b. 1956, s. 2001, m.	Lord Porchester, b. 1992
1748 I.	*Carrick (11th),* Arion Thomas Piers Hamilton Butler, b. 1975, s. 2008, m.	Hon. Piers E. T. L. B., b. 1979
1800 I.	° *Castle Stewart (8th),* Arthur Patrick Avondale Stuart, b. 1928, s. 1961, m.	Viscount Stuart, b. 1953
1814	°** *Cathcart (7th),* Charles Alan Andrew Cathcart, b. 1952, s. 1999, m.	Lord Greenock, b. 1986
1647 I.	*Cavan (13th),* Roger Cavan Lambart, b. 1944, s. 1988 (claim to the peerage not yet established)	Cavan C. E. L., b. 1957
1827	° *Cawdor (7th),* Colin Robert Vaughan Campbell, b. 1962, s. 1993, m.	Viscount Emlyn, b. 1998
1801	*Chichester (9th),* John Nicholas Pelham, b. 1944, s. 1944, m.	Richard A. H. P., b. 1952
1803 I.	** *Clancarty (9th),* Nicholas Power Richard Le Poer Trench, b. 1952, s. 1995, m.	None
1776 I.	*Clanwilliam (8th),* Patrick James Meade, b. 1960, s. 2009, m.	Lord Gillford, b. 1998
1776	*Clarendon (8th),* George Edward Laurence Villiers, b. 1976, s. 2009, m.	Lord Hyde, b. 2008
1620 I.	*Cork and Orrery (15th),* John Richard Boyle, b. 1945, s. 2003, m.	Viscount Dungarvan, b. 1978
1850	*Cottenham (9th),* Mark John Henry Pepys, b. 1983, s. 2000, m.	Hon. Sam R. P., b. 1986
1762 I.	** *Courtown (9th),* James Patrick Montagu Burgoyne Winthrop Stopford, b. 1954, s. 1975, m.	Viscount Stopford, b. 1988
1697	*Coventry (13th),* George William Coventry, b. 1939, s. 2004, m.	David D. S. C., b. 1973
1857	° *Cowley (7th),* Garret Graham Wellesley, b. 1934, s. 1975, m.	Viscount Dangan, b. 1965

1892	*Cranbrook (5th)*, Gathorne Gathorne-Hardy, *b.* 1933, *s.* 1978, *m.*	Lord Medway, *b.* 1968
1801	*Craven (9th)*, Benjamin Robert Joseph Craven, *b.* 1989, *s.* 1990	Rupert J. E. C., *b.* 1926
1398 S.	*Crawford (29th) and Balcarres (12th) (S. 1651) and Baron Balniel (life peerage, 1974)*, Robert Alexander Lindsay, KT, GCVO, PC, *b.* 1927, *s.* 1975, *m.* Premier Earl on Union Roll	Lord Balniel, *b.* 1958
1861	*Cromartie (5th)*, John Ruaridh Blunt Grant Mackenzie, *b.* 1948, *s.* 1989, *m.*	Viscount Tarbat, *b.* 1987
1901	*Cromer (4th)*, Evelyn Rowland Esmond Baring, *b.* 1946, *s.* 1991, *m.*	Viscount Errington, *b.* 1994
1633 S.	*Dalhousie (17th)*, James Hubert Ramsay, *b.* 1948, *s.* 1999, *m. Lord Steward*	Lord Ramsay, *b.* 1981
1725 I.	*Darnley (11th)*, Adam Ivo Stuart Bligh, *b.* 1941, *s.* 1980, *m.*	Lord Clifton, *b.* 1968
1711	*Dartmouth (10th)*, William Legge, MEP, *b.* 1949, *s.* 1997, *m.*	Hon. Rupert L., *b.* 1951
1761	° *De La Warr (11th)*, William Herbrand Sackville, *b.* 1948, *s.* 1988, *m.*	Lord Buckhurst, *b.* 1979
1622	*Denbigh (12th) and Desmond (11th) (I. 1622)*, Alexander Stephen Rudolph Feilding, *b.* 1970, *s.* 1995, *m.*	Viscount Feilding, *b.* 2005
1485	*Derby (19th)*, Edward Richard William Stanley, *b.* 1962, *s.* 1994, *m.*	Lord Stanley, *b.* 1998
1553	*Devon (19th)*, Charles Peregrine Courtenay, *b.* 1975, *s.* 2015, *m.*	Lord Courtenay, *b.* 2009
1800 I.	*Donoughmore (8th)*, Richard Michael John Hely-Hutchinson, *b.* 1927, *s.* 1981, *w.*	Viscount Suirdale, *b.* 1952
1661 I.	*Drogheda (12th)*, Henry Dermot Ponsonby Moore, *b.* 1937, *s.* 1989, *m.*	Viscount Moore, *b.* 1983
1837	*Ducie (7th)*, David Leslie Moreton, *b.* 1951, *s.* 1991, *m.*	Lord Moreton, *b.* 1981
1860	*Dudley (5th)*, William Humble David Jeremy Ward, *b.* 1947, *s.* 2013	Hon. Leander G. D. W., *b.* 1971
1660 S.	** *Dundee (12th)*, Alexander Henry Scrymgeour, *b.* 1949, *s.* 1983, *m.*	Lord Scrymgeour, *b.* 1982
1669 S.	*Dundonald (15th)*, Iain Alexander Douglas Blair Cochrane, *b.* 1961, *s.* 1986, *m.*	Lord Cochrane, *b.* 1991
1686 S.	*Dunmore (12th)*, Malcolm Kenneth Murray, *b.* 1946, *s.* 1995, *m.*	Hon. Geoffrey C. M., *b.* 1949
1833	*Durham (7th)*, Edward Richard Lambton, *b.* 1961, *s.* 2006, *m.*	Viscount Lambton, *b.* 1985
1643 S.	*Dysart (13th)*, John Peter Grant of Rothiemurchus, *b.* 1946, *s.* 2011, *m.*	Lord Huntingtower, *b.* 1977
1837	*Effingham (7th)*, David Mowbray Algernon Howard, *b.* 1939, *s.* 1996, *m.*	Lord Howard of Effingham, *b.* 1971
1507 S.	*Eglinton (18th) and Winton (9th) (S. 1600)*, Archibald George Montgomerie, *b.* 1939, *s.* 1966, *m.*	Lord Montgomerie, *b.* 1966
1821	*Eldon (5th)*, John Joseph Nicholas Scott, *b.* 1937, *s.* 1976, *m.*	Viscount Encombe, *b.* 1962
1633 S.	*Elgin (11th) and Kincardine (15th) (S. 1647)*, Andrew Douglas Alexander Thomas Bruce, KT, *b.* 1924, *s.* 1968, *m.*	Lord Bruce, *b.* 1961
1789 I.	*Enniskillen (7th)*, Andrew John Galbraith Cole, *b.* 1942, *s.* 1989, *m.*	Berkeley A. C., *b.* 1949
1789 I.	*Erne (6th)*, Henry George Victor John Crichton, KCVO, *b.* 1937, *s.* 1940, *m.*	Viscount Crichton, *b.* 1971
1452 S.	** *Erroll (24th)*, Merlin Sereld Victor Gilbert Hay, *b.* 1948, *s.* 1978, *m.* Hereditary Lord High Constable and Knight Marischal of Scotland	Lord Hay, *b.* 1984
1661	*Essex (11th)*, Frederick Paul de Vere Capell, *b.* 1944, *s.* 2005	William J. C., *b.* 1952
1711	° *Ferrers (14th)*, Robert William Saswalo Shirley, *b.* 1952, *s.* 2012, *m.*	Viscount Tamworth, *b.* 1984
1789	° *Fortescue (8th)*, Charles Hugh Richard Fortescue, *b.* 1951, *s.* 1993, *m.*	John A. F. F., *b.* 1955
1841	*Gainsborough (6th)*, Anthony Baptist Noel, *b.* 1950, *s.* 2009, *m.*	Viscount Campden, *b.* 1977
1623 S.	*Galloway (13th)*, Randolph Keith Reginald Stewart, *b.* 1928, *s.* 1978, *w.*	Andrew C. S., *b.* 1949
1703 S.	** *Glasgow (10th)*, Patrick Robin Archibald Boyle, *b.* 1939, *s.* 1984, *m.*	Viscount of Kelburn, *b.* 1978
1806 I.	*Gosford (7th)*, Charles David Nicholas Alexander John Sparrow Acheson, *b.* 1942, *s.* 1966, *m.*	Nicholas H. C. A., *b.* 1947
1945	*Gowrie (2nd)*, Alexander Patrick Greysteil Hore Ruthven, PC, *b.* 1939, *s.* 1955, *m.*	Viscount Ruthven of Canberra, *b.* 1964
1684 I.	*Granard (10th)*, Peter Arthur Edward Hastings Forbes, *b.* 1957, *s.* 1992, *m.*	Viscount Forbes, *b.* 1981
1833	° *Granville (6th)*, Granville George Fergus Leveson-Gower, *b.* 1959, *s.* 1996, *m.*	Lord Leveson, *b.* 1999
1806	° *Grey (7th)*, Philip Kent Grey, *b.* 1940, *s.* 2013, *m.*	Viscount Howick, *b.* 1968
1752	*Guilford (10th)*, Piers Edward Brownlow North, *b.* 1971, *s.* 1999, *m.*	Lord North, *b.* 2002
1619 S.	*Haddington (13th)*, John George Baillie-Hamilton, *b.* 1941, *s.* 1986, *m.*	Lord Binning, *b.* 1985
1919	° *Haig (3rd)*, Alexander Douglas Derrick Haig, *b.* 1961, *s.* 2009, *m.*	None
1944	*Halifax (3rd)*, Charles Edward Peter Neil Wood, *b.* 1944, *s.* 1980, *m.*	Lord Irwin, *b.* 1977
1754	*Hardwicke (10th)*, Joseph Philip Sebastian Yorke, *b.* 1971, *s.* 1974, *m.*	Viscount Royston, *b.* 2009
1812	*Harewood (8th)*, David Henry George Lascelles, *b.* 1950, *s.* 2011, *m.*	Viscount Lascelles, *b.* 1978
1742	*Harrington (12th)*, Charles Henry Leicester Stanhope, *b.* 1945, *s.* 2009, *m.*	Viscount Petersham, *b.* 1967
1809	*Harrowby (8th)*, Dudley Adrian Conroy Ryder, *b.* 1951, *s.* 2007, *m.*	Viscount Sandon, *b.* 1981
1605 S.	** *Home (15th)*, David Alexander Cospatrick Douglas-Home, KT, CVO, CBE, *b.* 1943, *s.* 1995, *m.*	Lord Dunglass, *b.* 1987
1821	° ** *Howe (7th)*, Frederick Richard Penn Curzon, PC, *b.* 1951, *s.* 1984, *m.*	Viscount Curzon, *b.* 1994
1529	*Huntingdon (16th)*, William Edward Robin Hood Hastings Bass, LVO, *b.* 1948, *s.* 1990, *m.*	Hon. Simon A. R. H. H. B., *b.* 1950
1885	*Iddesleigh (5th)*, John Stafford Northcote, *b.* 1957, *s.* 2004, *m.*	Viscount St Cyres, *b.* 1985
1756	*Ilchester (10th)*, Robin Maurice Fox-Strangways, *b.* 1942, *s.* 2006, *m.*	Lord Stavordale, *b.* 1972
1929	*Inchcape (4th)*, (Kenneth) Peter (Lyle) Mackay, *b.* 1943, *s.* 1994, *m.*	Viscount Glenapp, *b.* 1979
1919	*Iveagh (4th)*, Arthur Edward Rory Guinness, *b.* 1969, *s.* 1992, *m.*	Viscount Elveden, *b.* 2003
1925	° *Jellicoe (3rd)*, Patrick John Bernard Jellicoe, *b.* 1950, *s.* 2007	Hon. Nicholas C. J., *b.* 1953

1697	*Jersey (10th)*, George Francis William Child Villiers, *b.* 1976, *s.* 1998, *m.*	Viscount Villiers, *b.* 2015
1822 I.	*Kilmorey (6th)*, Sir Richard Francis Needham, PC, *b.* 1942, *s.* 1977, *m.* (Does not use title)	Viscount Newry and Mourne, *b.* 1966
1866	*Kimberley (5th)*, John Armine Wodehouse, *b.* 1951, *s.* 2002, *m.*	Lord Wodehouse, *b.* 1978
1768 I.	*Kingston (12th)*, Robert Charles Henry King-Tenison, *b.* 1969, *s.* 2002, *m.*	Viscount Kingsborough, *b.* 2000
1633 S.	** *Kinnoull (16th)*, Charles William Harley Hay, *b.* 1962, *s.* 2013, *m.*	Viscount Dupplin, *b.* 2011
1677 S.	*Kintore (14th)*, James William Falconer Keith, *b.* 1976, *s.* 2004, *m.*	Lord Inverurie, *b.* 2010
1624 S.	*Lauderdale (18th)*, Ian Maitland, *b.* 1937, *s.* 2008, *m.*	Viscount Maitland, *b.* 1965
1837	*Leicester (8th)*, Thomas Edward Coke, *b.* 1965, *s.* 2015, *m.*	Viscount Coke, *b.* 2003
1641 S.	*Leven (15th) and Melville (14th) (S. 1690)*, Alexander Ian Leslie Melville, *b.* 1984, *s.* 2012	Hon. Archibald R. L. M., *b.* 1957
1831	*Lichfield (6th)*, Thomas William Robert Hugh Anson, *b.* 1978, *s.* 2005, *m.*	Viscount Anson, *b.* 2011
1803 I.	*Limerick (7th)*, Edmund Christopher Pery, *b.* 1963, *s.* 2003, *m.*	Viscount Glentworth, *b.* 1991
1572	*Lincoln (19th)*, Robert Edward Fiennes-Clinton, *b.* 1972, *s.* 2001	Hon. William J. Howson, *b.* 1980
1633 S.	** *Lindsay (16th)*, James Randolph Lindesay-Bethune, *b.* 1955, *s.* 1989, *m.*	Viscount Garnock, *b.* 1990
1626	*Lindsey (14th) and Abingdon (9th) (1682)*, Richard Henry Rupert Bertie, *b.* 1931, *s.* 1963, *m.*	Lord Norreys, *b.* 1958
1776 I.	*Lisburne (9th)*, David John Francis Malet Vaughan, *b.* 1945, *s.* 2014, *m.*	Hon. Michael J. W. M. V., *b.* 1948
1822 I.	** *Listowel (6th)*, Francis Michael Hare, *b.* 1964, *s.* 1997, *m.*	Hon. Timothy P. H., *b.* 1966
1905	** *Liverpool (5th)*, Edward Peter Bertram Savile Foljambe, *b.* 1944, *s.* 1969, *m.*	Viscount Hawkesbury, *b.* 1972
1945	° *Lloyd George of Dwyfor (4th)*, David Richard Owen Lloyd George, *b.* 1951, *s.* 2010, *m.*	Viscount Gwynedd, *b.* 1986
1785 I.	*Longford (8th)*, Thomas Frank Dermot Pakenham, *b.* 1933, *s.* 2001, *m.* (Does not use title)	Edward M. P., *b.* 1970
1807	*Lonsdale (8th)*, Hugh Clayton Lowther, *b.* 1949, *s.* 2006, *m.*	Hon. William J. L., *b.* 1957
1633 S.	*Loudoun (15th)*, Simon Michael Abney-Hastings, *b.* 1974, *s.* 2012, *m.*	Hon. Marcus W. A.-H., *b.* 1981
1838	*Lovelace (5th)*, Peter Axel William Locke King, *b.* 1951, *s.* 1964, *m.*	None
1795 I.	*Lucan (7th)*, Richard John Bingham, *b.* 1934, *s.* 1964, *m.* (missing since 8 November 1974)	Lord Bingham, *b.* 1967
1880	** *Lytton (5th)*, John Peter Michael Scawen Lytton, *b.* 1950, *s.* 1985, *m.*	Viscount Knebworth, *b.* 1989
1721	*Macclesfield (9th)*, Richard Timothy George Mansfield Parker, *b.* 1943, *s.* 1992, *m.*	Hon. J. David G. P., *b.* 1945
1800	*Malmesbury (7th)*, James Carleton Harris, *b.* 1946, *s.* 2000, *m.*	Viscount FitzHarris, *b.* 1970
1776	*Mansfield and Mansfield (8th) (1792)*, William David Mungo James Murray, *b.* 1930, *s.* 1971, *m.*	Viscount Stormont, *b.* 1956
1565 S.	*Mar (14th) and Kellie (16th) (S. 1616) and Baron Erskine of Alloa Tower (life peerage, 2000)*, James Thorne Erskine, *b.* 1949, *s.* 1994, *m.*	Hon. Alexander D. E., *b.* 1952
1785 I.	*Mayo (11th)*, Charles Diarmuidh John Bourke, *b.* 1953, *s.* 2006, *m.*	Lord Naas, *b.* 1985
1627 I.	*Meath (15th)*, John Anthony Brabazon, *b.* 1941, *s.* 1998, *m.*	Lord Ardee, *b.* 1977
1766 I.	*Mexborough (8th)*, John Christopher George Savile, *b.* 1931, *s.* 1980, *m.*	Viscount Pollington, *b.* 1959
1813	*Minto (7th)*, Gilbert Timothy George Lariston Elliot-Murray-Kynynmound, *b.* 1953, *s.* 2005, *m.*	Viscount Melgund, *b.* 1984
1562 S.	*Moray (21st)*, John Douglas Stuart, *b.* 1966, *s.* 2011, *m.*	Lord Doune, *b.* 2002
1815	*Morley (6th)*, John St Aubyn Parker, KCVO, *b.* 1923, *s.* 1962, *m.*	Viscount Boringdon, *b.* 1956
1458 S.	*Morton (22nd)*, John Charles Sholto Douglas, *b.* 1927, *s.* 1976, *m.*	Lord Aberdour, *b.* 1952
1789	*Mount Edgcumbe (8th)*, Robert Charles Edgcumbe, *b.* 1939, *s.* 1982	Piers V. E., *b.* 1946
1805	° *Nelson (10th)*, Simon John Horatio Nelson, *b.* 1971, *s.* 2009, *m.*	Viscount Merton, *b.* 2010
1660 S.	*Newburgh (12th)*, Don Filippo Giambattista Camillo Francesco Aldo Maria Rospigliosi, *b.* 1942, *s.* 1986, *m.*	Princess Donna Benedetta F. M. R., *b.* 1974
1827 I.	*Norbury (7th)*, Richard James Graham-Toler, *b.* 1967, *s.* 2000	None
1806 I.	*Normanton (6th)*, Shaun James Christian Welbore Ellis Agar, *b.* 1945, *s.* 1967, *m.*	Viscount Somerton, *b.* 1982
1647 S.	*Northesk (15th)*, Patrick Charles Carnegy, *b.* 1940, *s.* 2010	Hon. Colin D. C., *b.* 1942
1801	*Onslow (8th)*, Rupert Charles William Bullard Onslow, *b.* 1967, *s.* 2011, *m.*	Anthony E. E. O., *b.* 1955
1696 S.	*Orkney (9th)*, (Oliver) Peter St John, *b.* 1938, *s.* 1998, *m.*	Viscount Kirkwall, *b.* 1969
1328 I.	*Ormonde and Ossory (I. 1527)*, The 25th/18th Earl (7th Marquess) died in 1988	†Viscount Mountgarret *b.* 1961 (*see* that title)
1925	** *Oxford and Asquith (3rd)*, Raymond Benedict Bartholomew Michael Asquith, OBE, *b.* 1952, *s.* 2011, *m.*	Viscount Asquith, *b.* 1979
1929	° ** *Peel (3rd)*, William James Robert Peel, GCVO, PC, *b.* 1947, *s.* 1969, *m.* Lord Chamberlain	Viscount Clanfield, *b.* 1976
1551	*Pembroke (18th) and Montgomery (15th) (1605)*, William Alexander Sidney Herbert, *b.* 1978, *s.* 2003, *m.*	Lord Herbert *b.* 2012
1605 S.	*Perth (18th)*, John Eric Drummond, *b.* 1935, *s.* 2002, *m.*	Viscount Strathallan, *b.* 1965
1905	*Plymouth (3rd)*, Other Robert Ivor Windsor-Clive, *b.* 1923, *s.* 1943, *m.*	Viscount Windsor, *b.* 1951
1785	*Portarlington (7th)*, George Lionel Yuill Seymour Dawson-Damer, *b.* 1938, *s.* 1959, *m.*	Viscount Carlow, *b.* 1965
1689	*Portland (12th)*, Count Timothy Charles Robert Noel Bentinck, *b.* 1953, *s.* 1997, *m.*	Viscount Woodstock, *b.* 1984

1743	Portsmouth (10th), Quentin Gerard Carew Wallop, b. 1954, s. 1984, m.	Viscount Lymington, b. 1981
1804	Powis (8th), John George Herbert, b. 1952, s. 1993, m.	Viscount Clive, b. 1979
1765	Radnor (9th), William Pleydell-Bouverie, b. 1955, s. 2008, m.	Viscount Folkestone, b. 1999
1831 I.	Ranfurly (7th), Gerald Françoys Needham Knox, b. 1929, s. 1988, m.	Viscount Northland, b. 1957
1771 I.	Roden (10th), Robert John Jocelyn, b. 1938, s. 1993, m.	Viscount Jocelyn, b. 1989
1801	Romney (8th), Julian Charles Marsham, b. 1948, s. 2004, m.	Viscount Marsham, b. 1977
1703 S.	Rosebery (7th), Neil Archibald Primrose, b. 1929, s. 1974, m.	Lord Dalmeny, b. 1967
1806 I.	Rosse (7th), William Brendan Parsons, b. 1936, s. 1979, m.	Lord Oxmantown, b. 1969
1801	** Rosslyn (7th), Peter St Clair-Erskine, CVO, QPM, b. 1958, s. 1977, m.	Lord Loughborough, b. 1986
1457 S.	Rothes (22nd), James Malcolm David Leslie, b. 1958, s. 2005, m.	Hon. Alexander J. L., b. 1962
1861	° Russell (7th), John Francis Russell, b. 1971, s. 2014, m.	None
1915	° St Aldwyn (3rd), Michael Henry Hicks Beach, b. 1950, s. 1992, m.	Hon. David S. H. B., b. 1955
1815	St Germans (10th), Peregrine Nicholas Eliot, b. 1941, s. 1988, m.	Lord Eliot, b. 2004
1660	** Sandwich (11th), John Edward Hollister Montagu, b. 1943, s. 1995, m.	Viscount Hinchingbrooke, b. 1969
1690	Scarbrough (13th), Richard Osbert Lumley, b. 1973, s. 2004, m.	Hon. Thomas H. L., b. 1980
1701 S.	Seafield (13th), Ian Derek Francis Ogilvie-Grant, b. 1939, s. 1969, m.	Viscount Reidhaven, b. 1963
1882	** Selborne (4th), John Roundell Palmer, GBE, b. 1940, s. 1971, m.	Viscount Wolmer, b. 1971
1646 S.	Selkirk (11th), Disclaimed for life 1994 (see Lord Selkirk of Douglas, Life Peers)	Master of Selkirk, b. 1978
1672	Shaftesbury (12th), Nicholas Edmund Anthony Ashley-Cooper, b. 1979, s. 2005, m.	Lord Ashley, b. 2011
1756 I.	Shannon (10th), Richard Henry John Boyle, b. 1960, s. 2013	Robert F. B., b. 1930
1442	** Shrewsbury and Waterford (22nd) (I. 1446), Charles Henry John Benedict Crofton Chetwynd Chetwynd-Talbot, b. 1952, s. 1980, m. Premier Earl of England and Ireland	Viscount Ingestre, b. 1978
1961	Snowdon (1st) and Baron Armstrong-Jones (life peerage, 1999), Antony Charles Robert Armstrong-Jones, GCVO, b. 1930, m.	Viscount Linley, b. 1961
1765	° Spencer (9th), Charles Edward Maurice Spencer, b. 1964, s. 1992, m.	Viscount Althorp, b. 1994
1703 S.	** Stair (14th), John David James Dalrymple, b. 1961, s. 1996, m.	Viscount Dalrymple, b. 2008
1984	Stockton (2nd), Alexander Daniel Alan Macmillan, b. 1943, s. 1986, m.	Viscount Macmillan of Ovenden, b. 1974
1821	Stradbroke (6th), Robert Keith Rous, b. 1937, s. 1983, m.	Viscount Dunwich, b. 1961
1847	Strafford (8th), Thomas Edmund Byng, b. 1936, s. 1984, m.	Viscount Enfield, b. 1964
1606 S.	Strathmore and Kinghorne (18th) (S. 1677), Michael Fergus Bowes Lyon, b. 1957, s. 1987, m.	Lord Glamis, b. 1986
1603	Suffolk (21st) and Berkshire (14th) (1626), Michael John James George Robert Howard, b. 1935, s. 1941, m.	Viscount Andover, b. 1974
1955	Swinton (3rd), Nicholas John Cunliffe-Lister, b. 1939, s. 2006, m.	Lord Masham b. 1970
1714	Tankerville (10th), Peter Grey Bennet, b. 1956, s. 1980	Adrian G. B., b. 1958
1822	° Temple of Stowe (9th), James Grenville Temple-Gore-Langton, b. 1955, s. 2013, m.	Hon. Robert C. T.-G.-L., b. 1957
1815	Verulam (7th), John Duncan Grimston, b. 1951, s. 1973, m.	Viscount Grimston, b. 1978
1729	° Waldegrave (13th), James Sherbrooke Waldegrave, b. 1940, s. 1995, m.	Viscount Chewton, b. 1986
1759	Warwick (9th) and Brooke (9th) (1746), Guy David Greville, b. 1957, s. 1996, m.	Lord Brooke, b. 1982
1633 S.	Wemyss (13th) and March (9th) (S. 1697), James Donald Charteris, b. 1948, s. 2008, m.	Lord Elcho, b. 1984
1621 I.	Westmeath (13th), William Anthony Nugent, b. 1928, s. 1971, m.	Sean C. W. N., b. 1965
1624	Westmorland (16th), Anthony David Francis Henry Fane, b. 1951, s. 1993, m.	Hon. Harry St C. F., b. 1953
1876	Wharncliffe (5th), Richard Alan Montagu Stuart Wortley, b. 1953, s. 1987, m.	Viscount Carlton, b. 1980
1801	Wilton (8th), Francis Egerton Grosvenor, b. 1934, s. 1999, m.	Viscount Grey de Wilton, b. 1959
1628	Winchilsea (17th) and Nottingham (12th) (1681), Daniel James Hatfield Finch Hatton, b. 1967, s. 1999, m.	Viscount Maidstone, b. 1998
1766 I.	° Winterton (8th), (Donald) David Turnour, b. 1943, s. 1991, m.	Robert C. T., b. 1950
1956	Woolton (3rd), Simon Frederick Marquis, b. 1958, s. 1969, m.	None
1837	Yarborough (8th), Charles John Pelham, b. 1963, s. 1991, m.	Lord Worsley, b. 1990

COUNTESSES IN THEIR OWN RIGHT

Style, The Rt. Hon. the Countess (of) _
    Envelope (formal), The Rt. Hon. the Countess (of) _; *(social),* The Countess (of) _. *Letter (formal),* Madam; *(social),*
    Lady _. *Spoken (formal),* Madam; *(social),* Lady _.
Husband, Untitled
Children's style, As for children of an Earl

Created	Title, order of succession, name, etc	Heir
c.1115 S.	** *Mar (31st),* Margaret of Mar, *b.* 1940, *s.* 1975, *m.* Premier Earldom of Scotland	Mistress of Mar, *b.* 1963
1947	° *Mountbatten of Burma (2nd),* Patricia Edwina Victoria Knatchbull, CBE, *b.* 1924, *s.* 1979, *w.*	Lord Romsey, (*also* Lord Brabourne (8th) *see* that title)
c.1235 S.	*Sutherland (24th),* Elizabeth Millicent Sutherland, *b.* 1921, *s.* 1963, *w.*	Lord Strathnaver, *b.* 1947

VISCOUNTS

Coronet, Sixteen silver balls

Style, The Rt. Hon. the Viscount _
    Envelope (formal), The Rt. Hon. the Viscount _; *(social),* The Viscount _. *Letter (formal),* My Lord; *(social),* Dear Lord
    _. *Spoken,* Lord _.
Wife's style, The Rt. Hon. the Viscountess _
    Envelope (formal), The Rt. Hon. the Viscountess _; *(social),* The Viscountess _. *Letter (formal),* Madam; *(social),* Dear
    Lady _. *Spoken,* Lady _.
Children's style, 'The Hon.' before forename and surname, as for Baron's children
In Scotland, the heir apparent to a Viscount may be styled 'The Master of _ (title of peer)'

Created	Title, order of succession, name, etc	Heir
1945	*Addison (4th),* William Matthew Wand Addison, *b.* 1945, *s.* 1992, *m.*	Hon. Paul W. A., *b.* 1973
1946	*Alanbrooke (3rd),* Alan Victor Harold Brooke, *b.* 1932, *s.* 1972	None
1919	*Allenby (4th),* Henry Jaffray Hynman Allenby, *b.* 1968, *s.* 2014, *m.*	Hon. Harry M. E. A., *b.* 2000
1911	*Allendale (4th),* Wentworth Peter Ismay Beaumont, *b.* 1948, *s.* 2002, *m.*	Hon. Wentworth A. I. B., *b.* 1979
1642 S.	*of Arbuthnott (17th),* John Keith Oxley Arbuthnott, *b.* 1950, *s.* 2012, *m.*	Master of Arbuthnott, *b.* 1977
1751 I.	*Ashbrook (11th),* Michael Llowarch Warburton Flower, *b.* 1935, *s.* 1995, *m.*	Hon. Rowland F. W. F., *b.* 1975
1917	** *Astor (4th),* William Waldorf Astor, *b.* 1951, *s.* 1966, *m.*	Hon. William W. A., *b.* 1979
1781 I.	*Bangor (8th),* William Maxwell David Ward, *b.* 1948, *s.* 1993, *m.*	Hon. E. Nicholas W., *b.* 1953
1925	*Bearsted (5th),* Nicholas Alan Samuel, *b.* 1950, *s.* 1996, *m.*	Hon. Harry R. S., *b.* 1988
1963	*Blakenham (2nd),* Michael John Hare, *b.* 1938, *s.* 1982, *m.*	Hon. Caspar J. H., *b.* 1972
1935	*Bledisloe (4th),* Rupert Edward Ludlow Bathurst, *b.* 1964, *s.* 2009, *m.*	Hon. Benjamin B., *b.* 2004
1712	*Bolingbroke (9th) and St John (10th) (1716),* Nicholas Alexander Mowbray St John, *b.* 1974, *s.* 2011, *m.*	German A. St J., *b.* 1980
1960	*Boyd of Merton (2nd),* Simon Donald Rupert Neville Lennox-Boyd, *b.* 1939, *s.* 1983, *m.*	Hon. Benjamin A. L.-B., *b.* 1964
1717 I.	*Boyne (11th),* Gustavus Michael Stucley Hamilton-Russell, *b.* 1965, *s.* 1995, *m.*	Hon. Gustavus A. E. H.-R., *b.* 1999
1929	*Brentford (4th),* Crispin William Joynson-Hicks, *b.* 1933, *s.* 1983, *m.*	Hon. Paul W. J.-H., MBE, *b.* 1971
1929	** *Bridgeman (3rd),* Robin John Orlando Bridgeman, *b.* 1930, *s.* 1982, *m.*	Hon. Luke R. O. B., *b.* 1971
1868	*Bridport (4th) and 7th Duke, Bronte in Sicily, 1799,* Alexander Nelson Hood, *b.* 1948, *s.* 1969, *m.*	Hon. Peregrine A. N. H., *b.* 1974
1952	** *Brookeborough (3rd),* Alan Henry Brooke, *b.* 1952, *s.* 1987, *m.*	Hon. Christopher A. B., *b.* 1954
1933	*Buckmaster (4th),* Adrian Charles Buckmaster, *b.* 1949, *s.* 2007, *m.*	Hon. Andrew N. B., *b.* 1980
1939	*Caldecote (3rd),* Piers James Hampden Inskip, *b.* 1947, *s.* 1999, *m.*	Hon. Thomas J. H. I., *b.* 1985
1941	*Camrose (4th),* Adrian Michael Berry, *b.* 1937, *s.* 2001, *m.*	Hon. Jonathan W. B., *b.* 1970
1954	*Chandos (3rd) and Baron Lyttelton of Aldershot (life peerage, 2000),* Thomas Orlando Lyttelton, *b.* 1953, *s.* 1980, *m.*	Hon. Oliver A. L., *b.* 1986

1665 I.	*Charlemont (15th),* John Dodd Caulfeild, *b.* 1966, *s.* 2001, *m.*	Hon. Shane A. C., *b.* 1996
1921	*Chelmsford (4th)* Frederic Corin Piers Thesiger, *b.* 1962, *s.* 1999, *m.*	Hon. Frederic T. *b.* 2006
1717 I.	*Chetwynd (11th),* Adam Douglas Chetwynd, *b.* 1969, *s.* 2015, *m.*	Hon. Connor A. C., *b.* 2011
1911	*Chilston (4th),* Alastair George Akers-Douglas, *b.* 1946, *s.* 1982, *m.*	Hon. Oliver I. A.-D., *b.* 1973
1902	*Churchill (3rd) and 5th UK Baron Churchill (1815),* Victor George Spencer, OBE, *b.* 1934, *s.* 1973	To Barony only, Richard H. R. S., *b.* 1926
1718	*Cobham (12th),* Christopher Charles Lyttelton, *b.* 1947, *s.* 2006, *m.*	Hon. Oliver C. L., *b.* 1976
1902	** *Colville of Culross (5th),* Charles Mark Townshend Colville, *b.* 1959, *s.* 2010	Master of Colville, *b.* 1961
1826	*Combermere (6th),* Thomas Robert Wellington Stapleton-Cotton, *b.* 1969, *s.* 2000, *m.*	Hon. Laszlo M. W. S.-C., *b.* 2010
1917	*Cowdray (4th),* Michael Orlando Weetman Pearson, *b.* 1944, *s.* 1995, *m.*	Hon. Peregrine J. D. P., *b.* 1994
1927	** *Craigavon (3rd),* Janric Fraser Craig, *b.* 1944, *s.* 1974	None
1943	*Daventry (4th),* James Edward FitzRoy Newdegate, *b.* 1960, *s.* 2000, *m.*	Hon. Humphrey J. F. N., *b.* 1995
1937	*Davidson (3rd),* Malcolm William Mackenzie Davidson, *b.* 1934, *s.* 2012, *m.*	Hon. John N. A. D., *b.* 1971
1956	*De L'Isle (2nd),* Philip John Algernon Sidney, MBE, *b.* 1945, *s.* 1991, *m.*	Hon. Philip W. E. S., *b.* 1985
1776 I.	*de Vesci (7th),* Thomas Eustace Vesey, *b.* 1955, *s.* 1983, *m.*	Hon. Oliver I. V., *b.* 1991
1917	*Devonport (3rd),* Terence Kearley, *b.* 1944, *s.* 1973, *m.*	Chester D. H. K., *b.* 1932
1964	*Dilhorne (2nd),* John Mervyn Manningham-Buller, *b.* 1932, *s.* 1980, *m.*	Hon. James E. M.-B., *b.* 1956
1622 I.	*Dillon (22nd),* Henry Benedict Charles Dillon, *b.* 1973, *s.* 1982	Thomas A. L. D., *b.* 1983
1785 I.	*Doneraile (10th),* Richard Allen St Leger, *b.* 1946, *s.* 1983, *m.*	Hon. Nathaniel W. R. St J. St L., *b.* 1971
1680 I.	*Downe (12th),* Richard Henry Dawnay, *b.* 1967, *s.* 2002	Thomas P. D., *b.* 1978
1959	*Dunrossil (3rd),* Andrew William Reginald Morrison, *b.* 1953, *s.* 2000, *m.*	Hon. Callum A. B. M., *b.* 1994
1964	** *Eccles (2nd),* John Dawson Eccles, CBE, *b.* 1931, *s.* 1999, *m.*	Hon. William D. E., *b.* 1960
1897	*Esher (5th),* Christopher Lionel Baliol Brett, *b.* 1936, *s.* 2004, *m.*	Hon. Matthew C. A. B., *b.* 1963
1816	*Exmouth (10th),* Paul Edward Pellew, *b.* 1940, *s.* 1970, *m.*	Hon. Edward F. P., *b.* 1978
1620 S.	** *of Falkland (15th),* Lucius Edward William Plantagenet Cary, *b.* 1935, *s.* 1984, *m. Premier Scottish Viscount on the Roll*	Master of Falkland, *b.* 1963
1720	*Falmouth (9th),* George Hugh Boscawen, *b.* 1919, *s.* 1962, *w.*	Hon. Evelyn A. H. B., *b.* 1955
1720 I.	*Gage (8th),* (Henry) Nicolas Gage, *b.* 1934, *s.* 1993, *m.*	Hon. Henry W. G., *b.* 1975
1727 I.	*Galway (12th),* George Rupert Monckton-Arundell, *b.* 1922, *s.* 1980, *m.*	Hon. J. Philip M., *b.* 1952
1478 I.	*Gormanston (17th),* Jenico Nicholas Dudley Preston, *b.* 1939, *s.* 1940, *m. Premier Viscount of Ireland*	Hon. Jenico F. T. P., *b.* 1974
1816 I.	*Gort (9th),* Foley Robert Standish Prendergast Vereker, *b.* 1951, *s.* 1995, *m.*	Hon. Robert F. P. V., *b.* 1993
1900	** *Goschen (4th),* Giles John Harry Goschen, *b.* 1965, *s.* 1977, *m.*	Hon. Alexander J. E. G., *b.* 2001
1849	*Gough (5th),* Shane Hugh Maryon Gough, *b.* 1941, *s.* 1951	None
1929	*Hailsham (3rd) and Baron Hogg (life peerage, 2015),* Douglas Martin Hogg, PC, QC, *b.* 1945, *s.* 2001, *m.*	Hon. Quintin J. N. M. H., *b.* 1973
1891	*Hambleden (5th),* William Henry Bernard Smith, *b.* 1955, *s.* 2012, *m.*	Hon. Bernardo J. S., *b.* 1957
1884	*Hampden (7th),* Francis Anthony Brand, *b.* 1970, *s.* 2008, *m.*	Hon. Lucian A. B., *b.* 2005
1936	** *Hanworth (3rd),* David Stephen Geoffrey Pollock, *b.* 1946, *s.* 1996, *m.*	Harold W. C. P., *b.* 1988
1791 I.	*Harberton (11th),* Henry Robert Pomeroy, *b.* 1958, *s.* 2004, *m.*	Hon. Patrick C. P., *b.* 1995
1846	*Hardinge (8th),* Thomas Henry de Montarville Hardinge, *b.* 1993, *s.* 2014	Hon. Jamie A. D. H., *b.* 1996
1791 I.	*Hawarden (9th),* (Robert) Connan Wyndham Leslie Maude, *b.* 1961, *s.* 1991, *m.*	Hon. Varian J. C. E. M., *b.* 1997
1960	*Head (2nd),* Richard Antony Head, *b.* 1937, *s.* 1983, *m.*	Hon. Henry J. H., *b.* 1980
1550	*Hereford (19th),* Charles Robin De Bohun Devereux, *b.* 1975, *s.* 2004, *m. Premier Viscount of England*	Hon. Henry W. de B. D., *b.* 2015
1842	*Hill (9th),* Peter David Raymond Charles Clegg-Hill, *b.* 1945, *s.* 2003, *m.*	Hon. Michael C. D. C.-H., *b.* 1988
1796	*Hood (8th),* Henry Lyttleton Alexander Hood, *b.* 1958, *s.* 1999, *m.*	Hon. Archibald L. S. H., *b.* 1993
1945	*Kemsley (3rd),* Richard Gomer Berry, *b.* 1951, *s.* 1999, *m.*	Hon. Luke G. B., *b.* 1998
1911	*Knollys (3rd),* David Francis Dudley Knollys, *b.* 1931, *s.* 1966, *m.*	Hon. Patrick N. M. K., *b.* 1962
1895	*Knutsford (6th),* Michael Holland-Hibbert, *b.* 1926, *s.* 1986, *m.*	Hon. Henry T. H.-H., *b.* 1959
1954	*Leathers (3rd),* Christopher Graeme Leathers, *b.* 1941, *s.* 1996, *m.*	Hon. James F. L., *b.* 1969
1781 I.	*Lifford (9th),* (Edward) James Wingfield Hewitt, *b.* 1949, *s.* 1987, *m.*	Hon. James T. W. H., *b.* 1979
1921	*Long (4th),* Richard Gerard Long, CBE, *b.* 1929, *s.* 1967, *m.*	Hon. James R. L., *b.* 1960
1957	*Mackintosh of Halifax (3rd),* (John) Clive Mackintosh, *b.* 1958, *s.* 1980, *m.*	Hon. Thomas H. G. M., *b.* 1985
1955	*Malvern (3rd),* Ashley Kevin Godfrey Huggins, *b.* 1949, *s.* 1978	Hon. M. James H., *b.* 1928
1945	*Marchwood (3rd),* David George Staveley Penny, *b.* 1936, *s.* 1979, *w.*	Hon. Peter G. W. P., *b.* 1965
1942	*Margesson (3rd),* Richard Francis David Margesson, *b.* 1960, *s.* 2014, *m.*	None
1660 I.	*Massereene (14th) and Ferrard (7th) (I. 1797),* John David Clotworthy Whyte-Melville Foster Skeffington, *b.* 1940, *s.* 1992, *m.*	Hon. Charles J. C. W.-M. F. S., *b.* 1973
1802	*Melville (10th),* Robert Henry Kirkpatrick Dundas, *b.* 1984, *s.* 2011	Hon. James D. B. D., *b.* 1986
1916	*Mersey (5th) and 14th Lord Nairne (S. 1681),* Edward John Hallam Bigham, *b.* 1966, *s.* 2006, *m.*	Hon. David E. H. B., *b.* 1938 (to Viscountcy); Mistress of Nairne, *b.* 2003 (to Lordship of Nairne)

1717 I.	*Midleton (12th)*, Alan Henry Brodrick, *b.* 1949, *s.* 1988, *m.*	Hon. Ashley R. B., *b.* 1980
1962	*Mills (3rd)*, Christopher Philip Roger Mills, *b.* 1956, *s.* 1988, *m.*	None
1716 I.	*Molesworth (12th)*, Robert Bysse Kelham Molesworth, *b.* 1959, *s.* 1997	Hon. William J. C. M., *b.* 1960
1801 I.	*Monck (7th)*, Charles Stanley Monck, *b.* 1953, *s.* 1982 (Does not use title)	Hon. George S. M., *b.* 1957
1957	*Monckton of Brenchley (3rd)*, Christopher Walter Monckton, *b.* 1952, *s.* 2006, *m.*	Hon. Timothy D. R. M., *b.* 1955
1946	*Montgomery of Alamein (2nd)*, David Bernard Montgomery, CMG, CBE, *b.* 1928, *s.* 1976, *m.*	Hon. Henry D. M., *b.* 1954
1550 I.	*Mountgarret (18th)*, Piers James Richard Butler, *b.* 1961, *s.* 2004, *m.*	Hon. Edmund H. R. B., *b.* 1962
1952	*Norwich (2nd)*, John Julius Cooper, CVO, *b.* 1929, *s.* 1954, *m.*	Hon. Jason C. D. B. C., *b.* 1959
1651 S.	*of Oxfuird (14th)*, Ian Arthur Alexander Makgill, *b.* 1969, *s.* 2003, *m.*	Master of Oxfuird, *b.* 2012
1873	*Portman (10th)*, Christopher Edward Berkeley Portman, *b.* 1958, *s.* 1999, *m.*	Hon. Luke O. B. P., *b.* 1984
1743 I.	*Powerscourt (11th)*, Mervyn Anthony Wingfield, *b.* 1963, *s.* 2015, *m.*	Hon. Guy C. P. W., *b.* 1940
1900	** *Ridley (5th)*, Matthew White Ridley, *b.* 1958, *s.* 2012, *m.*	Hon. Matthew W. R., *b.* 1993
1960	*Rochdale (3rd)*, Jonathan Hugo Durival Kemp, *b.* 1961, *s.* 2015, *m.*	George T. K., *b.* 2001
1919	*Rothermere (4th)*, (Harold) Jonathan Esmond Vere Harmsworth, *b.* 1967, *s.* 1998, *m.*	Hon. Vere R. J. H. H., *b.* 1994
1937	*Runciman of Doxford (3rd)*, Walter Garrison Runciman (Garry), CBE, *b.* 1934, *s.* 1989, *m.*	Hon. David W. R., *b.* 1967
1918	*St Davids (4th)*, Rhodri Colwyn Philipps, *b.* 1966, *s.* 2009, *m.*	Hon. Roland A. J. E. P., *b.* 1970
1801	*St Vincent (8th)*, Edward Robert James Jervis, *b.* 1951, *s.* 2006, *m.*	Hon. James R. A. J., *b.* 1982
1937	*Samuel (5th)*, Jonathan Herbert Samuel, *b.* 1965, *s.* 2014, *m.*	Hon. Benjamin A. S., *b.* 1983
1911	*Scarsdale (4th)*, Peter Ghislain Nathaniel Curzon, *b.* 1949, *s.* 2000, *m.*	Hon. David J. N. C., *b.* 1958
1905	*Selby (6th)*, Christopher Rolf Thomas Gully, *b.* 1993, *s.* 2001	Hon. (James) Edward H. G. G., *b.* 1945
1805	*Sidmouth (8th)*, Jeremy Francis Addington, *b.* 1947, *s.* 2005, *w.*	Hon. John A., *b.* 1990
1940	** *Simon (3rd)*, Jan David Simon, *b.* 1940, *s.* 1993, *m.*	None
1960	** *Slim (2nd)*, John Douglas Slim, OBE, *b.* 1927, *s.* 1970, *m.*	Hon. Mark W. R. S., *b.* 1960
1954	*Soulbury (4th)*, Oliver Peter Ramsbotham, *b.* 1943, *s.* 2010, *m.*	Hon. Edward H. R., *b.* 1966
1776 I.	*Southwell (7th)*, Pyers Anthony Joseph Southwell, *b.* 1930, *s.* 1960, *m.*	Hon. Richard A. P. S., *b.* 1956
1942	*Stansgate (3rd)*, Stephen Michael Wedgwood Benn, *b.* 1951, *s.* 2014, *m.*	Hon. Daniel J. W. B., *b.* 1991
1959	*Stuart of Findhorn (3rd)*, Dominic Stuart, *b.* 1948, *s.* 1999, *m.*	Hon. Andrew M. S., *b.* 1957
1957	*Tenby (3rd)*, William Lloyd George, *b.* 1927, *s.* 1983, *m.*	Hon. Timothy H. G. L. G., *b.* 1962
1952	*Thurso (3rd)*, John Archibald Sinclair, PC, *b.* 1953, *s.* 1995, *m.*	Hon. James A. R. S., *b.* 1984
1721	*Torrington (11th)*, Timothy Howard St George Byng, *b.* 1943, *s.* 1961, *m.*	Colin H. Cranmer-Byng, *b.* 1960
1936	** *Trenchard (3rd)*, Hugh Trenchard, *b.* 1951, *s.* 1987, *m.*	Hon. Alexander T. T., *b.* 1978
1921	** *Ullswater (2nd)*, Nicholas James Christopher Lowther, LVO, PC, *b.* 1942, *s.* 1949, *m.*	Hon. Benjamin J. L., *b.* 1975
1642 I.	*Valentia (16th)*, Frances William Dighton Annesley, *b.* 1959, *s.* 2005, *m.*	Hon. Peter J. A., *b.* 1967
1952	** *Waverley (3rd)*, John Desmond Forbes Anderson, *b.* 1949, *s.* 1990, *m.*	Hon. Forbes A. R. A., *b.* 1996
1938	*Weir (3rd)*, William Kenneth James Weir, *b.* 1933, *s.* 1975, *m.*	Hon. James W. H. W., *b.* 1965
1918	*Wimborne (4th)*, Ivor Mervyn Vigors Guest, *b.* 1968, *s.* 1993	Hon. Julian J. G., *b.* 1945
1923	** *Younger of Leckie (5th)*, James Edward George Younger, *b.* 1955, *s.* 2003, *m.*	Hon. Alexander W. G. Y., *b.* 1993

BARONS/LORDS

Coronet, Six silver balls

Style, The Rt. Hon. the Lord _
 Envelope (formal), The Rt. Hon. Lord _; *(social)*, The Lord _. *Letter (formal)*, My Lord; *(social)*, Dear Lord _. *Spoken*, Lord _.
In the Peerage of Scotland there is no rank of Baron; the equivalent rank is Lord of Parliament and Scottish peers should always be styled 'Lord', never 'Baron'.
Wife's style, The Rt. Hon. the Lady _
 Envelope (formal), The Rt. Hon. Lady _; *(social)*, The Lady _. *Letter (formal)*, My Lady; *(social)*, Dear Lady _. *Spoken*, Lady _
Children's style, 'The Hon.' before forename (F_) and surname (S_)
 Envelope, The Hon. F_ S_. *Letter*, Dear Mr/Miss/Mrs S_. *Spoken*, Mr/Miss/Mrs S_
In Scotland, the heir apparent to a Lord may be styled 'The Master of _ (title of peer)'

Created	*Title, order of succession, name, etc*	*Heir*
1911	*Aberconway (4th)*, (Henry) Charles McLaren, *b.* 1948, *s.* 2003, *m.*	Hon. Charles S. M., *b.* 1984
1873	** *Aberdare (5th)*, Alastair John Lyndhurst Bruce, *b.* 1947, *s.* 2005, *m.*	Hon. Hector M. N. B., *b.* 1974

1835	*Abinger (9th)*, James Harry Scarlett, *b.* 1959, *s.* 2002, *m.*	Hon. Peter R. S., *b.* 1961
1869	*Acton (5th)*, John Charles Ferdinand Harold Lyon-Dalberg-Acton, *b.* 1966, *s.* 2010, *m.*	Hon. John C. L.-D.-A., *b.* 1943
1887	** *Addington (6th)*, Dominic Bryce Hubbard, *b.* 1963, *s.* 1982, *m.*	Hon. Michael W. L. H., *b.* 1965
1896	*Aldenham (6th) and Hunsdon of Hunsdon (4th) (1923)*, Vicary Tyser Gibbs, *b.* 1948, *s.* 1986, *m.*	Hon. Humphrey W. F. G., *b.* 1989
1962	*Aldington (2nd)*, Charles Harold Stuart Low, *b.* 1948, *s.* 2000, *m.*	Hon. Philip T. A. L., *b.* 1990
1945	*Altrincham (3rd)*, Anthony Ulick David Dundas Grigg, *b.* 1934, *s.* 2001, *m.*	Hon. (Edward) Sebastian G., *b.* 1965
1929	*Alvingham (2nd)*, Maj.-Gen. Robert Guy Eardley Yerburgh, CBE, *b.* 1926, *s.* 1955, *m.*	Capt. Hon. Robert R. G. Y., *b.* 1956
1892	*Amherst of Hackney (5th)*, Hugh William Amherst Cecil, *b.* 1968, *s.* 2009, *m.*	Hon. Jack W. A. C., *b.* 2001
1881	*Ampthill (5th)*, David Whitney Erskine Russell, *b.* 1947, *s.* 2011, *m.*	Hon. Anthony J. M. R., *b.* 1952
1947	*Amwell (3rd)*, Keith Norman Montague, *b.* 1943, *s.* 1990, *m.*	Hon. Ian K. M., *b.* 1973
1863	*Annaly (6th)*, Luke Richard White, *b.* 1954, *s.* 1990, *m.*	Hon. Luke H. W., *b.* 1990
1885	*Ashbourne (4th)*, Edward Barry Greynville Gibson, *b.* 1933, *s.* 1983, *m.*	Hon. Edward C. d'O. G., *b.* 1967
1835	*Ashburton (7th)*, John Francis Harcourt Baring, KG, KCVO, *b.* 1928, *s.* 1991, *m.*	Hon. Mark F. R. B., *b.* 1958
1892	*Ashcombe (5th)*, Mark Edward Cubitt, *b.* 1964, *s.* 2013, *m.*	Hon. Richard R. A. C., *b.* 1995
1911	** *Ashton of Hyde (4th)*, Thomas Henry Ashton, *b.* 1958, *s.* 2008, *m.*	Hon. John E. A., *b.* 1966
1800 I.	*Ashtown (8th)*, Roderick Nigel Godolphin Trench, *b.* 1944, *s.* 2010, *m.*	Hon. Timothy R. H. T., *b.* 1968
1956	** *Astor of Hever (3rd)*, John Jacob Astor, PC, *b.* 1946, *s.* 1984, *m.*	Hon. Charles G. J. A., *b.* 1990
1789 I.	*Auckland (10th) and Auckland (10th) (1793)*, Robert Ian Burnard Eden, *b.* 1962, *s.* 1997, *m.*	Henry V. E., *b.* 1958
1313	*Audley,* Barony in abeyance between three co-heiresses since 1997	
1900	** *Avebury (4th)*, Eric Reginald Lubbock, *b.* 1928, *s.* 1971, *m.*	Hon. Lyulph A. J. L., *b.* 1954
1718 I.	*Aylmer (14th)*, (Anthony) Julian Aylmer, *b.* 1951, *s.* 2006, *m.*	Hon. Michael H. A., *b.* 1991
1929	*Baden-Powell (3rd)*, Robert Crause Baden-Powell, *b.* 1936, *s.* 1962, *w.*	Hon. David M. B.-P., *b.* 1940
1780	*Bagot (10th)*, (Charles Hugh) Shaun Bagot, *b.* 1944, *s.* 2001, *m.*	Richard C. V. B., *b.* 1941
1953	*Baillieu (3rd)*, James William Latham Baillieu, *b.* 1950, *s.* 1973, *m.*	Hon. Robert L. B., *b.* 1979
1607 S.	*Balfour of Burleigh (8th)*, Robert Bruce, *b.* 1927, *s.* 1967, *m.*	Hon. Victoria B., *b.* 1973
1924	*Banbury of Southam (3rd)*, Charles William Banbury, *b.* 1953, *s.* 1981, *m.*	None
1698	*Barnard (11th)*, Harry John Neville Vane, TD, *b.* 1923, *s.* 1964	Hon. Henry F. C. V., *b.* 1959
1887	*Basing (6th)*, Stuart Anthony Whitfield Sclater-Booth, *b.* 1969, *s.* 2007, *m.*	Hon. Luke W. S.-B., *b.* 2000
1917	*Beaverbrook (3rd)*, Maxwell William Humphrey Aitken, *b.* 1951, *s.* 1985, *m.*	Hon. Maxwell F. A., *b.* 1977
1647 S.	*Belhaven and Stenton (13th)*, Robert Anthony Carmichael Hamilton, *b.* 1927, *s.* 1961, *m.*	Master of Belhaven, *b.* 1953
1848 I.	*Bellew (8th)*, Bryan Edward Bellew, *b.* 1943, *s.* 2010, *m.*	Hon. Anthony R. B. B., *b.* 1972
1856	*Belper (5th)*, Richard Henry Strutt, *b.* 1941, *s.* 1999, *m.*	Hon. Michael H. S., *b.* 1969
1421	*Berkeley (18th) and Gueterbock (life peerage, 2000)*, Anthony Fitzhardinge Gueterbock, OBE, *b.* 1939, *s.* 1992, *m.*	Hon. Thomas F. G., *b.* 1969
1922	*Bethell (5th)*, James Nicholas Bethell, *b.* 1967, *s.* 2007, *m.*	Hon. Jacob N. D. B., *b.* 2006
1938	*Bicester (4th)*, Hugh Charles Vivian Smith, *b.* 1934, *s.* 2014	Charles J. V. S., *b.* 1963
1903	*Biddulph (5th)*, (Anthony) Nicholas Colin Maitland Biddulph, *b.* 1959, *s.* 1988, *m.*	Hon. Robert J. M. B., *b.* 1994
1958	*Birkett (3rd)*, Thomas Birkett, *b.* 1982, *s.* 2015	None
1907	*Blyth (5th)*, James Audley Ian Blyth, *b.* 1970, *s.* 2009, *m.*	Hon. Hugo A. J. B., *b.* 2006
1797	*Bolton (8th)*, Harry Algar Nigel Orde-Powlett, *b.* 1954, *s.* 2001, *m.*	Hon. Thomas O.-P., MC, *b.* 1979
1452 S.	*Borthwick (24th)*, John Hugh Borthwick, *b.* 1940, *s.* 1996, *m.*	Hon. James H. A. B. of Glengelt, *b.* 1940
1922	** *Borwick (5th)*, (Geoffrey Robert) James Borwick, *b.* 1955, *s.* 2007, *m.*	Hon. Edwin D. W. B., *b.* 1984
1761	*Boston (11th)*, George William Eustace Boteler Irby, *b.* 1971, *s.* 2007, *m.*	Hon. Thomas W. G. B. I., *b.* 1999
1942	** *Brabazon of Tara (3rd)*, Ivon Anthony Moore-Brabazon, PC, *b.* 1946, *s.* 1974, *m.*	Hon. Benjamin R. M.-B., *b.* 1983
1880	*Brabourne (8th)*, Norton Louis Philip Knatchbull, *b.* 1947, *s.* 2005, *m.* (*also* Lord Romsey heir to Countess Mountbatten of Burma, *see* that title)	Hon. Nicholas L. C. N. K., *b.* 1981
1925	*Bradbury (3rd)*, John Bradbury, *b.* 1940, *s.* 1994, *m.*	Hon. John B., *b.* 1973
1962	*Brain (3rd)*, Michael Cottrell Brain, *b.* 1928, *s.* 2014, *m.*	Hon. Thomas R. B., *b.* 1965
1938	*Brassey of Apethorpe (4th)*, Edward Brassey, *b.* 1964, *s.* 2015, *m.*	Hon. Christian B., *b.* 2003
1788	*Braybrooke (10th)*, Robin Henry Charles Neville, *b.* 1932, *s.* 1990, *m.*	Richard R. N., *b.* 1977
1957	** *Bridges (2nd)*, Thomas Edward Bridges, GCMG, *b.* 1927, *s.* 1969, *m.*	Hon. Mark T. B., CVO, *b.* 1954
1945	*Broadbridge (4th)*, Martin Hugh Broadbridge, *b.* 1929, *s.* 2000, *w.*	Hon. Richard J. M. B., *b.* 1959
1933	*Brocket (3rd)*, Charles Ronald George Nall-Cain, *b.* 1952, *s.* 1967, *w.*	Hon. Alexander C. C. N.-C., *b.* 1984
1860	** *Brougham and Vaux (5th)*, Michael John Brougham, CBE, *b.* 1938, *s.* 1967	Hon. Charles W. B., *b.* 1971
1776	*Brownlow (7th)*, Edward John Peregrine Cust, *b.* 1936, *s.* 1978, *m.*	Hon. Peregrine E. Q. C., *b.* 1974
1942	*Bruntisfield (3rd)*, Michael John Victor Warrender, *b.* 1949, *s.* 2007, *m.*	Hon. John M. P. C. W., *b.* 1996

1950	*Burden (4th),* Fraser William Elsworth Burden, *b.* 1964, *s.* 2000, *m.*	Hon. Ian S. B., *b.* 1967
1529	*Burgh (8th),* (Alexander) Gregory Disney Leith, *b.* 1958, *s.* 2001, *m.*	Hon. Alexander J. S. L., *b.* 1986
1903	*Burnham (7th),* Harry Frederick Alan Lawson, *b.* 1968, *s.* 2005	None
1897	*Burton (4th),* Evan Michael Ronald Baillie, *b.* 1949, *s.* 2013, *m.*	Hon. James E. B., *b.* 1975
1643	*Byron (13th),* Robert James Byron, *b.* 1950, *s.* 1989, *m.*	Hon. Charles R. G. B., *b.* 1990
1937	*Cadman (3rd),* John Anthony Cadman, *b.* 1938, *s.* 1966, *m.*	Hon. Nicholas A. J. C., *b.* 1977
1945	*Calverley (3rd),* Charles Rodney Muff, *b.* 1946, *s.* 1971	Hon. Jonathan E. Brown, *b.* 1975
1383	*Camoys (7th),* (Ralph) Thomas Campion George Sherman Stonor, GCVO, PC, *b.* 1940, *s.* 1976, *m.*	Hon. R. William R. T. S., *b.* 1974
1715 I.	*Carbery (12th),* Michael Peter Evans-Freke, *b.* 1942, *s.* 2012, *m.*	Hon. Dominic R. C. E.-F., *b.* 1969
1834 I.	*Carew (7th) and Carew (7th) (1838),* Patrick Thomas Conolly-Carew, *b.* 1938, *s.* 1994, *m.*	Hon. William P. C.-C., *b.* 1973
1916	*Carnock (5th),* Adam Nicolson, *b.* 1957, *s.* 2008, *m.*	Hon. Thomas N., *b.* 1984
1796 I.	*Carrington (6th) and Carrington (6th) (1797) and Carington of Upton (life peerage, 1999),* Peter Alexander Rupert Carington, KG, GCMG, CH, MC, PC, *b.* 1919, *s.* 1938, *w.*	Hon. Rupert F. J. C., *b.* 1948
1812 I.	*Castlemaine (8th),* Roland Thomas John Handcock, MBE, *b.* 1943, *s.* 1973, *m.*	Hon. Ronan M. E. H., *b.* 1989
1936	*Catto (3rd),* Innes Gordon Catto, *b.* 1950, *s.* 2001, *m.*	Hon. Alexander G. C., *b.* 1952
1918	*Cawley (4th),* John Francis Cawley, *b.* 1946, *s.* 2001, *m.*	Hon. William R. H. C., *b.* 1981
1858	*Chesham (7th),* Charles Gray Compton Cavendish, *b.* 1974, *s.* 2009, *m.*	Hon. Oliver N. B. C., *b.* 2007
1945	*Chetwode (2nd),* Philip Chetwode, *b.* 1937, *s.* 1950, *m.*	Hon. Roger C., *b.* 1968
1945	*Chorley (2nd),* Roger Richard Edward Chorley, *b.* 1930, *s.* 1978, *m.*	Hon. Nicholas R. D. C., *b.* 1966
1858	*Churston (5th),* John Francis Yarde-Buller, *b.* 1934, *s.* 1991, *m.*	Hon. Benjamin F. A. Y.-B., *b.* 1974
1800 I.	*Clanmorris (8th),* Simon John Ward Bingham, *b.* 1937, *s.* 1988, *m.*	Robert D. de B. B., *b.* 1942
1672	*Clifford of Chudleigh (14th),* Thomas Hugh Clifford, *b.* 1948, *s.* 1988, *m.*	Hon. Alexander T. H. C., *b.* 1985
1299	*Clinton (22nd),* Gerard Nevile Mark Fane Trefusis, *b.* 1934, *s.* 1965, *m.*	Hon. Charles P. R. F. T., *b.* 1962
1955	*Clitheroe (2nd),* Ralph John Assheton, *b.* 1929, *s.* 1984, *m.*	Hon. Ralph C. A., *b.* 1962
1919	*Clwyd (4th),* (John) Murray Roberts, *b.* 1971, *s.* 2006	Hon. Jeremy T. R., *b.* 1973
1948	*Clydesmuir (3rd),* David Ronald Colville, *b.* 1949, *s.* 1996, *m.*	Hon. Richard C., *b.* 1980
1960	*Cobbold (2nd),* David Antony Fromanteel Lytton Cobbold, *b.* 1937, *s.* 1987, *m.*	Hon. Henry F. L. C., *b.* 1962
1919	*Cochrane of Cults (4th),* (Ralph Henry) Vere Cochrane, *b.* 1926, *s.* 1990, *m.*	Hon. Thomas H. V. C., *b.* 1957
1954	*Coleraine (2nd),* (James) Martin (Bonar) Law, *b.* 1931, *s.* 1980, *m.*	Hon. James P. B. L., *b.* 1975
1873	*Coleridge (5th),* William Duke Coleridge, *b.* 1937, *s.* 1984, *m.*	Hon. James D. C., *b.* 1967
1946	*Colgrain (4th),* Alastair Colin Leckie Campbell, *b.* 1951, *s.* 2008, *m.*	Hon. Thomas C. D. C., *b.* 1984
1917	** *Colwyn (3rd),* (Ian) Anthony Hamilton-Smith, CBE, *b.* 1942, *s.* 1966, *m.*	Hon. Craig P. H.-S., *b.* 1968
1956	*Colyton (2nd),* Alisdair John Munro Hopkinson, *b.* 1958, *s.* 1996, *m.*	Hon. James P. M. H., *b.* 1983
1841	*Congleton (8th),* Christopher Patrick Parnell, *b.* 1930, *s.* 1967, *m.*	Hon. John P. C. P., *b.* 1959
1927	*Cornwallis (4th),* Fiennes Wykeham Jeremy Cornwallis, *b.* 1946, *s.* 2010, *m.*	Hon. Fiennes A. W. M. C., *b.* 1987
1874	*Cottesloe (5th),* John Tapling Fremantle, *b.* 1927, *s.* 1994, *w.*	Hon. Thomas F. H. F., *b.* 1966
1929	*Craigmyle (4th),* Thomas Columba Shaw, *b.* 1960, *s.* 1998, *m.*	Hon. Alexander F. S., *b.* 1988
1899	*Cranworth (3rd),* Philip Bertram Gurdon, *b.* 1940, *s.* 1964, *m.*	Hon. Sacha W. R. G., *b.* 1970
1959	** *Crathorne (2nd),* Charles James Dugdale, KCVO, *b.* 1939, *s.* 1977, *w.*	Hon. Thomas A. J. D., *b.* 1977
1892	*Crawshaw (5th),* David Gerald Brooks, *b.* 1934, *s.* 1997, *m.*	Hon. John P. B., *b.* 1938
1940	*Croft (3rd),* Bernard William Henry Page Croft, *b.* 1949, *s.* 1997, *m.*	None
1797 I.	*Crofton (8th),* Edward Harry Piers Crofton, *b.* 1988, *s.* 2007	Hon. Charles M. G. C., *b.* 1988
1375	** *Cromwell (7th),* Godfrey John Bewicke-Copley, *b.* 1960, *s.* 1982, *m.*	Hon. David G. B.-C., *b.* 1997
1947	*Crook (3rd),* Robert Douglas Edwin Crook, *b.* 1955, *s.* 2001, *m.*	Hon. Matthew R. C., *b.* 1990
1920	*Cullen of Ashbourne (3rd),* Edmund Willoughby Marsham Cokayne, *b.* 1916, *s.* 2000, *w.*	Michael J. C., *b.* 1950
1914	*Cunliffe (3rd),* Roger Cunliffe, *b.* 1932, *s.* 1963, *m.*	Hon. Henry C., *b.* 1962
1332	*Darcy de Knayth (19th),* Caspar David Ingrams, *b.* 1962, *s.* 2008, *m.*	Hon. Thomas R. I., *b.* 1999
1927	*Daresbury (4th),* Peter Gilbert Greenall, *b.* 1953, *s.* 1996, *m.*	Hon. Thomas E. G., *b.* 1984
1924	*Darling (3rd),* (Robert) Julian Henry Darling, *b.* 1944, *s.* 2003, *m.*	Hon. Robert J. C. D., *b.* 1972
1946	*Darwen (4th),* Paul Davies, *b.* 1962, *s.* 2011	Hon. Benjamin D., *b.* 1966
1932	*Davies (3rd),* David Davies, *b.* 1940, *s.* 1944, *m.*	Hon. David D. D., *b.* 1975
1812 I.	*Decies (7th),* Marcus Hugh Tristram de la Poer Beresford, *b.* 1948, *s.* 1992, *m.*	Hon. Robert M. D. de la P. B., *b.* 1988
1299	*de Clifford (27th),* John Edward Southwell Russell, *b.* 1928, *s.* 1982, *m.*	Miles E. S. R., *b.* 1966
1851	*De Freyne (8th),* Fulke Charles Arthur John French, *b.* 1957, *s.* 2009, *m.*	Hon. Alexander J. C. F., *b.* 1988
1821	*Delamere (5th),* Hugh George Cholmondeley, *b.* 1934, *s.* 1979, *m.*	Hon. Thomas P. G. C., *b.* 1968
1838	** *de Mauley (7th),* Rupert Charles Ponsonby, *b.* 1957, *s.* 2002, *m.*	Ashley G. P., *b.* 1959
1937	** *Denham (2nd),* Bertram Stanley Mitford Bowyer, KBE, PC, *b.* 1927, *s.* 1948, *m.*	Hon. Richard G. G. B., *b.* 1959

1834	*Denman (6th),* Richard Thomas Stewart Denman, *b.* 1946, *s.* 2012, *m.*	Hon. Robert D., *b.* 1995
1887	*De Ramsey (4th),* John Ailwyn Fellowes, *b.* 1942, *s.* 1993, *m.*	Hon. Freddie J. F., *b.* 1978
1264	*de Ros (28th),* Peter Trevor Maxwell, *b.* 1958, *s.* 1983, *m. Premier Baron of England*	Hon. Finbar J. M., *b.* 1988
1881	*Derwent (5th),* Robin Evelyn Leo Vanden-Bempde-Johnstone, LVO, *b.* 1930, *s.* 1986, *m.*	Hon. Francis P. H. V.-B.-J., *b.* 1965
1831	*de Saumarez (7th),* Eric Douglas Saumarez, *b.* 1956, *s.* 1991, *m.*	Hon. Victor T. S., *b.* 1956
1910	*de Villiers (4th),* Alexander Charles de Villiers, *b.* 1940, *s.* 2001, *m.*	None
1930	*Dickinson (2nd),* Richard Clavering Hyett Dickinson, *b.* 1926, *s.* 1943, *m.*	Hon. Martin H. D., *b.* 1961
1620 I.	*Digby (12th) and Digby (5th) (1765),* Edward Henry Kenelm Digby, KCVO, *b.* 1924, *s.* 1964, *m.*	Hon. Henry N. K. D., *b.* 1954
1615	*Dormer (17th),* Geoffrey Henry Dormer, *b.* 1920, *s.* 1995, *m.*	Hon. William R. D., *b.* 1960
1943	*Dowding (3rd),* Piers Hugh Tremenheere Dowding, *b.* 1948, *s.* 1992, *m.*	Hon. Mark D. J. D., *b.* 1949
1439	*Dudley (15th),* Jim Anthony Hill Wallace, *b.* 1930, *s.* 2002, *m.*	Hon. Jeremy W. G. W., *b.* 1964
1800 I.	*Dufferin and Clandeboye (11th),* John Francis Blackwood, *b.* 1944, *s.* 1991 (claim to the peerage not yet established), *m.*	Hon. Francis S. B., *b.* 1979
1929	*Dulverton (3rd),* (Gilbert) Michael Hamilton Wills, *b.* 1944, *s.* 1992, *m.*	Hon. Robert A. H. W., *b.* 1983
1800 I.	*Dunalley (7th),* Henry Francis Cornelius Prittie, *b.* 1948, *s.* 1992, *m.*	Hon. Joel H. P., *b.* 1981
1324 I.	*Dunboyne (30th),* Richard Pierce Theobald Butler, *b.* 1983, *s.* 2013, *m.*	Michael J. B., *b.* 1944
1892	*Dunleath (6th),* Brian Henry Mulholland, *b.* 1950, *s.* 1997, *m.*	Hon. Andrew H. M., *b.* 1981
1439 I.	*Dunsany (21st),* Randal Plunkett, *b.* 1983, *s.* 2011	Hon. Oliver P., *b.* 1985
1780	*Dynevor (10th),* Hugo Griffith Uryan Rhys, *b.* 1966, *s.* 2008	Robert D. A. R., *b.* 1963
1963	*Egremont (2nd) and Leconfield (7th) (1859),* John Max Henry Scawen Wyndham, *b.* 1948, *s.* 1972, *m.*	Hon. George R. V. W., *b.* 1983
1643 S.	*Elibank (14th),* Alan D'Ardis Erskine-Murray, *b.* 1923, *s.* 1973, *w.*	Master of Elibank, *b.* 1964
1802	*Ellenborough (9th),* Rupert Edward Henry Law, *b.* 1955, *s.* 2013, *m.*	Hon. James R. T. L., *b.* 1983
1509 S.	*Elphinstone (19th) and Elphinstone (5th) (1885),* Alexander Mountstuart Elphinstone, *b.* 1980, *s.* 1994, *m.*	Master of Elphinstone, *b.* 2011
1934 **	*Elton (2nd),* Rodney Elton, TD, *b.* 1930, *s.* 1973, *m.*	Hon. Edward P. E., *b.* 1966
1627 S.	*Fairfax of Cameron (14th),* Nicholas John Albert Fairfax, *b.* 1956, *s.* 1964, *m.*	Hon. Edward N. T. F., *b.* 1984
1961	*Fairhaven (3rd),* Ailwyn Henry George Broughton, *b.* 1936, *s.* 1973, *m.*	Maj. Hon. James H. A. B., *b.* 1963
1916	*Faringdon (3rd),* Charles Michael Henderson, KCVO, *b.* 1937, *s.* 1977, *m.*	Hon. James H. H., *b.* 1961
1756 I.	*Farnham (13th),* Simon Kenlis Maxwell, *b.* 1933, *s.* 2001, *w.*	Hon. Robin S. M., *b.* 1965
1856 I.	*Fermoy (6th),* Maurice Burke Roche, *b.* 1967, *s.* 1984, *m.*	Hon. E. Hugh B. R., *b.* 1972
1826	*Feversham (7th),* Jasper Orlando Slingsby Duncombe, *b.* 1968, *s.* 2009	Hon. Jake B. D., *b.* 1972
1798 I.	*ffrench (8th),* Robuck John Peter Charles Mario ffrench, *b.* 1956, *s.* 1986, *m.*	None
1909	*Fisher (4th),* Patrick Vavasseur Fisher, *b.* 1953, *s.* 2012, *m.*	Hon. Benjamin C. V. F., *b.* 1986
1295	*Fitzwalter (22nd),* Julian Brook Plumptre, *b.* 1952, *s.* 2004, *m.*	Hon. Edward B. P., *b.* 1989
1776	*Foley (9th),* Thomas Henry Foley, *b.* 1961, *s.* 2012	Rupert T. F., *b.* 1970
1445 S.	*Forbes (23rd),* Malcolm Nigel Forbes, *b.* 1946, *s.* 2013, *m. Premier Lord of Scotland*	Master of Forbes, *b.* 1970
1821	*Forester (9th),* Charles Richard George Weld-Forester, *b.* 1975, *s.* 2004, *m.*	Hon. Brook G. P. W.-F., *b.* 2014
1922	*Forres (4th),* Alastair Stephen Grant Williamson, *b.* 1946, *s.* 1978, *m.*	Hon. George A. M. W., *b.* 1972
1917	*Forteviot (4th),* John James Evelyn Dewar, *b.* 1938, *s.* 1993, *w.*	Hon. Alexander J. E. D., *b.* 1971
1951 **	*Freyberg (3rd),* Valerian Bernard Freyberg, *b.* 1970, *s.* 1993, *m.*	Hon. Joseph J. F., *b.* 2007
1917	*Gainford (4th),* George Pease, *b.* 1926, *s.* 2013, *m.*	Hon. Adrian C. P., *b.* 1960
1818 I.	*Garvagh (6th),* Spencer George Stratford de Redcliffe Canning, *b.* 1953, *s.* 2013, *w.*	Hon. Stratford G. E. de R. C., *b.* 1990
1942 **	*Geddes (3rd),* Euan Michael Ross Geddes, *b.* 1937, *s.* 1975, *m.*	Hon. James G. N. G., *b.* 1969
1876	*Gerard (5th),* Anthony Robert Hugo Gerard, *b.* 1949, *s.* 1992, *m.*	Hon. Rupert B. C. G., *b.* 1981
1824	*Gifford (6th),* Anthony Maurice Gifford, QC, *b.* 1940, *s.* 1961, *m.*	Hon. Thomas A. G., *b.* 1967
1917	*Gisborough (3rd),* Thomas Richard John Long Chaloner, *b.* 1927, *s.* 1951, *m.*	Hon. T. Peregrine L. C., *b.* 1961
1960	*Gladwyn (2nd),* Miles Alvery Gladwyn Jebb, *b.* 1930, *s.* 1996	None
1899	*Glanusk (5th),* Christopher Russell Bailey, *b.* 1942, *s.* 1997, *m.*	Hon. Charles H. B., *b.* 1976
1918 **	*Glenarthur (4th),* Simon Mark Arthur, *b.* 1944, *s.* 1976, *m.*	Hon. Edward A. A., *b.* 1973
1911	*Glenconner (4th),* Cody Charles Edward Tennant, *b.* 1994, *s.* 2010	Euan L. T., *b.* 1983
1964	*Glendevon (3rd),* Jonathan Charles Hope, *b.* 1952, *s.* 2009	None
1922	*Glendyne (4th),* John Nivison, *b.* 1960, *s.* 2008	None
1939 **	*Glentoran (3rd),* (Thomas) Robin (Valerian) Dixon, CBE, *b.* 1935, *s.* 1995, *m.*	Hon. Daniel G. D., *b.* 1959
1909	*Gorell (5th),* John Picton Gorell Barnes, *b.* 1959, *s.* 2007, *m.*	Hon. Oliver G. B., *b.* 1993
1953 **	*Grantchester (3rd),* Christopher John Suenson-Taylor, *b.* 1951, *s.* 1995, *m.*	Hon. Jesse D. S.-T., *b.* 1977
1782	*Grantley (8th),* Richard William Brinsley Norton, *b.* 1956, *s.* 1995	Hon. Francis J. H. N., *b.* 1960
1794 I.	*Graves (10th),* Timothy Evelyn Graves, *b.* 1960, *s.* 2002, *m.*	None
1445 S.	*Gray (23rd),* Andrew Godfrey Diarmid Stuart Campbell-Gray, *b.* 1964, *s.* 2003, *m.*	Master of Gray, *b.* 1996
1950	*Greenhill (3rd),* Malcolm Greenhill, *b.* 1924, *s.* 1989	None
1927 **	*Greenway (4th),* Ambrose Charles Drexel Greenway, *b.* 1941, *s.* 1975, *m.*	Hon. Nigel P. G., *b.* 1944

1902	*Grenfell (3rd) and Grenfell of Kilvey (life peerage, 2000)*, Julian Pascoe Francis St Leger Grenfell, *b.* 1935, *s.* 1976, *m.*	Richard A. St L. G., *b.* 1966
1944	*Gretton (4th)*, John Lysander Gretton, *b.* 1975, *s.* 1989	Hon. John F. B. G., *b.* 2008
1397	*Grey of Codnor (6th)*, Richard Henry Cornwall-Legh, *b.* 1936, *s.* 1996, *m.*	Hon. Richard S. C. C.-L., *b.* 1976
1955	*Gridley (3rd)*, Richard David Arnold Gridley, *b.* 1956, *s.* 1996, *m.*	Peter A. C. G., *b.* 1940
1964	*Grimston of Westbury (3rd)*, Robert John Sylvester Grimston, *b.* 1951, *s.* 2003, *m.*	Hon. Gerald C. W. G., *b.* 1953
1886	*Grimthorpe (5th)*, Edward John Beckett, *b.* 1954, *s.* 2003, *m.*	Hon. Harry M. B., *b.* 1993
1945	*Hacking (3rd)*, Douglas David Hacking, *b.* 1938, *s.* 1971, *m.*	Hon. Douglas F. H., *b.* 1968
1950	*Haden-Guest (5th)*, Christopher Haden-Guest, *b.* 1948, *s.* 1996, *m.*	Hon. Nicholas H.-G., *b.* 1951
1886	*Hamilton of Dalzell (5th)*, Gavin Goulburn Hamilton, *b.* 1968, *s.* 2006, *m.*	Hon. Francis A. J. G. H., *b.* 2009
1874	*Hampton (7th)*, John Humphrey Arnott Pakington, *b.* 1964, *s.* 2003, *m.*	Hon. Charles R. C. P., *b.* 2005
1939	*Hankey (3rd)*, Donald Robin Alers Hankey, *b.* 1938, *s.* 1996, *m.*	Hon. Alexander M. A. H., *b.* 1947
1958	*Harding of Petherton (2nd)*, John Charles Harding, *b.* 1928, *s.* 1989, *w.*	Hon. William A. J. H., *b.* 1969
1910	*Hardinge of Penshurst (4th)*, Julian Alexander Hardinge, *b.* 1945, *s.* 1997	Hon. Hugh F. H., *b.* 1948
1876	*Harlech (6th)*, Francis David Ormsby-Gore, *b.* 1954, *s.* 1985, *m.*	Hon. Jasset D. C. O.-G., *b.* 1986
1939	*Harmsworth (3rd)*, Thomas Harold Raymond Harmsworth, *b.* 1939, *s.* 1990, *m.*	Hon. Dominic M. E. H., *b.* 1973
1815	*Harris (8th)*, Anthony Harris, *b.* 1942, *s.* 1996, *m.*	Rear-Adm. Michael G. T. H., *b.* 1941
1954	*Harvey of Tasburgh (3rd)*, Charles John Giuseppe Harvey, *b.* 1951, *s.* 2010, *m.*	Hon. John H., *b.* 1993
1295	*Hastings (23rd)*, Delaval Thomas Harold Astley, *b.* 1960, *s.* 2007, *m.*	Hon. Jacob A. A., *b.* 1991
1835	*Hatherton (8th)*, Edward Charles Littleton, *b.* 1950, *s.* 1985, *m.*	Hon. Thomas E. L., *b.* 1977
1776 M.	*Hawke (12th)*, William Martin Theodore Hawke, *b.* 1995, *s.* 2010	None
1927	*Hayter (4th)*, George William Michael Chubb, *b.* 1943, *s.* 2003, *m.*	Hon. Thomas F. F. C., *b.* 1986
1945	*Hazlerigg (3rd)*, Arthur Grey Hazlerigg, *b.* 1951, *s.* 2002, *m.*	Hon. Arthur W. G. H. *b.* 1987
1943	*Hemingford (3rd)*, (Dennis) Nicholas Herbert, *b.* 1934, *s.* 1982, *m.*	Hon. Christopher D. C. H., *b.* 1973
1906	*Hemphill (6th)*, Charles Andrew Martyn Martyn-Hemphill, *b.* 1954, *s.* 2012, *m.*	Hon. Richard P. L. M.-H., *b.* 1990
1799 I.	** *Henley (8th) and Northington (6th) (1885)*, Oliver Michael Robert Eden, PC, *b.* 1953, *s.* 1977, *m.*	Hon. John W. O. E., *b.* 1988
1800 I.	*Henniker (9th) and Hartismere (6th) (1866)*, Mark Ian Philip Chandos Henniker-Major, *b.* 1947, *s.* 2004, *m.*	Hon. Edward G. M. H.-M., *b.* 1985
1461	*Herbert (19th)*, David John Seyfried Herbert, *b.* 1952, *s.* 2002, *m.* Title called out of abeyance 2002	Hon. Oliver R. S. H., *b.* 1976
1935	*Hesketh (3rd)*, Thomas Alexander Fermor-Hesketh, KBE, PC, *b.* 1950, *s.* 1955, *m.*	Hon. Frederick H. F.-H., *b.* 1988
1828	*Heytesbury (7th)*, James William Holmes à Court, *b.* 1967, *s.* 2004, *m.*	Peter M. H.. H. à. C., *b.* 1968
1886	*Hindlip (6th)*, Charles Henry Allsopp, *b.* 1940, *s.* 1993, *w.*	Hon. Henry W. A., *b.* 1973
1950	*Hives (3rd)*, Matthew Peter Hives, *b.* 1971, *s.* 1997	Hon. Michael B. H., *b.* 1926
1912	*Hollenden (4th)*, Ian Hampden Hope-Morley, *b.* 1946, *s.* 1999, *m.*	Hon. Edward H.-M., *b.* 1981
1897	*Holm Patrick (4th)*, Hans James David Hamilton, *b.* 1955, *s.* 1991, *m.*	Hon. Ion H. J. H., *b.* 1956
1797 I.	*Hotham (8th)*, Henry Durand Hotham, *b.* 1940, *s.* 1967, *m.*	Hon. William B. H., *b.* 1972
1881	*Hothfield (6th)*, Anthony Charles Sackville Tufton, *b.* 1939, *s.* 1991, *m.*	Hon. William S. T., *b.* 1977
1930	*Howard of Penrith (3rd)*, Philip Esme Howard, *b.* 1945, *s.* 1999, *m.*	Hon. Thomas Philip H., *b.* 1974
1960	*Howick of Glendale (2nd)*, Charles Evelyn Baring, *b.* 1937, *s.* 1973, *m.*	Hon. David E. C. B., *b.* 1975
1796 I.	*Huntingfield (7th)*, Joshua Charles Vanneck, *b.* 1954, *s.* 1994, *w.*	Hon. Gerard C. A. V., *b.* 1985
1866	** *Hylton (5th)*, Raymond Hervey Jolliffe, *b.* 1932, *s.* 1967, *m.*	Hon. William H. M. J., *b.* 1967
1933	*Iliffe (3rd)*, Robert Peter Richard Iliffe, *b.* 1944, *s.* 1996, *m.*	Hon. Edward R. I., *b.* 1968
1543 I.	*Inchiquin (18th)*, Conor Myles John O'Brien, *b.* 1943, *s.* 1982, *m.*	Conor J. A. O'B., *b.* 1952
1962	*Inchyra (3rd)*, Christian James Charles Hoyer Millar, *b.* 1962, *s.* 2011, *m.*	Hon. Jake C. R. M., *b.* 1996
1964	** *Inglewood (2nd)*, (William) Richard Fletcher-Vane, *b.* 1951, *s.* 1989, *m.*	Hon. Henry W. F. F.-V., *b.* 1990
1919	*Inverforth (4th)*, Andrew Peter Weir, *b.* 1966, *s.* 1982	Hon. Benjamin A. W., *b.* 1997
1941	*Ironside (2nd)*, Edmund Oslac Ironside, *b.* 1924, *s.* 1959, *m.*	Hon. Charles E. G. I., *b.* 1956
1952	*Jeffreys (3rd)*, Christopher Henry Mark Jeffreys, *b.* 1957, *s.* 1986, *m.*	Hon. Arthur M. H. J., *b.* 1989
1906	*Joicey (5th)*, James Michael Joicey, *b.* 1953, *s.* 1993, *m.*	Hon. William J. J., *b.* 1990
1937	*Kenilworth (4th)*, (John) Randle Siddeley, *b.* 1954, *s.* 1981, *m.*	Hon. William R. J. S., *b.* 1992
1935	*Kennet (3rd)*, William Aldus Thoby Young, *b.* 1957, *s.* 2009, *m.*	Hon. Archibald W. K. Y., *b.* 1992
1776 I.	*Kensington (8th) and Kensington (5th) (1886)*, Hugh Ivor Edwardes, *b.* 1933, *s.* 1981, *m.*	Hon. W. Owen A. E., *b.* 1964
1951	*Kenswood (2nd)*, John Michael Howard Whitfield, *b.* 1930, *s.* 1963, *m.*	Hon. Michael C. W., *b.* 1955
1788	*Kenyon (6th)*, Lloyd Tyrell-Kenyon, *b.* 1947, *s.* 1993, *m.*	Hon. Lloyd N. T.-K., *b.* 1972
1947	*Kershaw (4th)*, Edward John Kershaw, *b.* 1936, *s.* 1962, *m.*	Hon. John C. E. K., *b.* 1971
1943	*Keyes (3rd)*, Charles William Packe Keyes, *b.* 1951, *s.* 2005, *m.*	Hon. (Leopold R.) J. K., *b.* 1956
1909	*Kilbracken (4th)*, Christopher John Godley, *b.* 1945, *s.* 2006, *m.*	Hon. James J. G., *b.* 1972

1900	*Killanin (4th)*, (George) Redmond Fitzpatrick Morris, *b.* 1947, *s.* 1999, *m.*	Hon. Luke M. G. M., *b.* 1975
1943	*Killearn (3rd)*, Victor Miles George Aldous Lampson, *b.* 1941, *s.* 1996, *w.*	Hon. Miles H. M. L., *b.* 1977
1789 I.	*Kilmaine (8th)*, John Francis Sandford Browne, *b.* 1983, *s.* 2013	Revd Aubrey R. C. B., *b.* 1931
1831	*Kilmarnock (8th)*, Dr Robin Jordan Boyd, *b.* 1941, *s.* 2009, *m.*	Hon. Simon J. B., *b.* 1978
1941	*Kindersley (4th)*, Rupert John Molesworth Kindersley, *b.* 1955, *s.* 2013, *m.*	Hon. Frederick H. M. K., *b.* 1987
1223 I.	*Kingsale (36th)*, Nevinson Mark de Courcy, *b.* 1958, *s.* 2005, *m. Premier Baron of Ireland*	Joseph K. C. de C., *b.* 1955
1902	*Kinross (5th)*, Christopher Patrick Balfour, *b.* 1949, *s.* 1985, *m.*	Hon. Alan I. B., *b.* 1978
1951	*Kirkwood (3rd)*, David Harvie Kirkwood, PHD, *b.* 1931, *s.* 1970, *m.*	Hon. James S. K., *b.* 1937
1800 I.	*Langford (9th)*, Col. Geoffrey Alexander Rowley-Conwy, OBE, *b.* 1912, *s.* 1953, *m.*	Hon. Owain G. R.-C., *b.* 1958
1942	*Latham (2nd)*, Dominic Charles Latham, *b.* 1954, *s.* 1970	Anthony M. L., *b.* 1954
1431	*Latymer (9th)*, Crispin James Alan Nevill Money-Coutts, *b.* 1955, *s.* 2003, *m.*	Hon. Drummond W. T. M.-C., *b.* 1986
1869	*Lawrence (5th)*, David John Downer Lawrence, *b.* 1937, *s.* 1968	None
1947	*Layton (3rd)*, Geoffrey Michael Layton, *b.* 1947, *s.* 1989, *m.*	Jonathan F. L., *b.* 1942
1839	*Leigh (6th)*, Christopher Dudley Piers Leigh, *b.* 1960, *s.* 2003, *m.*	Hon. Rupert D. L., *b.* 1994
1962	*Leighton of St Mellons (3rd)*, Robert William Henry Leighton Seager, *b.* 1955, *s.* 1998, *m.*	Hon. Simon J. L. S., *b.* 1957
1797	*Lilford (8th)*, Mark Vernon Powys, *b.* 1975, *s.* 2005	Robert C. L. P., *b.* 1930
1945	*Lindsay of Birker (3rd)*, James Francis Lindsay, *b.* 1945, *s.* 1994, *m.*	Alexander S. L., *b.* 1940
1758 I.	*Lisle (9th)*, (John) Nicholas Geoffrey Lysaght, *b.* 1960, *s.* 2003	Hon. David J. L., *b.* 1963
1850	*Londesborough (9th)*, Richard John Denison, *b.* 1959, *s.* 1968, *m.*	Hon. James F. D., *b.* 1990
1541 I.	*Louth (17th)*, Jonathan Oliver Plunkett, *b* 1952, *s.* 2013	Hon. Matthew O. P., *b.* 1982
1458 S.	*Lovat (16th) and Lovat (5th) (1837)*, Simon Fraser, *b.* 1977, *s.* 1995	Hon. Jack F., *b.* 1984
1946	*Lucas of Chilworth (3rd)*, Simon William Lucas, *b.* 1957, *s.* 2001, *m.*	Hon. John R. M. L., *b.* 1995
1663	** *Lucas (11th) and Dingwall (14th) (S. 1609)*, Ralph Matthew Palmer, *b.* 1951, *s.* 1991, *m.*	Hon. Lewis E. P., *b.* 1987
1929	*Luke (3rd)*, Arthur Charles St John Lawson Johnston, *b.* 1933, *s.* 1996, *m.*	Hon. Ian J. St J. L. J., *b.* 1963
1914	** *Lyell (3rd)*, Charles Lyell, *b.* 1939, *s.* 1943	None
1859	*Lyveden (7th)*, Jack Leslie Vernon, *b.* 1938, *s.* 1999, *m.*	Hon. Colin R. V., *b.* 1967
1959	*MacAndrew (3rd)*, Christopher Anthony Colin MacAndrew, *b.* 1945, *s.* 1989, *m.*	Hon. Oliver C. J. M., *b.* 1983
1776 I.	*Macdonald (8th)*, Godfrey James Macdonald of Macdonald, *b.* 1947, *s.* 1970, *m.*	Hon. Godfrey E. H. T. M., *b.* 1982
1937	*McGowan (4th)*, Harry John Charles McGowan, *b.* 1971, *s.* 2003, *m.*	Hon. Dominic J. W. M., *b.* 1951
1922	*Maclay (3rd)*, Joseph Paton Maclay, *b.* 1942, *s.* 1969, *m.*	Hon. Joseph P. M., *b.* 1977
1955	*McNair (3rd)*, Duncan James McNair, *b.* 1947, *s.* 1989, *m.*	Hon. William S. A. M., *b.* 1958
1951	*Macpherson of Drumochter (3rd)*, James Anthony Macpherson, *b.* 1979, *s.* 2008, *m.*	Hon. Daniel T. M., *b.* 2013
1937	** *Mancroft (3rd)*, Benjamin Lloyd Stormont Mancroft, *b.* 1957, *s.* 1987, *m.*	Hon. Arthur L. S. M., *b.* 1995
1807	*Manners (6th)*, John Hugh Robert Manners, *b.* 1956, *s.* 2008, *m.*	Hon. John A. D. M., *b.* 2011
1922	*Manton (4th)*, Miles Ronald Marcus Watson, *b.* 1958, *s.* 2003, *m.*	Hon. Thomas N. C. D. W., *b.* 1985
1908	*Marchamley (4th)*, William Francis Whiteley, *b.* 1968, *s.* 1994, *m.*	Hon. Leon W., *b.* 2004
1965	*Margadale (3rd)*, Alastair John Morrison, *b.* 1958, *s.* 2003, *m.*	Hon. Declan J. M., *b.* 1993
1961	*Marks of Broughton (3rd)*, Simon Richard Marks, *b.* 1950, *s.* 1998, *m.*	Hon. Michael M., *b.* 1989
1964	*Martonmere (2nd)*, John Stephen Robinson, *b.* 1963, *s.* 1989	Hon. James I. R., *b.* 2003
1776 I.	*Massy (10th)*, David Hamon Somerset Massy, *b.* 1947, *s.* 1995	Hon. John H. M., *b.* 1950
1935	*May (4th)*, Jasper Bertram St John May, *b.* 1965, *s.* 2006	None
1928	*Melchett (4th)*, Peter Robert Henry Mond, *b.* 1948, *s.* 1973	None
1925	*Merrivale (4th)*, Derek John Philip Duke, *b.* 1948, *s.* 2007, *m.*	Hon. Thomas D., *b.* 1980
1911	*Merthyr (5th)*, David Trevor Lewis, *b.* 1977, *s.* 2015, *m.*	Hon. Peter H. L., *b.* 1937
1919	*Meston (3rd)*, James Meston, QC, *b.* 1950, *s.* 1984, *m.*	Hon. Thomas J. D. M., *b.* 1977
1838	*Methuen (8th)*, James Paul Archibald Methuen-Campbell, *b.* 1952, *s.* 2014	Thomas R. M. M.-C., *b.* 1977
1711	*Middleton (13th)*, Michael Charles James Willoughby, *b.* 1948, *s.* 2011, *m.*	Hon. James W. M. W., *b.* 1976
1939	*Milford (4th)*, Guy Wogan Philipps, QC, *b.* 1961, *s.* 1999, *m.*	Hon. Archie S. P., *b.* 1997
1933	*Milne (4th)*, George Alexander Milne, *b.* 1941, *s.* 2005	Hon. Iain C. L. M., *b.* 1949
1951	*Milner of Leeds (3rd)*, Richard James Milner, *b.* 1959, *s.* 2003, *m.*	None
1947	*Milverton (2nd)*, Revd Fraser Arthur Richard Richards, *b.* 1930, *s.* 1978, *m.*	Hon. Michael H. R., *b.* 1936
1873	*Moncreiff (6th)*, Rhoderick Harry Wellwood Moncreiff, *b.* 1954, *s.* 2002, *m.*	Hon. Harry J. W. M., *b.* 1986
1884	*Monk Bretton (3rd)*, John Charles Dodson, *b.* 1924, *s.* 1933, *m.*	Hon. Christopher M. D., *b.* 1958
1885	*Monkswell (5th)*, Gerard Collier, *b.* 1947, *s.* 1984, *m.*	Hon. James A. C., *b.* 1977
1728	*Monson (12th)*, Nicholas John Monson, *b.* 1955, *s.* 2011, *m.*	Hon. Andrew A. J. M., *b.* 1959
1885	*Montagu of Beaulieu (4th)*, Ralph Douglas-Scott-Montagu, *b.* 1961, *s.* 2015, *m.*	Hon. Jonathan D. D.-S.-M., *b.* 1975
1839	*Monteagle of Brandon (7th)*, Charles James Spring Rice, *b.* 1953, *s.* 2013, *m.*	Hon. Michael S. R., *b.* 1935
1943	*Moran (3rd)*, James McMoran Wilson, *b.* 1952, *s.* 2014, *m.*	Hon. David A. M. W., *b.* 1990

1918	*Morris (4th)*, Thomas Anthony Salmon Morris, *b.* 1982, *s.* 2011	Hon. John M. M., *b.* 1983
1950	*Morris of Kenwood (3rd)*, Jonathan David Morris, *b.* 1968, *s.* 2004, *m.*	Hon. Benjamin J. M., *b.* 1998
1831	*Mostyn (7th)*, Gregory Philip Roger Lloyd-Mostyn, *b.* 1984, *s.* 2011	Roger Hugh L.-M., *b.* 1941
1933	*Mottistone (6th)*, Christopher David Peter Seely, *b.* 1974, *s.* 2013	Hon. Richard W. A. S., *b.* 1988
1945	** *Mountevans (4th)*, Jeffrey Richard de Corban Evans, *b.* 1948, *s.* 2014, *m.*	Hon. Alexander R. A. E., *b.* 1975
1283	*Mowbray (27th), Segrave (28th) (1295) and Stourton (24th) (1448)*, Edward William Stephen Stourton, *b.* 1953, *s.* 2006, *m.*	Hon. James C. P. S., *b.* 1991
1932	*Moyne (3rd)*, Jonathan Bryan Guinness, *b.* 1930, *s.* 1992, *m.*	Hon. Valentine G. B. G., *b.* 1959
1929	** *Moynihan (4th)*, Colin Berkeley Moynihan, *b.* 1955, *s.* 1997, *m.*	Hon. Nicholas E. B. M., *b.* 1994
1781 I.	*Muskerry (9th)*, Robert Fitzmaurice Deane, *b.* 1948, *s.* 1988, *m.*	Hon. Jonathan F. D., *b.* 1986
1627 S.	*Napier (15th) and Ettrick (6th) (1872)*, Francis David Charles Napier, *b.* 1962, *s.* 2012, *m.*	Master of Napier, *b.* 1996
1868	*Napier of Magdala (6th)*, Robert Alan Napier, *b.* 1940, *s.* 1987, *m.*	Hon. James R. N., *b.* 1966
1940	*Nathan (3rd)*, Rupert Harry Bernard Nathan, *b.* 1957, *s.* 2007, *m.*	None
1960	*Nelson of Stafford (4th)*, Alistair William Henry Nelson, *b.* 1973, *s.* 2006, *m.*	Hon. James J. N., *b.* 1947
1959	*Netherthorpe (3rd)*, James Frederick Turner, *b.* 1964, *s.* 1982, *m.*	Hon. Andrew J. E. T., *b.* 1993
1946	*Newall (2nd)*, Francis Storer Eaton Newall, *b.* 1930, *s.* 1963, *m.*	Hon. Richard H. E. N., *b.* 1961
1776 I.	*Newborough (8th)*, Robert Vaughan Wynn, *b.* 1949, *s.* 1998, *m.*	Antony C. V. W., *b.* 1949
1892	*Newton (5th)*, Richard Thomas Legh, *b.* 1950, *s.* 1992, *m.*	Hon. Piers R. L., *b.* 1979
1930	*Noel-Buxton (4th)*, Charles Connal Noel-Buxton, *b.* 1975, *s.* 2013, *m.*	Hon. Simon C. N.-B., *b.* 1943
1957	*Norrie (2nd)*, (George) Willoughby Moke Norrie, *b.* 1936, *s.* 1977, *m.*	Hon. Mark W. J. N., *b.* 1972
1884	** *Northbourne (5th)*, Christopher George Walter James, *b.* 1926, *s.* 1982, *m.*	Hon. Charles W. H. J., *b.* 1960
1866	** *Northbrook (6th)*, Francis Thomas Baring, *b.* 1954, *s.* 1990, *m.*	To the Baronetcy, Peter B., *b.* 1939
1878	*Norton (8th)*, James Nigel Arden Adderley, *b.* 1947, *s.* 1993, *m.*	Hon. Edward J. A. A., *b.* 1982
1906	*Nunburnholme (6th)*, Stephen Charles Yanath Wilson, *b.* 1973, *s.* 2000	Hon. David M. W., *b.* 1954
1950	*Ogmore (3rd)*, Morgan Rees-Williams, *b.* 1937, *s.* 2004, *m.*	Hon. Tudor D. R.-W., *b.* 1991
1870	*O'Hagan (4th)*, Charles Towneley Strachey, *b.* 1945, *s.* 1961, *m.*	Hon. Richard T. S., *b.* 1950
1868	*O'Neill (4th)*, Raymond Arthur Clanaboy O'Neill, KCVO, TD, *b.* 1933, *s.* 1944, *m.*	Hon. Shane S. C. O'N., *b.* 1965
1836 I.	*Oranmore and Browne (5th) and Mereworth (3rd) (1926)*, Dominick Geoffrey Thomas Browne, *b.* 1929, *s.* 2002	Shaun D. B., *b.* 1964
1933	** *Palmer (4th)*, Adrian Bailie Nottage Palmer, *b.* 1951, *s.* 1990, *m.*	Hon. Hugo B. R. P., *b.* 1980
1914	*Parmoor (5th)*, Michael Leonard Seddon Cripps, *b.* 1942, *s.* 2008, *m.*	Hon. Henry W. A. C., *b.* 1976
1937	*Pender (3rd)*, John Willoughby Denison-Pender, *b.* 1933, *s.* 1965, *w.*	Hon. Henry J. R. D.-P., *b.* 1968
1866	*Penrhyn (7th)*, Simon Douglas-Pennant, *b.* 1938, *s.* 2003, *m.*	Hon. Edward S. D.-P., *b.* 1966
1603	*Petre (18th)*, John Patrick Lionel Petre, *b.* 1942, *s.* 1989, *m.*	Hon. Dominic W. P., *b.* 1966
1918	*Phillimore (5th)*, Francis Stephen Phillimore, *b.* 1944, *s.* 1994, *m.*	Hon. Tristan A. S. P., *b.* 1977
1945	*Piercy (3rd)*, James William Piercy, *b.* 1946, *s.* 1981	Hon. Mark E. P. P., *b.* 1953
1827	*Plunket (9th)*, Tyrone Shaun Terence Plunket, *b.* 1966, *s.* 2013, *m.*	Hon. Rory P. R. P., *b.* 2001
1831	*Poltimore (7th)*, Mark Coplestone Bampfylde, *b.* 1957, *s.* 1978, *m.*	Hon. Henry A. W. B., *b.* 1985
1690 S.	*Polwarth (11th)*, Andrew Walter Hepburne-Scott, *b.* 1947, *s.* 2005, *m.*	Master of Polwarth, *b.* 1973
1930	*Ponsonby of Shulbrede (4th) and Ponsonby of Roehampton (life peerage, 2000)*, Frederick Matthew Thomas Ponsonby, *b.* 1958, *s.* 1990, *m.*	Hon. Cameron J. J. P., *b.* 1995
1958	*Poole (2nd)*, David Charles Poole, *b.* 1945, *s.* 1993, *m.*	Hon. Oliver J. P., *b.* 1972
1852	*Raglan (6th)*, Geoffrey Somerset, *b.* 1932, *s.* 2010, *m.*	Inigo A. F. S., *b.* 2004
1932	*Rankeillour (5th)*, Michael Richard Hope, *b.* 1940, *s.* 2005, *m.*	James F. H., *b.* 1968
1953	*Rathcavan (3rd)*, Hugh Detmar Torrens O'Neill, *b.* 1939, *s.* 1994, *m.*	Hon. François H. N. O'N., *b.* 1984
1916	*Rathcreedan (3rd)*, Christopher John Norton, *b.* 1949, *s.* 1990, *m.*	Hon. Adam G. N., *b.* 1952
1868 I.	*Rathdonnell (5th)*, Thomas Benjamin McClintock-Bunbury, *b.* 1938, *s.* 1959, *m.*	Hon. William L. M.-B., *b.* 1966
1911	*Ravensdale (3rd)*, Nicholas Mosley, MC, *b.* 1923, *s.* 1966, *m.*	Daniel N. M., *b.* 1982
1821	*Ravensworth (9th)*, Thomas Arthur Hamish Liddell, *b.* 1954, *s.* 2004, *m.*	Hon. Henry A. T. L., *b.* 1987
1821	*Rayleigh (6th)*, John Gerald Strutt, *b.* 1960, *s.* 1988, *m.*	Hon. John F. S., *b.* 1993
1937	** *Rea (3rd)*, John Nicolas Rea, MD, *b.* 1928, *s.* 1981, *m.*	Hon. Matthew J. R., *b.* 1956
1628 S.	*Reay (15th)*, Aeneas Simon Mackay, *b.* 1965, *s.* 2013, *m.*	Master of Reay, *b.* 2010
1902	*Redesdale (6th) and Mitford (life peerage, 2000)*, Rupert Bertram Mitford, *b.* 1967, *s.* 1991, *m.*	Hon. Bertram D. M., *b.* 2000
1940	*Reith (2nd)*, Christopher John Reith, *b.* 1928, *s.* 1971, *m.* Disclaimed for life 1972.	Hon. James H. J. R., *b.* 1971
1928	*Remnant (3rd)*, James Wogan Remnant, CVO, *b.* 1930, *s.* 1967, *m.*	Hon. Philip J. R., CBE, *b.* 1954
1806 I.	*Rendlesham (9th)*, Charles William Brooke Thellusson, *b.* 1954, *s.* 1999, *m.*	Hon. Peter R. T., *b.* 1920
1933	*Rennell (4th)*, James Roderick David Tremayne Rodd, *b.* 1978, *s.* 2006	None
1964	*Renwick (2nd)*, Harry Andrew Renwick, *b.* 1935, *s.* 1973, *m.*	Hon. Robert J. R., *b.* 1966
1885	*Revelstoke (7th)*, Alexander Rupert Baring, *b.* 1970, *s.* 2012	Hon. Thomas J. B., *b.* 1971
1905	*Ritchie of Dundee (6th)*, Charles Rupert Rendall Ritchie, *b.* 1958, *s.* 2008, *m.*	Hon. Sebastian R., *b.* 2004
1935	*Riverdale (3rd)*, Anthony Robert Balfour, *b.* 1960, *s.* 1998	Arthur M. B., *b.* 1938

1961	*Robertson of Oakridge (3rd)*, William Brian Elworthy Robertson, *b.* 1975, *s.* 2009, *m.*	None
1938	*Roborough (4th)*, Massey John Henry Lopes, *b.* 1969, *s.* 2015, *m.*	Hon. Henry M. P. L., *b.* 1997
1931	*Rochester (2nd)*, Foster Charles Lowry Lamb, *b.* 1916, *s.* 1955, *w.*	Hon. David C. L., *b.* 1944
1934	*Rockley (4th)*, Anthony Robert Cecil, *b.* 1961, *s.* 2011, *m.*	Hon. William E. C., *b.* 1996
1782 M.	*Rodney (11th)*, John George Brydges Rodney, *b.* 1999, *s.* 2011	Nicholas S. H. R., *b.* 1947
1651 S.	*Rollo (14th) and Dunning (5th) (1869)*, David Eric Howard Rollo, *b.* 1943, *s.* 1997, *m.*	Master of Rollo, *b.* 1972
1959	*Rootes (3rd)*, Nicholas Geoffrey Rootes, *b.* 1951, *s.* 1992, *m.*	William B. R., *b.* 1944
1796 I.	*Rossmore (7th) and Rossmore (6th) (1838)*, William Warner Westenra, *b.* 1931, *s.* 1958, *m.*	Hon. Benedict W. W., *b.* 1983
1939 **	*Rotherwick (3rd)*, (Herbert) Robin Cayzer, *b.* 1954, *s.* 1996, *m.*	Hon. H. Robin C., *b.* 1989
1885	*Rothschild (4th)*, (Nathaniel Charles) Jacob Rothschild, OM, GBE, *b.* 1936, *s.* 1990, *m.*	Hon. Nathaniel P. V. J. R., *b.* 1971
1911	*Rowallan (4th)*, John Polson Cameron Corbett, *b.* 1947, *s.* 1993, *m.*	Hon. Jason W. P. C. C., *b.* 1972
1947	*Rugby (3rd)*, Robert Charles Maffey, *b.* 1951, *s.* 1990, *m.*	Hon. Timothy J. H. M., *b.* 1975
1919 **	*Russell of Liverpool (3rd)*, Simon Gordon Jared Russell, *b.* 1952, *s.* 1981, *m.*	Hon. Edward C. S. R., *b.* 1985
1876	*Sackville (7th)*, Robert Bertrand Sackville-West, *b.* 1958, *s.* 2004, *m.*	Hon. Arthur S-W., *b.* 2000
1964	*St Helens (2nd)*, Richard Francis Hughes-Young, *b.* 1945, *s.* 1980, *m.*	Hon. Henry T. H.-Y., *b.* 1986
1559 **	*St John of Bletso (21st)*, Anthony Tudor St John, *b.* 1957, *s.* 1978, *m.*	Hon. Oliver B. St J., *b.* 1995
1887	*St Levan (5th)*, James Piers Southwell St Aubyn, *b.* 1950, *s.* 2013, *m.*	Hon. Hugh J. St A., *b.* 1983
1885	*St Oswald (6th)*, Charles Rowland Andrew Winn, *b.* 1959, *s.* 1999, *m.*	Hon. Rowland C. S. H. W., *b.* 1986
1960	*Sanderson of Ayot (2nd)*, Alan Lindsay Sanderson, *b.* 1931, *s.* 1971, *m.* Disclaimed for life 1971.	Hon. Michael S., *b.* 1959
1945	*Sandford (3rd)*, James John Mowbray Edmondson, *b.* 1949, *s.* 2009, *m.*	Hon. Devon J. E., *b.* 1986
1871	*Sandhurst (6th)*, Guy Rees John Mansfield, QC, *b.* 1949, *s.* 2002, *m.*	Hon. Edward J. M., *b.* 1982
1888	*Savile (4th)*, John Anthony Thornhill Lumley-Savile, *b.* 1947, *s.* 2008, *m.*	Hon. James G. A. L-S., *b.* 1975
1447	*Saye and Sele (21st)*, Nathaniel Thomas Allen Fiennes, *b.* 1920, *s.* 1968, *m.*	Hon. Martin G. F., *b.* 1961
1826	*Seaford (6th)*, Colin Humphrey Felton Ellis, *b.* 1946, *s.* 1999, *m.*	Hon. Benjamin F. T. E., *b.* 1976
1932 **	*Selsdon (3rd)*, Malcolm McEacharn Mitchell-Thomson, *b.* 1937, *s.* 1963, *m.*	Hon. Callum M. M. M.-T., *b.* 1969
1489 S.	*Sempill (21st)*, James William Stuart Whitemore Sempill, *b.* 1949, *s.* 1995, *m.*	Master of Sempill, *b.* 1979
1916	*Shaughnessy (5th)*, Charles George Patrick Shaughnessy, *b.* 1955, *s.* 2007, *m.*	David J. S., *b.* 1957
1946	*Shepherd (3rd)*, Graham George Shepherd, *b.* 1949, *s.* 2001, *m.*	Hon. Patrick M. S., *b.* 1980
1964	*Sherfield (3rd)*, Dwight William Makins, *b.* 1951, *s.* 2006, *m.*	None
1902	*Shuttleworth (5th)*, Charles Geoffrey Nicholas Kay-Shuttleworth, KCVO, *b.* 1948, *s.* 1975, *m.*	Hon. Thomas E. K.-S., *b.* 1976
1950	*Silkin (3rd)*, Christopher Lewis Silkin, *b.* 1947, *s.* 2001. Disclaimed for life 2002.	Rory L. S., *b.* 1954
1963	*Silsoe (3rd)*, Simon Rupert Trustram Eve *b.* 1966, *s.* 2005	Hon. Peter N. T. E., *b.* 1930
1947	*Simon of Wythenshawe (3rd)*, Matthew Simon, *b.* 1955, *s.* 2002, *m.*	Michael B. S., *b.* 1970
1449 S.	*Sinclair (18th)*, Matthew Murray Kennedy St Clair *b.* 1968, *s.* 2004, *m.*	Master of Sinclair, *b.* 2007
1957	*Sinclair of Cleeve (3rd)*, John Lawrence Robert Sinclair, *b.* 1953, *s.* 1985	None
1919	*Sinha (6th)*, Arup Kumar Sinha, *b.* 1966, *s.* 1999	Hon. Dilip K. S., *b.* 1967
1828 **	*Skelmersdale (7th)*, Roger Bootle-Wilbraham, *b.* 1945, *s.* 1973, *m.*	Hon. Andrew B.-W., *b.* 1977
1916	*Somerleyton (4th)*, Hugh Francis Saville Crossley, *b.* 1971, *s.* 2012, *m.*	Hon. John de B. T. S. C., *b.* 2010
1784	*Somers (9th)*, Philip Sebastian Somers Cocks, *b.* 1948, *s.* 1995	Jonathan B. C., *b.* 1985
1780	*Southampton (7th)*, Edward Charles FitzRoy, *b.* 1955, *s.* 2015, *m.*	Hon. Charles E. M. F., *b.* 1983
1959	*Spens (4th)*, Patrick Nathaniel George Spens, *b.* 1968, *s.* 2001, *m.*	Hon. Peter L. S., *b.* 2000
1640	*Stafford (15th)*, Francis Melfort William Fitzherbert, *b.* 1954, *s.* 1986, *m.*	Hon. Benjamin J. B. F., *b.* 1983
1938	*Stamp (4th)*, Trevor Charles Bosworth Stamp, MD, *b.* 1935, *s.* 1987, *m.*	Hon. Nicholas C. T. S., *b.* 1978
1839	*Stanley of Alderley (9th)*, *Sheffield (9th) (I. 1738) and Eddisbury (8th) (1848)*, Richard Oliver Stanley, *b.* 1956, *s.* 2013, *m.*	Hon. Charles E. S., *b.* 1960
1318	*Strabolgi (12th)*, Andrew David Whitley Kenworthy, *b.* 1967, *s.* 2010, *m.*	Hon. Joel B. K., *b.* 2004
1628	*Strange (17th)*, Adam Humphrey Drummond of Megginch, *b.* 1953, *s.* 2005, *m.*	Hon. John A. H. D. of M. *b.* 1992
1955	*Strathalmond (3rd)*, William Roberton Fraser, *b.* 1947, *s.* 1976, *m.*	Hon. William G. F., *b.* 1976
1936	*Strathcarron (3rd)*, Ian David Patrick Macpherson, *b.* 1949, *s.* 2006, *m.*	Hon. Rory D. A. M., *b.* 1982
1955 **	*Strathclyde (2nd)*, Thomas Galloway Dunlop du Roy de Blicquy Galbraith, CH, PC, *b.* 1960, *s.* 1985, *m.*	Hon. Charles W. du R. de B. G., *b.* 1962
1900	*Strathcona and Mount Royal (4th)*, Donald Euan Palmer Howard, *b.* 1923, *s.* 1959, *m.*	Hon. D. Alexander S. H., *b.* 1961
1836	*Stratheden (7th) and Campbell (7th) (1841)*, David Anthony Campbell, *b.* 1963, *s.* 2011, *m.*	None
1884	*Strathspey (6th)*, James Patrick Trevor Grant of Grant, *b.* 1943, *s.* 1992, *m.*	Hon. Michael P. F. G., *b.* 1953
1838	*Sudeley (7th)*, Merlin Charles Sainthill Hanbury-Tracy, *b.* 1939, *s.* 1941	Nicholas E. J. H.-T., *b.* 1959

1786	*Suffield (12th)*, Charles Anthony Assheton Harbord-Hamond, *b.* 1953, *s.* 2011, *m.*	Hon. John E. R. H.-H., *b.* 1956
1893	*Swansea (5th)*, Richard Anthony Hussey Vivian, *b.* 1957, *s.* 2005, *m.*	Hon. James H. H. V., *b.* 1999
1907	*Swaythling (5th)*, Charles Edgar Samuel Montagu, *b.* 1954, *s.* 1998, *m.*	Rupert A. S. M., *b.* 1965
1919	** *Swinfen (3rd)*, Roger Mynors Swinfen Eady, *b.* 1938, *s.* 1977, *m.*	Hon. Charles R. P. S. E., *b.* 1971
1831 I.	*Talbot of Malahide (10th)*, Reginald John Richard Arundell, *b.* 1931, *s.* 1987, *m.*	Hon. Richard J. T. A., *b.* 1957
1946	*Tedder (3rd)*, Robin John Tedder, *b.* 1955, *s.* 1994, *m.*	Hon. Benjamin J. T., *b.* 1985
1884	*Tennyson (6th)*, David Harold Alexander Tennyson, *b.* 1960, *s.* 2006	Alan J. D. T., *b.* 1965
1918	*Terrington (6th)*, Christopher Richard James Woodhouse, MB, *b.* 1946, *s.* 2001, *m.*	Hon. Jack H. L. W., *b.* 1978
1940	*Teviot (2nd)*, Charles John Kerr, *b.* 1934, *s.* 1968, *m.*	Hon. Charles R. K., *b.* 1971
1616	*Teynham (20th)*, John Christopher Ingham Roper-Curzon, *b.* 1928, *s.* 1972, *m.*	Hon. David J. H. I. R.-C., *b.* 1965
1964	*Thomson of Fleet (3rd)*, David Kenneth Roy Thomson, *b.* 1957, *s.* 2006, *m.*	Hon. Benjamin T., *b.* 2006
1792	** *Thurlow (9th)*, Roualeyn Robert Hovell-Thurlow-Cumming-Bruce, *b.* 1952, *s.* 2013, *m.*	Hon. Nicholas E. H.-T.-C.-B., *b.* 1986
1876	*Tollemache (5th)*, Timothy John Edward Tollemache, KCVO, *b.* 1939, *s.* 1975, *m.*	Hon. Edward J. H. T., *b.* 1976
1564 S.	*Torphichen (15th)*, James Andrew Douglas Sandilands, *b.* 1946, *s.* 1975, *m.*	Robert P. S., *b.* 1950
1947	** *Trefgarne (2nd)*, David Garro Trefgarne, PC, *b.* 1941, *s.* 1960, *m.*	Hon. George G. T., *b.* 1970
1921	*Trevethin (5th) and Oaksey (3rd) (1947)*, Patrick John Tristram Lawrence, QC, *b.* 1960, *s.* 2012, *m.*	Hon. Oliver J. T. L., *b.* 1990
1880	*Trevor (5th)*, Marke Charles Hill-Trevor, *b.* 1970, *s.* 1997, *m.*	Hon. Iain R. H.-T., *b.* 1971
1461 I.	*Trimlestown (21st)*, Raymond Charles Barnewall, *b.* 1930, *s.* 1997	None
1940	*Tryon (3rd)*, Anthony George Merrik Tryon, OBE, *b.* 1940, *s.* 1976, *w.*	Hon. Charles G. B. T., *b.* 1976
1935	*Tweedsmuir (4th)*, John William de l'Aigle (Toby) Buchan, *b.* 1950, *s.* 2008, *m.*	Hon. John A. G. B., *b.* 1986
1523	*Vaux of Harrowden (12th)*, Richard Hubert Gordon Gilbey, *b.* 1965, *s.* 2014, *m.*	Hon. Alexander J. C. G., *b.* 2000
1800 I.	*Ventry (8th)*, Andrew Wesley Daubeny de Moleyns, *b.* 1943, *s.* 1987, *m.*	Hon. Francis W. D. de M., *b.* 1965
1762	*Vernon (11th)*, Anthony William Vernon-Harcourt, *b.* 1939, *s.* 2000, *m.*	Hon. Simon A. V-H., *b.* 1969
1922	*Vestey (3rd)*, Samuel George Armstrong Vestey, KCVO, *b.* 1941, *s.* 1954, *m.*	Hon. William G. V., *b.* 1983
1841	*Vivian (7th)*, Charles Crespigny Hussey Vivian, *b.* 1966, *s.* 2004	Thomas C. B. V., *b.* 1971
1934	*Wakehurst (3rd)*, (John) Christopher Loder, *b.* 1925, *s.* 1970, *m.*	Hon. Timothy W. L., *b.* 1958
1723	** *Walpole (10th) and Walpole of Wolterton (8th) (1756)*, Robert Horatio Walpole, *b.* 1938, *s.* 1989, *m.*	Hon. Jonathan R. H. W., *b.* 1967
1780	*Walsingham (9th)*, John de Grey, MC, *b.* 1925, *s.* 1965, *m.*	Hon. Robert de. G., *b.* 1969
1936	*Wardington (3rd)*, William Simon Pease, *b.* 1925, *s.* 2005, *m.*	None
1792 I.	*Waterpark (8th)*, Roderick Alexander Cavendish, *b.* 1959, *s.* 2013, *m.*	Hon. Luke F. C., *b.* 1990
1942	*Wedgwood (5th)*, Antony John Wedgwood, *b.* 1944, *s.* 2014, *m.*	Hon. Josiah T. A. W., *b.* 1978
1861	*Westbury (6th)*, Richard Nicholas Bethell, MBE, *b.* 1950, *s.* 2001, *m.*	Hon. Alexander B., *b.* 1986
1944	*Westwood (3rd)*, (William) Gavin Westwood, *b.* 1944, *s.* 1991, *m.*	Hon. W. Fergus W., *b.* 1972
1544/5	*Wharton (12th)*, Myles Christopher David Robertson, *b.* 1964, *s.* 2000, *m.*	Hon. Meghan Z. M. R., *b.* 2006
1935	*Wigram (2nd)*, (George) Neville (Clive) Wigram, MC, *b.* 1915, *s.* 1960, *w.*	Maj. Hon. Andrew F. C. W., MVO, *b.* 1949
1491	** *Willoughby de Broke (21st)*, Leopold David Verney, *b.* 1938, *s.* 1986, *m.*	Hon. Rupert G. V., *b.* 1966
1937	*Windlesham (4th)*, James Rupert Hennessy, *b.* 1968, *s.* 2010, *m.*	Hon. George R. J. H., *b.* 2006
1951	*Wise (3rd)*, Christopher John Clayton Wise, *b.* 1949, *s.* 2012	Hon. Martin H. W., *b.* 1950
1869	*Wolverton (8th)*, Miles John Glyn, *b.* 1966, *s.* 2011	Jonathan C. G., *b.* 1990
1928	*Wraxall (3rd)*, Eustace Hubert Beilby Gibbs, KCVO, CMG, *b.* 1929, *s.* 2001, *m.*	Hon. Anthony H. G., *b.* 1958
1915	*Wrenbury (4th)*, William Edwards Buckley, *b.* 1966, *s.* 2014, *m.*	Hon. Jamie P. B., *b.* 2001
1838	*Wrottesley (6th)*, Clifton Hugh Lancelot de Verdon Wrottesley, *b.* 1968, *s.* 1977, *m.*	Hon. Victor E. F. de V. W., *b.* 2004
1829	*Wynford (9th)*, John Philip Robert Best, *b.* 1950, *s.* 2002, *m.*	Hon. Harry R. F. B., *b.* 1987
1308	*Zouche (18th)*, James Assheton Frankland, *b.* 1943, *s.* 1965, *m.*	Hon. William T. A. F., *b.* 1984

BARONESSES/LADIES IN THEIR OWN RIGHT

Style, The Rt. Hon. the Lady _ , *or* The Rt. Hon. the Baroness _ , according to her preference. Either style may be used, except in the case of Scottish titles (indicated by S.), which are not baronies (*see* page 44) and whose holders are always addressed as Lady.

Envelope, may be addressed in same way as a Baron's wife or, if she prefers *(formal),* The Rt. Hon. the Baroness _;   *(social),* The Baroness _. Otherwise as for a Baron's wife

Husband, Untitled

Children's style, As for children of a Baron

Created	Title, order of succession, name, etc	Heir
1664	*Arlington (11th),* Jennifer Jane Forwood, *b.* 1939, *s.* 1999, *w.* Title called out of abeyance 1999	Hon. Patrick J. D. F., *b.* 1967
1455	*Berners (16th),* Pamela Vivien Kirkham, *b.* 1929, *s.* 1995, *m.* Title called out of abeyance 1995	Hon. Rupert W. T. K., *b.* 1953
1529	*Braye (8th),* Mary Penelope Aubrey-Fletcher, *b.* 1941, *s.* 1985, *m.*	Linda K. C. Fothergill, *b.* 1930
1321	*Dacre (29th),* Emily Beamish, *b.* 1983, *s.* 2014, *m.*	Three co-heiresses
1283	*Fauconberg (10th) and Conyers (16th) (1509),* Baronies in abeyance between two co-heiresses since 2013	
1490 S.	*Herries of Terregles (15th),* Mary Katharine Mumford, DCVO, *b.* 1940, *s.* 2014, *w.*	Marchioness of Lothian, *b.* 1945
1597	*Howard de Walden (10th),* Mary Hazel Caridwen Czernin, *b.* 1935, *s.* 2004, *m.* Title called out of abeyance 2004	Hon. Peter J. J. C., *b.* 1966
1602 S.	*Kinloss (13th),* Teresa Mary Nugent Freeman-Grenville, *b.* 1957, *s.* 2012	Mistress of Kinloss, *b.* 1960
1445 S.	*Saltoun (20th),* Flora Marjory Fraser, *b.* 1930, *s.* 1979, *w.*	Hon. Katharine I. M. I. F., *b.* 1957
1313	*Willoughby de Eresby (27th),* (Nancy) Jane Marie Heathcote-Drummond-Willoughby, *b.* 1934, *s.* 1983	Two co-heirs

LIFE PEERS

Style, The Rt. Hon. the Lord _ /The Rt. Hon. the Lady _ , *or* The Rt. Hon. the Baroness _ , according to her preference *Envelope (formal),* The Rt. Hon. Lord _/Lady_/ Baroness_; *(social),* The Lord _/Lady_/Baroness_ *Letter (formal),* My Lord/Lady; *(social),* Dear Lord/ Lady _. *Spoken,* Lord/Lady _
Wife's style, The Rt. Hon. the Lady _
Husband, Untitled
Children's style, 'The Hon.' before forename (F_) and surname (S_)
   Envelope, The Hon. F_ S_. *Letter,* Dear Mr/Miss/Mrs S_. *Spoken,* Mr/Miss/Mrs S_

NEW LIFE PEERAGES

1 September 2014 to 31 August 2015:
Dr Rosalind Altmann; Rt. Hon. James Arbuthnot; Rt. Hon. Gregory Barker; Rt. Hon. Sir Alan Beith; Rt. Hon. David Blunkett; Sharon Bowles; James Bridges, MBE; Sir Malcolm Bruce; Lorely Burt; Rt. Hon. Sir Menzies Campbell, CH, CBE, QC; Rt. Hon. Alistair Darling; Andrew Dunlop; Sir Jonathan Evans, KCB; Catherine Fall; Rt. Hon. Lynne Featherstone; Simone Finn; Rt. Hon. Don Foster; Stephen Gilbert; Sir Andrew Green, KCMG; Rt. Hon. William Hague; Viscount Hailsham; Rt. Hon. Peter Hain; William Hay; Robert Hayward, OBE; Rt. Hon. Dame Tessa Jowell, DBE; Richard Keen, QC; Sir Robert Kerslake; Rt. Hon. Andrew Lansley; Spencer Livermore; James Lupton, CBE; Ruby McGregor-Smith, CBE; Anne McIntosh; Rt. Hon. Francis Maude, Michelle Mone, OBE; TD; Rt. Hon. Peter Murphy; Jonny Oates; Terence O'Neill; James O'Shaughnessy; Emma Pidding, CBE; Stuart Polak, CBE; Cllr Gary Porter; Rt. Hon. Dame Dawn Primarolo, DBE; David Prior; Cllr Elizabeth Redfern; Rt. Hon. Andrew Robathan; Kate Rock; Sir Robert Rogers, KCB; Cllr Jane Scott, OBE; Shas Sheehan; Kevin Shinkwin; Philip Smith, CBE; Philippa Stroud; Rt. Hon. Sir Andrew Stunell, OBE; Dorothy Thornhill, MBE; Dave Watts; Rt. Hon. David Willetts; Alison Wolf, CBE; Rt. Hon. Sir George Young, Bt., CH

SYMBOLS
* Hereditary peer who has been granted a life peerage. For further details, please refer to the Hereditary Peers section. For example, life peer *Balniel* can be found under his hereditary title *Earl of Crawford and Balcarres*
§ Members of the Judiciary currently disqualified from sitting or voting in the House of Lords until they retire from that office. For further information *see* Law Courts and Offices
‡ Title not confirmed at time of going to press
¶ Peer who has permanently resigned from the House of Lords

CREATED UNDER THE APPELLATE JURISDICTION ACT 1876 (AS AMENDED)

BARONS
Created
2004   *Brown of Eaton-under-Heywood,* Simon Denis Brown, PC, *b.* 1937, *m.*
1991   *Browne-Wilkinson,* Nicolas Christopher Henry Browne-Wilkinson, PC, *b.* 1930, *m.*
2004   *Carswell,* Robert Douglas Carswell, PC, *b.* 1934, *m.*

2009   *Collins of Mapesbury,* Lawrence Antony Collins, PC, *b.* 1941
1986   *Goff of Chieveley,* Robert Lionel Archibald Goff, PC, *b.* 1926, *m.*
1995   *Hoffmann,* Leonard Hubert Hoffmann, PC, *b.* 1934, *m.*
1997   *Hutton,* (James) Brian (Edward) Hutton, PC, *b.* 1931, *m.*
2009   §*Kerr of Tonaghmore,* Brian Francis Kerr, PC, *b.* 1948, *m.*
1993   ¶*Lloyd of Berwick,* Anthony John Leslie Lloyd, PC, *b.* 1929, *m.*
2005   §*Mance,* Jonathan Hugh Mance, PC, *b.* 1943, *m.*
1998   *Millett,* Peter Julian Millett, PC, *b.* 1932, *m.*
2007   §*Neuberger of Abbotsbury,* David Edmond Neuberger, PC, *b.* 1948, *m.*
1994   *Nicholls of Birkenhead,* Donald James Nicholls, PC, *b.* 1933, *m.*
1999   *Phillips of Worth Matravers,* Nicholas Addison Phillips, KG, PC, *b.* 1938, *m.*
1997   *Saville of Newdigate,* Mark Oliver Saville, PC, *b.* 1936, *m.*
2000   *Scott of Foscote,* Richard Rashleigh Folliott Scott, PC, *b.* 1934, *m.*
1995   *Steyn,* Johan van Zyl Steyn, PC, *b.* 1932, *m.*
2003   *Walker of Gestingthorpe,* Robert Walker, PC, *b.* 1938, *m.*
1992   *Woolf,* Harry Kenneth Woolf, CH, PC, *b.* 1933, *m.*

BARONESSES
2004   §*Hale of Richmond,* Brenda Marjorie Hale, DBE, PC, *b.* 1945, *m.*

CREATED UNDER THE LIFE PEERAGES ACT 1958

BARONS
Created
2001   *Adebowale,* Victor Olufemi Adebowale, CBE, *b.* 1962
2005   *Adonis,* Andrew Adonis, PC, *b.* 1963, *m.*
2011   *Ahmad of Wimbledon,* Tariq Mahmood Ahmad, *b.* 1968, *m.*
1998   *Ahmed,* Nazir Ahmed, *b.* 1957, *m.*
1996   *Alderdice,* John Thomas Alderdice, *b.* 1955, *m.*
2010   *Allan of Hallam,* Richard Beecroft Allan, *b.* 1966
2013   *Allen of Kensington,* Charles Lamb Allen, CBE, *b.* 1957
1998   *Alli,* Waheed Alli, *b.* 1964
2004   *Alliance,* David Alliance, CBE, *b.* 1932
1997   *Alton of Liverpool,* David Patrick Paul Alton, *b.* 1951, *m.*
2005   *Anderson of Swansea,* Donald Anderson, PC, *b.* 1939, *m.*
2015   ‡*Arbuthnot,* James Arbuthnot, PC, *b.* 1952, *m.*
1992   *Archer of Weston-super-Mare,* Jeffrey Howard Archer, *b.* 1940, *m.*
1988   *Armstrong of Ilminster,* Robert Temple Armstrong, GCB, CVO, *b.* 1927, *m.*
1999   **Armstrong-Jones,* Earl of Snowdon, GCVO, *b.* 1930, *m.* (*see* Hereditary Peers)
2000   ¶*Ashcroft,* Michael Anthony Ashcroft, KCMG, PC, *b.* 1946, *m.*

2001	*Ashdown of Norton-sub-Hamdon,* Jeremy John Durham (Paddy) Ashdown, GCMG, KBE, CH, PC, *b.* 1941, *m.*	2001	*Browne of Madingley,* Edmund John Phillip Browne, *b.* 1948
1998	*Bach,* William Stephen Goulden Bach, *b.* 1946, *m.*	2015	‡*Bruce,* Malcolm Gray Bruce, *b.* 1944, *m.*
1997	¶*Bagri,* Raj Kumar Bagri, CBE, *b.* 1930, *m.*	2006	*Burnett,* John Patrick Aubone Burnett, *b.* 1945, *m.*
1997	*Baker of Dorking,* Kenneth Wilfred Baker, CH, PC, *b.* 1934, *m.*	1998	*Burns,* Terence Burns, GCB, *b.* 1944, *m.*
2013	*Balfe,* Richard Andrew Balfe, *b.* 1944, *m.*	1998	*Butler of Brockwell,* (Frederick Edward) Robin Butler, KG, GCB, CVO, PC, *b.* 1938, *m.*
1974	**Balniel,* The Earl of Crawford and Balcarres, KT, GCVO, PC *b.* 1927, *m.* (*see* Hereditary Peers)	2014	*Callanan,* Martin John Callanan, *b.* 1961, *m.*
2013	*Bamford,* Anthony Paul Bamford, *b.* 1945, *m.*	2004	*Cameron of Dillington,* Ewen (James Hanning) Cameron, *b.* 1949, *m.*
1992	*Barber of Tewkesbury,* Derek Coates Barber, *b.* 1918, *m.*	1984	*Cameron of Lochbroom,* Kenneth John Cameron, PC, *b.* 1931, *m.*
2015	‡*Barker,* Gregory Barker, PC, *b.* 1966, *m.*	2015	‡*Campbell,* (Walter) Menzies Campbell, CH, CBE, QC, *b.* 1941, *m.*
1997	*Bassam of Brighton,* (John) Steven Bassam, PC, *b.* 1953	2001	*Campbell-Savours,* Dale Norman Campbell-Savours, *b.* 1943, *m.*
2008	*Bates,* Michael Walton Bates, PC, *b.* 1961	2002	*Carey of Clifton,* Rt. Revd George Leonard Carey, PC, Royal Victorian Chain, *b.* 1935, *m.*
2010	*Beecham,* Jeremy Hugh Beecham, *b.* 1944, *m.*	
2015	‡*Beith,* Alan James Beith, PC, *b.* 1943, *m.*	1999	**Carington of Upton,* Lord Carrington, KG, GCMG, CH, MC, PC, *b.* 1919, *w.* (*see* Hereditary Peers)
1998	*Bell,* Timothy John Leigh Bell, *b.* 1941, *m.*	
2013	*Berkeley of Knighton,* Michael Fitzhardinge Berkeley, CBE, *b.* 1948, *m.*	1999	*Carlile of Berriew,* Alexander Charles Carlile, QC, *b.* 1948, *m.*
2001	*Best,* Richard Stuart Best, OBE, *b.* 1945, *m.*	2013	*Carrington of Fulham,* Matthew Hadrian Marshall Carrington, *b.* 1947, *m.*
2007	*Bew,* Prof. Paul Anthony Elliott Bew, *b.* 1950, *m.*	
2001	*Bhatia,* Amirali Alibhai Bhatia, OBE, *b.* 1932, *m.*	2008	*Carter of Barnes,* Stephen Andrew Carter, CBE, *b.* 1964, *m.*
2004	*Bhattacharyya,* Prof. (Sushantha) Kumar Bhattacharyya, CBE *b.* 1932, *m.*	2004	*Carter of Coles,* Patrick Robert Carter, *b.* 1946, *m.*
2010	*Bichard,* Michael George Bichard, KCB, *b.* 1947	2014	*Cashman,* Michael Maurice Cashman, CBE, *b.* 1950
2006	*Bilimoria,* Karan Faridoon Bilimoria, CBE, *b.* 1961, *m.*	1990	*Cavendish of Furness,* (Richard) Hugh Cavendish, *b.* 1941, *m.*
2000	*Birt,* John Francis Hodgess Birt, *b.* 1944, *m.*	1996	*Chadlington,* Peter Selwyn Gummer, *b.* 1942, *m.*
2010	*Black of Brentwood,* Guy Vaughan Black, *b.* 1964, *m.*	1964	*Chalfont,* (Alun) Arthur Gwynne Jones, OBE, MC, PC, *b.* 1919, *w.*
2001	*Black of Crossharbour,* Conrad Moffat Black, PC (Canadian), *b.* 1944, *m.*	2005	*Chidgey,* David William George Chidgey, *b.* 1942, *m.*
1997	*Blackwell,* Norman Roy Blackwell, *b.* 1952, *m.*	1998	*Christopher,* Anthony Martin Grosvenor Christopher, CBE, *b.* 1925, *m.*
2010	*Blair of Boughton,* Ian Warwick Blair, QPM, *b.* 1953, *m.*	2001	*Clark of Windermere,* David George Clark, PC, PHD, *b.* 1939, *m.*
2011	*Blencathra,* David John Maclean, PC, *b.* 1953	1998	*Clarke of Hampstead,* Anthony James Clarke, CBE, *b.* 1932, *m.*
2015	‡*Blunkett,* David Blunkett, PC, *b.* 1947, *m.*	
1995	*Blyth of Rowington,* James Blyth, *b.* 1940, *m.*	2009	§*Clarke of Stone-Cum-Ebony,* Anthony Peter Clarke, PC, *b.* 1943, *m.*
2010	*Boateng,* Paul Yaw Boateng, PC, *b.* 1951, *m.*	
1996	*Borrie,* Gordon Johnson Borrie, QC, *b.* 1931, *w.*	1998	*Clement-Jones,* Timothy Francis Clement-Jones, CBE, *b.* 1949, *m.*
2010	*Boswell of Aynho,* Timothy Eric Boswell, *b.* 1942, *m.*	1990	*Clinton-Davis,* Stanley Clinton Clinton-Davis, PC, *b.* 1928, *m.*
2013	*Bourne of Aberystwyth,* Nicholas Henry Bourne, *b.* 1952	2000	*Coe,* Sebastian Newbold Coe, CH, KBE, *b.* 1956, *m.*
1996	*Bowness,* Peter Spencer Bowness, CBE, *b.* 1943, *m.*	2011	*Collins of Highbury,* Raymond Edward Harry Collins, *b.* 1954
2003	*Boyce,* Michael Boyce, KG, GCB, OBE, *b.* 1943, *m.*	
2006	§*Boyd of Duncansby,* Colin David Boyd, PC, *b.* 1953, *m.*	2001	*Condon,* Paul Leslie Condon, QPM, *b.* 1947, *m.*
2006	*Bradley,* Keith John Charles Bradley, PC, *b.* 1950, *m.*	2014	*Cooper of Windrush,* Andrew Timothy Cooper, *b.* 1963, *m.*
1999	*Bradshaw,* William Peter Bradshaw, *b.* 1936, *m.*	1997	*Cope of Berkeley,* John Ambrose Cope, PC, *b.* 1937, *m.*
1998	*Bragg,* Melvyn Bragg, *b.* 1939, *m.*	
1987	*Bramall,* Edwin Noel Westby Bramall, KG, GCB, OBE, MC, *b.* 1923, *w.*	2010	*Cormack,* Patrick Thomas Cormack, *b.* 1939, *m.*
2000	*Brennan,* Daniel Joseph Brennan, QC, *b.* 1942, *m.*	2006	*Cotter,* Brian Joseph Michael Cotter, *b.* 1939, *m.*
2015	*Bridges of Headley,* James George Robert Bridges, MBE, *b.* 1970, *m.*	1991	*Craig of Radley,* David Brownrigg Craig, GCB, OBE, *b.* 1929, *m.*
1976	*Briggs,* Asa Briggs, FBA, *b.* 1921, *m.*	1987	*Crickhowell,* (Roger) Nicholas Edwards, PC, *b.* 1934, *m.*
2004	*Broers,* Prof. Alec (Nigel) Broers, *b.* 1938, *m.*	
1997	*Brooke of Alverthorpe,* Clive Brooke, *b.* 1942, *m.*	2006	*Crisp,* (Edmund) Nigel (Ramsay) Crisp, KCB, *b.* 1952, *m.*
2001	*Brooke of Sutton Mandeville,* Peter Leonard Brooke, CH, PC, *b.* 1934, *m.*	2003	*Cullen of Whitekirk,* William Douglas Cullen, KT, PC, *b.* 1935, *m.*
1998	*Brookman,* David Keith Brookman, *b.* 1937, *m.*	
1979	*Brooks of Tremorfa,* John Edward Brooks, *b.* 1927, *m.*	2005	*Cunningham of Felling,* John Anderson Cunningham, PC, *b.* 1939, *m.*
2006	*Browne of Belmont,* Wallace Hamilton Browne, *b.* 1947	1996	*Currie of Marylebone,* David Anthony Currie, *b.* 1946, *m.*
2010	*Browne of Ladyton,* Desmond Henry Browne, PC, *b.* 1952	

2011   *Curry of Kirkharle,* Donald Thomas Younger Curry, CBE, *b.* 1944, *m.*

2011   *Dannatt,* (Francis) Richard Dannatt, GCB, CBE, MC, *b.* 1950, *m.*

2015   ‡*Darling,* Alistair Maclean Darling, PC, *b.* 1953, *m.*

2007   *Darzi of Denham,* Ara Warkes Darzi, KBE, PC, *b.* 1960, *m.*

2006   *Davidson of Glen Clova,* Neil Forbes Davidson, QC, *b.* 1950, *m.*

2009   *Davies of Abersoch,* Evan Mervyn Davies, CBE, *b.* 1952, *m.*

1997   *Davies of Coity,* (David) Garfield Davies, CBE, *b.* 1935, *m.*

1997   *Davies of Oldham,* Bryan Davies, PC, *b.* 1939, *m.*

2010   *Davies of Stamford,* John Quentin Davies, *b.* 1944, *m.*

2006   *Dear,* Geoffrey (James) Dear, QPM, *b.* 1937, *m.*

2010   *Deben,* John Selwyn Gummer, PC, *b.* 1939, *m.*

2012   *Deighton,* Paul Clive Deighton, KBE, *b.* 1956, *m.*

1991   *Desai,* Prof. Meghnad Jagdishchandra Desai, PHD, *b.* 1940, *m.*

1997   *Dholakia,* Navnit Dholakia, OBE, PC, *b.* 1937, *m.*

1997   *Dixon,* Donald Dixon, PC, *b.* 1929, *m.*

1993   *Dixon-Smith,* Robert William Dixon-Smith, *b.* 1934, *m.*

2010   *Dobbs,* Michael John Dobbs, *b.* 1948, *m.*

1985   *Donoughue,* Bernard Donoughue, DPHIL, *b.* 1934

2004   *Drayson,* Paul Rudd Drayson, PC, *b.* 1960, *m.*

1994   *Dubs,* Alfred Dubs, *b.* 1932, *m.*

2015   *Dunlop,* Andrew James Dunlop, *b.* 1959, *m.*

2004   *Dykes,* Hugh John Maxwell Dykes, *b.* 1939, *m.*

1995   *Eames,* Rt. Revd Robert Henry Alexander Eames, OM, PHD, *b.* 1937, *m.*

1992   *Eatwell,* John Leonard Eatwell, PHD, *b.* 1945

1983   ¶*Eden of Winton,* John Benedict Eden, PC, *b.* 1925, *m.*

2011   ¶*Edmiston,* Robert Norman Edmiston, *b.* 1946, *m.*

1999   *Elder,* Thomas Murray Elder, *b.* 1950

1992   *Elis-Thomas,* Dafydd Elis Elis-Thomas, PC, *b.* 1946, *m.*

1981   *Elystan-Morgan,* Dafydd Elystan Elystan-Morgan, *b.* 1932, *w.*

2011   *Empey,* Reginald Norman Morgan Empey, OBE, *b.* 1947, *m.*

2000   *Erskine of Alloa Tower,* Earl of Mar and Kellie, *b.* 1949, *m.* (*see* Hereditary Peers)

1997   ¶*Evans of Parkside,* John Evans, *b.* 1930, *m.*

2000   *Evans of Temple Guiting,* Matthew Evans, CBE, *b.* 1941, *m.*

1998   *Evans of Watford,* David Charles Evans, *b.* 1942, *m.*

2014   *Evans of Weardale,* Jonathan Douglas Evans, KCB, *b.* 1958

1983   *Ezra,* Derek Ezra, MBE, *b.* 1919, *m.*

1997   *Falconer of Thoroton,* Charles Leslie Falconer, PC, QC, *b.* 1951, *m.*

2014   *Farmer,* Michael Stahel Farmer, *b.* 1944, *m.*

1999   *Faulkner of Worcester,* Richard Oliver Faulkner, *b.* 1946, *m.*

2010   *Faulks,* Edward Peter Lawless Faulks, QC, *b.* 1950, *m.*

2001   *Fearn,* Ronald Cyril Fearn, OBE, *b.* 1931, *m.*

1996   *Feldman,* Basil Feldman, *b.* 1926, *m.*

2010   *Feldman of Elstree,* Andrew Simon Feldman, PC, *b.* 1966, *m.*

1999   *Fellowes,* Robert Fellowes, GCB, GCVO, PC, *b.* 1941, *m.*

2011   *Fellowes of West Stafford,* Julian Alexander Fellowes, *b.* 1949, *m.*

1999   *Filkin,* David Geoffrey Nigel Filkin, CBE, *b.* 1944

2011   *Fink,* Stanley Fink, *b.* 1957, *m.*

2013   *Finkelstein,* Daniel William Finkelstein, OBE, *b.* 1962, *m.*

2011   *Flight,* Howard Emerson Flight, *b.* 1948, *m.*

1999   *Forsyth of Drumlean,* Michael Bruce Forsyth, PC, *b.* 1954, *m.*

2015   ‡*Foster,* Donald Michael Ellison Foster, PC, *b.* 1947, *m.*

2005   *Foster of Bishop Auckland,* Derek Foster, PC, *b.* 1937, *m.*

1999   ¶*Foster of Thames Bank,* Norman Robert Foster, OM, *b.* 1935, *m.*

2005   *Foulkes of Cumnock,* George Foulkes, PC, *b.* 1942, *m.*

2001   *Fowler,* (Peter) Norman Fowler, PC, *b.* 1938, *m.*

2014   *Fox,* Christopher Francis Fox, *b.* 1957, *m.*

2011   *Framlingham,* Michael Nicholson Lord, *b.* 1938, *m.*

1997   *Freeman,* Roger Norman Freeman, PC, *b.* 1942, *m.*

2009   *Freud,* David Anthony Freud, PC, *b.* 1950 *m.*

2010   *Gardiner of Kimble,* John Gardiner, *b.* 1956, *m.*

1997   *Garel-Jones,* (William Armand) Thomas Tristan Garel-Jones, PC, *b.* 1941, *m.*

1999   *Gascoyne-Cecil,* The Marquess of Salisbury, KCVO, PC, *b.* 1946, *m.* (*see* Hereditary Peers)

2010   *German,* Michael James German, OBE, *b.* 1945, *m.*

2004   *Giddens,* Prof. Anthony Giddens, *b.* 1938, *m.*

2015   ‡*Gilbert,* Stephen Gilbert

2011   *Glasman,* Maurice Mark Glasman, *b.* 1961, *m.*

2011   *Glendonbrook,* Michael David Bishop, CBE, *b.* 1942

2014   *Goddard of Stockport,* David Goddard, *b.* 1952

2011   *Gold,* David Laurence Gold, *b.* 1951, *m.*

1999   *Goldsmith,* Peter Henry Goldsmith, PC, QC, *b.* 1950, *m.*

1997   ¶*Goodhart,* William Howard Goodhart, QC, *b.* 1933, *m.*

2005   *Goodlad,* Alastair Robertson Goodlad, KCMG, *b.* 1943, *m.*

1997   *Gordon of Strathblane,* James Stuart Gordon, CBE, *b.* 1936, *m.*

1999   *Grabiner,* Anthony Stephen Grabiner, QC, *b.* 1945, *m.*

2011   *Grade of Yarmouth,* Michael Ian Grade, CBE, *b.* 1943, *m.*

1983   *Graham of Edmonton,* (Thomas) Edward Graham, PC, *b.* 1925, *m.*

2000   *Greaves,* Anthony Robert Greaves, *b.* 1942, *m.*

2014   *Green of Deddington,* Andrew Fleming Green, KCMG, *b.* 1941, *m.*

2010   *Green of Hurstpierpoint,* Stephen Keith Green, *b.* 1948, *m.*

2000   ¶*Grenfell of Kilvey,* Lord Grenfell, *b.* 1935, *m.* (*see* Hereditary Peers)

2004   *Griffiths of Burry Port,* Revd Dr Leslie John Griffiths, *b.* 1942, *m.*

1991   *Griffiths of Fforestfach,* Brian Griffiths, *b.* 1941, *m.*

2001   *Grocott,* Bruce Joseph Grocott, PC, *b.* 1940, *m.*

2000   *Gueterbock,* Lord Berkeley, OBE, *b.* 1939, *m.* (*see* Hereditary Peers)

2000   *Guthrie of Craigiebank,* Charles Ronald Llewelyn Guthrie, GCB, LVO, OBE, *b.* 1938, *m.*

1995   *Habgood,* Rt. Revd John Stapylton Habgood, PC, PHD, *b.* 1927, *m.*

2015   ‡*Hague,* William Jefferson Hague, PC, *b.* 1961, *m.*

2015   ‡*Hain,* Peter Gerald Hain, PC, *b.* 1950, *m.*

2010   *Hall of Birkenhead,* Anthony William Hall, CBE, *b.* 1951, *m.*

2007   *Hameed,* Dr Khalid Hameed, *b.* 1941, *m.*

2005   *Hamilton of Epsom,* Archibald Gavin Hamilton, PC,
      b. 1941, *m.*
2001   *Hannay of Chiswick,* David Hugh Alexander
      Hannay, GCMG, CH, *b.* 1935, *w.*
1998   *Hanningfield,* Paul Edward Winston White, *b.* 1940
1997   *Hardie,* Andrew Rutherford Hardie, PC, QC,
      b. 1946, *m.*
2006   *Harries of Pentregarth,* Rt. Revd Richard Douglas
      Harries, *b.* 1936, *m.*
1998   *Harris of Haringey,* (Jonathan) Toby Harris,
      b. 1953, *m.*
1996   *Harris of Peckham,* Philip Charles Harris, *b.* 1942, *m.*
1999   *Harrison,* Lyndon Henry Arthur Harrison,
      b. 1947, *m.*
2004   *Hart of Chilton,* Garry Richard Rushby Hart,
      b. 1940, *m.*
1993   *Haskel,* Simon Haskel, *b.* 1934, *m.*
1998   *Haskins,* Christopher Robin Haskins, *b.* 1937, *m.*
2005   *Hastings of Scarisbrick,* Michael John Hastings,
      CBE, *b.* 1958, *m.*
1997   *Hattersley,* Roy Sidney George Hattersley, PC,
      b. 1932
2013   *Haughey,* William Haughey, OBE, *b.* 1956, *m.*
2004   *Haworth,* Alan Robert Haworth, *b.* 1948, *m.*
2014   *Hay of Ballyore,* William Alexander Hay, *b.* 1950, *m.*
2015   ‡*Hayward,* Robert Antony Hayward, OBE, *b.* 1949
1992   *Healey,* Denis Winston Healey, CH, MBE, PC,
      b. 1917, *w.*
2010   *Hennessy of Nympsfield,* Prof. Peter John Hennessy,
      b. 1947, *m.*
2001   *Heseltine,* Michael Ray Dibdin Heseltine, CH, PC,
      b. 1933, *m.*
1997   *Higgins,* Terence Langley Higgins, KBE, PC,
      b. 1928, *m.*
2010   *Hill of Oareford,* Jonathan Hopkin Hill, CBE, PC,
      b. 1960, *m.*
2000   *Hodgson of Astley Abbotts,* Robin Granville
      Hodgson, CBE, *b.* 1942, *m.*
2015   **‡Hogg,* Viscount Hailsham, PC, QC, *b.* 1945, *m.*
      (*see* Hereditary Peers)
1991   *Hollick,* Clive Richard Hollick, *b.* 1945, *m.*
2013   *Holmes of Richmond,* Christopher Holmes, MBE,
      b. 1971
1995   *Hope of Craighead,* (James Arthur) David Hope,
      KT, PC, *b.* 1938, *m.*
2005   ¶*Hope of Thornes,* Rt. Revd David Michael Hope,
      KCVO, PC, *b.* 1940
2013   *Horam,* John Rhodes Horam, *b.* 1939, *m.*
2010   *Howard of Lympne,* Michael Howard, CH, PC, QC,
      b. 1941, *m.*
2004   *Howard of Rising,* Greville Patrick Charles Howard,
      b. 1941, *m.*
2005   *Howarth of Newport,* Alan Thomas Howarth, CBE,
      PC, *b.* 1944
1992   ¶*Howe of Aberavon,* (Richard Edward) Geoffrey
      Howe, CH, PC, QC, *b.* 1926, *m.*
1997   *Howell of Guildford,* David Arthur Russell Howell,
      PC, *b.* 1936, *m.*
1978   *Howie of Troon,* William Howie, *b.* 1924, *w.*
1997   *Hoyle,* (Eric) Douglas Harvey Hoyle, *b.* 1930, *w.*
1997   *Hughes of Woodside,* Robert Hughes, *b.* 1932, *m.*
2000   *Hunt of Chesterton,* Julian Charles Roland Hunt,
      CBE, *b.* 1941, *m.*
1997   *Hunt of Kings Heath,* Philip Alexander Hunt, OBE,
      PC, *b.* 1949, *m.*
1997   *Hunt of Wirral,* David James Fletcher Hunt, MBE,
      PC, *b.* 1942, *m.*
1997   *Hurd of Westwell,* Douglas Richard Hurd, CH,
      CBE, PC, *b.* 1930, *w.*

2011   *Hussain,* Qurban Hussain, *b.* 1956, *m.*
1978   *Hutchinson of Lullington,* Jeremy Nicolas
      Hutchinson, QC, *b.* 1915, *w.*
2010   *Hutton of Furness,* John Matthew Patrick Hutton,
      PC, *b.* 1955, *m.*
1999   *Imbert,* Peter Michael Imbert, CVO, QPM,
      b. 1933, *m.*
1997   *Inge,* Peter Anthony Inge, KG, GCB, PC,
      b. 1935, *m.*
1987   *Irvine of Lairg,* Alexander Andrew Mackay Irvine,
      PC, QC, *b.* 1940, *m.*
2006   *James of Blackheath,* David Noel James, CBE,
      b. 1937, *m.*
1997   *Janner of Braunstone,* Greville Ewan Janner, QC,
      b. 1928, *w.*
2007   *Janvrin,* Robin Berry Janvrin, GCB, GCVO, PC,
      b. 1946, *m.*
2006   *Jay of Ewelme,* Michael (Hastings) Jay, GCMG,
      b. 1946, *m.*
1987   ¶*Jenkin of Roding,* (Charles) Patrick (Fleeming)
      Jenkin, PC, *b.* 1926, *m.*
2000   ¶*Joffe,* Joel Goodman Joffe, CBE, *b.* 1932, *m.*
2001   *Jones,* (Stephen) Barry Jones, *b.* 1937, *m.*
2007   *Jones of Birmingham,* Digby Marritt Jones, *b.* 1955, *m.*
2005   *Jones of Cheltenham,* Nigel David Jones, *b.* 1948, *m.*
1997   *Jopling,* (Thomas) Michael Jopling, PC, *b.* 1930, *m.*
2000   *Jordan,* William Brian Jordan, CBE, *b.* 1936, *m.*
1991   *Judd,* Frank Ashcroft Judd, *b.* 1935, *m.*
2008   *Judge,* Igor Judge, PC, *b.* 1941, *m.*
2010   *Kakkar,* Prof. Ajay Kumar Kakkar, PC, *b.* 1964
2004   *Kalms,* Harold Stanley Kalms, *b.* 1931, *m.*
2015   *Keen of Elie,* richard Sanderson Keen, QC,
      b. 1954, *m.*
2010   *Kennedy of Southwark,* Roy Francis Kennedy,
      b. 1962
2004   *Kerr of Kinlochard,* John (Olav) Kerr, GCMG,
      b. 1942, *m.*
2010   **Kerr of Monteviot,* Marquess of Lothian (Michael
      Ancram), PC, QC, *b.* 1945, *m.* (*see* Hereditary
      Peers)
2015   *Kerslake,* Robert Walter Kerslake, *b.* 1955, *m.*
2011   *Kestenbaum,* Jonathan Andrew Kestenbaum,
      b. 1959, *m.*
2001   *Kilclooney,* John David Taylor, PC (NI), *b.* 1937, *m.*
1996   *Kilpatrick of Kincraig,* Robert Kilpatrick, CBE,
      b. 1926, *m.*
2001   *King of Bridgwater,* Thomas Jeremy King, CH, PC,
      b. 1933, *m.*
2013   *King of Lothbury,* Mervyn Allister King, KG, GBE,
      b. 1948
2005   *Kinnock,* Neil Gordon Kinnock, PC, *b.* 1942, *m.*
1999   *Kirkham,* Graham Kirkham, *b.* 1944, *m.*
1975   *Kirkhill,* John Farquharson Smith, *b.* 1930, *m.*
2005   *Kirkwood of Kirkhope,* Archibald Johnstone
      Kirkwood, *b.* 1946, *m.*
2010   *Knight of Weymouth,* James Philip Knight, PC,
      b. 1965, *m.*
2007   *Krebs,* Prof. John (Richard) Krebs, FRS, *b.* 1945, *m.*
2004   ¶*Laidlaw,* Irvine Alan Stewart Laidlaw, *b.* 1942, *m.*
1999   *Laird,* John Dunn Laird, *b.* 1944, *m.*
1998   *Laming,* (William) Herbert Laming, PC, CBE,
      b. 1936, *w.*
1998   *Lamont of Lerwick,* Norman Stewart Hughson
      Lamont, PC, *b.* 1942, *m.*
1997   *Lang of Monkton,* Ian Bruce Lang, PC, *b.* 1940, *m.*
2015   ‡*Lansley,* Andrew David Lansley, PC, CBE,
      b. 1956, *m.*
1992   *Lawson of Blaby,* Nigel Lawson, PC, *b.* 1932, *m.*
2000   *Layard,* Peter Richard Grenville Layard, *b.* 1934, *m.*

1999   *Lea of Crondall,* David Edward Lea, OBE, *b.* 1937

2006   *Leach of Fairford,* Charles Guy Rodney Leach, *b.* 1934, *m.*

2006   *Lee of Trafford,* John Robert Louis Lee, *b.* 1942, *m.*

2013   *Leigh of Hurley,* Howard Darryl Leigh, *b.* 1959, *m.*

2004   *Leitch,* Alexander Park Leitch, *b.* 1947, *m.*

2014   *Lennie,* Christopher John Lennie, *b.* 1953, *m.*

1993   *Lester of Herne Hill,* Anthony Paul Lester, QC, *b.* 1936, *m.*

1997   *Levene of Portsoken,* Peter Keith Levene, KBE, *b.* 1941, *m.*

1997   *Levy,* Michael Abraham Levy, *b.* 1944, *m.*

2010   *Lexden,* Alistair Basil Cooke, OBE, *b.* 1945

2010   *Liddle,* Roger John Liddle, *b.* 1947, *m.*

2010   *Lingfield,* Robert George Alexander Balchin, *b.* 1942, *m.*

1999   *Lipsey,* David Lawrence Lipsey, *b.* 1948, *m.*

2014   *Lisvane,* Robert James Rogers, KCB, *b.* 1950, *m.*

2015   ‡*Livermore,* Spencer Livermore, *b.* 1975

2013   *Livingston of Parkhead,* Ian Paul Livingston, *b.* 1964, *m.*

1997   *Lloyd-Webber,* Andrew Lloyd Webber, *b.* 1948, *m.*

2011   *Loomba,* Rajinder Paul Loomba, CBE, *b.* 1943, *m.*

2006   *Low of Dalston,* Prof. Colin MacKenzie Low, CBE, *b.* 1942, *m.*

2000   *Luce,* Richard Napier Luce, KG, GCVO, PC, *b.* 1936, *m.*

2015   ‡*Lupton,* James Roger Crompton Lupton, CBE, *b.* 1955, *m.*

2000   **Lyttelton of Aldershot,* The Viscount Chandos, *b.* 1953, *m.* (*see* Hereditary Peers)

2010   *McAvoy,* Thomas McLaughlin McAvoy, PC, *b.* 1943, *m.*

1976   *McCluskey,* John Herbert McCluskey, *b.* 1929, *m.*

1989   *McColl of Dulwich,* Ian McColl, CBE, FRCS, FRCSE, *b.* 1933, *m.*

2010   *McConnell of Glenscorrodale,* Dr Jack Wilson McConnell, PC, *b.* 1960, *m.*

2010   *Macdonald of River Glaven,* Kenneth Donald John Macdonald, QC, *b.* 1953, *m.*

1998   *Macdonald of Tradeston,* Angus John Macdonald, CBE, PC, *b.* 1940, *m.*

2010   *McFall of Alcluith,* John Francis McFall, PC, *b.* 1944, *m.*

1991   *Macfarlane of Bearsden,* Norman Somerville Macfarlane, KT, FRSE, *b.* 1926, *m.*

2001   *MacGregor of Pulham Market,* John Roddick Russell MacGregor, CBE, PC, *b.* 1937, *m.*

1979   *Mackay of Clashfern,* James Peter Hymers Mackay, KT, PC, FRSE, *b.* 1927, *m.*

1995   *Mackay of Drumadoon,* Donald Sage Mackay, PC, *b.* 1946, *m.*

1998   *MacKenzie of Culkein,* Hector Uisdean MacKenzie, *b.* 1940

1999   *Mackenzie of Framwellgate,* Brian Mackenzie, OBE, *b.* 1943, *m.*

2004   *McKenzie of Luton,* William David McKenzie, *b.* 1946, *m.*

1996   *MacLaurin of Knebworth,* Ian Charter MacLaurin, *b.* 1937, *m.*

2001   *Maclennan of Rogart,* Robert Adam Ross Maclennan, PC, *b.* 1936, *m.*

1995   *McNally,* Tom McNally, PC, *b.* 1943, *m.*

2011   *Magan of Castletown,* George Morgan Magan, *b.* 1945, *m.*

2001   *Maginnis of Drumglass,* Kenneth Wiggins Maginnis, *b.* 1938, *m.*

2007   *Malloch-Brown,* George Mark Malloch Brown, KCMG, PC, *b.* 1953, *m.*

2008   *Mandelson,* Peter Benjamin Mandelson, PC, *b.* 1953

2011   *Marks of Henley-on-Thames,* Jonathan Clive Marks, QC, *b.* 1952, *m.*

2006   *Marland,* Jonathan Peter Marland, *b.* 1956, *m.*

1991   *Marlesford,* Mark Shuldham Schreiber, *b.* 1931, *m.*

2009   *Martin of Springburn,* Michael Martin, PC, *b.* 1945, *m.*

2015   *Maude of Horsham,* Francis Anthony Aylmer Maude, PC, TD, *b.* 1953, *m.*

2005   *Mawhinney,* Brian Stanley Mawhinney, PC, *b.* 1940, *m.*

2007   *Mawson,* Revd Andrew Mawson, OBE, *b.* 1954, *m.*

2004   *Maxton,* John Alston Maxton, *b.* 1936, *m.*

2001   *May of Oxford,* Robert McCredie May, OM, *b.* 1936, *m.*

1997   ¶*Mayhew of Twysden,* Patrick Barnabas Burke Mayhew, PC, QC, *b.* 1929, *m.*

2013   *Mendelsohn,* Jonathan Neil Mendelsohn, *b.* 1966, *m.*

2000   *Mitchell,* Parry Andrew Mitchell, *b.* 1943, *m.*

2000   **Mitford,* Lord Redesdale, *b.* 1967, *m.* (*see* Hereditary Peers)

2008   *Mogg,* John (Frederick) Mogg, KCMG, *b.* 1943 *m.*

2010   *Monks,* John Stephen Monks, *b.* 1945, *m.*

2005   *Moonie,* Dr. Lewis George Moonie, *b.* 1947, *m.*

1992   *Moore of Lower Marsh,* John Edward Michael Moore, PC, *b.* 1937, *w.*

2000   *Morgan,* Kenneth Owen Morgan, *b.* 1934, *m.*

2001   *Morris of Aberavon,* John Morris, KG, PC, QC, *b.* 1931, *m.*

2006   *Morris of Handsworth,* William Manuel Morris, *b.* 1938, *m.*

2006   *Morrow,* Maurice George Morrow, *b.* 1948, *m.*

2015   ‡*Murphy,* Paul Peter Murphy, PC, *b.* 1948

2008   *Myners,* Paul Myners, CBE, *b.* 1948, *m.*

1997   *Naseby,* Michael Wolfgang Laurence Morris, PC, *b.* 1936, *m.*

2013   *Nash,* John Alfred Stoddard Nash, *b.* 1949

1997   *Neill of Bladen,* (Francis) Patrick Neill, QC, *b.* 1926, *m.*

1997   *Newby,* Richard Mark Newby, PC, OBE, *b.* 1953, *m.*

1994   ¶*Nickson,* David Wigley Nickson, KBE, FRSE, *b.* 1929, *m.*

2011   *Noon,* Gulam Kaderbhoy Noon, MBE, *b.* 1936, *m.*

1998   *Norton of Louth,* Philip Norton, *b.* 1951

2000   *Oakeshott of Seagrove Bay,* Matthew Alan Oakeshott, *b.* 1947, *m.*

2015   ‡*Oates,* Jonathan Oates, *b.* 1969, *c.p.*

2012   *O'Donnell,* Augustine Thomas (Gus) O'Donnell, GCB, *b.* 1952, *m.*

2005   *O'Neill of Clackmannan,* Martin John O'Neill, *b.* 1945, *m.*

2015   *O'Neill of Gatley,* Terence James O'Neill, PC, *b.* 1957, *m.*

2015   ‡*O'Shaughnessy,* James O'Shaughnessy

2001   *Ouseley,* Herman George Ouseley, *b.* 1945, *m.*

1992   *Owen,* David Anthony Llewellyn Owen, CH, PC, *b.* 1938, *m.*

1999   *Oxburgh,* Ernest Ronald Oxburgh, KBE, FRS, PHD, *b.* 1934, *m.*

2013   *Paddick,* Brian Leonard Paddick, *b.* 1958, *m.*

2011   *Palmer of Childs Hill,* Monroe Edward Palmer, OBE, *b.* 1938, *m.*

1991   *Palumbo,* Peter Garth Palumbo, *b.* 1935, *m.*

2013   *Palumbo of Southwark,* James Rudolph Palumbo, *b.* 1963

2008   *Pannick,* David Philip Pannick, QC, *b.* 1956, *m.*

2000   *Parekh,* Bhikhu Chhotalal Parekh, *b.* 1935, *m.*

1992 ¶*Parkinson,* Cecil Edward Parkinson, PC, *b.* 1931, *m.*

1999 *Patel,* Narendra Babubhai Patel, KT, *b.* 1938

2000 *Patel of Blackburn,* Adam Hafejee Patel, *b.* 1940

2006 *Patel of Bradford,* Prof. Kamlesh Kumar Patel, OBE, *b.* 1960 *m.*

1997 *Patten,* John Haggitt Charles Patten, PC, *b.* 1945, *m.*

2005 *Patten of Barnes,* Christopher Francis Patten, CH, PC, *b.* 1944, *m.*

1996 *Paul,* Swraj Paul, PC, *b.* 1931, *m.*

1990 *Pearson of Rannoch,* Malcolm Everard MacLaren Pearson, *b.* 1942, *m.*

2001 *Pendry,* Thomas Pendry, PC, *b.* 1934, *m.*

1987 *Peston,* Maurice Harry Peston, *b.* 1931, *m.*

1998 ¶*Phillips of Sudbury,* Andrew Wyndham Phillips, OBE, *b.* 1939, *m.*

1992 *Plant of Highfield,* Prof. Raymond Plant, PHD, *b.* 1945, *m.*

1987 *Plumb,* (Charles) Henry Plumb, *b.* 1925, *m.*

2015 ‡*Polak,* Stuart Polak, CBE

2000 **Ponsonby of Roehampton,* Lord Ponsonby of Shulbrede, *b.* 1958, *m.* (*see* Hereditary Peers)

2010 *Popat,* Dolar Amarshi Popat, *b.* 1953, *m.*

2015 ‡*Porter,* Gary Porter

2000 *Powell of Bayswater,* Charles David Powell, KCMG, *b.* 1941

2010 *Prescott,* John Leslie Prescott, *b.* 1938, *m.*

1987 *Prior,* James Michael Leathes Prior, PC, *b.* 1927, *m.*

2015 *Prior of Brampton,* David Gifford Leathes Prior, *b.* 1954, *m.*

1982 ¶*Prys-Davies,* Gwilym Prys Prys-Davies, *b.* 1923, *m.*

2013 *Purvis of Tweed,* Jeremy Purvis, *b.* 1974

1997 *Puttnam,* David Terence Puttnam, CBE, *b.* 1941, *m.*

1994 *Quirk,* Prof. (Charles) Randolph Quirk, CBE, FBA, *b.* 1920, *m.*

2001 *Radice,* Giles Heneage Radice, PC, *b.* 1936

2005 *Ramsbotham,* David John Ramsbotham, GCB, CBE, *b.* 1934, *m.*

2004 *Rana,* Dr Diljit Singh Rana, MBE, *b.* 1938, *m.*

1997 *Razzall,* (Edward) Timothy Razzall, CBE, *b.* 1943, *m.*

2005 *Rees of Ludlow,* Prof. Martin John Rees, OM, *b.* 1942, *m.*

2010 *Reid of Cardowan,* Dr John Reid, PC, *b.* 1947, *m.*

1991 *Renfrew of Kaimsthorn,* (Andrew) Colin Renfrew, FBA, *b.* 1937, *m.*

1999 *Rennard,* Christopher John Rennard, MBE, *b.* 1960

1997 *Renton of Mount Harry,* (Ronald) Timothy Renton, PC, *b.* 1932, *m.*

1997 *Renwick of Clifton,* Robin William Renwick, KCMG, *b.* 1937, *m.*

2010 *Ribeiro,* Bernard Francisco Ribeiro, CBE, *b.* 1944, *m.*

1990 *Richard,* Ivor Seward Richard, PC, QC, *b.* 1932, *m.*

2014 *Richards of Herstmonceux,* David Julian Richards, GCB, CBE, DSO, *b.* 1952, *m.*

2010 *Risby,* Richard John Grenville Spring, *b.* 1946, *m.*

1992 *Rix,* Brian Norman Roger Rix, CBE, *b.* 1924, *w.*

2015 ‡*Robathan,* Andrew Robathan, PC, *b.* 1951, *m.*

2004 *Roberts of Llandudno,* Revd John Roger Roberts, *b.* 1935, *m.*

1999 *Robertson of Port Ellen,* George Islay MacNeill Robertson, KT, GCMG, PC, *b.* 1946, *m.*

1992 *Rodgers of Quarry Bank,* William Thomas Rodgers, PC, *b.* 1928, *w.*

1999 *Rogan,* Dennis Robert David Rogan, *b.* 1942, *m.*

1996 *Rogers of Riverside,* Richard George Rogers, CH, RA, RIBA, *b.* 1933, *m.*

2001 *Rooker,* Jeffrey William Rooker, PC, *b.* 1941, *m.*

2000 ¶*Roper,* John Francis Hodgess Roper, PC, *b.* 1935, *m.*

2014 *Rose of Monewden,* Stuart Alan Ransom Rose, *b.* 1949

2004 *Rosser,* Richard Andrew Rosser, *b.* 1944, *m.*

2006 *Rowe-Beddoe,* David (Sydney) Rowe-Beddoe, *b.* 1937, *m.*

2004 *Rowlands,* Edward Rowlands, CBE, *b.* 1940, *m.*

1997 *Ryder of Wensum,* Richard Andrew Ryder, OBE, PC, *b.* 1949, *m.*

1996 *Saatchi,* Maurice Saatchi, *b.* 1946, *w.*

2009 *Sacks,* Chief Rabbi Dr Jonathan Henry Sacks, *b.* 1948, *m.*

1989 *Sainsbury of Preston Candover,* John Davan Sainsbury, KG, *b.* 1927, *m.*

1997 *Sainsbury of Turville,* David John Sainsbury, *b.* 1940, *m.*

1997 ¶*Sandberg,* Michael Graham Ruddock Sandberg, CBE, *b.* 1927, *m.*

1985 *Sanderson of Bowden,* Charles Russell Sanderson, *b.* 1933, *m.*

2010 *Sassoon,* James Meyer Sassoon, *b.* 1955, *m.*

1998 *Sawyer,* Lawrence (Tom) Sawyer, *b.* 1943

2014 *Scriven,* Paul James Scriven, *b.* 1966

1997 *Selkirk of Douglas,* James Alexander Douglas-Hamilton, PC, QC, *b.* 1942, *m.*

1996 ¶*Sewel,* John Buttifant Sewel, CBE, *b.* 1946

2010 *Sharkey,* John Kevin Sharkey, *b.* 1947, *m.*

1999 ¶*Sharman,* Colin Morven Sharman, OBE, *b.* 1943, *m.*

1994 ¶*Shaw of Northstead,* Michael Norman Shaw, *b.* 1920, *m.*

2006 *Sheikh,* Mohamed Iltaf Sheikh, *b.* 1941, *m.*

2001 ¶*Sheldon,* Robert Edward Sheldon, PC, *b.* 1923, *m.*

2013 *Sherbourne of Didsbury,* Stephen Ashley Sherbourne, CBE, *b.* 1945

2015 ‡*Shinkwin,* Kevin Shinkwin

2010 *Shipley,* John Warren Shipley, OBE, *b.* 1946

2000 *Shutt of Greetland,* David Trevor Shutt, OBE, PC, *b.* 1942

1997 *Simon of Highbury,* David Alec Gwyn Simon, CBE, *b.* 1939, *m.*

1997 ¶*Simpson of Dunkeld,* George Simpson, *b.* 1942, *m.*

2011 *Singh of Wimbledon,* Indarjit Singh, CBE, *b.* 1932, *m.*

1991 *Skidelsky,* Robert Jacob Alexander Skidelsky, DPHIL, *b.* 1939, *m.*

2015 ‡*Smith,* Philip Smith, CBE

1997 *Smith of Clifton,* Trevor Arthur Smith, *b.* 1937, *m.*

2005 *Smith of Finsbury,* Christopher Robert Smith, PC, *b.* 1951

2008 *Smith of Kelvin,* Robert (Haldane) Smith, KT, *b.* 1944, *m.*

1999 *Smith of Leigh,* Peter Richard Charles Smith, *b.* 1945, *m.*

2004 *Snape,* Peter Charles Snape, *b.* 1942

2005 *Soley,* Clive Stafford Soley, *b.* 1939

1990 *Soulsby of Swaffham Prior,* Ernest Jackson Lawson Soulsby, PHD, *b.* 1926, *w.*

2010 *Spicer,* (William) Michael Hardy Spicer, PC, *b.* 1943, *m.*

1997 *Steel of Aikwood,* David Martin Scott Steel, KT, KBE, PC, *b.* 1938, *m.*

2011 *Stephen,* Nicol Ross Stephen, *b.* 1960, *m.*

1991 *Sterling of Plaistow,* Jeffrey Maurice Sterling, GCVO, CBE, *b.* 1934, *m.*

2007 *Stern of Brentford,* Nicholas Herbert Stern, *b.* 1946, *m.*

2005 *Stevens of Kirkwhelpington,* John Arthur Stevens, QPM, *b.* 1942, *m.*

1987   *Stevens of Ludgate,* David Robert Stevens, *b.* 1936, *m.*

2010   *Stevenson of Balmacara,* Robert Wilfrid Stevenson, *b.* 1947, *m.*

1999   *Stevenson of Coddenham,* Henry Dennistoun Stevenson, CBE, *b.* 1945, *m.*

1992   *Stewartby,* (Bernard Harold) Ian (Halley) Stewart, RD, PC, FBA, FRSE, *b.* 1935, *m.*

2011   *Stirrup,* Graham Eric Stirrup, KG, GCB, AFC, *b.* 1949, *m.*

1983   *Stoddart of Swindon,* David Leonard Stoddart, *b.* 1926, *m.*

1997   *Stone of Blackheath,* Andrew Zelig Stone, *b.* 1942, *m.*

2011   *Stoneham of Droxford,* Benjamin Russell Mackintosh Stoneham, *b.* 1940, *m.*

2011   *Storey,* Michael John Storey, CBE, *b.* 1949

2011   *Strasburger,* Paul Cline Strasburger, *b.* 1946

2015   ‡*Stunell,* Andrew Stunell, PC, OBE, *b.* 1942, *m.*

2009   *Sugar,* Alan Michael Sugar, *b.* 1947, *m.*

2014   *Suri,* Ranbir Singh Suri, *b.* 1935

2001   *Sutherland of Houndwood,* Stewart Ross Sutherland, KT, *b.* 1941, *m.*

1971   *Tanlaw,* Simon Brooke Mackay, *b.* 1934, *m.*

1996   *Taverne,* Dick Taverne, QC, *b.* 1928, *m.*

1978   *Taylor of Blackburn,* Thomas Taylor, CBE, *b.* 1929, *m.*

2010   *Taylor of Goss Moor,* Matthew Owen John Taylor, *b.* 1963, *m.*

2006   *Taylor of Holbeach,* John Derek Taylor, PC, CBE, *b.* 1943, *m.*

1996   *Taylor of Warwick,* John David Beckett Taylor, *b.* 1952, *m.*

1992   *Tebbit,* Norman Beresford Tebbit, CH, PC, *b.* 1931, *m.*

2001   *Temple-Morris,* Peter Temple-Morris, *b.* 1938, *m.*

2006   *Teverson,* Robin Teverson, *b.* 1952, *m.*

2013   § *Thomas of Cwmgiedd,* Roger John Laugharne Thomas, PC, *b.* 1947, *m., Lord Chief Justice of England and Wales*

1996   *Thomas of Gresford,* Donald Martin Thomas, OBE, QC, *b.* 1937, *m.*

1997   *Thomas of Macclesfield,* Terence James Thomas, CBE, *b.* 1937, *m.*

1981   *Thomas of Swynnerton,* Hugh Swynnerton Thomas, *b.* 1931, *m.*

1990   ¶*Tombs,* Francis Leonard Tombs, FENG, *b.* 1924, *w.*

1998   *Tomlinson,* John Edward Tomlinson, *b.* 1939

1994   *Tope,* Graham Norman Tope, CBE, *b.* 1943, *m.*

1981   *Tordoff,* Geoffrey Johnson Tordoff, *b.* 1928, *m.*

2010   *Touhig,* James Donnelly Touhig, PC, *b.* 1947, *m.*

2012   *Trees,* Alexander John Trees, PHD, *b.* 1946, *m.*

2004   *Triesman,* David Maxim Triesman, *b.* 1943

2006   *Trimble,* William David Trimble, PC, *b.* 1944, *m.*

2010   *True,* Nicholas Edward True, CBE, *b.* 1951, *m.*

2004   *Truscott,* Dr Peter Derek Truscott, *b.* 1959, *m.*

1993   *Tugendhat,* Christopher Samuel Tugendhat, *b.* 1937, *m.*

2004   *Tunnicliffe,* Denis Tunnicliffe, CBE, *b.* 1943, *m.*

2000   *Turnberg,* Leslie Arnold Turnberg, MD, *b.* 1934, *m.*

2005   *Turnbull,* Andrew Turnbull, KCB, CVO, *b.* 1945, *m.*

2005   *Turner of Ecchinswell,* (Jonathan) Adair Turner, *b.* 1955, *m.*

2005   *Tyler,* Paul Archer Tyler, PC, CBE, *b.* 1941, *m.*

2004   *Vallance of Tummel,* Iain (David Thomas) Vallance, *b.* 1943, *m.*

2013   *Verjee,* Rumi Verjee, CBE, *b.* 1957

1996   *Vincent of Coleshill,* Richard Frederick Vincent, GBE, KCB, DSO, *b.* 1931, *m.*

1985   *Vinson,* Nigel Vinson, LVO, *b.* 1931, *m.*

1990   ¶*Waddington,* David Charles Waddington, GCVO, PC, QC, *b.* 1929, *m.*

1990   *Wade of Chorlton,* (William) Oulton Wade, *b.* 1932, *m.*

1992   *Wakeham,* John Wakeham, PC, *b.* 1932, *m.*

1999   *Waldegrave of North Hill,* William Arthur Waldegrave, PC, *b.* 1946, *m.*

2007   *Walker of Aldringham,* Michael John Dawson Walker, GCB, CMG, CBE, *b.* 1944, *m.*

1995   *Wallace of Saltaire,* William John Lawrence Wallace, PC, PHD, *b.* 1941, *m.*

2007   *Wallace of Tankerness,* James Robert Wallace, PC, QC, *b.* 1954, *m.*

1989   *Walton of Detchant,* John Nicholas Walton, TD, FRCP, *b.* 1922, *w.*

1998   *Warner,* Norman Reginald Warner, PC, *b.* 1940, *m.*

2011   *Wasserman,* Gordon Joshua Wasserman, *b.* 1938

1997   *Watson of Invergowrie,* Michael Goodall Watson, *b.* 1949, *m.*

1999   *Watson of Richmond,* Alan John Watson, CBE, *b.* 1941, *m.*

2015   ‡*Watts,* David Leonard Watts, *b.* 1951, *m.*

2010   *Wei,* Nathanael Ming-Yan Wei, *b.* 1977, *m.*

1976   *Weidenfeld,* (Arthur) George Weidenfeld, GBE, *b.* 1919, *m.*

2007   *West of Spithead,* Alan William John West, GCB, DSC, PC, *b.* 1948, *m.*

2013   *Whitby,* Michael John Whitby, *b.* 1948

1996   *Whitty,* John Lawrence (Larry) Whitty, PC, *b.* 1943, *m.*

2011   *Wigley,* Dafydd Wynne Wigley, PC, *b.* 1943, *m.*

2015   ‡*Willetts,* David Lindsay Willetts, *b.* 1956, *m.*

2010   *Williams of Baglan,* Michael Charles Williams, *b.* 1949

1985   *Williams of Elvel,* Charles Cuthbert Powell Williams, CBE, PC, *b.* 1933, *m.*

2013   *Williams of Oystermouth,* Rt. Revd Rowan Douglas Williams, PC, Royal Victorian Chain, DPHIL, *b.* 1950, *m.*

2010   *Willis of Knaresborough,* George Philip Willis, *b.* 1941, *m.*

2010   *Wills,* Michael David Wills, PC, *b.* 1952, *m.*

2002   *Wilson of Dinton,* Richard Thomas James Wilson, GCB, *b.* 1942, *m.*

1992   *Wilson of Tillyorn,* David Clive Wilson, KT, GCMG, PHD, *b.* 1935, *m.*

1995   *Winston,* Robert Maurice Lipson Winston, FRCOG, *b.* 1940, *m.*

2010   *Wolfson of Aspley Guise,* Simon Adam Wolfson, *b.* 1967, *m.*

1991   *Wolfson of Sunningdale,* David Wolfson, *b.* 1935, *m.*

2011   *Wood of Anfield,* Stewart Martin Wood, *b.* 1968, *m.*

1999   *Woolmer of Leeds,* Kenneth John Woolmer, *b.* 1940, *m.*

2013   *Wrigglesworth,* Ian William Wrigglesworth, *b.* 1939, *m.*

1994   *Wright of Richmond,* Patrick Richard Henry Wright, GCMG, *b.* 1931, *m.*

2015   ‡*Young,* George Samuel Knatchbull Young, Bt., CH, PC, *b.* 1941, *m.*

1984   *Young of Graffham,* David Ivor Young, CH, PC, *b.* 1932, *m.*

2004   *Young of Norwood Green,* Anthony (Ian) Young, *b.* 1942, *m.*

BARONESSES
Created

2005   *Adams of Craigielea,* Katherine Patricia Irene
       Adams, *b.* 1947, *w.*
2007   *Afshar,* Prof. Haleh Afshar, OBE, *b.* 1944, *m.*
2015   *Altmann,* Dr Rosalind Miriam Altmann, CBE,
       b. 1956, *m.*
1997   *Amos,* Valerie Ann Amos, PC, *b.* 1954
2000   *Andrews,* Elizabeth Kay Andrews, OBE,
       b. 1943, *m.*
1996   *Anelay of St Johns,* Joyce Anne Anelay, DBE, PC,
       b. 1947, *m.*
2010   *Armstrong of Hill Top,* Hilary Jane Armstrong, PC,
       b. 1945, *m.*
1999   *Ashton of Upholland,* Catherine Margaret Ashton,
       GCMG, PC, *b.* 1956, *m.*
2011   *Bakewell,* Joan Dawson Bakewell, DBE, *b.* 1933
2013   *Bakewell of Hardington Mandeville,* Catherine
       Mary Bakewell, MBE, *b.* 1949
1999   *Barker,* Elizabeth Jean Barker, *b.* 1961
2010   *Benjamin,* Floella Karen Yunies Benjamin, OBE,
       b. 1949, *m.*
2011   *Berridge,* Elizabeth Rose Berridge, *b.* 1972
2000   *Billingham,* Angela Theodora Billingham, DPHIL,
       b. 1939, *w.*
1987   *Blackstone,* Tessa Ann Vosper Blackstone, PC, PHD,
       b. 1942
1999   *Blood,* May Blood, MBE, *b.* 1938
2004   *Bonham-Carter of Yarnbury,* Jane Bonham Carter,
       b. 1957, *w.*
2000   *Boothroyd,* Betty Boothroyd, OM, PC, *b.* 1929
2005   *Bottomley of Nettlestone,* Virginia Hilda Brunette
       Maxwell Bottomley, PC, *b.* 1948, *m.*
2015   ‡*Bowles,* Sharon Margaret Bowles, *b.* 1953, *m.*
2014   *Brady,* Karren Rita Brady, CBE, *b.* 1969, *m.*
2011   *Brinton,* Sarah Virginia Brinton, *b.* 1955, *m.*
2010   *Browning,* Angela Frances Browning, *b.* 1946, *m.*
2015   ‡*Burt,* Lorely Jane Burt, *b.* 1954, *m.*
1998   *Buscombe,* Peta Jane Buscombe, *b.* 1954, *m.*
2006   *Butler-Sloss,* (Ann) Elizabeth (Oldfield) Butler-Sloss,
       GBE, PC *b.* 1933, *m.*
1996   *Byford,* Hazel Byford, DBE, *b.* 1941, *w.*
2008   *Campbell of Loughborough,* Susan Catherine
       Campbell, CBE, *b.* 1948
2007   *Campbell of Surbiton,* Jane Susan Campbell, DBE,
       b. 1959, *m.*
1992   *Chalker of Wallasey,* Lynda Chalker, PC, *b.* 1942
2014   *Chisholm of Owlpen,* Caroline Elizabeth (Carlyn)
       Chisholm, *b.* 1951, *m.*
2005   §*Clark of Calton,* Dr Lynda Margaret Clark, PC,
       b. 1949
2000   *Cohen of Pimlico,* Janet Cohen, *b.* 1940, *m.*
2005   *Corston,* Jean Ann Corston, PC, *b.* 1942, *w.*
2007   *Coussins,* Jean Coussins, *b.* 1950
1982   *Cox,* Caroline Anne Cox, *b.* 1937, *m.*
1998   *Crawley,* Christine Mary Crawley, *b.* 1950, *m.*
1990   *Cumberlege,* Julia Frances Cumberlege, CBE,
       b. 1943, *m.*
1993   *Dean of Thornton-le-Fylde,* Brenda Dean, PC,
       b. 1943, *m.*
2005   *Deech,* Ruth Lynn Deech, DBE, *b.* 1943, *m.*
2010   *Donaghy,* Rita Margaret Donaghy, CBE, *b.* 1944, *m.*
2010   *Doocey,* Elizabeth Deirdre Doocey, OBE,
       b. 1948, *m.*
2010   *Drake,* Jean Lesley Patricia Drake, CBE, *b.* 1948
2004   *D'Souza,* Dr Frances Gertrude Claire D'Souza,
       CMG, PC, *b.* 1944, *m. Lord Speaker*
1990   ¶*Dunn,* Lydia Selina Dunn, DBE, *b.* 1940, *m.*
2010   *Eaton,* Ellen Margaret Eaton, DBE, *b.* 1942, *m.*

1990   *Eccles of Moulton,* Diana Catherine Eccles, *b.*
       1933, *m.*
1997   *Emerton,* Audrey Caroline Emerton, DBE, *b.* 1935
2014   *Evans of Bowes Park,* Natalie Jessica Evans,
       b. 1975, *m.*
1974   *Falkender,* Marcia Matilda Falkender, CBE, *b.* 1932
2004   *Falkner of Margravine,* Kishwer Falkner, *b.* 1955, *m.*
2015   ‡*Fall,* Catherine Fall
1994   *Farrington of Ribbleton,* Josephine Farrington,
       b. 1940, *m.*
2015   ‡*Featherstone,* Lynne Featherstone, PC, *b.* 1951
2001   *Finlay of Llandaff,* Ilora Gillian Finlay, *b.* 1949, *m.*
2015   ‡*Finn,* Simone Finn
1990   *Flather,* Shreela Flather, *b.* 1934, *m.*
1997   *Fookes,* Janet Evelyn Fookes, DBE, *b.* 1936
2006   *Ford,* Margaret Anne Ford, *b.* 1957, *m.*
2005   *Fritchie,* Irene Tordoff Fritchie, DBE, *b.* 1942, *m.*
1999   *Gale,* Anita Gale, *b.* 1940
2007   *Garden of Frognal,* Susan Elizabeth Garden, PC,
       b. 1944, *w.*
1981   *Gardner of Parkes,* (Rachel) Trixie (Anne) Gardner,
       b. 1927, *w.*
2000   *Gibson of Market Rasen,* Anne Gibson, OBE,
       b. 1940, *m.*
2013   *Goldie,* Annabel MacNicholl Goldie, MSP, *b.* 1950
2001   *Golding,* Llinos Golding, *b.* 1933, *m.*
1998   *Goudie,* Mary Teresa Goudie, MSP, *b.* 1946, *m.*
1993   *Gould of Potternewton,* Joyce Brenda Gould,
       b. 1932, *m.*
2001   *Greenfield,* Susan Adele Greenfield, CBE,
       b. 1950, *m.*
2000   *Greengross,* Sally Ralea Greengross, OBE,
       b. 1935, *m.*
2013   *Grender,* Rosalind Mary Grender, MBE, *b.* 1962
2010   *Grey-Thompson,* Tanni Carys Davina
       Grey-Thompson, DBE, *b.* 1969, *m.*
1991   *Hamwee,* Sally Rachel Hamwee, *b.* 1947
1999   *Hanham,* Joan Brownlow Hanham, CBE, *b.* 1939, *m.*
2014   *Harding of Winscombe,* Diana Mary (Dido)
       Harding, *b.* 1967, *m.*
1999   *Harris of Richmond,* Angela Felicity Harris, *b.* 1944
1996   *Hayman,* Helene Valerie Hayman, GBE, PC,
       b. 1949, *m.*
2010   *Hayter of Kentish Town,* Dr Dianne Hayter,
       b. 1949, *m.*
2014   *Helic,* Arminka Helic, *b.* 1968
2010   *Healy of Primrose Hill,* Anna Healy, *b.* 1955, *m.*
2004   *Henig,* Ruth Beatrice Henig, CBE, *b.* 1943, *m.*
2011   *Heyhoe-Flint,* Rachel Heyhoe Flint, OBE,
       b. 1939, *m.*
1991   *Hilton of Eggardon,* Jennifer Hilton, QPM, *b.* 1936
2013   *Hodgson of Abinger,* Fiona Ferelith Hodgson, CBE,
       b. 1954, *m.*
1995   *Hogg,* Sarah Elizabeth Mary Hogg, *b.* 1946, *m.*
2010   *Hollins,* Prof. Sheila Clare Hollins, *b.* 1946, *m.*
1990   *Hollis of Heigham,* Patricia Lesley Hollis, PC,
       DPHIL, *b.* 1941, *m.*
1985   *Hooper,* Gloria Dorothy Hooper, CMG, *b.* 1939
2001   *Howarth of Breckland,* Valerie Georgina Howarth,
       OBE, *b.* 1940
2001   *Howe of Idlicote,* Elspeth Rosamond Morton Howe,
       CBE, *b.* 1932, *m.*
1999   *Howells of St Davids,* Rosalind Patricia-Anne
       Howells, *b.* 1931, *m.*
2010   *Hughes of Stretford,* Beverley Hughes, PC,
       b. 1950, *m.*
2013   *Humphreys,* Christine Mary Humphreys, *b.* 1947
2010   *Hussein-Ece,* Meral Hussein Ece, OBE, *b.* 1953
2014   *Janke,* Barbara Lilian Janke, *b.* 1947, *m.*

1992   *Jay of Paddington,* Margaret Ann Jay, PC, *b.* 1939, *m.*

2011   *Jenkin of Kennington,* Anne Caroline Jenkin,
        b. 1955, *m.*

2010   *Jolly,* Judith Anne Jolly, *b.* 1951, *m.*

2013   *Jones of Moulsecoomb,* Jennifer Helen Jones,
        b. 1949

2006   *Jones of Whitchurch,* Margaret Beryl Jones, *b.* 1955

2015   ‡*Jowell,* Tessa Jane Helen Douglas Jowell, DBE,
        PC, *b.* 1947, *m.*

2013   *Kennedy of Cradley,* Alicia Pamela Kennedy,
        b. 1969, *m.*

1997   *Kennedy of the Shaws,* Helena Ann Kennedy, QC,
        b. 1950, *m.*

2012   *Kidron,* Beeban Tania Kidron, OBE, *b.* 1961 *m.*

2011   *King of Bow,* Oona Tamsyn King, *b.* 1967, *m.*

2006   *Kingsmill,* Denise Patricia Byrne Kingsmill, CBE,
        b. 1947, *m.*

2009   *Kinnock of Holyhead,* Glenys Elizabeth Kinnock,
        b. 1944, *m.*

1997   *Knight of Collingtree,* (Joan Christabel) Jill Knight,
        DBE, *b.* 1927, *w.*

2010   *Kramer,* Susan Veronica Kramer, PC, *b.* 1950, *w.*

2013   *Lane-Fox of Soho,* Martha Lane Fox, CBE, *b.* 1973

2013   *Lawrence of Clarendon,* Doreen Delceita Lawrence,
        OBE, *b.* 1952

2010   *Liddell of Coatdyke,* Helen Lawrie Liddell, PC,
        b. 1950, *m.*

1997   *Linklater of Butterstone,* Veronica Linklater,
        b. 1943, *m.*

2011   *Lister of Burtersett,* Margot Ruth Aline Lister, CBE,
        b. 1949, *m.*

1978   *Lockwood,* Betty Lockwood, *b.* 1924, *w.*

1997   *Ludford,* Sarah Ann Ludford, *b.* 1951

2004   *McDonagh,* Margaret Josephine McDonagh,
        b. 1961

2015   ‡*McGregor-Smith,* Ruby McGregor-Smith, CBE

2015   ‡*McIntosh,* Anne Caroline Ballingall McIntosh,
        b. 1954, *m.*

1999   *McIntosh of Hudnall,* Genista Mary McIntosh,
        b. 1946

1997   *Maddock,* Diana Margaret Maddock, *b.* 1945, *m.*

1991   *Mallalieu,* Ann Mallalieu, QC, *b.* 1945

2008   *Manningham-Buller,* Elizabeth (Lydia)
        Manningham-Buller, LG, DCB, *b.* 1948, *m.*

2013   *Manzoor,* Zahida Parveen Manzoor, CBE,
        b. 1958, *m.*

1970   *Masham of Ilton,* Susan Lilian Primrose Cunliffe-
        Lister, *b.* 1935, *w.*

1999   *Massey of Darwen,* Doreen Elizabeth Massey,
        b. 1938, *m.*

2006   *Meacher,* Molly Christine Meacher, *b.* 1940, *m.*

1998   *Miller of Chilthorne Domer,* Susan Elizabeth Miller,
        b. 1954

2014   *Mobarik,* Nosheena Shaheen Mobarik, CBE,
        b. 1957, *m.*

2015   ‡*Mone,* Michelle Mone, OBE, *b.* 1971

2004   *Morgan of Drefelin,* Delyth Jane Morgan,
        b. 1961, *m.*

2011   *Morgan of Ely,* Mair Eluned Morgan, *b.* 1967, *m.*

2001   *Morgan of Huyton,* Sally Morgan, *b.* 1959, *m.*

2004   *Morris of Bolton,* Patricia Morris, OBE, *b.* 1953

2005   *Morris of Yardley,* Estelle Morris, PC, *b.* 1952

2004   *Murphy,* Elaine Murphy, *b.* 1947, *m.*

2004   *Neuberger,* Rabbi Julia (Babette Sarah) Neuberger,
        DBE, *b.* 1950, *m.*

2007   *Neville-Jones,* (Lilian) Pauline Neville-Jones,
        DCMG, PC, *b.* 1939

2013   *Neville-Rolfe,* Lucy Jeanne Neville-Rolfe, DBE,
        CMG, *b.* 1953, *m.*

2010   *Newlove,* Helen Margaret Newlove, b. 1961, *w.*

1997   *Nicholson of Winterbourne,* Emma Harriet
        Nicholson, *b.* 1941, *m.*

1982   *Nicol,* Olive Mary Wendy Nicol, *b.* 1923, *m.*

2000   *Noakes,* Sheila Valerie Masters, DBE, *b.* 1949, *m.*

2000   *Northover,* Lindsay Patricia Granshaw, PC, *b.* 1954

2010   *Nye,* Susan Nye, *b.* 1955, *m.*

1991   *O'Cathain,* Detta O'Cathain, OBE, *b.* 1938, *w.*

2009   *O'Loan,* Nuala Patricia O'Loan, DBE, *b.* 1951, *m.*

1999   *O'Neill of Bengarve,* Onora Sylvia O'Neill, CH,
        CBE, FRS, FBA, *b.* 1941

1989   *Oppenheim-Barnes,* Sally Oppenheim-Barnes, PC,
        b. 1930, *m.*

2006   *Paisley of St George's,* Eileen Emily Paisley,
        b. 1931, *w.*

2010   *Parminter,* Kathryn Jane Parminter, *b.* 1964, *m.*

1991   *Perry of Southwark,* Pauline Perry, *b.* 1931, *m.*

2015   ‡*Pidding,* Emma Pidding, CBE

2014   *Pinnock,* Kathryn Mary Pinnock, *b.* 1946, *m.*

1997   *Pitkeathley,* Jill Elizabeth Pitkeathley, OBE,
        b. 1940

1999   *Prashar,* Usha Kumari Prashar, CBE, PC,
        b. 1948, *m.*

2015   ‡*Primarolo,* Dawn Primarolo, DBE, PC,
        b. 1954, *m.*

2004   *Prosser,* Margaret Theresa Prosser, OBE, *b.* 1937

2006   *Quin,* Joyce Gwendoline Quin, PC *b.* 1944

1996   *Ramsay of Cartvale,* Margaret Mildred (Meta)
        Ramsay, *b.* 1936

2011   *Randerson,* Jennifer Elizabeth Randerson,
        b. 1948, *m.*

1994   *Rawlings,* Patricia Elizabeth Rawlings, *b.* 1939

2014   *Rebuck,* Gail Ruth Rebuck, DBE, *b.* 1952, *m.*

2015   ‡*Redfern,* Elizabeth Redfern

1998   *Richardson of Calow,* Kathleen Margaret
        Richardson, OBE, *b.* 1938, *m.*

2015   ‡*Rock,* Kate Rock, *m.*

2004   *Royall of Blaisdon,* Janet Anne Royall, PC,
        b. 1955, *m.*

1997   *Scotland of Asthal,* Patricia Janet Scotland, PC, QC,
        b. 1955, *m.*

2015   ‡*Scott,* Jane Antoinette Scott, OBE, *b.* 1947, *m.*

2000   *Scott of Needham Market,* Rosalind Carol Scott,
        b. 1957

1991   *Seccombe,* Joan Anna Dalziel Seccombe, DBE,
        b. 1930, *m.*

2010   *Shackleton of Belgravia,* Fiona Sara Shackleton,
        LVO, *b.* 1956, *m.*

1998   *Sharp of Guildford,* Margaret Lucy Sharp,
        b. 1938, *m.*

1973   *Sharples,* Pamela Sharples, *b.* 1923, *w.*

2015   ‡*Sheehan,* Shas Sheehan, *b.* 1959, *m.*

2005   *Shephard of Northwold,* Gillian Patricia Shephard,
        PC, *b.* 1940, *m.*

2010   *Sherlock,* Maeve Christina Mary Sherlock, OBE,
        b. 1960

2014   *Shields,* Joanna Shields, OBE, b. 1962, *m.*

2010   *Smith of Basildon,* Angela Evans Smith, PC,
        b. 1959, *m.*

1995   *Smith of Gilmorehill,* Elizabeth Margaret Smith,
        b. 1940, *w.*

2014   *Smith of Newnham,* Dr Julie Elizabeth Smith,
        b. 1969

2010   *Stedman-Scott,* Deborah Stedman-Scott, OBE,
        b. 1955

1999   *Stern,* Vivien Helen Stern, CBE, *b.* 1941

2011   *Stowell of Beeston,* Tina Wendy Stowell, PC, MBE,
        b. 1967

2015   ‡*Stroud,* Philippa Stroud, *b.* 1965

2013 *Suttie*, Alison Mary Suttie, *b.* 1968

1996 *Symons of Vernham Dean*, Elizabeth Conway Symons, PC, *b.* 1951, *m.*

2005 *Taylor of Bolton*, Winifred Ann Taylor, PC, *b.* 1947, *m.*

1994 *Thomas of Walliswood*, Susan Petronella Thomas, OBE, *b.* 1935, *m.*

2006 *Thomas of Winchester*, Celia Marjorie Thomas, MBE, *b.* 1945

2015 ‡*Thornhill*, Dorothy Thornhill, MBE, *b.* 1955, *m.*

1998 *Thornton*, (Dorothea) Glenys Thornton, *b.* 1952, *m.*

2005 *Tonge*, Dr. Jennifer Louise Tonge, *b.* 1941, *m.*

1980 *Trumpington*, Jean Alys Barker, DCVO, PC, *b.* 1922, *w.*

1985 *Turner of Camden*, Muriel Winifred Turner, *b.* 1927, *m.*

2011 *Tyler of Enfield*, Claire Tyler, *b.* 1957

1998 *Uddin*, Manzila Pola Uddin, *b.* 1959, *m.*

2007 *Vadera*, Shriti Vadera, PC, *b.* 1962

2005 *Valentine*, Josephine Clare Valentine, *b.* 1958, *m.*

2006 *Verma*, Sandip Verma, *b.* 1959, *m.*

2004 *Wall of New Barnet*, Margaret Mary Wall, *b.* 1941, *m.*

2000 *Walmsley*, Joan Margaret Walmsley, *b.* 1943

1985 ¶*Warnock*, Helen Mary Warnock, DBE, *b.* 1924, *w.*

2007 *Warsi*, Sayeeda Hussain Warsi, PC, *b.* 1971

1999 *Warwick of Undercliffe*, Diana Mary Warwick, *b.* 1945, *m.*

2010 *Wheatcroft*, Patience Jane Wheatcroft, *b.* 1951, *m.*

2010 *Wheeler*, Margaret Eileen Joyce Wheeler, MBE, *b.* 1949

1999 *Whitaker*, Janet Alison Whitaker, *b.* 1936

1996 *Wilcox*, Judith Ann Wilcox, *b.* 1940, *w.*

1999 ¶*Wilkins*, Rosalie Catherine Wilkins, *b.* 1946

1993 *Williams of Crosby*, Shirley Vivien Teresa Brittain Williams, PC, *b.* 1930, *w.*

2013 *Williams of Trafford*, Susan Frances Maria Williams, *b.* 1967, *m.*

2014 *Wolf of Dulwich*, Alison Margaret Wolf, CBE, *b.* 1949, *m.*

2011 *Worthington*, Bryony Katherine Worthington, *b.* 1971, *m.*

2004 *Young of Hornsey*, Prof. Margaret Omolola Young, OBE, *b.* 1951, *m.*

1997 *Young of Old Scone*, Barbara Scott Young, *b.* 1948

COURTESY TITLES

The heir apparent to a Duke, Marquess or Earl uses the highest of his father's other titles as a courtesy title. For example, the Marquess of Blandford is heir to the Dukedom of Marlborough, and Viscount Amberley to the Earldom of Russell. Titles of second heirs (when in use) are also given, and the courtesy title of the father of a second heir is indicated by * eg Earl of Mornington, eldest son of *Marquess of Douro.

The holder of a courtesy title is not styled 'the Most Hon.' or 'the Rt. Hon.', and in correspondence 'the' is omitted before the title. The heir apparent to a Scottish title may use the title 'Master'.

MARQUESSES

*Blandford – *Marlborough*, D.
Bowmont and Cessford – *Roxburghe*, D.
Douglas and Clydesdale – *Hamilton and Brandon*, D.
*Douro – *Wellington*, D.
Graham – *Montrose*, D.
Granby – *Rutland*, D.
*Hamilton – *Abercorn*, D.
Lorne – *Argyll*, D.
Stafford – *Sutherland*, D.
Tavistock – *Bedford*, D.
Tullibardine – *Atholl*, D.
*Worcester – *Beaufort*, D.

EARLS

*Aboyne – *Huntly*, M.
Altamont – *Sligo*, M.
Arundel and Surrey – *Norfolk*, D.
Bective – *Headfort*, M.
Belfast – *Donegall*, M.
Brecknock – *Camden*, M.
*Burford – *St Albans*, D.
*Burlington – *Devonshire*, D.
*Cardigan – *Ailesbury*, M.
*Cassilis – *Ailsa*, M.
Compton – *Northampton*, M.
*Dalkeith – *Buccleuch*, D.
Dumfries – *Bute*, M.
Euston – *Grafton*, D.
Glamorgan – **Worcester*, M.
Grosvenor – *Westminster*, D.

*Haddo – *Aberdeen and Temair*, M.
Hillsborough – *Downshire*, M.
*Hopetoun – *Linlithgow*, M.
Kerry – *Lansdowne*, M.
*March and Kinrara – *Richmond*, D.
Medina – *Milford Haven*, M.
*Mount Charles – *Conyngham*, M.
Mornington – **Douro*, M.
Mulgrave – *Normanby*, M.
Percy – *Northumberland*, D.
Rocksavage – *Cholmondeley*, M.
Ronaldshay – *Zetland*, M.
*St Andrews – *Kent*, D.
Southesk – *Fife*, D.
*Tyrone – *Waterford*, M.
*Ulster – *Gloucester*, D.
Uxbridge – *Anglesey*, M.
*Wiltshire – *Winchester*, M.
Yarmouth – *Hertford*, M.

VISCOUNTS

Aithrie – **Hopetoun*, E.
Alexander – *Caledon*, E.
Althorp – *Spencer*, E.
Andover – *Suffolk and Berkshire*, E.
Anson – *Lichfield*, E.
Asquith – *Oxford and Asquith*, E.
Boringdon – *Morley*, E.

Borodale – *Beatty*, E.
Bury – *Albemarle*, E.
Campden – *Gainsborough*, E.
Carlow – *Portarlington*, E.
Carlton – *Wharncliffe*, E.
Chelsea – *Cadogan*, E.
Chewton – *Waldegrave*, E.
Clanfield – *Peel*, E.
Clive – *Powis*, E.
Coke – *Leicester*, E.
Corry – *Belmore*, E.
Corvedale – *Baldwin of Bewdley*, E.
Cranborne – *Salisbury*, M.
Crichton – *Erne*, E.
Curzon – *Howe*, E.
Dalrymple – *Stair*, E.
Dangan – *Cowley*, E.
Drumlanrig – *Queensberry*, M.
Duncannon – *Bessborough*, E.
Dungarvan – *Cork and Orrery*, E.
Dunluce – *Antrim*, E.
Dunwich – *Stradbroke*, E.
Dupplin – *Kinnoull*, E.
Elveden – *Iveagh*, E.
Emlyn – *Cawdor*, E
Encombe – *Eldon*, E.
Enfield – *Strafford*, E.
Erleigh – *Reading*, M.
Errington – *Cromer*, E.
Feilding – *Denbigh and Desmond*, E.

FitzHarris – *Malmesbury*, E.
Folkestone – *Radnor*, E.
Forbes – *Granard*, E.
Formartine – **Haddo*, E.
Garmoyle – *Cairns*, E.
Garnock – *Lindsay*, E.
Glenapp – *Inchcape*, E.
Glentworth – *Limerick*, E.
Glerawly – *Annesley*, E.
Grey de Wilton – *Wilton*, E.
Grimstone – *Verulam*, E.
Gwynedd – *Lloyd George of Dwyfor*, E.
Hawkesbury – *Liverpool*, E.
Hinchingbrooke – *Sandwich*, E.
Howick – *Grey*, E.
Ikerrin – *Carrick*, E.
Ingestre – *Shrewsbury*, E.
Jocelyn – *Roden*, E.
Kelburn – *Glasgow*, E.
Kingsborough – *Kingston*, E.
Kirkwall – *Orkney*, E.
Knebworth – *Lytton*, E.
Lambton – *Durham*, E.
Lascelles – *Harewood*, E.
Linley – *Snowdon*, E.
Lymington – *Portsmouth*, E.
Macmillan of Ovenden – *Stockton*, E.
Maidstone – *Winchilsea*, E
Maitland – *Lauderdale*, E.
Mandeville – *Manchester*, D.
Marsham – *Romney*, E.
Melgund – *Minto*, E.

Merton – *Nelson, E.*
Moore – *Drogheda, E.*
Newport – *Bradford, E.*
Northland – *Ranfurly, E*
Newry and Mourne – *Kilmorey, E.*
Petersham – *Harrington, E.*
Pollington – *Mexborough, E*
Raynham – *Townshend, M.*
Reidhaven – *Seafield, E.*
Royston – *Hardwicke, E.*
Ruthven of Canberra – *Gowrie, E.*
St Cyres – *Iddesleigh, E.*
Sandon – *Harrowby, E.*
Savernake – **Cardigan, E.*
Severn – *Wessex, E.*
Slane – **Mount Charles, E.*
Somerton – *Normanton, E.*
Stopford – *Courtown, E.*
Stormont – *Mansfield, E.*
Strabane – **Hamilton, M.*
Strathallan – *Perth, E.*
Stuart – *Castle Stewart, E.*
Suirdale – *Donoughmore, E.*
Tamworth – *Ferrers, E.*
Tarbat – *Cromartie, E.*

Villiers – *Jersey, E.*
Weymouth – *Bath, M.*
Windsor – *Plymouth, E.*
Wolmer – *Selborne, E.*
Woodstock – *Portland, E.*

BARONS (LORDS)
Aberdour – *Morton, E.*
Apsley – *Bathurst, E.*
Ardee – *Meath, E.*
Ashley – *Shaftesbury, E.*
Balniel – *Crawford and Balcarres, E.*
Berriedale – *Caithness, E.*
Bingham – *Lucan, E.*
Binning – *Haddington, E.*
Brooke – *Warwick, E.*
Bruce – *Elgin, E.*
Buckhurst – *De La Warr, E.*
Burghley – *Exeter, M.*
Cardross – *Buchan, E.*
Cavendish – **Burlington, E.*
Clifton – *Darnley, E.*
Cochrane – *Dundonald, E.*
Courtenay – *Devon, E.*
Culloden – **Ulster, E.*
Dalmeny – *Rosebery, E.*

Doune – *Moray, E.*
Downpatrick – **St Andrews, E.*
Dunglass – *Home, E.*
Elcho – *Wemyss and March, E.*
Eliot – *St Germans, E.*
Gillford – *Clanwilliam, E.*
Glamis – *Strathmore, E.*
Greenock – *Cathcart, E.*
Guernsey – *Aylesford, E.*
Hay – *Erroll, E.*
Herbert – *Pembroke and Montgomery, E.*
Howard of Effingham – *Effingham, E.*
Huntingtower – *Dysart, E.*
Hyde – *Clarendon, E.*
Inverurie – *Kintore, E.*
Irwin – *Halifax, E.*
Johnstone – *Annandale and Hartfell, E.*
Leveson – *Granville, E*
Loughborough – *Rosslyn, E.*
Masham – *Swinton, E.*
Medway – *Cranbrook, E.*

Montgomerie – *Eglinton and Winton, E.*
Moreton – *Ducie, E.*
Naas – *Mayo, E.*
Norreys – *Lindsey and Abingdon, E.*
North – *Guilford, E.*
Ogilvy – *Airlie, E.*
Oxmantown – *Rosse, E.*
Porchester – *Carnarvon, E.*
Ramsay – *Dalhousie, E.*
Romsey – *Mountbatten of Burma, C.*
St John – **Wiltshire, E.*
Scrymgeour – *Dundee, E.*
Settrington – **March and Kinrara, E.*
Seymour – *Somerset, D.*
Stanley – *Derby, E.*
Stavordale – *Ilchester, E.*
Strathavon – **Aboyne, E.*
Strathnaver – *Sutherland, C.*
Vere of Hanworth – **Burford, E.*
Wodehouse – *Kimberley, E*
Worsley – *Yarborough, E.*

PEERS' SURNAMES

The following symbols indicate the rank of the peer holding each title:

C.	Countess
D.	Duke
E.	Earl
M.	Marquess
V.	Viscount
*	Life Peer

Where no designation is given, the title is that of a hereditary Baron or Baroness.

Abney-Hastings – *Loudoun, E.*
Acheson – *Gosford, E.*
Adams – *A. of Craigielea**
Adderley – *Norton*
Addington – *Sidmouth, V.*
Agar – *Normanton, E.*
Ahmad – *A. of Wimbledon**
Aitken – *Beaverbrook*
Akers-Douglas – *Chilston, V.*
Alexander – *A. of Tunis, E.*
Alexander – *Caledon, E.*
Allan – *A. of Hallam**
Allen – *A. of Kensington**
Allsopp – *Hindlip*
Alton – *A. of Liverpool**
Anderson – *A. of Swansea**
Anderson – *Waverley, V.*
Anelay – *A. of St Johns**
Annesley – *Valentia, V.*
Anson – *Lichfield, E.*
Archer – *A. of Weston-super-Mare**
Armstrong – *A. of Hill Top**
Armstrong – *A. of Ilminster**

Armstrong-Jones – *Snowdon, E.*
Arthur – *Glenarthur*
Arundell – *Talbot of Malahide*
Ashdown – *A. of Norton-sub-Hamdon**
Ashley-Cooper – *Shaftesbury, E.*
Ashton – *A. of Hyde*
Ashton – *A. of Upholland**
Asquith – *Oxford and Asquith, E.*
Assheton – *Clitheroe*
Astley – *Hastings*
Astor – *A. of Hever*
Aubrey-Fletcher – *Braye*
Bailey – *Glanusk*
Baillie – *Burton*
Baillie Hamilton – *Haddington, E.*
Baker – *B. of Dorking**
Bakewell – *B. of Hardington Mandeville**
Balchin – *Lingfield**
Baldwin – *B. of Bewdley, E.*
Balfour – *Kinross*
Balfour – *Riverdale*
Bampfylde – *Poltimore*
Banbury – *B. of Southam*
Barber – *B. of Tewkesbury**
Baring – *Ashburton*
Baring – *Cromer, E.*
Baring – *Howick of Glendale*
Baring – *Northbrook*
Baring – *Revelstoke*
Barker – *Trumpington**

Barnes – *Gorell*
Barnewall – *Trimlestown*
Bassam – *B. of Brighton**
Bathurst – *Bledisloe, V.*
Beamish – *Dacre*
Beauclerk – *St Albans, D.*
Beaumont – *Allendale, V.*
Beckett – *Grimthorpe*
Benn – *Stansgate, V.*
Bennet – *Tankerville, E.*
Bentinck – *Portland, E.*
Beresford – *Decies*
Beresford – *Waterford, M.*
Berkeley – *B. of Knighton**
Berry – *Camrose, V.*
Berry – *Kemsley, V.*
Bertie – *Lindsey and Abingdon, E.*
Best – *Wynford*
Bethell – *Westbury*
Bewicke-Copley – *Cromwell*
Bigham – *Mersey, V.*
Bingham – *Clanmorris*
Bingham – *Lucan, E.*
Bishop – *Glendonbrook**
Black – *B. of Brentwood**
Black – *B. of Crossharbour**
Blackwood – *Dufferin and Clandeboye*
Blair – *B. of Boughton**
Bligh – *Darnley, E.*
Blyth – *B. of Rowington**
Bonham Carter – *B.-C. of Yarnbury**
Bootle-Wilbraham – *Skelmersdale*
Boscawen – *Falmouth, V.*
Boswell – *B. of Aynho**

Bottomley – *B. of Nettlestone**
Bourke – *Mayo, E.*
Bourne – *B. of Aberystwyth**
Bowes Lyon – *Strathmore and Kinghorne, E.*
Bowyer – *Denham*
Boyd – *B. of Duncansby**
Boyd – *Kilmarnock*
Boyle – *Cork and Orrery, E.*
Boyle – *Glasgow, E.*
Boyle – *Shannon, E.*
Brabazon – *Meath, E.*
Brand – *Hampden, V.*
Brassey – *B. of Apethorpe*
Brett – *Esher, V.*
Bridgeman – *Bradford, E.*
Brodrick – *Midleton, V.*
Brooke – *Alanbrooke, V.*
Brooke – *B. of Alverthorpe**
Brooke – *B. of Sutton Mandeville**
Brooke – *Brookeborough, V.*
Brooks – *B. of Tremorfa**
Brooks – *Crawshaw*
Brougham – *Brougham and Vaux*
Broughton – *Fairhaven*
Brown – *B. of Eaton-under-Heywood**
Browne – *B. of Belmont**
Browne – *B. of Ladyton**
Browne – *B. of Madingley**
Browne – *Kilmaine*
Browne – *Oranmore and Browne*
Browne – *Sligo, M.*
Bruce – *Aberdare*

Bruce – *Balfour of Burleigh*
Bruce – *Elgin and Kincardine, E.*
Brudenell-Bruce – *Ailesbury, M.*
Buchan – *Tweedsmuir*
Buckley – *Wrenbury*
Butler – *B. of Brockwell**
Butler – *Carrick, E.*
Butler – *Dunboyne*
Butler – *Mountgarret, V.*
Byng – *Strafford, E.*
Byng – *Torrington, V.*
Cameron – *C. of Dillington**
Cameron – *C. of Lochbroom**
Campbell – *Argyll, D.*
Campbell – *C. of Loughborough**
Campbell – *C. of Surbiton**
Campbell – *Cawdor, E.*
Campbell – *Colgrain*
Campbell – *Stratheden and Campbell*
Campbell-Gray – *Gray*
Canning – *Garvagh*
Capell – *Essex, E.*
Carey – *C. of Clifton**
Carington – *Carrington*
Carlile – *C. of Berriew**
Carnegie – *Fife, D.*
Carnegy – *Northesk, E.*
Carrington – *C. of Fulham**
Carter – *C. of Barnes**
Carter – *C. of Coles**
Cary – *Falkland, V.*
Caulfeild – *Charlemont, V.*
Cavendish – *C. of Furness**
Cavendish – *Chesham*
Cavendish – *Devonshire, D.*
Cavendish – *Waterpark*
Cayzer – *Rotherwick*
Cecil – *Amherst of Hackney*
Cecil – *Exeter, M.*
Cecil – *Rockley*
Chalker – *C. of Wallasey**
Chaloner – *Gisborough*
Charteris – *Wemyss and March, E.*
Chetwynd-Talbot – *Shrewsbury and Waterford, E.*
Chichester – *Donegall, M.*
Child Villiers – *Jersey, E.*
Chisholm – *C. of Owlpen**
Cholmondeley – *Delamere*
Chubb – *Hayter*
Clark – *C. of Calton**
Clarke – *C. of Hampstead**
Clarke – *C. of Stone-Cum-Ebony**
Clegg-Hill – *Hill, V.*
Clifford – *C. of Chudleigh*
Cochrane – *C. of Cults*
Cochrane – *Dundonald, E.*
Cocks – *Somers*
Cohen – *C. of Pimlico**
Cokayne – *Cullen of Ashbourne*

Coke – *Leicester, E.*
Cole – *Enniskillen, E.*
Collier – *Monkswell*
Collins – *C. of Highbury**
Collins – *C. of Mapesbury**
Colville – *Clydesmuir*
Colville – *C. of Culross, V.*
Compton – *Northampton, M.*
Conolly-Carew – *Carew*
Cooke – *Lexden**
Cooper – *C. of Windrush**
Cooper – *Norwich, V.*
Cope – *C. of Berkeley**
Corbett – *Rowallan*
Cornwall-Legh – *Grey of Codnor*
Courtenay – *Devon, E.*
Craig – *C. of Radley**
Craig – *Craigavon, V.*
Crichton – *Erne, E.*
Crichton-Stuart – *Bute, M.*
Cripps – *Parmoor*
Crossley – *Somerleyton*
Cubitt – *Ashcombe*
Cunliffe-Lister – *Masham of Ilton**
Cunliffe-Lister – *Swinton, E.*
Cunningham – *C. of Felling**
Currie – *C. of Marylebone**
Curry – *C. of Kirkharle**
Curzon – *Howe, E.*
Curzon – *Scarsdale, V.*
Cust – *Brownlow*
Czernin – *Howard de Walden*
Dalrymple – *Stair, E.*
Darzi – *D. of Denham**
Daubeny de Moleyns – *Ventry*
Davidson – *D. of Glen Clova**
Davies – *Darwen*
Davies – *D. of Abersoch**
Davies – *D. of Coity**
Davies – *D. of Oldham**
Davies – *D. of Stamford**
Dawnay – *Downe, V.*
Dawson-Damer – *Portarlington, E.*
Dean – *D. of Thornton-le-Fylde**
Deane – *Muskerry*
de Courcy – *Kingsale*
de Grey – *Walsingham*
Denison – *Londesborough*
Denison-Pender – *Pender*
Devereux – *Hereford, V.*
Dewar – *Forteviot*
Dixon – *Glentoran*
Dodson – *Monk Bretton*
Douglas – *Morton, E.*
Douglas – *Queensberry, M.*
Douglas-Hamilton – *Hamilton and Brandon, D.*
Douglas-Hamilton – *Selkirk, E.*
Douglas-Hamilton – *Selkirk of Douglas**
Douglas-Home – *Home, E.*

Douglas-Pennant – *Penrhyn*
Douglas-Scott-Montagu – *Montagu of Beaulieu*
Drummond – *Perth, E.*
Drummond of Megginch – *Strange*
Dugdale – *Crathorne*
Duke – *Merrivale*
Duncombe – *Feversham*
Dundas – *Melville, V.*
Dundas – *Zetland, M.*
Eady – *Swinfen*
Eccles – *E. of Moulton**
Ece – *Hussein-Ece**
Eden – *Auckland*
Eden – *E. of Winton**
Eden – *Henley*
Edgcumbe – *Mount Edgcumbe, E.*
Edmondson – *Sandford*
Edwardes – *Kensington*
Edwards – *Crickhowell**
Egerton – *Sutherland, D.*
Eliot – *St Germans, E.*
Elliot-Murray-Kynynmound – *Minto, E.*
Ellis – *Seaford*
Erskine – *Buchan, E.*
Erskine – *Mar and Kellie, E.*
Erskine-Murray – *Elibank*
Evans – *E. of Bowes Park**
Evans – *E. of Parkside**
Evans – *E. of Temple Guiting**
Evans – *E. of Watford**
Evans – *E. of Weardale**
Evans – *Mountevans*
Evans-Freke – *Carbery*
Eve – *Silsoe*
Fairfax – *F. of Cameron*
Falconer – *F. of Thoroton**
Falkner – *F. of Margravine**
Fane – *Westmorland, E.*
Farrington – *F. of Ribbleton**
Faulkner – *F. of Worcester**
Feilding – *Denbigh and Desmond, E.*
Feldman – *F. of Elstree**
Fellowes – *De Ramsey*
Fellowes – *F. of West Stafford**
Fermor-Hesketh – *Hesketh*
Fiennes – *Saye and Sele*
Fiennes-Clinton – *Lincoln, E.*
Finch Hatton – *Winchilsea and Nottingham, E.*
Finch-Knightley – *Aylesford, E.*
Finlay – *F. of Llandaff**
Fitzalan-Howard – *Norfolk, D.*
FitzGerald – *Leinster, D.*
Fitzherbert – *Stafford*
FitzRoy – *Grafton, D.*
FitzRoy – *Southampton*
FitzRoy Newdegate – *Daventry, V.*
Fletcher-Vane – *Inglewood*

Flower – *Ashbrook, V.*
Foljambe – *Liverpool, E.*
Forbes – *Granard, E*
Forsyth – *F. of Drumlean**
Forwood – *Arlington*
Foster – *F. of Thames Bank**
Foulkes – *F. of Cumnock**
Fox-Strangways – *Ilchester, E.*
Frankland – *Zouche*
Fraser – *Lovat*
Fraser – *Saltoun*
Fraser – *Strathalmond*
Freeman-Grenville – *Kinloss*
Fremantle – *Cottesloe*
French – *De Freyne*
Galbraith – *Strathclyde*
Garden – *G. of Frognal**
Gardiner – *G. of Kimble**
Gardner – *G. of Parkes**
Gascoyne-Cecil – *Salisbury, M.*
Gathorne-Hardy – *Cranbrook, E.*
Gibbs – *Aldenham*
Gibbs – *Wraxall*
Gibson – *Ashbourne*
Gibson – *G. of Market Rasen**
Gilbey – *Vaux of Harrowden*
Glyn – *Wolverton*
Goddard – *G. of Stockport**
Godley – *Kilbracken*
Goff – *G. of Chieveley**
Golding – *G. of Newcastle-under-Lyme**
Gordon – *Aberdeen, M.*
Gordon – *G. of Strathblane**
Gordon – *Huntly, M.*
Gordon Lennox – *Richmond, Gordon and Lennox, D.*
Gore – *Arran, E.*
Gould – *G. of Potternewton**
Grade – *G. of Yarmouth**
Graham – *G. of Edmonton**
Graham – *Montrose, D.*
Graham-Toler – *Norbury, E.*
Granshaw – *Northover**
Grant of Grant – *Strathspey*
Grant of Rothiemurchus – *Dysart, E.*
Green – *G. of Deddington**
Green – *G. of Hurstpierpoint**
Greenall – *Daresbury*
Greville – *Warwick and Brooke, E.*
Griffiths – *G. of Burry Port**
Griffiths – *G. of Fforestfach**
Grigg – *Altrincham*
Grimston – *G. of Westbury*
Grimston – *Verulam, E.*
Grosvenor – *Westminster, D.*
Grosvenor – *Wilton, E.*
Guest – *Wimborne, V.*
Gueterbock – *Berkeley*
Guinness – *Iveagh, E.*
Guinness – *Moyne*

Macmillan – *Stockton, E.*
Macpherson – *M. of Drumochter*
Macpherson – *Strathcarron*
Maffey – *Rugby*
Magan – *M. of Castletown**
Maginnis – *M. of Drumglass**
Maitland – *Lauderdale, E.*
Makgill – *Oxfuird, V.*
Makins – *Sherfield*
Manners – *Rutland, D.*
Manningham-Buller – *Dilhorne, V.*
Mansfield – *Sandhurst*
Marks – *M. of Broughton*
Marks – *M. of Henley-on-Thames**
Marquis – *Woolton, E.*
Marsham – *Romney, E.*
Martin – *M. of Springburn**
Martyn-Hemphill – *Hemphill*
Massey – *M. of Darwen**
Masters – *Noakes**
Maude – *Hawarden, V.*
Maxwell – *de Ros*
Maxwell – *Farnham*
May – *M. of Oxford**
Mayhew – *M. of Twysden**
Meade – *Clanwilliam, E.*
Mercer Nairne Petty-Fitzmaurice – *Lansdowne, M.*
Methuen-Campbell – *Methuen*
Millar – *Inchyra*
Miller – *M. of Chilthorne Domer**
Milner – *M. of Leeds*
Mitchell-Thomson – *Selsdon*
Mitford – *Redesdale*
Monckton – *M. of Brenchley, V.*
Monckton-Arundell – *Galway, V.*
Mond – *Melchett*
Money-Coutts – *Latymer*
Montagu – *Manchester, D.*
Montagu – *Sandwich, E.*
Montagu – *Swaythling*
Montagu Douglas Scott – *Buccleuch and Queensberry, D.*
Montagu Stuart Wortley – *Wharncliffe, E.*
Montague – *Amwell*
Montgomerie – *Eglinton and Winton, E.*
Montgomery – *M. of Alamein, V.*
Moore – *Drogheda, E.*
Moore – *M. of Lower Marsh**
Moore-Brabazon – *Brabazon of Tara*
Moreton – *Ducie, E.*
Morgan – *M. of Drefelin**
Morgan – *M. of Ely**
Morgan – *M. of Huyton**
Morris – *Killanin*

Morris – *M. of Aberavon**
Morris – *M. of Bolton**
Morris – *M. of Handsworth**
Morris – *M. of Kenwood*
Morris – *M. of Yardley**
Morris – *Naseby**
Morrison – *Dunrossil, V.*
Morrison – *Margadale*
Mosley – *Ravensdale*
Mountbatten – *Milford Haven, M.*
Muff – *Calverley*
Mulholland – *Dunleath*
Mumford – *Herries of Terregles*
Murray – *Atholl, D.*
Murray – *Dunmore, E.*
Murray – *Mansfield and Mansfield, E.*
Nall-Cain – *Brocket*
Napier – *Napier and Ettrick*
Napier – *N. of Magdala*
Needham – *Kilmorey, E.*
Neill – *N. of Bladen**
Nelson – *N. of Stafford*
Neuberger – *N. of Abbotsbury**
Nevill – *Abergavenny, M.*
Neville – *Braybrooke*
Nicholls – *N. of Birkenhead**
Nicholson – *Carnock*
Nicholson – *N. of Winterbourne**
Nivison – *Glendyne*
Noel – *Gainsborough, E.*
North – *Guilford, E.*
Northcote – *Iddesleigh, E.*
Norton – *Grantley*
Norton – *N. of Louth**
Norton – *Rathcreedan*
Nugent – *Westmeath, E.*
Oakeshott – *O. of Seagrove Bay**
O'Brien – *Inchiquin*
Ogilvie-Grant – *Seafield, E.*
Ogilvy – *Airlie, E.*
O'Neill – *O'N. of Bengarve**
O'Neill – *O'N. of Clackmannan**
O'Neill – *Rathcavan*
Orde-Powlett – *Bolton*
Ormsby-Gore – *Harlech*
Paget – *Anglesey, M.*
Paisley – *P. of St George's**
Pakenham – *Longford, E.*
Pakington – *Hampton*
Palmer – *Lucas and Dingwall*
Palmer – *P. of Childs Hill**
Palmer – *Selborne, E.*
Palumbo – *P. of Southwark**
Parker – *Macclesfield, E.*
Parker – *Morley, E.*
Parnell – *Congleton*
Parsons – *Rosse, E.*
Patel – *P. of Blackburn**
Patel – *P. of Bradford**
Patten – *P. of Barnes**
Paulet – *Winchester, M.*

Pearson – *Cowdray, V.*
Pearson – *P. of Rannoch**
Pease – *Gainford*
Pease – *Wardington*
Pelham – *Chichester, E.*
Pelham – *Yarborough, E.*
Pellew – *Exmouth, V.*
Penny – *Marchwood, V.*
Pepys – *Cottenham, E.*
Percy – *Northumberland, D.*
Perry – *P. of Southwark**
Pery – *Limerick, E.*
Philipps – *Milford*
Philipps – *St Davids, V.*
Phillips – *P. of Sudbury**
Phillips – *P. of Worth Matravers**
Phipps – *Normanby, M.*
Plant – *P. of Highfield**
Pleydell-Bouverie – *Radnor, E.*
Plumptre – *Fitzwalter*
Plunkett – *Dunsany*
Plunkett – *Louth*
Pollock – *Hanworth, V.*
Pomeroy – *Harberton, V.*
Ponsonby – *Bessborough, E.*
Ponsonby – *de Mauley*
Ponsonby – *P. of Shulbrede*
Powell – *P. of Bayswater**
Powys – *Lilford*
Pratt – *Camden, M.*
Preston – *Gormanston, V.*
Primrose – *Rosebery, E.*
Prittie – *Dunalley*
Purvis – *P. of Tweed**
Ramsay – *Dalhousie, E.*
Ramsay – *R. of Cartvale**
Ramsbotham – *Soulbury, V.*
Rees – *R. of Ludlow**
Rees-Williams – *Ogmore*
Reid – *R. of Cardowan**
Renfrew – *R. of Kaimsthorn**
Renton – *R. of Mount Harry**
Renwick – *R. of Clifton**
Rhys – *Dynevor*
Richards – *Milverton*
Richards – *R. of Herstmonceux**
Richardson – *R. of Calow**
Ritchie – *R. of Dundee*
Roberts – *Clwyd*
Roberts – *R. of Llandudno**
Robertson – *R. of Oakridge*
Robertson – *R. of Port Ellen**
Robertson – *Wharton*
Robinson – *Martonmere*
Roche – *Fermoy*
Rodd – *Rennell*
Rodgers – *R. of Quarry Bank**
Rogers – *Lisvane**
Rogers – *R. of Riverside**
Roper-Curzon – *Teynham*
Rose – *R. of Monewden**
Rospigliosi – *Newburgh, E.*
Rous – *Stradbroke, E.*

Rowley-Conwy – *Langford*
Royall – *R. of Blaisdon**
Runciman – *R. of Doxford, V.*
Russell – *Ampthill*
Russell – *Bedford, D.*
Russell – *de Clifford*
Russell – *R. of Liverpool*
Ryder – *Harrowby, E.*
Ryder – *R. of Wensum**
Sackville – *De La Warr, E.*
Sackville-West – *Sackville*
Sainsbury – *S. of Preston Candover**
Sainsbury – *S. of Turville**
St Aubyn – *St Levan*
St Clair – *Sinclair*
St Clair-Erskine – *Rosslyn, E.*
St John – *Bolingbroke and St John, V.*
St John – *St John of Bletso*
St Leger – *Doneraile, V.*
Samuel – *Bearsted, V.*
Sanderson – *S. of Ayot*
Sanderson – *S. of Bowden**
Sandilands – *Torphichen*
Saumarez – *de Saumarez*
Savile – *Mexborough, E.*
Saville – *S. of Newdigate**
Scarlett – *Abinger*
Schreiber – *Marlesford**
Sclater-Booth – *Basing*
Scotland – *S. of Asthal**
Scott – *Eldon, E.*
Scott – *S. of Foscote**
Scott – *S. of Needham Market**
Scrymgeour – *Dundee, E.*
Seager – *Leighton of St Mellons*
Seely – *Mottistone*
Seymour – *Hertford, M.*
Seymour – *Somerset, D.*
Shackleton – *S. of Belgravia**
Sharp – *S. of Guildford**
Shaw – *Craigmyle*
Shaw – *S. of Northstead**
Shephard – *S. of Northwold**
Sherbourne – *S. of Didsbury**
Shirley – *Ferrers, E.*
Shutt – *S. of Greetland**
Siddeley – *Kenilworth*
Sidney – *De L'Isle, V.*
Simon – *S. of Highbury**
Simon – *S. of Wythenshawe*
Simpson – *S. of Dunkeld**
Sinclair – *Caithness, E.*
Sinclair – *S. of Cleeve*
Sinclair – *Thurso, V.*
Singh – *S. of Wimbledon**
Skeffington – *Massereene and Ferrard, V.*
Smith – *Bicester*
Smith – *Hambleden, V.*
Smith – *Kirkhill**
Smith – *S. of Basildon**
Smith – *S. of Clifton**
Smith – *S. of Finsbury**

Smith – S. of Gilmorehill*
Smith – S. of Kelvin*
Smith – S. of Leigh*
Smith – S. of Newnham*
Somerset – Beaufort, D.
Somerset – Raglan
Soulsby – S. of Swaffham
    Prior*
Spencer – Churchill, V.
Spencer-Churchill –
    Marlborough, D.
Spring – Risby*
Spring Rice – Monteagle of
    Brandon
Stanhope – Harrington, E.
Stanley – Derby, E.
Stanley – S. of Alderley and
    Sheffield
Stapleton-Cotton –
    Combermere, V.
Steel – S. of Aikwood*
Sterling – S. of Plaistow*
Stern – S. of Brentford*
Stevens – S. of
    Kirkwhelpington*
Stevens – S. of Ludgate*
Stevenson – S. of Balmacara*
Stevenson – S. of
    Coddenham*
Stewart – Galloway, E.
Stewart – Stewartby*
Stoddart – S. of Swindon*
Stone – S. of Blackheath*
Stoneham – S. of Droxford*
Stonor – Camoys
Stopford – Courtown, E.
Stourton – Mowbray,
    Segrave and S.
Stowell – S. of Beeston*
Strachey – O'Hagan
Strutt – Belper
Strutt – Rayleigh
Stuart – Castle Stewart, E.
Stuart – Moray, E.

Stuart – S. of Findhorn, V.
Suenson-Taylor –
    Grantchester
Sutherland – S. of
    Houndwood*
Symons – S. of Vernham
    Dean*
Taylor – Kilclooney*
Taylor – T. of Blackburn*
Taylor – T. of Bolton*
Taylor – T. of Goss Moor*
Taylor – T. of Holbeach*
Taylor – T. of Warwick*
Taylour – Headfort, M.
Temple-Gore-Langton –
    Temple of Stowe, E.
Tennant – Glenconner
Thellusson – Rendlesham
Thesiger – Chelmsford, V.
Thomas – T. of Cwmgiedd*
Thomas – T. of Gresford*
Thomas – T. of
    Macclesfield*
Thomas – T. of Swynnerton*
Thomas – T. of Walliswood*
Thomas – T. of Winchester*
Thomson – T. of Fleet
Thynn – Bath, M.
Tottenham – Ely, M.
Trefusis – Clinton
Trench – Ashtown
Tufton – Hothfield
Turner – Netherthorpe
Turner – T. of Camden*
Turner – T. of Ecchinswell*
Turnour – Winterton, E.
Tyler – T. of Enfield*
Tyrell-Kenyon – Kenyon
Vallance – V. of Tummel*
Vanden-Bempde-Johnstone
    – Derwent
Vane – Barnard
Vane-Tempest-Stewart –
    Londonderry, M.

Vanneck – Huntingfield
Vaughan – Lisburne, E.
Vereker – Gort, V.
Verney – Willoughby de
    Broke
Vernon – Lyveden
Vesey – de Vesci, V.
Villiers – Clarendon, E.
Vincent – V. of Coleshill*
Vivian – Swansea
Wade – W. of Chorlton*
Waldegrave – W. of North
    Hill*
Walker – W. of Aldringham*
Walker – W. of
    Gestingthorpe*
Wall – W. of New Barnet*
Wallace – Dudley
Wallace – W. of Saltaire*
Wallace – W. of Tankerness*
Wallop – Portsmouth, E.
Walton – W. of Detchant*
Ward – Bangor, V.
Ward – Dudley, E.
Warrender – Bruntisfield
Warwick – W. of
    Undercliffe*
Watson – Manton
Watson – W. of Invergowrie*
Watson – W. of Richmond*
Webber – Lloyd-Webber*
Weir – Inverforth
Weld-Forester – Forester
Wellesley – Cowley, E.
Wellesley – Wellington, D.
West – W. of Spithead*
Westenra – Rossmore
White – Annaly
White – Hanningfield*
Whiteley – Marchamley
Whitfield – Kenswood
Williams – W. of Baglan*
Williams – W. of Crosby*
Williams – W. of Elvel*

Williams – W. of
    Oystermouth*
Williams – W. of Trafford*
Williamson – Forres
Willis – W. of
    Knaresborough*
Willoughby – Middleton
Wills – Dulverton
Wilson – Moran
Wilson – Nunburnholme
Wilson – W. of Dinton*
Wilson – W. of Tillyorn*
Windsor – Gloucester, D.
Windsor – Kent, D.
Windsor-Clive –
    Plymouth, E.
Wingfield – Powerscourt, V.
Winn – St Oswald
Wodehouse – Kimberley, E.
Wolf – W. of Dulwich*
Wolfson – W. of Aspley
    Guise*
Wolfson – W. of
    Sunningdale*
Wood – Halifax, E.
Wood – W. of Anfield*
Woodhouse – Terrington
Woolmer – W. of Leeds*
Wright – W. of Richmond*
Wyndham – Egremont and
    Leconfield
Wynn – Newborough
Yarde-Buller – Churston
Yerburgh – Alvingham
Yorke – Hardwicke, E.
Young – Kennet
Young – Y. of Graffham*
Young – Y. of Hornsey*
Young – Y. of Norwood
    Green*
Young – Y. of Old Scone*
Younger – Y. of Leckie, V.

LORDS SPIRITUAL

The Lords Spiritual are the Archbishops of Canterbury and York and 24 other diocesan bishops of the Church of England. The Bishops of London, Durham and Winchester always have seats in the House of Lords; the other 21 seats were previously filled by the remaining diocesan bishops in order of seniority. However, the Lords Spiritual (Women) Act 2015 provides for vacancies among the remaning 21 places to be filled by any female diocesan bishop in office at the time and, only if there is no female diocesan bishop, by the longest serving male diocesan bishop. The provision will remain in place for ten years from 2015, equivalent to two fixed-term parliaments. At the end of this period, the provision under the Act will end and the previous arrangements under which vacancies are filled according to length of service as a diocesan bishop will be restored.

The Bishop of Sodor and Man and the Bishop of Gibraltar in Europe are not eligible to sit in the House of Lords.

ARCHBISHOPS

Style, The Most Revd and Rt. Hon. the Lord Archbishop of_
Addressed as Archbishop *or* Your Grace

INTRODUCED TO HOUSE OF LORDS
2012   *Canterbury* (105th), Justin Portal Welby, *b.* 1956, *m., cons.* 2011, *elected* 2012, *trans.* 2013
2006   *York* (97th), John Mugabi Tucker Sentamu, PHD, *b.* 1949, *m., cons.* 1996, *elected* 2002, *trans.* 2005

BISHOPS

Style, The Rt. Revd the Lord Bishop of _
Addressed as Bishop *or* My Lord
elected date of confirmation as diocesan bishop

INTRODUCED TO HOUSE OF LORDS
as at November 2015

1996   *London* (132nd), Richard John Carew Chartres, KCVO, PC, *b.* 1947, *m., cons.* 1992, *elected* 1995
2014   *Durham* (74th), Paul Roger Butler, *b.* 1955, *m., cons.* 2004, *elected* 2009, *trans.* 2014
2012   *Winchester* (97th), Timothy John Dakin, *b.* 1958, *m., cons.* 2012, *elected* 2012
2001   *Chester* (40th), Peter Robert Forster, PHD, *b.* 1950, *m., cons.* 1996, *elected* 1996
2004   *Norwich* (71st), Graham Richard James, *b.* 1951, *m., cons.* 1993, *elected* 1999
2009   *Bristol* (55th), Michael Arthur Hill, *b.* 1949, *m., cons.* 1998, *elected* 2003
2010   *Derby* (7th), Alastair Llewellyn John Redfern, PHD, *b.* 1948, *m., cons.* 1997, *elected* 2005
2010   *Birmingham* (9th), David Andrew Urquhart, *b.* 1952, *cons.* 2000, *elected* 2006
2012   *Worcester* (113th), John Geoffrey Inge, PHD, *b.* 1955, *m., cons.* 2003, *elected* 2007
2013   *Coventry* (9th), Christopher John Cocksworth, PHD, *b.* 1959, *m., cons.* 2008, *elected* 2008
2013   *Truro* (15th), Timothy Martin Thornton, *b.* 1957, *m., cons.* 2001, *elected* 2008
2013   *Sheffield* (7th), Stephen John Lindsey Croft, PHD, *b.* 1957, *m., cons.* 2009, *elected* 2009
2013   *Carlisle* (66th), James William Scobie Newcome, *b.* 1953, *m., cons.* 2002, *elected* 2009
2013   *St Albans* (10th), Alan Gregory Clayton Smith, PHD, *b.* 1957, *cons.* 2001, *elected* 2009
2014   *Peterborough* (38th), Donald Spargo Allister, *b.* 1952, *m., cons.* 2010, *elected* 2010
2014   *Portsmouth* (9th), Christopher Richard James Foster, *b.* 1953, *m., cons.* 2001, *elected* 2010
2014   *Chelmsford* (10th), Stephen Geoffrey Cottrell, *b.* 1958, *m., cons.* 2004, *elected* 2010
2014   *Rochester* (107th), James Henry Langstaff, *b.* 1956, *m., cons.* 2004, *elected* 2010
2014   *Ely* (69th), Stephen David Conway, *b.* 1957, *cons.* 2006, *elected* 2010
2014   *Southwark* (10th), Christopher Thomas James Chessun, *b.* 1956, *cons.* 2005, *elected* 2011
2014   *Leeds* (1st), Nicholas Baines, *b.* 1957, *m., cons.* 2003, *elected* 2014
2015   *Salisbury* (78th), Nicholas Roderick Holtam, *b.* 1954, *m., cons.* 2011, *elected* 2011
2015   *Gloucester* (41st), Rachel Treweek, *b.* 1963, *m., cons.* 2015, *elected* 2015
2015   *Lincoln* (71st), Christopher Lowson, *b.* 1953, *m., cons.* 2011, *elected* 2011

BISHOPS AWAITING SEATS, in order of seniority
as at November 2015

Chichester (103rd), Martin Clive Warner, PHD, *b.* 1958, *cons.* 2010, *elected* 2012
Blackburn (9th), Julian Tudor Henderson, *b.* 1954, *m., cons.* 2013, *elected* 2013
Manchester (12th), David Stuart Walker, *b.* 1957, *m., cons.* 2000, *elected* 2013
Bath and Wells (79th), Peter Hancock, *b.* 1955, *m., cons.* 2010, *elected* 2014
Exeter (71st), Robert Ronald Atwell, *b.* 1954, *cons.* 2008, *elected* 2014
Liverpool (8th), Paul Bayes, *b.* 1953, *m., cons.* 2010, *elected* 2014
Hereford (105th), Richard Michael Cokayne Frith, *b.* 1949, *m., cons.* 1998, *elected* 2014
Guildford (10th), Andrew John Watson, *b.* 1961, *m., cons.* 2008, *elected* 2014
St Edmundsbury and Ipswich (11th), Martin Alan Seeley, *b.* 1954, *m., cons.* 2015, *elected* 2015
Southwell and Nottingham (12th), Paul Gavin Williams, *b.* 1968, *m., cons.* 2009, *elected* 2015
Newcastle (12th), Christine Elizabeth Hardman, *b.* 1951, *m., cons.* 2015, *elected* 2015
Oxford (43rd), vacant
Leicester (7th), vacant
Lichfield (99th), vacant

ORDERS OF CHIVALRY

THE MOST NOBLE ORDER OF THE GARTER (1348)

KG
Ribbon, Blue
Motto, Honi soit qui mal y pense
(Shame on him who thinks evil of it)

The number of Knights and Ladies Companion is limited to 24

SOVEREIGN OF THE ORDER
The Queen

LADIES OF THE ORDER
HRH The Princess Royal, 1994
HRH Princess Alexandra, The Hon. Lady Ogilvy, 2003

ROYAL KNIGHTS
HRH The Prince Philip, Duke of Edinburgh, 1947
HRH The Prince of Wales, 1958
HRH The Duke of Kent, 1985
HRH The Duke of Gloucester, 1997
HRH The Duke of York, 2006
HRH The Earl of Wessex, 2006
HRH The Duke of Cambridge, 2008

EXTRA KNIGHTS COMPANION AND LADIES
Grand Duke Jean of Luxembourg, 1972
HM The Queen of Denmark, 1979
HM The King of Sweden, 1983
HM King Juan Carlos, 1988
HRH Princess Beatrix of the Netherlands, 1989
HIM The Emperor of Japan, 1998
HM The King of Norway, 2001

KNIGHTS AND LADIES COMPANION
Lord Carrington, 1985
Lord Bramall, 1990
Lord Sainsbury of Preston Candover, 1992
Lord Ashburton, 1994
Sir Ninian Stephen, 1994
Sir Timothy Colman, 1996
Duke of Abercorn, 1999
Sir William Gladstone, 1999
Lord Inge, 2001
Sir Anthony Acland, 2001
Duke of Westminster, 2003
Lord Butler of Brockwell, 2003
Lord Morris of Aberavon, 2003
Sir John Major, 2005
Lord Luce, 2008

Sir Thomas Dunne, 2008
Lord Phillips of Worth Matravers, 2011
Lord Boyce, 2011
Lord Stirrup, 2013
Baroness Manningham-Buller, 2014
Lord King of Lothbury, 2014

Prelate, Bishop of Winchester
Chancellor, Duke of Abercorn, KG
Register, Dean of Windsor
Garter King of Arms, Thomas Woodcock, CVO
Gentleman Usher of the Black Rod, Lt.-Gen. David Leakey, CMG, CBE
Secretary, Patric Dickinson, LVO

THE MOST ANCIENT AND MOST NOBLE ORDER OF THE THISTLE (REVIVED 1687)

KT
Ribbon, Green
Motto, Nemo me impune lacessit
(No one provokes me with impunity)

The number of Knights and Ladies of the Thistle is limited to 16

SOVEREIGN OF THE ORDER
The Queen

ROYAL KNIGHTS
HRH The Prince Philip, Duke of Edinburgh, 1952
HRH The Prince of Wales, Duke of Rothesay, 1977
HRH The Duke of Cambridge, Earl of Strathearn, 2012

ROYAL LADY OF THE ORDER
HRH The Princess Royal, 2000

KNIGHTS AND LADIES
Earl of Elgin and Kincardine, 1981
Earl of Airlie, 1985
Earl of Crawford and Balcarres, 1996
Lady Marion Fraser, 1996
Lord Macfarlane of Bearsden, 1996
Lord Mackay of Clashfern, 1997
Lord Wilson of Tillyorn, 2000
Lord Sutherland of Houndwood, 2002
Sir Eric Anderson, 2002
Lord Steel of Aikwood, 2004
Lord Robertson of Port Ellen, 2004
Lord Cullen of Whitekirk, 2007
Lord Hope of Craighead, 2009
Lord Patel, 2009

Earl of Home, 2013
Lord Smith of Kelvin, 2013

Chancellor, Earl of Airlie, KT, GCVO, PC
Dean, Very Revd Prof. Iain Torrance, TD
Secretary, Mrs C. Roads, LVO
Lord Lyon King of Arms, Dr Joseph Morrow
Gentleman Usher of the Green Rod, Rear-Adm. Christopher Layman, CB, DSO, LVO

THE MOST HONOURABLE ORDER OF THE BATH (1725)

GCB *Military* GCB *Civil*

GCB	Knight (or Dame) Grand Cross
KCB	Knight Commander
DCB	Dame Commander
CB	Companion

Ribbon, Crimson
Motto, Tria juncta in uno
(Three joined in one)

Remodelled 1815, and enlarged many times since. The order is divided into civil and military divisions. Women became eligible for the order from 1 January 1971.

THE SOVEREIGN

GREAT MASTER AND FIRST OR PRINCIPAL KNIGHT GRAND CROSS
HRH The Prince of Wales, KG, KT, GCB, OM

Dean of the Order, Dean of Westminster
Bath King of Arms, Admiral of the Fleet, the Lord Boyce, KG, GCB, OBE
Registrar and Secretary, Rear-Adm. Iain Henderson, CB, CBE
Genealogist, Thomas Woodcock, CVO
Gentleman Usher of the Scarlet Rod, Maj.-Gen. Charles Vyvyan, CB, CBE
Deputy Secretary, Secretary of the Central Chancery of the Orders of Knighthood
Chancery, Central Chancery of the Orders of Knighthood, St James's Palace, London SW1A 1BH

THE ORDER OF MERIT (1902)

OM *Military*   OM *Civil*

OM
Ribbon, Blue and crimson

This order is designed as a special distinction for eminent men and women without conferring a knighthood upon them. The order is limited in numbers to 24, with the addition of foreign honorary members.

THE SOVEREIGN

HRH The Prince Philip, Duke of
    Edinburgh, 1968
Sir Michael Atiyah, 1992
Sir Aaron Klug, 1995
Lord Foster of Thames Bank, 1997
Prof. Sir Roger Penrose, 2000
Sir Tom Stoppard, 2000
HRH The Prince of Wales, 2002
Lord May of Oxford, 2002
Lord Rothschild, 2002
Sir David Attenborough, 2005
Baroness Boothroyd, 2005
Sir Michael Howard, 2005
Sir Timothy Berners-Lee, KBE, 2007
Lord Eames, 2007
Lord Rees of Ludlow, 2007
Rt. Hon. Jean Chrétien, QC, 2009
Robert Neil MacGregor, 2010
Hon. John Howard, 2012
David Hockney, 2012
Sir Simon Rattle, 2013
Prof. Sir Magdi Yacoub, 2013

Secretary and Registrar, Lord Fellowes,
    GCB, GCVO, PC, QSO
Chancery, Central Chancery of the Orders
    of Knighthood, St James's Palace,
    London SW1A 1BH

THE MOST DISTINGUISHED ORDER OF ST MICHAEL AND ST GEORGE (1818)

GCMG   KCMG

GCMG   Knight (or Dame) Grand
            Cross
KCMG   Knight Commander
DCMG   Dame Commander
CMG   Companion

Ribbon, Saxon blue, with scarlet centre
Motto, Auspicium melioris aevi
(Token of a better age)

THE SOVEREIGN

GRAND MASTER
HRH The Duke of Kent, KG, GCMG,
    GCVO, ADC

Prelate, Rt. Revd David Urquhart
Chancellor, Lord Robertson of Port
    Ellen, KT, GCMG, PC
Secretary, Permanent Under-Secretary
    of State at the Foreign and
    Commonwealth Office and Head of
    the Diplomatic Service
Registrar, Sir David Manning, GCMG,
    CVO
King of Arms, Sir Jeremy Greenstock,
    GCMG
Gentleman Usher of the Blue Rod, vacant
Dean, Dean of St Paul's
Deputy Secretary, Secretary of the
    Central Chancery of the Orders of
    Knighthood
Hon. Genealogist, Timothy Duke
Chancery, Central Chancery of the Orders
    of Knighthood, St James's Palace,
    London SW1A 1BH

THE IMPERIAL ORDER OF THE CROWN OF INDIA (1877) FOR LADIES

CI

Badge, the royal cipher of Queen Victoria in jewels within an oval, surmounted by an heraldic crown and attached to a bow of light blue watered ribbon, edged white

The honour does not confer any rank or title upon the recipient

No conferments have been made since 1947

HM The Queen, 1947

THE ROYAL VICTORIAN ORDER (1896)

GCVO   KCVO

GCVO   Knight or Dame Grand
            Cross
KCVO   Knight Commander
DCVO   Dame Commander
CVO   Commander
LVO   Lieutenant
MVO   Member

Ribbon, Blue, with red and white edges
Motto, Victoria

THE SOVEREIGN
GRAND MASTER
HRH The Princess Royal, KG, KT,
    GCVO

Chancellor, Lord Chamberlain
Secretary, Keeper of the Privy Purse
Registrar, Secretary of the Central
    Chancery of the Orders of
    Knighthood
Chaplain, Chaplain of the Queen's
    Chapel of the Savoy
Hon. Genealogist, David White

THE MOST EXCELLENT ORDER OF THE BRITISH EMPIRE (1917)

GBE   KBE

The order was divided into military and civil divisions in December 1918

GBE	Knight or Dame Grand Cross
KBE	Knight Commander
DBE	Dame Commander
CBE	Commander
OBE	Officer
MBE	Member

Ribbon, Rose pink edged with pearl grey with vertical pearl stripe in centre (military division); without vertical pearl stripe (civil division)
Motto, For God and the Empire

THE SOVEREIGN

GRAND MASTER
HRH The Prince Philip, Duke of Edinburgh, KG, KT, OM, GBE, PC

Prelate, Bishop of London
King of Arms, vacant
Registrar, Secretary of the Central Chancery of the Orders of Knighthood
Secretary, Secretary of the Cabinet and Head of the Home Civil Service
Dean, Dean of St Paul's
Lady Usher of the Purple Rod, Dame Amelia Chilcott Fawcett, DBE
Chancery, Central Chancery of the Orders of Knighthood, St James's Palace, London SW1A 1BH

ORDER OF THE COMPANIONS OF HONOUR (1917)

CH

Ribbon, Carmine, with gold edges

This order consists of one class only and carries with it no title. The number of awards is limited to 65 (excluding honorary members).

Anthony, John, 1981
Ashdown of Norton-sub-Hamdon, Lord, 2015
Attenborough, Sir David, 1995
Baker, Dame Janet, 1993
Baker of Dorking, Lord, 1992
Birtwistle, Sir Harrison, 2000
Brenner, Sydney, 1986
Brook, Peter, 1998
Brooke of Sutton Mandeville, Lord, 1992
Campbell, Sir Menzies, 2013
Carrington, Lord, 1983
Clarke, Kenneth, 2014
Coe, Lord, 2012
De Chastelain, Gen. John, 1999
Dench, Dame Judi, 2005
Hannay of Chiswick, Lord, 2003
Hawking, Prof. Stephen, 1989
Healey, Lord, 1979
Heseltine, Lord, 1997
Higgs, Prof. Peter, 2012
Hockney, David, 1997
Hodgkin, Sir Howard, 2002
Howard, Sir Michael, 2002
Howard of Lympne, Lord, 2011
Howe of Aberavon, Lord, 1996
Hurd of Westwell, Lord, 1995
King of Bridgwater, Lord, 1992
Lovelock, Prof. James, 2002
McKellen, Sir Ian Murray, 2008
McKenzie, Prof. Dan Peter, 2003
Major, Sir John, 1998
Marriner, Sir Neville, 2015
Maxwell Davies, Sir Peter, 2013
O'Neill of Bengarve, Baroness, 2013
Owen, Lord, 1994
Patten of Barnes, Lord, 1997
Peters, Dame Mary, 2015
Riley, Bridget, 1998
Rogers of Riverside, Lord, 2008
Serota, Sir Nicholas, 2013
Smith, Dame Margaret (Maggie), 2014
Somare, Sir Michael, 1978
Strathclyde, Lord, 2013
Tebbit, Lord, 1987
Woolf, Lord, 2015
Young, Sir George, 2012
Young of Graffham, Lord, 2015

Honorary Members, Prof. Amartya Sen, 2000; Bernard Haitink, 2002
Secretary and Registrar, Secretary of the Central Chancery of the Orders of Knighthood

THE DISTINGUISHED SERVICE ORDER (1886)

DSO

Ribbon, Red, with blue edges

Bestowed in recognition of especial services in action of commissioned officers in the Navy, Army and Royal Air Force and (since 1942) Mercantile Marine. The members are Companions only. A bar may be awarded for any additional act of service.

THE IMPERIAL SERVICE ORDER (1902)

ISO

Ribbon, Crimson, with blue centre

Appointment as companion of this order is open to members of the civil services whose eligibility is determined by the grade they hold. The order consists of the sovereign and companions to a number not exceeding 1,900, of whom 1,300 may belong to the home civil services and 600 to overseas civil services. The then prime minister announced in March 1993 that he would make no further recommendations for appointments to the order.

Secretary, Head of the Home Civil Service
Registrar, Secretary of the Central Chancery of the Orders of Knighthood

THE ROYAL VICTORIAN CHAIN (1902)

It confers no precedence on its holders

HM THE QUEEN

HM The King of Thailand, 1960
HM The Queen of Denmark, 1974
HM The King of Sweden, 1975
HRH Princess Beatrix of the Netherlands, 1982
Gen. Antonio Eanes, 1985
HM King Juan Carlos, 1986
HM The King of Norway, 1994
Earl of Airlie, 1997
Rt. Revd and Rt. Hon. Lord Carey of Clifton, 2002
HRH Prince Philip, Duke of Edinburgh, 2007
HM The Sultan of Oman, 2010
Rt. Revd and Rt. Hon. Lord Williams of Oystermouth, 2012

BARONETAGE AND KNIGHTAGE

BARONETS

Style, 'Sir' before forename and surname, followed by 'Bt'.
  Envelope, Sir F_ S_, Bt. *Letter (formal)*, Dear Sir; *(social)*, Dear Sir F_. *Spoken*, Sir F_
Wife's style, 'Lady' followed by surname
  Envelope, Lady S_. *Letter (formal)*, Dear Madam; *(social)*, Dear Lady S_. *Spoken*, Lady S_
Style of Baronetess, 'Dame' before forename and surname, followed by 'Btss.' (*see also* Dames)

There are five different creations of baronetcies: Baronets of England (creations dating from 1611); Baronets of Ireland (creations dating from 1619); Baronets of Scotland or Nova Scotia (creations dating from 1625); Baronets of Great Britain (creations after the Act of Union 1707 which combined the kingdoms of England and Scotland); and Baronets of the United Kingdom (creations after the union of Great Britain and Ireland in 1801).

Badge of Baronets of the United Kingdom   *Badge of Baronets of Nova Scotia*

Badge of Ulster

The patent of creation limits the destination of a baronetcy, usually to male descendants of the first baronet. In some cases, however, special remainders have allowed baronetcies to pass, in the absence of sons, to another relative. In the case of baronetcies of Scotland or Nova Scotia, a special remainder of 'heirs male and of tailzie' allows the baronetcy to descend to heirs general, including women. There are four existing Scottish baronetcies with such a remainder.

The Official Roll of the Baronetage is kept at the Crown Office and maintained by the Registrar and Assistant Registrar of the Baronetage. Anyone who considers that he or she is entitled to be entered on the roll may apply through the Crown Office to prove their succession. Every person succeeding to a baronetcy must exhibit proofs of succession to the Lord Chancellor. A person whose name is not entered on the official roll will not be addressed or mentioned by the title of baronet or baronetess in any official document, nor will he or she be accorded precedence as a baronet or baronetess.

BARONETCIES EXTINCT SINCE THE LAST EDITION
Dodds (cr. 1964); Hawley (cr. 1795)

OFFICIAL ROLL OF THE BARONETAGE, Crown Office, House of Lords, London SW1A 0PW T 020-7219 2632
Registrar, Ian Denyer, MVO
Assistant Registrar, Grant Bavister

KNIGHTS

Style, 'Sir' before forename and surname, followed by appropriate post-nominal initials if a Knight Grand Cross or Knight Commander
  Envelope, Sir F_ S_. *Letter (formal)*, Dear Sir; *(social)*, Dear Sir F_. *Spoken*, Sir F_
Wife's style, 'Lady' followed by surname
  Envelope, Lady S_. *Letter (formal)*, Dear Madam; *(social)*, Dear Lady S_. *Spoken*, Lady S_

The prefix 'Sir' is not used by knights who are clerics of the Church of England, who do not receive the accolade. Their wives are entitled to precedence as the wife of a knight but not to the style of 'Lady'.

ORDERS OF KNIGHTHOOD
Knight Grand Cross and Knight Commander are the higher classes of the Orders of Chivalry (*see* Orders of Chivalry). Honorary knighthoods of these orders may be conferred on men who are citizens of countries of which the Queen is not head of state. As a rule, the prefix 'Sir' is not used by honorary knights.

KNIGHTS BACHELOR

The Knights Bachelor do not constitute a royal order, but comprise the surviving representation of the ancient state orders of knighthood. The Register of Knights Bachelor, instituted by James I in the 17th century, lapsed, and in 1908 a voluntary association under the title of the Society of Knights (now the Imperial Society of Knights Bachelor) was formed with the primary objectives of continuing the various registers dating from 1257 and obtaining the uniform registration of every created Knight Bachelor. In 1926 a design for a badge to be worn by Knights Bachelor was approved and adopted; in 1974 a neck badge and miniature were added.

THE IMPERIAL SOCIETY OF KNIGHTS BACHELOR, Magnesia House, 56 Playhouse Yard, London EC4V 5EX
Knight Principal, Sir Colin Berry
Prelate, Rt. Revd and Rt. Hon. Bishop of London
Registrar, Sir Gavyn Arthur
Hon. Treasurer, Sir Jeremy Elwes, CBE
Clerk to the Council, Col. Simon Doughty

LIST OF BARONETS AND KNIGHTS *as at 31 August 2015*

†	Not registered on the Official Roll of the Baronetage at the time of going to press
( )	The date of creation of the baronetcy is given in parentheses
I	Baronet of Ireland
NS	Baronet of Nova Scotia
S	Baronet of Scotland

A full entry in italic type indicates that the recipient of a knighthood died during the year in which the honour was conferred. The name is included for purposes of record. Peers are not included in this list.

Aaronson, Sir Michael John, Kt., CBE

Abbott, *Adm.* Sir Peter Charles, GBE, KCB

†Abdy, Sir Robert Etienne Eric, Bt. (1850)

Abed, *Dr* Sir Fazle Hasan, KCMG

Acher, Sir Gerald, Kt., CBE, LVO

Ackroyd, Sir Timothy Robert Whyte, Bt. (1956)

Acland, Sir Antony Arthur, KG, GCMG, GCVO

Acland, *Lt.-Col.* Sir (Christopher) Guy (Dyke), Bt. (1890), MVO

†Acland, Sir Dominic Dyke, Bt. (1678)

Adam, Sir Kenneth Hugo, Kt., OBE

Adams, Sir Geoffrey Doyne, KCMG

Adams, Sir William James, KCMG

Adsetts, Sir William Norman, Kt., OBE

Adye, Sir John Anthony, KCMG

Aga Khan IV, HH Prince Karim, KBE

Agnew, Sir Crispin Hamlyn, Bt. (S. 1629)

Agnew, Sir George Anthony, Bt. (1895)

Agnew, Sir Rudolph Ion Joseph, Kt.

Agnew, Sir Theodore, Kt.

Agnew-Somerville, Sir James Lockett Charles, Bt. (1957)

Ah Koy, Sir James Michael, KBE

Aikens, *Rt. Hon.* Sir Richard John Pearson, Kt.

Ainslie, Sir Charles Benedict, Kt., CBE

†Ainsworth, Sir Anthony Thomas Hugh, Bt. (1917)

Aird, Sir (George) John, Bt. (1901)

Airy, *Maj.-Gen.* Sir Christopher John, KCVO, CBE

Aitchison, Sir Charles Walter de Lancey, Bt. (1938)

Ajegbo, Sir Keith Onyema, Kt., OBE

Akenhead, *Hon.* Sir Robert, Kt.

Akers-Jones, Sir David, KBE, CMG

Alberti, *Prof.* Sir Kurt George Matthew Mayer, Kt.

Albu, Sir George, Bt. (1912)

Alcock, *Air Chief Marshal* Sir (Robert James) Michael, GCB, KBE

Aldous, *Rt. Hon.* Sir William, Kt.

Aldridge, Sir Rodney Malcolm, Kt., OBE

Alexander, *Rt. Hon.* Sir Daniel (Grian), Kt.

Alexander, Sir Douglas, Bt. (1921)

Alexander, Sir Richard, Bt. (1945)

Alghanim, Sir Kutayba Yusuf, KCMG

Allan, *Hon.* Sir Alexander Claud Stuart, KCB

Allen, Sir Errol Newton Fitzrose, KCMG

Allen, *Prof.* Sir Geoffrey, Kt., PHD, FRS

Allen, Sir John Derek, Kt., CBE

Allen, Sir Mark John Spurgeon, Kt., CMG

Allen, *Hon.* Sir Peter Austin Philip Jermyn, Kt.

Allen, Sir Thomas Boaz, Kt., CBE

Allen, *Hon.* Sir William Clifford, KCMG

Allen, Sir William Guilford, Kt.

Alleyne, Sir George Allanmoore Ogarren, Kt.

Alleyne, *Revd* John Olpherts Campbell, Bt. (1769)

Allinson, Sir (Walter) Leonard, KCVO, CMG

Alliott, *Hon.* Sir John Downes, Kt.

Allison, *Air Chief Marshal* Sir John Shakespeare, KCB, CBE

Amess, Sir David Anthony Andrew, Kt.

Amet, *Hon.* Sir Arnold Karibone, Kt.

Amory, Sir Ian Heathcoat, Bt. (1874)

Anderson, *Dr* Sir James Iain Walker, Kt., CBE

Anderson, Sir John Anthony, KBE

Anderson, Sir Leith Reinsford Steven, Kt., CBE

Anderson, *Prof.* Sir Roy Malcolm, Kt.

Anderson, *Air Marshal* Sir Timothy Michael, KCB, DSO

Anderson, Sir (William) Eric Kinloch, KT

Anderton, Sir (Cyril) James, Kt., CBE, QPM

Andrew, Sir Robert John, KCB

Andrew, Sir Warwick, Kt.

Andrews, Sir Derek Henry, KCB, CBE

Andrews, Sir Ian Charles Franklin, Kt., CBE, TD

Angest, Sir Henry, Kt.

Annesley, Sir Hugh Norman, Kt., QPM

Anson, Sir John, KCB

Anson, *Rear-Adm.* Sir Peter, Bt. (1831), CB

Anstruther, Sir Sebastian Paten Campbell, Bt. (S. 1694 and S. 1700)

Anstruther-Gough-Calthorpe, Sir Euan Hamilton, Bt. (1929)

Antrobus, Sir Edward Philip, Bt. (1815)

Appleyard, Sir Leonard Vincent, KCMG

Appleyard, Sir Raymond Kenelm, KBE

Arbib, Sir Martyn, Kt.

Arbuthnot, Sir Keith Robert Charles, Bt. (1823)

Arbuthnot, Sir William Reierson, Bt. (1964)

Arbuthnott, *Prof.* Sir John Peebles, Kt., PHD, FRSE

†Archdale, Sir Nicholas Edward, Bt. (1928)

Arculus, Sir Ronald, KCMG, KCVO

Arculus, Sir Thomas David Guy, Kt.

Armitage, *Air Chief Marshal* Sir Michael John, KCB, CBE

Armitt, Sir John Alexander, Kt., CBE

Armour, *Prof.* Sir James, Kt., CBE

Armstrong, Sir Christopher John Edmund Stuart, Bt. (1841), MBE

Armstrong, Sir Patrick John, Kt., CBE

Armstrong, Sir Richard, Kt., CBE

Armytage, Sir John Martin, Bt. (1738)

Arnold, *Hon.* Sir Richard David, Kt.

Arnold, Sir Thomas Richard, Kt.

Arnott, Sir Alexander John Maxwell, Bt. (1896)

†Arthur, Sir Benjamin Nathan, Bt. (1841)

Arthur, Sir Gavyn Farr, Kt.

Arthur, *Lt.-Gen.* Sir (John) Norman Stewart, KCB, CVO

Arthur, Sir Michael Anthony, KCMG

Arulkumaran, *Prof.* Sir Sabaratnam, Kt.

Asbridge, Sir Jonathan Elliott, Kt.

Ash, *Prof.* Sir Eric Albert, Kt., CBE, FRS, FRENG

Ashburnham, Sir James Fleetwood, Bt. (1661)

Ashmore, *Admiral of the Fleet* Sir Edward Beckwith, GCB, DSC

Ashworth, *Dr* Sir John Michael, Kt.

Aske, Sir Robert John Bingham, Bt. (1922)

Askew, Sir Bryan, Kt.

Asquith, *Hon.* Sir Dominic Anthony Gerard, KCMG

Astill, *Hon.* Sir Michael John, Kt.

Astley-Cooper, Sir Alexander Paston, Bt. (1821)

Astwood, *Hon.* Sir James Rufus, KBE

Atcherley, Sir Harold Winter, Kt.

Atiyah, Sir Michael Francis, Kt., OM, PHD, FRS

Atkins, *Rt. Hon.* Sir Robert James, Kt.

Atkinson, *Prof.* Sir Anthony Barnes, Kt.

Atkinson, Sir Frederick John, KCB

Atkinson, Sir William Samuel, Kt.

Atopare, Sir Sailas, GCMG

Attenborough, Sir David Frederick, Kt., OM, CH, CVO, CBE, FRS

Aubrey-Fletcher, Sir Henry Egerton, Bt. (1782)

Audland, Sir Christopher John, KCMG

Augier, *Prof.* Sir Fitzroy Richard, Kt.

Auld, *Rt. Hon.* Sir Robin Ernest, Kt.

Austin, Sir Anthony Leonard, Bt. (1894)

Austin, *Air Marshal* Sir Roger Mark, KCB, AFC

Austen-Smith, *Air Marshal* Sir Roy David, KBE, CB, CVO, DFC

Avei, Sir Moi, KBE

Ayaz, *Dr* Sir Iftikhar Ahmad, KBE

Ayckbourn, Sir Alan, Kt., CBE

Aykroyd, Sir Henry Robert George, Bt. (1920)

Aykroyd, Sir James Alexander Frederic, Bt. (1929)
Aylmer, Sir Richard John, Bt. (I. 1622)
Aylward, *Prof.* Sir Mansel, Kt., CB
Aynsley-Green, *Prof.* Sir Albert, Kt.

Bacha, Sir Bhinod, Kt., CMG
Backhouse, Sir Alfred James Stott, Bt. (1901)
Bacon, Sir Nicholas Hickman Ponsonby, Bt., OBE (1611 and 1627), *Premier Baronet of England*
Baddeley, Sir John Wolsey Beresford, Bt. (1922)
Badge, Sir Peter Gilmour Noto, Kt.
Baer, Sir Jack Mervyn Frank, Kt.
Bagge, Sir (John) Jeremy Picton, Bt. (1867)
Baggott, Sir Matthew David, Kt., CBE, QPM
Bagnall, *Air Chief Marshal* Sir Anthony, GBE, KCB
Bai, Sir Brown, KBE
Bailey, Sir Alan Marshall, KCB
Bailey, Sir Brian Harry, Kt., OBE
Bailey, Sir John Bilsland, KCB
Bailey, Sir John Richard, Bt. (1919)
Bailhache, Sir Philip Martin, Kt.
Baillie, Sir Adrian Louis, Bt. (1823)
Bain, *Prof.* Sir George Sayers, Kt.
Baird, Sir Charles William Stuart, Bt. (1809)
†Baird, Sir James Andrew Gardiner, Bt. (S. 1695)
Baird, *Air Marshal* Sir John Alexander, KBE
Baird, *Vice-Adm.* Sir Thomas Henry Eustace, KCB
Bairsto, *Air Marshal* Sir Peter Edward, KBE, CB
Baker, Sir Bryan William, Kt.
Baker, *Hon.* Sir Jeremy Russell, Kt.
Baker, *Prof.* Sir John Hamilton, Kt., QC
Baker, Sir John William, Kt., CBE
Baker, *Hon.* Sir Jonathan Leslie, Kt.
Baker, *Rt. Hon.* Sir (Thomas) Scott (Gillespie), Kt.
Baldry, Sir Antony Brian, Kt.
Baldwin, *Prof.* Sir Jack Edward, Kt., FRS
Ball, Sir Christopher John Elinger, Kt.
Ball, *Prof.* Sir John Macleod, Kt.
Ball, Sir Richard Bentley, Bt. (1911)
Ball, *Prof.* Sir Robert James, Kt., PHD
Ballantyne, *Dr* Sir Frederick Nathaniel, GCMG
Band, *Adm.* Sir Jonathon, GCB
Banham, Sir John Michael Middlecott, Kt.
Bannerman, Sir David Gordon, Bt. (S. 1682), OBE
Bannister, Sir Roger Gilbert, Kt., CBE, DM, FRCP
Barber, Sir Brendan, Kt.
Barber, Sir Michael Bayldon, Kt.
Barber, Sir (Thomas) David, Bt. (1960)
Barclay, Sir Robert Colraine, Bt. (S. 1668)
Barclay, Sir David Rowat, Kt.
Barclay, Sir Frederick Hugh, Kt.
Barder, Sir Brian Leon, KCMG
Baring, Sir John Francis, Bt. (1911)
Barker, Sir Colin, Kt.

Barker, *Hon.* Sir (Richard) Ian, Kt.
Barling, *Hon.* Sir Gerald Edward, Kt.
Barlow, Sir Christopher Hilaro, Bt. (1803)
Barlow, Sir Frank, Kt., CBE
Barlow, Sir James Alan, Bt. (1902)
Barlow, Sir John Kemp, Bt. (1907)
Barnes, *The Most Revd* Brian James, KBE
Barnes, Sir (James) David (Francis), Kt., CBE
Barnett, *Hon.* Sir Michael Lancelot Patrick, Kt.
Barnett, *Prof.* Sir Richard Robert, Kt.
Barnewall, Sir Reginald Robert, Bt. (I. 1623)
Baron, Sir Thomas, Kt., CBE
†Barran, Sir John Ruthven, Bt. (1895)
Barrett, Sir Stephen Jeremy, KCMG
Barrett-Lennard, Sir Peter John, Bt. (1801)
Barrington, Sir Benjamin, Bt. (1831)
Barrington, Sir Nicholas John, KCMG, CVO
Barrington-Ward, *Rt. Revd* Simon, KCMG
Barron, Sir Donald James, Kt.
Barron, *Rt. Hon.* Sir Kevin, Kt.
Barrons, *Gen.* Sir Richard, KCB, CBE, ADC
Barrow, Sir Anthony John Grenfell, Bt. (1835)
Barrow, Sir Timothy Earle, KCMG, LVO, MBE
Barry, Sir (Lawrence) Edward (Anthony Tress), Bt. (1899)
Barter, Sir Peter Leslie Charles, Kt., OBE
Bartlett, Sir Andrew Alan, Bt. (1913)
Barttelot, *Col.* Sir Brian Walter de Stopham, Bt. (1875), OBE
Bate, *Prof.* Sir Andrew Jonathan, Kt., CBE
Bates, Sir James Geoffrey, Bt. (1880)
Bates, Sir Richard Dawson Hoult, Bt. (1937)
Bateson, *Prof.* Sir Patrick, Kt.
Bather, Sir John Knollys, KCVO
Batho, Sir Peter Ghislain, Bt. (1928)
Bathurst, *Admiral of the Fleet* Sir (David) Benjamin, GCB
Battersby, *Prof.* Sir Alan Rushton, Kt., FRS
Battishill, Sir Anthony Michael William, GCB
Baulcombe, *Prof.* Sir David Charles, Kt., FRS
Baxendell, Sir Peter Brian, Kt., CBE, FRENG
Bayley, Sir Hugh Nigel Edward, Kt.
Bayne, Sir Nicholas Peter, KCMG
Baynes, Sir Christopher Rory, Bt. (1801)
Bazalgette, Sir Peter Lytton, Kt.
Bazley, Sir Thomas John Sebastian, Bt. (1869)
Beach, *Gen.* Sir (William Gerald) Hugh, GBE, KCB, MC
Beache, *Hon.* Sir Vincent Ian, KCMG
Beale, *Lt.-Gen.* Sir Peter John, KBE, FRCP
Beamish, Sir Adrian John, KCMG
Bean, *Dr* Sir Charles Richard, Kt.

Bean, *Rt. Hon.* Sir David Michael, Kt.
Bear, Sir Michael David, Kt.
Beatson, *Rt. Hon.* Sir Jack, Kt.
Beavis, *Air Chief Marshal* Sir Michael Gordon, KCB, CBE, AFC
Beck, Sir Edgar Philip, Kt.
Beckett, Sir Richard Gervase, Bt. (1921), QC
Beckwith, Sir John Lionel, Kt., CBE
Beddington, *Prof.* Sir John Rex, Kt., CMG
Beecham, Sir Robert Adrian, Bt. (1914)
Beetham, *Marshal of the Royal Air Force* Sir Michael James, GCB, CBE, DFC, AFC
Beevor, Sir Thomas Agnew, Bt. (1784)
Beldam, *Rt. Hon.* Sir (Alexander) Roy (Asplan), Kt.
Belgrave, *HE* Sir Elliott Fitzroy, GCMG
Bell, Sir David Charles Maurice, Kt.
Bell, Sir David Robert, KCB
Bell, *Prof.* Sir John Irving, GBE
Bell, Sir John Lowthian, Bt. (1885)
Bell, *Prof.* Sir Peter Robert Frank, Kt.
Bell, *Hon.* Sir Rodger, Kt.
Bellamy, *Hon.* Sir Christopher William, Kt.
Bellingham, Sir Anthony Edward Norman, Bt. (1796)
Bender, Sir Brian Geoffrey, KCB
Benn, Sir (James) Jonathan, Bt. (1914)
Bennett, *Air Vice-Marshal* Sir Erik Peter, KBE, CB
Bennett, *Hon.* Sir Hugh Peter Derwyn, Kt.
Bennett, *Gen.* Sir Phillip Harvey, KBE, DSO
Bennett, Sir Ronald Wilfrid Murdoch, Bt. (1929)
Benson, Sir Christopher John, Kt.
Beresford, Sir (Alexander) Paul, Kt.
Beresford-Peirse, Sir Henry Njers de la Poer, Bt. (1814)
Berghuser, *Hon.* Sir Eric, Kt., MBE
Beringer, *Prof.* Sir John Evelyn, Kt., CBE
Berman, Sir Franklin Delow, KCMG
Berners-Lee, Sir Timothy John, OM, KBE, FRS
Bernard, Sir Dallas Edmund, Bt. (1954)
Berney, Sir Julian Reedham Stuart, Bt. (1620)
Bernstein, Sir Howard, Kt.
Berragan, *Lt.-Gen.* Sir Gerald William, KBE, CB
Berridge, *Prof.* Sir Michael John, Kt., FRS
Berriman, Sir David, Kt.
Berry, *Prof.* Sir Colin Leonard, Kt., FRCPATH
Berry, *Prof.* Sir Michael Victor, Kt., FRS
Berthoud, Sir Martin Seymour, KCVO, CMG
Berwick, *Prof.* Sir George Thomas, Kt., CBE
Best-Shaw, Sir Thomas Joshua, Bt. (1665)
Bethel, Sir Baltron Benjamin, KCMG
Bethlehem, Sir Daniel, KCMG
Bett, Sir Michael, Kt., CBE
Bettison, Sir Norman George, Kt., QPM

Bevan, Sir James David, KCMG

Bevan, Sir Martyn Evan Evans, Bt. (1958)

Bevan, Sir Nicolas, Kt., CB

Bevan, Sir Timothy Hugh, Kt.

Beverley, *Lt.-Gen.* Sir Henry York La Roche, KCB, OBE, RM

Bhadeshia, *Prof.* Sir Harshad Kumar Dharamshi, Kt., FRS

Bibby, Sir Michael James, Bt. (1959)

Bickersteth, *Rt. Revd* John Monier, KCVO

Biddulph, Sir Ian D'Olier, Bt. (1664)

Biggam, Sir Robin Adair, Kt.

Bilas, Sir Angmai Simon, Kt., OBE

Bill, *Lt.-Gen.* Sir David Robert, KCB

Billière, *Gen.* Sir Peter Edgar de la Cour de la, KCB, KBE, DSO, MC

Bindman, Sir Geoffrey Lionel, Kt.

Bingham, *Hon.* Sir Eardley Max, Kt.

Birch, Sir John Allan, KCVO, CMG

Birch, Sir Roger, Kt., CBE, QPM

Bird, *Prof.* Sir Adrian Peter, Kt., CBE, FRS, FRSE

Bird, Sir Richard Geoffrey Chapman, Bt. (1922)

Birkett, Sir Peter, Kt.

Birkin, Sir John Christian William, Bt. (1905)

Birkin, Sir (John) Derek, Kt., TD

Birkmyre, Sir James, Bt. (1921)

Birrell, Sir James Drake, Kt.

Birss, *Hon.* Sir Colin Ian, Kt.

Birt, Sir Michael, Kt.

Birtwistle, Sir Harrison, Kt., CH

Bischoff, Sir Winfried Franz Wilhelm, Kt.

Black, *Adm.* Sir (John) Jeremy, GBE, KCB, DSO

Black, Sir Robert David, Bt. (1922)

Blackburn, *Vice-Adm.* Sir David Anthony James, KCVO, CB

Blackburne, *Hon.* Sir William Anthony, Kt.

Blackett, Sir Hugh Francis, Bt. (1673)

Blackham, *Vice-Adm.* Sir Jeremy Joe, KCB

Blackman, Sir Frank Milton, KCVO, OBE

†Blair, Sir Patrick David Hunter, Bt. (1786)

Blair, *Hon.* Sir William James Lynton, Kt.

Blake, Sir Anthony Teilo Bruce, Bt. (I. 1622)

Blake, Sir Francis Michael, Bt. (1907)

Blake, *Hon.* Sir Nicholas John Gorrod, Kt.

Blake, Sir Peter Thomas, Kt., CBE

Blake, Sir Quentin Saxby, Kt., CBE

Blakemore, *Prof.* Sir Colin Brian, Kt., FRS

Blaker, Sir John, Bt. (1919)

Blakiston, Sir Ferguson Arthur James, Bt. (1763)

Blanch, Sir Malcolm, KCVO

Bland, Sir (Francis) Christopher (Buchan), Kt.

Bland, *Lt.-Col.* Sir Simon Claud Michael, KCVO

Blank, Sir Maurice Victor, Kt.

Blatherwick, Sir David Elliott Spiby, KCMG, OBE

Blelloch, Sir John Nial Henderson, KCB

Blennerhassett, Sir (Marmaduke) Adrian Francis William, Bt. (1809)

Blewitt, *Maj.* Sir Shane Gabriel Basil, GCVO

Blofeld, *Hon.* Sir John Christopher Calthorpe, Kt.

Blois, Sir Charles Nicholas Gervase, Bt. (1686)

Blom-Cooper, Sir Louis Jacques, Kt., QC

Blomefield, Sir Thomas Charles Peregrine, Bt. (1807)

Bundell, *Prof.* Sir Richard William, Kt., CBE, FBA

Bloom, *Prof.* Sir Stephen Robert, Kt.

Bloomfield, Sir Kenneth Percy, KCB

Blundell, *Prof.* Sir Richard William, Kt., CBE, FBA

Blundell, Sir Thomas Leon, Kt., FRS

†Blunden, Sir Hubert Chisholm, Bt. (I. 1766)

Blunt, Sir David Richard Reginald Harvey, Bt. (1720)

Blyth, Sir Charles (Chay), Kt., CBE, BEM

Boardman, *Prof.* Sir John, Kt., FSA, FBA

Bodey, *Hon.* Sir David Roderick Lessiter, Kt.

Bodmer, Sir Walter Fred, Kt., PHD, FRS

Body, Sir Richard Bernard Frank Stewart, Kt.

Bogle, Sir Nigel, Kt.

Bogan, Sir Nagora, KBE

Boileau, Sir Nicolas Edmond George, Bt. (1838)

Boles, Sir Richard Fortescue, Bt. (1922)

Bona, Sir Kina, KBE

Bonallack, Sir Michael Francis, Kt., OBE

Bond, Sir John Reginald Hartnell, Kt.

Bond, *Prof.* Sir Michael Richard, Kt., FRCPSYCH, FRCPGLAS, FRCSE

Bone, *Prof.* Sir (James) Drummond, Kt., FRSE

Bone, Sir Roger Bridgland, KCMG

Bonfield, Sir Peter Leahy, Kt., CBE, FRENG

Bonham, Sir George Martin Antony, Bt. (1852)

Bonington, Sir Christian John Storey, Kt., CVO, CBE

Bonsor, Sir Nicholas Cosmo, Bt. (1925)

Boord, Sir Nicolas John Charles, Bt. (1896)

Boorman, *Lt.-Gen.* Sir Derek, KCB

Booth, Sir Clive, Kt.

Booth, Sir Douglas Allen, Bt. (1916)

Boothby, Sir Brooke Charles, Bt. (1660)

Bore, Sir Albert, Kt.

Boreel, Sir Stephan Gerard, Bt. (1645)

Borthwick, Sir Anthony Thomas, Bt. (1908)

Borysiewicz, *Prof.* Sir Leszek Krzysztof, Kt.

Bosher, Sir Robin, Kt.

Bossom, *Hon.* Sir Clive, Bt. (1953)

Bostock, Sir David John, KCMG

Boswell, *Lt.-Gen.* Sir Alexander Crawford Simpson, KCB, CBE

Botham, Sir Ian Terence, Kt., OBE

Bottomley, Sir Peter James, Kt.

Bottoms, *Prof.* Sir Anthony Edward, Kt.

Boughey, Sir John George Fletcher, Bt. (1798)

Boulton, Sir Clifford John, GCB

†Boulton, Sir John Gibson, Bt. (1944)

Bouraga, Sir Phillip, KBE

Bourn, Sir John Bryant, KCB

Bowater, Sir Euan David Vansittart, Bt. (1939)

†Bowater, Sir Michael Patrick, Bt. (1914)

Bowden, Sir Andrew, Kt., MBE

Bowden, Sir Nicholas Richard, Bt. (1915)

Bowen, Sir Barry Manfield, KCMG

Bowen, Sir Geoffrey Fraser, Kt.

Bowen, Sir George Edward Michael, Bt. (1921)

Bowes Lyon, Sir Simon Alexander, KCVO

Bowlby, Sir Richard Peregrine Longstaff, Bt. (1923)

Bowman, Sir Edwin Geoffrey, KCB

Bowman, Sir Jeffery Haverstock, Kt.

Bowness, Sir Alan, Kt., CBE

Bowyer-Smyth, Sir Thomas Weyland, Bt. (1661)

Boyce, Sir Graham Hugh, KCMG

Boyce, Sir Robert Charles Leslie, Bt. (1952)

Boyd, Sir Alexander Walter, Bt. (1916)

Boyd, Sir John Dixon Iklé, KCMG

Boyd, Sir Michael, Kt.

Boyd, *Prof.* Sir Robert David Hugh, Kt.

Boyd-Carpenter, Sir (Marsom) Henry, KCVO

Boyd-Carpenter, *Lt.-Gen. Hon.* Sir Thomas Patrick John, KBE

Boyle, *Prof.* Sir Roger Michael, Kt., CBE

Boyle, Sir Simon Hugh Patrick, KCVO

Boyle, Sir Stephen Gurney, Bt. (1904)

Bracewell-Smith, Sir Charles, Bt. (1947)

Bradbeer, Sir John Derek Richardson, Kt., OBE, TD

Bradford, Sir Edward Alexander Slade, Bt. (1902)

Bradshaw, *Lt-Gen.* Sir Adrian, KCB, OBE

Brady, *Prof.* Sir John Michael, Kt., FRS

Brailsford, Sir David John, Kt., CBE

Braithwaite, Sir Rodric Quentin, GCMG

Bramley, *Prof.* Sir Paul Anthony, Kt.

Branagh, Sir Kenneth Charles, Kt.

Branson, Sir Richard Charles Nicholas, Kt.

Braithwaite, *Rt. Hon.* Sir Nicholas Alexander, Kt., OBE

Bratza, *Hon.* Sir Nicolas Dušan, Kt.

Breckenridge, *Prof.* Sir Alasdair Muir, Kt., CBE

Brennan, *Hon.* Sir (Francis) Gerard, KBE

Brenton, Sir Anthony Russell, KCMG

Brewer, Sir David William, Kt., CMG

Brierley, Sir Ronald Alfred, Kt.

Briggs, *Rt. Hon.* Sir Michael Townley Featherstone, Kt.

Brighouse, *Prof.* Sir Timothy Robert Peter, Kt.

Bright, Sir Graham Frank James, Kt.

Bright, Sir Keith, Kt.

Brigstocke, *Adm.* Sir John Richard, KCB

Brinckman, Sir Theodore George Roderick, Bt. (1831)

†Brisco, Sir Campbell Howard, Bt. (1782)

Briscoe, Sir Brian Anthony, Kt.

Briscoe, Sir John Geoffrey James, Bt. (1910)

Brittan, Sir Samuel, Kt.

Britton, Sir Paul John James, Kt., CB

†Broadbent, Sir Andrew George, Bt. (1893)

Broadbent, Sir Richard John, KCB

Brocklebank, Sir Aubrey Thomas, Bt. (1885)

Brodie, Sir Benjamin David Ross, Bt. (1834)

Bromhead, Sir John Desmond Gonville, Bt. (1806)

Bromley, Sir Michael Roger, KBE

Bromley, Sir Rupert Charles, Bt. (1757)

Bromley-Davenport, Sir William Arthur, KCVO

Brook, *Prof.* Sir Richard John, Kt. OBE

Brooke, Sir Alistair Weston, Bt. (1919)

Brooke, Sir Francis George Windham, Bt. (1903)

Brooke, *Rt. Hon.* Sir Henry, Kt.

Brooke, Sir Richard Christopher, Bt. (1662)

Brooke, Sir Rodney George, Kt., CBE

Brooking, Sir Trevor David, Kt., CBE

Brooksbank, Sir (Edward) Nicholas, Bt. (1919)

Broomfield, Sir Nigel Hugh Robert Allen, KCMG

†Broughton, Sir David Delves, Bt. (1661)

Broughton, Sir Martin Faulkner, Kt.

Broun, Sir Wayne Hercules, Bt. (S. 1686)

Brown, Sir (Austen) Patrick, KCB

Brown, *Adm.* Sir Brian Thomas, KCB, CBE

Brown, Sir David, Kt.

Brown, *Hon.* Sir Douglas Dunlop, Kt.

Brown, Sir Ewan, Kt., CBE

Brown, Sir George Francis Richmond, Bt. (1863)

Brown, Sir Mervyn, KCMG, OBE

Brown, Sir Peter Randolph, Kt.

Brown, *Rt. Hon.* Sir Stephen, GBE

Brown, Sir Stephen David Reid, KCVO

Brownrigg, Sir Nicholas (Gawen), Bt. (1816)

Browse, *Prof.* Sir Norman Leslie, Kt., MD, FRCS

Bruce, Sir (Francis) Michael Ian, Bt. (S. 1628)

Bruce-Clifton, Sir Hervey Hamish Peter, Bt. (1804)

Bruce-Gardner, Sir Robert Henry, Bt. (1945)

Brunner, Sir Hugo Laurence Joseph, KCVO

Brunner, Sir John Henry Kilian, Bt. (1895)

Brunton, Sir Gordon Charles, Kt.

†Brunton, Sir James Lauder, Bt. (1908)

Bryant, *Air Chief Marshal* Sir Simon, KCB, CBE, ADC

Bubb, Sir Stephen John Limrick, Kt.

Buchan-Hepburn, Sir John Alastair Trant Kidd, Bt. (1815)

Buchanan, Sir Andrew George, Bt. (1878), KCVO

Buchanan-Jardine, Sir John Christopher Rupert, Bt. (1885)

Buckland, Sir Ross, Kt.

Buckley, *Dr* Sir George William, Kt.

Buckley, Sir Michael Sidney, Kt.

Buckley, *Lt.-Cdr.* Sir (Peter) Richard, KCVO

Buckley, *Hon.* Sir Roger John, Kt.

Bucknall, *Lt-Gen.* Sir James Jeffrey Corfield, KCB, CBE

†Buckworth-Herne-Soame, Sir Richard John, Bt. (1697)

Budd, Sir Alan Peter, GBE

Budd, Sir Colin Richard, KCMG

Bull, Sir George Jeffrey, Kt.

Bull, Sir Simeon George, Bt. (1922)

Bullock, Sir Stephen Michael, Kt.

Bultin, Sir Bato, Kt., MBE

Bunbury, Sir Michael William, Bt. (1681), KCVO

Bunyard, Sir Robert Sidney, Kt., CBE, QPM

Burbidge, Sir Peter Dudley, Bt. (1916)

Burden, Sir Anthony Thomas, Kt., QPM

Burdett, Sir Savile Aylmer, Bt. (1665)

Burgen, Sir Arnold Stanley Vincent, Kt., FRS

Burgess, Sir (Joseph) Stuart, Kt., CBE, PHD, FRSC

Burgess, *Prof.* Sir Robert George, Kt.

Burke, Sir James Stanley Gilbert, Bt. (I. 1797)

Burke, Sir (Thomas) Kerry, Kt.

Burn, *Prof.* Sir John, Kt.

Burns, *Rt. Hon.* Sir Simon Hugh McGuigan, Kt.

Burnell-Nugent, *Vice-Adm.* Sir James Michael, KCB, CBE, ADC

Burnett, Sir Charles David, Bt., (1913)

Burnett, *Rt. Hon.* Sir Ian Duncan, Kt.

Burnett, Sir Walter John, Kt.

Burney, Sir Nigel Dennistoun, Bt. (1921)

Burns, *Dr* Sir Henry, Kt.

Burns, Sir (Robert) Andrew, KCMG

Burnton, *Rt. Hon.* Sir Stanley Jeffrey, Kt.

Burrell, Sir Charles Raymond, Bt. (1774)

Burridge, *Air Chief Marshal* Sir Brian Kevin, KCB, CBE, ADC

Burt, Sir Peter Alexander, Kt.

Burton, *Lt.-Gen.* Sir Edmund Fortescue Gerard, KBE

Burton, Sir Graham Stuart, KCMG

Burton, *Hon.* Sir Michael John, Kt.

Burton, Sir Michael St Edmund, KCVO, CMG

Butler, *Hon.* Sir Arlington Griffith, KCMG

Butler, *Dr* Sir David Edgeworth, Kt., CBE

Butler, Sir Percy James, Kt., CBE

Butler, Sir Reginald Richard Michael, Bt. (1922)

Butler, Sir Richard Pierce, Bt. (I. 1628)

Butterfield, *Hon.* Sir Alexander Neil Logie, Kt.

Butterfill, Sir John Valentine, Kt.

Buxton, Sir Crispin Charles Gerard, Bt. (1840)

Buxton, *Rt. Hon.* Sir Richard Joseph, Kt.

Buzzard, Sir Anthony Farquhar, Bt. (1929)

Byatt, Sir Ian Charles Rayner, Kt.

Byford, Sir Lawrence, Kt., CBE, QPM

Byron, *Rt. Hon.* Sir Charles Michael Dennis, Kt.

Cable, *Rt. Hon.* Sir (John) Vincent, Kt., PHD

†Cable-Alexander, Sir Patrick Desmond William, Bt. (1809)

Cadbury, Sir (Nicholas) Dominic, Kt.

Cadogan, *Prof.* Sir John Ivan George, Kt., CBE, FRS, FRSE

Cahn, Sir Albert Jonas, Bt. (1934)

Cahn, Sir Andrew Thomas, KCMG

Caine, Sir Michael (Maurice Micklewhite), Kt., CBE

Caines, Sir John, KCB

Cairns, *Very Revd* John Ballantyne, KCVO

Caldwell, Sir Edward George, KCB

Callaghan, Sir William Henry, Kt.

Callan, Sir Ivan Roy, KCVO, CMG

Callman, *His Hon.* Sir Clive Vernon, Kt.

Calman, *Prof.* Sir Kenneth Charles, KCB, MD, FRCP, FRCS, FRSE

Calne, *Prof.* Sir Roy Yorke, Kt., FRS

Calvert-Smith, Sir David, Kt., QC

Cameron, Sir Hugh Roy Graham, Kt., QPM

Campbell, *Prof.* Sir Colin Murray, Kt.

Campbell, Sir Ian Tofts, Kt., CBE, VRD

Campbell, Sir Ilay Mark, Bt. (1808)

Campbell, Sir James Alexander Moffat Bain, Bt. (S. 1668)

Campbell, Sir Lachlan Philip Kemeys, Bt. (1815)

Campbell, *Dr.* Sir Philip Henry Montgomery, Kt.

Campbell, Sir Roderick Duncan Hamilton, Bt. (1831)

Campbell, Sir Robin Auchinbreck, Bt. (S. 1628)

Campbell, *Dr* Sir Simon Fraser, Kt., CBE

Campbell, *Rt. Hon.* Sir William Anthony, Kt.

Campbell-Orde, Sir John Alexander, Bt. (1790)

Cannadine, *Prof.* Sir David Nicholas, Kt.

Capewell, *Lt-Gen.* Sir David Andrew, KCB, OBE, RM

†Carden, Sir Christopher Robert, Bt. (1887)

†Carden, Sir John Craven, Bt. (I. 1787)

Carew, Sir Rivers Verain, Bt. (1661)

Carey, Sir de Vic Graham, Kt.

Carleton-Smith, *Maj.-Gen.* Sir Michael Edward, Kt., CBE

Carlisle, Sir James Beethoven, GCMG

Carlisle, Sir John Michael, Kt.

Carlisle, Sir Kenneth Melville, Kt.

Carnegie, Sir Roderick Howard, Kt.

Carnwath, *Rt. Hon.* Sir Robert John Anderson, Kt., CVO (Lord Carnwath of Notting Hill)

Carr, *Very Revd Dr* Arthur Wesley, KCVO

Carr, Sir Peter Derek, Kt., CBE

Carr, Sir Roger Martyn, Kt.

Carrick, *Hon.* Sir John Leslie, KCMG

Carrick, Sir Roger John, KCMG, LVO

Carruthers, Sir Ian James, Kt., OBE

Carsberg, *Prof.* Sir Bryan Victor, Kt.

Carter, Sir Andrew Nicholas, Kt., OBE

Carter, Sir David Anthony, Kt.

Carter, *Prof.* Sir David Craig, Kt., FRCSE, FRCSGLAS, FRCPE

Carter, Sir John Alexander, Kt.

Carter, Sir John Gordon Thomas, Kt.

Carter, *Lt-Gen.* Sir Nicholas Patrick, KCB, CBE, DSO

Cartledge, Sir Bryan George, KCMG

Caruna, *Hon.* Sir Peter Richard, KCMG, QC

†Cary, Sir Nicholas Robert Hugh, Bt. (1955)

Cash, Sir Andrew John, Kt., OBE

Cash, Sir William Nigel Paul, Kt.

Cass, Sir Geoffrey Arthur, Kt.

Cassel, Sir Timothy Felix Harold, Bt. (1920)

Cassels, Sir John Seton, Kt., CB

Cassels, *Adm.* Sir Simon Alastair Cassillis, KCB, CBE

Cassidi, *Adm.* Sir (Arthur) Desmond, GCB

Castell, Sir William Martin, Kt.

Catto, *Prof.* Sir Graeme Robertson Dawson, Kt.

Cave, Sir John Charles, Bt. (1896)

Cave-Browne-Cave, Sir John Robert Charles, Bt. (1641)

Cayley, Sir Digby William David, Bt. (1661)

Cazalet, *Hon.* Sir Edward Stephen, Kt.

Cazalet, Sir Peter Grenville, Kt.

Cecil, *Rear-Adm.* Sir (Oswald) Nigel Amherst, KBE, CB

Chadwick, *Rt. Hon.* Sir John Murray, Kt.

Chadwick, Sir Joshua Kenneth Burton, Bt. (1935)

Chadwyck-Healey, Sir Charles Edward, Bt. (1919)

Chakrabarti, Sir Sumantra, KCB

Chalmers, Sir Iain Geoffrey, Kt.

Chalmers, Sir Neil Robert, Kt.

Chalstrey, Sir (Leonard) John, Kt., MD, FRCS

Chan, *Rt. Hon.* Sir Julius, GCMG, KBE

Chan, Sir Thomas Kok, Kt., OBE

Chance, Sir (George) Jeremy ffolliott, Bt. (1900)

Chandler, Sir Colin Michael, Kt.

Chantler, *Prof.* Sir Cyril, Kt., MD, FRCP

Chaplin, Sir Malcolm Hilbery, Kt., CBE

Chapman, Sir David Robert Macgowan, Bt. (1958)

Chapman, Sir Frank, Kt.

Chapman, Sir George Alan, Kt.

Chapple, *Field Marshal* Sir John Lyon, GCB, CBE

Charles, *Hon.* Sir Arthur William Hessin, Kt.

Charlton, Sir Robert (Bobby), Kt., CBE

Charnley, Sir (William) John, Kt., CB, FRENG

Chartres, *Rt. Revd and Rt. Hon.* Richard John Carew, KCVO

†Chaytor, Sir Bruce Gordon, Bt. (1831)

Checketts, *Sqn. Ldr.* Sir David John, KCVO

Checkland, Sir Michael, Kt.

Cheshire, Sir Ian Michael, Kt.

Cheshire, *Air Chief Marshal* Sir John Anthony, KBE, CB

Chessells, Sir Arthur David (Tim), Kt.

†Chetwynd, Sir Peter James Talbot, Bt. (1795)

Cheyne, Sir Patrick John Lister, Bt. (1908)

Chichester, Sir James Henry Edward, Bt. (1641)

Chichester-Clark, Sir Robin, Kt.

Chilcot, *Rt. Hon.* Sir John Anthony, GCB

Child, Sir (Coles John) Jeremy, Bt. (1919)

Chilwell, *Hon.* Sir Muir Fitzherbert, Kt.

Chinn, Sir Trevor Edwin, Kt., CVO

†Chinubhai, Sir Prashat, Bt. (1913)

Chipperfield, *Prof.* Sir David Alan, Kt., CBE

Chipperfield, Sir Geoffrey Howes, KCB

Chisholm, Sir John Alexander Raymond, Kt., FRENG

†Chitty, Sir Andrew Edward Willes, Bt. (1924)

Cholmeley, Sir Hugh John Frederick Sebastian, Bt. (1806)

Chow, Sir Chung Kong, Kt.

Chow, Sir Henry Francis, Kt., OBE

Christopher, Sir Duncan Robin Carmichael, KBE, CMG

Chung, Sir Sze-yuen, GBE, FRENG

Clark, *Prof.* Sir Christopher Munro, Kt.

Clark, Sir Francis Drake, Bt. (1886)

Clark, Sir John Arnold, Kt.

Clark, Sir Jonathan George, Bt. (1917)

Clark, Sir Terence Joseph, KBE, CMG, CVO

Clark, Sir Timothy Charles, KBE

Clarke, Sir (Charles Mansfield) Tobias, Bt. (1831)

Clarke, *Rt. Hon.* Sir Christopher Simon Courtenay Stephenson, Kt.

Clarke, *Hon.* Sir David Clive, Kt.

Clarke, Sir Jonathan Dennis, Kt.

Clarke, Sir Paul Robert Virgo, KCVO

Clarke, Sir Robert Cyril, Kt.

Clarke, Sir Rupert Grant Alexander, Bt. (1882)

Clay, Sir Edward, KCMG

Clay, Sir Richard Henry, Bt. (1841)

Clayton, Sir David Robert, Bt. (1732)

Cleaver, Sir Anthony Brian, Kt.

Clementi, Sir David Cecil, Kt.

Clerk, Sir Robert Maxwell, Bt. (S. 1679), OBE

Clerke, Sir Francis Ludlow Longueville, Bt. (1660)

Clifford, Sir Roger Joseph, Bt. (1887)

Clifford, Sir Timothy Peter Plint, Kt.

Coates, Sir Anthony Robert Milnes, Bt. (1911)

Coates, Sir David Frederick Charlton, Bt. (1921)

Coats, Sir Alastair Francis Stuart, Bt. (1905)

Cobb, *Hon.* Sir Stephen William Scott, Kt.

Cochrane, Sir (Henry) Marc (Sursock), Bt. (1903)

†Cockburn, Sir Charles Christopher, Bt. (S. 1671)

Cockburn-Campbell, Sir Alexander Thomas, Bt. (1821)

Cockell, Sir Merrick, Kt.

Cockshaw, Sir Alan, Kt., FRENG

Codrington, Sir Christopher George Wayne, Bt. (1876)

Codrington, Sir Giles Peter, Bt. (1721)

Codron, Sir Michael Victor, Kt., CBE

Coghill, Sir Patrick Kendal Farley, Bt. (1778)

Coghlin, *Rt. Hon.* Sir Patrick, Kt.

Cohen, Sir Ivor Harold, Kt., CBE, TD

Cohen, *Prof.* Sir Philip, Kt., PHD, FRS

Cohen, Sir Ronald, Kt.

Cole, Sir (Robert) William, Kt.

Coleman, Sir Robert John, KCMG

Coleridge, *Hon.* Sir Paul James Duke, Kt.

Coles, Sir (Arthur) John, GCMG

Colfox, Sir Philip John, Bt. (1939)

Collas, Sir Richard John, Kt.

Collett, Sir Ian Seymour, Bt. (1934)

Collier, Sir Paul, Kt., CBE

Collins, Sir Alan Stanley, KCVO, CMG

Collins, *Hon.* Sir Andrew David, Kt.

Collins, Sir Bryan Thomas Alfred, Kt., OBE, QFSM

Collins, Sir John Alexander, Kt

Collins, Sir Kenneth Darlington, Kt.

Collins, *Dr* Sir Kevan Arthur, Kt.

Collins, *Prof.* Sir Rory Edwards, Kt.

Collyear, Sir John Gowen, Kt.

Colman, *Hon.* Sir Anthony David, Kt.

Colman, Sir Michael Jeremiah, Bt. (1907)

Colman, Sir Timothy, KG

Colquhoun of Luss, Sir Malcolm Rory, Bt. (1786)

Colt, Sir Edward William Dutton, (1694)

Colthurst, Sir Charles St John, Bt. (I. 1744)

Conant, Sir John Ernest Michael, Bt. (1954)

Conner, *Rt. Revd* David John, KCVO

Connery, Sir Sean, Kt.

Connor, Sir William Joseph, Kt.

Conran, Sir Terence Orby, Kt.

Cons, *Hon.* Sir Derek, Kt.

Constantinou, Sir Kosta George, Kt., OBE

Constantinou, Sir Theophilus George, Kt., CBE

Conway, *Prof.* Sir Gordon Richard, KCMG, FRS

Cook, Sir Christopher Wymondham Rayner Herbert, Bt. (1886)

Cook, *Prof.* Sir Peter Frederic Chester, Kt.

Cooke, *Col.* Sir David William Perceval, Bt. (1661)

Cooke, *Hon.* Sir Jeremy Lionel, Kt.

Cooke, *Prof.* Sir Ronald Urwick, Kt.

Cooksey, Sir David James Scott, GBE

Cooper, *Prof.* Sir Cary Lynn, Kt., CBE

Cooper, *Gen.* Sir George Leslie Conroy, GCB, MC

Cooper, Sir Richard Adrian, Bt. (1905)

Cooper, Sir Robert Francis, KCMG, MVO

Cooper, *Maj.-Gen.* Sir Simon Christie, GCVO

Cooper, Sir William Daniel Charles, Bt. (1863)

Coote, Sir Christopher John, Bt. (I. 1621), *Premier Baronet of Ireland*

Copisarow, Sir Alcon Charles, Kt.

Corbett, *Maj.-Gen.* Sir Robert John Swan, KCVO, CB

Cordy-Simpson, *Lt.-Gen.* Sir Roderick Alexander, KBE, CB

Corfield, Sir Kenneth George, Kt., FRENG

Corness, Sir Colin Ross, Kt.

Corry, Sir James Michael, Bt. (1885)

Cortazzi, Sir (Henry Arthur) Hugh, GCMG

Cory, Sir (Clinton Charles) Donald, Bt. (1919)

Cory-Wright, Sir Richard Michael, Bt. (1903)

Cossons, Sir Neil, Kt., OBE

Cotter, Sir Patrick Laurence Delaval, Bt. (I. 1763)

Cotterell, Sir John Henry Geers, Bt. (1805)

†Cotts, Sir Richard Crichton Mitchell, Bt. (1921)

Coulson, *Hon.* Sir Peter David William, Kt.

Couper, Sir James George, Bt. (1841)

Courtenay, Sir Thomas Daniel, Kt.

Cousins, *Air Chief Marshal* Sir David, KCB, AFC

Coville, *Air Marshal* Sir Christopher Charles Cotton, KCB

Cowan, *Gen.* Sir Samuel, KCB, CBE

Coward, *Lt-Gen.* Sir Gary Robert, KBE, CB, OBE

Coward, *Vice-Adm.* Sir John Francis, KCB, DSO

Cowper-Coles, Sir Sherard Louis, KCMG, LVO

Cox, Sir Alan George, Kt., CBE

Cox, *Prof.* Sir David Roxbee, Kt.

Cox, Sir George Edwin, Kt.

Craft, *Prof.* Sir Alan William, Kt.

Cragnolini, Sir Luciano, Kt.

Craig, Sir (Albert) James (Macqueen), GCMG

Craig-Cooper, Sir (Frederick Howard) Michael, Kt., CBE, TD

Crane, *Prof.* Sir Peter Robert, Kt.

Cranston, *Hon.* Sir Ross Frederick, Kt.

Craufurd, Sir Robert James, Bt. (1781)

Craven, Sir John Anthony, Kt.

Craven, Sir Philip Lee, Kt., MBE

Crawford, *Prof.* Sir Frederick William, Kt., FRENG

Crawford, Sir Robert William Kenneth, Kt. CBE

Crawley-Boevey, Sir Thomas Michael Blake, Bt. (1784)

Cresswell, *Hon.* Sir Peter John, Kt.

Crew, Sir (Michael) Edward, Kt., QPM

Crewe, *Prof.* Sir Ivor Martin, Kt.

Crisp, Sir John Charles, Bt. (1913)

Critchett, Sir Charles George Montague, Bt. (1908)

Crittin, *Hon.* Sir John Luke, KBE

Croft, Sir Owen Glendower, Bt. (1671)

Croft, Sir Thomas Stephen Hutton, Bt. (1818)

†Crofton, Sir Hugh Denis, Bt. (1801)

†Crofton, Sir Julian Malby, Bt. (1838)

Crombie, Sir Alexander, Kt.

Crompton, Sir Dan, Kt., CBE, QPM

Cropper, Sir James Anthony, KCVO

Crossley, Sir Sloan Nicholas, Bt. (1909)

Crowe, Sir Brian Lee, KCMG

Cruickshank, Sir Donald Gordon, Kt.

Cruthers, Sir James Winter, Kt.

Cubie, *Dr* Sir Andrew, Kt., CBE

Cubitt, Sir Hugh Guy, Kt., CBE

Cubitt, *Maj.-Gen.* Sir William George, KCVO, CBE

Cullen, Sir (Edward) John, Kt., FRENG

Culme-Seymour, Sir Michael Patrick, Bt. (1809)

Culpin, Sir Robert Paul, Kt.

Cummins, Sir Michael John Austin, Kt.

Cunliffe, *Prof.* Sir Barrington, Kt., CBE

Cunliffe, Sir David Ellis, Bt. (1759)

Cunliffe, Sir Jonathan Stephen, Kt., CB

Cunliffe-Owen, Sir Hugo Dudley, Bt. (1920)

Cunningham, *Lt.-Gen.* Sir Hugh Patrick, KBE

Cunningham, *Prof.* Sir John, KCVO

Cunningham, Sir Roger Keith, Kt., CBE

Cunningham, Sir Thomas Anthony, Kt.

Cunynghame, Sir Andrew David Francis, Bt. (S. 1702)

†Currie, Sir Bradley Mark Higgins, Bt. (1847)

Curtain, Sir Michael, KBE

Curtis, Sir Barry John, Kt.

Curtis, *Hon.* Sir Richard Herbert, Kt.

Curtis, Sir Edward Philip, Bt. (1802)

Cuschieri, *Prof.* Sir Alfred, Kt.

Dain, Sir David John Michael, KCVO

Dales, Sir Richard Nigel, KCVO

Dalrymple-Hay, Sir Malcolm John Robert, Bt. (1798)

†Dalrymple-White, Sir Jan Hew, Bt. (1926)

Dalton, Sir David Nigel, Kt.

Dalton, *Vice-Adm.* Sir Geoffrey Thomas James Oliver, GCB

Dalton, Sir Richard John, KCMG

Dalton, *Air Chief Marshal* Sir Stephen Gary George, GCB

Dalyell, Sir Tam (Thomas), Bt. (NS 1685)

Dancer, Sir Eric, KCVO, CBE

Dangoor, Sir Naim Eliahou, Kt., CBE

Daniel, Sir John Sagar, Kt., DSC

Darell, Sir Guy Jeffrey Adair, Bt. (1795)

Darrington, Sir Michael John, Kt.

Darroch, Sir Nigel Kim, KCMG

Dasgupta, *Prof.* Sir Partha Sarathi, Kt.

Dashwood, *Prof.* Sir (Arthur) Alan, KCMG, CBE, QC

Dashwood, Sir Edward John Francis, Bt. (1707), *Premier Baronet of Great Britain*

Dashwood, Sir Frederick George Mahon, Bt. (1684)

Daunt, Sir Timothy Lewis Achilles, KCMG

David, *His Hon.* Sir Robin (Robert) Daniel George, Kt.

Davidson, Sir Martin Stuart, KCMG

Davies, *Prof.* Sir David Evan Naughton, Kt., CBE, FRS, FRENG

Davies, Sir David John, Kt.

Davies, Sir Frank John, Kt., CBE

Davies, *Prof.* Sir Graeme John, Kt., FRENG

Davies, Sir John Howard, Kt.

Davies, Sir John Michael, KCB

Davies, Sir Rhys Everson, Kt., QC

Davis, Sir Andrew Frank, Kt., CBE

Davis, Sir Crispin Henry Lamert, Kt.

Davis, Sir John Gilbert, Bt. (1946)

Davis, Sir Michael Lawrence, Kt.

Davis, *Rt. Hon.* Sir Nigel Anthony Lambert, Kt.

Davis, Sir Peter John, Kt.

Davis, *Hon.* Sir William Easthorpe, Kt., QC

Davis-Goff, Sir Robert (William), Bt. (1905)

†Davson, Sir George Trenchard Simon, Bt. (1927)

Dawanincura, Sir John Norbert, Kt., OBE

Dawbarn, Sir Simon Yelverton, KCVO, CMG

Dawson, *Hon.* Sir Daryl Michael, KBE, CB

Dawson, Sir Nicholas Antony Trevor, Bt. (1920)

Dawtry, Sir Alan (Graham), Kt., CBE, TD

Day, Sir Barry Stuart, Kt., OBE

Day, *Air Chief Marshal* Sir John Romney, KCB, OBE, ADC

Day, Sir (Judson) Graham, Kt.

Day, Sir Michael John, Kt., OBE

Day, Sir Simon James, Kt.

Day-Lewis, Sir Daniel Michael Blake, Kt.

Deane, *Hon.* Sir William Patrick, KBE

Dearlove, Sir Richard Billing, KCMG, OBE

†Debenham, Sir Thomas Adam, Bt. (1931)

de Deney, Sir Geoffrey Ivor, KCVO

Deegan, Sir Michael, Kt., CBE

Deeny, *Hon.* Sir Donnell Justin Patrick, Kt.

De Haan, Sir Roger Michael, Kt., CBE

De Halpert, *Rear-Adm.* Sir Jeremy Michael, KCVO, CB

de Hoghton, Sir (Richard) Bernard (Cuthbert), Bt. (1611)

De la Bère, Sir Cameron, Bt. (1953)

de la Rue, Sir Andrew George Ilay, Bt. (1898)

Dellow, Sir John Albert, Kt., CBE

Delves, *Lt.-Gen.* Sir Cedric Norman George, KBE

Denholm, Sir John Ferguson (Ian), Kt., CBE

Denison-Smith, *Lt.-Gen.* Sir Anthony Arthur, KBE

Denny, Sir Charles Alistair Maurice, Bt. (1913)

†Denny, Sir Piers Anthony de Waltham, Bt. (I. 1782)

Derbyshire, Sir Andrew George, Kt.

De Silva, *Rt. Hon.* Sir (George) Desmond Lorenz, Kt., QC

de Trafford, Sir John Humphrey, Bt. (1841)

Devane, Sir Ciaran Gearoid, Kt.

Deverell, *Lt-Gen.* Sir Christopher Michael, KCB, MBE

Deverell, *Gen.* Sir John Freegard, KCB, OBE

De Ville, Sir Harold Godfrey Oscar, Kt., CBE

Devine, *Prof.* Sir Thomas Martin, Kt., OBE, FRSE

Devitt, Sir James Hugh Thomas, Bt. (1916)

de Waal, Sir (Constant Henrik) Henry, KCB, QC

Dewey, Sir Anthony Hugh, Bt. (1917)

De Witt, Sir Ronald Wayne, Kt.

Diamond, *Prof.* Sir Ian David, Kt., FRSE

Dick-Lauder, Sir Piers Robert, Bt. (S. 1690)

Dilke, Revd Charles John Wentworth, Bt. (1862)

Dilnot, Sir Andrew William, Kt., CBE

Dillon, Sir Andrew Patrick, Kt., CBE

Dilley, Sir Philip Graham, Kt.

Dillwyn-Venables-Llewelyn, Sir John Michael, Bt. (1890)

Dingemans, *Hon.* Sir James Michael, Kt.

Dixon, Sir Jeremy, Kt.

Dixon, Sir Jonathan Mark, Bt. (1919)

Dixon, *Dr* Sir Michael, Kt.

Dixon, Sir Peter John Bellett, Kt.

Djanogly, Sir Harry Ari Simon, Kt., CBE

Dobson, *Vice-Adm.* Sir David Stuart, KBE

Dollery, Sir Colin Terence, Kt.

Don-Wauchope, Sir Roger (Hamilton), Bt. (S. 1667)

Donald, Sir Alan Ewen, KCMG

Donaldson, *Prof.* Sir Liam Joseph, Kt.

Donaldson, *Prof.* Sir Simon Kirwan, Kt.

Donne, Sir John Christopher, Kt.

Donnelly, Sir Joseph Brian, KBE, CMG

Dorman, Sir Philip Henry Keppel, Bt. (1923)

Douglas, *Prof.* Sir Neil James, Kt.

Douglas, *Hon.* Sir Roger Owen, Kt.

Dove, *Hon.* Sir Ian Williams, Kt., QC

Dowell, Sir Anthony James, Kt., CBE

Dowling, Sir Robert, Kt.

Downes, *Prof.* Sir Charles Peter, Kt., OBE, FRSE

Downey, Sir Gordon Stanley, KCB

Doyle, Sir Reginald Derek Henry, Kt., CBE

D'Oyly, Sir Hadley Gregory Bt. (1663)

Drewry, *Lt.-Gen.* Sir Christopher Francis, KCB, CBE

Drinkwater, Sir John Muir, Kt., QC

Dryden, Sir John Stephen Gyles, Bt. (1733 and 1795)

Duberly, Sir Archibald Hugh, KCVO, CBE

du Cann, *Rt. Hon.* Sir Edward Dillon Lott, KBE

Duckworth, Sir James Edward Dyce, Bt. (1909)

du Cros, Sir Julian Claude Arthur Mallet, Bt. (1916)

Dudley-Williams, Sir Alastair Edgcumbe James, Bt. (1964)

Duff, *Prof.* Sir Gordon William, Kt.

Duff-Gordon, Sir Andrew Cosmo Lewis, Bt. (1813)

Duffell, *Lt.-Gen.* Sir Peter Royson, KCB, CBE, MC

Duffy, Sir (Albert) (Edward) Patrick, Kt., PHD

†Dugdale, Sir (William) Matthew Stratford, Bt. (1936)

Duggin, Sir Thomas Joseph, Kt.

Dunbar, Sir Archibald Ranulph, Bt. (S. 1700)

Dunbar, Sir James Michael, Bt. (S. 1694)

Dunbar, Sir Robert Drummond Cospatrick, Bt. (S. 1698)

Dunbar of Hempriggs, Sir Richard Francis, Bt. (S. 1706)

Dunbar-Nasmith, *Prof.* Sir James Duncan, Kt., CBE

Duncan, Sir James Blair, Kt.

Dunford, *Dr* Sir John Ernest, Kt., OBE

Dunlop, Sir Thomas, Bt. (1916)

Dunne, Sir Martin, KCVO

Dunne, Sir Thomas Raymond, KG, KCVO

Dunning, Sir Simon William Patrick, Bt. (1930)

Dunnington-Jefferson, Sir John Alexander, Bt. (1958)

Dunstone, Sir Charles William, Kt., CVO

Dunt, *Vice-Adm.* Sir John Hugh, KCB

Duntze, Sir Daniel Evans, Bt. (1774)

Dupre, Sir Tumun, Kt., MBE

Durand, Sir Edward Alan Christopher David Percy, Bt. (1892)

Durant, Sir (Robert) Anthony (Bevis), Kt.

Durie, Sir David Robert Campbell, KCMG

Durrant, Sir William Alexander Estridge, Bt. (1784)

Duthie, Sir Robert Grieve (Robin), Kt., CBE

Dutton, *Lt.-Gen.* Sir James Benjamin, KCB, CBE

Dwyer, Sir Joseph Anthony, Kt.

Dyke, Sir David William Hart, Bt. (1677)

Dymock, *Vice-Adm.* Sir Anthony Knox, KBE, CB

Dyson, Sir James, Kt., CBE (Lord Dyson)

Dyson, *Rt. Hon.* Sir John Anthony, Kt.

Eady, *Hon.* Sir David, Kt.

†Eardley-Wilmot, Sir Benjamin John Assheton, Bt. (1821)

Earle, Sir (Hardman) George (Algernon), Bt. (1869)

Eastwood, *Prof.* Sir David Stephen, Kt.

Eaton, *Adm.* Sir Kenneth John, GBE, KCB

Eberle, *Adm.* Sir James Henry Fuller, GCB

Ebrahim, Sir (Mahomed) Currimbhoy, Bt. (1910)

Eddington, Sir Roderick Ian, Kt.

Eder, *Hon.* Sir Henry Bernard, Kt.

Edis, *Hon.* Sir Andrew Jeremy Coulter, Kt., QC

Edge, *Capt.* Sir (Philip) Malcolm, KCVO

†Edge, Sir William, Bt. (1937)

Edmonstone, Sir Archibald Bruce Charles, Bt. (1774)

Edward, *Rt. Hon.* Sir David Alexander Ogilvy, KCMG

Edwardes, Sir Michael Owen, Kt.

Edwards, Sir Christopher John Churchill, Bt. (1866)

Edwards, *Prof.* Sir Christopher Richard Watkin, Kt.

Edwards, Sir Gareth Owen, Kt., CBE

Edwards, Sir Llewellyn Roy, Kt.

Edwards, *Prof.* Sir Michael, OBE

Edwards, Sir Robert Paul, Kt.

†Edwards-Moss, Sir David John, Bt. (1868)

Edwards-Stuart, *Hon.* Sir Antony James Cobham, Kt.

Egan, Sir John Leopold, Kt.

Egerton, Sir William de Malpas, Bt. (1617)

Ehrman, Sir William Geoffrey, KCMG

Eichelbaum, *Rt. Hon.* Sir Thomas, GBE

Elder, Sir Mark Philip, Kt., CBE

Eldon, Sir Stewart Graham, KCMG, OBE

Elias, *Rt. Hon.* Sir Patrick, Kt.

Eliott of Stobs, Sir Charles Joseph Alexander, Bt. (S. 1666)

Elliot, Sir Gerald Henry, Kt.

Elliott, Sir Clive Christopher Hugh, Bt. (1917)

Elliott, Sir David Murray, KCMG, CB

Elliott, *Prof.* Sir John Huxtable, Kt., FBA

Elliott, *Prof.* Sir Roger James, Kt., FRS

Ellis, Sir Herbert Douglas, Kt., OBE

Ellis, Sir Vernon James, Kt.

Ellwood, Sir Peter Brian, Kt., CBE

†Elphinstone, Sir Alexander, Bt. (S. 1701)

Elphinstone, Sir John Howard Main, Bt. (1816)

Elton, Sir Arnold, Kt., CBE

Elton, Sir Charles Abraham Grierson, Bt. (1717)

Elvidge, Sir John, KCB

Elwes, *Dr* Sir Henry William, KCVO

Elwes, Sir Jeremy Vernon, Kt., CBE

Elwood, Sir Brian George Conway, Kt., CBE

Elworthy, *Air Cdre. Hon.* Sir Timothy Charles, KCVO, CBE

Enderby, *Prof.* Sir John Edwin, Kt. CBE, FRS

Engle, Sir George Lawrence Jose, KCB, QC

English, Sir Terence Alexander Hawthorne, KBE, FRCS

Ennals, Sir Paul Martin, Kt., CBE

Epstein, *Prof.* Sir (Michael) Anthony, Kt., CBE, FRS

Errington, *Col.* Sir Geoffrey Frederick, Bt. (1963), OBE

Erskine, Sir (Thomas) Peter Neil, Bt. (1821)

Erskine-Hill, Sir Alexander Rodger, Bt. (1945)

Esmonde, Sir Thomas Francis Grattan, Bt. (I. 1629)

Esplen, Sir John Graham, Bt. (1921)

Esquivel, *Rt. Hon.* Sir Manuel, KCMG

Essenhigh, *Adm.* Sir Nigel Richard, GCB

Etherington, Sir Stuart James, Kt.

Etherton, *Rt. Hon.* Sir Terence Michael Elkan Barnet, Kt.

Evans, Sir Anthony Adney, Bt. (1920)

Evans, *Rt. Hon.* Sir Anthony Howell Meurig, Kt., RD

Evans, *Prof.* Sir Christopher Thomas, Kt., OBE

Evans, *Air Chief Marshal* Sir David George, GCB, CBE

Evans, *Hon.* Sir David Roderick, Kt.

Evans, Sir Harold Matthew, Kt.

Evans, *Prof.* Sir John Grimley, Kt., FRCP

Evans, Sir John Stanley, Kt., QPM

Evans, *Prof.* Sir Martin John, Kt., FRS

Evans, Sir Richard Harry, Kt., CBE

Evans, *Prof.* Sir Richard John, Kt.

Evans, Sir Robert, Kt., CBE, FRENG

Evans-Lombe, *Hon.* Sir Edward Christopher, Kt.

†Evans-Tipping, Sir David Gwynne, Bt. (1913)

Everard, Sir Henry Peter Charles, Bt. (1911)

Everington, *Dr.* Sir Anthony Herbert, Kt., OBE

Every, Sir Henry John Michael, Bt. (1641)

Ewart, Sir William Michael, Bt. (1887)

Eyre, Sir Reginald Edwin, Kt.

Eyre, Sir Richard Charles Hastings, Kt., CBE

Fagge, Sir John Christopher Frederick, Bt. (1660)

Fahy, Sir Peter, Kt., QPM

Fairbairn, Sir (James) Brooke, Bt. (1869)

Fairlie-Cuninghame, Sir Robert Henry, Bt. (S. 1630)

Fairweather, Sir Patrick Stanislaus, KCMG

Faldo, Sir Nicholas Alexander, Kt., MBE

†Falkiner, Sir Benjamin Simon Patrick, Bt. (I. 1778)

Fall, Sir Brian James Proetel, GCVO, KCMG

Fang, *Prof.* Sir Harry, Kt., CBE

Fareed, Sir Djamil Sheik, Kt.

Farmer, Sir Thomas, Kt., CVO, CBE

Farquhar, Sir Michael Fitzroy Henry, Bt. (1796)

Farquharson, Sir Angus Durie Miller, KCVO, OBE

Farrell, Sir Terence, Kt., CBE

Farrer, Sir (Charles) Matthew, GCVO

Farrington, Sir Henry William, Bt. (1818)

Fat, Sir (Maxime) Edouard (Lim Man) Lim, Kt.

Faulkner, Sir (James) Dennis (Compton), Kt., CBE, VRD

Fay, Sir (Humphrey) Michael Gerard, Kt.

Fayrer, Sir John Lang Macpherson, Bt. (1896)

Feachem, *Prof.* Sir Richard George Andrew, KBE

Fean, Sir Thomas Vincent, KCVO

Feilden, Sir Henry Rudyard, Bt. (1846)

Feldmann, *Prof.* Sir Marc, Kt.

Fell, Sir David, KCB

Fender, Sir Brian Edward Frederick, Kt., CMG, PHD

Fenn, Sir Nicholas Maxted, GCMG

Fenwick, Sir Leonard Raymond, Kt., CBE

Fergus, Sir Howard Archibald, KBE

Ferguson, Sir Alexander Chapman, Kt., CBE

Ferguson-Davie, Sir Michael, Bt. (1847)

Fergusson of Kilkerran, Sir Charles, Bt. (S. 1703)

Fergusson, Sir Ewan Alastair John, GCMG, GCVO

Ferris, *Hon.* Sir Francis Mursell, Kt., TD

Fersht, *Prof.* Sir Alan Roy, Kt., FRS

ffolkes, Sir Robert Francis Alexander, Bt. (1774), OBE

Field, Sir Malcolm David, Kt.

Field, *Hon.* Sir Richard Alan, Kt.

Fielding, Sir Leslie, KCMG

Fields, Sir Allan Clifford, KCMG

Fieldsend, *Hon.* Sir John Charles Rowell, KBE

Fiennes, Sir Ranulph Twisleton-Wykeham, Bt. (1916), OBE

Figgis, Sir Anthony St John Howard, KCVO, CMG

Finch, Sir Robert Gerard, Kt.

Finlay, Sir David Ronald James Bell, Bt. (1964)

Finlayson, Sir Garet Orlando, KCMG, OBE

Fish, *Hon.* Sir David Royden, Kt.

†Fison, Sir Charles William, Bt. (1905)

FitzGerald, Sir Adrian James Andrew, Bt. (1880)

†Fitzgerald, *Revd* Daniel Patrick, Bt. (1903)

FitzHerbert, Sir Richard Ranulph, Bt. (1784)

Fitzpatrick, *Air Marshal* Sir John Bernard, KBE, CB

Flanagan, Sir Ronald, GBE, QPM

Flaux, *Hon.* Sir Julian Martin, Kt.

Floud, *Prof.* Sir Roderick Castle, Kt.

Floyd, *Rt. Hon.* Sir Christopher David, Kt.

Floyd, Sir Giles Henry Charles, Bt. (1816)

Foley, *Lt.-Gen.* Sir John Paul, KCB, OBE, MC

Follett, *Prof.* Sir Brian Keith, Kt., FRS

Forbes of Craigievar, Sir Andrew Iain Ochoncar, Bt. (S. 1630)

Forbes, *Adm.* Sir Ian Andrew, KCB, CBE

Forbes, Sir James Thomas Stewart, Bt. (1823)

Forbes, *Vice-Adm.* Sir John Morrison, KCB

Forbes, *Hon.* Sir Thayne John, Kt.

†Forbes Adam, Revd Stephen Timothy Beilby, Bt. (1917)

Forbes-Leith, Sir George Ian David, Bt. (1923)

Ford, *Lt.-Col.* Sir Andrew Charles, KCVO

Ford, Sir Andrew Russell, Bt. (1929)

Ford, Sir David Robert, KBE, LVO

Ford, Sir John Archibald, KCMG, MC

Ford, *Gen.* Sir Robert Cyril, GCB, CBE

Forestier-Walker, Sir Michael Leolin, Bt. (1835)

Forrest, *Prof.* Sir (Andrew) Patrick (McEwen), Kt.

Forsyth-Johnson, Sir Bruce Joseph, Kt., CBE (Bruce Forsyth)

Forte, *Hon.* Sir Rocco John Vincent, Kt.

Forwood, Sir Peter Noel, Bt. (1895)

Foskett, *Hon.* Sir David Robert, Kt.

Foster, Sir Andrew William, Kt.

Foster, *Prof.* Sir Christopher David, Kt.

†Foster, Sir Saxby Gregory, Bt. (1930)

Foulkes, Sir Arthur Alexander, GCMG

Fountain, *Hon.* Sir Cyril Stanley Smith, Kt.

Fowke, Sir David Frederick Gustavus, Bt. (1814)

Fowler, Sir (Edward) Michael Coulson, Kt.

Fox, Sir Christopher, Kt., QPM

Fox, Sir Paul Leonard, Kt., CBE

Francis, Sir Horace William Alexander, Kt., CBE, FRENG

Francis, Sir Robert Anthony, Kt., QC

Frank, Sir Robert Andrew, Bt. (1920)

Franklin, Sir Michael David Milroy, KCB, CMG

Fraser, Sir Charles Annand, KCVO

Fraser, Sir Iain Michael Duncan, Bt. (1943)

Fraser, Sir James Murdo, KBE

Fraser, Sir Simon James, KCMG

Fraser, Sir William Kerr, GCB

Frayling, *Prof.* Sir Christopher John, Kt.

Frederick, Sir Christopher St John, Bt. (1723)

Freedman, *Rt. Hon. Prof.* Sir Lawrence David, KCMG, CBE

Freeman, Sir James Robin, Bt. (1945)

French, *Air Marshal* Sir Joseph Charles, KCB, CBE

Frere, *Vice-Adm.* Sir Richard Tobias, KCB

Fretwell, Sir (Major) John (Emsley), GCMG

Friend *Prof.* Sir Richard Henry, Kt.

Froggatt, Sir Peter, Kt.

Fry, Sir Graham Holbrook, KCMG

Fry, *Lt.-Gen.* Sir Robert Allan, KCB, CBE

Fry, *Dr* Sir Roger Gordon, Kt., OBE

Fulford, *Rt. Hon.* Sir Adrian Bruce, Kt.

Fuller, Sir James Henry Fleetwood, Bt. (1910)

Fulton, *Lt.-Gen.* Sir Robert Henry Gervase, KBE

Furness, Sir Stephen Roberts, Bt. (1913)

Gage, *Rt. Hon.* Sir William Marcus, Kt., QC

Gains, Sir John Christopher, Kt.

Gainsford, Sir Ian Derek, Kt.

Gale, Sir Roger James, Kt.

Galsworthy, Sir Anthony Charles, KCMG

Galway, Sir James, Kt., OBE

Gamble, Sir David Hugh Norman, Bt. (1897)

Gambon, Sir Michael John, Kt., CBE

Gammell, Sir William Benjamin Bowring, Kt.

Gardiner, Sir John Eliot, Kt., CBE

Gardner, *Prof.* Sir Richard Lavenham, Kt.

Gardner, Sir Roy Alan, Kt.

Garland, *Hon.* Sir Patrick Neville, Kt.

Garland, *Hon.* Sir Ransley Victor, KBE

Garland, *Dr* Sir Trevor, KBE

Garnett, *Adm.* Sir Ian David Graham, KCB

Garnier, Sir Edward Henry, Kt., QC

Garnier, *Rear-Adm.* Sir John, KCVO, CBE

Garrard, Sir David Eardley, Kt.

Garrett, Sir Anthony Peter, Kt., CBE

Garrick, Sir Ronald, Kt., CBE, FRENG

Garthwaite, Sir (William) Mark (Charles), Bt. (1919)

Gass, Sir Simon Lawrance, KCMG, CVO

Geidt, *Rt. Hon.* Sir Christopher, KCB, KCVO, OBE

Geim, *Prof.* Sir Andre Konstantin, Kt.

Geno, Sir Makena Viora, KBE

Gent, Sir Christopher Charles, Kt.

George, *Prof.* Sir Charles Frederick, Kt., MD, FRCP

George, Sir Richard William, Kt., CVO

Gerken, *Vice-Adm.* Sir Robert William Frank, KCB, CBE

Gershon, Sir Peter Oliver, Kt., CBE

Gethin, Sir Richard Joseph St Lawrence, Bt. (I. 1665)

Gibbings, Sir Peter Walter, Kt.

Gibbons, Sir William Edward Doran, Bt. (1752)

Gibbs, *Hon.* Sir Richard John Hedley, Kt.

Gibbs, Sir Roger Geoffrey, Kt.

†Gibson, *Revd* Christopher Herbert, Bt. (1931)

Gibson, Sir Ian, Kt., CBE

Gibson, Sir Kenneth Archibald, Kt.

Gibson, *Rt. Hon.* Sir Peter Leslie, Kt.

Gibson-Craig-Carmichael, Sir David Peter William, Bt. (S. 1702 and 1831)

Gieve, Sir Edward John Watson, KCB

Giffard, Sir (Charles) Sydney (Rycroft), KCMG

Gifford, Sir Michael Roger, Kt.

Gilbart, *Hon.* Sir Andrew James, Kt., QC

Gilbart-Denham, *Lt.-Col.* Sir Seymour Vivian, KCVO

Gilbert, *Air Chief Marshal* Sir Joseph Alfred, KCB, CBE

†Gilbey, Sir Walter Gavin, Bt. (1893)

Gill, Sir Anthony Keith, Kt.

Gill, Sir Robin Denys, KCVO

Gillam, Sir Patrick John, Kt.

Gillen, *Hon.* Sir John de Winter, Kt.

Gillett, Sir Nicholas Danvers Penrose, Bt. (1959)

Gillinson, Sir Clive Daniel, Kt., CBE

Gilmore, *Prof.* Sir Ian Thomas, Kt.

Gilmour, *Hon.* Sir David Robert, Bt. (1926)

Gilmour, Sir John Nicholas, Bt. (1897)

Gina, Sir Lloyd Maepeza, KBE

Giordano, Sir Richard Vincent, KBE

Girolami, Sir Paul, Kt.

Girvan, *Rt. Hon.* Sir (Frederick) Paul, Kt.

Gladstone, Sir (Erskine) William, Bt. (1846), KG

Glean, Sir Carlyle Arnold, GCMG

Glidewell, *Rt. Hon.* Sir Iain Derek Laing, Kt.

Globe, *Hon.* Sir Henry Brian, Kt.

Glover, Sir Victor Joseph Patrick, Kt.

Glyn, Sir Richard Lindsay, Bt. (1759 and 1800)

Gobbo, Sir James Augustine, Kt., AC

Goldberg, *Prof.* Sir David Paul Brandes, Kt.

Goldring, *Rt. Hon.* Sir John Bernard, Kt.

Gomersall, Sir Stephen John, KCMG

Gonsalves-Sabola, *Hon.* Sir Joaquim Claudino, Kt

Gooch, Sir Arthur Brian Sherlock Heywood, Bt. (1746)

Gooch, Sir Miles Peter, Bt. (1866)

Good, Sir John James Griffen, Kt. CBE

Goodall, Sir (Arthur) David Saunders, GCMG

Goodall, *Air Marshal* Sir Roderick Harvey, KBE, CB, AFC

Goode, *Prof.* Sir Royston Miles, Kt., CBE, QC

Goodenough, Sir Anthony Michael, KCMG

Goodenough, Sir William McLernon, Bt. (1943)

Goodhart, Sir Robert Anthony Gordon, Bt. (1911)

Goodison, Sir Nicholas Proctor, Kt.

Goodman, Sir Patrick Ledger, Kt., CBE

Goodson, Sir Alan Reginald, Bt. (1922)

Goodwin, Sir Frederick, KBE

Goold, Sir George William, Bt. (1801)

Gordon, Sir Donald, Kt.

Gordon, Sir Gerald Henry, Kt., CBE, QC

Gordon, Sir Robert James, Bt. (S. 1706)

Gordon-Cumming, Sir Alexander Penrose, Bt. (1804)

Gore, Sir Hugh Frederick Corbet, Bt. (I. 1622)

Gore-Booth, Sir Josslyn Henry Robert, Bt. (I. 1760)

Goring, Sir William Burton Nigel, Bt. (1678)

Gormley, Sir Antony Mark David, Kt., OBE

Gormley, Sir Paul Brendan, KCMG, MBE

Goschen, Sir (Edward) Alexander, Bt. (1916)

Gosling, Sir (Frederick) Donald, KCVO

Goss, *Hon.* Sir James Richard William, Kt., QC

Goulden, Sir (Peter) John, GCMG

Goulding, Sir (William) Lingard Walter, Bt. (1904)

Gourlay, Sir Simon Alexander, Kt.

Gowans, Sir James Learmonth, Kt., CBE, FRCP, FRS

Gowers, *Prof.* Sir William Timothy, Kt.

Gozney, Sir Richard Hugh Turton, KCMG

Graaff, Sir De Villiers, Bt. (1911)

Graham, Sir Alexander Michael, GBE

Graham, Sir James Bellingham, Bt. (1662)

Graham, Sir James Fergus Surtees, Bt. (1783)

Graham, Sir James Thompson, Kt., CMG

Graham, Sir John Alexander Noble, Bt. (1906), GCMG

Graham, Sir John Alistair, Kt.

Graham, Sir John Moodie, Bt. (1964)

Graham, Sir Peter, KCB, QC

Graham, *Lt.-Gen.* Sir Peter Walter, KCB, CBE

†Graham, Sir Ralph Stuart, Bt. (1629)

Graham-Moon, Sir Peter Wilfred Giles, Bt. (1855)

Graham-Smith, *Prof.* Sir Francis, Kt.

Grange, Sir Kenneth Henry, Kt., CBE

Grant, Sir Archibald, Bt. (S. 1705)

Grant, Sir Ian David, Kt., CBE

Grant, Sir (John) Anthony, Kt.

Grant, Sir John Douglas Kelso, KCMG

Grant, *Prof.* Sir Malcolm John, Kt., CBE

Grant, Sir Patrick Alexander Benedict, Bt. (S. 1688)

Grant, Sir Paul Joseph Patrick, Kt.

Grant, *Lt.-Gen.* Sir Scott Carnegie, KCB

Grant-Suttie, Sir James Edward, Bt. (S. 1702)

Granville-Chapman, *Gen.* Sir Timothy John, GBE, KCB, ADC

Grattan-Bellew, Sir Henry Charles, Bt. (1838)

Gray, Sir Bernard Peter, Kt.

Gray, *Hon.* Sir Charles Anthony St John, Kt.

Gray, Sir Charles Ireland, Kt., CBE

Gray, *Prof.* Sir Denis John Pereira, Kt., OBE, FRCGP

Gray, *Dr.* Sir John Armstrong Muir, Kt., CBE

Gray, Sir Robert McDowall (Robin), Kt.

Gray, Sir William Hume, Bt. (1917)

Graydon, *Air Chief Marshal* Sir Michael James, GCB, CBE

Grayson, Sir Jeremy Brian Vincent Harrington, Bt. (1922)

Green, Sir Allan David, KCB, QC

Green, Sir Edward Patrick Lycett, Bt. (1886)

Green, Sir Gregory David, KCMG

Green, *Hon.* Sir Guy Stephen Montague, KBE

Green, *Prof.* Sir Malcolm, Kt.

Green, *Hon.* Sir Nicholas Nigel, Kt., QC

Green, Sir Owen Whitley, Kt.

Green, Sir Philip Green, Kt.

Green-Price, Sir Robert John, Bt. (1874)

Greenaway, *Prof.* Sir David, Kt.
Greenaway, Sir Thomas Edward Burdick, Bt. (1933)
Greenbury, Sir Richard, Kt.
Greener, Sir Anthony Armitage, Kt.
Greengross, Sir Alan David, Kt.
Greenstock, Sir Jeremy Quentin, GCMG
Greenwell, Sir Edward Bernard, Bt. (1906)
Greenwood, *Prof.* Sir Brian Mellor, Kt., CBE
Greenwood, *Prof.* Sir Christopher John, Kt., CMG
Gregory, *Prof.* Sir Michael John, Kt., CBE
Gregson, Sir Peter John, Kt.
Gregson, Sir Peter Lewis, GCB
Grey, Sir Anthony Dysart, Bt. (1814)
Griffiths, Sir Michael, Kt.
Grigson, *Hon.* Sir Geoffrey Douglas, Kt.
Grimshaw, Sir Nicholas Thomas, Kt., CBE
Grimstone, Sir Gerald Edgar, Kt.
Grimwade, Sir Andrew Sheppard, Kt., CBE
Grose, *Vice-Adm.* Sir Alan, KBE
Gross, *Rt. Hon.* Sir Peter Henry, Kt.
Grossart, Sir Angus McFarlane McLeod, Kt., CBE
Grotrian, Sir Philip Christian Brent, Bt. (1934)
Grove, Sir Charles Gerald, Bt. (1874)
Grundy, Sir Mark, Kt.
Guinness, Sir Howard Christian Sheldon, Kt., VRD
Guinness, Sir John Ralph Sidney, Kt., CB
Guinness, Sir Kenelm Edward Lee, Bt. (1867)
Guise, Sir Christopher James, Bt. (1783)
Gull, Sir Rupert William Cameron, Bt. (1872)
Gumbs, Sir Emile Rudolph, Kt.
Gunn, Sir Robert Norman, Kt.
Gunning, Sir Charles Theodore, Bt. (1778)
Gunston, Sir John Wellesley, Bt. (1938)
Gurdon, *Prof.* Sir John Bertrand, Kt., DPHIL, FRS
Guthrie, Sir Malcolm Connop, Bt. (1936)

Haddacks, *Vice-Adm.* Sir Paul Kenneth, KCB
Haddon-Cave, *Hon.* Sir Charles Anthony, Kt.
Hadlee, Sir Richard John, Kt., MBE
Hagart-Alexander, Sir Claud, Bt. (1886)
Haines, *Prof.* Sir Andrew Paul, Kt.
Haji-Ioannou, Sir Stelios, Kt.
Halberg, Sir Murray Gordon, Kt., MBE
Hall, *Dr* Sir Andrew James, Kt.
Hall, Sir David Christopher, Bt. (1923)
Hall, *Prof.* Sir David Michael Baldock, Kt.
Hall, Sir Ernest, Kt., OBE
Hall, Sir Geoffrey, Kt.
Hall, Sir Graham Joseph, Kt.
Hall, Sir Iain Robert, Kt.

Hall, Sir John, Kt.
Hall, Sir John Bernard, Bt. (1919)
Hall, Sir John Douglas Hoste, Bt. (S. 1687)
Hall, HE *Prof.* Sir Kenneth Octavius, GCMG
Hall, Sir Peter Edward, KBE, CMG
Hall, Sir Peter Reginald Frederick, Kt., CBE
Hall, *Revd* Wesley Winfield, Kt.
Hall, Sir William Joseph, KCVO
Halpern, Sir Ralph Mark, Kt.
Halsey, *Revd* John Walter Brooke, Bt. (1920)
Halstead, Sir Ronald, Kt., CBE
Hamblen, *Hon.* Sir Nicholas Archibald, Kt.
Hambling, Sir Herbert Peter Hugh, Bt. (1924)
Hamilton, Sir Andrew Caradoc, Bt. (S. 1646)
Hamilton, Sir Nigel, KCB
Hamilton-Dalrymple, *Maj.* Sir Hew Fleetwood, Bt. (S. 1698), GCVO
Hamilton-Spencer-Smith, Sir John, Bt. (1804)
Hammick, Sir Jeremy Charles, Bt. (1834)
Hammond, Sir Anthony Hilgrove, KCB, QC
Hampel, Sir Ronald Claus, Kt.
Hampson, Sir Stuart, Kt.
Hampton, Sir (Leslie) Geoffrey, Kt.
Hampton, Sir Philip Roy, Kt.
Hanbury-Tenison, Sir Richard, KCVO
Hanham, Sir William John Edward, Bt. (1667)
Hankes-Drielsma, Sir Claude Dunbar, KCVO
Hanley, *Rt. Hon.* Sir Jeremy James, KCMG
Hanmer, Sir Wyndham Richard Guy, Bt. (1774)
Hannam, Sir John Gordon, Kt.
Hanson, Sir (Charles) Rupert (Patrick), Bt. (1918)
Hanson, Sir John Gilbert, KCMG, CBE
Harcourt-Smith, *Air Chief Marshal* Sir David, GBE, KCB, DFC
Hardie Boys, *Rt. Hon.* Sir Michael, GCMG
Harding, Sir George William, KCMG, CVO
Harding, *Marshal of the Royal Air Force* Sir Peter Robin, GCB
Hardy, Sir David William, Kt.
Hardy, Sir James Gilbert, Kt., OBE
Hardy, Sir Richard Charles Chandos, Bt. (1876)
Hare, Sir David, Kt., FRSL
Hare, Sir Nicholas Patrick, Bt. (1818)
Haren, *Dr* Sir Patrick Hugh, Kt.
Harford, Sir Mark John, Bt. (1934)
Harington, Sir Nicholas John, Bt. (1611)
Harkness, *Very Revd* James, KCVO, CB, OBE
Harley, *Gen.* Sir Alexander George Hamilton, KBE, CB
Harman, *Hon.* Sir Jeremiah LeRoy, Kt.
Harman, Sir John Andrew, Kt.
Harmsworth, Sir Hildebrand Harold, Bt. (1922)

Harper, *Air Marshal* Sir Christopher Nigel, KBE
Harper, Sir Ewan William, Kt., CBE
Harper, *Prof.* Sir Peter Stanley, Kt., CBE
Harris, Sir Christopher John Ashford, Bt. (1932)
Harris, *Air Marshal* Sir John Hulme, KCB, CBE
Harris, *Prof.* Sir Martin Best, Kt., CBE
Harris, Sir Michael Frank, Kt.
Harris, Sir (Theodore) Wilson, Kt.
Harris, Sir Thomas George, KBE, CMG
Harrison, *Prof.* Sir Brian Howard, Kt.
Harrison, Sir David, Kt., CBE, FRENG
Harrison, *Hon.* Sir Michael Guy Vicat, Kt.
Harrison, Sir Michael James Harwood, Bt. (1961)
Harrison, Sir (Robert) Colin, Bt. (1922)
Harrison, Sir Terence, Kt., FRENG
Harrop, Sir Peter John, KCB
Hart, *Hon.* Sir Anthony Ronald, Kt.
Hart, Sir Graham Allan, KCB
Hartwell, Sir (Francis) Anthony Charles Peter, Bt. (1805)
Harvey, Sir Charles Richard Musgrave, Bt. (1933)
Harvey, Sir Nicholas Barton, Kt.
Harvie, Sir John Smith, Kt., CBE
Harvie-Watt, Sir James, Bt. (1945)
Harwood, Sir Ronald, Kt., CBE
Haselhurst, *Rt. Hon.* Sir Alan Gordon Barraclough, Kt.
Haskard, Sir Cosmo Dugal Patrick Thomas, KCMG, MBE
Hastie, *Cdre* Sir Robert Cameron, KCVO, CBE, RD
Hastings, Sir Max Macdonald, Kt.
Hastings, *Dr* Sir William George, Kt., CBE
Hatter, Sir Maurice, Kt.
Havelock-Allan, Sir (Anthony) Mark David, Bt. (1858)
Hawkes, Sir John Garry, Kt., CBE
Hawkhead, Sir Anthony Gerard, Kt., CBE
Hawkins, Sir Richard Caesar, Bt. (1778)
Hawley, Sir James Appleton, KCVO, TD
Haworth, Sir Philip, Bt. (1911)
Hay, Sir David Russell, Kt., CBE, FRCP, MD
Hay, Sir John Erroll Audley, Bt. (S. 1663)
†Hay, Sir Ronald Frederick Hamilton, Bt. (S. 1703)
Hayden, *Hon.* Sir Anthony Paul, Kt.
Hayes, Sir Brian, Kt., CBE, QPM
Hayes, Sir Brian David, GCB
Hayman-Joyce, *Lt.-Gen.* Sir Robert John, KCB, CBE
Hayter, Sir Paul David Grenville, KCB, LVO
Head, Sir Patrick, Kt.
Head, Sir Richard Douglas Somerville, Bt. (1838)
Heald, Sir Oliver, Kt.
Heap, Sir Peter William, KCMG
Heap, *Prof.* Sir Robert Brian, Kt., CBE, FRS

Hearne, Sir Graham James, Kt., CBE

†Heathcote, Sir Mark Simon Robert, Bt. (1733), OBE

†Heathcote, Sir Timothy Gilbert, Bt. (1733)

Heatley, Sir Peter, Kt., CBE

Heber-Percy, Sir Algernon Eustace Hugh, KCVO

Hedley Hon. Sir Mark, Kt.

Hegarty, Sir John Kevin, Kt.

Heiser, Sir Terence Michael, GCB

Heller, Sir Michael Aron, Kt.

Henderson, Sir Denys Hartley, Kt.

Henderson, Hon. Sir Launcelot Dinadan James, Kt.

Henderson, Maj. Sir Richard Yates, KCVO

Hendry, Prof. Sir David Forbes, Kt.

Hendy, Sir Peter Gerard, Kt., CBE

Hennessy, Sir James Patrick Ivan, KBE, CMG

†Henniker, Sir Adrian Chandos, Bt. (1813)

Henniker-Heaton, Sir Yvo Robert, Bt. (1912)

Henriques, Hon. Sir Richard Henry Quixano, Kt.

Henry, Sir Lenworth George, Kt., CBE

†Henry, Sir Patrick Denis, Bt. (1923)

Henshaw, Sir David George, Kt.

Herbecq, Sir John Edward, KCB

Herbert, Adm. Sir Peter Geoffrey Marshall, KCB, OBE

Heron, Sir Conrad Frederick, KCB, OBE

Heron-Maxwell, Sir Nigel Mellor, Bt. (S. 1683)

Hervey, Sir Roger Blaise Ramsay, KCVO, CMG

Hervey-Bathurst, Sir Frederick William John, Bt. (1818)

Heseltine, Rt. Hon. Sir William Frederick Payne, GCB, GCVO

Hewetson, Sir Christopher Raynor, Kt., TD

Hewett, Sir Richard Mark John, Bt. (1813)

Hewitt, Sir (Cyrus) Lenox (Simson), Kt., OBE

Hewitt, Sir Nicholas Charles Joseph, Bt. (1921)

Heygate, Sir Richard John Gage, Bt. (1831)

Heywood, Sir Jeremy John, KCB, CVO

Heywood, Sir Peter, Bt. (1838)

Hickey, Sir John Tongri, Kt., CBE

Hickinbottom, Hon. Sir Gary Robert, Kt.

Hickman, Sir (Richard) Glenn, Bt. (1903)

Hicks, Sir Robert, Kt.

Hidden, Hon. Sir Anthony Brian, Kt.

Hielscher, Sir Leo Arthur, Kt.

Higgins, Sir David Hartmann, Kt.

Higgins, Rt. Hon. Sir Malachy Joseph, Kt.

Hildyard, Hon. Sir Robert Henry Thoroton, Kt.

Hill, Sir Brian John, Kt.

Hill, Rt. Revd Dr. Christopher John, KCVO

Hill, Prof. Sir Geoffrey William, Kt.

Hill, Sir James Frederick, Bt. (1917)

Hill, Sir John Alfred Rowley, Bt. (I. 1779)

Hill, Vice-Adm. Sir Robert Charles Finch, KBE, FRENG

Hill-Norton, Vice-Adm. Hon. Sir Nicholas John, KCB

Hill-Wood, Sir Samuel Thomas, Bt. (1921)

Hillhouse, Sir (Robert) Russell, KCB

Hillier, Air Marshal Sir Stephen John, KCB, CBE, DFC

Hills, Sir John Robert, Kt., CBE

Hilly, Sir Francis Billy, KCMG

Hine, Air Chief Marshal Sir Patrick Bardon, GCB, GBE

Hintze, Sir Michael, Kt.

Hirsch, Prof. Sir Peter Bernhard, Kt., PHD, FRS

Hirst, Sir Michael William, Kt.

Hoare, Prof. Sir Charles Anthony Richard, Kt., FRS

Hoare, Sir Charles James, Bt. (I. 1784)

Hoare, Sir David John, Bt. (1786)

Hobart, Sir John Vere, Bt. (1914)

Hobbs, Maj.-Gen. Sir Michael Frederick, KCVO, CBE

Hobhouse, Sir Charles John Spinney, Bt. (1812)

Hobson, Sir Ronald, KCVO

†Hodge, Sir Andrew Rowland, Bt. (1921)

Hodge, Sir James William, KCVO, CMG

Hodgkin, Sir (Gordon) Howard (Eliot), Kt., CH, CBE

Hodgkinson, Sir Michael Stewart, Kt.

Hodson, Sir Michael Robin Adderley, Bt. (I. 1789)

Hogan-Howe, Sir Bernard, Kt., QPM

Hogg, Sir Christopher Anthony, Kt.

Hogg, Sir Piers Michael James, Bt. (1846)

Hohn, Sir Christopher, KCMG

Holcroft, Sir Charles Anthony Culcheth, Bt. (1921)

Holden, Sir John David, Bt. (1919)

Holden, Sir Paul, Bt. (1893)

Holden-Brown, Sir Derrick, Kt.

Holder, Sir John Henry, Bt. (1898)

Holderness, Sir Martin William, Bt. (1920)

Holdgate, Sir Martin Wyatt, Kt., CB, PHD

Holgate, Hon. Sir David John, Kt., QC

Holland, Hon. Sir Alan Douglas, Kt.

Holland, Hon. Sir Christopher John, Kt.

Holland, Sir Geoffrey, KCB

Holland, Sir John Anthony, Kt.

Holliday, Prof. Sir Frederick George Thomas, Kt., CBE, FRSE

Holm, Sir Ian (Holm Cuthbert), Kt., CBE

Holman, Hon. Sir (Edward) James, Kt.

Holman, Prof. Sir John Stranger, Kt.

Holmes, Sir John Eaton, GCVO, KBE, CMG

Holroyd, Sir Michael De Courcy Fraser, Kt., CBE

Holroyde, Hon. Sir Timothy Victor, Kt.

Home, Sir William Dundas, Bt. (S. 1671)

Honywood, Sir Filmer Courtenay William, Bt. (1660)

†Hood, Sir John Joseph Harold, Bt. (1922)

Hooper, Rt. Hon. Sir Anthony, Kt.

Hope, Sir Alexander Archibald Douglas, Bt. (S. 1628)

Hope-Dunbar, Sir David, Bt. (S. 1664)

Hopkin, Prof. Sir Deian Rhys, Kt.

Hopkin, Sir Royston Oliver, KCMG

Hopkins, Sir Anthony Philip, Kt., CBE

Hopkins, Sir Michael John, Kt., CBE, RA, RIBA

Hopwood, Prof. Sir David Alan, Kt., FRS

Hordern, Rt. Hon. Sir Peter Maudslay, Kt.

Horlick, Vice-Adm. Sir Edwin John, KBE, FRENG

Horlick, Sir James Cunliffe William, Bt. (1914)

Horn-Smith, Sir Julian Michael, Kt.

Horne, Sir Alan Gray Antony, Bt. (1929)

Horne, Dr Sir Alistair Allan, Kt. CBE

Horner, Hon. Sir Thomas Mark, Kt.

Horsbrugh-Porter, Sir Andrew Alexander Marshall, Bt. (1902)

Horsfall, Sir Edward John Wright, Bt. (1909)

Hort, Sir Andrew Edwin Fenton, Bt. (1767)

Hosker, Sir Gerald Albery, KCB, QC

Hoskins, Prof. Sir Brian John, Kt. CBE, FRS

Hoskyns, Sir Robin Chevallier, Bt. (1676)

Hotung, Sir Joseph Edward, Kt.

Houghton, Gen. Sir John Nicholas Reynolds, GCB, CBE

Houghton, Sir John Theodore, Kt., CBE, FRS

Houghton, Sir Stephen Geoffrey, Kt., CBE

Houldsworth, Sir Richard Thomas Reginald, Bt. (1887)

Hourston, Sir Gordon Minto, Kt.

Housden, Sir Peter James, KCB

House, Sir Stephen, Kt., QPM

Houssemayne du Boulay, Sir Roger William, KCVO, CMG

Houstoun-Boswall, Sir (Thomas) Alford, Bt. (1836)

Howard, Sir David Howarth Seymour, Bt. (1955)

Howard, Prof. Sir Michael Eliot, Kt., OM, CH, CBE, MC

Howard-Lawson, Sir John Philip, Bt. (1841)

Howarth, Sir (James) Gerald Douglas, Kt.

Howells, Sir Eric Waldo Benjamin, Kt., CBE

Howes, Sir Christopher Kingston, KCVO, CB

Howlett, Gen. Sir Geoffrey Hugh Whitby, KBE, MC

Hoy, Sir Christopher Andrew, Kt., MBE

Hugh-Jones, Sir Wynn Normington, Kt., LVO

Hughes, *Rt. Hon.* Sir Anthony Philip Gilson, Kt. (Lord Hughes of Ombersley)

Hughes, *Rt. Hon.* Sir Simon Henry Ward, Kt.

Hughes, Sir Thomas Collingwood, Bt. (1773)

Hughes, Sir Trevor Poulton, KCB

Hughes-Hallett, Sir Thomas Michael Sydney, Kt.

Hughes-Morgan, Sir (Ian) Parry David, Bt. (1925)

Hull, *Prof.* Sir David, Kt.

Hulse, Sir Edward Jeremy Westrow, Bt. (1739)

Hum, Sir Christopher Owen, KCMG

Humphreys, *Prof.* Sir Colin John, Kt., CBE

Hunt, Sir John Leonard, Kt.

Hunt, *Dr* Sir Richard Timothy, Kt.

Hunt-Davis, *Brig.* Sir Miles Garth, GCVO, CBE

Hunte, *Dr* Sir Julian Robert, KCMG, OBE

Hunter, Sir Alistair John, KCMG

Hunter, *Prof.* Sir Laurence Colvin, Kt., CBE, FRSE

Hunter, *Dr* Sir Philip John, Kt., CBE

Hunter, Sir Thomas Blane, Kt.

Huntington-Whiteley, Sir John Miles, Bt. (1918)

Hurn, Sir (Francis) Roger, Kt.

Hurst, Sir Geoffrey Charles, Kt., MBE

Hurt, Sir John Vincent, Kt., CBE

Husbands, Sir Clifford Straugh, GCMG

Hutchison, *Rt. Hon.* Sir Michael, Kt.

Hutchison, Sir Peter Craft, Bt. (1956), CBE

Hutchison, Sir Robert, Bt. (1939)

Hutt, Sir Dexter Walter, Kt.

Huxtable, *Gen.* Sir Charles Richard, KCB, CBE

Hytner, Sir Nicholas, Kt.

Iacobescu, Sir George, Kt., CBE

Ibbotson, *Vice-Adm.* Sir Richard Jeffrey, KBE, CB, DSC

Imbert-Terry, Sir Michael Edward Stanley, Bt. (1917)

Imray, Sir Colin Henry, KBE, CMG

Ingham, Sir Bernard, Kt.

Ingilby, Sir Thomas Colvin William, Bt. (1866)

Inglis of Glencorse, Sir Roderick John, Bt. (S. 1703)

Ingram, Sir James Herbert Charles, Bt. (1893)

Innes, Sir Alastair Charles Deverell, Bt. (NS 1686)

Innes of Edingight, Sir Malcolm Rognvald, KCVO

Innes, Sir Peter Alexander Berowald, Bt. (S. 1628)

Insall, Sir Donald William, Kt., CBE

Ipatas, *Hon.* Peter, KBE

Irvine, Sir Donald Hamilton, Kt., CBE, MD, FRCGP

Irving, *Prof.* Sir Miles Horsfall, Kt., MD, FRCS, FRCSE

Irwin, *Lt.-Gen.* Sir Alistair Stuart Hastings, KCB, CBE

Irwin, *Hon.* Sir Stephen John, Kt.

Isaacs, Sir Jeremy Israel, Kt.

Isham, Sir Norman Murray Crawford, Bt. (1627), OBE

Italeli, *HE* Sir Iakoba Taeia, GCMG

Ive, Sir Jonathan Paul, KBE

Ivory, Sir Brian Gammell, Kt., CBE

Jack, Sir Malcolm Roy, KCB

Jack, *Hon.* Sir Raymond Evan, Kt.

Jackling, Sir Roger Tustin, KCB, CBE

Jackson, Sir Barry Trevor, Kt.

Jackson, Sir Kenneth Joseph, Kt.

Jackson, *Gen.* Sir Michael David, GCB, CBE

Jackson, Sir Michael Roland, Bt. (1902)

†Jackson, Sir Neil Keith, Bt. (1815)

Jackson, Sir Nicholas Fane St George, Bt. (1913)

Jackson, *Hon.* Sir Peter Arthur Brian, Kt.

Jackson, *Rt. Hon.* Sir Rupert Matthew, Kt.

Jackson, Sir (William) Roland Cedric, Bt. (1869)

Jacob, *Rt. Hon.* Sir Robert Raphael Hayim (Robin), Kt.

Jacobi, Sir Derek George, Kt., CBE

Jacobs, Sir Cecil Albert, Kt., CBE

Jacobs, *Rt. Hon.* Sir Francis Geoffrey, KCMG, QC

Jacobs, *Hon.* Sir Kenneth Sydney, KBE

Jacomb, Sir Martin Wakefield, Kt.

Jaffray, Sir William Otho, Bt. (1892)

Jagger, Sir Michael Philip, Kt.

James, Sir Jeffrey Russell, KBE

James, Sir John Nigel Courtenay, KCVO, CBE

Jardine, Sir Andrew Colin Douglas, Bt. (1916)

Jardine of Applegirth, Sir William Murray, Bt. (S. 1672)

Jarman, *Prof.* Sir Brian, Kt., OBE

Jarratt, Sir Alexander Anthony, Kt., CB

Jawara, *Hon.* Sir Dawda Kairaba, Kt.

Jay, Sir Antony Rupert, Kt., CVO

Jay, *Hon.* Sir Robert Maurice, Kt.

Jeewoolall, Sir Ramesh, Kt.

Jeffrey, Sir Thomas Baird, Kt., CB

Jeffrey, Sir William Alexander, KCB

Jeffreys, *Prof.* Sir Alec John, Kt., FRS

Jeffries, *Hon.* Sir John Francis, Kt.

Jehangir, Sir Cowasji, Bt. (1908)

Jejeebhoy, Sir Jehangir, Bt. (1857)

Jenkins, Sir Brian Garton, GBE

Jenkins, Sir Elgar Spencer, Kt., OBE

Jenkins, Sir James Christopher, KCB, QC

Jenkins, Sir John, KCMG, LVO

Jenkins, *Dr* Sir Karl William Pamp, Kt., CBE

Jenkins, Sir Michael Nicholas Howard, Kt., OBE

Jenkins, Sir Paul Christopher, KCB

Jenkins, Sir Simon, Kt.

Jenkinson, Sir John Banks, Bt. (1661)

Jenks, Sir (Richard) Peter, Bt. (1932)

Jenner, *Air Marshal* Sir Timothy Ivo, KCB

Jennings, Sir John Southwood, Kt., CBE, FRSE

Jennings, Sir Peter Neville Wake, Kt., CVO

Jephcott, Sir David Welbourn, Bt. (1962)

Jessel, Sir Charles John, Bt. (1883)

Jewkes, Sir Gordon Wesley, KCMG

Job, Sir Peter James Denton, Kt.

John, Sir David Glyndwr, KCMG

John, Sir Elton Hercules (Reginald Kenneth Dwight), Kt., CBE

Johns, *Vice-Adm.* Sir Adrian James, KCB, CBE, ADC

Johns, *Air Chief Marshal* Sir Richard Edward, GCB, KCVO, CBE

Johnson, Sir Colpoys Guy, Bt. (1755)

Johnson, *Gen.* Sir Garry Dene, KCB, OBE, MC

Johnson, Sir John Rodney, KCMG

†Johnson, Sir Patrick Eliot, Bt. (1818)

Johnson, *Hon.* Sir Robert Lionel, Kt.

Johnson-Ferguson, Sir Ian Edward, Bt. (1906)

Johnston, *Lt.-Gen.* Sir Maurice Robert, KCB, CVO, OBE

Johnston, Sir Thomas Alexander, Bt. (S. 1626)

Johnston, Sir William Ian Ridley, Kt., CBE, QPM

Johnstone, Sir Geoffrey Adams Dinwiddie, KCMG

Johnstone, Sir (George) Richard Douglas, Bt. (S. 1700)

Johnstone, Sir (John) Raymond, Kt., CBE

Jolliffe, Sir Anthony Stuart, GBE

Jolly, Sir Arthur Richard, KCMG

Jonas, Sir John Peter, Kt., CBE

Jones, Sir Alan Jeffrey, Kt.

Jones, Sir David Charles, Kt., CBE

Jones, Sir Derek William, KCB

Jones, Sir Harry George, Kt., CBE

Jones, Sir John Francis, Kt.

Jones, Sir Kenneth Lloyd, Kt., QPM

Jones, Sir Lyndon, Kt.

Jones, Sir Mark Ellis Powell, Kt.

Jones, Sir (Owen) Trevor, Kt.

Jones, *Vice-Adm.* Sir Philip Andrew, KCB

Jones, Sir Richard Anthony Lloyd, KCB

Jones, Sir Robert Edward, Kt.

Jones, Sir Roger Spencer, Kt., OBE

Jones, Sir Simon Warley Frederick Benton, Bt. (1919)

†Joseph, *Hon.* Sir James Samuel, Bt. (1943)

Jowell, *Prof.* Sir Jeffrey Lionel, KCMG, QC

Jowitt, *Hon.* Sir Edwin Frank, Kt.

Judge, Sir Paul Rupert, Kt.

Jugnauth, *Rt. Hon.* Sir Anerood, KCMG

Jungius, *Vice-Adm.* Sir James George, KBE

Kaberry, *Hon.* Sir Christopher Donald, Bt. (1960)

Kabui, Sir Frank Utu Ofagioro, GCMG, OBE

Kadoorie, *Hon.* Sir Michael David, Kt.

Kakaraya, Sir Pato, KBE

Kamit, Sir Leonard Wilson, Kt., CBE

Kao, *Prof.* Sir Charles Kuen, KBE

Kapoor, Sir Anish Mikhail, Kt., CBE

Kaputin, Sir John Rumet, KBE, CMG

Kaufman, *Rt. Hon.* Sir Gerald Bernard, Kt.

Kavali, Sir Thomas, Kt., OBE

Kay, *Rt. Hon.* Sir Maurice Ralph, Kt.

Kaye, Sir Paul Henry Gordon, Bt. (1923)

Keane, Sir John Charles, Bt. (1801)

Kearney, *Hon.* Sir William John Francis, Kt., CBE

Keegan, *Dr* Sir Donal Arthur John, KCVO, OBE

Keehan, *Hon.* Sir Michael Joseph, Kt.

Keene, *Rt. Hon.* Sir David Wolfe, Kt.

Keith, *Hon.* Sir Brian Richard, Kt.

Keith, *Rt. Hon.* Sir Kenneth, KBE

†Kellett, Sir Stanley Charles, Bt. (1801)

Kelly, Sir Christopher William, KCB

Kelly, Sir David Robert Corbett, Kt., CBE

Kemakeza, Sir Allan, Kt.

Kemball, *Air Marshal* Sir (Richard) John, KCB, CBE

Kemp-Welch, Sir John, Kt.

Kendall, Sir Peter Ashley, Kt.

Kenilorea, *Rt. Hon.* Sir Peter, KBE

Kennaway, Sir John Lawrence, Bt. (1791)

Kennedy, Sir Francis, KCMG, CBE

†Kennedy, Sir George Matthew Rae, Bt. (1836)

Kennedy, *Hon.* Sir Ian Alexander, Kt.

Kennedy, *Prof.* Sir Ian McColl, Kt.

Kennedy, *Rt. Hon.* Sir Paul Joseph Morrow, Kt.

Kenny, Sir Anthony John Patrick, Kt., DPHIL, DLITT, FBA

Kenny, *Gen.* Sir Brian Leslie Graham, GCB, CBE

Kenny, Sir Paul Stephen, Kt.

Kentridge, Sir Sydney Woolf, KCMG, QC

Kenyon, Sir Nicholas Roger, Kt., CBE

Keogh, *Prof.* Sir Bruce Edward, KBE

Kere, *Dr* Sir Nathan, KCMG

Kere, *Adm.* Sir John BevKere *Hon.* Sir Nathan, KCMGerley, GCB

Kerr, Sir Ronald James, Kt., CB

Kerr, *Hon.* Sir Timothy Julian, Kt., QC

Kershaw, *Prof.* Sir Ian, Kt.

Keswick, Sir Henry Neville Lindley, Kt.

Keswick, Sir John Chippendale Lindley, Kt.

Kevau, *Prof.* Sir Isi Henao, Kt., CBE

Khaw, *Prof.* Sir Peng Tee, Kt.

Kibble, *Prof.* Sir Thomas Walter Bannerman, Kt., CBE, FRS

Kikau, *Ratu* Sir Jone Latianara, KBE

Kimber, Sir Rupert Edward Watkin, Bt. (1904)

King, *Prof.* Sir David Anthony, Kt., FRS

King, Sir James Henry Rupert, Bt. (1888)

King, Sir Julian Beresford, KCVO, CMG

King, *Hon.* Sir Timothy Roger Alan, Kt.

King, Sir Wayne Alexander, Bt. (1815)

Kingman, *Prof.* Sir John Frank Charles, Kt., FRS

Kingsley, Sir Ben, Kt.

Kinloch, Sir David, Bt. (S. 1686)

Kinloch, Sir David Oliphant, Bt. (1873)

Kipalan, Sir Albert, Kt.

Kirch, Sir David Roderick, KBE

Kirkpatrick, Sir Ivone Elliott, Bt. (S. 1685)

Kiszely, *Lt.-Gen.* Sir John Panton, KCB, MC

Kitchin, *Rt. Hon.* Sir David James Tyson, Kt.

Kitson, *Gen.* Sir Frank Edward, GBE, KCB, MC

Kitson, Sir Timothy Peter Geoffrey, Kt.

Kleinwort, Sir Richard Drake, Bt. (1909)

Klug, Sir Aaron, Kt., OM

Knight, *Rt. Hon.* Sir Gregory, Kt.

Knight, Sir Kenneth John, Kt., CBE, QFSM

Knight, *Air Chief Marshal* Sir Michael William Patrick, KCB, AFC

Knight, *Prof.* Sir Peter, Kt.

Knill, Sir Thomas John Pugin Bartholomew, Bt. (1893)

Knowles, Sir Charles Francis, Bt. (1765)

Knowles, Sir Durward Randolph, Kt., OBE

Knowles, Sir Nigel Graham, Kt.

Knowles, *Hon.* Sir Robin St John, Kt.

Knox, Sir David Laidlaw, Kt.

Knox-Johnston, Sir William Robert Patrick (Sir Robin), Kt., CBE, RD

Kohn, *Dr* Sir Ralph, Kt.

Koraea, Sir Thomas, Kt.

Kornberg, *Prof.* Sir Hans Leo, Kt., DSc, SCD, PHD, FRS

Korowi, Sir Wiwa, GCMG

Kroto, *Prof.* Sir Harold Walter, Kt., FRS

Kulukundis, Sir Elias George (Eddie), Kt., OBE

Kulunga, Sir Toami, Kt., OBE, QPM

Kwok-Po Li, *Dr* Sir David, Kt., OBE

Lachmann, *Prof.* Sir Peter Julius, Kt.

Lacon, Sir, Edmund Richard Vere, Bt. (1818)

Lacy, Sir Patrick Brian Finucane, Bt. (1921)

Laing, Sir (John) Martin (Kirby), Kt., CBE

Laird, Sir Gavin Harry, Kt., CBE

Lake, Sir Edward Geoffrey, Bt. (1711)

Lakin, Sir Richard Anthony, Bt. (1909)

Lamb, Sir Albert Thomas, KBE, CMG, DFC

Lamb, *Lt.-Gen.* Sir Graeme Cameron Maxwell, KBE, CMG, DSO

Lambert, *Vice-Adm.* Sir Paul, KCB

†Lambert, Sir Peter John Biddulph, Bt. (1711)

Lambert, Sir Richard Peter, Kt.

Lampl, Sir Peter, Kt., OBE

Lamport, Sir Stephen Mark Jeffrey, KCVO

Landale, Sir David William Neil, KCVO

Landau, Sir Dennis Marcus, Kt.

Lander, Sir Stephen James, KCB

Lane, Prof. Sir David Philip, Kt.

Langham, Sir John Stephen, Bt. (1660)

Langlands, Sir Robert Alan, Kt.

Langley, *Hon.* Sir Gordon Julian Hugh, Kt.

Langrishe, Sir James Hercules, Bt. (I. 1777)

Langstaff, *Hon.* Sir Brian Frederick James, Kt.

Lankester, Sir Timothy Patrick, KCB

Lapli, Sir John Ini, GCMG

Lapthorne, Sir Richard Douglas, Kt., CBE

Large, Sir Andrew McLeod Brooks, Kt.

Latasi, *Rt. Hon.* Sir Kamuta, KCMG, OBE

Latham, *Rt. Hon.* Sir David Nicholas Ramsey, Kt.

Latham, Sir Michael Anthony, Kt.

Latham, Sir Richard Thomas Paul, Bt. (1919)

Latimer, Sir Graham Stanley, KBE

Latour-Adrien, *Hon.* Sir Maurice, Kt.

Laughton, Sir Anthony Seymour, Kt.

Laurence, *Vice-Adm.* Sir Timothy James Hamilton, KCVO, CB, ADC

Laurie, Sir Robert Bayley Emilius, Bt. (1834)

Lauterpacht, Sir Elihu, Kt., CBE, QC

Lawler, Sir Peter James, Kt., OBE

†Lawrence, Sir Aubrey Lyttelton Simon, Bt. (1867)

Lawrence, Sir Clive Wyndham, Bt. (1906)

Lawrence, Sir Edmund Wickham, GCMG, OBE

Lawrence, Sir Henry Peter, Bt. (1858)

Lawrence, Sir Ivan John, Kt., QC

Lawrence-Jones, Sir Christopher, Bt. (1831)

Laws, *Rt. Hon.* Sir John Grant McKenzie, Kt.

Laws, Sir Stephen Charles, KCB

Lawson, Sir Charles John Patrick, Bt. (1900)

Lawson, *Gen.* Sir Richard George, KCB, DSO, OBE

Lawson-Tancred, Sir Andrew Peter, Bt. (1662)

Lawton, *Prof.* Sir John Hartley, Kt., CBE, FRS

Layard, *Adm.* Sir Michael Henry Gordon, KCB, CBE

Lea, Sir Thomas William, Bt. (1892)

Leahy, Sir Daniel Joseph, Kt.

Leahy, Sir John Henry Gladstone, KCMG

Leahy, Sir Terence Patrick, Kt.

Learmont, *Gen.* Sir John Hartley, KCB, CBE

Leaver, Sir Christopher, GBE

Le Cheminant, *Air Chief Marshal* Sir Peter de Lacey, GBE, KCB, DFC

Lechler, *Prof.* Sir Robert Ian, Kt.

Lechmere, Sir Nicholas Anthony Hungerford, Bt. (1818)

†Leeds, Sir John Charles Hildyard, Bt. (1812)

Lees, Sir David Bryan, Kt.

Lees, Sir Thomas Edward, Bt. (1897)

Lees, Sir Thomas Harcourt Ivor, Bt. (1804)

Lees, Sir (William) Antony Clare, Bt. (1937)

Leese, Sir Richard Charles, Kt., CBE

Leeson, *Air Marshal* Sir Kevin James, KCB, CBE

le Fleming, Sir David Kelland, Bt. (1705)

Legard, Sir Charles Thomas, Bt. (1660)

Legg, Sir Thomas Stuart, KCB, QC

Leggatt, *Rt. Hon.* Sir Andrew Peter, Kt.

Leggatt, *Hon.* George Andrew Midsomer, Kt.

Leggett, *Prof.* Sir Anthony James, KBE

Le Grand, *Prof.* Sir Julian Ernest, Kt.

Leigh, Sir Edward Julian Egerton, Kt.

Leigh, Sir Geoffrey Norman, Kt.

Leigh, *Dr* Sir Michael, KCMG

Leigh, Sir Richard Henry, Bt. (1918)

Leighton, Sir John Mark Nicholas, Kt.

Leighton, Sir Michael John Bryan, Bt. (1693)

Leith-Buchanan, Sir Gordon Kelly McNicol, Bt. (1775)

Le Marchant, Sir Francis Arthur, Bt. (1841)

Lennox-Boyd, *Hon.* Sir Mark Alexander, Kt.

Leon, Sir John Ronald, Bt. (1911)

Lepping, Sir George Geria Dennis, GCMG, MBE

Leslie, Sir John Norman Ide, Bt. (1876)

Lester, Sir James Theodore, Kt.

Lethbridge, Sir Thomas Periam Hector Noel, Bt. (1804)

Lever, Sir Jeremy Frederick, KCMG, QC

Lever, Sir Paul, KCMG

Lever, Sir (Tresham) Christopher Arthur Lindsay, Bt. (1911)

Leveson, *Rt. Hon.* Sir Brian Henry, Kt.

Levi, Sir Wasangula Noel, Kt., CBE

Levinge, Sir Richard George Robin, Bt. (I. 1704)

Lewinton, Sir Christopher, Kt.

Lewis, *Hon.* Sir Clive Buckland, Kt.

Lewis, Sir David Thomas Rowell, Kt.

Lewis, Sir John Anthony, Kt., OBE

Lewis, Sir Leigh Warren, KCB

Lewis, Sir Terence Murray, Kt., OBE, GM, QPM

Lewison, *Rt. Hon.* Sir Kim Martin Jordan, Kt.

Ley, Sir Ian Francis, Bt. (1905)

Li, Sir Ka-Shing, KBE

Lickiss, Sir Michael Gillam, Kt.

Liddington, Sir Bruce, Kt.

Lightman, *Hon.* Sir Gavin Anthony, Kt.

Lighton, Sir Thomas Hamilton, Bt. (I. 1791)

Likierman, *Prof.* Sir John Andrew, Kt.

Lilleyman, *Prof.* Sir John Stuart, Kt.

Lindblom, *Hon.* Sir Keith John, Kt.

†Lindsay, Sir James Martin Evelyn, Bt. (1962)

Lindsay, *Hon.* Sir John Edmund Frederic, Kt.

†Lindsay-Hogg, Sir Michael Edward, Bt. (1905)

Lipton, Sir Stuart Anthony, Kt.

Lipworth, Sir (Maurice) Sydney, Kt.

Lister-Kaye, Sir John Phillip Lister, Bt. (1812)

Lithgow, Sir William James, Bt. (1925)

Llewellyn, Sir Roderic Victor, Bt. (1922)

Llewellyn-Smith, *Prof.* Sir Christopher Hubert, Kt.

Lloyd, *Prof.* Sir Geoffrey Ernest Richard, Kt., FBA

Lloyd, Sir Nicholas Markley, Kt.

Lloyd, *Rt. Hon.* Sir Peter Robert Cable, Kt.

Lloyd, Sir Richard Ernest Butler, Bt. (1960)

Lloyd, *Rt. Hon.* Sir Timothy Andrew Wigram, Kt.

Lloyd-Edwards, *Capt.* Sir Norman, KCVO, RD

Lloyd Jones, *Rt. Hon.* Sir David, Kt.

Loader, Air Marshal Sir Clive Robert, KCB, OBE

Lobban, Sir Iain Robert, KCMG, CB

Lockett, Sir Michael Vernon, KCVO

Lockhead, Sir Moir, Kt., OBE

Loder, Sir Edmund Jeune, Bt. (1887)

Logan, Sir David Brian Carleton, KCMG

Longley, *Hon.* Sir Hartman Godfrey, Kt.

Longmore, *Rt. Hon.* Sir Andrew Centlivres, Kt.

Lorimer, Sir (Thomas) Desmond, Kt.

Los, *Hon.* Sir Kubulan, Kt., CBE

Loughran, Sir Gerald Finbar, KCB

Lourdenadin, Sir Ninian Mogan, KCMG, KBE

Lovill, Sir John Roger, Kt., CBE

Lowa, *Rt. Revd* Sir Samson, KBE

Lowe, *Air Chief Marshal* Sir Douglas Charles, GCB, DFC, AFC

Lowe, Sir Frank Budge, Kt.

Lowe, Sir Philip Martin, KCMG

Lowe, Sir Thomas William Gordon, Bt. (1918)

Lowson, Sir Ian Patrick, Bt. (1951)

Lowther, *Col.* Sir Charles Douglas, Bt. (1824)

Loyd, Sir Julian St John, KCVO

Lu, Sir Tseng Chi, Kt.

Lucas, *Prof.* Sir Colin Renshaw, Kt.

Lucas, Sir Thomas Edward, Bt. (1887)

Lucas-Tooth, Sir (Hugh) John, Bt. (1920)

Luff, Sir Peter James, Kt.

Lumsden, Sir David James, Kt.

Lushington, Sir John Richard Castleman, Bt. (1791)

Lyall Grant, Sir Mark Justin, KCMG

Lyle, Sir Gavin Archibald, Bt. (1929)

Lynch-Blosse, *Capt.* Sir Richard Hely, Bt. (I. 1622)

Lynch-Robinson, Sir Dominick Christopher, Bt. (1920)

Lyne, *Rt. Hon.* Sir Roderic Michael John, KBE, CMG

Lyons, Sir John, Kt.

Lyons, Sir Michael Thomas, Kt.

McAllister, Sir Ian Gerald, Kt., CBE

McAlpine, Sir William Hepburn, Bt. (1918)

McCaffrey, Sir Thomas Daniel, Kt.

McCamley, Sir Graham Edward, KBE

McCarthy, Sir Callum, Kt.

McCartney, *Rt. Hon.* Sir Ian, Kt.

McCartney, Sir (James) Paul, Kt., MBE

Macartney, Sir John Ralph, Bt. (I. 1799)

McClement, *Vice-Admiral* Sir Timothy Pentreath, KCB, OBE

McClintock, Sir Eric Paul, Kt.

McCloskey, *Hon.* Sir John Bernard, Kt.

McColl, Sir Colin Hugh Verel, KCMG

McColl, *Gen.* Sir John Chalmers, KCB, CBE, DSO

McCollum, *Rt. Hon.* Sir William, Kt.

McCombe, *Rt. Hon.* Sir Richard George Bramwell, Kt.

McConnell, Sir Robert Shean, Bt. (1900)

†McCowan, Sir David William, Bt. (1934)

MacCulloch, *Prof.* Sir Diarmaid Ninian John, Kt.

McCulloch, *Rt. Revd* Nigel Simeon, KCVO

McCullough, *Hon.* Sir (Iain) Charles (Robert), Kt.

MacDermott, *Rt. Hon.* Sir John Clarke, Kt.

Macdonald, Sir Alasdair Uist, Kt., CBE

MacDonald, *Hon.* Sir Alistair William, Kt., QC

McDonald of Sleat, Sir Ian Godfrey Bosville, Bt. (S. 1625)

McDonald, *Prof.* Sir James, Kt.

Macdonald, Sir Kenneth Carmichael, KCB

McDonald, Sir Simon Gerard, KCMG, KCVO

McDonald, Sir Trevor, Kt., OBE

McDowell, Sir Eric Wallace, Kt., CBE

MacDuff, *Hon.* Sir Alistair Geoffrey, Kt.

Mace, *Lt.-Gen.* Sir John Airth, KBE, CB

McEwen, Sir John Roderick Hugh, Bt. (1953)

MacFadyen *Air Marshal* Sir Ian David, KCVO, CB, OBE

McFarland, Sir John Talbot, Bt. (1914)

MacFarlane, *Prof.* Sir Alistair George James, Kt., CBE, FRS

McFarlane, *Rt. Hon.* Sir Andrew Ewart, Kt.

Macfarlane, Sir (David) Neil, Kt.

McGeechan, Sir Ian Robert, Kt., OBE

McGrath, Sir Brian Henry, GCVO

Macgregor, Sir Ian Grant, Bt. (1828)

MacGregor of MacGregor, Sir Malcolm Gregor Charles, Bt. (1795)

McGrigor, Sir James Angus Rhoderick Neil, Bt. (1831)

McIntosh, Sir Neil William David, Kt., CBE

McIntosh, Sir Ronald Robert Duncan, KCB

McIntyre, Sir Donald Conroy, Kt., CBE

McIntyre, Sir Meredith Alister, Kt.

Mackay, *Hon.* Sir Colin Crichton, Kt.

MacKay, *Prof.* Sir Donald Iain, Kt.

MacKay, Sir Francis Henry, Kt.

McKay, Sir Neil Stuart, Kt., CB

McKay, Sir William Robert, KCB

Mackay-Dick, *Maj.-Gen.* Sir Iain Charles, KCVO, MBE

Mackechnie, Sir Alistair John, Kt.

McKellen, Sir Ian Murray, Kt., CH, CBE

Mackenzie, Sir (James William) Guy, Bt. (1890)

Mackenzie, *Gen.* Sir Jeremy John George, GCB, OBE

†Mackenzie, Sir Peter Douglas, Bt. (S. 1673)

†Mackenzie, Sir Roderick McQuhae, Bt. (S. 1703)

Mackeson, Sir Rupert Henry, Bt. (1954)

McKillop, Sir Thomas Fulton Wilson, Kt.

McKinnon, *Rt. Hon.* Sir Donald Charles, GCVO

McKinnon, Sir James, Kt.

McKinnon, *Hon.* Sir Stuart Neil, Kt.

Mackintosh, Sir Cameron Anthony, Kt.

Mackworth, Sir Digby (John), Bt. (1776)

McLaughlin, Sir Richard, Kt.

Maclean of Dunconnell, Sir Charles Edward, Bt. (1957)

Maclean, *Hon.* Sir Lachlan Hector Charles, Bt., CVO (NS 1631)

Maclean, Sir Murdo, Kt.

†McLeod, Sir James Roderick Charles, Bt. (1925)

MacLeod, Sir (John) Maxwell Norman, Bt. (1924)

Macleod, Sir (Nathaniel William) Hamish, KBE

McLintock, Sir Michael William, Bt. (1934)

McLoughlin, Sir Francis, Kt., CBE

Maclure, Sir John Robert Spencer, Bt. (1898)

McMahon, Sir Brian Patrick, Bt. (1817)

McMahon, Sir Christopher William, Kt.

McMaster, Sir Brian John, Kt., CBE

McMichael, *Prof.* Sir Andrew James, Kt., FRS

MacMillan *Very Rvd.* Gilleasbuig Iain, KCVO

McMillan, Sir Iain Macleod, Kt., CBE

Macmillan, *Dr* Sir James Loy, Kt., CBE

MacMillan, *Lt.-Gen.* Sir John Richard Alexander, KCB, CBE

McMullin, *Rt. Hon.* Sir Duncan Wallace, Kt.

McMurtry, Sir David, Kt., CBE

Macnaghten, Sir Malcolm Francis, Bt. (1836)

McNair-Wilson, Sir Patrick Michael Ernest David, Kt.

Macnaughton, *Prof.* Sir Malcolm Campbell, Kt.

McNee, Sir David Blackstock, Kt., QPM

McNulty, Sir (Robert William) Roy, Kt., CBE

MacPhail, Sir Bruce Dugald, Kt.

Macpherson, Sir Nicholas Ian, GCB

Macpherson of Cluny, *Hon.* Sir William Alan, Kt., TD

McQuarrie, Sir Albert, Kt.

MacRae, Sir (Alastair) Christopher (Donald Summerhayes), KCMG

Macready, Sir Charles Nevil, Bt. (1923)

MacSween, *Prof.* Sir Roderick Norman McIver, Kt.

Mactaggart, Sir John Auld, Bt. (1938)

McVicar, Sir David, Kt.

McWilliam, Sir Michael Douglas, KCMG

McWilliams, Sir Francis, GBE

Madden, Sir Charles Jonathan, Bt. (1919)

Madden, Sir David Christopher Andrew, KCMG

Maddison, *Hon.* Sir David George, Kt.

Madejski, Sir John Robert, Kt., OBE

Madel, Sir (William) David, Kt.

Magee, Sir Ian Bernard Vaughan, Kt., CB

Magnus, Sir Laurence Henry Philip, Bt. (1917)

Maguire, *Hon.* Sir Paul Richard, Kt.

Mahon, Sir William Walter, Bt. (1819), LVO

Maiden, Sir Colin James, Kt., DPHIL

Maini, *Prof.* Sir Ravinder Nath, Kt.

Maino, Sir Charles, KBE

†Maitland, Sir Charles Alexander, Bt. (1818)

Major, *Rt. Hon.* Sir John, KG, CH

Malbon, *Vice-Adm.* Sir Fabian Michael, KBE

Malcolm, Sir Alexander James Elton, Bt. (S. 1665), OBE

Malcolm, *Dr* Noel Robert, Kt., FBA

Males, *Hon.* Sir Stephen Martin, Kt.

Malet, Sir Harry Douglas St Lo, Bt. (1791)

Mallaby, Sir Christopher Leslie George, GCMG, GCVO

Mallick, *Prof.* Sir Netar Prakash, Kt.

Mallinson, Sir William James, Bt. (1935)

Malpas, Sir Robert, Kt., CBE

Mancham, Sir James Richard Marie, KBE

Mander, Sir (Charles) Nicholas, Bt. (1911)

Manduell, Sir John, Kt., CBE

Mann, *Hon.* Sir George Anthony, Kt.

Mann, Sir Rupert Edward, Bt. (1905)

Manning, Sir David Geoffrey, GCMG, KCVO

Mano, Sir Koitaga, Kt., MBE

Mans, *Lt-Gen.* Sir Mark Francis Noel, KCB, CBE

Mansel, Sir Philip, Bt. (1622)

Mansfield, *Prof.* Sir Peter, Kt.

Manuella, Sir Tulaga, GCMG, MBE

Mara, Sir Nambuga, KBE

Margetson, Sir John William Denys, KCMG

Margetts, Sir Robert John, Kt., CBE

Markesinis, *Prof.* Sir Basil Spyridonos, Kt. QC

Markham, *Prof.* Sir Alexander Fred, Kt.

Markham, Sir (Arthur) David, Bt. (1911)

Marling, Sir Charles William Somerset, Bt. (1882)

Marmot, Prof. Sir Michael Gideon, Kt.

Marr, Sir Leslie Lynn, Bt. (1919)

Marriner, Sir Neville, Kt., CBE, CH

†Marsden, Sir Tadgh Orlando Denton, Bt. (1924)

Marsh, *Prof.* Sir John Stanley, Kt., CBE

Marshall, Sir Michael John, Kt., CBE

Marshall, *Prof.* Sir (Oshley) Roy, Kt., CBE

Marshall, Sir Peter Harold Reginald, KCMG

Marshall, *Prof. Emeritus* Sir Woodville Kemble, Kt.

Martin, Sir Clive Haydon, Kt., OBE

Martin, Sir George Henry, Kt., CBE

Martin, Sir Gregory Michael Gerard, Kt.

Martin, *Prof.* Sir Laurence Woodward, Kt.

Martin, Sir (Robert) Bruce, Kt., QC

Marychurch, Sir Peter Harvey, KCMG

Masefield, Sir Charles Beech Gordon, Kt.

Mason, *Hon.* Sir Anthony Frank, KBE

Mason, *Prof.* Sir David Kean, Kt., CBE

Mason, Sir Peter James, KBE

Mason, *Prof.* Sir Ronald, KCB, FRS

Massey, *Vice-Adm.* Sir Alan, KCB, CBE, ADC

Massie, Sir Herbert William, Kt., CBE

Matane, HE Sir Paulias Nguna, GCMG, OBE

Matheson of Matheson, Sir Fergus John, Bt. (1882)

Mathews, *Vice-Adm.* Sir Andrew David Hugh, KCB

Mathewson, Sir George Ross, Kt., CBE, PHD, FRSE

Matthews, Sir Terence Hedley, Kt., OBE

Maughan, Sir Deryck, Kt.

Mawer, Sir Philip John Courtney, Kt.

Maxwell, Sir Michael Eustace George, Bt. (S. 1681)

Maxwell Davies, Sir Peter, Kt., CH, CBE

Maxwell Macdonald (formerly Stirling-Maxwell), Sir John Ronald, Bt. (NS 1682)

Maxwell-Scott, Sir Dominic James, Bt. (1642)

May, *Rt. Hon.* Sir Anthony Tristram Kenneth, Kt.

Mayall, *Lt-Gen.* Sir Simon Vincent, KBE, CB

Mayfield, Sir Andrew Charles, Kt.

Meadow, *Prof.* Sir (Samuel) Roy, Kt., FRCP, FRCPE

Meale, Sir Joseph Alan, Kt.

Medlycott, Sir Mervyn Tregonwell, Bt. (1808)

Meeran, *His Hon.* Sir Goolam Hoosen Kader, Kt.

Meldrum, Sir Graham, Kt., CBE, QFSM

Melhuish, Sir Michael Ramsay, KBE, CMG

Mellars, *Prof.* Sir Paul Anthony, Kt., FBA

Mellon, Sir James, KCMG

Melmoth, Sir Graham John, Kt.

Melville, *Prof.* Sir David, Kt., CBE

Merifield, Sir Anthony James, KCVO, CB

Metcalf, *Prof.* Sir David Harry, Kt., CBE

†Meyer, Sir (Anthony) Ashley Frank, Bt. (1910)

Meyer, Sir Christopher John Rome, KCMG

†Meyrick, Sir Timothy Thomas Charlton, Bt. (1880)

Miakwe, *Hon.* Sir Akepa, KBE

Michael, Sir Duncan, Kt.

Michael, *Dr* Sir Jonathan, Kt.

Michael, Sir Peter Colin, Kt., CBE

Michels, Sir David Michael Charles, Kt.

Middleton, Sir John Maxwell, Kt.

Middleton, Sir Peter Edward, GCB

Miers, Sir (Henry) David Alastair Capel, KBE, CMG

Milbank, Sir Anthony Frederick, Bt. (1882)

Milborne-Swinnerton-Pilkington, Sir Thomas Henry, Bt. (S. 1635)

Milburn, Sir Anthony Rupert, Bt. (1905)

†Miles, Sir Philip John, Bt. (1859)

Millais, Sir Geoffrey Richard Everett, Bt. (1885)

Millar, *Prof.* Sir Fergus Graham Burtholme, Kt.

Miller, Sir Albert Joel, KCMG, LVO, MBE, QPM, CPM

Miller, Sir Donald John, Kt., FRSE, FRENG

Miller, *Air Marshal* Sir Graham Anthony, KBE

Miller, Sir Anthony Thomas, Bt. (1705)

Miller, Sir Jonathan Wolfe, Kt., CBE

Miller, Sir Peter North, Kt.

Miller, Sir Robin Robert William, Kt.

Miller, Sir Ronald Andrew Baird, Kt., CBE

Miller of Glenlee, Sir Stephen William Macdonald, Bt. (1788)

Mills, Sir Ian, Kt.

Mills, Sir Jonathan Edward Harland (John), Kt., FRSE

Mills, Sir Keith Edward, GBE

Mills, Sir Peter Frederick Leighton, Bt. (1921)

Milman, Sir David Patrick, Bt. (1800)

Milne, Sir John Drummond, Kt.

Milne-Watson, Sir Andrew Michael, Bt. (1937)

Milner, Sir Timothy William Lycett, Bt. (1717)

Mirrlees, *Prof.* Sir James Alexander, Kt., FBA

Mitchell, *Rt. Hon.* Sir James FitzAllen, KCMG

Mitchell, *Very Revd* Patrick Reynolds, KCVO

Mitchell, *Hon.* Sir Stephen George, Kt.

Mitting, *Hon.* Sir John Edward, Kt.

Moate, Sir Roger Denis, Kt.

Moberly, Sir Patrick Hamilton, KCMG

Moffat, Sir Brian Scott, Kt., OBE

Moir, Sir Christopher Ernest, Bt. (1916)

Molesworth-St Aubyn, Sir William, Bt. (1689)

†Molony, Sir Peter John, Bt. (1925)

Moncada, *Prof.* Sir Salvador, Kt.

Montagu, Sir Nicholas Lionel John, KCB

Montagu-Pollock, Sir Giles Hampden, Bt. (1872)

Montague, Sir Adrian Alastair, Kt., CBE

Montgomery, Sir (Basil Henry) David, Bt. (1801), CVO

Montgomery, *Vice-Adm.* Sir Charles Percival Ross, KBE, ADC

Montgomery-Cuninghame, Sir John Christopher Foggo, Bt. (NS 1672)

Moody-Stuart, Sir Mark, KCMG

Moollan, Sir Abdool Hamid Adam, Kt.

†Moon, Sir Roger, Bt. (1887)

Moor, *Hon.* Sir Philip Drury, Kt.

Moorcroft, Sir William, KBE

Moore, *Most Revd* Desmond Charles, KBE

Moore, Sir Francis Thomas, Kt.

Moore, Sir John Michael, KCVO, CB, DSC

Moore, *Vice Adm.* Sir Michael Antony Claës, KBE, LVO

Moore, *Prof.* Sir Norman Winfrid, Bt. (1919)

Moore, Sir Roger George, KBE

Moore, Sir William Roger Clotworthy, Bt. (1932), TD

Moore-Bick, *Rt. Hon.* Sir Martin James, Kt.

Moores, Sir Peter, Kt., CBE

Morauta, Sir Mekere, KCMG

Mordaunt, Sir Richard Nigel Charles, Bt. (1611)

Morgan, *Vice-Adm.* Sir Charles Christopher, KBE

Morgan, *Rt. Hon.* Sir (Charles) Declan, Kt.

Morgan, Sir Graham, Kt.

Morgan, *Hon.* Sir Paul Hyacinth, Kt.

Morison, *Hon.* Sir Thomas Richard Atkin, Kt.

Moritz, Sir Michael Jonathan, KBE

Morland, *Hon.* Sir Michael, Kt.

Morland, Sir Robert Kenelm, Kt.

†Morris, Sir Allan Lindsay, Bt. (1806)

Morris, Sir Andrew Valentine, Kt., OBE

Morris, *Air Marshal* Sir Arnold Alec, KBE, CB

Morris, Sir Derek James, Kt.

Morris, Sir Keith Elliot Hedley, KBE, CMG

Morris, *Prof.* Sir Peter John, Kt.

Morris, Sir Trefor Alfred, Kt., CBE, QPM

Morrison, Sir (Alexander) Fraser, Kt., CBE

Morrison, Sir George Ivan, Kt., OBE

Morrison, Sir Kenneth Duncan, Kt., CBE

Morrison-Bell, Sir William Hollin Dayrell, Bt. (1905)

Morrison-Low, Sir Richard Walter, Bt. (1908)

Morritt, *Rt. Hon.* Sir (Robert) Andrew, Kt., CVO

Morse, Sir Amyas Charles Edward, KCB

Morse, Sir Christopher Jeremy, KCMG

Moses, *Rt. Hon.* Sir Alan George, Kt.

Moses, *Very Revd* Dr John Henry, KCVO

Moss, Sir David Joseph, KCVO, CMG

Moss, Sir Stephen Alan, Kt.

Moss, Sir Stirling Craufurd, Kt., OBE

Mostyn, *Hon.* Sir Nicholas Anthony Joseph Ghislain, Kt.

Mostyn, Sir William Basil John, Bt. (1670)

Motion, Sir Andrew, Kt.

†Mott, Sir David Hugh, Bt. (1930)

Mottram, Sir Richard Clive, GCB

†Mount, Sir (William Robert) Ferdinand, Bt. (1921)

Mountain, Sir Edward Brian Stanford, Bt. (1922)

Mowbray, Sir John Robert, Bt. (1880)

Moylan, *Hon.* Sir Andrew John Gregory, Kt.

Moynihan, *Dr* Sir Daniel, Kt.

†Muir, Sir Richard James Kay, Bt. (1892)

Muir-Mackenzie, Sir Alexander Alwyne Henry Charles Brinton, Bt. (1805)

Mulcahy, Sir Geoffrey John, Kt.

Mummery, *Rt. Hon.* Sir John Frank, Kt.

Munby, *Rt. Hon.* Sir James Lawrence, Kt.

Munro, Sir Alan Gordon, KCMG

†Munro, Sir Ian Kenneth, Bt. (S. 1634)

Munro, Sir Keith Gordon Ian, Bt. (1825)

Muria, *Hon.* Sir Gilbert John Baptist, Kt.

Murphy, Sir Jonathan Michael, Kt., QPM

Murray, Sir David Edward, Kt.

Murray, *Rt. Hon.* Sir Donald Bruce, Kt.

Murray, Sir Nigel Andrew Digby, Bt. (S. 1628)

Murray, Sir Patrick Ian Keith, Bt. (S. 1673)

Murray, Sir Robert Sydney, Kt., CBE

Murray, Sir Robin MacGregor, Kt.

†Murray, Sir Rowland William, Bt. (S. 1630)

Musgrave, Sir Christopher John Shane, Bt. (I. 1782)

Musgrave, Sir Christopher Patrick Charles, Bt. (1611)

Myers, Sir Derek John, Kt.

Myers, *Prof.* Sir Rupert Horace, KBE

Mynors, Sir Richard Baskerville, Bt. (1964)

Naipaul, Sir Vidiadhar Surajprasad, Kt.

Nairn, Sir Michael, Bt. (1904)

Naish, Sir (Charles) David, Kt.

Nalau, Sir Jerry Kasip, KBE

Nall, Sir Edward William Joseph Bt. (1954)

Namaliu, *Rt. Hon.* Sir Rabbie Langanai, KCMG

Napier, Sir Charles Joseph, Bt. (1867)

Napier, Sir John Archibald Lennox, Bt. (S. 1627)

Narey, Sir Martin James, Kt.

Naylor, Sir Robert, Kt.

Naylor-Leyland, Sir Philip Vyvyan, Bt. (1895)

Neal, Sir Eric James, Kt., CVO

Neale, Sir Gerrard Anthony, Kt.

Neave, Sir Paul Arundell, Bt. (1795)

Neill, *Rt. Hon.* Sir Brian Thomas, Kt.

Neill, Sir (James) Hugh, KCVO, CBE, TD

†Nelson, Sir Jamie Charles Vernon Hope, Bt. (1912)

Nelson, *Hon.* Sir Robert Franklyn, Kt.

New, *Maj.-Gen.* Sir Laurence Anthony Wallis, Kt., CB, CBE

Newbigging, Sir David Kennedy, Kt., OBE

Newby, *Prof.* Sir Howard Joseph, Kt., CBE

Newey, *Hon.* Sir Guy Richard, Kt.

Newington, Sir Michael John, KCMG

Newman, Sir Francis Hugh Cecil, Bt. (1912)

Newman, Sir Geoffrey Robert, Bt. (1836)

Newman, *Hon.* Sir George Michael, Kt.

Newman, Sir Kenneth Leslie, GBE, QPM

Newman, *Vice-Adm.* Sir Roy Thomas, KCB

Newman Taylor, *Prof.* Sir Anthony John, Kt., CBE

Newsam, Sir Peter Anthony, Kt.

Newson-Smith, Sir Peter Frank Graham, Bt. (1944)

Newton, *Revd* George Peter Howgill, Bt. (1900)

Newton, Sir John Garnar, Bt. (1924)

Newton, *Lt-Gen.* Sir Paul Raymond, KBE

Newton, *Hon.* Sir Roderick Brian, Kt.

Nice, Sir Geoffrey, Kt., QC

Nickell, *Prof.* Sir Stephen John, Kt., CBE, FBA

Nicol, *Hon.* Sir Andrew George Lindsay, Kt.

Nichol, Sir Duncan Kirkbride, Kt., CBE

Nicholas, Sir David, Kt., CBE

Nicholas, Sir John William, KCVO, CMG

Nicholls, Sir Nigel Hamilton, KCVO, CBE

Nichols, Sir Richard Everard, Kt.

Nicholson, Sir Bryan Hubert, GBE, Kt.

Nicholson, Sir Charles Christian, Bt. (1912)

Nicholson, Sir David, KCB, CBE

Nicholson, *Rt. Hon.* Sir Michael, Kt.

Nicholson, Sir Paul Douglas, KCVO, Kt.

Nicholson, Sir Robin Buchanan, Kt., PHD, FRS, FRENG

Nicoll, Sir William, KCMG

Nightingale, Sir Charles Manners Gamaliel, Bt. (1628)

Nixon, Sir Simon Michael Christopher, Bt. (1906)

Noble, Sir David Brunel, Bt. (1902)

Noble, Sir Timothy Peter, Bt. (1923)

Nombri, Sir Joseph Karl, Kt., ISO, BEM

Norman, Sir Nigel James, Bt. (1915)

Norman, Sir Ronald, Kt., OBE

Norman, Sir Torquil Patrick Alexander, Kt., CBE

Normington, Sir David John, GCB

Norrington, Sir Roger Arthur Carver, Kt., CBE

Norris, *Hon.* Sir Alastair Hubert, Kt.

Norriss, *Air Marshal* Sir Peter Coulson, KBE, CB, AFC

North, *Air Marshal.* Sir Barry Mark, KCB, OBE

North, Sir Peter Machin, Kt., CBE, QC, DCL, FBA

North, Sir Thomas Lindsay, Kt.

North, Sir (William) Jonathan (Frederick), Bt. (1920)

Norton, Barry, Kt.

Norton, *Maj.-Gen.* Sir George Pemberton Ross, KCVO, CBE

Norton-Griffiths, Sir John, Bt. (1922)

Nossal, Sir Gustav Joseph Victor, Kt., CBE

Nott, *Rt. Hon.* Sir John William Frederic, KCB

Nourse, *Rt. Hon.* Sir Martin Charles, Kt.

Novoselov, *Prof.* Sir Konstantin, Kt.

Nugee, *Hon.* Sir Chrisstopher George, Kt.

†Nugent, Sir Christopher George Ridley, Bt. (1806)

Nugent, Sir Nicholas Myles John, Bt. (I. 1795)

Nugent, Sir (Walter) Richard Middleton, Bt. (1831)

Nunn, Sir Trevor Robert, Kt., CBE

Nunneley, Sir Charles Kenneth Roylance, Kt.

Nursaw, Sir James, KCB, QC

Nurse, Sir Paul Maxime, Kt.

Nuttall, Sir Harry, Bt. (1922)

Nutting, Sir John Grenfell, Bt. (1903), QC

Oakeley, Sir John Digby Atholl, Bt. (1790)

Oakes, Sir Christopher, Bt. (1939)

Oakshott, Sir Thomas Hendrie, Bt. (1959)

O'Brien, Sir Robert Stephen, Kt., CBE

O'Brien, Sir Timothy John, Bt. (1849)

O'Brien, Sir William, Kt.

O'Brien, *Adm.* Sir William Donough, KCB, DSC

O'Connell, Sir Bernard, Kt.

O'Connell, Sir Maurice James Donagh MacCarthy, Bt. (1869)

O'Connor, Sir Denis Francis, Kt., CBE, QPM

Odell, Sir Stanley John, Kt.

Odgers, Sir Graeme David William, Kt.

O'Donnell, Sir Christopher John, Kt.

O'Donoghue, *Lt.-Gen.* Sir Kevin, KCB, CBE

O'Dowd, Sir David Joseph, Kt., CBE, QPM

Ogden, *Dr* Sir Peter James, Kt.

Ogden, Sir Robert, Kt., CBE

Ogilvy, Sir Francis Gilbert Arthur, Bt. (S. 1626)

Ogilvy-Wedderburn, Sir Andrew John Alexander, Bt. (1803)

Ogio, *HE* Sir Michael, GCMG, CBE

Ognall, *Hon.* Sir Harry Henry, Kt.

Ohlson, Sir Brian Eric Christopher, Bt. (1920)

Oldham, *Dr* Sir John, Kt., OBE

Oliver, Sir James Michael Yorrick, Kt.

Oliver, Sir Stephen John Lindsay, Kt., QC

O'Hara *Hon.* Sir John Ailbe

†O'Loghlen, Sir Michael, Bt. (1838)

Olver, Sir Richard Lake, Kt.

Omand, Sir David Bruce, GCB

Ondaatje, Sir Christopher, Kt., CBE

O'Nions, Prof. Sir Robert Keith, Kt., FRS, PHD

Onslow, Sir Richard Paul Atherton, Bt. (1797)

Oppenheimer, Sir Michael Bernard Grenville, Bt. (1921)

Oppenshaw, Sir Charles Peter Lawford, Kt., QC

O'Rahilly, *Prof.* Sir Stephen Patrick, Kt., FRS

Orde, Sir Hugh Stephen Roden, Kt., OBE, QPM

O'Regan, *Dr* Sir Stephen Gerard (Tipene), Kt.

O'Reilly, Sir Anthony John Francis, Kt.

O'Reilly, *Prof.* Sir John James, Kt.

Orr, Sir John, Kt., OBE

Orr-Ewing, Sir (Alistair) Simon, Bt. (1963)

Orr-Ewing, Sir Archibald Donald, Bt. (1886)

Osborn, Sir John Holbrook, Kt.

Osborn, Sir Richard Henry Danvers, Bt. (1662)

Osborne, Sir Peter George, Bt. (I. 1629)

O'Shea, *Prof.* Sir Timothy Michael Martin, Kt.

Osmotherly, Sir Edward Benjamin Crofton, Kt., CB

Oswald, Sir (William Richard) Michael, KCVO

Ottaway *Rt. Hon.* Sir Richard Geoffrey James, Kt.

Otton, Sir Geoffrey John, KCB

Otton, *Rt. Hon.* Sir Philip Howard, Kt.

Oulton, Sir Antony Derek Maxwell, GCB, QC

Ouseley, *Hon.* Sir Brian Walter, Kt.

Outram, Sir Alan James, Bt. (1858)

Owen, Sir Geoffrey, Kt.

Owen, *Prof.* Sir Michaael John, Kt.

Owen, *Hon.* Sir Robert Michael, Kt.

Owen-Jones, Sir Lindsay Harwood, KBE

Packer, Sir Richard John, KCB

Paget, Sir Julian Tolver, Bt. (1871), CVO

Paget, Sir Richard Herbert, Bt. (1886)

Paice, *Rt. Hon.* Sir James Edward Thornton, Kt.

Paine, Sir Christopher Hammon, Kt., FRCP, FRCR

Pakenham, *Hon.* Sir Michael Aiden, KBE, CMG

Palin, *Air Chief Marshal* Sir Roger Hewlett, KCB, OBE

Palmer, Sir Albert Rocky, Kt.

Palmer, Sir (Charles) Mark, Bt. (1886)

Palmer, Sir Geoffrey Christopher John, Bt. (1660)

Palmer, *Rt. Hon.* Sir Geoffrey Winston Russell, KCMG

Palmer, *Prof.* Sir Godfrey Henry Oliver, Kt., OBE

Palmer, Sir John Edward Somerset, Bt. (1791)

Palmer, *Maj.-Gen.* Sir (Joseph) Michael, KCVO

Palmer, Sir Reginald Oswald, GCMG, MBE

Paniguian, Sir Richard Leon, Kt., CBE

Panter, Sir Howard Hugh, Kt.

Pappano, Sir Antonio, Kt.

Parbo, Sir Arvi Hillar, Kt.

Park, *Hon.* Sir Andrew Edward Wilson, Kt.

Parker, Sir Alan, Kt.

Parker, Sir Alan William, Kt., CBE

Parker, *Rt. Hon.* Sir Jonathan Frederic, Kt.

Parker, *Hon.* Sir Kenneth Blades, Kt.

Parker, *Maj.* Sir Michael John, KCVO, CBE

Parker, *Gen.* Sir Nicholas Ralph, KCB, CBE

Parker, Sir Richard (William) Hyde, Bt. (1681)

Parker, Sir (Thomas) John, GBE

Parker, Sir William Peter Brian, Bt. (1844)

Parkes, Sir Edward Walter, Kt., FRENG

Parkinson, Sir Michael, Kt., CBE

Parry, *Prof.* Sir Eldryd Hugh Owen, KCMG, OBE

Parry, Sir Emyr Jones, GCMG

Parry-Evans, *Air Chief Marshal* Sir David, GCB, CBE

Parsons, Sir John Christopher, KCVO

Parsons, Sir Richard Edmund (Clement Fownes), KCMG

Partridge, Sir Michael John Anthony, KCB

Partridge, Sir Nicholas Wyndham, Kt., OBE

Pascoe, *Gen.* Sir Robert Alan, KCB, MBE

Pasley, Sir Robert Killigrew Sabine, Bt. (1794)

Paston-Bedingfeld, Sir Henry Edgar, Bt. (1661)

Paterson, Sir Dennis Craig, Kt.

Patey, Sir William Charters, KCMG

Patten, *Rt. Hon.* Sir Nicholas John, Kt.

Pattie, *Rt. Hon.* Sir Geoffrey Edwin, Kt.

Pattison, *Prof.* Sir John Ridley, Kt., DM, FRCPATH

Pattullo, Sir (David) Bruce, Kt., CBE

Pauncefort-Duncombe, Sir David Philip Henry, Bt. (1859)

Payne, *Prof.* Sir David Neil, Kt., CBE, FRS

Peace, Sir John Wilfrid, Kt.

Peach, Sir Leonard Harry, Kt.

Peach, *Air Chief Marshal* Sir Stuart William, KCB, CBE

Pearce, Sir (Daniel Norton) Idris, Kt., CBE, TD

Pearse, Sir Brian Gerald, Kt.

Pearson, Sir Francis Nicholas Fraser, Bt. (1964)

Pearson, Sir Keith, Kt.

Pearson, *Gen.* Sir Thomas Cecil Hook, KCB, CBE, DSO

Peart, *Prof.* Sir William Stanley, Kt., MD, FRS

Pease, Sir Joseph Gurney, Bt. (1882)

Pease, Sir Richard Thorn, Bt. (1920)

Peat, Sir Gerrard Charles, KCVO

Peat, Sir Michael Charles Gerrard, GCVO

Peckham, *Prof.* Sir Michael John, Kt.,

Peek, Sir Richard Grenville, Bt. (1874)

Pelgen, Sir Harry Friedrich, Kt., MBE

Pelham, *Dr* Sir Hugh Reginald Brentnall, Kt., FRS

Pelly, Sir Richard John, Bt. (1840)

Pendry, *Prof.* Sir John Brian, Kt., FRS

Penny, *Dr* Nicholas Beaver, Kt., FBA

Penrose, *Prof.* Sir Roger, Kt., OM, FRS

Penry-Davey, *Hon.* Sir David Herbert, Kt.

Pepper, *Dr.* Sir David Edwin, KCMG

Pepper, *Prof.* Sir Michael, Kt.

Pepys, *Prof.* Sir Mark Brian, Kt.

Perowne, *Vice-Adm.* Sir James Francis, KBE

Perring, Sir John Raymond, Bt. (1963)

Perris, Sir David (Arthur), Kt., MBE

Perry, Sir David Howard, KCB

Perry, Sir Michael Sydney, GBE

Pervez, Sir Mohammed Anwar, Kt., OBE

Peters, *Prof.* Sir David Keith, Kt., FRCP

Pethica, *Prof.* Sir John Bernard, Kt., FRS

Petit, Sir Dinshaw Manockjee, Bt. (1890)

Peto, Sir Francis Michael Morton, Bt. (1855)

Peto, Sir Henry Christopher Morton Bampfylde, Bt. (1927)

Peto, *Prof.* Sir Richard, Kt., FRS

Petrie, Sir Peter Charles, Bt. (1918), CMG

Pettigrew, Sir Russell Hilton, Kt.

†Philipson-Stow, Sir (Robert) Matthew. Bt. (1907)

Phillips, Sir (Gerald) Hayden, GCB

Phillips, Sir John David, Kt., QPM

Phillips, Sir Jonathan, KCB

Phillips, Sir Peter John, Kt., OBE

Phillips, Sir Robin Francis, Bt. (1912)

Phillips *Hon.* Sir Stephen Edmund, Kt.

Phillips, Sir Tom Richard Vaughan, KCMG

Pickard, Sir (John) Michael, Kt.

Picken, *Hon.* Sir Simon Derek, Kt., QC

Pickles, *Rt. Hon.* Sir Eric Jack, Kt.

Pickthorn, Sir James Francis Mann, Bt. (1959)

Pidgeon, Sir John Allan Stewart, Kt.

†Piers, Sir James Desmond, Bt. (I. 1661)

Piggott-Brown, Sir William Brian, Bt. (1903)

Pigot, Sir George Hugh, Bt. (1764)

Pigott, *Lt.-Gen.* Sir Anthony David, KCB, CBE

Pigott, Sir Berkeley Henry Sebastian, Bt. (1808)

Pike, *Lt.-Gen.* Sir Hew William Royston, KCB, DSO, MBE

Pike, Sir Michael Edmund, KCVO, CMG

Pile, Sir Anthony John Devereux, Bt. (1900)

Pilditch, Sir John Richard, Bt. (1929)

Pill, *Rt. Hon.* Sir Malcolm Thomas, Kt.

Pilling, Sir Joseph Grant, KCB

Pinsent, Sir Matthew Clive, Kt., CBE

†Pinsent, Sir Thomas Benjamin Roy, Kt.

Pirmohamed, *Prof.* Sir Hussein Munir, Kt.

Pissarides, *Prof.* Sir Christopher Antoniou, Kt., FBA

Pitcher, Sir Desmond Henry, Kt.

Pitchers, *Hon.* Sir Christopher (John), Kt.

Pitchford, *Rt. Hon.* Sir Christopher John, Kt.

Pitoi, Sir Sere, Kt., CBE

Pitt, Sir Michael Edward, Kt.

Plastow, Sir David Arnold Stuart, Kt.

Platt, Sir Martin Philip, Bt. (1959)

Pledger, *Air Chief Marshal* Sir Malcolm David, KCB, OBE, AFC

Plender, *Hon.* Sir Richard Owen, Kt.

Plumbly, Sir Derek John, KCMG

Pocock, *Dr* Sir Andrew John, KCMG

Pohai, Sir Timothy, Kt., MBE

Pole, Sir John Chandos, Bt. (1791)

Poliakoff, *Prof.* Sir Martyn, Kt., CBE

Pole, Sir (John) Richard (Walter Reginald) Carew, Bt. (1628)

Polkinghorne, *Revd Canon* John Charlton, KBE

Pollard, Sir Charles, Kt.

†Pollen, Sir Richard John Hungerford, Bt. (1795)

Pollock, Sir George Frederick, Bt. (1866)

Pomeroy, Sir Brian Walter, Kt., CBE

Ponder, *Prof.* Sir Bruce Anthony John, Kt.

Ponsonby, Sir Charles Ashley, Bt. (1956)

Poon, Sir Dickson, Kt., CBE

Poore, Sir Roger Ricardo, Bt. (1795)

Popplewell, *Hon.* Sir Andrew John, Kt.

Popplewell, *Hon.* Sir Oliver Bury, Kt.

†Porritt, *Hon.* Sir Jonathon Espie, Bt. (1963), CBE

Portal, Sir Jonathan Francis, Bt. (1901)

Porter, *Prof.* Sir Keith Macdonald, Kt.

Potter, *Rt. Hon.* Sir Mark Howard, Kt.

Pound, Sir John David, Bt. (1905)

Povey, Sir Keith, Kt., QPM

Powell, Sir John Christopher, Kt.

Powell, Sir Nicholas Folliott Douglas, Bt. (1897)

Power, Sir Alastair John Cecil, Bt. (1924)

Pownall, Sir Michael Graham, KCB

Prance, *Prof.* Sir Ghillean Tolmie, Kt., FRS

Prendergast, Sir (Walter) Kieran, KCVO, CMG

Prescott, Sir Mark, Bt. (1938)

Preston, Sir Philip Charles Henry Hulton, Bt. (1815)

Prevost, Sir Christopher Gerald, Bt. (1805)

Price, Sir Francis Caradoc Rose, Bt. (1815)

Price, Sir Frank Leslie, Kt.

†Prichard-Jones, Sir David John Walter, Bt. (1910)

Priestly, Sir Julian Gordon, KCMG

†Primrose, Sir John Ure, Bt. (1903)

Pringle, *Hon.* Sir John Kenneth, Kt.

†Pringle, Sir Simon Robert, Bt. (S. 1683)

Proby, Sir William Henry, Bt. (1952)

Proctor-Beauchamp, Sir Christopher Radstock, Bt. (1745)

Prosser, Sir David John, Kt.

Prosser, Sir Ian Maurice Gray, Kt.

Pryke, Sir Christopher Dudley, Bt. (1926)

Puapua, *Rt. Hon.* Sir Tomasi, GCMG, KBE

Pulford, *Air Marshal* Sir Andrew Douglas, KCB, CBE

Purves, Sir William, Kt., CBE, DSO

Purvis, *Vice-Adm.* Sir Neville, KCB

Quan, Sir Henry (Francis), KBE

Quilter, Sir Guy Raymond Cuthbert, Bt. (1897)

Radcliffe, Sir Sebastian Everard, Bt. (1813)

Radda, *Prof.* Sir George Karoly, Kt., CBE, FRS

Rae, Sir William, Kt., QPM

Raeburn, Sir Michael Edward Norman, Bt. (1923)

Rake, Sir Michael Derek Vaughan, Kt.

Ralli, Sir David Charles, Bt. (1912)

Ramakrishnan, *Dr* Sir Venkatraman, Kt.

Ramdanee, Sir Mookteswar Baboolall Kailash, Kt.

Ramphal, Sir Shridath Surendranath, GCMG

Ramphul, Sir Baalkhristna, Kt.

Ramphul, Sir Indurduth, Kt.

Ramsay, Sir Alexander William Burnett, Bt. (1806)

Ramsay, Sir Allan John (Hepple), KBE, CMG

Ramsay-Fairfax-Lucy, Sir Edmund John William Hugh, Bt. (1836)

Ramsden, Sir David Edward John, Kt., CBE

Ramsden, Sir John Charles Josslyn, Bt. (1689)

Ramsey, *Dr* Sir Frank Cuthbert, KCMG

Ramsey, *Hon.* Sir Vivian Arthur, Kt.

Randall, *Rt. Hon.* Sir (Alexander) John, Kt.

Rankin, Sir Ian Niall, Bt. (1898)

Rasch, Sir Simon Anthony Carne, Bt. (1903)

Rashleigh, Sir Richard Harry, Bt. (1831)

Ratcliffe, *Prof.* Sir Peter John, Kt., FRS

Ratford, Sir David John Edward, KCMG, CVO

Rattee, *Hon.* Sir Donald Keith, Kt.

Rattle, Sir Simon Dennis, Kt., OM, CBE

Rawlins, *Hon.* Sir Hugh Anthony, Kt.

Rawlins, *Prof.* Sir Michael David, Kt., FRCP, FRCPED

Rawlinson, Sir Anthony Henry John, Bt. (1891)

Rea, *Prof.* Sir Desmond, Kt., OBE

Read, *Prof.* Sir David John, Kt.

Reardon-Smith, Sir (William) Antony (John), Bt. (1920)

Reddaway, Sir David Norman, KCMG, MBE

Redgrave, Sir Steven Geoffrey, Kt., CBE

Redmayne, Sir Giles Martin, Bt. (1964)

Redmond, Sir Anthony Gerard, Kt.

Redwood, Sir Peter Boverton, Bt. (1911)

Reed, *Prof.* Sir Alec Edward, Kt., CBE

Reedie, Sir Craig Collins, Kt., CBE

Rees, Sir David Allan, Kt., PHD, DSC, FRS

Rees, Sir Richard Ellis Meuric, Kt., CBE

Reffell, *Adm.* Sir Derek Roy, KCB

Reich, Sir Erich Arieh, Kt.

Reid, Sir Alexander James, Bt. (1897)

Reid, Sir David Edward, Kt.

Reid, *Rt. Hon.* Sir George, Kt.

Reid, Sir (Philip) Alan, GCVO

Reid, Sir Robert Paul, Kt.

Reid, Sir William Kennedy, KCB

Reiher, Sir Frederick Bernard Carl, KCMG, KBE

Reilly, *Lt.-Gen.* Sir Jeremy Calcott, KCB, DSO

Renals, Sir Stanley, Bt. (1895)

Renouf, Sir Clement William Bailey, Kt.

Renshaw, Sir John David Bine, Bt. (1903)

Renwick, Sir Richard Eustace, Bt. (1921)

†Reynolds, Sir James Francis, Bt. (1923)

Reynolds, Sir Peter William John, Kt., CBE

Rhodes, Sir John Christopher Douglas, Bt. (1919)

Rice, *Prof.* Sir Charles Duncan, Kt.

Rice, *Maj.-Gen.* Sir Desmond Hind Garrett, KCVO, CBE

Rice, Sir Timothy Miles Bindon, Kt.

Richard, Sir Cliff, Kt., OBE

Richards, Sir Brian Mansel, Kt., CBE, PHD

Richards, *Hon.* Sir David Anthony Stewart, Kt.

Richards, Sir David Gerald, Kt.

Richards, Sir Francis Neville, KCMG, CVO

Richards, *Prof.* Sir Michael Adrian, Kt., CBE

Richards, Sir Rex Edward, Kt., DSC, FRS

Richards, *Rt. Hon.* Sir Stephen Price, Kt.

Richardson, Sir Anthony Lewis, Bt. (1924)

Richardson, Sir John Patrick, KBE

Richardson, Sir Thomas Legh, KCMG

Richardson-Bunbury, Sir (Richard David) Michael, Bt. (I. 1787)

Richmond, Sir David Frank, KBE, CMG

Richmond, *Prof.* Sir Mark Henry, Kt., FRS

Ricketts, Sir Peter Forbes, GCMG, GCVO

Ricketts, Sir Stephen Tristram, Bt. (1828)

Ricks, *Prof.* Sir Christopher Bruce, Kt.

Riddell, Sir Walter John, Bt. (S. 1628)

Ridgway, *Lt.-Gen.* Sir Andrew Peter, KBE, CB

Ridley, Sir Adam (Nicholas), Kt.

Ridley, Sir Michael Kershaw, KCVO

Rifkind, *Rt. Hon.* Sir Malcolm Leslie, KCMG

Rigby, Sir Anthony John, Bt. (1929)

Rigby, Sir Peter, Kt.

Rimer, *Rt. Hon.* Sir Colin Percy Farquharson, Kt.

Ripley, Sir William Hugh, Bt. (1880)

Ritako, Sir Thomas Baha, Kt., MBE

Ritblat, Sir John Henry, Kt.

Ritchie, *Prof.* Sir Lewis Duthie, Kt., OBE

Rivett-Carnac, Sir Jonathan James, Bt. (1836)

Rix, *Rt. Hon.* Sir Bernard Anthony, Kt.

Robb, Sir John Weddell, Kt.

Roberts, Sir Derek Harry, Kt., CBE, FRS, FRENG

Roberts, *Prof.* Sir Edward Adam, KCMG

Roberts, Sir Gilbert Howland Rookehurst, Bt. (1809)

Roberts, Sir Hugh Ashley, GCVO

Roberts, Sir Ivor Anthony, KCMG

Roberts, *Dr* Sir Richard John, Kt.

Roberts, Sir Samuel, Bt. (1919)

Roberts, *Maj.-Gen.* Sir Sebastian John Lechmere, KCVO, OBE

†Roberts-Buchanan, Sir James Elton Denby, Bt. (1909)

Robertson, Sir Simon Manwaring, Kt.

Robins, Sir Ralph Harry, Kt., FRENG

Robinson, Sir Anthony, Kt.

Robinson, Sir Bruce, KCB

†Robinson, Sir Christopher Philipse, Bt. (1854)

Robinson, Sir Gerrard Jude, Kt.

Robinson, Sir Ian, Kt.

Robinson, Sir John James Michael Laud, Bt. (1660)

Robinson, *Dr* Sir Kenneth, Kt.

Robinson, Sir Peter Frank, Bt. (1908)

Robson, Sir John Adam, KCMG

Robson, Sir Stephen Arthur, Kt., CB

Roch, *Rt. Hon.* Sir John Ormond, Kt.

Roche, Sir David O'Grady, Bt. (1838)

Roche, Sir Henry John, Kt.

Rodgers, Sir (Andrew) Piers (Wingate Aikin-Sneath), Bt. (1964)

Rodley, *Prof.* Sir Nigel, KBE

Rogers, *Air Chief Marshal* Sir John Robson, KCB, CBE

Rogers, Sir Peter, Kt.

Rollo, *Lt.-Gen.* Sir William Raoul, KCB, CBE

Ropner, Sir John Bruce Woollacott, Bt. (1952)

Ropner, Sir Robert Clinton, Bt. (1904)

Rose, Sir Arthur James, Kt., CBE

Rose, *Rt. Hon.* Sir Christopher Dudley Roger, Kt.

Rose, Sir Clive Martin, GCMG

Rose, Sir David Lancaster, Bt. (1874)

Rose, *Gen.* Sir (Hugh) Michael, KCB, CBE, DSO, QGM

Rose, Sir John Edward Victor, Kt.

Rose, Sir Julian Day, Bt. (1872 and 1909)

Rosenthal, Sir Norman Leon, Kt.

Ross, *Maj.* Sir Andrew Charles Paterson, Bt. (1960)

Ross, *Lt.-Gen.* Sir Robert Jeremy, KCB, OBE

Ross, *Lt.-Col.* Sir Walter Hugh Malcolm, GCVO, OBE

Ross, Sir Walter Robert Alexander, KCVO

Rossi, Sir Hugh Alexis Louis, Kt.

Roth, *Hon.* Sir Peter Marcel, Kt.

Rothschild, Sir Evelyn Robert Adrian de, Kt.

Rove, *Revd* Ikan, KBE

Rowe, *Rear-Adm.* Sir Patrick Barton, KCVO, CBE
Rowe-Ham, Sir David Kenneth, GBE
Rowland, Sir Geoffrey Robert, Kt.
Rowland, Sir (John) David, Kt.
Rowley, Sir Richard Charles, Bt. (1786 and 1836)
Rowling, Sir John Reginald, Kt.
Rowlinson, *Prof.* Sir John Shipley, Kt., FRS
Royce, *Hon.* Sir Roger John, Kt.
Royden, Sir Christopher John, Bt. (1905)
Rubin, *Prof.* Sir Peter Charles, Kt.
Rudd, Sir (Anthony) Nigel (Russell), Kt.
Ruddock, Sir Paul, Kt.
Rudge, Sir Alan Walter, Kt., CBE, FRS
Rugge-Price, Sir James Keith Peter, Bt. (1804)
Ruggles-Brise, Sir Timothy Edward, Bt. (1935)
Rumbold, Sir Henry John Sebastian, Bt. (1779)
Rushdie, Sir (Ahmed) Salman, Kt.
†Russell, Sir (Arthur) Mervyn, Bt. (1812)
Russell, Sir Charles Dominic, Bt. (1916)
Russell, Sir George, Kt., CBE
Russell, Sir Muir, KCB
Russell, Sir Robert, Kt.
Rutter, *Prof.* Sir Michael Llewellyn, Kt., CBE, MD, FRS
Ryan, Sir Derek Gerald, Bt. (1919)
Rycroft, Sir Richard John, Bt. (1784)
Ryder, *Rt. Hon.* Sir Ernest Nigel, Kt., TD

Sacranie, Sir Iqbal Abdul Karim Mussa, Kt., OBE
Sainsbury, *Rt. Hon.* Sir Timothy Alan Davan, Kt.
St Clair-Ford, Sir Robin Sam, Bt. (1793)
St George, Sir John Avenel Bligh, Bt. (I. 1766)
St John-Mildmay, Sir Walter John Hugh, Bt. (1772)
St Omer, *Hon. Dr* Sir Dunstan Gerbert Raphael, KCMG
Sainty, Sir John Christopher, KCB
Sakora, *Hon.* Sir Bernard Berekia, KBE
Sales, *Rt. Hon.* Sir Philip James, Kt.
Salika, Sir Gibuna Gibbs, KBE
Salisbury, Sir Robert William, Kt.
Salt, Sir Patrick MacDonnell, Bt. (1869)
Salt, Sir (Thomas) Michael John, Bt. (1899)
Salusbury-Trelawny, Sir John William Richard, Bt. (1628)
Salz, Sir Anthony Michael Vaughan, Kt.
Samani, *Prof.* Sir Nilesh Jayantilal, Kt.
Sampson, Sir Colin, Kt., CBE, QPM
Samuel, Sir John Michael Glen, Bt. (1898)
Samuelson, Sir James Francis, Bt. (1884)
Samuelson, Sir Sydney Wylie, Kt., CBE
Samworth, Sir David Chetwode, Kt., CBE

Sanders, Sir Robert Tait, KBE, CMG
Sanders, Sir Ronald Michael, KCMG
Sanderson, Sir Frank Linton, Bt. (1920)
Sands, Sir Roger Blakemore, KCB
Sants, Sir Hector William Hepburn, Kt.
Sarei, Sir Alexis Holyweek, Kt., CBE
Sargent, Sir William Desmond, Kt., CBE
Satchwell, Sir Kevin Joseph, Kt.
Saunders, Sir Bruce Joshua, KBE
Saunders, *Hon.* Sir John Henry Boulton, Kt.
Savill, *Prof.* Sir John Stewart, Kt.
Savory, Sir Michael Berry, Kt.
Sawers, Sir Robert John, GCMG
Saxby, *Prof.* Sir Robin Keith, Kt.
Scarlett, Sir John McLeod, KCMG, OBE
Schiemann, *Rt. Hon.* Sir Konrad Hermann Theodor, Kt.
Schiff, Sir András, Kt.
Scholar, Sir Michael Charles, KCB
Scholey, Sir David Gerald, Kt., CBE
Schubert, Sir Sydney, Kt.
Scipio, Sir Hudson Rupert, Kt.
Scott, Sir Anthony Percy, Bt. (1913)
Scott, Sir David Richard Alexander, Kt., CBE
Scott, *Prof.* Sir George Peter, Kt.
Scott, Sir James Jervoise, Bt. (1962)
Scott, Sir John Hamilton, KCVO
Scott, Sir Kenneth Bertram Adam, KCVO, CMG
Scott, Sir Oliver Christopher Anderson, Bt. (1909)
Scott, *Prof.* Sir Philip John, KBE
Scott, Sir Ridley, Kt.
Scott, Sir Robert David Hillyer, Kt.
Scott, Sir Walter John, Bt. (1907)
Scott-Lee, Sir Paul Joseph, Kt., QPM
Seale, Sir Clarence David, Kt.
Seale, Sir John Henry, Bt. (1838)
Sealy, Sir Austen Llewellyn, Kt.
Sebastian, Sir Cuthbert Montraville, GCMG, OBE
†Sebright, Sir Rufus Hugo Giles, Bt. (1626)
Seccombe, Sir (William) Vernon Stephen, Kt.
Seconde, Sir Reginald Louis, KCMG, CVO
Sedley, *Rt. Hon.* Sir Stephen John, Kt.
Seely, Sir Nigel Edward, Bt. (1896)
Seeto, Sir Ling James, Kt., MBE
Seeyave, Sir Rene Sow Choung, Kt., CBE
Seldon, *Dr* Sir Anthony Francis, Kt.
Semple, Sir John Laughlin, KCB
Sergeant, Sir Patrick, Kt.
Serota, *Hon.* Sir Nicholas Andrew, Kt., CH
Setchell, Sir Marcus Edward, KCVO
†Seton, Sir Charles Wallace, Bt. (S. 1683)
Seton, Sir Iain Bruce, Bt. (S. 1663)
Severne, *Air Vice-Marshal* Sir John de Milt, KCVO, OBE, AFC
Seymour, Sir Julian Roger, Kt., CBE
Shadbolt, *Prof.* Sir Nigel Richard, Kt.
Shaffer, Sir Peter Levin, Kt., CBE
Shakerley, Sir Nicholas Simon Adam, Bt. (1838)

Shakespeare, Sir Thomas William, Bt. (1942)
Sharp, Sir Adrian, Bt. (1922)
Sharp, Sir Leslie, Kt., QPM
Sharp, Sir Sheridan Christopher Robin, Bt. (1920)
Sharples, Sir James, Kt., QPM
Shaw, Sir Charles De Vere, Bt. (1821)
Shaw, *Prof.* Sir John Calman, Kt., CBE
Shaw, Sir Neil McGowan, Kt.
Shaw-Stewart, Sir Ludovic Houston, Bt. (S. 1667)
Shebbeare, Sir Thomas Andrew, KCVO
Sheehy, Sir Patrick, Kt.
Sheffield, Sir Reginald Adrian Berkeley, Bt. (1755)
Shehadie, Sir Nicholas Michael, Kt., OBE
Sheil, *Rt. Hon.* Sir John, Kt.
Sheinwald, Sir Nigel Elton, GCMG
Shelley, Sir John Richard, Bt. (1611)
Shepherd, Sir Colin Ryley, Kt.
Shepherd, Sir John Alan, KCVO, CMG
Shepherd, Sir Richard Charles Scrimgeour, Kt.
Sher, Sir Antony, KBE
Sherlock, Sir Nigel, KCVO, OBE
Sherston-Baker, Sir Robert George Humphrey, Bt. (1796)
Shiffner, Sir Henry David, Bt. (1818)
Shinwell, Sir (Maurice) Adrian, Kt.
Shirreff, *Gen.* Sir Alexander Richard David, KCB, CBE
Shock, Sir Maurice, Kt.
Shortridge, Sir Jon Deacon, KCB
Shuckburgh, Sir James Rupert Charles, Bt. (1660)
Sieff, *Hon.* Sir David, Kt.
Silber, *Rt. Hon.* Sir Stephen Robert, Kt.
Silk, Sir Evan Paul, KCB
†Simeon, Sir Stephen George Barrington, Bt. (1815)
Simmonds, *Rt. Hon. Dr* Sir Kennedy Alphonse, KCMG
Simmons, *Air Marshal* Sir Michael George, KCB, AFC
Simmons, Sir Stanley Clifford, Kt.
Simms, Sir Neville Ian, Kt., FRENG
Simon, *Hon.* Sir Peregrine Charles Hugh, Kt.
Simonet, Sir Louis Marcel Pierre, Kt., CBE
Simpson, Sir Peter Austin, Kt., OBE
Simpson, *Dr* Sir Peter Jeffery, Kt.
Sims, Sir Roger Edward, Kt.
Sinclair, Sir Clive Marles, Kt.
Sinclair, Sir Robert John, Kt.
Sinclair, Sir William Robert Francis, Bt. (S. 1704)
Sinclair-Lockhart, Sir Simon John Edward Francis, Bt. (S. 1636)
Singer, *Hon.* Sir Jan Peter, Kt.
Singh, *His Hon.* Sir Mota, Kt., QC
Singh, Sir Pritpal, Kt.
Singh, *Hon.* Sir Rabinder, Kt.
Singleton, Sir Roger, Kt., CBE
Sione, Sir Tomu Malaefone, GCMG, OBE
Sissons, *Prof.* Sir (John Gerald) Patrick, Kt.
†Sitwell, Sir George Reresby Sacheverell, Bt. (1808)

Skeggs, Sir Clifford George, Kt.

Skehel, Sir John James, Kt., FRS

Skingsley, *Air Chief Marshal* Sir Anthony Gerald, GBE, KCB

Skinner, Sir (Thomas) Keith (Hewitt), Bt. (1912)

Skipwith, Sir Patrick Alexander d'Estoteville, Bt. (1622)

Slack, Sir William Willatt, KCVO, FRCS

Slade, Sir Benjamin Julian Alfred, Bt. (1831)

Slade, *Rt. Hon.* Sir Christopher John, Kt.

Slaney, *Prof.* Sir Geoffrey, KBE

Slater, *Adm.* Sir John (Jock) Cunningham Kirkwood, GCB, LVO

Sleight, Sir Richard, Bt. (1920)

Smiley, *Lt.-Col.* Sir John Philip, Bt. (1903)

Smith, *Prof.* Sir Adrian Frederick Melhuish, Kt., FRS

Smith, *Hon.* Sir Andrew Charles, Kt.

Smith, Sir Andrew Thomas, Bt. (1897)

Smith, *Prof.* Sir David Cecil, Kt., FRS

Smith, Sir David Iser, KCVO

Smith, Sir Dudley (Gordon), Kt.

Smith, *Prof.* Sir Eric Brian, Kt., PHD

Smith, Sir John Alfred, Kt., QPM

Smith, Sir Joseph William Grenville, Kt.

Smith, Sir Kevin, Kt., CBE

Smith, Sir Martin Gregory, Kt.

Smith, Sir Michael John Llewellyn, KCVO, CMG

Smith, Sir (Norman) Brian, Kt., CBE, PHD

Smith, Sir Paul Brierley, Kt., CBE

Smith, *Hon.* Sir Peter (Winston), Kt.

Smith, Sir Robert Courtney, Kt., CBE

Smith, Sir Robert Hill, Bt. (1945)

Smith, *Gen.* Sir Rupert Anthony, KCB, DSO, OBE, QGM

Smith, Sir Steven Murray, Kt.

Smith-Dodsworth, Sir David John, Bt. (1784)

Smith-Gordon, Sir (Lionel) Eldred (Peter), Bt. (1838)

Smith-Marriott, Sir Peter Francis, Bt. (1774)

Smurfit, *Dr.* Sir Michael William Joseph, KBE

Smyth, Sir Timothy John, Bt. (1956)

Snowden, *Prof.* Sir Christopher Maxwell, Kt.

Snowden, *Hon.* Sir Richard Andrew, Kt., QC

Snyder, Sir Michael John, Kt.

Soames, *Rt. Hon.* Sir (Arthur) Nicholas Winston, Kt.

Soar, *Adm.* Sir Trevor Alan, KCB, OBE

Sobers, Sir Garfield St Auburn, Kt.

Solomon, Sir Harry, Kt.

Somare, *Rt. Hon.* Sir Michael Thomas, GCMG, CH

Somerville, *Brig.* Sir John Nicholas, Kt., CBE

Songo, Sir Bernard Paul, Kt., CMG, OBE

Sorabji, *Prof.* Sir Richard Rustom Kharsedji, Kt., CBE

Sorrell, Sir John William, Kt., CBE

Sorrell, Sir Martin Stuart, Kt.

Sosa, Sir Manuel, Kt.

Soulsby, Sir Peter Alfred, Kt.

Soutar, *Air Marshal* Sir Charles John Williamson, KBE

Souter, Sir Brian, Kt.

Southby, Sir John Richard Bilbe, Bt. (1937)

Southern, *Prof.* Sir Edwin Mellor, Kt.

Southgate, Sir Colin Grieve, Kt.

Southgate, Sir William David, Kt.

Southward, *Dr* Sir Nigel Ralph, KCVO

Sowrey, *Air Marshal* Sir Frederick Beresford, KCB, CBE, AFC

Sparrow, Sir John, Kt.

Spearman, Sir Alexander Young Richard Mainwaring, Bt. (1840)

Speed, Sir (Herbert) Keith, Kt., RD

Spencer, Sir Derek Harold, Kt., QC

Spencer, *Vice-Adm.* Sir Peter, KCB

Spencer, *Hon.* Sir Robin Godfrey, Kt.

Spencer-Nairn, Sir Robert Arnold, Bt. (1933)

Spicer, Sir Nicholas Adrian Albert, Bt. (1906)

Spiegelhalter *Prof.* Sir David John, Kt., OBE, FRS

Spiers, Sir Donald Maurice, Kt., CB, TD

Spooner, Sir James Douglas, Kt.

Spring, Sir Dryden Thomas, Kt.

Spurling, Sir John Damian, KCVO, OBE

Squire, *Air Chief Marshal* Sir Peter Ted, GCB, DFC, AFC, ADC

Stadlen, *Hon.* Sir Nicholas Felix, Kt.

Stagg, Sir Charles Richard Vernon, KCMG

Staite, Sir Richard John, Kt., OBE

Stamer, Sir Peter Tomlinson, Bt. (1809)

Stanhope, *Adm.* Sir Mark, GCB, OBE, ADC

Stanier, Sir Beville Douglas, Bt. (1917)

Stanley, *Rt. Hon.* Sir John Paul, Kt.

Starkey, Sir John Philip, Bt. (1935)

Starmer, Sir Keir, KCB, QC

Stear, *Air Chief Marshal* Sir Michael James Douglas, KCB, CBE

Steel, *Vice-Adm.* Sir David George, KBE

Steel, *Hon.* Sir David William, Kt.

Steer, Sir Alan William, Kt.

Stephen, *Rt. Hon.* Sir Ninian Martin, KG, GCMG, GCVO, KBE

Stephens, Sir (Edwin) Barrie, Kt.

Stephens, Sir Jonathan Andrew de Sievrac, KCB

Stephens, Sir William Benjamin Synge, Kt.

Stephenson, Sir Henry Upton, Bt. (1936)

Stephenson, Sir Paul Robert, Kt., QPM

Sterling, Sir Michael John Howard, Kt.

Sternberg, Sir Sigmund, Kt.

Stevenson, Sir Hugh Alexander, Kt.

Stevenson, Sir Simpson, Kt.

Stewart, Sir Alan d'Arcy, Bt. (I. 1623)

Stewart, Sir Brian John, Kt., CBE

Stewart, Sir David James Henderson, Bt. (1957)

Stewart, Sir David John Christopher, Bt. (1803)

Stewart, Sir James Moray, KCB

Stewart, Sir (John) Simon (Watson), Bt. (1920)

Stewart, Sir John Young, Kt., OBE

Stewart, Sir Patrick, Kt., OBE

Stewart, *Lt.-Col.* Sir Robert Christie, KCVO, CBE, TD

Stewart, Sir Robin Alastair, Bt. (1960)

Stewart, *Hon.* Sir Stephen Paul, Kt.

Stewart, *Prof.* Sir William Duncan Paterson, Kt., FRS, FRSE

Stewart-Clark, Sir John, Bt. (1918)

Stewart-Richardson, Sir Simon Alaisdair, Bt. (S. 1630)

Stilgoe, Sir Richard Henry Simpson, Kt., OBE

Stirling, Sir Angus Duncan Aeneas, Kt.

Stirling of Garden, *Col.* Sir James, KCVO, CBE, TD

Stirling-Hamilton, Sir Malcolm William Bruce, Bt. (S. 1673)

Stockdale, Sir Thomas Minshull, Bt. (1960)

Stoddart, *Prof.* Sir James Fraser, Kt.

Stone, Sir Christopher, Kt.

Stonhouse, *Revd* Michael Philip, Bt. (1628 and 1670)

Stonor, *Air Marshal* Sir Thomas Henry, KCB

Stoppard, Sir Thomas, Kt., OM, CBE

Storey, *Hon.* Sir Richard, Bt., CBE (1960)

Stothard, Sir Peter Michael, Kt.

Stott, Sir Adrian George Ellingham, Bt. (1920)

Stoute, Sir Michael Ronald, Kt.

Stracey, Sir John Simon, Bt. (1818)

Strachan, Sir Curtis Victor, Kt., CVO

Strachan, Sir Hew Francis Anthony, Kt.

Strachey, Sir Charles, Bt. (1801)

Straker, Sir Louis Hilton, KCMG

Strang Steel, Sir (Fiennes) Michael, Bt. (1938), CBE

Stratton, *Prof.* Sir Michael Rudolf, Kt., FRS

Street, *Hon.* Sir Laurence Whistler, KCMG

Streeton, Sir Terence George, KBE, CMG

Strickland-Constable, Sir Frederic, Bt. (1641)

Stringer, Sir Donald Edgar, Kt., CBE

Stringer, Sir Howard, Kt.

Strong, Sir Roy Colin, Kt., PHD, FSA

Stronge, Sir James Anselan Maxwell, Bt. (1803)

Stuart, Sir James Keith, Kt.

Stuart, Sir Kenneth Lamonte, Kt.

†Stuart, Sir Phillip Luttrell, Bt. (1660)

†Stuart-Forbes, Sir William Daniel, Bt. (S. 1626)

Stuart-Menteth, Sir Charles Greaves, Bt. (1838)

Stuart-Paul, *Air Marshal* Sir Ronald Ian, KBE

Stuart-Smith, *Hon.* Sir Jeremy Hugh, Kt.

Stuart-Smith, *Rt. Hon.* Sir Murray, KCMG, Kt.

Stubbs, Sir William Hamilton, Kt., PHD

Stucley, *Lt.* Sir Hugh George Coplestone Bampfylde, Bt. (1859)

Studd, Sir Edward Fairfax, Bt. (1929)

Studholme, Sir Henry William, Bt. (1956)

Stunell, *Rt. Hon.* Sir Robert Andrew, Kt., OBE

Sturridge, Sir Nicholas Anthony, KCVO

Stuttard, Sir John Boothman, Kt.

†Style, Sir William Frederick, Bt. (1627)

Sullivan, *Rt. Hon.* Sir Jeremy Mirth, Kt.

Sullivan, Sir Richard Arthur, Bt. (1804)

Sulston, Sir John Edward, Kt.

Sunderland, Sir John Michael, Kt.

Supperstone, *Hon.* Sir Michael Alan, Kt.

Sutherland, Sir John Brewer, Bt. (1921)

Sutherland, Sir William George MacKenzie, Kt.

Sutton, Sir Richard Lexington, Bt. (1772)

Swan, Sir Conrad Marshall John Fisher, KCVO, PHD

Swan, Sir John William David, KBE

Swann, Sir Michael Christopher, Bt. (1906), TD

Sweeney, Sir George, Kt.

Sweeney, *Hon.* Sir Nigel Hamilton, Kt.

Sweeting, *Prof.* Sir Martin Nicholas, Kt., OBE, FRS

Swinburn, *Lt.-Gen.* Sir Richard Hull, KCB

Swinnerton-Dyer, *Prof.* Sir (Henry) Peter (Francis), Bt. (1678), KBE, FRS

Swinton, *Maj.-Gen.* Sir John, KCVO, OBE

Swire, Sir Adrian Christopher, Kt.

Swire, Sir John Anthony, Kt., CBE

Sykes, Sir David Michael, Bt. (1921)

Sykes, Sir Francis John Badcock, Bt. (1781)

Sykes, Sir Hugh Ridley, Kt.

Sykes, *Prof.* Sir (Malcolm) Keith, Kt.

Sykes, Sir Richard, Kt.

Sykes, Sir Tatton Christopher Mark, Bt. (1783)

Symons, *Vice-Adm.* Sir Patrick Jeremy, KBE

†Synge, Sir Allen James Edward, Bt. (1801)

Tang, Sir David Wing-cheung, KBE

Tanner, Sir David Whitlock, Kt., CBE

Tapps-Gervis-Meyrick, Sir George Christopher Cadafael, Bt. (1791)

Tapsell, *Rt. Hon.* Sir Peter Hannay Bailey, Kt.

†Tate, Sir Edward Nicolas, Bt. (1898)

Taureka, *Dr* Sir Reubeh, KBE

Tauvasa, Sir Joseph James, KBE

Taylor, Sir Cyril Julian Hebden, GBE

Taylor, Sir Edward Macmillan (Teddy), Kt.

Taylor, Sir Hugh Henderson, KCB

Taylor, *Rt. Revd* John Bernard, KCVO

Taylor, *Dr* Sir John Michael, Kt., OBE

Taylor, *Prof.* Sir Martin John, Kt., FRS

Taylor, Sir Nicholas Richard Stuart, Bt. (1917)

Taylor, *Prof.* Sir William, Kt., CBE

Taylor, Sir William George, Kt.

Teagle, *Vice-Adm.* Sir Somerford Francis, KBE

Teare, *Hon.* Sir Nigel John Martin, Kt.

Teasdale, *Prof.* Sir Graham Michael, Kt.

Tebbit, Sir Kevin Reginald, KCB, CMG

Temple, *Prof.* Sir John Graham, Kt.

Temple, Sir Richard Carnac Chartier, Bt. (1876)

Temu, *Hon. Dr* Sir Puka, KBE, CMG

Tennyson-D'Eyncourt, Sir Mark Gervais, Bt. (1930)

Terry, *Air Marshal* Sir Colin George, KBE, CB

Terry, *Air Chief Marshal* Sir Peter David George, GCB, AFC

Thatcher, *Hon.* Sir Mark, Bt. (1990)

Thomas, Sir David John Godfrey, Bt. (1694)

Thomas, Sir Derek Morison David, KCMG

Thomas, *Prof.* Sir Eric Jackson, Kt.

Thomas, Sir Gilbert Stanley, Kt., OBE

Thomas, Sir Jeremy Cashel, KCMG

Thomas, Sir (John) Alan, Kt.

Thomas, *Prof.* Sir John Meurig, Kt., FRS

Thomas, Sir Keith Vivian, Kt.

Thomas, *Dr* Sir Leton Felix, KCMG, CBE

Thomas, Sir Philip Lloyd, KCVO, CMG

Thomas, Sir Quentin Jeremy, Kt., CB

Thomas, *Rt. Hon.* Sir Swinton Barclay, Kt.

Thomas, Sir William Michael, Bt. (1919)

Thompson, Sir Christopher Peile, Bt. (1890)

Thompson, Sir Clive Malcolm, Kt.

Thompson, Sir David Albert, KCMG

Thompson, *Prof.* Sir Michael Warwick, Kt., DSc

Thompson, Sir Nicholas Annesley, Bt. (1963)

Thompson, Sir Nigel Cooper, KCMG, CBE

Thompson, Sir Paul Anthony, Bt. (1963)

Thompson, Sir Peter Anthony, Kt.

Thompson, *Dr* Sir Richard Paul Hepworth, KCVO

Thompson, Sir Thomas d'Eyncourt John, Bt. (1806)

Thomson, Sir Adam McClure, KCMG

Thomson, Sir (Frederick Douglas) David, Bt. (1929)

Thomson, Sir John Adam, GCMG

Thomson, Sir Mark Wilfrid Home, Bt. (1925)

Thorne, Sir Neil Gordon, Kt., OBE, TD

Thornton, *Air Marshal* Sir Barry Michael, KCB

Thornton, Sir (George) Malcolm, Kt.

†Thorold, Sir (Anthony) Oliver, Bt. (1642)

Thorpe, *Rt. Hon.* Sir Mathew Alexander, Kt.

Thrift, *Prof.* Sir Nigel John, Kt.

Thurecht, Sir Ramon Richard, Kt., OBE

Thwaites, Sir Bryan, Kt., PHD

Tickell, Sir Crispin Charles Cervantes, GCMG, KCVO

Tidmarsh, Sir James Napier, KCVO, MBE

Tilt, Sir Robin Richard, Kt.

Tiltman, Sir John Hessell, KCVO

Timmins, *Col.* Sir John Bradford, KCVO, OBE, TD

Tims, Sir Michael David, KCVO

Tindle, Sir Ray Stanley, Kt., CBE

Tirvengadum, Sir Harry Krishnan, Kt.

Tjoeng, Sir James Neng, KBE

Tod, *Vice-Adm.* Sir Jonathan James Richard, KCB, CBE

Todd, *Prof.* Sir David, Kt., CBE

Toka, Sir Mahuru Dadi, Kt., MBE

Tollemache, Sir Lyonel Humphry John, Bt. (1793)

Tomkys, Sir (William) Roger, KCMG

Tomlinson, *Prof.* Sir Bernard Evans, Kt., CBE

Tomlinson, Sir John Rowland, Kt., CBE

Tomlinson, Sir Michael John, Kt., CBE

Tomlinson, *Rt. Hon.* Sir Stephen Miles, Kt.

Tooke, *Prof.* Sir John Edward, Kt.

Tooley, Sir John, Kt.

ToRobert, Sir Henry Thomas, KBE

Torpy, *Air Chief Marshal* Sir Glenn Lester, GCB, CBE, DSO

Torry, Sir Peter James, GCVO, KCMG

Touche, Sir Anthony George, Bt. (1920)

Touche, Sir Rodney Gordon, Bt. (1962)

Toulson, *Rt. Hon.* Sir Roger Grenfell, Kt. (Lord Toulson)

Tovadek, Sir Martin, Kt. CMG

Tovey, Sir Brian John Maynard, KCMG

Tovua, Sir Paul Joshua, KCMG

ToVue, Sir Ronald, Kt., OBE

Towneley, Sir Simon Peter Edmund Cosmo William, KCVO

Townsley, Sir John Arthur, Kt.

Traill, Sir Alan Towers, GBE

Trawen, Sir Andrew Sean, Kt., CMG, MBE

Trainor, *Prof.* Sir Richard Hughes, KBE

Treacher, *Adm.* Sir John Devereux, KCB

Treacy, *Rt. Hon.* Sir Colman Maurice, Kt.

Treacy, *Hon.* Sir (James Mary) Seamus, Kt.

Treitel, *Prof.* Sir Guenter Heinz, Kt., FBA, QC

Trescowthick, Sir Donald Henry, KBE

†Trevelyan, Sir Andrew John, Bt. (1662 and 1874)

Trezise, Sir Kenneth Bruce, Kt., OBE

Trippier, Sir David Austin, Kt., RD

Tritton, Sir Jeremy Ernest, Bt. (1905)

Trollope, Sir Anthony Simon, Bt. (1642)

Trotman-Dickenson, Sir Aubrey Fiennes, Kt.

Trotter, Sir Neville Guthrie, Kt.

Troubridge, Sir Thomas Richard, Bt. (1799)

Trousdell, *Lt.-Gen.* Sir Philip Charles Cornwallis, KBE, CB

Truscott, Sir Ralph Eric Nicholson, Bt. (1909)

Tsang, Sir Donald Yam-keun, KBE

Tuck, Sir Bruce Adolph Reginald, Bt. (1910)

Tucker, Sir Paul, Kt.

Tucker, *Hon.* Sir Richard Howard, Kt.

Tuckey, *Rt. Hon.* Sir Simon Lane, Kt.

Tugendhat, *Hon.* Sir Michael George, Kt.

Tuite, Sir Christopher Hugh, Bt. (I. 1622), PHD

Tuivaga, Sir Timoci Uluiburotu, Kt.

Tully, Sir William Mark, KBE

Tunstall, Sir Craig, Kt.

Tupper, Sir Charles Hibbert, Bt. (1888)

Turbott, Sir Ian Graham, Kt., CMG, CVO

Turing, Sir John Dermot, Bt. (S. 1638)

Turner, *Hon.* Sir Mark George, Kt.

Turner, *Hon.* Sir Michael John, Kt.

Turnquest, Sir Orville Alton, GCMG, QC

Tusa, Sir John, Kt.

Tweedie, *Prof.* Sir David Philip, Kt.

Tyrwhitt, Sir Reginald Thomas Newman, Bt. (1919)

Udny-Lister, Sir Edward Julian, Kt.

Ullman, Sir Anthony, Kt.

Underhill, *Rt. Hon.* Sir Nicholas Edward, Kt.

Underwood, *Prof.* Sir James Cressee Elphinstone, Kt.

Unwin, Sir (James) Brian, KCB

Ure, Sir John Burns, KCMG, LVO

Urquhart, Sir Brian Edward, KCMG, MBE

Urwick, Sir Alan Bedford, KCVO, CMG

Usher, Sir Andrew John, Bt. (1899)

Utting, Sir William Benjamin, Kt., CB

Vardy, Sir Peter, Kt.

Varney, Sir David Robert, Kt.

Vassar-Smith, Sir John Rathbone, Bt. (1917)

Vavasour, Sir Eric Michael Joseph Marmaduke, Bt. (1828)

Veness, Sir David, Kt., CBE, QPM

Venner, Sir Kenneth Dwight Vincent, KBE

Vereker, Sir John Michael Medlicott, KCB

Verey, Sir David John, Kt.

Verity, Sir Gary Keith, Kt.

Verney, Sir Edmund Ralph, Bt. (1818)

†Verney, Sir John Sebastian, Bt. (1946)

Vernon, Sir James William, Bt. (1914)

Vestey, Sir Paul Edmund, Bt. (1921)

Vickers, *Prof.* Sir Brian William, Kt.

Vickers, Sir John Stuart, Kt.

Vickers, *Lt.-Gen.* Sir Richard Maurice Hilton, KCB, CVO, OBE

Vickers, Sir Roger Henry, KCVO

Viggers, *Lt-Gen.* Sir Frederick Richard, KCB, CMG, MBE

Viggers, Sir Peter John, Kt.

Vincent, Sir William Percy Maxwell, Bt. (1936)

Vineall, Sir Anthony John Patrick, Kt.

Virdee, *Prof.* Sir Tejinder Singh, Kt.

Vos, *Rt. Hon.* Sir Geoffrey Michael, Kt.

†Vyvyan, Sir Ralph Ferrers Alexander, Bt. (1645)

Waena, Sir Nathaniel Rahumaea, GCMG

Waine, *Rt. Revd* John, KCVO

Waite, *Rt. Hon.* Sir John Douglas, Kt.

Waka, Sir Lucas Joseph, Kt., OBE

Wake, Sir Hereward, Bt. (1621), MC

Wakefield, Sir (Edward) Humphry (Tyrell), Bt. (1962)

Wakefield, Sir Norman Edward, Kt.

Wakeford, Sir Geoffrey Michael Montgomery, Kt., OBE

Wakeham, *Prof.* Sir William Arnot, Kt.

†Wakeley, Sir Nicholas Jeremy, Bt. (1952)

Wald, *Prof.* Sir Nicholas John, Kt.

Wales, Sir Robert Andrew, Kt.

Waley-Cohen, Sir Stephen Harry, Bt. (1961)

Walford, Sir Christopher Rupert, Kt.

Walker, *Gen.* Sir Antony Kenneth Frederick, KCB

Walker, Sir Christopher Robert Baldwin, Bt. (1856)

Walker, Sir David Alan, Kt.

Walker, *Air Vice-Marshal* Sir David Allan, KCVO, OBE

Walker, Sir Harold Berners, KCMG

Walker, Sir John Ernest, Kt., DPHIL, FRS

Walker, *Air Marshal* Sir John Robert, KCB, CBE, AFC

Walker, Sir Miles Rawstron, Kt., CBE

Walker, Sir Patrick Jeremy, KCB

Walker, *Hon.* Sir Paul James, Kt.

Walker, Sir Rodney Myerscough, Kt.

Walker, Sir Roy Edward, Bt. (1906)

Walker, *Hon.* Sir Timothy Edward, Kt.

Walker, Sir Victor Stewart Heron, Bt. (1868)

Walker-Okeover, Sir Andrew Peter Monro, Bt. (1886)

Walker-Smith, *Hon.* Sir John Jonah, Bt. (1960)

Wall, Sir (John) Stephen, GCMG, LVO

Wall, *Rt. Hon.* Sir Nicholas Peter Rathbone, Kt.

Wall, *Gen.* Sir Peter Anthony, GCB, CBE, ADC

Wallace, *Lt.-Gen.* Sir Christopher Brooke Quentin, KBE

Wallace, *Prof.* Sir David James, Kt., CBE, FRS

Waller, *Rt. Hon.* Sir (George) Mark, Kt.

Waller, Sir John Michael, Bt. (I. 1780)

Wallis, Sir Peter Gordon, KCVO

Wallis, Sir Timothy William, Kt.

Walmsley, *Vice-Adm.* Sir Robert, KCB

Walport, *Dr* Sir Mark Jeremy, Kt.

†Walsham, Sir Gerald Percy Robert, Bt. (1831)

Walters, Sir Dennis Murray, Kt., MBE

Walters, Sir Frederick Donald, Kt.

Walters, Sir Peter Ingram, Kt.

Wamiri, Sir Akapite, KBE

Warby, *Hon.* Sir Mark David John, Kt., QC

Ward, *Rt. Hon.* Sir Alan Hylton, Kt.

Ward, Sir Austin, Kt., QC

Ward, *Hon.* Sir (Frederik) Gordon (Roy), Kt., OBE

Ward, *Prof.* Sir John MacQueen, Kt., CBE

Ward, Sir Joseph James Laffey, Bt. (1911)

Ward, Sir Timothy James, Kt.

Wardale, Sir Geoffrey Charles, KCB

Wardlaw, Sir Henry Justin, Bt. (NS. 1631)

Waring, Sir (Alfred) Holburt, Bt. (1935)

Warmington, Sir Rupert Marshall, Bt. (1908)

Warner, Sir Gerald Chierici, KCMG

Warner, Sir Philip Courtenay Thomas, Bt. (1910)

Warren, Sir David Alexander, KCMG

Warren, Sir (Frederick) Miles, KBE

Warren, Sir Kenneth Robin, Kt.

Warren, Sir Nicholas Roger, Kt.

Wass, Sir Douglas William Gretton, GCB

Waterlow, Sir Christopher Rupert, Bt. (1873)

Waterlow, Sir (Thomas) James, Bt. (1930)

Waters, *Gen.* Sir (Charles) John, GCB, CBE

Waters, Sir (Thomas) Neil (Morris), Kt.

Waterworth, Sir Alan William, KCVO

Wates, Sir Christopher Stephen, Kt.

Watson, Sir Graham Robert, Kt.

Watson, Sir (James) Andrew, Bt. (1866)

Watson, *Prof.* Sir Robert Tony, Kt., CMG

Watson, Sir Ronald Matthew, Kt., CBE

Watson, Sir Simon Conran Hamilton, Bt. (1895)

Watt, *Gen.* Sir Charles Redmond, KCB, KCVO, CBE, ADC

Watts, Sir Philip Beverley, KCMG

Weatherall, *Prof.* Sir David John, Kt., FRS

Weatherall, *Vice-Adm.* Sir James Lamb, KCVO, KBE

Weatherup, *Hon.* Sir Ronald Eccles, Kt.

Webb, *Prof.* Sir Adrian Leonard, Kt.

Webb-Carter, *Maj.-Gen.* Sir Evelyn John, KCVO, OBE

Webster, *Vice-Adm.* Sir John Morrison, KCB

Wedgwood, Sir Ralph Nicholas, Bt. (1942)

Weekes, Sir Everton DeCourcey, KCMG, OBE

Weinberg, Sir Mark Aubrey, Kt.

Weir, *Hon.* Sir Reginald George, Kt.

Weir, Sir Roderick Bignell, Kt.

Welby, Sir (Richard) Bruno Gregory, Bt. (1801)

Welch, Sir John Reader, Bt. (1957)

Weldon, Sir Anthony William, Bt. (I. 1723)

Wellend, *Prof.* Sir Mark Edward, Kt.

Weller, *Prof.* Sir Ian Vincent Derrick, Kt.

Weller, Sir Nicholas John, Kt.

†Wells, Sir Christopher Charles, Bt. (1944)

Wells, Sir John Julius, Kt.

Wells, Sir William Henry Weston, Kt., FRICS

Wesker, Sir Arnold, Kt.

Wessely, *Prof.* Sir Simon Charles, Kt.

Westmacott, Sir Peter John, KCMG

Weston, Sir Michael Charles Swift, KCMG, CVO

Weston, Sir (Philip) John, KCMG

Whalen, Sir Geoffrey Henry, Kt., CBE

Wheeler, *Rt. Hon.* Sir John Daniel, Kt.

Wheeler, Sir John Frederick, Bt. (1920)

Wheeler, *Gen.* Sir Roger Neil, GCB, CBE

Wheeler-Booth, Sir Michael Addison John, KCB

Wheler, Sir Trevor Woodford, Bt. (1660)

Whitaker, Sir John James Ingham (Jack), Bt. (1936)

Whitbread, Sir Samuel Charles, KCVO

Whitchurch, Sir Graeme Ian, Kt., OBE

White, Sir Adrian Edwin, Kt., CBE

White, *Prof.* Sir Christopher John, Kt., CVO

White, Sir Christopher Robert Meadows, Bt. (1937)

White, Sir David (David Jason), Kt., OBE

White, Sir David Harry, Kt.

White, Sir George Stanley James, Bt. (1904)

White, Sir John Woolmer, Bt. (1922)

White, Sir Nicholas Peter Archibald, Bt. (1802)

White, Sir Willard Wentworth, Kt., CBE

White-Spunner, *Lt.-Gen.* Sir Barnabas William Benjamin, KCB, CBE

Whitehead, Sir Philip Henry Rathbone, Bt. (1889)

Whiteley, *Gen.* Sir Peter John Frederick, GCB, OBE, RM

Whitfield, Sir William, Kt., CBE

Whitmore, Sir Clive Anthony, GCB, CVO

Whitmore, Sir John Henry Douglas, Bt. (1954)

Whitson, Sir Keith Roderick, Kt.

Whittam Smith, Sir Andreas, Kt., CBE

Wickerson, Sir John Michael, Kt.

Wicks, Sir Nigel Leonard, GCB, CVO, CBE

Wigan, Sir Michael Iain, Bt. (1898)

Wiggin, Sir Richard Edward John, Bt. (1892)

Wiggins, Sir Bradley Marc, Kt., CBE

Wigram, Sir John Woolmore, Bt. (1805)

Wilbraham, Sir Richard Baker, Bt. (1776)

Wild, Sir John Ralston, Kt., CBE

Wiles, *Prof.* Sir Andrew John, KBE

Wilkie, *Hon.* Sir Alan Fraser, Kt.

Wilkins, Sir Michael, Kt.

Wilkinson, Sir (David) Graham (Brook) Bt. (1941)

Wilkinson, *Prof.* Sir Denys Haigh, Kt., FRS

Willcocks, Sir David Valentine, Kt., CBE, MC

Willcocks, *Lt.-Gen.* Sir Michael Alan, KCB, CVO

Williams, Sir Anthony Geraint, Bt. (1953)

Williams, Sir (Arthur) Gareth Ludovic Emrys Rhys, Bt. (1918)

Williams, Sir Charles Othniel, Kt.

Williams, Sir Daniel Charles, GCMG, QC

Williams, Sir David Reeve, Kt., CBE

Williams, Sir Donald Mark, Bt. (1866)

Williams, *Prof.* Sir (Edward) Dillwyn, Kt., FRCP

Williams, Sir Francis Owen Garbett, Kt., CBE

Williams, *Hon.* Sir (John) Griffith, Kt.

Williams, Sir (Lawrence) Hugh, Bt. (1798)

Williams, Sir Nicholas Stephen, Kt.

Williams, *Prof.* Sir Norman Stanley, Kt.

Williams, Sir Paul Michael, Kt., OBE

Williams, Sir Peter Michael, Kt.

Williams, Sir (Robert) Philip Nathaniel, Bt. (1915)

Williams, *HE Dr* Sir Rodney Errey Lawrence, GCMG

Williams, *Prof.* Sir Roger, Kt.

Williams, Sir (William) Maxwell (Harries), Kt.

Williams, *Hon.* Sir Wyn Lewis, Kt.

Williams-Bulkeley, Sir Richard Thomas, Bt. (1661)

Williams-Wynn, Sir David Watkin, Bt. (1688)

Williamson, Sir George Malcolm, Kt.

Williamson, *Marshal of the Royal Air Force* Sir Keith Alec, GCB, AFC

Williamson, Sir Robert Brian, Kt., CBE

Willink, Sir Edward Daniel, Bt. (1957)

Wills, Sir David James Vernon, Bt. (1923)

Wills, Sir David Seton, Bt. (1904)

Wilmot, Sir David, Kt., QPM

Wilmot, Sir Henry Robert, Bt. (1759)

Wilmut, *Prof.* Sir Ian, Kt., OBE

Wilsey, *Gen.* Sir John Finlay Willasey, GCB, CBE

Wilshaw, Sir Michael, Kt.

Wilson, *Prof.* Sir Alan Geoffrey, Kt.

Wilson, *Vice-Adm.* Sir Barry Nigel, KCB

Wilson, Sir David Mackenzie, Kt.

Wilson, Sir James William Douglas, Bt. (1906)

Wilson, *Brig.* Sir Mathew John Anthony, Bt. (1874), OBE, MC

Wilson, *Rt. Hon.* Sir Nicholas Allan Roy, Kt. (Wilson of Culworth)

Wilson, *Prof.* Sir Robert James Timothy, Kt.

Wilson, Sir Robert Peter, KCMG

Wilson, *Air Chief Marshal* Sir (Ronald) Andrew (Fellowes), KCB, AFC

Wilson, Sir Thomas David, Bt. (1920)

Wingate, *Capt.* Sir Miles Buckley, KCVO

Winkley, Sir David Ross, Kt.

Winnington, Sir Anthony Edward, Bt. (1755)

Winship, Sir Peter James Joseph, Kt., CBE

Winsor, Sir Thomas Philip, Kt.

Winter, *Dr* Sir Gregory Winter, Kt., CBE

Winterton, Sir Nicholas Raymond, Kt.

Wiseman, Sir John William, Bt. (1628)

Witty, Sir Andrew, Kt.

Wolfendale, *Prof.* Sir Arnold Whittaker, Kt., FRS

Wolseley, Sir Charles Garnet Richard Mark, Bt. (1628)

†Wolseley, Sir James Douglas, Bt. (I. 1745)

†Wombwell, Sir George Philip Frederick, Bt. (1778)

Womersley, Sir Peter John Walter, Bt. (1945)

Woo, Sir Leo Joseph, Kt., MBE

Woo, Sir Po-Shing, Kt.

Wood, Sir Andrew Marley, GCMG

Wood, Sir Anthony John Page, Bt. (1837)

Wood, Sir Ian Clark, Kt., CBE

Wood, Sir James Sebastian Lamin, KCMG

Wood, Sir Martin Francis, Kt., OBE

Wood, Sir Michael Charles, KCMG

Wood, *Hon.* Sir Roderic Lionel James, Kt.

Woodard, *Rear Adm.* Sir Robert Nathaniel, KCVO

Woodhead, *Vice-Adm.* Sir (Anthony) Peter, KCB

Woods, *Prof.* Sir Kent Linton, Kt.

Woods, Sir Robert Kynnersley, Kt., CBE

Woodward, Sir Clive Ronald, Kt., OBE

Woodward, Sir Thomas Jones (Tom Jones), Kt., OBE

Wootton, Sir David Hugh, Kt.

Worsley, Sir William Ralph, Bt. (1838)

Worsthorne, Sir Peregrine Gerard, Kt.

Worthington, Sir Mark, Kt., OBE

Wratten, *Air Chief Marshal* Sir William John, GEE, CB, AFC

Wraxall, Sir Charles Frederick Lascelles, Bt. (1813)

Wrey, Sir George Richard Bourchier, Bt. (1628)

Wright, Sir Allan Frederick, KBE

Wright, Sir David John, GCMG, LVO

Wright, *Hon.* Sir (John) Michael, Kt.

Wright, *Prof.* Sir Nicholas Alcwyn, Kt.

Wright, Sir Peter Robert, Kt., CBE

Wright, *Air Marshal* Sir Robert Alfred, KBE, AFC

Wright, Sir Stephen John Leadbetter, KCMG

Wrightson, Sir Charles Mark Garmondsway, Bt. (1900)

Wrigley, *Prof.* Sir Edward Anthony (Sir Tony), Kt., PHD, PBA

Wrixon-Becher, Sir John William Michael, Bt. (1831)

Wroughton, Sir Philip Lavallin, KCVO

Wu, Sir Gordon Ying Sheung, KCMG

Wynne, Sir Graham Robert, Kt., CBE

Yacoub, *Prof.* Sir Magdi Habib, Kt., OM, FRCS

Yaki, Sir Roy, KBE

Yang, *Hon.* Sir Ti Liang, Kt.

Yarrow, Sir Eric Grant, Bt. (1916), MBE

Yassaie, *Dr* Sir Hossein, Kt.

Yocklunn, Sir John (Soong Chung), KCVO

Yoo Foo, Sir (François) Henri, Kt.

Young, Sir Brian Walter Mark, Kt.

Young, Sir Colville Norbert, GCMG, MBE

Young, Sir Dennis Charles, KCMG
Young, Sir Jimmy Leslie Ronald, Kt., CBE
Young, Sir John Kenyon Roe, Bt. (1821)
Young, Sir John Robertson, GCMG
Young, Sir Leslie Clarence, Kt., CBE
Young, Sir Nicholas Charles, Kt.
Young, Sir Robin Urquhart, KCB
Young, Sir Roger William, Kt.

Young, Sir Stephen Stewart Templeton, Bt. (1945)
Young, Sir William Neil, Bt. (1769)
Younger, *Capt.* Sir John David Bingham, KCVO
Younger, Sir Julian William Richard, Bt. (1911)
Yuwi, Sir Matiabe, KBE

Zacca, *Rt. Hon.* Sir Edward, KCMG

Zambellas, *Adm.* Sir George Michael, KCB, DSC
Zeeman, *Prof.* Sir (Erik) Christopher, Kt., FRS
Zissman, Sir Bernard Philip, Kt.
Zunz, Sir Gerhard Jacob (Jack), Kt., FRENG
Zurenuoc, Sir Manasupe Zure, Kt., OBE
Zurenuoc, Sir Zibang, KBE

THE ORDER OF ST JOHN

THE MOST VENERABLE ORDER OF THE HOSPITAL OF ST JOHN OF JERUSALEM (1888)

GCStJ	Bailiff/Dame Grand Cross
KStJ	Knight of Justice/Grace
DStJ	Dame of Justice/Grace
CStJ	Commander
OStJ	Officer
SBStJ	Serving Brother
SSStJ	Serving Sister

Motto, Pro Fide, Pro Utilitate Hominum
(For the faith and in the service of humanity)

The Order of St John, founded in the early 12th century in Jerusalem, was a religious order with a particular duty to care for the sick. In Britain the order was dissolved by Henry VIII in 1540 but the British branch was revived in the early 19th century. The branch was not accepted by the Grand Magistracy of the Order in Rome but its search for a role in the tradition of the hospitallers led to the founding of the St John Ambulance Association in 1877 and later the St John Ambulance Brigade; in 1882 the St John Ophthalmic Hospital was founded in Jerusalem. A royal charter was granted in 1888 establishing the Order of St John as a British Order of Chivalry with the sovereign as its head.

Since October 1999 the whole order worldwide has been governed by a Grand Council which includes a representative from each of the 11 priories (England, Scotland, Wales, Hong Kong, Kenya, Singapore, South Africa, New Zealand, Canada, Australia and the USA). In addition there are also five commanderies in Northern Ireland, Jersey, Guernsey, the Isle of Man and Western Australia. There are also branches in about 30 other Commonwealth countries. Apart from St John Ambulance, the Order is also responsible for the Eye Hospital in Jerusalem. Admission to the order is usually conferred in recognition of service to either one of these institutions. Membership does not confer any rank, style, title or precedence on a recipient.

SOVEREIGN HEAD OF THE ORDER
HM The Queen

GRAND PRIOR
HRH The Duke of Gloucester, KG, GCVO

Lord Prior, vacant
Prelate, vacant
Sub Prior, Stuart Shilson, LVO
Chancellor, Patrick Burgess, OBE
Secretary General, vacant
International Office, 3 Charterhouse Mews, London EC1M 6BB
T 020-7251 3292 **W** www.stjohninternational.org

DAMES

Style, 'Dame' before forename and surname, followed by appropriate post-nominal initials. Where such an award is made to a lady already in possession of a higher title, the appropriate initials follow her name
Envelope, Dame F_ S_, followed by appropriate post-nominal letters. *Letter (formal),* Dear Madam; *(social),* Dear Dame F_. *Spoken,* Dame F_
Husband, Untitled

Dame Grand Cross and Dame Commander are the higher classes for women of the Order of the Bath, the Order of St Michael and St George, the Royal Victorian Order, and the Order of the British Empire. Dames Grand Cross rank after the wives of Baronets and before the wives of Knights Grand Cross. Dames Commanders rank after the wives of Knights Grand Cross and before the wives of Knights Commanders.

Honorary damehoods may be conferred on women who are citizens of countries of which the Queen is not head of state.

LIST OF DAMES *As at 31 August 2015*

Women peers in their own right and life peers are not included in this list. Female members of the royal family are not included in this list; details of the orders they hold can be found within the Royal Family section.

If a dame has a double barrelled or hyphenated surname, she is listed under the first element of the name.

Abaijah, Dame Josephine, DBE
Abramsky, Dame Jennifer Gita, DBE
Acland Hood Gass, Lady (Elizabeth Periam), DCVO
Airlie, The Countess of, DCVO
Alexander, Dame Helen Anne, DBE
Allen, *Prof.* Dame Ingrid Victoria, DBE
Andrews, *Hon.* Dame Geraldine Mary, DBE
Andrews, Dame Julie, DBE
Angiolini, *Rt. Hon.* Dame Elish, DBE, QC
Anglesey, Shirley, Marchioness of, DBE
Anson, Lady (Elizabeth Audrey), DBE
Anstee, Dame Margaret Joan, DCMG
Archer, *Dr* Dame Mary Doreen, DBE
Arden, *Rt. Hon.* Dame Mary Howarth (Mrs Mance), DBE
Ashcroft, *Prof.* Dame Frances Mary, DBE, FRS
Asplin, *Hon.* Dame Sarah Jane (Mrs Sherwin), DBE
Atkins, Dame Eileen, DBE
August, Dame Kathryn, DBE
Bacon, Dame Patricia Anne, DBE
Bailey, *Prof.* Dame Susan Mary, DBE
Baker, Dame Janet Abbott (Mrs Shelley), CH, DBE
Barbour, Dame Margaret (Mrs Ash), DBE
Barker, Dame Katharine Mary, DBE
Barker-Welch, *Hon.* Dame Maizie Irene, DBE
Barrow, Dame Jocelyn Anita (Mrs Downer), DBE
Barstow, Dame Josephine Clare (Mrs Anderson), DBE
Bassey, Dame Shirley, DBE
Beasley, *Prof.* Dame Christine Joan, DBE
Beaurepaire, Dame Beryl Edith, DBE
Beckett, *Rt. Hon.* Dame Margaret Mary, DBE
Beer, *Prof.* Dame Gillian Patricia Kempster, DBE, FBA
Begg, Dame Anne, DBE
Beral, *Prof.* Dame Valerie, DBE
Bertschinger, *Dr* Dame Claire, DBE
Bevan, Dame Yasmin, DBE
Bewley, Dame Beulah Rosemary, DBE

Bibby, Dame Enid, DBE
Black, *Prof.* Dame Carol Mary, DBE
Black, *Rt. Hon.* Dame Jill Margaret, DBE
Blackadder, Dame Elizabeth Violet, DBE
Blaize, Dame Venetia Ursula, DBE
Blaxland, Dame Helen Frances, DBE
Blume, Dame Hilary Sharon Braverman, DBE
Booth, *Hon.* Dame Margaret Myfanwy Wood, DBE
Bourne, Dame Susan Mary (Mrs Bourne), DBE
Bowe, *Dr* Dame (Mary) Colette, DBE
Bowtell, Dame Ann Elizabeth, DCB
Braddock, *Dr* Dame Christine, DBE
Brain, Dame Margaret Anne (Mrs Wheeler), DBE
Breakwell, *Prof.* Dame Glynis Marie, DBE
Brennan, Dame Maureen, DBE
Brennan, Dame Ursula, DCB
Brewer, *Dr* Dame Nicola Mary, DCMG
Bridges, Dame Mary Patricia, DBE
Brindley, Dame Lynne Janie, DBE
Brittan, Dame Diana (Lady Brittan of Spennithorne), DBE
Brooke, *Rt. Hon.* Dame Annette (Lesley), DBE
Browne, Lady Moyra Blanche Madeleine, DBE
Bruce, Dame Susan Margaret, DBE
Bruce, *Prof.* Dame Victoria Geraldine, DBE, FBA, FRSE
Buckland, Dame Yvonne Helen Elaine, DBE
Burnell, *Prof.* Dame Susan Jocelyn Bell, DBE
Burslem, Dame Alexandra Vivien, DBE
Butler, Dame Rosemary Janet Mair, DBE
Byatt, Dame Antonia Susan, DBE, FRSL
Caldicott, Dame Fiona, DBE, FRCP, FRCPSYCH
Cairncross, Dame Frances Anne, DBE, FRSE
Cameron, *Prof.* Dame Averil Millicent, DBE
Campbell-Preston, Dame Frances Olivia, DCVO
Carnall, Dame Ruth, DBE
Carnwath, Dame Alison Jane, DBE
Carr, *Hon.* Dame Sue Lascelles (Mrs Birch), DBE
Cartwright, Dame Silvia Rose, DBE
Clark, *Prof.* Dame Jill MacLeod, DBE
Clark, *Prof.* Dame (Margaret) June, DBE, PHD
Cleverdon, Dame Julia Charity, DCVO, CBE
Coates, Dame Sally, DBE
Collarbone, Dame Patricia, DBE
Collins, Dame Joan Henrietta, DBE
Contreras, *Prof.* Dame Marcela, DBE
Corner, *Prof.* Dame Jessica Lois, DBE
Corsar, *Hon.* Dame Mary Drummond, DBE
Coward, Dame Pamela Sarah, DBE
Cowley, *Prof.* Dame Sarah Ann, DBE
Cox, *Hon.* Dame Laura Mary, DBE
Cramp, *Prof.* Dame Rosemary Jean, DBE
Cullum, *Prof.* Dame Nicola Anne, DBE
Dacon, Dame Monica Jessie, DBE, CMG
Davies, *Prof.* Dame Kay Elizabeth, DBE
Davies, Dame Laura Jane, DBE
Davies, *Hon.* Dame Nicola Velfor, DBE
Davies, *Prof.* Dame Sally Claire, DBE
Davies, Dame Wendy Patricia, DBE
Davis, Dame Karlene Cecile, DBE
Dawson, *Prof.* Dame Sandra Jane Noble, DBE
De Souza, Dame Rachel Mary, DBE
Dell, Dame Miriam Patricia, DBE
Dench, Dame Judith Olivia (Mrs Williams), CH, DBE
Descartes, Dame Marie Selipha Sesenne, DBE, BEM
Dethridge, Dame Kate, DBE

Digby, The Lady, DBE
Dobbs, *Hon.* Dame Linda Penelope, DBE
Docherty, Dame Jacqueline, DBE
Donald, *Prof.* Dame Athene Margaret, DBE, FRS
Dowling, *Prof.* Dame Ann Patricia, DBE
Duffield, Dame Vivien Louise, DBE
Duffy, Dame Carol Ann, DBE
Dumont, Dame Ivy Leona, DCMG
Dunnell, Dame Karen, DCB
Dyche, Dame Rachael Mary, DBE
Elcoat, Dame Catherine Elizabeth, DBE
Ellis, Dame Diana Margaret (Mrs Ellis), DBE
Ellison, Dame Jill, DBE
Elton, Dame Susan Richenda (Lady Elton), DCVO
Engel, Dame Pauline Frances (Sister Pauline Engel), DBE
Esteve-Coll, Dame Elizabeth Anne Loosemore, DBE
Evans, Dame Anne Elizabeth Jane, DBE
Evans, Dame Madeline Glynne Dervel, DBE, CMG
Evans, Dame Oremi, DBE
Fagan, Dame (Florence) Mary, DCVO
Farnham, Dame Marion (Lady Farnham), DCVO
Fawcett, Dame Amelia Chilcott, DBE
Fielding, Dame Pauline, DBE
Finch, *Prof.* Dame Janet Valerie, DBE
Fisher, Dame Jacqueline, DBE
Forgan, Dame Elizabeth Anne Lucy, DBE
Fradd, Dame Elizabeth, DBE
Fraser, Lady Antonia, DBE
Fraser, Dame Dorothy Rita, DBE
Fry, Dame Margaret Louise, DBE
Furse, Dame Clara Hedwig Frances, DBE
Gaymer, Dame Janet Marion, DBE, QC
Ghosh, Dame Helen Frances, DCB
Gibb, Dame Moira Margaret, DBE
Glenn, *Prof.* Dame Hazel Gillian, DBE
Glennie, *Dr* Dame Evelyn Elizabeth Ann, DBE
Gloster, *Rt. Hon.* Dame Elizabeth (Lady Popplewell), DBE
Glover, Dame Audrey Frances, DBE, CMG
Glover, *Prof.* Dame Lesley Anne, DBE, FRSE
Goad, Dame Sarah Jane Frances, DCVO
Goodall, *Dr* Dame (Valerie) Jane, DBE
Goodfellow, *Prof.* Dame Julia Mary, DBE
Gordon, Dame Minita Elmira, GCMG, GCVO
Gordon, *Hon.* Dame Pamela Felicity, DBE
Gow, Dame Jane Elizabeth (Mrs Whiteley), DBE
Grafton, Ann, The Duchess of, GCVO
Grant, Dame Mavis, DBE
Green, Dame Pauline, DBE
Grey, Dame Beryl Elizabeth (Mrs Svenson), DBE
Griffiths, Dame Anne, DCVO
Grimthorpe, Elizabeth, The Lady, DCVO
Guilfoyle, Dame Margaret Georgina Constance, DBE
Guthardt, *Revd Dr* Dame Phyllis Myra, DBE
Hadid, Dame Zaha, DBE
Hakin, *Dr* Dame Barbara Ann, DBE
Hall, *Prof.* Dame Wendy, DBE
Hallett, *Rt. Hon.* Dame Heather Carol, DBE
Hallett, Dame Nancy Karen, DBE
Harbison, Dame Joan Irene, DBE
Harper, Dame Elizabeth Margaret Way, DBE
Harris, Dame Pauline (Lady Harris of Peckham), DBE
Harris, Dame Philippa Jill Olivier, DBE
Hassan, Dame Anna Patricia Lucy, DBE
Hay, Dame Barbara Logan, DCMG, MBE
Henderson, Dame Fiona Douglas, DCVO
Hercus, *Hon.* Dame (Margaret) Ann, DCMG
Higgins, *Prof.* Dame Joan Margaret, DBE
Higgins, *Prof.* Dame Julia Stretton, DBE, FRS
Higgins, *Prof.* Dame Rosalyn, DBE, QC

Hill, *Air Cdre* Dame Felicity Barbara, DBE
Hill, *Prof.* Dame Judith Eileen, DBE
Hine, Dame Deirdre Joan, DBE, FRCP
Hodge, *Rt. Hon.* Lady Margaret (Eve), DBE
Hodgson, Dame Patricia Anne, DBE
Hogg, *Hon.* Dame Mary Claire (Mrs Koops), DBE
Holborow, Lady Mary Christina, DCVO
Hollows, Dame Sharon, DBE
Holmes, Dame Kelly, DBE
Holroyd, Lady (Margaret Drabble), DBE
Holt, Dame Denise Mary, DCMG
Hoodless, Dame Elisabeth Anne, DBE
Hoyles, *Prof.* Dame Celia Mary, DBE
Hufton, *Prof.* Dame Olwen, DBE
Humphrey, *Prof.* Dame Caroline (Lady Rees of Ludlow), DBE
Husband, *Prof.* Dame Janet Elizabeth Siarey, DBE
Hussey, Dame Susan Katharine (Lady Hussey of North Bradley), GCVO
Hutton, Dame Deirdre Mary, DBE
Hyde, Dame Helen, DBE
Imison, Dame Tamsyn, DBE
Ion, *Dr* Dame Susan Elizabeth, DBE
Isaacs, Dame Albertha Madeline, DBE
James, Dame Naomi Christine (Mrs Haythorne), DBE
Jenkins, Dame (Mary) Jennifer (Lady Jenkins of Hillhead), DBE
John, Dame Susan, DBE
Johnson, *Prof.* Dame Anne Mandall, DBE
Jones, Dame Gwyneth (Mrs Haberfeld-Jones), DBE
Jordan, *Prof.* Dame Carole, DBE
Joseph, Dame Monica Theresa, DBE
Jowell, *Rt. Hon.* Dame Tessa Jane, DBE
Julius, *Dr* Dame DeAnne Shirley, DCMG, CBE
Karika, Dame Pauline Margaret Rakera George (Mrs Taripo), DBE
Keeble, *Dr* Dame Reena, DBE
Keegan, Dame Elizabeth Mary, DBE
Keegan, Dame Geraldine Mary Marcella, DBE
Keith, Dame Penelope Anne Constance (Mrs Timson), DBE
Kekedo, Dame Rosalina Violet, DBE
Kelleher, Dame Joan, DBE
Kelly, Dame Barbara Mary, DBE
Kelly, Dame Lorna May Boreland, DBE
Kendrick, Dame Fiona Marie, DBE
Kershaw, Dame Janet Elizabeth Murray (Dame Betty), DBE
Kettlewell, *Comdt.* Dame Marion Mildred, DBE
Kharas, Dame Zarine, DBE
Khemka, Dame Asha, DBE
Kidu, Lady, DBE
King, *Rt. Hon.* Dame Eleanor Warwick, DBE
King, *Prof.* Dame Julia Elizabeth, DBE
Kinnair, Dame Donna, DBE
Kirby, Dame Carolyn Emma, DBE
Kirby, Dame Georgina Kamiria, DBE
Kirwan, *Prof.* Dame Frances Clare, DBE, FRS
Kramer, *Prof.* Dame Leonie Judith, DBE
La Grenade, *HE* Dame Cécile Ellen Fleurette, GCMG, OBE
Laine, Dame Cleo (Clementine) Dinah (Lady Dankworth), DBE
Laing, *Hon.* Dame Elisabeth Mary Caroline, DBE
Lake-Tack, *HE* Dame Louise Agnetha, GCMG
Lamb, Dame Dawn Ruth, DBE
Lang, *Hon.* Dame Beverley Ann Macnaughton, DBE
Lansbury Shaw, Dame Angela Brigid, DBE
Lavender, *Prof.* Dame Tina, DBE
Leather, Dame Susan Catherine, DBE
Lee, *Prof.* Dame Hermione, DBE
Legge-Bourke, *Hon.* Dame Elizabeth Shân Josephine, DCVO
Leslie, Dame Alison Mariot, DCMG

Leslie, Dame Ann Elizabeth Mary, DBE
Lewis, Dame Edna Leofrida (Lady Lewis), DBE
Lively, Dame Penelope Margaret, DBE
Lott, Dame Felicity Ann Emwhyla (Mrs Woolf), DBE
Louisy, Dame (Calliopa) Pearlette, GCMG
Lynn, Dame Vera (Mrs Lewis), DBE
Lynne, Dame Gillian Barbara, DBE
MacArthur, Dame Ellen Patricia, DBE
Macdonald, Dame Mary Beaton, DBE
McDonald, Dame Mavis, DCB
McGowan, *Hon.* Dame Maura Patricia, DBE
McGuire, *Rt. Hon.* Dame Anne Catherine, DBE
MacIntyre, *Prof.* Dame Sarah Jane, DBE
Macmillan of Ovenden, Katharine, Viscountess, DBE
Macur, *Rt. Hon.* Dame Julia Wendy, DBE
McVittie, Dame Joan Christine, DBE
Mayhew, Jonas, Dame Judith, DBE
Major, Dame Malvina Lorraine (Mrs Fleming), DBE
Major, Dame Norma Christina Elizabeth, DBE
Makin, *Dr* Dame Pamela Louise, DBE
Mantel, *Dr.* Dame Hiliary Mary, DBE
Marsden, *Dr* Dame Rosalind Mary, DCMG
Marsh, Dame Mary Elizabeth, DBE
Mason, Dame Monica Margaret, DBE
Matheson, Dame Jilian Norma, DCB
Mellor, Dame Julie Thérèse Mellor, DBE
Metge, *Dr* Dame (Alice) Joan, DBE
Middleton, Dame Elaine Madoline, DCMG, MBE
Mills, *Prof.* Dame Anne Jane, DCMG, CBE
Mirren, Dame Helen, DBE
Monroe, *Prof.* Dame Barbara, DBE
Moore, Dame Julie, DBE
Moores, Dame Yvonne, DBE
Morgan, *Dr* Dame Gillian Margaret, DBE
Morris, Dame Sylvia Ann, DBE
Morrison, *Hon.* Dame Mary Anne, GCVO
Muirhead, Dame Lorna Elizabeth Fox, DBE
Mullally, *Rt. Revd* Dame Sarah Elisabeth, DBE
Murray, Dame Jennifer Susan, DBE
Nelson, *Prof.* Dame Janet Laughland, DBE
Nelson-Taylor, Dame Nicola Jane, DBE
Neville, Dame Elizabeth, DBE, QPM
Newell, Dame Priscilla Jane, DBE
O'Brien, Dame Una, DCB
Ogilvie, Dame Bridget Margaret, DBE, PHD, DSc
Oliver, Dame Gillian Frances, DBE
Owers, Dame Anne Elizabeth (Mrs Cook), DBE
Oxenbury, Dame Shirley Ann, DBE
Palmer, Dame Felicity Joan, DBE
Paraskeva, *Rt. Hon.* Dame Janet, DBE
Park, Dame Merle Florence (Mrs Bloch), DBE
Parker, *Hon.* Dame Judith Mary Frances, DBE
Partridge, *Prof.* Dame Linda, DBE
Patel, Dame Indira, DBE
Paterson, Dame Vicki, DBE
Patterson, *Hon.* Dame Frances Silvia, DBE
Pauffley, *Hon.* Dame Anna Evelyn Hamilton, DBE
Peacock, Dame Alison Margaret, DBE
Pearce, *Prof.* Dame Shirley, DBE
Penhaligon, Dame Annette (Mrs Egerton), DBE
Pereira, *Hon.* Dame Janice Mesadis, DBE
Perkins, Dame Mary Lesley, DBE
Peters, Dame Mary Elizabeth, DBE, CH
Pienaar, Dame Erica, DBE
Pindling, Lady (Marguerite Matilda), GCMG
Platt, Dame Denise, DBE
Plotnikoff, Dame Joyce Evelyn, DBE
Plowright, Dame Joan Ann, DBE
Plunket Greene, Dame Barbara Mary, DBE

Poole, Dame Avril Anne Barker, DBE
Porter, Dame Shirley (Lady Porter), DBE
Powell, Dame Sally Ann Vickers, DBE
Pringle, Dame Anne Fyfe, DCMG
Proudman, *Hon.* Dame Sonia Rosemary Susan, DBE
Pugh, *Dr* Dame Gillian Mary, DBE
Quinn, Dame Sheila Margaret Imelda, DBE
Rafferty, *Rt. Hon.* Dame Anne Judith, DBE
Rantzen, Dame Esther Louise (Mrs Wilcox), DBE
Rawson, *Prof.* Dame Jessica Mary, DBE
Rees, *Prof.* Dame Judith Anne, DBE
Rees, *Prof.* Dame Lesley Howard, DBE
Rees, *Prof.* Dame Teresa Lesley, DBE
Reeves, Dame Helen May, DBE
Rego, Dame Paula Figueiroa, DBE
Reid, Dame Seona Elizabeth, DBE
Reynolds, Dame Fiona Claire, DBE
Rhodes, Dame Zandra Lindsey, DBE
Richard, Dame Alison (Fettes), DBE
Richardson, Dame Mary, DBE
Rigg, Dame Diana, DBE
Rimington, Dame Stella, DCB
Ritterman, Dame Janet, DBE
Roberts, Dame Jane Elisabeth, DBE
Roberts, *Hon.* Dame Jennifer Mary, DBE
Roberts, *Hon.* Dame Priscilla Jane Stephanie (Lady Roberts),
    DCVO
Robins, Dame Ruth Laura, DBE
Robinson, *Prof.* Dame Carol Vivien, DBE
Robottom, Dame Marlene, DBE
Roe, Dame Marion Audrey, DBE
Roe, Dame Raigh Edith, DBE
Ronson, Dame Gail, DBE
Rose, *Hon.* Dame Vivien Judith, DBE
Ross-Wawrzynski, Dame Dana (Mrs Ross-Wawrzynski), DBE
Rothwell, *Prof.* Dame Nancy Jane, DBE
Ruddock, *Rt. Hon.* Dame Joan Mary, DBE
Runciman of Doxford, The Viscountess, DBE
Russell, *Hon.* Dame Alison Hunter, DBE
Russell, *Dr* Dame Philippa Margaret, DBE
Sackler, Dame Theresa, DBE
Salas, Dame Margaret Laurence, DBE
Salmond, *Prof.* Dame Mary Anne, DBE
Savill, Dame Rosalind Joy, DBE
Sawyer, *Rt. Hon.* Dame Joan Augusta, DBE
Scardino, Dame Marjorie, DBE
Scott, Dame Catherine Margaret (Mrs Denton), DBE
Scott Thomas, Dame Kristin, DBE
Seward, Dame Margaret Helen Elizabeth, DBE
Shafik, *Dr.* Dame Nemat Talaat, DBE
Sharp, *Rt. Hon.* Dame Victoria Madeleine, DBE
Shaw, *Prof.* Dame Pamela Jean, DBE
Sheldrick, *Dr* Dame Daphne Marjorie, DBE
Shirley, Dame Stephanie, DBE
Shovelton, Dame Helena, DBE
Sibley, Dame Antoinette (Mrs Corbett), DBE
Sills, *Prof.* Dame Eileen, DBE
Silver, *Dr* Dame Ruth Muldoon, DBE
Simler, *Hon.* Dame Ingrid Ann (Mrs Bernstein), DBE
Slade, *Hon.* Dame Elizabeth Ann, DBE
Slingo, *Prof.* Dame Julia Mary, DBE
Smith, Dame Dela, DBE
Smith, *Rt. Hon.* Dame Janet Hilary (Mrs Mathieson), DBE
Smith, *Hon.* Dame Jennifer Meredith, DBE
Smith, Dame Margaret Natalie (Maggie) (Mrs Cross),
    CH, DBE
Southgate, *Prof.* Dame Lesley Jill, DBE
Spencer, Dame Rosemary Jane, DCMG
Steel, *Hon.* Dame (Anne) Heather (Mrs Beattie), DBE

Stocking, Dame Barbara Mary, DBE
Storey, Dame Sarah Joanne, DBE
Strachan, Dame Valerie Patricia Marie, DCB
Strathern, *Prof.* Dame Anne Marilyn, DBE
Street, Dame Susan Ruth, DCB
Stringer, *Prof.* Dame Joan Kathleen, DBE
Sutherland, Dame Veronica Evelyn, DBE, CMG
Suzman, Dame Janet, DBE
Swift, *Hon.* Dame Caroline Jane (Mrs Openshaw), DBE
Symmonds, Dame Olga Patricia, DBE
Tanner, *Dr* Dame Mary Elizabeth, DBE
Taylor, Dame Meg, DBE
Te Kanawa, Dame Kiri Janette, DBE
Theis, *Hon.* Dame Lucy Morgan, DBE
Thirlwall, *Hon.* Dame Kathryn Mary, DBE
Thomas, *Prof.* Dame Jean Olwen, DBE
Thomas, Dame Maureen Elizabeth (Lady Thomas), DBE
Thompson, Dame Ila Dianne, DBE
Thornton, *Prof.* Dame Janet Maureen, DBE
Tickell, Dame Clare Oriana, DBE
Tinson, Dame Sue, DBE
Tizard, Dame Catherine Anne, GCMG, GCVO, DBE
Tokiel, Dame Rosa, DBE
Trotter, Dame Janet Olive, DBE
Turner-Warwick, Dame Margaret Elizabeth Harvey, DBE, FRCP, FRCPED
Twelftree, Dame Marcia, DBE
Uchida, Dame Mitsuko, DBE

Uprichard, Dame Mary Elizabeth, DBE
Varley, Dame Joan Fleetwood, DBE
Wagner, Dame Gillian Mary Millicent (Lady Wagner), DBE
Wall, Dame (Alice) Anne, (Mrs Michael Wall), DCVO
Wallace, *Prof.* Dame Helen Sarah, DBE, CMG
Wallis, Dame Sheila Ann, DBE
Walter, Dame Harriet Mary, DBE
Warner, *Prof.* Dame Marina Sarah, DBE, FBA
Waterhouse, Dr Dame Rachel Elizabeth, DBE
Waterman, *Dr* Dame Fanny, DBE
Watkinson, Dame Angela Eileen, DBE
Webb, *Prof.* Dame Patricia, DBE
Weir, Dame Gillian Constance (Mrs Phelps), DBE
Weller, Dame Rita, DBE
Weston, Dame Margaret Kate, DBE
Westwood, Dame Vivienne Isabel, DBE
Whitehead, *Hon.* Dame Annabel Alice Hoyer, DCVO
Williams, Dame Josephine, DBE
Willmot, Dame Glenis, DBE
Wilson, Dame Jacqueline, DBE
Wilson-Barnett, *Prof.* Dame Jenifer, DBE
Winstone, Dame Dorothy Gertrude, DBE, CMG
Wolfson de Botton, Dame Janet (Mrs Wolfson de Botton), DBE
Wong Yick-ming, Dame Rosanna, DBE
Woolf, Dame Catherine Fiona, DBE
Zaffar, Dame Naila, DBE

DECORATIONS AND MEDALS

PRINCIPAL DECORATIONS AND MEDALS
IN ORDER OF WEAR

VICTORIA CROSS (VC), 1856 (*see* below)
GEORGE CROSS (GC), 1940 (*see* below)

BRITISH ORDERS OF KNIGHTHOOD (*see also* Orders of Chivalry)
Order of the Garter
Order of the Thistle
Order of St Patrick
Order of the Bath
Order of Merit
Order of the Star of India
Order of St Michael and George
Order of the Indian Empire
Order of the Crown of India
Royal Victorian Order (Classes I, II and III)
Order of the British Empire (Classes I, II and III)
Order of the Companions of Honour
Distinguished Service Order
Royal Victorian Order (Class IV)
Order of the British Empire (Class IV)
Imperial Service Order
Royal Victorian Order (Class V)
Order of the British Empire (Class V)

BARONET'S BADGE

KNIGHT BACHELOR'S BADGE

INDIAN ORDER OF MERIT (MILITARY)

DECORATIONS
Conspicuous Gallantry Cross (CGC), 1995
Royal Red Cross Class I (RRC), 1883
Distinguished Service Cross (DSC), 1914
Military Cross (MC), December 1914
Distinguished Flying Cross (DFC), 1918
Air Force Cross (AFC), 1918
Royal Red Cross Class II (ARRC)
Order of British India
Kaisar-i-Hind Medal
Order of St John

MEDALS FOR GALLANTRY AND DISTINGUISHED CONDUCT
Union of South Africa Queen's Medal for Bravery, in Gold
Distinguished Conduct Medal (DCM), 1854
Conspicuous Gallantry Medal (CGM), 1874
Conspicuous Gallantry Medal (Flying)
George Medal (GM), 1940
Queen's Police Medal for Gallantry
Queen's Fire Service Medal for Gallantry
Royal West African Frontier Force Distinguished Conduct Medal
King's African Rifles Distinguished Conduct Medal
Indian Distinguished Service Medal
Union of South Africa Queen's Medal for Bravery, in Silver
Distinguished Service Medal (DSM), 1914
Military Medal (MM), 1916
Distinguished Flying Medal (DFM), 1918
Air Force Medal (AFM)
Constabulary Medal (Ireland)

Medal for Saving Life at Sea (Sea Gallantry Medal)
Indian Order of Merit (Civil)
Indian Police Medal for Gallantry
Ceylon Police Medal for Gallantry
Sierra Leone Police Medal for Gallantry
Sierra Leone Fire Brigades Medal for Gallantry
Overseas Territories Police Medal for Gallantry
Queen's Gallantry Medal (QGM), 1974
Royal Victorian Medal (RVM), Gold, Silver and Bronze
British Empire Medal (BEM)
Canada Medal
Queen's Police Medal for Distinguished Service (QPM)
Queen's Fire Service Medal for Distinguished Service (QFSM)
Queen's Volunteer Reserves Medal
Queen's Medal for Chiefs

CAMPAIGN MEDALS AND STARS
Including authorised United Nations, European Community/Union and North Atlantic Treaty Organisation medals (in order of date of campaign for which awarded)

Iraq Reconstruction Service Medal
Civilian Service Medal (Afghanistan)

POLAR MEDALS (in order of date)

IMPERIAL SERVICE MEDAL

POLICE MEDALS FOR VALUABLE SERVICE
Indian Police Medal for Meritorious Service
Ceylon Police Medal for Merit
Sierra Leone Police Medal for Meritorious Service
Sierra Leone Fire Brigades Medal for Meritorious Service
Overseas Territories Police Medal for Meritorious Service

BADGE OF HONOUR

JUBILEE, CORONATION AND DURBAR MEDALS
Queen Victoria, King Edward VII, King George V, King George VI, Queen Elizabeth II, Visit Commemoration and Long and Faithful Service Medals

EFFICIENCY AND LONG SERVICE DECORATIONS AND MEDALS
Medal for Meritorious Service
Accumulated Campaign Service Medal
Medal for Long Service and Good Conduct (Military)
Naval Long Service and Good Conduct Medal
Medal for Meritorious Service (Royal Navy 1918–28)
Indian Long Service and Good Conduct Medal
Indian Meritorious Service Medal
Royal Marines Meritorious Service Medal (1849–1947)
Royal Air Force Meritorious Service Medal (1918–1928)
Royal Air Force Long Service and Good Conduct Medal
Medal for Long Service and Good Conduct (Ulster Defence Regiment)
Indian Long Service and Good Conduct Medal
Royal West African Frontier Force Long Service and Good Conduct Medal
Royal Sierra Leone Military Forces Long Service and Good Conduct Medal
King's African Rifles Long Service and Good Conduct Medal

Indian Meritorious Service Medal
Police Long Service and Good Conduct Medal
Fire Brigade Long Service and Good Conduct Medal
African Police Medal for Meritorious Service
Royal Canadian Mounted Police Long Service Medal
Ceylon Police Long Service Medal
Ceylon Fire Services Long Service Medal
Sierra Leone Police Long Service Medal
Overseas Territories Police Long Service Medal
Sierra Leone Fire Brigades Long Service Medal
Mauritius Police Long Service and Good Conduct Medal
Mauritius Fire Services Long Service and Good Conduct Medal
Mauritius Prisons Service Long Service and Good Conduct Medal
Overseas Territories Fire Brigades Long Service Medal
Overseas Territories Prison Service Medal
Hong Kong Disciplined Services Medal
Army Emergency Reserve Decoration (ERD)
Volunteer Officers' Decoration (VD)
Volunteer Long Service Medal
Volunteer Officers' Decoration (for India and the Colonies)
Volunteer Long Service Medal (for India and the Colonies)
Colonial Auxiliary Forces Officers' Decoration
Colonial Auxiliary Forces Long Service Medal
Medal for Good Shooting (Naval)
Militia Long Service Medal
Imperial Yeomanry Long Service Medal
Territorial Decoration (TD), 1908
Ceylon Armed Services Long Service Medal
Efficiency Decoration (ED)
Territorial Efficiency Medal
Efficiency Medal
Special Reserve Long Service and Good Conduct Medal
Decoration for Officers of the Royal Navy Reserve (RD), 1910
Decoration for Officers of the Royal Naval Volunteer Reserve (VRD)
Royal Naval Reserve Long Service and Good Conduct Medal
Royal Naval Volunteer Reserve Long Service and Good Conduct Medal
Royal Naval Auxiliary Sick Berth Reserve Long Service and Good Conduct Medal
Royal Fleet Reserve Long Service and Good Conduct Medal
Royal Naval Wireless Auxiliary Reserve Long Service and Good Conduct Medal
Royal Naval Auxiliary Service Medal
Air Efficiency Award (AE), 1942
Volunteer Reserves Service Medal
Ulster Defence Regiment Medal
Northern Ireland Home Service Medal
Queen's Medal (for Champion Shots of the RN and RM)
Queen's Medal (for Champion Shots of the New Zealand Naval Forces)
Queen's Medal (for Champion Shots in the Military Forces)
Queen's Medal (for Champion Shots of the Air Forces)
Cadet Forces Medal, 1950
HM Coastguard Long Service and Good Conduct Medal
Special Constabulary Long Service Medal
Canadian Forces Decoration
Royal Observer Corps Medal
Civil Defence Long Service Medal
Ambulance Service (Emergency Duties) Long Service and Good Conduct Medal
Royal Fleet Auxiliary Service Medal
Prison Services (Operational Duties) Long Service and Good Conduct Medal
Jersey Honorary Police Long Service and Good Conduct Medal
Merchant Navy Medal for Meritorious Service
Ebola Medal for Service in West Africa
Rhodesia Medal

Royal Ulster Constabulary Service Medal
Northern Ireland Prison Service Medal
Union of South Africa Commemoration Medal
Indian Independence Medal
Pakistan Medal
Ceylon Armed Services Inauguration Medal
Ceylon Police Independence Medal (1948)
Sierra Leone Independence Medal
Jamaica Independence Medal
Uganda Independence Medal
Malawi Independence Medal
Fiji Independence Medal
Papua New Guinea Independence Medal
Solomon Islands Independence Medal
Service Medal of the Order of St John
Badge of the Order of the League of Mercy
Voluntary Medical Service Medal (1932)
Women's Royal Voluntary Service Medal
South African Medal for War Services
Overseas Territories Special Constabulary Medal

HONORARY MEMBERSHIP OF COMMONWEALTH ORDERS

OTHER COMMONWEALTH MEMBERS' ORDERS, DECORATIONS AND MEDALS

FOREIGN ORDERS

FOREIGN DECORATIONS

FOREIGN MEDALS

THE VICTORIA CROSS (1856)
FOR CONSPICUOUS BRAVERY

VC

Ribbon, Crimson, for all Services (until 1918 it was blue for the Royal Navy)

Instituted on 29 January 1856, the Victoria Cross was awarded retrospectively to 1854, the first being held by Lt C. D. Lucas, RN, for bravery in the Baltic Sea on 21 June 1854 (gazetted 24 February 1857). The first 62 crosses were presented by Queen Victoria in Hyde Park, London, on 26 June 1857.

The Victoria Cross is worn before all other decorations, on the left breast, and consists of a cross-pattée of bronze, 3.8cm in diameter, with the royal crown surmounted by a lion in the centre, and beneath there is the inscription For Valour. Holders of the VC currently receive a tax-free annuity of £2,149, irrespective of need or other conditions. In 1911, the right to receive the cross was extended to Indian soldiers, and in 1920 to matrons, sisters and nurses, the staff of the nursing services and other services pertaining to hospitals and nursing, and to civilians of either sex regularly or temporarily under the orders, direction or supervision of the naval, military, or air forces of the crown.

SURVIVING RECIPIENTS OF THE VICTORIA CROSS
as at 31 August 2015

Apiata, Cpl. B. H., VC (New Zealand Special Air Service) 2004 Afghanistan

Beharry, *LSgt.* J. G., VC (Princess of Wales's Royal Regiment)
2005 *Iraq*
Cruickshank, *Flt. Lt.* J. A., VC (RAFVR)
1944 *World War*
Donaldson, *Cpl.* M. G. S., VC (Australian Special Air Service)
2008 *Afghanistan*
Keighran, *Cpl.* D. A., VC (Royal Australian Regiment)
2012 *Afghanistan*
Leakey, *Lance Cpl.* J. M., VC (Parachute Regiment)
2015 *Afghanistan*
Payne, *WO* K., VC, DSC (USA) (Australian Army Training
Team)
1969 *Vietnam*
Rambahadur Limbu, *Capt.,* VC, MVO (10th Princess Mary's
Gurkha Rifles)
1965 *Sarawak*
Roberts-Smith, *Cpl.* B., VC (Australian Special Air Service)
2010 *Afghanistan*
Speakman, *Sgt.* W., VC (Black Watch, attached KOSB)
1951 *Korea*

THE GEORGE CROSS (1940)
FOR GALLANTRY

GC

Ribbon, Dark blue, threaded through a bar adorned with
laurel leaves
Instituted 24 September 1940 (with amendments,
3 November 1942)

The George Cross is worn before all other decorations
(except the VC) on the left breast (when worn by a woman it
may be worn on the left shoulder from a ribbon of the same
width and colour fashioned into a bow). It consists of a plain
silver cross with four equal limbs, the cross having in the
centre a circular medallion bearing a design showing St
George and the Dragon. The inscription *For Gallantry*
appears round the medallion and in the angle of each limb of
the cross is the royal cypher 'G VI' forming a circle
concentric with the medallion. The reverse is plain and bears
the name of the recipient and the date of the award. The
cross is suspended by a ring from a bar adorned with laurel
leaves on dark blue ribbon 3.8cm wide.

The cross is intended primarily for civilians; awards to the
fighting services are confined to actions for which purely
military honours are not normally granted. It is awarded only
for acts of the greatest heroism or of the most conspicuous
courage in circumstances of extreme danger. From 1 April
1965, holders of the cross have received a tax-free annuity,
which is currently £2,149. The cross has twice been awarded
collectively rather than to an individual: to Malta (1942) and
the Royal Ulster Constabulary (1999).

In October 1971 all surviving holders of the Albert Medal
and the Edward Medal exchanged those decorations for the
George Cross.

SURVIVING RECIPIENTS OF THE GEORGE CROSS
as at 31 August 2015

If the recipient originally received the Albert Medal (AM) or
the Edward Medal (EM), this is indicated by the initials in
parentheses.

Bamford, J., GC, 1952
Beaton, J., GC, CVO, 1974
Croucher, *Lance Cpl.* M., GC, 2008
Finney, C., GC, 2003
Flintoff, H. H., GC (EM), 1944
Gledhill, A. J., GC, 1967
Gregson, J. S., GC (AM), 1943
Haberfield, *Csgt.* K. H., GC, 2005
Hughes, *WO2* K. S., GC, 2010
Johnson, *WO1 (SSM)* B., GC, 1990
Kinne, D. G., GC, 1954
Lowe, A. R., GC (AM), 1949
Norton, *Maj.* P. A., GC, 2006
Pratt, M. K., GC, 1978
Purves, Mrs M., GC (AM), 1949
Raweng, Awang anak, GC, 1951
Shephard, S. J., GC, 2014
Stevens, H. W., GC, 1958
Walker, C., GC, 1972
Wooding, E. A., GC (AM), 1945

THE ELIZABETH CROSS (2009)

EC

Instituted 1 July 2009

The Elizabeth Cross consists of a silver cross with a laurel
wreath passing between the arms, which bear the floral
symbols of England (rose), Scotland (thistle), Ireland
(shamrock) and Wales (daffodil). The centre of the cross bears
the royal cypher and the reverse is inscribed with the name
of the person for whom it is in honour. The cross is
accompanied by a memorial scroll and a miniature.

The cross was created to commemorate UK armed forces
personnel who have died on operations or as a result of an
act of terrorism. It may be granted to and worn by the next of
kin of any eligible personnel who died from 1 January 1948
to date. It offers the wearer no precedence. Those that are
eligible include the next of kin of personnel who died while
serving on a medal earning operation, as a result of an act of
terrorism, or on a non-medal earning operation where death
was caused by the inherent high risk of the task.

The Elizabeth Cross is not intended as a posthumous
medal for the fallen but as an emblem of national recognition
of the loss and sacrifice made by the personnel and their
families.

CHIEFS OF CLANS IN SCOTLAND

Only chiefs of whole Names or Clans are included, except certain special instances (marked *) who, though not chiefs of a whole Name, were or are for some reason (eg the Macdonald forfeiture) independent. Under decision (*Campbell-Gray,* 1950) that a bearer of a 'double or triple-barrelled' surname cannot be held chief of a part of such, several others cannot be included in the list at present.

THE ROYAL HOUSE: HM The Queen

AGNEW: Sir Crispin Agnew of Lochnaw, Bt., QC
ANSTRUTHER: Tobias Anstruther of Anstruther and Balcaskie
ARBUTHNOTT: Viscount of Arbuthnott
BANNERMAN: Sir David Bannerman of Elsick, Bt.
BARCLAY: Peter C. Barclay of Towie Barclay and of that Ilk
BORTHWICK: Lord Borthwick
BOYLE: Earl of Glasgow
BRODIE: Alexander Brodie of Brodie
BROUN OF COLSTOUN: Sir Wayne Broun of Colstoun, Bt.
BRUCE: Earl of Elgin and Kincardine, KT
BUCHAN: David Buchan of Auchmacoy
BURNETT: James C. A. Burnett of Leys
CAMERON: Donald Cameron of Lochiel
CAMPBELL: Duke of Argyll
CARMICHAEL: Richard Carmichael of Carmichael
CARNEGIE: Duke of Fife
CATHCART: Earl Cathcart
CHARTERIS: Earl of Wemyss and March
CLAN CHATTAN: K. Mackintosh of Clan Chattan
CHISHOLM: Hamish Chisholm of Chisholm (*The Chisholm*)
COCHRANE: Earl of Dundonald
COLQUHOUN: Sir Malcolm Rory Colquhoun of Luss, Bt.
CRANSTOUN: David Cranstoun of that Ilk
CUMMING: Sir Alastair Cumming of Altyre, Bt.
DARROCH: Duncan Darroch of Gourock
DEWAR: Michael Dewar of that Ilk and Vogrie
DRUMMOND: Earl of Perth
DUNBAR: Sir James Dunbar of Mochrum, Bt.
DUNDAS: David Dundas of Dundas
DURIE: Andrew Durie of Durie, CBE
ELIOTT: Mrs Margaret Eliott of Redheugh
ERSKINE: Earl of Mar and Kellie
FARQUHARSON: Capt. Alwyne Farquharson of Invercauld, MC
FERGUSSON: Sir Charles Fergusson of Kilkerran, Bt.
FORBES: Lord Forbes
FORSYTH: Alistair Forsyth of that Ilk
FRASER: Lady Saltoun
*FRASER (OF LOVAT): Lord Lovat
GAYRE: Reinold Gayre of Gayre and Nigg
GORDON: Marquess of Huntly
GRAHAM: Duke of Montrose
GRANT: Lord Strathspey
GUTHRIE: Alexander Guthrie of Guthrie
HAIG: Earl Haig
HALDANE: Martin Haldane of Gleneagles
HANNAY: David Hannay of Kirkdale and of that Ilk
HAY: Earl of Erroll

HENDERSON: Alistair Henderson of Fordell
HUNTER: Pauline Hunter of Hunterston
IRVINE OF DRUM: David Irvine of Drum
JARDINE: Sir William Jardine of Applegirth, Bt.
JOHNSTONE: Earl of Annandale and Hartfell
KEITH: Earl of Kintore
KENNEDY: Marquess of Ailsa
KERR: Marquess of Lothian, PC
KINCAID: Madam Arabella Kincaid of Kincaid
LAMONT: Revd Peter Lamont of that Ilk
LEASK: Jonathan Leask of that Ilk
LENNOX: Edward Lennox of that Ilk
LESLIE: Earl of Rothes
LINDSAY: Earl of Crawford and Balcarres, KT, GCVO, PC
LIVINGSTONE (or MACLEA): Niall Livingstone of the Bachuil
LOCKHART: Angus Lockhart of the Lee
LUMSDEN: Gillem Lumsden of that Ilk and Blanerne
MACALESTER: William St J. McAlester of Loup and Kennox
MACARTHUR: John MacArthur of that Ilk
MCBAIN: James H. McBain of McBain
MACDONALD: Lord Macdonald (*The Macdonald of Macdonald*)
*MACDONALD OF CLANRANALD: Ranald Macdonald of Clanranald
*MACDONALD OF KEPPOCH: Ranald MacDonald of Keppoch
*MACDONALD OF SLEAT (CLAN HUSTEAIN): Sir Ian Macdonald of Sleat, Bt.
*MACDONELL OF GLENGARRY: Ranald MacDonell of Glengarry
MACDOUGALL: Morag MacDougall of MacDougall
MACDOWALL: Fergus Macdowall of Garthland
MACGREGOR: Sir Malcolm MacGregor of MacGregor, Bt.
MACINTYRE: Donald MacIntyre of Glenoe
MACKAY: Lord Reay
MACKENZIE: Earl of Cromartie
MACKINNON: Anne Mackinnon of Mackinnon
MACKINTOSH: John Mackintosh of Mackintosh (*The Mackintosh of Mackintosh*)
MACLACHLAN: Euan MacLachlan of MacLachlan
MACLAREN: Donald MacLaren of MacLaren and Achleskine
MACLEAN: Hon. Sir Lachlan Maclean of Duart, Bt., CVO
MACLENNAN: Ruaraidh MacLennan of MacLennan
MACLEOD: Hugh MacLeod of MacLeod
MACMILLAN: George MacMillan of MacMillan

MACNAB: James W. A. Macnab of Macnab (*The Macnab*)
MACNAGHTEN: Sir Malcolm Macnaghten of Macnaghten and Dundarave, Bt.
MACNEACAIL: John Macneacail of Macneacail and Scorrybreac
MACNEIL OF BARRA: Rory Macneil of Barra (*The Macneil of Barra*)
MACPHERSON: Hon. Sir William Macpherson of Cluny, TD
MACTAVISH: Steven MacTavish of Dunardry
MACTHOMAS: Andrew MacThomas of Finegand
MAITLAND: Earl of Lauderdale
MAKGILL: Viscount of Oxfuird
MALCOLM (MACCALLUM): Robin N. L. Malcolm of Poltalloch
MAR: Countess of Mar
MARJORIBANKS: Andrew Marjoribanks of that Ilk
MATHESON: Maj. Sir Fergus Matheson of Matheson, Bt.
MENZIES: David Menzies of Menzies
MOFFAT: Madam Moffat of that Ilk
MONCREIFFE: Hon. Peregrine Moncreiffe of that Ilk
MONTGOMERIE: Earl of Eglinton and Winton
MORRISON: Dr John Ruairidh Morrison of Ruchdi
MUNRO: Hector Munro of Foulis
MURRAY: Duke of Atholl
NESBITT (or NISBET): Mark Nesbitt of that Ilk
OGILVY: Earl of Airlie, KT, GCVO, PC
OLIPHANT: Richard Oliphant of that Ilk
RAMSAY: Earl of Dalhousie
RIDDELL: Sir Walter Riddell of Riddell, Bt.
ROBERTSON: Alexander Robertson of Struan (*Struan-Robertson*)
ROLLO: Lord Rollo
ROSS: David Ross of that Ilk and Balnagowan
RUTHVEN: Earl of Gowrie, PC
SCOTT: Duke of Buccleuch and Queensberry, KBE
SCRYMGEOUR: Earl of Dundee
SEMPILL: Lord Sempill
SHAW: John Shaw of Tordarroch
SINCLAIR: Earl of Caithness, PC
SKENE: Danus Skene of Skene
STIRLING: Fraser Stirling of Cader
STRANGE: Maj. Timothy Strange of Balcaskie
SUTHERLAND: Countess of Sutherland
SWINTON: John Swinton of that Ilk
TROTTER: Alexander Trotter of Mortonhall, CVO
URQUHART: Wilkins F. Urquhart of Urquhart
WALLACE: Ian Wallace of that Ilk
WEDDERBURN: Master of Dundee
WEMYSS: Michael Wemyss of that Ilk

THE PRIVY COUNCIL

The sovereign in council, or Privy Council, was the chief source of executive power until the system of cabinet government developed in the 18th century. Now the Privy Council's main functions are to advise the sovereign and to exercise its own statutory responsibilities independent of the sovereign in council.

Membership of the Privy Council is automatic upon appointment to certain government and judicial positions in the UK, eg cabinet ministers must be Privy Counsellors and are sworn in on first assuming office. Membership is also accorded by the Queen to eminent people in the UK and independent countries of the Commonwealth of which she is Queen, on the recommendation of the prime minister. Membership of the council is retained for life, except for very occasional removals.

The administrative functions of the Privy Council are carried out by the Privy Council Office under the direction of the president of the council, who is always a member of the cabinet. (*See also* Parliament)
President of the Council, Rt. Hon. Chris Grayling, MP
Clerk of the Council, Richard Tilbrook

Style The Right (or Rt.) Hon._
  *Envelope, The Right (or Rt.) Hon. F_ S_*
  *Letter, Dear Mr/Miss/Mrs S_*
  *Spoken, Mr/Miss/Mrs S_*
It is incorrect to use the letters PC after the name in conjunction with the prefix The Rt. Hon., unless the Privy Counsellor is a peer below the rank of Marquess and so is styled The Rt. Hon. because of his/her rank.

MEMBERS *as at August 2015*

HRH The Duke of Edinburgh, 1951
HRH The Prince of Wales, 1977

Abernethy, *Hon.* Lord (Alastair Cameron), 2005
Adonis, Lord, 2009
Aikens, Sir Richard, 2008
Ainsworth, Robert, 2005
Airlie, Earl of, 1984
Aldous, Sir William, 1995
Alebua, Ezekiel, 1988
Alexander, Douglas, 2005
Alexander, Sir Danny, 2010
Amos, Baroness, 2003
Anderson of Swansea, Lord, 2000
Anelay of St Johns, Baroness, 2009
Angiolini, Dame Elish, 2006
Anthony, Douglas, 1971
Arbuthnot, Lord, 1998
Arden, Dame Mary, 2000
Armstrong of Hill Top, Baroness, 1999
Arthur, *Hon.* Owen, 1995
Ashdown of Norton-sub-Hamdon, Lord, 1989
Ashcroft, Lord, 2012
Ashton of Upholland, Baroness, 2006
Astor of Hever, Lord, 2015
Atkins, Sir Robert, 1995
Auld, Sir Robin, 1995
Baker, Norman, 2014
Baker, Sir Thomas, 2002
Baker of Dorking, Lord, 1984
Baldry, Sir Tony, 2013
Balls, Ed, 2007
Barker, Lord, 2012
Barron, Sir Kevin, 2001
Bassam of Brighton, Lord, 2009
Bates, Lord, 2015
Battle, John, 2002
Bean, Sir David, 2014
Beatson, Sir Jack, 2013
Beckett, Dame Margaret, 1993
Beith, Lord, 1992
Beldam, Sir Roy, 1989
Benn, Hilary, 2003
Bercow, John, 2009

Birch, William, 1992
Black, Dame Jill, 2011
Blackstone, Baroness, 2001
Blair, Anthony, 1994
Blanchard, Peter, 1998
Blears, Hazel, 2005
Blencathra, Lord, 1995
Blunkett, Lord, 1997
Boateng, Lord, 1999
Bolger, James, 1991
Bonomy, *Hon.* Lord (Iain Bonomy), 2010
Boothroyd, Baroness, 1992
Bottomley of Nettlestone, Baroness, 1992
Boyd of Duncansby, Lord, 2000
Brabazon of Tara, Lord, 2013
Bracadale, *Hon.* Lord (Alistair Campbell), 2013
Bradley, Lord, 2001
Bradshaw, Ben, 2009
Brake, Thomas, 2011
Brathwaite, Sir Nicholas, 1991
Briggs, Sir Michael, 2013
Brodie, *Hon.* Lord (Philip Brodie), 2013
Brokenshire, James, 2015
Brooke, Annette, 2014
Brooke, Sir Henry, 1996
Brooke of Sutton Mandeville, Lord, 1988
Brown, Gordon, 1996
Brown, Nicholas, 1997
Brown, Sir Stephen, 1983
Brown of Eaton-under-Heywood, Lord, 1992
Browne of Ladyton, Lord, 2005
Browne-Wilkinson, Lord, 1983
Bruce, Sir Malcolm, 2006
Burnett, Sir Ian, 2014
Burnham, Andy, 2007
Burns, Simon, 2011
Burnton, Sir Stanley, 2008
Burstow, Paul, 2012
Burt, Alistair, 2013
Butler of Brockwell, Lord, 2004

Butler-Sloss, Baroness, 1988
Buxton, Sir Richard, 1997
Byers, Stephen, 1998
Byrne, Liam, 2008
Byron, Sir Dennis, 2004
Cable, Sir Vincent, 2010
Caborn, Richard, 1999
Caithness, Earl of, 1990
Cameron, David, 2005
Cameron of Lochbroom, Lord, 1984
Camoys, Lord, 1997
Campbell, Alan, 2014
Campbell, Lord, 1999
Campbell, Sir William, 1999
Canterbury, Archbishop of, 2013
Carey of Clifton, Lord, 1991
Carloway, *Hon.* Lord (Colin Sutherland), 2008
Carmichael, Alistair, 2010
Carnwath of Notting Hill, Lord, 2002
Carrington, Lord, 1959
Carswell, Lord, 1993
Chadwick, Sir John, 1997
Chalfont, Lord, 1964
Chalker of Wallasey, Baroness, 1987
Chan, Sir Julius, 1981
Chilcot, Sir John, 2004
Christie, Perry, 2004
Clark, Greg, 2010
Clark, Helen, 1990
Clark of Carlton, Baroness, 2013
Clark of Windermere, Lord, 1997
Clarke, Charles, 2001
Clarke, Sir Christopher, 2013
Clarke, Kenneth, 1984
Clarke, *Hon.* Lord (Matthew Clarke), 2008
Clarke, Thomas, 1997
Clarke of Stone-Cum-Ebony, Lord, 1998
Clegg, Nicholas, 2008
Clinton-Davis, Lord, 1998
Clwyd, Ann, 2004
Coghlin, Sir Patrick, 2009
Collins of Mapesbury, Lord, 2007
Cooper, Yvette, 2007

Cope of Berkeley, Lord, 1988
Corston, Baroness, 2003
Cosgrove, *Hon.* Lady (Hazel Cosgrove), 2003
Coulsfield, *Hon.* Lord (John Coulsfield), 2000
Crabb, Stephen, 2014
Crawford and Balcarres, Earl of, 1972
Creech, *Hon.* Wyatt, 1999
Crickhowell, Lord, 1979
Cullen of Whitekirk, Lord, 1997
Cunningham of Felling, Lord, 1993
Curry, David, 1996
Darling, Lord, 1997
Darzi of Denham, Lord, 2009
Davey, Edward, 2012
Davies, Denzil, 1978
Davies, Ronald, 1997
Davies of Oldham, Lord, 2006
Davis, David, 1997
Davis, Sir Nigel, 2011
Davis, Terence, 1999
de la Bastide, Michael, 2004
de Silva, Sir Desmond, 2011
Dean of Thornton-le-Fylde, Baroness, 1998
Deben, Lord, 1985
Denham, John, 2000
Denham, Lord, 1981
Dholakia, Lord, 2010
Dixon, Lord, 1996
Dobson, Frank, 1997
Dodds, Nigel, 2010
Donaldson, Jeffrey, 2007
Dorrell, Stephen, 1994
Dorrian, *Hon.* Lady (Leona Dorrian), 2013
Douglas, *Dr* Denzil, 2011
Drayson, Lord, 2008
Drummond Young, *Hon.* Lord (James Drummond Young), 2013
D'Souza, Baroness, 2009
du Cann, Sir Edward, 1964
Duncan, Alan, 2010
Duncan Smith, Iain, 2001
Dyson, Lord, 2001
Eassie, *Hon.* Lord (Ronald Mackay), 2006
East, Paul, 1998
Eden of Winton, Lord, 1972
Edward, Sir David, 2005
Eggar, Timothy, 1995
Eichelbaum, Sir Thomas, 1989
Elias, Sir Patrick, 2009
Elias, *Hon.* Dame, Sian, 1999
Elis-Thomas, Lord, 2004
Emslie, *Hon.* Lord (George Emslie), 2011
Esquivel, Manuel, 1986
Etherton, Sir Terence, 2008
Evans, Sir Anthony, 1992
Evennett, David, 2015
Falconer of Thoroton, Lord, 2003
Fallon, Michael, 2012
Featherstone, Baroness, 2014
Feldman of Elstree, Lord, 2015
Fellowes, Lord, 1990
Fergusson, Alexander, 2010
Field, Frank, 1997

Flint, Caroline, 2008
Floyd, Sir Christopher, 2013
Forsyth of Drumlean, Lord, 1995
Foster, Lord, 2010
Foster of Bishop Auckland, Lord, 1993
Foulkes of Cumnock, Lord, 2002
Fowler, Lord, 1979
Fox, Liam, 2010
Francois, Mark, 2010
Freedman, Sir Lawrence, 2009
Freeman, Lord, 1993
Freud, Lord, 2015
Fulford, Sir Adrian, 2013
Gage, Sir William, 2004
Garden of Frognal, Baroness, 2015
Garel-Jones, Lord, 1992
Garnier, Sir Edward, 2015
Geidt, Sir Christopher, 2007
George, Bruce, 2000
Gibson, Sir Peter, 1993
Gill, *Hon.* Lord (Brian Gill), 2002
Gillan, Cheryl, 2010
Gillen, Sir John, 2014
Girvan, Sir (Frederick) Paul, 2007
Glidewell, Sir Iain, 1985
Gloster, Dame Elizabeth, 2013
Goff of Chieveley, Lord, 1982
Goldring, Sir John, 2008
Goldsmith, Lord, 2002
Goodlad, Lord, 1992
Gove, Michael, 2010
Gowrie, Earl of, 1984
Graham, Sir Douglas, 1998
Graham of Edmonton, Lord, 1998
Grayling, Chris, 2010
Green, Damian, 2012
Greening, Justine, 2011
Grieve, Dominic, 2010
Grocott, Lord, 2002
Gross, Sir Peter, 2011
Habgood, Lord, 1983
Hague, Lord, 1995
Hailsham, Viscount, 1992
Hain, Lord, 2001
Hale of Richmond, Baroness, 1999
Halfron, Robert, 2015
Hallett, Dame Heather, 2005
Hamilton, *Hon.* Lord (Arthur Hamilton), 2002
Hamilton of Epsom, Lord, 1991
Hammond, Philip, 2010
Hancock, Matthew, 2014
Hands, Gregory, 2014
Hanley, Sir Jeremy, 1994
Hanson, David, 2007
Hardie, Lord, 1997
Hardie Boys, Sir Michael, 1989
Harman, Harriet, 1997
Harper, Mark, 2015
Haselhurst, Sir Alan, 1999
Hattersley, Lord, 1975
Hayes, John, 2013
Hayman, Baroness, 2000
Healey, John, 2008
Healey, Lord, 1964
Heath, David, 2015
Heathcoat-Amory, David, 1996
Hendry, Charles, 2015
Henley, Lord, 2013

Henry, John, 1996
Herbert, Nick, 2010
Heseltine, Lord, 1979
Heseltine, Sir William, 1986
Hesketh, Lord, 1991
Hewitt, Patricia, 2001
Higgins, Lord, 1979
Higgins, Sir Malachy, 2007
Hill, Keith, 2003
Hill of Oareford, Lord, 2013
Hodge, Lord, 2013
Hodge, Margaret, 2003
Hoffmann, Lord, 1992
Hollis of Heigham, Baroness, 1999
Hoon, Geoffrey, 1999
Hooper, Sir Anthony, 2004
Hope of Craighead, Lord, 1989
Hope of Thornes, Lord, 1991
Hordern, Sir Peter, 1993
Howard of Lympne, Lord, 1990
Howarth, George, 2005
Howarth of Newport, Lord, 2000
Howe, Earl, 2013
Howe of Aberavon, Lord, 1972
Howell of Guildford, Lord, 1979
Howells, Kim, 2009
Hoyle, Lindsay, 2013
Hughes, Simon, 2010
Hughes of Ombersley, Lord, 2006
Hughes of Stretford, Baroness, 2004
Hunt, Jeremy, 2010
Hunt, Jonathon, 1989
Hunt of Kings Heath, Lord, 2009
Hunt of Wirral, Lord, 1990
Hurd of Westwell, Lord, 1982
Hutchison, Sir Michael, 1995
Hutton, Lord, 1988
Hutton of Furness, Lord, 2001
Inge, Lord, 2004
Ingraham, Hubert, 1993
Ingram, Adam, 1999
Irvine of Lairg, Lord, 1997
Jack, Michael, 1997
Jackson, Sir Rupert, 2008
Jacob, Sir Robert, 2004
Jacobs, Francis, 2005
Janvrin, Lord, 1998
Javid, Sajid, 2014
Jay of Paddington, Baroness, 1998
Jenkin of Roding, Lord, 1973
Johnson, Alan, 2003
Jones, Carwyn, 2010
Jones, David, 2012
Jones, Lord, 1999
Jopling, Lord, 1979
Jowell, Baroness, 1998
Judge, Lord, 1996
Jugnauth, Sir Anerood, 1987
Kakkar, Lord, 2014
Kaufman, Sir Gerald, 1978
Kay, Sir Maurice, 2004
Keene, Sir David, 2000
Keith, Sir Kenneth, 1998
Kelly, Ruth, 2004
Kenilorea, Sir Peter, 1979
Kennedy, Jane, 2003
Kennedy, Sir Paul, 1992
Kerr of Tonaghmore, Lord, 2004
Khan, Sadiq, 2009

King, Dame Eleanor, 2014
King of Bridgwater, Lord, 1979
Kingarth, *Hon.* Lord (Derek Emslie), 2006
Kinnock, Lord, 1983
Kirkwood, *Hon.* Lord (Ian Kirkwood), 2000
Kitchin, Sir David, 2011
Knight, Sir Gregory, 1995
Knight of Weymouth, Lord, 2008
Kramer, Baroness, 2014
Lamb, Norman, 2014
Laming, Lord, 2014
Lammy, David, 2008
Lamont of Lerwick, Lord, 1986
Lang of Monkton, Lord, 1990
Lansley, Lord, 2010
Latasi, Sir Kamuta, 1996
Latham, Sir David, 2000
Laws, David, 2010
Laws, Sir John, 1999
Lawson of Blaby, Lord, 1981
Leggatt, Sir Andrew, 1990
Letwin, Oliver, 2002
Leveson, Sir Brian, 2006
Lewis, Dr Julian, 2015
Lewison, Sir Kim, 2011
Liddell of Coatdyke, Baroness, 1998
Lidington, David, 2010
Lilley, Peter, 1990
Llewellyn, Edward, 2015
Lloyd of Berwick, Lord, 1984
Lloyd, Sir Peter, 1994
Lloyd, Sir Timothy, 2005
Lloyd Jones, Sir David, 2012
Llwyd, Elfyn, 2011
London, Bishop of, 1995
Longmore, Sir Andrew, 2001
Lothian, Marquess of, 1996
Luce, Lord, 1986
Lyne, Sir Roderic, 2009
McAvoy, Lord, 2003
McCartney, Sir Ian, 1999
McCollum, Sir Liam, 1997
McCombe, Sir Richard, 2012
McConnell of Glenscorrodale, Lord, 2001
MacDermott, Sir John, 1987
Macdonald of Tradeston, Lord, 1999
McFadden, Patrick, 2008
McFall of Alcluith, Lord, 2004
McFarlane, Sir Andrew, 2011
MacGregor of Pulham Market, Lord, 1985
McGuire, Dame Anne, 2008
Mackay, Andrew, 1998
Mackay of Clashfern, Lord, 1979
Mackay of Drumadoon, Lord, 1996
McKinnon, Sir Donald, 1992
Maclean, *Hon.* Lord (Ranald MacLean), 2001
McLeish, Henry, 2000
Maclennan of Rogart, Lord, 1997
McLoughlin, Patrick, 2005
McMullin, Sir Duncan, 1980
McNally, Lord, 2005
McNulty, Anthony, 2007
Mactaggart, Fiona, 2015
Macur, Dame Julia, 2013

McVey, Esther, 2014
Major, Sir John, 1987
Malcolm, *Hon.* Lord (Colin Campbell), 2015
Malloch-Brown, Lord, 2007
Mance, Lord, 1999
Mandelson, Lord, 1998
Marnoch, *Hon.* Lord (Michael Marnoch), 2001
Martin of Springburn, Lord, 2000
Marwick, Tricia, 2012
Mates, Michael, 2004
Maude of Horsham, Lord, 1992
Mawhinney, Lord, 1994
May, Sir Anthony, 1998
May, Theresa, 2003
Mayhew of Twysden, Lord, 1986
Meacher, Michael, 1997
Mellor, David, 1990
Menzies, *Hon.* Lord (Duncan Menzies), 2012
Michael, Alun, 1998
Milburn, Alan, 1998
Miliband, David, 2005
Miliband, Ed, 2007
Miller, Maria, 2012
Millett, Lord, 1994
Milton, Anne, 2015
Mitchell, Andrew, 2010
Mitchell, Sir James, 1985
Mitchell, Dr Keith, 2004
Moore, Michael, 1990
Moore, Michael, 2010
Moore of Lower Marsh, Lord, 1986
Moore-Bick, Sir Martin, 2005
Morgan, Sir Declan, 2009
Morgan, Nicky, 2014
Morgan, Rhodri, 2000
Morris of Aberavon, Lord, 1970
Morris of Yardley, Baroness, 1999
Morritt, Sir Robert, 1994
Moses, Sir Alan, 2005
Moyle, Roland, 1978
Mulholland, Frank, 2011
Mummery, Sir John, 1996
Munby, Sir James, 2009
Mundell, David, 2010
Murphy, James, 2008
Murphy, Lord, 1999
Murray, *Hon.* Lord (Ronald Murray), 1974
Murray, Sir Donald, 1989
Musa, Wilbert, 2005
Namaliu, Sir Rabbie, 1989
Naseby, Lord, 1994
Needham, Sir Richard, 1994
Neill, Sir Brian, 1985
Neuberger of Abbotsbury, Lord, 2004
Neville-Jones, Baroness, 2010
Newby, Lord, 2014
Nicholls of Birkenhead, Lord, 1995
Nicholson, Sir Michael, 1995
Nimmo Smith, *Hon.* Lord (William Nimmo Smith), 2005
Northover, Baroness, 2015
Nott, Sir John, 1979
Nourse, Sir Martin, 1985
O'Brien, Mike, 2009
O'Brien, Stephen, 2013

O'Donnell, Turlough, 1979
Oppenheim-Barnes, Baroness, 1979
Osborne, George, 2010
Osborne, *Hon.* Lord (Kenneth Osborne), 2001
Ottaway, Sir Richard, 2013
Otton, Sir Philip, 1995
Owen, Lord, 1976
Paeniu, Bikenibeu, 1991
Paice, Sir James, 2010
Palmer, Sir Geoffrey, 1986
Paraskeva, Dame Janet, 2010
Parker, Sir Jonathan, 2000
Parkinson, Lord, 1981
Patel, Priti, 2015
Paterson, Owen, 2010
Paton, *Hon.* Lady (Ann Paton), 2007
Patten, Lord, 1990
Patten, Sir Nicholas, 2009
Patten of Barnes, Lord, 1989
Patterson, Percival, 1993
Pattie, Sir Geoffrey, 1987
Paul, Lord, 2009
Peel, Earl, 2006
Pendry, Lord, 2000
Penning, Mike, 2014
Penrose, *Hon.* Lord (George Penrose), 2000
Peters, Winston, 1998
Philip, *Hon.* Lord (Alexander Philip), 2005
Phillips of Worth Matravers, Lord, 1995
Pickles, Sir Eric, 2010
Pill, Sir Malcolm, 1995
Pitchford, Sir Christopher, 2010
Portillo, Michael, 1992
Potter, Sir Mark, 1996
Prashar, Baroness, 2009
Primarolo, Baroness, 2002
Prior, Lord, 1970
Puapua, Sir Tomasi, 1982
Purnell, James, 2007
Quin, Baroness, 1998
Radice, Lord, 1999
Rafferty, Dame Anne, 2011
Ramsden, James, 1963
Randall, Sir John, 2010
Raynsford, Nick, 2001
Redwood, John, 1993
Reed, Lord, 2008
Reid, Sir George, 2004
Reid of Cardowan, Lord, 1998
Renton of Mount Harry, Lord, 1989
Richard, Lord, 1993
Richards, Sir Stephen, 2005
Riddell, Peter, 2010
Rifkind, Sir Malcolm, 1986
Rimer, Sir Colin, 2007
Rix, Sir Bernard, 2000
Robathan, Lord, 2010
Robertson, Hugh, 2012
Robertson of Port Ellen, Lord, 1997
Robinson, Peter, 2007
Roch, Sir John, 1993
Rodgers of Quarry Bank, Lord, 1975
Rooker, Lord, 1999
Roper, Lord, 2005
Rose, Sir Christopher, 1992

Ross, *Hon.* Lord (Donald MacArthur), 1985
Royall of Blaisdon, Baroness, 2008
Rudd, Amber, 2015
Ruddock, Dame Joan, 2010
Ryan, Joan, 2007
Ryder, Sir Ernest, 2013
Ryder of Wensum, Lord, 1990
Sainsbury, Sir Timothy, 1992
Sales, Sir Philip, 2014
Salisbury, Marquess of, 1994
Salmond, Alex, 2007
Sandiford, Erskine, 1989
Saville of Newdigate, Lord, 1994
Sawyer, Dame Joan, 2004
Schiemann, Sir Konrad, 1995
Scotland of Asthal, Baroness, 2001
Scott of Foscote, Lord, 1991
Seaga, Edward, 1981
Sedley, Sir Stephen, 1999
Selkirk of Douglas, Lord, 1996
Shapps, Grant, 2010
Sharp, Dame Victoria, 2013
Sheldon, Lord, 1977
Shephard of Northwold, Baroness, 1992
Sheil, Sir John, 2005
Shipley, Jennifer, 1998
Short, Clare, 1997
Shutt of Greetland, Lord, 2009
Simmonds, Sir Kennedy, 1984
Simmonds, Mark, 2014
Simpson, Keith, 2015
Sinclair, Ian, 1977
Slade, Sir Christopher, 1982
Smith, Andrew, 1997
Smith, Dame Janet, 2002
Smith, *Hon.* Lady (Anne Smith), 2013
Smith, Jacqueline, 2003
Smith of Basildon, Baroness, 2009
Smith of Finsbury, Lord, 1997
Soames, *Hon.* (Arthur) Nicholas, 2011
Somare, Sir Michael, 1977
Soubry, Anna, 2015
Spellar, John, 2001
Spelman, Caroline, 2010

Spicer, Lord, 2013
Stanley, Sir John, 1984
Steel of Aikwood, Lord, 1977
Stephen, Sir Ninian, 1979
Stewartby, Lord, 1989
Steyn, Lord, 1992
Stowell of Beeston, Baroness, 2014
Strang, Gavin, 1997
Strathclyde, Lord, 1995
Straw, Jack, 1997
Stuart, Freundel, 2013
Stuart-Smith, Sir Murray, 1988
Stunnell, Lord, 2012
Sturgeon, Nicola, 2014
Sullivan, Sir Jeremy, 2009
Sumption, Lord, 2011
Sutherland, *Hon.* Lord (Ranald Sutherland), 2000
Swayne, Desmond, 2011
Swire, Hugo, 2010
Symons of Vernham Dean, Baroness, 2001
Tapsell, Sir Peter, 2011
Taylor of Bolton, Baroness, 1997
Taylor of Holbeach, Lord, 2014
Tebbit, Lord, 1981
Thomas, Edmund, 1996
Thomas, Sir Swinton, 1994
Thomas of Cwmgiedd, Lord, 2003
Thorpe, Sir Matthew, 1995
Thurso, Viscount, 2014
Timms, Stephen, 2006
Tipping, Andrew, 1998
Tizard, Robert, 1986
Tomlinson, Sir Stephen, 2011
Touhig, Lord, 2006
Toulson, Lord, 2007
Treacy, Sir Colman, 2012
Trefgarne, Lord, 1989
Trimble, Lord, 1997
Trumpington, Baroness, 1992
Truss, Elizabeth, 2014
Tuckey, Sir Simon, 1998
Tyler, Lord, 2014
Tyrie, Andrew, 2015
Ullswater, Viscount, 1994

Underhill, Sir Nicholas, 2013
Upton, Simon, 1999
Vadera, Baroness, 2009
Vaz, Keith, 2006
Villiers, Theresa, 2010
Vos, Sir Geoffrey, 2013
Waddington, Lord, 1987
Waite, Sir John, 1993
Wakeham, Lord, 1983
Waldegrave of North Hill, Lord, 1990
Walker of Gestingthorpe, Lord, 1997
Wall, Sir Nicholas, 2004
Wallace of Saltaire, Lord, 2012
Wallace of Tankerness, Lord, 2000
Waller, Sir Mark, 1996
Ward, Sir Alan, 1995
Warner, Lord, 2006
Warsi, Baroness, 2010
Webb, Steve, 2014
West of Spithead, Lord, 2010
Wheatley, *Hon.* Lord (John Wheatley) 2007
Wheeler, Sir John, 1993
Whittingdale, John, 2015
Whitty, Lord, 2005
Widdecombe, Ann, 1997
Wigley, Lord, 1997
Willetts, Lord, 2010
Williams of Crosby, Baroness, 1974
Williams of Elvel, Lord, 2013
Williams of Oystermouth, Lord, 2002
Williamson, Gavin, 2015
Willott, Jennifer, 2014
Wills, Lord, 2008
Wilson, Brian, 2003
Wilson of Culworth, Lord, 2005
Winterton, Rosie, 2006
Wingti, Paias, 1987
Woodward, Shaun, 2007
Woolf, Lord, 1986
Wright, Jeremy, 2014
York, Archbishop of, 2005
Young, Lord, 1993
Young of Graffham, Lord, 1984
Zacca, Edward, 1992

PRIVY COUNCIL OF NORTHERN IRELAND

The Privy Council of Northern Ireland had responsibilities in Northern Ireland similar to those of the Privy Council in Great Britain until the Northern Ireland Act 1974. Membership of the Privy Council of Northern Ireland is retained for life. Since the Northern Ireland Constitution Act 1973 no further appointments have been made. The postnominal initials PC (NI) are used to differentiate its members from those of the Privy Council.

MEMBERS *as at August 2015*
Bailie, Robin, 1971
Bleakley, David, 1971
Dobson, John, 1969
Kilclooney, Lord, 1970

PARLIAMENT

The UK constitution is not contained in any single document but has evolved over time, formed by statute, common law and convention. A constitutional monarchy, the UK is governed by ministers of the crown in the name of the sovereign, who is head both of the state and of the government.

The organs of government are the legislature (parliament), the executive and the judiciary. The executive comprises HM government (the cabinet and other ministers), government departments and local authorities (see Government Departments, Public Bodies and Local Government). The judiciary (see Law Courts and Offices) pronounces on the law, both written and unwritten, interprets statutes and is responsible for the enforcement of the law; the judiciary is independent of both the legislature and the executive.

THE MONARCHY

The sovereign personifies the state and is, in law, an integral part of the legislature, head of the executive, head of the judiciary, commander-in-chief of all armed forces of the crown and supreme governor of the Church of England. In the Channel Islands and the Isle of Man, which are crown dependencies, the sovereign is represented by a lieutenant-governor. In the member states of the Commonwealth of which the sovereign is head of state, her representative is a governor-general; in UK overseas territories the sovereign is usually represented by a governor, who is responsible to the British government.

Although in practice the powers of the monarchy are now very limited, and restricted mainly to the advisory and ceremonial, there are important acts of government which require the participation of the sovereign. These include summoning, proroguing and dissolving parliament, giving royal assent to bills passed by parliament, appointing important office-holders, eg government ministers, judges, bishops and governors, conferring peerages, knighthoods and other honours, and granting pardon to a person wrongly convicted of a crime. The sovereign appoints the prime minister; by convention this office is held by the leader of the political party which enjoys, or can secure, a majority of votes in the House of Commons. In international affairs the sovereign, as head of state, has the power to declare war and make peace, to recognise foreign states and governments, to conclude treaties and to annex or cede territory. However, as the sovereign entrusts executive power to ministers of the crown and acts on the advice of her ministers, which she cannot ignore, royal prerogative powers are in practice exercised by ministers, who are responsible to parliament.

Ministerial responsibility does not diminish the sovereign's importance to the smooth working of government. She holds meetings of the Privy Council (see below), gives audiences to her ministers and other officials at home and overseas, receives accounts of cabinet decisions, reads dispatches and signs state papers; she must be informed and consulted on every aspect of national life; and she must show complete impartiality.

COUNSELLORS OF STATE

If the sovereign travels abroad for more than a few days or suffers from a temporary illness, it is necessary to appoint members of the royal family, known as counsellors of state, under letters patent to carry out the chief functions of the monarch, including the holding of Privy Councils and giving royal assent to acts passed by parliament. The normal procedure is to appoint three or four members of the royal family among those members remaining in the UK, provided they are over 21. There are currently five counsellors of state.

In the event of the sovereign on accession being under the age of 18 years, or by infirmity of mind or body, rendered incapable of performing the royal functions, provision is made for a regency.

THE PRIVY COUNCIL

The sovereign in council, or Privy Council, was the chief source of executive power until the system of cabinet government developed. Its main function today is to advise the sovereign on the approval of various statutory functions and acts of the royal prerogative. These powers are exercised through orders in council and royal proclamations, approved by the Queen at meetings of the Privy Council. The council is also able to exercise a number of statutory duties without approval from the sovereign, including powers of supervision over the registering bodies for the medical and allied professions. These duties are exercised through orders of council.

Although appointment as a privy counsellor is for life, only those who are currently government ministers are involved in the day-to-day business of the council. A full council is summoned only on the death of the sovereign or when the sovereign announces his or her intention to marry. (For a full list of privy counsellors, see the Privy Council section.)

There are a number of advisory Privy Council committees whose meetings the sovereign does not attend. Some are prerogative committees, such as those dealing with legislative matters submitted by the legislatures of the Channel Islands and the Isle of Man or with applications for charters of incorporation; and some are provided for by statute, eg those for the universities of Oxford and Cambridge and some Scottish universities.

Administrative work is carried out by the Privy Council Office under the direction of the Lord President of the Council, a cabinet minister.

JUDICIAL COMMITTEE OF THE PRIVY COUNCIL
Supreme Court Building, Parliament Square, London SW1P 3BD
T 020-7960 1500 W www.jcpc.uk

The Judicial Committee of the Privy Council is the court of final appeal from courts of the UK dependencies, courts of independent Commonwealth countries which have retained the right of appeal and courts of the Channel Islands and the Isle of Man. It also hears very occasional appeals from a number of ancient and ecclesiastical courts.

The committee is composed of privy counsellors who hold, or have held, high judicial office. Only three or five judges hear each case, and these are usually justices of the supreme court.
Chief Executive, Jenny Rowe, CB

PARLIAMENT

Parliament is the supreme law-making authority and can legislate for the UK as a whole or for any parts of it separately (the Channel Islands and the Isle of Man are crown dependencies and not part of the UK). The main functions of parliament are to pass laws, to enable the government to raise taxes and to scrutinise government policy and administration, particularly proposals for expenditure. International treaties and agreements are customarily presented to parliament before ratification.

Parliament can trace its roots to two characteristics of Anglo-Saxon rule: the *witan* (a meeting of the king, nobles and advisors) and the *moot* (county meetings where local matters were discussed). However, it was the parliament that Simon de Montfort called in 1265 that is accepted as the forerunner to modern parliament, as it included non-noble representatives from counties, cities and towns alongside the nobility. The nucleus of early parliaments at the beginning of the 14th century were the officers of the king's household and the king's judges, joined by such ecclesiastical and lay magnates as the king might summon to form a prototype 'House of Lords', and occasionally by the knights of the shires, burgesses and proctors of the lower clergy. By the end of Edward III's reign a 'House of Commons' was beginning to appear; the first known Speaker was elected in 1377.

Parliamentary procedure is based on custom and precedent, partly formulated in the standing orders of both houses of parliament. Each house has the right to control its own internal proceedings and to commit for contempt. The system of debate in the two houses is similar; when a motion has been moved, the Speaker proposes the question as the subject of a debate. Members speak from wherever they have been sitting. Questions are decided by a vote on a simple majority. Draft legislation is introduced, in either house, as a bill. Bills can be introduced by a government minister or a private member, but in practice the majority of bills which become law are introduced by the government. To become law, a bill must be passed by each house (for parliamentary stages, *see* Parliamentary Information) and then sent to the sovereign for the royal assent, after which it becomes an act of parliament.

Proceedings of both houses are public, except on extremely rare occasions. The minutes (called *Votes and Proceedings in the Commons,* and *Minutes of Proceedings in the Lords)* and the speeches *(The Official Report of Parliamentary Debates,* Hansard) are published daily. Proceedings are also recorded for transmission on radio and television and stored in the Parliamentary Recording Unit before transfer to the National Sound Archive. Television cameras have been allowed into the House of Lords since 1985 and into the House of Commons since 1989; committee meetings may also be televised.

The Fixed Term Parliament Act 2011 fixed the duration of a parliament at five years in normal circumstances, the term being reckoned from the date given on the writs for the new parliament. The term of a parliament has been prolonged by legislation in such rare circumstances as the two World Wars (31 January 1911 to 25 November 1918; 26 November 1935 to 15 June 1945). The life of a parliament is divided into sessions, usually of one year in length, beginning and ending most often in May.

DEVOLUTION
The Scottish parliament and the National Assembly for Wales have legislative power over all devolved matters, ie matters not reserved to Westminster or otherwise outside its powers. The Northern Ireland Assembly has legislative authority in the fields previously administered by the Northern Ireland departments. The assembly was suspended in October 2002 and dissolved in April 2003, before being reinstated on 8 May 2007. For further information, *see* Devolved Government.

THE HOUSE OF LORDS
London SW1A 0PW
T 020-7219 3107
E hlinfo@parliament.uk W www.parliament.uk

The House of Lords is the second chamber, or 'Upper House', of the UK's bicameral parliament. Until the beginning of the 20th century, the House of Lords had considerable power, being able to veto any bill submitted to it by the House of Commons. Since the introduction of the Parliament Acts 1911 and 1949, however, it has no powers over money bills and its power of veto over public legislation has been reduced over time to the power to delay bills for up to one session of parliament (usually one year). Today the main functions of the House of Lords are to contribute to the legislative process, to act as a check on the government, and to provide a forum of expertise. Its judicial role as final court of appeal ended in 2009 with the establishment of a new UK Supreme Court (*see* Law Courts and Offices section).

The House of Lords has a number of select committees. Some relate to the internal affairs of the house – such as its management and administration – while others carry out important investigative work on matters of public interest. The main committees are: the Communications Committee; the Constitution Committee; the Economic Affairs Committee; the European Union Committee; and the Science and Technology Committee. House of Lords' investigative committees look at broad issues and do not mirror government departments as the select committees in the House of Commons do.

The Constitutional Reform Act 2005 significantly altered the judicial function of the House of Lords and the role of the Lord Chancellor as a judge and its presiding officer. The Lord Chancellor is no longer the presiding officer of the House of Lords nor head of the judiciary in England and Wales, but remains a cabinet minister (the Lord Chancellor and Secretary of State for Justice), and is currently a member of the House of Commons. The function of the presiding officer of the House of Lords was devolved to the newly created post of the Speaker of the House of Lords, commonly known as Lord Speaker. The first Lord Speaker elected by the House was the Rt. Hon. Baroness Hayman on 4 July 2006.

Membership of the House of Lords comprises mainly of life peers created under the Life Peerages Act 1958, along with 92 hereditary peers and a small number of Lords of Appeal in Ordinary, ie law lords, who were created under the Appellate Jurisdiction Act 1876*. The Archbishops of Canterbury and York, the Bishops of London, Durham and Winchester, and the 21 senior diocesan bishops of the Church of England are also members.

The House of Lords Act 1999 provides for 92 hereditary peers to remain in the House of Lords until further reform of the House has been carried out. Of these, 75 (42 Conservative, 28 crossbench, three Liberal Democrat and two Labour) are elected by hereditary peers in their political party or crossbench grouping. In addition, 15 office holders were elected by the whole house. Two hereditary peers with royal duties, the Earl Marshal and the Lord Great Chamberlain, have also remained members. Since November 2002 by-elections have been held to fill vacancies left by deaths of hereditary peers and are now held within three months following the permanent retirement of an elected hereditary peer; the by-elections take place under the Alternative Vote System and must occur within three months of the death of the hereditary peer (*see also* The Peerage).

Peers are disqualified from sitting in the house if they are:
• aliens, ie any peer who is not a British citizen, a Commonwealth citizen (under the British Nationality Act 1981) or a citizen of the Republic of Ireland

- under the age of 21
- undischarged bankrupts or, in Scotland, those whose estate is sequestered
- holders of a disqualifying judicial office
- members of the European parliament
- convicted of treason

Bishops cease to be members of the house when they retire.

Members who do not wish to attend sittings of the House of Lords may apply for leave of absence for the duration of a parliament. Since the passage of the House of Lords Reform Act 2014, members of the House may also retire permanently by giving notice in writing to the Clerk of the Parliaments.

Members of the House of Lords, who are not paid a salary, may claim a daily allowance of £300 (or may elect to claim a reduced daily allowance of £150) per sitting day – but only if they attend a sitting of the House and/or committee proceedings.

* Although the office of Lord of Appeal in Ordinary no longer exists, law lords created under the Appellate Jurisdiction Act 1876 remain members of the House. Those in office at the time of the establishment of the Supreme Court became justices of the UK Supreme Court and are not permitted to sit or vote in the House of Lords until they retire.

COMPOSITION *as at 1 September 2015*

Archbishops and bishops	25
Life peers under the Appellate Jurisdiction Act 1876 and the Life Peerages Act 1958	664
Peers under the House of Lords Act 1999	86
Total	775

STATE OF THE PARTIES *as at 1 September 2015†*

Conservative	225
Labour	211
Liberal Democrat	101
Crossbench	176
Archbishops and bishops	25
Non-affiliated	20
Other parties	17
Total	775

† Excluding 34 peers on leave of absence and eight disqualified as senior members of the judiciary

HOUSE OF LORDS PAY FOR SENIOR STAFF 2015–16

Senior staff are placed in the following pay bands according to their level of responsibility and taking account of other factors such as experience and marketability.

Judicial group 4	£176,226
Senior band 3	£104,000–£139,829
Senior band 2	£85,000–£124,845
Senior band 1A	£69,000–£105,560
Senior band 1	£63,500–£93,380
Band A1	£60,824–£74,998
Band A2	£49,329–£61,741

OFFICERS AND OFFICIALS

The house is presided over by the Lord Speaker, whose powers differ from those of the Speaker of the House of Commons. The Lord Speaker has no power to rule on matters of order because the House of Lords is self-regulating. The maintenance of the rules of debate is the responsibility of all the members who are present.

A panel of deputy speakers is appointed by Royal Commission. The first deputy speaker is the Chair of Committees, a salaried officer of the house appointed at the beginning of each session. He or she chairs a number of 'domestic' committees relating to the internal affairs of the house . The first deputy speaker is assisted by a panel of deputy chairs, headed by the salaried Principal Deputy Chair of Committees, who is also chair of the European Union Committee of the house.

The Clerk of the Parliaments is the accounting officer and the chief permanent official responsible for the administration of the house. The Gentleman Usher of the Black Rod is responsible for security and other services and also has royal duties as secretary to the Lord Great Chamberlain.

Lord Speaker (£101,664), Rt. Hon. Baroness D'Souza, CMG

Chair of Committees (£84,524), Rt. Hon. Lord Laming, CBE

Principal Deputy Chair of Committees (£79,076), Lord Boswell of Aynho

Clerk of the Parliaments (Judicial Group 4), David Beamish

Clerk Assistant (Senior Band 3), Edward Ollard

Reading Clerk and Clerk of the Overseas Office (Senior Band 3), Simon Burton

Gentleman Usher of the Black Rod and Serjeant-at-Arms (Senior Band 2), Lt.-Gen. David Leakey, CMG, CBE

Yeoman Usher of the Black Rod and Deputy Serjeant-at-Arms (Band A1), Neil Baverstock

Commissioner for Lords' Standards, Paul Kernagham, CBE, QPM

Counsel to the Chair of Committees (Senior Band 2), Peter Milledge; P. Hardy

Registrar of Lords' Interests (Senior Band 1A), Brendan Keith

Clerk of Committees (Senior Band 2), Dr F. P. Tudor

Legal Adviser to the Human Rights Committee (Senior Band 2), Murray Hunt

Director of Information Services and Librarian (Senior Band 2), Dr Elizabeth Hallam Smith

Director of Facilities (Senior Band 2), Carl Woodall

Finance Director (Senior Band 1A), Andrew Makower

Director of Parliamentary Digital Service (Senior Band 1A), Rob Greig

Director of Human Resources (Senior Band 1A), Tom Mohan

Clerk of Legislation (Senior Band 1A), Jake Vaughan

Principal Clerk of Select Committees (Senior Band 1A), Christopher Johnson, DPHIL

Director of Parliamentary Archives (Senior Band 1), Adrian Brown

LORD GREAT CHAMBERLAIN'S OFFICE

Lord Great Chamberlain, Marquess of Cholmondeley, KCVO

Secretary to the Lord Great Chamberlain, Lt.-Gen. David Leakey, CMG, CBE

SELECT COMMITTEES

The main House of Lords select committees, as at July 2015, are as follows:

Administration and Works – Chair, Rt. Hon. Lord Laming, CBE; *Clerk,* Chris Atkinson

Communications – Chair, Lord Best, OBE; *Clerk,* Anna Murphy

Constitution – Chair, Lord Lang of Monkton, PC; *Clerk,* Antony Willott

Delegated Powers and Regulatory Reform – Chair, Baroness Fookes, DBE; *Clerk,* Christine Salmon Percival

Economic Affairs – Chair, Lord Hollick; *Clerk,* Ayeesha Waller

Equality Act 2010 and Disability – Chair, Baroness Deech, DBE; *Clerk,* Michael Collon

European Union – Chair, Lord Boswell of Aynho; *Principal Clerk,* Christopher Johnson, DPHIL; *Clerk,* Stuart Stoner

European Union – Sub-committees:

Energy and Environment – Chair, Baroness Scott of Needham Market; *Clerk,* Patrick Milner

External Affairs – Chair, Lord Tugendhat; *Clerk,* Eva George

Financial Affairs – Chair, Baroness Falkner of Margravine; *Clerk,* John Turner

Home Affairs – Chair, Baroness Prashar; *Clerk,* Theodore Pembroke

Internal Market – Chair, Lord Whitty; *Clerk,* Alicia Cunningham

Justice – Chair, Baroness Kennedy of the Shaws; *Clerk,* Megan Conway

House – Chair, Baroness D'Souza, CMG, PC; *Clerk,* Rob Whiteway

Hybrid Instruments – Chair, Rt. Hon. Lord Laming, CBE; *Clerk,* vacant

Information – Chair, Baroness Donaghy, CBE; *Clerk,*

Liaison – Chair, Rt. Hon. Lord Laming, CBE; *Clerk,* Philippa Tudor

National Policy for the Built Environment – Chair, Baroness O'Cathain, OBE; *Clerk,* Matthew Smith

Privileges and Conduct – Chair, Rt. Hon. Lord Laming, CBE; *Clerk,* Chloe Mawson

Procedure – Chair, Rt. Hon. Lord Laming, CBE; *Clerk,* Chloe Mawson

Refreshment – Chair, Rt. Hon. Lord Laming, CBE; *Clerk,* Chris Atkinson

Science and Technology – Chair, Earl of Selborne, GBE; *Clerk,* Chris Clarke

Secondary Legislation Scrutiny – Chair, Lord Trefgarne, PC; *Clerk,* vacant

Selection Committee – Chair, Rt. Hon. Lord Laming, CBE; *Clerk,* vacant

Sexual Violence in Conflict – Chair, Baroness Nicholson of Winterbourne; *Clerk,* Aaron Speer

Social Mobility – Chair, Baroness Corston, PC; *Clerk,* Luke Hussey

Standing Orders (Private Bills) – Chair, Rt. Hon. Lord Laming, CBE; *Clerk,* vacant

Joint Committees:
Consolidation Bills
Human Rights
National Security Strategy
Palace of Westminster
Statutory Instruments – Chair, Derek Twigg; *Clerk,* Amelia Aspden

THE HOUSE OF COMMONS

London SW1A 0AA
T 020-7219 3000 W www.parliament.uk

HOUSE OF COMMONS INFORMATION OFFICE

14 Tothill Street, London SW1H 9NB
T 020-7219 4272 E hcinfo@parliament.uk

The members of the House of Commons are elected by universal adult suffrage. For electoral purposes, the UK is divided into constituencies, each of which returns one member to the House of Commons, the member being the candidate who obtains the largest number of votes cast in the constituency. To ensure equitable representation, the four Boundary Commissions keep constituency boundaries under review and recommend any redistribution of seats which may seem necessary because of population movements etc. At the 2010 general election the number of seats increased from 646 to 650. Of the present 650 seats, there are 533 for England, 40 for Wales, 59 for Scotland and 18 for Northern Ireland.

NUMBER OF SEATS IN THE HOUSE OF COMMONS BY COUNTRY

	2005	2015
England	529	533
Wales	40	40
Scotland	59	59
Northern Ireland	18	18
Total	646	650

ELECTIONS

Elections are by secret ballot, each elector casting one vote; voting is not compulsory. (For entitlement to vote in parliamentary elections, *see* Legal Notes.) When a seat becomes vacant between general elections, a by-election is held.

British subjects and citizens of the Irish Republic can stand for election as MPs provided they are 18 or over and not subject to disqualification. Those disqualified from sitting in the house include:
• undischarged bankrupts
• people sentenced to more than one year's imprisonment
• members of the House of Lords (but hereditary peers not sitting in the Lords are eligible)
• holders of certain offices listed in the House of Commons Disqualification Act 1975, eg members of the judiciary, civil service, regular armed forces, police forces, some local government officers and some members of public corporations and government commissions

A candidate does not require any party backing but his or her nomination for election must be supported by the signatures of ten people registered in the constituency. A candidate must also deposit £500 with the returning officer, which is forfeit if the candidate does not receive more than 5 per cent of the votes cast. All election expenses at a general election, except the candidate's personal expenses, are subject to a statutory limit of £8,700, plus six pence for each elector in a borough constituency or nine pence for each elector in a county constituency.

See pages 128–173 for an alphabetical list of MPs and results of the general election in 2015.

STATE OF THE PARTIES *as at 1 September 2015**

Party	Seats
Conservative	330
Labour	232
Scottish National Party	56
Democratic Unionist Party	8
Liberal Democrats	8
Sinn Fein (have not taken their seats)	4
Plaid Cymru	3
Social Democratic & Labour Party	3
Ulster Unionist Party	2
Green	1
Independent	1
The Speaker	1
UK Independence Party	1
Total	650

* Working majority of 16; 330 Conservative MPs less all other parties (exlcuding the speaker, deputy speakers and Sinn Fein)

BUSINESS

The week's business of the house is outlined each Thursday by the leader of the house, after consultation between the chief government whip and the chief opposition whip. A quarter to a third of the time will be taken up by the government's legislative programme and the rest by other business. As a rule, bills likely to raise political controversy are introduced in the Commons before going on to the Lords, and the Commons claims exclusive control in respect of national taxation and expenditure. Bills such as the finance bill, which imposes taxation, and the consolidated fund bills, which authorise expenditure, must begin in the Commons. A bill of which the financial provisions are subsidiary may begin in the Lords, and the Commons may waive its rights in regard to Lords' amendments affecting finance.

The Commons has a public register of MPs' financial and certain other interests; this is published annually as a House of Commons paper. Members must also disclose any relevant financial interest or benefit in a matter before the house when taking part in a debate, in certain other proceedings of the house, or in consultations with other MPs, with ministers or with civil servants.

MEMBERS' PAY AND ALLOWANCES

Since 1911 members of the House of Commons have received salary payments; facilities for free travel were introduced in 1924. Salary rates for the last 30 years are as follows:

1985 Jan	£16,904	2000 Apr	£48,371
1986 Jan	17,702	2001 Apr	49,822
1987 Jan	18,500	2002 Apr	55,118
1988 Jan	22,548	2003 Apr	56,358
1989 Jan	24,107	2004 Apr	57,485
1990 Jan	26,701	2005 Apr	59,095
1991 Jan	28,970	2006 Apr	59,686
1992 Jan	30,854	2007 Apr	61,181
1993 Jan	30,854	2008 Apr	63,291
1994 Jan	31,687	2009 Apr	64,766
1995 Jan	33,189	2010 Apr	65,738
1996 Jan	34,085	2011 Apr	65,738
1996 Jul	43,000	2012 Apr	65,738
1997 Apr	43,860	2013 Apr	66,396
1998 Apr	45,066	2014 Apr	67,060
1999 Apr	47,008	2015 May	74,000

The Independent Parliamentary Standards Authority (IPSA) was established under the Parliamentary Standards Act 2009 and is responsible for the independent regulation and administration of the MPs' Scheme of Business Costs and Expenses, as well as for paying the salaries of MPs and their staff members. Since May 2011, the IPSA has also been responsible for determining MPs' pay and setting the level of any increase to their salary.

For 2015–16, the office costs expenditure budget is £26,050 for London area MPs and £23,400 for non-London area MPs. The maximum annual staff budget for London area MPs is £147,000 and £140,000 for non-London area MPs.

Since 1972 MPs have been able to claim reimbursement for the additional cost of staying overnight away from their main residence while on parliamentary business. This is not payable to London area MPs and those MPs who reside in 'grace and favour' accommodation. Accommodation expenses for MPs claiming rental payments in the London area is capped at £20,600 a year; outside of the London area each constituency is banded according to rental values in the area and capped accordingly; annual caps range from £10,400 to £15,650 across five bands. For MPs who own their own homes, mortgage interest and associated expenses up to £8,850 are payable.

For ministerial salaries see Government Departments.

MEMBERS' PENSIONS

Pension arrangements for MPs were first introduced in 1964. Under the Parliamentary Contributory Pension Fund CARE (career-averaged revalued earnings) scheme, MPs receive a pension on retirement based upon accumulating proportions of pensionable earnings over each year of membership. MPs contributions are payable at a rate of 11.09 per cent of pay. Exchequer contributions are paid at a rate recommended by the Government Actuary and meet the balance of the cost of providing MPs' retirement benefits. Pensions are normally payable upon retirement at age 65 to those who are no longer MPs. Abated pensions may be payable to members aged 55 or over. Pensions are also payable to spouses and other qualifying partners of deceased scheme members at the rate of three-eighths of the deceased member's pension. In the case of members who are in service, an enhanced spouse's or partner's pension and a lump sum equal to two times pensionable salary is payable. There are also provisions in place for dependants and MPs of any age who retire due to ill health. All pensions are CPI index-linked.

HOUSE OF COMMONS PAY BANDS FOR SENIOR STAFF

Senior Staff are placed in the following Senior Civil Service pay bands. These pay bands apply to the most senior staff in departments and agencies.

Pay Band 1	£63,500–£93,380
Pay Band 1A	£67,600–£105,560
Pay Band 2	£85,000–£124,845
Pay Band 3	£104,000–£139,829

OFFICERS AND OFFICIALS

The House of Commons is presided over by the Speaker, who has considerable powers to maintain order. A deputy speaker, called the Chairman of Ways and Means, and two deputy chairs may preside over sittings of the House of Commons; they are elected by the house, and, like the Speaker, neither speak nor vote other than in their official capacity.

The staff of the house are employed by a commission chaired by the Speaker. The heads of the six House of Commons departments are permanent officers of the house, not MPs. The Clerk of the House is the principal adviser to the Speaker on the privileges and procedures of the house, the conduct of the business of the house, and committees. The Serjeant-at-Arms is responsible for security and ceremonial functions of the house.

Speaker (£142,826)*, Rt. Hon. John Bercow, MP
Chairman of Ways and Means (£107,108), Rt. Hon. Lindsay Hoyle, MP
First Deputy Chairman of Ways and Means (£102,098), Eleanor Laing, MP
Second Deputy Chairman of Ways and Means (£102,098), Natascha Engel, MP
House of Commons Commission, Rt, Hon. John Bercow, MP (chair); Sir Paul Beresford, MP; Angela Eagle, MP; Rt. Hon. Chris Grayling, MP
Secretary of the Commission, Robert Twigger

* Salaries in parentheses are the maximum available. The Speaker and Deputies have opted not to take the statutory increases awarded to them each year as office holders.

OFFICE OF THE SPEAKER

Speaker's Secretary, Peter Barratt
Assistant Secretary to the Speaker, Ian Davies, MBE
Trainbearer, Jim Davey
Speaker's Counsel, Michael Carpenter, CB
Chaplain to the Speaker, Revd Rose Hudson-Wilkin

OFFICE OF THE CLERK OF THE HOUSE

Clerk of the House, David Natzler
Private Secretary, Lloyd Owen

PARLIAMENTARY COMMISSIONER FOR STANDARDS

Parliamentary Commissioner for Standards, Kathryn Hudson
Registrar of Members' Financial Interests, Heather Wood

PARLIAMENTARY SECURITY DIRECTOR

Parliamentary Security Director, Paul Martin, CBE
Deputy Parliamentary Security Director, Emily Baldock

OFFICE OF THE CHAIRMAN OF WAYS AND MEANS

Secretary to the Chairman of Ways and Means, Joanna Dodd

GOVERNANCE OFFICE
Head of Office, Tom Goldsmith
Corportate Risk Management Facilitator, Rachel Harrison
Head of Central Communications, Marianne Cwynarski
Head of Internal Audit, Paul Dillon-Robinson
Head of Parliamentary Programme and Project Assurance,
    Jane Rumsam
Strategy, Planning and Performance Manager, Jane Hough

DEPARTMENT OF CHAMBER AND COMMITTEE
SERVICES
Acting Clerk Assistant and Acting Director General,
    Jacqy Sharpe
Director of Departmental Services, Elizabeth Hunt

OVERSEAS OFFICE
Principal Clerk, Crispin Poyser
Delegation Secretary, Nick Wright
Inward Visits Manager, Alison Game, MBE
National Parliament Representative (Brussels), Alison Grove

COMMITTEE OFFICE
Clerk of Committees, Andrew Kennon
Principal Clerk of Select Committees, Mark Hutton; Colin Lee;
    Simon Patrick
Business Managers, Anita Fuki; Richard Dawson
Operations Manager, Karen Saunders

DEPARTMENTAL SELECT COMMITTEES
Backbench Business – Chair, Ian Mearns; *Clerk,* Mike
    Hennessy
Business, Innovation and Skills – Chair, Iain Wright;
    Clerk, Jessica Montgomery
Communities and Local Government – Chair, Clive Betts;
    Clerk, Dr Anna Dickson
Culture, Media and Sport – Chair, Jesse Norman;
    Clerk, Elizabeth Flood
Defence – Chair, Dr Julian Lewis; *Clerk,* James Davies
Education – Chair, Neil Carmichael; *Clerk,* Lynn Gardner
Energy and Climate Change – Chair, Angus Brendan MacNeil;
    Clerk, Dr Farrah Bhatti
Environment, Food and Rural Affairs – Chair, Neil Parish;
    Clerks, David Weir
Foreign Affairs – Chair, Crispin Blunt; *Clerk,* Kenneth Fox
Health – Chair, Dr Sarah Wollaston; *Clerk,* Huw Yardley
High Speed Rail Bill – Chair, Robert Syms; *Clerk,* Neil
    Caulfield
Home Affairs – Chair, Keith Vaz; *Clerk,* Carol Oxborough
International Development – Chair, Stephen Twigg; *Clerk,*
    Kate Emms
Justice – Chair, Robert Neill; *Clerk,* Nick Walker
Northern Ireland Affairs – Chair, Laurence Robertson;
    Clerk, Mike Clark
Procedure – Chair, Charles Walker; *Clerk,* Martyn Atkins
Science and Technology – Chair, Nicola Blackwood; *Clerk,*
    Simon Fiander
Scottish Affairs – Chair, Pete Wishart; *Clerk,* Jyoti Chandola
Standards – Chair, Kevin Barron; *Clerk,* Eve Samson
Statutory Instruments – Chair, Derek Twigg; *Clerk,* Amelia
    Aspden
Transport – Chair, Louise Ellman; *Clerk,* Gordon Clarke
Treasury – Chair, Andrew Tyrie; *Clerk,* James Rhys
Welsh Affairs – Chair, David Davies; *Clerk,* Richard Ward
Women and Equalities – Chair, Maria Miller; *Clerk,* Gosia
    McBride
Work and Pensions – Chair, Frank Field; *Clerk,* Adam
    Mellows-Facer

DOMESTIC COMMITTEES
Administration – Chair, Sir Paul Beresford; Clerks, Sarah
    Heath; Helen Wood
Finance – Chair, Nicholas Brown; *Clerk,* Robert Twigger
Members' Expenses – Chair, vacant; *Clerk,* Robert Twigger

OTHER COMMITTEES
Environmental Audit – Chair, Huw Irranca-Davies;
    Clerk, David Slater
Liaison – Chair, vacant; *Clerk,* Andrew Kennon
Petitions Committee – Chair, Helen Jones; *Clerk,* Anne-Marie
    Griffiths
Public Accounts – Chair, Meg Hillier; *Clerk,* Sarah Petit
Public Administration and Constitutional Affairs – Chair,
    Bernard Jenkin; *Clerks,* Dr Rebecca Davies; Sian
    Woodward
Regulatory Reform – Chair, vacant; *Clerk,* Jessica Montgomery
European Scrutiny Committee – Chair, Sir William Cash;
    Clerk, Sarah Davies

SCRUTINY UNIT
Head of Unit, Jessica Mulley
Deputy Head of Unit, Larry Honeysett

VOTE OFFICE
Deliverer of the Vote, Catherine Fogarty
Deputy Deliverer of the Vote, Owen Sweeney
Head of Procedural Publishing, Tom McVeagh
Procedural Publishing Operations Manager, Stuart Miller

CHAMBER BUSINESS DIRECTORATE
Acting Clerk of Legislation, Liam Laurence Smyth
Principal Clerks
    Table Office, Philippa Helme
    Journals, Paul Evans
    Bills, Matthew Hamlyn

OFFICIAL REPORT DIRECTORATE
Editor, Lorraine Sutherland
Deputy Editor, Alex Newton
Director of Broadcasting, John Angeli

SERJEANT-AT-ARMS DIRECTORATE
Serjeant-at-Arms, Lawrence Ward
Deputy Serjeant-at-Arms, Richard Latham
Assistant Serjeant-at-Arms, Lesley Scott

OFFICE OF SPEAKER'S COUNSEL
Speaker's Counsel and Head of Legal Services Office, Michael
    Carpenter, CB
Counsel for European Legislation, Arnold Ridout
Assistant Counsel for European Legislation, Joanne Dee
Counsel for Domestic Legislation, Peter Davis
Deputy Counsel for Domestic Legislation, Peter Brooksbank;
    Philip Davies; Daniel Greenberg
Principal Assistant Counsel, Helen Emes
Legal Assistants, Ami Cochrane; Emma Johnston

DEPARTMENT OF FACILITIES
Director-General, John Borley, CB
Director of Business Management, Della Herd
Acting Parliamentary Director of Estates, Brian Finnimore
Director of Accommodation and Logistics Services, Fiona
    Channon
Director of Facilities Finance, Philip Collins
Executive Officer, Katie Phelan-Molloy
Director of Catering Services, Richard Tapner-Evans
Operations Manager, Robert Gibbs
Executive Chef, Mark Hill

DEPARTMENT OF FINANCE
Director of Finance, Myfanwy Barrett
Chief Accountant, Alex Mills
Head of Financial Planning, Amanda Colledge
Head of Financial Accounting, Debra Shirtcliffe
Head of Financial Services, Sam Rao

DEPARTMENT OF HUMAN RESOURCES AND CHANGE
Director-General of HR and Change, Andrew J. Walker
Director of HR Services, Alix Langley
Occupational Health and Wellbeing Manager, Anne Mossop
Head of Safety, Dr Marianne McDougall

DEPARTMENT OF INFORMATION SERVICES
Director-General and Librarian, Penny Young
Director of Service Delivery, John Benger
Head of Central Support Services, Grahame Allen
Curator of Works of Art, Malcolm Hay
Head of Customer Services, Dr Patsy Richards

PARLIAMENTARY INFORMATION AND COMMUNICATION TECHNOLOGY (ICT)
Director of Parliamentary Digital Service, Rob Greig
Director of Technology, Steve O'Connor
Director of Operations and Members Services, Rob Sanders
Director of Resources, Tracey Jessup
Director of Programmes and Projects, Steven Mark
Head of the Web and Intranet Service, Tracy Green

OTHER PRINCIPAL OFFICERS
Clerk of the Crown in Chancery, Dame Ursula Brennan
Parliamentary and Health Service Ombudsman, Dame Julie
  Mellor

NATIONAL AUDIT OFFICE
157–197 Buckingham Palace Road, London SW1W 9SP
T 020-7798 7000
E enquiries@nao.gsi.gov.uk W www.nao.org.uk

The National Audit Office came into existence under the National Audit Act 1983 to replace and continue the work of the former Exchequer and Audit Department. The act reinforced the office's total financial and operational independence from the government and brought its head, the Comptroller and Auditor-General, into a closer relationship with parliament as an officer of the House of Commons.

The National Audit Office (NAO) scrutinises public spending on behalf of parliament, helping it to hold government departments to account and helping public service managers improve performance and service delivery. The NAO audits the financial statements of all government departments and a wide range of other public bodies. It regularly publishes 'value for money' reports on the efficiency and effectiveness of how public resources are used.
Comptroller and Auditor-General, Amyas Morse
Assistant Auditors-General, Sue Higgins; Sally Howes; Martin
  Sinclair; John Thorpe
Chief Operating Officer, Michael Whitehouse

PARLIAMENTARY INFORMATION

The following is a short glossary of aspects of the work of parliament. Unless otherwise stated, references are to House of Commons procedures.

BILL – Proposed legislation is termed a bill. The stages of a public bill (for private bills, *see* below) in the House of Commons are as follows:

First reading: This stage introduces the legislation to the house and, for government bills, merely constitutes an order to have the bill printed.

Second reading: The debate on the principles of the bill.

Committee stage: The detailed examination of a bill, clause by clause. In most cases this takes place in a public bill committee, or the whole house may act as a committee. Public bill committees may take evidence before embarking on detailed scrutiny of the bill. Very rarely, a bill may be examined by a select committee.

Report stage: Detailed review of a bill as amended in committee, on the floor of the house, and an opportunity to make further changes.

Third reading: Final debate on the full bill in the Commons.

Public bills go through the same stages in the House of Lords, but with important differences: the committee stage is taken in committee of the whole house or in a grand committee, in which any peer may participate. There are no time limits, all amendments are debated, and further amendments can be made at third reading.

A bill may start in either house, and has to pass through both houses to become law. Both houses have to agree the final text of a bill, so that amendments made by the second house are then considered in the originating house, and if not agreed, sent back or themselves amended, until agreement is reached.

CHILTERN HUNDREDS – A nominal office of profit under the crown, the acceptance of which requires an MP to vacate his/her seat. The Manor of Northstead is similar. These are the only means by which an MP may resign.

CONSOLIDATED FUND BILL – A bill to authorise the issue of money to maintain government services. The bill is dealt with without debate.

EARLY DAY MOTION – A motion put on the notice paper by an MP without, in general, the real prospect of its being debated. Such motions are expressions of back-bench opinion.

FATHER OF THE HOUSE – The MP whose continuous service in the House of Commons is the longest. The present Father of the House is the Rt. Hon. Sir Gerald Kaufman, MP.

GRAND COMMITTEES – There are three grand committees in the House of Commons, one each for Northern Ireland, Scotland and Wales; they consider matters relating specifically to that country. In the House of Lords, bills may be sent to a grand committee instead of a committee of the whole house (*see also* Bill).

HOURS OF MEETING – The House of Commons normally meets on Mondays at 2.30pm, Tuesdays and Wednesdays at 11.30am, Thursdays at 9.30am and some Fridays at 9.30am. (*See also* Westminster Hall Sittings, below.) The House of Lords normally meets at 2.30pm Mondays and Tuesdays, 3pm on Wednesdays and at 11am on Thursdays. The House of Lords occasionally sits on Fridays at 10am.

LEADER OF THE OPPOSITION – In 1937 the office of leader of the opposition was recognised and a salary was assigned to the post. In 2015–16 this is £135,776 (including a parliamentary salary of £74,000). The present leader of the opposition is the Rt. Hon. Jeremy Corbyn, MP.

THE LORD CHANCELLOR – The office of Lord High Chancellor of Great Britain was significantly altered by the Constitutional Reform Act 2005. Previously, the Lord Chancellor was (*ex officio*) the Speaker of the House of Lords, and took part in debates and voted in divisions in the House of Lords. The Department for Constitutional Affairs was created in 2003, and became the Ministry of Justice in 2007, incorporating most of the responsibilities of the Lord Chancellor's department. The role of Speaker has been transferred to the post of Lord Speaker. The Constitutional

Reform Act 2005 also brought to an end the Lord Chancellor's role as head of the judiciary. A Judicial Appointments Commission was created in April 2006, and a supreme court (separate from the House of Lords) was established in 2009.

THE LORD GREAT CHAMBERLAIN – The Lord Great Chamberlain is a Great Officer of State, the office being hereditary since the grant of Henry I to the family of De Vere, Earls of Oxford. It is now a joint hereditary office rotating on the death of the sovereign between the Cholmondeley, Carington and Ancaster families.

The Lord Great Chamberlain, currently the Marquess of Cholmondeley, is responsible for the royal apartments in the Palace of Westminster, the Royal Gallery, the administration of the Chapel of St Mary Undercroft and, in conjunction with the Lord Speaker and the Speaker of the House of Commons, Westminster Hall. The Lord Great Chamberlain has the right to perform specific services at a coronation and has particular responsibility for the internal administrative arrangements within the House of Lords for state openings of parliament.

THE LORD SPEAKER – The first Lord Speaker of the House of Lords, the Rt. Hon. Baroness Hayman, took up office on 4 July 2006. The Lord Speaker is independent of the government and elected by members of the House of Lords rather than appointed by the prime minister. Although the Lord Speaker's primary role is to preside over proceedings in the House of Lords, she does not have the same powers as the Speaker of the House of Commons. For example, the Lord Speaker is not responsible for maintaining order during debates, as this is the responsibility of the house as a whole. The Lord Speaker sits in the Lords on one of the woolsacks, which are couches covered in red cloth and stuffed with wool.

OPPOSITION DAY – A day on which the topic for debate is chosen by the opposition. There are 20 such days in a normal session. On 17 days, subjects are chosen by the leader of the opposition; on the remaining three days by the leader of the next largest opposition party.

PARLIAMENT ACTS 1911 AND 1949 – Under these acts, bills may become law without the consent of the Lords, though the House of Lords has the power to delay a public bill for a parliamentary session.

PRIME MINISTER'S QUESTIONS – The prime minister answers questions from 12 to 12.30pm on Wednesdays.

PRIVATE BILL – A bill promoted by a body or an individual to give powers additional to, or in conflict with, the general law, and to which a special procedure applies to enable people affected to object.

PRIVATE MEMBER'S BILL – A public bill promoted by an MP or peer who is not a member of the government.

PRIVATE NOTICE QUESTION – A question adjudged of urgent importance on submission to the Speaker (in the Lords, the Lord Speaker), answered at the end of oral questions.

PRIVILEGE – The House of Commons has rights and immunities to protect it from obstruction in carrying out its duties. These are known as parliamentary privilege and enable Members of Parliament to debate freely. The most important privilege is that of freedom of speech. MPs cannot be prosecuted for sedition or sued for libel or slander over anything said during proceedings in the house. This enables them to raise in the house questions affecting the public good which might be difficult to raise outside owing to the possibility of legal action against them. The House of Lords has similar privileges.

QUESTION TIME – Oral questions are answered by ministers in the Commons from 2.30 to 3.30pm on Mondays, 11.30am to 12.30pm on Tuesdays and

Wednesdays, and 9.30 to 10.30am on Thursdays. Questions are also taken for half an hour at the start of the Lords sittings.

ROYAL ASSENT – The royal assent is signified by letters patent to such bills and measures as have passed both Houses of Parliament (or bills which have been passed under the Parliament Acts 1911 and 1949). The sovereign has not given royal assent in person since 1854. On occasion, for instance in the prorogation of parliament, royal assent may be pronounced to the two houses by Lords Commissioners. More usually royal assent is notified to each house sitting separately in accordance with the Royal Assent Act 1967. The old French formulae for royal assent are then endorsed on the acts by the Clerk of the Parliaments.

The power to withhold assent resides with the sovereign but has not been exercised in the UK since 1707.

SELECT COMMITTEES – Consisting usually of 10 to 15 members of all parties, select committees are a means used by both houses in order to investigate certain matters.

Most select committees in the House of Commons are tied to departments: each committee investigates subjects within a government department's remit. There are other select committees dealing with matters such as public accounts (ie the spending by the government of money voted by parliament) and European legislation, and also committees advising on procedures and domestic administration of the house. Major select committees usually take evidence in public; their evidence and reports are published on the parliament website and in hard copy by The Stationery Office (TSO). House of Commons select committees are reconstituted after a general election.

In the House of Lords, select committees do not mirror government departments but cover broader issues. There is a select committee on the European Union (EU), which has six sub-committees dealing with specific areas of EU policy, a select committee on science and technology, a select committee on economic affairs and also one on the constitution. There is also a select committee on delegated powers and regulatory reform and one on privileges and conduct. In addition, *ad hoc* select committees have been set up from time to time to investigate specific subjects. There are also joint committees of the two houses, eg the committees on statutory instruments and on human rights.

THE SPEAKER – The Speaker of the House of Commons is the spokesperson and chair of the Chamber. He or she is elected by the house at the beginning of each parliament or when the previous Speaker retires or dies. The Speaker neither speaks in debates nor votes in divisions except when the voting is equal.

VACANT SEATS – When a vacancy occurs in the House of Commons during a session of parliament, the writ for the by-election is moved by a whip of the party to which the member whose seat has been vacated belonged. If the house is in recess, the Speaker can issue a warrant for a writ, should two members certify to him that a seat is vacant.

WESTMINSTER HALL SITTINGS – Following a report by the Modernisation of the House of Commons Select Committee, the Commons decided in May 1999 to set up a second debating forum. It is known as 'Westminster Hall' and sittings are in the Grand Committee Room on some Mondays from 4.30pm to 7.30pm, Tuesdays and Wednesdays from 9.30am to 11.30am and from 2pm to 5pm, and Thursdays from 1.30pm to 4.30pm. Sittings are open to the public at the times indicated.

WHIPS – In order to secure the attendance of members of a particular party in parliament, particularly on the occasion of an important vote, whips (originally known as 'whippers-in') are appointed. The written appeal or circular letter issued by them is also known as a 'whip', its urgency being denoted by the number of times it is underlined. Failure to respond to a three-line whip is tantamount in the Commons to secession (at any rate temporarily) from the party. Whips are provided with office accommodation in both houses, and government and some opposition whips receive salaries from public funds.

PARLIAMENTARY ARCHIVES
Houses of Parliament, London SW1A 0PW
T 020-7219 3074 E archives@parliament.uk
W www.parliament.uk/archives

Since 1497, the records of parliament have been kept within the Palace of Westminster. They are in the custody of the Clerk of Parliaments. In 1946 the House of Lords Record Office, which became the Parliamentary Archives in 2006, was established to supervise their preservation and their availability to the public. Some 3 million documents are preserved, including acts of parliament from 1497, journals of the House of Lords from 1510, minutes and committee proceedings from 1610, and papers laid before parliament from 1531. Among the records are the Petition of Right, the death warrant of Charles I, the Declaration of Breda, and the Bill of Rights. Records are made available through a public search room.
Director of the Parliamentary Archives, Adrian Brown

GOVERNMENT OFFICE

The government is the body of ministers responsible for the administration of national affairs, determining policy and introducing into parliament any legislation necessary to give effect to government policy. The majority of ministers are members of the House of Commons but members of the House of Lords, or of neither house, may also hold ministerial responsibility. The prime minister is, by current convention, always a member of the House of Commons.

THE PRIME MINISTER
The office of prime minister, which had been in existence for nearly 200 years, was officially recognised in 1905 and its holder was granted a place in the table of precedence. The prime minister, by tradition also First Lord of the Treasury and Minister for the Civil Service, is appointed by the sovereign and is usually the leader of the party which enjoys, or can secure, a majority in the House of Commons. Other ministers are appointed by the sovereign on the recommendation of the prime minister, who also allocates functions among ministers and has the power to dismiss ministers from their posts.

The prime minister informs the sovereign on state and political matters, advises on the dissolution of parliament, and makes recommendations for important crown appointments, ie the award of honours, etc.

As the chair of cabinet meetings and leader of a political party, the prime minister is responsible for translating party policy into government activity. As leader of the government, the prime minister is responsible to parliament and to the electorate for the policies and their implementation.

The prime minister also represents the nation in international affairs, eg summit conferences.

THE CABINET
The cabinet developed during the 18th century as an inner committee of the Privy Council, which was the chief source of executive power until that time. The cabinet is composed of about 20 ministers chosen by the prime minister, usually the heads of government departments (generally known as secretaries of state unless they have a special title, eg Chancellor of the Exchequer), the leaders of the two houses of parliament, and the holders of various traditional offices.

The cabinet's functions are the final determination of policy, control of government and coordination of government departments. The exercise of its functions is dependent upon the incumbent party's (or parties') majority support in the House of Commons. Cabinet meetings are held in private, taking place once or twice a week during parliamentary sittings and less often during a recess. Proceedings are confidential, the members being bound by their oath as privy counsellors not to disclose information about the proceedings.

The convention of collective responsibility means that the cabinet acts unanimously even when cabinet ministers do not all agree on a subject. The policies of departmental ministers must be consistent with the policies of the government as a whole, and once the government's policy has been decided, each minister is expected to support it or resign.

The convention of ministerial responsibility holds a minister, as the political head of his or her department, accountable to parliament for the department's work. Departmental ministers usually decide all matters within their responsibility, although on matters of political importance they normally consult their colleagues collectively. A decision by a departmental minister is binding on the government as a whole.

POLITICAL PARTIES

Before the reign of William and Mary, the principal officers of state were chosen by and were responsible to the sovereign alone, and not to parliament or the nation at large. Such officers acted sometimes in concert with one another but more often independently, and the fall of one did not, of necessity, involve that of others, although all were liable to be dismissed at any moment.

In 1693 the Earl of Sunderland recommended to William III the advisability of selecting a ministry from the political party which enjoyed a majority in the House of Commons, and the first united ministry was drawn in 1696 from the Whigs, to which party the king owed his throne. This group became known as the 'junto' and was regarded with suspicion as a novelty in the political life of the nation, being a small section meeting in secret apart from the main body of ministers. It may be regarded as the forerunner of the cabinet and in the course of time it led to the establishment of the principle of joint responsibility of ministers, so that internal disagreement caused a change of personnel or resignation of the whole body of ministers.

The accession of George I, who was unfamiliar with the English language, led to a disinclination on the part of the sovereign to preside at meetings of his ministers and caused the emergence of a prime minister, a position first acquired by Robert Walpole in 1721 and retained by him without interruption for 20 years and 326 days. The office of prime minister was formally recognised in 1905 when it was established by royal warrant.

DEVELOPMENT OF PARTIES
In 1828 the Whigs became known as Liberals, a name originally given by opponents to imply laxity of principles, but gradually accepted by the party to indicate its claim to be pioneers and champions of political reform and progressive legislation. In 1861 a Liberal Registration Association was founded and Liberal Associations became widespread. In 1877 a National Liberal Federation was formed, with its headquarters in London. The Liberal Party was in power for long periods during the second half of the 19th century and

for several years during the first quarter of the 20th century, but after a split in the party in 1931, the numbers elected remained small. In 1988 a majority of the Liberals agreed on a merger with the Social Democratic Party under the title Social and Liberal Democrats; since 1989 they have been known as the Liberal Democrats. A minority continue separately as the Liberal Party.

Soon after the change from Whig to Liberal, the Tory Party became known as Conservative, a name believed to have been invented by John Wilson Croker in 1830 and to have been generally adopted around the time of the passing of the Reform Act of 1832 – to indicate that the preservation of national institutions was the leading principle of the party. After the Home Rule crisis of 1886 the dissentient Liberals entered into a compact with the Conservatives, under which the latter undertook not to contest their seats, but a separate Liberal Unionist organisation was maintained until 1912, when it was united with the Conservatives.

Labour candidates for parliament made their first appearance at the general election of 1892, when there were 27 standing as Labour or Liberal-Labour. In 1900 the Labour Representation Committee (LRC) was set up in order to establish a distinct Labour group in parliament, with its own whips, its own policy, and a readiness to cooperate with any party which might be engaged in promoting legislation in the direct interests of labour. In 1906 the LRC became known as the Labour Party.

The Green Party was founded in 1973 and campaigns for social and environmental justice. The party began as 'People', was renamed the Ecology Party, and became the Green Party in 1985.

The UK Independence Party (UKIP) was founded in 1993 by members of the Anti-Federalist League. It is a right-wing populist party with one key policy – to leave the European Union. In the 2014 European elections, UKIP became the first party, other than the Conservatives or Labour to win a national election in over a century.

Plaid Cymru was founded in 1926 to provide an independent political voice for Wales and to campaign for self-government in Wales.

The Scottish National Party (SNP) was founded in 1934 to campaign for independence for Scotland and a referendum on the subject was held in September 2014 which culminated in a 'no' to independence result.

The Social Democratic and Labour Party (SDLP) was founded in 1970, emerging from the civil rights movement of the 1960s, with the aim of promoting reform, reconciliation and partnership across the sectarian divide in Northern Ireland, and of opposing violence from any quarter.

The Democratic Unionist Party (DUP) was founded in 1971 to resist moves by the Ulster Unionist Party which were considered a threat to the Union. Its aim is to maintain Northern Ireland as an integral part of the UK.

The Alliance Party of Northern Ireland was formed in 1970 as a non-sectarian unionist party.

Sinn Fein first emerged in the 1900s as a federation of nationalist clubs. It is a left-wing republican and labour party that seeks to end British governance in Ireland and achieve a 32-county republic.

GOVERNMENT AND OPPOSITION

The government is formed by the party which wins the largest number of seats in the House of Commons at a general election, or which has the support of a majority of members in the House of Commons. By tradition, the leader of the majority party is asked by the sovereign to form a government, while the largest minority party becomes the official opposition with its own leader and a shadow cabinet.

Leaders of the government and opposition sit on the front benches of the Commons with their supporters (the back-benchers) sitting behind them.

FINANCIAL SUPPORT

Financial support for opposition parties in the House of Commons was introduced in 1975 and is commonly known as Short Money, after Edward Short, the leader of the house at that time, who introduced the scheme. Short Money is only payable to those parties that secured either one seat or two seats and more than 150,000 votes at the previous general election, and is only intended to provide assistance for parliamentary duties. The amount payable is £16,956.86 for every seat won at the most recent general election plus £33.86 for every 200 votes gained by the party. Short Money approximations for 2015–16 are:

DUP	£166,000
Green	£212,000
Labour	£6,200,000
Liberal Democrats	£540,000
Plaid Cymru	£81,000
SDLP	£70,000
SNP	£1,200,000
UKIP	£650,000

* The sum paid to Sinn Fein and any other party that may choose not to take their seats in the House of Commons is calculated on the same basis as Short Money, but is known as Representative Money.

A specific allocation of around £777,500, for the leader of the opposition's office was introduced in April 1999.

Financial support for opposition parties in the House of Lords was introduced in 1996 and is commonly known as Cranborne Money, after former leader of the house, Viscount Cranborne.

The following list of political parties are those with at least one MP or sitting member of the House of Lords in the present parliament.

ALLIANCE PARTY OF NORTHERN IRELAND

88 University Street, Belfast BT7 1HE
T 028-9032 4274 E alliance@allianceparty.org
W www.allianceparty.org
Party Leader, David Ford
Deputy Party Leader, Naomi Long, MP
President, Andrew Muir
Chair, Neil Kelly

CONSERVATIVE PARTY

Conservative Campaign Headquarters, 4 Matthew Parker Street London SW1H 9HQ
T 020-7222 9000 W www.conservatives.com
Parliamentary Party Leader, Rt. Hon. David Cameron, MP
Leader in the Lords and Lord Privy Seal, Rt. Hon. Baroness Stowell of Beeston, MBE
Leader in the Commons and Lord President of the Council, Rt. Hon. Chris Grayling, MP
Deputy Leader in the Commons, Dr Thérèse Coffey, MP
Chair, Lord Feldman of Elstree
Party Treasurer, Michael Farmer

GREEN PARTY

Development House, 56–64 Leonard Street, London, EC2A 4LT
T 020-7549 0310 E office@greenparty.org.uk
W www.greenparty.org.uk
Party Leader, Natalie Bennett

Deputy Leaders, Shahrar Ali; Amelia Womack
Chair, Richard Mallender
Finance Coordinator, Michael Coffey

LABOUR PARTY
Labour Central, Kings Manor, Newcastle upon Tyne NE1 6PA
T 0845-092 2299 W www.labour.org.uk
General Secretary, Iain McNicol
General Secretary, Welsh Labour, Dave Hagendyk
General Secretary, Scottish Labour Party, Brian Roy

SHADOW CABINET *as at September 2015*
Leader of the Opposition, Rt. Hon. Jeremy Corbyn, MP
Deputy Leader, Tom Watson, MP
Chancellor of the Exchequer, John McDonnell, MP
Secretary of State for Foreign Affairs, Rt. Hon. Hilary Benn, MP
Secretary of State for the Home Department, Rt. Hon. Andy Burnham, MP
First Secretary of State for Business, Innovation and Skills, Angela Eagle, MP
Secretary of State for Communities and Local Government and Minister for Constitutional Convention, Jon Trickett, MP
Secretary of State for Culture, Media and Sport, Michael Dugher, MP
Secretary of State for Defence, Maria Eagle, MP
Secretary of State for Education, Lucy Powell, MP
Secretary of State for Energy and Climate Change, Lisa Nandy, MP
Secretary of State for Environment, Food and Rural Affairs, Kerry McCarthy, MP
Secretary of State for Health, Heidi Alexander, MP
Minister for Mental Health, Luciana Berger, MP
Minister for Housing and Planning, Rt. Hon. John Healey, MP
Secretary of State for International Development, Diane Abbott, MP
Lord Chancellor and Secretary of State for Justice, Rt. Hon. Lord Falconer of Thoroton, QC
Secretary of State for Northern Ireland, Vernon Coaker, MP
Secretary of State for Scotland, Ian Murray, MP
Secretary of State for Transport, Lilian Greenwood, MP
Chief Secretary to the Treasury, Seema Malhotra, MP
Minister for Women and Equalities, Kate Green, MP
Secretary of State for Wales, Nia Griffith, MP
Secretary of State for Work and Pensions, Owen Smith, MP
Minister for Young People and Voter Registration, Gloria De Piero, MP
Leader of the House of Commons, Chris Bryant, MP
Leader of the House of Lords, Rt. Hon. Baroness Smith of Basildon
Attorney-General, Catherine McKinnell, MP
Minister without Portfolio, Jonathan Ashworth, MP

LABOUR WHIPS
Commons Chief Whip, Rt. Hon. Rosie Winterton, MP
Lords Chief Whip, Rt. Hon. Lord Bassam of Brighton

LIBERAL DEMOCRATS
8–10 Great George Street, London SW1P 3AE
T 020-7022 0988 E info@libdems.org.uk W www.libdems.org.uk
Parliamentary Party Leader, Tim Farron, MP
Deputy Party Leader, Rt. Hon. Malcolm Bruce, MP
Leader in the Lords, Rt. Hon. Lord Wallace
President, Sarah Brinton
Chief Executive, Tim Gordon
Hon. Treasurer, Lord Wrigglesworth

NORTHERN IRELAND DEMOCRATIC UNIONIST PARTY
91 Dundela Avenue, Belfast BT4 3BU
T 028-9047 1155
E info@mydup.com W www.mydup.com
Parliamentary Party Leader, Rt. Hon. Peter Robinson, MLA
Deputy Leader, Rt. Hon Nigel Dodds, OBE, MP, MLA
Chair, Lord Morrow, MLA

PLAID CYMRU – THE PARTY OF WALES
Ty Gwynfor, Anson Court, Atlantic Wharf, Caerdydd CF10 4AL
T 029-2047 2272 E post@plaidcymru.org W www.partyof.wales
Party Leader, Leanne Wood, AM
Hon. Party President, Rt. Hon. Lord Wigley
Parliamentary Group Leader, Jonathan Edwards, MP
Chair, Dafydd Trystan Davies
Chief Executive, Rhuanedd Richards

SCOTTISH NATIONAL PARTY
Gordon Lamb House, 3 Jackson's Entry, Edinburgh EH8 8PJ
T 0800-633 5432 E info@snp.org W www.snp.org
Westminster Parliamentary Party Leader, Angus Robertson, MP
Westminster Parliamentary Party Chief Whip, Stewart Hosie, MP
*Scottish Parliamentary Party Leader and Leader of the SNP, Rt. Hon. Nicola Sturgeon, MSP
Deputy Leader and Deputy First Minister of Scotland, Stewart Hosie, MP
Party President, Ian Hudghton, MEP
National Treasurer, Colin Beattie, MSP
Chief Executive, Peter Murrell

SINN FEIN
53 Falls Road, Belfast BT12 4PD
T 028-9034 7350 E admin@sinnfein.ie W www.sinnfein.ie
Party President, Gerry Adams
Vice-President, Mary Lou McDonald
Chair, Declan Kearney

SOCIAL DEMOCRATIC AND LABOUR PARTY
121 Ormeau Road, Belfast BT7 1SH
T 028-9024 7700 E info@sdlp.ie W www.sdlp.ie
Parliamentary Party Leader, Dr Alisdair McDonnell, MP, MLA
Deputy Leader, Dolores Kelly, MLA
Party Whip, Pat Ramsey, MLA
Chair, Joe Byrne, MLA
Treasurer, Peter McEvoy

ULSTER UNIONIST PARTY
Strandtown Hall, 2–4 Belmont Road, Belfast BT4 2AN
T 028-9047 4630
E uup@uup.org W www.uup.org
Party Leader, Mike Nesbitt, MLA
Chair, Lord Empey of Shandon, OBE
Hon. Treasurer, Cllr Mark Cosgrove

UK INDEPENDENCE PARTY
Lexdrum House, King Charles Business Park, Newton Abbot, Devon TQ12 9BG
T 01626-831290
E mail@ukip.org W www.ukip.org
Party Leader, Nigel Farage, MEP
Deputy Leader, Paul Nuttall
Chair, Steve Crowther
Treasurer, Hugh Williams
Party Secretary, Matt Richardson

128

MEMBERS OF PARLIAMENT *as at May 2015*

* Denotes new MP in the 2015 parliament

Abbott, Diane (*b.* 1953) *Lab., Hackney North & Stoke Newington,* Maj. 24,008
Abrahams, Debbie (*b.* 1960) *Lab., Oldham East & Saddleworth,* Maj. 6,002
Adams, Nigel (*b.* 1966) *C., Selby & Ainsty,* Maj. 13,557
Afriyie, Adam (*b.* 1965) *C., Windsor,* Maj. 25,083
***Ahmed-Sheikh**, Tasmina (*b.* 1970) *SNP, Ochil & Perthshire South,* Maj. 10,168
Aldous, Peter (*b.* 1961) *C., Waveney,* Maj. 2,408
Alexander, Heidi (*b.* 1975) *Lab., Lewisham East,* Maj. 14,333
Ali, Rushanara (*b.* 1975) *Lab., Bethnal Green & Bow,* Maj. 24,317
***Allan**, Lucy (*b.* 1964) *C., Telford,* Maj. 730
Allen, Graham (*b.* 1953) *Lab., Nottingham North,* Maj. 11,860
***Allen**, Heidi (*b.* 1975) *C., Cambridgeshire South,* Maj. 20,594
Amess, Sir David (*b.* 1952) *C., Southend West,* Maj. 14,021
Anderson, David (*b.* 1953) *Lab., Blaydon,* Maj. 14,227
Andrew, Stuart (*b.* 1971) *C., Pudsey,* Maj. 4,501
***Ansell**, Caroline (*b.* 1972) *C., Eastbourne,* Maj. 733
***Argar**, Edward (*b.* 1977) *C., Charnwood,* Maj. 16,931
***Arkless**, Richard (*b.* 1975) *SNP, Dumfries & Galloway,* Maj. 6,514
Ashworth, Jonathan (*b.* 1978) *Lab. Co-op, Leicester South,* Maj. 17,865
***Atkins**, Victoria (*b.* 1976) *C., Louth & Horncastle,* Maj. 14,977
Austin, Ian (*b.* 1965) *Lab., Dudley North,* Maj. 4,181
Bacon, Richard (*b.* 1962) *C., Norfolk South,* Maj. 20,493
Bailey, Adrian (*b.* 1945) *Lab. Co-op, West Bromwich West,* Maj. 7,742
Baker, Steve (*b.* 1971) *C., Wycombe,* Maj. 14,856
Baldwin, Harriett (*b.* 1960) *C., Worcestershire West,* Maj. 22,578
Barclay, Steve (*b.* 1972) *C., Cambridgeshire North East,* Maj. 16,874
***Bardell**, Hannah (*b.* 1984) *SNP, Livingston,* Maj. 16,843
Baron, John (*b.* 1959) *C., Basildon & Billericay,* Maj. 12,482
Barron, Rt. Hon. Sir Kevin (*b.* 1946) *Lab., Rother Valley,* Maj. 7,297
Barwell, Gavin (*b.* 1972) *C., Croydon Central,* Maj. 165
Bebb, Guto (*b.* 1968) *C., Aberconwy,* Maj. 3,999
Beckett, Rt. Hon. Dame Margaret (*b.* 1943) *Lab., Derby South,* Maj. 8,828
Bellingham, Henry (*b.* 1955) *C., Norfolk North West,* Maj. 13,948
Benn, Rt. Hon. Hilary (*b.* 1953) *Lab., Leeds Central,* Maj. 16,967
Benyon, Richard (*b.* 1960) *C., Newbury,* Maj. 26,368
Bercow, Rt. Hon. John (*b.* 1963) *The Speaker, Buckingham,* Maj. 22,942
Beresford, Sir Paul (*b.* 1946) *C., Mole Valley,* Maj. 25,453
Berger, Luciana (*b.* 1981) *Lab. Co-op, Liverpool Wavertree,* Maj. 24,303
Berry, Jake (*b.* 1978) *C., Rossendale & Darwen,* Maj. 5,654
***Berry**, James (*b.* 1984) *C., Kingston & Surbiton,* Maj. 2,834
Betts, Clive (*b.* 1950) *Lab., Sheffield South East,* Maj. 12,311
Bingham, Andrew (*b.* 1962) *C., High Peak,* Maj. 4,894
***Black**, Mhairi (*b.* 1994) *SNP, Paisley & Renfrewshire South,* Maj. 5,684
***Blackford**, Ian (*b.* 1961) *SNP, Ross, Skye & Lochaber,* Maj. 5,124

Blackman, Bob (*b.* 1956) *C., Harrow East,* Maj. 4,757
***Blackman**, Kirsty (*b.* 1986) *SNP, Aberdeen North,* Maj. 13,396
Blackman-Woods, Dr Roberta (*b.* 1957) *Lab., Durham, City of,* Maj. 11,439
Blackwood, Nicola (*b.* 1979) *C., Oxford West & Abingdon,* Maj. 9,582
Blenkinsop, Tom (*b.* 1980) *Lab., Middlesbrough South & Cleveland East,* Maj. 2,268
Blomfield, Paul (*b.* 1953) *Lab., Sheffield Central,* Maj. 17,309
Blunt, Crispin (*b.* 1960) *C., Reigate,* Maj. 22,334
Boles, Nick (*b.* 1965) *C., Grantham & Stamford,* Maj. 18,989
Bone, Peter (*b.* 1952) *C., Wellingborough,* Maj. 16,397
***Borwick**, Lady (Victoria) (*b.* 1956) *C., Kensington,* Maj. 7,361
***Boswell**, Phil (*b.* 1963) *SNP, Coatbridge, Chryston & Bellshill,* Maj. 11,501
Bottomley, Sir Peter (*b.* 1944) *C., Worthing West,* Maj. 16,855
Bradley, Karen (*b.* 1970) *C., Staffordshire Moorlands,* Maj. 10,174
Bradshaw, Rt. Hon. Ben (*b.* 1960) *Lab., Exeter,* Maj. 7,183
Brady, Graham (*b.* 1967) *C., Altrincham & Sale West,* Maj. 13,290
***Brady**, Mickey (*b.* 1950) *SF, Newry & Armagh,* Maj. 4,176
Brake, Rt. Hon. Tom (*b.* 1962) *LD, Carshalton & Wallington,* Maj. 1,510
Brazier, Julian (*b.* 1953) *C., Canterbury,* Maj. 9,798
Brennan, Kevin (*b.* 1959) *Lab., Cardiff West,* Maj. 6,789
Bridgen, Andrew (*b.* 1964) *C., Leicestershire North West,* Maj. 11,373
Brine, Steve (*b.* 1974) *C., Winchester,* Maj. 16,914
***Brock**, Deidre (*b.* 1961) *SNP, Edinburgh North & Leith,* Maj. 5,597
Brokenshire, James (*b.* 1968) *C., Old Bexley & Sidcup,* Maj. 15,803
***Brown**, Alan (*b.* 1970) *SNP, Kilmarnock & Loudoun,* Maj. 13,638
Brown, Lyn (*b.* 1960) *Lab., West Ham,* Maj. 27,986
Brown, Rt. Hon. Nicholas (*b.* 1950) *Lab., Newcastle upon Tyne East,* Maj. 12,494
Bruce, Fiona (*b.* 1957) *C., Congleton,* Maj. 16,773
Bryant, Chris (*b.* 1962) *Lab., Rhondda,* Maj. 7,455
Buck, Karen (*b.* 1958) *Lab., Westminster North,* Maj. 1,977
Buckland, Robert (*b.* 1968) *C., Swindon South,* Maj. 5,785
Burden, Richard (*b.* 1954) *Lab., Birmingham Northfield,* Maj. 2,509
***Burgon**, Richard (*b.* 1980) *Lab., Leeds East,* Maj. 12,533
Burnham, Rt. Hon. Andy (*b.* 1970) *Lab., Leigh,* Maj. 14,096
Burns, Conor (*b.* 1972) *C., Bournemouth West,* Maj. 12,410
Burns, Rt. Hon. Sir Simon (*b.* 1952) *C., Chelmsford,* Maj. 18,250
Burrowes, David (*b.* 1969) *C., Enfield Southgate,* Maj. 4,753
Burt, Rt. Hon. Alistair (*b.* 1955) *C., Bedfordshire North East,* Maj. 25,644
***Butler**, Dawn (*b.* 1969) *Lab., Brent Central,* Maj. 19,649
Byrne, Rt. Hon. Liam (*b.* 1970) *Lab., Birmingham Hodge Hill,* Maj. 23,362
***Cadbury**, Ruth (*b.* 1959) *Lab., Brentford & Isleworth,* Maj. 465
Cairns, Alun (*b.* 1970) *C., Vale of Glamorgan,* Maj. 6,880
Cameron, Rt. Hon. David (*b.* 1966) *C., Witney,* Maj. 25,155
***Cameron**, Dr Lisa (*b.* 1972) *SNP, East Kilbride, Strathaven & Lesmahagow,* Maj. 16,527
Campbell, Rt. Hon. Alan (*b.* 1957) *Lab., Tynemouth,* Maj. 8,240

Campbell, Gregory (*b.* 1953) *DUP, Londonderry East,* Maj. 7,804

Campbell, Ronnie (*b.* 1943) *Lab., Blyth Valley,* Maj. 9,229

Carmichael, Rt. Hon. Alistair (*b.* 1965) *LD, Orkney & Shetland,* Maj. 817

Carmichael, Neil (*b.* 1961) *C., Stroud,* Maj. 4,866

Carswell, Douglas (*b.* 1971) *UKIP, Clacton,* Maj. 3,437

***Cartlidge**, James (*b.* 1974) *C., Suffolk South,* Maj. 17,545

Cash, Sir William (*b.* 1940) *C., Stone,* Maj. 16,250

***Caulfield**, Maria (*b.* 1974) *C., Lewes,* Maj. 1,083

***Chalk**, Alex (*b.* 1977) *C., Cheltenham,* Maj. 6,516

Champion, Sarah (*b.* 1969) *Lab., Rotherham,* Maj. 8,446

***Chapman**, Douglas (*b.* 1955) *SNP, Dunfermline & Fife West,* Maj. 10,352

Chapman, Jenny (*b.* 1973) *Lab., Darlington,* Maj. 3,158

***Cherry**, Joanna (*b.* 1966) *SNP, Edinburgh South West,* Maj. 8,135

Chishti, Rehman (*b.* 1978) *C., Gillingham & Rainham,* Maj. 10,530

Chope, Christopher (*b.* 1947) *C., Christchurch,* Maj. 18,224

***Churchill**, Jo (*b.* 1964) *C., Bury St Edmunds,* Maj. 21,301

Clark, Rt. Hon. Greg (*b.* 1967) *C., Tunbridge Wells,* Maj. 22,874

Clarke, Rt. Hon. Kenneth (*b.* 1940) *C., Rushcliffe,* Maj. 13,829

Clegg, Rt. Hon. Nick (*b.* 1967) *LD, Sheffield Hallam,* Maj. 2,353

***Cleverly**, James (*b.* 1969) *C., Braintree,* Maj. 17,610

Clifton-Brown, Geoffrey (*b.* 1953) *C., The Cotswolds,* Maj. 21,477

Clwyd, Rt. Hon. Ann (*b.* 1937) *Lab., Cynon Valley,* Maj. 9,406

Coaker, Vernon (*b.* 1953) *Lab., Gedling,* Maj. 2,986

Coffey, Ann (*b.* 1946) *Lab., Stockport,* Maj. 10,061

Coffey, Dr Thérèse (*b.* 1971) *C., Suffolk Coastal,* Maj. 18,842

Collins, Damian (*b.* 1974) *C., Folkestone & Hythe,* Maj. 13,797

Colvile, Oliver (*b.* 1959) *C., Plymouth Sutton & Devonport,* Maj. 523

***Cooper**, Julie (*b.* 1960) *Lab., Burnley,* Maj. 3,244

Cooper, Rosie (*b.* 1950) *Lab., Lancashire West,* Maj. 8,360

Cooper, Rt. Hon. Yvette (*b.* 1969) *Lab., Normanton, Pontefract & Castleford,* Maj. 15,428

Corbyn, Jeremy (*b.* 1949) *Lab., Islington North,* Maj. 21,194

***Costa**, Alberto (*b.* 1971) *C., Leicestershire South,* Maj. 16,824

***Cowan**, Ronnie (*b.* 1959) *SNP, Inverclyde,* Maj. 11,063

Cox, Geoffrey (*b.* 1960) *C., Devon West & Torridge,* Maj. 18,403

***Cox**, Jo (*b.* 1974) *Lab., Batley & Spen,* Maj. 6,057

***Coyle**, Neil (*b.* 1978) *Lab., Bermondsey & Old Southwark,* Maj. 4,489

Crabb, Rt. Hon. Stephen (*b.* 1973) *C., Preseli Pembrokeshire,* Maj. 4,969

Crausby, David (*b.* 1946) *Lab., Bolton North East,* Maj. 4,377

***Crawley**, Angela (*b.* 1987) *SNP, Lanark & Hamilton East,* Maj. 10,100

Creagh, Mary (*b.* 1967) *Lab., Wakefield,* Maj. 2,613

Creasy, Stella (*b.* 1977) *Lab. Co-op, Walthamstow,* Maj. 23,195

Crouch, Tracey (*b.* 1975) *C., Chatham & Aylesford,* Maj. 11,455

Cruddas, Jon (*b.* 1965) *Lab., Dagenham & Rainham,* Maj. 4,980

Cryer, John (*b.* 1964) *Lab., Leyton & Wanstead,* Maj. 14,919

***Cummins**, Judith (*b.* 1967) *Lab., Bradford South,* Maj. 6,450

Cunningham, Alex (*b.* 1955) *Lab., Stockton North,* Maj. 8,367

Cunningham, Jim (*b.* 1941) *Lab., Coventry South,* Maj. 3,188

Dakin, Nic (*b.* 1955) *Lab., Scunthorpe,* Maj. 3,134

Danczuk, Simon (*b.* 1966) *Lab., Rochdale,* Maj. 12,442

David, Wayne (*b.* 1957) *Lab., Caerphilly,* Maj. 10,073

***Davies**, Byron (*b.* 1952) *C., Gower,* Maj. 27

***Davies**, Chris (*b.* 1967) *C., Brecon & Radnorshire,* Maj. 5,102

Davies, David (*b.* 1970) *C., Monmouth,* Maj. 10,982

Davies, Geraint (*b.* 1960) *Lab. Co-op, Swansea West,* Maj. 7,036

Davies, Glyn (*b.* 1944) *C., Montgomeryshire,* Maj. 5,325

***Davies**, James (*b.* 1980) *C., Vale of Clwyd,* Maj. 237

***Davies**, Mims (*b.* 1975) *C., Eastleigh,* Maj. 9,147

Davies, Philip (*b.* 1972) *C., Shipley,* Maj. 9,624

Davis, Rt. Hon. David (*b.* 1948) *C., Haltemprice & Howden,* Maj. 16,195

***Day**, Martyn (*b.* 1971) *SNP, Linlithgow & Falkirk East,* Maj. 12,934

De Piero, Gloria (*b.* 1972) *Lab., Ashfield,* Maj. 8,820

***Debbonaire**, Thangam (*b.* 1966) *Lab., Bristol West,* Maj. 5,673

Dinenage, Caroline (*b.* 1971) *C., Gosport,* Maj. 17,098

Djanogly, Jonathan (*b.* 1965) *C., Huntingdon,* Maj. 19,404

***Docherty**, Martin (*b.* 1971) *SNP, Dunbartonshire West,* Maj. 14,171

Dodds, Rt. Hon. Nigel (*b.* 1958) *DUP, Belfast North,* Maj. 5,326

Doherty, Pat (*b.* 1945) *SF, Tyrone West,* Maj. 10,060

Donaldson, Rt. Hon. Jeffrey (*b.* 1962) *DUP, Lagan Valley,* Maj. 13,000

***Donaldson**, Stuart (*b.* 1992) *SNP, Aberdeenshire West & Kincardine,* Maj. 7,033

***Donelan**, Michelle (*b.* 1984) *C., Chippenham,* Maj. 10,076

Dorries, Nadine (*b.* 1958) *C., Bedfordshire Mid,* Maj. 23,327

***Double**, Steve (*b.* 1966) *C., St Austell & Newquay,* Maj. 8,173

Doughty, Stephen (*b.* 1980) *Lab. Co-op, Cardiff South & Penarth,* Maj. 7,453

Dowd, Jim (*b.* 1951) *Lab., Lewisham West & Penge,* Maj. 12,714

Dowd, Peter (*b.* 1957) *Lab., Bootle,* Maj. 28,704

***Dowden**, Oliver (*b.* 1978) *C., Hertsmere,* Maj. 18,461

Doyle-Price, Jackie (*b.* 1969) *C., Thurrock,* Maj. 536

Drax, Richard (*b.* 1958) *C., Dorset South,* Maj. 11,994

Dromey, Jack (*b.* 1948) *Lab., Birmingham Erdington,* Maj. 5,129

***Drummond**, Flick (*b.* 1962) *C., Portsmouth South,* Maj. 5,241

Duddridge, James (*b.* 1971) *C., Rochford & Southend East,* Maj. 9,476

Dugher, Michael (*b.* 1975) *Lab., Barnsley East,* Maj. 12,034

Duncan, Rt. Hon. Sir Alan (*b.* 1957) *C., Rutland & Melton,* Maj. 21,051

Duncan Smith, Rt. Hon. Iain (*b.* 1954) *C., Chingford & Woodford Green,* Maj. 8,386

Dunne, Philip (*b.* 1958) *C., Ludlow,* Maj. 18,929

Durkan, Mark (*b.* 1960) *SDLP, Foyle,* Maj. 6,046

Eagle, Angela (*b.* 1961) *Lab., Wallasey,* Maj. 16,348

Eagle, Maria (*b.* 1961) *Lab., Garston & Halewood,* Maj. 27,146

Edwards, Jonathan (*b.* 1976) *PC, Carmarthen East & Dinefwr,* Maj. 5,599

Efford, Clive (*b.* 1958) *Lab., Eltham,* Maj. 2,693

Elliott, Julie (*b.* 1963) *Lab., Sunderland Central,* Maj. 11,179

***Elliott**, Tom (*b.* 1963) *UUP, Fermanagh & South Tyrone,* Maj. 530

Ellis, Michael (*b.* 1967) *C., Northampton North,* Maj. 3,245

Ellison, Jane (*b.* 1964) *C., Battersea,* Maj. 7,938

Ellman, Louise (b. 1945) Lab. Co-op, Liverpool Riverside, Maj. 24,463

Ellwood, Tobias (b. 1966) C., Bournemouth East, Maj. 14,612

Elphicke, Charlie (b. 1971) C., Dover, Maj. 6,294

Engel, Natascha (b. 1967) Lab., Deputy Speaker, Derbyshire North East, Maj. 1,883

Esterson, Bill (b. 1966) Lab., Sefton Central, Maj. 11,846

Eustice, George (b. 1971) C., Camborne & Redruth, Maj. 7,004

Evans, Chris (b. 1976) Lab. Co-op, Islwyn, Maj. 10,404

Evans, Graham (b. 1963) C., Weaver Vale, Maj. 806

Evans, Nigel (b. 1957) C., Ribble Valley, Maj. 13,606

Evennett, Rt. Hon. David (b. 1949) C., Bexleyheath & Crayford, Maj. 9,192

Fabricant, Michael (b. 1950) C., Lichfield, Maj. 18,189

Fallon, Rt. Hon. Michael (b. 1952) C., Sevenoaks, Maj. 19,561

Farrelly, Paul (b. 1962) Lab., Newcastle-under-Lyme, Maj. 650

Farron, Tim (b. 1970) LD, Westmorland & Lonsdale, Maj. 8,949

*Fellows, Marion (b. 1949) SNP, Motherwell & Wishaw, Maj. 11,898

*Fernandes, Suella (b. 1980) C., Fareham, Maj. 22,262

*Ferrier, Margaret (b. 1960) SNP, Rutherglen & Hamilton West, Maj. 9,975

Field, Rt. Hon. Frank (b. 1942) Lab., Birkenhead, Maj. 20,652

Field, Rt. Hon. Mark (b. 1964) C., Cities of London & Westminster, Maj. 9,671

Fitzpatrick, Jim (b. 1952) Lab., Poplar & Limehouse, Maj. 16,924

Flello, Robert (b. 1966) Lab., Stoke-on-Trent South, Maj. 2,539

*Fletcher, Colleen (b. 1954) Lab., Coventry North East, Maj. 12,274

Flint, Rt. Hon. Caroline (b. 1961) Lab., Don Valley, Maj. 8,885

Flynn, Paul (b. 1935) Lab., Newport West, Maj. 3,510

*Foster, Kevin (b. 1978) C., Torbay, Maj. 3,286

Fovargue, Yvonne (b. 1956) Lab., Makerfield, Maj. 13,155

Fox, Rt. Hon. Dr Liam (b. 1961) C., Somerset North, Maj. 23,099

*Foxcroft, Vicky (b. 1977) Lab., Lewisham Deptford, Maj. 21,516

Francois, Rt. Hon. Mark (b. 1965) C., Rayleigh & Wickford, Maj. 17,230

*Frazer, Lucy (b. 1972) C., Cambridgeshire South East, Maj. 16,837

Freeman, George (b. 1967) C., Norfolk Mid, Maj. 17,276

Freer, Mike (b. 1960) C., Finchley & Golders Green, Maj. 5,662

Fuller, Richard (b. 1962) C., Bedford, Maj. 1,097

*Fysh, Marcus (b. 1970) C., Yeovil, Maj. 5,313

Gale, Sir Roger (b. 1943) C., Thanet North, Maj. 10,948

Gapes, Mike (b. 1952) Lab. Co-op, Ilford South, Maj. 19,777

Gardiner, Barry (b. 1957) Lab., Brent North, Maj. 10,834

Garnier, Rt. Hon. Sir Edward (b. 1952) C., Harborough, Maj. 19,632

Garnier, Mark (b. 1963) C., Wyre Forest, Maj. 12,871

Gauke, David (b. 1971) C., Hertfordshire South West, Maj. 23,263

*Gethins, Stephen (b. 1976) SNP, Fife North East, Maj. 4,344

*Ghani, Nusrat (b. 1972) C., Wealden, Maj. 22,967

Gibb, Nick (b. 1960) C., Bognor Regis & Littlehampton, Maj. 13,944

*Gibson, Patricia (b. 1968) SNP, Ayrshire North & Arran, Maj. 13,573

Gillan, Rt. Hon. Cheryl (b. 1952) C., Chesham & Amersham, Maj. 23,920

Glass, Pat (b. 1956) Lab., Durham North West, Maj. 10,056

Glen, John (b. 1974) C., Salisbury, Maj. 20,421

Glindon, Mary (b. 1957) Lab., Tyneside North, Maj. 17,194

Godsiff, Roger (b. 1946) Lab., Birmingham Hall Green, Maj. 19,818

Goldsmith, Zac (b. 1975) C., Richmond Park, Maj. 23,015

Goodman, Helen (b. 1958) Lab., Bishop Auckland, Maj. 3,508

Goodwill, Robert (b. 1956) C., Scarborough & Whitby, Maj. 6,200

Gove, Rt. Hon. Michael (b. 1967) C., Surrey Heath, Maj. 24,804

*Grady, Patrick (b. 1980) SNP, Glasgow North, Maj. 9,295

Graham, Richard (b. 1958) C., Gloucester, Maj. 7,251

Grant, Helen (b. 1961) C., Maidstone & The Weald, Maj. 10,709

*Grant, Peter (b. 1961) SNP, Glenrothes, Maj. 13,897

Gray, James (b. 1954) C., Wiltshire North, Maj. 21,046

*Gray, Neil (b. 1986) SNP, Airdrie & Shotts, Maj. 8,779

Grayling, Rt. Hon. Chris (b. 1962) C., Epsom & Ewell, Maj. 24,443

*Green, Chris (b. 1973) C., Bolton West, Maj. 801

Green, Rt. Hon. Damian (b. 1956) C., Ashford, Maj. 19,296

Green, Kate (b. 1960) Lab., Stretford & Urmston, Maj. 11,685

Greening, Rt. Hon. Justine (b. 1969) C., Putney, Maj. 10,180

Greenwood, Lilian (b. 1966) Lab., Nottingham South, Maj. 6,936

*Greenwood, Margaret (b. 1959) Lab., Wirral West, Maj. 417

Grieve, Rt. Hon. Dominic (b. 1956) C., Beaconsfield, Maj. 26,311

Griffith, Nia (b. 1956) Lab., Llanelli, Maj. 7,095

Griffiths, Andrew (b. 1970) C., Burton, Maj. 11,252

Gummer, Ben (b. 1978) C., Ipswich, Maj. 3,733

Gwynne, Andrew (b. 1974) Lab., Denton & Reddish, Maj. 10,511

Gyimah, Sam (b. 1976) C., Surrey East, Maj. 22,658

*Haigh, Louise (b. 1987) Lab., Sheffield Heeley, Maj. 12,954

Halfon, Rt. Hon. Robert (b. 1969) C., Harlow, Maj. 8,350

*Hall, Luke (b. 1986) C., Thornbury & Yate, Maj. 1,495

Hamilton, Fabian (b. 1955) Lab., Leeds North East, Maj. 7,250

Hammond, Rt. Hon. Philip (b. 1955) C., Runnymede & Weybridge, Maj. 22,134

Hammond, Stephen (b. 1962) C., Wimbledon, Maj. 12,619

Hancock, Rt. Hon. Matthew (b. 1978) C., Suffolk West, Maj. 14,984

Hands, Rt. Hon. Greg (b. 1965) C., Chelsea & Fulham, Maj. 16,022

Hanson, Rt. Hon. David (b. 1957) Lab., Delyn, Maj. 2,930

Harman, Rt. Hon. Harriet (b. 1950) Lab., Camberwell & Peckham, Maj. 25,824

Harper, Rt. Hon. Mark (b. 1970) C., Forest of Dean, Maj. 10,987

*Harpham, Harry (b. 1954) Lab., Sheffield Brightside & Hillsborough, Maj. 13,807

Harrington, Richard (b. 1957) C., Watford, Maj. 9,794

*Harris, Carolyn (b. 1960) Lab., Swansea East, Maj. 12,028

Harris, Rebecca (b. 1967) C., Castle Point, Maj. 8,934

Hart, Simon (b. 1963) C., Carmarthen West & Pembrokeshire South, Maj. 6,054

Haselhurst, Rt. Hon. Sir Alan (b. 1937) C., Saffron Walden, Maj. 24,991

*Hayes, Helen (b. 1974) Lab., Dulwich & West Norwood, Maj. 16,122

Lidington, Rt. Hon. David (b. 1956) C., Aylesbury,
Maj. 17,158
Lilley, Rt. Hon. Peter (b. 1943) C., Hitchin & Harpenden,
Maj. 20,055
*Long Bailey, Rebecca (b. 1979) Lab., Salford & Eccles,
Maj. 12,541
Lopresti, Jack (b. 1969) C., Filton & Bradley Stoke,
Maj. 9,838
Lord, Jonathan (b. 1962) C., Woking, Maj. 20,810
Loughton, Tim (b. 1962) C., Worthing East & Shoreham,
Maj. 14,949
Lucas, Caroline (b. 1960) Green, Brighton Pavilion,
Maj. 7,967
Lucas, Ian (b. 1960) Lab., Wrexham, Maj. 1,831
Lumley, Karen (b. 1964) C., Redditch, Maj. 7,054
*Lynch, Holly (b. 1986) Lab., Halifax, Maj. 428
McCabe, Steve (b. 1955) Lab., Birmingham Selly Oak,
Maj. 8,447
*McCaig, Callum (b. 1985) SNP, Aberdeen South,
Maj. 7,230
McCarthy, Kerry (b. 1965) Lab., Bristol East, Maj. 3,980
McCartney, Jason (b. 1968) C., Colne Valley, Maj. 5,378
McCartney, Karl (b. 1968) C., Lincoln, Maj. 1,443
McDonagh, Siobhain (b. 1960) Lab., Mitcham & Morden,
Maj. 16,922
McDonald, Andy (b. 1958) Lab., Middlesbrough,
Maj. 12,477
*McDonald, Stewart (b. 1986) SNP, Glasgow South,
Maj. 12,269
*McDonald, Stuart (b. 1978) SNP, Cumbernauld, Kilsyth &
Kirkintilloch East, Maj. 14,752
McDonnell, Dr Alasdair (b. 1949) SDLP, Belfast South,
Maj. 906
McDonnell, John (b. 1951) Lab., Hayes & Harlington,
Maj. 15,700
McFadden, Rt. Hon. Pat (b. 1965) Lab., Wolverhampton
South East, Maj. 10,778
*McGarry, Natalie (b. 1981) SNP, Glasgow East,
Maj. 10,387
*McGinn, Conor (b. 1984) Lab., St Helens North,
Maj. 17,291
McGovern, Alison (b. 1980) Lab., Wirral South, Maj. 4,599
*McInnes, Liz (b. 1959) Lab., Heywood & Middleton,
Maj. 5,299
*Mackinlay, Craig (b. 1967) C., Thanet South, Maj. 2,812
McKinnell, Catherine (b. 1976) Lab., Newcastle upon Tyne
North, Maj. 10,153
*Mackintosh, David (b. 1979) C., Northampton South,
Maj. 3,793
*McLaughlin, Anne (b. 1966) SNP, Glasgow North East,
Maj. 9,222
McLoughlin, Rt. Hon. Patrick (b. 1957) C., Derbyshire
Dales, Maj. 14,044
*McNally, John (b. 1951) SNP, Falkirk, Maj. 19,701
MacNeil, Angus (b. 1970) SNP, Na h-Eileanan an Iar,
Maj. 4,102
McPartland, Stephen (b. 1976) C., Stevenage, Maj. 4,955
Mactaggart, Rt. Hon. Fiona (b. 1953) Lab., Slough,
Maj. 7,336
*Madders, Justin (b. 1972) Lab., Ellesmere Port & Neston,
Maj. 6,275
Mahmood, Khalid (b. 1961) Lab., Birmingham Perry Barr,
Maj. 14,828
Mahmood, Shabana (b. 1980) Lab., Birmingham Ladywood,
Maj. 21,868
Main, Anne (b. 1957) C., St Albans, Maj. 12,732
*Mak, Alan (b. 1983) C., Havant, Maj. 13,920
Malhotra, Seema (b. 1972) Lab. Co-op, Feltham & Heston,
Maj. 11,463

*Malthouse, Kit (b. 1966) C., Hampshire North West,
Maj. 23,943
Mann, John (b. 1960) Lab., Bassetlaw, Maj. 8,843
*Mann, Scott (b. 1977) C., Cornwall North, Maj. 6,621
*Marris, Rob (b. 1955) Lab., Wolverhampton South West,
Maj. 801
Marsden, Gordon (b. 1953) Lab., Blackpool South,
Maj. 2,585
*Maskell, Rachael (b. 1972) Lab., Co-op, York Central,
Maj. 6,716
Maskey, Paul (b. 1967) SF, Belfast West, Maj. 12,365
*Matheson, Chris (b. 1968) Lab., Chester, City of, Maj. 93
*Mathias, Tania (b. 1964) C., Twickenham, Maj. 2,017
May, Rt. Hon. Theresa (b. 1956) C., Maidenhead,
Maj. 29,059
Maynard, Paul (b. 1975) C., Blackpool North & Cleveleys,
Maj. 3,340
Meacher, Rt. Hon. Michael (b. 1939) Lab., Oldham West &
Royton, Maj. 14,738
Meale, Sir Alan (b. 1949) Lab., Mansfield, Maj. 5,315
Mearns, Ian (b. 1957) Lab., Gateshead, Maj. 14,784
Menzies, Mark (b. 1971) C., Fylde, Maj. 13,224
*Mercer, Johnny (b. 1981) C., Plymouth Moor View,
Maj. 1,026
*Merriman, Huw (b. 1973) C., Bexhill & Battle,
Maj. 20,075
Metcalfe, Stephen (b. 1966) C., Basildon South & Thurrock
East, Maj. 7,691
Miliband, Rt. Hon. Edward (b. 1969) Lab., Doncaster North,
Maj. 11,780
Miller, Rt. Hon. Maria (b. 1964) C., Basingstoke, Maj. 11,063
*Milling, Amanda (b. 1975) C., Cannock Chase, Maj. 4,923
Mills, Nigel (b. 1974) C., Amber Valley, Maj. 4,205
Milton, Rt. Hon. Anne (b. 1955) C., Guildford,
Maj. 22,448
Mitchell, Rt. Hon. Andrew (b. 1956) C., Sutton Coldfield,
Maj. 16,417
Molloy, Francie (b. 1950) SF, Ulster Mid, Maj. 13,617
*Monaghan, Carol (b. 1972) SNP, Glasgow North West,
Maj. 10,364
*Monaghan, Dr Paul (b. 1966) SNP, Caithness, Sutherland &
Easter Ross, Maj. 3,844
Moon, Madeleine (b. 1950) Lab., Bridgend, Maj. 1,927
Mordaunt, Penny (b. 1973) C., Portsmouth North,
Maj. 10,537
Morden, Jessica (b. 1968) Lab., Newport East, Maj. 4,705
Morgan, Rt. Hon. Nicky (b. 1972) C., Loughborough,
Maj. 9,183
Morris, Anne Marie (b. 1957) C., Newton Abbot,
Maj. 11,288
Morris, David (b. 1966) C., Morecambe & Lunesdale,
Maj. 4,590
Morris, Grahame (b. 1961) Lab., Easington, Maj. 14,641
Morris, James (b. 1967) C., Halesowen & Rowley Regis,
Maj. 3,082
*Morton, Wendy (b. 1967) C., Aldridge-Brownhills,
Maj. 11,723
Mowat, David (b. 1957) C., Warrington South, Maj. 2,750
Mulholland, Greg (b. 1970) LD, Leeds North West,
Maj. 2,907
*Mullin, Roger (b. 1948) SNP, Kirkcaldy & Cowdenbeath,
Maj. 9,974
Mundell, Rt. Hon. David (b. 1962) C., Dumfriesshire,
Clydesdale & Tweeddale, Maj. 798
Murray, Ian (b. 1976) Lab., Edinburgh South, Maj. 2,637
Murray, Sheryll (b. 1956) C., Cornwall South East,
Maj. 16,995
Murrison, Dr Andrew (b. 1961) C., Wiltshire South West,
Maj. 18,168

Nandy, Lisa (*b. 1979*) *Lab., Wigan,* Maj. 14,236

Neill, Robert (*b. 1952*) *C., Bromley & Chislehurst,* Maj. 13,564

*****Newlands**, Gavin (*b. 1980*) *SNP, Paisley & Renfrewshire North,* Maj. 9,076

Newton, Sarah (*b. 1962*) *C., Truro & Falmouth,* Maj. 14,000

*****Nicolson**, John (*b. 1961*) *SNP, Dunbartonshire East,* Maj. 2,167

Nokes, Caroline (*b. 1972*) *C., Romsey & Southampton North,* Maj. 17,712

Norman, Jesse (*b. 1962*) *C., Hereford & Herefordshire South,* Maj. 16,890

Nuttall, David (*b. 1962*) *C., Bury North,* Maj. 378

Offord, Dr Matthew (*b. 1969*) *C., Hendon,* Maj. 3,724

*****O'Hara**, Brendan (*b. 1964*) *SNP, Argyll & Bute,* Maj. 8,473

*****Onn**, Melanie (*b. 1979*) *Lab., Great Grimsby,* Maj. 4,540

Onwurah, Chi (*b. 1965*) *Lab., Newcastle upon Tyne Central,* Maj. 12,673

Opperman, Guy (*b. 1965*) *C., Hexham,* Maj. 12,031

*****Osamor**, Kate (*b. 1968*) *Lab. Co-op, Edmonton,* Maj. 15,419

Osborne, Rt. Hon. George (*b. 1971*) *C., Tatton,* Maj. 18,241

*****Oswald**, Kirsten (*b. 1972*) *SNP, Renfrewshire East,* Maj. 3,718

Owen, Albert (*b. 1960*) *Lab., Ynys Mon,* Maj. 229

Paisley, Ian (*b. 1966*) *DUP, Antrim North,* Maj. 11,546

Parish, Neil (*b. 1956*) *C., Tiverton & Honiton,* Maj. 20,173

Patel, Rt. Hon. Priti (*b. 1972*) *C., Witham,* Maj. 19,554

Paterson, Rt. Hon. Owen (*b. 1956*) *C., Shropshire North,* Maj. 16,494

*****Paterson**, Steven (*b. 1975*) *SNP, Stirling,* Maj. 10,480

Pawsey, Mark (*b. 1957*) *C., Rugby,* Maj. 10,345

Pearce, Teresa (*b. 1955*) *Lab., Erith & Thamesmead,* Maj. 9,525

Penning, Rt. Hon. Mike (*b. 1957*) *C., Hemel Hempstead,* Maj. 14,420

*****Pennycook**, Matthew (*b. 1982*) *Lab., Greenwich & Woolwich,* Maj. 11,946

Penrose, John (*b. 1964*) *C., Weston-super-Mare,* Maj. 15,609

Percy, Andrew (*b. 1977*) *C., Brigg & Goole,* Maj. 11,176

Perkins, Toby (*b. 1970*) *Lab., Chesterfield,* Maj. 13,598

Perry, Claire (*b. 1964*) *C., Devizes,* Maj. 20,751

*****Phillips**, Jess (*b. 1981*) *Lab., Birmingham Yardley,* Maj. 6,595

Phillips, Stephen (*b. 1970*) *C., Sleaford & North Hykeham,* Maj. 24,115

Phillipson, Bridget (*b. 1983*) *Lab., Houghton & Sunderland South,* Maj. 12,938

*****Philp**, Chris (*b. 1976*) *C., Croydon South,* Maj. 17,140

Pickles, Rt. Hon. Sir Eric (*b. 1952*) *C., Brentwood & Ongar,* Maj. 21,810

Pincher, Christopher (*b. 1969*) *C., Tamworth,* Maj. 11,302

Poulter, Dr Daniel (*b. 1978*) *C., Suffolk Central & Ipswich North,* Maj. 20,144

Pound, Stephen (*b. 1948*) *Lab., Ealing North,* Maj. 12,326

*****Pow**, Rebecca (*b. 1960*) *C., Taunton Deane,* Maj. 15,491

Powell, Lucy (*b. 1974*) *Lab. Co-op, Manchester Central,* Maj. 21,639

*****Prentis**, Victoria (*b. 1971*) *C., Banbury,* Maj. 18,395

Prisk, Mark (*b. 1962*) *C., Hertford & Stortford,* Maj. 21,509

Pritchard, Mark (*b. 1966*) *C., The Wrekin,* Maj. 10,743

Pugh, Dr John (*b. 1948*) *LD, Southport,* Maj. 1,322

*****Pursglove**, Tom (*b. 1988*) *C., Corby,* Maj. 2,412

*****Quin**, Jeremy (*b. 1968*) *C., Horsham,* Maj. 24,658

*****Quince**, Will (*b. 1982*) *C., Colchester,* Maj. 5,575

Qureshi, Yasmin (*b. 1963*) *Lab., Bolton South East,* Maj. 10,928

Raab, Dominic (*b. 1974*) *C., Esher & Walton,* Maj. 28,616

*****Rayner**, Angela (*b. 1980*) *Lab., Ashton-under-Lyne,* Maj. 10,756

Redwood, Rt. Hon. John (*b. 1951*) *C., Wokingham,* Maj. 24,197

Reed, Jamie (*b. 1973*) *Lab., Copeland,* Maj. 2,564

Reed, Steve (*b. 1963*) *Lab. Co-op, Croydon North,* Maj. 21,364

*****Rees**, Christina (*b. 1954*) *Lab., Neath,* Maj. 9,548

Rees-Mogg, Jacob (*b. 1969*) *C., Somerset North East,* Maj. 12,749

Reeves, Rachel (*b. 1979*) *Lab., Leeds West,* Maj. 10,727

Reynolds, Emma (*b. 1977*) *Lab., Wolverhampton North East,* Maj. 5,495

Reynolds, Jonathan (*b. 1980*) *Lab. Co-op, Stalybridge & Hyde,* Maj. 6,686

*****Rimmer**, Marie (*b. 1947*) *Lab., St Helens South & Whiston,* Maj. 21,243

Ritchie, Margaret (*b. 1958*) *SDLP, Down South,* Maj. 5,891

Robertson, Angus (*b. 1969*) *SNP, Moray,* Maj. 9,065

Robertson, Laurence (*b. 1958*) *C., Tewkesbury,* Maj. 21,972

*****Robinson**, Gavin (*b. 1985*) *DUP, Belfast East,* Maj. 2,597

Robinson, Geoffrey (*b. 1938*) *Lab., Coventry North West,* Maj. 4,509

*****Robinson**, Mary (*b. 1955*) *C., Cheadle,* Maj. 6,453

Rosindell, Andrew (*b. 1966*) *C., Romford,* Maj. 13,859

Rotheram, Steve (*b. 1961*) *Lab., Liverpool Walton,* Maj. 27,777

Rudd, Rt. Hon. Amber (*b. 1963*) *C., Hastings & Rye,* Maj. 4,796

Rutley, David (*b. 1961*) *C., Macclesfield,* Maj. 14,811

*****Ryan**, Rt. Hon. Joan (*b. 1955*) *Lab., Enfield North,* Maj. 1,086

*****Salmond**, Alex (*b. 1954*) *SNP, Gordon,* Maj. 8,687

*****Sandbach**, Antoinette (*b. 1969*) *C., Eddisbury,* Maj. 12,974

*****Saville-Roberts**, Liz (*b. 1964*) *PC, Dwyfor Meirionnydd,* Maj. 5,261

*****Scully**, Paul (*b. 1968*) *C., Sutton & Cheam,* Maj. 3,921

Selous, Andrew (*b. 1962*) *C., Bedfordshire South West,* Maj. 17,813

*****Shah**, Naseem (*b. 1973*) *Lab., Bradford West,* Maj. 11,420

Shannon, Jim (*b. 1955*) *DUP, Strangford,* Maj. 10,185

Shapps, Rt. Hon. Grant (*b. 1968*) *C., Welwyn Hatfield,* Maj. 12,153

Sharma, Alok (*b. 1967*) *C., Reading West,* Maj. 6,650

Sharma, Virendra (*b. 1947*) *Lab., Ealing Southall,* Maj. 18,760

Sheerman, Barry (*b. 1940*) *Lab. Co-op, Huddersfield,* Maj. 7,345

Shelbrooke, Alec (*b. 1976*) *C., Elmet & Rothwell,* Maj. 8,490

*****Sheppard**, Tommy (*b. 1959*) *SNP, Edinburgh East,* Maj. 9,106

*****Sherriff**, Paula (*b. 1975*) *Lab., Dewsbury,* Maj. 1,451

Shuker, Gavin (*b. 1981*) *Lab. Co-op, Luton South,* Maj. 5,711

*****Siddiq**, Tulip (*b. 1982*) *Lab., Hampstead & Kilburn,* Maj. 1,138

Simpson, David (*b. 1959*) *DUP, Upper Bann,* Maj. 2,264

Simpson, Rt. Hon. Keith (*b. 1949*) *C., Broadland,* Maj. 16,838

Skidmore, Chris (*b. 1981*) *C., Kingswood,* Maj. 9,006

Skinner, Dennis (*b. 1932*) *Lab., Bolsover,* Maj. 11,778

Slaughter, Andy (*b. 1960*) *Lab., Hammersmith,* Maj. 6,518

*****Smeeth**, Ruth (*b. 1979*) *Lab., Stoke-on-Trent North,* Maj. 4,836

Smith, Rt. Hon. Andrew (*b. 1951*) *Lab., Oxford East,* Maj. 15,280

Smith, Angela (*b. 1961*) *Lab., Penistone & Stocksbridge,* Maj. 6,723

*Smith, Catherine (b. 1985) Lab., Lancaster & Fleetwood, Maj. 1,265

Smith, Chloe (b. 1982) C., Norwich North, Maj. 4,463

Smith, Henry (b. 1969) C., Crawley, Maj. 6,526

*Smith, Jeff (b. 1963) Lab., Manchester Withington, Maj. 14,873

Smith, Julian (b. 1971) C., Skipton & Ripon, Maj. 20,761

Smith, Nick (b. 1960) Lab., Blaenau Gwent, Maj. 12,703

Smith, Owen (b. 1970) Lab., Pontypridd, Maj. 8,985

*Smith, Royston (b. 1964) C., Southampton Itchen, Maj. 2,316

*Smyth, Karin (b. 1964) Lab., Bristol South, Maj. 7,128

Soames, Rt. Hon. Sir Nicholas (b. 1948) C., Sussex Mid, Maj. 24,286

*Solloway, Amanda (b. 1961) C., Derby North, Maj. 41

Soubry, Rt. Hon. Anna (b. 1956) C., Broxtowe, Maj. 4,287

Spellar, Rt. Hon. John (b. 1947) Lab., Warley, Maj. 14,702

Spelman, Rt. Hon. Caroline (b. 1958) C., Meriden, Maj. 18,795

Spencer, Mark (b. 1970) C., Sherwood, Maj. 4,647

*Starmer, Sir Keir (b. 1962) Lab., Holborn & St Pancras, Maj. 17,048

*Stephens, Christopher (b. 1973) SNP, Glasgow South West, Maj. 9,950

Stephenson, Andrew (b. 1981) C., Pendle, Maj. 5,453

*Stevens, Jo (b. 1966) Lab., Cardiff Central, Maj. 4,981

Stevenson, John (b. 1963) C., Carlisle, Maj. 2,774

Stewart, Bob (b. 1949) C., Beckenham, Maj. 18,471

Stewart, Iain (b. 1972) C., Milton Keynes South, Maj. 8,672

Stewart, Rory (b. 1973) C., Penrith & The Border, Maj. 19,894

Streeter, Gary (b. 1955) C., Devon South West, Maj. 20,109

*Streeting, Wes (b. 1983) Lab., Ilford North, Maj. 589

Stride, Mel (b. 1961) C., Devon Central, Maj. 21,265

Stringer, Graham (b. 1950) Lab., Blackley & Broughton, Maj. 16,874

Stuart, Gisela (b. 1955) Lab., Birmingham Edgbaston, Maj. 2,706

Stuart, Graham (b. 1962) C., Beverley & Holderness, Maj. 12,203

Sturdy, Julian (b. 1971) C., York Outer, Maj. 13,129

*Sunak, Rishi (b. 1980) C., Richmond (Yorks), Maj. 19,550

Swayne, Rt. Hon. Desmond (b. 1956) C., New Forest West, Maj. 20,604

Swire, Rt. Hon. Hugo (b. 1959) C., Devon East, Maj. 12,261

Syms, Robert (b. 1956) C., Poole, Maj. 15,789

Tami, Mark (b. 1963) Lab., Alyn & Deeside, Maj. 3,343

*Thewliss, Alison (b. 1982) SNP, Glasgow Central, Maj. 7,662

*Thomas, Derek (b. 1972) C., St Ives, Maj. 2,469

Thomas, Gareth (b. 1967) Lab. Co-op, Harrow West, Maj. 2,208

*Thomas-Symonds, Nick (b. 1980) Lab., Torfaen, Maj. 8,169

*Thompson, Owen (b. 1978) SNP, Midlothian, Maj. 9,859

*Thomson, Michelle (b. 1965) SNP, Edinburgh West, Maj. 3,210

Thornberry, Emily (b. 1960) Lab., Islington South & Finsbury, Maj. 12,708

*Throup, Maggie (b. 1957) C., Erewash, Maj. 3,584

Timms, Rt. Hon. Stephen (b. 1955) Lab., East Ham, Maj. 34,252

Timpson, Edward (b. 1973) C., Crewe & Nantwich, Maj. 3,620

*Tolhurst, Kelly (b. 1978) C., Rochester & Strood, Maj. 7,133

Tomlinson, Justin (b. 1976) C., Swindon North, Maj. 11,786

*Tomlinson, Michael (b. 1977) C., Dorset Mid & Poole North, Maj. 10,530

*Tracey, Craig (b. 1974) C., Warwickshire North, Maj. 2,973

Tredinnick, David (b. 1950) C., Bosworth, Maj. 10,988

*Trevelyan, Anne-Marie (b. 1969) C., Berwick-upon-Tweed, Maj. 4,914

Trickett, Jon (b. 1950) Lab., Hemsworth, Maj. 12,078

Truss, Rt. Hon. Elizabeth (b. 1975) C., Norfolk South West, Maj. 13,861

*Tugendhat, Tom (b. 1973) C., Tonbridge & Malling, Maj. 23,734

*Turley, Anna (b. 1978) Lab. Co-op, Redcar, Maj. 10,388

Turner, Andrew (b. 1953) C., Isle of Wight, Maj. 13,703

Turner, Karl (b. 1971) Lab., Hull East, Maj. 10,319

Twigg, Derek (b. 1959) Lab., Halton, Maj. 20,285

Twigg, Stephen (b. 1966) Lab. Co-op, Liverpool West Derby, Maj. 27,367

Tyrie, Rt. Hon. Andrew (b. 1957) C., Chichester, Maj. 24,413

Umunna, Chuka (b. 1978) Lab., Streatham, Maj. 13,934

Vaizey, Edward (b. 1969) C., Wantage, Maj. 21,749

Vara, Shailesh (b. 1960) C., Cambridgeshire North West, Maj. 19,795

Vaz, Rt. Hon. Keith (b. 1956) Lab., Leicester East, Maj. 18,352

Vaz, Valerie (b. 1954) Lab., Walsall South, Maj. 6,007

Vickers, Martin (b. 1950) C., Cleethorpes, Maj. 7,893

Villiers, Rt. Hon. Theresa (b. 1968) C., Chipping Barnet, Maj. 7,656

Walker, Charles (b. 1967) C., Broxbourne, Maj. 16,723

Walker, Robin (b. 1978) C., Worcester, Maj. 5,646

Wallace, Ben (b. 1970) C., Wyre & Preston North, Maj. 14,151

*Warburton, David (b. 1965) C., Somerton & Frome, Maj. 20,268

*Warman, Matt (b. 1981) C., Boston & Skegness, Maj. 4,336

Watkinson, Dame Angela (b. 1941) C., Hornchurch & Upminster, Maj. 13,074

Watson, Tom (b. 1967) Lab., West Bromwich East, Maj. 9,470

Weir, Mike (b. 1957) SNP, Angus, Maj. 11,230

*West, Catherine (b. 1966) Lab., Hornsey & Wood Green, Maj. 11,058

Wharton, James (b. 1984) C., Stockton South, Maj. 5,046

*Whately, Helen (b. 1976) C., Faversham & Kent Mid, Maj. 16,652

Wheeler, Heather (b. 1959) C., Derbyshire South, Maj. 11,471

White, Chris (b. 1967) C., Warwick & Leamington, Maj. 6,606

Whiteford, Dr Eilidh (b. 1969) SNP, Banff & Buchan, Maj. 14,339

Whitehead, Dr Alan (b. 1950) Lab., Southampton Test, Maj. 3,810

*Whitford, Dr Philippa (b. 1959) SNP, Ayrshire Central, Maj. 13,589

Whittaker, Craig (b. 1962) C., Calder Valley, Maj. 4,427

Whittingdale, Rt. Hon. John (b. 1959) C., Maldon, Maj. 22,070

Wiggin, Bill (b. 1966) C., Herefordshire North, Maj. 19,996

*Williams, Craig (b. 1985) C., Cardiff North, Maj. 2,137

Williams, Hywel (b. 1953) PC, Arfon, Maj. 3,668

Williams, Mark (b. 1966) LD, Ceredigion, Maj. 3,067

Williamson, Rt. Hon. Gavin (b. 1976) C., Staffordshire South, Maj. 20,371

*Wilson, Corri (b. 1963) SNP, Ayr, Carrick & Cumnock, Maj. 11,265

Wilson, Phil (b. 1959) Lab., Sedgefield, Maj. 6,843

Wilson, Rob (b. 1965) C., Reading East, Maj. 6,520

Wilson, Sammy (b. 1953) DUP, Antrim East, Maj. 5,795

Winnick, David (b. 1933) Lab., Walsall North, Maj. 1,937

Winterton, Rt. Hon. Rosie (*b.* 1958) *Lab., Doncaster Central,*
Maj. 10,093
Wishart, Pete (*b.* 1962) *SNP, Perth & Perthshire North,*
Maj. 9,641
Wollaston, Dr Sarah (*b.* 1962) *C., Totnes,* Maj. 18,285
*Wood, Mike (*b.* 1976) *C., Dudley South,* Maj. 4,270
Woodcock, John (*b.* 1978) *Lab. Co-op, Barrow & Furness,*
Maj. 795

*Wragg, William (*b.* 1987) *C., Hazel Grove,*
Maj. 6,552
Wright, Iain (*b.* 1972) *Lab., Hartlepool,* Maj. 3,024
Wright, Rt. Hon. Jeremy (*b.* 1972) *C., Kenilworth &
Southam,* Maj. 21,002
Zahawi, Nadhim (*b.* 1967) *C., Stratford-on-Avon,*
Maj. 22,876
*Zeichner, Daniel (*b.* 1956) *Lab., Cambridge,* Maj. 599

GENERAL ELECTION RESULTS

The results of voting in each of the 650 parliamentary constituencies at the general election of 7 May 2015 are given below.

KEY
* New MP
E. Electorate   T. Turnout

swing N/A Indicates a constituency for which the swing data cannot be calculated because one of the top two parties in the General Election 2015 did not field a candidate in the seat in 2010.

Abbreviations

30-50	The 30-50 Coalition
Above	Above and Beyond
Active Dem.	Movement for Active Democracy
AD	Apolitical Democrats
Alliance	Alliance Party of Northern Ireland
AP	All People's Party
APNI	APNI Party
Atom	Children of the Atom
AWP	Animal Welfare Party
Beer	Reduce Tax on Beer Party
Beer BS	Beer, Baccy and Scratchings Party
Birthday	The Birthday Party
BNP	British National Party
Bournemouth	Bournemouth Independent Alliance
Brit. Dem.	British Democratic Party
Brit. Ind.	British Independents
Bristol	Independents for Bristol
C.	Conservative
Campaign	Campaign Party
Change	Alter Change
Ch. M.	Christian Movement for Great Britain
Ch. P.	The Christian Party
CISTA	Cannabis is Safer than Alcohol
Class War	Class War
Comm.	Communist Party of Britain
Comm. Lge	Communist League
Community	Communities United Party
Consensus	Consensus
CPA	Christian People's Alliance
Croydon	Putting Croydon First
CSP	Common Sense Party
Dem. Ref.	Democratic Reform Party
Digital	Digital Democracy
DP	The Democratic Party
DUP	Democratic Unionist Party
Eccentric	The Eccentric Party of Great Britain
Elmo	Give Me Back Elmo
Eng. Dem.	English Democrats
EP	Europeans Party
FPT	Free Public Transport Party
FUKP	Free United Kingdom Party
Green	Green Party
Green Soc.	Alliance for Green Socialism
Guildford	Guildford Greenbelt Group
Hoi	Hoi Polloi Party
Hospital	Save Hartlepool Hospital
Humanity	Humanity

IASI	Independents Against Social Injustice
IE	Independence from Europe
Ind.	Independent
Ind. CHC	Independent Community and Health Concern
IPAP	The Independent Political Alliance Party
ISWSL	Independent Save Withybush Save Lives
IZB	Islam Zinda Baad Platform
JACP	Justice & Anti-Corruption Party
JMB	Justice for Men & Boys
Lab.	Labour
Lab. Co-op	Labour and Co-operative
LD	Liberal Democrat
Lib.	The Liberal Party
Lib. GB	Liberty Great Britain
Lincs Ind.	Lincolnshire Independents
Loony	Monster Raving Loony Party
LP	Land Party
LU	Left Unity
Magna Carta	Magna Carta Conservation Party Great Britain
Mainstream	Mainstream Party
Manston	Manston Airport Independent Party
MC	The Magna Carta Party
Meb. Ker.	Mebyon Kernow
Nat. Lib.	National Liberal Party
ND	No description
NE	The North East Party
New IC	New Independent Centralists
NF	National Front
NHAP	National Health Action Party
Northern	Northern Party
Patria	Patria
PBP	People Before Profit Alliance
PC	Plaid Cymru
Peace	Peace Party
PF	People First
Pilgrim	The Pilgrim Party
Pirate	Pirate Party UK
Plural	The Pluralist Party
Poole	The Party for Poole People Ltd
PPP	The Principles of Politics Party
PP UK	Population Party UK
PSP	Patriotic Socialist Party
Real	Keep It Real Party
Realist	The Realists' Party

Reality	We are the Reality Party
Reboot	Rebooting Democracy
Rep. Soc.	The Republican Socialist Party
Respect	The Respect Party
Restore	Restore the Family for Children's Sake
RFAC	Red Flag Anti-Corruption
Rochdale	Rochdale First Party
Roman	The Roman Party
S. New	Something New
Scot. Green	Scottish Green Party
SCP	Scottish Christian Party
SDLP	Social Democratic and Labour Party
SEP	Socialist Equality Party
SF	Sinn Fein
SNP	Scottish National Party
Soc.	Socialist Party
Soc. Dem.	Social Democratic Party
Soc. Lab.	Socialist Labour Party
Song	World Peace Through Song
Southport	The Southport Party
Speaker	The Speaker
SPGB	The Socialist Party of Great Britain
SSP	Scottish Socialist Party
TEP	The Evolution Party
Thanet	Party for a United Thanet
TSPP	The Sustainable Population Party
TUSC	Trade Unionist and Socialist Coalition
TUV	Traditional Unionist Voice
U Party	Universal Party
Ubuntu	Ubuntu
UKIP	UK Independence Party
UKPDP	UK Progressive Democracy Party
UUP	Ulster Unionist Party
Uttlesford	Residents for Uttlesford
Vapers	Vapers in Power
VAT	Reduce VAT in Sport
Wessex Reg.	Wessex Regionalists
Whig	Whig Party
Wigan	Wigan Independents
Worth	The New Society of Worth
WP	Workers' Party
WRP	Workers' Revolutionary Party
WVPTFP	War Veteran's Pro-Traditional Family Party
Yorks	Yorkshire First
Young	Young People's Party
Zeb	Al-Zebabist Nation of Ooog

PARLIAMENTARY CONSTITUENCIES AS AT 7 MAY 2015 GENERAL ELECTION

UK Turnout
E. 46,424,006 T. 30,697,845 (66.1%)

ENGLAND

ALDERSHOT
E. 72,434   T. 46,191 (63.77%)   C. hold
Gerald Howarth, C.   23,369
Gary Puffett, Lab.   8,468
Bill Walker, UKIP   8,253
Alan Hilliar, LD   4,076
Carl Hewitt, Green   2,025
C. majority 14,901 (32.26%)
1.18% swing C. to Lab.
(2010: C. majority 5,586 (12.31%))

ALDRIDGE-BROWNHILLS
E. 60,215   T. 39,497 (65.59%)   C. hold
*Wendy Morton, C.   20,558
John Fisher, Lab.   8,835
Anthony Thompson, UKIP   7,751
Ian Garrett, LD   1,330
Martyn Curzey, Green   826
Mark Beech, Loony   197
C. majority 11,723 (29.68%)
4.92% swing C. to Lab.
(2010: C. majority 15,266 (39.51%))

ALTRINCHAM & SALE WEST
E. 72,004   T. 50,517 (70.16%)   C. hold
Graham Brady, C.   26,771
James Wright, Lab.   13,481
Jane Brophy, LD   4,235
Chris Frost, UKIP   4,047
Nick Robertson-Brown, Green   1,983
C. majority 13,290 (26.31%)
0.11% swing C. to Lab.
(2010: C. majority 11,595 (23.47%))

AMBER VALLEY
E. 70,226   T. 45,717 (65.10%)   C. hold
Nigel Mills, C.   20,106
Kevin Gillott, Lab.   15,901
Stuart Bent, UKIP   7,263
Kate Smith, LD   1,360
John Devine, Green   1,087
C. majority 4,205 (9.20%)
4.02% swing Lab. to C.
(2010: C. majority 536 (1.17%))

ARUNDEL & SOUTH DOWNS
E. 77,272   T. 56,477 (73.09%)   C. hold
Nick Herbert, C.   34,331
Peter Grace, UKIP   8,154
Christopher Wellbelove, Lab.   6,324
Shweta Kapadia, LD   4,062
Isabel Thurston, Green   3,606
C. majority 26,177 (46.35%)
2.87% swing C. to UKIP
(2010: C. majority 16,691 (29.81%))

ASHFIELD
E. 77,126   T. 47,409 (61.47%)   Lab. hold
Gloria De Piero, Lab.   19,448
Helen Harrison, C.   10,628
Simon Ashcroft, UKIP   10,150
Philip Smith, LD   7,030
Mike Buchanan, JMB   153
Lab. majority 8,820 (18.60%)
3.55% swing C. to Lab.
(2010: Lab. majority 192 (0.40%))

ASHFORD
E. 85,189   T. 57,372 (67.35%)   C. hold
Damian Green, C.   30,094
Gerald O'Brien, UKIP   10,798
Brendan Chilton, Lab.   10,580
Debbie Enever, LD   3,433
Mandy Rossi, Green   2,467
C. majority 19,296 (33.63%)
7.98% swing C. to UKIP
(2010: C. majority 17,297 (31.34%))

ASHTON-UNDER-LYNE
E. 67,714   T. 38,918 (57.47%)   Lab. hold
*Angela Rayner, Lab.   19,366
Tracy Sutton, C.   8,610
Maurice Jackson, UKIP   8,468
Charlotte Hughes, Green   1,531
Carly Hicks, LD   943
Lab. majority 10,756 (27.64%)
1.99% swing C. to Lab.
(2010: Lab. majority 9,094 (23.66%))

AYLESBURY
E. 80,611   T. 55,419 (68.75%)   C. hold
David Lidington, C.   28,083
Chris Adams, UKIP   10,925
Will Cass, Lab.   8,391
Steven Lambert, LD   5,885
David Lyons, Green   2,135
C. majority 17,158 (30.96%)
7.21% swing C. to UKIP
(2010: C. majority 12,618 (23.73%))

BANBURY
E. 86,420   T. 58,008 (67.12%)   C. hold
*Victoria Prentis, C.   30,749
Sean Woodcock, Lab.   12,354
Dickie Bird, UKIP   8,050
John Howson, LD   3,440
Ian Middleton, Green   2,686
Roseanne Edwards, NHAP   729
C. majority 18,395 (31.71%)
0.97% swing C. to Lab.
(2010: C. majority 18,227 (32.41%))

BARKING
E. 74,004   T. 43,023 (58.14%)   Lab. hold
Margaret Hodge, Lab.   24,826
Roger Gravett, UKIP   9,554
Mina Rahman, C.   7,019
Tony Rablen, Green   879
Peter Wilcock, LD   562
Joseph Mambuliya, TUSC   183
Lab. majority 15,272 (35.50%)
7.98% swing Lab. to UKIP
(2010: Lab. majority 16,555 (36.51%))

BARNSLEY CENTRAL
E. 64,534   T. 36,560 (56.65%)   Lab. hold
Dan Jarvis, Lab.   20,376
Lee Hunter, UKIP   7,941
Kay Carter, C.   5,485
Michael Short, Green   938
David Ridgway, LD   770
Dave Gibson, TUSC   573
Ian Sutton, Eng. Dem.   477
Lab. majority 12,435 (34.01%)
4.29% swing Lab. to UKIP
(2010: Lab. majority 11,093 (29.98%))
(2011: Lab. majority 11,771 (48.60%))

BARNSLEY EAST
E. 69,135   T. 38,517 (55.71%)   Lab. hold
Michael Dugher, Lab.   21,079
Robert Swiffen, UKIP   9,045
Katharine Harborne, C.   5,622
Ruth Coleman-Taylor, LD   1,217
Tony Devoy, Yorks   647
Kevin Riddiough, Eng. Dem.   440
Ralph Dyson, TUSC   364
Billy Marsden, Vapers   103
Lab. majority 12,034 (31.24%)
5.65% swing Lab. to UKIP
(2010: Lab. majority 11,090 (28.89%))

BARROW & FURNESS
E. 68,338   T. 43,275 (63.32%)
                              Lab. Co-op hold
John Woodcock, Lab. Co-op   18,320
Simon Fell, C.   17,525
Nigel Cecil, UKIP   5,070
Clive Peaple, LD   1,169
Robert O'Hara, Green   1,061
Ian Jackson, Ind.   130
Lab. Co-op majority 795 (1.84%)
4.98% swing Lab. Co-op to C.
(2010: Lab. Co-op majority 5,208
(11.80%))

BASILDON & BILLERICAY
E. 68,459   T. 43,028 (62.85%)   C. hold
John Baron, C.   22,668
Gavin Callaghan, Lab.   10,186
George Konstantinidis, UKIP   8,538
Martin Thompson, LD   1,636
C. majority 12,482 (29.01%)
0.34% swing C. to Lab.
(2010: C. majority 12,338 (29.68%))

BASILDON SOUTH & THURROCK EAST
E. 73,210   T. 45,593 (62.28%)   C. hold
Stephen Metcalfe, C.   19,788
Ian Luder, UKIP   12,097
Mike Le-Surf, Lab.   11,493
Geoff Williams, LD   1,356
Kerry Smith, Ind.   401
None Of The Above X, ND   253
Stuart Hooper, Ind.   205
C. majority 7,691 (16.87%)
10.55% swing C. to UKIP
(2010: C. majority 5,772 (12.90%))

BASINGSTOKE
E. 79,662   T. 53,076 (66.63%)   C. hold
Maria Miller, C.   25,769
Paul Harvey, Lab.   14,706
Alan Stone, UKIP   8,290
Janice Spalding, LD   3,919
Omar Selim, Ind.   392
C. majority 11,063 (20.84%)
4.64% swing C. to Lab.
(2010: C. majority 13,176 (26.01%))

BASSETLAW
E. 77,480   T. 49,289 (63.62%)   Lab. hold
John Mann, Lab.   23,965
Sarah Downes, C.   15,122
David Scott, UKIP   7,865
Leon Duveen, LD   1,331
Kris Wragg, Green   1,006
Lab. majority 8,843 (17.94%)
0.69% swing C. to Lab.
(2010: Lab. majority 8,215 (16.57%))

BATH
E. 60,869   T. 47,167 (77.49%)   C. gain
*Ben Howlett, C.   17,833
Steve Bradley, LD   14,000
Ollie Middleton, Lab.   6,216
Dominic Tristram, Green   5,634
Julian Deverell, UKIP   2,922
Loraine Morgan-Brinkhurst, Ind.   499
Jenny Knight, Eng. Dem.   63
C. majority 3,833 (8.13%)
16.68% swing LD to C.
(2010: LD majority 11,883 (25.24%))

BATLEY & SPEN
E. 78,373   T. 50,479 (64.41%)   Lab. hold
*Jo Cox, Lab.   21,826
Imtiaz Ameen, C.   15,769
Aleks Lukic, UKIP   9,080
John Lawson, LD   2,396
Ian Bullock, Green   1,232
Dawn Wheelhouse, TUSC   123
Karl Varley, PSP   53
Lab. majority 6,057 (12.00%)
1.69% swing C. to Lab.
(2010: Lab. majority 4,406 (8.62%))

BATTERSEA
E. 76,106   T. 51,031 (67.05%)   C. hold
Jane Ellison, C.   26,730
Will Martindale, Lab.   18,792
Luke Taylor, LD   2,241
Joe Stuart, Green   1,682
Christopher Howe, UKIP   1,586
C. majority 7,938 (15.56%)
1.65% swing Lab. to C.
(2010: C. majority 5,977 (12.25%))

BEACONSFIELD
E. 76,380   T. 53,163 (69.60%)   C. hold
Dominic Grieve, C.   33,621
Tim Scott, UKIP   7,310
Tony Clements, Lab.   6,074
Peter Chapman, LD   3,927
Dave Hampton, Green   2,231
C. majority 26,311 (49.49%)
3.31% swing C. to UKIP
(2010: C. majority 21,782 (41.50%))

BECKENHAM
E. 67,436   T. 48,803 (72.37%)   C. hold
Bob Stewart, C.   27,955
Marina Ahmad, Lab.   9,484
Rob Bryant, UKIP   6,108
Anuja Prashar, LD   3,378
Ruth Fabricant, Green   1,878
C. majority 18,471 (37.85%)
2.78% swing C. to Lab.
(2010: C. majority 17,784 (37.29%))

BEDFORD
E. 69,311   T. 46,086 (66.49%)   C. hold
Richard Fuller, C.   19,625
Patrick Hall, Lab.   18,528
Charlie Smith, UKIP   4,434
Mahmud Henry Rogers, LD   1,958
Ben Foley, Green   1,412
Faruk Choudhury, Ind.   129
C. majority 1,097 (2.38%)
0.31% swing C. to Lab.
(2010: C. majority 1,353 (3.00%))

BEDFORDSHIRE MID
E. 81,144   T. 58,060 (71.55%)   C. hold
Nadine Dorries, C.   32,544
Charlynne Pullen, Lab.   9,217
Nigel Wickens, UKIP   8,966
Linda Jack, LD   4,193
Gareth Ellis, Green   2,462
Tim Ireland, Ind.   384
Ann Kelly, Loony   294
C. majority 23,327 (40.18%)
1.23% swing Lab. to C.
(2010: C. majority 15,152 (27.60%))

BEDFORDSHIRE NORTH EAST
E. 83,551   T. 58,672 (70.22%)   C. hold
Alistair Burt, C.   34,891
Saqhib Ali, Lab.   9,247
Adrianne Smyth, UKIP   8,579
Peter Morris, LD   3,418
Mark Bowler, Green   2,537
C. majority 25,644 (43.71%)
2.02% swing Lab. to C.
(2010: C. majority 18,942 (34.10%))

BEDFORDSHIRE SOUTH WEST
E. 79,664   T. 51,304 (64.40%)   C. hold
Andrew Selous, C.   28,212
Daniel Scott, Lab.   10,399
John Van Weenen, UKIP   7,941
Stephen Rutherford, LD   2,646
Emily Lawrence, Green   2,106
C. majority 17,813 (34.72%)
0.75% swing Lab. to C.
(2010: C. majority 16,649 (32.79%))

BERMONDSEY & OLD SOUTHWARK
E. 80,604   T. 51,424 (63.80%)   Lab. gain
*Neil Coyle, Lab.   22,146
Simon Hughes, LD   17,657
JP Floru, C.   6,051
Andrew Beadle, UKIP   3,254
William Lavin, Green   2,023
Kingsley Abrams, TUSC   142
Lucy Hall, Ind.   72
Donald Cole, AP   59
Steve Freeman, Rep. Soc.   20
Lab. majority 4,489 (8.73%)
13.92% swing LD to Lab.
(2010: LD majority 8,530 (19.10%))

BERWICK-UPON-TWEED
E. 58,098   T. 40,423 (69.58%)   C. gain
*Anne-Marie Trevelyan, C.   16,603
Julie Porksen, LD   11,689
Scott Dickinson, Lab.   6,042
Nigel Coghill-Marshall, UKIP   4,513
Rachael Roberts, Green   1,488
Neil Humphrey, Eng. Dem.   88
C. majority 4,914 (12.16%)
9.58% swing LD to C.
(2010: LD majority 2,690 (7.00%))

BETHNAL GREEN & BOW
E. 82,825   T. 52,924 (63.90%)   Lab. hold
Rushanara Ali, Lab.   32,387
Matt Smith, C.   8,070
Alistair Polson, Green   4,906
Paula McQueen, UKIP   3,219
Teena Lashmore, LD   2,395
Glyn Robbins, TUSC   949
M. Rowshan Ali, Community   356
Jonathan Dewey, CISTA   303
Alasdair Henderson, Whig   203
Elliot Ball, 30-50   78
Jason Pavlou, RFAC   58
Lab. majority 24,317 (45.95%)
8.47% swing C. to Lab.
(2010: Lab. majority 11,574 (22.82%))

BEVERLEY & HOLDERNESS
E. 80,822   T. 52,677 (65.18%)   C. hold
Graham Stuart, C.   25,363
Margaret Pinder, Lab.   13,160
Gary Shores, UKIP   8,794
Denis Healy, LD   2,900
Richard Howarth, Green   1,802
Lee Walton, Yorks   653
C. majority 12,203 (23.17%)
1.42% swing C. to Lab.
(2010: C. majority 12,987 (24.41%))

BEXHILL & BATTLE
E. 78,796   T. 55,218 (70.08%)   C. hold
*Huw Merriman, C.   30,245
Geoffrey Bastin, UKIP   10,170
Michelle Thew, Lab.   7,797
Rachel Sadler, LD   4,199
Jonathan Kent, Green   2,807
C. majority 20,075 (36.36%)
swing N/A
(2010: C. majority 12,880 (23.60%))

BEXLEYHEATH & CRAYFORD
E. 64,828   T. 43,685 (67.39%)   C. hold
David Evennett, C.   20,643
Stef Borella, Lab.   11,451
Chris Attard, UKIP   9,182
Richard Davis, LD   1,308
Stella Gardiner, Green   950
Maggi Young, Eng. Dem.   151
C. majority 9,192 (21.04%)
1.46% swing C. to Lab.
(2010: C. majority 10,344 (23.95%))

BIRKENHEAD
E. 62,438   T. 37,680 (60.35%)   Lab. hold
Frank Field, Lab.   26,468
Clark Vasey, C.   5,816
Wayne Harling, UKIP   3,838
Allan Brame, LD   1,396
Kenny Peers, Green   162
Lab. majority 20,652 (54.81%)
5.61% swing C. to Lab.
(2010: Lab. majority 15,395 (43.58%))

BIRMINGHAM EDGBASTON
E. 65,591   T. 41,293 (62.96%)   Lab. hold
Gisela Stuart, Lab.   18,518
Luke Evans, C.   15,812
Graham Short, UKIP   4,154
Phil Simpson, Green   1,371
Lee Dargue, LD   1,184
Gabriel Ukandu, Ch. P.   163
Henna Rai, Ind.   91
Lab. majority 2,706 (6.55%)
1.74% swing C. to Lab.
(2010: Lab. majority 1,274 (3.06%))

BIRMINGHAM ERDINGTON
E. 65,128   T. 34,684 (53.26%)   Lab. hold
Jack Dromey, Lab.   15,824
Robert Alden, C.   10,695
Andrew Garcarz, UKIP   6,040
Ann Holtom, LD   965
Joe Belcher, Green   948
Ted Woodley, TUSC   212
Lab. majority 5,129 (14.79%)
2.78% swing C. to Lab.
(2010: Lab. majority 3,277 (9.22%))

BIRMINGHAM HALL GREEN
E. 76,330   T. 47,046 (61.64%)   Lab. hold
Roger Godsiff, Lab.   28,147
James Bird, C.   8,329
Jerry Evans, LD   5,459
Elly Stanton, Green   2,200
Rashpal Mondair, UKIP   2,131
Shiraz Peer, Respect   780
Lab. majority 19,818 (42.12%)
12.12% swing C. to Lab.
(2010: Lab. majority 3,799 (7.80%))

BIRMINGHAM HODGE HILL
E. 75,302   T. 41,039 (54.50%)   Lab. hold
Liam Byrne, Lab.   28,069
Kieran Mullan, C.   4,707
Albert Duffen, UKIP   4,651
Phil Bennion, LD   2,624
Chris Nash, Green   835
Andy Chaffer, Comm.   153
Lab. majority 23,362 (56.93%)
8.28% swing C. to Lab.
(2010: Lab. majority 10,302 (24.26%))

BIRMINGHAM LADYWOOD
E. 68,128   T. 35,916 (52.72%)   Lab. hold
Shabana Mahmood, Lab.   26,444
Isabel Sigmac, C.   4,576
Clair Braund, UKIP   1,805
Margaret Okole, Green   1,501
Shazad Iqbal, LD   1,374
Timothy Burton, Lib. GB   216
Lab. majority 21,868 (60.89%)
8.57% swing C. to Lab.
(2010: Lab. majority 10,105 (28.20%))

BIRMINGHAM NORTHFIELD
E. 71,428   T. 42,461 (59.45%)   Lab. hold
Richard Burden, Lab.   17,673
Rachel Maclean, C.   15,164
Keith Rowe, UKIP   7,106
Steven Haynes, LD   1,349
Anna Masters, Green   1,169
Lab. majority 2,509 (5.91%)
0.37% swing Lab. to C.
(2010: Lab. majority 2,782 (6.65%))

BIRMINGHAM PERRY BARR
E. 69,943   T. 41,260 (58.99%)   Lab. hold
Khalid Mahmood, Lab.   23,697
Charlotte Hodivala, C.   8,869
Harjinder Singh, UKIP   5,032
Arjun Singh, LD   2,001
James Lovatt, Green   1,330
Robert Punton, TUSC   331
Lab. majority 14,828 (35.94%)
3.48% swing C. to Lab.
(2010: Lab. majority 11,908 (28.32%))

BIRMINGHAM SELLY OAK
E. 75,092   T. 45,294 (60.32%)   Lab. hold
Steve McCabe, Lab.   21.584
Alex Boulter, C.   13.137
Steven Brookes, UKIP   5.755
Colin Green, LD   2.517
Clare Thomas, Green   2.301
Lab. majority 8,447 (18.65%)
5.59% swing C. to Lab.
(2010: Lab. majority 3,482 (7.48%))

BIRMINGHAM YARDLEY
E. 72,146   T. 41,151 (57.04%)   Lab. gain
*Jess Phillips, Lab.   17,129
John Hemming, LD   10,534
Paul Clayton, UKIP   6,637
Arun Photay, C.   5,760
Grant Bishop, Green   698
Teval Stephens, Respect   187
Eamonn Flynn, TUSC   135
Peter Johnson, Soc. Dem.   71
Lab. majority 6,595 (16.03%)
11.69% swing LD to Lab.
(2010: LD majority 3,002 (7.35%))

BISHOP AUCKLAND
E. 66,089   T. 39,389 (59.60%)   Lab. hold
Helen Goodman, Lab.   16,307
Christopher Adams, C.   12,799
Rhys Burriss, UKIP   7,015
Stephen White, LD   1,723
Thom Robinson, Green   1,545
Lab. majority 3,508 (8.91%)
1.89% swing Lab. to C.
(2010: Lab. majority 5,218 (12.68%))

BLACKBURN
E. 73,265   T. 43,999 (60.05%)   Lab. hold
*Kate Hollern, Lab.   24,762
Bob Eastwood, C.   12,002
Dayle Taylor, UKIP   6,280
Gordon Lishman, LD   955
Lab. majority 12,760 (29.00%)
3.67% swing C. to Lab.
(2010: Lab. majority 9,856 (21.66%))

BLACKLEY & BROUGHTON
E. 71,900   T. 37,112 (51.62%)   Lab. hold
Graham Stringer, Lab.   22,982
Martin Power, UKIP   6,108
Michelle Tanfield-Johnson, C.   5,581
David Jones, Green   1,567
Richard Gadsden, LD   874
Lab. majority 16,874 (45.47%)
3.09% swing Lab. to UKIP
(2010: Lab. majority 12,303 (35.97%))

BLACKPOOL NORTH & CLEVELEYS
E. 62,469   T. 39,393 (63.06%)   C. hold
Paul Maynard, C.   17,508
Sam Rushworth, Lab.   14,168
Simon Noble, UKIP   5,823
Sue Close, LD   948
John Warnock, Green   889
James Walsh, Northern   57
C. majority 3,340 (8.48%)
1.59% swing Lab. to C.
(2010: C. majority 2,150 (5.30%))

BLACKPOOL SOUTH
E. 57,411   T. 32,436 (56.50%)   Lab. hold
Gordon Marsden, Lab.   13,548
Peter Anthony, C.   10,963
Peter Wood, UKIP   5,613
Duncan Royle, Green   841
Bill Greene, LD   743
Andy Higgins, Ind.   655
Lawrence Chard, Ind.   73
Lab. majority 2,585 (7.97%)
1.35% swing C. to Lab.
(2010: Lab. majority 1,851 (5.26%))

BLAYDON
E. 67,706   T. 44,936 (66.37%)   Lab. hold
David Anderson, Lab.   22,090
Mark Bell, UKIP   7,863
Alison Griffiths, C.   7,838
Jonathan Wallace, LD   5,497
Paul McNally, Green   1,648
Lab. majority 14,227 (31.66%)
swing N/A
(2010: Lab. majority 9,117 (20.30%))

BLYTH VALLEY
E. 63,958   T. 38,461 (60.13%)   Lab. hold
Ronnie Campbell, Lab.   17,813
Barry Elliott, UKIP   8,584
Greg Munro, C.   8,346
Philip Latham, LD   2,265
Dawn Furness, Green   1,453
Lab. majority 9,229 (24.00%)
8.09% swing Lab. to UKIP
(2010: Lab. majority 6,668 (17.29%))

BOGNOR REGIS & LITTLEHAMPTON
E. 73,095   T. 47,116 (64.46%)   C. hold
Nick Gibb, C.   24,185
Graham Jones, UKIP   10,241
Alan Butcher, Lab.   6,508
Francis Oppler, LD   4,240
Simon McDougall, Green   1,942
C. majority 13,944 (29.60%)
7.67% swing C. to UKIP
(2010: C. majority 13,063 (27.88%))

BOLSOVER
E. 71,976   T. 43,998 (61.13%)   Lab. hold
Dennis Skinner, Lab.   22,542
Peter Bedford, C.   10,764
Ray Calladine, UKIP   9,228
David Lomax, LD   1,464
Lab. majority 11,778 (26.77%)
0.67% swing C. to Lab.
(2010: Lab. majority 11,182 (25.42%))

BOLTON NORTH EAST
E. 67,901   T. 43,161 (63.56%)   Lab. hold
David Crausby, Lab.   18,541
James Daly, C.   14,164
Harry Lamb, UKIP   8,117
Stephen Rock, LD   1,236
Laura Diggle, Green   1,103
Lab. majority 4,377 (10.14%)
0.35% swing C. to Lab.
(2010: Lab. majority 4,084 (9.44%))

BOLTON SOUTH EAST
E. 69,692   T. 40,743 (58.46%)   Lab. hold
Yasmin Qureshi, Lab.   20,555
Jeff Armstrong, UKIP   9,627
Mudasir Dean, C.   8,289
Alan Johnson, Green   1,200
Darren Reynolds, LD   1,072
Lab. majority 10,928 (26.82%)
8.33% swing Lab. to UKIP
(2010: Lab. majority 8,634 (21.80%))

BOLTON WEST
E. 72,727   T. 48,592 (66.81%)   C. gain
*Chris Green, C.   19,744
Julie Hilling, Lab.   18,943
Bob Horsefield, UKIP   7,428
Andrew Martin, LD   1,947
Andy Smith, Ind.   321
John Vickers, TUSC   209
C. majority 801 (1.65%)
0.92% swing Lab. to C.
(2010: Lab. majority 92 (0.19%))

BOOTLE
E. 70,137   T. 45,152 (64.38%)   Lab. hold
*Peter Dowd, Lab.   33,619
Paul Nuttall, UKIP   4,915
Jade Marsden, C.   3,639
Lisa Tallis, Green   1,501
David Newman, LD   978
Pete Glover, TUSC   500
Lab. majority 28,704 (63.57%)
1.61% swing UKIP to Lab.
(2010: Lab. majority 21,181 (51.31%))

BOSTON & SKEGNESS
E. 67,834   T. 43,339 (63.89%)   C. hold
*Matt Warman, C.   18,981
Robin Hunter-Clarke, UKIP   14,645
Paul Kenny, Lab.   7,142
David Watts, LD   1,015
Victoria Percival, Green   800
Chris Pain, IE   324
Peter Johnson, ND   170
Lyn Luxton, Pilgrim   143
Robert West, BNP   119
C. majority 4,336 (10.00%)
14.99% swing C. to UKIP
(2010: C. majority 12,426 (28.81%))

BOSWORTH
E. 79,742   T. 53,582 (67.19%)   C. hold
David Tredinnick, C.   22,939
Michael Mullaney, LD   11,951
Chris Kealey, Lab.   9,354
David Sprason, UKIP   9,338
C. majority 10,988 (20.51%)
5.62% swing LD to C.
(2010: C. majority 5,032 (9.27%))

BOURNEMOUTH EAST
E. 71,956   T. 44,827 (62.30%)   C. hold
Tobias Ellwood, C.   22,060
Peter Stokes, Lab.   7,448
David Hughes, UKIP   7,401
Jon Nicholas, LD   3,752
Alasdair Keddie, Green   3,263
David Ross, Bournemouth   903
C. majority 14,612 (32.60%)
1.29% swing C. to Lab.
(2010: C. majority 7,728 (17.55%))

BOURNEMOUTH WEST
E. 72,082   T. 41,773 (57.95%)   C. hold
Conor Burns, C.   20,155
Martin Houlden, UKIP   7,745
David Stokes, Lab.   7,386
Mike Plummer, LD   3,281
Elizabeth McManus, Green   3,107
Dick Franklin, Patria   99
C. majority 12,410 (29.71%)
4.12% swing C. to UKIP
(2010: C. majority 5,583 (13.40%))

BRACKNELL
E. 78,131   T. 53,086 (67.94%)   C. hold
Phillip Lee, C.   29,606
James Walsh, Lab.   8,956
Richard Thomas, UKIP   8,339
Patrick Smith, LD   3,983
Derek Florey, Green   2,202
C. majority 20,650 (38.90%)
1.64% swing Lab. to C.
(2010: C. majority 15,704 (30.12%))

BRADFORD EAST
E. 66,123   T. 41,406 (62.62%)   Lab. gain
*Imran Hussain, Lab.   19,312
David Ward, LD   12,228
Iftikhar Ahmed, C.   4,682
Owais Rajput, UKIP   4,103
Dave Stevens, Green   871
James Lewthwaite, Brit. Dem.   210
Lab. majority 7,084 (17.11%)
9.01% swing LD to Lab.
(2010: LD majority 365 (0.90%))

BRADFORD SOUTH
E. 63,670   T. 37,600 (59.05%)   Lab. hold
*Judith Cummins, Lab.   16,328
Tanya Graham, C.   9,878
Jason Smith, UKIP   9,057
Andrew Robinson, Green   1,243
Andrew Tear, LD   1,094
Lab. majority 6,450 (17.15%)
2.49% swing C. to Lab.
(2010: Lab. majority 4,622 (12.16%))

BRADFORD WEST
E. 63,371   T. 40,290 (63.58%)   Lab. gain
*Naseem Shah, Lab.   19,977
George Galloway, Respect   8,557
George Grant, C.   6,160
Harry Boota, UKIP   3,140
Alun Griffiths, LD   1,173
Celia Hickson, Green   1,085
James Kirkcaldy, Ind.   100
Therese Hirst, Eng. Dem.   98
Lab. majority 11,420 (28.34%)
swing N/A
(2010: Lab. majority 5,763 (14.20%))
(2012: Respect majority 10,140 (30.90%))

BRAINTREE
E. 73,557   T. 50,283 (68.36%)   C. hold
*James Cleverly, C.   27,071
Richard Bingley, UKIP   9,461
Malcolm Fincken, Lab.   9,296
Matthew Klesel, LD   2,488
Paul Jeater, Green   1,564
Toby Pereira, Ind.   295
Paul Hooks, BNP   108
C. majority 17,610 (35.02%)
6.29% swing C. to UKIP
(2010: C. majority 16,121 (32.76%))

BRENT CENTRAL
E. 77,038   T. 47,032 (61.05%)   Lab. gain
*Dawn Butler, Lab.   29,216
Alan Mendoza, C.   9,567
Lauren Keith, LD   3,937
Shahrar Ali, Green   1,912
Stephen Priestley, UKIP   1,850
John Boyle, TUSC   235
Kamran Malik, Community   170
Noel Coonan, Ind.   145
Lab. majority 19,649 (41.78%)
28.36% swing LD to Lab.
(2010: LD majority 1,345 (2.97%))

BRENT NORTH
E. 82,196   T. 52,235 (63.55%)   Lab. hold
Barry Gardiner, Lab.   28,351
Luke Parker, C.   17,517
Paul Lorber, LD   2,607
Alan Craig, UKIP   2,024
Scott Bartle, Green   1,539
Elcena Jeffers, Ind.   197
Lab. majority 10,834 (20.74%)
2.70% swing C. to Lab.
(2010: Lab. majority 8,028 (15.35%))

BRENTFORD & ISLEWORTH
E. 84,557   T. 57,355 (67.83%)   Lab. gain
*Ruth Cadbury, Lab.   25,096
Mary Macleod, C.   24,631
Richard Hendron, UKIP   3,203
Joe Bourke, LD   2,305
Daniel Goldsmith, Green   2,120
Lab. majority 465 (0.81%)
2.23% swing C. to Lab.
(2010: C. majority 1,958 (3.64%))

BRENTWOOD & ONGAR
E. 72,461   T. 51,897 (71.62%)   C. hold
Eric Pickles, C.   30,534
Michael McGough, UKIP   8,724
Liam Preston, Lab.   6,492
David Kendall, LD   4,577
Reza Hossain, Green   1,397
Robin Tilbrook, Eng. Dem.   173
C. majority 21,810 (42.03%)
5.43% swing C. to UKIP
(2010: C. majority 16,921 (33.45%))

BRIDGWATER & SOMERSET WEST
E. 80,491   T. 54,447 (67.64%)   C. hold
Ian Liddell-Grainger, C.   25,020
Stephen Fitzgerald, UKIP   10,437
Mick Lerry, Lab.   9,589
Theodore Butt Phillip, LD   6,765
Julie Harvey-Smith, Green   2,636
C. majority 14,583 (26.78%)
6.86% swing C. to UKIP
(2010: C. majority 9,249 (16.97%))

BRIGG & GOOLE
E. 68,486   T. 43,270 (63.18%)   C. hold
Andrew Percy, C.   22,946
Jacky Crawford, Lab.   11,770
David Jeffreys, UKIP   6,694
Natalie Hurst, Green   915
Liz Leffman, LD   764
Trevor Dixon, Ind.   153
Ray Spalding, IE   28
C. majority 11,176 (25.83%)
7.05% swing Lab. to C.
(2010: C. majority 5,147 (11.73%))

BRIGHTON KEMPTOWN
E. 67,858   T. 45,306 (66.77%)   C. hold
Simon Kirby, C.   18,428
Nancy Platts, Lab.   17,738
Ian Buchanan, UKIP   4,446
Davy Jones, Green   3,187
Paul Chandler, LD   1,365
Jacqueline Shodeke, SPGB   73
Matt Taylor, Ind.   69
C. majority 690 (1.52%)
0.79% swing C. to Lab.
(2010: C. majority 1,328 (3.11%))

BRIGHTON PAVILION
E. 76,557   T. 54,676 (71.42%)   Green hold
Caroline Lucas, Green   22,871
Purna Sen, Lab.   14,904
Clarence Mitchell, C.   12,448
Nigel Carter, UKIP   2,724
Chris Bowers, LD   1,525
Nick Yeomans, Ind.   116
Howard Pilott, SPGB   88
Green majority 7,967 (14.57%)
6.08% swing Lab. to Green
(2010: Green majority 1,252 (2.42%))

BRISTOL EAST
E. 71,965   T. 46,213 (64.22%)   Lab. hold
Kerry McCarthy, Lab.   18,148
Theo Clarke, C.   14,168
James McMurray, UKIP   7,152
Lorraine Francis, Green   3,827
Abdul Malik, LD   2,689
Matt Gordon, TUSC   229
Lab. majority 3,980 (8.61%)
0.17% swing C. to Lab.
(2010: Lab. majority 3,722 (8.27%))

BRISTOL NORTH WEST
E. 76,626   T. 51,805 (67.61%)   C. hold
Charlotte Leslie, C.   22,767
Darren Jones, Lab.   17,823
Michael Frost, UKIP   4,889
Clare Campion-Smith, LD   3,214
Justin Quinnell, Green   2,952
Anne Lemon, TUSC   160
C. majority 4,944 (9.54%)
1.24% swing C. to Lab.
(2010: C. majority 3,274 (6.50%))

BRISTOL SOUTH
E. 81,996   T. 50,842 (62.01%)   Lab. hold
*Karin Smyth, Lab.   19,505
Isobel Grant, C.   12,377
Steve Wood, UKIP   8,381
Tony Dyer, Green   5,861
Mark Wright, LD   4,416
Tom Baldwin, TUSC   302
Lab. majority 7,128 (14.02%)
0.76% swing Lab. to C.
(2010: Lab. majority 4,734 (9.79%))

BRISTOL WEST
E. 89,198   T. 64,218 (71.99%)   Lab. gain
*Thangam Debbonaire, Lab.   22,900
Darren Hall, Green   17,227
Stephen Williams, LD   12,103
Claire Hiscott, C.   9,752
Paul Turner, UKIP   1,940
Dawn Parry, Bristol   204
Stewart Weston, LU   92
Lab. majority 5,673 (8.83%)
18.67% swing LD to Lab.
(2010: LD majority 11,366 (20.54%))

BROADLAND
E. 74,680   T. 53,089 (71.09%)   C. hold
Keith Simpson, C.   26,808
Chris Jones, Lab.   9,970
Stuart Agnew, UKIP   8,881
Steve Riley, LD   5,178
Andrew Boswell, Green   2,252
C. majority 16,838 (31.72%)
0.33% swing C. to Lab.
(2010: C. majority 7,292 (13.84%))

BROMLEY & CHISLEHURST
E. 65,476   T. 44,066 (67.30%)   C. hold
Robert Neill, C.   23,343
John Courtneidge, Lab.   9,779
Emmett Jenner, UKIP   6,285
Sam Webber, LD   2,836
Roisin Robertson, Green   1,823
C. majority 13,564 (30.78%)
3.09% swing C. to Lab.
(2010: C. majority 13,900 (31.56%))

BROMSGROVE
E. 73,329   T. 52,245 (71.25%)   C. hold
Sajid Javid, C.   28,133
Tom Ebbutt, Lab.   11,604
Stuart Cross, UKIP   8,163
Bart Ricketts, LD   2,616
Spoz Esposito, Green   1,729
C. majority 16,529 (31.64%)
4.87% swing Lab. to C.
(2010: C. majority 11,308 (21.90%))

BROXBOURNE
E. 72,944   T. 46,024 (63.09%)   C. hold
Charles Walker, C.   25,797
David Platt, UKIP   9,074
Edward Robinson, Lab.   8,470
Anthony Rowlands, LD   1,467
Russell Secker, Green   1,216
C. majority 16,723 (36.34%)
9.16% swing C. to UKIP
(2010: C. majority 18,804 (41.18%))

BROXTOWE
E. 71,865   T. 53,440 (74.36%)   C. hold
Anna Soubry, C.   24,163
Nick Palmer, Lab.   19,876
Frank Dunne, UKIP   5,674
Stan Heptinstall, LD   2,120
David Kirwan, Green   1,544
Ray Barry, JMB   63
C. majority 4,287 (8.02%)
3.64% swing Lab. to C.
(2010: C. majority 389 (0.74%))

BUCKINGHAM
E. 77,572   T. 53,692 (69.22%)
                             Speaker hold
John Bercow, Speaker   34,617
David Fowler, UKIP   11,675
Alan Francis, Green   7,400
Speaker majority 22,942 (42.73%)
swing N/A
(2010: Speaker majority 12,529 (25.92%))

BURNLEY
E. 64,486   T. 39,746 (61.64%)   Lab. gain
*Julie Cooper, Lab.   14,951
Gordon Birtwistle, LD   11,707
Tom Commis, UKIP   6,864
Sarah Cockburn-Price, C.   5,374
Mike Hargreaves, Green   850
Lab. majority 3,244 (8.16%)
6.25% swing LD to Lab.
(2010: LD majority 1,818 (4.34%))

BURTON
E. 75,300   T. 49,334 (65.52%)   C. hold
Andrew Griffiths, C.   24,736
Jon Wheale, Lab.   13,484
Mike Green, UKIP   8,658
David MacDonald, LD   1,232
Sam Patrone, Green   1,224
C. majority 11,252 (22.81%)
5.08% swing Lab. to C.
(2010: C. majority 6,304 (12.65%))

BURY NORTH
E. 67,580   T. 45,230 (66.93%)   C. hold
David Nuttall, C.   18,970
James Frith, Lab.   18,592
Ian Henderson, UKIP   5,595
John Southworth, Green   1,141
Richard Baum, LD   932
C. majority 378 (0.84%)
2.08% swing C. to Lab.
(2010: C. majority 2,243 (4.99%))

BURY ST EDMUNDS
E. 85,993   T. 59,341 (69.01%)   C. hold
*Jo Churchill, C.   31,815
Bill Edwards, Lab.   10,514
John Howlett, UKIP   8,739
Helen Geake, Green   4,692
David Chappell, LD   3,581
C. majority 21,301 (35.90%)
2.52% swing Lab. to C.
(2010: C. majority 12,380 (21.08%))

BURY SOUTH
E. 73,883   T. 47,215 (63.91%)   Lab. hold
Ivan Lewis, Lab.   21,272
Daniel Critchlow, C.   16,350
Seamus Martin, UKIP   6,299
Paul Ankers, LD   1,690
Glyn Heath, Green   1,434
Valerie Morris, Eng. Dem.   170
Lab. majority 4,922 (10.42%)
1.80% swing C. to Lab.
(2010: Lab. majority 3,292 (6.82%))

CALDER VALLEY
E. 77,753   T. 53,541 (68.86%)   C. hold
Craig Whittaker, C.   23,354
Josh Fenton-Glynn, Lab.   18,927
Paul Rogan, UKIP   5,950
Alisdair Calder McGregor, LD   2,666
Jenny Shepherd, Green   2,090
Rod Sutcliffe, Yorks   389
Joe Stead, Song   165
C. majority 4,427 (8.27%)
2.08% swing C. to Lab.
(2010: C. majority 6,431 (12.42%))

CAMBERWELL & PECKHAM
E. 80,507   T. 51,561 (64.05%)   Lab. hold
Harriet Harman, Lab.   32,614
Naomi Newstead, C.   6,790
Amelia Womack, Green   5,187
Yahaya Kiingi, LD   2,580
David Kurten, UKIP   2,413
Prem Goyal, AP   829
Rebecca Fox, NHAP   466
Nick Wrack, TUSC   292
Alex Robertson, CISTA   197
Joshua Ogunleye, WRP   107
Felicity Anscomb, Whig   86
Lab. majority 25,824 (50.08%)
1.96% swing C. to Lab.
(2010: Lab. majority 17,187 (36.84%))

CAMBORNE & REDRUTH
E. 66,944   T. 45,868 (68.52%)   C. hold
George Eustice, C.   18,452
Michael Foster, Lab.   11,448
Bob Smith, UKIP   6,776
Julia Goldsworthy, LD   5,687
Geoff Garbett, Green   2,608
Loveday Jenkin, Meb. Ker.   897
C. majority 7,004 (15.27%)
2.98% swing C. to Lab.
(2010: C. majority 66 (0.16%))

CAMBRIDGE
E. 83,384   T. 51,774 (62.09%)   Lab. gain
*Daniel Zeichner, Lab.   18,646
Julian Huppert, LD   18,047
Chamali Fernando, C.   8,117
Rupert Read, Green   4,109
Patrick O'Flynn, UKIP   2,668
Keith Garrett, Reboot   187
Lab. majority 599 (1.16%)
8.01% swing LD to Lab.
(2010: LD majority 6,792 (13.55%))

CAMBRIDGESHIRE NORTH EAST
E. 82,990   T. 51,780 (62.39%)   C. hold
Stephen Barclay, C.   28,524
Andrew Charalambous, UKIP   11,650
Ken Rustidge, Lab.   7,476
Lucy Nethsingha, LD   2,314
Helen Scott-Daniels, Green   1,816
C. majority 16,874 (32.59%)
6.54% swing C. to UKIP
(2010: C. majority 16,425 (31.43%))

CAMBRIDGESHIRE NORTH WEST
E. 91,783   T. 61,100 (66.57%)   C. hold
Shailesh Vara, C.   32,070
Peter Reeve, UKIP   12,275
Nick Thulbourn, Lab.   10,927
Nicholas Sandford, LD   3,479
Nicola Day, Green   2,159
Fay Belham, CPA   190
C. majority 19,795 (32.40%)
4.90% swing C. to UKIP
(2010: C. majority 16,677 (28.61%))

CAMBRIDGESHIRE SOUTH
E. 84,132   T. 61,540 (73.15%)   C. hold
*Heidi Allen, C.   31,454
Dan Greef, Lab.   10,860
Sebastian Kindersley, LD   9,368
Marion Mason, UKIP   6,010
Simon Saggers, Green   3,848
C. majority 20,594 (33.46%)
1.87% swing C. to Lab.
(2010: C. majority 7,838 (13.27%))

CAMBRIDGESHIRE SOUTH EAST
E. 84,570   T. 59,506 (70.36%)   C. hold
*Lucy Frazer, C.   28,845
Jonathan Chatfield, LD   12,008
Huw Jones, Lab.   9,013
Deborah Rennie, UKIP   6,593
Clive Semmens, Green   3,047
C. majority 16,837 (28.29%)
8.99% swing LD to C.
(2010: C. majority 5,946 (10.32%))

CANNOCK CHASE
E. 74,531   T. 47,099 (63.19%)   C. hold
*Amanda Milling, C.   20,811
Janos Toth, Lab.   15,888
Grahame Wiggin, UKIP   8,224
Ian Jackson, LD   1,270
Paul Woodhead, Green   906
C. majority 4,923 (10.45%)
1.72% swing Lab. to C.
(2010: C. majority 3,195 (7.01%))

CANTERBURY
E. 83,481   T. 53,465 (64.04%)   C. hold
Julian Brazier, C.   22,918
Hugh Lanning, Lab.   13,120
Jim Gascoyne, UKIP   7,289
James Flanagan, LD   6,227
Stuart Jeffery, Green   3,746
Robert Cox, SPGB   165
C. majority 9,798 (18.33%)
5.17% swing C. to Lab.
(2010: C. majority 6,048 (12.29%))

CARLISLE
E. 65,827   T. 42,587 (64.70%)   C. hold
John Stevenson, C.   18,873
Lee Sherriff, Lab.   16,099
Fiona Mills, UKIP   5,277
Helen Davison, Green   1,125
Loraine Birchall, LD   1,087
Alfred Okam, Ind.   126
C. majority 2,774 (6.51%)
2.25% swing Lab. to C.
(2010: C. majority 853 (2.02%))

CARSHALTON & WALLINGTON
E. 69,866   T. 47,613 (68.15%)   LD hold
Tom Brake, LD   16,603
Matthew Maxwell Scott, C.   15,093
Siobhan Tate, Lab.   7,150
Bill Main-Ian, UKIP   7,049
Ross Hemingway, Green   1,492
Ashley Dickenson, CPA   177
Richard Edmonds, NF   49
LD majority 1,510 (3.17%)
4.14% swing LD to C.
(2010: LD majority 5,260 (11.46%))

CASTLE POINT
E. 68,170   T. 45,450 (66.67%)   C. hold
Rebecca Harris, C.   23,112
Jamie Huntman, UKIP   14,178
Joe Cooke, Lab.   6,283
Dominic Ellis, Green   1,076
Sereena Davey, LD   801
C. majority 8,934 (19.66%)
swing N/A
(2010: C. majority 7,632 (16.95%))

CHARNWOOD
E. 77,269   T. 52,261 (67.64%)   C. hold
*Edward Argar, C.   28,384
Sean Kelly-Walsh, Lab.   11,453
Lynton Yates, UKIP   8,330
Simon Sansome, LD   3,605
Cathy Duffy, BNP   489
C. majority 16,931 (32.40%)
1.23% swing Lab. to C.
(2010: C. majority 15,029 (28.07%))

CHATHAM & AYLESFORD
E. 68,625   T. 43,073 (62.77%)   C. hold
Tracey Crouch, C.   21,614
Tristan Osborne, Lab.   10,159
Ian Wallace, UKIP   8,581
Thomas Quinton, LD   1,360
Luke Balnave, Green   1,101
John-Wesley Gibson, CPA   133
Ivor Riddell, TUSC   125
C. majority 11,455 (26.59%)
6.37% swing Lab. to C.
(2010: C. majority 6,069 (13.85%))

CHEADLE
E. 73,239   T. 53,095 (72.50%)   C. gain
*Mary Robinson, C.   22,889
Mark Hunter, LD   16,436
Martin Miller, Lab.   8,673
Shaun Hopkins, UKIP   4,423
Matthew Torbitt, Ind.   390
Drew Carswell, Above   208
Helen Bashford, IE   76
C. majority 6,453 (12.15%)
9.19% swing LD to C.
(2010: LD majority 3,272 (6.23%))

CHELMSFORD
E. 78,580   T. 53,817 (68.49%)   C. hold
Simon Burns, C.   27,732
Chris Vince, Lab.   9,482
Mark Gough, UKIP   7,652
Stephen Robinson, LD   6,394
Angela Thomson, Green   1,892
Henry Boyle, Lib.   665
C. majority 18,250 (33.91%)
0.65% swing C. to Lab.
(2010: C. majority 5,110 (9.36%))

CHELSEA & FULHAM
E. 63,478   T. 40,226 (63.37%)   C. hold
Greg Hands, C.   25,322
Alexandra Sanderson, Lab.   9,300
Simon Bailey, LD   2,091
Adrian Noble, UKIP   2,039
Guy Rubin, Green   1,474
C. majority 16,022 (39.83%)
1.06% swing C. to Lab.
(2010: C. majority 16,722 (41.96%))

CHELTENHAM
E. 77,286   T. 53,735 (69.53%)   C. gain
*Alex Chalk, C.   24,790
Martin Horwood, LD   18,274
Paul Gilbert, Lab.   3,902
Christina Simmonds, UKIP   3,808
Adam Van Coevorden, Green   2,689
Richard Lupson-Darnell, Ind.   272
C. majority 6,516 (12.13%)
10.72% swing LD to C.
(2010: LD majority 4,920 (9.32%))

CHESHAM & AMERSHAM
E. 73,423   T. 52,731 (71.82%)   C. hold
Cheryl Gillan, C.   31,138
Alan Stevens, UKIP   7,218
Benjamin Davies, Lab.   6,712
Kirsten Johnson, LD   4,761
Gill Walker, Green   2,902
C. majority 23,920 (45.36%)
5.47% swing C. to UKIP
(2010: C. majority 16,710 (31.86%))

CHESTER, CITY OF
E. 72,269   T. 51,161 (70.79%)   Lab. gain
*Chris Matheson, Lab.   22,118
Stephen Mosley, C.   22,025
Stephen Ingram, UKIP   4,148
Bob Thompson, LD   2,870
Lab. majority 93 (0.18%)
2.85% swing C. to Lab.
(2010: C. majority 2,583 (5.52%))

CHESTERFIELD
E. 72,078   T. 45,567 (63.22%)   Lab. hold
Toby Perkins, Lab.   21,829
Mark Vivis, C.   8,231
Stuart Yeowart, UKIP   7,523
Julia Cambridge, LD   6,301
Matthew Genn, Green   1,352
Matt Whale, TUSC   202
Tommy Holgate, Peace   129
Lab. majority 13,598 (29.84%)
3.27% swing C. to Lab.
(2010: Lab. majority 549 (1.20%))

CHICHESTER
E. 83,575   T. 57,139 (68.37%)   C. hold
Andrew Tyrie, C.   32,953
Andrew Moncreiff, UKIP   8,540
Mark Farwell, Lab.   6,933
Andrew Smith, LD   4,865
Jasper Richmond, Green   3,742
Andrew Emerson, Patria   106
C. majority 24,413 (42.73%)
2.90% swing C. to UKIP
(2010: C. majority 15,877 (27.96%))

CHINGFORD & WOODFORD GREEN
E. 66,691   T. 43,804 (65.68%)   C. hold
Iain Duncan Smith, C.   20,999
Bilal Mahmood, Lab.   12,613
Freddy Vachha, UKIP   5,644
Anne Crook, LD   2,400
Rebecca Tully, Green   1,854
Len Hockey, TUSC   241
Lisa McKenzie, Class War   53
C. majority 8,386 (19.14%)
5.46% swing C. to Lab.
(2010: C. majority 12,963 (30.07%))

CHIPPENHAM
E. 74,225   T. 55,407 (74.65%)   C. gain
*Michelle Donelan, C.   26,354
Duncan Hames, LD   16,278
Julia Reid, UKIP   5,884
Andy Newman, Lab.   4,561
Tina Johnston, Green   2,330
C. majority 10,076 (18.19%)
11.45% swing LD to C.
(2010: LD majority 2,470 (4.72%))

CHIPPING BARNET
E. 77,853   T. 53,013 (68.09%)   C. hold
Theresa Villiers, C.   25,759
Amy Trevethan, Lab.   18,103
Victor Kaye, UKIP   4,151
A Poppy, Green   2,501
Marisha Ray, LD   2,381
Mehdi Akhavan, ND   118
C. majority 7,656 (14.44%)
4.56% swing C. to Lab.
(2010: C. majority 11,927 (23.57%))

CHORLEY
E. 74,679   T. 51,712 (69.25%)   Lab. hold
Lindsay Hoyle, Lab.   23,322
Rob Loughenbury, C.   18,792
Mark Smith, UKIP   6,995
Stephen Fenn, LD   1,354
Alistair Straw, Green   1,111
Adrian Maudsley, Ind.   138
Lab. majority 4,530 (8.76%)
1.78% swing C. to Lab.
(2010: Lab. majority 2,593 (5.21%))

CHRISTCHURCH
E. 69,302   T. 49,707 (71.73%)   C. hold
Christopher Chope, C.   28,887
Robin Grey, UKIP   10,663
Andrew Satherley, Lab.   4,745
Andy Canning, LD   3,263
Shona Dunn, Green   2,149
C. majority 18,224 (36.66%)
5.64% swing C. to UKIP
(2010: C. majority 15,410 (31.18%))

CITIES OF LONDON & WESTMINSTER
E. 60,992   T. 36,185 (59.33%)   C. hold
Mark Field, C.   19,570
Nik Slingsby, Lab.   9,899
Belinda Brooks-Gordon, LD   2,521
Hugh Small, Green   1,953
Robert Stephenson, UKIP   1,894
Edouard-Henri Desforges, CISTA   160
Jill McLachlan, CPA   129
Adam Clifford, Class War   59
C. majority 9,671 (26.73%)
1.63% swing C. to Lab.
(2010: C. majority 11,076 (29.99%))

CLACTON
E. 68,936   T. 44,207 (64.13%)   UKIP hold
Douglas Carswell, UKIP   19,642
Giles Watling, C.   16,205
Tim Young, Lab.   6,364
Chris Southall, Green   1,184
David Grace, LD   812
UKIP majority 3,437 (7.77%)
swing N/A
(2010: C. majority 12,068 (27.99%))
(2014: UKIP majority 12,404 (35.10%))

CLEETHORPES
E. 70,514   T. 45,089 (63.94%)   C. hold
Martin Vickers, C.   21,026
Peter Keith, Lab.   13,133
Stephen Harness, UKIP   8,356
Roy Horobin, LD   1,346
Carol Thornton, Green   1,013
Malcolm Morland, TUSC   215
C. majority 7,893 (17.51%)
3.97% swing Lab. to C.
(2010: C. majority 4,298 (9.56%))

COLCHESTER
E. 74,203   T. 48,593 (65.49%)   C. gain
*Will Quince, C.   18,919
Bob Russell, LD   13,344
Jordan Newell, Lab.   7,852
John Pitts, UKIP   5,870
Mark Goacher, Green   2,499
Ken Scrimshaw, CPA   109
C. majority 5,575 (11.47%)
13.30% swing LD to C.
(2010: LD majority 6,982 (15.13%))

COLNE VALLEY
E. 82,510   T. 56,800 (68.84%)   C. hold
Jason McCartney, C.   25,246
Jane East, Lab.   19,868
Melanie Roberts, UKIP   5,734
Cahal Burke, LD   3,407
Chas Ball, Green   1,919
Paul Salveson, Yorks   572
Melodie Staniforth, ND   54
C. majority 5,378 (9.47%)
0.56% swing C. to Lab.
(2010: C. majority 4,837 (8.75%))

CONGLETON
E. 72,398   T. 50,976 (70.41%)   C. hold
Fiona Bruce, C.   27,164
Darren Price, Lab.   10,391
Lee Slaughter, UKIP   6,922
Peter Hirst, LD   4,623
Alec Heath, Green   1,876
C. majority 16,773 (32.90%)
2.17% swing Lab. to C.
(2010: C. majority 7,063 (13.91%))

COPELAND
E. 62,119   T. 39,631 (63.80%)   Lab. hold
Jamie Reed, Lab.   16,750
Stephen Haraldsen, C.   14,186
Michael Pye, UKIP   6,148
Danny Gallagher, LD   1,368
Allan Todd, Green   1,179
Lab. majority 2,564 (6.47%)
1.24% swing Lab. to C.
(2010: Lab. majority 3,833 (8.96%))

CORBY
E. 79,775   T. 56,174 (70.42%)   C. gain
*Tom Pursglove, C.   24,023
Andy Sawford, Lab. Co-op   21,611
Margot Parker, UKIP   7,708
Peter Harris, LD   1,458
Jonathan Hornett, Green   1,374
C. majority 2,412 (4.29%)
0.40% swing Lab. to C.
(2010: C. majority 1,895 (3.49%))
(2012: Lab. majority 7,791 (21.84%))

CORNWALL NORTH
E. 67,192   T. 48,245 (71.80%)   C. gain
*Scott Mann, C.   21,689
Dan Rogerson, LD   15,068
Julie Lingard, UKIP   6,121
John Whitby, Lab.   2,621
Amanda Pennington, Green   2,063
Jeremy Jefferies, Meb. Ker.   631
John Allman, Restore   52
C. majority 6,621 (13.72%)
10.91% swing LD to C.
(2010: LD majority 2,981 (6.36%))

CORNWALL SOUTH EAST
E. 71,071   T. 50,498 (71.05%)   C. hold
Sheryll Murray, C.   25,516
Phil Hutty, LD   8,521
Bradley Monk, UKIP   7,698
Declan Lloyd, Lab.   4,692
Martin Corney, Green   2,718
Andrew Long, Meb. Ker.   1,003
George Trubody, Ind.   350
C. majority 16,995 (33.65%)
13.58% swing LD to C.
(2010: C. majority 3,220 (6.49%))

COTSWOLDS, THE
E. 78,292   T. 56,667 (72.38%)   C. hold
Geoffrey Clifton-Brown, C.   32,045
Paul Hodgkinson, LD   10,568
Chris Harlow, UKIP   6,188
Manjinder Kang, Lab.   5,240
Penny Burgess, Green   2,626
C. majority 21,477 (37.90%)
7.22% swing LD to C.
(2010: C. majority 12,864 (23.46%))

COVENTRY NORTH EAST
E. 76,401   T. 42,231 (55.28%)   Lab. hold
*Colleen Fletcher, Lab.   22,025
Michelle Lowe, C.   9,751
Avtar Taggar, UKIP   6,278
Russell Field, LD   2,007
Matthew Handley, Green   1,245
Nicky Downes, TUSC   633
William Sidhu, Ch. M.   292
Lab. majority 12,274 (29.06%)
0.96% swing C. to Lab.
(2010: Lab. majority 11,775 (27.14%))

COVENTRY NORTH WEST
E. 74,597   T. 45,246 (60.65%)   Lab. hold
Geoffrey Robinson, Lab.   18,557
Parvez Akhtar, C.   14,048
Harjinder Singh Sehmi, UKIP   7,101
Laura Vesty, Green   1,961
Andrew Furse, LD   1,810
Dave Nellist, TUSC   1,769
Lab. majority 4,509 (9.97%)
1.77% swing Lab. to C.
(2010: Lab. majority 6,288 (13.51%))

COVENTRY SOUTH
E. 71,380 T. 43,699 (61.22%) Lab. hold
Jim Cunningham, Lab.   18,472
Gary Ridley, C.   15,284
Mark Taylor, UKIP   5,709
Greg Judge, LD   1,779
Benjamin Gallaher, Green   1,719
Judy Griffiths, TUSC   650
Chris Rooney, Mainstream   86
Lab. majority 3,188 (7.30%)
0.54% swing Lab. to C.
(2010: Lab. majority 3,845 (8.37%))

CRAWLEY
E. 73,940   T. 48,550 (65.66%) C. hold
Henry Smith, C.   22,829
Chris Oxlade, Lab.   16,303
Chris Brown, UKIP   6,979
Sarah Osborne, LD   1,339
Guy Hudson, Green   1,100
C. majority 6,526 (13.44%)
0.48% swing Lab. to C.
(2010: C. majority 5,928 (12.48%))

CREWE & NANTWICH
E. 74,039   T. 49,896 (67.39%) C. hold
Edward Timpson, C.   22,445
Adrian Heald, Lab.   18,825
Richard Lee, UKIP   7,252
Roy Wood, LD   1,374
C. majority 3,620 (7.26%)
2.29% swing C. to Lab.
(2010: C. majority 6,046 (11.84%))

CROYDON CENTRAL
E. 78,171   T. 52,941 (67.72%) C. hold
Gavin Barwell, C.   22,753
Sarah Jones, Lab.   22,588
Peter Staveley, UKIP   4,810
Esther Sutton, Green   1,454
James Robert Fearnley, LD   1,152
April Ashley, TUSC   127
Martin Camden, UKPDP   57
C. majority 165 (0.31%)
2.83% swing C. to Lab.
(2010: C. majority 2,969 (5.97%))

CROYDON NORTH
E. 85,951 T. 53,522 (62.27%)
                              Lab. Co-op hold
Steve Reed, Lab. Co-op   33,513
Vidhi Mohan, C.   12,149
Winston McKenzie, UKIP   2,899
Shasha Khan, Green   2,515
Joanna Corbin, LD   1,919
Glen Hart, TUSC   261
Lee Berks, Ind.   141
Ben Stevenson, Comm.   125
Lab. Co-op majority 21,364 (39.92%)
4.01% swing C. to Lab.
(2010: Lab. majority 16,483 (31.90%))
(2012: Lab. majority 11,761 (47.87%))

CROYDON SOUTH
E. 82,010   T. 57,712 (70.37%) C. hold
*Chris Philp, C.   31,448
Emily Benn, Lab.   14,308
Kathleen Garner, UKIP   6,068
Gill Hickson, LD   3,448
Peter Underwood, Green   2,154
Mark Samuel, Croydon   221
Jon Bigger, Class War   65
C. majority 17,140 (29.70%)
0.59% swing C. to Lab.
(2010: C. majority 15,818 (28.08%))

DAGENHAM & RAINHAM
E. 69,049   T. 43,050 (62.35%) Lab. hold
Jon Cruddas, Lab.   17,830
Peter Harris, UKIP   12,850
Julie Marson, C.   10,492
Kate Simpson, Green   806
Denise Capstick, LD   717
Tess Culnane, BNP   151
Terry London, ND   133
Kim Gandy, Eng. Dem.   71
Lab. majority 4,980 (11.57%)
12.58% swing Lab. to UKIP
(2010: Lab. majority 2,630 (5.95%))

DARLINGTON
E. 65,832 T. 41,141 (62.49%) Lab. hold
Jenny Chapman, Lab.   17,637
Peter Cuthbertson, C.   14,479
David Hodgson, UKIP   5,392
Anne-Marie Curry, LD   1,966
Michael Cherrington, Green   1,444
Alan Docherty, TUSC   223
Lab. majority 3,158 (7.68%)
0.11% swing Lab. to C.
(2010: Lab. majority 3,388 (7.90%))

DARTFORD
E. 76,686   T. 52,418 (68.35%) C. hold
Gareth Johnson, C.   25,670
Simon Thomson, Lab.   13,325
Elizabeth Jones, UKIP   10,434
Simon Beard, LD   1,454
Andy Blatchford, Green   1,324
Steve Uncles, Eng. Dem.   211
C. majority 12,345 (23.55%)
1.16% swing Lab. to C.
(2010: C. majority 10,628 (21.22%))

DAVENTRY
E. 72,753   T. 52,518 (72.19%) C. hold
Chris Heaton-Harris, C.   30,550
Abigail Campbell, Lab.   9,491
Michael Gerard, UKIP   8,296
Callum Delhoy, LD   2,352
Steve Whiffen, Green   1,829
C. majority 21,059 (40.10%)
0.31% swing C. to Lab.
(2010: C. majority 19,188 (37.06%))

DENTON & REDDISH
E. 66,574   T. 38,681 (58.10%) Lab. hold
Andrew Gwynne, Lab.   19,661
Lana Hempsall, C.   9,150
Andrew Fairfoull, UKIP   7,225
Nick Koopman, Green   1,466
Mark Jewell, LD   957
Victoria Lofas, Ind.   222
Lab. majority 10,511 (27.17%)
0.53% swing C. to Lab.
(2010: Lab. majority 9,831 (26.12%))

DERBY NORTH
E. 64,739   T. 44,745 (69.12%) C. gain
*Amanda Solloway, C.   16,402
Chris Williamson, Lab.   16,361
Tilly Ward, UKIP   6,532
Lucy Care, LD   3,832
Alice Mason-Power, Green   1,618
C. majority 41 (0.09%)
0.73% swing Lab. to C.
(2010: Lab. majority 613 (1.36%))

DERBY SOUTH
E. 70,247   T. 40,820 (58.11%) Lab. hold
Margaret Beckett, Lab.   20,007
Evonne Williams, C.   11,179
Victor Webb, UKIP   6,341
Joe Naitta, LD   1,717
David Foster, Green   1,208
Chris Fernandez, TUSC   225
David Gale, Brit. Ind.   143
Lab. majority 8,828 (21.63%)
3.38% swing C. to Lab.
(2010: Lab. majority 6,122 (14.86%))

DERBYSHIRE DALES
E. 63,470   T. 47,361 (74.62%) C. hold
Patrick McLoughlin, C.   24,805
Andy Botham, Lab.   10,761
John Young, UKIP   5,508
Benjamin Fearn, LD   3,965
Ian Wood, Green   2,173
Amila Y'Mech, Humanity   149
C. majority 14,044 (29.65%)
1.54% swing C. to Lab.
(2010: C. majority 13,866 (29.64%))

DERBYSHIRE MID
E. 67,576   T. 47,729 (70.63%) C. hold
Pauline Latham, C.   24,908
Nicola Heaton, Lab.   12,134
Martin Fitzpatrick, UKIP   6,497
Hilary Jones, LD   2,292
Sue MacFarlane, Green   1,898
C. majority 12,774 (26.76%)
1.46% swing Lab. to C.
(2010: C. majority 11,292 (23.85%))

DERBYSHIRE NORTH EAST
E. 71,456   T. 47,948 (67.10%) Lab. hold
Natascha Engel, Lab.   19,488
Lee Rowley, C.   17,605
James Bush, UKIP   7,631
David Batey, LD   2,004
David Kesteven, Green   1,059
Rob Lane, Ind.   161
Lab. majority 1,883 (3.93%)
0.64% swing Lab. to C.
(2010: Lab. majority 2,445 (5.20%))

DERBYSHIRE SOUTH
E. 74,395   T. 50,762 (68.23%) C. hold
Heather Wheeler, C.   25,066
Cheryl Pidgeon, Lab.   13,595
Alan Graves, UKIP   8,998
Lorraine Johnson, LD   1,887
Marianne Bamkin, Green   1,216
C. majority 11,471 (22.60%)
4.23% swing Lab. to C.
(2010: C. majority 7,128 (14.14%))

DEVIZES
E. 69,211   T. 49,006 (70.81%) C. hold
Claire Perry, C.   28,295
David Pollitt, UKIP   7,544
Chris Watts, Lab.   6,360
Manda Rigby, LD   3,954
Emma Dawnay, Green   2,853
C. majority 20,751 (42.34%)
4.12% swing C. to UKIP
(2010: C. majority 13,005 (28.06%))

DEVON CENTRAL
E. 72,737   T. 54,448 (74.86%)   C. hold
Mel Stride, C.   28,436
John Conway, UKIP   7,171
Lynne Richards, Lab.   6,985
Alex White, LD   6,643
Andy Williamson, Green   4,866
Arthur Price, Ind.   347
C. majority 21,265 (39.06%)
3.55% swing C. to UKIP
(2010: C. majority 9,230 (17.13%))

DEVON EAST
E. 74,224   T. 54,717 (73.72%)   C. hold
Hugo Swire, C.   25,401
Claire Wright, Ind.   13,140
Andrew Chapman, UKIP   6,870
Steve Race, Lab.   5,591
Stuart Mole, LD   3,715
C. majority 12,261 (22.41%)
swing N/A
(2010: C. majority 9,114 (17.17%))

DEVON NORTH
E. 74,737   T. 52,320 (70.01%)   C. gain
*Peter Heaton-Jones, C.   22,341
Nick Harvey, LD   15,405
Steve Crowther, UKIP   7,719
Mark Cann, Lab.   3,699
Ricky Knight, Green   3,018
Gerrard Sables, Comm.   138
C. majority 6,936 (13.26%)
12.30% swing LD to C.
(2010: LD majority 5,821 (11.34%))

DEVON SOUTH WEST
E. 71,035   T. 50,372 (70.91%)   C. hold
Gary Streeter, C.   28,500
Chaz Singh, Lab.   8,391
Robin Julian, UKIP   7,306
Tom Davies, LD   3,767
Win Scutt, Green   2,408
C. majority 20,109 (39.92%)
1.82% swing C. to Lab.
(2010: C. majority 15,874 (31.84%))

DEVON WEST & TORRIDGE
E. 78,582   T. 56,584 (72.01%)   C. hold
Geoffrey Cox, C.   28,774
Derek Sargent, UKIP   10,371
Paula Dolphin, LD   7,483
Mike Sparling, Lab.   6,015
Cathrine Simmons, Green   3,941
C. majority 18,403 (32.52%)
3.83% swing C. to UKIP
(2010: C. majority 2,957 (5.35%))

DEWSBURY
E. 79,765   T. 53,630 (67.24%)   Lab. gain
*Paula Sherriff, Lab.   22,406
Simon Reevell, C.   20,955
Mark Thackray, UKIP   6,649
Ednan Hussain, LD   1,924
Adrian Cruden, Green   1,366
Richard Carter, Yorks   236
Steve Hakes, CPA   94
Lab. majority 1,451 (2.71%)
2.77% swing C. to Lab.
(2010: C. majority 1,526 (2.83%))

DON VALLEY
E. 71,299   T. 42,486 (59.59%)   Lab. hold
Caroline Flint, Lab.   19,621
Carl Jackson, C.   10,736
Guy Aston, UKIP   9,963
Rene Paterson, LD   1,487
Steve Williams, TUSC   437
Louise Dutton, Eng. Dem.   242
Lab. majority 8,885 (20.91%)
6.32% swing C. to Lab.
(2010: Lab. majority 3,595 (8.28%))

DONCASTER CENTRAL
E. 71,136   T. 40,420 (56.82%)   Lab. hold
Rosie Winterton, Lab.   19,840
Chris Hodgson, UKIP   9,747
Zoe Metcalfe, C.   8,386
John Brown, LD   1,717
Mev Akram, TUSC   421
David Burnett, Eng. Dem.   309
Lab. majority 10,093 (24.97%)
5.66% swing Lab. to UKIP
(2010: Lab. majority 6,229 (14.92%))

DONCASTER NORTH
E. 70,898   T. 39,501 (55.72%)   Lab. hold
Ed Miliband, Lab.   20,708
Kim Parkinson, UKIP   8,928
Mark Fletcher, C.   7,235
Penny Baker, LD   1,005
Peter Kennedy, Green   757
David Allen, Eng. Dem.   448
Mary Jackson, TUSC   258
Nick The Flying Brick, Loony   162
Lab. majority 11,780 (29.82%)
6.59% swing Lab. to UKIP
(2010: Lab. majority 10,909 (26.30%))

DORSET MID & POOLE NORTH
E. 68,917   T. 46,499 (67.47%)   C. gain
*Michael Tomlinson, C.   23,639
Vikki Slade, LD   13,109
Richard Turner, UKIP   5,663
Patrick Canavan, Lab.   2,767
Mark Chivers, Green   1,321
C. majority 10,530 (22.65%)
11.61% swing LD to C.
(2010: LD majority 269 (0.57%))

DORSET NORTH
E. 74,576   T. 53,385 (71.58%)   C. hold
*Simon Hoare, C.   30,227
Steve Unwin, UKIP   9,109
Hugo Mieville, LD   6,226
Kim Fendley, Lab.   4,785
Richard Barrington, Green   3,038
C. majority 21,118 (39.56%)
3.15% swing C. to UKIP
(2010: C. majority 7,625 (14.08%))

DORSET SOUTH
E. 71,974   T. 48,597 (67.52%)   C. hold
Richard Drax, C.   23,756
Simon Bowkett, Lab.   11,762
Malcolm Shakesby, UKIP   7,304
Howard Legg, LD   2,901
Jane Burnet, Green   2,275
Mervyn Stewkesbury, Ind.   435
Andy Kirkwood, Active Dem.   164
C. majority 11,994 (24.68%)
4.94% swing Lab. to C.
(2010: C. majority 7,443 (14.79%))

DORSET WEST
E. 78,427   T. 56,458 (71.99%)   C. hold
Oliver Letwin, C.   28,329
Ros Kayes, LD   12,199
David Glossop, UKIP   7,055
Rachel Rogers, Lab.   5,633
Peter Barton, Green   3,242
C. majority 16,130 (28.57%)
10.86% swing LD to C.
(2010: C. majority 3,923 (6.84%))

DOVER
E. 72,929   T. 50,224 (68.87%)   C. hold
Charlie Elphicke, C.   21,737
Clair Hawkins, Lab.   15,443
David Little, UKIP   10,177
Sarah Smith, LD   1,572
Jolyon Trimingham, Green   1,295
C. majority 6,294 (12.53%)
1.03% swing Lab. to C.
(2010: C. majority 5,274 (10.47%))

DUDLEY NORTH
E. 60,718   T. 37,992 (62.57%)   Lab. hold
Ian Austin, Lab.   15,885
Les Jones, C.   11,704
Bill Etheridge, UKIP   9,113
Will Duckworth, Green   517
Mike Collins, LD   478
Rehan Afzal, APNI   156
Dave Pitt, TUSC   139
Lab. majority 4,181 (11.00%)
4.66% swing C. to Lab.
(2010: Lab. majority 649 (1.68%))

DUDLEY SOUTH
E. 60,363   T. 38,210 (63.30%)   C. hold
*Mike Wood, C.   16,723
Natasha Millward, Lab.   12,453
Paul Brothwood, UKIP   7,236
Vicky Duckworth, Green   970
Martin Turner, LD   828
C. majority 4,270 (11.18%)
0.54% swing Lab. to C.
(2010: C. majority 3,856 (10.10%))

DULWICH & WEST NORWOOD
E. 75,244   T. 51,362 (68.26%)   Lab. hold
*Helen Hayes, Lab.   27,772
Resham Kotecha, C.   11,650
James Barber, LD   5,055
Rashid Nix, Green   4,844
Rathy Alagaratnam, UKIP   1,606
Steve Nally, TUSC   248
David Lambert, Ind.   125
Amadu Kanumansa, AP   62
Lab. majority 16,122 (31.39%)
3.48% swing C. to Lab.
(2010: Lab. majority 9,365 (19.42%))

DURHAM, CITY OF
E. 68,741   T. 45,669 (66.44%)   Lab. hold
Roberta Blackman-Woods, Lab.   21,596
Rebecca Coulson, C.   10,157
Liam Clark, UKIP   5,232
Craig Martin, LD   5,153
Jonathan Elmer, Green   2,687
John Marshall, Ind.   649
Jon Collings, Ind.   195
Lab. majority 11,439 (25.05%)
2.99% swing Lab. to C.
(2010: Lab. majority 3,067 (6.63%))

DURHAM NORTH
E. 65,373   T. 40,146 (61.41%)   Lab. hold
Kevan Jones, Lab.   22,047
Laetitia Glossop, C.   8,403
Malcolm Bint, UKIP   6,404
Peter Maughan, LD   2,046
Vicki Nolan, Green   1,246
Lab. majority 13,644 (33.99%)
2.25% swing C. to Lab.
(2010: Lab. majority 12,076 (29.48%))

DURHAM NORTH WEST
E. 69,817   T. 42,818 (61.33%)   Lab. hold
Pat Glass, Lab.   20,074
Charlotte Haitham-Taylor, C.   10,018
Bruce Reid, UKIP   7,265
Owen Temple, LD   3,894
Mark Shilcock, Green   1,567
Lab. majority 10,056 (23.49%)
0.59% swing C. to Lab.
(2010: Lab. majority 7,612 (17.37%))

EALING CENTRAL & ACTON
E. 71,238   T. 50,894 (71.44%)   Lab. gain
*Rupa Huq, Lab.   22,002
Angie Bray, C.   21,728
Jon Ball, LD   3,106
Peter Florence, UKIP   1,926
Tom Sharman, Green   1,841
Jonathan Notley, Ind.   125
Scott Dore, WRP   73
Tammy Rendle, Above   54
Andrzej Rygielski, EP   39
Lab. majority 274 (0.54%)
4.21% swing C. to Lab.
(2010: C. majority 3,716 (7.87%))

EALING NORTH
E. 73,836   T. 48,510 (65.70%)   Lab. hold
Stephen Pound, Lab.   26,745
Thomas O'Malley, C.   14,419
Afzal Akram, UKIP   3,922
Meena Hans, Green   1,635
Kevin McNamara, LD   1,575
David Hofman, TUSC   214
Lab. majority 12,326 (25.41%)
2.95% swing C. to Lab.
(2010: Lab. majority 9,301 (19.51%))

EALING SOUTHALL
E. 65,495   T. 43,321 (66.14%)   Lab. hold
Virendra Sharma, Lab.   28,147
James Symes, C.   9,387
Jaspreet Mahal, Green   2,007
John Poynton, UKIP   1,769
Kavya Kaushik, LD   1,550
Jagdeesh Singh, Nat. Lib.   461
Lab. majority 18,760 (43.30%)
10.79% swing C. to Lab.
(2010: Lab. majority 9,291 (21.73%))

EASINGTON
E. 61,675   T. 34,624 (56.14%)   Lab. hold
Grahame Morris, Lab.   21,132
Jonathan Arnott, UKIP   6,491
Chris Hampsheir, C.   4,478
Luke Armstrong, LD   834
Susan McDonnell, NE   810
Martie Warin, Green   733
Steve Colborn, SPGB   146
Lab. majority 14,641 (42.29%)
5.99% swing Lab. to UKIP
(2010: Lab. majority 14,982 (42.91%))

EAST HAM
E. 87,378   T. 52,290 (59.84%)   Lab. hold
Stephen Timms, Lab.   40,563
Samir Jassal, C.   6,311
Daniel Oxley, UKIP   2,622
Tamsin Omond, Green   1,299
David Thorpe, LD   856
Mohammed Aslam, Community   409
Lois Austin, TUSC   230
Lab. majority 34,252 (65.50%)
5.13% swing C. to Lab.
(2010: Lab. majority 27,826 (55.24%))

EASTBOURNE
E. 78,262   T. 52,907 (67.60%)   C. gain
*Caroline Ansell, C.   20,934
Stephen Lloyd, LD   20,201
Nigel Jones, UKIP   6,139
Jake Lambert, Lab.   4,143
Andrew Durling, Green   1,351
Paul Howard, Ind.   139
C. majority 733 (1.39%)
3.99% swing LD to C.
(2010: LD majority 3,435 (6.59%))

EASTLEIGH
E. 79,609   T. 55,505 (69.72%)   C. gain
*Mims Davies, C.   23,464
Mike Thornton, LD   14,317
Patricia Culligan, UKIP   8,783
Mark Latham, Lab.   7,181
Ron Meldrum, Green   1,513
Ray Hall, Beer BS   133
Declan Clune, TUSC   114
C. majority 9,147 (16.48%)
11.84% swing LD to C.
(2010: LD majority 3,864 (7.20%))
(2013: LD majority 1,771 (4.26%))

EDDISBURY
E. 68,636   T. 47,352 (68.99%)   C. hold
*Antoinette Sandbach, C.   24,167
James Laing, Lab.   11,193
Rob Millington, UKIP   5,778
Ian Priestner, LD   4,289
Andrew Garman, Green   1,624
George Antar, CISTA   301
C. majority 12,974 (27.40%)
1.36% swing C. to Lab.
(2010: C. majority 13,255 (29.19%))

EDMONTON
E. 66,015   T. 41,338 (62.62%)
                             Lab. Co-op hold
*Kate Osamor, Lab. Co-op   25,388
Gonul Daniels, C.   9,969
Neville Watson, UKIP   3,366
Douglas Coker, Green   1,358
David Schmitz, LD   897
Lewis Peacock, TUSC   360
Lab. Co-op majority 15,419 (37.30%)
6.75% swing C. to Lab.
(2010: Lab. Co-op majority 9,613
(23.81%))

ELLESMERE PORT & NESTON
E. 68,134   T. 46,727 (68.58%)   Lab. hold
*Justin Madders, Lab.   22,316
Katherine Fletcher, C.   16,041
Jonathan Starkey, UKIP   5,594
Trish Derraugh, LD   1,563
Michelle Palmer, Green   990
Felicity Dowling, TUSC   192
John Dyer, ND   31
Lab. majority 6,275 (13.43%)
1.82% swing C. to Lab.
(2010: Lab. majority 4,331 (9.79%))

ELMET & ROTHWELL
E. 79,143   T. 57,797 (73.03%)   C. hold
Alec Shelbrooke, C.   27,978
Veronica King, Lab.   19,488
Paul Spivey, UKIP   6,430
Stewart Golton, LD   2,640
Dave Brooks, Green   1,261
C. majority 8,490 (14.69%)
3.29% swing Lab. to C.
(2010: C. majority 4,521 (8.10%))

ELTHAM
E. 63,998   T. 43,157 (67.43%)   Lab. hold
Clive Efford, Lab.   18,393
Spencer Drury, C.   15,700
Peter Whittle, UKIP   6,481
Alex Cunliffe, LD   1,308
James Parker, Green   1,275
Lab. majority 2,693 (6.24%)
1.14% swing C. to Lab.
(2010: Lab. majority 1,663 (3.96%))

ENFIELD NORTH
E. 68,119   T. 46,137 (67.73%)   Lab. gain
*Joan Ryan, Lab.   20,172
Nick de Bois, C.   19,086
Deborah Cairns, UKIP   4,133
David Flint, Green   1,303
Cara Jenkinson, LD   1,059
Yemi Awolola, CPA   207
Joe Simpson, TUSC   177
Lab. majority 1,086 (2.35%)
3.08% swing C. to Lab.
(2010: C. majority 1,692 (3.81%))

ENFIELD SOUTHGATE
E. 64,938   T. 45,812 (70.55%)   C. hold
David Burrowes, C.   22,624
Bambos Charalambous, Lab.   17,871
David Schofield, UKIP   2,109
Jean Robertson-Molloy, Green   1,690
Paul Smith, LD   1,518
C. majority 4,753 (10.38%)
3.41% swing C. to Lab.
(2010: C. majority 7,626 (17.19%))

EPPING FOREST
E. 73,545   T. 49,348 (67.10%)   C. hold
Eleanor Laing, C.   27,027
Andrew Smith, UKIP   9,049
Gareth Barrett, Lab.   7,962
Jon Whitehouse, LD   3,448
Anna Widdup, Green   1,782
Mark Wadsworth, Young   80
C. majority 17,978 (36.43%)
6.79% swing C. to UKIP
(2010: C. majority 15,131 (32.48%))

EPSOM & EWELL
E. 78,834   T. 57,143 (72.67%)   C. hold
Chris Grayling, C.   33,309
Sheila Carlson, Lab.   8,866
Robert Leach, UKIP   7,117
Stephen Gee, LD   5,002
Susan McGrath, Green   2,116
Lionel Blackman, Ind.   612
Gareth Harfoot, ND   121
C. majority 24,443 (42.78%)
0.75% swing C. to Lab.
(2010: C. majority 16,134 (29.36%))

EREWASH
E. 71,937   T. 48,322 (67.17%)   C. hold
*Maggie Throup, C.   20,636
Catherine Atkinson, Lab.   17,052
Philip Rose, UKIP   7,792
Martin Garnett, LD   1,658
Ralph Hierons, Green   1,184
C. majority 3,584 (7.42%)
1.08% swing Lab. to C.
(2010: C. majority 2,501 (5.25%))

ERITH & THAMESMEAD
E. 69,787   T. 42,617 (61.07%)   Lab. hold
Teresa Pearce, Lab.   21,209
Anna Firth, C.   11,684
Ronie Johnson, UKIP   7,368
Simon Waddington, LD   972
Ann Garrett, Green   941
Sidney Cordle, CPA   255
Graham Moore, Eng. Dem.   188
Lab. majority 9,525 (22.35%)
4.46% swing C. to Lab.
(2010: Lab. majority 5,703 (13.43%))

ESHER & WALTON
E. 79,894   T. 56,976 (71.31%)   C. hold
Dominic Raab, C.   35,845
Francis Eldergill, Lab.   7,229
Nicholas Wood, UKIP   5,551
Andrew Davis, LD   5,372
Olivia Palmer, Green   2,355
Matt Heenan, CISTA   396
Della Reynolds, Ind.   228
C. majority 28,616 (50.22%)
1.00% swing Lab. to C.
(2010: C. majority 18,593 (34.09%))

EXETER
E. 76,964   T. 54,018 (70.19%)   Lab. hold
Ben Bradshaw, Lab.   25,062
Dom Morris, C.   17,879
Keith Crawford, UKIP   5,075
Diana Moore, Green   3,491
Joel Mason, LD   2,321
Edmund Potts, TUSC   190
Lab. majority 7,183 (13.30%)
4.04% swing C. to Lab.
(2010: Lab. majority 2,721 (5.21%))

FAREHAM
E. 77,233   T. 54,700 (70.82%)   C. hold
*Suella Fernandes, C.   30,689
Malcolm Jones, UKIP   8,427
Stuart Rose, Lab.   7,800
Matt Winnington, LD   4,814
Miles Grindey, Green   2,129
Nick Gregory, Ind.   705
Harvey Hines, Ind.   136
C. majority 22,262 (40.70%)
5.23% swing C. to UKIP
(2010: C. majority 17,092 (31.45%))

FAVERSHAM & KENT MID
E. 69,523   T. 45,803 (65.88%)   C. hold
*Helen Whately, C.   24,895
Peter Edwards-Daem, UKIP   8,243
Michael Desmond, Lab.   7,403
David Naghi, LD   3,039
Tim Valentine, Green   1,768
Hairy Knorm Davidson, Loony   297
Gary Butler, Eng. Dem.   158
C. majority 16,652 (36.36%)
8.08% swing C. to UKIP
(2010: C. majority 17,088 (36.58%))

FELTHAM & HESTON
E. 82,328   T. 49,405 (60.01%)
                               Lab. Co-op hold
Seema Malhotra, Lab. Co-op   25,845
Simon Nayyar, C.   14,382
Peter Dul, UKIP   6,209
Roger Crouch, LD   1,579
Tony Firkins, Green   1,390
Lab. Co-op majority 11,463 (23.20%)
6.80% swing C. to Lab.
(2010: Lab. Co-op majority 4,658 (9.60%))
(2011: Lab. majority 6,203 (26.71%))

FILTON & BRADLEY STOKE
E. 70,722   T. 49,101 (69.43%)   C. hold
Jack Lopresti, C.   22,920
Ian Boulton, Lab.   13,082
Ben Walker, UKIP   7,261
Peter Bruce, LD   3,581
Diana Warner, Green   2,257
C. majority 9,838 (20.04%)
2.86% swing Lab. to C.
(2010: C. majority 6,914 (14.31%))

FINCHLEY & GOLDERS GREEN
E. 72,049   T. 50,759 (70.45%)   C. hold
Mike Freer, C.   25,835
Sarah Sackman, Lab.   20,173
Richard King, UKIP   1,732
Jonathan Davies, LD   1,662
Adele Ward, Green   1,357
C. majority 5,662 (11.15%)
0.58% swing C. to Lab.
(2010: C. majority 5,809 (12.32%))

FOLKESTONE & HYTHE
E. 83,612   T. 55,010 (65.79%)   C. hold
Damian Collins, C.   26,323
Harriet Yeo, UKIP   12,526
Claire Jeffrey, Lab.   7,939
Lynne Beaumont, LD   4,882
Martin Whybrow, Green   2,956
Seth Cruse, TUSC   244
Rohen Kapur, Young   72
Andy Thomas, SPGB   68
C. majority 13,797 (25.08%)
9.87% swing C. to UKIP
(2010: C. majority 10,122 (19.17%))

FOREST OF DEAN
E. 69,882   T. 49,520 (70.86%)   C. hold
Mark Harper, C.   23,191
Steve Parry-Hearn, Lab.   12,204
Steve Stanbury, UKIP   8,792
James Greenwood, Green   2,703
Christopher Coleman, LD   2,630
C. majority 10,987 (22.19%)
0.25% swing C. to Lab.
(2010: C. majority 11,064 (22.69%))

FYLDE
E. 65,679   T. 43,557 (66.32%)   C. hold
Mark Menzies, C.   21,406
Jed Sullivan, Lab.   8,182
Paul White, UKIP   5,569
Mike Hill, Ind.   5,166
Fred van Mierlo, LD   1,623
Bob Dennett, Green   1,381
Elizabeth Clarkson, Northern   230
C. majority 13,224 (30.36%)
1.07% swing C. to Lab.
(2010: C. majority 13,185 (30.18%))

GAINSBOROUGH
E. 73,212   T. 49,261 (67.29%)   C. hold
Edward Leigh, C.   25,949
David Prescott, Lab.   10,500
John Saxon, UKIP   7,727
Lesley Rollings, LD   3,290
Geoffrey Barnes, Green   1,290
Christopher Darcel, Lincs Ind.   505
C. majority 15,449 (31.36%)
1.14% swing C. to Lab.
(2010: C. majority 10,559 (21.44%))

GARSTON & HALEWOOD
E. 74,063   T. 48,983 (66.14%)   Lab. hold
Maria Eagle, Lab.   33,839
Martin Williams, C.   6,693
Carl Schears, UKIP   4,482
Anna Martin, LD   2,279
William Ward, Green   1,690
Lab. majority 27,146 (55.42%)
6.01% swing C. to Lab.
(2010: Lab. majority 16,877 (39.41%))

GATESHEAD
E. 63,910   T. 38,009 (59.47%)   Lab. hold
Ian Mearns, Lab.   21,549
John Tennant, UKIP   6,765
Thomas Smith, C.   5,562
Frank Hindle, LD   2,585
Andy Redfern, Green   1,548
Lab. majority 14,784 (38.90%)
6.18% swing Lab. to UKIP
(2010: Lab. majority 12,549 (32.80%))

GEDLING
E. 70,046   T. 47,998 (68.52%)   Lab. hold
Vernon Coaker, Lab.   20,307
Carolyn Abbott, C.   17,321
Lee Waters, UKIP   6,930
Robert Swift, LD   1,906
Jim Norris, Green   1,534
Lab. majority 2,986 (6.22%)
1.18% swing C. to Lab.
(2010: Lab. majority 1,859 (3.86%))

GILLINGHAM & RAINHAM
E. 72,609   T. 47,078 (64.84%)   C. hold
Rehman Chishti, C.   22,590
Paul Clark, Lab.   12,060
Mark Hanson, UKIP   9,199
Paul Chaplin, LD   1,707
Neil Williams, Green   1,133
Jacqui Berry, TUSC   273
Roger Peacock, ND   72
Mike Walters, ND   44
C. majority 10,530 (22.37%)
1.91% swing Lab. to C.
(2010: C. majority 8,680 (18.55%))

GLOUCESTER
E. 82,949   T. 52,575 (63.38%)   C. hold
Richard Graham, C.   23,837
Sophy Gardner, Lab.   16,586
Richard Ford, UKIP   7,497
Jeremy Hilton, LD   2,828
Jonathan Ingleby, Green   1,485
George Ridgeon, Loony   227
Sue Powell, TUSC   115
C. majority 7,251 (13.79%)
4.51% swing Lab. to C.
(2010: C. majority 2,420 (4.77%))

GOSPORT
E. 73,271   T. 47,665 (65.05%)   C. hold
Caroline Dinenage, C.   26,364
Christopher Wood, UKIP   9,266
Alan Durrant, Lab.   6,926
Rob Hylands, LD   3,298
Monica Cassidy, Green   1,707
Jeffrey Roberts, ND   104
C. majority 17,098 (35.87%)
6.36% swing C. to UKIP
(2010: C. majority 14,413 (30.71%))

GRANTHAM & STAMFORD
E. 81,151   T. 53,755 (66.24%)   C. hold
Nick Boles, C.   28,399
Marietta King, UKIP   9,410
Barrie Fairbairn, Lab.   9,070
Harrish Bisnauthsing, LD   3,263
Aidan Campbell, Green   1,872
Ian Selby, Ind.   1,017
Jan Hansen, Lincs Ind.   724
C. majority 18,989 (35.33%)
5.96% swing C. to UKIP
(2010: C. majority 14,826 (28.08%))

GRAVESHAM
E. 74,307   T. 50,149 (67.49%)   C. hold
Adam Holloway, C.   23,484
Tanmanjit Singh Dhesi, Lab.   15,114
Sean Marriott, UKIP   9,306
Mark Lindop, Green   1,124
Anne-Marie Bunting, LD   1,111
C. majority 8,370 (16.71%)
1.49% swing C. to Lab.
(2010: C. majority 9,312 (19.69%))

GREAT GRIMSBY
E. 58,484   T. 33,731 (57.68%)   Lab. hold
*Melanie Onn, Lab.   13,414
Marc Jones, C.   8,874
Victoria Ayling, UKIP   8,417
Steve Beasant, LD   1,680
Vicky Dunn, Green   783
Gary Calder, Ind.   390
Val O'Flynn, TUSC   173
Lab. majority 4,540 (13.46%)
5.65% swing C. to Lab.
(2010: Lab. majority 714 (2.17%))

GREAT YARMOUTH
E. 69,793   T. 44,469 (63.72%)   C. hold
Brandon Lewis, C.   19,089
Lara Norris, Lab.   12,935
Alan Grey, UKIP   10,270
James Joyce, LD   1,030
Harry Webb, Green   978
Samuel George Townley, CISTA   167
C. majority 6,154 (13.84%)
1.95% swing Lab. to C.
(2010: C. majority 4,276 (9.93%))

GREENWICH & WOOLWICH
E. 73,315   T. 46,716 (63.72%)   Lab. hold
*Matthew Pennycook, Lab.   24,384
Matt Hartley, C.   12,438
Ryan Acty, UKIP   3,888
Abideen Akinoshun, Green   2,991
Tom Holder, LD   2,645
Lynne Chamberlain, TUSC   370
Lab. majority 11,946 (25.57%)
0.46% swing C. to Lab.
(2010: Lab. majority 10,153 (24.65%))

GUILDFORD
E. 76,554   T. 53,986 (70.52%)   C. hold
Anne Milton, C.   30,802
Kelly-Marie Blundell, LD   8,354
Richard Wilson, Lab.   6,534
Harry Aldridge, UKIP   4,774
John Pletts, Green   2,558
Susan Parker, Guildford   538
John Morris, Peace   230
Gerri Smyth, CISTA   196
C. majority 22,448 (41.58%)
13.79% swing LD to C.
(2010: C. majority 7,782 (14.00%))

HACKNEY NORTH & STOKE
NEWINGTON
E. 83,195   T. 49,887 (59.96%)   Lab. hold
Diane Abbott, Lab.   31,357
Amy Gray, C.   7,349
Heather Finlay, Green   7,281
Simon de Deney, LD   2,492
Keith Fraser, UKIP   1,085
Jon Homan, AWP   221
Jonathan Silberman, Comm. Lge   102
Lab. majority 24,008 (48.12%)
3.85% swing C. to Lab.
(2010: Lab. majority 14,461 (31.11%))

HACKNEY SOUTH & SHOREDITCH
E. 79,962   T. 47,610 (59.54%)
                              Lab. Co-op hold
Meg Hillier, Lab. Co-op   30,663
Jack Tinley, C.   6,420
Charlotte George, Green   5,519
Ben Mathis, LD   2,186
Angus Small, UKIP   1,818
Brian Debus, TUSC   302
Paul Birch, CISTA   297
Taiwo Adewuyi, CPA   236
Russell Higgs, Ind.   78
Bill Rogers, WRP   63
Gordon Shrigley, Campaign   28
Lab. Co-op majority 24,243 (50.92%)
4.36% swing C. to Lab.
(2010: Lab. majority 14,288 (33.34%))

HALESOWEN & ROWLEY REGIS
E. 74,203   T. 43,818 (59.05%)   C. hold
James Morris, C.   18,933
Stephanie Peacock, Lab.   15,851
Dean Perks, UKIP   7,280
Peter Tyzack, LD   905
John Payne, Green   849
C. majority 3,082 (7.03%)
1.22% swing Lab. to C.
(2010: C. majority 2,023 (4.60%))

HALIFAX
E. 70,461   T. 43,753 (62.10%)   Lab. hold
*Holly Lynch, Lab.   17,506
Philip Allott, C.   17,078
Liz Phillips, UKIP   5,621
Mohammad Ilyas, LD   1,629
Gary Scott, Green   1,142
Asama Javed, Respect   465
Trevor Bendrien, Ch. P.   312
Lab. majority 428 (0.98%)
1.20% swing Lab. to C.
(2010: Lab. majority 1,472 (3.38%))

HALTEMPRICE & HOWDEN
E. 71,205   T. 48,757 (68.47%)   C. hold
David Davis, C.   26,414
Edward Hart, Lab.   10,219
John Kitchener, UKIP   6,781
Carl Minns, LD   3,055
Tim Greene, Green   1,809
Diana Wallis, Yorks   479
C. majority 16,195 (33.22%)
0.68% swing C. to Lab.
(2010: C. majority 11,602 (23.81%))

HALTON
E. 72,818   T. 45,023 (61.83%)   Lab. hold
Derek Twigg, Lab.   28,292
Matthew Lloyd, C.   8,007
Glyn Redican, UKIP   6,333
Ryan Bate, LD   1,097
David Melvin, Green   1,017
Vic Turton, Ind.   277
Lab. majority 20,285 (45.05%)
3.77% swing C. to Lab.
(2010: Lab. majority 15,504 (37.51%))

HAMMERSMITH
E. 72,254   T. 47,960 (66.38%)   Lab. hold
Andy Slaughter, Lab.   23,981
Charlie Dewhirst, C.   17,463
Millicent Scott, LD   2,224
David Akan, Green   2,105
Richard Wood, UKIP   2,105
Stephen Brennan, ND   82
Lab. majority 6,518 (13.59%)
3.06% swing C. to Lab.
(2010: Lab. majority 3,549 (7.48%))

HAMPSHIRE EAST
E. 72,600   T. 51,649 (71.14%)   C. hold
Damian Hinds, C.   31,334
Peter Baillie, UKIP   6,187
Richard Robinson, LD   5,732
Alex Wilks, Lab.   5,220
Peter Bisset, Green   3,176
C. majority 25,147 (48.69%)
2.61% swing C. to UKIP
(2010: C. majority 13,497 (26.30%))

HAMPSHIRE NORTH EAST
E. 74,025   T. 54,000 (72.95%)   C. hold
*Ranil Jayawardena, C.   35,573
Graham Cockarill, LD   5,657
Amran Hussain, Lab.   5,290
Robert Blay, UKIP   4,732
Andrew Johnston, Green   2,364
Mad Max Bobetsky, Loony   384
C. majority 29,916 (55.40%)
10.14% swing LD to C.
(2010: C. majority 18,597 (35.13%))

HAMPSHIRE NORTH WEST
E. 79,223   T. 55,195 (69.67%)   C. hold
*Kit Malthouse, C.   32,052
Sue Perkins, UKIP   8,109
Andrew Adams, Lab.   7,342
Alex Payton, LD   5,151
Dan Hill, Green   2,541
C. majority 23,943 (43.38%)
4.88% swing C. to UKIP
(2010: C. majority 18,583 (34.87%))

HAMPSTEAD & KILBURN
E. 80,241   T. 53,964 (67.25%)   Lab. hold
*Tulip Siddiq, Lab.	23,977
Simon Marcus, C.	22,839
Maajid Nawaz, LD	3,039
Rebecca Johnson, Green	2,387
Magnus Nielsen, UKIP	1,532
The Eurovisionary Carroll, Ind.	113
Robin Ellison, U Party	77

Lab. majority 1,138 (2.11%)
1.01% swing C. to Lab.
(2010: Lab. majority 42 (0.08%))

HARBOROUGH
E. 77,760   T. 52,471 (67.48%)   C. hold
Edward Garnier, C.	27,675
Sundip Meghani, Lab.	8,043
Mark Hunt, UKIP	7,539
Zuffar Haq, LD	7,037
Darren Woodiwiss, Green	2,177

C. majority 19,632 (37.41%)
0.59% swing Lab. to C.
(2010: C. majority 9,797 (17.83%))

HARLOW
E. 67,994   T. 44,251 (65.08%)   C. hold
Robert Halfon, C.	21,623
Suzy Stride, Lab.	13,273
Sam Stopplecamp, UKIP	7,208
Murray Sackwild, Green	954
Geoff Seeff, LD	904
David Brown, TUSC	174
Eddy Butler, Eng. Dem.	115

C. majority 8,350 (18.87%)
3.82% swing Lab. to C.
(2010: C. majority 4,925 (11.22%))

HARROGATE & KNARESBOROUGH
E. 77,379   T. 53,376 (68.98%)   C. hold
Andrew Jones, C.	28,153
Helen Flynn, LD	11,782
David Simister, UKIP	5,681
Jan Williams, Lab.	5,409
Shan Oakes, Green	2,351

C. majority 16,371 (30.67%)
14.36% swing LD to C.
(2010: C. majority 1,039 (1.96%))

HARROW EAST
E. 70,980   T. 49,000 (69.03%)   C. hold
Bob Blackman, C.	24,668
Uma Kumaran, Lab.	19,911
Aidan Powlesland, UKIP	2,333
Ross Barlow, LD	1,037
Emma Wallace, Green	846
Nana Asante, TUSC	205

C. majority 4,757 (9.71%)
1.31% swing Lab. to C.
(2010: C. majority 3,403 (7.09%))

HARROW WEST
E. 69,643 T. 46,603 (66.92%)
Lab. Co-op hold
Gareth Thomas, Lab. Co-op	21,885
Hannah David, C.	19,677
Mohammad Ali Bhatti, UKIP	2,047
Chris Noyce, LD	1,567
Rowan Langley, Green	1,310
Kailash Trivedi, Ind.	117

Lab. Co-op majority 2,208 (4.74%)
1.04% swing Lab. to C.
(2010: Lab. Co-op majority 3,143 (6.82%))

HARTLEPOOL
E. 69,516   T. 39,490 (56.81%)   Lab. hold
Iain Wright, Lab.	14,076
Phillip Broughton, UKIP	11,052
Richard Royal, C.	8,256
Stephen Picton, Ind.	2,954
Michael Holt, Green	1,341
Sandra Allison, Hospital	849
Hilary Allen, LD	761
John Hobbs, Ind.	201

Lab. majority 3,024 (7.66%)
13.93% swing Lab. to UKIP
(2010: Lab. majority 5,509 (14.41%))

HARWICH & ESSEX NORTH
E. 69,289   T. 48,432 (69.90%)   C. hold
Bernard Jenkin, C.	24,722
Edward Carlsson Browne, Lab.	9,548
Mark Hughes, UKIP	8,464
Dominic Graham, LD	3,576
Christopher Flossman, Green	2,122

C. majority 15,174 (31.33%)
2.17% swing Lab. to C.
(2010: C. majority 11,447 (23.36%))

HASTINGS & RYE
E. 75,095   T. 50,927 (67.82%)   C. hold
Amber Rudd, C.	22,686
Sarah Owen, Lab. Co-op	17,890
Andrew Michael, UKIP	6,786
Jake Bowers, Green	1,951
Nick Perry, LD	1,614

C. majority 4,796 (9.42%)
2.71% swing Lab. to C.
(2010: C. majority 1,993 (4.00%))

HAVANT
E. 70,573   T. 44,828 (63.52%)   C. hold
*Alan Mak, C.	23,159
John Perry, UKIP	9,239
Graham Giles, Lab.	7,149
Steve Sollitt, LD	2,929
Tim Dawes, Green	2,352

C. majority 13,920 (31.05%)
7.05% swing C. to UKIP
(2010: C. majority 12,160 (27.70%))

HAYES & HARLINGTON
E. 74,875   T. 45,056 (60.17%)   Lab. hold
John McDonnell, Lab.	26,843
Pearl Lewis, C.	11,143
Cliff Dixon, UKIP	5,388
Satnam Khalsa, LD	888
Alick Munro, Green	794

Lab. majority 15,700 (34.85%)
4.73% swing C. to Lab.
(2010: Lab. majority 10,824 (25.39%))

HAZEL GROVE
E. 63,098   T. 43,219 (68.50%)   C. gain
*William Wragg, C.	17,882
Lisa Smart, LD	11,330
Michael Taylor, Lab.	7,584
Darran Palmer, UKIP	5,283
Graham Reid, Green	1,140

C. majority 6,552 (15.16%)
15.17% swing LD to C.
(2010: LD majority 6,371 (15.18%))

HEMEL HEMPSTEAD
E. 74,616   T. 49,633 (66.52%)   C. hold
Mike Penning, C.	26,245
Tony Breslin, Lab.	11,825
Howard Koch, UKIP	7,249
Rabi Martins, LD	2,402
Alan Borgars, Green	1,660
Brian Hall, Ind.	252

C. majority 14,420 (29.05%)
0.05% swing C. to Lab.
(2010: C. majority 13,406 (27.10%))

HEMSWORTH
E. 72,714   T. 42,406 (58.32%)   Lab. hold
Jon Trickett, Lab.	21,772
Chris Pearson, C.	9,694
Steve Ashton, UKIP	8,565
Mary Macqueen, LD	1,357
Martin Roberts, Yorks	1,018

Lab. majority 12,078 (28.48%)
3.01% swing C. to Lab.
(2010: Lab. majority 9,844 (22.45%))

HENDON
E. 74,658   T. 49,630 (66.48%)   C. hold
Matthew Offord, C.	24,328
Andrew Dismore, Lab.	20,604
Raymond Shamash, UKIP	2,595
Alasdair Hill, LD	1,088
Ben Samuel, Green	1,015

C. majority 3,724 (7.50%)
3.64% swing Lab. to C.
(2010: C. majority 106 (0.23%))

HENLEY
E. 78,243   T. 55,236 (70.60%)   C. hold
John Howell, C.	32,292
Sam Juthani, Lab.	6,917
Susan Cooper, LD	6,205
Christopher Jones, UKIP	6,007
Mark Stevenson, Green	3,815

C. majority 25,375 (45.94%)
0.34% swing Lab. to C.
(2010: C. majority 16,588 (30.99%))

HEREFORD & HEREFORDSHIRE SOUTH
E. 70,711   T. 47,257 (66.83%)   C. hold
Jesse Norman, C.	24,844
Nigel Ely, UKIP	7,954
Anna Coda, Lab.	6,042
Lucy Hurds, LD	5,002
Diana Toynbee, Green	3,415

C. majority 16,890 (35.74%)
3.55% swing C. to UKIP
(2010: C. majority 2,481 (5.13%))

HEREFORDSHIRE NORTH
E. 66,683   T. 48,023 (72.02%)   C. hold
Bill Wiggin, C.	26,716
Jonathan Oakton, UKIP	6,720
Jeanie Falconer, LD	5,768
Sally Prentice, Lab.	5,478
Daisy Blench, Green	3,341

C. majority 19,996 (41.64%)
2.23% swing C. to UKIP
(2010: C. majority 9,887 (20.78%))

HERTFORD & STORTFORD
E. 78,906   T. 56,277 (71.32%)   C. hold
Mark Prisk, C.	31,593
Katherine Chibah, Lab.	10,084
Adrian Baker, UKIP	7,534
Michael Green, LD	4,385
Sophie Christophy, Green	2,681

C. majority 21,509 (38.22%)
0.93% swing C. to Lab.
(2010: C. majority 15,437 (27.88%))

HERTFORDSHIRE NORTH EAST
E. 73,944   T. 52,287 (70.71%)   C. hold
Oliver Heald, C.   28,949
Chris York, Lab.   9,869
William Compton, UKIP   6,728
Joe Jordan, LD   3,952
Mario May, Green   2,789
C. majority 19,080 (36.49%)
0.30% swing C. to Lab.
(2010: C. majority 15,194 (30.13%))

HERTFORDSHIRE SOUTH WEST
E. 79,666   T. 57,267 (71.88%)   C. hold
David Gauke, C.   32,608
Simon Diggins, Lab.   9,345
Mark Anderson, UKIP   6,603
Nigel Quinton, LD   5,872
Charlotte Pardy, Green   2,583
Graham Cartmell, CSP   256
C. majority 23,263 (40.62%)
1.05% swing C. to Lab.
(2010: C. majority 14,920 (26.29%))

HERTSMERE
E. 73,753   T. 50,091 (67.92%)   C. hold
*Oliver Dowden, C.   29,696
Richard Butler, Lab.   11,235
Frank Ward, UKIP   6,383
Sophie Bowler, LD   2,777
C. majority 18,461 (36.85%)
0.19% swing C. to Lab.
(2010: C. majority 17,605 (37.24%))

HEXHAM
E. 60,614   T. 43,345 (71.51%)   C. hold
Guy Opperman, C.   22,834
Liam Carr, Lab.   10,803
David Nicholson, UKIP   4,302
Jeff Reid, LD   2,961
Lee Williscroft-Ferris, Green   2,445
C. majority 12,031 (27.76%)
1.76% swing Lab. to C.
(2010: C. majority 5,788 (13.31%))

HEYWOOD & MIDDLETON
E. 79,989   T. 48,538 (60.68%)   Lab. hold
*Liz McInnes, Lab.   20,926
John Bickley, UKIP   15,627
Iain Gartside, C.   9,268
Anthony Smith, LD   1,607
Abi Jackson, Green   1,110
Lab. majority 5,299 (10.92%)
13.28% swing Lab. to UKIP
(2010: Lab. majority 5,971 (12.95%))
(2014: Lab. majority 617 (2.17%))

HIGH PEAK
E. 73,336   T. 50,789 (69.26%)   C. hold
Andrew Bingham, C.   22,836
Caitlin Bisknell, Lab.   17,942
Ian Guiver, UKIP   5,811
Stephen Worrall, LD   2,389
Charlotte Farrell, Green   1,811
C. majority 4,894 (9.64%)
0.17% swing Lab. to C.
(2010: C. majority 4,677 (9.29%))

HITCHIN & HARPENDEN
E. 74,839   T. 55,375 (73.99%)   C. hold
Peter Lilley, C.   31,488
Rachel Burgin, Lab.   11,433
John Stocker, UKIP   4,917
Pauline Pearce, LD   4,484
Richard Wise, Green   3,053
C. majority 20,055 (36.22%)
2.42% swing C. to Lab.
(2010: C. majority 15,271 (27.91%))

HOLBORN & ST PANCRAS
E. 86,864   T. 54,917 (63.22%)   Lab. hold
*Keir Starmer, Lab.   29,062
Will Blair, C.   12,014
Natalie Bennett, Green   7,013
Jill Fraser, LD   3,555
Maxine Spencer, UKIP   2,740
Shane O'Donnell, CISTA   252
Vanessa Hudson, AWP   173
David O'Sullivan, SEP   108
Lab. majority 17,048 (31.04%)
2.65% swing C. to Lab.
(2010: Lab. majority 9,942 (18.19%))

HORNCHURCH & UPMINSTER
E. 79,331   T. 55,236 (69.63%)   C. hold
Angela Watkinson, C.   27,051
Lawrence Webb, UKIP   13,977
Paul McGeary, Lab.   11,103
Jonathan Mitchell, LD   1,501
Melanie Collins, Green   1,411
Paul Borg, BNP   193
C. majority 13,074 (23.67%)
11.22% swing C. to UKIP
(2010: C. majority 16,371 (30.66%))

HORNSEY & WOOD GREEN
E. 79,241   T. 57,785 (72.92%)   Lab. gain
*Catherine West, Lab.   29,417
Lynne Featherstone, LD   18,359
Suhail Rahuja, C.   5,347
Gordon Peters, Green   3,146
Clive Morrison, UKIP   1,271
Helen Spiby-Vann, CPA   118
Frank Sweeney, WRP   82
Geoff Moseley, Hoi   45
Lab. majority 11,058 (19.14%)
15.81% swing LD to Lab.
(2010: LD majority 6,875 (12.49%))

HORSHAM
E. 78,181   T. 56,925 (72.81%)   C. hold
*Jeremy Quin, C.   32,627
Roger Arthur, UKIP   7,969
Morwen Millson, LD   6,647
Martyn Davis, Lab.   6,499
Darrin Green, Green   2,198
James Smith, S. New   375
Jim Duggan, Peace   307
Jim Rae, Ind.   303
C. majority 24,658 (43.32%)
2.17% swing C. to UKIP
(2010: C. majority 11,460 (20.52%))

HOUGHTON & SUNDERLAND SOUTH
E. 68,316   T. 38,489 (56.34%)   Lab. hold
Bridget Phillipson, Lab.   21,218
Richard Elvin, UKIP   8,280
Stewart Hay, C.   7,105
Alan Robinson, Green   1,095
Jim Murray, LD   791
Lab. majority 12,938 (33.61%)
7.01% swing Lab. to UKIP
(2010: Lab. majority 10,990 (28.91%))

HOVE
E. 73,505   T. 52,214 (71.03%)   Lab. gain
*Peter Kyle, Lab.   22,082
Graham Cox, C.   20,846
Christopher Hawtree, Green   3,569
Kevin Smith, UKIP   3,265
Peter Lambell, LD   1,861
Jenny Barnard-Langston, Ind.   322
Dave Hill, TUSC   144
The Dame Dixon, Loony   125
Lab. majority 1,236 (2.37%)
3.06% swing C. to Lab.
(2010: C. majority 1,868 (3.75%))

HUDDERSFIELD
E. 65,265   T. 40,478 (62.02%)
                          Lab. Co-op hold
Barry Sheerman, Lab. Co-op   18,186
Itrat Ali, C.   10,841
Rob Butler, UKIP   5,948
Andrew Cooper, Green   2,798
Zulfiqar Ali, LD   2,365
Mike Forster, TUSC   340
Lab. Co-op majority 7,345 (18.15%)
3.56% swing C. to Lab.
(2010: Lab. majority 4,472 (11.04%))

HULL EAST
E. 65,606   T. 35,144 (53.57%)   Lab. hold
Karl Turner, Lab.   18,180
Richard Barrett, UKIP   7,861
Christine Mackay, C.   5,593
David Nolan, LD   2,294
Sarah Walpole, Green   806
Martin Clayton, Yorks   270
Mike Cooper, NF   86
Val Hoodless, Soc. Dem.   54
Lab. majority 10,319 (29.36%)
5.27% swing Lab. to UKIP
(2010: Lab. majority 8,597 (25.15%))

HULL NORTH
E. 63,650   T. 35,336 (55.52%)   Lab. hold
Diana Johnson, Lab.   18,661
Sergi Singh, UKIP   5,762
Dehenna Davison, C.   5,306
Mike Ross, LD   3,175
Martin Deane, Green   2,066
Vicky Butler, Yorks   366
Lab. majority 12,899 (36.50%)
0.70% swing UKIP to Lab.
(2010: Lab. majority 641 (1.93%))

HULL WEST & HESSLE
E. 59,008   T. 31,803 (53.90%)   Lab. hold
Alan Johnson, Lab.   15,646
Paul Salvidge, UKIP   6,313
Jo Barker, C.   5,561
Claire Thomas, LD   3,169
Angela Needham, Green   943
Paul Spooner, TUSC   171
Lab. majority 9,333 (29.35%)
3.88% swing Lab. to UKIP
(2010: Lab. majority 5,742 (18.23%))

HUNTINGDON
E. 82,404   T. 55,926 (67.87%)   C. hold
Jonathan Djanogly, C.   29,652
Nik Johnson, Lab.   10,248
Paul Bullen, UKIP   9,473
Rod Cantrill, LD   4,375
Tom MacLennan, Green   2,178
C. majority 19,404 (34.70%)
1.57% swing C. to Lab.
(2010: C. majority 10,819 (19.94%))

HYNDBURN
E. 68,341   T. 42,887 (62.75%)   Lab. hold
Graham Jones, Lab.   18,076
Kevin Horkin, C.   13,676
Janet Brown, UKIP   9,154
Kerry Gormley, Green   1,122
Alison Firth, LD   859
Lab. majority 4,400 (10.26%)
1.51% swing C. to Lab.
(2010: Lab. majority 3,090 (7.24%))

ILFORD NORTH
E. 78,162 T. 48,932 (62.60%) Lab. gain
*Wes Streeting, Lab.   21,463
Lee Scott, C.   20,874
Philip Hyde, UKIP   4,355
Rich Clare, LD   1,130
David Reynolds, Green   1,023
Doris Osen, Ind.   87
Lab. majority 589 (1.20%)
6.35% swing C. to Lab.
(2010: C. majority 5,404 (11.49%))

ILFORD SOUTH
E. 95,023 T. 51,912 (54.63%)
                          Lab. Co-op hold
Mike Gapes, Lab. Co-op   33,232
Chris Chapman, C.   13,455
Amjad Khan, UKIP   2,705
RoseMary Warrington, Green   1,506
Ashburn Holder, LD   1,014
Lab. Co-op majority 19,777 (38.10%)
8.02% swing C. to Lab.
(2010: Lab. Co-op majority 11,287
(22.05%))

IPSWICH
E. 74,498 T. 48,694 (65.36%) C. hold
Ben Gummer, C.   21,794
David Ellesmere, Lab.   18,061
Maria Vigneau, UKIP   5,703
Barry Broom, Green   1,736
Chika Akinwale, LD   1,400
C. majority 3,733 (7.67%)
1.62% swing Lab. to C.
(2010: C. majority 2,079 (4.43%))

ISLE OF WIGHT
E. 108,804 T. 70,300 (64.61%) C. hold
Andrew Turner, C.   28,591
Iain McKie, UKIP   14,888
Vix Lowthion, Green   9,404
Stewart Blackmore, Lab.   8,984
David Goodall, LD   5,235
Ian Stephens, Ind.   3,198
C. majority 13,703 (19.49%)
11.87% swing C. to UKIP
(2010: C. majority 10,527 (14.98%))

ISLINGTON NORTH
E. 73,325 T. 49,234 (67.14%) Lab. hold
Jeremy Corbyn, Lab.   29,659
Alex Burghart, C.   8,465
Caroline Russell, Green   5,043
Julian Gregory, LD   3,984
Gregory Clough, UKIP   1,971
Bill Martin, SPGB   112
Lab. majority 21,194 (43.05%)
1.39% swing C. to Lab.
(2010: Lab. majority 12,401 (27.83%))

ISLINGTON SOUTH & FINSBURY
E. 68,127 T. 44,270 (64.98%) Lab. hold
Emily Thornberry, Lab.   22,547
Mark Lim, C.   9,839
Terry Stacy, LD   4,829
Pete Muswell, UKIP   3,375
Charlie Kiss, Green   3,371
Jay Kirton, CISTA   309
Lab. majority 12,708 (28.71%)
2.92% swing C. to Lab.
(2010: Lab. majority 3,569 (8.19%))

JARROW
E. 63,882 T. 38,564 (60.37%) Lab. hold
Stephen Hepburn, Lab.   21,464
Steven Harrison, UKIP   7,583
Nick Mason, C.   6,584
David Herbert, Green   1,310
Stan Collins, LD   1,238
Norman Hall, TUSC   385
Lab. majority 13,881 (35.99%)
swing N/A
(2010: Lab. majority 12,908 (33.28%))

KEIGHLEY
E. 68,865 T. 49,123 (71.33%) C. hold
Kris Hopkins, C.   21,766
John Grogan, Lab.   18,713
Paul Latham, UKIP   5,662
Ros Brown, Green   1,661
Gareth Epps, LD   1,321
C. majority 3,053 (6.22%)
0.03% swing Lab. to C.
(2010: C. majority 2,940 (6.16%))

KENILWORTH & SOUTHAM
E. 65,245 T. 48,791 (74.78%) C. hold
Jeremy Wright, C.   28,474
Bally Singh, Lab.   7,472
Harry Cottam, UKIP   5,467
Richard Dickson, LD   4,913
Rob Ballantyne, Green   1,956
Nick Blunderbuss Green, Loony   370
Jon Foster-Smith, Digital   139
C. majority 21,002 (43.04%)
1.91% swing Lab. to C.
(2010: C. majority 12,552 (25.92%))

KENSINGTON
E. 61,333 T. 34,828 (56.79%) C. gain
*Lady (Victoria) Borwick, C.   18,199
Rod Abouharb, Lab.   10,838
Robin McGhee, LD   1,962
Robina Rose, Green   1,765
Jack Bovill, UKIP   1,557
Tony Auguste, CISTA   211
Andrew Knight, AWP   158
Toby Abse, Green Soc.   115
Roland Courtenay, New IC   23
C. majority 7,361 (21.14%)
1.69% swing C. to Lab.
(2010: C. majority 8,616 (24.51%))

KETTERING
E. 70,155 T. 47,218 (67.31%) C. hold
Philip Hollobone, C.   24,467
Rhea Keehn, Lab.   11,877
Jonathan Bullock, UKIP   7,600
Rob Reeves, Green   1,633
Chris McGlynn, LD   1,490
Derek Hilling, Eng. Dem.   151
C. majority 12,590 (26.66%)
3.72% swing Lab. to C.
(2010: C. majority 9,094 (19.21%))

KINGSTON & SURBITON
E. 81,277 T. 59,253 (72.90%) C. gain
*James Berry, C.   23,249
Ed Davey, LD   20,415
Lee Godfrey, Lab.   8,574
Ben Roberts, UKIP   4,321
Clare Keogh, Green   2,322
Daniel Gill, CPA   198
Laurel Fogarty, TUSC   174
C. majority 2,834 (4.78%)
9.01% swing LD to C.
(2010: LD majority 7,560 (13.24%))

KINGSWOOD
E. 67,992 T. 48,125 (70.78%) C. hold
Chris Skidmore, C.   23,252
Jo McCarron, Lab.   14,246
Duncan Odgers, UKIP   7,133
Adam Boyden, LD   1,827
Cezara Nanu, Green   1,370
Julie Lake, BNP   164
Richard Worth, TUSC   84
Liam Bryan, Vapers   49
C. majority 9,006 (18.71%)
6.81% swing Lab. to C.
(2010: C. majority 2,445 (5.10%))

KNOWSLEY
E. 79,109 T. 50,728 (64.12%) Lab. hold
George Howarth, Lab.   39,628
Louise Bours, UKIP   4,973
Alice Bramall, C.   3,367
Carl Cashman, LD   1,490
Vikki Gregorich, Green   1,270
Lab. majority 34,655 (68.32%)
swing N/A
(2010: Lab. majority 25,686 (57.52%))

LANCASHIRE WEST
E. 70,945 T. 49,676 (70.02%) Lab. hold
Rosie Cooper, Lab.   24,474
Paul Greenall, C.   16,114
Jack Sen, UKIP   6,058
Ben Basson, Green   1,582
Daniel Lewis, LD   1,298
David Braid, WVPTFP   150
Lab. majority 8,360 (16.83%)
3.93% swing C. to Lab.
(2010: Lab. majority 4,343 (8.96%))

LANCASTER & FLEETWOOD
E. 60,883 T. 41,738 (68.55%) Lab. gain
*Cat Smith, Lab.   17,643
Eric Ollerenshaw, C.   16,378
Matthew Atkins, UKIP   4,060
Chris Coates, Green   2,093
Robin Long, LD   1,390
Harold Elletson, Northern   174
Lab. majority 1,265 (3.03%)
1.91% swing C. to Lab.
(2010: C. majority 333 (0.78%))

LEEDS CENTRAL
E. 81,799 T. 45,048 (55.07%) Lab. hold
Hilary Benn, Lab.   24,758
Nicola Wilson, C.   7,791
Luke Senior, UKIP   7,082
Michael Hayton, Green   3,558
Emma Spriggs, LD   1,529
Liz Kitching, TUSC   330
Lab. majority 16,967 (37.66%)
4.27% swing C. to Lab.
(2010: Lab. majority 10,645 (28.47%))

LEEDS EAST
E. 64,754 T. 38,196 (58.99%) Lab. hold
*Richard Burgon, Lab.   20,530
Ryan Stephenson, C.   7,997
Mark Maniatt, UKIP   7,256
Ed Sanderson, LD   1,296
Kate Bisson, Green   1,117
Lab. majority 12,533 (32.81%)
2.80% swing C. to Lab.
(2010: Lab. majority 10,293 (27.22%))

LEEDS NORTH EAST
E. 69,097   T. 48,291 (69.89%)   Lab. hold
Fabian Hamilton, Lab.   23,137
Simon Wilson, C.   15,887
Warren Hendon, UKIP   3,706
Aqila Choudhry, LD   2,569
Emma Carter, Green   2,541
Celia Foote, Green Soc.   451
Lab. majority 7,250 (15.01%)
2.73% swing C. to Lab.
(2010: Lab. majority 4,545 (9.56%))

LEEDS NORTH WEST
E. 61,974   T. 43,357 (69.96%)   LD hold
Greg Mulholland, LD   15,948
Alex Sobel, Lab.   13,041
Alex Story, C.   8,083
Tim Goodall, Green   3,042
Julian Metcalfe, UKIP   2,997
Bob Buxton, Yorks   143
Mike Davies, Green Soc.   79
Mark Flanagan, Above   24
LD majority 2,907 (6.70%)
9.90% swing LD to Lab.
(2010: LD majority 9,103 (20.93%))

LEEDS WEST
E. 64,950   T. 38,423 (59.16%)   Lab. hold
Rachel Reeves, Lab.   18,456
Alex Pierre-Traves, C.   7,729
Anne Murgatroyd, UKIP   7,104
Andrew Pointon, Green   3,217
Laura Coyle, LD   1,495
Matthew West, CISTA   217
Ben Mayor, TUSC   205
Lab. majority 10,727 (27.92%)
2.67% swing C. to Lab.
(2010: Lab. majority 7,016 (18.10%))

LEICESTER EAST
E. 75,430   T. 48,068 (63.73%)   Lab. hold
Keith Vaz, Lab.   29,386
Kishan Devani, C.   11,034
Susanna Steptoe, UKIP   4,290
Nimit Jethwa, Green   1,468
Dave Raval, LD   1,233
Michael Barker, TUSC   540
Tom Darwood, ND   117
Lab. majority 18,352 (38.18%)
4.42% swing C. to Lab.
(2010: Lab. majority 14,082 (29.34%))

LEICESTER SOUTH
E. 73,518   T. 45,962 (62.52%)
                          Lab. Co-op hold
Jon Ashworth, Lab. Co-op   27,473
Leon Hadji-Nikolaou, C.   9,628
Peter Stone, UKIP   3,832
Gabby Garcia, Green   2,533
Anita Prabhakar, LD   2,127
Andrew Walton, TUSC   349
Lab. Co-op majority 17,845 (38.87%)
7.32% swing C. to Lab.
(2010: Lab. majority 8,808 (18.69%))
(2011: Lab. majority 12,078 (35.34%))

LEICESTER WEST
E. 63,204   T. 34,522 (54.62%)   Lab. hold
Liz Kendall, Lab.   16,051
Paul Bessant, C.   8,848
Stuart Young, UKIP   5,950
Peter Hague, Green   1,878
Ian Bradwell, LD   1,507
Heather Rawling, TUSC   288
Lab. majority 7,203 (20.86%)
4.83% swing C. to Lab.
(2010: Lab. majority 4,017 (11.21%))

LEICESTERSHIRE NORTH WEST
E. 72,194   T. 51,548 (71.40%)   C. hold
Andrew Bridgen, C.   25,505
Jamie McMahon, Lab. Co-op   14,132
Andy McWilliam, UKIP   8,704
Mark Argent, LD   2,033
Benjamin Gravestock, Green   1,174
C. majority 11,373 (22.06%)
3.80% swing Lab. to C.
(2010: C. majority 7,511 (14.46%))

LEICESTERSHIRE SOUTH
E. 76,877   T. 53,926 (70.15%)   C. hold
*Alberto Costa, C.   28,700
Amanda Hack, Lab.   11,876
Barry Mahoney, UKIP   9,363
Geoffrey Welsh, LD   3,987
C. majority 16,824 (31.20%)
1.30% swing Lab. to C.
(2010: C. majority 15,524 (28.44%))

LEIGH
E. 75,974   T. 45,123 (59.39%)   Lab. hold
Andy Burnham, Lab.   24,312
Louisa Townson, C.   10,216
Les Leggett, UKIP   8,903
Bill Winlow, LD   1,150
Stephen Hall, TUSC   542
Lab. majority 14,096 (31.24%)
2.07% swing C. to Lab.
(2010: Lab. majority 12,011 (27.09%))

LEWES
E. 69,481   T. 50,540 (72.74%)   C. gain
*Maria Caulfield, C.   19,206
Norman Baker, LD   18,123
Ray Finch, UKIP   5,427
Lloyd Russell-Moyle, Lab.   5,000
Alfie Stirling, Green   2,784
C. majority 1,083 (2.14%)
8.70% swing LD to C.
(2010: LD majority 7,647 (15.27%))

LEWISHAM DEPTFORD
E. 73,426   T. 47,426 (64.59%)   Lab. hold
*Vicky Foxcroft, Lab.   28,572
Bim Afolami, C.   7,056
John Coughlin, Green   5,932
Michael Bukola, LD   2,497
Massimo Dimambro, UKIP   2,013
Helen Mercer, PBP   666
Malcolm Martin, CPA   300
Chris Flood, TUSC   286
Phillip Badger, Dem. Ref.   74
David Harvey, ND   30
Lab. majority 21,516 (45.37%)
2.57% swing C. to Lab.
(2010: Lab. majority 12,499 (30.32%))

LEWISHAM EAST
E. 73,428   T. 42,923 (58.46%)   Lab. hold
Heidi Alexander, Lab.   23,907
Peter Fortune, C.   9,574
Anne Marie Waters, UKIP   3,886
Julia Fletcher, LD   2,455
Storm Poorun, Green   2,429
Nick Long, PBP   390
Maureen Martin, CPA   282
Lab. majority 14,333 (33.39%)
6.97% swing C. to Lab.
(2010: Lab. majority 6,216 (14.90%))

LEWISHAM WEST & PENGE
E. 72,289   T. 48,125 (66.57%)   Lab. hold
Jim Dowd, Lab.   24,347
Russell Jackson, C.   11,633
Tom Chance, Green   4,077
Gary Harding, UKIP   3,764
Alex Feakes, LD   3,709
Martin Powell-Davies, TUSC   391
David Hansom, Ind.   160
George Whale, Lib. GB   44
Lab. majority 12,714 (26.42%)
5.42% swing C. to Lab.
(2010: Lab. majority 5,828 (12.94%))

LEYTON & WANSTEAD
E. 64,746   T. 40,705 (62.87%)   Lab. hold
John Cryer, Lab.   23,858
Matthew Scott, C.   8,939
Ashley Gunstock, Green   2,974
Rosamund Beattie, UKIP   2,341
Carl Quilliam, LD   2,304
Mahtab Aziz, Ind.   289
Lab. majority 14,919 (36.65%)
7.64% swing C. to Lab.
(2010: Lab. majority 6,416 (15.98%))

LICHFIELD
E. 83,339   T. 51,467 (61.76%)   C. hold
Michael Fabricant, C.   28,389
Chris Worsey, Lab.   10,200
John Rackham, UKIP   8,082
Paul Ray, LD   2,700
Robert Pass, Green   1,976
Andy Bennetts, Class War   120
C. majority 18,189 (35.34%)
0.39% swing Lab. to C.
(2010: C. majority 17,683 (34.29%))

LINCOLN
E. 74,121   T. 46,852 (63.21%)   C. hold
Karl McCartney, C.   19,976
Lucy Rigby, Lab.   18,533
Nick Smith, UKIP   5,721
Ross Pepper, LD   1,992
Elaine Smith, TUSC   344
Helen Powell, Lincs Ind.   286
C. majority 1,443 (3.08%)
0.38% swing Lab. to C.
(2010: C. majority 1,058 (2.31%))

LIVERPOOL RIVERSIDE
E. 70,950   T. 44,263 (62.39%)
                          Lab. Co-op hold
Louise Ellman, Lab. Co-op   29,835
Martin Dobson, Green   5,372
Jackson Ng, C.   4,245
Joe Chiffers, UKIP   2,510
Paul Childs, LD   1,719
Tony Mulhearn, TUSC   582
Lab. Co-op majority 24,463 (55.27%)
0.26% swing Lab. to Green
(2010: Lab. majority 14,173 (36.53%))

LIVERPOOL WALTON
E. 62,868   T. 38,403 (61.09%)   Lab. hold
Steve Rotheram, Lab.   31,222
Steve Flatman, UKIP   3,445
Norsheen Bhatti, C.   1,802
Jonathan Clatworthy, Green   956
Pat Moloney, LD   899
Alexander Karran, Ind.   56
Jonathan Dzon, Plural   23
Lab. majority 27,777 (72.33%)
1.49% swing UKIP to Lab.
(2010: Lab. majority 19,818 (57.72%))

LIVERPOOL WAVERTREE
E. 61,731 T. 40,974 (66.38%)
Lab. Co-op hold
Luciana Berger, Lab. Co-op	28,401
James Pearson, C.	4,098
Adam Heatherington, UKIP	3,375
Leo Evans, LD	2,454
Peter Cranie, Green	2,140
Dave Walsh, TUSC	362
Niamh McCarthy, Ind.	144

Lab. Co-op majority 24,303 (59.31%)
6.84% swing C. to Lab.
(2010: Lab. Co-op majority 7,167 (18.90%))

LIVERPOOL WEST DERBY
E. 63,875 T. 41,031 (64.24%)
Lab. Co-op hold
Stephen Twigg, Lab. Co-op	30,842
Neil Miney, UKIP	3,475
Ed McRandal, C.	2,710
Steve Radford, Lib.	2,049
Rebecca Lawson, Green	996
Paul Twigger, LD	959

Lab. Co-op majority 27,367 (66.70%)
2.80% swing UKIP to Lab.
(2010: Lab. Co-op majority 18,467 (51.61%))

LOUGHBOROUGH
E. 72,644 T. 52,020 (71.61%) C. hold
Nicky Morgan, C.	25,762
Matthew O'Callaghan, Lab.	16,579
Bill Piper, UKIP	5,704
Steve Coltman, LD	2,130
Matt Sisson, Green	1,845

C. majority 9,183 (17.65%)
5.28% swing Lab. to C.
(2010: C. majority 3,744 (7.09%))

LOUTH & HORNCASTLE
E. 74,280 T. 50,336 (67.77%) C. hold
*Victoria Atkins, C.	25,755
Colin Mair, UKIP	10,778
Matthew Brown, Lab.	9,077
Lisa Gabriel, LD	2,255
Romy Rayner, Green	1,549
Daniel Simpson, Lincs Ind.	659
Peter Hill, Loony	263

C. majority 14,977 (29.75%)
7.78% swing C. to UKIP
(2010: C. majority 13,871 (27.47%))

LUDLOW
E. 66,423 T. 48,063 (72.36%) C. hold
Philip Dunne, C.	26,093
David Kelly, UKIP	7,164
Charlotte Barnes, LD	6,469
Simon Slater, Lab.	5,902
Janet Phillips, Green	2,435

C. majority 18,929 (39.38%)
4.52% swing C. to UKIP
(2010: C. majority 9,749 (20.01%))

LUTON NORTH
E. 66,533 T. 42,571 (63.98%) Lab. hold
Kelvin Hopkins, Lab.	22,243
Dean Russell, C.	12,739
Allan White, UKIP	5,318
Aroosa Ulzaman, LD	1,299
Sofiya Ahmed, Green	972

Lab. majority 9,504 (22.33%)
2.42% swing C. to Lab.
(2010: Lab. majority 7,520 (17.48%))

LUTON SOUTH
E. 67,234 T. 42,216 (62.79%)
Lab. Co-op hold
Gavin Shuker, Lab. Co-op	18,660
Katie Redmond, C.	12,949
Yasin Rehman, UKIP	5,129
Ashuk Ahmed, LD	3,183
Simon Hall, Green	1,237
Attiq Malik, Ind.	900
Paul Weston, Lib. GB	158

Lab. Co-op majority 5,711 (13.53%)
4.01% swing C. to Lab.
(2010: Lab. Co-op majority 2,329 (5.52%))

MACCLESFIELD
E. 71,580 T. 49,598 (69.29%) C. hold
David Rutley, C.	26,063
Tim Roca, Lab.	11,252
Adrian Howard, UKIP	6,037
Neil Christian, LD	3,842
Joan Plimmer, Green	2,404

C. majority 14,811 (29.86%)
1.61% swing Lab. to C.
(2010: C. majority 11,959 (23.89%))

MAIDENHEAD
E. 74,963 T. 53,855 (71.84%) C. hold
Theresa May, C.	35,453
Charles Smith, Lab.	6,394
Tony Hill, LD	5,337
Herbie Crossman, UKIP	4,539
Emily Blyth, Green	1,915
Ian Taplin, Ind.	162
Joe Wilcox, Class War	55

C. majority 29,059 (53.96%)
0.79% swing Lab. to C.
(2010: C. majority 16,769 (31.22%))

MAIDSTONE & THE WEALD
E. 73,181 T. 50,010 (68.34%) C. hold
Helen Grant, C.	22,745
Jasper Gerard, LD	12,036
Eddie Powell, UKIP	7,930
Allen Simpson, Lab.	5,268
Hannah Patton, Green	1,396
Paul Hobday, NHAP	583
Robin Kinrade, Ind.	52

C. majority 10,709 (21.41%)
4.69% swing LD to C.
(2010: C. majority 5,889 (12.04%))

MAKERFIELD
E. 74,370 T. 44,788 (60.22%) Lab. hold
Yvonne Fovargue, Lab.	23,208
Andrew Collinson, UKIP	10,053
Zehra Zaidi, C.	8,752
John Skipworth, LD	1,639
Philip Mitchell, Green	1,136

Lab. majority 13,155 (29.37%)
swing N/A
(2010: Lab. majority 12,490 (28.53%))

MALDON
E. 69,455 T. 48,045 (69.17%) C. hold
John Whittingdale, C.	29,112
Beverley Acevedo, UKIP	7,042
Peter Edwards, Lab.	5,690
Ken Martin, Ind.	2,424
Zoe O'Connell, LD	2,157
Robert Graves, Green	1,504
John Marett, TSPP	116

C. majority 22,070 (45.94%)
4.40% swing C. to UKIP
(2010: C. majority 19,407 (40.52%))

MANCHESTER CENTRAL
E. 98,435 T. 45,331 (46.05%)
Lab. Co-op hold
Lucy Powell, Lab. Co-op	27,772
Xingang Wang, C.	6,133
Myles Power, UKIP	5,033
Kieran Turner-Dave, Green	3,838
John Reid, LD	1,867
Loz Kaye, Pirate	346
Alex Davidson, TUSC	270
Paul Davies, Comm. Lge	72

Lab. Co-op majority 21,639 (47.74%)
3.39% swing C. to Lab.
(2010: Lab. majority 10,439 (26.15%))
(2012: Lab. majority 9,936 (59.68%))

MANCHESTER GORTON
E. 72,959 T. 42,019 (57.59%) Lab. hold
Gerald Kaufman, Lab.	28,187
Laura Bannister, Green	4,108
Mo Afzal, C.	4,063
Phil Eckersley, UKIP	3,434
Dave Page, LD	1,782
Simon Hickman, TUSC	264
Cris Chesha, Pirate	181

Lab. majority 24,079 (57.31%)
4.96% swing Green to Lab.
(2010: Lab. majority 6,703 (17.49%))

MANCHESTER WITHINGTON
E. 80,590 T. 49,966 (62.00%) Lab. gain
*Jeff Smith, Lab.	26,843
John Leech, LD	11,970
Robert Manning, C.	4,872
Lucy Bannister, Green	4,048
Mark Davies, UKIP	2,172
Marcus Farmer, Ind.	61

Lab. majority 14,873 (29.77%)
16.99% swing LD to Lab.
(2010: LD majority 1,894 (4.21%))

MANSFIELD
E. 77,534 T. 47,193 (60.87%) Lab. hold
Sir Alan Meale, Lab.	18,603
Andrea Clarke, C.	13,288
Sid Pepper, UKIP	11,850
Tony Rogers, LD	1,642
Paul Frost, Green	1,486
Karen Seymour, TUSC	324

Lab. majority 5,315 (11.26%)
0.58% swing Lab. to C.
(2010: Lab. majority 6,012 (12.42%))

MEON VALLEY
E. 72,738 T. 51,717 (71.10%) C. hold
George Hollingbery, C.	31,578
Dave Alexander, UKIP	7,665
Gemma McKenna, Lab.	5,656
Chris Carrigan, LD	4,987
Diana Korchien, Green	1,831

C. majority 23,913 (46.24%)
3.55% swing C. to UKIP
(2010: C. majority 12,125 (23.66%))

MERIDEN
E. 81,079 T. 52,603 (64.88%) C. hold
Caroline Spelman, C.	28,791
Tom McNeil, Lab.	9,996
Mick Gee, UKIP	8,908
Ade Adeyemo, LD	2,638
Alison Gavin, Green	2,170
Chris Booth, IE	100

C. majority 18,795 (35.73%)
2.29% swing Lab. to C.
(2010: C. majority 16,253 (31.16%))

MIDDLESBROUGH
E. 61,868   T. 32,706 (52.86%)   Lab. hold
Andy McDonald, Lab.   18,584
Nigel Baker, UKIP   6,107
Simon Clarke, C.   5,388
Hannah Graham, Green   1,407
Richard Kilpatrick, LD   1,220
Lab. majority 12,477 (38.15%)
2.02% swing Lab. to UKIP
(2010: Lab. majority 8,689 (25.97%))
(2012: Lab. majority 8,211 (47.7%))

MIDDLESBROUGH SOUTH &
CLEVELAND EAST
E. 71,153   T. 45,677 (64.20%)   Lab. hold
Tom Blenkinsop, Lab.   19,193
Will Goodhand, C.   16,925
Steve Turner, UKIP   6,935
Ben Gibson, LD   1,564
Martin Brampton, Green   1,060
Lab. majority 2,268 (4.97%)
0.67% swing C. to Lab.
(2010: Lab. majority 1,677 (3.63%))

MILTON KEYNES NORTH
E. 84,892   T. 57,692 (67.96%)   C. hold
Mark Lancaster, C.   27,244
Emily Darlington, Lab.   17,491
David Reilly, UKIP   6,852
Paul Graham, LD   3,575
Jennifer Marklew, Green   2,255
Katie Simpson, TUSC   163
David Mortimer, Ind.   112
C. majority 9,753 (16.91%)
0.14% swing Lab. to C.
(2010: C. majority 8,961 (16.63%))

MILTON KEYNES SOUTH
E. 87,968   T. 59,019 (67.09%)   C. hold
Iain Stewart, C.   27,671
Andrew Pakes, Lab. Co-op   18,929
Vince Peddle, UKIP   7,803
Lisa Smith, LD   2,309
Samantha Pancheri, Green   1,936
Stephen Fulton, Ind.   255
Matthew Gibson, Real   116
C. majority 8,742 (14.81%)
2.71% swing Lab. to C.
(2010: C. majority 5,201 (9.40%))

MITCHAM & MORDEN
E. 68,474   T. 45,142 (65.93%)   Lab. hold
Siobhain McDonagh, Lab.   27,380
Paul Holmes, C.   10,458
Richard Hilton, UKIP   4,287
Mason Redding, Green   1,422
Diana Coman, LD   1,378
Des Coke, CPA   217
Lab. majority 16,922 (37.49%)
3.14% swing C. to Lab.
(2010: Lab. majority 13,666 (31.20%))

MOLE VALLEY
E. 74,317   T. 55,140 (74.20%)   C. hold
Paul Beresford, C.   33,434
Paul Kennedy, LD   7,981
Paul Oakley, UKIP   6,181
Len Amos, Lab.   4,565
Jacquetta Fewster, Green   2,979
C. majority 25,453 (46.16%)
8.67% swing LD to C.
(2010: C. majority 15,653 (28.81%))

MORECAMBE & LUNESDALE
E. 66,476   T. 43,242 (65.05%)   C. hold
David Morris, C.   19,691
Amina Lone, Lab.   15,101
Steve Ogden, UKIP   5,358
Matthew Severn, LD   1,612
Phil Chandler, Green   1,395
Michael Dawson, ND   85
C. majority 4,590 (10.61%)
4.31% swing Lab. to C.
(2010: C. majority 866 (1.99%))

MORLEY & OUTWOOD
E. 76,179   T. 48,250 (63.34%)   C. gain
*Andrea Jenkyns, C.   18,776
Ed Balls, Lab. Co-op   18,354
David Dews, UKIP   7,951
Rebecca Taylor, LD   1,426
Martin Hemingway, Green   1,264
Arnie Craven, Yorks   479
C. majority 422 (0.87%)
1.56% swing Lab. to C.
(2010: Lab. Co-op majority 1,101 (2.25%))

NEW FOREST EAST
E. 72,720   T. 49,447 (68.00%)   C. hold
Julian Lewis, C.   27,819
Roy Swales, UKIP   8,657
Andrew Pope, Lab.   6,018
Bruce Tennent, LD   4,626
Sally May, Green   2,327
C. majority 19,162 (38.75%)
4.53% swing C. to UKIP
(2010: C. majority 11,307 (22.60%))

NEW FOREST WEST
E. 68,465   T. 47,410 (69.25%)   C. hold
Desmond Swayne, C.   28,420
Paul Bailey, UKIP   7,816
Lena Samuels, Lab.   5,133
Imogen Shepherd-DuBey, LD   3,293
Janet Richards, Green   2,748
C. majority 20,604 (43.46%)
4.75% swing C. to UKIP
(2010: C. majority 16,896 (35.52%))

NEWARK
E. 73,724   T. 52,302 (70.94%)   C. hold
Robert Jenrick, C.   29,834
Michael Payne, Lab.   11,360
Brian Mapletoft, UKIP   6,294
David Dobbie, LD   2,385
Elayne Forster, Green   1,792
Helen Tyrer, Consensus   637
C. majority 18,474 (35.32%)
1.90% swing Lab. to C.
(2010: C. majority 16,152 (31.53%))
(2014: C. majority 7,403 (19.13%))

NEWBURY
E. 79,058   T. 57,300 (72.48%)   C. hold
Richard Benyon, C.   34,973
Judith Bunting, LD   8,605
Catherine Anderson, UKIP   6,195
Jonny Roberts, Lab.   4,837
Paul Field, Green   2,324
Peter Norman, AD   228
Barrie Singleton, Ind.   85
Andrew Stott, PSP   53
C. majority 26,368 (46.02%)
12.56% swing LD to C.
(2010: C. majority 12,248 (20.90%))

NEWCASTLE-UNDER-LYME
E. 66,752   T. 42,997 (64.41%)   Lab. hold
Paul Farrelly, Lab.   16,520
Tony Cox, C.   15,870
Phil Wood, UKIP   7,252
Ian Wilkes, LD   1,826
Sam Gibbons, Green   1,246
David Nixon, Ind.   283
Lab. majority 650 (1.51%)
1.04% swing Lab. to C.
(2010: Lab. majority 1,552 (3.59%))

NEWCASTLE UPON TYNE CENTRAL
E. 61,061   T. 35,085 (57.46%)   Lab. hold
Chi Onwurah, Lab.   19,301
Simon Kitchen, C.   6,628
Daniel Thompson, UKIP   5,214
Nick Cott, LD   2,218
Alexander Johnson, Green   1,724
Lab. majority 12,673 (36.12%)
4.76% swing C. to Lab.
(2010: Lab. majority 7,466 (21.86%))

NEWCASTLE UPON TYNE EAST
E. 74,112   T. 39,222 (52.92%)   Lab. hold
Nick Brown, Lab.   19,378
Duncan Crute, C.   6,884
David Robinson-Young, UKIP   4,910
Wendy Taylor, LD   4,332
Andrew Gray, Green   3,426
Paul Phillips, TUSC   170
Mollie Stevenson, Comm.   122
Lab. majority 12,494 (31.85%)
1.43% swing C. to Lab.
(2010: Lab. majority 4,453 (11.77%))

NEWCASTLE UPON TYNE NORTH
E. 67,267   T. 44,891 (66.74%)   Lab. hold
Catherine McKinnell, Lab.   20,689
Stephen Bates, C.   10,536
Tim Marron, UKIP   7,447
Anita Lower, LD   4,366
Alison Whalley, Green   1,515
Violet Rook, NE   338
Lab. majority 10,153 (22.62%)
0.05% swing Lab. to C.
(2010: Lab. majority 3,414 (7.77%))

NEWTON ABBOT
E. 69,743   T. 48,199 (69.11%)   C. hold
Anne Marie Morris, C.   22,794
Richard Younger-Ross, LD   11,506
Rod Peers, UKIP   6,726
Roy Freer, Lab.   4,736
Steven Smyth-Bonfield, Green   2,216
Sean Brogan, TUSC   221
C. majority 11,288 (23.42%)
11.17% swing LD to C.
(2010: C. majority 523 (1.08%))

NORFOLK MID
E. 76,975   T. 52,212 (67.83%)   C. hold
George Freeman, C.   27,206
Anna Coke, UKIP   9,930
Harry Clarke, Lab.   9,585
Paul Speed, LD   3,300
Simeon Jackson, Green   2,191
C. majority 17,276 (33.09%)
5.44% swing C. to UKIP
(2010: C. majority 13,856 (27.29%))

NORFOLK NORTH
E. 68,958   T. 49,414 (71.66%)   LD hold
Norman Lamb, LD   19,299
Ann Steward, C.   15,256
Michael Baker, UKIP   8,328
Denise Burke, Lab.   5,043
Michael Macartney-Filgate, Green   1,488
LD majority 4,043 (8.18%)
7.61% swing LD to C.
(2010: LD majority 11,626 (23.41%))

NORFOLK NORTH WEST
E. 72,400   T. 47,371 (65.43%)   C. hold
Henry Bellingham, C.   24,727
Jo Rust, Lab.   10,779
Toby Coke, UKIP   8,412
Michael de Whalley, Green   1,780
Hugh Lanham, LD   1,673
C. majority 13,948 (29.44%)
5.74% swing C. to Lab.
(2010: C. majority 14,810 (30.98%))

NORFOLK SOUTH
E. 78,885   T. 57,123 (72.41%)   C. hold
Richard Bacon, C.   30,995
Deborah Sacks, Lab.   10,502
Barry Cameron, UKIP   7,847
Jacqueline Howe, LD   4,689
Catherine Rowett, Green   3,090
C. majority 20,493 (35.88%)
0.14% swing C. to Lab.
(2010: C. majority 10,940 (19.89%))

NORFOLK SOUTH WEST
E. 76,970   T. 50,110 (65.10%)   C. hold
Elizabeth Truss, C.   25,515
Paul Smyth, UKIP   11,654
Peter Smith, Lab.   8,649
Rupert Moss-Eccardt, LD   2,217
Sandra Walmsley, Green   2,075
C. majority 13,861 (27.66%)
7.22% swing C. to UKIP
(2010: C. majority 13,140 (26.73%))

NORMANTON, PONTEFRACT &
CASTLEFORD
E. 82,592   T. 45,897 (55.57%)   Lab. hold
Yvette Cooper, Lab.   25,213
Nathan Garbutt, UKIP   9,785
Beth Prescott, C.   9,569
Edward McMillan-Scott, LD   1,330
Lab. majority 15,428 (33.61%)
swing N/A
(2010: Lab. majority 10,979 (23.74%))

NORTHAMPTON NORTH
E. 59,147   T. 39,411 (66.63%)   C. hold
Michael Ellis, C.   16,699
Sally Keeble, Lab.   13,454
Tom Rubython, UKIP   6,354
Tony Clarke, Green   1,503
Angela Paterson, LD   1,401
C. majority 3,245 (8.23%)
1.71% swing Lab. to C.
(2010: C. majority 1,936 (4.81%))

NORTHAMPTON SOUTH
E. 61,284   T. 38,884 (63.45%)   C. hold
*David Mackintosh, C.   16,163
Kevin McKeever, Lab.   12,370
Rose Gibbins, UKIP   7,114
Sadik Chaudhury, LD   1,673
Julie Hawkins, Green   1,403
Kevin Willsher, Ind.   161
C. majority 3,793 (9.75%)
2.82% swing C. to Lab.
(2010: C. majority 6,004 (15.40%))

NORTHAMPTONSHIRE SOUTH
E. 85,092   T. 60,862 (71.52%)   C. hold
Andrea Leadsom, C.   36,607
Lucy Mills, Lab.   10,191
Roger Clark, UKIP   8,204
Tom Snowdon, LD   3,613
Damon Boughen, Green   2,247
C. majority 26,416 (43.40%)
2.75% swing Lab. to C.
(2010: C. majority 20,478 (34.19%))

NORWICH NORTH
E. 65,136   T. 43,592 (66.92%)   C. hold
Chloe Smith, C.   19,052
Jessica Asato, Lab.   14,589
Glenn Tingle, UKIP   5,986
Adrian Holmes, Green   1,939
James Wright, LD   1,894
Mick Hardy, Ind.   132
C. majority 4,463 (10.24%)
0.54% swing Lab. to C.
(2010: C. majority 3,901 (9.16%))

NORWICH SOUTH
E. 74,875   T. 48,463 (64.73%)   Lab. gain
*Clive Lewis, Lab.   19,033
Lisa Townsend, C.   11,379
Lesley Grahame, Green   6,749
Simon Wright, LD   6,607
Steve Emmens, UKIP   4,539
David Peel, Class War   96
Cengiz Ceker, Ind.   60
Lab. majority 7,654 (15.79%)
13.15% swing LD to Lab.
(2010: LD majority 310 (0.65%))

NOTTINGHAM EAST
E. 60,464   T. 35,209 (58.23%)
                           Lab. Co-op hold
Chris Leslie, Lab. Co-op   19,208
Garry Hickton, C.   7,314
Fran Loi, UKIP   3,501
Antonia Zenkevitch, Green   3,473
Tadeusz Jones, LD   1,475
Seb Soar, Ind.   141
James Stephenson, Ind.   97
Lab. Co-op majority 11,894 (33.78%)
6.05% swing C. to Lab.
(2010: Lab. Co-op majority 6,969
(21.05%))

NOTTINGHAM NORTH
E. 65,918   T. 35,343 (53.62%)   Lab. hold
Graham Allen, Lab.   19,283
Louise Burfitt-Dons, C.   7,423
Stephen Crosby, UKIP   6,542
Katharina Boettge, Green   1,088
Tony Sutton, LD   847
Cathy Meadows, TUSC   160
Lab. majority 11,860 (33.56%)
4.91% swing C. to Lab.
(2010: Lab. majority 8,138 (23.74%))

NOTTINGHAM SOUTH
E. 68,987   T. 43,465 (63.00%)   Lab. hold
Lilian Greenwood, Lab.   20,697
Jane Hunt, C.   13,761
David Hollas, UKIP   4,900
Adam McGregor, Green   2,345
Deborah Newton-Cook, LD   1,532
Andrew Clayworth, TUSC   230
Lab. majority 6,936 (15.96%)
5.81% swing C. to Lab.
(2010: Lab. majority 1,772 (4.34%))

NUNEATON
E. 68,032   T. 45,749 (67.25%)   C. hold
Marcus Jones, C.   20,827
Vicky Fowler, Lab.   15,945
Alwyn Waine, UKIP   6,582
Keith Kondakor, Green   1,281
Christina Jebb, LD   816
Paul Reilly, TUSC   194
Stephen Paxton, Eng. Dem.   104
C. majority 4,882 (10.67%)
3.02% swing Lab. to C.
(2010: C. majority 2,069 (4.63%))

OLD BEXLEY & SIDCUP
E. 66,035   T. 46,748 (70.79%)   C. hold
James Brokenshire, C.   24,682
Ibrahim Mehmet, Lab.   8,879
Catherine Reilly, UKIP   8,528
Jennifer Keen, LD   1,644
Derek Moran, Green   1,336
Bob Gill, NHAP   1,216
Laurence Williams, Ch. P.   245
Nicola Finch, BNP   218
C. majority 15,803 (33.80%)
0.53% swing C. to Lab.
(2010: C. majority 15,857 (34.86%))

OLDHAM EAST & SADDLEWORTH
E. 72,005   T. 44,483 (61.78%)   Lab. hold
Debbie Abrahams, Lab.   17,529
Sajjad Hussain, C.   11,527
Peter Klonowski, UKIP   8,557
Richard Marbrow, LD   5,718
Miranda Meadowcroft, Green   1,152
Lab. majority 6,002 (13.49%)
4.04% swing C. to Lab.
(2010: Lab. majority 103 (0.23%))
(2011: Lab. majority 3,558 (10.23%))

OLDHAM WEST & ROYTON
E. 72,341   T. 43,137 (59.63%)   Lab. hold
Michael Meacher, Lab.   23,630
Francis Arbour, UKIP   8,892
Kamran Ghafoor, C.   8,187
Garth Harkness, LD   1,589
Simeon Hart, Green   839
Lab. majority 14,738 (34.17%)
4.03% swing Lab. to UKIP
(2010: Lab. majority 9,352 (21.79%))

ORPINGTON
E. 68,129   T. 49,032 (71.97%)   C. hold
Joseph Johnson, C.   28,152
Idham Ramadi, UKIP   8,173
Nigel de Gruchy, Lab.   7,645
Peter Brooks, LD   3,330
Tamara Galloway, Green   1,732
C. majority 19,979 (40.75%)
8.09% swing C. to UKIP
(2010: C. majority 17,200 (35.17%))

OXFORD EAST
E. 78,974   T. 50,689 (64.18%)   Lab. hold
Andrew Smith, Lab.   25,356
Melanie Magee, C.   10,076
Ann Duncan, Green   5,890
Alasdair Murray, LD   5,453
Ian Macdonald, UKIP   3,451
Chaka Artwell, Ind.   160
Mad Hatter, Loony   145
James Morbin, TUSC   108
Kevin Parkin, SPGB   50
Lab. majority 15,280 (30.14%)
3.25% swing C. to Lab.
(2010: Lab. majority 4,581 (8.87%))

OXFORD WEST & ABINGDON
E. 79,767   T. 57,247 (71.77%)   C. hold
Nicola Blackwood, C.   26,153
Layla Moran, LD   16,571
Sally Copley, Lab.   7,274
Alan Harris, UKIP   3,963
Larry Sanders, Green   2,497
Helen Salisbury, NHAP   723
Mike Foster, SPGB   66
C. majority 9,582 (16.74%)
8.21% swing LD to C.
(2010: C. majority 176 (0.31%))

PENDLE
E. 64,657   T. 44,448 (68.74%)   C. hold
Andrew Stephenson, C.   20,978
Azhar Ali, Lab.   15,525
Mick Waddington, UKIP   5,415
Graham Roach, LD   1,487
Laura Fisk, Green   1,043
C. majority 5,453 (12.27%)
2.15% swing Lab. to C.
(2010: C. majority 3,585 (7.96%))

PENISTONE & STOCKSBRIDGE
E. 71,048   T. 46,854 (65.95%)   Lab. hold
Angela Smith, Lab.   19,691
Steven Jackson, C.   12,968
Graeme Waddicar, UKIP   10,738
Rosalyn Gordon, LD   2,957
Colin Porter, Eng. Dem.   500
Lab. majority 6,723 (14.35%)
3.90% swing C. to Lab.
(2010: Lab. majority 3,049 (6.55%))

PENRITH & THE BORDER
E. 65,209   T. 43,921 (67.35%)   C. hold
Rory Stewart, C.   26,202
Lee Rushworth, Lab.   6,308
John Stanyer, UKIP   5,353
Neil Hughes, LD   3,745
Bryan Burrow, Green   2,313
C. majority 19,894 (45.29%)
2.42% swing Lab. to C.
(2010: C. majority 11,241 (24.93%))

PETERBOROUGH
E. 72,521   T. 47,075 (64.91%)   C. hold
Stewart Jackson, C.   18,684
Lisa Forbes, Lab.   16,759
Mary Herdman, UKIP   7,485
Darren Fower, LD   1,774
Darren Bisby-Boyd, Green   1,218
Chris Ash, Lib.   639
John Fox, Ind.   516
C. majority 1,925 (4.09%)
3.37% swing C. to Lab.
(2010: C. majority 4,861 (10.82%))

PLYMOUTH MOOR VIEW
E. 69,146   T. 42,606 (61.62%)   C. gain
*Johnny Mercer, C.   16,020
Alison Seabeck, Lab.   14,994
Penny Mills, UKIP   9,152
Stuart Bonar, LD   1,265
Ben Osborn, Green   1,023
Louise Parker, TUSC   152
C. majority 1,026 (2.41%)
3.12% swing Lab. to C.
(2010: Lab. majority 1,588 (3.82%))

PLYMOUTH SUTTON & DEVONPORT
E. 69,146   T. 47,963 (69.36%)   C. hold
Oliver Colvile, C.   18,120
Luke Pollard, Lab. Co-op   17,597
Roy Kettle, UKIP   6,731
Libby Brown, Green   3,401
Graham Reed, LD   2,008
Laura-Jane Rossington, Comm.   106
C. majority 523 (1.09%)
0.76% swing C. to Lab.
(2010: C. majority 1,149 (2.62%))

POOLE
E. 72,557   T. 47,393 (65.32%)   C. hold
Robert Syms, C.   23,745
David Young, UKIP   7,956
Helen Rosser, Lab.   6,102
Philip Eades, LD   5,572
Adrian Oliver, Green   2,198
Mark Howell, Poole   1,766
Ian Northover, ND   54
C. majority 15,789 (33.32%)
4.45% swing C. to UKIP
(2010: C. majority 7,541 (15.90%))

POPLAR & LIMEHOUSE
E. 82,076   T. 51,044 (62.19%)   Lab. hold
Jim Fitzpatrick, Lab.   29,886
Christopher Wilford, C.   12,962
Nicholas McQueen, UKIP   3,128
Maureen Childs, Green   2,463
Elaine Bagshaw, LD   2,149
Hugo Pierre, TUSC   367
Rene Mugenzi, RFAC   89
Lab. majority 16,924 (33.16%)
10.12% swing C. to Lab.
(2010: Lab. majority 6,030 (12.91%))

PORTSMOUTH NORTH
E. 73,105   T. 45,390 (62.09%)   C. hold
Penny Mordaunt, C.   21,343
John Ferrett, Lab.   10,806
Mike Fitzgerald, UKIP   8,660
Darren Sanders, LD   2,828
Gavin Ellis, Green   1,450
Jon Woods, TUSC   231
Steven George, JACP   72
C. majority 10,537 (23.21%)
3.35% swing Lab. to C.
(2010: C. majority 7,289 (16.52%))

PORTSMOUTH SOUTH
E. 71,639   T. 41,903 (58.49%)   C. gain
*Flick Drummond, C.   14,585
Gerald Vernon-Jackson, LD   9,344
Sue Castillon, Lab.   8,184
Steve Harris, UKIP   5,595
Ian McCulloch, Green   3,145
Mike Hancock, Ind.   716
Sean Hoyle, TUSC   235
Don Jerrard, JACP   99
C. majority 5,241 (12.51%)
12.55% swing LD to C.
(2010: LD majority 5,200 (12.60%))

PRESTON
E. 59,981 T. 33,469 (55.80%)
                          Lab. Co-op hold
Mark Hendrick, Lab. Co-op   18,755
Richard Holden, C.   6,688
James Barker, UKIP   5,139
Gemma Christie, Green   1,643
Jo Barton, LD   1,244
Lab. Co-op majority 12,067 (36.05%)
4.79% swing C. to Lab.
(2010: Lab. Co-op majority 7,733
(23.79%))

PUDSEY
E. 70,533   T. 50,927 (72.20%)   C. hold
Stuart Andrew, C.   23,637
Jamie Hanley, Lab.   19,136
Roger Tattersall, UKIP   4,689
Ryk Downes, LD   1,926
Claire Allen, Green   1,539
C. majority 4,501 (8.84%)
2.73% swing Lab. to C.
(2010: C. majority 1,659 (3.38%))

PUTNEY
E. 63,918   T. 42,813 (66.98%)   C. hold
Justine Greening, C.   23,018
Sheila Boswell, Lab.   12,838
Andy Hallett, LD   2,717
Chris Poole, Green   2,067
Tricia Ward, UKIP   1,989
Guy Dessoy, AWP   184
C. majority 10,180 (23.78%)
0.44% swing C. to Lab.
(2010: C. majority 10,053 (24.65%))

RAYLEIGH & WICKFORD
E. 77,870   T. 53,220 (68.34%)   C. hold
Mark Francois, C.   29,088
John Hayter, UKIP   11,858
David Hough, Lab.   6,705
Linda Kendall, Ind.   2,418
Mike Pitt, LD   1,622
Sarah Yapp, Green   1,529
C. majority 17,230 (32.38%)
10.60% swing C. to UKIP
(2010: C. majority 22,338 (42.68%))

READING EAST
E. 74,651   T. 50,494 (67.64%)   C. hold
Rob Wilson, C.   23,217
Matt Rodda, Lab.   16,697
Jenny Woods, LD   3,719
Christine Forrester, UKIP   3,647
Rob White, Green   3,214
C. majority 6,520 (12.91%)
2.09% swing C. to Lab.
(2010: C. majority 7,605 (15.21%))

READING WEST
E. 72,302   T. 48,404 (66.95%)   C. hold
Alok Sharma, C.   23,082
Victoria Groulef, Lab.   16,432
Malik Azam, UKIP   4,826
Meri O'Connell, LD   2,355
Miriam Kennet, Green   1,406
Suzie Ferguson, Ind.   156
Neil Adams, TUSC   83
Philip West, Roman   64
C. majority 6,650 (13.74%)
0.55% swing Lab. to C.
(2010: C. majority 6,004 (12.63%))

REDCAR
E. 64,825 T. 40,919 (63.12%)
                          Lab. Co-op gain
*Anna Turley, Lab. Co-op   17,946
Josh Mason, LD   7,558
Chris Gallacher, UKIP   7,516
Jacob Young, C.   6,630
Peter Pinkney, Green   880
Philip Lockey, NE   389
Lab. Co-op majority 10,388 (25.39%)
18.91% swing LD to Lab.
(2010: LD majority 5,214 (12.43%))

REDDITCH
E. 65,529   T. 44,098 (67.30%)   C. hold
Karen Lumley, C.   20,771
Rebecca Blake, Lab.   13,717
Peter Jewell, UKIP   7,133
Hilary Myers, LD   1,349
Kevin White, Green   960
Seth Colton, Ind.   168
C. majority 7,054 (16.00%)
1.39% swing Lab. to C.
(2010: C. majority 5,821 (13.22%))

REIGATE
E. 73,429   T. 51,349 (69.93%)   C. hold
Crispin Blunt, C.   29,151
Joseph Fox, UKIP   6,817
Ali Aklakul, Lab.   6,578
Anna Tarrant, LD   5,369
Jonathan Essex, Green   3,434
C. majority 22,334 (43.49%)
2.86% swing C. to UKIP
(2010: C. majority 13,591 (27.19%))

RIBBLE VALLEY
E. 77,873   T. 52,243 (67.09%)   C. hold
Nigel Evans, C.   25,404
David Hinder, Lab.   11,798
Shirley Parkinson, UKIP   8,250
Jackie Pearcey, LD   2,756
Graham Sowter, Green   2,193
David Brass, Ind.   1,498
Grace Astley, Ind.   288
Tony Johnson, IPAP   56
C. majority 13,606 (26.04%)
1.10% swing C. to Lab.
(2010: C. majority 14,769 (28.25%))

RICHMOND (YORKS)
E. 83,451   T. 53,999 (64.71%)   C. hold
*Rishi Sunak, C.   27,744
Matthew Cooke, UKIP   8,194
Mike Hill, Lab.   7,124
John Harris, LD   3,465
John Blackie, Ind.   3,348
Leslie Rowe, Green   2,313
Robin Scott, Ind.   1,811
C. majority 19,550 (36.20%)
swing N/A
(2010: C. majority 23,336 (43.69%))

RICHMOND PARK
E. 77,297   T. 59,101 (76.46%)   C. hold
Zac Goldsmith, C.   34,404
Robin Meltzer, LD   11,389
Sachin Patel, Lab.   7,296
Andree Frieze, Green   3,548
Sam Naz, UKIP   2,464
C. majority 23,015 (38.94%)
16.02% swing LD to C.
(2010: C. majority 4,091 (6.90%))

ROCHDALE
E. 79,170   T. 45,430 (57.38%)   Lab. hold
Simon Danczuk, Lab.   20,961
Mohammed Masud, UKIP   8,519
Azi Ahmed, C.   7,742
Andy Kelly, LD   4,667
Farooq Ahmed, Rochdale   1,535
Mark Hollinrake, Green   1,382
Kevin Bryan, NF   433
Mohammed Salim, IZB   191
Lab. majority 12,442 (27.39%)
2.32% swing Lab. to UKIP
(2010: Lab. majority 889 (1.94%))

ROCHESTER & STROOD
E. 79,000   T. 52,516 (66.48%)   C. gain
*Kelly Tolhurst, C.   23,142
Mark Reckless, UKIP   16,009
Naushabah Khan, Lab.   10,396
Clive Gregory, Green   1,516
Prue Bray, LD   1,251
Dan Burn, TUSC   202
C. majority 7,133 (13.58%)
swing N/A
(2010: C. majority 9,953 (20.75%))
(2014: UKIP majority 2,920 (7.29%))

ROCHFORD & SOUTHEND EAST
E. 71,935   T. 43,608 (60.62%)   C. hold
James Duddridge, C.   20,241
Ian Gilbert, Lab.   10,765
Floyd Waterworth, UKIP   8,948
Simon Cross, Green   2,195
Peter Gwizdala, LD   1,459
C. majority 9,476 (21.73%)
2.41% swing C. to Lab.
(2010: C. majority 11,050 (26.54%))

ROMFORD
E. 72,594   T. 49,178 (67.74%)   C. hold
Andrew Rosindell, C.   25,067
Gerard Batten, UKIP   11,208
Sam Gould, Lab.   10,268
Ian Sanderson, LD   1,413
Lorna Tooley, Green   1,222
C. majority 13,859 (28.18%)
11.71% swing C. to UKIP
(2010: C. majority 16,954 (36.48%))

ROMSEY & SOUTHAMPTON NORTH
E. 66,519   T. 48,398 (72.76%)   C. hold
Caroline Nokes, C.   26,285
Ben Nicholls, LD   8,573
Darren Paffey, Lab.   5,749
Sandra James, UKIP   5,511
Ian Callaghan, Green   2,280
C. majority 17,712 (36.60%)
14.05% swing LD to C.
(2010: C. majority 4,156 (8.49%))

ROSSENDALE & DARWEN
E. 84,011   T. 49,024 (58.35%)   C. hold
Jake Berry, C.   22,847
Will Straw, Lab.   17,193
Clive Balchin, UKIP   6,862
Karen Pollard-Rylance, Green   1,046
Afzal Anwar, LD   806
Kevin Scranage, Ind.   122
Simon Thomas, TUSC   103
Shaun Hargreaves, Northern   45
C. majority 5,654 (11.53%)
1.00% swing Lab. to C.
(2010: C. majority 4,493 (9.53%))

ROTHER VALLEY
E. 74,275   T. 47,019 (63.30%)   Lab. hold
Kevin Barron, Lab.   20,501
Allen Cowles, UKIP   13,204
Gareth Streeter, C.   10,945
Robert Teal, LD   1,992
Sharon Pilling, Eng. Dem.   377
Lab. majority 7,297 (15.52%)
9.92% swing Lab. to UKIP
(2010: Lab. majority 5,866 (12.55%))

ROTHERHAM
E. 63,698   T. 37,823 (59.38%)   Lab. hold
Sarah Champion, Lab.   19,860
Jane Collins, UKIP   11,414
Sebastian Lowe, C.   4,656
Janice Middleton, LD   1,093
Pat McLaughlin, TUSC   409
Adam Walker, BNP   225
Dean Walker, Eng. Dem.   166
Lab. majority 8,446 (22.33%)
8.19% swing Lab. to UKIP
(2010: Lab. majority 10,462 (27.89%))
(2012: Lab. majority 5,318 (24.79%))

RUGBY
E. 79,557   T. 49,006 (61.60%)   C. hold
Mark Pawsey, C.   24,040
Claire Edwards, Lab.   13,695
Gordon Davies, UKIP   6,855
Ed Goncalves, LD   2,776
Terence White, Green   1,415
Pete McLaren, TUSC   225
C. majority 10,345 (21.11%)
4.23% swing Lab. to C.
(2010: C. majority 6,000 (12.64%))

RUISLIP, NORTHWOOD & PINNER
E. 73,219   T. 51,222 (69.96%)   C. hold
Nick Hurd, C.   30,521
Michael Borio, Lab.   10,297
Gerard Barry, UKIP   5,598
Joshua Dixon, LD   2,537
Karen Pillai, Green   1,801
Wally Kennedy, TUSC   302
Sockalingam Yogalingam, Nat. Lib.   166
C. majority 20,224 (39.48%)
0.76% swing Lab. to C.
(2010: C. majority 19,060 (37.96%))

RUNNYMEDE & WEYBRIDGE
E. 73,744   T. 50,052 (67.87%)   C. hold
Philip Hammond, C.   29,901
Arran Neathey, Lab.   7,767
Joe Branco, UKIP   6,951
John Vincent, LD   3,362
Rustam Majainah, Green   2,071
C. majority 22,134 (44.22%)
0.86% swing Lab. to C.
(2010: C. majority 16,509 (34.29%))

RUSHCLIFFE
E. 73,294   T. 55,164 (75.26%)   C. hold
Kenneth Clarke, C.   28,354
David Mellen, Lab.   14,525
Matthew Faithfull, UKIP   5,943
Richard Mallender, Green   3,559
Bob Johnston, LD   2,783
C. majority 13,829 (25.07%)
2.69% swing C. to Lab.
(2010: C. majority 15,811 (29.45%))

RUTLAND & MELTON
E. 79,789   T. 54,603 (68.43%)   C. hold
Alan Duncan, C.   30,383
Richard Billington, UKIP   8,678
James Moore, Lab.   8,383
Ed Reynolds, LD   4,407
Alastair McQuillan, Green   2,325
Marilyn Gordon, Ind.   427
C. majority 21,705 (39.75%)
3.40% swing C. to UKIP
(2010: C. majority 14,000 (25.35%))

SAFFRON WALDEN
E. 80,615   T. 57,563 (71.40%)   C. hold
Sir Alan Haselhurst, C.   32,926
Peter Day, UKIP   7,935
Jane Berney, Lab.   6,791
Mike Hibbs, LD   6,079
Karmel Stannard, Green   2,174
Heather Asker, Uttlesford   1,658
C. majority 24,991 (43.42%)
3.98% swing C. to UKIP
(2010: C. majority 15,242 (28.03%))

ST ALBANS
E. 72,507   T. 54,433 (75.07%)   C. hold
Anne Main, C.   25,392
Kerry Pollard, Lab.   12,660
Sandy Walkington, LD   10,076
Chris Wright, UKIP   4,271
Jack Easton, Green   2,034
C. majority 12,732 (23.39%)
0.11% swing Lab. to C.
(2010: C. majority 2,305 (4.36%))

ST AUSTELL & NEWQUAY
E. 76,607   T. 50,361 (65.74%)   C. gain
*Stephen Double, C.   20,250
Stephen Gilbert, LD   12,077
David Mathews, UKIP   8,503
Deborah Hopkins, Lab.   5,150
Steve Slade, Green   2,318
Dick Cole, Meb. Ker.   2,063
C. majority 8,173 (16.23%)
9.50% swing LD to C.
(2010: LD majority 1,312 (2.78%))

ST HELENS NORTH
E. 75,262   T. 46,256 (61.46%)   Lab. hold
*Conor McGinn, Lab.   26,378
Paul Richardson, C.   9,087
Ian Smith, UKIP   6,983
Denise Aspinall, LD   2,046
Elizabeth Ward, Green   1,762
Lab. majority 17,291 (37.38%)
3.99% swing C. to Lab.
(2010: Lab. majority 13,101 (29.40%))

ST HELENS SOUTH & WHISTON
E. 77,720   T. 48,397 (62.27%)   Lab. hold
*Marie Rimmer, Lab.   28,950
Gillian Keegan, C.   7,707
John Beirne, UKIP   6,766
Brian Spencer, LD   2,737
James Chan, Green   2,237
Lab. majority 21,243 (43.89%)
4.42% swing C. to Lab.
(2010: Lab. majority 14,122 (30.65%))

ST IVES
E. 65,570   T. 48,312 (73.68%)   C. gain
*Derek Thomas, C.   18,491
Andrew George, LD   16,022
Graham Calderwood, UKIP   5,720
Cornelius Olivier, Lab.   4,510
Tim Andrewes, Green   3,051
Rob Simmons, Meb. Ker.   518
C. majority 2,469 (5.11%)
4.43% swing LD to C.
(2010: LD majority 1,719 (3.74%))

SALFORD & ECCLES
E. 74,290   T. 43,261 (58.23%)   Lab. hold
*Rebecca Long Bailey, Lab.   21,364
Greg Downes, C.   8,823
Paul Doyle, UKIP   7,806
Emma Van Dyke, Green   2,251
Charlie Briggs, LD   1,614
Bez Berry, Reality   703
Noreen Bailey, TUSC   517
Sam Clark, Pirate   183
Lab. majority 12,541 (28.99%)
4.67% swing C. to Lab.
(2010: Lab. majority 5,725 (13.78%))

SALISBURY
E. 69,590   T. 50,705 (72.86%)   C. hold
John Glen, C.   28,192
Tom Corbin, Lab.   7,771
Paul Martin, UKIP   6,152
Reetendra Nath Banerji, LD   5,099
Alison Craig, Green   2,762
King Arthur Pendragon, Ind.   729
C. majority 20,421 (40.27%)
0.66% swing C. to Lab.
(2010: C. majority 5,966 (12.31%))

SCARBOROUGH & WHITBY
E. 73,511   T. 47,739 (64.94%)   C. hold
Robert Goodwill, C.   20,613
Ian McInnes, Lab.   14,413
Samuel Cross, UKIP   8,162
David Malone, Green   2,185
Michael Beckett, LD   2,159
Juliet Boddington, Green Soc.   207
C. majority 6,200 (12.99%)
1.75% swing C. to Lab.
(2010: C. majority 8,130 (16.50%))

SCUNTHORPE
E. 64,010   T. 36,941 (57.71%)   Lab. hold
Nic Dakin, Lab.   15,393
Jo Gideon, C.   12,259
Stephen Howd, UKIP   6,329
Des Comerford, Ind.   1,097
Martin Dwyer, Green   887
Simon Dodd, LD   770
Paul Elsom, Ind.   206
Lab. majority 3,134 (8.48%)
0.80% swing C. to Lab.
(2010: Lab. majority 2,549 (6.88%))

SEDGEFIELD
E. 62,860   T. 38,716 (61.59%)   Lab. hold
Phil Wilson, Lab.   18,275
Scott Wood, C.   11,432
John Leathley, UKIP   6,426
Stephen Glenn, LD   1,370
Greg Robinson, Green   1,213
Lab. majority 6,843 (17.67%)
1.97% swing Lab. to C.
(2010: Lab. majority 8,696 (21.62%))

SEFTON CENTRAL
E. 67,746   T. 49,021 (72.36%)   Lab. hold
Bill Esterson, Lab.   26,359
Valerie Allen, C.   14,513
Tim Power, UKIP   4,879
Paula Keaveney, LD   2,086
Lindsay Melia, Green   1,184
Lab. majority 11,846 (24.17%)
8.10% swing C. to Lab.
(2010: Lab. majority 3,862 (7.97%))

SELBY & AINSTY
E. 76,082   T. 52,804 (69.40%)   C. hold
Nigel Adams, C.   27,725
Mark Hayes, Lab.   14,168
Colin Heath, UKIP   7,389
Nicola Turner, LD   1,920
Ian Richards, Green   1,465
Ian Wilson, TUSC   137
C. majority 13,557 (25.67%)
0.98% swing Lab. to C.
(2010: C. majority 12,265 (23.71%))

SEVENOAKS
E. 70,741   T. 50,124 (70.86%)   C. hold
Michael Fallon, C.   28,531
Steve Lindsay, UKIP   8,970
Chris Clark, Lab.   6,448
Alan Bullion, LD   3,937
Amelie Boleyn, Green   2,238
C. majority 19,561 (39.03%)
7.10% swing C. to UKIP
(2010: C. majority 17,515 (35.45%))

SHEFFIELD BRIGHTSIDE &
HILLSBOROUGH
E. 73,090   T. 40,053 (54.80%)   Lab. hold
*Harry Harpham, Lab.   22,663
John Booker, UKIP   8,856
Elise Dunweber, C.   4,407
Jonathan Harston, LD   1,802
Christine Gilligan Kubu, Green   1,712
Maxine Bowler, TUSC   442
Justin Saxton, Eng. Dem.   171
Lab. majority 13,807 (34.47%)
8.21% swing Lab. to UKIP
(2010: Lab. majority 13,632 (35.03%))

SHEFFIELD CENTRAL
E. 77,014   T. 44,173 (57.36%)   Lab. hold
Paul Blomfield, Lab.   24,308
Jillian Creasy, Green   6,999
Stephanie Roe, C.   4,917
Joe Otten, LD   4,278
Dominic Cook, UKIP   3,296
Steve Andrew, Comm.   119
Andy Halsall, Pirate   113
Elizabeth Breed, Eng. Dem.   68
Thom Brown, Above   42
Michael Driver, WRP   33
Lab. majority 17,309 (39.18%)
swing N/A
(2010: Lab. majority 165 (0.40%))

SHEFFIELD HALLAM
E. 73,658   T. 55,481 (75.32%)   LD hold
Nick Clegg, LD   22,215
Oliver Coppard, Lab.   19,862
Ian Walker, C.   7,544
Joseph Jenkins, UKIP   3,575
Peter Garbutt, Green   1,772
Carlton Reeve, Ind.   249
Steven Clegg, Eng. Dem.   167
Jim Stop the fiasco Wild, Ind.   97
LD majority 2,353 (4.24%)
16.55% swing LD to Lab.
(2010: LD majority 15,284 (29.89%))

SHEFFIELD HEELEY
E. 69,265   T. 42,048 (60.71%)   Lab. hold
*Louise Haigh, Lab.   20,269
Howard Denby, UKIP   7,315
Stephen Castens, C.   6,792
Simon Clement-Jones, LD   4,746
Rita Wilcock, Green   2,566
Alan Munro, TUSC   238
David Haslett, Eng. Dem.   122
Lab. majority 12,954 (30.81%)
4.02% swing Lab. to UKIP
(2010: Lab. majority 5,807 (14.21%))

SHEFFIELD SOUTH EAST
E. 70,422   T. 41,685 (59.19%)   Lab. hold
Clive Betts, Lab.   21,439
Steve Winstone, UKIP   9,128
Matt Sleat, C.   7,242
Gail Smith, LD   2,226
Linda Duckenfield, Green   1,117
Jen Battersby, CISTA   207
Ian Whitehouse, TUSC   185
Matthew Roberts, Eng. Dem.   141
Lab. majority 12,311 (29.53%)
7.31% swing Lab. to UKIP
(2010: Lab. majority 10,505 (25.37%))

SHERWOOD
E. 73,334   T. 50,698 (69.13%)   C. hold
Mark Spencer, C.   22,833
Leonie Mathers, Lab.   18,186
Sally Chadd, UKIP   7,399
Lydia Davies-Bright, Green   1,108
Dan Mosley, LD   1,094
Dave Perkins, Class War   78
C. majority 4,647 (9.17%)
4.36% swing Lab. to C.
(2010: C. majority 214 (0.44%))

SHIPLEY
E. 70,466   T. 50,542 (71.73%)   C. hold
Philip Davies, C.   25,269
Steve Clapcote, Lab.   15,645
Waqas Khan, UKIP   4,479
Kevin Warnes, Green   2,657
Andrew Martin, LD   1,949
Darren Hill, Yorks   543
C. majority 9,624 (19.04%)
0.54% swing C. to Lab.
(2010: C. majority 9,944 (20.12%))

SHREWSBURY & ATCHAM
E. 76,460   T. 54,102 (70.76%)   C. hold
Daniel Kawczynski, C.   24,628
Laura Davies, Lab.   15,063
Suzanne Evans, UKIP   7,813
Christine Tinker, LD   4,268
Emma Bullard, Green   2,247
Stirling McNeillie, Atom   83
C. majority 9,565 (17.68%)
2.85% swing C. to Lab.
(2010: C. majority 7,944 (14.98%))

SHROPSHIRE NORTH
E. 78,910   T. 52,573 (66.62%)   C. hold
Owen Paterson, C.   27,041
Graeme Currie, Lab.   10,547
Andrea Allen, UKIP   9,262
Tom Thornhill, LD   3,148
Duncan Kerr, Green   2,575
C. majority 16,494 (31.37%)
0.98% swing C. to Lab.
(2010: C. majority 15,828 (30.52%))

SITTINGBOURNE & SHEPPEY
E. 76,018   T. 49,378 (64.96%)   C. hold
Gordon Henderson, C.   24,425
Richard Palmer, UKIP   12,257
Guy Nicholson, Lab.   9,673
Keith Nevols, LD   1,563
Gary Miller, Green   1,185
Mad Mike Young, Loony   275
C. majority 12,168 (24.64%)
10.02% swing C. to UKIP
(2010: C. majority 12,383 (25.49%))

SKIPTON & RIPON
E. 76,243   T. 54,559 (71.56%)   C. hold
Julian Smith, C.   30,248
Malcolm Birks, Lab.   9,487
Alan Henderson, UKIP   7,651
Jacquie Bell, LD   4,057
Andy Brown, Green   3,116
C. majority 20,761 (38.05%)
1.25% swing C. to Lab.
(2010: C. majority 9,950 (18.18%))

SLEAFORD & NORTH HYKEHAM
E. 88,188   T. 61,944 (70.24%)   C. hold
Stephen Phillips, C.   34,805
Jason Pandya-Wood, Lab.   10,690
Steven Hopkins, UKIP   9,716
Matthew Holden, LD   3,500
Marianne Overton, Lincs Ind.   3,233
C. majority 24,115 (38.93%)
2.11% swing Lab. to C.
(2010: C. majority 19,905 (33.44%))

SLOUGH
E. 86,366   T. 48,275 (55.90%)   Lab. hold
Fiona Mactaggart, Lab.   23,421
Gurcharan Singh, C.   16,085
Diana Coad, UKIP   6,274
Tom McCann, LD   1,275
Julian Edmonds, Green   1,220
Lab. majority 7,336 (15.20%)
1.81% swing C. to Lab.
(2010: Lab. majority 5,523 (11.57%))

SOLIHULL
E. 77,251   T. 54,779 (70.91%)   C. gain
*Julian Knight, C.   26,956
Lorely Burt, LD   14,054
Phil Henrick, UKIP   6,361
Nigel Knowles, Lab.   5,693
Howard Allen, Green   1,632
Mike Nattrass, IE   50
Matthew Ward, DP   33
C. majority 12,902 (23.55%)
11.94% swing LD to C.
(2010: LD majority 175 (0.32%))

SOMERSET NORTH
E. 80,115   T. 58,942 (73.57%)   C. hold
Liam Fox, C.   31,540
Greg Chambers, Lab.   8,441
Ian Kealey, UKIP   7,669
Marcus Kravis, LD   7,486
David Derbyshire, Green   3,806
C. majority 23,099 (39.19%)
0.52% swing Lab. to C.
(2010: C. majority 7,862 (13.57%))

SOMERSET NORTH EAST
E. 69,380   T. 51,110 (73.67%)   C. hold
Jacob Rees-Mogg, C.   25,439
Todd Foreman, Lab.   12,690
Ernie Blaber, UKIP   6,150
Wera Hobhouse, LD   4,029
Katy Boyce, Green   2,802
C. majority 12,749 (24.94%)
7.67% swing Lab. to C.
(2010: C. majority 4,914 (9.60%))

SOMERTON & FROME
E. 83,527   T. 60,309 (72.20%)   C. gain
*David Warburton, C.   31,960
David Rendel, LD   11,692
Alan Dimmick, UKIP   6,439
Theo Simon, Green   5,434
David Oakensen, Lab.   4,419
Ian Angell, Ind.   365
C. majority 20,268 (33.61%)
18.30% swing LD to C.
(2010: LD majority 1,817 (3.00%))

SOUTH HOLLAND & THE DEEPINGS
E. 77,015   T. 49,207 (63.89%)   C. hold
John Hayes, C.   29,303
David Parsons, UKIP   10,736
Matthew Mahabadi, Lab.   6,122
Daniel Wilshire, Green   1,580
George Smid, LD   1,466
C. majority 18,567 (37.73%)
7.43% swing C. to UKIP
(2010: C. majority 21,880 (43.60%))

SOUTH RIBBLE
E. 76,489   T. 52,370 (68.47%)   C. hold
*Seema Kennedy, C.   24,313
Veronica Bennett, Lab.   18,368
David Gallagher, UKIP   7,377
Sue McGuire, LD   2,312
C. majority 5,945 (11.35%)
0.28% swing Lab. to C.
(2010: C. majority 5,554 (10.79%))

SOUTH SHIELDS
E. 62,730   T. 36,265 (57.81%)   Lab. hold
Emma Lewell-Buck, Lab.   18,589
Norman Dennis, UKIP   7,975
Robert Oliver, C.   6,021
Shirley Ford, Green   1,614
Lisa Nightingale, Ind.   1,427
Gita Gordon, LD   639
Lab. majority 10,614 (29.27%)
swing N/A
(2010: Lab. majority 11,109 (30.42%))
(2013: Lab. majority 6,505 (26.30%))

SOUTHAMPTON ITCHEN
E. 72,309   T. 44,710 (61.83%)   C. gain
*Royston Smith, C.   18,656
Rowenna Davis, Lab. Co-op   16,340
Kim Rose, UKIP   6,010
John Spottiswoode, Green   1,876
Eleanor Bell, LD   1,595
Sue Atkins, TUSC   233
C. majority 2,316 (5.18%)
2.81% swing Lab. to C.
(2010: Lab. majority 192 (0.43%))

SOUTHAMPTON TEST
E. 70,285   T. 43,652 (62.11%)   Lab. hold
Alan Whitehead, Lab.   18,017
Jeremy Moulton, C.   14,207
Pearline Hingston, UKIP   5,566
Angela Mawle, Green   2,568
Adrian Ford, LD   2,121
Chris Davis, Ind.   770
Nick Chaffey, TUSC   403
Lab. majority 3,810 (8.73%)
1.63% swing C. to Lab.
(2010: Lab. majority 2,413 (5.46%))

SOUTHEND WEST
E. 66,876   T. 44,509 (66.55%)   C. hold
David Amess, C.   22,175
Julian Ware-Lane, Lab.   8,154
Brian Otridge, UKIP   7,803
Paul Collins, LD   4,129
Jonathan Fuller, Green   2,083
Jeremy Moss, Eng. Dem.   165
C. majority 14,021 (31.50%)
0.57% swing C. to Lab.
(2010: C. majority 7,270 (16.67%))

SOUTHPORT
E. 67,328   T. 44,101 (65.50%)   LD hold
John Pugh, LD   13,652
Damien Moore, C.   12,330
Liz Savage, Lab.   8,468
Terry Durrance, UKIP   7,429
Laurence Rankin, Green   1,230
Jacqueline Barlow, Southport   992
LD majority 1,322 (3.00%)
5.38% swing LD to C.
(2010: LD majority 6,024 (13.77%))

SPELTHORNE
E. 71,592   T. 49,079 (68.55%)   C. hold
Kwasi Kwarteng, C.   24,386
Redvers Cunningham, UKIP   10,234
Rebecca Geach, Lab.   9,114
Rosie Shimell, LD   3,163
Paul Jacobs, Green   1,724
Juliet Griffith, ND   230
Paul Couchman, TUSC   228
C. majority 14,152 (28.84%)
4.87% swing C. to UKIP
(2010: C. majority 10,019 (21.18%))

STAFFORD
E. 68,705   T. 48,767 (70.98%)   C. hold
Jeremy Lefroy, C.   23,606
Kate Godfrey, Lab.   14,429
Edward Whitfield, UKIP   6,293
Karen Howell, NHAP   1,701
Mike Shone, Green   1,390
Keith Miller, LD   1,348
C. majority 9,177 (18.82%)
3.98% swing Lab. to C.
(2010: C. majority 5,460 (10.87%))

STAFFORDSHIRE MOORLANDS
E. 63,104   T. 42,587 (67.49%)   C. hold
Karen Bradley, C.   21,770
Trudie McGuinness, Lab.   11,596
George Langley-Poole, UKIP   6,236
John Redfern, LD   1,759
Brian Smith, Green   1,226
C. majority 10,174 (23.89%)
4.31% swing Lab. to C.
(2010: C. majority 6,689 (15.27%))

STAFFORDSHIRE SOUTH
E. 84,243   T. 49,598 (58.87%)   C. hold
Gavin Williamson, C.   29,478
Kevin McElduff, Lab.   9,107
Lyndon Jones, UKIP   8,267
Robert Woodthorpe Browne, LD   1,448
Claire McIlvenna, Green   1,298
C. majority 20,371 (41.07%)
4.09% swing Lab. to C.
(2010: C. majority 16,590 (32.89%))

STALYBRIDGE & HYDE
E. 69,081   T. 41,034 (59.40%)
                            Lab. Co-op hold
Jonathan Reynolds, Lab. Co-op   18,447
Martin Riley, C.   11,761
Angela McManus, UKIP   7,720
Jenny Ross, Green   1,850
Pete Flynn, LD   1,256
Lab. Co-op majority 6,686 (16.29%)
4.79% swing C. to Lab.
(2010: Lab. majority 2,744 (6.71%))

STEVENAGE
E. 70,597   T. 47,799 (67.71%)   C. hold
Stephen McPartland, C.   21,291
Sharon Taylor, Lab. Co-op   16,336
David Collins, UKIP   6,864
Susan Van De Ven, LD   1,582
Graham White, Green   1,369
Trevor Palmer, TUSC   175
Charles Vickers, Eng. Dem.   115
David Cox, Ind.   67
C. majority 4,955 (10.37%)
1.18% swing Lab. to C.
(2010: C. majority 3,578 (8.01%))

STOCKPORT
E. 63,931   T. 39,649 (62.02%)   Lab. hold
Ann Coffey, Lab.   19,771
Daniel Hamilton, C.   9,710
Steven Woolfe, UKIP   5,206
Daniel Hawthorne, LD   3,034
Gary Lawson, Green   1,753
John Pearson, LU   175
Lab. majority 10,061 (25.38%)
4.02% swing C. to Lab.
(2010: Lab. majority 6,784 (17.34%))

STOCKTON NORTH
E. 66,126   T. 39,571 (59.84%)   Lab. hold
Alex Cunningham, Lab.   19,436
Chris Daniels, C.   11,069
Mandy Boylett, UKIP   7,581
Anthony Sycamore, LD   884
John Tait, NE   601
Lab. majority 8,367 (21.14%)
2.12% swing C. to Lab.
(2010: Lab. majority 6,676 (16.90%))

STOCKTON SOUTH
E. 75,109   T. 51,797 (68.96%)   C. hold
James Wharton, C.   24,221
Louise Baldock, Lab. Co-op   19,175
Ted Strike, UKIP   5,480
Drew Durning, LD   1,366
Jacqui Lovell, Green   952
Steve Walmsley, IASI   603
C. majority 5,046 (9.74%)
4.54% swing Lab. to C.
(2010: C. majority 332 (0.66%))

STOKE-ON-TRENT CENTRAL
E. 62,250   T. 31,084 (49.93%)   Lab. hold
Tristram Hunt, Lab.   12,220
Mick Harold, UKIP   7,041
Liam Ascough, C.   7,008
Mark Breeze, Ind.   2,120
Zulfiqar Ali, LD   1,296
Jan Zablocki, Green   1,123
Ali Majid, CISTA   244
Paul Toussaint, Ubuntu   32
Lab. majority 5,179 (16.66%)
8.92% swing Lab. to UKIP
(2010: Lab. majority 5,566 (17.14%))

STOKE-ON-TRENT NORTH
E. 72,689   T. 38,654 (53.18%)   Lab. hold
*Ruth Smeeth, Lab.   15,429
Ben Adams, C.   10,593
Geoffrey Locke, UKIP   9,542
Paul Roberts, LD   1,137
Sean Adam, Green   1,091
John Millward, Ind.   508
Craig Pond, Ind.   354
Lab. majority 4,836 (12.51%)
3.99% swing Lab. to C.
(2010: Lab. majority 8,235 (20.49%))

STOKE-ON-TRENT SOUTH
E. 68,788   T. 39,107 (56.85%)   Lab. hold
Rob Flello, Lab.   15,319
Joe Rich, C.   12,780
Tariq Mahmood, UKIP   8,298
Peter Andras, LD   1,309
Luke Bellamy, Green   1,029
Matt Wright, TUSC   372
Lab. majority 2,539 (6.49%)
1.94% swing Lab. to C.
(2010: Lab. majority 4,130 (10.36%))

STONE
E. 67,339   T. 47,031 (69.84%)   C. hold
Bill Cash, C.   25,733
Sam Hale, Lab.   9,483
Andrew Illsley, UKIP   7,620
Martin Lewis, LD   2,473
Wenslie Naylon, Green   1,191
John Coutouvidis, Ind.   531
C. majority 16,250 (34.55%)
2.33% swing Lab. to C.
(2010: C. majority 13,292 (28.14%))

STOURBRIDGE
E. 69,077   T. 46,029 (66.63%)   C. hold
Margot James, C.   21,195
Pete Lowe, Lab.   14,501
James Carver, UKIP   7,774
Chris Bramall, LD   1,538
Christian Kiever, Green   1,021
C. majority 6,694 (14.54%)
1.81% swing Lab. to C.
(2010: C. majority 5,164 (10.93%))

STRATFORD-ON-AVON
E. 70,914   T. 51,459 (72.57%)   C. hold
Nadhim Zahawi, C.   29,674
Edward Fila, UKIP   6,798
Jeff Kenner, Lab.   6,677
Elizabeth Adams, LD   6,182
Dominic Giles, Green   2,128
C. majority 22,876 (44.45%)
1.72% swing C. to UKIP
(2010: C. majority 11,346 (22.45%))

STREATHAM
E. 78,673   T. 49,933 (63.47%)   Lab. hold
Chuka Umunna, Lab.   26,474
Kim Caddy, C.   12,540
Amna Ahmad, LD   4,491
Jonathan Bartley, Green   4,421
Bruce Machan, UKIP   1,602
Artificial Beast, CISTA   192
Unjum Mirza, TUSC   164
Deon Gayle, WRP   49
Lab. majority 13,934 (27.91%)
1.72% swing C. to Lab.
(2010: Lab. majority 3,259 (6.96%))

STRETFORD & URMSTON
E. 69,490   T. 46,386 (66.75%)   Lab. hold
Kate Green, Lab.   24,601
Lisa Cooke, C.   12,916
Kalvin Chapman, UKIP   5,068
Geraldine Coggins, Green   2,187
Louise Ankers, LD   1,362
Paul Bradley-Law, Whig   169
Paul Carson, PP UK   83
Lab. majority 11,685 (25.19%)
2.65% swing C. to Lab.
(2010: Lab. majority 8,935 (19.90%))

STROUD
E. 80,522   T. 60,819 (75.53%)   C. hold
Neil Carmichael, C.   27,813
David Drew, Lab. Co-op   22,947
Caroline Stephens, UKIP   4,848
Sarah Lunnon, Green   2,779
Adrian Walker-Smith, LD   2,086
Rich Wilson, Ind.   246
David Michael, FPT   100
C. majority 4,866 (8.00%)
2.88% swing Lab. to C.
(2010: C. majority 1,299 (2.24%))

SUFFOLK CENTRAL & IPSWICH
NORTH
E. 78,782   T. 54,089 (68.66%)   C. hold
Daniel Poulter, C.   30,317
Jack Abbott, Lab.   10,173
Mark Cole, UKIP   7,459
Jon Neal, LD   3,314
Rhodri Griffiths, Green   2,664
Tony Holyoak, Eng. Dem.   162
C. majority 20,144 (37.24%)
1.32% swing Lab. to C.
(2010: C. majority 13,786 (25.81%))

SUFFOLK COASTAL
E. 78,782   T. 55,594 (70.57%)   C. hold
Therese Coffey, C.   28,855
Russell Whiting, Lab.   10,013
Daryll Pitcher, UKIP   8,655
James Sandbach, LD   4,777
Rachel Smith-Lyte, Green   3,294
C. majority 18,842 (33.89%)
1.77% swing Lab. to C.
(2010: C. majority 9,128 (16.63%))

SUFFOLK SOUTH
E. 73,220   T. 51,907 (70.89%)   C. hold
*James Cartlidge, C.   27,546
Jane Basham, Lab.   10,001
Steven Whalley, UKIP   7,897
Grace Weaver, LD   4,044
Robert Lindsay, Green   2,253
Stephen Todd, CPA   166
C. majority 17,545 (33.80%)
0.19% swing Lab. to C.
(2010: C. majority 8,689 (16.90%))

SUFFOLK WEST
E. 76,197   T. 49,232 (64.61%)   C. hold
Matthew Hancock, C.   25,044
Julian Flood, UKIP   10,700
Michael Jefferys, Lab.   8,604
Elfreda Tealby-Watson, LD   2,465
Niall Pettitt, Green   1,779
C. majority 14,984 (30.44%)
6.85% swing C. to UKIP
(2010: C. majority 13,050 (27.14%))

SUNDERLAND CENTRAL
E. 72,933   T. 41,762 (57.26%)   Lab. hold
Julie Elliott, Lab.   20,959
Jeffrey Townsend, C.   9,780
Bryan Foster, UKIP   7,997
Rachel Featherstone, Green   1,706
Adrian Page, LD   1,105
Joseph Young, ND   215
Lab. majority 11,179 (26.77%)
5.47% swing C. to Lab.
(2010: Lab. majority 6,725 (15.84%))

SURREY EAST
E. 79,654   T. 56,103 (70.43%)   C. hold
Sam Gyimah, C.   32,211
Helena Windsor, UKIP   9,553
Matt Wilson, Lab.   6,627
David Lee, LD   5,189
Nicky Dodgson, Green   2,159
Sandy Pratt, Ind.   364
C. majority 22,658 (40.39%)
4.73% swing C. to UKIP
(2010: C. majority 16,874 (30.88%))

SURREY HEATH
E. 79,515   T. 54,431 (68.45%)   C. hold
Michael Gove, C.   32,582
Paul Chapman, UKIP   7,778
Laween Atroshi, Lab.   6,100
Ann-Marie Barker, LD   4,937
Kimberley Lawson, Green   2,400
Juliana Brimicombe, Ch. P.   361
Bob Smith, Ind.   273
C. majority 24,804 (45.57%)
2.88% swing C. to UKIP
(2010: C. majority 17,289 (31.81%))

SURREY SOUTH WEST
E. 77,050   T. 57,119 (74.13%)   C. hold
Jeremy Hunt, C.   34,199
Mark Webber, UKIP   5,643
Howard Kaye, Lab.   5,415
Louise Irvine, NHAP   4,851
Patrick Haveron, LD   3,586
Susan Ryland, Green   3,105
Paul Robinson, S. New   320
C. majority 28,556 (49.99%)
3.05% swing C. to UKIP
(2010: C. majority 16,318 (28.50%))

SUSSEX MID
E. 79,520   T. 57,492 (72.30%)   C. hold
Nicholas Soames, C.   32,268
Greg Mountain, UKIP   7,982
Toby Brothers, UKIP   6,898
Daisy Cooper, LD   6,604
Miranda Diboll, Green   2,453
Beki Adam, Ind.   958
Baron Von Thunderclap, Loony   329
C. majority 24,286 (42.24%)
0.94% swing C. to Lab.
(2010: C. majority 7,402 (13.25%))

SUTTON & CHEAM
E. 69,160   T. 49,905 (72.16%)   C. gain
*Paul Scully, C.   20,732
Paul Burstow, LD   16,811
Emily Brothers, Lab.   5,546
Angus Dalgleish, UKIP   5,341
Maeve Tomlinson, Green   1,051
Dave Ash, NHAP   345
Pauline Gorman, TUSC   79
C. majority 3,921 (7.86%)
5.59% swing LD to C.
(2010: LD majority 1,608 (3.31%))

SUTTON COLDFIELD
E. 74,956   T. 50,854 (67.85%)   C. hold
Andrew Mitchell, C.   27,782
Rob Pocock, Lab.   11,365
Marcus Brown, UKIP   7,489
Richard Brighton-Knight, LD   2,627
David Ratcliff, Green   1,426
Mark Sleigh, Ubuntu   165
C. majority 16,417 (32.28%)
0.67% swing C. to Lab.
(2010: C. majority 17,005 (33.61%))

SWINDON NORTH
E. 81,005   T. 52,242 (64.49%)   C. hold
Justin Tomlinson, C.   26,295
Mark Dempsey, Lab.   14,509
James Faulkner, UKIP   8,011
Poppy Hebden-Leeder, Green   1,723
Janet Ellard, LD   1,704
C. majority 11,786 (22.56%)
4.26% swing Lab. to C.
(2010: C. majority 7,060 (14.04%))

SWINDON SOUTH
E. 73,956   T. 49,263 (66.61%)   C. hold
Robert Buckland, C.   22,777
Anne Snelgrove, Lab.   16,992
John Short, UKIP   5,920
Damon Hooton, LD   1,817
Talis Kimberley-Fairbourn, Green   1,757
C. majority 5,785 (11.74%)
2.11% swing Lab. to C.
(2010: C. majority 3,544 (7.52%))

TAMWORTH
E. 71,912   T. 47,174 (65.60%)   C. hold
Christopher Pincher, C.   23,606
Carol Dean, Lab.   12,304
Jan Higgins, UKIP   8,727
Jenny Pinkett, LD   1,427
Nicola Holmes, Green   1,110
C. majority 11,302 (23.96%)
5.42% swing Lab. to C.
(2010: C. majority 6,090 (13.13%))

TATTON
E. 64,512   T. 45,298 (70.22%)   C. hold
George Osborne, C.   26,552
David Pinto-Duschinsky, Lab.   8,311
Stuart Hutton, UKIP   4,871
Gareth Wilson, LD   3,850
Tina Louise Rothery, Green   1,714
C. majority 18,241 (40.27%)
1.47% swing Lab. to C.
(2010: C. majority 14,487 (32.03%))

TAUNTON DEANE
E. 81,830   T. 57,887 (70.74%)   C. gain
*Rebecca Pow, C.   27,849
Rachel Gilmour, LD   12,358
Laura Bailhache, UKIP   6,921
Neil Guild, Lab.   5,347
Clive Martin, Green   2,630
Mike Rigby, Ind.   2,568
Stephen German, TUSC   118
Bruce Gauld, Ind.   96
C. majority 15,491 (26.76%)
16.81% swing LD to C.
(2010: LD majority 3,993 (6.87%))

TELFORD
E. 66,166   T. 40,645 (61.43%)   C. gain
*Lucy Allan, C.   16,094
David Wright, Lab.   15,364
Denis Allen, UKIP   7,330
Peter Hawkins, Green   930
Ian Croll, LD   927
C. majority 730 (1.80%)
2.08% swing Lab. to C.
(2010: Lab. majority 978 (2.37%))

TEWKESBURY
E. 78,500   T. 55,344 (70.50%)   C. hold
Laurence Robertson, C.   30,176
Ed Buxton, Lab.   8,204
Alistair Cameron, LD   7,629
Stuart Adair, UKIP   7,128
Jemma Clarke, Green   2,207
C. majority 21,972 (39.70%)
2.04% swing Lab. to C.
(2010: C. majority 6,310 (11.69%))

THANET NORTH
E. 70,504   T. 47,053 (66.74%)   C. hold
Roger Gale, C.   23,045
Piers Wauchope, UKIP   12,097
Frances Rehal, Lab.   8,411
Ed Targett, Green   1,719
George Cunningham, LD   1,645
Cemanthe McKenzie, Thanet   136
C. majority 10,948 (23.27%)
11.45% swing C. to UKIP
(2010: C. majority 13,528 (31.21%))

THANET SOUTH
E. 70,182   T. 49,401 (70.39%)   C. hold
*Craig Mackinlay, C.   18,838
Nigel Farage, UKIP   16,026
Will Scobie, Lab.   11,740
Ian Driver, Green   1,076
Russ Timpson, LD   932
Al Murray, FUKP   318
Ruth Bailey, Manston   191
Nigel Askew, Reality   126
Grahame Birchall, Thanet   63
Dean McCastree, Ind.   61
Zebadiah Abu-Obadiah, Zeb   30
C. majority 2,812 (5.69%)
18.40% swing C. to UKIP
(2010: C. majority 7,617 (16.58%))

THIRSK & MALTON
E. 77,451   T. 52,365 (67.61%)   C. hold
*Kevin Hollinrake, C.   27,545
Alan Avery, Lab.   8,089
Toby Horton, UKIP   7,805
Dinah Keal, LD   4,703
Chris Newsam, Green   2,404
John Clark, Lib.   1,127
Philip Tate, Ind.   692
C. majority 19,456 (37.15%)
1.08% swing C. to Lab.
(2010: C. majority 11,281 (29.58%))

THORNBURY & YATE
E. 65,884   T. 48,570 (73.72%)   C. gain
*Luke Hall, C.   19,924
Steve Webb, LD   18,429
Russ Martin, UKIP   5,126
Hadleigh Roberts, Lab.   3,775
Iain Hamilton, Green   1,316
C. majority 1,495 (3.08%)
8.92% swing LD to C.
(2010: LD majority 7,116 (14.76%))

THURROCK
E. 77,569   T. 49,564 (63.90%)   C. hold
Jackie Doyle-Price, C.   16,692
Polly Billington, Lab.   16,156
Tim Aker, UKIP   15,718
Rhodri Jamieson-Ball, LD   644
Jamie Barnes, CISTA   244
Daniel Munyambu, ND   79
Aba Kristilolu, AP   31
C. majority 536 (1.08%)
0.44% swing Lab. to C.
(2010: C. majority 92 (0.20%))

TIVERTON & HONITON
E. 76,270   T. 53,763 (70.49%)   C. hold
Neil Parish, C.   29,030
Graham Smith, UKIP   8,857
Caroline Kolek, Lab.   6,835
Stephen Kearney, LD   5,626
Paul Edwards, Green   3,415
C. majority 20,173 (37.52%)
3.41% swing C. to UKIP
(2010: C. majority 9,320 (16.98%))

TONBRIDGE & MALLING
E. 74,877   T. 53,670 (71.68%)   C. hold
*Thomas Tugendhat, C.   31,887
Robert Izzard, UKIP   8,153
Claire Leigh, Lab.   7,604
Mary Varrall, LD   3,660
Howard Porter, Green   2,366
C. majority 23,734 (44.22%)
4.99% swing C. to UKIP
(2010: C. majority 18,178 (35.43%))

TOOTING
E. 76,778   T. 53,529 (69.72%)   Lab. hold
Sadiq Khan, Lab.   25,263
Dan Watkins, C.   22,421
Esther Obiri-Darko, Green   2,201
Philip Ling, LD   2,107
Przemek Skwirczynski, UKIP   1,537
Lab. majority 2,842 (5.31%)
0.16% swing LD to Lab.
(2010: Lab. majority 2,524 (4.98%))

TORBAY
E. 76,259   T. 48,079 (63.05%)   C. gain
*Kevin Foster, C.   19,551
Adrian Sanders, LD   16,265
Tony McIntyre, UKIP   6,540
Su Maddock, Lab.   4,166
Paula Hermes, Green   1,557
C. majority 3,286 (6.83%)
7.56% swing LD to C.
(2010: LD majority 4,078 (8.29%))

TOTNES
E. 68,630   T. 47,097 (68.62%)   C. hold
Sarah Wollaston, C.   24,941
Justin Haque, UKIP   6,656
Nicky Williams, Lab.   5,988
Gill Coombs, Green   4,845
Julian Brazil, LD   4,667
C. majority 18,285 (38.82%)
0.50% swing C. to UKIP
(2010: C. majority 4,927 (10.30%))

TOTTENHAM
E. 70,809   T. 42,558 (60.10%)   Lab. hold
David Lammy, Lab.   28,654
Stefan Mrozinski, C.   5,090
Dee Searle, Green   3,931
Turhan Ozen, LD   1,756
Tariq Saeed, UKIP   1,512
Jenny Sutton, TUSC   1,324
Tania Mahmood, Peace   291
Lab. majority 23,564 (55.37%)
5.49% swing C. to Lab.
(2010: Lab. majority 16,931 (41.61%))

TRURO & FALMOUTH
E. 73,601   T. 51,544 (70.03%)   C. hold
Sarah Newton, C.   22,681
Simon Rix, LD   8,681
Stuart Roden, Lab.   7,814
John Hyslop, UKIP   5,967
Karen Westbrook, Green   4,483
Loic Rich, Ind.   792
Stephen Richardson, Meb. Ker.   563
Rik Evans, NHAP   526
Stanley Guffogg, PPP   37
C. majority 14,000 (27.16%)
13.13% swing LD to C.
(2010: C. majority 435 (0.89%))

TUNBRIDGE WELLS
E. 73,429   T. 51,428 (70.04%)   C. hold
Greg Clark, C.   30,181
Kevin Kerrigan, Lab.   7,307
Colin Nicholson, UKIP   6,481
James MacCleary, LD   4,342
Marie Jones, Green   2,659
Graham Naismith, Ind.   458
C. majority 22,874 (44.48%)
0.47% swing C. to Lab.
(2010: C. majority 15,576 (30.95%))

TWICKENHAM
E. 80,242   T. 62,004 (77.27%)   C. gain
*Tania Mathias, C.   25,580
Vince Cable, LD   23,563
Nick Grant, Lab.   7,129
Barry Edwards, UKIP   3,069
Tanya Williams, Green   2,463
Dominic Stockford, Ch. P.   174
David Wedgwood, MC   26
C. majority 2,017 (3.25%)
11.79% swing LD to C.
(2010: LD majority 12,140 (20.33%))

TYNEMOUTH
E. 77,523   T. 53,495 (69.01%)   Lab. hold
Alan Campbell, Lab.   25,791
Glenn Hall, C.   17,551
Gary Legg, UKIP   6,541
Julia Erskine, Green   2,017
John Paton-Day, LD   1,595
Lab. majority 8,240 (15.40%)
2.25% swing C. to Lab.
(2010: Lab. majority 5,739 (10.90%))

TYNESIDE NORTH
E. 79,286   T. 46,818 (59.05%)   Lab. hold
Mary Glindon, Lab.   26,191
Martin McGann, C.   8,997
Scott Hartley, UKIP   7,613
John Appleby, LD   2,075
Martin Collins, Green   1,442
Tim Wall, TUSC   304
Bob Batten, NF   191
Lab. majority 17,194 (36.73%)
2.21% swing C. to Lab.
(2010: Lab. majority 12,884 (27.76%))

UXBRIDGE & RUISLIP SOUTH
E. 70,634   T. 44,811 (63.44%)   C. hold
*Boris Johnson, C.   22,511
Chris Summers, Lab.   11,816
Jack Duffin, UKIP   6,346
Mike Cox, LD   2,215
Graham Lee, Green   1,414
Gary Harbord, TUSC   180
Jenny Thompson, Ind.   84
Howling Laud Hope, Loony   72
Sabrina Moosun, Community   52
Lord Toby Jug, Eccentric   50
Michael Doherty, Ind.   39
Jane Lawrence, Realist   18
James Jackson, ND   14
C. majority 10,695 (23.87%)
0.51% swing C. to Lab.
(2010: C. majority 11,216 (24.88%))

VAUXHALL
E. 81,698   T. 47,941 (58.68%)   Lab. hold
Kate Hoey, Lab.   25,778
James Bellis, C.   13,070
Gulnar Hasnain, Green   3,658
Adrian Hyyrylainen-Trett, LD   3,312
Ace Nnorom, UKIP   1,385
Mark Chapman, Pirate   201
Simon Hardy, LU   188
Louis Jensen, CISTA   164
Waleed Salman Ghani, Whig   103
Danny Lambert, SPGB   82
Lab. majority 12,708 (26.51%)
0.87% swing Lab. to C.
(2010: Lab. majority 10,651 (24.66%))

WAKEFIELD
E. 70,521   T. 42,973 (60.94%)   Lab hold
Mary Creagh, Lab.   17,301
Antony Calvert, C.   14,688
Alan Hazelhurst, UKIP   7,862
Finbarr Cronin, LD   1,483
Rebecca Thackray, Green   1,069
Mick Griffiths, TUSC   287
Elliot Barr, CISTA   283
Lab. majority 2,613 (6.08%)
1.23% swing C. to Lab.
(2010: Lab. majority 1,613 (3.63%))

WALLASEY
E. 65,495   T. 43,366 (66.21%)   Lab. hold
Angela Eagle, Lab.   26,176
Chris Clarkson, C.   9,828
Geoff Caton, UKIP   5,063
Julian Pratt, Green   1,288
Kris Brown, LD   1,011
Lab. majority 16,348 (37.70%)
8.64% swing C. to Lab.
(2010: Lab. majority 8,507 (20.42%))

WALSALL NORTH
E. 67,080   T. 36,883 (54.98%)   Lab. hold
David Winnick, Lab.   14,392
Douglas Hansen-Luke, C.   12,455
Liz Hazell, UKIP   8,122
Nigel Jones, LD   840
Pete Smith, TUSC   545
Mike Harrison, Green   529
Lab. majority 1,937 (5.25%)
1.26% swing C. to Lab.
(2010: Lab. majority 990 (2.74%))

WALSALL SOUTH
E. 67,743   T. 41,838 (61.76%)   Lab. hold
Valerie Vaz, Lab.   19,740
Sue Arnold, C.   13,733
Derek Bennett, UKIP   6,540
Charlotte Fletcher, Green   1,149
Joel Kenrick, LD   676
Lab. majority 6,007 (14.36%)
5.03% swing C. to Lab.
(2010: Lab. majority 1,755 (4.29%))

WALTHAMSTOW
E. 67,289   T. 41,796 (62.11%)
                                 Lab. Co-op hold
Stella Creasy, Lab. Co-op   28,779
Molly Samuel-Leport, C.   5,584
Michael Gold, Green   2,661
Paul Hillman, UKIP   2,507
Steven Cheung, LD   1,661
Nancy Taaffe, TUSC   394
Ellie Merton, ND   129
Jonty Leff, WRP   81
Lab. Co-op majority 23,195 (55.50%)
8.82% swing C. to Lab.
(2010: Lab. majority 9,478 (23.12%))

WANSBECK
E. 63,273   T. 38,528 (60.89%)   Lab. hold
Ian Lavery, Lab.   19,267
Chris Galley, C.   8,386
Melanie Hurst, UKIP   7,014
Tom Hancock, LD   2,407
Christopher Hedley, Green   1,454
Lab. majority 10,881 (28.24%)
0.03% swing Lab. to C.
(2010: Lab. majority 7,031 (18.37%))

WANTAGE
E. 83,516   T. 58,320 (69.83%)   C. hold
Ed Vaizey, C.   31,092
Stephen Webb, Lab.   9,343
Alex Meredith, UKIP   7,611
Lee Upcraft, UKIP   7,288
Kate Prendergast, Green   2,986
C. majority 21,749 (37.29%)
0.37% swing C. to Lab.
(2010: C. majority 13,547 (24.04%))

WARLEY
E. 63,740   T. 37,829 (59.35%)   Lab. hold
John Spellar, Lab.   22,012
Tom Williams, C.   7,310
Pete Durnell, UKIP   6,237
Robert Buckman, Green   1,465
Catherine Smith, LD   805
Lab. majority 14,702 (38.86%)
5.38% swing C. to Lab.
(2010: Lab. majority 10,756 (28.11%))

WARRINGTON NORTH
E. 72,632   T. 45,419 (62.53%)   Lab. hold
Helen Jones, Lab.   21,720
Richard Short, C.   12,797
Trevor Nicholls, UKIP   7,757
Stefan Krizanac, LD   1,881
Sarah Hayes, Green   1,264
Lab. majority 8,923 (19.65%)
2.17% swing C. to Lab.
(2010: Lab. majority 6,771 (15.32%))

WARRINGTON SOUTH
E. 85,566   T. 59,353 (69.37%)   C. hold
David Mowat, C.   25,928
Nick Bent, Lab.   23,178
Malcolm Lingley, UKIP   4,909
Bob Barr, LD   3,335
Stephanie Davies, Green   1,765
Kevin Bennett, TUSC   238
C. majority 2,750 (4.63%)
0.90% swing Lab. to C.
(2010: C. majority 1,553 (2.83%))

WARWICK & LEAMINGTON
E. 71,570   T. 50,581 (70.67%)   C. hold
Chris White, C.   24,249
Lynnette Kelly, Lab.   17,643
Alastair MacBrayne, UKIP   4,183
Haseeb Arif, LD   2,512
Azzees Minott, Green   1,994
C. majority 6,606 (13.06%)
2.95% swing Lab. to C.
(2010: C. majority 3,513 (7.16%))

WARWICKSHIRE NORTH
E. 70,152   T. 47,377 (67.53%)   C. hold
*Craig Tracey, C.   20,042
Mike O'Brien, Lab.   17,069
William Cash, UKIP   8,256
Alan Beddow, LD   978
Ian Bonner, Green   894
Eileen Hunter, TUSC   138
C. majority 2,973 (6.28%)
3.08% swing Lab. to C.
(2010: C. majority 54 (0.11%))

WASHINGTON & SUNDERLAND WEST
E. 68,188   T. 37,257 (54.64%)   Lab. hold
Sharon Hodgson, Lab.   20,478
Aileen Casey, UKIP   7,321
Bob Dhillon, C.   7,033
Anthony Murphy, Green   1,091
Dominic Haney, LD   993
Gary Duncan, TUSC   341
Lab. majority 13,157 (35.31%)
6.92% swing Lab. to UKIP
(2010: Lab. majority 11,458 (30.69%))

WATFORD
E. 84,270   T. 56,149 (66.63%)   C. hold
Richard Harrington, C.   24,400
Matt Turmaine, Lab.   14,606
Dorothy Thornhill, LD   10,152
Nick Lincoln, UKIP   5,481
Aidan Cottrell-Boyce, Green   1,332
Mark O'Connor, TUSC   178
C. majority 9,794 (17.44%)
4.61% swing Lab. to C.
(2010: C. majority 1,425 (2.58%))

WAVENEY
E. 80,171   T. 52,196 (65.11%)   C. hold
Peter Aldous, C.   22,104
Bob Blizzard, Lab.   19,696
Simon Tobin, UKIP   7,580
Graham Elliott, Green   1,761
Steve Gordon, LD   1,055
C. majority 2,408 (4.61%)
1.55% swing Lab. to C.
(2010: C. majority 769 (1.50%))

WEALDEN
E. 80,252   T. 57,017 (71.05%)   C. hold
*Nus Ghani, C.   32,508
Peter Griffiths, UKIP   9,541
Solomon Curtis, Lab.   6,165
Giles Goodall, LD   5,180
Mark Smith, Green   3,623
C. majority 22,967 (40.28%)
5.12% swing C. to UKIP
(2010: C. majority 17,179 (31.25%))

WEAVER VALE
E. 68,407   T. 46,867 (68.51%)   C. hold
Graham Evans, C.   20,227
Julia Tickridge, Lab.   19,421
Amos Wright, UKIP   4,547
Mary Di Mauro, LD   1,395
Chris Copeman, Green   1,183
Joseph Whyte, TUSC   94
C. majority 806 (1.72%)
0.27% swing C. to Lab.
(2010: C. majority 991 (2.25%))

WELLINGBOROUGH
E. 77,127   T. 50,430 (65.39%)   C. hold
Peter Bone, C.   26,265
Jonathan Munday, UKIP   9,868
Richard Garvie, Lab.   9,839
Chris Nelson, LD   2,240
Marion Turner-Hawes, Green   2,218
C. majority 16,397 (32.51%)
6.28% swing C. to UKIP
(2010: C. majority 11,787 (22.82%))

WELLS
E. 79,405   T. 56,904 (71.66%)   C. gain
*James Heappey, C.   26,247
Tessa Munt, LD   18,662
Helen Hims, UKIP   5,644
Chris Inchley, Lab.   3,780
Jon Cousins, Green   2,331
Paul Arnold, ND   83
Dave Dobbs, Birthday   81
Gypsy Watkins, Ind.   76
C. majority 7,585 (13.33%)
7.38% swing LD to C.
(2010: LD majority 800 (1.43%))

WELWYN HATFIELD
E. 73,264   T. 50,205 (68.53%)   C. hold
Grant Shapps, C.   25,281
Anawar Miah, Lab.   13,128
Arthur Stevens, UKIP   6,556
Hugh Annand, LD   3,140
Marc Scheimann, Green   1,742
Michael Green, Ind.   216
Richard Shattock, TUSC   142
C. majority 12,153 (24.21%)
5.69% swing C. to Lab.
(2010: C. majority 17,423 (35.58%))

WENTWORTH & DEARNE
E. 74,283   T. 43,189 (58.14%)   Lab. hold
John Healey, Lab.   24,571
Mike Hookem, UKIP   10,733
Michael Naughton, C.   6,441
Edwin Simpson, LD   1,135
Alan England, Eng. Dem.   309
Lab. majority 13,838 (32.04%)
5.23% swing Lab. to UKIP
(2010: Lab. majority 13,920 (33.06%))

WEST BROMWICH EAST
E. 63,641   T. 37,492 (58.91%)   Lab. hold
Tom Watson, Lab.   18,817
Olivia Seccombe, C.   9,347
Steve Latham, UKIP   7,949
Flo Clucas, LD   751
Barry Lim, Green   628
Lab. majority 9,470 (25.26%)
3.81% swing C. to Lab.
(2010: Lab. majority 6,696 (17.64%))

WEST BROMWICH WEST
E. 65,533   T. 35,026 (53.45%)
                            Lab. Co-op hold
Adrian Bailey, Lab. Co-op   16,578
Graham Eardley, UKIP   8,836
Paul Ratner, C.   8,365
Mark Redding, Green   697
Karen Trench, LD   550
Lab. Co-op majority 7,742 (22.10%)
9.26% swing Lab. to UKIP
(2010: Lab. majority 5,651 (15.62%))

WEST HAM
E. 90,634   T. 52,793 (58.25%)   Lab. hold
Lyn Brown, Lab.   36,132
Festus Akinbusoye, C.   8,146
Jamie McKenzie, UKIP   3,950
Rachel Collinson, Green   2,651
Paul Reynolds, LD   1,430
Andy Uzoka, CPA   369
Cydatty Bogie, Community   115
Lab. majority 27,986 (53.01%)
2.51% swing C. to Lab.
(2010: Lab. majority 22,534 (47.99%))

WESTMINSTER NORTH
E. 62,346   T. 39,514 (63.38%)   Lab. hold
Karen Buck, Lab.   18,504
Lindsey Hall, C.   16,527
Nigel Sussman, UKIP   1,489
Kirsty Allan, LD   1,457
Jennifer Nadel, Green   1,322
Gabriela Fajardo, Ch. P.   152
Nicholas Ward, Ind.   63
Lab. majority 1,977 (5.00%)
0.18% swing Lab. to C.
(2010: Lab. majority 2,126 (5.37%))

WESTMORLAND & LONSDALE
E. 65,857   T. 48,929 (74.30%)   LD hold
Tim Farron, LD   25,194
Ann Myatt, C.   16,245
Alan Piper, UKIP   3,031
John Bateson, Lab.   2,661
Chris Loynes, Green   1,798
LD majority 8,949 (18.29%)
2.76% swing LD to C.
(2010: LD majority 12,264 (23.82%))

WESTON-SUPER-MARE
E. 79,493   T. 52,552 (66.11%)   C. hold
John Penrose, C.   25,203
Tim Taylor, Lab.   9,594
Ernie Warrender, UKIP   9,366
John Munro, LD   5,486
Richard Lawson, Green   2,592
Ronald Lavelle, Eng. Dem.   311
C. majority 15,609 (29.70%)
1.83% swing C. to Lab.
(2010: C. majority 2,691 (5.10%))

WIGAN
E. 76,068   T. 45,293 (59.54%)   Lab. hold
Lisa Nandy, Lab.   23,625
Caroline Kerswell, C.   9,389
Mark Bradley, UKIP   8,818
Will Patterson, Green   1,273
Mark Clayton, LD   1,255
Gareth Fairhurst, Wigan   768
Brian Parr, Ind.   165
Lab. majority 14,236 (31.43%)
3.84% swing C. to Lab.
(2010: Lab. majority 10,487 (23.76%))

WILTSHIRE NORTH
E. 67,858   T. 50,556 (74.50%)   C. hold
James Gray, C.   28,938
Brian Mathew, LD   7,892
Patricia Bryant, UKIP   5,813
Peter Baldrey, Lab.   4,930
Phil Chamberlain, Green   2,350
Simon Killane, Ind.   390
Giles Wareham, Ind.   243
C. majority 21,046 (41.63%)
13.13% swing LD to C.
(2010: C. majority 7,483 (15.37%))

WILTSHIRE SOUTH WEST
E. 73,030   T. 51,643 (70.71%)   C. hold
Andrew Murrison, C.   27,198
Matthew Brown, UKIP   9,030
George Aylett, Lab.   6,948
Trevor Carbin, LD   5,482
Phil Randle, Green   2,985
C. majority 18,168 (35.18%)
5.50% swing C. to UKIP
(2010: C. majority 10,367 (21.15%))

WIMBLEDON
E. 65,853   T. 48,422 (73.53%)   C. hold
Stephen Hammond, C.   25,225
Andrew Judge, Lab.   12,606
Shas Sheehan, LD   6,129
Peter Bucklitsch, UKIP   2,476
Charles Barraball, Green   1,986
C. majority 12,619 (26.06%)
0.38% swing C. to Lab.
(2010: C. majority 11,408 (24.07%))

WINCHESTER
E. 74,119   T. 55,316 (74.63%)   C. hold
Steve Brine, C.   30,425
Jackie Porter, LD   13,511
Mark Chaloner, Lab.   4,613
Martin Lyon, UKIP   4,122
Michael Wilks, Green   2,645
C. majority 16,914 (30.58%)
12.56% swing LD to C.
(2010: C. majority 3,048 (5.45%))

WINDSOR
E. 74,119   T. 50,160 (67.67%)   C. hold
Adam Afriyie, C.   31,797
Fiona Dent, Lab.   6,714
Tariq Malik, UKIP   4,992
George Fussey, LD   4,323
Derek Wall, Green   1,834
Wisdom Da Costa, Ind.   500
C. majority 25,083 (50.01%)
0.47% swing C. to Lab.
(2010: C. majority 19,054 (38.42%))

WIRRAL SOUTH
E. 56,956 T. 41,837 (73.45%) Lab. hold
Alison McGovern, Lab.   20,165
John Bell, C.   15,566
David Scott, UKIP   3,737
Elizabeth Jewkes, LD   1,474
Paul Cartlidge, Green   895
Lab. majority 4,599 (10.99%)
4.83% swing C. to Lab.
(2010: Lab. majority 531 (1.33%))

WIRRAL WEST
E. 55,377 T. 41,858 (75.59%) Lab. gain
*Margaret Greenwood, Lab.   18,898
Esther McVey, C.   18,481
Hilary Jones, UKIP   2,772
Peter Reisdorf, LD   1,433
David James, ND   274
Lab. majority 417 (1.00%)
3.59% swing C. to Lab.
(2010: C. majority 2,436 (6.19%))

WITHAM
E. 67,090 T. 47,168 (70.31%) C. hold
Priti Patel, C.   27,123
Garry Cockrill, UKIP   7,569
John Clarke, Lab.   7,467
Jo Hayes, LD   2,891
James Abbott, Green   2,038
Doreen Scrimshaw, CPA   80
C. majority 19,554 (41.46%)
2.11% swing C. to UKIP
(2010: C. majority 15,196 (32.45%))

WITNEY
E. 79,767 T. 58,482 (73.32%) C. hold
David Cameron, C.   35,201
Duncan Enright, Lab.   10,046
Simon Strutt, UKIP   5,352
Andrew Graham, LD   3,953
Stuart Macdonald, Green   2,970
Clive Peedell, NHAP   616
Colin Bex, Wessex Reg.   110
Chris Tompson, Ind.   94
Vivien Saunders, VAT   56
Bobby Smith, Elmo   37
Deek Jackson, LP   35
Nathan Handley, ND   12
C. majority 25,155 (43.01%)
1.40% swing C. to Lab.
(2010: C. majority 22,740 (39.36%))

WOKING
E. 74,287 T. 51,964 (69.95%) C. hold
Jonathan Lord, C.   29,199
Jill Rawling, Lab.   8,389
Chris Took, LD   6,047
Rob Burberry, UKIP   5,873
Martin Robson, Green   2,109
Declan Wade, CISTA   229
Ruth Temple, Magna Carta   77
Angela Woolford, TEP   41
C. majority 20,810 (40.05%)
1.10% swing C. to Lab.
(2010: C. majority 6,807 (12.90%))

WOKINGHAM
E. 77,881 T. 55,999 (71.90%) C. hold
John Redwood, C.   32,329
Andy Croy, Lab.   8,132
Clive Jones, LD   7,572
Philip Cunnington, UKIP   5,516
Adrian Windisch, Green   2,092
Kaz Lokuciewski, Ind.   358
C. majority 24,197 (43.21%)
0.30% swing Lab. to C.
(2010: C. majority 13,492 (24.74%))

WOLVERHAMPTON NORTH EAST
E. 61,073 T. 34,003 (55.68%) Lab. hold
Emma Reynolds, Lab.   15,669
Darren Henry, C.   10,174
Star Etheridge, UKIP   6,524
Ian Jenkins, LD   935
Becky Cooper, Green   701
Lab. majority 5,495 (16.16%)
4.52% swing C. to Lab.
(2010: Lab. majority 2,484 (7.12%))

WOLVERHAMPTON SOUTH EAST
E. 62,561 T. 34,764 (55.57%) Lab. hold
Pat McFadden, Lab.   18,539
Suria Photay, C.   7,761
Barry Hodgson, UKIP   7,061
Ian Griffiths, LD   798
Geeta Kauldhar, Green   605
Lab. majority 10,778 (31.00%)
6.00% swing C. to Lab.
(2010: Lab. majority 6,593 (19.00%))

WOLVERHAMPTON SOUTH WEST
E. 60,375 T. 40,209 (66.60%) Lab. gain
*Rob Marris, Lab.   17,374
Paul Uppal, C.   16,573
David Everett, UKIP   4,310
Andrea Cantrill, Green   1,058
Neale Upstone, LD   845
Brian Booth, Ind.   49
Lab. majority 801 (1.99%)
1.86% swing C. to Lab.
(2010: C. majority 691 (1.72%))

WORCESTER
E. 71,003 T. 49,723 (70.03%) C. hold
Robin Walker, C.   22,534
Joy Squires, Lab.   16,888
James Goad, UKIP   6,378
Louis Stephen, Green   2,024
Federica Smith, LD   1,677
Pete McNally, TUSC   153
Mark Shuker, Ind.   69
C. majority 5,646 (11.35%)
2.63% swing Lab. to C.
(2010: C. majority 2,982 (6.09%))

WORCESTERSHIRE MID
E. 73,069 T. 52,225 (71.47%) C. hold
*Nigel Huddleston, C.   29,763
Richard Keel, UKIP   9,231
Robin Lunn, Lab.   7,548
Margaret Rowley, LD   3,750
Neil Franks, Green   1,933
C. majority 20,532 (39.31%)
4.61% swing C. to UKIP
(2010: C. majority 15,864 (31.15%))

WORCESTERSHIRE WEST
E. 73,415 T. 54,100 (73.69%) C. hold
Harriett Baldwin, C.   30,342
Richard Chamings, UKIP   7,764
Daniel Walton, Lab.   7,244
Dennis Wharton, LD   5,245
Julian Roskams, Green   3,505
C. majority 22,578 (41.73%)
2.33% swing C. to UKIP
(2010: C. majority 6,754 (12.49%))

WORKINGTON
E. 58,672 T. 38,463 (65.56%) Lab. hold
*Sue Hayman, Lab.   16,282
Rozila Kana, C.   11,596
Mark Jenkinson, UKIP   7,538
Phill Roberts, LD   1,708
Jill Perry, Green   1,149
Roy Ivinson, ND   190
Lab. majority 4,686 (12.18%)
0.26% swing C. to Lab.
(2010: Lab. majority 4,575 (11.65%))

WORSLEY & ECCLES SOUTH
E. 72,174 T. 42,048 (58.26%) Lab. hold
Barbara Keeley, Lab.   18,600
Iain Lindley, C.   12,654
Owen Hammond, UKIP   7,688
Christopher Bertenshaw, Green   1,242
Kate Clarkson, LD   1,100
Steve North, TUSC   380
Mags McNally, Reality   200
Geoffrey Berg, Ind.   184
Lab. majority 5,946 (14.14%)
1.87% swing C. to Lab.
(2010: Lab. majority 4,337 (10.40%))

WORTHING EAST & SHOREHAM
E. 74,272 T. 49,898 (67.18%) C. hold
Tim Loughton, C.   24,686
Tim Macpherson, Lab.   9,737
Mike Glennon, UKIP   8,267
Bob Smytherman, LD   3,360
James Doyle, Green   2,605
Carl Walker, NHAP   1,243
C. majority 14,949 (29.96%)
0.90% swing C. to Lab.
(2010: C. majority 11,105 (22.95%))

WORTHING WEST
E. 75,617 T. 50,763 (67.13%) C. hold
Peter Bottomley, C.   26,124
Tim Cross, UKIP   9,269
Jim Deen, Lab.   7,955
Hazel Thorpe, LD   4,477
David Aherne, Green   2,938
C. majority 16,855 (33.20%)
6.29% swing C. to UKIP
(2010: C. majority 11,729 (23.88%))

WREKIN, THE
E. 65,942 T. 45,437 (68.90%) C. hold
Mark Pritchard, C.   22,579
Katrina Gilman, Lab.   11,836
Jill Seymour, UKIP   7,620
Rod Keyes, LD   1,959
Cath Edwards, Green   1,443
C. majority 10,743 (23.64%)
1.54% swing Lab. to C.
(2010: C. majority 9,450 (20.56%))

WYCOMBE
E. 76,371 T. 51,439 (67.35%) C. hold
Steven Baker, C.   26,444
David Williams, Lab.   11,588
David Meacock, UKIP   5,198
Steve Guy, LD   4,546
Jem Bailey, Green   3,086
David Fitton, Ind.   577
C. majority 14,856 (28.88%)
1.24% swing C. to Lab.
(2010: C. majority 9,560 (19.85%))

WYRE & PRESTON NORTH
E. 70,697　T. 49,893 (70.57%)　C. hold
Ben Wallace, C.　26,528
Ben Whittingham, Lab.　12,377
Kate Walsh, UKIP　6,577
John Potter, LD　2,712
Anne Power, Green　1,699
C. majority 14,151 (28.36%)
1.36% swing C. to Lab.
(2010: C. majority 15,844 (30.88%))

WYRE FOREST
E. 77,451　T. 49,440 (63.83%)　C. hold
Mark Garnier, C.　22,394
Matt Lamb, Lab.　9,523
Michael Wrench, UKIP　7,967
Richard Taylor, Ind. CHC　7,211
Andy Crick, LD　1,228
Natalie McVey, Green　1,117
C. majority 12,871 (26.03%)
1.72% swing Lab. to C.
(2010: C. majority 2,643 (5.19%))

WYTHENSHAWE & SALE EAST
E. 75,980　T. 43,263 (56.94%)　Lab. hold
Mike Kane, Lab.　21,693
Fiona Green, C.　11,124
Lee Clayton, UKIP　6,354
Victor Chamberlain, LD　1,927
Jess Mayo, Green　1,658
Johnny Disco, Loony　292
Lynn Worthington, TUSC　215
Lab. majority 10,569 (24.43%)
2.92% swing C. to Lab.
(2010: Lab. majority 7,575 (18.59%))
(2014: Lab. majority 8,960 (37.54%))

YEOVIL
E. 82,446　T. 56,933 (69.05%)　C. gain
*Marcus Fysh, C.　24,178
David Laws, LD　18,865
Simon Smedley, UKIP　7,646
Sheena King, Lab.　4,053
Emily McIvor, Green　2,191
C. majority 5,313 (9.33%)
16.07% swing LD to C.
(2010: LD majority 13,036 (22.81%))

YORK CENTRAL
E. 75,351　T. 47,677 (63.27%)
Lab. Co-op hold
*Rachael Maskell, Lab. Co-op　20,212
Robert McIlveen, C.　13,496
Ken Guest, UKIP　4,795
Jonathan Tyler, Green　4,791
Nick Love, LD　3,804
Chris Whitwood, Yorks　291
Megan Ollerhead, TUSC　288
Lab. Co-op majority 6,716 (14.09%)
0.10% swing C. to Lab.
(2010: Lab. majority 6,451 (13.88%))

YORK OUTER
E. 78,561　T. 53,903 (68.61%)　C. hold
Julian Sturdy, C.　26,477
Joe Riches, Lab.　13,343
James Blanchard, LD　6,269
Paul Abbott, UKIP　5,251
Ginnie Shaw, Green　2,558
C. majority 13,129 (24.36%)
0.77% swing C. to Lab.
(2010: C. majority 3,688 (6.92%))

YORKSHIRE EAST
E. 81,030　T. 49,991 (61.69%)　C. hold
Greg Knight, C.　25,276
Kevin Hickson, Lab.　10,343
Stephanie Todd, UKIP　8,955
Robert Adamson, LD　2,966
Mark Maloney, Green　1,731
Stewart Arnold, Yorks　720
C. majority 14,933 (29.87%)
1.35% swing Lab. to C.
(2010: C. majority 13,486 (26.31%))

WALES

ABERAVON
E. 49,821　T. 31,523 (63.27%)　Lab. hold
*Stephen Kinnock, Lab.　15,416
Peter Bush, UKIP　4,971
Edward Yi He, C.　3,742
Duncan Higgitt, PC　3,663
Helen Ceri Clarke, LD　1,397
Captain Beany, Ind.　1,137
Jonathan Tier, Green　711
Andrew Jordan, Soc. Lab.　352
Owen Herbert, TUSC　134
Lab. majority 10,445 (33.13%)
8.60% swing Lab. to UKIP
(2010: Lab. majority 11,039 (35.66%))

ABERCONWY
E. 45,540　T. 30,148 (66.20%)　C. hold
Guto Bebb, C.　12,513
Mary Wimbury, Lab.　8,514
Dafydd Meurig, PC　3,536
Andrew Haigh, UKIP　3,467
Victor Babu, LD　1,391
Petra Haig, Green　727
C. majority 3,999 (13.26%)
0.96% swing Lab. to C.
(2010: C. majority 3,398 (11.34%))

ALYN & DEESIDE
E. 62,016　T. 41,314 (66.62%)　Lab. hold
Mark Tami, Lab.　16,540
Laura Knightly, C.　13,197
Blair Smillie, UKIP　7,260
Tudor Jones, LD　1,733
Jacqueline Hurst, PC　1,608
Alasdair Ibbotson, Green　976
Lab. majority 3,343 (8.09%)
0.39% swing C. to Lab.
(2010: Lab. majority 2,919 (7.31%))

ARFON
E. 40,492　T. 26,837 (66.28%)　PC hold
Hywel Williams, PC　11,790
Alun Pugh, Lab.　8,122
Anwen Barry, C.　3,521
Simon Wall, UKIP　2,277
Mohammed Shultan, LD　718
Kathrine Jones, Soc. Lab.　409
PC majority 3,668 (13.67%)
4.04% swing Lab. to PC
(2010: PC majority 1,455 (5.58%))

BLAENAU GWENT
E. 51,332　T. 31,683 (61.72%)　Lab. hold
Nick Smith, Lab.　18,380
Susan Boucher, UKIP　5,677
Tracey West, C.　3,419
Steffan Lewis, PC　2,849
Mark Pond, Green　738
Sam Rees, LD　620
Lab. majority 12,703 (40.09%)
5.40% swing Lab. to UKIP
(2010: Lab. majority 10,516 (32.46%))

BRECON & RADNORSHIRE
E. 54,311　T. 40,074 (73.79%)　C. gain
*Chris Davies, C.　16,453
Roger Williams, LD　11,351
Matthew Dorrance, Lab.　5,904
Darran Thomas, UKIP　3,338
Freddy Greaves, PC　1,767
Chris Carmichael, Green　1,261
C. majority 5,102 (12.73%)
11.19% swing LD to C.
(2010: LD majority 3,747 (9.65%))

BRIDGEND
E. 59,998　T. 39,453 (65.76%)　Lab. hold
Madeleine Moon, Lab.　14,624
Meirion Jenkins, C.　12,697
Caroline Jones, UKIP　5,911
James Radcliffe, PC　2,784
Anita Davies, LD　1,648
Les Tallon-Morris, Ind.　763
Tony White, Green　736
Aaron David, TUSC　118
David Elston, Pirate　106
Adam Lloyd, NF　66
Lab. majority 1,927 (4.88%)
0.51% swing Lab. to C.
(2010: Lab. majority 2,263 (5.90%))

CAERPHILLY
E. 62,793　T. 40,283 (64.15%)　Lab. hold
Wayne David, Lab.　17,864
Sam Gould, UKIP　7,791
Leo Docherty, C.　6,683
Beci Newton, PC　5,895
Katy Beddoe, Green　937
Aladdin Ayesh, LD　935
Jaime Davies, TUSC　178
Lab. majority 10,073 (25.01%)
8.61% swing Lab. to UKIP
(2010: Lab. majority 10,755 (27.58%))

CARDIFF CENTRAL
E. 57,454 T. 38,646 (67.26%) Lab. gain
*Jo Stevens, Lab.   15,462
Jenny Willott, LD   10,481
Richard Hopkin, C.   5,674
Anthony Raybould, UKIP   2,499
Christopher von Ruhland, Green   2,461
Martin Pollard, PC   1,925
Steve Williams, TUSC   110
Kazimir Hubert, Ind.   34
Lab. majority 4,981 (12.89%)
12.77% swing LD to Lab.
(2010: LD majority 4,576 (12.66%))

CARDIFF NORTH
E. 67,193 T. 51,151 (76.13%) C. hold
*Craig Williams, C.   21,709
Mari Williams, Lab.   19,572
Ethan Wilkinson, UKIP   3,953
Elin Walker Jones, PC   2,301
Elizabeth Clark, LD   1,953
Ruth Osner, Green   1,254
Jeff Green, Ch. P.   331
Shaun Jenkins, Change   78
C. majority 2,137 (4.18%)
1.89% swing Lab. to C.
(2010: C. majority 194 (0.41%))

CARDIFF SOUTH & PENARTH
E. 75,714 T. 46,667 (61.64%)
                          Lab. Co-op hold
Stephen Doughty, Lab. Co-op   19,966
Emma Warman, C.   12,513
John Rees-Evans, UKIP   6,423
Ben Foday, PC   3,443
Nigel Howells, LD   2,318
Anthony Slaughter, Green   1,746
Ross Saunders, TUSC   258
Lab. Co-op majority 7,453 (15.97%)
2.68% swing C. to Lab.
(2010: Lab. Co-op majority 4,710 (10.62%))
(2012: Lab. majority 5,334 (27.44%))

CARDIFF WEST
E. 66,758 43,792 (65.60%) Lab. hold
Kevin Brennan, Lab.   17,803
James Taghdissian, C.   11,014
Neil McEvoy, PC   6,096
Brian Morris, UKIP   4,923
Cadan ap Tomos, LD   2,069
Ken Barker, Green   1,704
Helen Jones, TUSC   183
Lab. majority 6,789 (15.50%)
1.95% swing C. to Lab.
(2010: Lab. majority 4,750 (11.60%))

CARMARTHEN EAST & DINEFWR
E. 55,750 T. 39,399 (70.67%) PC hold
Jonathan Edwards, PC   15,140
Calum Higgins, Lab.   9,541
Matthew Paul, C.   8,336
Norma Woodward, UKIP   4,363
Ben Rice, Green   1,091
Sara Lloyd-Williams, LD   928
PC majority 5,599 (14.21%)
2.53% swing Lab. to PC
(2010: PC majority 3,481 (9.16%))

CARMARTHEN WEST &
PEMBROKESHIRE SOUTH
E. 57,755 T. 40,350 (69.86%) C. hold
Simon Hart, C.   17,626
Delyth Evans, Lab.   11,572
John Atkinson, UKIP   4,698
Elwyn Williams, PC   4,201
Gary Tapley, Green   1,290
Selwyn Runnett, LD   963
C. majority 6,054 (15.00%)
3.28% swing Lab. to C.
(2010: C. majority 3,423 (8.45%))

CEREDIGION
E. 54,215 T. 37,416 (69.01%) LD hold
Mark Williams, LD   13,414
Mike Parker, PC   10,347
Henrietta Hensher, C.   4,123
Gethin James, UKIP   3,829
Huw Thomas, Lab.   3,615
Daniel Thompson, Green   2,088
LD majority 3,067 (8.20%)
6.78% swing LD to PC
(2010: LD majority 8,324 (21.76%))

CLWYD SOUTH
E. 54,996 T. 35,064 (63.76%) Lab. hold
Susan Elan Jones, Lab.   13,051
David Nicholls, C.   10,649
Mandy Jones, UKIP   5,480
Mabon ap Gwynfor, PC   3,620
Bruce Roberts, LD   1,349
Duncan Rees, Green   915
Lab. majority 2,402 (6.85%)
0.66% swing Lab. to C.
(2010: Lab. majority 2,834 (8.17%))

CLWYD WEST
E. 58,657 T. 38,028 (64.83%) C. hold
David Jones, C.   16,463
Gareth Thomas, Lab.   9,733
Warwick Nicholson, UKIP   4,988
Marc Jones, PC   4,651
Sarah Lesiter-Burgess, LD   1,387
Bob English, Soc. Lab.   612
Rory Jepson, Above   194
C. majority 6,730 (17.70%)
0.43% swing Lab. to C.
(2010: C. majority 6,419 (16.84%))

CYNON VALLEY
E. 51,421 T. 30,472 (59.26%) Lab. hold
Ann Clwyd, Lab.   14,532
Cerith Griffiths, PC   5,126
Rebecca Rees-Evans, UKIP   4,976
Keith Dewhurst, C.   3,676
Angharad Jones, LD   830
John Matthews, Green   799
Chris Beggs, Soc. Lab.   533
Lab. majority 9,406 (30.87%)
0.66% swing Lab. to PC
(2010: Lab. majority 9,617 (32.19%))

DELYN
E. 53,639 T. 37,457 (69.83%) Lab. hold
David Hanson, Lab.   15,187
Mark Isherwood, C.   12,257
Nigel Williams, UKIP   6,150
Paul Rowlinson, PC   1,803
Tom Rippeth, LD   1,380
Kay Roney, Green   680
Lab. majority 2,930 (7.82%)
0.84% swing C. to Lab.
(2010: Lab. majority 2,272 (6.14%))

DWYFOR MEIRIONNYDD
E. 44,395 T. 28,913 (65.13%) PC hold
*Liz Saville-Roberts, PC   11,811
Neil Fairlamb, C.   6,550
Mary Griffiths Clarke, Lab.   3,904
Christopher Gillibrand, UKIP   3,126
Louise Hughes, Ind.   1,388
Steve Churchman, LD   1,153
Marc Fothergill, Green   981
PC majority 5,261 (18.20%)
1.92% swing PC to C.
(2010: PC majority 6,367 (22.03%))

GOWER
E. 61,820 T. 42,758 (69.17%) C. gain
*Byron Davies, C.   15,862
Liz Evans, Lab.   15,835
Colin Beckett, UKIP   4,773
Darren Thomas, PC   3,051
Mike Sheehan, LD   1,552
Julia Marshall, Green   1,161
Baron Barnes Von Claptrap, Loony   253
Steve Roberts, Ind.   168
Mark Evans, TUSC   103
C. majority 27 (0.06%)
3.25% swing Lab. to C.
(2010: Lab. majority 2,683 (6.44%))

ISLWYN
E. 55,075 T. 35,401 (64.28%)
                          Lab. Co-op hold
Chris Evans, Lab. Co-op   17,336
Joe Smyth, UKIP   6,932
Laura Jones, C.   5,366
Lyn Ackerman, PC   3,794
Brendan D'Cruz, LD   950
Peter Varley, Green   659
Baron Von Magpie, Loony   213
Josh Rawcliffe, TUSC   151
Lab. Co-op majority 10,404 (29.39%)
8.56% swing Lab. to UKIP
(2010: Lab. Co-op majority 12,215
(35.21%))

LLANELLI
E. 59,314 T. 38,574 (65.03%) Lab. hold
Nia Griffith, Lab.   15,948
Vaughan Williams, PC   8,853
Ken Rees, UKIP   6,269
Selaine Saxby, C.   5,534
Cen Phillips, LD   751
Guy Smith, Green   689
Sian Caiach, PF   407
Scott Jones, TUSC   123
Lab. majority 7,095 (18.39%)
2.92% swing PC to Lab.
(2010: Lab. majority 4,701 (12.55%))

MERTHYR TYDFIL & RHYMNEY
E. 61,719 T. 32,715 (53.01%) Lab. hold
*Gerald Jones, Lab.   17,619
David Rowlands, UKIP   6,106
Bill Rees, C.   3,292
Rhayna Mann, PC   3,099
Bob Griffin, LD   1,351
Elspeth Parris, Green   603
Eddy Blanche, Ind.   459
Robert Griffiths, Comm.   186
Lab. majority 11,513 (35.19%)
2.88% swing Lab. to UKIP
(2010: Lab. majority 4,056 (12.64%))

MONMOUTH
E. 65,706   T. 47,462 (72.23%)   C. hold
David Davies, C.   23,701
Ruth Jones, Lab.   12,719
Gareth Dunn, UKIP   4,942
Veronica German, LD   2,496
Jonathan Clark, PC   1,875
Christopher Were, Green   1,629
Stephen Morris, Eng. Dem.   100
C. majority 10,982 (23.14%)
0.36% swing Lab. to C.
(2010: C. majority 10,425 (22.41%))

MONTGOMERYSHIRE
E. 48,491   T. 33,757 (69.61%)   C. hold
Glyn Davies, C.   15,204
Jane Dodds, LD   9,879
Des Parkinson, UKIP   3,769
Martyn Singleton, Lab.   1,900
Ann Griffith, PC   1,745
Richard Chaloner, Green   1,260
C. majority 5,325 (15.77%)
6.14% swing LD to C.
(2010: C. majority 1,184 (3.50%))

NEATH
E. 56,099   T. 37,135 (66.20%)   Lab. hold
*Christina Rees, Lab.   16,270
Daniel Thomas, PC   6,722
Richard Pritchard, UKIP   6,094
Ed Hastie, C.   5,691
Catrin Brock, Green   1,185
Clare Bentley, LD   1,173
Lab. majority 9,548 (25.71%)
0.31% swing Lab. to PC
(2010: Lab. majority 9,775 (26.33%))

NEWPORT EAST
E. 56,018   T. 35,108 (62.67%)   Lab. hold
Jessica Morden, Lab.   14,290
Natasha Asghar, C.   9,585
David Stock, UKIP   6,466
Paul Halliday, LD   2,251
Tony Salkeld, PC   1,231
David Mclean, Green   887
Shangara Singh Bhatoe, Soc. Lab.   398
Lab. majority 4,705 (13.40%)
0.30% swing Lab. to C.
(2010: Lab. majority 1,650 (4.79%))

NEWPORT WEST
E. 62,145   T. 40,347 (64.92%)   Lab. hold
Paul Flynn, Lab.   16,633
Nick Webb, C.   13,123
Gordon Norrie, UKIP   6,134
Simon Coopey, PC   1,604
Ed Townsend, LD   1,581
Pippa Bartolotti, Green   1,272
Lab. majority 3,510 (8.70%)
0.11% swing Lab. to C.
(2010: Lab. majority 3,544 (8.92%))

OGMORE
E. 55,320   T. 35,250 (63.72%)   Lab. hold
Huw Irranca-Davies, Lab.   18,663
Jane March, C.   5,620
Glenda Davies, UKIP   5,420
Tim Thomas, PC   3,556
Gerald Francis, LD   1,072
Laurie Brophy, Green   754
Emma Saunders, TUSC   165
Lab. majority 13,043 (37.00%)
0.61% swing Lab. to C.
(2010: Lab. majority 13,246 (38.23%))

PONTYPRIDD
E. 58,929   T. 37,882 (64.28%)   Lab. hold
Owen Smith, Lab.   15,554
Ann-Marie Mason, C.   6,569
Andrew Tomkinson, UKIP   5,085
Mike Powell, LD   4,904
Osian Lewis, PC   4,348
Katy Clay, Green   992
Damien Biggs, Soc. Lab.   332
Esther Pearson, TUSC   98
Lab. majority 8,985 (23.72%)
0.56% swing C. to Lab.
(2010: Lab. majority 2,785 (7.59%))

PRESELI PEMBROKESHIRE
E. 57,291   T. 40,556 (70.79%)   C. hold
Stephen Crabb, C.   16,383
Paul Miller, Lab.   11,414
Howard Lillyman, UKIP   4,257
Chris Overton, ISWSL   3,729
John Osmond, PC   2,518
Frances Bryant, Green   1,452
Nick Tregoning, LD   780
Rodney Maile, Worth   23
C. majority 4,969 (12.25%)
0.31% swing Lab. to C.
(2010: C. majority 4,605 (11.63%))

RHONDDA
E. 51,809   T. 31,538 (60.87%)   Lab. hold
Chris Bryant, Lab.   15,976
Shelley Rees-Owen, PC   8,521
Ron Hughes, UKIP   3,998
Lyn Hudson, C.   2,116
George Summers, LD   474
Lisa Rapado, Green   453
Lab. majority 7,455 (23.64%)
6.77% swing Lab. to PC
(2010: Lab. majority 11,553 (37.18%))

SWANSEA EAST
E. 58,011   T. 33,618 (57.95%)   Lab. hold
*Carolyn Harris, Lab.   17,807
Cliff Johnson, UKIP   5,779
Altaf Hussain, C.   5,142
Dic Jones, PC   3,498
Amina Jamal, LD   1,392
Lab. majority 12,028 (35.78%)
6.56% swing Lab. to UKIP
(2010: Lab. majority 10,838 (33.17%))

SWANSEA WEST
E. 58,776   T. 35,156 (59.81%)
                             Lab. Co-op hold
Geraint Davies, Lab. Co-op   14,967
Emma Lane, C.   7,931
Martyn Ford, UKIP   4,744
Chris Holley, LD   3,178
Harri Roberts, PC   2,266
Ashley Wakeling, Green   1,784
Ronnie Job, TUSC   159
Maxwell Rosser, Ind.   78
Brian Johnson, SPGB   49
Lab. Co-op majority 7,036 (20.01%)
3.08% swing C. to Lab.
(2010: Lab. majority 504 (1.42%))

TORFAEN
E. 61,896   T. 37,937 (61.29%)   Lab. hold
*Nick Thomas-Symonds, Lab.   16,938
Graham Smith, C.   8,769
Ken Beswick, UKIP   7,203
Boydd Hackley-Green, PC   2,169
Alison Willott, LD   1,271
Matt Cooke, Green   746
John Cox, Soc. Lab.   697
Mark Griffiths, Comm.   144
Lab. majority 8,169 (21.53%)
1.60% swing Lab. to C.
(2010: Lab. majority 9,306 (24.72%))

VALE OF CLWYD
E. 56,505   T. 35,261 (62.40%)   C. gain
*James Davies, C.   13,760
Chris Ruane, Lab.   13,523
Paul Davies-Cooke, UKIP   4,577
Mair Rowlands, PC   2,486
Gwyn Williams, LD   915
C. majority 237 (0.67%)
3.87% swing Lab. to C.
(2010: Lab. majority 2,509 (7.06%))

VALE OF GLAMORGAN
E. 72,187   T. 51,293 (71.06%)   C. hold
Alun Cairns, C.   23,607
Chris Elmore, Lab.   16,727
Kevin Mahoney, UKIP   5,489
Ian Johnson, PC   2,869
David Morgan, LD   1,309
Alan Armstrong, Green   1,054
Steve Reed, CISTA   238
C. majority 6,880 (13.41%)
2.28% swing Lab. to C.
(2010: C. majority 4,307 (8.85%))

WREXHAM
E. 50,992   T. 32,719 (64.16%)   Lab. hold
Ian Lucas, Lab.   12,181
Andrew Atkinson, C.   10,350
Niall Plevin-Kelly, UKIP   5,072
Carrie Harper, PC   2,501
Rob Walsh, LD   1,735
David Munnerley, Green   669
Brian Edwards, Ind.   211
Lab. majority 1,831 (5.60%)
2.94% swing Lab. to C.
(2010: Lab. majority 3,658 (11.09%))

YNYS MON
E. 49,944   T. 34,926 (69.93%)   Lab. hold
Albert Owen, Lab.   10,871
John Rowlands, PC   10,642
Michelle Willis, C.   7,393
Nathan Gill, UKIP   5,121
Mark Rosenthal, LD   751
Liz Screen, Soc. Lab.   148
Lab. majority 229 (0.66%)
3.24% swing Lab. to PC
(2010: Lab. majority 2,461 (7.14%))

SCOTLAND

ABERDEEN NORTH
E. 67,745   T. 43,936 (64.85%)   SNP gain
*Kirsty Blackman, SNP   24,793
Richard Baker, Lab. Co-op   11,397
Sanjoy Sen, C.   5,304
Euan Davidson, LD   2,050
Tyrinne Rutherford, TUSC   206
Christopher Willett, NF   186
SNP majority 13,396 (30.49%)
26.33% swing Lab. to SNP
(2010: Lab. majority 8,361 (22.18%))

ABERDEEN SOUTH
E. 68,056   T. 48,551 (71.34%)   SNP gain
*Callum McCaig, SNP   20,221
Anne Begg, Lab.   12,991
Ross Thomson, C.   11,087
Denis Rixon, LD   2,252
Dan Yeats, Scot. Green   964
Sandra Skinner, UKIP   897
Christopher Gray, Ind.   139
SNP majority 7,230 (14.89%)
19.78% swing Lab. to SNP
(2010: Lab. majority 3,506 (8.15%))

ABERDEENSHIRE WEST & KINCARDINE
E. 73,445   T. 55,196 (75.15%)   SNP gain
*Stuart Donaldson, SNP   22,949
Alexander Burnett, C.   15,916
Robert Smith, LD   11,812
Barry Black, Lab.   2,487
David Lansdell, UKIP   1,006
Richard Openshaw, Scot. Green   885
Graham Reid, Ind.   141
SNP majority 7,033 (12.74%)
21.46% swing LD to SNP
(2010: LD majority 3,684 (8.15%))

AIRDRIE & SHOTTS
E. 66,715   T. 44,286 (66.38%)   SNP gain
*Neil Gray, SNP   23,887
Pamela Nash, Lab.   15,108
Eric Holford, C.   3,389
Matt Williams, UKIP   1,088
John Love, LD   678
Deryck Beaumont, Ind.   136
SNP majority 8,779 (19.82%)
27.22% swing Lab. to SNP
(2010: Lab. majority 12,408 (34.61%))

ANGUS
E. 65,792   T. 44,485 (67.61%)   SNP hold
Mike Weir, SNP   24,130
Derek Wann, C.   12,900
Gerard McMahon, Lab.   3,919
Calum Walker, UKIP   1,355
Sanjay Samani, LD   1,216
David Mumford, Scot. Green   965
SNP majority 11,230 (25.24%)
8.30% swing C. to SNP
(2010: SNP majority 3,282 (8.65%))

ARGYLL & BUTE
E. 68,875   T. 51,883 (75.33%)   SNP gain
*Brendan O'Hara, SNP   22,959
Alan Reid, LD   14,486
Alastair Redman, C.   7,733
Mary Galbraith, Lab.   5,394
Caroline Santos, UKIP   1,311
SNP majority 8,473 (16.33%)
14.50% swing LD to SNP
(2010: LD majority 3,431 (7.59%))

AYR, CARRICK & CUMNOCK
E. 72,985   T. 52,209 (71.53%)   SNP gain
*Corri Wilson, SNP   25,492
Sandra Osborne, Lab.   14,227
Lee Lyons, C.   10,355
Joseph Adam-Smith, UKIP   1,280
Richard Brodie, LD   855
SNP majority 11,265 (21.58%)
25.34% swing Lab. to SNP
(2010: Lab. majority 9,911 (21.60%))

AYRSHIRE CENTRAL
E. 69,982   T. 50,774 (72.55%)   SNP gain
*Philippa Whitford, SNP   26,999
Brian Donohoe, Lab.   13,410
Marc Hope, C.   8,803
Gordon Bain, LD   917
Veronika Tudhope, Scot. Green   645
SNP majority 13,589 (26.76%)
27.71% swing Lab. to SNP
(2010: Lab. majority 12,007 (27.34%))

AYRSHIRE NORTH & ARRAN
E. 75,772   T. 53,869 (71.09%)   SNP gain
*Patricia Gibson, SNP   28,641
Katy Clark, Lab.   15,068
Jamie Greene, C.   7,968
Sharon McGonigal, UKIP   1,296
Ruby Kirkwood, LD   896
SNP majority 13,573 (25.20%)
23.33% swing Lab. to SNP
(2010: Lab. majority 9,895 (21.46%))

BANFF & BUCHAN
E. 68,609   T. 45,629 (66.51%)   SNP hold
Eilidh Whiteford, SNP   27,487
Alex Johnstone, C.   13,148
Sumon Hoque, Lab.   2,647
David Evans, LD   2,347
SNP majority 14,339 (31.43%)
10.48% swing C. to SNP
(2010: SNP majority 4,027 (10.47%))

BERWICKSHIRE, ROXBURGH & SELKIRK
E. 74,179   T. 55,038 (74.20%)   SNP gain
*Calum Kerr, SNP   20,145
John Lamont, C.   19,817
Michael Moore, LD   10,294
Kenryck Lloyd-Jones, Lab.   2,700
Peter Neilson, UKIP   1,316
Pauline Stewart, Scot. Green   631
Jesse Rae, Ind.   135
SNP majority 328 (0.60%)
27.04% swing LD to SNP
(2010: LD majority 5,675 (11.58%))

CAITHNESS, SUTHERLAND & EASTER ROSS
E. 47,558   T. 34,186 (71.88%)   SNP gain
*Paul Monaghan, SNP   15,831
John Thurso, LD   11,987
John Erskine, Lab.   3,061
Alastair Graham, C.   2,326
Ann Therese Murray, UKIP   981
SNP majority 3,844 (11.24%)
16.73% swing LD to SNP
(2010: LD majority 4,826 (16.78%))

COATBRIDGE, CHRYSTON & BELLSHILL
E. 73,813   T. 50,698 (68.68%)   SNP gain
*Phil Boswell, SNP   28,696
Tom Clarke, Lab.   17,195
Mhairi Fraser, C.   3,209
Scott Cairns, UKIP   1,049
Robert Simpson, LD   549
SNP majority 11,501 (22.69%)
36.22% swing Lab. to SNP
(2010: Lab. majority 20,714 (49.75%))

CUMBERNAULD, KILSYTH & KIRKINTILLOCH EAST
E. 67,009   T. 49,382 (73.69%)   SNP gain
*Stuart McDonald, SNP   29,572
Gregg McClymont, Lab.   14,820
Malcolm Mackay, C.   3,891
John Duncan, LD   1,099
SNP majority 14,752 (29.87%)
31.65% swing Lab. to SNP
(2010: Lab. majority 13,755 (33.43%))

DUMFRIES & GALLOWAY
E. 75,249   T. 56,602 (75.22%)   SNP gain
*Richard Arkless, SNP   23,440
Finlay Carson, C.   16,926
Russell Brown, Lab.   13,982
Geoff Siddall, UKIP   1,301
Andrew Metcalf, LD   953
SNP majority 6,514 (11.51%)
25.16% swing Lab. to SNP
(2010: Lab. majority 7,449 (14.28%))

DUMFRIESSHIRE, CLYDESDALE & TWEEDDALE
E. 68,483   T. 52,134 (76.13%)   C. hold
David Mundell, C.   20,759
Emma Harper, SNP   19,961
Archie Dryburgh, Lab.   7,711
Kevin Newton, UKIP   1,472
Amanda Kubie, LD   1,392
Jody Jamieson, Scot. Green   839
C. majority 798 (1.53%)
12.87% swing C. to SNP
(2010: C. majority 4,194 (9.14%))

DUNBARTONSHIRE EAST
E. 66,966   T. 54,871 (81.94%)   SNP gain
*John Nicolson, SNP   22,093
Jo Swinson, LD   19,926
Amanjit Jhund, Lab.   6,754
Andrew Polson, C.   4,727
Ross Greer, Scot. Green   804
Wilfred Arasaratnam, UKIP   567
SNP majority 2,167 (3.95%)
16.05% swing LD to SNP
(2010: LD majority 2,184 (4.55%))

DUNBARTONSHIRE WEST
E. 69,193   T. 51,141 (73.91%)   SNP gain
*Martin Docherty, SNP   30,198
Gemma Doyle, Lab. Co-op   16,027
Maurice Corry, C.   3,597
Aileen Morton, LD   816
Claire Muir, Ind.   503
SNP majority 14,171 (27.71%)
34.45% swing Lab. to SNP
(2010: Lab. Co-op majority 17,408 (41.19%))

DUNDEE EAST
E. 66,960 T. 48,185 (71.96%) SNP hold

Stewart Hosie, SNP	28,765
Lesley Brennan, Lab.	9,603
Bill Bowman, C.	7,206
Craig Duncan, LD	1,387
Helen Grayshan, Scot. Green	895
Lesley Parker-Hamilton, CISTA	225
Carlo Morelli, TUSC	104

SNP majority 19,162 (39.77%)
17.64% swing Lab. to SNP
(2010: SNP majority 1,821 (4.49%))

DUNDEE WEST
E. 66,287 T. 44,714 (67.46%) SNP gain

*Chris Law, SNP	27,684
Michael Marra, Lab.	10,592
Nicola Ross, C.	3,852
Pauline Hinchion, Scot. Green	1,225
Daniel Coleman, LD	1,057
Jim McFarlane, TUSC	304

SNP majority 17,092 (38.23%)
28.91% swing Lab. to SNP
(2010: Lab. majority 7,278 (19.60%))

DUNFERMLINE & FIFE WEST
E. 78,037 T. 55,890 (71.62%) SNP gain

*Douglas Chapman, SNP	28,096
Thomas Docherty, Lab.	17,744
James Reekie, C.	6,623
Gillian Cole-Hamilton, LD	2,232
Lewis Campbell, Scot. Green	1,195

SNP majority 10,352 (18.52%)
27.07% swing Lab. to SNP
(2010: Lab. majority 5,470 (11.18%))

EAST KILBRIDE, STRATHAVEN & LESMAHAGOW
E. 83,071 T. 60,539 (72.88%) SNP gain

*Lisa Cameron, SNP	33,678
Michael McCann, Lab.	17,151
Graham Simpson, C.	7,129
Robert Sale, UKIP	1,221
Paul McGarry, LD	1,042
John Houston, Ind.	318

SNP majority 16,527 (27.30%)
27.88% swing Lab. to SNP
(2010: Lab. majority 14,503 (28.47%))

EAST LOTHIAN
E. 79,481 T. 59,014 (74.25%) SNP gain

*George Kerevan, SNP	25,104
Fiona O'Donnell, Lab.	18,301
David Roach, C.	11,511
Ettie Spencer, LD	1,517
Jason Rose, Scot. Green	1,245
Oluf Marshall, UKIP	1,178
Mike Allan, Ind.	158

SNP majority 6,803 (11.53%)
20.04% swing Lab. to SNP
(2010: Lab. majority 12,258 (24.93%))

EDINBURGH EAST
E. 66,178 T. 47,089 (71.16%) SNP gain

*Tommy Sheppard, SNP	23,188
Sheila Gilmore, Lab.	14,082
James McMordie, C.	4,670
Peter McColl, Scot. Green	2,809
Karen Utting, LD	1,325
Oliver Corbishley, UKIP	898
Ayesha Saleem, TUSC	117

SNP majority 9,106 (19.34%)
21.18% swing Lab. to SNP
(2010: Lab. majority 9,181 (23.03%))

EDINBURGH NORTH & LEITH
E. 80,978 T. 58,008 (71.63%) SNP gain

*Deidre Brock, SNP	23,742
Mark Lazarowicz, Lab. Co-op	18,145
Iain McGill, C.	9,378
Sarah Beattie-Smith, Scot. Green	3,140
Martin Veart, LD	2,634
Alan Melville, UKIP	847
Bruce Whitehead, TUSC	122

SNP majority 5,597 (9.65%)
18.73% swing Lab. to SNP
(2010: Lab. Co-op majority 1,724 (3.64%))

EDINBURGH SOUTH
E. 65,846 T. 49,286 (74.85%) Lab. hold

Ian Murray, Lab.	19,293
Neil Hay, SNP	16,656
Miles Briggs, C.	8,626
Phyl Meyer, Scot. Green	2,090
Pramod Subbaraman, LD	1,823
Paul Marshall, UKIP	601
Colin Fox, SSP	197

Lab. majority 2,637 (5.35%)
swing N/A
(2010: Lab. majority 316 (0.72%))

EDINBURGH SOUTH WEST
E. 72,178 T. 51,602 (71.49%) SNP gain

*Joanna Cherry, SNP	22,168
Ricky Henderson, Lab.	14,033
Gordon Lindhurst, C.	10,444
Alan Doherty, Scot. Green	1,965
Daniel Farthing-Sykes, LD	1,920
Richard Lucas, UKIP	1,072

SNP majority 8,135 (15.76%)
23.22% swing Lab. to SNP
(2010: Lab. majority 8,447 (18.58%))

EDINBURGH WEST
E. 71,749 T. 54,858 (76.46%) SNP gain

*Michelle Thomson, SNP	21,378
Michael Crockart, LD	18,168
Lindsay Paterson, C.	6,732
Cammy Day, Lab.	6,425
Pat Black, Scot. Green	1,140
Otto Inglis, UKIP	1,015

SNP majority 3,210 (5.85%)
14.30% swing LD to SNP
(2010: LD majority 3,803 (8.19%))

FALKIRK
E. 83,380 T. 60,340 (72.37%) SNP gain

*John McNally, SNP	34,831
Karen Whitefield, Lab.	15,130
Alison Harris, C.	7,325
David Coburn, UKIP	1,829
Galen Milne, LD	1,225

SNP majority 19,701 (32.65%)
24.05% swing Lab. to SNP
(2010: Lab. majority 7,843 (15.45%))

FIFE NORTH EAST
E. 62,003 T. 45,263 (73.00%) SNP gain

*Stephen Gethins, SNP	18,523
Tim Brett, LD	14,179
Huw Bell, C.	7,373
Brian Thomson, Lab.	3,476
Andy Collins, Scot. Green	1,387
Mike Scott-Hayward, Ind.	325

SNP majority 4,344 (9.60%)
19.87% swing LD to SNP
(2010: LD majority 9,048 (22.58%))

GLASGOW CENTRAL
E. 70,945 T. 39,318 (55.42%) SNP gain

*Alison Thewliss, SNP	20,658
Anas Sarwar, Lab.	12,996
Simon Bone, C.	2,359
Cass MacGregor, Scot. Green	1,559
Stuart Maskell, UKIP	786
Chris Young, LD	612
James Marris, CISTA	171
Andrew Elliott, TUSC	119
Katie Rhodes, SEP	58

SNP majority 7,662 (19.49%)
27.00% swing Lab. to SNP
(2010: Lab. majority 10,551 (34.50%))

GLASGOW EAST
E. 70,378 T. 42,417 (60.27%) SNP gain

*Natalie McGarry, SNP	24,116
Margaret Curran, Lab.	13,729
Andy Morrison, C.	2,544
Arthur Thackeray, UKIP	1,105
Kim Long, Scot. Green	381
Gary McLelland, LD	318
Liam McLaughlan, SSP	224

SNP majority 10,387 (24.49%)
30.65% swing Lab. to SNP
(2010: Lab. majority 11,840 (36.81%))

GLASGOW NORTH
E. 58,875 T. 36,922 (62.71%) SNP gain

*Patrick Grady, SNP	19,610
Ann McKechin, Lab.	10,315
Lauren Hankinson, C.	2,901
Martin Bartos, Scot. Green	2,284
Jade O'Neil, LD	1,012
Jamie Robertson, UKIP	486
Angela McCormick, TUSC	160
Russell Benson, CISTA	154

SNP majority 9,295 (25.17%)
28.88% swing Lab. to SNP
(2010: Lab. majority 3,898 (13.16%))

GLASGOW NORTH EAST
E. 66,678 T. 37,857 (56.78%) SNP gain

*Anne McLaughlin, SNP	21,976
Willie Bain, Lab.	12,754
Annie Wells, C.	1,769
Zara Kitson, Scot. Green	615
Eileen Baxendale, LD	300
Geoff Johnson, CISTA	225
Jamie Cocozza, TUSC	218

SNP majority 9,222 (24.36%)
39.28% swing Lab. to SNP
(2010: Lab. majority 15,942 (54.21%))

GLASGOW NORTH WEST
E. 68,418 T. 43,854 (64.10%) SNP gain

*Carol Monaghan, SNP	23,908
John Robertson, Lab.	13,544
Roger Lewis, C.	3,692
James Harrison, LD	1,194
Moira Crawford, Scot. Green	1,167
Chris MacKenzie, CISTA	213
Zoe Streatfield, Comm.	136

SNP majority 10,364 (23.63%)
31.21% swing Lab. to SNP
(2010: Lab. majority 13,611 (38.25%))

GLASGOW SOUTH
E. 74,051 T. 48,778 (65.87%) SNP gain

*Stewart McDonald, SNP	26,773
Tom Harris, Lab.	14,504
Kyle Thornton, C.	4,752
Alastair Whitelaw, Scot. Green	1,431
Ewan Hoyle, LD	1,019
Brian Smith, TUSC	299

SNP majority 12,269 (25.15%)
28.36% swing Lab. to SNP
(2010: Lab. majority 12,658 (31.57%))

GLASGOW SOUTH WEST
E. 66,209 T. 40,921 (61.81%) SNP gain
*Christopher Stephens, SNP   23,388
Ian Davidson, Lab. Co-op   13,438
Gordon McCaskill, C.   2,036
Sarah Hemy, UKIP   970
Sean Templeton, Scot. Green   507
Isabel Nelson, LD   406
Bill Bonnar, SSP   176
SNP majority 9,950 (24.32%)
35.24% swing Lab. to SNP
(2010: Lab. Co-op majority 14,671
(46.16%))

GLENROTHES
E. 69,781 T. 47,598 (68.21%) SNP gain
*Peter Grant, SNP   28,459
Melanie Ward, Lab. Co-op   14,562
Alex Stewart-Clark, C.   3,685
Jane Ann Liston, LD   892
SNP majority 13,897 (29.20%)
34.90% swing Lab. to SNP
(2010: Lab. majority 16,448 (40.61%))

GORDON
E. 79,393 T. 58,161 (73.26%) SNP gain
*Alex Salmond, SNP   27,717
Christine Jardine, LD   19,030
Colin Clark, C.   6,807
Braden Davy, Lab.   3,441
Emily Santos, UKIP   1,166
SNP majority 8,687 (14.94%)
14.39% swing LD to SNP
(2010: LD majority 6,748 (13.83%))

INVERCLYDE
E. 59,350 T. 44,607 (75.16%) SNP gain
*Ronnie Cowan, SNP   24,585
Iain McKenzie, Lab.   13,522
George Jabbour, C.   4,446
John Watson, LD   1,106
Michael Burrows, UKIP   715
Craig Hamilton, CISTA   233
SNP majority 11,063 (24.80%)
31.63% swing Lab. to SNP
(2010: Lab. majority 14,426 (38.47%))
(2011: Lab. majority 5,838 (20.78%))

INVERNESS, NAIRN, BADENOCH &
STRATHSPEY
E. 77,268 T. 57,613 (74.56%) SNP gain
*Drew Hendry, SNP   28,838
Danny Alexander, LD   18,029
Mike Robb, Lab.   4,311
Edward Mountain, C.   3,410
Isla O'Reilly, Scot. Green   1,367
Les Durance, UKIP   1,236
Donald Boyd, SCP   422
SNP majority 10,809 (18.76%)
20.39% swing LD to SNP
(2010: LD majority 8,765 (18.61%))

KILMARNOCK & LOUDOUN
E. 75,233 T. 53,903 (71.65%) SNP gain
*Alan Brown, SNP   30,000
Cathy Jamieson, Lab. Co-op   16,362
Brian Whittle, C.   6,752
Rod Ackland, LD   789
SNP majority 13,638 (25.30%)
25.95% swing Lab. to SNP
(2010: Lab. Co-op majority 12,378
(26.59%))

KIRKCALDY & COWDENBEATH
E. 75,941 T. 52,892 (69.65%) SNP gain
*Roger Mullin, SNP   27,628
Kenny Selbie, Lab. Co-op   17,654
Dave Dempsey, C.   5,223
Jack Neill, UKIP   1,237
Callum Leslie, LD   1,150
SNP majority 9,974 (18.86%)
34.55% swing Lab. to SNP
(2010: Lab. majority 23,009 (50.24%))

LANARK & HAMILTON EAST
E. 78,846 T. 55,258 (70.08%) SNP gain
*Angela Crawley, SNP   26,976
Jim Hood, Lab.   16,876
Alex Allison, C.   8,772
Donald MacKay, UKIP   1,431
Gregg Cullen, LD   1,203
SNP majority 10,100 (18.28%)
23.61% swing Lab. to SNP
(2010: Lab. majority 13,478 (28.95%))

LINLITHGOW & FALKIRK EAST
E. 86,955 T. 61,597 (70.84%) SNP gain
*Martyn Day, SNP   32,055
Michael Connarty, Lab.   19,121
Sandy Batho, C.   7,384
Alistair Forrest, UKIP   1,682
Emma Farthing-Sykes, LD   1,252
Neil McIvor, NF   103
SNP majority 12,934 (21.00%)
22.70% swing Lab. to SNP
(2010: Lab. majority 12,553 (24.40%))

LIVINGSTON
E. 82,373 T. 57,547 (69.86%) SNP gain
*Hannah Bardell, SNP   32,736
Graeme Morrice, Lab.   15,893
Chris Donnelly, C.   5,929
Nathan Somerville, UKIP   1,757
Charles Dundas, LD   1,232
SNP majority 16,843 (29.27%)
25.90% swing Lab. to SNP
(2010: Lab. majority 10,791 (22.52%))

MIDLOTHIAN
E. 67,875 T. 48,331 (71.21%) SNP gain
*Owen Thompson, SNP   24,453
Kenny Young, Lab.   14,594
Michelle Ballantyne, C.   5,760
Ian Baxter, Scot. Green   1,219
Gordon Norrie, UKIP   1,173
Aisha Mir, LD   1,132
SNP majority 9,859 (20.40%)
23.39% swing Lab. to SNP
(2010: Lab. majority 10,349 (26.37%))

MORAY
E. 71,685 T. 49,280 (68.75%) SNP hold
Angus Robertson, SNP   24,384
Douglas Ross, C.   15,319
Sean Morton, Lab.   4,898
Robert Scorer, UKIP   1,939
Jamie Paterson, LD   1,395
James MacKessack-Leitch, Scot.
Green   1,345
SNP majority 9,065 (18.39%)
swing N/A
(2010: SNP majority 5,590 (13.63%))

MOTHERWELL & WISHAW
E. 70,269 T. 48,237 (68.65%) SNP gain
*Marion Fellows, SNP   27,275
Frank Roy, Lab.   15,377
Meghan Gallacher, C.   3,695
Neil Wilson, UKIP   1,289
Ross Laird, LD   601
SNP majority 11,898 (24.67%)
33.81% swing Lab. to SNP
(2010: Lab. majority 16,806 (42.96%))

NA H-EILEANAN AN IAR
E. 21,744 T. 15,938 (73.30%) SNP hold
Angus MacNeil, SNP   8,662
Alasdair Morrison, Lab.   4,560
Mark Brown, C.   1,215
John Cormack, SCP   1,045
Ruaraidh Ferguson, LD   456
SNP majority 4,102 (25.74%)
6.46% swing Lab. to SNP
(2010: SNP majority 1,885 (12.81%))

OCHIL & PERTHSHIRE SOUTH
E. 77,370 T. 57,871 (74.80%) SNP gain
*Tasmina Ahmed-Sheikh, SNP   26,620
Gordon Banks, Lab.   16,452
Luke Graham, C.   11,987
Iliyan Stefanov, LD   1,481
Martin Gray, UKIP   1,331
SNP majority 10,168 (17.57%)
13.92% swing Lab. to SNP
(2010: Lab. majority 5,187 (10.28%))

ORKNEY & SHETLAND
E. 34,551 T. 22,728 (65.78%) LD hold
Alistair Carmichael, LD   9,407
Danus Skene, SNP   8,590
Donald Cameron, C.   2,025
Gerry McGarvey, Lab.   1,624
Robert Smith, UKIP   1,082
LD majority 817 (3.59%)
23.91% swing LD to SNP
(2010: LD majority 9,928 (51.32%))

PAISLEY & RENFREWSHIRE NORTH
E. 66,206 T. 50,462 (76.22%) SNP gain
*Gavin Newlands, SNP   25,601
Jim Sheridan, Lab.   16,525
John Anderson, C.   6,183
James Speirs, LD   1,055
Ryan Morrison, Scot. Green   703
Andy Doyle, CISTA   202
Jim Halfpenny, TUSC   193
SNP majority 9,076 (17.99%)
26.47% swing Lab. to SNP
(2010: Lab. majority 15,280 (34.96%))

PAISLEY & RENFREWSHIRE SOUTH
E. 61,281 T. 46,226 (75.43%) SNP gain
*Mhairi Black, SNP   23,548
Douglas Alexander, Lab.   17,864
Fraser Galloway, C.   3,526
Eileen McCartin, LD   1,010
Sandra Webster, SSP   278
SNP majority 5,684 (12.30%)
26.92% swing Lab. to SNP
(2010: Lab. majority 16,614 (41.54%))

PERTH & PERTHSHIRE NORTH
E. 72,447 T. 54,200 (74.81%) SNP hold

Pete Wishart, SNP	27,379
Alexander Stewart, C.	17,738
Scott Nicholson, Lab.	4,413
Peter Barrett, LD	2,059
Louise Ramsay, Scot. Green	1,146
John Myles, UKIP	1,110
Xander McDade, Ind.	355

SNP majority 9,641 (17.79%)
4.36% swing C. to SNP
(2010: SNP majority 4,379 (9.07%))

RENFREWSHIRE EAST
E. 69,982 T. 56,730 (81.06%) SNP gain

*Kirsten Oswald, SNP	23,013
Jim Murphy, Lab.	19,295
David Montgomery, C.	12,465
Graeme Cowie, LD	1,069
Robert Malyn, UKIP	888

SNP majority 3,718 (6.55%)
24.23% swing Lab. to SNP
(2010: Lab. majority 10,420 (20.36%))

ROSS, SKYE & LOCHABER
E. 54,169 T. 41,811 (77.19%) SNP gain

*Ian Blackford, SNP	20,119
Charles Kennedy, LD	14,995
Lindsay McCallum, C.	2,598
Chris Conniff, Lab.	2,043
Anne Thomas, Scot. Green	1,051
Philip Anderson, UKIP	814
Ronnie Campbell, Ind.	191

SNP majority 5,124 (12.26%)
24.89% swing LD to SNP
(2010: LD majority 13,070 (37.52%))

RUTHERGLEN & HAMILTON WEST
E. 82,701 T. 57,615 (69.67%) SNP gain

*Margaret Ferrier, SNP	30,279
Tom Greatrex, Lab. Co-op	20,304
Taylor Muir, C.	4,350
Janice MacKay, UKIP	1,301
Tony Hughes, LD	1,045
Yvonne Maclean, CISTA	336

SNP majority 9,975 (17.31%)
31.01% swing Lab. to SNP
(2010: Lab. Co-op majority 21,002 (44.70%))

STIRLING
E. 67,236 T. 52,135 (77.54%) SNP gain

*Steven Paterson, SNP	23,783
Johanna Boyd, Lab.	13,303
Stephen Kerr, C.	12,051
Mark Ruskell, Scot. Green	1,606
Elisabeth Wilson, LD	1,392

SNP majority 10,480 (20.10%)
22.30% swing Lab. to SNP
(2010: Lab. majority 8,354 (17.85%))

NORTHERN IRELAND

ANTRIM EAST
E. 62,810 T. 33,497 (53.33%) DUP hold

Sammy Wilson, DUP	12,103
Roy Beggs, UUP	6,308
Stewart Dickson, Alliance	5,021
Noel Jordan, UKIP	3,660
Oliver McMullan, SF	2,314
Ruth Wilson, TUV	1,903
Margaret Anne McKillop, SDLP	1,639
Alex Wilson, C.	549

DUP majority 5,795 (17.30%)
swing N/A
(2010: DUP majority 6,770 (22.20%))

ANTRIM NORTH
E. 75,874 T. 41,907 (55.23%) DUP hold

Ian Paisley, DUP	18,107
Timothy Gaston, TUV	6,561
Daithi McKay, SF	5,143
Robin Swann, UUP	5,054
Declan O'Loan, SDLP	2,925
Jayne Dunlop, Alliance	2,351
Robert Hill, UKIP	1,341
Carol Freeman, C.	368
Thomas Palmer, Ind.	57

DUP majority 11,546 (27.55%)
1.03% swing DUP to TUV
(2010: DUP majority 12,558 (29.62%))

ANTRIM SOUTH
E. 67,423 T. 36,523 (54.17%) UUP gain

*Danny Kinahan, UUP	11,942
William McCrea, DUP	10,993
Declan Kearney, SF	4,699
Neil Kelly, Alliance	3,576
Roisin Lynch, SDLP	2,990
Richard Cairns, TUV	1,908
Alan Dunlop, C.	415

UUP majority 949 (2.60%)
swing N/A
(2010: DUP majority 1,183 (3.48%))

BELFAST EAST
E. 63,154 T. 39,682 (62.83%) DUP gain

*Gavin Robinson, DUP	19,575
Naomi Long, Alliance	16,978
Neil Wilson, C.	1,121
Ross Brown, Green	1,058
Niall O Donnghaile, SF	823
Mary Muldoon, SDLP	127

DUP majority 2,597 (6.54%)
5.49% swing Alliance to DUP
(2010: Alliance majority 1,533 (4.45%))

BELFAST NORTH
E. 68,552 T. 40,593 (59.21%) DUP hold

Nigel Dodds, DUP	19,096
Gerry Kelly, SF	13,770
Alban Maginness, SDLP	3,338
Jason O'Neill, Alliance	2,941
Gemma Weir, WP	919
Fra Hughes, Ind.	529

DUP majority 5,326 (13.12%)
3.55% swing SF to DUP
(2010: DUP majority 2,224 (6.01%))

BELFAST SOUTH
E. 64,912 T. 38,957 (60.02%) SDLP hold

Alasdair McDonnell, SDLP	9,560
Jonathan Bell, DUP	8,654
Paula Bradshaw, Alliance	6,711
Mairtin O Muilleoir, SF	5,402
Rodney McCune, UUP	3,549
Clare Bailey, Green	2,238
Bob Stoker, UKIP	1,900
Ben Manton, C.	582
Lily Kerr, WP	361

SDLP majority 906 (2.33%)
7.50% swing SDLP to DUP
(2010: SDLP majority 5,926 (17.33%))

BELFAST WEST
E. 62,685 T. 35,329 (56.36%) SF hold

Paul Maskey, SF	19,163
Gerry Carroll, PBP	6,798
Alex Attwood, SDLP	3,475
Frank McCoubrey, DUP	2,773
Bill Manwaring, UUP	1,088
Brian Higginson, UKIP	765
Gerard Catney, Alliance	636
John Lowry, WP	597
Paul Shea, C.	34

SF majority 12,365 (35.00%)
swing N/A
(2010: SF majority 17,579 (54.71%))
(2011: SF majority 13,123 (50.6%))

DOWN NORTH
E. 64,207 T. 35,947 (55.99%) Ind. hold

Lady (Sylvia) Hermon, Ind.	17,689
Alex Easton, DUP	8,487
Andrew Muir, Alliance	3,086
Steven Agnew, Green	1,958
Mark Brotherston, C.	1,593
Jonny Lavery, UKIP	1,482
William Cudworth, TUV	686
Tom Woolley, SDLP	355
Glenn Donnelly, CISTA	338
Therese McCartney, SF	273

Ind. majority 9,202 (25.60%)
swing N/A
(2010: Ind. majority 14,364 (42.90%))

DOWN SOUTH
E. 75,215 T. 42,697 (56.77%) SDLP hold

Margaret Ritchie, SDLP	18,077
Chris Hazzard, SF	12,186
Harold McKee, UUP	3,964
Jim Wells, DUP	3,486
Henry Reilly, UKIP	3,044
Martyn Todd, Alliance	1,622
Felicity Buchan, C.	318

SDLP majority 5,891 (13.80%)
2.98% swing SDLP to SF
(2010: SDLP majority 8,412 (19.75%))

FERMANAGH & SOUTH TYRONE
E. 70,106 T. 50,864 (72.55%) UUP gain

*Tom Elliott, UUP	23,608
Michelle Gildernew, SF	23,078
John Coyle, SDLP	2,732
Tanya Jones, Green	788
Hannah Su, Alliance	658

UUP majority 530 (1.04%)
swing N/A
(2010: SF majority 4 (0.01%))

FOYLE
E. 70,035 T. 37,002 (52.83%) SDLP hold

Mark Durkan, SDLP	17,725
Gearoid O hEara, SF	11,679
Gary Middleton, DUP	4,573
Julia Kee, UUP	1,226
David Hawthorne, Alliance	835
Kyle Thompson, UKIP	832
Hamish Badenoch, C.	132

SDLP majority 6,046 (16.34%)
1.80% swing SF to SDLP
(2010: SDLP majority 4,824 (12.73%))

LAGAN VALLEY
E. 71,140 T. 39,795 (55.94%) DUP hold
Jeffrey Donaldson, DUP	19,055
Alex Redpath, UUP	6,055
Trevor Lunn, Alliance	5,544
Pat Catney, SDLP	2,500
Alan Love, UKIP	2,200
Samuel Morrison, TUV	1,887
Jacqui McGeough, SF	1,144
Jonny Orr, Ind.	756
Helen Osborne, C.	654
DUP majority 13,000 (32.67%)
swing N/A
(2010: DUP majority 10,486 (28.70%))

LONDONDERRY EAST
E. 66,925 T. 34,714 (51.87%) DUP hold
Gregory Campbell, DUP	14,663
Caoimhe Archibald, SF	6,859
William McCandless, UUP	5,333
Gerry Mullan, SDLP	4,268
Yvonne Boyle, Alliance	2,642
Neil Paine, CISTA	527
Liz St Clair-Legge, C.	422
DUP majority 7,804 (22.48%)
3.58% swing SF to DUP
(2010: DUP majority 5,355 (15.32%))

NEWRY & ARMAGH
E. 77,622 T. 49,877 (64.26%) SF hold
*Mickey Brady, SF	20,488
Danny Kennedy, UUP	16,312
Justin McNulty, SDLP	12,026
Kate Nicholl, Alliance	841
Robert Rigby, C.	210
SF majority 4,176 (8.37%)
swing N/A
(2010: SF majority 8,331 (18.55%))

STRANGFORD
E. 64,286 T. 33,924 (52.77%) DUP hold
Jim Shannon, DUP	15,053
Robert Burgess, UUP	4,868
Kellie Armstrong, Alliance	4,687
Joe Boyle, SDLP	2,335
Joe Jordan, UKIP	2,237
Johnny Andrews, C.	2,167
Stephen Cooper, TUV	1,701
Sheila Bailie, SF	876
DUP majority 10,185 (30.02%)
swing N/A
(2010: DUP majority 5,876 (18.08%))

TYRONE WEST
E. 63,854 T. 38,654 (60.53%) SF hold
Pat Doherty, SF	16,807
Tom Buchanan, DUP	6,747
Daniel McCrossan, SDLP	6,444
Ross Hussey, UUP	6,144
Stephen Donnelly, Alliance	869
Ciaran McClean, Green	780
Barry Brown, CISTA	528
Claire-Louise Leyland, C.	169
Susan-Anne White, Ind.	166
SF majority 10,060 (26.03%)
1.32% swing SF to DUP
(2010: SF majority 10,685 (28.67%))

ULSTER MID
E. 67,831 T. 40,922 (60.33%) SF hold
Francie Molloy, SF	19,935
Sandra Overend, UUP	6,318
Ian McCrea, DUP	5,465
Malachy Quinn, SDLP	5,055
Gareth Ferguson, TUV	1,892
Alan Day, UKIP	863
Eric Bullick, Alliance	778
Hugh Scullion, WP	496
Lucille Nicholson, C.	120
SF majority 13,617 (33.28%)
swing N/A
(2010: SF majority 15,363 (37.62%))
(2013: SF majority 4,681 (12.58%))

UPPER BANN
E. 80,052 T. 47,219 (58.99%) DUP hold
David Simpson, DUP	15,430
Jo-Anne Dobson, UUP	13,166
Catherine Seeley, SF	11,593
Dolores Kelly, SDLP	4,238
Peter Lavery, Alliance	1,780
Martin Kelly, CISTA	460
Damien Harte, WP	351
Amandeep Singh Bhogal, C.	201
DUP majority 2,264 (4.79%)
swing N/A
(2010: DUP majority 3,361 (8.12%))

MANIFESTO COMMITMENTS

THE CONSERVATIVE PARTY MANIFESTO 2015

Below are selected key commitments made by the Conservative Party in their 2015 manifesto.

ECONOMY AND TAXATION
- Increase the income tax personal allowance to £12,500
- Increase the higher rate income tax threshold to £50,000
- Freeze income tax, national insurance and VAT rates for the duration of the next parliament
- Reduce government spending by 1 per cent in real terms for the first two years of the next parliament
- Increase annual tax charges paid by those with non-domiciled status
- Invest in infrastructure and devolve power to support industry growth and jobs in the English regions

HEALTH
- Provide an additional £8bn of real terms funding to NHS England over the five years to 2020
- Ensure everyone can access a GP and necessary hospital care seven days a week by 2020
- Guarantee same-day GP appointments for those aged 75 and over if they need one
- Continue to invest in the Cancer Drugs Fund and deliver earlier detection and diagnosis, and better treatment and care for cancer and dementia patients
- Increase funding for mental health care and enforce new access and waiting time standards for those with mental ill-health

EDUCATION
- Train an extra 17,500 maths and physics teachers over the next five years
- Create 3 million new apprenticeships
- Ensure there is no cap on university places
- Turn every 'failing' secondary school into an academy
- Support the delivery of free schools for parents and communities that want them

LAW AND ORDER
- Replace the Human Rights Act with a British Bill of Rights; curtailing the role of the European Court of Human Rights and making the UK Supreme Court arbiter of human rights matters in the UK
- Develop the role of Police and Crime Commissioners
- Prioritise victim support
- Deploy new technology to monitor offenders in the community and to bring persistent offenders to justice quickly
- Continue to reform the police and prison systems

SOCIETY
- Support museums, libraries, media, press freedom, creative industries and tourism
- Introduce three days a year paid volunteering leave for those in the public sector and with big companies
- Guarantee a place on the National Citizen Service scheme for every 16 and 17-year-old who wants one

- Build 200,000 new starter homes for first-time buyers aged under 40
- Increase the state pension by at least 2.5 per cent, in line with inflation, or in line with earnings – whichever is higher

IMMIGRATION
- Continue to work towards the goal of reducing annual net migration to under 100,000 a year*
- Maintain an annual cap of 20,700 on the number of skilled migrants who can come to the UK from outside the EU
- Reform welfare rules so that EU migrants have to be resident in the UK for at least four years before they can claim certain benefits or social housing
- End the provision of out of work benefits for all EU migrants
- Migrants will be required to leave the UK if they have not found a job within six months
- Enhance border security and strengthen the enforcement of immigration rules

* For the year ending December 2014 net migration stood at 318,000 (Source: ONS)

POLITICAL REFORM
- Maintain the Westminster Parliament as the UK's law-making body
- Give English MPs a veto over matters only affecting England
- Introduce a Scotland bill, to ensure that more than 50 per cent of the Scottish parliament's budget is funded from revenues raised in Scotland and also devolve further powers in welfare, taxation and spending to the Scottish parliament
- Devolve new powers to the Welsh Assembly, including control over its name, size, assembly electoral system and voting age
- Fully implement the Stormont House Agreement in Northern Ireland

ENVIRONMENT
- Establishing a new 'Blue Belt' category to protect marine habitats
- Spend £3bn over this parliament enhancing England's countryside
- Build 1,400 new flood defence schemes to protect 300,000 homes
- Work with the natural capital committee on a 25-year plan to restore the UK's biodiversity
- Phase-out public subsidies for new onshore wind farms

DEFENCE AND FOREIGN AFFAIRS
- Give the UK people a say in whether we should remain in the EU, with an 'in-out' referendum by 2017
- Work for peace and stability in Iraq and Syria; pursuing a comprehensive political and military strategy to defeat IS
- Uphold the sovereignty of Ukraine by continuing to reject Russia's illegal annexation of Crimea
- Invest at least £160bn in new military equipment over the next decade
- Spend 0.7 per cent of GNI on international development

POLITICAL PARTIES' KEY PLEDGES

Includes the political parties which are represented by at least one MP in the current parliament (*see* State of the Parties, page 120). The parties are ordered by number of seats held and then alphabetical order if tied.

CONSERVATIVES
- Eliminate the deficit and be running a surplus by the end of the parliament
- Provide an extra £8bn above inflation for the NHS by 2020
- Extend the right-to-buy scheme to housing association tenants in England
- Introduce legislation so that those working 30 hours a week on the minimum wage are not eligible for tax
- 30 hours of free childcare a week for working parents of all three- and four-year-olds
- Referendum on the UK's EU membership

LABOUR
- Cut the deficit every year; balance the books as soon as possible in next parliament
- An extra £2.5bn for the NHS, largely paid for by a mansion tax on properties valued at over £2m
- Increase the hourly minimum wage to more than £8 by 2019
- No increases in VAT, national insurance or basic and higher rates of income tax
- Access to childcare from 8am to 6pm for parents of primary school children
- A freeze on energy bills until 2017 and new powers to the energy regulator to reduce bills for winter 2015

SCOTTISH NATIONAL PARTY
- Increase government spending by 0.5 per cent a year to enable £140bn extra investment in the economy and public services
- Annual UK target of 100,000 affordable homes
- Increase the hourly minimum wage to £8.70 by 2020
- Restore the 50 per cent income tax rate for those earning over £150,000
- Build an alliance against the renewal of the Trident nuclear weapons system
- Retain the triple lock on pensions and protect the winter fuel allowance

DEMOCRATIC UNIONIST PARTY
- Grow the Northern Ireland economy by making the region an attractive option for foreign investment
- Deliver world class public services
- Create a society based on fairness and opportunity for everyone
- Make politics and government work better in Northern Ireland and enhance British identity

LIBERAL DEMOCRATS
- Balance the budget fairly through a mixture of cuts and taxes on higher earners
- Increase the tax-free allowance to £12,500
- Guarantee education funding for all from nursery age to 19 years and ensure every school-aged child is taught by a qualified teacher

- Invest £8bn in the NHS and bring mental health care in line with that provided for physical health
- Five new laws to protect the natural environment and fight climate change

SINN FEIN
- End austerity – negotiate an extra £1.5bn for job creation and strong public services in Northern Ireland
- Return economic powers for a fair recovery, including full control over income tax
- Fully implement the welfare protection outlined in the Stormont House Agreement
- Continue to campaign for a referendum on Irish unity

PLAID CYMRU
- Living wage for all employees by 2020
- Extra 1,000 doctors for Wales NHS
- Devolve control of the criminal justice system – including policing – to Wales
- Oppose renewal of the Trident nuclear weapons system
- Wales to get the same devolved powers and similar funding to Scotland – an additional £1.2bn a year

SOCIAL DEMOCRATIC AND LABOUR PARTY
- A Scottish-style commission on devolving fiscal powers to Northern Ireland
- A prosperity process rather than continued austerity
- VAT in the hospitality and tourism industry reduced to 5 per cent
- Opposition to further welfare spending cuts

ULSTER UNIONIST PARTY
- Reduce the rate of corporation tax in Northern Ireland to encourage economic growth and create tens of thousands of new jobs
- An integrated education system in Northern Ireland where children mix from age four to ensure against sectarianism
- Benchmark the performance of the NHS in Northern Ireland against the best performing aspects of the NHS in other parts of the UK
- Improve mental health and wellbeing

GREEN
- End austerity and restore the public sector, creating jobs that pay at least a living wage
- End privatisation of the NHS and re-nationalise the railways
- Work with other countries on climate change to ensure global temperature increases do not exceed 2°C
- Invest £85bn in a public programme of renewable fuel generation, flood defences and building insulation
- Provide 500,000 social homes for rent by 2020 and introduce rent caps

UK INDEPENDENCE PARTY
- Hold a referendum on the UK's membership of the European Union
- Limit immigration to 50,000 skilled workers a year and implement a five-year ban on unskilled immigration
- Provide an additional £3bn a year of funding for the NHS in England
- No tax on the minimum wage
- Meet the NATO target of spending 2 per cent of GDP on defence, and look to increase this target substantially

THE GOVERNMENT

as at 1 September 2015

THE CABINET

Prime Minister, First Lord of the Treasury and Minister for the Civil Service
Rt. Hon. David Cameron, MP
Chancellor of the Exchequer and First Secretary of State
Rt. Hon. George Osborne, MP
Secretary of State for Foreign and Commonwealth Affairs
Rt. Hon. Philip Hammond, MP
Secretary of State for the Home Department
Rt. Hon. Theresa May, MP
Lord Chancellor and Secretary of State for Justice
Rt. Hon. Michael Gove, MP
Secretary of State for Defence
Rt. Hon. Michael Fallon, MP
Secretary of State for Work and Pensions
Rt. Hon. Iain Duncan Smith, MP
Secretary of State for Health
Rt. Hon. Jeremy Hunt, MP
Lord President of the Council and Leader of the House of Commons
Rt. Hon. Chris Grayling, MP
Secretary of State for International Development
Rt. Hon. Justine Greening, MP
Secretary of State for Education and Minister for Women and Equalities
Rt. Hon. Nicky Morgan, MP
Lord Privy Seal and Leader of the House of Lords
Rt. Hon. Baroness Stowell of Beeston, MBE
Secretary of State for Transport
Rt. Hon. Patrick McLoughlin, MP
Secretary of State for Business, Innovation and Skills and President of the Board of Trade
Rt. Hon. Sajid Javid, MP
Secretary of State for Northern Ireland
Rt. Hon. Theresa Villiers, MP
Secretary of State for Environment
Rt. Hon. Theresa Villiers, MP
Secretary of State for Environment, Food and Rural Affairs
Rt. Hon. Elizabeth Truss, MP
Secretary of State for Communities and Local Government
Rt. Hon. Greg Clark, MP
Secretary of State for Wales
Rt. Hon. Stephen Crabb, MP
Chancellor of the Duchy of Lancaster
Rt. Hon. Oliver Letwin, MP
Secretary of State for Culture, Media and Sport
Rt. Hon. John Whittingdale, MP
Secretary of State for Scotland
David Mundell, MP
Secretary of State for Energy and Climate Change
Rt. Hon. Amber Rudd, MP

ALSO ATTENDING CABINET MEETINGS

Attorney-General
Rt. Hon. Jeremy Wright, QC, MP
Minister for the Cabinet Office and Paymaster General
Rt. Hon. Matthew Hancock, MP
Chief Secretary to the Treasury
Rt. Hon. Greg Hands, MP
Minister for Small Business, Industry and Enterprise
Rt. Hon. Anna Soubry, MP

Minister without Portfolio
Rt. Hon. Robert Halfon, MP
Parliamentary Secretary to the Treasury and Chief Whip
Rt. Hon. Mark Harper, MP
Minister of State at the Foreign and Commonwealth Office
Rt. Hon. Baroness Anelay of St Johns, DBE
Minister of State for Employment
Rt. Hon. Priti Patel, MP

LAW OFFICERS

Attorney-General
Rt. Hon. Jeremy Wright, QC, MP
Solicitor-General
Robert Buckland, QC, MP
Advocate-General for Scotland
Rt. Hon. Lord Keen of Elie, QC

MINISTERS OF STATE

Business, Innovation and Skills
Jo Johnson, MP
*Ed Vaizey, MP
†Rt. Hon. Lord Maude of Horsham
‡Nick Boles, MP
Communities and Local Government
Rt. Hon. Mark Francois, MP
Brandon Lewis, MP
Culture, Media and Sport
§Ed Vaizey, MP
Defence
Philip Dunne, MP
Penny Mordaunt, MP
Rt. Hon. Earl Howe
Education
§Nick Boles, MP
Nick Gibb, MP
Edward Timpson, MP
Energy and Climate Change
Andrea Leadsom, MP
Enivronment, Food and Rural Affairs
George Eustice, MP
Foreign and Commonwealth Office
Rt. Hon. David Lidington, MP
Rt. Hon. Hugo Swire, MP
§Rt. Hon. Lord Maude of Horsham
**Rt. Hon. Baroness Anelay of St Johns, DBE
Rt. Hon. Grant Shapps, MP
Health
Rt. Hon. Alistair Burt, MP
Home Office
Rt. Hon. Mike Penning, MP
Rt. Hon. John Hayes, MP
James Brokenshire, MP
Rt. Hon. Lord Bates
Justice
Rt. Hon. Mike Penning, MP
Rt. Hon. Lord Faulks, QC
International Development
Rt. Hon. Grant Shapps, MP
Rt. Hon. Desmond Swayne, TD, MP

Work and Pensions
Rt. Hon. Priti Patel, MP
Rt. Hon. Lord Freud
Baroness Altmann, CBE
UK Export Finance
**Lord Maude of Horsham

* position held jointly with the Department for Culture, Media and Sport
† position held jointly with the Foreign and Commonwealth Office (FCO)
‡ position held jointly with the Department for Education
§ position held jointly with the Department for Business, Innovation and Skills (BIS)
** position held jointly between the FCO and the BIS

UNDER-SECRETARIES OF STATE

Business, Innovation and Skills
*George Freeman, MP
Baroness Neville-Rolfe, DBE, CMG
Communities and Local Government
Marcus Jones, MP
James Wharton, MP
Baroness Williams of Trafford
Culture, Media and Sport
Richard Harrington, MP
Baroness Neville-Rolfe, DBE, CMG
Tracey Crouch, MP
Baroness Shields, OBE
Defence
Mark Lancaster, TD, MP
Julian Brazier, MP
Education
Caroline Dinenage, MP
Sam Gyimah, MP
Lord Nash
Energy and Climate Change
Lord Bourne of Aberystwyth
Environment, Food and Rural Affairs
Rory Stewart, MP
Foreign and Commonwealth Office
Tobias Ellwood, MP
Health
Ben Gummer, MP
Jane Ellison, MP
†George Freeman, MP
Lord Prior of Brampton
Home Office
Karen Bradley, MP
Lord Ahmad of Wimbledon
Richard Harrington, MP
International Development
Baroness Verma
Richard Harrington, MP
Justice
Caroline Dinenage, MP
Dominic Raab, MP
Andrew Selous, MP
Shailesh Vara, MP
Northern Ireland Office
Ben Wallace, MP
Scotland Office
Lord Dunlop
Transport
Robert Goodwill, MP
Claire Perry, MP

Andrew Jones, MP
Lord Ahmad of Wimbledon
Wales Office
Alun Cairns, MP
Lord Bourne of Aberystwyth
Work and Pensions
Justin Tomlinson, MP
Shailesh Vara, MP

* Jointly with the Department for Health
† Jointly with BIS

OTHER MINISTERS

Cabinet Office
Rob Wilson, MP *(Parliamentary Secretary)*
John Penrose, MP *(Parliamentary Secretary)*
Lord Bridges of Headley *(Parliamentary Secretary)*
Office of the Leader of the House of Commons
Thérèse Coffey, MP
(Parliamentary Secretary and Deputy Leader of the Commons)
Office of the Leader of the House of Lords
Rt. Hon. Earl Howe *(Deputy Leader of the House of Lords)*
Treasury
Damian Hinds, MP *(Exchequer Secretary)*
David Gauke, MP *(Financial Secretary)*
Harriet Baldwin, MP *(Economic Secretary)*
Lord O'Neill of Gatley *(Commercial Secretary)*

GOVERNMENT WHIPS

HOUSE OF LORDS
Lords Chief Whip and Captain of the Honourable Corps of Gentlemen-at-Arms
Lord Taylor of Holbeach, CBE
Deputy Chief Whip and Captain of the Queen's Bodyguard of the Yeomen of the Guard
Lord Gardiner of Kimble
Lords-in-Waiting
Lord Ashton of Hyde
Lord Bourne of Aberystwyth
Viscount Young of Leckie
Earl of Courtown
Baronesses-in-Waiting
Baroness Chisholm of Owlpen
Baroness Evans of Bowes Park

HOUSE OF COMMONS
Chief Whip and Parliamentary Secretary to the Treasury
Rt. Hon. Mark Harper, MP
Deputy Chief Whip and Treasurer of HM Household
Anne Milton, MP
Deputy Chief Whip and Comptroller of HM Household
Gavin Barwell, MP
Government Whip and Vice-Chamberlain of HM Household
Kris Hopkins, MP
Lords Commissioners of HM Treasury (Whips)
David Evennett, MP; John Penrose, *Alun Cairns, MP;
Charlie Elphicke, MP; Mel Stride, MP;
George Hollingberry, MP
Assistant Whips Guy Opperman, MP; Julian Smith, MP;
Margot James, MP; Sarah Newton, MP;
Stephen Barclay, MP; Simon Kirby, MP;
Jackie Doyle-Price, MP

* alongside role as Under-Secretary of State at the Wales Office

GOVERNMENT DEPARTMENTS

THE CIVIL SERVICE

The civil service helps the government develop and deliver its policies as effectively as possible. It works in three types of organisations – departments, executive agencies, and non-departmental government bodies (NDPBs). Under the Next Steps programme, launched in 1988, many semi-autonomous executive agencies were established to carry out much of the work of the civil service. Executive agencies operate within a framework set by the responsible minister which specifies policies, objectives and available resources. All executive agencies are set annual performance targets by their minister. Each agency has a chief executive, who is responsible for the day-to-day operations of the agency and who is accountable to the minister for the use of resources and for meeting the agency's targets. The minister accounts to parliament for the work of the agency.

There are currently 412,000 civil servants on a full-time equivalent (FTE) basis and 447,000 on a headcount basis. FTE is a measure that counts staff according to the proportion of full-time hours that they work. Almost three-quarters of all civil servants work outside London and the south-east. All government departments and executive agencies are responsible for their own pay and grading systems for civil servants outside the senior civil service.

SALARIES 2015–16

MINISTERIAL SALARIES from 31 July 2015 until May 2020

Ministers who are members of the House of Commons receive a parliamentary salary of £74,000 in addition to their ministerial salary.

Prime minister	£75,440
Cabinet minister (Commons)	£67,505
Cabinet minister (Lords)	£101,038
Minister of state (Commons)	£31,680
Minister of state (Lords)	£78,891
Parliamentary under-secretary (Commons)	£22,375
Parliamentary under-secretary (Lords)	£68,710

SPECIAL ADVISERS' SALARIES from 1 April 2015

Special advisers to government ministers are paid out of public funds; their salaries are negotiated individually, but are usually in the range of £40,352 to £106,864.

CIVIL SERVICE SALARIES from 1 April 2015

Senior Civil Servants	
Permanent secretary	£142,000–£200,000
Band 3	£105,000–£208,100
Band 2	£86,000–£162,500
Band 1	£63,000–£117,800

Staff are placed in pay bands according to their level of responsibility and taking account of other factors such as experience and marketability. Movement within and between bands is based on performance. Following the delegation of responsibility for pay and grading to government departments and agencies from 1 April 1996, it is no longer possible to show service-wide pay rates for staff outside the Senior Civil Service.

GOVERNMENT DEPARTMENTS

For more information on government departments, see
W www.gov.uk/government/ministers

ATTORNEY-GENERAL'S OFFICE

Attorney-General's Office, 20 Victoria Street, London SW1H 0NF
T 020-7271 2492 E correspondence@attorneygeneral.gsi.gov.uk
W www.gov.uk/government/organisations/attorney-generals-office

The law officers of the crown for England and Wales are the Attorney-General and the Solicitor-General. The Attorney-General, assisted by the Solicitor-General, is the chief legal adviser to the government and is also ultimately responsible for all crown litigation. He has overall responsibility for the work of the Law Officers' Departments (the Treasury Solicitor's Department, the Crown Prosecution Service – incorporating the Revenue and Customs Prosecutions Office – and the Serious Fraud Office, and HM Crown Prosecution Service Inspectorate). The Attorney-General also oversees the armed forces' prosecuting authority and the government legal service. He has a specific statutory duty to superintend the discharge of their duties by the Director of Public Prosecutions (who heads the Crown Prosecution Service) and the Director of the Serious Fraud Office. The Attorney-General has specific responsibilities for the enforcement of the criminal law and also performs certain public interest functions, eg protecting charities and appealing unduly lenient sentences. He also deals with questions of law arising in bills and with issues of legal policy.

Following the devolution of power to the Northern Ireland Assembly on 12 April 2010, the assembly now appoints the Attorney General for Northern Ireland. The Attorney General for England and Wales holds the office of Advocate General for Northern Ireland, with significantly reduced responsibilities in Northern Ireland.

Attorney-General, Rt. Hon. Jeremy Wright, QC, MP
Parliamentary Private Secretary, Rehman Chishti, MP
Solicitor-General, Robert Buckland, QC, MP
Director-General, Rowena Collins Rice

DEPARTMENT FOR BUSINESS, INNOVATION AND SKILLS

1 Victoria Street, London SW1H 0ET
T 020-7215 5000
W www.gov.uk/government/organisations/department-for-business-innovation-skills

The Department for Business, Innovation and Skills (BIS) was established in June 2009 by merging the Department for Business, Enterprise and Regulatory Reform and the Department for Innovation, Universities and Skills. BIS is the department for economic growth which invests in skills and education to promote trade, boost innovation and help people to start and grow a business. BIS also protects consumers and reduces the impact of regulation.

Secretary of State for Business, Innovation and Skills and
President of the Board of Trade, Rt. Hon. Sajid Javid, MP*

Parliamentary Private Secretary, John Glen, MP
Principal Private Secretary, Emma Squire
Senior Private Secretary, Emily Shirtcliff
Special Advisers, Nick King; Salma Shah; Daniel Gilbert
Minister of State, Jo Johnson, MP *(Universities and Science)*
Parliamentary Private Secretary, Anne Marie Morris, MP
Senior Private Secretary, Hannah Nicholls
Minister of State, Rt. Hon. Lord Maude of Horsham *(Trade and Investment)**
Senior Private Secretary, John Frew
Special Adviser, Simone Finn
Minister of State, Rt. Hon. Anna Soubry, MP *(Small Business, Industry and Enterprise)*
Parliamentary Private Secretary, Mark Pawsey, MP
Senior Private Secretary, Claire Rannard
Special Adviser, Elliott Burton
Minister of State, Ed Vaizey, MP *(Culture and the Digital Economy)†*
Parliamentary Private Secretary, Sheryll Murray, MP
Private Secretary, Jack Hindley
Minister of State, Nick Boles, MP *(Skills)‡*
Parliamentary Private Secretary, Anne Marie Morris, MP
Senior Private Secretary, Rose McNamee
Parliamentary Under-Secretary of State, George Freeman, MP *(Life Sciences)§*
Senior Private Secretary, Rebecca Molyneux
Parliamentary Under-Secretary of State, Baroness Neville-Rolfe, DBE, CMG *(Minister for Intellectual Property)†*
Private Secretary, Harriet Smith
Permanent Secretary, Martin Donnelly
Senior Private Secretary, Casey Malynn
Head of Parliamentary Unit, Georgina Holme-Skelton

* Jointly with UK Export Finance
† Jointly with the Department for Culture, Media and Sport
‡ Jointly with the Department for Education
§ Jointly with the Department of Health

DEPARTMENTAL BOARD
Chair, Rt. Hon. Sajid Javid, MP *(Secretary of State)*
Members, Sam Beckett *(Economics and Markets);* Gareth Davies *(Knowledge and Innovation);* Martin Donnelly *(Permanent Secretary);* Dominic Jermey *(Chief Executive, UK Trade and Investment);* Bernadette Kelly *(Business and Local Growth);* Philippa Lloyd *(People and Strategy);* Howard Orme *(Finance and Commercial);* Mark Russell *(Chief Executive, Shareholder Executive);* Rachel Sandby-Thomas, CB *(Enterprise and Skills and Legal)*
Non-Executive Members, Stephen Bligh; Allan Cook *(Lead);* Prof. Dame Ann Dowling, DBE; Juergen Maier; Dale Murray; Dalton Philips; Prof. Wendy Purcell

BETTER REGULATION EXECUTIVE
1 Victoria Street, London SW1 0ET
T 020-7215 5000 E betterregulation@bis.gsi.gov.uk
W www.gov.uk/government/policy-teams/better-regulation-executive

The Better Regulation Executive (BRE) is a joint BIS/Cabinet Office unit which leads on delivering the government's manifesto commitment to reduce the overall burden on business, in order to increase growth and create jobs. Each government department is however responsible for delivering its part of the deregulation agenda within the framework put in place by the BRE.
Non-Executive Chair, Lord Curry of Kirkharle, CBE
Chief Executive, Graham Turnock

SHAREHOLDER EXECUTIVE
1 Victoria Street, London SW1H 0ET
T 020-7215 5000
W www.shareholderexecutive.gov.uk

The Shareholder Executive was set up in September 2003 to work with other departments in government to improve the government's capabilities and performance as a shareholder, and to offer corporate finance expertise and advice across government. Its goal is to create a climate of ownership that, while challenging, is genuinely supportive and provides the framework for the 23 businesses under its remit to be successful. In addition, the Shareholder Executive's Government Property Unit is responsible for maximising value from the state's property portfolio.
Chair, Robert Swannell
Chief Executive, Mark Russell

CABINET OFFICE
70 Whitehall, London SW1A 2AS
T 020-7276 1234
W www.gov.uk/government/organisations/cabinet-office

The Cabinet Office, alongside the Treasury, sits at the centre of the government, with an overarching purpose of making government work better. It supports the prime minister and the cabinet, helping to ensure effective development, coordination and implementation of policy and operations across all government departments. The Cabinet Office also leads work to ensure that the Civil Service provides the most effective and efficient support to the government to meet its objectives. The department is headed by the Minister for the Cabinet Office.
Prime Minister, First Lord of the Treasury and Minister for the Civil Service, Rt. Hon. David Cameron, MP
Parliamentary Private Secretary, Gavin Williamson, MP
Principal Private Secretary, Chris Martin
Chancellor of the Duchy of Lancaster, Rt. Hon. Oliver Letwin, MP
Parliamentary Private Secretary, Alok Sharma, MP
Minister for the Cabinet Office and Paymaster General, Rt. Hon. Matthew Hancock, MP
Parliamentary Private Secretary, Gareth Johnson, MP
Principal Private Secretary, Athith Shetty
Private Secretaries, Helen Devanny, Miriam Laurance, Joe Taylor
Lord President of the Council, Rt. Hon. Chris Grayling, MP
Parliamentary Private Secretary, Mike Freer, MP
Minister for Civil Society, Rob Wilson, MP
Private Secretary, Elizabeth Jacobs
Minister for Constitutional Reform, John Penrose, MP
Parliamentary Secretary, Lord Bridges of Headley
Private Secretary, Luke Montague
Minister without Portfolio, Rt. Hon. Robert Halfon, MP
Parliamentary Private Secretary, Andrew Stephenson, MP
Head of the Civil Service and Cabinet Secretary, Sir Jeremy Heywood, KCB, CVO
Chief Executive of the Civil Service, John Manzoni
Permanent Secretary and First Parliamentary Counsel, Richard Heaton, CB
Chair of the Joint Intelligence Committee, Jon Day
National Security Adviser, Sir Kim Darroch
Head of European and Global Issues, Tom Scholar

MANAGEMENT BOARD
Chair, Rt. Hon. Francis Maude, MP
Board Members, Melanie Dawes *(Director-General, Economic and Domestic Affairs Secretariat);* Sue Gray

(Director-General, Propriety and Ethics Team, and Head of Private Offices Group); Richard Heaton, CB *(Permanent Secretary and First Parliamentary Counsel);* Sir Jeremy Heywood, KCB, CVO *(Cabinet Secretary);* Nick Hurd, MP *(Minister for Civil Society);* Bruce Mann, CB *(Finance Director)*
Non-Executive Directors, Lord Browne of Madingley; Ian Davis; Rona Fairhead; Dame Barbara Stocking, DBE

HONOURS AND APPOINTMENTS SECRETARIAT
Room G-39, Horse Guards Road, London SW1A 2HQ
T 020-7276 2777
Head, Richard Tilbrook

OFFICE OF THE LEADER OF THE HOUSE OF COMMONS
1 Horse Guards Road, London SW1A 2HQ
T 020-7276 1005 E commonsleader@cabinetoffice.gov.uk
W www.gov.uk/government/organisations/the-office-of-the-leader-of-the-house-of-commons

The Office of the Leader of the House of Commons is responsible for the arrangement of government business in the House of Commons and for planning and supervising the government's legislative programme. The Leader of the House of Commons upholds the rights and privileges of the house and acts as a spokesperson for the government as a whole.

The leader reports regularly to the cabinet on parliamentary business and the legislative programme. In his capacity as leader of the house, he is a member of the House of Commons Commission. He also chairs the cabinet committee on the legislative programme. As Lord President of the Council, he is a member of the cabinet and in charge of the Office of the Privy Council.

The Deputy Leader of the House of Commons supports the leader in handling the government's business in the house. He is responsible for monitoring MPs' and peers' correspondence.
Leader of the House of Commons and Lord Privy Seal, Rt. Hon. Chris Grayling, MP
Parliamentary Private Secretary, Mike Freer, MP
Head of Office, Mike Winter
Deputy Head of Office, Christine Hill
Assistant Private Secretaries, James Waddington *(Parliamentary Business);* Mark Fernandes *(Parliamentary Reform)*
Deputy Leader of the House of Commons, Dr Thérèse Coffey, MP
Private Secretary, Mark Fernandes

OFFICE OF THE LEADER OF THE HOUSE OF LORDS
House of Lords, London SW1A 0PW
T 020-7219 3200 E psleaderofthelords@cabinet-office.x.gsi.gov.uk
W www.gov.uk/government/organisations/office-of-the-leader-of-the-house-of-lords

The Office of the Leader of the House of Lords provides support to the leader in their parliamentary and ministerial duties, which include leading the government benches in the House of Lords; the delivery of the government's business in the Lords; taking part in formal ceremonies such as the state opening of parliament; and giving guidance to the House of Lords on matters of procedure and order.
Lord Privy Seal, Leader of the House of Lords, Rt. Hon. Baroness Stowell of Beeston, MBE
Parliamentary Private Secretary, Kwasi Kwarteng, MP
Deputy Leader of the House of Lords, Rt. Hon. Earl Howe

GOVERNMENT POLICY
PRIME MINISTER'S OFFICE
10 Downing Street, London SW1A 2AA
T 020-7930 4433
W www.number-10.gov.uk
Prime Minister, Rt. Hon. David Cameron, MP
Parliamentary Private Secretary, Gavin Williamson, MP
Principal Private Secretary, Chris Martin
Private Secretaries, Nigel Casey *(Foreign Affairs);* Kate Joseph *(Home Affairs);* Ed Whiting *(Foreign Affairs and Development)*
Speech Writer to the Prime Minister, Tim Kiddell
Director of Communications, Craig Oliver
Director of External Relations, Gabby Bertin
Director of Operations and Campaigns, Liz Sugg
Director of Strategy, Ameet Gill
Prime Minister's Official Spokesman, Helen Bower
Chief of Staff, Ed Llewellyn
Deputy Chief of Staff, Catherine Fall
Press Secretary to the Prime Minister, Graeme Wilson
Head of Policy Unit, Camilla Cavendish
Head of Implementation Unit, Antonia Romeo
Head of Corporate Services, Helen Lederer

CIVIL SERVICE REFORM
Director-General, Oliver Robbins, CB

ECONOMIC AND DOMESTIC AFFAIRS SECRETARIAT
Director-General, Antonia Romeo

IMPLEMENTATION GROUP
Executive Director, Simon Case

PRIVATE OFFICES GROUP
Director-General, Propriety and Ethics and Head of Private Offices Group, Sue Gray

UK GOVERNANCE GROUP
Second Permanent Secretary and Head of UK Governance Group, Philip Rycroft

CABINET OFFICE CORPORATE SERVICES
Executive Director, Government Communications, Alex Aiken
Finance Director, Guy Lester
Human Resources Directors, Crystal Akass; Ruth Bailey

NATIONAL SECURITY
Comprises the National Security Secretariat and the Joint Intelligence Organisation. The National Security Secretariat is responsible for providing policy advice to the National Security Council, where ministers discuss national security issues at a strategic level; coordinating and developing foreign and defence policy across government; coordinating policy, ethical and legal issues across the intelligence community, managing its funding and priorities, and dealing with the Intelligence and Security Committee which calls it to account; developing effective protective security policies and capabilities for government; improving the UK's resilience to respond to and recover from emergencies, and maintaining facilities for the effective coordination of government response to crises; and providing strategic leadership for cyber security in the UK, in line with the National Cyber Security Strategy.

NATIONAL SECURITY SECRETARIAT
National Security Adviser, Sir Mark Lyall Grant
Deputy National Security Adviser, Julian Miller, CB

JOINT INTELLIGENCE ORGANISATION
Chair, Joint Intelligence Committee, Jon Day

EFFICIENCY AND REFORM GROUP
Chief Procurement Officer, Bill Crothers, CB
Deputy Chief Procurement Officer, Sally Collier

INDEPENDENT OFFICES

CIVIL SERVICE COMMISSION
1 Horse Guards Road, London SW1A 2HQ
T 020-7271 0831
W http://civilservicecommission.independent.gov.uk

The Civil Service Commission regulates the requirement that selection for appointment to the Civil Service must be on merit on the basis of fair and open competition; the commission publishes its recruitment principles and audit departments and agencies' performance against these. Commissioners personally chair competitions for the most senior jobs in the civil service. In addition, the commission hears complaints from civil servants under the Civil Service Code.

The commission was established as a statutory body in November 2010 under the provisions of the Constitutional Reform and Governance Act 2010.
First Commissioner (part-time), Sir David Normington, GCB
Commissioners, Jonathan Baume; Kathryn Bishop; Andrew Flanagan; Dame Moira Gibb, DBE; Wanda Goldwag; Angela Sarkis, CBE

THE COMMISSIONER FOR PUBLIC APPOINTMENTS
G/8, 1 Horse Guards Road, London SW1A 2HQ
T 020-7271 0831 E publicappointments@csc.gsi.gov.uk
W http://publicappointmentscommissioner.independent.gov.uk

The Commissioner for Public Appointments is responsible for monitoring, regulating and reporting on ministerial appointments (including those made by Welsh government ministers) to public bodies. The commissioner can investigate complaints about the way in which appointments were made.
Commissioner for Public Appointments, Sir David Normington, GCB
Chief Executive Commission Secretariat, Clare Salters

OFFICE OF THE PARLIAMENTARY COUNSEL
1 Horse Guards Road, London SW1A 2HQ
T 02-7276 6586 E goodlaw@cabinet-office.gsi.gov.ukk
W www.gov.uk/government/organisations/office-of-the-parliamentary-counsel

The Office of the Parliamentary Counsel is a group of government lawyers who specialise in drafting government bills; advising departments on the rules and procedures of Parliament; reviewing orders and regulations which amend Acts of Parliament; and assisting the government on a range of legal and constitutional issues.
First Parliamentary Counsel, Richard Heaton, CB
Chief Executive, Jim Barron, CBE

DEPARTMENT FOR COMMUNITIES AND LOCAL GOVERNMENT
2 Marsham Street, London SW1P 4DF
T 0303-444 0000
W www.gov.uk/government/organisations/department-for-communities-and-local-government

The Department for Communities and Local Government was formed in May 2006 with a remit to promote community cohesion and prevent extremism, and was given responsibility for housing, urban regeneration and planning. It unites the communities and civil renewal functions previously undertaken by the Home Office, with responsibility for regeneration, neighbourhood renewal and local government (previously

held by the Office of the Deputy Prime Minister, which was abolished following a cabinet reshuffle in May 2006). The department ensures that the Fire and Rescue services have the resources they need to reduce the number of deaths from fire, promote fire prevention activity and respond swiftly to national emergencies. The department also has responsibility for equality policy on race and faith (functions that were previously split between several government departments).
Secretary of State for Communities and Local Government and Minister for Faith, Rt. Hon. Greg Clark, MP
Parliamentary Private Secretary, Henry Smith, MP
Principal Private Secretary, Alex Williams
Special Advisers, Megan Powell-Chandler; Jacob Willmer
Minister of State, Brandon Lewis, MP *(Housing and Planning)*
Parliamentary Private Secretary, Andrew Griffiths, MP
Private Secretary, Ruth Long
Minister of State, Rt. Hon. Mark Francois, MP *(Communities and Resilience)*
Parliamentary Private Secretary, Andrew Griffiths, MP
Private Secretary, Lucy Yates
Parliamentary Under-Secretary of State, Marcus Jones, MP *(Local Government)*
Private Secretary, Peter Fenn
Parliamentary Under-Secretary of State, James Wharton, MP *(Local Growth and the Northern Powerhouse)*
Private Secretary, Kerr McKendrick
Parliamentary Under-Secretary of State, Baroness Williams of Trafford
Private Secretary, Shamila Meadows

MANAGEMENT BOARD
Permanent Secretary, Melanie Dawes, CB
Members, Stephen Aldridge, CB; Dawn Brodrick, CB; Andrew Campbell, CB; Louise Casey, CB; Helen Edwards, CBE; David Hill; Jacinda Humphry; Peter Schofield
Non-Executive Members, Stephen Hay; Nick Markham; Grenville Turner; Sara Weller *(Lead)*

DEPARTMENT FOR CULTURE, MEDIA AND SPORT
100 Parliament Street, London SW1A 2BQ
T 020-7211 6000 E enquiries@culture.gov.uk
W www.gov.uk/government/organisations/department-for-culture-media-sport

The Department for Culture, Media and Sport (DCMS) was established in July 1997 and aims to improve the quality of life for all those in the UK through cultural and sporting activities while championing the tourism, creative and leisure industries. It is responsible for government policy relating to the arts, sport, the National Lottery, tourism, libraries, museums and galleries, broadcasting, creative industries – including film and the music industry – press freedom and regulation, licensing, gambling, the historic environment, telecommunications and online and media ownership and mergers.

The department is also responsible for 41 agencies and public bodies that help deliver the department's strategic aims and objectives, the listing of historic buildings and scheduling of ancient monuments, the export licensing of cultural goods, and the management of the Government Art Collection and the Royal Parks (its sole executive agency). It has the responsibility for humanitarian assistance in the event of a disaster, as well as for the organisation of the annual Remembrance Day ceremony at the Cenotaph. In September 2012, the Government Equalities Office became part of DCMS, having previously been part of the Home Office.
Secretary of State for Culture, Media and Sport, Rt. Hon. John Whittingdale, MP

Parliamentary Private Secretary, Heather Wheeler, MP
Principal Private Secretary, Ben Dean
Minister of State, Ed Vaizey, MP *(Culture and the Digital Economy)**
Parliamentary Private Secretary, Sheryll Murray, MP
Private Secretary, Jack Hindley
Parliamentary Under-Secretary of State, Tracey Crouch, MP *(Sport, Tourism and Heritage)*
Private Secretary, Philip Bland
Parliamentary Under-Secretary of State, Baroness Neville-Rolfe, DBE, CMG *(Minister for Intellectual Property)**
Private Secretary, Lizzie Glithero-West
Parliamentary Under-Secretary of State, Baroness Shields *(Internet Safety and Security)*
Private Secretary, Saskia Bradbury

*Jointly with the Department for Business, Innovation and Skills

MANAGEMENT BOARD
Permanent Secretary, Sue Owen
Members, Hugh Harris; Sarah Healey; Clare Pillman; Alison Pritchard; David Rossington; Chris Townsend; Andrea Young
Non-Executive Members, Ajay Chowdhury; Dr Tracy Long; Ruby McGregor-Smith, CBE; Sir David Verey

GOVERNMENT EQUALITIES OFFICE (GEO)
100 Parliament Street, London SW1A 2BQ T 020-7211 6000
E enquiries@culture.gsi.gov.uk
W www.gov.uk/government/organisations/government-equalities-office

The GEO is responsible for the government's overall strategy on equality. Its work includes leading the development of a more integrated approach on equality across government with the aim of improving equality and reducing discrimination and disadvantage for all. The office is also responsible for leading policy on gender equality, sexual orientation and transgender equality matters.
Minister for Women and Equality, Rt. Hon. Nicky Morgan, MP
Parliamentary Under-Secretary of State, Caroline Dinenage, MP *(Women, Equalities and Family Justice)*
Director, Alison Pritchard

MINISTRY OF DEFENCE
see Defence Chapter

DEPARTMENT FOR EDUCATION
Piccadilly Gate, Store Street, Manchester M1 2WD
T 0370-000 2288
W www.gov.uk/government/organisations/department-for-education

The Department for Education (DfE) was established in May 2010 in place of the Department for Children, Schools and Families (DCSF), in order to refocus the department on its core purpose of supporting teaching and learning. The department is responsible for education and children's services, while the Department for Business, Innovation and Skills is responsible for higher education. The DfE is supported by nine executive agencies and public bodies.
The department's objectives include the expansion of the academies programme, to allow schools to apply to become independent of their local authority, and the introduction of the free schools programme, to allow any suitable proposers, such as parents, businesses or charities, to set up their own school.
Secretary of State for Education and Minister for Women and Equalities, Rt. Hon. Nicky Morgan, MP
Parliamentary Private Secretary, Robin Walker, MP
Principal Private Secretary, Rose Pennells
Special Advisers, Lee Davis; George Looker; Luke Tryl

Minister of State, Nick Boles, MP *(Skills)**
Parliamentary Private Secretary, Anne Marie Morris, MP
Senior Private Secretary, Rose McNamee
Minister of State, Nick Gibb, MP *(Schools)*
Parliamentary Private Secretary, Stephen Metcalfe, MP
Private Secretary, Huw Leslie
Minister of State, Edward Timpson, MP *(Children and Families)*
Parliamentary Private Secretary, Stephen Metcalfe, MP
Private Secretary, Holly Jones
Parliamentary Under-Secretary of State, Lord Nash *(Schools)*
Private Secretary, Bonnie Wang
Parliamentary Under-Secretary of State, Caroline Dinenage, MP *(Women, Equalities and Family Justice)†*
Private Secretary, Ben Charnock
Parliamentary Under-Secretary of State, Sam Gyimah, MP *(Childcare and Education)*
Private Secretary, Hannah Maher

* Jointly with the Department for Business, Innovation and Skills
†Jointly with the Ministry of Justice

MANAGEMENT BOARD
Permanent Secretary, Chris Wormald
Members, Shona Dunn; Simon Fryer; Simon Judge; Paul Kissack; Peter Lauener; Andrew McCully; Tom Shinner
Non-Executive Members, Paul Marshall *(Lead);* David Meller; Marion Plant, OBE

DEPARTMENT OF ENERGY AND CLIMATE CHANGE
3 Whitehall Place, London SW1A 2AW
T 0300-060 4000 E correspondence@decc.gsi.gov.uk
W www.gov.uk/government/organisations/department-of-energy-climate-change

The Department of Energy and Climate Change (DECC) was formed in 2008 to ensure that the UK has secure, clean, affordable energy supplies and to promote international action to mitigate climate change. It is supported by nine agencies and public bodies.
Secretary of State for the Department of Energy and Climate Change, Rt. Hon. Amber Rudd, MP
Parliamentary Private Secretary, Paul Maynard, MP
Private Secretary, Tim Lord
Minister of State, Andrea Leadsom, MP
Parliamentary Private Secretary, Sheryll Murray, MP
Private Secretary, Stephen Burke
Parliamentary Under-Secretary of State, Lord Bourne of Aberystwyth*
Private Secretary, Edward Hogg
*Jointly with the Wales Office

MANAGEMENT BOARD
Permanent Secretary, Stephen Lovegrove
Members, Prof. John Loughhead *(Chief Scientific Adviser);* Clive Maxwell *(Director-General, Consumers and Households);* Angie Ridgwell *(Director-General, Finance and Corporate Services);* Jeremy Pocklington *(Director-General, Markets and Infrastructure);* Katrina Williams *(Director-General, International, Science and Resilience)*

DEPARTMENT FOR ENVIRONMENT, FOOD AND RURAL AFFAIRS
Nobel House, 17 Smith Square, London SW1P 3JR
T 03459-335577
E defra.helpline@defra.gsi.gov.uk
W www.gov.uk/government/organisations/department-for-environment-food-rural-affairs

The Department for Environment, Food and Rural Affairs (DEFRA) is responsible for government policy on the environment, rural matters and farming and food production. In association with the agriculture departments of the Scottish government, the National Assembly for Wales and the Northern Ireland Office, the department is responsible for negotiations in the EU on the common agricultural and fisheries policies, and for single European market questions relating to its responsibilities. Its remit includes international agricultural and food trade policy.

The department's five strategic priorities are climate change adaptation; sustainable consumption and production; the protection of natural resources and the countryside; sustainable rural communities; and sustainable farming and food, including animal health and welfare. DEFRA, which is supported by 34 executive agencies and public bodies, is also the lead government department for emergencies in animal and plant diseases, flooding, food and water supply, dealing with the consequences of a chemical, biological, radiological or nuclear incident, and other threats to the environment.

Secretary of State for Environment, Food and Rural Affairs,
  Rt. Hon. Elizabeth Truss, MP
Parliamentary Private Secretary, Mark Spencer, MP
Principal Private Secretary, Dr Jeremy Marlow
Senior Private Secretary, Stuart Colville
Private Secretaries, Emma Southard; Adam Stevens
Parliamentary Under-Secretary of State, Rory Stewart, MP
  *(Natural Environment, Floods and Water, Resource and
  Environmental Management, Rural Affairs, Lead
  responsibility for the Environment Agency, Natural England
  and the Forestry Commission and Deputy for the Secretary of
  State on Environment Council)*
Senior Private Secretary, Suzie Pinkett
Minister of State, George Eustice, MP *(Farming, Food and the
  Marine Environment)*
Parliamentary Private Secretary, Matthew Offord
Senior Private Secretary, Matthew Sabourin
Private Secretaries, Yasmin Hussain; James Turner; David How
Spokesman in the House of Lords, Lord Gardiner of Kimble
Permanent Secretary, Bronwyn Hill, CBE
Private Secretary, Linda Kiff

SUPERVISORY BOARD
Chair, Bronwyn Hill *(Permanent Secretary)*
Members, Betsy Bassis *(Chief Operating Officer);* Prof Ian
  Boyd *(Chief Scientific Adviser);* Alastair Bridges *(Finance);*
  Nick Joicey *(Strategy, International and Biosecurity);* Sonia
  Phippard *(Policy Delivery)*
Non-Executive Members, Catherine Doran; Iain Ferguson;
  Sir Tony Hawkhead, CBE; Paul Rew

FOREIGN AND COMMONWEALTH OFFICE

King Charles Street, London SW1A 2AH
T 020-7008 1500 E fcocorrespondence@fco.gov.uk
W www.gov.uk/government/organisations/foreign-commonwealth-office

The Foreign and Commonwealth Office (FCO) provides the means of communication between the British government and other governments – and international governmental organisations – on all matters falling within the field of international relations. The FCO employs over 14,000 people in nearly 270 places across the world through a network of embassies and consulates, which help to protect and promote national interests. FCO diplomats are skilled in understanding and influencing what is happening abroad, supporting British citizens who are travelling and living overseas, helping to manage migration into Britain, promoting British trade and other interests abroad and

encouraging foreign investment in the UK. The FCO is supported by 11 executive agencies and public bodies.

Secretary of State for Foreign and Commonwealth Affairs,
  Rt. Hon. Philip Hammond, MP
Parliamentary Private Secretary, Christopher Pincher, MP
Principal Private Secretary, Martin Reynolds
Special Advisers, Graham Hook; Hayden Allan; Duncan
  McCourt
Minister of State, Rt. Hon. David Lidington, MP *(Europe)*
Parliamentary Private Secretary, James Morris, MP
Private Secretary, Jennifer MacNaughton
Minister of State, Rt. Hon. Hugo Swire, MP
Parliamentary Private Secretary, Pauline Latham, MP
Private Secretary, Fergus Eckersley
Minister of State, Rt. Hon. Lord Maude of Horsham
  *(Trade and Investment)**
Private Secretary, Nick Whittingham
Minister of State, Rt. Hon. Baroness Anelay of St Johns,
  DBE
Private Secretary, Kate English
Minister of State, Rt. Hon. Grant Shapps, MP†
Private Secretary, Iain Griffiths
Parliamentary Under-Secretary of State, Tobias Ellwood, MP
Private Secretary, Sharon Wilkins
Special Representatives, Rt. Hon. Baroness Anelay of St Johns,
  DBE *(Prime Minister's Special Representative on Preventing
  Sexual Violence in Conflict);* Sir Andrew Burns *(Post-
  Holocaust Issues);* Rt. Hon. Sir Alan Duncan, MP *(Special
  Envoy to Oman and Yemen);* Owen Jenkins *(Afghanistan
  and Pakistan);* Matthew Cannell *(Sudan and South Sudan);*
  Sir David King *(Climate Change)*

* Jointly with the Department for Business, Innovation and Skills and UK Export Finance
†Jointly with the Department for International Development

BOARD
Permanent Under-Secretary and Head of the Diplomatic Service,
  Sir Simon Fraser, KCMG
Members, Deborah Bronnert; Sir Simon Gass *(Political);*
  Dominic Jermey, OBE *(Chief Executive, UK Trade and
  Investment);* Julian King, KCVO, CMG *(Economic and
  Consular);* Sara Mackintosh *(Defence and Intelligence)*
Non-Executive Members, Julia Bond; Prof. Robin Grimes;
  Sir Richard Lambert *(Lead);* Rudy Markham

DEPARTMENT OF HEALTH

Richmond House, 79 Whitehall, London SW1A 2NS
T 020-7210 4850
W https://www.gov.uk/government/organisations/department-of-health

The Department of Health (DH) leads, shapes and funds health and care in England, making sure people have the support, care and treatment they need and that this is delivered in a compassionate, respectful and dignified manner.

The DH leads across health and care by creating national policies and legislation to meet current and future challenges. It provides funding, assures the delivery and continuity of services and accounts to parliament in a way that represents the best interests of the patient, public and taxpayer. 26 executive agencies and public bodies support the DH.

Secretary of State for Health, Rt. Hon. Jeremy Hunt, MP
Parliamentary Private Secretary, Steve Brine, MP
Principal Private Secretary, Kristen McLeod
Private Secretary, Andrew Edmunds
Minister of State, Rt. Hon. Alistair Burt, MP *(Community and
  Social Care)*
Parliamentary Private Secretary, Karen Lumley

Private Secretary, Claire McAvinchey
Parliamentary Under-Secretary of State, Ben Gummer, MP
    (Care Quality)
Private Secretary, Alex Wallace
Parliamentary Under-Secretary of State, Jane Ellison, MP
    (Public Health)
Private Secretary, Kirsty Bell
Parliamentary Under-Secretary of State, Lord Prior of
    Brampton *(NHS Productivity)*
Private Secretary, Ilaria Regondi
Parliamentary Under-Secretary of State, George Freeman, MP
    (Life Sciences)*
Private Secretary, Rebecca Molyneux

* Jointly with the Department for Business, Innovation and Skills

DEPARTMENTAL BOARD
Chair, Rt. Hon. Jeremy Hunt, MP
Members, Rt. Hon. Alistair Burt MP; Will Cavendish
    (Innovation, Growth and Technology); Prof. Dame Sally
    Davies, DBE *(Chief Medical Officer);* Jane Ellison, MP;
    Tamara Finkelstein *(Chief Operating Officer);* Ben
    Gummer, MP; Felicity Harvey, CBE *(Public Health);*
    Charlie Massey *(Strategy and External Relations);* Dame
    Una O'Brien, DCB *(Permanent Secretary);* Dr Daniel
    Poulter, MP; Lord Prior; Jon Rouse *(Social Care, Local
    Government and Care Partnerships);* David Williams
    (Finance and NHS)
Non-Executive Members, Dr Catherine Bell; Gerry Murphy;
    Chris Pilling; Peter Sands *(Lead)*

HOME OFFICE
2 Marsham Street, London SW1P 4DF
T 020-7035 4848 E public.enquiries@homeoffice.gsi.gov.uk
W www.gov.uk/government/organisations/home-office

The Home Office deals with those internal affairs in
England and Wales which have not been assigned to other
government departments. The Secretary of State for the
Home Department is the link between the Queen and the
public, and exercises certain powers on her behalf, including
that of the royal pardon.

The Home Office aims to build a safe, just and tolerant
society and to maintain and enhance public security and
protection; to support and mobilise communities so that they
are able to shape policy and improvement for their locality,
overcome nuisance and anti-social behaviour, maintain and
enhance social cohesion and enjoy their homes and public
spaces peacefully; to deliver departmental policies and
responsibilities fairly, effectively and efficiently; and to make
the best use of resources. These objectives reflect the
priorities of the government and the home secretary in areas
of crime, citizenship and communities, namely to work on
the problems caused by illegal drug use; shape the alcohol
strategy, policy and licensing conditions; keep the UK safe
from the threat of terrorism; reduce and prevent crime, and
ensure people feel safe in their homes and communities;
secure the UK border and control immigration; consider
applications to enter and stay in the UK; issue passports and
visas; and to support visible, responsible and accountable
policing by empowering the public and freeing up the police
to fight crime.

The Home Office delivers these aims through the
immigration services, its 29 executive agencies and non-
departmental public bodies, and by working with partners
in private, public and voluntary sectors, individuals and
communities. The home secretary is also the link between the
UK government and the governments of the Channel Islands
and the Isle of Man.

Secretary of State for the Home Department, Rt. Hon. Theresa
    May, MP
Parliamentary Private Secretary, Michael Ellis, MP
Principal Private Secretary, Andrew Scurry
Special Advisers, Alex Dawson; Stephen Parkinson; Liz
    Sanderson
Minister of State, Mike Penning, MP *(Policing, Crime and
    Criminal Justice and Victims)**
Parliamentary Private Secretary, Chris White, MP
Private Secretary, Sarah Phillips
Minister of State, Rt. Hon. John Hayes, MP *(Security)*
Parliamentary Private Secretary, Chris White, MP
Minister of State, James Brokenshire, MP *(Immigration)*
Parliamentary Private Secretary, Craig Whittaker, MP
Private Secretary, Jon Rosenorn-Lanng
Minister of State, Rt. Hon. Lord Bates
Private Secretary, Moore Flannery
Parliamentary Under-Secretary of State, Karen Bradley, MP
    (Preventing Abuse and Exploitation)
Parliamentary Under-Secretary of State, Lord Ahmad of
    Wimbledon *(Countering Extremism)*

*Jointly with the Ministry of Justice

MANAGEMENT BOARD
Permanent Secretary, Mark Sedwill
Members, Mary Calam *(Crime and Policing Group);* Mandie
    Campbell *(Immigration Enforcement);* Charles Farr
    (Office for Security and Counter Terrorism); Peter Fish
    (Legal); Sir Charles Montgomery *(Border Force);* Mike
    Parsons *(Chief Operating Officer, Home Office);* Sarah
    Rapson *(UK Visas and Immigration);* Prof. Bernard
    Silverman *(Chief Scientific Adviser);* Peter Storr
    (International and Immigration Policy); Julie Taylor
    (Transformation); Mark Thomson *(HM Passport Office);*
    Kevin White, CB *(Human Resources);* Simon Wren
    (Communications)

DEPARTMENT FOR INTERNATIONAL DEVELOPMENT
22 Whitehall, London SW1A 2EG T 020-7023 0000
Abercrombie House, Eaglesham Road, East Kilbride, Glasgow
G75 8EA T 01355-844000
Public Enquiries 0845-300 4100 E enquiry@dfid.gov.uk
W www.gov.uk/government/organisations/department-for-
international-development

The Department for International Development (DFID) is
responsible for promoting sustainable development and
reducing poverty. The central focus of the government's
policy, based on the 1997, 2000, 2006 and 2009 white
papers on international development, is a commitment to
the internationally agreed Millennium Development Goals,
to be achieved by 2015. These seek to eradicate extreme
poverty and hunger; achieve universal primary education;
promote gender equality and empower women; reduce
child mortality; improve maternal health; combat HIV/AIDS,
malaria and other diseases; improve sanitation and access
to clean water; ensure environmental sustainability; and
encourage a global partnership for development.

DFID's assistance is concentrated in the poorest countries
of sub-Saharan Africa and Asia, but also contributes to
poverty reduction and sustainable development in middle-
income countries, including those in Latin America and
Eastern Europe. It also responds to overseas emergencies.
The department works in partnership with governments
of developing countries, charities, non-governmental
organisations and businesses. It also works with multilateral
institutions, including the World Bank, United Nations

agencies and the European Commission. The department, which is supported by two executive agencies and public bodies, has headquarters in London and East Kilbride, offices in many developing countries, and staff based in British embassies and high commissions around the world.
Secretary of State for International Development,
    Rt. Hon. Justine Greening, MP
Parliamentary Private Secretary, Andrew Bingham, MP
Principal Private Secretary, Jonathan Baxter
Special Advisers, Simon Bishop; Aline Nassif
Minister of State, Rt. Hon. Grant Shapps, MP*
Parliamentary Private Secretary, Charlotte Leslie, MP
Private Secretary, Vicky Seymour
Minister of State, Rt. Hon. Desmond Swayne, TD, MP
Parliamentary Private Secretary, Charlotte Leslie, MP
Private Secretary, Heather Opie
Parliamentary Under-Secretary of State, Baroness Verma
Private Secretary, Zoe Ware

*Jointly with the Foreign and Commonwealth Office

MANAGEMENT BOARD
Chair, Rt. Hon. Justine Greening, MP
Members, Richard Calvert *(Finance and Corporate Performance);* Nick Dyer *(acting Policy and Global Programmes);* Joy Hutcheon *(Country Programmes);* David Kennedy *(Economic Development);* Mark Lowcock *(Permanent Secretary);* Rt. Hon. Grant Shapps, MP; Rt. Hon. Desmond Swayne, TD, MP; Baroness Verma
Non-Executive Members, Vivienne Cox *(Lead);* Richard Keys; Tim Robinson; Eric Salama

CDC GROUP
123 Victoria Street, London SW1E 6DE
T 020-7963 4700 E enquiries@cdcgroup.com
W www.cdcgroup.com

Founded in 1948, CDC is the UK's Development Finance Institution wholly owned by the UK government. It invests to create jobs and build businesses in developing countries in Africa and South Asia. In 2014 CDC made 19 new investment commitments which totalled £296.8m across these regions. CDC is a public limited company with net assets of £3,369m.
Chair, Graham Wrigley
Chief Executive, Diana Noble

MINISTRY OF JUSTICE
102 Petty France, London SW1H 9AJ
T 020-3334 3555 E general.queries@justice.gsi.gov.uk
W www.gov.uk/government/organisations/ministry-of-justice

The Ministry of Justice (MoJ) was established in May 2007. MoJ is headed by the Lord Chancellor and Secretary of State for Justice who is responsible for improvements to the justice system so that it better serves the public. He is also responsible for some areas of constitutional policy (those not covered by the Deputy Prime Minister).
    The MoJ established five key priorities for 2014. These were to reduce reoffending by using the skills of the public, private and voluntary sectors; reduce youth crime by putting education at the centre of youth justice; build a prison system that delivers maximum value for money; reduce the cost of legal aid and ensure it helps those cases that genuinely require it; and to improve the way the courts are run and put the needs of victims first. The MoJ has a budget of around £9bn and is supported by 38 executive agencies and public bodies to achieve its targets.
    The Lord Chancellor and Secretary of State for Justice is the government minister responsible to parliament for the

judiciary, the court system and prisons and probation. The Lord Chief Justice has been the head of the judiciary since 2006.
    MoJ incorporates the National Offender Management Service; the HM Prison Service and the National Probation Service; Her Majesty's Courts and Tribunals Service; the Legal Aid Agency; and the Youth Justice Board.
    MoJ has several associated departments, non-departmental public bodies and executive agencies, including the National Archives and the Office of the Public Guardian.
Lord Chancellor and Secretary of State for Justice,
    Rt. Hon. Michael Gove, MP
Parliamentary Private Secretary, Robert Jenrick, MP
Principal Private Secretary, Amy Rees
Minister of State, Rt. Hon. Mike Penning, MP
    (Policing, Crime and Criminal Justice and Victims)
Parliamentary Private Secretary, Chris White, MP
Private Secretary, Marc Attwell
Minister of State, Lord Edward Faulks, QC *(Civil Justice)*
Private Secretary, Elaine Cobb
Parliamentary Under-Secretary of State, Shailesh Vara, MP
    (Courts and Legal Aid)
Private Secretary, Stephen Doney
Parliamentary Under-Secretary of State, Andrew Selous, MP
    (Prisons, Probation, Rehabilitation and Sentencing)
Private Secretary, Catherine Bennion
Parliamentary Under-Secretary of State, Caroline Dinenage,
    MP *(Women, Equalities and Family Justice)*†
Private Secretary, Ben Charnock
Parliamentary Under-Secretary of State, Dominic Raab, MP
    (Human Rights)
Private Secretary, Mary Jones

*Jointly with the Home Office
†Jointly with the Department for Education

MANAGEMENT BOARD
Permanent Secretary, Ursula Brennan
Members, Ann Beasley *(Director-General, Finance);* Matthew Coats *(Director-General, Legal Aid Agency and Corporate Services Group);* Catherine Lee *(Director-General, Law and Access to Justice Group);* Michael Spurr *(Chief Executive, National Offender Management Service)*
Non-Executive Member, Sir Theodore Agnew

NORTHERN IRELAND OFFICE
1 Horse Guards Road, London SW1A 2HQ
Stormont House, Stormont Estate, Belfast BT4 3SH
T 028-9052 0700 E nioweb.editor@nio.x.gsi.gov.uk
W www.gov.uk/government/organisations/northern-ireland-office

The Northern Ireland Office was established in 1972, when the Northern Ireland (Temporary Provisions) Act transferred the legislative and executive powers of the Northern Ireland parliament and government to the UK parliament and a secretary of state. Under the terms of the 1998 Good Friday Agreement, power was devolved to the Northern Ireland Assembly in 1999. The assembly took on responsibility for the relevant areas of work previously undertaken by the departments of the Northern Ireland Office, covering agriculture and rural development, the environment, regional development, social development, education, higher education, training and employment, enterprise, trade and investment, culture, arts and leisure, health, social services, public safety and finance and personnel. In October 2002 the Northern Ireland Assembly was suspended and Northern Ireland returned to direct rule, but despite repeated setbacks, devolution was restored on 8 May 2007. For further details, *see* Regional Government.

The Northern Ireland Office is supported by three executive agencies and public bodies and is currently responsible for overseeing the devolution settlement; representing Northern Ireland interests within the UK government and similarly representing the UK government in Northern Ireland; working in partnership with the Northern Ireland Executive for a stable, prosperous Northern Ireland; and supporting and implementing political agreements to increase stability.

Secretary of State for Northern Ireland, Rt. Hon. Theresa Villiers, MP
Parliamentary Private Secretary, Rebecca Harris, MP
Parliamentary Under-Secretary of State, Ben Wallace, MP
Private Secretary, Andy Monaghan
Permanent Secretary, Sir Jonathan Stephens

OFFICE OF THE ADVOCATE-GENERAL FOR SCOTLAND

Dover House, Whitehall, London SW1A 2AU
T 020-7270 6770
Office of the Solicitor to the Advocate-General, Victoria Quay, Edinburgh EH6 6QQ
T 0131-244 0359 E enquiries@advocategeneral.gsi.gov.uk
W www.gov.uk/government/organisations/office-of-the-advocate-general-for-scotland

The Advocate-General for Scotland is one of the three law officers of the crown, alongside the Attorney-General and the Solicitor-General for England and Wales. He is the legal adviser to the UK government on Scottish law and is supported by staff in the Office of the Advocate-General for Scotland. The office is divided into the Legal Secretariat, based mainly in London, and the Office of the Solicitor to the Advocate-General, based in Edinburgh.

The post was created as a consequence of the constitutional changes set out in the Scotland Act 1998, which created a devolved Scottish parliament. The Lord Advocate and the Solicitor-General for Scotland then became part of the Scottish government and the Advocate-General took over their previous role as legal adviser to the UK government on Scots law. *See also* Regional Government *and* Ministry of Justice.

Advocate-General for Scotland, Lord Keen of Elie, QC
Private Secretary, Craig Chalcraft

MANAGEMENT BOARD
Direcor and Solicitor, Michael Chalmers
Members, Jim Logie; Ruraidh Macniven; Fiona Robertson; Neil Taylor

SCOTLAND OFFICE

Dover House, Whitehall, London SW1A 2AU
1 Melville Crescent, Edinburgh EH3 7HW
T 0131-244 9010 E enquiries@scotlandoffice.gsi.gov.uk
W www.gov.uk/government/organisations/scotland-office

The Scotland Office is the department of the Secretary of State for Scotland which represents Scottish interests within the UK government in matters reserved to the UK parliament. The Secretary of State for Scotland maintains the stability of the devolution settlement for Scotland; delivers secondary legislation under the Scotland Act 1998; is responsible for the conduct and funding of the Scottish parliament elections; manages the Scottish vote provision and authorises the monthly payment of funds from the UK consolidated fund to the Scottish consolidated fund; and publishes regular information on the state of the Scottish economy.

Matters reserved to the UK parliament include the constitution, foreign affairs, defence, international development, the civil service, financial and economic matters, national security, immigration and nationality, misuse of drugs, trade and industry, various aspects of energy regulation (eg coal, electricity, oil, gas and nuclear energy), various aspects of transport, social security, employment, abortion, genetics, surrogacy, medicines, broadcasting and equal opportunities. Devolved matters include health and social work, education and training, local government and housing, justice and police, agriculture, forestry, fisheries, the environment, tourism, sports, heritage, economic development and internal transport. *See also* Regional Government *and* Ministry of Justice.

Secretary of State for Scotland, Rt. Hon. David Mundell, MP
Parliamentary Private Secretary, Iain Stewart, MP
Principal Private Secretary, Chris Flatt
Parliamentary Under-Secretary of State, Lord Dunlop
Private Secretary, Stephanie Sandison

MANAGEMENT BOARD
Director, Francesca Osowska, OBE
Members, Colin Faulkner; Chris Flatt; Helena Gray; Glenn Preston

DEPARTMENT FOR TRANSPORT

Great Minster House, 33 Horseferry Road, London SW1P 4DR
T 0300-330 3000
W www.gov.uk/government/organisations/department-for-transport

The Department for Transport (DfT) works with its agencies and partners to support the transport network that helps the UK's businessees and gets people and goods travelling around the country. The DfT plans and invests in transport infrastructure to keep the UK on the move. DFT is supported by 19 executive agencies and public bodies.

Secretary of State for Transport, Rt. Hon. Patrick McLoughlin, MP
Parliamentary Private Secretary, Stuart Andrew, MP
Principal Private Secretary, Phil West
Parliamentary Under-Secretary of State, Robert Goodwill, MP
Private Secretary, Alex Philpott
Parliamentary Under-Secretary of State, Andrew Jones, MP
Private Secretary, Rory Sedgley
Parliamentary Under-Secretary of State, Claire Perry, MP
Private Secretary, Matthew Eglinton
Parliamentary Under-Secretary of State, Lord Ahmad of Wimbledon
Private Secretary, Fiona Douglas
Permanent Secretary, Philip Rutnam
Private Secretary, Natalie Golding

MANAGEMENT BOARD
Chair, Rt. Hon. Patrick McLoughlin, MP *(Secretary of State)*
Members, Lord Ahmad of Wimbledon; Lucy Chadwick *(Director-General, International, Security and Environment);* John Dowie *(Director-General, Roads, Traffic and Local);* Robert Goodwill, MP; Andrew Jones, MP; Jonathan Moor, CBE *(Director-General, Resources and Strategy);* Clare Moriarty *(Director-General, Rail Executive);* Nick Olley *(General Counsel);* Claire Perry, MP; David Prout *(Director-General, High Speed 2);* Philip Rutnam *(Permanent Secretary)*

HM TREASURY

1 Horse Guards Road, London SW1A 2HQ
T 020-7270 5000 E public.enquiries@hmtreasury.gsi.gov.uk
W www.gov.uk/government/organisations/hm-treasury

HM Treasury is the country's economics and finance ministry, and is responsible for formulating and implementing the government's financial and economic policy. It aims to raise the rate of sustainable growth, boost prosperity, and provide the conditions necessary for universal economic and employment opportunities. The Office of the Lord High Treasurer has been continuously in commission for over 200 years. The Lord High Commissioners of HM Treasury are the First Lord of the Treasury (who is also the prime minister), the Chancellor of the Exchequer and five junior lords. This board of commissioners is assisted at present by the chief secretary, the parliamentary secretary (who is also the government chief whip in the House of Commons), the financial secretary, the economic secretary, the exchequer secretary and the commercial secretary. The prime minister as first lord is not primarily concerned with the day-to-day aspects of Treasury business; neither are the parliamentary secretary and the junior lords as government whips. Treasury business is managed by the Chancellor of the Exchequer and the other Treasury ministers, assisted by the permanent secretary.

The chief secretary is responsible for public expenditure, including spending reviews and strategic planning; in-year control; public-sector pay and pensions; Annually Managed Expenditure and welfare reform; efficiency in public services; procurement and capital investment. He also has responsibility for the Treasury's interest in devolution.

The financial secretary has responsibility for financial services policy including banking and financial services reform and regulation; financial stability; city competitiveness; wholesale and retail markets in the UK, Europe and internationally; and the Financial Services Authority. His other responsibilities include banking support; bank lending; UK Financial Investments; Equitable Life; and personal savings and pensions policy. He also provides support to the chancellor on EU and wider international finance issues.

The exchequer secretary is a title only used occasionally, normally when the post of paymaster-general is allocated to a minister outside of the Treasury (as it is at present; the Rt. Hon. Matthew Hancock, MP was appointed paymaster-general and minister of the Cabinet Office in May 2015). The exchequer secretary's responsibilities include strategic oversight of the UK tax system; corporate and small business taxation, with input from the commercial secretary; departmental minister for HM Revenue and Customs and the Valuation Office Agency; and lead minister on European and international tax issues.

The economic secretary's responsibilities include environmental issues such as taxation of transport, international climate change and energy; North Sea oil taxation; tax credits and child poverty; assisting the chief secretary on welfare reform; charities and the voluntary sector; excise duties and gambling; stamp duty land tax; EU Budget; the Royal Mint; and departmental minister for HM Treasury Group.

The role of commercial secretary was created in 2010. Responsibilities include enterprise and productivity; corporate finance; assisting the financial secretary on financial services, banking policy promoting the government's financial services policies and the competitiveness of the UK; asset freezing and financial crime; foreign exchange reserves and debt management policy; National Savings and Investments; and the Debt Management Office. The commercial secretary is also the treasury spokesperson in the House of Lords.

Prime Minister and First Lord of the Treasury, Rt. Hon. David Cameron, MP
Chancellor of the Exchequer, Rt. Hon. George Osborne, MP
Parliamentary Private Secretary, Chris Skidmore, MP
Principal Private Secretary, Clare Lombardelli
Private Secretary, Melanie Pitt
Special Advisers to the Chancellor of the Exchequer, James Chapman; Matt Cook; Thea Rogers
Council of Economic Advisers, Lisa Buckland; Richard Davies; Simon Glasson; Neil O'Brien; Eleanor Wolfson
Chief Secretary to the Treasury, Rt. Hon. Greg Hands, MP
Parliamentary Private Secretary, Jake Berry, MP
Private Secretary, Alex Furse
Special Adviser to the Chief Secretary, Jennifer Donnellan
Financial Secretary to the Treasury, David Gauke, MP
Parliamentary Private Secretary, Conor Burns, MP
Exchequer Secretary to the Treasury, Damian Hinds, MP
Private Secretary, David Pares
Economic Secretary to the Treasury, Harriet Baldwin, MP
Private Secretary, Luke Seaman
Commercial Secretary to the Treasury, Lord O'Neill of Gatley
Private Secretary, Zoe NcNulty
Lords Commissioners of HM Treasury (Whips), Alun Cairns, MP; Charlie Elphicke, MP; David Evennett, MP; George Hollingberry, MP; John Penrose, MP; Mel Stride, MP
Assistant Whips, Stephen Barclay, MP; Jackie Doyle-Price, MP; Margot James, MP; Simon Kirby, MP; Sarah Newton, MP; Guy Opperman, MP; Julian Smith, MP

MANAGEMENT BOARD

Chair, Sir Nicholas Macpherson, GCB *(Permanent Secretary)*
Executive Members, Mark Bowman *(Director-General, International and EU);* James Bowler *(Director-General, Tax and Welfare);* Julian Kelly *(Public Spending and Finance);* John Kingman *(Second Permanent Secretary);* Sir Dave Ramsden, CBE *(Chief Economic Adviser);* Charles Roxburgh *(Director-General, Financial Services)*

ROYAL MINT LTD

PO Box 500, Llantrisant, Pontyclun CF72 8YT
T 01443-222111 W www.royalmint.com

From 1975 the Royal Mint operated as a trading fund and was established as an executive agency in 1990. Since 2010 it has operated as Royal Mint Ltd, a company 100 per cent owned by HM Treasury, with an exclusive contract to supply all coinage for the UK.

The Royal Mint actively competes in world markets for a share of the available circulating coin business and about half of the coins and blanks it produces annually are exported. It is the leading export mint, accounting for around 15 per cent of the world market. The Royal Mint also manufactures special proof and uncirculated quality coins in gold, silver and other metals; military and civil decorations and medals; commemorative and prize medals; and royal and official seals.

Master of the Mint, Chancellor of the Exchequer *(ex officio)*
Chair, Peter Warry
Chief Executive, Adam Lawrence

UK EXPORT FINANCE

1 Horse Guards Road, London SW1A 2HQ
T 020-7271 8000 E contact-us@ukef.gsi.gov.uk
W www.gov.uk/government/organisations/uk-export-finance

UK Export Finance is the UK's export credit agency. It helps UK exporters by providing insurance to them and guarantees to banks to share the risks of providing export finance.

Additionally, it can make loans to overseas buyers of goods and services from the UK. UK Export Finance is the operating name of the Export Credits Guarantee Department.

The priorities of UK Export Finance are to fulfil its statutory remit to support exports; operate within the policy and financial objectives established by the government, which includes international obligations; and to recover the maximum amount of debt in respect of claims paid, taking account of the government's policy on debt forgiveness. It is supported by the Export Guarantees Advisory Council.

Secretary of State for Business, Innovation and Skills and President of the Board of Trade, Rt. Hon. Sajid Javid, MP*
Senior Private Secretary, Emily Shirtcliffe
Minister of State, Rt. Hon. Lord Maude of Horsham *(Trade and Investment)**†
Private Secretary, Nick Whittingham

*Jointly with the Department for Business, Innovation, and Skills
†Jointly with the Foreign and Commonwealth Office

MANAGEMENT BOARD
Members, Steve Dodgson *(Business Group);* Cameron Fox *(Finance);* David Godfrey *(Chief Executive);* David Havelock *(Credit Risk Group);* Lucy Wylde *(General Counsel)*
Non-Executive Members, Guy Beringer; Roger Lowe; Amin Mawji, OBE; Jane Owen; Sir Eric Peacock

WALES OFFICE
Gwydyr House, Whitehall, London SW1A 2NP
T 029-2092 4220 E correspondence@walesoffice.gsi.gov.uk
W www.gov.uk/wales-office

The Wales Office was established in 1999 when most of the powers of the Welsh Office were handed over to the National Assembly for Wales. It is the department of the Secretary of State for Wales, who is the key government figure liaising with the devolved government in Wales and who represents Welsh interests in the cabinet and parliament. The secretary of state has the right to attend and speak at sessions of the National Assembly (and must consult the assembly on the government's legislative programme). *See also* Regional Government *and* Ministry of Justice.

Secretary of State for Wales, Rt. Hon. Stephen Crabb, MP
Parliamentary Private Secretary, David Morris, MP
Special Adviser, Emily Poole
Parliamentary Under-Secretary of State, Alun Cairns, MP
Private Secretary, Elizabeth Allen
Parliamentary Under-Secretary of State, Lord Bourne of Aberystwyth*
Private Secretary, Elizabeth Allen
Director of Office, Glynne Jones

*Jointly with the Department of Energy and Climate Change

DEPARTMENT FOR WORK AND PENSIONS
Caxton House, Tothill Street, London SW1H 9NA
T 020-7340 4000 E ministers@dwp.gsi.gov.uk
W www.gov.uk/government/organisations/department-for-work-pensions

The Department for Work and Pensions was formed in June 2001 from parts of the former Department of Social Security, the Department for Education and Employment and the Employment Service. The department helps unemployed people of working age into work, helps employers to fill their vacancies and provides financial support to people unable to help themselves, through back-to-work programmes. The department also administers the child support system, social security benefits and the social fund. In addition, the department has reciprocal social security arrangements with other countries.

Secretary of State for Work and Pensions, Rt. Hon. Iain Duncan Smith, MP
Parliamentary Private Secretary, David Rutley, MP
Principal Private Secretary, Paul McComb
Private Secretaries, Rob Cook; David Slovak
Minister of State, Rt. Hon. Priti Patel, MP *(Employment)*
Parliamentary Private Secretary, Alec Shelbrooke, MP
Private Secretary, Mike Maynard
Assistant Private Secretaries, Tia Priest; Nicholas Slim; Sam Gilbert
Minister of State, Baroness Altmann, CBE *(Pensions)*
Private Secretary, Michael Dynan-Oakley
Assistant Private Secretaries, Yasna Reynolds; Victoria Olipliant; Ella Taylor
Parliamentary Under-Secretary, Justin Tomlinson, MP *(Disabled People)*
Private Secretary, Jack Goodwin
Assistant Private Secretaries, Heather Lockley; Frank Shields; Joanna Ziff
Minister of State, Lord Freud *(Welfare Reform)*
Private Secretary, Becky Richards
Assistant Private Secretaries, Gemma Alcorn; Chris Ramm; Sarah Gaskell
Permanent Secretary, Robert Devereux

MANAGEMENT BOARD
Permanent Secretary and Head of Department, Robert Devereux
Members, Debbie Alder *(Director-General, Human Resources);* Neil Couling, CBE *(Director-General, Universal Credit);* Kevin Cunnington *(Director-General, Digital Transformation);* Mike Driver *(Director-General, Finance);* Jeremy Moore *(Director-General, Strategy, Policy and Analysis);* Mayank Prakash *(Director-General, Technology);* Noel Shanahan, CB *(Director-General, Operations)*

EXECUTIVE AGENCIES

Executive agencies are well-defined business units that carry out services with a clear focus on delivering specific outputs within a framework of accountability to ministers. They can be set up or disbanded without legislation, and they are organisationally independent from the department they are answerable to. In the following list the agencies are shown in the accounts of their sponsor departments. Legally they act on behalf of the relevant secretary of state. Their chief executives also perform the role of accounting officers, which means they are responsible for the money spent by their organisations. Staff employed by agencies are civil servants.

DEPARTMENT FOR BUSINESS, INNOVATION AND SKILLS

COMPANIES HOUSE
Crown Way, Cardiff CF14 3UZ
T 0303-123 4500 E enquiries@companies-house.gov.uk
W www.companies-house.gov.uk

Companies House incorporates and dissolves companies, examines and stores company information delivered under the Companies Act and related legislation; and makes this information available to the public.

Registrar of Companies for England and Wales and Chief Executive, Tim Moss
Registrar of Companies for Scotland, Aoife Ann Martin
Registrar of Companies for Northern Ireland, Helen Shilliday

THE INSOLVENCY SERVICE
4 Abbey Orchard Street, London SW1P 2HT
T 020-7637 1110 E redundancyclaims@insolvency.gsi.gov.uk
W www.bis.gov.uk/insolvency

The role of the service includes administration and investigation of the affairs of bankrupts, individuals subject to debt relief orders, partnerships and companies in compulsory liquidation; dealing with the disqualification of directors in all corporate failures; authorising and regulating the insolvency profession; providing banking and investment services for bankruptcy and liquidation estate funds; assessing and paying statutory entitlement to redundancy payments when an employer cannot, or will not, pay its employees; and advising ministers on insolvency, redundancy and related issues. The service has around 1,700 staff, operating from 21 locations across Great Britain.
Inspector-General and Chief Executive, Sarah Albon
Deputy Chief Executive, Graham Horne

INTELLECTUAL PROPERTY OFFICE
Concept House, Cardiff Road, Newport NP10 8QQ
T 0300-300 2000 E information@ipo.gov.uk
W www.gov.uk/government/organisations/intellectual-property-office

The Intellectual Property Office (an operating name of the Patent Office) was set up in 1852 to act as the UK's sole office for the granting of patents. It was established as an executive agency in 1990 and became a trading fund in 1991. The office is responsible for the granting of intellectual property (IP) rights which include patents, trade marks, designs and copyright.
Comptroller-General and Chief Executive, John Alty

MET OFFICE
FitzRoy Road, Exeter, Devon EX1 3PB
T 01392-885680 E enquiries@metoffice.gov.uk
W www.metoffice.gov.uk

The Met Office is the UK's National Weather Service, operating as an executive agency of BIS, having transferred from the MoD in July 2011. It is a world leader in providing weather and climate services, using over 10 million weather observations a day, and employs more than 1,700 people at 60 locations throughout the world.
Chief Executive, Rob Varley
Chief Scientist, Prof. Julia Slingo, OBE

NATIONAL MEASUREMENT AND REGULATION OFFICE
Stanton Avenue, Teddington, Middx TW11 0JZ
T 020-8943 7272 E info@nmro.gov.uk
W www.gov.uk/nmro

The National Measurement and Regulation Office (NMRO), formerly the National Measurement Office, aims to simplify technical regulation for the benefit of British business. The work of the NMRO should reduce unnecessary costs and give businesses greater confidence to invest and grow.
Chief Executive (acting), Richard Sanders

SKILLS FUNDING AGENCY
Cheylesmore House, Quinton Road, Coventry CV1 2WT
T 0345-377 5000 E info@skillsfundingagency.bis.gov.uk
W www.gov.uk/sfa

The Skills Funding Agency (SFA) funds skills training for further education (FE) in England, including traineeships and apprenticeships. The SFA supports over 1,000 colleges, private training organisations and employers with more than £4bn of funding annually. It is responsible for giving colleges, training organisations and employers the right funding to help adults, young people, the unemployed and those with low skill levels the opportunity to obtain the skills they require for employment.
Chief Executive, Peter Lauener

UK SPACE AGENCY
Polaris House, North Star Avenue, Swindon, Wiltshire SN2 1SZ
T 020-7215 5000 E info@ukspaceagency.bis.gsi.gov.uk
W www.gov.uk/uk-space-agency

The UK Space Agency was established on 23 March 2010 and became an executive agency on 1 April 2011. It was created to provide a single voice for UK space ambitions, and is responsible for all strategic decisions on the UK civil space programme. Responsibilities of the UK Space Agency include coordinating UK civil space activity; supporting academic research; nurturing the UK space industry; raising the profile of UK space activities at home and abroad; working to increase understanding of space science and its practical benefits; and inspiring the next generation of UK scientists and engineers. It aims to capture 10 per cent of the global market for space by 2030.
Chief Executive, Dr David Parker

CABINET OFFICE

CROWN COMMERCIAL SERVICE
Floor 9, The Capital Building, Old Hall Street, Liverpool L3 9PP
T 0345-410 2222 E info@crowncommercial.gov.uk
W www.gov.uk/government/organisations/crown-commercial-service

The Crown Commercial Service (CCS) is an executive agency of the Cabinet Office, bringing together policy, advice and direct buying; providing commercial services to the public sector and saving money for the taxpayer. The CCS works with over 1,400 organisations in the public sector.
Chair, Ed Smith
Chief Executive, Sally Collier

DEPARTMENT FOR COMMUNITIES AND LOCAL GOVERNMENT

PLANNING INSPECTORATE
Temple Quay House, 2 The Square, Temple Quay, Bristol BS1 6PN
T 0303-444 5000 E enquiries@pins.gsi.gov.uk
W www.gov.uk/government/organisations/planning-inspectorate;
www.planningportal.gov.uk/planning/planninginspectorate

The main work of the inspectorate consists of national infrastructure planning under the Planning Act 2008 as amended by the Localism Act 2011, the processing of planning and enforcement appeals, and holding examinations into development plan documents. It also deals with listed building consent appeals; advertisement appeals; rights of way cases; cases arising from the Environmental Protection and Water acts, the Transport and Works Act 1992 and other highways legislation; and reporting on planning applications called in for decision by the Department for Communities and Local Government and the Welsh government.
Chief Executive, Simon Ridley

THE QUEEN ELIZABETH II CONFERENCE CENTRE
Broad Sanctuary, London SW1P 3EE
T 020-7798 4000 W www.qeiicentre.london

The centre provides secure conference facilities for national and international government and private sector use.
Chief Executive, Mark Taylor

DEPARTMENT FOR CULTURE, MEDIA AND SPORT

THE ROYAL PARKS
The Old Police House, Hyde Park, London W2 2UH
T 0300-061 2000 E hq@royalparks.gsi.gov.uk
W www.royalparks.org.uk

Royal Parks is responsible for maintaining and developing over 2,000 hectares (5,000 acres) of urban parkland contained within the eight royal parks in London: Bushy Park (with the Longford river); Green Park; Greenwich Park; Hyde Park; Kensington Gardens; Regent's Park (with Primrose Hill); Richmond Park and St James's Park.
Chief Executive, Andrew Scattergood

MINISTRY OF DEFENCE
see Defence chapter

DEPARTMENT FOR EDUCATION

THE EDUCATION FUNDING AGENCY
Sanctuary Buildings, 20 Great Smith Street, London SW1P 3BT
T 0370-000 2288
W www.gov.uk/government/organisations/education-funding-agency

Formed on 1 April 2012, the Education Funding Agency (EFA) is the DFE's delivery agency for funding and compliance. It manages £54m of funding each year to support all state-provided education for 8 million children aged 3 to 16, and 1.6 million young people aged 16 to 19. The EFA also supports the delivery of building and maintenance programmes for schools, academies, free schools and sixth-form colleges.
Chief Executive, Peter Lauener

NATIONAL COLLEGE FOR TEACHING AND LEADERSHIP
Piccadilly Gate, Store Street, Manchester M1 2WD
T 0370-000 2288 E enquiries@nationalcollege.org.uk
W www.gov.uk/government/organisations/national-college-for-teaching-and-leadership

On 1 April 2013 the National College merged with the Teaching Agency to become the National College for Teaching and Leadership. It has two key aims: improving the quality of the workforce; and helping schools to help each other to improve. It is also the awarding body for Qualified Teacher Status (QTS).
Chief Executive, Charlie Taylor

STANDARDS AND TESTING AGENCY
53–55 Butts Road, Earlsdon Park, Coventry CV1 3BH
T 0300-303 3013 E assessments@education.gov.uk
W www.gov.uk/government/organisations/standards-and-testing-agency

The Standards and Testing Agency (STA) opened on 1 October 2011 and is responsible for the development and delivery of all statutory assessments from early years to the end of Key Stage 2.
Chief Executive, Claire Burton

DEPARTMENT FOR ENVIRONMENT, FOOD AND RURAL AFFAIRS

ANIMAL AND PLANT HEALTH AGENCY
Woodham Lane, New Haw, Addlestone, Surrey KT15 3NB
T 01932-341 111 E apha.corporate_centre@apha.gsi.gov.uk
W www.gov.uk/government/organisations/animal-and-plant-health-agency

The Animal and Plant Health Agency (APHA) was launched on 1 October 2014. It merged the former Animal Health and Veterinary Laboratories Agency with parts of the Food and Environment Research Agency responsible for plant and bee health to create a single agency responsible for animal, plant and bee health.

APHA is responsible for identifying and controlling endemic and exotic diseases and pests in animals, plants and bees, and surveillance of new and emerging pests and diseases; scientific research in areas such as bacterial, viral, prion and parasitic diseases, vaccines and food safety and act as an international reference laboratory for many farm animal diseases; facilitating international trade in animals, products of animal origin, and plants; protecting endangered wildlife through licensing and registration; managing a programme of apiary inspections, diagnostics, research and development, training and advice; and regulating the safe disposal of animal by-products to reduce the risk of potentially dangerous substances entering the food chain.

The agency provides all or some of these services to DEFRA and the Scottish and Welsh governments.
Chief Executive, Chris Hadkiss

CENTRE FOR ENVIRONMENT, FISHERIES AND AQUACULTURE SCIENCE (CEFAS)
Pakefield Road, Lowestoft, Suffolk NR33 0HT
T 01502-562244 W www.cefas.gov.uk

Established in April 1997, the agency provides research and consultancy services in fisheries science and management, aquaculture, fish health and hygiene, environmental impact assessment, and environmental quality assessment.
Chief Executive, Tom Karsten

RURAL PAYMENTS AGENCY
PO Box 69, Reading RG1 3YD
T 0300-0200 301 E ruralpayments@defra.gsi.gov.uk
W www.gov.uk/government/organisations/rural-payments-agency

The RPA was established in 2001. It pays out over £2bn each year to support the farming and food sector and is responsible for Common Agricultural Policy (CAP) schemes in England. In addition it manages over 40 other rural economy and community schemes. It is also responsible for operating cattle tracing services across Great Britain; conducting inspections of farms, processing plants and fresh produce markets in England; and managing the Rural Land Register.
Chief Executive, Mark Grimshaw

VETERINARY MEDICINES DIRECTORATE
Woodham Lane, New Haw, Addlestone, Surrey KT15 3LS
T 01932-336911 E postmaster@vmd.defra.gsi.gov.uk
W www.gov.uk/government/organisations/veterinary-medicines-directorate

The Veterinary Medicines Directorate is responsible for all aspects of the authorisation and control of veterinary medicines, including post-authorisation surveillance of residues in animals and animal products. It is also responsible for the development and enforcement of legislation concerning veterinary medicines and the provision of policy advice to ministers.
Chief Executive, Prof. Pete Borriello

FOREIGN AND COMMONWEALTH OFFICE

FCO SERVICES
Hanslope Park, Milton Keynes MK19 7BH
T 01908-515 789 E fcoservices.customercontactcentre@fco.gov.uk
W www.fcoservices.gov.uk

FCO Services was established as an executive agency in April 2006 and became a trading fund in April 2008. It operates as the service delivery arm of the FCO, keeping their people, assets and information across the globe safe and secure from the threats they face. FCO Services also works with central government departments, law enforcement, HM government abroad, local government and the UK's critical national infrastructure.
Chief Executive, Danny Payne

WILTON PARK CONFERENCE CENTRE
Wiston House, Steyning, W. Sussex BN44 3DZ
T 01903-815020 W www.wiltonpark.org.uk

Wilton Park organises international affairs conferences and is hired out to government departments and commercial users.
Chair, Iain Ferguson
Chief Executive, Richard Burge

DEPARTMENT OF HEALTH

MEDICINES AND HEALTHCARE PRODUCTS REGULATORY AGENCY (MHRA)
151 Buckingham Palace Road, London SW1W 9SZ
E info@mhra.gsi.gov.uk
W www.gov.uk/government/organisations/medicines-and-healthcare-products-regulatory-agency

The MHRA is a centre of the Medicines and Healthcare Products Regulatory Agency which also includes the National Institute for Biological Standards and Control (NIBSC) and the Clinical Practice Research Datalink (CPRD). The MHRA is responsible for regulating all medicines and medical devices in the UK by ensuring they work and are acceptably safe.
Chair, Sir Michael Rawlins
Chief Executive, Dr Ian Hudson

PUBLIC HEALTH ENGLAND
Wellington House, 133–155 Waterloo Road, London SE1 8UG
T 020-7654 8000 E enquiries@phe.gov.uk
W www.gov.uk/government/organisations/public-health-england

Public Health England (PHE) began operating on 1 April 2013 with a remit to protect and improve the health and wellbeing of people within the UK, and reducing health inequalities. PHE employs 5,000 staff who are mostly scientists, researchers and public health professionals. It has 15 local centres and four regions in England and works closely with public health profesionals in Wales, Scotland, Northern Ireland and internationally.
Chair, Prof. David Heymann, CBE
Chief Executive, Duncan Selbie

MINISTRY OF JUSTICE

CRIMINAL INJURIES COMPENSATION AUTHORITY (CICA)
Tay House, 300 Bath Street, Glasgow G2 4LN
T 0300-003 3601
W www.gov.uk/goverment/organisations/criminal-injuries-compensation-authority

CICA is the executive agency responsible for administering the Criminal Injuries Compensation Scheme in England, Scotland and Wales (separate arrangements apply in Northern Ireland). CICA handles up to 40,000 applications for compensation each year, covering every aspect of compensation under the 1996, 2001 and 2008 Criminal Injuries Compensation Schemes. Appeals against decisions made by CICA can be put to the First-tier Tribunal (Criminal Injuries Compensation) *see* Tribunals.
Chief Executive, Carole Oatway

HER MAJESTY'S COURTS AND TRIBUNALS SERVICE
see Law Courts and Offices

LEGAL AID AGENCY
Berkley Way, Viking Business Park, Jarrow, South Tyneside NE31 1SF
T 0300-200 2020 E contactcivil@legalaid.gsi.gov.uk
W www.gov.uk/government/organisations/legal-aid-agency

The Legal Aid Agency provides civil and criminal legal aid and advice in England and Wales. Formed on 1 April 2013 as part of the Legal Aid, Sentencing and Punishment of Offenders Act 2012, the agency replaces the Legal Services Commission, a non-departmental public body of the MoJ.
Chief Executive, Matthew Coats

NATIONAL OFFENDER MANAGEMENT SERVICE
see The Prison Service

OFFICE OF THE PUBLIC GUARDIAN
PO Box 16185, Birmingham B2 2WH
T 0300-456 0300 E customerservices@publicguardian.gsi.gov.uk
W www.gov.uk/government/organisations/office-of-the-public-guardian

The Office of the Public Guardian (OPG) works within the Mental Capacity Act 2005 to support and protect those who lack the mental capacity to make decisions for themselves. It supports the Public Guardian in the registration of Enduring Powers of Attorney (EPA) and Lasting Powers of Attorney (LPA), and the supervision of deputies appointed by the Court of Protection. The OPG also has responsibility for investigating and acting on allegations of abuse by attorneys and deputies. The OPG's responsibility extends across England and Wales.
Chief Executive and Public Guardian, Alan Eccles, CBE

DEPARTMENT FOR TRANSPORT

DRIVER AND VEHICLE LICENSING AGENCY (DVLA)
Longview Road, Swansea SA6 7JL
W www.gov.uk/government/organisations/driver-and-vehicle-licensing-agency

The DVLA, established as an executive agency in 1990, maintains registers of drivers and vehicles in Great Britain. The information collated by the DVLA helps to improve road safety, reduce vehicle related crime, support environmental initiatives and limit vehicle tax evasion. The DVLA maintains over 45 million driver records and over 38 million vehicle records and collects over £6bn a year in vehicle tax.
Chief Executive, Oliver Morley

DRIVER AND VEHICLE STANDARDS AGENCY
Berkeley House, Croydon Street, Bristol BS5 0DA
T 0300-123 9000 E inform@vosa.gov.uk
W www.gov.uk/government/organisations/driver-and-vehicle-standards-agency

Formed by the merger of the Driving Standards Agency and the Vehicle and Operator Services Agency in 2014, the Driver and Vehicle Standards Agency (DVSA) is responsible for improving road safety in the UK by setting standards for driving and motorcycling, and ensuring drivers, vehicle

operators and MOT garages understand and comply with roadworthiness standards. It additionally provides a range of licensing, testing, education and enforcement services.
Chief Executive, Alastair Peoples

MARITIME AND COASTGUARD AGENCY
Spring Place, 105 Commercial Road, Southampton SO15 1EG
T 023-8032 9100
W www.gov.uk/government/organisations/maritime-and-coastguard-agency

The agency's aims are to prevent loss of life, continuously improve maritime safety and protect the marine environment.
Chief Executive, Sir Alan Massey
Chief Coastguard, Keith Oliver

VEHICLE CERTIFICATION AGENCY
1 Eastgate Office Centre, Eastgate Road, Bristol BS5 6XX
T 0300-330 5797 E enquiries@vca.gov.uk W www.dft.gov.uk/vca

The agency is the UK authority responsible for ensuring that new road vehicles, agricultural tractors, off-road vehicles and vehicle parts have been designed and constructed to meet internationally agreed standards of safety and environmental protection.
Chief Executive, Paul Markwick

HM TREASURY

UK DEBT MANAGEMENT OFFICE
Eastcheap Court, 11 Philpot Lane, London EC3M 8UD
T 020-7862 6500 W www.gov.uk/government/organisations/uk-debt-management-office

The UK Debt Management Office (DMO) was launched as an executive agency of HM Treasury in April 1998. The Chancellor of the Exchequer determines the policy and financial framework within which the DMO operates, but delegates operational decisions on debt and cash management and the day-to-day running of the office to the chief executive. The DMO's remit is to carry out the government's debt management policy of minimising financing costs over the long term, and to minimise the cost of offsetting the government's net cash flows over time, while operating at a level of risk approved by ministers in both cases. The DMO is also responsible for providing loans to local authorities through the Public Works Loan Board, and for managing the assets of certain public-sector bodies through the Commissioners for the Reduction of the National Debt.
Chief Executive, Robert Stheeman

NON-MINISTERIAL GOVERNMENT DEPARTMENTS

Non-ministerial government departments are part of central government but are not headed by a minister and are not funded by a sponsor department. They are created to implement specific legislation, but do not have the ability to change it. Departments may have links to a minister, but the minister is not responsible for the department's overall performance. Staff employed by non-ministerial departments are civil servants.

CHARITY COMMISSION
PO Box 1227, Liverpool L69 3UG
T 0845-300 0218
W www.gov.uk/government/organisations/charity-commission

The Charity Commission is established by law as the independent regulator and registrar of charities in England and Wales. Its aim is to provide the best possible regulation of these charities in order to ensure their legal compliance and increase their efficiency, accountability and effectiveness, as well as to encourage public trust and confidence in them. The commission maintains a register of over 160,000 charities. It is accountable to both parliament and the First-tier Tribunal (Charity), and the chamber of the Upper Tribunal or high court for decisions made in exercising the commission's legal powers. The Charity Commission has offices in London, Liverpool, Taunton and Newport.
Chair, William Shawcross, CVO
Chief Executive, Paula Sussex

COMPETITION AND MARKETS AUTHORITY
Victoria House, Southampton Row, London WC1B 4AD
T 020-3738 6000 E general.enquiries@cma.gsi.gov.uk
W www.gov.uk/cma

The Competition and Markets Authority (CMA) is the UK's primary competition and consumer authority. It is an independent non-ministerial government department with responsibility for carrying out investigations into mergers, markets and the regulated industries and enforcing competition and consumer law. From 1 April 2014 it took over the functions of the Competition Commission and the competition and certain consumer functions of the Office of Fair Trading under the Enterprise Act 2002, as amended by the Enterprise and Regulatory Reform Act 2013.
Chair, David Currie
Chief Executive, Alex Chisholm

CROWN PROSECUTION SERVICE
Rose Court, 2 Southwark Bridge Road, London SE1 9HS
T 020-3357 0000 E enquiries@cps.gsi.gov.uk
W www.cps.gov.uk

The Crown Prosecution Service (CPS) is the independent body responsible for prosecuting people in England and Wales. The CPS was established as a result of the Prosecution of Offences Act 1985. It works closely with the police to advise on lines of inquiry and to decide on appropriate charges and other disposals in all but minor cases. *See also* Law Courts and Offices.
Director of Public Prosecutions, Alison Saunders, CB
Chief Executive, Peter Lewis, CB

FOOD STANDARDS AGENCY
Aviation House, 125 Kingsway, London WC2B 6NH
T 020-7276 8829 E helpline@foodstandards.gsi.gov.uk
W www.food.gov.uk

Established in April 2000, the FSA is a UK-wide non-ministerial government body responsible for food safety and hygiene. The agency has the general function of developing policy in these areas and provides information and advice to the government, other public bodies and consumers. The FSA also works with local authorities to enforce food safety regulations and has staff working in UK meat plants to check that the requirements of the regulations are being met.
Chair, Tim Bennett
Chief Executive, Catherine Brown

FOOD STANDARDS AGENCY NORTHERN IRELAND, 10C Clarendon Road, Belfast BT1 3BG T 028-9041 7700 E infosani@foodstandards.gsi.gov.uk

FOOD STANDARDS AGENCY WALES, 11th Floor, South Gate House, Wood Street, Cardiff CF10 1EW T 029-2067 8999 E wales@foodstandards.gsi.gov.uk

FORESTRY COMMISSION

Silvan House, 231 Corstorphine Road, Edinburgh EH12 7AT
T 0300-067 4321 E enquiries@forestry.gsi.gov.uk
W www.forestry.gov.uk

The Forestry Commission is the government department responsible for forestry policy in England and Scotland. It is divided into Forestry Commission England and Forestry Commission Scotland, which report to forestry ministers (the Secretary of State for Environment, Food & Rural Affairs in the UK government, and to ministers in the Scottish government), to whom it is responsible for advice on and implementation of forestry policy. It has an agency, Forest Research, which carries out scientific research and technical development relevant to forestry. The public forests are managed through two additional executive agencies, known as Forest Enterprise England and Forest Enterprise Scotland.

On 1 April 2013 the functions of its Welsh division, Forestry Commission Wales, were subsumed into Natural Resources Wales, a new body established by the Welsh government to regulate and manage natural resources in Wales.

The commission's principal objectives are to protect and expand England's and Scotland's forests and woodlands; enhance the economic value of forest resources; conserve and improve the biodiversity, landscape and cultural heritage of forests and woodlands; develop opportunities for woodland recreation; and increase public understanding of, and community participation in, forestry. It does this by managing public forests in its care to implement these objectives; by supporting other woodland owners with grants, regulation, advice and tree felling licences; and, through its Forest Research agency, by carrying out scientific research and technical development in support of these objectives.

Chair (2014–17), Sir Harry Studholme, Bt.
Deputy Chair and Director, England, Ian Gambles
Forestry Commissioner, Scotland, Dr Bob McIntosh

FORESTRY COMMISSION ENGLAND, 620 Bristol Business Park, Coldharbour Lane, Bristol BS16 1EJ T 0117-906 6000
FORESTRY COMMISSION SCOTLAND, Silvan House, 231 Corstorphine Road, Edinburgh EH12 7AT T 0845-367 3787

GOVERNMENT ACTUARY'S DEPARTMENT

Finlaison House, 15–17 Furnival Street, London EC4A 1AB
T 020-7211 2601
Belford House, 59 Belford Road, Edinburgh EH4 3UE
T 0131-467 0324
E enquiries@gad.gov.uk W www.gov.uk/gad

The Government Actuary's Department (GAD) was established in 1919 and provides actuarial advice to the public sector in the UK and overseas, and also to the private sector, where consistent with government policy. The GAD provides advice on occupational pension schemes, social security and National Insurance, investment and strategic risk management, insurance analysis and advice, financial risk management, and healthcare financing.

Government Actuary, Martin Clarke
Deputy Government Actuaries, George Russell; Colin Wilson
Chief Actuaries, Sandra Bell; Ian Boonin; Tracey Cutler; Adrian Hale; Stephen Humphrey; Ken Kneller; Ian Rogers; Aidan Smith; Sue Vivian; Matt Wood

GOVERNMENT LEGAL DEPARTMENT

1 Kemble Street, London WC2B 4TS
T 020-7210 3000
E thetreasurysolicitor@governmentlegal.gov.uk
W www.gov.uk/gld

The Treasury Solicitor's Department became the Government Legal Department (GLD) on 1 April 2015. The department provides legal advice to government on the development, design and implementation of government policies and decisions, and represents the government in court. It is superintended by the Attorney-General. The permanent secretary of the GLD, the Treasury Solicitor, is also the Queen's Proctor, and is responsible for collecting ownerless goods *(bona vacantia)* on behalf of the crown.

HM Procurator-General and Treasury Solicitor, Jonathan Jones
Directors-General, Stephen Braviner-Roman; Peter Fish; Claire Johnston
Head of Bona Vacantia, Mayur Patel

HM REVENUE AND CUSTOMS (HMRC)

100 Parliament Street, London SW1A 2BQ
Income Tax Enquiries 0300-200 3300
National Insurance Enquiries 0300-200 3500
VAT Enquiries 0300-200 3700
W www.gov.uk/government/organisations/hm-revenue-customs

HMRC was formed following the integration of the Inland Revenue and HM Customs and Excise, which was made formal by parliament in April 2005. It collects and administers direct taxes (capital gains tax, corporation tax, income tax, inheritance tax and national insurance contributions) and indirect taxes (excise duties, insurance premium tax, petroleum revenue tax, stamp duty, stamp duty land tax, stamp duty reserve tax and value-added tax). HMRC also pays and administers child benefit, tax credits and the Child Trust Fund, in addition to being responsible for environmental taxes, national minimum wage enforcement, recovery of student loans, the climate change levy and landfill tax. HMRC also administers the Government Banking Service.

Chief Executive and Permanent Secretary, Lin Homer
Tax Assurance Commissioner and Second Permanent Secretary, Edward Troup

VALUATION OFFICE AGENCY

Wingate House, 93–107 Shaftesbury Avenue, London W1D 5BU
T 0300-050 0385 W www.voa.gov.uk

Established in 1991, the Valuation Office is an executive agency of HM Revenue and Customs. It is responsible for compiling and maintaining the business rating and council tax valuation lists for England and Wales; valuing property throughout Great Britain for the purposes of taxes administered by HMRC; providing statutory and non-statutory property valuation services in England, Wales and Scotland; and giving policy advice to ministers on property valuation matters. In April 2009 the VOA assumed responsibility for the functions of The Rent Service, which provided a rental valuation service to local authorities in England, and fair rent determinations for landlords and tenants.

Chief Executive, Penny Ciniewicz

LAND REGISTRY

Trafalgar House, 1 Bedford Park, Croydon CR0 2AQ
T 0300-006 0411
W www.gov.uk/government/organisations/land-registry

A government department and trading fund of BIS, Land Registry maintains the Land Register – the definitive source of information for more than 24 million property titles in England and Wales. The Land Register has been open to public inspection since 1990.

Chief Land Registrar and Chief Executive, Graham Farrant

NATIONAL ARCHIVES
NATIONAL ARCHIVES
Kew, Richmond, Surrey TW9 4DU
T 020-8876 3444 W www.nationalarchives.gov.uk

The National Archives is a non-ministerial government department of the Ministry of Justice. It incorporates the Public Record Office, Historical Manuscripts Commission, Office of Public Sector Information and Her Majesty's Stationery Office. As the official archive of the UK government, it preserves, protects and makes accessible the historical collection of official records.

The National Archives also manages digital information including the UK government web archive which contains over one billion digital documents, and devises solutions for keeping government records readable now and in the future.

The organisation administers the UK's public records system under the Public Records Acts of 1958 and 1967. The records it holds span 1,000 years – from the Domesday Book to the latest government papers to be released – and fill more than 167km (104 miles) of shelving.
Chief Executive and Keeper, Jeff James

NATIONAL CRIME AGENCY
Units 1–6 Citadel Place, Tinworth Street, London SE11 5EF
T 0370-496 7622 E communication@nca.x.gsi.gov.uk
W www.nationalcrimeagency.gov.uk

The National Crime Agency (NCA) is an operational crime fighting agency introduced under the Crime and Courts Act 2013, which became fully operational in October 2013. The NCA's remit is to fight organised crime, strengthen UK borders, tackle fraud and cyber crime and protect children and young people. The agency employs over 4,000 officers and provides leadership through its organised crime, border policing, economic crime and Child Exploitation and Online Protection Centre commands, the National Cyber Crime Unit and specialist capability teams.
Chair, Keith Bristow, QPM

NATIONAL SAVINGS AND INVESTMENTS
Glasgow G58 1SB
T 0500-007 007 W www.nsandi.com

NS&I (National Savings and Investments) came into being in 1861 when the Palmerston government set up the Post Office Savings Bank, a savings scheme which aimed to encourage ordinary wage earners 'to provide for themselves against adversity and ill health'. NS&I was established as a government department in 1969. It is responsible for the design, marketing and administration of savings and investment products for personal savers and investors. It has over 25 million customers and more than £110bn invested.
See also Banking and Finance, National Savings.
Chief Executive, Jane Platt, CBE

OFFICE OF GAS AND ELECTRICITY MARKETS (OFGEM)
9 Millbank, London SW1P 3GE
T 020-7901 7295 W www.ofgem.gov.uk

OFGEM is the regulator for Britain's gas and electricity industries. Its role is to protect and advance the interests of consumers by promoting competition where possible, and through regulation only where necessary. OFGEM operates under the direction and governance of the Gas and Electricity Markets Authority, which makes all major decisions and sets policy priorities for OFGEM. OFGEM's powers are provided for under the Gas Act 1986 and the Electricity Act 1989, as amended by the Utilities Act 2000. It also has enforcement powers under the Competition Act 1998 and the Enterprise Act 2002.
Chair, David Gray
Chief Executive, Dermot Nolan

OFFICE OF QUALIFICATIONS AND EXAMINATIONS REGULATION (OFQUAL)
Spring Place, Herald Avenue, Coventry CV5 6UB
T 0300-303 3344 E public.enquiries@ofqual.gov.uk
W www.gov.uk/government/organisations/ofqual

OFQUAL became the independent regulator of qualifications, examinations and assessments on 1 April 2010. It is responsible for maintaining standards, improving confidence and distributing information about qualifications and examinations, as well as regulating general and vocational qualifications in England and vocational qualifications in Northern Ireland.
Chief Executive, Glenys Stacey

OFFICE OF RAIL REGULATION
1 Kemble Street, London WC2B 4AN
T 020-7282 2000 E contact.cct@orr.gsi.gov.uk
W www.orr.gov.uk

The Office of the Rail and Road (ORR) is the operating name of the Office of Rail Regulation. The Office of Rail Regulation was established on 5 July 2004 under the Railways and Transport Safety Act 2003. It replaced the Office of the Rail Regulator.

On 1 April 2006, ORR assumed new responsibilities as a combined safety and economic regulator under the Railways Act 2005. It also has concurrent jurisdiction with the Competition and Market Authority under the Competition Act 1998 as the competition authority for the railways.

As the railway industry's independent health and safety and econimic regulator, its principal functions are to: ensure that Network Rail and HS1 manage the national network efficiently and in a way that meets the needs of its users; encourage continuous health and safety performance; secure compliance with relevant health and safety law, including taking enforcement action as necessary; develop policy and enhance relevant railway health and safety legislation; and license operators of railway assets, setting the terms for access by operators to the network and other railway facilities, and enforce competition and consumer law in the rail sector.

On 1 April 2015, under the Infrastructure Act 2015, ORR assumed responsibility for monitoring Highways England's management and development of the strategic road network – the motorways and main 'A' roads in England. In this role ORR ensures that the network is managed efficiently, safely and sustainably, for the benefit of road users and the public.

On 16 March 2015, ORR signed an agreement with the French rail regulator ARAF to establish a collaborative regulatory approach for consistent independent regulation across the Channel tunnel network.

ORR is led by a board appointed by the Secretary of State for Transport.
Chair, Anna Walker

OFFICE FOR STANDARDS IN EDUCATION, CHILDREN'S SERVICES AND SKILLS (OFSTED)
Piccadilly Gate, Store Street, Manchester M1 2WD
T 0300-123 1231 E enquiries@ofsted.gov.uk
W www.gov.uk/government/organisations/ofsted

Ofsted was established under the Education (Schools Act) 1992 and was relaunched on 1 April 2007 with a wider remit, bringing together four formerly separate inspectorates. It works to raise standards in services through the inspection

and regulation of care for children and young people, and inspects education and training for children of all ages. *See also* Education.
HM Chief Inspector, Sir Michael Wilshaw
Chair, David Hoare

ORDNANCE SURVEY

Adanac Drive, Southampton SO16 0AS
T 0845-605 0505
E customerservices@os.uk
W www.ordnancesurvey.co.uk

Ordnance Survey is the national mapping agency for Great Britain. It is a government department and executive agency operating as a trading fund since 1999.
Director-General and Chief Executive, Nigel Clifford

SERIOUS FRAUD OFFICE

2–4 Cockspur Street, London SW1Y 5BS
T 020-7239 7272 E public.enquiries@sfo.gsi.gov.uk
W www.sfo.gov.uk

The Serious Fraud Office is an independent government department that investigates and, where appropriate, prosecutes serious or complex fraud, bribery and corruption. It is part of the UK criminal justice system with jurisdiction over England, Wales and Northern Ireland but not Scotland, the Isle of Man or the Channel Islands. The office is headed by a director who is superintended by the Attorney-General.
Director, David Green, CB, QC

SUPREME COURT OF THE UNITED KINGDOM

see Law Courts and Offices

UK STATISTICS AUTHORITY

1 Drummond Gate, London SW1V 2QQ
T 0845-604 1857 E authority.enquiries@statistics.gsi.gov.uk
W www.statisticsauthority.gov.uk

The UK Statistics Authority was established on 1 April 2008 by the Statistics and Registration Service Act 2007 as an independent body operating at arm's length from government, reporting to the UK parliament and the devolved legislatures. Its overall objective is to promote and safeguard the production and publication of official statistics and ensure their quality and comprehensiveness. The authority's main functions are the oversight of the Office for National Statistics (ONS); monitoring and reporting on all UK official statistics, which includes around 30 central government departments and the devolved administrations; and the production of a code of practice for statistics and the assessment of official statistics against the code.

BOARD
Chair, Sir Andrew Dilnot, CBE
Board Members, Dr Dame Colette Bowe, DBE; Carolyn Fairbairn; Dame Moira Gibb, DBE; Prof. David Hand; Ed Humpherson *(Director-General, Regulation);* Dr David

Levy; John Pullinger *(National Statistician);* Prof. Sir Adrian Smith, FRS *(Deputy Chair, ONS);* Glen Watson *(Deputy National Statistician)*

OFFICE FOR NATIONAL STATISTICS (ONS)

Cardiff Road, Newport NP10 8XG
T 0845-601 3034 E info@statistics.gov.uk W www.ons.gov.uk

The ONS was created in 1996 by the merger of the Central Statistical Office and the Office of Population Censuses and Surveys. On 1 April 2008 it became the executive office of the UK Statistics Authority. As part of these changes, the office's responsibility for the General Register Office transferred to HM Passport Office of the Home Office.

The ONS is responsible for preparing, interpreting and publishing key statistics on the government, economy and society of the UK. Its key responsibilities include designing, managing and running the Census and providing statistics on health and other demographic matters in England and Wales; the production of the UK National Accounts and other economic indicators; the organisation of population censuses in England and Wales and surveys for government departments and public bodies.
National Statistician, John Pullinger
Director-Generals, Jonathan Athow; Heather Savory; Glen Watson

UK TRADE AND INVESTMENT

1 Victoria Street, London SW1H 0ET
T 020-7215 5000 E enquiries@ukti.gsi.gov.uk
W www.gov.uk/government/organisations/uk-trade-investment

UK Trade and Investment is a government organisation that helps UK-based companies succeed in international markets. It assists overseas companies to bring high quality investment to the UK economy.
Chief Executive, Dominic Jermey, OBE, CVO

WATER SERVICES REGULATION AUTHORITY (OFWAT)

Centre City Tower, 7 Hill Street, Birmingham B5 4UA
T 0121-644 7500 E mailbox@ofwat.gsi.gov.uk
W www.ofwat.gov.uk

OFWAT is the independent economic regulator of the water and sewerage companies in England and Wales. It is responsible for ensuring that the water industry in England and Wales provides household and business customers with a good quality service and value for money. This is done by ensuring that the companies provide customers with a good quality, efficient service at a fair price; limiting the prices companies can charge; monitoring the companies' performance and taking action, including enforcement, to protect customers' interests; settting the companies efficiency targets; making sure the companies deliver the best for consumers and the environment in the long term; and encouraging competition where it benefits consumers.
Chair, Jonson Cox
Chief Executive, Cathryn Ross

PUBLIC BODIES

The following section is a listing of public bodies and other civil service organisations: it is not a complete list of these organisations.

Whereas executive agencies are either part of a government department or are one in their own right (*see* Government Departments), public bodies carry out their functions to a greater or lesser extent at arm's length from central government. Ministers are ultimately responsible to parliament for the activities of the public bodies sponsored by their department and in almost all cases (except where there is separate statutory provision) ministers make the appointments to their boards. Departments are responsible for funding and ensuring good governance of their public bodies.

The term 'public body' is a general one which includes public corporations, such as the BBC; NHS bodies; and non-departmental public bodies (NDPBs).

In October 2010, the government announced proposals to drastically reform public bodies or 'quangos' (quasi-autonomous non-governmental organisations, another term for NDPBs). In total, 901 bodies were reviewed – 679 NDPBs and 222 other statutory bodies. Consequently, the government introduced the Public Bodies Bill, which received royal assent on 14 December 2011 and became the Public Bodies act 2011, allowing the government to abolish, merge or transfer the functions of the public bodies listed in the appropriate schedules to the Act.

ADJUDICATOR'S OFFICE
PO Box 10280, Nottingham NG2 9PF
T 0300-057 1111 W www.adjudicatorsoffice.gov.uk

The Adjudicator's Office investigates complaints from individuals and businesses about the way that HM Revenue and Customs, the Valuation Office Agency and the Insolvency Service have handled a person's affairs. The Adjudicator's Office will only consider a complaint after the respective organisation's internal complaints procedure has been exhausted.
The Adjudicator, Judy Clements, OBE

ADVISORY, CONCILIATION AND ARBITRATION SERVICE (ACAS)
22nd Floor, Euston Tower, 286 Euston Road, London NW1 3JJ
T 0300-123 1100 W www.acas.org.uk

The Advisory, Conciliation and Arbitration Service was set up under the Employment Protection Act 1975 (the provisions now being found in the Trade Union and Labour Relations (Consolidation) Act 1992).

ACAS is largely funded by the Department for Business, Innovation and Skills. A council sets its strategic direction, policies and priorities, and ensures that the agreed strategic objectives and targets are met. It consists of a chair and 11 employer, trade union and independent members, appointed by the Secretary of State for Business, Innovation and Skills.

ACAS aims to improve organisations and working life through better employment relations, to provide up-to-date information, independent advice and high-quality training, and to work with employers and employees to solve problems and improve performance.

ACAS has regional offices, in Birmingham, Bristol, Bury St Edmunds, Cardiff, Fleet, Glasgow, Leeds, Liverpool, Manchester, Newcastle upon Tyne and Nottingham. The head office is in London.
Chair, Sir Brendan Barber
Chief Executive, Anne Sharp

ADVISORY COUNCIL ON NATIONAL RECORDS AND ARCHIVES
The National Archives, Kew, Surrey TW9 4DU
T 020-8392 5337
W www.nationalarchives.gov.uk/advisorycouncil

The Advisory Council on National Records and Archives advises the Lord Chancellor on issues relating to public records that are over 30 years old including public access to them. The council meets four times a year, and its main task is to consider requests for the extended closure of public records; it also reaches decisions regarding government departments that want to keep records.

The Forum on Historical Manuscripts and Academic Research, a sub-committee of the Advisory Council, provides advice to the Lord Chancellor on matters relating to historical manuscripts, records and archives, other than public records.
Chair, Rt. Hon. Lord Dyson, PC *(Master of the Rolls)*

AGRICULTURE AND HORTICULTURE DEVELOPMENT BOARD
Stoneleigh Park, Kenilworth, Warwickshire CV8 2TL
T 02476-692051 E info@ahdb.org.uk W www.ahdb.org.uk

The Agriculture and Horticulture Development Board (AHDB) is funded by the agriculture and horticulture industries through statutory levies, with the duty to improve efficiency and competitiveness within six sectors: pig meat in England; milk in Great Britain; beef and lamb in England; commercial horticulture in Great Britain; cereals and oilseeds in the UK; and potatoes in Great Britain. The AHDB represents about 75 per cent of total UK agricultural output. Levies raised from the six sectors are ring-fenced to ensure that they can only be used to the benefit of the sectors from which they were raised.
Chair, Sir Peter Kendall
Independent members, Prof. Ian Crute, CBE; Will Lifford; George Lyon
Sector members, Gary Taylor, MBE *(horticulture);* Stuart Roberts *(beef and lamb);* Meryl Ward, MBE *(pig meat);* Fiona Fell *(potatoes);* Paul Temple *(cereals and oilseeds);* Gwyn Howells *(milk)*
Chief Executive, Jane King

ARCHITECTURE AND DESIGN SCOTLAND
Bakehouse Close, 146 Canongate, Edinburgh EH8 8DD
T 0131-556 6699
W www.ads.org.uk

Architecture and Design Scotland (A+DS) was established in 2005 by the Scottish government as the national champion for good architecture, urban design and planning in the built environment; it works with a wide range of organisations at national, regional and local levels.
Chair, Karen Anderson
Chief Executive, Jim MacDonald

ARMED FORCES' PAY REVIEW BODY

8th Floor, Fleetbank House, 2-6 Salisbury Square, London EC4Y 8JX
T 020-7211 8315 W www.ome.uk.com

The Armed Forces' Pay Review Body was appointed in 1971. It advises the prime minister and the Secretary of State for Defence on the pay and allowances of members of naval, military and air forces of the Crown.

Chair, John Steele

Members, Brendan Connor; Tim Flesher, CB; Paul Kernaghan, CBE, QPM; Judy McKnight, CBE; Ken Mayhew; Vilma Patterson, MBE; Jon Westbrook, CBE

ARTS COUNCIL ENGLAND

21 Bloomsbury Street, London WC1B 3HF
T 0845-300 6200 W www.artscouncil.org.uk

Arts Council England is the national development agency for the arts in England. Using public money from government and the National Lottery, it supports a range of artistic activities, including theatre, music, literature, dance, photography, digital art, carnival and crafts. Between 2015 and 2018, Arts Council England is investing £1.1bn of public money from the government and around £700m from the National Lottery.

The governing body, the national council, comprises 14 members, who are appointed by the Secretary of State for Culture, Media and Sport usually for a term of four years. There are also five councils, responsible for the agreement of area strategies, plans and priorities for action within the national framework.

National Council Chair, Sir Peter Bazalgette

National Council Members, Maria Balshaw; Matthew Bowcock, CBE; David Bryan; Prof. Jon Cook; Joe Docherty; Sheila Healy; David Joseph; Sir Nicholas Kenyon; Nazo Moosa; Peter Phillips; Alistair Spalding, CBE; Rosemary Squire, OBE; Veronica Wadley

Chief Executive, Darren Henley

ARTS COUNCIL OF NORTHERN IRELAND

77 Malone Road, Belfast BT9 6AQ
T 028-9038 5200 E info@artscouncil-ni.org
W www.artscouncil-ni.org

The Arts Council of Northern Ireland is the prime distributor of government funds in support of the arts in Northern Ireland. It is funded by the Department of Culture, Arts and Leisure and from National Lottery funds.

Chair, Bob Collins

Members, David Alderdice; Anna Carragher; Damien Coyle; Eibhlinn Ni Dhochartaigh; Noelle McAlinden; Katherine McCloskey; Prof. Ian Montgomery; Paul Mullan; Prof. Paul Seawright; Conor Shields; Brian Sore; Nisha Tandon; Dr Siún Hanrahan; Dr Leon Litvack

Chief Executive, Roisin McDonough

ARTS COUNCIL OF WALES

Bute Place, Cardiff CF10 5AL
T 0845-873 4900 E information@artscouncilofwales.org.uk
W www.artswales.org.uk

The Arts Council of Wales was established in 1994 by royal charter and is the development body for the arts in Wales. It funds arts organisations with funding from the Welsh government and is the distributor of National Lottery funds to the arts in Wales.

Chair, Prof. Dai Smith

Members, John Geraint; Michael Griffiths; Melanie Hawthorne; Dr Lesley Hodgson; Margaret Jervis, MBE; Marian Wyn Jones; Andrew Miller; Richard Turner; Alan Watkin; Prof. Gerwyn Wiliams; John Carey Williams; Dr Kate Woodward

Chief Executive, Nick Capaldi

AUDIT SCOTLAND

102 West Port, Edinburgh EH3 9DN
T 0131-625 1500 E info@audit-scotland.gov.uk
W www.audit-scotland.gov.uk

Audit Scotland was set up in 2000 to provide services to the Accounts Commission and the Auditor-General for Scotland. Together they help to ensure that public-sector bodies in Scotland are held accountable for the proper, efficient and effective use of public funds.

Audit Scotland's work covers about 200 bodies including local authorities; health boards; further education colleges; Scottish Water; the Scottish government; government agencies such as the Prison Service and non-departmental public bodies such as the Scottish Police Authority and the Scottish Fire and Rescue Service.

Audit Scotland carries out financial and regularity audits to ensure that public-sector bodies adhere to the highest standards of financial management and governance. It also carries out performance audits to ensure that these bodies achieve the best value for money. All of Audit Scotland's work in connection with local authorities is carried out for the Accounts Commission; its other work is undertaken for the Auditor-General.

Auditor-General, Caroline Gardner

Chair of the Accounts Commission, Douglas Sinclair

BANK OF ENGLAND

Threadneedle Street, London EC2R 8AH
T 020-7601 4444 E enquiries@bankofengland.co.uk
W www.bankofengland.co.uk

The Bank of England was incorporated in 1694 under royal charter. It was nationalised in 1946 under the Bank of England Act of that year which gave HM Treasury statutory powers over the bank. It is the banker of the government and it manages the issue of banknotes. Since 1998 it has been operationally independent and its Monetary Policy Committee has been responsible for setting short-term interest rates to meet the government's inflation target. Its responsibility for banking supervision was transferred to the Financial Services Authority in the same year. As the central reserve bank of the country, the Bank of England keeps the accounts of British banks, and of most overseas central banks; the larger banks and building societies are required to maintain with it a proportion of their cash resources. The bank's core purposes are monetary stability and financial stability. The Banking Act 2009 increased the responsibilities of the bank, including giving it a new financial stability objective and creating a special resolution regime for dealing with failing banks.

In 2013, through the Prudential Regulation Authority (PRA), the bank became responsible for the prudential regulation and supervision of banks, building societies, credit unions, insurers and major investment firms.

Governor, Mark Carney

Deputy Governors, Andrew Bailey; Dr Ben Broadbent; Sir John Cunliffe; Nemat Shafik

Court of Directors, The Governor; Anthony Habgood (Chair of Court); the Deputy Governors; Michael Cohrs; Bradley Fried; Tim Frost; Baroness Harding of Winscombe; Dave Prentis; Don Robert; John Stewart; Dorothy Thompson

Monetary Policy Committee, The Governor; Dr Ben Broadbent; Nemat Shafik; Sir Jon Cunliffe; Andy Haldane; Kristin Forbes; Prof. David Miles; Ian McCafferty; Dr Martin Weale

Financial Policy Committee, The Governor; Andrew Bailey; Dr Ben Broadbent; Sir John Cunliffe; Alex Brazier; Dame Clara Furse, DBE; Donald Kohn; Richard Sharp; Martin Taylor; Martin Wheatley
Chief Legal Adviser, Sonya Branch
Director for Banknotes and Chief Cashier, Victoria Cleland
The Auditor, Stephen Brown

BIG LOTTERY FUND

1 Plough Place, London EC4A 1DE
T 020-7211 1800 **Advice Line** 0845-410 2030
E general.enquiries@biglotteryfund.org.uk
W www.biglotteryfund.org.uk

The Big Lottery Fund is responsible for distributing 40 per cent of all funds raised for good causes by the National Lottery, amounting to around £650m to 12,000 projects a year across the UK. It is responsible for supporting health, education, environmental and charitable projects.
Chair, Peter Ainsworth
Vice-Chair, Tony Burton, CBE
Regional Chairs, Frank Hewitt *(Northern Ireland)*; Maureen McGinn *(Scotland)*; Nat Sloane, *(England)*; Sir Adrian Webb *(Wales)*
Chief Executive, Dawn Austwick

BOUNDARY COMMISSIONS

ENGLAND

2nd Floor, 35 Great Smith Street, London SW1P 3BQ
T 020-7276 1102
E information@boundarycommissionengland.gov.uk
W www.independent.gov.uk/boundarycommissionforengland
Deputy Chair, Hon. Mrs Justice Patterson

WALES

Hastings House, Fitzalan Court, Cardiff CF24 0BL
T 029-2046 4819 E bcomm.wales@wales.gsi.gov.uk
W www.bcomm-wales.gov.uk
Deputy Chair, Hon. Mr Justice Williams

SCOTLAND

Thistle House, 91 Haymarket Terrace, Edinburgh EH12 5HD
T 0131-538 7510 E bcs@scottishboundaries.gov.uk
W www.bcomm-scotland.gov.uk
Deputy Chair, Hon. Lord Woolman

NORTHERN IRELAND

Forestview, Purdy's Lane, Belfast BT8 7AR
T 028-9069 4800 E bcni@belfast.org.uk
W www.boundarycommission.org.uk
Deputy Chair, Hon. Mr Justice McCloskey

The commissions, established in 1944, are constituted under the Parliamentary Constituencies Act 1986 (as amended). The Speaker of the House of Commons is the *ex officio* chair of all four commissions in the UK.

The next reviews of UK parliament constituencies will be undertaken using the electoral register from 1 December 2015; these reviews must be submitted before 1 October 2018.

BRITISH BROADCASTING CORPORATION (BBC)

BBC Broadcasting House, Portland Place, London W1A 1AA
W www.bbc.co.uk

The BBC was incorporated under royal charter in 1926 as successor to the British Broadcasting Company Ltd. The BBC's current charter, which came into force on 1 January 2007

and extends to 31 December 2016, recognises the BBC's editorial independence and sets out its public purposes. The BBC Trust was formed under the new charter and replaces the Board of Governors; it sets the strategic direction of the BBC and has a duty to represent the interests of licence fee payers. The chair, vice-chair and other trustees are appointed by the Queen-in-Council. The BBC is financed by television licence revenue and by grant-in-aid from parliament for the World Service (radio). *See* Broadcasting.

BBC TRUST MEMBERS

Chair, Rona Fairhead
National Trustees, Mark Florman *(England)*; Aideen McGinley, OBE *(Northern Ireland)*; Bill Matthews *(Scotland)*; Elan Closs Stephens *(Wales)*
Trustees, Sonita Alleyne, OBE; Richard Ayre; Sir Roger Carr; Mark Damazer; Nicholas Prettejohn; Suzanna Taverne; Lord Williams of Baglan

EXECUTIVE BOARD

Director-General, Lord Hall of Birkenhead
Directors, Helen Boaden *(Radio)*; Anne Bulford, OBE *(Finance and Operations)*; Danny Cohen *(Television)*; Tim Davie *(CEO: BBC Worldwide, Director: Global)*; James Harding *(News and Current Affairs)*; Rt. Hon. James Purnell *(Strategy & Digital)*
Non-Executive Directors, Simon Burke; Sir Nicholas Hytner; Dharmish Mistry; Alice Perkins; Dame Fiona Reynolds, DBE; Sir Howard Stringer

STATION CONTROLLERS

BBC1, Charlotte Moore
BBC2 and BBC4, Kim Shillinglaw
BBC3, Damian Kavanagh
BBC News Channel, Sam Taylor
BBC Parliament, Peter Knowles
BBC Northern Ireland, Peter Johnston
BBC Scotland, Ken MacQuarrie
BBC Wales, Rhodri Talfan-Davies
CBBC, Cheryl Taylor
CBeebies, Kay Benbow
Radio 1 and 1Xtra, Ben Cooper
Radio 2, 6 Music and Asian Network, Bob Shennan
Radio 3, vacant
Radio 4, Gwyneth Williams
Radio 5 Live and 5 Live Sports Extra, Jonathan Wall

BRITISH COUNCIL

Bridgewater House, 58 Whitworth Street, Manchester M1 6BB
T 0161-957 7755 E general.enquiries@britishcouncil.org
W www.britishcouncil.org

The British Council was established in 1934, incorporated by royal charter in 1940 and granted a supplemental charter in 1993. It is an independent, non-political organisation which promotes Britain abroad and is the UK's international organisation for educational and cultural relations. The British Council is represented in over 200 towns and cities in over 100 countries.
Chair, Sir Vernon Ellis
Chief Executive, Sir Ciarán Devne

BRITISH FILM INSTITUTE

21 Stephen Street, London W1T 1LN
T 020-7255 1444 W www.bfi.org.uk

The BFI, established in 1933, offers opportunities for people throughout the UK to experience, learn and discover more about the world of film and moving image culture. It incorporates the BFI National Archive, the BFI Reuben

Library, BFI Southbank, BFI Distribution, the annual BFI London Film Festival as well as the BFI London Lesbian and Gay Film Festival, and the BFI IMAX cinema. It also publishes the monthly *Sight and Sound* magazine and provides advice and support for regional cinemas and film festivals across the UK.

Following the closure of the UK Film Council in April 2011, the BFI became the lead body for film in the UK, in charge of allocating lottery money for the development and production of new British films.
Chair, Greg Dyke
Chief Executive, Amanda Nevill

BRITISH LIBRARY
96 Euston Road, London NW1 2DB
T 0843-208 1144 E customer-services@bl.uk
W www.bl.uk

The British Library was established in 1973. It is the UK's national library and one of the world's greatest research libraries. It aims to serve scholarship, research, industry, commerce and all other major users of information. The Library's collection has developed over 250 years and exceeds 150 million separate items, including books, journals, manuscripts, maps, stamps, music, patents, newspapers and sound recordings in all written and spoken languages. The library is now based at three sites: London (St Pancras and Colindale) and Boston Spa, W. Yorks. The library's sponsoring department is the Department for Culture, Media and Sport. Up to 10 million people visit the British Library website every year, where up to 4 million digitised collection items are available to view.

BRITISH LIBRARY BOARD
Chair, Rt. Hon. Baroness Blackstone
Members, David Barclay; Dr Robert Black, CBE, FRSE; Jonathan Callaway; Tracey Chevalier, FRSL; Martin Dickson; Rt. Hon. Lord Fellowes, GCB, GCVO; Roly Keating; Dr Stephen Page; Patrick Plant; Sir John Ritblat; Dr Simon Thurley, CBE; Prof. Dame Helen Wallace

EXECUTIVE
Chief Executive, Roly Keating
Director, Collections, Caroline Brazier
Chief Operating Officer, Phil Spence

BRITISH LIBRARY NEWSPAPERS
Colindale Avenue, London NW9 5HE
T 020-7412 7353

BRITISH LIBRARY, BOSTON SPA
Boston Spa, Wetherby, W. Yorks LS23 7BQ
T 01937-546070

BRITISH MUSEUM
Great Russell Street, London WC1B 3DG
T 020-7323 8000 E information@britishmuseum.org
W www.britishmuseum.org

The British Museum houses the national collection of antiquities, ethnography, coins and paper money, medals, prints and drawings. The British Museum dates from 7 June 1753, when parliament approved the holding of a public lottery to raise funds for the purchase of the collections of Sir Hans Sloane and the Harleian manuscripts, and for their proper housing and maintenance. The building (Montagu House) was opened in 1759. The existing buildings were erected between 1823 and the present day, and the original collection has increased to its current dimensions by gifts and purchases. Total government grant-in-aid for 2014–15 is £43.2m.

Chair, Sir Richard Lambert
Trustees, Karen Armstrong; Hon. Nigel Boardman; Cheryl Carolus; Patricia Cumper, MBE; Dame Liz Forgan, DBE; Prof. Clive Gamble; Penny Hughes, CBE; Sir George Iacobescu, CBE; Wasfi Kani, OBE; Sir Richard Lambert; James Lupton, CBE; Sir Deryck Maughan; John Micklethwait; Sir Paul Nurse, PRS; Gavin Patterson; Grayson Perry, CBE; Rt. Hon. Lord Sassoon, KT; Prof. Amartya Sen; Ahdaf Soueif; Lord Stern of Brentford, FBA; Lord Turner of Ecchinswell; Baroness Wheatcroft

OFFICERS
Director, Neil MacGregor, OM, FSA
Deputy Directors, Joanna Mackle; Jonathan Williams; Christopher Yates; Marilyn Standley

KEEPERS
Keeper of Africa, Oceania and the Americas, Lissant Bolton
Keeper of Ancient Egypt and Sudan, Neal Spencer
Keeper of Asia, Jane Portal
Keeper of Coins and Medals, Philip Attwood
Keeper of Greece and Rome, J. Lesley Fitton
Keeper of the Middle East, Jonathan Tubb
Keeper of Britain, Europe and Prehistory, Roger Bland
Keeper of Prints and Drawings, Hugo Chapman

BRITISH PHARMACOPOEIA COMMISSION
151 Buckingham Palace Road, London SW1W 9SZ
T 020-3080 6561 E bpcom@mhra.gsi.gov.uk
W www.pharmacopoeia.com

The British Pharmacopoeia Commission sets standards for medicinal products used in human and veterinary medicines and is responsible for publication of the *British Pharmacopoeia* (a publicly available statement of the standard that a medicinal substance or product must meet throughout its shelf-life), the *British Pharmacopoeia (Veterinary)* and the *British Approved Names.* It has 17 members, including two lay members, who are appointed on behalf of the Secretary of State for Health by the Department of Health.
Chair, Prof. Kevin Taylor
Vice-Chair, Prof. A. Davidson
Secretary and Scientific Director, Dr Samantha Atkinson

CARE QUALITY COMMISSION
Citygate, Gallowgate, Newcastle upon Tyne NE1 4PA
T 0300-061 6161 E enquiries@cqc.org.uk W www.cqc.org.uk

The Care Quality Commission (CQC) is the independent regulator of health and adult social care services in England, ensuring health and social care services provide people with safe, effective, compassionate, high-quality care and encouraging them to improve. CQC monitors, inspects and regulates services to make sure they meet fundamental standards of quality and safety and publishes performance ratings to help people choose care.
Chair, Hon. David Prior
Board Members, Prof. Louis Appleby; Paul Rew; Sir Robert Francis, QC; Anna Bradley; Camilla Cavendish; Paul Corrigan; Dr Jennifer Dixon; Michael Mire; Kay Sheldon
Chief Executive, David Behan, CBE

CENTRAL ARBITRATION COMMITTEE
22nd Floor, Euston Tower, 286 Euston Road, London NW1 3JJ
T 020-7904 2300 E enquiries@cac.gov.uk W www.cac.gov.uk

The Central Arbitration Committee (CAC) is a permanent independent body with statutory powers whose main function is to adjudicate on applications relating to the statutory recognition and de-recognition of trade unions for

collective bargaining purposes, where such recognition or de-recognition cannot be agreed voluntarily. In addition, the CAC has a statutory role in determining disputes between trade unions and employers over the disclosure of information for collective bargaining purposes, and in resolving applications and complaints under the information and consultation regulations, and performs a similar role in relation to the legislation on the European Works Council, European companies, European cooperative societies and cross-border mergers. The CAC and its predecessors have also provided voluntary arbitration in collective disputes, but this role has not been used for some years.
Chair, Sir Michael Burton
Chief Executive, Simon Gouldstone

CERTIFICATION OFFICE FOR TRADE UNIONS AND EMPLOYERS' ASSOCIATIONS

Euston Tower, 286 Euston Road, London NW1 3JJ
T 020-7210 3734 E info@certoffice.org
W www.gov.uk/certificationofficer

The Certification Office is an independent statutory authority. The Certification Officer is appointed by the Secretary of State for Business, Innovation and Skills and is responsible for maintaining a list of trade unions and employers' associations; ensuring compliance with statutory requirements and keeping available for public inspection annual returns from trade unions and employers' associations; determining complaints concerning trade union elections, certain ballots and certain breaches of trade union rules; ensuring observance of statutory requirements governing mergers between trade unions and employers' associations; overseeing the political funds and finances of trade unions and employers' associations; and for certifying the independence of trade unions.
Certification Officer, David Cockburn

CHURCH COMMISSIONERS

Church House, Great Smith Street, London SW1P 3AZ
T 020-7898 1000 E commissioners.enquiry@churchofengland.org
W www.churchofengland.org/about-us/structure/churchcommissioners

The Church Commissioners were established in 1948 by the amalgamation of Queen Anne's Bounty (established 1704) and the Ecclesiastical Commissioners (established 1836). They are responsible for the management of some of the Church of England's assets, the income from which is predominantly used to help pay for the stipend and pension of the clergy and to support the church's work throughout the country. The commissioners own UK and global company shares, over 43,000ha (106,000 acres) of agricultural land, a residential estate in central London, and commercial property across Great Britain, plus an interest in overseas property via managed funds. They also carry out administrative duties in connection with pastoral reorganisation and closed churches.

The 33 commissioners are: the Archbishops of Canterbury and of York; eleven people elected by the General Synod, comprising four bishops, three clergy and four lay persons; three Church Estates Commissioners; two cathedral deans; nine people appointed by the crown and the archbishops; six holders of state office, comprising the Prime Minister, the Lord Chancellor, the Lord President of the Council, the Secretary of State for Culture, Media and Sport, the Speaker of the House of Commons and the Lord Speaker.

CHURCH ESTATES COMMISSIONERS
First, Andreas Whittam Smith, CBE
Second, Rt. Hon. Caroline Spelman, MP
Third, Andrew Mackie

OFFICERS
Chief Executive, Andrew Brown
Official Solicitor, Stephen Slack

COAL AUTHORITY

200 Lichfield Lane, Mansfield, Notts NG18 4RG
T 01623-637000 E thecoalauthority@coal.gov.uk
W coal.decc.gov.uk/coalauthority

The Coal Authority was established under the Coal Industry Act 1994 to manage certain functions previously undertaken by British Coal, including ownership of unworked coal. It is responsible for licensing coal mining operations and for providing information on coal reserves and past and future coal mining. It settles subsidence damage claims which are not the responsibility of licensed coal mining operators. It deals with the management and disposal of property, and with surface hazards such as abandoned coal mine entries and mine water discharges. The Coal Authority's powers were extended alongside the Energy Act 2011 to enable it to deal with metal mine subsidence issues and deliver a metal mine water treatment programme when the necessary funding is made available.
Chair, Stephen Dingle
Chief Executive, Philip Lawrence

COMMITTEE ON STANDARDS IN PUBLIC LIFE

1 Horseguards Road, London SW1A 2HQ
T 020-7271 2948 E public@public-standards.gov.uk
W www.gov.uk/government/organisations/the-committee-on-standards-in-public-life

The Committee on Standards in Public Life (CSPL) was set up in October 1994. It is formed of 9 people appointed by the prime minister, comprising the chair, three political members nominated by the leaders of the three main political parties and five independent members. The CSPL advises the prime minister on ethical standards across the whole of public life in the UK. It monitors and reports on issues relating to the standards of conduct of all public office holders. It is responsible for promoting the 7 principles of public life, being: selflessness; integrity; objectivity; accountability; openness; honesty; and leadership.
Chair, Lord Bew
Members, Lord Alderdice; Rt. Hon. Dame Margaret Beckett, DBE, MP; Carolyn Fairbairn; David Prince, CBE; Patricia Moberly; Sheila Drew Smith, OBE; Richard Thomas; Dame Angela Watkinson, DBE, MP

COMMONWEALTH WAR GRAVES COMMISSION

2 Marlow Road, Maidenhead, Berks SL6 7DX
T 01628-634221 W www.cwgc.org

The Commonwealth War Graves Commission (formerly Imperial War Graves Commission) was founded by royal charter in 1917. It is responsible for the commemoration of around 1.7 million members of the forces of the Commonwealth who lost their lives in the two world wars. More than one million graves are maintained in over 23,000 burial grounds across 153 countries. Over three-quarters of a million men and women who have no known grave or who were cremated are commemorated by name on memorials built by the commission.

The funds of the commission are derived from the six participating governments: the UK, Canada, Australia, New Zealand, South Africa and India.
President, HRH the Duke of Kent, KG, GCMG, GCVO, ADC

Chair, Secretary of State for Defence (UK)
Vice-Chair, Air Chief Marshal Sir Joe French, KCB, CBE
Members, High Commissioners in London for Australia, Canada, India, New Zealand and South Africa; Edward Chaplin, CMG, OBE; Robert Fox, MBE; Kevan Jones, MP; Hon. Ros Kelly; Vice-Adm. Sir Tim Laurence, KCVO, CB; Lt.-Gen. Sir William Rollo, KCB, CBE; Keith Simpson, MP; Prof. Sir Hew Strachan, FRSE
Director-General and Secretary to the Commission, Victoria Wallace
Director of Legal Services, Gillian Stedman

COMPETITION SERVICE

Victoria House, Bloomsbury Place, London WC1A 2EB
T 020-7979 7979 E info@catribunal.org.uk
W www.catribunal.org.uk

The Competition Service is the financial corporate body by which the Competition Appeal Tribunal is administered and through which it receives funding for the performance of its judicial functions.
Registrar, Charles Dhanowa, OBE, QC

CONSUMER COUNCIL FOR WATER

7th Floor, Embassy House, 60 Church Street, Birmingham B3 2DJ
T 0121-345 1000 E enquiries@ccwater.org.uk
W www.ccwater.org.uk

The Consumer Council for Water was established in 2005 under the Water Act 2003 to represent consumers' interests in respect of price, service and value for money from their water and sewerage services, and to investigate complaints from customers about their water company. There are four regional committees in England and one in Wales.
Chair, Alan Lovell

CORPORATION OF TRINITY HOUSE

Trinity House, Tower Hill, London EC3N 4DH
T 020-7481 6900 E enquiries@thls.org
W www.trinityhouse.co.uk

The Corporation of Trinity House of Deptford Strond is the UK's largest-endowed maritime charity, established formally by Royal Charter by Henry VIII in 1514, with statutory duties as the General Lighthouse Authority (GLA) for England, Wales, the Channel Islands and Gibraltar. Its remit is to assist the safe passage of a variety of vessels through some of the busiest sea-lanes in the world; it does this by deploying and maintaining approximately 600 aids to navigation, ranging from lighthouses to a satellite navigation service. The corporation also has certain statutory jurisdiction over aids to navigation maintained by local harbour authorities and is responsible for marking or dispersing wrecks dangerous to navigation, except those occurring within port limits or wrecks of HM ships.

The statutory duties of Trinity House are funded by the General Lighthouse Fund, which is provided from light dues levied on ships calling at ports of the UK and the Republic of Ireland. The corporation is a deep-sea pilotage authority, authorised by the Secretary of State for Transport to license deep-sea pilots. In addition Trinity House is a charitable organisation that maintains a number of retirement homes for mariners and their dependants, funds a four-year training scheme for those seeking a career in the merchant navy, and also dispenses grants to a wide range of maritime charities. The charity work is wholly funded by its own activities.

The corporation is controlled by a court of 31 Elder Brethren; a separate board controls the Lighthouse Service. The Elder Brethren also act as nautical assessors in marine cases in the Admiralty Division of the High Court.

ELDER BRETHREN
Master, HRH the Princess Royal, KG, KT, GCVO
Deputy Master, Capt. Ian McNaught
Wardens, Simon Sherrard *(Rental)*; Capt. Nigel Palmer, OBE *(Nether)*
Elder Brethren, HRH the Duke of Edinburgh, KG, KT, OM, GBE; HRH the Prince of Wales, KG, KT, GCB; HRH the Duke of York, KG, GCVO, ADC; Capt. Roger Barker; Adm. Lord Boyce, KG, GCB, OBE; Lord Browne of Madingley; Capt. John Burton-Hall, RD; Lord Carrington, KG, GCMG, CH, PC; Viscount Cobham; Capt. Sir Malcolm Edge, KCVO; Capt. Ian Gibb, MBE; Capt. Duncan Glass, OBE; Capt. Stephen Gobbi; Lord Greenway; Rear-Adm. Sir Jeremy de Halpert, KCVO, CB; Capt. Nigel Hope, RD; Lord Mackay of Clashfern, KT; Sir John Major, KG, CH; Capt. Peter Mason, CBE; Cdre. Peter Melson, CVO, CBE, RN; Capt. David Orr; Sir John Parker, GBE; Douglas Potter; Capt. Nigel Pryke; Capt. Derek Richards, RD; Lord Robertson of Port Ellen, KT, GCMG, PC; Rear-Adm. Sir Patrick Rowe, KCVO, CBE; Cdre. James Scorer; Adm. Sir Jock Slater, GCB, LVO; Cdre. David Squire, CBE, RFA; Rear-Adm. Lord Sterling of Plaistow, GCVO, CBE, RNR; Capt. Colin Stewart, LVO; Sir Adrian Swire, KT, AE; Capt. Sir Miles Wingate, KCVO; Capt. Thomas Woodfield, OBE; Capt. Richard Woodman, LVO; Rear-Adm. David Snelson, CB; Cdre. William Walworth, CBE

OFFICERS
Secretary, Cdr Graham Hockley, RN
Director of Finance & Support Services, Jerry Wedge
Director of Navigational Requirements, Capt. Roger Barker
Director of Operations, vacant

CREATIVE SCOTLAND

Waverley Gate, 2–4 Waterloo Place, Edinburgh EH1 3EG
T 0330-333 2000 E enquiries@creativescotland.com
W www.creativescotland.com

Creative Scotland is the organisation tasked with leading the development of the arts, creative and screen industries across Scotland. It was created in 2010 as an amalgamation of the Scottish Arts Council and Scottish Screen, and it encourages and sustains the arts through investment in the form of grants, bursaries, loans and equity. It aims to invest in talent; artistic production; audiences, access and participation; and the cultural economy. Total Scottish government grant-in-aid for 2015–16 is £50m.
Chair, Richard Findlay
Board, Steve Grimmond; Sandra Gunn; Prof. Robin MacPherson; May Miller; Fergus Muir; Barclay Price; Richard Scott; Dr Gary West; Ruth Wishart
Chief Executive, Janet Archer

CRIMINAL CASES REVIEW COMMISSION

5 St Philip's Place, Birmingham B3 2PW
T 0121-233 1473 E info@ccrc.x.gsi.gov.uk
W www.ccrc.gov.uk

The Criminal Cases Review Commission is the independent body set up under the Criminal Appeal Act 1995. It is a non-departmental public body reporting to parliament via the Lord Chancellor and Secretary of State for Justice. It is responsible for investigating possible miscarriages of justice in England, Wales and Northern Ireland, and deciding whether or not to refer cases back to an appeal court. Members of the commission are appointed in accordance with the Commissioner for Public Appointments' code of practice.

Chair, Richard Foster, CBE
Members, Liz Calderbank; Jim England; Julie Goulding;
    Celia Hughes; Stephen Leach, CB; Alexandra Marks;
    Dr Sharon Persaud; Andrew Rennison; David Smith;
    Ewen Smith; Ranjit Sondhi
Chief Executive, Karen Kneller

CROFTING COMMISSION
Great Glen House, Leachkin Road, Inverness IV3 8NW
T 01463-663439 E info@crofting.scotland.gov.uk
W www.crofting.scotland.gov.uk

The Crofting Commission was established on 1 April 2012,
taking over the regulation of crofting from the Crofters
Commission. The aim of the Crofting Commission is to
regulate crofting, to promote the occupancy of crofts, active
land use, and shared management of the land by crofters, as
a means of sustaining and enhancing rural communities in
Scotland.
Chief Executive, Catriona Maclean

CROWN ESTATE
16 New Burlington Place, London W1S 2HX
T 020-7851 5000 E enquiries@thecrownestate.co.uk
W www.thecrownestate.co.uk

The Crown Estate is part of the hereditary possessions of
the sovereign 'in right of the crown', managed under the
provisions of the Crown Estate Act 1961. It had a capital
value of £9.9bn in 2014, and includes substantial blocks
of urban property, primarily in London, almost 144,000
hectares (356,000 acres) of rural land, over half of the
foreshore, and the seabed out to the 12 nautical mile
territorial limit throughout the UK. The Crown Estate has a
duty to maintain and enhance the capital value of estate and
the income obtained from it. Under the terms of the act, the
estate pays its revenue surplus to the Treasury every year.
Chair and First Commissioner, Sir Stuart Hampson
Chief Executive and Second Commissioner, Alison Nimmo,
    CBE, FRICS

DISCLOSURE AND BARRING SERVICE
PO Box 3961, Wootton Bassett SN4 4HF
T 0300-020 0190 E customerservices@dbs.gsi.gov.uk
W https://www.gov.uk/government/organisations/disclosure-and-
barring-service

The Disclosure and Barring Service (DBS) is an executive
non-departmental public body of the Home Office. It helps
employers make safer recruitment decisions and prevent
unsuitable people from working with vulnerable groups,
including children. It was formed on 1 December 2012
and replaced the Criminal Records Bureau (CRB) and
Independent Safeguarding Authority (ISA). The DBS is
responsible for the children's barred list and adults' barred
list for England, Wales and Northern Ireland.
Chair, Bill Griffiths
Chief Executive, Adriènne Kelbie

ENVIRONMENT AGENCY
PO Box 544, Rotherham S60 1BY
T 0370-850 6506 E enquiries@environment-agency.gov.uk,
Incident Hotline 0800-807060
W www.environment-agency.gov.uk

Established in 1996 under the Environment Act 1995, the
Environment Agency is a non-departmental public body
sponsored by the Department for Environment, Food and
Rural Affairs. On 1 April 2013, Natural Resources Wales
took over the Environment Agency's responsibilities in
Wales. Around 70 per cent of the agency's funding is from
the government, with the rest raised from various charging
schemes. The agency is responsible for pollution prevention
and control in England and for the management and use
of water resources, including flood defences, fisheries and
navigation. Its remit also includes: scrutinising potentially
hazardous business operations; helping businesses to use
resources more efficiently; taking action against those who
do not take environmental responsibilities seriously;
looking after wildlife; working with farmers; helping people
get the most out of their environment; and improving the
quality of inner city areas and parks by restoring rivers and
lakes.

The Environment Agency has head offices in Bristol and
London has offices across England divided into 16 regions.
Its total grant-in-aid for 2015–16 is £738m.
Chair, Sir Philip Dilley
Deputy Chair, Emma Howard Boyd
Board Members, Peter Ainsworth; Karen Burrows;
    Clive Elphick; Lynne Frostick; Richard Leafe; Richard
    MacDonald; John Varley; Gill Weeks
Chief Executive, Dr Paul Leinster, CBE

EQUALITY AND HUMAN RIGHTS COMMISSION
Arndale House, The Arndale Centre, Manchester M4 3AQ
T 0161-829 8100 E correspondence@equalityhumanrights.com
W www.equalityhumanrights.com

The Equality and Human Rights Commission (EHRC) is a
statutory body, established under the Equality Act 2006 and
launched in October 2007. It inherited the responsibilities
of the Commission for Racial Equality, the Disability Rights
Commission and the Equal Opportunities Commission.
The EHRC's purpose is to reduce inequality, eliminate
discrimination, strengthen relations between people, and
promote and protect human rights. It enforces equality
legislation on age, disability and health, gender, race, religion
and belief, sexual orientation or transgender status, and
encourages compliance with the Human Rights Act 1998
throughout England, Wales and Scotland.
Chair, Baroness O'Neill of Bengarve, CH, CBE, PHD
Deputy Chair, Caroline Waters, OBE
Commissioners, Sarah Anderson, CBE; Evelyn Asante-
    Mensah, OBE; Ann Beynon, OBE *(Wales Commissioner)*;
    Laura Carstensen; Lord Holmes of Richmond, MBE
    (Disability Commissioner); Kaliani Lyle *(Scotland
    Commissioner)*; Prof. Sarwan Singh; Sarah Veale, CBE;
    Susan Johnson, OBE; Lorna McGregor
Chief Executive, Mark Hammond

EQUALITY COMMISSION FOR NORTHERN IRELAND
Equality House, 7–9 Shaftesbury Square, Belfast BT2 7DP
T 028-9050 0600 Textphone 028-9050 0589
E information@equalityni.org W www.equalityni.org

The Equality Commission was set up in 1999 under the
Northern Ireland Act 1998 and is responsible for promoting
equality, keeping the relevant legislation under review,
eliminating discrimination on the grounds of race, disability,
sexual orientation, gender (including marital and civil
partner status, gender reassignment, pregnancy and
maternity), age, religion and political opinion and for
overseeing the statutory duties on public authorities to
promote equality of opportunity and good relations.
Chief Commissioner, Dr Michael Wardlow
Deputy Chief Commissioner, Revd Dr Lesley Carroll
Chief Executive, Evelyn Collins, CBE, FRSA

GAMBLING COMMISSION

Victoria Square House, Victoria Square, Birmingham B2 4BP
T 0121-230 6666 E info@gamblingcommission.gov.uk
W www.gamblingcommission.gov.uk

The Gambling Commission was established under the Gambling Act 2005, and took over the role previously occupied by the Gaming Board for Great Britain in regulating and licensing all commercial gambling – apart from spread betting and the National Lottery – ie casinos, bingo, betting, remote gambling, gaming machines and lotteries. It also advises local and central government on related issues, and is responsible for the protection of children and the vulnerable from being harmed by gambling. In October 2013, the Gambling Commission took over all the responsibilities of the National Lottery Commission in regulating the National Lottery. The commission is sponsored by the Department for Culture, Media and Sport, with its work funded by licence fees paid by the gambling industry.
Chair, Philip Graf, CBE
Chief Executive, Jenny Williams

HEALTH AND SAFETY EXECUTIVE

Redgrave Court, Merton Road, Bootle, Merseyside L20 7HS
T 0845-300 9923 W www.hse.gov.uk

The Health and Safety Commission (HSC) and the Health and Safety Executive (HSE) merged on 1 April 2008 to form a single national regulatory body – the HSE – responsible for promoting the cause of better health and safety at work. The HSE is sponsored by the Department for Work and Pensions.

HSE regulates all industrial and commercial sectors except operations in the air and at sea. This includes agriculture, construction, manufacturing, services, transport, mines, offshore oil and gas, quarries and major hazard sites in chemicals and petrochemicals.

HSE is responsible for developing and enforcing health and safety law; providing guidance and advice; commissioning research; conducting inspections and accident and ill-health investigations; developing standards; and licensing or approving some work activities such as asbestos removal. The HSE's nuclear directorate merged with a number of other bodies on 1 April 2011 to form the Office for Nuclear Regulation, an agency of the HSE.
Chair, Judith Hackitt, CBE
Board Members, Nick Baldwin; Jonathan Baume; George Brechin; Isobel Garner; Paul Kenny; John Morgan; Frances Outram; Sarah Pinch; Martyn Thomas; Sarah Veale, CBE
Chief Executive, Richard Judge

HER MAJESTY'S OFFICERS OF ARMS

COLLEGE OF ARMS (HERALDS' COLLEGE)
130 Queen Victoria Street, London EC4V 4BT
T 020-7248 2762 E enquiries@college-of-arms.gov.uk
W www.college-of-arms.gov.uk

The Sovereign's Officers of Arms (Kings, Heralds and Pursuivants of Arms) were first incorporated by Richard III in 1484. The powers vested by the crown in the Earl Marshal (the Duke of Norfolk) with regard to state ceremonial are largely exercised through the college. The college is also the official repository of the arms and pedigrees of English, Welsh, Northern Irish and Commonwealth (except Canadian) families and their descendants, and its records include official copies of the records of the Ulster King of Arms, the originals of which remain in Dublin. The 13 officers of the college specialise in genealogical and heraldic work for their respective clients.

Arms have long been, and still are, granted by letters patent from the Kings of Arms. A right to arms can only be established by the registration in the official records of the College of Arms of a pedigree showing direct male line descent from an ancestor already appearing therein as being entitled to arms, or by making application through the College of Arms for a grant of arms. Grants are made to corporations as well as to individuals.
Earl Marshal, the Duke of Norfolk

KINGS OF ARMS
Garter, Thomas Woodcock, CVO, FSA
Clarenceux, Patric Dickinson, LVO
Norroy and Ulster, Timothy Duke

HERALDS
Chester, vacant
Lancaster, Robert Noel
Windsor, William Hunt, TD
Somerset (and Registrar), David White
Richmond (and Earl Marshal's Secretary), Clive Cheesman, FSA
York, Michael O'Donoghue

PURSUIVANTS
Portcullis, Hon. Christopher Fletcher-Vane
Rouge Croix, John Allen-Petrie

COURT OF THE LORD LYON

HM New Register House, Edinburgh EH1 3YT
T 0131-556 7255 W www.lyon-court.com

Her Majesty's Officers of Arms in Scotland perform ceremonial duties and in addition may be consulted by members of the public on heraldic and genealogical matters in a professional capacity.

KING OF ARMS
Lord Lyon King of Arms, Dr Joseph Morrow

HERALDS
Rothesay, Sir Crispin Agnew of Lochnaw, Bt., QC
Snawdoun, Elizabeth Roads, LVO, FSA, FSA SCOT
Marchmont, Hon. Adam Bruce, WS

PURSUIVANTS
Ormond, Mark Dennis
Dingwall, Yvonne Holton
Unicorn, John Malden

EXTRAORDINARY OFFICERS
Orkney Herald Extraordinary, Sir Malcolm Innes of Edingight, KCVO, WS
Angus Herald Extraordinary, Robin Blair, CVO, WS
Islay Herald Extraordinary, David Sellar, MVO
Ross Herald Extraordinary, Charles Burnett, FSA SCOT

HIGHLANDS AND ISLANDS ENTERPRISE

Fraser House, Friar's Lane, Inverness IV1 1BA
T 01463-234171 E info@hient.co.uk W www.hie.co.uk

Highlands and Islands Enterprise (HIE) was set up under the Enterprise and New Towns (Scotland) Act 1991. Its role is to deliver community and economic development in line with the Scottish government economic strategy. It focuses on four priorities: supporting businesses and social enterprises; strengthening communities and fragile areas; developing growth sectors; and creating the conditions for a competitive and low carbon region. HIE's draft budget for 2015–16 is £97.7m.
Chair, Prof. Lorne Crerar
Chief Executive, Alex Paterson

HISTORIC ENGLAND

1 Waterhouse Square, 138–142 Holborn, London EC1N 2ST
T 020-7973 3700 E customers@historicengland.org.uk
W www.historicengland.org.uk

Historic England was established as an executive non-departmental public body on 1 April 2015, having previously been known as English Heritage (following the National Heritage Act 1983). Its remit is to look after England's historic environment and has five key objectives: to champion historic places; to identify and protect England's heritage; to support change, including giving advice on over 20,000 applications for planning permission or listed building consent; to understand historic places; and to provide expertise at a local level. In 2015–16 Historic England will receive £88.5m in grant-in-aid from the Department for Culture, Media and Sport.

Chair, Sir Laurie Magnus
Commissioners, Lynda Addison, OBE; Sally Balcombe; Alex Balfour; Prof. Martin Daunton; Prof. Michael Fulford, CBE; Victoria Harley; Martin Moore; Michael Morrison; Baroness Young of Hornsey, OBE
Chief Executive, Duncan Wilson, OBE

HISTORIC ROYAL PALACES

Apartment 39A, Hampton Court Palace, Surrey KT8 9AU
T 0844-482 7777 E operators@hrp.org.uk W www.hrp.org.uk

Historic Royal Palaces was established in 1998 as a royal charter body with charitable status and is contracted by the Secretary of State for Culture, Media and Sport to manage the palaces on his behalf. The palaces – the Tower of London, Hampton Court Palace, the Banqueting House, Kensington Palace and Kew Palace – are owned by the Queen on behalf of the nation. Since 1 April 2014, Historic Royal Palaces is also responsible for the management of Hillsborough Castle in Northern Ireland under contract with the Secretary of State for Northern Ireland.

The organisation is governed by a board comprising a chair and 11 non-executive trustees. The chief executive is accountable to the board of trustees and ultimately to parliament. Historic Royal Palaces receives no funding from the government or the Crown.

TRUSTEES

Chair, Rupert Gavin
Appointed by the Queen, Val Gooding, CBE; Sir Trevor McDonald, OBE; Jonathan Marsden, CVO, FSA; Mike Stephens
Appointed by the Secretary of State, Dawn Austwick, OBE; Prof. Sir David Cannadine; Bruce Carnegie-Brown; Liz Cleaver; Jane Kennedy; Louise Wilson, FRSA
Ex officio, Gen. Lord Dannatt, GCB, CBE, MC *(159th Constable of the Tower of London)*

OFFICER
Chief Executive, Michael Day, CVO

HOMES AND COMMUNITIES AGENCY

Fry Building, 2 Marsham Street, London W1T 7BN
T 0300-500 1234 E mail@homesandcommunities.gsi.gov.uk
W www.gov.uk/hca

The Homes and Communities Agency (HCA) is the national housing regeneration agency for England. The HCA invests mostly in building new homes, but also in creating employment floorspace nationwide. The HCA also brings forward public land for development and increases the speed with which it is made available.

Chair, Robert Napier, CBE
Chief Executive, Andy Rose

HUMAN TISSUE AUTHORITY (HTA)

151 Buckingham Palace Road, London SW1W 9SZ
T 020-7269 1900 E enquiries@hta.gov.uk
W www.hta.gov.uk

The Human Tissue Authority (HTA) was established on 1 April 2005 under the Human Tissue Act 2004, and is sponsored and part-funded by the Department of Health. It regulates organisations that remove, store and use tissue for research, medical treatment, post-mortem examination, teaching and display in public. The HTA also gives approval for organ and bone marrow donations from living people. Under the EU tissues and cells directives, the HTA is one of the two designated competent authorities for the UK responsible for regulating tissues and cells. The HTA is also the sole competent authority for the UK under the EU organ donation directive.

Chair, Sharmila Nebhrajani, OBE
Chief Executive, Allan Marriott-Smith

IMPERIAL WAR MUSEUMS (IWM)

Lambeth Road, London SE1 6HZ
T 020-7416 5000 E mail@iwm.org.uk
W www.iwm.org.uk

IWM is the world's leading authority on conflict and its impact, focusing on Britain, its former empire and the Commonwealth, from the First World War to the present. IWM aims to enrich people's understanding of the causes, course and consequences of war and conflict.

IWM comprises the organisation's flagship, IWM London; IWM North in Trafford, Manchester; IWM Duxford in Cambridgeshire; the Churchill War Rooms in Whitehall; and HMS *Belfast* in the Pool of London.

The total grant-in-aid for 2015–16 is £19.8m.

OFFICERS

President, HRH the Duke of Kent, KG, GCMG, GCVO, ADC
Chair, Sir Francis Richards, KCMG, CVO
Trustees, Rt. Hon. Lord Ashcroft, KCMG; Rear-Adm. Amjad Hussain, CB; Dame Judith Mayhew, DBE; Air Chief Marshal Sir Stuart Peach, KCB, CBE, FRAES; Sir John Scarlett, KCMG, OBE; Prof. Sir Hew Strachan, FRSE; Tamsin Todd; Peter Watkins, CBE; Matthew Westerman; Sir Nick Williams; HE Hon. Alexander Downer; HE Gordon Campbell; HE Ranjan Mathai; HE Hon. Sir Lockwood Smith; HE Syed Ibne Abbas; HE Obed Mlaba; HE Dr Chris Nonis
Director-General, Diane Lees, CBE
Directors, Jon Card *(Executive Director of Collections and Governance);* Samantha Heywood *(Director of Special Projects);* Phil Reed *(Director of Museums and Executive Vice President American Air Museum);* Graeme Etheridge *(Change Director)*

INFORMATION COMMISSIONER'S OFFICE

Wycliffe House, Water Lane, Wilmslow, Cheshire SK9 5AF
T 0303-123 1113 W www.ico.org.uk

The Information Commissioner's Office (ICO) oversees and enforces the Freedom of Information Act 2000 and the Data Protection Act 1998, with the objective of promoting public access to official information and protecting personal information.

The Data Protection Act 1998 sets out rules for the processing of personal information and applies to records held on computers and some paper files. The Freedom of Information Act 2000 is designed to help end the culture of unnecessary secrecy and open up the inner workings of the public sector to citizens and businesses.

The ICO also enforces and oversees the privacy and electronic communications regulations 2003 and the environmental regulations 2004. It also has limited responsibilities under the INSPIRE regulations 2009.

The Information Commissioner reports annually to parliament on the performance of his/her functions under the acts and has obligations to assess breaches of the acts. As of April 2010, the ICO has been able to fine organisations up to £500,000 for serious breaches of the Data Protection Act. The budget for 2013–14 was £20m.

Information Commissioner, Christopher Graham

INDUSTRIAL INJURIES ADVISORY COUNCIL

First Floor, Caxton House, Tothill Street, London SW1H 9NA
T 020-7449 5618 E iiac@dwp.gsi.gov.uk
W www.gov.uk/iiac

The Industrial Injuries Advisory Council was established under the National Insurance (Industrial Injuries) Act 1946, which came into effect on 5 July 1948. Statutory provisions governing its work are set out in the Social Security Administration Act 1992 and corresponding Northern Ireland legislation. The council currently consists of 17 independent members, including a chair, appointed by the Secretary of State for Work and Pensions, and has three roles: to advise on the prescription of diseases; to consider and advise on draft regulations and proposals concerning the industrial injuries disablement benefit scheme referred to it by the Secretary of State for Work and Pensions or the Department for Social Development in Northern Ireland; and to advise on any other matter concerning the scheme or its administration.

Chair, Prof. Keith Palmer

JOINT NATURE CONSERVATION COMMITTEE

Monkstone House, City Road, Peterborough PE1 1JY
T 01733-562626 E comment@jncc.gov.uk
W www.jncc.defra.gov.uk

The committee was established under the Environmental Protection Act 1990 and was reconstituted by the Natural Environment and Rural Communities Act 2006. It advises the government and devolved administrations on UK and international nature conservation issues. Its work contributes to maintaining and enriching biological diversity, conserving geological features and sustaining natural systems.

Chair, Prof. Chris Gilligan
Chief Executive, Marcus Yeo

LAW COMMISSION

1st Floor, Tower, 52 Queen Anne's Gate, London SW1H 9AG
T 020-3334 0200 E enquiries@lawcommission.gsi.gov.uk
W www.lawcom.gov.uk

The Law Commission was set up under the Law Commissions Act 1965 to make proposals to the government for the examination of the law in England and Wales and for its revision where it is unsuited for modern requirements, obscure or otherwise unsatisfactory. It recommends to the lord chancellor programmes for the examination of different branches of the law and suggests whether the examination should be carried out by the commission itself or by some other body. The commission is also responsible for the preparation of Consolidation and Statute Law (Repeals) Bills.

Chair, Rt. Hon. Lord Justice David Bean
Commissioners, Prof. Nicholas Hopkins; Stephen Lewis; Prof. David Ormerod QC; Nicholas Paines, QC
Chief Executive, Elaine Lorimer

NATIONAL ARMY MUSEUM

Royal Hospital Road, London SW3 4HT
T 020-7730 0717 E info@nam.ac.uk
W www.nam.ac.uk

The National Army Museum explores the impact of the British Army on the story of Britain, Europe and the world. It was established by royal charter in 1960 and moved to its current site in Chelsea in 1970. The museum houses a wide array of artefacts, paintings, photographs, uniforms and equipment. The museum is closed for major refurbishment until late 2016.

Chair, General Sir Richard Shirreff, KCB, CBE
Council Members, Keith Baldwin; Patrick Bradley; Algy Cluff; Brig. Douglas Erskine Crum; Rt. Hon. Lord Hamilton of Epsom; Prof. William Philpott; Lt.-Gen Sir Barney White-Spunner, KCB, CBE; Caroline Wyatt, CB, CBE; Deborah Younger
Director-General, Janice Murray, FRSA

NATIONAL GALLERIES OF SCOTLAND

73 Belford Road, Edinburgh EH4 3DS
T 0131-624 6200 E enquiries@nationalgalleries.org
W www.nationalgalleries.org

The National Galleries of Scotland comprise three galleries in Edinburgh: the National Gallery of Scotland, the Scottish National Portrait Gallery and the Scottish National Gallery of Modern Art. There are also partner galleries at Paxton House, Berwickshire, and Duff House, Banffshire.

TRUSTEES
Chair, Ben Thomson
Trustees, Tricia Bey; Alistair Dodds; Edward Green; Benny Higgins; Lesley Knox; Prof. Nicholas Pearce; Tari Lang; Catherine Muirden; Willy Watt; Nicky Wilson

OFFICERS
Director-General, Sir John Leighton
Directors, Christopher Baker *(Scottish National Portrait Gallery);* Michael Clarke, CBE *(National Gallery of Scotland);* Nicola Catterall *(Chief Operating Officer);* Dr Simon Groom *(Scottish National Gallery of Modern Art);* Jacqueline Ridge *(Keeper of Conservation)*

NATIONAL GALLERY

Trafalgar Square, London WC2N 5DN
T 020-7747 2885 E information@ng-london.org.uk
W www.nationalgallery.org.uk

The National Gallery, which houses a collection of paintings in the western European tradition from the 13th to the 20th century, was founded in 1824, following a parliamentary grant of £60,000 for the purchase and exhibition of the Angerstein collection of pictures. The present site was first occupied in 1838; an extension to the north of the building with a public entrance in Orange Street was opened in 1975; the Sainsbury Wing was opened in 1991; and the Getty Entrance opened off Trafalgar Square at the east end of the main building in 2004. Total government grant-in-aid for 2015–16 is £24.17m.

BOARD OF TRUSTEES
Chair, Mark Getty
Trustees, Lance Batchelor; Gautam Dalal; Prof. Dexter Dalwood; Lady Heseltine; Sir Michael Hintze; Prof. Anya Hurlbert; Lord King of Lothbury, KG, GBE, FBA; John Nelson; Hannah Rothschild; Charles Sebag-Montefiore; Monisha Shah; John Singer; Caroline Thomson

OFFICERS
Director, Dr Sir Nicholas Penny
Director of Public Engagement and Deputy Director, Dr Susan Foister
Director of Finance and Operations, Chris Walker
Director of Collections, Dr Ashok Roy

NATIONAL HERITAGE MEMORIAL FUND

7 Holbein Place, London SW1W 8NR
T 020-7591 6044 E NHMF_Enquiries@nhmf.org.uk
W www.nhmf.org.uk

The National Heritage Memorial Fund was set up under the National Heritage Act 1980 in memory of people who have given their lives for the United Kingdom. The fund provides grants to organisations based in the UK, mainly so that they can buy items of outstanding interest and of importance to the national heritage. These must either be at risk or have a memorial character. The fund is administered by a chair and 14 trustees who are appointed by the prime minister.

The National Heritage Memorial Fund receives an annual grant from the Department for Culture, Media and Sport. Under the National Lottery etc Act 1993, the trustees of the fund became responsible for the distribution of funds for both the National Heritage Memorial Fund and the Heritage Lottery Fund.

Chair, Sir Peter Luff
Trustees, David Heathcoat-Amory; Jim Dixon; Dr Angela Dean; Sandie Dawe, CBE; Sir Roger De Haan; Perdita Hunt, OBE; Steve Miller; Richard Morris, OBE; Atul Patel; Dame Seona Reid, DBE; Virginia Tandy, OBE; Dr Tom Tew
Chief Executive, Carole Souter, CBE

NATIONAL LIBRARY OF SCOTLAND

George IV Bridge, Edinburgh EH1 1EW
T 0131-623 3700 E enquiries@nls.uk W www.nls.uk

The library, which was founded as the Advocates' Library in 1682, became the National Library of Scotland (NLS) in 1925. Funded by the Scottish government, it contains about 24 million printed items: two million maps, 25,000 newspaper and magazine titles and over 100,000 manuscripts, including the John Murray Archive. The library receives around 300,000 new items every year and has material in 490 languages. It has an unrivalled Scottish collection as well as online catalogues and digital resources which can be accessed through the NLS website. Material can be consulted in the reading rooms, which are open to anyone with a valid library card.

The National Library of Scotland Act 2012 modernised the make-up and responsibilities of the board of trustees. At present there are 14, one of whom is nominated by the Faculty of Advocates. All of them are appointed by the Scottish ministers.

Chair, James Boyle
National Librarian and Chief Executive, Dr John Scally
Heads of Department, John Coll *(Access);* Graeme Forbes *(Ingest);* Anthony Gillespie *(Finance);* Murat Guven *(Resources);* Alexandra Miller *(Communications and Enterprise);* Robin Smith *(Collections and Interpretation)*

NATIONAL LIBRARY OF WALES/ LLYFRGELL GENEDLAETHOL CYMRU

Aberystwyth, Ceredigion, Wales SY23 3BU
T 01970-632800 W www.llgc.org.uk

The National Library of Wales was founded by royal charter in 1907, and is funded by the Welsh government. It contains about five million printed books, 40,000 manuscripts, four million deeds and documents, numerous maps, prints and drawings, and a sound and moving image collection. It specialises in manuscripts and books relating to Wales and the Celtic peoples. It is the repository for pre-1858 Welsh probate records, manorial records and tithe documents, and certain legal records. Admission is by reader's ticket to the reading rooms but entry to the exhibition programme is free.

Total grant-in-aid from the Welsh government for 2014–15 was £15.13m.

Trustees, Lord Aberdare; Tricia Carter *(Vice-President);* Philip Cooper; Susan Davies; Roy Evans; Sir Deian Hopkin *(President);* Colin John *(Treasurer);* Wyn Penri Jones; Enid Morgan; Roy Roberts; David Hugh Thomas; Michael Trickey; Gareth Haulfryn Williams; Huw Williams
Librarian and Chief Executive, Aled Gruffydd Jones

NATIONAL MUSEUM OF THE ROYAL NAVY

HM Naval Base (PP66), Portsmouth PO1 3NH
T 023-9272 7574
W www.nmrn.org.uk

The National Museum of the Royal Navy comprises six museums: HMS *Victory,* the National Museum of the Royal Navy Portsmouth, the Fleet Air Arm Museum, the Royal Navy Submarine Museum, the Royal Marines Museum and Explosion! Museum of Naval Firepower. The Fleet Air Museum is located at RNAS Yeovilton, Somerset, while the other four are situated in Portsmouth and Gosport.

Chair, Adm. Sir Jonathon Band, GCB
Trustees, M. Bedingfield; John Brookes, OBE; Prof. John Craven, CBE; Sir Robert Crawford, CBE; Neil Davidson, FCA; Lieut.-Gen. Sir Robert Fulton, KBE; M. Gambazzi; Vice-Adm. Sir Adrian Johns, KCB, CBE, ADC; Rear-Adm. Terry Loughran, CB; Vice-Adm. Sir Tim McClement, KCB, OBE; Kim Marshall; Tim Schadla-Hall; Dr Caroline Williams, C. Wilson
Director-General, Prof. Dominic Tweddle

NATIONAL MUSEUM WALES/AMGUEDDFA CYMRU

Cathays Park, Cardiff CF10 3NP
T 029-2039 7951
W www.museumwales.ac.uk

National Museum Wales – Amgueddfa Cymru (also known as Amgueddfa Cymru) is the body that runs Wales's seven national museums. It comprises National Museum Cardiff; St Fagans: National History Museum; Big Pit: National Coal Museum, Blaenafon; National Roman Legion Museum, Caerleon; National Slate Museum, Llanberis; National Wool Museum, Dre-fach Felindre; National Waterfront Museum, Swansea; and National Collections Centre, Nantgarw. Total funding from the Welsh government for 2014–15 was £26m.

Trustees, Elisabeth Elias *(President);* Dr Haydn Ellis Edwards *(Vice President);* Laurence Pavelin, CBE *(Treasurer);* Baroness Andrews, OBE; Prof. Tony Atkins; Dr Carol Bell; Miriam Hazell Griffiths; Dr Glenda Jones; Emeritus Prof. R. Gareth Wyn Jones, FLSW; Dr Hywel Ceri Jones, CMG; Christina Macaulay; Prof. Robert Pickard; Victoria Mary Provis; Keshav Singhal, MBE
Director-General, David Anderson

NATIONAL MUSEUMS LIVERPOOL

127 Dale Street, Liverpool L2 2JH
T 0151-207 0001 W www.liverpoolmuseums.org.uk

National Museums Liverpool is a group of museums and collections including the World Museum, the Merseyside Maritime Museum (also home to the Border Force National

Museum), the Lady Lever Art Gallery, the Walker Art Gallery, Sudley House, the International Slavery Museum and the Museum of Liverpool.

Chair, Prof. Phil Redmond, CBE

Trustees, Carmel Booth; Laura Carstensen; Clive Elphick; Andrew McCluskey; Philip Price; Dr Nicola Thorp

Director, Dr David Fleming, OBE

Director of Art Galleries, Sandra Penketh

Director, World Museum Liverpool, Steve Judd

Director, Museum of Liverpool, Janet Dugdale

Head of International Slavery Museum, Dr Richard Benjamin

NATIONAL MUSEUMS NORTHERN IRELAND

Cultra, Holywood, Northern Ireland BT18 0EU
T 0845-608 0000 W www.nmni.com

Across three unique sites National Museums Northern Ireland cares for and presents inspirational collections reflecting the creativity, innovation, history, culture and people of Northern Ireland and beyond.

Together the Ulster Museum, Ulster Folk and Transport Museum and Ulster American Folk Park offer a unique opportunity to experience the heritage and way of life of Northern Ireland.

Chair, Miceal McCoy

Trustees, Prof. Michael Catto; Prof. Garth Earls; Prof. Karen Fleming; Hazel Francey; Daphne Harshaw; Dr Rosemary Kelly; Dr Leon Litvack; Alan McFarland; Dr George McIlroy; Catherine Molloy; Annette Moor; Joseph Rice; Dr Margaret Ward

Chief Executive (acting), Jude Helliker

NATIONAL MUSEUMS SCOTLAND

Chambers Street, Edinburgh EH1 1JF
T 0300-123 6789 E info@nms.ac.uk W www.nms.ac.uk

National Museums Scotland provides advice, expertise and support to the museums community across Scotland, and undertakes fieldwork that often involves collaboration at local, national and international levels. National Museums Scotland comprises the National Museum of Scotland, the National War Museum, the National Museum of Rural Life, the National Museum of Flight and the National Museums Collection Centre. Its collections represent more than two centuries of collecting and include Scottish and classical archaeology, decorative and applied arts, world cultures and social history and science, technology and the natural world.

Up to 15 trustees can be appointed by the Minister for Culture and External Affairs for a term of four years, and may serve a second term.

Chair, Bruce Minto

Trustees, Dr Isabel Bruce, OBE, FRSSA; Prof. Chris Breward; Gordon Drummond; Chris Fletcher; Dr Anna Gregor, CBE, FRCR, FRCP; Andrew Holmes; Dr Brian Lang, FRSE; Lynda Logan; Dr Catriona Macdonald; Miller McLean, FCIBS, FIB; Prof. Walter Nimmo, FRCA, FRCP, FRSE; James Troughton, RIBA; Eilidh Wiseman

Director, Dr Gordon Rintoul

NATIONAL PORTRAIT GALLERY

St Martin's Place, London WC2H 0HE
T 020-7306 0055 W www.npg.org.uk

The National Portrait Gallery was formed after a grant was made in 1856 to form a gallery of the portraits of the most eminent persons in British history. Today the gallery collects portraits of those who have made, or are making, a significant contribution to British history and culture. The collection includes works across all media, from painting and sculpture to photography and digital portraits. The gallery stages a range of exhibitions, displays, talks and events throughout the year which explore the nature of portraiture. The present building was opened in 1896 and the Ondaatje Wing (including the Balcony Gallery, Tudor Gallery, Digital Space, Ondaatje Wing Theatre and roof-top Portrait Restaurant) opened in May 2000. There are three principle partnerships displaying portraits at Montacute House, Beningbrough Hall and Bodelwyddan Castle. Total government grant-in-aid for 2015–16 is £6.74m.

BOARD OF TRUSTEES

Chair, Sir William Proby, Bt., CBE

Trustees, Dr Brian Allen; Allegra Berman; Prof. Dame Carol Black, DBE; Dr Rosalind P. Blakesley; Dr Augustus Casely-Hayford; Kim Evans, OBE; Rt. Hon. Nick Clegg, MP; Rt. Hon. Lord Janvrin, GCB, GCVO, QSO; Christopher Le Brun, PRA; Mary McCartney; David Ross; Stephan Shakespeare; Marina Warner, CBE, FBA

Director, Dr Nicholas Cullinan

NATURAL ENGLAND

4th Floor, Foss House, King's Pool, 1-2 Peasholme Green, York YO1 7PX
T 0300-060 6000 E enquiries@naturalengland.org.uk
W www.gov.uk/natural-england

Natural England is the government's adviser on the natural environment, providing practical scientific advice on how to look after England's landscapes and wildlife.

The organisation's remit is to ensure sustainable stewardship of the land and sea so that people and nature can thrive.

Natural England works with farmers and land managers; business and industry; planners and developers; national and local government; charities and conservationists; interest groups and local communities to help them improve their local environment.

Chair, Andrew Sells

Chief Executive, James Cross

NATURAL HISTORY MUSEUM

Cromwell Road, London SW7 5BD
T 020-7942 5000 W www.nhm.ac.uk

The Natural History Museum, which houses 80 million natural history specimens, originates from the natural history departments of the British Museum, which grew extensively during the 19th century; in 1860 it was agreed that the natural history collections should be separated from the British Museum's collections of books, manuscripts and antiquities. Part of the site of the 1862 International Exhibition in South Kensington was acquired for the new museum, and the museum opened to the public in 1881. In 1963 the Natural History Museum became completely independent with its own board of trustees. The Natural History Museum at Tring, bequeathed by the second Lord Rothschild, has formed part of the museum since 1937. The Geological Museum merged with the Natural History Museum in 1985. In September 2009 the Natural History Museum opened the Darwin Centre, which contains public galleries, a high-tech interactive area known as the Attenborough Studio, scientific research facilities and storage for 28 million zoological specimens, 17 million entomology specimens and three million botanical specimens. Total government grant-in-aid for 2015–16 is £41.9m

Chair, Lord Green of Hurstpierpoint

Trustees, Prof. Sir Roy Anderson, FRS, FMEDSCI; Prof. Sir John Beddington, CMG, FRS; Prof. David Drewry; Prof. Christopher Gilligan; Prof. Sir John Holman; Dr

Derek Langslow, CBE; Hilary Newiss; Simon Patterson; Prof. Stephen Sparks, FRS, CBE; Dr Kim Winser, OBE
Museum Director, Dr Michael Dixon
Directors, Neil Greenwood *(Finance and Corporate Services);* Dr Justin Morris *(Public Engagement);* Prof. Ian Owens *(Science)*

NATURAL RESOURCES WALES
Ty Cambria, 29 Newport Road, Cardiff CF24 0TP
T 0300-065 3000 E enquiries@naturalresourceswales.gov.uk
W www.naturalresources.wales

Natural Resources Wales is the principal adviser to the Welsh government on the environment. It became operational on 1 April 2013 following a merger of the Countryside Council for Wales, Environment Agency Wales and the Forestry Commission Wales. It is responsible for ensuring that the natural resources of Wales are sustainably maintained, enhanced and used; now and in the future.
Chair, Prof. Peter Matthews, FRSC, FCIWEM, FIWO
Board Members, Harry Legge-Bourke; Revd Hywel Davies; Dr Ruth Hall; Dr Madeleine Havard; Andy Middleton; Nigel Reader, CBE; Prof. Lynda Warren; Sir Paul Williams, OBE
Chief Executive, Dr Emyr Roberts

NHS PAY REVIEW BODY
8th Floor, Fleetbank House, 2-6 Salisbury Square, London EC4Y 8JX
T 020-7211 8295 W www.gov.uk/government/organisations/nhs-pay-review-body

The NHS Pay Review Body (NHSPRB) makes recommendations to the prime minister, Secretary of State for Health and ministers in Scotland, Wales and Northern Ireland on the remuneration of all paid staff under agenda for change and employed in the NHS. The review body was established in 1983 for nurses and allied health professionals. Its remit has since expanded to cover over 1.8 million staff; ie almost all staff in the NHS, with the exception of dentists, doctors and very senior managers.
Chair, Jerry Cope
Members, Prof. David Blackaby; Joan Ingram; Graham Jagger; Colin Kennedy; Janet Rubin, MBE; Prof. Anna Vignoles

NORTHERN IRELAND HUMAN RIGHTS COMMISSION
Temple Court, 39 North Street, Belfast BT1 1NA
T 028-9024 3987 E information@nihrc.org W www.nihrc.org

The Northern Ireland Human Rights Commission is a non-departmental public body, established by the Northern Ireland Act 1998 and set up in March 1999. Its purpose is to protect and promote human rights in Northern Ireland. Its main functions include reviewing the law and practice relating to human rights, advising government and the Northern Ireland Assembly, and promoting an awareness of human rights. It can also investigate human rights violations and take cases to court. The members of the commission are appointed by the Secretary of State for Northern Ireland.
Chief Commissioner, Les Allamby
Commissioners, John Corey; Christine Collins; Milton Kerr, QPM; Grainia Long; Alan McBride; Marion Reynolds; Paul Yam
Director, Virginia McVea

NORTHERN LIGHTHOUSE BOARD
84 George Street, Edinburgh EH2 3DA
T 0131-473 3100 E enquiries@nlb.org.uk W www.nlb.org.uk

The Northern Lighthouse Board is the general lighthouse authority for Scotland and the Isle of Man and owes its origin to an act of parliament passed in 1786. At present there are 19 commissioners who operate under the Merchant Shipping Act 1995.

The commissioners control 206 lighthouses, many lighted and unlighted buoys, a DGPS (differential global positioning system) station and an ELORAN (long-range navigation) system. *See also* Transport.
Chair, Capt. Alistair Mackenzie
Commissioners, Lord Advocate; Solicitor-General for Scotland; Lord Provosts of Edinburgh, Glasgow and Aberdeen; Convener of Highland Council; Convener of Argyll and Bute Council; Sheriffs-Principal of North Strathclyde, Tayside, Central and Fife, Grampian, Highlands and Islands, South Strathclyde, Dumfries and Galloway, Lothians and Borders and Glasgow and Strathkelvin; Capt. Alastair Beveridge; Capt. Michael Brew; Graham Crerar; Capt. H. Michael Close; John Ross, CBE
Chief Executive, Mike Bullock, MBE

NUCLEAR DECOMMISSIONING AUTHORITY
Herdus House, Westlakes Science and Technology Park, Moor Row, Cumbria CA24 3HU
T 01925-802077 E enquiries@nda.gov.uk W www.nda.gov.uk

The Nuclear Decommissioning Authority (NDA) was created under the Energy Act 2004. It is a strategic authority that owns 19 sites and associated civil nuclear liabilities and assets of the public sector, previously under the control of the UK Energy Authority and British Nuclear Fuels. The NDA's responsibilities include decommissioning and cleaning up civil nuclear facilities; ensuring the safe management of waste products, both radioactive and non-radioactive; implementing government policy on the long-term management of nuclear waste; and developing UK-wide low-level waste strategy plans.

Total planned expenditure for 2015–16 is £3.31bn, with total grant-in-aid standing at £2.09bn. The remaining £1.22bn will come from commercial operations.
Chair, Stephen Henwood
Chief Executive, John Clarke

OFFICE FOR BUDGET RESPONSIBILITY
20 Victoria Street, London SW1H 0NF
T 020-7271 2520 E obrenquiries@obr.gsi.gov.uk
W budgetresponsibility.org.uk

The Office for Budget Responsibility (OBR) was created in 2010 to provide independent and authoritative analysis of the UK's public finances. It has four main roles: producing forecasts for the economy and public finances; judging progress towards the government's fiscal targets; assessing the long-term sustainability of the public finances; and scrutinising HM Treasury's costing of tax and welfare spending measures.
Chair, Robert Chote
Committee Members, Steve Nickell, CBE; Graham Parker, CBE

OFFICE OF COMMUNICATIONS (OFCOM)
Riverside House, 2A Southwark Bridge Road, London SE1 9HA
T 0300-123 3000 W www.ofcom.org.uk

OFCOM was established in 2003 under the Office of Communications Act 2002 as the independent regulator and competition authority for the UK communications industries with responsibility for television, radio, telecommunications and wireless communications services.

Following the passing of the Postal Services Act 2011, OFCOM has assumed regulatory responsibility for postal services from Postcomm, the Postal Services Commission.

Chair, Dame Patricia Hodgson, DBE
Deputy Chair, Baroness Noakes, DBE
Board Members, Dame Lynne Brindley, DBE; Tim Gardam;
   Stephen Hill; Graham Mather; Mike McTighe; Jonathan
   Oxley; Dr Stephen Unger
Chief Executive, Sharon White

OFFICE OF TAX SIMPLIFICATION

HM Treasury, 1 Horse Guards Road, London SW1A 2HQ
E ots@ots.gsi.gov.uk W www.gov.uk/government/organisations/
office-of-tax-simplification

The chancellor and exchequer secretary to HM Treasury
launched the Office of Tax Simplification (OTS) on 20 July
2010 to provide the government with independent advice on
simplifying the UK tax system. The OTS is an independent
office of HM Treasury that provides the government with
independent advice on simplifying the UK tax system. It
carries out projects investigating complex areas of the tax
system and makes recommendations to the chancellor in
reports which are published on its website.
Chair, Rt. Hon. Michael Jack
Tax Director, John Whiting

OFFICE OF MANPOWER ECONOMICS (OME)

8th Floor, Fleetbank House, 2–6 Salisbury Square, London EC4Y 8JX
T 020-7211 8165 W www.gov.uk/government/organisations/
office-of-manpower-economics

The Office of Manpower Economics (OME) was established
in 1971. It is an independent non-statutory organisation
which is responsible for servicing eight independent review
bodies which make recommendations impacting 2.5m
workers – around 45 per cent of public sector staff – and
a pay bill of £100bn.
OME Director, Martin Williams
Directors, Jenny Eastabrook *(National Crime Agency
   Remuneration Review Body, Police Remuneration Review
   Body, and School Teachers' Review Body);* Margaret McEvoy
   (Chief Economist and Research and Analysis Group); Stuart
   Sarson *(Prison Service Pay Review Body and Armed Forces'
   Pay Review Body);* Ffiona Kyte *(Senior Salaries Review Body,
   NHS Pay Review Body, and Review Body on Doctors' and
   Dentists' Remuneration)*

PARADES COMMISSION

Andras House, 60 Great Victoria Street, Belfast BT2 7BB
T 028-9089 5900 E info@paradescommissionni.org
W www.paradescommission.org

The Parades Commission was set up under the Public
Processions (Northern Ireland) Act 1998. Its function
is to encourage and facilitate local accommodation of
contentious parades; where this is not possible, the
commission is empowered to make legal determinations
about such parades, which may include imposing conditions
on aspects of the notified parade (such as restrictions on
routes/areas and exclusion of certain groups with a record of
bad behaviour).
   The chair and members are appointed by the Secretary of
State for Northern Ireland; the membership must, as far as is
practicable, be representative of the community in Northern
Ireland.
Chair, Anne Henderson
Members, Sarah Havlin; Paul Hutchinson; Colin Kennedy;
   Frances McCartney; Anne Marshall

PAROLE BOARD FOR ENGLAND AND WALES

52 Queen Anne's Gate, London SW1H 9AG
T 020-3334 4402 E info@paroleboard.gsi.gov.uk
W www.gov.uk/government/organisations/parole-board

The Parole Board was established in 1968 under the
Criminal Justice Act 1967 and became an independent
executive non-departmental public body on 1 July 1996
under the Criminal Justice and Public Order Act 1994. It is
the body that protects the public by making risk assessments
about prisoners to decide who may safely be released into
the community and who must remain in, or be returned
to, custody. Board decisions are taken at two main types of
panels of up to three members: 'paper panels' for the majority
of cases, or oral hearings for decisions concerning prisoners
serving life or indeterminate sentences for public protection.
The budget for 2014–15 was £14.2m.
Chair, Sir David Calvert-Smith
Chief Executive, Claire Bassett

PAROLE BOARD FOR SCOTLAND

Saughton House, Broomhouse Drive, Edinburgh EH11 3XD
T 0131-244 8373
E paroleboardforscotlandexecutive@scotland.gsi.gov.uk
W www.scottishparoleboard.gov.uk

The board directs and advises the Scottish ministers on the
release of prisoners on licence, and related matters.
Chair, John Watt

PENSION PROTECTION FUND (PPF)

Renaissance, 12 Dingwall Road, Croydon CR0 2NA
T 0845-600 2541 E information@ppf.gsi.gov.uk
W www.pensionprotectionfund.org.uk

The PPF became operational in 2005. It was established to
pay compensation to members of eligible defined-benefit
pension schemes where a qualifying insolvency event in
relation to the employer occurs and where there is a lack of
sufficient assets in the pension scheme. The PPF also
administers the Financial Assistance Scheme, which helps
members whose schemes wound-up before 2005. It is also
responsible for the Fraud Compensation Fund (which
provides compensation to occupational pension schemes that
suffer a loss that can be attributed to dishonesty). The chair
and board of the PPF are appointed by, and accountable to,
the Secretary of State for Work and Pensions, and are
responsible for paying compensation, calculating annual
levies (which help fund the PPF), and setting and overseeing
investment strategy.
Chair, Lady Judge, CBE
Chief Executive, Alan Rubenstein

PENSIONS REGULATOR

Napier House, Trafalgar Place, Brighton BN1 4DW
T 0845-600 0707 E customersupport@tpr.gov.uk
W www.thepensionsregulator.gov.uk

The Pensions Regulator was established in 2005 as the
regulator of work-based pension schemes in the UK,
replacing the Occupational Pensions Regulatory Authority
(OPRA). It aims to protect the benefits of occupational and
personal pension scheme members by working with trustees,
employers, pension providers and advisors. The regulator's
work focuses on encouraging better management and
administration of schemes, ensuring that final salary schemes
have a sensible funding plan, and encouraging money
purchase schemes to provide members with the information

that they need to make informed choices about their pension fund. The Pensions Act 2004 and the Pensions Act 2008 gave the regulator a range of powers which can be used to protect scheme members, but a strong emphasis is placed on educating and enabling those responsible for managing pension schemes, and powers are used only where necessary. The regulator offers three free online resources to help trustees, employers, professionals and advisors understand their role, duties and obligations.

Chair, Mark Boyle
Chief Executive, Lesley Titcomb

POLICE ADVISORY BOARD FOR ENGLAND AND WALES

Home Office, 6th Floor Fry, 2 Marsham Street, London SW1P 4DF
T 020-7271 0472 W www.gov.uk/government/organisations/police-advisory-board-for-england-and-wales

The Police Advisory Board for England and Wales was established in 1965 and provides advice to the home secretary on general questions affecting the police in England and Wales. It also considers draft regulations which the secretary of state proposes to make with respect to matters other than hours of duty, leave, pay and allowances or the issue, use and return of police clothing, personal equipment and other effects.

Independent Chair, Elizabeth France
Independent Deputy Chair, Prof. Gillian Morris

PRISON SERVICE PAY REVIEW BODY

8th Floor, Fleetbank House, 2-6 Salisbury Square, London EC4Y 8JX
T 020-7211 8259 W www.gov.uk/government/organisations/prison-services-pay-review-body

The Prison Service Pay Review Body was set up in 2001. It makes independent recommendations on the pay of prison governors, operational managers, prison officers and related grades for the Prison Service in England and Wales and for the Northern Ireland Prison Service.

Chair, Dr Peter Knight, CBE
Members, Prof. John Beath; Nicholas Caton; Elaine Hartin; Karen Heaton; Esmond Lindop; Peter Maddison, QPM

PRIVY COUNCIL OFFICE

2 Carlton Gardens, London SW1Y 5AA
T 020-7747 5310 E pcosecretariat@pco.gov.uk
W http://privycouncil.independent.gov.uk

The primary function of the office is to act as the secretariat to the Privy Council. It is responsible for the arrangements leading to the making of all royal proclamations and orders in council; for certain formalities connected with ministerial changes; for considering applications for the granting (or amendment) of royal charters; for the scrutiny and approval of by-laws and statutes of chartered institutions and of the governing instruments of universities and colleges; and for the appointment of high sheriffs and Privy Council appointments to governing bodies. Under the relevant acts, the office is responsible for the approval of certain regulations and rules made by the regulatory bodies of the medical and certain allied professions.

The Lord President of the Council is the ministerial head of the office and presides at meetings of the Privy Council. The Clerk of the Council is the administrative head of the Privy Council office.

Lord President of the Council and Leader of the House of Commons, Rt. Hon. Chris Grayling, MP
Clerk of the Council, Richard Tilbrook

Head of Secretariat and Deputy Clerk, Ceri King
Deputy Clerk, Christopher Berry

REVIEW BODY ON DOCTORS' AND DENTISTS' REMUNERATION

8th Floor, Fleetbank House, 2-6 Salisbury Square, London EC4Y 8JX
T 020-7211 8809
W www.gov.uk/government/organisations/review-body-on-doctors-and-dentists-remuneration

The Review Body on Doctors' and Dentists' Remuneration was set up in 1971. It advises the prime minister, first ministers in Scotland, Wales and Northern Ireland, and the ministers for Health, in England, Scotland, Wales and Northern Ireland on the remuneration of doctors and dentists taking any part in the National Health Service.

Chair, Prof. Paul Curnan
Members, Lucinda Bolton; Mark Butler; John Glennie, OBE; Alan Henry, OBE; Prof. Kevin Lee; Prof. Steve Thompson; Nigel Turner, OBE

ROYAL AIR FORCE MUSEUM

Grahame Park Way, London NW9 5LL
T 020-8205 2266 E london@rafmuseum.org
W www.rafmuseum.org.uk

The museum has two sites, one at the former airfield at Hendon and the second at Cosford, in the West Midlands, both of which illustrate the development of aviation from before the Wright brothers to the present-day RAF. The museum's collection across both sites consists of over 170 aircraft, as well as artefacts, aviation memorabilia, fine art and photographs.

Chair, Air Chief Marshal Sir Glenn Torpy, GCB, CBE, DSO
Trustees, Dr Carol Cole; Brendan Connor; Alan Coppin; Dr Rodney Eastwood, MBE; Rt. Hon. Lord Hutton of Furness; Gerry Grimstone; Richard Holman; Hon. John Michaelson; Andrew Reid; Michael Schindler; Robin Southwell; Alan Spence; Malcolm G. F. White, OBE
Director-General, Air Vice-Marshal Peter Dye, OBE
Chief Executive, Maggie Appleton, MBE

ROYAL BOTANIC GARDEN EDINBURGH

20A Inverleith Row, Edinburgh EH3 5LR
T 0131-552 7171 W www.rbge.org.uk

The Royal Botanic Garden Edinburgh (RBGE) originated as the Physic Garden, established in 1670 beside the Palace of Holyroodhouse. The garden moved to its present 28ha site at Inverleith, Edinburgh, in 1821. There are also three regional gardens: Benmore Botanic Garden, near Dunoon, Argyll; Logan Botanic Garden, near Stranraer, Wigtownshire; and Dawyck Botanic Garden, near Stobo, Peeblesshire. Since 1986 RBGE has been administered by a board of trustees established under the National Heritage (Scotland) Act 1985. It receives an annual grant from the Scottish government's Rural and Environmental Research and Analysis Directorate.

The RBGE is an international centre for scientific research on plant diversity and for horticulture education and conservation. It has an extensive library, a herbarium with almost three million preserved plant specimens, and over 15,000 species in the living collections.

Chair, Sir Muir Russell, KCB, FRSE
Trustees, Prof. Beverley Glover; Prof. Iain Gordon, FRSE; Patricia Henton, FRSE; Angela McNaught; Prof. Thomas Meagher; Diana Murray; Tim Rollinson, CBE; Prof. Ian Wall, FRSE
Regius Keeper and Queen's Botanist in Scotland, Simon Milne, MBE

ROYAL BOTANIC GARDENS, KEW

Kew Gardens, Richmond, Surrey TW9 3AB
T 020-8332 5655 E info@kew.org
Wakehurst, Ardingly, W. Sussex RH17 6TN
T 01444-894066
E wakehurstinfo@kew.org W www.kew.org

Kew Gardens was originally laid out as a private garden for the now demolished White House for George III's mother, Princess Augusta, in 1759. The gardens were much enlarged in the 19th century, notably by the inclusion of the grounds of the former Richmond Lodge. In 1965 Kew acquired the gardens at Wakehurst on a long lease from the National Trust. Under the National Heritage Act 1983 a board of trustees was set up to administer the gardens, which in 1984 became an independent body supported by grant-in-aid from the Department for Environment, Food and Rural Affairs.

The functions of RBG, Kew are to carry out research into plant sciences, to disseminate knowledge about plants and to provide the public with the opportunity to gain knowledge and enjoyment from the gardens' collections. There are extensive national reference collections of living and preserved plants and a comprehensive library and archive. The main emphasis is on plant conservation and biodiversity; Wakehurst houses the Millennium Seed Bank Partnership, which is the largest *ex situ* conservation project in the world – its aim is to save seed from 25 per cent of the earth's wild plant species by 2020.

Chair, Marcus Agius

Trustees, Catherine Dugmore; Valerie Gooding; Ian Karet; Dr Geoffrey Hawtin; Sir Henry Keswick; George Loudon; Sir Derek Myers; Prof. Malcolm Press; Prof. Nicola Spence; Jennifer Ullman
Director, Richard Deverell

ROYAL COMMISSION ON THE ANCIENT AND HISTORICAL MONUMENTS OF SCOTLAND

John Sinclair House, 16 Bernard Terrace, Edinburgh EH8 9NX
T 0131-662 1456 W www.rcahms.gov.uk

The Royal Commission on the Ancient and Historical Monuments of Scotland (RCAHMS) was established by a royal warrant in 1908, which was revised in 1992, and is appointed to provide for the collecting, recording and interpretation of information on the architectural, industrial, archaeological and maritime heritage of Scotland, to give a picture of the human influence on Scotland's places from the earliest times to the present day. It is funded by the Scottish government. More than 15 million items, including photographs, maps, drawings and documents, are available through the search room, and online databases provide access to over 600,000 images and information on 300,000 buildings and sites. RCAHMS also holds Scotland's national collection of historical aerial photography as well as The Aerial Reconnaissance Archives (TARA) of international wartime photography.

Chair, Prof. John Hume, OBE, FSA SCOT

Commissioners, Dr Kate Byrne, FRSA; Tom Dawson, FSA SCOT; Mark Hopton, FSA SCOT; Dr Jeremy Huggett, FSA, FSA SCOT; Prof. John Hunter, OBE, FSA, FSA SCOT; Paul Jardine; Dr Gordon Masterton, OBE, FICE, FIES; Jude Quartson-Mochrie; Elspeth Reid
Chief Executive, Diana Murray, FSA, FSA SCOT

ROYAL COMMISSION ON THE ANCIENT AND HISTORICAL MONUMENTS OF WALES

Crown Building, Plas Crug, Aberystwyth SY23 1NJ
T 01970-621200 E nmr.wales@rcahmw.gov.uk
W www.rcahmw.gov.uk

The Royal Commission on the Ancient and Historical Monuments of Wales, established in 1908, is the investigation body and national archive for the historic environment of Wales. It has the lead role in ensuring that Wales's archaeological, built and maritime heritage is authoritatively recorded, and seeks to promote the understanding and appreciation of this heritage nationally and internationally. The commission is funded by the Welsh government.

Chair, Dr Eurwyn Wiliam, FSA

Vice-Chair, Henry Owen-John, FSA

Commissioners, Catherine S. Hardman; Jonathan Hudson; Thomas O. S. Lloyd, OBE, FSA; Dr Mark Redknap, FSA; Prof. Christopher Williams, FRHISTS
Chief Executive. Christopher Catling

ROYAL MUSEUMS GREENWICH

National Maritime Museum, Greenwich, London SE10 9NF
T 020-8858 4422 W www.rmg.co.uk

Royal Museums Greenwich comprises the National Maritime Museum, the Queen's House and the Royal Observatory Greenwich. It also works in collaboration with the Cutty Sark Trust. The National Maritime Museum provides information on the maritime history of Great Britain and is the largest institution of its kind in the world, with over two million items in its collections related to seafaring, navigation and astronomy. Originally the home of Charles I's Queen, Henrietta Maria, the Queen's House was designed by Inigo Jones and built between 1616–18, although it was structurally altered between 1629–35. It now contains a fine-art collection. The Royal Observatory, Greenwich is the home of Greenwich Mean Time and the prime meridian of the world. It also contains London's only planetarium, Harrison's timekeepers and the UK's largest refracting telescope.

Director, Kevin Fewster, FRSA

Chair, Sir Charles Dunstone

Trustees, Eleanor Boddington; Sir Robert Crawford, CBE; Linda Hutchinson; Prof. Christopher Lintott; Joyce Bridges, CBE; Carol Marlow; Jonathan Ofer; Eric Reynolds; Gerald Russell; Prof. Alison Bashford; Jeremy Penn; Adm. Sir Mark Stanhope, GCB, OBE

SCHOOL TEACHERS' REVIEW BODY

8th Floor, Fleetbank House, 2-6 Salisbury Square, London EC4Y 8JX
T 020-7211 8463
W www.gov.uk/government/organisations/school-teachers-review-body

The School Teachers' Review Body was set up under the School Teachers' Pay and Conditions Act 1991. It is required to examine and report on such matters relating to the statutory conditions of employment of school teachers in England and Wales as may be referred to it by the education secretary.

Chair, Dr Patricia Rice

Members, Peter Batley; Jonathan Crossley-Holland; Daniel Flint; Ken Clark; Debbie Meech; Jill Pullen; Mike Redhouse

SCIENCE MUSEUM

Exhibition Road, London SW7 2DD
T 0870-870 4868 E info@sciencemuseum.org.uk
W www.sciencemuseum.org.uk

The Science Museum, part of the Science Museum Group (SMG), houses the national collections of science, technology, industry and medicine. The museum began as the science collection of the South Kensington Museum and first opened in 1857. In 1883 it acquired the collections of the Patent Museum and in 1909 the science collections were transferred to the new Science Museum, leaving the art collections with the Victoria and Albert Museum. The Wellcome Wing was opened in July 2000.

The SMG also incorporates the National Railway Museum, York; the National Media Museum, Bradford; Locomotion: the National Railway Museum at Shildon; and the Museum of Science and Industry, Manchester.

Total government grant-in-aid for 2015–16 is £38.87m.

Chair, Dame Mary Archer

Trustees, Howard Covington; Matthew D'Ancona; Prof. Dame Athene Donald, DBE, FRS; Lord Faulkner of Worcester; Sharon Flood; Prof. Russell Foster, CBE; Andreas Goss; Lord Grade of Yarmouth, CBE; Prof. Ludmilla Jordanova; Simon Linnett; Prof. Averil Macdonald; Prof. David Phoenix, OBE; Dr Gill Samuels, CBE; Anton Valk, CBE; Dame Fiona Woolf, CBE; Rt. Hon. David Willetts

Director of SMG, Ian Blatchford

Director of Science Museum, Ian Blatchford

Director of Museum of Science & Industry, Sally MacDonald

Director of National Media Museum, Jo Quinton-Tulloch

Director of National Railway Museum, Paul Kirkman

SCOTTISH CRIMINAL CASES REVIEW COMMISSION

5th Floor, Portland House, 17 Renfield Street, Glasgow G2 5AH
T 0141-270 7030 E info@sccrc.org.uk W www.sccrc.org.uk

The commission is a non-departmental public body, funded by the Scottish Government Criminal Justice Directorate, and established by Act of Parliament in April 1999. It assumed the role previously performed by the Secretary of State for Scotland to consider alleged miscarriages of justice in Scotland and refer cases meeting the relevant criteria to the high court for determination. Members are appointed by the Queen on the recommendation of the first minister; senior executive staff are appointed by the commission.

Chair, Jean Couper, CBE

Members, Gerrard Bann; Peter Ferguson, QC; Prof. George Irving, CBE; Frances McMenamin, QC

Chief Executive, Gerard Sinclair

SCOTTISH ENTERPRISE

Atrium Court, 50 Waterloo Street, Glasgow G2 6HQ
T 0845-607 8787 E enquiries@scotent.co.uk
W www.scottish-enterprise.com

Scottish Enterprise was established in 1991 and its purpose is to stimulate the sustainable growth of Scotland's economy. It is mainly funded by the Scottish government and is responsible to the Scottish ministers. Working in partnership with the private and public sectors, Scottish Enterprise will invest £321.2m in 2015–16 to further the development of Scotland's economy by helping ambitious and innovative businesses grow and become more successful. Scottish Enterprise is particularly interested in supporting companies that provide renewable energy, encourage trade overseas, increase innovation, and those that will help Scotland become a low-carbon economy. Its grant-in-aid allocation (capital and resource allocation) for 2015–16 is £243.5m.

Chair, Crawford Gillies

Chief Executive, Dr Lena Wilson

SCOTTISH ENVIRONMENT PROTECTION AGENCY (SEPA)

Erskine Court, Castle Business Park, Stirling FK9 4TZ
T 0300-099 6699
W www.sepa.org.uk

SEPA was established in 1996 and is the public body responsible for environmental protection in Scotland. It regulates potential pollution to land, air and water; the storage, transport and disposal of controlled waste; and the safekeeping and disposal of radioactive materials. It does this within a complex legislative framework of acts of parliament, EU directives and regulations, granting licences to operations of industrial processes and waste disposal. SEPA also operates Floodline (T 0845-988 1188), a public service providing information on the possible risk of flooding 24 hours a day, 365 days a year.

Chair, David Sigsworth

Chief Executive, Terry A'Hearn

Directors, Calum MacDonald *(Operations);* David Pirie *(Science and Strategy)*

SCOTTISH LAW COMMISSION

140 Causewayside, Edinburgh EH9 1PR
T 0131-668 2131 E info@scotlawcom.gsi.gov.uk
W www.scotlawcom.gov.uk

The Scottish Law Commission, established in 1965, keeps the law in Scotland under review and makes proposals for its development and reform. It is responsible to the Scottish ministers through the Scottish government justice directorate.

Chair (part-time), Hon. Lord Pentland

Chief Executive, Malcolm McMillan

Commissioners, C. Drummond; D. Johnston, QC; Prof. H. MacQueen; Dr A. Steven

SCOTTISH LEGAL AID BOARD

Thistle House, 91 Haymarket Terrace, Edinburgh EH12 5HE
T 0131-226 7061 **Helpline** 0845-122 8686
E general@slab.org.uk W www.slab.org.uk

The Scottish Legal Aid Board was set up under the Legal Aid (Scotland) Act 1986 to manage legal aid in Scotland. It reports to the Scottish government. Board members are appointed by Scottish ministers.

Chair, Iain Robertson, CBE

Members, Les Campbell; Rani Dhir; Alastair Kinroy, QC; Denise Loney; Ray MacFarlane; Vincent McGovern; Bill McQueen, CBE; Ros Micklem; Derek Ogg, QC; Sheriff Ray Small; Graham Watson

Chief Executive, Lindsay Montgomery, CBE

SCOTTISH NATURAL HERITAGE (SNH)

Great Glen House, Leachkin Road, Inverness IV3 8NW
T 01463-725000 E enquiries@snh.gov.uk
W www.snh.org.uk

SNH was established in 1992 under the Natural Heritage (Scotland) Act 1991. It is the government's adviser on all aspects of nature and landscape across Scotland and its role is to help the public understand, value and enjoy Scotland's nature, as well as to support those people and organisations that manage it.

Chair, Ian Ross

Acting Chief Executive, Susan Davies

Directors, Nick Halfhide *(Operations);* Andrew Bachell *(Policy and Advice);* Joe Moore *(Corporate Services)*

SEAFISH

18 Logie Mill, Logie Green Road, Edinburgh EH7 4HS
T 0131-558 3331 E seafish@seafish.co.uk
W www.seafish.org

Established under the Fisheries Act 1981, Seafish works with all sectors of the UK seafood industry to satisfy consumers, raise standards, improve efficiency and secure a sustainable and profitable future. Services range from research and development, economic consulting, market research and training and accreditation through to legislative advice for the seafood industry. It is sponsored by the four UK fisheries departments, which appoint the board, and is funded by a levy on seafood.

Chair, Elaine Hayes
Chief Executive, Dr Paul Williams

SECURITY AND INTELLIGENCE SERVICES

GOVERNMENT COMMUNICATIONS HEADQUARTERS (GCHQ)

Hubble Road, Cheltenham GL51 0EX
T 01242-221491 W www.gchq.gov.uk

GCHQ produces signals intelligence in support of national security and the UK's economic wellbeing, and in the prevention or detection of serious crime. Additionally, GCHQ's Information Security arm, CESG, is the national technical authority for information assurance, and provides advice and assistance to government departments, the armed forces and other national infrastructure bodies on the security of their communications and information systems. GCHQ was placed on a statutory footing by the Intelligence Services Act 1994 and is headed by a director who is directly accountable to the foreign secretary.

Director, Robert Hannigan, CMG

SECRET INTELLIGENCE SERVICE (MI6)

PO Box 1300, London SE1 1BD
W www.sis.gov.uk

Established in 1909 as the Foreign Section of the Secret Service Bureau, the Secret Intelligence Service produces secret intelligence in support of the government's security, defence, foreign and economic policies. It was placed on a statutory footing by the Intelligence Services Act 1994 and is headed by a chief, known as 'C', who is directly accountable to the foreign secretary.

Chief, Alex Younger

SECURITY SERVICE (MI5)

PO Box 3255, London SW1P 1AE
T 020-7930 9000 W www.mi5.gov.uk

The Security Service is responsible for security intelligence work against covertly organised threats to the UK. It is organised into seven branches, each with dedicated areas of responsibility, which include countering terrorism, espionage and the proliferation of weapons of mass destruction. The Security Service also provides security advice to a wide range of organisations to help reduce vulnerability to threats from individuals, groups or countries hostile to UK interests. The home secretary has parliamentary accountability for the Security Service. There is a network of regional offices around the UK plus a Northern Ireland headquarters.

Director-General, Andrew Parker

SENIOR SALARIES REVIEW BODY

8th Floor, Fleetbank House, 2-6 Salisbury Square, London EC4Y 8JX
T 020-7211 8315 W www.ome.uk.com

The Senior Salaries Review Body (formerly the Top Salaries Review Body) was set up in 1971 to advise the prime minister on the remuneration of the judiciary, senior civil servants, senior officers of the armed forces and very senior managers in the NHS. In 1993 its remit was extended to cover the pay, pensions and allowances of MPs, ministers and others whose pay is determined by the Ministerial and Other Salaries Act 1975, and also the allowances of peers. If asked, it advises on the pay of officers and members of the devolved parliament and assemblies.

Chair, Dr Martin Read, DPHIL, FIET
Members, Margaret Edwards; Dame Hazel Genn, DBE, QC; David Lebrecht; John Steele

STUDENT LOANS COMPANY LTD

100 Bothwell Street, Glasgow G2 7JD
T 0141-306 2000 W www.slc.co.uk

The Student Loans Company (SLC) is owned by the Department for Business, Innovation and Skills and the Secretary of State for Scotland. It processes and administers financial assistance, in the form of grants and loans, for undergraduates who have secured a place at university or college. The SLC also provides loans for tuition fees, which are paid directly to the university or college. In the year 2013–14 the SLC supported around 1.43 million students.

Chair, Christian Brodie
Chief Executive, Mick Laverty

TATE

W www.tate.org.uk

TATE BRITAIN

Millbank, London SW1P 4RG
T 020-7887 8888 E visiting.britain@tate.org.uk

TATE MODERN

Bankside, London SE1 9TG
T 020-7887 8888 E visiting.modern@tate.org.uk

TATE LIVERPOOL

Albert Dock, Liverpool L3 4BB
T 0151-702 7400 E visiting.liverpool@tate.org.uk

TATE ST IVES

Porthmeor Beach, St Ives, Cornwall TR26 1TG
T 01736-796226 E visiting.stives@tate.org.uk

Tate comprises four art galleries: Tate Britain and Tate Modern in London, Tate Liverpool and Tate St Ives.

Tate Britain, which opened in 1897, displays the national collection of British art from 1500 to the present day – with special attention and dedicated space given to Blake, Turner and Constable. A £45m renovation of Tate Britain was completed in 2013.

Opened in May 2000, Tate Modern displays the Tate collection of international modern art dating from 1900 to the present day. It includes works by Dalí, Picasso, Matisse and Warhol as well as many contemporary works. It is housed in the former Bankside Power Station in London, which was redesigned by the Swiss architects Herzog and de Meuron.

Tate Liverpool opened in 1988 and houses mainly 20th-century art and Tate St Ives, which features work by artists from and working in St Ives and includes the Barbara Hepworth Museum and Sculpture Garden, opened in 1993.

BOARD OF TRUSTEES
Chair, Lord Browne of Madingley
Trustees, John Akomfrah; Lionel Barber; Tom Bloxham, MBE; Mala Gaonkar; Maja Hoffman; Lisa Milroy; Elisabeth Murdoch; Franck Petitgas; Dame Seona Reid, DBE; Hannah Rothschild; Monisha Shah; Gareth Thomas; Stephen Witherford

OFFICERS
Director, Tate, Sir Nicholas Serota, CH
Directors, Dr Penelope Curtis *(Tate Britain);* Chris Dercon
(Tate Modern); Caroline Collier *(Tate National);* Andrea
Nixon *(Tate Liverpool);* Mark Osterfield *(Tate St Ives)*

TOURISM BODIES
Visit Britain, Visit Scotland, Visit Wales and the Northern
Ireland Tourist Board are responsible for developing and
marketing the tourist industry in their respective regions.
Visit Wales is not listed here as it is part of the Welsh
government, within the Department for Heritage, and not a
public body.

VISITBRITAIN
Sanctuary Buildings, 20 Great Smith Street, London SW1P 3BT
T 020-7578 1000 E industry.relations@visitbritain.org
W www.visitbritain.com
Chair, Christopher Rodrigues, CBE
Chief Executive, Sally Balcombe

VISIT SCOTLAND
Ocean Point One, 94 Ocean Drive, Edinburgh EH6 6JH
T 0131-472 2222
E info@visitscotland.com W www.visitscotland.com
Chair, Dr Mike Cantlay, OBE
Chief Executive, Malcolm Roughead, OBE

NORTHERN IRELAND TOURIST BOARD
St. Anne's Court, 59 North Street, Belfast BT1 1NB
T 028-9023 1221 E info@tourismni.com W www.nitb.com
Chair, Terence Brannigan
Chief Executive, John McGrillen

TRANSPORT FOR LONDON (TFL)
Windsor House, 42–50 Victoria Street, London SW1H 0TL
E enquire@tfl.gov.uk W www.tfl.gov.uk

TfL was created in July 2000 and is the integrated body
responsible for the capital's transport system. Its role is to
implement the Mayor of London's transport strategy and
manage the transport services across London for which the
mayor has responsibility. These services include London's
buses, London Underground, London Overground, the
Docklands Light Railway (DLR), Tramlink, London River
Services and Victoria Coach Station. TfL also runs the
Emirates Air Line and the London Transport Museum. In
a joint venture with the Department for Transport, TfL is
responsible for the construction of Crossrail - a new railway
linking Maidenhead and Heathrow in the west, to Shenfield
and Abbey Wood in the east. The central section of Crossrail
is expected to be completed by the end of 2018.

TfL is responsible for managing the Congestion Charging
scheme and for maintaining 360 miles (580km) of main
roads and all of London's 6,000+ traffic lights. It also
regulates the city's taxis and private hire vehicles. TfL runs
the Santander Cycle Hire scheme, allowing customers to hire
a bicycle from £2, and the Dial-a-ride scheme, a door-to-
door service for disabled people unable to use buses, trams or
the London Underground.
Chair, Boris Johnson
Members, Peter Anderson; Sir John Armitt, CBE;
   Sir Brendan Barber; Richard Barnes; Charles Belcher;
   Roger Burnley; Brian Cooke; Isabel Dedring *(Deputy
   Chair);* Baroness Grey-Thompson, DBE; Angela Knight;
   Michael Liebreich; Eva Lindholm; Daniel Moylan;
   Bob Oddy; Keith Williams; Steve Wright, MBE
Commissioner, Mike Brown

UK ATOMIC ENERGY AUTHORITY
Culham Science Centre, Abingdon, Oxfordshire OX14 3DB
T 01235-528822 W www.gov.uk/government/organisations/uk-
atomic-energy-authority

The UK Atomic Energy Authority (UKAEA) was established
by the Atomic Energy Authority Act 1954 and took
over responsibility for the research and development of the
civil nuclear power programme. The UKAEA reports to
the Department for Business, Innovation and Skills and is
responsible for managing UK fusion research including
operating the Joint European Torus (JET) on behalf of
the UKAEA's European partners at its site in Culham,
Oxfordshire. In October 2009, as part of the government's
Operation Efficiency Programme, the authority sold its
commercial arm, UKAEA Limited; as a result, the UKAEA no
longer provides nuclear decommissioning services.
Chair, Prof. Roger Cashmore, CMG, FRS
Chief Executive, Prof. Steven Cowley

UK SPORT
21 Bloomsbury Street, London WC1B 3HF
T 020-7211 5100 E info@uksport.gov.uk W www.uksport.gov.uk

UK Sport was established by royal charter in 1997 and is
accountable to parliament through the Department for
Culture, Media and Sport. Its mission is to lead sport in the
UK to world-class success. This means working with partner
organisations to deliver medals at the Olympic and
Paralympic Games and organising, bidding for and staging
major sporting events in the UK; increasing the UK's
sporting activity and influence overseas; and promoting
sporting conduct, ethics and diversity in society. UK Sport
is funded by a mix of grant-in-aid and National Lottery
income. For 2014–15 projected grant-in-aid and National
Lottery funding amounted to approximately £111m.
Chair, Rod Carr, CBE
Chief Executive, Liz Nicholl, OBE

VICTORIA AND ALBERT MUSEUM
Cromwell Road, London SW7 2RL
T 020-7942 2000 W www.vam.ac.uk

The Victoria and Albert Museum (V&A) is the national
museum of art, design and performance. It descends directly
from the Museum of Manufactures, which opened in
Marlborough House in 1852 after the Great Exhibition of
1851. The museum was moved in 1857 to become part of
the South Kensington Museum. It was renamed the Victoria
and Albert Museum in 1899. It also houses the National Art
Library and Print Room.

The museum's collections span over 5,000 years of human
creativity, including paintings, sculpture, architecture,
ceramics, furniture, fashion and textiles, theatre and
performance, photography, glass, jewellery and metalwork.
Materials relating to childhood are displayed at the V&A
Museum of Childhood at Bethnal Green, which opened in
1872 and is the most important surviving example of the
type of glass and iron construction used by Joseph Paxton
for the Great Exhibition. The V&A also houses the National
Art Library which holds over 950,000 books dedicated to
the study of fine and decorative arts from around the world.
Chair, Nicholas Coleridge, CBE
Trustees, Joao Baptista; Mark Damazer, CBE; Prof. Margot
   Finn; Andrew Hochhauser, QC; Stephen McGuckin;
   Dame Theresa Sackler, DBE; Mark Sebba; Caroline Silver;
   Sir John Sorrell; Dr Paul Thompson; Edmund de Waal,
   OBE; Prof. Evelyn Welch
Director, Prof. Martin Roth

WALLACE COLLECTION
Hertford House, Manchester Square, London W1U 3BN
T 020-7563 9500 E collections@wallacecollection.org
W www.wallacecollection.org

The Wallace Collection was bequeathed to the nation by the widow of Sir Richard Wallace, in 1897, and Hertford House was subsequently acquired by the government. The collection contains works by Titian and Rembrandt, and includes porcelain, furniture and an array of arms and armour.

Chair, António Horta Osório
Trustees, Prof. Jasper Conran, OBE; Prof. Frances Corner, OBE; Duke of Devonshire, KCVO, CBE; Jennifer Eady, QC; Rupert Hambro; Jagdip Jagpal; Denise Lewis; Jessica Pulay; Sir Hugh Roberts, GCVO, FSA; Kate de Rothschild Agius; Dr Ashok Roy; Adrian Sassoon; Timothy Schrofer
Director, Dr Christoph Vogtherr

WALES

WELSH GOVERNMENT

Cathays Park, Cardiff CF10 3NQ
T 0845-010 3300 W http://wales.gov.uk

The Welsh government is the devolved government of Wales. It is accountable to the National Assembly for Wales, the Welsh legislature which represents the interests of the people of Wales, and makes laws for Wales. The Welsh government and the National Assembly for Wales were established as separate institutions under the Government of Wales Act 2006.

The Welsh government comprises the first minister, who is usually the leader of the largest party in the National Assembly for Wales; up to 14 ministers and deputy ministers; and a counsel general (the chief legal adviser).

Following the referendum on 3 March 2011 on granting further law-making powers to the National Assembly, the Welsh government's functions now include the ability to propose bills to the National Assembly on subjects within 20 set areas of policy. Subject to limitations prescribed by the Government of Wales Act 2006, acts of the National Assembly may make any provision that could be made by act of parliament. The 20 areas of responsibility devolved to the National Assembly for Wales (and within which Welsh ministers exercise executive functions) are: agriculture, fisheries, forestry and rural development; ancient monuments and historic buildings; culture; economic development; education and training; environment; fire and rescue services and promotion of fire safety; food; health and health services; highways and transport; housing; local government; the National Assembly for Wales; public administration; social welfare; sport and recreation; tourism; town and county planning; water and flood defence; and the Welsh language.
First Minister of Wales, Rt. Hon. Carwyn Jones, AM
Minister for Communities and Tackling Poverty, Lesley Griffiths, AM
Minister for Economy, Science and Transport, Edwina Hart, MBE, AM
Minister for Education and Skills, Huw Lewis, AM
Minister for Finance and Government Business, Jane Hutt, AM
Minister for Health and Social Services, Mark Drakeford, AM
Minister for Natural Resources, Carl Sargeant, AM
Minister for Public Services, Leighton Andrews, AM
Deputy Minister for Health, Vaughan Gething, AM
Deputy Minister for Culture, Sport and Tourism, Ken Skates, AM
Deputy Minister for Farming and Food, Rebecca Evans, AM
Deputy Minister for Skills and Technology, Julie James, AM
Counsel General of Wales, Theodore Huckle, QC
Chief Whip, Janice Gregory, AM

MANAGEMENT BOARD

Permanent Secretary, Sir Derek Jones, KCB
Director-General, Finance and Corporate Services, Michael Hearty
Director-General, Economy, Science and Transport, James Price
Director-General, Education and Skills, Owen Evans
Director-General, Health, Social Services and Children and Chief Executive of NHS Wales, Andrew Goodall
Director-General, Local Government and Communities, Dr June Milligan
Director-General, People, Places and Corporate Services, Bernard Galton

Director-General, Natural Resources, Gareth Jones
Non-Executive Directors, Elan Closs Stephens; James Turner; Adrian Webb

DEPARTMENTS

Department for Education and Skills
Department for Health and Social Services
Department for Economy, Science and Transport
Department for Finance and Corporate Services
Department for Local Government and Communities
Department for Natural Resources
Permanent Secretary's Division (Office of the First Minister; Legal Services Department; European and External Affairs Division; Constitutional Affairs and Inter-governmental Relations Division)
Sustainable Futures

ASSEMBLY COMMITTEES

Children, Young People and Education
Communities, Equality and Local Government
Constitutional and Legislative Affairs
Enterprise and Business
Environment and Sustainability
Finance
Health and Social Care
Petitions
Public Accounts
Scrutiny of the First Minister
Standards of Conduct

ASSEMBLY COMMISSION

The Assembly Commission was created under the Government of Wales Act 2006 to ensure that the assembly is provided with the property, staff and services required for it to carry out its functions. The commission also sets the National Assembly's strategic aims, objectives, standards and values. The Assembly Commission consists of the presiding officer, plus four other assembly members, one nominated by each of the four party groups. The five commissioners are accountable to the National Assembly.
Presiding Officer, Dame Rosemary Butler, DBE, AM
Commissioners, Peter Black, Angela Burns, Rhodri Glyn Thomas, Sandy Mewies
Chief Executive and Clerk of the Assembly, Claire Clancy

NATIONAL ASSEMBLY FOR WALES

Cardiff Bay, Cardiff CF99 1NA
T 0845-010 5500 W www.assemblywales.org

In July 1997 the government announced plans to establish a National Assembly for Wales. In a referendum in September 1997 about 50 per cent of the electorate voted, of whom 50.3 per cent voted in favour of a national assembly. Elections are held every four years and the first election took place on 6 May 1999. The fourth election took place on 5 May 2011. There has been a minority Labour administration since the 2011 elections.

National Assembly members are elected using the additional member system. Voters are given two votes: one for a constituency member and one for a regional member. The constituency members are elected under the first-past-the-post system, also used to elect constituency members to the London Assembly. Four regional members in each of the five constituencies are then chosen from party lists or independent candidates using a form of proportional representation.

Until 2007 the National Assembly for Wales was a corporate body comprising both the executive and legislative branches of government. It had no primary law-making powers and only had responsibility for exercising and implementing ministerial functions which had previously been vested in the Secretary of State for Wales.

The Government of Wales Act 2006 introduced a radical change to the functions and status of the National Assembly for Wales. With effect from 25 May 2007 the act formally separated the National Assembly for Wales (the legislature – made up of 60 elected assembly members) and the Welsh government (the executive – comprising the first minister, Welsh ministers, deputy Welsh ministers and the counsel general). It also made changes to the electoral process: candidates are no longer permitted to stand as both constituency and regional members. The act enabled the National Assembly for Wales to formulate its own legislation (assembly measures) on the 20 devolved areas for which it has responsibility (*see* Welsh government); the assembly was given legislative competence (the legal authority to pass measures) on a case-by-case basis by the UK parliament.

The act also included a mechanism that would allow for full transfer of legislative powers relating to all devolved matters to the National Assembly, provided that the people of Wales voted for such a proposal in a referendum. In a referendum held on 3 March 2011, 63.5 per cent voted in favour of giving the National Assembly full legislative powers for all devolved matters. The National Assembly for Wales can now pass legislation (assembly acts) on the 20 devolved areas for which it has responsibility. An assembly act has the same powers as an act of the UK parliament and may be proposed by the Welsh government, assembly committees, an assembly member or the assembly commission.

The National Assembly for Wales also scrutinises and monitors the Welsh government. It meets in plenary in the Senedd debating chamber. The 60 assembly members examine and approve assembly bills and approve certain items of subordinate legislation; approve the Welsh government and assembly commission's budget; hold Welsh ministers to account; and analyse and debate their decisions and policies.

Presiding Officer, Dame Rosemary Butler, DBE, AM
Deputy Presiding Officer, David Melding, AM

SALARIES 2015–16	
First Minister*	£80,870
Minister/Presiding Officer*	£41,949
Deputy Minister/Deputy Presiding Officer*	£26,385
Assembly Member (AM)†	£54,391

* Also receives the assembly member salary
† Reduced by two-thirds if the member is also an MP or an MEP

MEMBERS OF THE NATIONAL ASSEMBLY FOR WALES
as at 1 September 2015

Andrews, Leighton, *Lab.*, Rhondda, Maj. 6,739
Antoniw, Mick, *Lab.*, Pontypridd, Maj. 7,694
ap Iorwerth, Rhun, *PC, Ynys Môn*, Maj. 9,166
Asghar, Mohammad, *C, South Wales East region*
Black, Peter, *LD, South Wales West region*
Burns, Angela, *C, Carmarthen West and South Pembrokeshire*, Maj. 1,504
Butler, Dame Rosemary, DBE, *Lab., Newport West*, Maj. 4,220
Chapman, Christine, *Lab., Cynon Valley*, Maj. 6,515
Cuthbert, Jeff, *Lab., Caerphilly*, Maj. 4,924

Davies, Alun, *Lab., Blaenau Gwent*, Maj. 9,120
Davies, Andrew R. T., *C, South Wales Central region*
Davies, Jocelyn, *PC, South Wales East region*
Davies, Keith, *Lab., Llanelli*, Maj. 80
Davies, Paul, *C, Preseli Pembrokeshire*, Maj. 2,175
Davies, Suzy, *C, South Wales West region*
Drakeford, Mark, *Lab., Cardiff West*, Maj. 5,901
Elis-Thomas, Rt. Hon. Lord, *PC, Dwyfor Meirionnydd*, Maj. 5,417
Evans, Rebecca, *Lab., Mid and West Wales region*
Finch-Saunders, Janet, *C, Aberconwy*, Maj. 1,567
George, Russell, *C, Montgomeryshire*, Maj. 2,324
Gething, Vaughan, *Lab., Cardiff South and Penarth*, Maj. 6,259
Graham, William, *C, South Wales East region*
Gregory, Janice, *Lab., Ogmore*, Maj. 9,576
Griffiths, John, *Lab., Newport East*, Maj. 5,388
Griffiths, Lesley, *Lab., Wrexham*, Maj. 3,337
Hart, Edwina, *Lab., Gower*, Maj. 4,864
Haworth, Janet, *C, North Wales region*
Hedges, Mike, *Lab., Swansea East*, Maj. 8,281
Hussain, Altaf, *C. South Wales West region*
Hutt, Jane, *Lab., Vale of Glamorgan*, Maj. 3,775
Huws Gruffydd, Llyr, *PC, North Wales region*
Isherwood, Mark, *C, North Wales region*
James, Julie, *Lab., Swansea West*, Maj. 4,654
Jenkins, Bethan, *PC, South Wales West region*
Jones, Alun Ffred, *PC, Arfon*, Maj. 5,394
Jones, Ann, *Lab., Vale of Clwyd*, Maj. 4,011
Jones, Rt. Hon. Carwyn, *Lab., Bridgend*, Maj. 6,775
Jones, Elin, *PC, Ceredigion*, Maj. 1,777
Lewis, Huw, *Lab., Merthyr Tydfil and Rhymney*, Maj. 7,051
Melding, David, *C, South Wales Central region*
Mewies, Sandra, *Lab., Delyn*, Maj. 2,881
Millar, Darren, *C, Clwyd West*, Maj. 4,248
Morgan, Julie, *Lab., Cardiff North*, Maj. 1,782
Neagle, Lynne, *Lab., Torfaen*, Maj. 6,088
Parrott, Eluned, *LD, South Wales Central region*
Powell, William, *LD, Mid and West Wales region*
Price, Gwyn, *Lab., Islwyn*, Maj. 7,589
Ramsay, Nicholas, *C, Monmouth*, Maj. 6,117
Rathbone, Jenny, *Lab., Cardiff Central*, Maj. 38
Rees, David, *Lab., Aberavon*, Maj. 9,311
Roberts, Aled, *LD, North Wales region*
Sargeant, Carl, *Lab., Alyn and Deeside*, Maj. 5,581
Skates, Ken, *Lab., Clwyd South*, Maj. 2,659
Thomas, Gwenda, *Lab., Neath*, Maj. 6,390
Thomas, Rhodri Glyn, *PC, Carmarthen East and Dinefwr*, Maj. 4,148
Thomas, Simon, *PC, Mid and West Wales region*
Watson, Joyce, *Lab., Mid and West Wales region*
Whittle, Lindsay, *PC, South Wales East region*
Williams, Kirsty, *LD, Brecon and Radnorshire*, Maj. 2,757
Wood, Leanne, *PC, South Wales Central region*

STATE OF THE PARTIES
as at 1 September 2015

	Constituency AMs	Regional AMs	AM total
Labour (Lab.)	28*	2	30
Conservative (C.)	6	8†	14
Plaid Cymru (PC)	5	6	11
Liberal Democrats (LD)	1	4	5
Total	40	20	60

* Includes the Presiding Officer
† Includes the Deputy Presiding Officer

NATIONAL ASSEMBLY ELECTION RESULTS
As at 5 May 2011
E. Electorate T. Turnout
See General Election Results for a list of party abbreviations

CONSTITUENCIES
E. 2,289,555 T. 41.5%

ABERAVON (S. WALES WEST)
E. 50,754 T. 18,879 (37.20%)
David Rees, Lab.	12,104
Paul Nicholls-Jones, PC	2,793
Tamojen Morgan, C.	2,704
Helen Ceri Clarke, LD	1,278

Lab. majority 9,311 (49.32%)
8.65% swing PC to Lab.

ABERCONWY (WALES N.)
E. 44,978 T. 20,288 (45.11%)
Janet Finch-Saunders, C.	6,888
Iwan Huws, PC	5,321
Eifion Wyn Williams, Lab.	5,206
Mike Priestley, LD	2,873

C. majority 1,567 (7.72%)
7.95% swing PC to C.

ALYN AND DEESIDE (WALES N.)
E. 61,751 T. 22,769 (36.87%)
Carl Sargeant, Lab.	11,978
John Bell, C.	6,397
Pete Williams, LD	1,725
Shane Brennan, PC	1,710
Michael Whitby, BNP	959

Lab. majority 5,581 (24.51%)
4.29% swing C. to Lab.

ARFON (WALES N.)
E. 41,093 T. 17,664 (42.99%)
Alun Ffred Jones, PC	10,024
Christina Rees, Lab.	4,630
Aled Davies, C.	2,209
Rhys Jones, LD	801

PC majority 5,394 (30.54%)
2.45% swing Lab. to PC

BLAENAU GWENT
(S. WALES EAST)
E. 53,230 T. 20,211 (37.97%)
Alun Davies, Lab.	12,926
Jayne Sullivan, Ind.	3,806
Darren Jones, PC	1,098
Bob Hayward, C.	1,066
Brian Urch, BNP	948
Martin Blakeborough, LD	367

Lab. majority 9,120 (45.12%)
33.95% swing Ind. to Lab.

BRECON AND RADNORSHIRE
(WALES MID AND W.)
E. 53,546 T. 28,348 (52.94%)
Kirsty Williams, LD	12,201
Chris Davies, C.	9,444
Christopher Lloyd, Lab.	4,797
Gary Price, PC	1,906

LD majority 2,757 (9.73%)
4.45% swing LD to C.

BRIDGEND (S. WALES WEST)
E. 59,104 T. 24,035 (40.67%)
Carwyn Jones, Lab.	13,499
Alex Williams, C.	6,724
Tim Thomas, PC	2,076
Briony Davies, LD	1,736

Lab. majority 6,775 (28.19%)
8.89% swing C. to Lab.

CAERPHILLY (S. WALES EAST)
E. 62,049 T. 25,570 (41.21%)
Jeff Cuthbert, Lab.	12,521
Ron Davies, PC	7,597
Owen Meredith, C.	3,368
Kay David, LD	1,062
Anthony King, BNP	1,022

Lab. majority 4,924 (19.26%)
5.25% swing PC to Lab.

CARDIFF CENTRAL
(S. WALES CENTRAL)
E. 64,347 T. 23,628 (36.72%)
Jenny Rathbone, Lab.	8,954
Nigel Howells, LD	8,916
Matt Smith, C.	3,559
Chris Williams, PC	1,690
Mathab Khan, Ind.	509

Lab. majority 38 (0.16%)
14.74% swing LD to Lab.

CARDIFF NORTH
(S. WALES CENTRAL)
E. 66,934 T. 34,431 (51.44%)
Julie Morgan, Lab.	16,384
Jonathan Morgan, C.	14,602
Ben Foday, PC	1,850
Matt Smith, LD	1,595

Lab. majority 1,782 (5.18%)
9.77% swing C. to Lab.

CARDIFF SOUTH AND PENARTH
(S. WALES CENTRAL)
E. 75,038 T. 27,479 (36.62%)
Vaughan Gething, Lab.	13,814
Ben Gray, C.	7,555
Liz Musa, PC	3,324
Sian Cliff, LD	2,786

Lab. majority 6,259 (22.78%)
6.24% swing C. to Lab.

CARDIFF WEST
(S. WALES CENTRAL)
E. 64,219 T. 27,726 (43.17%)
Mark Drakeford, Lab.	13,067
Craig Williams, C.	7,167
Neil McEvoy, PC	5,551
David Morgan, LD	1,942

Lab. majority 5,901 (21.28%)
3.77% C. to Lab.

CARMARTHEN EAST AND
DINEFWR (WALES MID AND W.)
E. 54,243 T. 27,828 (51.30%)
Rhodri Glyn Thomas, PC	12,501
Anthony Jones, Lab.	8,353
Henrietta Hensher, C.	5,635
Will Griffiths, LD	1,339

PC majority 4,148 (14.91%)
7.01% swing PC to Lab.

CARMARTHEN WEST AND
SOUTH PEMBROKESHIRE
(WALES MID AND W.)
E. 58,435 T. 28,156 (48.18%)
Angela Burns, C.	10,095
Christine Gwyther, Lab.	8,591
Nerys Evans, PC	8,373
Selwyn Runnett, LD	1,097

C. majority 1,504 (5.34%)
2.50% swing Lab. to C.

CEREDIGION
(WALES MID AND W.)
E. 56,983 T. 29,076 (51.03%)
Elin Jones, PC	12,020
Liz Evans, LD	10,243
Luke Evetts, C.	2,755
Richard Boudier, Lab.	2,544
Chris Simpson, Green	1,514

PC majority 1,777 (6.11%)
3.51% swing PC to LD

CLWYD SOUTH (WALES N.)
E. 54,499 T. 19,498 (37.59%)
Ken Skates, Lab.	8,500
Paul Rogers, C.	5,841
Mabon ap Gwynfor, PC	3,719
Bruce Roberts, LD	1,977

Lab. majority 2,659 (13.27%)
3.77% swing C. to Lab.

CLWYD WEST (WALES N.)
E. 57,980 T. 25,153 (43.38%)
Darren Millar, C.	10,890
Crispin Jones, Lab.	6,642
Eifion Lloyd Jones, PC	5,775
Brian Cossey, LD	1,846

C. majority 4,248 (16.89%)
5.40% swing Lab. to C.

CYNON VALLEY
(S. WALES CENTRAL)
E. 52,133 T. 18,760 (35.98%)
Christine Chapman, Lab.	11,626
Dafydd Trystan Davies, PC	5,111
Dan Saxton, C.	1,531
Ian Walton, LD	492

Lab. majority 6,515 (34.73%)
2.96% swing PC to Lab.

DELYN (WALES N.)
E. 53,996 T. 23,194 (42.96%)
Sandy Mewies, Lab.	10,695
Matt Wright, C.	7,814
Carrie Harper, PC	2,918
Michele Jones, LD	1,767

Lab. majority 2,881 (12.42%)
5.03% swing C. to Lab.

DWYFOR MEIRONNYDD (WALES MID AND W.)
E. 44,669 T. 20,743 (46.44%)
Dafydd Elis-Thomas, PC	9,656
Simon Baynes, C.	4,239
Louise Hughes, Llais Gwynedd	3,225
Martyn Stuart Singleton, Lab.	2,623
Steven William Churchman, LD	1,000

PC majority 5,417 (26.11%)
6.99% swing PC to C.

GOWER (S. WALES WEST)
E. 61,909 T. 26,773 (43.25%)
Edwina Hart, Lab.	12,866
Caroline Jones, C.	8,002
Darren Price, PC	3,249
Peter May, LD	2,656

Lab. majority 4,864 (18.17%)
6.92% swing C. to Lab.

ISLWYN (S. WALES EAST)
E. 54,893 T. 20,908 (38.09%)
Gwyn Price, Lab.	12,116
Steffan Lewis, PC	4,527
David Chipp, C.	2,497
Peter Whalley, BNP	1,115
Tom Sullivan, LD	653

Lab. majority 7,589 (36.30%)
10.09% swing PC to Lab.

LLANELLI (WALES MID AND W.)
E. 58,838 T. 26,070 (44.31%)
Keith Davies, Lab.	10,359
Helen Mary Jones, PC	10,279
Andrew Morgan, C.	2,880
Sian Caiach, Putting Llanelli First	2,004
Cheryl Philpott, LD	548

Lab. majority 80 (0.31%)
7.19% swing PC to Lab.

MERTHYR TYDFIL AND RHYMNEY (S. WALES EAST)
E. 55,031 T. 19,320 (35.11%)
Huw Lewis, Lab.	10,483
Tony Rogers, Ind.	3,432
Amy Kitcher, LD	2,480
Noel Turner, PC	1,701
Chris O'Brien, C.	1,224

Lab. majority 7,051 (36.50%)
0.14% swing Ind. to Lab.

MONMOUTH (S. WALES EAST)
E. 64,857 T. 30,001 (46.26%)
Nick Ramsay, C.	15,087
Mark Whitcutt, Lab.	8,970
Janet Ellard, LD	2,937
Fiona Cross, PC	2,263
Steve Uncles, Eng. Dem.	744

C. majority 6,117 (20.39%)
4.13% swing C. to Lab.

MONTGOMERYSHIRE (WALES MID AND W.)
E. 48,675 T. 22,933 (47.11%)
Russell George, C.	10,026
Wyn Williams, LD	7,702
Nick Colbourne, Lab.	2,609
David Senior, PC	2,596

C. majority 2,324 (10.13%)
9.50% swing LD to C.

NEATH (S. WALES WEST)
E. 57,533 T. 23,849 (41.45%)
Gwenda Thomas, Lab.	12,736
Alun Llewelyn, PC	6,346
Alex Powell, C.	2,780
Michael Green, BNP	1,004
Mathew McCarthy, LD	983

Lab. majority 6,390 (26.79%)
9.54% swing PC to Lab.

NEWPORT EAST (S. WALES EAST)
E. 55,120 T. 19,460 (35.30%)
John Griffiths, Lab.	9,888
Nick Webb, C.	4,500
Ed Townsend, LD	3,703
Chris Paul, PC	1,369

Lab. majority 5,388 (27.69%)
9.11% swing C. to Lab.

NEWPORT WEST (S. WALES EAST)
E. 63,180 T. 23,014 (36.43%)
Rosemary Butler, Lab.	12,011
David Williams, C.	7,791
Lyndon Binding, PC	1,626
Liz Newton, LD	1,586

Lab. majority 4,220 (18.34%)
6.21% swing C. to Lab.

OGMORE (S. WALES WEST)
E. 55,442 T. 20,264 (36.55%)
Janice Gregory, Lab.	12,955
Danny Clark, PC	3,379
Martyn Hughes, C.	2,945
Gerald Francis, LD	985

Lab. majority 9,576 (47.26%)
6.28% swing PC to Lab.

PONTYPRIDD (S. WALES CENTRAL)
E. 60,028 T. 23,333 (38.87%)
Mick Antoniw, Lab.	11,864
Michael Powell, LD	4,170
Joel James, C.	3,659
Ioan Bellin, PC	3,139
Ken Owen, ND	501

Lab. majority 7,694 (32.97%)
9.28% swing LD to Lab.

PRESELI PEMBROKESHIRE (WALES MID AND W.)
E. 57,758 T. 27,218 (47.12%)
Paul Davies, C.	11,541
Terry Mills (Lab.)	9,366
Rhys Sinnett, PC	4,226
Rob Kilmister, LD	2,085

C. majority 2,175 (7.99%)
1.58% swing C. to Lab.

RHONDDA (S. WALES CENTRAL)
E. 52,532 T. 20,027 (38.12%)
Leighton Andrews, Lab.	12,650
Sarah Evans-Fear, PC	5,911
James Jeffreys, C.	969
George Summers, LD	497

Lab. majority 6,739 (33.65%)
2.77% swing PC to Lab.

SWANSEA EAST (S. WALES WEST)
E. 60,246 T. 18,910 (58.36%)
Mike Hedges, Lab.	11,035
Daniel Boucher, C.	2,754
Dic Jones, PC	2,346
Sam Samuel, LD.	1,673
Joanne Shannon, BNP	1,102

Lab. majority 8,281 (43.79%)
6.05% swing C. to Lab.

SWANSEA WEST (S. WALES WEST)
E. 62,345 T. 21,805 (34.97%)
Julie James, Lab.	9,885
Steve Jenkins, C.	5,231
Rob Speht, LD	3,654
Carl Harris, PC	3,035

Lab. majority 4,654 (21.34%)
4.09% swing C. to Lab.

TORFAEN (S. WALES EAST)
E. 61,126 T. 22,328 (36.53%)
Lynne Neagle, Lab.	10,318
Elizabeth Haynes, Ind.	4,230
Natasha Asghar, C.	3,306
Jeff Rees, PC	2,716
Susan Harwood, BNP	906
Will Griffiths, LD	852

Lab. majority 6,088 (27.27%)
0.52% swing Lab. to Ind.

VALE OF CLWYD (WALES N.)
E. 56,232 T. 23,056 (41.00%)
Ann Jones, Lab.	11,691
Ian Gunning, C.	7,680
Alun Lloyd Jones, PC	2,597
Heather Prydderch, LD	1,088

Lab. majority 4,011 (17.40%)
8.49% swing C. to Lab.

VALE OF GLAMORGAN (S. WALES CENTRAL)
E. 71,602 T. 33,254 (46.80%)
Jane Hutt, Lab.	15,746
Angela Jones-Evans, C.	11,971
Ian Johnson, PC	4,024
Damian Chick, LD	1,513

Lab. majority 3,775 (11.35%)
5.55% swing C. to Lab.

WREXHAM (WALES N.)
E. 53,516 T. 18,687 (34.92%)
Lesley Griffiths, Lab.	8,368
John Marek, C.	5,031
Bill Brereton	2,692
Marc Jones, PC	2,596

Lab. majority 3,337 (17.86%)
3.15% swing C. to Lab.

YNYS MON (WALES N.)
E. 49,431 T. 24,067 (48.69%)
Ieuan Wyn Jones, PC	9,969
Paul Williams, C.	7,032
Joe Lock, Lab.	6,307
Rhys Taylor, LD	759

PC majority 2,937 (12.20%)
7.27% swing PC to C.

REGIONS
E. 2,289,555 T. 41.4%

MID AND WEST WALES
E. 433,147 T. 210,352 (48.56%)

PC	56,384	(26.7%)
C.	52,905	(25.1%)
Lab.	47,348	(22.5%)
LD	26,847	(12.7%)
UKIP	9,211	(4.4%)
Green	8,660	(4.1%)
Soc. Lab.	3,951	(1.9%)
BNP	2,821	(1.3%)
Welsh Christian Party	1,630	(0.8%)
Comm. Brit.	595	(0.3%)

PC majority 3,479 (1.65%)
3.25% swing PC to C. (2007 PC majority 17,652)

ADDITIONAL MEMBERS
Rebecca Evans, *Lab.*   William Powell, *LD*
Joyce Watson, *Lab.*   Simon Thomas, *PC*

NORTH WALES
E. 473,296 T. 194,798 (41.16%)

Lab.	62,677	(32.2%)
C.	52,201	(26.8%)
PC	41,701	(21.4%)
LD	11,507	(5.9%)
UKIP	9,608	(4.9%)
Soc. Lab.	4,895	(2.5%)
BNP	4,785	(2.5%)
Green	4,406	(2.3%)
Welsh Christian Party	1,401	(0.7%)
Ind.	1,094	(0.6%)
Comm. Brit.	523	(0.3%)

Lab. majority 10,476 (5.38%)
5.05% swing PC to Lab. (2007 Lab. majority 1,273)

ADDITIONAL MEMBERS
Mark Isherwood, *C.*   Aled Roberts, *LD*
Antoinette Sandbach, *C.*   Llyr Huws Griffiths, *PC*

SOUTH WALES CENTRAL
E. 506,293 T. 208,333 (41.15%)

Lab.	85,445	(41.0%)
C.	45,751	(22.0%)
PC	28,606	(13.7%)
LD	16,514	(7.9%)
Green	10,774	(5.2%)
UKIP	8,292	(4.0%)
Soc. Lab.	4,690	(2.3%)
BNP	3,805	(1.8%)
Welsh Christian Party	1,873	(0.9%)
Loony	1,237	(0.6%)
TUSC	830	(0.4%)
Comm. Brit.	516	(0.2%)

Lab. majority 39,694 (19.05%)
6.55% swing LD to C. (2007 Lab. majority 25,652)

ADDITIONAL MEMBERS
David Melding, *C.*   Leanne Wood, *PC*
Andrew Davies, *C.*   John Dixon, *LD*

SOUTH WALES EAST
E. 469,486 T. 181,024 (38.56%)

Lab.	82,699	(45.7%)
C.	35,459	(19.6%)
PC	21,851	(12.1%)
LD	10,798	(6.0%)
UKIP	9,526	(5.3%)
BNP	6,485	(3.6%)
Green	4,857	(2.7%)
Soc. Lab.	4,427	(2.4%)
Welsh Christian Party	2,441	(1.3%)
Eng. Dem.	1,904	(1.1%)
Comm. Brit.	578	(0.3%)

Lab. majority 47,240 (26.10%)
5.95% swing LD to Lab. (2007 Lab. majority 30,063)

ADDITIONAL MEMBERS
William Graham, *C.*   Jocelyn Davies, *PC*
Mohammad Asghar, *C.*   Lindsay Whittle, *PC*

SOUTH WALES WEST
E. 407,333 T. 154,381 (37.90%)

Lab.	71,766	(46.5%)
Con.	27,457	(17.8%)
PC	21,258	(13.8%)
LD	10,683	(6.9%)
UKIP	6,619	(4.3%)
Soc. Lab.	5,057	(3.3%)
BNP	4,714	(3.1%)
Green	3,952	(2.6%)
Welsh Christian Party	1,602	(1.0%)
TUSC	809	(0.5%)
Comm. Brit.	464	(0.3%)

Lab. majority 44,309 (28.70%)
8.10% swing LD to Lab. (2007 Lab. majority 29,528)

ADDITIONAL MEMBERS
Suzy Davies, *C.*   Peter Black, *LD*
Byron Davies, *C.*   Bethan Jenkins, *PC*

SCOTLAND

SCOTTISH GOVERNMENT

Andrew's House, Regent Road, Edinburgh EH1 3DG
T 0300-244 4000
E ceu@scotland.gsi.gov.uk W www.gov.scot

The devolved government for Scotland is responsible for most of the issues of day-to-day concern to the people of Scotland, including health, education, justice, rural affairs and transport.

The Scottish government was known as the Scottish executive when it was established in 1999, following the first elections to the Scottish parliament. There has been a majority Scottish National Party administration since the elections in May 2011.

The government is led by a first minister who is nominated by the parliament and in turn appoints the other Scottish ministers who make up the cabinet.

Civil servants in Scotland are accountable to Scottish ministers, who are themselves accountable to the Scottish parliament.

CABINET

First Minister, Rt. Hon. Nicola Sturgeon, MSP
Deputy First Minister and Cabinet Secretary for Finance, Constitution and Economy, John Swinney, MSP
Cabinet Secretary for Infrastructure, Investment and Cities, Keith Brown, MSP
Cabinet Secretary for Culture, Europe and External Affairs, Fiona Hyslop, MSP
Cabinet Secretary for Education and Lifelong Learning, Angela Constance, MSP
Cabinet Secretary for Health and Wellbeing, Shona Robison, MSP
Cabinet Secretary for Rural Affairs and the Environment, Richard Lochhead, MSP
Cabinet Secretary for Justice, Michael Matheson, MSP
Cabinet Secretary for Social Justice, Communities and Pensioners' Rights, Angela Constance, MSP
Cabinet Secretary for Fair Work, Skills and Training, Roseanna Cunningham
Minister for Children and Young People, Aileen Campbell, MSP
Minister for Community Safety and Legal Affairs, Paul Wheelhouse, MSP
Minister for Business, Energy, and Tourism, Fergus Ewing, MSP
Minister for Environment, Climate Change and Land Reform, Aileen McLeod, MSP
Minister for Europe and International Development, Humza Yousaf, MSP
Minister for Housing and Welfare, Margaret Burgess, MSP
Minister for Learning, Science and Scotland's Languages, Alasdair Allan, MSP
Minister for Local Government and Community Empowerment, Marco Biagi, MSP
Minister for Parliamentary Business, Joe Fitzpatrick, MSP
Minister for Public Health, Maureen Watt, MSP
Minister for Transport and Islands, Derek Mackay, MSP
Minister for Youth and Women's Employment, Annabelle Ewing, MSP
Minister for Sport and Health Improvement, Jamies Hepburn, MSP

LAW OFFICERS

Lord Advocate, Frank Mulholland, QC
Solicitor-General for Scotland, Lesley Thomson

STRATEGIC BOARD

Permanent Secretary, Leslie Evans
Director-General Communities, Sarah Davidson
Director-General, Enterprise, Environment and Digital, Graeme Dickson
Director-General, Finance, Alyson Stafford
Director-General, Health and Social Care, Paul Gray
Director-General, Learning and Justice, Paul Johnston
Director-General, Strategy and External Affairs, Ken Thomson

GOVERNMENT DEPARTMENTS

DIRECTOR-GENERAL ENTERPRISE, ENVIRONMENT AND INNOVATION

St Andrew's House, Edinburgh EH1 3DG
Directorates: Agriculture, Food and Rural Affairs; Chief Scientific Adviser for Rural Affairs and the Environment; Chief Economist; Economic Development; Energy and Climate Change; Environment and Forestry; Marine Scotland; Scottish Development International
Director-General, Graeme Dickson
Executive Agencies
Accountant in Bankruptcy
Drinking Water Quality Regulator
James Hutton Institute
Moredun Research Institute
Scottish Agricultural College
Transport Scotland
Waterwatch Scotland

DIRECTOR-GENERAL FINANCE

Victoria Quay, Edinburgh EH6 6QQ
Directorates: Legal Services (Solicitor to the Scottish Government), Financial Management; Financial Strategy; Office of the Scottish Parliamentary Counsel; Scottish Procurement and Commercial; Internal Audit
Director-General, Alyson Stafford
Executive Agencies
Audit Scotland
Scottish Public Pensions Agency

DIRECTOR-GENERAL COMMUNITIES

Saughton House, Broomhouse Drive, Edinburgh, EH11 3XD
Directorates: Digital; Housing, Regeneration and Welfare; Local Government and Communities
Director-General, Sarah Davidson
Executive Agency
Scottish Housing Regulator

DIRECTOR-GENERAL HEALTH AND SOCIAL CARE

St Andrew's House, Regent Road, Edinburgh EH1 3DG
Directorates: Chief Medical Officer; Chief Nursing Officer; Children and Families; Finance, eHealth and Analytics; Health and Social Care Integration; Healthcare Quality and Strategy; Office of the Director-General Health and Social Care and Chief Executive NHS Scotland; Performance and Delivery; Population Health Improvement
Director-General Health and Social Care and Chief Executive NHS Scotland, Paul Gray
Executive Agencies
Disclosure Scotland
Scottish Children's Reporters Administration

DIRECTOR-GENERAL LEARNING AND JUSTICE

St Andrew's House, Edinburgh EH1 3DG

Directorates: Advance Learning and Science; Education Analytical Services; Fair Work; Justice; Learning; Safer Communities
Director-General, Paul Johnston
Executive Agencies
Education Scotland
HM Chief Inspector of Prosecution in Scotland
HM Inspectorate of Constabulary
HM Inspectorate of Prisons
Inspectorate of Prosecution in Scotland
Justices of the Peace Advisory Committee
Scottish Prison Service
Student Awards Agency for Scotland
Visiting Committees for Scottish Penal Establishments

DIRECTOR-GENERAL STRATEGY AND EXTERNAL AFFAIRS
St Andrew's House, Edinburgh EH1 3DG
Directorates: Communications and Ministerial Support; Culture, Europe and External Affairs; People; Strategy and Constitution
Executive Agency
Historic Scotland

NON-MINISTERIAL DEPARTMENTS

FOOD STANDARDS SCOTLAND
Pilgrim House, Old Ford Road, Aberdeen AB11 5RL
T 01224-285100
Chief Executive, Geoff Ogle

NATIONAL RECORDS OF SCOTLAND
General Register House, 2 Princes Street, Edinburgh EH1 3YY
T 0131-535 1314 W www.nationalrecordsofscotland.gov.uk
Registrar General and Keeper of the Records of Scotland, Tim Ellis

OFFICE OF THE SCOTTISH CHARITY REGULATOR
2nd Floor, Quadrant House, 9 Riverside Drive, Dundee DD1 4NY
T 01382-220446 W www.oscr.org.uk
Chief Executive, David Robb

REGISTERS OF SCOTLAND
Meadowbank House, 153 London Road, Edinburgh, Midlothian EH8 7AU T 0845-607 0161 W www.ros.gov.uk
Keeper, Sheenagh Adams

REVENUE SCOTLAND
PO Box 24068, Victoria Quay, Edinburgh EH6 9BR
T 0300-020 0310 W www.revenue.scot
Chief Executive, Eleanor Emberson

SCOTTISH COURTS AND TRIBUNALS SERVICE
Saughton House, Broomhouse Drive, Edinburgh EH11 3XD
T 0131-444 3352 W www.scotcourts.gov.uk
Chief Executive, Eric McQueen

SCOTTISH HOUSING REGULATOR
Highlander House, 58 Waterloo Street, Glasgow G2 7DA
T 0141-271 3810 W www.scottishhousingregulator.gov.uk
Chief Executive, Michael Cameron

SCOTTISH PARLIAMENT
Edinburgh EH99 1SP
T 0131-348 5000/ 0800-092 7500
E sp.info@scottish.parliament.uk
W www.scottish.parliament.uk

In July 1997 the government announced plans to establish a Scottish parliament. In a referendum on 11 September 1997 about 60 per cent of the electorate voted. Of those who voted, 74.3 per cent voted in favour of the parliament and 63.5 per cent voted in support of granting the parliament having tax-raising powers. Elections are normally held every four years, but the current session is scheduled to last five years in order to avoid it falling at the same time as the UK General Election 2015. The first elections were held on 6 May 1999, when around 59 per cent of the electorate voted. The first meeting was held on 12 May 1999 and the Scottish parliament was officially opened on 1 July 1999 at the Assembly Hall, Edinburgh. A new building to house the parliament was opened, in the presence of the Queen, at Holyrood on 9 October 2004. On 5 May 2011 the fourth elections to the Scottish parliament took place.

The Scottish parliament normally 129 members (including the presiding officer), comprising 73 constituency members and 56 additional regional members, mainly from party lists. There are currently 128 members –until the Scottish parliament elections in May 2016 – following the death of Margo MacDonald, who was an independent regional MSP, in 2014. It can introduce primary legislation and has the power to raise or lower the basic rate of income tax by up to three pence in the pound. Members of the Scottish parliament are elected using the additional member system, the same system used to elect London Assembly and Welsh Assembly members.

The areas for which the Scottish parliament is responsible include: civil and criminal justice; education; health; environment; economic development; local government; housing; police; fire services; planning; financial assistance to industry; tourism; heritage and the arts; agriculture; social work; sports; public registers and records; forestry; food standards; and some aspects of transport.

SALARIES *as at 1 April 2015*	
First Minister*	£85,598
Cabinet Secretary	£44,406
Lord Advocate*	£58,013
Solicitor-General for Scotland*	£41,95˙
Minister*	£27,816
MSP†	£59,089
Presiding Officer*	£44,406
Deputy Presiding Officer*	£27,816

* In addition to the MSP salary
† Reduced by two-thirds if the member is also an MP or an MEP

MEMBERS OF THE SCOTTISH PARLIAMENT
as at 1 September 2015
Adam, George, *SNP, Paisley,* Maj. 248
Adamson, Clare, *SNP, Central Scotland region*
Allan, Alasdair, *SNP, Na h-Eileanan an Iar,* Maj. 4,772
Allard, Christian, *SNP, North East Scotland region*
Baillie, Jackie, *Lab., Dumbarton,* Maj. 1,639
Baker, Claire, *Lab., Mid Scotland and Fife region*
Baker, Richard, *Lab., North East Scotland region*
Baxter, Jayne, *Lab., Mid Scotland and Fife region*
Beamish, Claudia, *Lab., South Scotland region*
Beattie, Colin, *SNP, Midlothian North and Musselburgh,* Maj. 2,996
Biagi, Marco, *SNP, Edinburgh Central,* Maj. 237
Bibby, Neil, *Lab., West Scotland region*
Boyack, Sarah, *Lab., Lothian region*
Brodie, Chic, *SNP, South Scotland region*
Brown, Gavin, *C., Lothian region*
Brown, Keith, *SNP, Clackmannanshire and Dunblane,* Maj. 3,609
Buchanan, Cameron, *C., Lothian region*
Burgess, Margaret, *SNP, Cunninghame South,* Maj. 2,348
Campbell, Aileen, *SNP, Clydesdale,* Maj. 4,216
Campbell, Roderick, *SNP, North East Fife,* Maj. 2,592
Carlaw, Jackson, *C., West Scotland region*

Chisholm, Malcolm, *Lab., Edinburgh Northern and Leith,* Maj. 595

Coffey, Willie, *SNP, Kilmarnock and Irvine Valley,* Maj. 5,993

Constance, Angela, *SNP, Almond Valley,* Maj. 5,542

Crawford, Bruce, *SNP, Stirling,* Maj. 5,671

Cunningham, Roseanna, *SNP, Perthshire South and Kinross-shire,* Maj. 7,166

Davidson, Ruth, *C., Glasgow region*

Dey, Graeme, *SNP, Angus South,* Maj. 10,583

Don, Nigel, *SNP, Angus North and Mearns,* Maj. 7,286

Doris, Bob, *SNP, Glasgow region*

Dornan, James, *SNP, Glasgow Cathcart,* Maj. 1,592

Dugdale, Kezia, *Lab., Lothian region*

Eadie, Jim, *SNP, Edinburgh Southern,* Maj. 693

Ewing, Annabelle, *SNP, Mid Scotland and Fife region*

Ewing, Fergus, *SNP, Inverness and Nairn,* Maj. 9,745

Fabiani, Linda, *SNP, East Kilbride,* Maj. 1,949

Fee, Mary, *Lab., West Scotland region*

Ferguson, Patricia, *Lab., Glasgow Maryhill and Springburn,* Maj. 1,252

Fergusson, Rt. Hon. Alex, *C., Galloway and West Dumfries,* Maj. 862

Findlay, Neil, *Lab., Lothian region*

Finnie, John, *Ind., Highlands and Islands region*

FitzPatrick, Joe, *SNP, Dundee City West,* Maj. 6,405

Fraser, Murdo, *C., Mid Scotland and Fife region*

Gibson, Kenneth, *SNP, Cunninghame North,* Maj. 6,117

Gibson, Rob, *SNP, Caithness, Sutherland and Ross,* Maj. 7,458

Goldie, Baroness, *C., West Scotland region*

Grahame, Christine, *SNP, Midlothian South, Tweeddale and Lauderdale,* Maj. 4,924

Grant, Rhoda, *Lab., Highlands and Islands region*

Gray, Iain, *Lab., East Lothian,* Maj. 151

Griffin, Mark, *Lab., Central Scotland region*

Harvie, Patrick, *Green, Glasgow region*

Henry, Hugh, *Lab., Renfrewshire South,* Maj. 2,577

Hepburn, Jamie, *SNP, Cumbernauld and Kilsyth,* Maj. 3,459

Hilton, Cara, *Lab., Dunfermline,* Maj. 2,873

Hume, Jim, *LD, South Scotland region*

Hyslop, Fiona, *SNP, Linlithgow,* Maj. 4,091

Ingram, Adam, *SNP, Carrick, Cumnock and Doon Valley,* Maj. 2,581

Johnstone, Alex, *C., North East Scotland region*

Johnstone, Alison, *Green, Lothian region*

Keir, Colin, *SNP, Edinburgh West,* Maj. 2,689

Kelly, James, *Lab., Rutherglen,* Maj. 1,779

Kidd, Bill, *SNP, Glasgow Anniesland,* Maj. 7

Lamont, Johann, *Lab., Glasgow Pollok,* Maj. 623

Lamont, John, *C., Ettrick, Roxburgh and Berwickshire,* Maj. 5,334

Lochhead, Richard, *SNP, Moray,* Maj. 10,944

Lyle, Richard, *SNP, Central Scotland region*

McAlpine, Joan, *SNP, South Scotland region*

McArthur, Liam, *LD, Orkney,* Maj. 860

MacAskill, Kenny, *SNP, Edinburgh Eastern,* Maj. 2,233

McCulloch, Margaret, *Lab., Central Scotland region*

MacDonald, Angus, *SNP, Falkirk East,* Maj. 3,535

MacDonald, Gordon, *SNP, Edinburgh Pentlands,* Maj. 1,758

Macdonald, Lewis, *Lab., North East Scotland region*

McDonald, Mark, *SNP, Aberdeen Donside,* Maj. 2,025

McDougall, Margaret, *Lab., West Scotland region*

McGrigor, Jamie, *C., Highlands and Islands region*

McInnes, Alison, *LD, North East Scotland region*

Macintosh, Ken, *Lab., Eastwood,* Maj. 2,012

Mackay, Derek, *SNP Renfrewshire North and West,* Maj. 1,564

McKelvie, Christina, *SNP, Hamilton, Larkhall and Stonehouse,* Maj. 2,213

MacKenzie, Mike, *SNP, Highlands and Islands region*

McLeod, Aileen, *SNP, South Scotland region*

McLeod, Fiona, *SNP, Strathkelvin and Bearsden,* Maj. 1,802

McMahon, Michael, *Lab., Uddingston and Bellshill,* Maj. 714

McMahon, Siobhan, *Lab., Central Scotland region*

McMillan, Stuart, *SNP, West Scotland region*

McNeil, Duncan, *Lab., Greenock and Inverclyde,* Maj. 511

McTaggart, Anne, *Lab., Glasgow region*

Malik, Hanzala, *Lab., Glasgow region*

Marra, Jenny, *Lab., North East Scotland region*

Martin, Paul, *Lab., Glasgow Provan,* Maj. 2,079

Marwick, Rt. Hon. Tricia, *SNP, Mid Fife and Glenrothes,* Maj. 4,188

Mason, John, *SNP, Glasgow Shettleston,* Maj. 586

Matheson, Michael, *SNP, Falkirk West,* Maj. 5,745

Maxwell, Stewart, *SNP, West Scotland region*

Milne, Nanette, *C, North East Scotland region*

Mitchell, Margaret, *C, Central Scotland region*

Murray, Elaine, *Lab., Dumfriesshire,* Maj. 3,156

Neil, Alex, *SNP, Airdrie and Shotts,* Maj. 2,001

Paterson, Gil, *SNP, Clydebank and Milngavie,* Maj. 714

Pearson, Graeme, *Lab, South Scotland region*

Pentland, John, *Lab., Motherwell and Wishaw,* Maj. 587

Rennie, Willie, *LD, Mid Scotland and Fife region*

Robertson, Dennis, *SNP, Aberdeenshire West,* Maj. 4,112

Robison, Shona, *SNP, Dundee City East,* Maj. 10,679

Rowley, Alex, *Lab., Cowdenbeath,* Maj. 5,488

Russell, Michael, *SNP, Argyll and Bute,* Maj. 8,543

Salmond, Rt. Hon. Alex, *SNP, Aberdeenshire East,* Maj. 15,295

Scanlon, Mary, *C., Highlands and Islands region*

Scott, John, *C., Ayr,* Maj. 1,113

Scott, Tavish, *LD, Shetland Islands,* Maj. 1,617

Simpson, Richard, *Lab., Mid Scotland and Fife region*

Smith, Drew, *Lab., Glasgow region*

Smith, Elaine, *Lab., Coatbridge and Chryston,* Maj. 2,741

Smith, Liz, *C., Mid Scotland and Fife region*

Stevenson, Stewart, *SNP, Banffshire and Buchan Coast,* Maj. 12,220

Stewart, David, *Lab., Highlands and Islands region*

Stewart, Kevin, *SNP, Aberdeen Central,* Maj. 617

Sturgeon, Nicola, *SNP, Glasgow Southside,* Maj. 4,349

Swinney, John, *SNP, Perthshire North,* Maj. 10,353

Thompson, Dave, *SNP, Skye, Lochaber and Badenoch,* Maj. 4,995

Torrance, David, *SNP, Kirkcaldy,* Maj. 182

Urquhart, Jean, *Ind., Highlands and Islands region*

Watt, Maureen, *SNP, Aberdeen South and North Kincardine,* Maj. 6,323

Wheelhouse, Paul, *SNP, South Scotland region*

White, Sandra, *SNP, Glasgow Kelvin,* Maj. 882

Wilson, John, *Ind., Central Scotland region*

Yousaf, Humza, *SNP, Glasgow region*

STATE OF THE PARTIES
as at 1 September 2015

	Constituency MSPs	Regional MSPs	Total
Scottish National Party (SNP)	51	13	64
Scottish Labour Party (Lab.)	16	22	38
Scottish Conservative and Unionist Party (C.)	3	12	15
Scottish Liberal Democrats (LD)	2	3	5
Scottish Green Party (Green)	0	2	2
Independent (Ind.)	0	3	3
*Presiding Officer	1	0	1
Total	73	55	128

*The presiding officer was elected as a constituency member for the SNP but has no party affiliation while in post

The Presiding Officer, Rt. Hon. Tricia Marwick, MSP
Deputy Presiding Officers, John Scott, MSP *(C.);* Elaine Smith, MSP *(Lab.)*

SCOTTISH PARLIAMENT ELECTION RESULTS
as at 5 May 2011
Electorate (E.) 3,985,161 Turnout (T.) 50.4%
See General Election Results for a list of party abbreviations

ABERDEEN CENTRAL
(Scotland North East Region)
E. 57,396 T. 25,149 (43.82%)
Kevin Stewart, SNP	10,058
Lewis Macdonald, Lab.	9,441
Sandy Wallace, C.	3,100
Sheila Thomson, LD	2,349
Mike Phillips, NF	201

SNP majority 617 (2.45%)
0.54% swing Lab. to SNP

ABERDEEN DONSIDE
(Scotland North East Region)
E. 56,145 T. 26,761 (47.66%)
Brian Adam, SNP	14,790
Barney Crockett, Lab.	7,615
Ross Thomson, C.	2,166
Millie McLeod, LD.	1,606
David Henderson, Ind.	371
Christopher Willett, NF	213

SNP majority 7,175 (26.81%)
6.87% swing Lab. to SNP

ABERDEEN SOUTH & KINCARDINE NORTH
(Scotland North East Region)
E. 54,338 T. 28,697 (52.81%)
Maureen Watt, SNP	11,947
Greg Williams, Lab.	5,624
John Sleigh, LD	4,994
Stewart Whyte, C.	4,058

SNP majority 6,323 (22.03%)
15.77% swing LD to SNP

ABERDEENSHIRE EAST
(Scotland North East Region)
E. 57,591 T. 30,286 (52.59%)
Alex Salmond, SNP	19,533
Alison McInnes, LD	4,238
Geordie Burnett Stuart, C.	4,211
Peter Smyth, Lab.	2,304

SNP majority 15,295 (50.5%)
19.53% swing LD to SNP

ABERDEENSHIRE WEST
(Scotland North East Region)
E. 53,779 T. 28,636 (53.25%)
Dennis Robertson, SNP	12,186
Mike Rumbles, LD	8,074
Nanette Milne, C.	6,027
Jean Morrison, Lab.	2,349

SNP majority 4,112 (14.36%)
13.45% swing LD to SNP

AIRDRIE & SHOTTS
(Scotland Central Region)
E. 51,336 T. 23,894 (46.54%)
Alex Neil, SNP	11,984
Karen Whitefield, Lab.	9,983
Robert Crozier, C.	1,396
John Love, LD	531

SNP majority 2,001 (8.37%)
5.50% swing Lab. to SNP

ALMOND VALLEY
(Lothian Region)
E. 59,896 T. 30,737 (51.32%)
Angela Constance, SNP	16,704
Lawrence Fitzpatrick, Lab.	11,162
Andrew Hardie, C.	1,886
Emma Sykes, LD	656
Neil McIvor, NF	329

SNP majority 5,542 (18.03%)
9.01% swing Lab. to SNP

ANGUS NORTH & MEARNS
(Scotland North East Region)
E. 52,124 T. 24,920 (47.81%)
Nigel Don, SNP	13,660
Alex Johnstone, C.	6,374
Kevin Hutchens, Lab.	3,160
Sanjay Samani, LD	1,726

SNP majority 7,286 (29.24%)
4.15% swing C. to SNP

ANGUS SOUTH
(Scotland North East Region)
E. 54,922 T. 27,643 (50.33%)
Graeme Dey, SNP	16,164
Hughie Campbell Adamson, C.	5,581
William Campbell, Lab.	3,703
David Fairweather, AIR	1,321
Clive Sneddon, LD	874

SNP majority 10,583 (38.28%)
9.31% swing C. to SNP

ARGYLL & BUTE
(Highlands and Islands Region)
E. 49,028 T. 26,476 (54.00%)
Michael Russell, SNP	13,390
Jamie McGrigor, C.	4,847
Mick Rice, Lab.	4,041
Alison Hay, LD	3,220
George Doyle, Ind.	542
George White, Lib.	436

SNP majority 8,543 (32.27%)
8.52% swing C. to SNP

AYR
(Scotland South Region)
E. 61,563 T. 33,373 (54.21%)
John Scott, C.	12,997
Chic Brodie, SNP	11,884
Gordon McKenzie, Lab.	7,779
Eileen Taylor, LD	713

C. majority 1,113 (3.34%)
5.16% swing C. to SNP

BANFFSHIRE & BUCHAN COAST
(Scotland North East Region)
E. 53,698 T. 25,004 (46.56%)
Stewart Stevenson, SNP	16,812
Michael Watt, C.	4,592
Alan Duffill, Lab.	2,642
Galen Milne, LD	958

SNP majority 12,220 (48.87%)
3.48% swing C. to SNP

CAITHNESS, SUTHERLAND & ROSS
(Highlands and Islands Region)
E. 55,116 T. 28,600 (51.89%)
Rob Gibson, SNP	13,843
Robbie Rowantree, LD	6,385
John MacKay, Lab.	5,438
Edward Mountain, C.	2,934

SNP majority 7,458 (26.08%)
17.32% swing LD to SNP

CARRICK, CUMNOCK & DOON VALLEY
(Scotland South Region)
E. 59,368 T. 28,703 (48.35%)
Adam Ingram, SNP	13,250
Richard Leonard, Lab.	10,669
Peter Kennerley, C.	4,160
Andrew Chamberlain, LD	624

SNP majority 2,581 (8.99%)
11.77% swing Lab. to SNP

CLACKMANNANSHIRE & DUNBLANE
(Mid Scotland and Fife Region)
E. 49,415 T. 27,416 (55.48%)
Keith Brown, SNP	13,253
Richard Simpson, Lab.	9,644
Callum Campbell, C.	3,501
Tim Brett, LD	1,018

SNP majority 3,609 (13.16%)
5.20% swing Lab. to SNP

CLYDEBANK & MILNGAVIE
(Scotland West Region)
E. 53,018 T. 28,369 (53.51%)
Gils Paterson, SNP	12,278
Des McNulty, Lab.	11,564
Alice Struthers, C.	2,758
John Duncan, LD	1,769

SD majority 714 (2.52%)
6.56% swing Lab. to SNP

CLYDESDALE
(Scotland South Region)
E. 56,828 T. 29,937 (52.68%)
Aileen Campbell, SNP	14,931
Karen Gillon, Lab.	10,715
Colin McGavigan, C.	4,291

SNP majority 4,216 (14.08%)
8.89% swing Lab. to SNP

COATBRIDGE & CHRYSTON
(Scotland Central Region)
E. 51,206 T. 23,279 (45.46%)
Elaine Smith, Lab.	12,161
John Wilson, SNP	9,420
Jason Lingiah, C.	1,317
Rod Ackland, LD	381

Lab. majority 2,741 (11.77%)
3.28% swing Lab. to SNP

COWDENBEATH
(Mid Scotland and Fife Region)
E. 54,284 T. 25,670 (47.29%)
Helen Eadie, Lab.	11,926
Ian Chisholm, SNP	10,679
Belinda Don, C.	1,792
Keith Legg, LD	997
Mike Heenan, Land Party	276

Lab. majority 1,247 (4.86%)
4.85% swing Lab. to SNP

CUMBERNAULD & KILSYTH
(Scotland Central Region)
E. 48,006 T. 25,254 (52.61%)
Jamie Hepburn, SNP	13,595
Cathie Craigie, Lab.	10,136
James Boswell, C.	1,156
Martin Oliver, LD	367

SNP majority 3,459 (13.7%)
10.79% Lab. to SNP

CUNNINGHAME NORTH
(Scotland West Region)
E. 56,548 T. 29,536 (52.23%)
Kenneth Gibson, SNP	15,539
Allan Wilson, Lab.	9,422
Maurice Golden, C.	4,032
Mallika Punukollu, LD	543

SNP majority 6,117 (20.71%)
10.29% swing Lab. to SNP

CUNNINGHAME SOUTH
(Scotland South Region)
E. 50,926 T. 22,056 (43.31%)
Margaret Burgess, SNP	10,993
Irene Oldfather, Lab.	8,645
Alistair Haw, C.	1,871
Ruby Kirkwood, LD	547

SNP majority 2,348 (10.65%)
9.93% swing Lab. to SNP

DUMBARTON
(Scotland West Region)
E. 53,470 T. 28,508 (53.32%)
Jackie Baillie, Lab.	12,562
Iain Robertson, SNP	10,923
Graham Smith, C.	3,395
Helen Watt, LD	858
George Rice, Ind.	770

Lab. majority 1,639 (5.75%)
0.24% swing SNP to Lab.

DUMFRIESSHIRE
(Scotland South Region)
E. 59,716 T. 31,895 (53.41%)
Elaine Murray, Lab.	12,624
Gill Dykes, C.	9,468
Aileen Orr, SNP	8,384
Richard Brodie, LD	1,419

Lab. majority 3,156 (9.89%)
5.99% swing C. to Lab.

DUNDEE EAST
(Scotland North East Region)
E. 54,404 T. 25,753 (47.34%)
Shona Robison, SNP	16,541
Mohammed Asif, Lab.	5,862
Brian Docherty, C.	2,550
Allan Petrie, LD	800

SNP majority 10,679 (41.47%)
12.47% swing Lab. to SNP

DUNDEE WEST
(Scotland North East Region)
E. 53,841 T. 24,461 (45.43%)
Joe Fitzpatrick, SNP	14,089
Richard McCready, Lab.	7,684
Colin Stewart, C.	1,625
Alison Burns, LD	1,063

SNP majority 6,405 (26.18%)
8.88% swing Lab. to SNP

DUNFERMLINE
(Scotland Mid and Fife Region)
E. 55,479 T. 29,299 (52.81%)
Bill Walker, SNP	11,010
Alex Rowley, Lab.	10,420
Jim Tolson, LD	5,776
James Reekie, C.	2,093

SNP majority 599 (2.01%)
13.41% swing LD to SNP

EAST KILBRIDE
(Scotland Central Region)
E. 58,251 T. 29,911 (51.35%)
Linda Fabiani, SNP	14,359
Andy Kerr, Lab.	12,410
Graham Simpson, C.	2,260
Douglas Herbison, LD	468
John Houston, Ind.	414

SNP majority 1,949 (6.52%)
6.64% swing Lab. to SNP

EAST LOTHIAN
(Scotland South Region)
E. 56,333 T. 32,177 (57.12%)
Iain Gray, Lab.	12,536
David Berry, SNP	12,385
Derek Brownlee, C.	5,344
Ettie Spencer, LD	1,912

Lab. majority 151 (0.47%)
3.12% swing Lab. to SNP

EASTWOOD
(Scotland West Region)
E. 50,476 T. 31,924 (63.25%)
Ken Macintosh, Lab.	12,662
Jackson Carlaw, C.	10,650
Stewart Maxwell, SNP	7,777
Gordon Cochrane, LD	835

Lab. majority 2,012 (6.3%)
8.74% swing C. to Lab.

EDINBURGH CENTRAL
(Lothian Region)
E. 53,606 T. 29,014 (54.12%)
Marco Biagi, SNP	9,480
Sarah Boyack, Lab.	9,243
Alex Cole-Hamilton, LD	5,937
Iain McGill, C.	4,354

SNP majority 237 (0.82%)
10.16% swing Lab. to SNP

EDINBURGH EASTERN
(Lothian Region)
E. 55,773 T. 30,728 (55.09%)
Kenny MacAskill, SNP	14,552
Ewan Aitken, Lab.	12,319
Cameron Buchanan, C.	2,630
Martin Veart, LD	1,227

SNP majority 2,233 (7.27%)
4.53% swing Lab. to SNP

EDINBURGH NORTHERN & LEITH
(Lothian Region)
E. 59,138 T. 30,885 (52.23%)
Malcolm Chisholm, Lab.	12,858
Shirley-Anne Somerville, SNP	12,263
Sheila Low, C.	2,928
Don Farthing, LD	2,836

Lab. majority 595 (1.93%)
2.66% swing Lab. to SNP

EDINBURGH PENTLANDS
(Lothian Region)
E. 52,620 T. 30,049 (57.11%)
Gordon MacDonald, SNP	11,197
David McLetchie, C.	9,439
Ricky Henderson, Lab.	7,993
Simon Clark, LD	1,420

SNP majority 1,758 (5.85%)
7.42% swing C. to SNP

EDINBURGH SOUTHERN
(Lothian Region)
E. 54,868 T. 33,796 (61.60%)
Jim Eadie, SNP	9,947
Paul Godzik, Lab.	9,254
Mike Pringle, LD	8,297
Gavin Brown, C.	6,298

SNP majority 693 (2.05%)
12.06% swing LD to SNP

EDINBURGH WESTERN
(Lothian Region)
E. 56,338 T. 33,452 (59.38%)
Colin Keir, SNP	11,965
Margaret Smith, LD	9,276
Lesley Hinds, Lab.	7,164
Gordon Lindhurst, C.	5,047

SNP majority 2,689 (8.04%)
12.60% swing LD to SNP

ETTRICK, ROXBURGH & BERWICKSHIRE
(Scotland South Region)
E. 54,327 T. 28,816 (53.04%)
John Lamont, C.	12,933
Paul Wheelhouse, SNP	7,599
Euan Robson, LD	4,990
Rab Stewart, Lab.	2,986
Jesse Rae, Ind.	308

C. majority 5,334 (18.51%)
1.39% swing C. to SNP

FALKIRK EAST
(Scotland Central Region)
E. 56,408 T. 28,168 (49.94%)
Angus MacDonald, SNP	14,302
Cathy Peattie, Lab.	10,767
Lynn Munro, C.	2,372
Ross Laird, LD	727

SNP majority 3,535 (12.55%)
9.33% swing Lab. to SNP

FALKIRK WEST
(Scotland Central Region)
E. 55,739 T. 28,199 (50.59%)

Michael Matheson, SNP	15,607
Dennis Goldie, Lab.	9,862
Allan Finnie, C.	2,086
Callum Chomczuk, LD	644

SNP majority 5,745 (20.37%)
8.91% swing Lab. to SNP

FIFE MID & GLENROTHES
(Scotland Mid and Fife Region)
E. 53,701 T. 26,313 (49.0%)

Tricia Marwick, SNP	13,761
Claire Baker, Lab.	9,573
Allan Smith, C.	1,676
Jim Parker, ASPP	673
Callum Leslie, LD	630

SNP majority 4,188 (15.92%)
3.43% swing Lab. to SNP

FIFE NORTH EAST
(Scotland Mid and Fife Region)
E. 58,858 T. 29,676 (50.42%)

Roderick Campbell, SNP	11,029
Iain Smith, LD	8,437
Miles Briggs, C.	5,618
Colin Davidson, Lab.	3,613
Mike Scott-Hayward, UKIP	979

SNP majority 2,592 (8.73%)
15.02% swing LD to SNP

GALLOWAY & WEST DUMFRIES
(Scotland South Region)
E. 56,611 T. 29,997 (52.99%)

Alex Fergusson, C.	11,071
Aileen McLeod, SNP	10,209
Willie Scobie, Lab.	7,954
Joe Rosiejak, LD	763

C. majority 862 (2.87%)
2.40% swing C. to SNP

GLASGOW ANNIESLAND
(Glasgow Region)
E. 55,411 T. 23,918 (43.16%)

Bill Kidd, SNP	10,329
Bill Butler, Lab.	10,322
Matthew Smith, C.	2,011
Paul McGarry, LD	1,000
Marc Livingstone, Comm. Brit.	256

SNP majority 7 (0.03%)
10.09% swing Lab. to SNP

GLASGOW CATHCART
(Glasgow Region)
E. 58,525 T. 26,222 (44.8%)

James Dornan, SNP	11,918
Charlie Gordon, Lab.	10,326
Richard Sullivan, C.	2,410
Eileen Baxendale, LD	1,118
John McKee, Ind.	450

SNP majority 1,592 (6.07%)
6.53% swing Lab. to SNP

GLASGOW KELVIN
(Glasgow Region)
E. 61,893 T. 24,548 (39.66%)

Sandra White, SNP	10,640
Pauline McNeil, Lab.	9,758
Natalie McKee, LD	1,900
Ruth Davidson, C.	1,845
Tom Muirhead, Ind.	405

SNP majority 882 (3.59%)
4.03% swing Lab. to SNP

GLASGOW MARYHILL & SPRINGBURN
(Glasgow Region)
E. 56,622 T. 20,531 (36.26%)

Patricia Ferguson, Lab.	9,884
Bob Doris, SNP	8,592
Stephanie Murray, C.	1,222
Sophie Bridger, LD	833

Lab. majority 1,292 (6.29%)
5.43% swing Lab. to SNP

GLASGOW POLLOK
(Glasgow Region)
E. 58,429 T. 22,915 (39.22%)

Johann Lamont, Lab.	10,875
Chris Stephens, SNP	10,252
Andrew Morrison, C.	1,298
Isabel Nelson, LD	490

Lab. majority 623 (2.72%)
8.53% swing Lab. to SNP

GLASGOW PROVAN
(Glasgow Region)
E. 55,118 T. 19,185 (34.81%)

Paul Martin, Lab.	10,037
Anne McLaughlin, SNP	7,958
Majid Hussain, C.	777
Michael O'Donnell, LD	413

Lab. majority 2,079 (10.84%)
8.68% swing Lab. to SNP

GLASGOW SHETTLESTON
(Glasgow Region)
E. 55,874 T. 21,204 (37.95%)

John Mason, SNP	10,128
Frank McAveety, Lab.	9,542
David Wilson, C.	1,163
Ruaraidh Dobson, LD	371

SNP majority 586 (2.76%)
12.61% swing Lab. to SNP

GLASGOW SOUTHSIDE
(Glasgow Region)
E. 52,325 T. 22,608 (43.21%)

Nicola Sturgeon, SNP	12,306
Stephen Curran, Lab.	7,957
David Meikle, C.	1,733
Kenneth Elder, LD	612

SNP majority 4,349 (19.24%)
9.68% swing Lab. to SNP

GREENOCK & INVERCLYDE
(Scotland West Region)
E. 56,989 T. 28,298 (49.50%)

Duncan McNeil, Lab.	12,387
Stuart McMillan, SNP	11,876
Graeme Brooks, C.	2,011
Ross Finnie, LD	1,934

Lab. majority 511 (1.81%)
6.90% swing Lab. to SNP

HAMILTON, LARKHALL & STONEHOUSE
(Scotland Central Region)
E. 56,123 T. 25,354 (45.18%)

Christina McKelvie, SNP	12,202
Tom McCabe, Lab.	9,989
Margaret Mitchell, C.	2,547
Ewan Hoyle, LD	616

SNP majority 2,213 (8.73%)
10.99% swing Lab. to SNP

INVERNESS & NAIRN
(Highlands and Islands Region)
E. 62,168 T. 32,731 (52.65%)

Fergus Ewing, SNP	16,870
David Stewart, Lab.	7,125
Mary Scanlon, C.	3,797
Christine Jardine, LD	3,763
Donald Boyd, Christian Party	646
Ross Durance, UKIP	530

SNP majority 9,745 (29.77%)
4.85% swing Lab. to SNP

KILMARNOCK & IRVINE VALLEY
(Scotland Central Region)
E. 63,257 T. 31,858 (50.36%)

Willie Coffey, SNP	16,964
Matt McLaughlin, Lab.	10,971
Grant Fergusson, C.	3,309
Robbie Simpson, LD	614

SNP majority 5,993 (18.81%)
7.40% swing Lab. to SNP

KIRKCALDY
(Scotland Mid and Fife Region)
E. 60,079 T. 27,803 (46.28%)

David Torrance, SNP	12,579
Marilyn Livingstone, Lab.	12,397
Ian McFarlane, C.	2,007
John Mainland, LD	820

SNP majority 182 (0.65%)
6.19% swing Lab. to SNP

LINLITHGOW
(Lothian Region)
E. 65,025 T. 34,182 (52.57%)

Fiona Hyslop, SNP	17,027
Mary Mulligan, Lab.	12,936
Christopher Donnelly, C.	2,646
Jennifer Lang, LD	1,015
Mike Coyle, NF	558

SNP majority 4,091 (11.97%)
6.42% swing Lab. to SNP

MIDLOTHIAN NORTH &
MUSSELBURGH
(Lothian Region)
E. 58,246 T. 29,818 (51.19%)

Colin Beattie, SNP	14,079
Bernard Harkins, Lab.	11,083
Scott Douglas, C.	2,541
Ian Younger, LD	1,254
Alan Hay, Ind.	861

SNP majority 2,996 (10.05%)
7.61% swing Lab. to SNP

MIDLOTHIAN SOUTH,
TWEEDDALE & LAUDERDALE
(Lothian Region)
E. 57,781 T. 31,841 (55.11%)

Christine Grahame, SNP	13,855
Jeremy Purvis, LD	8,931
Ian Miller, Lab.	5,312
Peter Duncan, C.	3,743

SNP majority 4,924 (15.46%)
5.87% swing LD to SNP

MORAY
(Highlands and Islands Region)
E. 56,215 T. 28,596 (50.87%)

Richard Lochhead, SNP	16,817
Douglas Ross, C.	5,873
Kieron Green, Lab.	3,580
Jamie Paterson, LD	1,327
Donald Gatt, UKIP	999

SNP majority 10,944 (38.27%)
6.19% swing C. to SNP

MOTHERWELL & WISHAW
(Scotland Central Region)
E. 53,610 T. 24,451 (45.61%)

John Pentland, Lab.	10,713
Clare Adamson, SNP	10,126
Bob Burgess, C.	1,753
John Swinburne, ASPP	945
Tom Selfridge, Christian Party	547
Beverley Hope, LD	367

Lab. majority 587 (2.4%)
10.20% swing Lab. to SNP

NA H-EILEANAN AN IAR
(Highlands and Islands Region)
E. 21,834 T. 13,011 (59.59%)

Alasdair Allan, SNP	8,496
Donald Crichton, Lab.	3,724
Charlie McGrigor, C.	563
Peter Morrison, LD	228

SNP majority 4,772 (36.68%)
15.82% swing Lab. to SNP

ORKNEY
(Highlands and Islands Region)
E. 16,393 T. 8,152 (49.73%)

Liam McArthur, LD	2,912
James Stockan, Ind.	2,052
George Adam, SNP	2,044
Jamie Halcro Johnston, C.	686
William Sharkey, Lab.	458

LD majority 860 (10.55%)
17.70% swing LD to Ind.

PAISLEY
(Scotland West Region)
E. 52,066 T. 25,590 (49.15%)

George Adam, SNP	10,913
Evan Williams, Lab.	10,665
Malcolm MacAskill, C.	2,229
Eileen McCartin, LD	1,783

SNP majority 248 (0.97%)
7.80% swing Lab. to SNP

PERTHSHIRE NORTH
(Scotland and Mid Fife Region)
E. 53,412 T. 29,953 (56.08%)

John Swinney, SNP	18,219
Murdo Fraser, C.	7,866
Pete Cheema, Lab.	2,672
Victor Clements, LD	1,196

SNP majority 10,353 (34.56%)
6.53% swing C. to SNP

PERTHSHIRE SOUTH &
KINROSS-SHIRE
(Scotland and Mid Fife Region)
E. 58,093 T. 31,216 (53.73%)

Roseanna Cunningham, SNP	16,073
Liz Smith, C.	8,907
Tricia Duncan, Lab.	3,980
Willie Robertson, LD	2,256

SNP majority 7,166 (22.96%)
9.25% swing C. to SNP

RENFREWSHIRE NORTH & WEST
(Scotland West Region)
E. 49,060 T. 27,495 (56.04%)

Derek Mackay, SNP	11,510
Stuart Clark, Lab.	9,946
Annabel Goldie, C.	5,489
Andrew Page, LD	550

SNP majority 1,564 (5.69%)
8.42% swing Lab. to SNP

RENFREWSHIRE SOUTH
(Scotland West Region)
E. 50,221 T. 26,908 (53.58%)

Hugh Henry, Lab.	12,933
Andrew Doig, SNP	10,356
Alistair Campbell, C.	2,917
Gordon Anderson, LD	702

Lab. majority 2,577 (9.58%)
5.41% swing Lab. to SNP

RUTHERGLEN
(Glasgow Region)
E. 57,777 T. 27,122 (46.94%)

James Kelly, Lab.	12,489
Jim McGuigan, SNP	10,710
Martyn McIntyre, C.	2,096
Lisa Strachan, LD	1,174
Caroline Johnstone, Ind.	633

Lab. majority 1,779 (6.56%)
7.43% swing Lab. to SNP

SHETLAND ISLANDS
(Highlands and Islands Region)
E. 17,505 T. 9,391 (53.65%)

Tavish Scott, LD	4,462
Billy Fox, Ind.	2,845
Jean Urquhart, SNP	1,134
Jamie Kerr, Lab.	620
Sandy Cross, C.	330

LD majority 1,617 (17.22%)
5.5% swing LD to Ind.

SKYE, LOCHABER & BADENOCH
(Highlands and Islands Region)
E. 57,024 T. 31,915 (55.97%)

Dave Thompson, SNP	14,737
Alan MacRae, LD	9,742
Linda Stewart, Lab.	4,112
Kerensa Carr, C.	2,834
Ronnie Campbell, Ind.	490

SNP majority 4,995 (15.65%)
12.97% swing LD to SNP

STIRLING
(Scotland and Mid Fife Region)
E. 51,458 T. 30,406 (59.09%)

Bruce Crawford, SNP	14,859
John Hendry, Lab.	9,188
Neil Benny, C.	4,610
Graham Reed, LD	1,296
Jack Black, Ind.	454

SNP majority 5,671 (18.65%)
9.93% swing Lab. to SNP

STRATHKELVIN & BEARSDEN
(Scotland West Region)
E. 59,323 T. 33,752 (56.90%)

Fiona McLeod, SNP	14,258
David Whitton, Lab.	12,456
Jean Turner, Ind.	6,742
Stephanie Fraser, C.	4,438
Gordon Macdonald, LD	2,600

SNP majority 1,802 (5.34%)
7.69% swing Lab. to SNP

UDDINGSTON & BELLSHILL
(Central Scotland Region)
E. 55,584 T. 24,995 (44.97%)

Michael McMahon, Lab.	11,531
Richard Lyle, SNP	10,817
Mark Brown, C.	2,117
Fraser Macgregor, LD	530

Lab majority 714 (2.86%)
9.04% swing Lab. to SNP

REGIONS
E. 3,985,161 T. 50.4%

GLASGOW
E. 514,393 T. 208,712 (40.57%)

SNP	83,109	(39.8%)
Lab.	73,031	(35.0%)
C.	12,749	(6.1%)
Green	12,454	(6.0%)
Respect	6,972	(3.3%)
LD	5,312	(2.5%)
ASPP	3,750	(1.8%)
BNP	2,424	(1.2%)
Socialist Labour	2,276	(1.1%)
Christian Party	1,501	(0.7%)
Scottish Unionist Party	1,447	(0.7%)
SSP	1,362	(0.7%)
UKIP	1,123	(0.5%)
Pirate	581	(0.3%)
Ind. Johnstone	338	(0.2%)
SHP	283	(0.1%)

Lab. majority 10,078 (4.83%)
8.04% swing Lab. to SNP (2007 Lab. majority 23,006)

ADDITIONAL MEMBERS
Humza Yousaf, SNP
Bob Doris, SNP
Hanzala Malik, Lab.
Drew Smith, Lab.
Anne McTaggert, Lab.
Ruth Davidson, C.
Patrick Harvie, Green

HIGHLANDS AND ISLANDS
E. 337,588 T. 179,010 (53.03%)

SNP	85,082	(47.5%)
Lab.	25,884	(14.5%)
C.	21,729	(12.1%)
LD	20,843	(11.6%)
Green	9,076	(5.1%)
Christian Party	3,541	(2%)
UKIP	3,372	(1.9%)
ASPP	2,770	(1.5%)
Ban Bankers Bonuses	1,764	(1%)
Lib.	1,696	(0.9%)
Soc. Lab.	1,406	(0.8%)
BNP	1,134	(0.6%)
SSP	509	(0.3%)
Solidarity	204	(0.1%)

SNP majority 59,198 (33.07%)
8.16% swing Lab. to SNP (2007 SNP majority 26,978)

ADDITIONAL MEMBERS
John Finnie, SNP
Jean Urquhart, SNP
Mike MacKenzie, SNP
Rhoda Grant, Lab.
David Stewart, Lab.
Jamie McGrigor, C.
Mary Scanlon, C.

LOTHIAN
E. 515,978 T. 283,203 (54.89%)

SNP	110,953	(39.2%)
Lab.	70,544	(24.9%)
C.	33,019	(11.7%)
Green	21,505	(7.6%)
Ind. MacDonald	18,732	(6.6%)
LD	15,588	(5.5%)
ASPP	3,218	(1.1%)
BNP	1,978	(0.7%)
UKIP	1,822	(0.6%)
Soc. Lab.	1,681	(0.6%)
SSP	1,183	(0.4%)
Christian Party	914	(0.3%)
Lib.	697	(0.2%)
CPA	553	(0.2%)
Solidarity	327	(0.1%)
Ind. Hogg	294	(0.1%)
Ind. O'Neill	134	(0.1%)
Ind. Brown	61	(0.1%)

SNP majority 40,409 (14.27%)
7.0% swing Lab. to SNP (2007 SNP majority 524)

ADDITIONAL MEMBERS
Sarah Boyack, Lab.
Kezia Dugdale, Lab.
Neil Findlay, Lab.
David McLetchie, C.
Gavin Brown, C.
Alison Johnstone, Green
Margo MacDonald, Ind.

SCOTLAND CENTRAL
E. 497,737 T. 233,560 (46.92%)

SNP	108,261	(46.4%)
Lab.	82,459	(35.3%)
C.	14,870	(6.4%)
ASPP	5,793	(2.5%)
Green	5,634	(2.4%)
LD	3,318	(1.4%)
Christian Party	3,173	(1.4%)
Soci. Lab.	2,483	(1.1%)
BNP	2,214	(0.9%)
Scottish Unionist Party	1,555	(0.7%)
UKIP	1,263	(0.5%)
Ind. O'Donnell	821	(0.4%)
SSP	820	(0.4%)
Solidarity	559	(0.2%)
SHP	337	(0.1%)

Lab. majority 25,802 (11.05%)
10.08% swing Lab. to SNP (2007 Lab. majority 23,386)

ADDITIONAL MEMBERS
Richard Lyle, SNP
John Wilson, SNP
Clare Adamson, SNP
Siobhan McMahon, Lab.
Mark Griffin, Lab.
Margaret McCulloch, Lab.
Margaret Mitchell, C.

SCOTLAND MID AND FIFE
E. 503,559 T. 258,163 (51.27%)

SNP	116,691	(45.2%)
Lab.	64,623	(25.0%)
C.	36,458	(14.1%)
LD	15,103	(5.9%)
Green	10,914	(4.2%)
ASPP	4,113	(1.6%)
UKIP	2,838	(1.1%)
Soc. Lab.	1,771	(0.7%)
BNP	1,726	(0.7%)
Ind. Rodger	1,466	(0.6%)
SSP	834	(0.3%)
Christian Party	786	(0.3%)
CPA	638	(0.2%)
Solidarity	202	(0.1%)

SNP majority 52,068 (10.9%)
7.43% swing Lab. to SNP (2007 Lab. majority 18,168)

ADDITIONAL MEMBERS
Annabelle Ewing, *SNP*
John Park, *Lab.*
Claire Baker, *Lab.*
Richard Simpson, *Lab.*
Murdo Fraser, *C.*
Liz Smith, *C.*
Willie Rennie, *LD*

SCOTLAND NORTH EAST
E. 550,162 T. 267,045 (48.54%)

SNP	140,749	(52.7%)
Lab.	43,893	(16.4%)
C.	37,681	(14.1%)
LD	18,178	(6.8%)
Green	10,407	(3.9%)
ASPP	4,420	(1.7%)
UKIP	2,477	(0.9%)
Christian Party	2,159	(0.8%)
BNP	1,925	(0.7%)
Soc. Lab.	1,459	(0.5%)
Ind. Cox	758	(0.3%)
NF	640	(0.2%)
AIR	471	(0.2%)
Solidarity	286	(0.1%)
Ind. Henderson	237	(0.1%)
Ind. McBride	190	(0.1%)

SNP majority 96,856 (36.27%)
7.68% swing Lab. to SNP (2007 SNP majority 53,140)

ADDITIONAL MEMBERS
Mark McDonald, *SNP*
Richard Baker, *Lab.*
Jenny Marra, *Lab.*
Lewis McDonald, *Lab.*
Alex Johnstone, *C.*
Nanette Milne, *C.*
Alison McInnes, *LD*

SCOTLAND SOUTH
E. 529,682 T. 278,987 (52.67%)

SNP	114,270	(41.0%)
Lab.	70,595	(25.3%)
C.	54,352	(19.5%)
LD	15,096	(5.4%)
Green	8,656	(3.1%)
ASPP	4,418	(1.6%)
UKIP	3,243	(1.2%)
Soc. Lab.	2,906	(1.0%)
BNP	2,017	(0.7%)
Christian Party	1,924	(0.7%)
Solidarity	813	(0.3%)
SSP	697	(0.2%)

SNP majority 43,675 (15.66%)
7.95% swing Lab. to SNP (2007 Lab. majority 2,709)

ADDITIONAL MEMBERS
Joan McAlpine, *SNP*
Aileen McLeod, *SNP*
Paul Wheelhouse, *SNP*
Chic Brodie, *SNP*
Claudia Beamish, *Lab.*
Graeme Pearson, *Lab.*
Jim Hume, *LD*

SCOTLAND WEST
E. 536,062 T. 282,371 (52.68%)

SNP	117,306	(41.5%)
Lab.	92,530	(32.8%)
C.	35,995	(12.7%)
LD	9,148	(3.2%)
Green	8,414	(3.0%)
ASPP	4,771	(1.7%)
Soc. Lab.	2,865	(1.0%)
Christian Party	2,468	(0.9%)
BNP	2,162	(0.8%)
UKIP	2,000	(0.7%)
SSP	1,752	(0.6%)
Ban Bankers Bonuses	1,204	(0.4%)
Pirate	850	(0.3%)
Ind. Vassie	460	(0.2%)
Solidarity	446	(0.2%)

SNP majority 24,776 (8.77%)
7.4% swing Lab. to SNP (2007 Lab. majority 15,772)

ADDITIONAL MEMBERS
Stewart Maxwell, *SNP*
Stuart McMillan, *SNP*
Mary Fee, *Lab.*
Neil Bibby, *Lab.*
Margaret McDougall, *Lab.*
Annabel Goldie, *C.*
Jackson Carlaw, *C.*

THE SCOTTISH REFERENDUM

THE ROAD TO REFERENDUM

Following the establishment of a majority Scottish National Party (SNP) government at Holyrood in May 2011, the SNP officially launched its independence bid at its annual party conference in October the same year. In May 2012 the UK government published the results of the Scottish referendum consultation, which showed strong levels of support for a single clear question on independence. On 25 May 2012 the 'Yes Scotland' campaign launched with the aim of encouraging 1 million Scots to sign a declaration of independence prior to a referendum.

THE EDINBURGH AGREEMENT
A series of talks between the Scottish government's deputy first minister Nicola Sturgeon and the Secretary of State for Scotland Michael Moore resulted in the Edinburgh Agreement. The agreement was signed by prime minister David Cameron and first minister Alex Salmond on 15 October 2012 and set out a timetable for a referendum vote to be held in autumn 2014.

SHOULD SCOTLAND BE AN INDEPENDENT COUNTRY?
On 30 January 2013 the wording of the independence referendum question was finalised as a simple yes/no question: 'Should Scotland be an independent country?'

THOSE AGED 16 GET TO VOTE
On 12 March 2013 the Scottish independence referendum (franchise) bill was brought before parliament to ensure that all those aged 16 and over on the date of the referendum were entitled to vote.

THE DATE IS SET
On the 21 March 2013 the date of the referendum was revealed as 18 September 2014. On 26 November 2013 Alex Salmond launched his government's independence blueprint, a 667-page white paper entitled *Scotland's Future: Your guide to an independent Scotland*. On 13 February 2014 the UK Chancellor of the Exchequer, George Osborne ruled out a formal currency union in the event of independence. The formal 16-week campaign period, during which the amount of money registered campaigners can spend was limited, began at the start of May 2014.

REFERENDUM RESULTS *18 September 2014*

SHOULD SCOTLAND BE AN INDEPENDENT COUNTRY?

NO	YES
2,001,926 votes	1,617,989 votes
(55.3%)	(44.7%)
Turnout 84.6%	

PERCENTAGE OF VOTE BY REGION
Only four of the 32 Scottish local authority areas voted in favour of independence: Dundee City, Glasgow, North Lanarkshire and West Dunbartonshire.

Local Authority Area	No (%)	Yes (%)
Aberdeen City	58.6	41.4
Aberdeenshire	60.4	39.6
Angus	56.3	43.7
Argyll and Bute	58.5	41.5
Clackmannanshire	53.8	46.2
Dumfries and Galloway	65.7	34.3
Dundee City	42.7	57.3
East Ayrshire	52.8	47.2
East Dunbartonshire	61.2	38.8
East Lothian	61.7	38.3
East Renfrewshire	63.2	36.8
Edinburgh City	61.1	38.9
Falkirk	53.5	46.5
Fife	55.0	45.0
Glasgow City	46.5	53.5
Highland	52.9	47.1
Inverclyde	50.1	49.9
Midlothian	56.3	43.7
Moray	57.6	42.4
North Ayrshire	51.0	49.0
North Lanarkshire	48.9	51.1
Orkney	67.2	32.8
Perth and Kinross	60.2	39.8
Renfrewshire	52.8	47.2
Scottish Borders	66.6	33.4
Shetland	63.7	36.3
South Ayrshire	57.9	42.1
South Lanarkshire	54.7	45.3
Stirling	59.8	40.2
West Dunbartonshire	46.0	54.0
Western Isles (Eilean Siar)	53.4	46.5
West Lothian	55.2	44.3

NORTHERN IRELAND

NORTHERN IRELAND EXECUTIVE
Stormont Castle, Stormont, Belfast BT4 3TT
T 028-9052 8400
W www.northernireland.gov.uk

The first minister and deputy first minister head the executive committee of ministers and, acting jointly, determine the total number of ministers in the executive. First and deputy first ministers are elected by Northern Ireland assembly members through a formula of parallel consent that requires a majority of designated unionists, a majority of designated nationalists and a majority of the whole assembly to vote in favour. The parties elected to the assembly select ministerial portfolios in proportion to party strengths using the d'Hondt nominating procedure.

The executive committee includes five DUP ministers, four SF ministers, two Alliance members, one Social Democratic and Labour Party minister and one Ulster Unionist minister alongside the acting first minister Arlene Foster, MLA of the DUP and the deputy first minister, Martin McGuinness, MLA, of SF.

EXECUTIVE COMMITTEE
Acting First Minister, Arlene Foster, MLA
Deputy First Minister, Martin McGuinness, MLA
Junior Ministers, Jennifer McCann, MLA; Michelle McIlveen, MLA
Minister for Agriculture and Rural Development, Michelle O'Neill, MLA
Minister for Culture, Arts and Leisure, Carál Ní Chuilín, MLA
Minister for Education, John O'Dowd, MLA
Minister for Employment and Learning, Dr Stephen Farry, MLA
Minister for Enterprise, Trade and Investment, Jonathan Bell, MLA
Minister for Environment, Mark Durkan, MLA
Minister for Finance and Personnel, Arlene Foster, MLA
Minister for Health, Social Services and Public Safety, Simon Hamilton, MLA
Minister for Justice, David Ford, MLA
Minister for Regional Development, vacant
Minister for Social Development, Mervyn Storey, MLA

OFFICE OF THE FIRST MINISTER AND DEPUTY FIRST MINISTER
Stormont Castle, Stormont, Belfast BT4 3TT
T 028-9052 8400 W www.ofmdfmni.gov.uk

DEPARTMENT OF AGRICULTURE AND RURAL DEVELOPMENT
Dundonald House, Upper Newtownards Road, Belfast BT4 3SB
T 028-9052 0100 W www.dardni.gov.uk

EXECUTIVE AGENCIES
Forest Service
Rivers Agency

DEPARTMENT OF CULTURE, ARTS AND LEISURE
Causeway Exchange, 1–7 Bedford Street, Belfast BT1 7FB
T 028-9025 8825 W www.dcalni.gov.uk

DEPARTMENT OF EDUCATION
Rathgael House, Balloo Road, Bangor, Co. Down BT19 7PR
T 028-9127 9279 W www.deni.gov.uk

DEPARTMENT FOR EMPLOYMENT AND LEARNING
Adelaide House, 39–49 Adelaide Street, Belfast BT2 8FD
T 028-9025 7777 W www.delni.gov.uk

DEPARTMENT OF ENTERPRISE, TRADE AND INVESTMENT
Netherleigh, Massey Avenue, Belfast BT4 2JP T 028-9052 9900
W www.detini.gov.uk

DEPARTMENT OF THE ENVIRONMENT
Goodwood House, 45–58 May Street, Belfast BT1 4NN
W www.doeni.gov.uk

EXECUTIVE AGENCIES
Driver and Vehicle Agency (DVA)
NI Environment Agency (NIEA)

DEPARTMENT OF FINANCE AND PERSONNEL
Rathgael House, Balloo Road, Bangor BT19 7NA T 028-9185 8111
W www.dfpni.gov.uk

EXECUTIVE AGENCIES
Northern Ireland Statistics and Research Agency (NISRA)

DEPARTMENT OF HEALTH, SOCIAL SERVICES AND PUBLIC SAFETY
Castle Buildings, Stormont, Belfast BT4 3SJ T 028-9052 0500
W www.dhsspsni.gov.uk

DEPARTMENT OF JUSTICE
Block B, Castle Buildings, Stormont Estate, Belfast BT4 3SG
T 028-9076 3000 W www.dojni.gov.uk

EXECUTIVE AGENCIES
Forensic Service Northern Ireland
Legal Services Agency
Northern Ireland Courts and Tribunals Service
Northern Ireland Prison Service
Youth Justice Agency

DEPARTMENT FOR REGIONAL DEVELOPMENT
Clarence Court, 10–18 Adelaide Street, Belfast BT2 8GB
T 028-9054 0540 W www.drdni.gov.uk

DEPARTMENT FOR SOCIAL DEVELOPMENT
Lighthouse Building, 1 Cromac Place, Gasworks Business Park, Ormeau Road, Belfast BT7 2JB T 028-9082 9000
W www.dsdni.gov.uk

EXECUTIVE AGENCIES
Northern Ireland Central Investment Fund for Charities

NORTHERN IRELAND AUDIT OFFICE
106 University Street, Belfast BT7 1EU
T 028-9025 1000 E info@niauditoffice.gov.uk
W www.niauditoffice.gov.uk
Comptroller and Auditor-General, Kieran Donnelly

NORTHERN IRELAND AUTHORITY FOR UTILITY REGULATION
Queens House, 14 Queen Street, Belfast BT1 6ED
T 028-9031 1575 E info@uregni.gov.uk W www.uregni.gov.uk
Chair, Dr Bill Emery

NORTHERN IRELAND ASSEMBLY

Parliament Buildings, Stormont, Belfast BT4 3XX
T 028-9052 1137 E info@niassembly.gov.uk
W www.niassembly.gov.uk

The Northern Ireland Assembly was established as a result of the Belfast Agreement (also known as the Good Friday Agreement) in April 1998. The agreement was endorsed through a referendum held in May 1998 and subsequently given legal force through the Northern Ireland Act 1998.

The Northern Ireland Assembly has full legislative and executive authority for all matters that are the responsibility of the government's Northern Ireland departments – known as transferred matters. Excepted and reserved matters are defined in schedules 2 and 3 of the Northern Ireland Act 1998 and remain the responsibility of UK parliament.

The first assembly election occurred on 25 June 1998 and the 108 members elected met for the first time on 1 July 1998. Members of the Northern Ireland Assembly are elected by the single transferable vote system from 18 constituencies – six per constituency. Under the single transferable vote system every voter has a single vote that can be transferred from one candidate to another. Voters number their candidates in order of preference. Where candidates reach their quota of votes and are elected, surplus votes are transferred to other candidates according to the next preference on each voter's ballot slip. The candidate in each round with the fewest votes is eliminated and their surplus votes are redistributed according to the voter's next preference. The process is repeated until the required number of members are elected.

On 29 November 1999 the assembly appointed ten ministers as well as the chairs and deputy chairs for the ten statutory departmental committees. Devolution of powers to the Northern Ireland Assembly occurred on 2 December 1999, following several delays concerned with Sinn Fein's inclusion in the executive while Irish Republican Army (IRA) weapons were yet to be decommissioned.

Since the devolution of powers, the assembly has been suspended by the Secretary of State for Northern Ireland on four occasions. The first was between 11 February and 30 May 2000, with two 24-hour suspensions on 10 August and 22 September 2001 – all owing to a lack of progress in decommissioning. The final suspension took place on 14 October 2002 after unionists walked out of the executive following a police raid on Sinn Fein's office investigating alleged intelligence gathering.

The assembly was formally dissolved in April 2003 in anticipation of an election, which eventually took place on 26 November 2003. The results of the election changed the balance of power between the political parties, with an increase in the number of seats held by the Democratic Unionist Party (DUP) and Sinn Fein (SF), so that they became the largest parties. The assembly was restored to a state of suspension following the November election while political parties engaged in a review of the Belfast Agreement aimed at fully restoring the devolved institutions.

In July 2005 the leadership of the IRA formally ordered an end to its armed campaign; it authorised a representative to engage with the Independent International Commission on Decommissioning in order to verifiably put the arms beyond use. On 26 September 2005 General John de Chastelain, the chair of the commission, along with two independent church witnesses confirmed that the IRA's entire arsenal of weapons had been decommissioned.

Following the passing of the Northern Ireland Act 2006 the secretary of state created a non-legislative fixed-term assembly, whose membership consisted of the 108 members elected in the 2003 election. It first met on 15 May 2006 with the remit of making preparations for the restoration of devolved government; its discussions informed the next round of talks called by the British and Irish governments held at St Andrews. The St Andrews agreement of 13 October 2006 led to the establishment of the transitional assembly.

The Northern Ireland (St Andrews Agreement) Act 2006 set out a timetable to restore devolution, and also set the date for the third election to the assembly as 7 March 2007. The DUP and SF again had the largest number of Members of the Legislative Assembly (MLAs) elected, and although the initial restoration deadline of 26 March was missed, the leaders of the DUP and SF (Revd Dr Ian Paisley, MP, MLA and Gerry Adams, MLA, respectively) took part in a historic meeting and made a joint commitment to establish an executive committee in the assembly to which devolved powers were restored on 8 May 2007. After completing a full four-year mandate, new assembly elections took place on 5 May 2011 to elect the 108 members of the legislative assembly.

SALARIES	
	2015–16
First Minister/Deputy First Minister	£120,000
Minister	£86,000
MLA	£48,000

NORTHERN IRELAND ASSEMBLY MEMBERS

* Previously MLA for another party
as at June 2015

Agnew, Steven, *Green, North Down*
Allister, Jim, *TUV, North Antrim*
Anderson, Sydney, *DUP, Upper Bann*
Attwood, Alex, *SDLP, Belfast West*
Beggs, Roy, *UUP, East Antrim*
Bell, Jonathan, *DUP, Strangford*
Boylan, Cathal, *SF, Newry and Armagh*
Boyle, Michaela, *SF, West Tyrone*
Bradley, Dominic, *SDLP, Newry and Armagh*
Bradley, Paula, *DUP, Belfast North*
Brady, Mickey, *SF, Newry and Armagh*
Buchanan, Thomas, *DUP, West Tyrone*
Byrne, Joe, *SDLP, West Tyrone*
Cameron, Pam, *DUP, South Antrim*
Campbell, Gregory, *DUP, East Londonderry*
Clarke, Trevor, *DUP, South Antrim*
Cochrane, Judith, *Alliance, Belfast East*
Copeland, Michael, *UUP, Belfast East*
Craig, Jonathan, *DUP, Lagan Valley*
Cree, Leslie, *UUP, North Down*
Dallat, John, *SDLP, East Londonderry*
Dickson, Stewart, *Alliance, East Antrim*
Dobson, Jo-Anne, *UUP, Upper Bann*
Douglas, Sammy, *DUP, Belfast East*
Dunne, Gordon, *DUP, North Down*
Durkan, Mark, *SDLP, Foyle*
Easton, Alex, *DUP, North Down*
Eastwood, Colum, *SDLP, Foyle*
Elliot, Tom, *UUP, Fermanagh and South Tyrone*
Farry, Stephen, *Alliance, North Down*
Fearon, Megan, *SF, Newry and Armagh*
Flanagan, Phil, *SF, Fermanagh and South Tyrone*
Ford, David, *Alliance, South Antrim*
Foster, Arlene, *DUP, Fermanagh and South Tyrone*
Frew, Paul, *DUP, North Antrim*
Gardiner, Samuel, *UUP, Upper Bann*
Girvan, Paul, *DUP, South Antrim*
Givan, Paul, *DUP, Lagan Valley*

Hale, Brenda, *DUP, Lagan Valley*
Hamilton, Simon, *DUP, Strangford*
Hazzard, Chris, *SF, South Down*
Hilditch, David, *DUP, East Antrim*
Humphrey, William, *DUP, Belfast North*
Hussey, Ross, *UUP, West Tyrone*
Irwin, William, *DUP, Newry and Armagh*
Kelly, Dolores, *SDLP, Upper Bann*
Kelly, Gerry, *SF, Belfast North*
Kennedy, Danny, *UUP, Newry and Armagh*
Kinahan, Danny, *UUP, South Antrim*
Lo, Anna, *Alliance, Belfast South*
Lunn, Trevor, *Alliance, Lagan Valley*
Lynch, Sean, *SF, Fermanagh and South Tyrone*
Lyttle, Chris, *Alliance, Belfast East*
Maginness, Alban, *SDLP, Belfast North*
Maskey, Alex, *SF, Belfast South*
McAleer, Declan, *SF, West Tyrone*
*McCallister, John, *NI21, South Down*
McCann, Fra, *SF, Belfast West*
McCann, Jennifer, *SF, Belfast West*
McCarthy, Kieran, *Alliance, Strangford*
McCartney, Raymond, *SF, Foyle*
McCausland, Nelson, *DUP, Belfast North*
McCorley, Rosaleen, *SF, Belfast West*
*McCrea, Basil, *NI21, Lagan Valley*
McCrea, Ian, *DUP, Mid Ulster*
McDonnell, Dr Alasdair, *SDLP, Belfast South*
McElduff, Barry, *SF, West Tyrone*
McGahan, Bronwyn, *SF, Fermanagh and South Tyrone*
McGimpsey, Michael, *UUP, Belfast South*
McGlone, Patsy, *SDLP, Mid Ulster*
McGuinness, Martin, *SF, Mid Ulster*
McIlveen, David, *DUP, North Antrim*
McIlveen, Michelle, *DUP, Strangford*
McKay, Daithi, *SF, North Antrim*
McKevitt, Karen, *SDLP, South Down*
McKinney, Fearghal, *SDLP, Belfast South*
McLaughlin, Maeve, *SF, Foyle*
McLaughlin, Mitchel, *SF, South Antrim*
McMullan, Oliver, *SF, East Antrim*
*McNarry, David, *UKIP, Strangford*
McQuillan, Adrian, *DUP, East Londonderry*

Middleton, **Gary,** *DUP, Foyle*
Milne, Ian, *SF, Mid Ulster*
Morrow, Lord, *DUP, Fermanagh and South Tyrone*
Moutray, Stephen, *DUP, Upper Bann*
Murphy, Conor, *SF, Newry and Armagh*
Nesbitt, Mike, *UUP, Strangford*
Newton, Robin, *DUP, Belfast East*
Ni Chuilin, Caral, *SF, Belfast North*
O'Dowd, John, *SF, Upper Bann*
O'Neill, Michelle, *SF, Mid Ulster*
O hOisin, Cathal, *SF, East Londonderry*
Overend, Sandra, *UUP, Mid Ulster*
Poots, Edwin, *DUP, Lagan Valley*
Ramsey, Pat, *SDLP, Foyle*
Ramsey, Sue, *SF, Belfast West*
Robinson, George, *DUP, East Londonderry*
Robinson, Rt. Hon. Peter, *DUP, Belfast East*
Rodgers, Sean, *SDLP, South Down*
Ross, Alastair, *DUP, East Antrim*
Ruane, Caitriona, *SF, South Down*
Sheehan, Pat, *SF, Belfast West*
Spratt, Jimmy, *DUP, Belfast South*
Storey, Mervyn, *DUP, North Antrim*
Sugden, Claire, *Ind., East Londonderry*
Swann, Robin, *UUP, North Antrim*
Weir, Peter, *DUP, North Down*
Wells, Jim, *DUP, South Down*
Wilson, Sammy, *DUP, East Antrim*

STATE OF THE PARTIES *as at 1 September 2014*

Party	Seats
Democratic Unionist Party (DUP)	38
Sinn Fein (SF)	29
Social Democratic and Labour Party (SDLP)	14
Ulster Unionist Party (UUP)	13
Alliance Party (Alliance)	8
NI21	2
Green Party	1
Independent (Ind.)	1
Traditional Unionist Voice (TUV)	1
UK Independence Party (UKIP)	1
Total	108

NORTHERN IRELAND ASSEMBLY ELECTION RESULTS

As at 5 May 2011
E. 1,210,009 T. 55.64%

E. Electorate T. Turnout
First = first-preference votes
Final = final total for that candidate, after all necessary transfers of lower-preference votes
R. = round
* = eliminated last
See General Election Results for a list of party abbreviations

ANTRIM EAST
E. 61,617 T. 29,430 (47.76%)

	First	Final	Elected (R.)
Sammy Wilson, DUP	7,181	7,181	First (1)
David Hilditch, DUP	3,288	4,219	Second (2)
Roy Beggs, UUP	3,042	4,194	Fifth (9)
Stewart Dickson, Alliance	2,889	4,777	Fourth (9)
Oliver McMullan, SF	2,369	3,389	Sixth (10)
*Rodney McCune, UUP	1,851	2,890	
Gerardine Mulvenna, Alliance	1,620		
Alastair Ross, DUP	1,608	4,267	Third (6)
Ruth Wilson, TUV	1,346		
Justin McCamphill, SDLP	1,333		
Gordon Lyons, DUP	1,321		
Daniel Donnelly, Green	664		
Steven Moore, BNP	511		

ANTRIM NORTH
E. 74,760 T. 40,983 (54.82%)

	First	Final	Elected (R.)
Paul Frew, DUP	6,581	6,581	First (1)
Daithi McKay, SF	6,152	6,152	Second (1)
Mervyn Storey, DUP	6,083	6,083	Third (1)
Jim Allister, TUV	4,061	5,430	Sixth (9)
*Declan O'Loan, SDLP	3,682	4,816	
David McIlveen, DUP	3,275	6,594	Fourth (8)
Evelyne Robinson, DUP	3,256		
Robin Swann, UUP	2,518	5,557	Fifth (9)
Bill Kennedy, UUP	2,189		
Jayne Dunlop, Alliance	1,848		
Audrey Patterson, TUV	668		

ANTRIM SOUTH
E. 65,231 T. 32,652 (50.06%)

	First	Final	Elected (R.)
Paul Girvan, DUP	4,844	4,844	First (1)
Mitchel McLaughlin, SF	4,662	4,662	Second (1)
Trevor Clarke, UUP	4,607	4,607	Third (1)
David Ford, Alliance	4,554	4,660	Fourth (2)
Danny Kinahan, UUP	3,445	5,585	Fifth (3)
*Thomas Burns, SDLP	3,406	3,591	
Pam Lewis, DUP	2,866	4,668	Sixth (4)
Adrian Cochrane-Watson, UUP	2,285		
Mel Lucas, TUV	1,091		
Stephen Parkes, BNP	404		

BELFAST EAST
E. 61,263 T. 32,828 (53.59%)

	First	Final	Elected (R.)
Peter Robinson, DUP	9,149	9,149	First (1)
Judith Cochrane, Alliance	4,329	4,755	Third (7)
Chris Lyttle, Alliance	4,183	4,696	Fourth (9)
Sammy Douglas, DUP	2,668	4,783	Fifth (11)
Robin Newton, DUP	2,436	4,801	Second (2)
Michael Copeland, UUP	2,194	3,723	Sixth (11)
*Dawn Purvis, Ind.	1,702	2,789	
Brian Ervine, PUP	1,493		
Niall O'Donnghaile, SF	1,030		
Philip Robinson, UUP	943		
Harry Toan, TUV	712		
Martin Gregg, Green	572		
Ann Cooper, BNP	337		
Magdalena Wolska, SDLP	250		
Tommy Black, SP	201		
Kevin McNally, WP	102		
Stephen Stewart, Ind.	46		

BELFAST NORTH
E. 68,119 T. 34,280 (50.32%)

	First	Final	Elected (R.)
Gerry Kelly, SF	6,674	6,674	First (1)
Nelson McCausland, DUP	5,200	5,200	Second (1)
Alban Maginness, SDLP	4,025	5,004	Fourth (6)
William Humphrey, DUP	3,724	4,332	Fifth (7)
Paula Bradley, DUP	3,488	4,065	Sixth (7)
Caral Ni Chuilin, SF	2,999	4,868	Third (6)
*Fred Cobain, UUP	2,758	3,623	
Billy Webb, Alliance	2,096		
Raymond McCord, Ind.	1,176		
JJ Magee, SF	998		
John Lavery, WP	332		

BELFAST SOUTH
E. 62,484 T. 32,752 (52.42%)

	First	Final	Elected (R.)
Anna Lo, Alliance	6,390	6,390	First (1)
Dr Alasdair McDonnell, SDLP	4,527	4,916	Second (2)
Jimmy Spratt, DUP	4,045	4,281	Sixth (5)
Alex Maskey, SF	4,038	4,452	Fourth (5)
*Ruth Patterson, DUP	3,800	4,163	
Connall McDevitt, SDLP	3,191	4,445	Fifth (5)
Michael McGimpsey, UUP	2,988	4,622	Third (5)
Mark Finlay, UUP	1,394		
Claire Bailey, Green	889		
Brian Faloon, PBP	414		
Paddy Meehan, SP	234		
Nico Torregrosa, UKIP	234		
Paddy Lynn, WP	135		
Charles Smyth, Pro-Capitalism	29		

BELFAST WEST
E. 61,520 T. 35,618 (57.89%)

	First	Final	Elected (R.)
Paul Maskey, SF	5,343	5,343	First (1)
Jennifer McCann, SF	5,239	5,239	Second (1)
Fra McCann, SF	4,481	5,167	Third (10)
Sue Ramsey, SF	4,116	4,823	Fifth (11)
Alex Attwood, SDLP	3,765	5,152	Fourth (10)
Pat Sheehan, SF	3,723	4,327	Sixth (11)
*Brian Kingston, DUP	2,587	3,867	
Gerry Carroll, PBP	1,661		
Bill Manwaring, UUP	1,471		
Colin Keenan, SDLP	802		
John Lowry, WP	586		
Pat Lawlor, SP	384		
Dan McGuinness, Alliance	365		
Brian Pelan, Ind.	122		

DOWN NORTH
E. 62,170 T. 28,528 (45.89%)

	First	Final	Elected (R.)
Alex Easton, DUP	5,175	5,175	First (1)
Gordon Dunne, DUP	3,741	4,121	Second (2)
Peter Weir, DUP	3,496	4,101	Third (2)
Stephen Farry, Alliance	3,131	4,078	Fourth (10)
Steven Agnew, Green	2,207	3,229	Sixth (11)
*Anne Wilson, Alliance	2,100	3,130	
Alan McFarland, Ind.	1,879		
Alan Chambers, Ind.	1,765		
Leslie Cree, UUP	1,585	4,015	Fifth (10)
Colin Breen, UUP	1,343		
Liam Logan, SDLP	768		
Fred McGlade, UKIP	615		
Conor Keenan, SF	293		

DOWN SOUTH
E. 73,240 T. 42,551 (58.10%)

	First	Final	Elected (R.)
Margaret Ritchie, SDLP	8,506	8,506	First (1)
Catriona Ruane, SF	5,955	6,192	Second (2)
Jim Wells, DUP	5,200	6,543	Third (5)
John McCallister, UUP	4,409	6,240	Fourth (6)
Willie Clarke, SF	3,882	6,777	Fifth (7)
Karen McKevitt, SDLP	3,758	5,347	Sixth (9)
Naomi Bailie, SF	3,050		
*Eamonn O'Neill, SDLP	2,663	4,883	
Henry Reilly, UKIP	2,332		
Cadogan Enright, Green	1,107		
David Griffin, Alliance	864		

FERMANAGH AND SOUTH TYRONE
E. 70,985 T. 48,949 (68.96%)

	First	Final	Elected (R.)
Michelle Gildernew, SF	9,110	9,110	First (1)
Tom Elliott, UUP	6,896	6,896	Second (1)
Arlene Foster, DUP	6,876	6,876	Third (3)
Sean Lynch, SF	5,146	6,476	Fifth (6)
Phil Flanagan, SF	5,082	6,137	Sixth (6)
Maurice Morrow, DUP	4,844	7,229	Fourth (5)
*Tommy Gallagher, SDLP	4,606	6,075	
Kenny Donaldson, UUP	2,366		
Alex Elliott, TUV	1,231		
Pat Cox, Ind.	997		
Hannah Su, Alliance	845		

FOYLE
E. 68,663 T. 39,686 (57.80%)

	First	Final	Elected (R.)
William Hay, DUP	7,154	7,154	First (1)
Martina Anderson, SF	6,950	6,950	Second (1)
Mark Durkan, SDLP	4,970	5,794	Third (4)
Raymond McCartney, SF	3,638	6,245	Fourth (7)
Pat Ramsey, SDLP	3,138	4,876	Sixth (7)
*Eamonn McCann (PBP)	3,120	3,916	
Colum Eastwood, SDLP	2,967	5,563	Fifth (7)
Pol Callaghan, SDLP	2,624		
Paul Fleming, SF	2,612		
Paul McFadden, Ind.	1,280		
Keith McGrellis, Alliance	334		
Terry Doherty, Ind.	60		

LAGAN VALLEY
E. 67,532 T. 35,842 (53.07%)

	First	Final	Elected (R.)
Edwin Poots, DUP	7,329	7,329	First (1)
Basil McCrea, UUP	5,771	5,771	Second (1)
Trevor Lunn, Alliance	4,389	5,120	Fourth (6)
Paul Givan, DUP	4,352	5,518	Fifth (7)
Jonathan Craig, DUP	4,263	5,081	Third (5)
Brenda Hale, DUP	2,910	4,791	Sixth (7)
*Pat Catney, SDLP	2,165	3,406	
Mark Hill, UUP	1,482		
Mary-Kate Quinn, SF	1,203		
Lyle Rea, TUV	1,031		
Conor Quinn, Green	592		

LONDONDERRY EAST
E. 65,226 T. 35,303 (54.12%)

	First	Final	Elected (R.)
Gregory Campbell, DUP	6,319	6,319	First (1)
Cathal O hOisin, SF	4,681	4,962	Third (6)
George Robinson, DUP	3,855	4,823	Fourth (7)
David McClarty (Ind.)	3,003	4,405	Fifth (7)
John Dallat, SDLP	2,967	5,207	Second (6)
Bernadette Archibald, SF	2,639		
Adrian McQuillan, DUP	2,633	3,782	Sixth (7)
Thomas Conway	2,222		
Barney Fitzpatrick, Alliance	1,905		
Boyd Douglas, TUV	1,568		
Lesley Macaulay, UUP	1,472		
*David Harding, UUP	1,458	3,460	

NEWRY AND ARMAGH
E. 77,544 T. 47,562 (61.34%)

	First	Final	Elected (R.)
Conor Murphy, SF	9,127	9,127	First (1)
Danny Kennedy, UUP	8,718	8,718	Second (1)
Dominic Bradley, SDLP	7,123	7,123	Third (1)
Cathal Boylan, SF	6,614	8,092	Fourth (2)
William Irwin, DUP	6,101	7,502	Fifth (3)
*Thomas O'Hanlon, SDLP	3,825	5,014	
Mickey Brady, SF	3,254	5,625	Sixth (6)
Barrie Halliday, TUV	830		
David Murphy, Alliance	734		
Robert Woods, UKIP	98		
James Malone, ND	90		

STRANGFORD
E. 62,178 T. 30,186 (48.55%)

	First	Final	Elected (R.)
Michelle McIlveen, DUP	4,573	4,573	First (1)
Kieran McCarthy, Alliance	4,284	4,284	Second (1)
Jonathan Bell, DUP	4,265	4,265	Third (1)
Simon Hamilton, DUP	3,456	5,745	Fourth (5)
Mike Nesbitt, UUP	3,273	4,072	Fifth (6)
David McNarry, UUP	2,733	3,767	Sixth (6)
*Joe Boyle, SDLP	2,525	3,308	
Billy Walker, DUP	2,175		
Mickey Coogan, SF	902		
Terry Williams, TUV	841		
Cecil Andrews, UKIP	601		

TYRONE WEST
E. 62,970 T. 40,323 (64.04%)

	First	Final	Elected (R.)
Barry McElduff, SF	6,008	6,008	First (1)
Pat Doherty, SF	5,630	5,630	Second (1)
Michaela Boyle, SF	5,053	7,792	Third (4)
Tom Buchanan, DUP	5,027	5,162	Fifth (5)
Ross Hussey, UUP	4,072	4,398	Sixth (5)
*Allan Bresland, DUP	4,059	4,124	
Joe Byrne, SDLP	3,353	5,321	Fourth (5)
Declan McAleer, SF	3,008		
Paddy McGowan, Ind.	1,145		
Eugene McMenamin, Ind.	1,096		
Eric Bullick, Ind.	852		

ULSTER MID
E. 66,602 T. 43,522 (65.35%)

	First	Final	Elected (R.)
Martin McGuinness, SF	8,957	8,957	First (1)
Ian McCrea, DUP	7,127	7,127	Second (1)
Michelle O'Neill, SF	5,178	5,735	Sixth (7)
Patsy McGlone, SDLP	5,065	6,110	Third (5)
Sandra Overend, UUP	4,409	7,130	Fourth (6)
Francie Molloy, SF	4,263	5,191	Fifth (7)
*Ian Milne, SF	2,635	4,412	
Walter Millar, TUV	2,075		
Austin Kelly, SDLP	1,214		
Hugh McCloy, Ind.	933		
Michael McDonald, Alliance	398		
Harry Hutchinson, PBP	243		
Gary McCann, Ind.	241		

UPPER BANN
E. 77,905 T. 43,113 (55.34%)

	First	Final	Elected (R.)
John O'Dowd, SF	6,649	6,649	First (1)
Sydney Anderson, DUP	5,584	6,163	Second (5)
Stephen Moutray, DUP	5,645	6,085	Third (5)
*Johnny McGibbon, SF	4,879	5,438	
Dolores Kelly, SDLP	4,846	5,787	Sixth (7)
Sam Gardiner, UUP	3,676	6,012	Fourth (7)
Colin McCusker, UUP	3,402		
Joanne Dobson, UUP	3,348	5,827	Fifth (7)
Harry Hamilton, Alliance	1,979		
David Vance, TUV	1,026		
Sheila McQuaid, Alliance	786		
Barbara Trotter, UKIP	272		

REGIONAL GOVERNMENT

LONDON

GREATER LONDON AUTHORITY (GLA)
City Hall, The Queen's Walk, London SE1 2AA
T 020-7983 4000 E mayor@london.gov.uk
W www.london.gov.uk

On 7 May 1998 London voted in favour of the formation of the Greater London Authority (GLA). The first elections to the GLA took place on 4 May 2000 and the new authority took over its responsibilities on 3 July 2000. In July 2002 the GLA moved to one of London's most spectacular buildings, newly built on a brownfield site on the south bank of the Thames, adjacent to Tower Bridge. The fourth and most recent election to the GLA took place on 3 May 2012.

The structure and objectives of the GLA stem from its main areas of responsibility: transport, policing, fire and emergency planning, economic development, planning, culture and health. There are four functional bodies which form part of the wider GLA group and report to the GLA: the Mayor's Office for Policing and Crime (MOPAC), Transport for London (TfL), the London Fire and Emergency Planning Authority (LFEPA) and the London Legacy Development Corporation, established in 2012.

The GLA consists of a directly elected mayor, the Mayor of London, and a separately elected assembly, the London Assembly. The mayor has the key role in decision making, with the assembly responsible for regulating and scrutinising these decisions, and investigating issues of importance to Londoners. In addition, the GLA has around 600 permanent staff to support the activities of the mayor and the assembly, which are overseen by a head of paid service. The mayor may appoint two political advisers and not more than ten other members of staff, though he does not necessarily exercise this power, but he does not appoint the chief executive, the monitoring officer or the chief finance officer. These must be appointed jointly by the assembly and the mayor.

Every aspect of the assembly and its activities must be open to public scrutiny and therefore accountable. The assembly holds the mayor to account through scrutiny of his strategies, decisions and actions. Mayor's Question Time, conducted on ten occasions a year at City Hall, is carried out by direct questioning at assembly meetings and by conducting detailed investigations in committee.

People's Question Time, held twice a year, and Talk London (W www.talklondon.london.gov.uk) give Londoners the chance to question and express their opinions to the mayor and the assembly about plans, priorities and policies for London.

The role of the mayor can be broken down into a number of key areas:
• to represent and promote London at home and abroad and speak up for Londoners
• to devise strategies and plans to tackle London-wide issues, such as crime, transport, housing, planning, economic development and regeneration, environment, public services, society and culture, sport and health; and to set budgets for TfL, MOPAC, LFEPA and the London Legacy Development Corporation
• the mayor is chair of TfL, and is responsible for the Metropolitan Police's priorities and performance

The role of the assembly can be broken down into a number of key areas:
• to hold the mayor to account by examining his decisions and actions
• to have the power to amend the mayor's budget by a majority of two-thirds
• to have the power to summon the mayor, senior staff of the GLA and functional bodies
• to investigate issues of London-wide significance and make proposals to appropriate stakeholders
• to examine the work of MOPAC and to review the police and crime plan for London through the Police and Crime Committee

Mayor, Boris Johnson
Deputy Mayors, Roger Evans, AM *(Statutory Deputy Mayor);* Richard Blakeway *(Housing, Land and Property);* Isabel Dedring *(Transport);* Stephen Greenhalgh *(Policing and Crime);* Sir Edward Lister *(Policy and Planning, and Chief of Staff);* Munira Mirza *(Education and Culture);* Matthew Pencharz *(Environment and Energy)*
Chair of the London Assembly, Jennette Arnold, OBE, AM
Deputy Chair of the Assembly, Tony Arbour, AM

ELECTIONS AND VOTING SYSTEMS
The assembly is elected every four years at the same time as the mayor, and consists of 25 members. There is one member from each of the 14 GLA constituencies topped up with 11 London-wide members who are either representatives of political parties or individuals standing as independent candidates. The last election was on 3 May 2012.

Two distinct voting systems are used to appoint the existing mayor and the assembly. The mayor is elected using the supplementary vote system (SVS). With SVS, electors have two votes: one to give a first choice for mayor and one to give a second choice; they cannot vote twice for the same candidate. If one candidate gets more than half of all the first-choice votes, he or she becomes mayor. If no candidate gets more than half of the first-choice votes, the two candidates with the most first-choice votes remain in the election and all the other candidates drop out. The second-choice votes on the ballot papers for the candidates who are then counted. Where these second-choice votes are for the two remaining candidates they are added to the first-choice votes these candidates already have. The candidate with the most first- and second-choice votes combined becomes the Mayor of London.

The assembly is appointed using the additional member system (AMS). Under AMS, electors have two votes. The first vote is for a constituency candidate. The second vote is for a party list or individual candidate contesting the London-wide assembly seats. The 14 constituency members are elected under the first-past-the-post system, the same system used in general and local elections. Electors vote for one candidate and the candidate with the most votes wins. The additional members are drawn from party lists or are independent candidates who stand as London members; they are chosen using a form of proportional representation.

The Greater London Returning Officer (GLRO) is the independent official responsible for running the election in London. He is supported in this by returning officers in each of the 14 London constituencies.
GLRO, Jeff Jacobs

TRANSPORT FOR LONDON (TFL)

TfL is the integrated body responsible for London's transport system. Its role is to implement the mayor's transport strategy for London and manage transport services across the capital for which the mayor has responsibility. TfL is directed by a management board whose members are chosen for their understanding of transport matters and are appointed by the mayor, who chairs the board. TfL's role is:

- to manage the London Underground, buses, Croydon Tramlink, London Overground and the Docklands Light Railway (DLR)
- to manage a 580km network of main roads and all 6,000 of London's traffic lights
- to regulate taxis and minicabs
- to run the London River Services, Victoria Coach Station and London Transport Museum
- to help to coordinate the Dial-a-Ride, Capital Call and Taxicard schemes for door-to-door services for transport users with mobility problems

The London Borough Councils maintain the role of highway and traffic authorities for 95 per cent of London's roads. A congestion charge for motorists driving into central London between the hours of 7am and 6.30pm, Monday to Friday (excluding public holidays) was introduced on 17 February 2003. On 19 February 2007, the charge zone roughly doubled in size after a westward expansion and the charging hours were shortened, to finish at 6pm. On 4 January 2011, the westward expansion was removed from the charging zone and an automated payment system was also introduced. As at September 2015 the daily congestion charge was £11.50 (£10.50 if paid via the automated service).

TfL introduced a low emission zone (LEZ) for London on 4 February 2008 which is in constant operation. Following tougher emissions standards introduced on 3 January 2012 there is a daily charge for polluting vehicles entering the zone (which covers most of Greater London) that do not meet Euro 3 or Euro 4 emissions standards. With the exception of minibuses, vehicles over three-and-a-half tonnes such as lorries, buses and coaches, face a daily charge of £200. Vehicles up to three-and-a-half tonnes and minibuses (with more than eight passenger seats) up to five tonnes pay a daily charge of £100. For further information see W www.tfl.gov.uk/lez

Since 2 January 2009, Londoners over pensionable age (or over 60 if born before 1950) and those with eligible disabilities are entitled to free travel on the capital's transport network at any time. War veterans who are receiving ongoing payments under the war pensions scheme, or those receiving guaranteed income payments under the armed forces compensation scheme can travel free at any time on bus, underground, DLR, tram and London Overground services and at certain times on National Rail services.

In the summer of 2010, the London cycle hire scheme launched with 6,000 new bicycles for hire from 400 docking stations across eight boroughs, the City and the Royal parks. The scheme has been expanded and there are now around 10,000 bicycles available and over 700 docking stations.
Commissioner of TfL (interim), Mike Brown, MVO

MAYOR'S OFFICE FOR POLICING AND CRIME (MOPAC)

The Mayor's Office for Policing and Crime (MOPAC) was set up in response to the Police Reform and Social Responsibility Act 2011, replacing the Metropolitan Police Authority. MOPAC is headed by the mayor, or the appointed statutory deputy mayor for policing and crime. Operational responsibility for policing in London belongs to the Metropolitan Police Commissioner. The major areas of focus of MOPAC are:

- operational policing and crime reduction including counter terrorism
- ensuring the Metropolitan Police effectively reduce gang crime and violence in London and coordinating support for communities and local organisations to prevent gang activities
- criminal justice, including preventing reoffending, reducing crime and decreasing demand within the criminal justice system in addition to reducing alcohol and drug abuse.

The Police and Crime Committee consisting of nine elected members of the London Assembly scrutinises the work of MOPAC and meets regularly to hold to account the Deputy Mayor for Policing and Crime.
Deputy Mayor for Policing and Crime, Stephen Greenhalgh

LONDON FIRE AND EMERGENCY PLANNING AUTHORITY (LFEPA)

In July 2000 the London Fire and Civil Defence Authority became the London Fire and Emergency Planning Authority. It consists of 17 members, eight drawn from the assembly, seven from the London boroughs and two mayoral appointees. The role of the LFEPA is:

- to set the strategy for the provision of fire services
- to ensure that the fire brigade can meet all the normal requirements efficiently
- to ensure that effective arrangements are made for the fire brigade to receive emergency calls and deal with them promptly
- to ensure members of the fire brigade are properly trained and equipped
- to ensure that information useful to the development of the fire brigades is gathered
- to ensure arrangements for advice and guidance on fire protection are made

Chair, Gareth Bacon

LONDON LEGACY DEVELOPMENT CORPORATION

Following the London 2012 Olympic Games, the London Legacy Development Corporation was made responsible for the long-term planning, development, management and maintenance of the Queen Elizabeth Olympic Park (formerly the Olympic Park) and its facilities. The organisation is tasked with transforming the area into a thriving neighbourhood.
Chair, Neale Coleman, CBE

SALARIES *as at August 2015*	
Mayor	£143,911
Chief of Staff and Deputy Mayor of Policy and Planning	£168,924
Deputy Mayors	
Housing, Land and Property	£146,245
Transport	£146,245
Policing and Crime	£146,245
Education and Culture	£145,345
Environment and Energy	£107,017
Statutory Deputy Mayor	£99,188
Chair of the Assembly	£66,168
Assembly Member	£55,161

LONDON ASSEMBLY COMMITTEES
Chair, Audit Panel, Valerie Shawcross, CBE
Chair, Budget and Performance Committee, John Biggs
Chair, Budget Monitoring Sub-Committee, John Biggs
Chair, Confirmation Hearings Committee, various
Chair, Devolution Working Group, Darren Johnson
Chair, Economy Committee, Fiona Twycross
Chair, Education Panel, Jennette Arnold, OBE

Chair, *Environment Committee,* Darren Johnson
Chair, *GLA Oversight Committee,* Len Duvall
Chair, *Health Committee,* Dr Onkar Sahota
Chair, *Housing Committee,* Tom Copley, AM
Chair, *Online Crime Working Group,* Roger Evans
Chair, *Planning Committee,* Nicky Gavron
Chair, *Police and Crime Committee,* Joanne McCartney
Chair, *Regeneration Committee,* Gareth Bacon
Chair, *Transport Committee,* Valerie Shawcross, CBE

LONDON ASSEMBLY MEMBERS
as at 3 May 2012
Arbour, Tony, *C., South West,* Maj. 19,262
Arnold, Jennette, *Lab. North East,* Maj. 66,188
Bacon, Gareth, *C., London List*
Biggs, John, *Lab., City and East,* Maj. 82,744
Boff, Andrew, *C., London List*
Borwick, Victoria, *C., London List*
Cleverly, James, *C., Bexley and Bromley,* Maj. 47,768
Copley, Tom, *Lab. London List*
Dismore, Andrew, *Lab., Barnet and Camden,* Maj. 21,299
Duvall, Len, *Lab., Greenwich and Lewisham,* Maj. 38,037
Evans, Roger, *C., Havering and Redbridge,* Maj. 3,899
Gavron, Nicky, *Lab., London List*
Johnson, Darren, *Green, London List*
Jones, Jenny, *Green, London List*
Knight, Stephen, *LD, London List*
Malthouse, Kit, *C., West Central,* Maj. 29,131
McCartney, Joanne, *Lab., Enfield and Haringey,* Maj. 36,741
O'Connell, Steve, *C., Croydon and Sutton,* Maj. 9,418
Pidgeon, Caroline, *LD, London List*
Qureshi, Murad, *Lab., London List*
Sahota, Dr Onkar, *Lab., Ealing and Hillingdon,* Maj. 3,110
Shah, Navin, *Lab., Brent and Harrow,* Maj. 29,796
Shawcross, Valerie, *Lab., Lambeth and Southwark,* Maj. 52,702
Tracey, Richard, *C., Merton and Wandsworth,* Maj. 9,981
Twycross, Fiona, *Lab., London List*

STATE OF THE PARTIES *as at 3 May 2012*

Party	Seats
Conservative (C.)	9
Labour (Lab.)	12
Liberal Democrats (LD)	2
Green	2

MAYORAL ELECTION RESULTS
as at 3 May 2012

Electorate 5,910,460   Turnout 38%

Change in turnout from 2008: -7.33%
Good votes: 1st choice 2,208,475 (98.21%); 2nd choice 1,763,009 (79.83%)
Rejected votes: 1st choice 40,210 (1.79%); 2nd choice 445,466 (20.17%)

First	Party	Votes	%
Boris Johnson	C.	971,931	44.01
Ken Livingstone	Lab.	889,918	40.30
Jenny Jones	Green	98,913	4.48
Brian Paddick	LD	91,774	4.16
Siobhan Benita	Ind.	83,914	3.80
Lawrence Webb	UKIP	43,274	1.96
Carlos Cortiglia	BNP	28,751	1.30

Second	Party	Votes	%
Brian Paddick	LD	363,692	20.63
Jenny Jones	Green	363,193	20.60
Ken Livingstone	Lab.	335,398	19.02
Boris Johnson	C.	253,709	14.39
Siobhan Benita	Ind.	212,412	12.05
Lawrence Webb	UKIP	161,252	9.15
Carlos Cortiglia	BNP	73,353	4.16

LONDON ASSEMBLY ELECTION RESULTS
as at 3 May 2012
E. Electorate T. Turnout
See General Election Results for a list of party abbreviations

CONSTITUENCIES
E. 5,910,460 T. 38%

BARNET AND CAMDEN
E. 446,248 T. 38%
Andrew Dismore, Lab.	74,677
Brian Coleman, C.	53,378
Audrey Poppy, Green	17,904
Chris Richards, LD	13,800
Michael Corby, UKIP	7,331

Lab. majority 21,299

BEXLEY AND BROMLEY
E. 447,465 T. 38.1%
James Cleverly, C.	88,482
Josie Channer, Lab.	40,714
Sam Webber, LD,	11,396
David Cobum, UKIP	10,771
Jonathan Rooks, Green	9,209
Donna Treanor, BNP	7,563

C. majority 47,768

BRENT AND HARROW
E. 389,737 T. 38%
Navin Shah, Lab.	70,400
Sachin Rajput, C.	40,604
Charlotte Henry, LD	15,690
Shahrar Ali, Green	10,546
Mick McGough, UKIP	7,830

Lab. majority 29,796

CITY AND EAST
E. 500,427 T. 34.8%
John Biggs, Lab.	107,667
John Moss, C.	24,923
Chris Smith, Green	10,891
Richard Macmillan, LD	7,351
Paul Borg, BNP	7,031
Kamran Malik, CUP	6,774
Steven Woolfe, UKIP	5,243
Paul Davies, Comm. Lge	1,108

Lab. majority 82,744

CROYDON AND SUTTON
E. 436,451 T. 35.7%
Stephen O'Connell, C.	60,152
Louisa Woodley, Lab.	50,734
Abigail Lock, LD	21,889
Winston McKenzie, UKIP	10,757
Gordon Ross, Green	10,287

C. majority 9,418

EALING AND HILLINGDON
E. 439,143 T. 37.9%
Onkar Sahota, Lab.	65,584
Richard Barnes, C.	62,474
Michael Cox, LD	11,805
Mike Harling, Green	10,877
Helen Knight, UKIP	6,750
Dave Furness, BNP	4,284
Ian Edward, NF	2,035

Lab. majority 3,110

ENFIELD AND HARINGEY
E. 383,623 T. 38.3%
Joanne McCartney, Lab.	74,034
Andy Hemsted, C.	37,293
Dawn Barnes, LD	13,601
Peter Krakowiak, Green	12,278
Peter Staveley, UKIP	4,298
Marie Nicholas, BNP	3,081

Lab. majority 36,741

GREENWICH AND LEWISHAM
E. 359,742 T. 37.2%
Len Duvall, Lab.	65,366
Alex Wilson, C.	27,329
Roger Sedgley, Green	12,427
John Russell, LD	9,393
Barbara Raymond, PBP	6,873
Paul Oakley, UKIP	4,997
Roberta Woods, BNP	3,551
Tess Culnane, NF	1,816

Lab. majority 38,037

HAVERING AND REDBRIDGE
E. 389,814 T. 36.9%
Roger Evans, C.	53,285
Mandy Richards, Lab.	49,386
Lawrence Webb, UKIP	9,471
Melvin Brown, RAL	8,239
Farrukh Islam, LD	6,435
Robert Taylor, BNP	5,234
Haroon Saad, Green	5,207
Mark Twiddy, Eng. Dem.	2,573
Richard Edmonds, NF	1,936

C. majority 3,899

LAMBETH AND SOUTHWARK
E. 422,981 T. 37.8%
Valerie Shawcross, Lab.	83,239
Michael Mitchell, C.	30,537
Rob Blackie, LD	18,359
Jonathan Bartley, Green	18,144
James Fluss, UKIP	4,395
Daniel Lambert, Soc.	2,938

Lab. majority 52,702

MERTON AND WANDSWORTH
E. 376,365 T. 40.9%
Richard Tracey, C.	65,197
Leonie Cooper, Lab.	55,216
Lisa Smart, LD	11,904
Roy Vickery, Green	11,307
Mazhar Manzoor, UKIP	3,717
Thamilini Kulendran, Ind.	2,424
James Martin, Soc.	1,343

C. majority 9,981

NORTH EAST
E. 499,418 T. 39.1%
Jennette Arnold, Lab.	101,902
Naomi Newstead, C.	35,714
Caroline Allen, Green	29,677
Farooq Qureshi, LD	13,237
Paul Wiffen, UKIP	6,623
Ijaz Hayat, Ind.	4,842

Lab. majority 66,188

SOUTH WEST
E. 437,945 T. 40.2%
Tony Arbour, C.	69,151
Lisa Homan, Lab.	49,889
Munira Wilson, LD	28,947
Daniel Goldsmith, Green	17,070
Jeff Bolter, UKIP	8,505

C. majority 19,262

WEST CENTRAL
E. 381,101 T. 39.2%
Kit Malthouse, C.	73,761
Todd Foreman, Lab.	44,630
Susanna Rustin, Green	12,799
Layla Moran, LD	10,035
Elizabeth Jones, UKIP	5,161

C. majority 29,131

LONDON-WIDE MEMBERS

Conservative	*Labour Party*
Gareth Bacon	Tom Copley
Andrew Boff	Nicky Gavron
Victoria Borwick	Murad Qureshi
	Fiona Twycross

Green Party	*Liberal Democrat*
Darren Johnson	Stephen Knight
Jenny Jones	Caroline Pidgeon

EUROPEAN PARLIAMENT

European parliament elections take place at five-yearly intervals; the first direct elections to the parliament were held in 1979. In mainland Britain, members of the European parliament (MEPs) were elected in all constituencies on a first-past-the-post basis until 1999, when a regional system of proportional representation was introduced; in Northern Ireland three MEPs have been elected by the single transferable vote system of proportional representation since 1979. Under the terms of the Lisbon Treaty, the UK gained an extra seat in December 2011, taking the total to 73. This seat was added to the West Midlands region and filled by the highest-ranked losing candidate standing for the region in the 2009 European parliament elections.

At the 2014 European parliament elections all UK MEPs were elected under a 'closed-list' regional system of proportional representation, with England being divided into nine regions (residents of Gibraltar vote in the South West region) and Scotland, Wales and Northern Ireland each constituting a single region each. Parties submitted a list of candidates for each region in their own order of preference. Votes were cast for a party or an independent candidate, and the first seat in each region was allocated to the party or candidate with the highest number of votes. The rest of the seats in each region were then allocated broadly in proportion to each party's share of the vote. Each region returned the following number of members: East Midlands, 5; Eastern, 7; London, 8; North East, 3; North West, 8; South East, 10; South West, 6; West Midlands, 7; Yorkshire and the Humber, 6; Wales, 4; Northern Ireland, 3; Scotland, 6.

If a vacancy occurs due to the resignation or death of an MEP, it is filled by the next available person on that party's list. If an independent MEP resigns or dies, a by-election is held. Where an MEP leaves the party on whose list he/she was elected, there is no requirement to resign the post of MEP.

British subjects and nationals of member states of the European Union are eligible for election to the European parliament provided they are aged 18 or over and not subject to disqualification. Since 1994, eligible citizens have had the right to vote in elections to the European parliament in the UK as long as they are entered on the electoral register.

In July 2009 an MEP statute introduced a uniform salary for all MEPs, set at a rate of 38.5 per cent of the basic salary of a European court of justice judge. As at May 2015 this equated an annual salary of €96,246.36 (approximately £68,000, depending on the monthly exchange rate). Member states can also subject the salary to national taxes. In the UK the salary is taxed by HM Revenue and Customs in order to bring the total tax paid up to the level of taxation payable by a UK resident.

The 2014 UK component of the European parliament was won by UKIP, who claimed 24 seats. It was the first time a party other than the Conservatives or Labour had won the largest number of seats in a general election since the December 1910 general election.

The next elections to the European parliament will take place in 2019. For further information visit the UK's European parliament website (W www.europarl.org.uk).

UK MEMBERS *as at June 2015*

* Denotes membership of the last European parliament
† Previously sat as a member of the Conservative party
‡ Previously sat as a member of UKIP
§ Previously sat as a member of UCUNF

*Agnew, Stuart (b. 1949), UKIP, Eastern
Aker, Tim (b. 1985), UKIP, Eastern
Anderson, Lucy, Lab., London
*Anderson, Martina (b. 1962), SF, Northern Ireland
Arnott, Jonathan (b. 1981), UKIP, North East
*Ashworth, Richard (b. 1947), C., South East
Atkinson, Janice (b. 1962), Ind., South East
Bashir, Amjad (b. 1952), UKIP, Yorkshire and the Humber
*Batten, Gerard (b. 1954), UKIP, London
*Bearder, Catherine (b. 1949), LD, South East
Bours, Louise (b. 1968), UKIP, North West
Brannen, Paul (b. 1962), Lab., North East
*‡Campbell Bannerman, David (b. 1960), C., Eastern
Carver, Jim (b. 1969), UKIP, West Midlands
Coburn, David (b. 1958), UKIP, Scotland
Collins, Jane (b. 1962), UKIP, Yorkshire and the Humber
Corbett, Richard (b. 1955), Lab., Yorkshire and the Humber
Dalton, Daniel (b. 1974), C., West Midlands
Dance, Seb (b. 1981), Lab., London
*Dartmouth, Earl of (b. 1949), UKIP, South West
*Deva, Nirj (b. 1948), C., South East
Dodds, Anneliese (b. 1978), Lab., South East
*Dodds, Diane (b. 1958), DUP, Northern Ireland
Duncan, Ian (b. 1973), C., Scotland
Etheridge, Bill (b. 1970), UKIP, West Midlands
*Evans, Jill (b. 1959), PC, Wales
*Farage, Nigel (b. 1964), UKIP, South East
Finch, Ray (b. 1963), UKIP, South East
*Ford, Vicky (b. 1967), C., Eastern
*Foster, Jacqueline (b. 1947), C., North West
*Fox, Ashley (b. 1969), C., South West
Gill, Nathan (b. 1973), UKIP, Wales
Gill, Neena (b. 1957), Lab., West Midlands
*Girling, Julie (b. 1956), C., South West
Griffin, Theresa (b. 1962), Lab., North West
*Hannan, Daniel (b. 1971), C., South East
*†Helmer, Roger (b. 1944), UKIP, East Midlands
*Honeyball, Mary (b. 1952), Lab., London
Hookem, Mike (b. 1953), UKIP, Yorkshire and the Humber
*Howitt, Richard (b. 1961), Lab., Eastern
*Hudghton, Ian (b. 1951), SNP, Scotland
James, Diane (b. 1959), UKIP, South East
*Kamall, Dr Syed (b. 1967), C., London
*Karim, Sajjad (b. 1970), C., North West
Khan, Afzal (b. 1960), Lab., North West
*Kirkhope, Timothy (b. 1945), C., Yorkshire and the Humber
Kirton-Darling, Judith (b. 1977), Lab., North East
*Lambert, Jean (b. 1950), Green, London
Lewer, Andrew (b. 1971), C., East Midlands
*McAvan, Linda (b. 1962), Lab., Yorkshire and the Humber
*McClarkin, Emma (b. 1978), C., East Midlands
*McIntyre, Anthea (b. 1954), C., West Midlands
*Martin, David (b. 1954), Lab., Scotland
Moody, Clare (b. 1965), Lab., South West
*Moraes, Claude (b. 1965), Lab., London
*Nicholson, James (b. 1945), UUP, Northern Ireland
*Nuttall, Paul (b. 1976), UKIP, North West
O'Flynn, Patrick (b. 1965), UKIP, Eastern
Parker, Margaret (b. 1943), UKIP, East Midlands
Reid, Julia (b. 1952), UKIP, South West
Scott Cato, Molly (b. 1963), Green, South West
Seymour, Jill (b. 1958), UKIP, West Midlands
Simon, Siôn (b. 1968), Lab., West Midlands
*Smith, Alyn (b. 1973), SNP, Scotland

*Stihler, Catherine (b. 1973), Lab., Scotland
*Swinburne, Dr Kay (b. 1967), C., Wales
*Tannock, Dr Charles (b. 1957), C., London
*Taylor, Keith (b. 1953), Green, South East
*Van Orden, Geoffrey (b. 1945), C., Eastern
*Vaughan, Derek (b. 1961), Lab., Wales
Ward, Julie (b. 1957), Lab., North West
*Willmott, Glenis (b. 1951), Lab., East Midlands
Woolfe, Steven (b. 1967), UKIP, North West

STATE OF THE PARTIES as at June 2015

Party	Seats
UK Independence Party (UKIP)	24
Labour (Lab.)	20
Conservative (C.)	19
Green Party (Green)	3
Scottish National Party (SNP)	2
Others*	5
Total	73

* The Democratic Unionist Party (DUP), Liberal Democrats (LD), Plaid Cymru (PC), the Ulster Unionist Party (UUP) and Sinn Fein (SF) have one seat each.

UK REGIONS as at 22 May 2014 election

Abbreviations

4FP	4 Freedoms Party (UK EPP)
AIFE	An Independence from Europe
AW	Animal Welfare
BF	Britain First
CPA	Christian Peoples Alliance
EP	Europeans Party
Harmony	Harmony Party
Liberty	Liberty GB
NLP	National Liberal Party
NI21	NI21
No2EU	No2EU Yes to Democracy
Peace	Peace Party
Roman	Roman Party
SGB	Socialist Party of Great Britain
SLP	Socialist Labour Party
TUV	Traditional Unionist Voice (NI)
UUP	Ulster Unionist Party
WDR	We Demand a Referendum
Your	YOURvoice
YF	Yorkshire First

For other abbreviations, see UK General Election Results.

E. 46,615,585   T. 35.32%

EASTERN
(Bedfordshire, Cambridgeshire, Essex, Hertfordshire, Luton, Norfolk, Peterborough, Southend-on-Sea, Suffolk, Thurrock)

E. 4,369,382	T. 36.19%
UKIP	542,812 (34.5%)
C.	446,569 (28.4%)
Lab.	271,601 (17.2%)
Green	133,331 (8.5%)
LD	108,010 (6.9%)
AIFE	26,564 (1.7%)
Eng. Dem.	16,497 (1.0%)
BNP	12,465 (0.8%)
CPA	11,627 (0.7%)
No2EU	4,870 (0.3%)
UKIP majority	96,243

(June 2009, C. maj. 186,410)

MEMBERS ELECTED
1. P. O'Flynn, UKIP 2. *V. Ford, C.
3. *R. Howitt, Lab. 4. *S. Agnew, UKIP
5. *G. Van Orden, C. 6. T. Aker, UKIP
7. *‡ D. Campbell Bannerman, C.

EAST MIDLANDS
(Derby, Derbyshire, Leicester, Leicestershire, Lincolnshire, Northamptonshire, Nottingham, Nottinghamshire, Rutland)

E. 3,437,794	T. 32.6%
UKIP	368,734 (32.9%)
C.	291,270 (26.0%)
Lab.	279,363 (24.9%)
Green	67,066 (6.0%)
LD	60,773 (5.4%)
AIFE	21,384 (1.9%)
BNP	18,326 (1.6%)
Eng. Dem.	11,612 (1.0%)
Harmony	2,194 (0.2%)
UKIP majority	77,464

(June 2009, C. maj. 163,330)

MEMBERS ELECTED
1. *†R. Helmer, UKIP 2.*E. McClarkin, C. 3. *G. Willmott, Lab. 4. M. Parker, UKIP 5. A. Lewer, C.

LONDON

E. 5,490,248	T. 40.5%
Lab.	806,959 (36.7%)
C.	495,639 (22.5%)
UKIP	371,133 (16.9%)
Green	196,419 (8.9%)
LD	148,013 (6.7%)
4FP	28,014 (1.3%)
AIFE	26,675 (1.2%)
CPA	23,702 (1.1%)
NHA	23,253 (1.1%)
AW	21,092 (1.0%)
BNP	19,246 (0.9%)
EP	10,712 (0.5%)
Eng. Dem.	10,142 (0.5%)
CUP	6,951 (0.3%)
NLP	6,736 (0.3%)
No2EU	3,804 (0.2%)
Harmony	1,985 (0.1%)
Lab. majority	311,320

(June 2009, C. maj. 106,447)

MEMBERS ELECTED
1. *C. Moraes, Lab. 2. *S. Kamall, C.
3. *M. Honeyball, Lab. 4. *G. Batten, UKIP 5. L. Anderson, Lab.
6. *C. Tannock, C. 7. S. Dance, Lab.
8. *J. Lambert, Green

NORTH EAST
(Co. Durham, Darlington, Hartlepool, Middlesbrough, Northumberland, Redcar and Cleveland, Stockton-on-Tees, Tyne and Wear)

E. 1,968,780	T. 31.0%
Lab.	221,988 (36.5%)
UKIP	177,660 (29.2%)
C.	107,733 (17.7%)
LD	36,093 (5.9%)
Green	31,605 (5.2%)
AIFE	13,934 (2.3%)
BNP	10,360 (1.7%)
Eng. Dem.	9,279 (1.5%)
Lab. majority	44,328

(June 2009, Lab. maj. 30,427)

MEMBERS ELECTED
1. J. Darling, Lab. 2. J. Arnott, UKIP
3. P. Brannen, Lab.

NORTHERN IRELAND
(Northern Ireland forms a three-member seat with a single transferable vote system)

E. 1,225,771	T. 51.84%
	1st Pref. Votes
Martina Anderson, SF	159,813 (25.5%)
Diane Dodds, DUP	131,163 (20.9%)
Jim Nicholson, UUP	83,438 (13.3%)
Alex Attwood, SDLP	81,594 (13%)
Jim Allister, TUV	75,806 (12.1%)
Anna Lo, Alliance	44,432 (7.1%)
Henry Reilly, UKIP	24,584 (3.9%)
Ross Brown, Green	10,598 (1.7%)
Tina McKenzie, NI21	10,553 (1.7%)
Mark Brotherston, C.	4,144 (0.7%)

MEMBERS ELECTED
1. *M. Anderson, SF 2. *D. Dodds, DUP 3. *§ J. Nicholson, UUP

NORTH WEST
(Blackburn-with-Darwen, Blackpool, Cheshire, Cumbria, Greater Manchester, Halton, Lancashire, Merseyside, Warrington)

E. 5,267,777		T. 33.68%
Lab.	594,063	(33.9%)
UKIP	481,932	(27.5%)
C.	351,985	(20.1%)
Green	123,075	(7.0%)
LD	105,487	(6.0%)
BNP	32,826	(1.9%)
AIFE	26,731	(1.5%)
Eng. Dem.	19,522	(1.1%)
Pirate	8,597	(0.5%)
No2EU	5,402	(0.3%)
SEP	5,067	(0.3%)
Lab. majority		112,131

(June 2009, C. maj. 86,343)

MEMBERS ELECTED
1. T. Griffin, *Lab.* 2.*P. Nuttall, *UKIP*
3. *J. Foster, *C.* 4. A. Khan, *Lab.*
5. L. Bours, *UKIP* 6. J. Ward, *Lab.*
7. *S. Karim, *C.* 8. S. Woolfe, *UKIP*

SCOTLAND

E. 4,016,735		T. 33.5%
SNP	389,503	(29.0%)
Lab.	348,219	(25.9%)
C.	231,330	(17.2%)
UKIP	140,534	(10.5%)
Green	108,305	(8.7%)
LD	95,319	(7.1%)
BF	13,639	(1.0%)
BNP	10,216	(0.8%)
No2EU	6,418	(0.5%)
SNP majority		41,284

(June 2009, SNP. maj. 91,154)

MEMBERS ELECTED
1. *I. Hudghton, *SNP* 2. *D. Martin, *Lab.* 3. I. Duncan, *C.* 4. *A. Smith, *SNP*
5. *C. Stihler, *Lab.* 6. D. Coburn, *UKIP*

SOUTH EAST
(Bracknell Forest, Brighton and Hove, Buckinghamshire, East Sussex, Hampshire, Isle of Wight, Kent, Medway, Milton Keynes, Newbury, Oxfordshire, Portsmouth, Reading, Slough, Southampton, Surrey, West Sussex, Windsor and Maidenhead, Wokingham)

E. 6,441,003		T. 36.46%
UKIP	751,439	(32.1%)
C.	723,571	(31.0%)
Lab.	342,775	(14.7%)
Green	211,706	(9.1%)
LD	187,876	(8.0%)

AIFE	45,199	(1.9%)
Eng. Dem.	17,771	(0.8%)
BNP	16,909	(0.7%)
CPA	14,893	(0.6%)
Peace	10,130	(0.4%)
SGB	5,454	(0.2%)
Roman	2,997	(0.1%)
Your	2,932	(0.1%)
Liberty	2,494	(0.1%)
Harmony	1,904	(0.1%)
UKIP majority		27,868

(June 2009, C. maj. 372,286)

MEMBERS ELECTED
1. *N. Farage, *UKIP* 2. *D. Hannan, *C.*
3. J. Atkinson, *UKIP* 4. *N. Deva, *C.*
5. A. Dodds, *Lab.* 6. D. James, *UKIP*
7. *R. Ashworth, *C.* 8. *K.Taylor, *Green*
9. * C. Bearder, *LD* 10. R. Finch, *UKIP*

SOUTH WEST
(Bath and North East Somerset, Bournemouth, Bristol, Cornwall, Devon, Dorset, Gloucestershire, North Somerset, Plymouth, Poole, Somerset, South Gloucestershire, Swindon, Torbay, Wiltshire, Isles of Scilly, Gibraltar)

E. 4,059,889		T. 37.03%
UKIP	484,184	(32.3%)
C.	433,151	(28.9%)
Lab.	206,124	(13.8%)
Green	166,447	(11.1%)
LD	160,376	(10.7%)
AIFE	23,169	(1.6%)
Eng. Dem.	15,081	(1.0%)
BNP	10,910	(0.7%)
UKIP majority		51,033

(June 2009, C. maj. 126,627)

MEMBERS ELECTED
1. *W. Dartmouth, *UKIP* 2. *A. Fox, *C.*
3. J. Reid, *UKIP* 4. *J. Girling, *C.*
5. C. Moody, *Lab.* 6. M. Scott Cato, *Green*

WALES

E. 2,327,175		T. 31.50%
Lab.	206,332	(28.2%)
UKIP	201,983	(27.6%)
C.	127,742	(17.4%)
PC	111,864	(15.3%)
Green	33,275	(4.5%)
LD	28,930	(4.0%)
BNP	7,655	(1.0%)
BF	6,633	(0.9%)
SLP	4,459	(0.6%)
No2EU	2,803	(0.4%)
SGB	1,384	(0.2%)
Lab. majority		4,349

(June 2004, Lab. maj. 120,039)

MEMBERS ELECTED
1. *D. Vaughan, *Lab.* 2. N. Gill, *UKIP*
3. *K. Swinburne, *C.* 4. *J. Evans, *PC*

WEST MIDLANDS
(Herefordshire, Shropshire, Staffordshire, Stoke-on-Trent, Telford and Wrekin, Warwickshire, West Midlands Metropolitan area, Worcestershire)

E. 4,105,305		T. 33.31%
UKIP	428,010	(28.1%)
Lab.	363,033	(21.3%)
C.	330,470	(17.0%)
LD	75,648	(12.0%)
Green	71,464	(8.6%)
AIFE	27,171	(6.2%)
WDR	23,426	(2.3%)
BNP	20,643	(1.3%)
Eng. Dem.	12,832	(1.0%)
No2EU	4,653	(0.9%)
Harmony	1,857	(0.6%)
UKIP majority		64,977

(June 2009, C. maj. 96,016)

MEMBERS ELECTED
1. J Seymour, *UKIP* 2. N. Gill, *Lab.*
3. *P. Bradbourn, *C.* 4. J. Carver, *UKIP*
5. S. Simon, *Lab.* 6. *A. McIntyre, *C.*
7. B. Etheridge, *UKIP*

YORKSHIRE AND THE HUMBER
(East Riding of Yorkshire, Kingston-upon-Hull, North East Lincolnshire, North Lincolnshire, North Yorkshire, South Yorkshire, West Yorkshire, York)

E. 3,905,726		T. 33.2%
UKIP	403,630	(31.1%)
Lab.	380,189	(29.3%)
C	248,945	(19.2%)
Green	102,282	(7.9%)
LD	81,108	(6.3%)
AIFE	24,297	(1.9%)
BNP	20,138	(1.6%)
YF	19,017	(1.5%)
Eng. Dem.	13,288	(1.0%)
No2EU	3,807	(0.3%)
UKIP majority		23,441

(June 2009, C. maj. 69,793)

MEMBERS ELECTED
1. J. Collins, *UKIP* 2. *L. McAvan, *Lab.*
3. *T. Kirkhope, *C.* 4. A. Bashir, *UKIP*
5. R. Corbett, *Lab.* 6. M. Hookem, *UKIP*

LOCAL GOVERNMENT

Major changes in local government were introduced in England and Wales in 1974 and in Scotland in 1975 by the Local Government Act 1972 and the Local Government (Scotland) Act 1973. Further significant alterations were made in England by the Local Government Acts of 1985, 1992 and 2000.

The structure in England was based on two tiers of local authorities (county councils and district councils) in the non-metropolitan areas; and a single tier of metropolitan councils in the six metropolitan areas of England and London borough councils in London.

Following reviews of the structure of local government in England by the Local Government Commission (now the Boundary Commission for England), 46 unitary (all-purpose) authorities were created between April 1995 and April 1998 to cover certain areas in the non-metropolitan counties. The remaining county areas continue to have two tiers of local authorities. The county and district councils in the Isle of Wight were replaced by a single unitary authority on 1 April 1995; the former counties of Avon, Cleveland, Humberside and Berkshire were replaced by unitary authorities; and Hereford & Worcester was replaced by a new county council for Worcestershire (with district councils) and a unitary authority for Herefordshire. On 1 April 2009 the county areas of Cornwall, Durham, Northumberland, Shropshire and Wiltshire were given unitary status and two new unitary authorities were created for Bedfordshire (Bedford and Central Bedfordshire) and Cheshire (Cheshire East and Cheshire West & Chester) replacing the two-tier county/district system in these areas.

The Local Government (Wales) Act 1994 and the Local Government etc (Scotland) Act 1994 abolished the two-tier structure in Wales and Scotland with effect from 1 April 1996, replacing it with a single tier of unitary authorities. In June 2015 the Welsh government published a proposal to reduce the number of local authorities in Wales from 22 to eight or nine.

In Northern Ireland a reform programme to reduce the number of local authorities from 26 to 11 began in 2012 when legislation finalising the boundaries of the new 11 local government district authorities was approved by the Northern Ireland Assembly. The Local Government Act (Northern Ireland) 2014 received royal assent on 12 May 2014, providing the legislative framework for the 11 new councils. On 1 April 2015 additional functions, that were previously the responsibility of the Northern Ireland executive, fully transferred to the new district authorities.

ELECTIONS

Local elections are normally held on the first Thursday in May. Generally, all citizens of the UK, the Republic of Ireland, Commonwealth and other European Union citizens who are 18 years or over and resident on the qualifying date in the area for which the election is being held, are entitled to vote at local government elections. A register of electors is prepared and published annually by local electoral registration officers.

A returning officer has the overall responsibility for an election. Voting takes place at polling stations, arranged by the local authority and under the supervision of a presiding officer specially appointed for the purpose. Candidates, who are subject to various statutory qualifications and disqualifications designed to ensure that they are suitable to hold office, must be nominated by electors for the electoral area concerned.

In England, the Local Government Boundary Commission for England is responsible for carrying out periodic reviews of electoral arrangements, to consider whether the boundaries of wards or divisions within a local authority need to be altered to take account of changes in electorate; structural reviews, to consider whether a single, unitary authority should be established in an area instead of an existing two-tier system; and administrative boundary reviews of district or county authorities.

The Local Democracy and Boundary Commission for Wales, the Local Government Boundary Commission for Scotland and the local government boundary commissioner for Northern Ireland (appointed when required by the Boundary Commission for Northern Ireland) are responsible for reviewing the electoral arrangements and boundaries of local authorities within their respective regions.

The Local Government Act 2000 provided for the secretary of state to change the frequency and phasing of elections in England and Wales.

LOCAL GOVERNMENT BOUNDARY COMMISSION FOR ENGLAND, 14th Floor, Millbank Tower, London SW1P 4QP T 0330-500 1525 E reviews@lgbce.org.uk W www.lgbce.org.uk

LOCAL DEMOCRACY AND BOUNDARY COMMISSION FOR WALES, Ground Floor, Hastings House, Fitzalan Court, Cardiff CF24 0BL T 029-2046 4819 E ldbc.wales@wales.gsi.gov.uk W www.lgbc-wales.gov.uk

LOCAL GOVERNMENT BOUNDARY COMMISSION FOR SCOTLAND, Thistle House, 91 Haymarket Terrace, Edinburgh EH12 5HD T 0131-538 7510 E lgbcs@scottishboundaries.gov.uk W www.lgbc-scotland.gov.uk

BOUNDARY COMMISSION FOR NORTHERN IRELAND, Stormont House, Stormont Estate, Belfast BT4 3SH T 028-9069 4800 E bcni@belfast.org.uk W www.boundarycommission.org.uk

INTERNAL ORGANISATION

The council as a whole is the final decision-making body within any authority. Councils are free to a great extent to make their own internal organisational arrangements. The Local Government Act, given royal assent on 28 July 2000, allows councils to adopt one of three broad categories of constitution which include a separate executive:
• A directly elected mayor with a cabinet selected by that mayor
• A cabinet, either elected by the council or appointed by its leader
• A directly elected mayor and council manager
Normally, questions of policy are settled by the full council, while the administration of the various services is the responsibility of committees of councillors. Day-to-day decisions are delegated to the council's officers, who act within the policies laid down by the councillors.

FINANCE

Local government in England, Wales and Scotland is financed from four sources: council tax, non-domestic rates, government grants and income from fees and charges for services.

COUNCIL TAX

Council tax is a local tax levied by each local council. Liability for the council tax bill usually falls on the owner-occupier or tenant of a dwelling which is their sole or main residence. Council tax bills may be reduced because of the personal circumstances of people resident in a property and there are discounts in the case of dwellings occupied by fewer than two adults.

In England, unitary and metropolitan authorities are responsible for collecting their own council tax. In areas where there are two tiers of local authority, each county and district authority sets its own council tax rate; the district authorities collect the combined council tax and the county councils claim their share from the district councils' collection funds. In Wales, each unitary authority sets its own council tax rate and is responsible for collection. In Scotland, each local authority sets its own rate of council tax.

The tax relates to the value of the dwelling. In England and Scotland each dwelling is placed in one of eight valuation bands, ranging from A to H, based on the property's estimated market value as at 1 April 1991. In Wales there are nine bands, ranging from A to I, based on the estimated market value of property as at 1 April 2003.

The valuation bands and ranges of values in England, Wales and Scotland are:

England

A	Up to £40,000	E	£88,001–£120,000
B	£40,001–£52,000	F	£120,001–£160,000
C	£52,001–£68,000	G	£160,001–£320,000
D	£68,001–£88,000	H	Over £320,001

Wales

A	Up to £44,000	F	£162,001–£223,000
B	£44,001–£65,000	G	£223,001–£324,000
C	£65,001–£91,000	H	£324,001–£424,000
D	£91,001–£123,000	I	Over £424,001
E	£123,001–£162,000		

Scotland

A	Up to £27,000	E	£58,001–£80,000
B	£27,001–£35,000	F	£80,001–£106,000
C	£35,001–£45,000	G	£106,001–£212,000
D	£45,001–£58,000	H	Over £212,001

The council tax within a local area varies between the different bands according to proportions laid down by law. The charge attributable to each band as a proportion of the Band D charge set by the council is approximately:

A	67%	F	144%
B	78%	G	167%
C	89%	H	200%
D	100%	I	233%*
E	122%		

* Wales only

The average Band D council tax bill for each authority area is given in the tables starting on page 264. There may be variations from the given figure within each district council area because of different parish or community precepts being levied.

NON-DOMESTIC RATES

Non-domestic (business) rates are collected by billing authorities; these are the district councils in those areas of England with two tiers of local government and are unitary authorities in other parts of England, in Wales and in Scotland. In respect of England and Wales, the Local Government Finance Act 1988 provides for liability for rates to be assessed on the basis of a poundage (multiplier) tax on the rateable value of property (hereditaments). Separate multipliers are set by the Department for Communities and Local Government (CLG) in England, the Welsh government and the Scottish government. Rates are collected by the billing authority for the area where a property is located. Rate income collected by billing authorities is paid into a national non-domestic rating (NNDR) pool and redistributed to individual authorities on the basis of the adult population figure as prescribed by CLG, the Welsh government or the Scottish government. The rates pools are maintained separately in England, Wales and Scotland. Actual payment of rates in certain cases is subject to transitional arrangements, to phase in the larger increases and reductions in rates resulting from the effects of the latest revaluation.

Rateable values for the 2010 rating lists for England, Wales and Scotland came into effect on 1 April 2010. They are derived from the rental value of property as at 1 April 2003 and determined on certain statutory assumptions by the Valuation Office Agency in England and Wales, and by local area assessors in Scotland. New property which is added to the list, and significant changes to existing property, necessitate amendments to the rateable value on the same basis. Rating lists (valuation rolls in Scotland) remain in force until the next general revaluation, which usually take place every five years to reflect changes in the property market. The next revaluations for England, Wales and Scotland are scheduled for 2017.

A revaluation of non-domestic properties in Northern Ireland was completed at the start of 2015 and since 1 April 2015 the rateable value of all non-domestic properties in Northern Ireland is based on the rental value of the property as at 1 April 2013; there is no date scheduled for the next revaluation.

Certain types of property are exempt from rates, eg agricultural land and buildings, certain businesses and some places of public religious worship. Charities and other non-profit-making organisations may receive full or partial relief and relief schemes for small businesses are available in England, Wales, Scotland and Northern Ireland. Empty commercial property in England and Wales is exempt from business rates for the first three months that the property is vacant (six months for some types of property such as industrial premises and listed buildings), after which full business rates are normally payable. In Scotland an empty commercial property is exempt from business rates for the first three months and entitled to a 10 per cent discount thereafter, except for empty industrial and listed buildings and properties with a rateable value of less than £1,700, which are entirely exempt.

COMPLAINTS

ENGLAND

In England the Local Government Ombudsman investigates complaints of injustice arising from maladministration by local authorities and certain other bodies. The Local Government Ombudsman will not usually consider a complaint unless the local authority concerned has had an opportunity to investigate and reply to a complainant.

LOCAL GOVERNMENT OMBUDSMAN, PO Box 4771, Coventry CV4 0EH T 0300-061 0614 W www.lgo.org.uk
Ombudsman, Dr Jane Martin

WALES

The office of Public Services Ombudsman for Wales came into force on 1 April 2006, incorporating the functions of the Local Government Ombudsman for Wales.

PUBLIC SERVICES OMBUDSMAN FOR WALES,
1 Ffordd yr Hen Gae, Pencoed CF35 5LJ T 0300-790 0203
W www.ombudsman-wales.org.uk
Ombudsman, Nick Bennett

SCOTLAND

The Scottish Public Services Ombudsman is responsible for complaints regarding the maladministration of local government in Scotland.

SCOTTISH PUBLIC SERVICES OMBUDSMAN,
4 Melville Street, Edinburgh EH3 7NS T 0800-377 7330
W www.spso.org.uk
Ombudsman, Jim Martin

NORTHERN IRELAND

The Northern Ireland Ombudsman (also known as the Northern Ireland Commissioner for Complaints) fulfils a similar function in Northern Ireland, investigating complaints about local authorities and certain public bodies. Complaints are made to the relevant local authority in the first instance but may also be made directly to the ombudsman.

NORTHERN IRELAND COMMISSIONER FOR
COMPLAINTS, 33 Wellington Place, Belfast BT1 6HN
T 028-9023 3821 E ombudsman@ni-ombudsman.org.uk
W www.ni-ombudsman.org.uk
Ombudsman, Dr Tom Frawley, CBE

THE QUEEN'S REPRESENTATIVES

The lord-lieutenant of a county is the permanent local representative of the Crown in that county. The appointment of lord-lieutenants is now regulated by the Lieutenancies Act 1997. They are appointed by the sovereign on the recommendation of the prime minister. The retirement age is 75. The office of lord-lieutenant dates from 1551, and its holder was originally responsible for maintaining order and for local defence in the county. The duties of the post include attending on royalty during official visits to the county, performing certain duties in connection with the armed forces (and in particular the reserve forces), and making presentations of honours and awards on behalf of the Crown. In England, Wales and Northern Ireland, the lord-lieutenant usually also holds the office of *Custos Rotulorum.* As such, he or she acts as head of the county's commission of the peace (which recommends the appointment of magistrates).

The office of sheriff (from the Old English *shire-reeve*) of a county was created in the tenth century. The sheriff was the special nominee of the sovereign, and the office reached the peak of its influence under the Norman kings. The Provisions of Oxford (1258) laid down a yearly tenure of office. Since the mid-16th century the office has been purely civil, with military duties taken over by the lord-lieutenant of the county. The sheriff (commonly known as 'high sheriff') attends on royalty during official visits to the county, acts as the returning officer during parliamentary elections in county constituencies, attends the opening ceremony when a high court judge goes on circuit, executes high court writs, and appoints under-sheriffs to act as deputies. The appointments and duties of the sheriffs in England and Wales are laid down by the Sheriffs Act 1887.

The serving high sheriff submits a list of names of possible future sheriffs to a tribunal, which chooses three names to put to the sovereign. The tribunal nominates the high sheriff annually on 12 November and the sovereign picks the name of the sheriff to succeed in the following year. The term of office runs from 25 March to the following 24 March (the civil and legal year before 1752). No person may be chosen twice in three years if there is any other suitable person in the county.

CIVIC DIGNITIES

District councils in England and local councils in Wales may petition for a royal charter granting borough or 'city' status to the council.

In England and Wales the chair of a borough or county borough council may be called a mayor, and the chair of a city council may be called a lord mayor (if lord mayoralty has been conferred on that city). Parish councils in England and community councils in Wales may call themselves 'town councils', in which case their chair is the town mayor.

In Scotland the chair of a local council may be known as a convenor; a provost is the mayoral equivalent. The chair of the councils for the cities of Aberdeen, Dundee, Edinburgh and Glasgow are lord provosts.

ENGLAND

There are 27 counties, divided into 201 districts, 55 unitary authorities (plus the Isles of Scilly) and 36 metropolitan boroughs.

The populations of most of the unitary authorities are in the range of 100,000 to 300,000. The district councils have populations broadly in the range of 60,000 to 150,000; some, however, have larger populations, because of the need to avoid dividing large towns, and some in mainly rural areas have smaller populations.

The main conurbations outside Greater London – Tyne and Wear, West Midlands, Merseyside, Greater Manchester, West Yorkshire and South Yorkshire – are divided into 36 metropolitan boroughs, most of which have a population of over 200,000.

ELECTIONS

For districts, counties and for 8,810 parishes, there are elected councils, consisting of directly elected councillors. The councillors elect one of their number as chair annually.

In general, councils can have whole council elections, elections by thirds or elections by halves. However all metropolitan authorities must hold elections by thirds. The electoral cycle of any new unitary authority is specified in the appropriate statutory order under which it is established.

FUNCTIONS

In areas with a two-tier system of local governance, functions are divided between the district and county authorities, with those functions affecting the larger area or population generally being the responsibility of the county council. A few functions continue to be exercised over the larger area by joint bodies, made up of councillors from each authority within the area.

Generally the allocation of functions is as follows:
County councils: education; strategic planning; traffic, transport and highways; fire service; consumer protection; refuse disposal; smallholdings; social care; libraries
District councils: local planning; housing; highways (maintenance of certain urban roads and off-street car parks); building regulations; environmental health; refuse collection; cemeteries and crematoria; collection of council tax and non-domestic rates
Unitary and metropolitan councils: their functions are all those listed above, except that the fire service is exercised by a joint body

Concurrently by county and district councils: recreation (parks, playing fields, swimming pools); museums; encouragement of the arts, tourism and industry

PARISH COUNCILS

Parish or town councils are the most local tier of government in England. There are currently around 10,000 parishes in England, of which around 8,810 have councils. Since 15 February 2008 local councils have been able to create new parish councils without seeking approval from the government. Around 80 per cent of parish councils represent populations of less than 2,500; parishes with no parish council can be grouped with neighbouring parishes under a common parish council. A parish council comprises at least five members, the number being fixed by the district council. Elections are held every four years, at the time of the election of the district councillor for the ward including the parish. Full parish councils must be formed for those parishes with more than 999 electors – below this number, parish meetings comprising the electors of the parish must be held at least twice a year.

Parish council functions include: allotments; encouragement of arts and crafts; community halls, recreational facilities (eg open spaces, swimming pools), cemeteries and crematoria; and many minor functions. They must also be given an opportunity to comment on planning applications. They may, like county and district councils, spend limited sums for the general benefit of the parish. They levy a precept on the district councils for their funds. Parish precepts for 2015–16 totalled £409m, an increase of 5.2 per cent on 2014–15.

FINANCE

Local government revenue expenditure is budgeted to be £9.54bn in 2015–16; of this £24.7bn is to be raised through council tax, £11.9bn from the business rate retention scheme and £56.6bn from government grants. The remainder will be drawn down from local authority reserves.

Since April 2013 local authorities retain a share of business rates and keep the growth on that share (the 'rate retention scheme'). Revenue support grant is paid to local authorities to enable all authorities in the same class to broadly set the same council tax; in 2015–16 revenue support grant totals £9.5bn. In addition central government pays specific grants in support of revenue expenditure on particular services. Police grant totals £7.4bn in 2015–16.

In England, the average council tax per dwelling for 2014–15 is £1,051. The average council tax bill for a Band D dwelling (occupied by two adults, including parish precepts) for 2015–16 is £1,484, an increase of 1.1 per cent from 2014–15. The average Band D council tax is £1,547 in shire districts, £1,451 in metropolitan areas, £1,520 in unitary authority areas and £1,298 in London. Since 2006–7 the London figure has included a levy to fund the 2012 Olympic Games, which equates to a £20 a year increase on a Band D council tax. This levy is expected to continue until 2016–17.

The non-domestic rating multiplier for England for 2015–16 is 49.3p (48.0p for small businesses). The City of London is able to set a different multiplier from the rest of England; for 2015–16 this is 49.7p (48.4p for small businesses).

Under the Local Government and Housing Act 1989, local authorities have four main ways of paying for capital expenditure: borrowing and other forms of extended credit; capital grants from central government towards some types of capital expenditure; 'usable' capital receipts from the sale of land, houses and other assets; and revenue.

The amount of capital expenditure which a local authority can finance by borrowing (or other forms of credit) is effectively limited by the credit approvals issued to it by central government. Most credit approvals can be used for any kind of local authority capital expenditure; these are known as basic credit approvals. Others (supplementary credit approvals) can be used only for the kind of expenditure specified in the approval, and so are often given to fund particular projects or services.

Local authorities can use all capital receipts from the sale of property or assets for capital spending, except in the case of sales of council houses. Generally, the 'usable' part of a local authority's capital receipts consists of 25 per cent of receipts from the sale of council houses and 50 per cent of other housing assets such as shops or vacant land. The balance has to be set aside as provision for repaying debt and meeting other credit liabilities.

EXPENDITURE

Budgeted revenue expenditure for 2015–16 is:

Service	£ million
*Education	34,976
Highways and transport	4,922
Social care	21,779
Public health	3,321
Housing (excluding HRA)	1,742
Cultural, environment and planning	8,695
Police	10,951
Fire and rescue	2,080
Central services	3,112
Mandatory housing benefits	21,094
Other services	281
Less appropriations from accumulated absences account	(6)
Net current expenditure	113,089
Capital financing	4,463
Capital expenditure charged to revenue account	1,320
Discretionary non-domestic rate relief	–
Bad debt provision	57
Flood defence payments to Environment Agency	30
Private Finance Initiative schemes	4
Carbon Reduction Commitment	25
Less adjustments permitted by regulation	(20)
Less interest receipts	(793)
Less specific grants outside AEF	(22,427)
Less Business Rates Supplement	(223)
Less Community Infrastructure Levy	(87)
REVENUE EXPENDITURE	95,437

HRA = Housing Revenue Account

AEF = aggregate external finance

* Education expenditure is not comparable to previous years due to a number of schools becoming centrally funded academies

LONDON

The Greater London Council was abolished in 1986 and London was divided into 32 borough councils, which have a status similar to the metropolitan borough councils in the rest of England, and the City of London Corporation.

In March 1998 the government announced proposals for a Greater London Authority (GLA) covering the area of the 32 London boroughs and the City of London, which would comprise a directly elected mayor and a 25-member assembly. A referendum was held in London on 7 May 1998 and 72 per cent of voters balloted in favour of the GLA. A London mayor was elected on 4 May 2000 and the authority assumed its responsibilities on 3 July 2000 (*see also* Regional Government).

LONDON BOROUGH COUNCILS

The London boroughs have whole council elections every four years, in the year immediately following the county council election year. The most recent elections took place on 22 May 2014.

The borough councils have responsibility for the following functions: building regulations, cemeteries and crematoria, consumer protection, education, youth employment, environmental health, electoral registration, food, drugs, housing, leisure services, libraries, local planning, local roads, museums, parking, recreation (parks, playing fields, swimming pools), refuse collection and street cleaning, social services, town planning and traffic management.

CITY OF LONDON CORPORATION

The City of London Corporation is the local authority for the City of London. Its legal definition is the 'Mayor and Commonalty and Citizens of the City of London'. It is governed by the court of common council, which consists of the lord mayor, 25 other aldermen and 100 common councilmen. The lord mayor and two sheriffs are nominated annually by the City guilds (the livery companies) and elected by the court of aldermen. Aldermen and councilmen are elected from the 25 wards into which the City is divided; councilmen must stand for re-election annually. The council is a legislative assembly, and there are no political parties.

The corporation has the same functions as the London borough councils. In addition, it runs the City of London Police; is the health authority for the Port of London; has health control of animal imports throughout Greater London, including at Heathrow airport; owns and manages public open spaces throughout Greater London; runs the central criminal court; and runs Billingsgate, New Spitalfields and Smithfield markets.

THE CITY GUILDS (LIVERY COMPANIES)

The livery companies of the City of London grew out of early medieval religious fraternities and began to emerge as trade and craft guilds, retaining their religious aspect, in the 12th century. From the early 14th century, only members of the trade and craft guilds could call themselves citizens of the City of London. The guilds began to be called livery companies, because of the distinctive livery worn by the most prosperous guild members on ceremonial occasions, in the late 15th century.

By the early 19th century the power of the companies within their trades had begun to wane, but those wearing the livery of a company continued to play an important role in the government of the City of London. Liverymen still have the right to nominate the lord mayor and sheriffs, and most members of the court of common council are liverymen.

WALES

The Local Government (Wales) Act 1994 abolished the two-tier structure of eight county and 37 district councils which had existed since 1974, and replaced it, from 1 April 1996, with 22 unitary authorities. The new authorities were elected in May 1995. Each unitary authority inherited all the functions of the previous county and district councils, except fire services (which are provided by three combined fire authorities, composed of representatives from the unitary authorities) and national parks (which are the responsibility of three independent national park authorities). In June 2015 the Welsh government published plans to reduce the number of local authorities from 22 to eight or nine.

COMMUNITY COUNCILS

In Wales communities are the equivalent of parishes in England. Unlike England, where many areas are not in any parish, communities have been established for the whole of Wales, approximately 865 communities in all. Community meetings may be convened as and when desired.

Community or town councils exist in around 730 of the communities and further councils may be established at the request of a community meeting. Community councils have broadly the same range of powers as English parish councils. Community councillors are elected for a term of four years.

ELECTIONS

Elections take place every four years; the last elections took place in May 2012.

FINANCE

Total budgeted revenue expenditure for 2015–16 is £7.8bn, a decrease of 1.6 per cent on 2014–15. Total budget requirement, which excludes expenditure financed by specific and special government grants and any use of reserves, is £6bn. This comprises revenue support grant of £3.3bn, support from the national non-domestic rate pool of £1bn, police grant of £221m and £1.6bn to be raised through council tax. The non-domestic rating multiplier for Wales for 2015–16 is 48.2p. The average Band D council tax levied in Wales for 2015–16 is £1,328, comprising unitary authorities £1,088, police and crime commissioners £211 and community councils £29.

EXPENDITURE

Local authority budgeted revenue expenditure for 2015–16 is:

Service	£ million
Education	2,555.1
Social services	1,639.0
Council fund housing	1,141.2
Local environmental services	377.8
Roads and transport	286.5
Libraries, culture, heritage, sport and recreation	218.6
Planning, economic and community development	80.6
Council tax collection	36.2
Debt financing	338.3
Central administrative and other revenue expenditure	313.3
Police	666.9
Fire	144.8
National parks	14.5
Gross revenue expenditure	7,812.8
Less specific and special government grants	(1,935.1)
Net revenue expenditure	5,877.7
Less appropriations from reserves	(84.5)
Council tax reduction scheme	255.7
BUDGET REQUIREMENT	6,048.9

SCOTLAND

The Local Government etc (Scotland) Act 1994 abolished the two-tier structure of nine regional and 53 district councils which had existed since 1975 and replaced it, from 1 April 1996, with 29 unitary authorities on the mainland; the three islands councils remained. The new authorities were elected in April 1995.

In July 1999 the Scottish parliament assumed responsibility for legislation on local government.

ELECTIONS

The unitary authorities consist of directly elected councillors. The Scottish Local Government (Elections) Act 2002 moved elections from a three-year to a four-year cycle, but to avoid the local authority elections coinciding with the Scottish parliament elections in May 2011, the last local authority elections took place in May 2012.

FUNCTIONS

The functions of the councils and islands councils are: education; social work; strategic planning; the provision of infrastructure such as roads; consumer protection; flood prevention; coast protection; valuation and rating; the police and fire services; civil defence; electoral registration; public transport; registration of births, deaths and marriages; housing; leisure and recreation; development and building control; environmental health; licensing; allotments; public conveniences; and the administration of district courts.

COMMUNITY COUNCILS

Scottish community councils differ from those in England and Wales. Their purpose as defined in statute is to ascertain and express the views of the communities they represent, and to take in the interests of their communities such action as appears to be expedient or practicable. Around 1,200 community councils have been established under schemes drawn up by local authorities in Scotland.

FINANCE

Budgeted total revenue support for 2015–16 is £10.0bn, comprising £7.1bn general resource grant, non-domestic rate income of £2.8bn and specific revenue grants of £90.9m. The non-domestic rate multiplier or poundage for 2015–16 is 48.0p. Larger businesses in 2015–16 (rateable value in excess of £35,000) pay a poundage supplement of 1.3p, which contributes towards the cost of the small business bonus scheme. Non-domestic properties with a rateable value of £18,000 or less may be eligible for non-domestic rates relief – ranging from 25 to 100 per cent – from the small business bonus scheme. The average Band D council tax for 2015–16 is £1,149.

EXPENDITURE

Local authority budgeted net expenditure for 2015–16 is:

Service	£ million
Education	4,764.7
Cultural and related services	583.2
Social work services	3,106.3
Roads and transport	457.7
Environmental services	680.7
Planning and development services	278.8
Other	2,005.7
TOTAL	11,877.1

NORTHERN IRELAND

In 2012 a reform programme began to reduce the number of district councils from 26 to 11. The Local Government Act (Northern Ireland) received royal assent on 12 May 2014 providing new governance arrangements for local councils and made transitional provisions for the transfer of staff, assets and liabilities etc to the new 11 councils. On 1 April 2015 additional functions, that were previously the responsibility of the Northern Ireland executive, fully transferred to the new district authorities.

ELECTIONS

Elections to the 11 councils took place on 22 May 2014.

FUNCTIONS

The councils are responsible for approving business and financial plans, setting domestic and non-domestic rates. From April 2016 councils will also be responsible for urban regeneration and community development.

The district councils are responsible for:

Direct Service Provision of a wide range of local services, including: building control-inspection and the regulation of new buildings; byelaw enforcement; cemeteries; community centres; cultural facilities; dog control; environmental health; food safety; health and safety; local economic development; local planning; off-street parking (except park and ride schemes); parks, open spaces and playgrounds; public conveniences; recycling and waste management; registration of births, deaths and marriages; sport, leisure and recreational facilities; and street cleaning. District councils also have a role in community development and safety; sports development; summer schemes; and tourism.

Representation: nominating representatives to sit as members of the various statutory bodies responsible for the administration of regional services such as education, health and social services, libraries and road safety committees

FINANCE

Government in Northern Ireland is part-funded by a system of rates, which supplement the Northern Ireland budget from the UK government. The ratepayer receives a combined tax bill consisting of the regional rate, set by the Northern Ireland executive, and the district rate, which is set by each district council. The regional and district rates are both collected by the Land and Property Services Agency (formerly the Rate Collection Agency). The product of the district rates is paid over to each council while the product of the regional rate supports expenditure by the departments of the executive and assembly.

Since April 2007 domestic rates bills have been based on the capital value of a property, rather than the rental value. The capital value is defined as the price the property might reasonably be expected to realise had it been sold on the open market on 1 January 2005. Non-domestic rates bills are based on 2001 rental values.

Rate bills are calculated by multiplying the property's net annual rental value (in the case of non-domestic property), or capital value (in the case of domestic property), by the regional and district rate poundages respectively.

For 2015–16 the overall average domestic poundage is 0.7490p compared to 0.7387p in 2014–15. The overall average non-domestic rate poundage in 2015–16 is 55.47p compared to 59.17p in 2014–15.

POLITICAL COMPOSITION OF LOCAL COUNCILS

as at May 2015

Abbreviations

All.	Alliance
BNP	British National Party
C.	Conservative
DUP	Democratic Unionist Party
Green	Green
Ind.	Independent
Ind. Un.	Independent Unionist
Lab.	Labour
LD	Liberal Democrat
Lib.	Liberal
O.	Other
PC	Plaid Cymru
PUP	Progressive Unionist Party of Northern Ireland
R.	Residents Associations/Ratepayers
SD	Social Democrat
SDLP	Social Democratic and Labour Party
SF	Sinn Fein
SNP	Scottish National Party
Soc.	Socialist
TUV	Traditional Unionist Voice
UKIP	UK Independence Party
UUP	Ulster Unionist Party
v.	vacant

Total number of seats is given in parentheses after council name.

ENGLAND

COUNTY COUNCILS

Buckinghamshire (49)	C. 37; LD 4; UKIP 4; Ind. 2; Lab. 1; O. 1
Cambridgeshire (69)	C. 33; LD 13; UKIP 11; Lab. 8; Ind. 4
Cumbria (84)	Lab. 36; C. 26; LD 15; Ind. 5; O. 2; v. 2
Derbyshire (64)	Lab. 43; C. 17; LD 3; v. 1
Devon (62)	C. 38; LD 9; Lab. 7; UKIP 4; Ind. 3; Green 1
Dorset (45)	C. 27; LD 12; Lab. 5; UKIP. 1
East Sussex (49)	C. 20; LD 10; Lab. 7; UKIP 7; Ind. 3; O. 2
Essex (75)	C. 44; Lab. 9; LD 9; UKIP 6; O. 4; Green 2; Ind. 1
Gloucestershire (53)	C. 24; LD 14; Lab. 9; UKIP 3; Green 1; Ind. 1; O. 1
Hampshire (78)	C. 46; LD 16; UKIP 9; Lab. 4; Ind. 2; O. 1
Hertfordshire (77)	C. 46; LD 16; Lab. 15
Kent (84)	C. 46; UKIP 16; Lab. 13; LD 7; Green 1; Ind. 1
Lancashire (84)	Lab. 39; C. 35; LD 6; Ind. 3; Green 1
Leicestershire (55)	C. 30; LD 13; Lab. 10; UKIP 2
Lincolnshire (77)	C. 34; Lab. 12; UKIP 12; O. 11; LD 4; Ind. 3; v. 1
Norfolk (84)	C. 40; UKIP 14; Lab. 13; LD 10; Green 4; O. 1; v. 2
North Yorkshire (72)	C. 45; Ind. 10; Lab. 7; LD 6; Lib. 2; UKIP 2
Northamptonshire (57)	C. 36; Lab. 11; LD 6; UKIP 3; Ind. 1
Nottinghamshire (67)	Lab. 32; C. 21; LD 7; O. 4; Ind. 3
Oxfordshire (63)	C. 31; Lab. 15; LD 11; Ind. 4; Green 2
Somerset (55)	C. 31; LD 15; Lab. 3; Ind. 3; UKIP 3
Staffordshire (62)	C. 34; Lab. 23; O. 3; Ind. 1; UKIP 1
Suffolk (75)	C. 38; Lab. 15; UKIP 9; LD 7; Ind. 4; Green 2
Surrey (81)	C. 58; LD. 9; R. 9; UKIP 3; Green 1; Lab. 1
Warwickshire (62)	C. 26; Lab. 22; LD 9; Ind. 3; Green 2
West Sussex (71)	C. 44; UKIP 10; LD 7; Lab. 6; Ind. 4
Worcestershire (57)	C. 31; Lab. 11; LD 4; Ind. 3; O. 3; Green 2; UKIP 2; R. 1

DISTRICT COUNCILS

Adur (30)	C. 21; UKIP 6; Ind. 2; Lab. 1
Allerdale (56)	Lab. 28; C. 17; Ind. 4; O. 4; UKIP 3
Amber Valley (45)	C. 24; Lab. 23
Arun (54)	C. 42; LD 5; UKIP 4; Ind. 2; Lab. 1
Ashfield (35)	Lab. 22; LD 5; C. 4; Ind. 3; O. 1
Ashford (43)	C. 34; Lab. 4; Ind. 3; LD 1; UKIP 1
Aylesbury Vale (59)	C. 43; LD 9; UKIP 4; Lab. 2; Ind. 1
Babergh (43)	C. 31; Ind. 8; LD 3; Lab. 1
Barrow-in-Furness (36)	Lab. 27; C. 9
Basildon (42)	C. 18; UKIP 11; Lab. 9; O. 2; Green 1; LD 1
Basingstoke and Deane (60)	C. 32; Lab. 17; LD 7; Ind. 4
Bassetlaw (48)	Lab. 33; C. 12; Ind. 3
Blaby (39)	C. 29; Lab. 6; LD 4
Bolsover (37)	Lab. 32; Ind. 4; O. 1
Boston (30)	C. 13; UKIP 12; Ind. 2; Lab. 2; O. 1
Braintree (49)	C. 44; Lab. 2; R. 2; Green 1
Breckland (49)	C. 42; UKIP 4; Lab. 2; Ind. 1
Brentwood (37)	C. 23; LD 11; Lab. 2; Ind. 1
Broadland (47)	C. 43; LD 4
Bromsgrove (31)	C. 18; Lab. 7; Ind. 3; R. 3
Broxbourne (30)	C. 24; Lab. 3; O. 2; UKIP 1
Broxtowe (44)	C. 27; Lab. 12; LD 4; Ind. 1
Burnley (45)	Lab. 30; LD 10; C. 5
Cambridge (42)	Lab. 24; LD 14; Ind. 2; C. 1; Green 1
Cannock Chase (41)	Lab. 22; C. 12; UKIP 5; Ind. 1; LD 1
Canterbury (39)	C. 31; Lab. 3; LD 3; UKIP 2
Carlisle (52)	Lab. 29; C. 20; Ind. 2; LD 1
Castle Point (41)	C. 23; O. 13; UKIP 3; Ind. 2
Charnwood (52)	C. 41; Lab. 9; Ind. 1; LD 1
Chelmsford (57)	C. 52; LD 5
Cheltenham (40)	LD 24; C. 11; O. 4; Ind. 1
Cherwell (50)	C. 41; Lab. 7; LD 1; Ind. 1; O. 1
Chesterfield (48)	Lab. 34; LD 11; Ind. 2; UKIP 1
Chichester (48)	C. 42; Ind. 3; LD 3
Chiltern (40)	C. 35; LD 3; Ind. 2
Chorley (47)	Lab. 31; C. 14; Ind. 2
Christchurch (24)	C. 21; Ind. 2; UKIP 1

Colchester (60) C. 27; LD 20; Lab. 9; O. 4
Copeland (51) Lab. 29; C. 17; Ind. 5
Corby (29) Lab. 24; C. 5
Cotswolds (34) C. 24; LD 10
Craven (30) C. 20; Ind. 6; LD 2; Lab. 1; UKIP 1
Crawley (37) Lab. 19; C. 18
Dacorum (51) C. 46; LD 3; Lab. 2
Dartford (44) C. 34; Lab. 7; R. 3
Daventry (36) C. 31; Lab. 2; UKIP 2; LD 1
Derbyshire Dales (39) C. 29; Lab. 5; LD 3; Ind. 1; O. 1
Dover (45) C. 25; Lab. 17; UKIP 3
East Cambridgeshire (39) C. 36; LD 2; Ind. 1
East Devon (59) C. 37; Ind. 15; LD 6; O. 1
East Dorset (29) C. 25; LD 3; Ind. 1
East Hampshire (44) C. 42; LD 2
East Hertfordshire (50) C. 50
East Lindsey (55) C. 33; UKIP 8; Ind. 6; Lab. 4; O. 3; LD 1
East Northamptonshire (40) C. 37; Ind. 2; LD 1
East Staffordshire (39) C. 25; Lab. 12; LD 1; UKIP 1
Eastbourne (27) LD 18; C. 9
Eastleigh (44) LD 38; C. 6
Eden (38) C. 21; Ind. 10; LD 7
Elmbridge (60) C. 33; R. 19; LD 7; O. 1
Epping Forest (58) C. 38; R. 12; LD 3; Ind. 2; UKIP 2; Green 1
Epsom and Ewell (38) R. 31; C. 4; Lab. 3
Erewash (47) C. 30; Lab. 17
Exeter (40) Lab. 29; C. 10; LD 1
Fareham (31) C. 24; LD 4; Ind. 2; UKIP 1
Fenland (39) C. 34; Ind. 3; LD 2
Forest Heath (27) C. 23; Ind. 2; Lab. 1; LD 1
Forest of Dean (48) C. 21; Lab. 13; UKIP 7; Ind. 5; Green 2
Fylde (51) C. 32; Ind. 12; LD 2; O. 2; R. 2; Lab. 1
Gedling (41) Lab. 25; C. 15; LD 1
Gloucester (36) C. 20; Lab. 9; LD 7
Gosport (34) C. 21; Lab. 6; LD 6; UKIP 1
Gravesham (44) C. 23; Lab. 21
Great Yarmouth (39) C. 14; Lab. 14; UKIP 10; Ind. 1
Guildford (48) C. 35; LD 9; O. 3; Lab. 1
Hambleton (28) C. 27; UKIP 1
Harborough (37) C. 29; LD 8
Harlow (33) Lab. 19; C. 12; UKIP 2
Harrogate (54) C. 35; LD 15; Ind. 2; O. 2
Hart (33) C. 16; LD 8; O. 8; Ind. 1
Hastings (32) Lab. 24; C. 8
Havant (38) C. 31; Lab. 4; UKIP 2; LD 1
Hertsmere (39) C. 37; Lab. 2
High Peak (43) C. 23; Lab. 17; LD 2; Ind. 1
Hinckley and Bosworth (34) C. 21; LD 12; Lab. 1
Horsham (44) C. 39; LD 4; Ind. 1
Huntingdonshire (52) C. 35; Ind. 5; UKIP 5; LD 4; Lab. 2; O. 1
Hyndburn (34) Lab. 25; C. 7; UKIP 2
Ipswich (48) Lab. 31; C. 15; LD 2
Kettering (36) C. 25; Lab. 7; Ind. 1; v. 3
King's Lynn and West Norfolk (62) C. 50; Lab. 10; Ind. 2
Lancaster (60) Lab. 29; C. 19; Green 9; Ind. 2; O. 1
Lewes (41) C. 24; LD 11; Green 3; Ind. 2; UKIP 1
Lichfield (47) C. 41; Lab. 4; LD 1; UKIP 1
Lincoln City (33) Lab. 27; C. 6

Maidstone (55) C. 25; LD 20; Ind. 6; Lab. 2; UKIP 2
Maldon (31) C. 28; Ind. 2; UKIP 1
Malvern Hills (38) C. 23; Ind. 7; LD 5; Green 3
Mansfield (36) Lab. 18; Ind. 16; UKIP 2
Melton (28) C. 26; Ind. 2
Mendip (47) C. 32; LD 11; Green 3; Ind. 1
Mid Devon (42) C. 28; Ind. 6; LD 5; UKIP 2; Lib. 1
Mid Suffolk (40) C. 29; Green 5; LD 4; Ind. 2
Mid Sussex (54) C. 54
Mole Valley (41) C. 23; LD 10; Ind. 6; v. 2
New Forest (60) C. 58; LD 2
Newark and Sherwood (39) C. 24; Lab. 12; Ind. 3
Newcastle-under-Lyme (60) Lab. 28; C. 20; LD 5; Ind. 4; UKIP 2; Green 1
North Devon (43) C. 19; LD 12; Ind. 10; O. 1; UKIP 1
North Dorset (33) C. 27; LD 4; Ind. 2
North East Derbyshire (53) Lab. 34; C. 18; Ind. 1
North Hertfordshire (49) C. 36; Lab. 11; LD 2
North Kesteven (43) C. 28; O. 15
North Norfolk (48) C. 33; LD 15
North Warwickshire (35) C. 22; Lab. 13
North West Leicestershire (38) C. 25; Lab. 10; Ind. 2; LD 1
Northampton (45) C. 26; Lab. 17; LD 2
Norwich (39) Lab. 22; Green 14; LD 3
Nuneaton and Bedworth (34) Lab. 28; C. 3; Green 2; Ind. 1
Oadby and Wigston (26) LD 19; C. 6; Lab. 1
Oxford (48) Lab. 33; LD 8; Green 6; Ind. 1
Pendle (49) C. 19; Lab. 18; LD 11; BNP 1
Preston (57) Lab. 32; C. 19; LD 5; Ind. 1
Purbeck (25) C. 20; LD 4; Ind. 1
Redditch (29) Lab. 15; C. 13; UKIP 1
Reigate and Banstead (51) C. 40; R. 7; Green 2; LD 1; UKIP 1
Ribble Valley (40) C. 35; LD 4; Lab. 1
Richmondshire (34) C. 21; Ind. 11; LD 2
Rochford (39) C. 28; Green 4; UKIP 3; LD 2; Lab. 1; O. 1
Rossendale (36) Lab. 19; C. 15; Ind. 1; O. 1
Rother (38) C. 31; O. 3; LD 2; Ind. 1; Lab. 1
Rugby (42) C. 22; Lab. 9; LD 8; Ind. 3
Runnymede (42) C. 36; R. 6
Rushcliffe (44) C. 34; Lab. 4; Green 2; Ind. 2; LD 2
Rushmoor (39) C. 26; Lab. 11; UKIP 2
Ryedale (30) C. 20; Ind. 5; Lib. 3; LD 2
St Albans (58) C. 32; LD 16; Lab. 8; Green 1; Ind. 1
St Edmundsbury (45) C. 36; UKIP 4; Ind. 2; Lab. 2; Green 1; Ind. 1
Scarborough (50) C. 26; Lab. 14; UKIP 5; Ind. 3; Green 2
Sedgemoor (48) C. 35; Lab. 10; UKIP 2; LD 1
Selby (31) C. 22; Lab. 8; Ind. 1
Sevenoaks (54) C. 49; LD 2; Ind. 1; Lab. 1; UKIP 1
Shepway (30) C. 22; UKIP 7; Lab. 1
South Bucks (28) C. 27; Ind. 1
South Cambridgeshire (57) C. 38; LD 11; Ind. 7; Lab. 1
South Derbyshire (36) C. 24; Lab. 12
South Hams (31) C. 25; Green 3; LD 2; Lab. 1
South Holland (37) C. 28; Ind. 7; UKIP 2

South Kesteven (58) C. 45; Ind. 5; Lab. 3; O. 2; UKIP 1; v. 2
South Lakeland (51) LD 32; C. 15; Lab. 3; Ind. 1
South Norfolk (46) C. 40; LD 6
South Northamptonshire C. 35; Lab. 4; LD 3 (42)
South Oxfordshire (36) C. 33; Lab. 1; LD 1; R 1
South Ribble (50) C. 29; Lab. 19; LD 2
South Somerset (60) LD 29; C. 28; Ind. 3
South Staffordshire (49) C. 43; Ind. 4; Lab. 1; UKIP 1
Spelthorne (39) C. 35; LD 3; Lab. 1
Stafford (40) C. 29; Lab. 9; Ind. 2
Staffordshire Moorlands C. 41; Lab. 7; O. 6; LD 2 (56)
Stevenage (39) Lab. 30; C. 6; LD 3
Stratford-on-Avon (36) C. 31; LD 3; Ind. 1; Lab. 1
Stroud (51) C. 23; Lab. 18; Green 6; LD 3; O. 1
Suffolk Coastal (42) C. 37; Ind. 2; LD 2; Lab. 1
Surrey Heath (40) C. 36; Ind. 2; Lab. 1; LD 1
Swale (47) C. 32; UKIP 9; Lab. 4; Ind. 2
Tamworth (30) C. 18; Lab. 11; UKIP 1
Tandridge (42) C. 35; LD 6; Ind. 1
Taunton Deane (56) C. 36; LD 14; Ind. 3; Lab. 2; UKIP 1
Teignbridge (46) C. 30; LD 11; Ind. 5
Tendring (60) C. 23; UKIP 16; Ind. 11; Lab. 4; R. 3; LD 1; O. 1; v. 1
Test Valley (48) C. 38; LD 9; Ind. 1
Tewkesbury (38) C. 33; Ind. 2; LD 2; O. 1
Thanet (56) UKIP 33; C. 18; Lab. 4; Ind. 1
Three Rivers (39) LD 19; C. 17; Lab. 3
Tonbridge and Malling C. 48; LD 4; Ind. 2 (54)
Torridge (36) C. 19; O. 10; UKIP 7
Tunbridge Wells (48) C. 42; LD 3; Lab. 2; Ind. 1
Uttlesford (39) C. 23; O. 9; LD 6; Ind. 1
Vale of White Horse (38) C. 29; LD 9
Warwick (46) C. 31; Lab. 9; R. 3; LD 2; Green 1
Watford (36) LD 18; Lab. 13; C. 5
Waveney (48) C. 27; Lab. 20; Green 1
Waverley (57) C. 53; R. 3; Ind. 1
Wealden (55) C. 50; Ind. 5
Wellingborough (36) C. 27; Lab. 9
Welwyn and C. 31; Lab. 15; LD 2 Hatfield (48)
West Devon (31) C. 21; Ind. 9; LD 1
West Dorset (42) C. 30; LD 12
West Lancashire (54) Lab. 30; C. 23; O. 1
West Lindsey (36) C. 24; LD 7; Lab. 3; Ind. 2
West Oxfordshire (49) C. 40; Lab. 4; LD 4; Ind. 1
West Somerset (28) C. 21; Ind. 3; UKIP 3; Lab. 1
Weymouth and Portland C. 14; Lab. 13; LD 6; Ind. 3 (36)
Winchester (57) C. 33; LD 22; Lab. 2
Woking (36) C. 24; LD 9; Lab. 2; Ind. 1
Worcester (35) C. 19; Lab. 15; Green 1
Worthing (37) C. 30; LD 4; UKIP 2; Green 1
Wychavon (45) C. 38; LD 5; UKIP 1; v. 1
Wycombe (60) C. 47; Lab. 6; O. 3; Ind. 2; LD 1; UKIP 1
Wyre (50) C. 36; Lab. 14
Wyre Forest (33) C. 23; Ind. 5; Lab. 3; LD 1; UKIP 1

LONDON BOROUGH COUNCILS

Barking and Dagenham Lab. 51 (51)
Barnet (63) C. 32; Lab. 30; LD 1

Bexley (63) C. 45; Lab. 15; UKIP 3
Brent (63) Lab. 56; C. 6; LD 1
Bromley (60) C. 51; Lab. 7; UKIP 2
Camden (54) Lab. 40; C. 12; Green 1; LD 1
Croydon (70) Lab. 40; C. 30
Ealing (69) Lab. 53; C. 12; LD 4
Enfield (63) Lab. 39; C. 22; Ind. 2
Greenwich (51) Lab. 43; C. 8
Hackney (57) Lab. 50; C. 4; LD 3
Hammersmith and Lab. 26; C. 20 Fulham (46)
Haringey (57) Lab. 48; LD 9
Harrow (63) Lab. 34; C. 26; Ind. 2; LD 1
Havering (54) Ind. 24; C. 22; UKIP 7; Lab. 1
Hillingdon (65) C. 42; Lab. 23
Hounslow (60) Lab. 47; C. 11; Ind. 1; v. 1
Islington (48) Lab. 47; Green 1
Kensington and Chelsea C. 37; Lab. 12; LD 1 (50)
Kingston upon Thames C. 28; LD 18; Lab. 2 (48)
Lambeth (63) Lab. 59; C. 3; Green 1
Lewisham (55) Lab. 54; Green 1
Merton (60) Lab. 36; C. 20; R. 3; O. 1
Newham (60) Lab. 60
Redbridge (63) Lab. 35; C. 25; LD 3
Richmond upon Thames C. 39; LD 15 (54)
Southwark (63) Lab. 48; LD 13; C. 2
Sutton (54) LD 43; C. 8; Ind. 2; v. 1
Tower Hamlets (45) Lab. 22; Ind. 17; C. 5; v. 1
Waltham Forest (60) Lab. 44; C. 16
Wandsworth (60) C. 39; Lab. 19; O. 2
Westminster (60) C. 44; Lab. 16

METROPOLITAN BOROUGHS

Barnsley (63) Lab. 55; C. 4; Ind. 4
Birmingham (120) Lab. 79; C. 30; LD 11
Bolton (60) Lab. 39; C. 15; LD 3; UKIP 3
Bradford (90) Lab. 46; C. 23; LD 9; O. 8; Green 3; Ind. 1
Bury (51) Lab. 35; C. 12; LD 2; Green 1; Ind. 1
Calderdale (51) Lab. 24; C. 21; LD 5; Ind. 1
Coventry (54) Lab. 41; C. 13
Doncaster (63) Lab. 42; C. 8; O. 3; UKIP 2; Ind. 1
Dudley (72) Lab. 38; C. 25; UKIP 7; Green 1; Ind. 1
Gateshead (66) Lab. 56; LD 10
Kirklees (69) Lab. 34; C. 18; LD 10; Green 4; Ind. 3
Knowsley (63) Lab. 63
Leeds (99) Lab. 63; C. 19; LD 9; O. 5; Green 3
Liverpool (90) Lab. 81; Green 4; LD 2; O. 2; Ind. 1
Manchester (96) Lab. 96
Newcastle-upon-Tyne Lab. 53; LD 22; Ind. 3 (78)
North Tyneside (60) Lab. 49; C. 9; LD 2
Oldham (60) Lab. 45; LD 10; C. 2; UKIP 2; Ind. 1
Rochdale (60) Lab. 47; C. 11; LD 2
Rotherham (63) Lab. 48; UKIP 12; Ind. 2; C. 1
St Helens (48) Lab. 42; C. 3; LD 3
Salford (60) Lab. 52; C. 8
Sandwell (72) Lab. 68; Ind. 2; UKIP 1; v. 1
Sefton (66) Lab. 42; LD 16; C. 7; O. 1
Sheffield (84) Lab. 59; LD 17; Green 4; UKIP 4

Solihull (51)	C. 32; Green 9; LD 6; UKIP 2; Ind. 1; Lab. 1
South Tyneside (54)	Lab. 52; C. 1; Ind. 1
Stockport (63)	LD 26; Lab. 21; C. 13; Ind. 3
Sunderland (75)	Lab. 66; C. 6; Ind. 3
Tameside (57)	Lab. 52; C. 5
Trafford (63)	C. 34; Lab. 26; LD 3
Wakefield (63)	Lab. 53; C. 6; Ind. 2; UKIP 2
Walsall (60)	Lab. 27; C. 25; UKIP 3; Ind. 2; LD 2; O. 1
Wigan (75)	Lab. 64; Ind. 8; C. 3
Wirral (66)	Lab. 38; C. 21; LD 5; Green 1; Ind. 1
Wolverhampton (60)	Lab. 48; C. 10; LD 1; UKIP 1

UNITARY COUNCILS

Bath and North East Somerset (65)	C. 37; LD 15; Lab. 6; Ind. 5; Green 2
Bedford (40)	C. 15; Lab. 14; LD 9; Ind. 2
Blackburn with Darwen (64)	Lab. 47; C. 14; LD 3
Blackpool (42)	Lab. 29; C. 13; LD 1; v. 1
Bournemouth (54)	C. 51; Green 1; Ind. 1; UKIP 1
Bracknell Forest (42)	C. 41; Lab. 1
Brighton and Hove (54)	Lab. 23; C. 20; Green 11
Bristol (70)	Lab. 30; C. 16; Green 14; LD 9; UKIP 1
Central Bedfordshire (59)	C. 53; Ind. 3; Lab. 2; LD 1
Cheshire East (82)	C. 53; Lab. 16; O. 7; R. 3; LD 2; Ind. 1
Cheshire West and Chester (75)	Lab. 38; C. 36; Ind. 1
Cornwall (123)	LD 37; Ind. 36; C. 29; Lab. 8; UKIP 6; O. 5; Green 1; v. 1
Darlington (50)	Lab. 29; C. 17; LD 3; Ind. 1
Derby (51)	Lab. 27; C. 14; LD 7; UKIP 2; Ind. 1
Durham (126)	Lab. 96; Ind. 17; LD 9; C. 4
East Riding of Yorkshire (67)	C. 51; Lab. 6; Ind. 5; UKIP 3; LD 2
Halton (56)	Lab. 52; LD 2; C. 2
Hartlepool (33)	Lab. 22; C. 3; Ind. 3; O. 3; UKIP 2
Herefordshire (58)	C. 27; Ind. 13; O. 13; LD 3; Green 2
*Isles of Scilly (21)	Ind. 19; v. 2
Isle of Wight (40)	Ind. 21; C. 14; Lab. 2; UKIP 2; LD 1
Kingston-upon-Hull (59)	Lab. 40; LD 15; C. 2; O. 1; UKIP 1
Leicester (54)	Lab. 52; C. 1; LD 1
Luton (48)	Lab. 35; LD 8; C. 5
Medway (55)	C. 36; Lab. 15; UKIP 3; Ind. 1
Middlesbrough (47)	Lab. 34; O. 6; C. 4; Ind. 3
Milton Keynes (57)	Lab. 23; C. 22; LD 12
North East Lincolnshire (42)	Lab. 19; C. 10; UKIP 9; LD 3; v. 1
North Lincolnshire (43)	C. 26; Lab. 17
North Somerset (50)	C. 36; Ind. 7; LD 4; Lab. 3
Northumberland (68)	Lab. 32; C. 21; LD 10; Ind. 2; O. 2; v. 1
Nottingham (55)	Lab. 52; C. 3
Peterborough (57)	C. 26; Lab. 12; Ind. 6; O. 4; LD 4; UKIP 4; v. 1
Plymouth (57)	Lab. 28; C. 26; UKIP 3
Poole (42)	C. 32; LD 6; O. 3; UKIP 1
Portsmouth (42)	C. 18; LD 15; Lab. 4; UKIP 4; Ind. 1

Reading (46)	Lab. 31; C. 10; Green 3; LD 2
Redcar and Cleveland (59)	Lab. 29; LD 11; C. 10; Ind. 8; UKIP 1
Rutland (26)	C. 17; Ind. 7; LD 2
Shropshire (74)	C. 47; LD 13; Lab. 9; O. 4; Ind. 1
Slough (42)	Lab. 30; C. 10; UKIP 2
South Gloucestershire (70)	C. 40; LD 16; Lab. 14
Southampton (48)	Lab. 25; C. 20; O. 2; Ind. 1
Southend-on-Sea (51)	C. 22; Ind. 11; Lab. 9; LD 4; O. 3; UKIP 2
Stockton-on-Tees (56)	Lab. 32; C. 13; O. 10; LD 1
Stoke-on-Trent (44)	Lab. 21; Ind. 14; C. 7; UKIP 2
Swindon (57)	C. 32; Lab. 23; LD 2
Telford and Wrekin (54)	Lab. 27; C. 22; LD 3; Ind. 2
Thurrock (49)	Lab. 18; C. 17; UKIP 12; Ind. 2
Torbay (37)	C. 26; LD 7; Ind. 3; UKIP 1
Warrington (57)	Lab. 42; LD 9; C. 5; O. 1
West Berkshire (52)	C. 48; LD 4
Wiltshire (98)	C. 60; LD 21; Ind. 12; Lab. 4; UKIP 1
Windsor and Maidenhead (57)	C. 54; R. 2; LD 1
Wokingham (54)	C. 47; LD 5; Ind. 1; Lab. 1
York (47)	Lab. 15; C. 14; LD 12; Green 4; Ind. 2

* Thirteen councillors are elected by the residents of the isle of St Mary's and two councillors each are elected by the residents of the four other islands (Bryher, St Agnes, St Martins and Tresco)

WALES

Blaenau Gwent (42)	Lab. 32; Ind. 10
Bridgend (54)	Lab. 38; Ind. 11; LD 3; C. 1; PC 1
Caerphilly (73)	Lab. 47; PC 20; Ind. 3; v. 3
Cardiff (80)	Lab. 51; LD 15; C. 9; PC 3; Ind. 2
Carmarthenshire (74)	PC 29; Lab. 22; Ind. 21; O. 2
Ceredigion (42)	PC 19; Ind. 11; LD 7; O. 5
Conwy (59)	Ind. 19; C. 13; PC 12; Lab. 11; LD 4
Denbighshire (47)	Lab. 18; Ind. 13; C. 8; PC 8
Flintshire (70)	Lab. 33; O. 17; C. 8; Ind. 6; LD 6
Gwynedd (75)	PC 37; Ind. 18; O. 12; Lab. 5; LD 2; v. 1
Merthyr Tydfil (33)	Lab. 25; Ind. 8
Monmouthshire (43)	C. 19; Lab. 11; Ind. 10; LD 3
Neath Port Talbot (64)	Lab. 50; PC 8; Ind. 6
Newport (50)	Lab. 37; C. 10; Ind. 2; LD 1
Pembrokeshire (60)	Ind. 31; O. 16; Lab. 6; PC 4; C. 3
Powys (73)	O. 35; Ind. 13; C. 11; LD 8; Lab. 6
Rhondda Cynon Taff (75)	Lab. 60; PC 9; Ind. 4; C. 1; LD 1
Swansea (72)	Lab. 48; LD 12; Ind. 8; C. 4
Torfaen (44)	Lab. 30; Ind. 8; C. 4; PC 2
Vale of Glamorgan (47)	Lab. 21; C. 12; PC 6; Ind. 4; O. 3; UKIP 1
Wrexham (52)	Ind. 27; Lab. 13; O. 5; LD 5; PC 2
Ynys Mon (Isle of Anglesey) (30)	Ind. 12; PC 12; O. 3; Lab. 2; LD 1

SCOTLAND

Aberdeen (43)	Lab. 17; SNP 13; LD 5; Ind. 3; C. 2; O. 1; v. 2
Aberdeenshire (68)	SNP 28; C. 13; Ind. 13; LD 11; Lab. 2; Green 1
Angus (29)	SNP 14; Ind. 9; C. 4; LD 1; Lab. 1

Argyll and Bute (36)	Ind. 17; SNP 9; C. 4; LD 4; Lab. 1; O. 1
Clackmannanshire (18)	Lab. 8; SNP 8; C. 1; Ind. 1
Dumfries and Galloway (47)	Lab. 15; C. 14; SNP 10; Ind. 5; O. 3
Dundee (29)	SNP 16; Lab. 10; C. 1; Ind. 1; LD 1
East Ayrshire (32)	SNP 15; Lab. 14; C. 2; Ind. 1
East Dunbartonshire (24)	Lab. 9; SNP 8; LD 3; C. 2; Ind. 2
East Lothian (23)	Lab. 10; SNP 8; C. 3; Ind. 2
East Renfrewshire (20)	Lab. 8; C. 6; SNP 4; Ind. 2
Edinburgh (58)	Lab. 20; SNP 17; C. 11; Green 6; LD 3; Ind. 1
Eilean Siar (Western Isles) (31)	Ind. 23; SNP 6; Lab. 2
Falkirk (31)	Lab. 14; SNP 12; Ind. 3; C. 2
Fife (78)	Lab. 33; SNP 27; LD 10; Ind. 4; C. 3; O. 1
Glasgow (79)	Lab. 45; SNP 27; Green 5; C. 1; LD 1
Highland (80)	Ind. 32; SNP 21; LD 11; Lab. 8; O. 8
Inverclyde (20)	Lab. 9; SNP 6; Ind. 2; LD 2; C. 1
Midlothian (18)	Lab. 8; SNP 8; Green 1; Ind. 1
Moray (26)	SNP 11; Ind. 10; C. 3; Lab. 2
North Ayrshire (30)	SNP 12; Lab. 11; Ind. 6; C. 1
North Lanarkshire (70)	Lab. 43; SNP 21; Ind. 6
Orkney Islands (21)	Ind. 18; O. 3
Perth and Kinross (41)	SNP 18; C. 10; LD 5; Lab. 4; Ind. 4
Renfrewshire (40)	Lab. 22; SNP 15; C. 1; Ind. 1; LD 1
Scottish Borders (34)	Ind. 10; C. 9; SNP 9; LD 6
Shetland Islands (22)	Ind. 22
South Ayrshire (30)	C. 10; Lab. 9; SNP 9; Ind. 2
South Lanarkshire (67)	Lab. 38; SNP 21; C. 3; Ind. 3; LD 1; O. 1
Stirling (22)	SNP 9; Lab. 8; C. 4; Green 1
West Dunbartonshire (22)	Lab. 12; SNP 6; Ind. 3; O. 1
West Lothian (33)	Lab. 16; SNP 15; C. 1; Ind. 1

NORTHERN IRELAND

Antrim and Newtownabbey (40)	DUP 15; UUP 11; All. 4; SDLP 4; SF 3; TUV 2; v. 1
Armagh, Banbridge and Craigavon (41)	DUP 13; UUP 12; SF 8; SDLP 6 Ind. 1; UKIP 1
Belfast (60)	SF 19; DUP 13; All. 8; SDLP 7; UUP 7; PUP 3; Green 1; O. 1; TUV 1
Causeway Coast and Glens (40)	DUP 11; UUP 9; SF 7; SDLP 6; TUV 3; All. 1; Ind. 1; Ind. Un. 1; PUP 1
Derry and Strabane (40)	SF 16; SDLP 10; DUP 8; Ind. 4; UUP 2
Fermanagh and Omagh (40)	SF 17; UUP 9; SDLP 8; DUP 5; Ind. 1
Lisburn and Castlereagh (40)	DUP 20; UUP 8; All. 7; SDLP 3; O. 1; TUV 1
Mid and East Antrim (40)	DUP 18; UUP 10; TUV 5; All. 3; SF 3; Ind. 2; SDLP 1; UKIP 1
Mid Ulster (40)	SF 18; DUP 8; UUP 7; SDLP 6; Ind. 1
Newry, Mourne and Down (41)	SF 14; SDLP 13; Ind. 5; DUP 4; UUP 3; All. 1; UKIP 1
North Down and Ards (40)	DUP 17; UUP 9; All. 7; Ind. 3; Green 2; SDLP 1; TUV 1

ENGLAND

The country of England lies between 55° 46′ and 49° 57′ 30″ N. latitude (from a few miles north of the mouth of the Tweed to the Lizard), and between 1° 46′ E. and 5° 43′ W. longitude (from Lowestoft to Land's End). England is bounded on the north by the Cheviot Hills; on the south by the English Channel; on the east by the Straits of Dover (Pas de Calais) and the North Sea; and on the west by the Atlantic Ocean, Wales and the Irish Sea. It has a total area of 130,432 sq. km (50,360 sq. miles): land 130,279 sq. km (50,301 sq. miles); inland water 153 sq. km (59 sq. miles).

POPULATION
The population at the 2011 census was 53,012,456 (men 26,069,148; women 26,943,308). The average density of the population in 2011 was 406 persons per sq. km (1,053 per sq. mile).

FLAG
The flag of England is the cross of St George, a red cross on a white field (cross gules in a field argent). The cross of St George, the patron saint of England, has been used since the 13th century.

RELIEF
There is a marked division between the upland and lowland areas of England. In the extreme north the Cheviot Hills (highest point, the Cheviot, 815m/2,674ft) form a natural boundary with Scotland. Running south from the Cheviots, though divided from them by the Tyne Gap, is the Pennine range (highest point, Cross Fell, 893m/2,930ft), the main orological feature of the country. The Pennines culminate in the Peak District of Derbyshire (Kinder Scout, 636m/2,088ft). West of the Pennines are the Cumbrian mountains, which include Scafell Pike (978m/3,210ft), the highest peak in England, and to the east are the Yorkshire Moors, their highest point being Urra Moor (454m/1,490ft).

In the west, the foothills of the Welsh mountains extend into the bordering English counties of Shropshire (the Wrekin, 407m/1,334ft; Long Mynd, 516m/1,694ft) and Hereford and Worcester (the Malvern Hills – Worcestershire Beacon, 425m/1,394ft). Extensive areas of highland and moorland are also to be found in the south-western peninsula formed by Somerset, Devon and Cornwall, principally Exmoor (Dunkery Beacon, 519m/1,704ft), Dartmoor (High Willhays, 621m/2,038ft) and Bodmin Moor (Brown Willy, 420m/1,377ft). Ranges of low, undulating hills run across the south of the country, including the Cotswolds in the Midlands and south-west, the Chilterns to the north of London, and the North (Kent) and South (Sussex) Downs of the south-east coastal areas.

The lowlands of England lie in the Vale of York, East Anglia and the area around the Wash. The lowest-lying are the Cambridgeshire Fens in the valleys of the Great Ouse and the river Nene, which are below sea-level in places. Since the 17th century extensive drainage has brought much of the Fens under cultivation. The North Sea coast between the Thames and the Humber, low-lying and formed of sand and shingle for the most part, is subject to erosion and defences against further incursion have been built along many stretches.

HYDROGRAPHY
The Severn is the longest river in Great Britain, rising on the north-eastern slopes of Plynlimon (Wales) and entering England in Shropshire, with a total length of 354km (220 miles) from its source to its outflow into the Bristol Channel, where it receives the Bristol Avon on the east and the Wye on the west; its other tributaries are the Vyrnwy, Tern, Stour, Teme and Upper (or Warwickshire) Avon. The Severn is tidal below Gloucester, and a high bore or tidal wave sometimes reverses the flow as high as Tewkesbury (21.75km/13.5 miles above Gloucester). The scenery of the greater part of the river is very picturesque, and the Severn is a noted salmon river, with some of its tributaries being famous for trout. Navigation is assisted by the Gloucester and Berkeley Ship Canal (26km/16.25 miles), which admits vessels of 350 tons to Gloucester. The Severn Tunnel was begun in 1873 and completed in 1886 at a cost of £2m and after many difficulties caused by flooding. It is 7km (4 miles 628 yards) in length (of which 3.67km/2.25 miles are under the river). The Severn road bridge between Haysgate, Gwent, and Almondsbury, Glos, with a centre span of 988m (3,240ft), was opened in 1966.

The longest river wholly in England is the Thames, with a total length of 346km (215 miles) from its source in the Cotswold hills to the Nore, and is navigable by ocean-going ships to London Bridge. The Thames is tidal to Teddington (111km/69 miles from its mouth) and forms county boundaries almost throughout its course; on its banks are situated London, Windsor Castle, Eton College and Oxford University. Of the remaining English rivers, those flowing into the North Sea are the Tyne, Wear, Tees, Ouse and Trent from the Pennine Range, the Great Ouse (257km/160 miles), which rises in Northamptonshire, and the Orwell and Stour from the hills of East Anglia. Flowing into the English Channel are the Sussex Ouse from the Weald, the Itchen from the Hampshire hills, and the Axe, Teign, Dart, Tamar and Exe from the Devonian hills. Flowing into the Irish Sea are the Mersey, Ribble and Eden from the western slopes of the Pennines and the Derwent from the Cumbrian mountains.

The English Lakes, notable for their picturesque scenery and poetic associations, lie in Cumbria's Lake District; the largest are Windermere (14.7 sq. km/5.7 sq. miles), Ullswater (8.8 sq. km/3.4 sq. miles) and Derwent Water (5.3 sq. km/2.0 sq. miles).

ISLANDS
The Isle of Wight is separated from Hampshire by the Solent. The capital, Newport, stands at the head of the estuary of the Medina, and Cowes (at the mouth) is the chief port. Other centres are Ryde, Sandown, Shanklin, Ventnor, Freshwater, Yarmouth, Totland Bay, Seaview and Bembridge.

Lundy (the name is derived from the Old Norse for 'puffin island'), 18km (11 miles) north-west of Hartland Point, Devon, is around 5km (3 miles) long and almost 1km (half a mile) wide on average, with a total area of around 452 hectares (1,116 acres), and a population of 27. It became the property of the National Trust in 1969 and is now principally a bird sanctuary and the UK's first marine conservation zone.

The Isles of Scilly comprise around 140 islands and skerries (total area, 10 sq. km/6 sq. miles) situated 45 km (28 miles) south-west of Land's End in Cornwall. Only five are inhabited: St Mary's, St Agnes, Bryher, Tresco and St Martin's. The population at the 2011 census was 2,200. The entire group has been designated an Area of Outstanding Natural Beauty because of its unique flora and fauna. Tourism and the winter/spring flower trade for the home market form the basis of the economy of the islands. The island group is a recognised rural development area.

EARLY HISTORY

Archaeological evidence suggests that England has been inhabited since at least the Palaeolithic period, though the extent of the various Palaeolithic cultures was dependent upon the degree of glaciation. The succeeding Neolithic and Bronze Age cultures have left abundant remains throughout the country; the best-known of these are the henges and stone circles of Stonehenge (ten miles north of Salisbury, Wilts) and Avebury (Wilts), both of which are believed to have been of religious significance. In the latter part of the Bronze Age the Goidels, a people of the Celtic race, invaded the country and brought with them Celtic civilisation and dialects; as a result place names in England bear witness to the spread of the invasion across the whole region.

THE ROMAN CONQUEST

The Roman conquest of Gaul (57–50 BC) brought Britain into close contact with Roman civilisation, but although Julius Caesar raided the south of Britain in 55 and 54 BC, conquest was not undertaken until nearly 100 years later. In AD 43 the Emperor Claudius dispatched Aulus Plautius, with a well-equipped force of 40,000, and himself followed with reinforcements in the same year. Success was delayed by the resistance of Caratacus (Caractacus), the British leader from AD 48–51, who was finally captured and sent to Rome, and by a great revolt in AD 61 led by Boudicca (Boadicea), Queen of the Iceni, but the south of Britain was secured by AD 70, and Wales and the area north to the Tyne by about AD 80.

In AD 122, the Emperor Hadrian visited Britain and built a continuous rampart, since known as Hadrian's Wall, from Wallsend to Bowness (Tyne to Solway). The work was entrusted by the Emperor Hadrian to Aulus Platorius Nepos, legate of Britain from AD 122 to 126, and it was intended to form the northern frontier of the Roman Empire.

The Romans administered Britain as a province under a governor, with a well-defined system of local government, each Roman municipality ruling itself and its surrounding territory, while London was the centre of the road system and the seat of the financial officials of the Province of Britain. Colchester, Lincoln, York, Gloucester and St Albans stand on the sites of five Roman municipalities, and at Wroxeter, Caerleon, Chester, Lincoln and York were at various times the sites of legionary fortresses. Well-preserved Roman towns have been uncovered at or near Silchester *(Calleva Atrebatum)*, ten miles south of Reading, Wroxeter *(Viroconium Cornoviorum)*, near Shrewsbury, and St Albans *(Verulamium)* in Hertfordshire.

Four main groups of roads radiated from London, and a fifth (the Fosse) ran obliquely from Lincoln through Leicester, Cirencester and Bath to Exeter. Of the four groups radiating from London, one ran south-east to Canterbury and the coast of Kent, a second to Silchester and thence to parts of western Britain and south Wales, a third (later known as Watling Street) ran through St Albans to Chester, with various branches, and the fourth reached Colchester, Lincoln, York and the eastern counties.

In the fourth century Britain was subjected to raids along the east coast by Saxon pirates, which led to the establishment of a system of coastal defences from the Wash to Southampton Water, with forts at Brancaster, Burgh Castle (Yarmouth), Walton (Felixstowe), Bradwell, Reculver, Richborough, Dover, Lympne, Pevensey and Porchester (Portsmouth). The Irish (Scoti) and Picts in the north were also becoming more aggressive and from around AD 350 incursions became more frequent and more formidable. As the Roman Empire came increasingly under attack towards the end of the fourth century, many troops were removed from Britain for service in other parts of the empire. The island was eventually cut off from Rome by the Teutonic conquest of Gaul, and with the withdrawal of the last Roman garrison early in the fifth century, the Romano-British were left to themselves.

SAXON SETTLEMENT

According to legend, the British King Vortigern called in the Saxons to defend his lands against the Picts. The Saxon chieftains Hengist and Horsa landed at Ebbsfleet, Kent, and established themselves in the Isle of Thanet, but the events during the one-and-a-half centuries between the final break with Rome and the re-establishment of Christianity are unclear. However, it would appear that over the course of this period the raids turned into large-scale settlement by invaders traditionally known as Angles (England north of the Wash and East Anglia), Saxons (Essex and southern England) and Jutes (Kent and the Weald), which pushed the Romano-British into the mountainous areas of the north and west. Celtic culture outside Wales and Cornwall survives only in topographical names. Various kingdoms established at this time attempted to claim overlordship of the whole country, hegemony finally being achieved by Wessex (with the capital at Winchester) in the ninth century. This century also saw the beginning of raids by the Vikings (Danes), which were resisted by Alfred the Great (871–899), who fixed a limit on the advance of Danish settlement by the Treaty of Wedmore (878), giving them the area north and east of Watling Street on the condition that they adopt Christianity.

In the tenth century the kings of Wessex recovered the whole of England from the Danes, but subsequent rulers were unable to resist a second wave of invaders. England paid tribute *(Danegeld)* for many years, and was invaded in 1013 by the Danes and ruled by Danish kings (including Cnut) from 1016 until 1042, when Edward the Confessor was recalled from exile in Normandy. On Edward's death in 1066 Harold Godwinson (brother-in-law of Edward and son of Earl Godwin of Wessex) was chosen to be King of England. After defeating (at Stamford Bridge, Yorkshire, 25 September 1066) an invading army under Harald Hadraada, King of Norway (aided by the outlawed Earl Tostig of Northumbria, Harold's brother), Harold was himself defeated at the Battle of Hastings on 14 October 1066, and the Norman conquest secured the throne of England for Duke William of Normandy, a cousin of Edward the Confessor.

CHRISTIANITY

Christianity reached the Roman province of Britain from Gaul in the third century (or possibly earlier). Alban, traditionally Britain's first martyr, was put to death as a Christian during the persecution of Diocletian (22 June 303) at his native town *Verulamium,* and the bishops of *Londinium, Eboracum* (York), and *Lindum* (Lincoln) attended the Council of Arles in 314. However, the Anglo-Saxon invasions submerged the Christian religion in England until the sixth century: conversion was undertaken in the north from 563 by Celtic missionaries from Ireland led by St Columba, and in the south by a mission sent from Rome in 597 which was led by St Augustine, who became the first archbishop of Canterbury. England appears to have been converted again by the end of the seventh century and followed, after the Council of Whitby in 663, the practices of the Roman Church, which brought the kingdom into the mainstream of European thought and culture.

PRINCIPAL CITIES

There are 51 cities in England and space constraints prevent us from including profiles of them all. Below is a selection of

England's principal cities with the date on which city status was conferred in parentheses. Other cities are Bradford (pre-1900), Chelmsford (2012), Chichester (pre-1900), Coventry (pre-1900), Derby (1977), Ely (pre-1900), Exeter (pre-1900), Gloucester (pre-1900), Hereford (pre-1900), Kingston-upon-Hull (pre-1900), Lancaster (1937), Lichfield (pre-1900), London (pre-1900), Peterborough (pre-1900), Plymouth (1928), Portsmouth (1926), Preston (2002), Ripon (pre-1900), Salford (1926), Stoke-on-Trent (1925), Sunderland (1992), Truro (pre-1900), Wakefield (pre-1900), Wells (pre-1900), Westminster (pre-1900), Wolverhampton (2000) and Worcester (pre-1900).

Certain cities have also been granted a lord mayoralty – this grant confers no additional powers or functions and is purely honorific. Cities with lord mayors are Birmingham, Bradford, Bristol, Canterbury, Chester, Coventry, Exeter, Kingston-upon-Hull, Leeds, Leicester, Liverpool, London, Manchester, Newcastle-upon-Tyne, Norwich, Nottingham, Oxford, Plymouth, Portsmouth, Sheffield, Stoke-on-Trent, Westminster and York.

BATH (PRE-1900)

Bath stands on the river Avon between the Cotswold hills to the north and the Mendips to the south, and was originally a small Roman town *(Aquae Sulis)* with a baths and temple complex built around naturally occurring hot springs. In the early 18th century Bath became England's premier spa town where the rich and celebrated members of fashionable society gathered to 'take the waters' and enjoy the town's theatres and concert rooms. During this period the architect John Wood laid the foundations of a new Georgian city built using the honey-coloured stone for which Bath is famous today. Since 1987 the city has been listed as a UNESCO World Heritage Site.

Contemporary Bath is a thriving tourist destination and remains a leading cultural, religious and historical centre with many art galleries and historic sites including the Pump Room (1790); the Royal Crescent (1767); the Circus (1754); the 18th-century Assembly Rooms (housing the Museum of Costume); Pulteney Bridge (1771); the Guildhall and the Abbey, now over 500 years old, which is built on the site of a Saxon monastery. In 2006 the Bath Thermae Spa was completed and the hot springs reopened to the public for the first time since 1978.

BIRMINGHAM (PRE-1900)

Birmingham is Britain's second largest city, with a population of over one million. The generally accepted derivation of 'Birmingham' is the *ham* (dwelling-place) of the *ing* (family) of *Beorma*, presumed to have been Saxon. During the Industrial Revolution the town grew into a major manufacturing centre, known as the 'city of a thousand trades', and in 1889 was granted city status. By the 18th century, Birmingham was the main European producer of items such as buckles, medals and coins. Today, around 40 per cent of all the UK's handmade jewellery is produced in Birmingham's Jewellery Quarter. Another product of the Industrial Revolution are the city's 34 miles (56km) of canals.

Recent developments include Millennium Point, which houses Thinktank, the Birmingham science museum, and Brindleyplace, a development of shops, offices and leisure facilities on a former industrial site clustered around canals. In 2003 the Bullring shopping centre was officially opened as part of the city's urban regeneration programme.

The principal buildings are the Town Hall (1834–50), the Council House (1879), Victoria Law Courts (1891), the University of Birmingham (1906–9), the 13th-century Church of St Martin in the Bull Ring (rebuilt 1873), the cathedral (formerly St Philip's Church) (1711), the Roman Catholic cathedral of St Chad (1839–41), the Assay Office (1773), the Rotunda (1964) and the National Exhibition Centre (1976).

BRIGHTON AND HOVE (2000)

Brighton and Hove is situated on the south coast of England, around 96 km (60 miles) south of London. Originally a fishing village called Brighthelmstone, it was transformed into a fashionable seaside resort in the 18th century when Dr Richard Russell popularised the benefits of his 'sea-water cure'; as one of the closest beaches to London, Brighton began to attract wealthy visitors. One of these was the Prince Regent (the future King George IV), who first visited in 1783 and became so fond of the city that in 1807 he bought the former farmhouse he had been renting, and gradually turned it into Brighton's most recognisable building, the Royal Pavilion. The Pavilion is renowned for its Indo-Saracenic exterior, featuring minarets and an enormous central dome designed by John Nash, combined with the lavish chinoiserie of Frederick Crace's and Robert Jones' interiors. Queen Victoria sold the Pavilion to Brighton's municipal authority in 1850.

Brighton and Hove's Regency heritage can also be seen in the numerous elegant squares and crescents designed by Amon Wilds and Augustin Busby that dominate the seafront.

BRISTOL (PRE-1900)

Bristol was a royal borough before the Norman conquest. The earliest form of the name is *Bricgstow*. Due to the city's position close to the mouth of the River Avon, it was an important location for marine trade for centuries and prospered greatly from the transatlantic slave trade during the 18th century.

The principal buildings include the 12th-century Cathedral with Norman chapter house and gateway; the 14th-century Church of St Mary Redcliffe; Wesley's Chapel, Broadmead; the Merchant Venturers' Almshouses; the Council House (1956); the Guildhall; the Exchange (erected from the designs of John Wood in 1743); Cabot Tower; the University and Clifton College.

The Clifton Suspension Bridge, with a span of 214m (702ft) over the Avon, was projected by Isambard Kingdom Brunel in 1836 but was not completed until 1864. Brunel's SS *Great Britain,* the first ocean-going propeller-driven ship, now forms a museum at the Western Dockyard, from where she was originally launched in 1843. The docks themselves have been extensively restored and redeveloped; the 19th-century two-storey former tea warehouse is now the Arnolfini centre for contemporary arts, and an 18th-century sail-loft houses the Architecture Centre. On Princes Wharf, 1950s transit sheds have been renovated and converted into the museum of Bristol, M Shed, which opened in 2011.

CAMBRIDGE (1951)

Cambridge, a settlement far older than its ancient university, lies on the River Cam (or Granta). Its industries include technology research and development, and biotechnology. Among its open spaces are Jesus Green, Sheep's Green, Coe Fen, Parker's Piece, Christ's Pieces, the University Botanic Garden, and the 'Backs' – lawns and gardens through which the Cam winds behind the principal line of college buildings. Historical sites east of the Cam include King's Parade, Great St Mary's Church, Gibbs' Senate House and King's College Chapel.

University and college buildings provide the outstanding features of Cambridge's architecture but several churches (especially St Bene't's, the oldest building in the city, and Holy Sepulchre or the Round Church) are also notable. The

Guildhall (1937) stands on a site of which at least part has held municipal buildings since 1224. In 2009 the University of Cambridge celebrated its 800th anniversary.

CANTERBURY (PRE-1900)

Canterbury, seat of the Archbishop of Canterbury, the primate of the Church of England, dates back to prehistoric times. It was the Roman *Durovernum Cantiacorum* and the Saxon *Cant-wara-byrig* (stronghold of the men of Kent). It was here in 597 that St Augustine began the conversion of the English to Christianity, when Ethelbert, King of Kent, was baptised.

Of the Benedictine St Augustine's Abbey, burial place of the Jutish kings of Kent, only ruins remain. According to Bede, St Martin's Church, on the eastern outskirts of the city, was the place of worship of Queen Bertha, the Christian wife of King Ethelbert, before the advent of St Augustine.

In 1170 the rivalry of Church and State culminated in the murder of Archbishop Thomas Becket in Canterbury Cathedral, by Henry II's knights. His shrine became a great centre of pilgrimage, as described in Chaucer's *Canterbury Tales*. After the Reformation pilgrimages ceased, but the prosperity of the city was strengthened by an influx of Huguenot refugees, who introduced weaving. The poet and playwright Christopher Marlowe was born and raised in Canterbury and the city is home to the 1,200-seat Marlowe Theatre, which reopened to the public in 2011, following an extensive £25m rebuild.

The cathedral, its architecture ranging from the 11th to the 15th centuries, is famous worldwide. Visitors are attracted particularly to the Martyrdom, the Black Prince's Tomb and the Warriors' Chapel.

The medieval city walls are built on Roman foundations and the 14th-century West Gate is one of the finest buildings of its kind in the country.

CHESTER (PRE-1900)

Chester is situated on the River Dee. Its recorded history dates from the first century when the Romans founded the fortress of *Deva*. The city's name is derived from the Latin *castra* (a camp or encampment). During the Middle Ages, Chester was the principal port of north-west England but declined with the silting of the Dee estuary and competition from Liverpool. The city was also an important military centre, notably during Edward I's Welsh campaigns and the Elizabethan Irish campaigns. During the Civil War, Chester supported the King and was besieged from 1643 to 1646. Chester's first charter was granted c.1175 and the city was incorporated in 1506. The office of sheriff is the earliest created in the country (1120s), and in 1992 the mayor, who also enjoys the title 'Admiral of the Dee', was made a lord mayor.

The city's architectural features include the city walls (an almost complete two-mile circuit), the unique 13th-century Rows (covered galleries above the street-level shops), the Victorian Gothic town hall (1869), the castle (rebuilt 1788 and 1822) and numerous half-timbered buildings. The cathedral was a Benedictine abbey until the dissolution of the monasteries. Chester racecourse is the oldest racecourse in Britain, believed to have origins in the 13th century. The first recorded horserace was in 1539, during the reign of Henry VIII. Chester also houses the ruins of a Roman amphitheatre, built in the late first century AD.

DURHAM (PRE-1900)

The city of Durham's prominent Norman cathedral and castle are set high on a wooded peninsula overlooking the river Wear. The cathedral was founded as a shrine for the body of St Cuthbert in 995. The present building dates from 1093 and among its many treasures is the tomb of the Venerable Bede (673–735). Durham's prince bishops had unique powers up to 1836, being lay rulers as well as religious leaders. As a palatinate, Durham could have its own army, nobility, coinage and courts. The castle was the main seat of the prince bishops for nearly 800 years; it is now used as a college by the University of Durham. The university, founded in the early 19th century on the initiative of Bishop William Van Mildert, is England's third oldest.

Annual events include Durham's regatta in June (claimed to be the oldest rowing event in Britain) and the annual Gala (formerly Durham Miners' Gala) in July. Durham County Cricket Club was established in 1882.

LEEDS (PRE-1900)

Leeds, situated in the lower Aire valley, was first incorporated by Charles I in 1626. The earliest forms of the name are *Loidis* or *Ledes*, the origins of which are obscure.

The principal buildings are the Civic Hall (1933), the Town Hall (1858), the Municipal Buildings and Art Gallery (1884) with the Henry Moore Gallery (1982), the Corn Exchange (1863) and the University. The parish church of St Peter was rebuilt in 1841 and granted minster status in 2012. The 17th-century St John's Church has a fine interior with a famous English Renaissance screen; the last remaining 18th-century church in the city is Holy Trinity in Boar Lane (1727). Kirkstall Abbey (about three miles from the centre of the city), founded by Henry de Lacy in 1152, is one of the most complete examples of a Cistercian house now remaining. The Royal Armouries Museum forms part of a group of museums that house the national collection of antique arms and armour. The Grand Theatre and Opera House is home to Northern Ballet and Opera North.

LEICESTER (1919)

Leicester is situated in central England. The city was an important Roman settlement and also one of the five 'burghs' or boroughs of the Danelaw. In 1485 Richard III was buried in Leicester following his death at the nearby Battle of Bosworth. In 1589 Queen Elizabeth I granted a charter to the city and the ancient title was confirmed by letters patent in 1919.

The textile industry was responsible for Leicester's early expansion and the city still maintains a strong manufacturing base. Cotton mills and factories are now undergoing extensive regeneration and are being converted into offices, apartments, bars and restaurants. The principal buildings include the two universities (the University of Leicester and De Montfort University), as well as the Town Hall, the 13th-century Guildhall, De Montfort Hall, Leicester Cathedral, the Jewry Wall (the UK's highest standing Roman wall), St Nicholas Church and St Mary de Castro church. The motte and Great Hall of Leicester can be seen from the castle gardens, situated next to the River Soar.

LINCOLN (PRE-1900)

Situated 64km (40 miles) inland on the river Witham, Lincoln derives its name from a contraction of *Lindum Colonia*, the settlement founded in AD 48 by the Romans to command the crossing of Ermine Street and Fosse Way. Sections of the third-century Roman city wall can be seen, including an extant gateway (Newport Arch). The Romans also drained the surrounding fenland and created a canal system, laying the foundations of Lincoln's agricultural prosperity and also the city's importance in the medieval wool trade as a port and staple town.

As one of the five 'burghs' or boroughs of the Danelaw, Lincoln was an important trading centre in the ninth and tenth centuries and prosperity from the wool trade lasted until the 14th century. This wealth enabled local merchants to build parish churches, of which three survive, and there are also remains of a 12th-century Jewish community. However, the removal of the staple to Boston in 1369 heralded a decline, from which the city only recovered fully in the 19th century, when improved fen drainage made Lincoln agriculturally important. Improved canal and rail links led to industrial development, mainly in the manufacture of machinery and engineering products.

The castle was built shortly after the Norman Conquest and is unusual in having two mounds; on one motte stands a keep (Lucy's Tower) added in the 12th century. It currently houses one of the four surviving copies of the Magna Carta. The cathedral was begun c.1073 but was mostly destroyed by fire and earthquake in the 12th century. Rebuilding was begun by St Hugh and completed over a century later. Other notable architectural features are the 12th-century High Bridge, the oldest in Britain still to carry buildings, and the Guildhall, situated above the 15th-century Stonebow gateway.

LIVERPOOL (PRE-1900)

Liverpool, on the north bank of the river Mersey, 5km (3 miles) from the Irish Sea, is the UK's foremost port for Atlantic trade.

There are 2,100 acres of dockland on both sides of the river and the Gladstone and Royal Seaforth Docks can accommodate tanker-sized vessels. Liverpool Free Port was opened in 1984.

Liverpool was created a free borough in 1207 and was given city status in 1880. From the early 18th century it expanded rapidly with the growth of industrialisation and the transatlantic slave trade. Surviving buildings from this period include the Bluecoat Chambers (1717, formerly the Bluecoat School), and the Town Hall (1754, rebuilt to the original design 1795). Notable from the 19th and 20th centuries are the Anglican cathedral (built from the designs of Sir Giles Gilbert Scott, it took 74 years to construct), and the Catholic Metropolitan Cathedral (designed by Sir Frederick Gibberd, consecrated 1967). Both of these cathedrals are situated on Hope Street, named after the merchant William Hope, which is the only street in the UK with a cathedral at either end. The refurbished Albert Dock (designed by Jesse Hartley) contains the Merseyside Maritime Museum, the International Slavery Museum, the Beatles Story and the Tate Liverpool art gallery. The Museum of Liverpool opened in 2011.

MANCHESTER (PRE-1900)

Manchester (the *Mamucium* of the Romans, who occupied it in AD 79) is a commercial and industrial centre connected with the sea by the Manchester Ship Canal, 57km (35.5 miles) long, opened in 1894, and accommodating ships up to 15,000 tons. During the Industrial Revolution the city had a thriving cotton industry and by 1853 there were over 100 cotton mills which dominated the city's landscape.

The principal buildings are the Town Hall, erected in 1877 from the designs of Alfred Waterhouse, with a large extension of 1938; the Royal Exchange (1869, enlarged 1921); the Central Library (1934); Heaton Hall; the 17th-century Chetham Library; the Rylands Library (1900), which includes the Althorp collection; the university precinct; the 15th-century cathedral (formerly the parish church); the Manchester Central conference and exhibition centre and the Bridgewater Hall (1996) concert venue. Manchester is the home of the Hallé Orchestra, the Royal Northern College of Music, the Royal Exchange Theatre and numerous public art galleries.

The town received its first charter of incorporation in 1838 and was created a city in 1853.

NEWCASTLE UPON TYNE (PRE-1900)

Newcastle upon Tyne, on the north bank of the River Tyne, is 13km (8 miles) from the North Sea. A cathedral and university city, it is the administrative, commercial and cultural centre for north-east England and the principal port.

The principal buildings include the Castle Keep (12th century), Black Gate (13th century), Blackfriars (13th century), West Walls (13th century), St Nicholas's Cathedral (15th century, fine lantern tower), St Andrew's Church (12th–14th century), St John's (14th–15th century), All Saints (1786 by Stephenson), St Mary's Roman Catholic Cathedral (1844), Trinity House (17th century), Sandhill (16th-century houses), Guildhall (Georgian), Grey Street (1834–9), Central Station (1846–50) and the Central Library (1969). Open spaces include the Town Moor (927 acres).

Numerous bridges span the Tyne at Newcastle, including the Tyne Bridge (1928) and the tilting Millennium Bridge (2001) which links the city with Gateshead to the south.

The city's name is derived from the 'new castle' (1080) erected as a defence against the Scots. In 1265 defensive walls over two miles in length were built around the city as further protection; parts of these walls remain today and can be found to the west of the city centre.

NORWICH (PRE-1900)

Norwich grew from an early Anglo-Saxon settlement near the confluence of the rivers Yare and Wensum, and now serves as the provincial capital for the predominantly agricultural region of East Anglia. The name is thought to relate to the most northerly of a group of Anglo-Saxon villages or *wics*. The city's first known charter was granted in 1158 by Henry II.

Norwich serves its surrounding area as a market town and commercial centre. From the 14th century until the Industrial Revolution, Norwich was the regional centre of the woollen industry. Now the biggest single industry is financial services and principal trades are engineering, printing and shoemaking. The University of East Anglia is on the city's western boundary and admitted its first students in 1963. Norwich is accessible to seagoing vessels by means of the river Yare, entered at Great Yarmouth, 32km (20 miles) to the east.

Among many historic buildings are the cathedral (completed in the 12th century and surmounted by a 15th-century spire 96m (315ft) in height); the keep of the Norman castle (now a museum and art gallery); the 15th-century flint-walled Guildhall; some 30 medieval parish churches; St Andrew's and Blackfriars' Halls; the Tudor houses preserved in Elm Hill and the Georgian Assembly House.

NOTTINGHAM (PRE-1900)

Nottingham stands on the river Trent. *Snotingaham* or *Notingeham*, the 'homestead of the people of Snot', is the Anglo-Saxon name for the Celtic settlement of *Tigguocobauc*, or the house of caves. In 878, Nottingham became one of the five 'burghs' or boroughs of the Danelaw. William the Conqueror ordered the construction of Nottingham Castle, while the town itself developed rapidly under Norman rule. Its laws and rights were formally recognised by Henry II's charter in 1155. The castle became a favoured residence of King John. In 1642 Charles I raised his personal standard at Nottingham Castle at the start of the Civil War.

Architecturally, Nottingham has a wealth of notable buildings, particularly those designed in the Victorian era by T. C. Hine and Watson Fothergill. The city council owns the castle, of Norman origin but restored in 1878, Wollaton Hall (1580–8), Newstead Abbey (once the home of Lord Byron), the Guildhall (1888) and the Council House (1929). St Mary's, St Peter's and St Nicholas' churches are of interest, as is the Roman Catholic cathedral (Pugin, 1842–4). Nottingham was granted city status in 1897.

OXFORD (PRE-1900)

Oxford is a university city, an important industrial centre and a market town.

Oxford is known for its architecture, its oldest specimens being the reputedly Saxon tower of St Michael's Church, the remains of the Norman castle and city walls, and the Norman church at Iffley. It also has many Gothic buildings, such as the Divinity Schools, the Old Library at Merton College, William of Wykeham's New College, Magdalen and Christ Church colleges and many other college buildings. Later centuries are represented by the Laudian quadrangle at St John's College, the Renaissance Sheldonian Theatre by Sir Christopher Wren, Trinity College Chapel, All Saints Church, Hawksmoor's mock-Gothic at All Souls College, and the 18th-century Queen's College. In addition to individual buildings, High Street and Radcliffe Square both form interesting architectural compositions. Most of the colleges have gardens, those of Magdalen, New College, St John's and Worcester being the largest.

The Oxford University Museum of Natural History, renowned for its spectacular neo-gothic architecture, houses the university's scientific collections of zoological, entomological and geological specimens and is attached to the neighbouring Pitt Rivers Museum, which houses ethnographic and archaeological objects from around the world. The Ashmolean is the city's museum of art and archaeology and Modern Art Oxford hosts a programme of contemporary art exhibitions.

ST ALBANS (PRE-1900)

The origins of St Albans, situated on the river Ver, stem from the Roman town of *Verulamium*. Named after the first Christian martyr in Britain, who was executed there, St Albans has developed around the Norman abbey and cathedral church (consecrated 1115), which was built partly of materials from the old Roman city. The museums house Iron Age and Roman artefacts and the Roman theatre, unique in Britain, has a stage as opposed to an amphitheatre. Archaeological excavations in the city centre have revealed evidence of pre-Roman, Saxon and medieval occupation.

The town's significance grew to the extent that it was a signatory and venue for the drafting of the Magna Carta. It was also the scene of riots during the Peasants' Revolt, the French King John was imprisoned there after the Battle of Poitiers, and heavy fighting took place there during the Wars of the Roses.

Previously controlled by the Abbot, the town achieved a charter in 1553 and city status in 1877. The street market, first established in 1553, is still an important feature of the city, as are many hotels and inns, surviving from the days when St Albans was an important coach stop. St Albans is also noted for its Clock Tower, built between 1403 and 1412, the only remaining medieval town belfry in England.

SALISBURY (PRE-1900)

The history of Salisbury centres around the cathedral and cathedral close. The city evolved from an Iron Age camp a mile to the north of its current position which was strengthened by the Romans and called *Serviodunum*. The Normans built a castle and cathedral on the site and renamed it Sarum. In 1220 Bishop Richard Poore and the architect Elias de Derham decided to build a new Gothic-style cathedral. The cathedral was completed 38 years later and a community known as New Sarum, now called Salisbury, grew around it. Originally the cathedral had a squat tower; the 123m (404ft) spire that makes the cathedral the tallest medieval structure in the world was added c.1315. A walled close with houses for the clergy was built around the cathedral; the Medieval Hall still stands today, alongside buildings dating from the 13th to the 20th century, including some designed by Sir Christopher Wren.

A prosperous wool and cloth trade allowed Salisbury to flourish until the 17th century. When the wool trade declined new crafts were established, including cutlery, leather and basket work, saddlery, lacemaking, joinery and malting. By 1750 it had become an important road junction and coaching centre and in the Victorian era the railways enabled a new age of expansion and prosperity.

SHEFFIELD (PRE-1900)

Sheffield is situated at the confluence of the rivers Sheaf, Porter, Rivelin and Loxley with the river Don and was created a city in 1893.

The parish church of St Peter and St Paul, founded in the 12th century, became the cathedral church of the diocese of Sheffield in 1914. The Roman Catholic Cathedral Church of St Marie (founded 1847) was created a cathedral for the new diocese of Hallam in 1980; parts of the present building date from c.1435. The principal buildings are the Town Hall (1897), the Cutlers' Hall (1832), City Hall (1932), Graves Art Gallery (1934), Mappin Art Gallery, the Crucible Theatre and the restored Lyceum theatre, which dates from 1897 and was reopened in 1990. Three major sporting and entertainment venues were opened between 1990 and 1991: Sheffield Arena, Don Valley Stadium (closed 2013) and Pond's Forge. The Millennium Galleries opened in 2001. The Leadmill, Sheffield's longest-running independent live music venue, opened in 1980.

SOUTHAMPTON (1964)

Southampton is a major seaport on the south coast of England, situated between the mouths of the Test and Itchen rivers. Southampton's natural deep-water harbour has made the area an important settlement since the Romans built the first port (known as *Clausentum*) in the first century, and Southampton's port has witnessed several important departures, including those of Henry V in 1415 for the Battle of Agincourt, the *Mayflower* in 1620, and the RMS *Titanic* in 1912.

The city's strategic importance, not only as a seaport but also as a centre for aircraft production, meant that it was heavily bombed during the Second World War. However, many historically significant structures remain, including the Wool House, dating from 1417 and now used as the Maritime Museum; parts of the Norman city walls, which are among the most complete in the UK; the Bargate, which was originally the main gateway into the city; God's House Tower, now the Museum of Archaeology; St Michael's, the city's oldest church; and the Tudor Merchants Hall.

WINCHESTER (PRE-1900)

Winchester, the ancient capital of England, is situated on the river Itchen. The city is rich in architecture of all types, and especially notable is the cathedral. Built in 1079–93 the cathedral exhibits examples of Norman, early English and Perpendicular styles and is the burial place of author Jane Austen. Winchester College, founded in 1382, is one of the country's most famous public schools, and the original building (1393) remains largely unaltered. St Cross Hospital, another great medieval foundation, lies one mile south of the city. The almshouses were founded in 1136 by Bishop Henry de Blois, and Cardinal Henry Beaufort added a new almshouse of 'Noble Poverty' in 1446. The chapel and dwellings are of great architectural interest, and visitors may still receive the 'Wayfarer's Dole' of bread and ale, a tradition now 900 years old.

Excavations have done much to clarify the origins and development of Winchester. Part of the forum and several of the streets from the Roman town have been discovered. Excavations in the cathedral close have uncovered the entire site of the Anglo-Saxon cathedral (known as the Old Minster) and parts of the New Minster which was built by Alfred the Great's son, Edward the Elder, and is the burial place of the Alfredian dynasty. The original burial place of St Swithun, before his remains were translated to a site in the present cathedral, was also uncovered.

Excavations in other parts of the city have cast much light on Norman Winchester, notably on the site of the Royal Castle (adjacent to which the new Law Courts have been built) and in the grounds of Wolvesey Castle, where the great house built by Bishops Giffard and Henry de Blois in the 12th century has been uncovered. The Great Hall, built by Henry III between 1222 and 1236, survives and houses the Arthurian Round Table.

YORK (PRE-1900)

The city of York is an archiepiscopal seat. Its recorded history dates from AD 71, when the Roman Ninth Legion established a base under Petilius Cerealis that would later become the fortress of *Eburacum,* or *Eboracum.* In Anglo-Saxon times the city was the royal and ecclesiastical centre of Northumbria, and after capture by a Viking army in AD 866 it became the capital of the Viking kingdom of Jorvik. By the 14th century the city had become a great mercantile centre, mainly because of its control of the wool trade, and was used as the chief base against the Scots. Under the Tudors its fortunes declined, although Henry VIII made it the headquarters of the Council of the North. Excavations on many sites, including Coppergate, have greatly expanded knowledge of Roman, Viking and medieval urban life.

The city is rich in examples of architecture of all periods. The earliest church was built in AD 627 and, from the 12th to 15th centuries, the present Minster was built in a succession of styles.

LORD-LIEUTENANTS AND HIGH SHERIFFS

Area	Lord-Lieutenant	High Sheriff (2015–16)
Bedfordshire	Helen Nellis	The Countess of Erroll
Berkshire	James Puxley	David Albermarle Bertie
Bristol	Mary Prior, MBE	Dr Rosalind Kennedy
Buckinghamshire	Sir Henry Aubrey-Fletcher, Bt.	Anna Skelton
Cambridgeshire	Sir Hugh Duberly, KCVO, CBE	Capt. Victor Lucas
Cheshire	David Briggs, MBE	Charles Holroyd, CBE
Cornwall	Col. Edward Bolitho, OBE	Anthony Fortescue
Cumbria	Claire Hensman	Samuel Rayner
Derbyshire	William Tucker	Oliver Stephenson
Devon	David Fursdon	Adm. Sir James Burnell-Nugent, KCB, CBE
Dorset	Angus Campbell	Jennifer Coombs
Durham	Susan Snowdon	James Featherstone Fenwick
East Riding of Yorkshire	Hon. Susan Cunliffe-Lister	James Dick, OBE
East Sussex	Peter Field	Juliet Smith
Essex	Lord Petre	Gerald Thompson
Gloucestershire	Dame Janet Trotter, DBE	Roger Head
Greater London	Kenneth Olisa, OBE	Dr Ghazala Afzal
Greater Manchester	Warren Smith	Mrs Sharman Birtles
Hampshire	Nigel Atkinson	Lady Portal, MBE
Herefordshire	Countess of Darnley	Edward Harley
Hertfordshire	Countess of Verulam	Jonathan Gosselin Trower
Isle of Wight	Maj.-Gen. Martin White, CB, CBE	Ronald Holland
Kent	Viscount De L'Isle, MBE	William Alexander
Lancashire	Lord Shuttleworth, KCVO	Amanda Parker
Leicestershire	Lady Gretton	Gordon Arthur
Lincolnshire	Toby Dennis	Air Vice-Marshal Hector Mackay, CB, OBE, AFC
Merseyside	Dame Lorna Fox Muirhead, DBE	Robert Owen
Norfolk	Richard Jewson	Nicholas Hedley Pratt
North Yorkshire	Barry Dodd, CBE	Charles Forbes Adam
Northamptonshire	David Laing	Dr Ahmed Mukhtar
Northumberland	Duchess of Northumberland	Lucy Maxwell Carroll
Nottinghamshire	Sir John Peace	Dr Jaswant Bilkhu
Oxfordshire	Tim Stevenson, OBE	Thomas Birch Reynardson
Rutland	Dr Laurence Howard, OBE	Andrew Brown Williamson-Noble
Shropshire	Sir Algernon Heber-Percy, KCVO	David Stacey
Somerset	Anne Maw	Hon. Mrs James Nelson
South Yorkshire	Andrew Coombe	John Holt
Staffordshire	Ian Dudson, CBE	John Leavesley
Suffolk	Countess of Euston	Judith Shallow
Surrey	Michael More-Molyneux	Elizabeth Stafford Kennedy
Tyne and Wear	Susan Winfield, OBE	Kathryn Hay Winksell, OBE
Warwickshire	Timothy Cox	Janet Bell-Smith
West Midlands	vacant	Edward Turpie, MBE
West Sussex	Susan Pyper	Denise Patterson
West Yorkshire	Dr Ingrid Roscoe	Edmund Anderson
Wiltshire	Sarah Troughton	Lady Gooch
Worcestershire	Lt.-Col. Patrick Holcroft, LVO, OBE	Sir Anthony Winnington, Bt.

COUNTY COUNCILS

Council & Administrative Headquarters	Telephone	Population*	Council Tax†	Chief Executive‡
Buckinghamshire, Aylesbury	01296-395000	521,922	£1,116	Chris Williams
Cambridgeshire, Cambridge	0345-045 5200	639,818	£1,144	Mark Lloyd
Cumbria, Carlisle	01228-606060	497,874	£1,185	Diane Wood
Derbyshire, Matlock	01629-580000	779,804	£1,120	Ian Stephenson
Devon, Exeter	0345-155 1015	765,302	£1,161	Phil Norrey
Dorset, Dorchester	01305-221000	418,269	£1,215	Debbie Ward
East Sussex, Lewes	0345-608 0190	539,766	£1,204	Becky Shaw
Essex, Chelmsford	0845-7430 430	1,431,953	£1,087	vacant
Gloucestershire, Gloucester	01452-425000	611,332	£1,091	Peter Bungard
Hampshire, Winchester	0300-555 1375	1,346,136	£1,038	Andrew Smith, OBE
Hertfordshire, Hertford	0300-123 4040	1,154,766	£1,141	John Wood
Kent, Maidstone	0300-041 4141	1,510,354	£1,090	David Cockburn
Lancashire, Preston	0300-123 6701	1,184,735	£1,130	Jo Turton
Leicestershire, Leicester	0116-232 3232	667,905	£1,084	John Sinnott
Lincolnshire, Lincoln	01522-552222	731,516	£1,086	Tony McArdle
Norfolk, Norwich	0344-800 8020	877,710	£1,145	Wendy Thomson
North Yorkshire, Northallerton	01609-780780	601,536	£1,100	Richard Flinton
Northamptonshire, Northampton	0300-126 1000	714,392	£1,069	Paul Blantern
Nottinghamshire, Nottingham	0115-982 3823	801,390	£1,241	Anthony May
Oxfordshire, Oxford	01865-792422	672,516	£1,232	Joanna Simons
Somerset, Taunton	0300-123 2224	541,609	£1,027	Patrick Flaherty
Staffordshire, Stafford	0300-111 8000	860,165	£1,047	John Henderson, CB
Suffolk, Ipswich	0345-606 6067	738,512	£1,127	Deborah Cadman
Surrey, Kingston upon Thames	0345-600 9009	1,161,256	£1,220	David McNulty
Warwickshire, Warwick	01926-410410	551,594	£1,201	Jim Graham
West Sussex, Chichester	01243-777100	828,398	£1,162	Diane Ashby
Worcestershire, Worcester	01905-763763	575,421	£1,080	Clare Marchant

* Source: Office for National Statistics – Mid-2014 Population Estimates (Crown copyright)

† Average 2015–16 Band D council tax in the county area exclusive of precepts for fire authorities and Police Crime Commissioners. County councils claim their share of the combined council tax from the collection funds of the district authorities within their area. Average Band D council tax bills for the billing authority are given on the following pages

‡ Or equivalent postholder

LONDON BOROUGH COUNCILS

Council	Telephone	Population*	Council Tax‡	Chief Executive‡
Barking and Dagenham	020-8592 4500	198,294	£1,332	Chris Naylor
Barnet	020-8359 2000	374,915	£1,397	Andrew Travers
Bexley	020-8303 7777	239,865	£1,446	Will Tuckley
Brent	020-8937 1234	320,762	£1,354	Christine Gilbert (acting)
Bromley	020-8464 3333	321,278	£1,325	Doug Patterson
Camden	020-7974 4444	234,846	£1,337	Mike Cooke
CITY OF LONDON CORPORATION	020-7606 3030	8,072	£943	John Barradell, OBE
Croydon	020-8726 6000	376,040	£1,466	Nathan Elvery
Ealing	020-8825 5000	342,118	£1,355	Martin Smith
Enfield	020-8379 1000	324,574	£1,395	Rob Leak
Greenwich	020-8854 8888	268,678	£1,276	John Comber
Hackney	020-8356 5000	263,150	£1,293	Tim Shields
Hammersmith and Fulham	020-8748 3020	178,365	£1,023	Nigel Pallace
Haringey	020-8489 0000	267,541	£1,479	Nick Walkley
Harrow	020-8863 5611	246,011	£1,529	Michael Lockwood
Havering	01708-434343	245,974	£1,514	Cheryl Coppell
Hillingdon	01895-250111	292,690	£1,408	Fran Beasley
Hounslow	020-8583 2000	265,568	£1,375	Mary Harpley
Islington	020-7527 2000	221,030	£1,276	Lesley Seary
Kensington and Chelsea	020-7361 3000	156,190	£1,078	Nicholas Holgate
Kingston upon Thames	020-8547 5000	169,958	£1,675	Bruce McDonald
Lambeth	020-7926 1000	318,216	£1,239	Sean Harriss
Lewisham	020-8314 6000	291,933	£1,355	Barry Quirk, CBE
Merton	020-8274 4901	203,515	£1,401	Ged Curran
Newham	020-8430 2000	324,322	£1,241	Kim Bromley-Derry
Redbridge	020-8554 5000	293,055	£1,391	Roger Hampson
Richmond upon Thames	020-8891 1411	193,585	£1,582	Gillian Norton
Southwark	020-7525 5000	302,538	£1,207	Eleanor Kelly
Sutton	020-8770 5000	198,134	£1,459	Niall Bolger
Tower Hamlets	020-7364 5000	284,015	£1,181	Stephen Halsey
Waltham Forest	020-8496 3000	268,020	£1,447	Martin Esom
Wandsworth	020-8871 6000	312,145	£683	Paul Martin
WESTMINSTER	020-7641 6000	233,292	£674	Charlie Parker

DISTRICT COUNCILS

District Council	Telephone	Population*	Council Tax‡	Chief Executive‡
Adur	01903-239999	63,176	£1,596	Alex Bailey
Allerdale	01900-702702	96,471	£1,613	Ian Frost
Amber Valley	01773-570222	123,942	£1,559	Julian Townsend
Arun	01903-737500	154,414	£1,531	Nigel Lynn
Ashfield	01623-450000	122,508	£1,669	Robert Mitchell
Ashford	01233-331111	123,285	£1,482	John Bunnett
Aylesbury Vale	01296-585858	184,560	£1,551	Andrew Grant
Babergh	01473-822801	88,845	£1,516	Charlie Adan
Barrow-in-Furness	01229-876543	67,648	£1,619	Phil Huck
Basildon	01268-533333	180,521	£1,560	Bala Mahendran
Basingstoke and Deane	01256-844844	172,870	£1,379	Melbourne Barrett
Bassetlaw	01909-533533	114,143	£1,676	Neil Taylor
Blaby	0116-275 0555	95,851	£1,548	Sandra Whiles
Bolsover	01246-242424	77,155	£1,635	Wesley Lumley
Boston	01205-314200	66,458	£1,471	Phil Drury
Braintree	01376-552525	149,985	£1,494	Nicola Beach
Breckland	01362-656870	133,986	£1,500	Anna Graves
Brentwood	01277-312500	75,645	£1,480	Philip Ruck
Broadland	01603-431133	125,961	£1,533	Phil Kirby
Bromsgrove	01527-881288	95,485	£1,564	Kevin Dicks
Broxbourne	01992-785555	95,748	£1,402	Jeff Stack
Broxtowe	0115-917 7777	111,780	£1,674	Ruth Hyde, OBE
Burnley	01282-425011	87,291	£1,630	Pam Smith
CAMBRIDGE	01223-457000	128,515	£1,567	Antoinette Jackson
Cannock Chase	01543-462621	98,549	£1,516	Tony McGovern
CANTERBURY	01227-862000	157,649	£1,509	Colin Carmichael
CARLISLE	01228-817000	108,022	£1,605	Jason Gooding
Castle Point	01268-882200	88,907	£1,542	David Marchant
Charnwood	01509-263151	173,545	£1,502	Geoffrey Parker
CHELMSFORD	01245-606606	171,633	£1,508	Steve Packham
Cheltenham	01242-262626	116,495	£1,490	Andrew North
Cherwell	01295-252535	144,494	£1,604	Sue Smith
Chesterfield	01246-345345	104,288	£1,522	Huw Bowen
Chichester	01243-785166	115,527	£1,495	Diane Shepherd
Chiltern	01494-729000	93,972	£1,561	Alan Goodrum
Chorley	01257-515151	111,607	£1,547	Gary Hall
Christchurch	01202-495000	48,895	£1,657	David McIntosh
Colchester	01206-282222	180,420	£1,497	Adrian Pritchard
Copeland	0845-054 8600	69,832	£1,630	Paul Walker
Corby	01536-464000	65,434	£1,452	Norman Stronach
Cotswold	01285-623000	84,637	£1,486	David Neudegg
Craven	01756-700600	55,696	£1,585	Paul Shevlin
Crawley	01293-438000	109,883	£1,494	Lee Harris
Dacorum	01442-228000	149,741	£1,480	Sally Marshall
Dartford	01322-343434	102,234	£1,504	Graham Harris
Daventry	01327-871100	79,036	£1,475	Ian Vincent
Derbyshire Dales	01629-761100	71,281	£1,600	Dorcas Bunton
Dover	01304-821199	113,066	£1,537	Nadeem Aziz
East Cambridgeshire	01353-665555	86,685	£1,591	John Hill
East Devon	01395-516551	136,374	£1,573	Mark Williams
East Dorset	01202-886201	88,186	£1,720	David McIntosh
East Hampshire	01730-266551	117,483	£1,458	Sandy Hopkins
East Hertfordshire	01279-655261	143,021	£1,508	vacant
East Lindsey	01507-601111	137,623	£1,443	Stuart Davy
East Northamptonshire	01832-742000	88,872	£1,482	David Oliver
East Staffordshire	01283-508000	115,663	£1,504	Andy O'Brien
Eastbourne	01323-410000	101,547	£1,657	Robert Cottrill
Eastleigh	023-8068 8000	128,877	£1,450	Nick Tustian
Eden	01768-817817	52,630	£1,614	Robin Hooper
Elmbridge	01372-474474	132,769	£1,639	Robert Moran
Epping Forest	01992-564000	128,777	£1,511	Glen Chipp
Epsom and Ewell	01372-732000	78,318	£1,613	Frances Rutter
Erewash	0115-907 2244	114,048	£1,537	Jeremy Jaroszek
EXETER	01392-277888	124,328	£1,544	Karime Hassan
Fareham	01329-236100	114,331	£1,397	Peter Grimwood
Fenland	01354-654321	97,732	£1,671	Paul Medd
Forest Heath	01638-719000	62,812	£1,520	Ian Gallin
Forest of Dean	01594-810000	83,674	£1,525	Sue Pangbourne
Fylde	01253-658658	77,042	£1,568	Allan Oldfield
Gedling	0115-901 3901	115,638	£1,658	John Robinson

District Council	Telephone	Population*	Council Tax‡	Chief Executive‡
GLOUCESTER	01452-396396	125,649	£1,485	–
Gosport	023-9258 4242	84,287	£1,459	Ian Lycett
Gravesham	01474-564422	105,261	£1,497	David Hughes
Great Yarmouth	01493-856100	98,172	£1,512	Gordon Mitchell
Guildford	01483-505050	142,958	£1,613	Sue Sturgeon
Hambleton	01619-779977	89,828	£1,504	Phillip Morton
Harborough	01858-828282	88,008	£1,523	Beverley Jolly & Norman Proudfoot
Harlow	01279-446655	84,564	£1,563	Malcolm Morley
Harrogate	01423-500600	157,267	£1,608	Wallace Sampson
Hart	01252-622122	93,325	£1,470	Patricia Hughes & Daryl Phillips
Hastings	01424-451066	91,093	£1,673	Neil Dart
Havant	023-9244 6019	122,210	£1,449	Sandy Hopkins
Hertsmere	020-8207 2277	102,427	£1,470	Donald Graham
High Peak	0345-129 7777	91,364	£1,556	Simon Baker
Hinckley and Bosworth	01455-238141	107,722	£1,480	Steve Atkinson
Horsham	01403-215100	134,158	£1,489	Tom Crowley
Huntingdonshire	01480-388388	173,605	£1,609	Jo Lancaster
Hyndburn	01254-388111	80,208	£1,585	David Welsby
Ipswich	01473-432000	134,966	£1,625	Russell Williams
Kettering	01536-410333	96,945	£1,484	David Cook, MBE
King's Lynn and West Norfolk	01553-616200	150,026	£1,516	Ray Harding
LANCASTER	01524-582000	141,277	£1,571	Mark Cullinan
Lewes	01273-471600	100,229	£1,702	Jenny Rowlands
Lichfield	01543-308000	102,093	£1,488	Diane Tilley
LINCOLN	01522-881188	96,202	£1,533	Angela Andrews (acting)
Maidstone	01622-602000	161,819	£1,568	Alison Broom
Maldon	01621-854477	62,767	£1,523	Fiona Marshall
Malvern Hills	01684-862151	75,911	£1,538	Jack Hegarty
Mansfield	01623-463463	105,893	£1,677	Ruth Marlow
Melton	01664-502502	50,969	£1,535	Lynn Aisbett
Mendip	0300-3038588	110,844	£1,496	Stuart Brown
Mid Devon	01884-255255	79,198	£1,633	Kevin Finan
Mid Suffolk	01449-720711	99,121	£1,514	Charlie Adan
Mid Sussex	01444-458166	144,377	£1,515	Kathryn Hall
Mole Valley	01306-885001	86,234	£1,601	Yvonne Rees
New Forest	023-8028 5000	178,907	£1,482	David Yates
Newark and Sherwood	01636-650000	117,758	£1,718	Andrew Muter
Newcastle-under-Lyme	01782-717717	126,052	£1,479	John Sellgren
North Devon	01271-327711	94,059	£1,623	Mike Mansell
North Dorset	01258-454111	70,043	£1,675	Matt Prosser
North East Derbyshire	01246-231111	99,352	£1,635	Wes Lumley
North Hertfordshire	01462-474000	131,046	£1,517	David Scholes
North Kesteven	01529-414155	111,046	£1,502	Ian Fytche
North Norfolk	01263-513811	102,867	£1,540	Sheila Oxtoby
North Warwickshire	01827-715341	62,468	£1,641	Jerry Hutchinson
North West Leicestershire	01530-454545	95,882	£1,552	Christine Fisher
Northampton	0300-330 7000	219,495	£1,494	David Kennedy
NORWICH	0344-980 3333	137,472	£1,593	Laura McGillivray
Nuneaton and Bedworth	024-7637 6376	126,174	£1,601	Alan Franks
Oadby and Wigston	0116-288 8961	55,928	£1,527	Mark Hall
OXFORD	01865-249811	157,997	£1,679	Peter Sloman
Pendle	01282-661661	89,840	£1,624	Dean Langton
PRESTON	01772-906900	140,452	£1,644	Lorraine Norris
Purbeck	01929-556561	45,679	£1,713	Steve Mackenzie
Redditch	01527-64252	84,471	£1,560	Kevin Dicks
Reigate and Banstead	01737-276000	143,094	£1,647	John Jory
Ribble Valley	01200-425111	58,091	£1,511	Marshall Scott
Richmondshire	01748-829100	52,729	£1,607	Tony Clark
Rochford	01702-318111	84,776	£1,549	Amar Dave
Rossendale	01706-217777	69,168	£1,610	Stuart Sugarman
Rother	01424-787000	92,130	£1,649	Malcolm Johnston & Anthony Leonard
Rugby	01788-533533	102,500	£1,578	Ian Davis & Adam Norburn
Runnymede	01932-838383	84,584	£1,580	Paul Turrell
Rushcliffe	0115-981 9911	113,670	£1,670	Allen Graham
Rushmoor	01252-398398	95,296	£1,441	Andrew Colver
Ryedale	01653-600666	52,655	£1,592	Janet Waggott
ST ALBANS	01727-866100	144,834	£1,497	James Blake
St Edmundsbury	01284-763233	112,073	£1,519	Ian Gallin
Scarborough	01723-232323	108,006	£1,610	Jim Dillon

District Council	Telephone	Population*	Council Tax‡	Chief Executive‡
Sedgemoor	0845-408 2540	119,057	£1,472	Mr Kerry Rickards
Selby	01757-705101	85,355	£1,592	Mary Weastell
Sevenoaks	01732-227000	117,811	£1,575	Dr Pav Ramewal
Shepway	01303-853000	109,452	£1,593	Alistair Stewart
South Bucks	01895-837200	68,512	£1,541	Alan Goodrum
South Cambridgeshire	0345-045 0500	153,281	£1,591	Jean Hunter
South Derbyshire	01283-595795	98,374	£1,536	Frank McArdle
South Hams	01803-861234	84,108	£1,601	Alan Robinson & Tracy Winser
South Holland	01775-761161	90,419	£1,471	Anna Graves
South Kesteven	01476-406080	137,981	£1,455	Beverly Agass
South Lakeland	01539-733333	103,271	£1,605	Lawrence Conway
South Norfolk	01508-533633	129,226	£1,551	Sandra Dinneen
South Northamptonshire	01327-322322	88,164	£1,511	Sue Smith
South Oxfordshire	01235-520202	137,015	£1,585	David Buckle
South Ribble	01772-421491	109,077	£1,570	Mike Nuttall
South Somerset	01935-462462	164,569	£1,502	Mark Williams
South Staffordshire	01902-696000	110,692	£1,439	Steve Winterflood
Spelthorne	01784-451499	98,106	£1,618	Roberto Tambini
Stafford	01785-619000	132,241	£1,457	Ian Thompson
Staffordshire Moorlands	0345-605 3010	97,763	£1,477	Simon Baker
Stevenage	01438-242242	85,997	£1,477	Scott Crudgington
Stratford-on-Avon	01789-267575	121,056	£1,572	Paul Lankester
Stroud	01453-766321	115,093	£1,555	David Hagg
Suffolk Coastal	01394-383789	124,776	£1,503	Stephen Baker
Surrey Heath	01276-707100	87,533	£1,651	Karen Whelan
Swale	01795-417850	140,836	£1,489	Abdool Kara
Tamworth	01827-709709	77,112	£1,452	Tony Goodwin
Tandridge	01883-722000	85,374	£1,649	Louise Round
Taunton Deane	01823-356356	112,817	£1,433	Penny James
Teignbridge	01626-361101	127,357	£1,613	Nicola Bulbeck
Tendring	01255-686868	139,916	£1,479	Ian Davidson
Test Valley	01264-368000	119,332	£1,415	Roger Tetstall
Tewkesbury	01684-295010	85,784	£1,452	Michael Dawson
Thanet	01843-577000	138,410	£1,539	Madeline Homer
Three Rivers	01923-776611	90,423	£1,486	Dr Steven Halls
Tonbridge and Malling	01732-844522	124,426	£1,539	Julie Beilby
Torridge	01237-428700	65,618	£1,602	Jenny Wallace
Tunbridge Wells	01892-526121	116,105	£1,513	William Benson
Uttlesford	01799-510510	84,042	£1,513	John Mitchell
Vale of White Horse	01235-520202	124,852	£1,576	David Buckle
Warwick	01926-410410	139,396	£1,560	Chris Elliott
Watford	01923-226400	95,505	£1,539	Manny Lewis
Waveney	01502-562111	115,919	£1,461	Stephen Baker
Waverley	01483-523333	122,860	£1,646	Paul Wenham
Wealden	01323-443322	154,767	£1,698	Charles Lant
Wellingborough	01933-229777	76,446	£1,421	John Campbell
Welwyn & Hatfield	01707-357000	116,024	£1,524	Michel Saminaden
West Devon	01822-813600	54,260	£1,678	Sophie Hosking & Steve Jordan
West Dorset	01305-251010	100,474	£1,680	Matt Prosser
West Lancashire	01695-577177	111,940	£1,552	Gill Rowe & Kim Webber
West Lindsey	01427-676676	91,787	£1,530	Manjeet Gill
West Oxfordshire	01993-861000	108,158	£1,552	Elaine Nicklin
West Somerset	01643-703704	34,322	£1,486	Penny James
Weymouth and Portland	01305-838000	64,992	£1,756	Matt Prosser
WINCHESTER	01962-840222	119,218	£1,452	Simon Eden
Woking	01483-755855	99,426	£1,652	Ray Morgan, OBE
WORCESTER	01905-722233	100,842	£1,512	Lesley Meagher (acting)
Worthing	01903-239999	106,863	£1,522	Alex Bailey
Wychavon	01386-565000	119,752	£1,497	Jack Hegarty
Wycombe	01494-461000	174,878	£1,505	Karen Satterford
Wyre	01253-891000	108,742	£1,548	Garry Payne
Wyre Forest	01562-732928	98,960	£1,563	Ian Miller

METROPOLITAN BOROUGH COUNCILS

Metropolitan Borough Council	Telephone	Population*	Council Tax‡	Chief Executive‡
Barnsley	01226-770770	237,843	£1,470	Diana Terris
BIRMINGHAM	0121-303 1111	1,101,360	£1,320	Mark Rogers
Bolton	01204-333333	280,439	£1,492	Paul Najsarek
BRADFORD	01274-432001	528,155	£1,361	Kersten England
Bury	0161-253 5000	187,474	£1,514	Mike Owen *(acting)*
Calderdale	01422-288001	207,376	£1,459	Merran McRae
COVENTRY	0500-834 333	337,428	£1,537	Martin Reeves
Doncaster	01302-736000	304,185	£1,384	Johanna Miller
Dudley	0300-555 2345	315,799	£1,287	Sarah Norman
Gateshead	0191-433 3000	200,505	£1,634	Jane Robinson
Kirklees	01484-221000	431,020	£1,471	Adrian Lythgo
Knowsley	0151-489 6000	146,407	£1,507	Mike Harden
LEEDS	0113-222 4444	766,399	£1,375	Tom Riordan
LIVERPOOL	0151-233 3000	473,073	£1,616	Ged Fitzgerald
MANCHESTER	0161-234 5000	520,215	£1,382	Sir Howard Bernstein
NEWCASTLE UPON TYNE	0191-278 7878	289,835	£1,545	Pat Ritchie
North Tyneside	0191-643 5991	202,744	£1,491	Patrick Melia
Oldham	0161-770 3000	228,765	£1,607	Carolyn Wilkins
Rochdale	01706-647474	212,962	£1,540	Steve Rumbelow
Rotherham	01709-382121	260,070	£1,526	Stella Manzie, CBE
St Helens	01744-676789	177,188	£1,451	Carole Hudson, CBE
SALFORD	0161-794 4711	242,040	£1,536	Jim Taylor
Sandwell	0121-569 2200	316,719	£1,337	Jan Britton
Sefton	0151-922 4040	273,531	£1,560	Margaret Carney
SHEFFIELD	0114-273 4567	563,749	£1,526	John Mothersole
Solihull	0121-704 8001	209,890	£1,351	Nick Page
South Tyneside	0191-427 7000	148,740	£1,480	Martin Swales
Stockport	0161-480 4949	286,755	£1,607	Eamonn Boylan
SUNDERLAND	0191-520 5555	276,889	£1,350	Dave Smith
Tameside	0161-342 8355	220,771	£1,443	Steven Pleasant
Trafford	0161-912 2000	232,458	£1,316	Theresa Grant
WAKEFIELD	0845-850 6506	331,379	£1,393	Joanne Roney, OBE
Walsall	01922-650000	274,173	£1,600	Paul Sheehan
Wigan	01942-244991	320,975	£1,403	Donna Hall
Wirral	0151-606 2000	320,914	£1,509	Eric Robinson
WOLVERHAMPTON	01902-551155	252,987	£1,531	Keith Ireland

UNITARY COUNCILS

Unitary Council	Telephone	Population*	Council Tax‡	Chief Executive‡
Bath and North East Somerset	01225-477000	182,021	£1,479	Dr Jo Farrar
Bedford	01234-267422	163,924	£1,599	Philip Simpkins
Blackburn with Darwen	01254-585585	146,743	£1,495	Harry Catherall
Blackpool	01253-477477	140,501	£1,530	Neil Jack
Bournemouth	01202-451451	191,390	£1,499	Tony Williams
Bracknell Forest	01344-352000	118,025	£1,383	Timothy Wheadon
BRIGHTON AND HOVE	01273-290000	281,076	£1,569	Penny Thompson, CBE
BRISTOL	0117-922 2000	442,474	£1,660	Nicola Yates
Central Bedfordshire	0300-300 8000	269,076	£1,688	Richard Carr
Cheshire East	0300-123 5500	374,179	£1,483	Mike Suarez
Cheshire West and Chester	0300-123 8123	332,210	£1,525	Steve Robinson
Cornwall	0300-123 4100	545,335	£1,550	Andrew Kerr
Darlington	01325-380651	105,367	£1,524	Ada Burns
DERBY	01332-293111	252,463	£1,432	Paul Robison (acting)
DURHAM	0300-026000	517,773	£1,675	George Garlick
East Riding of Yorkshire	01482-393939	337,115	£1,518	Nigel Pearson
Halton	0303-333 4300	126,354	£1,433	David Parr
Hartlepool	01429-266522	92,590	£1,696	Gill Alexander
Herefordshire	01432-260000	187,160	£1,584	Alastair Neill
Isle of Wight	01983-821000	139,105	£1,547	Dave Burbage
Isles of Scilly§	01720-424000	2,280	£1,241	Theo Leijser
KINGSTON-UPON-HULL	01482-609100	257,710	£1,420	Darryl Stephenson
LEICESTER	0116-254 1000	337,653	£1,542	Andy Keeling
Luton	01582-546000	210,962	£1,514	Trevor Holden
Medway	01634-333333	274,015	£1,410	Neil Davies
Middlesbrough	01642-245432	139,119	£1,657	Mike Robinson
Milton Keynes	01908-691691	259,245	£1,451	Carole Mills
North East Lincolnshire	01472-313131	159,804	£1,569	Rob Walsh
North Lincolnshire	01724-296296	169,247	£1,571	Simon Driver
North Somerset	01934-888888	208,154	£1,459	Mike Jackson
Northumberland	0345-600 6400	315,987	£1,591	Steven Mason
NOTTINGHAM	0115-915 5555	314,268	£1,709	Ian Curryer
PETERBOROUGH	01733-747474	190,461	£1,383	Gillian Beasley
PLYMOUTH	01752-668000	261,546	£1,568	Tracey Lee
Poole	01202-633633	150,109	£1,465	Andrew Flockhart (acting)
PORTSMOUTH	023-9282 2251	209,085	£1,390	David Williams
Reading	0118-937 3787	160,825	£1,589	Ian Wardle
Redcar and Cleveland	0164-277 4774	135,042	£1,668	Amanda Skelton
Rutland	01572-722577	38,022	£1,710	Helen Briggs
Shropshire	0345-678 9000	310,121	£1,504	Clive Wright
Slough	01753-475111	144,575	£1,403	Ruth Bagley, OBE
South Gloucestershire	01454-868009	271,556	£1,550	Amanda Deeks
SOUTHAMPTON	023-8083 3000	245,290	£1,532	Dawn Baxendale
Southend-on-Sea	01702-215000	177,931	£1,380	Robert Tinlin
Stockton-on-Tees	01642-393939	194,119	£1,627	Neil Schneider
STOKE-ON-TRENT	01782-234567	251,027	£1,430	John van de Laarschot
Swindon	01793-463000	215,799	£1,404	Gavin Jones
Telford and Wrekin	01952-380000	169,440	£1,492	Richard Partington
Thurrock	01375-652652	163,270	£1,338	David Bull (acting)
Torbay	01803-201201	132,984	£1,514	Steve Parrock
Warrington	01925-443322	206,428	£1,456	Steven Broomhead
West Berkshire	01635-42400	155,732	£1,546	Nick Carter
Wiltshire	0300-456 0100	483,143	£1,534	C. Brand, C. Godfrey & M. Rae
Windsor and Maidenhead	01628-683800	147,400	£1,150	Alison Alexander
Wokingham	0118-974 6000	159,097	£1,525	Andy Couldrick
YORK	01904-551550	204,439	£1,453	Kersten England

* *Source:* Office for National Statistics – *Mid-2014 Population Estimates* (Crown copyright)
‡ Average Band D council tax bill for 2015–16
‡ Or equivalent postholder
§ Under the Isles of Scilly Clause the council has additional functions to other unitary authorities
Councils in CAPITAL LETTERS have city status

MAP OF COUNCILS IN ENGLAND

1	Stockton-on-Tees	22	Walsall
2	Middlesbrough	23	Sandwell
3	Blackpool	24	Dudley
4	Blackburn	25	Birmingham
	with Darwen	26	Solihull
5	Bolton	27	Coventry
6	Bury	28	Peterborough
7	Rochdale	29	South Glos
8	Salford	30	Bristol
9	Oldham	31	Bath and
10	Liverpool		NE Somerset
11	Knowsley	32	Windsor and
12	St Helens		Maidenhead
13	Halton	33	Slough
14	Warrington	34	Reading
15	Trafford	35	Wokingham
16	Manchester	36	Bracknell Forest
17	Tameside	37	Thurrock
18	Stockport	38	Southend
19	Nottingham	39	Medway
20	Telford and	40	Plymouth
	Wrekin	41	Torbay
21	Wolverhampton	42	Bournemouth

LONDON

1	Hillingdon	18	Kensington and Chelsea
2	Harrow	19	City of Westminster
3	Barnet	20	City of London
4	Enfield	21	Tower Hamlets
5	Waltham Forest	22	Richmond upon Thames
6	Redbridge	23	Wandsworth
7	Barking and Dagenham	24	Lambeth
8	Havering	25	Southwark
9	Ealing	26	Lewisham
10	Brent	27	Greenwich
11	Camden	28	Bexley
12	Haringey	29	Kingston upon Thames
13	Islington	30	Merton
14	Hackney	31	Sutton
15	Newham	32	Croydon
16	Hounslow	33	Bromley
17	Hammersmith and Fulham		

LONDON

THE CITY OF LONDON CORPORATION

The City of London is the historic centre at the heart of London known as 'the square mile', around which the vast metropolis has grown over the centuries. The City's residential population was 7,400 at the 2011 census and in addition, around 400,000 people work in the City. The civic government is carried on by the City of London Corporation through the court of Common Council.

The City is an international financial and business centre, generating about £30bn a year for the British economy. It includes the head offices of the principal banks, insurance companies and mercantile houses, in addition to buildings ranging from the historic Roman Wall and the 15th-century Guildhall, to the massive splendour of St Paul's Cathedral and the architectural beauty of Wren's spires.

The City of London was described by Tacitus in AD 62 as 'a busy emporium for trade and traders'. Under the Romans it became an important administration centre and hub of the road system. Little is known of London in Saxon times, when it formed part of the kingdom of the East Saxons. In 886 Alfred recovered London from the Danes and reconstituted it a burgh under his son-in-law. In 1066 the citizens submitted to William the Conqueror who in 1067 granted them a charter, which is still preserved, establishing them in the rights and privileges they had hitherto enjoyed.

THE MAYORALTY
The mayoralty was probably established about 1189, the first mayor being Henry Fitz Ailwyn who filled the office for 23 years and was succeeded by Fitz Alan (1212–14). A new charter was granted by King John in 1215, directing the mayor to be chosen annually, which has been done ever since, though in early times the same individual often held the office more than once. A familiar instance is that of 'Whittington, thrice Lord Mayor of London' (in reality four times: 1397, 1398, 1406 and 1419); and many modern cases have occurred. The earliest instance of the phrase 'lord mayor' in English is in 1414. It was used more generally in the latter part of the 15th century and became invariable from 1535 onwards. At Michaelmas the liverymen in Common Hall choose two aldermen who have served the office of sheriff for presentation to the Court of Aldermen, and one is chosen to be lord mayor for the following mayoral year.

LORD MAYOR'S DAY
The lord mayor of London was previously elected on the feast of St Simon and St Jude (28 October), and from the time of Edward I, at least, was presented to the King or to the Barons of the Exchequer on the following day, unless that day was a Sunday. The day of election was altered to 16 October in 1346, and after some further changes was fixed for Michaelmas Day in 1546, but the ceremonies of admittance and swearing-in of the lord mayor continued to take place on 28 and 29 October respectively until 1751. In 1752, at the reform of the calendar, the lord mayor was continued in office until 8 November, the 'new style' equivalent of 28 October. The lord mayor is now presented to the lord chief justice at the royal courts of justice on the second Saturday in November to make the final declaration of office, having been sworn in at Guildhall on the preceding day. The procession to the royal courts of justice is popularly known as the Lord Mayor's Show.

REPRESENTATIVES
Aldermen are mentioned in the 11th century and their office is of Saxon origin. They were elected annually between 1377 and 1394, when an act of parliament of Richard II directed them to be chosen for life. Aldermen now serve a six-year term of office before submitting themselves for re-election.

The Common Council was, at an early date, substituted for a popular assembly called the *Folkmote*. At first only two representatives were sent from each ward, but now each of the City's 25 wards is represented by an alderman and at least two Common Councilmen (the number depending on the size of the ward). Common Councilmen are elected every four years.

OFFICERS
Sheriffs were Saxon officers; their predecessors were the *wic-reeves* and *portreeves* of London and Middlesex. At first they were officers of the Crown, and were named by the Barons of the Exchequer; but Henry I (in 1132) gave the citizens permission to choose their own sheriffs, and the annual election of sheriffs became fully operative under King John's charter of 1199. The citizens lost this privilege, as far as the election of the sheriff of Middlesex was concerned, by the Local Government Act 1888; but the liverymen continue to choose two sheriffs of the City of London, who are appointed on Midsummer Day and take office at Michaelmas.

The office of chamberlain is an ancient one, the first contemporary record of which is 1237. The town clerk (or common clerk) is first mentioned in 1274.

ACTIVITIES
The work of the City of London Corporation is assigned to a number of committees which present reports to the Court of Common Council. These committees are: Audit and Risk Management; Barbican Centre; Barbican Residential; Board of Governors of the City of London Freeman's School, the City of London School, the City of London School for Girls and the Guildhall School of Music and Drama; City Bridge Trust; Community and Children's Services; Culture Heritage and Libraries; Education; Epping Forest and Commons; Establishment; Finance; Freedom Applications; Gresham (City Side); Guildhall Improvement; Hampstead Heath, Highgate Wood and Queen's Park; Health and Wellbeing; Investment; Licensing; Livery; Markets; Open Spaces and City Gardens; Pensions Board; Planning and Transportation; Police; Policy and Resources; Port Health and Environmental Services; Standards Committees; and West Ham Park.

The City's estate, in the possession of which the City of London Corporation differs from other municipalities, is managed by the City Lands and Bridge House Estates Committee, the chairmanship of which carries with it the title of chief commoner.

The Honourable the Irish Society, which manages the City Corporation's estates in Ulster, consists of a governor and five other aldermen, the recorder, and 19 common councilmen, of whom one is elected deputy governor.

THE LORD MAYOR 2015–16
The Rt. Hon. the Lord Mayor, Lord Mountevans*
Private Secretary, William Chapman
* Provisional at time of going to press

THE SHERIFFS 2015–16
Alderman Charles Bowman (Lime Street); Dr Christine Rigden

OFFICERS, ETC
Town Clerk, John Barradell
Chamberlain, Peter Kane
Chief Commoner (2015), Deputy William Dove, OBE
Clerk, The Honourable the Irish Society, C. Fisher

THE ALDERMEN
with office held and date of appointment to that office

Name and Ward	Common Councilman	Alderman	Sheriff	Lord Mayor
Sir David Howard, Bt., *Cornhill*	1972	1986	1997	2000
Ian Luder, *Castle Baynard*	1998	2005	2007	2008
Nicholas Anstee, *Aldersgate*	1987	1996	2003	2009
Sir Michael Bear, *Portsoken*	2003	2005	2007	2010
Sir David Wootton, *Langbourn*	2002	2005	2009	2011
Sir Roger Gifford, *Cordwainer*	–	2004	2008	2012
Dame Fiona Woolf, DBE, *Candlewick*	–	2007	2010	2013
Alan Yarrow, *Bridge & Bridge Wt.*	–	2007	2011	2014
Lord Mountevans, *Cheap*	–	2007	2012	2015

All the above have passed the Civic Chair

Dr Andrew Parmley, *Vintry*	1992	2001	2014	
Alison Gowman, *Dowgate*	1991	2002	–	
Gordon Haines, *Queenhithe*	–	2004	–	
Jeffrey Evans, *Cheap*	–	2007	2012	
Sir Paul Judge, *Tower*	–	2007	2013	
David Graves, *Cripplegate*	–	2008	–	
John Garbutt, *Walbrook*	–	2009	–	
Neil Redcliffe, *Bishopsgate*	–	2009	–	
Peter Hewitt, *Aldgate*	–	2012	–	
Timothy Hailes, *Bassishaw*	–	2013	–	
Julian Malins, QC, *Farringdon Wt.*	–	2013	–	
Matthew Richardson, *Billingsgate*	2009	2012	–	
William Russell, *Bread Street*	–	2013	–	
Peter Estlin, *Coleman Street*	–	2013	–	
Charles Bowman, *Lime Street*	–	2013	–	
Timothy Hailes, *Bassishaw*	–	2013	–	
Julian Malins, QC, *Farringdon Wt.*	1981	2013	–	
Prof. Michael Mainelli, *Broad Street*	–	2013	–	
Vincent Keaveny, *Farringdon Wn*	–	2013	–	
Peter Estlin, *Coleman Street*	–	2013	–	

THE COMMON COUNCIL
Deputy: each common councilman so described serves as deputy to the alderman of her/his ward.

Abrahams, G. C. (2000)	*Farringdon Wt.*
Absalom, *Deputy* J. D. (1994)	*Farringdon Wt.*
Anderson, R. K. (2013)	*Aldersgate*
Bain-Stewart, A. (2005)	*Farringdon Wn.*
Barker, *Deputy* J. A., OBE (1981)	*Cripplegate Wn.*
Barrow, *Deputy* D. (2007)	*Aldgate*
Bennett, *Deputy* J. A. (2005)	*Broad Street*
Benstead-Smith, N. M. (2014)	*Cheap*
Boden, C. P. (2013)	*Castle Baynard*
Boleat, M. J. (2002)	*Cordwainer*
Bottomley, K. D. F. (2015)	*Bridge & Bridge Wt.*
Bradshaw, D. J. (1991)	*Cripplegate Wn.*
Campbell-Taylor, Revd W. G. (2014)	*Portsoken*
Cassidy, *Deputy* M. J., CBE (1980)	*Coleman Street*
Chadwick, R. A. H. (1994)	*Tower*
Challis, N. K. (2005)	*Castle Baynard*
Chapman, *Deputy* J. D. (2006)	*Langbourn*
Colthurst, H. N. A. (2013)	*Lime Street*
Cotgrove, D. (1991)	*Lime Street*
De Sausmarez, H. J. (2015)	*Candlewick*
Deane, *Deputy* A. J. C. (2011)	*Farringdon Wt.*
Dostalova, K. (2013)	*Farringdon Wn.*
Dove, *Deputy* W. H., OBE (1993)	*Bishopsgate Wt.*
Duckworth, S. D., OBE (2000)	*Bishopsgate Wn.*
Dudley, Revd Dr M. R. (2002)	*Aldersgate*
Dunphy, P. G. (2009)	*Cornhill*
Edham, E. (2014)	*Castle Baynard*
Eskenzi, *Deputy* A. N., CBE (1970)	*Farringdon Wn.*
Everett, K. M. (1984)	*Candlewick*
Fernandes, S. A. (2009)	*Coleman Street*
Fletcher, J. W. (2011)	*Portsoken*
Fraser, S. J., CBE (1993)	*Coleman Street*
Fraser, *Deputy* W. B., OBE (1981)	*Vintry*
Fredericks, M. B. (2008)	*Tower*
Frew, L. (2013)	*Walbrook*
Gillon, G. M. F. (1995)	*Cordwainer*
Ginsburg, *Deputy* S. (1990)	*Bishopsgate Wn.*
Haines, *Deputy* Revd S. D. (2005)	*Cornhill*
Harris, B. N. (2004)	*Bridge & Bridge Wt.*
Harrower, G. G. (2015)	*Bassishaw*
Haywood, C. M. (2013)	*Broad Street*
Hoffman, T. D. D. (2002)	*Vintry*
Holmes, A. (2013)	*Farringdon Wn.*
Howard, *Deputy* R. P. S. (2011)	*Lime Street*
Hudson, M. (2007)	*Castle Baynard*
Hyde, W. (2011)	*Bishopsgate Wt.*
Ingham Clark, J. (2013)	*Billingsgate*
James, Clare (2008)	*Farringdon Wn.*
Jones, G. P., QC (2013)	*Farringdon Wt.*
Jones, *Deputy* H. L. M. (2004)	*Portsoken*
King, *Deputy* A. J. N. (1999)	*Queenhithe*
Lawrence, G. A. (2002)	*Farringdon Wt.*
Littlechild, V. (2009)	*Cripplegate Wn.*
Lodge, O. A. W., TD (2009)	*Bread Street*
Lord, C. E., OBE (2001)	*Farringdon Wt.*
Lumley, Prof. J. S. P. (2013)	*Aldersgate*
McGuinness, *Deputy* C. S. (1997)	*Castle Baynard*
McMurtie, A. S. (2013)	*Coleman Street*
Martinelli, P. N. (2009)	*Farringdon Wt.*
Mayhew, J. P. (1996)	*Aldersgate*
Mead, W. (1997)	*Farringdon Wt.*
Merrett, R. A. (2009)	*Bassishaw*

Mooney, B. D. F. (1998)	*Queenhithe*
Moore, G. W. (2009)	*Cripplegate Wt.*
Morris, H. F. (2008)	*Aldgate*
Moss, *Deputy* A. M. (2013)	*Cheap*
Moys, S. D. (2001)	*Aldgate*
Nash, *Deputy* J. C., OBE (1983)	*Aldersgate*
Newman, B. P., CBE (1989)	*Aldersgate*
Packham, G. D. (2013)	*Castle Baynard*
Patel, D. (2013)	*Aldgate*
Pembroke, A. M. F. (1978)	*Cheap*
Pleasance, J. L. (2013)	*Langbourn*
Pollard, *Deputy* J. H. G. (2002)	*Dowgate*
Price, E. C. L. (2013)	*Farringdon Wt.*
Priest, H. J. S. (2009)	*Castle Baynard*
Pulman, *Deputy* G. A. G. (1983)	*Tower*
Punter, C. (1993)	*Cripplegate Wt.*
Quilter, S. D. (1998)	*Cripplegate Wt.*
Regan, *Deputy* R. D., OBE (1998)	*Farringdon Wn.*
Regis, D. (2009)	*Portsoken*
Richardson, A. F. M. (2013)	*Farringdon Wt.*
Rogula, E. (2008)	*Lime Street*
Rounding, V. (2011)	*Farringdon Wn.*
Scott, J. G. S. (1999)	*Broad Street*
Seaton, I. (2009)	*Cornhill*
Shilson, *Deputy*, G. R. E., DPHIL (2009)	*Bread Street*
Simons, J. L. (2004)	*Castle Baynard*
Sleigh, T. C. C. (2013)	*Bishopsgate Wt.*
Smith, G. M. (2013)	*Farringdon Wn.*
Snyder, *Deputy* Sir Michael (1986)	*Cordwainer*
Starling, A. M. (2006)	*Cripplegate Wn.*
Streeter, P. T. (2013)	*Bishopsgate Wn.*
Thompson, D. J. (2004)	*Aldgate*
Thomson, *Deputy* J. M. D. (2013)	*Walbrook*
Tomlinson, *Deputy* J. (2004)	*Cripplegate Wt.*
Tumbridge, J. R. (2009)	*Tower*
Welbank, *Deputy* M., MBE (2005)	*Billingsgate*
Wheatley, M. R. P. H. D. (2013)	*Dowgate*
Woodhouse, P. (2013)	*Langbourn*

THE CITY GUILDS (LIVERY COMPANIES)

The constitution of the livery companies has been unchanged for centuries. There are three ranks of membership: freemen, liverymen and assistants. A person can become a freeman by patrimony (through a parent having been a freeman); by servitude (through having served an apprenticeship to a freeman); or by redemption (by purchase).

Election to the livery is the prerogative of the company, who can elect any of its freemen as liverymen. Assistants are usually elected from the livery and form a Court of Assistants which is the governing body of the company. The master (in some companies called the prime warden) is elected annually from the assistants.

The register for 2015–16 lists 25,510 liverymen of the guilds entitled to vote at elections at Common Hall.

The order of precedence, omitting extinct companies, is given in parentheses after the name of each company in the list below. In certain companies the election of master or prime warden for the year does not take place until the autumn. In such cases the master or prime warden for 2014–15, rather than 2015–16, is given.

THE TWELVE GREAT COMPANIES
In order of civic precedence

MERCERS *(1)*. *Hall*, Mercers' Hall, Ironmonger Lane, London EC2V 8HE *Livery*, 247. *Clerk*, Menna McGregor *Master*, Timothy Haywood, CBE

GROCERS *(2)*. *Hall*, Grocers' Hall, Princes Street, London EC2R 8AD *Livery*, 348. *Clerk*, Brig. Robert Pridham, OBE *Master*, Charles McAndrew

DRAPERS *(3)*. *Hall*, Drapers' Hall, Throgmorton Avenue, London EC2N 2DQ *Livery*, 317. *Clerk*, Col. Richard Winstanley, OBE *Master*, John Giffard, CBE, QPM

FISHMONGERS *(4)*. *Hall*, Fishmongers' Hall, London Bridge, London EC4R 9EL *Livery*, 388. *Clerk*, Maj.-Gen. Colin Boag, CB, CBE *Prime Warden*, Michael McLaren

GOLDSMITHS *(5)*. *Hall*, Goldsmiths' Hall, Foster Lane, London EC2V 6BN *Livery*, 285. *Clerk*, Rear-Adm. Richard Melly *Prime Warden*, Timothy Schroder

MERCHANT TAYLORS *(6/7)*. *Hall*, Merchant Taylors' Hall, 30 Threadneedle Street, London EC2R 8JB *Livery*, 340. *Clerk*, Rear-Adm. Nicholas Harris, CB, MBE *Master*, P. T. E. Massey

SKINNERS *(6/7)*. *Hall*, Skinners' Hall, 8 Dowgate Hill, London EC4R 2SP *Livery*, 400. *Clerk*, Maj.-Gen. Brian Plummer, CBE *Master*, The Hon. Emmeline Winterbotham

HABERDASHERS *(8)*. *Hall*, Haberdashers' Hall, 18 West Smithfield, London EC1A 9HQ *Livery*, 320. *Clerk*, Cdre Philip Thicknesse, RN *Master*, Audley Twiston-Davies

SALTERS *(9)*. *Hall*, Salters' Hall, 4 Fore Street, London EC2Y 5DE *Livery*, 176. *Clerk*, Capt. David Morris, RN *Master*, Col. David Woodd

IRONMONGERS *(10)*. *Hall*, Ironmongers' Hall, 1 Shaftesbury Place, London EC2Y 8AA *Livery*, 146. *Clerk*, Col. Hamon Massey *Master*, George Bastin

VINTNERS *(11)*. *Hall*, Vintners' Hall, Upper Thames Street, London EC4V 3BG *Livery*, 369. *Clerk*, Brig. Jonathan Bourne-May *Master*, Simon Leschallas

CLOTHWORKERS *(12)*. *Hall*, Clothworkers' Hall, Dunster Court, Mincing Lane, London EC3R 7AH *Livery*, 200. *Clerk*, Mr Andrew Blessley *Master*, Melville Haggard

OTHER CITY GUILDS
In alphabetical order

ACTUARIES *(91)*. Cheapside House, 138 Cheapside, London EC2V 6BW *Livery*, 220. *Clerk*, David Johnson *Master*, Peter Thompson

AIR PILOTS AND AIR NAVIGATORS *(81)*. *Hall*, Cobham House, 9 Warwick Court, Gray's Inn, London WC1R 5DJ *Livery*, 600. *Clerk*, Paul Tacon *Grand Master*, HRH the Duke of York, KG, GCVO, ADC(P) *Master*, Sqn Ldr Chris Ford

APOTHECARIES *(58)*. *Hall*, Apothecaries' Hall, 14 Black Friars Lane, London EC4V 6EJ *Livery*, 1,215. *Clerk*, A. Wallington-Smith *Master*, Dr R. N. Palmer

ARBITRATORS *(93)*. 98 Elm Road, Kingston-upon-Thames, Surrey KT2 6HU *Livery*, 180. *Clerk*, Elinor Pritchard *Master*, Michael Goodridge, MBE

ARMOURERS AND BRASIERS *(22)*. *Hall*, Armourers' Hall, 81 Coleman Street, London EC2R 5BJ *Livery*, 130. *Clerk*, Peter Bateman *Master*, Col. David Wynne Davies

ART SCHOLARS *(110)*. Furniture Makers' Hall, 12 Austin Friars, London EC2N 2HE *Livery*, 85. *Clerk*, Georgina Gough *Master*, Alistair Leslie

BAKERS *(19)*. *Hall*, Bakers' Hall, 9 Harp Lane, London EC3R 6DP *Livery*, 350. *Clerk*, Cdre Martin Westwood *Master*, Colin Reese, QC

BARBERS *(17)*. *Hall*, Barber-Surgeons' Hall, Monkwell Square, Wood Street, London EC2Y 5BL *Livery*, 220. *Clerk*, Col. Peter Durrant, MBE *Master*, Geoffrey Preston

BASKETMAKERS *(52)*. 56 Victoria Way, Liphook, Hampshire GU30 7NJ *Livery*, 300. *Clerk*, Fiona Janczur *Prime Warden*, Richard Boucher-Giles

BLACKSMITHS *(40)*. 9 Little Trinity Lane, London EC4V 2AD *Livery*, 246. *Clerk*, Wg Cdr M. A. Heath *Prime Warden*, Nigel Whitehead

BOWYERS *(38)*. 46 The Haydens, Tonbridge, Kent TN9 1NS, *Livery*, 88. *Clerk*, Brian Francois *Master*, Revd John Hayton, TD

BREWERS *(14)*. *Hall*, Brewers' Hall, Aldermanbury Square, London EC2V 7HR *Livery*, 200. *Clerk*, Col. Michael O'Dwyer, OBE *Master*, Miles Jenner, DL

BRODERERS *(48)*. Ember House, 35–37 Creek Road, East Molesey, Surrey KT8 9BE *Livery*, 126. *Clerk*, Peter J. C. Crouch *Master*, Nicholas Bagshawe

BUILDERS MERCHANTS *(88)*. 4 College Hill, London EC4R 2RB *Livery*, 208. *Clerk*, T. Statham *Master*, Leo Martin

BUTCHERS *(24)*. *Hall*, Butchers' Hall, 87 Bartholomew Close, London EC1A 7EB *Livery*, 638. *Clerk*, Maj.-Gen. J. S. Mason, MBE *Master*, Patricia Dart

CARMEN *(77)*. Five Kings House, 1 Queen Street Place, London EC4R 1QS *Livery*, 500. *Clerk*, Walter Gill *Master*, Mark Roderick Winton Griffiths

CARPENTERS *(26)*. *Hall*, Carpenters' Hall, 1 Throgmorton Avenue, London EC2N 2JJ *Livery*, 150. *Clerk*, Brig. Tim Gregson, MBE *Master*, Michael Neal

CHARTERED ACCOUNTANTS *(86)*. Larksfield, Kent Hatch Road, Crockham Hill, Edenbridge, Kent TN8 6SX *Livery*, 365. *Clerk*, Peter Dickinson *Master*, David Illingworth

CHARTERED ARCHITECTS *(98)*. 164 Stockbridge Road, Winchester SO22 6RW *Livery*, 165. *Clerk*, Ian Head *Master*, Dr Geoffrey Purves

CHARTERED SECRETARIES AND ADMINISTRATORS *(87)*. 3rd Floor, Saddlers' House, 40 Gutter Lane, London EC2V 6BR *Livery*, 240. *Clerk*, Erica Lee *Master*, Patricia Day

CHARTERED SURVEYORS *(85)*. 75 Meadway Drive, Horsell, Woking, Surrey GU21 4TF *Livery*, 365. *Clerk*, Amanda Jackson *Master*, Graham Chase

CLOCKMAKERS *(61)*. 1 Throgmorton Avenue, London EC2N 2BY *Livery*, 289. *Clerk*, Lt.-Col. Oliver Bartrum, MBE *Master*, Philip Whyte

COACHMAKERS AND COACH-HARNESS MAKERS *(72)*. The Old Barn, Church Lane, Glentham Market Rasen, Lincolnshire LN8 2EL *Livery*, 500. *Clerk*, Cdr Mark Leaning, RN *Master*, Michael Kimber

CONSTRUCTORS *(99)*. 5 Delft Close, Locks Heath, Southampton SO31 7TQ *Livery*, 145. *Clerk*, Kim Tyrrell *Master*, Graeme Monteith

COOKS *(35)*. 18 Solent Drive, Warsash, Southampton SO31 9HB *Livery*, 75. *Clerk*, Vice-Adm. P. J. Wilkinson, CB, CVO *Master*, Donald Hodgson

COOPERS *(36)*. *Hall*, Coopers' Hall, 13 Devonshire Square, London EC2M 4TH *Livery*, 260. *Clerk*, Lt.-Col. Adrian Carroll *Master*, Vivian Bairstow

CORDWAINERS *(27)*. Clothworkers' Hall, Dunster Court, Mincing Lane, London EC3R 7AH *Livery*, 182. *Clerk*, John Miller *Master*, John Rubinstein

CURRIERS *(29)*. Oak Lodge, 4 Greenhill Lane, Wimborne, Dorset BH21 2RN *Livery*, 105. *Clerk*, Adrian Rafferty *Master*, J. Allen

CUTLERS *(18)*. *Hall*, Cutlers' Hall, Warwick Lane, London EC4M 7BR *Livery*, 100. *Clerk*, Rupert Meacher *Master*, J. C. W. Wichtowski

DISTILLERS *(69)*. 1 The Sanctuary, Westminster, London SW1P 3JT *Livery*, 260. *Clerk*, Edward Macey-Dare *Master*, Douglas Morton

DYERS *(13)*. *Hall*, Dyers' Hall, 10 Dowgate Hill, London EC4R 2ST *Livery*, 136. *Clerk*, J. R. Vaizey *Prime Warden*, A. C. S. Macpherson

EDUCATORS *(109)*. 8 Little Trinity Lane, London EC4V 2AN *Livery*, 275. *Clerk*, Dr Misha Hebel *Master*, John Leighfield, CBE

ENGINEERS *(94)*. Wax Chandlers' Hall, 6 Gresham Street, London EC2V 7AD *Livery*, 320. *Clerk*, A. G. Willenbruch *Master*, Air Vice-Marshal P. J. O'Reilly, CB

ENVIRONMENTAL CLEANERS *(97)*. 64 Ravensfield Gardens, Epsom, Surrey KT19 0SR *Livery*, 185. *Clerk*, Maureen Marden *Master*, Timothy Doyle

FAN MAKERS *(76)*. Skinners' Hall, 8 Dowgate Hill, London EC4R 2SP *Livery*, 180. *Clerk*, Martin Davies *Master*, John Naylor

FARMERS *(80)*. *Hall*, The Farmers' and Fletchers' Hall, 3 Cloth Street, London EC1A 7LD *Livery*, 350. *Clerk*, Col. David King, OBE *Master*, A. J. Alston

FARRIERS *(55)*. 19 Queen Street, Chipperfield, Kings Langley, Herts WD4 9BT *Livery*, 351. *Clerk*, Charlotte Clifford *Master*, Guy Hurst

FELTMAKERS *(63)*. Post Cottage, Greywell, Hook, Hants RG29 1DA *Livery*, 190. *Clerk*, Maj. J. T. H. Coombs *Master*, Peter Simeons

FIREFIGHTERS *(103)*. The Insurance Hall, 20 Aldermanbury, London EC2V 7GF *Livery*, 121. *Clerk*, Steven Tamcken *Master*, Ron Murray

FLETCHERS *(39)*. *Hall*, The Farmers' and Fletchers' Hall, 3 Cloth Street, London EC1A 7LD *Livery*, 143. *Clerk*, Kate Pink *Master*, Adrian Knight

FOUNDERS *(33)*. *Hall*, Founders' Hall, 1 Cloth Fair, London EC1A 7JQ *Livery*, 175. *Clerk*, J. P. Knight *Master*, P. A. Draycott

FRAMEWORK KNITTERS *(64)*. The Grange, Kimcote, Lutterworth LE17 5RU *Livery*, 200. *Clerk*, Capt. Shaun Mackaness *Master*, David Miller

FRUITERERS *(45)*. Chapelstones, 84 High Street, Codford St Mary, Warminster BA12 0ND *Livery*, 283. *Clerk*, Lt.-Col. L. French *Master*, R. Best

FUELLERS *(95)*. Skinners' Hall, 8 Dowgate Hill, London EC4R 2SP *Livery*, 141. *Clerk*, Cdre Bill Walworth *Master*, Neville Chamberlain, CBE

FURNITURE MAKERS *(83)*. *Hall*, Furniture Makers' Hall, 12 Austin Friars, London EC2N 2HE *Livery*, 205. *Clerk*, Jonny Westbrooke *Master*, David Dewing

GARDENERS *(66)*. 25 Luke Street, London EC2A 4AR *Livery*, 298. *Clerk*, Maj. Jeremy Herrtage *Master*, Bernard Williams

GIRDLERS *(23)*. *Hall*, Girdlers' Hall, Basinghall Avenue, London EC2V 5DD *Livery*, 80. *Clerk*, Brig. Ian Rees *Master*, Patrick Reeve

GLASS SELLERS *(71)*. 17 The Ryde, Hatfield, Herts AL9 5DQ *Livery*, 230. *Clerk*, Caroline Gillett *Master*, William Knocker

GLAZIERS AND PAINTERS OF GLASS *(53)*. *Hall*, Glaziers' Hall, 9 Montague Close, London SE1 9DD *Livery*, 292. *Clerk*, Cdr Andrew Gordon-Lennox, RN *Master*, Duncan Gee

GLOVERS *(62)*. Seniors Farmhouse, Semley, Shaftesbury, Dorset SP7 9AX *Livery*, 245. *Clerk*, Lt.-Col. Mark Butler *Master*, Michael Orr

GOLD AND SILVER WYRE DRAWERS *(74)*. 9A Prince of Wales Mansions, Prince of Wales Drive, London SW11 4BG *Livery*, 280. *Clerk*, Cdr. R. House *Master*, Michael F. Powell

GUNMAKERS *(73)*. The Proof House, 48–50 Commercial Road, London E1 1LP *Livery*, 350. *Clerk*, John Allen *Master*, J. F. Jackman

HACKNEY CARRIAGE DRIVERS *(104)*. 25 The Grove, Parkfield, Latimer, Bucks HP5 1UE *Livery*, 105. *Clerk*, Mary Whitworth *Master*, Colin Evans

HORNERS *(54)*. 12 Coltsfoot Close, Ixworth, Suffolk IP31 2NJ *Livery*, 225. *Clerk*, Jonathan Mead *Master*, Raymond Layard

INFORMATION TECHNOLOGISTS *(100)*. *Hall*, Information Technologists' Hall, 39A Bartholomew Close, London EC1A 7JN *Livery*, 349. *Clerk*, Mike Jenkins *Master*, Nicholas Birtles

INNHOLDERS *(32)*. *Hall*, Innholders' Hall, 30 College Street, London EC4R 2RH *Livery*, 150. *Clerk*, Dougal Bulger *Master*, Julia Sibley, MBE

INSURERS *(92)*. Insurance Hall, 20 Aldermanbury, London EC2V 7HY *Livery*, 341. *Clerk*, Sarah Clark *Master*, Andrew Hubbard, FCA

INTERNATIONAL BANKERS *(106)*. 12 Austin Friars, London EC2N 2HE *Livery*, 223. *Clerk*, Nicholas Westgarth *Master*, Michael Llewelyn-Jones

JOINERS AND CEILERS *(41)*. 75 Meadway Drive, Horsell, Woking, Surrey GU21 4TF *Livery*, 115. *Clerk*, Amanda Jackson *Master*, Mark Snelling

LAUNDERERS *(89)*. *Hall*, Launderers' Hall, 9 Montague Close, London Bridge, London SE1 9DD *Livery*, 175. *Clerk*, Margaret Campbell *Master*, Paul Higgs

LEATHERSELLERS *(15)*. 21 Garlick Hill, London EC4V 2AU *Livery*, 150. *Clerk*, Brig. David Santa-Olalla, DSO, MC *Master*, His Hon. Anthony Thornton, QC

LIGHTMONGERS *(96)*. 1 Manor House Garden, High Street, Wanstead, London E11 2RU *Livery*, 168. *Clerk*, Phillip Hyde *Master*, Rod Bennion

LORINERS *(57)*. 30 Elm Park, Royal Wootton Bassett, Wiltshire SN4 7TA *Livery*, 400. *Clerk*, Honor Page *Master*, Graham Flight

MAKERS OF PLAYING CARDS *(75)*. 256 St David's Square, London E14 3WE *Livery*, 147. *Clerk*, David Barrett *Master*, Capt. Michael Davis-Marks, OBE

MANAGEMENT CONSULTANTS *(105)*. Skinners' Hall, 8 Dowgate Hill, London EC4R 2SP *Livery*, 197. *Clerk*, Julie Fox *Master*, David Peregrine-Jones

MARKETORS *(90)*. Plaisterers' Hall, One London Wall, London EC2Y 5JU *Livery*, 250. *Clerk*, John Hammond *Master*, Andrew Marsden

MASONS *(30)*. 8 Little Trinity Lane. London EC4V 2AN *Livery*, 163. *Clerk*, Maj. Giles Clapp *Master*, William Gloyn

MASTER MARINERS *(78)*. *Hall*, HQS Wellington, Temple Stairs, Victoria Embankment, London WC2R 2PN *Livery*, 160. *Clerk*, Cdre Angus Menzies, RN *Master*, Capt. Jim Conybeare

MUSICIANS *(50)*. 1 Speed Highwalk, Barbican, London EC2Y BDX *Livery*, 420. *Clerk*, Hugh Lloyd *Master*, Kathleen Duncan, OBE

NEEDLEMAKERS *(65)*. PO Box 3682, Windsor, Berkshire SL4 3WR *Livery*, 200. *Clerk*, Philip Grant *Master*, Geoffrey Lewis, FRICS

PAINTER-STAINERS *(28)*. *Hall*, Painters' Hall, 9 Little Trinity Lane, London EC2V 2AD *Livery*, 310. *Clerk*, C. J. Twyman *Master*, A. J. Ward

PATTENMAKERS *(70)*. 3 The High Street, Sutton Valence, Kent ME17 3AG *Livery*, 200. *Clerk*, Col. R. W. Murfin, TD *Master*, Nicholas Andrews

PAVIORS *(56)*. Paviors' House, Charter House, Charterhouse Square, London EC1M 6AN *Livery*, 285. *Clerk*, John Freestone *Master*, Terry Last

PEWTERERS *(16)*. *Hall*, Pewterers' Hall, Oat Lane, London EC2V 7DE *Livery*, 98. *Clerk*, Capt. Paddy Watson, RN *Master*, Mark Chambers

PLAISTERERS *(46)*. *Hall*, Plaisterers' Hall, 1 London Wall, London EC2Y 5JU *Livery*, 236. *Clerk*, Nigel Bamping *Master*, Bill Mahoney

PLUMBERS *(31)*. Wax Chandlers' Hall, 6 Gresham Street, London EC2V 7AD *Livery*, 360. *Clerk*, Air Cdre Paul Nash, OBE *Master*, Stephen Hodkinson

POULTERS *(34)*. 57 Cullum Welch House, Golden Lane Estate, London EC17 0SH *Livery*, 204. *Clerk*, Vernon Ashford *Master*, Rowland Hughes

SADDLERS *(25)*. *Hall*, Saddlers' Hall, 40 Gutter Lane, London EC2V 6BR *Livery*, 75. *Clerk*, Col. Nigel Lithgow, CBE *Master*, C. E. Barclay

SCIENTIFIC INSTRUMENT MAKERS *(84)*. 9 Montague Close, London SE1 9DD *Livery*, 185. *Clerk*, N. J. Watson *Master*, C. J. Sawyer

SCRIVENERS *(44)*. HQS Wellington, Temple Stairs, Victoria Embankment, London WC2R 2PN *Livery*, 191. *Clerk*, Giles Cole *Master*, Jeremy Burgess

SECURITY PROFESSIONALS *(108)*. 34 Tye Green, Glemsford, Suffolk CO10 7RG *Livery*, 150. *Clerk*, Patricia Boswell *Master*, Stewart Seymour, CSyP

SHIPWRIGHTS *(59)*. Ironmongers Hall, Shaftesbury Place, London EC2Y 8AA *Livery*, 450. *Clerk*, Lt.-Col. Richard Cole-Mackintosh *Prime Warden*, Douglas Barrow, PC *Grand Master*, HRH the Prince of Wales, KG, KT, GCB

SOLICITORS *(79)*. 4 College Hill, London EC4R 2RB *Livery*, 350. *Clerk*, Neil Cameron *Master*, Dame Fiona Woolf

SPECTACLE MAKERS *(60)*. Apothecaries' Hall, Black Friars Lane, London EC4V 6EL *Livery*, 400. *Clerk*, Helen Perkins, FCIS, FCSI *Master*, Edward Middleton, FCA

STATIONERS AND NEWSPAPER MAKERS *(47)*. *Hall*, Stationers' Hall, Ave Maria Lane, London EC4M 7DD *Livery*, 540. *Clerk*, William Alden, MBE *Master*, Helen Esmonde

TALLOW CHANDLERS *(21)*. *Hall*, Tallow Chandlers' Hall, 4 Dowgate Hill, London EC4R 2SH *Livery*, 180. *Clerk*, Brig. D. Homer, MBE *Master*, Nicholas Bull, FCA

TAX ADVISERS *(107)*. 191 West End Road, Ruislip, Middx HA4 6LD *Freemen*, 145. *Clerk*, Paul Herbage, MBE *Master*, Anthony Thomas

TIN PLATE WORKERS (ALIAS WIRE WORKERS) *(67)*. PO Box 71002, London W4 9FH *Livery*, 200. *Clerk*, Piers Baker *Master*, Ian Makowski

TOBACCO PIPE MAKERS AND TOBACCO BLENDERS *(82)*. 14 Montpelier Road, Sutton, Surrey SM1 4QE *Livery*, 138. *Clerk*, Sandra Stocker *Master*, Christopher Allen

TURNERS *(51)*. Skinner's Hall, 8 Dowgate Hill, London EC4R 2SP *Livery*, 186. *Clerk*, Alex Robertson *Master*, Nicholas Edwards

TYLERS AND BRICKLAYERS *(37)*. 3 Farmers' Way, Seer Green, Bucks HP9 2YY *Livery*, 158. *Clerk*, John Brooks *Master*, Tom Rider

UPHOLDERS *(49)*. E clerk@upholders.co.uk *Livery*, 175. *Clerk*, Susan Nevard *Master*, Wynne Gilham

WATER CONSERVATORS *(102)*. The Lark, 2 Bell Lane, Worlington, Bury St Edmunds, Suffolk IP28 8SE *Livery*, 212. *Clerk*, Ralph Riley *Master*, Peter Hall

WAX CHANDLERS *(20)*. *Hall*, Wax Chandlers' Hall, 6 Gresham Street, London EC2V 7AD *Livery*, 110. *Clerk*, Georgina Brown *Master*, Dr Andrew Mair

WEAVERS *(42)*. Saddlers' House, Gutter Lane, London EC2V 6BR *Livery*, 125. *Clerk*, John Snowdon *Upper Bailiff*, John Nugee

WHEELWRIGHTS *(68)*. 16 Gordon Avenue, Twickenham TW1 1NQ *Livery*, 220. *Clerk*, Bridget Hynard *Master*, G. I. A. Armfield

WOOLMEN *(43)*. 52 Cumberland Drive, Bexleyheath, Kent DA7 5LB *Livery*, 150. *Clerk*, Maj. Steve Wake *Master*, John Brewer

WORLD TRADERS *(101)*. 13 Hall Gardens, Colney Heath, St. Albans, Herts AL4 0QF *Livery*, 240. *Clerk*, Mrs Gaye Duffy *Master*, Wendy Hyde, C.C.

PARISH CLERKS *(No Livery*)*. Acreholt, 33 Medstead Road, Beech, Alton, Hants GU34 4AD *Members*, 91. *Clerk*, Alana Coombes *Master*, Martin Woods

WATERMEN AND LIGHTERMEN *(No Livery*)*. *Hall*, Watermen's Hall, 16–18 St Mary at Hill, London EC3R 8EF *Craft Owning Freemen*, 381. *Clerk*, Colin Middlemiss *Master*, Richard Springford

* Parish Clerks and Watermen and Lightermen have requested to remain with no livery

WALES

Cymru

The principality of Wales (Cymru) occupies the extreme west of the central southern portion of the island of Great Britain, with a total area of 20,778 sq. km (8,022 sq. miles): land 20,733 sq. km (8,005 sq. miles); inland water 45 sq. km (17 sq. miles). It is bordered in the north by the Irish Sea, in the south by the Bristol Channel, in the east by the English counties of Cheshire West and Chester, Shropshire, Herefordshire and Gloucestershire, and in the west by St George's Channel.

Across the Menai Straits is Ynys Mon (Isle of Anglesey) (715 sq. km/276 sq. miles), communication with which is facilitated by the Menai Suspension Bridge (305m/1,000ft long) built by Telford in 1826, and by the Britannia Bridge (351m/1,151ft), a two-tier road and rail truss arch design, rebuilt in 1972 after a fire destroyed the original tubular railway bridge built by Stephenson in 1850. Holyhead harbour, on Holy Isle (north-west of Anglesey), provides ferry services to Dublin (113km/70 miles).

POPULATION
The population at the 2011 census was 3,063,456 (men 1,504,228; women 1,559,228). The average density of population in 2011 was 147 persons per sq. km (382 per sq. mile).

RELIEF
Wales is a country of extensive tracts of high plateau and shorter stretches of mountain ranges deeply dissected by river valleys. Lower-lying ground is largely confined to the coastal belt and the lower parts of the valleys. The highest mountains are those of Snowdonia in the north-west (Snowdon, 1,085m/3,559ft and Aran Fawddwy, 906m/2,971ft). Snowdonia is also home to Cader Idris (Pen y Gadair, 892m/2,928ft). Other high peaks are to be found in the Cambrian range (Plynlimon, 752m/2,467ft), and the Black Mountains, Brecon Beacons and Black Forest ranges in the south-east (Pen y Fan, 886m/2,906ft; Waun Fâch, 811m/2,660ft; Carmarthen Van, 802m/2,630ft).

HYDROGRAPHY
The principal river in Wales is the Severn, which flows from the slopes of Plynlimon to the English border. The Wye (209km/130 miles) also rises on the slopes of Plynlimon. The Usk (90km/56 miles) flows into the Bristol Channel through Gwent. The Dee (113km/70 miles) rises in Bala Lake and flows through the Vale of Llangollen, where an aqueduct (built by Telford in 1805) carries the Pontcysyllte branch of the Shropshire Union Canal across the valley. The estuary of the Dee is the navigable portion; it is 23km (14 miles) in length and about 8km (5 miles) in breadth. The Towy (109km/68 miles), Teifi (80km/50 miles), Taff (64km/40 miles), Dovey (48km/30 miles), Taf (40km/25 miles) and Conway (39km/24 miles) are wholly Welsh rivers.

The largest natural lake is Bala (Llyn Tegid) in Gwynedd, nearly 7km (4 miles) long and 1.6km (1 mile) wide. Lake Vyrnwy is an artificial reservoir, about the size of Bala, and forms the water supply of Liverpool; Birmingham's water is supplied from reservoirs in the Elan and Claerwen valleys.

WELSH LANGUAGE
According to the 2011 census results, the percentage of people aged three years and over who are able to speak Welsh is:

Blaenau Gwent	7.8	Neath Port Talbot	15.3
Bridgend	9.7	Newport	9.3
Caerphilly	11.2	Pembrokeshire	19.2
Cardiff	11.1	Powys	18.6
Carmarthenshire	43.9	Rhondda Cynon Taf	12.3
Ceredigion	47.3	Swansea	11.4
Conwy	27.4	Torfaen	9.8
Denbighshire	24.6	Vale of Glamorgan	10.8
Flintshire	13.2	Wrexham	12.9
Gwynedd	65.4	Ynys Mon	
Merthyr Tydfil	8.9	(Isle of Anglesey)	57.2
Monmouthshire	9.9	*Total in Wales*	19.0

FLAG
The flag of Wales, the Red Dragon *(Y Ddraig Goch)*, is a red dragon on a field divided white over green (per fess argent and vert a dragon passant gules). The flag was augmented in 1953 by a royal badge on a shield encircled with a riband bearing the words *Ddraig Goch Ddyry Cychwyn* and imperially crowned, but this augmented flag is rarely used.

EARLY HISTORY

The earliest inhabitants of whom there is any record appear to have been subdued or exterminated by the Goidels (a people of Celtic race) in the Bronze Age. A further invasion of Celtic Brythons and Belgae followed in the ensuing Iron Age. The Roman conquest of southern Britain and Wales was for some time successfully opposed by Caratacus (Caractacus or Caradog), chieftain of the Catuvellauni and son of Cunobelinus (Cymbeline). South-east Wales was subjugated and the legionary fortress at Caerleon-on-Usk established by around AD 75–7; the conquest of Wales was completed by Agricola around AD 78. Communications were opened up by the construction of military roads from Chester to Caerleon-on-Usk and Caerwent, and from Chester to Conwy (and thence to Carmarthen and Neath). Christianity was introduced in the fourth century, during the Roman occupation.

ANGLO-SAXON ATTACKS
The Anglo-Saxon invaders of southern Britain drove the Celts into the mountain stronghold of Wales, and into Strathclyde (Cumberland and south-west Scotland) and Cornwall, giving them the name of *Waelisc* (Welsh), meaning 'foreign'. The West Saxons' victory of Deorham (AD 577) isolated Wales from Cornwall and the battle of Chester (AD 613) cut off communication with Strathclyde and northern Britain. In the eighth century the boundaries of the Welsh were further restricted by the annexations of Offa, King of Mercia, and counter-attacks were largely prevented by the construction of an artificial boundary from the Dee to the Wye (Offa's Dyke).

In the ninth century Rhodri Mawr (844–878) united the country and successfully resisted further incursions of the Saxons by land and raids of Norse and Danish pirates by sea, but at his death his three provinces of Gwynedd (north), Powys (central) and Deheubarth (south) were divided among his three sons, Anarawd, Mervyn and Cadell. Cadell's son Hywel Dda ruled a large part of Wales and codified its laws but the provinces were not united again until the rule of Llewelyn ap Seisyllt (husband of the heiress of Gwynedd) from 1018 to 1023.

THE NORMAN CONQUEST
After the Norman conquest of England, William I created palatine counties along the Welsh frontier, and the Norman barons began to make encroachments into Welsh territory. The Welsh princes recovered many of their losses during the civil wars of Stephen's reign (1135–54), and in the early 13th century Owen Gruffydd, prince of Gwynedd, was the dominant figure in Wales. Under Llywelyn ap Iorwerth (1194–1240) the Welsh united in powerful resistance to English incursions and Llywelyn's privileges and de facto independence were recognised in the Magna Carta. His grandson, Llywelyn ap Gruffydd, was the last native prince; he was killed in 1282 during hostilities between the Welsh and English, allowing Edward I of England to establish his authority over the country. On 7 February 1301, Edward of Caernarvon, son of Edward I, was created Prince of Wales, a title subsequently borne by the eldest son of the sovereign.

Strong Welsh national feeling continued, expressed in the early 15th century in the rising led by Owain Glyndwr, but the situation was altered by the accession to the English throne in 1485 of Henry VII of the Welsh House of Tudor. Wales was politically annexed by England under the Act of Union of 1535, which extended English laws to the principality and gave it parliamentary representation for the first time.

EISTEDDFOD
The Welsh are a distinct nation, with a language and literature of their own; the national bardic festival (Eisteddfod), instituted by Prince Rhys ap Griffith in 1176, is still held annually.

PRINCIPAL CITIES

There are six cities in Wales (with date city status conferred): Bangor (pre-1900), Cardiff (1905), Newport (2002), St Asaph (2012), St David's (1994) and Swansea (1969).

Cardiff and Swansea have also been granted lord mayoralities.

CARDIFF
Cardiff (Caerdydd), at the mouth of the rivers Taff, Rhymney and Ely, is the capital city of Wales and at the 2011 census had a population of 346,090. The city has changed dramatically in recent years following the regeneration of Cardiff Bay and construction of a barrage, which has created a permanent freshwater lake and waterfront for the city. As the capital city, Cardiff is home to the National Assembly for Wales and is a major administrative, retail, business and cultural centre.

The city is home to many fine buildings, including the City Hall, Cardiff Castle, Llandaff Cathedral, the National Museum of Wales, university buildings, law courts and the Temple of Peace and Health. The Millennium Stadium opened in 1999 and has hosted high-profile events since 2001.

SWANSEA
Swansea (Abertawe) is a seaport with a population of 239,023 at the 2011 census. The Gower peninsula was brought within the city boundary under local government reform in 1974.

The principal buildings are the Norman castle (rebuilt c.1330), the Royal Institution of South Wales, founded in 1835 (including library), the University of Wales Swansea at Singleton and the Guildhall, containing Frank Brangwyn's British Empire panels. The Dylan Thomas Centre, formerly the old Guildhall, was restored in 1995. More recent buildings include the County Hall, the Maritime Quarter Marina, the Wales National Pool and the National Waterfront Museum.

Swansea was chartered by the Earl of Warwick (1158–84), and further charters were granted by King John, Henry III, Edward II, Edward III and James II, Oliver Cromwell and the Marcher Lord William de Breos. It was formally invested with city status in 1969.

LORD-LIEUTENANTS AND HIGH SHERIFFS

Area	Lord-Lieutenant	High Sheriff (2015–16)
Clwyd	Henry Fetherstonhaugh, OBE	Janet Evans
Dyfed	Hon. Robin Lewis, OBE	James Lewis
Gwent	Sir Simon Boyle, KCVO	Lt.-Col. Andrew Tuggey
Gwynedd	Edmund Bailey	Dr Elizabeth Nesbit Andrews, MBE
Mid Glamorgan	Kate Thomas, CVO	Jayne James
Powys	Hon. Dame Elizabeth Legge-Bourke, DCVO	Lt.-Col. Michael Ledston Lewis
South Glamorgan	Dr Peter Beck, MD, FRCP	Prof. Heather Stevens, CBE
West Glamorgan	D. Byron Lewis	Robert Redfern

LOCAL COUNCILS

Council	Administrative Headquarters	Telephone	Population*	Council Tax†	Chief Executive
Blaenau Gwent	Ebbw Vale	01495-311556	69,674	£1,635	David Waggett
Bridgend	Bridgend	01656-643643	141,214	£1,483	Darren Mepham
Caerphilly	Hengoed	01443-815588	179,941	£1,215	Chris Burns
CARDIFF	Cardiff	029-2087 2087	354,294	£1,224	Paul Orders
Carmarthenshire	Carmarthen	01267-234567	184,898	£1,348	Mark James, CBE
Ceredigion	Aberaeron	01545-570881	75,425	£1,300	Bronwen Morgan
Conwy	Conwy	01492-574000	116,287	£1,286	Iwan Davies
Denbighshire	Ruthin	01824-706101	94,791	£1,422	Dr Mohammed Mehmet
Flintshire	Mold	01352-752121	153,804	£1,301	Colin Everett
Gwynedd	Caernarfon	01766-771000	122,273	£1,430	Dilwyn Williams
Merthyr Tydfil	Merthyr Tydfil	01685-725000	59,065	£1,554	Gareth Chapman
Monmouthshire	Cwmbran	01633-644644	92,336	£1,349	Paul Matthews
Neath Port Talbot	Port Talbot	01639-686868	140,490	£1,609	Steven Phillips
NEWPORT	Newport	01633-656656	146,841	£1,154	Will Godfrey
Pembrokeshire	Haverfordwest	01437-764551	123,666	£1,029	Ian Westley
Powys	Llandrindod Wells	01597-827460	132,675	£1,287	Jeremy Patterson
Rhondda Cynon Taff	Tonypandy	01443-425005	236,888	£1,519	Steve Merritt
SWANSEA	Swansea	01792-636000	241,297	£1,342	Jack Straw
Torfaen	Pontypool	01495-762200	91,609	£1,352	Alison Ward
Vale of Glamorgan	Barry	01446-700111	127,685	£1,312	Neil Moore
Wrexham	Wrexham	01978-292000	136,714	£1,276	Dr Helen Paterson
Ynys Mon (Isle of Anglesey)	Ynys Mon	01248-750057	70,169	£1,296	vacant

* *Source:* Office for National Statistics – *Mid-2014 Population Estimates* (Crown copyright)
† Average Band D council tax bill 2015–16
Councils in CAPITAL LETTERS have city status

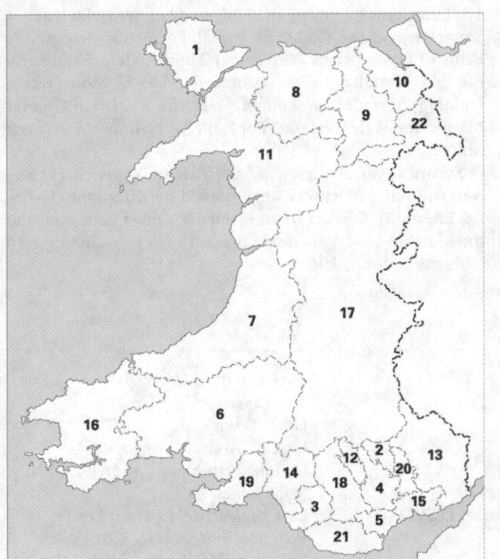

Key	Council	Key	Council
1	Anglesey (Ynys Mon)	12	Merthyr Tydfil
2	Blaenau Gwent	13	Monmouthshire
3	Bridgend	14	Neath Port Talbot
4	Caerphilly	15	Newport
5	Cardiff	16	Pembrokeshire
6	Carmarthenshire	17	Powys
7	Ceredigion	18	Rhondda Cynon Taff
8	Conwy	19	Swansea
9	Denbighshire	20	Torfaen
10	Flintshire	21	Vale of Glamorgan
11	Gwynedd	22	Wrexham

SCOTLAND

Scotland occupies the northern portion of the main island of Great Britain and includes the Inner and Outer Hebrides, Orkney, Shetland and many other islands. It lies between 60° 51' 30" and 54° 38' N. latitude and between 1° 45' 32" and 6° 14' W. longitude, with England to the south-east, the North Channel and the Irish Sea to the south-west, the Atlantic Ocean on the north and west, and the North Sea on the east.

The greatest length of the mainland (Cape Wrath to the Mull of Galloway) is 441km (274 miles), and the greatest breadth (Buchan Ness to Applecross) is 248km (154 miles). The customary measurement of the island of Great Britain is from the site of John o' Groats house, near Duncansby Head, Caithness, to Land's End, Cornwall, a total distance of 970km (603 miles) in a straight line and approximately 1,448km (900 miles) by road.

The total area of Scotland is 78,807 sq. km (30,427 sq. miles): land 77,907 sq. km (30,080 sq. miles), inland water 900 sq. km (347 sq. miles).

POPULATION
The population at the 2011 census was 5,295,403 (men 2,567,444; women 2,727,959). The average density of the population in 2011 was 67 persons per sq. km (174 per sq. mile).

RELIEF
There are three natural orographic divisions of Scotland. The southern uplands have their highest points in Merrick (843m/2,766ft), Rhinns of Kells (814m/2,669ft) and Cairnsmuir of Carsphairn (797m/2,614ft), in the west; and the Tweedsmuir Hills in the east (Broad Law 840m/2,756ft; Dollar Law 817m/2,682ft; Hartfell 808m/2,651ft).

The central lowlands, formed by the valleys of the Clyde, Forth and Tay, divide the southern uplands from the Highlands, which extend from close to the extreme north of the mainland to the central lowlands, and are divided into a northern and a southern system by the Great Glen.

The Grampian Mountains, the southern Highland system, include in the west Ben Nevis (1,343m/4,406ft), the highest point in the British Isles, and in the east the Cairngorm Mountains (Ben Macdui 1,309m/4,296ft; Braeriach 1,295m/4,248ft; Cairn Gorm 1,245m/4,084ft). The north-west Highlands contain the mountains of Wester and Easter Ross (Carn Eige 1,183m/3,880ft; Sgurr na Lapaich 1,151m/3,775ft).

Created, like the central lowlands, by a major geological fault, the Great Glen (97km/60 miles long) runs between Inverness and Fort William, and contains Loch Ness, Loch Oich and Loch Lochy. These are linked to each other and to the north-east and south-west coasts of Scotland by the Caledonian Canal, providing a navigable passage between the Moray Firth and the Inner Hebrides.

HYDROGRAPHY
The western coast is fragmented by peninsulas and islands, and indented by fjords (sea-lochs), the longest of which is Loch Fyne (68km/42 miles long) in Argyll. Although the east coast tends to be less fractured and lower, there are several great drowned inlets (firths), including the Firth of Forth, Firth of Tay and the Moray Firth, as well as the Firth of Clyde in the west.

The lochs are the principal hydrographic feature. The largest in Scotland and in Britain is Loch Lomond (70 sq. km/

27 sq. miles), in the Grampian valleys, and the longest and deepest is Loch Ness (39km/24 miles long and 244m/800ft deep), in the Great Glen.

The longest river is the Tay (188km/117 miles), noted for its salmon. It flows into the North Sea, with Dundee on the estuary, which is spanned by the Tay Bridge (3,136m/10,289ft) opened in 1887 and the Tay Road Bridge (2,245m/7,365ft) opened in 1966. Other noted salmon rivers are the Dee (145km/90 miles) which flows into the North Sea at Aberdeen, and the Spey (177km/110 miles), the swiftest flowing river in the British Isles, which flows into the Moray Firth. The Tweed, which gave its name to the woollen cloth produced along its banks, marks in the lower stretches of its 154km (96 mile) course the border between Scotland and England.

The most important river commercially is the Clyde (171km/106 miles), formed by the junction of the Daer and Portrail water, which flows through the city of Glasgow to the Firth of Clyde. During its course it passes over the picturesque Falls of Clyde, Bonnington Linn (9m/30ft), Corra Linn (26m/84ft), Dundaff Linn (3m/10ft) and Stonebyres Linn (24m/80ft), above and below Lanark. The Forth (106km/66 miles), upon which stands Edinburgh, the capital, is spanned by the Forth Railway Bridge (1890), which is 1,625m (5,330ft) long, and the Forth Road Bridge (1964), which has a total length of 1,876m (6,156ft) (over water) and a single span of 914m (3,000ft).

The highest waterfall in Scotland, and the British Isles, is Eas a'Chùal Aluinn with a total height of 201m (658ft), which falls from Glas Bheinn in Sutherland. The Falls of Glomach, on a head-stream of the Elchaig in Wester Ross, have a drop of 113m (370ft).

GAELIC LANGUAGE
According to the 2011 census, 1.1 per cent (58,000 people) of the population of Scotland aged three and over were able to speak the Scottish form of Gaelic. This was a slight decrease from the 1.2 per cent recorded at the 2001 census.

LOWLAND SCOTTISH LANGUAGE
Several regional lowland Scottish dialects, known variously as Scots, Lallans or Doric, are widely spoken. According to the 2011 census, 43 per cent of the population of Scotland aged three and over stated they could do one or a combination of read, write, speak or understand Scots. A question on Scots was not included in the 2001 census.

FLAG
The flag of Scotland is known as the Saltire. It is a white diagonal cross on a blue field (saltire argent in a field azure) and represents St Andrew, the patron saint of Scotland.

THE SCOTTISH ISLANDS

ORKNEY
The Orkney Islands (total area 972 sq. km/376 sq. miles) lie about 10km (six miles) north of the mainland, separated from it by the Pentland Firth. Of the 90 islands and islets (holms and skerries) in the group, about one-third are inhabited.

The total population at the 2011 census was 21,349; the 2011 populations of the islands shown here include those of smaller islands forming part of the same council district.

Mainland, 17,162	Inner Holm, 1
Auskerry, 4	North Ronaldsay, 72
Burray, 409	Papa Westray, 90
Eday, 160	Rousay, 216
Egilsay, 26	Sanday, 494
Flotta, 8	Shapinsay, 307
Gairsay, 3	South Ronaldsay, 909
Graemsay, 28	Stronsay, 349
Holm of Grimbister, 3	Westray, 588
Hoy, 419	Wyre, 29

The islands are rich in prehistoric and Scandinavian remains, the most notable being the Stone Age village of Skara Brae, the burial chamber of Maes Howe, the many brochs (towers) and the 12th-century St Magnus Cathedral. Scapa Flow, between the Mainland and Hoy, was the war station of the British Grand Fleet from 1914 to 1919 and the scene of the scuttling of the surrendered German High Seas Fleet (21 June 1919).

Most of the islands are low-lying and fertile, and farming (principally beef cattle) is the main industry. Flotta, to the south of Scapa Flow, is the site of the oil terminal for the Piper, Claymore and Tartan fields in the North Sea.

The capital is Kirkwall (population 7,045) situated on Mainland.

SHETLAND

The Shetland Islands have a total area of 1,427 sq. km (551 sq. miles) and had a population at the 2011 census of 23,167. They lie about 80km (50 miles) north of the Orkneys, with Fair Isle about half way between the two groups. Out Stack, off Muckle Flugga, 1.6km (one mile) north of Unst, is the most northerly part of the British Isles (60° 51′ 30″ N. lat.).

There are over 100 islands, of which 16 are inhabited. Populations at the 2011 census were:

Mainland, 18,765	Muckle Roe, 130
Bressay, 368	Papa Stour, 15
Bruray, 24	Trondra, 135
East Burra, 76	Unst, 632
Fair Isle, 68	Vaila, 2
Fetlar, 61	West Burra, 776
Foula, 38	Whalsay, 1,061
Housay, 50	Yell, 966

Shetland's many archaeological sites include Jarlshof, Mousa and Clickhimin, and its long connection with Scandinavia has resulted in a strong Norse influence on its place names and dialect.

Industries include fishing, knitwear and farming. In addition to the fishing fleet there are fish processing factories, and the traditional handknitting of Fair Isle and Unst is now supplemented with machine-knitted garments. Farming is mainly crofting, with sheep being raised on the moorland and hills of the islands. Latterly the islands have become a centre of the North Sea oil industry, with pipelines from the Brent and Ninian fields running to the terminal at Sullom Voe, the largest of its kind in Europe.

The capital is Lerwick (population 6,958) situated on Mainland. Lerwick is the main centre for supply services for offshore oil exploration and development.

THE HEBRIDES

Until the late 13th century the Hebrides included other Scottish islands in the Firth of Clyde, the peninsula of Kintyre (Argyll), the Isle of Man and the (Irish) Isle of Rathlin. The origin of the name is probably the Greek *Eboudai*, latinised as *Hebudes* by Pliny, and corrupted to its present form. The Norwegian name *Sudreyjar* (Southern Islands) was latinised as *Sodorenses,* a name that survives in the Anglican bishopric of Sodor and Man.

There are over 500 islands and islets, of which about 100 are inhabited, though mountainous terrain and extensive peat bogs mean that only a fraction of the total area is under cultivation. Stone, Bronze and Iron Age settlement has left many remains, including those at Callanish on Lewis, and Norse colonisation influenced language, customs and place names. Occupations include farming (mostly crofting and stock-raising), fishing and the manufacture of tweeds and other woollens. Tourism is also an important part of the economy.

The Inner Hebrides lie off the west coast of Scotland and are relatively close to the mainland. The largest and best-known is Skye (area 1,665 sq. km/643 sq. miles; pop. 10,008; chief town, Portree), which contains the Cuillin Hills (Sgurr Alasdair, 993m/3,257ft), Bla Bheinn (928m/3,046ft), the Storr (719m/2,358ft) and the Red Hills (Beinn na Caillich, 732m/2,403ft). Other islands in the Highland council area include Raasay (pop. 161), Eigg (pop. 83), Muck (pop. 27) and Rhum (pop. 22).

Further south the Inner Hebridean islands include Arran (pop. 4,629), containing Goat Fell (874m/2,868ft); Coll (pop. 195) and Tiree (pop. 653); Colonsay (pop. 124) and Oronsay (pop. 8); Easdale (pop. 59); Gigha (pop. 163); Islay (area 608 sq. km/235 sq. miles; pop. 3,228); Jura (area 414 sq. km/160 sq. miles; pop. 196), with a range of hills culminating in the Paps of Jura (Beinn-an-Oir, 785m/2,576ft, and Beinn Chaolais, 755m/2,477ft); Lismore (pop. 192); Luing (pop. 195); and Mull (area 950 sq. km/367 sq. miles; pop. 2,800; chief town Tobermory), containing Ben More (967m/3,171ft).

The Outer Hebrides, separated from the mainland by the Minch, now form the Eilean Siar (Western Isles) council area (area 2,897 sq. km/1,119 sq. miles; pop. 27,684). The main islands are Lewis with Harris (area 1,994 sq. km/770 sq. miles, pop. 21,031), whose chief town, Stornoway, is the administrative headquarters; North Uist (pop. 1,254); South Uist (pop. 1,754); Benbecula (pop. 1,303) and Barra (pop. 1,174). Other inhabited islands include Great Bernera (252), Berneray (138), Eriskay (143), Grimsay (169), Scalpay (291) and Vatersay (90).

EARLY HISTORY

There is evidence of human settlement in Scotland dating from the third millennium BC, the earliest settlers being Mesolithic hunters and fishermen. Early in the second millennium BC, Neolithic farmers began to cultivate crops and rear livestock; their settlements were on the west coast and in the north, and included Skara Brae and Maeshowe (Orkney). Settlement by the early Bronze Age 'Beaker Folk', so-called from the shape of their drinking vessels, in eastern Scotland dates from about 1800 BC. Further settlement is believed to have occurred from 700 BC onwards, as tribes were displaced from further south by new incursions from the Continent and the Roman invasions from AD 43.

Julius Agricola, the Roman governor of Britain AD 77–84, extended the Roman conquests in Britain by advancing into Caledonia, culminating with a victory at Mons Graupius, probably in AD 84; he was recalled to Rome shortly afterwards and his forward policy was not pursued. Hadrian's Wall, mostly completed by AD 30, marked the northern frontier of the Roman empire except for the period between about AD 144 and 190 when the frontier moved north to the Forth-Clyde isthmus and a turf wall, the Antonine Wall, was manned.

After the Roman withdrawal from Britain, there were centuries of warfare between the Picts, Scots, Britons, Angles and Vikings. The Picts, generally accepted to be descended from the indigenous Iron Age people of northern Scotland, occupied the area north of the Forth. The Scots, a Gaelic-speaking people of northern Ireland, colonised the area of Argyll and Bute (the kingdom of Dalriada) in the fifth century AD and then expanded eastwards and northwards. The Britons, speaking a Brythonic Celtic language, colonised Scotland from the south from the first century BC; they lost control of south-eastern Scotland (incorporated into the kingdom of Northumbria) to the Angles in the early seventh century but retained Strathclyde (south-western Scotland and Cumbria). Viking raids from the late eighth century were followed by Norse settlement in the western and northern isles, Argyll, Caithness and Sutherland from the mid-ninth century onwards.

UNIFICATION
The union of the areas which now comprise Scotland began in AD 843 when Kenneth MacAlpin, king of the Scots from c.834, also became king of the Picts, joining the two lands to form the kingdom of Alba (comprising Scotland north of a line between the Forth and Clyde rivers). Lothian, the eastern part of the area between the Forth and the Tweed, seems to have been leased to Kenneth II of Alba (reigned 971–995) by Edgar of England c.973, and Scottish possession was confirmed by Malcolm II's victory over a Northumbrian army at Carham c.1016. At about this time Malcolm II (reigned 1005–34) placed his grandson Duncan on the throne of the British kingdom of Strathclyde, bringing under Scots rule virtually all of what is now Scotland.

The Norse possessions were incorporated into the kingdom of Scotland from the 12th century onwards. An uprising in the mid-12th century drove the Norse from most of mainland Argyll. The Hebrides were ceded to Scotland by the Treaty of Perth in 1266 after a Norwegian expedition in 1263 failed to maintain Norse authority over the islands. Orkney and Shetland fell to Scotland in 1468–9 as a pledge for the unpaid dowry of Margaret of Denmark, wife of James III, although Danish claims of suzerainty were relinquished only with the marriage of Anne of Denmark to James VI in 1590.

From the 11th century, there were frequent wars between Scotland and England over territory and the extent of England's political influence. The failure of the Scottish royal line with the death of Margaret of Norway in 1290 led to disputes over the throne which were resolved by the adjudication of Edward I of England. He awarded the throne to John Balliol in 1292 but Balliol's refusal to be a puppet king led to war. Balliol surrendered to Edward I in 1296 and Edward attempted to rule Scotland himself. Resistance to Scotland's loss of independence was led by William Wallace, who defeated the English at Stirling Bridge (1297), and Robert Bruce, crowned in 1306, who held most of Scotland by 1311 and routed Edward II's army at Bannockburn (1314). England recognised the independence of Scotland in the Treaty of Northampton in 1328. Subsequent clashes include the disastrous battle of Flodden (1513) in which James IV and many of his nobles fell.

THE UNION
In 1603 James VI of Scotland succeeded Elizabeth I on the throne of England (his mother, Mary Queen of Scots, was the great-granddaughter of Henry VII), his successors reigning as sovereigns of Great Britain. Political union of the two countries did not occur until 1707.

THE JACOBITE REVOLTS
After the abdication (by flight) in 1688 of James VII and II, the crown devolved upon William III (grandson of Charles I) and Mary II (elder daughter of James VII and II). In 1689 Graham of Claverhouse roused the Highlands on behalf of James VII and II, but died after a military success at Killiecrankie.

After the death of Anne (younger daughter of James VII and II), the throne devolved upon George I (great-grandson of James VI and I). In 1715, armed risings on behalf of James Stuart (the Old Pretender, son of James VII and II) led to the indecisive battle of Sheriffmuir, and the Jacobite movement died down until 1745, when Charles Stuart (the Young Pretender) defeated the Royalist troops at Prestonpans and advanced to Derby (1746). From Derby, the adherents of 'James VIII and III' (the title claimed for his father by Charles Stuart) fell back on the defensive and were finally crushed at Culloden (16 April 1746) by an army led by the Duke of Cumberland, son of George II.

PRINCIPAL CITIES

ABERDEEN
Aberdeen, 209km (130 miles) north-east of Edinburgh, received its charter as a Royal Burgh in 1124. Scotland's third largest city, Aberdeen lies between two rivers, the Dee and the Don, facing the North Sea; the city has a strong maritime history and is today a major centre for offshore oil exploration and production. It is also an ancient university town and distinguished research centre. Other industries include engineering, food processing, textiles, paper manufacturing and chemicals.

Places of interest include King's College, St Machar's Cathedral, Brig o' Balgownie, Duthie Park and Winter Gardens, Hazlehead Park, the Kirk of St Nicholas, Mercat Cross, Marischal College and Marischal Museum, Provost Skene's House, Aberdeen Art Gallery, Gordon Highlanders Museum, Satrosphere Science Centre, and Aberdeen Maritime Museum.

DUNDEE
The Royal Burgh of Dundee is situated on the north bank of the Tay estuary. The city's port and dock installations are important to the offshore oil industry and the airport also provides servicing facilities. Principal industries include textiles, biotechnology and digital media, lasers, printing, tyre manufacture, food processing, engineering and tourism.

The unique City Churches – three churches under one roof, together with the 15th-century St Mary's Tower – are the most prominent architectural feature. Dundee is home to two historic ships: the Dundee-built RRS *Discovery* which took Capt. Scott to the Antarctic lies alongside Discovery Quay, and the frigate *Unicorn,* the only British-built wooden warship still afloat, is moored in Victoria Dock. Places of interest include Mills Public Observatory, the Tay road and rail bridges, Dundee Contemporary Arts centre, McManus Galleries, Claypotts Castle, Broughty Castle, Verdant Works (textile heritage centre) and the Sensation Science Centre.

EDINBURGH
Edinburgh is the capital city and seat of government in Scotland. The new Scottish parliament building designed by Enric Miralles was completed in 2004 and is open to visitors. The city is built on a group of hills and both the Old and New Towns are inscribed on the UNESCO World Cultural and Natural Heritage List for their cultural significance.

Other places of interest include the castle, which houses the Stone of Scone and also includes St Margaret's Chapel, the oldest building in Edinburgh, and near it, the Scottish National War Memorial; the Palace of Holyroodhouse, the Queen's official residence in Scotland; Parliament House, the present seat of the judicature; Princes Street; three universities (Edinburgh, Heriot-Watt, Napier); St Giles' Cathedral; St Mary's (Scottish Episcopal) Cathedral (Sir George Gilbert Scott); the General Register House (Robert Adam); the National and Signet libraries; the National Gallery of Scotland; the Royal Scottish Academy; the Scottish National Portrait Gallery and the Edinburgh International Conference Centre.

GLASGOW

Glasgow, a Royal Burgh, is Scotland's largest city and its principal commercial and industrial centre. The city occupies the north and south banks of the Clyde, formerly one of the chief commercial estuaries in the world. The main industries include engineering, electronics, finance, chemicals and printing. The city is also a key tourist and conference destination.

The chief buildings are the 13th-century Gothic cathedral, the university (Sir George Gilbert Scott), the City Chambers, the Royal Concert Hall, St Mungo Museum of Religious Life and Art, Pollok House, the School of Art (Charles Rennie Mackintosh), Kelvingrove Art Gallery and Museum, the Gallery of Modern Art, the Riverside Museum: Scotland's Museum of Transport and Travel (Zaha Hadid), the Burrell Collection museum and the Mitchell Library. The city is home to the Royal Scottish National Orchestra, Scottish Opera, Scottish Ballet, BBC Scotland and Scottish Television (STV).

INVERNESS

Inverness was granted city status in 2000. The city's name is derived from the Gaelic for 'the mouth of the Ness', referring to the river on which it lies. Inverness is recorded as being at the junction of trade routes since AD 565. Today the city is the main administrative centre for the north of Scotland and is the capital of the Highlands. Tourism is one of the city's main industries.

Among the city's most notable buildings is Abertarff House, built in 1593 and the oldest secular building remaining in Inverness. Balnain House, built as a town house in 1726, is a fine example of early Georgian architecture. The Old High Church, on St Michael's Mount, is the original parish church of Inverness and is built on the site of the earliest Christian church in the city. Parts of the church date back to the 14th century.

Stirling was granted city status in 2002 and Perth in 2012. Aberdeen, Dundee, Edinburgh and Glasgow have also been granted lord mayoralty/lord provostship.

LORD-LIEUTENANTS

Title	Name
Aberdeen City*	Lord Provost George Adam
Aberdeenshire	James Ingleby
Angus	Georgiana Osborne
Argyll and Bute	Patrick Stewart, MBE
Ayrshire and Arran	John Duncan, QPM
Banffshire	Clare Russell
Berwickshire	Jeannna Swan
Caithness	M. Anne Dunnett
Clackmannanshire	Lt.-Col. John Stewart
Dumfries	Jean Tulloch
Dunbartonshire	Rear-Adm. Michael Gregory, OBE
Dundee City*	Lord Provost Robert Duncan
East Lothian	Maj. Michael Williams, MBE
Edinburgh City*	Rt. Hon. Lord Provost Donald Wilson
Eilean Siar (Western Isles)	Alexander Matheson, OBE
Fife	Robert Balfour
Glasgow City*	Rt. Hon. Lord Provost Sadie Docherty
Inverness	Donald Cameron of Lochiel
Kincardineshire	Carol Kinghorn
Lanarkshire	Mushtaq Ahmad, OBE
Midlothian	Sir Robert Maxwell Clerk, Bt., OBE
Moray	Lt.-Col. Grenville Shaw Johnston, OBE, TD
Nairn	Ewen Brodie of Lethen, CVO
Orkney	Bill Spence
Perth and Kinross	Brig. Melville Jameson, CBE
Renfrewshire	Guy Clark
Ross and Cromarty	Janet Bowen
Roxburgh, Ettrick and Lauderdale	Capt. Hon. Gerald Maitland-Carew
Shetland	Robert Hunter
Stirling and Falkirk	Marjory McLachlan
Sutherland	Dr Monica Main
The Stewartry of Kirkcudbright	Lt.-Col. Sir Malcolm Ross, GCVO, OBE
Tweeddale	Prof. Sir Hew Strachan
West Lothian	Isobel Brydie, MBE
Wigtown	John Ross

* The Lord Provosts of the four cities of Aberdeen, Dundee, Edinburgh and Glasgow are Lord-Lieutenants *ex officio* for those districts

LOCAL COUNCILS

Council	Administrative Headquarters	Telephone	Population*	Council Tax†	Chief Executive
ABERDEEN	Aberdeen	01224-522000	228,990	£1,230	Angela Scott
Aberdeenshire	Aberdeen	08456-081207	260,500	£1,141	Jim Savege
Angus	Forfar	0845-277 7778	116,660	£1,072	Richard Stiff
Argyll and Bute	Lochgilphead	01546-602127	87,660	£1,178	Sally Loudon
Clackmannanshire	Alloa	01259-450000	51,190	£1,148	Elaine McPherson
Dumfries and Galloway	Dumfries	030-3333 3000	149,940	£1,049	Gavin Stevenson
DUNDEE	Dundee	01382-434000	148,260	£1,211	David Martin
East Ayrshire	Kilmarnock	01563-576000	122,150	£1,189	Fiona Lees
East Dunbartonshire	Kirkintilloch	0300-123 4510	106,730	£1,142	Gerry Cornes
East Lothian	Haddington	01620-827827	102,050	£1,118	Angela Leitch
East Renfrewshire	Giffnock	0141-577 3000	92,380	£1,126	Lorraine McMillan
EDINBURGH	Edinburgh	0131-200 2000	492,680	£1,169	Dame Sue Bruce, DBE
Eilean Siar (Western Isles)	Stornoway	01851-703773	27,250	£1,024	Malcolm Burr
Falkirk	Falkirk	01324-506070	157,640	£1,070	Mary Pitcaithly, OBE
Fife	Glenrothes	0345-155 0000	367,260	£1,118	Steve Grimmond
GLASGOW	Glasgow	0141-287 2000	599,650	£1,213	Annemarie O'Donnell
Highland	Inverness	01349-886606	233,100	£1,163	Steve Barron
Inverclyde	Greenock	01475-717171	79,860	£1,198	John Mundell
Midlothian	Dalkeith	0131-270 7500	86,210	£1,210	Kenneth Lawrie
Moray	Elgin	01343-543451	94,750	£1,135	Roddy Burns
North Ayrshire	Irvine	0845-603 0590	136,450	£1,152	Elma Murray
North Lanarkshire	Motherwell	01698-403200	337,950	£1,098	Gavin Whitefield
Orkney	Kirkwall	01856-873535	21,590	£1,037	Alistair Buchan
Perth and Kinross	Perth	01738-475000	148,880	£1,158	Bernadette Malone
Renfrewshire	Paisley	0300-300 0300	174,230	£1,165	Sandra Black
Scottish Borders	Melrose	01835-824000	114,030	£1,084	Tracey Logan
Shetland	Lerwick	01595-693535	23,230	£1,053	Mark Boden
South Ayrshire	Ayr	0300-123 0900	112,510	£1,154	Eileen Howat
South Lanarkshire	Hamilton	0303-123 1015	315,360	£1,101	Lindsay Freeland
STIRLING	Stirling	0845-277 7000	91,580	£1,197	Stewart Carruth
West Dunbartonshire	Dumbarton	01389-737000	89,730	£1,163	Joyce White
West Lothian	Livingston	01506-280000	177,150	£1,128	Graham Hope

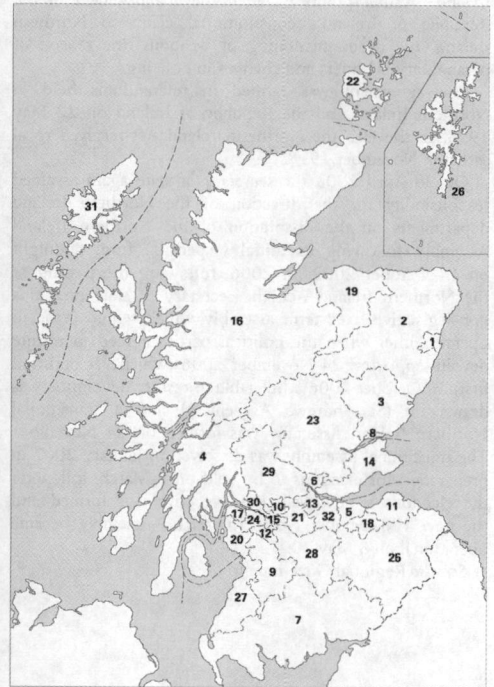

Key	Council	Key	Council
1	Aberdeen City	17	Inverclyde
2	Aberdeenshire	18	Midlothian
3	Angus	19	Moray
4	Argyll and Bute	20	North Ayrshire
5	City of Edinburgh	21	North Lanarkshire
6	Clackmannanshire	22	Orkney
7	Dumfries and Galloway	23	Perth and Kinross
8	Dundee City	24	Renfrewshire
9	East Ayrshire	25	Scottish Borders
10	East Dunbartonshire	26	Shetland
11	East Lothian	27	South Ayrshire
12	East Renfrewshire	28	South Lanarkshire
13	Falkirk	29	Stirling
14	Fife	30	West Dunbartonshire
15	Glasgow City	31	Western Isles (Eilean Siar)
16	Highland	32	West Lothian

* *Source:* Office for National Statistics – *Mid-2014 Population Estimates* (Crown copyright)
† Average Band D council tax bill 2015–16
Councils in CAPITAL LETTERS have city status

NORTHERN IRELAND

Northern Ireland has a total area of 14,149 sq. km (5,463 sq. miles): land, 13,576 sq. km (5,242 sq. miles); inland water, 573 sq. km (221 sq. miles).

The population of Northern Ireland at the 2011 census was 1,810,863 (men 887,323; women 923,540). The average density of population in 2011 was 128 persons per sq. km (331 per sq. mile).

FLAG
The official national flag of Northern Ireland is the Union Flag.

PRINCIPAL CITIES

In addition to Belfast and Londonderry, three other places in Northern Ireland have been granted city status: Armagh (1994), Lisburn (2002) and Newry (2002).

BELFAST
Belfast, the administrative centre of Northern Ireland, is situated at the mouth of the River Lagan at its entrance to Belfast Lough. The city grew to be a great industrial centre, owing to its easy access by sea to Scottish coal and iron.

The principal buildings are of a relatively young age and include the parliament buildings at Stormont, the City Hall, Waterfront Hall, the Law Courts, the Public Library and the Museum and Art Gallery. In March 2012, a new museum, Titanic Belfast, opened on the banks of the Lagan River – the site where RMS *Titanic* was built and launched. The museum forms the centrepiece of a new mixed-use maritime quarter.

Belfast received its first charter of incorporation in 1613 and was created a city in 1888; the title of lord mayor was conferred in 1892.

LONDONDERRY
Londonderry (originally Derry) is situated on the River Foyle, and has important associations with the City of London. The Irish Society was created by the City of London in 1610, and under its royal charter of 1613 it fortified the city and was for a long time closely associated with its administration. Because of this connection the city was incorporated in 1613 under the new name of Londonderry.

The city is famous for the great siege of 1688–9, when for 105 days the town held out against the forces of James II. The city walls are still intact and form a circuit of 1.6 km (one mile) around the old city.

Interesting buildings are the Protestant cathedral of St Columb's (1633) and the Guildhall, reconstructed in 1912 and containing a number of beautiful stained glass windows, many of which were presented by the livery companies of London.

CONSTITUTIONAL HISTORY

Northern Ireland is subject to the same fundamental constitutional provisions which apply to the rest of the UK. It had its own parliament and government from 1921 to 1972, but after increasing civil unrest the Northern Ireland (Temporary Provisions) Act 1972 transferred the legislative and executive powers of the Northern Ireland parliament and government to the UK parliament and a secretary of state. The Northern Ireland Constitution Act 1973 provided for devolution in Northern Ireland through an assembly and executive, but a power-sharing executive formed by the Northern Ireland political parties in January 1974 collapsed in May 1974. Following the collapse of the power-sharing executive Northern Ireland returned to direct rule governance under the provisions of the Northern Ireland Act 1974, placing the Northern Ireland department under the direction and control of the Northern Ireland secretary.

In December 1993 the British and Irish governments published the Joint Declaration, complementing their political talks and making clear that any settlement would need to be founded on principles of democracy and consent.

On 12 January 1998 the British and Irish governments issued a joint document, *Propositions on Heads of Agreement*, proposing the establishment of various new cross-border bodies; further proposals were presented on 27 January. A draft peace settlement was issued by the talks' chairman, US Senator George Mitchell, on 6 April 1998 but was rejected by the Unionists the following day. On 10 April agreement was reached between the British and Irish governments and the eight Northern Ireland political parties still involved in the talks (the Good Friday Agreement). The agreement provided for an elected Northern Ireland Assembly, a North/South Ministerial Council, and a British-Irish Council comprising representatives of the British, Irish, Channel Islands and Isle of Man governments and members of the new assemblies for Scotland, Wales and Northern Ireland. Further points included the abandonment of the Republic of Ireland's constitutional claim to Northern Ireland, the decommissioning of weapons, the release of paramilitary prisoners and changes in policing.

The agreement was ratified in referendums held in Northern Ireland and the Republic of Ireland on 22 May 1998. In the UK, the Northern Ireland Act received royal assent in November 1998.

On 28 April 2003 the secretary of state again assumed responsibility for the direction of the Northern Ireland departments on the dissolution of the Northern Ireland Assembly, following its initial suspension from midnight on 14 October 2002. In 2006, following the passing of the Northern Ireland Act, the secretary of state created a non-legislative fixed-term assembly which would cease to operate either when the political parties agreed to restore devolution, or on 24 November 2006 (whichever occurred first). In October 2006 a timetable to restore devolution was drawn up (St Andrews Agreement) and a transitional Northern Ireland Assembly was formed on 24 November. The transitional assembly was dissolved in January 2007 in preparation for elections to be held on 7 March; following the elections a power-sharing executive was formed and the new 108-member Northern Ireland Assembly became operational on 8 May 2007.

See also Regional Government.

LORD-LIEUTENANTS AND HIGH SHERIFFS

County	Lord-Lieutenant	High Sheriff (2015)
Antrim	Joan Christie, OBE	John Pinkerton
Armagh	Earl of Caledon, KCVO	Anna Shepherd
Belfast City	Fionnuala Mary Jay-O'Boyle, CBE	Councillor Gareth McKee
Down	David Lindsay	Patrick Cross
Fermanagh	Viscount Brookeborough	Hope Kerr
Londonderry	Denis Desmond, CBE	Helen Mark
Londonderry City	Dr Angela Josepha Garvey	Mrs Harvinder Torney
Tyrone	Robert Scott, OBE	Dr Lisheen Webb

LOCAL COUNCILS

Council	Telephone	Population*	Chief Executive
Antrim & Newtownabbey	028-9448 1311	139,966	Jacqui Dixon
Armagh, Banbridge & Craigavon	0300-030 0900	205,711	Roger Wilson
Belfast	028-9027 0549	336,830	Suzanne Wylie
Causeway Coast & Glens	028-7034 7034	142,303	David Jackson, MBE
Derry & Strabane	028-7138 2204	149,198	John Kelpie
Fermanagh & Omagh	0300-303 1777	114,992	Brendan Hegarty
Lisburn & Castlereagh	028-9250 9250	138,627	Theresa Donaldson
Mid & East Antrim	028-9335 8000	136,642	Anne Donaghy
Mid Ulster	0300-013 2132	142,895	Anthony Tohill
Newry, Mourne & Down	028-3031 3037	175,403	Liam Hannaway
North Down & Ards	0300-013 3333	157,930	Stephen Reid

* Source: NISRA – Mid-year Population Estimates 2014

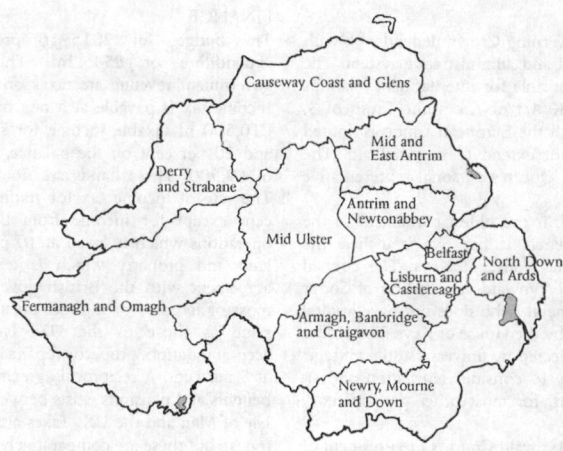

THE ISLE OF MAN

Ellan Vannin

The Isle of Man is an island situated in the Irish Sea, at latitude 54° 3'–54° 25' N. and longitude 4° 18'–4° 47' W., nearly equidistant from England, Scotland and Ireland. Although the early inhabitants were of Celtic origin, the Isle of Man was part of the Norwegian Kingdom of the Hebrides until 1266, when this was ceded to Scotland. Subsequently granted to the Stanleys (Earls of Derby) in the 15th century and later to the Dukes of Atholl, it was brought under the administration of the Crown in 1765. The island forms the bishopric of Sodor and Man.

The total land area is 572 sq. km (221 sq. miles). The 2011 census showed a resident population of 84,497 (men, 41,971; women, 42,526). The main language in use is English. Around 1,660 people are able to speak the Manx Gaelic language.

CAPITAL – ΨDouglas; population, 27,938 (2011). ΨCastletown (3,097) is the ancient capital; the other towns are ΨPeel (5,093) and ΨRamsey (7,821)

FLAG – A red flag charged with three conjoined armoured legs in white and gold

NATIONAL DAY – 5 July (Tynwald Day)

GOVERNMENT

The Isle of Man is a self-governing Crown dependency, with its own parliamentary, legal and administrative system. The British government is responsible for international relations and defence. Under the UK Act of Accession, Protocol 3, the island's relationship with the European Union is limited to trade alone and does not extend to financial aid. The Lieutenant-Governor is the Queen's personal representative on the island.

The legislature, Tynwald, is the oldest parliament in the world in continuous existence. It has two branches: the Legislative Council and the House of Keys. The council consists of the President of Tynwald, the Bishop of Sodor and Man, the Attorney-General (who does not have a vote) and eight members elected by the House of Keys. The House of Keys has 24 members, elected by universal adult suffrage. The branches sit separately to consider legislation and sit together, as Tynwald Court, for most other parliamentary purposes.

The presiding officer of Tynwald Court is the President of Tynwald, elected by the members, who also presides over sittings of the Legislative Council. The presiding officer of the House of Keys is the Speaker, who is elected by members of the house.

The principal members of the Manx government are the chief minister and eight departmental ministers, who comprise the Council of Ministers.

Lieutenant-Governor, HE Adam Wood
President of Tynwald, Hon. Clare Christian

Speaker, House of Keys, Hon. Steve Rodan, SHK
The First Deemster and Clerk of the Rolls, His Hon. David Doyle
Clerk of Tynwald, Secretary to the House of Keys and Counsel to the Speaker, Roger Phillips
Clerk of the Legislative Council and Deputy Clerk of Tynwald, Jonathan King
Attorney-General, Stephen Harding
Chief Minister, Hon. Allan Bell, MHK
Chief Secretary, Will Greenhow

ECONOMY

Much of the income generated in the island is earned in the services sector with financial and professional services accounting for 43 per cent of the national income. E-gaming is also a significant sector, contributing 13.5 per cent to the national income. Under the terms of protocol 3, the island has tariff-free access to EU markets for the products of its engineering, farming and fishing industries.

In May 2015 the island's unemployment rate was 1.7 per cent and the rate of inflation (RPI) was 2.1 per cent.

FINANCE

The budget for 2015–16 provides for net revenue expenditure of £545.2m. The principal sources of government revenue are taxes on income and expenditure. Income tax is payable at a rate of 10 per cent on the first £10,500 of taxable income for single resident individuals and 20 per cent on the balance, after personal allowances of £9,500. These bands are doubled for married couples. The rate of income tax for trading companies is zero per cent except for income from banking and major retail operations which is taxed at 10 per cent, and income from land and property which is taxed at 20 per cent. By agreement with the British government, the island keeps most of its rates of indirect taxation (VAT and duties) the same as those in the UK. However, VAT on tourist accommodation, property, repairs and renovations is charged at 5 per cent. A reciprocal agreement on national insurance benefits and pensions exists between the governments of the Isle of Man and the UK. Taxes are also charged on property (rates), but these are comparatively low.

The major government expenditure items are social care, health and education, which account for 50 per cent of the government budget. The island makes an annual contribution to the UK for defence and other external services.

The island has a special relationship with the European Union and neither contributes money to nor receives funds from the EU budget.

Ψ = sea port

THE CHANNEL ISLANDS

The Channel Islands, situated off the north-west coast of France (at a distance of 16km (10 miles) at their closest point), are the only portions of the Dukedom of Normandy still belonging to the Crown, to which they have been attached since the Norman Conquest of 1066. They were the only British territory to come under German occupation during the Second World War, following invasion on 30 June and 1 July 1940. Guernsey and Jersey were relieved by British forces on 9 May 1945, Sark on 10 May 1945 and Alderney on 16 May 1945; 9 May (Liberation Day) is now observed as a bank and public holiday in Guernsey and Jersey.

The islands consist of Jersey (11,630ha/28,717 acres), Guernsey (6,340ha/15,654 acres), and the dependencies of Guernsey: Alderney (795ha/1,962 acres), Brecqhou (30ha/74 acres), Great Sark (419ha/1,035 acres), Little Sark (97ha/239 acres), Herm (130ha/320 acres), Jethou (18ha/44 acres) and Lihou (15ha/38 acres) – a total of 19,474ha/48,083 acres, or 195 sq. km/75 sq. miles.

The 2011 census (taken in March) showed the population of Jersey as 97,857. Guernsey did not complete the same census, but the most recent official records for Guernsey and Alderney estimated the populations at 62,732 and 1,903 respectively. Sark's population is estimated to be around 600. The official language is English but French is often used for ceremonial purposes. In country districts of Jersey and Guernsey and throughout Sark a Norman-French *patois* is also in use, though to a lesser extent.

GOVERNMENT

The islands are Crown dependencies with their own legislative assemblies (the States of Jersey and the States of Alderney, the States of Deliberation in Guernsey and the Chief Pleas in Sark), systems of local administration and law, and their own courts. *Projets de Loi* (Acts) passed by the States require the sanction of the Queen-in-council. The UK government is responsible for defence and international relations, although the islands are increasingly entering into agreements with other countries in their own right. The Channel Islands are not members of the European Union but, under protocol 3 of the UK's Treaty of Accession, have trading rights with the free movement of goods within the EU. A common customs tariff, levies and agricultural and import measures apply to trade between the islands and non-member countries.

In both Jersey and Guernsey bailiwicks the Lieutenant-Governor and Commander-in-Chief, who is appointed by the Crown, is the personal representative of the Queen and the official channel of communication between the Crown (via the Privy Council) and the islands' governments.

The head of government in both Jersey and Guernsey is the Chief Minister. Jersey has a ministerial system of government; the executive comprises the Council of Ministers and consists of a chief minister and ten other ministers. The ministers are assisted by up to ten assistant ministers. Members of the States who are not in the executive are able to sit on a number of scrutiny panels and the Public Accounts Committee to examine the policy of the executive and hold ministers to account. Guernsey is administered by a number of departments and committees. There are ten States departments with mandated responsibilities, each department is constituted of a minister and four members of the States. Each of the ministers has a seat on the Policy Council

which is presided over by the Chief Minister. The States of Deliberation, the island's parliamentary assembly, is the overarching executive. There are also five parliamentary committees, each led by a chair, responsible for scrutinising policy, finance and legislation, parliamentary procedural matters and public sector pay negotiations. Alderney has a legislature comprising a President and ten members elected by universal suffrage. Sark has a directly elected legislature of 28 members *(conseillers)* who serve on a number of committees.

Justice is administered by the royal courts of Jersey and Guernsey, each consisting of the bailiff and 12 elected jurats. The bailiffs of Jersey and Guernsey, appointed by the Crown, are presidents of the royal courts of their respective islands. Each bailiff is the *ex-officio* presiding officer in their respective parliaments and, by convention, the civic head.

Each bailiwick constitutes a deanery under the administration of the Diocese of Winchester. Since January 2014 episcopal oversight for the Channel Islands has been delegated, on a temporary basis, to the Bishop of Dover (Diocese of Canterbury).

ECONOMY

A mild climate and good soil have led to the development of intensive systems of agriculture and horticulture, which form a significant part of the economy. Equally important are earnings from tourism and banking and finance: the low rates of income and corporation tax and the absence of death duties make the islands an important offshore financial centre. The financial services sector contributes over 50 per cent of GDP in Jersey and around 40 per cent in Guernsey. In addition, there is no VAT or equivalent tax in Guernsey and only small goods and services tax in Jersey (5 per cent since 1 June 2011). The Channel Islands stock exchange is located in Guernsey, which also has a thriving e-gaming sector.

Principal exports are agricultural produce and flowers; imports are chiefly machinery, manufactured goods, food, fuel and chemicals. Trade with the UK is regarded as internal.

British currency is legal tender in the Channel Islands but each bailiwick issues its own coins and notes (*see* Currency section). They also issue their own postage stamps; UK stamps are not valid.

JERSEY

Lieutenant-Governor and Commander-in-Chief of Jersey,
    HE Gen. Sir John McColl, KCB, CBE, DSO, *apptd* 2011
Chief of Staff, Maj. Justin Oldridge
Bailiff of Jersey, William J. Bailhache
Deputy Bailiff, Timothy J. Le Cocq
Attorney-General, Robert J. MacRae, QC
Receiver-General, David Pett
Solicitor-General, Mark Temple
Greffier of the States, Michael N. de la Haye, OBE
States Treasurer, Richard Bell
Chief Minister, Senator Ian Gorst

FINANCE	2013	2014
Revenue income	£1,283,412,000	£1,158,308,000
Revenue expenditure	£1,004,863,000	£1,151,886,000
Capital expenditure	£51,507,000	£65,484,000

CHIEF TOWN – ΨSt Helier, on the south coast
FLAG – A white field charged with a red saltire cross, and the arms of Jersey in the upper centre

GUERNSEY AND DEPENDENCIES

Lieutenant-Governor and Commander-in-Chief of the Bailiwick of Guernsey and its Dependencies, vacant
Presiding Officer of the Royal Court and of the States of Deliberation, Bailiff Richard Collas
Deputy Presiding Officer of the Royal Court and States of Deliberation, Deputy Bailiff Richard McMahon, QC
HM Procureur and Receiver-General (Attorney-General), Howard Roberts, QC
HM Comptroller (Solicitor-General), Megan Pullum, QC

GUERNSEY
Chief Minister, Deputy Jonathan Le Tocq
Chief Executive, Paul Whitfield

FINANCE	2013	2014
Revenue income	£361,257,000	£384,550,000
Revenue expenditure	£345,698,000	£355,900,000
Capital expenditure	£13,362,000	£7,300,000

CHIEF TOWNS – ΨSt Peter Port, on the east coast of Guernsey; St Anne on Alderney

FLAG – White, bearing a red cross of St George, with a gold cross of Normandy overall in the centre

ALDERNEY
President of the States, Stuart Trought
Chief Executive, Victor Brownlees
Greffier, Sarah Kelly

SARK
Sark was the last European territory to abolish feudal parliamentary representation. Elections for a democratic legislative assembly took place in December 2008, with the *conseillers* taking their seats in the newly constituted Chief Pleas in January 2009.
Seigneur of Sark, John Beaumont, OBE
Seneschal, Jeremy la Trobe-Bateman
President, Lt.-Col. Reg Guille, MBE
Greffier, Trevor Hamon

OTHER DEPENDENCIES
Herm and Lihou are owned by the States of Guernsey; Herm is leased, Lihou is uninhabited. Jethou is leased by the Crown to the States of Guernsey and is sub-let by the States. Brecqhou is within the legislative and judicial territory of Sark.

Ψ = seaport

LAW COURTS AND OFFICES

SUPREME COURT OF THE UNITED KINGDOM

The Supreme Court of the United Kingdom is the highest domestic judicial authority; it replaced the appellate committee of the House of Lords (the house functioning in its judicial capacity) on 1 October 2009. It is the final court of appeal for cases heard in Great Britain and Northern Ireland (except for criminal cases from Scotland). Cases concerning the interpretation and application of European Union law, including preliminary rulings requested by British courts and tribunals, which are decided by the Court of Justice of the European Union (CJEU) (see European Union), and the supreme court can make a reference to the CJEU in appropriate cases. Additionally, in giving effect to rights contained in the European Convention on Human Rights, the supreme court must take account of any decision of the European Court of Human Rights.

The supreme court also assumed jurisdiction in relation to devolution matters under the Scotland Act 1998 (now partly superseded by the Scotland Act 2012), the Northern Ireland Act 1988 and the Government of Wales Act 2006; these powers were transferred from the Judicial Committee of the Privy Council. Ten of the 12 Lords of Appeal in Ordinary (Law Lords) from the House of Lords transferred to the 12-member supreme court when it came into operation (at the same time one law lord retired and another was appointed Master of the Rolls). All new justices of the supreme court are now appointed by an independent selection commission, and, although styled Rt. Hon. Lord, are not members of the House of Lords. Peers who are members of the judiciary are disqualified from sitting or voting in the House of Lords until they retire from their judicial office. See Life Peers (page 60) for a list of such peers (§).

President of the Supreme Court (£220,655), Rt. Hon. Lord Neuberger of Abbotsbury, *born* 1948, *apptd* 2012
Deputy President of the Supreme Court (£213,125), Rt. Hon. Lady Hale of Richmond, *born* 1945, *apptd* 2013

JUSTICES OF THE SUPREME COURT *as at September 2015* (each £213,125)
Style, The Rt. Hon. Lord/Lady–

Rt. Hon. Lord Mance, *born* 1943, *apptd* 2005
Rt. Hon. Lord Kerr of Tonaghmore, *born* 1948, *apptd* 2009
Rt. Hon. Lord Clarke of Stone-cum-Ebony, *born* 1943, *apptd* 2009
Rt. Hon. Lord Wilson of Culworth, *born* 1945, *apptd* 2011
Rt. Hon. Lord Sumption, *born* 1948, *apptd* 2012
Rt. Hon. Lord Reed, *born* 1956, *apptd* 2012
Rt. Hon. Lord Carnwath of Notting Hill, CVO, *born* 1945, *apptd* 2012
Rt. Hon. Lord Hughes of Ombersley, *born* 1948, *apptd* 2013
Rt. Hon. Lord Toulson, *born* 1946, *apptd* 2013
Rt. Hon. Lord Hodge, *born* 1953, *apptd* 2013

UNITED KINGDOM SUPREME COURT
Parliament Square, London SW1P 3BD T 020-7960 1900
Chief Executive, Mark Ormerod, CB

JUDICATURE OF ENGLAND AND WALES

The legal system in England and Wales is divided into criminal law and civil law. Criminal law is concerned with acts harmful to the community and the rules laid down by the state for the benefit of citizens, whereas civil law governs the relationships and transactions between individuals. Administrative law is a kind of civil law usually concerning the interaction of individuals and the state, and most cases are heard in tribunals specific to the subject (see Tribunals section). Scotland and Northern Ireland possess legal systems that differ from the system in England and Wales in law, judicial procedure and court structure, but retain the distinction between criminal and civil law.

Under the provisions of the Criminal Appeal Act 1995, a commission was set up to direct and supervise investigations into possible miscarriages of justice and to refer cases to the appeal courts on the grounds of conviction and sentence; these functions were formerly the responsibility of the home secretary.

SENIOR COURTS OF ENGLAND AND WALES
The senior courts of England and Wales (until September 2009 known as the supreme court of judicature of England and Wales) comprise the high court, the crown court and the court of appeal. The President of the Courts of England and Wales, a new title given to the Lord Chief Justice under the Constitutional Reform Act 2005, is the head of the judiciary.

The high court was created in 1875 and combined many previously separate courts. Sittings are held at the royal courts of justice in London or at around 120 district registries outside the capital. It is the superior civil court and is split into three divisions – the chancery division, the Queen's bench division and the family division – each of which is further divided. The chancery division is headed by the Chancellor of the High Court and is concerned mainly with equity, trusts, tax and bankruptcy, while also including two specialist courts, the patents court and the companies court. The Queen's bench division (QBD) is the largest of the three divisions, and is headed by its own president. It deals with common law (ie tort, contract, debt and personal injuries), some tax law, eg VAT tribunal appeals, and encompasses the admiralty court and the commercial court. The QBD also administers the technology and construction court. The family division was created in 1970 and is headed by its own president, who is also Head of Family Justice, and hears cases concerning divorce, access to and custody of children, and other family matters. The divisional court of the high court sits in the family and chancery divisions, and hears appeals from the magistrates' courts and county courts.

The crown court was set up in 1972 and sits at 77 centres throughout England and Wales. It deals with more serious (indictable) criminal offences, which are triable before a judge and jury, including treason, murder, rape, kidnapping, armed robbery and Official Secrets Act offences. It also handles cases transferred from the magistrates' courts where the magistrate decides his or her own power of sentence is inadequate, or where someone appeals against a magistrate's decision, or in a case that is triable 'either way' where the accused has chosen a jury trial. The crown court centres are divided into three tiers: high court judges, circuit judges and sometimes recorders (part-time circuit judges), sit in first-tier centres, hearing the most serious criminal offences (eg murder, treason, rape, manslaughter) and some civil high court cases. The second-tier centres are presided over by high court judges, circuit judges or recorders and also deal with the most serious criminal cases. Third-tier courts deal with the remaining criminal offences, with circuit judges or recorders presiding.

HIERARCHY OF ENGLISH AND WELSH COURTS

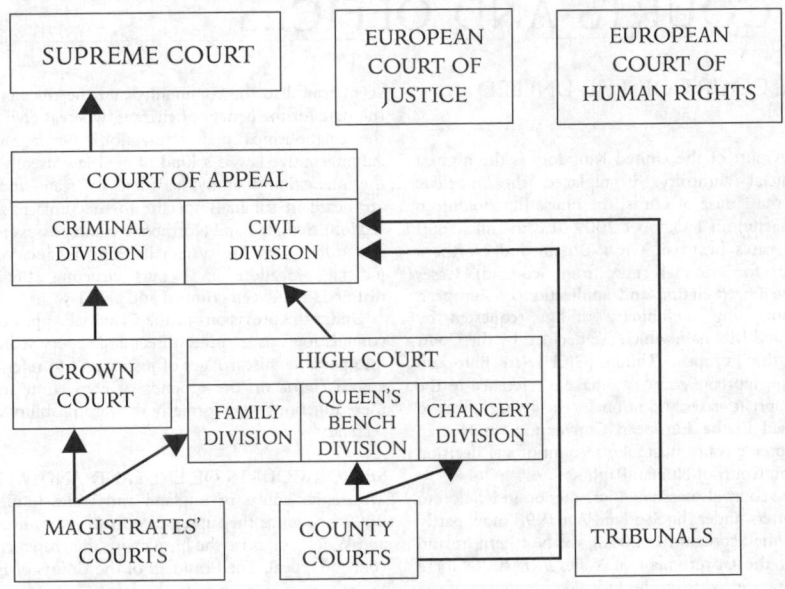

The court of appeal hears appeals against both fact and law, and was last restructured in 1966 when it replaced the court of criminal appeal. It is split into the civil division (which hears appeals from the high court, tribunals and in certain cases, the county courts) and the criminal division (which hears appeals from the crown court). Cases are heard by Lords Justices of Appeal and high court judges if deemed suitable for reconsideration.

The Constitutional Reform Act 2005 instigated several key changes to the judiciary in England and Wales. These included the establishment of the independent supreme court, which opened in October 2009; the reform of the post of Lord Chancellor, transferring its judicial functions to the President of the Courts of England and Wales; a duty on government ministers to uphold the independence of the judiciary by barring them from trying to influence judicial decisions through any special access to judges; the formation of a fully transparent and independent Judicial Appointments Commission that is responsible for selecting candidates to recommend for judicial appointment to the Lord Chancellor and Secretary of State for Justice; and the creation of the post of Judicial Appointments and Conduct Ombudsman.

CRIMINAL CASES

In criminal matters the decision to prosecute (in the majority of cases) rests with the Crown Prosecution Service (CPS), which is the independent prosecuting body in England and Wales. The CPS is headed by the director of public prosecutions, who works under the superintendence of the Attorney-General. Certain categories of offence continue to require the Attorney-General's consent for prosecution.

Most minor criminal cases (summary offences) are dealt with in magistrates' courts, usually by a bench of three unpaid lay magistrates (justices of the peace) sitting without a jury and assisted on points of law and procedure by a legally trained clerk. As at 1 April 2015, there were around 23,000 justices of the peace. In some courts a full-time, salaried and legally qualified district judge (magistrates' court) – formerly known as a stipendiary judge – presides alone. There are 138 district judges and 115 deputy district judges operating

in around 330 magistrates' courts in England and Wales. Magistrates' courts oversee the completion of 90 per cent of all criminal cases. Magistrates' courts also house some family proceedings courts (which deal with relationship breakdown and childcare cases) and youth courts. Cases of medium seriousness (known as 'offences triable either way') where the defendant pleads not guilty can be heard in the crown court for a trial by jury, if the defendant so chooses. Preliminary proceedings in a serious case to decide whether there is evidence to justify committal for trial in the crown court are dealt with in the magistrates' courts.

The 77 centres that the crown court sits in are divided into seven regions. There are 640 circuit judges and 1,031 recorders (part-time circuit judges); they must sit a minimum of 15 days per year and are usually subject to a maximum of 30. A jury is present in all trials that are contested.

Appeals from magistrates' courts against sentence or conviction are made to the crown court, and appeals upon a point of law are made to the high court, which may ultimately be appealed to the supreme court. Appeals from the crown court, either against sentence or conviction, are made to the court of appeal (criminal division). Again, these appeals may be brought to the supreme court if a point of law is contested, and if the house considers it is of sufficient importance.

CIVIL CASES

Most minor civil cases – including contract, tort (especially personal injuries), property, divorce and other family matters, bankruptcy etc – are dealt with by the county courts, of which there are 216 (see W www.justice.gov.uk for further details). Cases are heard by circuit judges, recorders or district judges. For cases involving small claims (with certain exceptions, where the amount claimed is £5,000 or less) there are informal and simplified procedures designed to enable parties to present their cases themselves without recourse to lawyers. Where there are financial limits on county court jurisdiction, claims that exceed those limits may be tried in the county courts with the consent of the parties, subject to the court's agreement, or in certain circumstances on transfer from the high court. Outside London, bankruptcy proceedings can be heard in designated county courts. Magistrates' courts also deal with certain classes of civil case, and committees of magistrates license public houses, clubs and betting shops. For the implementation of the Children Act 1989, a new structure of hearing centres was set up in 1991 for family proceedings cases, involving magistrates' courts (family proceedings courts), divorce county courts, family hearing centres and care centres.

Appeals in certain family matters heard in the family proceedings courts go to the family division of the high court. Appeals from county courts may be heard in the court of appeal (civil division) or the high court, and may go on to the supreme court.

CORONERS' COURTS
The coroners' courts investigate violent and unnatural deaths or sudden deaths where the cause is unknown. Doctors, the police, various public authorities or members of the public may bring cases before a local coroner (a senior lawyer or doctor), in order to determine whether further criminal investigation is necessary. Where a death is sudden and the cause is unknown, the coroner may order a post-mortem examination to determine the cause of death rather than hold an inquest in court. An inquest must be held, however, if a person died in a violent or unnatural way, or died in prison or other unusual circumstances. If the coroner suspects murder, manslaughter or infanticide, he or she must summon a jury.

SENIOR JUDICIARY OF ENGLAND AND WALES
Lord Chief Justice of England and Wales and Head of Criminal Justice (£247,112), Rt. Hon. Lord Thomas of Cwmgiedd, *born* 1947, *apptd* 2013
Master of the Rolls and Head of Civil Justice (£220,655), Rt. Hon. Lord Dyson, *born* 1943, *apptd* 2012
President of the Queen's Bench Division (£213,125), Rt. Hon. Sir Brian Leveson, *born* 1949, *apptd* 2013
President of the Family Division and Head of Family Justice (£213,125), Rt. Hon. Sir James Munby, *born* 1948, *apptd* 2013
Chancellor of the High Court (£213,125), Rt. Hon. Sir Terence Etherton, *born* 1951, *apptd* 2013

SENIOR COURTS OF ENGLAND AND WALES
COURT OF APPEAL
Presiding Judge, Criminal Division, Lord Chief Justice of England and Wales
Presiding Judge, Civil Division, Master of the Rolls
Vice-President, Civil Division (£202,668), Rt. Hon. Sir Martin Moore-Bick, *born* 1946, *apptd* 2014
Vice-President, Criminal Division (£202,668), Rt. Hon. Dame Heather Hallett, DBE, *born* 1949, *apptd* 2013

LORD JUSTICES OF APPEAL *as at September 2015* (each £202,668)
Style, The Rt. Hon. Lord/Lady Justice [surname]

Rt. Hon. Sir John Laws, *born* 1945, *apptd* 1999
Rt. Hon. Dame Mary Arden, DBE, *born* 1947, *apptd* 2000
Rt. Hon. Sir Andrew Longmore, *born* 1944, *apptd* 2001
Rt. Hon. Sir Martin Moore-Bick, *born* 1948, *apptd* 2005
Rt. Hon. Sir Stephen Richards, *born* 1950, *apptd* 2005
Rt. Hon. Dame Heather Hallett, DBE, *born* 1949, *apptd* 2005
Rt. Hon. Sir Rupert Jackson, *born* 1948, *apptd* 2008
Rt. Hon. Sir Richard Aikens, *born* 1948, *apptd* 2008
Rt. Hon. Sir Jeremy Sullivan, *born* 1945, *apptd* 2009

Rt. Hon. Sir Patrick Elias, *born* 1947, *apptd* 2009
Rt. Hon. Sir Nicholas Patten, *born* 1950, *apptd* 2009
Rt. Hon. Sir Christopher Pitchford, *born* 1947, *apptd* 2010
Rt. Hon. Dame Jill Black, DBE, *born* 1954, *apptd* 2010
Rt. Hon. Sir Stephen Tomlinson, *born* 1952, *apptd* 2010
Rt. Hon. Sir Peter Gross, *born* 1952, *apptd* 2010
Rt. Hon. Dame Anne Rafferty, DBE, *born* 1950, *apptd* 2011
Rt. Hon. Sir Andrew McFarlane, *born* 1954, *apptd* 2011
Rt. Hon. Sir Nigel Davis, *born* 1951, *apptd* 2011
Rt. Hon. Sir Kim Lewison, *born* 1952, *apptd* 2011
Rt. Hon. Sir David Kitchin, *born* 1955, *apptd* 2011
Rt. Hon. Sir David Lloyd Jones, *born* 1952, *apptd* 2012
Rt. Hon. Sir Colman Treacy, *born* 1949, *apptd* 2012
Rt. Hon. Sir Richard McCombe, *born* 1952, *apptd* 2012
Rt. Hon. Sir Jack Beatson, *born* 1948, *apptd* 2013
Rt. Hon. Dame Elizabeth Gloster, DBE, *born* 1949, *apptd* 2013
Rt. Hon. Sir Ernest Ryder, TD, *born* 1957, *apptd* 2013
Rt. Hon. Sir Nicholas Underhill, *born* 1952, *apptd* 2013
Rt. Hon. Sir Michael Briggs, *born* 1954, *apptd* 2013
Rt. Hon. Sir Christopher Floyd, *born* 1951, *apptd* 2013
Rt. Hon. Sir Adrian Fulford, *born* 1953, *apptd* 2013
Rt. Hon. Dame Julia Macur, DBE, *born* 1957, *apptd* 2013
Rt. Hon. Sir Christopher Clarke, *born* 1947, *apptd* 2013
Rt. Hon. Dame Victoria Sharp, DBE, *born* 1956, *apptd* 2013
Rt. Hon. Sir Geoffrey Vos, *born* 1855, *apptd* 2013
Rt. Hon. Sir David Bean, *born* 1954, *apptd* 2014
Rt. Hon. Dame Eleanor King, DBE, *born* 1957, *apptd* 2014
Rt. Hon. Sir Ian Burnett, *born* 1958, *apptd* 2014
Rt. Hon. Sir Philip Sales, *born* 1962, *apptd* 2014
Ex Officio Judges, Lord Chief Justice of England and Wales; Master of the Rolls; President of the Queen's Bench Division; President of the Family Division; Chancellor of the High Court

COURTS-MARTIAL APPEAL COURT
Judges, Lord Chief Justice of England and Wales; Master of the Rolls; Lord Justices of Appeal; Judges of the High Court of Justice

HIGH COURT
CHANCERY DIVISION
Chancellor of the High Court (£213,125), Rt. Hon. Sir Terence Etherton, *born* 1951, *apptd* 2013
Personal Secretary, Elaine Harbert
Legal Secretary, Vannina Ettori
Clerk, Amanda Collins

JUDGES *as at September 2015* (each £177,988)
Style, The Hon. Mr/Mrs Justice [surname]

Hon. Sir Peter Smith, *born* 1952, *apptd* 2002
Hon. Sir David Richards, *born* 1951, *apptd* 2003
Hon. Sir George Mann, *born* 1951, *apptd* 2004
Hon. Sir Nicholas Warren, *born* 1949, *apptd* 2005
Hon. Sir Launcelot Henderson, *born* 1951, *apptd* 2007
Hon. Sir Paul Morgan, *born* 1952, *apptd* 2007
Hon. Sir Alastair Norris, *born* 1950, *apptd* 2007
Hon. Sir Gerald Barling, *born* 1949, *apptd* 2007
Hon. Dame Sonia Proudman, DBE, *born* 1949, *apptd* 2008
Hon. Sir Richard Arnold, *born* 1961, *apptd* 2008
Hon. Sir Peter Roth, *born* 1952, *apptd* 2009
Hon. Sir Guy Newey, *born* 1959, *apptd* 2010
Hon. Sir Robert Hildyard, *born* 1952, *apptd* 2011
Hon. Dame Sarah Asplin, DBE, *born* 1959, *apptd* 2012
Hon. Sir Colin Birss, *born* 1964, *apptd* 2013
Hon. Dame Vivien Rose, DBE, *born* 1960, *apptd* 2013
Hon. Sir Christopher Nugee, *born* 1959, *apptd* 2013
Hon. Sir Andrew Snowden, *born* 1962, *apptd* 2015

The Chancery Division also includes three specialist courts: the Companies Court, the Patents Court and the Bankruptcy Court.

QUEEN'S BENCH DIVISION
President (£213,125), Rt. Hon. Sir Brian Leveson, *born* 1949, *apptd* 2013
Vice-President (£202,668), Rt. Hon. Sir Nigel Davis, *born* 1951, *apptd* 2014

JUDGES *as at September 2015* (each £177,988)
Style, The Hon. Mr/Mrs Justice [surname]

Hon. Sir Andrew Collins, *born* 1942, *apptd* 1994
Hon. Sir William Charles, *born* 1948, *apptd* 1998
Hon. Sir Michael Burton, *born* 1946, *apptd* 1998
Hon. Sir Andrew Smith, *born* 1947, *apptd* 2000
Hon. Sir Duncan Ouseley, *born* 1950, *apptd* 2000
Hon. Sir John Mitting, *born* 1947, *apptd* 2001
Hon. Sir Jeremy Cooke, *born* 1949, *apptd* 2001
Hon. Sir Peregrine Simon, *born* 1950, *apptd* 2002
Hon. Dame Laura Cox, DBE, *born* 1951, *apptd* 2002
Hon. Sir Alan Wilkie, *born* 1947, *apptd* 2004
Hon. Sir Paul Walker, *born* 1954, *apptd* 2004
Hon. Sir Charles Openshaw, *born* 1947, *apptd* 2005
Hon. Dame Caroline Swift, DBE, *born* 1955, *apptd* 2005
Hon. Sir Brian Langstaff, *born* 1948, *apptd* 2005
Hon. Sir Stephen Irwin, *born* 1953, *apptd* 2006
Hon. Sir Nigel Teare, *born* 1952, *apptd* 2006
Hon. Sir Wyn Williams, *born* 1951, *apptd* 2007
Hon. Sir Timothy King, *born* 1949, *apptd* 2007
Hon. Sir John Saunders, *born* 1949, *apptd* 2007
Hon. Sir Julian Flaux, *born* 1955, *apptd* 2007
Hon. Sir David Foskett, *born* 1949, *apptd* 2007
Hon. Sir Robert Akenhead, *born* 1949, *apptd* 2007
Hon. Sir Nicholas Blake, *born* 1949, *apptd* 2007
Hon. Sir Ross Cranston, *born* 1948, *apptd* 2007
Hon. Sir Peter Coulson, *born* 1958, *apptd* 2008
Hon. Sir William Blair, *born* 1950, *apptd* 2008
Hon. Sir Nigel Sweeney, *born* 1954, *apptd* 2008
Hon. Dame Elizabeth Slade, DBE, *born* 1949, *apptd* 2008
Hon. Sir Nicholas Hamblen, *born* 1957, *apptd* 2008
Hon. Sir Gary Hickinbottom, *born* 1955, *apptd* 2009
Hon. Sir Timothy Holroyde, *born* 1955, *apptd* 2009
Hon. Sir Andrew Nicol, *born* 1951, *apptd* 2009
Hon. Sir Kenneth Parker, *born* 1945, *apptd* 2009
Hon. Sir Antony Edwards-Stuart, *born* 1946, *apptd* 2009
Hon. Dame Nicola Davies, DBE, *born* 1953, *apptd* 2010
Hon. Dame Kathryn Thirlwall, DBE, *born* 1957, *apptd* 2010
Hon. Sir Michael Supperstone, *born* 1950, *apptd* 2010
Hon. Sir Robin Spencer, *born* 1955, *apptd* 2010
Hon. Sir Keith Lindblom, *born* 1956, *apptd* 2010
Hon. Sir Henry Globe, *born* 1949, *apptd* 2011
Hon. Sir Andrew Popplewell, *born* 1959, *apptd* 2011
Hon. Sir Rabinder Singh, *born* 1964, *apptd* 2011
Hon. Dame Beverley Lang, DBE, *born* 1955, *apptd* 2011
Hon. Sir Charles Haddon-Cave, *born* 1956, *apptd* 2011
Hon. Sir Stephen Males, *born* 1955, *apptd* 2012
Hon. Sir Jeremy Stuart-Smith, *born* 1955, *apptd* 2012
Hon. Sir George Leggatt, *born* 1957, *apptd* 2012
Hon. Sir Mark Turner, *born* 1959, *apptd* 2013
Hon. Sir Jeremy Baker, *born* 1958, *apptd* 2013
Hon. Sir Stephen Stewart, *born* 1953, *apptd* 2013
Hon. Sir Robert Jay, QC, *born* 1959, *apptd* 2013
Hon. Sir James Dingemans, *born* 1964, *apptd* 2013
Hon. Sir Clive Lewis, *born* 1960, *apptd* 2013
Hon. Dame Sue Carr, DBE, *born* 1964, *apptd* 2013
Hon. Sir Stephen Phillips, *born* 1961, *apptd* 2013
Hon. Dame Geraldine Andrews, DBE, *born* 1959, *apptd* 2013

Hon. Dame Frances Patterson, DBE, *born* 1955, *apptd* 2013
Hon. Sir Nicholas Green, QC, *born* 1958, *apptd* 2013
Hon. Dame Ingrid Simler, DBE, *born* 1963, *apptd* 2013
Hon. Dame Elisabeth Laing, DBE, *born* 1956, *apptd* 2014
Hon. Sir William Davis, QC, *born* 1954, *apptd* 2014
Hon. Sir Mark Warby, QC, *born* 1958, *apptd* 2014
Hon. Sir Andrew Edis, *born* 1957, *apptd* 2014
Hon. Dame Maura McGowan, *born* 1957, *apptd* 2014
Hon. Sir James Goss, *born* 1953, *apptd* 2014
Hon. Sir Robin Knowles, *born* 1960, *apptd* 2014
Hon. Sir Ian Dove, *born* 1963, *apptd* 2014
Hon. Sir Andrew Gilbart, *born* 1950, *apptd* 2014
Hon. Sir David Holgate, *born* 1956, *apptd* 2014
Hon. Sir Timothy Kerr, *born* 1958, *apptd* 2015
Hon. Sir Simon Picken, *born* 1966, *apptd* 2015

The Queen's Bench Division also includes the Divisional Court, the Admiralty Court, Commercial Court and Technology and Construction Court.

FAMILY DIVISION
President (£213,125), Rt. Hon. Sir James Munby, *born* 1948, *apptd* 2013
Secretary, Mrs Sarah Leung
Clerk, George Pitchley

JUDGES *as at September 2015* (each £177,988)
Style, The Hon. Mr/Mrs Justice [surname]

Hon. Sir Edward Holman, *born* 1947, *apptd* 1995
Hon. Dame Mary Hogg, DBE, *born* 1947, *apptd* 1995
Hon. Sir David Bodey, *born* 1947, *apptd* 1999
Hon. Dame Anna Pauffley, DBE, *born* 1956, *apptd* 2003
Hon. Sir Roderic Wood, *born* 1951, *apptd* 2004
Hon. Sir Andrew Moylan, *born* 1953, *apptd* 2007
Hon. Dame Judith Parker, DBE, *born* 1950, *apptd* 2008
Hon. Sir Jonathan Baker, *born* 1955, *apptd* 2009
Hon. Sir Nicholas Mostyn, *born* 1957, *apptd* 2010
Hon. Sir Peter Arthur Jackson, *born* 1955, *apptd* 2010
Hon. Dame Lucy Theis, DBE, *born* 1960, *apptd* 2010
Hon. Sir Philip Moor, *born* 1959, *apptd* 2011
Hon. Sir Stephen Cobb, *born* 1960, *apptd* 2013
Hon. Sir Michael Keehan, *born* 1960, *apptd* 2013
Hon. Sir Anthony Hayden, *born* 1961, *apptd* 2013
Hon. Dame Alison Russell, DBE, *born* 1958, *apptd* 2014
Hon. Roderick Newton, *born* 1958, *apptd* 2014
Hon. Dame Jennifer Roberts, *born* 1953, *apptd* 2014
Hon. Sir Alistair MacDonald, *born* 1970, *apptd* 2015

DEPARTMENTS AND OFFICES OF THE SENIOR COURTS OF ENGLAND AND WALES
Royal Courts of Justice, London WC2A 2LL
T 020-7947 6000

ADMINISTRATIVE COURT OFFICE
T 020-7947 6655
Judge in charge of the Administrative Court (£177,988), Hon. Sir Duncan Ouseley
Master of the Crown Office, and Queen's Coroner and Attorney (£106,040), M. Egan, QC
Deputy Master of the Crown Office, Mrs L. G. Knapman
Court Manager, Miss A. Lee

ADMIRALTY, COMMERCIAL AND LONDON MERCANTILE COURT
Ground Floor, 7 Rolls Buildings, London EC4A 1NL
T 020-7947 6112
Registrar (£106,040), J. Kay, QC
Admiralty Marshal, M. Parker
Admiralty Court Manager, W. Lusty

Judge in charge of the Commercial Court (£177,988), Hon. Sir Julian Flaux
Commercial Court Senior Lists Officer, J. Kelly

BANKRUPTCY AND COMPANIES COURT REGISTRY
7 Rolls Building, Fetter Lane, London EC4A 1NL T 020-7947 6294
Chief Registrar (132,184), S. Baister
Bankruptcy Registrars (£106,040), S. Barber; Briggs; C. Derrett; C. Jones
Court Manager, T. Pollen

CENTRAL OFFICE OF THE QUEEN'S BENCH DIVISION
Senior Master and Queen's Remembrancer (£132,184), B. Fontaine
Masters of the Queen's Bench Division (£106,040), J. D. Cook; R. Eastman; Gidden; J. K. Kay, QC; Leslie; V. McCloud; R. R. Roberts; B. Yoxall
Court Manager, Miss A. Lee

CHANCERY CHAMBERS
7 Rolls Building, Fetter Lane, London EC4A 1NL T 020-7947 7391
Chief Master (£132,184), M. Marsh
Masters Chancery (£106,040), T. J. Bowles; J. E. Clark; N. S. Price; P. R. Teverson
Court Manager, T. Pollen

COSTS OFFICE
T 020-7947 6423
Senior Costs Judge (£132,184), A. Gordon-Saker
Masters of the Senior Courts (£106,040), C. D. N. Campbell; P. Haworth; C. Leonard; J. E. O'Hare; J. Rowley; J. Simons
Court Manager, S. Christou

COURT OF APPEAL CIVIL DIVISION
T 020-7947 6915
Deputy Registrars, Marie Bancroft-Rimmer; Sally Meacher
Court Manager, Miss K. Langan

COURT OF APPEAL CRIMINAL DIVISION
T 020-7947 6011
Registrar (£106,040), M. Egan, QC
Deputy Registrar, Mrs L. G. Knapman
Court Manager, Miss C. Brownbill

COURT OF PROTECTION
First Avenue House, 42–49 High Holborn, London WC1V 6NP
T 0300-456 4600
Senior Judge (£132,184), D. Lush
Court Manager, J. Matthews

ELECTION PETITIONS OFFICE
Room E113, Royal Courts of Justice, Strand, London WC2A 2LL
T 020-7947 6877

The office accepts petitions and deals with all matters relating to the questioning of parliamentary, European parliament, local government and parish elections, and with applications for relief under the 'representation of the people' legislation.
Prescribed Officer, The Senior Master and Senior Remembrancer (£132,184), B. Fontaine
Chief Clerk, Geraint Evans

EXAMINERS OF THE COURT
Empowered to take examination of witnesses in all divisions of the High Court.

PRINCIPAL REGISTRY (FAMILY DIVISION)
First Avenue House, 42–49 High Holborn, London WC1V 6NP
T 020-7421 8594
Senior District Judge (£132,184), P. Waller
District Judges (£106,040), Mrs A. Aitken; Ms Y. Gibson; Mrs L. Gordon-Saker; Harper; Ms H. Macgregor; R. Robinson; C. Simmonds

TECHNOLOGY AND CONSTRUCTION COURT (TCC)
Ground Floor, 7 Rolls Building, Fetter Lane, London EC4A 1NL
T 020-7947 7156
Judge in charge of the TCC (£177,988), Hon. Mr Justice Edwards-Stuart
Court Manager, W. Lusty
List Officer, S. Gibbon

COURT FUNDS OFFICE
Glasgow G58 1AB T 0300-020 0199

The Court Funds Office (CFO), established in 1726, provides a banking and administration service for the civil courts throughout England and Wales, including the High Court.
Head of CFO, Eddie Bloomfield

OFFICIAL SOLICITOR AND PUBLIC TRUSTEE
Victory House, 30–34 Kingsway, London WC2B 6EX

The Official Solicitor and the Public Trustee are independent statutory office holders. Their office (OSPT) is an arms-length body of the Ministry of Justice that exists to support their work. The Official Solicitor provides access to the justice system to those who are vulnerable by virtue of minority or lack of mental capacity. The Public Trustee acts as executor or administrator of estates and as the appointed trustee of settlements, providing an effective executor and trustee service of last resort.
Official Solicitor to the Senior Courts, Alistair Pitblado
Public Trustee, Eddie Bloomfield

PROBATE SERVICE
London Probate Department
PRFD, 7th Floor, First Avenue House, 42–49 High Holborn, London WC1V 6NP T 020-7421 8500
Probate Manager, Ms T. Constantinou

DISTRICT PROBATE REGISTRIES
Birmingham District
Brighton District
Bristol District
Cardiff District (Wales)
Ipswich District
Leeds District
Liverpool District
Manchester District
Newcastle District
Oxford District
Winchester District

JUDGE ADVOCATES GENERAL
The Judge Advocate General is the judicial head of the Service justice system, and the leader of the judges who preside over trials in the court martial and other Service courts. The defendants are service personnel from the Royal Navy, the army and the Royal Air Force, and civilians accompanying them overseas.

JUDGE ADVOCATE GENERAL OF THE FORCES
9th Floor, Thomas More Building, Royal Courts of Justice, Strand, London WC2A 2LL
T 020-7218 8095
Judge Advocate General (£151,112), His Hon. Judge Blackett
Vice Judge Advocate General (£124,445), Michael Hunter
Assistant Judge Advocates General (£106,040), J. P. Camp;
    M. R. Elsom; R. D. Hill; A. M. Large; A. J. B. McGrigor;
    E. Peters
Style, Judge [surname]

HIGH COURT AND CROWN COURT CENTRES
First-tier centres deal with both civil and criminal cases and are served by high court and circuit judges. Second-tier centres deal with criminal cases only and are served by high court and circuit judges. Third-tier centres deal with criminal cases only and are served only by circuit judges.

LONDON REGION
First-tier – None
Second-tier – Central Criminal Court
Third-tier – Blackfriars, Croydon, Harrow, Inner London, Isleworth, Kingston upon Thames, Snaresbrook, Southwark, Wood Green, Woolwich
Delivery Director, Sheila Proudlock, 3rd Floor, Rose Court, 2 Southwark Bridge, London SE1 9HS

The high court (first-tier) in Greater London sits at the Royal Courts of Justice.

MIDLANDS REGION
First-tier – Birmingham, Lincoln, Nottingham, Stafford, Warwick
Second-tier – Leicester, Northampton, Shrewsbury, Worcester, Wolverhampton
Third-tier – Coventry, Derby, Hereford, Stoke on Trent
Delivery Director, Lucy Garrod, 6th Floor, Temple Court, Bull Street, Birmingham B4 6WF

NORTH-EAST REGION
First-tier – Leeds, Newcastle upon Tyne, Sheffield, Teesside
Second-tier – Bradford, York
Third-tier – Doncaster, Durham, Kingston upon Hull, Great Grimsby
Delivery Director, Mark Swales, 17th Floor, West Riding House, Albion Street, Leeds LS1 5AA T 0113-251 1204

NORTH-WEST REGION
First-tier – Carlisle, Chester, Liverpool, Manchester (Crown Square), Preston
Third-tier – Barrow in Furness, Bolton, Burnley, Knutsford, Lancaster, Manchester (Minshull Street), Warrington
Delivery Director, Gill Hague, Manchester Civil Justice Centre, 1 Bridge Street West, Manchester M60 1UR T 0161-240 5000

SOUTH-EAST REGION
First-tier – Cambridge, Chelmsford, Lewes, Norwich, Oxford
Second-tier – Guildford, Ipswich, Luton, Maidstone, Reading, St Albans
Third-tier – Aylesbury, Basildon, Canterbury, Chichester, Croydon, King's Lynn, Peterborough, Southend
Delivery Director, Chris Jennings, 9th Floor, 102 Petty France, London SW1H 9AJ T 020-3206 0627

SOUTH-WEST REGION
First-tier – Bristol, Exeter, Truro, Winchester
Second-tier – Dorchester & Weymouth, Gloucester, Plymouth

Third-tier – Barnstaple, Bournemouth, Newport (IoW), Portsmouth, Salisbury, Southampton, Swindon, Taunton
Delivery Director, Sandra Aston, PO Box 484, Queensway House, Weston-super-Mare, N. Somerset BS23 9BJ
T 01934 528668

WALES REGION
First-tier – Caernarfon, Cardiff, Merthyr Tydfil, Mold, Swansea
Second-tier – Carmarthen, Newport, Welshpool
Third-tier – Dolgellau, Haverfordwest
Delivery Director, Luigi Strinati, Wales Support Unit, 2nd Floor, Cardiff and Vale of Glamorgan Magistrates' Court, Fitzalan Place, Cardiff CF24 0RZ T 029-2067 8311

CIRCUIT JUDGES
Circuit judges are barristers of at least seven years' standing or recorders of at least five years' standing. Circuit judges serve in the county courts and the crown court.
Style, His/Her Hon. Judge [surname]
Senior Presiding Judge, Rt. Hon. Lord Justice Gross
Senior Circuit Judges, each £142,745
Circuit Judges at the Central Criminal Court, London (Old Bailey Judges), each £142,745
Circuit Judges, each £132,184

MIDLAND CIRCUIT
Presiding Judges, Hon. Mr Justice Haddon-Cave; Hon. Mrs Justice Thirlwall

NORTH-EASTERN CIRCUIT
Presiding Judges, Hon. Mr Justice Globe; Hon. Mr Justice Males

NORTHERN CIRCUIT
Presiding Judges, Hon. Mr Justice Holroyde; Hon. Mr Justice Turner

SOUTH-EASTERN CIRCUIT
Presiding Judges, Hon. Mr Justice Singh; Hon. Mr Justice Spencer; Hon. Mr Justice Stuart-Smith; Hon. Mr Justice Sweeney

WALES CIRCUIT
Presiding Judges, Hon. Mrs Justice Davies; Hon. Mr Justice Williams

WESTERN CIRCUIT
Presiding Judges, Hon. Mr Justice Dingemans; Hon. Mr Justice Teare

DISTRICT JUDGES
District judges, formerly known as registrars of the court, are solicitors of at least seven years' standing and serve in county courts.
District Judges, each £106,040

DISTRICT JUDGES (MAGISTRATES' COURTS)
District judges (magistrates' courts), formerly known as stipendiary magistrates, serve in magistrates courts where they hear criminal cases, youth cases and some civil proceedings. Many also hear family cases in the single family court. Some may be authorised to handle extradition proceedings and terrorist cases. District judges (magistrates' courts) are appointed following competition conducted by the Judicial Appointments Commission.
District Judges (Magistrates' Courts), each £106,040

OFFICE OF THE CHIEF MAGISTRATE
181 Marylebone Road, London NW1 5BR
T 020-3126 3100

The Chief Magistrate (senior district judge) is responsible for hearing many of the sensitive or complex cases – extradition and special jurisdiction cases in particular – in the magistrates' courts. The Chief Magistrate also supports and guides district judges (magistrates' court), and liaises with the senior judiciary and presiding judges on matters pertaining to magistrates' courts.

The Office of the Chief Magistrate provides administrative support to both the Chief Magistrate and to all the district judges sitting at magistrates' courts in England and Wales.
Chief Magistrate, Howard Riddle
Deputy Chief Magistrate, Emma Arbuthnot

CROWN PROSECUTION SERVICE
Rose Court, 2 Southwark Bridge Road, London SE1 9HS
T 020-3357 0000 E enquiries@cps.gsi.gov.uk W www.cps.gov.uk

The Crown Prosecution Service (CPS) is responsible for prosecuting cases investigated by the police in England and Wales, with the exception of cases conducted by the Serious Fraud Office and certain minor offences.

The CPS is headed by the director of public prosecutions (DPP), who works under the superintendence of the attorney-general. The service is divided into 13 areas across England and Wales, with each area led by a chief crown prosecutor.
Director of Public Prosecutions, Alison Saunders, CB
Chief Executive, Peter Lewis, CB
Chief Operating Officer, Jim Brisbane
Principal Legal Adviser, Alison Levitt, QC
Directors, Jim Brisbane *(Operations);* Helen Kershaw
(Private Office); Joanna Millington *(Communication);* Paul Staff *(Corporate Services and Finance);* Mark Summerfield *(Human Resources)*

CPS AREAS
EAST MIDLANDS, 2 King Edward Court, King Edward Street, Nottingham NG1 1EL T 0115-852 3300
Chief Crown Prosecutor, Steve Chappell
EASTERN, County House, 100 New London Road, Chelmsford, Essex CM2 0RG T 01245-455800
Chief Crown Prosecutor, Jenny Hopkins
LONDON, 5th Floor, Rose Court, 2 Southwark Bridge, London SE1 9HS T 020-3357 0000
Chief Crown Prosecutor, Baljit Ubhey, OBE
MERSEY–CHESHIRE, 2nd Floor, Walker House, Exchange Flags, Liverpool L2 3YL T 0151-239 6400
Chief Crown Prosecutor, Claire Lindley
NORTH EAST, St Ann's Quay, 112 Quayside, Newcastle Upon Tyne, NE1 3BD T 0191-260 4200
Chief Crown Prosecutor, Gerry Wareham
NORTH WEST, 1st Floor, Stocklund House, Castle Street, Carlisle CA3 8SY T 01228-882900
Chief Crown Prosecutor (acting), Ian Rushton
SOUTH EAST, Riding Gate House, 37 Old Dover Road, Canterbury, Kent CT1 3JG T 01227-866000
Chief Crown Prosecutor, Jaswant Narwal
SOUTH WEST, 5th Floor, Kite Wing, Temple Quay House, 2 The Square, Bristol BS1 6PN T 0117-930 2800
Chief Crown Prosecutor, Barry Hughes
THAMES AND CHILTERN, Eaton Court, 112 Oxford Road, Reading, Berks RG1 7LL T 0118-951 3600
Chief Crown Prosecutor, Adrian Foster
WALES, 20th Floor, Capital Tower, Greyfriars Road, Cardiff CF10 3PL T 029-2080 3800
Chief Crown Prosecutor, Ed Beltrami
WESSEX, 3rd Floor, Black Horse House, 8–10 Leigh Road, Eastleigh, Hants SO50 9FH T 02380-673 800
Chief Crown Prosecutor, Kate Brown
WEST MIDLANDS, Colmore Gate, 2 Colmore Row, Birmingham B3 2QA T 0121-262 1300
Chief Crown Prosecutor, Grace Ononiwu, OBE
YORKSHIRE AND HUMBERSIDE, 27 Park Place, Leeds LS1 2SZ T 0113-290 2700
Chief Crown Prosecutor, Martin Goldman

HER MAJESTY'S COURTS AND TRIBUNALS SERVICE
1st Floor, 102 Petty France, London SW1H 9AJ
W www.justice.gov.uk

Her Majesty's Courts Service and the Tribunals Service merged on 1 April 2011 to form HM Courts and Tribunals Service. It is an agency of the Ministry of Justice, operating as a partnership between the Lord Chancellor, the Lord Chief Justice and the Senior President of Tribunals. It is responsible for administering the criminal, civil and family courts and tribunals in England and Wales and non-devolved tribunals in Scotland and Northern Ireland.
Chief Executive, Natalie Ceeney

JUDICIAL APPOINTMENTS COMMISSION
1st Floor, Zone A, 102 Petty France, London SW1H 9AJ
T 020-3334 0123 E jaas@jac.gsi.gov.uk
W jjac.judiciary.gov.uk

The Judicial Appointments Commission was established as an independent non-departmental public body in April 2006 by the Constitutional Reform Act 2005. Its role is to select judicial office holders independently of government (a responsibility previously held by the Lord Chancellor) for courts and tribunals in England and Wales, and for some tribunals whose jurisdiction extends to Scotland or Northern Ireland. It has a statutory duty to encourage diversity in the range of persons available for selection and is sponsored by the Ministry of Justice and accountable to parliament through the Lord Chancellor. It is made up of 15 commissioners, including a chair.
Chair, Christopher Stephens
Commissioners, Martin Forde, QC; Debra van Gene; Prof. Emily Jackson; Prof. Noel Lloyd, CBE; Rt. Hon. Dame Julia Macur, DBE; Alexandra Marks; Katharine Rainsford; Lt.-Gen. Sir Andrew Ridgway, KBE, CB; Lucy Scott-Moncrieff, CBE; District Judge Simmonds; Dame Valerie Strachan, DCB; Hon. Sir Alan Wilkie
Chief Executive, Nigel Reeder

DIRECTORATE OF JUDICIAL OFFICES
The Judicial Office was established in April 2006 to support the judiciary in discharging its responsibilities under the Constitutional Reform Act 2005. It is led by a chief executive, who reports to the Lord Chief Justice rather than to ministers, and its work is directed by the judiciary rather than by the administration of the day. The Judicial Office incorporates the Judicial College, sponsorship of the Family and Civil Justice Councils, the Office for Judicial Complaints and Office of the Chief Coroner.

CHIEF EXECUTIVE'S OFFICE
T 020-7947 7598
Chief Executive, Jillian Kay

JUDICIAL COMMITTEE OF THE PRIVY COUNCIL

The Judicial Committee of the Privy Council is the final court of appeal for the United Kingdom overseas territories (*see* UK Overseas Territories section), crown dependencies and those independent Commonwealth countries which have retained this avenue of appeal and the sovereign base areas of Akrotiri and Dhekelia in Cyprus. The committee also hears appeals against pastoral schemes under the Pastoral Measure 1983, and deals with appeals from veterinary disciplinary bodies.

Until October 2009, the Judicial Committee of the Privy Council was the final arbiter in disputes as to the legal competence of matters done or proposed by the devolved legislative and executive authorities in Scotland, Wales and Northern Ireland. This is now the responsibility of the UK Supreme Court.

Between 1 April 2014 and 31 March 2015 the Judicial Committee heard a total of 58 appeals.

The members of the Judicial Committee are the justices of the supreme court, and Privy Counsellors who hold or have held high judicial office in the United Kingdom or in certain designated courts of Commonwealth countries from which appeals are taken to committee.

JUDICIAL COMMITTEE OF THE PRIVY COUNCIL
Parliament Square, London SW1A 2AJ T 020-7960 1500
W www.jcpc.uk
Registrar of the Privy Council, Louise di Mambro

SCOTTISH JUDICATURE

Scotland has a legal system separate from, and differing greatly from, the English legal system in enacted law, judicial procedure and the structure of courts.

In Scotland the system of public prosecution is headed by the Lord Advocate and is independent of the police, who have no say in the decision to prosecute. The Lord Advocate, discharging his functions through the Crown Office in Edinburgh, is responsible for prosecutions in the high court, sheriff courts and justice of the peace courts. Prosecutions in the high court are prepared by the Crown Office and conducted in court by one of the law officers, by an advocate-depute, or by a solicitor advocate. In the inferior courts the decision to prosecute is made and prosecution is preferred by procurators fiscal, who are lawyers and full-time civil servants subject to the directions of the Crown Office. A permanent legally qualified civil servant, known as the crown agent, is responsible for the running of the Crown Office and the organisation of the Procurator Fiscal Service, of which he or she is the head.

Scotland is divided into six sheriffdoms, each with a full-time sheriff principal. The sheriffdoms are further divided into sheriff court districts, each of which has a legally qualified resident sheriff or sheriffs, who are the judges of the court.

In criminal cases sheriffs principal and sheriffs have the same powers; sitting with a jury of 15 members, they may try more serious cases on indictment, or, sitting alone, may try lesser cases under summary procedure. Minor summary offences are dealt with in justice of the peace courts, which replaced district courts formerly operated by local authorities, and presided over by lay justices of the peace (of whom some 500 regularly sit in court) and, in Glasgow only, by stipendiary magistrates. Juvenile offenders (children under 16) may be brought before an informal children's hearing comprising three local lay people. The superior criminal court is the high court of justiciary which is both a trial and an appeal court. Cases on indictment are tried by a high court judge, sitting with a jury of 15, in Edinburgh and on circuit in other towns. Appeals from the lower courts against conviction or sentence are also heard by the high court,

which sits as an appeal court only in Edinburgh. There is no further appeal to the UK supreme court in criminal cases.

In civil cases the jurisdiction of the sheriff court extends to most kinds of action. Appeals against decisions of the sheriff may be made to the sheriff principal and thence to the court of session, or direct to the court of session, which sits only in Edinburgh. The court of session is divided into the inner and the outer house. The outer house is a court of first instance in which cases are heard by judges sitting singly, sometimes with a jury of 12. The inner house, itself subdivided into two divisions of equal status, is mainly an appeal court. Appeals may be made to the inner house from the outer house as well as from the sheriff court. An appeal may be made from the inner house to the UK supreme court.

The judges of the court of session are the same as those of the high court of justiciary, with the Lord President of the court of session also holding the office of Lord Justice General in the high court. Senators of the College of Justice are Lords Commissioners of Justiciary as well as judges of the court of session. On appointment, a senator takes a judicial title, which is retained for life. Although styled The Hon./Rt. Hon. Lord, the senator is not a peer, although some judges are peers in their own right.

The office of coroner does not exist in Scotland. The local procurator fiscal inquires privately into sudden or suspicious deaths and may report findings to the crown agent. In some cases a fatal accident inquiry may be held before the sheriff.

COURT OF SESSION AND HIGH COURT OF JUSTICIARY
The Lord President and Lord Justice General (£220,655),
Rt. Hon. Lord Gill, *born* 1942, *apptd* 2012
Private Secretary, P. Gilmour

INNER HOUSE
Lords of Session (each £202,668)

FIRST DIVISION
The Lord President

Rt. Hon. Lord Eassie (Ronald Mackay), *born* 1945,
  apptd 2006
Rt. Hon. Lord Menzies (Duncan Menzies), *born* 1953,
  apptd 2012
Rt. Hon. Lady Smith (Anne Smith), *born* 1955, *apptd* 2012
Rt. Hon. Lord Brodie (Philip Brodie), *born* 1950, *apptd* 2012
Rt. Hon. Lady Clark of Calton (Lynda Clark), *born* 1949,
  apptd 2013

SECOND DIVISION
Lord Justice Clerk (£213,125), Rt. Hon. Lord Carloway,
  born 1954, *apptd* 2012
Rt. Hon. Lady Paton (Ann Paton), *born* 1952, *apptd* 2007
Rt. Hon. Lady Dorrian (Leona Dorrian), *born* 1957, *apptd*
  2012
Rt. Hon. Lord Bracadale (Alistair Campbell), *born* 1949,
  apptd 2013
Rt. Hon. Lord Drummond Young (James Drummond Young),
  born 1950, *apptd* 2013
Rt. Hon. Lord Malcolm (Colin M. Campbell), *born* 1953,
  apptd 2007

OUTER HOUSE
Lords of Session (each £177,988)
Hon. Lord Glennie (Angus Glennie), *born* 1950, *apptd* 2005
Hon. Lord Kinclaven (Alexander F. Wylie), *born* 1951,
  apptd 2005
Hon. Lord Turnbull (Alan Turnbull), *born* 1958, *apptd* 2006

Hon. Lord Brailsford (Sidney Brailsford), *born* 1954, *apptd* 2006
Hon. Lord Uist (Roderick Macdonald), *born* 1951, *apptd* 2006
Hon. Lord Matthews (Hugh Matthews), *born* 1953, *apptd* 2007
Hon. Lord Woolman (Stephen Woolman), *born* 1953, *apptd* 2008
Hon. Lord Pentland (Paul Cullen), *born* 1957, *apptd* 2008
Hon. Lord Bannatyne (Iain Peebles), *born* 1954, *apptd* 2008
Hon. Lady Stacey (Valerie E. Stacey), *born* 1954, *apptd* 2009
Hon. Lord Tyre (Colin Tyre), *born* 1956, *apptd* 2010
Hon. Lord Doherty (Raymond Doherty), *born* 1958, *apptd* 2010
Hon. Lord Stewart (Angus Stewart), *born* 1946, *apptd* 2010
Rt. Hon. Lord Boyd of Duncansby (Colin Boyd), *born* 1953, *apptd* 2012
Hon. Lord Jones (Michael Jones), *born* 1948, *apptd* 2012
Hon. Lord Burns (David Burns), *born* 1952, *apptd* 2012
Hon. Lady Scott (Margaret Scott), *born* 1960, *apptd* 2012
Hon. Lady Wise (Morag Wise), *born* 1963, *apptd* 2013
Hon. Lord Armstrong (Iain Armstrong), *born* 1956, *apptd* 2013
Hon. Lady Rae (Rita Rae), *born* 1950, *apptd* 2014
Hon. Lady Wolffe (Sarah Wolffe), *apptd* 2014

COURT OF SESSION AND HIGH COURT OF JUSTICIARY

Parliament House, Parliament Square, Edinburgh EH1 1RQ
T 0131-225 2595

Principal Clerk of Session and Justiciary, G. Marwick
Deputy Principal Clerk of Session and Principal Extractor, G. Prentice
Deputy Principal Clerk of Justiciary, J. Moyes
Depute in Charge of Offices of Court, Y. Anderson
Officer in Charge of Justiciary Office, Roddy MacPherson
Keeper of the Rolls, G. Combe
Depute Clerks, D. Cullen; A. Hutchison; C. Reid
Appeal Manager, F. Merrilees
Clerking Service Manager, D. MacLeod
Depute Clerks of Session and Justiciary, L. Alexander; N. Boyle; R. Broome; G. Burton; Z. Conway; L. Curran; H. Fraser; A. Galloway; K. Keir; T. Kell; A. Lynch; N. Marchant; R. Martin; M. McGrane; G. McLeod; L. McNamara; L. Morgan; D. Morrison; C. Munn; K. Neal; R. Newlands; K. O'Hare; C. Scott; G. Scott; L. Sexto; C. Stark; P. Weir

JUDICIAL APPOINTMENTS BOARD FOR SCOTLAND

38–39 Drumsheugh Gardens, Edinburgh EH3 7SW
T 0131-528 5101 W www.judicialappointmentsscotland.org.uk

The board's remit is to provide the first minister with the names of candidates recommended for appointment to the posts of senator of the college of justice, chair of the Scottish Land Court, sheriff principal, sheriff and part-time sheriff.
Chair, Sir Muir Russell, KCB, FRSE

JUDICIAL OFFICE FOR SCOTLAND

Parliament House, Edinburgh EH1 1RQ
T 0131-240 6677 W www.scotland-judiciary.org.uk

The Judicial Office for Scotland came into being on 1 April 2010 as part of the changes introduced by the Judiciary and Courts (Scotland) Act 2008. It provides support for the Lord President in his role as head of the Scottish judiciary with responsibility for the training, welfare, deployment and conduct of judges and the efficient disposal of business in the courts.
Executive Director, Steve Humphreys

SCOTTISH COURT SERVICE

Saughton House, Broomhouse Drive, Edinburgh EH11 3XD
T 0131-444 3300 W www.scotcourts.gov.uk

The Scottish Court Service is responsible for the provision of staff, buildings and technology to support Scotland's courts, the independent judiciary, the courts' Rules Councils and the Office of the Public Guardian. On 1 April 2010 it was established by the Judiciary and Courts (Scotland) Act 2008 as an independent body, governed by a corporate board and chaired by the Lord President.
Chief Executive, Eric McQueen

SCOTTISH GOVERNMENT JUSTICE DIRECTORATE

Legal System Division, Room 2W, St Andrew's House, Edinburgh EH1 3DG
T 0131-556 8400

The Justice Directorate is responsible for the appointment of judges and sheriffs to meet the needs of the business of the supreme and sheriffs court in Scotland. It is also responsible for providing resources for the efficient administration of certain specialist courts and tribunals.
Director (acting), Neil Rennick

SCOTTISH LAND COURT

126 George Street, Edinburgh EH2 4HH
T 0131-271 4360

The court deals with disputes relating to agricultural and crofting land in Scotland.
Chair (£142,745), Hon. Lord McGhie (James McGhie), QC
Deputy Chair, R. J. Macleod
Members, A. Macdonald *(part-time)*; J. A. Smith *(part-time)*
Principal Clerk, Barbara Brown

SHERIFF COURT OF CHANCERY

27 Chambers Street, Edinburgh EH1 1LB
T 0131-225 2525

The court deals with service of heirs and completion of title in relation to heritable property.
Sheriff of Chancery, M. Stephen

SHERIFF COURTS

The majority of cases in Scotland are handled by one of the 39 sheriff courts. Criminal cases are heard by a sheriff and a jury (solemn procedure) but can be heard by a sheriff alone (summary procedure). Civil cases are heard by a single sheriff.

Scotland is split into six sheriffdoms, each headed by a sheriff principal.

SALARIES

Sheriff Principal, £142,745
Sheriff, £132,184

SHERIFFDOMS

GLASGOW AND STRATHKELVIN
  Sheriff Principal, C. A. L. Scott, QC
GRAMPIAN, HIGHLAND AND ISLANDS
  Sheriff Principal, D. C. W. Pyle
LOTHIAN AND BORDERS
  Sheriff Principal, M. M. Stephen, QC
NORTH STRATHCLYDE
  Sheriff Principal, D. L. Murray
SOUTH STRATHCLYDE, DUMFRIES AND GALLOWAY
  Sheriff Principal, I. R. Abercrombie, QC
TAYSIDE, CENTRAL AND FIFE
  Sheriff Principal, W. M. Lewis

JUSTICE OF THE PEACE COURTS

Justice of the peace courts replaced district courts and are a unique feature of Scotland's judicial system. Justices of the peace are lay magistrates who either sit alone, or in a bench of three, and deal with summary crimes such as speeding and careless driving. In court, justices have access to solicitors, who fulfill the role of legal advisers or clerks of court.

A justice of the peace court can be presided over by a stipendiary magistrate – a legally qualified solicitor or advocate who sits alone. They deal with more serious summary business similar to sheriffs, such as drink driving and assault. All sheriffs principal have powers to appoint stipendiary magistrates, but at present they have only been appointed in the justice of the peace court in the Sheriffdom of Glasgow and Strathkelvin.

CROWN OFFICE AND PROCURATOR FISCAL SERVICE

CROWN OFFICE
25 Chambers Street, Edinburgh EH1 1LA
T 01389-739557 W www.crownoffice.gov.uk
Chief Executive and Crown Agent, Catherine Dyer

PROCURATORS FISCAL

PAY BAND AND SALARY SCALE: £75,000–£162,500

NORTH FEDERATION
　Area Procurator Fiscal, Liam Murphy
EAST FEDERATION
　Area Procurator Fiscal, John Dunn
WEST FEDERATION
　Area Procurator Fiscal, David Harvie
NATIONAL FEDERATION
　Director of Serious Casework, John Logue

COURT OF THE LORD LYON

HM New Register House, Edinburgh EH1 3YT
T 0131-556 7255 W www.lyon-court.com

The Court of the Lord Lyon is the Scottish Court of Chivalry (including the genealogical jurisdiction of the *Ri-Sennachie* of Scotland's Celtic kings). The Lord Lyon King of Arms has jurisdiction, subject to appeal to the Court of Session and the House of Lords, in questions of heraldry and the right to bear arms. The court also administers the Public Register of All Arms and Bearings and the Public Register of All Genealogies in Scotland. Pedigrees are established by decrees of Lyon Court and by letters patent. As Royal Commissioner in Armory, the Lord Lyon grants patents of arms to virtuous and well-deserving Scots and to petitioners (personal or corporate) in the Queen's overseas realms of Scottish connection, and also issues birthbrieves. For information on Her Majesty's Officers of Arms in Scotland, *see* the Court of the Lord Lyon in the Public Bodies section.

Lord Lyon King of Arms, Dr Joseph J. Morrow
Lyon Clerk and Keeper of the Records, Mrs C. G. W. Roads, LVO, FSA SCOT, FSA
Procurator Fiscal, Alexander M. S. Green
Macer, Roderick Macpherson

NORTHERN IRELAND JUDICATURE

In Northern Ireland the legal system and the structure of courts closely resemble those of England and Wales; there are, however, often differences in enacted law.

The court of judicature of Northern Ireland comprises the court of appeal, the high court of justice and the crown court.

The practice and procedure of these courts is similar to that in England. The superior civil court is the high court of justice, from which an appeal lies to the Northern Ireland court of appeal; the UK supreme court is the final civil appeal court.

The crown court, served by high court and county court judges, deals with criminal trials on indictment. Cases are heard before a judge and, except those certified by the Director of Public Prosecutions under the Justice and Security Act 2007, a jury. Appeals from the crown court against conviction or sentence are heard by the Northern Ireland court of appeal; the UK supreme court is the final court of appeal.

The decision to prosecute in criminal cases in Northern Ireland rests with the Director of Public Prosecutions.

Minor criminal offences are dealt with in magistrates' courts by a legally qualified district judge (magistrates' courts) and, where an offender is under the age of 18, by youth courts each consisting of a district judge (magistrates' courts) and two lay magistrates (at least one of whom must be a woman). As at 1 June 2015 there were 210 lay magistrates in Northern Ireland. Appeals from magistrates' courts are heard by the county court, or by the court of appeal on a point of law or an issue as to jurisdiction.

Magistrates' courts in Northern Ireland can deal with certain classes of civil case but most minor civil cases are dealt with in county courts. Judgments of all civil courts are enforceable through a centralised procedure administered by the Enforcement of Judgments Office.

COURT OF JUDICATURE

The Royal Courts of Justice, Chichester Street, Belfast BT1 3JF
T 0300-200 7812
Lord Chief Justice of Northern Ireland (£220,655),
　Rt. Hon. Sir Declan Morgan, *born* 1952, *apptd* 2009
Principal Private Secretary, Laurene McAlpine

LORDS JUSTICES OF APPEAL (£202,668)
Style, The Rt. Hon. Lord Justice [surname]

Rt. Hon. Sir Paul Girvan, *born* 1948, *apptd* 2007
Rt. Hon. Sir Patrick Coghlin, *born* 1945, *apptd* 2008
Rt. Hon. Sir John Gillen, *born* 1947, *apptd* 2014

HIGH COURT JUDGES (£177,988)
Style, The Hon. Mr Justice [surname]

Hon. Sir Ronald Weatherup, *born* 1947, *apptd* 2001
Hon. Sir Reginald Weir, *born* 1947, *apptd* 2003
Hon. Sir Donnell Deeny, *born* 1950, *apptd* 2004
Hon. Sir Benjamin Stephens, *born* 1954, *apptd* 2007
Hon. Sir Seamus Treacy, *born* 1956, *apptd* 2007
Hon. Sir Bernard McCloskey, *born* 1956, *apptd* 2008
Hon. Sir Paul Maguire, *born* 1952, *apptd* 2012
Hon. Sir Mark Horner, *born* 1956, *apptd* 2012
Hon. Sir John O'Hara, *born* 1956, *apptd* 2013

MASTERS OF THE HIGH COURT (£106,040)
Master Bell, *apptd* 2006; Master Hardstaff, *apptd* 2014; Master Kelly, *apptd* 2005; Master McCorry, *apptd* 2011; Master Sweeney, *apptd* 2015; Master A. Wells, *apptd* 2013; Master H. Wells, *apptd* 2005

OFFICIAL SOLICITOR
Official Solicitor to the Court of Judicature, Miss B. M. Donnelly

COUNTY COURTS

JUDGES (£132,184†)
Style, His/Her Hon. Judge [surname]

Judge Babington; Judge Devlin; Judge Finnegan, QC; Judge Fowler, QC; Judge Grant; Judge Kerr, QC; Judge Kinney; Judge Lynch, QC; Judge McColgan; Judge McFarland; Judge McReynolds; Judge Marrinan; Judge Miller, QC; Judge Philpott, QC; Judge Ramsay; Judge Sherrard; Judge Smyth

† County court judges are paid £142,745 so long as they are required to carry out significantly different work from their counterparts elsewhere in the UK

RECORDERS
Belfast (£154,165), Judge McFarland
Londonderry (£142,745), Judge Babington

DISTRICT JUDGES (£106,040)
Only barristers and solicitors with ten years' standing are eligible to become district judges. There are four district judges in Northern Ireland.

MAGISTRATES' COURTS

DISTRICT JUDGES (MAGISTRATES' COURTS) (£106,040)
There are 21 district judges (magistrates' courts) in Northern Ireland.

NORTHERN IRELAND COURTS AND TRIBUNALS SERVICE
23–27 Oxford Street, Belfast BT1 3LA
T 0300-200 7812 **W** www.courtsni.gov.uk
Chief Executive, Ronnie Armour

CROWN SOLICITOR'S OFFICE
Royal Courts of Justice, Chichester Street, Belfast BT1 3JE
T 028-9054 2555
Crown Solicitor, J. Conn

PUBLIC PROSECUTION SERVICE
Linum Chambers, 2 Bedford Square, Belfast BT2 7ES
T 028-9089-7100 **W** www.ppsni.gov.uk
Director of Public Prosecutions, Barra McGrory, QC

TRIBUNALS

Information on all the tribunals listed here, with the exception of the independent tribunals and the tribunals based in Scotland, Wales and Northern Ireland, can be found on the Ministry of Justice website (W www.justice.gov.uk/tribunals).

HM COURTS AND TRIBUNALS SERVICE

102 Petty France, London SW1H 9AJ
W www.justice.gov.uk and
W https://courttribunalfinder.service.gov.uk

HM Courts Service and the Tribunals Service merged on 1 April 2011 to form HM Courts and Tribunals Service, an integrated agency providing support for the administration of justice in courts and tribunals. It is an agency within the Ministry of Justice, operating as a partnership between the Lord Chancellor, the Lord Chief Justice and the Senior President of Tribunals. It is responsible for the administration of the criminal, civil and family courts and tribunals in England and Wales and non-devolved tribunals in Scotland and Northern Ireland. The agency's work is overseen by a board headed by an independent chair working with non-executive, executive and judicial members.

A two-tier tribunal system, comprising the First-tier Tribunal and Upper Tribunal, was established on 3 November 2008 as a result of radical reform under the Tribunals, Courts and Enforcement Act 2007. Both of these tiers are split into a number of separate chambers. These chambers group together individual tribunals (also known as 'jurisdictions') which deal with similar work or require similar skills. Cases start in the First-tier Tribunal and there is a right of appeal to the Upper Tribunal. Some tribunals transferred to the new two-tier system immediately, with more transferring between 2009 and 2011. The exception is employment tribunals, which remain outside this structure. The Act also allowed legally qualified tribunal chairs and adjudicators to swear the judicial oath and become judges.
Senior President, Rt. Hon. Sir Ernest Ryder, TD
Chief Executive, Natalie Ceeney, CBE

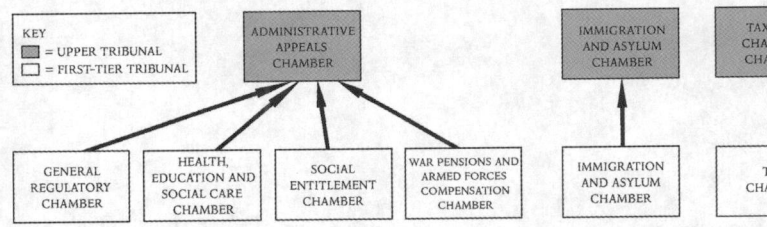

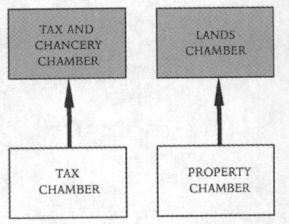

FIRST-TIER TRIBUNAL

The main function of the First-tier Tribunal is to hear appeals by citizens against decisions of the government. In most cases appeals are heard by a panel made up of one judge and two specialists in their relevant field, known as 'members'. Both judges and members are appointed through the Independent Judicial Appointments Commission. Most of the tribunals administered by central government are part of the First-tier Tribunal, which is split into seven separate chambers.

GENERAL REGULATORY CHAMBER

For all jurisdictions: General Regulatory Chamber, HMCTS, PO Box 9300, Leicester LE1 8DJ T 0300-123 4504
E grc@hmcts.gsi.gov.uk
Chamber President, Judge Lane*
Judicial Leads, Judge Brodrick (Transport); Judge McKenna (Charity)

*Acts as judicial lead for all jurisdictions with the exception of the ones specified above

CHARITY

Under the Charities Act 2011 (only applicable to England and Wales), First-tier Tribunal (Charity) hears appeals against the decisions of the Charity Commission, applications for the review of decisions made by the Charity Commission and considers references from the Attorney-General or the Charity Commission on points of law.

CLAIMS MANAGEMENT SERVICES

Under section 13 of the Compensation Act 2006, Claims Management Services hears appeals pertaining to decisions made by the claims regulator, such as the regulator's decision to cancel or suspend a claims management licence, refuse authorisation for claims managment services or add conditions to a claims management licence. Claims management services include all companies and individuals that offer a service for people hoping to claim compensation for personal injury, mis-sold financial products and services, redundancy, criminial or industrial injury and housing disrepair.

COMMUNITY RIGHT TO BID

The Community Right to Bid jurisdiction of the General Regulatory Chamber was established in January 2013 and hears appeals against review decisions made by local authorities to list your property as a community asset and give local communities the right to bid for it if you decide to sell. Individuals have the right to appeal against a listing decision under the Localism Act 2011 and the assets of community value (England) regulations 2012.

COPYRIGHT LICENSING

Under the copyright (regulation of relevant licensing bodies) regulations 2014 a copyright licensing body may appeal to a First-tier Tribunal (Copyright Licensing) against a government decision to fine or impose a code of conduct on their organisation.

ELECTRONIC COMMUNICATIONS AND POSTAL SERVICES

Hears appeals against decisions made by the Interception of Communications Commissioner under the Regulation of Investigatory Powers (Monetary Penalty Notices and Consents for Interceptions) Regulations 2011.

ENVIRONMENT

First-tier Tribunal (Environment) was created to decide appeals regarding civil sanctions made by environmental regulators. Established in April 2010, the jurisdiction of the tribunal extends to England and Wales.

ESTATE AGENTS

First-tier Tribunal (Estate Agents) hears appeals, under the Estate Agents Act 1979, against decisions made by the Office of Fair Trading pertaining to orders prohibiting a person from being employed as an estate agent when that person has been, for example, convicted of fraud or another offence involving dishonesty. The tribunal also hears appeals relating to decisions refusing to revoke or vary a prohibition order or warning order, as well as appeals regarding the issuing of a warning order when a person has not fulfilled their obligations under the Act.

EXAM BOARD

Under the Education Act 1997 regulated awarding organisations can appeal to the Exam Board tribunal if they disagree with a decision by OFQUAL or the Welsh government to impose a fine, the amount of the fine, or to recover the costs of taking enforcement action. The board is an independent tribunal and hears appeals across England and Wales.

FOOD

The food jurisdiction of the General Regulatory Chamber was established in January 2013 and hears appeals against some of the decisions taken by the Food Standards Agency, Department for Environment, Food and Rural Affairs and local authority trading standards departments. It also deals with appeals against decisions under the Fish Labelling (England) Regulations.

GAMBLING

First-tier Tribunal (Gambling) hears and decides appeals against decisions made by the Gambling Commission under the Gambling Act 2005.

IMMIGRATION SERVICES

First-tier Tribunal (Immigration Services) is an independent judicial body established in 2000. It hears appeals against decisions made by the Office of the Immigration Services Commissioner and considers disciplinary charges brought against immigration advisers by the Commissioner. The tribunal does not deal with immigration and asylum cases.

INFORMATION RIGHTS

First-tier Tribunal (Information Rights) determines appeals against notices issued by the Information Commissioner under the Freedom of Information Act 2000 and other regulations.

When a minister of the crown issues a certificate on the grounds of national security, the appeal must be transferred to the Administrative Appeals Chamber of the Upper Tribunal on receipt.

LETTING OR MANAGING AGENTS

First-tier Tribunal (Letting or Managing Agents) hears appeals against a decision by a local authority or the Trading Standards Office to impose a fine on an agent for not being a member of an approved complaints scheme or for not clearly publicising fees under The Redress Schemes for Lettings Agency Work and Property Management Work (Requirements to Belong to a Scheme etc) (England) Order 2014 and schedule 9 of the Consumer Rights Act 2015.

MICROCHIPPING DOGS

Established under the Microchipping of Dogs (England) Regulations 2015, appeals can be made to First-Tier Tribunal (Microchipping Dogs) against a decision by the Department for the Environment and Rural Affairs to ban or stop an individual from microchipping dogs or from running a database on microchipped dogs.

PENSIONS REGULATION

First-tier Tribunal (Pensions) hears appeals against decisions made by the Pensions Regulator under section 44 of the Pensions Act 2008. Appeals under section 102 of the Act are heard by the Tax and Chancery Chamber of the Upper Tribunal.

PROFESSIONAL REGULATION

The professional regulation jurisdiction hears appeals against decisions made by the Council for Licensed Conveyancers under the Legal Services Act 2007.

TRANSPORT

First-tier Tribunal (Transport) hears appeals against decisions made by the Registrar of Approved Driving Instructors under the Road Traffic Act 1988, Transport Act 2000 and the Motor Cars (Driving Instruction) Regulations 2005. Its jurisdiction covers England, Scotland and Wales.

HEALTH, EDUCATION AND SOCIAL CARE CHAMBER

Chamber President, His Hon. Judge Sycamore
Deputy Chamber Presidents, Judge Hinchliffe (Mental Health); Judge Tudur (Special Educational Needs and Disability, Care Standards and Primary Health Lists)

CARE STANDARDS

First-tier Tribunal (Care Standards), 1st Floor Darlington Magistrates' Court, Parkgate DL1 1RU
T 01325-289350 E cst@hmcts.gsi.gov.uk
First-tier Tribunal (Care Standards) was established under the Protection of Children Act 1999 and considers appeals in relation to decisions made by the Secretary of State for Education, the Secretary of State for Health, OFSTED, OFQUAL or the Care Council Wales about the inclusion of individuals' names on the list of those considered unsuitable to work with children or vulnerable adults, restrictions from teaching and employment in schools/further education institutions, and the registration of independent schools. It also deals with general registration decisions made about care homes, children's homes, childcare providers, nurses' agencies, social workers, residential family centres, independent hospitals and fostering agencies.

MENTAL HEALTH

PO Box 8793, 5th Floor, Leicester LE1 8BN
T 0300-123 2201 E mhrtenquiries@hmcts.gsi.gov.uk
The First-tier Tribunal (Mental Health) hears applications and references for people detained under the Mental Health Act 1983 (as amended by the Mental Health Act 2007). There are separate mental health tribunals for Wales and Scotland.

PRIMARY HEALTH LISTS

First-tier Tribunal (Primary Health Lists), 1st Floor Darlington Magistrates' Court, Parkgate DL1 1RU
T 01325-289350
First-tier Tribunal (Primary Health Lists) hears appeals against decisions made by the NHS Commissioning Board to not include, to remove or to change the conditions of inclusion for medical practitioners and providers on the NHS medical, dental, opthalmic or pharmaceutical lists.

SPECIAL EDUCATIONAL NEEDS AND DISABILITY

First-tier Tribunal (SEND), 1st Floor Darlington Magistrates' Court, Parkgate DL1 1RU

T 01325-289350 E sendistqueries@hmcts.gsi.gov.uk

First-tier Tribunal (Special Educational Needs and Disability) considers parents' appeals against the decisions of local authorities about children's special educational needs if parents cannot reach agreement with the local authority. It also considers claims of disability discrimination in schools.

IMMIGRATION AND ASYLUM CHAMBER

Chamber President, Judge Clements

PO Box 6987, Leicester LE1 6ZX

T 0300-123 1711 E customer.service@hmcts.gsi.gov.uk

The Immigration and Asylum Chamber is an independent tribunal dealing with appeals against decisions made by the Home Office concerning immigration, asylum and nationality matters.

PROPERTY CHAMBER

Chamber President, Judge McGrath

10 Alfred Place, London WC1E 7LR

T 020-7446 7700 E rplondon@hmcts.gsi.gov.uk

The First-tier Tribunal (Property Chamber) Residential Property serves the private-rented and leasehold property market in England by resolving disputes between leaseholders, tenants and landlords.

SOCIAL ENTITLEMENT CHAMBER

Chamber President, His Hon. Judge Aitken

Judicial Leads, His Hon. Judge Aitken (Social Security and Child Support); Sehba Storey (Asylum Support and Criminal Injuries Compensation)

ASYLUM SUPPORT

2nd Floor, Anchorage House, 2 Clove Crescent, London E14 2BE

T 020-7538 6171

First-tier Tribunal (Asylum Support) deals with appeals against decisions made by the Home Office. The Home Office decides whether asylum seekers, failed asylum seekers and/or their dependants are entitled to support and accommodation on the grounds of destitution, as provided by the Immigration and Asylum Act 1999. The tribunal can only consider appeals against a refusal or termination of support. It can, if appropriate, require the Secretary of State for the Home Department to reconsider the original decision, substitute the original decision with the tribunal's own decision or dismiss the appeal.

CRIMINAL INJURIES COMPENSATION

3rd Floor Wellington House, 134–136 Wellington Street, Glasgow G2 2XL T 0141-354 8555 E cic.enquiries@hmcts.gsi.gov.uk

First-tier Tribunal (Criminal Injuries Compensation) determines appeals against review decisions made by the Criminal Injuries Compensation Authority on applications for compensation made by victims of violent crime. It only considers appeals on claims made on or after 1 April 1996 under the Criminal Injuries Compensation Scheme.

SOCIAL SECURITY AND CHILD SUPPORT

England and Wales, T 0300-123 1142

Scotland, T 0141-354 8400

First-tier Tribunal (Social Security and Child Support) arranges and hears appeals against decisions made by the Department for Work and Pensions and HM Revenue and Customs regarding social security benefits. Appeals considered include those concerned with: attendance, bereavement and carer's allowances; child benefit; child support; the compensation recovery scheme (including NHS recovery claims); diffuse mesotheliomia and the industrial injuries disablement benefit payment schemes; income support; jobseeker's allowance; tax credits; universal credit; and vaccine damage payment.

TAX CHAMBER

Chamber President, Judge Bishopp

MP EXPENSES

PO Box 16972, Birmingham B16 6TZ

T 0300-123 1024 E taxappeals@hmcts.gsi.gov.uk

First-tier Tribunal (MP Expenses) hears appeals against certain decisions made by the Compliance Officer, an independent office holder appointed by the Independent Parliamentary Standards Authority, the organisation responsible for determining and paying MP expenses. Appeals can be made by current or former MPs under the Parliamentary Standards Act 2009. The jurisdiction is UK-wide.

TAX

PO Box 16972, Birmingham B4 6EQ

T 0300-123 1024 E taxappeals@hmcts.gsi.gov.uk

First-tier Tribunal (Tax) hears most appeals against decisions made by HM Revenue and Customs in relation to income tax, corporation tax, capital gains tax, inheritance tax, stamp duty land tax, statutory sick and maternity pay, national insurance contributions and VAT or duties. The tribunal also hears some appeals relating to goods seized by either HM Revenue and Customs or Border Force and against some decisions made by the National Crime Agency. Appeals can be made by individuals or organisations, single taxpayers or large multinational companies. The jurisdiction is UK-wide.

WAR PENSIONS AND ARMED FORCES COMPENSATION CHAMBER

Chamber President, Judge McKenna

5th Floor, Fox Court, 14 Gray's Inn Road, London WC1X 8HN

T 020-3206 0701 E armedforces.chamber@hmcts.gsi.gov.uk

The War Pensions and Armed Forces Compensation Chamber of the First-tier Tribunal hears appeals brought by ex-servicemen and women against decisions by Veterans UK regarding pensions, compensation and other amounts under the war pensions legislation for injuries sustained before 5 April 2005, and under the armed forces compensation scheme for injuries after that date.

UPPER TRIBUNAL

Comprising four separate chambers, the Upper Tribunal deals mostly with appeals from, and enforcement of, decisions taken by the First-tier Tribunal, but it also handles some cases that do not go through the First-tier Tribunal. Additionally, it has assumed some of the supervisory powers of the courts to deal with the actions of tribunals, government departments and some other public authorities. All the decision-makers of the Upper Tribunal are judges or expert members sitting in a panel chaired by a judge, and are specialists in the areas of law they handle. Over time their decisions are expected to build comprehensive case law for each area covered by the tribunals.

ADMINISTRATIVE APPEALS CHAMBER

Chamber President, Hon. Sir Willim Charles

General Enquiries, E adminappeals@hmcts.gsi.gov.uk

England and Wales, 5th Floor, 7 Rolls Buildings, London EC4A 1NL T 020-7071 5662

Scotland, George House, 126 George Street, Edinburgh EH2 4HH
    T 0131-271 4310

Northern Ireland, Tribunal Hearing Centre, 2nd Floor Royal Courts of Justice, Chichester Street, Belfast BT1 3JF
T 028-9072 4848

The Administrative Appeals Chamber considers appeals against most of the decisions of the following First-tier chambers: General Regulatory; Health, Education and Social Care; Social Entitlement; and War Pensions and Armed Forces Compensation. It also considers appeals against decisions of the Disclosure and Barring Service (England and Wales), Traffic Commissioners (England, Wales and Scotland) and appeals from decisions of a number of independent tribunals in Northern Ireland, Scotland and Wales. Its judges also decide Forfeiture Act references (England, Wales and Scotland).

IMMIGRATION AND ASYLUM CHAMBER
Chamber President, Hon. Sir Bernard McCloskey
15–25 Bream's Buildings, London EC4A 1DZ
T 0300-123 1711 E fieldhousecorrespondence@hmcts.gsi.gov.uk

The Immigration and Asylum Chamber hears appeals against decisions made by the Immigration and Asylum Chamber in the First-tier Tribunal relating to visa and asylum applications and the right to enter or stay in the UK. The chamber also deals with applications for judicial review of certain decisions made by the Home Office relating to immigration, asylum and human rights claims.

LANDS CHAMBER
Chamber President, Hon. Sir Keith Lindblom
5th Floor, 7 Rolls Buildings, London EC4A 1NL
T 020-7612 9710 E lands@hmcts.gsi.gov.uk

The Lands Chamber determines questions relating to the valuation of land, rating appeals from valuation tribunals, appeals from the First-tier (Property Chamber), applications to discharge or modify restrictions on the use of land, and compulsory purchase compensation. The tribunal may also arbitrate under a reference by consent.

TAX AND CHANCERY CHAMBER
Chamber President, Hon. Dame Vivien Rose, DBE
5th Floor, 7 Rolls Buildings, London EC4A 1NL
T 020-7612 9700 E uttc@hmcts.gsi.gov.uk

The Tax and Chancery Chamber hears appeals against decisions made by the First-tier Tribunal (Tax), the land registration division of the First-tier Tribunal (Property Chamber) and the General Regulatory Chamber in cases relating to charities. The chamber also hears appeals against decisions issued by the Financial Conduct Authority, the Prudential Regulation Authority, the Pensions Regulator, the Bank of England, HM Treasury and OFGEM.

SPECIAL IMMIGRATION APPEALS COMMISSION

15–25 Bream's Buildings, London EC4A 1DZ
T 0300-123 1711 E customer.service@hmcts.gsi.gov.uk

The commission was set up under the Special Immigration Appeals Commission Act 1997. It remains separate from the First-tier and Upper Tribunal structure but is part of HM Courts and Tribunals Service. Its main function is to consider appeals against orders for deportation or exclusion, or orders withdrawing or refusing British nationality, in cases which involve considerations of national security.
Chair, Hon. Sir Stephen Irwin

EMPLOYMENT TRIBUNALS

Employment Tribunal Central Office England and Wales, PO Box 10218, Leicester LE1 8EG **Public Enquiry Line**: 0300-123 1024

Employment Tribunal Central Office Scotland, PO Box 27105, Glasgow G2 9JR **Public Enquiry Line**: 0141-354 8574

Employment tribunals hear claims regarding matters of employment law, redundancy, dismissal, contract disputes, sexual, racial and disability discrimination and related areas of dispute which may arise in the workplace. A public register of judgments in England and Wales is held at Triton House, St Andrew's Street North, Bury St Edmunds, Suffolk IP33 1TR and in Scotland at the central office in Glasgow.
President (England and Wales), Brian Doyle
President (Scotland), Shona Simon

EMPLOYMENT APPEAL TRIBUNAL
Employment Appeal Tribunal England and Wales, 2nd Floor, Fleetbank House, 2–6 Salisbury Square, London EC4Y 8AE
T 020-7273 1041 E londoneat@hmcts.gsi.gov.uk
Employment Appeal Tribunal Scotland, 52 Melville Street, Edinburgh EH3 7HF T 0131-225 3963
E edinburgheat@hmcts.gsi.gov.uk

The Employment Appeal Tribunal hears appeals (on points of law only) arising from decisions made by employment tribunals.
President, Hon. Sir Brian Langstaff

SCOTTISH COURTS AND TRIBUNALS SERVICE

First Floor, Bothwell House, Hamilton Business Park, Caird Park, Hamilton ML3 0QA T 0800-345 7060 W www.scotland.gov.uk
Director of Tribunals Operations, Martin McKenna

The Scottish Courts and Tribunals Service currently provides administrative support for the following Scottish tribunals:

THE ADDITIONAL SUPPORT NEEDS TRIBUNAL FOR SCOTLAND, Europa Building, 450 Argyle Street, Glasgow G2 8LH T 0845-120 2906
E asntsinquiries@scotland.gsi.gov.uk
W www.asntscotland.gov.uk
President, May Dunsmuir
COUNCIL TAX REDUCTION REVIEW PANEL, Europa Building, 450 Argyle Street, Glasgow G2 8LH
T 0141-242 0223 E ctrrpadmin@scotland.gsi.gov.uk
W www.counciltaxreductionreview.scotland.gov.uk
Senior Convener, Donald Ferguson
HOMEOWNER HOUSING PANEL, Europa Building, 450 Argyle Street, Glasgow G2 8LH T 0141-242 0175
E hohpadmin@scotland.gsi.gov.uk
W www.hohp.scotland.gov.uk
President, Aileen Devanny
THE LANDS TRIBUNAL FOR SCOTLAND, George House, 126 George Street, Edinburgh EH2 4HH T 0131-271 4350
E mailbox@lands-tribunal-scotland.org.uk
W www.lands-tribunal-scotland.org.uk
President, Hon. Lord Minginish (Roderick MacLeod), QC
THE MENTAL HEALTH TRIBUNAL FOR SCOTLAND, Bothwell House, First Floor, Hamilton Business Park, Caird Park, Hamilton ML3 0QA T 0800-345 7060
E mhts@scotland.gsi.gov.uk W www.mhtscotland.gov.uk
President, Dr Joe Morrow
THE PENSIONS APPEAL TRIBUNAL SCOTLAND, George House, 126 George Street, Edinburgh EH2 4HH
T 0131-271 4340 E info@patscotland.org.uk
W www.patscotland.org.uk
President, Marion Caldwell, QC
THE PRIVATE RENTED HOUSING PANEL, Europa Building, 450 Argyle Street, Glasgow G2 8LH
T 0141-242 0142 E prhpadmin@scotland.gsi.gov.uk
W www.prhpscotland.gov.uk
President, Aileen Devanny

THE SCOTTISH CHARITY APPEALS PANEL,
George House, 126 George Street, Edinburgh EH2 4HH
T 0131-271 4340 E scap@scotland.gsi.gov.uk
W www.scap.gov.uk
Chairs, Aileen Devanny; Joseph Hughes; Gary McIlravey;
John Walker

NORTHERN IRELAND COURTS AND TRIBUNALS SERVICE

Laganside House, 23–27 Oxford Street, Belfast BT1 3LA
T 028-9032 8594 W www.courtsni.gov.uk
Lord Chief Justice of Northern Ireland, Rt. Hon. Sir Declan
Morgan

The Northern Ireland Courts and Tribunals Service currently
provides administrative support for the following Northern
Ireland tribunals:

THE APPEALS SERVICE, Cleaver House,
3 Donegall Square North, Belfast BT1 5GA
T 028-9051 8518 E appeals.service.belfast@dsdni.gov.uk
President of the Appeal Tribunals, John Duffy
THE CARE TRIBUNAL, 2nd Floor, Royal Courts of Justice,
Chichester Street, Belfast BT1 3JF T 028-9072 4857
E tribunalsunit@courtsni.gov.uk
Chair, Diane Drennan
THE CHARITY TRIBUNAL, 2nd Floor,
Royal Courts of Justice, Chichester Street, Belfast BT1 3JF
T 028-9072 4857 E tribunalsunit@courts.ni.gov.uk
President, Damien McMahon
CRIMINAL INJURIES COMPENSATION APPEALS
PANEL NORTHERN IRELAND, 2nd Floor,
Royal Courts of Justice, Chichester Street, Belfast BT1 3JF
T 028-9072 4823 E cicapnicustomer@courtsni.gov.uk
Chair, Patricia McKaigue
LANDS TRIBUNAL, 2nd Floor, Royal Courts of Justice,
Chichester Street, Belfast BT1 3JF T 028-9032 7703
E landstribunal@courtsni.gov.uk
Valuation Member, Henry Spence
MENTAL HEALTH REVIEW TRIBUNAL, 2nd Floor,
Royal Courts of Justice, Chichester Street, Belfast BT1 3JF
T 028-9072 4843 E tribunalsunit@courtsni.gov.uk
Chair, Attracta Wilson
NORTHERN IRELAND HEALTH AND SAFETY
TRIBUNAL, 2nd Floor, Royal Courts of Justice,
Chichester Street, Belfast BT1 3JF T 028-9072 4857
E tribunalsunit@courtsni.gov.uk
Chairs, James Leonard; Damian McMahon;
Petra Shiels
NORTHERN IRELAND TRAFFIC PENALTY
TRIBUNAL, 2nd Floor, Royal Courts of Justice,
Chichester Street, Belfast BT1 3JF T 028-9072 4888
E tribunalsunit@courtsni.gov.uk
Adjudicators, Michael Bready; Maura Hutchinson;
Julie McGrath; Patrick McGurgan
NORTHERN IRELAND VALUATION TRIBUNAL,
2nd Floor, Royal Courts of Justice, Chichester Street,
Belfast BT1 3JF T 028-9072 4857
E tribunalsunit@courtsni.gov.uk
President, James Leonard
OFFICE OF SOCIAL SECURITY COMMISSIONERS
AND CHILD SUPPORT COMMISSIONERS,
2nd Floor, Royal Courts of Justice, Chichester Street,
Belfast BT1 3JF T 028-9072 4883
E tribunalsunit@courtsni.gov.uk
Chief Commissioner, Dr Kenneth Mullan

PAROLE COMMISSIONERS FOR NORTHERN
IRELAND, Linum Chambers, 9th Floor, 2 Bedford Square,
Bedford Street, Belfast BT2 7ES T 028-9054 5900
E pcniinfo@dojni.x.gsi.gov.uk W www.parolecomni.org.uk
Chief Commissioner, Ms Christine Glenn
PENSIONS APPEAL COMMISSIONERS, 2nd Floor,
Royal Courts of Justice, Chichester Street, Belfast BT1 3JF
T 028-9072 4883 E tribunalsunit@courtsni.gov.uk
Chief Commissioner, Dr Kenneth Mullan
PENSIONS APPEAL TRIBUNAL, 2nd Floor,
Royal Courts of Justice, Chichester Street, Belfast BT1 3JF
T 028-9072 4883 E tribunalsunit@courtsni.gov.uk
President, Dr Kenneth Mullan
RENT ASSESSMENT PANEL, Cleaver House,
3 Donegall Square North, Belfast BT1 5GA T 028-9051 8518
E appeals.service.belfast@dsdni.gov.uk
SPECIAL EDUCATIONAL NEEDS AND DISABILITY
TRIBUNAL, 2nd Floor, Royal Courts of Justice,
Chichester Street, Belfast BT1 3JF T 028-9072 4887
E tribunalsunit@courtsni.gov.uk
President, Damian G. McCormick

INDEPENDENT TRIBUNALS

The following represents a selection of tribunals not
administered by HM Courts and Tribunals Service.

CIVIL AVIATION AUTHORITY
CAA House, 45–59 Kingsway, London WC2B 6TE
T 020-7379 7311 E infoservices@caa.co.uk
W www.caa.co.uk
The Civil Aviation Authority (CAA) does not have a separate
tribunal department as such, but for certain purposes the
CAA must conform to tribunal requirements, for example, to
deal with appeals against the refusal or revocation of aviation
licences and certificates issued by the CAA, and the
allocation of routes outside of the EU to airlines.
    The chair and five non-executive members who may sit
on panels for tribunal purposes are appointed by the
Secretary of State for Transport.
Chair, Dame Deirdre Hutton, DBE

COMPETITION APPEAL TRIBUNAL
Victoria House, Bloomsbury Place, London WC1A 2EB
T 020-7979 7979 E info@catribunal.org.uk
W www.catribunal.org.uk
The Competition Appeal Tribunal (CAT) is a specialist
tribunal established to hear certain cases in the sphere of UK
competition and economic regulatory law. It hears appeals
against decisions of the Competition and Markets Authority
(CMA) and the sectoral regulators in respect of infringements
of competition law and with respect to mergers and markets.
The CAT also has jurisdiction to award damages in respect
of infringements of EU or UK competition law and to hear
appeals against decisions of the Office of Communications
(OFCOM) in telecommunications matters.
President, Hon. Sir Peter Roth

COPYRIGHT TRIBUNAL
4 Abbey Orchard Street, London SW1P 2HT
T 020-7034 2836 E copyright.tribunal@ipo.gov.uk
W www.ipo.gov.uk/ctribunal
The Copyright Tribunal resolves disputes over the terms and
conditions of licences offered by, or licensing schemes
operated by, collective management organisations in the
copyright and related rights area. Its decisions are appealable
to the high court on points of law only.
Chair, Hon. Mr Justice Hacon

INDUSTRIAL TRIBUNALS AND THE FAIR EMPLOYMENT TRIBUNAL (NORTHERN IRELAND)

Killymeal House, 2 Cromac Quay, Ormeau Road, Belfast BT7 2JD
T 028-9032 7666 E mail@employmenttribunalsni.org
W www.employmenttribunalsni.co.uk

The industrial tribunal system in Northern Ireland was set up in 1965 and has a similar remit to the employment tribunals in the rest of the UK. There is also a Fair Employment Tribunal, which hears and determines individual cases of alleged religious or political discrimination in employment. Employers can appeal to the Fair Employment Tribunal if they consider the directions of the Equality Commission to be unreasonable, inappropriate or unnecessary, and the Equality Commission can make application to the tribunal for the enforcement of undertakings or directions with which an employer has not complied.

President, Eileen McBride

INVESTIGATORY POWERS TRIBUNAL

PO Box 33220, London SW1H 9ZQ
T 020-7035 3711 E info@ipt-uk.com W www.ipt-uk.com

The Investigatory Powers Tribunal replaced the Interception of Communications Tribunal, the Intelligence Services Tribunal, the Security Services Tribunal and the complaints function of the commissioner appointed under the Police Act 1997.

The Regulation of Investigatory Powers Act 2000 (RIPA) provides for a tribunal made up of senior members of the legal profession, independent of the government and appointed by the Queen, to consider all complaints against the intelligence services and those against public authorities in respect of powers covered by RIPA; and to consider proceedings brought under section 7 of the Human Rights Act 1998 against the intelligence services and law enforcement agencies in respect of these powers.

President, Sir Michael Burton

NATIONAL HEALTH SERVICE TRIBUNAL (SCOTLAND)

Anderson Strathern LLP, Lomond House, 9 George Square, Glasgow G2 1DY
T 0141-242 7974 E nhstribunal@nhs.net

The Scottish National Health Service Tribunal considers representations that the continued inclusion of a family health service practitioner (eg a doctor, dentist, optometrist or pharmacist) on a health board's list would be prejudicial to the efficiency of the service concerned, by virtue either of fraudulent practices or unsatisfactory personal or professional conduct. If this is established, the tribunal has the power to disqualify practitioners from working in the NHS family health services.

Chair, J. Michael Graham

SOLICITORS' DISCIPLINARY TRIBUNAL

5th Floor, Gate House, 1 Farringdon Street, London EC4M 7LG
T 020-7329 4808 E enquiries@solicitorsdt.com
W www.solicitorstribunal.org.uk

The Solicitors' Disciplinary Tribunal is an independent statutory body whose members are appointed by the Master of the Rolls. The tribunal adjudicates upon alleged breaches of the rules and regulations applicable to solicitors and their firms, including the Solicitors' Code of Conduct 2007. It also decides applications by former solicitors for restoration to the Roll.

President, Andrew Spooner

SOLICITORS' DISCIPLINE TRIBUNAL (SCOTTISH)

Unit 3.5, The Granary Business Centre, Coal Road, Cupar, Fife KY15 5YQ
T 01334-659088 E enquiries@ssdt.org.uk W www.ssdt.org.uk

The Scottish Solicitors' Discipline Tribunal is an independent statutory body with a panel of 24 members, 12 of whom are solicitors appointed by the Lord President of the Court of Session. Its principal function is to consider complaints of misconduct against solicitors in Scotland.

Chair, Alaistair Cockburn

TRAFFIC PENALTY TRIBUNAL

Springfield House, Water Lane, Wilmslow, Cheshire SK9 5BG
T 01625-445555 E info@trafficpenaltytribunal.gov.uk
W www.trafficpenaltytribunal.gov.uk

The Traffic Penalty Tribunal adjudicators consider appeals in relation to penalty charge notices issued by local authorities in England (outside London) and Wales for parking and bus lane contraventions and, additionally in Wales, moving traffic contraventions. The tribunal also considers appeals in relation to penalties issued by the Secretary of State for Transport for failing to pay a charge at the Dartford river crossing and by Durham County Council in the Durham congestion charging zone.

Chief Adjudicator, Caroline Sheppard

VALUATION TRIBUNAL FOR ENGLAND

2nd Floor, 120 Leman Street, London E1 8EU
T 020-7246 3900 W www.valuationtribunal.gov.uk

The Valuation Tribunal for England (VTE) came into being on 1 October 2009, replacing 56 valuation tribunals in England. Provision for the VTE was made in the Local Government and Public Involvement in Health Act 2007. The VTE hears appeals concerning council tax and non-domestic (business) rates, as well as a small number of appeals against drainage boards' assessments of drainage rates. A separate panel is constituted for each hearing, and consists of a chair and usually one or two other members.

The Valuation Tribunal Service (VTS) was created as a corporate body by the Local Government Act 2003, and is responsible for providing or arranging the services required for the operation of the Valuation Tribunal for England. The VTS board consists of a chair and members appointed by the secretary of state. The VTS is sponsored by the Department for Communities and Local Government.

President (VTE), Prof. Graham Zellick, CBE, QC
Chair (VTS), Anne Galbraith, CBE

VALUATION TRIBUNAL FOR WALES

Government Buildings, Block A (L1), Sarn Mynach, Llandudno Junction LL31 9RZ
T 0300-062 5350 E VTWalesnorth@vtw.gsi.gov.uk
W www.valuation-tribunals-wales.org.uk

The Valuation Tribunal for Wales (VTW) was established by the Valuation Tribunal for Wales Regulations 2010, and hears and determines appeals concerning council tax, non-domestic rating and drainage rates in Wales. The governing council, comprising the president, four regional representatives and one member who is appointed by the Welsh government, performs the management functions on behalf of the tribunal.

President, Miss C. Cobert

OMBUDSMAN SERVICES

The following section is a listing of selected ombudsman services. Ombudsmen are a free, independent and impartial means of resolving certain disputes outside of the courts. These disputes are, in the majority of cases, concerned with whether something has been badly or unfairly handled (for example owing to delay, neglect, inefficiency or failure to follow proper procedures). Most ombudsman schemes are established by statute; they cover various public and private bodies and generally examine matters only after the relevant body has been given a reasonable opportunity to deal with the complaint.

After conducting an investigation an ombudsman will usually issue a written report, which normally suggests a resolution to the dispute and often includes recommendations concerning the improvement of procedures.

OMBUDSMAN ASSOCIATION

56 Cambridge Road, Carshalton, Surrey SM5 3QS
T 020-8894 9272 E secretary@ombudsmanassociation.org
W www.ombudsmanassociation.org

The Ombudsman Association was established in 1994 and exists to provide information to the government, public bodies and the public about ombudsmen and other complaint-handling services in the UK and Ireland. An ombudsman scheme must meet four criteria in order to attain full Ombudsman Association membership: independence from the organisations the ombudsman has the power to investigate, fairness, effectiveness and public accountability. Complaint Handler membership is open to complaint-handling bodies that do not meet these criteria in full. Ombudsmen schemes from the UK, Ireland, British crown dependencies and overseas territories may apply to the Ombudsman Association for membership. The Ombudsman Association publishes a triannual newsletter containing news about ombudsmen and complaint-handling services in the UK, Ireland and overseas, along with topical articles of interest to members of the Association.
Chair, Lewis Shand Smith

The following is a selection of organisations that are members of the Ombudsman Association.

FINANCIAL OMBUDSMAN SERVICE

Exchange Tower, London E14 9SR
T 020-7964 1000 E complaint.info@financial-ombudsman.org.uk
W www.financial-ombudsman.org.uk

The Financial Ombudsman Service settles individual disputes between businesses providing financial services and their customers. The service answers around a million enquiries every year and deals with over 250,000 disputes. The service examines complaints about most financial matters, including banking, insurance, mortgages, pensions, savings, loans and credit cards. *See also* Banking and Finance.
Chief Ombudsman and Chief Executive, Caroline Wayman

HOUSING OMBUDSMAN SERVICE

81 Aldwych, London WC2B 4HN
T 0300-111 3000 E info@housing-ombudsman.org.uk
W www.housing-ombudsman.org.uk

The Housing Ombudsman Service was established in 1997 to deal with complaints and disputes involving tenants and housing associations and social landlords, certain private-sector landlords and managing agents. The ombudsman has a statutory jurisdiction over all registered social landlords in England. Private and other landlords can join the service on a voluntary basis. On 1 April 2013 a new Housing Ombudsman Service was launched with an extended jurisdiction covering all housing associations and local authorities.
Ombudsman, Denise Fowler

INDEPENDENT POLICE COMPLAINTS COMMISSION (IPCC)

90 High Holborn, London WC1V 6BH
T 0300-020 0096 E enquiries@ipcc.gsi.gov.uk
W www.ipcc.gov.uk

The IPCC succeeded the Police Complaints Authority in 2004. It was established under the Police Reform Act 2002. The IPCC is responsible for carrying out independent investigations into serious incidents or allegations of misconduct by those serving with the police in England and Wales. The IPCC's chair and commissioners must not have worked for the police in any capacity prior to their appointment. It has the power to initiate, undertake and oversee investigations and is also responsible for the way in which complaints are handled by local police forces. The IPCC is also responsible for serious complaints and conduct matters relating to staff at the National Crime Agency (NCA), Her Majesty's Revenue and Customs (HMRC), and the Home Office immigration and enforcement staff. In 2011 the IPCC became responsible for investigating allegations against the Police and Crime Commissioner for each police force area in England and Wales (established 2011) and against the equivalent for the Metropolitan Police, the Mayor's Office for Policing and Crime (MOPAC), set up in 2012.
Chair, Dame Anne Owers
Deputy Chairs, Rachel Cerfontyne; Sarah Green
Chief Executive, Lesley Longstone

LEGAL OMBUDSMAN

PO Box 6806, Wolverhampton WV1 9WJ
T 0300-555 0333 E enquiries@legalombudsman.org.uk
W www.legalombudsman.org.uk

The Legal Ombudsman was set up by the Office for Legal Complaints under the Legal Services Act 2007 and is the single body for all consumer legal complaints in England and Wales. It replaced the Office of the Legal Services Ombudsman in 2010. The Legal Ombudsman aims to resolve disputes between individuals and authorised legal practitioners, including barristers, law cost draftsmen, legal executives, licensed conveyancers, notaries, patent attorneys, probate practitioners, registered European lawyers, solicitors and trade mark attorneys. The Legal Ombudsman is an independent and impartial organisation and deals with various types of complaints against legal services, such as wills, family issues, personal injury and buying or selling a house.
Chief Ombudsman (acting), Kathryn King

LOCAL GOVERNMENT OMBUDSMAN

PO Box 4771, Coventry CV4 OEH
T 0300-061 0614 W www.lgo.org.uk

The Local Government Ombudsman deals with complaints about councils and service failure by local authorities, schools and care providers.

There are two ombudsmen in England, each with responsibility for different regions; they aim to provide satisfactory redress for complainants and better administration by the authorities. The ombudsmen investigate complaints about most council matters, including housing, planning, education, social care, housing benefit, transport and highways, environment and waste, and council tax. *See also* Local Government.

Local Government Ombudsman, Dr Jane Martin

NORTHERN IRELAND OMBUDSMAN

33 Wellington Place, Belfast BT1 6HN
T 028-9023 3821 E ombudsman@ni-ombudsman.org.uk
W www.ni-ombudsman.org.uk

The Northern Ireland Ombudsman (also known as the Assembly Ombudsman and the Northern Ireland Commissioner for Complaints) is appointed under legislation with powers to investigate complaints by people claiming to have sustained injustice arising from action taken by a Northern Ireland government department, their agencies or any other public body within his remit. Public bodies include all local authorities, education and library boards and organisations providing health and social care.

Ombudsman, Dr Tom Frawley, CBE
Deputy Ombudsman, Marie Anderson

OFFICE OF THE PENSIONS OMBUDSMAN

11 Belgrave Road, London SW1V 1RB
T 020-7630 2200 E enquiries@pensions-ombudsman.org.uk
W www.pensions-ombudsman.org.uk

The Pensions Ombudsman is appointed by the Secretary of State for Work and Pensions, under the Pension Schemes Act 1993 as amended by the Pensions Act 1995. He investigates and decides complaints and disputes about the way that personal and occupational pension schemes are run and between members of pensions schemes and their beneficiaries, employers, trustees, managers and scheme administrators. As the ombudsman for the Board of the Pension Protection Fund, he can deal with disputes about the decisions made by the board or the actions of their staff. He also deals with appeals against decisions made by the scheme manager under the Financial Assistance Scheme.

Pensions Ombudsman, Anthony Arter
Deputy Pensions Ombudsman, Karen Johnston

OMBUDSMAN SERVICES

The Brew House, Wilderspool Park, Greenalls Avenue,
Warrington WA4 6HL
W www.ombudsman-services.org

Ombudsman Services was founded in 2002 and provides independent dispute resolution for the communications, copyright licensing, energy and property sectors.

Ombudsman Services: Communications investigates complaints from consumers about companies which provide communication services to the public.

Ombudsman Services: Copyright Licensing helps to resolve complaints about bodies that either own or administer, on behalf of third parties, the licensing of copyright materials.

Ombudsman Services: Energy helps to resolve complaints from consumers about energy (gas and electricity companies). This service is also responsible for handling investigations concerning the government's Green Deal policy, which launched in 2013, and offers long-term loans towards energy-saving home improvements.

Ombudsman Services: Property investigates complaints from consumers about chartered surveying companies, surveyors, estate agents and other property professionals.

Chair, Dame Janet Finch
Chief Ombudsman, Lewis Shand Smith

OMBUDSMAN SERVICES: COMMUNICATIONS
PO Box 730, Warrington WA4 6WU
T 0330-440 1614

OMBUDSMAN SERVICES: COPYRIGHT LICENSING
PO Box 1124, Warrington WA4 9GH
T 0330-440 1601

OMBUDSMAN SERVICES: ENERGY
PO Box 966, Warrington WA4 9DF
T 0330-440 1624

OMBUDSMAN SERVICES: PROPERTY
PO Box 1021, Warrington WA4 9FE
T 0330-440 1634

PARLIAMENTARY AND HEALTH SERVICE OMBUDSMAN

Millbank Tower, Millbank, London SW1P 4QP
T 0345-015 4033
W www.ombudsman.org.uk

The Parliamentary Commissioner for Administration (commonly known as the Parliamentary Ombudsman) is independent of government and is an officer of Parliament. She is responsible for investigating complaints referred to her by MPs from members of the public who claim to have sustained injustice in consequence of maladministration by or on behalf of government departments and certain non-departmental public bodies in the UK. Certain types of action by government departments or bodies are excluded from investigation.

The Health Service Ombudsman is responsible for investigating complaints about services funded by the National Health Service in England that have not been dealt with by the service providers to the satisfaction of the complainant. This includes complaints about doctors, dentists, pharmacists and opticians. Complaints can be referred directly by the member of the public who claims to have sustained injustice or hardship in consequence of the failure in a service provided by a relevant organisation.

The two offices of the Parliamentary and Health Service Ombudsman are traditionally held by the same person.

Parliamentary Ombudsman and Health Service Ombudsman, Dame Julie Mellor, DBE

PRISONS AND PROBATION OMBUDSMAN

PO Box 70769, London SE1P 4XY
T 020-7633 4100 E mail@ppo.gsi.gov.uk
W www.ppo.gov.uk

The Prisons and Probation Ombudsman investigates complaints from prisoners, people on probation and immigration detainees, deaths of prisoners, residents of probation-service Approved Premises and those held in immigration removal centres. The ombudsman is appointed by the Secretary of State for Justice and works closely with the Ministry of Justice. All deaths that occur in prison are investigated and an anonymised fatal incident report is written after each investigation.

Ombudsman, Nigel Newcomen, CBE

PROPERTY OMBUDSMAN

Milford House, 43–55 Milford Street, Salisbury SP1 2BP
T 01722-333306
W www.tpos.co.uk

The Property Ombudsman (TPO) scheme was established in 1998 and provides a free, impartial and independent service for dealing with unresolved disputes between property agents and buyers, sellers, tenants and landlords of property in the UK.

The ombudsman's role is to consider complaints against the agents' obligation to act in accordance with the TPO codes of practice and to propose a full and final resolution to the dispute. Consumers are not bound by the Ombudsman's decision, but registered agents are.

With over 12,800 estate agent offices and 11,500 lettings offices registered, TPO is the primary dispute-resolution service for the property industry.
Ombudsman, Katrine Sporle, CBE

PUBLIC SERVICES OMBUDSMAN FOR WALES

1 Ffordd yr Hen Gae, Pencoed CF35 5LJ
T 0300-790 0203
W www.ombudsman-wales.org.uk

The office of Public Services Ombudsman for Wales was established, with effect from 1 April 2006, by the Public Services Ombudsman (Wales) Act 2005. The ombudsman, who is appointed by the Queen, investigates complaints of injustice caused by maladministration or service failure by public services such as the Assembly Commission (and public bodies sponsored by the assembly); Welsh government; National Health Service bodies, including GPs, family health service providers and hospitals; registered social landlords; local authorities, including community councils; fire and rescue authorities; police authorities; the Arts Council of Wales; national park authorities; and countryside and environmental organisations.
Ombudsman, Nick Bennett

REMOVALS INDUSTRY OMBUDSMAN SCHEME

PO Box 6412, Leighton Buzzard, Beds LU7 6EG
T 01525-850054 E ombudsman@removalsombudsman.co.uk
W www.removalsombudsman.org.uk

The Removals Industry Ombudsman Scheme was established to resolve disputes between removal companies that are members of the scheme and their clients, both domestic and commercial. It comprises a board of four members, only one of whom has any connection with the removals industry. The ombudsman investigates complaints such as breaches of contract, unprofessional conduct, delays, excessive charges or breaches in the code of practice. The National Guild of Removers and Storers is currently the principal member.
Ombudsman, Lynne Stone

SCOTTISH PUBLIC SERVICES OMBUDSMAN

4 Melville Street, Edinburgh EH3 7NS
T 0800-377 7330
W www.spso.org.uk

The Scottish Public Services Ombudsman (SPSO) was established in 2002. The SPSO is the final stage for complaints about public services in Scotland. Its service is free and independent. SPSO investigates complaints about the Scottish government, its agencies and departments; the Scottish Parliamentary Corporate Body; colleges and universities; councils; housing associations; NHS Scotland; prisons; some water and sewerage service providers; and most other Scottish public bodies. The ombudsman looks at complaints regarding poor service or administrative failure and can usually only look at those that have been through the formal complaints process of the organisation concerned. It also has a statutory function in improving complaints handling in public services, which it carries out through its Complaints Standards Authority.
Scottish Public Services Ombudsman, Jim Martin

WATERWAYS OMBUDSMAN

PO Box 854, Altrincham WA15 5JS
T 0161-980 4858 E enquiries@waterways-ombudsman.org
W www.waterways-ombudsman.org

Since July 2012, the Waterways Ombudsman has investigated complaints about the Canal and River Trust and its subsidiaries (such as British Waterways Marinas Limited). The ombudsman does not consider complaints about canals in Scotland, which are the responsibility of the Scottish Public Services Ombudsman.
Ombudsman, Andrew Walker

THE POLICE SERVICE

There are 45 police forces in the United Kingdom: 43 in England and Wales, including the Metropolitan Police and the City of London Police, Police Scotland and the Police Service of Northern Ireland. The Isle of Man, Jersey and Guernsey have their own forces responsible for policing in their respective islands and bailiwicks. The National Crime Agency, which became operational in October 2013, is responsible for preventing organised crime and strengthening UK borders.

Since 1964, police authorities – separate independent bodies for each police force – were responsible for the supervision of local policing in England and Wales. Following the government's white paper *Policing in the 21st Century* it was concluded that, in order to make the police more accountable, police authorities should be replaced with a directly elected commissioner for each force, supported by a police and crime panel. In November 2012, following the enactment of the Police Reform and Social Responsibility Act 2011, elections to install police and crime commissioners (PCCs) were held in 41 police force areas across England and Wales. The PCCs are responsible for appointing the chief constable of their force, establishing local priorities and setting budgets. The PCCs are not in place to run their local force but rather to hold them to account. The Mayor of London, supported by the Mayor's Office for Policing and Crime (MOPAC), acts as the PCC for the Metropolitan Police. The City of London Corporation acts as the police authority for the City of London Police.

In England the police and crime panels are made up of representatives from each local authority in a police force area. In Wales they are independent public bodies, established and maintained by the secretary of state, rather than local authority committees.

Under the Police and Fire Reform (Scotland) Act 2012, Police Scotland was established on 1 April 2013, merging the eight separate territorial police forces, the Scottish Crime and Drug Enforcement Agency and the Association of Chief Police Officers in Scotland. Responsible for policing the whole of Scotland, Police Scotland is the second largest force in the UK after the Metropolitan Police. The service is led by a chief constable who is supported by a team of four deputy constables, assistant chief constables and three directors. The Scottish Police Authority, established in October 2012, is responsible for maintaining policing, promoting policing principles, the continuous improvement of policing and holds the Chief Constable to account. In Northern Ireland, the Northern Ireland Policing Board, an independent public body consisting of 19 political and independent members, fulfils a similar role.

Police forces in England, Scotland and Wales are financed by central and local government grants and a precept on the council tax. The Police Service of Northern Ireland is wholly funded by central government.

The home secretary, the Scottish government and the Northern Ireland Minister of Justice are responsible for the organisation, administration and operation of the police service. They regulate police ranks, discipline, hours of duty and pay and allowances. All police forces are subject to inspection by HM Inspectorate of Constabulary, which reports to the home secretary and the Northern Ireland Minister of Justice. Police forces in Scotland are inspected by HM Inspectorate of Constabulary for Scotland which operates independently of the Scottish government.

COMPLAINTS

The Independent Police Complaints Commission (IPCC) was established under the Police Reform Act 2002. The IPCC is responsible for overseeing the whole of the police complaints system in England and Wales. It has the power to initiate, undertake and oversee investigations and is also responsible for the way in which complaints are handled by local police forces. In addition the IPCC is responsible for dealing with serious complaints and conduct matters relating to staff at the National Crime Agency, HM Revenue and Customs and Home Office immigration and enforcement staff. The most recent responsibility assigned to the IPCC is to decide whether investigations should be made regarding any allegations of criminal offence against MOPAC, the PCCs or their deputies.

Complaints about the police must first be recorded with the relevant police force; the local force will attempt to resolve complaints internally and an official investigation might not be required. Certain complaints, such as an allegation that an officer has seriously assaulted someone, are automatically referred to the IPCC. The IPCC or police force may refer the case to the Crown Prosecution Service, which will decide whether to bring criminal charges against the officer/s involved. An officer who is dismissed, required to resign or reduced in rank, whether as a result of a complaint or not, can appeal to a police appeals tribunal established by the relevant police authority.

On 1 April 2013, under the Police and Fire Reform (Scotland) Act 2012 which brought together Scotland's eight police services into the single Police Service of Scotland, the remit of the Police Complaints Commissioner for Scotland (PCCS) was expanded to include investigations into the most serious incidents concerning the police. To reflect this change, the PCCS was renamed the Police Investigations and Review Commissioner (PIRC).

The Police Ombudsman for Northern Ireland provides an independent police complaints system for Northern Ireland, dealing with all stages of the complaints procedure. Complaints that cannot be resolved informally are investigated and the ombudsman recommends a suitable course of action to the Chief Constable of the Police Service of Northern Ireland or the Northern Ireland Policing Board based on the investigation's findings. The ombudsman may recommend that a police officer be prosecuted, but the decision to prosecute a police officer rests with the Director of Public Prosecutions.

INDEPENDENT POLICE COMPLAINTS
COMMISSION, PO Box 473, Sale M33 0BW
T 0300-020 0096 E enquiries@ipcc.gsi.gov.uk
W www.ipcc.gov.uk
POLICE INVESTIGATIONS AND REVIEW
COMMISSIONER, Hamilton House, Hamilton Business Park,
Caird Park, Hamilton ML3 0QA T 0808-178 5577
E enquiries@pirc.gsi.gov.uk W www.pirc.scotland.gov.uk
Police Investigations and Review Commissioner,
Kate Frame
POLICE OMBUDSMAN FOR NORTHERN IRELAND,
New Cathedral Buildings, Writers' Square, 11 Church Street,
Belfast BT1 1PG T 028-9082 8600
E info@policeombudsman.org W www.policeombudsman.org
Police Ombudsman, Dr Michael Maguire

POLICE SERVICES

COLLEGE OF POLICING
Leamington Road, Ryton-on-Dunsmore, Coventry CV8 3EN
T 0800-496 3322 E contactus@college.pnn.police.uk
W www.college.police.uk

The College of Policing was established in December 2012 as the first professional body set up for policing. It works on behalf of the public to raise professional standards in policing and to assist forces to reduce crime and protect the public. It engages with the public through the Police and Crime Commissioners to ensure that it is responsive to the issues of greatest concern.

The government has designated the college as a centre for reviewing and testing practices and interventions to identify which are effective in reducing crime. It makes this information accessible for all in policing, particularly frontline practitioners. The college also supports continuous professional development and sets national standards for promotion and progression.

Chief Executive, Alex Marshall, QPM
Chair, Prof. Dame Shirley Pearce, DBE

NATIONAL CRIME AGENCY
Units 1–6 Citadel Place, Tinworth Street, London SE11 5EF
T 0370-496 7622
E communication@nca.x.gsi.gov.uk
W www.nationalcrimeagency.gov.uk

Established under the Crime and Courts Act 2013 the National Crime Agency (NCA) became fully operational in October 2013. The NCA is a non-ministerial government department.

In order to carry out its remit to fight organised crime, strengthen UK borders, tackle fraud and cyber crime and protect children and young people the agency is organised into four separate commands: Border Policing, Child Exploitation and Online Protection, Economic Crime and Organised Crime; and a specialist National Cyber Crime Unit.

The director-general has independent operational direction and control over the NCA's activities and, through the home secretary, is accountable to parliament.

Director-General, Keith Bristow, QPM

UK MISSING PERSONS BUREAU
Albert Day Building, Sunningdale Park, Ascot, Berks SL5 0QE
T 0845-000 5481 E missingpersonsbureau@nca.x.gsi.gov.uk
W www.missingpersons.police.uk

The UK Missing Persons Bureau, which is now part of the National Crime Agency, acts as the centre for the exchange of information connected with the search for missing persons nationally and internationally alongside the police and other related organisations. The unit focuses on cross-matching missing persons with unidentified persons or bodies by maintaining records, including a dental index of ante-mortem chartings of long-term missing persons and post-mortem chartings from unidentified bodies.

Information is supplied and collected for all persons who have been missing in the UK for over 72 hours (or fewer where police deem appropriate), foreign nationals reported missing in the UK, UK nationals reported missing abroad and all unidentified bodies and persons found within the UK.

SPECIALIST FORCES

BRITISH TRANSPORT POLICE
25 Camden Road, London NW1 9LN T 0800-405040
W www.btp.police.uk

Strength (March 2015), 2,876
British Transport Police is the national police force for the railways in England, Wales and Scotland, including the London Underground system, Docklands Light Railway, Glasgow Subway, Midland Metro tram system, Sunderland Metro, London Tramlink and the Emirates Air Line cable car. The chief constable reports to the British Transport Police Authority. The members of the authority are appointed by the transport secretary and include representatives from the rail industry as well as independent members. Officers are paid the same salary as those in other police forces.
Chief Constable, Paul Crowther, OBE

CIVIL NUCLEAR CONSTABULARY
Building F6, Culham Science Centre, Abingdon,
Oxfordshire OX14 3DB T 01235-466606
W www.gov.uk/government/organisations/civil-nuclear-constabulary

Strength (July 2015), c.1,500
The Civil Nuclear Constabulary (CNC) operates under the strategic direction of the Department of Energy and Climate Change. The CNC is a specialised armed force that protects civil nuclear sites and nuclear materials. The constabulary is responsible for policing UK civil nuclear industry facilities and for escorting nuclear material between establishments within the UK and worldwide.
Chief Constable, Michael Griffiths, CBE
Deputy Chief Constable, Simon Chesterton, QPM

MINISTRY OF DEFENCE POLICE
Ministry of Defence Police HQ, Wethersfield, Braintree, Essex
CM7 4AZ T 01371-854000 W www.mod.police.uk

Strength (July 2015), c.2,650
Part of the Ministry of Defence Police and Guarding Agency, the Ministry of Defence Police is a statutory civil police force with particular responsibility for the security and policing of the MoD environment. It contributes to the physical protection of property and personnel within its jurisdiction and provides a comprehensive police service to the MoD as a whole.
Chief Constable, Alf Hitchcock, QPM
Deputy Chief Constable, Gerard McAuley

THE SPECIAL CONSTABULARY
Darby House, 162 Bletchingley Road, Merstham, Surrey RH1 3DN
W www.policespecials.com

Strength (June 2015), c.20,000
The Special Constabulary is a force of trained volunteers who support and work with their local police force, usually for a minimum of 16 hours a month. Special constables are thoroughly grounded in the basic aspects of police work, such as self-defence, powers of arrest, common crimes and preparing evidence for court, before they can begin to carry out any police duties. Once they have completed their training, they have the same powers as a regular officer and wear a similar uniform.

POLICE FORCES

The telephone number for each local police force in England, Wales, Scotland and Northern Ireland is T 101

ENGLAND

Force	Strength†	Chief Constable	Police and Crime Commissioner
Avon and Somerset	2,716	John Long *(acting)*, QPM	Sue Mountstevens
Bedfordshire	1,161	Colette Paul, QPM	Olly Martins
Cambridgeshire	1,337	Simon Parr, QPM	Sir Graham Bright
Cheshire	1,878	Simon Byrne	John Dwyer
Cleveland	1,434	Jacqui Cheer, QPM	Barry Coppinger
Cumbria	1,137	Jeremy Graham	Richard Rhodes
Derbyshire	1,889	Mick Creedon, QPM	Alan Charles
Devon and Cornwall	3,073	Shaun Sawyer	Tony Hogg
Dorset	1,268	Debbie Simpson, QPM	Martyn Underhill
Durham	1,199	Mike Barton, QPM	Ron Hogg
Essex	3,090	Stephen Kavanagh	Nick Alston
Gloucestershire	1,178	Suzette Davenport	Martin Surl
Greater Manchester	6,749	Sir Peter Fahy, QPM	Tony Lloyd
Hampshire	3,283	Andy Marsh	Simon Hayes
Hertfordshire	1,923	Andy Bliss, QPM	David Lloyd
Humberside	1,760	Justine Curran, QPM	Matthew Grove
Kent	3,196	Alan Pughsley, QPM	Ann Barnes
Lancashire	3,059	Steve Finnigan, CBE, QPM	Clive Grunshaw
Leicestershire	2,072	Simon Cole, QPM	Sir Clive Loader
Lincolnshire	1,108	Neil Rhodes	Alan Hardwick
Merseyside	3,978	Sir Jon Murphy, QPM	Jane Kennedy
Norfolk	1,551	Simon Bailey	Stephen Bett
North Yorkshire	1,392	Dave Jones	Julia Mulligan
Northamptonshire	1,364	Adrian Lee	Adam Simmonds
Northumbria	3,506	Sue Sim	Vera Baird
Nottinghamshire	2,106	Chris Eyre, QPM	Paddy Tipping
South Yorkshire	2,690	David Crompton, QPM	Dr Alan Billings
Staffordshire	1,684	Jane Sawyers	Matthew Ellis
Suffolk	1,180	Douglas Paxton, QPM	Tim Passmore
Surrey	1,941	Lynne Owens, QPM	Kevin Hurley
Sussex	2,831	Giles York, QPM	Katy Bourne
Thames Valley	4,209	Sara Thornton, CBE, QPM	Anthony Stansfeld
Warwickshire	791	Andy Parker, QPM	Ron Ball
West Mercia	1,902	David Shaw	Bill Longmore
West Midlands	7,401	Chris Sims, OBE, QPM	David Jamieson
West Yorkshire	4,774	Mark Gilmore, QPM	Mark Burns-Williamson, OBE
Wiltshire	1,022	Patrick Geenty	Angus Macpherson
WALES			
Dyfed-Powys	1,094	Simon Prince, QPM	Christopher Salmon
Gwent	1,272	Jeffrey Farrar, QPM	Ian Johnston
North Wales	1,515	Mark Polin, QPM	Winston Roddick
South Wales	2,853	Peter Vaughan, QPM	Rt. Hon. Alun Michael
POLICE SCOTLAND	17,234	vacant	–
POLICE SERVICE OF NORTHERN IRELAND	7,791	George Hamilton, QPM	–

ISLANDS	Strength†	Chief Constable	Telephone
Isle of Man	210	Gary Roberts	01624-631212
States of Jersey	230	Mike Bowron, QPM	01534-612612
Guernsey	148	Patrick Rice	01481-725111

† Size of force (full-time equivalent) as at March 2015
Sources: R. Hazell & Co, Sweet & Maxwell *Police and Constabulary Almanac 2015*

LONDON FORCES

CITY OF LONDON POLICE
37 Wood Street, London EC2P 2NQ T 020-7601 2222
W www.cityoflondon.police.uk
Strength (March 2015), 750

The City of London has one of the most important financial centres in the world and the force has particular expertise in fraud investigation. The force concentrates on: economic crime, counter terrorism and community policing. It has a wholly elected police authority, the police committee of the City of London Corporation, which appoints the commissioner.

Commissioner, Adrian Leppard, QPM
Assistant Commissioner, Ian Dyson
Commanders, Wayne Chance *(Operations)*; Steve Head *(Economic Crime)*

METROPOLITAN POLICE SERVICE

New Scotland Yard, Broadway, London SW1H 0BG
T 020-7230 1212 W www.met.police.uk
Strength (March 2015), 39,548
Commissioner, Sir Bernard Hogan-Howe, QPM
Deputy Commissioner, Craig Mackey, QPM

The Metropolitan Police Service is divided into three main areas for operational purposes:
TERRITORIAL POLICING
Most of the day-to-day policing of London is carried out by 32 borough operational command units operating within the same boundaries as the London borough councils.
Assistant Commissioner, Helen King, QPM
SPECIALIST CRIME AND OPERATIONS (SC&O)
SC&O provides two main services: reducing the harm caused by serious crime and criminal networks and providing specialist policing services across London. SC&O provides specialist training to detectives, and conducts forensic examinations of crime scenes in the capital.
Assistant Commissioner, Patricia Gallan
SPECIALIST OPERATIONS
• *Counter Terrorism Command* is responsible for the prevention and disruption of terrorist activity, domestic extremism and related offences within London and nationally. It provides an explosives disposal and chemical, biological, radiological and nuclear capability in London, assists the security services in fulfilling their roles and provides a point of contact for international partners
• *Protection Command* is responsible for the protection and security of high-profile persons, including the royal family and the prime minister. It is also responsible for protecting royal residences and embassies, providing residential protection for visiting heads of state, heads of government and foreign ministers and advising the diplomatic community on security
• *Security Command* works with authorities at the Houses of Parliament to provide security for peers, MPs, employees and visitors to the Palace of Westminster. It is also responsible for policing Heathrow and London City airports
Assistant Commissioner, Mark Rowley, QPM
PROFESSIONALISM
The Directorate of Professionalism's key aims are to uphold and improve professional standards across the Metropolitan Police Service. The directorate works with the IPCC to establish good practice, reduce bureaucracy and review decision making. It also works with the Crown Prosecution Service to ensure timely and professional investigations of complaints and conduct matters.
Assistant Commissioner, Martin Hewitt

STAFF ASSOCIATIONS

Police officers are not permitted to join a trade union or to take strike action. All ranks have their own staff associations.
NATIONAL POLICE CHIEFS' COUNCIL (NPPC),
    10 Victoria Street, London SW1H 0NN T 020-7084 8950
    Chair, Sara Thornton

ENGLAND AND WALES

POLICE FEDERATION OF ENGLAND AND WALES,
    Federation House, Highbury Drive, Leatherhead,
    Surrey KT22 7UY T 01372-352000 W www.polfed.org
    General Secretary, Andy Fittes
POLICE SUPERINTENDENTS' ASSOCIATION OF
    ENGLAND AND WALES, 67A Reading Road, Pangbourne,
    Reading RG8 7JD T 0118-984 4005 W www.policesupers.com
    National Secretary, Chief Supt. Tim Jackson

SCOTLAND

ASSOCIATION OF SCOTTISH POLICE
    SUPERINTENDENTS, Scottish Police College,
    Tulliallan Castle, Kincardine, Fife FK10 4BE T 01259-732123
    W www.scottishpolicesupers.org.uk
    General Secretary, Craig Suttie
SCOTTISH POLICE FEDERATION, 5 Woodside Place,
    Glasgow G3 7QF T 0300-303 0027 W www.spf.org.uk
    General Secretary, Calum Steele

NORTHERN IRELAND

POLICE FEDERATION FOR NORTHERN IRELAND,
    77–79 Garnerville Road, Belfast BT4 2NX T 028-9076 4200
    W www.policefed-ni.org.uk
    Secretary, Marty Whittle
SUPERINTENDENTS' ASSOCIATION OF NORTHERN
    IRELAND, PSNI College, Garnerville Road, Belfast BT4 2NX
    T 028-9092 2201 W www.policesuperintendentsni.org
    Hon. Secretary, vacant

RATES OF PAY *from September 2015*

Chief Constables of Greater Manchester and	
West Midlands*	£186,954
Chief Constable	£133,983–£174,491
Deputy Chief Constable	£112,173–£143,334
Assistant Chief Constable and	
Commanders	£96,596–£109,055
Chief Superintendent	£79,557–£83,925
Superintendent Range *in rank on or after*	
1 April 2014	£64,188–£75,816
Superintendent *in rank before*	
1 April 2014‡	£64,188–£74,784
Chief Inspector‡	£53,358 (£55,485)–£55,554 (£57,675)†
Inspector‡	£48,207 (£50,319)–£52,290 (£54,420)†
Sergeant	£38,910–£42,285†
Constable *apptd on or after 1 April 2013*	£19,578–£37,626
Constable *apptd before 1 April 2013*	£23,964–£37,626†
Metropolitan Police	
Commissioner	£267,970
Deputy Commissioner	£221,229
City of London Police	
Commissioner	£165,777
Assistant Commissioner	£136,734
Police Scotland	
Chief Constable	£208,100
Deputy Chief Constable	£169,600
Assistant Chief Constable	£115,000
Police Service of Northern Ireland	
Chief Constable	£199,413
Deputy Chief Constable	£162,020

* Also applicable to the four Assistant Commissioners of the Metropolitan Police Service
† Officers on this pay point may additionally receive a competence-related threshold payment of £300 in 2015–16. This payment will be abolished from 1 April 2016
‡ London salary in parentheses. All other officers (not Metropolitan or City of London Commissioners) working in London receive an additional payment of £2,349 per annum

THE PRISON SERVICE

The prison services in the UK are the responsibility of the Secretary of State for Justice, the Scottish Secretary for Justice and the Minister of Justice in Northern Ireland. The chief executive (director-general in Northern Ireland), officers of the National Offender Management Service (NOMS), the Scottish Prison Service (SPS) and the Northern Ireland Prison Service are responsible for the day-to-day running of the system.

There are 122 prison establishments in England and Wales, 15 in Scotland and three in Northern Ireland. Convicted prisoners are classified according to their assessed security risk and are housed in establishments appropriate to that level of security. There are no open prisons in Northern Ireland. Female prisoners are housed in women's establishments or in separate wings of mixed prisons. Remand prisoners are, where possible, housed separately from convicted prisoners. Offenders under the age of 21 are usually detained in a Young Offender Institution, which may be a separate establishment or part of a prison. Appellant and failed asylum seekers are held in Immigration Removal Centres, or in separate units of other prisons.

Fourteen prisons are now run by the private sector in England and Wales, and in England, Wales and Scotland all escort services have been contracted out to private companies. In Scotland, two prisons (Kilmarnock and Addiewell) were built and financed by the private sector and are being operated by private contractors.

There are independent prison inspectorates in England, Wales and Scotland which report annually on conditions and the treatment of prisoners. The Chief Inspector of Criminal Justice in Northern Ireland and HM Inspectorate of Prisons for England and Wales perform an inspectorate role for prisons in Northern Ireland. Every prison establishment also has an independent monitoring board made up of local volunteers.

Any prisoner whose complaint is not satisfied by the internal complaints procedures may complain to the prisons and probation ombudsman for England and Wales, the Scottish public services ombudsman or the prisoner ombudsman for Northern Ireland. The prisons and probation inspectors, the prisons ombudsman and the independent monitoring boards report to the home secretary and to the Minister of Justice in Northern Ireland.

PRISON STATISTICS

The projected 'high scenario' prison population for 2020 in England and Wales is 98,900; the 'low scenario' is 81,400.

PRISON POPULATION (UK) as at June 2015

	Remand	Sentenced	Other
ENGLAND AND WALES	11,785	72,659	1,749
Male	11,159	69,404	1,726
Female	626	3,255	23
SCOTLAND*	1,365	6,062	–
Male	1,283	5,757	–
Female	82	305	–
N. IRELAND	373	1,292	0
Male	355	1,253	0
Female	18	39	0
UK TOTAL	13,523	80,013	1,749

* Figures from August 2015
Sources: MoJ; Scottish Prison Service; NI Prison Service

PRISON CAPACITY (ENGLAND AND WALES)
as at August 2015

Male prisoners	82,041
Female prisoners	3,910
Total	85,951
Useable operational capacity	88,242
Under home detention curfew supervision	2,127

Source: MoJ – Prisons and Probation Statistics

SENTENCED PRISON POPULATION BY SEX AND OFFENCE (ENGLAND AND WALES)
as at 30 June 2015

	Male	Female
Violence against the person	17,664	873
Sexual offences	11,402	88
Robbery	7,934	312
Theft offences	10,825	742
Criminal damage and arson	1,066	115
Fraud offences	1,227	182
Drugs offences	10,013	429
Possession of weapons	1,697	56
Public order offences	1,153	37
Miscellaneous crimes against society	3,008	217
Summary non-motoring	2,568	139
Summary motoring	374	7
Offence not recorded	379	45
Total	69,310	3,242

Source: MoJ – Prisons and Probation Statistics

SENTENCED POPULATION BY LENGTH OF SENTENCE (ENGLAND AND WALES)
as at 30 June 2015

	British	Other Nationalities or Not Recorded
Less than 12 months	5,347	843
12 months to less than 4 years	16,958	1,650
4 years to less than life	25,794	3,013
Indeterminate	11,020	1,033
Total*	59,119	6,539

* Figures do not include civil (non-criminal) prisoners or fine defaulters
Source: MoJ – Prisons and Probation Statistics

AVERAGE DAILY POPULATION BY TYPE OF CUSTODY 2014–15 (SCOTLAND)

Remand: sub total	1,525
Persons under sentence: sub total	6,205
Under 4 years	3,385
4 years and over	2,820
Total	7,730

Source: SPS – Annual Report and Accounts 2014–15

SUICIDES IN PRISON IN 2014 (ENGLAND AND WALES)

Total	82

Source: MoJ

THE PRISON SERVICES

NATIONAL OFFENDER MANAGEMENT SERVICE

Clive House, 70 Petty France, London SW1H 9EX
T 0300-047 6325 E public.enquiries@noms.gsi.gov.uk
W www.gov.uk/government/organisations/national-offender-management-service

HM Prison Service became part of the National Offender Management Service (NOMS) on 1 April 2008 as part of the reorganisation of the Ministry of Justice (MoJ).

SALARIES (ENGLAND AND WALES)
from 1 April 2015
All salary ranges given are for the average across England and Wales (includes inner and outer London salaries) and are based on a 37-hour-week inclusive of the required hours allowance (Governors, Deputy Governors and Heads of Function) or the additional 17 per cent unsocial hours payment for all other grades.

Governor	£63,411–£86,075
Deputy Governor	£44,972–£69,124
Head of Function	£38,569–£53,970
Custodial Manager	£29,562–£33,334
Supervising/Specialist Officer	£26,183–£29,221
Prison Officer	£20,545–£22,892
Operational Support Grade	£17,386–£18,622

THE NOMS BOARD
Chief Executive, Michael Spurr
Director of Commissioning and Commercial, Ian Blakeman
Director of Probation, Colin Allars
Director of National Operational Services, Digby Griffith
Director of Public Sector Prisons, Phil Copple
Director of Human Resources, Carol Carpenter
Director, National Offender Management Service in Wales, Sarah Payne
Director of Finance and Analysis, Andrew Emmett
Director of Digital and Change, Bryan Clarke
Director of Commissioning and Contract Management, Ian Porée

DEPUTY DIRECTORS OF CUSTODY
Paul Baker *(East Midlands and West Midlands);* Ian Barrow *(Wales);* Michelle Jarman-Howe *(Kent and Sussex);* Ian Mulholland *(Public Service Prisons);* Nick Pascoe *(London);* Neil Richards *(Yorkshire and Humberside);* Andy Rogers *(South-West);* Alan Scott *(North-West);* Adrian Smith *(East of England);* Claudia Sturt *(South-Central);* Alan Tallentire *(North-East);* Richard Vince *(High Security)*

OPERATING COSTS OF NOMS 2014–15
Staff costs	£1,864,683,000
Operating income	(£313,596,000)
Net operating costs (before tax)	£3,762,100,000
Net operating costs (after tax)	£3,761,676,000
Source: NOMS – *Annual Report 2014–15*

SCOTTISH PRISON SERVICE (SPS)

Calton House, 5 Redheughs Rigg, Edinburgh EH12 9HW
T 0131-244 8745 E gaolinfo@sps.pnn.gov.uk
W www.sps.gov.uk

SALARIES *from October 2015*
Governor in Charge	£62,160–£70,509
Deputy Governor	£50,323–£58,424
Head of Operations	£40,654–£48,579
Unit Manager	£32,778–£41,269
First Line Manager	£26,717–£34,430
Residential Officer	£22,427–£28,891
Operations Officer	£17,521–£22,245

SPS BOARD
Chief Executive, Colin McConnell
Directors, Ian Davidson *(Strategy and Innovation);* Eric Murch *(Operations);* Catherine Topley *(Corporate Services)*
Non-Executive Directors, S. Browell; A. Burns; H. McGuigan; A. Macmillan; J. Martin; S. Matheson, OBE; H. Monro; Z. Van Zwanenberg

OPERATING COSTS OF SPS 2014–15
Total income	(£7,491,000)
Total expenditure	£310,081,000
Staff costs	£163,029,000
Running costs	£115,513,000
Other current expenditure	£31,539,000
Operating cost	£302,590,000
Interest payable and similar charges	£11,181,000
Net operating cost	£313,771,000
Source: SPS – *Annual Report and Accounts 2014–15*

NORTHERN IRELAND PRISON SERVICE

Dundonald House, Upper Newtownards Road, Belfast BT4 3SU
T 028-9052 2922 E info@niprisonservice.gov.uk
W www.dojni.gov.uk

SALARIES *as at April 2015*
Governor 1	£74,747–£81,356
Governor in Charge	£64,900–£72,900
Head of Function	£53,300–£57,050
Head of Unit	£47,150–£51,055
Senior Prison Officer	£33,400–£38,000
Main Grade Prison Officer	£22,397–£30,406
Operational Support Grade	£20,297

SENIOR STAFF
Director-General, Sue McAllister
Executive, Mark Adam *(Human Resources and Corporate Services);* Brian McCaughey *(Rehabilitation);* Max Murray *(Estates Management)*

OPERATING COSTS OF NORTHERN IRELAND PRISON SERVICE 2013–14
Staff costs	£76,682,000
Net running costs	£31,706,000
Depreciation	£11,999,000
Operating expenditure	£120,387,000
Net operating costs for the year	£122,798,000
Source: NI Prison Service – *Annual Report and Accounts 2013–14*

PRISON ESTABLISHMENTS

ENGLAND AND WALES *as at June 2015*

Prison	Address	Capacity	Prisoners	Governor/Director
ALTCOURSE (private prison)	Liverpool L9 7WU	1,093	1,090	Dave Thompson
ASHFIELD (private prison)	Bristol BS16 9QJ	400	391	Ray Duckworth
*‡ASKHAM GRANGE	York YO23 3FT	128	87	Diane Pellew
‡AYLESBURY	Bucks HP20 1EH	444	383	Kevin Leggett
BEDFORD	Bedford MK40 1HG	506	489	Ian Blakeman
BELMARSH	London SE28 0EB	906	867	Phil Wragg
BIRMINGHAM	Birmingham B18 4AS	1,450	1,426	Peter Small
BLANTYRE HOUSE	Kent TN17 2NH	0	0	James Bourke
†‡BRINSFORD	Wolverhampton WV10 7PY	455	386	Carl Hardwick
‡BRISTOL	Bristol BS7 8PS	614	594	Andrea Albutt
‡BRIXTON	London SW2 5XF	798	795	Edmond Tullett
*BRONZEFIELD (private prison)	Middlesex TW15 3JZ	527	491	Charlotte Pattison-Rideout
BUCKLEY HALL	Lancs OL12 9DP	445	446	Susan Kennedy
BULLINGDON	Oxon OX25 1PZ	1,114	1,079	Ian Blakeman
BURE	Norfolk NR10 5GB	624	622	Sue Doolan
†CARDIFF	Cardiff CF24 0UG	820	815	Steve Cross
CHANNINGS WOOD	Devon TQ12 6DW	731	720	Gavin O'Malley
‡CHELMSFORD	Essex CM2 6LQ	745	690	Helen Carter
COLDINGLEY	Surrey GU24 9EX	519	516	Glenn Knight
‡COOKHAM WOOD	Kent ME1 3LU	188	173	Jonathan French
DARTMOOR	Devon PL20 6RR	660	633	Terry Witton
‡DEERBOLT	Co. Durham DL12 9BG	513	360	Gabrielle Lee
‡DONCASTER (private prison)	Doncaster DN5 8UX	1,145	1,107	John Biggin
DOVEGATE (private prison)	Staffs ST14 8XR	1,133	1,103	Craig Thomson
§DOVER	Kent CT17 9DR	401	370	Sara Pennington
*DOWNVIEW	Surrey SM2 5PD	0	0	Jonathan French
*‡DRAKE HALL	Staffs ST21 6LQ	340	300	Paul Newton
DURHAM	Durham DH1 3HU	995	948	Tim Allen
*‡EAST SUTTON PARK	Kent ME17 3DF	100	94	James Bourke
*‡EASTWOOD PARK	Glos GL12 8DB	363	330	Simon Beecroft
ELMLEY	Kent ME12 4DZ	1,175	1,152	Jim Carmichael
ERLESTOKE	Wilts SN10 5TU	524	514	Andy Rogers
†‡EXETER	Devon EX4 4EX	561	524	Jeannine Hendrick
FEATHERSTONE	Wolverhampton WV10 7PU	687	677	Deborah Butler
†‡FELTHAM	Middx TW13 4ND	594	496	Glenn Knight
FORD	W. Sussex BN18 0BX	524	512	Sharon Williams
‡FOREST BANK (private prison)	Manchester M27 8FB	1,460	1,434	Trevor Shortt
*FOSTON HALL	Derby DE65 5DN	345	290	Ken Kan
FRANKLAND	Durham DH1 5YD	844	834	Paddy Fox
FULL SUTTON	York YO41 1PS	616	585	Paul Foweather
GARTH	Preston PR26 8NE	773	795	Steve Lawrence
GARTREE	Leics LE16 7RP	708	710	Ian Telfer
†‡GLEN PARVA	Leicester LE18 4TN	728	554	Michael Wood
GRENDON/SPRING HILL	Bucks HP18 0TL	568	529	Jamie Bennett
‡GUYS MARSH	Dorset SP7 0AH	579	564	Duncan Burles
§HASLAR	Hampshire PO12 2AW	0	0	Paul Millett
HAVERIGG	Cumbria LA18 4NA	644	622	Tony Corcoran
HEWELL	Worcs B97 6QS	1,279	1,261	Nigel Atkinson
HIGH DOWN	Surrey SM2 5PJ	1,163	1,147	Ian Bickers
HIGHPOINT	Suffolk CB8 9YG	1,300	1,298	Nigel Smith
†‡HINDLEY	Lancs WN2 5TH	398	436	Peter Francis
‡HOLLESLEY BAY	Suffolk IP12 3JW	424	391	Declan Moore
*‡HOLLOWAY	London N7 0NU	591	518	Julia Killick
HOLME HOUSE	Stockton-on-Tees TS18 2QU	1,210	1,199	Jenny Mooney
‡HULL	Hull HU9 5LS	1,044	995	Norman Griffin
HUMBER	E. Yorks HU15	1,026	1,008	Ian Telfer
‡HUNTERCOMBE	Oxon RG9 5SB	430	427	Nigel Atkinson
ISIS	Thamesmead SE28 0NZ	622	614	Grahame Hawkings
ISLE OF WIGHT	Isle of Wight PO30 5RS	1,097	1,079	Andy Lattimore
KENNET	Merseyside L31 1HX	342	290	Steve Valentine
KIRKHAM	Lancs PR4 2RN	657	606	Graham Beck
KIRKLEVINGTON GRANGE	Cleveland TS15 9PA	283	274	Steve Robson
†‡LANCASTER FARMS	Lancaster LA1 3QZ	549	535	Derek Harrison
LEEDS	Leeds LS12 2TJ	1,212	1,189	Susan Kennedy
LEICESTER	Leicester LE2 7AJ	411	340	Ali Dodds
‡LEWES	E. Sussex BN7 1EA	722	649	Nigel Foote
LEYHILL	Glos GL12 8BT	527	494	Chantel King
LINCOLN	Lincoln LN2 4BD	729	643	Peter Wright
LINDHOLME	Doncaster DN7 6EE	1,010	990	Steve Robson
LITTLEHEY	Cambs PE28 0SR	1,219	1,210	David Taylor
LIVERPOOL	Liverpool L9 3DF	1,386	1,193	John Illingsworth
LONG LARTIN	Worcs WR11 8TZ	625	616	Nick Dann
*‡LOW NEWTON	Durham DH1 5YA	344	297	Alan Richer

Prison	Address	Capacity	Prisoners	Governor/Director
LOWDHAM GRANGE (private prison)	Notts NG14 7DA	920	914	Trish Mitchell
MAIDSTONE	Kent ME14 1UZ	600	599	Dave Atkinson
MANCHESTER	Manchester M60 9AH	1,286	1,090	Hannah Lane
‡MOORLAND/HATFIELD	Doncaster DN7 6BW	1,006	970	David Bamford
§MORTON HALL	Lincoln LN6 9PT	392	373	Karen Head
MOUNT	Herts HP3 0NZ	1,020	1,020	Steven Bradford
*‡NEW HALL	W. Yorks WF4 4XX	425	386	Diane Pellew
NORTH SEA CAMP	Lincs PE22 0QX	420	307	Paul Yates
‡NORTHUMBERLAND	Northumberland NE65 9XF	1,348	1,329	Matt Spencer
‡NORWICH	Norfolk NR1 4LU	769	737	Will Styles
NOTTINGHAM	Notts NG5 3AG	1,060	1,049	James Shanley
OAKWOOD	W. Midlands WV10 7QD	1,605	1,599	John McLaughlin
ONLEY	Warks CV23 8AP	747	720	Stephen Ruddy
†‡PARC (private prison)	Bridgend CF35 6AP	1,723	1,687	Janet Wallsgrove
‡PENTONVILLE	London N7 8TT	1,316	1,297	Kevin Reilly
*†PETERBOROUGH (private prison)	Peterborough PE3 7PD	1,252	1,188	Nick Leader
‡PORTLAND	Dorset DT5 1DL	531	486	James Lucas
PRESTON	Lancs PR1 5AB	790	707	Paul Holland
RANBY	Notts DN22 8EU	1,098	1,065	Susan Howard
RISLEY	Cheshire WA3 6BP	1,095	1,081	Jerry Spencer
‡ROCHESTER	Kent ME1 3QS	738	735	Andy Hudson
RYE HILL (private prison)	Warks CV23 8SZ	625	625	Dave Thompson, OBE
*SEND	Surrey GU23 7LJ	282	278	Dave Charity (acting)
STAFFORD	Stafford ST16 3AW	741	738	Bridie Oakes-Richards
STANDFORD HILL	Kent ME12 4AA	464	456	Sarah Coccia
STOCKEN	Leics LE15 7RD	713	683	Michael Wood
‡STOKE HEATH	Shropshire TF9 2JL	782	748	John Huntington
*‡STYAL	Cheshire SK9 4HR	485	471	John Hewitson
SUDBURY	Derbys DE6 5HW	600	447	Adrian Turner
SWALESIDE	Kent ME12 4AX	1,112	1,108	Sarah Coccia
†‡SWANSEA	Swansea SA1 3SR	455	429	Lauren Watson
‡SWINFEN HALL	Staffs WS14 9QS	594	578	Teresa Clarke
THAMESIDE	London SE28 0FJ	1,080	1,009	Guy Baulf
‡THORN CROSS	Cheshire WA4 4RL	381	339	Pia Sinha
USK/PRESCOED	Monmouthshire NP15 1XP	503	499	Steve Cross
VERNE	Dorset DT5 1EQ	580	491	David Ward
WAKEFIELD	W. Yorks WF2 9AG	730	722	Susan Howard
WANDSWORTH	London SW18 3HS	1,658	1,593	Kenny Brown
‡WARREN HILL	Suffolk IP12 3JW	212	157	Bev Bevan
WAYLAND	Norfolk IP25 6RL	1,015	1,000	Steve Rodford, OBE
WEALSTUN	W. Yorks LS23 7AZ	833	807	Andrew Dickinson
‡WERRINGTON	Stoke-on-Trent ST9 0DX	160	114	Babafemi Dada
‡WETHERBY	W. Yorks LS22 5ED	336	278	Sara Snell
WHATTON	Nottingham NG13 9FQ	841	838	Lynn Saunders
WHITEMOOR	Cambs PE15 0PR	458	447	Paul Cawkwell
WINCHESTER	Winchester SO22 5DF	685	681	David Rogers
WOODHILL	Bucks MK4 4DA	727	706	Rob Davis
WORMWOOD SCRUBS	London W12 0AE	1,279	1,241	Gary Monaghan
WYMOTT	Preston PR26 8LW	1,143	1,130	Terry Williams

SCOTLAND *as at July 2015*

Prison	Address	Average Daily	Maximum Number	Governor/Director
ADDIEWELL (private prison)	West Lothian EH55 8QA	700	710	Audrey Park
†BARLINNIE	Glasgow G33 2QX	1,303	1,433	Ian Whitehead
*†‡CORNTON VALE	Stirling FK9 5NU	213	264	Allister Purdie
†DUMFRIES	Dumfries DG2 9AX	174	186	Rhona Hotchkiss
†EDINBURGH	Edinburgh EH11 3LN	864	931	Teresa Medhurst
GLENOCHIL	Tullibody FK10 3AD	635	678	Nigel Ironside
GRAMPIAN	Aberdeenshire AB42 2YY	291	395	Jim Farish
†‡GREENOCK	Greenock PA16 9AH	235	248	William Stuart
*†INVERNESS	Inverness IV2 3HH	120	141	Andrew Hodge
†‡KILMARNOCK (private prison)	Kilmarnock KA1 5AA	501	518	Craig Thomson
LOW MOSS	Glasgow G64 2PZ	737	764	Sharanne Findley (acting)
OPEN ESTATE	Angus DD8 3QY	252	276	Jacqui Clinton
†PERTH	Perth PH2 8AT	643	689	Tom McMurchie (acting)
†‡POLMONT	Falkirk FK2 0AB	501	546	Sue Brookes
SHOTTS	Lanarkshire ML7 4LE	531	540	James Kerr

NORTHERN IRELAND *as at June 2015*

Prison	Address	Prisoners	Governor/Director
*†‡HYDEBANK WOOD	Belfast BT8 8NA	153	Austin Treacy
†§MAGHABERRY	Co. Antrim BT28 2NF	974	Pat Maguire
MAGILLIGAN	Co. Londonderry BT49 0LR	538	Alan Longwell

* Women's establishment or establishment with units for women; † Remand Centre or establishment with units for remand prisoners; ‡ Young Offender Institution or establishment with units for young offenders; § Immigration Removal Centre or establishment with units for immigration detainees

DEFENCE

The armed forces of the UK comprise the Royal Navy, the Army and the Royal Air Force (RAF). The Queen is Commander-in-Chief of all the armed forces. The Secretary of State for Defence is responsible for the formulation and content of defence policy and for providing the means by which it is conducted. The formal legal basis for the conduct of defence in the UK rests on a range of powers vested by statute and letters patent in the Defence Council, chaired by the Secretary of State for Defence. Beneath the ministers lies the top management of the Ministry of Defence (MoD), headed jointly by the Permanent Secretary and the Chief of Defence Staff. The Permanent Secretary is the government's principal civilian adviser on defence and has the primary responsibility for policy, finance, management and administration. The Permanent Secretary is also personally accountable to parliament for the expenditure of all public money allocated to defence purposes. The Chief of the Defence Staff is the professional head of the armed forces in the UK and the principal military adviser to the secretary of state and the government.

The Defence Board is the executive of the Defence Council. Chaired by the Permanent Secretary, it acts as the main executive board of the Ministry of Defence, providing senior level leadership and strategic management of defence.

The Central Staff, headed by the Vice-Chief of the Defence Staff and the Second Permanent Under-Secretary of State, is the policy core of the department. Defence Equipment and Support, headed by the Chief of Defence Materiel, is responsible for purchasing defence equipment and providing logistical support to the armed forces.

A permanent Joint Headquarters for the conduct of joint operations was set up at Northwood in 1996. The Joint Headquarters connects the policy and strategic functions of the MoD head office with the conduct of operations and is intended to strengthen the policy/executive division.

The UK pursues its defence and security policies through its membership of NATO (to which most of its armed forces are committed), the European Union, the Organisation for Security and Cooperation in Europe and the UN (see International Organisations section).

STRENGTH OF THE REGULAR ARMED FORCES

	Royal Navy	Army	RAF	All Services
1975 strength	76,200	167,100	95,000	338,300
2000 strength	42,850	110,050	54,720	207,620
2005 strength	39,940	109,290	51,870	201,100
2006 strength	39,390	107,730	48,730	195,850
2007 strength	38,850	106,340	45,480	190,670
2008 strength	38,560	104,980	43,370	186,910
2009 strength	38,340	106,700	43,560	188,600
2010 strength	38,730	108,920	44,050	191,700
2011 strength	37,660	106,240	42,460	186,360
2012 strength	35,540	104,250	40,000	179,800
2013 strength	33,960	99,730	37,030	170,710
2014 strength	33,330	91,070	35,230	159,630
2015 strength	32,740	87,060	33,930	153,720

Source: MoD – Defence Statistics (Tri-Service)

SERVICE PERSONNEL BY RANK AND GENDER 2015

	Males	Females
Officers	23,760	3,470
Other Ranks	114,410	12,080

Source: MoD – Defence Statistics (Tri-Service)

UK regular forces include trained and untrained personnel and nursing services, but exclude Gurkhas, full-time reserve service personnel, mobilised reservists and naval activated reservists. As at 1 April 2015 these groups provisionally numbered:

All Gurkhas	2,870
Full-time reserve service	3,750
Mobilised reservists	
Army	310
RAF	70
Naval activated reservists	30

Source: MoD – Defence Statistics (Tri-Service)

CIVILIAN PERSONNEL

2000 level	121,300
2001 level	118,200
2002 level	110,100
2003 level	107,600
2004 level	108,990
2005 level	107,680
2006 level	102,970
2007 level	95,790
2008 level	88,690
2009 level	86,620
2010 level	85,850
2011 level	83,060
2012 level	70,940
2013 level	65,400
2014 level	62,340
2015 level	58,200

Source: MoD – Defence Statistics (Tri-Service)

UK REGULAR FORCES: DEATHS

In 2014 there were a total of 68 deaths among the UK regular armed forces, of which 12 were serving in the Royal Navy and Royal Marines, 40 in the Army and 16 in the RAF. The largest single cause of death was land transport accidents, which accounted for 31 deaths (31 per cent of the total) in 2014. Cancer accounted for 15 deaths (22 per cent) and other accidents accounted for a further 12 deaths (18 per cent). For the first time since 2002, there were no deaths as a result of hostile action. Suicides and open verdicts accounted for six deaths.

NUMBER OF DEATHS AND MORTALITY RATES

	2010	2011	2012	2013	2014
Total number	187	132	130	86	68
Royal Navy	30	19	20	13	12
Army	136	98	95	63	40
RAF	21	15	15	10	16
Mortality rates per thousand					
Tri-service rate	0.97	0.69	0.72	0.50	0.42
Navy	0.77	0.52	0.59	0.42	0.35
Army	1.16	0.88	0.89	0.65	0.42
RAF	0.50	0.33	0.42	0.23	0.40

Source: MoD National Statistics

NUCLEAR FORCES
The Vanguard Class SSBN (ship submersible ballistic nuclear) provides the UK's strategic nuclear deterrent. Each Vanguard Class submarine is capable of carrying 16 Trident D5 missiles equipped with nuclear warheads.

There is a ballistic missile early warning system station at RAF Fylingdales in North Yorkshire.

ARMS CONTROL
The 1990 Conventional Armed Forces in Europe (CFE) Treaty, which commits all NATO and former Warsaw Pact members to limiting their holdings of five major classes of conventional weapons, has been adapted to reflect the changed geo-strategic environment and negotiations continue for its implementation. The Open Skies Treaty, which the UK signed in 1992 and entered into force in 2002, allows for the overflight of states parties by other states parties using unarmed observation aircraft.

The UN Convention on Certain Conventional Weapons (as amended 2001), which bans or restricts the use of specific types of weapons that are considered to cause unnecessary or unjustifiable suffering to combatants, or to affect civilians indiscriminately, was ratified by the UK in 1995. In 1968 the UK signed and ratified the Nuclear Non-Proliferation Treaty, which came into force in 1970 and was indefinitely and unconditionally extended in 1995. In 1996 the UK signed the Comprehensive Nuclear Test Ban Treaty and ratified it in 1998. The UK is a party to the 1972 Biological and Toxin Weapons Convention, which provides for a worldwide ban on biological weapons, and the 1993 Chemical Weapons Convention, which came into force in 1997 and provides for a verifiable worldwide ban on chemical weapons.

DEFENCE BUDGET DEPARTMENTAL EXPENDITURE
LIMITS £ billion

	2015–16
Resource DEL	28.1
Capital DEL	6.8
Total	34.9

Source: HM Treasury – Summer Budget 2015 (Crown copyright)

MINISTRY OF DEFENCE
Main Building, Whitehall, London SW1A 2HB
T 020-7218 9000
W www.gov.uk/government/organisations/ministry-of-defence

Secretary of State for Defence, Rt. Hon. Michael Fallon, MP
Parliamentary Private Secretary, Graham Evans, MP
Private Secretary, Luke Dearden
Special Advisers, Ben Mascall; James Wild
Minister of State (Defence Procurement), Philip Dunne, MP
Parliamentary Private Secretary, Oliver Colville, MP
Minister of State (Armed Forces), Penny Mordaunt, MP
Parliamentary Private Secretary, Oliver Colville, MP
Parliamentary Under-Secretary of State and Minister for
    Defence, Personnel and Veterans, Mark Lancaster, TD, MP
Parliamentary Under-Secretary of State and Minister for
    Reserves, Julian Brazier, MP
Private Secretary, Emma Frost
Parliamentary Under-Secretary of State and Lords Spokesman,
    Rt. Hon. Earl Howe

CHIEFS OF STAFF
Chief of the Defence Staff, Gen. Sir Nicholas Houghton, GCB, CBE, ADC
Vice Chief of the Defence Staff, Air Chief Marshal Sir Stuart Peach, KCB, CBE, ADC
Chief of the Naval Staff and First Sea Lord, Adm. Sir George Zambellas, KCB, DSC, ADC
Second Sea Lord, Rear-Adm. (Simon) Jonathan Woodcock, OBE
Chief of the General Staff, Gen. Sir Nicholas Carter, KCB, CBE, DSO, ADC
Assistant Chief of the General Staff, Maj.-Gen. David Cullen, OBE
Chief of the Air Staff, Air Chief Marshal Sir Andrew Pulford, KCB, CBE, ADC
Assistant Chief of the Air Staff, Air Vice-Marshal Richard Knighton

SENIOR OFFICIALS
Permanent Under-Secretary of State, Jon Thompson
Chief of Defence Materiel, Sir Bernard Gray
Chief Scientific Adviser, Prof. Vernon Gibson, FRS
Director-General Finance, Louise Tulett

THE DEFENCE COUNCIL
The Defence Council is chaired by the Secretary of State, and comprises the other ministers, the Permanent Under-Secretary, the Chief of Defence Staff and senior service officers and officials who head the armed services and the department's major corporate functions. It provides the formal legal basis for the conduct of UK defence through a range of powers vested in it by statute and letters patent.

THE DEFENCE BOARD
Chaired by the Secretary of State, the Defence Board is the main corporate board of the MoD, providing senior level leadership and strategic management of defence. The current membership of the Defence Board is: the Secretary of State; the Minister of State for Defence Procurement; the Permanent Secretary (the most senior civilian in the MoD); the Chief of Defence Staff (the professional head of the armed forces); the Vice-Chief of the Defence Staff (the chief operating officer for the armed forces element of defence business); the Chief of Defence Materiel (the head of Defence Equipment and Support); the Director-General Finance; and three non-executive members.

CENTRAL STAFF
Vice-Chief of the Defence Staff, Air Chief Marshal Sir Stuart Peach, KCB, CBE, ADC

JOINT FORCES COMMAND
Commander Joint Forces Command, Gen. Sir Richard Barrons, KCB, CBE, ADC
Chief of Joint Operations, Lt.-Gen. John Lorimer, MBE, DSO
Chief of Staff (Operations), Air Vice-Marshal Stuart Atha, DSO
Chief of Staff HQ, Rear-Adm. Paul Bennett, OBE

FLEET COMMAND
First Sea Lord, Adm. Sir George Zambellas, KCB, DSC, ADC
Fleet Commander and Deputy Chief of Naval Staff, Vice-Adm. Sir Philip Jones, KCB

NAVAL HOME COMMAND
Second Sea Lord, Rear-Adm. (Simon) Jonathan Woodcock, OBE

LAND FORCES
Commander Land Forces, Lt.-Gen. James Everard, CBE
Chief of Staff Land Forces, Maj.-Gen. Timothy Robinson, CBE

AIR COMMAND
Deputy Commander Operations, Air Marshal Greg Bagwell, CB, CBE
Deputy Commander Capability and Air Member for Personnel and Capability, Air Marshal Sir Barry North, OBE

DEFENCE EQUIPMENT AND SUPPORT
Chief of Defence Materiel, Sir Bernard Gray
Chief of Materiel (Fleet), Vice-Adm. Simon Lister, CB, OBE
Chief of Materiel (Land), Lt.-Gen. Sir Christopher Deverell, KCB, MBE
Chief of Materiel (Air), Air Marshal Sir Simon Bollom, CB

EXECUTIVE AGENCIES

DEFENCE ELECTRONICS AND COMPONENTS AGENCY
Welsh Road, Deeside, Flintshire CH5 2LS T 01244-847745
E decainfo@deca.mod.uk
W www.gov.uk/government/organisations/defence-electronics-and-components-agency
Director Support Services, Ian Doughty

DEFENCE SCIENCE AND TECHNOLOGY LABORATORY
Porton Down, Salisbury, Wiltshire SP4 0JQ T 01980-613000
E centralenquiries@dstl.gov.uk
W www.gov.uk/government/organisations/defence-science-and-technology-laboratory
Chief Executive, Jonathan Lyle

UK HYDROGRAPHIC OFFICE
Admiralty Way, Taunton, Somerset TA1 2DN T 01823-337900
E customerservices@ukho.gov.uk
W www.gov.uk/government/organisations/uk-hydrographic-office
Chief Executive, John Humphrey

ARMED FORCES TRAINING AND RECRUITMENT
Flag Officer Sea Training (FOST) is responsible for all Royal Navy and Royal Fleet Auxiliary operational sea training. FOST's International Defence Training provides the focal point for all aspects of naval training. Training is divided into five streams: Naval Core Training (responsible for new entry, command, leadership and management training); Royal Marine; Submarine; Surface and Aviation.

The Army Recruiting and Training Division (ARTD) is responsible for the four key areas of army training: soldier initial training, at the School of Infantry or at one of the army's four other facilities; officer initial training at the Royal Military Academy Sandhurst; trade training at one of the army's specialist facilities; and resettlement training for those about to leave the army. Trade training facilities include: the Armour Centre; the Infantry Battle School; the Infantry Training Centre, Catterick; the Royal School of Military Engineering and the Army Aviation Centre.

The Royal Air Force No. 22 (Training) Group exists to recruit RAF personnel and provide trained specialist personnel to the armed forces as a whole, such as providing the army air corps with trained helicopter pilots. The group is split into five areas: RAF College Cranwell; the Air Cadet Organisation (ACO); the Directorate of Flying Training (DFT); the Directorate of Ground Training; and the Defence College of Technical Training.

The Defence College of Technical Training provides technical training to all three services and includes the Defence School of Aeronautical Engineering (DSAE); the Defence School of Communications and Information Systems (DSCIS); the Defence School of Electronic and Mechanical Engineering (DSEME); and the Defence School of Marine Engineering (DSMarE).

USEFUL WEBSITES
W www.royalnavy.mod.uk
W www.army.mod.uk
W www.raf.mod.uk

THE ROYAL NAVY

In Order of Seniority

LORD HIGH ADMIRAL OF THE UNITED KINGDOM
HRH The Prince Philip, Duke of Edinburgh, KG, KT, OM, GBE, AC, QSO, PC, *apptd* 2011

ADMIRALS OF THE FLEET
HRH The Prince Philip, Duke of Edinburgh, KG, KT, OM, GBE, AC, QSO, PC, *apptd* 1953
Sir Edward Ashmore, GCB, DSC, *apptd* 1977
Sir Benjamin Bathurst, GCB, *apptd* 1995
HRH The Prince of Wales, KG, KT, GCB, OM, AK, QSO, PC, ADC, *apptd* 2012
Lord Boyce, KG, GCB, OBE, *apptd* 2014

ADMIRALS
(Former Chiefs or Vice Chiefs of Defence Staff and First Sea Lords who remain on the active list)
Slater, Sir Jock, GCB, LVO, *apptd* 1991
Abbott, Sir Peter, GBE, KCB, *apptd* 1995
Essenhigh, Sir Nigel, GCB, *apptd* 1998
West of Spithead, Lord, GCB, DSC, PC, *apptd* 2000

Band, Sir Jonathon, GCB, *apptd* 2002
Stanhope, Sir Mark, GCB, OBE, *apptd* 2004

ADMIRALS
HRH The Princess Royal, KG, KT, GCVO, QSO *(Cdre-in-Chief HM Naval Base Portsmouth)*
Zambellas, Sir George, KCB, DSC, ADC *(First Sea Lord and Chief of Naval Staff)*

VICE-ADMIRALS
HRH The Duke of York, KG, GCVO, ADC *(Adm. of the Sea Cadet Corps and Cdre-in-Chief Fleet Air Arm)*
Jones, Sir Philip, KCB *(Fleet Commander, Deputy Chief of Naval Staff and Chief Naval Warfare Officer)*
Hudson, Peter, CB, CBE *(Cdr Maritime Command)*
Corder, Ian, CB *(UK Military Representative to NATO and the EU)*
Lister, Simon, CB, OBE *(Chief of Materiel (Fleet), Chief of Fleet Support to the Navy Board and Chief Naval Engineering Officer)*
Potts, Duncan, CB *(Director-General Joint Force Development and Director Defence Academy)*
Woodcock, (Simon) Jonathan, OBE *(Second Sea Lord)*

REAR-ADMIRALS

Parr, Matthew, CB *(Cdr (Operations) and Rear-Adm. Submarines (Head of Fighting Arm))*

Fraser, Timothy, CB *(Assistant Chief of Defence Staff (Capability and Force Design))*

Parker, Henry *(Director Ship Acquisition and Deputy Director Ships)*

Beverstock, Mark *(Assistant Chief of Defence Staff (Nuclear and Chemical, Biological))*

Morse, James *(Assistant Chief of Naval Staff (Capability) and Controller of the Navy)*

Lowe, Timothy *(National Hydrographer and Deputy Chief Executive (Hydrography))*

Williams, Simon *(Naval Secretary and Assistant Chief of Naval Staff (Personnel))*

Bennett, Paul, OBE *(Chief of Staff Joint Forces Command)*

Wareham, Michael *(Director Submarines)*

Cree, Malcolm *(Chief of Staff (Integrated Change Programme))*

Ancona, Simon *(Assistant Chief of Defence Staff (Defence Engagement))*

Kingwell, John *(Director Concepts and Doctrine)*

Mackay, Graeme *(Director Carrier Strike)*

Clink, John, OBE *(Flag Officer Sea Training)*

Burton, Alexander *(Assistant Chief of Naval Staff (Surface Ships))*

Beckett, Keith CBE *(Chief Strategic Systems Executive)*

Radakin, Antony *(Cdr UK Maritime Forces and Rear-Adm. Surface Ships (Head of Fighting Arm))*

Stokes, Richard *(Assistant Chief of Naval Staff (Support))*

Weale, John, OBE *(Flag Officer Scotland and Northern Ireland and Assistant Chief of Naval Staff (Submarines))*

Blount, Keith, OBE *(Assistant Chief of Naval Staff (Aviation, Amphibious Capability and Carriers) and Rear-Adm. Fleet Air Arm (Head of Fighting Arm))*

McAlpine, Paul, OBE *(Deputy Cdr Strike Force NATO)*

Hine, Nicholas *(Assistant Chief of Naval Staff (Policy))*

MEDICAL

Walker, Alasdair, OBE, QHS *(Surgeon Rear-Adm., Director Medical Policy and Operational Capability and Medical Director General (Naval))*

ROYAL MARINES

CAPTAIN-GENERAL

HRH The Prince Philip, Duke of Edinburgh, KG, KT, OM, GBE, AC, QSO, PC

LIEUTENANT-GENERAL

Messenger, Gordon, CB, DSO*, OBE *(Deputy Chief of Defence Staff (Military Strategic Operations))*

Davis, Edward, CB, CBE *(Deputy Cdr Land Command, Izmir)*

MAJOR-GENERAL

Smith, Martin, MBE *(Cdr UK Amphibious Forces and Commandant-General Royal Marines)*

The Royal Marines were formed in 1664 and are part of the Naval Service. Their primary purpose is to conduct amphibious and land warfare. The principal operational units are:

• Three Commando Brigade, an amphibious all-arms brigade trained to operate in arduous environments (a core element of the UK's Joint Rapid Reaction Force). The commando units, 40 Commando, 42 Commando and 45 Commando each have a strength of around 700 and are based in Taunton, Plymouth and Arbroath, respectively. 43 Commando Fleet Protection Group is over 500 strong

and is based at HM Naval Base Clyde on the west coast of Scotland.

• 1 Assault Group, which has its headquarters located in Devonport, Plymouth is responsible for ten landing craft training squadron at Poole, Dorset and 11 amphibious trials and training squadron at Instow, Devon

The Royal Marines also provide detachments for warships and land-based naval parties as required.

ROYAL MARINES RESERVES (RMR)

The Royal Marines Reserve is a commando-trained volunteer force with the principal role, when mobilised, of supporting the Royal Marines. The RMR consists of approximately 600 trained ranks who are distributed between the four RMR centres in the UK. Approximately 10 per cent of the RMR are working with the regular corps on long-term attachments within all of the Royal Marines regular units.

OTHER PARTS OF THE NAVAL SERVICE

FLEET AIR ARM

The Fleet Air Arm (FAA) provides the Royal Navy with a multi-role aviation combat capability able to operate autonomously at short notice worldwide in all environments, over the sea and land. The FAA numbers some 6,200 people, which comprises 11.5 per cent of the total Royal Naval strength. It operates some 200 combat aircraft and more than 50 support/training aircraft.

ROYAL FLEET AUXILIARY SERVICE (RFA)

The Royal Fleet Auxiliary Service is a civilian-manned flotilla of 13 ships owned by the MoD. Its primary role is to supply the Royal Navy and host nations while at sea with fuel, ammunition, food and spares, enabling them to maintain operations away from their home ports. It also provides amphibious support and secure sea transport for military units and their equipment. The ships routinely support and embark Royal Naval Air Squadrons.

ROYAL NAVAL RESERVE (RNR)

The Royal Naval Reserve is an integral part of the Naval Service. It is a part-time force of 2,300 trained men and women who are deployed with the Royal Navy in times of tension, humanitarian crisis or conflict.

The Royal Naval Reserve has 18 units throughout the UK; 17 of these provide initial training while one other specialist unit, HMS *Ferret,* provides intelligence training. Basic training is provided at HMS *Raleigh,* Torpoint in Cornwall for ratings and at the Britannia Royal Naval College, Dartmouth in Devon for officers; both these and most other RNR courses are of two weeks' duration or less.

QUEEN ALEXANDRA'S ROYAL NAVAL NURSING SERVICE

The first nursing sisters were appointed to naval hospitals in 1884 and the Queen Alexandra's Royal Naval Nursing Service (QARNNS) gained its current title in 1902. Nursing ratings were introduced in 1960 and men were integrated into the service in 1982; QARNNS recruits qualified nurses as both officers and ratings, and student nurse training can be undertaken in the service.

Patron, HRH Princess Alexandra, the Hon. Lady Ogilvy, KG, GCVO

Head of the Naval Nursing Service, Capt. Steve Spencer, QHNS, QARNNS

HM FLEET
as at September 2015

Submarines

Vanguard Class	Vanguard, Vengeance, Victorious, Vigilant
Trafalgar Class	Talent, Torbay, Trenchant, Triumph
Astute Class	Astute, Ambush, Artful
Landing Platform Helicopter	Ocean
Landing Platform Dock	Albion, Bulwark

Destroyers

Type 45	Daring, Dauntless, Defender, Diamond, Dragon, Duncan

Frigates

Type 23	Argyll, Iron Duke, Kent, Lancaster, Monmouth, Montrose, Northumberland, Portland, Richmond, St Albans, Somerset, Sutherland, Westminster

Mine Warfare Vessels

Hunt Class	Atherstone, Brocklesby, Cattistock, Chiddingfold, Hurworth, Ledbury, Middleton, Quorn
Sandown Class	Bangor, Blyth, Grimsby, Pembroke, Penzance, Ramsey, Shoreham

Patrol Vessels

Archer Class P2000 Training Boats	Archer, Biter, Blazer, Charger, Dasher, Example, Exploit, Explorer, Express, Puncher, Pursuer, Raider, Ranger, Smiter, Tracker, Trumpeter
Gibraltar Squadron 16m Fast Patrol Boats	Sabre, Scimitar
River Class	Clyde, Mersey, Severn, Tyne

Survey Vessels

Ice Patrol Ships	Protector
Ocean Survey Vessel	Scott
Coastal Survey Vessel	Gleaner
Multi-Role Survey Vessels	Echo, Enterprise

ROYAL FLEET AUXILIARY

Landing Ship Dock (Auxiliary)	RFA Cardigan Bay, RFA Mounts Bay, RFA Lyme Bay
Wave Class	RFA Wave Knight, RFA Wave Ruler
Rover Class	RFA Black Rover, RFA Gold Rover
Leaf Class	RFA Orangeleaf
Fort Class	RFA Fort Austin, RFA Fort Rosalie, RFA Fort Victoria
Forward Repair Ship	RFA Diligence
Joint Casualty Treatment Ship/Maritime Afloat Training Capability	RFA Argus

---

THE ARMY

In Order of Seniority

THE QUEEN

FIELD MARSHALS
HRH The Prince Philip, Duke of Edinburgh, KG, KT, OM, GBE, AC, QSO, PC, *apptd* 1953
Lord Bramall, KG, GCB, OBE, MC, *apptd* 1982
Lord Vincent of Coleshill, GBE, KCB, DSO, *apptd* 1991

Sir John Chapple, GCB, CBE, *apptd* 1992
HRH The Duke of Kent, KG, GCMG, GCVO, ADC, *apptd* 1993
Lord Inge, KG, GCB, PC, *apptd* 1994
HRH The Prince of Wales, KG, KT, GCB, OM, AK, QSO, PC, ADC, *apptd* 2012
Lord Guthrie of Craigiebank, GCB, LVO, OBE, *apptd* 2012
Lord Walker of Aldringham, GCB, CMG, CBE, *apptd* 2014

FORMER CHIEFS OF STAFF
Gen. Sir Roger Wheeler, GCB, CBE, *apptd* 1997
Gen. Sir Mike Jackson, GCB, CBE, DSO, *apptd* 2003
Gen. Sir Timothy Granville-Chapman, GBE, KCB, *apptd* 2005
Gen. Lord Dannatt, GCB, CBE, MC, *apptd* 2006
Gen. Lord Richards of Herstmonceux, GCB, CBE, DSO, ADC, *apptd* 2009
Gen. Sir Peter Wall, GCB, CBE, *apptd* 2010

GENERALS
Houghton, Sir Nicholas, GCB, CBE, ADC *(Chief of the Defence Staff)*
Barrons, Sir Richard, KCB, CBE, ADC *(Cdr Joint Force Command)*
Bradshaw Sir Adrian, KCB, OBE *(Deputy Supreme Allied Cdr Europe)*
Carter, Sir Nicholas, KCB, CBE, DSO, ADC *(Chief of the General Staff)*

LIEUTENANT-GENERALS
Deverell, Sir Christopher, KCB, MBE *(Chief of Materiel (Land) and Quartermaster General)*
Berragan, Sir Gerald, KBE, CB *(pending retirement)*
Everard, J., CBE *(Cdr Land Forces)*
Gregory, A., CB *(Chief of Defence People)*
Lorimer, J., MBE, DSO *(Chief of Joint Operations, Permanent Joint HQ)*
Evans, T., CBE, DSO *(Cdr Allied Rapid Reaction Corps)*
Jones, P., CB, CBE *(Chief of Staff Supreme Allied Command Transformation)*
Poffley, M., OBE *(Deputy Chief of the General Staff)*
Beckett, T., CBE *(Defence Senior Adviser to the Middle East)*
Bashall, J., CBE *(Cdr Personnel and Support Command)*
Radford, T., OBE, DSO *(Deputy Cdr, Resolute Support)*

MAJOR-GENERALS
Foster, A., CMG, MBE *(Deputy Military Adviser UNHQ)*
Conway, M., CB *(pending retirement)*
Jaques, P., CBE *(Director Land Equipment, Defence Equipment and Support)*
Norton, Sir George, KCVO, CBE *(Deputy Cdr NATO Rapid Deployment Corps, Naples)*
Ashmore, N., OBE *(Military Secretary / General Officer Scotland)*

Cullen, D., CB, OBE *(Assistant Chief of the General Staff)*
Storrie, A., CBE *(Deputy Commandant, Royal College of Defence Studies)*
Pope, N., CBE *(Director Capability and Master of Signals)*
Rowan, J., OBE, QHS *(Director Army Medical Services)*
Carleton-Smith, M., CBE *(Director Strategy)*
Free, J., CBE *(Commandant Joint Services Command and Staff College)*
Nugee, R., CBE *(Assistant Chief of Defence Staff (Personnel Capability) and Defence Services Secretary)*
Weighill, R., CBE *(pending retirement)*
Munro, R., CBE, TD *(Deputy Cdr Land Forces (Reserves))*
Chiswell, J., CBE, MC *(appointment witheld)*
Smyth-Osbourne, E., CBE *(GOC London District and Maj.-Gen. Commanding the Household Division)*
Urch, T., CBE *(GOC Force Troops Command)*
Cripwell, R., CBE *(Head of British Defence Staff (USA)))*
Sanders, P., CBE, DSO *(GOC 3rd (UK) Division)*
Crackett, J., CB, TD *(Assistant Chief of Defence Staff (Reserves and Cadets))*
Hockenhull, J., OBE *(Director DC13, Defence Intelligence Staff)*
Nitsch, R., CBE *(Director Personnel)*
Skeates, S., CBE *(Standing Joint Force Cdr)*
Tickell, C., CBE *(Director Army Recruiting and Training)*
Semple, R., CBE *(Director Information)*
Felton, R., CBE *(Cdr Joint Helicopter Command)*
Talbot Rice, R. *(Head of Armoured Vehicle Programmes)*
Bathurst, B., CBE *(pending assignment)*
Dickinson, A., CBE *(Director Army Basing and Infrastructure)*
Welch, N., OBE *(Chief of Staff, HQ Allied Rapid Reaction Corps)*
Fattorini, C., *(Senior British Loan Service Officer (Oman))*
Coulter, D., QHC, CF *(Revd Doctor – Chaplain-General)*
Hooper, I. *(Director Service Operations, Information Systems and Services)*
Lawrence, J., CBE *(Director Joint Warfare)*
Patterson, J. *(Director Capability, Joint Forces Command)*
Bruce, R., DSO *(Deputy Cdr Combined Joint Task Force Kuwait)*
Fay, A., *(Assistant Chief of Defence Staff (Logistic Operations))*
Gaunt, M., *(Director Support)*
Hill, G., CBE *(GOC 1st (UK) Division)*
Robinson, T., CBE *(Chief of Staff Land Forces)*
Bramble, W., CBE *(Deputy Adviser Ministry of Interior, HQ Resolute Support)*
Stanford, R., MBE *(GOC Support Command)*
Cave, I., *(Deputy Chief of Staff (Plans), Joint Force Command Naples)*
Nanson, P., CBE *(Commandant Royal Military Academy Sandhurst)*

CONSTITUTION OF THE ARMY

The army consists of the Regular Army, the Regular Reserve and the Territorial Army (TA). It is commanded by the Chief of the General Staff, who is the professional Head of Service and Chair of the Executive Committee of the Army Board, which provides overall strategic policy and direction to the Commander Land Forces (formerly Commander-in-Chief, Land Forces). There are four subordinate commands that report to the Commander Land Forces: the Field Army; Support Command, headed by the Adjutant General; Force Development and Capability Command and the Joint Helicopter Command. The army is divided into functional arms and services, subdivided into regiments and corps (listed below in order of precedence). During 2008, as part of the Future Army Structure (FAS) reform programme, the infantry was re-structured into large multi-battalion regiments, which involved amalgamations and changes in

title for some regiments. The 2010 Strategic Defence and Security Review laid out the commitments expected of the UK Armed Forces and, as a result, Army 2020 was created to replace FAS. The main changes at divisional, brigade and unit level occurred largely between mid-2014 and mid-2015.

All enquiries with regard to records of serving personnel (Regular and Territorial Army) should be directed to The Army Personnel Centre Help Desk, Kentigern House, 65 Brown Street, Glasgow G2 8EX T 0845-600 9663. Enquirers should note that the Army is governed in the release of personal information by various acts of parliament.

ORDER OF PRECEDENCE OF CORPS AND REGIMENTS OF THE BRITISH ARMY

ARMS

HOUSEHOLD CAVALRY
The Life Guards
The Blues and Royals (Royal Horse Guards and 1st Dragoons)

ROYAL HORSE ARTILLERY
(when on parade, the Royal Horse Artillery take precedence over the Household Cavalry)

ROYAL ARMOURED CORPS
1st the Queen's Dragoon Guards
The Royal Scots Dragoon Guards (Carabiniers and Greys)
The Royal Dragoon Guards
The Queen's Royal Hussars (The Queen's Own and Royal Irish)
The Royal Lancers
The King's Royal Hussars
The Light Dragoons
Royal Tank Regiment

ROYAL REGIMENT OF ARTILLERY
(with the exception of the Royal Horse Artillery (*see* above))

CORPS OF ROYAL ENGINEERS

ROYAL CORPS OF SIGNALS

REGIMENTS OF FOOT GUARDS
Grenadier Guards
Coldstream Guards
Scots Guards
Irish Guards
Welsh Guards

REGIMENTS OF INFANTRY
The Royal Regiment of Scotland
The Princess of Wales's Royal Regiment (Queen and Royal Hampshire's)
The Duke of Lancaster's Regiment (King's, Lancashire and Border)
The Royal Regiment of Fusiliers
The Royal Anglian Regiment
The Rifles
The Yorkshire Regiment
The Mercian Regiment
The Royal Welsh
The Royal Irish Regiment
The Parachute Regiment
The Royal Gurkha Rifles

SPECIAL AIR SERVICE

ARMY AIR CORPS

SERVICES

ROYAL ARMY CHAPLAINS' DEPARTMENT
THE ROYAL LOGISTIC CORPS
ROYAL ARMY MEDICAL CORPS
CORPS OF ROYAL ELECTRICAL AND MECHANICAL
    ENGINEERS
ADJUTANT-GENERAL'S CORPS
ROYAL ARMY VETERINARY CORPS
SMALL ARMS SCHOOL CORPS
ROYAL ARMY DENTAL CORPS
INTELLIGENCE CORPS
ROYAL ARMY PHYSICAL TRAINING CORPS
QUEEN ALEXANDRA'S ROYAL ARMY NURSING
    CORPS
CORPS OF ARMY MUSIC

THE ROYAL MONMOUTHSHIRE ROYAL ENGINEERS
    (MILITIA) (THE ARMY RESERVE)

THE HONOURABLE ARTILLERY COMPANY (THE
    ARMY RESERVE)

REST OF THE ARMY RESERVE

THE ARMY RESERVE
The Army Reserve (formerly the Territorial Army (TA)) is
part of the UK's reserve land forces and provides support
to the regular army at home and overseas. The Army Reserve
is divided into three types of unit: national, regional, and
sponsored. Army Reserve soldiers serving in regional units

complete a minimum of 27 days training a year, comprising
some evenings, weekends and an annual two-week camp.
National units normally specialise in a specific role or trade,
such as logistics, IT, communications or medical services.
Members of national units have a lower level of training
commitment and complete 19 days training a year. Sponsored
reserves are individuals who will serve, as members of the
workforce of a company contracted to the MoD, in a
military capacity and have agreed to accept a reserve liability
to be called up for active service in a crisis. In 2012 the
Secretary of State for Defence issued a consultation paper
Future Reserves 2020: Delivering the Nation's Security Together,
which outlined plans to invest an additional £1.8bn in the
Reserve Forces over the next ten years, for the Reserve Forces
to be more integrated with the regular forces and to have a
more significant role within the armed forces as a whole.

**QUEEN ALEXANDRA'S ROYAL ARMY
NURSING CORPS**
The Queen Alexandra's Royal Army Nursing Corps
(QARANC) was founded in 1902 as Queen Alexandra's
Imperial Military Nursing Service and gained its present title
in 1949. The QARANC has trained nurses for the register
since 1950 and also trains and employs health care assistants
up to diploma level 3 in Health and Social Care. The
corps also recruits qualified nurses as officers and other ranks
and in 1992 male nurses already serving in the army were
transferred to the QARANC.
Colonel-in-Chief, HRH The Countess of Wessex, GCVO
Colonels Commandant, Col. Sue Bush; Col. Jane Davis, OBE,
    QVRM, TD

THE ROYAL AIR FORCE

In Order of Seniority

THE QUEEN
MARSHALS OF THE ROYAL AIR FORCE
HRH The Prince Philip, Duke of Edinburgh, KG, KT, OM,
    GBE, AC, QSO, PC, *apptd* 1953
HRH The Prince of Wales, KG, KT, GCB, OM, AK, QSO,
    PC, ADC, *apptd* 2012

FORMER CHIEFS OF THE AIR STAFF

MARSHALS OF THE ROYAL AIR FORCE
Sir Michael Beetham, GCB, CBE, DFC, AFC, *apptd* 1982
Sir Keith Williamson, GCB, AFC, *apptd* 1985
Lord Craig of Radley, GCB, OBE, *apptd* 1988
Lord Stirrup, KG, GCB, AFC, *apptd* 2003

AIR CHIEF MARSHALS
Sir Michael Graydon, GCB, CBE, *apptd* 1991
Sir Richard Johns, GCB, KCVO, OBE, *apptd* 1994
Sir Peter Squire, GCB, DFC, AFC, *apptd* 1999
Sir Glenn Torpy, GCB, CBE, DSO, *apptd* 2006
Sir Stephen Dalton, GCB, *apptd* 2009

AIR RANK LIST

AIR CHIEF MARSHALS
Peach, Sir Stuart, KCB, CBE, ADC *(Vice Chief of the Defence
    Staff)*
Pulford, Sir Andrew, KCB, CBE, ADC *(Chief of the AIr Staff)*

AIR MARSHALS
Harper, Sir Christopher, KBE *(Director-General International
    Military Staff)*
Garwood, R., CB, CBE, DFC *(Director-General of the
    Military Aviation Authority)*
Hillier, Sir Stephen, KCB, CBE, DFC *(Deputy Chief of the
    Defence Staff (Military Capability))*
Bollom, S., CB *(Chief of Materiel (Air) and Air Member for
    Materiel)*
Bagwell, G., CB, CBE *(Deputy Cdr Operations and Air
    Member for Operations)*
Stacey, G., CB, MBE *(Deputy Cdr Joint Force Command,
    Brunssum)*
North, Sir Barry, KCB, OBE *(Deputy Cdr Capability and Air
    Member for Personnel and Capability)*
Evans, C., CB, QHP *(Surgeon-General HQ Joint Medical
    Command)*
Osborne, P., CBE *(Chief of Defence Intelligence)*

AIR VICE-MARSHALS
Irvine, L., CB *(Director RAF Legal Services)*
Young, J., CB, OBE *(Director Technical, Defence Equipment
    and Support)*
Chaffey, J., QHC *(Chaplain Chief and Director-General
    Chaplaincy Services)*
Howard, G., CB *(Assistant Chief of the Defence Staff Logistics
    Operations)*
Atha, S., CB, DSO *(Chief of Staff (Operations), Permanent
    Joint HQ)*
Morrison, I., CBE *(Director-General, Saudi Armed Forces
    Project)*

Clark, M. *(Director Technical in the Military Aviation Authority)*

Farnell, G., CB, OBE *(General-Manager, NATO Eurofighter and Typhoon Management Agency)*

Atherton, P., OBE *(Director Operations, Military Aviation Authority)*

Brecht, M. *(Chief of Staff Capability, Air Command)*

Stringer, E., CBE *(Assistant Chief of the Defence Staff (Operations))*

Bishop, T., OBE *(Air Officer Commanding No. 38 Group)*

Evans, S., CBE *(Senior British Military Adviser to the United States Central Command, Tampa)*

Gray, S., OBE *(Director Combat Air, Defence Equipment and Support)*

Turner, A., CBE *(Air Officer Commanding No. 22 Group and Chief of Staff Training)*

Stubbs, D., OBE *(Chief of Staff Personnel and Air Secretary)*

West, M., CBE *(Director of Projects and Programme Delivery, Defence Infrastructure Organisation)*

Waterfall, G., CBE *(Air Officer Commanding No.1 Group)*

Neal, M., OBE *(Director Service Design, Information Services and Systems)*

Broadbridge, Hon. R., QHS *(Director Healthcare Delivery and Training)*

Wigston, M., CBE *(Commander British Forces Cyprus and Administer of the Sovereign Base Area)*

Knighton, R. *(Assistant Chief of the Air Staff)*

Parker, G., OBE *(Air Officer Commanding No. 2 Group)*

CONSTITUTION OF THE RAF

The RAF consists of a single command, Air Command, based at RAF High Wycombe. RAF Air Command was formed on 1 April 2007 from the amalgamation of Strike Command and Personnel and Training Command.

Air Command consists of three groups, each organised around specific operational duties. No. 1 Group is the coordinating organisation for the tactical fast-jet forces responsible for attack, offensive support and air defence operations. No. 2 Group provides air combat support including air transport and air-to-air refuelling; intelligence surveillance; targeting and reconnaissance; and force protection. No. 22 (Training) Group recruits personnel and provides trained specialist personnel to the RAF, as well as to the Royal Navy and the Army (*see also* Armed Forces Training and Recruitment).

RAF EQUIPMENT
AIRCRAFT

Combat Aircraft	Lightening II, Tornado GR4, Typhoon FGR4
Training Aircraft	Hawk T1, Hawk T2, King Air B200, Tucano T1, Tutor T1, Vigilant T1, Viking T1
Surveillance Aircraft	Reaper MQ9A RPAS, RC-135W Rivet Joint, Sentinel R1, E-3D Sentry AEW1, Shadow R1

HELICOPTERS

Helicopters	Chinook, Griffin HAR2, Merlin HC3, Puma HC2, Sea King HAR3/3A
Training Helicopters	Griffin HT1, Squirrel HT1

ROYAL AUXILIARY AIR FORCE

The Auxiliary Air Force was formed in 1924 to train an elite corps of civilians to serve their country in flying squadrons in their spare time. In 1947 the force was awarded the prefix 'royal' in recognition of its distinguished war service and the Sovereign's Colour for the RAuxAF was presented in 1989. The RAuxAF continues to recruit civilians who undertake military training in their spare time, with a standard minimum commitment of 27 days a year. With the amendments to the reserve service made under the Defence Reform Act 2014, reservists can now be employed to support the RAF across the full spectrum of military tasks. There are currently 27 squadrons with the RAuxAF, with a total establishment of just under 3,200 posts, with reservist posts being available in the majority of trades.

Air Commodore-in-Chief, HM The Queen

Honorary Inspector-General (Air Vice-Marshal) Royal Auxiliary Air Force, Lord Beaverbrook

Inspector Royal Auxiliary Air Force, Gp Capt. Gavin Hellard, ADC

PRINCESS MARY'S ROYAL AIR FORCE NURSING SERVICE

The Princess Mary's Royal Air Force Nursing Service (PMRAFNS) was formed on 1 June 1918 as the Royal Air Force Nursing Service. In June 1923, His Majesty King George V gave his royal assent for the Royal Air Force Nursing Service to be known as the Princess Mary's Royal Air Force Nursing Service. Men were integrated into the PMRAFNS in 1980.

Patron and Air Chief Commandant, HRH Princess Alexandra, The Hon. Lady Ogilvy, KG, GCVO

Director of Nursing Services and Matron-in-Chief, Gp Capt. Phil Spragg

SERVICE SALARIES

The following rates of pay apply from 1 April 2015 and are rounded to the nearest pound.

The pay rates shown are for army personnel. The rates also apply to personnel of equivalent rank and pay band in the other services (see below for table of relative ranks).

Rank	Annual salary
SECOND LIEUTENANT	£25,472
LIEUTENANT	
On appointment	£30,617
After 1 year in rank	£31,426
After 2 years in rank	£32,231
After 3 years in rank	£33,032
After 4 years in rank	£33,842
CAPTAIN	
On appointment	£39,236
After 1 year in rank	£40,287
After 2 years in rank	£41,351
After 3 years in rank	£42,419
After 4 years in rank	£43,474
After 5 years in rank	£44,538
After 6 years in rank	£45,592
After 7 years in rank	£46,131
After 8 years in rank	£46,660
MAJOR	
On appointment	£49,424
After 1 year in rank	£50,644
After 2 years in rank	£51,856
After 3 years in rank	£53,085
After 4 years in rank	£54,301
After 5 years in rank	£55,530
After 6 years in rank	£56,750
After 7 years in rank	£57,966
After 8 years in rank	£59,191
LIEUTENANT-COLONEL	
On appointment	£69,366
After 1 year in rank	£70,285
After 2 years in rank	£71,196
After 3 years in rank	£72,108
After 4 years in rank	£73,019
After 5 years in rank	£77,212
After 6 years in rank	£78,242
After 7 years in rank	£79,281
After 8 years in rank	£80,320
COLONEL	
On appointment	£84,037
After 1 year in rank	£85,079
After 2 years in rank	£86,124
After 3 years in rank	£87,166
After 4 years in rank	£88,207
After 5 years in rank	£89,248
After 6 years in rank	£90,290
After 7 years in rank	£91,335
After 8 years in rank	£92,381
BRIGADIER	
On appointment	£100,146
After 1 year in rank	£101,158
After 2 years in rank	£102,170
After 3 years in rank	£103,178
After 4 years in rank	£104,198

PAY SYSTEM FOR SENIOR MILITARY OFFICERS

Pay rates effective from 1 April 2015 for all military officers of 2* rank and above (excluding medical and dental officers). All pay rates are rounded to the nearest pound.

Rank	Annual salary
MAJOR-GENERAL (2*)	
Scale 1	£111,567
Scale 2	£113,747
Scale 3	£115,972
Scale 4	£118,241
Scale 5	£120,555
Scale 6	£122,914
LIEUTENANT-GENERAL (3*)	
Scale 1	£129,810
Scale 2	£136,174
Scale 3	£142,856
Scale 4	£148,468
Scale 5	£152,845
Scale 6	£157,355
GENERAL (4*)	
Scale 1	£170,292
Scale 2	£174,549
Scale 3	£178,913
Scale 4	£183,386
Scale 5	£187,054
Scale 6	£190,795

Field Marshal – appointments to this rank will not usually be made in peacetime. The salary for holders of the rank is equivalent to the salary of a 5-star General, a salary created only in times of war. In peacetime, the equivalent rank to Field Marshal is the Chief of the Defence Staff. From 1 April 2015, the annual salary range for the Chief of the Defence Staff is £245,338–£260,355.

OFFICERS COMMISSIONED FROM THE SENIOR RANKS

Rank	Annual salary
Level 15	£52,445
Level 14	£52,101
Level 13	£51,741
Level 12	£51,042
Level 11	£50,347
Level 10	£49,644
Level 9	£48,945
Level 8	£48,246
Level 7*	£47,373
Level 6	£46,834
Level 5	£46,287
Level 4†	£45,207
Level 3	£44,669
Level 2	£44,118
Level 1‡	£43,041

* Officers commissioned from the ranks with more than 15 years' service enter on level 7

† Officers commissioned from the ranks with between 12 and 15 years' service enter on level 4

‡ Officers commissioned from the ranks with less than 12 years' service enter on level 1

SOLDIERS' SALARIES

Under the Pay 2000 scheme, personnel are paid in either a high or low band in accordance with how their trade has been allocated to those bands at each rank. Pay is based on trade and rank, not on individual appointment, or in response to temporary changes in role.

Rates of pay effective from 1 April 2015 (rounded to the nearest pound) are:

Rank	Lower band	Higher band
PRIVATE		
Level 1	£18,125	£18,125
Level 2	£18,612	£19,498
Level 3	£19,099	£21,473
Level 4	£20,727	£22,531
LANCE CORPORAL (levels 5–7 also applicable to Privates)		
Level 5	£21,816	£24,913
Level 6	£22,188	£26,125
Level 7	£23,138	£27,324
Level 8	£24,197	£28,553
Level 9	£25,074	£29,947
CORPORAL		
Level 1	£27,324	£28,553
Level 2	£28,553	£29,947
Level 3	£29,947	£31,414
Level 4	£30,176	£32,147
Level 5	£30,413	£32,922
Level 6	£30,655	£33,604
Level 7	£30,879	£34,338
SERGEANT		
Level 1	£31,058	£33,897
Level 2	£31,871	£34,774
Level 3	£32,672	£35,655
Level 4	£33,003	£36,105
Level 5	£33,863	£36,808
Level 6	£35,032	£37,511
Level 7	£35,300	£38,215
STAFF SERGEANT		
Level 1	£34,380	£38,240
Level 2	£34,829	£39,164
Level 3	£35,961	£40,101
Level 4	£36,804	£41,029
WARRANT OFFICER II (levels 5–7 also applicable to Staff Sergeants)		
Level 5	£37,304	£41,961
Level 6	£38,990	£42,889
Level 7	£39,588	£43,508
Level 8	£40,101	£44,127
Level 9	£41,008	£44,758
WARRANT OFFICER I		
Level 1	£39,944	£43,546
Level 2	£40,719	£44,402
Level 3	£41,541	£45,165
Level 4	£42,364	£45,995
Level 5	£43,190	£46,817
Level 6	£44,402	£47,652
Level 7	£45,656	£48,381

RELATIVE RANK – ARMED FORCES

Royal Navy	Army	Royal Air Force
1 Admiral of the Fleet	1 Field Marshal	1 Marshal of the RAF
2 Admiral (Adm.)	2 General (Gen.)	2 Air Chief Marshal
3 Vice-Admiral (Vice-Adm.)	3 Lieutenant-General (Lt.-Gen.)	3 Air Marshal
4 Rear-Admiral (Rear-Adm.)	4 Major-General (Maj.-Gen.)	4 Air Vice-Marshal
5 Commodore (Cdre)	5 Brigadier (Brig.)	5 Air Commodore (Air Cdre)
6 Captain (Capt.)	6 Colonel (Col.)	6 Group Captain (Gp Capt.)
7 Commander (Cdr)	7 Lieutenant-Colonel (Lt.-Col.)	7 Wing Commander (Wg Cdr)
8 Lieutenant-Commander (Lt.-Cdr)	8 Major (Maj.)	8 Squadron Leader (Sqn Ldr)
9 Lieutenant (Lt.)	9 Captain (Capt.)	9 Flight Lieutenant (Flt Lt)
10 Sub-Lieutenant (Sub-Lt.)	10 Lieutenant (Lt.)	10 Flying Officer (FO)
11 Midshipman	11 Second Lieutenant (2nd Lt.)	11 Pilot Officer (PO)

SERVICE RETIRED PAY *on compulsory retirement*

Those that leave the service having served at least two years, but not long enough to qualify for the appropriate immediate pension, qualify for a preserved pension and terminal grant, both of which are payable from age 60, for service before 6 April 2006, and age 65 for service after 6 April 2006. The tax-free resettlement grants shown below are payable on release to those that have completed nine years' service (officers) or 12 years (other ranks).

The annual rates for army personnel are given. The rates also apply to personnel of equivalent rank in the other services, including the nursing services.

OFFICERS

The rates shown below are applicable to officers who give full pay service on the active list on or after 31 March 2015. Pensionable earnings for senior officers (*) is defined as the total amount of basic pay received during the year ending on the day prior to retirement, or the amount of basic pay received during any 12-month period within three years prior to retirement, whichever is the higher. Figures for senior officers are percentage rates of pensionable earnings on final salary arrangements on or after 31 March 2015.

No. of years reckonable service	Capt. and below	Major	Lt.-Col.	Colonel	Brigadier	Major-General*	Lieutenant-General*	General*
16	£12,994	£15,476	£20,291	£24,545	£29,118	—	—	—
17	£13,593	£16,211	£21,238	£25,671	£30,254	—	—	—
18	£14,192	£16,946	£22,365	£26,796	£31,389	—	—	—
19	£14,791	£17,681	£23,402	£27,922	£32,524	—	—	—
20	£15,389	£18,416	£24,439	£29,047	£33,659	—	—	—
21	£15,988	£19,151	£25,475	£30,173	£34,794	—	—	—
22	£16,587	£19,886	£26,512	£31,298	£35,930	—	—	—
23	£17,186	£20,622	£27,549	£32,424	£37,065	—	—	—
24	£17,785	£21,357	£28,586	£33,549	£38,200	38.5%	—	—
25	£18,384	£22,092	£29,623	£34,675	£39,335	39.7%	—	—
26	£18,983	£22,827	£30,660	£35,800	£40,471	40.8%	—	—
27	£19,582	£23,562	£31,697	£36,926	£41,606	42.0%	42.0%	—
28	£20,181	£24,297	£32,734	£38,052	£42,741	43.1%	43.1%	—
29	£20,780	£25,032	£33,771	£39,177	£43,876	44.3%	44.3%	—
30	£21,378	£25,767	£34,808	£40,303	£45,011	45.4%	45.4%	45.4%
31	£21,977	£26,502	£35,844	£41,428	£46,147	46.6%	46.6%	46.6%
32	£22,576	£27,238	£36,881	£42,554	£47,282	47.7%	47.7%	47.7%
33	£23,175	£27,973	£37,918	£43,679	£48,417	48.9%	48.9%	48.9%
34	£23,774	£28,708	£38,955	£44,805	£49,552	50.0%	50.0%	50.0%

WARRANT OFFICERS, NCOS AND PRIVATES
(Applicable to soldiers who give full pay service on or after 31 March 2015)

No. of years reckonable service	Below Corporal	Corporal	Sergeant	Staff Sergeant	Warrant Officer Level II	Warrant Officer Level I
22	£7,690	£9,920	£10,875	£12,388	£13,226	£14,064
23	£7,958	£10,266	£11,255	£12,821	£13,688	£14,555
24	£8,227	£10,612	£11,635	£13,253	£14,149	£15,045
25	£8,495	£10,958	£12,014	£13,685	£14,611	£15,536
26	£8,763	£11,305	£12,394	£14,118	£15,073	£16,027
27	£9,032	£11,651	£12,773	£14,550	£15,534	£16,518
28	£9,300	£11,997	£13,153	£14,983	£15,996	£17,009
29	£9,569	£12,343	£13,533	£15,415	£16,457	£17,500
30	£9,837	£12,690	£13,912	£15,847	£16,919	£17,991
31	£10,105	£13,036	£14,292	£16,280	£17,381	£18,482
32	£10,374	£13,382	£14,671	£16,712	£17,842	£18,973
33	£10,642	£13,728	£15,051	£17,145	£18,304	£19,463
34	£10,911	£14,075	£15,431	£17,577	£18,766	£19,954
35	£11,179	£14,421	£15,810	£18,010	£19,227	£20,445
36	£11,448	£14,767	£16,190	£18,442	£19,689	£20,936
37	£11,716	£15,113	£16,569	£18,874	£20,151	£21,427

GRANTS AND GRATUITIES

Terminal grants are in each case three times the rate of retired pay or pension. There are special rates of retired pay for certain other ranks not shown above. Lower rates are payable in cases of voluntary retirement.

A gratuity of £4,420 is payable for officers with short service commissions for each year completed. Resettlement grants are £15,197 for officers and £10,387 for other ranks.

EDUCATION

THE UK EDUCATION SYSTEM

The structure of the education system in the UK is a devolved matter with each of the countries of the UK having separate systems under separate governments. There are differences between the school systems in terms of the curriculum, examinations and final qualifications and, at university level, in terms of the nature of some degrees and in the matter of tuition fees. The systems in England, Wales and Northern Ireland are similar and have more in common with one another than the Scottish system, which differs significantly.

Education in England is overseen by the Department for Education (DfE) and the Department for Business, Innovation and Skills (BIS).

In Wales, responsibility for education lies with the Department for Education and Skills (DfES) within the Welsh government. Ministers in the Scottish government are responsible for education in Scotland, led by the directorates of Learning and Lifelong Learning, while in Northern Ireland responsibility lies with the Department of Education (DENI) and the Department for Employment and Learning (DELNI) within the Northern Ireland government.

DEPARTMENT FOR EDUCATION T 0370-000 2288
  W www.gov.uk/government/organisations/department-for-education

DEPARTMENT FOR BUSINESS, INNOVATION AND SKILLS T 020-7215 5000
  W www.gov.uk/government/organisations/department-for-business-innovation-skills

DEPARTMENT FOR EDUCATION AND SKILLS (DFES) T 0300-060 3300
  W www.wales.gov.uk/topics/educationandskills

SCOTTISH GOVERNMENT – EDUCATION
  T 0131-244 4000; 0300-244 4000
  W www.gov.scot/Topics/Education

DEPARTMENT OF EDUCATION (NI) T 028-9127 9279
  W www.deni.gov.uk

DEPARTMENT FOR EMPLOYMENT AND LEARNING (NI) T 028-9025 7777 W www.delni.gov.uk

RECENT DEVELOPMENTS

In England, reform of the national curriculum, initial teacher training and apprenticeships continued under the former coalition government. Since May 2015, the new Conservative government announced plans to replace maintenance grants for students in England with loans of up to £8,200 from 2016–17 and proposed a bill to raise standards and turn 'coasting' schools into academies. Elsewhere in the UK, there were also plans for curriculum and assessment change and proposals to raise standards. Changes made or announced include:

ENGLAND
- Since September 2015, Ofsted inspect good schools and further education and skills providers once every 3 years under a new short (one-day) inspection model. Inspectors focus on ensuring standards are being maintained and check that leaders have identified areas of concern and have the capacity to address them
- Pupils starting secondary school in September 2015 must study the English Baccalaureate (EBacc) subjects of English, maths, science, history or geography, and a language at GCSE

- The achievement of a level 5 on the new 1 to 9 grading scale at GCSE (a low B or high C under the old grading system) will be considered the new 'good pass' used to hold the government and schools to account
- A school behaviour expert will draw up plans to help teachers deal with low-level disruption in classrooms
- Six new core maths qualifications are to be included in school and college performance tables from 2017 and be part of the TechBacc measure from 2016
- A new college of teaching, revised standards for school leaders, a working group on improving initial teacher training and a review of standards for teaching assistants
- 'Degree apprenticeships', designed by industry and funded by BIS (two-thirds) and employers (one-third), will be available from September 2015 in thirteen subjects including chartered surveying, aerospace engineering and laboratory science
- The cap is lifted on university student numbers but controls are placed on some private higher education providers from 2015–16
- In Research Excellence Framework assessments, 30 per cent of UK university research was judged to be world-leading and 46 per cent internationally excellent. A complementary Teaching Excellence Framework is proposed to improve the standing of university teaching in England

WALES
- New curriculum and assessment changes set out in *Successful Futures* accepted in full. Children and young people will be supported to be ambitious, capable learners; enterprising, creative contributors; ethical, informed citizens of Wales and the world; and healthy, confident individuals. Implementation plans were due in autumn 2015
- Plans set out to revise professional teaching standards and drive up the quality of initial teacher training, by overhauling the teaching qualification and accreditation process
- Qualifications Wales, a new body to oversee qualifications, regulation and assessment in Wales, started work in September 2015
- New *Digital Competence Framework* will help schools embed digital competency into their teaching and learning from September 2016
- Financial incentives introduced (up to £20,000) for top graduates to study to teach the priority subjects of Welsh, Maths, Physics and Chemistry at secondary school level
- *Qualified for Life*, an education improvement plan for Wales up to 2020, sets out four strategic objectives: an excellent professional workforce; engaging curriculum; credible qualifications; education leaders improving the system
- Skills Implementation Plan launched to respond to the needs of local employers with industry-led skills and training solutions

SCOTLAND
- Funding pledges include £2m for 250 extra teacher training places, £2.7m for pre-school programmes to improve literacy, £1m to develop the early years workforce, a doubling of spending on early years and childcare and £12m for clinical research fellowships
- Creative industries skills investment plan announced, the latest in a series which since March 2014 has included: construction, chemical sciences, energy, highlands and

islands, engineering, life sciences, ICT and digital, finance and tourism
• Education (Scotland) Bill to place a statutory duty on councils to narrow the attainment gap, require councils and ministers to report on progress, promote Gaelic education and ensure teachers and school leaders are appropriately trained and qualified. A Masters qualification for headship introduced in 2015 will be mandatory for all new headteachers from 2018–19
• From 2015–16 all pupils should be studying for the new Higher qualifications

NORTHERN IRELAND
• Addition of £80m to the schools budget for 2015–16, and £2.5m to the pre-school education programme
• Practical assessments of science subjects will remain as part of the overall grade at A-level. The weighting of AS-levels will be changed to 40 per cent and A2 levels to 60 per cent
• New higher level apprenticeships in Finance and Accountancy and Applied Industrial and Life Science (equivalent to a Foundation degree) to be piloted as part of *Securing our Success* strategy

STATE SCHOOL SYSTEM

PRE-SCHOOL
Pre-school education is not compulsory. In England, a free place is available for every 3- and 4-year-old whose parents want one, although parents may use as little or as much of their entitlement as they choose. All 3- and 4-year-olds, and disadvantaged 2-year-olds, are entitled to 15 hours a week of free early education over 38 weeks of the year until they reach compulsory school age (the term following their fifth birthday). This is delivered flexibly over a minimum of two days each week during normal term times. Free places are funded by local authorities and are delivered by a range of providers in the maintained and non-maintained sectors – nursery schools; nursery classes in primary schools; private schools; private day nurseries; voluntary playgroups; pre-schools; and registered childminders. In order to receive funding, providers must be working towards the early learning goals and other features of the Early Years Foundation Stage curriculum, must be inspected on a regular basis by Ofsted and must meet any conditions set by the local authority.

In Wales, every child is entitled to receive free Foundation Phase education for a minimum of two hours a day from the term following their third birthday.

In Scotland, councils have a duty to provide a pre-school education for all 3- and 4-year-olds whose parents request one. Education authorities must offer each child at least 600 hours of free pre-school education a year, although they may provide more if they choose.

In Northern Ireland, the Department of Education aims to provide a funded place for all 3- and 4-year-old children in their final pre-school year. All places offer 2.5 hours a day, five days a week for at least 38 weeks a year.

PRIMARY AND SECONDARY SCHOOLS
By law, full-time education starts at the age of five for children in England, Scotland and Wales and at the age of four in Northern Ireland. In practice, most children in the UK start school before their fifth birthday: in England all children are entitled to a primary school place from the September after their fourth birthday.

Children in England are required to stay in education or training until the end of the academic year in which they turn 18 (from September 2015). In all other parts of the UK,

compulsory schooling ends at age 16, but children born between certain dates may leave school before their 16th birthday. Most young people stay in some form of education until 17 or 18.

Primary education consists mainly of infant schools for children aged 5 to 7, junior schools for those aged 7 to 11, and combined infant and junior schools for both age groups.

First schools in some parts of England cater for ages 5 to 10 as the first stage of a three-tier system of first (lower), middle and secondary (upper) schools. Scotland has only primary schools with no infant/junior division.

Children usually leave primary school and move on to secondary school at the age of 11 (or 12 in Scotland). In the few areas of England that have a three-tier system of schools, middle schools cater for children after they leave first schools for three to four years between the ages of 8 and 14, depending on the local authority.

Secondary schools cater for children aged 11 to 16 and, if they have a sixth form, for those who choose to stay on to the age of 18. From the age of 16, students may move instead to further education colleges or work-based training.

Most UK secondary schools are co-educational. The largest secondary schools have more than 1,500 pupils and around 60 per cent of secondary pupils in the UK are in schools that take more than 1,000 pupils.

Most state-maintained secondary schools in England, Wales and Scotland are comprehensive schools, which admit pupils without reference to ability. In England there remain some areas with grammar schools, catering for pupils aged 11 to 18, which select pupils on the basis of high academic ability. Over half of state secondary schools in England (61 per cent in January 2015) are now academies: academies are funded directly by the state rather than being maintained by local authorities. Northern Ireland still has 68 grammar schools; the 11-plus has been officially discontinued but schools, or consortia of schools, use their own unregulated entry tests.

More than 90 per cent of pupils in the UK attend publicly funded schools and receive free education. The rest attend privately funded 'independent' schools, which charge fees, or are educated at home.

The bulk of the UK government's expenditure on school education is through local authorities (Education and Library Boards (ELBs) in Northern Ireland), who pass on state funding to schools and other educational institutions.

SPECIAL EDUCATION
Schools and local authorities in England and Wales, Education and Library Boards (ELBs) in Northern Ireland and education authorities in Scotland are required to identify and secure provision for children with special educational needs and to involve parents in decisions. The majority of children with special educational needs are educated in ordinary mainstream schools, sometimes with supplementary help from outside specialists. Parents of children with special educational needs (referred to as additional support needs in Scotland) have a right of appeal to independent tribunals if their wishes are not met.

Special educational needs provision may be made in maintained special schools, special units attached to mainstream schools or in mainstream classes themselves, all funded by local authorities. There are also non-maintained special schools run by voluntary bodies, mainly charities, who may receive grants from central government for capital expenditure and equipment but whose other costs are met primarily from the fees charged to local authorities for pupils placed in the schools. Some independent schools also provide education wholly or mainly for children with special educational needs.

ADDITIONAL SUPPORT NEEDS TRIBUNALS FOR
SCOTLAND T 0845-120 2906 W www.asntscotland.gov.uk
FIRST-TIER TRIBUNAL (SPECIAL EDUCATIONAL
NEEDS AND DISABILITY) T 020-7843 6958
W www.gov.uk/special-educational-needs-disability-tribunal
INFORMATION ADVICE AND SUPPORT SERVICES
NETWORK FOR SEND E iassn@ncb.org.uk
W www.iassnetwork.org.uk
SPECIAL EDUCATIONAL NEEDS TRIBUNAL FOR
WALES T 01597-829800 W sentw.gov.uk

HOME EDUCATION

In England and Wales parents have the right to educate their
children at home and do not have to be qualified teachers to
do so. Home-educated children do not have to follow the
National Curriculum or take national tests nor do they need
a fixed timetable, formal lessons or to observe school hours,
days or terms. However, by law parents must ensure that
the home education provided is full-time and suitable for the
child's age, ability and aptitude and, if appropriate, for any
special educational needs. Parents have no legal obligation to
notify the local authority that a child is being educated at
home, but if they take a child out of school, they must notify
the school in writing and the school must report this to the
local authority. Local authorities can make informal enquiries
of parents to establish that a suitable education is being
provided. For children in special schools, parents must seek
the consent of the local authority before taking steps to
educate them at home.

In Northern Ireland, ELBs monitor the quality of home
provision and provide general guidance on appropriate
materials and exam types through regular home visits.

The home schooling law in Scotland is similar to that of
England. One difference, however, is that if parents wish to
take a child out of school they must have permission from the
local education authority.

HOME EDUCATION ADVISORY SERVICE
T 01707-371854 W www.heas.org.uk
HOME EDUCATION IN NORTHERN IRELAND
W www.hedni.org
SCHOOLHOUSE HOME EDUCATION ASSOCIATION
(SCOTLAND) T 01307-463120 W www.schoolhouse.org.uk

FURTHER EDUCATION

In the UK, further education (FE) is generally understood as
post-secondary education, ie any education undertaken after
an individual leaves school that is below higher education
level. FE therefore embraces a wide range of general and
vocational study undertaken by people of all ages from 16
upwards, full-time or part-time, who may be self-funded,
employer-funded or state-funded.

FE in the UK is often undertaken at further education
colleges, although some takes place on employers' premises.
Many of these colleges offer some courses at higher
education level; some FE colleges teach certain subjects to
14- to 16-year-olds under collaborative arrangements with
schools. Colleges' income comes from public funding,
student fees and work for and with employers.

HIGHER EDUCATION

Higher education (HE) in the UK describes courses of
study, provided in universities, specialist colleges of higher
education and in some FE colleges, where the level of
instruction is above that of A-level or equivalent exams.

All UK universities and colleges that provide HE are
autonomous bodies with their own internal systems of
governance. They are not owned by the state. However, most
receive a portion of their income from state funds distributed
by the separate HE funding councils for England, Scotland

and Wales, and the Department for Employment and
Learning in Northern Ireland. The rest of their income
comes from a number of sources including fees from home
and overseas students, government funding for research,
endowments and work with or for business.

EXPENDITURE

UK-MANAGED EXPENDITURE ON EDUCATION
(Real terms adjusted to 2014–15 price levels) £bn

2005–6	85.4	2010–11	97.9
2006–7	86.9	2011–12	91.4
2007–8	91.0	2012–13	90.0
2008–9	93.7	2013–14	90.4
2009–10	97.3	2014–15 (est)	84.3

Source: HM Treasury – Public Spending Statistics July 2015

SCHOOLS

ENGLAND AND WALES

In England and Wales, publicly funded schools are referred to
as 'state schools'. The four main categories of state school –
Community, Foundation, Voluntary-aided and Voluntary-
controlled – are maintained by local authorities, which have a
duty to ensure there is a suitable place for every school-age
child resident in their area. Each school has a governing
body, made up of volunteers elected or appointed by
parents, staff, the community and the local authority,
which is responsible for strategic management, ensuring
accountability, monitoring school performance, setting
budgets and appointing the headteacher and senior staff.
The headteacher is responsible for the school's day-to-day
management and operations and for decisions requiring
professional teaching expertise.

In *Community schools,* which are non-denominational, local
authorities are the employers of the staff, own the land and
buildings and set the admissions criteria.

In *Foundation schools,* the governing body employs the staff
and sets the admissions criteria. The land and buildings
are usually owned by the governing body or a charitable
foundation. A Foundation school may have a religious
character, although most do not. A *Trust school* is a distinct
type of foundation school that forms a charitable trust with
an outside partner – for example, a business, a university,
an educational charity or simply another school – that
shares the school's aspirations. The decision to become a
Trust school is taken by the governing body while taking
account of parents' views. Community schools can take on
Foundation status and set up a trust in a single process.

Most *Voluntary-aided schools* are religious schools founded
by Christian denominations or other faiths. As with
Foundation schools, the governing body employs the staff
and sets the admissions criteria, which may include priority
for members of the faith or denomination. The school
buildings and land are normally owned and provided by a
charitable foundation, often a religious organisation, which
appoints a majority of the school's governors and makes a
small contribution to major building costs.

Voluntary-controlled schools are similar to Voluntary-aided
schools in that they often have a particular religious ethos,
commonly Church of England, and the school land and
buildings are normally owned by a charity. However, as with
Community schools, the local authority employs the school's
staff, sets the admissions criteria and bears all the costs.

Among the local authority-maintained schools are some
with particular characteristics:
• *Community and Foundation special schools* cater for children
with specific special educational needs, which may include
physical disabilities or learning difficulties

- *Grammar schools* are secondary schools catering for pupils aged 11 to 18 that select all of their pupils based on academic ability. In England there are 164 grammar schools, concentrated in certain local authority areas. Wales has none
- *Maintained boarding schools* are state-funded and offer free tuition but charge fees for board and lodging

In Wales, Welsh-medium primary and secondary schools were first established in the 1950s and 1960s, originally in response to the wishes of Welsh-speaking parents who wanted their children to be educated through the medium of the Welsh language. Now, many children who are not from Welsh-speaking homes also attend Welsh-medium and bilingual schools throughout Wales. There are 444 Welsh-medium primary schools, where the main or sole medium of instruction is in the Welsh language, two Welsh-medium middle schools and 52 Welsh-medium secondary schools, where more than half of foundation subjects (other than English and Welsh) and religious education are taught wholly or partly in Welsh.

England now has increasing numbers of *Academies*. Those set-up before the Academies Act 2010 were sponsored by business, faith or voluntary groups who contributed to funding their land and buildings, while the government covered the running costs at a level comparable to other local schools. The Academies Act 2010 streamlined the process of becoming an academy, enabled high-performing schools to convert without a sponsor and allowed primary and special schools to become academies. All academies now receive funding from central government at the level they would have received if still maintained by their local authority, with extra funding only to cover those services the local authority no longer provides. Academies have greater freedoms over how they use their budgets, set staff pay and conditions and deliver the curriculum. As at June 2015 there were 4,675 open academies, of which 2,546 were primaries.

SCOTLAND

Most schools in Scotland, known as 'publicly funded' schools, are state-funded and charge no fees. Funding is met from resources raised by the Scottish local authorities and from an annual grant from the Scottish government. Scotland does not have school governing bodies like the rest of the UK: local authorities retain greater responsibility for the management and performance of publicly funded schools. Headteachers manage at least 80 per cent of a school's budget, covering staffing, furnishings, repairs, supplies, services and energy costs. Spending on new buildings, modernisation projects and equipment is financed by the local authority within the limits set by the Scottish government.

Scotland has 370 state-funded *faith schools,* the majority of which are Catholic. It has no grammar schools.

Integrated community schools form part of the Scottish government's strategy to promote social inclusion and to raise educational standards. They encourage closer and better joint working among education, health and social work agencies and professionals, greater pupil and parental involvement in schools, and improved support and service provision for vulnerable children and young people.

Scotland has a number of *grant-aided schools* that are independent of local authorities but supported financially by the Scottish government. These schools are managed by boards and most of them provide education for children and young people with special educational needs.

NORTHERN IRELAND

Most schools in Northern Ireland are maintained by the state and generally charge no fees, though fees may be charged in preparatory departments of some grammar schools. There are different types of state-funded schools, each under the control of management committees, which also employ the teachers.

Controlled schools (nursery, primary, special, secondary and grammar schools) are managed by Northern Ireland's five ELBs through boards of governors consisting of teachers, parents, members of the ELB and transferor representatives (mainly from the Protestant churches).

Catholic maintained schools (nursery, primary, special and secondary) are under the management of boards of governors consisting of teachers, parents and members nominated by the employing authority, the Council for Catholic Maintained Schools (CCMS).

Other maintained schools (primary, special and secondary) are, in the main, Irish-medium schools that provide education in an Irish-speaking environment. The Department of Education has a duty to encourage and facilitate the development of Irish-medium education. Northern Ireland has 29 standalone Irish-medium schools, most of them primary schools, and ten Irish-medium units attached to English-medium host schools.

Voluntary schools are mainly grammar schools, which select most pupils according to academic ability. They are managed by boards of governors consisting of teachers, parents and, in most cases, representatives from the Department of Education and the ELB.

Integrated schools (primary and secondary) educate pupils from both the Protestant and Catholic communities as well as those of other faiths and no faith; each school is managed by a board of governors. There are at present 62 integrated schools maintained by the state, 24 of which are controlled schools.

Since 2013 all pupils are guaranteed access to a wide range of courses, with a minimum of 24 courses at Key Stage 4, and 27 at post-16. At least one-third of the courses on offer will be academic and another third will be vocational. Schools work with other schools, FE colleges and other providers to widen the range of courses on offer.

INDEPENDENT SCHOOLS

Around 6 per cent of UK schoolchildren are educated by privately funded 'independent' schools that charge fees and set their own admissions policies. Independent schools are required to meet certain minimum standards but need not teach the National Curriculum. *See also* Independent Schools.

UK SCHOOLS BY CATEGORY (2013–14)

	England	Wales
*Maintained nursery schools	414	17
†Maintained primary and secondary schools	16,290	1,574
Community	9,342	–
Voluntary-aided	3,760	–
Voluntary-controlled	2,369	–
Foundation	961	–
Pupil Referral Units	371	–
Maintained Special schools	964	42
‡Non-maintained Special schools	69	–
‡Academies	3,827	–
Independent schools	2,411	66
Total	24,346	1,699

* Includes one direct grant school in England
† Includes four middle schools in Wales
‡ Includes City Technology Colleges, University Technology Colleges, studio schools and free schools; excludes voluntary and private pre-school education centres
Source: DfE; Welsh government

Scotland

Publicly funded schools	2,560
Primary	2,055
Secondary	363
Special	142
Independent schools	100
Total	2,660

Source: Scottish government

Northern Ireland

State-maintained nursery schools	96
State-maintained primary and secondary schools	1,035
Controlled	440
Voluntary	51
Catholic maintained	452
Other maintained	30
Integrated	62
Special schools	40
Independent schools	15
Total	1,186

Source: DENI

INSPECTION

ENGLAND

The Office for Standards in Education, Children's Services and Skills (Ofsted) is the main body responsible for inspecting education in English schools. As well as inspecting all publicly funded and some independent schools, Ofsted inspects a range of other services in England, including childcare, children's homes, pupil referral units, local authority children's services, further education, initial teacher training and publicly funded adult skills training.

Ofsted is an independent, non-ministerial government department that reports directly to parliament, headed by Her Majesty's Chief Inspector (HMCI). Ofsted is required to promote improvement in the public services that it inspects; ensure that these services focus on the interests of their users – children, parents, learners and employers; and see that these services are efficient, effective and promote value for money. A new 'common inspection regime' came into effect in September 2015 *(see* Recent Developments) to make inspections of different settings with similar age groups more coherent.

Ofsted publishes the findings of its inspection reports, its recommendations and statistical information on its website.
OFFICE FOR STANDARDS IN EDUCATION,
   CHILDREN'S SERVICES AND SKILLS T 0300-123 1231
   W www.gov.uk/government/organisations/ofsted

WALES

Estyn is the office of Her Majesty's Inspectorate for Education and Training in Wales. It is independent of, but funded by, the Welsh government and is led by Her Majesty's Chief Inspector of Education and Training in Wales.

Estyn's role is to inspect quality and standards in education and training in Wales, including in primary, secondary, special and independent schools, and pupil referral units, publicly funded nursery schools and settings, further education, adult community-based and work-based learning, local authorities and teacher education and training.

Estyn also provides advice on quality and standards in education and training to the Welsh government and others and its remit includes making public good practice based on inspection evidence. Estyn publishes the findings of its inspection reports, its recommendations and statistical information on its website.
HER MAJESTY'S INSPECTORATE FOR EDUCATION
   AND TRAINING IN WALES T 029-2044 6446
   W www.estyn.gov.uk

SCOTLAND

HM Inspectorate of Education (HMIE) merged with Learning and Teaching Scotland in July 2011 to become Education Scotland, an executive agency of the Scottish government. Education Scotland operates independently and impartially while being directly accountable to Scottish ministers for the standards of its work. The agency's core business is inspection and review. It is responsible for delivering measurable year-on-year improvements, with maximum efficiency, by promoting excellence, building on strengths, and identifying and addressing under-performance. Since August 2015, inspections take account of national expectations of progress in implementing Curriculum for Excellence (CfE).

Inspection reports and reviews, recommendations, examples of good practice and statistical information are published on Education Scotland's website.
EDUCATION SCOTLAND T 0141 282 5000
   W www.educationscotland.gov.uk

NORTHERN IRELAND

The Education and Training Inspectorate (ETINI) provides inspection services for the Department of Education and Employment and Learning Northern Ireland.

ETINI carries out inspections of all schools, pre-school services, special education, further education colleges, initial teacher training, training organisations, and curriculum advisory and support services. Since September 2013 regional colleges of further education have received four weeks' notification of inspection, while all other organisations have received two weeks' notification of inspection.

The inspectorate's role is to improve services and it provides evidence-based advice to ministers in order to assist in the formulation of policies. It publishes the findings of its inspection reports, its recommendations and statistical information on its website.
EDUCATION AND TRAINING INSPECTORATE
   T 028-9127 9726 W www.etini.gov.uk

THE NATIONAL CURRICULUM

ENGLAND

The National Curriculum, first introduced in 1988, is mandatory in all state schools for children from age 5 onwards.

Until age 5, or the end of Reception Year in primary school, children are in the Early Years Foundation Stage (EYFS), which has its own learning and development requirements for children in nursery and primary schools. Changes to the EYFS came into effect in 2012 and 2014. These included simplifying the statutory assessment of children's development at age five; reducing the number of early learning goals from 69 to 17; focusing on seven areas of learning and development (prime areas: communication and language, physical development and personal, social and emotional development; and specific areas: literacy, mathematics, understanding the world, and expressive arts and design) and, for parents, a new progress check at age two on their child's development.

Following the EYFS, the National Curriculum is organised into 'Key Stages', and sets out the core subjects that must be taught and the standards or attainment targets for each subject at each Key Stage.
• Key Stage 1 covers Years 1 and 2 of primary school, for children aged 5–7
• Key Stage 2 covers Years 3 to 6 of primary school, for children aged 7–11
• Key Stage 3 covers Years 7 to 9 of secondary school, for children aged 11–14
• Key Stage 4 covers Years 10 and 11 of secondary school, for children aged 14–16

Within the framework of the National Curriculum, schools may plan and organise teaching and learning in the way that best meets the needs of their pupils, but maintained schools are expected to follow the programmes of study associated with particular subjects. The programmes of study describe the subject knowledge, skills and understanding that pupils are expected to have developed by the end of each Key Stage.

The former coalition government brought in a new National Curriculum for England, to be taught in all maintained primary and secondary schools from September 2014, however pupils in Years 10 and 11 continued to be taught English, mathematics and science on the old programmes of study until new, more demanding GCSEs in these subjects were ready for them to take. Since September 2015 all maintained secondary schools in England have had to teach the Key Stage 4 programmes of study for English and mathematics in Year 10. From September 2015 they must teach the new programmes for English and mathematics in Year 11 and science in Year 10, and from September 2017 schools must teach all the programmes of study to all Key Stage 4 pupils.

KEY STAGES 1 AND 2 COMPULSORY SUBJECTS	
English	Design and technology
Mathematics	Geography
Science	History
Art and design	Music
Computing	Physical education

Foreign languages will be compulsory in Key Stage 2, but not Key Stage 1: schools can choose from French, German, Italian, Mandarin, Spanish, Latin or Ancient Greek.

In Key Stage 3, compulsory subjects include those listed above for Key Stage 2 (though the language taught should be a modern foreign language) plus citizenship.

Pupils in Key Stage 4 study a mix of compulsory and optional subjects in preparation for national examinations such as GCSEs. Pupils at this key stage also have to undertake careers education and work-related learning. In addition, schools must offer at least one subject from each of four 'entitlement' areas: arts (art and design, music, dance, drama and media arts); design and technology; humanities (history and geography); and modern foreign languages. To meet the entitlement requirements, schools must ensure that courses in these areas lead to approved qualifications, and allow pupils to take courses in all four areas if they wish to do so.

KEY STAGE 4 COMPULSORY SUBJECTS	
English	Citizenship
Mathematics	Computing
Science	Physical education

Schools must teach religious education (RE) at all key stages, although parents have the right to withdraw children for all or part of the RE curriculum. Secondary schools must provide sex and relationship education.

Statutory assessment must be undertaken for all pupils in publicly funded schools in the relevant years. It first takes place towards the end of the Early Years Foundation Stage, when children's level of development is compared to and recorded against a Foundation Stage Profile (this will no longer be a statutory requirement from September 2016). Pupils receive a phonics screening check at the end of the first year in Key Stage 1, repeated the following year if necessary. Teacher assessments in English, mathematics and science take place at the end of Key Stage 1 (Year 2) and Key Stage 2 (Year 6); at the end of Key Stage 3 (Year 9) teachers assess progress in all subjects being studied. National tests in

English and mathematics take place in Year 6. At Key Stage 4, national examinations are the main form of assessment.

The assessment process for English at the end of Key Stage 2 now involves three elements. Reading comprehension is assessed by an external national test. Written comprehension is subject only to teacher assessment. Grammar, punctuation and spelling are assessed by a new external test introduced in May 2013.

Each year the DfE publishes on its website performance tables covering every school, college and local authority. The primary school tables are based mainly on the results of the tests taken by children at the end of Key Stage 2 when they are usually aged 11; since 2010 teacher assessment results are also included. Pupils at the end of Key Stage 2 will take new-style tests in English, mathematics and science, based on the new National Curriculum, for the first-time in summer 2016. The tables for secondary schools and attainment post-16 rely mainly on the results of national examinations. All tables include indicators of the progress that pupils have made since their last assessment. From 2016 the tables will identify 'coasting' schools that are not pushing every pupil to reach their potential.

DEPARTMENT FOR EDUCATION T 0370-000 2288
  W www.education.gov.uk

WALES

Wales is reviewing its National Curriculum and assessment from Foundation Phase to Key Stage 4. An implementation plan for the curriculum and assessment changes set out in *Successful Futures (see* Recent Developments) was due in autumn 2015. *Successful Futures* states that the purpose of the curriculum in Wales should be that children and young people develop as:

• Ambitious, capable learners, ready to learn throughout their lives
• Enterprising, creative contributors, ready to play a full part in life and work
• Ethical, informed citizens of Wales and the world
• Healthy, confident individuals, ready to lead fulfilling lives as valued members of society

It also sets out that the new national curriculum in Wales for 3- to 16-year-olds should be organised into areas of learning and experience that establish the breadth of the curriculum. These areas should provide rich contexts for developing the four curriculum purposes, be internally coherent, employ distinctive ways of thinking, and have an identifiable core of disciplinary or instrumental knowledge. There should be seven areas of learning and experience: expressive arts; health and well-being; humanities; languages, literacy and communication; mathematics and numeracy; and science and technology. Cross-curricular, all teachers should be responsible for developing literacy, numeracy and digital competence.

Initially a Foundation Phase curriculum for 3- to 7-year-olds was introduced in September 2008. The emphasis is on learning-by-doing and children's skills and knowledge are planned across seven areas of learning. They are:

• Personal and social development, well-being and cultural diversity
• Language, literacy and communication skills
• Mathematical development
• Welsh language development
• Knowledge and understanding of the world
• Physical development
• Creative development

Full details of the Foundation Phase can be found in *Framework for Children's Learning for 3- to 7-year-olds in Wales*, available on the Welsh government website (*see* below).

Currently the National Curriculum is for 7- to 16-year-olds. Originally it was broadly similar to that of England, with distinctive characteristics for Wales reflected in the programmes of study. From September 2008 a revised school curriculum was implemented, consisting of the National Curriculum subjects together with non-statutory frameworks for personal and social education, the world of work, religious education and skills.

The National Curriculum in Wales includes the following subjects:
• *Key Stage 2* – English, Welsh, mathematics, science, design and technology, ICT, history, geography, art and design, music, and physical education
• *Key Stage 3* – as Key Stage 2, plus a modern foreign language
• *Key Stage 4* – English, Welsh, mathematics, science and physical education

Welsh is compulsory for pupils at all key stages, either as a first or as a second language. In 2010, 16.5 per cent of pupils were taught Welsh as a first language. In April 2012, the Minister for Education and Skills approved the implementation of an action plan to raise standards and attainment in Welsh second language education.

Statutory testing at the end of Key Stage 2 was removed for pupils in Wales from 2004–5. Only statutory teacher assessment remains. It is also done at the end of Key Stage 1 (in future, the Foundation Phase) and Key Stage 3, and is being strengthened by moderation and accreditation arrangements.

The new National Literacy and Numeracy Framework (LNF), outlining the skills 5- to 15-year-olds are expected to acquire, became statutory from September 2013. For literacy, this means children should become accomplished in reading for information, writing for information and expressing themselves fluently and grammatically in speech. In numeracy, children are expected to develop numerical reasoning and use number skills, measuring skills and data skills.

New national reading and numeracy tests for pupils in Years 2 to 9 took place for the first time in Wales in May 2013. The tests are designed to give teachers a clearer insight into a learner's development and progress, to allow them to intervene at an earlier stage if learners are falling behind.

The reading test includes a statutory 'core' test, and a set of optional test materials to help teachers to investigate learners' strengths and development needs in more depth.

The numeracy test is split into two papers: numerical procedures and numerical reasoning. The procedural paper consists of a set of questions designed to assess the basic, essential numeracy skills such as addition, multiplication and division.

The numerical reasoning paper was introduced in May 2014. It will assess learners' ability to find the most effective ways to solve everyday numeracy problems.

Learners in Welsh medium schools will take a reading test in Welsh only in Years 2 and 3, but in both English and Welsh from Year 4 onwards. Schools will have the option to use both tests in Year 3. Learners will take the numeracy test in either English or Welsh.

THE WELSH GOVERNMENT – EDUCATION AND SKILLS
W www.wales.gov.uk/topics/educationandskills/schoolshome/curriculuminwales/arevisedcurriculumforwales
W www.learning.wales.gov.uk

SCOTLAND

The curriculum in Scotland is not prescribed by statute but is the responsibility of education authorities and individual schools. However, schools and authorities are expected to follow the Scottish government's guidance on management and delivery of the curriculum.

Advice and guidance are provided by the Scottish government primarily through Education Scotland.

Scotland is now implementing *Curriculum for Excellence*, which aims to provide more autonomy for teachers, greater choice and opportunity for pupils and a single coherent curriculum for all children and young people aged 3 to 18.

The purpose of Curriculum for Excellence is encapsulated in 'the four capacities': to enable each child or young person to be a successful learner, a confident individual, a responsible citizen and an effective contributor. It focuses on providing a broad curriculum that develops skills for learning, skills for life and skills for work, with a sustained focus on literacy and numeracy. The period of education from pre-school through to the end of secondary stage 3, when pupils reach age 14, has the particular purpose of providing each young person in Scotland with this broad general education.

Curriculum for Excellence sets out 'experiences and outcomes', which describe broad areas of learning and what is to be achieved within them. They are:
• Expressive arts (including art and design, dance, drama, music)
• Health and wellbeing (including physical education, food and health, relationships and sexual health and mental, physical and social wellbeing)
• Languages
• Mathematics
• Religious and moral education
• Sciences
• Social studies (including history, geography, society and economy)
• Technologies (including business, computing, food and textiles, craft, design, engineering and graphics)

The experiences and outcomes are written at five levels with progression to examinations and qualifications during the senior phase, which covers secondary stages 4 to 6 when students are generally aged 14 to 17. The framework is designed to be flexible so that pupils can progress at their own pace.

Level	Stage
Early	The pre-school years and primary 1 (ages 3–5), or later for some
First	To the end of primary 4 (age 8), but earlier or later for some
Second	To the end of primary 7 (age 11), but earlier or later for some
Third and Fourth	Secondary 1 to secondary 3 (ages 12–14), but earlier for some. The fourth level experiences and outcomes are intended to provide possibilities for choice and young people's programmes will not include all of the fourth level outcomes
Senior phase	Secondary 4 to secondary 6 (ages 15–18), and college or other means of study

Under the new curriculum, assessment of students' progress and achievements from ages 3 to 15 is carried out by teachers who base their assessment judgments on a range of evidence rather than single assessment instruments such as tests. Teachers have access to an online National Assessment Resource (NAR), which provides a range of assessment material and national exemplars across the curriculum areas.

In the senior phase, young people aged 16 to 18, including those studying outside school, build up a portfolio of national qualifications, awarded by the Scottish Qualifications Authority (SQA).

Provision is made for teaching in Gaelic in many parts of Scotland and the number of pupils, from nursery to secondary, in Gaelic-medium education is growing.

EDUCATION SCOTLAND T 0141-282 5000
W www.educationscotland.gov.uk
SCOTTISH QUALIFICATIONS AUTHORITY
T 0845-279 1000 W www.sqa.org.uk

NORTHERN IRELAND

In September 2009 Northern Ireland put in place across Years 1 to 12 a revised statutory curriculum placing greater emphasis on developing skills and preparing young people for life and work.

This curriculum includes a new Foundation Stage to cover Years 1 and 2 of primary school, so as to allow a more appropriate learning style for the youngest pupils and to ease the transition from pre-school. Key Stage 1 covers primary Years 3 and 4, until children are 8, and Key Stage 2 covers primary Years 5, 6 and 7, until children are 11. Post-primary, Key Stage 3 covers Years 8, 9 and 10 and Key Stage 4 Years 11 and 12.

The current primary curriculum is made up of the following areas of learning:
• Language and literacy
• Mathematics and numeracy
• The arts
• The world around us
• Personal development and mutual understanding
• Physical education
• Religeous education

The current post-primary curriculum includes a new area of learning for life and work, made up of employability, personal development, local and global citizenship and home economics (at Key Stage 3). It is also made up of RE and the following areas of learning:
• Language and literacy
• Mathematics and numeracy
• Modern languages
• The arts
• Environment and society
• Physical education
• Science and technology

At Key Stage 4, there are nine areas of learning, but statutory requirements have been significantly reduced to: learning for life and work, physical education and RE. The aim is to provide greater choice and flexibility for pupils and allow them access to a wider range of academic and vocational courses provided under the revised curriculum's 'Entitlement Framework' (EF).

Since September 2013, schools have been required to provide pupils with access to at least 18 courses at Key Stage 4 and 21 courses at post-16. This increased to 24 and 27 courses respectively in September 2015. At least one third of the courses must be 'general' with one third 'applied'. The remaining third is at the discretion of each school. Individual pupils decide on the number and mix of courses they wish to follow.

RE is a compulsory part of the Northern Ireland curriculum, although parents have the right to withdraw their children from part or all of RE or collective worship. Schools have to provide RE in accordance with a core syllabus drawn up by the province's four main churches (Church of Ireland, Presbyterian, Methodist and Roman Catholic) and specified by the Department of Education.

Revised assessment and reporting arrangements were introduced when the curriculum was revised. The focus from Foundation to Key Stage 3 is on 'Assessment for Learning'. This programme includes classroom-based teacher assessment, computer-based assessment of literacy and numeracy and pupils deciding on their strengths and weaknesses and how they might progress to achieve their potential. Assessment information is given to parents in an annual report. Pupils at Key Stage 4 and beyond continue to be assessed through public examinations.

The Council for the Curriculum, Examinations and Assessment (CCEA), a non-departmental public body reporting to the Department of Education in Northern Ireland, is unique in the UK in combining the functions of a curriculum advisory body, an awarding body and a qualifications regulatory body. It advises the government on what should be taught in Northern Ireland's schools and colleges, ensures that the qualifications and examinations offered by awarding bodies in Northern Ireland are of an appropriate quality and standard and, as the leading awarding body itself, offers a range of qualifications including GCSEs, A-levels and AS-levels.

The CCEA hosts a dedicated curriculum website covering all aspects of the revised curriculum, assessment and reporting.

COUNCIL FOR THE CURRICULUM, EXAMINATIONS AND ASSESSMENT T 028-9026 1200 W www.ccea.org.uk
NORTHERN IRELAND CURRICULUM
T 028-9028 1200 W www.nicurriculum.org.uk

QUALIFICATIONS

ENGLAND, WALES AND NORTHERN IRELAND

There is a very wide range of public examinations and qualifications available, accredited by the Office of Qualifications and Examinations Regulation (OFQUAL) in England, the Department for Education and Skills (DfES) in Wales, and the Council for the Curriculum, Examinations and Assessment (CCEA) in Northern Ireland. Up-to-date information on all accredited qualifications and awarding bodies is available online at the Register of Regulated Qualifications website.

The qualifications frameworks group all accredited qualifications into levels, up to level 8. All the qualifications within a level place similar demands on individuals as learners. Entry level, for example, covers basic knowledge and skills in English, maths and ICT not geared towards specific occupations, level 3 includes qualifications such as A-levels which are appropriate for those wishing to go on to higher education, level 7 covers Master's degrees and vocational qualifications appropriate for senior professionals and managers and level 8 is equivalent to a doctorate.

Young people aged 14 to 19 in schools or (post-16) colleges or apprenticeships may gain academic qualifications such as GCSEs, AS-levels and A-levels; qualifications linked to particular career fields, like diplomas; vocational qualifications such as BTECs and NVQs; and functional key or basic skills qualifications.

The National Qualifications Framework (NQF) formerly used in England, Wales and Northern Ireland has now been replaced by the Qualifications and Credit Framework (QCF) for England and Northern Ireland and the Credit and Qualifications Framework for Wales (CQFW). There is also a Framework for Higher Education Qualifications (FHEQ) for England, Wales and Northern Ireland.

QUALIFICATIONS AND CREDIT FRAMEWORK (QCF)
This framework, originally designed for vocational qualifications, has now been broadened to include all accredited academic, vocational or other qualifications taken in schools, further education, higher education or elsewhere. The QCF goes from entry level up to level 8. Qualifications in the QCF are built up of units of learning, and every qualification or

unit recognised in the framework has a credit value, showing how long it takes to complete. One credit is equivalent to ten hours. As each unit and the credits can be transferred, the system enables learners to complete qualifications at their own pace. When an individual takes QCF units or qualifications, their learning is 'banked' and stored on their personal learner record.

QCF qualifications include GCSEs and A-levels; International Baccalaureate; BTEC courses; English for Speakers of Other Languages (ESOL); Skills for Life; Foundation Learning; National Vocational Qualifications (NVQs); Cambridge Nationals; Higher National Certificates (HNC); and Higher National Diplomas (HND).

FRAMEWORK FOR HIGHER EDUCATION QUALIFICATIONS (FHEQ)

This framework applies to degrees, diplomas, certificates and other academic awards (other than honorary degrees and higher doctorates) granted by a higher education provider in the exercise of its degree awarding powers. It starts at QCF level 4 and goes up to level 8 and includes the following qualifications: Certificate of Higher Education; Diploma of Higher Education; Bachelor's degrees; Master's degrees; and Doctoral degrees.

COUNCIL FOR THE CURRICULUM, EXAMINATIONS AND ASSESSMENT (NORTHERN IRELAND)
T 028-9026 1200 W www.ccea.org.uk

DEPARTMENT FOR EDUCATION AND SKILLS (DfES)
T 0300-0603300; 0845-010 3300

W http://wales.gov.uk/topics/educationandskills

REGISTER OF REGULATED QUALIFICATIONS
T 0300-303 3346 W http://register.ofqual.gov.uk

OFFICE OF QUALIFICATIONS AND EXAMINATIONS REGULATION (OFQUAL) T 0300-303 3344
W www.ofqual.gov.uk

GCSE

The vast majority of pupils in their last year of compulsory schooling in England, Wales and Northern Ireland take at least one General Certificate of Secondary Education (GCSE) exam, though GCSEs may be taken at any age. GCSEs assess the performance of pupils on a subject-specific basis and are mostly taken after a two-year course. They are available in more than 50 subjects, most of them academic subjects, though some, known as vocational or applied GCSEs, involve the study of a particular area of employment and the development of work-related skills. Some subjects are also offered as short-course qualifications, equivalent to half a standard GCSE, or as double awards, equivalent to two GCSEs.

For many years GCSEs have been assessed on coursework completed by students during the course as well as exams at the end and GCSE certificates have been awarded on an eight-point scale from A* to G. In most subjects two different papers, foundation and higher, are provided for different ranges of ability, with grades A*–D available to students taking the higher paper and grades C–G available from the foundation paper.

Major changes to GCSEs are taking place in England. From 2015, GCSEs no longer involve modules and coursework, just exams at the end of the two-year course. The pass mark will be higher and the qualifications will be graded 9 to 1, rather than A* to G. There will no longer be controlled assessments (coursework done under exam conditions) and final exams will be essay-based. Changes will initially be for nine core GCSE subjects. Revised GCSEs in English language, English literature and mathematics began in September 2015 and those in chemistry, biology, physics, science (double award), geography, history and modern foreign languages will be taught from September 2016. Revised GCSEs in art and design, computer science, citizenship, dance, design and technology, drama, music, physical education and religious studies will also be ready for teaching from September 2016. The remaining subjects will either be reformed for teaching from 2017 or withdrawn.
W www.gov.uk/government/collections/gcse-subject-content

All GCSE specifications, assessments and grading procedures are monitored by OFQUAL, DfES and the CCEA.

Since September 2010 the government has allowed state schools to offer pupils International GCSE (iGCSE) exams in key subjects including English, mathematics, science and ICT. The iGCSEs do not include coursework and some experts consider them more rigorous than traditional GCSEs.

GCE A-LEVEL AND AS-LEVEL

GCE (General Certificate of Education) Advanced levels (A-levels) are the qualifications used by most young people in England, Wales and Northern Ireland to gain entry to university.

A-levels are subject-based qualifications. They are mostly taken by UK students aged 16 to 19 over a two-year course in school sixth forms or at college, but can be taken at any age. They are available in more than 45, mostly academic, subjects, though there are some A-levels in vocational areas, often termed 'applied A-levels'.

Traditionally, A-level qualifications consists of two parts: advanced subsidiary (AS) and A2 units. The AS has traditionally been a standalone qualification normally consisting of two units, assessed at the standard expected for a learner half way through an A-level course, that together contribute 50 per cent towards the full A-level. The A2 is the second half of a full A-level qualification. It normally consists of two units, assessed at the standard expected for a learner at the end of a full A-level course, that together make-up the remaining 50 per cent of the full A-level qualification. Most units are assessed by examination. Each unit is graded A–E. Since 2010 an A* grade has been awarded to exceptional candidates.

An extended project was introduced in September 2008 as a separate qualification. It is a single piece of work on a topic of the student's own choosing that requires a high degree of planning, preparation, research and autonomous working. Awards are graded A–E and the extended project is accredited as half an A-level.

Since September 2013, students in England in their first or second year of A-level studies can no longer sit A-level exams in January. A-levels are still examined unit by unit, but all exams are taken in the summer.

From 2015, revised AS and A-levels are being introduced in phases until 2017. All assessment of the new A-levels will take place at the end of the two-year course and the AS will become an entirely standalone qualification rather than contributing to a full A-level qualification.

Since September 2015 students have been taught the new-style AS-level and A-level in art and design, biology, business, chemistry, computer science, economics, English language, English language and literature, English literature, history, physics, psychology and sociology. The new AS and A-levels in ancient languages, dance, drama and theatre, geography, modern foreign languages (French, German and Spanish), music, physical education and religious studies will be taught from September 2016.

Further subjects in the new AS and A-level will be ready for teaching from September 2017.
W www.gov.uk/government/collections/gce-as-and-a-level-subject-content

INTERNATIONAL BACCALAUREATE

The International Baccalaureate (IB) offers four educational programmes for students aged 3 to 19: IB primary years programme, IB middle years programme, IB diploma programme, IB career-related certificate.

Some 155 'IB World Schools' in the UK offer at least one IB programme.

The IB diploma programme for students aged 16 to 19 is based around detailed academic study of a wide range of subjects, including languages, the arts, science, maths, history and geography, this leads to a single qualification recognised by UK universities.

The IB diploma is made up of a compulsory 'core' plus six separate subjects where individuals have some choice over what they study. The compulsory core contains three elements: theory of knowledge; creativity, action and service; and a 4,000-word extended essay.

The diploma normally takes two years to complete and most of the assessment is done through externally marked examinations. Candidates are awarded points for each part of the programme, up to a maximum of 45. A candidate must score 24 points or more to achieve a full diploma.

Successfully completing the diploma earns points on the 'UCAS tariff', the UK system for allocating points to qualifications used for entry to higher education. An IB diploma total of 24 points is worth 260 UCAS points – the same as a B and two C grades at A-level. The maximum of 45 points earns 720 UCAS points – equivalent to six A-levels at grade A.

WELSH BACCALAUREATE

The Welsh Baccalaureate Qualification (WBQ), available for 14- to 19-year-olds in Wales, combines a compulsory core, which incorporates personal development skills, with options from existing academic and vocational qualifications, such as A-levels, GCSEs and NVQs, to make one broader award. The WBQ can be studied in English or Welsh, or a combination of the two. Candidates who meet the requirements of the compulsory core and options relevant to each level of the qualification are awarded the Welsh Baccalaureate Foundation, Intermediate or Advanced Diploma as appropriate.

WJEC (Welsh Joint Education Committee), which administers the WBQ, has also developed two new WBQs at level 1 and level 2 suitable for delivery over one year and with a particular focus on employability. These are currently only available as a pilot in some colleges or work-based learning providers.

A revised and more rigorous Welsh Baccalaureate has been taught since September 2015. It is based on a Skills Challenge Certificate, which will be graded, and supporting qualifications. The aim is to enable learners to develop and demonstrate an understanding of, and proficiency in, essential and employability skills: communication, numeracy, digital Literacy, planning and organisation, creativity and innovation, critical thinking and problem solving, and personal effectiveness. The emphasis is on applied and purposeful learning and opportunities for assessment in a range of real life contexts through three 'challenge briefs' and an individual project.

BTECS, OCR NATIONALS AND OTHER VOCATIONAL QUALIFICATIONS

Vocational qualifications can range from general qualifications where a person learns skills relevant to a variety of jobs, to specialist qualifications designed for a particular sector. They are available from several awarding bodies, such as City & Guilds, Edexcel and OCR, and can be taken at many different levels. All vocational and work-related qualifications fit into the Qualifications and Credit Framework (QCF).

BTEC qualifications and OCR Nationals are particular types of work-related qualifications, available in a wide range of subjects, including: art and design, business, health and social care, information technology, media, public services, science and sport. The qualifications offer a mix of theory and practice, can include work experience and can take be part of an Apprenticeship. They can be studied full-time at college or school, or part-time at college.

Learners complete a range of assignments, case studies and practical activities, as well as a portfolio of evidence that shows what work has been completed.

From 2016, the quality and assessment of all vocational courses offered by schools and colleges to 14- to 19-year-olds will be strengthened. The standards of reformed BTECs, along with Cambridge OCR National Certificates and Vocational Certificates (V-Certs), will equal those of GCSE A*–C grades. All vocational qualifications will be graded (previously many were simply pass/fail) and all will have a 25 per cent externally examined component.

NVQS

A National Vocational Qualification (NVQ) is a 'competence-based' qualification that is recognised by employers. Individuals learn practical, work-related tasks designed to help them develop the skills and knowledge to do a particular job effectively. NVQs can be taken in school, at college or by people already in work. There are more than 1,300 different NVQs available from the vast majority of business sectors. NVQs exist at levels 1 to 5 on the QCF. An NVQ qualification at level 2 or 3 can also be taken as part of an Apprenticeship.

FUNCTIONAL SKILLS

Functional skills qualifications were launched during 2010, for all learners aged 14 and above. They test practical skills that allow people to work confidently, effectively and independently in life, and are available only in England. Wales and Northern Ireland have literacy and numeracy qualifications known as 'essential skills'.

Following a review by OFQUAL, the functional skills qualifications in English and mathematics are changing. Assessment materials will be improved, the risk of malpractice will be reduced, standard setting procedures will be strengthened and there will be better evaluation of how well the qualifications meet user needs.

APPRENTICESHIPS

Apprenticeships combine on-the-job training with nationally recognised qualifications, allowing individuals to gain skills and qualifications while working and earning a wage. More than 200 different types of apprenticeships are available, offering over 1,500 job roles; they take between one and five years to complete. There are four levels available:

• Intermediate Apprenticeships – at level 2 on the National Qualifications Framework (NQF), they are equivalent to five good GCSE passes
• Advanced Apprenticeships – at level 3 on the NQF, they are equivalent to two A-level passes
• Higher Apprenticeships – lead to qualifications at NVQ Level 4 or, in some cases, a foundation degree
• Degree Apprenticeships – added in 2015 (see Recent Developments)

In England, the National Apprenticeship Service (NAS), launched in 2009, is responsible for the delivery of apprenticeships and provides an online vacancy matching system. In 2013–14, some 440,000 young people (53 per cent women and 47 per cent men) started apprenticeships in England. The Welsh government and the Department for

Employment and Learning (DEL) are responsible for the apprenticeship programmes in Wales and Northern Ireland respectively.

NATIONAL APPRENTICESHIP SERVICE (NAS)
T 02476-826482 W www.apprenticeships.gov.uk

SCOTLAND

Scotland has its own system of public examinations and qualifications. The Scottish Qualifications Authority (SQA) is Scotland's national body for qualifications, responsible for developing, accrediting, assessing and certificating all Scottish qualifications apart from university degrees and some professional body qualifications.

There are qualifications at all levels of attainment. Almost all school candidates gain SQA qualifications in the fourth year of secondary school and most obtain further qualifications in the fifth or sixth year or in further education colleges. Increasingly, people also take them in the workplace.

SQA, with partners such as Universities Scotland, has introduced the Scottish Credit and Qualifications Framework (SCQF) as a way of comparing and understanding Scottish qualifications. It includes qualifications across academic and vocational sectors and compares them by giving a level and credit points. There are 12 levels in the SCQF, level 1 being the least difficult and level 12 the most difficult. The number of SCQF credit points shows how much learning has to be done to achieve the qualification. For instance, one SCQF credit point equals about 10 hours of learning including assessment.

* Standard Grades are taken over the third and fourth years at secondary school. Students often choose to study seven or eight subjects, of which Mathematics and English are compulsory. There are three levels of study at Standard Grade: Foundation, General and Credit. Students usually sit exams at two levels – either Foundation/General or General/Credit – to ensure they have the best chance of achieving as high a grade as possible.
* National Units are the building blocks of National Courses, but they are also recognised qualifications in their own right and are designed to take approximately 40 hours of teaching time to complete.
* National Courses usually comprise three National Units and an externally marked assessment. National Courses are available at a number of levels including Access 1, Access 2, Access 3, Intermediate 1, Intermediate 2, Higher and Advanced Higher.
* Skills for Work courses encourage school pupils to become familiar with the world of work. They involve a strong element of learning through involvement in practical and vocational activities and develop knowledge, skills and experience that are related to employment. They are available at a number of levels and are frequently delivered in partnership between schools and colleges.
* Wider Achievement qualifications provide young people with the opportunity to have learning and skills formally recognised, whether developed in or outside the classroom. Available at a number of levels in subjects including Employability, Leadership and Enterprise, these qualifications help schools deliver skills for learning, life and work.
* Scottish Baccalaureates consist of a coherent group of Higher and Advanced Higher qualifications and, uniquely, an interdisciplinary project of candidates' own choosing which is marked at Advanced Higher level in one of four broad topics – languages, science, expressive arts or social studies. Aimed at high-achieving candidates in their sixth year, the Scottish Baccalaureate is designed to encourage personalised, in-depth study and interdisciplinary learning in the later stages of secondary school.

As part of the Curriculum for Excellence programme (see above) SQA has developed new National qualifications that became available in schools from August 2013, replacing Standard Grade, Intermediate and Access qualifications at all levels. New Higher qualifications became available from August 2014 and Advanced Higher qualifications will be available from August 2015:

SCQF Level	New national qualifications	Replaces
1 and 2	National 1 and 2	Access 1 and Access 2
3	National 3	Access 3 Standard Grade (Foundation Level)
4	National 4	Standard Grade (General Level) Intermediate 1
5	National 5	Standard Grade (Credit Level) Intermediate 2
6	Higher (new)	Higher
7	Advanced Higher (new)	Advanced Higher

All new qualifications will run concurrently with existing qualifications until 2015/16. Final results for existing Access, Intermediate, Higher and Advanced Higher qualifications were issued in August 2015.

SQA has also developed five new Awards – in modern languages, personal achievement, personal development, religion and wellbeing – that cover work from across different subject areas, and are shorter than traditional courses and recognise success across different levels of difficulty. These started in August 2012 and are marked and assessed by schools and colleges rather than by external assessment or exams. New Awards in Cycling and Scottish Studies began in August 2013.

SQA QUALIFICATIONS

HIGHER NATIONAL CERTIFICATES AND HIGHER NATIONAL DIPLOMAS

Higher National Certificates and Higher National Diplomas (HNCs and HNDs) are offered by colleges, some universities and many other training providers – including employers. Both HNCs and HNDs are comprised of Higher National Units and cover a wide range of subject areas. Many HNDs allow the holder entry to the second or third year of a degree course. HNCs are available at SCQF level 7, HNDs at level 8.

NATIONAL QUALIFICATION GROUP AWARDS

National Certificates and National Progression Awards are designed to prepare people for employment, career development or progression to more advanced study at HNC/HND level. They also aim to develop a range of transferable knowledge including core skills. These certificates are aimed at 16- to 18-year-olds or adults in full-time education and are at SCQF levels 2 to 6. Each one has specific aims relating to a subject or occupational area.

SCOTTISH VOCATIONAL QUALIFICATIONS

Scottish Vocational Qualifications (SVQs) are based on national standards drawn up by people from industry, commerce and education. Possession of an SVQ demonstrates ability to perform in a job to agreed national standards. Primarily delivered to candidates in full-time employment, SVQs are available at SCQF levels 4 to 12.

PROFESSIONAL DEVELOPMENT AWARDS

Professional Development Awards (PDAs) are designed to develop and deliver high-level skills in a sharp, flexible and focused way. They are for people already in work who wish to extend or broaden their skills. Candidates often take a

PDA after completing a degree or vocational qualification. PDAs are available at SCQF levels 6 to 12.

THE SCOTTISH QUALIFICATIONS AUTHORITY (SQA) T 0845-279 1000 W www.sqa.org.uk

SCOTTISH CREDIT AND QUALIFICATIONS FRAMEWORK (SCQF) T 0845-270 7371 W www.scqf.org.uk

FURTHER EDUCATION AND LIFELONG LEARNING

ENGLAND

The further education (FE) system in England provides a wide range of education and training opportunities for young people and adults. From the age of 16, young people who wish to remain in education, but not in a school setting, can undertake further education (including skills training) in an FE college. There are two main types of college in the FE sector: sixth form colleges and general further education (GFE) colleges. Some FE colleges focus on a particular area, such as art and design or agriculture and horticulture. Each institution decides its own range of subjects and courses. Students at FE colleges can study for a wide and growing range of academic and/or work-related qualifications, from entry level to higher education level.

Though the Department for Business, Innovation and Skills is responsible for the FE sector and for funding FE for adults (19 or over), the Department for Education funds all education and training for 16- to 18-year-olds.

The proportion of 16- to 18-year-olds in education or training has risen steadily over recent years. Those in full-time education increased to a high of 71.5 per cent in 2014, driven by increase in state-funded schools and higher education, and is expected to increase to 100 per cent in 2015 as the education-leaving age in England becomes 18. It is assumed that most of the additional students will go into FE or work-based training rather than staying on at school.

The 'September Guarantee', introduced in 2007, offers a place in post-16 education or training to all 16- and 17-year-olds who want one. In 2014, 93.2 per cent of 16- and 17-year-olds in England received an offer of a place. A new Education Funding Agency (EFA) was established in April 2012 as an executive agency of the Department for Education (DfE). It is responsible for education funding for 16- to 19-year-olds as well as academies.

The FE sector in England, as in other parts of the UK, also provides a range of opportunities for adults.

The Skills Funding Agency (SFA), part of the Department for Business, Innovation and Skills, is presently responsible for funding and regulating education and training for adults. It will invest government funding of around £3.86bn in FE and skills training places in 2015–16.

In November 2010, the government announced a new strategy for FE, including more adult apprenticeships (provision for 200,000 adults by 2014–15); fully funded training for 19- to 24-year-olds undertaking their first full level 2 (GCSE equivalent) or first level 3 qualification when they do not already have one; and fully funded basic skills for people who left school without basic skills in reading, writing and mathematics. 'Train to Gain', the programme that funded trainees sponsored by employers, was replaced in July 2011 by a programme focused on helping small employers to train low-skilled staff. This was followed in December 2011 by a plan to reform FE that focuses on students and in April 2012 by the creation of a National Careers Service.

In April 2013, the government announced plans to make the skills system more 'responsive' and to create new traineeships.

From 2014, Tech-levels will take as long to complete as A-Levels and will need to be endorsed by either a professional association or by five employers registered with Companies House. These qualifications will focus on hands-on practical training leading to recognised occupations for example in engineering, computing, accounting or hospitality.

Applied General Qualifications will take the same time to complete as AS-levels and will focus on broader study of a technical area, not directly linked to an occupation. These qualifications will need backing from three universities to count in the school and college performance tables.

A Tech-level along with a core maths qualification, for example AS-level maths, and an extended project will amount to an over-arching Technical Baccalaureate.

New Substantial Vocational Qualifications at level 2 will provide 16- to 19-year-old students seeking entry at a more basic level to a skilled trade or occupation with qualifications that are valued by employers.

There are currently 19 centres of training excellence called National Skills Academies, led, funded and designed by employers, in various stages of development. Each academy offers specialist training in a key sector of the economy, working in partnership with colleges, schools and independent training providers.

Among the many voluntary bodies providing adult education, the Workers' Educational Association (WEA) is the UK's largest, operating throughout England and Scotland. It provides part-time courses to adults in response to local need in community centres, village halls, schools, pubs or workplaces. Similar but separate WEA organisations operate in Wales and Northern Ireland.

The National Institute of Adult Continuing Education (NIACE), a charitable non-governmental organisation, promotes lifelong learning opportunities for adults in England and Wales.

NATIONAL INSTITUTE OF ADULT CONTINUING EDUCATION (NIACE) T 0116-204 4200 W www.niace.org.uk

THE SKILLS FUNDING AGENCY T 0345-377 5000 W www.gov.uk/government/organisations/skills-funding-agency

WORKERS' EDUCATIONAL ASSOCIATION (WEA) T 020-7426 3450 W www.wea.org.uk

WALES

In Wales, the aims and makeup of the FE system are similar to those outlined for England. The Welsh government funds a wide range of learning programmes for young people through its 15 FE colleges, and local authorities and private organisations. The Welsh government has set out plans to improve learning opportunities for all post-16 learners in the shortest possible time, to increase the engagement of disadvantaged young people in the learning process, and to transform the learning network to increase learner choice, reduce duplication of provision and encourage higher-quality learning and teaching in all post-16 provision. One goal is to ensure that, by 2015, 95 per cent of young people will be ready for high-skilled employment or higher education by the age of 25.

In Wales, responsibility for adult and continuing education lies with the Department for Education and Skills (DfES) within the Welsh government. Wales operates a range of programmes to support skills development, including subsidised work-based training courses for employees and the Workforce Development Programme, where employers can use the free services of experienced skills advisers to develop staff training plans.

COLLEGES WALES T 029-2052 2500 W www.collegeswales.ac.uk

COLEG HARLECH WEA T 01248-353254
W www.harlech.ac.uk/en
NIACE DYSGU CYMRU T 029-2037 0900
W www.niacedc.org.uk
WEA SOUTH WALES T 029-2023 5277
W www.swales.wea.org.uk

SCOTLAND

Following a series of mergers, Scotland now has 27 FE colleges (known simply as colleges) which are at the fore-front of lifelong learning, education, training and skills in Scotland. Colleges cater for the needs of learners both in and out of employment, at all stages in their lives from middle secondary school and earlier to retirement. Colleges' courses span much of the range of learning needs, from specialised vocational education and training through to general educational programmes. The level of provision ranges from essential life skills and provision for students with learning difficulties to HNCs and HNDs. Some colleges, notably those in the Highlands and Islands, also deliver degrees and postgraduate qualifications.

A shift in study patterns is taking place within the college sector as colleges concentrate on full-time courses aimed at helping people gain employment and no longer fund short courses lasting less than ten hours. Overall figures are stable but this change has led to a decline in part-time study and an increase in full-time study.

The Scottish Funding Council (SFC) is the statutory body responsible for funding teaching and learning provision, research and other activities in Scotland's colleges. Overall strategic direction for the sector is provided by the Lifelong Learning Directorate of the Scottish government, which provides annual guidance to the SFC and liaises closely with bodies such as Colleges Scotland, the Scottish Qualifications Authority and the FE colleges themselves to ensure that policies remain relevant and practical.

The Scottish government takes responsibility for community learning and development in Scotland while Skills Development Scotland, a non-departmental public body, is charged with improving Scotland's skills performance by linking skills supply and demand and helping people and organisations to learn, develop and make use of these skills to greater effect. ILA Scotland is a Scottish government scheme delivered by Skills Development Scotland that provides funding for training to individuals over the age of 16 with an income of less than £22,000 a year.

ILA SCOTLAND T 0800-917 8000
W www.myworldofwork.co.uk/section/funding
COLLEGES SCOTLAND T 01786-892100
W www.collegesscotland.ac.uk
SCOTTISH FUNDING COUNCIL T 0131-313 6500
W www.sfc.ac.uk
SKILLS DEVELOPMENT SCOTLAND T 0141-285 6000
W www.skillsdevelopmentscotland.co.uk

NORTHERN IRELAND

FE in Northern Ireland is provided through six regional multi-campus colleges and the College of Agriculture, Food and Rural Affairs (CAFRE). Most secondary schools also have a sixth form which students may attend for two additional years to complete their AS-levels and A-levels.

Colleges Northern Ireland (CNI) acts as the representative body for the six FE colleges which, like their counterparts in the rest of the UK, are independent corporate bodies each managed by their own governing body. The range of courses that they offer spans essential skills, a wide choice of vocational and academic programmes and higher education programmes. Most full-time students in the six colleges are aged 16 to 19, while most part-time students are over 19.

The Department for Employment and Learning (DELNI) is responsible for the policy, strategic development and financing of the statutory FE sector and for lifelong learning, and also provides support to a small number of non-statutory FE providers. The Educational Guidance Service for Adults (EGSA), an independent, not-for-profit organisation, has a network of local offices based across Northern Ireland which provide services to adult learners, learning advisers, providers, employers and others interested in improving access to learning for adults.

COLLEGES NORTHERN IRELAND (CNI)
T 028-9068 2296 W www.anic.ac.uk
THE EDUCATIONAL GUIDANCE SERVICE FOR
ADULTS W www.egsa.org.uk
WEA NORTHERN IRELAND T 028-9032 9718
W www.wea-ni.com

FINANCIAL SUPPORT

England has a bursary scheme of up to £1,200 a year for full-time 16- to 19-year-old students facing financial hardship. Two types of bursary exist: vulnerable student bursary and discretionary bursary. Help with transport costs is also possible for some students. This scheme replaced the Education Maintenance Allowance (EMA) which gave 16- to 19-year-olds from low-income families a weekly allowance to continue in education.

There are EMA schemes in Scotland, Wales and Northern Ireland, but with slightly different eligibility conditions. Students must apply to the EMA scheme for the part of the UK where they intend to study. In Northern Ireland 16- to 19-year-old students, who meet the relevant criteria, and live in a household that has an annual income of £20,500 or less a year (£22,500 if there is more than one young person in the household who qualifies for child benefit) automatically get £30 a week in 2015–16.

Colleges and learning providers award learner support funds directly to new students aged 19 and over.

Care to Learn is available in England to help young parents under the age of 20, who are caring for their own child or children while they are in some form of publicly funded learning (below higher education level), with the costs of childcare and travel. The scheme is not income assessed and pays up to £160 a week (£175 in London) to cover costs.

Dance and Drama Awards (DaDA) are state-funded scholarships for students over the age of 16 enrolled at one of 19 private dance and drama schools in England, who are taking specified courses at National Certificate or National Diploma level. Awards, based on household income, cover some of students' tuition fees and up to £5,185 maintenance in 2015–16.

Young people studying away from home because their chosen course is not available locally may qualify for the *Residential Support Scheme*.

Information and advice on funding support and applications are available from the Learner Support helpline (T 0800-121 8989) or on the GOV.UK website (*see* below).

Discretionary Support Funds (DSF) are available in colleges and school sixth forms to help students who have trouble meeting the costs of participating in further education.

In Wales, students aged 19 or over on FE courses may be eligible for the *Welsh Government Learning Grant FE* (previously the *Assembly Learning Grant for Further Education*). This is a means-tested payment of up to £1,500 for full-time students and up to £750 for those studying part-time. *Discretionary Financial Contingency Funds* are also available to all students in Wales suffering hardship and are administered by the institutions themselves.

In Scotland, FE students can apply to their college for discretionary support in the form of *Further Education*

Bursaries. These can include allowances for maintenance, travel, study, childcare and additional support needs. *Individual Learning Accounts* provide up to £200 for those with incomes of less than £22,000.

In Northern Ireland, FE students may be eligible for *Further Education Awards,* non-refundable assistance administered on behalf of the five Education and Library Boards by the Western Education and Library Board.

UK FE students over 18 whose costs are not fully met from the grants described above may also be eligible for *Professional and Career Development Loans.* These loans – also available to HE students – cover up to 80 per cent of course fees (up to 100 per cent for those unemployed for three months); other course costs, such as books, travel and childcare; and living expenses, such as rent, food and clothing (for those who are unemployed or working fewer than 30 hours a week). The loans, of between £300 and £10,000, are available from participating high street banks. The Skills Funding Agency (SFA) pays the interest on the loan while the student is studying and for one month afterwards. Once students complete their courses, they must pay interest at the rate fixed when they took out the loan, which will be competitive with other commercially available 'unsecured' personal loans.
CAREERS SCOTLAND W www.careers-
    scotland.org.uk/Education/Funding/Funding.asp
GOV.UK W www.gov.uk/further-education-courses/financial-help
STUDENT FINANCE WALES T 0845-602 8845
    W www.studentfinancewales.co.uk
WESTERN EDUCATION AND LIBRARY BOARD
    T 028-8241 1411 W www.welbni.org

HIGHER EDUCATION

Publicly funded higher education (HE) in the UK is provided in 334 universities, higher education colleges and other specialist HE institutions, and a significant number of FE colleges offering higher education courses.

The Higher Education Funding Council for England (HEFCE) funds teaching and research in 121 English higher education institutions (HEIs), of which 103 have university status, and 205 FE colleges.

The Higher Education Funding Council for Wales (HEFCW) distributes funding for HE in Wales through Wales's 10 HEIs and some FE colleges.

The Scottish Funding Council (SFC) – which is also responsible for FE in Scotland – is the national strategic body responsible for funding HE teaching and research in Scotland's 19 HEIs and 27 colleges.

In Northern Ireland, HE is provided by two universities, two university colleges, six regional institutes of further and higher education and the Open University (OU), which operates UK-wide. Unlike other parts of the UK, Northern Ireland has no higher education funding council; the Department for Employment and Learning fulfils that role.

All UK universities and a number of HE colleges award their own degrees and other HE qualifications. HE providers who do not have their own degree-awarding powers offer degrees under 'validation arrangements' with other institutions that do have those powers. The OU, for example, runs a validation service which enables a number of other institutions to award OU degrees, after the OU has assured itself that the academic standards of their courses are as high as the OU's own standards.

Each HE institution is responsible for the standards of the awards it makes and the quality of the education it provides to its students, and each has its own internal quality assurance procedures. External quality assurance for HE institutions throughout the UK is provided by the Quality Assurance Agency for Higher Education (QAA).

The QAA is independent of government, funded by subscriptions from all publicly funded UK universities and colleges of HE. Its main role is to safeguard the standards of HE qualifications. It does this by defining standards for HE through a framework known as the academic infrastructure. QAA carries out reviews of the quality of UK HE institutions via a system known as 'institutional audits'. QAA also advises government on a range of HE quality issues, including applications for the grant of degree-awarding powers. It publishes reports on its review activities on its website.
DEPARTMENT FOR EMPLOYMENT AND LEARNING
    T 028-9025 7777 W www.delni.gov.uk
HIGHER EDUCATION FUNDING COUNCIL FOR
    ENGLAND T 0117-931 7317 W www.hefce.ac.uk
HIGHER EDUCATION FUNDING COUNCIL FOR
    WALES T 029-2076 1861 W www.hefcw.ac.uk
SCOTTISH FUNDING COUNCIL T 0131-313 6500
    W www.sfc.ac.uk
THE QUALITY ASSURANCE AGENCY FOR HIGHER
    EDUCATION T 01452-557000 W www.qaa.ac.uk
See also Universities for information on the 2014 Research Excellence Framework (which replaced the Research Assessment Exercise) and listings of universities in the UK.

STUDENTS APPLYING TO UNIVERSITY			
	2014	2015	*Difference*
Total applicants	634,610	647,610	2%
Source: UCAS			

STUDENTS IN HIGHER EDUCATION (2013–14)*			
	Full-time	*Part-time*	*Total*
HE students	1,696,030	603,325	2,299,355
Postgraduate students	304,445	234,995	539,440
Undergraduate students	1,391,585	368,330	1,759,915
*Includes UK, EU and non-EU students			
Source: Higher Education Statistics Agency (HESA) 2014			

UK HIGHER EDUCATION QUALIFICATIONS AWARDED (2013–14)		
	Full-time	*Part-time*
First degrees	383,630	38,220
Other undergraduate qualifications	53,875	44,145
Postgraduate Certificate in Education (PGCE)	21,305	1,055
Other postgraduate qualifications	14,570	32,345
Total higher degrees including doctorates	146,900	41,770
Source: HESA 2014		

COURSES
HE institutions in the UK mainly offer courses leading to the following qualifications. These qualifications go from levels 4 to 8 on England's Qualifications and Credit Framework, levels 7 to 12 on Scotland's Credit and Qualifications Framework. Individual HEIs may not offer all of these.

Certificates of Higher Education (CertHE) are awarded after one year's full-time study (or equivalent). If available to students on longer courses, they certify that students have reached a minimum standard in their first year.

Diplomas of Higher Education (DipHE) and other *Higher Diplomas* are awarded after two to three years' full-time study (or equivalent). They certify that a student has achieved a minimum standard in first- and second-year courses and, in the case of nursing, third-year courses. They can often be used for entry to the third year of a related degree course.

Foundation degrees are awarded after two years of full-time study (or equivalent). These degrees combine academic study with work-based learning, and have been designed jointly by universities, colleges and employers with a particular area of work in mind. They are usually accepted as a basis for entry to the third year of a related degree course.

Bachelor's degrees, also referred to as *first degrees,* have different titles, Bachelor of Arts (BA) and Bachelor of Science (BSc) being the most common. In England, Wales and Northern Ireland most Bachelor's degree courses are 'with Honours' and awarded after three years of full-time study, although in some subjects the courses last longer. In Scotland, where young people often leave school and go to university a year younger, HE institutions typically offer Ordinary Bachelor's degrees after three years' study and Bachelor's degrees with Honours after four years. Honours degrees are graded as first, upper-second (2:1), lower second (2:2), or third. HEIs in England, Wales and Northern Ireland may allow students who fail the first year of an Honours degree by a small margin to transfer to an Ordinary degree course, if they have one. Ordinary degrees may also be awarded to Honours degree students who do not finish an Honours degree course but complete enough of it to earn a pass.

Postgraduate or *Higher degrees.* Graduates may go on to take *Master's degrees,* which involve one or two years' work and can be taught or research-based. They may also take one-year postgraduate diplomas and certificates, often linked to a specific profession, such as the *Postgraduate Certificate in Education* (PGCE) required to become a state school teacher. A *doctorate,* leading to a qualification such as Doctor of Philosophy – a PHD or DPHIL – usually involves at least three years of full-time research.

The framework for HE qualifications in England, Wales and Northern Ireland (FHEQ) and the framework for qualifications of HE institutions in Scotland, can both be found on the QAA website, which describes the achievement represented by HE qualifications.

ADMISSIONS

When preparing to apply to a university or other HE college, individuals can compare facts and figures on institutions and courses using the government's Unistats website. This includes details of students' views from the annual National Student Survey.

For the vast majority of full-time undergraduate courses, individuals need to apply online through UCAS, the organisation responsible for managing applications to HE courses in the UK. More than half a million people wanting to study at a university or college each year use this UCAS service, which has useful online tools to help students find the right course.

UCAS also provides two specialist applications services used by more than 50,000 people each year: the Conservatoires UK Admissions Service (CUKAS), for those applying to UK music conservatoires, and the Graduate Teacher Training Registry (GTTR), for postgraduate applications for initial teacher training courses in England and Wales and some in Scotland. Details of initial teacher training courses in Scotland can also be obtained from Universities Scotland and from Teach in Scotland, the website created by the Scottish government to promote teaching.

Each university or college sets its own entry requirements. These can be in terms of particular exam grades or total points on the 'UCAS tariff' (UCAS's system for allocating points to different qualifications on a common basis), or be non-academic, like having a health check. HEIs will make 'firm offers' to candidates who have already gained the qualifications they present for entry, and 'conditional offers'

to those who have yet to take their exams or obtain their results. Conditional offers often require a minimum level of achievement in a specified subject, for example '300 points to include grade A at A-level Chemistry'. If candidates' achievements are lower than specified in their conditional offers, the university or college may not accept them; then, if they still wish to go into HE, they need to find another institution through the UCAS 'clearing' process.

The OU conducts its own admissions. It is the UK's only university dedicated to distance learning and the UK's largest for part-time HE. Because it is designed to be 'open' to all, no qualifications are needed for entry to the majority of its courses.

Individuals can search over 58,000 UK postgraduate courses and research opportunities on UK graduate careers website Prospects. The application process for postgraduate places can vary between institutions. Most universities and colleges accept direct applications and many accept applications through UKPASS, a free, centralised online service run by UCAS that allows individuals to submit up to ten different applications, track their progress and attach supporting material, such as references.

UNISTATS W http://unistats.direct.gov.uk
UCAS T 0371-468 0468 W www.ucas.com
UNIVERSITIES SCOTLAND T 0131-226 1111
    W www.universities-scotland.ac.uk
TEACH IN SCOTLAND T 0845-345 4745
    W www.teachinginscotland.com
PROSPECTS T 0161-277 5200 W www.prospects.ac.uk
UKPASS T 0371-334 4447 W http://ukpass.ac.uk

TUITION FEES AND STUDENT SUPPORT
TUITION FEES

HE institutions in England, Wales and Northern Ireland are allowed to charge variable tuition fees for full-time HE courses. Although students from outside the EU can be charged the full cost of their courses, the amount that HEIs may charge students from the UK and other EU countries was capped from 2006 at £3,000 a year plus inflationary increases. From September 2012, universities have been able to charge up to £9,000 a year in tuition fees. The exact fee depends on the course studied and the institution attended. Full-time students do not have to pay their fees before or during their course, as tuition fee loans are available to cover the full cost; these do not have to be repaid until the student is working (*see* below).

In recent years, Scottish HE institutions have charged flat rate fees, set by the Scottish government, to undergraduate students classed as being ordinarily resident in England, Wales or Northern Ireland; though, as explained above, students can get repayable tuition fee loans to cover the cost. Since 2012 universities can set their own fees, up to £9,000 a year, for undergraduates starting courses. On average, Scottish universities have opted to charge £6,841. However, undergraduate students classed as being ordinarily resident in Scotland or another EU country do not have to pay tuition fees at Scottish HE institutions. All tuition fees are paid on their behalf by the Scottish government through the Student Awards Agency for Scotland (SAAS); students must apply for this funding every year.

In the July 2015 Budget it was announced that from 2017–18 universities with 'high quality' teaching will be able to raise tuition fees in-line with inflation.

STUDENT LOANS, GRANTS AND BURSARIES
ENGLAND

All students starting a full-time HE course in 2015–16 can apply through Student Finance England for financial support. Two student loans are available from the government: a *tuition fee loan* of up to £9,000 for 2015–16; and a *maintenance loan* (for students aged under 60) to help with living expenses of up to £5,740 for those living away from home (£8,009 if studying away from home in London) and £4,565 for those living with their parents during term time, or £6,820 if living and studying abroad for at least one term.

The tuition fee loan is not affected by household income and is paid directly to the relevant HE institution. A proportion (currently 65 per cent) of the maximum maintenance loan is available irrespective of household income while the rest depends on an income assessment. Student Finance England usually pays the money into the student's own bank account in three instalments, one at the start of each term.

Repayment of both loans does not start until the April after the student has left university or college, or before they are earning more than £21,000 a year.

At this point the individual's employer will deduct 9 per cent of any salary above the starting limit through the Pay As You Earn (PAYE) system. The self-employed make repayments through their tax returns. Someone earning £21,702 a year, the average starting salary for graduates entering full-time employment, will have to pay back £5.27 a week. Student loans accrue interest from the date they are paid out, up until they are repaid in full. Generally, the interest rate for student loans is set in September each year. The latest rate can be found online (W www.studentloanrepayment.co.uk/interest).

In 2015–16, full-time HE students with a household income of £25,000 or under can apply for a *maintenance grant* towards living expenses, which does not have to be repaid. The maximum grant available is £3,387 for the academic year. Those with a household income of £42,620 or under receive a partial grant. If a student is eligible for the maintenance grant, their maintenance loan is reduced by £1 for every £1 of maintenance grant that they are entitled to (up to a maximum of £1,354). This means that students from lower income households generally have less to repay when they finish studying and start work. Some students who claim means-tested state benefits, such as single parents and students with certain disabilities, are entitled to the *special support grant,* also worth up to £3,387, instead of the maintenance grant. If a student receives the special support grant it does not effect the amount of maintenance loan that he or she receives.

For all new full-time students starting HE from September 2016, maintenance grants are to be replaced by loans (*see* Recent Developments). Students whose family income is up to £42,620 will be able to apply from January 2016 for maintenance loans of up to £8,200 a year (£10,702 in London) – the maximum amount applying only to students with a household income of less than £25,000 a year. Special support grants will also be replaced by maintenance loans.

Students needing extra help may also be entitled to receive disabled students' allowance (DSA), adult dependants' grant, childcare grant or parents' learning allowance. These grants will remain available to full-time students starting HE from September 2016 at the 2015–16 levels. DSA is also available to part-time and postgraduate students.

Part-time Higher Education Students in England are entitled to tuition fee loans (which replaced grants) of up to £6,750 in 2015–16. Following government changes to student finance, the maximum universities and colleges can charge part-time students in tuition fees is £6,750. Part-time students who earn over £21,000 a year have to start paying back their loans after four years even if their course has not finished.

Details are available on the Student Finance England website (W www.gov.uk/student-finance/loans-and-grants). There is a student finance calculator on the website to work out what financial support is available.

Universities and other higher education providers offer their own grants and bursaries, with differing criteria. Bursaries do not have to be repaid. Students should always check with the institution they are planning to attend to find out what extra financial support may be available.

If the student's chosen HE institution runs the *additional fee support scheme,* it could provide extra financial help if the student is on a low income and in certain other circumstances. Help may also be available through the institution's *access to learning fund,* for students in financial difficulty.

WALES
Welsh students starting a full-time HE course in 2015–16 can apply through Student Finance Wales for the forms of financial support described below.

A similar system of tuition fee and maintenance loans and grants operates in Wales as in England but Welsh students can also receive a substantial tuition *fee grant.* Maximum maintenance loans are: up to £5,376 for students living away from home (£7,532 if studying away from home in London) and £4,162 for those living with their parents during term time. From September 2015, eligible Welsh students can access a non means-tested tuition fee loan of up to £3,810 and grant of up to £5,190 to cover the exact amount that the institution charges for a course.

Welsh-domiciled students may apply for an *Welsh government learning grant* of up to £5,161 to help meet general living costs. This is paid in three instalments, one at the start of each term, like the student maintenance loan. The amount that a student gets depends on household income. The maximum grant is available to those with a household income of £18,370 or under. Those with an income of £50,020 or under receive a partial grant.

There is also a *special support grant* for single parents, student parents or those with disabilities, which is worth up to £5,161 a year in 201–16. It is paid directly to students and is not offset against student loan borrowing.

Students needing extra help may also be entitled to adult dependants' grant, childcare grant, parents' learning allowance and disabled students' allowance. These grants may also be available to part-time students.

Students can use the student finance calculator on the Student Finance Wales website to work out what financial support they may be entitled to.

Welsh HE institutions also hold financial contingency funds to provide discretionary assistance to students experiencing financial difficulties.

From September 2015 part-time undergraduate higher education students studying at least 50 per cent of an equivalent full-time course are entitled to receive a fee loan of £2,625 (£6,750 for a course at a publicly funded university or college elsewhere in the UK, or £4,500 at a private university or college).

A *course grant* of up to £1,155 for books, travel and other course-related costs is available for part-time students. This course grant depends on household income.

Recipients must be studying at an average course intensity of at least 50 per cent to get it, as for the fee grant. The *course grant* is paid into the student's bank account in one lump sum. It is not usually available to those who already have a UK honours degree.

Continuing part-time students get a *fee grant* of up to £1,025, depending on their household income (partial fee grant is available for those with household incomes up to £25,435).

STUDENT FINANCE WALES T 0300-200 4050
W www.studentfinancewales.co.uk

SCOTLAND

All students starting a full-time HE course in 2015–16 can apply through the Student Awards Agency for Scotland for financial support. Living cost support is mainly provided through a *student loan*, the majority of which is income-assessed. The maximum loan for 2015–16 is £5,750.

The *young students' bursary* (YSB) is available to young students from low-income backgrounds and is non-repayable. Eligible students receive this bursary instead of part of the student loan, thus reducing their level of repayable debt. In 2015–16 the maximum annual support provided through YSB is £1,750 if household income is £17,000 or less a year.

The *independent students' bursary* (ISB) similarly replaces part of the loan and reduces repayable debt for low-income students classed as 'independent' of parental support. The maximum paid is £750 a year to those whose household income is £17,000 or less a year.

Travel expenses are included within the student loan. There are also *supplementary grants* available to certain categories of students such as lone parents (£2,640) and those with dependants (£1,305). Extra help is also available to those who have a disability, learning difficulty or mental health problem.

STUDENT AWARDS AGENCY FOR SCOTLAND
T 0300-555 0505
W www.saas.gov.uk/forms/funding_guide.pdf

NORTHERN IRELAND

All students starting a full-time HE course in 2015–16 can apply through Student Finance Northern Ireland for financial support. The arrangements for both full-time and part-time students are similar to those for England. The main difference is that the income-assessed *maintenance grant* (or *special support grant* for students on certain income-assessed benefits) for new full-time students studying at UK universities and colleges is worth up to £3,475 (for household incomes of £19,203 or less). Loans are available for living costs, £3,750 for study in Northern Ireland, £4,840 for study elsewhere in the UK (£6,780 in London) and £4,840 for study in the Republic of Ireland.

STUDENT FINANCE NORTHERN IRELAND
T 0300-100 0077 W www.studentfinanceni.co.uk

DISABLED STUDENTS' ALLOWANCES

Disabled Students' Allowances (DSAs) are grants available throughout the UK to help meet the extra course costs that students can face as a direct result of a disability, ongoing health condition, mental health condition or specific learning difficulty. They help disabled people to study in HE on an equal basis with other students. They are paid on top of the standard student finance package and do not have to be repaid. The amount that an individual gets depends on the type of extra help needed, not on household income. This amounts to £5,212 for specialist equipment for the entire course, non-medical helper allowance of £20,725 a year and a general allowance of £1,741 a year. Eligible individuals should apply as early as possible to the relevant UK awarding authority.

POSTGRADUATE AWARDS

In general, postgraduate students do not qualify for mandatory support like student loans. An exception to this is students taking a Postgraduate Certificate in Education (PGCE), who can qualify for the finance package usually available only to undergraduates. There are also bursaries available for social work and some medical students.

There is heavy competition for any postgraduate funding available. Individuals can search for postgraduate awards and scholarships on two websites: Hot Courses and Prospects.

They can also search for grants available from educational trusts, often reserved for students from poorer backgrounds or for those who have achieved academic excellence, on W www.gov.uk/grant-bursary-adult-learners or the Family Action website. Otherwise they need to fund their own fees and living expenses.

Postgraduates from Scotland can get £3,400 towards tuition fees but no support for living costs. In Northern Ireland, the Department for Employment and Learning and the Education and Library Boards provide postgraduate funding for certain courses. Postgraduate students with an impairment, health condition or learning difficulty can apply for disabled students' allowances (*see* above) for both taught courses and research places. For both full-time and part-time postgraduate students there is a single allowance of up to £10,362 a year.

DEPARTMENT FOR EMPLOYMENT AND LEARNING
(DELNI) T 028-9025 7777 W www.delni.gov.uk
FAMILY ACTION T 020-7254 6251 W www.family-action.org.uk
HOT COURSES W www.hotcourses.com
SCHOLARSHIP SEARCH W www.scholarship-search.org.uk
PROSPECTS W www.prospects.ac.uk
STUDENT AWARDS AGENCY FOR SCOTLAND (SAAS)
T 0300-555 0505 W www.student-support-saas.gov.uk

TEACHER TRAINING

See Professional Education.

EMPLOYEES AND SALARIES

EMPLOYEES

QUALIFIED TEACHERS IN MAINTAINED SCHOOLS
(NOVEMBER 2013–14)
Full-time equivalent, thousands

	England	Wales	Scotland	NI	UK
Nursery and primary schools	215.5*	13.7	24.2	8.2	261.6
Secondary schools	213.4*	12.6	23.0	9.4	258.4
Special schools	21.3	0.7	2.0	0.8	24.8
Total	450.2	27.0	49.2	18.4	544.8

* Includes academies and city technology colleges in England

SUPPORT STAFF IN MAINTAINED SCHOOLS,
ENGLAND AND WALES (2013–14)
Full-time equivalent, thousands

	England	Wales
Total support staff	398.8*	23.5
Teaching assistants	255.1	–
Other support staff	143.7*	–

* Includes academies and city technology colleges in England

ACADEMIC STAFF IN UK HIGHER EDUCATION
INSTITUTIONS (2013–14)

	Full-time	Part-time	Total
Professors	15,705	4,040	19,745
Non-professors	112,465	62,030	174,495
Teaching only	12,475	40,100	52,575
Teaching and research	77,170	17,310	94,480
Research only	37,455	8,130	45,585
Neither teaching nor research	1,075	535	1,610

Source: HESA 2014

SALARIES

State school teachers in England and Wales are employed by local authorities or the governing bodies of their schools. All teachers are eligible for membership of the Teachers' Pension Scheme.

There are teaching and learning responsibility payments for specific posts, special needs work and recruitment and retention factors which may be awarded at the discretion of the school governing body or the local authority. There are separate pay ranges for Headteachers and other school leaders. Academies are free to set their own salaries.

In 2014, the average salary for all full- and part-time classroom teachers was £34,300 (£100 less than in 2013). The average salary for all full- and part-time leadership group teachers was £56,500 in 2014 (£500 more than in 2013). Overall, the average salary for all teachers was the same, at £37,400, as in 2013.

In local authority maintained nursery and primary schools the average salary for all teachers was £33,100, compared with £31,600 in primary academies. The average salary for all classroom teachers in local authority maintained secondary schools was £36,300; an increase of £100 from 2013, whereas, in secondary academies, it was £35,100; a decrease of £200 from the 2013 average.

In 2013 every school was required to revise its pay and appraisal policies, setting out how pay progression would, in future, be linked to a teacher's performance. The first decisions on pay progression under the new provisions were decided in September 2014, based on appraisals at the end of the 2013–14 cycle. Also in September 2014, school governing bodies were given more flexibility, within the national pay ranges, to determine the pay of headteachers and other school leaders. The pay of school leaders ranges from £38,215 to £107,210 a year outside London and from £45,436 to £114,437 a year in Inner London.

After completing initial teacher training (ITT) and achieving qualified teacher status (QTS), newly qualified teachers (NQTs) in maintained schools can expect to start on a salary of £21,804 a year in England and Wales (or £27,270 in inner London). The current pay ranges for teachers in England and Wales are:

Main pay range (including NQTs)	
London fringe	£23,082–£33,244
Outer London	£25,623–£35,823
Inner London	£27,543–£37,119
Rest of England and Wales	£22,023–£32,187
Upper pay range	
London fringe	£35,927–£38,555
Outer London	£38,355–£41,274
Inner London	£42,332–£45,905
Rest of England and Wales	£34,869–£37,496

In March 2014 the Scottish Negotiating Committee for Teachers agreed a two-year pay deal, backdated to 1 April 2013. The agreement provides for pay increases of 1 per cent from 1 April 2013, followed by a 1 per cent increase from 1 April 2014. Teachers are paid on a seven-point scale where the entry point is for newly qualified teachers undertaking their probationary year. Experienced, ambitious teachers who

reach the top of the main pay scale are eligible to become chartered teachers and earn more on a separate pay spine. However, to do so they must study for further professional qualifications. Headteachers and deputies have a separate pay spine as do 'principals' or heads of department. Additional allowances are payable to teachers under a range of circumstances, such as working in distant islands and remote schools.

Salary scales for teachers in Scotland remain at 2014 levels:

Headteacher/deputy headteacher	£43,137–£84,201
Principal teacher	£38,034–£49,086
Chartered teacher	£35,964–£42,768
Main grade	£21,867–£34,887

Teachers in Northern Ireland have broadly similar payscales to teachers in England and Wales. Classroom teachers who take on teaching and learning responsibilities outside their normal classroom duties may be awarded one of five teaching allowances. A two-year pay freeze was imposed for 2011 and 2012, except for those earning £21,000 or less, who received an increase of at least £250 a year. A 1 per cent pay increase, across all salary scales, was awarded in September 2013. In July 2015 a further 1 per cent increase to salary scales was announced; this increase was backdated to September 2014. As at September 2015, salary scales in Northern Ireland stood at:

Principal (headteacher)	£43,231–£107,209
Classroom teacher (upper pay scale)	£34,868–£37,495
Classroom teacher (main pay scale)	£22,022–£32,187
Unqualified teacher	£14,121
Teaching allowances	£1,884–£12,150

Since 2007, most academic staff in HE across the UK are paid on a single national pay scale as a result of a national framework agreement negotiated by the HE unions and HE institutions. Staff are paid according to rates on a 51-point national pay spine and academic and academic-related staff are graded according to a national grading structure. In 2014–15 the pay spine ranged from £13,953 to £58,172. From August 2015 employers have proposed to raise pay by 1 per cent (and by between 1.2 per cent and 2.65 per cent from pay scale point 8 to 1), but union representatives have not accepted this offer. As HE institutions are autonomous employers, precise job grades and salaries may vary but the following table outlines salaries that typically tally with certain job roles in HE.

Principal lecturer	£47,328–£54,841
Senior lecturer	£37,394–£45,954
Lecturer	£31,342–£36,309
Junior researcher	£24,775–£30,434

UNIVERSITIES

The following is a list of universities, which are those institutions that have been granted degree-awarding powers by either a royal charter or an act of parliament, or have been permitted to use the word 'university' (or 'university college') by the Privy Council. There are other recognised bodies in the UK with degree-awarding powers, as well as institutions offering courses leading to a degree from a recognised body. Further information is available at W www.gov.uk/recognised-uk-degrees

Student figures represent the number of undergraduate (UG) and postgraduate (PG) students based on information available at July 2015.

For information on tuition fees and student loans, *see* Education, Higher Education.

RESEARCH EXCELLENCE FRAMEWORK

The research excellence framework (REF) is the new system for assessing the quality of research in UK higher education institutions. It replaced the research assessment exercise (RAE), last conducted in 2008. The 2014 REF was conducted jointly by the Higher Education Funding Council for England (HEFCE), the Scottish Funding Council (SFC), the Higher Education Funding Council for Wales (HEFCW) and the Department for Employment and Learning (DEL), Northern Ireland. The primary purpose of REF 2014 was to assess the quality of research and produce outcomes for each submission made by institutions. The table below shows the top five universities or specialist colleges for each discipline based on the mean average ranking of the overall quality of their research.

Subject	Universities or university colleges
Agriculture, Veterinary & Food Science	Aberdeen (1), Warwick (2), Glasgow (3), Stirling (4), Queen's Belfast (5)
Anthropology	Oxford (1), Manchester: Anthropology (2), Manchester: Development Studies (3), UEA (4), LSE (5)
Architecture	Bath (1), Glasgow (1), Cambridge (3), Sheffield (4), Loughborough (5)
Area Studies	LSE (1), Birmingham (2), Exeter (3), London Met (4), UEA (5), Aston (5)
Art & Design	Reading (1), Courtauld (2), Westminster (3), St Andrews (4), York (5)
Biological Sciences	Institute of Cancer Research (1), Dundee (2), Edinburgh (3), Imperial (4), Oxford (5), Sheffield (5), Newcastle (5)
Business & Management	LSE (1), Cambridge (2), Imperial (3), Oxford (4), London Business School (5)
Chemistry	Cambridge (1), Liverpool (2), Oxford (3), Bristol (4), Durham (5)
Classics	Cambridge (1), Durham (2), St Andrews (2), Oxford (4), Birmingham (5)
Clinical Medicine	Oxford (1), Cambridge (2), King's (3), Imperial (4), Institute of Cancer Research (4)
Computer Science	UCL (1), Warwick (2), Imperial (3), Manchester (4), Sheffield (5)
Dentistry, Nursing & Pharmacy	Sheffield (1), Swansea (2), Southampton (3), Cardiff (4), Nottingham (4)
Earth Systems & Environmental Sciences	Oxford (1), Bristol (2), Cambridge (3), Southampton (4), Leeds (5)
Economics	UCL (1), LSE (2), Oxford (3), Cambridge (4), Warwick (5)
Education	Oxford (1), King's (2), Nottingham (3), Sheffield (4), Cambridge (5), Durham (5), Cardiff (5)
Engineering (Civil & Construction)	Cardiff (1), Imperial (2), Dundee (3), Sheffield (4), Manchester (5)
Engineering (Electronic)	Cambridge (1), Oxford (2), Imperial: Electrical and Electronic (3), Imperial: Metallurgy & Materials (4), Leeds (5)
Engineering (General)	Cambridge (1), Imperial (2), Manchester (3), Birmingham (4), Leeds (4)
English	Warwick (1), York (2), Newcastle (3), Durham (4), Queen Mary (5)
Geography, Environment & Archaeology	Bristol (1), Cambridge (2), Royal Holloway (2), LSE (4), St Andrews (5)
History	Birmingham (1), York (2), Southampton (3), Sheffield (3), King's (5), Hertfordshire (5)
Law	King's (1), LSE (2), Durham (3), Ulster (4), UCL (5), York (5)
Maths	Oxford (1), Cambridge (2), Warwick (3), Imperial (4), Bristol (5), Lancaster (5)
Modern Languages	Queen Mary (1), Edinburgh (2), Kent (3), Queen Margaret (3), Southampton (5), Queen's Belfast (5)
Philosophy	Oxford (1), Birmingham (2), King's (3), Warwick (4), St Andrew's (5), LSE (5)
Physics	Strathclyde (1), Oxford (2), Edinburgh (3), Nottingham (3), St Andrews (3)
Politics & International Studies	Essex (1), LSE (2), Sheffield (3), Oxford (4), UCL (5)
Psychology, Psychiatry & Neuroscience	Oxford (1), Cardiff (1), Cambridge (3), York (4), Birkbeck (5)
Public Health, Health Services & Primary Care	Oxford (1), Imperial (2), Cambridge (3), Bristol (4), Queen Mary (5)
Social Work and Social Policy	Oxford (1), LSE (2), York (3), UEA (4), Kent (5)
Sociology	York (1), Manchester (2), Cardiff (3), Lancaster (4), Oxford (5)
Sports-related subjects	Bristol (1), Liverpool John Moores (2), Leeds (3), Birmingham (4), Bath (5)
Theology & Religious Studies	Durham (1), Birmingham (2), Lancaster (3), Leeds (3), UCL (3)

UNIVERSITY OF ABERDEEN (1495)

King's College, Aberdeen AB24 3FX T 01224-272000
W www.abdn.ac.uk
Fee: £9,000 *Students:* 10,375 UG; 3,450 PG
Chancellor, HRH the Duchess of Rothesay, GCVO
Vice-Chancellor, Prof. Sir Ian Diamond, FRSE
University Secretary, Caroline Inglis

UNIVERSITY OF ABERTAY DUNDEE (1994)
Bell Street, Dundee DD1 1HG **T** 01382-308000
W www.abertay.ac.uk
Fee: £7,250 *Students:* 4,345 UG; 410 PG
Chancellor, Lord Cullen of Whitekirk, KT, PC, FRSE
Vice-Chancellor, Prof. Nigel Seaton, FRENG
Registrar, Susan Campbell

ABERYSTWYTH UNIVERSITY (1872)
Penglais, Aberystwyth SY23 3FL **T** 01970-623111
W www.aber.ac.uk
Fee: £9,000 *Students:* 9,560 UG; 1,610 PG
Vice-Chancellor, Prof. April McMahon, FRSE, FBA
University Secretary, Geraint Pugh

ANGLIA RUSKIN UNIVERSITY (1992)
Chelmsford Campus, Bishop Hall Lane, Chelmsford CM1 1SQ
T 0845-271 3333 **W** www.anglia.ac.uk
Fee: £9,000 *Students:* 17,290 UG; 3,410 PG
Chancellor, Lord Ashcroft, KCMG, PC
Vice-Chancellor, Prof. Michael Thorne, PHD, FRSA
Secretary and Clerk, Stephen Bennett

ARTS UNIVERSITY BOURNEMOUTH (2012)
Wallisdown, Poole BH12 5HH **T** 01202-533011
W www.aub.ac.uk
Fee: £9,000 *Students:* 2,865 UG; 75 PG
Chancellor, Prof. Sir Christopher Frayling
Vice-Chancellor, Prof. Stuart Bartholomew, CBE
University Secretary, Jon Renyard

UNIVERSITY OF THE ARTS LONDON (2003)
Formerly The London Institute (1986), renamed 2004)
272 High Holborn, London WC1V 7EY **T** 020-7514 6000
W www.arts.ac.uk
Fee: £9,000 *Students:* 14,035 UG; 3,105 PG
Chancellor, Grayson Perry, CBE
Vice-Chancellor, Nigel Carrington
Secretary and Registrar, Stephen Marshall

COLLEGES
CAMBERWELL COLLEGE OF ARTS (1898)
40–65 Peckham Road, London SE5 8UF **T** 020-7514 6301
W www.arts.ac.uk/camberwell
Head of College, Prof. Chris Wainwright
CENTRAL SAINT MARTINS COLLEGE OF ART AND
DESIGN (1854)
Granary Building, 1 Granary Square, London N1C 4AA
T 020-7514 7444 **W** www.arts.ac.uk/csm
Head of College, Jeremy Till
CHELSEA COLLEGE OF ARTS (1895)
16 John Islip Street, London SW1P 4JU **T** 020-7514 7751
W www.arts.ac.uk/chelsea
Head of College, Prof. Chris Wainwright
LONDON COLLEGE OF COMMUNICATION (1894)
Elephant and Castle, London SE1 6SB **T** 020-7514 6500
W www.arts.ac.uk/lcc
Head of College, Natalie Brett
LONDON COLLEGE OF FASHION (1963)
20 John Prince's Street, London W1G 0BJ **T** 020-7514 7400
W www.arts.ac.uk/fashion
Head of College, Prof. Frances Corner, OBE
WIMBLEDON COLLEGE OF ART (1930)
Merton Hall Road, London SW19 3QA **T** 020-7514 9641
W www.arts.ac.uk/wimbledon
Head of College, Chris Wainwright

ASTON UNIVERSITY (1966)
Aston Triangle, Birmingham B4 7ET **T** 0121-204 3000
W www.aston.ac.uk

Fee: £9,000 *Students:* 8,130 UG; 2,855 PG
Chancellor, Sir John Sunderland
Vice-Chancellor, Prof. Dame Julia King, DBE, FRENG, FRSA
Registrar, Alison Levey

BANGOR UNIVERSITY (1884)
Gwynedd LL57 2DG **T** 01248-351151 **W** www.bangor.ac.uk
Fee: £9,000 *Students:* 8,030 UG; 2,615 PG
Vice-Chancellor, Prof. John Hughes
University Secretary, Dr Kevin Mundy

UNIVERSITY OF BATH (1966)
Claverton Down, Bath BA2 7AY **T** 01225-388388
W www.bath.ac.uk
Fee: £9,000 *Students:* 10,810 UG; 4,345 PG
Chancellor, HRH the Earl of Wessex, KG, GCVO
Vice-Chancellor, Prof. Dame Glynis Breakwell, DBE, FRSA
University Secretary, Mark Humphriss

BATH SPA UNIVERSITY (2005)
Newton Park, Newton St Loe, Bath BA2 9BN **T** 01225-875875
W www.bathspa.ac.uk
Fee: £9,000 *Students:* 5,220 UG; 1,990 PG
Vice-Chancellor, Prof. Christina Slade
Academic Registrar, Christopher Ellicott

UNIVERSITY OF BEDFORDSHIRE (1993)
University Square, Luton LU1 3JU **T** 01234-400400
W www.beds.ac.uk
Fee: £9,000 *Students:* 12,900 UG; 4,940 PG
Chancellor, Rt. Hon. John Bercow, MP
Vice-Chancellor, Bill Rammell
Registrar, Jenny Jenkin

UNIVERSITY OF BIRMINGHAM (1900)
Edgbaston, Birmingham B15 2TT **T** 0121-414 3344
W www.birmingham.ac.uk
Fee: £9,000 *Students:* 19,185 UG; 13,150 PG
Chancellor, Lord Bilimoria, CBE
Vice-Chancellor and Principal, Prof. Sir David Eastwood
Registrar and Secretary, Lee Sanders

BIRMINGHAM CITY UNIVERSITY (1992)
City North Campus, Birmingham B42 2SU **T** 0121-331 5000
W www.bcu.ac.uk
Fee: £9,000 *Students:* 18,770 UG; 3,770 PG
Chancellor, Lord Mayor of Birmingham (Raymond Hassall
 2015–16)
Vice-Chancellor, Prof. Cliff Allan
University Secretary, Ms Christine Abbott

UNIVERSITY COLLEGE BIRMINGHAM (2012)
Summer Rowe, Birmingham B3 1JB **T** 0121-604 1000
W www.ucb.ac.uk
Fee: £8,558 *Students:* 4,510 UG; 485 PG
Vice-Chancellor, Ray Linforth

BISHOP GROSSETESTE UNIVERSITY (2013)
Longdales Road, Lincoln LN1 3DY **T** 01522-527347
W www.bishopg.ac.uk
Fee: £9,000 *Students:* 1,730 UG; 670 PG
Chancellor, Dame Judith Mayhew, DBE
Vice-Chancellor, Revd. Canon Prof. Peter Neil
Registrar and University Secretary, Dr Anne Craven

UNIVERSITY OF BOLTON (2005)
Deane Road, Bolton BL3 5AB **T** 01204-900600
W www.bolton.ac.uk

Fee: £9,000 *Students:* 5,740 UG; 1,055 PG
Chancellor, Lord Justice Ryder, PC
Vice-Chancellor, Prof George Holmes
Registrar and Secretary, Sue Duncan

BOURNEMOUTH UNIVERSITY (1992)
Fern Barrow, Poole, Dorset BH12 5BB T 01202-524111
W www.bournemouth.ac.uk
Fee: £9,000 *Students:* 14,910 UG; 2,825 PG
Chancellor, Lord Phillips of Worth Matravers, KG, PC
Vice-Chancellor, Prof. John Vinney
Clerk, Deborah Wakeley

UNIVERSITY OF BRADFORD (1966)
Richmond Road, Bradford BD7 1DP T 01274-232323
W www.bradford.ac.uk
Fee: £9,000 *Students:* 9,775 UG; 2,730 PG
Chancellor, Kate Swann
Vice-Chancellor and Principal, Prof. Brian Cantor, CBE
University Secretary, Alison Jones

UNIVERSITY OF BRIGHTON (1992)
Mithras House, Lewes Road, Brighton BN2 4AT T 01273-600900
W www.brighton.ac.uk
Fee: £9,000 *Students:* 16,655 UG; 4,045 PG
Vice-Chancellor, Prof. Julian Crampton
Registrar, Carol Burns

UNIVERSITY OF BRISTOL (1909)
Senate House, Tyndall Avenue, Bristol BS8 1TH T 0117-928 9000
W www.bris.ac.uk
Fee: £9,000 *Students:* 14,930 UG; 5,190 PG
Chancellor, Baroness Hale of Richmond, DBE, PC
Vice-Chancellor, Prof. Hugh Brady
Registrar, Robin Geller

BRUNEL UNIVERSITY LONDON (1966)
Kingston Lane, Uxbridge, Middx UB8 3PH T 01895-274000
W www.brunel.ac.uk
Fee: £9,000 *Students:* 10,075 UG; 4,255 PG
Chancellor, Sir Richard Sykes
Vice-Chancellor, Prof. Julia Buckingham, PHD, DSc, FRSA

UNIVERSITY OF BUCKINGHAM (1983)
Buckingham MK18 1EG T 01280-814080
W www.buckingham.ac.uk
Fee: £6,444 *Students:* 1,260 UG; 985 PG
Chancellor, Lady Keswick
Vice-Chancellor, Sir Anthony Seldon, PHD, FRSA
Registrar, Anne Miller

BUCKS NEW UNIVERSITY (2007)
High Wycombe Campus, Queen Alexandra Road, High Wycombe
HP11 2JZ T 01494-522141 W www.bucks.ac.uk
Fee: £9,000 *Students:* 7,990. UG; 1,095 PG
Vice-Chancellor, Prof. Rebecca Bunting

UNIVERSITY OF CAMBRIDGE (1209)
The Old Schools, Trinity Lane, Cambridge CB2 1TN
T 01223-337733 W www.cam.ac.uk
Fee: £9,000 *Students:* 12,155 UG; 7,425 PG
Chancellor, Lord Sainsbury of Turville, FRS (King's)
Vice-Chancellor, Prof. Sir Leszek Borysiewicz, FRS
  (Wolfson)
High Steward, Lord Watson of Richmond, CBE (Jesus)
Deputy High Steward, Mrs A. Lonsdale, CBE (Murray
  Edwards)
Commissary, Lord Mackay of Clashfern, KT, PC, FRSE
  (Trinity)

Pro-Vice-Chancellors, Dr J. C. Barnes (Murray Edwards);
  Prof. L. F. Gladden, CBE, FRS (Trinity); Prof. D. Maskell,
  FMedSci (Wolfson); Prof. J. K. M. Sanders, FRS (Selwyn);
  Prof. G. J. Virgo (Downing); Prof. S. J. Young, FRENG
  (Emmanuel)
Proctors (2015–16), D. Goode (Wolfson); R. Taplin (Gonville
  and Caius)
Deputy Proctors (2015–16), J. M. Holmes (Queens');
  R. K. Taplin (Downing)
Orator, Dr R. J. E. Thompson (Selwyn)
Registrar, Dr J. W. Nicholls (Emmanuel)
Librarian, Mrs A. E. Jarvis (Wolfson)
Director of the Fitzwilliam Museum, T. Knox (Gonville and
  Caius)
Academic Secretary, G. P. Allen (Wolfson)
Director of Finance, A. M. Reid (Wolfson)
Executive Director of Development, Ms A. Traub
Esquire Bedells, Mrs N. Hardy (Jesus); Ms S. V. Scarlett
  (Lucy Cavendish)
University Advocate, C. F. Forsyth (Robinson)
Deputy University Advocate, J. K. Seymour (Sidney Sussex)

COLLEGES AND HALLS *with dates of foundation*
CHRIST'S (1505)
Master, Prof. F. P. Kelly, CBE, FRS
CHURCHILL (1960)
Master, Prof. Dame Athene Donald, DBE, FRS
CLARE (1326)
Master, Lord Grabiner, QC
CLARE HALL (1966)
President, Prof. D. J. Ibbetson, FBA
CORPUS CHRISTI (1352)
Master, S. Laing
DARWIN (1964)
Master, C. M. R. Fowler
DOWNING (1800)
Master, Prof. G. R. Grimmett
EMMANUEL (1584)
Master, Dame Fiona Reynolds, DBE
FITZWILLIAM (1966)
Master, Mrs N. M. Padfield
GIRTON (1869)
Mistress, Prof. S. J. Smith, FBA
GONVILLE AND CAIUS (1348)
Master, Prof. Sir Alan Fersht, FRS
HOMERTON (1976)
Principal, Prof. G. Ward
HUGHES HALL (1885)
President, Dr Anthony Freeling
JESUS (1496)
Master, Prof. I. H. White
KING'S (1441)
Provost, Prof. M. R. E. Proctor, FRS
LUCY CAVENDISH (1965)
President, Prof. J. M. Todd, OBE
MAGDALENE (1542)
Master, Rt. Revd Lord Williams of Oystermouth, PC, DPHIL,
  FBA
MURRAY EDWARDS (1954)
President, Dame Barbara Stocking, DBE
NEWNHAM (1871)
Principal, Prof. Dame Carol Black, DBE, FRCP
PEMBROKE (1347)
Master, Sir Richard Dearlove, KCMG, OBE
PETERHOUSE (1284)
Master, Prof. A. K. Dixon, FRCP
QUEENS' (1448)
President, Prof. Lord Eatwell
ROBINSON (1979)
Warden, Prof. A. D. Yates

ST CATHARINE'S (1473)
Master, Prof. Dame Jean Thomas, DBE, FRS
ST EDMUND'S (1896)
Master, Matthew Bullock
ST JOHN'S (1511)
Master, Prof. C. M. Dobson, FRS
SELWYN (1882)
Master, Roger Mosey
SIDNEY SUSSEX (1596)
Master, Prof. R. V. Penty
TRINITY (1546)
Master, Sir Gregory Winter, CBE, FRS
TRINITY HALL (1350)
Master, Revd. Dr Jeremy Morris
WOLFSON (1965)
President, Prof. Sir Richard Evans, FBA

CANTERBURY CHRIST CHURCH UNIVERSITY (2005)
North Holmes Road, Canterbury CT1 1QU T 01227-767700
W www.canterbury.ac.uk
Fee: £9,000 *Students:* 13,945 UG; 3,480 PG
Chancellor, Most Revd and Rt. Hon. Archbishop of Canterbury
Vice-Chancellor, Prof. Rama Thirunamachandran
Academic Registrar, Lorri Curri

CARDIFF METROPOLITAN UNIVERSITY (2011)
Western Avenue, Cardiff CF5 2YB T 029-2041 6138
W www.cardiffmet.ac.uk
Fee: £9,000 *Students:* 8,730 UG; 4,665 PG
Vice-Chancellor and Principal, Prof. Anthony Chapman

CARDIFF UNIVERSITY (1883)
Cardiff CF10 3XQ T 029-2087 4000 W www.cardiff.ac.uk
Fee: £9,000 *Students:* 21,495 UG; 8,635 PG
Chancellor, Prof. Sir Martin Evans, FRS
Vice-Chancellor, Prof. Colin Riordan
Chief Operating Officer, Jayne Dowden

UNIVERSITY OF CENTRAL LANCASHIRE (1992)
Preston PR1 2HE T 01772-201201 W www.uclan.ac.uk
Fee: £9,000 *Students:* 21,995 UG; 4,590 PG
Chancellor, Sir Richard Evans, CBE
Vice-Chancellor, Prof. Gerry Kelleher

UNIVERSITY OF CHESTER (2005)
Parkgate Road, Chester CH1 4BJ T 01244-511000
W www.chester.ac.uk
Fee: £9,000 *Students:* 10,725 UG; 4,015 PG
Chancellor, Duke of Westminster, KG, CB, CVO, OBE
Vice-Chancellor, Canon Prof. Tim Wheeler
Registrar, Jonathan Moores

UNIVERSITY OF CHICHESTER (2005)
College Lane, Chichester PO19 6PE T 01243-816000
W www.chi.ac.uk
Fee: £9,000 *Students:* 4,790 UG; 845 PG
Vice-Chancellor, Prof. Clive Behagg, PHD
Secretary, Isabel Cherrett

CITY UNIVERSITY LONDON (1966)
Northampton Square, London EC1V 0HB T 020-7040 5060
W www.city.ac.uk
Fee: £9,000 *Students:* 9,645 UG; 8,500 PG
Chancellor, Alan Yarrow
Vice-Chancellor, Prof. Paul Curran
Secretary, Frank Toop

COVENTRY UNIVERSITY (1992)
Priory Street, Coventry CV1 5FB T 024-7688 7688
W www.coventry.ac.uk
Fee: £9,000 *Students:* 20,310 UG; 5,525 PG
Chancellor, Sir John Egan
Vice-Chancellor, John Latham
Registrar, Kate Quantrell

CRANFIELD UNIVERSITY (1969)
Cranfield, Bedfordshire MK43 0AL T 01234-750111
W www.cranfield.ac.uk
Students: 4,205 PG (postgraduate only)
Chancellor, Baroness Young of Old Scone
Vice-Chancellor, Prof. Sir Peter Gregson

UNIVERSITY FOR THE CREATIVE ARTS (2008)
Falkner Road, Farnham GU9 7DS T 01252-722441
W www.ucreative.ac.uk
Fee: £9,000 *Students:* 4,825 UG; 255 PG
Chancellor, Dame Zandra Rhodes, DBE
Vice-Chancellor, Dr Simon Ofield-Kerr
University Secretary, Marion Wilks

UNIVERSITY OF CUMBRIA (2007)
Fusehill Street, Carlisle CA1 2HH T 01228-616234
W www.cumbria.ac.uk
Fee: £9,000 *Students:* 7,695 UG; 1,930 PG
Chancellor, Most Revd and Rt. Hon. Archbishop of York
Vice-Chancellor, Prof. Peter Strike
Registrar and Secretary, Neil Harris

DE MONTFORT UNIVERSITY (1992)
The Gateway, Leicester LE1 9BH T 0116-255 1551
W www.dmu.ac.uk
Fee: £9,000 *Students:* 16,410 UG; 3,235 PG
Chancellor, Lord Alli
Vice-Chancellor, Prof. Dominic Shellard

UNIVERSITY OF DERBY (1992)
Kedleston Road, Derby DE22 1GB T 01332-590500
W www.derby.ac.uk
Fee: £9,000 *Students:* 13,565 UG; 2,820 PG
Chancellor, Duke of Devonshire, KCVO, CBE
Vice-Chancellor, Prof. John Coyne
Registrar, June Hughes

UNIVERSITY OF DUNDEE (1967)
Nethergate, Dundee DD1 4HN T 01382-383000
W www.dundee.ac.uk
Fee: £9,000 *Students:* 10,310 UG; 4,883 PG
Chancellor, Lord Patel, KT, FRSE
Vice-Chancellor and Principal, Prof. Pete Downes, OBE, FRSE
University Secretary, Dr Jim McGeorge

DURHAM UNIVERSITY (1832)
The Palatine Centre, Stockton Road, Durham DH1 3LE
T 0191-334 2000 W www.dur.ac.uk
Fee: £9,000 *Students:* 12,540 UG; 4,655 PG
Chancellor, Sir Thomas Allen, CBE
Vice-Chancellor, Prof. Ray Hudson, DSc, DLITT, FBA
Registrar and Treasurer (acting), Paulina Lubacz

COLLEGES
COLLINGWOOD (1972)
Principal, Prof. J. Elliott
GREY (1959)
Master, Prof. T. Allen
HATFIELD (1846)
Master, Prof. T. P. Burt

JOHN SNOW (2001)
Principal, Prof. C. Summerbell
JOSEPHINE BUTLER (2006)
Principal, A. Simpson
ST AIDAN'S (1947)
Principal, Dr S. F. Frenk
ST CHAD'S (1904)
Principal, Revd Dr J. P. M. Cassidy
ST CUTHBERT'S SOCIETY (1888)
Principal, Prof. E. Archibald
ST HILD AND ST BEDE (1839)
Principal, Prof. A. Darnell
ST JOHN'S (1909)
Principal, Revd Dr D. Wilkinson
ST MARY'S (1899)
Principal, Prof. S. Hackett
STEPHENSON (2001)
Principal, Prof. J. Ashworth
TREVELYAN (1966)
Principal, Prof. H. M. Evans
UNIVERSITY (1832)
Master, Prof. D. Held
USTINOV (2003)
Principal, Prof. G. McGregor
VAN MILDERT (1965)
Principal, Prof. D. Harper

UNIVERSITY OF EAST ANGLIA (1963)
Norwich Research Park, Norwich NR4 7TJ **T** 01603-456161
W www.uea.ac.uk
Fee: £9,000 *Students:* 12,090 UG; 5,055 PG
Chancellor, Rose Tremain, CBE
Vice-Chancellor, Prof. David Richardson
Registrar and Secretary, Brian Summers

UNIVERSITY OF EAST LONDON (1898)
University Way, London E16 2RD **T** 020-8223 3000
W www.uel.ac.uk
Fee: £9,000 *Students:* 12,900 UG; 4,275 PG
Chancellor, Lord Noon, MBE
Vice-Chancellor, Prof. John Joughin
Deputy Vice-Chancellor, Dusty Amroliwala

EDGE HILL UNIVERSITY (2006)
St Helens Road, Ormskirk, Lancs L39 4QP **T** 01695-575171
W www.edgehill.ac.uk
Fee: £9,000 *Students:* 12,670 UG; 4,110 PG
Chancellor, Prof. Tanya Byron
Vice-Chancellor, Dr John Cater
University Secretary, Lynda Brady

UNIVERSITY OF EDINBURGH (1583)
Old College, South Bridge, Edinburgh EH8 9YL **T** 0131-650 1000
W www.ed.ac.uk
Fee: £9,000 *Students:* 19,015 UG; 3,605 PG
Chancellor, HRH the Princess Royal, KG, KT, GCVO
Vice-Chancellor and Principal, Prof. Sir Timothy O'Shea,
  FRSE
University Secretary, Sarah Smith

EDINBURGH NAPIER UNIVERSITY (1992)
Sighthill Campus, Edinburgh EH11 4BN **T** 0333-900 6040
W www.napier.ac.uk
Fee: £9,000 *Students:* 10,605 UG; 2,085 PG
Chancellor, Tim Waterstone
Vice-Chancellor, Prof. Andrea Nolan, OBE
Secretary, Dr Gerry Webber

UNIVERSITY OF ESSEX (1965)
Wivenhoe Park, Colchester CO4 3SQ **T** 01206-873333
W www.essex.ac.uk
Fee: £9,000 *Students:* 10,840 UG; 3,140 PG
Chancellor, Shami Chakrabarti, CBE
Vice-Chancellor, Prof. Anthony Forster, DPHIL
Registrar, Bryn Morris

UNIVERSITY OF EXETER (1955)
Stocker Road, Exeter EX4 4PY **T** 01392-661000
W www.exeter.ac.uk
Fee: £9,000 *Students:* 15,030 UG; 4,470 PG
Chancellor, Baroness Benjamin, OBE
Vice-Chancellor, Prof. Sir Steve Smith, PHD
Chief Operating Officer, Geoff Pringle

FALMOUTH UNIVERSITY (2012)
Falmouth Campus, Woodlane, Falmouth TR11 4RH
T 01326-211077 **W** www.falmouth.ac.uk
Fee: £9,000 *Students:* 3,715 UG; 300 PG
Chancellor, Dawn French
Vice-Chancellor, Prof. Anne Carlisle

UNIVERSITY OF GLASGOW (1451)
University Avenue, Glasgow G12 8QQ **T** 0141-330 2000
W www.gla.ac.uk
Fee: £9,000 *Students:* 19,850 UG; 7,540 PG
Chancellor, Prof. Sir Kenneth Calman, KCB, FRCS, FRSE
Vice-Chancellor, Prof. Anton Muscatelli, FRSE
Registrar, David Bennion

GLASGOW CALEDONIAN UNIVERSITY (1993)
City Campus, Cowcaddens Road, Glasgow G4 0BA
T 0141-331 3000 **W** www.gcu.ac.uk
Fee: £7,000 *Students:* 13,825 UG; 2,925 PG
Chancellor, Prof. Muhammad Yunus
Vice-Chancellor, Prof. Pamela Gillies, CBE, FRSE
University Secretary, Jan Hulme

UNIVERSITY OF GLOUCESTERSHIRE (2001)
The Park, Cheltenham GL50 2RH **T** 0844-801 0001
W www.glos.ac.uk
Fee: £9,000 *Students:* 6,710 UG; 1,260 PG
Chancellor, Baroness Fritchie, DBE
Vice-Chancellor, Stephen Marston
Registrar, Julie Thackray

GLYNDWR UNIVERSITY (2008)
Mold Road, Wrexham LL11 2AW **T** 01978-290666
W www.glyndwr.ac.uk
Fee: £8,450 *Students:* 7,100 UG; 1,305 PG
Chancellor, Sir John Shortridge, KCB
Vice-Chancellor, Prof. Graham Upton

UNIVERSITY OF GREENWICH (1992)
Old Royal Naval College, Park Row, London SE10 9LS
T 020-8331 8000 **W** www.gre.ac.uk
Fee: £9,000 *Students:* 17,020 UG; 4,930 PG
Chancellor, Baroness Scotland of Asthal, PC, QC
Vice-Chancellor, Prof. David Maguire
Secretary, Louise Nadal

HARPER ADAMS UNIVERSITY (2012)
Newport, Shropshire TF10 8NB **T** 01952-820280
W www.harper-adams.ac.uk
Fee: £9,000 *Students:* 4,415 UG; 385 PG
Chancellor, HRH the Princess Royal, KG, KT, GCVO
Vice-Chancellor, Dr David Llewellyn
University Secretary, Dr Catherine Baxter

HERIOT-WATT UNIVERSITY (1966)
Edinburgh EH14 4AS **T** 0131-449 5111 **W** www.hw.ac.uk
Fee: £9,000 *Students:* 7,315 UG; 3,575 PG
Chancellor, Dr Robert Buchan
Vice-Chancellor and Principal, Prof. Julian Jones, OBE,
FRSE
Secretary, Ann Marie Dalton

UNIVERSITY OF HERTFORDSHIRE (1992)
Hatfield AL10 9AB **T** 01707-284000 **W** www.herts.ac.uk
Fee: £9,000 *Students:* 19,760 UG; 5,535 PG
Chancellor, Marquess of Salisbury, KCVO, PC
Vice-Chancellor, Prof. Quintin McKellar, CBE
Registrar, Sue Grant

UNIVERSITY OF THE HIGHLANDS AND ISLANDS
(2011)
Ness Walk, Inverness IV3 5SQ **T** 01463-279000
W www.uhi.ac.uk
Fee: £9,000 *Students:* 7,000 UG; 465 PG
Chancellor, HRH the Princess Royal, KG, KT, GCVO
Vice-Chancellor, Prof. Clive Mulholland
University Secretary, Fiona Larg

UNIVERSITY OF HUDDERSFIELD (1992)
Queensgate, Huddersfield HD1 3DH **T** 01484-422288
W www.hud.ac.uk
Fee: £9,000 *Students:* 14,965 UG; 4,210 PG
Chancellor, Prof. Sir Patrick Stewart, OBE
Vice-Chancellor, Prof. Bob Cryan, CBE, PHD, DSc
University Secretary, Michaela Boryslawskyj

UNIVERSITY OF HULL (1927)
Cottingham Road, Hull HU6 7RX **T** 01482-346311
W www.hull.ac.uk
Fee: £9,000 *Students:* 14,285 UG; 3,730 PG
Chancellor, Baroness Bottomley of Nettlestone, PC
Vice-Chancellor, Prof. Calie Pistorius, PHD
Registrar, Jeannette Strachan

IMPERIAL COLLEGE LONDON (1907)
South Kensington, London SW7 2AZ **T** 020-7589 5111
W www.imperial.ac.uk
Fee: £9,000 *Students:* 8,885 UG; 7,340 PG
Rector, Alice Gast
Deputy Rector, Prof. Stephen Richardson
Registrar, John Neilson

KEELE UNIVERSITY (1962)
Keele, Staffs ST5 5BG **T** 01782-732000 **W** www.keele.ac.uk
Fee: £9,000 *Students:* 7,555 UG; 2,425 PG
Chancellor, Jonathon Porritt, CBE
Vice-Chancellor, Prof. Nick Foskett, PHD

UNIVERSITY OF KENT (1965)
Canterbury CT2 7NZ **T** 01227-764000 **W** www.kent.ac.uk
Fee: £9,000 *Students:* 15,200 UG; 3,805 PG
Chancellor, Gavin Esler
Vice-Chancellor, Prof. Dame Julia Goodfellow, DBE, PHD

KINGSTON UNIVERSITY (1992)
River House, 53–57 High Street, Kingston upon Thames
KT1 1LQ **T** 020-8417 9000 **W** www.kingston.ac.uk
Fee: £9,000 *Students:* 17,790 UG; 5,270 PG
Chancellor, Bonnie Greer, OBE
Vice-Chancellor, Prof. Julius Weinberg
Academic Registrar, Matthew Hilton

UNIVERSITY OF LANCASTER (1964)
Bailrigg, Lancaster LA1 4YW **T** 01524-65201
W www.lancaster.ac.uk
Fee: £9,000 *Students:* 9,410 UG; 3,670 PG
Chancellor, Rt. Hon. Alan Milburn
Vice-Chancellor, Prof. Mark E. Smith
University Secretary, Fiona Aiken

UNIVERSITY OF LEEDS (1904)
Leeds LS2 9JT **T** 0113-243 1751 **W** www.leeds.ac.uk
Fee: £9,000 *Students:* 23,265 UG; 7,710 PG
Chancellor, Lord Bragg
Vice-Chancellor, Sir Alan Langlands
Registrar, Roger Gair

LEEDS BECKETT UNIVERSITY (1992)
City Campus, Leeds LS1 3HE **T** 0113-812 0000
W www.leedsbeckett.ac.uk
Fee: £9,000 *Students:* 20,935 UG; 3,970 PG
Chancellor, Sir Bob Murray CBE
Vice-Chancellor, Prof. Susan Price
Secretary and Registrar, Jenny Share

LEEDS TRINITY UNIVERSITY (2012)
Brownberrie Lane, Leeds LS18 5HD **T** 0113-283 7100
W www.leedstrinity.ac.uk
Fee: £9,000 *Students:* 2,750 UG; 570 PG
Chancellor, Gabby Logan
Vice-Chancellor, Prof. Margaret House
Secretary, Howard Nelson

UNIVERSITY OF LEICESTER (1957)
University Road, Leicester LE1 7RH **T** 0116-252 2522
W www.le.ac.uk
Fee: £9,000 *Students:* 10,905 UG; 5,845 PG
Chancellor, Lord Grocott, PC
Vice-Chancellor, Prof. Paul Boyle, FBA, FRSE
Registrar, Dave Hall

UNIVERSITY OF LINCOLN (1992)
Brayford Pool, Lincoln LN6 7˜S **T** 01522-882000
W www.lincoln.ac.uk
Fee: £9,000 *Students:* 11,210 UG; 2,190 PG
Chancellor, Lord Adebowale, CBE
Vice-Chancellor, Prof. Mary Stuart
Registrar, Chris Spendlove

UNIVERSITY OF LIVERPOOL (1903)
Brownlow Hill, Liverpool L69 7ZX **T** 0151-794 2000
W www.liv.ac.uk
Fee: £9,000 *Students:* 16,860 UG; 4,490 PG
Chancellor, Sir David King, FRS
Vice-Chancellor, Prof. Janet Beer

LIVERPOOL HOPE UNIVERSITY (2005)
Hope Park, Liverpool L16 9JD **T** 0151-291 3000
W www.hope.ac.uk
Fee: £9,000 *Students:* 4,315 UG; 1,925 PG
Chancellor, Lord Guthrie of Craigiebank, GCB, LVO, OBE
Vice-Chancellor and Rector, Prof. Gerald Pillay
Registrar, Neil McLaughlin-Cook

LIVERPOOL JOHN MOORES UNIVERSITY (1992)
Kingsway House, 2nd Floor, Hatton Garden, Liverpool L3 2AJ
T 0151-231 2121 **W** www.ljmu.ac.uk
Fee: £9,000 *Students:* 18,450 UG; 2,865 PG
Chancellor, Rt. Hon. Sir Brian Leveson
Vice-Chancellor, Prof. Nigel Weatherill, DSc, FRENG
Secretary, Denise Tipping

UNIVERSITY OF LONDON (1836)
Senate House, Malet Street, London WC1E 7HU
T 020-7862 8000 W www.london.ac.uk
Fee: £9,000
Chancellor, HRH the Princess Royal, KG, KT, GCVO
Vice-Chancellor, Prof. Sir Adrian Smith, FRS
University Secretary, Chris Cobb

COLLEGES
BIRKBECK COLLEGE
Malet Street, London WC1E 7HX
Students: 10,805 UG; 4,740 PG
President, Baroness Bakewell, DBE
Master, Prof. David Latchman, CBE
COURTAULD INSTITUTE OF ART
Somerset House, Strand, London WC2R 0RN
Students: 155 UG; 305 PG
Director, Prof. Deborah Swallow
GOLDSMITHS COLLEGE
New Cross, London SE14 6NW
Students: 5,030 UG; 3,080 PG
Warden, Patrick Loughrey
HEYTHROP COLLEGE
Kensington Square, London W8 5HN
Students: 415 UG; 335 PG
Principal, Michael Holman, SJ
INSTITUTE OF CANCER RESEARCH
15 Cotswold Road, Sutton, Surrey SM2 5NG
Students: (postgraduate only) 290 PG
Chief Executive, Prof. Paul Workman
KING'S COLLEGE LONDON (includes Guy's, King's and
St Thomas's Schools of Medicine, Dentistry and Biomedical
Sciences)
Strand, London WC2R 2LS
Students: 16,410 UG; 11,235 PG
Principal, Prof. Edward Byrne
LONDON BUSINESS SCHOOL
Regent's Park, London NW1 4SA
Students: 1,905 PG (postgraduate only)
Dean, Prof. Sir Andrew Likierman
LONDON SCHOOL OF ECONOMICS AND POLITICAL
SCIENCE
Houghton Street, London WC2A 2AE
Students: 4,035 UG; 6,115 PG
Director, Prof. Craig Calhoun
LONDON SCHOOL OF HYGIENE AND TROPICAL
MEDICINE
Keppel Street, London WC1E 7HT
Students: (postgraduate only) 1,250 PG
Director, Prof. Peter Piot, CMG, PHD, MD
QUEEN MARY (incorporating St Bartholomew's and the
London School of Medicine and Dentistry)
Mile End Road, London E1 4NS
Students: 11,200 UG; 4,220 PG
Principal, Prof. Simon Gaskell
ROYAL ACADEMY OF MUSIC
Marylebone Road, London NW1 5HT
Students: 350 UG; 395 PG
Principal, Prof. Jonathan Freeman-Attwood
ROYAL CENTRAL SCHOOL OF SPEECH AND
DRAMA
Eton Avenue, London NW3 3HY
Students: 630 UG; 355 PG
President, Michael Grandage, CBE
Principal, Prof. Gavin Henderson, CBE
ROYAL HOLLOWAY
Egham Hill, Egham, Surrey TW20 0EX
Students: 7,160 UG; 2,515 PG
Principal, Prof. Paul Layzell

ROYAL VETERINARY COLLEGE
Royal College Street, London NW1 0TU
Students: 1,595 UG; 560 PG
Principal, Prof. Stuart Reid
ST GEORGE'S
Cranmer Terrace, London SW17 0RE
Students: 4,590 UG; 915 PG
Principal, Prof. Peter Kopelman
SCHOOL OF ADVANCED STUDY
Senate House, Malet Street, London WC1E 7HU
Dean and Chief Executive, Prof. Roger Kain, CBE, FBA
SCHOOL OF ORIENTAL AND AFRICAN STUDIES
Thornhaugh Street, Russell Square, London WC1H 0XG
Students: 2,975 UG; 2,435 PG
Director, Prof. Paul Webley
UNIVERSITY COLLEGE LONDON (including the
Institute of Neurology, Eastman Dental Institute, School of
Pharmacy and Institute of Education)
Gower Street, London WC1E 6BT
Students: 15,415 UG; 13,015 PG
Provost and President, Prof. Michael Arthur, FRCP, FMedScI
UNIVERSITY OF LONDON INSTITUTE IN PARIS
9–11 rue de Constantine, 75340 Paris Cedex 07, France
Dean, Prof. Andrew Hussey, OBE

INSTITUTES
INSTITUTE OF ADVANCED LEGAL STUDIES
Charles Clore House, 17 Russell Square, London WC1B 5DR
Director, Jules Winterton
INSTITUTE OF CLASSICAL STUDIES
Senate House, Malet Street, London WC1E 7HU
Director, Prof. Greg Woolf, FSA
INSTITUTE OF COMMONWEALTH STUDIES
Senate House, Malet Street, London WC1E 7HU
Director, Prof. Rick Rylance
INSTITUTE OF ENGLISH STUDIES
Senate House, Malet Street, London WC1E 7HU
Director, Prof. Philip Murphy
INSTITUTE OF HISTORICAL RESEARCH
Senate House, Malet Street, London WC1E 7HU
Director, Prof. Lawrence Goldman
INSTITUTE OF LATIN AMERICAN STUDIES
Senate House, Malet Street, London WC1E 7HU
Director, Prof. Linda Newson
INSTITUTE OF MODERN LANGUAGES RESEARCH
Senate House, Malet Street, London WC1E 7HU
Director, Prof. Catherine Davies
INSTITUTE OF MUSICAL RESEARCH
Senate House, Malet Street, London WC1E 7HU
Director, Dr Paul Archbold
INSTITUTE OF PHILOSOPHY
Senate House, Malet Street, London WC1E 7HU
Director, Prof. Barry Smith
WARBURG INSTITUTE
Woburn Square, London WC1H 0AB
Director, Prof. David Freedberg

LONDON METROPOLITAN UNIVERSITY (2002)
166–220 Holloway Road, London N7 8DB
T 020-7423 0000 W www.londonmet.ac.uk
Fee: £9,000 *Students:* 13,100 UG; 3,155 PG
Patron, HRH the Duke of York, KG, GCVO
Vice-Chancellor, Prof. John Raftery
University Secretary, Alison Wells

LONDON SOUTH BANK UNIVERSITY (1992)
103 Borough Road, London SE1 0AA T 020-7815 7815
W www.lsbu.ac.uk

Fee: £9,000 *Students:* 17,005 UG; 4,220 PG
Chancellor, Richard Farleigh
Vice-Chancellor, Prof. David Phoenix
University Secretary, James Stevenson

LOUGHBOROUGH UNIVERSITY (1966)
Epinal Way, Loughborough, Leics LE11 3TU T 01509-222222
W www.lboro.ac.uk
Fee: £9,000 *Students:* 12,005 UG; 3,955 PG
Chancellor, Sir Nigel Rudd
Vice-Chancellor and President, Prof. Robert Allison
Chief Operating Officer, Richard Taylor

UNIVERSITY OF MANCHESTER (2004)
(Formed by the amalgamation of Victoria University of
Manchester (1851; reorganised 1880 and 1903) and the
University of Manchester Institute of Science and
Technology (1824))
Oxford Road, Manchester M13 9PL T 0161-306 6000
W www.manchester.ac.uk
Fee: £9,000 *Students:* 26,485 UG; 11,440 PG
Chancellor, Tom Bloxham, MBE
Vice-Chancellor, Prof. Dame Nancy Rothwell, DBE, FRS
Registrar, Will Spinks

MANCHESTER METROPOLITAN UNIVERSITY (1992)
All Saints, Manchester M15 6BH T 0161-247 2000
W www.mmu.ac.uk
Fee: £9,000 *Students:* 26,635 UG; 5.525 PG
Chancellor, Dianne Thompson, CBE
Vice-Chancellor, Prof. John Brooks, DSc
Registrar, Karen Moore

MIDDLESEX UNIVERSITY (1992)
Hendon Campus, The Burroughs, London NW4 4BT
T 020-8411 5555 W www.mdx.ac.uk
Fee: £9,000 *Students:* 15,645 UG; 4,235 PG
Chancellor, Dame Janet Ritterman, DBE
Vice-Chancellor, Prof. Michael Driscoll

NEWCASTLE UNIVERSITY (1963)
Newcastle upon Tyne NE1 7RU T 0191-208 6000
W www.ncl.ac.uk
Fee: £9,000 *Students:* 16,290 UG; 6,120 PG
Chancellor, Prof. Sir Liam Donaldson
Vice-Chancellor, Prof. Chris Brink, FRS, DPHIL
Registrar, Dr John Hogan

NEWMAN UNIVERSITY, BIRMINGHAM (2013)
Genners Lane, Bartley Green, Birmingham B32 3NT
T 0121-476 1181 W www.newman.ac.uk
Fee: £9,000 *Students:* 2,250 UG; 603 PG
Vice-Chancellor, Prof. Peter Lutzeier
University Secretary, Heather Somerfield

UNIVERSITY OF NORTHAMPTON (2005)
Park Campus, Boughton Green Road, Northampton NN2 7AL
T 01604-735500 W www.northampton.ac.uk
Fee: £9,000 *Students:* 10,975 UG; 2,315 PG
Chancellor, David Laing
Vice-Chancellor, Prof. Nick Petford, PHD, DSc
Registrar, Jane Bunce

NORTHUMBRIA UNIVERSITY AT NEWCASTLE (1992)
Ellison Building, Ellison Place, Newcastle upon Tyne NE1 8ST
T 0191-232 6002 W www.northumbria.ac.uk
Fee: £9,000 *Students:* 23,065 UG; 4,500 PG
Chancellor, Lord Stevens of Kirkwhelpington, QPM
Vice-Chancellor, Prof. Andrew Wathey, DPHIL
Chief Operating Officer, Chris Reilly

NORWICH UNIVERSITY OF THE ARTS (2012)
Francis House, 3–7 Redwell Street, Norwich NR2 4SN
T 01603-610561 W www.nua ac.uk
Fee: £9,000 *Students:* 1,705 UG; 60 PG
Chancellor, Sir John Hurt, CBE
Vice-Chancellor, Prof. John Last
Registrar, Angela Tubb

UNIVERSITY OF NOTTINGHAM (1948)
University Park, Nottingham NG7 2RD T 0115-951 5151
W www.nottingham.ac.uk
Fee: £9,000 *Students:* 24,885 UG; 8,385 PG
Chancellor, Sir Andrew Witty
Vice-Chancellor, Prof. David Greenaway
Registrar, Dr Paul Greatrix

NOTTINGHAM TRENT UNIVERSITY (1992)
Burton Street, Nottingham NG1 4BU T 0115-941 8418
W www.ntu.ac.uk
Fee: £9,000 *Students:* 21,670 UG; 5,175 PG
Chancellor, Kevin Cahill, CBE
Vice-Chancellor, Prof. Edward Peck

OPEN UNIVERSITY (1969)
Walton Hall, Milton Keynes MK7 6AA T 01908-274066
W www.open.ac.uk
Fee: £6,000 *Students:* 138,605 UG; 12,230 PG
Chancellor, Baroness Lane-Fox of Soho, CBE
Vice-Chancellor, Peter Horrocks
University Secretary, Fraser Woodburn

UNIVERSITY OF OXFORD (*c.*12th century)
University Offices, Wellington Square, Oxford OX1 2JD
T 01865-270000 W www.ox.ac.uk
Fee: £9,000 *Students:* 16,655 UG; 9,250 PG
Chancellor, Lord Patten of Barnes, CH, PC (Balliol,
    St Antony's)
Vice-Chancellor, Prof. Louise Richardson, FRSE
Pro-Vice-Chancellors, Dr S. J. Goss (Wadham); Prof. W. James
    (Brasenose); Prof. S. L. Mapstone (St Hilda's); Prof. J. N. P.
    Rawlins (Wolfson); Prof. A. Trefethen (St Cross); Prof. I. A.
    Walmsley (St. Hugh's)
Registrar, Prof. E. G. McKendrick (Lady Margaret Hall)
Deputy Registrar, M. Sibly (St Anne's)
Public Orator, R. H. A. Jenkyns (Lady Margaret Hall)
Director of University Library Services and Bodley's Librarian,
    R. Ovenden (Balliol)
Director of the Ashmolean Museum, Dr A. Sturgis (Worcester)
Keeper of Archives, S. Bailey (Linacre)
Director of Estates, P. Goffin
Director of Finance, G. F. B. Kerr (Keble)

COLLEGES AND HALLS *with dates of foundation*
ALL SOULS (1438)
Warden, Prof. Sir John Vickers, FBA
BALLIOL (1263)
Master, Prof. Sir Drummond Bone, FRSE
BLACKFRIARS (1221)
Regent, Very Revd Dr Simon Gaine
BRASENOSE (1509)
Principal, John Bowers, QC
CAMPION HALL (1896)
Master, Revd James Hanvey
CHRIST CHURCH (1546)
Dean, Very Revd Christopher Lewis
CORPUS CHRISTI (1517)
President, Prof. Richard Carwardine, FBA
EXETER (1314)
Rector, Prof. Sir Rick Trainor, KBE

GREEN TEMPLETON (2008)
Principal, Prof. Denise Lievesley, CBE
HARRIS MANCHESTER (1889)
Principal, Revd Dr Ralph Waller, FRSE
HERTFORD (1740)
Principal, Will Hutton
JESUS (1571)
Principal, Prof. Sir Nigel Shadbolt, FRENG
KEBLE (1870)
Warden, Sir Jonathan Phillips, KCB
KELLOGG (1990)
President, Prof. Jonathan M. Michie
LADY MARGARET HALL (1878)
Principal, Alan Rusbridger
LINACRE (1962)
Principal, Dr Nick Brown
LINCOLN (1427)
Rector, Prof. Henry Woudhuysen, FBA
MAGDALEN (1458)
President, Prof. David Clary, FRS
MANSFIELD (1886)
Principal, Baroness Kennedy of the Shaws, QC
MERTON (1264)
Warden, Prof. Sir Martin Taylor, FRS
NEW COLLEGE (1379)
Warden, Prof. Curtis Price
NUFFIELD (1958)
Warden, Sir Andrew Dilnot, CBE
ORIEL (1326)
Provost, Moira Wallace, OBE
PEMBROKE (1624)
Master, Dame Lynne Brindley, DBE
QUEEN'S (1341)
Provost, Prof. Paul Madden, FRS, FRSE
REGENT'S PARK (1810)
Principal, Revd Dr Robert Ellis
ST ANNE'S (1878)
Principal, Tim Gardam
ST ANTONY'S (1953)
Warden, Prof. Margaret MacMillan
ST BENET'S HALL (1897)
Master, Prof. Werner Jeanrond
ST CATHERINE'S (1963)
Master, Prof. Roger Ainsworth
ST CROSS (1965)
Master, Sir Mark Jones, FRSE
ST EDMUND HALL (*c.*1278)
Principal, Prof. Keith Gull, CBE, FRS, FMedSci
ST HILDA'S (1893)
Principal, Prof. Sir Gordon Duff, FRCP, FRSE, FMedSci
ST HUGH'S (1886)
Principal, Rt. Hon. Dame Elish Angiolini, DBE, QC
ST JOHN'S (1555)
President, Prof. Margaret J. Snowling, FBA, FMedSci
ST PETER'S (1929)
Principal, Mark Damazer, CBE
ST STEPHEN'S HOUSE (1876)
Principal, Revd Dr Robin Ward
SOMERVILLE (1879)
Principal, Dr Alice Prochaska
TRINITY (1554)
President, Sir Ivor Roberts, KCMG
UNIVERSITY (1249)
Master, Sir Ivor Crewe
WADHAM (1610)
Warden, Lord Macdonald of River Glaven, QC
WOLFSON (1981)
President, Prof. Dame Hermione Lee, DBE, FBA, FRSL

WORCESTER (1714)
Provost, Prof. Sir Jonathan Bate, CBE, FBA, FRSL
WYCLIFFE HALL (1877)
Principal, Revd Michael Lloyd

OXFORD BROOKES UNIVERSITY (1992)
Gipsy Lane, Oxford OX3 0BP T 01865-741111
W www.brookes.ac.uk
Fee: £9,000 *Students:* 13,715 UG; 4,185 PG
Chancellor, Dr Katherine Granger, CBE
Vice-Chancellor, Prof. Alistair Fitt
Registrar, Paul Large

UNIVERSITY OF PLYMOUTH (1992)
Drake Circus, Plymouth PL4 8AA T 01752-600600
W www.plymouth.ac.uk
Fee: £9,000 *Students:* 23,585 UG; 3,345 PG
Chancellor, Lord Kestenbaum
Vice-Chancellor, Prof. David Coslett
University Secretary, Jane Hopkinson

UNIVERSITY OF PORTSMOUTH (1992)
University House, Winston Churchill Avenue, Portsmouth PO1 2UP
T 023-9284 8484 W www.port.ac.uk
Fee: £9,000 *Students:* 18,380 UG; 3,520 PG
Chancellor, Sandi Toksvig, OBE
Vice-Chancellor, Prof. Graham Galbraith, PHD
Registrar, Stephen Wiggins

QUEEN MARGARET UNIVERSITY (2007)
Musselburgh, Edinburgh EH21 6UU T 0131-474 0000
W www.qmu.ac.uk
Fee: £7,000 *Students:* 3,520 UG; 1,695 PG
Chancellor, Sir Tom Farmer, CVO, CBE
Vice-Chancellor, Prof. Petra Wend, FRSE
Secretary, Irene Hynd

QUEEN'S UNIVERSITY BELFAST (1908)
University Road, Belfast BT7 1NN T 028-9024 5133
W www.qub.ac.uk
Fee: £9,000 *Students:* 18,370 UG; 4,950 PG
Chancellor, Thomas Moran
Vice-Chancellor, Prof. Patrick Johnston
Registrar, James O'Kane

UNIVERSITY OF READING (1926)
Whiteknights, PO Box 217, Reading RG6 6AH T 0118-987 5123
W www.reading.ac.uk
Fee: £9,000 *Students:* 9,320 UG; 4,275 PG
Chancellor, Sir John Madejski, OBE
Vice-Chancellor, Sir David Bell, KCB
University Secretary, Dr Richard Messer

ROBERT GORDON UNIVERSITY (1992)
Schoolhill, Aberdeen AB10 1FR T 01224-262000
W www.rgu.ac.uk
Fee: £8,500 *Students:* 9,360 UG; 4,030 PG
Chancellor, Sir Ian Wood, CBE
Vice-Chancellor, Prof. Ferdinand von Prondzynski
Academic Registrar, Hilary Douglas

ROEHAMPTON UNIVERSITY (2004)
Erasmus House, Roehampton Lane, London SW15 5PU
T 020-8392 3000 W www.roehampton.ac.uk
Fee: £9,000 *Students:* 6,110 UG; 2,420 PG
Chancellor, Dame Jacqueline Wilson, DBE, FRSL
Vice-Chancellor, Prof. Paul O'Prey
Registrar, Laurence Benson

ROYAL AGRICULTURAL UNIVERSITY (2013)
Stroud Road, Cirencester GL7 6JS
T 01285-652531 W www.rau.ac.uk
Fee: £9,000 *Students:* 955 UG; 200 PG
Principal, Prof. Chris Gaskell
Secretary, Theresa Chapman

ROYAL COLLEGE OF ART (1967)
Kensington Gore, London SW7 2EU T 020-7590 4444
W www.rca.ac.uk
Students: 1,670 PG (postgraduate only)
Provost, Sir James Dyson, CBE, FRS, FRENG
Rector, Dr Paul Thompson
Registrar, Corinne Smith

ROYAL COLLEGE OF MUSIC (1882)
Prince Consort Road, London SW7 2BS T 020-7591 4300
W www.rcm.ac.uk
Fee: £9,000 *Students:* 415 UG; 375 PG
President, HRH the Prince of Wales, KG, KT, GCB, OM
Director, Prof. Colin Lawson
Registrar, Elly Taylor

UNIVERSITY OF ST ANDREWS (1413)
St Andrews, Fife KY16 9AJ T 01334-476161
W www.st-andrews.ac.uk
Fee: £9,000 *Students:* 7,610 UG; 2,125 PG
Chancellor, Rt. Hon. Sir Menzies Campbell, CH, CBE, QC
Vice-Chancellor and Principal, Prof. Louise Richardson,
    FRSE
Academic Registrar, Ester Ruskuc

UNIVERSITY OF ST MARK AND ST JOHN (2012)
Derriford Road, Plymouth PL6 8BH T 01752-636700
W www.marjon.ac.uk
Fee: £9,000 *Students:* 2,215 UG; 540 PG
Vice-Chancellor, Prof. Cara Aitchison
Secretary, Dr Karen Cook

UNIVERSITY OF SALFORD (1967)
The Crescent, Salford M5 4WT
T 0161-295 5000 W www.salford.ac.uk
Fee: £9,000 *Students:* 14,910 UG; 3,575 PG
Chancellor, Dr Irene Khan
Vice-Chancellor, Prof. Martin Hall

UNIVERSITY OF SHEFFIELD (1905)
Western Bank, Sheffield S10 2TN T 0114-222 2000
W www.sheffield.ac.uk
Fee: £9,000 *Students:* 18,590 UG; 8,010 PG
Chancellor, Sir Peter Middleton, GCB
Vice-Chancellor, Prof. Sir Keith Burnett, CBE, DPHIL, FRS
Registrar and Secretary, vacant

SHEFFIELD HALLAM UNIVERSITY (1992)
City Campus, Howard Street, Sheffield S1 1WB T 0114-225 5555
W www.shu.ac.uk
Fee: £9,000 *Students:* 25,985 UG; 7,115 PG
Chancellor, Prof. Lord Winston, FRCOG, FRCP, FMedSci
Vice-Chancellor, Prof. Philip Jones
Secretary and Registrar, Elizabeth Winders

UNIVERSITY OF SOUTH WALES (1992)
Pontypridd CF37 1DL T 0345-576 0101 W www.southwales.ac.uk
Fee: £9,000 *Students:* 23,890 UG; 5,310 PG
Chancellor, Rt. Revd and Rt. Hon. Lord Williams of
    Oystermouth, PC, DPHIL
Vice-Chancellor, Prof. Julie Lydon, OBE
University Secretary, William Callaway

UNIVERSITY OF SOUTHAMPTON (1952)
University Road, Southampton SO17 1BJ T 023-8059 5000
W www.southampton.ac.uk
Fee: £9,000 *Students:* 16,195 UG; 7,840 PG
Chancellor, Dame Helen Alexander, DBE
Vice-Chancellor, Prof. Don Nutbeam
Registrar, Tessa Harrison

SOUTHAMPTON SOLENT UNIVERSITY (2005)
East Park Terrace, Southampton SO14 0YN T 023-8031 9039
W www.solent.ac.uk
Fee: £9,000 *Students:* 11,285 UG; 440 PG
Chancellor, Adm. Lord West of Spithead, GCB, DSC, PC
Vice-Chancellor, Prof. Graham Baldwin

STAFFORDSHIRE UNIVERSITY (1992)
College Road, Stoke-on-Trent ST4 2DE T 01782-294000
W www.staffs.ac.uk
Fee: £9,000 *Students:* 16,490 UG; 3,655 PG
Chancellor, Lord Stafford
Vice-Chancellor, Prof. Michael Gunn
University Secretary, Ken Sproston

UNIVERSITY OF STIRLING (1967)
Stirling FK9 4LA T 01786-473171 W www.stir.ac.uk
Fee: £6,750 *Students:* 7,675 UG; 3,415 PG
Chancellor, James Naughtie, OBE
Vice-Chancellor, Prof. Gerry McCormac, FRSE
University Secretary, Eileen Schofield

UNIVERSITY OF STRATHCLYDE (1964)
16 Richmond Street, Glasgow G1 1XQ T 0141-552 4400
W www.strath.ac.uk
Fee: £9,000 *Students:* 14,070 UG; 5,920 PG
Chancellor, Lord Smith of Kelvin, KT
Vice-Chancellor, Prof. Sir Jim McDonald, FRSE,
    FRENG
Chief Operating Officer, Hugh Hall

UNIVERSITY OF SUNDERLAND (1992)
Edinburgh Building, Chester Road, Sunderland SR1 3SD
T 0191-515 2000 W www.sunderland.ac.uk
Fee: £8,750 *Students:* 12,255 UG; 3,765 PG
Chancellor, Steve Cram, MBE
Vice-Chancellor, Shirley Atkinson

UNIVERSITY OF SURREY (1966)
Guildford GU2 7XH T 01483-300800 W www.surrey.ac.uk
Fee: £9,000 *Students:* 10,035 UG; 4.030 PG
Chancellor, HRH the Duke of Kent, KG, GCMG, GCVO
Vice-Chancellor, Prof. Sir Christopher Snowden, FRS,
    FRENG
Registrar, Dr David Ashton

UNIVERSITY OF SUSSEX (1961)
Sussex House, Brighton BN1 9RH T 01273-606755
W www.sussex.ac.uk
Fee: £9,000 *Students:* 10,145 UG; 3,490 PG
Chancellor, Sanjeev Bhaskar, OBE
Vice-Chancellor, Prof. Michael Farthing, FRCP
Registrar, John Duffy

SWANSEA UNIVERSITY (1920)
Singleton Park, Swansea SA2 8PP T 01792-205678
W www.swansea.ac.uk
Fee: £9,000 *Students:* 12,405 UG; 2,415 PG
Chancellor, Rt. Hon. Rhodri Morgan
Vice-Chancellor, Prof. Richard Davies
Registrar, Raymond Ciborowski

TEESSIDE UNIVERSITY (1992)
Middlesbrough TS1 3BA T 01642-218121
W www.tees.ac.uk
Fee: £9,000 *Students:* 16,070 UG; 1,995 PG
Chancellor, Lord Sawyer
Vice-Chancellor, Prof. Paul Croney, CBE
University Secretary, Prof. Liz Holey

UNIVERSITY OF ULSTER (1984)
Cromore Road, Coleraine, Co. Londonderry BT52 1SA
T 028-7012 3456 W www.ulster.ac.uk
Fee: £6,200 *Students:* 20,335 UG; 5,865 PG
Chancellor, James Nesbitt
Vice-Chancellor, Prof. Alastair Adair
University Secretary, Eamon Mullan

UNIVERSITY OF WALES, TRINITY SAINT DAVID (1828)
Carmarthen Campus, Carmarthen SA31 3EP
T 01267-676767 W www.uwtsd.ac.uk
Fee: £9,000 *Students:* 9,280 UG; 2,040 PG
Chancellor, HRH the Prince of Wales, KG, KT, GCB, OM
Vice-Chancellor, Prof. Medwin Hughes

UNIVERSITY OF WARWICK (1965)
Coventry CV4 7AL T 024-7652 3523 W www.warwick.ac.uk
Fee: £9,000 *Students:* 14,725 UG; 10,520 PG
Chancellor, Sir Richard Lambert
Vice-Chancellor, Prof. Sir Nigel Thrift, PHD, DSc, FBA
Registrar, Ken Sloan

UNIVERSITY OF WEST LONDON (1992)
St Mary's Road, Ealing, London W5 5RF T 0800-036 8888
W www.uwl.ac.uk
Fee: £9,000 *Students:* 9,785 UG; 1,520 PG
Chancellor, Laurence Geller, CBE
Vice-Chancellor, Prof. Peter John
Registrar, Prof. Kathryn Mitchell

UNIVERSITY OF WESTMINSTER (1992)
309 Regent Street, London W1B 2HW T 020-7911 5000
W www.westminster.ac.uk
Fee: £9,000 *Students:* 15,733 UG; 4,460 PG
Chancellor, Lord Paul, PC
Vice-Chancellor and Rector, Prof. Geoffrey Petts
Registrar and Secretary, Suzanne Enright

UNIVERSITY OF THE WEST OF ENGLAND (1992)
Frenchay Campus, Coldharbour Lane, Bristol BS16 1QY
T 0117-965 6261 W www.uwe.ac.uk

Fee: £9,000 *Students:* 21,500 UG; 5,545 PG
Chancellor, Sir Ian Carruthers, OBE
Vice-Chancellor, Prof. Steve West

UNIVERSITY OF THE WEST OF SCOTLAND (2007)
(Formed by the merger of the University of Paisley (1992) with Bell College, Hamilton)
Paisley PA1 2BE T 0141-848 3000 W www.uws.ac.uk
Fee: £7,000 *Students:* 13,630 UG; 1,630 PG
Chancellor, Rt. Hon. Dame Elish Angiolini, DBE, QC
Vice-Chancellor and Principal, Prof. Craig Mahoney
Registrar and Secretary, Donna McMillan

UNIVERSITY OF WINCHESTER (2005)
Winchester SO22 4NR T 01962-841515 W www.winchester.ac.uk
Fee: £9,000 *Students:* 5,620 UG; 1,260 PG
Chancellor, Dame Mary Fagan, DCVO
Vice-Chancellor, Prof. Joy Carter
Director of Student Recruitment and Marketing, Dr Karen Pendlebury

UNIVERSITY OF WOLVERHAMPTON (1992)
Wulfruna Street, Wolverhampton WV1 1LY T 01902-321000
W www.wlv.ac.uk
Fee: £9,000 *Students:* 16,160 UG; 2,940 PG
Chancellor, Lord Paul, PC
Vice-Chancellor, Prof. Geoff Layer, OBE, FRSA
Registrar, Dr Emma Wedge

UNIVERSITY OF WORCESTER (2005)
Henwick Grove, Worcester WR2 6AJ T 01905-855000
W www.worcester.ac.uk
Fee: £9,000 *Students:* 8,885 UG; 1,410 PG
Chancellor, HRH the Duke of Gloucester, KG, GCVO
Vice-Chancellor, Prof. David Green
Registrar, John Ryan

UNIVERSITY OF YORK (1963)
Heslington, York YO10 5DD T 01904-320000 W www.york.ac.uk
Fee: £9,000 *Students:* 12,695 UG; 3,935 PG
Chancellor, Prof. Sir Malcolm Grant, CBE
Vice-Chancellor, Prof. Koen Lamberts, PHD
Registrar, Dr David Duncan, PHD

YORK ST JOHN UNIVERSITY (2006)
Lord Mayor's Walk, York YO31 7EX T 01904-624624
W www.yorksj.ac.uk
Fee: £9,000 *Students:* 5,535 UG; 885 PG
Chancellor, Most Revd and Rt. Hon. Archbishop of York
Vice-Chancellor, Prof. Karen Stanton
Registrar, Alison Kennel

PROFESSIONAL EDUCATION

The organisations selected below provide specialist training, conduct examinations or are responsible for maintaining a register of those with professional qualifications in their sector, thereby controlling entry into a profession.

EU RECOGNITION

It is possible for those with professional qualifications obtained in the UK to have these recognised in other European countries. Further information can be obtained from:
UK NARIC, Oriel House, Oriel Road, Cheltenham GL50 1XP
T 0871-330 7033 W www.ecctis.co.uk

ACCOUNTANCY

Salary range for chartered accountants:
Certified £25,000 (starting), rising to £26,000–£45,000+ (qualified), £40,000–£100,000+ at senior levels
Management £28,000 (starting), £61,000 (average), £46,000–£129,000+ at senior levels
Public finance £18,000–£30,000 (starting), £32,000–£65,000 (qualified), £80,000+ at senior levels

Chartered Accountancy trainees can be school-leavers or graduates. They usually undertake a three-year training contract with an approved employer culminating in professional exams provided by ICAEW, ICAS or ICAI. Success in the exams and membership of one of the professional bodies – which includes continuous professional development and regulation – allows them to use the designation 'chartered accountant' and the letters ACA, FCA or CA.

The Association of Chartered Certified Accountants (ACCA) is the global body for professional accountants. The ACCA aims to offer business-relevant qualifications to students in a range of business sectors and countries seeking a career in accountancy, finance and management. The ACCA Qualification consists of up to 14 examinations, practical experiences and a professional ethics module. Chartered certified accountants can use the designatory letters ACCA.

Chartered global management accountants focus on accounting for businesses, and most do not work in accountancy practices but in industry, commerce, not-for-profit and public-sector organisations. Graduates who have not studied a business or accounting degree must complete the Chartered Institute of Management Accountants (CIMA) Certificate in Business Accounting before progressing to the CIMA Professional Qualification, which requires three years of practical experience, nine examinations and a pass in the Institute's Test of Professional Competence in Management Accounting (TOPCIMA). In May 2011, CIMA and the American Institute of Certified Public Accountants (AICPA) agreed on the creation of a new professional designation, the Chartered Global Management Accountant (CGMA), which represents a worldwide standard of professional excellence in management accounting.

The Chartered Institute of Public Finance and Accountancy (CIPFA) is the professional body for people working in public finance. Chartered public finance accountants usually work for public bodies, but they can also work in the private sector. To gain chartered public finance accountant status (CPFA), trainees must complete a professional qualification in public sector accountancy. In addition, CIPFA also offers a postgraduate diploma for those already working in leadership positions.

ASSOCIATION OF CHARTERED CERTIFIED ACCOUNTANTS (ACCA), 29 Lincoln's Inn Fields, London WC2A 3EE T 0141-582 2000 E info@accaglobal.com W www.accaglobal.com
Chief Executive, Helen Brand
CHARTERED INSTITUTE OF MANAGEMENT ACCOUNTANTS (CIMA), 26 Chapter Street, London SW1P 4NP T 020-8849 2251
E cima.contact@cimaglobal.com W www.cimaglobal.com
Chief Executive, Charles Tilley
CHARTERED INSTITUTE OF PUBLIC FINANCE AND ACCOUNTANCY (CIPFA), 77 Mansell Street, London E1 8AN T 020-7543 5600 E customerliaison@cipfa.org W www.cipfa.org
Chief Executive, Rob Whiteman
INSTITUTE OF CHARTERED ACCOUNTANTS IN ENGLAND AND WALES (ICAEW), Chartered Accountants' Hall, Moorgate Place, London EC2R 6EA
T 020-7920 8100 E contactus@icaew.com W www.icaew.com
Chief Executive, Michael Izza
INSTITUTE OF CHARTERED ACCOUNTANTS IN IRELAND (ICAI), 47 Pearse Street, Dublin T 0353-1637 7200 W www.charteredaccountants.ie
Chief Executive, Pat Costello
INSTITUTE OF CHARTERED ACCOUNTANTS OF SCOTLAND (ICAS), CA House, 21 Haymarket Yards, Edinburgh EH12 5BH T 0131-347 0100 E enquiries@icas.org.uk W www.icas.com
Chief Executive, Anton Colella

ACTUARIAL SCIENCE

Salary range: £25,000–£35,000 for graduate trainees; £40,000–£55,000 after qualification; £60,000–£100,000+ for senior roles; £185,000+ for senior directors

Actuaries apply financial and statistical theories to solve business problems. These problems usually involve analysing future financial events in order to assess investment risks. To qualify, graduate trainees must complete 15 exams and three years worth of actuarial work-based training; most graduate trainees take between three and six years to qualify. Students can become Associate members of the Institute and Faculty of Actuaries (IFoA) and gain the right to describe themselves as an actuary and to use the letters AIA or AFA. Members of the profession who wish to continue their studies to an advanced level, or who specialise in a particular actuarial field, may take further specialist exams to qualify as a Fellow and bear the designations FIA or FFA.

The IFoA is the UK's chartered professional body dedicated to educating, developing and regulating actuaries based both in the UK and internationally. The IFoA represent and regulate their members and oversee their education at all stages of qualification and development throughout their careers.

The Financial Reporting Council (FRC) is the unified independent regulator for corporate reporting, auditing, actuarial practice, corporate governance and the professionalism of accountants and actuaries. The FRC's Board for Actuarial Standards sets and maintains technical actuarial standards independently of the profession, while the Professional Oversight Board of the FRC oversees the regulation of the accountancy and actuarial professions by their respective professional bodies. The Accountancy and

Actuarial Discipline Board operates an investigation and discipline scheme for members of the profession who wish to raise issues affecting UK public interest.

FINANCIAL REPORTING COUNCIL (FRC), 8th Floor, 125 London Wall, London EC2Y 5AS T 020-7492 2300
E enquiries@frc.org.uk W www.frc.org.uk
Chief Executive, Stephen Haddrill

INSTITUTE AND FACULTY OF ACTUARIES, Staple Inn Hall, High Holborn, London WC1V 7QJ T 020-7632 2100
W www.actuaries.org.uk
Chief Executive, Derek Cribb

ARCHITECTURE
Salary range: £15,000–£26,000 during training; newly registered £26,000–£35,000; project architect and senior roles £35,000–£80,000+

It takes a minimum of seven years to become an architect, involving three stages: a three-year first degree, a two-year second degree or diploma and two years of professional experience followed by the successful completion of a professional practice examination.

The Architects Registration Board (ARB) is the independent regulator for the profession. It was set up by an act of parliament in 1997 and is responsible for maintaining the register of UK architects, prescribing qualifications that lead to registration as an architect, investigating complaints about the conduct and competence of architects and ensuring that only those who are registered with ARB offer their services as an architect. It is only following registration with ARB that an architect can apply for chartered membership of the Royal Institute of British Architects (RIBA). RIBA, the UK body for architecture and the architectural profession, received its royal charter in 1837 and validates courses at over 40 schools of architecture in the UK; it also validates overseas courses. RIBA provides support and guidance for its members in the form of training, technical services and events and sets standards for the education of architects.

The Chartered Institute of Architectural Technologists is the international qualifying body for Chartered Architectural Technologists (MCIAT) and Architectural Technicians (TCIAT).

ARCHITECTS REGISTRATION BOARD (ARB) 8 Weymouth Street, London W1W 5BU T 020-7580 5861
E info@arb.org.uk W www.arb.org.uk
Registrar and Chief Executive, Karen Holmes

CHARTERED INSTITUTE OF ARCHITECTURAL TECHNOLOGISTS 397 City Road, London EC1V 1NH T 020-7278 2206 E info@ciat.org.uk W www.ciat.org.uk
Chief Executive, Francesca Berriman

ROYAL INCORPORATION OF ARCHITECTS IN SCOTLAND 15 Rutland Square, Edinburgh EH1 2BE T 0131-229 7545 E info@rias.org.uk W www.rias.org.uk
Secretary, Neil Baxter

ROYAL INSTITUTE OF BRITISH ARCHITECTS (RIBA) 66 Portland Place, London W1B 1AD T 020-7580 5533
E info@riba.org W www.architecture.com
Chief Executive, Harry Rich

ENGINEERING
Salary range:
Civil/structural £23,500–£32,000 (graduate); £40,000–£70,000 with experience (chartered status, in senior posts)
Chemical £29,500 average (graduate); £70,000+ (chartered)
Electrical £20,000–£25,000 (graduate); £28,000–£40,000 with experience; £40,000–£55,000+ (chartered)

The Engineering Council holds the national registers of Engineering Technicians (EngTech), Incorporated Engineers (IEng), Chartered Engineers (CEng) and Information and Communication Technology Technicians (ICTTech). It also sets and maintains the internationally recognised standards of competence and ethics that govern the award and retention of these titles.

To apply for the EngTech, IEng, CEng or ICTTech titles, an individual must be a member of one of the 36 engineering institutions and societies (listed below) currently licensed by the Engineering Council to assess candidates. Applicants must demonstrate that they possess a range of technical and personal competences and are committed to keeping these up-to-date.

ENGINEERING COUNCIL, Aldgate House, 33 Aldgate High Street, London EC3N 1EN T 020-3206 0500
E info@engc.org.uk W www.engc.org.uk
Chief Executive, Jon Prichard

LICENSED MEMBERS
BCS – The Chartered Institute for IT W www.bcs.org
British Institute of Non-Destructive Testing W www.bindt.org
Chartered Institute of Plumbing and Heating Engineering W www.ciphe.org.uk
Chartered Institution of Building Services Engineers W www.cibse.org
Chartered Institution of Highways and Transportation W www.ciht.org.uk
Chartered Institution of Water and Environmental Management W www.ciwem.org.uk
Energy Institute W www.energyinst.org
Institute of Acoustics W www.ioa.org.uk
Institute of Cast Metals Engineers W www.icme.org.uk
Institute of Healthcare Engineering and Estate Management W www.iheem.org.uk
Institute of Highway Engineers W www.theihe.org
Institute of Marine Engineering, Science and Technology W www.imarest.org
Institute of Materials, Minerals and Mining W www.iom3.org
Institute of Measurement and Control W www.instmc.org.uk
Institute of Physics W www.iop.org
Institute of Physics and Engineering in Medicine W www.ipem.ac.uk
Institute of Water W www.instituteofwater.org.uk
Institution of Agricultural Engineers W www.iagre.org
Institution of Chemical Engineers W www.icheme.org
Institution of Civil Engineers W www.ice.org.uk
Institution of Diesel and Gas Turbine Engineers W www.idgte.org
Institution of Engineering Designers W www.ied.org.uk
Institution of Engineering and Technology W www.theiet.org
Institution of Fire Engineers W www.ife.org.uk
Institution of Gas Engineers and Managers W www.igem.org.uk
Institution of Lighting Professionals W www.theilp.org.uk
Institution of Mechanical Engineers W www.imeche.org
Institution of Railway Signal Engineers W www.irse.org
Institution of Royal Engineers W www.instre.org
Institution of Structural Engineers W www.istructe.org
Nuclear Institute W www.nuclearinst.com
Royal Aeronautical Society W www.aerosociety.com
Royal Institution of Naval Architects W www.rina.org.uk
Society of Environmental Engineers W www.environmental.org.uk
Society of Operations Engineers W www.soe.org.uk
The Welding Institute W www.theweldinginstitute.com

HEALTHCARE
CHIROPRACTIC
Salary range: £20,000–£40,000 starting salary; with own practice £50,000–£70,000

Chiropractors diagnose and treat conditions caused by problems with joints, ligaments, tendons and nerves of the body. The General Chiropractic Council (GCC) is the independent statutory regulatory body for chiropractors and its role and remit is defined in the Chiropractors Act 1994. The GCC sets the criteria for the recognition of chiropractic degrees and for standards of proficiency and conduct. Details of the institutions offering degree programmes are available on the GCC website (see below). It is illegal for anyone in the UK to use the title 'chiropractor' unless registered with the GCC.

The British Chiropractic Association, Scottish Chiropractic Association, McTimoney Chiropractic Association and United Chiropractic Association are the representative bodies for the profession and are sources of further information.

BRITISH CHIROPRACTIC ASSOCIATION,
59 Castle Street, Reading RG1 7SN T 0118-950 5950
E enquiries@chiropractic-uk.co.uk
W www.chiropractic-uk.co.uk
Executive Director, Satjit Singh

GENERAL CHIROPRACTIC COUNCIL (GCC),
44 Wicklow Street, London WC1X 9HL T 020-7713 5155
E enquiries@gcc-uk.org W www.gcc-uk.org
Chief Executive and Registrar, David Howell, CB, OBE

SCOTTISH CHIROPRACTIC ASSOCIATION, 1 Chisholm Avenue, Bishopton, Renfrewshire PA7 5JH T 0141-404 0260
E admin@sca-chiropractic.org W www.sca-chiropractic.org
Administrator, Morag Cairns

DENTISTRY
Salary range: see Health: Employees and Salaries

The General Dental Council (GDC) is the organisation that regulates dental professionals in the UK. All dentists, dental hygienists, dental therapists, dental technicians, clinical dental technicians, dental nurses and orthodontic therapists must be registered with the GDC to work in the UK.

There are various different routes to qualify for registration as a dentist, including holding a degree from a UK university, completing the GDC's qualifying examination or holding a relevant European Economic Area or overseas diploma. The GDC's purpose is to protect the public through the regulation of UK dental professionals. It keeps up-to-date registers of dental professionals, works to set standards of dental practice, behaviour and education, and helps to protect patients by hearing complaints and taking action against professionals where necessary.

Founded in 1880, the British Dental Association (BDA) is the professional association and trade union for dentists in the UK. It represents dentists working in general practice, in community and hospital settings, in academia, research and the armed forces, and includes dental students.

BRITISH DENTAL ASSOCIATION (BDA),
64 Wimpole Street, London W1G 8YS T 020-7935 0875
E enquiries@bda.org W www.bda.org
Chief Executive, Peter Ward

GENERAL DENTAL COUNCIL (GDC), 37 Wimpole Street, London W1G 8DQ T 020-7167 6000 E information@gdc-uk.org
W www.gdc-uk.org
Chief Executive, Evlynne Gilvarry

MEDICINE
Salary range: see Health: Employees and Salaries

The General Medical Council (GMC) regulates medical education and training in the UK. This covers undergraduate study (usually five years), the two-year foundation programme taken by doctors directly after graduation and all subsequent postgraduate study, including specialty and GP training.

All doctors must be registered with the GMC, which is responsible for protecting the public. It does this by promoting high standards of medical education and training, fostering good medical practice, keeping a register of qualified doctors and taking action where a doctor's fitness to practise is in doubt. Doctors are eligible for full registration upon successful completion of the first year of training after graduation.

Following the foundation programme, many doctors undertake specialist training (provided by the colleges and faculties listed below) to become either a consultant or a GP. Once specialist training has been completed, doctors are awarded the Certificate of Completion of Training (CCT) and are eligible to be placed on either the GMC's specialist register or its GP register.

GENERAL MEDICAL COUNCIL (GMC), 350 Euston Road, London NW1 3JN T 0161-923 6602 E gmc@gmc-uk.org
W www.gmc-uk.org
Chief Executive, Niall Dickson

WORSHIPFUL SOCIETY OF APOTHECARIES OF LONDON, Black Friars Lane, London EC4V 6EJ
T 020-7236 1189 E clerk@apothecaries.org
W www.apothecaries.org
Master, Dr J. Moore-Gillon

SPECIALIST TRAINING COLLEGES AND FACULTIES
College of Emergency Medicine W www.rcem.ac.uk
Faculty of Pharmaceutical Medicine W www.fpm.org.uk
Faculty of Public Health W www.fph.org.uk
Royal College of Anaesthetists W www.rcoa.ac.uk
Royal College of General Practitioners W www.rcgp.org.uk
Royal College of Obstetricians and Gynaecologists
W www.rcog.org.uk
Royal College of Opthalmologists W www.rcophth.ac.uk
Royal College of Paediatrics and Child Health
W www.rcpch.ac.uk
Royal College of Pathologists W www.rcpath.org
Royal College of Physicians, London W www.rcplondon.ac.uk
Royal College of Physicians and Surgeons of Glasgow
W www.rcpsg.ac.uk
Royal College of Physicians of Edinburgh W www.rcpe.ac.uk
Royal College of Psychiatrists W www.rcpsych.ac.uk
Royal College of Radiologists W www.rcr.ac.uk
Royal College of Surgeons of Edinburgh W www.rcsed.ac.uk
Royal College of Surgeons of England W www.rcseng.ac.uk

MEDICINE, SUPPLEMENTARY PROFESSIONS
The standard of professional education for arts therapists, biomedical scientists, chiropodists and podiatrists, clinical scientists, dietitians, hearing aid dispensers, occupational therapists, operating department practitioners, orthoptists, paramedics, physiotherapists, practitioner psychologists, prosthetists and orthotists, radiographers, social workers in England and speech and language therapists are regulated by the Health and Care Professions Council (HCPC), which only registers those practitioners who meet certain standards of training, professional skills, behaviour and health. The HCPC can take action against professionals who do not meet these standards or falsely declare they are registered. Each profession regulated by the HCPC has at least one professional title that is protected by law.

HEALTH AND CARE PROFESSIONS COUNCIL (HCPC), Park House, 184 Kennington Park Road, London SE11 4BU
T 0845-300 6184 E registration@hcpc-uk.org
W www.hcpc-uk.org
Chief Executive and Registrar, Marc Seale

ART, DRAMA AND MUSIC THERAPIES
Salary range: £25,500–£34,500 (starting); £39,000–£47,000 with experience

An art, drama or music therapist encourages people to express their feelings and emotions through art, such as painting and drawing, drama or music. A postgraduate qualification in the relevant therapy is required. Details of accredited training programmes in the UK can be obtained from the following organisations:

BRITISH ASSOCIATION FOR MUSIC THERAPY,
   24–27 White Lion Street, London N1 9PD T 020-7837 6100
   E info@bamt.org W www.bamt.org
   Chair, Donald Wetherick
BRITISH ASSOCIATION OF ART THERAPISTS,
   24–27 White Lion Street, London N1 9PD T 020-7686 4216
   E info@baat.org W www.baat.org
   Chief Executive, Val Huet
BRITISH ASSOCIATION OF DRAMA THERAPISTS,
   Waverley, Battledown Approach, Cheltenham,
   Gloucestershire GL52 6RE T 0124-2235 5155
   E info@badth.org.uk W www.badth.org.uk
   Chair, John Hazlett Dickinson

BIOMEDICAL SCIENCES
Salary range: £21,000–£28,000 (starting); £25,700–£34,500 with experience; £30,700–40,500 for senior roles

The Institute of Biomedical Science (IBMS) is the professional body for biomedical scientists in the UK. Biomedical scientists carry out investigations on tissue and body fluid samples to diagnose disease and monitor the progress of a patient's treatment. The IBMS sets quality standards for the profession through training, education, assessments, examinations and continuous professional development.

INSTITUTE OF BIOMEDICAL SCIENCE (IBMS),
   12 Coldbath Square, London EC1R 5HL T 020-7713 0214
   E mail@ibms.org W www.ibms.org
   Chief Executive, Jill Rodney

CHIROPODY AND PODIATRY
Salary range: £21,500–£40,500

Chiropodists and podiatrists assess, diagnose and treat problems of the lower leg and foot. The Society of Chiropodists and Podiatrists is the professional body and trade union for the profession. Qualifications granted and degrees recognised by the society are approved by the HCPC. HCPC registration is required in order to use the titles chiropodist and podiatrist.

SOCIETY OF CHIROPODISTS AND PODIATRISTS,
   1 Fellmonger's Path, Tower Bridge Road, London SE1 3LY
   T 020-7234 8620 W www.scpod.org
   Chief Executive, Joanna Brown

CLINICAL SCIENCE
Salary range: £25,500–£97,000+

Clinical scientists conduct tests in laboratories in order to diagnose and manage disease. The Association of Clinical Scientists is responsible for setting the criteria for competence of applicants to the HCPC's register and to present a Certificate of Attainment to candidates following a successful assessment. This certificate will allow direct registration with the HCPC.

ASSOCIATION OF CLINICAL SCIENTISTS,
   c/o Association for Clinical Biochemistry, 130–132 Tooley Street,
   London SE1 2TU T 020-7940 8960 E info@assclinsci.org
   W www.assclinsci.org
   Chair, Prof. Richard Lerski

DIETETICS
Salary range: £21,500–£40,500

Dietitians advise patients on how to improve their health and counter specific health problems through diet. The British Dietetic Association, established in 1936, is the professional association for dietitians. Full membership is open to UK-registered dietitians, who must also be registered with the HCPC.

BRITISH DIETETIC ASSOCIATION, 5th Floor,
   Charles House, 148–149 Great Charles Street Queensway,
   Birmingham B3 3HT T 0121-200 8080 E info@bda.uk.com
   W www.bda.uk.com
   Chief Executive, Andy Burman

OCCUPATIONAL THERAPY
Salary range: £21,400–£40,500; £63,000–£79,000 for consultancy roles

Occupational therapists work with people who have physical, mental and/or social problems, either from birth or as a result of accident, illness or ageing, and aim to make them as independent as possible. The professional qualification and eligibility for registration may be obtained upon successful completion of a validated course in any of the educational institutions approved by the College of Occupational Therapists, which is the professional body for occupational therapy in the UK. The courses are normally degree-level and based in higher education institutions.

COLLEGE OF OCCUPATIONAL THERAPISTS,
   106–114 Borough High Street, London SE1 1LB
   T 020-7357 6480 W www.cot.org.uk
   Chief Executive, Julia Scott

MENTAL HEALTH
Salary range:
Clinical psychologist £25,800, rising to £45,700–£81,000+ at senior levels
Counselling psychologist £25,800–£34,500 (starting), rising to £30,700–£40,500 (qualified) and up to £81,600 at senior levels
Educational psychologist £22,000, rising to £46,000 (fully qualified) and up to £63,500 at senior levels
Psychotherapist £21,600–£28,000 (starting), rising to £47,500 with experience

Psychologists and counsellors are mental health professionals who can work in a range of settings including prisons, schools and hospitals. The British Psychological Society (BPS) is the representative body for psychology and psychologists in the UK. The BPS is responsible for the development, promotion and application of psychology for the public good. The Association of Educational Psychologists (AEP) represents the interests of educational psychologists. The British Association for Counselling and Psychotherapy (BACP) sets educational standards and provides professional support to counsellors, pyschotherapists and others working in counselling, pyschotherapy or counselling-related roles. The BPS website provides more information on the different specialisations that may be pursued by psychologists.

ASSOCIATION OF EDUCATIONAL PSYCHOLOGISTS
   (AEP), 4 The Riverside Centre, Frankland Lane, Durham
   DH1 5TA T 0191-384 9512 E enquiries@aep.org.uk
   W www.aep.org.uk
   General Secretary, Kate Fallon
BRITISH ASSOCIATION FOR COUNSELLING
AND PSYCHOTHERAPY (BACP), BACP House,
   15 St John's Business Park, Lutterworth, Leicestershire LE17 4HB
   T 01455-883300 E bacp@bacp.co.uk W www.bacp.co.uk
   President, Dr Michael Shooter, CBE

BRITISH PSYCHOLOGICAL SOCIETY (BPS),
St Andrews House, 48 Princess Road East, Leicester LE1 7DR
T 0116-254 9568 E enquiries@bps.org.uk W www.bps.org.uk
President, Prof. Jamie Hacker Hughes

ORTHOPTICS
Salary range: £21,500 (graduate), rising to £30,700–£81,500 in senior posts

Orthoptists undertake the diagnosis and treatment of all types of squint and other anomalies of binocular vision, working in close collaboration with ophthalmologists. The all-graduate workforce comes from three universities: the University of Liverpool, the University of Sheffield and Glasgow Caledonian University.
BRITISH AND IRISH ORTHOPTIC SOCIETY,
Salisbury House, Station Road, Cambridge CB1 2LA
T 01353-665541 E bios@orthoptics.org.uk
W www.orthoptics.org.uk
Chair, Lesley-Anne Baxter

PARAMEDICAL SERVICES
Salary range: £21,500–£34,500

Paramedics deal with accidents and emergencies, assessing patients and carrying out any specialist treatment and care needed in the first instance. The body that represents ambulance professionals is the College of Paramedics.
COLLEGE OF PARAMEDICS, The Exchange, Express Park,
Bristol Road, Bridgwater TA6 4RR T 01278-420014
E membership@collegeofparamedics.co.uk
W www.collegeofparamedics.co.uk
Chief Executive, Dave Hodge

PHYSIOTHERAPY
Salary range: £21,500–£40,500

Physiotherapists are concerned with movement and function and deal with problems arising from injury, illness and ageing. Full-time three- or four-year degree courses are available at around 36 higher education institutions in the UK. Information about courses leading to state registration is available from the Chartered Society of Physiotherapy.
CHARTERED SOCIETY OF PHYSIOTHERAPY,
14 Bedford Row, London WC1R 4ED T 020-7306 6666
W www.csp.org.uk
Chief Executive, Karen Middleton, CBE

PROSTHETICS AND ORTHOTICS
Salary range: £21,000 on qualification, up to £67,000 as a consultant

Prosthetists provide artificial limbs, while orthotists provide devices to support or control a part of the body. It is necessary to obtain an honours degree to become a prosthetist or orthotist. Training is centred at the University of Salford and the University of Strathclyde.
BRITISH ASSOCIATION OF PROSTHETISTS AND
ORTHOTISTS, Sir James Clark Building,
Abbey Mill Business Centre, Paisley PA1 1TJ T 0141-561 7217
E enquiries@bapo.com W www.bapo.com
Chair, Lynne Rowley

RADIOGRAPHY
Salary range: £21,000–£40,000, rising to £67,800 in senior posts

In order to practise both diagnostic and therapeutic radiography in the UK, it is necessary to have successfully completed a course of education and training recognised by the HCPC. Such courses are offered by around 24 universities throughout the UK and lead to the award of a degree in radiography. Further information is available from the Society and College of Radiographers, the trade union and professional body which represents the whole of the radiographic workforce in the UK.
SOCIETY AND COLLEGE OF RADIOGRAPHERS,
207 Providence Square, Mill Street, London SE1 2EW
T 020-7740 7200 W www.sor.org
Chief Executive, Richard Evans

SPEECH AND LANGUAGE THERAPY
Salary range: £21,500–£40,500

Speech and language therapists (SLTs) work with people with communication, swallowing, eating and drinking problems. The Royal College of Speech and Language Therapists is the professional body for speech and language therapists and support workers. Alongside the HCPC, it accredits education and training courses leading to qualification.
ROYAL COLLEGE OF SPEECH AND LANGUAGE
THERAPISTS, 2 White Hart Yard, London SE1 1NX
T 020-7378 1200 E info@rcslt.org W www.rcslt.org
Chief Executive, Kamini Gadhok, MBE

NURSING
Salary range: see Health: Employees and Salaries

In order to practise in the UK, all nurses and midwives must be registered with the Nursing and Midwifery Council (NMC). The NMC is a statutory regulatory body that establishes and maintains standards of education, training, conduct and performance for nursing and midwifery. Courses leading to registration are currently at a minimum of degree level. All take a minimum of three years if undertaken full-time. The NMC approves programmes run jointly by higher education institutions with their healthcare service partners who offer clinical placements. The nursing part of the register has four fields of practice: adult, children's (paediatric), learning disability and mental health nursing. In most cases students must select one specific field to study before applying to an institution. Some universities run courses which offer the simultaneous study of two nursing fields. In addition, those studying to become adult nurses gain experience of nursing in relation to medicine, surgery, maternity care and nursing in the home. The NMC also sets standards for programmes leading to registration as a midwife and a range of post-registration courses including specialist practice programmes, nurse prescribing and those for teachers of nursing and midwifery. The NMC has a part of the register for specialist community public health nurses and approves programmes for health visitors, occupational health nurses and school nurses.
The Royal College of Nursing is the largest professional union for nursing in the UK, representing qualified nurses, midwives, healthcare assistants and nursing students in the NHS and the independent sector.
NURSING AND MIDWIFERY COUNCIL (NMC),
23 Portland Place, London W1B 1PZ T 020-7637 7181
E communications@nmc-uk.org W www.nmc-uk.org
Chief Executive and Registrar, Dame Janet Finch
ROYAL COLLEGE OF NURSING,
20 Cavendish Square, London W1G 0RN
T 020-7409 3333 W www.rcn.org.uk
Chief Executive and General Secretary, Dr Peter Carter

OPTOMETRY AND DISPENSING OPTICS

Salary range:
Optometrist £17,000–£60,000+, up to £81,500 for consultant posts
Dispensing Optician £16,000–£35,000+

There are various routes to qualification as a dispensing optician. Qualification takes three years in total, and can be completed by combining a distance learning course or day release while working as a trainee under the supervision of a qualified and registered optician. Alternatively, students can do a two-year full-time course followed by one year of supervised practice with a qualified and registered optician. Training must be done at a training establishment approved by the regulatory body – the General Optical Council (GOC). There are five training establishments which are approved by the GOC: ABDO (Association of British Dispensing Opticians) College, Anglia Ruskin University, Bradford College, City and Islington College and Glasgow Caledonian University. After the completion of training to fit contact lenses and attaining the ABDO Level 6 certificate in contact lens practice qualification, a Contact Lens Optician may apply to be included in the GOC Speciality Register. Students are also able to complete a Foundation or Undergraduate degree in Ophthalmic Dispensing, offered by ABDO in conjunction with Canterbury Christ Church University. All routes are concluded by professional qualifying examinations, successful completion of which leads to the awarding of the Level 6 Fellowship Diploma of the Association of British Dispensing Opticians (FBDO) by ABDO. FBDO holders are able to register with the GOC following the awarding of their diploma, with registration being compulsory for all practising dispensing opticians.

Continuing Education and Training (CET) is a statutory requirement for all registered dispensing opticians and contact lens opticians to retain GOC registration.

ASSOCIATION OF BRITISH DISPENSING OPTICIANS (ABDO), Godmersham Park, Godmersham, Canterbury, Kent CT4 7DT T 01227-738 829 E general@abdo.org.uk W www.abdo.org.uk
General Secretary, Sir Anthony Garrett, CBE
COLLEGE OF OPTOMETRISTS, 42 Craven Street, London WC2N 5NG T 020-7839 6000
W www.college-optometrists.org
Chief Executive, Bryony Pawinska
GENERAL OPTICAL COUNCIL (GOC), 41 Harley Street, London W1G 8DJ T 020-7580 3898 E goc@optical.org
W www.optical.org
Chair, Gareth Hadley

OSTEOPATHY

Salary Range: £20,000–£100,000+

Osteopathy is a system of diagnosis and treatment for a wide range of conditions. It works with the structure and function of the body, and is based on the principle that the well-being of an individual depends on the skeleton, muscles, ligaments and connective tissues functioning smoothly together. The General Osteopathic Council (GOsC) regulates the practice of osteopathy in the UK and maintains a register of those entitled to practise. It is a criminal offence for anyone to describe themselves as an osteopath unless they are registered with the GOsC.

To gain entry to the register, applicants must hold a recognised qualification from an osteopathic education institute accredited by the GOsC; this involves a four- to five-year honours degree programme combined with clinical training.

GENERAL OSTEOPATHIC COUNCIL (GOsC), Osteopathy House, 176 Tower Bridge Road, London SE1 3LU
T 020-7357 6655 W www.osteopathy.org.uk
Chief Executive and Registrar, Tim Walker

PHARMACY

Salary range: £20,000–£68,000+

Pharmacists are involved in the preparation and use of medicines, from the discovery of their active ingredients to their use by patients. Pharmacists also monitor the effects of medicines, both for patient care and for research purposes.

The General Pharmaceutical Council (GPhC) is the independent regulatory body for pharmacists in England, Scotland and Wales, having taken over the regulating function of the Royal Pharmaceutical Society in 2010. The GPhC maintains the register of pharmacists, pharmacy technicians and pharmacy premises; it also sets national standards for training, ethics, proficiency and continuing professional development. The Pharmaceutical Society of Northern Ireland (PSNI) performs the same role in Northern Ireland. In order to register, students must complete a four-year degree in pharmacy that is accredited by either the GPhC or the PSNI, followed by one year of pre-registration training at an approved pharmacy; they must then pass an entrance examination.

GENERAL PHARMACEUTICAL COUNCIL (GPhC), 25 Canada Square, London, E14 5LQ T 020-3713 8000
W www.pharmacyregulation.org
Chief Executive and Registrar, Duncan Rudkin
PHARMACEUTICAL SOCIETY OF NORTHERN IRELAND (PSNI), 73 University Street, Belfast BT7 1HL
T 028-9032 6927 W www.psni.org.uk
Chief Executive, Trevor Patterson
ROYAL PHARMACEUTICAL SOCIETY, 66-68 East Smithfield, London, E1W 1AW T 020-7572 2737
E support@rpharms.com W www.rpharms.com
Chief Executive, Helen Gordon

INFORMATION MANAGEMENT

Salary range: Archivist £21,000–£30,000 (starting); £30,000–£55,000+ in senior posts
Information Officer £17,000–£28,000 (starting); £26,000–£50,000+ in senior posts
Librarian £19,500–£23,500 (newly qualified); £23,500–£32,000 (chartered); £50,000+ in senior posts

The Chartered Institute of Library and Information Professionals (CILIP) is the leading professional body for librarians, information specialists and knowledge managers. The Archives and Records Association is the professional body for archivists and record managers. The Association of Special Libraries and Information Bureau (ASLIB) is a member association for people who manage information and knowledge in organisations across all sectors. ASLIB provides its members with access to leading publications in information and knowledge management, networking opportunities and professional development.

ARCHIVES AND RECORDS ASSOCIATION, Prioryfield House, 20 Canon Street, Taunton, Somerset TA1 1SW T 01823-327077 E ara@archives.org.uk
W www.archives.org.uk
Chief Executive, John Chambers
ASLIB, Howard House, Wagon Lane, Bingley, W. Yorks BD16 1WA
T 01274-777700 E support@aslib.com W www.aslib.com
Director, Rebecca Marsh

CHARTERED INSTITUTE OF LIBRARY AND
INFORMATION PROFESSIONALS (CILIP),
7 Ridgmount Street, London WC1E 7AE **T** 020-7255 0500
E info@cilip.org.uk **W** www.cilip.org.uk
Chief Executive, Nick Poole

JOURNALISM

Salary range: £12,000–£15,000 (trainee); £22,250 for
established journalists, rising to £35,000–£40,000 for those
with over a decade's experience

The National Council for the Training of Journalists (NCTJ)
accredits 83 courses for journalists run by a number of
different education providers throughout the United
Kingdom; it also provides professional support to journalists.

The Broadcast Journalism Training Council (BJTC) is an
association of the UK's main broadcast journalism employers
and accredits courses in broadcast journalism.

BROADCAST JOURNALISM TRAINING COUNCIL
(BJTC), 130 East Hill, London, SW18 2HF
T 0845-600 8789 **E** sec@bjtc.org.uk **W** www.bjtc.org.uk
Chair, Jon Godel

NATIONAL COUNCIL FOR THE TRAINING OF
JOURNALISTS (NCTJ), The New Granary, Station Road,
Newport, Saffron Walden, Essex CB11 3PL **T** 01799-544014
E info@nctj.com **W** www.nctj.com
Chief Executive, Joanne Butcher

LAW

There are three types of practising lawyers: barristers,
notaries and solicitors. Solicitors tend to work as a group in
firms, and can be approached directly by individuals. They
advise on a variety of legal issues and must decide the most
appropriate course of action, if any. Notaries have all the
powers of a solicitor other than the conduct of litigation.
Most of them are primarily concerned with the preparation
and authentication of documents for use abroad. Barristers
are usually self-employed. If a solicitor believes that a
barrister is required, he or she will instruct one on behalf of
the client; the client will not have contact with the barrister
without the solicitor being present.

When specialist expertise is needed, barristers give
opinions on complex matters of law, and when clients require
representation in the higher courts (crown courts, the high
court, the court of appeal and the supreme court), barristers
provide a specialist advocacy service. However, solicitors –
who represent their clients in the lower courts such as
magistrates' courts and county courts – can also apply for
advocacy rights in the higher courts instead of briefing a
barrister.

THE BAR

Salary range: £12,000–£65,000 (pupillage); £25,000–
£300,000 (qualified); £1,000,000+ with ten years
experience

The governing body of the Bar of England and Wales is the
General Council of the Bar, also known as the Bar Council.
Since January 2006, the regulatory functions of the Bar
Council (including regulating the education and training
requirements for those wishing to enter the profession) have
been undertaken by the Bar Standards Board.

In the first (or 'academic') stage of training, aspiring
barristers must obtain a law degree of a good standard (at
least second class). Alternatively, those with a non-law degree
(at least second class) may complete a one-year full-time or
two-year part-time Common Professional Examination
(CPE) or Graduate Diploma in Law (GDL).

The second (vocational) stage is the completion of the
Bar Professional Training Course (BPTC), which is available
at a number of validated institutions in the UK and must be
applied for around one year in advance. All barristers must
join one of the four Inns of Court prior to commencing
the BPTC.

Students are 'called to the Bar' by their Inn after
completion of the vocational stage, but cannot practise as a
barrister until completion of the third stage, which is called
'pupillage'. Being called to the Bar does not entitle a person
to practise as a barrister – successful completion of pupillage
is now a prerequisite. Pupillage lasts for two six-month
periods: the 'non-practising six' and the 'practising six'. The
former consists of shadowing an experienced barrister, while
the latter involves appearing in court as a barrister.

Admission to the Bar of Northern Ireland is controlled
by the General Council of the Bar of Northern Ireland;
admission as an Advocate to the Scottish Bar is through the
Faculty of Advocates.

FACULTY OF ADVOCATES, Parliament House,
Edinburgh EH1 1RF **T** 0131-226 5071
W www.advocates.org.uk
Dean, Richard Keen, QC

GENERAL COUNCIL OF THE BAR (THE BAR
COUNCIL), 289–293 High Holborn, London WC1V 7HZ
T 020-7242 0082 **E** contactus@barcouncil.org.uk
W www.barcouncil.org.uk
Chief Executive, Stephen Crowne

BAR STANDARDS BOARD address as above
E contactus@barstandardsboard.org.uk
W www.barstandardsboard.org.uk
Chair of the Bar Council, Sir Andrew Burns, KCMG

GENERAL COUNCIL OF THE BAR OF NORTHERN
IRELAND, The Bar Library, 91 Chichester Street,
Belfast BT1 3JQ **T** 028-9024 1523 **E** contactc@barofni.com
W www.barlibrary.com
Chief Executive, David Mulholland

THE INNS OF COURT

HONOURABLE SOCIETY OF GRAY'S INN,
8 South Square, London WC1R 5ET **T** 020-7458 7800
W www.graysinn.org.uk
Under-Treasurer, Brig. Anthony Faith, CBE

HONOURABLE SOCIETY OF LINCOLN'S INN,
Treasury Office, Lincoln's Inn, London WC2A 3TL
T 020-7405 1393 **E** mail@lincolnsinn.org.uk
W www.lincolnsinn.org.uk
Under-Treasurer, Mary Kerr

HONOURABLE SOCIETY OF THE INNER TEMPLE,
Inner Temple, London EC4Y 7HL **T** 020-7797 8250
W www.innertemple.org.uk
Treasurer, Rt. Hon. Lord Justice Moore-Bick

HONOURABLE SOCIETY OF THE MIDDLE TEMPLE,
Middle Temple Lane, London EC4Y 9AT **T** 020-7427 4800
E members@middletemple.org.uk
W www.middletemple.org.uk
Chief Executive, Guy Perricone

NOTARIES PUBLIC

Notaries are qualified lawyers with a postgraduate diploma in
notarial practice. Once a potential notary has passed the
postgraduate diploma, they can petition the Court of
Faculties for a 'faculty'. After the faculty is granted, the
notary is able to practise; however, for the first two years this
must be under the supervision of an experienced notary. The
admission and regulation of notaries in England and Wales is
a statutory function of the Faculty Office. This jurisdiction
was confirmed by the Courts and Legal Services Act 1990.
The Notaries Society of England and Wales is the
representative body for practising notaries.

THE FACULTY OFFICE, 1 The Sanctuary, Westminster,
London SW1P 3JT T 020-7222 5381
E faculty.office@1thesanctuary.com
W www.facultyoffice.org.uk
Registrars, Peter Beesley; Howard Dellar
THE NOTARIES SOCIETY OF ENGLAND AND WALES,
PO Box 1023, Ipswich IP1 9XB
E admin@thenotariessociety.org.uk
W www.thenotariessociety.org.uk
Secretary, Christopher Vaughan

SOLICITORS

Salary range: Trainee solicitors paid at least the national minimum wage; £25,000–£75,000 after qualification; £100,000+ (associate or partner)

Graduates from any discipline can train to be a solicitor; however, if the undergraduate degree is not in law, a one-year conversion course – either the Common Professional Examination (CPE) or the Graduate Diploma in Law (GDL) – must be completed. The next stage, and the beginning of the vocational phase, is the Legal Practice Course (LPC), which takes one year and is obligatory for both law and non-law graduates. The LPC provides professional instruction for prospective solicitors and can be completed on a full-time or part-time basis. Trainee solicitors then enter the final stage, which is a paid period of supervised work that lasts two years for full-time contracts. The employer that provides the training contract must be authorised by the Solicitors Regulation Authority (SRA) (the regulatory body of the Law Society of England and Wales), the Law Society of Scotland or the Law Society of Northern Ireland. The SRA also monitors the training contract to ensure that it provides the trainee with the expertise to qualify as a solicitor.

Conveyancers are specialist property lawyers, dealing with the legal processes involved in transferring buildings, land and associated finances from one owner to another. This was the sole responsibility of solicitors until 1987 but under current legislation it is now possible for others to train as conveyancers.
COUNCIL FOR LICENSED CONVEYANCERS (CLC),
16 Glebe Road, Chelmsford, Essex CM1 1QG T 01245-349599
E clc@clc-uk.org W www.clc-uk.org
Chief Executive, Sheila Kumar
THE LAW SOCIETY OF ENGLAND AND WALES,
The Law Society's Hall, 113 Chancery Lane, London WC2A 1PL
T 020-7242 1222 W www.lawsociety.org.uk
Chief Executive, Catherine Dixon
LAW SOCIETY OF NORTHERN IRELAND,
96 Victoria Street, Belfast BT1 3GN T 028-9023 1614
W www.lawsoc-ni.org
Chief Executive, Alan Hunter
LAW SOCIETY OF SCOTLAND, 26 Drumsheugh Gardens,
Edinburgh EH3 7YR T 0131-226 7411
E lawscot@lawscot.org.uk W www.lawscot.org.uk
Chief Executive, Lorna Jack
SOLICITORS REGULATION AUTHORITY (SRA),
The Cube, 199 Wharfside Street, Birmingham B1 1RN
T 0370-606 2555 W www.sra.org.uk
Chief Executive, Paul Philip

SOCIAL WORK

Salary range: £25,000–£34,000 (starting), rising to £42,000 as an experienced manager; £57,000+ at senior levels

Social workers tend to specialise in either adult or children's services. The HCPC obtained regulatory responsibility from the General Social Care Council in August 2012 and is responsible for setting standards of conduct and practice for social care workers and their employers; regulating the workforce and social work education and training. A degree or postgraduate qualification is needed in order to become a social worker. For more information *see* Social Welfare.
HEALTH AND CARE PROFESSIONS COUNCIL (HCPC),
Park House, 184 Kennington Park Road, London SE11 4BU
T 0845-300 6184 W www.hcpc-uk.org
Chief Executive and Registrar, Marc Seale

SURVEYING

Salary range: £18,500–£22,000 (starting); £45,000 (senior); up to £100,000 (partners and directors)

The Royal Institution of Chartered Surveyors (RICS) is the professional body that represents and regulates property professionals including land surveyors, valuers, auctioneers, quantity surveyors and project managers. Entry to the institution, following completion of a RICS-accredited degree, is through completion of the Assessment of Professional Competence (APC), which involves a period of practical training concluded by a final assessment of competence. Entry as a technical surveyor requires completion of the Assessment of Technical Competence (ATC), which mirrors the format of the APC. The different levels of RICS membership are MRICS (member) or FRICS (fellow) for chartered surveyors, and AssocRICS for associate members.

Relevant courses can also be accredited by the Chartered Institute of Building (CIOB), which represents managers working in a range of construction disciplines. The CIOB offers four levels of membership to those who satisfy its requirements: FCIOB (fellow), MCIOB (member), ICIOB (incorporated) and ACIOB (associate).
CHARTERED INSTITUTE OF BUILDING (CIOB),
1 Arlington Square, Downshire Way, Bracknell RG12 1WA
T 01344-630700 E reception@ciob.org.uk W www.ciob.org.uk
Chief Executive, Chris Blythe
ROYAL INSTITUTION OF CHARTERED SURVEYORS
(RICS), RICS HQ, Parliament Square, London SW1P 3AD
T 024-7686 8555 E contactrics@rics.org W www.rics.org
Chief Executive, Sean Tompkins

TEACHING

Salary range: £22,000–£57,000; headteacher £43,000–£113,000 (for more detailed information *see* Education: Employees and Salaries)

The General Teaching Councils (GTCs) for Northern Ireland, Scotland and Wales maintain registers of qualified teachers in their respective countries, and registration is a legal requirement in order to teach in local authority schools. On 1 April 2013, the Teaching Agency merged with the National College to form the National College for Teaching and Leadership (NCTL), an executive agency of the Department for Education, which became the awarding body for Qualified Teacher Status (QTS). UCAS Teacher Training (UTT) has replaced the Graduate Teacher Training Registry (GTTR) as the body through which to apply for postgraduate teacher training in the UK. To become a qualified teacher, all entrants must have a degree and gain QTS, which includes a minimum of 24 weeks in at least two different schools and academic study of teaching. Another route is through School-centred Initial Teacher Training (SCITT), where practical, hands-on teacher training is delivered by experienced, practising teachers in their own government-approved school.

Many courses also award an academic qualification known as the Postgraduate Certificate in Education (PGCE) in England and Wales and the Professional Graduate Diploma in Education (PGDE) in Scotland. Once training is completed, applicants spend a year in school as a newly qualified teacher (NQT).

Teachers in Further Education (FE) need not have QTS, though new entrants to FE may be required to work towards a specified FE qualification by employers. A range of courses are offered and usually require one year of study in addition to 100 hours of teaching experience. Similarly, academic staff in Higher Education require no formal teaching qualification, but are expected to obtain a qualification that meets standards set by the Higher Education Academy.

Details of routes to gaining QTS are available in England from the NCTL, the Department for Education and UTT, in Wales from the Teacher Training & Education Recruitment Forum Wales, in Scotland from Teach in Scotland and in Northern Ireland from the Department of Education.

The College of Teachers, under the terms of its royal charter, provides professional qualifications and membership to teachers and those involved in education in the UK and overseas.

COLLEGE OF TEACHERS, Institute of Education, 20 Bedford Way, London WC1H 0AL T 020-7911 5536
W www.collegeofteachers.ac.uk
Chief Executive and Registrar, Angela McFarlane
DEPARTMENT OF EDUCATION NORTHERN IRELAND, Rathgael House, Balloo Road, Bangor BT19 7PR
T 028-9127 9279 E mail@deni.gov.uk W www.deni.gov.uk
Permanent Secretary, Paul Sweeney
GENERAL TEACHING COUNCIL FOR NORTHERN IRELAND, 3rd Floor, Albany House, 73–75 Great Victoria Street, Belfast BT2 7AF T 028-9033 3390
E info@gtcni.org.uk W www.gtcni.org.uk
Chair, Ivan Arbuthnot
GENERAL TEACHING COUNCIL FOR SCOTLAND, Clerwood House, 96 Clermiston Road, Edinburgh EH12 6UT
T 0131-314 6000 E gtcs@gtcs.org.uk W www.gtcs.org.uk
Chief Executive, Kenneth Muir
EDUCATION WORKFORCE COUNCIL, 9th Floor, Eastgate House, 35–43 Newport Road, Cardiff CF24 0AB
T 029-2046 0099 E information@ewc.wales
W www.ewc.wales
Chair, Hayden Llewellyn
UCAS TEACHER TRAINING (UTT), Rosehill, New Barn Lane, Cheltenham GL52 3LZ T 0371-468 0469
W www.ucas.com/teacher-training
Chief Executive, Mary Curnock Cook, OBE

HIGHER EDUCATION ACADEMY, Innovation Way, York Science Park, Heslington, York YO10 5BR T 01904-717500
E enquiries@heacademy.ac.uk W www.heacademy.ac.uk
Chief Executive, Prof. Stephanie Marshall
NATIONAL COLLEGE FOR TEACHING AND LEADERSHIP, Triumph Road, Nottingham NG8 1DH
T 0345-609 0009 E college.enquiries@bt.com
W www.nationalcollege.org.uk
Chief Executive, Charlie Taylor

VETERINARY MEDICINE
Salary range: £21,000–£53,000+

The regulatory body for veterinary surgeons in the UK is the Royal College of Veterinary Surgeons (RCVS), which keeps the register of those entitled to practise veterinary medicine, the register of veterinary nurses and veterinary practice premises (on behalf of the Veterinary Medicines Directorate). Holders of recognised degrees from any of the seven UK university veterinary schools that have been approved by the RCUS or from certain EU or overseas universities are entitled to be registered, and holders of certain other degrees may take a statutory membership examination. The UK's RCUS-approved veterinary schools are located at the University of Bristol, the University of Cambridge, the University of Edinburgh, the University of Glasgow, the University of Liverpool, the University of Nottingham and the Royal Veterinary College in London; all veterinary degrees last for five years except that offered at Cambridge, which lasts for six.

The British Veterinary Association is the national representative body for the UK veterinary profession. The British Veterinary Nursing Association is the professional body representing veterinary nurses.

BRITISH VETERINARY ASSOCIATION, 7 Mansfield Street, London W1G 9NQ T 020-7636 6541 E bvahq@bva.co.uk
W www.bva.co.uk
Chief Executive, David Calpin
BRITISH VETERINARY NURSING ASSOCIATION, 82 Greenway Business Centre, Harlow Business Park, Harlow CM19 5QE T 01279-408644 E bvna@bvna.co.uk
W www.bvna.org.uk
Honorary Secretary, Lucy Hayne
ROYAL COLLEGE OF VETERINARY SURGEONS (RCVS), Belgravia House, 62–64 Horseferry Road, London SW1P 2AF T 020-7222 2001 E info@rcvs.org.uk
W www.rcvs.org.uk
Registrar, Nick Stace

INDEPENDENT SCHOOLS

Independent schools (non-maintained mainstream schools) charge fees and are owned and managed under special trusts, with profits being used for the benefit of the schools concerned. In 2013–14 there were 2,497 non-maintained mainstream schools in the UK, educating around 623,000 pupils, or around 6.3 per cent of the total school-age population. The number of pupils at non-maintained mainstream schools as at January 2015 was:

UK	623,186
England	582,866
Wales	8,991
Scotland	30,687
Northern Ireland	642

The Independent Schools Council (ISC), formed in 1974, acts on behalf of the seven independent schools' associations which constitute it. These associations are:
Association of Governing Bodies of Independent Schools (AGBIS)
Girls' Schools Association (GSA)
Headmasters' & Headmistresses' Conference (HMC)
Independent Association of Prep Schools (IAPS)
Independent Schools Association (ISA)
Independent Schools' Bursars Association (ISBA)
The Society of Heads

In 2014–15 there were 517,113 pupils being educated in 1,267 schools in membership of associations within the Independent Schools Council (ISC). Most schools not in membership of an ISC association are likely to be privately owned. The Independent Schools Inspectorate (ISI) was demerged from ISC with effect from 1 January 2008 and is legally and operationally independent of ISC. ISI works as an accredited inspectorate of schools in membership of the ISC associations under a framework agreed with the Department for Education (DfE). A school must pass an ISI accreditation inspection to qualify for membership of an association within ISC.

In 2014 at GCSE 60.6 per cent of all exams taken by candidates in ISC associations' member schools achieved either an A* or A grade (compared to the national average of 21.3 per cent), and at A-level 19.2 per cent of entries were awarded an A* grade (national average, 8.2 per cent). In 2014–15 a total of 167,798 (33.3 per cent) pupils at schools in ISC associations received help with their fees, mainly in the form of bursaries and scholarships from the schools. ISC schools provided more than £700m of assistance with fees.

INDEPENDENT SCHOOLS COUNCIL
First Floor, 27 Queen Anne's Gate, London SW1H 9BU
T 020-7766 7070 W www.isc.co.uk

The list of schools below was compiled from the Independent Schools Yearbook 2014–15 (ed. Judy Mott, published by Bloomsbury Publishing) which includes schools whose heads are members of one of the ISC's five Heads' Associations. Further details are available online (W www.isyb.co.uk).

The fees shown below represent the upper limit payable for the year 2014–15.

School	Web Address	Termly Fees Day	Board	Head
ENGLAND				
Abbey Gate College, Cheshire	www.abbeygatecollege.co.uk	£3,677	–	Mrs T. Pollard
The Abbey School, Berks	www.theabbey.co.uk	£4,830	–	Mrs R. Dent
Abbots Bromley School, Staffs	www.abbotsbromley.net	£5,119	£8,575	Mrs V. Musgrave
Abbot's Hill School, Herts	www.abbotshill.herts.sch.uk	£5,444	–	Mrs E. Thomas
Abbotsholme School, Derbys	www.abbotsholme.co.uk	£6,735	£9,890	S. Fairclough
Abingdon School, Oxon	www.abingdon.org.uk	£5,550	£11,730	Miss O. Lusk
Ackworth School, W. Yorks	www.ackworthschool.com	£4,285	£7,703	A. Maree
Adcote School, Shrops	www.adcoteschool.co.uk	£4,573	£8,351	G. Wright
AKS, Lancs	www.arnoldkeqms.com	£3,264	–	M. Walton
Aldenham School, Herts	www.aldenham.com	£6,663	£9,707	J. Fowler
Alderley Edge School for Girls, Cheshire	www.aesg.co.uk	£3,426	–	Mrs S. Goff
Alleyn's School, London SE22	www.alleyns.org.uk	£5,529	–	Dr G. Savage
Ampleforth College, N. Yorks	www.college.ampleforth.org.uk	£7,047	£10,441	D. Lambon
Ardingly College, W. Sussex	www.ardingly.com	£7,505	£10,120	B. Figgis
Ashford School, Kent	www.ashfordschool.co.uk	£5,200	£10,450	M. Buchanan
Ashville College, N. Yorks	www.ashville.co.uk	£4,220	£8,420	D. Lauder
Austin Friars St Monica's School, Cumbria	www.austinfriars.cumbria.sch.uk	£4,193	–	M. Harris
Bablake School, W. Midlands	www.bablake.com	£3,400	–	J. Watson
Badminton School, Bristol	www.badmintonschool.co.uk	£5,810	£11,010	Mrs R. Tear
Bancroft's School, Essex	www.bancrofts.org	£5,016	–	Mrs M. Ireland
Barnard Castle School, Durham	www.barnardcastleschool.org.uk	£7,391	£4,117	A. Stevens
Bedales School, Hants	www.bedales.org.uk	£8,590	£10,930	K. Budge
Bede's Senior School, E. Sussex	www.bedes.org	£6,640	£10,055	Dr R. Maloney
Bedford Girls' School, Beds	www.bedfordgirlsschool.co.uk	£3,960	–	Miss J. MacKenzie
Bedford Modern School, Beds	www.bedmod.co.uk	£3,982	–	M. Hall

Bedford School, Beds	www.bedfordschool.org.uk	£5,708	£9,654	J. Hodgson
Bedstone College, Shrops	www.bedstone.org	£4,555	£8,255	D. Gajadharsingh
Beechwood Sacred Heart School, Kent	www.beechwood.org.uk	£5,312	£8,820	A. Lennon
Benenden School, Kent	www.benenden.kent.sch.uk	–	£11,150	Mrs S. Price
Berkhamsted School, Herts	www.berkhamstedschool.org	£6,180	£9,843	M. Steed
Bethany School, Kent	www.bethanyschool.org.uk	£5,457	£9,246	M. Healy
Birkdale School, S. Yorks	www.birkdaleschool.org.uk	£3,850	–	Dr P. Owen
Birkenhead School, Merseyside	www.birkenheadschool.co.uk	£3,580	–	D. Edmunds
Bishop's Stortford College, Herts	www.bishopsstortfordcollege.org	£5,484	£8,238	J. Gladwin
Blackheath High School, London SE3	www.blackheathhighschool.gdst.net	£4,693	–	Mrs C. Chandler-Thompson
Bloxham School, Oxon	www.bloxhamschool.com	£7,890	£10,195	P. Sanderson
Blundell's School, Devon	www.blundells.org	£6,545	£10,175	Mrs N. Huggett
Bolton School Boys' Division, Lancs	www.boltonschool.org/seniorboys	£3,632	–	P. Britton
Bolton School Girls' Division, Lancs	www.boltonschool.org/seniorgirls	£3,632	–	Miss S. Hincks
Bootham School, N. Yorks	www.boothamschool.com	£5,505	£9,495	J. Taylor
Bournemouth Collegiate School, Dorset	www.bournemouthcollegiateschool.co.uk	£4,400	£8,400	R. Slatford
Box Hill School, Surrey	www.boxhillschool.com	£5,700	£9,980	C. Lowde
Bradfield College, Berks	www.bradfieldcollege.org.uk	£8,880	£11,100	S. Henderson
Bradford Grammar School, W. Yorks	www.bradfordgrammar.com	£3,930	–	K. Riley
Brentwood School, Essex	www.brentwoodschool.co.uk	£5,331	£10,463	D. Davies
Brighton & Hove High School, E. Sussex	www.bhhs.gdst.net	£4,155	–	Ms J. Smith
Brighton College, E. Sussex	www.brightoncollege.net	£7,080	£11,320	R. Cairns
Bristol Grammar School, Bristol	www.bristolgrammarschool.co.uk	£4,365	–	R. MacKinnon
Bromley High School, Kent	www.bromleyhigh.gdst.net	£4,896	–	Mrs A. Drew
Bromsgrove School, Worcs	www.bromsgrove-school.co.uk	£4,845	£10,395	P. Clague
Bruton School for Girls, Somerset	www.brutonschool.co.uk	£4,850	£8,858	Mrs N. Botterill
Bryanston School, Dorset	www.bryanston.co.uk	£9,153	£11,162	Ms S. Thomas
Burgess Hill School for Girls, W. Sussex	www.burgesshill-school.com	£5,100	£9,000	Mrs K. Bell
Bury Grammar School Boys, Lancs	www.bgsboys.co.uk	£3,266	–	R. Marshall
Bury Grammar School Girls, Lancs	www.bgsg.bury.sch.uk	£3,266	–	Mrs R. Georghiou
Canford School, Dorset	www.canford.com	£7,954	£10,374	B. Vessey
Caterham School, Surrey	www.caterhamschool.co.uk	£5,361	£10,003	J. Thomas
Channing School, London N6	www.channing.co.uk	£5,340	–	Mrs B. Elliott
Charterhouse, Surrey	www.charterhouse.org.uk	£8,273	£11,415	R. Pleming
Cheadle Hulme School, Cheshire	www.cheadlehulmeschool.co.uk	£3,552	–	Miss L. Pearson
Cheltenham College, Glos	www.cheltenhamcollege.org	£8,496	£11,238	Dr A. Peterken
Cheltenham Ladies' College, Glos	www.cheltladiescollege.org	£8,039	£11,862	Ms E. Jardine-Young
Chetham's School of Music, Greater Manchester	www.chethams.com	–	–	Mrs C. Moreland
Chigwell School, Essex	www.chigwell-school.org	£5,115	£8,560	M. Punt
Christ's Hospital, W. Sussex	www.christs-hospital.org.uk	£6,400	£9,850	J. Franklin
Churcher's College, Hants	www.churcherscollege.com	£4,352	–	S. Williams
City of London Freemen's School, Surrey	www.clfs.surrey.sch.uk	£5,175	£8,370	P. MacDonald
City of London School, London EC4	www.clsb.org.uk	£4,771	–	Mrs S. Fletcher
City of London School for Girls, London EC2	www.clsg.org.uk	£4,803	–	Mrs E. Harrop
Claremont Fan Court School, Surrey	www.claremont-school.co.uk	£5,090	–	J. Insall-Reid
Claysmore School, Dorset	www.claysmore.com	£7,783	£10,639	M. Cooke
Clifton College, Bristol	www.cliftoncollege.com	£7,875	£11,450	M. Moore
Clifton High School, Bristol	www.cliftonhigh.bristol.sch.uk	£4,270	–	Dr A. Neill
Cobham Hall, Kent	www.cobhamhall.com	£6,526	£9,817	P. Mitchell
Cokethorpe School, Oxon	www.cokethorpe.org.uk	£5,550	–	D. Ettinger
Colfe's School, London SE12	www.colfes.com	£4,917	–	R. Russell
Colston's School, Bristol	www.colstons.bristol.sch.uk	£4,045	–	J. McCullough
Concord College, Shrops	www.concordcollegeuk.com	£4,182	£10,800	N. Hawkins
Cranford House School, Oxon	www.cranfordhouse.net	£5,020	–	Dr J. Raymond
Cranleigh, Surrey	www.cranleigh.org	£8,910	£10,930	M. Reader
Croydon High School, Surrey	www.croydonhigh.gdst.net	£4,818	–	Mrs D. Leonard
Culford School, Suffolk	www.culford.co.uk	£5,780	£9,330	J. Johnson-Munday
Dame Allan's Boys' School, Tyne and Wear	www.dameallans.co.uk	£3,756	–	Dr J. Hind
Dame Allan's Girls' School, Tyne and Wear	www.dameallans.co.uk	£3,756	–	Dr J. Hind

School	Website	Day fees	Boarding fees	Head
Dauntsey's School, Wilts	www.dauntseys.org	£5,600	£10,850	M. Lascelles
Dean Close School, Glos	www.deanclose.org.uk	£7,360	£10,680	J. Lancashire
Denstone College, Staffs	www.denstonecollege.org	£4,568	£7,954	D. Derbyshire
Derby Grammar School, Derbys	www.derbygrammar.co.uk	£3,916	–	R. Paine
Derby High School, Derbys	www.derbyhigh.derby.sch.uk	£3,760	–	Mrs D. Gould
Dodderhill School, Worcs	www.dodderhill.co.uk	£3,350	–	Mrs C. Mawston
Dover College, Kent	www.dovercollege.org.uk	£4,750	£9,300	G. Holden
d'Overbroeck's, Oxon	www.doverbroecks.com	£6,860	£10,560	S. Cohen
Downe House, Berks	www.downehouse.net	£7,910	£10,930	Mrs E. McKendrick
Dulwich College, London SE21	www.dulwich.org.uk	£5,801	£12,108	Dr J. Spence
Dunottar School, Surrey	www.dunottarschool.com	£4,700	–	Mrs R. Cole
Durham High School for Girls, Durham	www.dhsfg.org.uk	£3,750	–	Mrs L. Renwick
Durham School, Durham	www.durhamschool.co.uk	£5,280	£8,645	K. McLaughlin
Eastbourne College, E. Sussex	www.eastbourne-college.co.uk	£6,860	£10,410	S. Davies
Edgbaston High School, W. Midlands	www.edgbastonhigh.co.uk	£3,729	–	Dr R. Weeks
Ellesmere College, Shrops	www.ellesmere.com	£5,598	£9,717	B. Wignall
Eltham College, London SE9	www.eltham-college.org.uk	£4,916	–	G. Sanderson
Emanuel School, London SW11	www.emanuel.org.uk	£5,468	–	M. Hanley-Browne
Epsom College, Surrey	www.epsomcollege.org.uk	£7,335	£10,730	J. Piggott
Eton College, Berks	www.etoncollege.com	–	£11,478	A. Little
Ewell Castle School, Surrey	www.ewellcastle.co.uk	£4,560	–	P. Harris
Exeter School, Devon	www.exeterschool.org.uk	£3,765	–	R. Griffin
Farlington School, W. Sussex	www.farlingtonschool.net	£5,385	£8,890	Miss L. Higson
Farnborough Hill, Hants	www.farnborough-hill.org.uk	£4,230	–	Mrs S. Buckle
Farringtons School, Kent	www.farringtons.org.uk	£4,390	£8,610	Mrs D. Nancekievill
Felsted School, Essex	www.felsted.org	£6,975	£9,990	Dr M. Walker
Forest School, London E17	www.forest.org.uk	£5,238	–	Mrs S. Kerr-Dineen
Framlingham College, Suffolk	www.framcollege.co.uk	£5,929	£9,222	P. Taylor
Francis Holland School, London NW1	www.francisholland.org.uk	£5,560	–	Mrs V. Durham
Francis Holland School, London SW1	www.francisholland.org.uk	£5,790	–	Mrs L. Elphinstone
Frensham Heights, Surrey	www.frensham.org	£6,110	£9,045	A. Fisher
Friends' School, Essex	www.friends.org.uk	£5,305	£8,590	Mrs A. Chaudhri
Fulneck School, W. Yorks	www.fulneckschool.co.uk	£3,950	£7,425	Mrs D. Newman
Gateways School, W. Yorks	www.gatewaysschool.co.uk	£3,940	–	Dr T. Johnson
Giggleswick School, N. Yorks	www.giggleswick.org.uk	£6,769	£9,884	M. Turnbull
The Godolphin and Latymer School, London W6	www.godolphinandlatymer.com	£6,060	–	Mrs R. Mercer
The Godolphin School, Wilts	www.godolphin.org	£6,176	£9,359	Mrs E. Hattersley
The Grange School, Cheshire	www.grange.org.uk	£3,435	–	C. Jeffery
Greenacre School for Girls, Surrey	www.greenacre.surrey.sch.uk	£5,094	–	Mrs L. Redding
Gresham's School, Norfolk	www.greshams.com	£7,620	£10,230	D. Robb
Guildford High School, Surrey	www.guildfordhigh.surrey.sch.uk	£4,988	–	Mrs F. Boulton
The Haberdashers' Aske's Boys' School, Herts	www.habsboys.org.uk	£5,554	–	P. Hamilton
Haberdashers' Aske's School for Girls, Herts	www.habsgirls.org.uk	£4,834	–	Miss B. O'Connor
Haileybury, Herts	www.haileybury.com	£7,546	£10,046	J. Davies
Halliford School, Middx	www.hallifordschool.co.uk	£4,315	–	S. Wilson
Hampshire Collegiate School, Hants	www.hampshirecs.org.uk	£4,715	£8,874	Mrs E. Henry
Hampton School, Middx	www.hamptonschool.org.uk	£5,585	–	K. Knibbs
Harrogate Ladies' College, N. Yorks	www.hlc.org.uk	£4,935	£10,695	Mrs S. Brett
Harrow School, Middx	www.harrowschool.org.uk	–	£11,530	J. Hawkins
Headington School, Oxon	www.headington.org	£5,480	£10,700	Mrs C. Jordan
Heathfield School, Berks	www.heathfieldschool.net	£7,525	£10,750	Mrs J. Heywood
Hereford Cathedral School, Herefords	www.herefordcs.com	£4,213	–	P. Smith
Hethersett Old Hall School, Norfolk	www.hohs.co.uk	£4,300	£8,100	S. Crump
Highgate School, London N6	www.highgateschool.org.uk	£6,055	–	A. Pettitt
Hill House School, S. Yorks	www.hillhouse.doncaster.sch.uk	£3,670	–	D. Holland
Hull Collegiate School, E. Yorks	www.hullcollegiateschool.co.uk	£3,571	–	Mrs R. Glover
Hurstpierpoint College, W. Sussex	www.hppc.co.uk	£6,975	£10,375	T. Manly
Hymers College, E. Yorks	www.hymerscollege.co.uk	£3,333	–	D. Elstone
Immanuel College, Herts	www.immanuelcollege.co.uk	£4,999	–	C. Dormer
Ipswich High School, Suffolk	www.ipswichhighschool.co.uk	£4,107	–	Ms O. Carlin
Ipswich School, Suffolk	www.ipswich.suffolk.sch.uk	£4,351	£8,054	N. Weaver

James Allen's Girls' School (JAGS), London SE22	www.jags.org.uk	£5,080	–	Mrs M. Gibbs
The John Lyon School, Middx	www.johnlyon.org	£5,188	–	Miss K. Haynes
Kent College, Kent	www.kentcollege.com	£5,613	£10,358	Dr D. Lamper
Kent College Pembury, Kent	www.kent-college.co.uk	£6,515	£9,633	Mrs S. Huang
Kimbolton School, Cambs	www.kimbolton.cambs.sch.uk	£4,615	£7,685	J. Belbin
King Edward VI High School for Girls, W. Midlands	www.kehs.org.uk	£3,750	–	Mrs A. Clark
King Edward VI School, Hants	www.kes.hants.sch.uk	£4,605	–	A. Thould
King Edward's School, Somerset	www.kesbath.com	£4,200	–	M. Boden
King Edward's School, W. Midlands	www.kes.org.uk	£3,860	–	J. Claughton
King Edward's, Surrey	www.kesw.org	£6,650	£9,500	J. Attwater
King Henry VIII School, W. Midlands	www.khviii.com	£3,400	–	J. Slack
King William's College, Isle of Man	www.kwc.im	£6,773	£9,860	M. Humphreys
Kingham Hill School, Oxon	www.kinghamhill.org.uk	£5,680	£9,490	Revd N. Seward
King's College School, London SW19	www.kcs.org.uk	£6,485	–	A. Halls
King's College, Somerset	www.kings-taunton.co.uk	£6,650	£9,800	R. Biggs
King's High School, Warwicks	www.kingshighwarwick.co.uk	£3,623	–	Mrs E. Surber
King's School, Somerset	www.kingsbruton.com	£6,868	£9,642	I. Wilmshurst
The King's School, Kent	www.kings-school.co.uk	£8,430	£11,120	P. Roberts
The King's School, Cheshire	www.kingschester.co.uk	£3,986	–	C. Ramsey
King's Ely, Cambs	www.kingsely.org	£6,177	£8,942	Mrs S. Freestone
The King's School, Glos	www.thekingsschool.co.uk	£5,895	–	A. Macnaughton
The King's School, Cheshire	www.kingsmac.co.uk	£3,770	–	Dr S. Hyde
King's Rochester, Kent	www.kings-rochester.co.uk	£5,680	£9,225	J. Walker
The King's School, Worcs	www.ksw.org.uk	£4,021	–	M. Armstrong
Kingsley School, Devon	www.kingsleyschoolbideford.co.uk	£4,170	£9,770	S. Woolcott
The Kingsley School, Warwicks	www.thekingsleyschool.com	£3,820	–	Ms H. Owens
Kingston Grammar School, Surrey	www.kgs.org.uk	£5,535	–	S. Lehec
Kingswood School, Somerset	www.kingswood.bath.sch.uk	£4,465	£9,624	S. Morris
Kirkham Grammar School, Lancs	www.kirkhamgrammar.co.uk	£3,338	£6,340	R. Laithwaite
The Lady Eleanor Holles School, Middx	www.lehs.org.uk	£5,800	–	Mrs H. Hanbury
Lancing College, W. Sussex	www.lancingcollege.co.uk	£7,480	£10,650	D. Oliver
Langley School, Norfolk	www.langleyschool.co.uk	£4,395	£8,930	D. Findlay
Latymer Upper School, London W6	www.latymer-upper.org	£5,770	–	D. Goodhew
Lavant House, W. Sussex	www.lavanthouse.org.uk	£4,500	£7,100	Mrs C. Horton
The Grammar School at Leeds, W. Yorks	www.gsal.org.uk	£4,038	–	M. Gibbons
Leicester Grammar School, Leics	www.leicestergrammar.org.uk	£3,859	–	C. King
Leicester High School for Girls, Leics	www.leicesterhigh.co.uk	£3,625	–	A. Whelpdale
Leighton Park School, Berks	www.leightonpark.com	£6,548	£10,197	N. Williams
Leweston School, Dorset	www.leweston.co.uk	£5,928	£9,576	A. Aylward
The Leys, Cambs	www.theleys.net	£6,395	£9,610	M. Priestley
Lichfield Cathedral School, Staffs	www.lichfieldcathedralschool.com	£6,450	£6,110	Mrs S. Hannam
Lincoln Minster School, Lincs	www.lincolnminsterschool.co.uk	£4,159	£9,952	C. Rickart
Longridge Towers School, Northumberland	www.lts.org.uk	£3,992	£8,132	T. Manning
Lord Wandsworth College, Hants	www.lordwandsworth.org	£6,840	£9,660	F. Livingstone
Loughborough Grammar School, Leics	www.lesgrammar.org	£3,682	£7,969	P. Fisher
Loughborough High School, Leics	www.leshigh.org	£3,553	–	Mrs G. Byrom
Luckley House School, Berks	www.luckleyhouseschool.org	£5,029	£8,801	Mrs J. Tudor
LVS Ascot (The Licensed Victuallers' School), Berks	www.lvs.ascot.sch.uk	£5,128	£9,010	Mrs C. Cunniffe
Magdalen College School, Oxon	www.mcsoxford.org	£5,140	–	Dr T. Hands
Malvern College, Worcs	www.malverncollege.org.uk	£7,558	£11,801	A. Clark
The Manchester Grammar School, Greater Manchester	www.mgs.org	£3,800	–	Dr M. Boulton
Manchester High School for Girls, Greater Manchester	www.manchesterhigh.co.uk	£3,546	–	Mrs A. Hewitt
Manor House School, Surrey	www.manorhouseschool.org	£5,050	–	Miss Z. Axton
The Marist Senior School, Berks	www.themaristschools.com	£4,200	–	K. McCloskey
Marlborough College, Wilts	www.marlboroughcollege.org	£9,375	£11,030	J. Leigh
Marymount International School, Surrey	www.marymountlondon.com	£6,890	£11,635	Ms S. Gallagher
Mayfield School, E. Sussex	www.mayfieldgirls.org	£6,250	£10,000	Miss A. Beary

School	Website			Head
The Maynard School, Devon	www.maynard.co.uk	£3,906	–	Ms B. Hughes
Merchant Taylors' Boys' School, Merseyside	www.merchanttaylors.com	£3,508	–	D. Cook
Merchant Taylors' Girls' School, Merseyside	www.merchanttaylors.com	£3,508	–	Mrs L. Robinson
Merchant Taylors' School, Middx	www.mtsn.org.uk	£6,017	–	S. Everson
Mill Hill School, London NW7	www.millhill.org.uk	£6,082	£9,609	Dr D. Luckett
Millfield, Somerset	millfieldschool.com	£7,500	£11,150	C. Considine
Milton Abbey School, Dorset	www.miltonabbey.co.uk	£5,495	£10,690	M. Bashaarat
Moira House Girls School, E. Sussex	www.moirahouse.co.uk	£5,110	£9,900	J. Sheridan
Monkton Combe School, Somerset	www.monktoncombeschool.com	£6,312	£9,772	R. Backhouse
More House School, London SW1	www.morehouse.org.uk	£5,500	–	Mrs A. Leach
Moreton Hall, Shrops	www.moretonhall.org	£8,320	£10,100	J. Forster
Mount Kelly, Devon	www.mountkelly.com	£5,330	£9,310	M. Semmence
Mount St Mary's College, Derbys	www.msmcollege.com	£3,490	£8,704	Dr N. Cuddihy
The Mount School, N. Yorks	www.mountschoolyork.co.uk	£5,515	£8,729	Ms J. Lodrick
New Hall School, Essex	www.newhallschool.co.uk	£5,739	£8,811	Mrs K. Jeffrey
Newcastle High School for Girls, Tyne and Wear	www.newcastlehigh.gdst.net	£3,896	–	Mrs H. French
Newcastle School for Boys, Tyne and Wear	www.newcastleschool.co.uk	£3,910	–	D. Tickner
Newcastle-under-Lyme School, Staffs	www.nuls.org.uk	£3,626	–	N. Rugg
North Cestrian Grammar School, Cheshire	www.ncgs.co.uk	£3,142	–	L. Bergin
North London Collegiate School, Middx	www.nlcs.org.uk	£5,875	–	Mrs B. McCabe
Northampton High School, Northants	www.northamptonhigh.gdst.net	£4,335	–	Mrs S. Dixon
Northwood College for Girls, Middx	www.northwoodcollege.gdst.net	£4,982	–	Miss J. Pain
Norwich High School, Norfolk	www.norwichhigh.gdst.net	£4,119	–	J. Morrow
Norwich School, Norfolk	www.norwich-school.org.uk	£4,565	–	S. Griffiths
Notre Dame School, Surrey	www.notredame.co.uk	£4,875	–	D. Plummer
Notting Hill and Ealing High School, London W13	www.nhehs.gdst.net	£5,250	–	Ms L. Hunt
Nottingham Girls' High School, Notts	www.nottinghamgirlshigh.gdst.net	£3,932	–	Mrs S. Gorham
Nottingham High School, Notts	www.nottinghamhigh.co.uk	£4,281	–	K. Fear
Oakham School, Rutland	www.oakham.rutland.sch.uk	£5,990	£9,980	N. Lashbrook
Ockbrook School, Derbys	www.ockbrooksch.co.uk	£3,755	£7,135	T. Brooksby
Oldham Hulme Grammar School, Lancs	www.ohgs.co.uk	£3,345	–	C. Mairs
The Oratory School, Oxon	www.oratory.co.uk	£7,450	£10,245	C. Dytor
Oswestry School, Shrops	www.oswestryschool.org.uk	£4,610	£8,595	J. Noad
Oundle School, Northants	www.oundleschool.org.uk	£6,875	£10,720	C. Bush
Our Lady's Abingdon Senior School, Oxon	www.olab.org.uk	£4,348	–	S. Oliver
Oxford High School, Oxon	www.oxfordhigh.gdst.net	£4,341	–	Mrs J. Carlisle
Palmers Green High School, London N21	www.pghs.co.uk	£4,465	–	Mrs C. Edmundson
Pangbourne College, Berks	www.pangbournecollege.com	£7,193	£10,172	T. Garnier
The Perse Upper School, Cambs	www.perse.co.uk	£4,970	–	E. Elliott
The Peterborough School, Cambs	www.thepeterboroughschool.co.uk	£4,526	–	A. Meadows
Pipers Corner School, Bucks	www.piperscorner.co.uk	£5,100	–	Mrs H. Ness-Gifford
Pitsford School, Northants	www.pitsfordschool.com	£4,333	–	N. Toone
Plymouth College, Devon	www.plymouthcollege.com	£4,920	£9,420	J. Standen
Pocklington School, E. Yorks	www.pocklingtonschool.com	£4,296	£8,099	M. Ronan
Portland Place School, London W1	www.portland-place.co.uk	£6,035	–	D. Hyman
The Portsmouth Grammar School, Hants	www.pgs.org.uk	£4,567	–	J. Priory
Portsmouth High School, Hants	www.portsmouthhigh.co.uk	£4,089	–	Mrs J. Prescott
Princess Helena College, Herts	www.princesshelenacollege.co.uk	£5,995	£9,705	Mrs S. Wallace-Woodroffe
Princethorpe College, Warwicks	www.princethorpe.co.uk	£3,536	–	E. Hester
Prior Park College, Somerset	www.thepriorfoundation.com	£4,975	£9,210	J. Murphy-O'Connor
Prior's Field, Surrey	www.priorsfieldschool.com	£5,395	£8,910	Mrs J. Roseblade
The Purcell School, Herts	www.purcell-school.org	£8,259	£10,562	D. Thomas
Putney High School, London SW15	www.putneyhigh.gdst.net	£5,290	–	Dr D. Lodge
Queen Anne's School, Berks	www.qas.org.uk	£6,770	£9,975	Mrs J. Harrington

Queen Elizabeth's Hospital (QEH), Bristol	www.qehbristol.co.uk	£4,231	–	S. Holliday
Queen Margaret's School, N. Yorks	www.queenmargarets.com	£6,125	£9,530	Mrs J. Miles
Queen Mary's School, N. Yorks	www.queenmarys.org	£5,390	£6,990	R. Johnston
Queen's College, London, London W1	www.qcl.org.uk	£5,410	–	Dr F. Ramsey
Queen's College, Somerset	www.queenscollege.org.uk	£5,470	£10,050	C. Alcock
Queen's Gate School, London SW7	www.queensgate.org.uk	£5,850	–	Mrs R. Kamaryc
Queenswood School, Herts	www.queenswood.org	£8,150	£10,750	Mrs P. Edgar
Radley College, Oxon	www.radley.org.uk	–	£11,075	J. Moule
Ratcliffe College, Leics	www.ratcliffe-college.co.uk	£4,955	£8,748	G. Lloyd
The Read School, N. Yorks	www.readschool.co.uk	£3,580	£8,610	J. Sweetman
Reading Blue Coat School, Berks	www.rbcs.org.uk	£4,860	–	M. Windsor
The Red Maids' School, Bristol	www.redmaids.co.uk	£4,090	–	Mrs I. Tobias
Redland High School for Girls, Bristol	www.redlandhigh.com	£3,880	–	Mrs C. Bateson
Reed's School, Surrey	www.reeds.surrey.sch.uk	£7,315	£9,680	M. Hoskins
Reigate Grammar School, Surrey	www.reigategrammar.org	£5,330	–	S. Fenton
Rendcomb College, Glos	www.rendcombcollege.org.uk	£6,910	£9,505	R. Martin
Repton School, Derbys	www.repton.org.uk	£7,825	£10,547	Mrs S. Tennant
Rishworth School, W. Yorks	www.rishworth-school.co.uk	£3,795	£8,160	A. Gloag
Roedean School, E. Sussex	www.roedean.co.uk	£6,300	£11,200	O. Blond
Rossall School, Lancs	www.rossallschool.org.uk	£4,060	£11,500	Ms E. Purves
Royal Grammar School, Surrey	www.rgs-guildford.co.uk	£5,100	–	Dr J. Cox
Royal Grammar School, Tyne and Wear	www.rgs.newcastle.sch.uk	£3,731	–	Dr B. Trafford
RGS Worcester, Worcs	www.rgsw.org.uk	£3,620	–	J. Pitt
The Royal High School Bath, Somerset	www.royalhighbath.gdst.net	£4,050	£8,499	Mrs J. Duncan
The Royal Hospital School, Suffolk	www.royalhospitalschool.org	£4,730	£9,070	J. Lockwood
The Royal Masonic School for Girls, Herts	www.royalmasonic.herts.sch.uk	£4,970	£8,600	Mrs D. Rose
Royal Russell School, Surrey	www.royalrussell.co.uk	£5,295	£10,475	C. Hutchinson
The Royal School, Wolverhampton, W. Midlands	www.theroyalschool.co.uk	£4,410	£9,610	M. Heywood
Rugby School, Warwicks	www.rugbyschool.net	£6,698	£10,675	P. Green
Ryde School with Upper Chine, Isle of Wight	www.rydeschool.org.uk	£3,850	£8,105	M. Waldron
Rye St Antony, Oxon	www.ryestantony.co.uk	£4,475	£7,355	Miss A. Jones
St Albans High School for Girls, Herts	www.stahs.org.uk	£4,825	–	Mrs J. Brown
St Albans School, Herts	www.st-albans.herts.sch.uk	£5,292	–	J. Gillespie
St Augustine's Priory School, London W5	www.saintaugustinespriory.org.uk	£4,200	–	Mrs S. Raffray
St Bede's College, Greater Manchester	www.stbedescollege.co.uk	£3,300	–	R. Robson
St Benedict's School, London W5	www.stbenedicts.org.uk	£4,620	–	C. Cleugh
St Catherine's School, Surrey	www.stcatherines.info	£5,535	£9,115	Mrs A. Phillips
St Catherine's School, Middx	www.stcatherineschool.co.uk	£4,405	–	Sr P. Thomas
St Christopher School, Herts	www.stchris.co.uk	£5,615	£9,935	R. Palmer
St Columba's College, Herts	www.stcolumbascollege.org	£4,390	–	D. Buxton
St Dominic's Brewood, Staffs	www.stdominicsbrewood.co.uk	£3,875	£7,167	H. Trump
St Dominic's Priory School, Staffs	www.stdominicspriory.co.uk	£3,482	£8,000	Mrs R. Harrison
St Dunstan's College, London SE6	www.stdunstans.org.uk	£5,020	–	N. Hewlett
St Edmund's College, Herts	www.stedmundscollege.org	£5,238	£8,836	P. Durn
St Edmund's School, Kent	www.stedmunds.org.uk	£6,217	£9,927	Mrs L. Moelwyn-Hughes
St Edward's, Oxford, Oxon	www.stedwardsoxford.org	£8,891	£11,111	S. Jones
St Edward's School, Glos	www.stedwards.co.uk	£4,900	–	Mrs P. Clayfield
Saint Felix School, Suffolk	www.stfelix.co.uk	£4,845	£8,465	Miss M. D'Alcorn
St Gabriel's, Berks	www.stgabriels.co.uk	£4,960	–	A. Jones
St George's College, Surrey	www.stgeorgesweybridge.com	£5,550	–	J. Peake
St George's School, W. Midlands	www.sgse.co.uk	£3,255	–	G. Neal
St George's, Ascot, Berks	www.stgeorges-ascot.org.uk	£6,750	£10,375	Mrs R. Owens
St Helen & St Katharine, Oxon	www.shsk.org.uk	£4,510	–	Mrs R. Dougall
St Helen's School, Middx	www.sthelens.london	£4,977	–	Dr M. Short
St James Senior Boys' School, Surrey	www.stjamesboys.co.uk	£5,090	£7,260	D. Brazier
St James Senior Girls' School, London W14	www.stjamesgirls.co.uk	£5,400	–	Mrs S. Labram

St John's College, Hants	www.stjohnscollege.co.uk	£3,550	£8,240	G. Best
St John's School, Surrey	www.stjohnsleatherhead.co.uk	£7,155	£9,035	M. Collier
St Joseph's College, Suffolk	www.stjos.co.uk	£4,365	£9,420	Mrs D. Clarke
St Lawrence College, Kent	www.slcuk.com	£5,643	£9,985	A. Spencer
St Margaret's School, Herts	www.stmargaretsbushey.co.uk	£4,910	£9,200	Mrs R. Hardy
St Margaret's School, London NW3	www.st-margarets.co.uk	£4,020	–	M. Webster
St Martha's, Herts	www.st-marthas.co.uk	£4,345	–	M. Burke
Saint Martin's, W. Midlands	www.saintmartins-school.com	£3,749	–	Miss N. Edgar
St Mary's Calne, Wilts	www.stmaryscalne.org	£8,450	£11,300	Dr F. Kirk
St Mary's School, Cambs	www.stmaryscambridge.co.uk	£4,638	£9,902	Ms C. Avery
St Mary's School, Essex	www.stmaryscolchester.org.uk	£4,100	–	Mrs H. Vipond
St Mary's College, Merseyside	www.stmarys.ac	£3,338	–	M. Kennedy
St Mary's School, Bucks	www.stmarysschool.co.uk	£4,652	–	Mrs J. Ross
St Mary's School Ascot, Berks	www.st-marys-ascot.co.uk	£7,800	£10,950	Mrs M. Breen
St Mary's School, Dorset	www.st-marys-shaftesbury.co.uk	£6,195	£8,990	R. James
St Nicholas' School, Hants	www.st-nicholas.hants.sch.uk	£4,265	–	Mrs A. Whatmough
St Paul's Girls' School, London W6	www.spgs.org	£6,958	–	Ms C. Farr
St Paul's School, London SW13	www.stpaulsschool.org.uk	£7,264	£10,880	M. Bailey
St Peter's School, York, N. Yorks	www.stpetersyork.org.uk	£5,310	£8,770	L. Winkley
St Swithun's School, Hants	www.stswithuns.com	£6,150	£9,855	Ms J. Gandee
Scarborough College N. Yorks	www.scarboroughcollege.co.uk	£4,331	£8,110	Mrs I. Nixon
Seaford College, W. Sussex	www.seaford.org	£6,150	£9,690	J. Green
Sevenoaks School, Kent	www.sevenoaksschool.org	£7,554	£11,526	Mrs C. Ricks
Shebbear College, Devon	www.shebbearcollege.co.uk	£3,950	£7,790	S. Weale
Sheffield High School, S. Yorks	www.sheffieldhighschool.org.uk	£3,805	–	Mrs V. Dunsford
Sherborne Girls, Dorset	www.sherborne.com	£7,505	£10,330	Mrs J. Dwyer
Sherborne School, Dorset	www.sherborne.org	£8,865	£10,950	R. Barlow
Shiplake College, Oxon	www.shiplake.org.uk	£6,450	£9,560	A. Davies
Shrewsbury High School, Shrops	www.shrewsburyhigh.gdst.net	£4,136	–	M. Getty
Shrewsbury School, Shrops	www.shrewsbury.org.uk	£7,385	£10,545	M. Turner
Sibford School, Oxon	www.sibfordschool.co.uk	£4,400	£8,549	M. Goodwin
Sidcot School, Somerset	www.sidcot.org.uk	£5,200	£9,340	I. Kilpatrick
Silcoates School, W. Yorks	www.silcoates.org.uk	£4,210	–	D. Wideman
Solihull School, W. Midlands	www.solsch.org.uk	£3,741	–	D. Lloyd
South Hampstead High School, London NW3	www.shhs.gdst.net	£5,074	–	Miss H. Pike
Stafford Grammar School, Staffs	www.staffordgrammar.co.uk	£3,666	–	M. Darley
Stamford High School, Lincs	www.ses.lincs.sch.uk	£4,482	£8,303	S. Roberts
Stamford School, Lincs	www.ses.lincs.sch.uk	£4,482	£8,303	S. Roberts
The Stephen Perse Foundation, Cambs	www.stephenperse.com	£5,135	–	Miss P. Kelleher
Stockport Grammar School, Cheshire	www.stockportgrammar.co.uk	£3,450	–	A. Chicken
Stonar, Wilts	www.stonarschool.com	£4,965	£8,960	Dr S. Divall
Stonyhurst College, Lancs	www.stonyhurst.ac.uk	£5,628	£10,111	A. Johnson
Stover School, Devon	www.stover.co.uk	£3,996	£8,178	R. Notman
Stowe School, Bucks	www.stowe.co.uk	£7,770	£10,700	Dr A. Wallersteiner
Streatham & Clapham High School, London SW16	www.schs.gdst.net	£5,013	–	Dr M. Sachania
Sunderland High School, Tyne and Wear	www.sunderlandhigh.co.uk	£3,077	–	Dr A. Slater
Surbiton High School, Surrey	www.surbitonhigh.com	£4,931	–	Ms E. Haydon
Sutton High School, Surrey	www.suttonhigh.gdst.net	£4,929	–	Mrs K. Crouch
Sutton Valence School, Kent	www.svs.org.uk	£6,435	£9,885	B. Grindlay
Sydenham High School, London SE26	www.sydenhamhighschool.gdst.net	£4,864	–	Mrs K. Pullen
Talbot Heath, Dorset	www.talbotheath.org	£4,113	£7,250	Mrs A. Holloway
Taunton School, Somerset	www.tauntonschool.co.uk	£5,675	£10,600	Dr J. Newton
Tettenhall College, W. Midlands	www.tettenhallcollege.co.uk	£4,200	£8,833	D. Williams
Thetford Grammar School, Norfolk	www.thetgram.norfolk.sch.uk	£4,109	–	G. Price
Tonbridge School, Kent	www.tonbridge-school.co.uk	£8,790	£11,721	T. Haynes
Tormead School, Surrey	www.tormeadschool.org.uk	£4,550	–	Mrs C. Foord
Tring Park School for the Performing Arts, Herts	www.tringpark.com	£7,110	£10,640	S. Anderson
Trinity School, Surrey	www.trinity-school.org	£4,820	–	M. Bishop
Trinity School, Devon	www.trinityschool.co.uk	£3,785	£8,340	T. Waters
Truro High School for Girls, Cornwall	www.trurohigh.co.uk	£3,851	£7,438	Dr G. Moodie
Truro School, Cornwall	www.truroschool.com	£4,075	£7,900	A. Gordon-Brown
Tudor Hall, Oxon	www.tudorhallschool.com	£6,420	£10,070	Miss W. Griffiths

University College School, London NW3	www.ucs.org.uk	£5,945	–	M. Beard
Uppingham School, Rutland	www.uppingham.co.uk	£7,665	£10,950	R. Harman
Walthamstow Hall, Kent	www.walthamstow-hall.co.uk	£5,750	–	Mrs J. Milner
Warminster School, Wilts	www.warminsterschool.org.uk	£4,650	£8,875	M. Mortimer
Warwick School, Warwicks	www.warwickschool.org	£3,791	£8,090	A. Lock
Welbeck - The Defence Sixth Form College, Leics	www.dsfc.ac.uk	–	–	J. Middleton
Wellingborough School, Northants	www.wellingboroughschool.org	£4,473	–	G. Bowe
Wellington College, Berks	www.wellingtoncollege.org.uk	£8,350	£11,375	Dr A. Seldon
Wellington School, Somerset	www.wellington-school.org.uk	£4,553	£9,395	H. Price
Wells Cathedral School, Somerset	www.wells-cathedral-school.com	£5,547	£9,283	Mrs E. Cairncross
West Buckland School, Devon	www.westbuckland.devon.com	£4,420	£8,200	J. Vick
Westfield School, Tyne and Wear	www.westfield.newcastle.sch.uk	£3,915	–	Mrs C. Jawaheer
Westholme School, Lancs	www.westholmeschool.com	£3,200	–	Mrs L. Horner
Westminster School, London SW1	www.westminster.org.uk	£8,456	£11,264	P. Derham
Westonbirt School, Glos	www.westonbirt.org	£7,100	£10,995	Mrs N. Dangerfield
Whitgift School, Surrey	www.whitgift.co.uk	£5,780	£11,132	Dr C. Barnett
Wimbledon High School, London SW19	www.wimbledonhigh.gdst.net	£5,250	–	Mrs J. Lunnon
Winchester College, Hants	www.winchestercollege.org	–	£11,580	R. Townsend
Windermere School, Cumbria	www.windermereschool.co.uk	£5,378	£9,632	I. Lavender
Wisbech Grammar School, Cambs	WisbechGrammar.com	£3,885	–	C. Staley
Withington Girls' School, Greater Manchester	www.wgs.org	£3,600	–	Mrs S. Marks
Woldingham School, Surrey	www.woldinghamschool.co.uk	£6,965	£11,225	Mrs J. Triffitt
Wolverhampton Grammar School, W. Midlands	www.wgs.org.uk	£4,085	–	Mrs K. Crewe-Read
Woodbridge School, Suffolk	www.woodbridge.suffolk.sch.uk	£4,944	£9,167	N. Tetley
Woodhouse Grove School, W. Yorks	www.woodhousegrove.co.uk	£3,940	£8,020	D. Humphreys
Worksop College, Notts	www.wsnl.co.uk	£5,410	£8,650	G. Horgan
Worth School, W. Sussex	www.worthschool.co.uk	£7,085	£9,990	G. Carminati
Wrekin College, Shrops	www.wrekincollege.com	–	–	Dr H. Griffiths
Wychwood School, Oxon	www.wychwoodschool.org	£4,550	£7,150	Mrs A. Johnson
Wycliffe College, Glos	www.wycliffe.co.uk	£5,995	£9,850	Mrs M. Burnet Ward
Wycombe Abbey, Bucks	www.wycombeabbey.com	£8,645	£11,525	Mrs R. Wilkinson
Wykeham House School, Hants	www.wykehamhouse.com	£3,990	–	Mrs L. Clarke
Yarm School, Cleveland	www.yarmschool.org	£3,867	–	D. Dunn
The Yehudi Menuhin School, Surrey	www.yehudimenuhinschool.co.uk	–	–	Dr R. Hillier

WALES

The Cathedral School Llandaff, Cardiff	www.cathedral-school.co.uk	£3,740	–	S. Morris
Christ College, Brecon	www.christcollegebrecon.com	£5,395	£8,335	Mrs E. Taylor
Haberdashers' Monmouth School for Girls, Monmouth	www.habs-monmouth.org	£4,419	£9,085	Mrs C. Pascoe
Howell's School Llandaff, Cardiff	www.howells-cardiff.gdst.net	£4,169	–	Mrs S. Davis
Monmouth School, Monmouth	www.habs-monmouth.org	£4,729	£9,085	Dr S. Connors
Rougemont School, Newport	www.rougemontschool.co.uk	£3,996	–	R. Carnevale
Ruthin School, Ruthin	www.ruthinschool.co.uk	£3,917	£8,167	T. Belfield
Rydal Penrhos School, Colwyn Bay	www.rydalpenrhos.com	£5,070	£10,105	P. Lee-Browne

SCOTLAND

Dollar Academy, Dollar	www.dollaracademy.org.uk	£3,678	£8,508	D. Knapman
The High School of Dundee, Dundee	www.highschoolofdundee.org.uk	£3,690	–	Dr J. Halliday
The Edinburgh Academy, Edinburgh	www.edinburghacademy.org.uk	£4,164	–	M. Longmore
Fettes College, Edinburgh	www.fettes.com	£7,730	£10,060	M. Spens
George Heriot's School, Edinburgh	www.george-heriots.com	£3,565	–	C. Wyllie
The Glasgow Academy, Glasgow	www.theglasgowacademy.org.uk	£3,468	–	P. Brodie
The High School of Glasgow, Glasgow	www.glasgowhigh.com	£3,659	–	C. Mair
Glenalmond College, Perth	www.glenalmondcollege.co.uk	£6,880	£10,100	G. Woods
Hutchesons' Grammar School, Glasgow	www.hutchesons.org	£3,477	–	Dr K. Greig
Kelvinside Academy, Glasgow	www.kelvinsideacademy.org.uk	£3,720	–	R. Karling
Kilgraston, Bridge of Earn	www.kilgraston.com	£5,225	£8,925	Mrs D. MacGinty
Lomond School, Helensburgh	www.lomondschool.com	£3,454	£7,670	Mrs J. Urquhart
Loretto School, Musselburgh	www.loretto.com	£6,670	£9,820	G. Hawley
The Mary Erskine School, Edinburgh	www.esms.org.uk	£3,355	£6,731	J. Gray

Merchiston Castle School, Edinburgh	www.merchiston.co.uk	£7,015	£9,520	A. Hunter
Morrison's Academy, Crieff	www.morrisonsacademy.org	£3,790	–	G. Pengelley
Robert Gordon's College, Aberdeen	www.rgc.aberdeen.sch.uk	£3,870	–	S. Mills
St Aloysius' College, Glasgow	www.staloysius.org	£3,438	–	J. Browne
St Columba's School, Kilmacolm	www.st-columbas.org	£3,533	–	D. Girdwood
St Leonards School, St Andrews	www.stleonards-fife.org	£3,999	£9,753	Dr M. Carslaw
St Margaret's School for Girls, Aberdeen	www.st-margaret.aberdeen.sch.uk	£3,734	–	Miss A. Tomlinson
Stewart's Melville College, Edinburgh	www.esms.org.uk	£3,355	£6,563	J. Gray
Strathallan School, Perth	www.strathallan.co.uk	£6,570	£9,682	B. Thompson

NORTHERN IRELAND

Bangor Grammar School, Bangor	www.bangorgrammarschool.com	–	–	Mrs E. Huddleson
Belfast Royal Academy, Belfast	www.belfastroyalacademy.com	£47	–	J. Dickson
Campbell College, Belfast	www.campbellcollege.co.uk	£2,460	£5,740	R. Robinson
The Royal School Dungannon, Dungannon	www.royaldungannon.com	£50	£5,117	D. Burnett

CHANNEL ISLANDS

Elizabeth College, Guernsey	www.elizabethcollege.gg	£3,205	–	G. Hartley
Victoria College, Jersey	www.victoriacollege.je	£1,612	–	A. Watkins

NATIONAL ACADEMIES OF SCHOLARSHIP

The national academies are self-governing bodies whose members are elected as a result of achievement and distinction in the academy's field. Within their discipline, the academies provide advice, support education and exceptional scholars, stimulate debate, promote UK research worldwide and collaborate with international counterparts.

Three of the national academies – the Royal Society, the British Academy and the Royal Academy of Engineering – receive grant-in-aid funding from the Department for Business, Innovation and Skills (BIS). The Academy of Medical Sciences receives core funding from the Department of Health and since 2014 an additional programme grant (£0.47m in 2015–16) from BIS. The Royal Society of Edinburgh is aided by funds provided by the Scottish government. In addition to government funding, the national academies generate additional income from donations, membership contributions, trading and investments.

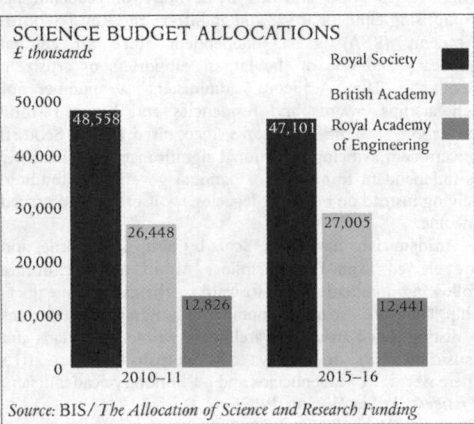

SCIENCE BUDGET ALLOCATIONS
£ thousands

Source: BIS/ The Allocation of Science and Research Funding

ACADEMY OF MEDICAL SCIENCES (1998)
41 Portland Place, London W1B 1QH
T 020-3176 2150 W www.acmedsci.ac.uk

Founded in 1998, the Academy of Medical Sciences is the independent body in the UK representing the diversity of medical science. The Academy seeks to improve health through research, as well as to promote medical science and its translation into benefits for society.

The academy is self-governing and receives funding from a variety of sources, including the fellowship, charitable donations, government and industry.

Fellows are elected from a broad range of medical sciences: biomedical, clinical and population based. The academy includes in its remit veterinary medicine, dentistry, nursing, medical law, economics, sociology and ethics. Elections are from nominations put forward by existing fellows.

As at May 2015 there were 1,094 fellows and 39 honorary fellows.
President, Prof. Sir John Tooke, PMEDSCI
Executive Director, Dr Helen Munn

BRITISH ACADEMY (1902)
10–11 Carlton House Terrace, London SW1Y 5AH
T 020-7969 5200 W www.britac.ac.uk

The British Academy is an independent, self-governing learned society for the promotion of the humanities and social sciences. It was founded in 1901 and granted a royal charter in 1902. The British Academy supports advanced academic research and is a channel for the government's support of research in those disciplines.

The fellows are scholars who have attained distinction in one of the branches of study that the academy exists to promote. Candidates must be nominated by existing fellows. There are around 930 fellows, 20 honorary fellows and 300 corresponding fellows overseas.
President, Lord Stern of Brentford
Chief Executive, Alun Evans

ROYAL ACADEMY OF ENGINEERING (1976)
3 Carlton House Terrace, London SW1Y 5DG
T 020-7766 0600 W www.raeng.org.uk

The Royal Academy of Engineering was established as the Fellowship of Engineering in 1976. It was granted a royal charter in 1983 and its present title in 1992. It is an independent, self-governing body whose object is the pursuit, encouragement and maintenance of excellence in the whole field of engineering, in order to promote the advancement of the science, art and practice of engineering for the benefit of the public.

Election to the fellowship is by invitation only, from nominations supported by the body of fellows. There are around 1,370 fellows, 42 honorary fellows and 102 international fellows. The Duke of Edinburgh is the senior fellow and the Princess Royal and the Duke of Kent are both royal fellows.
President, Dame Ann Dowling, DBE, FRENG, FRS
Chief Executive, Philip Greenish, CBE

ROYAL SOCIETY (1660)
6–9 Carlton House Terrace, London SW1Y 5AG
T 020-7451 2500 W www.royalsociety.org

The Royal Society is an independent academy promoting the natural and applied sciences. Founded in 1660 and granted a royal charter in 1662, the society has three roles: as the UK academy of science, as a learned society and as a funding agency. It is an independent, self-governing body under a royal charter, promoting and advancing all fields of physical and biological sciences, of mathematics and engineering, medical and agricultural sciences and their application.

Fellows are elected for their contributions to science, both in fundamental research resulting in greater understanding, and also in leading and directing scientific and technological progress in industry and research establishments. Each year up to 52 new fellows, who must be citizens or residents of the Commonwealth or Ireland, and up to ten foreign members may be elected. In addition one honorary fellow may also be elected annually from those not eligible for election as fellows or foreign members. There are around 1,430 fellows, 165 foreign members and six honorary members covering all scientific disciplines. The Queen is the patron of the Royal Society, and there are also six royal fellows.

President, Sir Venkatraman Ramakrishnan
Executive Director, Dr Julie Maxton

ROYAL SOCIETY OF EDINBURGH (1783)

22–26 George Street, Edinburgh EH2 2PQ
T 0131-240 5000 W www.royalsoced.org.uk

The Royal Society of Edinburgh (RSE) is an educational charity and Scotland's national academy. An independent body with charitable status, its multidisciplinary membership represents a knowledge resource for the people of Scotland. Granted its royal charter in 1783 for the 'advancement of learning and useful knowledge', the society organises conferences, debates and lectures; conducts independent inquiries; facilitates international collaboration and show-cases the country's research and development capabilities; provides educational activities for primary and secondary school students; and awards prizes and medals. The society also awards over £2m annually to Scotland's top researchers and entrepreneurs working in Scotland.

As at May 2015 there were 1,606 fellows, comprising 1,463 fellows, 70 honorary fellows and 73 corresponding fellows overseas.

President, Prof. Dame Jocelyn Bell Burnell, DBE, FRS, FRSE
General Secretary, Prof. Alan Alexander, OBE, FRSE

PRIVATELY FUNDED ARTS ACADEMIES

The Royal Academy and the Royal Scottish Academy support the visual arts community in the UK, hold educational events and promote interest in the arts. They are entirely privately funded through contributions by 'friends' (regular donors who receive benefits such as free entry, previews and magazines), bequests, corporate donations and exhibitions.

ROYAL ACADEMY OF ARTS (1768)

Burlington House, Piccadilly, London W1J 0BD
T 020-7300 8000 W www.royalacademy.org.uk

Founded by George III in 1768, the Royal Academy of Arts is an independent, self-governing society devoted to the encouragement and promotion of the fine arts.

Membership of the academy is limited to 80 academicians, all of whom are either painters, engravers, printmakers, draughtsmen, sculptors or architects. There must always be at least 14 sculptors, 12 architects and eight printmakers among the academicians. Candidates must be professionally active in the UK and are nominated and elected by the existing academicians. The members are known as royal academicians (RAs) and are responsible for both the governance and direction of the academy. When RAs reach the age of 75, they become senior academicians and can no longer serve as officers or on the committees.

The title of honorary academician is awarded to a small number of distinguished artists who are not resident in the UK; as at April 2015, there were 29 honorary academicians. Unlike the RAs, they do not take part in the governance of the academy and are unable to vote.

President, Christopher Le Brun, PRA
Secretary and Chief Executive, Dr Charles Saumarez Smith, CBE

ROYAL SCOTTISH ACADEMY (1838)

The Mound, Edinburgh EH2 2EL
T 0131-225 6671 W www.royalscottishacademy.org

Founded in 1826 and led by a body of academicians comprising eminent artists and architects, the Royal Scottish Academy (RSA) is an independent voice for cultural advocacy and one of the largest supporters of artists in Scotland. The Academy administers a number of scholarships, awards and residencies and has a historic collection of Scottish artworks, recognised by the Scottish government as being of national significance. The Academy is independent from local or national government funding, relying instead on bequests, legacies, sponsorship and earned income.

Academicians have to be Scots by birth or domicile, and are elected from the disciplines of art and architecure following nominations put forward by the existing member-ship. There are also a small number of honorary academicians – distinguished artists and architects, writers, historians and musicians – who do not have to be Scottish. As at May 2015 there were 111 academicians and 31 honorary academicians.

President, Arthur Watson, PRSA
Secretary, Marion Smith, RSA
Treasurer, Gareth Fisher, RSA

RESEARCH COUNCILS

The government funds basic and applied civil science research, mostly through seven research councils, which are established under royal charter and supported by the Department for Business, Innovation and Skills (BIS). Research Councils UK is the strategic partnership of these seven councils* (for further information *see* W www.rcuk.ac.uk). The councils support research and training in universities and other higher education and research facilities.

The science budget, administered by BIS, is the main source of public sector funding for research councils, with further public funds provided through the Large Facilities Capital Fund and the Higher Education Innovation Fund. Additional funds may also be provided by other government departments, devolved administrations, the European Commission and other international bodies. The councils also receive income for research specifically commissioned by government departments and the private sector, and income from charitable sources.

GOVERNMENT SCIENCE BUDGET
£ thousand

	2014–15	2015–16
Arts and Humanities Research Council	98,521	98,300
Biotechnology and Biological Sciences Research Council	391,271	432,300
Economic and Social Research Council	166,186	178,400
Engineering and Physical Sciences Research Council	780,150	898,100
Medical Research Council	649,370	810,000
Natural Environment Research Council	347,929	365,000
Science and Technology Facilities Council*	527,708	612,300
Higher Education Innovation Fund (HEIF)†	113,000	113,800

* Includes cross-council facilities and international subscriptions, which are managed by STFC on behalf of all research councils
† The research contribution to the HEIF, the Higher Education Funding Council for England (HEFCE) can add additional funding
Source: BIS – The Allocation of Science and Research Funding 2015/16

ARTS AND HUMANITIES RESEARCH COUNCIL*
Polaris House, North Star Avenue, Swindon SN2 1FL
T 01793-416000 W www.ahrc.ac.uk

The AHRC is the successor organisation to the Arts and Humanities Research Board and was incorporated by royal charter and established in 2005. It provides funding for postgraduate training and research in the arts and humanities; in any one year, the AHRC makes approximately 700 research awards and around 2,000 postgraduate scholarships. Awards are made after a rigorous peer review system, which ensures the quality of applications.
Chair, Prof. Sir Drummond Bone, FRSE
Chief Executive, Prof. Rick Rylance, FRSA

BIOTECHNOLOGY AND BIOLOGICAL SCIENCES RESEARCH COUNCIL*
Polaris House, North Star Avenue, Swindon SN2 1UH
T 01793-413200 W www.bbsrc.ac.uk

Established by royal charter in 1994, the BBSRC is the UK funding agency for research in the non-clinical life sciences. It funds research into how all living organisms function and behave, benefiting the agriculture, food, health, pharmaceutical and chemical sectors. To deliver its mission, the BBSRC supports research and training in universities and research centres throughout the UK, including providing strategic research grants to the institutes listed below. In June 2015, the institutes founded the National Institutes of Bioscience (NIB) partnership in order to increase the impact of bioscience research and to strengthen the UK's reputation in the field.
Chair, Prof. Sir Tom Blundell
Chief Executive, Prof. Jackie Hunter

INSTITUTES
BABRAHAM INSTITUTE, Babraham Hall, Babraham, Cambridge CB22 3AT T 01223-496000
Director, Prof. Michael Wakelam
GENOME ANALYSIS CENTRE, Norwich Research Park, Colney, Norwich NR4 7UH T 01603-450861
Director, Dr Mario Caccamo
INSTITUTE FOR BIOLOGICAL, ENVIRONMENTAL AND RURAL SCIENCES (ABERYSTWYTH UNIVERSITY), Penglais, Aberystwyth SY23 3DA T 01970-621986
Director, Prof. Mike Gooding
INSTITUTE OF FOOD RESEARCH, Norwich Research Park, Colney Lane, Norwich NR4 7UA T 01603-255000
Director, Prof. Ian Charles
JOHN INNES CENTRE, Norwich Research Park, Colney, Norwich NR4 7UH T 01603-450000
Director, Prof. Dale Sanders
PIRBRIGHT INSTITUTE, Pirbright Laboratory, Ash Road, Pirbright, Surrey GU24 0NF T 01483-232441
Director, Prof. John Fazakerley
ROSLIN INSTITUTE (UNIVERSITY OF EDINBURGH), Easter Bush, Midlothian EH25 9RG T 0131-651 9100
Director, Prof. David Hume
ROTHAMSTED RESEARCH, Harpenden, Herts AL5 2JQ T 01582-763133
Director, Prof. Achim Dobermann

ECONOMIC AND SOCIAL RESEARCH COUNCIL*
Polaris House, North Star Avenue, Swindon SN2 1UJ
T 01793-413000 E comms@esrc.ac.uk
W www.esrc.ac.uk

The ESRC was established by royal charter in 1965 as an organisation for funding and promoting research and post-graduate training in the social sciences. It also provides advice, disseminates knowledge and promotes public understanding in these areas. The ESRC provides core funding to the centres listed below.
Chair, Dr Alan Gillespie, CBE
Chief Executive, Prof. Jane Elliott

RESEARCH CENTRES
CENTRE FOR CLIMATE CHANGE, ECONOMICS AND POLICY, LSE, Houghton Street, London WC2A 2AE T 020-7107 5433
Directors, Dr Simon Dietz; Prof. Andy Gouldson

CENTRE FOR CORPUS APPROACHES TO SOCIAL SCIENCE (CASS), FASS Building, Lancaster University, Lancaster, Lancashire LA1 4YW E CASS@lancs.ac.uk
Director, Prof. Tony McEnery
CENTRE FOR LANGUAGE AND COMMUNICATIVE DEVELOPMENT, University of Manchester, Manchester M13 9PL T 0161-275 7342
Director, Prof. Elena Lieven
CENTRE FOR LONGITUDINAL STUDIES, Institute of Education, 20 Bedford Way, London WC1H 0AL T 020-7612 6875
Director (acting), Prof. Alissa Goodman
CENTRE FOR MACROECONOMICS, LSE, Houghton Street, London WC2A 2AE T 020-3486 2818
Directors, Prof. Wouter Den Haan; Prof. Morten Ravn
CENTRE FOR MAINTAINING FUNCTION AND WELLBEING IN LATER LIFE, Bangor University, Holyhead Road, Bangor LL57 2PZ T 01248-383968
Director, Bob Woods
CENTRE FOR MICRODATA METHODS AND PRACTICE, Institute for Fiscal Studies, 7 Ridgmount Street, London WC1E 7AE T 020-7291 4800
Director, Andrew Chesher
CENTRE ON DYNAMICS OF ETHNICITY, University of Manchester, Oxford Road, Manchester M13 9PL T 0161-275 4579
Director, Prof. James
NATIONAL CENTRE FOR RESEARCH METHODS, Social Sciences, Room 4139, Murray Building, University of Southampton, Southampton SO17 1BJ T 0238-059 8199
Director, Prof. Patrick Sturgis
SYSTEMIC RISK CENTRE, LSE, Houghton Street, London WC2A 2AE E scr@lse.ac.uk
Directors, Dr Jon Danielsson; Dr Jean-Pierre Zigrand
TAX ADMINISTRATION RESEARCH CENTRE, University of Exeter, Streatham Court, Rennes Drive, Exeter EX4 4ST T 01392-726286
Director, Prof. Gareth Myles
UK ENERGY RESEARCH CENTRE, 11 Princes Gardens, London SW7 1NA T 020-7594 1574
Director, Jim Watson

ENGINEERING AND PHYSICAL SCIENCES RESEARCH COUNCIL*
Polaris House, North Star Avenue, Swindon SN2 1ET
T 01793-444000 W www.epsrc.ac.uk

Formed in 1994 by royal charter, the EPSRC is the UK government's main agency for funding research and training in engineering and the physical sciences in universities and other organisations throughout the UK. It also provides advice, disseminates knowledge and promotes public understanding in these areas.
Chair, Paul Golby, FRENG
Chief Executive, Prof. Philip Nelson, FRENG

MEDICAL RESEARCH COUNCIL*
Polaris House, North Star Avenue, Swindon SN2 1FL
T 01793-416200 W www.mrc.ac.uk

The MRC is a publicly funded organisation dedicated to improving human health. The MRC supports research across the entire spectrum of medical sciences, in universities, hospitals, centres and institutes.
Chair, Donald Brydon, CBE
Chief Executive, Prof. Sir John Savill
Chair, Infections and Immunity Board, Prof. Paul Moss
Chair, Molecular and Cellular Medicine Board, Prof. Patrick Maxwell

Chair, Neurosciences and Mental Health Board, Prof. Hugh Perry
Chair, Population Health Sciences Group, Prof. Debbie Lawlor
Chair, Population and Systems Medicine Board, Prof. David Lomas

MRC UNITS, CENTRES AND INSTITUTES
Asthma UK Centre in Allergic Mechanisms of Asthma
W www.asthma-allergy.ac.uk
Behavioural and Clinical Neuroscience Institute (BCNI)
W http://research.psychol.cam.ac.uk/~bcni
Biostatistics Unit W www.mrc-bsu.cam.ac.uk
Brain Network Dynamics Unit W www.mrcbndu.ox.ac.uk
Cancer Unit W www.mrc-cu.cam.ac.uk
Centre for Brain Ageing and Vitality W www.ncl.ac.uk/cbav
Centre for Cognitive Ageing and Cognitive Epidemiology
W www.ccace.ed.ac.uk
Centre for Developmental Neurobiology
W www.kcl.ac.uk/oppn/depts/devneuro
Centre for Drug Safety Science W www.liv.ac.uk/drug-safety
Centre for Environment and Health
W www.environment-health.ac.uk
Centre for Genomics and Global Health W www.cggh.org
Centre for Immune Regulation W www.birmingham.ac.uk/research/activity/mds/centres/mrc-immune
Centre for Inflammation Research W www.cir.ed.ac.uk
Centre for Integrated Research into Musculoskeletal Ageing
W www.cimauk.org
Centre for Medical Molecular Virology
W www.ucl.ac.uk/infection-immunity/mrc_ucl-centre
Centre for Molecular Bacteriology and Infection
W www3.imperial.ac.uk/cmbi
Centre for Mouse Genetics W www.rc-harwell.ac.uk
Centre for Musculoskeletal Ageing Research
W www.birmingham.ac.uk/generic/mrc-aruk
Centre for Musculoskeletal Health and Work
W www.mrc.soton.ac.uk/cmhw
Centre for Neuromuscular Diseases W www.cnmd.ac.uk
Centre for Neuropsychiatric Genetics and Genomics
W http://medicine.cardiff.ac.uk/cngg
Centre for Outbreak Analysis and Modelling
W www1.imperial.ac.uk/medicine/about/institutes/outbreaks
Centre for Regenerative Medicine W www.crm.ed.ac.uk
Centre for Reproductive Health (CRH)
W www.crh.ed.ac.uk
Centre for Transplantation W http://transplantation.kcl.ac.uk
Centre for Virus Research
W www.gla.ac.uk/researchinstitutes/iii/cvr
Clinical Sciences Center W www.csc.mrc.ac.uk
Clinical Trial Services and Epidemiological Studies Unit
W www.ctsu.ox.ac.uk
Clinical Trials Unit W www.ctu.mrc.ac.uk
Cognition and Brain Sciences Unit W www.mrc-cbu.cam.ac.uk
Epidemiology Unit W www.mrc-epid.cam.ac.uk
Francis Crick Institute W www.crick.ac.uk
Functional Genomics Unit W www.mrcfgu.ox.ac.uk
Genome Damage and Stability Centre W www.sussex.ac.uk/gdsc
Human Genetics Unit W www.hgu.mrc.ac.uk
Human Immunology Unit
W www.imm.ox.ac.uk/mrc-human-immunology-unit
Human Nutrition Research Unit W www.mrc-hnr.cam.ac.uk
Institute of Genetics and Molecular Medicine
W www.igmm.ac.uk
Institute of Hearing Research W www.ihr.mrc.ac.uk
Institute of Radiation Oncology and Biology
W www.rob.ox.ac.uk
Integrative Epidemiology Unit
W www.bristol.ac.uk/integrative-epidemiology

Laboratory of Molecular Biology W www2.mrc-lmb.cam.ac.uk
Laboratory for Molecular Cell Biology W www.ucl.ac.uk/lmcb
Lifecourse Epidemiology Unit W www.mrc.soton.ac.uk
Lifelong Health and Ageing Unit W www.nshd.mrc.ac.uk
Metabolic Diseases Unit W www.mrc-cord.org
Mitochondrial Biology Unit W www.mrc-mbu.cam.ac.uk
Molecular Haemotology Unit
  W www.imm.ox.ac.uk/mrc-molecular-haematology-unit
National Institute for Medical Research (NIMR)
  W www.nimr.mrc.ac.uk
Prion Unit W www.prion.ucl.ac.uk
Protein Phosphorylation and Ubiquitylation Unit
  W www.ppu.mrc.ac.uk
Research Complex at Harwell (RCaH) W www.rc-harwell.ac.uk
Scottish Collaboration for Public Health Research and Policy
  W www.scphrp.ac.uk
Social and Public Health Sciences Unit W www.sphsu.mrc.ac.uk
Social, Genetic and Developmental Psychiatry Centre
  W www.kcl.ac.uk/iop/depts/mrc
Stem Cell Institute W www.stemcells.cam.ac.uk
Toxicology Unit W www.tox.mrc.ac.uk
Weatherall Institute of Molecular Medicine (WIMM)
  W www.imm.ox.ac.uk

MRC The Gambia W www.mrc.gm
Uganda Research Unit on AIDS W www.mrcuganda.org

NATIONAL PHYSICAL LABORATORY
Hampton Road, Teddington, Middx TW11 0LW
T 020-8977 3222 W www.npl.co.uk

The National Physical Laboratory (NPL) was established in 1900 and is the UK's national measurement institute. On 1 January 2015 it became a wholly owned government company, part of the Department for Business, Innovation and Skills. It develops, maintains and disseminates national measurement standards for physical quantities such as mass, length, time, temperature, voltage and force. It also conducts underpinning research on engineering materials and information technology, and disseminates good measurement practice.
Chief Executive, Dr Peter Thompson

ASSOCIATION OF INNOVATION, RESEARCH AND TECHNOLOGY ORGANISATIONS LIMITED (AIRTO)
T 020-8943 6600 E enquiries@airto.co.uk W www.airto.co.uk

AIRTO is a membership body, based at the NPL, for organisations operating in the UK's innovation, research and technology sector and represents around 80 per cent of organisations in this sector. AIRTO's members deliver vital innovation and knowledge transfer services which include applied and collaborative research and development (frequently in conjunction with universities), consultancy, technology validation and testing, incubation of commercialisation opportunities and early stage financing. AIRTO members have a combined turnover of over £5.5bn from clients inside and outside the UK, and together employ over 47,000 scientists, technologists and engineers. For a full list of members, *see* AIRTO's website.
President, Prof. Richard Brook, OBE, FRENG

NATURAL ENVIRONMENT RESEARCH COUNCIL*
Polaris House, North Star Avenue, Swindon SN2 1EU
T 01793-411500 W www.nerc.ac.uk

NERC is the leading funder of independent research, training and innovation in environmental science in the UK. Its work covers the full range of atmospheric, earth, biological, terrestrial and aquatic sciences. NERC invests public money in research exploring how we can sustainably benefit from our natural resources, predict and respond to natural hazards and understand environmental change. NERC works closely with policymakers and industry to support sustainable economic growth in the UK and around the world.
Chair, Sir Anthony Cleaver
Chief Executive, Prof. Duncan Wingham

RESEARCH CENTRES
BRITISH ANTARCTIC SURVEY, High Cross, Madingley Road, Cambridge CB3 0ET T 01223-221400
  Director, Prof. Jane Francis
BRITISH GEOLOGICAL SURVEY, Kingsley Dunham Centre, Keyworth, Nottingham NG12 5GG T 0115-936 3100
  Executive Director, Prof. John Ludden
CENTRE FOR ECOLOGY AND HYDROLOGY, Maclean Building, Benson Lane, Crowmarsh Gifford, Wallingford OX10 8BB T 01491-838800
  Director, Prof. Mark J. Bailey
NATIONAL CENTRE FOR ATMOSPHERIC SCIENCE, NCAS Headquarters, School of Earth and Environment, University of Leeds, Leeds LS2 9JT T 0113-343 6408
  Director, Prof. Stephen Mobbs
NATIONAL CENTRE FOR EARTH OBSERVATION, Michael Atiyah Building, University of Leicester, University Road, Leicester LE1 7RH T 0116-252 2016
  Director, Prof. John Remedios
NATIONAL OCEANOGRAPHY CENTRE, University of Southampton Waterfront Campus, European Way, Southampton SO14 3ZH T 023-8059 6666
  Director, Prof. Ed Hill, OBE

SCIENCE AND TECHNOLOGY FACILITIES COUNCIL*
Polaris House, North Star Avenue, Swindon SN2 1SZ
T 01793-442000 W www.stfc.ac.uk

Formed by royal charter in 2007, through the merger of the Council for the Central Laboratory of the Research Councils and the Particle Physics and Astronomy Research Council, the STFC is a non-departmental public body reporting to BIS.

The STFC invests in large national and international research facilities, while delivering science and technology expertise for the UK. The council is involved in research projects such as the Diamond Light Source Synchrotron and the Large Hadron Collider, and develops new areas of science and technology. The EPSRC has transferred its responsibility for nuclear physics to the STFC.
Chair, Prof. Michael Sterling, FRENG
Chief Executive, Prof. John Womersley

RESEARCH CENTRES
BOULBY UNDERGROUND SCIENCE FACILITY, Boulby Mine, Loftus, Saltburn-by-the-Sea, Cleveland TS13 4UZ T 01287-646300
CHILBOLTON OBSERVATORY, Chilbolton, Stockbridge, Hampshire SO20 6BJ T 01264-860391
DARESBURY LABORATORY, SciTech Daresbury, Warrington WA4 4AD T 01925-603000
RUTHERFORD APPLETON LABORATORY, Harwell Oxford, Didcot OX11 0QX T 01235-445000
UK ASTRONOMY TECHNOLOGY CENTRE, Royal Observatory Edinburgh, Blackford Hill, Edinburgh EH9 3HJ T 0131-668 8100

HEALTH

NATIONAL HEALTH SERVICE

The National Health Service (NHS) came into being on 5 July 1948 under the National Health Service Act 1946, covering England and Wales and, under separate legislation, Scotland and Northern Ireland. The NHS is now administered by the Secretary of State for Health (in England), the Welsh government, the Scottish government and the Northern Ireland Executive.

The function of the NHS is to provide a comprehensive health service designed to secure improvement in the physical and mental health of the people and to prevent, diagnose and treat illness. It was founded on the principle that treatment should be provided according to clinical need rather than ability to pay, and should be free at the point of delivery.

Hospital, mental, dental, nursing, ophthalmic and ambulance services and facilities for the care of expectant and nursing mothers and young children are provided by the NHS to meet all reasonable requirements. Rehabilitation services such as occupational therapy, physiotherapy, speech therapy and surgical and medical appliances are supplied where appropriate. Specialists and consultants who work in NHS hospitals can also engage in private practice, including the treatment of their private patients in NHS hospitals.

STRUCTURE

The structure of the NHS remained relatively stable for the first 30 years of its existence. In 1974, a three-tier management structure comprising regional health authorities, area health authorities and district management teams was introduced in England, and the NHS became responsible for community health services. In 1979, area health authorities were abolished and district management teams were replaced by district health authorities.

The National Health Service and Community Care Act 1990 provided for more streamlined regional health authorities and district health authorities, and for the establishment of family health services authorities (FHSAs) and NHS trusts. The concept of the 'internal market' was introduced into health care, whereby care was provided through NHS contracts where health authorities or boards and GP fundholders (the purchasers) were responsible for buying health care from hospitals, non-fundholding GPs, community services and ambulance services (the providers). The Act also paved the way for the community care reforms, which were introduced in April 1993, and changed the way care is administered for older people, the mentally ill, the physically disabled and people with learning disabilities.

ENGLAND

Under the Health and Social Care Act 2012, which gained royal assent in March 2012, the NHS in England is undergoing a complete operational and budgetary restructure at a cost of approximately £1.4bn. The full implementation of all the changes will not be complete for some time.

Hospitals will be extensively affected by the overhaul, with the cap on income from private hospital patients rising from 1.5 per cent to 49 per cent. All hospitals will become foundation trusts, competing for treatment contracts from clinical commissioning groups (CCGs).

On 1 April 2013 the new commissioning board, NHS England, took on full statutory responsibilities; at the same time, strategic health authorities (SHAs) and primary care trusts (PCTs) which, alongside the Department of Health (DoH), had been responsible for NHS planning and delivery, were abolished. NHS England is an executive non-departmental public body of the DoH with a remit to:
• provide national leadership to improve the quality of care
• oversee the operation of clinical commissioning groups
• allocate resources to clinical commissioning groups
• commission primary care and specialist services

The secretary of state has ultimate responsibility for the provision of a comprehensive health service in England and for ensuring the system works to its optimum capacity to meet the needs of its patients. The DoH is responsible for strategic leadership of the health and social care systems, but will cease to be the headquarters of the NHS, nor will it directly manage any NHS organisations.

In October 2014, NHS England published *Five Year Forward View* which committed the organisation to further change, including additional decentralisation and a greater emphasis on out-of-hospital care and preventative medicine.

NHS ENGLAND, PO Box 16738, Redditch B97 9PT
T 0300-311 2233 W www.england.nhs.uk
Chief Executive, Simon Stevens

CLINICAL COMMISSIONING GROUPS (CCGS)

On 1 April 2013, PCTs, which controlled 80 per cent of the NHS budget and commissioned most NHS services, were abolished. They were replaced with CCGs which took on many of the functions of the PCTs in addition to some functions previously assumed by the Department of Health. All GP practices now belong to a CCG which also includes other health professionals, such as nurses. CCGs commission most services, including:
• mental health and learning disability services
• planned hospital care
• rehabilitative care
• urgent and emergency care (including out-of-hours)
• most community health services

CCGs can commission any service provider that meets NHS standards and costs. These can be NHS hospitals, social enterprises, charities, or private-sector providers. There are 210 CCGs, which together are responsible for around 60 per cent of the NHS budget, around £69bn in 2015–16. In April 2015, 64 CCGs were approved to take on the additional responsibility for commissioning GP services within their area.

HEALTH AND WELLBEING BOARDS

Every upper-tier local authority hasestablished a health and wellbeing board to act as a forum for local commissioners across the NHS, social care, public health and other services. The 152 boards are intended to:
• encourage integrated commissioning of health and social care services
• increase democratic input into strategic decisions about health and wellbeing services
• strengthen working relationships between health and social care

PUBLIC HEALTH ENGLAND (PHE)

This new organisation was established on 1 April 2013. It provides national leadership and expert services to support public health and also works with local government and the NHS to respond to emergencies. PHE's responsibilities are to:

- coordinate a national public health service
- support the public to make healthier choices
- provide leadership to the public health delivery system
- support the development of the public health workforce

REGULATION

Since the restructuring of the NHS in England began in April 2013, some elements of the regulation system have changed. Responsibility for the regulation of particular aspects of care is shared across a number of different bodies, including the Care Quality Commission (CQC), Monitor, and individual professional regulatory bodies, such as the General Medical Council, Nursing and Midwifery Council, General Dental Council and the Health and Care Professions Council.

CARE QUALITY COMMISSION (CQC)

The CQC regulates all health and social care services in England, including those provided by the NHS, local authorities, private companies or voluntary organisations. In addition it protects the interests of people detained under the Mental Health Act. The CQC ensures that all essential standards of quality and safety are met where care is provided, from hospitals to private care homes. By law all NHS providers (such as hospitals and ambulance services) must register with the CQC to show they are protecting people from the risk of infection. The CQC possesses a range of legal powers and duties and will take action if providers do not meet essential standards of quality or safety.

MONITOR

Monitor is the sector regulator for health services in England. Their job is to protect and promote the interests of patients. Monitor's aim is to promote competition, regulate prices and ensure the continuity of services for NHS foundation trusts. Under the new structure, most NHS providers need to be registered with both the CQC and Monitor to be able to legally provide services.

HEALTHWATCH

Healthwatch England was established in October 2012 following the restructuring of the NHS. The organisation functions at a national and local level as an independent consumer body, gathering and representing the views of the public about health and social care services in England.
CARE QUALITY COMMISSION, Finsbury Tower,
  103–105 Bunhill Row, London EC1Y 8TG T 03000-616161
  W www.cqc.org.uk
  Chief Executive, David Behan
MONITOR, Wellington House, 133–155 Waterloo Road,
  London SE1 8UG T 020-3747 0000
  W www.monitor-nhsft.gov.uk
  Chief Executive, Dr David Bennett
HEALTHWATCH, Citygate, Gallowgate, Newcastle upon Tyne
  NE1 4PA T 03000-683000 W www.healthwatch.co.uk
  Chief Executive, Dr Katherine Rake, OBE

AUTHORITIES AND TRUSTS

Overseen by the NHS Trust Development Authority all NHS trusts are expected to eventually become foundation trusts.

ACUTE TRUSTS

Hospitals in England are managed by acute trusts. There are 161 acute trusts, of which 102 have foundation trust status. Acute trusts ensure hospitals provide high-quality healthcare and spend money efficiently. They employ a large sector of the NHS workforce, including doctors, nurses, pharmacists, midwives, and health visitors. Acute trusts also employ those in supplementary medical professions, such as physiotherapists, radiographers and podiatrists, in addition to many other non-medical staff.

AMBULANCE TRUSTS

There are 10 ambulance services (five foundation trusts) in England, providing emergency services to healthcare.

CLINICAL SENATES AND STRATEGIC CLINICAL NETWORKS

Clinical senates are advisory groups of experts from across health and social care. There are 12 senates covering England comprising clinical leaders from across the healthcare system, in addition to members from social care and public health.

There are 12 strategic clinical networks across England, comprising groups of clinical experts covering a particular disease, patient or professional group. They offer advice to CCGs and NHS England.

Neither organisation is a statutory body, and although they comment on CCG plans to NHS England, they are unable to veto them.

FOUNDATION TRUSTS

NHS foundation trusts are independent legal entities with unique governance arrangements. Each NHS foundation trust has a duty to consult and involve a board of governors in the strategic planning of its organisation. They have financial freedoms and can raise capital from both the public and private sectors within borrowing limits determined by projected cash flows and based on affordability. They are overseen by Monitor.

MENTAL HEALTH TRUSTS

There are 59 mental health trusts in England, 43 of which have foundation trust status. They provide health and social care services for people with mental health problems.

NHS TRUST DEVELOPMENT AUTHORITY (TDA)

Following the abolition of SHAs in 2013, the TDA became responsible for overseeing the performance, management and governance of NHS trusts, including clinical quality, and managing their progress towards foundation trust status.

SPECIAL HEALTH AUTHORITIES

There are 12 Special health authorities with a nationwide remit, including:
- The National Blood and Transplant Authority
- NHS Business Services Authority
- NHS Litigation Authority

WALES

The NHS Wales was reorganised according to Welsh Assembly commitments laid out in the *One Wales* strategy which came into effect in October 2009. There are now seven local health boards (LHBs) that are responsible for delivering all health care services within a geographical area, rather than the trust and local health board system that existed previously. Community health councils (CHCs) are statutory lay bodies that represent the public for the health service in their region. There are currently eight CHCs.

NHS TRUSTS

There are three NHS trusts in Wales. The Welsh Ambulance Services NHS Trust is for emergency services; the Velindre NHS Trust offers specialist services in cancer care; while Public Health Wales serves as a unified public health organisation for Wales.

LOCAL HEALTH BOARDS

The websites of the seven LHBs, and contact details for community health councils and NHS trusts, are available in

the *NHS Wales Directory* on the NHS Wales website
(W www.wales.nhs.uk).

ABERTAWE BRO MORGANNWG UNIVERSITY
  HEALTH BOARD, One Talbot Gateway, Baglan Energy Park,
  Baglan, Port Talbot SA12 7BR **T** 01639-683344
  Chief Executive, Paul Roberts

ANEURIN BEVAN HEALTH BOARD, Headquarters,
  Lodge Road, Caerleon, Newport NP18 3XQ **T** 01873-732732
  Chief Executive, Judith Paget

BETSI CADWALADR UNIVERSITY HEALTH BOARD,
  Ysbyty Gwynedd, Penrhosgarnedd, Bangor, Gwynedd
  LL57 2PW **T** 01248-384384
  Chief Executive (interim), Simon Dean

CARDIFF AND VALE UNIVERSITY HEALTH BOARD,
  Cardigan House, University Hospital of Wales, Heath Park,
  Cardiff CF14 4XW **T** 029-2074 7747
  Chief Executive, Adam Cairns

CWM TAF HEALTH BOARD, Ynysmeurig House,
  Navigation Park, Abercynon CF45 4SN **T** 01443-744800
  Chief Executive, Allison Williams

HYWEL DDA HEALTH BOARD, Corporate Offices,
  Ystwyth Building, Hafan Derwen, Jobswell Road, Carmarthen
  SA31 3BB **T** 01267-235151
  Chief Executive, Steve Moore

POWYS TEACHING HEALTH BOARD, Mansion House,
  Bronllys, Brecon, Powys LD3 0LS **T** 01874-771661
  Chief Executive, Carol Shillabeer

SCOTLAND

The Scottish government Health Directorate is responsible
both for NHS Scotland and for the development and
implementation of health and community care policy. The
chief executive of NHS Scotland leads the central
management of the NHS, is accountable to ministers for the
efficiency and performance of the service and heads the
Health Department which oversees the work of the 14
regional health boards. These boards provide strategic
management for the entire local NHS system and are
responsible for ensuring that services are delivered effectively
and efficiently.

In addition to the 14 regional health boards there are a
further seven special boards and one public health body,
which provide national services, such as the Scottish
ambulance service and NHS Health Scotland. Healthcare
Improvement Scotland, was formed on 1 April 2011 by the
Public Services Reform Act 2010 to improve the quality of
Scottish healthcare.

REGIONAL HEALTH BOARDS

AYRSHIRE AND ARRAN, Eglinton House, Ailsa Hospital,
  Dalmellington Road, Ayr KA6 6AB **T** 0800-169 1441
  W www.nhsaaa.net
  Chief Executive, John Burns

BORDERS, Borders General Hospital, Melrose, Roxburghshire
  TD6 9DA **T** 01896-826000 **W** www.nhsborders.org.uk
  Chief Executive, Jane Davidson

DUMFRIES AND GALLOWAY, Ryan North, Crichton Hall,
  Dumfries DG1 4TG **T** 01387-246246
  W www.nhsdg.scot.nhs.uk
  Chief Executive, Jeff Ace

EILEAN SIAR (WESTERN ISLES), 37 South Beach Street,
  Stornoway, Isle of Lewis HS1 2BB **T** 01851-702997
  W www.wihb.scot.nhs.uk
  Chief Executive, Gordon Jamieson

FIFE, Hayfield House, Hayfield Road, Kirkcaldy, Fife KY2 5AH
  T 01592-643355 **W** www.nhsfife.org
  Chief Executive, John Wilson

FORTH VALLEY, Carseview House, Castle Business Park, Stirling
  FK9 4SW **T** 01786-463031 **W** www.nhsforthvalley.com
  Chief Executive, Jane Grant

GRAMPIAN, Summerfield House, 2 Eday Road, Aberdeen
  AB15 6RE **T** 0845-456 6000 **W** www.nhsgrampian.org
  Chief Executive, Malcolm Wright

GREATER GLASGOW AND CLYDE, J B Russell House,
  Gartnavel Royal Hospital Campus, 1055 Great Western Road,
  Glasgow G12 0XH **T** 0141-201 4444 **W** www.nhsgg.org.uk
  Chief Executive, Robert Calderwood

HIGHLAND, Assynt House, Beechwood Park, Inverness IV2 3BW
  T 01463-717123 **W** www.nhshighland.scot.nhs.uk
  Chief Executive, Elaine Mead

LANARKSHIRE, Kirklands, Fallside Road, Bothwell G71 8BB
  T 01236-748748 **W** www.nhslanarkshire.org.uk
  Chief Executive, Calum Campbell

LOTHIAN, Waverley Gate, 2–4 Waterloo Place, Edinburgh
  EH1 3EG **T** 0131-536 9000 **W** www.nhslothian.scot.nhs.uk
  Chief Executive, Tim Davison

ORKNEY, Garden House, New Scapa Road, Kirkwall, Orkney
  KW15 1BQ **T** 01856-888000 **W** www.ohb.scot.nhs.uk
  Chief Executive, Cathie Cowan

SHETLAND, Upper Floor Montfield, Burgh Road, Lerwick
  ZE1 0LA **T** 01595-743060 **W** www.shb.scot.nhs.uk
  Chief Executive, Ralph Roberts

TAYSIDE, Level 10, Ninewells Hospital, Dundee DD1 9SY
  T 01382-660111 **W** www.nhstayside.scot.nhs.uk
  Chief Executive, Lesley McLay

NORTHERN IRELAND

On 1 April 2009 the four health and social services boards in
Northern Ireland were replaced by a single health and social
care board for the whole of Northern Ireland. The new board
together with its local commissioning groups (whose
boundaries are subject to review pending the outcome of
local government reform) are responsible for improving the
health and social wellbeing of people in the area for which
they are responsible, planning and commissioning services,
and coordinating the delivery of services in a cost-effective
manner.

HEALTH AND SOCIAL CARE BOARD,
  12–22 Linenhall Street, Belfast BT2 8BS **T** 030-0555 0115
  W www.hscboard.hscni.net
  Chief Executive, Valerie Watts

FINANCE

The NHS is still funded mainly through general taxation,
although in recent years more reliance has been placed on
the NHS element of national insurance contributions, patient
charges and other sources of income.

Funding for NHS England was set at £98.84bn for 2015–
16. Expenditure for the NHS in Wales, Scotland and
Northern Ireland is set by the devolved governments.

EMPLOYEES AND SALARIES

NHS HEALTH SERVICE STAFF 2015 (ENGLAND)
Full-time equivalent

All hospital, community and dental staff	1,218,911
Consultants	43,766
Registrars	39,976
Qualified nursing and midwifery staff	357,548
Qualified scientific, therapeutic and technical staff	155,603

Source: Health and Social Care Information Centre *NHS Hospital and Community Health Service: Monthly Workforce Statistics*

SALARIES

Many general practitioners (GPs) are self-employed and hold contracts, either on their own or as part of a Clinical Commissioning Group (CCG). The profit of GPs varies according to the services they provide for their patients and the way they choose to provide these services. Salaried GPs who are part of a CCG earn between £55,412 and £83,617. Most NHS dentists are self-employed contractors. A contract for dentists was introduced on 1 April 2006 which provides dentists with an annual income in return for carrying out an agreed amount, or units, of work. A salaried dentist employed by the NHS, who works mainly with community dental services earn between £38,095 and £81,480.

BASIC SALARIES FOR HOSPITAL MEDICAL AND DENTAL STAFF
from 1 April 2015
From 1 April 2015 to 31 March 2016 staff who are on the top salary in their pay band will receive a non-consolidated lump sum, payable in monthly instalments, of either 1 or 2 per cent of their basic pay dependent on the length of time they have been on the top salary in their pay band. The figures below do not include merit awards, discretionary points or banding supplements.

Consultant (2003 contract)	£75,249–£101,451
Specialist registrar	£31,301–£47,175
Speciality registrar (full)	£30,002–£47,175
Speciality registrar (fixed term)	£30,002–£39,693
Foundation house officer year 2	£28,076–£31,748
Foundation house officer year 1	£22,636–£25,461

NURSES
From 1 December 2004 the *Agenda for Change* pay system was introduced throughout the UK for all NHS staff with the exception of medical and dental staff, doctors in public health medicine and the community health service. Nurses' salaries are incorporated in the *Agenda for Change* nine pay band structure, which provides additional payments for flexible working such as providing out-of-hours services, working weekends and nights and being on-call. There is also additional payments for those staff who work in high-cost areas such as London.

SALARIES FOR NURSES AND MIDWIVES
from 1 April 2015

Nurse/Midwife consultant	£39,632–£67,805
Modern matron	£39,632–£47,559
Nurse advanced/team manager	£31,072–£40,964
Midwife higher level	£31,072–£40,964
Nurse specialist/team leader	£26,041–£34,876
Hospital/community midwife	£26,041–£34,876
Registered nurse/entry level midwife*	£21,692–£28,180

*Starting salaries in Wales and Norther Ireland are currently the same as in England. The starting salary in Scotland is £21,602

HEALTH SERVICES

PRIMARY CARE
Primary care comprises the services provided by general practitioners, community health centres, pharmacies, dental practices and opticians. Primary nursing care includes the work carried out by practice nurses, community nurses, community midwives and health visitors.

PRIMARY MEDICAL SERVICES
In England, primary medical services (PMS) are provided by 66,846 registerd GPs, working in around 8,000 GP practices, with 56.6 million registered patients.

In Wales, responsibility for primary medical services rests with local health boards (LHBs), in Scotland with the 14 regional health boards and in Northern Ireland with the health and social care board.

Any vocationally trained doctor may provide general or personal medical services. GPs may also have private fee-paying patients, but not if that patient is already an NHS patient on that doctor's patient list.

A person who is ordinarily resident in the UK is eligible to register with a GP (or PMS provider) for free primary care treatment. Should a patient have difficulty in registering with a doctor, he or she should contact the local CCG for help. When a person is away from home he/she can still access primary care treatment from a GP if they ask to be treated as a temporary resident. In an emergency any doctor in the service will give treatment and advice.

GPs or CCGs are responsible for the care of their patients 24 hours a day, seven days a week, but can fulfil the terms of their contract by delegating or transferring responsibility for out-of-hours care to an accredited provider.

In addition, NHS walk-in centres (WICs) throughout England are usually open seven days a week, from early in the morning until late in the evening. They are nurse-led and provide treatment for minor illnesses and injuries, health information and self-help advice. Some WICs are not able to treat young children.

HEALTH COSTS
Some people are exempt from, or entitled to help with, health costs such as prescription charges, ophthalmic and dental costs, and in some cases help towards travel costs to and from hospital.

The following list is intended as a general guide to those who may be entitled to help, or who are exempt from some of the charges relating to the above:

• children under 16 and young people in full-time education who are under 19
• people aged 60 or over
• pregnant women and women who have had a baby in the last 12 months and have a valid maternity exemption certificate (MatEx)
• people, or their partners, who are in receipt of income support, income-based jobseeker's allowance and/or income-based employment and support allowance
• people in receipt of the pension credit
• diagnosed glaucoma patients, people who have been advised by an ophthalmologist that they are at risk of glaucoma and people aged 40 or over who have an immediate family member who is a diagnosed glaucoma patient
• NHS in-patients
• NHS out-patients for all prescribed contraceptives, medication given at a hospital, NHS walk-in centre, personally administered by a GP or supplied at a hospital or primary care trust clinic for the treatment of tuberculosis or a sexually transmissible infection
• out-patients of the NHS Hospital Dental Service
• people registered blind or partially sighted
• people who need complex lenses
• war pensioners whose treatment/prescription is for their accepted disablement and who have a valid exemption certificate
• people who are entitled to, or named on, a valid NHS tax credit exemption or HC2 certificate
• people who have a medical exemption (MedEx) certificate, including those with cancer or diabetes

People in other circumstances may also be eligible for help; *see* booklet HC12 (England) and HCS2 (Scotland) for further information.

WALES

On 1 April 2007 all prescription charges (including those for medical supports and appliances and wigs) for people living in Wales were abolished. The above guide still applies for NHS dental and optical charges although all people aged under 25 living in Wales are also entitled to free dental examinations.

SCOTLAND

On 1 April 2011 all prescription charges in Scotland were abolished. Those entitled to free prescriptions in Scotland include patients registered with a Scottish GP and receiving a prescription from a Scottish pharmacy, and Scottish patients who have an English GP and an entitlement card.

NORTHERN IRELAND

On 1 April 2010 all prescription charges in Northern Ireland were abolished. All prescriptions dispensed in Northern Ireland are free, even for patients visiting from England, Wales or Scotland.

PHARMACEUTICAL SERVICES

Patients may obtain medicines and appliances under the NHS from any pharmacy whose owner has entered into arrangements with the CCG to provide this service. There are also some suppliers who only provide special appliances. In rural areas, where access to a pharmacy may be difficult, patients may be able to obtain medicines, etc, from a dispensing doctor.

In England, a charge of £8.20 is payable for each item supplied (except for contraceptives for which there is no charge), unless the patient is exempt and the declaration on the back of the prescription form is completed. Prescription prepayment certificates (£29.10 valid for three months, £104 valid for a year) may be purchased by those patients not entitled to exemption who require frequent prescriptions.

DENTAL SERVICES

Dentists, like doctors, may take part in the NHS and also have private patients. Dentists are responsible to the local health provider in whose areas they provide services. Patients may go to any dentist who is taking part in the NHS and is willing to accept them. There is a three-tier payment system based on the individual course of treatment required.

NHS DENTAL CHARGES
from 1 April 2015

	England/Wales
Band 1* – Examination, diagnosis, preventive care (eg x-rays, scale and polish)	£18.80/£13.50
Band 2 – Band 1 + basic additional treatment (eg fillings and extractions)	£51.30/£43.00
Band 3 – Bands 1 and 2 + all other treatment (eg crowns, dentures and bridges)	£222.50/£185.00

* Urgent and out-of-hours treatment is also charged at this payment tier

The cost of individual treatment plans should be known prior to treatment and some dental practices may require payment in advance. There is no charge for writing a prescription or removing stitches and only one charge is payable for each course of treatment even if more than one visit to the dentist is required. If additional treatment is required within two months of visiting the dentist and this is covered by the course of treatment most recently paid for (eg payment was made for the second tier of treatment but an additional filling is required) then this will be provided free of charge.

SCOTLAND AND NORTHERN IRELAND

Scotland and Northern Ireland have yet to simplify their charging systems. NHS dental patients pay 80 per cent of the cost of the individual items of treatment provided up to a maximum of £384. Patients in Scotland are entitled to free basic and extensive examinations.

GENERAL OPHTHALMIC SERVICES

General ophthalmic services are administered by local health providers. Testing of sight may be carried out by any ophthalmic medical practitioner or ophthalmic optician (optometrist). The optician must give the prescription to the patient, who can take this to any supplier of glasses to have them dispensed. Only registered opticians can supply glasses to children and to people registered as blind or partially sighted.

Free eyesight tests and help towards the cost are available to people in certain circumstances. Help is also available for the purchase of glasses or contact lenses (*see* Health Costs). In Scotland eye examinations, which include a sight test, are free to all UK residents. Help is also available for the purchase of glasses or contact lenses to those entitled to help with health costs in the same way it is available to those in England and Wales.

CHILD HEALTH SERVICES

Pre-school services at GP surgeries or child health clinics provide regular monitoring of children's physical, mental and emotional health and development and advise parents on their children's health and welfare.

NHS 111, NHS DIRECT AND NHS 24

NHS Direct Wales is a website and 24-hour nurse-led advice telephone service for Wales. It provides medical advice as well as directing people to the appropriate part of the NHS for treatment if necessary (T 0845 46 47 W www.nhsdirect.wales.nhs.uk). NHS Direct had also operated in England but closed on 31 March 2014. Non-urgent 24-hour nurse-led advice in England can be accessed via the NHS 111 service (T 111).

NHS 24 provides an equivalent service for Scotland (T 0845-424 2424 W www.nhs24.com).

SECONDARY CARE AND OTHER SERVICES

HOSPITALS

NHS hospitals provide acute and specialist care services, treating conditions which normally cannot be dealt with by primary care specialists, and provide for medical emergencies.

NUMBER OF BEDS 2014–15

	Average daily	
	available beds	occupation of beds
England	137,088	121,391
Wales*	11,241	9,653
Scotland*	16,059	13,650
Northern Ireland	6,034	5,020

* Figures are for 2013–14
Sources: NHS England, Welsh government, ISD Scotland, NI Direct

HOSPITAL CHARGES

Acute or foundation trusts can provide hospital accommodation in single rooms or small wards, if not required for patients who need privacy for medical reasons. The patient is still an NHS patient, but there may be a charge for these additional facilities. Acute or foundation trusts can charge for certain patient services that are considered to be additional treatments over and above the normal hospital service provision. There is no blanket policy to cover this and each case is considered in the light of the patient's clinical need. However, if an item or service is considered to be an integral part of a patient's treatment by their clinician, then a charge should not be made.

In some NHS hospitals, accommodation and services are available for the treatment of private patients where it does not interfere with care for NHS patients. Income generated by treating private patients is then put back into local NHS services. Private patients undertake to pay the full costs of medical treatment, accommodation, medication and other related services. Charges for private patients are set locally.

WAITING LISTS
England
For June 2015, 328,565 referral to treatment (RTT) patients started admitted treatment and 970,070 started non-admitted treatment. Of the admitted patients, 90 per cent were treated within 18 weeks, and for non-admitted patients 92 per cent were treated within 18 weeks.
Wales
In June 2015, 76.9 per cent of 90,012 patients were treated within 26 weeks and 89.1 per cent were treated within 36 weeks of the date the referral letter was received in the hospital. There are also operational standards for maximum waiting times for first out-patient appointments and in-patient or day-case treatment but these are not set targets. The standards are 14 weeks for in-patient or day case treatment, and ten weeks for a first out-patient appointment.
Scotland
In March 2015, 88.5 per cent of patients on an 18 week referral to treatment pathway were reported as being seen within 18 weeks, a decrease from 89.6 per cent in March 2014.
Northern Ireland
From March 2015 the aim was for at least 70 per cent of patients to wait no longer than nine weeks for a first out-patient appointment, with no patient waiting longer than 18 weeks. The total number of people waiting for a first out-patient appointment at the end of March 2015 was 191,779, of these 56.3 per cent had been waiting over nine weeks, compared with just 31.3 per cent at the end of March 2014. The number of people waiting for in-patient treatment at the end of March 2015 was 57,934 – of these, 48 per cent had been waiting for more than 13 weeks.

AMBULANCE SERVICE
The NHS provides emergency ambulance services free of charge via the 999 emergency telephone service. Air ambulances, provided through local charities and partially funded by the NHS, are used throughout the UK. They assist with cases where access may be difficult or heavy traffic could hinder road progress. Non-emergency ambulance services are provided free to patients who are deemed to require them on medical grounds.

Since 1 April 2001 all services have had a system of call prioritisation. Since 2013–14, ambulances have been expected to reach Red 1 – calls requiring a defibrillator – and Red 2 emergency calls within eight minutes, at least 75 per cent of the time. Non-emergency calls are categorised as Green 1, 2, 3 or 4, with category Green 4 calls being the least serious. Green calls are generally responded to between 20 minutes and one hour.

In April 2015, the NHS employed 18,798 qualified ambulance staff in England earning between £19,027 (ambulance practitioner) and £34,876 (senior paramedic).

BLOOD AND TRANSPLANT SERVICES
There are four national bodies which coordinate the blood donor programme and transplant and related services in the UK. Donors give blood at local centres on a voluntary basis.
NHS BLOOD AND TRANSPLANT, Oak House, Reeds Crescent, Watford, Herts WD24 4QN **T** 0300-123 2323 **W** www.nhsbt.nhs.uk
WELSH BLOOD SERVICE, Ely Valley Road, Talbot Green, Pontyclun CF72 9WB **T** 01443-622000 **W** www.welsh-blood.org.uk
SCOTTISH NATIONAL BLOOD TRANSFUSION SERVICE, 21 Ellen's Glen Road, Edinburgh EH17 7QT **T** 0131-314536 5510 **W** www.scotblood.co.uk
NORTHERN IRELAND BLOOD TRANSFUSION SERVICE, Lisburn Road, Belfast BT9 7TS **T** 028-9032 1414 **W** www.nibts.org

HOSPICES
Hospice or palliative care may be available for patients with life-threatening illnesses. It may be provided at the patient's home in a voluntary or NHS hospice or in hospital, and is intended to ensure the best possible quality of life for the patient, and to provide help and support to both the patient and the patient's family. The National Council for Palliative Care coordinates NHS and voluntary services in England, Wales and Northern Ireland; the Scottish Partnership for Palliative Care performs the same function in Scotland.
NATIONAL COUNCIL FOR PALLIATIVE CARE, The Fitzpatrick Building, 188–194 York Way, London N7 9AS **T** 020-7697 1520 **W** www.ncpc.org.uk
SCOTTISH PARTNERSHIP FOR PALLIATIVE CARE, CBC House, 24 Canning Street, Edinburgh EH3 8EG **T** 0131-272 2735 **W** www.palliativecarescotland.org.uk

COMPLAINTS

Patient advice and liaison services (PALS) have been established for every NHS and PCT in England. PALS can give advice on local complaints procedure, or resolve concerns informally. If the case is not resolved locally or the complainant is not satisfied with the way a local NHS body or practice has dealt with their complaint, they may approach the Parliamentary and Health Service Ombudsman in England, the Scottish Public Services Ombudsman, Public Services Ombudsman for Wales or the Northern Ireland Commissioner for Complaints.

HEALTH ADVICE AND MEDICAL TREATMENT ABROAD

IMMUNISATION
Country-by-country guidance is set out on the website **W** www.fitfortravel.nhs.uk.

RECIPROCAL ARRANGEMENTS
The European Health Insurance Card (EHIC) allows UK residents access to state-provided health care while temporarily travelling in all European Economic Area countries and Switzerland either free or at a reduced cost. A card is free, valid for up to five years and should be obtained before travelling. Applications can be made by telephone (**T** 0300 330 1350) online (**W** www.ehic.org.uk) or by post (a form is available from the post office).

The UK also has bilateral agreements with several other countries, including Australia and New Zealand, for the free provision of urgent medical treatment.

European Economic Area nationals visiting the UK and visitors from other countries with which the UK has bilateral health care agreements are able to receive emergency health care on the NHS on the same terms as available to UK residents.

SOCIAL WELFARE

SOCIAL SERVICES

The Secretary of State for Health (in England), the Welsh government, the Scottish government and the Secretary of State for Northern Ireland are responsible, under the Local Authority Social Services Act 1970, for the provision of social services for older people, disabled people, families and children, and those with mental disorders. Personal social services are administered by local authorities according to policies, with standards set by central and devolved government. Each authority has a director and a committee responsible for the social services functions placed upon them. Local authorities provide, enable and commission care after assessing the needs of their population. The private and voluntary sectors also play an important role in the delivery of social services, and an estimated 7 million people in the UK provide substantial regular care for a member of their family.

The Care Quality Commission (CQC) was established in April 2009, bringing together the independent regulation of health, mental health and adult social care. Prior to 1 April 2009 this work was carried out by three separate organisations: the Healthcare Commission, the Mental Health Act Commission and the Commission for Social Care Inspection. The CQC is responsible for the registration of health and social care providers, the monitoring and inspection of all health and adult social care, issuing fines, public warnings or closures if standards are not met and for undertaking regular performance reviews. Since April 2007 the Office for Standards in Education, Children's Services and Skills (Ofsted) has been responsible for inspecting and regulating all care services for children and young people in England. Both Ofsted and CQC collate information on local care services and make this information available to the public.

The Care and Social Services Inspectorate Wales (CSSIW), an operationally independent part of the Welsh government, is responsible for the regulation and inspection of all social care services in Wales. A new unified body, the Care Inspectorate, was established on 1 April 2011, replacing the Scottish Commission for the Regulation of Care (the Care Commission) and is now the independent care services regulator for Scotland.

The Department of Health, Social Services and Public Safety is responsible for social care in Northern Ireland.

CARE QUALITY COMMISSION (CQC), Citygate, Gallowgate, Newcastle upon Tyne NE1 4PA T 0300-061 6161 W www.cqc.org.uk

OFFICE FOR STANDARDS IN EDUCATION, CHILDREN'S SERVICES AND SKILLS (Ofsted), Piccadilly Gate, Store Street, Manchester M1 2WD T 0300-123 1231 E enquiries@ofsted.gov.uk W www.ofsted.gov.uk

CARE AND SOCIAL SERVICES INSPECTORATE WALES (CSSIW), Welsh Government Office, Rhydcar Business Park, Merthyr Tydfil CF48 1UZ T 0300-790 0126 E cssiw@wales.gsi.gov.uk W www.cssiw.org.uk

CARE INSPECTORATE, Compass House, 11 Riverside Drive, Dundee DD1 4NY T 0845-600 9527 E enquiries@careinspectorate.com W www.scswis.com

DEPARTMENT OF HEALTH, SOCIAL SERVICES AND PUBLIC SAFETY, Castle Buildings, Stormont, Belfast BT4 3SQ T 028-9052 0500 E webmaster@dhsspsni.gov.uk W www.dhsspsni.gov.uk

STAFF

Total Social Services Staff (England, full-time)	130,100
Community	42,933
Residential	29,923
Other	26,020
Domiciliary	18,214
Day	13,010

Source: Health and Social Care Information Centre 2015

OLDER PEOPLE

Services for older people are designed to enable them to remain living in their own homes for as long as possible. Local authority services include advice, domestic help, meals in the home, alterations to the home to aid mobility, emergency alarm systems, day and/or night attendants, laundry services and the provision of day centres and recreational facilities. Charges may be made for these services. Respite care may also be provided in order to allow carers temporary relief from their responsibilities.

Local authorities and the private sector also provide 'sheltered housing' for older people, sometimes with resident wardens.

If an older person is admitted to a residential home, charges are made according to a means test; if the person cannot afford to pay, the costs are met by the local authority.

DISABLED PEOPLE

Services for disabled people are designed to enable them to remain living in their own homes wherever possible. Local authority services include advice, adaptations to the home, meals in the home, help with personal care, occupational therapy, educational facilities and recreational facilities. Respite care may also be provided in order to allow carers temporary relief from their responsibilities.

Special housing may be available for disabled people who can live independently, and residential accommodation for those who cannot.

FAMILIES AND CHILDREN

Local authorities are required to provide services aimed at safeguarding the welfare of children in need and, wherever possible, allowing them to be brought up by their families. Services include advice, counselling, help in the home and the provision of family centres. Many authorities also provide short-term refuge accommodation for women and children.

DAY CARE

In allocating day care places to children, local authorities give priority to children with special needs, whether in terms of their health, learning abilities or social needs. Since September 2001, Ofsted has been responsible for the regulation and registration of all early years childcare and education provision in England (previously the responsibility of the local authorities). All day care and childminding services that care for children under eight years of age for more than two hours a day must register with Ofsted and are inspected at least every two years. As at 31 March 2015, there were 89,117 providers in England.

CHILD PROTECTION

Children considered to be at risk of physical injury, neglect or sexual abuse are placed on the local authority's child protection register. Local authority social services staff, schools, health visitors and other agencies work together to prevent and detect cases of abuse. As at 31 March 2014, there was a total of 56,231 children on child protection registers or subject to a child protection plan in the UK. In England, there were 48,300 children on child protection registers, of these, 20,980 were at risk of neglect, 4,770 of physical abuse, 2,210 of sexual abuse and 15,870 of emotional abuse. At 31 March (July in Scotland) 2014 there were 3,135 children on child protection registers in Wales, 2,882 in Scotland and 1,914 in Northern Ireland.

LOCAL AUTHORITY CARE

Local authorities are required to provide accommodation for children who have no parents or guardians or whose parents or guardians are unable or unwilling to care for them. A family proceedings court may also issue a care order where a child is being neglected or abused, or is not attending school; the court must be satisfied that this would positively contribute to the well-being of the child.

The welfare of children in local authority care must be properly safeguarded. Children may be placed with foster families, who receive payments to cover the expenses of caring for the child or children, or in residential care.

Children's homes may be run by the local authority or by the private or voluntary sectors; all homes are subject to inspection procedures. As at 31 March 2014, 68,840 children in the UK were in the care of local authorities, of these, 51,340 were in foster placements and 6,360 were in children's homes, hostels or secure units.

ADOPTION

Local authorities are required to provide an adoption service, either directly or via approved voluntary societies. In 2013–14, 5,050 children in local authority care were adopted.

PEOPLE WITH LEARNING DISABILITIES

Services for people with learning disabilities are designed to enable them to remain living in the community wherever possible. Local authority services include short-term care, support in the home, the provision of day care centres, and help with other activities outside the home. Residential care is provided for the severely or profoundly disabled.

MENTALLY ILL PEOPLE

Under the care programme approach, mentally ill people should be assessed by specialist services and receive a care plan. A key worker should be appointed for each patient and regular reviews of the person's progress should be conducted. Local authorities provide help and advice to mentally ill people and their families, and places in day centres and social centres. Social workers can apply for a mentally disturbed person to be compulsorily detained in hospital. Where appropriate, mentally ill people are provided with accommodation in special hospitals, local authority accommodation, or at homes run by private or voluntary organisations. Patients who have been discharged from hospitals may be placed on a supervision register.

NATIONAL INSURANCE

The National Insurance (NI) scheme operates under the Social Security Contributions and Benefits Act 1992 and the Social Security Administration Act 1992, and orders and regulations made thereunder. The scheme is financed by contributions payable by earners, employers and others (*see* below). Money collected under the scheme is used to finance the National Insurance Fund (from which contributory benefits are paid) and to contribute to the cost of the National Health Service.

NATIONAL INSURANCE FUND

Estimated receipts, payments and statement of balances of the National Insurance Fund for 2015–16:

Receipts	£ million
Net national insurance contributions	86,265
Compensation from the Consolidated Fund for statutory sick, maternity, paternity and adoption pay recoveries	2,545
Income from investments	95
State scheme premiums	49
Other receipts	34
TOTAL RECEIPTS	88,989

Payments	£ million
Benefits	
At present rates	93,780
Increase due to proposed rate changes	1,966
Personal and stakeholder pensions contracted-out rebates	0
Administration costs	939
Redundancy fund payments	330
Transfer to Northern Ireland	386
Other payments	175
TOTAL PAYMENTS	97,576

Balances	£ million
Balance at the beginning of the year	17,965
Excess of receipts over payments	(8,587)
BALANCE AT END OF YEAR	9,378

CONTRIBUTIONS

There are six classes of National Insurance contributions (NICs):

Class 1	paid by employees and their employers
Class 1A	paid by employers who provide employees with certain benefits in kind for private use, such as company cars
Class 1B	paid by employers who enter into a pay as you earn (PAYE) settlement agreement (PSA) with HM Revenue and Customs
Class 2	paid by self-employed people
Class 3	voluntary contributions paid to protect entitlement to the state pension for those who do not pay enough NI contributions in another class
Class 4	paid by the self-employed on their taxable profits over a set limit. These are normally paid by self-employed people in addition to class 2 contributions. Class 4 contributions do not count towards benefits.

The lower and upper earnings limits and the percentage rates referred to below apply from April 2015 to April 2016.

CLASS 1

Class 1 contributions are paid where a person:
• is an employed earner (employee), office holder (eg company director) or employed under a contract of service in Great Britain or Northern Ireland
• is 16 or over and under state pension age
• earns at or above the earnings threshold of £155 per week (including overtime pay, bonus, commission, etc, without deduction of superannuation contributions)

Class 1 contributions are made up of primary and secondary contributions. Primary contributions are those paid by the employee and these are deducted from earnings by the employer. Since 6 April 2001 the employee's and employer's earnings thresholds have been the same and are referred to as the earnings threshold. Primary contributions are not paid on earnings below the earnings threshold of £155 per week. However, between the lower earnings limit of £112 per week and the earnings threshold of £155 per week, NI contributions are treated as having been paid to protect the benefit entitlement position of lower earners. Contributions are payable at the rate of 12 per cent on earnings between the earnings threshold and the upper earnings limit of £815 per week (10.6 per cent for contracted-out employment). Above the upper earnings limit 2 per cent is payable.

Some married women or widows pay a reduced rate of 5.85 per cent on earnings between the earnings threshold and upper earnings limits and 2 per cent above this. It is no longer possible to elect to pay the reduced rate but those who had reduced liability before 12 May 1977 may retain it for as long as certain conditions are met.

Secondary contributions are paid by employers of employed earners at the rate of 13.8 per cent on all earnings above the earnings threshold of £155 per week. There is no upper earnings limit for employers' contributions. Employers operating contracted-out salary related schemes pay reduced contributions of 10.4 per cent. The contracted-out rate applies only to that portion of earnings between the earnings threshold and the upper earnings limit. Employers' contributions below and above those respective limits are assessed at the appropriate not contracted-out rate.

CLASS 2
Class 2 contributions are paid where a person is self-employed and is 16 or over and under state pension age. Contributions are paid at a flat rate of £2.80 per week regardless of the amount earned. However, those with earnings of less than £5,965 a year can apply for small earnings exception. Those granted exemption from class 2 contributions may pay class 2 or class 3 contributions voluntarily. Self-employed earners (whether or not they pay class 2 contributions) may also be liable to pay class 4 contributions based on profits. There are special rules for those who are concurrently employed and self-employed.

Married women and widows can no longer choose not to pay class 2 contributions but those who elected not to pay class 2 contributions before 12 May 1977 may retain the right for as long as certain conditions are met.

Class 2 contributions are collected by the national insurance contributions department of HM Revenue and Customs (HMRC), by direct debit or quarterly bills.

CLASS 3
Class 3 contributions are voluntary flat-rate contributions of £14.10 per week payable by persons over the age of 16 who would otherwise be unable to qualify for retirement pension and certain other benefits because they have an insufficient record of class 1 or class 2 contributions. This may include those who are not working, those not liable for class 1 or class 2 contributions, or those excepted from class 2 contributions. Married women and widows who on or before 11 May 1977 elected not to pay class 1 (full rate) or class 2 contributions cannot pay class 3 contributions while they retain this right. Class 3 contributions are collected by HMRC by quarterly bills or direct debit.

CLASS 4
Self-employed people whose profits and gains are over £8,060 a year pay class 4 contributions in addition to class 2 contributions. This applies to self-employed earners over 16 and under the state pension age. Class 4 contributions are calculated at 9 per cent of annual profits or gains between £8,060 and £42,385 and 2 per cent above. Class 4 contributions are assessed and collected by HMRC. It is possible, in some circumstances, to apply for exceptions from liability to pay class 4 contributions or to have the amount of contribution reduced.

PENSIONS

Many people will qualify for a state pension; however, there are further pension choices available, such as workplace, personal and stakeholder pensions. There are also other non-pension savings and investment options. The following section provides background information on existing pension schemes.

STATE PENSION
From April 2016, the system of basic and additional state pension will be replaced with a new scheme for people reaching state pension age after that date (ie men born on or after 6 April 1951, and women born on or after 6 April 1953).

Current pensioners and those reaching state pension age before the introduction of the new state pension will continue to receive their state pension in line with existing rules. Information about the new state pension can be found online: (W www.gov.uk/new-state-pension).

Currently the state pension does not have to be claimed at state pension age, people can delay claiming it to earn weekly state pension or a lump sum payment. Different rules apply to the new scheme from 6 April 2016. People will only earn weekly new state pension if they delay their claim.

CURRENT STATE PENSION SCHEME
The current system consists of:
• basic state pension
• additional state pension
People may be able to get both or either when they reach state pension age and meet the qualifying conditions.

Basic State Pension
The amount of basic state pension paid is dependent on the number of 'qualifying years' a person has established during their working life. In 2015–16, the full basic state pension is £115.95 a week (*see also* Benefits, State Pension: Categories A and B).

Working Life
The working life is from the start of the tax year (6 April) in which a person reaches 16 to the end of the tax year (5 April) before the one in which they reach state pension age (*see* State Pension Age).

Qualifying Years
A 'qualifying year' is a tax year in which a person has sufficient earnings upon which they have paid, are treated as having paid, or have been credited with national insurance (NI) contributions (*see* National Insurance Credits).

From 6 April 2010 to 5 April 2016, a person who has 30 qualifying years will be entitled to a full basic state pension. Someone with less than 30 qualifying years will be entitled to a proportion of the full basic state pension based on the number of qualifying years they have. Just one qualifying year, achieved through paid or credited contributions, will give entitlement to the basic state pension worth one-thirtieth of the full basic state pension.

Until 6 April 2010, women normally needed 39 qualifying years for a full basic state pension (£115.95 in 2015–16) and men normally needed 44 qualifying years. A reduced-rate basic state pension was payable if the number of qualifying years was less than 90 per cent of the working life, but to receive any basic state pension at all, a person must have had enough qualifying years, normally 10 or 11, to receive a basic state pension of at least 25 per cent of the full rate.

The full rate of the new state pension will be finalised closer to its introduction. It will be set at a level that is above the basic level of means-tested support, the standard minimum guarantee in pension credit (£151.20 in 2015–16 for a single person).

The amounts of state pension people will receive under the new system will also be based on their NI record, with NI contributors or credits made prior to 6 April 2016 recognised under transitional arrangements.

NI contributions and credits will be used to calculate a 'starting amount' under the new system. An individual's starting amount will be the higher of either:
• the value of NI contributions under the current state pension rules (basic state pension, additional state pension and graduated retirement benefit)
• the value of NI contributions if the new state pension had been in place at the start of their working life

A deduction may be made to these amounts for periods an individual was contracted out of the additional state pension before 6 April 2016.

A minimum of 10 qualifying years will usually be needed to get any new state pension.

National Insurance Credits
Those in receipt of carer's allowance, working tax credit (with a disability element), jobseeker's allowance, incapacity benefit, employment support allowance, unemployability supplement, statutory sick pay, statutory maternity pay or statutory adoption pay may have class 1 NI contributions credited to them each week. People may also get credits if they are unemployed and looking for work or too sick to work, even if they are not in receipt of any benefit, although the credits must be applied for in these circumstances. Since April 2010, spouses and civil partners of members of HM forces may get credits if they are on an accompanied assignment outside the UK. A new measure will allow those who reach state pension age on or after 6 April 2016 to apply for NI credits for periods before April 2010 during which they were married to, or in a civil partnership with, a member of HM forces and accompanied them on a posting outside the UK. Persons undertaking certain training courses or jury service or who have been wrongly imprisoned for a conviction which is quashed on appeal may also get class 1 NI credits for each week they fulfil certain conditions. Class 1 credits may also be available to men approaching state pension age. Until 5 April 2010, these credits were awarded for the tax years in which they reached age 60 and continued until age 64, if they were not liable to pay contributions and were not absent from the UK for more than six months in any tax year. Since 6 April 2010 these credits are being phased out in line with the increase in women's state pension age. Class 1 NI credits count toward all future contributory benefits. A class 3 NI credit for basic state pension and bereavement benefit purposes is awarded, where required, for each week the working tax credit (without a disability element) has been received or child benefit, for a child under 12, has been received. Class 3 credits may also be awarded, on application, to approved foster carers and people caring for at least 20 hours a week. Since 6 April 2011, class 3 credits have been available to adults under state pension age who care for a family member under 12. In certain cases people may also get a credit towards their state second pension.

State Pension Age
State pension age is currently 65 for men born before 6 December 1953 and 60 for women born before 6 April 1950. Women's state pension age will equalise with men's at 65 in 2018 and this will increase to age 66 for both men and women by October 2020. The Pensions Act 2014 makes provision for a regular review of state pension age. Reviews will take place at least once every six years and will take into account up-to-date life expectancy data and the findings of an independently led review, which will consider wider factors such as variation in life expectancy and employment opportunities for older workers. Further information can be obtained from the online state pension calculator (W www.gov.uk/calculate-state-pension).

Using the NI Contribution Record of Another Person to Claim a State Pension
Married people or civil partners whose own NI record is incomplete may get a lower-rate basic state pension calculated using their partner's NI contribution record. This can be up to £69.50 a week in 2015–16, including any basic state pension of their own. Married men, members of married same-sex couples and civil partners may only qualify if their spouse or civil partner was born on or after 6 April 1950 (this rule does not apply to a married woman whose spouse has legally changed gender from male to female during the marriage). Widows, widowers, surviving civil partners, and people who are divorced or whose civil partnership has been dissolved may qualify for up to a full basic state pension based on their late or ex-spouse's/civil partner's NI contributions.

People who reach state pension age before 6 April 2016 will continue to be able to use these provisions, even if their spouse or civil partner reaches state pension age on or after that date. However, contributions their spouse or civil partner pays, or is credited with, following implementation of the new system will only count towards their own state pension. This means that only the NI record of the spouse or civil partner up to and including 2015–16 will be used to calculate any derived entitlement.

People reaching state pension age on or after 6 April 2016 will not be able to claim state pension on their spouse's or civil partner's NI record. There will be special arrangements for women who had opted to pay the married women's and widows reduced rate contributions before May 1977.

Non-contributory State Pensions
A non-contributory state pension may be payable to those aged 80 or over who live in England, Scotland or Wales, and have done so for a total of ten years or more for any continuous period in the 20 years after their 60th birthday, if they are not entitled to another category of state pension, or are entitled to one below the rate of £69.50 a week in 2015–16 (*see also* Benefits, State Pension for people aged 80 and over).

Graduated Retirement Benefit
Graduated Retirement Benefit (GRB) is based on the amount of graduated NI contributions paid into the GRB scheme between April 1961 and April 1975 (*see also* Benefits, Graduated Retirement Benefit). It is normally paid as an increase to a main state pension. For those reaching state pension age under the new state pension rules, it will be included in the calculation of their basic amount.

Home Responsibilities Protection
From 6 April 1978 until 5 April 2010, it was possible for people who had low income or were unable to work because they cared for children or a sick or disabled person at home to reduce the number of qualifying years required for basic state pension. This was called home responsibilities protection (HRP); the number of years for which HRP was given was deducted from the number of qualifying years needed. HRP could, in some cases, also qualify the recipient

for additional state pension. From April 2003 to April 2010 HRP was also available to approved foster carers.

From 6 April 2010, HRP was replaced by weekly credits for parents and carers. A class 3 national insurance credit is given, where eligible, towards basic state pension and bereavement benefits for spouses and civil partners. An earnings factor credit towards additional state pension is also awarded. Any years of HRP accrued before 6 April 2010 have been converted into qualifying years of credits for people reaching state pension age after that date, up to a maximum of 22 years for basic state pension purposes.

Additional State Pension

The amount of additional state pension paid depends on the amount of earnings a person has, or is treated as having, between the lower and upper earnings limits (from April 2009, the upper accruals point replaced the upper earnings limit for additional pension) for each complete tax year between 6 April 1978 (when the scheme started) and the tax year before they reach state pension age. The right to additional state pension does not depend on the person's right to basic state pension.

From 1978 to 2002, additional state pension was called the State Earnings-Related Pension Scheme (SERPS). SERPS covered all earnings by employees from 6 April 1978 to 5 April 1997 on which standard rate class 1 NI contributions had been paid, and earnings between 6 April 1997 and 5 April 2002 if the standard rate class 1 NI contributions had been contracted-in.

In 2002, SERPS was reformed through the state second pension, by improving the pension available to low and moderate earners and extending access to certain carers and people with long-term illness or disability. If earnings on which class 1 NI contributions have been paid or can be treated as paid are above the annual NI lower earnings limit (£5,824 for 2015–16) but below the statutory low earnings threshold (£15,300 for 2015–16), the state second pension regards this as earnings of £15,300 and it is treated as equivalent. Certain carers and people with long-term illness and disability will be considered as having earned at the low earnings threshold for each complete tax year since 2002–3 even if they do not work at all, or earn less than the annual NI lower earnings limit.

The amount of additional state pension paid also depends on when a person reaches state pension age; changes phased in from 6 April 1999 mean that pensions are calculated differently from that date.

Additional State Pension Inheritance

Men or women widowed before 6 October 2002 may inherit all of their late spouse's SERPS pension. From 6 October 2002, the maximum percentage of SERPS pension that a person can inherit from a late spouse or civil partner depends on their late spouse's or civil partner's date of birth:

Maximum SERPS entitlement	d.o.b (men)	d.o.b (women)
100%	5/10/37 or earlier	5/10/42 or earlier
90%	6/10/37 to 5/10/39	6/10/42 to 5/10/44
80%	6/10/39 to 5/10/41	6/10/44 to 5/10/46
70%	6/10/41 to 5/10/43	6/10/46 to 5/10/48
60%	6/10/43 to 5/10/45	6/10/48 to 5/7/50
50%	6/10/45 or later	6/7/50 or later

The maximum state second pension a person can inherit from a spouse or civil partner is 50 per cent. If a person is bereaved before they have reached their state pension age, inherited SERPS or state second pension can be paid as part of widowed parent's allowance (in the case of a person who has dependent children) or otherwise only from state pension age. If they remarry or form a new civil partnership before

state pension age they lose the right to inherit any state pension.

New State Pension Inheritance

A person who reaches state pension age before 6 April 2016 will still be able to inherit additional state pension under the existing rules. However, if their late spouse or civil partner reaches state pension age on or after that date, the amount they can inherit will be based on the deceased's contributions up to 5 April 2016 only.

A person reaching state pension age on or after 6 April 2016 whose deceased spouse or civil partner reached state pension age or died before that date will be able to inherit additional state pension under the current rules. If the deceased spouse or civil partner is also in the new state pension the survivor may inherit half of any 'protected payment'. A person will have a protected payment if their state pension calculated under current rules is more than the full rate of new state pension at April 2016. The protected payment is the amount of the excess.

In order for a person reaching state pension age on or after 6 April 2016 to qualify for an inherited amount the marriage or civil partnership must have begun before that date; and, in the case of a person widowed under state pension age, they must not remarry or form a new civil partnership before state pension age.

State Pension Statements

The Department for Work and Pensions provide state pension statements. These statements give an estimate of the state pension an individual may get based on their current NI contribution record (W www.gov.uk/state-pension-statement).

There is also an online state pension calculator. Individuals can use this to find out their state pension age and, based on information they provide, get an estimate of their basic state pension (W www.gov.uk/calculate-state-pension).

PRIVATE PENSIONS

CONTRACTED-OUT PENSIONS

'Contracting-out' means leaving the additional state pension and joining a workplace, company or occupational pension scheme to build up benefits into an alternative pension scheme.

Contracting-Out with an Occupational Pension Scheme

An occupational pension scheme is an arrangement some employers set up to give their employees a pension when they retire. The government is gradually introducing a requirement for all employers to provide their workers with a workplace pension. All employers will be included by 2018.

Providing that a company pension scheme meets certain conditions, it can be used to contract employees out of the additional state pension. Employees who join a scheme that is contracted-out will automatically be contracted-out of the additional state pension.

Employers providing such contracted-out schemes pay a lower rate of National Insurance contributions for those employees who join their schemes, and employees themselves also pay reduced-rate contributions.

Contracted-Out Salary-Related (COSR) Scheme

• these schemes (also known as contracted-out defined benefit (DB) or final salary schemes) provide a pension related to earnings and the length of pensionable service
• any notional additional state pension built up from 6 April 1978 to 5 April 1997 will be reduced by the amount of guaranteed minimum pension (GMP) accrued during that period (the contracted-out deduction). GMP is payable at 65 for men and 60 for women

• since 6 April 1997 these schemes no longer provide a GMP. Instead, as a condition of contracting-out they have to ensure that the benefits provided are at least as good as a prescribed standard (known as the Reference Scheme Test)
• when someone contracts-out of the additional state pension through these schemes, both the scheme member and the employer pay a reduced rate of NI contributions (known as the contracted-out rebate) to compensate for the additional state pension given up

Changes to contracted-out pensions from 2012
The rules for contracting-out of the additional state pension changed from 6 April 2012. The changes means contracting-out will not be possible through:
• a money purchase (defined contribution) occupational pension scheme
• a personal pension or stakeholder pension
From that date, employees have not been able to contract-out of the state second pension on a money purchase basis. Anyone contracted-out through this basis from that date was automatically contracted back into the additional state pension. Those rights built up before the abolition date will be used to provide pension benefits. These changes have not affected contracting-out via a salary-related occupational pension scheme. However, the introduction of the single-tier pension scheme in April 2016 will close the additional state pension for those reaching state pension age after this date, and contracting out on a DB basis will end.

STAKEHOLDER PENSION SCHEMES
Introduced in 2001, stakeholder pensions are available to everyone but are principally for moderate earners who do not have access to a good value company pension scheme. Stakeholder pensions must meet minimum standards to make sure they are flexible, portable and annual management charges are capped. The minimum contribution is £20.

As with personal pensions it is possible to invest up to £3,600 (including tax relief) into stakeholder pensions each year without evidence of earnings. Contributions can be made on someone else's behalf, eg a non-working partner.

AUTOMATIC ENROLMENT INTO WORKPLACE PENSIONS
Since October 2012, employers must automatically enrol their workers who meet the age and earnings criteria into a workplace pension. This applies to people who are not already in a workplace pension scheme and who:
• earn over £10,000 per annum
• are aged 22 or over
• are under state pension age
• work in the UK
Employees who meet the above requirements are entitled to opt out of the scheme if they wish to. If remains in the scheme, they, together with their employer, will pay into it every month. The government will also contribute through tax relief. Further information is available at W www.gov.uk/workplace-pensions

COMPLAINTS
The Pensions Advisory Service provides information and guidance to members of the public, on state, company, personal and stakeholder schemes. They also help any member of the public who has a problem, complaint or dispute with their occupational or personal pensions.

There are two bodies for pension complaints. The Financial Ombudsman Service deals with complaints which predominantly concern the sale and/or marketing of occupational, stakeholder and personal pensions. The Pensions Ombudsman deals with complaints which pre-dominantly concern the management (after sale or marketing) of occupational, stakeholder and personal pensions.

The Pensions Regulator is the UK regulator for work-based pension schemes; it concentrates its resources on schemes where there is the greatest risk to the security of members' benefits, promotes good administration practice for all work-based schemes and works with trustees, employers and professional advisers to put things right when necessary.

WAR PENSIONS AND THE ARMED FORCES COMPENSATION SCHEME
Veterans UK is part of the Ministry of Defence. It was formed on 1 April 2007 to provide services to both serving personnel and veterans.

Veterans UK is responsible for the administration of the war pensions scheme and the armed forces compensation scheme (AFCS) to members of the armed forces in respect of disablement or death due to service. There is also a scheme for civilians and civil defence workers in respect of the Second World War, and other schemes for groups such as merchant seamen and Polish armed forces who served under British command during the Second World War. They are also responsible for the administration of the armed forces pension scheme (AFPS), which provides occupational pensions for ex-service personnel *(see* Defence).

THE WAR PENSIONS SCHEME
War disablement pension is awarded for the disabling effects of any injury, wound or disease which was the result of, or was aggravated by, service in the armed forces prior to 6 April 2005. Claims are only considered once the person has left the armed forces. The amount of pension paid depends on the severity of disablement, which is assessed by comparing the health of the claimant with that of a healthy person of the same age and sex. The person's earning capacity or occupation are not taken into account in this assessment. A pension is awarded if the person has a disablement of 20 per cent or more and a lump sum is usually payable to those with a disablement of less than 20 per cent. No award is made for noise-induced sensorineural hearing loss where the assessment of disablement is less than 20 per cent. Where an assessment of disablement is at 40 per cent or more, an age addition is automatically given when the pensioner reaches 65.

A pension is payable to war widows, widowers and surviving civil partners where the spouse's or civil partner's death was due to, or hastened by, service in the armed forces prior to 6 April 2005 or where the spouse or civil partner was in receipt of a war disablement pension constant attendance allowance (or would have been if not in hospital) at the time of death. A pension is also payable to widows, widowers or surviving civil partners if the spouse or civil partner was receiving the war disablement pension at the 80 per cent rate or higher in conjunction with unemployability supplement at the time of death. War widows, widowers and surviving civil partners receive a standard rank-related rate, but a lower weekly rate is payable to war widows, widowers and surviving civil partners of personnel of the rank of Major or below who are under the age of 40, without children and capable of maintaining themselves. This is increased to the standard rate at age 40. Allowances are paid for children and adult dependants. An age allowance is automatically given when the widow, widower or surviving civil partner reaches 65 and increased at ages 70 and 80.

Pensioners living overseas receive the same pension rates as those living in the UK. All war disablement pensions and allowances and pensions for war widows, widowers and surviving civil partners are tax-free in the UK; this does not always apply in overseas countries due to different tax laws.

SUPPLEMENTARY ALLOWANCES

A number of supplementary allowances may be awarded to a war pensioner and are intended to meet various needs. The principal supplementary allowances are unemployability supplement, allowance for lowered standard of occupation, constant attendance allowance and war pensions mobility supplement. Others include exceptionally severe disablement allowance, severe disablement occupational allowance, treatment allowance, comforts allowance, clothing allowance, age allowance and widow/widower/surviving civil partner's age allowance. Rent and children's allowances are also available with pensions for war widows, widowers and surviving civil partners.

ARMED FORCES COMPENSATION SCHEME

The armed forces compensation scheme (AFCS) became effective on 6 April 2005 and covers all regular (including Gurkhas) and reserve personnel whose injury, ill health or death is caused predominantly by service on or after 6 April 2005. There are time limits under this scheme and generally claims must be made within seven years of the injury occurring or from first seeking medical advice about an illness. There are some exceptions to this time limit, the main one being for a late-onset illness. Claims for a late-onset illness can be made at any time after the event to which it relates, providing the claim is made within three years of medical advice being sought.

The AFCS provides compensation where service in the armed forces is the only or predominant cause of injury, illness or death. Any other personal accident cover held by the individual is not taken into account when determining an AFCS award. Under the terms of the scheme a tax-free lump sum is payable to service or ex-service personnel based on a 15-level tariff, graduated according to the seriousness of the injury. If multiple injuries are sustained in the same incident compensation for each injury, up to the scheme maximum, is awarded. For those with the most serious injuries and illness a tax-free, index-linked monthly payment – a guaranteed income payment or GIP – is paid for life from the point of discharge. A survivor's GIP (SGIP) will also be paid to surviving spouses, civil partners and unmarried partners who meet certain criteria. GIP and SGIP are calculated by multiplying the pensionable pay of the service person by a factor that depends on the age at the person's last birthday. The younger the person, the higher the factor, because there are more years to normal retirement age.

ARMED FORCES INDEPENDENCE PAYMENT

Armed forces independence payment (AFIP) is designed to provide financial support for service personnel and veterans who have been seriously injured to cover the extra costs they may incur as a result of their injury. It is administered by Veterans UK as part of AFCS although payments are made by the Department for Work and Pensions (DWP). It is non-taxable and non-means-tested.

Service personnel and veterans awarded a GIP of 50 per cent or higher under the AFCS are eligible. Those eligible for AFIP are not required to undergo an assessment and will keep the payment for as long as they are entitled to receive a GIP of 50 per cent or higher.

DEPARTMENT FOR WORK AND PENSIONS BENEFITS

Payments under the AFCS and the war pensions scheme may affect income related benefits from the DWP. In particular any supplementary allowances in payment with war pensions. Any state pension for which a war widow, widower or surviving civil partner qualifies for on their own NI contribution record can be paid in addition to monies received under the war pensions scheme.

CLAIMS AND QUESTIONS

Further information on the war pensions scheme, the AFCS and the nearest Veterans' Welfare Office can be obtained from Veterans UK (T 0808-191 4218, if calling from the UK or, if living overseas, T (+44) (1253) 866-043).

VETERANS UK, Norcross Lane, Thornton-Cleveleys FY5 3WP
   E veterans-uk@mod.uk
   W www.gov.uk/government/organisations/veterans-uk

TAX CREDITS

Tax credits are administered by HM Revenue and Customs (HMRC). They are based on an individual's or couple's household income and current circumstances. Adjustments can be made during the year to reflect changes in income and/or circumstances. Further information regarding the qualifying conditions for tax credits, how to claim and the rates payable is available online on the HMRC website (W www.hmrc.gov.uk/taxcredits).

WORKING TAX CREDIT

Working tax credit is a payment from the government to support people on low incomes. It may be claimed by:
• those aged 25 or over who work at least 30 hours a week
• those aged 16 or over who work at least 16 hours a week, who are responsible for a child or young person, or have a disability that puts them at a disadvantage of getting a job
• those aged 60 or over, who work at least 16 hours a week
• couples who are responsible for a child or young person, who work at least 24 hours per week between them with one partner working at least 16 hours a week

The amount received depends on the circumstances and number of hours worked a week.

WORKING TAX CREDIT FOR INDIVIDUALS WITHOUT CHILDREN 2015–16

The amounts shown in the table below, presume a single person is over 25 years of age and working 30 or more hours a week, that a couple includes one person over 25 years of age who is working 30 or more hours a week and that a single adult with a disability is over 16 years of age and working 16–29 hours a week.

Annual Income/Status	Tax Credit per annum
£5,500	
*Single	–
*Couple	–
Single adult with a disability	£4,935
£9,850	
Single	£1,370
Couple	£3,380
Single adult with a disability	£3,530
£10,000	
Single	£1,305
Couple	£3,320
Single adult with a disability	£3,465
£12,000	
Single	£485
Couple	£2,500
Single adult with a disability	£2,645
£16,000	
Single	–
Couple	£860
Single adult with a disability	£1,005

* No amounts are shown here as this income would be under the minimum wage for 2015–16 of £5,491.20 per annum for an adult (aged 21 and above) working 16 hours a week (six months at £6.50/hour (minimum wage October 2014 to September 2015), plus six months at £6.70 (minimum wage from October 2015))

CHILDCARE
In families with children where a lone parent works at least 16 hours a week, or couples who work at least 24 hours a week between them with one partner working at least 16 hours a week, or where one partner works at least 16 hours a week and the other is disabled, an in-patient in hospital, or in prison, the family is entitled to the childcare element of working tax credit. Depending on circumstances this payment can contribute up to £175 of childcare costs for one child and up to £300 a week for two or more children. Families can only claim if they use an approved or registered childcare provider.

CHILD TAX CREDIT
Child tax credit combines all income-related support for children and is paid direct to the main carer. The credit is made up of a main 'family' payment with additional payments for each extra child in the household, for children with a disability and an extra payment for children who are severely disabled. Child tax credit is available to households where:
• there is at least one dependant under 16
• there is at least one dependant between 16 and 20 who is in relevant education or training or is registered for work, education or training with an approved body

BENEFITS

The following is intended as a general guide to the benefits system. Conditions of entitlement and benefit rates change annually and all prospective claimants should check exact entitlements and rates of benefit directly with their local Jobcentre Plus office, pension centre or online (W www.gov.uk). Leaflets relating to the various benefits and contribution conditions for different benefits are available from local Jobcentre Plus offices.

UNIVERSAL CREDIT
From 29 April 2013, Universal Credit began to gradually be introduced in certain areas of the country. Universal Credit is a single new payment for those looking for work or on a low income. Universal Credit will eventually replace:
• Income-based jobseekers allowance
• Income-related employment support allowance
• Income support
• Child tax credit
• Working tax credit
• Housing benefit
For more information go to W www.gov.uk/universalcredit

CONTRIBUTORY BENEFITS
Entitlement to contributory benefits depends on national insurance contribution conditions being satisfied either by the claimant or by someone on the claimant's behalf (depending on the kind of benefit). The class or classes of national insurance contribution relevant to each benefit are:

Jobseeker's allowance (contribution-based)	Class 1
Employment and Support Allowance (contributory)	Class 1 or 2
Widow's benefit and bereavement benefit	Class 1, 2 or 3
State pensions, categories A and B	Class 1, 2 or 3

The system of contribution conditions relates to yearly levels of earnings on which national insurance (NI) contributions have been paid.

JOBSEEKER'S ALLOWANCE
Jobseeker's allowance (JSA) replaced unemployment benefit and income support for unemployed people under state pension age from 7 October 1996. There are two routes of entitlement. Contribution-based JSA is paid at a personal rate (i.e. additional benefit for dependants is not paid) to those who have made sufficient NI contributions in two particular tax years. Savings and partner's earnings are not taken into account and payment can be made for up to six months. Rates of JSA correspond to income support rates.

Claims are made through Jobcentre Plus. A person wishing to claim JSA must generally be unemployed or working on average less than 16 hours a week, capable of work and available for any work which he or she can reasonably be expected to do, usually for at least 40 hours a week. The claimant must agree and sign a 'jobseeker's agreement', which will set out his or her plans to find work, and must actively seek work. If the claimant refuses work or training the benefit may be sanctioned for between one and 26 weeks.

A person will be sanctioned from JSA for up to 26 weeks if he or she has left a job voluntarily without just cause or through misconduct. In these circumstances, it may be possible to receive hardship payments, particularly where the claimant or the claimant's family is vulnerable, eg if sick or pregnant, or with children or caring responsibilities.

Weekly Rates from April 2015

Person aged 18–24	£57.90
Person aged 25 to state pension age*	£73.10

* Since October 2003 people aged between 60 and state pension age can choose to claim pension credits instead of JSA

EMPLOYMENT AND SUPPORT ALLOWANCE
From 27 October 2008, employment and support allowance (ESA) replaced incapacity benefit and income support paid on the grounds of incapacity or disability. The benefit consists of two strands, contribution-based benefit and income-related benefit, so that people no longer need to make two claims for benefit in order to gain their full entitlement. Contributory ESA is available to those who have limited capability for work but cannot get statutory sick pay from their employer. Those over pensionable age are not entitled to ESA. Apart from those who qualify under the special provisions for people incapacitated in youth, entitlement to contributory ESA is based on a person's NI contribution record. In order to qualify for contributory ESA, two contribution conditions, based on the last three years before the tax year in which benefit is claimed, must be satisfied. The amount of contributory ESA payable may be reduced where the person receives more than a specified amount of occupational or personal pension. Contributory ESA is paid only in respect of the person claiming the benefit – there are no additional amounts for dependants.

At the outset, new claimants are paid a basic allowance (the same rate as jobseeker's allowance) for 13 weeks while their medical condition is assessed and a work capability assessment is conducted. Following the completion of the assessment phase those claimants capable of engaging in work-related activities will receive a work-related activity component on top of the basic rate. The work-related activity component can be subject to sanctions if the claimant does not engage in the conditionality requirements without good reason. The maximum sanction is equal to the value of the work-related activity component of the benefit.

Those with the most severe health conditions or disabilities will receive the support component, which is more than the work-related activity component. Claimants in receipt of the support component are not required to engage in work-related activities, although they can volunteer to do so or undertake permitted work if their condition allows.

Weekly Rates from April 2015

ESA plus work-related activity component	up to £102.15
ESA plus support component	up to £109.30

BEREAVEMENT BENEFITS

Bereavement benefits replaced widow's benefit on 9 April 2001. Those claiming widow's benefit before this date will continue to receive it under the old scheme for as long as they qualify. The new system provides bereavement benefits for widows, widowers and, from 5 December 2005, surviving civil partners (providing that their deceased spouse or civil partner paid NI contributions). The new system offers benefits in three forms:

• *Bereavement payment* – may be received by a man or woman who is under the state pension age at the time of their spouse or civil partner's death, or whose husband, wife or civil partner was not entitled to a category A retirement pension when he or she died. It is a single tax-free lump sum of £2,000 payable immediately on widowhood or loss of a civil partner

• *Widowed parent's allowance* – a taxable benefit payable to the surviving partner if he or she is entitled or treated as entitled to child benefit, or to a widow if she is expecting her husband's baby at the time of his death

• *Bereavement allowance* – a taxable weekly benefit paid for 52 weeks after the spouse or civil partner's death. If aged over 55 and under state pension age the full allowance is payable, if aged between 45 and 54 a percentage of the full rate is paid. A widow, widower or surviving civil partner may receive this allowance if his or her widowed parent's allowance ends before 52 weeks

It is not possible to receive widowed parent's allowance and bereavement allowance at the same time. Bereavement benefits and widow's benefit, in any form, cease upon remarriage or a new civil partnership or are suspended during a period of cohabitation as partners without being legally married or in a civil partnership.

Weekly Rates from April 2015

Bereavement payment (lump sum)	£2,000
Widowed parent's allowance (or widowed mother's allowance)	£112.55
Bereavement allowance (or widow's pension), full entitlement (aged 55 and over at time of spouse's or civil partner's death)	£112.55

Amount of bereavement allowance (or widow's pension) by age of widow/widower or surviving civil partner at spouse's or civil partner's death:

aged 54	£104.67
aged 53	£96.79
aged 52	£88.91
aged 51	£81.04
aged 50	£73.16
aged 49	£65.28
aged 48	£57.40
aged 47	£49.52
aged 46	£41.64
aged 45	£33.77

STATE PENSION: CATEGORIES A AND B

Category A pension is payable for life to men and women who reach state pension age, who satisfy the contributions conditions and who claim for it. Category B pension may be payable to married women, married men and civil partners who are not entitled to a basic state pension on their own NI contributions or whose own basic state pension entitlement is less than £69.50 a week in 2015–16. It is based on their wife's, husband's or civil partner's NI contributions and is payable when both members of the couple have reached state pension age. Married men and civil partners may only be able to qualify for a category B pension if their wife or civil partner was born on or after 6 April 1950. Category B pension is also payable to widows, widowers and surviving civil partners who are bereaved before state pension age if they were previously entitled to widowed parent's allowance or bereavement allowance based on their late spouse's or civil partner's NI contributions. If they were receiving widowed parent's allowance on reaching state pension age, they could qualify for a category B pension payable at the same rate as their widowed parent's allowance comprising a basic pension, plus, if applicable, the appropriate share of their late spouse's or late civil partner's additional state pension. If their widowed parent's allowance had stopped before they reached state pension age, or they had been getting bereavement allowance at any time before state pension age, their category B pension will consist of inheritable additional state pension only. No basic state pension is included, although they may qualify for a basic state pension or have their own basic state pension improved by substituting their late spouse's or late civil partner's NI records for their own.

Widows who are bereaved when over state pension age can qualify for a category B pension regardless of the age of their husband when he died. This is payable at the same rate as the basic state pension the widow's late husband was entitled to (or would have been entitled to) at the time of his death. It can also be paid to widowers and civil partners who are bereaved when over state pension age if their wife or civil partner had reached state pension age when they died. Widowers and surviving civil partners who reached state pension age on or after 6 April 2010 and bereaved when over state pension age can qualify for a category B pension regardless of the age of their wife or civil partner when they died.

Where a person is entitled to both a category A and category B pension then they can be combined to give a composite pension, but this cannot be more than the full rate pension. Where a person is entitled to more than one category A or category B pension then only one can be paid. In such cases the person can choose which to get; if no choice is made, the most favourable one is paid.

A person may defer claiming their pension beyond state pension age. In doing so they may earn increments which will increase the weekly amount paid by 1 per cent per five weeks of deferral (equivalent to 10.4 per cent/year) when they claim their state pension. If a person delays claiming for at least 12 months they are given the option of a one-off taxable lump sum, instead of a pension increase, based on the weekly pension deferred, plus interest of at least 2 per cent above the Bank of England base rate. Since 6 April 2010, a category B pension has been treated independently of the spouse's or partner's pension. It is possible to take a category B pension even if the spouse or partner has deferred theirs.

It is no longer possible to claim an increase on a state pension for another adult (known as adult dependency increase). Those who received the increase before April 2010 can keep receiving it until the conditions are no longer met or until 5 April 2020, whichever is first.

Provision for children is made through child tax credits. An age addition of 25p a week is payable with a state pension if a pensioner is aged 80 or over.

Since 1989 pensioners have been allowed to have unlimited earnings without affecting their state pension. *See* Pensions.

Weekly Rates from April 2015

Category A or B pension for a single person	£115.95
Category B pension based on husband's/wife's/ civil partner's NI contributions	£69.50

GRADUATED RETIREMENT BENEFIT

Graduated retirement benefit (GRB) is based on the amount of graduated NI contributions paid into the GRB scheme between April 1961 and April 1975; however, it is still paid in addition to any state pension to those who made the relevant contributions. A person will receive graduated retirement benefit based on their own contributions, even if not entitled to a basic state pension. Widows, widowers and surviving civil partners may inherit half of their deceased spouse's or civil partner's entitlement, but none that the deceased spouse or civil partner may have been eligible for from a former spouse or civil partner. If a person defers making a claim beyond state pension age, they may earn an increase or a one-off lump sum payment in respect of their deferred graduated retirement benefit; calculated in the same way as for category A or B state pension.

NON-CONTRIBUTORY BENEFITS
These benefits are paid from general taxation and are not dependent on NI contributions.

JOBSEEKER'S ALLOWANCE (INCOME-BASED)
Those who do not qualify for contribution-based jobseeker's allowance (JSA), those who have exhausted their entitlement to contribution-based JSA or those for whom contribution-based JSA provides insufficient income may qualify for income-based JSA. The amount paid depends on age, whether they are single or a couple and amount of income and savings. To get income-based JSA the claimant must usually be aged 18 or over but below state pension age, although there are some exceptions for 16- or 17-year-olds. Since April 2003, child dependants have been provided for through the child tax credit system.

The rules of entitlement are the same as for contribution-based JSA.

If one person in a couple was born after 28 October 1957 and neither person in the couple has responsibility for a child or children, then the couple will have to make a joint claim for JSA if they wish to receive income-based JSA.

Weekly Rates from April 2015

Person aged 18–24	£57.90
Person aged 25 to state pension age	£73.10
Couple, both aged 18 to state pension age	£114.85

MATERNITY ALLOWANCE
Maternity allowance (MA) is a benefit available for pregnant women who cannot get statutory maternity pay (SMP) from their employer or have been employed/self-employed during or close to their pregnancy. In order to qualify for payment, a woman must have been employed and/or self-employed for at least 26 weeks in the 66-week period up to and including the week before the baby is due (test period). These weeks do not have to be in a row and any part weeks worked will count towards the 26 weeks. She must also have an average weekly earning of at least £30 (maternity allowance threshold) over any 13 weeks of the woman's choice within the test period.

Self-employed women who pay class 2 NI contributions or who hold a small earnings exception certificate are deemed to have enough earnings to qualify for MA.

A woman can choose to start receiving MA from the 11th week before the week in which the baby is due (if she stops work before then) up to the day following the day of birth. The exact date MA starts will depend on when the woman stops work to have her baby or if the baby is born before she stops work. However, where the woman is absent from work wholly or partly due to her pregnancy in the four weeks before the week the baby is due to be born, MA will start the day following the first day of absence from work. MA is paid for a maximum of 39 weeks.

Women who are not eligible for statutory maternity pay or the higher amount of MA may be eligible for a reduced rate of MA for a 14-week period. For example, women who take part in the business of their self-employed spouse or civil partner, for at least 26 weeks in the 66 weeks before their baby is due, and the work they do is unpaid.

Weekly Rate from April 2015

Standard rate	£139.58 or 90 per cent of the woman's average weekly earnings if less than £139.58
14-week reduced rate	£27

CHILD BENEFIT
Child benefit is payable for virtually all children aged under 16 and for those aged 16 and 17 if they are in relevant education or training or are registered for work, education or training with an approved body.

Weekly Rates at April 2015

Eldest/only child	£20.70
Each subsequent child	£13.70

GUARDIAN'S ALLOWANCE
Guardian's allowance is payable to a person who is bringing up a child or young person because the child's parents have died, or in some circumstances, where only one parent has died. To receive the allowance the person must be in receipt of child benefit for the child or young person, although they do not have to be the child's legal guardian.

Weekly Rate (in addition to child benefit) from April 2015

Each child	£16.55

CARER'S ALLOWANCE
Carer's allowance (CA) is a benefit payable to people who spend at least 35 hours a week caring for a severely disabled person. To qualify for CA a person must be caring for someone in receipt of one of the following benefits:
• attendance allowance
• personal independence payment
• constant attendance allowance, paid at not less than the normal maximum rate with an industrial injuries disablement payment or basic (full-day) rate, under the industrial injuries or war pension schemes.
• armed forces independence payment (AFIP)

Weekly Rate from April 2015

Carer's allowance	£62.10

ATTENDANCE ALLOWANCE
This may be payable to people aged 65 or over who need help with personal care because they are physically or mentally disabled, and who have needed help for a period of at least six months. Attendance allowance has two rates: the lower rate is for day or night care, and the higher rate is for day and night care. People not expected to live for more than six months because of a progressive disease can receive the highest rate of attendance allowance straight away.

Weekly Rates from April 2015

Higher rate	£82.30
Lower rate	£55.10

PERSONAL INDEPENDENCE PAYMENT (PIP)
Personal independence payment (PIP) replaced disability living allowance (DLA) for people aged 16 to 64 on 8 April 2013. PIP has two components: the daily living component and the mobility component, with each offering two different benefit rates: standard and enhanced. Whether one or both components are claimed depends on the requirements of the individual. Claimants are assessed on their

ability to carry out everyday activities, with the majority of claims evaluated via an interview. Claimants with a terminal illness automatically receive the enhanced daily living component.

Weekly Rates from April 2015
Daily living component

Standard	£55.10
Enhanced	£82.30

Mobility component

Standard	£21.80
Enhanced	£57.45

STATE PENSION FOR PEOPLE AGED 80 AND OVER

A state pension, also referred to as category D pension, is provided for people aged 80 and over if they are not entitled to another category of state pension or are entitled to a state pension that is less than £69.50 a week. The person must also live in Great Britain and have done so for a period of ten years or more in any continuous 20-year period since their 60th birthday.

Weekly Rate from April 2015

Single person	£69.50
Age addition	£0.25

INCOME SUPPORT

Broadly speaking income support is a benefit for those between age 16 and the age they can receive pension credit, whose income is below a certain level, who work on average less than 16 hours a week and who are:
• bringing up children alone
• registered sick or disabled
• a student who is also a lone parent or disabled
• caring for someone who is sick or elderly

Income support is not payable if the claimant, or claimant and partner, have capital or savings in excess of £16,000 – and deductions are made for capital and savings in excess of £6,000. For people permanently in residential care and nursing homes deductions apply for capital over £10,000.

Sums payable depend on fixed allowances laid down by law for people in different circumstances. If both partners are eligible for income support, either may claim it for the couple. People receiving income support may be able to receive housing benefit, help with mortgage or home loan interest and help with healthcare. They may also be eligible for help with exceptional expenses from the Social Fund. Special rates may apply to some people living in residential care or nursing homes.

INCOME SUPPORT PREMIUMS

Income support premiums are extra weekly payments for those with additional needs. People qualifying for more than one premium will normally only receive the highest single premium for which they qualify. However, family premium, disabled child premium, severe disability premium and carer premium are payable in addition to other premiums.

Child tax credit replaced premiums for people with children for all new income support claims from 6 April 2004. People with children who were already in receipt of income support in April 2004 and have not claimed child tax credit may qualify for:
• the family premium if they have at least one child
• the disabled child premium if they have a child who receives disability living allowance or is registered blind
• the enhanced disability child premium if they have a child in receipt of the higher rate disability living allowance care component

Carers may qualify for:
• the carer premium if they or their partner are in receipt of carer's allowance

Long-term sick or disabled people may qualify for:
• the disability premium if they or their partner are receiving certain benefits because they are disabled or cannot work; are registered blind; or if the claimant has been incapable of work or receiving statutory sick pay for at least 364 days (196 days if the person is terminally ill), including periods of incapacity separated by eight weeks or less
• the severe disability premium if the person lives alone and receives the middle or higher rate of disability living allowance care component and no one receives carer's allowance for caring for that person
• the enhanced disability premium if the person is in receipt of the higher rate disability living allowance care component

People with a partner aged over 60 may qualify for:
• the pensioner premium

WEEKLY RATES OF INCOME SUPPORT
from April 2015

Single person

aged 16–24	£57.90
aged 25+	£73.10
aged 16–17 and a single parent	£57.90
aged 18+ and a single parent	£73.10

Couples

Both under 18	£57.90
Both under 18, in certain circumstances	£87.50
One under 18, one aged 18–24	£57.90
One under 18, one aged 25+	£73.10
Both aged 18+	£114.85

Premiums

Carer premium	£34.60
Severe disability premium	£61.85
Enhanced disability premium	
Single person	£15.75
Couples	£22.60
Pensioner premium (couple)	£116.00

PENSION CREDIT

Pension credit was introduced on 6 October 2003 and replaced income support for those aged 60 and over. Between April 2010 and April 2020 the pension credit qualifying age is increasing from 60 to 65 alongside the increase in women's state pension age.

There are two elements to pension credit:

THE GUARANTEE CREDIT

The guarantee credit guarantees a minimum income of £151.20 for single people and £230.85 for couples, with additional elements for people who have:
• eligible housing costs
• severe disabilities
• caring responsibilities

Income from state pension, private pensions, earnings, working tax credit and certain benefits are taken into account when calculating the pension credit. For savings and capital in excess of £10,000, £1 for every £500 or part of £500 held is taken into account as income when working out entitlement to pension credit.

People receiving the guarantee credit element of pension credit will be able to receive housing benefit, council tax benefit and help with healthcare costs.

Weekly Rates from April 2015
Additional amount for severe disability

Single person	£61.85
Couple (one qualifies)	£61.85
Couple (both qualify)	£123.70
Additional amount for carers	£34.60

THE SAVINGS CREDIT

Single people aged 65 or over (and couples where one member is 65 or over) may be entitled to a savings credit which provides additional support for pensioners who have made modest provision towards their retirement. The savings credit is calculated by taking into account any qualifying income above the savings credit threshold. For 2015–16 the threshold is £126.50 for single people and £201.80 for couples. The maximum savings credit is £14.82 a week (£17.43 a week for couples).

Income that qualifies towards the savings credit includes state pensions, earnings, second pensions and income taken into account from capital above £10,000.

Some people will be entitled to the guarantee credit, some to the savings credit and some to both.

Where only the savings credit is in payment, people need to claim standard housing benefit or council tax benefit. Although local authorities take any savings credit into account in the housing benefit or council tax benefit assessment, for people aged 65 and over housing benefit or council tax benefit is enhanced to ensure that gains in pension credit are not depleted.

HOUSING BENEFIT

Housing benefit is designed to help people with rent (including rent for accommodation in guesthouses, lodgings or hostels). It does not cover mortgage payments. The amount of benefit paid depends on:
• the income of the claimant, and partner if there is one, including earned income, unearned income (any other income including some other benefits) and savings
• number of dependants
• certain extra needs of the claimant, partner or any dependants
• number and gross income of people sharing the home who are not dependent on the claimant
• how much rent is paid

Housing benefit is not payable if the claimant, or claimant and partner, have savings in excess of £16,000. The amount of benefit is affected if savings held exceed £6,000 (£10,000 for people living in residential care and nursing homes). Housing benefit is not paid for meals, fuel or certain service charges that may be included in the rent. Deductions are also made for most non-dependants who live in the same accommodation as the claimant (and their partner). If the claimant is living with a partner or civil partner there can only be one claim.

The maximum amount of benefit (which is not necessarily the same as the amount of rent paid) may be paid where the claimant is in receipt of income support, income-based jobseeker's allowance, the guarantee element of pension credit or where the claimant's income is less than the amount allowed for their needs. Any income over that allowed for their needs will mean that their benefit is reduced.

LOCAL HOUSING ALLOWANCE

Local housing allowance (LHA), which was rolled out nationally from 7 April 2008, is a way of calculating the rent element of housing benefit based on the area in which a person lives and household size. It affects people in the deregulated private rented sector who make a new claim for housing benefit or existing recipients who move address. LHA ensures that tenants in similar circumstances in the same area receive the same amount of financial support for their housing costs. It does not affect the way a person's income or capital is taken into account. LHA is paid to the tenant rather than the landlord in most circumstances. A weekly limit on payments is now in place so LHA does not exceed:
• £260.64 for a one bedroom property
• £302.33 for a two bedroom property
• £354.46 for a three bedroom property
• £417.02 for a four bedroom property

COUNCIL TAX REDUCTION

From April 2013, council tax benefit was replaced by council tax reduction. Nearly all the rules that apply to housing benefit apply to council tax reduction, which helps people on low incomes to pay council tax bills. The amount payable depends on how much council tax is paid and who lives with the claimant. The benefit may be available to those receiving income support, income-based jobseeker's allowance, the guarantee element of pension credit or to those whose income is less than that allowed for their needs. Any income over that allowed for their needs will mean that they will receive less help with their council tax reduction. Deductions are made for non-dependants.

A full council tax bill is based on at least two adults living in a home. Residents may receive a 25 per cent reduction on their bill if they count as an adult for council tax and live on their own. If the property is the resident's main home and there is no-one who counts as an adult, the reduction is 50 per cent.

THE SOCIAL FUND

REGULATED PAYMENTS
Sure Start Maternity Grant

Sure start maternity grant (SSMG) is a one-off payment of £500 to help people on low incomes pay for essential items for new babies that are expected, born, adopted, the subject of a parental order (following a surrogate birth) or, in certain circumstances, the subject of a residency order. SSMG can be claimed any time from within 11 weeks of the expected birth and up to three months after the birth, adoption or date of parental or residency order. Those eligible are people in receipt of income support, income-based jobseeker's allowance, pension credit, child tax credit at a rate higher than the family element or working tax credit where a disability or severe disability element is in payment. Since 11 April 2011, new rules have been applied for babies due, born or adopted on this date. These are that SSMG is only available if there are no other children under 16 in the family or in the case of a dependent child's new baby, SSMG is only available if the dependent is under the age of 20 and has no other children.

Funeral Payments

Payable to help cover the necessary cost of burial or cremation, a new burial plot with an exclusive right of burial (where burial is chosen), certain other expenses, and up to £700 for any other funeral expenses, such as the funeral director's fees, the coffin or flowers. Those eligible are people receiving income support, income-based jobseeker's allowance, pension credit, child tax credit at a higher rate than the family element, working tax credit where a disability or severe disability element is in payment, council tax benefit or housing benefit who have good reason for taking responsibility for the funeral expenses. These payments are recoverable from any estate of the deceased.

Cold Weather Payments

A payment of £25 per seven-day period between 1 November and 31 March when the average temperature is recorded at or forecast to be 0°C or below over seven consecutive days in the qualifying person's area. Payments are made to people on pension credit or child tax credit with a disability element, those on income support whose benefit includes a pensioner or disability premium, and those on income-based jobseeker's allowance or employment and support allowance who have a child who is disabled or under the age of five. Payments are made automatically and do not have to be repaid.

Winter Fuel Payments
For 2015–16 the winter fuel payment is set at £200 for households with someone aged 62–79 and £300 for households with someone aged 80 or over. The rate paid is based on the person's age and circumstances in the 'qualifying week' between 21 and 27 September 2015. The majority of eligible people are paid automatically before Christmas, although a few need to claim. Payments do not have to be repaid.

Christmas Bonus
The Christmas bonus is a one-off tax-free £10 payment made before Christmas to those people in receipt of a qualifying benefit in the qualifying week.

DISCRETIONARY PAYMENTS
Community Care Grants
These are intended to help people in Northern Ireland (they are no longer available in the rest of the UK) in receipt of income support, income-based jobseeker's allowance or employment and support allowance, pension credit, or payments on account of such benefits (or those likely to receive these benefits within the next six weeks because they are leaving residential or institutional accommodation) to live as independently as possible in the community; ease exceptional pressures on families; care for a prisoner or young offender released on temporary licence; help people set up home as part of a resettlement programme and/or assist with certain travelling expenses. They do not have to be repaid.

Budgeting Loans
These are interest-free loans to people who have been receiving income support, income-based jobseeker's allowance or employment and support allowance, pension credit or payments on account of such benefits for at least 26 weeks, for intermittent expenses that may be difficult to budget for. The smallest amount available to borrow is £100.

Crisis Loans
These are interest-free loans available to anyone in Northern Ireland aged 16 or over (they are no longer available in the rest of the UK), whether receiving benefits or not, who is without resources in an emergency or due to a disaster, where there is no other means of preventing serious damage or serious risk to their or their family members' health or safety.

SAVINGS
Savings over £500 (£1,000 for people aged 62 or over) are taken into account for community care grants and savings of £1,000 (£2,000 for people aged 62 or over) are taken into account for budgeting loans. All savings are taken into account for crisis loans. Savings are not taken into account for sure start maternity grant, funeral payments, cold weather payments, winter fuel payments or the Christmas bonus.

INDUSTRIAL INJURIES AND DISABLEMENT BENEFITS
The Industrial Injuries Scheme, administered under the Social Security Contributions and Benefits Act 1992, provides a range of benefits designed to compensate for disablement resulting from an industrial accident (ie an accident arising out of and in the course of an earner's employment) or from a prescribed disease due to the nature of a person's employment. Those who are self-employed are not covered by this scheme.

INDUSTRIAL INJURIES DISABLEMENT BENEFIT
A person may be able to claim industrial injuries disablement benefit if they are ill or disabled due to an accident or incident that happened at work or in connection with work in England, Scotland or Wales. The amount of benefit awarded depends on the person's age and the degree of disability as assessed by a doctor.

The benefit is payable whether the person works or not and those who are incapable of work are entitled to draw other benefits, such as statutory sick pay or incapacity benefit, in addition to industrial injuries disablement benefit. It may also be possible to claim the following allowances:
- reduced earnings allowance for those who are unable to return to their regular work or work of the same standard and who had their accident (or whose disease started) before 1 October 1990. At state pension age this is converted to retirement allowance
- constant attendance allowance for those with a disablement of 100 per cent who need constant care. There are four rates of allowance depending on how much care the person needs
- exceptionally severe disablement allowance can be claimed in addition to constant care attendance allowance at one of the higher rates for those who need constant care permanently

Weekly Rates of Benefit from April 2015

Degree of disablement	Aged 18+ or with dependants
100 per cent	£168.00
90	£151.20
80	£134.40
70	£117.60
60	£100.80
50	£84.00
40	£67.20
30	£50.40
20	£33.60
Unemployability supplement	£103.85
Reduced earnings allowance (maximum)	£67.20
Retirement allowance (maximum)	£16.80
Constant attendance allowance (normal maximum rate)	£67.20
Exceptionally severe disablement allowance	£67.20

OTHER BENEFITS
People who are disabled because of an accident or disease that was the result of work that they did before 5 July 1948 are not entitled to industrial injuries disablement benefit. They may, however, be entitled to payment under the Workmen's Compensation Scheme or the Pneumoconiosis, Byssinosis and Miscellaneous Diseases Benefit Scheme. People who suffer from certain industrial diseases caused by dust can make a claim for an additional payment under the Pneumoconiosis Act 1979 if they are unable to get damages from the employer who caused or contributed to the disease.

Diffuse Mesothelioma Payments (2008 Scheme)
Since 1 October 2008 any person suffering from the asbestos-related disease, diffuse mesothelioma, who is unable to make a claim under the Pneumoconiosis Act 1979, have not received payment in respect of the disease from an employer, via a civil claim or elsewhere, and are not entitled to compensation from a MoD scheme, can claim a one-off

lump sum payment. The scheme covers people whose exposure to asbestos occurred in the UK and was not as a result of their work as an employee (ie they lived near a factory using asbestos). The amount paid depends on the age of the person when the disease was diagnosed, or the date of the claim if the diagnosis date is not known. The current rate is £85,580 for those aged 37 and under to £13,295 for persons aged 77 and over. From 1 October 2009 claims must be received within 12 months of the date of diagnosis. If the sufferer has died, their dependants may be able to claim, but must do so within 12 months of the date of death.

CLAIMS AND QUESTIONS

Entitlement to benefit and regulated Social Fund payments is determined by a decision maker on behalf of the Secretary of State for the Department for Work and Pensions. A claimant who is dissatisfied with that decision can ask for an explanation. He or she can dispute the decision by applying to have it revised or, in particular circumstances, superseded. The claimant can appeal to the First Tier-tribunal (Social Security and Child Support). There is a further right of appeal to the Administrative and Appeals Chamber of the Upper Tribunal (see Tribunals).

Decisions on claims and applications for housing benefit and council tax benefit are made by local authorities. The explanation, dispute and appeals process is the same as for other benefits.

All decisions on applications to the discretionary Social Fund are made by Jobcentre Plus Social Fund decision makers. Applicants can ask for a review of the decision within 28 days of the date on the decision letter. As above, the claimant has a right of appeal to the First-tier Tribunal (Social Security and Child Support).

EMPLOYER PAYMENTS

STATUTORY MATERNITY PAY

Employers pay statutory maternity pay (SMP) to pregnant women who have been employed by them full or part-time continuously for at least 26 weeks into the 15th week before the week the baby is due, and whose earnings on average at least equal the lower earnings limit applied to NI contributions (£112 a week if the end of the qualifying week is in the 2015–16 tax year). SMP can be paid for a maximum period of up to 39 weeks. If the qualifying conditions are met women will receive a payment of 90 per cent of their average earnings for the first six weeks, followed by 33 weeks at £139.58 or 90 per cent of the woman's average weekly earnings if this is less than £139.58. SMP can be paid, at the earliest, 11 weeks before the week in which the baby is due, up to the day following the birth. Women can decide when they wish their maternity leave and pay to start and can work until the baby is born. However, where the woman is absent from work wholly or partly due to her pregnancy in the four weeks before the week the baby is due to be born, SMP will start the day following the first day of absence from work.

Employers are reimbursed for 92 per cent of the SMP they pay. Small employers with annual gross NI payments of £45,000 or less recover 103 per cent of the SMP paid out.

STATUTORY PATERNITY PAY

Ordinary Statutory Paternity Pay

Employers pay ordinary statutory paternity pay (OSPP) to employees who are taking leave when a child is born or placed for adoption. To qualify the employee must:
• have responsibility for the child's upbringing
• be the biological father of the child (or the child's adopter), or the spouse/civil partner/partner of the mother or adopter
• have been employed by the same employer for at least 26 weeks ending with the 15th week before the baby is due

(or the week in which the adopter is notified of having been matched with a child)
• continue working for the employer up to the child's birth (or placement for adoption)
• be earning an average of at least £112 a week (before tax)
Employees who meet these conditions receive payment of £139.58 or 90 per cent of the employee's average weekly earnings if this is less than £139.58. The employee can choose to be paid for one or two consecutive weeks. The earliest the OSPP period can begin is the date of the child's birth or placement for adoption. The OSPP period must be completed within eight weeks of that date. OSPP is not payable for any week in which the employee works. Employers are reimbursed in the same way as for statutory maternity pay.

ADDITIONAL PATERNITY LEAVE AND PAY

Regulations introduced on 6 April 2010 give parents greater flexibility in how they use their maternity and paternity provisions. For births from 3 April 2011, additional paternity leave (APL) entitles eligible fathers to take up to 26 weeks' additional paternity leave, allowing for up to a total of one year's leave to be shared between the couple. APL entitlement requires the mother to have returned to work; it must also be taken between 20 weeks and one year after the child is born. APL may be paid if taken during the mother's statutory maternity pay period or maternity allowance period.

The APL entitlement will also apply to husbands, partners or civil partners who are not the child's father but expect to have the main responsibility (apart from the mother) for the child's upbringing.

The current rate of additional statutory paternity pay is £139.58 a week or 90 per cent of the emplyee's average weekly earnings if this is less than £139.58.

STATUTORY ADOPTION PAY

Employers pay statutory adoption pay (SAP) to employees taking adoption leave from their employers. To qualify for SAP the employee must:
• be newly matched with a child by an adoption agency
• have been employed by the same employer for at least 26 weeks ending the week in which they have been notified of being matched with a child
• be earning an average of at least £112 a week (before tax)
Employees who meet these conditions receive payment of £139.58 or 90 per cent of their average weekly earnings if this is less than £139.58 for up to 39 weeks. The earliest SAP can be paid from is two weeks before the expected date of placement; the latest it can start is the date of the child's placement. Where a couple adopt a child, only one of them may receive SAP, the other may be able to receive statutory paternity pay if they meet the eligibility criteria. Employers are reimbursed in the same way as for statutory maternity pay.

The additional paternity leave entitlement (see above) will also apply to adoptions where adoptive parents are notified of a match on or after 3 April 2011.

STATUTORY SICK PAY

Employers pay statutory sick pay (SSP) for up to a maximum of 28 weeks to any employee incapable of work for four or more consecutive days. Employees must have done some work under their contract of service and have average weekly earnings of at least £112 from April 2014. SSP is a daily payment and is usually paid for the days that an employee would normally work, these days are known as qualifying days. SSP is not paid for the first three qualifying days in a period of sickness. SSP is paid at £88.45 per week and is subject to PAYE and NI contributions. Employees who cannot obtain SSP may be able to claim incapacity benefit. Employers may be able to recover some SSP costs.

THE WATER INDUSTRY

In the UK, the water industry provides clean and safe drinking water for homes and businesses to over 63 million people and has an annual turnover of around £10bn. It supplies around 17 billion litres of water a day to domestic and commercial customers and collects and treats more than 16 billion litres of wastewater a day. It also manages assets that include around 1,400 water treatment and 9,350 wastewater treatment works, 550 impounding reservoirs, over 6,500 service reservoirs/water towers and 800,000km of water mains and sewers.

Water services in England and Wales are provided by private companies. In Scotland and Northern Ireland there are single authorities, Scottish Water and Northern Ireland Water, that are publicly owned companies answerable to their respective governments. In drinking water quality tests carried out in 2013 by the Drinking Water Inspectorate, the water industry in England and Wales achieved 99.97 per cent compliance with the standards required by the EU Drinking Water Directive; Scotland achieved 99.86 per cent and Northern Ireland 99.81 per cent.

Water UK is the industry association that represents all UK water and wastewater service suppliers at national and European level and is funded directly by its members, who are the service suppliers for England, Scotland, Wales and Northern Ireland; every member has a seat on the Water UK Council.

WATER UK, 3rd Floor, 36 Broadway, London SW1H 0BH
T 020-7344 1844 W www.water.org.uk
Chief Executive, Pamela Taylor, OBE

ENGLAND AND WALES

In England and Wales, the Secretary of State for Environment, Food and Rural Affairs and the Welsh government have overall responsibility for water policy and oversee environmental standards for the water industry.

The statutory consumer representative body for water services is the Consumer Council for Water.

CONSUMER COUNCIL FOR WATER, 1st Floor,
Victoria Square House, Victoria Square, Birmingham B2 4AJ
T 0121-345 1000 E enquiries@ccwater.org.uk
W www.ccwater.org.uk

REGULATORY BODIES

The Water Services Regulation Authority (OFWAT) was established in 1989 when the water and sewerage industry in England and Wales was privatised. Its statutory role and duties are laid out under the Water Industry Act 1991 and it is the independent economic regulator of the water and sewerage companies in England and Wales. OFWAT's main duties are to ensure that the companies can finance and carry out their statutory functions and to protect the interests of water customers. OFWAT is a non-ministerial government department headed by a board following a change in legislation introduced by the Water Act 2003.

Under the Competition Act 1998, from 1 March 2000 the Competition Appeal Tribunal has heard appeals against the regulator's decisions regarding anti-competitive agreements and abuse of a dominant position in the marketplace. The Water Act 2003 placed a new duty on OFWAT to contribute to the achievement of sustainable development.

The Environment Agency has statutory duties and powers in relation to water resources, pollution control, flood defence, fisheries, recreation, conservation and navigation in England and Wales. It is also responsible for issuing permits, licences, consents and registrations such as industrial licences to extract water and fishing licences.

The Drinking Water Inspectorate (DWI) is the drinking water quality regulator for England and Wales, responsible for assessing the quality of the drinking water supplied by the water companies and investigating any incidents affecting drinking water quality, initiating prosecution where necessary. The DWI science and strategy group provides scientific advice on drinking water policy issues to DEFRA and the Welsh government.

OFWAT, Centre City Tower, 7 Hill Street, Birmingham B5 4UA
T 0121-644 7500 E mailbox@ofwat.gsi.gov.uk
W www.ofwat.gov.uk
Chair, Jonson Cox
Chief Executive, Cathryn Ross

METHODS OF CHARGING

In England and Wales, most domestic customers still pay for domestic water supply and sewerage services through charges based on the rateable value of their property. OFWAT estimated that the proportion of household customers in England and Wales to have metered supplies was around 50 per cent in 2014–15. Nearly all non-household customers are charged according to consumption.

Under the Water Industry Act 1999, water companies can continue basing their charges on the old rateable value of the property. Domestic customers can continue paying on an unmeasured basis unless they choose to pay according to consumption. After having a meter installed (which is free of charge), a customer can revert to unmeasured charging within 12 months. However, water companies may charge by meter for new homes, or homes where there is a high discretionary use of water. Domestic, school and hospital customers cannot be disconnected for non-payment.

In December 2014, OFWAT finalised its 2014 price review decisions for household water bills for the five-year period to 2020. With the exception of Bristol Water, all the water and sewerage, and water only companies confirmed acceptance of OFWAT's price decisions by the 12 February 2015 deadline. This means that average bills for water and waste-water customers in England and Wales will decrease by around 5 per cent, before adjustments for inflation, between 2015 and 2020; an average decrease of around £20, from £396 to £376 per annum.

AVERAGE HOUSEHOLD BILLS 2014–20 *(£)*

WATER AND SEWERAGE COMPANIES

	2014–15 (£)	2019–20 (£)	5-year change (%)
Anglian	431	390	−10
Dwr Cymru	440	416	−5
Northumbrian	388	382	−1
Severn Trent	333	316	−5
South West	545	506	−7
Southern	437	403	−8
Thames*	370	353	−5
United Utilities	410	398	−3
Wessex	485	442	−9
Yorkshire	373	361	−3

* Includes the cost for the preparatory works to build the Thames Tideway Tunnel – a 25km sewer to resolve the problem of too much sewage overflowing into the River Thames

WATER ONLY COMPANIES

	2014–15	2019–20	5-year change
	(£)	(£)	(%)
Affinity	176	163	–7
Bristol*	202	160	–21
Dee Valley	152	149	–2
Portsmouth	97	96	–1
Bournemouth	153	134	–12
South East	201	194	–3
South Staffordshire	141	135	–4
Sutton and East Surrey	186	180	–3

* Bristol Water has referred OFWAT's price decision to the Competition Markets Authority

Source: OFWAT

SCOTLAND

In 2002 the three existing water authorities in Scotland (East of Scotland Water, North of Scotland Water and West of Scotland Water) merged to form Scottish Water. Scottish Water, which serves more than 2.4 million households and provides 1.3 billion litres of water per day while removing 847 million litres of waste water, is a public sector company, structured and managed like a private company, but remains answerable to the Scottish parliament. Scottish Water is regulated by the Water Industry Commission for Scotland (established under the Water Services (Scotland) Act 2005), the Scottish Environment Protection Agency (SEPA) and the Drinking Water Quality Regulator for Scotland. The Water Industry Commissioner is responsible for regulating all aspects of economic and customer service performance, including water and sewerage charges. SEPA, created under the Environment Act 1995, is responsible for environmental issues, including controlling pollution and promoting the cleanliness of Scotland's rivers, lochs and coastal waters. The Public Services Reform (Scotland) Act 2010 transferred the complaints handling function of Waterwatch Scotland regarding Scottish Water, to the Scottish Public Services Ombudsman. Consumer Futures represented the views and interests of Scottish Water customers but became part of Citizens Advice Scotland in 2014.

METHODS OF CHARGING

Scottish Water sets charges for domestic and non-domestic water and sewerage provision through charges schemes which are regulated by the Water Industry Commission for Scotland. In February 2004 the harmonisation of all household charges across the country was completed following the merger of the separate authorities under Scottish Water. In November 2014 the Water Industry Commission for Scotland published *The Strategic Review of Charges 2015–2021*, stating that annual price rises would not increase at a rate higher than that of consumer price inflation during this six-year period. For the year 2015–16, the combined service charge, covering the water supply and waste water collection, increased by 1.6 per cent; resulting in an annual average household bill of £346.

CITIZENS ADVICE SCOTLAND, T 0808-800 9060
  W www.cas.org.uk
DRINKING WATER QUALITY REGULATOR FOR
  SCOTLAND, Area 1-D South, Victoria Quay,
  Edinburgh EH6 6QQ T 0131-244 0190 W www.dwqr.org.uk
SCOTTISH ENVIRONMENT PROTECTION AGENCY,
  Erskine Court, Castle Business Park, Stirling FK9 4TZ
  T 01786-457700 W www.sepa.org.uk
SCOTTISH WATER, Castle House, 6 Castle Drive,
  Dunfermline KY11 8GG T 0345-601 8855
  W www.scottishwater.co.uk
  Chief Executive, Douglas Millican

WATER INDUSTRY COMMISSION FOR SCOTLAND,
  First Floor, Moray House, Forthside Way, Stirling FK8 1QZ
  T 01786-430200 W www.watercommission.co.uk

NORTHERN IRELAND

Formerly an executive agency of the Department for Regional Development, Northern Ireland Water is a government-owned company but with substantial independence from government. Northern Ireland Water was set up as a result of government reform of water and sewerage services in April 2007. It is responsible for policy and coordination with regard to the supply, distribution and cleanliness of water, and the provision and maintenance of sewerage services. The Northern Ireland Authority for Utility Regulation (known as the Utility Regulator) is responsible for regulating the water services provided by Northern Ireland Water. The Drinking Water Inspectorate, a unit in the Northern Ireland Environment Agency (NIEA), regulates drinking water quality. Another NIEA unit, the Water Management Unit, has responsibility for the protection of the aquatic environment. The Consumer Council for Northern Ireland is the consumer representative body for water services.

METHODS OF CHARGING

The water and sewerage used by domestic customers in Northern Ireland is currently paid for by the Department for Regional Development (DRD), a system which will continue at least through the end of 2015; however the future of the subsidy is uncertain. Non-domestic customers in Northern Ireland became subject to water and sewerage charges and trade effluent charges where applicable in April 2008.

CONSUMER COUNCIL FOR NORTHERN IRELAND,
  Seatem House, 28–32 Alfred Street, Belfast BT2 8EN
  T 028-9025 1600 W www.consumercouncil.org.uk
NORTHERN IRELAND AUTHORITY FOR UTILITY
  REGULATION, Queens House, 14 Queen Street, Belfast
  BT1 6ED T 028-9031 1575 W www.uregni.gov.uk
NORTHERN IRELAND WATER, PO Box 1026, Belfast
  BT1 9DJ T 0345-744 0088 W www.niwater.com
  Chief Executive, Sara Venning

WATER SERVICE COMPANIES

(* *associate member of Water UK*)

AFFINITY WATER, Tamblin Way, Hatfield, Herts AL10 9EZ
  T 01707-268111 W www.affinitywater.co.uk
ALBION WATER LTD, Forest House, 3–5 Horndean Road,
  Bracknell RG12 0XQ T 0330-024 2020
  W www.albionwater.co.uk
ANGLIAN WATER SERVICES LTD, PO Box 10642, Harlow
  CM20 9HA T 03457-919155 W www.anglianwater.co.uk
BOURNEMOUTH WATER, George Jessel House,
  Francis Avenue, Bournemouth, Dorset BH11 8NX
  T 01202-590059 W www.bournemouthwater.co.uk
BRISTOL WATER PLC, Bridgwater Road, Bristol BS13 7AT
  T 0345-702 3797 W www.bristolwater.co.uk
CAMBRIDGE WATER PLC, 90 Fulbourn Road, Cambridge
  CB1 9JN T 01223-706050 W www.cambridge-water.co.uk
*CHOLDERTON & DISTRICT WATER COMPANY LTD,
  Estate Office, Cholderton, Salisbury, Wiltshire SP4 0DR
  T 01980-629203 W www.choldertonwater.co.uk
DEE VALLEY WATER PLC, Packsaddle, Wrexham Road,
  Rhostyllen, Wrexham LL14 4EH T 01978-846946
  W www.deevalleywater.co.uk
DWR CYMRU (WELSH WATER), Pentwyn Road, Nelson,
  Treharris, Mid Glamorgan CF46 6LY T 0800-052 0145
  W www.dwrcymru.co.uk

ESSEX & SUFFOLK WATER PLC (subsidiary of Northumbrian Water Ltd), Customer Centre, PO Box 292, Durham DH1 9TX **T** 0845-782 0111 **W** www.eswater.co.uk

NORTHUMBRIAN WATER LTD, Abbey Road, Pity Me, Durham DH1 5FJ **T** 0845-604 7468 **W** www.nwl.co.uk

PORTSMOUTH WATER PLC, PO Box 8, West Street, Havant, Hants PO9 1LG **T** 023-9249 9888 **W** www.portsmouthwater.co.uk

SEVERN TRENT WATER LTD, 2 St Johns Street, Coventry CV1 2LZ **T** 024-7771 5000 **W** www.stwater.co.uk

SOUTH EAST WATER LTD, Rocfort Road, Snodland, Kent ME6 5AH **T** 0333-000 0001 **W** www.southeastwater.co.uk

SOUTH STAFFORDSHIRE WATER PLC, Green Lane, Walsall WS2 7PD **T** 0845-607 0456 **W** www.south-staffs-water.co.uk

SOUTH WEST WATER LTD, Peninsula House, Rydon Lane, Exeter EX2 7HR **T** 01392-443020 **W** www.southwestwater.co.uk

SOUTHERN WATER SERVICES LTD, PO Box 41, Worthing BN13 3NZ **T** 01903-264444 **W** www.southernwater.co.uk

SUTTON AND EAST SURREY WATER PLC, London Road, Redhill, Surrey RH1 1LJ **T** 01737-772000 **W** www.waterplc.com

THAMES WATER UTILITIES LTD, PO Box 286, Swindon SN38 2RA **T** 0800-980 8800 **W** www.thameswater.co.uk

UNITED UTILITIES WATER PLC, Haweswater House, Lingley Mere Business Park, Great Sankey, Warrington WA5 3LP **T** 0845-746 2200 **W** www.unitedutilities.com

WESSEX WATER SERVICES LTD, Claverton Down, Bath BA2 7WW **T** 01225-526000 **W** www.wessexwater.co.uk

YORKSHIRE WATER SERVICES LTD, Western House, Western Way, Bradford BD6 2LZ **T** 01274-691111 **W** www.yorkshirewater.com

ISLAND WATER AUTHORITIES
(not members of Water UK)

COUNCIL OF THE ISLES OF SCILLY, Town Hall, St Mary's, Isles of Scilly TR21 0LW **T** 01720-424000 **W** www.scilly.gov.uk

GUERNSEY WATER, PO Box 30, Brickfield House, St Andrew, Guernsey GY1 3AS **T** 01481-239500 **W** www.water.gg

MANX UTILITIES, PO Box 177, Douglas, Isle of Man IM99 1PS **T** 01624-687687 **W** www.manxutilities.im

JERSEY WATER, PO Box 69, Mulcaster House, Westmount Road, St Helier, Jersey JE1 1DG **T** 01534-707300 **W** www.jerseywater.je

ENERGY

The main primary sources of energy in Britain are coal, oil, natural gas, renewables and nuclear power. The main secondary sources are electricity, coke and smokeless fuels and petroleum products. The UK was a net importer of fuels in the 1970s, however as a result of growth in oil and gas production from the North Sea, the UK became a net exporter of energy for most of the 1980s. Output decreased in the late 1980s following the Piper Alpha disaster until the mid-1990s, after which the UK again became a net exporter. Since 2004, the UK reverted back to become a net importer of energy. In 2014, the UK net import gap decreased to 94 million tonnes of oil equivalent – from 102 million tonnes of oil equivalent in the previous year – accounting for 46.2 per cent of the total energy used in the UK. In value terms, on an Overseas Trade Statistics (OTS) basis, the total fuel deficit for 2014 was £13.7bn, 25 per cent less than in 2013, due to substantial reduction in crude oil and natural gas prices. The deficit of crude oil and petroleum products, on the same basis, in 2014 was £5.8bn (1.1 per cent more than in 2013) compared with a £2.2bn surplus in 2004. The Department of Energy and Climate Change (DECC) is responsible for promoting energy efficiency.

INDIGENOUS PRODUCTION OF PRIMARY FUELS
Million tonnes of oil equivalent

	2013	2014
Primary oils	44.5	43.7
Natural gas	36.5	36.6
Primary electricity	18.5	17.5
Coal	8.0	7.3
Bioenergy and waste	7.5	7.9
Total	115.0	113.0

Source: DECC

INLAND ENERGY CONSUMPTION BY PRIMARY FUEL
Million tonnes of oil equivalent, temperature adjusted

	2013	2014
Natural gas	70.5	69.6
Petroleum	66.1	65.8
Coal	38.3	33.4
Nuclear electricity	15.4	13.9
Bioenergy and waste	9.4	10.7
Wind and hydro electricity	3.0	3.6
Net Imports	1.2	1.8
Total	203.9	198.8

Source: DECC

TRADE IN FUELS AND RELATED MATERIALS (2014)

	Quantity, million tonnes of oil equivalent	Value £m
Imports		
Crude oil	51.0	21,553
Petroleum products	33.3	16,455
Natural gas	41.0	6,750
Coal and other solid fuel	26.2	2,539
Electricity	2.0	1,022
Total	153.6	48,319
Exports		
Crude oil	41.5	18,160
Petroleum products	30.2	14,080
Natural gas	11.0	2,106
Coal and other solid fuel	0.6	118
Electricity	0.2	123
Total	83.5	34,587

Source: HMRC/DECC, ONS

OIL

Until the 1960s Britain imported almost all its oil supplies. In 1969 oil was discovered in the Arbroath field in the North Sea. The first oilfield to be brought into production was Argyll in 1975, and since the mid-1970s Britain has been a major producer of crude oil.

To date, the UK has produced around 3.6 billion tonnes of oil. It is estimated that there are around 716 million tonnes remaining to be produced. Licences for exploration and production are granted to companies by the DECC. As at July 2015, 678 offshore production licences and 138 onshore petroleum exploration and development licences had been awarded. At the end of 2014, there were a total of 338 offshore oil and gas fields in production. Total UK oil production peaked in 1999 but is now declining. Production stood at 39.9 million tonnes in 2014, just under a third of the 1999 level. Profits from oil production are subject to a special tax regime with different taxes applying depending on the date of approval of each field.

DRILLING ACTIVITY (2014)
by number of wells started

	Offshore	Onshore
Exploration	14	0
Appraisal	18	0
Exploration and appraisal	32	8
Development	126	11

Source: DECC

INDIGENOUS PRODUCTION AND REFINERY RECEIPTS
Thousand tonnes

	2013	2014
Indigenous production	40,646	39,928
Crude oil	38,456	37,474
*NGLs	2,190	2,453
Refinery receipts	65,687	60,823

* Natural Gas Liquids: condensates and petroleum gases derived at onshore treatment plants
Source: DECC

DELIVERIES OF PETROLEUM PRODUCTS FOR INLAND CONSUMPTION BY ENERGY USE
Thousand tonnes

	2013	2014
Transport	47,222	47,648
Industry	4,016	4,033
Domestic	2,580	2,299
Other	1,365	1,379
Total	55,183	55,359

Source: DECC

COAL

Mines were in private ownership until 1947 when they were nationalised and came under the management of the National Coal Board, later the British Coal Corporation. The corporation held a near monopoly on coal production until 1994 when the industry was restructured. Under the Coal Industry Act 1994, the Coal Authority was established to take over ownership of coal reserves and to issue licences to private mining companies. The Coal Authority is also responsible for the physical legacy of mining, eg subsidence damage claims that are not the responsibility of licensees, and for holding and making available all existing records. It also publishes current data on the coal industry on its website (W www.gov.uk/government/organisations/the-coal-authority).

The mines owned by the British Coal Corporation were sold as five separate businesses in 1994 and coal production is now undertaken entirely in the private sector. Coal output was around 50 million tonnes a year in 1994 but has since declined. In 2014, coal output stood at around 11.6 million tonnes. Deep mine production decreased by 9.9 per cent in 2014 due to the closure of a number of mines and geological conditions at some others. Surface mine production also decreased by 7.2 per cent due to geological conditions at some mines and the liquidation of Scottish Coal Company. As at 31 December 2014, there were ten deep mines and 22 surface mines in production in the UK.

The main consumer of coal in the UK is the electricity supply industry. Coal still supplies over a third of the UK's electricity needs but as indigenous production has declined, imports have continued to make up the shortfall and now represent around 86 per cent of UK coal supply, 42 per cent of which is currently supplied from Russia.

UK government policy is to meet the long-term challenges posed by climate change while continuing to ensure secure, clean and affordable energy. Coal's availability, flexibility and reliability compared to other sources mean that it is expected to continue to play an important role in the future generating mix, but its carbon emissions will need to be managed through the introduction of abatement technologies including carbon capture and storage (CCS).

CCS attempts to mitigate the effects of global warming by capturing the carbon dioxide emissions from power stations that burn fossil fuels, preventing the gas from being released into the atmosphere, and storing it in underground geological formations. CCS is still in its infancy and only through its successful demonstration and development will it be possible for coal to remain a part of a low-carbon UK energy mix. The government is committed to public sector investment in CCS technology on four power stations and has made it clear that there can be no new coal power stations in England and Wales without CCS on a defined amount of capacity. As part of a wider package of reforms to the electricity market, the government will also be introducing an Emissions Performance Standard, which will limit the emissions from new fossil fuel power stations.

COAL PRODUCTION AND FOREIGN TRADE
Thousand tonnes

	2013	2014
Surface mining	8,679	7,962
Deep-mined	4,089	3,685
Imports	49,402	41,765
Exports	(593)	(425)
*Total supply	60,248	48,658
Total demand	60,425	48,500

* Includes an estimate for slurry and stock change
Source: DECC

INLAND COAL USE
Thousand tonnes

	2013	2014
Fuel producers		
Electricity generators	50,041	38,400
Coke manufacture	5,288	4,977
Blast furnaces	1,411	1,513
Heat generation	609	516
Patent fuel manufacture	259	259
Final consumption		
Industry	2,134	2,241
Transport	14	13
Domestic	636	547
Public administration	22	23
Commercial	5	5
Agriculture	0	0
Miscellaneous	7	6

Source: DECC

GAS

From the late 18th century gas in Britain was produced from coal. In the 1960s town gas began to be produced from oil-based feedstocks using imported oil. In 1965 gas was discovered in the North Sea in the West Sole field, which became the first gasfield in production in 1967, and from the late 1960s natural gas began to replace town gas. From October 1998 Britain was connected to the continental European gas system via a pipeline from Bacton, Norfolk to Zeebrugge, Belgium. Gas is transported through 278,000km of mains pipeline including 7,600km of high-pressure gas pipelines owned and operated in the UK by National Grid Gas plc.

The gas industry in Britain was nationalised in 1949 and operated as the Gas Council. The Gas Council was replaced by the British Gas Corporation in 1972 and the industry became more centralised. The British Gas Corporation was privatised in 1986 as British Gas plc. In 1993 the Monopolies and Mergers Commission found that British Gas's integrated business in Great Britain as a gas trader and the owner of the gas transportation system could operate against the public interest. In February 1997, British Gas demerged its trading arm to become two separate companies, BG plc and Centrica plc. BG Group, as the company is now known, is an international natural gas company whose principal business is finding and developing gas reserves and building gas markets. Its core operations are located in the UK, South America, Egypt, Trinidad and Tobago, Kazakhstan and India. Centrica runs the trading and services operations under the British Gas brand name in Great Britain. In October 2000 BG demerged its pipeline business, Transco, which became part of Lattice Group, finally merging with the National Grid Group in 2002 to become National Grid Transco plc.

In July 2005 National Grid Transco plc changed its name to National Grid plc and Transco plc became National Grid Gas plc. In the same year National Grid Gas also completed the sale of four of its eight gas distribution networks. The distribution networks transport gas at lower pressures, which eventually supply the consumers such as domestic customers. The Scotland and south-east of England networks were sold to Scotia Gas Networks. The Wales and south-west network was sold to Wales & West Utilities and the network in the north-east to Northern Gas Networks. This was the biggest change in the corporate structure of gas infrastructure since privatisation in 1986.

Competition was gradually introduced into the industrial gas market from 1986. Supply of gas to the domestic market was opened to companies other than British Gas, starting in

April 1996 with a pilot project in the West Country and Wales, with the rest of the UK following soon after.

Declines in UK indigenous gas production and increasing demand led to the UK becoming a net importer of gas once more in 2004. With the depletion of the UK Continental Shelf reserves, UK gas production has seen growing rates of decline. As part of the Energy Act 2008, the government planned to strengthen regulation of the offshore gas supply infrastructure, to allow private sector investment to help maintain UK energy supplies.

BG GROUP PLC, Thames Valley Park Drive, Reading RG6 1PT
T 0118-935 3222 W www.bg-group.com
Chief Executive, Helge Lund

CENTRICA PLC, Millstream, Maidenhead Road, Windsor,
Berkshire SL4 5GD T 01753-494000 W www.centrica.com
Chair, Rick Haythornthwaite
Chief Executive, Iain Conn

NATIONAL GRID PLC, National Grid House, Warwick
Technology Park, Gallows Hill, Warwick CV34 6DA
T 01926-653000 W www.nationalgrid.com
Chair, Sir Peter Gershon, CBE
Chief Executive, Steve Holliday

UK GAS CONSUMPTION BY INDUSTRY
GWh

	2013	2014
Domestic	342,501	278,101
Industry	93,005	92,493
Public administration	44,419	36,969
Commercial	57,791	48,443
Agriculture	1,096	886
Non-energy use	5,598	5,430
Miscellaneous	12,065	10,079
Total gas consumption	556,475	472,401

Source: DECC

ELECTRICITY

The first power station in Britain generating electricity for public supply began operating in 1882. In the 1930s a national transmission grid was developed and it was reconstructed and extended in the 1950s and 1960s. Power stations were operated by the Central Electricity Generating Board.

Under the Electricity Act 1989, 12 regional electricity companies, responsible for the distribution of electricity from the national grid to consumers, were formed from the former area electricity boards in England and Wales. Four companies were formed from the Central Electricity Generating Board: three generating companies (National Power plc, Nuclear Electric plc and Powergen plc) and the National Grid Company plc, which owned and operated the transmission system in England and Wales. National Power and Powergen were floated on the stock market in 1991.

National Power was demerged in October 2000 to form two separate companies: International Power plc and Innogy plc, which manages the bulk of National Power's UK assets. Nuclear Electric was split into two parts in 1996.

The National Grid Company was floated on the stock market in 1995 and formed a new holding company, National Grid Group. National Grid Group completed a merger with Lattice in 2002 to form National Grid Transco, a public limited company (*see* Gas).

Following privatisation, generators and suppliers in England and Wales traded via the Electricity Pool. A competitive wholesale trading market known as NETA (New Electricity Trading Arrangements) replaced the Electricity Pool in March 2001, and was extended to include Scotland via the British Electricity Transmissions and Trading Arrangements (BETTA) in 2005. As part of BETTA, National Grid became the system operator for all transmission. The introduction of competition into the domestic electricity market was completed in May 1999. Since competition was introduced, over 19 million of Britain's 28 million electricity customers have switched their supplier.

In Scotland, three new companies were formed under the Electricity Act 1989: Scottish Power plc and Scottish Hydro-Electric plc, which were responsible for generation, transmission, distribution and supply; and Scottish Nuclear Ltd. Scottish Power and Scottish Hydro-Electric were floated on the stock market in 1991. Scottish Hydro-Electric merged with Southern Electric in 1998 to become Scottish and Southern Energy plc. Scottish Nuclear was incorporated into British Energy in 1996. BETTA opened the Scottish market to the same competition that had applied in England and Wales.

In Northern Ireland, Northern Ireland Electricity plc (NIE) was set up in 1993 under a 1991 Order in Council. In 1993 it was floated on the stock market and in 1998 it became part of the Viridian Group and was responsible for distribution and supply until NIE was sold to ESB Independent Energy in December 2010. In June 2010, Airtricity became the first new electricity supplier since the Northern Ireland electricity market was opened to competition in 2007.

On 12 July 2011, the government published *Planning Our Electric Future: a White Paper for Secure, Affordable and Low-carbon Electricity* in response to the challenges set by increasing electricity demands. It was agreed that extensive investment is needed to update the grid and build new power stations. Currently, 16 per cent of the UK electricity supply comes from nuclear reactors. While nuclear power stations will close gradually over the next decade, with only one expected to produce power beyond 2025, there are plans in place for a new generation of reactors to be built, potentially running by 2018.

On 30 September 2003 the Electricity Association, the industry's main trade association, was replaced with three separate trade bodies: the Association of Electricity Producers; the Energy Networks Association; and the Energy Retail Association. In April 2012, following a merger between the Association of Electricity Producers, the Energy Retail Association and the UK Business Council for Sustainable Energy, Energy UK – the new trade association for the gas and electricity sector – was established.

ENERGY NETWORKS ASSOCIATION, 6th floor,
Dean Bradley House, 52 Horseferry Road, London SW1P 2AF
T 020-7706 5100 W www.energynetworks.org
Chief Executive, David Smith
ENERGY UK, Charles House, 5–11 Regent Street,
London SW1Y 4LR T 020-7930 9390 W www.energy-uk.org.uk
Chief Executive, Lawrence Slade

ELECTRICITY PRODUCTION, SUPPLY AND CONSUMPTION
GWh

	2013	2014
Electricity produced		
Nuclear	70,607	63,748
Hydro	4,702	5,885
Wind, wave and solar photovoltaics	30,417	36,068
Coal	130,768	100,707
Oil	2,091	1,881
Gas	96,028	100,928
Other renewables	18,159	22,702
Other	3,493	4,125
Total	356,265	336,045
Electricity supplied		
Production	356,264	336,043
*Other sources	2,904	2,883
Imports	17,533	23,230
Exports	(3,103)	(2,720)
Total	373,598	359,436
Electricity consumed		
Industry	97,669	93,373
Transport	4,268	4,259
Other	215,040	205,777
Domestic	113,445	108,881
Public administration	18,820	18,203
Commercial	78,901	74,965
Agriculture	3,874	3,728
Total	316,977	303,409

* Pumped storage production

Source: DECC

GAS AND ELECTRICITY SUPPLIERS

With the gas and electricity markets open, most suppliers offer their customers both services. The majority of gas/electricity companies have become part of larger multi-utility companies, often operating internationally.

As part of measures to reduce the UK's carbon output, the government has outlined plans to introduce 'smart meters' to all UK homes. Smart meters perform the traditional meter function of measuring energy consumption, in addition to more advanced functions such as allowing energy suppliers to communicate directly with their customers and removing the need for meter readings and bill estimates. The meters also allow domestic customers to have direct access to energy consumption information.

The following list comprises a selection of suppliers offering gas and electricity. Organisations in italics are subsidiaries of the companies listed in capital letters directly above.

ENGLAND, SCOTLAND AND WALES
CENTRICA PLC, Millstream, Maidenhead Road, Windsor, Berkshire SL4 5GD T 01753-494000 W www.centrica.com
British Gas, PO Box 4805, Worthing BN11 9QW T 0800-048 0202 W www.britishgas.co.uk
EDF ENERGY, Osprey House, Osprey Road, Exeter, EX2 7WN T 0800-056 7777 W www.edfenergy.com
E.ON, 6th Floor, 100 Pall Mall, London SW1Y 5NQ T 024-7618 3843 W www.eonenergy.com
NORTHERN POWERGRID, Houghton le Spring DH4 7LA T 0845-070 7172 W www.northernpowergrid.com
NPOWER, PO Box 93, Peterlee SR8 2XX T 0800-073 3000 W www.npower.com
SCOTTISHPOWER, PO Box 8729, Bellshill ML4 3YD T 0845-270 0700 W www.scottishpower.co.uk
SSE PLC, Inveralmond House, 200 Dunkeld Road, Perth PH1 3AQ T 0800-980 8831 W www.sse.com
Scottish Hydro, T 0800-980 8754 W www.hydro.co.uk
Southern Electric, T 0800-980 8476 W www.southern-electric.co.uk
SWALEC, T 0800-980 9041 W www.swalec.co.uk

NORTHERN IRELAND
AIRTRICITY (a member of Scottish and Southern Energy), Red Oak South, South County Business Park, Leopardstown, Dublin 18 T 0345-864 3546 W www.sseairtricity.com
ELECTRIC IRELAND, Forsyth House, Cromac Square, Belfast BT2 8LA T 0845-600 5335 W www.electricireland.ie
VIRIDIAN GROUP PLC, Greenwood House, 64 Newforge Lane, Belfast BT9 5NF T 028-9066 8416 W www.viridiangroup.co.uk
Energia, 3rd Floor, Mill House, Ashtowngate, Navan Road, Dublin 15 T 1850-363744 W www.energia.ie

REGULATION OF THE GAS AND ELECTRICITY INDUSTRIES

The Office of the Gas and Electricity Markets (OFGEM) regulates the gas and electricity industries in Great Britain. It was formed in 1999 by the merger of the Office of Gas Supply and the Office of Electricity Regulation. OFGEM's overriding aim is to protect and promote the interests of all gas and electricity customers by promoting competition and regulating monopolies. It is governed by an authority and its powers are provided for under the Gas Act 1986, the Electricity Act 1989, the Competition Act 1998, the Utilities Act 2000 and the Enterprise Act 2002. Energywatch was the independent gas and electricity watchdog, set up in November 2000 through the Utility Act to protect and promote the interests of gas and electricity consumers. In October 2008 Energywatch merged with Postwatch and the National Consumer Council to form a new advocacy body, Consumer Focus. In October 2010, the government announced that Consumer Focus would be abolished and some of its functions would transfer to Citizens Advice, Citizens Advice Scotland and the Consumer Council for Northern Ireland. This transfer began in April 2013 and full responsibility was transferred to Citizens Advice following the abolishment of Consumer Focus on 1 April 2014.

CITIZENS ADVICE, 3rd Floor North, 200 Aldersgate Street, London EC1A 4HD T 0300-023 1231 W www.citizensadvice.org.uk
CITIZENS ADVICE SCOTLAND, 1st Floor, Spectrum House, 2 Powderhall Road, Edinburgh EH7 4GB T 0808-800 9060 W www.cas.org.uk
CONSUMER COUNCIL FOR NORTHERN IRELAND, 116 Holywood Road, Belfast BT4 1NY T 028-9067 2488 W www.consumercouncil.org.uk
THE OFFICE OF THE GAS AND ELECTRCITY MARKETS (OFGEM), 9 Millbank, London SW1 3GE T 020-7901 7000 W www.ofgem.gov.uk

NUCLEAR POWER

Nuclear reactors began to supply electricity to the national grid in 1956. Nuclear power is currently generated in the UK at nine sites: one magnox reactor (Wylfa 1, possible generation extension to December 2015) following the closure of Oldbury nuclear power station in February 2012, seven advanced gas-cooled reactors (AGR) and one pressurised water reactor (PWR), Sizewell 'B' in Suffolk. The AGRs and PWR are owned by a private company, EDF Energy, while the magnox reactor is state-owned by the Nuclear Decommissioning Authority. The first of a series of new-generation plants is expected to come on-line around

2018; all but one of the current sites (Sizewell 'B') will be shut down by 2035.

In April 2005 the responsibility for the decommissioning of civil nuclear reactors and other nuclear facilities used in research and development was handed to the Nuclear Decommissioning Authority (NDA). The NDA is a non-departmental public body, funded mainly by the DECC. The total planned expenditure for the NDA in 2015–16 was £3.31bn. Until April 2007, UK Nirex was responsible for the disposal of intermediate and some low-level nuclear waste. After this date Nirex was integrated into the NDA and renamed the Radioactive Waste Management directorate.

There are currently 17 nuclear sites owned by the NDA that are in various stages of decommissioning, including the world's first commercial power station at Calder Hall on the Sellafield site in Cumbria. The decommissioning of these sites is scheduled for completion within the next 15 to 20 years. In the case of the Dounreay research facility in Scotland, controls on access to contaminated land are expected to remain in place until around 2300.

In 2014 electricity supplied from nuclear sources accounted for 18.9 per cent of the total electricity supply. The 2008 Energy bill paved the way for the construction of up to ten new nuclear power stations by 2020. Eight sites have been assessed as potentially suitable for the development of new power stations in England and Wales before the end of 2025. A number of factors have led to government backing for nuclear power: domestic gas supplies are running low; oil and gas prices are high; carbon emissions must be cut to comply with EU legislation and meet global climate change targets; and a number of coal-fired power stations that fail to meet clean air requirements are due to be closed.

Nuclear power has its advantages: reactors emit virtually no carbon dioxide and uranium prices remain relatively steady. However, the advantages of low emissions are countered by the high costs of construction and difficulties in disposing of nuclear waste. Currently, the only method is to store it securely until it has slowly decayed to safe levels. Public distrust persists despite the advances in safety technology.

SAFETY AND REGULATION
The Office for Nuclear Regulation (ONR), a public corporation of the Department for Work and Pensions, is the nuclear industry's regulator. Operations at the 37 UK nuclear power stations are governed by a site licence which is issued under the Nuclear Installations Act. The ONR monitors compliance and has the jurisdiction to close down a reactor if the terms of the licence are breached. The DECC is responsible for security at all the UK's nuclear power stations, which are policed by the Civil Nuclear Constabulary, a specialised armed force created in April 2005. In 2009 Magnox Electric Ltd was found guilty of breaking the Radioactive Substances Act 2003: it had left a radioactive leak on a holding tank at Bradwell power station, Essex, unchecked for 14 years.

RENEWABLE SOURCES

Renewable sources of energy principally include biofuels, hydro, wind and solar. Renewable sources produced 14.3 million tonnes of oil equivalent for primary energy usage in 2014; of this, 10.1 million tonnes was used to generate electricity, 2.9 million tonnes to generate heat and 1.2 million tonnes was used as transport fuels. In 2014, the UK generated 19.1 per cent of its total electricity production from renewable sources, compared with 14.9 per cent in 2013. Heat from renewable sources increased by 4.6 per cent during 2014 to 2.7 million tonnes of oil equivalent. Overall,

in 2014 renewable energy accounted for 7 per cent of final energy consumption as measured using the 2009 Renewable Energy Directive (RED) methodology, an increase from 5.6 per cent in 2013. Averaged over 2013 and 2014, the UK has now achieved 6.3 per cent renewable energy, in excess of the interim target which was set at 5.4 per cent.

The government's principal mechanisms for developing renewable energy sources are the Renewables Obligation (RO) and the Renewable Heat Incentive (RHI). The RO aims to increase the contribution of electricity from renewables in the UK. There are seperate RO schemes for England and Wales, Scotland and Northern Ireland. For both England and Wales and Scotland, the RO was set so that 15.4 per cent of licensed electricity sales should be from renewable sources eligible for the RO by 2015/16 – 6.3 per cent in Northern Ireland. In 2014, renewable sources accounted for 19.8 per cent of sales on an RO basis, an increase from 15.6 per cent in 2013.

A Renewables Obligation has been in place in England and Wales since April 2002 to give incentives to generators to supply progressively higher levels of renewable energy over time. These measures included exempting renewable energy sources from the climate change levy, capital grants, enhanced research funding and regional planning to meet renewables targets.

In addition to the RO, in April 2010, the government launched a Feed-in Tariff (FIT) scheme in Great Britain to encourage the uptake of small-scale low carbon electricity generation technologies, principally renewables such as solar photovoltaics, wind and hydro-electricity.

The RHI was originally introduced in November 2011 to provide a long-term financial incentive to support the uptake of renewable heat in the non-domestic sector. In April 2014, the RHI was extended to cover the domestic sector replacing the renewable heat premium payment scheme which closed in March 2013. Participants of the scheme receive tarifff payments for the heat generated from an eligible renewable heating system which is heating a single dwelling.

The government approved an EU-wide agreement in March 2007 to generate 20 per cent of energy production from renewable sources by 2020. It has since negotiated down the national share in this target to 15 per cent of energy production by 2020. In July 2009 the government published a Renewable Energy Strategy in order to meet this target. Other impediments to the expansion of renewable energy production include planning restrictions, rising raw material prices, and the possible redirection of funds to develop CCS technology and nuclear energy sources.

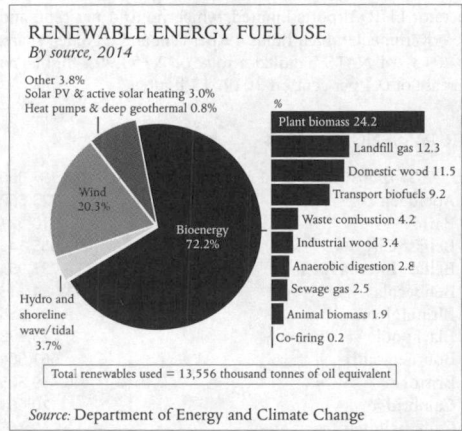

RENEWABLE ENERGY FUEL USE
By source, 2014

Other 3.8%
Solar PV & active solar heating 3.0%
Heat pumps & deep geothermal 0.8%

Wind 20.3%

Bioenergy 72.2%

Hydro and shoreline wave/tidal 3.7%

%	
Plant biomass	24.2
Landfill gas	12.3
Domestic wood	11.5
Transport biofuels	9.2
Waste combustion	4.2
Industrial wood	3.4
Anaerobic digestion	2.8
Sewage gas	2.5
Animal biomass	1.9
Co-firing	0.2

Total renewables used = 13,556 thousand tonnes of oil equivalent

Source: Department of Energy and Climate Change

TRANSPORT

CIVIL AVIATION

Since the privatisation of British Airways in 1987, UK airlines have been operated entirely by the private sector. In 2014, total capacity of British airlines amounted to 50.5 billion tonne-km, of which 41 billion tonne-km was on scheduled services. UK airlines carried around 141 million passengers; 125 million on scheduled services and 16 million on charter flights. Passenger traffic through UK airports increased by 0.44 per cent in 2014. Traffic at the six main London area airports (Gatwick, Heathrow, London City, Luton, Southend and Stansted) increased by 5 per cent over 2014 and other UK regional airports saw an increase of 3 per cent.

Leading British airlines include British Airways, EasyJet, Monarch, Thomas Cook Airlines, Thomson Airways and Virgin Atlantic. Irish airline Ryanair also operates frequent flights from the UK.

There are around 140 licensed civil aerodromes in Britain, with Heathrow and Gatwick handling the highest volume of passengers.

The Civil Aviation Authority (CAA), an independent statutory body, is responsible for the regulation of UK airlines. This includes economic and airspace regulation, air safety, consumer protection and environmental research and consultancy. All commercial airline companies must be granted an air operator's certificate, which is issued by the CAA to operators meeting the required safety standards. The CAA issues airport safety licences, which must be obtained by any airport used for public transport and training flights. All British-registered aircraft must be granted an airworthiness certificate, and the CAA issues professional licences to pilots, flight crew, ground engineers and air traffic controllers. The CAA also manages the Air Travel Organiser's Licence (ATOL), the UK's principal travel protection scheme. The CAA's costs are met entirely from charges on those whom it regulates; there is no direct government funding of the CAA's work.

The Transport Act 2000 separated the CAA from its subsidiary, National Air Traffic Services (NATS), which provides air traffic control services to aircraft flying in UK airspace and over the eastern part of the North Atlantic. NATS is a public private partnership (PPP) between the Airline Group (a consortium of UK airlines), which holds 42 per cent of the shares; NATS staff, who hold 5 per cent; UK airport operator LHR Airports Limited, which holds 4 per cent, and the government, which holds 49 per cent and a golden share. In 2013–14 NATS handled a total of 2,153,995 flights, an increase of 0.4 per cent on 2012–13 figures.

AIR PASSENGERS 2014

All UK Airports: Total	238,557,866
Aberdeen	3,723,662
Barra	10,521
Belfast City	2,555,145
Belfast International	4,033,954
Benbecula	31,213
Birmingham	9,705,955
Blackpool	223,998
Bournemouth	661,584
Bristol	6,339,805
Cambridge	20,663
Campbeltown	9,365
Cardiff	1,023,932
City of Derry (Eglinton)	350,257
Doncaster Sheffield	724,885
Dundee	22,069
Durham Tees Valley	142,379
East Midlands	4,510,544
Edinburgh	10,160,004
Exeter	767,404
Gatwick	38,103,667
Glasgow	7,715,988
Gloucestershire	15,172
Heathrow	73,405,330
Humberside	239,173
Inverness	612,725
Islay	27,659
Isle of Man	729,703
Isles of Scilly (St Mary's)	90,944
Kent International	12,508
Kirkwall	161,347
Lands End (St Just)	44,475
Leeds Bradford	2,274,474
Lerwick (Tingwall)	3,739
Liverpool	3,986,654
London City	3,647,824
Luton	10,484,938
Lydd	1,227
Manchester	21,989,682
Newcastle	4,516,739
Newquay	221,047
Norwich	458,968
Oxford (Kidlington)	1,194
Prestwick	913,685
Scatsta	279,799
Shoreham	452
Southampton	1,831,700
Southend	1,102,358
Stansted	19,965,093
Stornoway	129,481
Sumburgh	264,521
Tiree	9,322
Wick	28,145
Channel Islands Airports: Total	2,451,626
Alderney	61,317
Guernsey	894,602
Jersey	1,495,707

Source: Civil Aviation Authority

CAA, CAA House, 45–59 Kingsway, London WC2B 6TE
T 020-7379 7311 W www.caa.co.uk

Heathrow Airport	T 0844-335 1801
Gatwick Airport	T 0844-892 0322
Manchester Airport	T 0871-271 0711
Stansted Airport	T 0844-335 1803

BRITISH AIRLINES
BRITISH AIRWAYS, PO Box 365, Waterside, Harmondsworth UB7 0GB T 0844-493 0787 W www.britishairways.com
EASYJET, Hangar 89, London Luton Airport LU2 9PF T 0330-365 5000 W www.easyjet.com
MONARCH, Prospect House, Prospect Way, London Luton Airport LU2 9NU T 0333-003 0100 W www.monarch.co.uk

THOMAS COOK AIRLINES, Thomas Cook Business Park,
   Coningsby Road, Peterborough PE3 8SB T 01733-224 800
   W www.thomascook.com
THOMSON AIRWAYS, Wigmore House, Wigmore Place,
   Wigmore Lane, Luton, Beds LU2 9TN T 0203-451 2688
   W www.thomson.co.uk
VIRGIN ATLANTIC, The Office, Manor Royal, Crawley,
   W. Sussex RH10 9NU T 0344-811 0000
   W www.virgin-atlantic.com

RAILWAYS

The railway network in Britain was developed by private companies in the 19th century. In 1948 the main railway companies were nationalised and were run by a public authority, the British Transport Commission. The commission was replaced by the British Railways Board in 1963, operating as British Rail. On 1 April 1994, responsibility for managing the track and railway infrastructure passed to a newly formed company, Railtrack plc. In October 2001 Railtrack was put into administration under the Railways Act 1993. In October 2002 Railtrack was taken out of administration and replaced by the not-for-profit company Network Rail. The British Railways Board continued as operator of all train services until 1996–7, when they were sold or franchised to the private sector.
The Strategic Rail Authority (SRA) was created to provide strategic leadership to the rail industry and formally came into being on 1 February 2001 following the passing of the Transport Act 2000. In January 2002 it published its first strategic plan, setting out the strategic priorities for Britain's railways over the next ten years. In addition to its coordinating role, the SRA was responsible for allocating government funding to the railways and awarding and monitoring the franchises for operating rail services.

On 15 July 2004 the transport secretary announced a new structure for the rail industry in the white paper *The Future of Rail*. These proposals were implemented under the Railways Act 2005, which abolished the SRA, passing most of its functions to the Department for Transport; established the Rail Passengers Council as a single national body, dissolving the regional committees; and gave devolved governments in Scotland and Wales more say in decisions at a local level. In addition, responsibility for railway safety regulation was transferred to the Office of Rail Regulation from the Health and Safety Executive.

OFFICE OF RAIL AND ROAD
The Office of Rail and Road (ORR), previously known as the Office of Rail Regulation, was established on 5 July 2004 by the Railways and Transport Safety Act 2003, replacing the Office of the Rail Regulator. In April 2015 it acquired responsibility for monitoring Highways England in addition to its existing role as the railway industry's economic and safety regulator and changed its name to better reflect its functions. The ORR regulates Network Rail's stewardship of the national network, licenses operators, approves network access agreements, and enforces domestic competition law. The ORR is led by a board appointed by the Secretary of State for Transport and chaired by Anna Walker.

SERVICES
For privatisation, under the Railways Act 1993, domestic passenger services were divided into 25 train operating units, which were franchised to private sector operators via a competitive tendering process. The train operators formed the Association of Train Operating Companies (ATOC) to act as the official voice of the passenger rail industry and provide its members with a range of services enabling them to comply with conditions imposed on them through their franchise agreements and operating licences.

As at July 2015 there were 25 passenger train operating companies: Abellio Greater Anglia, Arriva Trains Wales, c2c, Caledonian Sleeper, Chiltern Railways, CrossCountry, East Midlands Trains, Eurostar, First Great Western, First Hull Trains, First TransPennine Express, Grand Central, Great Northern, Heathrow Express, London Midland, London Overground, Merseyrail, Northern, ScotRail, South West Trains, Southeastern, Southern, Thameslink, Virgin Trains and Virgin Trains East Coast.

Network Rail publishes a national timetable which contains details of rail services operated over the UK network and sea ferry services which provide connections with Ireland, the Isle of Man, the Isle of Wight, the Channel Islands and some European destinations.

The national rail enquiries service offers information about train times and fares for any part of the country, Transport for London (TfL) provides London-specific travel information for all modes of travel and Eurostar provides information for international channel tunnel rail services:

NATIONAL RAIL ENQUIRIES
T 0345-748 4950 W www.nationalrail.co.uk
TRANSPORT FOR LONDON
T 0343-222 1234 W www.tfl.gov.uk
EUROSTAR
T 03432-186186 W www.eurostar.com

TRANSPORT FOCUS AND LONDON TRAVELWATCH
Previously known as Passenger Focus, Transport Focus is the national consumer watchdog for bus, tram, coach and rail passengers in England. Under The Infrastructure Act 2015 Transport Focus's role was expanded to also represent users of the strategic road network. The entity is funded by the Department for Transport and is an executive non-departmental public body.

Established in July 2000, London TravelWatch is the operating name of the official watchdog organisation representing the interests of transport users in and around the capital. Officially known as the London Transport Users' Committee, it is sponsored and funded by the London Assembly and is independent of the transport operators. London TravelWatch represents users of buses, the Underground, river and rail services in and around London, including Eurostar and Heathrow Express, Croydon Tramlink and the Docklands Light Railway. The interests of pedestrians, cyclists and motorists are also represented, as are those of taxi users.

FREIGHT
On privatisation in 1996, British Rail's bulk freight operations were sold to North and South Railways – subsequently called English, Welsh and Scottish Railways (EWS). In 2007, EWS was bought by Deutsche Bahn and in January 2009 was re-named DB Schenker. The other major companies in the rail freight sector are: Colas Rail, Direct Rail Services, Freightliner and GB Railfreight (GBRf). In 2014–15 freight moved by rail amounted to 22.2 billion tonne-kilometres, a 2.2 per cent decrease from 2013–14.

NETWORK RAIL
Network Rail is responsible for the tracks, bridges, tunnels, level crossings, viaducts and 18 main stations that form Britain's rail network. In addition to providing the timetables for the passenger and freight operators, Network Rail is also responsible for all the signalling and electrical control equipment needed to operate the rail network and for monitoring and reporting performance across the industry.

In September 2014, Network Rail was reclassified as a public body after being privately run since 2002 as a commercial business which was directly accountable to its members. The members had similar rights to those of shareholders in a public company except they did not receive dividends or share capital and thereby had no financial interest in Network Rail. On 1 July 2015 the 46 public members were dismissed and the company is now accountable directly to parliament through the Secretary of State for Transport. Network Rail is regulated by the ORR and all of its profits are reinvested into maintaining and upgrading the rail infrastructure. In 2014–15 a total of 1,656 million passenger journeys were made on the rail network.

ASSOCIATION OF TRAIN OPERATING COMPANIES,
ATOC Ltd, 2nd Floor, 200 Aldersgate Street, London EC1A 4HD
T 020-7841 8000 W www.atoc.org
LONDON TRAVELWATCH, 169 Union Street, London
SE1 0LL T 020-3176 2999 W www.londontravelwatch.org.uk
NETWORK RAIL, 1 Eversholt Street, London NW1 2DN
T 020-7557 8000 W www.networkrail.co.uk
OFFICE OF RAIL REGULATION, 1 Kemble Street,
London WC2B 4AN T 020-7282 2018 W www.orr.gov.uk
TRANSPORT FOCUS, 2-6 Salisbury Square, London EC4Y 8JX
T 0300-123 0860 W www.transportfocus.org.uk

RAIL SAFETY
On 1 April 2006 responsibility for health and safety policy and enforcement on the railways transferred from the Health and Safety Executive to the Office of Rail Regulation (ORR).

In 2014–15 a total of 39 passengers, railway staff and other members of the public were fatally injured in all rail incidents (excluding suicides), compared with 37 in 2013–14.

ACCIDENTS ON RAILWAYS

	2013–14	2014–15
Rail incident fatalities	37	39
Passengers	4	3
Railway employees	3	3
Public	30	33
Rail incident major injuries	498	521
Passengers	276	296
Railway employees	177	175
Public	45	50

SUICIDES AND ATTEMPTED SUICIDES 2014–15
Fatalities	293
Major Injuries	38

Source: RSSB – Annual Safety Performance Report 2014–15

OTHER RAIL SYSTEMS
Responsibility for the London Underground passed from the government to the Mayor and Transport for London on 15 July 2003, with a public-private partnership already in place. Plans for a public-private partnership for London Underground were pushed through by the government in February 2002 despite opposition from the Mayor of London and a range of transport organisations. Under the PPP, long-term contracts with private companies were estimated to enable around £16bn to be invested in renewing and upgrading the London Underground's infrastructure over 15 years. In July 2007, Metronet, which was responsible for two of three PPP contracts, went into administration; TfL took over both contracts. Responsibility for stations, trains, operations, signalling and safety remains in the public sector. In 2014–15 there were more than 1,300 million passenger journeys on the London Underground.

In addition to Glasgow Subway, which is classified as an underground system (13 million passenger journeys in

2014–15), Britain has eight other light rail and tram systems: Blackpool Tramway, Docklands Light Railway (DLR), London Tramlink, Manchester Metrolink, Midland Metro, Nottingham Express Transit (NET), Sheffield Supertram and Tyne and Wear Metro.

In 2014–15 there were 240 million passenger light rail and tram journeys in Great Britain; an increase of 5.6 per cent on 2013–14 figures.

THE CHANNEL TUNNEL
The earliest recorded scheme for a submarine transport connection between Britain and France was in 1802. Tunnelling began simultaneously on both sides of the Channel three times: in 1881, in the early 1970s, and on 1 December 1987, when construction workers bored the first of the three tunnels which form the Channel Tunnel. Engineers 'holed through' the first tunnel (the service tunnel) on 1 December 1990 and tunnelling was completed in June 1991. The tunnel was officially inaugurated by the Queen and President Mitterrand of France on 6 May 1994.

The submarine link comprises two rail tunnels, each carrying trains in one direction, which measure 7.6m (24.93ft) in diameter. Between them lies a smaller service tunnel, measuring 4.8m (15.75ft) in diameter. The service tunnel is linked to the rail tunnels by 130 cross-passages for maintenance and safety purposes. The tunnels are 50km (31 miles) long, 38km (24 miles) of which is under the seabed at an average depth of 40m (132ft). The rail terminals are situated at Folkestone and Calais, and the tunnels go underground at Shakespeare Cliff, Dover and Sangatte, west of Calais.

RAIL LINKS
The British Channel Tunnel Rail Link route runs from Folkestone to St Pancras station, London, with intermediate stations at Ashford and Ebbsfleet in Kent and more recently, Stratford International.

Construction of the rail link was financed by the private sector with a substantial government contribution. A private sector consortium, London and Continental Railways Ltd (LCR), comprising Union Railways and the UK operator of Eurostar, owns the rail link and was responsible for its design and construction. The rail link was constructed in two phases: phase one, from the Channel Tunnel to Fawkham Junction, Kent, began in October 1998 and opened to fare-paying passengers on 28 September 2003; phase two, from Southfleet Junction to St Pancras, was completed in November 2007.

There are direct services from the UK to Calais, Disneyland Paris, Lille and Paris in France and Brussels in Belgium. There are also direct services to Avignon in the south of France between July and September and during the winter months (December to April) to the French Alps. High-speed trains also run from Lille to the south of France.

Eurostar, the high-speed passenger train service, connects London with Paris in 2 hours 15 minutes, Brussels in 1 hour 51 minutes and Lille in 1 hour 20 minutes. There are Eurostar terminals at London St Pancras, Ashford and Ebbsfleet in Kent, Paris Gare Du Nord and Lille in France, and Brussels-South in Belgium.

ROADS

HIGHWAY AUTHORITIES
The powers and responsibilities of highway authorities in England and Wales are set out in the Highways Act 1980; for Scotland there is separate legislation.

Responsibility for motorways and other trunk roads in Great Britain rests in England with the Secretary of State for

Transport, in Scotland with the Scottish government, and in Wales with the Welsh government. The highway authority for non-trunk roads in England, Wales and Scotland is, in general, the local authority in whose area the roads lie. With the establishment of the Greater London Authority in July 2000, Transport for London became the highway authority for roads in London.

In Northern Ireland the Department for Regional Development is the statutory road authority responsible for public roads and their maintenance and construction; the Transport NI executive agency (formerly known as the Roads Service) carries out these functions on behalf of the department.

FINANCE

In England all aspects of trunk road and motorway funding are provided directly by the government to Highways England, which operates, maintains and improves a network of motorways and trunk roads around 6,920km (4,300 miles) long, on behalf of the secretary of state. Since 2001 the length of the network that the Highways England is responsible for has been decreasing owing to a policy of de-trunking, which transfers responsibility for non-core roads to local authorities. For the financial year 2015–16 Highways England's total budget, excluding depreciation, is £2,854m: £979m for maintenance, £1,036m for major schemes and the remainder for traffic management, technology improvements, other programmes and administration costs.

Government support for local authority capital expenditure on roads and other transport infrastructure is provided through grant and credit approvals as part of the Local Transport Plan (LTP). Local authorities bid for resources on the basis of a five-year programme built around delivering integrated transport strategies. As well as covering the structural maintenance of local roads and the construction of major new road schemes, LTP funding also includes smaller-scale safety and traffic management measures with associated improvements to public transport, cyclists and pedestrians.

Total expenditure by the Welsh government in 2014–15 to improve and maintain the motorway and trunk road network in Wales was £271.7m. Total budgeted expenditure for the motorway and trunk road network in 2015–16 is £275.3m.

Since 1 July 1999 all decisions on Scottish transport expenditure have been devolved to the Scottish government. Total expenditure on motorways and trunk roads in Scotland during 2014–15 was £717.5m.

In Northern Ireland total expenditure by the Roads Service on all roads in 2014–15 was £178.4m, with £88m spent on trunk roads and motorways. Planned expenditure for 2015–16 is £97.1m, of which £69.9m is allocated for trunk roads and motorways.

The Transport Act 2000 gave English and Welsh local authorities (outside London) powers to introduce road-user charging or workplace parking levy schemes. The act requires that the net revenue raised is used to improve local transport services and facilities for at least ten years. The aim is to reduce congestion and encourage greater use of alternative modes of transport. Schemes developed by local authorities require government approval. The UK's first toll road, the M6 Toll, opened in December 2003 and runs for 43.5km (27 miles) around Birmingham from junction 3a to junction 11a on the M6.

Charging schemes in London are allowed under the 1999 Greater London Authority Act. The Central London Congestion Charge Scheme began on 17 February 2003 (see also Regional Government).

ROAD LENGTHS 2014
Miles

	England	Wales	Scotland	Great Britain
Major Roads	20,085	2,600	6,384	29,071
Motorways	1,893	88	284	2,265
Minor Roads	165,858	18,387	30,246	214,491
Total	187,838	21,075	36,914	245,827

Source: Department for Transport

BUSES

The majority of bus services outside London are provided on a commercial basis by private operators. Local authorities have powers to subsidise services where needs are not being met by a commercial service.

Since April 2008 men and women who have attained the state pension age and disabled people who qualify under the categories listed in the Transport Act 2000 have been able to travel for free on any local bus across England between 9.30am and 11pm Monday to Friday and all day on weekends and bank holidays. Local authorities recompense operators for the reduced fare revenue. The age of eligibility for concessionary travel currently stands at 60 but will increase in line with the state pension age, which is expected to reach 65 by 2018. A similar scheme operates in Wales and within London, although there is no time restriction. In Scotland, people aged 60 and over and disabled people have been able to travel for free on any local or long-distance bus since April 2006.

In London, Transport for London (TfL) has overall responsibility for setting routes, service standards and fares for the bus network. Almost all routes are competitively tendered to commercial operators.

In Northern Ireland, passenger transport services are provided by Ulsterbus and Metro (formerly Citybus), two wholly owned subsidiaries of the Northern Ireland Transport Holding Company. Along with Northern Ireland Railways, Ulsterbus and Metro operate under the brand name of Translink and are publicly owned. Ulsterbus is responsible for virtually all bus services in Northern Ireland except Belfast city services, which are operated by Metro. People living in Northern Ireland aged 65 and over can travel on buses and trains for free once they have obtained a Senior Citizen SmartPass from Translink.

LOCAL BUS PASSENGER JOURNEYS 2014–15

	No. of journeys (millions)
England	4,700
London	2,390
Scotland	420
Wales	100
Total	5,220

Source: Department for Transport

TAXIS AND PRIVATE HIRE VEHICLES

A taxi is a public transport vehicle with fewer than nine passenger seats, which is licensed to 'ply for hire'. This distinguishes taxis from private hire vehicles (PHVs) which must be booked in advance through an operator. In London, taxis and private hire vehicles are licensed by the Public Carriage Office (PCO), part of TfL. There are currently around 22,500 taxis and 62,800 PHVs licensed in London. Outside London, local authorities are responsible for the licensing of taxis and private hire vehicles operational in their respective administrative areas. At the end of March 2015 there were 76,100 licensed taxis and 166,100 PHVs in England. In 2014 there were 34,519 taxis and PHVs licensed in Scotland.

ROAD TRAFFIC BY VEHICLE TYPE (GREAT BRITAIN) 2014

	Million vehicle miles
All motor vehicles	311,100
Cars	244,500
Light goods vehicles	45,000
Heavy goods vehicles	16,000
Buses and coaches	2,800
Motorcycles	2,800
Pedal cycles	3,200

Source: Department for Transport

ROAD SAFETY

In May 2011, the government published *The Strategic Framework for Road Safety* which identified key indicators at national and local level intended to monitor the progress towards improving safety and decreasing the number of fatalities and seriously injured casualties on Great Britain's roads.

The key findings from the Department for Transport's 2014 annual road casualty report found that the number of people killed in road accidents reported to the police had increased, by 4 per cent, from 1,713 in 2013 to 1,775 in 2014; it is the third lowest figure after 2012 and 2013. The total number of reported casualties in Great Britain (slight injuries, serious injuries and fatalities) also increased by 6 per cent, from 183,670 in 2013 to 194,477 in 2014. Total reported child casualties (0–15 years) increased by 6 per cent in 2014 to 16,727, with the number of children killed or seriously injured also increasing by 5 per cent to 2,082 in 2014.

ROAD ACCIDENT CASUALTIES 2014

	Killed	Serious	Slight	Total
Average for 2005–9	2,816	27,225	216,010	246,050
England	1,472	19,953	153,604	175,029
Wales	103	1,160	6,945	8,208
Scotland	200	1,694	9,346	11,290
Great Britain	1,775	22,807	169,895	194,477

Source: Department for Transport

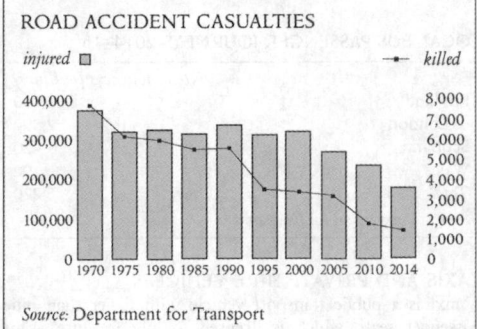

ROAD ACCIDENT CASUALTIES

injured □   killed

Source: Department for Transport

DRIVING LICENCES

It is necessary to hold a valid full licence in order to drive unaccompanied on public roads in the UK. Learner drivers must obtain a provisional driving licence before starting to learn to drive and must then pass theory and practical tests to obtain a full driving licence.

There are separate tests for driving motorcycles, cars, passenger-carrying vehicles (PCVs) and large goods vehicles

(LGVs). Drivers must hold full car entitlement before they can apply for PCV or LGV entitlements.

The Driver and Vehicle Licensing Agency (DVLA) ceased the issue of paper licences in March 2000, but those currently in circulation will remain valid until they expire or the details on them change. The photocard driving licence was introduced to comply with the second EC directive on driving licences. This requires a photograph of the driver to be included on all UK licences issued from July 2001. The photocard licence must be renewed every ten years, with fines of up to £1,000 for failure to do so.

To apply for a first photocard driving licence, individuals are required to either apply online or complete the form *Application for a Driving Licence* (D1) and submit by post.

The minimum age for driving motor cars, light goods vehicles up to 3.5 tonnes and motorcycles is 17 (moped, 16). Since June 1997, drivers who collect six or more penalty points within two years of qualifying lose their licence and are required to take another test. Forms and leaflets are available from post offices and online (W www.gov.uk/ dvlaforms or W www.gov.uk/government/organisations/driver- and-vehicle-licensing-agency).

The DVLA is responsible for issuing driving licences, registering and licensing vehicles, and collecting excise duty in Great Britain. The Driver and Vehicle Agency (DVA), has similar responsibilities in Northern Ireland.

DRIVING LICENCE FEES
As at August 2015

	online fee / postal fee*
Provisional licence	
Car, motorcycle or moped	£34/£43
Bus or lorry	Free
After disqualification until passing re-test	Free
Changing a provisional licence to a full licence	Free
Renewal	
Renewing an expired licence (must be renewed every 10 years)	£14/£17
At age 70 and over	Free
For medical reasons	Free
Bus or lorry driver entitlement	Free
After disqualification	£65
After disqualification for some drink driving offences†	£90
After revocation (under the New Drivers Act)	£50
Replacing a lost, stolen, defaced or destroyed licence	£20/£20
Adding an entitlement to a full licence	Free
Removing expired endorsements	£20
Exchanging	
a paper licence for a photocard licence‡	£20/£20
a full Northern Ireland licence for a full GB licence	Free
a full GB licence for a full EU/EEA or other foreign licence (including Channel Islands and Isle of Man)	Free
a full EU/EEA or other foreign licence (including Channel Islands and Isle of Man) for a full GB licence	£43
Changing	
name or address (existing licence must be surrendered)†	Free
photo	£14/£17

* Not all services are available online; in these instances just the postal fee is shown. Licence fees differ in Northern Ireland (W www.nidirect.gov.uk/the-cost-of-a-driving-licence).
† For an alcohol-related offence where the DVLA need to arrange medical enquiries
‡ If a paper licence is exchanged for a photocard at the same time as name or address details are changed there is no charge

DRIVING TESTS

The Driver and Vehicle Standards Agency (DVSA) is responsible for improving road safety in Great Britain by setting standards for driving and motorcycling and making sure drivers, vehicle operators and MOT garages understand and follow roadworthiness standards. The agency also provides a range of licensing, testing, education and enforcement services.

DRIVING TESTS TAKEN AND PASSED
April 2014–March 2015

	Number Taken	Percentage Passed
Practical Test		
Car	1,532,504	46.9
Motorcycle Module 1	52,005	69.7
Motorcycle Module 2	49,194	70.2
LGV/PCV	63,392	55.5
Driver CPC*	20,709	87.6
Theory Test		
Car	1,680,268	51.0
Motorcycle	62,807	74.1
LGV/PCV		
Multiple choice	49,908	66.4
Hazard perception	44,309	79.1
Driver CPC*	33,393	61.6

LGV = Large goods vehicle; PCV = Passenger-carrying vehicle
* Driver Certificate of Professional Competence – legal requirement for all professional bus, coach and lorry drivers
Source: DVSA

The theory and practical driving tests can be booked online (W www.gov.uk/book-practical-driving-test) or by phone (T 0300-200 1122).

DRIVING TEST FEES (WEEKDAY/EVENING* AND WEEKEND)
As at July 2015

Theory tests	
Car and motorcycle	£25.00
Bus and lorry	
Multiple choice	£28.00
Hazard perception	£12.00
Driver CPC	£24.00
Practical tests	
Car	£62.00/£75.00
Tractor and other specialist vehicles	£62.00/£75.00
Motorcycle	
Module 1 (off-road)	£15.50/£15.50
Module 2 (on-road)	£75.00/£88.50
Lorry and bus	£115.00/£141.00
Driver CPC	£55.00/£63.00
Car and trailer	£115.00/£141.00
Extended tests for disqualified drivers	
Car	£124.00/£150.00
Motorcycle Module 1 (on-road)	£150.00/£177.00

* After 4.30pm

VEHICLE LICENCES

Registration and first licensing of vehicles is through local offices of the DVLA in Swansea. Local facilities for relicensing are available at any post office which deals with vehicle licensing. Applicants will need to take their vehicle registration document (V5C) or, if this is not available, the applicant must complete form V62. Forms are available at post offices and online (W www.gov.uk/dvlaforms)

MOTOR VEHICLES LICENSED (GREAT BRITAIN)
As at 31 March 2015

	Thousands
All cars	29,766
Light goods vehicles	3,508
Motorcycles	1,205
Heavy goods vehicles	473
Buses and coaches	163
Other vehicles*	696
Total	35,811

* Includes rear diggers, lift trucks, rollers, ambulances, Hackney Carriages, three-wheelers and agricultural vehicles
Source: Department for Transport

VEHICLE EXCISE DUTY

Details of the present duties chargeable on motor vehicles are available at post offices and online (W www.gov.uk/government/publications/rates-of-vehicle-tax-v149). The Vehicle Excise and Registration Act 1994 provides *inter alia* that any vehicle kept on a public road but not used on roads is chargeable to excise duty as if it were in use. All non-commercial vehicles constructed before 1 January 1973 are exempt from vehicle excise duty. Any vehicle licensed on or after 31 January 1998, not in use and not kept on public roads must be registered as SORN (Statutory Off Road Notification) to be exempted from vehicle excise duty. From 1 January 2004 the registered keeper of a vehicle remains responsible for taxing a vehicle or making a SORN declaration until that liability is formally transferred to a new keeper.

RATES OF DUTY *from 1 April 2015*

	6 months	12 months
Cars registered before 1 March 2001		
Under 1,549cc	£79.75	£145.00
Over 1,549cc	£126.50	£230.00
Light goods vehicles registered on or after 1 March 2001		
	£123.75	£225.00
Euro 4 light goods vehicles registered between 1 March 2003		
and 31 December 2006	£77.00	£140.00
Euro 5 light goods vehicles registered between 1 January 2009		
and 31 December 2010	£77.00	£140.00
Motorcycles (with or without sidecar)		
Not over 150cc	–	£17.00
151–400cc	–	£38.00
401–600cc	£32.45	£59.00
600cc+	£44.55	£81.00
Tricycles		
Not over 150cc	–	£17.00
All others	£44.55	£81.00

MOT TESTING

Cars, motorcycles, motor caravans, light goods and dual-purpose vehicles more than three years old must be covered by a current MOT test certificate. However, some vehicles (ie minibuses, ambulances and taxis) may require a certificate at one year old. All certificates must be renewed annually. Only MOT testing stations showing a blue sign with three triangles and an official 'MOT: Test: Fees and Appeals' poster may carry out an approved MOT. The MOT testing scheme is administered by the Driver and Vehicle Standards Agency (DVSA) on behalf of the Secretary of State for Transport.

RATES OF DUTY *from 1 April 2015*
All rates of duty can also be paid by direct debit – the 6-month direct debit rate is slightly cheaper than the non-direct debit rate listed below. There is also the option to pay vehicle duty by direct debit monthly installments.

Cars registered on or after 1 March 2001 and first-year* rates

Band	CO_2 Emissions (g/km)	Petrol and Diesel Car				Alternative Fuel Car			
		6 months	12 months			6 months	12 months		
A	Up to 100	–	£0.00			–	£0.00		
B	101–110	–	£20.00			–	£10.00		
C	111–120	–	£30.00			–	£20.00		
D	121–130	£60.50	£110.00			£55.00	£100.00		
E	131–140	£71.50	£130.00			£66.00	£120.00		
F	141–150	£79.75	£145.00			£74.25	£135.00		
G	151–165	£99.00	£180.00			£93.50	£170.00		
H	166–175	£112.75	£205.00	(£295.00)		£107.25	£195.00	(£285.00)	
I	176–185	£123.75	£225.00	(£350.00)		£118.25	£215.00	(£340.00)	
J	186–200	£145.75	£265.00	(£490.00)		£140.25	£255.00	(£480.00)	
K†	201–225	£159.50	£290.00	(£640.00)		£154.00	£280.00	(£630.00)	
L	226–255	£269.50	£490.00	(£870.00)		£264.00	£480.00	(£860.00)	
M	255+	£277.75	£505.00	(£1,100.00)		£272.25	£495.00	(£1,090.00)	

* First-year rates (figures in parentheses) are payable for some vehicles' first tax disc taken out at first registration
† Includes cars that have a CO_2 emission figure over 225g/km but were registered before 23 March 2006

A fee is payable to MOT testing stations. The current maximum fees are:

For cars, private hire and public service vehicles, motor caravans, dual purpose vehicles, ambulances and taxis (all up to eight passenger seats)	£54.85
For motorcycles	£29.65
For motorcycles with sidecar	£37.80
For three-wheeled vehicles (up to 450kg unladen weight)	£37.80
*Private passenger vehicles and ambulances with:	
9–12 passenger seats	£57.30 (£64.00)
13–16 passenger seats	£59.55 (£80.50)
16+ passenger seats	£80.65 (£124.50)
Goods vehicles (3,000–3,500kg)	£58.60

* Figures in parentheses include seatbelt installation check

SHIPPING AND PORTS

Sea trade has always played a central role in Britain's economy. By the 17th century Britain had built up a substantial merchant fleet and by the early 20th century it dominated the world shipping industry. Between 1997 and 2009, the size and tonnage of the UK-registered trading fleet saw substantial growth however between 2009 and 2014 this had begun to slow and decrease. By the end of 2014 the number of ships in the UK-flagged merchant fleet had increased by 20 per cent while gross tonnage had more than quadrupled since 1999. The UK-flagged merchant fleet now constitutes 0.8 per cent of the world merchant fleet in terms of vessels and 1.1 per cent in terms of gross tonnage.

Freight is carried by liner and bulk services, almost all scheduled liner services being containerised. About 95 per cent by weight of Britain's overseas trade is carried by sea; this amounts to 75 per cent of its total value. Passengers and vehicles are carried by roll-on, roll-off ferries, hovercraft, hydrofoils and high-speed catamarans. There were around 43 million ferry passengers in 2013, of whom 22 million travelled internationally.

Lloyd's of London provides the most comprehensive shipping intelligence service in the world. *Lloyd's Shipping Index,* published daily, lists some 25,000 ocean-going vessels and gives the latest known report of each.

PORTS

There are more than 650 ports in Great Britain for which statutory harbour powers have been granted. Over 100 of these are active in cargo trade. The largest ports in terms of freight tonnage in 2014 were Grimsby and Immingham (59 million tonnes), London (44 million tonnes), Tees and Hartlepool (40 million tonnes), Southampton (37 million tonnes), Milford Haven (34 million tonnes), Liverpool (31 million tonnes), Felixstowe (28 million tonnes), Dover (28 million tonnes) and Forth (25 million tonnes). Belfast (17 million tonnes) is the principal freight port in Northern Ireland.

Broadly speaking, ports are owned and operated by private companies, local authorities or self-owning bodies, known as trust ports. The largest operator is Associated British Ports which owns 21 ports. Port traffic results show that 503 million tonnes were handled by UK ports in 2014, remaining stable compared to the previous year's.

MARINE SAFETY

The Maritime and Coastguard Agency (MCA) is an executive agency of the Department for Transport responsible for implementing the government's maritime safety policy in the UK and works to prevent the loss of life on the coast and at sea.

HM Coastguard maintains a 24-hour search and rescue response and coordination capability for the whole of the UK coast and the internationally agreed search and rescue region. HM Coastguard is responsible for mobilising and organising resources in response to people in distress at sea, or at risk of injury or death on the UK's cliffs or shoreline.

The MCA also inspects and surveys ships to ensure that they are meeting UK and international safety rules, provides certification to seafarers, registers vessels and responds to pollution from shipping and offshore installations.

Locations hazardous to shipping in coastal waters are marked by lighthouses and other lights and buoys. The lighthouse authorities are the Corporation of Trinity House (for England, Wales and the Channel Islands), the Northern Lighthouse Board (for Scotland and the Isle of Man), and the Commissioners of Irish Lights (for Northern Ireland and the Republic of Ireland). Trinity House maintains 66 lighthouses, eight light vessels/floats, 450 buoys, 21 beacons, 52 radar beacons, eight DGPS (differential global positioning system) stations* and three AIS (automatic identification system) stations. The Northern Lighthouse Board maintains 206 lighthouses, 165 buoys, 26 beacons, 29 radar beacons, 35 AIS stations, four DGPS stations and one LORAN (long-range navigation) station; and Irish Lights looks after 71 lighthouses, 117 buoys, 24 beacons, and three DGPS stations, with AIS in operation on 37 lighthouses.

Harbour authorities are responsible for pilotage within their harbour areas; and the Ports Act 1991 provides for the transfer of lights and buoys to harbour authorities where these are used mainly for local navigation.

* DGPS is a satellite-based navigation system

UK-OWNED TRADING VESSELS
500 gross tons and over, as at end 2014

Type of vessel	No.	Gross tonnage
Tankers	98	3,684,000
Fully cellular container	100	5,009,000
Dry bulk carriers	74	2,955,000
Ro-Ro (passenger and cargo)	85	1,293,000
Passenger	30	1,642,000
Other general cargo	95	446,000
Specialised carriers	26	1,249,000
All vessels	508	16,278,000

Source: Department for Transport

UK SEA PASSENGER* MOVEMENTS 2013

Type of journey	No. of passenger movements
International	
Ro-Ro Passengers on short sea routes	20,490,000
Passengers on cruises beginning or ending at UK ports*	1,906,000
Passengers on long sea journeys	34,000
Total	22,430,000

* Passengers are included at both departure and arrival if their journeys begin and end at a UK seaport
Source: Department for Transport

UK SHIPPING FORECAST AREAS

Weather bulletins for shipping are broadcast daily on BBC Radio 4 at 00h 48m, 05h 20m, 12h 01m and 17h 54m. All transmissions are broadcast on long wave at 1515m (198kHz) and the 00h 48m and 05h 20m transmissions are also broadcast on FM. The bulletins consist of a gale warning summary, general synopsis, sea-area forecasts and coastal station reports. In addition, gale warnings are broadcast at the first available programme break after receipt. If this does not coincide with a news bulletin, the warning is repeated after the next news bulletin. Shipping forecasts and gale warnings are also available on the Met Office and BBC Weather websites.

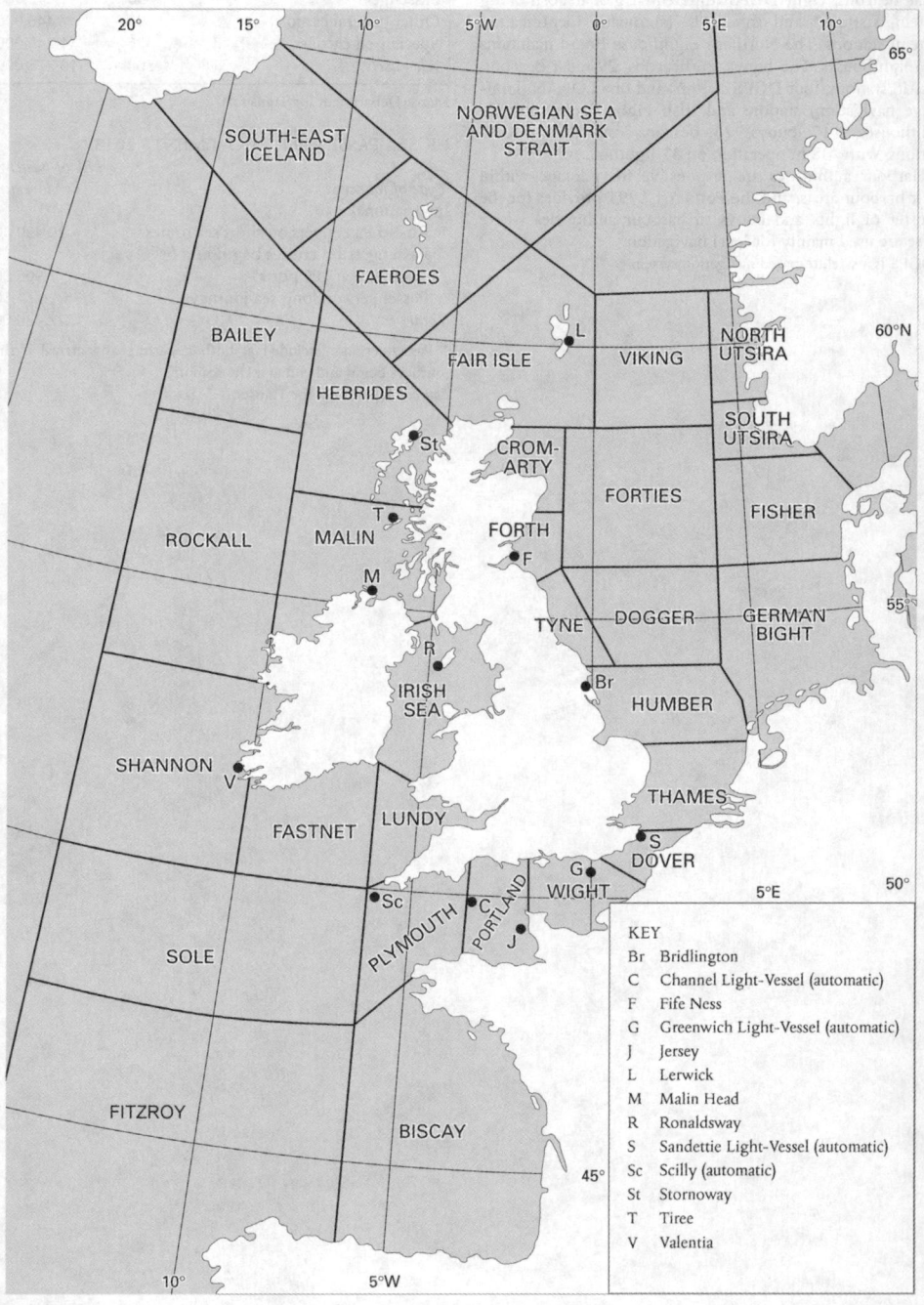

KEY
Br   Bridlington
C   Channel Light-Vessel (automatic)
F   Fife Ness
G   Greenwich Light-Vessel (automatic)
J   Jersey
L   Lerwick
M   Malin Head
R   Ronaldsway
S   Sandettie Light-Vessel (automatic)
Sc   Scilly (automatic)
St   Stornoway
T   Tiree
V   Valentia

RELIGION IN THE UK

The 2011 census in England and Wales included a voluntary question on religion; 92.8 per cent of the population chose to answer the question. Christianity remained the largest religion, despite a decrease of 4 million people from the 2001 census, to 33.2 million adherents, or 59.3 per cent of the population. The second largest religious group were Muslims with 2.7 million people identifying themselves as such, an increase of 1.2 million since 2001. The number of people reporting that they had 'no religion' was 14.1 million, around a quarter of the population. Of those reporting that they had no religion, the majority identified themselves as white (93 per cent) and born in the UK (also 93 per cent); in terms of age, the largest demographic were those aged 20 to 24 (1.4 million or 10 per cent). More than 240,000 people listed 'other religion' on the census, which included, among many others, 176,632 Jedi Knights, 56,620 Pagans and 39,061 Spiritualists. Norwich remained the city with the highest proportion reporting no religion (42.5 per cent), while London was the most diverse region with the largest proportion of people classifying themselves as Buddhist, Hindu, Jewish and Muslim. Knowsley, in Merseyside, was the local authority with the highest proportion of Christians at 80.9 per cent, while Tower Hamlets in London had the highest population of Muslims at 34.5 per cent.

In Northern Ireland, the religion question was phrased differently; 738,033 (41 per cent) identified themselves as Roman Catholic, 752,555 (42 per cent) as 'Protestant and other Christian', 14,859 (0.8 per cent) belonged to an 'other religion' and 183,164 (10 per cent) stated they had no religion.

CENSUS 2011 RESULTS – RELIGION IN ENGLAND, WALES AND SCOTLAND*

	thousands	per cent
Christian	36,093	58.8
Buddhist	261	0.4
Hindu	833	1.4
Jewish	269	0.4
Muslim	2,783	4.5
Sikh	432	0.7
Other religion	256	0.4
All religions	40,927	66.6
No religion	16,038	26.1
Not stated	4,406	7.2
All no religion/not stated	20,444	33.3
TOTAL	61,371	100

* Figures from the 2011 census for Northern Ireland did not contain a full breakdown of each major religion
Source: Census 2011

INTER-CHURCH AND INTER-FAITH COOPERATION

The main umbrella body for the Christian churches in the UK is Churches Together in Britain and Ireland. There are also ecumenical bodies in each of the constituent countries of the UK: Churches Together in England, Action of Churches Together in Scotland, CYTUN (Churches Together in Wales), and the Irish Council of Churches. The Free Churches Group (formerly the Free Churches Council), which is closely associated with Churches Together in England, represents most of the free churches in England and Wales, and the Evangelical Alliance represents evangelical Christians.

The Inter Faith Network for the United Kingdom promotes cooperation between faiths, and the Council of Christians and Jews works to improve relations between the two religions. Churches Together in Britain and Ireland also has a commission on inter-faith relations.

ACTION OF CHURCHES TOGETHER IN SCOTLAND, Inglewood House, Alloa, Clackmannanshire FK10 2HU
T 01259-216980 W www.acts-scotland.org
General Secretary, Revd Matthew Ross

CHURCHES TOGETHER IN BRITAIN AND IRELAND, 39 Ecclestone Square, London SW1V 1BX T 0845-680 6851
E info@ctbi.org.uk W www.ctbi.org.uk
General Secretary, Revd Bob Fyffe

CHURCHES TOGETHER IN ENGLAND, 27 Tavistock Square, London WC1H 9HH T 020-7529 8131
E office@cte.org.uk W www.cte.org.uk
General Secretary, Revd Dr David Cornick

COUNCIL OF CHRISTIANS AND JEWS, Collaboration House, 77–79 Charlotte Street, London W1T 4PW T 020-3515 3003 E cjrelations@ccj.org.uk
W www.ccj.org.uk
Director, Jane Clements

CYTUN (CHURCHES TOGETHER IN WALES), 58 Richmond Road, Cardiff CF24 3UR T 029-2046 4204
E post@cytun.org.uk W www.cytun.org.uk
Chief Executive, Revd Canon Aled Edwards, OBE

EVANGELICAL ALLIANCE, 176 Copenhagen Street, London N1 0ST T 020-7520 3830 E info@eauk.org
W www.eauk.org
General Director, Steve Clifford

FREE CHURCHES GROUP, 27 Tavistock Square, London WC1H 9HH T 020-3651 8334 E info@freechurches.org.uk
W www.freechurches.org.uk
Secretary, vacant

INTERFAITH NETWORK FOR THE UK, 2 Grosvenor Gardens, London SW1W 0DH T 020-7730 0410
W www.interfaith.org.uk
Director, Dr Harriet Crabtree

IRISH COUNCIL OF CHURCHES, Inter-Church Centre, 48 Elmwood Avenue, Belfast BT9 6AZ T 028-9066 3145
E info@irishchurches.org W www.irishchurches.org
Executive Officer, Mervyn McCullagh

RELIGIONS AND BELIEFS

BAHA'I FAITH
Baha'u'llah ('Glory of God'), the founder of the Baha'i faith, was born in Iran in 1817. He was imprisoned in 1852 for advocating the teachings of the Bab ('Gate'), a prophet who was martyred in 1850. Baha'u'llah was persecuted and sent into successive stages of exile, first to Baghdad – where in 1863 he announced that he was the 'promised one' foretold by the Bab – and then to Constantinople, Adrianople and eventually Acre, in present day Israel. He died in 1892 and was succeeded by his son, Abdu'l-Baha, as head of the Baha'i faith, under whose guidance the faith spread to Europe and North America. He was in turn succeeded by Shoghi Effendi, his grandson, who oversaw the establishment of the administrative order and the spread of the faith around the world until his death in 1957. The Universal House

of Justice, an elected international governing council, was formed in 1963 in accordance with Baha'u'llah's teachings.

The Baha'i faith espouses the oneness of humanity and of religion and teaches that there is only one God, whose will has been revealed to mankind by a series of messengers, such as Zoroaster, Abraham, Moses, Buddha, Krishna, Christ, Muhammad, the Bab and Baha'u'llah, who were seen as the founders of separate religions, but whose common purpose was to bring God's message to mankind. The Baha'i faith attributes the differences in teachings between religions to humanity's changing needs. Baha'i teachings include that all races and both sexes are equal and deserving of equal opportunities and treatment, that education is a fundamental right and that extremes of wealth and poverty should be eliminated. In addition, the faith exhorts mankind to establish a world federal system to promote peace and unity.

In an effort to translate these principles into action, Baha'is have initiated an educational process across the world that seeks to raise the capacity of people of all ages and from all backgrounds to contribute towards the betterment of society. There is no clergy; each local community elects a local spiritual assembly to tend to its administrative needs. A national spiritual assembly is elected annually by locally elected delegates, and every five years the national spiritual assemblies meet together to elect the Universal House of Justice, the supreme international governing body of the Baha'i Faith. Worldwide there are over 13,000 local spiritual assemblies and more than 5 million members.

BAHA'I COMMUNITY OF THE UK, 27 Rutland Gate, London SW7 1PD T 020-7584 2566 E nsa@bahai.org.uk W www.bahai.org.uk
Director, Office of Public Affairs, Dr Kishan Manocha

BUDDHISM

Buddhism originated in what is now the Bihar area of northern India in the teachings of Siddhartha Gautama, who became the *Buddha* ('Enlightened One'). In the Thai or Suriyakati calendar the beginning of the Buddhist era is dated from the death of Buddha; the year 2015 is therefore 2558 by the Thai Buddhist reckoning.

Fundamental to Buddhism is the concept of rebirth, whereby each life carries with it the consequences of the conduct of earlier lives (known as the law of *karma)* and this cycle of death and rebirth is broken only when the state of *nirvana* has been reached. Buddhism steers a middle path between belief in personal continuity and the belief that death results in total extinction.

While doctrine does not have a pivotal position in Buddhism, a statement of four 'Noble Truths' is common to all its schools and varieties. These are: suffering is inescapable in even the most fortunate of existences; craving is the root cause of suffering; abandonment of the selfish mindset is the way to end suffering; and bodily and mental discipline, accompanied by the cultivation of wisdom and compassion, provides the spiritual path ('Noble Eightfold Path') to accomplish this. Buddhists deny the idea of a creator and prefer to emphasise the practical aspects of moral and spiritual development.

The schools of Buddhism can be broadly divided into three: *Theravada,* the generally monastic-led tradition practised in Sri Lanka and South East Asia; *Mahayana,* the philosophical and popular traditions of the Far East; and *Esoteric,* the Tantric-derived traditions found in Tibet and Mongolia and, to a lesser extent, China and Japan. The extensive Theravada scriptures are contained in the *Pali Canon,* which dates in its written form from the first century BC. Mahayana and Esoteric schools have Sanskrit-derived translations of these plus many more additional scriptures as well as exegetical material.

In the East the new and full moons and the lunar quarter days were (and to a certain extent, still are) significant in determining the religious calendar. Most private homes contain a shrine where offerings, worship and other spiritual practices (such as meditation, chanting or mantra recitation) take place on a daily basis. Buddhist festivals vary according to local traditions within the different schools and there is little uniformity – even in commemorating the birth, enlightenment and death of the Buddha.

There is no governing authority for Buddhism in the UK. Communities representing all schools of Buddhism operate independently. The Buddhist Society was established in 1924; it runs courses, lectures and meditation groups, and publishes books about Buddhism. The Network of Buddhist Organisations was founded in 1993 to promote fellowship and dialogue between Buddhist organisations and to facilitate cooperation in matters of common interest.

There are estimated to be at least 375 million Buddhists worldwide. Of the 248,000 Buddhists in England and Wales (according to the 2011 census), 72,000 are white British (the majority are converts), 49,000 Chinese, 93,000 'other Asian' and 36,000 are 'other ethnic'.

THE BUDDHIST SOCIETY, 58 Eccleston Square, London SW1V 1PH T 020-7834 5858
E info@thebuddhistsociety.org W www.thebuddhistsociety.org
LONDON BUDDHIST CENTRE, 51 Roman Road, London E2 0HU T 020-8981 1225 E info@lbc.org.uk
W www.lbc.org.uk
Chair, Dharmachari Jnanavaca
THE NETWORK OF BUDDHIST ORGANISATIONS, PO Box 4147, Maidenhead SL60 1DN T 0845-345 8978
E secretary@nbo.org.uk W www.nbo.org.uk
THE OFFICE OF TIBET, Tibet House, 1 Culworth Street, London NW8 7AF T 020-7722 5378 E info@otlondon.org
W www.tibet.org
Representative of HH the Dalai Lama, Chonpel Tsering
SOKA GAKKAI UK, Taplow Court Grand Cultural Centre, Cliveden Road, Taplow, Berkshire SL6 0ER T 01628-773163
W www.sgi-uk.org

CHRISTIANITY

Christianity is a monotheistic faith based on the person and teachings of Jesus Christ, and all Christian denominations claim his authority. Central to its teaching is the concept of God and his son Jesus Christ, who was crucified and resurrected in order to enable mankind to attain salvation.

The Jewish scriptures predicted the coming of a *Messiah,* an 'anointed one', who would bring salvation. To Christians, Jesus of Nazareth, a Jewish rabbi (teacher) who was born in Palestine, was the promised Messiah. Jesus' birth, teachings, crucifixion and subsequent resurrection are recorded in the *Gospels,* which, together with other scriptures that summarise Christian belief, form the *New Testament.* This, together with the Hebrew scriptures – entitled the *Old Testament* by Christians – makes up the Bible, the sacred texts of Christianity.

Christians believe that sin distanced mankind from God, and that Jesus was the son of God, sent to redeem mankind from sin by his death. In addition, many believe that Jesus will return again at some future date, triumph over evil and establish a kingdom on earth, thus inaugurating a new age. The Gospel assures Christians that those who believe in Jesus and obey his teachings will be forgiven their sins and will be resurrected from the dead.

The Apostles were Jesus' first converts and are recognised by Christians as the founders of the Christian community. Early Christianity spread rapidly throughout the eastern provinces of the Roman Empire but was subjected to great persecution until AD 313, when Emperor Constantine's

Edict of Toleration confirmed its right to exist. Christianity was established as the religion of the Roman Empire in AD 381.

Between AD 325 and 787 there were seven Oecumenical Councils at which bishops from the entire Christian world assembled to resolve various doctrinal disputes. The estrangement between East and West began after Constantine moved the centre of the Roman Empire from Rome to Constantinople, and it grew after the division of the Roman Empire into eastern and western halves. Linguistic and cultural differences between Greek East and Latin West served to encourage separate ecclesiastical developments which became pronounced in the tenth and early 11th centuries. Administration of the church was divided between five ancient patriarchates: Rome and all the West, Constantinople (the imperial city – the 'New Rome'), Jerusalem and all of Palestine, Antioch and all the East, and Alexandria and all of Africa. Of these, only Rome was in the Latin West and after the schism in 1054, Rome developed a structure of authority centralised on the Papacy, while the Orthodox East maintained the style of localised administration. Papal authority over the doctrine and jurisdiction of the church in Western Europe was unrivalled after the split with the Eastern Orthodox Church until the Protestant Reformation in the 16th century.

Christian practices vary widely between different Christian churches, but prayer, charity and giving (for the maintenance of the church buildings, for the work of the church, and to those in need) are common to all. In addition, certain days of observance, ie the Sabbath, Easter and Christmas, are celebrated by most Christians. The Orthodox, Roman Catholic and Anglican churches celebrate many more days of observance, based on saints and significant events in the life of Jesus. The belief in sacraments, physical signs believed to have been ordained by Jesus Christ to symbolise and convey spiritual gifts, varies greatly between Christian denominations; baptism and the Eucharist are practised by most Christians. Baptism, symbolising repentance and faith in Jesus, is an act marking entry into the Christian community; the Eucharist, the ritual re-enactment of the Last Supper, Jesus' final meal with his disciples, is also practised by most denominations. Other sacraments, such as anointing the sick, the laying on of hands to symbolise the passing on of the office of priesthood or to heal the sick, and speaking in tongues, where it is believed that the person is possessed by the Holy Spirit, are less common. In denominations where infant baptism is practised, confirmation (where the person confirms the commitments made on their behalf in infancy) is common. Matrimony and the ordination of priests are also widely believed to be sacraments. Many Protestants regard only baptism and the Eucharist to be sacraments; the Quakers and the Salvation Army reject the use of sacraments.

See Churches for contact details of the Church of England, the Roman Catholic Church and other Christian churches in the UK.

HINDUISM

Hinduism has no historical founder but had become highly developed in India by c.2500 BC. Its adherents originally called themselves Aryans; Muslim invaders first called the Aryans 'Hindus' (derived from 'Sindhu', the name of the river Indus) in the eighth century.

Most Hindus hold that satya (truthfulness), honesty, sincerity and devotion to God are essential for good living. They believe in one supreme spirit (Brahman), and in the transmigration of atman (the soul). Most Hindus accept the doctrine of karma (consequences of actions), the concept of samsara (successive lives) and the possibility of all atmans achieving moksha (liberation from samsara) through jnana

(knowledge), yoga (meditation), karma (work or action) and bhakti (devotion).

Most Hindus offer worship to murtis (images of deities) representing different incarnations or aspects of Brahman, and follow their dharma (religious and social duty) according to the traditions of their varna (social class), ashrama (stage in life), jaiti (caste) and kula (family).

Hinduism's sacred texts are divided into shruti ('that which is heard'), including the Vedas, and smriti ('that which is remembered'), including the Ramayana, the Mahabharata, the Puranas (ancient myths), and the sacred law books. Most Hindus recognise the authority of the Vedas, the oldest holy books, and accept the philosophical teachings of the Upanishads, the Vedanta Sutras and the Bhagavad-Gita.

Hindus believe Brahman to be omniscient, omnipotent, limitless and all-pervading. Brahman is usually worshipped in its deity form. Brahma, Vishnu and Shiva are the most important deities or aspects of Brahman worshipped by Hindus; their respective consorts are Saraswati, Lakshmi and Durga or Parvati, also known as Shakti. There are believed to have been ten avatars (incarnations) of Vishnu, of whom the most important are Rama and Krishna. Other popular gods are Ganesha, Hanuman and Subrahmanyam. All Hindu gods are seen as aspects of the supreme spirit (Brahman), not as competing deities.

Orthodox Hindus revere all gods and goddesses equally, but there are many denominations, including the Hare-Krishna movement (ISKCon), the Arya Samaj and the Swaminarayan Hindu mission, in which worship is concentrated on one deity. The guru (spiritual teacher) is seen as the source of spiritual guidance.

Hinduism does not have a centrally trained and ordained priesthood. The pronouncements of the shankaracharyas (heads of monasteries) of Shringeri, Puri, Dwarka and Badrinath are heeded by the orthodox but may be ignored by the various sects.

The commonest form of worship is puja, in which water, flowers, food, fruit, incense and light are offered to the deity. Puja may be done either in a home shrine or a mandir (temple). Many British Hindus celebrate samskars (purification rites), to name a baby, for the sacred thread (an initiation ceremony), marriage and cremation.

The largest communities of Hindus in Britain are in Leicester, London, Birmingham and Bradford, and developed as a result of immigration from India, eastern Africa and Sri Lanka.

There are an estimated 800 million Hindus worldwide; there are around 817,000 adherents, according to the 2011 census in England and Wales, and around 135 temples in the UK.

ARYA SAMAJ LONDON, 69 Argyle Road, London W13 0LY
T 020-8991 1732 E aryasamajlondon@yahoo.co.uk
W aryasamajlondon.org.uk
General Secretary, Amrit Lal Bhardwaj

BHARATIYA VIDYA BHAVAN, 4A Castletown Road, London W14 9HE T 020-7381 3086 E info@bhavan.net
W www.bhavan.net
Executive Director, Dr M. N. Nandakumara

INTERNATIONAL SOCIETY FOR KRISHNA CONSCIOUSNESS (ISKCON), Bhaktivedanta Manor, Dharam Marg, Hilfield Lane, Aldenham, Watford, Herts WD25 8EZ T 01923-851000 E info@krishnatemple.com
W www.krishnatemple.com
Temple President, Sruti Dharma Das

NATIONAL COUNCIL OF HINDU TEMPLES (UK), c/o Shree Sanatan Mandir, 84 Weymouth Street, Leicester LE4 6FQ T 0776-317 8628 E info@nchtuk.org
W www.nchtuk.org
General Secretary, Satish K. Sharma

SWAMINARAYAN HINDU MISSION (SHRI
SWAMINARAYAN MANDIR), 105–119 Brentfield Road,
London NW10 8LD T 020-8965 2651
E info@londonmandir.baps.org W www.mandir.org

HUMANISM

Humanism traces its roots back to ancient times, with
Chinese, Greek, Indian and Roman philosophers expressing
Humanist ideas some 2,500 years ago. Confucius, the
Chinese philosopher who lived c.500 BC, believed that
religious observances should be replaced with moral values
as the basis of social and political order and that 'the true
way' is based on reason and humanity. He also stressed the
importance of benevolence and respect for others, and
believed that the individual situation should be considered
rather than the global application of traditional rules.

Humanists believe that there is no God or other
supernatural being, that humans have only one life
(Humanists do not believe in an afterlife or reincarnation)
and that humans can live ethical and fulfilling lives without
religious beliefs through a moral code derived from a
shared history, personal experience and thought. There are
no sacred Humanist texts. Particular emphasis is placed on
science as the only reliable source of knowledge of the
universe. Many Humanists recognise a need for ceremonies
to mark important occasions in life and the British Humanist
Association has a network of celebrants who are trained and
accredited to conduct baby namings, weddings and funerals.
The British Humanist Association's campaigns for a secular
state (a state based on freedom of religious or non-religious
belief with no privileges for any particular set of beliefs)
are based on equality and human rights. The association
also campaigns for inclusive schools that meet the needs
of all parents and pupils, regardless of their religious or
non-religious beliefs. According to figures from the 2011
census, there are just over 15,000 Humanists in England and
Wales.

BRITISH HUMANIST ASSOCIATION, 39 Moreland Street,
London EC1V 8BB T 020-7324 3060 E info@humanism.org.uk
W www.humanism.org.uk
Chief Executive, Andrew Copson

ISLAM

Islam (which means 'peace arising from submission to the
will of Allah' in Arabic) is a monotheistic religion which was
taught in Arabia by the Prophet Muhammad, who was born
in Mecca (Al-Makkah) in 570 AD. Islam spread to Egypt,
north Africa, Spain and the borders of China in the century
following the Prophet's death, and is now the predominant
religion in Indonesia, the near and Middle East, northern and
parts of western Africa, Pakistan, Bangladesh, Malaysia and
some of the former Soviet republics. There are also large
Muslim communities in other countries.

For Muslims (adherents of Islam), there is one God *(Allah)*,
who holds absolute power. Muslims believe that Allah's
commands were revealed to mankind through the prophets,
who include Abraham, Moses and Jesus, but that Allah's
message was gradually corrupted until revealed finally and in
perfect form to Muhammad through the angel *Jibril* (Gabriel)
over a period of 23 years. This last, incorruptible message is
said to have been recorded in the *Qur'an* (Koran), which
contains 114 divisions called *surahs,* each made up of *ayahs* of
various lengths, and is held to be the essence of all previous
scriptures. The *Ahadith* are the records of the Prophet
Muhammad's deeds and sayings (the *Sunnah*) as practised
and recounted by his immediate followers. A culture and a
system of law and theology gradually developed to form
a distinctive Islamic civilisation. Islam makes no distinction
between sacred and worldly affairs and provides rules for

every aspect of human life. The *Shariah* is the sacred law of
Islam based primarily upon prescriptions derived from the
Qur'an and the *Sunnah* of the Prophet.

The 'five pillars of Islam' are *shahadah* (a declaration of
faith in the oneness and supremacy of Allah and the
messengership of Muhammad); *salat* (formal prayer, to be
performed five times a day facing the *Ka'bah* (the most sacred
shrine in the holy city of Mecca)); *zakat* (welfare due, paid
annually on all savings at the rate of 2.5 per cent); *sawm*
(fasting during the month of Ramadan from dawn until
sunset); and *hajj* (pilgrimage to Mecca made once in a lifetime
if the believer is financially and physically able). Some
Muslims would add *jihad* as the sixth pillar (striving for the
cause of good and resistance to evil).

Two main groups developed among Muslims. *Sunni*
Muslims accept the legitimacy of Muhammad's first four
caliphs (successors as head of the Muslim community) and
of the authority of the Muslim community as a whole. About
90 per cent of Muslims are Sunni Muslims.

Shi'ites recognise only Muhammad's son-in-law Ali as his
rightful successor and the *Imams* (descendants of Ali, not to
be confused with *imams,* who are prayer leaders or religious
teachers) as the principal legitimate religious authority. The
largest group within Shi'ism is *Twelver Shi'ism*, which has
been the official school of law and theology in Iran since the
16th century; other subsects include the *Ismailis,* the *Druze*
and the *Alawis,* the latter two differing considerably from
the main body of Muslims. The *Ibadis* of Oman are neither
Sunni nor Shia, deriving from the strictly observant *Khariji*
(Seceders). There is no organised priesthood, but learned
men such as imams, *ulama,* and *ayatollahs* are accorded great
respect. The *Sufis* are the mystics of Islam. Mosques are
centres for worship and teaching and also for social and
welfare activities.

Islam was first recorded in western Europe in the eighth
century AD when 800 years of Muslim rule began in Spain.
Later, Islam spread to eastern Europe. More recently, Muslims
came to Europe from Africa, the Middle East and Asia in the
late 19th century. Both the Sunni and Shia traditions are
represented in Britain, but the majority of Muslims in Britain
adhere to Sunni Islam. Efforts to establish a representative
national body for Muslims in Britain resulted in the
founding, in 1997, of the Muslim Council of Britain. In
addition, there are many other Muslim organisations in the
UK. There are around 1.6 billion Muslims worldwide, with
around 2.8 million adherents in England, Wales and Scotland
and about 1,500 mosques in the UK.

ISLAMIC CULTURAL CENTRE – THE LONDON
CENTRAL MOSQUE, 146 Park Road, London NW8 7RG
T 020-7724 3363 E info@iccuk.org W www.iccuk.org
Director-General, Dr Ahmad Al-Dubayan
MUSLIM COUNCIL OF BRITAIN, PO Box 57330,
London E1 2WJ T 0845-262 6786 E admin@mcb.org.uk
W www.mcb.org.uk
Secretary-General, Dr Shuja Shafi
MUSLIM LAW (SHARIAH) COUNCIL UK, PO Box 851,
Wembley, Middx HA9 1BE T 0771-265 4880
E msraza@shariahcouncil.org W www.shariahcouncil.org
Chair, Dr Sheikh Gamal Solaiman Manna
MUSLIM WORLD LEAGUE LONDON, 46 Goodge Street,
London W1T 4LU T 020-7636 7568 E infor@mwllo.org.uk
W www.mwllo.org.uk
Director, Dr Ahmed Makhdoom

JAINISM

Jainism traces its history to Vardhamana Jnatriputra, known
as *Tirthankara Mahavira* ('the Great Hero') whose traditional
dates were 599–527 BC. Jains believe he was the last of the
current era in a series of 24 *Jinas* (those who overcome all

passions and desires) or *Tirthankaras* (those who show a way across the ocean of life) stretching back to remote antiquity. Born to a noble family in north-eastern India (presently the state of Bihar), he renounced the world for the life of a wandering ascetic and after 12 years of austerity and meditation he attained enlightenment. He then preached his message until, at the age of 72, he left the mortal world and achieved total liberation *(moksha)* from the cycle of death and rebirth.

Jains declare that the Hindu rituals of transferring merit are not acceptable as each living being is responsible for its own actions. They recognise some of the minor deities of the Hindu pantheon, but the supreme objects of worship are the Tirthankaras. The pious Jain does not ask favours from the Tirthankaras, but seeks to emulate their example in his or her own life.

Jains believe that the universe is eternal and self-subsisting, that there is no omnipotent creator God ruling it and the destiny of the individual is in his or her own hands. *Karma,* the fruit of past actions, is believed to determine the place of every living being and rebirth may be in the heavens, on earth as a human, an animal or other lower being, or in the hells. The ultimate goal of existence for Jains is *moksha,* a state of perfect knowledge and tranquillity for each individual soul, which can be achieved only by gaining enlightenment.

The Jainist path to liberation is defined by the three jewels: *Samyak Darshan* (right perception), *Samyak Jnana* (right knowledge) and *Samyak Charitra* (right conduct). Of the five fundamental precepts of the Jains, *Ahimsa* (non-injury to any form of being, in any mode: thought, speech or action) is the first and foremost, and was popularised by Gandhi as *Ahimsa paramo dharma* (non-violence is the supreme religion).

The largest population of Jains can be found in India but there are approximately 30,000 Jains in Britain, with sizeable communities in North America, East Africa, Australia and smaller groups in many other countries.

INSTITUTE OF JAINOLOGY, Unit 18, Silicon Business Centre, 28 Wadsworth Road, Perivale, Greenford, Middx UB6 7JZ **T** 020-8997 2300 **E** info@jainology.org **W** www.jainology.org
Deputy Chair, Dr Harshad Sanghrajka

JUDAISM

Judaism is the oldest monotheistic faith. The primary text of Judaism is the Hebrew bible or *Tanakh,* which records how the descendants of Abraham were led by Moses out of their slavery in Egypt to Mount Sinai where God's law *(Torah)* was revealed to them as the chosen people. The *Talmud,* which consists of commentaries on the *Mishnah* (the first text of rabbinical Judaism), is also held to be authoritative, and may be divided into two main categories: the *halakah* (dealing with legal and ritual matters) and the *aggadah* (dealing with theological and ethical matters not directly concerned with the regulation of conduct). The *midrash* comprises rabbinic writings containing biblical interpretations in the spirit of the aggadah. The halakah has become a source of division: orthodox Jews regard Jewish law as derived from God and therefore unalterable; progressive Jews seek to interpret it in the light of contemporary considerations; and conservative Jews aim to maintain most of the traditional rituals but to allow changes in accordance with tradition. Reconstructionist Judaism, a 20th-century movement, regards Judaism as a culture rather than a theological system and accepts all forms of Jewish practice.

The family is the basic unit of Jewish ritual, with the synagogue playing an important role as the centre for public worship and religious study. A synagogue is led by a group of laymen who are elected to office. The Rabbi is primarily a teacher and spiritual guide. The *Sabbath* is the central religious observance. Most British Jews are descendants of either the *Ashkenazim* of central and eastern Europe or the *Sephardim* of Spain, Portugal and the Middle East.

The Chief Rabbi of the United Hebrew Congregations of the Commonwealth is appointed by a Chief Rabbinate Conference, and is the rabbinical authority of the mainstream Orthodox sector of the Ashkenazi Jewish community, the largest body of which is the United Synagogue. His formal ecclesiastical authority is not recognised by the Reform Synagogues of Great Britain (the largest progressive group), the Union of Liberal and Progressive Synagogues, the Spanish and Portuguese Jews' Congregation or the Assembly of Masorti Synagogues. He is, however, generally recognised both outside the Jewish community and within it as the public religious representative of the totality of British Jewry. The Chief Rabbi is President of the London *Beth Din* (Court of Judgment), a rabbinic court. The *Dayanim* (Judges) adjudicate in disputes or on matters of Jewish law and tradition; they also oversee dietary law administration, marriage, divorce and issues of personal status.

The Board of Deputies of British Jews, established in 1760, is the representative body of British Jewry. The basis of representation is through the election of deputies by synagogues and communal organisations. It protects and promotes the interests of British Jewry, acts as the central voice of the community and seeks to counter anti-Jewish discrimination and anti-Semitic activities.

There are approximately 13.9 million Jews worldwide; in the UK there are an estimated 290,000 adherents and over 400 synagogues.

OFFICE OF THE CHIEF RABBI, 305 Ballards Lane, London N12 8GB **T** 020-8343 6301 **E** info@chiefrabbi.org **W** www.chiefrabbi.org
Chief Rabbi, Ephraim Mirvis
BETH DIN (COURT OF THE CHIEF RABBI), 305 Ballards Lane, London N12 8GB **T** 020-8343 6270 **E** info@bethdin.org.uk **W** www.theus.org.uk
Registrar, David Frei
Dayanim, Yonason Abraham; Menachem Gelley *(Rosh Beth Din);* Ivan Binstock; Shmuel Simons
MASORTI JUDAISM, Alexander House, 3 Shakespeare Road, London N3 1XE **T** 020-8349 6650 **E** enquiries@masorti.org.uk **W** www.masorti.org.uk
Executive Director, Matt Plen
BOARD OF DEPUTIES OF BRITISH JEWS, 37 Kentish Town, London NW1 8NX **T** 020-7543 5400 **E** info@bod.org.uk **W** www.bod.org.uk
Chief Executive, Gillian Merron
FEDERATION OF SYNAGOGUES, 65 Watford Way, London NW4 3AQ **T** 020-8202 2263 **E** info@federationofsynagogues.com **W** www.federationofsynagogues.com
Chief Executive, Rabbi Ari Lazarus
LIBERAL JUDAISM, The Montagu Centre, 21 Maple Street, London W1T 4BE **T** 020-7580 1663 **W** www.liberaljudaism.org
Chief Executive, Rabbi Danny Rich
THE MOVEMENT FOR REFORM JUDAISM, The Sternberg Centre for Judaism, 80 East End Road, London N3 2SY **T** 020-8349 5640 **E** admin@reformjudaism.org.uk **W** www.reformjudaism.org.uk
Senior Rabbi, Laura Janner-Klausner
SPANISH AND PORTUGUESE JEWS' CONGREGATION, 2 Ashworth Road, London W9 1JY **T** 020-7289 2573 **E** admin@spsyn.org.uk **W** www.sandp.org.uk
Adminstrator, Alison Rosen
UNION OF ORTHODOX HEBREW CONGREGATIONS, 140 Stamford Hill, London N16 6QT **T** 020-8802 6226
Executive Coordinator, Chanoch Kesselman

UNITED SYNAGOGUE HEAD OFFICE, Adler House,
735 High Road, London N12 0US T 020-8343 8989
W www.theus.org.uk
Chief Executive, Dr Stephen Wilson

PAGANISM

Paganism draws on the ideas of the Celtic people of pre-Roman Europe and is closely linked to Druidism. The first historical record of Druidry comes from classical Greek and Roman writers of the third century BC, who noted the existence of Druids among a people called the Keltoi who inhabited central and southern Europe. The word druid may derive from the Indo-European 'dreo-vid', meaning 'one who knows the truth'. In practice it was probably understood to mean something like 'wise-one' or 'philosopher-priest'.

Paganism is a pantheistic nature-worshipping religion which incorporates beliefs and ritual practices from ancient times. Pagans place much emphasis on the natural world and the ongoing cycle of life and death is central to their beliefs. Most Pagans believe that they are part of nature and not separate from, or superior to it, and seek to live in a way that minimises harm to the natural environment (the word Pagan derives from the Latin *Paganus,* meaning 'rural'). Paganism strongly emphasises the equality of the sexes, with women playing a prominent role in the modern Pagan movement and goddess worship featuring in most ceremonies. Paganism cannot be defined by any principal beliefs because it is shaped by each individual's experiences.

The Pagan Federation was founded in 1971 to provide information on Paganism, campaigns on issues which affect Paganism and provides support to members of the Pagan community. Within the UK the Pagan Federation is divided into 13 districts each with a district manager, regional and local coordinators. Local meetings are called 'moots' and take place in private homes, pubs or coffee bars. The Pagan Federation publishes a quarterly journal, *Pagan Dawn,* formerly *The Wiccan* (founded in 1968). The federation also publishes other material, arranges members-only and public events and maintains personal contact by letter with individual members and the wider Pagan community. Regional gatherings and conferences are held throughout the year.

THE PAGAN FEDERATION, BM Box 7097, London
WC1N 3XX E info@paganfederation.co.uk
W www.paganfed.org
President, Mike Stygal

SIKHISM

The Sikh religion dates from the birth of Guru Nanak in the Punjab in 1469. 'Guru' means teacher but in Sikh tradition has come to represent the divine presence of God giving inner spiritual guidance. Nanak's role as the human vessel of the divine guru was passed on to nine successors, the last of whom (Guru Gobind Singh) died in 1708. The immortal guru is now held to reside in the sacred scripture, *Guru Granth Sahib,* and so to be present in all Sikh gatherings.

Guru Nanak taught that there is one God and that different religions are like different roads leading to the same destination. He condemned religious conflict, ritualism and caste prejudices. The fifth Guru, Guru Arjan Dev, largely compiled the Sikh Holy scripture, a collection of hymns *(gurbani)* known as the *Adi Granth.* It includes the writings of the first five gurus and the ninth guru, and selected writings of Hindu and Muslim saints whose views are in accord with the gurus' teachings. Guru Arjan Dev also built the Golden Temple at Amritsar, the centre of Sikhism. The tenth guru, Guru Gobind Singh, passed on the guruship to the sacred scripture, Guru Granth Sahib, and founded the *Khalsa,* an order intended to fight against tyranny and injustice. Male initiates to the order added 'Singh' to their given names and

women added 'Kaur'. Guru Gobind Singh also made the wearing of five symbols obligatory: *kaccha* (a special undergarment), *kara* (a steel bangle), *kirpan* (a small sword), *kesh* (long unshorn hair, and consequently the wearing of a turban) and *kangha* (a comb). These practices are still compulsory for those Sikhs who are initiated into the Khalsa (the *Amritdharis*). Those who do not seek initiation are known as *Sehajdharis.*

There are no professional priests in Sikhism; anyone with a reasonable proficiency in the Punjabi language can conduct a service. Worship can be offered individually or communally, and in a private house or a *gurdwara* (temple). Sikhs are forbidden to eat meat prepared by ritual slaughter; they are also asked to abstain from smoking, alcohol and other intoxicants. Such abstention is compulsory for the Amritdharis.

There are about 24 million Sikhs worldwide and, according to the 2011 census, there are 432,000 adherents in England, Wales and Scotland. Every gurdwara manages its own affairs; there is no central body in the UK. The Sikh Missionary Society provides an information service.

SIKH MISSIONARY SOCIETY UK, 10 Featherstone Road,
Southall, Middx UB2 5AA T 020-8574 1902
E info@sikhmissionarysociety.org
W www.sikhmissionarysociety.org
Hon. General Secretary, Bahadur Singh

ZOROASTRIANISM

Zoroastrians are followers of the Iranian prophet Spitaman Zarathushtra (or Zoroaster in its hellenised form) who lived *c.*1200–1500 BC. Zoroastrians were persecuted in Iran following the Arab invasion of Persia in the seventh century AD and a group (who are known as Parsis) migrated to India in the ninth century AD to avoid harassment and persecution. Zarathushtra's words are recorded in 17 hymns called the *Gathas,* which, together with other scriptures, form the *Avesta.*

Zoroastrianism teaches that there is one God, *Ahura Mazda* ('Wise Lord'), and that all creation stems ultimately from God; the Gathas teach that human beings have free will, are responsible for their own actions and can choose between good and evil. It is believed that choosing *Asha* (truth or righteousness), with the aid of *Vohu Manah* (good mind), leads to happiness for the individual and society, whereas choosing evil leads to unhappiness and conflict. The *Gathas* also encourage hard work, good deeds and charitable acts. Zoroastrians believe that after death the immortal soul is judged by God, and is then sent to paradise or hell, where it will stay until the end of time to be resurrected for the final judgment.

In Zoroastrian places of worship, an urn containing fire is the central feature; the fire symbolises purity, light and truth and is a visible symbol of the *Fravashi* or *Farohar* (spirit), the presence of Ahura Mazda in every human being. Zoroastrians respect nature and much importance is attached to cultivating land and protecting air, earth and water.

The Zoroastrian Trust Funds of Europe is the main body for Zoroastrians in the UK. Founded in 1861 as the Religious Funds of the Zoroastrians of Europe, it disseminates information on the Zoroastrian faith, provides a place of worship and maintains separate burial grounds for Zoroastrians. It also holds religious and social functions and provides assistance to Zoroastrians as considered necessary, including the provision of loans and grants to students of Zoroastrianism, and participates in inter-faith educational activities.

There are approximately 150,000 Zoroastrians worldwide, of which around 4,000 reside in England and Wales, mainly in London and the South East.

ZOROASTRIAN TRUST FUNDS OF EUROPE, Zoroastrian
Centre, 440 Alexandra Avenue, Harrow, Middx HA2 9TL
T 020-8866 0765 E secretary@ztfe.com W www.ztfe.com
President, Malcolm Deboo

CHURCHES

There are two established (ie state) churches in the UK: the Church of England and the Church of Scotland. There are no established churches in Wales or Northern Ireland, though the Church in Wales, the Scottish Episcopal Church and the Church of Ireland are members of the Anglican Communion.

CHURCH OF ENGLAND

The Church of England is divided into the two provinces of Canterbury and York, each under an archbishop. The two provinces are subdivided into 42 dioceses, the newest of which came into existence on 20 April 2014. The new diocese is known as West Yorkshire and the Dales – officially entitled the Diocese of Leeds – and was formed by the amalgamation of the former dioceses of Bradford, Ripon and Leeds and Wakefield.

Legislative provision for the Church of England is made by the General Synod, established in 1970. It also discusses and expresses opinion on any other matter of religious or public interest. The General Synod has 467 members in total, divided between three houses: the House of Bishops, the House of Clergy and the House of Laity. It is presided over jointly by the Archbishops of Canterbury and York and normally meets twice a year. The synod has the power, delegated by parliament, to frame statute law (known as a 'measure') on any matter concerning the Church of England. A measure must be laid before both houses of parliament, who may accept or reject it but cannot amend it. Once accepted the measure is submitted for royal assent and then has the full force of law. In addition to the General Synod, there are synods at diocesan level. The entire General Synod is re-elected once every five years. The tenth General Synod was inaugurated by the Queen on 23 November 2015.

The Archbishops' Council was established in January 1999. Its creation was the result of changes to the Church of England's national structure proposed in 1995 and subsequently approved by the synod and parliament. The council's purpose, set out in the National Institutions Measure 1998, is 'to coordinate, promote and further the work and mission of the Church of England'. It reports to the General Synod. The Archbishops' Council comprises the Archbishops of Canterbury and York, ex officio, the prolocutors elected by the convocations of Canterbury and York, the chair and vice-chair of the House of Laity, two bishops, two clergy and two lay persons elected by their respective houses of the General Synod, the Church Estates Commissioner, and up to six persons appointed jointly by the two archbishops.

There are also a number of national boards, councils and other bodies working on matters such as social responsibility, mission, Christian unity and education, which report to the General Synod through the Archbishops' Council.

GENERAL SYNOD OF THE CHURCH OF ENGLAND/ ARCHBISHOPS' COUNCIL, Church House, Great Smith Street, London SW1P 3NZ T 020-7898 1000
Secretary-General, William Fittall

THE ORDINATION AND CONSECRATION OF WOMEN
The canon making it possible for women to be ordained to the priesthood was promulgated in the General Synod in February 1994 and the first 32 women priests were ordained on 12 March 1994.

On 14 July 2014 the General Synod approved the Bishops and Priests (Consecration and Ordination of Women) Measure which makes provision for the consecration of women as bishops and for the continuation of provision for the ordination of women. The Revd Elizabeth Lane was consecrated as the first female bishop on 26 January 2015 when she became Bishop Suffragan of Stockport in the diocese of Chester. The first female diocesan bishop, Rachel Treweek, was consecrated as the 41st Bishop of Gloucester on 22 July 2015.

PORVOO DECLARATION
The Porvoo Declaration was approved by the General Synod of the Church of England in July 1995. Churches that approve the declaration regard baptised members of each other's churches as members of their own, and allow free interchange of episcopally ordained ministers within the rules of each church.

MEMBERSHIP AND MINISTRY
In 2013, 132,990 people were baptised, 49,690 people were married in parish churches, the Church of England had an electoral roll membership of 1.2 million, and each week an average 1.01 million people attended services. As at December 2013 there were 15,799 churches and places of worship. As at December 2012* there were 358 senior clergy (including bishops, archdeacons and cathedral clergy); 7,195 full-time parochial stipendiary clergy; 245 full-time non-parochial stipendiary clergy; 3,148 self-supporting ministers; 1,520 chaplains and other ministers; 262 lay workers and Church Army evangelists; 6,623 licensed readers and 2,777 readers with permission to officiate and active emeriti; and approximately 5,700 active retired ordained clergy.

	Full-time Equivalent Diocesan Clergy 2012*		Electoral Roll Membership
	Male	Female	2013
Bath and Wells	144	53	32,400
Birmingham	115	48	15,100
Blackburn	148	20	29,300
†Bradford	69	18	9,900
Bristol	86	19	14,300
Canterbury	105	27	18,900
Carlisle	98	26	19,400
Chelmsford	265	89	43,400
Chester	168	56	38,600
Chichester	253	22	48,400
Coventry	99	18	15,300
Derby	104	45	15,900
Durham	132	33	20,500
Ely	81	46	17,900
Europe	110	14	9,600
Exeter	168	38	28,400
Gloucester	93	32	22,200
Guildford	136	34	29,500
Hereford	57	33	15,600
Leicester	95	41	16,000
Lichfield	241	51	37,600
Lincoln	112	35	22,500
Liverpool	150	56	23,500
London	450	80	68,300
Manchester	158	66	29,200

	Full-time Equivalent Diocesan Clergy 2012*		Electoral Roll Membership
	Male	Female	2013
Newcastle	88	28	15,200
Norwich	145	37	17,900
Oxford	293	98	51,900
Peterborough	100	37	18,500
Portsmouth	76	22	16,200
†Ripon and Leeds	81	40	15,000
Rochester	158	42	25,500
St Albans	168	71	32,500
St Edmundsbury and Ipswich	94	39	20,700
Salisbury	142	50	36,300
Sheffield	107	38	15,300
Sodor and Man	13	2	2,200
Southwark	264	82	46,700
Southwell and Nottingham	92	43	16,900
Truro	73	21	15,200
†Wakefield	100	35	16,100
Winchester	137	33	36,700
Worcester	86	27	15,500
York	163	36	29,100
‡Total	6,017	1,781	1,085,600

* 2013 figures for the ministry were not available from the Church of England at the time of going to press

† Now part of the new Diocese of Yorkshire and the Dales (also known as the Diocese of Leeds)

‡ Figures are rounded to the nearest 10 and may not add up as a result.

STIPENDS

	2015–16
Archbishop of Canterbury	£77,810
Archbishop of York	£66,680
Bishop of London	£61,120*
Other diocesan bishops	£42,240*
Suffragan bishops	£34,460*
Assistant bishops (full-time)	£33,350*
Deans	£34,460*
Archdeacons	£33,670*
Residentiary canons	£26,660†
Incumbents and clergy of similar status	£24,690†

* For those appointed on or after 1 April 2004; transitional arrangements are in place for those appointed prior to this date

† National stipend benchmark: adjusted regionally to reflect variations in the cost of living

CANTERBURY
105TH ARCHBISHOP AND PRIMATE OF ALL ENGLAND
Most Revd and Rt. Hon. Justin Welby, cons. 2011, apptd 2013; Lambeth Palace, London SE1 7JU
Signs Justin Cantuar:

BISHOPS SUFFRAGAN
*Dover, Rt. Revd Trevor Willmott, cons. 2002, apptd 2009; Upway, St Martin's Hill, Canterbury, Kent CT1 1PR
Ebbsfleet, Rt. Revd Jonathan Goodall, cons. 2013, apptd 2013; Hill House, Treetops, The Mount, Caversham, Reading RG4 7RE
Richborough, Rt. Revd Norman Banks, cons. 2011, apptd 2011; Parkside House, Abbey Mill Lane, St Albans AL3 4HE

*Temporarily responsible for episcopal oversight of the Channel Islands as Assistant Bishop of Winchester

DEAN
Very Revd Robert Willis, apptd 2001

Organist, D. Flood, FRCO, apptd 1988

ARCHDEACONS
Ashford, Ven. Philip Down, apptd 2011
Canterbury, Ven. Sheila Watson, apptd 2007
Maidstone, Ven. Stephen Taylor, apptd 2011

Vicar-General of Province and Diocese, Chancellor Sheila Cameron, QC
Commissary-General, Morag Ellis, QC
Joint Registrars of the Province, Canon John Rees; Stephen Slack
Diocesan Registrar and Legal Adviser, Owen Carew Jones
Diocesan Secretary, Julian Hills, Diocesan House, Lady Wootton's Green, Canterbury CT1 1NQ T 01227-459401

YORK
97TH ARCHBISHOP AND PRIMATE OF ENGLAND
Most Revd and Rt. Hon. Dr John Sentamu, cons. 1996, trans. 2005; Bishopthorpe, York YO23 2GE
Signs Sentamu Ebor:

BISHOPS SUFFRAGAN
Hull, Rt. Revd Alison White, cons. 2015, apptd 2015; Hullen House, Woodfield Lane, Hessle, Hull HU13 0ES
Selby, Rt. Revd John Thomson, cons. 2014, apptd 2014; 6 Pinfold Garth, Malton YO17 7XQ
Whitby, Rt. Revd Paul Fergson, cons. 2014, apptd 2014; 21 Thornton Road, Stainton TS8 9DS

PRINCIPAL EPISCOPAL VISITOR
Beverley, Rt. Revd Glyn Webster, cons. 2013, apptd 2013; Holy Trinity Rectory, Micklegate, York YO1 6LE

DEAN
Very Revd Vivienne Faull, apptd 2012

Director of Music, Robert Sharpe, apptd 2008

ARCHDEACONS
Cleveland, Ven. Samantha Rushton, apptd 2015
East Riding, Ven. Andy Broom, apptd 2014
York, Ven. Sarah Bullock, apptd 2013

Chancellor of the Diocese, His Hon. Judge Collier, QC, apptd 2006
Registrar and Legal Secretary, Caroline Mockford
Diocesan Secretary, Peter Warry, Diocesan House, Aviator Court, Clifton Moor, York YO30 4WJ T 01904-699500

LONDON (CANTERBURY)
132ND BISHOP
Rt. Revd and Rt. Hon. Richard Chartres, KCVO, cons. 1992, apptd 1995; The Old Deanery, Dean's Court, London EC4V 5AA
Signs Richard Londin:

AREA BISHOPS
Edmonton, vacant
Kensington, vacant
Stepney, Rt. Revd Adrian Newman, cons. 2011, apptd 2011; 63 Coburn Road, London E3 2DB
Willesden, Rt. Revd Peter Broadbent, cons. 2001, apptd 2001; 173 Willesden Lane, London NW6 7YN

BISHOP SUFFRAGAN
Fulham, Rt. Revd Jonathan Baker, cons. 2011, apptd 2013; The Old Deanery, Dean's Court, London EC4V 5AA

DEAN OF ST PAUL'S
Very Revd Dr David Ison, PHD, apptd 2012; Parkside House, Abbey Mill Lane, St Albans AL3 4HE

Director of Music, Andrew Carwood, apptd 2007

ARCHDEACONS
Charing Cross, vacant
Hackney, vacant
Hampstead, Ven. Luke Miller, *apptd* 2010
London, vacant
Middlesex, Ven. Stephan Welch, *apptd* 2006
Northolt, Ven. Duncan Green, *apptd* 2013

Chancellor, Nigel Seed, QC, *apptd* 2002
Registrar and Legal Secretary, Paul Morris
Diocesan Secretary, Andrew Brookes, London
   Diocesan House, 36 Causton Street, London SW1P 4AU
   T 020-7932 1100

DURHAM *(YORK)*
74TH BISHOP
Rt. Revd Paul Butler, *cons.* 2004, *trans.* 2013; Auckland Castle,
   Bishop Auckland DL14 7NR
   Signs Paul Dunelm:

BISHOP SUFFRAGAN
Jarrow, Rt. Revd Mark Bryant, *cons.* 2007, *apptd* 2007;
   Bishop's House, 25 Ivy Lane, Low Fell, Gateshead NE9 6QD

DEAN
Very Revd Michael Sadgrove, *apptd* 2003

Organist, James Lancelot, FRCO, *apptd* 1985

ARCHDEACONS
Auckland, Ven. Nicholas Barker, *apptd* 2007
Durham, Ven. Ian Jagger, *apptd* 2006
Sunderland, Ven. Stuart Bain, *apptd* 2002

Chancellor, His Hon. Judge Bursell, QC, *apptd* 1989
Registrar and Legal Secretary, Hilary Monckton-Milnes
Diocesan Secretary, Andrew Thurston, Diocesan Office,
   Auckland Castle, Bishop Auckland DL14 7QJ
   T 01388-660010

WINCHESTER *(CANTERBURY)*
97TH BISHOP
Rt. Revd Tim Dakin, *cons.* 2012, *apptd* 2011; Wolvesey,
   Winchester SO23 9ND
   Signs Tim Winton:

BISHOPS SUFFRAGAN
Basingstoke, Rt. Revd David Williams, *cons.* 2014,
   apptd 2014; Bishop's Office, Old Alresford Place, Alresford,
   Hants SO24 9DH
Southampton, Rt. Revd Jonathan Frost, *cons.* 2010,
   apptd 2010; Bishop's House, St Mary's Church Close,
   Wessex Lane, Southampton SO18 2ST

DEANS
Dean of Winchester, Very Revd James Atwell, *apptd* 2005
Dean of Jersey (A Peculiar), Very Revd Robert Key,
   apptd 2005
Dean of Guernsey (A Peculiar), vacant
Director of Music, Andrew Lumsden, *apptd* 2002

ARCHDEACONS
Bournemouth, Ven. Dr Peter Rouch, *apptd* 2011
Winchester, Ven. Michael Harley, *apptd* 2009

Chancellor, His Hon. Judge Clark, QC, *apptd* 1993
Acting Registrar and Legal Secretary, Sue de Candole
Chief Executive, Andrew Robinson, Old Alresford Place,
   Alresford, Hants SO24 9DH T 01962-737300

BATH AND WELLS *(CANTERBURY)*
79TH BISHOP
Rt. Revd Peter Hancock, *cons.* 2010, *apptd* 2014; The Bishop's
   Palace, Wells, Somerset BA5 2PD
   Signs Peter Bath & Wells:

BISHOP SUFFRAGAN
Taunton, vacant

DEAN
Very Revd John Clarke, *apptd* 2004

Organist, Matthew Owens, *apptd* 2005

ARCHDEACONS
Bath, Ven. Andrew Piggott, *apptd* 2005
Taunton, Ven. John Reed, *apptd* 1999
Wells, Ven. Nicola Sullivan, *apptd* 2006

Chancellor, Timothy Briden, *apptd* 1993
Registrar and Legal Secretary, Roland Callaby
Diocesan Secretary, Nick May, The Old Deanery, St Andrew's
   Street, Wells, Somerset BA5 2UG T 01749-670777

BIRMINGHAM *(CANTERBURY)*
9TH BISHOP
Rt. Revd David Urquhart, *cons.* 2000, *apptd* 2006; Bishop's
   Croft, Old Church Road, Harborne, Birmingham B17 0BG
   Signs David Birmingham:

BISHOP SUFFRAGAN
Aston, vacant

DEAN
Very Revd Catherine Ogle, *apptd* 2010

Director of Music, Marcus Huxley, FRCO, *apptd* 1986

ARCHDEACONS
Aston, Ven. Simon Heathfield, *apptd* 2014
Birmingham, Ven. Hayward Osborne, *apptd* 2001

Chancellor, Mark Powell, QC, *apptd* 2012
Registrar and Legal Secretary, Hugh Carslake
Diocesan Secretary, Andrew Halstead, 1 Colmore Row,
   Birmingham B3 2BJ T 0121-426 0400

BLACKBURN *(YORK)*
9TH BISHOP
Rt. Revd Julian Henderson, *cons.* 2013, *apptd* 2013;
   Bishop's House, Ribchester Road, Blackburn BB1 9EF
   Signs Julian Blackburn

BISHOPS SUFFRAGAN
Burnley, Rt. Revd Philip North, *cons.* 2015, *apptd* 2015;
   Dean House, 449 Padiham Road, Burnley BB12 6TE
Lancaster, Rt. Revd Geoffrey Pearson, *cons.* 2006,
   apptd 2006; The Vicarage, Whinney Brow Lane, Shireshead,
   Forton, Preston PR3 0AE

DEAN
Very Revd Christopher Armstrong, *apptd* 2001

Organist and Director of Music, Samuel Holden

ARCHDEACON
Blackburn, vacant
Lancaster, Ven. Michael Everitt, *apptd* 2011

Chancellor, His Hon. Judge Bullimore, *apptd* 1990
Registrar and Legal Secretary, Stephen Crossley

Diocesan Secretary, Graeme Pollard, Diocesan Office, Clayton House, Walker Office Park, Blackburn BB1 5AA
T 01254-503070

BRISTOL *(CANTERBURY)*
55TH BISHOP
Rt. Revd Michael Hill, *cons.* 1998, *apptd* 2003;
58A High Street, Winterbourne, Bristol BS36 1JQ
Signs Michael Bristol

BISHOP SUFFRAGAN
Swindon, Rt. Revd Dr Lee Rayfield, *cons.* 2005, *apptd* 2005;
Mark House, Field Rise, Swindon, Wiltshire SN1 4HP

DEAN
Very Revd David Hoyle, *apptd* 2010

Organist and Director of Music, Mark Lee, *apptd* 1998

ARCHDEACONS
Bristol, vacant
Malmesbury, Ven. Christine Froude, *apptd* 2011

Chancellor, The Worshipful Revd Justin Gau
Registrar and Legal Secretary, Roland Callaby
Diocesan Secretary, Oliver Home, First Floor, Hillside House,
1500 Parkway North, Stoke Gifford, Bristol BS34 8YU
T 0117-9060100

CARLISLE *(YORK)*
67TH BISHOP
Rt. Revd James Newcome, *cons.* 2002, *apptd* 2009;
Bishop's House, Ambleside Road, Keswick CA12 4DD
Signs James Carliol

BISHOP SUFFRAGAN
Penrith, Rt. Revd Robert Freeman, *cons.* 2011, *apptd* 2011;
Holm Croft, Castle Road, Kendal, Cumbria LA9 7AU

DEAN
Very Revd Mark Boyling, *apptd* 2004

Organist, Jeremy Suter, FRCO, *apptd* 1991

ARCHDEACONS
Carlisle, Ven. Kevin Roberts, *apptd* 2009
West Cumberland, Ven. Dr Richard Pratt, *apptd* 2009
Westmorland and Furness, Ven. Penny Driver, *apptd* 2012

Chancellor, Geoffrey Tattersall, QC, *apptd* 2003
Registrar and Legal Secretary, Jane Lowdon
Diocesan Secretary, Derek Hurton, Church House, West Walls,
Carlisle CA3 8UE T 01228-522573

CHELMSFORD *(CANTERBURY)*
10TH BISHOP
Rt. Revd Stephen Cottrell, *cons.* 2004, *apptd* 2010;
Bishopscourt, Main Road, Margaretting, Ingatestone,
Essex CM4 0HD
Signs Stephen Chelmsford

BISHOPS SUFFRAGAN
Barking, Rt. Revd Peter Hill, *cons.* 2014, *apptd* 2014;
Barking Lodge, Verulam Avenue, London E17 8ES
Bradwell, Rt. Revd John Wraw, *cons.* 2012, *apptd* 2012;
Bishop's House, Orsett Road, Horndon-on-the-Hill,
Stanford-le-Hope, Essex SS17 8NS
Colchester, Rt. Revd Roger Morris, *cons.* 2014, *apptd* 2014;
1 Fitzwater Road, Colchester, Essex CO3 3SS

DEAN
Very Revd Nicholas Henshall, *apptd* 2013

Director of Music, James Davy, *apptd* 2012

ARCHDEACONS
Barking, Ven. Dr John Perumbalath, *apptd* 2013
Chelmsford, Ven. David Lowman, *apptd* 2013
Colchester, Ven. Annette Cooper, *apptd* 2004
Harlow, Ven. Martin Webster, *apptd* 2009
Southend, Ven. Mina Smallman, *apptd* 2013
Stansted, Ven. Robin King, *apptd* 2013
West Ham, Ven. Elwin Cockett, *apptd* 2007

Chancellor, George Pulman, QC, *apptd* 2001
Registrar and Legal Secretary, Aiden Hargreaves-Smith
Chief Executive, John Ball, 53 New Street, Chelmsford,
Essex CM1 1AT T 01245-294400

CHESTER *(YORK)*
40TH BISHOP
Rt. Revd Peter Forster, PHD, *cons.* 1996, *apptd* 1996;
Bishop's House, Abbey Square, Chester CH1 2JD
Signs Peter Cestr:

BISHOPS SUFFRAGAN
Birkenhead, Rt. Revd Keith Sinclair, *cons.* 2007, *apptd* 2007;
Bishop's Lodge, 67 Bidston Road, Prenton CH43 6TR
Stockport, Rt. Revd Elizabeth Lane, *cons.* 2015, *apptd* 2015;
Bishop's Lodge, Back Lane, Dunham, Altrincham WA14 4SG

DEAN
Very Revd Dr Gordon McPhate, *apptd* 2002

Organist and Director of Music, Philip Rushforth, FRCO,
apptd 2008

ARCHDEACONS
Chester, Ven. Dr Michael Gilbertson, *apptd* 2010
Macclesfield, Ven. Ian Bishop, *apptd* 2011

Chancellor, His Hon. Judge Turner, QC, *apptd* 1998
Registrar and Legal Secretary, Helen McFall
Diocesan Secretary, George Colville, Church House,
5500 Daresbury Park, Daresbury, Warrington WA4 4GE
T 01928-718834

CHICHESTER *(CANTERBURY)*
103RD BISHOP
Rt. Revd Dr Martin Warner, *cons.* 2010, *apptd* 2012;
The Palace, Chichester PO19 1PY
Signs Martin Cicestr:

BISHOPS SUFFRAGAN
Horsham, Rt. Revd Mark Sowerby, *cons.* 2009, *apptd* 2009;
21 Guildford Road, Horsham, W. Sussex RH12 1LU
Lewes, Rt. Revd Richard Jackson, *cons.* 2014, *apptd* 2014;
c/o Church House, 211 New Church Road, Hove BN3 4ED

DEAN
Very Revd Stephen Waine, *apptd* 2015

Organist, Charles Harrison, *apptd* 2014

ARCHDEACONS
Brighton and Lewes, Ven. Martin Lloyd Williams, *apptd* 2015
Chichester, Ven. Douglas McKittrick, *apptd* 2002
Horsham, Ven. Fiona Windsor, *apptd* 2014
Hastings, Ven. Philip Jones, *apptd* 2005

Chancellor, Prof. Mark Hill, QC
Registrar and Legal Secretary, Matthew Chinery

Diocesan Secretary, Gabrielle Higgins, Diocesan Church House, 211 New Church Road, Hove, E. Sussex BN3 4ED
T 01273-421021

COVENTRY *(CANTERBURY)*
9TH BISHOP
Rt. Revd Dr Christopher Cocksworth, *cons.* 2008, *apptd* 2008; The Bishop's House, 23 Davenport Road, Coventry CV5 6PW
Signs Christopher Coventry

BISHOP SUFFRAGAN
Warwick, Rt. Revd John Stroyan, *cons.* 2005, *apptd* 2005; Warwick House, 139 Kenilworth Road, Coventry CV4 7AP

DEAN
Very Revd John Witcombe, *apptd* 2013

Director of Music, Mr Kerry Beaumont, *apptd* 2006

ARCHDEACONS
Coventry, Ven. John Green, CB, *apptd* 2013
Warwick, Ven. Morris Rodham, *apptd* 2010

Chancellor, Stephen Eyre, *apptd* 2009
Registrar and Legal Secretary, Mary Allanson
Diocesan Secretary, Simon Lloyd, Cathedral & Diocesan Offices, 1 Hilltop, Coventry CV1 5AB T 024-7652 1200

DERBY *(CANTERBURY)*
7TH BISHOP
Rt. Revd Dr Alastair Redfern, *cons.* 1997, *apptd* 2005; The Bishop's House, 6 King Street, Duffield, Belper, Derbyshire DE56 4EU
Signs Alastair Derby

BISHOP SUFFRAGAN
Repton, vacant

DEAN
Very Revd Dr John Davies, *apptd* 2010

Organist, Hugh Morris, *apptd* 2015

ARCHDEACONS
Chesterfield, Ven. Christine Wilson, *apptd* 2010
Derby, Ven. Dr Christopher Cunliffe, *apptd* 2006

Chancellor, His Hon. Judge Bullimore, *apptd* 1981
Registrar and Legal Secretary, Mrs Nadine Waldron
Diocesan Secretary, Maureen Cole, Derby Church House, Full Street, Derby DE1 3DR T 01332-388650

ELY *(CANTERBURY)*
69TH BISHOP
Rt. Revd Stephen Conway, *cons.* 2006, *apptd* 2011; The Bishop's House, Ely CB7 4DW
Signs Stephen Ely

BISHOP SUFFRAGAN
Huntingdon, Rt. Revd David Thomson, DPHIL, *cons.* 2008, *apptd* 2008; 14 Lynn Road, Ely, Cambs CB6 1DA

DEAN
Very Revd Mark Bonney, *apptd* 2012

Director of Music, Paul Trepte, FRCO, *apptd* 1991

ARCHDEACONS
Cambridge, Ven. Alex Hughes, *apptd* 2014
Huntingdon and Wisbech, Ven. Hugh McCurdy, *apptd* 2005

Chancellor, His Hon. Judge Leonard, QC
Registrar, Howard Dellar
Diocesan Secretary, Paul Evans, Bishop Woodford House, Barton Road, Ely, Cambs CB7 4DX T 01353-652702

EXETER *(CANTERBURY)*
71ST BISHOP
Rt. Revd Robert Atwell, *cons.* 2008, *apptd* 2014; The Palace, Exeter EX1 1HY
Signs Robert Exon:

BISHOPS SUFFRAGAN
Crediton, Rt. Revd Dame Sarah Mullally, DBE, *cons.* 2015, *apptd* 2015; 32 The Avenue, Tiverton EX16 4HW
Plymouth, Rt. Revd Nick McKinnel, *cons.* 2012, *trans.* 2015; 108 Molesworth Road, Stoke, Plymouth PL3 4AQ

DEAN
Very Revd Jonathan Draper, *apptd* 2012

Director of Music, Andrew Millington, *apptd* 1999

ARCHDEACONS
Barnstaple, Ven. Mark Butchers, *apptd* 2015
Exeter, Ven. Christopher Futcher, *apptd* 2012
Plymouth, Ven. Ian Chandler, *apptd* 2010
Totnes, Ven. Douglas Dettmer, *apptd* 2015

Chancellor, Hon. Sir Andrew McFarlane
Registrar and Legal Secretary, M. Follett
Diocesan Secretary, Mark Beedell, The Old Deanery, The Cloisters, Exeter EX1 1HS T 01392-272686

GIBRALTAR IN EUROPE *(CANTERBURY)*
4TH BISHOP
Rt. Revd Robert Innes, PHD, *cons.* 2014, *apptd* 2014; 47, rue Capitaine Crespel – boite 49, 1050 Brussels, Belgium

BISHOP SUFFRAGAN
In Europe, Rt. Revd David Hamid, *cons.* 2002, *apptd* 2002; 14 Tufton Street, London SW1P 3QZ

Dean, Cathedral Church of the Holy Trinity, Gibraltar, Very Revd Dr John Paddock

Chancellor, Pro-Cathedral of St Paul, Valletta, Malta, Canon Simon Godfrey
Chancellor, Pro-Cathedral of the Holy Trinity, Brussels, Belgium, Revd Dr Paul Vrolijk

ARCHDEACONS
Eastern, Ven. Patrick Curran
North-West Europe, Canon Meurig Williams *(acting)*
France, Ven. Ian Naylor
Gibraltar, Canon Geoffrey Johnston *(acting)*
Italy, Ven. Jonathan Boardman
Germany and Northern Europe, Ven. Peter Potter *(acting)*
Switzerland, Ven. Peter Potter

Chancellor, Prof. Mark Hill, QC
Registrar and Legal Secretary, Aiden Hargreaves-Smith
Diocesan Secretary, Adrian Mumford, 14 Tufton Street, London SW1P 3QZ T 020-7898 1155

GLOUCESTER *(CANTERBURY)*
41ST BISHOP
Rt. Revd Rachel Treweek, *cons.* 2015, *apptd* 2015; 2 College Green, Gloucester GL1 2LR
Signs Rachel Gloucestr

BISHOP SUFFRAGAN
Tewkesbury, Rt. Revd Martyn Snow, *cons.* 2013, *apptd* 2013; 2 College Green, Gloucester GL1 2LR

DEAN
Very Revd Stephen Lake, *apptd* 2011

Director of Music, Adrian Partington, *apptd* 2007

ARCHDEACONS
Cheltenham, Ven. Robert Springett, *apptd* 2010
Gloucester, Ven. Jackie Searle, *apptd* 2012

Chancellor and Vicar-General, June Rodgers, *apptd* 1990
Registrar and Legal Secretary, Jos Moule
Diocesan Secretary, Ben Preece Smith, Church House,
    College Green, Gloucester GL1 2LY T 01452-410022

GUILDFORD *(CANTERBURY)*
10TH BISHOP
Rt. Revd Andrew Watson, *cons.* 2008, *apptd* 2014;
    Willow Grange, Woking Road, Guildford, Surrey GU4 7QS
    Signs Andrew Guildford

BISHOP SUFFRAGAN
Dorking, vacant

DEAN
Very Revd Dianna Gwilliams, *apptd* 2013

Organist, Katherine Dienes-Williams, *apptd* 2007

ARCHDEACONS
Dorking, Ven. Paul Bryer, *apptd* 2014
Surrey, Ven. Stuart Beake, *apptd* 2005

Chancellor, Andrew Jordan
Registrars and Legal Secretaries, Lee Coley; Howard
    Dellar
Diocesan Secretary, vacant, Diocesan House, Quarry Street,
    Guildford GU1 3XG T 01483-790300

HEREFORD *(CANTERBURY)*
105TH BISHOP
Rt. Revd Richard Frith, cons. 1998, apptd 2014;
    Bishop's House, The Palace, Hereford HR4 9BN
    Signs Richard Hereford

BISHOP SUFFRAGAN
Ludlow, Rt. Revd Alistair Magowan, *cons.* 2009, *apptd* 2009;
    Bishop's House, Corvedale Road, Craven Arms,
    Shropshire SY7 9BT

DEAN
Very Revd Michael Tavinor, *apptd* 2002

Organist and Director of Music, Geraint Bowen, FRCO,
    apptd 2001

ARCHDEACONS
Hereford, Ven. Paddy Benson, *apptd* 2011
Ludlow, Rt. Revd Alistair Magowan, *apptd* 2009

Chancellor, His Hon. Judge Kaye, QC
Registrar and Legal Secretary, Howard Dellar
Diocesan Secretary, John Clark, The Palace, Hereford HR4 9BL
    T 01432-373300

LEICESTER *(CANTERBURY)*
7TH BISHOP
vacant

ASSISTANT BISHOP
Rt. Revd Christopher Boyle, *cons.* 2000, *apptd* 2009;
    St Martins House, 7 Peacock Lane, Leicester LE1 5PZ

DEAN
Very Revd David Monteith, *apptd* 2013

Director of Music, Dr Christopher Johns

ARCHDEACONS
Leicester, Ven. Timothy Stratford, *apptd* 2012
Loughborough, Ven. David Newman, *apptd* 2009

Chancellor, Mark Blackett-Ord
Registrar and Legal Secretary, Revd Trevor Kirkman
Diocesan Secretary, Carol Gibbons, St Martin's House,
    7 Peacock Lane, Leicester LE1 5PZ T 0116-261 5200

LICHFIELD *(CANTERBURY)*
99TH BISHOP
vacant

BISHOPS SUFFRAGAN
Shrewsbury, Rt. Revd Mark Rylands, *cons.* 2009,
    apptd 2009; Athlone House, 66 London Road,
    Shrewsbury SY2 6PG
Stafford, Rt. Revd Geoffrey Annas, *cons.* 2010, *apptd* 2010;
    Ash Garth, Broughton Crescent, Barlaston, Stoke-on-Trent
    ST12 9DD
Wolverhampton, Rt. Revd Clive Gregory, *cons.* 2007,
    apptd 2007; 61 Richmond Road, Wolverhampton WV3 9JH

DEAN
Very Revd Adrian Dorber, *apptd* 2005

Directors of Music, Ben and Cathy Lamb, *apptd* 2010
Organist, Martyn Rawles, *apptd* 2010

ARCHDEACONS
Lichfield, Ven. Simon Baker, *apptd* 2013
Salop, Ven. Paul Thomas, *apptd* 2011
Stoke-on-Trent, Ven. Matthew Parker, *apptd* 2013
Walsall, Ven. Dr Susan Weller, *apptd* 2015

Chancellor, His Hon. Judge Stephen Eyre, QC, *apptd* 2012
Registrar and Legal Secretary, N. Blackie
Diocesan Secretary, Julie Jones, St Mary's House, The Close,
    Lichfield, Staffs WS13 7LD T 01543-306030

LINCOLN *(CANTERBURY)*
72ND BISHOP
Rt. Revd Christopher Lowson, *cons.* 2011, *apptd* 2011;
    Bishop's Office, The Old Palace, Minster Yard, Lincoln LN2 1PU
    Signs Christopher Lincoln

BISHOPS SUFFRAGAN
Grantham, vacant
Grimsby, Rt. Revd Dr David Court, *cons.* 2014, *apptd* 2014;
    The Old Palace, Minster Yard, Lincoln LN2 1PU

DEAN
Very Revd Philip Buckler, *apptd* 2007

Director of Music, Aric Prentice, *apptd* 2003

ARCHDEACONS
Boston, Ven. Dr Justine Allain Chapman, *apptd* 2013
Lincoln, Ven. Timothy Barker, *apptd* 2009
Stow and Lindsey, vacant

Chancellor, His Hon. Judge Bishop
Registrar and Legal Secretary, Julie Robinson
Diocesan Secretary, Angela Sibson, OBE, Edward King House,
    Minster Yard, Lincoln LN2 1PU T 01522-504050

LIVERPOOL *(YORK)*
8TH BISHOP
Rt. Revd Paul Bayes, *cons.* 2010, *apptd* 2014; Bishop's Lodge,
Woolton Park, Liverpool L25 6DT
Signs Paul Liverpool

BISHOP SUFFRAGAN
Warrington, Rt. Revd Richard Blackburn, *cons.* 2009,
apptd 2009; 34 Central Avenue, Eccleston Park,
Liverpool L34 2QP

DEAN
Very Revd Pete Wilcox, *apptd* 2012

Director of Music, David Poulter, *apptd* 2008

ARCHDEACONS
Liverpool, Ven. Richard Panter, *apptd* 2002
Warrington, vacant

Chancellor, Hon. Sir Mark Hedley
Registrar and Legal Secretary, Howard Dellar
Diocesan Secretary, Mike Eastwood, St James House,
20 St James Street, Liverpool L1 7BY **T** 0151-709 9722

MANCHESTER *(YORK)*
12TH BISHOP
Rt. Revd Dr David Walker, *cons.* 2000, *apptd* 2013;
Bishopscourt, Bury New Road, Salford M7 4LE
Signs David Manchester

BISHOPS SUFFRAGAN
Bolton, Rt. Revd Christopher Edmondson, *cons.* 2008,
apptd 2008; Bishop's Lodge, Walkden Road, Worsley,
Manchester M28 2WH
Middleton, Rt. Revd Mark Davies, *cons.* 2008, *apptd* 2008;
The Hollies, Manchester Road, Rochdale OL11 3QY

DEAN
Very Revd Rogers Govender, *apptd* 2006

Organist, Christopher Stokes, *apptd* 1992

ARCHDEACONS
Bolton, Ven. David Bailey, *apptd* 2008
Manchester, Ven. Mark Ashcroft, *apptd* 2009
Rochdale, Ven. Cherry Vann, *apptd* 2008
Salford, Ven. David Sharples, *apptd* 2009

Chancellor, Geoffrey Tattersall, QC
Registrar and Legal Secretary, Jane Monks
Diocesan Secretary, Martin Miller, Diocesan Church House,
90 Deansgate, Manchester M3 2GH **T** 0161-828 1400

NEWCASTLE *(YORK)*
12TH BISHOP
Rt. Revd Christine Elizabeth Hardman, *cons.* 2015,
apptd 2015
Signs Christine Newcastle

ASSISTANT BISHOP
Rt. Revd Frank White, *cons.* 2002, *apptd* 2010

DEAN
Very Revd Christopher C. Dalliston, *apptd* 2003

Director of Music, Michael Stoddart, *apptd* 2009

ARCHDEACONS
Lindisfarne, Ven. Dr Peter Robinson, *apptd* 2008
Northumberland, Ven. Geoffrey Miller, *apptd* 2004

Chancellor, Euan Duff, *apptd* 2013
Registrar and Legal Secretary, Jane Lowdon
Diocesan Secretary, Shane Waddle, Church House,
St John's Terrace, North Shields NE29 6HS **T** 0191-270 4100

NORWICH *(CANTERBURY)*
71ST BISHOP
Rt. Revd Graham R. James, *cons.* 1993, *apptd* 2000;
Bishop's House, Norwich NR3 1SB
Signs Graham Norvic:

BISHOPS SUFFRAGAN
Lynn, Rt. Revd Jonathan Meyrick, *cons.* 2011, *apptd* 2011;
The Old Vicarage, Castle Acre, King's Lynn PE32 2AA
Thetford, Rt. Revd Alan Winton, PHD, *cons.* 2009,
apptd 2009; The Red House, 53 Norwich Road, Stoke Holy
Cross, Norwich NR14 8AB

DEAN
Very Revd Jane Hedges, *apptd* 2014

Master of Music, Ashley Grote, *apptd* 2012

ARCHDEACONS
Lynn, Ven. John Ashe, *apptd* 2009
Norfolk, Ven. Steven Betts, *apptd* 2012
Norwich, Ven. Jan McFarlane, *apptd* 2008

Chancellor, Ruth Arlow, *apptd* 2012
Registrar and Legal Secretary, Stuart Jones
Diocesan Secretary, Richard Butler, Diocesan House,
109 Dereham Road, Easton, Norwich, Norfolk NR9 5ES
T 01603-880853

OXFORD *(CANTERBURY)*
43RD BISHOP
vacant

AREA BISHOPS
Buckingham, Rt. Revd Dr Alan Wilson, *cons.* 2003,
apptd 2003; Sheridan, Grimms Hill, Great Missenden,
Bucks HP16 9BD
Dorchester, Rt. Revd Colin Fletcher, *cons.* 2000, *apptd* 2000;
Arran House, Sandy Lane, Yarnton, Oxon OX5 1PB
Reading, Rt. Revd Andrew Proud, *cons.* 2011, *apptd* 2011;
Bishop's House, Tidmarsh Lane, Tidmarsh, Reading RG8 8HA

DEAN OF CHRIST CHURCH
Very Revd Martyn Percy, PHD, *apptd* 2014

Organist, Dr Stephen Darlington, FRCO, *apptd* 1985

ARCHDEACONS
Berkshire, Ven. Olivia Graham, *apptd* 2013
Buckingham, Ven. Karen Gorham, *apptd* 2007
Oxford, Ven. Martin Gorick, *apptd* 2013

Chancellor, Revd Alex McGregor, *apptd* 2013
Registrar and Legal Secretary, Revd Canon John Rees
Diocesan Secretary, Rosemary Pearce, Diocesan Church House,
North Hinksey, Oxford OX2 0NB **T** 01865-208202

PETERBOROUGH *(CANTERBURY)*
38TH BISHOP
Rt. Revd Donald Allister, *cons.* 2010, *apptd* 2009;
Bishop's Lodging, The Palace, Peterborough PE1 1YA
Signs Donald Petriburg:

BISHOP SUFFRAGAN
Brixworth, Rt. Revd John Holbrook, *cons.* 2011, *apptd* 2011;
Orchard Acre, 11 North Street, Mears Ashby, Northants
NN6 0DW

DEAN
Very Revd Charles Taylor, *apptd* 2007

Director of Music, Stephen Grahl, *apptd* 2014

ARCHDEACONS
Northampton, Ven. Richard Ormston, *apptd* 2014
Oakham, Ven. Gordon Steele, *apptd* 2012

Chancellor, David Pittaway, QC, *apptd* 2005
Registrar and Legal Secretary, Anna Spriggs
Diocesan Secretary, Andrew Roberts, Diocesan Office,
    The Palace, Peterborough PE1 1YB **T** 01733-887000

PORTSMOUTH *(CANTERBURY)*
9TH BISHOP
Rt. Revd Christopher Foster, *cons.* 2010, *apptd* 2010;
    Bishopsgrove, 26 Osborn Road, Fareham, Hants PO16 7DQ
    Signs Christopher Portsmouth

DEAN
Very Revd David Brindley, *apptd* 2002

Organist, David Price, *apptd* 1996

ARCHDEACONS
Isle of Wight, Ven. Peter Sutton, *apptd* 2012
Portsdown, Ven. Joanne Grenfell, *apptd* 2013
The Meon, Ven. Gavin Collins, *apptd* 2011

Chancellor, His Hon. Judge Waller, CBE
Registrar and Legal Secretary, Hilary Tyler
Diocesan Secretary, Wendy Kennedy, Diocesan Offices, 1st Floor,
    Peninsular House, Wharf Road, Portsmouth PO2 8HB
    T 023-9289 9664

ROCHESTER *(CANTERBURY)*
107TH BISHOP
Rt. Revd James Langstaff, *cons.* 2004, *apptd* 2010;
    Bishopscourt, 24 St Margaret's Street, Rochester ME1 1TS
    Signs, James Roffen:

BISHOP SUFFRAGAN
Tonbridge, Rt. Revd Dr Brian Castle, *cons.* 2002, *apptd* 2002;
    Bishop's Lodge, 48 St Botolph's Road, Sevenoaks TN13 3AG

DEAN
vacant

Director of Music, Scott Farrell, *apptd* 2008

ARCHDEACONS
Bromley & Bexley, Ven. Dr Paul Wright, *apptd* 2003
Rochester, Ven. Simon Burton-Jones, *apptd* 2010
Tonbridge, Ven. Clive Mansell, *apptd* 2002

Chancellor, The Worshipful John Gallagher
Registrar and Legal Secretary, Owen Carew-Jones
Diocesan Secretary, Geoff Marsh, St Nicholas Church, Boley Hill,
    Rochester ME1 1SL **T** 01634-560000

ST ALBANS *(CANTERBURY)*
10TH BISHOP
Rt. Revd Dr Alan Smith, *cons.* 2001, *apptd* 2009, *trans.*
    2009; Abbey Gate House, St Albans AL3 4HD
    Signs Alan St Albans

BISHOPS SUFFRAGAN
Bedford, Rt. Revd Richard Atkinson, OBE, *cons.* 2012,
    apptd 2012; Bishop's Lodge, Bedford Road, Cardington,
    Bedford MK44 3SS

Hertford, Rt. Revd Michael Beasley, *cons.* 2015, *apptd* 2015;
    Bishopswood, 3 Stobarts Close, Knebworth SG3 6ND

DEAN
Very Revd Dr Jeffrey John, *apptd* 2004

Organist, Andrew Lucas, *apptd* 1998

ARCHDEACONS
Bedford, Ven. Paul Hughes, *apptd* 2004
Hertford, Ven. Dr Trevor Jones, *apptd* 1997
St Albans, Ven. Jonathan Smith, *apptd* 2008

Chancellor, Roger Kaye, *apptd* 2002
Registrar and Legal Secretary, Lee Coley
Diocesan Secretary, Susan Pope, Holywell Lodge, 41 Holywell Hill,
    St Albans AL1 1HE **T** 01727-854532

ST EDMUNDSBURY AND IPSWICH
(CANTERBURY)
11TH BISHOP
Rt. Revd Martin Seeley, *cons.* 2015, *apptd* 2015;
    The Bishop's House, 4 Park Road, Ipswich IP1 3ST
    Signs Martin St Edmundsbury and Ipswich

BISHOP SUFFRAGAN
Dunwich, vacant

DEAN
Very Revd Frances Ward, *apptd* 2010

Director of Music, James Thomas, *apptd* 1997

ARCHDEACONS
Sudbury, Ven. Dr David Jenkins, *apptd* 2010
Suffolk, Ven. Ian Morgan, *apptd* 2012

Chancellor, David Etherington, QC
Registrar and Legal Secretary, James Hall
Diocesan Secretary, Nicholas Edgell, Diocesan Office,
    St Nicholas Centre, 4 Cutler Street, Ipswich IP1 1UQ
    T 01473-298500

SALISBURY *(CANTERBURY)*
78TH BISHOP
Rt. Revd Nicholas Holtam, *cons.* 2011, *apptd* 2011;
    South Canonry, 71 The Close, Salisbury SP1 2ER
    Signs Nicholas Sarum

BISHOPS SUFFRAGAN
Ramsbury, Rt. Revd Edward Condry, DPHIL, *cons.* 2012,
    apptd 2012; Bishop's Office, Southbroom House,
    London Road, Devizes SN10 1LT
Sherborne, vacant

DEAN
Very Revd June Osborne, *apptd* 2004

Organist, David Halls, *apptd* 2005

ARCHDEACONS
Dorset, Ven. Antony Macrow-Wood, *apptd* 2015
Sarum, Ven. Alan Jeans, *apptd* 2003
Sherborne, Ven. Paul Taylor, *apptd* 2004
Wilts, Ven. Ruth Worsley, *apptd* 2012

Chancellor, His Hon. Judge Wiggs, *apptd* 1997
Acting Registrar and Legal Secretary, Sue de Candole
Diocesan Secretary, Lucinda Herklots, Church House,
    Crane Street, Salisbury SP1 2QB **T** 01722-411922

SHEFFIELD *(YORK)*
7TH BISHOP
Rt. Revd Steven Croft, PHD, *cons.* 2009, *apptd* 2008;
Bishopscroft, Snaithing Lane, Sheffield S10 3LG
Signs Steven Sheffield

BISHOP SUFFRAGAN
Doncaster, Rt. Revd Peter Burrows, *cons.* 2012, *apptd* 2011;
Doncaster House, Church Lane, Fishlake, Doncaster DN7 5JW

DEAN
Very Revd Peter Bradley, *apptd* 2003

Master of Music, Neil Taylor, *apptd* 1997

ARCHDEACONS
Doncaster, Ven. Steve Wilcockson, *apptd* 2012
Sheffield and Rotherham, Ven. Malcolm Chamberlain,
apptd 2013

Chancellor, Her Hon. Judge Sarah Singleton, QC, *apptd* 2014
Registrar and Legal Secretary, Andrew Vidler
Diocesan Secretary, Malcolm Fair, Church House,
95–99 Effingham Street, Rotherham S65 1BL T 01709-309100

SODOR AND MAN *(YORK)*
81ST BISHOP
Rt. Revd Robert Paterson, *cons.* 2008, *apptd* 2008;
Thie yn Aspick, 4 The Falls, Douglas, Isle of Man IM4 4PZ
Signs Robert Sodor as Mannin

ARCHDEACON OF MAN
Ven. Andrew Brown, *apptd* 2011

Vicar-General and Chancellor, Geoffrey Tattersall, QC
Registrar, Lionel Lennox
Diocesan Secretary, Andrew Swithinbank, Thie yn Aspick,
4 The Falls, Douglas, Isle of Man IM4 4PZ T 07624-314590

SOUTHWARK *(CANTERBURY)*
10TH BISHOP
Rt. Revd Christopher Chessun, *cons.* 2005, *apptd* 2011;
Trinity House, 4 Chapel Court, Borough High Street,
London SE1 1HW
Signs Christopher Southwark

AREA BISHOPS
Croydon, Rt. Revd Jonathan Clark, *cons.* 2012, *apptd* 2012;
St Matthew's House, 100 George Street, London CR0 1PE
Kingston upon Thames, Rt. Revd Dr Richard Cheetham,
cons. 2002, *apptd* 2002; 620 Kingston Road, Raynes Park,
London SW20 8DN
Woolwich, Rt. Revd Dr Michael Ipgrave, OBE, *cons.* 2012,
apptd 2012; Trinity House, 4 Chapel Court, Borough High
Street, London SE1 1HW

DEAN
Very Revd Andrew Nunn, *apptd* 2011

Organist, Peter Wright, FRCO, *apptd* 1989

ARCHDEACONS
Croydon, Ven. Christopher Skilton, *apptd* 2013
Lambeth, Ven. Simon Gates, *apptd* 2013
Lewisham & Greenwich, Ven. Alastair Cutting, *apptd* 2013
Reigate, Ven. Daniel Kajumba, *apptd* 2001
Southwark, Ven. Dr Jane Steen, *apptd* 2013
Wandsworth, vacant

Chancellor, Philip Petchey
Registrar and Legal Secretary, Paul Morris

Diocesan Secretary, Ruth Martin, Trinity House, 4 Chapel Court,
Borough High Street, London SE1 1HW T 020-7939 9400

SOUTHWELL AND NOTTINGHAM *(YORK)*
12TH BISHOP
Rt. Revd Paul Williams, *cons.* 2009, *trans.* 2015;
Bishop's Manor, Southwell, Nottinghamshire NG25 0JR
Signs Paul Southwell and Nottingham

BISHOP SUFFRAGAN
Sherwood, Rt. Revd Anthony Porter, *cons.* 2006, *apptd* 2006;
Jubilee House, Westgate, Southwell NG25 0JH

DEAN
vacant

Organist, Paul Hale, *apptd* 1989

ARCHDEACONS
Newark, Ven. David Picken, *apptd* 2012
Nottingham, Ven. Sarah Clark, *apptd* 2014

Chancellor, Linda Box, *apptd* 2005
Registrar and Legal Secretary, Amanda Redgate
Chief Executive, Nigel Spraggins, Jubilee House, Westgate,
Southwell, Notts NG25 0JH T 01636-814331

TRURO *(CANTERBURY)*
15TH BISHOP
Rt. Revd Tim Thornton, *cons.* 2001, *apptd* 2008; Lis Escop,
Truro TR3 6QQ
Signs Tim Truro

BISHOP SUFFRAGAN
St Germans, Rt. Revd Christopher Goldsmith, DPHIL,
cons. 2013, *apptd* 2013; Vounder, Tresillian, Truro TR2 4BW

DEAN
Very Revd Roger Bush, *apptd* 2012

Organist and Director of Music, Chris Gray, *apptd* 2008

ARCHDEACONS
Bodmin, Ven. Audrey Elkington, *apptd* 2011
Cornwall, Ven. Bill Stuart-White, *apptd* 2012

Chancellor, Timothy Briden, *apptd* 1998
Registrar and Legal Secretary, Martin Follett
Diocesan Secretary, Esther Pollard, Church House, Woodlands
Court, Truro Business Park, Threemilestone, Truro TR4 9NH
T 01872-274351

WEST YORKSHIRE AND THE DALES* *(YORK)*
1ST BISHOP OF LEEDS*
Rt. Revd Nicholas Baines, *cons.* 2003, *apptd* 2014;
Hollin House, Weetwood Avenue, Leeds LS16 5NG
Signs Nicholas Leeds

AREA BISHOPS
Bradford, Rt. Revd Toby Howarth, *cons.* 2014, *apptd* 2014;
c/o Bradford Cathedral, 1 Stott Hill, Bradford BD1 4EH
Huddersfield, Rt. Revd Jonathan Gibbs, *cons.* 2014,
apptd 2014; 2 Bullace Trees Lane, Roberttown WF15 7PF
Ripon, Rt. Revd James Bell, *cons.* 2004, *apptd* 2014;
Thistledown, Main Street, Exelby, Bedale DL8 2HD
Wakefield, Rt. Revd Anthony Robinson, *cons.* 2002,
apptd 2014; Pontefract House 181A Manygates Lane,
Sandal, Wakefield WF2 7DR

SUFFRAGAN BISHOP
Richmond, Rt. Revd Paul Slater, *cons.* 2015, *apptd* 2015

DEANS
Bradford, Very Revd Jerry Lepine, *apptd* 2013
Ripon, Very Revd John Dobson, *apptd* 2014
Wakefield, Very Revd Jonathan Greener, *apptd* 2007

Directors of Music, Andrew Bryden (Ripon), *apptd* 2003;
    Thomas Moore (Wakefield), *apptd* 2010; Alexander
    Woodrow (Bradford), *apptd* 2012

ARCHDEACONS
Bradford, Ven. Dr David Lee, *apptd* 2004
Halifax, Ven. Dr Anne Dawtry, *apptd* 2011
Leeds, Ven. Paul Hooper, *apptd* 2012
Richmond, vacant
Pontefract, Ven. Peter Townley, *apptd* 2008

Chancellor, Prof. Mark Hill, QC
Registrars and Legal Secretaries, Peter Foskett
Diocesan Secretaries, Debbie Child; Ashley Ellis
Bradfield Office, Kadugli House, Elmsley St, Steeton, Keighly,
    W. Yorks BD20 6SE **T** 01535-650555
Leeds Office, St Mary's Street, Leeds LS9 7DP **T** 0113-2000540
Wakefield Office, Church House, 1 South Parade, Wakefield
    WF1 1LP **T** 01924-371802

* The official name of the diocese is The Diocese of Leeds

WORCESTER *(CANTERBURY)*
113TH BISHOP
Rt. Revd Dr John Inge, *cons.* 2003, *apptd* 2007; The Bishop's
    Office, The Old Palace, Deansway, Worcester WR1 2JE
Signs John Wigorn

SUFFRAGAN BISHOP
Dudley, Rt. Revd Graham Usher, *cons.* 2014, *apptd* 2014;
    Bishop's House, 60 Bishop's Walk, Cradley Heath,
    West Midlands B64 7RH

DEAN
Very Revd Peter Atkinson, *apptd* 2006

Organist, Dr Peter Nardone, *apptd* 2012

ARCHDEACONS
Dudley, Ven. Nikki Groarke, *apptd* 2014
Worcester, Ven. Robert Jones, *apptd* 2014

Chancellor, Charles Mynors, *apptd* 1999
Registrar and Legal Secretary, Michael Huskinson
Diocesan Secretary, Robert Higham, The Old Palace, Deansway,
    Worcester WR1 2JE **T** 01905-20537

ROYAL PECULIARS
WESTMINSTER
The Collegiate Church of St Peter
Dean, Very Revd Dr John Hall
Canon Steward, Revd Canon Jane Sinclair
Chapter Clerk, Receiver-General and Registrar, Sir Stephen
    Lamport, KCVO, Chapter Office, 20 Dean's Yard,
    London SW1P 3PA
Organist, James O'Donnell, *apptd* 1999
Legal Secretary, Christopher Vyse, *apptd* 2000

WINDSOR
The Queen's Free Chapel of St George within Her Castle of
    Windsor
Dean, Rt. Revd David Conner, KCVO, *apptd* 1998
Chapter Clerk, Charlotte Manley, LVO, OBE, *apptd* 2003;
    Chapter Office, The Cloisters, Windsor Castle, Windsor,
    Berks SL4 1NJ
Director of Music, James Vivian, *apptd* 2013

OTHER ANGLICAN CHURCHES

THE CHURCH IN WALES
The Anglican Church was the established church in Wales
from the 16th century until 1920, when the estrangement of
the majority of Welsh people from Anglicanism resulted in
disestablishment. Since then the Church in Wales has been
an autonomous province consisting of six sees. The bishops
are elected by an electoral college comprising elected lay and
clerical members, who also elect one of the diocesan bishops
as Archbishop of Wales.

The legislative body of the Church in Wales is the
Governing Body, which has 144 members divided between
the three orders of bishops, clergy and laity. Its president is
the Archbishop of Wales and it meets twice annually. Its
decisions are binding upon all members of the church. The
church's property and finances are the responsibility of
the Representative Body. There are 53,262 members of the
Church in Wales, with 443 stipendiary clergy and 836
parishes.

THE REPRESENTATIVE BODY OF THE CHURCH IN
    WALES, 39 Cathedral Road, Cardiff CF11 9XF
    T 029-2034 8200 *Secretary,* John Shirley
12TH ARCHBISHOP OF WALES, Most Revd Dr Barry
    Morgan (Bishop of Llandaff), *elected* 2003
    Signs Barry Cambrensis

BISHOPS
Bangor (81st), Rt. Revd Andrew John, *b.* 1964, *cons.* 2008,
    elected 2008; Ty'r Esgob, Bangor, Gwynedd LL57 2SS
    Signs Andrew Bangor. *Stipendiary clergy,* 49
Llandaff (102nd), Most Revd Dr Barry Morgan (*also*
    Archbishop of Wales), *b.* 1947, *cons.* 1993, *trans.* 1999;
    Llys Esgob, The Cathedral Green, Llandaff, Cardiff CF5 2YE
    Signs Barry Cambrensis. *Stipendiary clergy,* 111
Monmouth (10th), Rt. Revd Richard Pain, *b.* 1956,
    cons. 2013, *elected* 2013; Bishopstow, Stow Hill,
    Newport NP20 4EA *Signs* Richard Monmouth.
    Stipendiary clergy, 87
St Asaph (76th), Rt. Revd Gregory Cameron, *b.* 1959,
    cons. 2009, *elected* 2009; Esgobty, Upper Denbigh Road,
    St Asaph, Denbighshire LL17 0TW *Signs* Gregory Llanelwy.
    Stipendiary clergy, 100
St David's (128th), Rt. Revd (John) Wyn Evans, *b.* 1946,
    cons. 2008, *elected* 2008; Llys Esgob, Abergwili,
    Carmarthen SA31 2JG *Signs* Wyn St Davids.
    Stipendiary clergy, 98
Swansea and Brecon (9th), Rt. Revd John Davies, *b.* 1953,
    cons. 2008, *elected* 2008; Ely Tower, Castle Square,
    Brecon, Powys LD3 9DJ
    Signs John Swansea & Brecon. *Stipendiary clergy,* 65

The stipend for a diocesan bishop of the Church in Wales is
£42,587 a year for 2015–16.

SCOTTISH EPISCOPAL CHURCH
The Scottish Episcopal Church was founded after the Act
of Settlement (1690) established the presbyterian nature of
the Church of Scotland. The Scottish Episcopal Church is
a member of the worldwide Anglican Communion. The
governing authority is the General Synod, which consists of
the Church's seven bishops, the conveners of the provincial
Standing Committee, the conveners of the boards, the
Church's representatives on the Anglican Consultative
Council and 124 elected members (62 from the clergy and
62 from the laity). The General Synod meets once a year. The
bishop who convenes and presides at meetings of the General
Synod is called the 'primus' and is elected by his fellow
bishops.

There are 32,634 members of the Scottish Episcopal Church, seven bishops, around 500 serving clergy and 300 churches and places of worship.

THE GENERAL SYNOD OF THE SCOTTISH EPISCOPAL CHURCH, 21 Grosvenor Crescent, Edinburgh EH12 5EE T 0131-225 6357 W www.scotland.anglican.org
Secretary-General, John Stuart

PRIMUS OF THE SCOTTISH EPISCOPAL CHURCH, Most Revd David Chillingworth (Bishop of St Andrews, Dunkeld and Dunblane), *elected* 2009

BISHOPS

Aberdeen and Orkney, Rt. Revd Dr Bob Gillies, *b.* 1951, *cons.* 2007, *elected* 2007. *Clergy,* 55

Argyll and the Isles, Rt. Revd Kevin Pearson, *b.* 1954, *cons.* 2011, *elected* 2010. *Clergy,* 28

Brechin, Rt. Revd Dr Nigel Peyton, *b.* 1951, *cons.* 2011, *elected* 2011. *Clergy,* 34

Edinburgh, Rt. Revd Dr John Armes, *b.* 1955, *cons.* 2012, *elected* 2012. *Clergy,* 163

Glasgow and Galloway, Rt. Revd Dr Gregor Duncan, *b.* 1950, *cons.* 2010, *elected* 2010. *Clergy,* 116

Moray, Ross and Caithness, Rt. Revd Mark Strange, *b.* 1961, *cons.* 2007, *elected* 2007. *Clergy,* 61

St Andrews, Dunkeld and Dunblane, Most Revd David Chillingworth, *b.* 1951, *cons.* 2005, *elected* 2005. *Clergy,* 78

The minimum stipend of a diocesan bishop of the Scottish Episcopal Church for 2015 is £37,035 (ie 1.5 times the standard clergy stipend of £24,690).

CHURCH OF IRELAND

The Anglican Church was the established church in Ireland from the 16th century but never secured the allegiance of the majority and was disestablished in 1871. The Church of Ireland is divided into the provinces of Armagh and Dublin, each under an archbishop. The provinces are subdivided into 12 dioceses.

The legislative body is the General Synod, which has 660 members in total, divided between the House of Bishops (12 members) and the House of Representatives (216 clergy and 432 laity). The Archbishop of Armagh is elected by the House of Bishops; other episcopal elections are made by an electoral college.

There are around 378,000 members of the Church of Ireland, 249, in Northern Ireland and 129,000 in the Republic of Ireland. There are two archbishops, ten bishops and 437 stipendiary clergy.

CENTRAL OFFICE, Church of Ireland House, Church Avenue, Rathmines, Dublin 6 T (+353) (1) 497 8422
Chief Officer and Secretary of the Representative Church Body, Adrian Clements

PROVINCE OF ARMAGH

Archbishop of Armagh, Primate of all Ireland and Metropolitan, Most Revd Richard Clarke, PHD, *b.* 1949, *cons.* 1996, *trans.* 2012. *Clergy,* 40

BISHOPS

Clogher, Rt. Revd John McDowell, *b.* 1956, *cons.* 2011, *apptd* 2011. *Clergy,* 26

Connor, Rt. Revd Alan Abernethy, *b.* 1957, *cons.* 2007, *apptd* 2007. *Clergy,* 72

Derry and Raphoe, Rt. Revd Kenneth Good, *b.* 1952, *cons.* 2002, *apptd* 2002. *Clergy,* 44

Down and Dromore, Rt. Revd Harold Miller, *b.* 1950, *cons.* 1997, *apptd* 1997. *Clergy,* 81

Kilmore, Elphin and Ardagh, Rt. Revd Ferran Glenfield, *b.* 1954, *cons.* 2013, *apptd* 2013. *Clergy,* 18

Tuam, Killala and Achonry, Rt. Revd Patrick Rooke, *b.* 1955, *cons.* 2011, *apptd* 2011. *Clergy,* 8

PROVINCE OF DUBLIN

Archbishop of Dublin, Bishop of Glendalough, Primate of Ireland and Metropolitan, Most Revd Michael Jackson, PHD, DPHIL, *b.* 1956, *cons.* 2002, *trans.* 2011. *Clergy,* 63

BISHOPS

Cashel and Ossory, Rt. Revd Michael Burrows, *b.* 1961, *cons.* 2006, *apptd* 2006. *Clergy,* 35

Cork, Cloyne and Ross, Rt. Revd Paul Colton, PHD, *b.* 1960, *cons.* 1999, *apptd* 1999. *Clergy,* 22

Limerick and Killaloe, Rt. Revd Kenneth Kearon, *b.* 1953, *cons.* 2015, *apptd* 2014. *Clergy,* 11

Meath and Kildare, Most Revd Patricia Storey, *b.* 1960, *cons.* 2013, *apptd* 2013. *Clergy,* 17

OVERSEAS

PRIMATES

Primate and Archbishop of Aotearoa, New Zealand and Polynesia, Most Revd William Turei

Primate of Australia, Most Revd Phillip Freir

Primate of Brazil, Most Revd Francisco De Assis Da Silva

Archbishop of the Province of Burundi, Most Revd Bernard Ntahoturi

Primate of Canada, Most Revd Frederick Hiltz

Archbishop of the Province of Central Africa, Most Revd Albert Chama

Primate of the Central Region of America, Most Revd Sturdie Downs

Archbishop of the Province of Congo, Most Revd Kahwa Henri Isingoma

Archbishop of Hong Kong Sheng Kung Hui, Most Revd Dr Paul Kwong

Archbishop of the Province of the Indian Ocean, Most Revd Ian Ernest

Primate of Japan (Nippon Sei Ko Kai), Most Revd Nathaniel Makoto Uematsu

Archbishop of Jerusalem and the Middle East, Most Revd Dr Mouneer Anis

Primate and Archbishop of All Kenya, Most Revd Dr Eliud Wabukala

Primate of Korea, Most Revd Paul Kim

Archbishop of Melanesia, Most Revd David Vunagi

Presiding Bishop of Mexico, Most Revd Francisco Moreno

Archbishop of the Province of Myanmar (Burma), Most Revd Stephen Oo

Metropolitan and Primate of All Nigeria, Most Revd Nicholas Okoh

Archbishop of Papua New Guinea, Rt. Revd Clyde Igara

Prime Bishop of the Philippines, Most Revd Renato Mag-Gay Abibico

Archbishop of the Province of Rwanda, Most Revd Dr Onesphore Rwaje

Archbishop of the Province of South East Asia, Most Revd Bolly Lapok

Primate of Southern Africa, Most Revd Dr Thabo Makgoba

Presiding Bishop of South America, Most Revd Hector Zavala Muñoz

Archbishop of the Province of South Sudan and Sudan, Most Revd Dr Daniel Deng Bul Yak

Archbishop of Tanzania, Most Revd Jacob Chimeledya

Archbishop of the Province of Uganda, Most Revd Stanley Ntagali

Presiding Bishop of the USA, Most Revd Katharine Schori

Primate and Metropolitan of the Province of West Africa, Most Revd Dr Daniel Sarfo
Archbishop of the Province of the West Indies, Most Revd Dr John Holder

OTHER CHURCHES AND EXTRA-PROVINCIAL DIOCESES

Anglican Church of Bermuda, extra-provincial to Canterbury
Bishop, Rt. Revd Nicholas Dill
Church of Ceylon, extra-provincial to Canterbury
Bishop of Colombo, Rt. Revd Dhiloraj Canagasabey
Bishop of Kurunagala, vacant
Episcopal Church of Cuba, Rt. Revd Griselda Del Carpio
Falkland Islands, extra-provincial to Canterbury
Bishop, Rt. Revd Nigel Stock (Bishop to the Forces)
Lusitanian Church (Portuguese Episcopal Church), extra-provincial to Canterbury
Bishop, Rt. Revd Jose Cabral
Reformed Episcopal Church of Spain, extra-provincial to Canterbury
Bishop, Rt. Revd Carlos López-Lozano

MODERATION OF CHURCHES IN FULL COMMUNION WITH THE ANGLICAN COMMUNION

Church of Bangladesh, Most Revd Paul Sarkar
Church of North India, Most Revd Pradeep Samantaroy
Church of South India, Most Revd Govada Dyvasirvadam
Church of Pakistan, Most Revd Samuel Azariah

CHURCH OF SCOTLAND

The Church of Scotland is the national church of Scotland. The church is reformed in doctrine, and presbyterian in constitution; ie based on a hierarchy of courts of ministers and elders and, since 1990, of members of a diaconate. At local level the Kirk Session consists of the parish minister and ruling elders. At district level the presbyteries, of which there are 44 in Britain, consist of all the ministers in the district, one ruling elder from each congregation, and those members of the diaconate who qualify for membership. The General Assembly is the supreme authority, and is presided over by a Moderator chosen annually by the Assembly. The sovereign, if not present in person, is represented by a Lord High Commissioner who is appointed each year by the Crown.

The Church of Scotland has around 400,000 members and 800 parish ministers. The majority of parishes are in Scotland, but there are also churches in England, Europe and overseas.

Lord High Commissioner (2015–16), Lord Hope of Craighead, KT, PC
Moderator of the General Assembly (2015–16), Rt. Revd Dr Angus Morrison
Principal Clerk, Revd John Chalmers
Depute Clerk, Revd George Whyte
Procurator, Laura Dunlop, QC
Law Agent and Solicitor of the Church, Janette Wilson
Parliamentary Officer, Chloe Clemmons
General Treasurer, Iain Grimmond
Secretary, Church and Society Council, Revd Ewan Aitken
CHURCH OFFICE, 121 George Street, Edinburgh EH2 4YN
T 0131-225 5722

PRESBYTERIES AND CLERKS

Aberdeen, Revd George Cowie; Revd John Ferguson
Abernethy, Catherine Buchan
Angus, Revd Mike Goss
Annandale and Eskdale, Revd Bryan Haston
Ardrossan, Alan Saunderson
Argyll, Ian MacLagan
Ayr, Revd Kenneth Elliott
Buchan, George Berstan
Caithness, Revd Ronald Johnstone
Dumbarton, Revd David Clark
Dumfries and Kirkcudbright, Revd William Hogg
Dundee, Revd James Wilson
Dunfermline, Revd Elizabeth Kenny
Dunkeld and Meigle, Revd John Russell
Duns, Helen Longmuir
Edinburgh, Revd Dr George Whyte
England, Revd Dr Pete Mills
Europe, Revd Jim Sharp
Falkirk, Revd Robert Allan
Glasgow, Very Revd William Hewitt
Gordon, Revd Euan Glen
Greenock and Paisley, Revd Dr Peter McEnhill
Hamilton, Revd Shaw Paterson
Inverness, Revd Reginald Campbell
Irvine and Kilmarnock, Steuart Dey
Jedburgh, Revd W. Frank Campbell
Kincardine and Deeside, Revd Hugh Conkey
Kirkcaldy, Revd Rosemary Frew
Lanark, Revd Helen Jamieson
Lewis, Revd Thomas Sinclair
Lochaber, Ella Gill
Lochcarron-Skye, Revd Allan Macarthur
Lothian, John McCulloch
Melrose and Peebles, Revd Victoria Linford
Moray, Revd Robert Anderson
Orkney, David Baker
Perth, Revd Alan Reid
Ross, Ronald Gunstone
St Andrews, Revd James Redpath
Shetland, Revd Charles Greig
Stirling, Revd Alex Millar
Sutherland, Mary Stobo
Uist, Wilson McKinlay
West Lothian, Revd Duncan Shaw
Wigtown and Stranraer, vacant

The stipends for ministers in the Church of Scotland in 2015 range from £26,119–£32,098, depending on length of service.

ROMAN CATHOLIC CHURCH

The Roman Catholic Church is a worldwide Christian church acknowledging as its head the Bishop of Rome, known as the Pope (father). Despite its widespread usage, 'Pope' is actually an unofficial term. The *Annuario Pontificio,* (Pontifical Yearbook) lists eight official titles: Bishop of Rome, Vicar of Jesus Christ, Successor of the Prince of the Apostles, Supreme Pontiff of the Universal Church, Primate of Italy, Archbishop and Metropolitan of the Roman Province, Sovereign of the State of the Vatican City and Servant of the Servants of God.

The Pope leads a communion of followers of Christ, who believe they continue His presence in the world as servants of faith, hope and love to all society. The Pope is held to be the successor of St Peter and thus invested with the power which was entrusted to St Peter by Jesus Christ. A direct line of succession is therefore claimed from the earliest Christian communities. With the fall of the Roman Empire the Pope also became an important political leader. His territory is now limited to the 0.44 sq. km (0.17 sq. miles) of the Vatican City State, created to provide some independence to the Pope from Italy and other nations. The episcopal jurisdiction of the Roman Catholic Church is called the Holy See.

The Pope exercises spiritual authority over the church with the advice and assistance of the Sacred College of Cardinals, the supreme council of the church. The number of cardinals was fixed at 70 by Pope Sixtus V in 1586 but has increased steadily since the pontificate of John XXIII. On 28 February 2013, the date of Pope Benedict XVI's resignation, there were 207 cardinals.

Following the death or resignation of the Pope, the members of the College of Cardinals under the age of 80 are called to the Vatican to elect a successor. They are known as cardinal electors and form an assembly called the conclave. The conclave, which comprised 115 cardinal electors when it convened in March 2013, conducts a secret ballot in complete seclusion to elect the next Pope. A two-thirds majority is necessary before the vote can be accepted as final. When a cardinal receives the necessary number of votes, the Dean of the Sacred College formally asks him if he will accept election and the name by which he wishes to be known. On his acceptance of the office of Supreme Pontiff, the conclave is dissolved and the first Cardinal Deacon announces the election to the assembled crowd in St Peter's Square.

The Pope has full legislative, judicial and administrative power over the whole Roman Catholic Church. He is aided in his administration by the curia, which is made up of a number of departments. The Secretariat of State is the central office for carrying out the Pope's instructions and is presided over by the Cardinal Secretary of State. It maintains relations with the departments of the curia, with the episcopate, with the representatives of the Holy See in various countries, governments and private persons. The congregations and pontifical councils are the Pope's ministries and include departments such as the Congregation for the Doctrine of Faith, whose field of competence concerns faith and morals; the Congregation for the Clergy and the Congregation for the Evangelisation of Peoples, the Pontifical Council for the Family and the Pontifical Council for the Promotion of Christian Unity.

The Holy See, composed of the Pope and those who help him in his mission for the church, is recognised by the Conventions of Vienna as an international moral body. Apostolic nuncios are the Pope's diplomatic representatives; in countries where no formal diplomatic relations exist between the Holy See and that country, the papal representative is known as an apostolic delegate.

According to the 2014 Pontifical Yearbook the number of Roman Catholics worldwide was 1,229 million at the end of 2012; the number of bishops was 5,133 and there were 414,313 priests.

SUPREME PONTIFF
His Holiness Pope Francis (Jorge Mario Bergoglio), *born* Buenos Aires, Argentina, 17 December 1936; *ordained priest* 13 December 1969; *appointed Archbishop* (of Buenos Aires), 28 February 1998; *created Cardinal* 21 February 2001; *assumed pontificate* 13 March 2013

PONTIFF EMERITUS
His Holiness Pope Benedict XVI (Joseph Ratzinger), *born* Bavaria, Germany, 16 April 1927; *ordained priest* 29 June 1951; *appointed Archbishop* (of Munich), 24 March 1977; *created Cardinal* 27 June 1977; *assumed pontificate* 19 April 2005; *resigned pontificate* 28 February 2013

SECRETARIAT OF STATE
Secretary of State, His Eminence Cardinal Pietro Parolin
First Section (General Affairs), Most Revd Giovanni Angelo Becciu (Titular Archbishop of Roselle)
Second Section (Relations with Other States), Most Revd Paul Gallagher (Titular Archbishop of Hodelm)

BISHOPS' CONFERENCE
The Catholic Bishops' Conference of England and Wales is the permanent assembly of Catholic Bishops and Ordinaries in the two member countries. The membership of the Conference comprises the Archbishops, Bishops and Auxiliary Bishops of the 22 Dioceses within England and Wales, the Bishop of the Forces (Military Ordinariate), the Apostolic Eparch of the Ukrainian Church in Great Britain, the Ordinary of the Personal Ordinariate of Our Lady of Walsingham, and the Apostolic Prefect of the Falkland Islands. The Conference is headed by a president and vice-president. There are six departments, each with an episcopal chair: Education and Formation, Christian Life and Worship, Christian Responsibility and Citizenship, Dialogue and Unity, Evangelisation and Catechesis, and International Affairs.

The Bishops' Conference Standing Committee is made up of two directly elected bishops in addition to the Metropolitan Archbishops and chairs from each of the above departments. The committee has general responsibility for continuity of policy between the plenary sessions of the conference, preparing the conference agenda and implementing its decisions.

The administration of the Bishops' Conference is funded by a levy on each diocese, according to income. A general secretariat in London coordinates and supervises the Bishops' Conference administration activities. There are also other agencies and consultative bodies affiliated to the conference.

The Bishops' Conference of Scotland is the permanently constituted assembly of the eight bishops of Scotland. The conference is headed by the president (Most Revd Philip Tartaglia, Archbishop of Glasgow). The conference establishes various agencies which perform advisory functions in relation to the conference. The more important of these agencies are called commissions; each one is headed by a bishop president who, with the other members of the commissions, are appointed by the conference.

The Irish Catholic Bishops' Conference (also known as the Irish Episcopal Conference) has as its president the Most Revd Eamon Martin (Archbishop of Armagh). Its membership comprises all the archbishops and bishops of Ireland. It appoints various commissions and agencies to assist with the work of the Catholic Church in Ireland.

The Catholic Church in the UK has over 900,000 mass attendees, 5,500 priests and 4,550 churches.

Bishops' Conferences secretariats:
ENGLAND AND WALES, 39 Eccleston Square, London SW1V 1BX T 020-7630 8220 W www.cbcew.org.uk
General Secretary, Revd Christopher Thomas
SCOTLAND, 64 Aitken Street, Airdrie ML6 6LT T 01236-764061 W www.bcos.org.uk
General Secretary, Mgr Hugh Bradley
IRELAND, Columba Centre, Maynooth, County Kildare T (+353) (1) 505 3000 E columbacentre@iecon.ie W www.catholicbishops.ie
Episcopal Secretary, Most Revd Kieran O'Reilly (Archbishop of Cashel and Emly)
Executive Secretary, Mgr Gearóid Dullea

GREAT BRITAIN
APOSTOLIC NUNCIO TO GREAT BRITAIN
Most Revd Antonio Mennini, 54 Parkside, London SW19 5NE
T 020-8944 7189

ENGLAND AND WALES
THE MOST REVD ARCHBISHOPS
Westminster, Cardinal Vincent Nichols, *cons.* 1992, *apptd* 2009 *Archbishop Emeritus,* Cardinal Cormac Murphy-O'Connor, *cons.* 1977, *elevated* 2001 *Auxiliaries,* John Sherrington, *cons.* 2011; Nicholas

Hudson, *cons.* 2014. *Clergy*, 318. *Archbishop's House*, Ambrosden Avenue, London SW1P 1QJ T 020-7798 9033

Birmingham, Bernard Longley, *cons.* 2003, *apptd* 2009 *Auxiliaries*, William Kenney, *cons.* 1987; David McGough, *cons.* 2005; Robert Byrne, *cons.* 2014. *Clergy*, 430. *Archbishop's House*, 8 Shadwell Street, Birmingham B4 6EY T 0121-236 9090

Cardiff, George Stack, *cons.* 2001, *apptd* 2011. *Clergy*, 47. *Archbishop's House*, 43 Cathedral Road, Cardiff CF11 9HD T 029-2022 0411

Liverpool, Malcolm McMahon, *cons.* 2000, *apptd* 2014 *Auxiliary*, Thomas Williams, *cons.* 2003. *Clergy*, 402. *Liverpool Archdiocesan Centre for Evangelisation*, Croxteth Drive, Sefton Park, Liverpool L17 1AA T 0151-522 1000

Southwark, Peter Smith, *cons.* 1995, *apptd* 2010 *Auxiliaries*, Patrick Lynch, *cons.* 2006; Paul Hendricks, *cons.* 2006. *Clergy*, 366. *Archbishop's House*, 150 St George's Road, London SE1 6HX T 020-7928 2495

THE RT. REVD BISHOPS

Arundel and Brighton, Michael Moth, *cons.* 2015, *apptd* 2015. *Clergy*, 95. *Bishop's House*, The Upper Drive, Hove, E. Sussex BN3 6NB T 01273-506387

Brentwood, Alan Williams, *cons.* 2014, *apptd* 2014. *Clergy*, 170. *Bishop's Office*, Cathedral House, Ingrave Road, Brentwood, Essex CM15 8AT T 01277-232266

Clifton, Declan Lang, *cons.* 2001, *apptd* 2001. *Clergy*, 153. *Bishop's House*, St Ambrose, North Road, Leigh Woods, Bristol BS8 3PW T 0117-973 3072

East Anglia, Alan Hopes, *cons.* 2003, *apptd* 2013. *Clergy*, 129. *Diocesan Curia*, The White House, 21 Upgate, Poringland, Norwich NR14 7SH T 01508-492202

Hallam, Ralph Heskett, *cons.* 2010, *apptd* 2014. *Clergy*, 71. *Bishop's House*, 75 Norfolk Road, Sheffield S2 2SZ T 0114-278 7988

Hexham and Newcastle, Seamus Cunningham, *cons.* 2009, *apptd* 2009. *Clergy*, 164. *Bishop's House*, East Denton Hall, 800 West Road, Newcastle upon Tyne NE5 2BJ T 0191-228 0003

Lancaster, Michael Campbell, *cons.* 2008, *apptd* 2009. *Clergy*, 97. *Bishop's Office*, The Pastoral Centre, Balmoral Road, Lancaster LA1 3BT T 01524-596050

Leeds, Marcus Stock. *Clergy*, 193. *Diocesan Curia*, Hinsley Hall, 62 Headingley Lane, Leeds LS6 2BX T 0113-230 4533

Menevia (Wales), Tom Burns, *cons.* 2002, *apptd* 2008. *Clergy*, 60. *Diocesan Office*, 27 Convent Street, Swansea SA1 2BX T 01792-644017

Middlesbrough, Terence Drainey, *cons.* 2008, *apptd* 2007. *Clergy*, 83. *Diocesan Curia*, 50A The Avenue, Linthorpe, Middlesbrough TS5 6QT T 01642-850505

Northampton, Peter Doyle, *cons.* 2005, *apptd* 2005. *Clergy*, 116. *Bishop's House*, Marriott Street, Northampton NN2 6AW T 01604-715635

Nottingham, vacant. *Clergy*, 166. *Bishop's House*, 27 Cavendish Road East, The Park, Nottingham NG7 1BB T 0115-947 4786

Plymouth, Mark O'Toole, *cons.* 2014, *apptd* 2013. *Clergy*, 50. *Bishop's House*, 45 Cecil Street, Plymouth PL1 5HW T 01752-224414

Portsmouth, Philip Egan, *cons.* 2012, *apptd* 2012. *Clergy*, 214. *Bishop's House*, Bishop Crispian Way, Portsmouth, Hants PO1 3HG T 023-9282 0894

Salford, John Arnold, *cons.* 2006, *trans.* 2014. *Clergy*, 218. *Diocesan Curia*, Wardley Hall, Worsley, Manchester M28 2ND T 0161-794 2825

Shrewsbury, Mark Davies, *cons.* 2010, *apptd* 2010. *Clergy* 112. *Diocesan Curia*, 2 Park Road South, Prenton, Wirral CH43 4UX T 0151-652 9855

Wrexham (Wales), Peter Brignall, *cons.* 2012, *apptd* 2012. *Clergy*, 16. *Bishop's House*, Sontley Road, Wrexham LL13 7EW T 01978-262726

SCOTLAND
THE MOST REVD ARCHBISHOPS

St Andrews and Edinburgh, Leo Cushley, *cons.* 2013, *apptd* 2013. *Archbishop Emeritus*, HE Cardinal Keith O'Brien, *cons.* 1985, *elevated* 2003. *Clergy*, 50. *Archdiocesan Offices*, 100 Strathearn Road, Edinburgh EH9 1BB T 0131-623 8900

Glasgow, Philip Tartaglia, *cons.* 2005, *elevated* 2012. *Clergy*, 198. *Diocesan Curia*, 196 Clyde Street, Glasgow G1 4JY T 0141-226 5898

THE RT. REVD BISHOPS

Aberdeen, Hugh Gilbert, *cons.* 2011, *apptd* 2011. *Clergy*, 47. *Bishop's House*, 3 Queen's Cross, Aberdeen AB15 4XU T 01224-319154

Argyll and the Isles, vacant. *Clergy*, 32. *Diocesan Office* Bishop's House, Esplanade, Oban, Argyll PA34 5AB T 01631-567436

Dunkeld, Stephen Robson, *cons.* 2012, *apptd* 2013. *Clergy*, 43. *Diocesan Curia*, 24–28 Lawside Road, Dundee DD3 6XY T 01382-225453

Galloway, William Nolan, *cons.* 2015, *apptd* 2014. *Clergy*, 19. *Diocesan Office*, 8 Corsehill Road, Ayr KA7 2ST T 01292-266750

Motherwell, Joseph Toal, *cons.* 2008, *trans.* 2014. *Clergy*, 123. *Diocesan Curia*, Coursington Road, Motherwell ML1 1PP T 01698-269114

Paisley, John Keenan, *cons.* 2014, *apptd* 2014. *Clergy*, 75. *Diocesan Curia*, Cathedral Precincts, Incle Street, Paisley PA1 1HR T 0141-847 6131

BISHOPRIC OF THE FORCES
vacant.
Administration, RC Bishopric of the Forces, Wellington House, St Omer Barracks, Thornhill Road, Aldershot, Hants GU11 2BG T 01252-348234

IRELAND
There is one hierarchy for the whole of Ireland. Several of the dioceses have territory partly in the Republic of Ireland and partly in Northern Ireland.

APOSTOLIC NUNCIO TO IRELAND
Most Revd Charles John Brown (Titular Archbishop of Aquileia), 183 Navan Road, Dublin 7 T (+353) (1) 838 0577

THE MOST REVD ARCHBISHOPS

Armagh, Eamon Martin (*also* Primate of all Ireland), *cons.* 2013, *apptd* 2014. *Clergy*, 135. *Bishop's Residence*, Ara Coeli, Cathedral Road, Armagh BT61 7QY T 028-3752 5103

Cashel and Emly, Kieran O'Reilly, *cons.* 2010, *trans.* 2015. *Clergy*, 83. *Archbishop's House*, Thurles, Co. Tipperary T (+353) (504) 21512

Dublin, Diarmuid Martin, *cons.* 1999, *apptd* Coadjutor Archbishop 2003, *succeeded as Archbishop* 2004. *Archbishop Emeritus*, HE Cardinal Desmond Connell, *cons.* 1988, *elevated* 2001. *Auxiliaries*, Eamonn Walsh, *cons.* 1990; Raymond Field, *cons.* 1997. *Clergy*, 389. *Archbishop's House*, Drumcondra, Dublin 9 T (+353) (1) 837 9253

Tuam, Dr Michael Neary, *cons.* 1992, *apptd* 1995. *Clergy*, 110. *Archbishop's House*, Tuam, Co. Galway T (+353) (93) 24166

THE MOST REVD BISHOPS

Achonry, Brendan Kelly, *cons.* 2008, *apptd* 2007. *Clergy,* 50.
 Bishop's House, Edmondstown, Ballaghaderreen, Co.
 Roscommon **T** (+353) (94) 986 0021

Ardagh and Clonmacnois, Francis Duffy, *cons.* 2013,
 apptd 2013. *Clergy,* 60. *Diocesan Office,* St Michael's,
 Ballinalee Road, Longford, Co. Longford **T** (+353) (43) 334 6432

Clogher, Liam MacDaid, *cons.* 2010, *apptd* 2010. *Clergy,* 74.
 Bishop's House, Monaghan **T** (+353) (47) 81019

Clonfert, John Kirby, *cons.* 1988, *apptd* 1988. *Clergy,* 37.
 Bishop's House, Coorheen, Loughrea, Co. Galway
 T (+353) (91) 841560

Cloyne, William Crean, *cons.* 2013, *apptd* 2013. *Clergy,* 126.
 Diocesan Office, Cobh, Co. Cork **T** (+353) (21) 481 1430

Cork and Ross, John Buckley, *cons.* 1984, *apptd* 1998.
 Clergy, 133. *Diocesan Office,* Cork and Ross Offices,
 Redemption Road, Cork **T** (+353) (21) 430 1717

Derry, Donal McKeown, *cons.* 2001, *apptd* 2014.
 Clergy, 108. *Bishop's House,* St Eugene's Cathedral,
 Derry BT48 9AP **T** 028-7126 2302

Down and Connor, Noel Treanor, *cons.* 2008, *apptd* 2008.
 Auxiliary, Anthony Farquhar, *cons.* 1983. *Clergy,* 199.
 Bishop's Residence, Lisbreen, 73 Somerton Road, Belfast,
 Co. Antrim BT15 4DE **T** 028-9077 6185

Dromore, John McAreavey, *cons.* 1999, *apptd* 1999.
 Clergy, 33. *Bishop's House,* 44 Armagh Road, Newry,
 Co. Down BT35 6PN **T** 028-3026 2444

Elphin, Kevin Doran, *cons.* 2014, *apptd* 2014. *Clergy,* 66.
 Bishop's House, Temple St, St Mary's, Sligo
 T (+353) (71) 915 0106

Ferns, Denis Brennan, *cons.* 2006, *apptd* 2006. *Clergy,* 88.
 Bishop's House, Summerhill, Wexford **T** (+353) (53) 912 2177

Galway, Kilmacduagh and Kilfenora, Martin Drennan,
 cons. 1997, *apptd* 2005. *Clergy,* 57. *Diocesan Office,*
 The Cathedral, Galway **T** (+353) (91) 563566

Kerry, Ray Browne, *cons.* 2013, *apptd* 2013. *Clergy,* 88.
 Bishop's House, Killarney, Co. Kerry **T** (+353) (64) 663 1168

Kildare and Leighlin, Denis Nulty, *cons.* 2013, *apptd* 2013.
 Clergy, 72. *Bishop's House,* Old Dublin Road, Carlow Town
 T (+353) (59) 917 6725

Killala, John Fleming, *cons.* 2002, *apptd* 2002. *Clergy,* 40.
 Bishop's House, Ballina, Co. Mayo **T** (+353) (96) 21518

Killaloe, vacant. *Clergy,* 95. *Diocesan Office,* Westbourne,
 Ennis, Co. Clare **T** (+353) (65) 682 8638

Kilmore, Leo O'Reilly, *cons.* 1997, *apptd* 1998. *Clergy,* 67.
 Bishop's House, Cullies, Cavan, Co. Cavan
 T (+353) (49) 433 1496

Limerick, Brendan Leahy, *cons.* 2013, *apptd* 2013.
 Clergy, 109. *Diocesan Office,* Social Service Centre,
 Henry Street, Limerick **T** (+353) (61) 315856

Meath, Michael Smith, *cons.* 1984, *apptd* 1990. *Clergy,* 120.
 Bishop's House, Dublin Road, Mullingar, Co. Westmeath
 T (+353) (44) 934 8841

Ossory, Séamus Freeman, *cons.* 2007, *apptd* 2007. *Clergy,* 81.
 Diocesan Office, James's Street, Kilkenny
 T (+353) (56) 776 2448

Raphoe, Dr Philip Boyce, *cons.* 1995, *apptd* 1995. *Clergy,* 80.
 Bishop's House, Ard Adhamhnáin, Letterkenny, Co. Donegal
 T (+353) (74) 912 1208

Waterford and Lismore, Alphonsus Cullinan, *cons.* 2015,
 apptd 2015. *Clergy,* 114. *Bishop's House,* John's Hill,
 Waterford **T** (+353) (51) 874463

OTHER CHURCHES IN THE UK

ASSOCIATED PRESBYTERIAN CHURCHES OF SCOTLAND

The Associated Presbyterian Churches came into being in 1989 as a result of a division within the Free Presbyterian Church of Scotland. The Associated Presbyterian Churches is reformed and evangelistic in nature and emphasises the importance of doctrine based primarily on the Bible and secondly on the Westminster Confession of Faith. There are an estimated 500 members, 8 ministers and 18 congregations in Scotland. There are also congregations in Canada.

ASSOCIATED PRESBYTERIAN CHURCHES OF
 SCOTLAND, 64 Roxburgh Road, Wick KW1 5HP
 T 01955-928075 **W** www.apchurches.org
 Presbytery Clerk, Revd Ross Macaskill

BAPTIST CHURCH

Baptists trace their origins to John Smyth, who in 1609 in Amsterdam reinstituted the baptism of conscious believers as the basis of the fellowship of a gathered church. Members of Smyth's church established the first Baptist church in England in 1612. They came to be known as 'General' Baptists and their theology was Arminian, whereas a later group of Calvinists who adopted the baptism of believers came to be known as 'Particular' Baptists. The two sections of the Baptists were united into one body, the Baptist Union of Great Britain and Ireland, in 1891. In 1988 the title was changed to the Baptist Union of Great Britain.

Baptists emphasise the complete autonomy of the local church, although individual churches are linked in various kinds of associations. There are international bodies (such as the Baptist World Alliance) and national bodies, but some Baptist churches belong to neither. However, in Great Britain the majority of churches and associations belong to the Baptist Union of Great Britain. There are also Baptist Unions in Wales, Scotland and Ireland, which are much smaller than the Baptist Union of Great Britain, and there is some overlap of membership.

There are currently around 135,000 members, 2,500 ministers and 2,084 churches associated with the Baptist Union of Great Britain. The Baptist Union of Great Britain is one of the founder members of the European Baptist Federation (1948) and the Baptist World Alliance (1905); the latter represents 42 million members worldwide.

In the Baptist Union of Wales (Undeb Bedyddwyr Cymru) there are 11,355 members, 88 pastors and 386 churches, including those in England.

In the Baptist Union of Scotland there are 11,500 members and 165 churches.

BAPTIST UNION OF GREAT BRITAIN, Baptist House,
 PO Box 44, 129 Broadway, Didcot, Oxon OX11 8RT
 T 01235-517700 **W** www.baptist.org.uk
 President (2015–16), Revd Jenni Entrican
 General Secretary, Revd Lynn Green

BAPTIST UNION OF WALES, Y Llwyfan, College Road,
 Carmarthen SA31 3EQ **T** 01267-245660
 E judith@bedyddwyrcymru.co.uk **W** www.buw.org.uk
 President of the English Assembly (2015–16), Revd Peter
  Thomas
 President of the Welsh Assembly (2015–16), Revd I. Elfryn
  Jones
 General Secretary of the Baptist Union of Wales, Revd Judith
  Morris

BAPTIST UNION OF SCOTLAND, 48 Speirs Wharf, Glasgow
 G4 9TH **T** 0141-423 6169 **E** admin@scottishbaptist.org.uk
 General Director, Revd A. Donaldson

THE BRETHREN

The Brethren was founded in Dublin in 1827–8, basing itself on the structures and practices of the early church and rejecting denominationalism and clericalism. Many groups sprang up; the group at Plymouth became the best known, resulting in its designation by others as the 'Plymouth

Brethren'. Early worship had a prescribed form but quickly assumed an unstructured, non-liturgical format.

There are services devoted to worship, usually involving the breaking of bread, and separate preaching meetings. There is no salaried ministry.

A theological dispute led in 1848 to schism between the Open Brethren and the Closed or Exclusive Brethren, each branch later suffering further divisions.

Open Brethren churches are run by appointed elders and are completely independent, but freely cooperate with each other. Exclusive Brethren churches believe in a universal fellowship between congregations. They do not have appointed elders, but use respected members of their congregation to perform certain administrative functions.

The Brethren are established throughout the UK, Ireland, Europe, India, Africa and Australasia. In the UK there are over 70,000 members, 1,250 assembly halls and over 200 full-time Bible teachers, evangelists and administrators. There are a number of publishing houses that publish Brethren-related literature. Chapter Two is the main supplier of such literature in the UK; it also has a Brethren history archive which is available for use by appointment.

CHAPTER TWO, 3 Conduit Mews, London SE18 7AP

T 020-8316 5389 E info@chaptertwobooks.org.uk

W www.chaptertwobooks.org.uk

CONGREGATIONAL FEDERATION

The Congregational Federation was founded by members of Congregational churches in England and Wales who did not join the United Reformed Church in 1972. There are also churches in Scotland and France affiliated to the federation. The federation exists to encourage congregations of believers to worship in free assembly, but it has no authority over them and emphasises their right to independence and self-governance.

The federation has 7,060 members, 187 accredited ministers and 265 churches in England, Wales and Scotland.

CONGREGATIONAL FEDERATION, 8 Castle Gate,

Nottingham NG1 7AS T 0115-911 1460

E admin@congregational.org.uk

W www.congregational.org.uk

President of the Federation (2015–16), Betty Bentham

General Secretary, Yvonne Campbell

FELLOWSHIP OF INDEPENDENT EVANGELICAL CHURCHES

The Fellowship of Independent Evangelical Churches (FIEC) was founded by Revd E. J. Poole-Connor (1872–1962) in 1922. In 1923 the fellowship published its first register of non-denominational pastors, evangelists and congregations who had accepted the doctrinal basis for the fellowship.

Members of the fellowship have two primary convictions: firstly to defend the evangelical faith, and secondly that evangelicalism is the bond that unites the fellowship, rather than forms of worship or church government.

The FIEC exists to promote the welfare of non-denominational Bible churches and to give expression to the fundamental doctrines of evangelical Christianity. It supports individual churches by gathering and disseminating information and resources and advising churches on current theological, moral, social and practical issues.

There are currently 516 churches affiliated to the fellowship.

FELLOWSHIP OF INDEPENDENT EVANGELICAL CHURCHES, 39 The Point, Market Harborough,

Leics LE16 7QU T 01858-434540 E admin@fiec.org.uk

W www.fiec.org.uk

National Director, John Stevens

FREE CHURCH OF ENGLAND

The Free Church of England, otherwise called the Reformed Episcopal Church, is an independent episcopal church, constituted according to the historic faith, tradition and practice of the Church of England. Its roots lie in the 18th century, but it started to grow significantly from the 1840s onwards, as clergy and congregations joined it from the established church in protest against the Oxford Movement. The historic episcopate was conferred on the English church in 1876 through bishops of the Reformed Episcopal Church (which had broken away from the Protestant Episcopal Church in the USA in 1873). A branch of the Reformed Episcopal Church was founded in the UK and this merged with the Free Church of England in 1927 to create the present church. The Orders of the Free Church of England are recognised by the Church of England.

Worship is according to the *Book of Common Prayer* and some modern liturgy is permissable. Only men are ordained to the orders of deacon, presbyter and bishop.

The Free Church of England has two dioceses, 19 congregations and around 900 members in England. There is one congregation in St Petersburg, Russia and three congregations and six missions in Brazil.

THE FREE CHURCH OF ENGLAND, 329 Wolverhampton Road West, Willenhall, W. Midlands WV13 2RL

T 01902-607335 W www.fcofe.org.uk

Bishop Primus, Rt. Revd Dr John Fenwick (Bishop of the Northern Diocese)

General Secretary, Rt. Revd Paul Hunt (Bishop of the Southern Diocese)

FREE CHURCH OF SCOTLAND

The Free Church of Scotland was formed in 1843 when over 400 ministers withdrew from the Church of Scotland as a result of interference in the internal affairs of the church by the civil authorities. In 1900, all but 26 ministers joined with others to form the United Free Church (most of which rejoined the Church of Scotland in 1929). In 1904 the remaining 26 ministers were recognised by the House of Lords as continuing the Free Church of Scotland.

The church maintains strict adherence to the Westminster Confession of Faith (1648) and accepts the Bible as the sole rule of faith and conduct. Its general assembly meets annually. It also has links with reformed churches overseas. The Free Church of Scotland has about 12,000 members, 90 ministers and 100 congregations.

FREE CHURCH OF SCOTLAND, 15 North Bank Street,

The Mound, Edinburgh EH1 2LS T 0131-226 5286

E offices@freechurchofscotland.org.uk W www.freechurch.org

Chief Administrative Officer, Rod Morrison

FREE PRESBYTERIAN CHURCH OF SCOTLAND

The Free Presbyterian Church of Scotland was formed in 1893 by two ministers of the Free Church of Scotland who refused to accept a Declaratory Act passed by the Free Church General Assembly in 1892. The Free Presbyterian Church of Scotland is Calvinistic in doctrine and emphasises observance of the Sabbath. It adheres strictly to the Westminster Confession of Faith (1648).

The church has about 700 members in Scotland. It has 17 ministers and 40 churches in the UK.

FREE PRESBYTERIAN CHURCH OF SCOTLAND,

133 Woodlands Road, Glasgow G3 6LE

E outreach@fpchurch.org.uk W www.fpchurch.org.uk

Moderator (2015–16), Revd Keith Watkins

Clerk of the Synod, Revd John MacLeod

HOLY APOSTOLIC CATHOLIC ASSYRIAN CHURCH OF THE EAST

The Holy Apostolic Catholic Assyrian Church of the East traces its beginnings to the middle of the first century. It spread from Upper Mesopotamia throughout the territories of the Persian Empire. The Assyrian Church of the East became theologically separated from the rest of the Christian community following the Council of Ephesus in 431. The church is headed by the Catholicos Patriarch and is episcopal in government. The liturgical language is Syriac (Aramaic). The Assyrian Church of the East and the Roman Catholic Church agreed a common Christological declaration in 1994, and a process of dialogue between the Assyrian Church of the East and the Chaldean Catholic Church, which is in communion with Rome but shares the Syriac liturgy, was instituted in 1996.

The church has around 325,000 members in the Middle East, India, Russia, Europe, North America and Australasia. In Great Britain there is one parish, which is situated in London. The church in Great Britain forms part of the Diocese of Europe under HG Mar Odisho Oraham.

HOLY APOSTOLIC CATHOLIC ASSYRIAN CHURCH OF THE EAST, St Mary's Church, Westminster Road, Hanwell, London W7 3TU T 020-8567 1814

INDEPENDENT METHODIST CHURCHES

The Independent Methodist Churches were formed in 1805 and remained independent when the Methodist Church in Great Britain was formed in 1932. They are mainly concentrated in the industrial areas of the north of England.

The churches are Methodist in doctrine but their organisation is congregational. All the churches are members of the Independent Methodist Connexion of Churches. The controlling body of the Connexion is the Annual Meeting, to which churches send delegates. The Connexional President is elected every two years. Between annual meetings the affairs of the Connexion are handled by the Connexional Committee and departmental committees. Ministers are appointed by the churches and trained through the Connexion. The ministry is open to both men and women.

There are 1,600 members, 70 ministers and 74 churches in Great Britain.

INDEPENDENT METHODIST RESOURCE CENTRE, The Resource Centre, Fleet Street, Wigan WN5 0DS T 01942-223526 E resourcecentre@imcgb.org.uk W www.imcgb.org.uk
President, Ken McDermott
General Secretary, Brian Rowney

LUTHERAN CHURCH

Lutheranism is based on the teachings of Martin Luther, the German leader of the Protestant Reformation. The authority of the scriptures is held to be supreme over church tradition. The teachings of Lutheranism are explained in detail in 16th-century confessional writings, particularly the Augsburg Confession. Lutheranism is one of the largest Protestant denominations and it is particularly strong in northern Europe and the USA. Some Lutheran churches are episcopal, while others have a synodal form of organisation; unity is based on doctrine rather than structure. Most Lutheran churches are members of the Lutheran World Federation, based in Geneva.

Lutheran services in Great Britain are held in 15 languages to serve members of different nationalities. Services usually follow ancient liturgies. English-language congregations are members either of the Lutheran Church in Great Britain or of the Evangelical Lutheran Church of England. The Lutheran Church in Great Britain and other Lutheran churches in Britain are members of the Lutheran Council of Great Britain, which represents them and coordinates their common work.

There are around 70 million Lutherans worldwide, with around 180,000 members in Great Britain.

THE LUTHERAN COUNCIL OF GREAT BRITAIN, 30 Thanet Street, London WC1H 9QH T 020-7388 4044 E enquiries@lutheran.org.uk W www.lutheran.org.uk
Chair, Revd Torbjorn Holt

METHODIST CHURCH

The Methodist movement started in England in 1729 when the Revd John Wesley, an Anglican priest, and his brother Charles met with others in Oxford and resolved to conduct their lives by 'rule and method'. In 1739 the Wesleys began evangelistic preaching and the first Methodist chapel was founded in Bristol in the same year. In 1744 the first annual conference was held, at which the Articles of Religion were drawn up. Doctrinal emphases included repentance, faith, the assurance of salvation, social concern and the priesthood of all believers. After John Wesley's death in 1791 the Methodists withdrew from the established church to form the Methodist Church. Methodists gradually drifted into many groups, but in 1932 the Wesleyan Methodist Church, the United Methodist Church and the Primitive Methodist Church united to form the Methodist Church of Great Britain.

The governing body is the Conference. The Conference meets annually and consists of two parts: the ministerial and representative sessions. The Methodist Church is structured as a 'Connexion' of churches, circuits and districts. The local churches in a defined area form a circuit, and a number of these circuits make up each of the 31 districts. There are around 80 million Methodists worldwide. In Great Britain there are nearly 230,000 members, 3,680 presbyters, 171 Deacons and 5,023 churches.

THE METHODIST CHURCH OF GREAT BRITAIN, Methodist Church House, 25 Marylebone Road, London NW1 5JR T 020-7486 5502 E helpdesk@methodistchurch.org.uk W www.methodist.org.uk
President of the Conference (2015–16), Revd Steve Wild
General Secretary and Secretary of the Conference, Revd Gareth Powell

THE METHODIST CHURCH IN IRELAND
The Methodist Church in Ireland is autonomous but has close links with British Methodism. It has a community roll of 47,401, members, 123 ministers, 280 lay preachers and 221 churches.

METHODIST CHURCH IN IRELAND, 1 Fountainville Avenue, Belfast BT9 6AN T 028-9032 4554 E secretary@irishmethodist.org W www.irishmethodist.org
President (2015–16), Revd Brian Anderson
Secretary, Revd John Stephens

ORTHODOX CHURCHES

EASTERN ORTHODOX CHURCH
The Eastern (or Byzantine) Orthodox Church is a communion of self-governing Christian churches that recognises the honorary primacy of the Ecumenical Patriarch of Constantinople.

The position of Orthodox Christians is that the faith was fully defined during the period of the Oecumenical Councils. In doctrine it is strongly trinitarian, and stresses the mystery and importance of the sacraments. It is episcopal in government. The structure of the Orthodox Christian year differs from that of western churches.

Orthodox Christians throughout the world are estimated to number about 300 million; there are around 300,000 in the UK.

GREEK ORTHODOX CHURCH (PATRIARCHATE OF ANTIOCH)

The church is led by John X, Patriarch of Antioch, who was enthroned in February 2013. The UK forms part of the Archdiocese of the British Isles and Ireland. There are 15 parishes in the UK and the Republic of Ireland, including St George's Cathedral in London, and 27 clergy.

ANTIOCHIAN ORTHODOX DEANERY OF THE UK
    AND IRELAND, 29 Willis Road, Cale Green, Stockport,
    Cheshire SK3 8HQ T 0161-476 4847
    E father.gregory@.gmail.com
    W www.antiochian-orthodox.co.uk
    Dean, Archpriest Fr. Gregory Hallam

GREEK ORTHODOX CHURCH (PATRIARCHATE OF CONSTANTINOPLE)

The presence of Greek Orthodox Christians in Britain dates back at least to 1677 when Archbishop Joseph Geogirenes of Samos fled from Turkish persecution and came to London. The present Greek cathedral in Moscow Road, Bayswater, was opened for public worship in 1879, and the Diocese of Thyateira and Great Britain was established in 1922. There are now around 100 parishes and one monastery in the UK, served by one archbishop, three bishops and around 120 clergy.

THE PATRIARCHATE OF CONSTANTINOPLE IN
    GREAT BRITAIN, Archdiocese of Thyateira and Great
    Britain, Thyateira House, 5 Craven Hill, London W2 3EN
    T 020-7224 9301 E mail@thyateira.org.uk
    W www.thyateira.org.uk
    Archbishop, Gregorios of Thyateira and Great Britain

THE RUSSIAN ORTHODOX CHURCH (PATRIARCHATE OF MOSCOW)

The records of Russian Orthodox Church activities in Britain date from the visit to England of Tsar Peter I in the early 18th century. Clergy were sent from Russia to serve the chapel established to minister to the staff of the Imperial Russian Embassy in London.

In 2007, after an 80-year division, the Russian Orthodox Church Outside Russia agreed to become an autonomous part of the Russian Orthodox Church, Patriarchate of Moscow. The reunification agreement was signed by Patriarch Alexy II, 15th Patriarch of Moscow and All Russia and Metropolitan Laurus, leader of the Russian Orthodox Church Outside Russia on 17 May at a ceremony at Christ the Saviour Cathedral in Moscow. Patriarch Alexy II died on 5 December 2008. Metropolitan Kirill of Smolensk and Kaliningrad was enthroned as the 16th Patriarch of Moscow and All Russia on 1 February 2009, having been elected by a secret ballot of clergy on 27 January 2009.

The diocese of Sourozh is the diocese of the Russian Orthodox Church in Great Britain and Ireland and is led by Archbishop Elisey of Sourozh.

DIOCESE OF SOUROZH, Diocesan Office, Cathedral of the
    Dormition of the Mother of God and All Saints, 67 Ennismore
    Gardens, London SW7 1NH T 020-7584 0096
    W www.sourozh.org
    Diocesan Hierarch, Archbishop Elisey of Sourozh

SERBIAN ORTHODOX CHURCH (PATRIARCHATE OF SERBIA)

There are seven parishes in Great Britain and around 4,000 members. Great Britain is part of the Diocese of Great Britain and Scandinavia, which is led by Bishop Dositey. The church can be contacted via the church of St Sava in London.

SERBIAN ORTHODOX CHURCH IN GREAT BRITAIN,
    Church of Saint Sava, 89 Lancaster Road, London W11 1QQ
    T 020-7727 8367 E crkva@spclondon.org
    W www.spclondon.org
    Archpriest, Very Revd Goran Spaic

OTHER NATIONALITIES

The Patriarchates of Romania and Bulgaria (Diocese of Western Europe) have memberships estimated at 20,000 and 2,000 respectively, while the Georgian Orthodox Church has around 500 members. The Belarusian (membership estimated at 2,400) and Latvian (membership of around 100).

ORIENTAL ORTHODOX CHURCHES

The term 'Oriental Orthodox Churches' is now generally used to describe a group of six ancient eastern churches (Armenian, Coptic, Eritrean, Ethiopian, Indian (Malankara) and Syrian) which rejected the Christological definition of the Council of Chalcedon (AD 451). There are around 50 million members worldwide of the Oriental Orthodox Churches and over 20,000 in the UK.

ARMENIAN ORTHODOX CHURCH (CATHOLICOSATE OF ETCHMIADZIN)

The Armenian Orthodox Church is led by HH Karekin II, Catholics of All Armenians.

ARMENIAN CHURCH OF GREAT BRITAIN, The
    Armenian Vicarage, Iverna Gardens, London W8 6TP
    T 020-7937 0152 E information@armenianchurch.org.uk
    W www.armenianchurch.co.uk
    Primate, vacant

COPTIC ORTHODOX CHURCH

The Coptic Orthodox Church is headed by Pope Tawadros II, who was appointed in November 2012. There are three dioceses in the UK: the Midlands, led by HG Bishop Missael; Ireland, Scotland and north-east England, led by HG Bishop Antony; and the Papal Diocese which is led by HG Bishop Angaelos and covers all the remaining parishes in the UK.

CATHEDRAL OF ST GEORGE AT THE COPTIC
    ORTHODOX CHURCH CENTRE, Shephalbury Manor,
    Broadhall Way, Stevenage, Herts SG2 8NP T 020-7993 9001
    E admin@copticcentre.com W www.copticcentre.com
    Bishop, HG Bishop Angaelos

BRITISH ORTHODOX CHURCH

The British Orthodox Church is canonically part of the Coptic Orthodox Patriarchate of Alexandria. As it ministers to British people, all of its services are in English.

THE BRITISH ORTHODOX CHURCH, 10 Heathwood
    Gardens, Charlton, London SE7 8EP T 020-8854 3090
    E info@britishorthodox.org W www.britishorthodox.org
    Metropolitan, Abba Seraphim

ERITREAN ORTHODOX TEWAHEDO CHURCH

The Eritrean Orthodox Church was granted independence in 1994 by Pope Shenouda III, following the declaration of Eritrea's independence from Ethiopia in 1993. In 2006, the Eritrean government removed the third patriarch, Abune Antonios, from office and imprisoned him; the government replaced him with Abune Dioskoros in 2007, although the Oriental Orthodox Churches continue to recognise Antonios as the rightful patriarch. The diocesan bishop for North America, Europe and the Middle East is HG Abune Makarios.

ETHIOPIAN ORTHODOX TAWAHEDO CHURCH

The Ethiopian Orthodox Church was administratively part of the Coptic Orthodox Church of Alexandria until 1959, when it was granted its own patriarch by the Coptic Orthodox Pope of Alexandria and Patriarch of All Africa, Cyril VI. The church in London was established in 1976.

ETHIOPIAN ORTHODOX TAWAHEDO CHURCH,
    Re'ese Adbarat Saint Mary of Debre Tsion, 1 St Philip Street,
    London SW8 3RT T 020-7819 9857
    E info@debretsionlondon.org W www.debretsionlondon.org
    Priest-in-charge, Archimandrite Aba Girma Kebede

INDIAN ORTHODOX CHURCH
The Indian Orthodox Church, also known as the Malankara Orthodox Church, traces its origins to the first century. The head of the Malankara Orthodox Church is HH Baselios Mar Thoma Paulose II. The mother church of all the parishes in the UK and the Republic of Ireland is St Gregorios Church in London. The London parish has around 280 families as practising members.
INDIAN ORTHODOX CHURCH, St Gregorios Indian
  Orthodox Church, Cranfield Road, Brockley, London SE4 1UF
  T 020-8691 9456 E ioclondon@gmail.com
  W www.indian-orthodox.co.uk
  Diocesan Metropolitan, HG Dr Mathews Mar Thimothios
  Vicar, Revd Fr Thomas P. John

SYRIAN ORTHODOX CHURCH
The Syrian (Syriac) Orthodox Church of Antioch is an Oriental Orthodox Church based in the Eastern Mediterranean headed by HH Moran Mor Ignatius Aphrem II. The Patriarchate Vicariate in the UK is represented by HE Archbishop Mor Athanasius Toma Dawood.
SYRIAN ORTHODOX CHURCH IN THE UK,
  St Thomas Cathedral, 7–11 Armstrong Road, London W3 7JL
  T 020-8749 5834 E enquiry-uk@syrianorthodoxchurch.net
  W www.syrianorthodoxchurch.net
  Archbishop, HE Mor Athanasius Toma Dawood

PENTECOSTAL CHURCHES
Pentecostalism is inspired by the descent of the Holy Spirit upon the apostles at Pentecost. The movement began in Los Angeles, USA, in 1906 and is characterised by baptism with the Holy Spirit, divine healing, speaking in tongues (glossolalia) and a literal interpretation of the scriptures.
The Pentecostal movement in Britain dates from 1907. Initially, groups of Pentecostalists were led by laymen and did not organise formally. However, in 1915 the Elim Foursquare Gospel Alliance (more commonly called the Elim Pentecostal Church) was founded in Ireland by George Jeffreys and currently has about 550 churches, 68,500 adherents and 650 accredited ministers. In 1924 about 70 independent assemblies formed a fellowship called Assemblies of God in Great Britain and Ireland, which now incorporates around 570 churches, around 75,000 adherents and 1,015 ministers.
The Apostolic Church grew out of the 1904–5 Christian revivals in South Wales and was established in 1916. The Apostolic Church has around 110 churches, 7,180 adherents and 115 ministers in the UK. The New Testament Church of God was established in England in 1953 and has over 125 congregations, nearly 30,000 members and over 300 ministers across England and Wales.
In recent years many aspects of Pentecostalism have been adopted by the growing charismatic movement within the Roman Catholic, Protestant and Eastern Orthodox churches. There are about 105 million Pentecostalists worldwide, with over 350,000 adherents in the UK.
THE APOSTOLIC CHURCH, PO Box 51298, London
  SE11 9AJ T 020-7587 1802 E admin@apostolic-church.org
  W www.apostolic-church.org
  National Leader, Emmanuel Mbakwe
ASSEMBLIES OF GOD, National Ministry Centre, Mattersey,
  Doncaster DN10 5HD T 017-7781 7663 E info@aog.org.uk
  W www.aog.org.uk
  National Leader, John Partington
THE ELIM PENTECOSTAL CHURCH, Elim International
  Centre, De Walden Road, West Malvern, Worcestershire
  WR14 4DF T 0345-302 6750 E info@elimhq.net
  W www.elim.org.uk
  General Superintendent, Revd John Glass

THE NEW TESTAMENT CHURCH OF GOD, National
  Office, 3 Cheyne Walk, Northampton NN1 5PT
  T 01604-824222 W www.ntcg.org.uk
  Administrative Bishop, Donald Bolt

PRESBYTERIAN CHURCH IN IRELAND
Irish Presbyterianism traces its origins back to the Plantation of Ulster in 1606, when English and Scottish Protestants began to settle on the land confiscated from the Irish chieftains. The first presbytery was established in Ulster in 1642 by chaplains of a Scottish army that had been sent to crush a Catholic rebellion in 1641.
The Presbyterian Church in Ireland is reformed in doctrine and belongs to the World Alliance of Reformed Churches. Structurally, the 545 congregations are grouped in 19 presbyteries under the General Assembly. This body meets annually and is presided over by a moderator who is elected for one year. The ongoing work of the church is undertaken by 12 boards under which there are specialist committees.
There are over 240,000 members of Irish presbyterian churches in Ireland and Northern Ireland.
THE PRESBYTERIAN CHURCH IN IRELAND, Assembly
  Buildings, 2–10 Fisherwick Place, Belfast BT1 6DW
  T 028-9032 2284 E info@presbyterianireland.org
  W www.presbyterianireland.org
  Moderator (2015–16), Rt. Revd Ian McNie
  Clerk of Assembly and General Secretary, Revd Trevor
  Gribben

PRESBYTERIAN CHURCH OF WALES
The Presbyterian Church of Wales or Calvinistic Methodist Church of Wales is Calvinistic in doctrine and presbyterian in constitution. It was formed in 1811 when Welsh Calvinists severed the relationship with the established church by ordaining their own ministers. It secured its own confession of faith in 1823 and a Constitutional Deed in 1826, and since 1864 the General Assembly has met annually, presided over by a moderator elected for a year. The doctrine and constitutional structure of the Presbyterian Church of Wales was confirmed by act of parliament in 1931–2.
The Church has 25,000 members, 58 ministers and 653 congregations.
THE PRESBYTERIAN CHURCH OF WALES,
  Tabernacle Chapel, 81 Merthyr Road, Whitchurch,
  Cardiff CF14 1DD T 029-2062 7465
  E swyddfa.office@ebcpcw.org.uk W www.ebcpcw.org.uk
  Moderator (2014–15), Revd Neil Kirkham
  General Secretary, Revd Meirion Morris

RELIGIOUS SOCIETY OF FRIENDS (QUAKERS)
Quakerism is a religious denomination which was founded in the 17th century by George Fox and others in an attempt to revive what they saw as the original 'primitive Christianity'. The movement, at first called Friends of the Truth, started in the Midlands, Yorkshire and north-west England, but there are now Quakers all over the UK and in 36 countries around the world. The colony of Pennsylvania, founded by William Penn, was originally a Quaker settlement.
Quakers place an emphasis on the experience of God in daily life rather than on sacraments or religious occasions. There is no church calendar. Worship is largely silent and there are no appointed ministers; the responsibility for conducting a meeting is shared equally among those present. Religious tolerance and social reform have always been important to Quakers, together with a commitment to peace and non-violence in resolving disputes.

There are more than 23,000 'friends' or Quakers in Great Britain. There are around 475 places where Quaker meetings are held, many of them Quaker-owned Friends Meeting Houses. The Britain Yearly Meeting is the name given to the central organisation of Quakers in Britain.

THE RELIGIOUS SOCIETY OF FRIENDS (QUAKERS) IN BRITAIN, Friends House, 173–177 Euston Road, London NW1 2BJ **T** 020-7663 1000 **E** enquiries@quaker.org.uk **W** www.quaker.org.uk
Recording Clerk, Paul Parker

SALVATION ARMY

The Salvation Army is an international Christian organisation working in 126 countries worldwide. As a church and registered charity, The Salvation Army is funded through donations from its members, the general public and, where appropriate, government grants. The Salvation Army was founded by Methodists William and Catherine Booth in the East End of London in 1865 and marked its 150th anniversary on 2 July 2015. It now has around 40,000 members and 1,067 Salvation Army Officers (full-time ministers) in the UK. There are over 700 local church and community centres, 62 residential support centres for homeless people, 16 care homes for older people and six substance-misuse centres. It also runs a clothing recycling programme, charity shops, foodbanks, a prison-visiting service and a family-tracing service. In 1878 it adopted a quasi-military command structure intended to inspire and regulate its endeavours and to reflect its view that the church was engaged in spiritual warfare.

UK TERRITORIAL HEADQUARTERS, 101 Newington Causeway, London SE1 6BN **T** 020-7367 4500 **E** info@salvationarmy.org.uk **W** www.salvationarmy.org.uk
UK Territorial Commander, Commissioner Clive Adams

SEVENTH-DAY ADVENTIST CHURCH

The Seventh-day Adventist Church is a worldwide Christian church marked by its observance of Saturday as the Sabbath and by its emphasis on the imminent second coming of Jesus Christ. Adventists summarise their faith in '28 fundamental beliefs'. The church grew out of the Millerite movement in the USA during the mid-19th century and was formally established in 1863. The church has an ethnically and culturally diverse worldwide membership of over 17 million. In the UK and Ireland there are 34,048 members worshipping in around 300 churches and companies.

BRITISH UNION CONFERENCE OF SEVENTH-DAY ADVENTISTS, Stanborough Park, Watford WD25 9JZ **T** 01923-672251 **E** info@adventist.org.uk **W** www.adventist.org.uk
President, Pastor Ian Sweeney

THE (SWEDENBORGIAN) NEW CHURCH

The New Church is based on the teachings of the 18th-century Swedish scientist and theologian Emanuel Swedenborg (1688–1772), who believed that Jesus Christ appeared to him and instructed him to reveal the spiritual meaning of the Bible. He claimed to have visions of the spiritual world, including heaven and hell, and conversations with angels and spirits. He published several theological works, including descriptions of the spiritual world and a Bible commentary.

Swedenborgians believe that the second coming of Jesus Christ is taking place, being not an actual physical reappearance of Christ, but rather his return in spirit. It is also believed that concurrent with our life on earth is life in a parallel spiritual world, of which we are usually unconscious until death. There are around 30,000 Swedenborgians worldwide, with around 600 members, 18 churches and five ministers in the UK.

THE GENERAL CONFERENCE OF THE NEW CHURCH, Purley Chase Centre, Purley Chase Lane, Mancetter, Warwickshire CV9 2RQ **T** 01827-712370 **W** www.generalconference.org.uk
Company Secretary, Zoë Brooks

UNDEB YR ANNIBYNWYR CYMRAEG

Undeb Yr Annibynwyr Cymraeg (the Union of Welsh Independents) was formed in 1872 and is a voluntary association of Welsh Congregational churches and personal members. It is mainly Welsh-speaking. Congregationalism in Wales dates back to 1639 when the first Welsh Congregational church was opened in Gwent. Member churches are traditionally congregationalist in organisation and Calvinistic in doctrine, although a wide range of interpretations are permitted. Each church has complete independence in the governance and administration of its affairs.

The Union has around 24,000 members, 80 ministers and 440 member churches.

UNDEB YR ANNIBYNWYR CYMRAEG, 5 Axis Court, Riverside Business Park, Swansea Vale, Swansea SA7 0AJ **T** 01792-795888 **E** undeb@annibynwyr.org **W** www.annibynwyr.org
President of the Union (2014–16), Revd Dr R. Alun Evans
General Secretary, Revd Dr Geraint Tudur

UNITED REFORMED CHURCH

The United Reformed Church (URC) was first formed by the union of most of the Congregational churches in England and Wales with the Presbyterian Church of England in 1972. It is Calvinistic in doctrine, and its followers form independent self-governing congregations bound under God by covenant, a principle laid down in the writings of Robert Browne (1550–1633). From the late 16th century the movement was driven underground by persecution, but the cause was defended at the Westminster Assembly in 1643 and the Savoy Declaration of 1658 laid down its principles. Congregational churches formed county associations for mutual support and in 1832 these associations merged to form the Congregational Union of England and Wales.

In the 1960s there was close cooperation locally and nationally between congregational and presbyterian churches. This led to union negotiations and a Scheme of Union, supported by an act of parliament in 1972. In 1981 a further unification took place, with the Reformed Association of Churches of Christ becoming part of the URC. In 2000 a third union took place, with the Congregational Union of Scotland. At its basis the URC reflects local church initiative and responsibility with a conciliar pattern of oversight.

The URC is divided into 13 synods, each with a synod moderator. There are around 1,500 churches which serve around 58,000 adults and around 41,000 children and young people. There are around 550 ministers in active service.

The General Assembly is the central body, and comprises around 400 representatives, mainly appointed by the synods, of which half are lay persons and half are ministers. Since 2010 the General Assembly has met biennially to elect two moderators (one lay and one ordained), who then become the public representatives of the URC.

UNITED REFORMED CHURCH, 86 Tavistock Place, London WC1H 9RT **T** 020-7916 2020 **E** urc@urc.org.uk **W** www.urc.org.uk
Moderators of the General Assembly 2016–18, Revd Kevin Watson; Alan Yates
General Secretary, Revd John Proctor

WESLEYAN REFORM UNION

The Wesleyan Reform Union was founded by Methodists who left or were expelled from Wesleyan Methodism in 1849 following a period of internal conflict. Its doctrine is conservative evangelical and its organisation is congregational, each church having complete independence in the government and administration of its affairs. The union has around 1,540 members, 20 ministers and 96 churches.

THE WESLEYAN REFORM UNION,
Wesleyan Reform Church House, 123 Queen Street,
Sheffield S1 2DU T 0114-272 1938 E gen.sec@thewru.co.uk
W www.thewru.com
President (2015–16), Andy Wilcock
General Secretary, Revd Colin Braithwaite

NON-TRINITARIAN CHURCHES

CHRISTADELPHIAN

Christadelphians believe that the Bible is the word of God and that it reveals both God's dealings with mankind in the past and his plans for the future. These plans centre on the work of Jesus Christ, who it is believed will return to Earth to establish God's kingdom. The Christadelphian group was founded in the USA in the 1850s by the Englishman, Dr John Thomas.

THE CHRISTADELPHIAN MAGAZINE AND
PUBLISHING ASSOCIATION, 404 Shaftmoor Lane,
Hall Green, Birmingham B28 8SZ T 0121-777 6328
W www.thechristadelphian.com

CHURCH OF CHRIST, SCIENTIST

The Church of Christ, Scientist was founded by Mary Baker Eddy in the USA in 1879 to 'reinstate primitive Christianity and its lost element of healing'. Christian Science teaches the need for spiritual regeneration and salvation from sin, but it is best known for its reliance on prayer alone in the healing of sickness. Adherents believe that such healing is the result of divine laws, or divine science, and is in direct line with that practised by Jesus Christ (revered, not as God, but as the son of God) and by the early Christian church.

The denomination consists of The First Church of Christ, Scientist, in Boston, Massachusetts, USA ('The Mother Church') and its branch churches in almost 80 countries worldwide. The Bible and Mary Baker Eddy's book, *Science and Health with Key to the Scriptures,* are used for daily spiritual guidance and healing by all members and are read at services. There are no clergy; those engaged in full-time healing are called Christian Science practitioners, of whom there are around 1,500 worldwide. The church also publishes *The Christian Science Monitor.*

No membership figures are available, since Mary Baker Eddy felt that numbers are no measure of spiritual vitality and ruled that such statistics should not be published. There are almost 2,000 branch churches worldwide.

CHRISTIAN SCIENCE COMMITTEE ON
PUBLICATION, 90 Long Acre, London WC2E 9RZ
T 020-8150 0245 E londoncs@csps.com
W www.christianscience.co.uk
District Manager for the UK and Ireland, Tony Lobl

CHURCH OF JESUS CHRIST OF LATTER-DAY SAINTS

The Church of Jesus Christ of Latter-day Saints ('Mormons') was founded in New York State, USA, in 1830, and came to Britain in 1837. The oldest continuous congregation of the church is in Preston, Lancashire.

Mormons are Christians who claim to belong to the 'restored church' of Jesus Christ. They believe that true Christianity died when the last original apostle died, but that it was given back to the world by God and Jesus Christ through Joseph Smith, the church's founder and first president. They accept and use the Bible as scripture, but believe in continuing revelation from God; Mormons also use additional scriptures, including *The Book of Mormon: Another Testament of Jesus Christ.* The importance of the family is central to the church's beliefs and practices. Church members set aside Monday evenings as family home evenings when Christian family values are taught. Polygamy was formally discontinued in 1890.

The church has no paid ministry: local congregations are headed by a leader chosen from among their number. The world governing body, based in Utah, USA, is led by a president, believed to be the chosen prophet, and his two counsellors. There are over 15 million members worldwide, with 186,193 members and 335 congregations in the UK.

THE CHURCH OF JESUS CHRIST OF LATTER-DAY
SAINTS, UK Headquarters, 751 Warwick Road, Solihull,
W. Midlands B91 3DQ T 0121-712 1200
W www.mormonnewsroom.org.uk

JEHOVAH'S WITNESSES

The movement now known as Jehovah's Witnesses grew from a Bible study group formed by Charles Taze Russell in 1872 in Pennsylvania, USA. In 1896 it adopted the name of the Watch Tower Bible and Tract Society, and in 1931 its members became known as Jehovah's Witnesses.

Jehovah's (God's) Witnesses believe in the Bible as the word of God, and consider it to be inspired and historically accurate. They take the scriptures literally, except where there are obvious indications that they are figurative or symbolic, and reject the doctrine of the Trinity. Witnesses also believe that all those approved of by Jehovah will have eternal life on a cleansed and beautified earth; only 144,000 will go to heaven to rule with Jesus Christ. They believe that the second coming of Christ began in 1914, that his thousand-year reign over the earth is imminent, and that armageddon (a final battle in which evil will be defeated) will precede Christ's rule of peace. Jehovah's Witnesses refuse to take part in military service and do not accept blood transfusions.

The eight-member world governing body is based in New York, USA. There is no paid ministry, but each congregation has elders assigned to look after various duties and every Witness takes part in the public ministry in their neighbourhood. There are 7.97 million Jehovah's Witnesses worldwide, with around 136,000 Witnesses in Great Britain organised into around 1,500 congregations.

BRITISH HEADQUARTERS, The Ridgeway,
London NW7 1RN T 020-8906 2211 W www.jw.org

UNITARIAN AND FREE CHRISTIAN CHURCHES

Unitarian communities first became established in Poland and Transylvania in the 16th century. The first avowedly Unitarian place of worship in the British Isles opened in London in 1774. The General Assembly of Unitarian and Free Christian Churches came into existence in 1928 as the result of the amalgamation of two earlier organisations.

There are around 3,400 Unitarians in Great Britain in 170 self-governing congregations and fellowship groups.

GENERAL ASSEMBLY OF UNITARIAN AND FREE
CHRISTIAN CHURCHES, Essex Hall, 1–6 Essex Street,
London WC2R 3HY T 020-7240 2384 E info@unitarian.org.uk
W www.unitarian.org.uk
President (2015–16), John Clifford

COMMUNICATIONS

POSTAL SERVICES

Royal Mail was privatised on 15 October 2013 when it was listed on the London Stock Exchange. Royal Mail Holdings plc owns Royal Mail Group Ltd – which operates Royal Mail, Parcelforce Worldwide and General Logistics Systems (GLS). The Post Office remains wholly state-owned.

Royal Mail is the sole provider of the 'universal service': postal products and associated minimum service standards that must be available to all addresses in the UK. In 2014 Royal Mail collected and delivered 1,068 million parcels and 13,342 million letters to 29 million addresses across the UK. Compared with 2013, the amount of parcels collected and delivered remained the same, but the amount of letters decreased slightly by 4 per cent.

Following the passing of the Postal Services Act 2011, the Office of Communications (OFCOM) assumed regulatory responsibility for postal services. OFCOM's primary responsibility is to secure the provision of a universal postal service with regard to its financial sustainability.

ROYAL MAIL GROUP LTD, 100 Victoria Embankment, London EC4Y 0HQ T 0345-774 0740
W www.royalmailgroup.com
OFCOM, Riverside House, 2A Southwark Bridge Road, London SE1 9HA T 0207-981 3000 W www.ofcom.org.uk

PRICING IN PROPORTION
Since 2006 Royal Mail has priced mail according to its size as well as its weight. The system is intended to reflect the fact that larger, bulkier items cost more to handle than smaller, lighter ones. There are five basic categories of correspondence:

LETTER: *Length* up to 240mm, *width* up to 165mm, *thickness* up to 5mm, *weight* up to 100g; eg most cards and postcards
LARGE LETTER: *Length* up to 353mm, *width* up to 250mm, *thickness* up to 25mm, *weight* up to 750g; eg most A4 documents and magazines
SMALL PARCEL: *Length* up to 450mm, *width* up to 350mm, *thickness* up to 160mm, *weight* up to 2kg, eg books, clothes and gifts
MEDIUM PARCEL: *Length* up to 610mm, *width* up to 460mm, *thickness* up to 460mm, *weight* up to 20kg; eg gifts, shoes, heavy or bulky items
LARGE PARCEL (Parcelforce Worldwide): *Length* up to 150cm, with a combined length and width of less than 300cm, *weight* up to 30kg

For rolled and cylinder shaped parcels, eg posters and prints, the length of the item plus twice the diameter must not exceed 104cm, with the greatest dimension being no more than 90cm. Rolled and cylinder shaped parcels which measure up to 450mm in length and 80mm in diameter and which do not exceed 2kg can be sent as small parcels. Items larger than those listed above can only be sent via Parcelforce Worldwide as large parcels.

INLAND POSTAL SERVICES
Following are details of a number of popular postal services along with prices correct as at April 2015. For a full list of prices *see* W www.royalmail.com

FIRST AND SECOND CLASS

Format	Maximum weight	First class	Second class
Letter/postcard	100g	£0.63	£0.54
Large letter	100g	£0.95	£0.74
	250g	£1.26	£1.19
	500g	£1.68	£1.51
	750g	£2.42	£2.05
Small parcel	1,000g	£3.30	£2.80
	2,000g	£5.45	£2.80
Medium parcel	1,000g	£5.65	£4.89
	2,000g	£8.90	£4.89
	5,000g	£15.85	£13.75
	10,000g	£21.90	£20.25
	20,000g	£33.40	£28.55

First class post is normally delivered on the following working day and second class within three working days. Prices are exempt from VAT.

LARGE PARCEL RATES (PARCELFORCE WORLDWIDE)

Maximum weight	Lowest tariff*
2kg	£11.99
5kg	£12.98
10kg	£16.40
15kg	£23.14
20kg	£28.51
25kg	£39.64
30kg	£43.78

* The rate listed includes VAT and is for delivery within two working days

OVERSEAS POSTAL SERVICES
For charging purposes Royal Mail divides the world into four zones: UK, Europe, World Zone 1 and World Zone 2. There is a complete listing on the Royal Mail website (W www.royalmail.com/international-zones)

Europe: Albania, Andorra, Armenia, Austria, Azerbaijan, Azores, Balearic Islands, Belarus, Belgium, Bosnia and Hercegovina, Bulgaria, Canary Islands, Corsica, Croatia, Cyprus, Czech Rep., Denmark, Estonia, Finland, France, Georgia, Germany, Gibraltar, Greece, Greenland, Hungary, Iceland, Ireland, Italy, Kazakhstan, Kosovo, Kyrgyzstan, Latvia, Liechtenstein, Lithuania, Luxembourg, Macedonia, Malta, Moldova, Monaco, Montenegro, Netherlands, Norway, Poland, Portugal, Romania, Russia, San Marino, Serbia, Slovakia, Slovenia, Spain, Sweden, Switzerland, Tajikistan, Turkey, Turkmenistan, Ukraine, Uzbekistan

World Zone 1: N. America, S. America, Africa, the Middle East, the Far East and S. E. Asia

World Zone 2: Australia, British Indian Ocean Territory, Fiji, French Polynesia, Kiribati, Laos, Macau, Nauru, New Caledonia, New Zealand, Palau, Papua New Guinea, Pitcairn Islands, Singapore, Solomon Islands, Tonga, Tuvalu, Samoa

INTERNATIONAL ECONOMY MAIL RATES*

Maximum weight	Standard tariff
Letters up to 100g†	
10g	£0.85
20g	£0.85
100g	£1.37

* Formerly Surface Mail
† Can only be sent by International Economy to destinations outside of Europe

Maximum weight	Large letters	Small parcels and printed papers
100g	£2.38	£3.25
250g	£3.63	£3.75
500g	£5.08	£5.30
750g	£6.53	£6.65
1,000g	–	£8.06
2,000g	–	£13.26

Printed papers only add £1.15 for each additional 250g, or part thereof, up to 5,000g

INTERNATIONAL STANDARD MAIL RATES*

Weight up to and including	Europe	World Zone 1	World Zone 2
Letters			
10g	£1.00	£1.00	£1.00
20g	£1.00	£1.33	£1.33
100g	£1.52	£2.25	£2.25
Large letters			
100g	£2.45	£3.15	£3.30
250g	£3.70	£4.75	£5.05
500g	£5.15	£7.45	£7.90
750g	£6.60	£10.15	£10.75
Small parcels and printed papers			
100g	£3.45	£4.10	£4.45
250g	£3.95	£5.00	£5.45
500g	£5.50	£7.70	£8.45
750g	£6.85	£10.30	£11.15
1,000g	£8.26	£12.95	£13.90
2,000g	£13.46	£19.75	£21.50

Printed papers only add £1.15 for Europe, £1.70 for World Zone 1 or £1.90 for World Zone 2 for each additional 250g, or part thereof, up to 5,000g
* Formerly Airmail

SPECIAL DELIVERY SERVICES

INTERNATIONAL TRACKED AND SIGNED FOR SERVICES
There are various services available: *International Tracked & Signed* provides full end-to-end tracking, signature on delivery and online delivery confirmation to 53 destinations; *International Tracked* provides the same, but without a signature on delivery, to 39 destinations; and International Signed is tracked within the UK, a signature is taken on delivery and is available to 180 destinations. All Tracked and Signed For services deliver to Europe within 3–5 working days, and worldwide within 5–7 working days. Proof of posting and compensation up to £50 is provided as standard. Additional compensation up to £250 can be provided for an extra fee.

SAME DAY
A courier service which provides same day delivery of urgent items in most places in the UK. With collection within the hour of booking, satellite tracking, delivery confirmation and automatic compensation up to £2,500, and for an additional fee, up to £20,000, the service is charged for on a loaded mile basis T 0330-088 5522

SIGNED FOR
A service which offers proof of delivery including a signature from the receiver and compensation cover up to £50. The first class service is delivered the next working day and prices vary from £1.73 to £34.50 depending on the size and weight of the item. The second class service allows two to three working days for delivery with charges of £1.64 to £29.65.

SPECIAL DELIVERY GUARANTEED
A guaranteed next working day delivery service by 9am or 1pm with a refund option guaranteed for late delivery. With many options available, Royal Mail offers a full list of prices online W www.royalmail.com/personal/uk-delivery/special-delivery

OTHER SERVICES

KEEPSAFE
Mail is held for up to two months while the addressee is away, and is delivered when the addressee returns. Prices start at £13.10 for 17 days up to £43.40 for 66 days.

PASSPORT CHECK & SEND
For a fee of £9.75 passport applications are checked to ensure they meet the requirements set by HM Passport Office and are dispatched by special delivery. For further information *see* W www.postoffice.co.uk

POST OFFICE BOX
A Post Office (PO) Box provides a short and memorable alternative address. Mail is held at a local delivery office until the addressee is ready to collect it, or delivered to a street address for an extra fee. Prices start at £144.00 for six months or £252.00 for a year.

POSTCODE FINDER
Customers can search an online database to find UK postcodes and addresses. For more information *see* Royal Mail's postcode finder W www.royalmail.com/postcode-finder

REDELIVERY
Customers can request a redelivery of an item for up to 18 days if it was unable to be delivered. A 48-hour notice period is required for redelivery or the item can be held at the recipient's local Post Office branch for a fee of £0.70 upon collection in addition to proof of identity and the original delivery notification card.

REDIRECTION
Customers may arrange the redirection of their mail via post, at the Post Office or online, subject to verification of their identity. The service is available for 0–3 months, 3–6 months or 6–12 months at varying prices depending on the location of delivery. A full price list is available at W www.royalmail.com/personal/receiving-mail/redirection

TRACK AND TRACE
An online service for customers to track the progress of items sent using any special delivery tracked and signed for service. It is accessible from W www.royalmail.com/track-your-item

CONTACTS
Parcelforce Worldwide
    T 0344-800 4466 W www.parcelforce.com
Post Office enquiries T 0345-611 2970 W www.postoffice.co.uk
Postcode enquiry line T 0906-302 1222/ 0845-711 1222

TELECOMMUNICATIONS

Mobile network technology has improved dramatically since the launch in 1985 of the first-generation global system for mobile communications (GSM), which offered little or no data capability. In 1992 Vodafone launched a new GSM network, usually referred to as 2G or second generation, which used digital encoding and allowed voice and low-speed data communications. This technology was extended, via the enhanced data transfer rate of 2.5G, to 3G – a family of mobile standards that provide high bandwidth support to applications such as voice- and video-calling, high-speed data transfer, television streaming and full internet access. Most recently, a 4G superfast mobile spectrum was rolled out, which delivers speeds of up to 100 megabits per second (Mbps), allowing for faster download speeds on a range of devices. In February 2015, OFCOM stated that 5G data connections could be available in the UK by 2020.

FOURTH GENERATION (4G) AND WI-FI

In March 2011 OFCOM announced plans for the auction of additional spectrum (the airwaves on which all communications rely) to provide the necessary capacity for 4G technology in the UK. OFCOM originally aimed to begin the auction in early 2012, but following a consultation regarding the proposals in 2011, the auction did not take place until February 2013. The spectrum was auctioned in two bands – 800 MHz and 2.6 GHz – which lie within the 'sweetspot', the frequency in greatest demand. This combination of low and high frequencies provides the potential to cope with high demand of 4G services. The auction raised £2.34bn for HM Treasury, less than the £3.5bn that was forecast by the Office for Budget Responsibility, and considerably less than the 3G auction in 2000 which raised £22bn. The winning bidders for the distribution of 4G mobile broadband were Everything Everywhere (EE), Hutchison 3G UK (3), Niche Spectrum Ventures (a BT subsidiary), Telefonica (O2) and Vodafone.

4G coverage is expected to cover 98 per cent of the UK population indoors and above that when outdoors. The speeds offered by 4G are approximately five to ten times faster than 3G networks which allows for higher quality and faster streaming of media such as TV and films. The UK population in more rural areas, that was often outside 3G coverage, should also be able to access mobile broadband through the 4G spectrum.

EE was the first operator to launch 4G in late 2012 and by April 2013 the service was available in ten cities where the broadband speed was doubled to more than 20Mbps. O2 and Vodafone subsequently launched their 4G networks in late August 2013 while 3 began their service in December 2013. As at April 2015 EE, the largest network provider of 4G, had rolled out 4G coverage to around 510 towns and cities, covering over 80 per cent of the UK population.

The number of Wi-Fi hotspots around the world continued to increase in 2014 with 47.7 million public hotspots worldwide – the equivalent of one for every 150 people. France was ranked the most connected country with 13,096,824 hotspots, the USA second with 9,858,246, while the UK was third with 5,611,944 – one for every 11 people. There is Wi-Fi access at 150 London Underground stations, available in ticket halls, corridors and platforms. Additionally Wi-Fi is also available at 56 London Overground stations.

FIXED-LINE SERVICES

Fixed-line services saw a slight increase in 2013 to 33.38 million connections in the UK from 33.20 million in 2012. However, fixed voice call minutes continued to decline, from 103 billion minutes in 2012 to 92 billion minutes in 2013, a steady decline from the 141 billion minutes recorded in 2008. Business customers continued to gravitate towards the use of mobile phones, emails and voice over internet protocol (VoIP) services such as Skype, with a decline of 0.4 million (6 per cent) to 8.3 million in the number of business lines in 2013.

The decrease in the number of business lines was offset slightly by a small increase in the number of residential lines which rose by 0.6 million (2.0 per cent) to 25.0 million in 2013. The increase is most likely due to the increasing number of households and the necessity of most UK households to have a fixed line in order to access fixed broadband services. The average cost of a residential fixed broadband connection increased in 2013 to £16.96 (3.7 per cent) due to the continued take-up of superfast broadband services. In turn, the average headline speed increased by 5.8Mbps to 17.8Mbps, while users who invested in higher speed packages, including superfast services received a headline speed of up to 30Mbps or more. Superfast broadband connections, of which there were none in 2009, increased to 5.6 million connections, from 3.2 million in 2012.

MOBILE COMMUNICATIONS

OFCOM reported the first decrease in UK mobile subscriptions with 83.1 million active at the end of 2013, compared with 83.4 million at the end of 2012. There was a 20 per cent increase in smartphone ownership with 61 per cent of adults in the UK owning one at the start of 2014. There was a large reduction in the number of outgoing SMS messages sent in 2013, with 129.9 billion messages sent compared to 171.9 billion in 2012. The decline in text messaging is likely to be a result of the of the increasing number of smartphones being used for communication, with social media platforms and instant messaging services such as WhatsApp and iMessenger, often pre-installed, providing alternatives to SMS.

It was estimated that over 6 million 4G mobile subscriptions were active in the UK at the end of March 2014 which represented 8 per cent of active mobile subscriptions. This was a dramatic increase in 4G subscriptions of which there were only 318,000 at the start of 2013. At the end of 2013 there were an estimated 55 million UK mobile data connections, including machine-to-machine (M2M); the majority of this was due to an increase in the number of handsets used to access data services, up by 6.2 million (16.1 per cent) to 44.5 million as a result of increased smartphone ownership.

MOBILE DATA USAGE

The proportion of adults who browsed the web, used email, downloaded apps and used instant messaging all increased

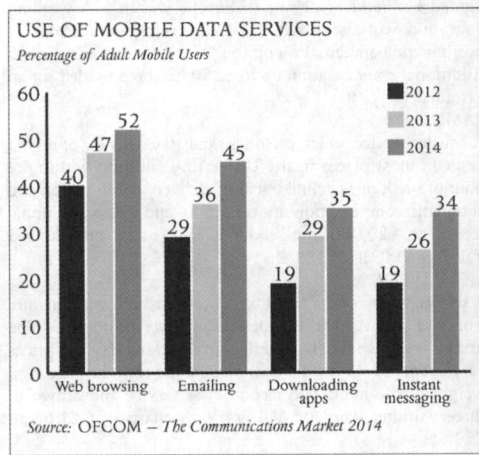

SMARTPHONE OWNERSHIP BY AGE
Percentage

Source: OFCOM – The Communications Market 2014

USE OF MOBILE DATA SERVICES
Percentage of Adult Mobile Users

Source: OFCOM – The Communications Market 2014

at the start of 2014; 52 per cent of mobile users said they browsed the internet on their mobile phone in the first quarter of 2014, an 11 per cent increase compared to the same period in 2013. Between the 2013 and 2014 the number of mobile users who downloaded apps increased from 29 to 35 per cent while those using instant messaging increased from 26 to 34 per cent.

HEALTH
In 1999 the Independent Expert Group on Mobile Phones (IEGMP) was established to examine the possible effects on health of mobile phones, base stations and transmitters. The main findings of the IEGMP's report *Mobile Phones and Health,* published in May 2000, were:
- exposure to radio frequency radiation below guideline levels did not cause adverse health effects to the general population
- the use of mobile phones by drivers of any vehicle can increase the chance of accidents
- the widespread use of mobile phones by children for non-essential calls should be discouraged because if there are unrecognised adverse health effects children may be more vulnerable
- there is no general risk to the health of people living near to base stations on the basis that exposures are expected to be much lower than guidelines set by the International Commission on Non-Ionising Radiation Protection

The government set up the Mobile Telecommunications Health and Research (MTHR) programme in 2001 to undertake independent research into the possible health risks from mobile telephone technology. The MTHR programme published its report in September 2007 concluding that, in the short term, neither mobile phones nor base stations have been found to be associated with any biological or adverse health effects. An international cohort study into the possible long-term health effects of mobile phone use was launched by the MTHR in April 2010. The study is known as COSMOS and aims to follow the health of 250,000 mobile phone users from five countries over 20 to 30 years. The full 2007 report and details of COSMOS can be found on the MTHR and COSMOS websites (W www.mthr.org.uk; www.ukcosmos.org).

A national measurement programme, to ensure that emissions from mobile phone base stations do not exceed the ICNIRP guideline levels, is overseen by OFCOM and annual audits of these levels can be found on the sitefinder part of its website. The Health Protection Agency (HPA), part of Public Health England from 1 April 2013, is responsible for providing information and advice in relation to the health effects of electromagnetic fields, including those emitted from mobile phones and base stations. In April 2012, the HPA's independent Advisory Group on Non-ionising Radiation published a report concluding that there was no convincing evidence that mobile phone technologies cause adverse effects on human health.

SAFETY WHILE DRIVING
Under legislation that came into effect in December 2003 it is illegal for drivers to use a hand-held mobile phone while driving. Since February 2007, under the Road Safety Act 2006, the fixed penalty for using a hand-held mobile device while driving is £100 and three penalty points. The same fixed penalty can also be issued to a driver for not having proper control of a vehicle while using a hands-free device. If the police or driver chooses to take the case to court rather than issue or accept a fixed penalty notice, the driver may be disqualified from driving in addition to a maximum fine of £1,000 for car drivers and £2,500 for drivers of buses, coaches or heavy goods vehicles. The only exceptions for using a mobile phone while driving are to call the emergency services, or when the driver is safely parked.

REGULATION
Under the Communications Act 2003, OFCOM is the independent regulator and competition authority for the UK communications industries, with responsibilities across television, radio, telecommunications and wireless communications services. Competition in the communications market is also regulated by the Office of Fair Trading, although OFCOM takes the lead in competition investigations in the UK market. The Competition Appeal Tribunal hears appeals against OFCOM's decisions, and price-related appeals are referred to the Competition Commission.

CONTACTS
OFCOM, Riverside House, 2A Southwark Bridge Road, London SE1 9HA T 020-7981 3000 W www.ofcom.org.uk

INTERNET

In 2014, 22 million households in Great Britain had internet access. This represented 84 per cent of households, up from 83 per cent in 2013. Of the households with internet access, 91 per cent used a fixed broadband connection.

In 2014 68 per cent of adults reported that they had used a device such as a mobile phone, portable computer (tablet or laptop) or other handheld device to access the internet 'on the go' (away from the home or workplace). Of these, 58 per cent used a mobile phone or smart phone, 43 per cent used a portable computer and 15 per cent used an ebook reader or other handheld device.

Over a four-year period between 2010–14, the number of adults who accessed the internet using a mobile phone more than doubled from 24 per cent to 58 per cent, with 96 per cent of those aged 16 to 24 reporting that they used their mobile phone to access the internet in 2014. The dramatic increase in these figures is predominantly due to the ownership of smartphones with enhanced technology to facilitate easier internet access.

In 2014, 54 per cent of all adults (aged 16+) used social networking sites such as Facebook and Twitter with 91 per cent of those aged 16 to 24 using these media platforms as a form of internet communication. For this age range, social networking has replaced sending emails as the most popular internet activity.

The youngest demographic represented, aged 16 to 24, were proportionally the largest users of many of the available internet activities, due to their familiarity with internet usage from an early age. This age group were most likely to engage in online activities including social networking, blogging, or downloading games, films or music. Those aged 25 to 34 engaged in more established activities such as personal banking and shopping – the latter saw a small increase in demand, with 74 per cent of adults buying goods or services online in 2014. A rise in internet shopping was also evident among those aged over 65, as 40 per cent made purchases online, over twice as many as in 2008.

There were 4 million households with no internet access in 2014, the majority (53 per cent) stating they did not need it. Of the households with no internet connection, 32 per cent indicated that this was due to a lack of computer skills, while other reasons included equipment costs (12 per cent) and access costs (11 per cent).

In 2014, 38 million adults (76 per cent) accessed the internet daily, 21 million more than in 2006, when directly comparable records began.

TOP TEN BROADBAND SUBSCRIBERS BY COUNTRY
fixed lines

Country (2013 position)	Number of Subscribers 2014
1. China (all territories) (1)	201,000,000
2. USA (2)	97,000,000
3. Japan (3)	36,000,000
4. Germany (4)	29,000,000
5. France (6)	26,000,000
6. Russia (5)	25,000,000
7. UK (7)	24,000,000
8. Brazil (8)	23,000,000
9. South Korea (9)	19,000,000
10. Mexico (*)	17,000,000

* Not in the 2013 Top Ten

Sources: Office for National Statistics – *Internet Access – Households and Individuals, 2014* (Crown Copyright); Point Topic

GLOSSARY OF TERMS

The following is a list of selected internet terms. It is by no means exhaustive but is intended to cover those that the average computer user might encounter.

BANNER AD: An advertisement on a web page that links to a corresponding website when clicked.

BLOG: Short for 'web log' – an online personal journal that is frequently updated and intended to be read by the public. Blogs are kept by 'bloggers' and are commonly available as RSS feeds.

BOOKMARKS: A method of storing links or automatic pathways within web browsers which allow a user to quickly return to a webpage. Referred to as 'Favourites' in Internet Explorer.

BROWSER: Typically refers to a 'web browser' program that allows a computer user to view web page content on their computer, eg Firefox, Internet Explorer or Safari.

CLICK-THROUGH: The number of times a web user 'clicks through' a paid advertisement link to the corresponding website.

CLOUD COMPUTING: The use of IT resources as an on-demand service across a network; through cloud computing, software, advanced computation and archived information can be accessed remotely, without the user needing local dedicated hardware.

COOKIE: A piece of information placed on a user's hard disk by a web server. Cookies contain data about the user's activity on a website, and are returned to the server whenever a browser makes further requests. They are important for remembering information such as login and registration details, 'shopping cart' data, user preferences etc, and are often set to expire after a fixed period.

DOMAIN: A set of words or letters, separated by dots, used to identify an internet server, eg www.whitakers almanack.com, where 'www' denotes a web (http) server, 'whitakersalmanack' denotes the organisation name and 'com' denotes that the organisation is a company.

FIREWALL: A protection system designed to prevent unauthorised access to or from a private network.

FTP: File Transfer Protocol – a set of network rules enabling a user to exchange files with a remote server.

HACKER: A person who attempts to break or 'hack' into websites. Motives typically involve the desire to procure personal information such as addresses, passwords or credit card details. Hackers may also delete code or incorporate traces of malicious code to damage the functionality of a website.

HIT: A single request from a web browser for a single item from a web server. In order for a web browser to display a page that contains three graphics, four 'hits' would occur at the server: one for the HTML page and one for each of the three graphics. Therefore the number of hits on a website is not synonymous with the number of visitors.

HTML: HyperText Mark-up Language – a programming language used to denote or mark up how an internet page should be presented to a user from an HTTP server via a web browser.

HTTP: HyperText Transfer Protocol – an internet protocol whereby a web server sends web pages, images and files to a web browser.

HYPERLINK: A piece of specially coded text that users can click on to navigate to the web page, or element of a web page, associated with that link's code. Links are typically distinguished through the use of bold, underlined or differently coloured text.

JAVA: A programming language used widely on the internet.

MALWARE: A combination of the words 'malicious' and 'software'. Malware is software designed with the intention of infiltrating a computer and damaging its system.

OPEN-SOURCE: Describes a computer program that has its source code (the instructions that make up a program) freely available for viewing and modification.

PAGERANK: A link analysis algorithm used by search engines that assigns a numerical value based on a website's relevance and reputation. In general, a site with a higher pagerank has more traffic than a site with a lower one.

PHISHING: The fraudulent practice of sending emails to acquire personal information by masquerading as a legitimate company.

PODCAST: A form of audio and video broadcasting using the internet. Although the word is a portmanteau of 'iPod' and broadcasting, podcasting does not require the use of an iPod. A podcaster creates a list of files and makes it available in the RSS 2.0 format. The list can then be obtained using podcast 'retriever' software which makes the files available to digital devices (including iPods); users may then listen or watch at their convenience.

RSS FEED: Rich Site Summary or RDF Site Summary or Real Simple Syndication – a commonly used protocol for syndication and sharing of content, originally developed to facilitate the syndication of news articles, now widely used to share the content of blogs.

SEO: Search engine optimisation – the process of optimising the content of a web page to ensure that it is indexed by search engines.

SERVER: A node on a network that provides service to the terminals on the network. These computers have higher hardware specifications, ie more resources and greater speed, in order to handle large amounts of data.

SOCIAL NETWORKING: The practice of using a web-hosted service such as Facebook or Twitter to upload and share content and build friendship networks.

SPAM: A term used for unsolicited, generally junk, email.

TRAFFIC: The number of visitors to a website.

TWITTER: An online microblogging service that allows users to stay connected through the exchange of 140-character posts, known as 'tweets'.

URL: Uniform Resource Locator – address of a file accessible on the internet, eg http://www.whitakersalmanack.com

USER-GENERATED CONTENT (UGC): Refers to various media content produced or primarily influenced by end-users, as opposed to traditional media producers such as licensed broadcasters and production companies. These forms of media include digital video, blogging, podcasting, mobile phone photography and wikis.

CONSERVATION AND HERITAGE

NATIONAL PARKS

© Natural England

ENGLAND AND WALES
There are nine national parks in England, and three in Wales. In addition, the Norfolk and Suffolk Broads are considered to have equivalent status to a national park. Under the National Parks and Access to the Countryside Act 1949, as clarified by the Natural Environment and Rural Communities Act 2006, the two purposes of the national parks are to conserve and enhance the parks' natural beauty, wildlife and cultural heritage, and to promote opportunities for the understanding and enjoyment of the special qualities of national parks by the public. If there is a conflict between the two purposes, then conservation takes precedence.

Natural England is the statutory body that has the power to designate national parks in England, and Natural Resources Wales (formerly Countryside Council for Wales) is responsible for national parks in Wales. Designations in England are confirmed by the Secretary of State for Environment, Food and Rural Affairs and those in Wales by the Welsh government. The designation of a national park does not affect the ownership of the land or remove the rights of the local community. The majority of the land in the national parks is owned by private landowners (around 75 per cent) or by bodies such as the National Trust and the Forestry Commission. The national park authorities own only a small percentage of the land themselves.

The Environment Act 1995 replaced the existing national park boards and committees with free-standing national park authorities (NPAs). NPAs are the sole local planning authorities for their areas and as such influence land use and development, and deal with planning applications. NPAs are responsible for carrying out the statutory purposes of national parks stated above.

In pursuing these purposes they have a statutory duty to seek to foster the economic and social well-being of the communities within national parks. The NPAs publish management plans setting out overarching policies for their area and appoint their own officers and staff.

The Broads Authority was established under the Norfolk and Suffolk Broads Act 1988 and meets the requirement for the authority to have a navigation function in addition to a regard for the needs of agriculture, forestry and the economic and social interests of those who live or work in the Broads.

MEMBERSHIP
Membership of English NPAs comprises local authority appointees, members directly appointed by the Secretary of State for Environment, Food and Rural Affairs and members appointed by the secretary after consultation with local parishes. Under the Natural Environment and Rural Communities Act 2006 every district, county or unitary authority with land in a national park is entitled to appoint at least one member unless it chooses to opt out. The total number of local authority and parish members must exceed the number of national members.

Northumberland, Pembrokeshire Coast and Snowdonia NPAs have 18 members; Dartmoor has 19; the Lake District and North York Moors have 20; the Broads has 21; Exmoor, the New Forest and Yorkshire Dales have 22; Brecon Beacons 24; South Downs 27; and the Peak District 30.

In Wales, two-thirds of NPA members are appointed by the constituent local authorities and one-third by the Welsh government, advised by Natural Resources Wales.

FUNDING
Core funding for the English NPAs and the Broads Authority is provided by central government through the Department for Environment, Food and Rural Affairs (DEFRA) National Park Grant. For 2015–16 a total of £44.7m was allocated.

In Wales, the three national parks are funded by the Welsh government and their constituent local authorities. Total budgeted revenue expenditure for 2015–16 was £14.5m.

All NPAs and the Broads Authority can take advantage of grants from other bodies including lottery and European grants.

The national parks (with date that designation was confirmed) are:

BRECON BEACONS (1957), Powys (66 per cent)/ Carmarthenshire/Rhondda, Cynon and Taff/Merthyr Tydfil/Blaenau Gwent/Monmouthshire, 1,344 sq. km/ 519 sq. miles – The park is centred on the Brecon Beacons mountain range, which includes the three highest mountains in southern Britain (Pen y Fan, Corn Du and Cribyn), but also includes the valleys of the rivers Usk and Wye, the Black Mountains to the east and the Black Mountain to the west. There are information centres at the visitor centre at Libanus (near Brecon), Abergavenny and Llandovery, as well as the Waterfalls Centre in Pontneddfechan.
National Park Authority, Plas y Ffynnon, Cambrian Way, Brecon, Powys LD3 7HP T 01874-624437 W www.beacons-npa.gov.uk
Chief Executive, John Cook

BROADS (1989), Norfolk/Suffolk, 303 sq. km/117 sq. miles – The Broads are located between Norwich and Great Yarmouth on the flood plains of the six rivers flowing through the area to the sea. The area is one of fens, winding waterways, woodland and marsh. The 60 or so broads are man-made, and many are connected to the rivers by dykes, providing over 200km (125 miles) of navigable waterways. There are information centres at Hoveton, Whitlingham Country Park and How Hill National Nature Reserve. There are yacht stations at Norwich, Reedham and Great Yarmouth.
Broads Authority, Yare House, 62–64 Thorpe Road, Norwich NR1 1RY T 01603-610734 W www.broads-authority.gov.uk
Chief Executive, Dr John Packman
DARTMOOR (1951), Devon, 953 sq. km/368 sq. miles – The park consists of moorland and rocky granite tors, and is rich in prehistoric remains. There are visitor centres at Haytor, Princetown (main visitor centre) and Postbridge.
National Park Authority, Parke, Bovey Tracey, Devon TQ13 9JQ T 01626-832093 E hq@dartmoor.gov.uk W www.dartmoor.gov.uk
Chief Executive, Kevin Bishop
EXMOOR (1954), Somerset (71 per cent)/Devon, 694 sq. km/268 sq. miles – Exmoor is a moorland plateau inhabited by wild Exmoor ponies and red deer. There are many ancient remains and burial mounds. There are national park centres at Dunster, Dulverton and Lynmouth.
National Park Authority, Exmoor House, Dulverton, Somerset TA22 9HL T 01398-323665 E info@exmoor-nationalpark.gov.uk W www.exmoor-nationalpark.gov.uk
Chief Executive, Dr Nigel Stone
LAKE DISTRICT (1951), Cumbria, 2,292 sq. km/885 sq. miles – The Lake District includes England's highest mountains (Scafell Pike, Helvellyn and Skiddaw) but it is most famous for its glaciated lakes. There are national park information centres at Bowness-on-Windermere, Keswick, Ullswater and a visitor centre at Brockhole, Windermere.
National Park Authority, Murley Moss, Oxenholme Road, Kendal, Cumbria LA9 7RL T 01539-724555 E hq@lakedistrict.gov.uk W www.lakedistrict.gov.uk
Chief Executive, Richard Leafe
NEW FOREST (2005), Hampshire, 570 sq. km/220 sq. miles – The forest has been protected since 1079 when it was declared a royal hunting forest. The area consists of forest, ancient woodland, heathland, farmland, coastal saltmarsh and mudflats. Much of the forest is managed by the Forestry Commission, which provides several campsites. There is a visitor centre at Lyndhurst.
National Park Authority, Town Hall, Avenue Road, Lymington, Hants SO41 9ZG T 01590-646600
E enquiries@newforestnpa.gov.uk W www.newforestnpa.gov.uk
Chief Executive, Alison Barnes
NORTH YORK MOORS (1952), North Yorkshire (96 per cent)/Redcar and Cleveland, 1,434 sq. km/554 sq. miles – The park consists of woodland, moorland and coast, and includes the Hambleton Hills and the Cleveland Way. There are visitor centres at Danby and Sutton Bank.
National Park Authority, The Old Vicarage, Bondgate, Helmsley, York YO62 5BP T 01439-772700
E general@northyorkmoors.org.uk W www.northyorkmoors.org.uk
Chief Executive, Andy Wilson
NORTHUMBERLAND (1956), Northumberland, 1,048 sq. km/404 sq. miles – The park is an area of hill country, comprising open moorland, blanket bogs and very small patches of ancient woodland, stretching from Hadrian's Wall to the Scottish border. There is an information centre at Once Brewed.
National Park Authority, Eastburn, South Park, Hexham, Northumberland NE46 1BS T 01434-605555
E enquiries@nnpa.org.uk
W www.northumberlandnationalpark.org.uk
Chief Executive, Tony Gates

PEAK DISTRICT (1951), Derbyshire (64 per cent)/ Staffordshire/South Yorkshire/Cheshire/West Yorkshire/ Greater Manchester, 1,437 sq. km/555 sq. miles – The Peak District includes the gritstone moors of the Dark Peak, the limestone dales of the White Peak and the crags and rolling farmland of the South West Peak. There are information centres at Bakewell, Castleton, Edale and Upper Derwent.
National Park Authority, Aldern House, Baslow Road, Bakewell, Derbyshire DE45 1AE T 01629-816200
E customer.service@peakdistrict.gov.uk
W www.peakdistrict.gov.uk
Chief Executive, Sarah Fowler
PEMBROKESHIRE COAST (1952 and 1995), Pembrokeshire, 621 sq. km/236 sq. miles – The park includes cliffs, moorland and a number of islands, including Skomer and Ramsey. There are information centres in Newport and Tenby and a gallery and visitor centre, Oriel y Parc, in St Davids. The park also manages Castell Henllys Iron Age Village and Carew Castle and Tidal Mill.
National Park Authority, Llanion Park, Pembroke Dock, Pembrokeshire SA72 6DY T 0845-345 7275
E info@pembrokeshirecoast.org.uk
W www.pembrokeshirecoast.org.uk
Chief Executive, Tegryn Jones
SNOWDONIA/ERYRI (1951), Gwynedd/Conwy, 2,176 sq. km/840 sq. miles – Snowdonia, which takes its name from Snowdon, is an area of deep valleys and rugged mountains. There are information centres at Aberdyfi, Beddgelert, Betws y Coed and Dolgellau.
National Park Authority, Penrhyndeudraeth, Gwynedd LL48 6LF T 01766-770274 E parc@snowdonia-npa.gov.uk
W www.snowdonia-npa.gov.uk
Chief Executive, Emyr Williams
THE SOUTH DOWNS (2010), West Sussex/Hampshire, 1,624 sq. km/627 sq. miles – The South Downs contains a diversity of natural habitats, including flower-studded chalk grassland, ancient woodland, flood meadow, lowland heath and rare chalk heathland. There are visitor centres at Beachy Head, Queen Elizabeth Country Park in Hampshire and Seven Sisters Country Park in East Sussex.
National Park Authority, North Street, Midhurst, W. Sussex GU29 9DH T 01730-814810 W www.southdowns.gov.uk
Chief Executive, Trevor Beattie
YORKSHIRE DALES (1954), North Yorkshire (88 per cent)/Cumbria, 1,769 sq. km/683 sq. miles – The Yorkshire Dales is composed primarily of limestone overlaid in places by millstone grit. The three peaks of Ingleborough, Whernside and Pen-y-ghent are within the park. There are information centres at Grassington, Hawes, Aysgarth Falls, Malham and Reeth.
National Park Authority, Yoredale, Bainbridge, Leyburn, N. Yorks DL8 3EL T 0300-456 0030 E info@yorkshiredales.org.uk
W www.yorkshiredales.org.uk
Chief Executive, David Butterworth

SCOTLAND

On 9 August 2000 the national parks (Scotland) bill received royal assent, giving parliament the ability to create national parks in Scotland. The Act gives Scottish parks wider powers than in England and Wales, including statutory responsibilities for the local economy and rural communities. The board of the Cairngorms NPA comprises 19 members; seven appointed by the Scottish ministers, a further seven nominated to the board by the five local authorities in the park area and five locally elected members. The board of Loch Lomond and the Trossachs NPA comprises 17 members; six appointed by the Scottish ministers, a further six nominated by local authorities within the park boundaries and five elected via a postal ballot of the local electorate. In Scotland, the national parks are central government bodies and are wholly funded by the Scottish government. The draft budget for 2015–16 totalled £12.5m.

CAIRNGORMS (2003), North-East Scotland, 4,528 sq. km/1,748 sq. miles – The Cairngorms national park is the largest in the UK, covering around 6 per cent of Scotland. It displays a vast collection of landforms, including five of the six highest mountains in the UK and contains 25 per cent of Britain's threatened species. The near natural woodlands contain remnants of the original ancient Caledonian pine forest. There are nine visitor centres within the park.
National Park Authority, 14 The Square, Grantown-on-Spey, Morayshire PH26 3HG T 01479-873535
E enquiries@cairngorms.co.uk W www.cairngorms.co.uk
Chief Executive, Grant Moir
LOCH LOMOND AND THE TROSSACHS (2002), Argyll and Bute/Perth and Kinross/Stirling/West Dunbartonshire, 1,865 sq. km/720 sq. miles – The park boundaries encompass lochs, rivers, forests, 21 mountains above 914m (3,000ft) including Ben More and a further 19 mountains between 762m (2,500ft) and 914m (3,000ft). There is a national park centre in Balmaha. There are also seven visitor centres administered by VisitScotland.
National Park Authority, Carrochan, Carrochan Road, Balloch G83 8EG T 01389-722600 E info@lochlomond-trossachs.org
W www.lochlomond-trossachs.org
Chief Executive, Gordon Watson

NORTHERN IRELAND
There is a power to designate national parks in Northern Ireland under the Nature Conservation and Amenity Lands Order (Northern Ireland) 1985, but there are currently no national parks in Northern Ireland.

AREAS OF OUTSTANDING NATURAL BEAUTY

ENGLAND AND WALES
Under the National Parks and Access to the Countryside Act 1949, provision was made for the designation of areas of outstanding natural beauty (AONBs). Natural England is responsible for AONBs in England and Natural Resources Wales for the Welsh AONBs. Designations in England are confirmed by the Secretary of State for Environment, Food and Rural Affairs and those in Wales by the Welsh government. The Countryside and Rights of Way (CROW) Act 2000 placed greater responsibility on local authorities to protect AONBs and made it a statutory duty for relevant authorities to produce a management plan for their AONB area. The CROW Act also provided for the creation of conservation boards for larger and more complex AONBs.

The primary objective of the AONB designation is to conserve and enhance the natural beauty of the area. Where an AONB has a conservation board, it has the additional purpose of increasing public understanding and enjoyment of the special qualities of the area; the board has greater weight should there be a conflict of interests between the two. In addition, the board is also required to foster the economic and social well-being of the local communities but without incurring significant expenditure in doing so. Overall responsibility for AONBs lies with the relevant local authorities or conservation board. To coordinate planning and management responsibilities between local authorities in whose area they fall, AONBs are overseen by a joint advisory committee (or similar body) which includes representatives from the local authorities, landowners, farmers, residents and conservation and recreation groups. Core funding for AONBs is provided by central government through DEFRA, local authorities and Natural Resources Wales.

The 38 AONBs (with date designation confirmed) are:

ARNSIDE AND SILVERDALE (1972), Cumbria/Lancashire, 75 sq. km/29 sq. miles
BLACKDOWN HILLS (1991), Devon/Somerset, 370 sq. km/143 sq. miles
CANNOCK CHASE (1958), Staffordshire, 68 sq. km/26 sq. miles
CHICHESTER HARBOUR (1964), Hampshire/West Sussex, 74 sq. km/29 sq. miles
CHILTERNS (1965; extended 1990), Bedfordshire/Buckinghamshire/Herefordshire/Oxfordshire, 839 sq. km/324 sq. miles
CLWYDIAN RANGE AND DEE VALLEY (1985; extended 2011), Denbighshire/Flintshire, 389 sq. km/150 sq. miles
CORNWALL (1959; Camel Estuary 1983), 958 sq. km/370 sq. miles
COTSWOLDS (1966; extended 1990), Gloucestershire/Oxfordshire/Warwickshire/Wiltshire/Worcestershire, 2,046 sq. km/790 sq. miles
CRANBORNE CHASE AND WEST WILTSHIRE DOWNS (1983), Dorset/Hampshire/Somerset/Wiltshire, 983 sq. km/380 sq. miles
DEDHAM VALE (1970; extended 1978, 1991), Essex/Suffolk, 90 sq. km/35 sq. miles
DORSET (1959), Dorset/Somerset, 1,129 sq. km/436 sq. miles
EAST DEVON (1963), 268 sq. km/103 sq. miles
FOREST OF BOWLAND (1964), Lancashire/North Yorkshire, 803 sq. km/310 sq. miles
GOWER (1956), Swansea, 188 sq. km/73 sq. miles
HIGH WEALD (1983), East Sussex/Kent/Surrey/West Sussex, 1,461 sq. km/564 sq. miles
HOWARDIAN HILLS (1987), North Yorkshire, 204 sq. km/79 sq. miles
ISLE OF WIGHT (1963), 189 sq. km/73 sq. miles
ISLES OF SCILLY (1976), 16 sq. km/6 sq. miles
KENT DOWNS (1968), 878 sq. km/339 sq. miles
LINCOLNSHIRE WOLDS (1973), 558 sq. km/215 sq. miles
LLYN (1957), Gwynedd, 155 sq. km/60 sq. miles
MALVERN HILLS (1959), Gloucestershire/Worcestershire, 105 sq. km/41 sq. miles
MENDIP HILLS (1972; extended 1989), Somerset, 198 sq. km/76 sq. miles
NIDDERDALE (1994), North Yorkshire, 603 sq. km/233 sq. miles
NORFOLK COAST (1968), 451 sq. km/174 sq. miles
NORTH DEVON (1960), 171 sq. km/66 sq. miles
NORTH PENNINES (1988), Cumbria/Durham/North Yorkshire/Northumberland, 1,983 sq. km/766 sq. miles
NORTH WESSEX DOWNS (1972), Hampshire/Oxfordshire/Wiltshire, 1,730 sq. km/668 sq. miles
NORTHUMBERLAND COAST (1958), 138 sq. km/64 sq. miles
QUANTOCK HILLS (1957), Somerset, 99 sq. km/38 sq. miles
SHROPSHIRE HILLS (1959), 804 sq. km/310 sq. miles
SOLWAY COAST (1964), Cumbria, 115 sq. km/44 sq. miles
SOUTH DEVON (1960), 337 sq. km/130 sq. miles
SUFFOLK COAST AND HEATHS (1970), 403 sq. km/156 sq. miles
SURREY HILLS (1958), 419 sq. km/162 sq. miles
TAMAR VALLEY (1995), Cornwall/Devon, 190 sq. km/73 sq. miles
WYE VALLEY (1971), Gloucestershire/Herefordshire/Monmouthshire, 326 sq. km/126 sq. miles
YNYS MON (ISLE OF ANGLESEY) (1967), 221 sq. km/85 sq. miles

NORTHERN IRELAND

The Department of the Environment for Northern Ireland, with advice from the Council for Nature Conservation and the Countryside, designates AONBs in Northern Ireland. Dates given are those of designation.

ANTRIM COAST AND GLENS (1988), Co. Antrim, 725 sq. km/280 sq. miles
BINEVENAGH (2006), Co. Londonderry, 166 sq. km/ 64 sq. miles
CAUSEWAY COAST (1989), Co. Antrim, 42 sq. km/ 16 sq. miles
LAGAN VALLEY (1965), Co. Down, 39 sq. km/15 sq. miles
MOURNE (1986), Co. Down, 580 sq. km/224 sq. miles
RING OF GULLION (1991), Co. Armagh, 153 sq. km/ 59 sq. miles
SPERRIN (1968; extended 2008), Co. Tyrone/Co. Londonderry, 1,182 sq. km/456 sq. miles
STRANGFORD LOUGH AND LECALE (2010), Co. Down, 528 sq. km/204 sq. miles

NATIONAL SCENIC AREAS

In Scotland, national scenic areas have a broadly equivalent status to AONBs. Scottish Natural Heritage recognises areas of national scenic significance. At the beginning of June 2015 there were 40, covering a land area of 1,021,600 hectares (2,524,400 acres) and a marine area of 359,500 hectares (888,300 acres).

Development within national scenic areas is dealt with by local authorities, who are required to consult Scottish Natural Heritage concerning certain categories of development. Disagreements between Scottish Natural Heritage and local authorities are referred to the Scottish government. Land management uses can also be modified in the interest of scenic conservation.

ASSYNT-COIGACH, Highland, 90,200ha/222,884 acres
BEN NEVIS AND GLEN COE, Highland, 101,600ha/ 251,053 acres
CAIRNGORM MOUNTAINS, Highland/Aberdeenshire/ Moray, 67,200ha/166,051 acres
CUILLIN HILLS, Highland, 21,900ha/54,115 acres
DEESIDE AND LOCHNAGAR, Aberdeenshire, 40,000ha/ 98,840 acres
DORNOCH FIRTH, Highland, 7,500ha/18,532 acres
EAST STEWARTRY COAST, Dumfries and Galloway, 4,500ha/11,119 acres
EILDON AND LEADERFOOT, Borders, 3,600ha/ 8,896 acres
FLEET VALLEY, Dumfries and Galloway, 5,300ha/ 13,096 acres
GLEN AFFRIC, Highland, 19,300ha/47,690 acres
GLEN STRATHFARRAR, Highland, 3,800ha/9,390 acres
HOY AND WEST MAINLAND, Orkney Islands, 14,800ha/ 36,571 acres
JURA, Argyll and Bute, 21,800ha/53,868 acres
KINTAIL, Highland, 15,500ha/38,300 acres
KNAPDALE, Argyll and Bute, 19,800ha/48,926 acres
KNOYDART, Highland, 39,500ha/97,604 acres
KYLE OF TONGUE, Highland, 18,500ha/45,713 acres
KYLES OF BUTE, Argyll and Bute, 4,400ha/10,872 acres
LOCH LOMOND, Argyll and Bute, 27,400ha/67,705 acres
LOCH NA KEAL, Mull, Argyll and Bute, 12,700ha/ 31,382 acres
LOCH RANNOCH AND GLEN LYON, Perthshire and Kinross, 48,400ha/119,596 acres
LOCH SHIEL, Highland, 13,400ha/33,111 acres
LOCH TUMMEL, Perthshire and Kinross, 9,200ha/ 22,733 acres
LYNN OF LORN, Argyll and Bute, 4,800ha/11,861 acres
MORAR, MOIDART AND ARDNAMURCHAN, Highland, 13,500ha/33,358 acres
NITH ESTUARY, Dumfries and Galloway, 9,300ha/ 22,980 acres
NORTH ARRAN, North Ayrshire, 23,800ha/58,810 acres
NORTH-WEST SUTHERLAND, Highland, 20,500ha/ 50,655 acres
RIVER EARN, Perthshire and Kinross, 3,000ha/7,413 acres
RIVER TAY, Perthshire and Kinross, 5,600ha/13,838 acres
ST KILDA, Eilean Siar (Western Isles), 900ha/2,224 acres
SCARBA, LUNGA AND THE GARVELLACHS, Argyll and Bute, 1,900ha/4,695 acres
SHETLAND, Shetland Isles, 11,600ha/28,664 acres
SMALL ISLANDS, Highland, 15,500ha/38,300 acres
SOUTH LEWIS, HARRIS AND NORTH UIST, Eilean Siar (Western Isles), 109,600ha/270,822 acres
SOUTH UIST MACHAIR, Eilean Siar (Western Isles), 6,100ha/15,073 acres
THE TROSSACHS, Stirling, 4,600ha/11,367 acres
TROTTERNISH, Highland, 5,000ha/12,355 acres
UPPER TWEEDDALE, Borders, 10,500ha/25,945 acres
WESTER ROSS, Highland, 145,300ha/359,036 acres

THE NATIONAL FOREST

The National Forest is one of the UK's biggest environmental projects, creating a forest across 518.5 sq. km (200.2 sq. miles) of Derbyshire, Leicestershire and Staffordshire. Since the early 1990s, more than 8.5 million trees have been planted to create 7,000ha of new woodland landscapes. Forest cover has increased from 6 per cent to 20 per cent, with the aim of eventually covering approximately one-third of the designated area.

Since its establishment in 1995, the National Forest leads the project and is responsible for delivery of the government-approved National Forest Strategy, sponsored by DEFRA. Priorities include continued forest creation and management, economic development of the area for recreation and tourism, and engaging local communities in the forest to improve quality of life.

NATIONAL FOREST COMPANY, Bath Yard, Moira, Swadlincote, Derbyshire DE12 6BA T 01283-551211
E enquiries@nationalforest.org W www.nationalforest.org
Chief Executive, John Everitt

SITES OF SPECIAL SCIENTIFIC INTEREST

Site of Special Scientific Interest (SSSI) is a legal notification applied to land in England, Scotland or Wales which Natural England (NE), Scottish Natural Heritage (SNH) or the Natural Resources Wales (NRW) identifies as being of special interest because of its flora, fauna, geological, geomorphological or physiographical features. In some cases, SSSIs are managed as nature reserves.

NE, SNH and NRW must notify the designation of an SSSI to the local planning authority, every owner/occupier of the land, and the environment secretary, the Scottish ministers or the National Assembly for Wales. Forestry and agricultural departments and a number of other interested parties are also formally notified.

Objections to the notification of an SSSI can be made and ultimately considered at a full meeting of the Council of NE or NRW. In Scotland an objection will be dealt with by the main board of SNH or an appropriate subgroup.

The protection of these sites depends on the cooperation of individual landowners and occupiers. Owner/occupiers must consult NE, SNH or NRW and gain written consent before they can undertake certain listed activities on the site. Funds are available through management agreements and grants to assist owners and occupiers in conserving sites' interests. Sites can also be protected by management schemes, management notices and other enforcement mechanisms. As a last resort a site can be purchased.

SSSIs in Britain as at June 2015:

	Number	Hectares	Acres
England	4,129	1,082,984	2,676,112
Scotland	1,423	1,022,350	2,526,282
Wales	1,062	261,902	647,173

NORTHERN IRELAND
In Northern Ireland 360 areas of special scientific interest (ASSIs) have been declared by the Department of the Environment for Northern Ireland.

NATIONAL NATURE RESERVES

National Nature Reserves are defined in the National Parks and Access to the Countryside Act 1949 as modified by the Natural Environment and Rural Communities Act 2006. National Nature Reserves may be managed solely for the purpose of conservation, or for both the purposes of conservation and recreation, providing this does not compromise the conservation purpose.

NE, SNH or NRW can declare as a national nature reserve land which is held and managed as a nature reserve under an agreement; land held and managed by NE, SNH or NRW; or land held and managed as a nature reserve by an approved body. NE, SNH or NRW can make by-laws to protect reserves from undesirable activities; these are subject to confirmation by the Secretary of State for Environment, Food and Rural Affairs, the National Assembly for Wales or the Scottish ministers.

National nature reserves in Britain as at June 2015:

	Number	Hectares	Acres
England	226	93,616	231,330
Scotland	51	128,202	316,793
Wales	76	25,561	63,162

NORTHERN IRELAND
Nature reserves are established and managed by the Department of the Environment for Northern Ireland, with advice from the Council for Nature Conservation and the Countryside. Nature reserves are declared under the Nature Conservation and Amenity Lands (Northern Ireland) Order 1985; to date, 47 nature reserves have been declared.

LOCAL NATURE RESERVES

Local Nature Reserves are defined in the National Parks and Access to the Countryside Act 1949 (as amended by the Natural Environment and Rural Communities Act 2006) as land designated for the study and preservation of flora and fauna, or of geological or physiographical features. Local Nature Reserves also have a statutory obligation to provide opportunities for the enjoyment of nature or open air recreation, providing this does not compromise the conservation purpose of the reserve. Local authorities in England, Scotland and Wales have the power to acquire, declare and manage reserves in consultation with NE, SNH and NRW. There is similar legislation in Northern Ireland, where the consulting organisation is the Environment Agency.

Any organisation, such as water companies, educational trusts, local amenity groups and charitable nature conservation bodies, such as wildlife trusts, may manage local nature reserves, provided that a local authority has a legal interest in the land. This means that the local authority must either own it, lease it or have a management agreement with the landowner.

Designated local nature reserves in Britain as at June 2015:

	Number	Hectares	Acres
England	1,574	38,967	96,287
Scotland	72	10,724	26,500
Wales	94	8,793	21,727

There are 24 local nature reserves in Northern Ireland.

FOREST RESERVES

The Forestry Commission is the government department responsible for forestry policy throughout Great Britain. Forestry is a devolved matter, with the separate Forestry Commissions for England, Scotland and Wales reporting directly to their appropriate minister. The equivalent body in Northern Ireland is the Forest Service, an agency of the Department of Agriculture and Rural Development for Northern Ireland. The Forestry Commission in each country is led by a director who is also a member of the GB Board of Commissioners. As at March 2014, UK woodland certified by the Forestry Commission (including Forestry Commission-managed woodland) amounted to around 1,377,000ha (3,402,641 acres): 349,000ha (862,398 acres) in England, 141,000ha (348,419 acres) in Wales, 822,000ha (2,031,206 acres) in Scotland and 65,000ha (160,619 acres) in Northern Ireland. For more information, see W www.forestry.gov.uk

There are 35 forest nature reserves in Northern Ireland, covering 1,737 hectares (4,292 acres), designated and administered by the Forest Service. There are also 16 national nature reserves on Forest Service-owned property.

MARINE NATURE RESERVES

Marine protected areas provide protection for marine flora and fauna, and geological and physiographical features on land covered by tidal waters or parts of the sea in or adjacent to the UK. These areas also provide opportunities for study and research.

ENGLAND AND WALES
The Marine and Coastal Access Act 2009 created a new kind of statutory protection for marine protected areas in England and Wales, marine conservation zones (MCZs), which are designed to increase the protection of species and habitats deemed to be of national importance. The Secretary of State for Environment, Food and Rural Affairs and the National Assembly for Wales have the power to designate MCZs. Individual MCZs can have varying levels of protection: some include specific activities that are appropriately managed, while others prohibit all damaging and disturbing activities. The act converted the waters around Lundy Island, a former marine protected area, to MCZ status in 2010.

In 2009, Natural England and the Joint Nature Conservation Committee (JNCC) gave sea-users and stake-holders the ability to recommend potential MCZs to the UK government by establishing four regional projects. In September 2011, these projects recommended 127 MCZs, which were reviewed by Natural England and the JNCC. On 21 November 2013, the government announced the creation of 27 new MCZs, covering an area of around 9,700 sq. km, to protect wildlife including seahorses, coral reefs and oyster beds from dredging and bottom-trawling. A public consultation on the designation of an additional 23 MCZs, covering an area of 10,810 sq. km, closed in April 2015 with the results for the designations due in 2016. The 27 MCZs (with date designation confirmed) are:

Inshore Sites
ALN ESTUARY (2013), Northumberland, 0.39 sq. km
BLACKWATER, CROUCH, ROACH AND COLNE
    ESTUARIES (2013), Essex, 284 sq. km
BEACHY HEAD WEST (2013), E. Sussex, 24 sq. km
CHESIL BEACH AND STENNIS LEDGES (2013), Dorset,
    37 sq. km
CUMBRIA COAST (2013), Cumbria, 18 sq. km
FOLKESTONE POMERANIA (2013), Kent, 34 sq. km
FYLDE (2013), Lancs, 260 sq. km
ISLES OF SCILLY (2013), 30 sq. km
KINGMERE (2013), Sussex, 47 sq. km
LUNDY (2010 and 2013), Bristol Channel, 31 sq. km
THE MANACLES (2013), Cornwall, 3.5 sq. km
MEDWAY ESTUARY (2013), Kent, 60 sq. km
PADSTOW BAY AND SURROUNDS (2013), Cornwall,
    90 sq. km
PAGHAM HARBOUR (2013), Sussex, 3 sq. km
POOLE ROCKS (2013), Dorset, 4 sq. km
SKERRIES BANK AND SURROUNDS (2013), Devon,
    250 sq. km
SOUTH DORSET (2013), 193 sq. km
TAMAR ESTUARY, Devon/Cornwall (2013), 15 sq. km
THANET COAST (2013), Kent, 64 sq. km
TORBAY (2013), Devon, 20 sq. km
UPPER FOWEY AND PONT PILL (2013), Cornwall,
    2 sq. km
WHITSAND AND LOOE BAY (2013), Cornwall, 52 sq. km
Offshore Sites
THE CANYONS (2013), Cornwall, 661 sq. km
EAST OF HAIG FRAS (2013), Cornwall, 400 sq. km
NORTH EAST OF FARNES DEEP (2013),
    Northumberland, 492 sq. km
SOUTH-WEST DEEPS (WEST) (2013), Cornwall, 1,800
    sq. km
SWALLOW SAND (2013), Northumberland, 4,746 sq. km

SCOTLAND
In July 2014, under the Marine (Scotland) Act 2010, the
Scottish government designated 17 marine protected areas
(MPAs) in Scottish inshore territorial waters (Clyde Sea Sill;
East Caithness Cliffs; Fetlar to Haroldswick; Loch Creran;
Loch Sunart; Loch Sunart to the Sound of Jura; Loch Sween;
Lochs Duich, Long and Alsh; Monarch Isles; Mousa to
Boddam; Noss Head; Papa Westray; Small Isles; South Arran;
Upper Loch Fyne and Loch Goil; Wester Ross; and Wyre
and Rousay Sounds). A further 13, also in July 2014, were
designated in offshore waters under the UK Marine and
Coastal Access Act 2009. These are: Central Fladen; East of
Gannet and Montrose Fields; Faroe–Shetland Sponge Belt;
Firth of Forth Banks Complex; Geikie Slide and Hebridean
Slope; Hatton–Rockall Basin; North-east Faroe Shetland
Channel; North-west Orkney; Norwegian Sediment
Boundary Plain; Rosemary Bank Seamount; Barra Fan and
Hebrides Terrace Seamount; Turbot Bank; and West
Shetland Shelf.

NORTHERN IRELAND
The Marine Act (Northern Ireland) 2013 includes provisions
for establishing Marine Conservation Zones (MCZs), as well
as a system of marine planning, fisheries management and
marine licensing. MCZs may be designated for various
purposes including the conservation of marine species and
habitats, taking fully into account any economic, cultural or
social consequences of doing so. The Act also allows the NI
Department of the Environment to make byelaws to protect
MCZs from damage caused by unregulated activities such
as anchoring, kite surfing or jet skiing. It is an offence to

intentionally or recklessly destroy or damage a protected
feature of an MCZ.

Strangford Lough was Northern Ireland's only marine
nature reserve, establised in 1995 under the Nature
Conservation and Amenity Lands Order (Northern Ireland)
1985, but it was redesignated as Northern Ireland's first
MCZ on the introduction of the Marine Act (Northern
Ireland) 2013.

INTERNATIONAL CONVENTIONS

The UK is party to a number of international conventions.

BERN CONVENTION
The 1979 Bern Convention on the Conservation of
European Wildlife and Natural Habitats came into force in
the UK in June 1982. There are 51 contracting parties and
a number of other states attend meetings as observers.

The aims are to conserve wild flora and fauna and their
habitats, especially where this requires the cooperation of
several countries, and to promote such cooperation. The
convention imposes legal obligations on contracting parties,
protecting over 500 wild plant species and more than 1,000
wild animal species.

All parties to the convention must promote national
conservation policies and take account of the conservation of
wild flora and fauna when setting planning and development
policies. Reports on contracting parties' conservation policies
must be submitted to the standing committee every four
years.

SECRETARIAT OF THE BERN CONVENTION
    STANDING COMMITTEE, Council of Europe,
    Avenue de L'Europe, 67075 Strasbourg-Cedex, France
    W www.coe.int/bernconvention

BIOLOGICAL DIVERSITY
The UK ratified the Convention on Biological Diversity
(CBD) in June 1994. As at July 2015 there were 196 parties
to the convention.

There are seven programmes addressing agricultural
biodiversity, marine and coastal biodiversity and the
biodiversity of inland waters, dry and sub-humid lands,
islands, mountains and forests. On 29 January 2000 the
Conference of the Parties adopted a supplementary
agreement to the convention known as the Cartagena
Protocol on Biosafety. The protocol seeks to protect
biological diversity from potential risks that may be posed by
introducing modified living organisms, resulting from
biotechnology, into the environment. As at July 2015, 170
countries were party to the protocol; the UK joined on 17
February 2004. The Nagoya Protocol on Access and Benefit-
sharing was adopted in October 2010 and entered into force
on 12 October 2014. It provides international rules and
procedure on liability and redress for damage to biodiversity
resulting from living modified organisms. As at July 2015,
59 countries were party to the protocol.

The UK Biodiversity Action Plan (UKBAP), published in
1994, was the UK government's response to the CBD at the
1992 Rio Earth Summit. The UK Post-2010 Biodiversity
Framework replaced UKBAP when it was published in 2012
by DEFRA and the devolved administrations. The framework
covers the period 2011–20 and forms the UK government's
response to the strategic plan of the CBD. It includes five
internationally agreed strategic goals to be achieved by
2020: to address the underlying causes of biodiversity loss
by making biodiversity a mainstream issue across government
and society; to reduce the direct pressures on biodiversity and
promote sustainable use; to safeguard ecosystems, species and
genetic diversity; to enhance the benefits to all from

biodiversity and ecosystem services; and to enhance implementation through participatory planning, knowledge management and capacity building. The list of priority species and habitats under the biodiversity framework covers 1,150 species and 65 habitats.

Secretariat of the Convention on Biological Diversity, 413, Saint Jacques Street, Suite 800, Montreal, QC H2Y 1N9 Canada T +1514-288 2220 E secretariat@cbd.int W www.cbd.int

JNCC, Monkstone House, City Road, Peterborough PE1 1JY T 01733-555948 W www.jncc.defra.gov.uk

BONN CONVENTION

The 1979 Convention on Conservation of Migratory Species of Wild Animals (also known as the CMS or Bonn Convention) came into force in the UK in October 1985. As at 1 July 2015, 120 countries were party to the convention.

It requires the protection of listed endangered migratory species and encourages international agreements covering these and other threatened species.

Seven agreements have been concluded to date under the convention. They aim to conserve seals in the Wadden Sea; bat populations in Europe; small cetaceans of the Baltic, north-east Atlantic, Irish and North Seas; cetaceans of the Mediterranean Sea, Black Sea and contiguous Atlantic area; African-Eurasian migratory waterbirds; albatrosses and petrels; and gorillas and their habitats. A further 19 memorandums of understanding have been agreed for the Siberian crane, slender-billed curlew, marine turtles of the Atlantic coast of Africa, Indian Ocean and South East Asia, the middle-European population of the great bustard, bukhara deer, aquatic warbler, West-African populations of the African elephant, saiga antelope, cetaceans of the Pacific Islands, dugongs (large marine mammals), eastern-Atlantic populations of the Mediterranean monk seals, ruddy-headed goose, grassland birds of southern South America, birds of prey of Africa and Eurasia, small cetaceans and manatees of West Africa, sharks, huemuls (Andean deer) and high Andean flamingoes. In addition, there are three special species initiatives: the central Asian flyway, the central Asian mammals initiative and Sahelo–Saharan megafauna plan.

UNEP/CMS SECRETARIAT, Platz der Vereinten Nationen 1, 53113 Bonn, Germany T (+49) (228) 815 2401 E secretariat@cms.int W www.cms.int

CITES

The 1973 Convention on International Trade in Endangered Species of Wild Fauna and Flora (CITES), which entered into force in 1975, is an agreement between governments to ensure that international trade in specimens of wild animals and plants does not threaten their survival. The convention came into force in the UK in October 1976 and there are currently 181 member countries. Countries party to the convention ban commercial international trade in an agreed list of endangered species and regulate and monitor trade in other species that might become endangered. The convention accords varying degrees of protection to more than 35,000 species of animals and plants whether they are traded as live specimens or as products derived from them.

The Conference of the Parties to CITES meets every two to three years to review the convention's implementation. The Animal and Plant Health Agency at the Department for Environment, Food and Rural Affairs carries out the government's responsibilities under CITES.

CITES is implemented in the EU through a series of EC regulations known as the Wildlife Trade Regulations.

CITES SECRETARIAT, International Environment House, 11 Chemin des Anémones, CH-1219 Châtelaine, Geneva, Switzerland T (+41) (22) 917 8139/40 E info@cites.org W www.cites.org

INTERNATIONAL WHALING COMMISSION

The International Convention for the Regulation of Whaling was signed in Washington DC in 1946 and currently has 88 member countries.

The measures in the convention provide for the complete protection of certain species; designate specified areas as whale sanctuaries; set limits on the numbers and size of whales which may be taken; prescribe open and closed seasons and areas for whaling; and prohibit the capture of suckling calves and female whales accompanied by calves. The International Whaling Commission meets annually to review and revise these measures.

THE INTERNATIONAL WHALING COMMISSION, The Red House, 135 Station Road, Impington, Cambridge, Cambridgeshire CB24 9NP T 01223-233 971 W www.iwc.int

OSPAR

The Convention for the Protection of the Marine Environment of the North-East Atlantic (the OSPAR Convention) was adopted in Paris, France in September 1992 and entered into force in March 1998. The OSPAR Convention replaced both the Oslo Convention (1972) and the Paris Convention (1974), with the intention of providing a comprehensive approach to addressing all sources of pollution which may affect the maritime area, and matters relating to the protection of the maritime environment. An annex on biodiversity and ecosystems was adopted in 1998 to cover non-polluting human activities that can adversely affect the sea.

Fifteen countries plus the European Union are party to the convention; the UK ratified OSPAR in 1998. The OSPAR Commission makes decisions and recommendations and sets out actions to be taken by the contracting parties. The OSPAR Secretariat administers the work under the convention, coordinates the work of the contracting parties and runs the formal meeting schedule of OSPAR.

OSPAR SECRETARIAT, Victoria House, 37–63 Southampton Row, London WC1B 4DA T 020-7430 5200 E secretariat@ospar.org W www.ospar.org

RAMSAR CONVENTION

The 1971 Convention on Wetlands of National Importance, called the Ramsar Convention, is an inter-governmental treaty that provides for the conservation and sustainable use of wetlands and their resources. The Convention entered into force in the UK in 1976.

Governments that are contracting parties to the convention must designate wetlands for inclusion in the List of Wetlands of International Importance (the 'Ramsar List') and include wetland conservation considerations in their land-use planning. As at May 2015, the Convention's 168 contracting parties had designated 2,208 wetland sites, covering 210,734,269 hectares. The UK currently has 170 designated sites covering 1,278,930 hectares.

The contracting parties meet every three years to assess progress. The 13th Meeting of the Conference of the Contracting Parties to the Ramsar Convention on Wetlands will take place in Dubai, UAE in 2018.

At the 12th meeting of the Convention, held in Uruguay in June 2015, a new Ramsar Strategic Plan was adopted for the years 2016–24. The four priorities central to the new plan are: to address the factors driving the loss and degradation of wetlands; to renew country commitment to conserve and protect the Ramsar site network; to promote wise use of wetlands and to restore wetlands that are relevant for biodiversity conservation, disaster risk reduction, livelihoods and climate change mitigation; and to improve the implementation of the Convention.

RAMSAR CONVENTION SECRETARIAT, Rue Mauverney 28, CH-1196 Gland, Switzerland T (+41) (22) 999 0170 E ramsar@ramsar.org W www.ramsar.org

UK LEGISLATION

The Wildlife and Countryside Act 1981 gives legal protection to a wide range of wild animals and plants. Every five years the statutory nature conservation agencies (Natural England, Natural Resources Wales and Scottish Natural Heritage), working jointly through the JNCC, are required to review schedules 5 (animals, other than birds) and 8 (plants) of the Wildlife and Countryside Act 1981. They make recommendations to the Secretary of State for Environment, Food and Rural Affairs, the National Assembly for Wales and the Scottish government for changes to these schedules. The most recent variations of schedules 5 and 8 for England came into effect on 1 October 2011, following the fifth quinquennial review. The sixth review is currently underway.

Under section 9 of the act it is an offence to kill, injure, take, possess or sell (whether alive or dead) any wild animal included in schedule 5 of the act and to disturb its place of shelter and protection or to destroy that place. However certain species listed on schedule 5 are protected against some, but not all, of these activities.

Under section 13 of the act it is illegal without a licence to pick, uproot, sell or destroy plants listed in schedule 8. Since January 2001, under the Countryside and Rights of Way Act 2000, persons found guilty of an offence under part 1 of the Wildlife and Countryside Act 1981 face a maximum penalty of up to £5,000 and/or up to a six-month custodial sentence per specimen.

BIRDS

The act lays down a close season for birds (listed on Schedule 2, part 1) from 1 February to 31 August inclusive, each year. Variations to these dates are made for:

Black grouse – 10 December to 20 August (10 December–1 September for Somerset, Devon and New Forest)
Capercaillie – 1 February to 30 September (England and Wales only)
Grey partridge – 1 February to 1 September
Pheasant – 1 February to 1 October
Ptarmigan and Red grouse – 10 December to 12 August
Red-legged partridge – 1 February to 1 September
Snipe – 1 February to 11 August
Woodcock – 1 February to 30 September (England and Wales); 1 February to 31 August (Scotland)
Birds listed on schedule 2, part 1 (below high water mark) (see below) – 21 February to 31 August
Wild duck and wild geese, in or over any area below the high-water mark of ordinary spring tides – 21 February to 31 August
Sundays and Christmas Day in Scotland, and Sundays for any area of England or Wales prescribed by the Secretary of State.

Birds listed on schedule 2, part 1, which may be killed or taken outside the close season are: capercaillie (England and Wales only); coot; certain wild duck (gadwall, goldeneye, mallard, Northern pintail, common pochard, Northern shoveler, teal, tufted duck, Eurasian wigeon); certain wild geese (Canada, greylag, pink-footed, white-fronted (in England and Wales only); golden plover; moorhen; snipe; and woodcock.

Section 16 of the 1981 act allows licences to be issued on either an individual or general basis, to allow the killing, taking and sale of certain birds for specified reasons such as public health and safety. All other wild birds are fully protected by law throughout the year.

ANIMALS PROTECTED BY SCHEDULE 5

Adder *(Vipera berus)*
Anemone, Ivell's Sea *(Edwardsia ivelli)*
Anemone, Starlet Sea *(Nematosella vectensis)*
Bat, Horseshoe, all species *(Rhinolophidae)*
Bat, Typical, all species *(Vespertilionidae)*
Beetle *(Hypebaeus flavipes)*
Beetle, Bembridge Water *(Paracymus aeneus)*
Beetle, Lesser Silver Water *(Hydrochara caraboides)*
Beetle, Mire Pill *(Curimopsis nigrita)*
Beetle, Moccas *(Hypebaeus flavipes)*
Beetle, Rainbow Leaf *(Chrysolina cerealis)*
Beetle, Spangled Water *(Graphoderus zonatus)*
Beetle, Stag *(Lucanus cervus)*
Beetle, Violet Click *(Limoniscus violaceus)*
Beetle, Water *(Paracymus aeneus)*
Burbot *(Lota lota)*
Butterfly, Adonis Blue *(Lysandra bellargus)*
Butterfly, Black Hairstreak *(Strymonidia pruni)*
Butterfly, Brown Hairstreak *(Thecla betulae)*
Butterfly, Chalkhill Blue *(Lysandra coridon)*
Butterfly, Chequered Skipper *(Carterocephalus palaemon)*
Butterfly, Duke of Burgundy Fritillary *(Hamearis lucina)*
Butterfly, Glanville Fritillary *(Melitaea cinxia)*
Butterfly, Heath Fritillary *(Mellicta athalia or Melitaea athalia)*
Butterfly, High Brown Fritillary *(Argynnis adippe)*
Butterfly, Large Blue *(Maculinea arion)*
Butterfly, Large Copper *(Lycaena dispar)*
Butterfly, Large Heath *(Coenonympha tullia)*
Butterfly, Large Tortoiseshell *(Nymphalis polychloros)*
Butterfly, Lulworth Skipper *(Thymelicus acteon)*
Butterfly, Marsh Fritillary *(Eurodryas aurinia)*
Butterfly, Mountain Ringlet *(Erebia epiphron)*
Butterfly, Northern Brown Argus *(Aricia artaxerxes)*
Butterfly, Pearl-bordered Fritillary *(Boloria euphrosyne)*
Butterfly, Purple Emperor *(Apatura iris)*
Butterfly, Silver Spotted Skipper *(Hesperia comma)*
Butterfly, Silver-studded Blue *(Plebejus argus)*
Butterfly, Small Blue *(Cupido minimus)*
Butterfly, Swallowtail *(Papilio machaon)*
Butterfly, White Letter Hairstreak *(Stymonida w-album)*
Butterfly, Wood White *(Leptidea sinapis)*
Cat, Wild *(Felis silvestris)*
Cicada, New Forest *(Cicadetta montana)*
Crayfish, Atlantic Stream *(Austropotamobius pallipes)*
Cricket, Field *(Gryllus campestris)*
Cricket, Mole *(Gryllotalpa gryllotalpa)*
Cricket, Wart-biter *(Decticus verrucivorus)*
Damselfly, Southern *(Coenagrion mercuriale)*
Dolphin, all species *(Cetacea)*
Dormouse *(Muscardinus avellanarius)*
Dragonfly, Norfolk Aeshna *(Aeshna isosceles)*
Frog, Common *(Rana temporaria)*
Frog, Pool, Northern Clade *(Pelophylax lessonae)*
Goby, Couch's *(Gobius couchii)*
Goby, Giant *(Gobius cobitis)*
Hatchet Shell, Northern *(Thyasira gouldi)*
Hydroid, Marine *(Clavopsella navis)*
Lagoon Snail, De Folin's *(Caecum armoricum)*
Lagoon Worm, Tentacled *(Alkmaria romijni)*
Leech, Medicinal *(Hirudo medicinalis)*
Lizard, Sand *(Lacerta agilis)*
Lizard, Viviparous *(Lacerta vivipara)*
Marten, Pine *(Martes martes)*
Moth, Barberry Carpet *(Pareulype berberata)*
Moth, Black-veined *(Siona lineata or Idaea lineata)*
Moth, Fiery Clearwing *(Bembecia chrysidiformis)*
Moth, Fisher's Estuarine *(Gortyna borelii)*

Moth, New Forest Burnet *(Zygaena viciae)*
Moth, Reddish Buff *(Acosmetia caliginosa)*
Moth, Slender Scotch Burnet *(Zygaena loti)*
Moth, Sussex Emerald *(Thalera fimbrialis)*
Moth, Talisker Burnet *(Zygaena lonicerae)*
Mussel, Fan *(Atrina fragilis)*
Mussel, Freshwater Pearl *(Margaritifera margaritifera)*
Newt, Great Crested (or Warty) *(Triturus cristatus)*
Newt, Palmate *(Triturus helveticus)*
Newt, Smooth *(Triturus vulgaris)*
Otter, Common *(Lutra lutra)*
Porpoise, all species *(Cetacea)*
Sandworm, Lagoon *(Armandia cirrhosa)*
Sea Fan, Pink *(Eunicella verrucosa)*
Sea Slug, Lagoon *(Tenellia adspersa)*
Sea-mat, Trembling *(Victorella pavida)*
Seahorse, Short Snouted (England only) *(Hippocampus hippocampus)*
Seahorse, Spiny (England only) *(Hippocampus guttulatus)*
Shad, Allis *(Alosa alosa)*
Shad, Twaite *(Alosa fallax)*
Shark, Angel (England only) *(Squatina squatina)*
Shark, Basking *(Cetorhinus maximus)*
Shrimp, Fairy *(Chirocephalus diaphanus)*
Shrimp, Lagoon Sand *(Gammarus insensibilis)*
Shrimp, Tadpole (Apus) *(Triops cancriformis)*
Skate, White *(Rostroraja alba)*
Slow-worm *(Anguis fragilis)*
Snail, Glutinous *(Myxas glutinosa)*
Snail, Roman (England only) *(Helix pomatia)*
Snail, Sandbowl *(Catinella arenaria)*
Snake, Grass *(Natrix natrix or Natrix helvetica)*
Snake, Smooth *(Coronella austriaca)*
Spider, Fen Raft *(Dolomedes plantarius)*
Spider, Ladybird *(Eresus niger)*
Squirrel, Red *(Sciurus vulgaris)*
Sturgeon *(Acipenser sturio)*
Toad, Common *(Bufo bufo)*
Toad, Natterjack *(Bufo calamita)*
Turtle, Flatback *(Cheloniidae/Natator Depressus)*
Turtle, Green Sea *(Chelonia mydas)*
Turtle, Hawksbill *(Eretmochelys imbricate)*
Turtle, Kemp's Ridley Sea *(Lepidochelys kempii)*
Turtle, Leatherback Sea *(Dermochelys coriacea)*
Turtle, Loggerhead Sea *(Caretta caretta)*
Turtle, Olive Ridley *(Lepidochelys olivacea)*
Vendace *(Coregonus albula)*
Vole, Water *(Arvicola terrestris)*
Walrus *(Odobenus rosmarus)*
Whale, all species *(Cetacea)*
Whitefish *(Coregonus lavaretus)*

PLANTS PROTECTED BY SCHEDULE 8

Adder's Tongue, Least *(Ophioglossum lusitanicum)*
Alison, Small *(Alyssum alyssoides)*
Anomodon, Long-leaved *(Anomodon longifolius)*
Beech-lichen, New Forest *(Enterographa elaborata)*
Blackwort *(Southbya nigrella)*
Bluebell *(Hyacinthoides non-scripta)*
Bolete, Royal *(Boletus regius)*
Broomrape, Bedstraw *(Orobanche caryophyllacea)*
Broomrape, Oxtongue *(Orobanche loricata)*
Broomrape, Thistle *(Orobanche reticulata)*
Cabbage, Lundy *(Rhynchosinapis wrightii)*
Calamint, Wood *(Calamintha sylvatica)*
Caloplaca, Snow *(Caloplaca nivalis)*
Catapyrenium, Tree *(Catapyrenium psoromoides)*
Catchfly, Alpine *(Lychnis alpina)*
Catillaria, Laurer's *(Catellaria laureri)*

Centaury, Slender *(Centaurium tenuiflorum)*
Cinquefoil, Rock *(Potentilla rupestris)*
Cladonia, Convoluted *(Cladonia convoluta)*
Cladonia, Upright Mountain *(Cladonia stricta)*
Clary, Meadow *(Salvia pratensis)*
Club-rush, Triangular *(Scirpus triquetrus)*
Colt's-foot, Purple *(Homogyne alpina)*
Cotoneaster, Wild *(Cotoneaster integerrimus)*
Cottongrass, Slender *(Eriophorum gracile)*
Cow-wheat, Field *(Melampyrum arvense)*
Crocus, Sand *(Romulea columnae)*
Crystalwort, Lizard *(Riccia bifurca)*
Cudweed, Broad-leaved *(Filago pyramidata)*
Cudweed, Jersey *(Gnaphalium luteoalbum)*
Cudweed, Red-tipped *(Filago lutescens)*
Cut-grass *(Leersia oryzoides)*
Diapensia *(Diapensia lapponica)*
Dock, Shore *(Rumex rupestris)*
Earwort, Marsh *(Jamesoniella undulifolia)*
Eryngo, Field *(Eryngium campestre)*
Fern, Dickie's Bladder *(Cystopteris dickieana)*
Fern, Killarney *(Trichomanes speciosum)*
Flapwort, Norfolk *(Leiocolea rutheana)*
Fleabane, Alpine *(Erigeron borealis)*
Fleabane, Small *(Pulicaria vulgaris)*
Fleawort, South Stack *(Tephroseris integrifolia ssp maritima)*
Frostwort, Pointed *(Gymnomitrion apiculatum)*
Fungus, Hedgehog *(Hericium erinaceum)*
Galingale, Brown *(Cyperus fuscus)*
Gentian, Alpine *(Gentiana nivalis)*
Gentian, Dune *(Gentianella uliginosa)*
Gentian, Early *(Gentianella anglica)*
Gentian, Fringed *(Gentianella ciliata)*
Gentian, Spring *(Gentiana verna)*
Germander, Cut-leaved *(Teucrium botrys)*
Germander, Water *(Teucrium scordium)*
Gladiolus, Wild *(Gladiolus illyricus)*
Goblin Lights *(Catolechia wahlenbergii)*
Goosefoot, Stinking *(Chenopodium vulvaria)*
Grass-poly *(Lythrum hyssopifolia)*
Grimmia, Blunt-leaved *(Grimmia unicolor)*
Gyalecta, Elm *(Gyalecta ulmi)*
Hare's-ear, Sickle-leaved *(Bupleurum falcatum)*
Hare's-ear, Small *(Bupleurum baldense)*
Hawk's-beard, Stinking *(Crepis foetida)*
Hawkweed, Northroe *(Hieracium northroense)*
Hawkweed, Shetland *(Hieracium zetlandicum)*
Hawkweed, Weak-leaved *(Hieracium attenuatifolium)*
Heath, Blue *(Phyllodoce caerulea)*
Helleborine, Red *(Cephalanthera rubra)*
Horsetail, Branched *(Equisetum ramosissimum)*
Hound's-tongue, Green *(Cynoglossum germanicum)*
Knawel, Perennial *(Scleranthus perennis)*
Knotgrass, Sea *(Polygonum maritimum)*
Lady's-slipper *(Cypripedium calceolus)*
Lecanora, Tarn *(Lecanora archariana)*
Lecidea, Copper *(Lecidea inops)*
Leek, Round-headed *(Allium sphaerocephalon)*
Lettuce, Least *(Lactuca saligna)*
Lichen, Arctic Kidney *(Nephroma arcticum)*
Lichen, Ciliate Strap *(Heterodermia leucomelos)*
Lichen, Coralloid Rosette *(Heterodermia propagulifera)*
Lichen, Ear-lobed Dog *(Peltigera lepidophora)*
Lichen, Forked Hair *(Bryoria furcellata)*
Lichen, Golden Hair *(Teloschistes flavicans)*
Lichen, Orange-fruited Elm *(Caloplaca luteoalba)*
Lichen, River Jelly *(Collema dichotomum)*
Lichen, Scaly Breck *(Squamarina lentigera)*
Lichen, Starry Breck *(Buellia asterella)*

Lily, Snowdon *(Lloydia serotina)*
Liverwort, Lindenberg's Leafy *(Adelanthus lindenbergianus)*
Lungwort, Tree *(Lobaria pulmonaria)*
Marsh-mallow, Rough *(Althaea hirsuta)*
Marshwort, Creeping *(Apium repens)*
Milk-parsley, Cambridge *(Selinum carvifolia)*
Moss *(Drepanocladius vernicosus)*
Moss, Alpine Copper *(Mielichoferia mielichoferi)*
Moss, Baltic Bog *(Sphagnum balticum)*
Moss, Blue Dew *(Saelania glaucescens)*
Moss, Blunt-leaved Bristle *(Orthotrichum obtusifolium)*
Moss, Bright Green Cave *(Cyclodictyon laetevirens)*
Moss, Cordate Beard *(Barbula cordata)*
Moss, Cornish Path *(Ditrichum cornubicum)*
Moss, Derbyshire Feather *(Thamnobryum angustifolium)*
Moss, Flamingo *(Desmatodon cernuus)*
Moss, Glaucous Beard *(Barbula glauca)*
Moss, Green Shield *(Buxbaumia viridis)*
Moss, Hair Silk *(Plagiothecium piliferum)*
Moss, Knothole *(Zygodon forsteri)*
Moss, Large Yellow Feather *(Scorpidium turgescens)*
Moss, Millimetre *(Micromitrium tenerum)*
Moss, Multi-fruited River *(Cryphaea lamyana)*
Moss, Nowell's Limestone *(Zygodon gracilis)*
Moss, Polar Feather *(Hygrohypnum polare)*
Moss, Rigid Apple *(Bartramia stricta)*
Moss, Round-leaved Feather *(Rhyncostegium rotundifolium)*
Moss, Schleicher's Thread *(Bryum schleicheri)*
Moss, Slender Green Feather *(Drepanocladus vernicosus)*
Moss, Triangular Pygmy *(Acaulon triquetrum)*
Moss, Vaucher's Feather *(Hypnum vaucheri)*
Mudwort, Welsh *(Limosella australis)*
Naiad, Holly-leaved *(Najas marina)*
Naiad, Slender *(Najas flexilis)*
Nail, Rock *(Calicium corynellum)*
Orache, Stalked *(Halimione pedunculata)*
Orchid, Early Spider *(Ophrys sphegodes)*
Orchid, Fen *(Liparis loeselii)*
Orchid, Ghost *(Epipogium aphyllum)*
Orchid, Lapland Marsh *(Dactylorhiza lapponica)*
Orchid, Late Spider *(Ophrys fuciflora)*
Orchid, Lizard *(Himantoglossum hircinum)*
Orchid, Military *(Orchis militaris)*
Orchid, Monkey *(Orchis simia)*
Pannaria, Caledonia *(Panneria ignobilis)*
Parmelia, New Forest *(Parmelia minarum)*
Parmentaria, Oil Stain *(Parmentaria chilensis)*
Pear, Plymouth *(Pyrus cordata)*
Penny-cress, Perfoliate *(Thlaspi perfoliatum)*
Pennyroyal *(Mentha pulegium)*
Pertusaria, Alpine Moss *(Pertusaria bryontha)*
Petalwort *(Petallophyllum ralfsi)*
Physcia, Southern Grey *(Physcia tribacioides)*
Pigmyweed *(Crassula aquatica)*
Pine, Ground *(Ajuga chamaepitys)*
Pink, Cheddar *(Dianthus gratianopolitanus)*
Pink, Childing *(Petroraghia nanteuilii)*
Pink, Deptford (England and Wales only) *(Dianthus armeria)*
Polypore, Oak *(Buglossoporus pulvinus)*
Pseudocyphellaria, Ragged *(Pseudocyphellaria lacerata)*
Psora, Rusty Alpine *(Psora rubiformis)*
Puffball, Sandy Stilt *(Battarraea phalloides)*
Ragwort, Fen *(Senecio paludosus)*
Ramping-fumitory, Martin's *(Fumaria martinii)*
Rampion, Spiked *(Phyteuma spicatum)*
Restharrow, Small *(Ononis reclinata)*
Rock-cress, Alpine *(Arabis alpina)*
Rock-cress, Bristol *(Arabis stricta)*
Rustwort, Western *(Marsupella profunda)*

Sandwort, Norwegian *(Arenaria norvegica)*
Sandwort, Teesdale *(Minuartia stricta)*
Saxifrage, Drooping *(Saxifraga cernua)*
Saxifrage, Tufted *(Saxifraga cespitosa)*
Saxifrage, Yellow Marsh *(Saxifrage hirulus)*
Solenopsora, Serpentine *(Solenopsora liparina)*
Solomon's-seal, Whorled *(Polygonatum verticillatum)*
Sow-thistle, Alpine *(Cicerbita alpina)*
Spearwort, Adder's-tongue *(Ranunculus ophioglossifolius)*
Speedwell, Fingered *(Veronica triphyllos)*
Speedwell, Spiked *(Veronica spicata)*
Spike-rush, Dwarf *(Eleocharis parvula)*
Star-of-Bethlehem, Early *(Gagea bohemica)*
Starfruit *(Damasonium alisma)*
Stonewort, Bearded *(Chara canescens)*
Stonewort, Foxtail *(Lamprothamnium papulosum)*
Strapwort *(Corrigiola litoralis)*
Sulphur-tresses, Alpine *(Alectoria ochroleuca)*
Turpswort *(Geocalyx graveolens)*
Violet, Fen *(Viola persicifolia)*
Viper's-grass *(Scorzonera humilis)*
Water-plantain, Floating *(Luronium natans)*
Water-plantain, Ribbon-leaved *(Alisma gramineum)*
Wood-sedge, Starved *(Carex depauperata)*
Woodsia, Alpine *(Woodsia alpina)*
Woodsia, Oblong *(Woodsia ilvenis)*
Wormwood, Field *(Artemisia campestris)*
Woundwort, Downy *(Stachys germanica)*
Woundwort, Limestone *(Stachys alpina)*
Yellow-rattle, Greater *(Rhinanthus serotinus)*

WORLD HERITAGE SITES

The Convention Concerning the Protection of the World Cultural and Natural Heritage was adopted by the United Nations Educational, Scientific and Cultural Organization (UNESCO) in 1972 and ratified by the UK in 1984. As at July 2015, 191 states were party to the convention. The convention provides for the identification, protection and conservation of cultural and natural sites of outstanding universal value.

Cultural sites may be:
• an extraordinary exponent of human creative genius
• sites representing architectural and technological innovation or cultural interchange
• sites of artistic, historic, aesthetic, archaeological, scientific, ethnologic or anthropologic value
• 'cultural landscapes', ie sites whose characteristics are marked by significant interactions between human populations and their natural environment
• exceptional examples of a traditional settlement or land- or sea-use, especially those threatened by irreversible changes.
• unique or exceptional examples of a cultural tradition or a civilisation either still present or extinct

Natural sites may be:
• those displaying critical periods of earth's history
• superlative examples of on-going ecological and biological processes in the evolution of ecosystems
• those exhibiting remarkable natural beauty and aesthetic significance or those where extraordinary natural phenomena are witnessed
• the habitat of threatened species and plants

Governments which are party to the convention nominate sites in their country for inclusion in the World Heritage List. Nominations are considered by the World Heritage Committee, an inter-governmental committee composed of 21 representatives of the parties to the convention. The committee is advised by the International Council on

Monuments and Sites (ICOMOS), the International Centre for the Study of the Preservation and Restoration of Cultural Property (ICCROM) and the International Union for the Conservation of Nature (IUCN). ICOMOS evaluates and reports on proposed cultural and mixed sites, ICCROM provides expert advice and training on how to conserve and restore cultural property and IUCN provides technical evaluations of natural heritage sites and reports on the state of conservation of listed sites.

A prerequisite for inclusion in the World Heritage List is the existence of an effective legal protection system in the country in which the site is situated and a detailed management plan to ensure the conservation of the site. Inclusion in the list does not confer any greater degree of protection on the site than that offered by the national protection framework.

If a site is considered to be in serious danger of decay or damage, the committee may add it to the World Heritage in Danger List. Sites on this list may benefit from particular attention or emergency measures to allay threats and allow them to retain their world heritage status, or in extreme cases of damage or neglect they may lose their world heritage status completely. As at July 2015, there were 48 sites on the World Heritage in Danger List, with the most recent additions including the Old City of Sana'a in Yemen and Hatra in Iraq.

Financial support for the conservation of sites on the World Heritage List is provided by the World Heritage Fund, administered by the World Heritage Committee. The fund's income is derived from compulsory and voluntary contributions from the states party to the convention and from private donations.

WORLD HERITAGE CENTRE, UNESCO, 7 Place de Fontenoy, 75352 Paris 07 SP, France E wh-info@unesco.org W whc.unesco.org

DESIGNATED SITES

As at 8 July 2015, following the 39th session of the World Heritage Committee, 1,031 sites across 163 countries were on the World Heritage List. Of these, 26 are in the UK and three in British overseas territories; 24 are listed for their cultural significance (†), four for their natural significance (*) and one for both cultural and natural significance. Liverpool's Maritime Mercantile City is the only UK site on the List of World Heritage in Danger. The year in which sites were designated appears in the first set of parentheses. The number in the second set of parentheses denotes the position of each site on the map below.

UNITED KINGDOM
†Bath – the city (1987). (1)
†Blaenarvon industrial landscape, Wales (2000). (2)
†Blenheim Palace and Park, Oxfordshire (1987). (3)
†Canterbury Cathedral, St Augustine's Abbey, St Martin's Church, Kent (1988). (4)
†Castle and town walls of King Edward I, north Wales – Beaumaris, Caernarfon Castle, Conwy Castle, Harlech Castle (1986). (5)
†Cornwall and west Devon mining landscape (2006). (6)
†Derwent Valley Mills, Derbyshire (2001). (7)
*Dorset and east Devon coast (2001). (8)
†Durham Cathedral and Castle (1986). (9)
†Edinburgh old and new towns (1995). (10)
†Forth Bridge, Firth of Forth, Scotland (2015). (26)

†Frontiers of the Roman Empire– Hadrian's Wall, northern England; Antonine Wall, central Scotland (1987, 2005, 2008). (11)
*Giant's Causeway and Causeway coast, Co. Antrim (1986). (12)
†Greenwich, London – maritime Greenwich, including the Royal Naval College, Old Royal Observatory, Queen's House, town centre (1997). (13)
†Heart of Neolithic Orkney (1999). (14)
†Ironbridge Gorge, Shropshire – the world's first iron bridge and other early industrial sites (1986). (15)
†Liverpool – six areas of the maritime mercantile city (2004). (16)
†New Lanark, South Lanarkshire, Scotland (2001). (17)
†Pontcysyllte Aqueduct and Canal, Wrexham, Wales (2009). (18)
†Royal Botanic Gardens, Kew (2003). (19)
†*St Kilda, Eilean Siar (Western Isles) (1986). (20)
†Saltaire, West Yorkshire (2001). (21)
†Stonehenge, Avebury and related megalithic sites, Wiltshire (1986). (22)
†Studley Royal Park, Fountains Abbey, St Mary's Church, N. Yorkshire (1986). (23)
†Tower of London (1988). (24)
†Westminster Abbey, Palace of Westminster, St Margaret's Church, London (1987). (25)

BRITISH OVERSEAS TERRITORIES
*Henderson Island, Pitcairn Islands, South Pacific Ocean (1988)
*Gough Island and Inaccessible Island (part of Tristan da Cunha), South Atlantic Ocean (1995)
†Historic town of St George and related fortifications, Bermuda (2000)

WORLD HERITAGE SITES IN THE UK

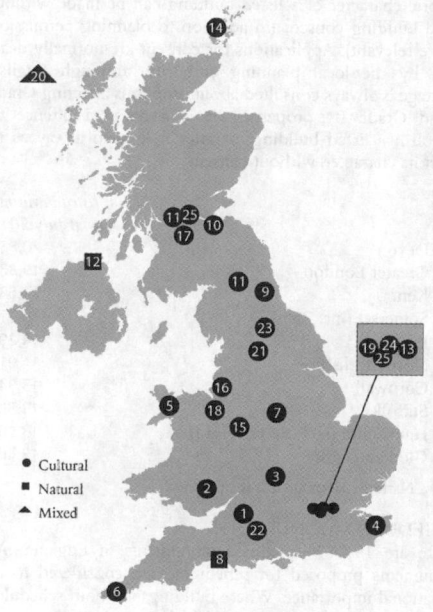

● Cultural
■ Natural
▲ Mixed

HISTORIC BUILDINGS AND MONUMENTS

ENGLAND

Under the Planning (Listed Buildings and Conservation Areas) Act 1990, the Secretary of State for Culture, Media and Sport has a statutory duty to approve lists of buildings or groups of buildings in England which are of special architectural or historic interest. In November 2009 responsibility for compiling the list of buildings was passed to English Heritage. Under the Ancient Monuments and Archaeological Areas Act 1979 as amended by the National Heritage Act 1983, the secretary of state is also responsible for compiling a schedule of ancient monuments. Decisions are taken on the advice of English Heritage. In April 2005 responsibility for the administration of the listing system was transferred from the secretary of state to English Heritage. In April 2011, English Heritage launched the National Heritage List for England, a searchable database of all nationally designated heritage assets (W www.historicengland.org.uk/listing/the-list).

LISTED BUILDINGS

Listed buildings are classified into Grade I, Grade II* and Grade II. There are 376,099 listed buildings in England, of which approximately 90 per cent are Grade II listed. Almost all pre-1700 buildings are listed, as are most buildings of 1700 to 1840. English Heritage carries out thematic surveys of particular types of buildings with a view to making recommendations for listing. The main purpose of listing is to ensure that care is taken in deciding the future of a building. No changes which affect the architectural or historic character of a listed building can be made without listed building consent (in addition to planning permission where relevant). Applications for consent are normally dealt with by the local planning authority, although English Heritage is always consulted about proposals affecting Grade I and Grade II* properties. It is a criminal offence to demolish a listed building, or alter it in such a way as to affect its character, without consent.

Area	No. of listed buildings as at July 2015
1. Devon	20,856
2. Greater London	19,331
3. Kent	17,685
4. Somerset (inc. Bath)	16,119
5. Essex	14,294
6. North Yorkshire	14,011
7. Cornwall	13,946
8. Suffolk	13,583
9. Hampshire (inc. Isle of Wight)	13,562
10. Gloucestershire	13,463

Source: National Heritage List for England

SCHEDULED MONUMENTS

There are 19,717 scheduled monuments in England. All monuments proposed for scheduling are considered to be of national importance. Where buildings are both scheduled and listed, ancient monuments legislation takes precedence. The main purpose of scheduling a monument is to preserve it for the future and to protect it from damage, destruction or any unnecessary interference. Once a monument has been scheduled, scheduled monument consent is required before any works can be carried out. The scope of the control is more extensive and more detailed than that applied to listed buildings, but certain minor works, as detailed in the Ancient Monuments (Class Consents) Order 1994, may be carried out without consent. It is a criminal offence to carry out unauthorised work to scheduled monuments.

WALES

Under the Planning (Listed Buildings and Conservation Areas) Act 1990 and the Ancient Monuments and Archaeological Areas Act 1979, the National Assembly for Wales is responsible for listing buildings and scheduling monuments in Wales on the advice of Cadw (the Welsh government's historic environment division) and the Royal Commission on the Ancient and Historical Monuments of Wales (RCAHMW). The criteria for evaluating buildings are similar to those in England and the same listing system is used. As at March 2015, there were 29,966 listed buildings and 4,182 scheduled monuments in Wales.

SCOTLAND

Under the Planning (Listed Buildings and Conservation Areas) (Scotland) Act 1997 and the Ancient Monuments and Archaeological Areas Act 1979, Scottish ministers are responsible for listing buildings and scheduling monuments in Scotland on the advice of Historic Scotland and the Royal Commission on the Ancient and Historical Monuments of Scotland (RCAHMS). The criteria for evaluating buildings are similar to those in England but an A, B, C(S) categorisation is used. As at March 2015 there were 47,423 listed buildings and 8,183 scheduled monuments in Scotland.

NORTHERN IRELAND

Under the Planning (Northern Ireland) Order 1991 and the Historic Monuments and Archaeological Objects (Northern Ireland) Order 1995, the Northern Ireland Environment Agency (part of the Department of the Environment of the Northern Ireland) is responsible for listing buildings and scheduling monuments. The Historic Buildings Council for Northern Ireland and the relevant district council must be consulted on listing proposals, and the Historic Monuments Council for Northern Ireland must be consulted on scheduling proposals. The criteria for evaluating buildings are similar to those in England but an A, B+, B1 and B2 categorisation is used. As at March 2015 there were 8,621 listed buildings and 1,972 scheduled monuments in Northern Ireland.

ENGLAND

For more information on English Heritage properties, including those listed below, the official website is
W www.english-heritage.org.uk
For more information on National Trust properties in England, including those listed below, the official website is
W www.nationaltrust.org.uk
KEY
(EH) English Heritage property
(NT) National Trust property
* UNESCO World Heritage Site (see also World Heritage Sites)

A LA RONDE (NT), Exmouth, Devon EX8 5BD T 01395-265514
　Unique 16-sided house completed c.1796

ALNWICK CASTLE, Alnwick, Northumberland NE66 1NQ
T 01665-511100 W www.alnwickcastle.com
Seat of the Dukes of Northumberland since 1309; Italian
Renaissance-style interior; gardens with spectacular water
features

ALTHORP, Northants NN7 4HQ T 01604-770006
W www.spencerofalthorp.com
Spencer family seat; permanent Diana, Princess of Wales
exhibition

ANGLESEY ABBEY (NT), Lode, Cambs CB25 9EJ
T 01223-810080
Jacobean house (c.1600) with gardens and a working
watermill (Lode Mill) on the site of a 12th-century priory;
fine furnishings and a unique clock collection

APSLEY HOUSE (EH), London W1J 7NT T 020-7499 5676
Built by Robert Adam 1771–8, home of the Dukes of
Wellington since 1817 and known as 'No. 1 London';
collection of fine and decorative arts

ARUNDEL CASTLE, Arundel, W. Sussex BN18 9AB
T 01903-882173 W www.arundelcastle.org
Castle dating from the Norman Conquest; seat of the
Dukes of Norfolk

AVEBURY (EH/NT), Wilts SN8 1RF T 01672-539250
Remains of stone circles constructed 4,000 years ago
enclosing part of the later village of Avebury

BANQUETING HOUSE, Whitehall, London SW1A 2ER
T 0844-482 7777 W www.hrp.org.uk/banquetinghouse
Designed by Inigo Jones in 1619; ceiling paintings by
Rubens; site of the execution of Charles I

BASILDON PARK (NT), Reading, Berks RG8 9NR
T 01491-672382
Palladian mansion built in 1776–83 by John Carr

BATTLE ABBEY (EH), Battle, E. Sussex TN33 0AD
T 01424-775705
Remains of the abbey founded by William the Conqueror
on the site of the Battle of Hastings

BEESTON CASTLE (EH), Cheshire CW6 9TX
T 01829-260464
Built in the 13th century by Ranulf, sixth Earl of Chester
on the site of an Iron Age hillfort

BELVOIR CASTLE, Grantham, Lincs NG32 1PE
T 01476-871002 W www.belvoircastle.com
Seat of the Dukes of Rutland; 19th-century Gothic-style
castle; notable art collection

BERKELEY CASTLE, Glos GL13 9BQ T 01453-810303
W www.berkeley-castle.com
Completed late 12th century; site of the murder of
Edward II (1327)

BIRDOSWALD ROMAN FORT (EH), Brampton,
Cumbria CA8 7DD T 01697-747602
Stretch of Hadrian's Wall with Roman wall fort, turret and
milecastle

*BLENHEIM PALACE, Woodstock, Oxon OX20 1PP
T 01993-810530 W www.blenheimpalace.com
Seat of the Dukes of Marlborough and Winston
Churchill's birthplace; house designed by Vanbrugh;
landscaped parkland by Capability Brown

BLICKLING ESTATE (NT), Blickling, Norfolk NR11 6NF
T 01263-738030
Jacobean house with state rooms; extensive gardens,
temple and 18th-century orangery

BODIAM CASTLE (NT), Bodiam, E. Sussex TN32 5UA
T 01580-830196
Well-preserved medieval moated castle built in 1385

BOLSOVER CASTLE (EH), Bolsover, Derbys S44 6PR
T 01246-822844
17th-century castle on site of medieval fortress

BOSCOBEL HOUSE (EH), Bishops Wood, Shrops ST19 9AR
T 01902-850244

Timber-framed 17th-century hunting lodge; refuge of
fugitive Charles II from parliamentary troops

BOUGHTON HOUSE, Kettering, Northants NN14 1BJ
T 01536-515731 W www.boughtonhouse.org.uk
17th-century house with French-style additions; home of
the Dukes of Buccleuch and Queensbury

BOWOOD HOUSE, Calne, Wilts SN11 0LZ T 01249-812102
W www.bowood.org/bowood-house
18th-century house in Capability Brown park, featuring
Robert Adam orangery and renowned pinetum and
arboretum

BUCKFAST ABBEY, Buckfastleigh, Devon TQ11 0EE
T 01364-645500 W www.buckfast.org.uk
Benedictine monastery on medieval foundations

BUCKINGHAM PALACE, London SW1A 1AA
T 020-7766 7300 W www.royalcollection.org.uk
Purchased by George III in 1761, and the Sovereign's
official London residence since 1837; 19 state rooms,
including the Throne Room, and Queen's Gallery

BUCKLAND ABBEY (NT), Yelverton, Devon PL20 6EY
T 01822-853607
13th-century Cistercian monastery; home of Sir Francis
Drake

BURGHLEY HOUSE, Stamford, Lincs PE9 3JY T 01780-752451
W www.burghley.co.uk
Late Elizabethan house built by William Cecil, first Lord
Burghley

CARISBROOKE CASTLE (EH), Newport, Isle of Wight
PO30 1XY T 01983-523112
W www.carisbrookecastlemuseum.org.uk
Norman castle; museum; prison of Charles I 1647–8

CARLISLE CASTLE (EH), Carlisle, Cumbria CA3 8UR
T 01228-591922
Medieval castle; prison of Mary Queen of Scots

CASTLE ACRE PRIORY (EH), King's Lynn, Norfolk PE32 2XD
T 01760-755394
Remains include 12th-century church and prior's
lodgings

CASTLE DROGO (NT), Drewsteignton, Devon EX6 6PB
T 01647-433306
Granite castle designed by Lutyens in 1911

CASTLE HOWARD, N. Yorks YO60 7DA T 01653-648333
W www.castlehoward.co.uk
Designed by Vanbrugh 1699–1726; mausoleum designed
by Hawksmoor

CASTLE RISING CASTLE (EH), King's Lynn, Norfolk
PE31 6AH T 01553-631330 W www.castlerising.co.uk
12th-century keep with gatehouse and bridge, surrounded
by 20 acres of defensive earthworks

CHARLES DARWIN'S HOUSE (DOWN HOUSE) (EH),
Downe, Kent BR6 7JT T 01689-859119
The family home where Darwin wrote *On the Origin of
Species*

CHARTWELL (NT), Westerham, Kent TN16 1PS
T 01732-868381
Home and studio of Sir Winston Churchill

CHATSWORTH, Bakewell, Derbys DE45 1PP T 01246-565300
W www.chatsworth.org
Tudor mansion set in magnificent parkland; seat of the
Dukes of Devonshire

CHESTERS ROMAN FORT (EH), Chollerford,
Northumberland NE46 4EU T 01434-681379
Roman cavalry fort built to guard Hadrian's Wall

CHYSAUSTER ANCIENT VILLAGE (EH), Penzance,
Cornwall TR20 8XA T 07831-757934
Remains of nearly 2,000-year-old Celtic settlement; eight
stone-walled homesteads

CLANDON PARK (NT), West Clandon, Guildford, Surrey
GU4 7RQ T 01483-222502 W www.clandonpark.co.uk

18th-century Palladian mansion and gardens, which contain a Maori meeting house, brought back from New Zealand in 1892

CLIFFORD'S TOWER (EH), York YO1 9SA T 01904-646940
13th-century keep built on a mound; remains of a castle built by William the Conqueror

CORBRIDGE ROMAN SITE (EH), Corbridge, Northumberland NE45 5NT T 01434-632349
Excavated central area of a Roman garrison town

CORFE CASTLE (NT), Wareham, Dorset BH20 5EZ
T 01929-481294
Former royal castle dating from the 11th century and partially ruined during the English Civil War

CROFT CASTLE AND PARKLAND (NT), Yarpole, Herefordshire HR6 9PW T 01568-780246
17th-century quadrangular manor house with Georgian-Gothic interior; built close to ruin of pre-Conquest border castle

DEAL CASTLE (EH), Deal, Kent CT14 7BA T 01304-372762
Largest of the coastal defence forts built by Henry VIII; shaped like a rose with six inner and outer bastions

*DERWENT VALLEY MILLS, Belper, Derbyshire
T 01629-536831 W www.derwentvalleymills.org
Series of 18th- and 19th-century cotton mills; birthplace of the modern factory

DOVER CASTLE (EH), Dover, Kent CT16 1HU T 01304-211067
Castle with Roman, Saxon and Norman features; tunnels used as wartime operations rooms

DR JOHNSON'S HOUSE, Gough Square, London EC4A 3DE
T 020-7353 3745 W www.drjohnsonshouse.org
Home of Samuel Johnson 1748–59

DUNSTANBURGH CASTLE (EH/NT), Craster, nr Alnwick, Northumberland NE66 3TT T 01665-576231
14th-century castle ruins on a cliff with a substantial twin-towered gatehouse-keep

ELTHAM PALACE (EH), Eltham, London SE9 5QE
T 02082-94 2548
Art Deco house next to remains of medieval palace once occupied by Henry VIII; moated gardens

FARLEIGH HUNGERFORD CASTLE (EH), Bath, Somerset BA2 7RS T 01225-754026
Late 14th-century castle with inner and outer courts; chapel with rare medieval wall paintings

FARNHAM CASTLE KEEP (EH), Farnham, Surrey GU9 0AG
T 01252-721194 W www.farnhamcastle.com
Large 12th-century castle keep with motte and bailey wall

FISHBOURNE ROMAN PALACE, Fishbourne, Chichester, W. Sussex PO19 3QR T 01243-785859
W www.sussexpast.co.uk
Excavated Roman palace with largest collection of in-situ mosaics in Britain

*FOUNTAINS ABBEY (NT), nr Ripon, N. Yorks HG4 3DY
T 01765-608888
Ruined Cistercian monastery and corn mill; site includes Studley Royal, a Georgian water garden and deer park

FRAMLINGHAM CASTLE (EH), Framlingham, Suffolk IP13 9BP T 0870-333 1181
Castle (c.1200) with high curtain walls enclosing an almshouse (1639); once the refuge of Mary Tudor

FURNESS ABBEY (EH), Barrow-in-Furness, Cumbria LA13 0PJ
T 01229-823420
Remains of church and cloister buildings founded in 1123

GLASTONBURY ABBEY, Glastonbury, Somerset BA6 9EL
T 01458-832267 W www.glastonburyabbey.com
12th-century abbey destroyed by fire in 1184 and later rebuilt; ruined in 1539 during dissolution of monasteries; site of an early Christian settlement

GOODRICH CASTLE (EH), Ross-on-Wye, Herefordshire HR9 6HY T 01600-890538

Remains of 12th- and 13th-century castle; contains a famous mortar that ruined the castle in 1646

GREENWAY (NT), nr Brixham, Devon TQ5 0ES
T 01803-842382
Agatha Christie's holiday home which inspired several of the settings in her books, including the murder in *Dead Man's Folly;* large woodland; walled garden

GREENWICH, London SE10 9NF W www.visitgreenwich.org.uk
Former Royal Observatory (founded 1675) housing the time ball and zero meridian of longitude; the Queen's House, designed for Queen Anne, wife of James I, by Inigo Jones; Painted Hall and neoclassical Chapel (Old Royal Naval College)

GRIMES GRAVES (EH), Brandon, Norfolk IP26 5DE
T 01842-810656
Neolithic flint mines; one shaft can be descended

GUILDHALL, London EC2V 7HH T 020-7332 1313
W www.guildhall.cityoflondon.gov.uk
Centre of civic government of the City built c.1441; facade built 1788–9

HADDON HALL, Bakewell, Derbys DE45 1LA T 01629-812855
W www.haddonhall.co.uk
Well-preserved 12th-century manor house

HAILES ABBEY (EH), Cheltenham, Glos GL54 5PB
T 01242-602398
Ruins of a 13th-century Cistercian monastery

HAM HOUSE AND GARDEN (NT), Richmond-upon-Thames, Surrey TW10 7RS T 020-8940 1950
Stuart house with lavish interiors and formal gardens

HAMPTON COURT PALACE, East Molesey, Surrey KT8 9AU
T 0844-482 7777 W www.hrp.org.uk
16th-century palace originally built for Cardinal Wolsey with 17th- and 18th-century additions by Wren; Royal Tennis Court and world-renowned maze

HARDWICK HALL (NT), Chesterfield, Derbys S44 5QJ
T 01246-850430
Elizabethan house built for Bess of Hardwick

HARDY'S BIRTHPLACE (NT), Higher Bockhampton, Dorset DT2 8QJ T 01305-262366
Birthplace and home of Thomas Hardy

HAREWOOD HOUSE, Harewood, W. Yorks LS17 9LG
T 0113-218 1010 W www.harewood.org
18th-century house designed by John Carr and Robert Adam; park by Capability Brown

HATFIELD HOUSE, Hatfield, Herts AL9 5NQ T 01707-287010
W www.hatfield-house.co.uk
Jacobean house built by Robert Cecil; features surviving wing of Royal Palace of Hatfield (c.1485), the childhood home of Elizabeth I

HELMSLEY CASTLE (EH), Helmsley, N. Yorks YO62 5AB
T 01439-770442
12th-century keep and curtain wall with 16th-century buildings; spectacular earthwork defences

HEVER CASTLE, nr Edenbridge, Kent TN8 7NG
T 01732-865224 W www.hevercastle.co.uk
13th-century double-moated castle; childhood home of Anne Boleyn

HIGH CROSS HOUSE (NT), nr Totnes, Devon TQ9 6ED
T 01803-842382
Celebrated Modernist house containing original Bauhaus furniture

HOLKHAM HALL, Wells-next-the-Sea, Norfolk NR23 1AB
T 01328-710227 W www.holkham.co.uk
Palladian mansion; notable fine art collection

HOUSESTEADS ROMAN FORT (EH), Hexham, Northumberland NE47 6NN T 01434-344363
Excavated Roman infantry fort on Hadrian's Wall with museum

*IRONBRIDGE GORGE, Ironbridge, Shropshire
W www.ironbridgeguide.info
Important Industrial Revolution site, featuring the world's first iron bridge

KEDLESTON HALL (NT), Derbys DE22 5JH T 01332-842191
Palladian mansion built 1759–65; complete Robert Adam interiors; museum of Asian artefacts

KELMSCOTT MANOR, nr Lechlade, Glos GL7 3HJ
T 01367-252486 W www.kelmscottmanor.org.uk
Built c.1600; summer home of William Morris, with products of Morris and Co.

KENILWORTH CASTLE (EH), Kenilworth, Warks CV8 1NE
T 01926-852078
Largest castle ruin in England; Norman keep with 13th-century outer walls

KENSINGTON PALACE, Kensington Gardens, London W8 4PX
T 0844-482 7777 W www.hrp.org.uk
Built in 1605 and enlarged by Wren; birthplace of Queen Victoria

KENWOOD HOUSE (EH), Hampstead Lane, London NW3 7JR
T 020-7973 3416
Neoclassical villa housing the Iveagh bequest of paintings and furniture

KEW PALACE, Richmond-upon-Thames, Surrey TW9 3AB
T 0844-482 7777 W www.hrp.org.uk
Red-brick mansion (c.1631); includes Queen Charlotte's Cottage, used by King George III and family as a summerhouse

KINGSTON LACY (NT), Wimborne Minster, Dorset BH21 4EA
T 01202-883402
17th-century mansion with 19th-century alterations; important art collection

KNEBWORTH HOUSE, Knebworth, Herts SG3 6PY
T 01438-812661 W www.knebworthhouse.com
Tudor manor house concealed by 19th-century Gothic decoration; Lutyens gardens

KNOLE (NT), Sevenoaks, Kent TN15 0RP T 01732-462100
House built in 1456 set in 1,000-acre deer park; fine art and furniture collection; birthplace of Vita Sackville-West

LAMBETH PALACE, London SE1 7JU T 020-7898 1200
W www.archbishopofcanterbury.org
Official residence of the Archbishop of Canterbury since the 13th century

LANERCOST PRIORY (EH), Brampton, Cumbria CA8 2HQ
T 01697-73030 W www.lanercostpriory.org.uk
The nave of the Augustinian priory's church, c.1166, is still used; remains of other claustral buildings

LANHYDROCK (NT), Bodmin, Cornwall PL30 5AD
T 01208-265950
House dating from the 17th century; 50 rooms, including kitchen and nursery

LEEDS CASTLE, nr Maidstone, Kent ME17 1PL
T 01622-765400 W www.leeds-castle.com
Castle dating from the 12th century, situated on two islands in a lake; used as a royal palace by Henry VIII

LEVENS HALL, Kendal, Cumbria LA8 0PD T 01539-560321
W www.levenshall.co.uk
Elizabethan house with unique topiary garden (1694); steam engine collection

LINCOLN CASTLE, Lincoln, Lincs LN1 3AA T 01522-782040
W www.lincolncastle.com
Built by William the Conqueror in 1068 on a Roman site; one of only two double-motted castles in Britain

LINDISFARNE PRIORY (EH), Holy Island, Northumberland
TD15 2RX T 01289-389200
Founded in AD 635; re-established in the 12th century as a Benedictine priory, now ruined

LITTLE MORETON HALL (NT), Congleton, Cheshire
CW12 4SD T 01260-272018
Iconic timber-framed moated Tudor manor house with knot garden

LONGLEAT HOUSE, Warminster, Wilts BA12 7NW
T 01985-844400 W www.longleat.co.uk
Elizabethan house in Italian Renaissance style; Capability Brown parkland with lakes; safari park

LULLINGSTONE ROMAN VILLA (EH), Eynsford, Kent
DA4 0JA T 01322-863467
Large villa occupied for much of the Roman period; fine mosaics and unique Christian paintings

MIDDLEHAM CASTLE (EH), Middleham, N. Yorks DL8 4QG
T 01969-623899
12th-century keep within later fortifications; childhood home of Richard III

MONTACUTE HOUSE (NT), Montacute, Somerset TA15 6XP
T 01935-823289
Elizabethan mansion with National Portrait Gallery collection of portraits from the period

MOUNT GRACE PRIORY (EH), Northallerton, N. Yorks
DL6 3JG T 01609-883494
Carthusian priory with remains of monastic buildings

OLD SARUM (EH), Salisbury, Wilts SP1 3SD T 01722-335398
Iron Age hill fort enclosing remains of Norman castle and cathedral

ORFORD CASTLE (EH), Orford, Suffolk IP12 2ND
T 01394-450472
Polygonal tower keep of c.1170 and remains of coastal defence castle built by Henry II

OSBORNE HOUSE (EH), East Cowes, Isle of Wight PO32 6JX
T 01983-200022
Queen Victoria's seaside residence; built by Thomas Cubitt in Italian Renaissance style; summer house, Swiss Cottage and museum

OSTERLEY PARK (NT), Isleworth, Middx TW7 4RB
T 020-8232 5050
18th-century neoclassical mansion with Tudor stable block

PENDENNIS CASTLE (EH), Falmouth, Cornwall TR11 4LP
Well-preserved 16th-century coastal defence castle

PENSHURST PLACE, Penshurst, Kent TN11 8DG
T 01892-870307 W www.penshurstplace.com
Medieval house featuring Baron's Hall (1341) and gardens (1346); toy museum

PETWORTH HOUSE (NT), Petworth, W. Sussex GU28 0AE
T 01798-343929
Late 17th-century house set in Capability Brown landscaped deer park; fine art collection

PEVENSEY CASTLE (EH), Pevensey, E. Sussex BN24 5LE
T 01323-762604
Walls of a fourth-century Roman fort; remains of an 11th-century castle

PEVERIL CASTLE (EH), Castleton, Derbys S33 8WQ
T 01433-620613
Remains of a 12th-century castle defended on two sides by precipitous rocks

POLESDEN LACEY (NT), nr Dorking, Surrey RH5 6BD
T 01372-452048
Regency villa remodelled in the Edwardian era; fine paintings and furnishings; walled rose garden

PORTCHESTER CASTLE (EH), Portchester, Hants PO16 9QW
T 02392-378291
Walls of a late Roman fort enclosing a Norman keep and an Augustinian priory church

POWDERHAM CASTLE, Kenton, Devon EX6 8JQ
T 01626-890243 W www.powderham.co.uk
Medieval castle with 18th- and 19th-century alterations, including James Wyatt music room

RABY CASTLE, Staindrop, Co. Durham DL2 3AH
T 01833-660202 W www.rabycastle.com
14th-century castle with walled gardens

RAGLEY HALL, Alcester, Warks B49 5NJ T 01789-762090
W www.ragleyhall.com
17th-century Palladian house with gardens and lake

RICHBOROUGH ROMAN FORT (EH), Richborough, Kent
CT13 9JW T 01304-612013
Remains of a Roman Saxon Shore fortress; landing-site of
the Claudian invasion in AD 43

RICHMOND CASTLE (EH), Richmond, N. Yorks DL10 4QW
T 01748-822493
12th-century keep with 11th-century curtain wall

RIEVAULX ABBEY (EH), nr Helmsley, N. Yorks YO62 5LB
T 01439-798228
Remains of a Cistercian abbey founded c.1132

ROCHESTER CASTLE (EH), Rochester, Kent ME1 1SW
T 01634-335882
11th-century castle partly on the Roman city wall, with a
well-preserved square keep of c.1127

ROCKINGHAM CASTLE, Market Harborough, Leics LE16 8TH
T 01536-770240 W www.rockinghamcastle.com
Built by William the Conqueror; formal gardens and
400-year-old 'elephant' hedge

ROMAN BATHS, Pump Room, Stall Street, Bath BA1 1LZ
T 01225-477785 W www.romanbaths.co.uk
Extensive remains of a Roman temple and bathing complex
which still flows with natural thermal water; museum

ROYAL PAVILION, Brighton BN1 1EE T 03000-290900
W www.brighton-hove-rpml.org.uk
Unique palace of George IV, in indo-gothic style with
chinoiserie interiors and Regency gardens

ST AUGUSTINE'S ABBEY (EH), Canterbury, Kent CT1 1PF
T 01227-767345
Remains of Benedictine monastery founded c.597

ST MAWES CASTLE (EH), St Mawes, Cornwall TR2 5DE
T 01326-270526
Coastal defence castle built by Henry VIII

ST MICHAEL'S MOUNT (NT), Marazion, Cornwall TR17 0HS
T 01736-710265 W www.stmichaelsmount.co.uk
12th-century church and castle with later additions,
situated on an iconic rocky island

*SALTAIRE VILLAGE, nr Shipley, W. Yorks
W www.saltairevillage.info
Victorian industrial village founded by mill owner Titus
Salt for his workers see also World Heritage Sites

SANDRINGHAM, Norfolk PE35 6EN T 01485-545400
W www.sandringhamestate.co.uk
The Queen's private residence; neo-Jacobean house built
in 1870 with gardens and country park

SCARBOROUGH CASTLE (EH), Scarborough, N. Yorks
YO11 1HY T 01723-372451
Remains of 12th-century keep and curtain walls

SHERBORNE CASTLE, Sherborne, Dorset DT9 5NR
T 01935-812072 W www.sherbornecastle.com
16th-century castle built by Sir Walter Raleigh set in
Capability Brown landscaped gardens

SHUGBOROUGH ESTATE (NT), Milford, Staffs ST17 0XB
T 0845-459 8900 W www.shugborough.org.uk
Late 17th century house in 18th-century park with
monuments, temples and pavilions in the Greek Revival
style; seat of the Earls of Lichfield

SKIPTON CASTLE, Skipton, N. Yorks BD23 1AW
T 01756-792442 W www.skiptoncastle.co.uk
Well-preserved D-shaped medieval castle with six round
towers and inner courtyard

SMALLHYTHE PLACE (NT), Tenterden, Kent TN30 7NG
T 01580-762334
Half-timbered 16th-century house

*STONEHENGE (EH), nr Amesbury, Wilts SP4 7DE
T 01722-343830
World-famous prehistoric monument comprising
concentric stone circles surrounded by a ditch and bank

STONOR PARK, Henley-on-Thames, Oxon RG9 6HF
T 01491-638587 W www.stonor.com
Medieval house with Georgian facade; refuge for Catholic
recusants after the Reformation

STOURHEAD (NT), Stourton, Wilts BA12 6QD
T 01747-841152
18th-century Palladian mansion with world-renowned
landscape gardens; King Alfred's Tower

STRATFIELD SAYE HOUSE, Hants RG7 2BT T 01256-882694
W www.stratfield-saye.co.uk
House built 1630–40; home of the Dukes of Wellington
since 1817

STRATFORD-UPON-AVON, Warks T 01789-868191
W www.stratford-upon-avon.co.uk
Shakespeare's Birthplace Trust with Shakespeare Centre;
Anne Hathaway's Cottage; Holy Trinity Church, where
Shakespeare is buried

SUDELEY CASTLE, Winchcombe, Glos GL54 5JD
T 01242-604244 W www.sudeleycastle.co.uk
Castle built in 1442; once owned by Richard III and
former home to Catherine Parr, sixth wife of Henry VIII;
restored in the 19th century

SULGRAVE MANOR, nr Banbury, Oxon OX17 2SD
T 01295-760205 W www.sulgravemanor.org.uk
Home of George Washington's family

SUTTON HOUSE (NT), Hackney, London E9 6JQ
T 020-8986 2264
Tudor house, built in 1535 by Sir Ralph Sadleir

SYON HOUSE, Brentford, Middx TW8 8JF T 020-8560 0882
W www.syonpark.co.uk
Built on the site of a former monastery; Robert Adam
interior; Capability Brown park

TINTAGEL CASTLE (EH), Tintagel, Cornwall PL34 0HE
T 01840-770328
13th-century cliff-top castle and 5th–6th-century Celtic
settlement; linked with Arthurian legend

TOWER OF LONDON, London EC3N 4AB T 0844-482 7777
W www.hrp.org.uk
Royal palace and fortress begun by William the Conqueror
in 1078; houses the Crown Jewels

TYNEMOUTH PRIORY AND CASTLE (EH), Tyne and Wear
NE30 4BZ T 0191-257 1090
Remains of a Benedictine priory, founded c.1090, moated
castle-towers, a gatehouse and keep on Saxon monastic
site

UPPARK (NT), South Harting, W. Sussex GU31 5QR
T 01730-825415
17th-century house, restored after fire; Fetherstonhaugh
art collection; 18th-century dolls' house

WALMER CASTLE (EH), Walmer, Kent CT14 7LJ
T 01304-364288
One of Henry VIII's coastal defence castles, now the
residence of the Lord Warden of the Cinque Ports

WARKWORTH CASTLE (EH), Warkworth, Northumberland
NE65 0UJ T 01665-711423
14th-century keep amid earlier ruins, with hermitage
upstream

WHITBY ABBEY (EH), Whitby, N. Yorks YO22 4JT
T 01947-603568
Remains of Norman church on the site of a monastery
founded in AD 657

WILTON HOUSE, nr Salisbury, Wilts SP2 0BJ T 01722-746714
W www.wiltonhouse.com
17th-century house on the site of a Tudor house and
ninth-century nunnery; Palladian bridge

WINDSOR CASTLE, Windsor, Berks SL4 1NJ T 020-7766 7304
W www.royalcollection.org.uk
Official residence of the Queen; oldest royal residence still
in regular use; largest inhabited castle in the world. Also St
George's Chapel; Queen Mary's Dolls' House

WOBURN ABBEY, Woburn, Beds MK17 9WA T 01525-290333
W www.woburn.co.uk
Built on the site of a Cistercian abbey; seat of the Dukes of
Bedford; art collection; antiques centre

WROXETER ROMAN CITY (EH), nr Shrewsbury, Shropshire
SY5 6PH T 01743-761330
Second-century public baths and part of the forum of the
Roman town of *Viroconium*

WALES

For more information on Cadw properties, including those
listed below, the official website is W www.cadw.wales.gov.uk
For more information on National Trust properties in Wales,
including those listed below, the official website is
W www.nationaltrust.org.uk
KEY
(C) Property of Cadw: Welsh Historic Monuments
(NT) National Trust property
* UNESCO World Heritage Site (*see also* World Heritage
Sites)

*BEAUMARIS CASTLE (C), Anglesey LL58 8AP
T 01248-810361
Concentrically planned 13th-century castle, still virtually
intact

*BLAENAVON, Church Road, Blaenavon NP4 9AS T
01495-742333 W www.visitblaenavon.co.uk
18th- and 19th-century industrial landscape associated
with coal and iron production

CAERLEON ROMAN BATHS AND AMPHITHEATRE (C),
Newport NP18 1AE T 01633-422518
Rare example of a legionary bath-house and late
first-century arena surrounded by bank for spectators

*CAERNARFON CASTLE (C), Gwynedd LL55 2AY
T 01286-677617 W www.caernafon-castle.co.uk
Huge fortress with polygonal towers built between 1283
and 1330, initially for King Edward I of England; setting
for the investiture of Prince Charles in 1969

CAERPHILLY CASTLE (C), Caerphilly CF83 1JD
T 029-2088 3143
Concentrically planned castle (c.1270) notable for its scale
and use of water defences

CARDIFF CASTLE, Cardiff CF10 3RB T 029-2087 8100
W www.cardiffcastle.com
Norman keep built on site of Roman fort; 'fairytale'
gothic-revival mansion added in the 19th century

CASTELL COCH (C), Tongwynlais, Cardiff CF15 7JS
T 029-2081 0101
'Fairytale'-style castle, rebuilt 1875–90 on medieval
foundations

CHEPSTOW CASTLE (C), Monmouthshire NP16 5EY
T 01291-624065
Rectangular keep amid extensive fortifications; developed
throughout the Middle Ages

*CONWY CASTLE (C), Gwynedd LL32 8AY T 01492-592358
Built for Edward I in 1283–7 on narrow rocky outcrop;
features eight towers and two barbicans

CRICCIETH CASTLE (C), Gwynedd LL52 0DP
T 01766-522227
Native Welsh 13th-century castle, taken and altered by
Edward I and Edward II

DENBIGH CASTLE (C), Denbighshire LL16 3NB
T 01745-813385

Remains of the castle (begun 1282), including
triple-towered gatehouses

DYFFRYN GARDENS (NT), St Nicholas, Cardiff CF5 6SU
T 029-2059 3328
Edwardian gardens designed by Thomas Mawson,
overlooked by a grand Edwardian mansion

*HARLECH CASTLE (C), Gwynedd LL46 2YH T 01766-780552
Well-preserved castle, constructed 1283–95, on an
outcrop above the former shoreline; withstood seven-year
siege 1461–8

PEMBROKE CASTLE, Pembrokeshire SA71 4LA
T 01646-684585 W www.pembroke-castle.co.uk
Castle founded in 1093; Great Tower built in late 12th
century; birthplace of King Henry VII

PENRHYN CASTLE (NT), Bangor, Gwynedd LL57 4HN
T 01248-353084
Neo-Norman castle built in the 19th century; railway and
dolls' museums; private art collection

*PONTCYSYLLTE AQUEDUCT AND CANAL, Trevor,
Wrexham LL20 7TG T 01978-292015
W www.pontcysyllte.com
Longest and highest aqueduct in Great Britain; designed
by Thomas Telford and finished in 1805

POWIS CASTLE (NT), Welshpool, Powys SY21 8RF
T 01938-551944
Medieval castle with interior in variety of styles;
17th-century gardens; Clive of India museum

RAGLAN CASTLE (C), Monmouthshire NP15 2BT
T 01291-690228
Remains of 15th-century castle with moated hexagonal
keep

ST DAVIDS BISHOP'S PALACE (C), Pembrokeshire SA62 6PE
T 01437-720517
Remains of residence of Bishops of St Davids built
1328–47

TINTERN ABBEY (C), nr Chepstow, Monmouthshire NP16 6SE
T 01291-689251
Remains of 13th-century church and conventual buildings
of a 12th-century Cistercian monastery

TRETOWER COURT AND CASTLE (C), nr Crickhowell,
Powys NP8 1RD T 01874-730279
Medieval manor house rebuilt in the 15th century, with
remains of 12th-century castle near by

SCOTLAND

For more information on Historic Scotland properties,
including those listed below, the official website is
W www.historic-scotland.gov.uk
For more information on National Trust for Scotland
properties, including those listed below, the official website is
W www.nts.org.uk
KEY
(HS) Historic Scotland property
(NTS) National Trust for Scotland property
* Part of the Heart of Neolithic Orkney UNESCO World
Heritage Site

ABBOTSFORD HOUSE, Melrose, Roxburghshire TD6 9BQ
T 01896-752043 W www.scottsabbotsford.co.uk
Home of Sir Walter Scott; features historic Scottish relics
and formal gardens

BALMORAL CASTLE, Ballater, Aberdeenshire AB35 5TB
T 01339-742534 W www.balmoralcastle.com
Baronial-style castle built for Victoria and Albert; the
Queen's private residence

BLACKHOUSE, ARNOL (HS), Lewis, Western Isles HS2 9DB
T 01851-710395
Traditional Lewis thatched house

BLAIR CASTLE, Blair Atholl, Perthshire PH18 5TL
T 01796-481207 W www.blair-castle.co.uk
Mid-18th-century mansion with 13th-century tower; seat
of the Dukes and Earls of Atholl

BOWHILL, Selkirk, Scottish Borders TD7 5ET T 01750-22204
W www.bowhillhouse.co.uk
Present house dates mainly from 1812; Seat of the Dukes
of Buccleuch and Queensberry; fine collection of
paintings

BROUGH OF BIRSAY (HS), Orkney KW17 2LX
T 01856-841815
Remains of Norse and Pictish village on the tidal island of
Birsay

CAERLAVEROCK CASTLE (HS), Glencaple, Dumfries and
Galloway DG1 4RU T 01387-770244
Unique triangular 13th-century moated castle with
classical Renaissance additions

CAIRNPAPPLE HILL (HS), Torphichen, West Lothian
T 01506-634622
Neolithic ceremonial site and Bronze Age burial chambers

CALANAIS STANDING STONES (HS), Lewis, Western Isles
HS2 9DY T 01851-621422
Standing stones in a cross-shaped setting, dating from
between 2900 and 2600 BC

CATERTHUNS (BROWN AND WHITE) (HS), Menmuir,
nr Brechin, Angus
Two large Iron Age hill forts

CAWDOR CASTLE, Nairn, Moray IV12 5RD T 01667-404401
W www.cawdorcastle.com
14th-century keep with 15th- and 17th-century additions

CLAVA CAIRNS (HS), nr Inverness, Inverness-shire IV2 5EU
T 01667-460232
Bronze Age cemetery complex of cairns and standing
stones

CRATHES CASTLE (NTS), nr Banchory, Aberdeenshire
AB31 5QJ T 0845-643 9215
16th-century baronial castle in woodland, fields and
gardens

CULZEAN CASTLE (NTS), Maybole, Ayrshire KA19 8LE
T 01655-884455
18th-century Robert Adam castle with oval staircase and
circular saloon

DRYBURGH ABBEY (HS), nr Melrose, Roxburghshire TD6 0RQ
T 01835-822381
12th-century abbey containing the tomb of Sir Walter
Scott

DUNVEGAN CASTLE, Skye IV55 8WF T 01470-521206
W www.dunvegancastle.com
13th-century castle with later additions; home of the
chiefs of the Clan MacLeod

EDINBURGH CASTLE (HS), EH1 2NG T 0131-225 9846
W www.edinburghcastle.gov.uk
Fortress perched on extinct volcano; includes the Scottish
Crown Jewels, Scottish National War Memorial, Scottish
United Services Museum

EDZELL CASTLE (HS), nr Brechin, Angus DD9 7UE
T 01356-648631
Ruined 16th-century tower house on medieval
foundations; early 17th-century walled garden

EILEAN DONAN CASTLE, Dornie, Ross and Cromarty
IV40 8DX T 01599-555202 W www.eileandonancastle.com
13th-century castle situated at the meeting point of three
sea lochs; Jacobite relics

ELGIN CATHEDRAL (HS), Moray IV30 1HU T 01343-547171
13th-century cathedral and octagonal chapterhouse

FLOORS CASTLE, Kelso, Roxburghshire TD5 7SF
T 01573-223333 W www.floorscastle.com
Largest inhabited castle in Scotland; seat of the Dukes of
Roxburghe; built in the 1720s by William Adam

FORT GEORGE (HS), Ardersier, Inverness-shire IV2 7TD
T 01667-460232
18th-century fort; still a working army barracks

GLAMIS CASTLE, Forfar, Angus DD8 1RJ T 01307-840393
W www.glamis-castle.co.uk
Seat of the Lyon family (later Earls of Strathmore and
Kinghorne) since 1372; the setting for Shakepeare's
Macbeth

GLASGOW CATHEDRAL (HS), Lanarkshire G4 0QZ
T 0141-552 8198 W www.glasgowcathedral.org.uk
Late 12th-century cathedral with vaulted crypt

GLENELG BROCHS (HS), Glenelg, Ross and Cromarty
T 01667-460232
Two broch towers (Dun Telve and Dun Troddan) with
well-preserved structural features

HOPETOUN HOUSE, South Queensferry, West Lothian
EH30 9SL T 0131-331 2451 W www.hopetoun.co.uk
Designed by Sir William Bruce in 1699 and enlarged by
William Adam 1721–48

HUNTLY CASTLE (HS), Aberdeenshire AB54 4SH
T 01466-793191
Ruin of a 16th- and 17th-century baronial residence

INVERARAY CASTLE, Argyll PA32 8XE T 01499-302203
W www.inveraray-castle.com
Gothic-style 18th-century castle designed by William
Adam and Roger Morris; seat of the Dukes of Argyll

IONA ABBEY (HS), Iona, Inner Hebrides PA76 6SQ
T 01681-700512
Monastery founded by St Columba in AD 563

JARLSHOF (HS), Sumburgh Head, Shetland ZE3 9JN
T 01950-460112
Prehistoric settlement with later ninth-century Norse
additions

JEDBURGH ABBEY (HS), Scottish Borders TD8 6JQ
T 01835-863925
Ruined Augustinian abbey founded *c*.1138

KISIMUL CASTLE (HS), Castlebay, Barra, Western Isles
HS9 5UZ T 01871-810313
Medieval island home of the Clan MacNeil

LINLITHGOW PALACE (HS), Kirkgate, Linlithgow, West
Lothian EH49 7AL T 01506-842896
Ruined royal palace, founded in 1424, set in park;
birthplace of James V and Mary, Queen of Scots

*MAESHOWE (HS), Stenness, Orkney KW16 3HH
T 01856-761606
Neolithic chambered tomb with Viking runes

MEIGLE SCULPTURED STONES (HS), Meigle, Perthshire
PH12 8SB T 01828-640612
Twenty-six carved Pictish stones dating from the late
8th to the late 10th centuries

MELROSE ABBEY (HS), Melrose, Roxburghshire TD6 9LG
T 01896-822562
Ruin of Cistercian abbey founded *c*.1136 by David I;
museum of medieval objects

MOUSA BROCH (HS), Island of Mousa, Shetland ZE2 9HP
Finest surviving Iron Age broch tower

NEW ABBEY CORN MILL (HS), Dumfriesshire DG2 8BX
T 01387-850260
Working water-powered mill built in the late 18th
century

*NEW LANARK, South Lanarkshire ML11 9DB
T 01555-661 345
18th-century village built around a cotton mill

PALACE OF HOLYROODHOUSE, Edinburgh EH8 8DX
T 0131-556 5100 W www.royalcollection.org.uk
The Queen's official Scottish residence; home to Mary,
Queen of Scots; main part of the palace built 1671–9
close to ruined 12th-century Augustinian abbey

*RING O' BRODGAR (HS), Stenness, Orkney KW16
T 01856-841815
Neolithic circle of upright stones surrounded by circular ditch

ROSSLYN CHAPEL, Roslin, Midlothian EH25 9PU
T 0131-440 2159 W www.rosslynchapel.org.uk
Historic church built between 1446 and 1484 with unique stone carvings

ST ANDREWS CASTLE AND CATHEDRAL (HS), Fife
KY16 9AR (castle); 9QL (cathedral) T 01334-477196 (castle);
01334-472563 (cathedral)
Ruins of 13th-century castle, the former residence of bishops of St Andrews, and remains of the largest cathedral in Scotland; museum

SCONE PALACE, Perth, Perthshire PH2 6BD T 01738-552300
Georgian-Gothic house built 1802–12

*SKARA BRAE (HS), nr Stromness, Orkney KW16 3LR
T 01856-841815
Neolithic village with adjacent replica house

SMAILHOLM TOWER (HS), nr Kelso, Roxburghshire TD5 7PG
T 01573-460365
Well-preserved 15th-century tower-house

STIRLING CASTLE (HS), Stirlingshire FK8 1EJ
T 01786-450000 W www.stirlingcastle.gov.uk
Great Hall and gatehouse built for James IV c.1500; palace built for James V in 1538; site of coronations including Mary, Queen of Scots

*STONES OF STENNESS, Stenness, Orkney T 01856 841815
Four surviving Neolithic standing stones and the uprights of a three-stone dolmen

TANTALLON CASTLE (HS), North Berwick, East Lothian
EH39 5PN T 01620-892727
Ruined 14th-century curtain wall with towers

THREAVE CASTLE (HS), Castle Douglas, Kirkcudbrightshire
DG7 1TJ T 07711-223101
Ruined late 14th-century tower on an island; accessible only by boat

URQUHART CASTLE (HS), Drumnadrochit, Inverness-shire
IV63 6XJ T 01456-450551
13th-century castle remains on the banks of Loch Ness

NORTHERN IRELAND

For the Northern Ireland Environment Agency, the official website is W www.doeni.gov.uk/niea
For more information on National Trust properties in Northern Ireland, including those listed below, the official website is W www.nationaltrust.org.uk

KEY
(NIEA) Property in the care of the Northern Ireland Environment Agency
(NT) National Trust property

CARRICKFERGUS CASTLE (NIEA), Carrickfergus, Co.
Antrim BT38 7BG T 028-9335 1273
Castle built in 1177 and taken by King John in 1210; garrisoned until 1928

CASTLE COOLE (NT), Enniskillen, Co. Fermanagh BT74 6JY
T 028-6632 2690
18th-century neoclassical mansion in parkland; designed by James Wyatt

CASTLE WARD (NT), Strangford, Co. Down BT30 7LS
T 028-4488 1204
18th-century house with Classical and Gothic facades

DEVENISH MONASTIC SITE (NIEA), nr Enniskillen, Co.
Fermanagh T 028-6862 1588
Island monastery founded in the sixth century by St Molaise; church dating from 13th century

DOWNHILL DEMESNE AND HEZLETT HOUSE (NT),
Castlerock, Co. Londonderry BT51 4RP T 028-7084 8728
Ruins of 18th-century mansion and a 17th century cottage in landscaped estate including Mussenden Temple

DUNLUCE CASTLE (NIEA), Bushmills, Co. Antrim BT57 8UY
T 028-2073 1938
Ruins of medieval stronghold of the McDonnells

FLORENCE COURT (NT), Enniskillen, Co. Fermanagh
BT92 1DB T 028-6634 8249
Mid-18th-century house with Rococo decoration

GREY ABBEY (NIEA), Greyabbey, Co. Down BT22 2NQ
T 028-9181 1491
Substantial remains of a Cistercian abbey founded in 1193 set in landscaped parkland

MOUNT STEWART (NT), Newtownards, Co. Down BT22 2AD
T 028-4278 8387
18th-century house; octagonal Temple of the Winds

NENDRUM MONASTIC SITE (NIEA), Mahee Island,
Co. Down T 028-9054 3037
Island monastery founded in the fifth century by St Machaoi

PATTERSON'S SPADE MILL (NT), Templepatrick, Co. Antrim
BT39 0AP T 028-9443 3619
Last working water-driven spade mill in the UK

TULLY CASTLE (NIEA), Co. Fermanagh T 028-6862 1588
Fortified house and bawn built c.1619

MUSEUMS AND GALLERIES

There are approximately 2,500 museums and galleries in the UK. As of February 2015, 1,581 of these were fully accredited by Arts Council England. Accreditation indicates that the museum or gallery has an appropriate constitution, is soundly financed, has adequate collection management standards and public services and has access to professional curatorial advice. A further 149 museums and galleries have applied for, or are in the process of obtaining accreditation, and these applications are assessed by either Arts Council England; CyMAL: Museums, Archives and Libraries Wales; Museums Galleries Scotland or the Northern Ireland Museums Council.

The following is a selection of museums and art galleries in the UK. Opening hours and admission charges vary. Further information about museums and galleries in the UK is available from the Museums Association (W www.museumsassociation.org T 020-7566 7800).

W www.culture24.org.uk includes a database of all the museums and galleries in the UK.

ENGLAND

* England's national museums and galleries, which receive funding from a government department, such as the DCMS or MoD. These institutions are deemed to have collections of national importance, and the government is able to call upon their staff for expert advice

ALTON
Jane Austen's House Museum, Chawton, Hants GU34 1SD
 T 01420-83262 W www.jane-austens-house-museum.org.uk
 17th-century house which tells the author's story
BARNARD CASTLE
The Bowes Museum, Co. Durham DL12 8NP T 01833-690606
 W www.bowesmuseum.org.uk
 Public gallery in a French châteaux style featuring archaeology, fashion and ceramics. Houses one of the largest collections of Spanish art in the country
BATH
American Museum, Claverton Manor BA2 7BD T 01225-460503
 W www.americanmuseum.org
 American decorative arts from the 17th to 20th centuries; American heritage exhibition
Fashion Museum, Bennett Street BA1 2QH T 01225-477789
 W www.museumofcostume.co.uk
 Fashion from the 17th century to the present day
Victoria Art Gallery, Bridge Street BA2 4AT T 01225-477233
 W www.victoriagal.org.uk
 European Old Masters and British art since the 15th century
BEAMISH
Beamish Museum, Co. Durham DH9 0RG T 0191-370 4000
 W www.beamish.org.uk
 Living working museum of a northern town during Georgian, Victorian and Edwardian times
BEAULIEU
National Motor Museum, Hants SO42 7ZN T 01590-612345
 W www.beaulieu.co.uk
 National motor museum within the New Forest national park
BIRMINGHAM
Aston Hall, Trinity Road B6 6JD T 0121-675 4722
 W www.birminghammuseums.org.uk/aston
 Jacobean House containing paintings, furniture and tapestries from the 17th to 19th centuries

Barber Institute of Fine Arts, University of Birmingham, Edgbaston
 B15 2TS T 0121-414 7333 W www.barber.org.uk
 Extensive coin collection; fine arts, including Old Masters
Birmingham Museum and Art Gallery, Chamberlain Square
 B3 3DH T 0121-303 1966 W www.bmag.org.uk
 Includes notable collection of Pre-Raphaelite art
Museum of the Jewellery Quarter, Vyse Street, Hockley B18 6HA
 T 0121-554 3598
 W www.birminghammuseums.org.uk/jewellery
 Preserved jewellery workshop
Thinktank, Curzon Street B4 7XG T 0121-202 2222
 W www.thinktank.ac
 Science museum featuring over 200 hands-on displays and a Planetarium
BOURNEMOUTH
Russell-Cotes Art Gallery and Museum, East Cliff Promenade
 BH1 3AA T 01202-451858
 W www.russell-cotes.bournemouth.gov.uk
 Seaside villa housing 19th- and 20th-century art and sculptures from around the world
BOVINGTON
Tank Museum, Dorset BH20 6JG T 01929-405096
 W www.tankmuseum.org
 Collection of 200 tanks from their invention in 1915 to the modern conflict in Afghanistan
BRADFORD
Bradford Industrial Museum, Moorside Mills, Moorside Road, Eccleshill BD2 3HP T 01274-435900
 W www.bradfordmuseums.org
 Steam power, machinery and motor vehicle exhibits
Cartwright Hall Art Gallery, Lister Park BD9 4NS
 T 01274-431212 W www.bradfordmuseums.org
 British 19th- and 20th-century fine art, contemporary prints and south Asian art
National Media Museum, BD1 1NQ T 0844-856 3797
 W www.nationalmediamuseum.org.uk
 Photography, film and television interactive exhibits; features an IMAX cinema and the only permanent Cinerama screen in Europe
BRIGHTON
Booth Museum of Natural History, Dyke Road BN1 5AA
 T 03000-290900
 W www.brightonmuseums.org.uk/booth
 Zoology, botany and geology collections; British birds in recreated habitats
Brighton Museum and Art Gallery, Royal Pavilion Gardens
 BN1 1EE T 03000-290900
 W www.brightonmuseums.org.uk/brighton
 Includes fine art and design, fashion, world art; Sussex history
BRISTOL
Arnolfini, Narrow Quay BS1 4QA T 0117-917 2300
 W www.arnolfini.org.uk
 Experimental contemporary visual arts, dance, performance, music; talks and workshops
Blaise Castle House Museum, Henbury Road BS10 7QS
 T 0117-903 9818 W www.bristol.gov.uk/node/2869
 18th-century mansion; social history collections
Bristol Museum and Art Gallery, Queen's Road BS8 1RL
 T 0117-922 3571 W www.bristol.gov.uk/node/2904
 Includes Victorian, Edwardian and French fine art; archaeology, local history and natural sciencies

M Shed, Prince's Wharf BS1 4RN **T** 0117-352 6600
W www.mshed.org
The story of Bristol's heritage of engineering, transport, music and industry

CAMBRIDGE
Fitzwilliam Museum, Trumpington Street CB2 1RB
T 01223-332900 **W** www.fitzmuseum.cam.ac.uk
Antiquities, fine and applied arts, clocks, ceramics, manuscripts, furniture, sculpture, coins and medals
*Imperial War Museum Duxford, Duxford CB22 4QR
T 01223-835000 **W** duxford.iwm.org.uk
Displays of military and civil aircraft, tanks and naval exhibits
Museum of Archaeology and Anthropology, Downing Street CB2 3DZ **T** 01223-333516 **W** www.maa.cam.ac.uk
Global archaeological and anthropological collections; photography and modern art collections
Sedgwick Museum of Earth Sciences, Downing Street CB2 3EQ
T 01223-333456 **W** www.sedgwickmuseum.org
Extensive geological collection
Whipple Museum of the History of Science, Free School Lane CB2 3RH **T** 01223-330906 **W** www.hps.cam.ac.uk/whipple
Scientific instruments from the 14th century to the present

CARLISLE
Tullie House Museum and Art Gallery, Castle Street CA3 8TP
T 01228-618718 **W** www.tulliehouse.co.uk
Prehistoric archaeology, Hadrian's Wall; Viking and medieval Cumbria, and the social history of Carlisle

CHATHAM
The Historic Dockyard, ME4 4TE **T** 01634-823800
W www.thedockyard.co.uk
Maritime attractions including HMS *Cavalier*, the UK's last Second World War destroyer
Royal Engineers Museum, Prince Arthur Road, Gillingham ME4 4UG **T** 01634-822839 **W** www.re-museum.co.uk
Regimental history, ethnography, decorative art and photography

CHELTENHAM
Art Gallery and Museum, Clarence Street GL50 3JT
T 01242-237431 **W** www.cheltenhammuseum.org.uk
Arts and crafts, local heroes, fine art and natural history

CHESTER
Grosvenor Museum, Grosvenor Street CH1 2DD **T** 01244-972120
W www.grosvenormuseum.co.uk
Roman collections, natural history, art, Chester silver, local history and costume

CHICHESTER
Weald and Downland Open Air Museum, Singleton PO18 0EU
T 01243-811363 **W** www.wealddown.co.uk
Rebuilt vernacular buildings from south-east England; includes medieval houses and a working watermill; craft demonstrations, Tudor kitchen and cooking

COLCHESTER
Colchester Castle Museum, Castle Park CO1 1TJ **T** 01206-282939
W www.visitcolchester.com
Largest Norman keep in Europe standing on foundations of the Roman Temple of Claudius

COVENTRY
Coventry Transport Museum, Hales Street CV1 1JD
T 024-7623 4270 **W** www.transport-museum.com
Extensive collection of motor vehicles and bicycles; land speed record-holding car
Herbert Art Gallery and Museum, Jordan Well CV1 5QP
T 024-7623 7521 **W** www.theherbert.org
Local history, archaeology, industry and visual arts

DERBY
Derby Museum and Art Gallery, The Strand DE1 1BS
T 01332-641901
W www.derbymuseums.org/museumartgallery
Includes paintings by Joseph Wright of Derby, origins of Derby and military history
Derby Silk Mill, Silk Mill Lane DE1 3AF **T** 01332-255308
W wwww.derbymuseums.org/locations/the-silk-mill
Built on the site of the world's first factory; wildlife gallery, fine art, Bonnie Prince Charlie Room
Pickford's House Museum, Friar Gate DE1 1DA **T** 01332-715181
W www.derbymuseums.org/pickfords-house
Georgian town house designed by architect Joseph Pickford; museum of Georgian life and costume

DEVIZES
Wiltshire Heritage Museum, Long Street SN10 1NS
T 01380-727369 **W** www.wiltshiremuseum.org.uk
Natural and local history; art gallery; archaeological finds from prehistoric, Roman and Saxon sites

DORCHESTER
Dorset County Museum, High West Street DT1 1XA
T 01305-262735 **W** www.dorsetcountymuseum.org
Includes a collection of Thomas Hardy's manuscripts, books, notebooks and drawings; local history, geology and Roman mosaics

DOVER
Dover Museum, Market Square CT16 1PH **T** 01304-201066
W www.dovermuseum.co.uk
Contains the Dover Bronze Age Boat Gallery and archaeological finds from Bronze Age, Roman and Saxon sites

EXETER
Royal Albert Memorial Museum and Art Gallery, Queen Street EX4 3RX **T** 01392-265858 **W** www.rammuseum.org.uk
Natural history; archaeology; worldwide fine and decorative art including Exeter silver

GATESHEAD
Baltic Centre for Contemporary Art, South Shore Road NE8 3BA
T 0191-478 1810 **W** www.balticmill.com
Contemporary art exhibitions and events
Shipley Art Gallery, Prince Consort Road NE8 4JB
T 0191-477 1495 **W** www.twmuseums.org.uk/shipley
Contemporary crafts

GAYDON
Heritage Motor Centre, Banbury Road, Warks CV35 0BJ
T 01926-641188 **W** www.heritage-motor-centre.co.uk
The world's largest collection of British cars with nearly 300 vehicles spanning the classic, vintage and veteran eras

GLOUCESTER
Gloucester Waterways Museum, Gloucester Docks GL1 2EH
T 01452-318200
W www.canalrivertrust.org.uk/gloucester-waterways-museum
200-year history of Britain's canals and inland waterways

GOSPORT
Royal Navy Submarine Museum, Haslar Jetty Road, Hants PO12 2AS **T** 023-9251 0354 **W** www.submarine-museum.co.uk
Underwater warfare exhibition, including submarines HMS *Alliance* and HMS *Holland 1* – the Royal Navy's first submarine

GRASMERE
Dove Cottage and the *Wordsworth Museum*, Cumbria LA22 9SH
T 015394-35544 **W** www.wordsworth.org.uk
William Wordsworth's manuscripts, home and garden

HOVE
Hove Museum and Art Gallery, New Church Road BN3 4AB
T 03000-290900 **W** www.brightonmuseums.org.uk/hove
Toys, cinema, local history and fine art collections

HULL
Ferens Art Gallery, Queen Victoria Square HU1 3RA
T 01482-300300 **W** www.hullcc.gov.uk/ferens
European Old Masters, Victorian, Edwardian and contemporary British art

Hull Maritime Museum, Queen Victoria Square HU1 3DX
  T 01482-300300 W www.hullcc.gov.uk
  Hull's maritime heritage including whaling, fishing,
  navigation and merchant trade

HUNTINGDON

The Cromwell Museum, Grammar School Walk PE29 3LF
  T 01480-375830 W www.cambridgeshire.gov.uk/info/20011/
  archives_archaeology_and_museums/24/cromwell_museum
  Portraits and memorabilia relating to Oliver Cromwell

IPSWICH

Christchurch Mansion and *Wolsey Art Gallery*, Christchurch
  Park IP4 2BE T 01473-433554 W www.cimuseums.org.uk
  Tudor house with paintings by Gainsborough, Constable
  and other Suffolk artists; furniture and 18th-century
  ceramics; temporary exhibitions

KEIGHLEY

The Brontë Parsonage Museum, Haworth, W. Yorks BD22 8DR
  T 01535-642323 W www.bronte.org.uk
  The former home of the literary Brontë sisters

KESWICK

Pencil Museum, Southey Works CA12 5NG T 01768-773626
  W www.pencilmuseum.co.uk
  500-year history of the pencil; demonstration events and
  workshops throughout the year

LEEDS

Armley Mills, Leeds Industrial Museum, Canal Road, Armley
  LS12 2QF T 0113-263 7861 W www.leeds.gov.uk/armleymills
  Once the world's largest woollen mill, now a museum for
  textiles and Leeds' industrial heritage

Leeds Art Gallery, The Headrow LS1 3AA T 0113-247 8256
  W www.leeds.gov.uk/artgallery
  Includes English watercolours, sculpture, contemporary art
  and prints from the region's artists

Royal Armouries Museum, Armouries Drive LS10 1LT
  T 0113-220 1999 W www.royalarmouries.org
  National collection of over 8,500 items of arms and
  armour from BC to present over five galleries: War,
  Tournament, Oriental, Self Defence and Hunting

LEICESTER

Jewry Wall Museum, St Nicholas Circle LE1 4LB T 0116-225 4971
  W www.leicester.gov.uk
  Archaeology; Roman Jewry Wall and baths; mosaics

New Walk Museum and Art Gallery, 53 New Walk LE1 7EA
  T 0116-255 4900 W www.leicester.gov.uk
  Natural and cultural history; ancient Egypt gallery;
  European art and decorative arts

LINCOLN

The Collection, Danes Terrace LN2 1LP T 01522-782040
  W www.thecollectionmuseum.com
  Artefacts from the Stone Age to the Roman, Viking and
  Medieval eras; adjacent art gallery; collections of
  contemporary art and craft, sculpture, porcelain, clocks
  and watches

Museum of Lincolnshire Life, Burton Road LN1 3LY
  T 01522-782040
  W www.lincolnshire.gov.uk/museumoflincolnshirelife
  Social history; agricultural, industrial, military and
  commercial exhibits

LIVERPOOL

International Slavery Museum, Albert Dock L3 4AX
  T 0151-478 4499 W www.liverpoolmuseums.org.uk/ism
  Explores historical and contemporary aspects of slavery

Lady Lever Art Gallery, Wirral CH62 5EQ T 0151-478 4136
  W www.liverpoolmuseums.org.uk/ladylever
  Paintings, furniture and porcelain

Merseyside Maritime Museum, Albert Dock L3 4AQ
  T 0151-478 4499 W www.liverpoolmuseums.org.uk/maritime
  Floating exhibits, working displays and craft
  demonstrations; incorporates the *UK Border Agency
  National Museum*

Museum of Liverpool, Pier Head L3 1DG T 0151-478 4545
  W www.liverpoolmuseums.org.uk/mol
  Explores the significance of the city's geography, history
  and culture

Sudley House, Mossley Hill Road L18 8BX T 0151-478 4016
  W www.liverpoolmuseums.org.uk/sudley
  Late 18th- and 19th-century paintings in former
  shipowner's home

Tate Liverpool, Albert Dock L3 4BB T 0151-1702 7400
  W www.tate.org.uk/liverpool
  20th-century paintings and sculpture

Walker Art Gallery, William Brown Street L3 8EL
  T 0151-478 4199 W www.liverpoolmuseums.org.uk/walker
  Paintings from the 13th century to the present day

World Museum Liverpool, William Brown Street L3 8EN
  T 0151-478 4393 W www.liverpoolmuseums.org.uk/wml
  Includes Egyptian mummies, weapons and classical
  sculpture; planetarium, aquarium, vivarium and natural
  history centre

LONDON: GALLERIES

Barbican Art Gallery, Barbican Centre, Silk Street EC2Y 8DS
  T 020-7638 4141 W www.barbican.org.uk
  Art, music, theatre, dance and film exhibitions

Courtauld Institute of Art Gallery, Somerset House, Strand
  WC2R 0RN T 020-7848 2526 W www.courtauld.ac.uk
  Impressionist and post-impressionist paintings

Dennis Severs' House, 18 Folgate Street E1 6BX T 020-7247013
  W www.dennissevershouse.co.uk
  Candlelit recreation of a Huguenot silk weaver's home

Dulwich Picture Gallery, Gallery Road SE21 7AD
  T 020-8693 5254 W www.dulwichpicturegallery.org.uk
  England's first public art gallery; designed by Sir John
  Soane to house 17th- and 18th-century paintings

Estorick Collection of Modern Italian Art, Canonbury Square
  N1 2AN T 020-7704 9522 W www.estorickcollection.com
  Early 20th-century Italian drawings, paintings, sculptures
  and etchings, with an emphasis on Futurism

Hayward Gallery, Belvedere Road SE1 8XX T 020-7960 4200
  W www.southbankcentre.co.uk
  Temporary exhibitions

National Gallery, Trafalgar Square WC2N 5DN T 020-7747 2885
  W www.nationalgallery.org.uk
  Western painting from the 13th to 19th centuries; early
  Renaissance collection in the Sainsbury Wing

National Portrait Gallery, St Martin's Place WC2H 0HE
  T 020-7306 0055 W www.npg.org.uk
  Portraits of eminent people in British history

Photographers' Gallery, Ramillies Street W1F 7LW
  T 020-7087 9300 W www.thephotographersgallery.org.uk
  Temporary exhibitions; permanent camera obscura

The Queen's Gallery, Buckingham Palace SW1A 1AA
  T 020-7766 7300 W www.royalcollection.org.uk
  Art from the Royal Collection

Royal Academy of Arts, Burlington House, Piccadilly W1J 0BD
  T 020-7300 8000 W www.royalacademy.org.uk
  British art since 1750 and temporary exhibitions; annual
  Summer Exhibition

Saatchi Gallery, Duke of York's HQ, King's Road SW3 4RY
  T 020-7823 2363 W www.saatchi-gallery.co.uk
  Contemporary art including paintings, photographs,
  sculpture and installations

Serpentine Gallery, Kensington Gardens W2 3XA
  T 020-7402 6075 W www.serpentinegallery.org
  Temporary exhibitions of British and international
  contemporary art

Tate Britain, Millbank SW1P 4RG T 020-7887 8888
  W www.tate.org.uk/britain
  British art from the 16th century to the present;
  international modern art

*Tate Modern, Bankside SE1 9TG T 020-7887 8888
W www.tate.org.uk/modern
International modern art from 1900 to the present

*Wallace Collection, Manchester Square W1U 3BN
T 020-7563 9500 W www.wallacecollection.org
Old Masters; French 18th-century paintings, furniture, armour, porcelain, clocks and sculpture

Whitechapel Art Gallery, Whitechapel High Street E1 7QX
T 020-7522 7888 W www.whitechapelgallery.org
Temporary exhibitions of modern art

LONDON: MUSEUMS

Bank of England Museum, Threadneedle Street EC2R 8AH
(entrance on Bartholomew Lane) T 020-7601 5545
W www.bankofengland.co.uk/museum
History of the Bank of England since 1694

*British Museum, Great Russell Street WC1B 3DG
T 020-7323 8299 W www.britishmuseum.org
Collection of art and antiquities spanning 2 million years of human history; temporary exhibitions; houses the Elgin Marbles from the Parthenon

Brunel Museum, Rotherhithe SE16 4LF T 020-7231 3840
W www.brunel-museum.org.uk
Explores the engineering achievements of Isambard Kingdom Brunel and his father, Marc Brunel

Cartoon Museum, Little Russell Street WC1A 2HH
T 020-7580 8155 W www.cartoonmuseum.org
British cartoons, caricature and comic art from the 18th century to the present

Charles Dickens Museum, Doughty Street WC1N 2LX
T 020-7405 2127 W www.dickensmuseum.com
Dickens's home from 1837–9; manuscripts, personal items and paintings

*Churchill War Rooms, King Charles Street SW1A 2AQ
T 020-7930 6961 W cwr.iwm.org.uk
Underground rooms used by Churchill and the government during the Second World War

Cutty Sark, King William Walk SE10 9HT T 020-8858 4422
W www.rmg.co.uk/cuttysark
The world's last remaining tea clipper; re-opened in April 2012 following extensive restoration

Design Museum, Shad Thames SE1 2YD T 020-7403 6933
W www.designmuseum.org
The development of design and the mass-production of consumer objects

Firepower, the Royal Artillery Museum, Royal Arsenal, Woolwich
SE18 6ST T 020-8855 7755 W www.firepower.org.uk
The history and development of artillery over the last 700 years including the collections of the Royal Regiment of Artillery

Garden Museum, Lambeth Palace Road SE1 7LB T 020-7401 8865
W www.gardenmuseum.org.uk
History and development of gardens and gardening; temporary exhibitions, symposia and events

Geffrye Museum, Kingsland Road E2 8EA T 020-7739 9893
W www.geffrye-museum.org.uk
English urban domestic interiors from 1600 to the present day; also paintings, furniture, decorative arts, walled herb garden and period garden rooms

*HMS Belfast, The Queen's Walk SE1 2JH T 020-7940 6300
W hmsbelfast.iwm.org.uk
Life and work on board a Second World War cruiser

*Horniman Museum, London Road SE23 3PQ T 020-8699 1872
W www.horniman.ac.uk
Museum of anthropology, musical instruments and natural history; aquarium; reference library; gardens

*Imperial War Museum, Lambeth Road SE1 6HZ
T 020-7416 5000 W www.iwm.org.ukc
All aspects of the two World Wars and other military operations involving Britain and the Commonwealth since 1914

Jewish Museum, Albert Street NW1 7NB T 020-7284 7384
W www.jewishmuseum.org.uk
Jewish life, history, art and religion

London Metropolitan Archives, Northampton Road EC1R 0HB
T 020-7332 3820 W www.cityoflondon.gov.uk/lma
Material on the history of London and its people dating from 1067 to the present day

London Museum of Water and Steam, Green Dragon Lane TW8
0EN T 020-8568 4757 W www.waterandsteam.org.uk
Large collection of steam engines; reopened in 2014 after refurbishment

London Transport Museum, Covent Garden Piazza WC2E 7BB
T 020-7379 6344 W www.ltmuseum.co.uk
Vehicles, photographs and graphic art relating to the history of transport in London

MCC Museum, Lord's Cricket Ground, St John's Wood NW8 8QN
T 020-7616 8595 W www.lords.org/mcc
Cricket exhibits including the Ashes, kits, paintings and W. G. Grace exhibit; guided tours by appointment

*Museum of Childhood (V&A), Cambridge Heath Road E2 9PA
T 020-8983 5200 W www.museumofchildhood.org.uk
Toys, games and exhibits relating to the social history of childhood from the 17th century to the present

*Museum of London, London Wall EC2Y 5HN T 020-7001 9844
W www.museumoflondon.org.uk
History of London from prehistoric times to the present day; Galleries of Modern London

Museum of London Docklands, West India Quay, Canary Wharf
E14 4AL T 020-7001 9844
W www.museumoflondon.org.uk/docklands
Explores the story of London's river, port and people over 2,000 years; includes the London Sugar Slavery Gallery

National Archives Museum, Kew TW9 4DU T 020-8876 3444
W www.nationalarchives.gov.uk/museum
Displays treasures from the archives, including the Domesday Book and Magna Carta

*National Army Museum, Royal Hospital Road SW3 4HT
T 020-7730 0717 W www.nam.ac.uk
Five-hundred-year history of the British soldier; exhibits include model of the Battle of Waterloo and recreated First World War trench

*National Maritime Museum, Romney Road SE10 9NF
T 020-8858 4422
W www.rmg.co.uk/national-maritime-museum
Maritime history of Britain; collections include globes, clocks, telescopes and paintings; comprises the main building, the Royal Observatory and the Queen's House

*Natural History Museum, Cromwell Road SW7 5BD
T 020-7942 5000 W www.nhm.ac.uk
Natural history collections and interactive Darwin Centre

Petrie Museum of Egyptian Archaeology, University College
London, Malet Place WC1E 6BT T 020-7679 2884
W www.ucl.ac.uk/museums/petrie
Egyptian and Sudanese archaeology featuring around 80,000 objects

*Royal Air Force Museum, Hendon NW9 5LL T 020-8205 2266
W www.rafmuseum.org.uk
Aviation from before the Wright brothers to the present

Royal Mews, Buckingham Palace SW1W 1QH T 020-7766 7302
W www.royalcollection.org.uk/visit/royalmews
State vehicles, including the Queen's gold state coach; home to the Queen's horses; guided tours

*Science Museum, Exhibition Road SW7 2DD T 0870 870 4868
W www.sciencemuseum.org.uk
Science, technology, industry and medicine exhibitions; children's interactive gallery; IMAX cinema

Shakespeare's Globe Exhibition, New Globe Walk, Bankside
SE1 9DT T 020-7902 1400 W www.shakespearesglobe.com
Recreation of Elizabethan theatre using 16th-century techniques; includes a tour of the theatre

Sir John Soane's Museum, Lincoln's Inn Fields WC2A 3BP
T 020-7405 2107 W www.soane.org
Art and antiquities collected by Soane throughout his
lifetime; authentic Georgian and Victorian interior

Tower Bridge Exhibition, SE1 2UP T 020-7403 3761
W www.towerbridge.org.uk
History of the bridge and display of Victorian steam
machinery; panoramic views from walkways

Victoria and Albert Museum, Cromwell Road SW7 2RL
T 020-7942 2000 W www.vam.ac.uk
Includes the National Art Library and the Gilbert
Collection; fine and applied art and design; furniture,
glass, textiles, theatre and dress collections; temporary
exhibitions

Wellcome Collection, Euston Road NW1 2BE T 020-7611 2222
W www.wellcomecollection.org
Contemporary and historic exhibitions and collections
including the Wellcome Library

Wimbledon Lawn Tennis Museum, Church Road SW19 5AE
T 020-8944 1066 W www.wimbledon.com/museum
Tennis trophies, fashion and memorabilia; view of Centre
Court

MALTON
Eden Camp, N. Yorks YO17 6RT T 01653-697777
W www.edencamp.co.uk
Restored POW camp and Second World War memorabilia

MANCHESTER
Gallery of Costume, Platt Hall, Rusholme M14 5LL
T 0161-245 7245 W www.manchestergalleries.org
Exhibits from the 17th century to the present day

Imperial War Museum North, Trafford Wharf Road M17 1TZ
T 0161-836 4000 W www.iwm.org.uk/north
History of war from the 20th century to the present

Manchester Art Gallery, Mosley Street M2 3JL T 0161-235 8888
W www.manchestergalleries.org
European fine and decorative art from the 17th to 20th
centuries

Manchester Museum, Oxford Road M13 9PL T 0161-275 2648
W www.museum.manchester.ac.uk
Collections include decorative arts, natural history and
zoology; three Ancient Worlds galleries

Museum of Science and Industry, Liverpool Road, Castlefield
M3 4FP T 0161-832 2244 W www.mosi.org.uk
On site of world's oldest passenger railway station;
galleries relating to space, energy, power, transport,
aviation, textiles and social history

National Football Museum, Cathedral Gardens M4 3BG
T 0161-605 8200 W www.nationalfootballmuseum.com
Home to the FIFA, FA and Football League collections
including the 1966 World Cup final ball

People's History Museum, Left Bank, Spinningfields M3 3ER
T 0161-838 9190 W www.phm.org.uk
History of British political and working life

Whitworth Art Gallery, Oxford Road M15 6ER T 0161-275 7450
W www.whitworth.manchester.ac.uk
Fine and modern art, wallpapers, prints, textiles and
sculptures

MILTON KEYNES
Bletchley Park National Codes Centre, Bucks MK3 6EB
T 01908-640404 W www.bletchleypark.org
Home of British codebreaking during the Second World
War; Enigma machine; computer museum and Alan Turing
gallery

MONKWEARMOUTH
Monkwearmouth Station Museum, North Bridge Street,
Sunderland SR5 1AP T 0191-567 7075
W www.seeitdoitsunderland.co.uk/monkwearmouth-station-
museum
Victorian train station; interactive galleries

NEWCASTLE UPON TYNE
Discovery Museum, Blandford Square NE1 4JA T 0191-232 6789
W www.twmuseums.org.uk/discovery
Science and industry, local history, fashion; Tyneside's
maritime history; digital jukebox of 2,000 film and TV
titles from the BFI National Archive

Great North Museum: Hancock, Barras Bridge NE2 4PT
T 0191-222 6765
W www.twmuseums.org.uk/greatnorthmuseum
Natural and ancient history; planetarium; Living Planet
display incorporates live animal tanks and aquaria

Laing Art Gallery, New Bridge Street NE1 8AG T 0191-232 7734
W www.twmuseums.org.uk/laing
19th and 20th century art including local painters;
ceramics, glass, Japanese decrotive arts and prints

NEWMARKET
National Horseracing Museum, High Street CB8 8JH
T 01638-667333 W www.nhrm.co.uk
The story of people and horses involved in racing;
temporary exhibitions

NORTH SHIELDS
Stephenson Railway Museum, Middle Engine Lane NE29 8DX
T 0191-200 7146 W www.twmuseums.org.uk/stephenson
Locomotive engines and rolling stock; open April through
November and school holidays outside this period

NOTTINGHAM
Museum of Nottingham Life, Brewhouse Yard, Castle Boulevard
NG7 1FB T 0115-876 1400 W www.nottinghamcity.gov.uk
Social history from the 17th to 20th centuries

Natural History Museum, Wollaton Hall, Wollaton NG8 2AE
T 0115-876 3100 W www.nottinghamcity.gov.uk
Geology, botany and zoology specimens housed in an
Elizabethan mansion

Nottingham Castle and Art Gallery, Lenton Road NG1 6EL
T 0115-876 1400
W www.mynottingham.gov.uk/nottinghamcastle
Paintings, ceramics, silver, glass and jewellery; history of
Nottingham

OXFORD
Ashmolean Museum, Beaumont Street OX1 2PH T 01865-278000
W www.ashmolean.org
Art and archaeology including Egyptian, Minoan,
Anglo-Saxon and Chinese exhibits; largest collection of
Raphael drawings in the world

Modern Art Oxford, Pembroke Street OX1 1BP T 01865-722733
W www.modernartoxford.org.uk
Temporary exhibitions

Museum of the History of Science, Broad Street OX1 3AZ
T 01865-277280 W www.mhs.ox.ac.uk
Displays include early scientific instruments, chemical
apparatus, clocks and watches

Oxford University Museum of Natural History, Parks Road
OX1 3PW T 01865-272950 W www.oum.ox.ac.uk
Entomology, geology, mineralogy and petrology, and
zoology

Pitt Rivers Museum, South Parks Road OX1 3PP T 01865-270927
W www.prm.ox.ac.uk
Anthropological and archaeological artefacts

PLYMOUTH
City Museum and Art Gallery, Drake Circus PL4 8AJ
T 01752-304774 W www.plymouthmuseum.gov.uk
Local and natural history; ceramics; silver; Old Masters;
world artefacts; temporary exhibitions

PORTSMOUTH
Charles Dickens Birthplace, Old Commercial Road PO1 4QL
T 023-9282 1879 W www.charlesdickensbirthplace.co.uk
Reproduction Regency house; Dickens memorabilia

D-Day Museum, Clarence Esplanade, Southsea PO5 3NT
T 023-9282 6722 W www.ddaymuseum.co.uk
Includes the Overlord embroidery

Portsmouth Historic Dockyard, HM Naval Base PO1 3LJ
T 023-9283 9766 W www.historicdockyard.co.uk
Incorporates the *National Museum of the Royal Navy*
(PO1 3NH T 023-9272 7574 W www.nmrn.org.uk), *HMS Victory* – restoration work open to the public (PO1 3NH
T 023-9283 9766 W www.hms-victory.com), *HMS Warrior*
(PO1 3QX T 023-9277 8600 W www.hmswarrior.org), *Mary Rose* (PO1 3LX T 023-9281 2931 W www.maryrose.org) and *Action Stations* (PO1 3LJ T 023-9289 3338
W www.actionstations.org)
History of the Royal Navy and of the dockyard; warships and technology spanning 500 years

PRESTON
Harris Museum and Art Gallery, Market Square PR1 2PP
T 01772-258248 W www.harrismuseum.org.uk
British art since the 18th century; ceramics, glass, costume and local history; contemporary exhibitions

ST ALBANS
Verulamium Museum, St Michael's Street AL3 4SW
T 01727-751814 W www.stalbansmuseums.org.uk
Remains of Iron Age settlement and the third-largest city in Roman Britain; moving to a new site in 2017

ST IVES
Tate St Ives, Porthmeor Beach, Cornwall TR26 1TG
T 01736-796226 W www.tate.org.uk/stives
Modern art, much by artists associated with St Ives; includes the Barbara Hepworth Museum and Sculpture Garden; open after 2014 part closure

SALISBURY
Salisbury & South Wiltshire Museum, The Close SP1 2EN
T 01722-332151 W www.salisburymuseum.org.uk
Local history and archaeology; Stonehenge exhibits

SHEFFIELD
Graves Gallery, Surrey Street S1 1XZ T 0114-278 2600
W www.museums-sheffield.org.uk
Twentieth-century British art; European art spanning four centuries
Millennium Galleries, Arundel Gate S1 2PP T 0114-278 2600
W www.museums-sheffield.org.uk
Incorporates four different galleries: the Special Exhibition Gallery, the Craft and Design Gallery, the Metalwork Gallery and the Ruskin Gallery, which houses John Ruskin's collection of paintings, drawings, books and medieval manuscripts
Weston Park Museum, Western Bank S10 2TP T 0114-278 2600
W www.museums-sheffield.org.uk
World and local history; art and temporary exhibitions

SOUTHAMPTON
City Art Gallery, Commercial Road SO14 7LP T 023-8083 3007
W www.southampton.gov.uk/art
Western art from the Renaissance to the present
SeaCity Museum, Havelock Road SO14 7FY T 023-8083 3007
W www.seacitymuseum.co.uk
Opened in 2012, the museum tells the story of the city's maritime past and present

SOUTH SHIELDS
Arbeia Roman Fort, Baring Street NE33 2BB T 0191-456 1369
W www.twmuseums.org.uk/arbeia
Excavated ruins; reconstructions of original buildings
South Shields Museum and Art Gallery, Ocean Road NE33 2JA
T 0191-456 8740 W www.twmuseums.org.uk/southshields
South Tyneside history; interactive art gallery

STOKE-ON-TRENT
Etruria Industrial Museum, Lower Bedford Street ST4 7AF
T 01782-233144 W www.etruriamuseum.org.uk
Britain's sole surviving steam-powered potter's mill
Gladstone Pottery Museum, Uttoxeter Road, Longton ST3 1PQ
T 01782-237777 W www.stokemuseums.org.uk/visit/gpm
The last complete Victorian pottery factory in Britain

Potteries Museum and Art Gallery, Bethesda Street ST1 3DW
T 01782-232323 W www.stokemuseums.org.uk/pmag
Pottery, china and porcelain collections and a Mark XVI Spitfire
The Wedgwood Museum, Barlaston ST12 9ER T 01782-371902
W www.wedgwoodmuseum.org.uk
The story of Josiah Wedgwood and the company he founded

SUNDERLAND
Sunderland Museum and Winter Gardens, Burdon Road SR1 1PP
T 0191-553 2323
W www.seeitdoitsunderland.co.uk/sunderland-museum-winter-gardens
Fine and decorative art, local history and gardens

TELFORD
Ironbridge Gorge Museums, TF8 7DQ T 01952-433424
W www.ironbridge.org.uk
Ten museums including The Museum of the Gorge; The Iron Bridge and Tollhouse; Blists Hill (late Victorian working town); Brosely Pipeworks; Coalbrookdale Museum of Iron; Coalport China Museum; Jackfield Tile Museum; Tar Tunnel; Darby Houses

WAKEFIELD
Hepworth Wakefield, Gallery Walk WF1 5AW T 01924-247360
W www.hepworthwakefield.org
Historic and modern art; temporary exhibitions of contemporary art
National Coal Mining Museum for England, New Road, Overton WF4 4RH T 01924-848806 W www.ncm.org.uk
Includes underground tours of one of Britain's oldest working mines
Yorkshire Sculpture Park, West Bretton WF4 4LG T 01924-832631
W www.ysp.co.uk
Open-air sculpture gallery including works by Henry Moore, Barbara Hepworth and others in 500 acres of parkland

WEYBRIDGE
Brooklands Museum, Brooklands Road KT13 0QN
T 01932-857381 W www.brooklandsmuseum.com
Birthplace of British motorsport; world's first purpose-built motor racing circuit

WILMSLOW
Quarry Bank Mill and Styal Estate, Wilmslow SK9 4LA
T 01625-527468 W www.quarrybankmill.org.uk
Europe's most powerful working waterwheel owned by the National Trust illustrating history of cotton industry; costumed guides at restored Apprentice House

WINCHESTER
Winchester Science Centre and Planetarium, Telegraph Way, Hants SO21 1HZ T 01962-863791
W www.winchestersciencecentre.org
Interactive science centre and planetarium

WORCESTER
City Art Gallery and Museum, Foregate Street WR1 1DT
T 01905-25371
W www.whub.org.uk/cms/museums-worcestershire/mag.aspx
Includes the Regimental museum, 19th-century chemist shop and changing art exhibitions
Museum of Worcester Porcelain, Severn Street WR1 2ND
T 01905-21247 W www.worcesterporcelainmuseum.org.uk
Worcester porcelain from 1751 to the present day

WROUGHTON
Science Museum, Wilts SN4 9LT T 01793-846200
W www.sciencemuseum.org.uk/wroughton
Object stores closed to the public due to redevelopment work; Library and Archive are open to the public by appointment

YEOVIL
Fleet Air Arm Museum, RNAS Yeovilton, Somerset BA22 8HT
T 01935-840565 W www.fleetairarm.com
History of naval aviation; historic aircraft, including
Concorde 002
YORK
Beningbrough Hall, Beningbrough YO30 1DD
T 01904-472027
W www.nationaltrust.org.uk/beningbrough-hall
18th-century house with portraits from the National
Portrait Gallery; parklands and gardens
JORVIK Viking Centre, Coppergate YO1 9WT T 01904-615505
W www.jorvik-viking-centre.co.uk
Reconstruction of Viking York based on archaeological
evidence
National Railway Museum, Leeman Road YO26 4XJ
T 0844-815 3139 W www.nrm.org.uk
Includes locomotives, rolling stock and carriages
York Art Gallery, Exhibition Square, YO1 7EW T 01904 687687
W www.yorkartgallery.org
600 years of British and European painting; ceramics
and sculpture
York Castle Museum, Eye of York YO1 9RY T 01904-687687
W www.yorkcastlemuseum.org.uk
Includes Kirkgate, a reconstructed Victorian street;
costume and military collections
Yorkshire Museum, Museum Gardens YO1 7FR T 01904-687687
W www.yorkshiremuseum.org.uk
Yorkshire life from Roman to medieval times; geology and
biology; York observatory

WALES

* Members of National Museum Wales, a public body that receives
its funding through grant-in-aid from the Welsh Assembly

ABERYSTWYTH
Ceredigion Museum, Terrace Road SY23 2AQ T 01970-633088
W www.museum.ceredigion.gov.uk
Local history, housed in a restored Edwardian theatre
Silver Mountain Experience, Ponterwyd SY23 3AB
T 01970-890620 W www.silvermountainexperience.co.uk
Tours of an 18th-century silver mine, with interactive
challenges and games for children
BLAENAFON
Big Pit National Coal Museum, Torfaen NP4 9XP
T 029-2057 3650 W www.museumwales.ac.uk/en/bigpit
Colliery with an underground tour and exhibitions of
modern mining equipment
BODELWYDDAN
Bodelwyddan Castle, Denbighshire LL18 5YA T 01745-584060
W www.bodelwyddan-castle.co.uk
Art gallery within an historic house; features temporary art
exhibits
CAERLEON
National Roman Legion Museum, NP18 1AE T 029-2057 3550
W www.museumwales.ac.uk/en/roman
Features the oldest recorded piece of writing in Wales;
pottery, Roman era gemstones
CARDIFF
National Museum Cardiff, Cathays Park CF10 3NP
T 029-2057 3000 W www.museumwales.ac.uk/en/cardiff
Houses Wales's national art, archaeology and natural
history collections
St Fagans: National History Museum, St Fagans CF5 6XB
T 029-2057 3500 W www.museumwales.ac.uk/en/stfagans
Open-air museum with re-erected buildings, agricultural
equipment and costume

TECHNIQUEST, Stuart Street CF10 5BW T 029-2047 5475
W www.techniquest.org
Interactive science exhibits, planetarium and science
theatre
CRICCIETH
Lloyd George Museum, Llanystumdwy LL52 0SH T 01766-522071
W www.gwynedd.gov.uk
Childhood home of David Lloyd George
DRE-FACH FELINDRE
National Wool Museum, Llandysul SA44 5UP T 029-2057 3070
W www.museumwales.ac.uk/en/wool
Exhibitions, a working woollen mill and craft workshops
LLANBERIS
National Slate Museum, Gwynedd LL55 4TY T 029-2057 3700
W www.museumwales.ac.uk/en/slate
Former slate quarry with original machinery and plant;
slate crafts demonstrations; working waterwheel
LLANDRINDOD WELLS
National Cycle Collection, Automobile Palace, Temple Street
LD1 5DL T 01597-825531 W www.cyclemuseum.org.uk
Approximately 250 bicycles on display, from 1819 to the
present
PRESTEIGNE
Judge's Lodging Museum, Broad Street LD8 2AD T 01544-260650
W www.judgeslodging.org.uk
Restored apartments, courtroom, cells and servants'
quarters
SWANSEA
National Waterfront Museum, Oystermouth Road SA1 3RD
T 029-2057 3600 W www.museumwales.ac.uk/en/swansea
Wales during the Industrial Revolution
Swansea Museum, Victoria Road SA1 1SN T 01792-653763
W www.swansea.gov.uk/swanseamuseum
Paintings, Egyptian artifacts, transport and nautical
collections; war time Swansea
TENBY
Tenby Museum and Art Gallery, Castle Hill SA70 7BP
T 01834-842809 W www.tenbymuseum.org.uk
Local archaeology, history, geology and art

SCOTLAND

* Members of National Museums of Scotland or National Galleries
of Scotland, which are non-departmental public bodies funded by,
and accountable to, the Scottish government

ABERDEEN
Aberdeen Art Gallery, Schoolhill AB10 1FQ T 01224-523700
W www.aagm.co.uk
Paintings, sculptures and graphics; temporary exhibitions
Aberdeen Maritime Museum, Shiprow AB11 5BY T 01224-337700
W www.aagm.co.uk
Maritime history, including shipbuilding and North Sea oil
AYR
Robert Burns Birthplace Museum, Murdoch's Lone,
Alloway KA7 4PQ T 0844-493 2601
W www.burnsmuseum.org.uk
Comprises Burns Cottage, birthplace of the poet, gardens
and a museum
EDINBURGH
Britannia, Leith EH6 6JJ T 0131-555 5566
W www.royalyachtbritannia.co.uk
Former royal yacht with royal barge and royal family
picture gallery
City Art Centre, Market Street EH1 1DE T 0131-529 3993
W www.edinburghmuseums.org.uk
Rolling programme of exhibitions including historic and
modern photography; contemporary art, design and
architecture

Museum of Childhood, High Street EH1 1TG **T** 0131-529 4142
W www.edinburghmuseums.org.uk
Toys, games, clothes and exhibits relating to the social
history of childhood
Museum of Edinburgh, Canongate, Royal Mile EH8 8DD
T 0131-529 4143 **W** www.edinburghmuseums.org.uk
Local history, silver, glass and Scottish pottery
**Museum of Flight,* East Fortune Airfield, East Lothian EH39 5LF
T 0300-123 6789 **W** www.nms.ac.uk/flight
Aviation from the early 20th century to the present
**National Museum of Scotland,* Chambers Street EH1 1JF
T 0300-123 6789 **W** www.nms.ac.uk/scotland
Scottish history; world cultures; natural world; art and
design; science and technology
**National War Museum of Scotland,* Edinburgh Castle EH1 2NG
T 0300-123 6789 **W** www.nms.ac.uk/war
Scotland's military history housed within Edinburgh
Castle
Scottish National Gallery,* The Mound EH2 2EL **T 0131-624 6200
W www.nationalgalleries.org
Fine art from the early Renaissance to the end of the 19th
century
**Scottish National Gallery of Modern Art,* Belford Road EH4 3DR
T 0131-624 6200 **W** www.nationalgalleries.org
Contemporary art featuring British, French and Russian
collections; outdoor sculpture park
**Scottish National Portrait Gallery,* Queen Street EH2 1JD
T 0131-624 6200 **W** www.nationalgalleries.org/portraitgallery
Portraits of eminent people in Scottish history;
Photography Gallery; Victorian Library
The Writers' Museum, Lady Stair's Close EH1 2PA
T 0131-529 4901 **W** www.edinburghmuseums.org.uk
Exhibitions relating to Robert Burns, Sir Walter Scott and
Robert Louis Stevenson
FORT WILLIAM
West Highland Museum, Cameron Square PH33 6AJ
T 01397-702169 **W** www.westhighlandmuseum.org.uk
Highland life; Victorian and Jacobite collections
GLASGOW
Burrell Collection, Pollokshaws Road G43 1AT **T** 0141-287 2550
W www.glasgowlife.org.uk/museums
Paintings by major artists; medieval art, Chinese and
Islamic art
Gallery of Modern Art, Royal Exchange Square G1 3AH
T 0141-287 3050 **W** www.glasgowlife.org.uk/museums
Collection of contemporary Scottish and world art
Hunterian, University of Glasgow G12 8QQ **T** 0141-330 4221
W www.gla.ac.uk/hunterian
Rennie Mackintosh and Whistler collections; coins;
Scottish paintings; Pacific ethnographic collection;
archaeology; medicine
Kelvingrove Art Gallery & Museum, Argyle Street G3 8AG
T 0141-276 9599 **W** www.glasgowlife.org.uk/museums
Includes Old Masters; natural history; arms and armour
Museum of Piping, McPhater Street G4 0HW **T** 0141-353 0220
W www.thepipingcentre.co.uk
The history and origins of bagpiping
**Museum of Rural Life,* Philipshill Road, East Kilbride G76 9HR
T 0300-123 6789 **W** www.nms.ac.uk/rural
History of rural life and work

People's Palace and Winter Gardens, Glasgow Green G40 1AT
T 0141-276 0788 **W** www.glasgowlife.org.uk/museums
Social history of Glasgow since 1750
Riverside Museum, 100 Pointhouse Place G3 8RS
T 0141-287 2720 **W** www.glasgowlife.org.uk/museums
Scotland's museum of transport and travel; the Tall Ship
Glenlee, a Clyde-built sailing ship, is berthed alongside
St Mungo Museum of Religious Art and Life, Castle Street G4 0RH
T 0141-276 1625 **W** www.glasgowlife.org.uk/museums
Exhibits detailing the world's major religions; oldest Zen
garden in Britain

NORTHERN IRELAND

* Members of National Museums Northern Ireland, a non-
departmental public body of the Northern Ireland Office

ARMAGH
**Armagh County Museum,* The Mall East BT61 9BE
T 028-3752 3070 **W** www.nmni.com/acm
Local history; fine art; archaeology; crafts
BANGOR
North Down Museum, Town Hall BT20 4BT **T** 028-9127 1200
W www.northdownmuseum.com
Presents the history of North Down, including its
early-Christian monastery and Plantation-era maps
BELFAST
Titanic Belfast, Queen's Road, Titanic Quarter BT3 9EP
T 028-9076 6386 **W** www.titanicbelfast.com
The story of RMS *Titanic* from her conception to demise;
Shipyard ride and ocean exploration centre
Ulster Museum,* Botanic Gardens BT9 5AB **T 028-9044 0000
W www.nmni.com/um
Irish antiquities; natural and local history; fine and applied
arts
W5,* Odyssey, Queen's Quay BT3 9QQ **T 028-9046 7700
W www.w5online.co.uk
Interactive science and technology centre
HOLYWOOD
**Ulster Folk and Transport Museum,* Cultra BT18 0EU
T 028-9042 8428 **W** www.nmni.com/uftm
Open-air museum with original buildings from Ulster
town and rural life *c.*1900; indoor galleries including Irish
rail and road transport
LONDONDERRY
The Tower Museum, Union Hall Place BT48 6LU **T** 028-7137 2411
W www.derrycity.gov.uk/museums/tower-museum
Tells the story of Ireland through the history of
Londonderry
NEWTOWNARDS
The Somme Heritage Centre, Bangor Road BT23 7PH
T 028-9182 3202 **W** www.sommeassociation.com
Commemorates the part played by Irish forces in the First
World War
OMAGH
**Ulster American Folk Park,* Castletown, Co. Tyrone BT78 5QU
T 028-8224 3292 **W** www.nmni.com/uafp
Open-air museum telling the story of Ulster's emigrants to
America; restored or recreated dwellings and workshops;
ship and dockside gallery

SIGHTS OF LONDON

For historic buildings, museums and galleries in London, *see* the Historic Buildings and Monuments, and Museums and Galleries sections.

BRIDGES

The bridges over the Thames in London, from east to west, are:

Tower Bridge (268m/880ft by 18m/60ft), architect: Horace Jones, engineer: John Wolfe Barry, opened 1894

London Bridge (262m/860ft by 32m/105ft), original 13th-century stone bridge rebuilt and opened 1831 (engineer: John Rennie), reconstructed in Arizona when current London Bridge opened 1973 (architect: Lord Holford, engineer: Mott, Hay and Anderson)

Cannon Street Railway Bridge (261m/855ft), engineers: John Hawkshaw and John Wolfe Barry, originally named Alexandra Bridge, opened 1866; renovated 1979–82

Southwark Bridge (244m/800ft by 17m/56ft), engineer: John Rennie, originally named Queen Street Bridge, opened 1819; rebuilt 1912–21 (architect: Ernest George, engineer: Mott, Hay and Anderson)

Millennium Bridge (325m/1,066ft by 4m/13ft), architect: Foster and Partners, engineer: Ove Arup and Partners, opened 2000; reopened after modification 2002

Blackfriars Railway Bridge (284m/933ft), engineers: John Wolfe Barry and Henri Marc Brunel, orginally named St Paul's Railway Bridge, opened 1886

Blackfriars Bridge (294m/963ft by 32m/105ft), engineer: Robert Mylne, opened 1769; rebuilt 1869 (engineer: Joseph Cubitt); widened 1909

Waterloo Bridge (366m/1,200ft by 24m/80ft), engineer: John Rennie, opened 1817; rebuilt 1945 (architect: Sir Giles Gilbert Scott, engineer: Rendel, Palmer and Triton)

Golden Jubilee Bridges (325m/1,066ft by 4.7m/15ft), architect: Lifschutz Davidson, engineer: WSP Group, opened 2002; commonly known as the Hungerford Footbridges

Hungerford Railway Bridge (366m/1,200ft), engineer: Isambard Kingdom Brunel, suspension bridge opened 1845; present railway bridge opened 1864 (engineer: John Hawkshaw); widened in 1886

Westminster Bridge (228m/748ft by 26m/85ft), engineer: Charles Labelye, opened 1750; rebuilt 1862 (architect: Charles Barry, engineer: Thomas Page)

Lambeth Bridge (237m/776ft by 18m/60ft), engineer: Peter W. Barlow, original suspension bridge opened 1862; current structure opened 1932 (architect: Reginald Blomfield, engineer: George W. Humphreys)

Vauxhall Bridge (231m/759ft by 24m/80ft), engineer: James Walker, opened 1816; redesigned and opened 1906 (architect: William Edward Riley, engineers: Alexander Binnie and Maurice Fitzmaurice)

Grosvenor Railway Bridge (213m/699ft), engineer: John Fowler, opened 1860; rebuilt 1965; also known as the Victoria Railway Bridge

Chelsea Bridge (213m/699ft by 25m/83ft), original suspension bridge opened 1858 (engineer: Thomas Page); rebuilt 1937 (architects: George Topham Forrest and E. P. Wheeler, engineer: Rendel, Palmer and Triton)

Albert Bridge (216m/710ft by 12m/40ft), engineer: Rowland M. Ordish, opened 1873; restructured 1884 (engineer: Joseph Bazalgette); strengthened 1971–3

Battersea Bridge (204m/670ft by 17m/56ft), engineer: Henry Holland, opened 1771; rebuilt 1890 (engineer: Joseph Bazalgette)

Battersea Railway Bridge (204m/670ft), engineer: William Baker, opened 1863; also known as Cremorne Bridge

Wandsworth Bridge (189m/619ft by 18m/60ft), engineer: Julian Tolmé, opened 1873; rebuilt 1940 (architect: E. P. Wheeler, engineer: T. Pierson Frank)

Putney Railway Bridge (229m/750ft), engineers: W. H. Thomas and William Jacomb, opened 1889; also known as the Fulham Railway Bridge or the Iron Bridge – it has no official name

Putney Bridge (213m/699ft by 23m/74ft), architect: Jacob Ackworth, original wooden bridge opened 1729; current granite structure completed in 1886 (engineer: Joseph Bazalgette). The starting point of the Boat Race.

Hammersmith Bridge (210m/688ft by 10m/33ft), engineer: William Tierney Clarke; the first suspension bridge in London, originally built 1827; rebuilt 1887 (engineer: Joseph Bazalgette)

Barnes Railway Bridge (also footbridge, 110m/360ft), engineer: Joseph Locke, opened 1849; rebuilt 1895 (engineers: London and South Western Railway); the original structure stands unused

Chiswick Bridge (137m/450ft by 21m/70ft), architect: Herbert Baker, engineer: Alfred Dryland, opened 1933. The bridge marks the end point of the Boat Race.

Kew Railway Bridge (175m/575ft), engineer: W. R. Galbraith, opened 1869

Kew Bridge (110m/360ft by 17m/56ft), engineer: Robert Tunstall, original timber bridge built 1759; replaced by a Portland stone structure in 1789 (engineer: James Paine); current granite bridge renamed King Edward VII Bridge in 1903, but still known as Kew Bridge (engineers: John Wolfe Barry and Cuthbert Brereton)

Richmond Lock (91m/300ft by 11m/36ft), engineer: F. G. M. Stoney, lock and footbridge opened 1894

Twickenham Bridge (85m/280ft by 21m/70ft), architect: Maxwell Ayrton, engineer: Alfred Dryland, opened 1933

Richmond Railway Bridge (91m/300ft), engineer: Joseph Locke, opened 1848; rebuilt 1906–8 (engineer: J. W. Jacomb-Hood)

Richmond Bridge (85m/280ft by 10m/33ft), architect: James Paine, engineer: Kenton Couse, built 1777; widened 1939

Teddington Lock (198m/650ft), engineer: G. Pooley, two footbridges opened 1889; marks the end of the tidal reach of the Thames

Kingston Railway Bridge architects: J. E. Errington and W. R. Galbraith, engineer: Thomas Brassey, opened 1863

Kingston Bridge (116m/382ft), engineer: Edward Lapidge, built 1825–8; widened 1911–14 (engineers: Basil Mott and David Hay) and 1999–2001

Hampton Court Bridge, engineers: Samuel Stevens and Benjamin Ludgator, built 1753; replaced by iron bridge 1865; present bridge opened 1933 (architect: Edwin Lutyens, engineer: W. P. Robinson)

CEMETERIES

In 1832, in response to the overcrowding of burial grounds in London, the government authorised the establishment of seven non-denominational cemeteries that would encircle the city. These large cemeteries, known as the 'magnificent seven', were seen by many Victorian families as places in which to demonstrate their wealth and stature, and as a result there are some highly ornate graves and tombs.

THE MAGNIFICENT SEVEN

Abney Park, Stoke Newington, N16 (13ha/32 acres), established 1840; tomb of William and Catherine Booth, founders of the Salvation Army, and memorials to many nonconformists and dissenters

Brompton, Old Brompton Road, SW10 (16.5ha/40 acres), established 1840; graves of Sir Henry Cole, Emmeline Pankhurst, John Wisden

Highgate, Swains Lane, N6 (15ha/38 acres), established 1839; graves of Douglas Adams, George Eliot, Eric Hobsbawm, Michael Faraday, Karl Marx, Ralph Miliband and Christina Rossetti

Kensal Green, Harrow Road, W10 (29ha/72 acres), established 1833; tombs of Charles Babbage, Isambard Kingdom Brunel, Wilkie Collins, George Cruikshank, Tom Hood, Leigh Hunt, Harold Pinter, William Makepeace Thackeray, Anthony Trollope

Nunhead, Linden Grove, SE15 (21ha/52 acres), established 1840; closed in 1969, restored and opened for burials

Tower Hamlets, Southern Grove, E3 (11ha/27 acres), established 1841, 350,000 interments; bombed heavily during the Second World War and closed to burials in 1966; now a nature reserve

West Norwood Cemetery and Crematorium, Norwood High Street, SE27 (17ha/42 acres), established 1837; tombs of C. W. Alcock, Mrs Beeton, Sir Henry Tate and Joseph Whitaker (*Whitaker's Almanack*)

OTHER CEMETERIES

Bunhill Fields, City Road, EC1 (1.6ha/4 acres), 17th-century nonconformist burial ground containing the graves of William Blake, John Bunyan and Daniel Defoe

City of London Cemetery and Crematorium, Aldersbrook Road, E12 (81ha/200 acres), established 1856; grave of Bobby Moore

Golders Green Crematorium, Hoop Lane, NW11 (5ha/12 acres), established 1902; retains the ashes of Kingsley Amis, Lionel Bart, Enid Blyton, Marc Bolan, Sigmund Freud, Keith Moon, Ivor Novello, Bram Stoker and H. G. Wells

Hampstead, Fortune Green Road, NW6 (10.5ha/26 acres), established 1876; graves of Alan Coren, Kate Greenaway, Joseph Lister and Marie Lloyd

MARKETS

Billingsgate, Trafalgar Way, E14 (fish), a market site for over 1,000 years, with the Lower Thames Street site dating from 1876; moved to the Isle of Dogs in 1982; owned and run by the City of London Corporation

Borough, Southwark Street, SE1 (vegetables, fruit, meat, dairy, bread), established on present site in 1756; privately owned and run

Brick Lane, E1 (jewellery, vintage clothes, bric-a-brac, food), open Sunday

Brixton, SW9 (African-Caribbean food, music, clothing), open Monday to Saturday

Broadway, E8 (food, fashion, crafts), re-established in 2004, open Saturday

Camden Lock, NW1 (second-hand clothing, jewellery, alternative fashion, crafts), established in 1973

Columbia Road, E2 (flowers), dates from 19th century; became dedicated flower market in the 20th century

Covent Garden, WC2 (antiques, handicrafts, jewellery, clothing, food), originally a fruit and vegetable market (*see* New Covent Garden market); it has been trading in its current form since 1980

Grays, Davies Street, W1K (antiques), indoor market in listed building, established 1977

Greenwich, SE10 (crafts, fashion, food), market revived in the 1980s

Leadenhall, Gracechurch Street, EC3V (meat, poultry, cheese, clothing), site of market since 14th century; present hall built 1881; owned and run by the City of London Corporation

New Covent Garden, SW8 (wholesale vegetables, fruit, flowers), established in 1670 under a charter of Charles II; relocated from central London in 1974

New Spitalfields, E10 (vegetables, fruit), established 1682, modernised 1928, moved out of the City to Leyton in 1991

Old Spitalfields, E1 (arts, crafts, books, clothes, organic food, antiques), continues to trade on the original Spitalfields site on Commercial Street

Petticoat Lane, Middlesex Street, E1, a market has existed on the site for over 500 years, now a Sunday morning market selling almost anything

Portobello Road, W11, originally for herbs and horse-trading from 1870; became famous for antiques after the closure of the Caledonian Market in 1948

Smithfield, EC1 (meat, poultry), built 1866–8, refurbished 1993–4; the site of St Bartholomew's Fair from 12th to 19th century; owned and run by the City of London Corporation

MONUMENTS

CENOTAPH

Whitehall, SW1. The Cenotaph (from the Greek meaning 'empty tomb') was built to commemorate 'The Glorious Dead' and is a memorial to all ranks of the sea, land and air forces who gave their lives in the service of the Empire during the First World War. Designed by Sir Edwin Lutyens and constructed in plaster as a temporary memorial in 1919, it was replaced by a permanent structure of Portland stone and unveiled by George V on 11 November 1920, Armistice Day. An additional inscription was made in 1946 to commemorate those who gave their lives in the Second World War

FOURTH PLINTH

Trafalgar Square, WC2. The fourth plinth (1841) was designed for an equestrian statue that was never built due to lack of funds. From 1999 temporary works have been displayed on the plinth including *Ecce Homo* (Mark Wallinger), *Monument* (Rachel Whiteread), *Alison Lapper Pregnant* (Marc Quinn), *One & Other* (Antony Gormley) and *Hahn/Cock* (Katharina Fritsch). Since March 2015 *Gift Horse* (Hans Haacke), depicting a skeletal, riderless horse, has occupied the plinth. This will be followed in 2016 by *Really Good* (David Shrigley).

LONDON MONUMENT

(Commonly called the Monument), Monument Street. EC3. Built to designs by Sir Christopher Wren and Robert Hooke between 1671 and 1677, the Monument commemorates the Great Fire of London, which broke out in Pudding Lane on 2 September 1666. The fluted Doric column is 36.6m (120ft) high, the moulded cylinder above the balcony supporting a flaming vase of gilt bronze is an additional 12.8m (42ft), and the column is based on a square plinth 12.2m (40ft) high (with fine carvings on the west face), making a total height of 61.6m (202ft) – the tallest isolated stone column in the world, with views of London from a gallery at the top (311 steps)

OTHER MONUMENTS
(sculptor's name in parentheses):
7 July Memorial (Carmody Groarke), Hyde Park
Viscount Alanbrooke (Roberts-Jones), Whitehall
Albert Memorial (Scott), Kensington Gore
Battle of Britain (Day), Victoria Embankment
Beatty (Wheeler), Trafalgar Square
Belgian Gratitude (setting by Blomfield, statue by Rousseau), Victoria Embankment
Boadicea (or *Boudicca*), *Queen of the Iceni* (Thornycroft), Westminster Bridge
Brunel (Marochetti), Victoria Embankment
Burghers of Calais (Rodin), Victoria Tower Gardens, Westminster
Burns (Steell), Embankment Gardens
Canada Memorial (Granche), Green Park
Carlyle (Boehm), Chelsea Embankment
Cavalry (Jones), Hyde Park
Edith Cavell (Frampton), St Martin's Place
Charles I (Le Sueur), Trafalgar Square
Charles II (Gibbons), Royal Hospital, Chelsea
Churchill (Roberts-Jones), Parliament Square
Cleopatra's Needle (20.9m/68.5ft high, *c.*1500 BC, erected in London in 1878; the sphinxes are Victorian), Thames Embankment
Clive (Tweed), King Charles Street
Captain Cook (Brock), The Mall
Oliver Cromwell (Thornycroft), outside Westminster Hall
Cunningham (Belsky), Trafalgar Square
Gen. Charles de Gaulle (Conner), Carlton Gardens
Diana, Princess of Wales Memorial Fountain (Gustafson Porter), Hyde Park
Disraeli, Earl of Beaconsfield (Raggi), Parliament Square
Lord Dowding (Winter), Strand
Duke of Cambridge (Jones), Whitehall
Duke of York (37.8m/124ft column, with statue by Westmacott), Carlton House Terrace
Edward VII (Mackennal), Waterloo Place
Elizabeth I (Kerwin, 1586, oldest outdoor statue in London; from Ludgate), Fleet Street
Eros (Shaftesbury Memorial) (Gilbert), Piccadilly Circus
Marechal/Marshall Foch (Mallisard, copy of one in Cassel, France), Grosvenor Gardens
Charles James Fox (Westmacott), Bloomsbury Square
Yuri Gagarin (Novikov, copy of Russian statue), The Mall
Mahatma Gandhi (Jackson), Parliament Square
George III (Cotes Wyatt), Cockspur Street
George IV (Chantrey), Trafalgar Square
George V (Reid Dick and Scott), Old Palace Yard
George VI (McMillan), Carlton Gardens
Gladstone (Thornycroft), Strand
Guards' (Crimea; Bell), Waterloo Place
Guards Division (Ledward, figures, Bradshaw, cenotaph), Horse Guards' Parade
Haig (Hardiman), Whitehall
Sir Arthur (Bomber) Harris (Winter), Strand
Gen. Henry Havelock (Behnes), Trafalgar Square
International Brigades Memorial (Spanish Civil War) (Ian Walters), Jubilee Gardens, South Bank
Irving (Brock), north side of National Portrait Gallery
Isis (Gudgeon), Hyde Park
James II (Gibbons), Trafalgar Square
Jellicoe (McMillan), Trafalgar Square
Samuel Johnson (Fitzgerald), opposite St Clement Danes
Kitchener (Tweed), Horse Guards' Parade
Abraham Lincoln (Saint-Gaudens, copy of one in Chicago), Parliament Square
Mandela (Walters), Parliament Square
Milton (Montford), St Giles, Cripplegate
Mountbatten (Belsky), Foreign Office Green

Gen. Charles James Napier (Adams), Trafalgar Square
Nelson (Railton), Trafalgar Square, with Landseer's lions (cast from guns recovered from the wreck of the *Royal George*)
Florence Nightingale (Walker), Waterloo Place
Palmerston (Woolner), Parliament Square
Sir Keith Park (Johnson), Waterloo Place
Peel (Noble), Parliament Square
Pitt (Chantrey), Hanover Square
Portal (Nemon), Embankment Gardens
Prince Albert (Bacon), Holborn Circus
Queen Elizabeth Gate (Lund and Wynne), Hyde Park Corner
Queen Mother (Jackson), Carlton Gardens
Raleigh (McMillan), Greenwich
Richard I (Coeur de Lion) (Marochetti), Old Palace Yard
Roberts (Bates), Horse Guards' Parade
Franklin D. Roosevelt (Reid Dick), Grosvenor Square
Royal Air Force (Blomfield), Victoria Embankment
Royal Air Force Bomber Command Memorial (O'Connor), Green Park
Royal Artillery (Great War) (Jagger and Pearson), Hyde Park Corner
Royal Artillery (South Africa) (Colton), The Mall
Captain Scott (Lady Scott), Waterloo Place
Shackleton (Jagger), Kensington Gore
Shakespeare (Fontana, copy of one by Scheemakers in Westminster Abbey), Leicester Square
Smuts (Epstein), Parliament Square
Sullivan (Goscombe John), Victoria Embankment
Trenchard (McMillan), Victoria Embankment
Victoria Memorial (Webb and Brock), in front of Buckingham Palace
Raoul Wallenberg (Jackson), Great Cumberland Place
George Washington (Houdon copy), Trafalgar Square
Wellington (Boehm), Hyde Park Corner
Wellington (Chantrey), outside Royal Exchange
John Wesley (Adams Acton), City Road
Westminster School (Crimea) (Scott), Broad Sanctuary
William III (Bacon), St James's Square
Wolseley (Goscombe John), Horse Guards' Parade

PARKS, GARDENS AND OPEN SPACES

CITY OF LONDON CORPORATION OPEN SPACES
W www.cityoflondon.gov.uk
Ashtead Common (202ha/500 acres), Surrey
Burnham Beeches and *Fleet Wood* (220ha/540 acres), Bucks. Acquired by the City of London for the benefit of the public in 1880, Fleet Wood (26ha/65 acres) being presented in 1921
Coulsdon Common (51ha/127 acres), Surrey
Epping Forest (2,476ha/6,118 acres), Essex. Acquired by the City of London in 1878 and opened to the public in 1882. The Queen Elizabeth Hunting Lodge, built for Henry VIII in 1543, lies at the edge of the forest. The present forest is 19.3km (12 miles) long by around 3km (2 miles) wide, approximately one-tenth of its original area
*Epping Forest Buffer Land (718ha/1,774 acres), Waltham Abbey/Epping
Farthing Downs and New Hill (95ha/235 acres), Surrey
Hampstead Heath (275ha/680 acres), NW3. Including Golders Hill (15ha/36 acres) and Parliament Hill (110ha/271 acres)
Highgate Wood (28ha/70 acres), N6/N10
Kenley Common (56ha/139 acres), Surrey
Queen's Park (12ha/30 acres), NW6
Riddlesdown (43ha/104 acres), Surrey
Spring Park (20ha/50 acres), Kent
Stoke Common (80ha/198 acres), Bucks. Ownership was transferred to the City of London in 2007

West Ham Park (31ha/77 acres), E15

West Wickham Common (10ha/26 acres), Kent

Also over 150 smaller open spaces within the City of London, including *Finsbury Circus* and *St Dunstan-in-the-East*

* Includes Copped Hall Park, Woodredon Estate and Warlies Park

OTHER PARKS AND GARDENS

CHELSEA PHYSIC GARDEN, 66 Royal Hospital Road SW3 4HS T 020-7352 5646 W www.chelseaphysicgarden.co.uk
A garden of general botanical research and education, maintaining a wide range of rare and unusual plants; established in 1673 by the Society of Apothecaries

HAMPTON COURT PARK AND GARDENS (304ha/750 acres), Surrey KT8 9AU T 0844-482 7777 W www.hrp.org.uk
Also known as Home Park, the park lies beyond the palace's formal gardens. It contains a herd of deer and a 750-year-old oak tree from the original park

HOLLAND PARK (22ha/54 acres), Ilchester Place W8 T 020-7361 3000 W www.rbkc.gov.uk The largest park in the Royal Borough of Kensington and Chelsea, includes the Kyoto Garden

KEW, ROYAL BOTANIC GARDENS (120ha/300 acres), Richmond, Surrey TW9 3AB T 020-8332 5655 W www.kew.org
Founded in 1759 and declared a UNESCO World Heritage Site in 2003

THAMES BARRIER PARK (9ha/22acres), North Woolwich Road E16 2HP T 020-7476 3741 Opened in 2000, landscaped gardens with spectacular views of the Thames Barrier

ROYAL PARKS

W www.royalparks.org.uk

Bushy Park (450ha/1,099 acres), Middx. Adjoins Hampton Court; contains an avenue of horse-chestnuts enclosed in a fourfold avenue of limes planted by William III

Green Park (19ha/47 acres), W1. Between Piccadilly and St James's Park, with Constitution Hill leading to Hyde Park Corner

Greenwich Park (74ha/183 acres), SE10. Enclosed by Humphrey, Duke of Gloucester, and laid out by Charles II from the designs of Le Nôtre. On a hill in Greenwich Park is the Royal Observatory (founded 1675). Its buildings are now managed by the National Maritime Museum (T 020-8858 4422 W www.rmg.co.uk) and the earliest building is named Flamsteed House, after John Flamsteed (1646–1719), the first astronomer royal

Hyde Park (142ha/350 acres), W1/W2. From Park Lane to Kensington Gardens and incorporating the Serpentine lake, Apsley House, the Achilles Statue, Rotten Row and the Ladies' Mile; fine gateway at Hyde Park Corner. To the north-east is Marble Arch, originally erected by George IV at the entrance to Buckingham Palace and re-erected in the present position in 1851. At Hyde Park Corner stands Wellington Arch, built in 1825–7, it opened to the public in 2012 following major renovation

Kensington Gardens (111ha/275 acres), W2/W8. From the western boundary of Hyde Park to Kensington Palace; contains the Albert Memorial, Serpentine Gallery and Peter Pan statue

The Regent's Park and *Primrose Hill* (197ha/487 acres), NW1. From Marylebone Road to Primrose Hill surrounded by the Outer Circle; divided by the Broad Walk leading to the Zoological Gardens

Richmond Park (1,000ha/2,500 acres), Surrey. Designated a National Nature Reserve, a Site of Special Scientific Interest and a Special Area of Conservation

St James's Park (23ha/58 acres), SW1. From Whitehall to Buckingham Palace; ornamental lake of 4.9ha (12 acres); the Mall leads from Admiralty Arch to Buckingham Palace

PLACES OF HISTORICAL AND CULTURAL INTEREST

1 Canada Square

Canary Wharf E14 5AB T 020-7418 2000

W www.canarywharf.com

Also known as 'Canary Wharf', the steel and glass skyscraper is designed to sway 35cm in the strongest winds

20 Fenchurch Street

W www.20fenchurchstreet.co.uk

Designed by architect Rafael Viñoly the skyscraper was completed in March 2014 and is nicknamed the 'Walkie-Talkie' because of its shape. The top three floors include a large viewing platform and are open to the public

30 St Mary Axe

EC3A 8EP W www.30stmaryaxe.com

Completed in 2004 and commonly known as the 'Gherkin', each of the floors rotates five degrees from the one below

122 Leadenhall Street

EC3V 4AB W www.theleadenhallbuilding.com

The distinctive 225m (737ft) asymmetrical Leadenhall Building, designed by architects Rogers Stirk Harbour & Partners, was completed in 2014

Alexandra Palace

Alexandra Palace Way N22 7AY T 020-8365 2121

W www.alexandrapalace.com

The Victorian palace was severely damaged by fire in 1980 but was restored, and reopened in 1988. Alexandra Palace now provides modern facilities for exhibitions, conferences, banquets and leisure activities. There is a winter ice rink, a boating lake and a conservation area

Barbican Centre

Silk Street EC2Y 8DS T 020-7638 4141

W www.barbican.org.uk

Owned, funded and managed by the City of London Corporation, the Barbican Centre opened in 1982 and houses the Barbican Theatre, a studio theatre called The Pit and the Barbican Hall; it is also home to the London Symphony Orchestra. There are three cinemas, six conference rooms, two art galleries, a sculpture court, a lending library, trade and banqueting facilities and a conservatory

British Library

St Pancras, 96 Euston Road NW1 2DB T 0843-208 1144

W www.bl.uk

The largest building constructed in the UK in the 20th century with basements extending 24.5m underground. Holdings include the *Magna Carta*, the Gutenburg Bible, Shakespeare's First Folio, Beatles manuscripts and the first edition of *The Times* from 1788. Holds temporary exhibitions on a range of topics

Central Criminal Court

Old Bailey EC4M 7EH T 020-7248 3277

W www.cityoflondon.gov.uk

The highest criminal court in the UK, the 'Old Bailey' is located on the site of the old Newgate Prison. Trials held here have included those of Oscar Wilde, Dr Crippen and the Yorkshire Ripper. The courthouse has been rebuilt several times since 1674; Edward VII officially opened the current neo-baroque building in 1907

Charterhouse

Charterhouse Square EC1M 6AN T 020-7253 9503

W www.thecharterhouse.org

A Carthusian monastery from 1371 to 1538, purchased in 1611 by Thomas Sutton, who endowed it as a residence for aged men 'of gentle birth' and a school for poor scholars (removed to Godalming in 1872)

Downing Street
SW1 **W** www.number10.gov.uk
Number 10 Downing Street is the official town residence of the prime minister, number 11 of the Chancellor of the Exchequer and number 12 is the office of the government whips. The street was named after Sir George Downing, Bt., soldier and diplomat, who was MP for Morpeth 1660–84

George Inn
The George Inn Yard SE1 1NH **T** 020-7407 2056
W www.nationaltrust.org.uk/george-inn
The last galleried inn in London, built in 1677. Now owned by the National Trust and run as an ordinary public house

Horse Guards
Whitehall SW1
Archway and offices built about 1753. The changing of the guard takes place daily at 11am (10am on Sundays) and the inspection at 4pm. Only those with the Queen's permission may drive through the gates and archway into *Horse Guards Parade,* where the colour is 'trooped' on the Queen's official birthday

HOUSES OF PARLIAMENT **W** www.parliament.uk
House of Commons, Westminster SW1A 0AA **T** 020-7219 4272
House of Lords, Westminster SW1A 0PW **T** 020-7219 3107
The royal palace of Westminster, originally built by Edward the Confessor, was the normal meeting place of Parliament from about 1340. St Stephen's Chapel was used from about 1550 for the meetings of the House of Commons, which had previously been held in the Chapter House or Refectory of Westminster Abbey. The House of Lords met in an apartment of the royal palace. The fire of 1834 destroyed much of the palace, and the present Houses of Parliament were erected on the site from the designs of Sir Charles Barry and Augustus Welby Pugin between 1840 and 1867. The chamber of the House of Commons was destroyed by bombing in 1941, and a new chamber designed by Sir Giles Gilbert Scott was used for the first time in 1950. *Westminster Hall and the Crypt Chapel* was the only part of the old palace of Westminster to survive the fire of 1834. It was built by William II from 1097 to 1099 and altered by Richard II between 1394 and 1399. The hammerbeam roof of carved oak dates from 1396–8. The Hall was the scene of the trial of Charles I. *The Victoria Tower* of the House of Lords is 98.5m (323ft) high and *The Clock Tower* of the House of Commons is 96.3m (316ft) high and contains 'Big Ben', the hour bell said to be named after Sir Benjamin Hall, First Commissioner of Works when the original bell was cast in 1856. This bell, which weighed 16 tons 11 cwt, was found to be cracked in 1857. The present bell (13.5 tons) is a recasting of the original and was first brought into use in 1859. The dials of the clock are 7m (23ft) in diameter, the hands being 2.7m (9ft) and 4.3m (14ft) long (including balance piece).

During session, tours of the Houses of Parliament are only available to UK residents who have made advance arrangements through an MP or peer. Overseas visitors are no longer provided with permits to tour the Houses of Parliament during session, although they can tour on Saturdays and during the summer opening and attend debates for both houses in the Strangers' Galleries. During the summer recess, tickets for tours of the Houses of Parliament can be booked by telephone (**T** 0844-847 1672) or bought on site at the ticket office on Abingdon Green opposite Parliament and the Victoria Tower Gardens. The Strangers' Gallery of the House of Commons is open to the public when the house is sitting. To acquire tickets in advance, UK residents should write to their local MP and overseas visitors should apply to their embassy or high commission in the UK for a permit. If none of these arrangements has been made, visitors should join the public queue outside St Stephen's Entrance, where there is also a queue for entry to the House of Lords Gallery

INNS OF COURT
The Inns of Court are ancient unincorporated bodies of lawyers which for more than five centuries have had the power to call to the Bar those of their members who have qualified for the rank or degree of Barrister-at-Law. There are four Inns of Court as well as many lesser inns:

Lincoln's Inn, WC2A 3TL **T** 020-7405 1393
W www.lincolnsinn.org.uk
The most ancient of the inns with records dating back to 1422. The hall and library buildings are from 1845, although the library is first mentioned in 1474; the old hall (late 15th century) and the chapel were rebuilt *c.*1619–23

Inner Temple, King's Bench Walk EC4Y 7HL **T** 020-7797 8250
W www.innertemple.org.uk
Middle Temple, Middle Temple Lane EC4Y 9BT
T 020-7427 4800 **W** www.middletemple.org.uk
Records for the Inner and Middle Temple date back to the beginning of the 16th century. The site was originally occupied by the Order of Knights Templar *c.*1160–1312. The two inns have separate halls thought to have been formed *c.*1350. The division between the two societies was formalised in 1732 with Temple Church and the Masters House remaining in common. The Inner Temple Garden is normally open to the public on weekdays between 12.30pm and 3pm

Temple Church, EC4Y 7BB **T** 020-7353 8559
W www.templechurch.com
The nave forms one of five remaining round churches in England

Gray's Inn, South Square WC1R 5ET **T** 020-7458 7800
W www.graysinn.info
Founded early 14th century; hall 1556–8
No other 'Inns' are active, but there are remains of *Staple Inn,* a gabled front on Holborn (opposite Gray's Inn Road). *Clement's Inn* (near St Clement Danes Church), *Clifford's Inn,* Fleet Street, and *Thavies Inn,* Holborn Circus, are all rebuilt. *Serjeants' Inn,* Fleet Street, and another (demolished 1910) of the same name in Chancery Lane, were composed of Serjeants-at-Law, the last of whom died in 1922

Institute of Contemporary Arts
The Mall SW1Y 5AH **T** 020-7930 3647 **W** www.ica.org.uk
Exhibitions of modern art in the fields of film, theatre, new media and the visual arts

Lloyd's
Lime Street EC3M 7HA **T** 020-7327 1000 **W** www.lloyds.com
International insurance market which evolved during the 17th century from Lloyd's Coffee House. The present building was opened for business in May 1986, and houses the Lutine Bell. Underwriting is on three floors with a total area of 10,591 sq. m (114,000 sq. ft). The Lloyd's building is not open to the general public

London Central Mosque and the Islamic Cultural Centre
Park Road NW8 7RG **T** 020-7724 3363 **W** www.iccuk.org
The focus for London's Muslims; established in 1944 but not completed until 1977, the mosque can accommodate about 5,000 worshippers; guided tours are available

London Eye
South Bank SE1 7PB **T** 0870-990 8883 **W** www.londoneye.com
Opened in March 2000 as London's millennium landmark, this 137m (450ft) observation wheel is the tallest cantilevered observation wheel in the world. The wheel provides a 30-minute ride offering panoramic views of the capital

London Zoo
Regent's Park NW1 4RY **T** 0844-225 1826 **W** www.zsl.org

Madame Tussauds
Marylebone Road NW1 5LR **T** 0871-894 3000
W www.madametussauds.com
Waxwork exhibition

Mansion House
Cannon Street EC4N 8BH **T** 020-7626 2500
W www.cityoflondon.gov.uk
The official residence of the Lord Mayor. Built in the 18th century in the Palladian style. Open to groups by appointment only

Marlborough House
Pall Mall SW1Y 5HX **T** 020-7747 6500
W www.thecommonwealth.org
Built by Wren for the first Duke of Marlborough and completed in 1711, the house reverted to the Crown in 1835. In 1863 it became the London house of the Prince of Wales and was the London home of Queen Mary until her death in 1953. In 1959 Marlborough House was given by the Queen as the headquarters for the Commonwealth Secretariat and it was opened as such in 1965. The Queen's Chapel, Marlborough Gate, was begun in 1623 from the designs of Inigo Jones for the Infanta Maria of Spain, and completed for Queen Henrietta Maria. Marlborough House is not open to the public

Neasden Temple
BAPS Shri Swaminarayan Mandir, Brentfield Road, Neasden
NW10 8LD **T** 020-8965 2651 **W** http://londonmandir.baps.org
The first and largest traditional Hindu Mandir outside of India; opened in 1995

Port of London
Port of London Authority, Royal Pier Road, Kent DA12 2BG
T 01474-562200 **W** www.pla.co.uk
The Port of London covers the tidal section of the river Thames from Teddington to the seaward limit (the outer Tongue buoy and the Sunk light vessel), a distance of 150km (93 miles). The governing body is the Port of London Authority (PLA). Cargo is handled at privately operated riverside terminals between Fulham and Canvey Island, including the enclosed dock at Tilbury, 40km (25 miles) below London Bridge. Passenger vessels and cruise liners can be handled at moorings at Greenwich, Tower Bridge and Tilbury

Queen Elizabeth Olympic Park
Stratford E20 **T** 0800-072 2110
W www.queenelizabetholympicpark.co.uk
Built for the London 2012 Olympic and Paralympic Games, the park, which included the Olympic Stadium, Velodrome and Aquatics Centre has been redeveloped to provide 227ha (560 acres) of parkland with play areas, outside arts and theatre spaces, waterways and wetlands. The north of the park, which includes the Copper Box Arena sport venue, re-opened to the public in 2013. The south of the park, which re-opened in April 2014, incorporates three venues for arts and sports events and the *ArcelorMittal Orbit,* designed by Sir Anish Kapoor and Cecil Balmond; it is the UK's tallest sculpture (114.5m/376ft) and has two accessible observation floors

Roman Remains
The city wall of Roman *Londinium* was largely rebuilt during the medieval period but sections may be seen near the White Tower in the Tower of London; at Tower Hill; at Coopers' Row; at All Hallows, London Wall, its vestry being built on the remains of a semi-circular Roman bastion; at St Alphage, London Wall, showing a succession of building repairs from the Roman until the late medieval period; and at St Giles, Cripplegate. Sections of the great forum and basilica, more than 165 sq. m (1,776 sq. ft),

have been encountered during excavations in the area of Leadenhall, Gracechurch Street and Lombard Street. Traces of Roman activity along the river include a massive riverside wall built in the late Roman period, and a succession of Roman timber quays along Lower and Upper Thames Street. Finds from these sites can be seen at the Museum of London.

Other major buildings are the amphitheatre at Guildhall, remains of bath-buildings in Upper and Lower Thames Street, and the temple of Mithras in Walbrook

Royal Albert Hall
Kensington Gore SW7 2AP **T** 0845-401 5045
W www.royalalberthall.com
The elliptical hall, one of the largest in the world, was completed in 1871; since 1941 it has been the venue each summer for the Promenade Concerts founded in 1895 by Sir Henry Wood. Other events include pop and classical music concerts, dance, opera, sporting events, conferences and banquets

Royal Courts of Justice
Strand WC2A 2LL **T** 020-7947 7726 **W** www.justice.gov.uk
Victorian Gothic building that is home to the high court. Visitors are free to watch proceedings

Royal Hospital, Chelsea
Royal Hospital Road SW3 4SR **T** 020-7881 5200
W www.chelsea-pensioners.co.uk
Founded by Charles II in 1682, and built by Wren; opened in 1692 for old and disabled soldiers. The extensive grounds include the former Ranelagh Gardens and are the venue for the Chelsea Flower Show each May

Royal Naval College
Greenwich SE10 9NN **T** 020-8269 4747 **W** www.ornc.org
The building was the Greenwich Hospital until 1869. It was built by Charles II, largely from designs by John Webb, and by Queen Mary II and William III, from designs by Wren. It stands on the site of an ancient abbey, a royal house and Greenwich Palace, which was constructed by Henry VII. Henry VIII, Mary I and Elizabeth I were born in the royal palace and Edward VI died there

Royal Opera House
Covent Garden WC2E 9DD **T** 020-7240 1200
W www.roh.org.uk
Home of The Royal Ballet (1931) and The Royal Opera (1946). The Royal Opera House is the third theatre to be built on the site, opening 1858; the first was opened in 1732

St James's Palace
Pall Mall SW1A 1BQ **W** www.royal.gov.uk
Built by Henry VIII, only the Gatehouse and Presence Chamber remain; later alterations were made by Wren and Kent. Representatives of foreign powers are still accredited 'to the Court of St James's'. *Clarence House* (1825), the official London residence of the Prince of Wales and his sons, stands within the St James's Palace estate

St Paul's Cathedral
St Paul's Churchyard EC4M 8AD **T** 020-7246 8350
W www.stpauls.co.uk
Built 1675–1710. The cross on the dome is 111m (365ft) above ground level, the inner cupola 66.4m (218ft) above the floor. 'Great Paul' in the south-west tower weighs nearly 17 tons. The organ by Father Smith (enlarged by Willis and rebuilt by Mander) is in a case carved by Grinling Gibbons, who also carved the choir stalls

Shakespeare's Globe
New Globe Walk SE1 9DT **T** 020-7902 1400
W www.shakespearesglobe.com
Reconstructed in 1997, the open-air playhouse is a unique resource for the works of William Shakespeare through perfomance and education; a new indoor replica Jacobean theatre staged its first public performance in January 2014

Shard

London Bridge SE1 T 020-7493 5311 W www.the-shard.com

Completed in May 2012, the skyscraper stands at 310m (1,016ft) and possesses a unique facade of 11,000 glass panels and a 360-degree viewing gallery

Somerset House

Strand WC2R 1LA T 020-7845 4600

W www.somersethouse.org.uk

The river facade (183m/600ft long) was built in 1776–1801 from the designs of Sir William Chambers; the eastern extension, which houses part of King's College, was built by Smirke in 1829–35. Somerset House was the property of Lord Protector Somerset, at whose attainder in 1552 the palace passed to the Crown, and it was a royal residence until 1692. Somerset House has recently undergone extensive renovation and is home to the Embankment Galleries and the Courtauld Gallery. Open-air concerts and ice-skating (Dec–Jan) are held in the courtyard

SOUTH BANK, SE1

Arts complex on the south bank of the river Thames which consists of:

BFI Southbank T 020-7928 3232 W www.bfi.org.uk

Opened in 1952 and administered by the British Film Institute, has four auditoria of varying capacities. Venue for the annual London Film Festival.

The *Royal Festival Hall* T 020-7960 4200

W www.southbankcentre.co.uk

Opened in 1951 for the Festival of Britain, adjacent are the *Queen Elizabeth Hall,* the *Purcell Room* and the *Hayward Gallery*

The *Royal National Theatre,* T 020-7452 3000

W www.nationaltheatre.org.uk

Opened in 1976; comprises the Olivier, the Lyttelton and Dorfman theatres. The Cottesloe Theatre closed in February 2013 and, following refurbishment reopened in 2014 as the Dorfman Theatre

Southwark Cathedral

London Bridge SE1 9DA T 020-7367 6700

W www.cathedral.southwark.anglican.org

Mainly 13th century, but the nave is largely rebuilt. The tomb of John Gower (1330–1408) is between the Bunyan and Chaucer memorial windows in the north aisle; Shakespeare's effigy, backed by a view of Southwark and the Globe Theatre, is in the south aisle; the tomb of Bishop Andrewes (d.1626) is near the screen. The Lady Chapel was the scene of the consistory courts of the reign of Mary (Gardiner and Bonner) and is still used as a consistory court. John Harvard, after whom Harvard University is named, was baptised here in 1607, and the chapel by the north choir aisle is his memorial chapel

Thames Embankments

Sir Joseph Bazalgette (1819–91) constructed the *Victoria Embankment,* on the north side from Westminster to Blackfriars for the Metropolitan Board of Works, 1864–70; (the seats, of which the supports of some are a kneeling camel, laden with spicery, and of others a winged sphinx, were presented by the Grocers' Company and by W. H. Smith, MP, in 1874); the *Albert Embankment,* on the south side from Westminster Bridge to Vauxhall, 1866–9, and the Chelsea Embankment, 1871–4. The total cost exceeded £2m. Bazalgette also inaugurated the London main drainage system, 1858–65. A medallion *(Flumini vincula posuit)* has been placed on a pier of the *Victoria Embankment* to commemorate the engineer

Thames Flood Barrier

W www.environment-agency.gov.uk

Officially opened in May 1984, though first used in February 1983, the barrier consists of ten rising sector gates which span approximately 520m from bank to bank of the Thames at Woolwich Reach. When not in use the gates lie horizontally, allowing shipping to navigate the river normally; when the barrier is closed, the gates turn through 90 degrees to stand vertically more than 50 feet above the river bed. The barrier took eight years to complete and can be raised within about 90 minutes

Trafalgar Tavern

Park Row, Greenwich SE10 9NW T 020-8858 2909

W www.trafalgartavern.co.uk

Regency-period riverside public house built in 1837. Charles Dickens and William Gladstone were patrons

Wembley Stadium

Wembley HA9 0WS T 0844-980 8001

W www.wembleystadium.com

The second largest stadium in Europe; hosts major sporting events and music concerts

Westminster Abbey

SW1P 3PA T 020-7222 5152 W www.westminster-abbey.org

Founded as a Benedictine monastery over 1,000 years ago, the church was rebuilt by Edward the Confessor in 1065 and again by Henry III in the 13th century. The abbey is the resting place for monarchs including Edward I, Henry III, Henry V, Henry VII, Elizabeth I, Mary I and Mary, Queen of Scots, and has been the setting of coronations since that of William the Conqueror in 1066. In Poets' Corner there are memorials to many literary figures, and many scientists and musicians are also remembered here. The grave of the Unknown Warrior is to be found in the nave

Westminster Cathedral

Francis Street SW1P 1QW T 020-7798 9055

W www.westminstercathedral.org.uk

Roman Catholic cathedral built 1895–1903 from the designs of John Francis Bentley. The campanile is 83m (273ft) high

Wimbledon All England Lawn Tennis Club

Church Road SW19 5AE T 020-8944 1066

W www.wimbledon.com

Venue for the Wimbledon Championships. Includes the Wimbledon Lawn Tennis Museum

HALLMARKS

Hallmarks are the symbols stamped on gold, silver, palladium or platinum articles to indicate that they have been tested at an official Assay Office and that they conform to one of the legal standards. The marking of gold and silver articles to identify the maker was instituted in England in 1363 under a statute of Edward III. In 1478 the Assay Office in Goldsmiths' Hall was established and all gold and silversmiths were required to bring their wares to be date-marked by the Hall, hence the term 'hallmarked'.

With certain exceptions, all gold, silver, palladium or platinum articles are required by law to be hallmarked before they are offered for sale. Current hallmarking requirements come under the UK Hallmarking Act 1973 and subsequent amendments. The act is built around the principle of description, where it is an offence for any person to apply to an unhallmarked article a description indicating that it is wholly or partly made of gold, silver, palladium or platinum. There is an exemption by weight: compulsory hallmarks are not needed on gold and palladium under 1g, silver under 7.78g and platinum under 0.5g. Also, some descriptions, such as rolled gold and gold plate, are permissible. The British Hallmarking Council is a statutory body created as a result of the Hallmarking Act. It ensures adequate provision for assaying and hallmarking, supervises the assay offices and ensures the enforcement of hallmarking legislation. The four assay offices at London, Birmingham, Sheffield and Edinburgh operate under the act.

BRITISH HALLMARKING COUNCIL Secretariat, 1 Colmore Square, Birmingham B4 6AA T 0870-763 1455
W www.gov.uk/government/organisations/british-hallmarking-council

COMPULSORY MARKS

Since January 1999 UK hallmarks have consisted of three compulsory symbols – the sponsor's mark, the millesimal fineness (purity) mark and the assay office mark. The distinction between UK and foreign articles has been removed, and more finenesses are now legal, reflecting the more common finenesses elsewhere in Europe.

SPONSOR'S MARK
Formerly known as the maker's mark, the sponsor's mark was instituted in England in 1363. Originally a device such as a bird or fleur-de-lis, now it consists of a combination of at least two initials (usually a shortened form of the manufacturer's name) and a shield design. The London Assay Office offers 45 standard shield designs but other designs are possible by arrangement.

MILLESIMAL FINENESS MARK
The millesimal fineness (purity) mark indicates the number of parts per thousand of pure metal in the alloy. The current finenesses allowed in the UK are:

Gold	999; 990; 916.6 (22 carat); 750 (18 carat); 585 (14 carat); 375 (9 carat)
Silver	999; 958.4 (Britannia); 925 (sterling); 800
Palladium	999; 950; 500
Platinum	999; 950; 900; 850

ASSAY OFFICE MARK
This mark identifies the particular assay office at which the article was tested and marked. The British assay offices are:

 LONDON, Goldsmiths' Hall, Gutter Lane, London EC2V 8AQ T 020-7606 8971
W www.thegoldsmiths.co.uk

 BIRMINGHAM, FO Box 151, Newhall Street, Birmingham B3 1SB T 0121-236 6951
W www.theassayoffice.co.uk

 SHEFFIELD, Guardians' Hall, Beulah Road, Hillsborough, Sheffield S6 2AN T 0114-231 2121
W www.assayoffice.co.uk

 EDINBURGH, Goldsmiths' Hall, 24 Broughton Street, Edinburgh EH1 3RH T 0131-556 1144
W www.edinburghassayoffice.co.uk

Assay offices formerly existed in other towns, eg Chester, Exeter, Glasgow, Newcastle, Norwich and York, each having its own distinguishing mark

OPTIONAL MARKS

Since 1999 traditional pictorial marks such as a crown for gold, the Britannia for 958 silver, the lion passant for 925 silver (lion rampant in Scotland) and the orb for 950 platinum may be added voluntarily to the millesimal mark. In 2010 a pictorial mark for 950 palladium was introduced.

 Gold – a crown

 Britannia silver

 Sterling silver (England)

 Sterling silver (Scotland)

 Platinum – an orb

 Palladium – the Greek goddess Pallas Athene

OTHER MARKS

FOREIGN GOODS
Foreign goods imported into the UK are required to be hallmarked before sale, unless they already bear a convention mark (*see* below) or a hallmark struck by an independent assay office in the European Economic Area which is deemed to be equivalent to a UK hallmark.

The following are the assay office marks used for gold imported articles until the end of 1998. For silver and platinum the symbols remain the same but the shields differ in shape.

 London

 Birmingham

 Sheffield

 Edinburgh

CONVENTION HALLMARKS
The UK has been a signatory to the International Convention on Hallmarks since 1972. A convention hallmark struck by the UK assay offices is recognised by all member countries in the convention and, similarly, convention marks from member countries are legally recognised in the UK. There are currently 19 members of the hallmarking convention: Austria, Cyprus, Czech Republic, Denmark, Finland, Hungary, Ireland, Israel, Latvia, Lithuania, the

Netherlands, Norway, Poland, Portugal, Slovakia, Slovenia, Sweden, Switzerland, and the UK.

A convention hallmark comprises four marks: a sponsor's mark, a common control mark, a fineness mark, and an assay office mark.

Examples of common control marks (figures differ according to fineness, but the style of each mark remains the same for each article):

GOLD	SILVER	PALLADIUM	PLATINUM

COMMEMORATIVE MARKS

There are other marks to commemorate special events: the silver jubilee of King George V and Queen Mary in 1935, the coronation of Queen Elizabeth II in 1953, her silver jubilee in 1977, and her golden jubilee in 2002. During 1999 and 2000 there was a voluntary additional Millennium Mark. A mark to commemorate the Queen's diamond jubilee in 2012 was available from July 2011 to October 2012:

   Diamond Jubilee Hallmark

DATE LETTER

The date letter shows the year in which an article was assayed and hallmarked. Each alphabetical cycle has a distinctive style of lettering or shape of shield. The date letters were different at the various assay offices and the particular office must be established from the assay office mark before reference is made to tables of date letters. Date letter marks became voluntary from 1 January 1999.

The table which follows shows one specimen shield and letter used by the London Assay Office on silver articles for each alphabetical cycle from 1498. The same letters are found on gold articles but the surrounding shield may differ. Until 1 January 1975 two calendar years are given for each specimen date letter as the letter changed annually in May on St Dunstan's Day (the patron saint of silversmiths). Since 1 January 1975, each date letter has indicated a calendar year from January to December and each office has used the same style of date letter and shield for all articles:

LONDON (GOLDSMITHS' HALL) DATE LETTERS FROM 1498

	from	to		from	to
	1498–9	1517–18		1756–7	1775–6
	1518–19	1537–8		1776–7	1795–6
	1538–9	1557–8		1796–7	1815–16
	1558–9	1577–8		1816–17	1835–6
	1578–9	1597–8		1836–7	1855–6
	1598–9	1617–18		1856–7	1875–6
	1618–19	1637–8		1876–7 (A to M square shield, N to Z as shown)	1895–6
	1638–9	1657–8		1896–7	1915–16
	1658–9	1677–8		1916–17	1935–6
	1678–9	1696–7		1936–7	1955–6
	1697 (from March, 1697 only)	1715–16		1956–7	1974
	1716–17	1735–6		1975	1999
	1736–7	1738–9		2000	
	1739–40	1755–6			

BRITISH CURRENCY

The unit of currency is the pound sterling (£) of 100 pence. The decimal system was introduced on 15 February 1971.

COIN

Gold Coins	Bi-colour Coins‡
One hundred pounds £100*	Two pounds £2
Fifty pounds £50*	Nickel-Brass Coins
Twenty-five pounds £25*	Two pounds £2 (pre-1997)§
Ten pounds £10*	One pound £1
Five pounds £5	
Two pounds £2	Cupro-Nickel Coins
Sovereign £1	Crown £5 (since 1990)§
Half-sovereign 50p	50 pence 50p
	Crown 25p (pre-1990)§
Silver Coins	20 pence 20p
(Britannia coins*)	
Two pounds £2	Nickel-plated Steel Coins ℂ
One pound £1	10 pence 10p
50 pence 50p	5 pence 5p
Twenty pence 20p	
	Bronze Coins
Maundy Money†	2 pence 2p
Fourpence 4p	1 penny 1p
Threepence 3p	
Twopence 2p	Copper-plated Steel Coins**
Penny 1p	2 pence 2p
	1 penny 1p

* Britannia coins: gold bullion introduced 1987; silver, 1997
† Ceremonial money given annually by the sovereign on Maundy Thursday to as many elderly men and women as there are years in the sovereign's age
‡ Cupro-nickel centre and nickel-brass outer ring
§ Commemorative coins; not intended for general circulation
ℂ Pre-2012 the 10p and 5p coins were struck in cupro-nickel
** Since September 1992, although in 1998 the 2p was struck in both copper-plated steel and bronze

GOLD COIN

Gold ceased to circulate during the First World War. Since then controls on buying, selling and holding gold coin have been imposed at various times but have subsequently been revoked. Under the Exchange Control (Gold Coins Exemption) Order 1979, gold coins may now be imported and exported without restriction, except gold coins which are more than 50 years old and valued at a sum in excess of £8,000; these cannot be exported without specific authorisation from the Department for Business, Innovation and Skills.

Value Added Taxation on the sale of gold coins was revoked in 2000.

SILVER COIN

Prior to 1920 silver coins were struck from sterling silver, an alloy of which 925 parts in 1,000 were silver. In 1920 the proportion of silver was reduced to 500 parts. Since 1947 all 'silver' coins, except Maundy money, have been struck from cupro-nickel, an alloy of 75 parts copper and 25 parts nickel, except for the 20p, composed of 84 parts copper, 16 parts nickel. Maundy coins continue to be struck from sterling silver.

BRONZE COIN

Bronze, introduced in 1860 to replace copper, is an alloy consisting mainly of copper with small amounts of zinc and tin. Bronze was replaced by copper-plated steel in September 1992 with the exception of 1998 when the 2p was made in both copper-plated steel and bronze.

LEGAL TENDER AND VALUE IN CIRCULATION
as at 31 March 2014

Denomination	Legal up to	Face value (£m est)
Gold*	any amount	–
£2	any amount	832
£1	any amount	1,553
50p	£10	474
20p	£10	553
10p	£5	163
5p	£5	192
2p	20p	131
1p	20p	113

* Dated 1838 onwards, if not below least current weight

£5 (Crown since 1990) and 25p (Crown pre-1990) up to £10 are also legal tender but are only redeemable at the Post Office.

The following coins have ceased to be legal tender:

Farthing	31 Dec 1960
Halfpenny (½d)	31 Jul 1969
Half-crown	31 Dec 1969
Threepence	31 Aug 1971
Penny (1d)	31 Aug 1971
Sixpence	30 Jun 1980
Halfpenny (½p)	31 Dec 1984
Old 5 pence	31 Dec 1990
Old 10 pence	30 Jun 1993
Old 50 pence	28 Feb 1998

The Channel Islands and the Isle of Man issue their own coinage, which is legal tender only in the island of issue.

COIN STANDARDS

	Metal	Standard weight (g)	Standard diameter (mm)
1p	bronze	3.56	20.3
1p	copper-plated steel	3.56	20.3
2p	bronze	7.12	25.9
2p	copper-plated steel	7.12	25.9
5p	nickel-plated steel	3.25	18.0
10p	nickel-plated steel	6.5	24.5
20p	cupro-nickel	5.0	21.4
25p Crown	cupro-nickel	28.28	38.6
50p	cupro-nickel	8.00	27.3
£1	nickel-brass	9.5	22.5
£2	nickel-brass	15.98	28.4
£2	cupro-nickel, nickel-brass	12.00	28.4
£5 Crown	cupro-nickel	28.28	38.6

The 'remedy' is the amount of variation from standard permitted in weight and fineness of coins when first issued from the Royal Mint.

THE TRIAL OF THE PYX

The Trial of the Pyx is the examination by a jury to ascertain that coins made by the Royal Mint, which have been set aside in the pyx (or box), are of the proper weight, diameter and composition required by law. The trial is held annually, presided over by the Queen's Remembrancer, with a jury of freemen of the Company of Goldsmiths.

BANKNOTES

Bank of England notes are issued in denominations of £5, £10, £20 and £50 for the amount of the fiduciary note issue, and are legal tender in England and Wales. No £1 notes have been issued since 1984 and in March 1998 the outstanding notes were written off in accordance with the provision of the Currency Act 1983.

The current E series of notes was introduced from June 1990, replacing the D series (*see* below). A new-style £20 note, the first in series F, was introduced in March 2007. A £50 note, the second in the F series, and the first banknote issued by the Bank of England to feature two portraits on the reverse, was issued in November 2011. The historical figures portrayed in these series are:

£5	May 2002–date	Elizabeth Fry
£5	Jun 1990–2003	George Stephenson*
£10	Nov 2000–date	Charles Darwin
£10	Apr 1992–2003	Charles Dickens*
£20	Mar 2007–date	Adam Smith
£20	Jun 1999–2010	Sir Edward Elgar*
£20	Jun 1991–2001	Michael Faraday*
£50	Nov 2011–date	Matthew Boulton and James Watt
£50	Apr 1994–2014	Sir John Houblon*

* These notes have been withdrawn from circulation

NOTE CIRCULATION

Note circulation is highest at the two peak spending periods of the year: around Christmas and during the summer holiday period.

The value of notes in circulation (£ million) at the end of February 2014 and 2015 was:

	2014	2015
£5	1,540	1,601
£10	7,182	7,371
£20	36,483	38,912
£50	11,025	11,788
Other notes*	3,967	4,118
Total	60,198	63,789

* Includes higher value notes used as backing for the note issues of authorised banks in Scotland and Northern Ireland

LEGAL TENDER

Banknotes which are no longer legal tender are payable when presented at the head office of the Bank of England in London.

The white notes for £10, £20, £50, £100, £500 and £1,000, which were issued until April 1943, ceased to be legal tender in May 1945, and the white £5 note in March 1946.

The white £5 note issued between October 1945 and September 1956, the £5 notes issued between 1957 and

1963 (bearing a portrait of Britannia) and the first series to bear a portrait of the Queen, issued between 1963 and 1971, ceased to be legal tender in March 1961, June 1967 and September 1973 respectively.

The series of £1 notes issued during the years 1928 to 1960 and the 10 shilling notes issued from 1928 to 1961 (those without the royal portrait) ceased to be legal tender in May and October 1962 respectively. The £1 note first issued in March 1960 (bearing on the back a representation of Britannia) and the £10 note first issued in February 1964 (bearing a lion on the back), both bearing a portrait of the Queen on the front, ceased to be legal tender in June 1979. The £1 note first issued in 1978 ceased to be legal tender on 11 March 1988. The 10 shilling note was replaced by the 50p coin in October 1969, and ceased to be legal tender on 21 November 1970.

The D series of banknotes was introduced from 1970 and ceased to be legal tender from the dates shown below. The predominant identifying feature of each note was the portrayal on the back of a prominent figure from British history:

£1	Feb 1978–Mar 1988	Sir Isaac Newton
£5	Nov 1971–Nov 1991	Duke of Wellington
£10	Feb 1975–May 1994	Florence Nightingale
£20	Jul 1970–Mar 1993	William Shakespeare
£50	Mar 1981–Sep 1996	Sir Christopher Wren

The £1 coin was introduced on 21 April 1983 to replace the £1 note.

OTHER BANKNOTES

Scotland – Banknotes are issued by three Scottish banks. The Royal Bank of Scotland issues notes for £1, £5, £10, £20, £50 and £100. Bank of Scotland and the Clydesdale Bank issue notes for £5, £10, £20, £50 and £100. Scottish notes are not legal tender in the UK but they are an authorised currency.

Northern Ireland – Banknotes are issued by four banks in Northern Ireland. The Bank of Ireland and the Ulster Bank issue notes for £5, £10, £20, £50 and £100. The First Trust Bank issue notes for £10, £20, £50 and £100 and Danske Bank (formerly Northern Bank) issue notes for £10 and £20. Northern Ireland notes are not legal tender in the UK but they are an authorised currency.

Channel Islands – The States of Guernsey issues its own currency notes and coinage. The notes are for £1, £5, £10, £20 and £50, and the coins are for 1p, 2p, 5p, 10p, 20p, 50p, £1 and £2. The States of Jersey issues its own currency notes and coinage. The notes are for £1, £5, £10, £20, £50 and £100, and the coins are for 1p, 2p, 5p, 10p, 20p, 50p, £1 and £2.

The Isle of Man – The Isle of Man government issues notes for £1, £5, £10, £20 and £50. Although these notes are only legal tender in the Isle of Man, they may be exchanged at face value at certain UK banks at their discretion. The Isle of Man issues coins for 1p, 2p, 5p, 10p, 20p, 50p, £1, £2 and £5.

Although none of the series of notes specified above is legal tender in the UK, they are generally accepted by banks irrespective of their place of issue. At one time banks made a commission charge for handling Scottish and Irish notes but this was abolished some years ago.

BANKING AND PERSONAL FINANCE

There are two main types of deposit-taking institutions: banks and building societies, although National Savings and Investments also provides savings products. Banks and building societies are regulated by the Prudential Regulation Authority, part of the Bank of England (*see* Financial Services Regulation), and National Savings and Investments is accountable to HM Treasury.

The main institutions within the British banking system are the Bank of England (the central bank), retail banks, investment banks and overseas banks. In its role as the central bank, the Bank of England acts as banker to the government and as a note-issuing authority; it also oversees the efficient functioning of payment and settlement systems.

Since May 1997, the Bank of England has had operational responsibility for monetary policy. At monthly meetings of its monetary policy committee the Bank sets the interest rate at which it will lend to the money markets.

OFFICIAL INTEREST RATES 2005–15

4 August 2005	4.50%
3 August 2006	4.75%
9 November 2006	5.00%
11 January 2007	5.25%
10 May 2007	5.50%
5 July 2007	5.75%
6 December 2007	5.50%
7 February 2008	5.25%
10 April 2008	5.00%
8 October 2008	4.50%
6 November 2008	3.00%
4 December 2008	2.00%
8 January 2009	1.50%
5 February 2009	1.00%
5 March 2009	0.50%

RETAIL BANKING

Retail banks offer a wide variety of financial services to individuals and companies, including current and deposit accounts, loan and overdraft facilities, credit and debit cards, investment services, pensions, insurance and mortgages. All banks offer internet and telephone banking facilities and the majority also offer traditional branch services.

The Financial Ombudsman Service provides independent and impartial arbitration in disputes between banks and their customers (*see* Financial Services Regulation).

PAYMENT CLEARINGS

The Payment Systems Regulator (PSR), a subsidiary of the Financial Conduct Authority (*see* Financial Services Regulation), is the economic regulator for the payment systems industry in the UK. Funded by an annual levy on the firms it regulates, it was established on 1 April 2015. The PSR's statutory objectives are:

• to ensure that payment systems are operated and developed in a way that considers and promotes the interests of all the businesses and consumers that use them
• to promote effective competition in the markets for payment systems and services – between operators, payment service providers and infrastructure providers
• to promote development and innovation in payment systems, in particular the infrastructure used to operate these systems

DESIGNATED PAYMENT SYSTEMS
The PSR can only use its regulatory powers in relation to payment systems designated by HM Treasury, which regularly reviews this list. The current designated payment systems are: BACS, C&C (Cheque & Credit Clearing Company), CHAPS, Faster Payments Scheme (FPS), LINK, Northern Ireland Cheque Clearing (NICC), MasterCard, Visa Europe (Visa).

PSR, 25 The North Colonnade, Canary Wharf, London E14 5HS
T 020-7066 1000 E contactus@psr.org.uk W www.psr.org.uk

GLOSSARY OF FINANCIAL TERMS

AER (ANNUAL EQUIVALENT RATE) – A notional rate quoted on savings and investment products which demonstrates the return on interest, when compounded and paid annually.

APR (ANNUAL PERCENTAGE RATE) – Calculates the total amount of interest payable over the whole term of a product (such as investment or loan), allowing consumers to compare rival products on a like-for-like basis. Companies offering loans, credit cards, mortgages or overdrafts are required by law to provide the APR rate. Where typical APR is shown, it refers to the company's typical borrower and so is given as a best example; rate and costs may vary depending on individual circumstances.

ANNUITY – A type of insurance policy that provides regular income in exchange for a lump sum. The annuity can be bought from a company other than the existing pension provider.

MAJOR RETAIL BANKS' FINANCIAL RESULTS 2014

Bank group	Profit/(loss) before taxation £ million	Profit/(loss) after taxation £ million	Total assets £ million
Barclays Bank	2,309	854	1,358,693
Cooperative Bank	(264)	(225)	37,583
HSBC Bank	1,953	1,389	797,853
Lloyds Banking Group	1,762	1,499	854,896
RBS Group	2,643	(2,711)	1,050,763
Santander UK	1,399	1,110	275,977
TSB Banking Group	170	135	27,171
Virgin Money Group	34	9	26,537

ASU – Accident, sickness and unemployment insurance taken out by a borrower to protect against being unable to work for these reasons. The policy will usually pay a percentage of the normal monthly mortgage repayment if the borrower is unable to work.

ATM (AUTOMATED TELLER MACHINES) – Commonly referred to as cash machines. Users can access their bank accounts using a card for simple transactions such as withdrawing money and viewing an account balance. Some banks and independent ATM deployers charge for transactions.

BANKER'S DRAFT – A cheque drawn on a bank against a cash deposit. Considered to be a secure way of receiving money in instances where a cheque could 'bounce' or where it is not desirable to receive cash.

BASE RATE – The interest rate set by the Bank of England at which it will lend to financial institutions. This acts as a benchmark for all other interest rates.

BASIS POINT – Unit of measure (usually one-hundredth of a percentage point) used to express movements in interest rates, foreign rates or bond yields.

BUY-TO-LET – The purchase of a residential property for the sole purpose of letting to a tenant. Not all lenders provide mortgage finance for this purpose. Buy-to-let lenders assess projected rental income (typical expectations are between 125 and 130 per cent of the monthly interest payment) in addition to, or instead of, the borrower's income. Buy-to-let mortgages are available as either interest only or repayment.

CAPITAL GAIN/LOSS – Increase/decrease in the value of a capital asset when it is sold or transferred compared to its initial worth.

CAPPED RATE MORTGAGE – The interest rate applied to a loan is guaranteed not to rise above a certain rate for a set period of time; the rate can therefore fall but will not rise above the capped rate. The level at which the cap is fixed is usually higher than for a fixed rate mortgage for a comparable period of time. The lender normally imposes early redemption penalties within the first few years.

CASH CARD – Issued by banks and building societies for withdrawing cash from ATMs.

CHARGE CARD – Charge cards, eg American Express and Diners Club, can be used in a similar way to credit cards but the debt must be settled in full each month.

CHIP AND PIN CARD – A credit/debit card which incorporates an embedded chip containing unique owner details. When used with a PIN, such cards offer greater security as they are less prone to fraud. Since 14 February 2006, most card transactions in the UK have required the use of a chip and pin card.

CREDIT CARD – Normally issued with a credit limit, credit cards can be used for purchases until the limit is reached. There is normally an interest-free period on the outstanding balance of up to 56 days. Charges can be avoided if the balance is paid off in full within the interest-free period. Alternatively part of the balance can be paid and in most cases there is a minimum amount set by the issuer (normally a percentage of the outstanding balance) which must be paid on a monthly basis. Some card issuers charge an annual fee and most issuers belong to at least one major credit card network, eg Mastercard or Visa.

CREDIT RATING – Overall credit worthiness of a borrower based on information from a credit reference agency, such as Experian or Equifax, which holds details of credit agreements, payment records, county court judgements etc for all adults in the UK. This information is supplied to lenders who use it in their credit scoring or underwriting systems to calculate the risk of granting a loan to an individual and the probability that it will be repaid. Each lender sets their own criteria for credit worthiness and may accept or reject a credit application based on an individual's credit rating.

CRITICAL ILLNESS COVER – Insurance that covers borrowers against critical illnesses such as stroke, heart attack or cancer and is designed to protect mortgage or other loan payments.

DEBIT CARD – Debit cards were introduced on a large scale in the UK in the mid-1980s, replacing cash and cheques to purchase goods and services. They can be used to withdraw cash from ATMs in the UK and abroad and may also function as a cheque guarantee card. Funds are automatically withdrawn from an individual's bank account after making a purchase and no interest is charged.

DIRECT DEBIT – An instruction from a customer to their bank, which authorises the payee to charge costs to the customer's bank account.

DISCOUNTED MORTGAGE – Discounted mortgages guarantee an interest rate set at a margin below the standard variable rate for a period of time. The discounted rate will move up or down with the standard variable rate, but the payment rate will retain the agreed differential below the standard variable rate. The lender normally imposes early redemption penalties within the first few years.

EARLY REDEMPTION PENALTY – *see* Redemption Penalty

ENDOWMENT MORTGAGE – Only the interest on a property loan is paid back to the lender each month as long as an endowment life insurance policy is taken out for an agreed amount of time, typically 25 years. When the policy matures the lender will take repayment of the money owed on the property loan and any surplus goes to the policyholder. If the endowment policy shows a shortfall on projected returns, the policy holder must make further provision to pay off the mortgage.

EQUITY – When applied to real estate, equity is the difference between the value of a property and the amount outstanding on any loan secured against it. Negative equity occurs when the loan is greater than the market value of the property.

FIXED RATE MORTGAGE – A repayment mortgage where the interest rate on the loan is fixed for a set amount of time, normally a period of between one and ten years. The interest rate does not vary with changes to the base rate resulting in the monthly mortgage payment remaining the same for the duration of the fixed period. The lender normally imposes early redemption penalties within the first few years.

ISA (INDIVIDUAL SAVINGS ACCOUNT) – A means by which investors can save (in a cash ISA) and invest (in a stocks and shares ISA) without paying any tax on the proceeds. There are limits on the amount that can be invested during any given tax year (*see* Taxation).

INTEREST ONLY MORTGAGE – Only interest is paid by the borrower and capital remains constant for the term of the loan. The onus is on the borrower to make provision to repay the capital at the end of the term. This is usually achieved through an investment vehicle such as an endowment policy or pension.

LOAN TO VALUE (LTV) – This is the ratio between the size of a mortgage loan sought and the mortgage lender's valuation. On a loan of £55,000, for example, on a property valued at £100,000 the loan to value is 55 per cent. This means that there is sufficient equity in the property for the lender to be reassured that if interest or capital repayments were stopped, it could sell the property and recoup the money owed. Fewer options are available to borrowers requiring high LTV.

LONDON INTERBANK OFFERED RATE (LIBOR) – Is the interest rate that London banks charge when lending to one another on the wholesale money market. LIBOR is set by supply and demand of money as banks lend to each other in order to balance their books on a daily basis.

MIG (MORTGAGE INDEMNITY GUARANTEE) – An insurance for the lender paid by the borrower on high LTV mortgages (typically more than 90 per cent). It is a policy designed to protect the lender against loss in the event of the borrower defaulting or ceasing to repay a mortgage and is usually paid as a one-off premium or can be added to the value of the loan. It offers no protection to the borrower. Not all lenders charge MIG premiums.

OVERDRAFT – An 'authorised' overdraft is an arrangement made between customer and bank allowing the balance of the customer's account to go below zero; interest is normally charged at an agreed rate and sometimes an arrangement fee is charged. If the negative balance exceeds the agreed terms or a prior arrangement for an overdraft facility has not been made (an 'unauthorised' overdraft) then additional penalty fees may be charged and higher interest rates may apply. Interest-free overdrafts are available for customers in certain circumstances, such as full-time higher education students and recent graduates.

PERSONAL PENSION PLAN (PPP) – Designed for the self-employed or those in non-pensionable employment. Contributions made to a PPP are exempt from tax and the retirement age may be selected at any time from age 50 to 75. Up to 25 per cent of the pension fund may be taken as a tax-free cash sum on retirement.

PHISHING – A fraudulent attempt to obtain bank account details and security codes through an email. The email purports to come from a *bona fide* bank or building society and attempts to steer the recipient, usually under the pretext that the banking institution is updating its security arrangements, to a website which requests personal details.

PIN (PERSONAL IDENTIFICATION NUMBER) – A PIN is issued alongside a cash card to allow the user to access a bank account via an ATM. PINs are also issued with smart, credit and debit cards and, since 14 February 2006, have been compulsory as a security measure in the majority of purchases.

PORTABLE MORTGAGE – A mortgage product that can be transferred to a different property in the event of a house move. Preferable where early redemption penalties are charged.

REDEMPTION PENALTY – A charge levied for paying off a loan, debt balance or mortgage before a date agreed with the lender.

REPAYMENT MORTGAGE – In contrast to the interest only mortgage, the monthly repayment includes an element of the capital sum borrowed in addition to the interest charged.

SHARE – A share is a divided-up unit of the value of a company. If a company is worth £100m, and there are 50 million shares in issue, then each share is worth £2 (usually listed as pence). As the overall value of the company fluctuates so does the share price.

STANDING ORDER – An instruction made by the customer to their bank, which allows the transfer of a set amount to a payee at regular intervals.

UNIT TRUST – A 'pooled' fund of assets, usually shares, owned by a number of individuals. Managed by professional, authorised fund-management groups, unit trusts have traditionally delivered better returns than average cash deposits, but do rise and fall in value as their underlying investment varies in value.

VARIABLE RATE MORTGAGE – Repayment mortgages where the interest rate set by the lender increases or decreases in relation to the base interest rate which can result in fluctuating monthly repayments.

WITH-PROFITS – Usually applies to pensions, endowments, savings schemes or bonds. The intention is to smooth out the rises and falls in the stock market for the benefit of the investor. Actuaries working for the insurance company, or fund managers, hold back some profits in good years in order to make up the difference in years when shares perform badly.

BANK FAMILY TREE

Includes the major retail banks operating in the UK as at April 2015. Financial results for these banks are given on page 485. Building societies are only included in instances where they demutualised to become a bank.

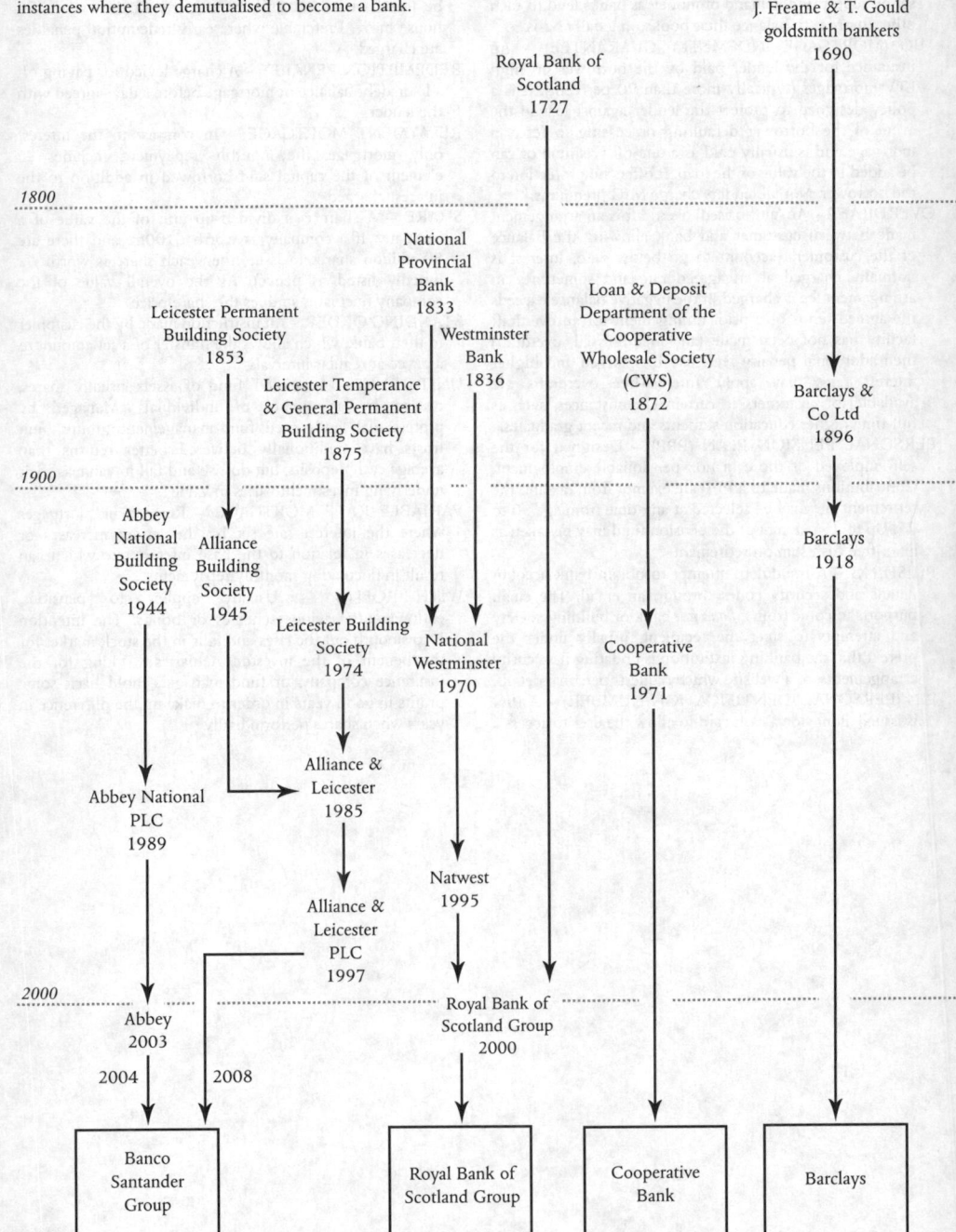

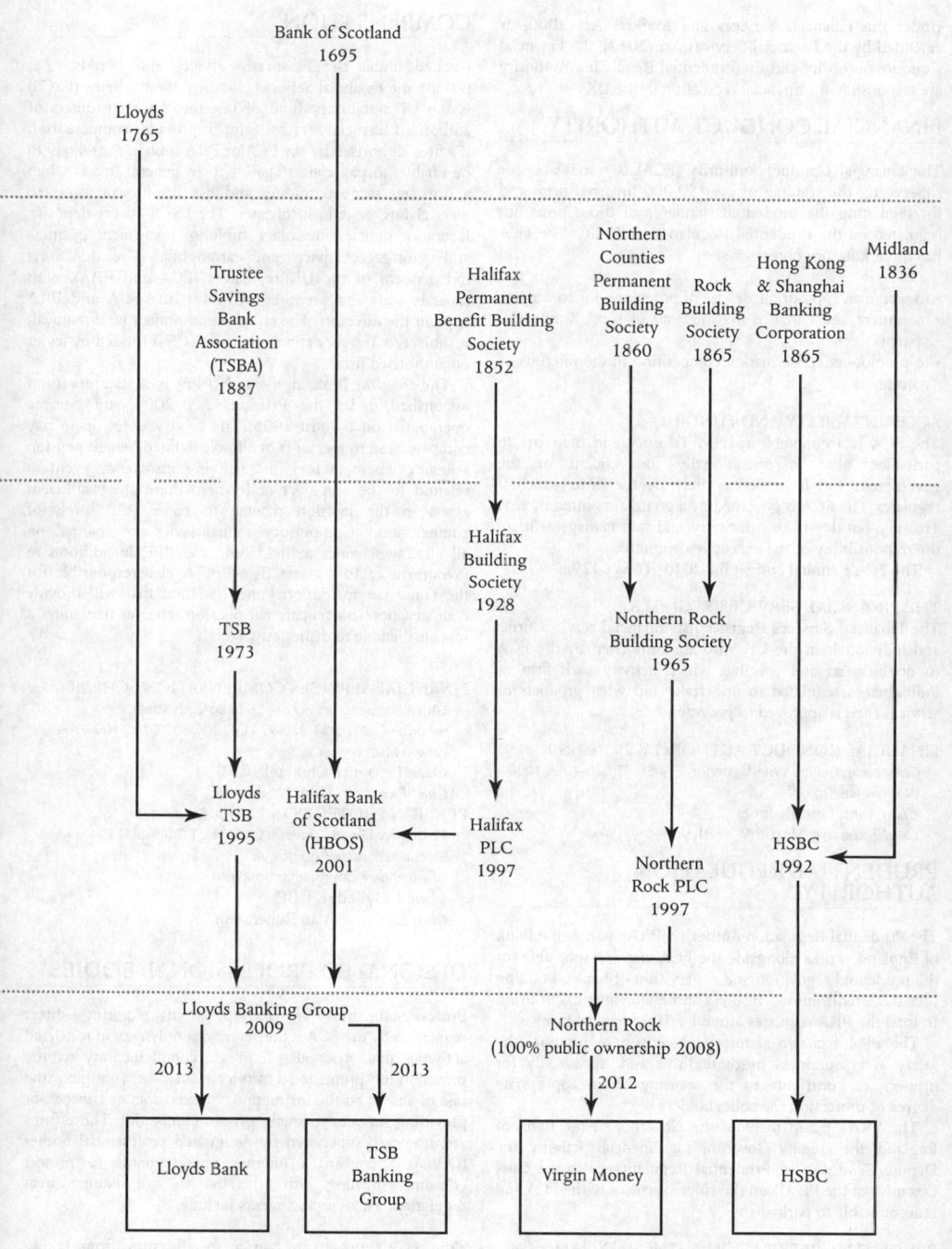

FINANCIAL SERVICES REGULATION

Under the Financial Services and Markets Act 2000, as amended by the Financial Services Act (2012), the Financial Conduct Authority and the Prudential Regulation Authority are responsible for financial regulation in the UK.

FINANCIAL CONDUCT AUTHORITY

The Financial Conduct Authority (FCA) is responsible for supervising the conduct of over 50,000 financial firms and for regulating the prudential standards of those firms not regulated by the Prudential Regulation authority. The FCA has three statutory objectives:

• to secure an appropriate degree of protection for consumers
• to protect and enhance the integrity of the UK financial system
• to promote effective market competition in the interests of consumers

ACCOUNTABILITY AND FUNDING
The FCA is accountable to HM Treasury and therefore to parliament, but is operationally independent of the government and is funded entirely by the firms which it regulates. The FCA is governed by a board appointed by HM Treasury, but day-to-day decisions and staff management are the responsibility of the executive committee.

The FCA's annual budget for 2015–16 is £479m.

THE FINANCIAL SERVICES REGISTER
The Financial Services Register lists financial services firms and individuals in the UK who are authorised by the FCA to do business and specifies which activity each firm or individual is regulated to undertake and what products or services each is approved to provide.

FINANCIAL CONDUCT AUTHORITY, 25 The North Colonnade, Canary Wharf, London E14 5HS T 020-7066 1000
W www.fca.org.uk
Chair, John Griffith-Jones
Chief Executive, Martin Wheatley

PRUDENTIAL REGULATION AUTHORITY

The Prudential Regulation Authority (PRA), part of the Bank of England, works alongside the FCA and is responsible for the prudential regulation and supervision of banks, building societies, credit unions, insurers and major investment firms. In total the PRA regulates around 1,700 financial firms.

The PRA has two statutory objectives: to promote the safety and soundness of these firms and, specifically for insurers, to contribute to the securing of an appropriate degree of protection for policyholders.

The PRA's board includes the Governor of the Bank of England, the Deputy Governor for Financial Stability, the Deputy Governor for Prudential Regulation (also the chief executive of the PRA) and the chief executive of the FCA and is accountable to parliament.

PRUDENTIAL REGULATION AUTHORITY, 20 Moorgate, London EC2R 6DA T 020-7601 4444
E enquiries@bankofengland.co.uk
W www.bankofengland.co.uk/pra
Chief Executive, Andrew Bailey

COMPENSATION

Created under the Financial Services and Markets Act (2000), the Financial Services Compensation Scheme (FSCS) is the UK's statutory fund of last resort for customers of authorised financial services firms. It provides compensation if a firm authorised by the FCA or PRA is unable, or likely to be unable, to pay claims against it. In general this is when a firm has stopped trading and has insufficient assets to meet claims, or is in insolvency. The FSCS covers deposits, insurance policies, insurance broking, investment business and mortgage advice and arranging. The FSCS is independent of the UK regulators (FCA and PRA), with separate staff and premises. However, the FCA and PRA appoint the directors. The chair's appointment (and removal) is subject to Treasury approval. The FSCS is funded by levies on authorised firms.

The Pension Protection Fund (PPF) is a statutory fund established under the Pensions Act 2004 and became operational on 6 April 2005. The fund was set up to pay compensation to members of eligible defined benefit pension schemes, where there is a qualifying insolvency event in relation to the employer and where there are insufficient assets in the pension scheme to cover PPF levels of compensation. Compulsory annual levies are charged on all eligible schemes to help fund the PPF, in addition to investment of PPF assets. The PPF is also responsible for the Fraud Compensation Fund – a fund that will provide compensation to occupational pension schemes that suffer a loss attributable to dishonesty.

FINANCIAL SERVICES COMPENSATION SCHEME, 10th Floor, Beaufort House, 15 St Botolph Street, London EC3A 7QU T 020-7741 4100/0800-678 1100
W www.fscs.org.uk
Chair, Lawrence Churchill, CBE
Chief Executive, Mark Neale
PENSION PROTECTION FUND, Renaissance, 12 Dingwall Road, Croydon CR0 2NA T 0845-600 2541
E information@ppf.gsi.gov.uk
W www.pensionprotectionfund.org.uk
Chair, Lady Judge, CBE
Chief Executive, Alan Rubenstein

DESIGNATED PROFESSIONAL BODIES

Professional firms are exempt from requiring direct regulation by the FCA if they carry out only certain restricted activities that arise out of, or are complementary to, the provision of professional services, such as arranging the sale of shares on the instructions of executors or trustees, or providing services to small, private companies. These firms are, however, supervised by designated professional bodies (DPBs). There are a number of safeguards to protect consumers dealing with firms that do not require direct regulation. These arrangements include:

• the FCA's power to ban a specific firm from taking advantage of the exemption and to restrict the regulated activities permitted to the firms
• rules which require professional firms to ensure that their clients are aware that they are not authorised persons

• a requirement for the DPBs to supervise and regulate the firms and inform the FCA on how the professional firms carry on their regulated activities

See Professional Education section for contact details of the following DPBs:

Association of Chartered Certified Accountants
Council for Licensed Conveyancers
Institute of Actuaries
Institute of Chartered Accountants in England and Wales
Institute of Chartered Accountants in Ireland
Institute of Chartered Accountants of Scotland
Law Society of England and Wales
Law Society of Northern Ireland
Law Society of Scotland
Royal Institution of Chartered Surveyors

RECOGNISED INVESTMENT EXCHANGES

The FCA currently supervises eight recognised investment exchanges (RIEs) in the UK; recognition confers an exemption from the need to be authorised to carry out regulated activities in the UK. The RIEs are organised markets on which member firms can trade investments such as equities and derivatives. The RIEs are listed with their year of recognition in parentheses:

BATS TRADING (2013), 6th Floor 10 Lower Street, London EC3R 6AF **T** 020-7012 8900 **W** www.batstrading.co.uk
CME EUROPE LTD (2014), 1 New Change, London EC4M 9AF **T** 020-3379 3700 **W** www.cmegroup.com/europe
EURONEXT LONDON LTD (2014), Juxon House, 100 St. Paul's Churchyard, London EC4M 8BU **T** 020-7280 6850 **W** www.euronext.com
ICAP SECURITIES & DERIVATIVES EXCHANGE LTD (2007), 2 Broadgate, London EC2M 7UR **T** 020-7050 7650 **W** www.isdx.com
ICE FUTURES EUROPE (2015), 5th Floor Milton Gate, 60 Chiswell Street, London EC1Y 4SA **T** 020-7065 7700 **W** www.theice.com
LIFFE ADMINISTRATION AND MANAGEMENT (2001), Milton Gate, 60 Chiswell Street, London EC1Y 4SA **T** 020-7065 7700 **W** www.intercontinentalexchange.com
LONDON METAL EXCHANGE (2001), 56 Leadenhall Street, London EC3A 2BJ **T** 020-7264 5555 **W** www.lme.co.uk
LONDON STOCK EXCHANGE (2001), 10 Paternoster Square, London EC4M 7LS **T** 020-7797 1000 **W** www.londonstockexchange.com

RECOGNISED CLEARING HOUSES

The Bank of England is responsible for recognising and supervising recognised clearing houses (RCHs), which organise the settlement of transactions on recognised investment exchanges. There are currently five RCHs in the UK:

CME CLEARING EUROPE (2010), 1 New Change, London EC4M 9AF **T** 020-3379 3700 **W** www.cmeclearingeurope.co.uk
EUROCLEAR UK AND IRELAND (2001), 33 Cannon Street, London EC4M 5SB **T** 020-7849 0000 **W** www.euroclear.com/en.html
ICE CLEAR EUROPE (2008), 5th Floor, Milton Gate, 60 Chiswell Street, London EC1Y 4SA **T** 020-7065 7600 **W** www.theice.com/clear_europe

LCH (LONDON CLEARING HOUSE) CLEARNET (2001), Aldgate House, 33 Aldgate High Street, London EC3N 1EA **T** 020-7426 7000 **W** www.lchclearnet.com
LME (LONDON METAL EXCHANGE) CLEAR (2014), 56 Leadenhall Street, London EC3A 2BJ **T** 020-7264 5555 **W** www.lme.co.uk

OMBUDSMAN SCHEMES

The Financial Ombudsman Service was set up by the Financial Services and Markets Act 2000 to provide consumers with a free, independent service for resolving disputes with authorised financial firms. The Financial Ombudsman Service can consider complaints about most financial matters including: banking; credit cards and store cards; financial advice; hire purchase and pawnbroking; insurance; loans and credit; money transfer; mortgages; payday lending and debt collecting; payment protection insurance; pensions; savings and investments; stocks, shares, unit trusts and bonds.

Complainants must first complain to the firm involved. They do not have to accept the ombudsman's decision and are free to go to court if they wish, but if a decision is accepted, it is binding for both the complainant and the firm.

The Pensions Ombudsman can investigate and decide complaints and disputes regarding the way occupational and personal pension schemes are administered and managed. The Pensions Ombudsman is also the Ombudsman for the Pension Protection Fund (PPF) and the Financial Assistance Scheme (which offers help to those who were a member of an under-funded defined benefit pension scheme that started to wind-up in specific financial circumstances between 1 January 1997 and 5 April 2005).

FINANCIAL OMBUDSMAN SERVICE, Exchange Tower, London E14 9SR **Helpline** 0800-023 4567 **T** 020-7964 1000 **E** complaint.info@financial-ombudsman.org.uk **W** www.financial-ombudsman.org.uk
Chief Executive and Chief Ombudsman, Caroline Wayman
PENSIONS OMBUDSMAN, 11 Belgrave Road, London SW1V 1RB **T** 020-7630 2200 **E** enquiries@pensions-ombudsman.org.uk **W** www.pensions-ombudsman.org.uk
Pensions Ombudsman, Tony King
Deputy Pensions Ombudsman, Jane Irvine

PANEL ON TAKEOVERS AND MERGERS

The Panel on Takeovers and Mergers is an independent body, established in 1968, whose main functions are to issue and administer the City code and to ensure equality of treatment and opportunity for all shareholders in takeover bids and mergers. The panel's statutory functions are set out in the Companies Act 2006.

The panel comprises up to 35 members drawn from major financial and business institutions. The chair, deputy chair and up to 20 other members are nominated by the panel's own nomination committee. The remaining members are nominated by professional bodies representing the banking, insurance, investment, pension and accountancy industries, the Association for Financial Markets in Europe and the CBI.

PANEL ON TAKEOVERS AND MERGERS, 10 Paternoster Square, London EC4M 7DY **T** 020-7382 9026 **E** info@thetakeoverpanel.org.uk **W** www.thetakeoverpanel.org.uk
Chair, Sir Gordon Langley

NATIONAL SAVINGS AND INVESTMENTS

NS&I (National Savings and Investments) is an executive agency of HM Treasury and one of the UK's largest financial providers, with over 25 million customers and over £100bn invested. NS&I offers savings and investment products to personal savers and investors and the money is used to manage the national debt. When people invest in NS&I they are lending money to the government which pays them interest or prizes in return. All products are financially secure because they are guaranteed by HM Treasury.

TAX-FREE PRODUCTS

SAVINGS CERTIFICATES

Index-linked Saving Certificates
Otherwise known as inflation-beating savings, index-linked saving certificates are fixed rate investments that pay tax-free returns guaranteed to be above inflation. They are sold in limited issues with a minimum and maximum investment.

Fixed Interest Saving Certificates
Fixed interest saving certificates are fixed rate investments that pay tax-free returns. They are sold in limited issues with a minimum and maximum investment.

PREMIUM BONDS
Introduced in 1956, premium bonds enable savers to enter a regular draw for tax-free prizes, while retaining the right to get their money back. A sum equivalent to interest on each bond is put into a prize fund and distributed by monthly prize draws. The prizes are drawn by ERNIE (electronic random number indicator equipment) and are free of all UK income tax and capital gains tax. Two £1m jackpots are drawn each month in addition to other tax-free prizes ranging in value from £25 to £100,000.

Bonds are in units of £1, with a minimum purchase of £100 (£50 if the purchase is by standing order), up to a maximum holding limit of £40,000 per person. Bonds become eligible for prizes once they have been held for one clear calendar month following the month of purchase. Each £1 unit can win only one prize per draw, but it will be awarded the highest for which it is drawn. Bonds remain eligible for prizes until they are repaid.

The scheme offers a facility to reinvest prize wins automatically. Upon completion of an automatic prize reinvestment mandate, holders receive new bonds which are immediately eligible for future prize draws. Bonds can only be held in the name of an individual and not by organisations.

CHILDREN'S BONDS
Children's bonus bonds were introduced in 1991. In September 2012 changes were made to the product; including a change in name to Children's Bonds, which reflects the way interest is paid. Any amount between £25 and £3,000 can be invested and interest is added at a fixed rate each year for five years. The minimum holding is £25 and the maximum holding is £3,000 per child per issue. They can be bought by parents, guardians and grandparents (including great grandparents) for any child under 16, but the investment must be managed by a parent or guardian. All returns are totally exempt from UK income tax.

INDIVIDUAL SAVINGS ACCOUNTS
Since April 1999 NS&I has offered cash individual savings accounts (ISAs). Its Direct ISA, launched in April 2006, can be opened and managed online and by telephone with a minimum investment of £1 and a maximum investment of £15,240 in the 2015–16 tax year. Interest for the Direct ISA is calculated daily and is free of tax.

OTHER PRODUCTS

GUARANTEED EQUITY BONDS
Guaranteed equity bonds are five-year investments where the returns are linked to the performance of the FTSE-100 index with a guarantee that the original capital invested will be returned even if the FTSE-100 index falls over the five years. They are sold in limited issues with a minimum investment of £1,000 and a maximum of £1m. The returns are subject to income tax on maturity, unless they are held in a self-invested pension plan (SIPP).

SAVINGS AND INVESTMENT ACCOUNTS
The direct saver account was launched in March 2010. Customers are able to invest between £1 and £2m per person. The account can be managed online or by telephone. Interest is paid without deduction of tax at source.

The investment account is a postal-only account which pays tiered rates of interest. It can be opened with a minimum balance of £20 and has a maximum limit of £1m. The interest is paid without deduction of tax at source.

INCOME BONDS
NS&I income bonds were introduced in 1982. They are suitable for those who want to receive regular pay-ments of interest while preserving the full cash value of their capital. The minimum holding for each investment is £500 and the maximum £1m per person. A variable rate of interest is calculated on a day-to-day basis and paid monthly. Interest is taxable but is paid without deduction of tax at source.

GUARANTEED INCOME BONDS
Guaranteed income bonds were introduced in February 2008 and changes were made to the product in September 2012. They are designed for those who want to receive regular monthly payments of interest while preserving the full cash value of their capital. There is a minimum and maximum holding per person, per issue. Joint investors can combine their allowance to invest up to double the maximum individual holding per issue. A fixed rate of interest is calculated on a day-to-day basis and paid monthly. Interest is taxable and tax is deducted at source. They are sold in limited issues.

GUARANTEED GROWTH BONDS
Guaranteed growth bonds were introduced in February 2008 and changes were made to the product in September 2012. As for Guaranteed income bonds, there is a minimum and maximum holding per person, per issue and joint investors can combine their allowance to invest up to double the maximum individual holding per issue. A fixed rate of interest is calculated on a day-to-day basis and is paid annually on the anniversary of the date of investment. Interest is taxable and tax is deducted at source. They are sold in limited issues.

FURTHER INFORMATION
Further information regarding products and their current availability can be obtained online (W www.nsandi.com) and by telephone (T 0500-007007).

THE NATIONAL DEBT

HISTORY

The early 1700s saw the meteoric rise of the banking and financial markets in Great Britain, with the emerging stock market revolving around government funds. The ability to raise money by means of creating debt through the issue of bills and bonds heralded the beginning of the national debt.

The war years of 1914–18 saw an increase in the national debt from £650m at the start of the war to £7,500m by 1919. The Treasury developed new expertise in foreign exchange, currency, credit and price control in order to manage the post-war economy. The slump of the 1930s necessitated the restructuring of the UK economy following the Second World War (the national debt stood at £21bn by its end) and the emphasis was placed on economic planning and financial relations.

The relatively high period of inflation in the 1970s and 1980s led to the rise of the national debt in nominal terms from £36bn in 1972 to £197bn in 1987 and then to £419bn in March 1998. Although in nominal terms the national debt has risen sharply in recent years, as a percentage of GDP it has decreased dramatically since the end of the Second World War, when it stood at 250 per cent of GDP (for current figures, *see* table below).

THE UK DEBT MANAGEMENT OFFICE

The decision in 1997 to transfer monetary policy to the Bank of England, while the Treasury retained control of fiscal policy, led to the creation of the UK Debt Management Office (DMO) as an executive agency of HM Treasury in April 1998. Initially the DMO was responsible only for the management of government marketable debt and for issuing gilts. In April 2000 responsibility for exchequer cash management and for issuing Treasury bills (short-dated securities with maturities of less than one year) was transferred from the Bank of England to the DMO. The national debt also includes the (non-marketable) liabilities of National Savings and Investments and other public sector and foreign currency debt.

In 2002 the operations of the long-standing statutory functions of the Public Works Loan Board, which lends capital to local authorities, and the Commissioners for the Reduction of the National Debt, which manages the investment portfolios of certain public funds, were integrated within the DMO (*see also* Government Departments).

UK PUBLIC SECTOR NET DEBT

	£ billion	per cent of GDP
2013–14 (outturn)	1,402	79.1
2014–15 (forecast)	1,479	80.4
2015–16 (forecast)	1,533	80.2

Source: HM Treasury: *Budget 2015* (Crown copyright)

THE LONDON STOCK EXCHANGE

The London Stock Exchange Group (LSEG) serves the needs of companies by providing facilities for raising capital. It also operates marketplaces for members to trade financial instruments, including equities, bonds and derivatives, on behalf of investors and institutions such as pension funds and insurers.

LSEG's key subsidiary companies are the London Stock Exchange, Borsa Italiana, MTS (an electronic platform for the trading of European government and corporate bonds), Turquoise (a trading platform for European equities) and FTSE (a global index provider).

Headquartered in London, with significant operations in Italy, France, North America and Sri Lanka, the group employs around 2,800 people.

HISTORY

The London Stock Exchange is one of the world's oldest stock exchanges, dating back more than 300 years to its origins in the coffee houses of 17th-century London. It was formally established as a membership organisation in 1801.

MAJOR DEVELOPMENTS

'BIG BANG'
In 1986 a package of reforms which are now known as 'Big Bang' transformed the London Stock Exchange and the City of London, liberalising the way in which banks and stock-broking firms operated and facilitating greater foreign investment. The London Stock Exchange ceased granting voting rights to individual members and became a private company. The 'Big Bang' also saw the start of a move towards fully electronic trading and the closure of the trading floor.

INTRODUCTION OF SETS
In October 1997, the Exchange introduced SETS, its electronic order book. The system enhanced the efficiency and transparency of trading on the Exchange, allowing trades to be executed automatically and anonymously rather than negotiated by telephone.

DEMUTUALISATION AND LISTING
The London Stock Exchange demutualised in 2000 and listed on its own main market in 2001.

MERGER WITH BORSA ITALIANA
In October 2007 the London Stock Exchange merged with the Italian stock exchange, Borsa Italiana, creating London Stock Exchange Group (LSEG).

DIVERSIFICATION
Since 2009 LSEG has diversified its business beyond the listing and trading of UK and Italian equities:

- In 2009 LSEG purchased Sri Lankan technology company MillenniumIT which provides technology to stock exchanges, brokerages and regulators around the world. It also supplies the trading technology to LSEG's own markets
- In 2010 LSEG acquired a majority stake in Turquoise, a platform facilitating the trading of stocks listed in 18 European countries and the USA
- In 2011 LSEG became the owner of FTSE, the international business which creates and manages over 200,000 financial indices
- In 2013 LSEG purchased a majority stake in LCH (London Clearing House) Clearnet (see also Financial Services Regulation, Recognised Clearing Houses)

UK EQUITY MARKETS

LSEG offers a range of listing options for companies, according to their size, history and requirements:

- The Main Market has the highest standards of regulation and disclosure obligations and is overseen by the UK Listing Authority (UKLA), a division of the Financial Conduct Authority (FCA). A Main Market listing enables established companies to raise capital, widen their investor base and have their shares traded alongside global peers. They are also eligible for inclusion in key indices, such as the FTSE 100 and the FTSE 250
- The Alternative Investment Market (AIM), established in June 1995, is specially designed to meet the needs of small and growing companies. It enables them to raise capital and broaden their investor base in a more flexible regulatory environment, while still being traded on an internationally recognised market. AIM companies retain an experienced Nominated Adviser (or 'Nomad') firm, which is responsible for ensuring the company's suitability for the market
- The Professional Securities Market (PSM), established in July 2005, allows companies to target professional investors only, on a market that offers greater flexibility in accounting standards
- The Specialist Fund Market (SFM), established in November 2007, is a market for highly specialised investment entities, such as hedge funds or private equity funds, that wish to target institutional investors only

As at April 2015 there were 5,191 companies listed on LSEG's primary markets, with a combined market value of £1,891,386m: 1,557 on the Main Market (1,218 on the UK main market and 339 on the international main market), 3,591 on the AIM, 15 on the PSM and 28 entities on the SFM.

LONDON STOCK EXCHANGE, 10 Paternoster Square, London EC4M 7LS T 020-7797 1000
W www.lseg.com
Chair, Chris Gibson-Smith, PHD
Chief Executive, Xavier Rolet

ECONOMIC STATISTICS

THE BUDGET (SUMMER 2015)

GOVERNMENT EXPENDITURE

DEPARTMENTAL EXPENDITURE LIMITS £ billion

	Plans 2015–16
Resource DEL	
Education	53.5
NHS (Health)	111.9
Transport	2.3
Business, Innovation and Skills	13.1
CLG Communities	2.5
CLG Local Government	10.6
Home Office	10.2
Justice	6.3
Law Officers' Departments	0.5
Defence	28.1
Foreign and Commonwealth Office	1.8
International Development	7.4
Energy and Climate Change	1.4
Environment, Food and Rural Affairs	1.6
Culture, Media and Sport	1.1
Work and Pensions	6.3
Scotland	25.5
Wales	12.9
Northern Ireland	9.6
Chancellor's departments	3.5
Cabinet Office	2.5
Small and Independent bodies	1.6
Reserve	2.0
Special reserve	0.2
Adjustment for budget exchange	(0.5)
TOTAL RESOURCE DEL	316.1
*OBR Allowance for shortfall	(1.0)
OBR Resource DEL	315.1
Capital DEL	
Education	4.7
NHS (Health)	4.6
Transport	6.1
Business, Innovation and Skills	3.8
CLG Communities	5.3
CLG Local Government	0.0
Home Office	0.4
Justice	0.3
Law Officers' Departments	0.0
Defence	6.8
Foreign and Commonwealth Office	0.1
International Development	2.6
Energy and Climate Change	2.5
Environment, Food and Rural Affairs	0.5
Culture, Media and Sport	0.4
Work and Pensions	0.2
Scotland	3.1
Wales	1.5
Northern Ireland	1.1
Chancellor's departments	0.3
Cabinet Office	0.4
Small and Independent bodies	0.1
Reserve	0.9
Special reserve	0.1
Adjustment for budget exchange	(1.6)
TOTAL CAPITAL DEL	44.4
*OBR Allowance for shortfall	(2.0)
OBR Capital DEL	42.4
TOTAL DEL	360.5

* OBR = Office for Budget Responsibility

Source: HM Treasury – *Summer Budget 2015* (Crown copyright)

TOTAL MANAGED EXPENDITURE £ billion

	Plans 2015–16	Plans 2016–17	Plans 2017–18
Current Expenditure			
Resource Annually Managed Expenditure (AME)	337.9	344.3	358.6
Resource DEL	315.1	–	–
Ring-fenced depreciation	22.3	–	–
Resource DEL, including depreciation	–	341.4	339.7
Capital Expenditure			
Capital AME	24.7	26.0	26.3
Capital DEL	42.4	42.6	43.3
TOTAL MANAGED EXPENDITURE	742.3	754.3	768.0
Total Managed Expenditure (% GDP)	39.6%	38.7%	37.8%

Source: HM Treasury – *Summer Budget 2015* (Crown copyright)

GOVERNMENT RECEIPTS £ billion

	Outturn 2014–15	Forecast 2015–16	Forecast 2016–17
Income tax (gross of tax credits)[1]	163.7	170.2	184.8
Pay as you earn	140.0	145.2	155.1
Self assessment	23.6	25.3	31.3
National insurance contributions (NICs)	110.3	114.8	125.8
Value added tax	111.3	115.9	119.2
Corporation tax	42.9	43.1	43.4
Petroleum revenue tax	0.1	0.0	(0.1)
Fuel duties	27.2	27.1	27.3
Business rates	27.3	28.0	29.0
Council tax	27.9	28.4	29.0
VAT refunds	13.7	13.6	13.8
Capital gains tax	5.6	6.4	7.4
Inheritance tax	3.8	4.2	4.6
Stamp duty land tax	10.9	11.5	12.6
Stamp taxes on shares	2.9	3.2	3.3
Tobacco duties	9.3	9.1	9.0
Spirits duties	3.0	3.2	3.2
Wine duties	3.8	4.0	4.1
Beer and cider duties	3.6	3.5	3.4
Air passenger duty	3.2	3.1	3.2
Insurance premium tax	3.0	3.5	4.5
Climate change levy	1.6	2.3	2.4
Other HMRC taxes[2]	6.6	6.9	6.9
Vehicle excise duties	5.9	5.6	5.5
Bank levy	2.8	3.7	3.1
Bank surcharge	0.0	0.0	0.9
Licence fee receipts	3.1	3.1	3.2
Enviromental levies	3.6	6.0	7.3
EU ETS* Auction recipts	0.4	0.3	0.3
Scottish taxes	0.0	0.6	0.7
Diverted profits tax	0.0	0.0	0.3
Other taxes	6.2	7.1	7.1
Total Taxes	603.6	628.9	665.2

Less own resources			
contribution to EU	(3.0)	(3.1)	(3.2)
Interest and dividends	5.8	5.8	6.6
Gross operating surplus	36.9	39.2	41.1
Other receipts	3.0	2.0	1.5
CURRENT RECEIPTS	646.4	672.8	711.2
UK oil and gas revenues[3]	2.2	0.7	0.5

* ETS = Emissions Trading System
[1] Income tax includes PAYE and Self Assessment receipts, and also includes tax on savings income and other minor income tax components
[2] Consists of landfill tax (excluding Scotland from 2015–16), aggregates levy, betting and gaming duties, and customs duties and levies
[3] Consists of offshore corporation tax and petroleum revenue tax
Source: HM Treasury – *Summer Budget 2015* (Crown copyright)

TRADE

TRADE IN GOODS £ million

	Exports	Imports	Balance
2008	251,565	345,826	(94,261)
2009	227,727	310,660	(82,933)
2010	265,243	363,828	(98,585)
2011	298,421	398,513	(100,092)
2012	300,457	409,157	(108,700)
2013	304,756	412,646	(107,890)
2014	292,867	412,472	(119,605)

Source: ONS (Crown copyright)

BALANCE OF PAYMENTS, 2014

Current Account	£ million
Trade in goods and services	
Trade in goods	(119,605)
Trade in services	85,863
Total trade in goods and services	(33,742)
Income	
Compensation of employees	(440)
Investment income	(37,747)
Other	(567)
Total income	(38,754)
Total secondary income	(25,424)
TOTAL (CURRENT BALANCE)	(97,920)

Source: ONS (Crown copyright)

UK EMPLOYMENT

DISTRIBUTION OF THE WORKFORCE

	Mar 2014	Mar 2015
Workforce jobs	33,051,000	33,673,000
HM forces	167,000	161,000
Self-employment jobs	4,529,000	4,370,000
Employees jobs	28,334,000	29,124,000
Government-supported trainees	21,000	19,000

Source: ONS – *Labour Market Statistics 2015* (Crown copyright)

EMPLOYED AND UNEMPLOYED BY GENDER
thousands

	Apr–Jun 2014		Apr–Jun 2015	
	Male	*Female*	*Male*	*Female*
EMPLOYED				
All aged 16+	16,326	14,355	16,499	14,535
UNEMPLOYED				
All aged 16+	2,074	930	1,852	838

Source: ONS – *Labour Market Statistics 2015* (Crown copyright)

UK GDP GROWTH
volume % change on previous quarter

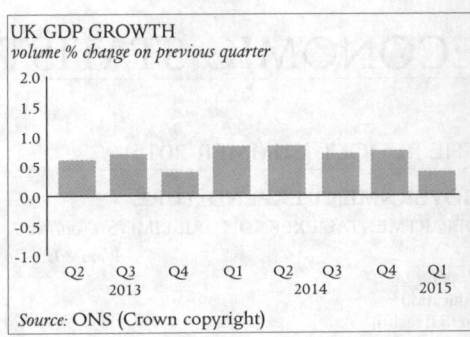

Source: ONS (Crown copyright)

DURATION OF UNEMPLOYMENT, APR–JUN 2015

All unemployed	1,852,000
Less than 6 months	971,000
6 months–1 year	305,000
1 year +	575,000 (31.1% of total)

Source: ONS – *Labour Market Statistics 2015* (Crown copyright)

MEDIAN EARNINGS, 2014

	All	Male	Female
Median gross annual earnings* *(£, thousands)*	27.2	29.4	23.9
Median gross weekly earnings *(£)*	518.0	557.08	461.90
Median hourly earnings, excluding overtime *(£)*	13.08	13.59	12.31

* Full-time
Source: ONS (Crown copyright)

LABOUR STOPPAGES BY DURATION, 2014

Under 5 days	92
5–10 days	6
11–20 days	0
21–30 days	0
31–50	0
50+	0
All stoppages	98

Source: ONS (Crown copyright)

LABOUR DISPUTES BY INDUSTRY, 2014

Industry Group	Working Days Lost
Manufacturing	7,600
Sewage, waste and water supply	400
Construction	2,800
Transport, storage and communication	24,900
Financial, insurance and administration	6,500
Public administration and defence	390,300
Education	312,800
Human health and social work	36,300
Arts entertainment	800

Source: ONS (Crown copyright)

TRADE UNIONS

Year	No. of unions	Total membership
2011–12	172	7,261,210
2012–13	166	7,197,415
2013–14	166	7,086,116
2014–15	160	7,010,527

Source: Annual Report of the Certification Officer 2014–15

COST OF LIVING AND INFLATION RATES

The first cost of living index to be calculated took July 1914 as 100 and was based on the pattern of expenditure of working-class families in 1914. The cost of living index was superseded in 1947 by the general index of retail prices (RPI), although the older term is still popularly applied.

The Harmonised Index of Consumer Prices (HICP) was introduced in 1997 to enable comparisons within the European Union using an agreed methodology. In 2003 the National Statistician renamed the HICP the Consumer Prices Index (CPI) to reflect its role as the main target measure of inflation for macroeconomic purposes. In March 2013 CPIH, an additional index which includes owner-occupiers' housing costs, was introduced.

The RPI and indices based on it continue to be published alongside the CPI. Private-sector pensions and index-linked gilts continue to be calculated with reference to RPI or its derivatives.

CPI AND RPI

The CPI and RPI measure the changes month by month in the average level of prices of goods and services purchased by households in the UK. The indices are compiled using a selection of around 700 goods and services, and the prices charged for these items are collected at regular intervals at about 140 locations throughout the country. The Office for National Statistics (ONS) reviews the components of the indices once a year to reflect changes in consumer preferences and the establishment of new products. The table below shows changes made by the ONS to the CPI 'shopping basket' in 2015.

The CPI excludes a number of items that are included in the RPI, mainly related to housing, such as council tax, and a range of owner-occupier housing costs, such as mortgage

payments. The CPI covers all private households, whereas the RPI excludes the top 4 per cent by income and pensioner households which derive at least three-quarters of their income from state benefits. The two indices use different methodologies to combine the prices of goods and services, which means that since 1996 the CPI inflation measure is less than the RPI inflation measure.

INFLATION RATE

The 12-monthly percentage change in the 'all items' index of the RPI or CPI is referred to as the rate of inflation. As the most familiar measure of inflation, the RPI is often referred to as the 'headline rate of inflation'. The CPI is the main measure of inflation for macroeconomic purposes and forms the basis of the government's inflation target, which is currently 2 per cent. The percentage change in prices between any two months/years can be obtained using this formula:

$$\frac{\text{Later date RPI/CPI} - \text{Earlier date RPI/CPI}}{\text{Earlier date RPI/CPI}} \times 100$$

For example, to find the CPI rate of inflation for 2006, using the annual averages for 2005 and 2006:

$$\frac{102.3 - 100.0}{100.0} \times 100 = 2.3$$

From 14 February 2006 the reference year for the CPI was re-based to 2005=100 to improve price comparison clarity across the EU. None of the underlying data, from which the re-referenced series was calculated, was revised. Historical

CHANGES TO THE 'SHOPPING BASKET' OF GOODS AND SERVICES IN 2015

The table below shows changes to the CPI* basket of goods and services made by the ONS in 2015 in order to reflect changes in consumer preferences and the establishment of new products.

Goods and services group	Removed items	New items
Alcoholic beverage	–	bottled speciality beer/ale
Audio-visual equipment	–	headphones
Cultural services	–	games consoles online subscription services; music streaming subscription services
Financial services	foreign exchange commission	
Food	frozen pizza; home killed beef (braising steak); oven-ready joint; yoghurt drink	chilled pizza; liver; melon; oven-ready gammon or pork joint; protein powder; sweet potato
Gardens & pets	cut flowers (lilies)	–
Maintenance of dwelling	white emulsion paint	non-white emulsion paint
Operation of personal transport equipment	satellite navigation device	
Telephone equipment	–	mobile phone accessory
Tobacco	–	electronic cigarette refills/liquid

* RPI goods and services are grouped together under different classifications

rates of change (such as annual inflation figures), calculated from the re-based rounded index levels, were revised due to the effect of rounding. The CPI rate of inflation figure given in the table below may differ by plus or minus 0.1 percentage points from the figure calculated by the above equation. The change of reference period and revision due to rounding does not apply to the RPI, which remains unchanged.

The RPI and CPI figures are published on either the second or third Tuesday of each month in an indices bulletin on the ONS website (W www.ons.gov.uk).

PURCHASING POWER OF THE POUND

Changes in the internal purchasing power of the pound may be defined as the 'inverse' of changes in the level of prices:

when prices go up, the amount which can be purchased with a given sum of money goes down. To find the purchasing power of the pound in one month or year, given that it was 100p in a previous month or year, the calculation would be:

$$100p \times \frac{\text{Earlier month/year RPI}}{\text{Later month/year RPI}}$$

Thus, if the purchasing power of the pound is taken to be 100p in 1975, the comparable purchasing power in 2000 would be:

$$100p \times \frac{34.2}{170.3} = 20.1p$$

For longer term comparisons, it has been the practice to use an index which has been constructed by linking together the RPI for the period 1962 to date; an index derived from the consumers' expenditure deflator for the period 1938 to 1962; and the pre-war 'cost of living' index for the period 1914 to 1938. This long-term index enables the internal purchasing power of the pound to be calculated for any year from 1914 onwards. It should be noted that these figures can only be approximate.

	Annual average RPI (1987 = 100)	Purchasing power of £ (1998 = 1.00)	Annual average CPI (2005 = 100)*	Annual average CPIH (2005=100)	Rate of inflation (RPI/CPI/CPIH)
1914	2.8	58.18			
1915	3.5	46.54			
1920	7.0	23.27			
1925	5.0	32.58			
1930	4.5	36.20			
1935	4.0	40.72			
1938	4.4	37.02			
There are no official figures for 1939–45					
1946	7.4	22.01			
1950	9.0	18.10			
1955	11.2	14.54			
1960	12.6	12.93			
1965	14.8	11.00			
1970	18.5	8.80			
1975	34.2	4.76			
1980	66.8	2.44	18.0		
1985	94.6	1.72	6.1		
1990	126.1	1.29	71.5		9.5/7.0
1995	149.1	1.09	86.0		3.5/2.6
1998	162.9	1.00	91.1		3.4/1.6
2000	170.3	0.96	93.1		3.0/0.8
2005	192.0	0.85	100.0	100.0	2.8/2.1
2006	198.1	0.82	102.3	102.3	3.2/2.3/2.3
2007	206.6	0.79	104.7	104.6	4.3/2.3/2.2
2008	214.8	0.76	108.5	108.1	4.0/3.6/3.4
2009	213.7	0.76	110.8	110.3	−0.5/2.2/2.0
2010	223.6	0.73	114.5	113.4	4.6/3.3/2.9
2011	235.2	0.69	119.6	118.0	5.2/4.5/4.1
2012	242.7	0.67	123.0	121.2	3.2/2.8/2.7
2013	250.1	0.65	126.1	124.1	3.0/2.6/2.4
2014	256.0	0.64	128.0	125.8	2.4/1.5/1.4

* In accordance with an EU Commission regulation, all published CPI figures were re-based to 2005=100 with effect from 14 February 2006, replacing the 1996=100 series

INSURANCE

AUTHORISATION AND REGULATION OF INSURANCE COMPANIES

Since April 2013, under the Financial Services Act 2012, the prudential supervision of banks and insurers is the responsibility of the Prudential Regulation Authority (PRA), an operationally independent subsidiary of the Bank of England. The Financial Conduct Authority (FCA) is responsible for consumer protection and markets oversight. All life insurers, general insurers, reinsurers, insurance and reinsurance brokers, financial advisers and composite firms are statutorily regulated. See also Financial Services Regulation.

Firms wishing to effect or carry out contracts of insurance must apply for authorisation to do so. The PRA assesses applicant insurers from a prudential perspective, using the same framework that is employed for supervision of existing insurers. The FCA then assesses applicants from a conduct perspective. Although the PRA manages the authorisation process, an insurer will be granted authorisation only where both the FCA and the PRA are satisfied that an insurer meets the relevant requirements.

As at July 2014 there were over 1,300 insurance organisations and friendly societies with authorisation to transact one or more classes of insurance business in the UK. However, the single European insurance market, established in 1994, gave insurers authorised in any other European Union country automatic UK authorisation without further formality. The number of insurers operating within the single European market has been decreasing since 2010 and currently stands at around 5,300.

COMPLAINTS

Disputes between consumers and financial businesses can be referred to the Financial Ombudsman Service (FOS). Consumers with a complaint about any form of money matter, including insurance, mortgages, savings and credit, must firstly take the matter to the highest level within the provider. If it remains unresolved and it involves an amount below £150,000 (£100,000 for complaints received before 1 January 2012), it can be referred, free of charge, to the FOS, which examines the facts of a complaint and delivers a decision binding on the provider (but not the consumer). Small businesses with a turnover of up to €2m (£1.7m) and fewer than ten employees also have access to the scheme. In 2013, 74 per cent of new complaints about financial serivces companies related to payment protection insurance. Other types of insurance, such as motor, buildings and life insurance, accounted for just 7 per cent of the complaints received. See also Financial Services Regulation.

ASSOCIATION OF BRITISH INSURERS

Over 90 per cent of the domestic business of UK insurance companies is transacted by the 250 members of the Association of British Insurers (ABI). The ABI is a trade association which protects and promotes the interests of all its insurance company members. Only insurers authorised in the EU are eligible for membership. Brokers, intermediaries, financial advisers and claims handlers may not join the ABI but may have their own trade associations.

ASSOCIATION OF BRITISH INSURERS (ABI),
51 Gresham Street, London EC2V 7HQ T 020-7600 3333
W www.abi.org.uk
Chair, Paul Evans
Director-General, Huw Evans

BALANCE OF PAYMENTS

The financial services industry contributes 8 per cent to the UK's gross domestic product (GDP). In 2013 insurance sector net exports totalled £10.2bn.

WORLDWIDE MARKET

The UK insurance industry is the largest in Europe and currently the third largest in the world behind the USA and Japan. China has the fastest growing insurance market and is expected to overtake the UK in the next few years.

Market	Premium income ($bn)	Percentage of total
USA	1,787	34.6
Japan	532	10.3
UK	330	6.4

TAKEOVERS AND MERGERS

As predicted, 2014 saw an increase in mergers and acquisitions as excess capital and pressure to sell non-core assets drove an upsurge in activity.

In January 2014 Co-operative Insurance ended speculation that it would sell its general business arm by confirming that it was no longer for sale.

In April new RSA (Royal Insurance and Sun Alliance) chief executive Stephen Hester began a series of disposals designed to focus RSA's operations on UK, Ireland, Scandinavia and Latin America. It began with the sale of RSA's Baltic and Polish operations and was followed by sales of businesses in Canada, China, Hong Kong, India, Italy and Singapore. By the end of the year sales had topped £500m.

Standard Life also disposed of an overseas operation when it sold its Canadian unit to Canada's largest life insurer, Manulife Financial for £2.2bn in cash.

December 2014 saw the largest deal involving UK companies in six years when AVIVA took over Friends Life in a £5.6bn deal. The combined group will have around 16 million UK customers and assets of over £330bn.

INDUSTRY ISSUES

Since 2002 the European Commission (EC) has been formulating plans for Solvency II, which aims to establish an EU-wide set of requirements for capital adequacy and management standards, modernising and consolidating a large number of EU directives known as Solvency I which was established in the 1970s. Solvency II will codify 14 EU insurance directives. Agreement was finally reached in November 2014 and the agreed implementation date of 1 January 2016 looks very likely. However there are a number of objections and concerns to be ironed out, particularly the effect on American subsidiaries of UK companies, who may find themselves at a disadvantage with local competitors because of the 'equivalency' requirements.

GENERAL INSURANCE

The period of extreme weather and serious flooding between 23 December 2013 and 28 February 2014 brought the subject of flooding, flood protection and the continuance of cover for homes in high flood risk areas back to the top of the agenda. This period saw nearly 19,000 flood claims totalling £451m and over 448,000 storm damage claims costing nearly £650m.

Even before these events, agreement had been reached between the UK government and insurers for a not-for-profit flood reinsurance fund ('Flood Re') owned and managed by the insurance industry to ensure domestic properties in high risk areas continued to receive affordable cover for flooding. During 2014 the industry and government continued work on the finer details, and the Water Act 2014 received royal assent on 24 May 2014.

In August 2014, insurers voiced serious concerns about the government's proposals to reform the Riot (Damages) Act 1886. At present, under the act, compensation is paid by the police to homeowners and businesses who suffer riot damage to their property or possessions if they have no insurance or are under insured. There is no limit on the amount of compensation payable. Insurers are also able to claim under the act for any payments made to customers – this has meant that they have not needed to charge policyholders for riot cover. Under the new proposals businesses with a turnover over £2m and most car owners would be excluded from claiming which would mean premium increases for those people who buy insurance and no compensation at all for the uninsured.

The fight against general insurance fraud continued with several motor insurance initiatives. In December 2014 a new service called My Licence was launched by the Motor Insurers' Bureau and the Driver and Vehicle Licensing Agency. The initiative was developed in partnership with the Association of British Insurers and the Department for Transport. The scheme allows motor insurers to ask applicants for their driving licence number, which will then allow them to access the DVLA's driver database to acquire a complete and accurate record of the applicants' entitlements, endorsements and any convictions. This will eliminate withholding of information on motoring convictions. A survey during the year highlighted that over 3,500 motor insurance applications a week contain incorrect details on endorsements and convictions. Motor insurance was the biggest area for fraud in 2013, with nearly 60,000 fraudulent claims discovered, an increase of 34 per cent on 2012.

Another area of concern for motor insurers was the increase in claims for 'whiplash' (soft tissue injury). An estimated £2bn a year is paid in claims of this nature; it is very difficult to verify the extent of a claimant's injury which makes these claims open to exploitation by fraudsters. To combat this, the Ministry of Justice have established a new body, MedCo, which runs an IT system that provides an independently and randomly selected choice of appropriately accredited medical experts or medical reporting organisations from which a solicitor can choose who to instruct to examine a claim. The MedCo system launched on 6 April 2015 ending the practice of lawyers and claimants using their own experts and ensuring that it is no longer possible for claimant lawyers to source reports from an individual or organisation with which they have a financial link. It is hoped that the system will deter those aiming to cheat the system.

Overall, insurance frauds totalling £1.3bn were detected in 2014, an increase of 18 per cent.

Despite the rise in fraud, the cost of motor insurance decreased in 2014 by around 4 per cent. An average motorist is now paying £372 a year for motor cover. Home buildings and contents policies also saw decreases with an average buildings policy reduced by 6 per cent to £230 a year and an average home contents policy decreasing by 5 per cent to £124 a year.

With the notable exception of weather related and business interruption claims, most other classes of business saw claims payments decrease in 2014. Fire and theft claims reduced by 9 per cent and 4.2 per cent respectively and subsidence claims decreased by around 2 per cent.

LONDON INSURANCE MARKET

The London Insurance Market is a unique wholesale marketplace and a distinct, separate sector of the UK insurance and reinsurance industry. It is the world's leading market for internationally traded insurance and reinsurance, its business comprising mainly overseas non-life large and high-exposure risks. It is the only place in the world where all 20 of the world's largest insurance companies have an office. The market is centred on the square mile of the City of London, which provides the required financial, banking, legal and other support services. Around 58 per cent of London market business is transacted at Lloyd's of London, the remainder through insurance companies and protection and indemnity clubs. In 2013 the market had a written gross premium income of around £60bn. Around 200 Lloyd's brokers service the market.

The trade association for the international insurers and reinsurers writing primarily non-marine insurance and all classes of reinsurance business in the London market is the International Underwriting Association (IUA).

INTERNATIONAL UNDERWRITING ASSOCIATION,
London Underwriting Centre, 3 Minster Court, Mincing Lane, London EC3R 7DD **T** 020-7617 4444 **W** www.iua.co.uk
Chair, Malcolm Newman
Chief Executive, Dave Matcham

BRITISH INSURANCE COMPANIES

The following insurance company figures refer to members and certain non-members of the ABI.

CLAIMS STATISTICS *(£m)*

	2010	2011	2012	2013	2014
Theft	529	603	554	472	452
Fire	1,072	1,156	995	1,051	952
Weather	707	618	1,087	703	1,029
Domestic subsidence	171	158	114	101	99
Business interruption	180	161	161	100	127
Total	2,659	2,696	2,911	2,427	2,659

WORLDWIDE GENERAL BUSINESS TRADING RESULTS *(£m)*

	2012	2013
Net written premiums	46,825	50,154
Underwriting results	778	1,444
Investment income	2,822	1,219
Overall trading profit	3,600	2,663
Profit as percentage of premium income	7.7	5.3

WORLDWIDE GENERAL BUSINESS UNDERWRITING RESULTS *(£m)*

	2012			2013		
	UK	Overseas	Total	UK	Overseas	Total
Motor						
Premiums	11,569	4,837	16,406	10,960	5,260	16,220
Profit (loss)	(301)	204	(97)	(53)	194	141
Percentage of premiums	(2.6)	4.2	(0.6)	(0.5)	3.7	0.9
Non-motor						
Premiums	19,507	7,947	27,454	19,845	10,976	30,821
Profit (loss)	159	468	627	866	196	1,062
Percentage of premiums	0.8	5.9	2.3	4.4	1.8	3.4

NET PREMIUM INCOME BY SECTOR *(£m)*

	2012		2013	
	UK	Overseas	UK	Overseas
Motor	11,556	4,837	10,960	5,260
Non-motor	19,504	7,947	19,845	10,976
Marine, aviation and transport	1,187	495	1,130	762
Reinsurance	848	355	830	387
Total general business	33,095	13,634	32,765	17,385
Ordinary long-term	121,056	38,122	119,678	43,423
TOTAL	154,151	51,756	152,443	60,808

LLOYD'S OF LONDON

Lloyd's of London is an international market for almost all types of general insurance. Lloyd's currently has the capacity to accept insurance premiums of around £26bn. Much of this business comes from outside the UK and makes a valuable contribution to the balance of payments.

A policy is underwritten at Lloyd's by a mixture of private and corporate members. Specialist underwriters accept insurance risks at Lloyd's on behalf of members (referred to as 'Names') grouped in syndicates. There are currently 94 syndicates of varying sizes, each managed by one of the 59 underwriting agents approved by the Council of Lloyd's.

Members divide into three categories: corporate organisations, individuals who have no limit to their liability for losses, and those who have an agreed limit (known as NameCos).

Lloyd's is incorporated by an act of parliament (Lloyd's Acts 1871 onwards) and is governed by an 18-person council, made up of six working, six external and six nominated members. The structure immediately below this changed when, in 2002, Lloyd's members voted at an extraordinary general meeting to implement a new franchise system for the market with the aim of improving profitability. The first move was the introduction of a new governance structure, replacing the Lloyd's Market Board and the Lloyd's Regulatory Board with an 11-person Lloyd's Franchise Board. Four main committees report to this board.

The corporation is a non-profit making body chiefly financed by its members' subscriptions. It provides the premises, administrative staff and services for Lloyd's underwriting syndicates. It does not, however, assume corporate liability for the risks accepted by its members. Individual members are responsible to the full extent of their personal means for their underwriting affairs unless they have converted to limited liability companies.

Lloyd's syndicates have no direct contact with the public. All business is transacted through insurance brokers accredited by the Corporation of Lloyd's. In addition, non-Lloyd's brokers in the UK, when guaranteed by Lloyd's brokers, are able to deal directly with Lloyd's motor syndicates, a facility that has made the Lloyd's market more accessible to the insuring public.

Under the Financial Services and Markets Act 2000, Lloyds is regulated by the FCA and the PRA. However, in situations where Lloyd's internal regulatory and compensation arrangements are more far-reaching – as for example with the Lloyd's Central Fund which safeguards claim payments to policyholders – the regulatory role is delegated to the Council of Lloyd's.

DEVELOPMENTS IN 2014

Despite predictions of a softening market and the possible impact of low interest rates, Lloyd's recorded another outstanding year with profits of £3.2bn, matching the figure for 2013. The combined ratio – the sum of losses incurred plus operating expenses expressed as a percentage of earned premium – was 88.1 per cent and the return on capital was 14.7 per cent. Gross written premiums decreased very slightly over 2013 to £25.28bn.

A major factor in the results for the past two years has been the absence of serious catastrophes, particularly no major hurricane damage. This situation cannot continue indefinitely and with premium levels under pressure and low investment returns the possibility of price rises remain. However, there is also intense competition, which may reduce their effect.

Only the motor and aviation accounts recorded losses during the year although the aviation figure was small (£8m) and the motor loss was reduced to £69m from £87m in 2013.

LLOYD'S OF LONDON, One Lime Street, London EC3M 7HA

T 020-7327 1000 W www.lloyds.com

Chair, John Nelson

Chief Executive, Inga Beale

LLOYD'S MEMBERSHIP

	2013	2014
Individual	529	447
Corporate	1,623	1,686

LLOYD'S SEGMENTAL RESULTS 2014 *(£m)*

	Gross premiums written	Net earned premium	Result
Reinsurance	8,497	6,680	1,250
Casualty	4,963	3,939	81
Property	6,281	4,572	577
Marine	2,142	1,759	85
Motor	1,213	1,082	(69)
Energy	1,533	1,093	189
Aviation	582	377	(8)
Life	72	73	5
Total from syndicate operations	25,283	19,575	2,110

LIFE AND LONG-TERM INSURANCE AND PENSIONS

At the end of 2013 life and pensions providers may have expected that the year ahead would bring a period of relative calm and consolidation entering into the second year of auto-enrolment into workplace pensions and the second year of the new 'twin peaks' regulatory system, despite the inevitable review of fees charged and further internal preparations for the start of Solvency II (see Industry Issues). The period before a General Election often sees a reduction in the number of new government initiatives but the spring of 2014 proved to be far from quiet.

In March, the UK life insurance industry was rocked by three regulatory announcements that temporarily knocked billions off the market value of insurers. These developments may have long-term consequences for the industry and for some types of business.

Firstly, the UK government announced a cap on the charges that companies can impose on workplace pensions (auto-enrolment). The proposed cap was lower than many companies were already charging, and it was thought that some companies would struggle to operate profitably with charges at the proposed level. Secondly, the media reportage of an FCA review into legacy products or 'zombie funds'. These are products like personal pensions, endowments and whole life insurance policies, that are in funds that are now closed. The policies date from the 1970s to 2000 and the review will examine whether or not customers are getting a fair deal, particularly on exit fees.

Initially, the announcement caused serious concern in the markets, especially for the insurers who specialise in closed-book business. Following criticism from the ABI and the Chancellor of the Exchequer, the FCA clarified that the review was much less intrusive than had been reported and ordered an enquiry into the way the announcement had been handled. The markets subsequently recovered.

The most far-reaching of the three developments came in the Budget when the chancellor announced that anyone aged 55 or over, who held a pension based on how much had been paid in, a defined contribution (DC) scheme, would no longer be forced to buy an annuity with their pension pot. Instead savers would be free to take the proceeds and invest or spend them as they see fit. This change represented one of the biggest adjustments to the UK pension regime for almost a century and posed a significant challenge to major players in the annuity field.

As the year went on concerns emerged about whether consumers would use the government's free advice service or take adequate advice elsewhere, before making a decision on what to do with their pension pot. There is also a potential problem with fraudsters offering dubious investment vehicles or advice. The new rules came into effect on 6 April 2015 and the industry faces challenges in making annuities an attractive option and developing new products for the released funds.

PAYMENTS TO POLICYHOLDERS (£m)

	2012	2013
Payments to UK policyholders	152,177	160,615
Payments to overseas policyholders	30,034	30,551
Total	182,211	191,166

WORLDWIDE LONG-TERM PREMIUM INCOME (£m)

	2009	2010	2011	2012	2013
UK Life Insurance					
Regular Premium	7,990	7,455	6,717	6,058	5,419
Single Premium	12,346	11,786	9,290	8,622	4,525
Total	20,336	19,241	16,007	14,680	9,944
Individual Pensions					
Regular Premium	9,629	10,651	11,155	12,554	11,199
Single Premium	18,095	17,567	16,123	16,392	12,936
Total	27,724	28,218	27,278	28,946	24,135
Occupational Pensions					
Regular Premium	5,599	4,340	3,809	3,270	4,744
Single Premium	63,388	59,693	67,995	67,566	75,827
Total	68,987	64,033	71,804	70,836	80,571
Other (eg income protection, long-term care)	1,473	1,482	1,456	1,764	1,457
TOTAL UK PREMIUM INCOME	118,520	112,974	116,545	116,226	116,107
Overseas Premium Income					
Regular Premium	11,240	11,971	11,654	11,881	12,782
Single Premium	29,212	29,885	26,873	28,857	31,425
Total	40,452	41,856	38,527	40,738	44,207
TOTAL WORLDWIDE PREMIUM INCOME	158,972	154,830	155,072	156,964	160,314

PRIVATE MEDICAL INSURANCE

	2009	2010	2011	2012	2013
Number of people covered (thousand)	5,938	5,841	5,668	5,611	5,143
Corporate	4,384	4,305	4,232	4,210	3,787
Personal	1,554	1,536	1,436	1,401	1,356
Gross Earned Premiums (£m)	3,444	3,614	3,548	3,625	3,597
Corporate	1,838	1,982	1,929	2,010	1,982
Personal	1,606	1,632	1,619	1,615	1,615
Gross Claims Incurred (£m)	2,679	2,858	2,727	2,770	2,674

TAXATION

The government raises money to pay for public services such as education, health and the social security system through tax. Each year the Chancellor of the Exchequer's budget sets out how much it will cost to provide these services and how much tax is therefore needed to pay for them. HM Revenue and Customs (HMRC) is the government department that collects it. There are several different types of tax. The varieties that individuals may have to pay include income tax payable on earnings, pensions, state benefits, savings and investments; capital gains tax (CGT) payable on the disposal of certain assets; inheritance tax (IHT) payable on estates upon death and certain lifetime gifts; stamp duty payable when purchasing property and shares; and value added tax (VAT) payable on goods and services, plus certain other duties such as fuel duty on petrol and excise duty on alcohol and tobacco. Government funds are also raised from companies and small businesses through corporation tax.

New taxation measures and changes to the administration of the taxation system are normally announced by the incumbent Chancellor of the Exchequer in either the government's autumn statement or its annual Budget which is delivered in the Spring.

The government has a stated policy of investing manpower and funding into reducing tax evasion and avoidance by both individuals and companies. Information and updates on the latest measures can be found on the government's website (W www.gov.uk/government/policies/reducing-tax-evasion-and-avoidance).

The government also has an ongoing drive to simplify the UK tax system via the Office of Tax Simplification (OTS). Details of the OTS and its work can also be found on the government's website (W www.gov.uk/government/organisations/office-of-tax-simplification). The OTS welcomes views from individuals and can be contacted via email (E ots@ots.gsi.gov.uk).

HELP AND INFORMATION ON TAXATION
For information and help on any aspect of personal taxation individuals may contact their local tax office or call the HMRC helpline (T 0300-200 3300).

HMRC closed its network of enquiry centres in the first half of 2014 because visitor numbers had dropped dramatically. To help the estimated 1.5 million customers identified as needing extra help to get their taxes and entitlements right, HMRC introduced a new service offering more in-depth support on the phone and a mobile advisory service if a face-to-face appointment is required.

The HMRC website (W www.gov.uk/government/organisations/hm-revenue-customs) provides wide-ranging information online. All HMRC forms, leaflets and guides are listed on, and can be downloaded from, the website or ordered by telephone. A list of all HMRC telephone helplines and order lines is also on the website. Those most relevant to topics covered in this section on taxation are included at pertinent points throughout.

INCOME TAX

Income tax is levied on different sorts of income. Not all types of income are taxable, however, and individuals are only taxed on their 'taxable income' above a certain level. Reliefs and allowances can also reduce or, in some cases, cancel out an individual's income tax bill.

An individual's taxable income is assessed each tax year, starting on 6 April and ending on 5 April the following year.

The information below relates specifically to the year of assessment 2015–16, ending on 5 April 2016, and has only limited application to earlier years. Changes due to come into operation at a later date are briefly mentioned where information is available. Types of income that are taxable include:

- earnings from employment or self-employment
- most pensions income including state, company and personal pensions
- interest on most savings
- income (dividends) from shares
- income from property
- income received from a trust
- certain state benefits
- an individual's share of any joint income

There are certain sorts of income on which individuals never pay tax. These are ignored altogether when working out how much income tax an individual may need to pay. Types of income that are not taxable include:

- certain state benefits and tax credits such as child benefit, working tax credit, child tax credit, pension credit, attendance allowance, personal independence payment, housing benefit and maternity allowance
- winter fuel payments
- income from National Savings and Investments savings certificates
- interest, dividends and other income from various tax-free investments, notably individual savings accounts (ISAs)
- premium bond and national lottery prizes

PERSONAL ALLOWANCE
Every individual resident in the UK has a 'personal allowance' for tax purposes. This is the amount of taxable income that an individual can earn or receive each year tax-free. This tax year (2015–16) the basic personal allowance or tax-free amount is £10,600, an increase of £600 from the 2014–15 figure of £10,000. Individuals may be entitled to a higher personal allowance if they were born before 6 April 1938. As previously announced, the cash value of date-of-birth related allowances are now frozen until they eventually align with the basic personal allowance. The government's plan, as announced in the 2015 Budget, is to have a single personal allowance for all taxpayers regardless of age from 2016–17.

Income tax is only due on an individual's taxable income that is above his or her tax-free allowance. Husbands and wives are taxed separately, with each entitled to his or her personal allowance. Each spouse may obtain other allowances and reliefs where the required conditions are satisfied.

Since 2013–14, the amount of an individual's personal allowance has depended on their date of birth and their total income received from all taxable sources for the tax year. For 2015–16, there are two date-of-birth related levels of personal allowance. Everyone born after 6 April 1938 receives an allowance of £10,600 a year while those born before this date receive £10,660.

If an individual born before 5 April 1948 has an income over the £27,700 'income limit' for age-related allowances but not more than £100,000, their age-related allowance reduces by half the amount (£1 for every £2) he or she has over the £27,700 limit, until the basic rate allowance for those born after 5 April 1948 is reached.

Since April 2010 all three levels of personal allowance have been subject to a single income limit of £100,000, meaning that the personal allowance is reduced for individuals with an 'adjusted net income' (*see* below) over £100,000. Those individuals with an 'adjusted net income' below or equal to the £100,000 limit are entitled to the full amount of personal allowance. However, where an individual's adjusted net income is above the £100,000 limit, their personal allowance is reduced by half the amount (£1 for every £2) they have over that limit, irrespective of their age or date of birth, until their personal allowance is reduced to nil.

An individual's 'adjusted net income' is calculated in a series of steps. The starting point is 'net income', which is the total of the individual's income subject to income tax less specified deductions such as payments made gross to pension schemes. This net income is then reduced by the grossed-up amount of the individual's Gift Aid contributions to charities and the grossed-up amount of the individual's pension contributions that have received tax relief at source. The final step is to add back any relief for payments to trade unions or police organisations deducted in arriving at the individual's net income. The result is the individual's adjusted net income.

From April 2015 some married couples and civil partners, made up of one non-taxpayer and one basic-rate taxpayer, became eligible for the new marriage allowance, which allows them to share some of the non-taxpayer's unused annual income tax allowance. In the 2015–16 tax year, the new allowance allows a spouse or civil partner with an income less than £10,600 to transfer up to £1,060 of their unused personal allowance to their higher-income partner. So long as the person receiving the transfer is a basic-rate taxpayer, which, in most cases, means having an income of between £10,601 and £42,385, this transferable tax allowance is worth up to £212 in 2015–16.

INCOME TAX ALLOWANCES

	2014–15	2015–16
Personal Allowance		
Those born after 5 April 1948	£10,000	£10,600
Those born between 6 April 1938 and 5 April 1948	£10,500	£10,600
Those born before 6 April 1938	£10,660	£10,660
Income limit for personal allowance	£100,000	£100,000
Income limit for personal allowances (born before 6 April 1948)	£27,000	£27,000
Transferable tax allowance for married couples and civil partners	—	£1,060

BLIND PERSON'S ALLOWANCE

If an individual is registered blind or is unable to perform any work for which eyesight is essential, he or she can claim blind person's allowance, an extra amount of tax-free income added to the personal allowance. In 2015–16 the blind person's allowance is £2,290. It is the same for everyone who can claim it, whatever his or her age or level of income. If an individual is married or in a civil partnership and cannot use all of his or her blind person's allowance because of insufficient income, the unused part of the allowance can be passed to the spouse or civil partner.

CALCULATING INCOME TAX DUE

Individuals' liability to pay income tax is determined by establishing their level of taxable income for the year. For married couples and civil partners, income must be allocated between the couple by reference to the individual who is beneficially entitled to that income. Where income arises from jointly held assets, it is normally apportioned equally between the partners. If, however, the beneficial interests in jointly held assets are not equal, in most cases couples can make a special declaration to have income apportioned by reference to the actual interests in that income.

To work out an individual's liability for tax, his or her taxable income must be allocated between three different types: earned income (excluding income from savings and dividends); income from savings; and company dividends from shares and other equity-based investments.

After the tax-free personal allowance plus any deductible allowances and reliefs have been taken into account, the amount of tax an individual pays is calculated using different tax rates and a series of tax bands. The tax band applies to an individual's income after tax allowances and any reliefs have been taken into account. Individuals are not taxed on all of their income.

For the tax year 2015–16, the basic rate of income tax is 20 per cent (20 pence in the pound) and the higher rate is 40 per cent (40 pence in the pound). The additional rate is 45 per cent (45 pence in the pound).

The starting rate of tax for savings income such as bank or building society interest was reduced from 10 per cent to nil from April 2015 and the maximum amount of taxable savings income that can be eligible for this starting rate was increased from £2,880 to £5,000. If an individual's taxable non-savings income is above £5,000, the zero per cent starting rate for savings is not available for their savings income.

For 2015–16 the basic rate limit above which tax is payable at the higher rate of 40 per cent is £31,785 and the higher rate limit, above which tax is payable at the additional rate of 45 per cent, remains at £150,000.

INCOME TAX RATES (PER CENT) AND TAX BANDS FOR 2015–16

Band	Earned income	Band	Savings	Dividends
£0–£31,785	20%	£0–£5,000*	0%	10%
£31,785+	40%	£5,000–£31,785	20%	10%
£150,000+	45%	£31,785+	40%	32.5%
		£150,000+	45%	37.5%

* If an individual's taxable non-savings income is above £5,000 the 20 per cent tax band applies to savings income from £0–£31,785

The first calculation is applied to earned income which includes income from employment or self-employment, most pension income and rental income plus the value of a wide range of employee fringe benefits such as company cars, living accommodation and private medical insurance (for more information on fringe benefits, *see* later section on payment of income tax). In working out the amount of an individual's net taxable earnings, all expenses incurred 'wholly, exclusively and necessarily' in the performance of his or her work duties, together with the cost of business travel, may be deducted. Fees and subscriptions to certain professional bodies may also be deducted. Redundancy payments and other sums paid on the termination of an employment are assessable income, but the first £30,000 is normally tax-free provided the payment is not linked with the recipient's retirement or performance.

The first £31,785 of taxable income remaining after the tax-free allowance plus any deductible allowances and reliefs have been taken into account, is taxed at the basic rate of 20 per cent. Taxable income between £31,785 and £150,000 is taxed at the higher rate of 40 per cent. Taxable income above £150,000 is taxed at the additional rate of 45 per cent.

Savings and dividends income is added to an individual's other taxable income and taxed last. This means that tax on such sorts of income is based on an individual's highest income tax band.

It was announced in the 2015 Budget that the basic rate limit will be increased to £31,900 for 2016–17 amd £32,300 for 2017–18.

SAVINGS INCOME

The second calculation is applied to any income from savings received by an individual. The appropriate rate at which it must be taxed is determined by adding income from savings to an individual's other taxable income, excluding dividends.

There is a zero per cent starting rate for savings income only, with a limit of £5,000. If an individual's taxable non-savings income exceeds this limit, the zero per cent savings rate is not applicable. Savings income above £5,000 and below the £31,785 basic rate limit is taxable at 20 per cent. Savings income between £31,785 and £150,000 is taxable at 40 per cent. Savings income over £150,000 is taxed at 45 per cent. If savings income falls on both sides of a tax band, the relevant amounts are taxed at the rates for each tax band.

Most savings income, such as interest paid on bank and building society accounts, already has tax at a rate of 20 per cent deducted from it 'at source' – that is, before it is paid out to individuals. This is confirmed by the entry 'net interest' on bank and building society statements.

Higher rate taxpayers whose income is sufficient to pay 40 or 45 per cent tax on their savings income must let their tax office know what savings income they have received so that the extra tax they owe can be collected.

Non-taxpayers – ie individuals, including most children, whose taxable income is less than their tax allowances – can register to have their savings interest paid 'gross' without any tax being deducted from it at source. To do this, they must complete form R85, available at all banks and building societies. Parents or guardians need to fill in this form on behalf of those under 16.

The eligibility rules for completing a form R85 changed from April 2015. Previously an R85 could be completed only by a saver whose total taxable income for the tax year was below their tax-free personal allowance. From 6 April 2015, a saver who is unlikely to be liable for tax on any of their savings income in the tax year can complete an R85 and register to receive interest without tax deducted even if they pay tax on other (non-savings) income. In practice, this means that if a saver's total taxable income is expected to be below the total of their tax-free personal allowance plus the £5,000 starting rate for savings, they can register to have interest paid on their accounts without tax deducted using form R85. For individuals who are unsure whether they are eligible to register to have their savings interest paid gross, HMRC offers an 'R85 checker' on its website (W www.hmrc.gov.uk/tools/r85/r85-2015.htm).

Non-taxpayers who have already had tax deducted from their savings interest can claim it back from HMRC by filling in form R40. For help or information about registering to get interest paid tax-free or to claim tax back on savings interest, individuals may visit W www.gov.uk/apply-tax-free-interest-on-savings or call a dedicated helpline on T 0300-200 3312.

It was announced in the 2015 Budget that from April 2016, a new tax-free personal savings allowance of £1,000 (or £500 for higher rate taxpayers) would be introduced on the interest individuals earn on savings. The result will be that 95 per cent of individuals will not have to pay tax on the first £1,000 (£500 for higher rate taxpayers) of interest they earn on their savings. A basic rate taxpayer with a total income up to £42,700 a year will be eligible for the £1,000 tax-free savings allowance. A higher rate taxpayer earning from £42,701 to £150,000 will be eligible for a £500 tax-free savings allowance. From April 2016 banks and building societies will stop automatically taking 20 per cent in income tax from the interest earned on standard savings accounts and will pay gross interest instead. This means that non-taxpayers, including most children and many pensioners, will no longer have to fill out form R85 (described above) in order to get their savings interest paid tax free.

DIVIDEND INCOME

The third and final income tax calculation is on UK dividends, which means income from shares in UK companies and other share-based investments including unit trusts and open-ended investment companies (OEICs).

Dividend tax rates differ from those on savings income. The rate that an individual pays on his or her dividends depends on the amount of his or her overall taxable income (after allowances). Dividend income at or below the £31,785 basic rate tax limit is taxable at 10 per cent, between £31,785 and £150,000 at 32.5 per cent, and above £150,000 at 37.5 per cent.

When dividends are paid, a voucher is sent that shows the dividend paid and the amount of associated 'tax credit'. Companies pay dividends out of profits on which they have already paid or are due to pay tax. The tax credit takes account of this and is available to the shareholder to offset against any income tax that may be due on their dividend income. The dividend paid represents 90 per cent of their dividend income. The remaining 10 per cent is made up of the tax credit. In other words the tax credit represents 10 per cent of the dividend income.

Individuals who pay tax at the basic rate have no tax to pay on their dividend income because the tax liability is 10 per cent – the same amount as the tax credit. Higher rate taxpayers pay a total of 32.5 per cent tax on dividend income above the £31,865 basic rate tax limit, but because the first 10 per cent of the tax due on their dividend income is already covered by the tax credit, in practice they owe only 22.5 per cent. For the same reason, additional rate taxpayers who pay a total of 37.5 per cent on dividend income above the £150,000 additional rate tax limit, owe only 27.5 per cent in practice.

Non-taxpayers cannot claim the 10 per cent tax credit. This is because income tax has not been deducted from the dividends paid to them. The view is that they have simply been given a 10 per cent credit against any income tax due.

If there is significant change to an individual's savings or other income, whatever his or her current tax bracket, it is the individual's responsibility to contact the relevant tax office immediately, even if he or she does not normally complete a tax return. This enables the tax office to work out whether extra or less tax should be paid.

INDIVIDUAL SAVINGS ACCOUNTS

There is a small selection of savings and investment products that are tax-free. This means that there is no tax to pay on any income generated in the form of interest or dividends, nor on any increase in the value of the capital invested. Their tax-efficient status has been granted by the government in order to give people an incentive to save more. For this reason there are usually limits and restrictions on the amount of money an individual may invest in such savings and investments. Individual savings accounts (ISAs) are the best known among tax-efficient savings and investments. Individuals can use an ISA to save cash, or invest in stocks and shares.

To be eligible to invest in ISAs and receive all profits free of tax, individuals must be UK residents and be aged 18 or over (over 16 for cash ISAs). An ISA must be in an individual's name and cannot be held jointly with another person.

Major changes to ISAs announced in the 2014 Budget, took effect from 1 July 2014. For the 2014–15 tax year individuals could save up to £11,880 each tax year in an adult ISA and could invest in two separate ISAs each tax year: a cash ISA and a stocks and shares ISA (an umbrella term covering investments in unit trusts, company shares, bonds, investment-type life insurance etc). Up to £5,940 of an individual's ISA allowance could be saved in one cash ISA with one provider. The remainder of the £11,880 could be invested in one stocks and shares ISA with either the same or a different provider. Alternatively an individual could open a single stocks and shares ISA and invest the full £11,880.

ISA savers had the option to transfer some or all of the money they had saved in previous tax years in cash ISAs to their stocks and shares ISA without affecting their annual ISA investment allowance. They could also choose to transfer all the money they had saved to date in a cash ISA in the current tax year to a stocks and shares ISA. However, the rules did not allow the reverse; that is, the transfer of monies saved in a stocks and shares ISA to a cash ISA.

On 1 July 2014 ISAs were reformed into a simpler product and overall annual subscription limit for these accounts was increased to £15,000 for 2014–15 and it was raised again to £15,240 for 2015–16. Since July 2014 individuals aged 18 or over can hold any combination of cash or stocks and shares in an ISA. Individuals aged 16 to 18 also have a full ISA allowance, £15,240 for 2015–16, but are restricted to cash-only ISAs.

ISA savers can now choose to subscribe their full allowance to a cash account where previously only 50 per cent of the allowance could be saved in cash. Investors also now have the right to transfer their investments from a stocks and shares to a cash account if they wish. There have also been consequential changes to the rules on the investments that can be held in a ISA, so that a wider range of securities, including certain retail bonds with less than five years before maturity, can be invested.

Further flexibility for ISAs was announced in the 2015 Budget. Instead of only being able to make deposits totalling £15,240, in the 2015–16 tax year, individuals can now take out their money from an ISA and put it back in without losing their ISA tax benefits as long as the repayment is made in the same tax year as the withdrawal.

From December 2014 there was a change in the law to allow spouses and civil partners to inherit their partner's ISA benefits after death. It had previously been the case that when an ISA saver died, their ISA tax advantages died with them, even if they were saving as a couple. Since April 2015, surviving spouses and civil partners are now able to invest as much into their own ISA as their spouse or civil partner used to have, in addition to their normal annual ISA limit.

There are also annual savings limits on the amount that can be invested in long-term, tax-free savings accounts for children called Junior ISAs. Parents or guardians with parental responsibility can open Junior ISAs for children aged under 18 who live in the UK. The Junior ISA investment limit for 2015–16 is £4,080 per child. However, while parents can open and manage Junior ISAs for their children, the invested money belongs to the child who can take control of their account when they are 16 and withdraw the money when they are 18. Children aged 16 and 17 can open their own Junior ISA as well as an adult cash ISA. Junior ISAs automatically turn into an adult ISA when the child turns 18.

It was announced in the 2015 Budget that with effect from 1 July 2015 the list of qualifying investments for ISAs would be extended to include listed bonds issued by cooperative societies, community benefit societies and SME (small and medium-sized enterprise) securities that are admitted to trading on a recognised stock exchange. The government is also consulting on further extending this list of qualifying investments to include debt securities and equity securities offiered via crowd funding platforms.

It was also announced in the 2015 Budget that new Help to Buy ISAs would be introduced to help individuals save a deposit towards buying their first home. From autumn 2015, aspiring first-time buyers aged 16 or over may save up to £200 a month in a Help to Buy ISA and the government will boost their savings by 25 per cent; £50 for every £200 saved, up to a maximum bonus of £3,000 per person. If, therefore, an individual saves £12,000, the government bonus will boost their total savings to £15,000. Savers can start an account with a lump-sum deposit of up to £1,000. The minimum savings to qualify for the scheme are £1,600, but there is no monthly minimum investment. Savings held in a Help to Buy ISA can be accessed at any time but the government payment is only added if and when the savings are used as a deposit on a home in the UK. The bonus is available on home purchases of up to £450,000 in London and up to £250,000 outside London.

Further details about ISAs are available via the HMRC's savings helpline (T 0300-200 3312).

DEDUCTIBLE ALLOWANCES AND RELIEF

Income taxpayers may be entitled to certain tax-deductible allowances and reliefs as well as their personal allowances. Examples include the married couple's allowance and maintenance payments relief, (see below). Unlike the tax-free allowances, these are not amounts of income that an individual can receive tax-free but amounts by which their tax bill can be reduced.

MARRIED COUPLE'S ALLOWANCE

A married couple's allowance (MCA) is available to taxpayers who are married or are in a civil partnership only where one or other partner was born before 6 April 1935. Eligible couples can start to claim the MCA from the year of marriage or civil partnership registration.

The MCA is restricted to give relief at a fixed rate of 10 per cent, which means that – unlike the personal allowance – it is not income that can be received without paying tax. Instead, it reduces an individual's tax bill by up to a fixed amount calculated as 10 per cent of the amount of the allowance to which they are entitled.

In 2015–16, the MCA is £8,355 at 10 per cent, worth up to £835.50 off a couple's tax bill. The MCA is made up of two parts. There is a minimum amount (£3,220 in 2015–16) which will always be due. The remaining amount (£8,355 in 2015–16) can be reduced if the husband's income exceeds certain limits.

The husband will normally receive the allowance, but the couple can jointly decide which of them will get the minimum amount of the allowance. Alternatively, they can decide to have the minimum amount of the allowance split equally between them. They must inform their tax office of their decision before the start of the new tax year in which they want the decision to take effect. Once this is done, the change will apply until the couple decides to alter it. The remaining part of the allowance must go to the husband unless he lacks sufficient income to use it.

If an individual does not have enough income to use all of his or her share of the MCA, the tax office can transfer the unused part of it to his or her spouse or civil partner.

Like the personal allowance, the MCA can be gradually reduced at the rate of £1 of the allowance for every £2 of income above the income limit (£27,700 in 2015–16). The amount of MCA can only be affected by the husband's income, and it only starts to be affected if his personal allowance has already been reduced back to the basic level for people born after 5 April 1948. The wife's income never affects the amount of MCA. Whatever the level of the husband's income, the MCA can never be reduced below the minimum amount: in 2015–16 this is £3,220 at 10 per cent.

The same system of allowance allocation applies to civil partners based on the income of the highest earner.

MAINTENANCE PAYMENTS RELIEF

An allowance is available to reduce an individual's tax bill for maintenance payments he or she makes to his or her ex-spouse or former civil partner in certain circumstances. To be eligible one or other partner must have been born before 6 April 1935; the couple must be legally separated or divorced; the maintenance payments being made must be under a court order; and the payments must be for the maintenance of an ex spouse or former civil partner (provided he or she is not now remarried or in a new civil partnership) or for children who are under 21. For the tax year 2015–16, this allowance can reduce an individual's tax bill by:

- 10 per cent of £3,220 (maximum £322) – this applies where an individual makes maintenance payments of £3,220 or more a year
- 10 per cent of the amount the individual has actually paid – this applies where an individual makes maintenance payments of less than £3,220 a year

An individual cannot claim a tax reduction for any voluntary payments he or she makes for a child, ex-spouse or former civil partner. To claim maintenance payments relief, individuals should contact their tax office.

CHARITABLE DONATION

A number of charitable donations qualify for tax relief. Individuals can increase the value of regular or one-off charitable gifts of money, however small, by using the Gift Aid scheme that allows charities or community amateur sports clubs (CASCs) to reclaim 20 per cent basic rate tax relief on donations they receive. If a taxpayer gives £10 using Gift Aid, for example, the donation is worth £12.50 to the charity or CASC.

Individuals who pay 40 per cent higher rate income tax can claim back the difference between the 40 per cent and the 20 per cent basic rate of income tax on the total (gross) value of their donations. For example, a 40 per cent tax payer donates £100; the total value of this donation to the charity or CASC is £125, of which the individual can claim back 20 per cent (£25) for themselves. Similarly, those who pay 45 per cent additional rate income tax can claim back the difference between the 45 per cent and the 20 per cent basic rate on the total (gross) value of their donations. On a £100 donation, this means they can claim back £31.25.

In order to make a Gift Aid donation, individuals need to make a Gift Aid declaration. The charity or CASC will normally ask an individual to complete a simple form. One form can cover every gift made to the same charity or CASC for whatever period chosen, including both gifts made in the past and in the future. In April 2013 the government introduced a new scheme where charities are able to claim a Gift Aid-type tax refund on small, ad-hoc donations up to a total of £5,000 a year per charity, without the need for donors to fill in any forms at all. This means Gift Aid can be claimed on the contents of collecting tins, for example. If a charity collects the full £5,000, it will get £1,250 back.

Individuals can use Gift Aid provided the amount of income tax and/or capital gains tax they have paid in the tax year in which their donations are made is at least equal to the amount of basic rate tax the charity or CASC is reclaiming on their gifts. It is the responsibility of the individual to make sure this is the case. If an individual makes Gift Aid donations and has not paid sufficient tax, they may have to pay the shortfall to HMRC. The Gift Aid scheme is not suitable for non-taxpayers.

Individuals who complete a tax return and are due a tax refund can ask HMRC to treat all or part of it as a Gift Aid donation.

For employees or those in receipt of an occupational pension, a tax-efficient way of making regular donations to charities is to use the payroll giving scheme. It allows the donations to be paid from a salary or pension before income tax is deducted. This effectively reduces the cost of giving for donors, which may allow them to give more.

For example, it costs a basic-rate taxpayer only £8 in take-home pay to give £10 to charity from their pre-tax pay. Where a donor pays 40 per cent higher rate tax, that same £10 donation costs the taxpayer £6 and for donors who pay the additional 45 per cent rate tax, it costs £5.50.

Anyone who pays tax through the pay as you earn (PAYE) system (see Payment of Income Tax) can give to any charity of their choosing in this way, providing their employer or pension provider offers the payroll giving scheme. There is no limit to the amount individuals can donate.

A reduced rate of inheritance tax (IHT) applies where an individual, in their will, leaves 10 per cent or more of their net estate to charity. In such cases the current IHT 40 per cent rate is reduced to 36 per cent. The reduced rate applies where death occurred on or after 6 April 2012.

Details of tax-efficient charitable giving methods can be found at W www.gov.uk/donating-to-charity

TAX RELIEF ON PENSION CONTRIBUTIONS

Pensions are long-term investments designed to help ensure that people have enough income in retirement. The government encourages individuals to save towards a pension by offering tax relief on their contributions. Tax relief reduces an individual's tax bill or increases their pension fund.

The way tax relief is given on pension contributions depends on whether an individual pays into a company, public service or personal pension scheme.

For employees who pay into a company or public service pension scheme, most employers take the pension contributions from the employee's pay before deducting tax, which means that the individual – whether they pay income tax at the basic or higher rate – gets full tax relief straight away. Some employers, however, use the same method of paying pension contributions as that used by personal pension scheme payers described below.

Individuals who pay into a personal pension scheme make contributions from their net salary; that is, after tax has been deducted. For each pound that individuals contribute to their pension from net salary, the pension provider claims tax back from the government at the basic rate of 20 per cent and reinvests it on behalf of the individual into the scheme. In practice this means that for every £80 an individual pays into their pension, they receive £100 in their pension fund.

Higher rate taxpayers currently get 40 per cent tax relief on money they put into a pension. On contributions made from net salary, the first 20 per cent is claimed back from HMRC by the pension scheme in the same way as for a lower rate taxpayer. It is then up to individuals to claim back the other 20 per cent from their tax office, either when they fill in their annual tax return or by telephone or letter. In a similar fashion, individuals subject to the 45 per cent additional rate of income tax can get 45 per cent tax relief on their pension contributions.

Most providers of retirement annuities, which are a type of personal pension scheme set up before July 1988, do not offer a 'tax relief at source' scheme whereby they claim back tax at the basic rate, as is the case with more modern personal pensions. In such cases, contributing individuals need to claim the tax relief they are due through their tax return or by telephoning or writing to HMRC.

Non-taxpayers can still pay into a personal pension scheme and benefit from 20 per cent basic rate relief on the first £2,880 a year they contribute. In practice this means that the government tops up their £2,880 contribution to make it £3,600 which is the current universal pension allowance. Such pension contributions may be made on behalf of a non-taxpayer by another individual. An individual may, for example, contribute to a pension on behalf of a husband, wife, civil partner, child or grandchild. Tax relief will be added to their contribution at the basic rate, again on up to £2,880 a year benefiting the recipient, but their own tax bill will not be affected.

In any one tax year, individuals can get tax relief on pension contributions made into any number and type of registered pension schemes of 100 per cent of their annual earnings, irrespective of age, up to a maximum 'annual allowance'. For the tax year 2015–16 the annual allowance is £40,000. Individuals pay tax at 40 per cent on any contributions they make above the annual allowance. Everyone also has a 'lifetime allowance' (£1.25m in 2015–16) which means taxpayers can save up to a total of £1.25m in their pension fund and still get tax relief at their highest income tax rate on all of their contributions.

It was announced in the 2015 Budget that the pensions lifetime allowance would be reduced from £1.25m to £1m from April 2016. A protection regime will be introduced alongside the reduction to protect pension savers who think they may be affected by this change.

For information on pensions and tax relief visit W www. gov.uk/browse/working. Another useful source of information and advice is The Pensions Advisory Service (TPAS), an independent voluntary organisation grant-aided by the Department for Work and Pensions at W www.pensions advisoryservice.org.uk; its Pensions Helpline is on T 0300-123 1047.

PAYMENT OF INCOME TAX
Employees have their income tax deducted from their wages throughout the year by their employer who sends it on to HMRC. Those in receipt of a company pension have their due tax deducted in the same way by their pension provider. This system of collecting income tax is known as 'pay as you earn' (PAYE).

BENEFITS IN KIND
The PAYE system is also used to collect tax on certain fringe benefits or 'benefits in kind' that employees or directors receive from their employer, but are not included in their salary. These include company cars, private medical insurance paid for by the employer or cheap or free loans from the employer. Some fringe benefits are tax-free, including employer-paid contributions into an employee's pension fund, cheap or free canteen meals, works buses, in-house sports facilities, reasonable relocation expenses, provision of a mobile phone and workplace nursery places provided for the children of employees. For taxable fringe benefits, tax is paid on the 'taxable value' of the benefit.

Employers submit returns for individual employees earning at or above the £8,500 per annum threshold (including the value of expenses and benefits) to the tax office on the form P11D, with details of any fringe benefits they have been given. For those earning less than the £8,500 threshold (part-time employees) a P9D form is submitted. Employees should get a copy of this form by 6 July following the end of the tax year and must enter the value of the fringe benefits they have received on their tax return for the relevant year, even if tax has already been paid on them under PAYE. Fringe benefits may be taxed under PAYE by being offset against personal tax allowances in an individual's PAYE code. Otherwise tax will be collected after the end of the tax year by the issue of an assessment on the fringe benefits.

SELF-ASSESSMENT
Individuals who are not on PAYE, notably the self-employed, need to complete a self-assessment tax return each year, in paper form or online (W www.gov.uk/log-in-file-self-assessment-tax-return), and pay any income tax owed in twice-yearly instalments. Some individuals with more complex tax affairs such as those who earn money from rents or investments above a certain level may also need to fill out a self-assessment return, even if they are on PAYE. HMRC uses the figures supplied on the tax return to work out the individual's tax bill, or they can choose to work it out themselves. It is called 'self-assessment' because individuals are responsible for making sure the details they provide are correct.

Tax returns are usually sent out in early April, following the end of the tax year to which they apply. They may also go out at other times, for example if an individual wants to claim an allowance or repayment or to register for self-assessment for the first time.

Individuals with simple tax affairs may receive a short four-page return. Those with more complex affairs must fill out a full return that has 12 core pages plus extra pages, depending on the sorts of income received.

Central to the self-assessment system is the requirement for individuals to contact their tax office if they do not receive a self-assessment return but think they should or if their financial circumstances change. Individuals have six months from when the tax year ends to report any new income, for example. If an individual becomes self-employed, they have three months after the calendar month in which they began self-employed work to let HMRC know. This can be done by telephoning the helpline number for the newly self-employed on T 0300-200 3504.

TAX RETURN FILING AND PAYMENT DEADLINES
There are also key deadlines for filing (sending in) completed tax returns and paying the tax due. Failure to do so can incur penalties, interest charges and surcharges.

KEY FILING DATES FOR SELF-ASSESSMENT RETURNS

Date	Why the date is important
31 Oct*	Deadline for filing paper returns* for tax year ending the previous 5 April
30 Dec	Deadline for online filing where the amount owed for tax year ending the previous 5 April is less than £3,000 and the taxpayer wants HMRC to collect any tax due through their PAYE tax code
31 Jan†	Deadline for online filing of returns for tax year ending the previous 5 April

* Or three months from the date the return was requested if this was after 31 July

† Or three months from the date the return was requested if this was after 31 October

KEY SELF-ASSESSMENT PAYMENT DATES

Date	What payment is due?
31 Jan	Deadline for paying the balance of any tax owed – the 'balancing payment' – for the tax year ending the previous 5 April. It is also the date by which a taxpayer must make any first 'payment on account' (advance payment) for the current tax year. For example, on 31 January 2016 a taxpayer may have to pay both the balancing payment for the year 2015–16 and the first payment on account for 2016–17.
31 Jul	Deadline for making a second payment on account for the current tax year

LATE FILING AND PAYMENT PENALTIES

Late filing of tax returns incurs an automatic £100 penalty although individuals may appeal against the penalty if they have a reasonable excuse. For late filing of 2014–15 tax returns the following penalties also apply:

- Over three months late – £10 each day, up to a maximum of £900, in addition to the penalty above
- Over six months late – an additional £300 or 5 per cent of the tax due, whichever is the higher, in addition to the penalty above
- Over 12 months late – a further £300 or 5 per cent of the tax due, whichever is the higher. In serious cases HMRC reserve the right to ask for 100 per cent of the tax due instead. In both instances this is in addition to the penalty above

Late payment of tax owing for 2014–15 incurs the following penalties:

- Over 30 days – 5 per cent of the tax unpaid at that date
- Over six months – an additional 5 per cent of the tax unpaid at that date
- Over 12 months – a further 5 per cent of the tax unpaid at that date

Interest is due on all outstanding amounts, including any unpaid penalties, until payment is received in full.

It was announced in the 2015 Budget that the government intends to abolish the annual tax return for millions of individuals and small businesses through the introduction of digital tax accounts as part of its aim to modernise and simplify the taxation system. The government says that by early 2016, 10 million individuals (and 5 million small businesses) will have access to their own digital tax account which will bring together all of a taxpayer's details in one secure place akin to an online bank account. By the end of this parliament, the expectation is that every individual and small business in the UK will have one. Individuals will be able to register, file, pay and update their information at any time of the year using a digital device of their choice.

TAX CREDITS

Child tax credit, working tax credit and the new universal credit are paid to qualifying individuals. Although the titles of these credits incorporates the word 'tax', they do not affect the amount of income tax payable or repayable. They are forms of social security benefits. See Social Welfare.

CAPITAL GAINS TAX

Capital gains tax (CGT) is a tax on the gain or profit that an individual makes when they sell, give away or otherwise dispose of an asset – that is, something they own such as shares, land or buildings. An individual potentially has to pay CGT on gains they make from any disposal of assets during a tax year. There is, however, a tax-free allowance and some additional reliefs that may reduce an individual's CGT bill. The following information relates to the tax year 2015–16 ending on 5 April 2016.

CGT is paid by individuals who are either resident or ordinarily resident in the UK for the tax year, executors or administrators – 'personal representatives' – responsible for a deceased person's financial affairs and trustees of a settlement. Non-residents are not usually liable to CGT unless they carry on a business in the UK through a branch or agency. However, from April 2015, the government introduced a CGT charge on future gains made by non-residents disposing of UK residential property. Special CGT rules apply to individuals who used to live and work in the UK but have since left the country.

CAPITAL GAINS CHARGEABLE TO CGT

Typically, individuals have made a gain if they sell an asset for more than they paid for it. It is the gain that is taxed, not the amount the individual receives for the asset. For example, a man buys shares for £1,000 and later sells them for £3,000. He has made a gain of £2,000 (£3,000 less £1,000). If someone gives an asset away, the gain will be based on the difference between what the asset was worth when originally acquired compared with its worth at the time of disposal. The same is true when an asset is sold for less than its full worth in order to give away part of the value. For example, a woman buys a property for £120,000 and three years later, when the property's market value has risen to £180,000, she gives it to her son. The son may pay nothing for the property or pay less than its true worth, eg £100,000. Either way, she has made a gain of £60,000 (£180,000 less £120,000).

If an individual disposes of an asset he or she received as a gift, the gain is worked out according to the market value of the asset when it was received. For example, a man gives his sister a painting worth £8,000. She pays nothing for it. Later she sells the painting for £10,000. For CGT purposes, she is treated as making a gain of £2,000 (£10,000 less £8,000). If an individual inherits an asset, the estate of the person who died does not pay CGT at the time. If the inheritor later disposes of the asset, the gain is worked out by looking at the market value at the time of the death. For example, a woman acquires some shares for £5,000 and leaves them to her niece when she dies. No CGT is payable at the time of death when the shares are worth £8,000. Later the niece sells the shares for £10,000. She has made a gain of £2,000 (£10,000 less £8,000).

Individuals may also have to pay CGT if they dispose of part of an asset or exchange one asset for another. Similarly, CGT may be payable if an individual receives a capital sum of money from an asset without disposing of it, for example where he or she receives compensation when an asset is damaged.

Assets that may lead to a CGT charge when they are disposed of include:

- shares in a company
- units in a unit trust
- land and buildings (though not normally an individual's main home – see 'disposal of a home' section for details)
- higher value jewellery, paintings, antiques and other personal effects assets used in business such as goodwill

EXEMPT GAINS

Certain kinds of assets do not give rise to a chargeable gain when they are disposed of. Assets exempt from CGT include:

- an individual's private car
- an individual's main home, if certain conditions are met
- tax-free investments such as assets held in an ISA
- UK government gilts or 'bonds'

- personal belongings including jewellery, paintings and antiques individually worth £6,000 or less
- cash in sterling or foreign currency held for an individual for his/her family's own personal use
- betting, lottery or pools winnings
- personal injury compensation

DISPOSAL OF A HOME: PRIVATE RESIDENCE RELIEF

When an individual sells their own home they automatically qualify for private residence relief which means they do not have to pay any CGT provided that:

- the property has been their only home or main residence since they bought it, and
- they have used it as their home and for no other purpose

Even if an individual has not lived in the property for all of the time that they owned it, they may still be entitled to the full relief.

Under the relief rules, the final 18 months of ownership are always treated as if the individual lived in the property even if they did not. This means that if an individual moves out of one home and into a new one, they have up to 18 months in which to sell their former home without incurring any CGT on the sale proceeds. This 'final period of exemption' was halved from 36 months to the current 18 months in April 2014.

Full relief is granted to individuals when they sell their home if they could not live in it for periods because they were working abroad. Full relief is also granted if an individual is prevented from living in the home for periods totalling a maximum of four years because their job requires them to work elsewhere in the UK. In both cases however, for the property to qualify for full relief, the general rule is that it must have been the individual's only or main home both before and after they worked away.

Individuals can also get full relief when they sell their home if they have lived away from it for reasons other than working away provided all of the following apply:

- they were not living away from the home for more than three years in total during the time they owned the property
- they were not entitled to private residence relief on any other property during that time
- the property was their only or main home both before and after they lived elsewhere

There are instances when individuals may not get the full amount of private residence relief when they sell their home. These include if:

- the garden or grounds, including the site of the house, are larger than 5,000 square metres
- any part of the home has been used exclusively for business purposes
- all or part of the home has been let out (or more than one lodger has been taken in at a time). The owner may, however, be entitled to another form of CGT relief – letting relief – instead
- the main reason the property was bought was to make a profit from a quick sale

If an individual lives in – not just owns – more than one property, they can 'nominate' which should be treated as their main home for private residence relief purposes. Married couples or those in a civil partnership must make such a nomination jointly as they are only entitled to private residence relief on one house between them.

It was announced in the 2014 Budget that, from April 2015, this ability to nominate which home should qualify for private residence relief will cease. Instead it will be decided on objective grounds which of an individual's two or more homes is indeed their main or primary residence.

Certain other kinds of disposal similarly do not give rise to a chargeable gain. For example, individuals who are married or in a civil partnership and who live together may sell or give assets to their spouse or civil partner without having to pay CGT. Individuals may not, however, give or sell assets cheaply to their children without having to consider CGT. There is no CGT to pay on assets given to a registered charity.

CALCULATING CGT

CGT is worked out for each tax year and is charged on the total of an individual's taxable gains after taking into account certain costs and reliefs that can reduce or defer chargeable gains, allowable losses made on assets to which CGT normally applies and an annual exempt (tax-free) amount that applies to every individual. If the total of an individual's net gains in a tax year is less than the annual exempt amount (AEA), the individual will not have to pay CGT. For the tax year 2015–16 the AEA is £11,100. If an individual's net gains are more than the AEA, they pay CGT on the excess. Should any part of the exemption remain unused, this cannot be carried forward to a future year.

There are certain reliefs available that may eliminate, reduce or defer CGT. Some reliefs are available to many people while others are available only in special circumstances. Some reliefs are given automatically while others are given only if they are claimed. Some of the costs of buying, selling and improving assets may be deducted from total gains when working out an individual's chargeable gain.

RATES OF TAX

The net gains remaining, if any, calculated after subtracting the AEA, deducting costs and taking into account all CGT reliefs, incur liability to capital gains tax. Individuals pay CGT at a rate of 18 per cent on gains up to the unused amount of the basic rate income tax band (if any) and at 28 per cent on gains above that amount. The CGT rate charged to trustees and personal representatives is 28 per cent.

CGT for 2015–16 is due for payment in full on 31 January 2017. If payment is delayed, interest or surcharges may be imposed. A husband and wife or registered civil partners who live together are separately assessed for CGT. Each partner must independently calculate his or her gains and losses with each entitled to the AEA of £11,100 for 2015–16.

VALUATION OF ASSETS

The disposal proceeds – ie the amount received as consideration for the disposal of an asset – are the sum used to establish the gain or loss once certain allowable costs have been deducted. In most cases this is straightforward because the disposal proceeds are the amount actually received for disposing of the asset. This may include cash payable now or in the future and the value of any asset received in exchange for the asset disposed of. However, in certain circumstances, the disposal proceeds may not accurately reflect the value of the asset and the individual may be treated as disposing of an asset for an amount other than the actual amount (if any) that they received. This applies, in particular, where an asset is transferred as a gift or sold for a price known to be below market value. Disposal proceeds in such transactions are deemed to be equal to the market value of the asset at the time it was disposed of rather than the actual amount (if any) received for it.

Market value represents the price that an asset might reasonably be expected to fetch upon sale in the open market.

In the case of unquoted shares or securities, it is to be assumed that the hypothetical purchaser in the open market would have available all the information that a prudent prospective purchaser of shares or securities might reasonably require if that person were proposing to purchase them from a willing vendor by private treaty and at arm's length. The market value of unquoted shares or securities will often be established following negotiations with the specialist HMRC Shares and Assets Valuation department. The valuation of land and interests in land in the UK is dealt with by the Valuation Office Agency. Special rules apply to determine the market value of shares quoted on the London Stock Exchange.

ALLOWABLE COSTS

When working out a chargeable gain, once the actual or notional disposal proceeds have been determined, certain allowable costs may be deducted. There is a general rule that no costs that could be taken into account when working out income or losses for income tax purposes may be deducted. Subject to this, allowable costs are:

- acquisition costs – the actual amount spent on acquiring the asset or, in certain circumstances, the equivalent market value
- incidental costs of acquiring the asset such as fees paid for professional advice, valuation costs, stamp duty and advertising costs to find a seller
- enhancement costs – incurred for the purpose of enhancing the value of the asset (not including normal maintenance and repair costs)
- expenditure on defending or establishing a person's rights over the asset
- incidental costs of disposing of the asset such as fees paid for professional advice, valuation costs, stamp duty and advertising costs to find a buyer

If an individual disposes of part of his or her interest in an asset, or part of a holding of shares of the same class in the same company, or part of a holding of units in the same unit trust, he or she can deduct part of the allowable costs of the asset or holding when working out the chargeable gain. Allowable costs may also be reduced by some reliefs.

ENTREPRENEURS' RELIEF

Entrepreneurs' Relief allows individuals in business and some trustees to claim relief on the first £10m of gains made on the disposal of any of the following: all or part of a business; the assets of a business after it has ceased; and shares in a company. The relief is available to taxpayers as individuals if they are in business, for example as a sole trader or as a partner in a trading business, or if they hold shares in their own personal trading company. This relief is not available for companies.

Depending on the type of disposal, certain qualifying conditions need to be met throughout a qualifying one-year period. For example, if an individual is selling all or part of their business, they must have owned the business during a one-year period that ends on the date of the disposal.

Recent changes include a condition announced at Budget 2015 which prevents claims to entrepreneurs' relief in respect of gains on disposals of privately-held assets used in a business unless they are associated with a significant material disposal, that is to say a disposal of at least a 5 per cent shareholding in the company or of at least a 5 per cent share in the assets of the partnership carrying the business. This condition has effect for disposals on or after 18 March 2015.

Where Entrepreneurs' Relief applies, qualifying gains liable to CGT are charged at 10 per cent. An individual can make claims for this relief on more than one occasion as long as the lifetime total of all their claims does not exceed £10m of gains qualifying for relief.

BUSINESS ASSET ROLL-OVER RELIEF

When certain types of business asset are sold or disposed of and the proceeds reinvested in new qualifying trading assets, business asset roll-over relief makes it possible to 'roll-over' or postpone the payment of any CGT that would normally be due. The gain is deducted from the base cost of the new asset and only becomes chargeable to CGT on the eventual disposal of that replacement asset unless a further roll-over situation then develops. Full relief is available if all the proceeds from the original asset are reinvested in the qualifying replacement asset.

For example, a trader sells a freehold office for £75,000 and makes a gain of £30,000. All of the proceeds are reinvested in a new freehold business premises costing £90,000. The trader can postpone the whole of the £30,000 gain made on the sale of the old office, as all of the proceeds have been reinvested. When the trader eventually sells the new business premises and the CGT bill becomes payable, the cost of the new premises will be treated as £60,000 (£90,000 less the £30,000 gain).

If only part of the proceeds from the disposal of an old asset is reinvested in a new one, it may still be possible to postpone paying tax on part of the gain until the eventual disposal of the new asset.

Relief is only available if the acquisition of the new asset takes place within a period between 12 months before, and 36 months after, the disposal of the old asset. However, HMRC may extend this time limit at their discretion where there is a clear intention to acquire a replacement asset. The most common types of business assets that qualify for roll-over relief are land, buildings occupied and used for the purposes of trade, and fixed plant and machinery. Assets used for the commercial letting of furnished holiday accommodation qualify if certain conditions are satisfied.

GIFTS HOLD-OVER RELIEF

The gift of an asset is treated as a disposal made for a consideration equal to market value, with a corresponding acquisition by the transferee at an identical value. In the case of gifts of business assets made by individuals and a limited range of trustees, a form of hold-over relief may be available. This relief, which must be claimed, in effect enables liability for CGT to be deferred and passed to the person to whom the gift is made. Relief is limited to the transfer of certain assets including the following:

- gifts of assets used for the purposes of a business carried on by the donor or his or her personal company
- gifts of shares in trading companies that are not listed on a stock exchange
- gifts of shares or securities in the donor's personal trading company
- gifts of agricultural land and buildings that would qualify for inheritance tax agricultural property relief
- gifts that are chargeable transfers for inheritance tax purposes
- certain types of gifts that are specifically exempt from inheritance tax

Hold-over relief is automatically due on certain sorts of gifts including gifts to charities and community amateur sports clubs, and gifts of works of art where certain undertakings have been given. There are certain rules to prevent gifts hold-over relief being used for tax-avoidance purposes. For example, restrictions may apply where an individual gifts assets to trustees administering a trust in which the individual retains an interest or the assets transferred comprise a dwelling-house. Subject to these exceptions, the effect of a valid claim for hold-over relief is similar to a claim for roll-over relief on the disposal of business assets.

OTHER CGT RELIEFS

There are certain other CGT reliefs available on the disposal of property, shares and business assets. For detailed information on all CGT reliefs and for more general guidance on CGT visit W www.gov.uk/personal-tax/capital-gains-tax

REPORTING AND PAYING CGT

Individuals are responsible for telling HMRC about capital gains on which they have to pay tax. Individuals who receive a self-assessment tax return may report capital gains by filling in the capital gains supplementary pages – the return explains how to obtain these pages if needed.

Individuals who do not normally complete a tax return but who need to report capital gains or losses should contact their local tax office.

There is a time limit for claiming capital losses. The deadline is four years from 31 January after the end of the tax year in which the loss was made.

INHERITANCE TAX

Inheritance tax (IHT) is a tax on the value of a person's estate on death and on certain gifts made by an individual during his or her lifetime, usually payable within six months of death. Broadly speaking, a person's estate is everything he or she owned at the time of death including property, possessions, money and investments, less his or her debts. Not everyone pays IHT. It only applies if the taxable value of an estate is above the current IHT threshold. If an estate, including any assets held in trust and gifts made within seven years of death, is less than the threshold, no IHT will be due.

The nil-rate band for 2015–16 is £329,000, the first increase since the nil-rate band was frozen at £325,000 in 2010.

A claim can be made to transfer any unused IHT nil-rate band on a person's death to the estate of their surviving spouse or civil partner. This applies where the IHT nil-rate band of the first deceased spouse or civil partner was not fully used in calculating the IHT liability of their estate. When the surviving spouse or civil partner dies, the unused amount may be added to their own nil-rate band (*see* below for details).

IHT used to be something only very wealthy individuals needed to consider. This is no longer the case. The fact that the IHT threshold has not kept pace with house price inflation in recent years means that the estates of some 'ordinary' taxpayers are now liable for IHT purely because of the value of their home. However, there are a number of ways that individuals – while still alive – can legally reduce the IHT bill that will apply to their estates on death. Several valuable IHT exemptions are available (explained further below) which allow individuals to pass on assets during their lifetime or in their will without any IHT being due. Detailed information on IHT is available at W www.gov.uk/inheritance-tax Further help is also available from the Probate and Inheritance Helpline (T 0300-123 1072).

DOMICILE

Liability to IHT depends on an individual's domicile at the time of any gift or on death. Domicile is a complex legal concept and what follows explains some of the main issues. An individual is domiciled in the country where he or she has a permanent home. Domicile is different from nationality or residence, and an individual can only have one domicile at any given time.

A 'domicile of origin' is normally acquired from the individual's father on birth, though this may not be the country in which he or she is born. For example, a child born in Germany while his or her father is working there, but whose permanent home is in the UK, will have the UK as his or her domicile of origin. Until a person legally changes his or her domicile, it will be the same as that of the person on whom they are legally dependent.

Individuals can legally acquire a new domicile – a 'domicile of choice' – from the age of 16 by leaving the current country of domicile and settling in another country and providing strong evidence of intention to live there permanently or indefinitely. Women who were married before 1974 acquired their husband's domicile and still retain it until they legally acquire a new domicile.

For IHT purposes, there is a concept of 'deemed domicile'. This means that even if a person is not domiciled in the UK under general law, he or she is treated as domiciled in the UK at the time of a transfer (ie at the time of a lifetime gift or on death) if he or she (a) was domiciled in the UK within the three years immediately before the transfer, or (b) was 'resident' in the UK in at least 17 of the 20 income tax years of assessment ending with the year in which a transfer is made. Where a person is domiciled, or treated as domiciled, in the UK at the time of a gift or on death, the location of assets is immaterial and full liability to IHT arises. A non-UK domiciled individual is also liable to IHT but only on chargeable property in the UK.

The assets of husband and wife and registered civil partners are not merged for IHT purposes, except that the IHT value of assets owned by one spouse or civil partner may be affected if the other also owns similar assets (eg shares in the same company or a share in their jointly owned house). Each spouse or partner is treated as a separate individual entitled to receive the benefit of his or her exemptions, reliefs and rates of tax.

IHT EXEMPTIONS

There are some important exemptions that allow individuals to legally pass assets on to others, both before and after their death – without being subject to IHT.

Exempt Beneficiaries

Assets can be given away to certain people and organisations without any IHT having to be paid. These gifts, which are exempt whether individuals make them during their lifetime or in their will, include gifts to:

- a husband, wife or civil partner, even if the couple is legally separated (but not if they are divorced or the civil partnership has dissolved). Note that gifts to an unmarried partner or a partner with whom the donor has not formed a civil partnership are not exempt
- a 'qualifying' charity established in the EU or another specified country
- some national institutions, including national museums, universities and the National Trust
- UK political parties

Annual Exemption

The first £3,000 of gifts made each tax year by each individual is exempt from IHT. If this exemption is not used, or not wholly used in any year, the balance may be carried forward to the following year only. A couple, therefore, may give away a total of £6,000 per tax year between them or £12,000 if they have not used their previous year's annual exemptions.

Wedding Gifts / Civil Partnership Ceremony Gifts

Some gifts are exempt from IHT because of the type of gift or reason for making it. Wedding or civil partnership ceremony gifts made to either of the couple are exempt from IHT up to certain amounts:

- gifts by a parent, £5,000
- gifts by a grandparent or other relative, £2,500
- gifts by anyone else, £1,000

The gift must be made on or shortly before the date of the wedding or civil partnership ceremony. If the ceremony is called off but the gift is made, this exemption will not apply.

Small Gifts

An individual can make small gifts, up to the value of £250, to any number of people in any one tax year without them being liable for IHT. However, a larger sum such as £500 cannot be given and exemption claimed for the first £250. In addition, this exemption cannot be used with any other exemption when giving to the same person. For example, a parent cannot combine a 'small gifts exemption' with a 'wedding/civil partnership ceremony gift exemption' to give a child £5,250 when he or she gets married or forms a civil partnership. Neither may an individual combine a 'small gifts exemption' with the 'annual exemption' to give someone £3,250. Note that it is possible to use the 'annual exemption' with any other exemption, such as the 'wedding/civil partnership ceremony gift exemption'. For example, if a child marries or forms a civil partnership, the parent can give him or her a total IHT-free gift of £8,000 by combining £5,000 under the wedding/civil partnership gift exemption and £3,000 under the annual exemption.

Normal Expenditure

Any gifts made out of individuals' after-tax income (not capital) are exempt from IHT if they are part of their normal expenditure and do not result in a fall in their standard of living. These can include regular payments to someone, such as an allowance or gifts for Christmas or a birthday and regular premiums paid on a life insurance policy for someone else.

Maintenance Gifts

An individual can make IHT-free maintenance payments to his or her spouse or registered civil partner, ex-spouse or former civil partner, relatives dependent because of old age or infirmity, and children (including adopted children and step-children) who are under 18 or in full-time education.

POTENTIALLY EXEMPT TRANSFERS

If an individual makes a gift to either another individual or certain types of trust and it is not covered by one of the above exemptions, it is known as a 'potentially exempt transfer' (PET). A PET is only free of IHT on two strict conditions: (a) the gift must be made at least seven years before the donor's death. If the donor does not survive seven years after making the gift, it will be liable for IHT and (b) the gift must be made as a true gift with no strings attached (technically known as a 'gift with reservation of benefit'). This means that the donor must give up all rights to the gift and stop benefiting from it in any way.

If a gift is made and the donor does retain some benefit from it then it will still count as part of his or her estate no matter how long he or she lives after making it. For example, a father could make a lifetime gift of his home to his child. However, HMRC would not accept this as a true gift if the father continued to live in the home (unless he paid his child a full commercial rent to do so) because he would be considered to still have a material interest in the gifted home. Its value, therefore, would still be liable for IHT.

In some circumstances a gift with strings attached might give rise to an income tax charge on the donor based on the value of the benefit he or she retains. In this case the donor

can choose whether to pay the income tax or have the gift treated as a gift with reservation.

CHARGEABLE TRANSFERS

Any remaining lifetime gifts that are not (potentially or otherwise) exempt transfers are chargeable transfers or 'chargeable gifts', meaning that they incur liability to IHT. Chargeable transfers comprise mainly gifts to or from companies and gifts to particular types of trust. There is an immediate claim for IHT on chargeable gifts, and additional tax may be payable if the donor dies within seven years of making a chargeable gift.

DEATH

Immediately before the time of death an individual is deemed to make a transfer of value. This transfer will comprise the value of assets forming part of the deceased's estate after subtracting most liabilities. Any exempt transfers may be excluded such as transfers for the benefit of a surviving spouse or civil partner, and charities. Death may also trigger three additional liabilities:

- a PET made within the seven years before the death loses its potential status and becomes chargeable to IHT
- the value of gifts made with reservation may incur liability if any benefit was enjoyed within the seven years before the death
- additional tax may become payable for chargeable lifetime transfers made within the seven years before the death

The 'personal representative' (the person nominated to handle the affairs of the deceased person) arranges to value the estate and pay any IHT that is due. One or more personal representatives can be nominated in a person's will, in which case they are known as the 'executors'. If a person dies without leaving a will a court can nominate the personal representative, who is then known as the 'administrator'. Valuing the deceased person's estate is one of the first things his or her personal representative needs to do. The representative will not normally be able to take over management of the estate (called 'applying for probate') until all or some of any IHT that is due has been paid.

VALUATIONS

When valuing a deceased person's estate all assets (property, possessions and money) owned at the time of death and certain assets given away during the seven years before death must be included. The valuation must accurately reflect what those assets would reasonably fetch in the open market at the date of death. The value of all of the assets that the deceased owned should include:

- his or her share of any assets owned jointly with someone else, for example a house owned with a partner
- any assets that are held in a trust, from which the deceased had the right to benefit
- any assets given away, but in which he or she kept an interest (gifts with reservation)
- PETs given away within the last seven years

Most estate assets can be valued quite easily, for example money in bank accounts or stocks and shares. In other instances the help of a professional valuer may be needed. Advice on how to value different assets including joint or trust assets is available at W www.gov.uk/valuing-estate-of-someone-who-died When valuing an estate, special relief is made available for certain assets. The two main reliefs are business relief and agricultural property relief, outlined below. Once all assets have been valued, the next step is to deduct from the total assets everything that the deceased person owed such as unpaid bills, outstanding mortgages and other loans plus their funeral expenses.

The value of all of the assets, less the deductible debts, is their estate. IHT is only payable on any value above £329,000 for the tax year 2015–16 at the current rate of 40 per cent.

A new reduced rate of IHT was introduced at the beginning of the 2012–13 tax year to encourage individuals to pledge part of their estate to charity on death. Where 10 per cent or more of a deceased's net estate (after deducting IHT exemptions, reliefs and the nil-rate band) is left to charity, the 40 per cent rate is reduced to 36 per cent.

RELIEF FOR SELECTED ASSETS
Agricultural Property
If an individual owns agricultural property and it is part of a working farm, it is possible to pass on some of this property free of IHT, either during that individual's lifetime or on their death. Agricultural property generally includes land or pasture used in the growing of crops or intensive rearing of animals for food consumption. It can also include farmhouses and farm cottages. The agricultural property can be owner-occupied or let. Relief is only due if the transferor has owned the property and it has been occupied for agricultural purposes for a minimum period.

The chargeable value transferred, either on a lifetime gift or on death, must be determined. This value may then be reduced by a percentage. Depending on the type of property, it will normally qualify for relief of 100 per cent.

Business Relief
Business relief is available on transfers of certain types of business and of business assets if they qualify as relevant business property and the transferor has owned them for a minimum period. The relief can be claimed for transfers made during the person's lifetime or on their death. Where the chargeable value transferred is attributable to relevant business property, the business relief reduces that value by a percentage of either 50 or 100 per cent, depending on the type of asset. Business relief may be claimed on relevant business property including property and buildings or assets such as unlisted shares or machinery.

It is a general requirement that the property must have been retained for a period of two years before the transfer or death, and restrictions may be necessary if the property has not been used wholly for business purposes. The same property cannot obtain both business property relief and the relief available for agricultural property.

CALCULATION OF TAX PAYABLE
The calculation of IHT payable adopts the use of a cumulative or 'running' total. Looking back seven years from the death the chargeable value of gifts in that period is added to the total value of the estate at death. The gifts will use up all or part of the inheritance tax threshold (the 'nil-rate band' above which IHT becomes payable) first.

Lifetime Chargeable Transfers
The value transferred by lifetime chargeable transfers must be added to the seven-year running total to calculate whether any IHT is due. If the nil-rate band is exceeded, tax will be imposed on the excess at the rate of 20 per cent. However, if the donor dies within a period of seven years from the date of the chargeable lifetime transfer, additional tax may be due. This is calculated by applying tax at the full rate of 40 per cent in substitution for the rate of 20 per cent previously used. The amount of tax is then reduced to a percentage by applying tapering relief. This percentage is governed by the number of years from the date of the lifetime gift to the date of death, as follows:

PERIOD OF YEARS BEFORE DEATH

Not more than 3	100%
More than 3 but not more than 4	80%
More than 4 but not more than 5	60%
More than 5 but not more than 6	40%
More than 6 but not more than 7	20%

Should this exercise produce liability greater than that previously paid at the 20 per cent rate on the lifetime transfer, additional tax, representing the difference, must be paid. Where the calculation shows an amount falling below tax paid on the lifetime transfer, no additional liability can arise nor will the shortfall become repayable.

Tapering relief is, of course, only available if the calculation discloses a liability to IHT. There is no liability if the lifetime transfer falls within the nil-rate band.

Potentially Exempt Transfers
Where a PET loses immunity from liability to IHT because the donor dies within seven years of making the transfer, the value transferred enters into the running total. Any liability to IHT will be calculated by applying the full rate of 40 per cent, reduced to the percentage governed by tapering relief if the original transfer occurred more than three years before death. Again, liability to IHT can only arise if the nil-rate band is exceeded.

Death
On death, IHT is due on the value of the deceased's estate plus the running total of gifts made in the seven years before death if these come to more than the nil-rate band. IHT is then charged at the full rate of 40 per cent on the amount in excess of the nil-rate band.

Settled Property and Trusts
Trusts are special legal arrangements that can be used by individuals to control how their assets are distributed to their beneficiaries and minimise their IHT liability. Complex rules apply to establish IHT liability on settled property which includes property held in trust, and individuals are advised to take expert legal advice when setting up trusts.

RATES OF TAX
There are four rates:

- a nil-rate
- a lifetime rate of 20 per cent
- a full rate of 40 per cent
- a reduced rate of 36 per cent applicable to taxable estates where 10 per cent of the net estate has been left to charity (see above)

After being frozen for several years the nil-rate band has increased by 1 per cent to £329,000 for 2015–16. Any excess over this level is taxable at 20 per cent, 40 per cent or 36 per cent as the case may be.

TRANSFER OF NIL-RATE BAND
Transfers of property between spouses or civil partners are generally exempt from IHT. This means that someone who dies leaving some or all of their property to their spouse or civil partner may not have fully used up their nil-rate band. Under rules introduced in autumn 2007, any nil-rate band unused on the first death can be used when the surviving spouse or civil partner dies. A transfer of unused nil-rate band from a deceased spouse or civil partner (no matter what the date of their death) may be made to the estate of their surviving spouse or civil partner.

Where a valid claim to transfer unused nil-rate band is made, the nil-rate band that is available when the surviving spouse or civil partner dies is increased by the proportion of the nil-rate band unused on the first death. For example, if on the first death the chargeable estate is £150,000 and the nil-rate band is £300,000, 50 per cent of the nil-rate band would be unused. If the nil-rate band when the survivor dies is £329,000, then that would be increased by 50 per cent to £493,500. The amount of the nil-rate band that can be transferred does not depend on the value of the first spouse or civil partner's estate. Whatever proportion of the nil-rate band is unused on the first death is available for transfer to the survivor.

The amount of additional nil-rate band that can be accumulated by any one surviving spouse or civil partner is limited to the value of the nil-rate band in force at the time of their death. This may be relevant where a person dies having survived more than one spouse or civil partner.

Where these rules have effect, personal representatives do not have to claim for the unused nil-rate band to be transferred at the time of the first death. Any claims for transfer of unused nil-rate band amounts are made by the personal representatives of the estate of the second spouse or civil partner to die when they make an IHT return.

Guidance on how to transfer the nil-rate band can be found at W www.gov.uk/inheritance-tax/leaving-assets-spouse-civil-partner

PAYMENT OF TAX
IHT is normally due six months after the end of the month in which the death occurs or the chargeable transaction takes place. This is referred to as the 'due date'. Tax on some assets such as business property, certain shares and securities and land and buildings (including the deceased person's home) can be deferred and paid in equal instalments over ten years, though interest will be charged in most cases. If IHT is due on lifetime gifts and transfers, the person or transferee who received the gift or assets is normally liable to pay the IHT, though any IHT already paid at the time of a transfer into a trust or company will be taken into account. If tax owed is not paid by the due date, interest is charged on any unpaid IHT, no matter what caused the delay in payment.

It has been announced that HMRC will be investing in a new online service to support the administration of IHT. This will do away with the need to complete paper forms and enable individuals to proceed with their application for probate and submit IHT accounts online. It is anticipated that the new online service will become available in 2016.

CORPORATION TAX

Corporation tax is a tax on a company's profits, including all its income and gains. This tax is payable by UK resident companies and by non-resident companies carrying on a trade in the UK through a permanent establishment. The following comments are confined to companies resident in the UK. The word 'company' is also used to include:

- members' clubs, societies and associations
- trade associations
- housing associations
- groups of individuals carrying on a business but not as a partnership (for example, cooperatives)

A company's taxable income is charged by reference to income or gains arising in its 'accounting period', which is normally 12 months long. In some circumstances accounting periods can be shorter than 12 months, but never longer. The

accounting period is also normally the period for which a company's accounts are drawn up, but the two periods do not have to coincide.

If a company is liable to pay corporation tax on its profits, several things must be done. HMRC must be informed that the company exists and is liable for tax. A self-assessment company tax return plus full accounts and calculation of tax liability must be filed by the statutory filing date, normally 12 months after the end of the accounting period. Companies have to work out their own tax liability and have to pay their tax without prior assessment by HMRC. Records of all company expenditure and income must be kept in order to work out the tax liability correctly. Companies are liable to penalties if they fail to carry out these obligations.

A radically simpler way for small self-employed businesses, such as sole traders and partnerships, to calculate their tax was introduced with effect from the 2013–14 tax year. Such businesses with receipts of up to £81,000 are able to work out their income on a cash basis and use simplified expenses rules, rather than having to follow the rules for larger businesses. Limited companies and limited liability partnerships can not use cash basis. If a small business uses cash basis accounting and the business grows during the tax year, it can stay in the scheme up to a total business income of £162,000 a year.

Corporation tax information is available at W www.gov.uk/browse/business/business-tax and companies may file their company tax returns online (W www.gov.uk/file-your-company-accounts-and-tax-return).

RATE OF TAX
The rate of corporation tax is fixed for a financial year starting on 1 April and ending on the following 31 March. If a company's accounting period does not coincide with the financial year, its profits must be apportioned between the financial years and the tax rates for each financial year applied to those profits. The corporation tax liability is the total tax for both financial years.

A major change to corporation tax rates, first announced in the 2013 Budget, was brought in for the tax year 2015–16. For many years previously, corporation tax rates were based on three thresholds. Small companies with taxable profits up to £300,000 were taxed at the small profits rate: 20 per cent for 2014–15 and 2013–14. Companies with taxable profits between £300,001 and £1,500,000 were taxed at the marginal rate: 21.25 per cent in 2014–15 and 23.75 per cent in 2013–14. Companies with taxable profits over £1,500,000 were taxed at the main rate of corporation tax: 21 per cent for 2014–15 and 23 per cent for 2013–14.

From 1 April 2015, the main rate of corporation tax was reduced to 20 per cent, thereby unifying the small profits rate and the main rate, eliminating marginal relief and giving UK companies a single 20 per cent rate of corporation tax.

CORPORATION TAX ON PROFITS

£ per year	2015–16	2014–15
£0–£300,000	20%	20%
£300,001–£1,500,000	20%	Marginal relief
£1,500,001 or more	20%	21%

CAPITAL ALLOWANCES
Businesses can claim tax allowances, called capital allowances, on certain purchases or investments. This means that a proportion of these costs can be deducted from a business' taxable profits and reduce its tax bill. Capital

allowances are currently available on plant and machinery, buildings, and research and development. The amount of the allowance depends on what is being claimed for.

Detailed information on capital allowances is available at W www.gov.uk/capital-allowances/overview

PAYMENT OF TAX

Corporation tax liabilities are normally due and payable in a single lump sum not later than nine months and one day after the end of the accounting period. For 'large' companies – those with profits over £1.5m – there is a requirement to pay corporation tax in four quarterly instalments. Where a company is a member of a group, the profits of the entire group must be merged to establish whether the company is 'large'.

HMRC runs a Business Payment Support Service (BPSS) which allows businesses facing temporary financial difficulties more time to pay their tax bills. Traders concerned about their ability to meet corporation tax, VAT or other payments owed to HMRC can call the Business Payment Support Line (T 0300-200 3835) seven days a week. This helpline is for new enquiries only, not for traders who have already been contacted by HMRC about an overdue payment. For details of the service visit W www.gov.uk/government/organisations/hm-revenue-customs/contact/business-payment-support-service

CAPITAL GAINS

Chargeable gains arising to a company are calculated in a manner similar to that used for individuals. However, companies are not entitled to the CGT annual exemption. Companies do not suffer CGT on chargeable gains but incur liability to corporation tax instead. Tax is due on the full chargeable gain of an accounting period after subtracting relief for any losses.

GROUPS OF COMPANIES

Each company within a group is separately charged corporation tax on profits, gains and income. However, where one group member realises a loss for which special rules apply, other than a capital loss, a claim may be made to offset the deficiency against profits of some other member of the same group. The transfer of capital assets from one member of a group to a fellow member will usually incur no liability to tax on chargeable gains.

SPORTS CLUBS

Though corporation tax is payable by unincorporated associations, including most sports clubs on their profits, a substantial exemption from liability to corporation tax is available to qualifying registered community amateur sports clubs (CASCs). Sports clubs that are registered as CASCs are exempt from liability to corporation tax on:

• profits from trading where the turnover of the trade is less than £30,000 in a 12-month period
• income from letting property where the gross rental income is less than £20,000 in a 12-month period
• bank and building society interest received
• chargeable gains
• any Gift Aid donations

All of the exemptions depend upon the club having been a registered CASC for the whole of the relevant accounting period and the income or gains being used only for qualifying purposes. If the club has only been a registered CASC for part of an accounting period the exemption amounts of £50,000 (for trading) and £30,000 (for income from property) are reduced proportionately. Only interest and gains received after the club is registered are exempted.

Some of the rules for CASCs changed on 1 April 2015. Full details can be found at W www.gov.uk/government/publications/community-amateur-sports-clubs-detailed-guidance-notes

Charities are also generally exempt from corporation tax where they operate through a company structure.

VALUE ADDED TAX

Value added tax (VAT) is a tax on consumer expenditure charged when an individual buys goods and services in the European Union, including the UK. It is normally included in the sale price of goods and services and paid at the point of purchase. Each EU country has its own rate of VAT. From a business point of view, VAT is charged on most business transactions involving the supply of goods and services by a registered trader in the UK and Isle of Man. It is also charged on goods and some services imported from places outside the EU and on goods and some services coming into the UK from the other EU countries. VAT is administered by HMRC. A wide range of information on VAT, including VAT forms, is available online (W www.gov.uk/business-tax/vat). HMRC also runs a VAT Enquiries helpline (T 0300-200 3700).

RATES OF TAX

There are three rates of VAT in the UK. The standard rate, payable on most goods and services in the UK, is 20 per cent.

The reduced rate – currently 5 per cent – is payable on certain goods and services including, for example, domestic fuel and power, children's car seats, women's sanitary products, contraceptive products, smoking cessation products and the installation of energy-saving materials such as wall insulation and solar panels.

A zero, or nil, rate applies to certain items including, for example, children's clothes, books, newspapers, most food and drink, and drugs and aids for disabled people. There are numerous exceptions to the zero-rated categories, however. While most food and drink is zero-rated, items including ice creams, chocolates, sweets, potato crisps and alcoholic drinks are not. Neither are drinks or items sold for consumption in a restaurant or cafe. Takeaway cold items such as sandwiches are zero-rated, while takeaway hot foods like fish and chips are not.

REGISTRATION

All traders, including professional persons and companies, must register for VAT if they are making 'taxable supplies' of a value exceeding stated limits. All goods and services that are VAT-rated are defined as 'taxable supplies' including zero-rated items which must be included when calculating the total value of a trader's taxable supplies – his or her 'taxable turnover'. The limits that govern mandatory registration are amended periodically.

An unregistered trader must register for VAT if:

• at the end of any month the total value of his or her taxable turnover (not just profit) for the past 12 months or less is more than the current VAT threshold of £82,000
and
• at any time he or she has reasonable grounds to expect that his or her taxable turnover will be more than the current registration threshold of £82,000 in the next 30 days alone

To register for VAT, one or more forms must be completed and sent to HMRC within 30 days of any of the above. Basic VAT registration can currently be completed online (W https://online.hmrc.gov.uk/registration/). Traders who do not register at the correct time can be fined. Traders must charge VAT on their taxable supplies from the date they first need to be registered. Traders who only supply zero-rated goods may not have to register for VAT even if their taxable turnover goes above the registration threshold. However, a trader in this position must inform HMRC first and apply to be 'exempt from registration'. A trader whose taxable turnover does not reach the mandatory registration limit may choose to register for VAT voluntarily if what he or she does counts as a business for VAT purposes. This step may be thought advisable to recover input tax (see below) or to compete with other registered traders. Registered traders may submit an application for deregistration if their taxable turnover subsequently falls. An application for deregistration can be made if the taxable turnover for the year beginning on the application date is not expected to exceed £80,000.

INPUT TAX

Registered traders suffer input tax when buying in goods or services for the purposes of their business. It is the VAT that traders pay out to their suppliers on goods and services coming *in* to their business. Relief can usually be obtained for input tax suffered, either by setting that tax against output tax due or by repayment. Most items of input tax can be relieved in this manner. Where a registered trader makes both exempt supplies and taxable supplies to his customers or clients, there may be some restriction in the amount of input tax that can be recovered.

OUTPUT TAX

When making a taxable supply of goods or services, registered traders must account for output tax, if any, on the value of that supply. Output tax is the term used to describe the VAT on the goods and services that they supply or sell – the VAT on supplies going *out* of the business and collected from customers on each sale made. Usually the price charged by the registered trader will be increased by adding VAT, but failure to make the required addition will not remove liability to account for output tax. The liability to account for output tax, and also relief for input tax, may be affected where a trader is using a special secondhand goods scheme.

EXEMPT SUPPLIES

VAT is not chargeable on certain goods and services because the law deems them 'exempt' from VAT. These include the provision of burial and cremation facilities, insurance, loans of money, certain types of education and training and some property transactions. The granting of a lease to occupy land or the sale of land will usually comprise an exempt supply, for example, but there are numerous exceptions. Exempt supplies do not enter into the calculation of taxable turnover that governs liability to mandatory registration (see above). Such supplies made by a registered trader may, however, limit the amount of input tax that can be relieved. It is for this reason that the exemption may be useful.

COLLECTION OF TAX

Registered traders submit VAT returns for accounting periods usually of three months in duration, but arrangements can be made to submit returns on a monthly basis. Very large traders must account for tax on a monthly basis, but this does not affect the three-monthly return. The return will show both the output tax due for supplies made by the trader in the accounting period and also the input tax for which relief is claimed. If the output tax exceeds input tax the balance must be remitted with the VAT return. Where input tax suffered exceeds the output tax due, the registered trader may claim the excess from HMRC.

This basis for collecting tax explains the structure of VAT. Where supplies are made between registered traders the supplier will account for an amount of tax that will usually be identical to the tax recovered by the person to whom the supply is made. However, where the supply is made to a person who is not a registered trader there can be no recovery of input tax and it is on this person that the final burden of VAT eventually falls. Where goods are acquired by a UK trader from a supplier within the EU, the trader must also account for the tax due on acquisition. There are a number of simplified arrangements to make VAT accounting easier for businesses, particularly small businesses, and there is advice on the HMRC website about how to choose the most appropriate scheme for a business:

Cash Accounting
This scheme allows businesses to only pay VAT on the basis of payments received from their customers rather than on invoice dates or time of supply. It can therefore be useful for businesses with cash flow problems that cannot pay their VAT as a result. Businesses may use the cash accounting scheme if taxable turnover is under £1.35m. There is no need to apply for the scheme – eligible businesses may start using it at the beginning of a new tax period. If a trader opts to use this scheme, he or she can do so until the taxable turnover reaches £1.6m.

Annual Accounting
If taxable turnover is under £1.35m a year, the trader may join the annual accounting scheme which allows them to make nine monthly or three quarterly instalments during the year based on an estimate of their total annual VAT bill. At the end of the year they submit a single return and any balance due. The advantages of this scheme for businesses are easier budgeting and cash flow planning because fixed payments are spread regularly throughout the year. Once a trader has joined the annual accounting scheme, membership may continue until the annual taxable turnover reaches £1.6m.

Flat Rate Scheme
This scheme allows small businesses with an annual taxable turnover of less than £150,000 to save on administration by paying VAT as a set flat percentage of their annual turnover instead of accounting internally for VAT on each individual 'in and out'. The percentage rate used is governed by the trade sector into which the business falls. The scheme can no longer be used once annual income exceeds £230,000.

Retail Schemes
There are special schemes that offer retailers an alternative if it is impractical for them to issue invoices for a large number of supplies direct to the public. These schemes include a provision to claim relief from VAT on bad debts where goods or services are supplied to a customer who does not pay for them.

VAT FACT SUMMARY
from 1 April 2015

Standard rate	20%
Reduced rate	5%
Registration (last 12 months or next 30 days)	£82,000
Deregistration (next 12 months under)	£80,000
Cash accounting scheme – up to	£1,350,000
Flat rate scheme – up to	£150,000
Annual accounting scheme – up to	£1,350,000

STAMP DUTY

For the majority of people, contact with stamp duty arises when they buy a property. Stamp duty is payable by the buyer as a way of raising revenue for the government based on the purchase price of a property, stocks and shares. This section aims to provide a broad overview of stamp duty as it may affect the average person.

STAMP DUTY LAND TAX

Stamp duty land tax was introduced on 1 December 2003 and covers the purchase of houses, flats and other land, buildings and certain leases in the UK.

Before 1 December 2003 property purchasers had to submit documents providing all details of the purchase to the Stamp Office for 'stamping'. The purchaser's solicitor or licensed conveyancer would then send the stamped documentation to the appropriate land registry to register ownership of the property. Under stamp duty land tax, purchasers do not have to send documents for stamping. Instead, a land transaction return form SDLT1, which contains all information regarding the purchase that is relevant to HMRC, is signed by the purchaser. Buyers of property are responsible for completing the land transaction return and payment of stamp duty, though the solicitor or licensed conveyancer acting for them in a land transaction will normally complete the relevant paperwork. Once HMRC has received the completed land transaction return and the payment of any stamp duty due, a certificate will be issued that enables a solicitor or licensed conveyancer to register the property in the new owner's name at the Land Registry.

The threshold for notification of residential property is currently £40,000. This means that taxpayers entering into a transaction involving residential or non-residential property where the chargeable consideration is less than £40,000 do not need to notify HMRC about the transaction.

Since 1 April 2015 stamp duty has no longer applied to land transactions in Scotland. These are now subject to land and buildings transaction tax, details of which can be found online (W www.gov.uk/sdlt-scottish-transactions).

RATES OF STAMP DUTY LAND TAX

Stamp duty is charged at different rates and has thresholds for different types of property and different values of transaction. The tax rate and payment threshold can vary according to whether the property is in residential or non-residential use and whether it is freehold or leasehold.

The government amended the rates and changed the calculation of stamp duty on purchases of residential property on 4 December 2014.

Previously, stamp duty was charged at a single rate for the entire price of a property. When assessing how much stamp duty was payable, the entire purchase price had to be taken into account so that the relevant stamp duty rate was paid on the whole sum, not just on the amount over each tax threshold. For example, on a property bought for £250,000, 1 per cent (£2,500) was payable in stamp duty. On a property bought for £250,001, however, 3 per cent of the whole price (£7,500) was payable.

Since 4 December 2014, however, stamp duty on purchases of residential property has been charged at increasing rates for each portion of the price.

For 2015–16, stamp duty is payable at the following rates on a residential property purchase: nothing on the first £125,000 of the property price; 2 per cent on the next £125,000; 5 per cent on the next £675,000; 10 per cent on the next £575,000 and 12 per cent on the rest.

For example, on a property bought for £275,000, a total of £3,750 is payable in stamp duty. This is made up of: nothing on the first £125,000, £2,500 (2 per cent) on the next £125,000 and £1,250 (5 per cent) on the remaining £25,000.

Stamp duty on residential property purchases 2015–16:

Portion of the transaction value	Stamp duty is charged at
Up to £125,000	zero
Between £125,001 and £250,000	2 per cent
Between £250,001 and £925,000	5 per cent
Between £925,001 and £1,500,000	10 per cent
Over £150,000,000	12 per cent

Stamp duty is charged at 15 per cent on residential properties costing more than £500,000 bought by bodies such as companies and collective investment schemes, though there are some exceptions. For example, stamp duty is payable based on the new rates and bands in the table above where the property is used for a property rental business.

On purchases of non-residential and mixed-use properties, stamp duty is payable at the following rates:

• nothing on the property price, premium or value up to £150,000 (annual rent less than £1,000)
• 1 per cent on properties up to £150,000 (annual rent £1,000 or more)
• 1 per cent on properties between £150,001 and £250,000 (rent £1,000 or more)
• 3 per cent on properties between £250,001 and £500,000 (rent £1,000 or more)
• 4 per cent on properties over £500,000 (rent £1,000 or more)

To work out the amount of stamp duty payable on residential or non-residential property, a stamp duty land tax calculator is available online (W www.hmrc.gov.uk/tools/sdlt/land-and-property.htm).

STAMP DUTY RESERVE TAX

Stamp duty or stamp duty reserve tax (SDRT) is payable at the rate of 0.5 per cent when shares are purchased. Stamp duty is payable when the shares are transferred using a stock transfer form, whereas SDRT is payable on 'paperless' share transactions where the shares are transferred electronically without using a stock transfer form. Most share transactions nowadays are paperless and settled by stockbrokers through CREST (the electronic settlement and registration system). SDRT therefore now accounts for the majority of taxation collected on share transactions effected through the London Stock Exchange.

The flat rate of 0.5 per cent is based on the amount paid for the shares, not what they are worth. If, for example, shares are bought for £2,000, £10 SDRT is payable, whatever the value of the shares themselves. If shares are transferred for free, no SDRT is payable.

A higher rate of 1.5 per cent is payable where shares are transferred into a 'depositary receipt scheme' or a 'clearance service'. These are special arrangements where the shares are held by a third party.

CREST automatically deducts the SDRT and sends it to HMRC. A stockbroker will settle up with CREST for the cost of the shares and the SDRT and then bill the purchaser for these and the broker's fees. If shares are not purchased through CREST, the stamp duty must be paid by the purchaser to HMRC.

UK stamp duty or SDRT is not payable on the purchase of foreign shares, though there may be foreign taxes to pay. SDRT is already accounted for in the price paid for units in unit trusts or shares in open-ended investment companies.

HELP AND INFORMATION

Further information on stamp duty land tax and SDRT is available via the stamp taxes helpline on T 0300-200 3510 or the government information website (W www.gov.uk).

LEGAL NOTES

These notes outline certain aspects of the law as they might affect the average person. They are intended only as a broad guideline and are by no means definitive. The law is constantly changing so expert advice should always be taken. In some cases, sources of further information are given in these notes.

It is always advisable to consult a solicitor without delay. Anyone who does not have a solicitor can contact the following for assistance in finding one: Citizens Advice (W www.citizensadvice.org.uk), the Community Legal Service (W www.gov.uk) or the Law Society of England and Wales. For assistance in Scotland, contact Citizens Advice Scotland (W www.cas.org.uk) or the Law Society of Scotland.

Legal aid schemes exist to make the help of a lawyer available to those who would not otherwise be able to afford one. Entitlement for most types of legal aid depends on an individual's means but a solicitor or Citizens Advice will be able to advise on this.

LAW SOCIETY OF ENGLAND AND WALES,
113 Chancery Lane, London WC2A 1PL T 020-7242 1222
W www.lawsociety.org.uk
LAW SOCIETY OF SCOTLAND, 26 Drumsheugh Gardens,
Edinburgh EH3 7YR T 0131-226 7411 W www.lawscot.org.uk

ABORTION

Abortion is governed by the Abortion Act 1967. Under its provisions, a legally induced abortion must be:
• performed by a registered medical practitioner
• carried out in an NHS hospital or other approved premises
• certified by two registered medical practitioners as justified on one or more of the following grounds:
(a) that the pregnancy has not exceeded its 24th week and that the continuance of the pregnancy would involve risk, greater than if the pregnancy were terminated, of injury to the physical or mental health of the pregnant woman or any existing children of her family
(b) that the termination is necessary to prevent grave permanent injury to the physical or mental health of the pregnant woman
(c) that the continuance of the pregnancy would involve risk to the life of the pregnant woman, greater than if the pregnancy were terminated
(d) that there is a substantial risk that if the child were born it would suffer from such physical or mental abnormalities as to be seriously handicapped.
In determining whether the continuance of a pregnancy would involve such risk of injury to health as is mentioned in grounds (a) or (b), account may be taken of the pregnant woman's actual or reasonably foreseeable environment.

The requirements relating to the opinion of two registered medical practitioners and to the performance of the abortion at an NHS hospital or other approved place cease to apply in circumstances where a registered medical practitioner is of the opinion, formed in good faith, that a termination is immediately necessary to save the life, or to prevent grave permanent injury to the physical or mental health, of the pregnant woman.

The Abortion Act 1967 does not apply to Northern Ireland, where abortion is not legal.

FAMILY PLANNING ASSOCIATION (UK),
23–28 Penn Street, London N1 5DL T 020-7608 5240
W www.fpa.org.uk

BRITISH PREGNANCY ADVISORY SERVICE (BPAS),
20 Timothys Bridge Road, Stratford-upon-Avon CV37 9BF
T 0345-365 5050 W www.bpas.org

ADOPTION OF CHILDREN

The Adoption and Children Act 2002 reformed the framework for domestic and intercountry adoption in England and Wales and some parts of it extend to Scotland and Northern Ireland. The Children and Adoption Act 2006, recently amended by the Children and Families Act 2014, introduced further provisions for adoptions involving a foreign element.

WHO MAY APPLY FOR AN ADOPTION ORDER
A couple (whether married or two people living as partners in an enduring family relationship) may apply for an adoption order where both of them are over 21 or where one is only 18 but the natural parent and the other is 21. An adoption order may be made for one applicant where that person is 21 and: a) the court is satisfied that person is the partner of a parent of the person to be adopted; or b) they are not married and are not civil partners; or c) married or in a civil partnership but they are separated from their spouse or civil partner and living apart with the separation likely to be permanent; or d) their spouse/civil partner is either unable to be found, or their spouse/civil partner is incapable by reason of ill-health of making an application. There are certain qualifying conditions an applicant must meet, eg residency in the British Isles.

ARRANGING AN ADOPTION
Adoptions may generally only be arranged by an adoption agency or by way of an order from the high court; breach of the restrictions on who may arrange an adoption would constitute a criminal offence. When deciding whether a child should be placed for adoption, the court or adoption agency must consider all the factors set out in the 'welfare checklist' – the paramount consideration being the child's welfare, throughout his or her life. These factors include the child's wishes, needs, age, sex, background and any harm which the child has suffered or is likely to suffer. At all times, the court or adoption agency must bear in mind that delay is likely to prejudice a child's welfare.

ADOPTION ORDER
Once an adoption has been arranged, a court order is necessary to make it legal; this may be obtained from the high court, county court or magistrates' court (including the family proceedings court). An adoption order may not be given unless the court is satisfied that the consent of the child's natural parents (or guardians) has been given correctly. Consent can be dispensed with on two grounds: where the parent or guardian cannot be found or is incapable of giving consent, or where the welfare of the child so demands.

An adoption order extinguishes the parental responsibility that a person other than the adopters (or adopter) has for the child. Where an order is made on the application of the partner of the parent, that parent keeps parental responsibility. Once adopted, the child has the same status as a child born to the adoptive parents, but may lose rights to the estates of those losing their parental responsibility.

REGISTRATION AND CERTIFICATES
All adoption orders made in England and Wales are required to be registered in the Adopted Children Register which also

contains particulars of children adopted under registrable foreign adoptions. The General Register Office keeps this register from which certificates may be obtained in a similar way to birth certificates. The General Register Office also has equivalents in Scotland and Northern Ireland.

TRACING NATURAL PARENTS OR CHILDREN WHO HAVE BEEN ADOPTED

An adult adopted person may apply to the Registrar-General to obtain a certified copy of his/her birth certificate. Adoption agencies and adoption support agencies should provide services to adopted persons to assist them in obtaining information about their adoption and facilitate contact with their relatives. There is an Adoption Contact Register which provides a safe and confidential way for birth parents and other relatives to assure an adopted person that contact would be welcome. The BAAF (see below) can provide addresses of organisations which offer advice, information and counselling to adopted people, adoptive parents and people who have had their children adopted.

BRITISH ASSOCIATION FOR ADOPTION AND FOSTERING (BAAF), Saffron House, 6–10 Kirby Street, London EC1N 8TS T 020-7421 2600 W www.baaf.org.uk

SCOTLAND

The relevant legislation is the Adoption and Children (Scotland) Act 2007 which came into force on 28 September 2009. In addition, adoptions with a foreign element are governed by the Adoptions with a Foreign Element (Scotland) Regulations 2009. Pre-2009 adoptions are governed by Part IV of the Adoption (Scotland) Act 1978. The provisions of the 2007 act are similar to those described above. In Scotland, petitions for adoption are made to the sheriff court or the court of session.

BRITISH ASSOCIATION FOR ADOPTION AND FOSTERING (BAAF), BAAF Scottish Centre, 113 Rose Street, Edinburgh EH2 3DT T 0131-226 9270

BIRTHS (REGISTRATION)

It is the duty of the parents of a child born in England or Wales to register the birth within 42 days of the date of birth at the register office in the district in which the baby was born. If it is inconvenient to go to the district where the birth took place, the information for the registration may be given to a registrar in another district, who will send your details to the appropriate register office. Failure to register the birth within 42 days without reasonable cause may leave the parents liable to a penalty. If a birth has not been registered within 12 months of its occurrence it is possible for the late registration of the birth to be authorised by the Registrar-General, provided documentary evidence of the precise date and place of birth are satisfactory.

Births that take place in England may only be registered in English, but births that take place in Wales may be registered bilingually in Welsh and English. In order to do this, the details must be given in Welsh and the registrar must be able to understand and write in Welsh.

If the parents of the child were married to each other at the time of the birth (or conception), either the mother or the father may register the birth alone. If the parents were not married to each other at the time of the child's birth (or conception), the father's particulars may be entered in the register only where he attends the register office with the mother and they sign the birth register together. Where an unmarried parent is unable to attend the register office, either parent may submit to the registrar a statutory declaration on Form 16 (or Form 16W for births which took place in Wales) acknowledging the father's paternity (this form may be obtained from any registrar in England or Wales or online at W www.gro.gov.uk); alternatively a parental responsibility agreement or appropriate court order may be produced to the registrar.

If the father's details are not included in the birth register, it may be possible to re-register the birth at a later date. If the parents do not register the birth of their child the following people may do so:

- an occupier of the house or an administrative member of staff of the hospital where the child was born
- a person who was present at the birth
- a person who is responsible for the child

Upon registration of the birth a short certificate is issued. It may be possible to register the birth while still at hospital. Hospitals will advise individually whether this is possible.

SAME-SEX COUPLES

Male couples must get a parental order from the court before they can be registered as parents. Female couples can include both of their names on the child's birth certificate when registering the birth; however the rules differ depending on whether or not they are in a civil partnership.

In the case of female civil partners, either woman can register the birth on her own if all of the following are true:

- the mother had the child by donor insemination or fertility treatment
- she was in a civil partnership at the time of the treatment
- her civil partner is the child's legal parent

When a mother is not in a civil partnership, her partner can be seen as the child's second parent if both women:

- are treated together in the UK by a licensed clinic
- have made a 'parenthood agreement'

However, for both parents' details to be recorded on the birth certificate, the parents must do one of the following:

- register the birth jointly
- complete a 'statutory declaration of acknowledgement of parentage' form and one parents takes the signed form when she registers the birth
- get a document from the court (eg a court order) giving the second female parent parental responsibility and one parent shows the document when she registers the birth

BIRTHS ABROAD

There are certain countries where birth registrations may be made for British citizens overseas (for more details on British citizenship see below). The British consul or high commission may register the births and issue certificates which are then sent to the General Register Office. If a birth is registered by the British consul or high commission, the registration would show the person's claim to British citizenship, British overseas territories citizenship or British overseas citizenship. All consular birth registrations are now performed at the Foreign and Commonwealth Office's facility.

SCOTLAND

In Scotland the birth of a child must be registered within 21 days at the registration office of any registration district in Scotland.

If the child is born, either in or out of Scotland, on a ship, aircraft or land vehicle that ends its journey at any place in Scotland, the child, in most cases, will be registered as if born in that place.

CERTIFICATES OF BIRTHS, DEATHS OR MARRIAGES

Certificates of births, marriages and deaths that have taken place in England and Wales since 1837 can be obtained from the General Register Office (GRO).

Marriage or death certificates may also be obtained from the minister of the church in which the marriage or funeral took place. Any register office can advise about the best way to obtain certificates.

The fees for certificates are:

Online application:
• full certificate of birth, marriage, death or adoption, £9.25
• full certificate of birth, marriage, death or adoption with GRO reference supplied, £9.25

By postal/phone/fax application:
• full certificate of birth, marriage, death or adoption, £9.25
• full certificate of birth, marriage, death or adoption with GRO reference supplied, £9.25
• extra copies of the same birth, marriage or death certificate issued at the same time, £9.25

A priority service is available for an additional fee.

A complete set of the GRO indexes including births, deaths and marriages, civil partnerships, adoptions and provisional indexes for births and deaths up to March 2015 are available at the British Library, City of Westminster Archives Centre, Manchester Central Library, Newcastle City Library, Library of Birmingham, Bridgend Reference and Information Library and Plymouth Central Library. Copies of GRO indexes may also be held at some libraries, family history societies, local records offices and The Church of Jesus Christ of Latter Day Saints family history centres. Some organisations may not hold a complete record of indexes and a small fee may be charged by some of them. GRO indexes are also available online.

The Society of Genealogists has many records of baptisms, marriages and deaths prior to 1837.

SCOTLAND

Certificates of births, deaths or marriages that have taken place in Scotland since 1855 can be obtained from the National Records of Scotland (formerly the General Register Office for Scotland) or from the appropriate local registrar.

Applicable fees – local registrar:
• each extract or abbreviated certificate of birth, death, marriage, civil partnership or adoption within a month of registration, £10.00
• each extract or abbreviated certificate of birth, death, marriage, civil partnership or adoption outwith a month of registration, £15.00

A priority service is available for an additional fee.

The National Records of Scotland also keeps the Register of Divorces (including decrees of declaration of nullity of marriage), and holds parish registers dating from before 1855.

Applicable fees – National Records of Scotland:
• personal application, or postal, telephone or fax order: £15.00

A priority service for a response within 24 hours is available for an additional fee of £15.00.

A search of birth, death and marriage records including records of Church of Scotland parishes and other statutory records can be done at the Scotland's People Centre. There are also indexes to some of the old parish registers death and burial records in the library at the centre and indexes and images of census records from 1841–1911 are available. The charges for such searches are as follows:
• full or part-day search pass, £15.00
• Quarterly search pass, £490.00
• annual search pass, £1,450.00

Online searching is also available. For more information, visit W www.scotlandspeople.gov.uk.

THE GENERAL REGISTER OFFICE, General Register Office, Certificate Services Section, PO Box 2, Southport PR8 2JD
T 0300-123 1837 W www.gro.gov.uk/gro/content/certificates

THE NATIONAL RECORDS OF SCOTLAND, New Register House, 3 West Register Street, Edinburgh EH1 3YT
T 0131-334 0380 W www.nrscotland.gov.uk
SCOTLAND'S PEOPLE CENTRE, General Register House, 2 Princes Street, Edinburgh EH1 3YY T 0131-314 4300
W www.scotlandspeoplehub.gov.uk
THE SOCIETY OF GENEALOGISTS, 14 Charterhouse Buildings, Goswell Road, London EC1M 7BA T 020-7251 8799
W www.sog.org.uk

BRITISH NATIONALITY

There are different types of British nationality status: British citizenship; British overseas citizenship; British national (overseas); British overseas territories citizenship; British protected persons; and British subjects. The most widely held of these is British citizenship. Everyone born in the UK before 1 January 1983 became a British citizen when the British Nationality Act 1981 came into force, with the exception of children born to certain diplomatic staff working in the UK at the time. Individuals born outside the UK before 1 January 1983 but who at that date were citizens of the UK and colonies and had a right of abode in the UK also became British citizens. British citizens have the right to live permanently in the UK and are free to leave and re-enter the UK at any time.

A person born on or after 1 January 1983 in the UK (including, for this purpose, the Channel Islands and the Isle of Man) is entitled to British citizenship if he/she falls into one of the following categories:
• he/she has a parent who is a British citizen
• he/she has a parent who is settled in the UK
• he/she is a newborn infant found abandoned in the UK
• his/her parents subsequently settle in the UK or become British citizens and an application is made before he/she is 18
• he/she lives in the UK for the first ten years of his/her life and is not absent for more than 90 days in each of those years
• he/she is adopted in the UK and one of the adopters is a British citizen
• the home secretary consents to his/her registration while he/she is a minor
• if he/she has always been stateless and lives in the UK for a period of five years before his/her 22nd birthday
• if he/she has been born on or after 13 January 2010 to a parent who is a member of the UK armed forces
• if he/she has been born on or after 13 January 2010 and a parent becomes a member of the UK armed forces, and an application is made before he/she is 18

A person born outside the UK may acquire British citizenship if he/she falls into one of the following categories:
• he/she has a parent who is a British citizen otherwise than by descent, eg a parent who was born in the UK
• he/she has a parent who is a British citizen serving the crown or a European community institution overseas and was recruited to that service in the UK (including qualifying territories for those born on or after 21 May 2002) or in the European Community (for services within an EU institution); or if the applicant himself/herself has at any time been in crown, or similar, service under the government of a British overseas territory
• if he/she has been born on or after 13 January 2010 to a parent who is a member of the UK armed forces serving outside the UK and qualifying territories, is of good character and (if he/she is a minor at the time of application) all parents then alive consent in signed writing
• the home secretary consents to his/her registration while he/she is a minor

- he/she is a British overseas territories citizen, a British overseas citizen, a British subject or a British protected person and has been lawfully resident in the UK for five years
- he/she is a British overseas territories citizen who acquired that citizenship from a connection with Gibraltar
- he/she is adopted or naturalised

Where parents are married, the status of either may confer citizenship on their child. Since July 2006, both parents are able to pass on nationality even if they are not married, provided that there is satisfactory evidence of paternity. For children born before July 2006, it must be shown that there is parental consent and that the child would have an automatic claim to citizenship or entitlement to registration had the parents been married. Where parents are not married, the status of the mother determines the child's citizenship.

Under the 1981 act, Commonwealth citizens and citizens of the Republic of Ireland were entitled to registration as British citizens before 1 January 1983. In 1983, citizens of the Falkland Islands were granted British citizenship.

Renunciation of British citizenship must be registered with the home secretary and will be revoked if no new citizenship or nationality is acquired within six months. If the renunciation was required in order to retain or acquire another citizenship or nationality, the citizenship may be reacquired only once. If the renunciation was for another reason, the home secretary may allow reacquisition more than once, depending on the circumstances. The secretary of state may deprive a person of a citizenship status if he or she is satisfied that the person has done anything seriously prejudicial to the vital interests of the UK, or a British overseas territory, unless making the order would have the effect of rendering such a person stateless. A person may also be deprived of a citizenship status which results from his registration or naturalisation if the secretary of state is satisfied that the registration or naturalisation was obtained by fraud, false representation or concealment of a material fact.

BRITISH DEPENDENT TERRITORIES CITIZENSHIP
Since 26 February 2002, this category of nationality no longer exists and has been replaced by British overseas territory citizenship.

If a person had this class of nationality only by reason of a connection to the territory of Hong Kong, they lost it automatically when Hong Kong was returned to the People's Republic of China. However, if after 30 June 1997, they had no other nationality and would have become stateless, or were born after 30 June 1997 and would have been born stateless (but had a parent who was a British national (overseas) or a British overseas citizen), they became a British overseas citizen.

BRITISH OVERSEAS CITIZENSHIP
Under the 1981 act, as amended by the British Overseas Territories Act 2002, this type of citizenship was conferred on any UK and colonies citizens who did not become either a British citizen or a British overseas territories citizen on 1 January 1983 and as such is now, for most purposes, only acquired by persons who would otherwise be stateless.

BRITISH OVERSEAS TERRITORIES CITIZENSHIP
This category of nationality replaced British dependent territories citizenship. Most commonly, this form of nationality is acquired where, after 31 December 1982, a person was a citizen of the UK and colonies and did not become a British citizen, and that person, and their parents or grandparents, were born, registered or naturalised in the specified British overseas territory. However, on 21 May 2002, people became British citizens if they had British overseas territories citizenship by connection with any British overseas territory, except for the sovereign base areas of Akrotiri and Dhekelia in Cyprus.

RESIDUAL CATEGORIES
British subjects, British protected persons and British nationals (overseas) may be entitled to registration as British citizens on completion of five years' legal residence in the UK.

Citizens of the Republic of Ireland who were also British subjects before 1 January 1949 can retain that status if they fulfil certain conditions.

EUROPEAN UNION CITIZENSHIP
British citizens (including Gibraltarians who are registered for this purpose) are also EU citizens and are entitled to travel freely to other EU countries to work, study, reside and set up a business. EU citizens have the same rights with respect to the UK.

NATURALISATION
Naturalisation is granted at the discretion of the home secretary. The basic requirements are lawful residence in the UK in the five years immediately preceding application (three years if the applicant is married to, or is the civil partner of a British citizen), good character, adequate knowledge of the English, Welsh or Scottish Gaelic language, passing the UK citizenship test and an intention to reside permanently in the UK.

STATUS OF ALIENS
Aliens, being persons without any of the above forms of British nationality, may not hold public office or vote in Britain and they may not own a British ship or aircraft. Citizens of the Republic of Ireland and Commonwealth citizens are not deemed to be aliens. Certain provisions of the Immigration and Asylum Act 1999 make provision about immigration and asylum and about procedures in connection with marriage by superintendent registrar's certificate.

CONSUMER LAW

SALE OF GOODS
A sale of goods contract is the most common type of contract. It is governed by the Sale of Goods Act 1979 (as amended by the Sale and Supply of Goods Act 1994). The act provides protection for buyers by implying terms into every sale of goods contract. These terms include:
- where the seller sells goods by reference to a description, an implied term that the goods will match that description and, where the sale is by sample and description, it will not be sufficient that the bulk of the goods correspond with the sample if the goods do not also correspond with the description
- where goods are sold by a business seller, an implied term that the goods will be of satisfactory quality ie they meet the standard that a reasonable person would regard as satisfactory, taking into account any description of the goods, the price, and all other relevant circumstances. The quality of the goods includes their state and condition, relevant aspects being whether they are fit for all the purposes for which such goods are commonly supplied, their appearance and finish, freedom from minor defects and their safety and durability. This term will not be implied, however, if a buyer has examined the goods (including in a sale by sample) and should have noticed the defect or if the seller specifically drew the buyer's attention to the defect

• where goods are sold by a business seller, an implied term that the goods are reasonably fit for any purpose made known to the seller by the buyer (either expressly or by implication), unless it is shown that the buyer does not rely on the seller's judgment, or it is not reasonable for him/her to do so

Some of the above terms can be excluded from contracts by the seller. The seller's right to do this is, however, restricted by the Unfair Contract Terms Act 1977. The act offers more protection to a buyer who 'deals as a consumer' (that is where the seller is selling in the course of a business, the goods are of a type ordinarily bought for private use and the goods are bought by a buyer who is not a business buyer) and does not allow for the implied terms described above to be excluded. In a sale of second-hand goods by auction (at which individuals have the opportunity of attending the sale in person), a buyer does not deal as a consumer.

HIRE-PURCHASE AGREEMENTS
Terms similar to those implied in contracts of sales of goods are implied into contracts of hire-purchase, under the Supply of Goods (Implied Terms) Act 1973. The 1977 act limits the exclusion of these implied terms as before.

SUPPLY OF GOODS AND SERVICES
Under the Supply of Goods and Services Act 1982, similar terms are also implied in other types of contract under which ownership of goods passes, and contracts for the hire of goods (though not hire-purchase agreements). These types of contracts have additional implied terms:
• that the supplier will use reasonable care and skill in carrying out the service
• that the supplier will carry out the service in a reasonable time (unless the time has been agreed)
• that the supplier will make a reasonable charge (unless the charge has already been agreed)
The 1977 act limits the exclusion of these implied terms in a similar manner as before.

UNFAIR TERMS
The Unfair Terms in Consumer Contracts Regulations 1999 apply to contracts between business sellers (or suppliers of goods and services) and consumers. Where the terms have not been individually negotiated (ie where the terms were drafted in advance so that the consumer was unable to influence those terms), a term will be deemed unfair if it operates to the detriment of the consumer (ie causes a significant imbalance in the parties' rights and obligations arising under the contract). An unfair term does not bind the consumer but the contract may continue to bind the parties if it is capable of existing without the unfair term. The regulations contain a non-exhaustive list of terms that are regarded as potentially unfair. When a term does not fall into such a category, whether it will be regarded as fair or not will depend on many factors, including the nature of the goods or services, the surrounding circumstances (such as the bargaining strength of both parties) and the other terms in the contract. The Consumer Rights Act 2015 (see below) replaces the 1999 regulations.

CONSUMER PROTECTION
The Consumer Protection from Unfair Trading Regulations 2008 (CPRs) replaced much previous consumer protection regulation, including the majority of the Trade Descriptions Act 1968. The CPRs prohibit 31 specific practices, including pyramid schemes. In addition the CPRs prohibit business sellers from making misleading actions and misleading omissions, which cause, or are likely to cause, the average consumer to take a different transactional decision. There is also a general duty not to trade unfairly. The CPRs were amended by the Consumer Protection (Amendment) Regulations 2014, which entered into force on 1 October 2014 and introduced a new direct civil right of redress for consumers against businesses for misleading and aggressive practices, as well as extending the CPRs to cover misleading and aggressive demands for payment.

Under the Consumer Protection Act 1987, producers of goods are liable for any injury, death or damage to any property exceeding £275 caused by a defect in their product (subject to certain defences).

Consumers are also afforded protection under the Consumer Contracts (Information, Cancellation and Additional Charges) Regulations 2013, which came into force on 13 June 2014.

The Consumer Rights Act 2015, which received royal assent on 26 March 2015, consolidates many of the key provisions within existing consumer rights legislation, including the Sale of Goods Act 1979, the Supply of Goods (Implied Terms) Act 1973 and the Supply of Goods and Services Act 1982. The Act also revokes the Unfair Terms in Consumer Contracts Regulations 1999, whose relevant provisions now form part of the 2015 Act. The Act also provides a new section on digital goods. The main provisions of the Consumer Rights Act came into force in October 2015.

CONSUMER CREDIT
In matters relating to the provision of credit (or the supply of goods on hire or hire-purchase), consumers are also protected by the Consumer Credit Act 1974 (as amended by the Consumer Credit Act 2006). The act was most recently amended by a number of statutory instruments made under the Financial Services and Markets Act 2000. These came into force on 1 April 2014 and represent a major overhaul of the consumer credit regime which was carried out in order to implement the recent EU Consumer Credit Directive. Under the new regime, responsibility for consumer credit regulation has been transferred from the Office of Fair Trading (OFT), which has ceased to exist, to the Financial Conduct Authority (FCA). Previously, a licence issued by the OFT was required in order to conduct a consumer credit, consumer hire or an ancillary credit business, subject to certain exemptions. The requirement to obtain a licence from the OFT has been replaced by the need to obtain authorisation from the FCA to carry out a consumer credit 'regulated' activity, likewise subject to certain exemptions. Provisions of the 1974 Act as amended include:
• in order for a creditor to enforce a regulated agreement, the agreement must comply with certain formalities and must be properly executed. An improperly executed regulated agreement is enforceable only on an order of the court. The debtor must also be given specified information by the creditor or his/her broker or agent during the negotiations which take place before the signing of the agreement. The agreement must also state certain information to ensure that the debtor or hirer is aware of the rights and duties conferred or imposed on him/her and the protection and remedies available to him/her under the act
• the right to withdraw from or cancel some contracts depending on the circumstances. For example, subject to certain exceptions, a borrower may withdraw from a regulated credit agreement within 14 days without giving any reason. The exceptions include agreements for credit exceeding £60,260 and agreements secured on land. The right to withdraw applies only to the credit agreement itself and not to goods or services purchased with it. The borrower must also repay the credit and any interest

- if the debtor is in breach of the agreement, the creditor must serve a default notice before taking any action such as repossessing the goods
- if the agreement is a hire purchase or conditional sale agreement, the creditor cannot repossess the goods without a court order if the debtor has paid one third of the total price of the goods
- in agreements where the relationship between the creditor and the debtor is unfair to the debtor, the court may alter or set aside some of the terms of the agreement

It is intended that the statutory basis of consumer credit regulation, under the 1974 Act, will be replaced by a rules-based approach under the new regime. The FCA will be reviewing the stautory framework over the next few years and will develop rule-based alternatives where possible.

SCOTLAND

The legislation governing the sale and supply of goods applies to Scotland as follows:

- the Sale of Goods Act 1979 applies with some modifications and it has been amended by the Sale and Supply of Goods Act 1994
- the Supply of Goods (Implied Terms) Act 1973 applies
- the Supply of Goods and Services Act 1982 does not extend to Scotland but some of its provisions were introduced by the Sale and Supply of Goods Act 1994
- only Parts II and III of the Unfair Contract Terms Act 1977 apply
- the Trade Descriptions Act 1968 applies with minor modifications
- the Consumer Credit Act 1974 applies
- the Consumer Credit Act 2006 applies
- the Consumer Protection Act 1987 applies
- the General Product Safety Regulations 2005 apply
- the Unfair Terms in Consumer Contracts Regulations 1999 apply
- the Unfair Terms in Consumer Contracts (Amendment) Regulations 2001 apply
- the Consumer Protection (Distance Selling) Regulations 2000 apply
- the Sale and Supply of Goods to Consumers Regulations 2002 apply
- the Consumer Protection from Unfair Trading Regulations 2008 apply

PROCEEDINGS AGAINST THE CROWN

Until 1947, proceedings against the Crown were generally possible only by a procedure known as a petition of right, which put the private litigant at a considerable disadvantage. The Crown Proceedings Act 1947 placed the Crown (not the sovereign in his/her private capacity, but as the embodiment of the state) largely in the same position as a private individual and made proceedings in the high court involving the Crown subject to the same rules as any other case. The act did not, however, extinguish or limit the Crown's prerogative or statutory powers, and it continued the immunity of HM ships and aircraft. It also left certain Crown privileges unaffected. The act largely abolished the special procedures which previously applied to civil proceedings by and against the Crown. Civil proceedings may be initiated against the appropriate government department or, if there is doubt regarding which is the appropriate department, against the attorney-general.

In Scotland proceedings against the Crown founded on breach of contract could be taken before the 1947 act and no special procedures applied. The Crown could, however, claim certain special pleas. The 1947 act applies in part to Scotland and brings the practice of the two countries as

closely together as the different legal systems permit. As a result of the Scotland Act 1998, actions against government departments should be raised against the Lord Advocate or the advocate-general. Actions should be raised against the Lord Advocate where the department involved administers a devolved matter. Devolved matters include agriculture, education, housing, local government, health and justice. Actions should be raised against the advocate-general where the department is dealing with a reserved matter. Reserved matters include defence, foreign affairs and social security.

DEATHS

WHEN A DEATH OCCURS

If the death (including stillbirth) was expected, the doctor who attended the deceased during their final illness should be contacted. If the death was sudden or unexpected, the family doctor (if known) and police should be contacted. If the cause of death is quite clear, the doctor will provide:

- a medical certificate that shows the cause of death
- a formal notice that states that the doctor has signed the medical certificate and that explains how to get the death registered
- if the death was known to be caused by a natural illness but the doctor wishes to know more about the cause of death, he/she may ask the relatives for permission to carry out a post-mortem examination

In England and Wales a coroner is responsible for investigating deaths occurring:

- when there is no doctor who can issue a medical certificate of cause of death
- no doctor has treated the deceased during his or her last illness or when the doctor attending the patient did not see him or her within 14 days before death, or after death
- the death occurred during an operation or before recovery from the effect of an anaesthetic
- the death was sudden and unexplained or attended by suspicious circumstances
- the death might be due to an industrial injury or disease, or to accident, violence, neglect or abortion
- the death occurred in prison or in police custody

The doctor will write on the formal notice that the death has been referred to the coroner; if the post-mortem shows that death was due to natural causes, the coroner may issue a notification which gives the cause of death so that the death can be registered. If the cause of death was violent or unnatural, is still undetermined after a post-mortem, or took place in prison or police custody, the coroner must hold an inquest. The coroner must hold an inquest in these circumstances even if the death occurred abroad (and the body has been returned to England or Wales).

In Scotland the office of coroner does not exist. The local procurator fiscal inquires into sudden or suspicious deaths. A fatal accident inquiry will be held before the sheriff where the death has resulted from an accident during the course of the employment of the person who has died, or where the person who has died was in legal custody, or where the Lord Advocate deems it in the public interest that an inquiry be held.

REGISTERING A DEATH

In England and Wales the death can be registered at any register office, although if it is registered by the registrar of births and deaths for the district in which it occurred, the necessary documents can be obtained on the same day. A death which occurs in Scotland can be registered in any registration district in Scotland. Information concerning a death can be given before any registrar of births and deaths in England and Wales. The registrar will pass the relevant details to the registrar for the district where the death occurred, who will then register the death.

In England and Wales the death must normally be registered within five days (unless the registrar says this period can be extended); in Scotland within eight days. If the death has been referred to the coroner/local procurator fiscal it cannot be registered until the registrar has received authority from the coroner/local procurator fiscal to do so. Failure to register a death involves a penalty in England and Wales and may lead to a court decree being granted by a sheriff in Scotland. A stillbirth normally needs to be registered within 42 days, and at the latest within three months. In many cases this can be done at the hospital or at the local register office. In Scotland this must be done within 21 days.

If the death occurred at a house or hospital, the death may be registered by:
• any relative of the deceased
• any person present at the death
• the owner or occupier of the house or hospital if he/she knew of the occurrence of the death
• any person making the funeral arrangements with the funeral director
• an administrator from the hospital
• in Scotland, the deceased's executor or legal representative
For deaths that took place elsewhere, the death may be registered by:
• any relative of the deceased
• someone present at the death
• someone who found the body
• a person in charge of the body
• any person making the funeral arrangements with the funeral director
The majority of deaths are registered by a relative of the deceased. The registrar would normally allow one of the other listed persons to register the death only if there were no relatives available.

The person registering the death should take the medical certificate of the cause of death (signed by a doctor) with them; it is also useful, though not essential, to take the deceased's birth and marriage/civil partnership certificates, council tax bill, driving licence, passport, NHS medical card, pension documentation and life assurance details. The details given to the registrar must be absolutely correct, otherwise it may be difficult to change them later. The person registering the death should check the entry carefully before it is signed. The registrar will issue a certificate for burial or cremation, and a certificate of registration of death (commonly known as a 'death certificate' which is issued for social security purposes if the deceased received a state pension or benefits) – both free of charge. A death certificate is a certified copy of the entry in the death register; copies can be provided on payment of a fee and may be required for the following purposes, in particular by the executor or administrator when sorting out the deceased's affairs:
• the will
• bank and building society accounts
• savings bank certificates and premium bonds
• insurance policies
• pension claims
If the death occurred abroad or on a foreign ship or aircraft, the death should be registered according to the local regulations of the relevant country and a death certificate should be obtained. In many countries the death can also be registered with the British consulate in that country and a record will be kept at the General Register Office. This avoids the expense of bringing the body back.

After 12 months (three months in Scotland) of death or the finding of a dead body, no death can be registered without the written authority of the registrar-general.

BURIAL AND CREMATION

In most circumstances in England and Wales a certificate for burial or cremation must be obtained from the registrar before the burial or cremation can take place. If the death has been referred to the coroner, an order for burial or a certificate for cremation must be obtained. In Scotland a body may be buried (but not cremated) before the death is registered.

Funeral costs can normally be repaid out of the deceased's estate and should be given priority over any other claims. If the deceased has left a will it may contain directions concerning the funeral; however, these directions need not be followed by the executor.

The deceased's papers should also indicate whether a grave space had already been arranged. This information will be contained in a document known as a 'Deed of Grant'. Most town churchyards and many suburban churchyards are no longer open for burial because they are full. Most cemeteries are non-denominational and may be owned by local authorities or private companies; fees vary.

If the body is to be cremated, an application form, two cremation certificates (for which there is a charge) or a certificate for cremation if the death was referred to the coroner, and a certificate signed by the medical referee must be completed in addition to the certificate for burial or cremation (the form is not required if the coroner has issued a certificate for cremation). All the forms are available from the funeral director or crematorium. Most crematoria are run by local authorities; the fees can include the medical referee's fee and the use of the chapel. Ashes may be scattered, buried in a churchyard or cemetery, or kept.

The registrar must be notified of the date, place and means of disposal of the body within 96 hours (England and Wales) or three days (Scotland).

If the death occurred abroad or on a foreign ship or aircraft, a local burial or cremation may be arranged. If the body is to be brought back to England or Wales, a death certificate from the relevant country or an authorisation for the removal of the body from the country of death from the coroner or relevant authority, together with a certificate of embalming, will be required. The British consulate can help to arrange this documentation. To arrange a funeral in England or Wales, an authenticated translation of a foreign death certificate or a death certificate issued in Scotland or Northern Ireland which must show the cause of death, is needed, together with a certificate of no liability to register from the registrar in England and Wales in whose sub-district it is intended to bury or cremate the body. If it is intended to cremate the body, a cremation order will be required from the Home Office or a certificate for cremation. If the body is to be cremated in Scotland, an order from the Scottish government Health Department must be obtained.

THE GENERAL REGISTER OFFICE, General Register Office, PO Box 2, Southport PR8 2JD T 0300-123 1837 W www.gro.gov.uk/gro/content/certificates
THE NATIONAL RECORDS OF SCOTLAND, New Register House, 3 West Register Street, Edinburgh EH1 3YT
T 0131-334 0380 W www.nrscotland.gov.uk

DIVORCE, DISSOLUTION AND RELATED MATTERS

Divorce is the legal process which ends a marriage. The process is the same whether the parties are of the opposite or same sex pursuant to the Marriage (Same Sex Couples) Act 2013. Dissolution is a similar process which ends a civil partnership. Divorce and dissolution should be distinguished from judicial separation which does not legally dissolve the marriage/civil partnership but removes the legal requirement for a married couple to live together.

DIVORCE

An application for a matrimonial order for divorce may only be presented to the court after one year of marriage and it must be based on matters which occurred within that time. The spouse who lodges this document is known as the 'petitioner' throughout the divorce proceedings and the other spouse is the 'respondent'.

Whether the English court may or may not have jurisdiction to deal with any divorce will depend on where the parties spent their married life and whether or not one party has retained the residence in Engalnd (and Wales). If there is a dispute as to which of two jurisdictions should host the divorce, where the two jurisdictions likely to be relevant are EU countries then the usual rule is that the divocrce takes place in the country where the petition is filed first. The exception to this rule is Denmark, which opted out of the EU regulation which determines forums in this way.

If the two countries are not within the EU, or one of them is Denmark, then the forum of divorce may be determined by which is the more appropriate or convenient. An election of a country in a pre-nupital agreement can be very important in resolving that dispute, although it cannot override the 'first in time' rule between EU countries (except Denmark) referred to above (save in the case of maintenance claims).

Some EU countries have signed up to a convention which would allow a couple to elect a choice of law even in EU countries whereby one country would be required to apply the law of another. For the time being, England has not signed up to that convention, and would apply English law only, though that may change in time.

There is only one ground for divorce, namely that the marriage has broken down irretrievably. This ground must be 'proved' by one of the following facts:
• the respondent has committed adultery and the petitioner finds it intolerable to live with him/her
• the respondent has behaved in such a way that the petitioner cannot reasonably be expected to live with him/her
• the respondent has deserted the petitioner for a continuous period of at least two years
• the two spouses have lived apart for at least two years and the respondent agrees to a divorce
• the two spouses have lived apart for at least five years
If the court is satisfied that the petitioner has proved one of those facts then it must grant a decree nisi (*see* below) unless it is satisfied that the marriage has not broken down.

DECREE NISI

If the judge is satisfied that the petitioner has proved the contents of the divorce petition, a date will be set for the pronouncement of the decree nisi in open court. The decree nisi is a preliminary decree of divorce; the marriage will not be legally dissolved until the decree absolute. Neither party needs to attend and all the proceedings up to this point are usually carried out on paper.

DECREE ABSOLUTE

The final step in the divorce procedure is to obtain a decree absolute which formally ends the marriage. The petitioner can apply for this six weeks and one day after the date of the decree nisi. If the petitioner does not apply the respondent can apply, but only after three months from the earliest date on which the petitioner could have applied.

A decree absolute will not usually be granted until the parties have agreed, or the court has dealt with, the parties' financial situation (*see* below for details of financial provision).

DISSOLUTION OF CIVIL PARTNERSHIPS

The legal process for dissolution of a civil partnership follows a model closely based on divorce. Irretrievable breakdown of the partnership is the sole ground for dissolution. The facts to be proved to establish this are the same as for divorce, with the exception of adultery which, due to its legal definition, can only apply to opposite sex couples. Adultery can, however, be used as an example of unreasonable behaviour.

FINANCIAL RELIEF ANCILLARY TO DIVORCE, NULLITY AND JUDICIAL SEPARATION

Following a petition for divorce, nullity or judicial separation, it is open to either spouse or former spouse to make a claim for financial provision provided they have not remarried. It is common practice for such an application to be made at the same time, or shortly after, a divorce petition has been issued. The courts have wide powers to make financial provision where a marriage breaks down. Orders can be made for:
• spousal maintenance (periodical payments) which can be capitalised into a lump sum
• lump sum payments
• adjustment or transfer of interests in property
• adjustment of interests in trusts and settlements
• orders relating to pensions

EXERCISE OF THE COURT'S POWERS TO ORDER FINANCIAL PROVISION

The court must exercise its powers so as to achieve an outcome which is fair between the parties, although it has a wide discretion in determining what is a fair financial outcome. It will consider the worldwide assets of both parties, whether liquid or illiquid. In exercising its discretion, the court has to consider a range of statutory factors including:
• the income, earning capacity, property and other financial resources which either party has or is likely to have in the foreseeable future, including, in the case of earning capacity, any increase in that capacity which it would in the opinion of the court be reasonable to expect a party to the marriage to take steps to acquire
• the financial needs, obligations and responsibilities which each of the parties to the marriage has or is likely to have in the foreseeable future
• the standard of living enjoyed by the family before the breakdown of the marriage
• the age of each party to the marriage and the duration of the marriage
• any physical or mental disability of either of the parties to the marriage
• the contribution which each of the parties has made or is likely to make in the foreseeable future to the welfare of the family, including any contribution by looking after the home or caring for the family
• the conduct of each of the parties, if that conduct is such that it would in the opinion of the court be inequitable to disregard it
• the value to each of the parties to the marriage of any benefit which, by reason of the dissolution of that marriage, that party will lose the chance of acquiring
When considering the above factors, the court must give paramount consideration to the welfare of any child of the family.

The court has a wide discretion in considering these factors in order to achieve an outcome it considers to be fair. The court's approach changed dramatically following the House of Lords decision of *White v White* in October 2000 where it was said that, after providing for the parties' reasonable ideas the remaining assets should be shared.

In the House of Lords cases of Miller and McFarlane the court refined the thinking in the White case to say that the court should strive to achieve a fair result by considering three strands:
• the needs of the parties going forward
• compensation for any economic disparity between the parties (such as where one party has sacrificed their career to become a full-time parent)
• sharing

In October 2010, the supreme court gave judgment in *Radmacher v Granatino* which made it clear that a person now entering into a pre-nuptial agreement will be considered to have intended to be held to that agreement. However, the court will still be able to decide as to whether the agreement is fair and whether the terms setting out the financial provision on divorce should be enforced in whole or in part. The supreme court gave some guidelines on when a pre-nuptial agreement would be considered 'fair', but ultimately it depends on the facts of the individual case.

The Law Commission's Marital Property, Needs and Agreements Report, published in February 2014, proposed the introduction of 'qualifying nuptial agreements' which would be enforceable contracts allowing couples to make binding agreements concerning the financial consequences of divorce or dissolution. In order for an agreement to qualify, certain procedural safeguards would need to be met. Agreements could not be used by parties to contract out of meeting the financial needs of the other or of any children. The report is currently awaiting the government's response.

FINANCIAL PROVISION ON DISSOLUTION OF A CIVIL PARTNERSHIP

The Civil Partnership Act 2004 makes provisions for financial relief for civil partners generally and extends the same rights and responsibilities invoked by marriage. Again the court must consider a number of factors when exercising its discretion and must take into account all of the circumstances of the case while giving first consideration to the welfare of any child of the family who is under 18. The list of statutory factors the court must consider resemble those for marriage and it is likely that the interpretation of these factors will be based on the courts' interpretation of the factors relating to marriage.

COHABITING COUPLES

There is no such thing as a common law spouse. Unmarried couples do not benefit from the same statutory protection afforded to married couples. Instead, the rights of cohabitees are based on property law and trust interests. Therefore, it is advisable to consider entering into a contract, or 'cohabitation agreement', which establishes how money and property should be divided in the event of a relationship breakdown.

The cohabitation rights bill 2013–14, which sought to introduce certain protections for cohabitees during their lifetime and on death, was introduced in October 2013 but made no progress. Thus, cohabitation agreements continue to be governed by the same general principles of property, trust, and contract law.

FINANCIAL PROVISION FOR CHILDREN

All parents are under a legal obligation to support their children financially. A parent who does not have day-to-day care of a child is under a duty to pay child maintenance to the parent who does.

Parents can arrange child maintenance themselves or through the Child Maintenance Service (CMS), (formerly the Child Support Agency (CSA)).

There are three different methods of calculating child support under the child Maintenance schemes:
• the 'old' scheme (for all applications up until March 2003
• the net income scheme (for post-March 2003 applications)
• the gross income scheme for all new applications since 25 November 2013

By 2017, all child maintenance calculations will be dealt with under the gross income scheme. CMS uses the paying parent's gross annual income from the latest available tax year as a starting point to work out child maintencance with reference to the gross income maximum of £156,000. Once the gross income information is received, the CMS applies a specific formula to work out the level of child maintenance payable.

Under the gross income scheme, it is mandatory for parents to have a conversation with the Child Maintenance Options (CMO) team to discuss their choices and consider alternatives before they proceed with their application. The CMO will discuss the various options available to parents if they cannot agree a so-called 'family-based arrangement' between themselves:
• 'Direct Pay' (known as 'Maintenance Direct' under a CSA arrangement) which enables parents to keep control of making and receiving payments. The statutory service works out the payment amounts for parents but will not be involved in other areas, such as collection and enforcement
• 'Collect and Pay' (known as the 'calculation and collection services' under a CSA arrangement) whereby the CSA or CMS calculates how much maintenance the paying parent owes. If payments aren't made on time, a range of enforcement actions can be taken

Within 72 hours of a payment being missed, the CMS will contact the paying parent to seek continuing payments. Where there is persistent non-payment, the CMS is able to take money directly from the paying parent, either from their earnings or bank account, or to take court action.

Provision is also made under Schedule 1 of the Children Act 1989 for unmarried parents to apply to the court for lump sum and property adjustment orders and, in limited circumstances, orders for child maintenance.

SCOTLAND

Although some provisions are similar to those for England and Wales, there is separate legislation for Scotland covering nullity of marriage, judicial separation, divorce and ancillary matters. The principal legislation in relation to family law in Scotland is the Family Law (Scotland) Act 1985. The Family Law (Scotland) Act 2006 came in to force on 4 May 2006, and introduced reforms to various aspects of Scottish family law. The following is confined to major points on which the law in Scotland differs from that of England and Wales.

An action for judicial separation or divorce may be raised in the court of session; it may also be raised in the sheriff court if either party was resident in the sheriffdom for 40 days immediately before the date of the action or for 40 days ending not more than 40 days before the date of the action and has no known residence in Scotland at that date. The fee for starting a divorce petition in the sheriff court is £141.

The grounds for raising an action of divorce in Scotland are set down in The Divorce (Scotland) Act 1976 and have been subject to reform in terms of the 2006 act. The current grounds for divorce are:
• the defender has committed adultery. When adultery is cited as proof that the marriage has broken down irretrievably, it is not necessary in Scotland to prove that it is also intolerable for the pursuer to live with the defender
• the defender's behaviour is such that the pursuer cannot reasonably be expected to cohabit with the defender

- there has been no cohabitation between the parties for one year prior to the raising of the action for divorce, and the defender consents to the granting of decree of divorce
- there has been no cohabitation between the parties for two years prior to the raising of the action for divorce
- an interim gender recognition certificate under the Gender Recognition Act 2004 has, after the date of marriage, been issued to either party to the marriage. However, as a result of changes under the Marriage and Civil Partnership (Scotland) Act 2014, this ground of divorce will sometimes not be available where a full gender recognition certificate has been issued under the 2004 Act.

The previously available ground of desertion was abolished by the 2006 Act.

A simplified procedure for 'do-it-yourself divorce' was introduced in 1983 for certain divorces. If the action is based on one or two years' separation and will not be opposed or because a gender recognition certificate has been issued; there are no children under 16; no financial claims; there is no sign that the applicant's spouse is unable to manage his or her affairs through mental illness or handicap; and there are no other court proceedings underway which might result in the end of the marriage, the applicant can access the appropriate forms to enable him or her to proceed on the Scottish Courts website. The fee is £107 as at 1 April 2014, however the applicant may be exempt from paying the fee if they are in receipt of certain benefits; or if legal advice and assistance is being provided by a solicitor in terms of the Legal Aid (Scotland) Act 1986.

Where a divorce action has been raised, it may be put on hold for a variety of reasons. In all actions for divorce an extract decree, which brings the marriage to an end, will be made available 14 days after the divorce has been granted. Unlike in England, there is no decree nisi, only a final decree of divorce. Parties must ensure that all financial issues have been resolved prior to divorce, as it is not possible to seek further financial provision after divorce has been granted.

FINANCIAL PROVISION

In relation to financial provision on divorce, the first, and most important, principle is fair sharing of the matrimonial property. There is a presumption that fair share means an equal share of the matrimonial property, which can be departed from if justified by special circumstances. In terms of Scots law matrimonial property is defined as all property acquired by either spouse from the date of marriage up to the date of separation. Property acquired before the marriage is not deemed to be matrimonial unless it was acquired for use by the parties as a family home or as furniture for that home. Property acquired after the date of separation is not matrimonial property. Any property acquired by either of the parties by way of gift or inheritance during the marriage is excluded and does not form part of the matrimonial property.

When considering whether to make an award of financial provision a court shall also take account of any economic advantage derived by either party to the marriage as a result of contributions, financial or otherwise, by the other, and of any economic disadvantage suffered by either party for the benefit of the other party. The court must also ensure that the economic burden of caring for a child under the age of 16 is shared fairly between the parties.

A court can also consider making an order requiring one party to pay the other party a periodical allowance for a certain period of time following divorce. Such an order may be appropriate in cases where there is insufficient capital to effect a fair sharing of the matrimonial property. Orders for periodical allowance are uncommon, as courts will favour a 'clean break' where possible.

CHILDREN

The court has the power to award a residence order in respect of any children of the marriage or to make an order regulating the child's contact with the non-resident parent. The court will only make such orders if it is deemed better for the child to do so than to make no order at all, and the welfare of the children is of paramount importance. The fact that a spouse has caused the breakdown of the marriage does not in itself preclude him/her from being awarded residence.

NULLITY

An action for 'declaration of nullity' can be brought if someone with a legitimate interest is able to show that the marriage is void or voidable. The action can only be brought in the court of session. Although the grounds on which a marriage may be void or voidable are similar to those on which a marriage can be declared invalid in England, there are some differences. Where a spouse is capable of sexual intercourse but refuses to consummate the marriage, this is not a ground for nullity in Scots law, though it could be a ground for divorce. Where a spouse was suffering from venereal disease at the time of marriage and the other spouse did not know, this is not a ground for nullity in Scots law, neither is the fact that a wife was pregnant by another man at the time of marriage without the knowledge of her husband.

COHABITING COUPLES

The law in Scotland now provides certain financial and property rights for cohabiting couples in terms of the Family Law (Scotland) Act 2006, or 'the 2006 Act'. The relevant 2006 Act provisions do not place cohabitants in Scotland on an equal footing with married couples or civil partners, but provide some rights for cohabitants in the event that the relationship is terminated by separation or death. The provisions relate to couples who cease to cohabit after 4 May 2006.

The legislation provides for a presumption that most contents of the home shared by the cohabitants are owned in equal shares. A former cohabitant can also seek financial provision on termination of the relationship in the form of a capital payment if they can successfully demonstrate that they have been financially disadvantaged, and that conversely the other cohabitant has been financially advantaged, as a consequence of contributions made (financial or otherwise). An order can also be made in respect of the economic burden of caring for a child of whom the cohabitants are the parents. Such a claim must be made no later than one year after the day on which the cohabitants cease to cohabit.

The 2006 Act also provides that a cohabitant may make a claim on their partner's estate in the event of that partner's death, providing that there is no will. A claim of this nature must be made no later than six months after the date of the partner's death.

THE CENTRAL FAMILY COURT, First Avenue House,
    42–49 High Holborn, London WC1 6NP T 0207-421 8594
THE COURT OF SESSION, Parliament House, Parliament
    Square, Edinburgh EH1 1RQ T 0131-225 2595
    W www.scotcourts.gov.uk
THE CHILD SUPPORT AGENCY, T 0345-713 3133
    W www.csa.gov.uk

EMPLOYMENT LAW

EMPLOYEES

A fundamental distinction in UK employment law is that drawn between an employee and someone who is self-employed. Further, there is an important, intermediate category introduced by legislation: 'workers' covers all employees but also catches others who do not have full employment status. An 'employee' is someone who has entered into or works under a contract of employment, while a 'worker' has entered into or works under a contract whereby he undertakes to do or perform personally any work or services for another party whose status is not that of a client or customer. Whether or not someone is an employee or a worker as opposed to being genuinely self-employed is an important and complex question, for it determines that person's statutory rights and protections. For certain purposes, such as protection against discrimination, protection extends to some genuinely self-employed people as well as workers and employees.

The greater the level of control that the employer has over the work carried out, the greater the depth of integration of the employee in the employer's business, and the closer the obligations to provide and perform work between the parties, the more likely it is that the parties will be employer and employee.

PAY AND CONDITIONS
The Employment Rights Act 1996 consolidated the statutory provisions relating to employees' rights. Employers must give each employee employed for one month or more a written statement containing the following information:
• names of employer and employee
• date when employment began and the date on which the employee's period of *continuous* employment began (taking into account any employment with a previous employer which counts towards that period)
• the scale, rate or other method of calculating remuneration and intervals at which it will be paid
• job title or description of job
• hours and the permitted place(s) of work and, where there are several such places, the address of the employer
• holiday entitlement and holiday pay
• provisions concerning incapacity for work due to sickness and injury, including provisions for sick pay
• details of pension scheme(s)
• length of notice the employee is obliged to give and entitled to receive in order to terminate the contract of employment
• if the employment is not intended to be permanent, the period for which it is expected to continue or, if it is for a fixed term, the end date of the contract
• details of any collective agreement (including the parties to the agreement) which directly affects the terms of employment
• details of disciplinary and grievance procedures (including the individual to whom a complaint should be made and the process of making that complaint)
• if the employee is to work outside the UK for more than one month, the period of such work and the currency in which payment is made and any additional remuneration or benefits payable to them
• a note stating whether a contracting-out certificate is in force
This must be given to the employee within two months of the start of their employment.

If the employer does not provide the written statement within two months (or a statement of any changes to these particulars within one month of the changes being made) then the employee can complain to an employment tribunal, which can specify the information that the employer should have given. When, in the context of an employee's successful tribunal claim, the employer is also found to have been in breach of the duty to provide the written statement at the time proceedings were commenced, the tribunal must award the employee two weeks' pay, and may award four weeks' pay, subject to the statutory cap, unless it would be unjust or inequitable to do so.

The Working Time Regulations 1998, the National Minimum Wage Act 1998, Employment Relations Act 1999, the Employment Act 2002 and the Employment Act 2008 now supplement the 1996 act.

FLEXIBLE WORKING
The Flexible Working Regulations 2014 gives all employees, from 30 June 2014, the right to apply for flexible working after working for the same employer for at least 26 weeks. An employer must consider and decide upon a request within three months and must have a sound business reason for rejecting any request. If an application under the act is not dealt with in accordance with a prescribed procedure, or is rejected on other than specific grounds, the employee may complain to an employment tribunal.

SICK PAY
Employees absent from work through illness or injury are entitled to receive Statutory Sick Pay (SSP) from the employer from the fourth day of absence for a maximum period of 28 weeks. The right to SSP will cease where an employee has had linked periods of sickness that have spanned a period of three years.

MATERNITY AND PARENTAL RIGHTS
Under the Employment Relations Act 1999, the Employment Act 2002, the Maternity and Parental Leave Regulations 1999 (as amended in 2002 and 2006), the Paternity and Adoption Leave Regulations 2002 and 2003, the Additional Paternity Leave Regulations 2010 and the Shared Parental Leave Regulations 2014, both men and women are entitled to take leave when they become a parent (including by adoption). Women are protected from discrimination, detriment or dismissal by reason of their pregnancy or maternity, including discrimination by association and by perception. Men and adoptive parents are protected from suffering a detriment or dismissal for taking paternity, adoption or parental leave.

Any woman who needs to attend an antenatal appointment on the advice of a registered medical professional is entitled to paid leave from work to attend. All pregnant women are entitled to a maximum period of maternity leave of 52 weeks. This comprises 26 weeks' ordinary maternity leave, followed immediately by 26 weeks' additional maternity leave. A woman who takes ordinary maternity leave normally has the right to return to the job in which she was employed before her absence. If she takes additional maternity leave, she is entitled to return to the same job or, if that is not reasonably practicable, to another job that is suitable and appropriate for her to do. There is a two-week period of compulsory maternity leave, immediately following the birth of the child, wherein the employer is not permitted to allow the mother to work.

A woman will qualify for Statutory Maternity Pay (SMP), which is payable for up to 39 weeks, if she has been continuously employed for not less than 26 weeks prior to the 15th week before the expected week of childbirth. For further information *see* Social Welfare, Employer Payments.

Employees are entitled to adoption leave and adoption pay (at the same rates as SMP) subject to fulfilment of similar criteria to those in relation to maternity leave and pay, but note that there is a 26-week qualifying period for adoption leave. Where a couple is adopting a child, either one (but not both) of the parents may take adoption leave, and the other may take paternity leave.

Certain employees are entitled to paternity leave on the birth or adoption of a child. To be eligible, the employee must be the child's father, or the partner of the mother or adopter, and meet other conditions. These conditions are, firstly, that they must have been continuously employed for not less than 26 weeks prior to the 15th week before the expected week of childbirth (or, in the case of adoptions, 26 weeks ending with the week in which notification of the adoption match is given) and, secondly, that the employee must have or expect to have responsibility for the upbringing of the child. The employee may take either one week's leave, or two consecutive weeks' leave. This leave may be taken at any time between the date of the child's birth (or placement for adoption) and 56 days later. A statutory payment is available during this period.

For births and adoptions from 3 April 2011 but before 5 April 2015, an eligible employee has been able to take additional paternity leave at the end of the mother's or adopter's leave period provided the child is at least 20 weeks old or was placed for adoption at least 20 weeks previously. The maximum period of leave is 26 weeks and leave cannot extend beyond the child's first birthday.

For births on or after 5 April 2015, eligible parents are entitled to shared parental leave (SPL) whereby they will be able to share a pot of leave of up to 50 weeks and 27 weeks of pay, after the initial two weeks of maternity leave that is compulsory for the mother. During that 50 week period, parents can decide to be off work at the same time and/or take it in turns to have periods of leave to look after their child. To be eligible, the employee must be the child's mother, father, partner of the mother or adopter, and must have worked for the same employer for not less than 26 weeks prior to the 15th week before the expected week of childbirth (or, in case of adoptions, 26 weeks ending with the week in which notification of the adoption match is given). The amount of leave available is calculated using the mother's entitlement to maternity leave. If a mother reduces maternity leave she and/or her partner may opt to take SPL for the remaining weeks. On taking SPL, a woman will be entitled to statutory shared parental pay at the same rate as SMP.

For more information *see* Social Welfare, Employer Payments.

Any employee with one year's service who has, or expects to have, responsibility for a child may take parental leave to care for the child. Each parent is entitled to a total of 18 weeks parental leave for each child or adopted child. This leave must be taken (at the rate of no more than four weeks a year, and in blocks of whole weeks only) before the child's 18th birthday.

SUNDAY TRADING
The Sunday Trading Act 1994 allows shops to open on Sunday. The Employment Rights Act 1996 gives shop workers and betting workers the right not to be dismissed, selected for redundancy or to suffer any detriment (such as the denial of overtime, promotion or training) if they refuse to work on Sundays. This does not apply to those who, under their contracts, are employed to work on Sundays.

TERMINATION OF EMPLOYMENT
An employee may be dismissed without notice if guilty of gross misconduct but in other cases a period of notice must be given by the employer. The minimum periods of notice specified in the Employment Rights Act 1996 are:
• one week if the employee has been continuously employed for one month or more but for less than two years
• one week for each complete year of continuous employment, if the employee has been employed for two years or more, up to a maximum of 12 weeks' notice
• longer periods apply if these are specified in the contract of employment
If an employee is dismissed with less notice than he/she is entitled to by statute, or under their contract if longer, he/she

will have a wrongful dismissal claim (unless the employer paid the employee in lieu of notice in accordance with a contractual provision entitling it to do so). This claim for wrongful dismissal can be brought by the employee either in the civil courts or the employment tribunal, but if brought in the tribunal the maximum amount that can be awarded is £25,000.

REDUNDANCY
An employee dismissed because of redundancy may be entitled to redundancy pay. This applies if:
• the employment commenced before 6 April 2012 and the employee has at least one year's continuous service or the employment commenced on or after 6 April 2012 and the employee has at least two years' continuous service
• the employee is dismissed by the employer by reason of redundancy (this can include cases of voluntary redundancy)
Redundancy can mean closure of the entire business, closure of a particular site of the business, or a reduction in the need for employees to carry out work of a particular kind.

An employee may not be entitled to a redundancy payment if offered a suitable alternative job by the same employer. The amount of statutory redundancy pay depends on the length of service, age, and their earnings, subject to a weekly maximum of (currently) £475. The maximum payment that can be awarded is £14,250. The redundancy payment is guaranteed by the government in cases where the employer becomes insolvent.

UNFAIR DISMISSAL
Complaints of unfair dismissal are dealt with by an employment tribunal. Any employee whose employment commenced before 6 April 2012 with at least one year's continuous service or any employee whose employment commenced on or after 6 April 2012 with at least two year's continuous service (subject to exceptions, including in relation to whistleblowers – *see* below) can make a complaint to the tribunal. At the tribunal, it is for the employee to show that the employer dismissed them either expressly or constructively and it is for the employer to prove that the dismissal was due to one or more potentially fair reasons: a statutory restriction preventing the continuation of the employee's contract; the employee's capability or qualifications for the job he/she was employed to do; the employee's conduct; redundancy; or some other substantial reason.

If the employer succeeds in showing this, the tribunal must then decide whether the employer acted reasonably in dismissing the employee for that reason. If the employee is found to have been unfairly dismissed, the tribunal can order that he/she be reinstated, re-engaged or compensated. Any person believing that they may have been unfairly dismissed should contact their local Citizens Advice bureau or seek legal advice. A claim must be brought within three months of the date of effective termination of employment.

The normal maximum compensatory award for unfair dismissal is £78,335 (as at April 2015). If the dismissal occurred after 6 April 2009 and the employer unreasonably failed to follow the ACAS Code of Practice on Disciplinary and Grievance Procedures in carrying out the dismissal, the tribunal may increase the employee's compensation by up to 25 per cent.

WHISTLEBLOWING
Under the whistleblowing legislation (Public Interest Disclosure Act 1998, which inserted provisions into the Employment Rights Act 1996) dismissal of an employee is automatically unfair if the reason or principal reason for

the dismissal is that the employee has made a protected disclosure. The legislation also makes it unlawful to subject workers (a broad category that includes employees and certain other individuals, such as agency workers) who have made a protected disclosure to any detriment on the ground that they have done so.

For a disclosure to qualify for protection, the claimant must show that he or she has disclosed information, which in his or her reasonable belief tends to show one or more of the following six categories of wrongdoing: criminal offences; breach of any legal obligation; miscarriages of justice; danger to the health and safety of any individual; damage to the environment; or the deliberate concealing of information about any of the other categories. The malpractices can be past, present, prospective or merely alleged.

A qualifying disclosure will only be protected if the manner of the disclosure fulfils certain conditions, which varies according to the type of disclosure. With effect from 25 June 2013, there is no requirement for the disclosure to have been made in 'good faith', although where it appears to the tribunal that the protected disclosure was not made in good faith, the tribunal may reduce any compensatory award it makes by up to 25 per cent if it considers that it is just and equitable to do so in all the circumstances.

Any whistleblower claim in the employment tribunal must normally be brought within three months of the date of dismissal or other act leading to a detriment.

An individual does not need to have been working with the employer for any particular period of time to be able to bring such a claim and compensation is uncapped (and can include an amount for injury to feelings).

DISCRIMINATION
Discrimination in employment on the grounds of sex (including gender reassignment), sexual orientation, being pregnant or on maternity leave, race, colour, nationality, ethnic or national origins, religion or belief, marital or civil partnership status, age or disability is unlawful. Discrimination legislation generally covers direct discrimination, indirect discrimination, harassment and victimisation. Only in limited circumstances can such discrimination be justified (rendering it lawful).

An individual does not need to be employed for any particular period of time to be able to claim discrimination (discrimination can be alleged at the recruitment phase), and discrimination compensation is uncapped (and can include an amount for injury to feelings). These features distinguish the discrimination laws from, for example, the unfair dismissal laws.

The Equality Act 2010 was passed on 8 April 2010 and the main provisions came into force on 1 October 2010. The Act unifies several pieces of discrimination legislation, providing one definition of direct discrimination, indirect discrimination, harassment and victimisation. The Equality Act applies to those employed in Great Britain but not to employees in Northern Ireland or (subject to EC exceptions) to those who work mainly abroad, and provides that:

- it is unlawful to discriminate on the grounds of sex, gender reassignment or marital/civil partner status, being pregnant or on maternity leave, including discrimination by association and by perception. This covers all aspects of employment (including advertising for jobs), but there are some limited exceptions, such as where the essential nature of the job requires it to be given to someone of a particular sex, or where decency and privacy requires it. The act entitles men and women to equality of remuneration for equivalent work or work of the same value
- individuals have the right not to be discriminated against on the grounds of race, colour, nationality, or ethnic or national origins and this applies to all aspects of employment. Employers may also take lawful positive action, including in relation to recruitment and promotion
- discrimination against a disabled person in all aspects of employment is unlawful. This includes protecting carers from discrimination by association with the disabled persons that they look after. In certain circumstances, the employer may show that the less favourable treatment is justified and so does not constitute discrimination. The act also imposes a duty on employers to make 'reasonable adjustments' to the arrangements and physical features of the workplace if these place disabled people at a substantial disadvantage compared with those who are not disabled. The definition of a 'disabled person' is wide and includes people diagnosed with HIV, cancer and multiple sclerosis
- discrimination against a person on the grounds of religion or belief (or lack of belief) including discrimination by association and by perception, in all aspects of employment, is unlawful
- discrimination against an individual on the grounds of sexual orientation, including discrimination by association and by perception, in all aspects of employment, is unlawful
- age discrimination in the workplace is unlawful, and an employer may no longer dismiss an employee by reason of retirement once they have reached a certain age. However, it is lawful to discriminate because of age in relation to benefits based on length of service, redundancy pay, national minimum wage and insurance benefits.

The responsibility for monitoring equality in society rests with the Equality and Human Rights Commission.

In Northern Ireland similar provisions exist to those that were in force in Great Britain prior to the coming into force of the Equality Act but are contained in separate legislation (although the Disability Discrimination Act does extend to Northern Ireland).

In Northern Ireland there is one combined body working towards equality and eliminating discrimination, the Equality Commission for Northern Ireland.

WORKING TIME
The Working Time Regulations 1998 impose rules that limit working hours and provide for rest breaks and holidays. The regulations apply to workers and so cover not only employees but also other individuals who undertake to perform personally any work or services (eg freelancers). The regulations are complex and subject to various exceptions and qualifications but the basic provisions relating to adult day workers are as follows:

- No worker is permitted to work more than an average of 48 hours per week (unless they have made a genuine voluntary opt-out of this limit – it is not sufficient to make it a term of the contract that the worker opts out), and a worker is entitled to, but is not required to take, the following breaks:
- 11 consecutive hours' uninterrupted rest in every 24-hour period
- an uninterrupted rest period of 24 hours in each 7-day period or 48 hours in each fortnight (in addition to the daily rest period)
- 20 minutes' rest break provided that the working day is longer than 6 hours
- 5.6 weeks' paid annual leave (28 days full-time). This equates to 4 weeks plus public holidays

There are specific provisions relating to night work, young workers (ie those over school leaving age but under 18) and a variety of workers in specialised sectors (such as off-shore oil rig workers).

HUMAN RIGHTS

On 2 October 2000 the Human Rights Act 1998 came into force in the UK. This act incorporates the European Convention on Human Rights into the law of the UK. The main principles of the act are as follows:

- all legislation must be interpreted and given effect by the courts as compatible with the Convention so far as it is possible to do so. Before the second reading of a new bill the minister responsible for the bill must provide a statement regarding its compatibility with the Human Rights Act
- subordinate legislation (eg statutory instruments) which is incompatible with the Convention can be struck down by the courts
- primary legislation (eg an act of parliament) which is incompatible with the Convention cannot be struck down by a court, but the higher courts can make a declaration of incompatibility which is a signal to parliament to change the law
- all public authorities (including courts and tribunals) must not act in a way which is incompatible with the Convention
- individuals whose Convention rights have been infringed by a public authority may bring proceedings against that authority, but the act is not intended to create new rights as between individuals

The main human rights protected by the Convention are the right to life (article 2); protection from torture and inhuman or degrading treatment (article 3); protection from slavery or forced labour (article 4); the right to liberty and security of the person (article 5); the right to a fair trial (article 6); the right not to be subject to retrospective criminal offences (article 7); the right to respect for private and family life (article 8); freedom of thought, conscience and religion (article 9); freedom of expression (article 10); freedom of peaceful association and assembly (article 11); the right to marry and found a family (article 12); protection from discrimination (article 14); the right to property (article 1 protocol No.1); the right to education (article 2 protocol No.1); and the right to free elections (article 3 protocol No.1). Most of the Convention rights are subject to limitations which deem the breach of the right acceptable on the basis it is 'necessary in a democratic society'.

Human rights are also enshrined in the common law (of tort). Although this is of historical significance, the common law (for example the duty of confidentiality) remains especially important regarding violations of human rights that occur between private parties, where the Human Rights Act 1998 does not apply.

PARENTAL RESPONSIBILITY

The Children Act 1989 (as amended by the Children and Families Act 2014) gives both the mother and father parental responsibility for the child if the parents are married to each other at the time of the child's birth. If the parents are not married, only the mother has parental responsibility. The father may acquire it in accordance with the provisions of section 4 of the Children Act 1989. He can do this in one of several ways, including: by being registered as the father on the child's birth certificate with the consent of the mother (only for fathers of children born after 1 December 2003, following changes to the Adoption and Children Act 2002); by applying to the court for a parental responsibility order; by entering into a parental responsibility agreement with the mother which must be in the prescribed form; or by marrying the mother of the child.

Following changes to the Children Act 1989 (introduced by the Children and Families Act 2014), if a court makes a child arrangements order in favour of a father, providing that the child lives with that father, the court must make a parental responsibility order in his favour. If the child arrangements order provides that the child spend time or otherwise have contact with the father, the court must consider whether to make a parental responsibility order (residence orders were replaced by child arrangement orders under the Children and Families Act 2014, but if obtained prior to 22 April 2014 are still valid).

Where a child's parent, who has parental responsibility, marries or enters into a civil partnership with a person who is not the child's parent, the child's parent(s) with parental responsibility can agree for the step-parent to have parental responsibility, or the step-parent may acquire parental responsibility by order of the court (section 4A(1) Children Act 1989).

If a child is born to female civil partners or female same-sex spouses as a result of IVF or AID treatment received after 5 April 2009, both individuals will have parental responsibility for that child. From 1 September 2009 a female, who is not in a civil partnership or same-sex marriage with the mother at the date of the child's birth, but is the child's other parent (under the Human Fertilisation and Embryology Act 2008), can acquire parental responsibility in the same way as set out above in relation to a father. Parental responsibility will also be acquired if the mother and the child's other parent enter into a civil partnership or (from 13 March 2014) a same-sex marriage after the child's date of birth.

Since 6 April 2010, following surrogacy arrangements, the court can order that a parental order is made in favour of the surrogate couple if at least one of them is a biological parent.

Where the court makes a child arrangements order and a person (who is not the parent or guardian of the child) is named in the order as a person with whom the child is to spend time or otherwise have contact (but not named as a person with whom the child is to live), the court may provide in the order for that person to have parental responsibility for the child.

An adoption order gives parental responsibility for the child to the adopters. It extinguishes parental responsibility that any person had for the child immediately before the making of the order.

In Scotland, the relevant legislation is the Children (Scotland) Act 1995, which gives the mother parental rights and responsibilities for her child whether or not she is married to the child's father. A father who is married to the mother, either at the time of the child's conception or subsequently, will also have automatic parental rights and responsibilities. Section 23 of the 2006 act provides that an unmarried father will obtain automatic parental responsibilities and rights if he is registered as the father on the child's birth certificate. For unmarried fathers who are not named on the birth certificate, or whose children were born before the 2006 act came into force, it is possible to acquire parental responsibilities and rights by applying to the court or by entering into a parental responsibilities and rights agreement with the mother. The father of any child, regardless of parental rights, has a duty to aliment that child until he/she is 18 (or under 25 if the child is still at an educational establishment or training for employment or for a trade, profession or vocation).

LEGITIMATION
Under the Legitimacy Act 1976, an illegitimate person automatically becomes legitimate when his/her parents marry. This applies even where one of the parents was married to a third person at the time of the birth. In such cases it is necessary to re-register the birth of the child.

In Scotland, the status of illegitimacy has been abolished by section 21 of the 2006 act. The Law Reform Act 1987 reformed the law so as to remove so far as possible the legal disadvantages of illegitimacy.

JURY SERVICE

In England and Wales, the law concerning juries is largely consolidated in the Juries Act 1974 (as amended by the Criminal Justice and Courts Act 2015). In England and Wales, a person charged with a serious criminal offence is entitled to have their trial heard by a jury in a crown court, except in cases where there is a danger of jury tampering or where jury tampering has taken place.

In civil cases, there is a right to a jury in the Queen's Bench Division of the high court in cases where the person applying for a jury has been accused of fraud, as well as in cases of malicious prosecution or false imprisonment. The same applies to the county court. In all other cases in the Queen's Bench Division only the judge has discretion to order trial with a jury, though such an order is seldom made. In the chancery division of the high court a jury is never used. The same is true in the family division of the high court.

No right to a jury trial exists in Scotland, although more serious offences are heard before a jury. In England and Wales criminal cases and civil cases in the high court are generally heard by a jury of 12 members, but in the county court the jury is smaller, normally consisting of eight members. In the event that a juror is excused the trial can proceed so long as there are at least seven remaining jurors in the county court and nine in the case of the high court or crown court. At an inquest, there must be at least seven and no more than 11 members. In Scotland there are 12 members of a jury in a civil case in the court of session and certain sheriff court cases, and 15 in a criminal trial in the high court of justiciary. Jurors are normally asked to serve for ten working days, during which time they could sit on more than one case. Jurors selected for longer cases are expected to sit for the duration of the trial.

In England and Wales, every 'registered' parliamentary or local government elector between the ages of 18 and 70 (the Criminal Justice and Courts Act has amended the maximum age to 75, although this provision is not in force at the time of writing) who has lived in the UK (including, for this purpose, the Channel Islands and the Isle of Man) for any period of at least five years since reaching the age of 13 is qualified to serve on a jury unless he/she is 'mentally disordered' or disqualified.

Those disqualified from jury service include:
- those who have at any time been sentenced by a court in the UK (including, for this purpose, the Channel Islands and the Isle of Man) to a term of imprisonment or youth custody of five years or more
- those who have within the previous ten years served any part of a sentence of imprisonment, youth custody or detention, been detained in a young offenders' institution, received a suspended sentence of imprisonment or order for detention, or received a community order
- those who are on bail in criminal proceedings
- those who have been convicted of a jury misconduct offence

The court has the discretion to excuse a juror from service, or defer the date of service, if the juror can show there is good reason why he/she should be excused from attending or good reason why his/her attendance should be deferred. It is an offence (punishable by a fine) to fail to attend when summoned, to serve knowing that you are disqualified from service, or to make false representations in an attempt to evade service. If a juror fails to turn up for service, or attends but cannot serve due to being under the influence of drink or drugs, this is punishable as contempt of court. Any party can object to any juror if he/she can show cause to the trial judge.

It may be appropriate for a judge to excuse a juror from a particular case if he is personally concerned in the facts of the particular case, or closely connected with a party to the proceedings or with a prospective witness. The judge may also discharge any juror who, from a mental or physical incapacity, temporary or permanent, or alternatively due to linguistic difficulties, cannot pay proper attention to the evidence.

An individual juror (or the entire jury) can be discharged if it is shown that they or any of their number have, among other things, separated from the rest of the jury without the leave of the court; talked to any person out of court who is not a member of the jury; determined the verdict of the trial by drawing lots; come to a compromise on the verdict; been drunk, or otherwise incapacitated, while carrying out their duties as a juror; exerted improper pressure on the other members of the jury (eg harassment or bullying); declined to take part in the jury's functions; displayed actual or apparent bias (eg racism, sexism or other discriminatory or deliberate hostility); or inadvertently possessed knowledge of the bad character of a party to the proceedings which has not been adduced as evidence in the proceedings. The factual situations that arise are many, and include falling asleep during the trial, asking friends on Facebook for help in making a decision, consulting an ouija board in the course of deliberations, making telephone calls after retirement, and lunching with a barrister not connected with the proceedings.

The Criminal Justice and Courts Act 2015 has introduced four new offences of juror misconduct with a penalty of up to two years in prison. A juror commits an offence if he: (a) intentionally seeks information during a trial where he knows, or ought to reasonably know, that the information sought is or may be relevant to the case; (b) passes on to another juror information obtained through such research; (c) engages in conduct from which it may reasonably be concluded that he intends to try the issue otherwise than on the basis of the evidence presented in the proceedings on the issue; and (d) discloses information about the jury's deliberations, subject to specified exceptions. A person who has been convicted of one of the above offences within the last 10 years will be disqualified from jury duty. A judge now has a discretionary power to order members of a jury to surrender their electronic communication devices for a period of time, and a court security officer is authorised to search a juror for a device that a judge has ordered be surrendered.

In England and Wales, the jury's verdict need not be unanimous. In criminal proceedings, and civil proceedings in the high court, the agreement of 10 jurors will suffice when there are not fewer than 11 people on the jury (or 9 in a jury of 10). In civil proceedings in the county court the agreement of seven or eight jurors will suffice. Where a majority verdict is given, the court must be satisfied that the jury had reasonable time to consider its verdict based on the nature and complexity of the case. In criminal proceedings this must be no less than two hours and ten minutes (allowing time for the jury to settle after retiring).

A juror is immune from prosecution or civil claim in respect of anything said or done by him or her in the discharge of their office. It is an offence for a juror to disclose what happened in the jury room even after the trial is over. A juror may claim travelling expenses, a subsistence allowance and an allowance for other financial loss (eg loss of earnings or benefits, fees paid to carers or child-minders) up to a stated limit. For more information on jury service, visit
W www.gov.uk/jury-service/overview

SCOTLAND

Qualification criteria for jury service in Scotland are similar to those in England and Wales, except that members of the judiciary are ineligible for ten years after ceasing to hold their post, and others concerned with the administration of justice are only eligible for service five years after ceasing to hold office. Certain persons have the right to apply to be excused – full-time members of the medical, dental, nursing, veterinary and pharmaceutical professions, full-time members of the armed forces, ministers of religion, persons who have served on a jury within the previous five years, members of the Scottish parliament, members of the Scottish government, junior Scottish ministers and those aged 71 years or over. Those who are incapable by reason of a mental disorder may also be excused. Such an application will be accepted if the application is made within 7 days of the person being notified that they may have to serve. For civil trials there is an age limit of 65 years. Those convicted of a crime and sentenced to a period of imprisonment of 5 years or more are automatically disqualified. The maximum fine for a person serving on a jury while knowing himself/herself to be ineligible is £1,000. The maximum fine for failing to attend without good cause in criminal trials is also £1,000, however in civil proceedings the maximum fine is £200.

HER MAJESTY'S COURTS AND TRIBUNALS SERVICE,
102 Petty France, London SW1H 9AJ T 0845-456 8770
JURY CENTRAL SUMMONING BUREAU,
Freepost LON 19669, Pocock Street, London SE1 0YG
T 0845-803 8003 E jurysummoning@hmcts.gsi.gov.uk
SCOTTISH COURTS SERVICE, Saughton House,
Broomhouse Drive, Edinburgh EH11 3XD T 0131-444 3300
W www.scotcourts.gov.uk
THE CLERK OF JUSTICIARY, High Court of Justiciary,
Lawnmarket, Edinburgh EH2 2NS T 0131-240 6900

LANDLORD AND TENANT

RESIDENTIAL LETTINGS

The provisions outlined here apply only where the tenant lives in a separate dwelling from the landlord and where the dwelling is the tenant's only or main home. It does not apply to licensees such as lodgers, guests or service occupiers.

The 1996 Housing Act radically changed certain aspects of the legislation referred to below; in particular, the grant of assured and assured shorthold tenancies under the Housing Act 1988.

ASSURED SHORTHOLD TENANCIES

If a tenancy was granted on or after 15 January 1989 and before 28 February 1997, the tenant would have an assured tenancy unless the landlord served notice under section 20 in the prescribed form prior to the commencement of the tenancy, stating that the tenancy is to be an assured shorthold tenancy and the tenancy is for a minimum fixed term period of six months (see below). An assured tenancy gives that tenant greater security. The tenant could, for example, stay in possession of the dwelling for as long as the tenant observed the terms of the tenancy. The landlord cannot obtain possession from such a tenant unless the landlord can establish a specific ground for possession (set out in the Housing Act 1988) and obtains a court order. The rent payable is that agreed with the landlord at the start of the tenancy. The landlord has the right to increase the rent annually by serving a notice. If that happens the tenant can apply to have the rent fixed by the rent assessment committee of the local authority. The tenant or the landlord may request that the committee sets the rent in line with open market rents for that type of property.

Under the Housing Act 1996, all new lettings (below an annual rent threshold of £100,000 since October 2010) entered into on or after 28 February 1997 (for whatever term) will be assured shorthold tenancies unless the landlord serves a notice stating that the tenancy is not to be an assured shorthold tenancy. This means that the landlord is entitled to possession at the end of the tenancy provided he serves a notice under section 21 Housing Act 1988 and commences the proceedings in accordance with the correct procedure. The landlord must obtain a court order, however, to obtain possession if the tenant refuses to vacate at the end of the tenancy. If the tenancy is an assured shorthold tenancy, the court must grant the order.

REGULATED TENANCIES

Before the Housing Act 1988 came into force on 15 January 1989 there were regulated tenancies; some are still in existence and are protected by the Rent Act 1977. Under this act it is possible for the landlord or the tenant to apply to the local rent officer to have a 'fair' rent registered. The fair rent is then the maximum rent payable.

SECURE TENANCIES

Secure tenancies are generally given to tenants of local authorities, housing associations (before 15 January 1989) and certain other bodies. This gives the tenant security of tenure unless the terms of the agreement are broken by the tenant and it is reasonable to make an order for possession. Those with secure tenancies may have the right to buy their property. In practice this right is generally only available to council tenants.

The Prevention of Social Housing Fraud Act came into force in October 2013. It creates criminal offences for unlawful sub-letting by secure and assured tenants of social housing.

AGRICULTURAL PROPERTY

Tenancies in agricultural properties are governed by the Agricultural Holdings Act 1986, the Agricultural Tenancies Act 1995 (both amended by the Regulatory Reform (Agricultural Tenancies) (England and Wales) Order 2006), the Tribunals, Courts and Enforcement Act 2007, the Legal Services Act 2007 and the Rent (Agriculture) Act 1976, which give similar protections to those described above, eg security of tenure, right to compensation for disturbance, etc. Similar provisions are applied to Scotland by the Agricultural Holdings (Scotland) Act 2003 for those leases entered into on or after 27 November 2003. The Agricultural Holdings (Scotland) Act 1991 continues to apply to those leases in Scotland entered into prior to this date and in certain other circumstances outlined by the 2003 act. However, one distinction to note between the 1991 act and the 2003 act is that those leases governed by the former have full security of tenure, subject to certain exceptions, whereas leases under the 2003 act are fixed term arrangements of various durations.

EVICTION

The Protection from Eviction Act 1977 (as amended by the Housing Act 1988 and Nationality, Immigration and Asylum Act 2002) sets out the procedure a landlord must follow in order to obtain possession of property. It is unlawful for a landlord to evict a tenant otherwise than in accordance with the law. For common law tenancies and for Rent Act tenants a notice to quit in the prescribed form giving 28 days notice is required. For secure and assured tenancies a notice seeking possession must be served. It is unlawful for the landlord to evict a person by putting their belongings on to the street, by changing the locks and so on. It is also unlawful for a landlord to harass a tenant in any way in order to persuade him/her to give up the tenancy. The tenant may be able to obtain an injunction to restrain the actions of the landlord and get back into the property and be awarded damages.

LANDLORD RESPONSIBILITIES
Under the Landlord and Tenant Act 1985, where the term of the lease is less than seven years, the landlord is responsible for maintaining the structure and exterior of the property, for sanitation, for heating and hot water, and all installations for the supply of water, gas and electricity.

While the responsibility of maintaining the premises remains intact, since July 2012 landlords are no longer permitted to enter the rental premises for the purpose of viewing their state and condition. This power of entry was revoked by the Protection of Freedoms Act 2012.

LEASEHOLDERS
Strictly speaking, leaseholders have bought a long lease rather than a property and in certain limited circumstances the landlord can end the tenancy. Under the Leasehold Reform Act 1967 (as amended by the Housing Acts 1969, 1974, 1980 and 1985), leaseholders of houses may have the right to buy the freehold or to take an extended lease for a term of 50 years. This applies to leases where the term of the lease is over 21 years, at a low rent, and where the leaseholder has occupied the house as his/her only or main residence for the last two years, or for a total of two years over the last ten. The tenant must give the landlord written notice of his desire to acquire the freehold or extend the leasehold.

The Leasehold Reform, Housing and Urban Development Act came into force in 1993 and allows the leaseholders of flats in certain circumstances to buy the freehold of the building in which they live.

Responsibility for maintenance of the structure, exterior and interior of the building should be set out in the lease. Usually the upkeep of the interior of his/her part of the property is the responsibility of the leaseholder, and responsibility for the structure, exterior and common interior areas is shared between the freeholder and the leaseholder(s).

If leaseholders are dissatisfied with charges made in respect of lease extensions, they are entitled to have their situation evaluated by the Leasehold Valuation Tribunal.

The Commonhold and Leasehold Reform Act 2002 makes provision for the freehold estate in land to be registered as commonhold land and for the legal interest in the land to be vested in a 'commonhold association' ie a private limited company.

BUSINESS LETTINGS
The Landlord and Tenant Acts 1927 and 1954 (as amended) give security of tenure to the tenants of most business premises. The landlord can only evict the tenant on one of the grounds laid down in the 1954 act, and in some cases where the landlord repossesses the property the tenant may be entitled to compensation.

SCOTLAND
In Scotland assured and short assured tenancies exist for residential lettings entered into after 2 January 1989 and are similar to assured shorthold tenancies in England and Wales. The relevant legislation is the Housing (Scotland) Act 1988.

Most tenancies created before 2 January 1989 were regulated tenancies and the Rent (Scotland) Act 1984 still applies where these exist. The act defines, among other things, the circumstances in which a landlord can increase the rent when improvements are made to the property. The provisions of the Rent Act do not apply to tenancies where the landlord is the Crown, a local authority or a housing corporation.

The Antisocial Behaviour etc (Scotland) Act 2004 provides that all private landlords letting property in Scotland must register with the local authority in which the let property is situated, unless the landlord is a local authority, or a registered social landlord. Exceptions also apply to holiday lets, owner-occupied accommodation and agricultural holdings. The act applies to partnerships, trusts and companies as well as to individuals.

Tenancy Deposit Schemes (Scotland) Regulations 2011 require that a landlord must pay deposits taken from tenants into an approved scheme and ensure that the money is held by an approved scheme for the duration of the tenancy. Evidence of registration with the relevant local authority in terms of the 2004 Act must be provided when the deposit is paid over.

Landlords who provide an assured or short assured tenancy must provide new tenants with a Tenant Information P ack. The tenant Information pack includes information on the Repairing Standard, and its provision satisfies the separate obligation of a landlord to provide a tenant with written information about the landlord's duty to repair and maintain in terms of the Housing (Scotland) Act 2006.

The Housing (Scotland) Acts of 1987 and 2001 relate to local authority and registered social landlord responsibilities for housing, the right to buy, and local authority secured tenancies. The provisions are broadly similar to England and Wales. The Housing (Scotland) Act 2010 is now in force. This reforms right-to-buy provisions, modernises social housing regulation, introduces the Scottish social housing charter and replaces the regulatory framework established by the 2001 act.

In Scotland, business premises are not controlled by statute to the same extent as in England and Wales, although the Tenancy of Shops (Scotland) Act 1949 gives some security to tenants of shops. Tenants of shops can apply to the sheriff, within 21 days of being served a notice to quit, for a renewal of tenancy if threatened with eviction. This application may be dismissed on various grounds, including where the landlord has offered to sell the property to the tenant at an agreed price or, in the absence of agreement as to price, at a price fixed by a single arbiter appointed by the parties or the sheriff. The act extends to properties where the Crown or government departments are the landlords or the tenants.

Under the Leases Act 1449 the landlord's successors (either purchasers or creditors) are bound by the agreement made with any tenants so long as the following conditions are met:
- the lease, if for more than one year, must be in writing
- there must be a rent
- there must be a term of expiry
- the tenant must have entered into possession
- the subjects of the lease must be land
- the landlord, if owner, must be the proprietor with a recorded title, ie the title deeds recorded in the Register of Sasines or registered in the Land Register

On 28 November 2015 certain leases which were granted for more than 175 years and under which the rent does not exceed £100 a year. will convert to heritable titles. Therefore the tenants under these leases will become the owners of the property. Conversion of the lease will be automatic, provided certain conditions are met, unless the tenant opts out. It is possible for the landlord to claim compensation for their loss of income.

LEGAL AID

The Access to Justice Act 1999 transformed what used to be known as the Legal Aid system. The Legal Aid Board was replaced by the Legal Services Commission, which was responsible for the development and administration of two legal funding schemes in England and Wales, namely the Criminal Defence Service and the Community Legal Service. The Criminal Defence Service assisted people who were under police investigation or facing criminal charges. The Community Legal Service was designed to increase access to legal information and advice by involving a much wider network of funders and providers in giving publicly funded legal services. In Scotland, provision of legal aid is governed by the Legal Aid (Scotland) Act 1986, the Legal Profession and Legal Aid (Scotland) Act 2007 and the Scottish Civil Justice Council and Criminal Legal Assistance Act 2013, and administered by the Scottish Legal Aid Board.

Under the Legal Aid, Sentencing and Punishment of Offenders Act 2012 (LASPO), which came into force on 1 April 2013, the Legal Services Commission was abolished and replaced by the newly created Legal Aid Agency. The act has also limited the areas of law that fall within the scope of legal aid funding, especially those related to civil legal services. However, the act does include provisions for funding in exceptional cases, such as where failure to provide legal aid would result in a violation of an individual's human rights or where providing legal aid would serve a wider public interest. Further, the act allows for areas of law to be added or omitted from the scope of legal aid independently, without subsequent legislation.

LASPO took whole areas of law out of scope for legal aid; some areas only qualify if they meet certain criteria. Broadly, the following categories of cases are now out of such scope: (a) family cases where there is no proof of domestic violence, forced marriage or child abduction; (b) immigration cases that do not involve asylum or detention; (c) housing and debt matters unless they constitute an immediate risk to the home; (d) welfare benefit cases except appeals to the upper tribunal or high court; (e) almost all clinical negligence cases; and (f) employment cases that do not involve human trafficking or a contravention of the Equality Act 2010.

LEGAL AID AGENCY,
W www.gov.uk/government/organisations/legal-aid-agency

CIVIL LEGAL AID
From 1 January 2000, only organisations (such as solicitors or Citizens Advice) with a contract with the Legal Services Commission (now Legal Aid Agency) have been able to give initial help in any civil matter. Moreover, from that date decisions about funding were devolved from the Legal Services Commission to contracted organisations in relation to any level of publicly funded service in family and immigration cases. For other types of case, applications for public funding are made through a solicitor (or other contracted legal services providers) in much the same way as the former Legal Aid.

Under the civil funding scheme there are broadly six levels of service available:
• legal help
• help at court
• family help – either family help (lower) or family help (higher)
• legal representation – either investigative help or full representation
• family mediation
• such other services as authorised by specific orders

ELIGIBILITY
Eligibility for funding from the Legal Aid Agency depends broadly on five factors:
• the level of service sought (*see* above)
• whether the applicant qualifies financially

• the merits of the applicant's case
• a costs-benefits analysis (if the costs are likely to outweigh any benefit that might be gained from the proceedings, funding may be refused)
• whether there is any public interest in the case being litigated (ie whether the case has a wider public interest beyond that of the parties involved, eg a human rights case)
The limits on capital and income above which a person is not entitled to public funding vary with the type of service sought.

LASPO has abolished capital passporting, meaning that all applicants are subject to the same capital test regardless of whether or not they are receiving benefits. The 2012 act also amended the merits criteria so that legal aid may be refused where the case is suitable for alternative funding, such as Conditional Fee Agreements.

CONTRIBUTIONS
Some of those who qualify for Legal Aid Agency funding will have to contribute towards their legal costs. Contributions must be paid by anyone who has a disposable income or disposable capital exceeding a prescribed amount. The rules relating to applicable contributions are complex and detailed information can be obtained from the Legal Aid Agency.

STATUTORY CHARGE
A statutory charge is made if a person keeps or gains money or property in a case for which they have received legal aid. This means that the amount paid by the Legal Aid Agency fund on their behalf is deducted from the amount that the person receives. This does not apply if the court has ordered that the costs be paid by the other party (unless the amount paid by the other party does not cover all of the costs). In certain circumstances, the Legal Aid Agency may waive or postpone payment.

CONTINGENCY OR CONDITIONAL FEES
This system was introduced by the Courts and Legal Services Act 1990. It can offer legal representation on a 'no win, no fee' basis. It provides an alternative form of assistance, especially for those cases which are ineligible for funding by the Legal Aid Agency. The main area for such work is in the field of personal injuries.

Not all solicitors offer such a scheme and different solicitors may well have different terms. The effect of the agreement is that solicitors may not make any charges, or may waive some of their charges, until the case is concluded successfully. If a case is won then the losing party will usually have to pay towards costs, with the winning party contributing around one third.

SCOTLAND
Civil legal aid is available for cases in the following:
• the sheriff courts
• the court of session
• the supreme court
• the lands valuation appeal court
• the Scottish land court
• the Lands Tribunal for Scotland
• the Employment Appeal Tribunals
• the Proscribed Organisations Appeal Commission
• certain appeals before the Social Security Commissioners
Civil legal aid is not available for election petitions, small claims, simplified divorce procedures or petitions by a debtor for his own sequestration. In defamation actions additional criteria must be met in order for legal aid to be available.

Eligibility for civil legal aid is assessed in a similar way to that in England and Wales, though the financial limits differ in some respects. A person shall be eligible for civil legal aid if their disposable income does not exceed £26,239 a year. A person may be refused civil aid if their disposable capital exceeds £13,017 and it appears to the Legal Aid board that they can afford to pay without legal aid. Additionally:

- if disposable capital is between £7,853 and £13,017, the applicant will be required to pay a contribution which will be equal to the difference between £7,853 and their disposable capital
- if disposable income is between £3,522 and £11,540, a contribution of one third of the difference between £3,522 and the disposable income may be payable
- if disposable income is between £11,541 and £15,743, one third of the difference between £3,522 and £11,540 plus half the difference between £11,541 and the disposable income may be payable
- if disposable income is between £15,744 and £26,239, a contribution of the following: one third of the difference between £3,522 and £11,540, plus half the difference between £11,541 and £15,743, plus all the remaining disposable income between £15,744 and £26,239 – will be payable

CRIMINAL LEGAL AID

The Legal Aid Agency provides defendants facing criminal charges with free legal representation if they pass a merits test and a means test.

Criminal legal aid covers the cost of preparing a case and legal representation in criminal proceedings. It is also available for appeals against verdicts or sentences in magistrates' courts, the crown court or the court of appeal. It is not available for bringing a private prosecution in a criminal court.

If granted criminal legal aid, either the person may choose their own solicitor or the court will assign one. Contributions to the legal costs may be required. The rules relating to applicable contributions are complex and detailed information can be obtained from the Legal Aid Agency.

DUTY SOLICITORS

LASPO also provides for free initial advice and initial assistance to anyone questioned by the police (whether under arrest or helping the police with their enquiries). No means test or contributions are required for this.

SCOTLAND

Legal advice and assistance operates in a similar way in Scotland. A person is eligible:

- if disposable income does not exceed £245 a week. If disposable income is between £105 and £245 a week, contributions are payable
- if disposable capital does not exceed £1,716 (if the person has dependent relatives, the savings allowance is higher)
- if receiving income support or income-related job seeker's allowance they qualify automatically provided their disposable capital is not over the limit

The procedure for application for criminal legal aid depends on the circumstances of each case. In solemn cases (more serious cases, such as murder) heard before a jury, a person is automatically entitled to criminal legal aid until they are given bail or placed in custody. Thereafter, it is for the court to decide whether to grant legal aid. The court will do this if the person accused cannot meet the expenses of the case without undue hardship on him or his dependants. In less serious cases the procedure depends on whether the person is in custody:

- anyone taken into custody has the right to free legal aid from the duty solicitor up to and including the first court appearance
- if the person is not in custody and wishes to plead guilty, they are not entitled to criminal legal aid but may be entitled to legal advice and assistance, including assistance by way of representation

However, regardless of whether the person is in custody if they wish to plead not guilty, they can apply for criminal legal aid. This must be done within 14 days of the first court appearance at which they made the plea

The criteria used to assess whether or not criminal legal aid should be granted is similar to the criteria for England and Wales. When meeting with your solicitor, take evidence of your financial position such as details of savings, bank statements, pay slips, pension book or benefits book.

Under the relevant provisions of the Scottish Civil Justice Council and Criminal Legal Assistance Act 2013, a person in receipt of criminal legal aid or criminal assistance by way of representation, will be required, in most circumstances, to make contributions where their weekly disposable income is £82 or above or if their disposable capital is £750 or more. The Scottish government has delayed the implementation of these provisions and no timetable has yet been proposed.

THE SCOTTISH LEGAL AID BOARD, Thistle House, 91 Haymarket Terrace, Edinburgh EH12 5HE T 0131-226 7061 W www.slab.org.uk

MARRIAGE

Any two persons may marry provided that:

- they are at least 16 years old on the day of the marriage (in England and Wales persons under the age of 18 must generally obtain the consent of their parents or guardian; if consent is refused an appeal may be made to the high court, the county court or a court of summary jurisdiction)
- they are not related to one another in a way which would prevent their marrying
- they are unmarried (a person who has already been married must produce documentary evidence that the previous marriage has been ended by death, divorce or annulment)
- they are capable of understanding the nature of a marriage ceremony and of consenting to marriage

It is now lawful for same sex couples to marry by way of civil or religious ceremony following the passing of the Marriage (Same Sex Couples) Act 2013, which came into force in March 2014. In addition, an existing marriage will now be able to continue where one or both parties change their legal gender and both parties wish to remain married. The Act also makes provision for civil partners to convert their civil partnership into a marriage if they wish to do so.

The parties should check the marriage will be recognised as valid in their home country if either is not a British citizen.

DEGREES OF RELATIONSHIP

A marriage between persons within the prohibited degrees of consanguinity, affinity or adoption is void.

Neither party may marry his or her parent, child, grandparent, grandchild, sibling, parent's sibling, sibling's child, adoptive parent, former adoptive parent, adoptive child or former adoptive child. All references to siblings include half-brothers/sisters.

Under the Marriage (Prohibited Degrees of Relationship) Act 1986, some exceptions to the law permit a person to marry certain step-relatives or in-laws.

In addition to the above, a person may not marry a child of their former civil partner, a child of a former spouse, the former civil partner of a grandparent, the former civil partner of a parent, the former spouse of a grandparent, the former spouse of a parent, the grandchild of a former civil partner or the grandchild of a former spouse, unless that relationship is the only reason they cannot marry and both persons are over 21 and the younger party has not at any time before attaining the age of 18 been a child of the family in relation to the other party.

ENGLAND AND WALES

TYPES OF MARRIAGE CEREMONY

It is possible to marry by either religious or civil ceremony. A religious ceremony can take place at a church or chapel of the Church of England or the Church in Wales, or at any other place of worship which has been formally registered by the Registrar-General. Same-sex marriages can also take place in a religious building, provided that the premises have been registered for the marriage of same-sex couples and the relevant governing authority in relation to the building has provided written consent. It is not possible, however, for same-sex marriages to take place in an Anglican church.

A civil ceremony can take place at a register office, a venue approved by the local authority or any religious premises where permission has been given by the relevant organisation and is approved by the local authority.

An application for an approved premises licence must be made by the owners or trustees of the building concerned; it cannot be made by the prospective marriage couple. Approved premises must be regularly open to the public so that the marriage can be witnessed; the venue must be deemed to be a permanent and immovable structure. Open-air ceremonies are prohibited.

Non-Anglican marriages may also be solemnised following the issue of a Registrar-General's licence in unregistered premises where one of the parties is seriously ill, is not expected to recover, and cannot be moved to registered premises. Detained and housebound persons may be married at their place of residence.

MARRIAGE IN THE CHURCH OF ENGLAND OR THE CHURCH IN WALES

Marriage by banns

The marriage can take place in a parish in which one of the parties lives, or in a church in another parish if it is the usual place of worship of either or both of the parties. Further to regulations introduced in October 2008 also, marriages can also take place in a parish where one of the parties was baptised or prepared for confirmation (but not if combined rite); a parish where one of the parties lived or attended worship for six months or more; a parish where one of the parents of either of the parties lived for six months or more; a parish where one of the parents of either of the parties has attended public worship for six months or more in the child's lifetime; or a parish where the parents or grandparents of either of the parties were married. The banns (ie the announcement of the marriage ceremony) must be called in the parish in which the marriage is to take place on three Sundays before the day of the ceremony; if either or both of the parties lives in a different parish the banns must also be called there. After three months the banns are no longer valid. The minister will not perform the marriage unless satisfied that the banns have been properly called.

Marriage by common licence

The vicar who is to conduct the marriage will arrange for a common licence to be issued by the diocesan bishop; this dispenses with the necessity for banns. One of the parties must have lived in the parish for 15 days immediately before the grant of the licence or must usually worship at the parish church or authorised chapel of that parish. Eligibility requirements vary from diocese to diocese, but it is not normally required that the parties should have been baptised. The licence is valid for three months.

Marriage by special licence

A special licence is granted by the Archbishop of Canterbury where a party has a genuine connection to a particular church or chapel but does not satisfy the legal requirements to marry there. The parties are usually required to demonstrate that they have a worshipping connection to the church or chapel. The special licence will expire after three months. Application must be made to the registrar of the Faculty Office: 1 The Sanctuary, London SW1P 3JT T 020-7222 5381.

Marriage by certificate

The marriage can be conducted on the authority of a superintendent registrar's certificates, provided that the consent of the minister of the church or chapel where the marriage is to take place is obtained. One of the parties must live in the parish or must usually worship at the church/chapel.

MARRIAGE BY OTHER RELIGIOUS CEREMONY

One of the parties must normally live in the registration district where the marriage is to take place. If the building where the parties wish to be married has not been registered, the couple can still have a religious ceremony there, but will also need to have a separate civil ceremony for the marriage to be valid. If the building is registered, in addition to giving notice to the superintendent registrar it may also be necessary to book a registrar, or authorised person to be present at the ceremony.

CIVIL MARRIAGE

A marriage may be solemnised at any register office, registered building or approved premises in England and Wales, without either of the parties being resident in the same district. The superintendent registrar of the district should be contacted, and, if the marriage is to take place at approved premises, the necessary arrangements at the venue must also be made.

NOTICE OF MARRIAGE

Where a marriage is intended to take place on the authority of a superintendent registrar's certificates, a notice of the marriage must be given in person to the superintendent registrar of the relevant district.

Both parties must have lived in a registration district in England or Wales for at least seven days immediately before giving notice personally at the local register office. If they live in different registration districts, notice must be given in both districts by the respective party in person. The marriage can take place in any register office or other approved premises in England and Wales no sooner than 28 days after notice has been given, when the superintendent registrar issues a certificate

A notice of marriage is valid for 12 months, unless it is for the marriage of a detained or housebound person, when it will usually only be accepted within three months of publication. Notice for marriages taking place within the Church of England or Church of Wales are also only valid for three months following publication. It should be possible to make an advance (provisional) booking 12 months before the ceremony. In this case it is still necessary to give formal notice three months before the marriage. When giving notice of the marriage it is necessary to produce official proof, if relevant, that any previous marriage has ended in divorce or death by producing a certified copy of the decree absolute or death certificate; it is also necessary for each of the parties to provide evidence of name and surname, date of birth, place of residence and nationality, for example, with a passport or birth certificate. If either party is under 18 years old, evidence of consent by their parent or guardian is required. There are special procedures for those wishing to get married in the UK that are subject to immigration control; the register office will be able to advise on these.

SOLEMNISATION OF THE MARRIAGE

On the day of the wedding there must be at least two other people present who are prepared to act as witnesses and sign the marriage register. A registrar of marriages must be present at a marriage in a register office or at approved premises, but an authorised person may act in the capacity of registrar in a registered building.

If the marriage takes place at approved premises, the room must be separate from any other activity on the premises at the time of the ceremony, and no food or drink can be sold or consumed in the room during the ceremony or for one hour beforehand.

The marriage must be solemnised with open doors. At some time during the ceremony the parties must make a declaration that they know of no legal impediment to the marriage and they must also say the contracting words; the declaratory and contracting words may vary according to the form of service. A civil marriage cannot contain any religious aspects, but it may be possible for non-religious music and/or readings to be included. It may also be possible to embellish the marriage vows taken by the couple.

CIVIL FEES

Notice and registration of Marriage at a Register Office
By superintendent registrar's certificate, £35 per person for the notice of the marriage (which is not refundable if the marriage does not in fact take place) and £46 for the registration of the marriage.

Marriage at a Register Office/Approved Premises
Fees for marriage at a register office are set by the local authority responsible. An additional fee will also be payable for the registrar's attendance at the marriage on an approved premises. This is also set locally by the local authority responsible. A further charge is likely to be made by the owners of the building for the use of the premises. For marriages taking place in a religious building other than the Church of England or Church of Wales, an additional fee of £84 is payable for the registrar's attendance at the marriage unless an 'Authorised Person' appointed by the trustees of the building has agreed to register the marriage. Additional fees may be charged by the trustees of the building for the wedding and by the person who performs the ceremony.

ECCLESIASTICAL FEES

(Church of England and Church in Wales)
Marriage by banns
For publication of banns, £28*
For certificate of banns issued at time of publication, £13*
For marriage service, £413*
For marriage certificate at time of registration £4 and £10 thereafter
* These fees are revised from 1 January each calendar year. Some may not apply to the Church in Wales

SCOTLAND
REGULAR MARRIAGES

A regular marriage is one which is celebrated by a minister of religion or authorised registrar or other celebrant. Each of the parties must complete a marriage notice form and return it to the district registrar for the area in which they are to be married, irrespective of where they live, within the three month period prior to the date of the marriage and not later than 29 days prior to that date. The district registrar must then enter the date of receipt and certain details in a marriage book kept for this purpose, and must also enter the names of the parties and the proposed date of marriage in a list which is displayed in a conspicuous place at the registration office until the date of the marriage has passed. All persons wishing to enter into a regular marriage in Scotland must follow the same preliminary procedure regardless of whether they intend to have a religious or civil ceremony. Before the marriage ceremony takes place any person may submit an objection in writing to the district registrar.

A marriage schedule, which is prepared by the registrar, will be issued to one or both of the parties in person up to seven days before a religious marriage; for a civil marriage the schedule will be available at the ceremony. The schedule must be handed to the celebrant before the ceremony starts and it must be signed immediately after the wedding. For religious marriages the schedule must be sent within three days by the parties to the district registrar who must register the marriage as soon as possible thereafter. In civil marriages, the district registrar must register the marriage as soon as possible.

The authority to conduct a religious marriage is deemed to be vested in the authorised celebrant rather than the building in which it takes place; open-air religious ceremonies are therefore permissible in Scotland.

From 10 June 2002 it has been possible, under the Marriage (Scotland) Act 2002, for venues or couples to apply to the local council for a licence to allow a civil ceremony to take place at a venue other than a registration office. To obtain further information, a venue or couple should contact the district registrar in the area they wish to marry.

MARRIAGE BY COHABITATION WITH HABIT AND REPUTE

Prior to the enactment of the Family Law (Scotland) Act 2006, if two people had lived together constantly as husband and wife and were generally held to be such by the neighbourhood and among their friends and relations, a presumption could arise from which marriage could be inferred. Before such a marriage could be registered, however, a decree of declarator of marriage had to be obtained from the court of session. Section 3 of the 2006 act provides that it will no longer be possible for a marriage to be constituted by cohabitation with habit and repute, but it will still be possible for couples whose period of cohabitation began before commencement of the 2006 act to seek a declarator under the old rule of law.

SAME-SEX MARRIAGES

On 12 March 2014 the Scottish government passed the Marriage and Civil Partnership (Scotland) Act 2014. This permits same-sex couples to get married, either in a civil ceremony or a 'religious or belief' ceremony where the religious or belief body has opted-in to solemnising same-sex marriage. Also, certain same-sex couples who have entered into a civil partnership have the option under the Act to change their civil partnership to a marriage.

It is still possible for same-sex couples to enter into a civil partnership and this may be a 'religious or belief' civil partnership if the religious or belief body has agreed to perform these.

CIVIL FEES

The fee for submitting a notice of marriage to the district registrar is £30.00 per person. Solemnisation of a civil marriage costs £55.00, while the extract of the entry in the register of marriages attracts a fee of £10.00. The costs of religious marriage ceremonies can vary.

THE GENERAL REGISTER OFFICE, PO Box 2,
  Southport PR8 2JD **T** 0845-603 7788
  W www.gro.gov.uk/gro/content/certificates
THE NATIONAL RECORDS OF SCOTLAND,
  New Register House, 2 Princes Street, Edinburgh EH1 3YY
  T 0131-314 0380 **W** www.nrsscotland.gov.uk

TOWN AND COUNTRY PLANNING

There are a number of acts governing the development of land and buildings in England and Wales and advice should always be sought from Citizens Advice or the local planning authority before undertaking building works on any land or property. If development takes place which requires planning permission without permission being given, enforcement action may take place and the situation may need to be rectified. Planning law in Scotland is similar but certain Scotland-specific legislation applies so advice should always be sought.

PLANNING PERMISSION

Planning permission is needed if the work involves:
- making a material change in use, such as dividing off part of the house or garden so that it can be used as a separate home or dividing off part of the house for commercial use, eg for a workshop
- going against the terms of the original planning permission, eg there may be a restriction on fences in front gardens on an open-plan estate
- building, engineering or mining, except for the permitted developments below
- new or wider access to a main road
- additions or extensions to flats or maisonettes
- work which might obstruct the view of road users

Planning permission is not needed to carry out internal alterations or work which does not affect the external appearance of the building, and are not works for making good war damage or works begun after 5 December 1968 for the alteration of a building by providing additional space in it underground.

Under regulations which came into effect on 1 October 2008, there are certain types of development for which the Secretary of State for the Environment, Food and Rural Affairs has granted general permissions (permitted development rights). These include house extensions and additions, outbuildings and garages, other ancillary garden buildings such as swimming pools or ponds, and laying patios, paths or driveways for domestic use. All developments are subject to a number of conditions.

Before carrying out any of the above permitted developments you should contact your local planning authority to find out whether the general permission has been modified in your area. For more information, visit W www.planningportal.gov.uk

OTHER RESTRICTIONS

It may be necessary to obtain other types of permissions before carrying out any development. These permissions are separate from planning permission and apply regardless of whether or not planning permission is needed, eg:
- building regulations will probably apply if a new building is to be erected, if an existing one is to be altered or extended, or if the work involves building over a drain or sewer. The building control department of the local authority will advise on this
- any alterations to a listed building or the grounds of a listed building must be approved by the local authority. Listing will include not only the main building but everything in the curtilage of the building
- local authority approval is necessary if a building (or, in some circumstances, gates, walls, fences or railings) in a conservation area is to be demolished; each local authority keeps a register of all local buildings that are in conservation areas
- many trees are protected by tree preservation orders and must not be pruned or taken down without local authority consent
- bats and many other species are protected, and Natural England, Natural Resources Wales or Scottish Natural Heritage must be notified before any work is carried out that will affect the habitat of protected species, eg timber treatment, renovation or extensions of lofts
- developments in areas with special designations, such as National Parks, Areas of Outstanding Natural Beauty, National Scenic Areas or in the Norfolk or Suffolk Broads, are subject to greater restrictions. The local planning authority will advise or refer enquirers to the relevant authority

There may also be restrictions contained in the title to the property which require you to get someone else's agreement before carrying out certain developments, and which should be considered when works are planned.

VOTERS' QUALIFICATIONS

Those entitled to vote at parliamentary, and local government elections are those who, at the date of taking the poll, are:
- on the electoral roll
- aged 18 years or older
- British citizens, Commonwealth citizens or citizens of the Irish Republic who are resident in the UK
- those who suffer from no other legal bar to voting (eg prisoners). It should be noted that there is some uncertainty regarding the future of the legal bar on prisoners' voting following a decision taken by the European Court of Human Rights
- in Northern Ireland electors must have been resident in Northern Ireland during the whole of the three-month period prior to the relevant date
- citizens of any EU member state may vote in local elections if they meet the criteria listed above (save for the nationality requirements)

British citizens resident abroad are entitled to vote, provided they have been registered to vote in the UK within the last 15 years, as overseas electors in domestic parliamentary elections in the constituency in which they were last resident if they are on the electoral roll of the relevant constituency. Members of the armed forces and their spouses or civil partners, Crown servants and employees of the British Council who are overseas, along with their spouses and civil partners, are entitled to vote regardless of how long they have been abroad. British citizens who had never been registered as an elector in the UK are not eligible to register as an overseas voter unless they left the UK before they were 18, providing they left the country no more than 15 years ago. Overseas electors may opt to vote by proxy or by postal vote. Overseas voters may not vote in local government elections.

The main categories of people who are not entitled to vote at general elections are:
- sitting peers in the House of Lords
- convicted persons detained in pursuance of their sentences (though remand prisoners, unconvicted prisoners and civil prisoners can vote if on the electoral register. This is currently subject to review, as detailed above
- those convicted within the previous five years of corrupt or illegal election practices
- EU citizens (who may only vote in EU and local government elections)

Under the Representation of the Peoples Act 2000, several new groups of people are permitted to vote for the first time. These include: people who live on barges; people in mental health hospitals (other than those with criminal convictions) and homeless people who have made a 'declaration of local connection'.

REGISTERING TO VOTE

Voters must be entered on an electoral register. The Electoral Registration Officer (ERO) for each council area is responsible for preparing and publishing the register for his area by 1 December each year. Names may be added to the register to reflect changes in people's circumstances as they occur and each month during December to August, the ERO publishes a list of alterations to the published register.

On 10 May 2012, the government introduced the electoral registration and administration bill, which received royal assent on 31 January 2013. The act replaced household registration with individual elector registration, meaning each elector must apply individually to be registered to vote. Individuals will also be asked for identifying information such as date of birth and national insurance number. The act also introduced a number of changes relating to electoral administration and the conduct of elections. Anyone failing to supply information to the ERO when requested, or supplying false information, may be fined by up to £1,000. Further, the ERO may impose a civil penalty on those who fail to make an application for registration when required to do so by the ERO. Application forms and more information are available from the Electoral Commission (W www.aboutmyvote.co.uk).

VOTING

Voting is not compulsory in the UK. Those who wish to vote do so in person at the allotted polling station. Postal votes are now available to anyone on request and you do not need to give a reason for using a postal vote.

A proxy (whereby the voter nominates someone to vote in person on their behalf) can be appointed to act in a specific election, for a specified period of time or indefinitely. For the appointment of an indefinite or long-term proxy, the voter needs to specify physical employment, study reasons or a disability to explain why they are making an application. With proxy votes where a particular election is specified, the voter needs to provide details of the circumstances by which they cannot reasonably be expected to go to the polling station. Applications for a proxy are normally available up to six working days before an election, but should the voter fall ill on election day, it is possible to appoint a proxy up until polling day.

WILLS

A will is used to appoint executors (who will administer the estate), give directions as to the disposal of the body, appoint guardians for children and determine how and to whom property is to be passed. A well-drafted will can operate to reduce the level of inheritance tax which the estate pays. It is best to have a will drawn up by a solicitor, but if a solicitor is not employed the following points must be taken into account:

- if possible the will must not be prepared on behalf of another person by someone who is to benefit from it or who is a close relative of a major beneficiary
- the language used must be clear and unambiguous and it is better to avoid the use of legal terms where the same thing can be expressed in plain language
- it is better to rewrite the whole document if a mistake is made. If necessary, alterations can be made by striking through the words with a pen, and the signature or initials of the testator and the witnesses must be put in the margin opposite the alteration. No alteration of any kind should be made after the will has been executed
- if the person later wishes to change the will or part of it, it is better to write a new will revoking the old. The use of codicils (documents written as supplements or containing modifications to the will) should be left to a solicitor
- the will should be typed or printed, or if handwritten be legible and preferably in ink

The form of a will varies to suit different cases – a solicitor will be able to advise as to wording, however, 'DIY' will-writing kits can be purchased from good stationery shops and many banks offer a will-writing service.

LAPSED LEGATEES

If a person who has been left property in a will dies before the person who made the will, the gift fails and will pass to the person entitled to everything not otherwise disposed of (the residuary estate). If the beneficiary of the residuary estate dies before the person who made the will, the gift of the residuary estate also fails and passes to the closest relative(s) of the testator in accordance with the intestacy rules.

It is always better to draw up a new will if a beneficiary predeceases the person who made the will.

EXECUTORS

It is usual to appoint two executors, although one is sufficient. No more than four persons can deal with the estate of the person who has died. The name and address of each executor should be given in full (the addresses are not essential but including them adds clarity to the document). Executors should be 18 years of age or over. An executor may be a beneficiary of the will.

WITNESSES

A person who is a beneficiary of a will, or the spouse or civil partner of a beneficiary at the time the will is signed, must not act as a witness or else he/she will be unable to take his/her gift. There is nothing preventing the spouse or civil partner of the person making the will from acting as a witness, but as it is rare for a spouse or civil partner not to benefit from the will of his/her spouse or civil partner, an independent witness is usually better.

It is also better that a person does not act as an executor and as a witness, as he/she can take no benefit (including remuneration) under a will to which he/she is witness. In relation to deaths on or after 1 February 2001, however, a professional executor who is also a witness can receive payments due to him or her under a term in the will for services provided as executor.

The identity of the witnesses should be made as explicit as possible, such as by stating their names, addresses, and occupations.

EXECUTION OF A WILL

The person making the will should sign his/her name in the presence of the two witnesses. It is advisable to sign at the foot of the document, so as to avoid uncertainty about the testator's intention. The witnesses must then sign their names while the person making the will looks on. If this procedure is not adhered to, the will may be considered invalid. There are certain exceptional circumstances where these rules are relaxed, eg where the person may be too ill to sign.

CAPACITY TO MAKE A WILL

Anyone aged 18 or over can make a will. However, if there is any suspicion that the person making the will is not, through reasons of infirmity or age, fully in command of his/her faculties, it is advisable to arrange for a medical practitioner to examine the person making the will at the time it is to be executed (to verify his/her mental capacity and to record that medical opinion in writing), and to ask the examining practitioner to act as a witness. If a person is not mentally able to make a will, the court may do this for him/her by virtue of the Mental Capacity Act 2005.

REVOCATION

A will may be revoked or cancelled in a number of ways:

- a later will revokes an earlier one if it says so; otherwise the earlier will is by implication revoked by the later one to the extent that it contradicts or repeats the earlier one
- a will is revoked if the physical document on which it is written is destroyed by the person whose will it is. There must be an intention to revoke the will and an act of destruction. It may not be sufficient to obliterate the will with a pen
- a will is revoked by the testator making a written declaration to this effect executed in the same way as a will
- a will is also revoked when the person marries or forms a civil partnership, unless it is clear from the will that the person intended the will to stand after that particular marriage or civil partnership. A will is not revoked, however, by the conversion of a civil partnership to a marriage
- where a marriage or civil partnership ends in divorce or dissolution or is annulled or declared void, gifts to the spouse or civil partner and the appointment of the spouse or civil partner as executor fail unless the will says that this is not to happen. A former spouse or civil partner is treated as having predeceased the testator. A separation does not change the effect of a married person or civil partner's will.

PROBATE AND LETTERS OF ADMINISTRATION

Probate is granted to the executors named in a will and once granted, the executors are obliged to carry out the instructions of the will. Letters of administration are granted where no executor is named in a will or is willing or able to act or where there is no will or no valid will; this gives a person, often the next of kin, similar powers and duties to those of an executor.

Applications for probate or for letters of administration can be made to the Principal Registry of the Family Division, to a district probate registry or to a probate sub-registry. Applicants will need the following documents: the Probate Application Form; the original will and codicils (if any) and three copies; a certificate of death; oath for executors or administrators; and the appropriate tax form (an 'IHT 205' if no inheritance tax is owed; otherwise an 'IHT 400' and 'IHT 421'), in addition to a cheque for the relevant probate fee. Certain property, up to the value of £5,000, may be disposed of without a grant of probate or letters of administration, as can assets that do not pass under the will such as jointly owned assets which pass automatically on the death of one of the joint holders to the survivor.

WHERE TO FIND A PROVED WILL

Since 1858 wills which have been proved, that is wills on which probate or letters of administration have been granted, must have been proved at the Principal Registry of the Family Division or at a district probate registry. The Lord Chancellor has power to direct where the original documents are kept but most are filed where they were proved and may be inspected there and a copy obtained. The Principal Registry also holds copies of all wills proved at district probate registries and these may be inspected at First Avenue House, High Holborn, London. An index of all grants, both of probate and of letters of administration, is compiled by the Principal Registry and may be seen either at the Principal Registry or at a district probate registry.

It is also possible to discover when a grant of probate or letters of administration is issued by requesting a standing search. In response to a request and for a small fee, a district probate registry will supply the names and addresses of executors or administrators and the registry in which the grant was made, of any grant in the estate of a specified person made in the previous 12 months or following six months.

PRINCIPAL REGISTRY (FAMILY DIVISION),
First Avenue House, 42–49 High Holborn, London WC1 6NP
T 020-7947 6000

INTESTACY

Intestacy occurs when someone dies without leaving a will or leaves a will which is invalid or which does not take effect for some reason. Intestacy can be partial, for instance, if there is a will which disposes of some but not all of the testator's property. In such cases the person's estate (property, possessions, other assets following the payment of debts) passes to certain members of the family. If a will has been written that disposes of only part of a person's property, these rules apply to the part which is undisposed of.

Some types of property do not follow the intestacy rules, for example, property held as joint tenants, insurance policies taken out for specified individuals or assigned into trust during the testator's lifetime and death benefits under a pension scheme.

Following a lengthy review by the Law Commission, the intestacy rules changed on 1 October 2014.

If the person (intestate) leaves a spouse or a civil partner who survives for 28 days and children (legitimate, illegitimate and adopted children and other descendants), the estate is divided as follows:

- if the estate is worth more than £250,000, the spouse or civil partner takes the 'personal chattels' (household articles, including cars, but nothing used for business purposes), £250,000 and half of the rest of the estate absolutely
- the rest of the estate goes to the children*

If the intestate leaves a spouse or civil partner who survives for 28 days but no children, the spouse or civil partner will take the estate in its entirety, regardless of its value.

If there is no surviving spouse or civil partner, the estate is distributed among those who survive the intestate as follows (these provisions remained unchanged at 1 October 2014):

- to surviving children*, but if none to
- parents (equally, if both alive), but if none to
- brothers and sisters of the whole blood* (including issue of deceased ones), but if none to
- brothers and sisters of the half blood* (including issue of deceased ones), but if none to
- grandparents (equally, if more than one), but if none to
- aunts and uncles of the whole blood*, but if none to
- aunts and uncles of the half blood*, but if none to
- the Crown, Duchy of Lancaster or the Duke of Cornwall (bona vacantia)

* To inherit, a member of these groups must survive the intestate and attain the age of 18, or marry under that age. If they die under the age of 18 (unless married under that age), their share goes to others, if any, in the same group. If any member of these groups predeceases the intestate leaving children, their share is divided equally among their children.

In England and Wales the provisions of the Inheritance (Provision for Family and Dependants) Act 1975 may allow other people to claim provision from the deceased's assets. This act also applies to cases where a will has been made and allows a person to apply to the court if they feel that the will or rules of intestacy (or both) do not make adequate

provision for them. The court can order payment from the deceased's assets or the transfer of property from them if the applicant's claim is accepted. The application must be made within six months of the grant of probate or letters of administration and the following people can make an application:
• the spouse or civil partner
• a former spouse or civil partner who has not remarried or formed a subsequent civil partnership
• a child of the deceased
• someone treated as a child of the deceased's family where the deceased stood in the role of a parent to the applicant
• someone maintained by the deceased
• someone who has cohabited for two years before the death in the same household as the deceased and as the husband or wife or civil partner of the deceased

SCOTLAND

In Scotland any person over 12 and of sound mind can make a will. The person making the will can only freely dispose of the heritage and what is known as the 'dead's part' of the estate because:
• the spouse or civil partner has the right to inherit one-third of the moveable estate if there are children or other descendants, and one-half of it if there are not
• children are entitled to one-third of the moveable estate if there is a surviving spouse or civil partner, and one-half of it if there is not

The remaining portion of the moveable estate is the dead's part, and legacies and bequests are payable from this. Debts are payable out of the whole estate before any division.

From August 1995, wills no longer needed to be 'holographed' and it is now only necessary to have one witness. The person making the will still needs to sign each page. It is better that the will is not witnessed by a beneficiary although the attestation would still be sound and the beneficiary would not have to relinquish the gift.

Subsequent marriage or civil partnership does not revoke a will but the birth of a child who is not provided for may do so. A will may be revoked by a subsequent will, either expressly or by implication, but in so far as the two can be read together both have effect. If a subsequent will is revoked, the earlier will may be revived provided it wasn't physically destroyed. However, the Scottish government has proposed changes to this in the succession (Scotland) bill which was introduced into the Scottish parliament in June 2015.

Wills may be registered in the sheriff court Books of the Sheriffdom in which the deceased lived or in the Books of Council and Session at the Registers of Scotland.

CONFIRMATION

Confirmation (the Scottish equivalent of probate) is obtained in the sheriff court of the sheriffdom in which the deceased was domiciled at the time of death. Executors are either 'nominate' (named by the deceased in the will) or 'dative' (appointed by the court in cases where no executor is named in a will or in cases of intestacy). Applicants for confirmation must first provide an inventory of the deceased's estate and a schedule of debts, with an affidavit. In estates under £36,000 gross, confirmation can be obtained under a simplified procedure at reduced fees, with no need for a solicitor. The local sheriff clerk's office can provide assistance.

PRINCIPAL REGISTRY (FAMILY DIVISION),
   First Avenue House, 42–49 High Holborn, London WC1 6NP
   T 020-7947 6000
REGISTERS OF SCOTLAND, Meadowbank House,
   153 London Road, Edinburgh EH8 7AU T 0845-607 0161

INTESTACY

The rules of distribution are contained in the Succession (Scotland) Act 1964 and are extended to include civil partners by the Civil Partnership Act 2004.

A surviving spouse or civil partner is entitled to 'prior rights'. Once the provisions of the Marriage and Civil Partnership Act 2014 come into force references to people who are or were married are to be read as referring to both opposite and same-sex marriage. Prior rights mean that if certain conditions are met the spouse or civil partner has the right to inherit:
• the matrimonial or family home up to a value of £473,000, or one matrimonial or family home if there is more than one, or, in certain circumstances, the value of the home
• the furnishings and contents of that home, up to the value of £29,000
• a cash sum of £50,000 if the deceased left children or other descendants, or £89,000 if not

These figures are increased from time to time by regulations.

Once prior rights have been satisfied legal rights are settled. Legal rights are:
• *Jus relicti(ae) and rights under the section 131 of the Civil Partnership Act 2004* – the right of a surviving spouse or civil partner to one-half of the net moveable estate, after satisfaction of prior rights, if there are no surviving children; if there are surviving children, the spouse or civil partner is entitled to one-third of the net moveable estate
• *Legitim and rights under the section 131 of the Civil Partnership Act 2004* – the right of surviving children to one-half of the net moveable estate if there is no surviving spouse or civil partner; if there is a surviving spouse or civil partner, the children are entitled to one-third of the net moveable estate after the satisfaction of prior rights

Once prior and legal rights have been satisfied, the remaining estate will be distributed in the following order:
• to descendants
• if no descendants, then to collaterals (ie brothers and sisters) and parents with each being entitled to half of the estate, or if only either parents or collaterals survive, the whole of the estate
• surviving spouse or civil partner
• if no collaterals, parents, spouse or civil partner, then to ascendants collaterals (ie aunts and uncles), and so on in an ascending scale
• if all lines of succession fail, the estate passes to the Crown

Relatives of the whole blood are preferred to relatives of the half blood. Also the right of representation, ie the right of the issue of a person who would have succeeded if he/she had survived the intestate applies.

The Family Law (Scotland) Act 2006 makes provision to allow an unmarried cohabitant to make a financial claim against the estate of a cohabitant who dies intestate. In general a claim must be made within six months of the deceased's death. The court must take into account certain factors when considering such a claim. If the claim is successful the court has the power to order payment of a capital sum and transfer of property.

INTELLECTUAL PROPERTY

Intellectual property is a broad term covering a number of legal rights provided by the government to help people protect their creative works and encourage further innovation. By using these legal rights people can own the things they create and control the way in which others use their innovations. Intellectual property owners can take legal action to stop others using their intellectual property, they can license their intellectual property to others or they can sell it on. Different types of intellectual property utilise different forms of protection including copyright, designs, patents and trade marks, which are all covered below in more detail.

CHANGES TO INTELLECTUAL PROPERTY LAW

- Reforms to the Copyright, Designs and Patents Act 1988 came into force on 1 June 2014 giving a number of sectors a legal framework suitable for the digital age, removing unnecessary regulations and enabling these sectors to better preserve and use copyright material. Under the reforms, disabled people and disability groups can make accessible copies of copyright material (eg music, film, books) when no commercial alternative exists, researchers benefit from the introduction of a new text and data mining exception for non-commercial research and schools, colleges and universities can obtain a licence to use copyright material on interactive whiteboards and in presentations without accidentally infringing copyright. An existing preservation exception was expanded to cover all types of copyright work, and now applies to museums and galleries as well as libraries and archives.
- A new online patent renewal service (W www.gov.uk/renew-patent) was launched on 1 July 2014; designed to make renewing over 400,000 patents each year simpler, quicker and cheaper for businesses and inventors
- The Intellectual Property Act 2014 came into effect on 1 October 2014. The Act modernised intellectual property law to help UK businesses better protect their rights. The Act also implemented reforms to design legislation and introduced a number of changes to patent law making it cheaper and easier to use and defend patents.

COPYRIGHT

Copyright protects all original literary, dramatic, musical and artistic works, as well as sound and film recordings and broadcasts. Among the works covered by copyright are novels, computer programs, newspaper articles, sculptures, technical drawings, websites, maps and photographs. Under copyright the creators of these works can control the various ways in which their material may be exploited, the rights broadly covering copying, adapting, issuing (including renting and lending) copies to the public, performing in public, and broadcasting the material. The transfer of copyright works to formats accessible to visually impaired persons without infringement of copyright was enacted in 2002.

Copyright protection in the UK is automatic and there is no official registration system. The creator of a work can help to protect it by including the copyright symbol ©, the name of the copyright owner, and the year in which the work was created. In addition, steps can be taken by the work's creator to provide evidence that he/she had the work at a particular time (eg by depositing a copy with a bank or solicitor). The main legislation is the Copyright, Designs and Patents Act 1988 (as amended). As a result of an EU directive effective from January 1996, the term of copyright protection for literary, dramatic, musical (including song lyrics and musical compositions) and artistic works lasts for 70 years after the death of the creator. For film, copyright lasts for 70 years after the director, authors of the screenplay and dialogue, or the composer of any music specially created for the film have all died. Sound recordings are protected for 50 years after their publication (or their first performance if they are not published), and broadcasts for 50 years from the end of the year in which the broadcast/transmission was made. The typographical arrangement of published editions remains under copyright protection for 25 years from the end of the year in which the particular edition was published.

The main international treaties protecting copyright are the Berne Convention for the Protection of Literary and Artistic Works (administered by the World Intellectual Property Organisation (WIPO)), the Rome Convention for the Protection of Performers, Producers of Phonograms and Broadcasting Organisations (administered by the United Nations Educational, Scientific and Cultural Organization (UNESCO), the International Labour Organisation and WIPO), the Geneva Phonograms Convention (administered by WIPO), and the Universal Copyright Convention (developed by UNESCO); the UK is a signatory to these conventions. Copyright material created by UK nationals or residents is protected in the countries that have signed one of the above-named conventions by the national law of that country. A list of participating countries may be obtained from the UK Intellectual Property Office. The World Trade Organisation's Trade-Related Aspects of Intellectual Property Rights (TRIPS) agreement, signed in 1995, may also provide copyright protection abroad.

Two treaties which strengthen and update international standards of protection, particularly in relation to new technologies, were agreed in December 1996: the WIPO Copyright Treaty, and the WIPO Performances and Phonograms Treaty. In May 2001 the European Union passed a new directive (which in 2003 became law in the UK) aimed at harmonising copyright law throughout the EU to take account of the internet and other technologies. More information can be found online (W www.ipo.gov.uk).

LICENSING

Use of copyright material without seeking permission in each instance may be permitted under 'blanket' licences available from national copyright licensing agencies. The International Federation of Reproduction Rights Organisations facilitates agreements between its member licensing agencies and on behalf of its members with organisations such as WIPO, UNESCO, the European Union and the Council of Europe. More information can be found online (W www.ifrro.org).

DESIGN PROTECTION

Design protection covers the outward appearance of an article and in the UK takes two forms: registered design and design right, which are not mutually exclusive. Registered design protects the aesthetic appearance of an article, including shape, configuration, pattern or ornament; artistic works such as sculptures are excluded, being generally protected by copyright. To achieve design protection the owner of the design must apply to the Intellectual Property Office. In order to qualify for protection, a design must be new and materially different from earlier UK published designs. Initial registration lasts for five years and can be extended in five-year increments to a maximum of 25 years.

The current legislation is the Registered Designs Act 1949 which has been amended several times, most recently by the Regulatory Reform Order 2006.

UK applicants wishing to protect their designs in the EU can do so by applying for a Registered Community Design with the Office for Harmonization in the Internal Market. Outside the EU separate applications must be made in each country in which protection is sought.

Design right is an automatic right which applies to the shape or configuration of articles and does not require registration. Unlike registered design, two-dimensional designs do not qualify for protection but designs of electronic circuits are protected by design right. Designs must be original and non-commonplace. The term of design right is ten years from first marketing of the design, or 15 years after the creation of the design, whichever is earlier. This right is effective only in the UK. After five years anyone is entitled to apply for a licence of right, which allows others to make and sell products copying the design. The current legislation is Part 3 of the Copyright, Designs and Patents Act 1988.

PATENTS

A patent is a document issued by the UK Intellectual Property Office relating to an invention. It gives the proprietor the right for a limited period to stop others from making, using, importing or selling the invention without the inventor's permission. In return the patentee pays a fee to cover the costs of processing the patent and publicly discloses details of the invention.

To qualify for a patent an invention must be new, must be functional or technical, must exhibit an inventive step, and must be capable of industrial application. The patent is valid for a maximum of 20 years from the date on which the application was filed, subject to payment of annual fees from the end of the fifth year.

The UK Intellectual Property Office, established in 1852, is responsible for ensuring that all stages of an application comply with the Patents Act 1977, and that the invention meets the criteria for a patent.

WIPO is responsible for administering many of the international conventions on intellectual property. The Patent Cooperation Treaty allows inventors to file a single application for patent rights in some or all of the contracting states. This application is searched by an International Searching Authority to confirm the invention is novel and that the same concept has not already been made publicly available. The application and search report are then published by the International Bureau of WIPO. It may also be the subject of an (optional) international preliminary examination. Applicants must then deal directly with the patent offices in the countries where they are seeking patent rights. The European Patent Convention allows inventors to obtain patent rights in all the contracting states by filing a single application with the European Patent Office. More information can be found online (W www.ipo.gov.uk).

RESEARCH DISCLOSURES

Research disclosures are publicly disclosed details of inventions. Once published, an invention is considered no longer novel and becomes 'prior art'. Publishing a disclosure is significantly cheaper than applying for a patent; however, unlike a patent, it does not entitle the author to exclusive rights to use or license the invention. Instead, research disclosures are primarily published to ensure the inventor the freedom to use the invention. This works because publishing legally prevents other parties from patenting the disclosed innovation and in the UK, patent law dictates that by disclosing details of an invention, even the inventor relinquishes their right to a patent.

In theory, publishing details of an invention anywhere should be enough to constitute a research disclosure. However, to be effective, a research disclosure needs to be published in a location which patent examiners will include in their prior art searches. To ensure global legal precedent it must be included in a publication with a recognised date stamp and made publicly available throughout the world.

Research Disclosure, established in 1960 and operated by Questel Ireland Ltd, is the primary publisher of research disclosures. It is the only disclosure service recognised by the Patent Cooperation Treaty as a mandatory search resource which must be consulted by the international search authorities. More information can be found online (W www.researchdisclosure.com).

TRADE MARKS

Trade marks are a means of identification, enabling traders to make their goods and services readily distinguishable from those supplied by others. Trade marks can take the form of words, a logo or a combination of both. Registration prevents other traders using the same or similar trade marks for similar products or services.

In the UK trade marks are registered at the UK Intellectual Property Office. In order to qualify for registration a trade mark must be capable of distinguishing its proprietor's goods or services from those of other undertakings; it should be non-deceptive, should not describe the goods and services or any characteristics of them, should not be contrary to law or morality and should not be similar or identical to any earlier trade marks for the same or similar goods or services. The owner of a registered trade mark may include an fi symbol next to it, and must renew their registration every ten years to keep it in force. The relevant current legislation is the Trade Marks Act 1994 (as amended).

It is possible to obtain an international trade mark registration, effective in 92 countries, under the Madrid system for the international registration of marks, to which the UK is party. British companies can obtain international trade mark registration in those countries party to the system through a single application to WIPO.

EU trade mark regulation is administered by the Office for Harmonization in the Internal Market (Trade Marks and Designs) in Alicante, Spain. The office registers Community trade marks, which are valid throughout the European Union. The registration of trade marks in individual member states continues in parallel with EU trade mark standards.

DOMAIN NAMES

An internet domain name (eg www.bloomsbury.com) has to be registered separately from a trade mark, and this can be done through a number of registrars which charge varying rates and compete for business. For each top-level domain name (eg uk.com), there is a central registry to store the unique internet names and addresses using that suffix. A list of accredited registrars can be found online (W www.icann.org).

CONTACTS

COPYRIGHT LICENSING AGENCY LTD, Saffron House, 6–10 Kirby Street, London EC1N 8TS T 020-7400 3100 W www.cla.co.uk

EUROPEAN PATENT OFFICE, 80298 Munich, Germany T (+49) 89 2399-0 W www.epo.org

INTELLECTUAL PROPERTY OFFICE, Concept House, Cardiff Road, Newport NP10 8QQ T 0300-300 2000 W www.ipo.gov.uk

WORLD INTELLECTUAL PROPERTY ORGANIZATION, 34 chemin des Colombettes, CH-1211 Geneva 20, Switzerland T (+41) 22 338 9111 W www.wipo.int

THE MEDIA

CROSS-MEDIA OWNERSHIP

The rules surrounding cross-media ownership were overhauled as part of the 2003 Communications Act. The act simplified and relaxed existing rules to encourage dispersion of ownership and new market entry while preventing the most influential media in any community being controlled by too narrow a range of interests. However, transfers and mergers are not solely subject to examination on competition grounds by the competition authorities. The Secretary of State for Culture, Media and Sport has a broad remit to decide if a transaction is permissible and can intervene on public interest grounds (relating both to newspapers and cross-media criteria, if broadcasting interests are also involved); the Secretary of State for Business, Innovation and Skills may also intervene in a media merger if it raises public interest considerations. The Office of Communications (OFCOM) has an advisory role in this context. Government and parliamentary assurances were given that any intervention into local newspaper transfers would be rare and exceptional. Following a request from the Secretary of State for Culture, Media and Sport in June 2010 for a removal of all restrictions from the ownership of local media, OFCOM recommended the liberalisation of local cross-media regulations to enable a single owner to control newspapers, a TV licence and radio stations in one area.

REGULATION

OFCOM is the regulator for the communication industries in the UK and has responsibility for television, radio, telecommunications and wireless communications services. OFCOM is required to report annually to parliament and exists to further the interests of consumers by balancing choice and competition with the duty to foster plurality; protect viewers and listeners and promote cultural diversity in the media; and to ensure full and fair competition between communications providers.

OFFICE OF COMMUNICATIONS (OFCOM)
Riverside House, 2A Southwark Bridge Road, London SE1 9HA
T 020-7981 3000 W www.ofcom.org.uk
Chief Executive, Sharon White

COMPLAINTS

Under the Communications Act 2003 OFCOM's licensees are obliged to adhere to the provisions of its codes (including advertising, programme standards, fairness, privacy and sponsorship). Complainants should contact the broadcaster in the first instance (details can be found on OFCOM's website); however, if the complainant wishes the complaint to be considered by OFCOM, it will do so. Complaints should be made within a reasonable time, as broadcasters are only required to keep recordings for the following periods: radio, 42 days; television, 90 days; and cable and satellite, 60 days. OFCOM can fine a broadcaster, revoke a licence or take programmes off the air. Since November 2004 complaints relating to individual advertisements on TV or radio have been dealt with by the Advertising Standards Authority.

ADVERTISING STANDARDS AUTHORITY
Mid City Place, 71 High Holborn, London WC1V 6QT
T 020-7492 2222 W www.asa.org.uk
Chief Executive, Guy Parker

TELEVISION

There are six major television broadcasters operating in the UK. Four of these – the BBC, ITV, Channel 4 and Channel 5 – launched as free-to-air analogue terrestrial networks. BSkyB and Virgin Media Television provide satellite television services.

Beginning as a radio station in 1922, the BBC is the oldest broadcaster in the world. The corporation began a London-only television service from Alexandra Palace in 1936 and achieved nationwide coverage 15 years later. A second station, BBC Two, was launched in 1964. The BBC's other free-to-air channels available in the UK comprise BBC Three, BBC Four, BBC One HD, BBC Two HD, BBC News, BBC Parliament and the children's channels, CBeebies and CBBC. BBC's iPlayer service was launced Christmas Day 2007 and allows users to view and listen to programress from the last seven days instantly, stream live television and download programmes on to a computer or mobile device for up to 30 days. An integrated service for radio was launched in June 2008. In 2009, iPlayer was extended to more than 20 devices, including mobile phones and games consoles, and a HD service was launched. The BBC services are funded by the licence fee. The corporation also has a commercial arm, BBC Worldwide, which was formed in 1994 and exists to maximise the value of the BBC's programme and publishing assets for the benefit of the licence payer. Its businesses include international programming distribution, magazines, other licensed products, live events and media monitoring.

The ITV (Independent Television) network began broadcasting in 1955 on Channel 3 in the London area, under the Television Act 1954 which made provision for commercial television in the UK. The ITV network originally comprised a number of independent licensees, the majority of which have now merged to form ITV plc. The network generates funds through broadcasting television advertisements. The ITV network channels now include ITV2, ITV3, ITV4, ITVBe and CiTV. ITV Player, similar to iPlayer, was launched December 2008. ITV Network Centre is wholly owned by the ITV companies and undertakes commissioning and scheduling of programmes shown across the ITV network and, as with the other terrestrial channels, 25 per cent of programmes must come from independent producers.

Channel 4 and S4C (Sianel Pedwar Cymru – Channel Four Wales) were launched in 1982 to provide programmes with a distinctive character that appeal to interests not catered for by ITV. Channel 4 has a remit to be innovative, experimental and distinctive. Although publicly owned, Channel 4 receives no public funding and is financed predominantly through advertising, but unlike ITV, Channel 4 is not shareholder-owned. It has expanded to create the stations E4, More4, Film4, 4Music and, in July 2012, catchup channel 4seven. All 4 is Channel 4's online service which enables viewers to download and revisit programmes from the last 30 days as well as access an older archive of footage. All 4 replaced Channel 4's first online platform 4oD (launched in 2006) in March 2015. S4/C, the Welsh language public service broadcaster, received annual funding from the Department for Culture, Media and Sport (DCMS), which was reduced by 93 per cent between 2010 and 2014; it now receives just under £7m a year. Amid funding concerns for the future of S4C, it was agreed that the BBC would fund most of S4C's activities from the licence fee, contributing £75.25m in 2015–16. S4C will remain independent and be entitled to receive UK government funding and generate its own revenue. The on-demand service is called S4C Clic.

Channel 5 began broadcasting in 1997. It was rebranded Five in 2002 but reverted to its original name, Channel 5, after the station was acquired by Northern & Shell in July 2010. Digital stations 5USA and 5* (formerly Five Life, then Fiver) were launched in October 2006. Demand Five is an online service, launched in June 2008, where viewers can watch and download content from the last 30 days.

BSkyB was formed after the merger in 1990 of Sky Television and British Sky Broadcasting. 21st Century Fox has a 39.14 per cent controlling stake in the company, which operates a satellite television service with 900 television channels, including Sky One and the Sky Sports and Sky Movies ranges. Sky Digital was launched on 1 October 1998. Its key selling points were the improvement in sound and picture quality and an increased number of channels, some of which were exclusive to Sky Digital. In 2001, Sky Digitial was rebranded to just 'Sky'. With the 2005 acquisition of Easynet, an internet access provider and network operator, BSkyB now offers voice over IP (VoIP) telephony, video on demand and internet-based TV. With a free box, Sky+ and Sky+ HD customers are able to pause and rewind live TV and record favourite programmes both at home or with a compatible device while on the move. In July 2010 BSkyB acquired Virgin Media Television, including its portfolio of channels such as Bravo and Challenge. On 13 November 2014 BSkyB paid 21st Century Fox £2.45bn and a 21 per cent stake in the National Geographic Channel to buy out Sky Italia; an 89.71 per cent stake in Sky Deutschland was also acquired for £4.44bn. The transaction will give BSkyB 20 million pay-TV customers across Europe. As at 30 July 2015, there were just over 12 million Sky customers in the UK.

In February 2011, a new version of OFCOM's Broadcasting Code came into force, permitting product placement for the first time in UK-produced television programmes. A large 'P' logo designed by OFCOM and broadcasters is displayed at the beginning and end of each programme containing product placement. The first instance of product placement occurred on 28 February 2011.

THE TELEVISION LICENCE
In the UK and its dependencies, a television licence is required to receive any publicly broadcast television service, regardless of its source, including commercial, satellite and cable programming. A TV licence registered to a home address allows the viewer to watch television on laptops, tablets and mobile phones outside the place of residence. If a viewer only watches catch-up TV, not live TV, using services such as BBC iPlayer, and this is the only means by which the viewer watches broadcasts, a television licence is not required.

The TV licence is classified as a tax, therefore non-payment is a criminal offence. A fine of up to £1,000 can be imposed on those successfully prosecuted. The TV licence is issued on behalf of the BBC as the licensing authority under the Communications Act 2003. In 2014–15 income from licence fees totalled £3,735m, a £9m increase on 2013–14. A six-year licence fee settlement was agreed in 2010 which froze the annual colour television licence fee at £145.50 until 2017. A black and white licence costs £49. Concessions are available for the elderly and people with disabilities. Further details can be found at W www.tvlicensing.co.uk/information

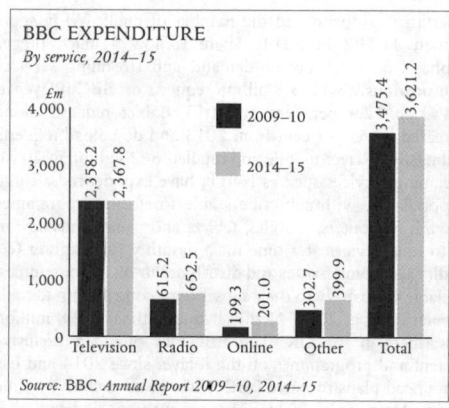

BBC EXPENDITURE
By service, 2014–15

Source: BBC *Annual Report 2009–10, 2014–15*

DIGITAL TELEVISION
The Broadcasting Act 1996 provided for the licensing of 20 or more digital terrestrial television (DTT) channels (on six frequency channels or 'multiplexes'). The first digital services went on air in autumn 1998.

In June 2002, following the collapse of ITV Digital, the digital terrestrial television licence was awarded to a consortium made up of the BBC, BSkyB and transmitter company Crown Castle by the Independent Television Commission. Freeview was launched on 30 October 2002: it now offers around 70 digital channels and 30 radio stations and requires the one-off purchase of a set-top box, but is subsequently free of charge with no subscription. In Autumn 2005 ITV and Channel 4 officially became shareholders, each taking a 20 per cent stake. As at July 2014, more than 20 million homes use Freeview on at least one set, amounting to around 30 per cent of UK households. Freeview additionally offers the UK's top six channels in HD, with a further 54 channels and 25 radio stations, including BBC News and Aljazeera, available to 70 per cent of UK homes since June 2014. There is an additional Freeview+ service which works in a similar fashion to Sky+. As at July 2014, 97 per cent of British homes had access to digital TV.

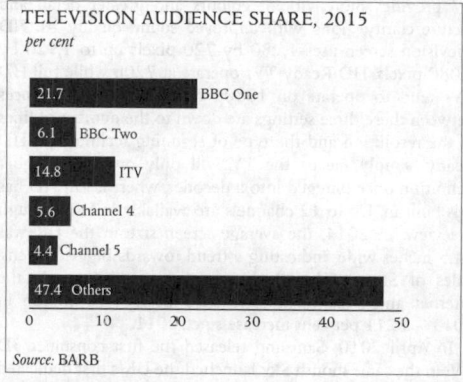

TELEVISION AUDIENCE SHARE, 2015
per cent

21.7	BBC One
6.1	BBC Two
14.8	ITV
5.6	Channel 4
4.4	Channel 5
47.4	Others

Source: BARB

RECENT DEVELOPMENTS
The internet has now firmly established itself as an alternative to live and programmed TV, particularly for those aged 16 to 34. Since the launch of 4oD in 2006 and BBC iPlayer in 2007, there has been a noticeable shift in the way viewers can watch their favourite programmes. Technological advancements have also contributed to this new phenomenon; more than half of the UK population e uses a tablet, nearly 75 per cent of UK homes have access to

superfast broadband and the number of public Wi-Fi spots reached 41,798 in 2014. There is now a much bigger emphasis on catch-up, on-demand and streaming services than previously, with 3.5 billion requests on BBC iPlayer in 2014, up 12.9 per cent on 2013. Tablet requests alone increased by 51 per cent from 2013 and download requests of the BBC iPlayer mobile app totalled 662 million in 2014. Streaming services such as Netflix have experienced a surge in popularity, with subscribers able to stream programmes through computers, mobiles, tablets and games consoles on up to four devices at a time for a monthly subscription fee. Netflix also commissions and distributes its own programmes, available exclusively to their subscribers, contributing to their popularity; as at 2014, Netflix had an estimated 2.8 million subscribers in the UK. The BBC has provided exclusive content and programmes on the iPlayer since 2014 and has announced plans to move BBC Three to an exclusive online service from early 2016. These transitions indicate that online catch-up and streaming services are now becoming competitive TV destinations in their own right.

Set-top boxes have also adapted to this viewing shift. YouView, in partnership with BBC, ITV, Channel Four, Channel Five, BT, Talk Talk and Arqiva, launched in July 2012. Subscribers are able to watch programmes (including on-demand), pause and rewind live TV and listen to digital radio via a hybrid set-top box connected to broadband. Originally envisaged as free-to-air, it has drawn criticism for tying customers into broadband services and subscriptions with BT and Talk Talk, with the one-off payment for the YouView box more expensive than the Freeview box. In June 2014, Freeview announced plans for a Freeview Connect service, which would provide catch-up services including iPlayer and 4oD as standard on smart TVs with broadband connections. It is seen as a free alternative to YouView, whereby viewers would still require a broadband connection but would not be tied to a specific provider. BBC, ITV and Channel Four announced they will substantially decrease their investment in YouView and instead invest a total of around £100m in the development of Freeview Connect.

Despite the rise in the popularity of tablets, traditional TV sets are still the most popular way to watch television. HD TV provides more vibrant colours and greater detail and picture clarity, along with improved sound quality. An HD television screen uses 1,280 by 720 pixels up to 1,920 by 1,080 pixels. HD Ready TVs operate at 720p while full HD TVs tend to operate on 1080p or 1080i; the differences between these three settings are down to the number of lines in the resolution and the type of scanning technology. 'HD Ready' simply means the TV will only operate a higher definition once plugged into a decoder, whereas full HD has this built in. Up to 12 channels are available in HD through Freeview. In 2014, the average screen size in the UK was 34.5 inches wide, indicating a trend towards bigger screens. Sales of Smart TVs, which can access apps, browse the internet and stream video, reached nearly 1.5 million in 2013 – a 211 per cent increase since 2011.

In April 2010, Samsung released the first consumer 3D TV; in the same month Sky launched the UK's first dedicated 3D channel. Several sporting events have been broadcast in 3D including the Wimbledon Championships. The BBC began a two-year 3D trial in 2011 but announced in July 2013 it would suspend 3D programming for an indefinite period of time due to a lack of public appetite for the technology. Of the estimated 1.5 million 3D TV sets in the UK, just 5 per cent used 3D to watch the Queen's Christmas Speech 2013.

In September 2012 OFCOM awarded its first local TV licences after announcing plans to broadcast 19 channels in total. In November 2013, Estuary TV, based in Grimsby, was the first to be launched. The government has backed the local TV initiative and the channels broadcast on channel 8 on Freeview in England and Northern Ireland and channel 26 in Scotland and Wales.

CONTACTS

THE BRITISH BROADCASTING CORPORATION
BBC Broadcasting House, Portland Place, London W1A 1AA
W www.bbc.co.uk
BBC North, Media City UK, Bridge House, Salford Quays, Manchester M50 2BH
Chair, Rona Fairhead
Director-General, Baron Hall of Birkenhead
BBC Worldwide, Television Centre, 101 Wood Lane, London W12 7FA **W** www.bbcworldwide.com

INDEPENDENT TELEVISION NETWORK
ITV Network Centre, 200 Gray's Inn Road, London WC1X 8HF
T 020-7156 6000 **W** www.itv.com
Chair, Archie Norman

INDEPENDENT TELEVISION NETWORK REGIONS
Anglia (eastern England), **W** www.itv.com/anglia
Border (Borders and the Isle of Man), **W** www.itv.com/border
Calendar (Yorkshire), **W** www.itv.com/calendar
Central (east, west and south Midlands), **W** www.itv.com/central
Channel (Channel Islands), **W** www.itv.com/channel
Granada (north-west England), **W** www.itv.com/granada
London **W** www.itv.com/london
Meridian (south and south-east England),
     W www.itv.com/meridian
STV (Scotland), **W** www.stv.tv
Tyne Tees (north-east England), **W** www.itv.com/tynetees
Ulster (Northern Ireland), **W** www.u.tv
Wales, **W** www.itv.com/wales
West, **W** www.itv.com/west

OTHER TELEVISION COMPANIES
Channel 4 Television, 124 Horseferry Road, London SW1P 2TX
     T 020-7396 4444 **W** www.channel4.com
Channel 5 Broadcasting Ltd, 10 Lower Thames Street, London EC3R 6EN **T** 020-8612 7700 **W** www.channel5.com
Independent Television News (ITN), 200 Gray's Inn Road, London WC1X 8XZ **T** 020-7833 3000 **W** www.itn.co.uk
Provides news programming for ITV and Channel 4.
Sianel Pedwar Cymru (S4/C), Parc Ty Glas, Llanishen, Cardiff CF14 5DU **T** 0870-600 4141 **W** www.s4c.co.uk

DIRECT BROADCASTING BY SATELLITE TELEVISION
British Sky Broadcasting Group PLC, Grant Way, Isleworth, Isleworth TW7 5QD **T** 033-3100 0333 **W** www.sky.com
Chair, Nicholas Ferguson, CBE

RADIO

UK domestic radio services are broadcast across three wavebands: FM, medium wave and long wave (used by BBC Radio 4). In the UK the FM waveband extends in frequency from 87.5MHz to 108MHz and the medium waveband from 531kHz to 1602kHz. A number of radio stations are broadcast in both analogue and digital as well as a growing number in digital alone. As at June 2014, the BBC Radio network controlled around 53.0 per cent of the listening market (*see* BBC Radio section), and the independent sector (*see* Independent Radio section) 44.4 per cent. As at June 2015, a listener tunes into an average of 21.7 hours of radio per week.

ESTIMATED RADIO AUDIENCE SHARE

	Apr–Jun 2013	Apr–Jun 2014	Percentage Apr–Jun 2015
BBC Radio 1	6.8	6.8	6.4
BBC Radio 2	17.2	17.7	17.6
BBC Radio 3	1.2	1.0	1.3
BBC Radio 4	12.1	11.6	11.7
BBC Radio Five Live	4.1	4.1	3.5
Five Live Sports Extra	0.3	0.3	0.6
BBC 6 Music	1.5	1.6	1.8
BBC Asian Network UK	0.3	0.3	0.4
1Xtra	0.5	0.5	0.5
BBC Local/Regional	8.3	7.7	7.5
BBC World Service	0.6	0.7	0.7
All BBC	53.9	53.3	53.0
All independent	43.7	43.2	44.4
All national independent	13.3	12.9	14.5
All local independent	30.4	30.3	29.8
Other	2.4	3.5	2.6

Source: RAJAR

DIGITAL RADIO

DAB (digital audio broadcasting) allows more services to be broadcast to a higher technical quality and provides the data facility for text and pictures. It was developed in a collaborative research project under the pan-European Eureka 147 initiative and has been adopted as a world standard by the International Telecommunication Union for new digital radio systems. The frequencies allocated for terrestrial digital radio in the UK are 174 to 239MHz. Additional spectrum (in the 'L-Band' range: 1452–1478MHz) was introduced in 2007.

Digital radio is available through digital radio sets, car radios, online, on games consoles and on mobile devices such as phones and tablets. An alternative method is to listen to digital radio through television sets via Freeview, cable or satellite.

The listening share via all digital platforms at the end of June 2014 was 37 per cent, the same as in June 2014. DAB accounts for 65 per cent of total digital listening, 17 per cent is online and 12 per cent on digital TV (DTV). In June 2009 the government published the white paper *Digital Britain*, which recommended that most services carried on the national and local DAB multiplexes should cease broadcasting on analogue radio by 2015, though the switch-off is now expected to take place between 2018 and 2020. Ultra-local radio, consisting of small independent and community stations, would continue to broadcast on FM. There are two criteria that must be met for digital migration to occur:
• at least 50 per cent of radio listening is digital
• national DAB coverage is comparable to FM coverage, and local DAB reaches 90 per cent of the population and all major roads

LICENSING

The Broadcasting Act 1996 provided for the licensing of digital radio services (on multiplexes, where a number of stations share one frequency to transmit their services). To allocate the multiplexes, OFCOM advertises licences for which interested parties can bid. Once the licence has been awarded, the new owner seeks out services to broadcast on the multiplex. The BBC has a separate national multiplex for its services. There are local multiplexes around the country, each broadcasting an average of seven services, plus the local BBC station.

INNOVATIONS

The internet offers a number of advantages compared to other digital platforms such as DAB including higher sound quality, a greater range of channel availability and flexibility in listening opportunity. Listeners can tune in to the majority of radio stations live on the internet or listen again online generally up to seven days after broadcast. DAB radio does not allow the same interactivity: the data is only able to travel one-way from broadcaster to listener whereas the internet allows a two-way flow of information.

Increase in WiFi hotspots also means listening to radio, podcasts and catch-up programmes is easy to do through tablets and mobile phones; 22 per cent of adults claim to listen to the radio via a mobile phone or tablet at least once a month, while the percentage for those aged 15 to 24 is noticeably higher at 34 per cent. The increase in music streaming services and radio-related apps has had a major effect on music discovery and sharing. In the UK in 2014 the number of streams a week averaged 285 million. Since 6 July 2014 the UK Official Charts Company has included streaming services in its compilation, with 100 streams the equivalent to one purchase.

Since 2005 most radio stations offer all or part of their programmes as downloadable files, known as podcasts, to listen to on computers, mobiles or tablets. Podcasting technology allows listeners to subscribe in order to receive automatically the latest episodes of regularly transmitted programmes as soon as they become available.

The relationship between radio stations and their audiences is also undergoing change. The quantity and availability of music on the internet has led to the creation of shows dedicated entirely to music sent in by listeners. Another new development in internet-based radio has been personalised radio stations, such as last.fm and Spotify. Last.fm 'recommends' songs based on the favourite artists and previous choices of the user. Spotify, available as an app on most smart phones and tablets as well as online, allows listeners access to the track, artist or genre of their choice, or to share and create playlists. It has seen steady growth in popularity since its launch in 2008, with over 20 million paying subscribers and over 75 million active users globally, as at June 2015. Spotify 'learns as you listen' and makes associated recommendations based on user choices. SoundCloud, founded in 2007, is an innovative 'sound platform' which enables users to upload their own music and recordings to share privately or publicly. Artists who upload their music are given a URL, allowing their music to be embedded anywhere, making it easier to share through social media platforms such as Twitter and Facebook. Users can also create their own playlists and link them to social media platforms. Radioplayer (W www.radioplayer.co.uk), a not-for-profit company backed by the BBC, Global Radio, Bauer Media and RadioCentre, allows audiences to listen to live and catch-up radio from one place. There are around 400 stations available and a 'recommended' service which offers station suggestions depending on location, what is trending and the type of music the user likes. Radioplayer launched as a mobile app in 2012 and a tablet app in 2013. Through the tablet app, users sample an average of 4.6 stations a week in comparison with just 2.1 for analogue users.

BBC RADIO

BBC Radio broadcasts network services to the UK, Isle of Man and the Channel Islands, with over 35 million listeners each week. There is also a tier of national services in Wales, Scotland and Northern Ireland and around 40 local radio stations in England and the Channel Islands. In Wales and Scotland there are also dedicated language services in Welsh and Gaelic respectively. The frequency allocated for digital BBC broadcasts is 225.648MHz.

BBC Radio, Broadcasting House, Portland Place, London W1A 1AA **W** www.bbc.co.uk/radio

BBC NETWORK RADIO STATIONS

Radio 1 (contemporary pop music and entertainment news) – 24 hours a day, *Frequencies:* 97–99 FM and digital

Radio 2 (popular music, entertainment, comedy and the arts) – 24 hours a day, *Frequencies:* 88–91 FM and digital

Radio 3 (classical music, classic drama, documentaries and features) – 24 hours a day, *Frequencies:* 90–93 FM and digital

Radio 4 (news, documentaries, drama, entertainment and cricket on long wave in season) – 5.20am–1am daily, with BBC World Service overnight, *Frequencies:* 92–95 FM/103–105 FM and 198 LW and digital

Radio Five Live (news and sport) – 24 hours a day, *Frequencies:* 909/693 MW and digital

Five Live Sports Extra (live sport) – schedule varies, digital only

6 Music (contemporary and classic pop and rock music) – 24 hours a day, digital only

Asian Network (news, music and sport) – 5am–1am, with Radio Five Live overnight, *Frequencies:* various MW frequencies in Midlands and digital

1Xtra (urban music: drum & bass, garage, hip hop, R&B) – 24 hours a day, digital only

BBC NATIONAL RADIO STATIONS

Radio Cymru (Welsh-language), *Frequencies: 92–105 FM* and digital

Radio Foyle, Frequencies: 93.1 FM and 792 MW and digital

Radio nan Gaidheal (Gaelic service), *Frequencies:* 103–105 FM and digital

Radio Scotland, Frequencies: 92–95 FM and 810 MW and digital. Local programmes for Orkney, Shetland and Highlands and Islands

Radio Ulster, Frequencies: 1341 MW and 92–95 FM and digital. Local programmes on Radio Foyle

Radio Wales, Frequencies: 657/882 MW and 93–104 FM and digital

BBC WORLD SERVICE

The BBC World Service broadcasts to an estimated weekly audience of 1.3 million people in the UK and 210 million worldwide, in 28 languages including English, and is now available in around 150 capital cities. It no longer broadcasts in Dutch, French for Europe, German, Hebrew, Italian, Japanese or Malay because it was found that most speakers of these languages preferred to listen to the English broadcasts. In 2006 services in ten languages (Bulgarian, Croatian, Czech, Greek, Hungarian, Kazakh, Polish, Slovak, Slovene and Thai) were terminated to provide funding for a new Arabic television channel, which was launched in March 2008. In August 2008 the BBC's Romanian World Service broadcasts were discontinued after 68 years. In January 2011 the BBC announced five more language services would be terminated: Albanian, Caribbean English, Macedonian, Portuguese for Africa and Serbian. The BBC World Service website offers interactive news services in 28 languages including English, Arabic, Chinese, Hindi, Persian, Portuguese for Brazil, Russian, Spanish and Urdu with audiostreaming available.

LANGUAGES

Arabic, Azeri, Bangla, Burmese, Cantonese, English, French, Hausa, Hindi, Indonesian, Kinyarwanda, Kirundi, Kyrgyz, Nepali, Pashto, Persian, Portuguese, Russian, Sinhala, Somali, Spanish, Swahili, Tamil, Turkish, Ukrainian, Urdu, Uzbek and Vietnamese.

UK frequencies: digital; overnight on BBC Radio 4.

BBC Learning English teaches English worldwide through radio, television and a wide range of published and online courses.

BBC Media Action is a registered charity established in 1999 by BBC World Service, known as the BBC World Service Trust until December 2011. It promotes development through the innovative use of the media in the developing world.

BBC Monitoring tracks the global media for the latest news reports emerging around the world.

BBC WORLD SERVICE, 1st Floor Brock House, 19 Langham Street, London W1A 1AA **W** www.bbc.co.uk/worldservice

INDEPENDENT RADIO

Until 1973, the BBC had a legal monopoly on radio broadcasting in the UK. During this time, the corporation's only competition came from pirate stations located abroad, such as Radio Luxembourg. Christopher Chataway, Minister for Post and Telecommunications, changed this by creating the first licences for commercial radio stations. The Independent Broadcasting Authority (IBA) awarded the first of these licences to the London Broadcasting Company (LBC) to provide London's news and information service. LBC was followed by Capital Radio, to offer the city's entertainment service, Radio Clyde in Glasgow and BRMB in Birmingham.

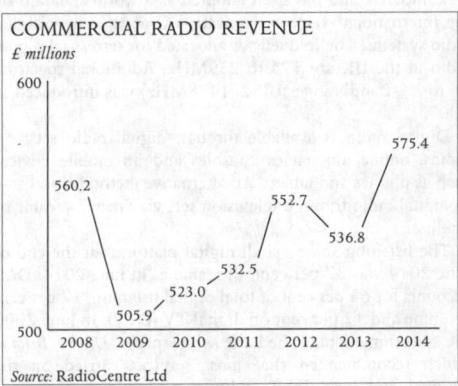

COMMERCIAL RADIO REVENUE
£ millions

600 — 560.2, 505.9, 523.0, 532.5, 552.7, 536.8, 575.4 (2008–2014)

Source: RadioCentre Ltd

The IBA was dissolved when the Broadcasting Act of 1990 de-regulated broadcasting, to be succeeded by the less rigid Radio Authority (RA). The RA began advertising new licences for the development of independent radio in January 1991. It awarded national and local radio, satellite and cable services licences, and long-term restricted service licences for stations serving non-commercial establishments such as hospitals and universities. The first national commercial digital multiplex licence was awarded in October 1998 and a number of local digital multiplex licences followed. At the end of 2003 the RA was replaced by OFCOM, which now carries out the licensing administration.

RadioCentre was formed in July 2006 as a result of the merger between the Radio Advertising Bureau (RAB) and the Commercial Radio Companies Association (CRCA), the former non-profit trade body for commercial radio companies in the UK, to operate essentially as a union for commercial radio stations.

RadioCentre, 6th Floor, 55 New Oxford Street, London WC1A 1BS **T** 020-7010 0600 **W** www.radiocentre.org

Chief Executive, Siobhan Kenny

THE PRESS

The newspaper and periodical press in the UK is large and diverse, catering for a wide variety of views and interests. There is no state control or censorship of the press; however, it is subject to the laws on publication.

The press is not state-subsidised and receives few tax concessions. The income of most newspapers and periodicals is derived largely from sales and from advertising. The Advertising Association reported that advertising revenue would return to growth in 2015 – only the second annual increase since 2007 – with UK national newspapers expecting to receive £1.42bn in advertising, reflecting a 1 per cent increase on 2014.

LEVESON REPORT

The Leveson Inquiry, established under the Inquiries Act 2005, was announced by the prime minister on 13 July 2011 to investigate the role of press and police in the *News of the World* phone-hacking scandal. Lord Justice Leveson was appointed as chair of the inquiry. The hearings began on 14 November 2011 and ended on 24 July 2012 following the testimonies of 650 witnesses.

The Leveson Report was published in late November 2012 and featured several broad and complex recommendations as to how the press should be regulated. The report generally recommended that the press should continue to be self-regulated, with the government allowed no direct power over what is published, and that a new press standards body, with a new code of conduct, should be established by legislation in order to ensure regulation is independent and effective. Lord Justice Leveson concluded that this arrangement should give the public confidence that their complaints would be dealt with seriously and ensure the press would be protected from interference.

SELF-REGULATION

Following the publication of the Leveson Report the Press Complaints Commission (PCC), which had been established in January 1991 as a non-statutory body to operate the press's self-regulation, was closed and replaced by the Independent Press Standards Organisation (IPSO) on 8 September 2014. While the majority of newspapers have signed up to the new regulator, several have not, including *The Guardian*, the *Financial Times*, *The Independent* and the *London Evening Standard*.

In 2013 a royal charter on press regulation was granted by the Privy Council to create a watchdog to oversee a new regulator. On 3 November 2014, a fully independent body, the Press Recognition Panel (PRP) was established to consider whether press regulators meet the criteria recommended in the Leveson Report and, if so, to afford these regulators official recognition.

IPSO has not sought recognition from the PRP, but another regulator, IMPRESS, established by a group of free speech campaigners, is aiming to become compliant with the requirements of the Leveson Report and announced in May 2015 its intention to seek recognition from the PRP.

INDEPENDENT PRESS STANDARDS ORGANISATION, Gate House, 1 Farringdon Street, London EC4M 7LH T 0300-123 2220 E inquiries@ipso.co.uk W www.ipso.co.uk *Chair*, Sir Alan Moses

PRESS RECOGNITION PANEL, 88 Wood Street, London EC2V 7RS W contact@pressrecognitionpanel.org.uk W www.pressrecognitionpanel.org.uk *Chair*, Dr David Wolfe, QC

NEWSPAPERS

Newspapers are mostly financially independent of any political party, though most adopt a political stance in their editorial comments, usually reflecting proprietorial influence. Ownership of the national and regional daily newspapers is concentrated in the hands of large corporations whose interests cover publishing and communications, although *The Guardian* and *The Observer* are owned by the Scott Trust, formed in 1936 to protect the financial and editorial independence of *The Guardian* in perpetuity. The rules on cross-media ownership, as amended by the Broadcasting Act 1996, which limited the extent to which newspaper organisations may become involved in broadcasting, have been relaxed by the Communications Act 2003: newspapers with over a 20 per cent share of national circulation may own national and/or local radio licences.

In October 2010, *The Independent* launched a concise newspaper, *i*, the first new daily newspaper since 1986. In July 2011, *News of the World* was closed by its parent company, News International, following accusations of phone-hacking. In February 2012 News International printed the first edition of *The Sun on Sunday*, a Sunday format of the daily tabloid paper *The Sun*. There are 14 daily and Sunday national papers and several hundred local papers that are published daily, weekly or twice-weekly. Scotland, Wales and Northern Ireland all have at least one daily and one Sunday national paper.

UK CIRCULATION

National Daily Newspapers	June 2014	June 2015	% +/−
The Sun	2,033,606	1,818,935	−10.56
Daily Mail	1,673,580	1,626,846	−2.79
Daily Mirror	958,675	855,987	−10.71
The Daily Telegraph	514,591	489,739	−4.83
Daily Express	479,703	432,565	−9.83
Daily Star	466,934	416,379	−10.83
The Times	393,531	389,409	−1.05
i	286,357	274,556	−4.12
Financial Times	220,532	214,256	−2.85
Daily Record	213,895	191,042	−10.68
The Guardian	185,312	171,218	−7.61
The Independent	63,506	57,930	−8.78

National Sunday Newspapers	June 2014	June 2015	% +/−
The Sun on Sunday	1,635,068	1,466,439	−10.31
The Mail on Sunday	1,528,562	1,434,018	−6.19
Sunday Mirror	922,491	815,766	−11.57
The Sunday Times	815,760	764,562	−6.28
Sunday Express	418,131	376,509	−9.95
The Sunday Telegraph	406,200	374,617	−7.78
The Sunday People	369,312	316,320	−14.35
Daily Star Sunday	294,944	257,859	−12.57
Sunday Mail	237,636	207,678	−12.61
Sunday Post	216,694	191,140	−11.79
The Observer	207,005	189,279	−8.56
The Independent on Sunday	100,102	97,218	−2.88

Source: Audit Bureau of Circulations Ltd

Newspapers are usually published in either broadsheet or smaller, tabloid format. The 'quality' daily papers – ie those providing detailed coverage of a wide range of public matters – have traditionally been broadsheets, the more populist newspapers tabloid. In 2004 this correlation between format and content was redefined when two traditionally broadsheet newspapers, *The Times* and *The Independent*, switched to tabloid-sized editions, while *The Guardian* launched a 'Berliner' format in September 2005. In October 2005 *The Independent on Sunday* became the first Sunday broadsheet to be published in the tabloid (or 'compact') size, and *The Observer*, like its daily counterpart *The Guardian*, began publishing in the Berliner format in January 2006.

NEWSPAPERS ONLINE

The demand to read news instantly and while on the move has increased the popularity of newspaper websites. Most newspapers now operate their own websites in line with their print editions, often including the same material as seen in daily printed editions but can also include video and audio features. Many articles and columns additionally have the option of reader contributions and debate. Certain newspapers charge a subscription fee to access their websites but the majority are free to browse.

NATIONAL PRESS WEBSITE DAILY AVERAGE BROWSERS

National Press Website	June 2014	June 2015	% +/−
MailOnline	10,912,083	13,635,561	24.96
theguardian.com	5,718,502	7,771,486	35.90
Mirror Group Nationals	2,680,547	4,265,187	59.12
Telegraph	3,901,515	4,097,915	5.03
The Independent	1,856,894	2,551,686	37.42
express.co.uk	705,976	1,028,026	45.62
dailystar.co.uk	524,986	769,101	46.50

Source: Audit Bureau of Circulations Ltd

NATIONAL DAILY NEWSPAPERS
DAILY EXPRESS
Northern & Shell Building, 10 Lower Thames Street, London EC3R 6EN T 020-8612 7000 W www.express.co.uk
Editor, Hugh Whittow
DAILY MAIL
Northcliffe House, 2 Derry Street, London W8 5TT
T 020-7938 6000 W www.dailymail.co.uk
Editor, Paul Dacre
DAILY MIRROR
1 Canada Square, Canary Wharf, London E14 5AP
T 020-7293 3000 W www.mirror.co.uk
Editor, Lloyd Embley
DAILY RECORD
1 Central Quay, Glasgow G3 8DA T 0141-309 3000
W www.dailyrecord.co.uk
Editor, Murray Foote
DAILY STAR
Northern & Shell Building, 10 Lower Thames Street, London EC3R 6EN T 020-8612 7000 W www.dailystar.co.uk
Editor, Dawn Neesom
THE DAILY TELEGRAPH
111 Buckingham Palace Road, London SW1W 0DT
T 020-7931 2000 W www.telegraph.co.uk
Editor, Chris Evans
FINANCIAL TIMES
1 Southwark Bridge, London SE1 9HL T 020-7873 3000
W www.ft.com
Editor, Lionel Barber

THE GUARDIAN
King's Place, 90 York Way, London N1 9GU T 020-3353 2000
W www.theguardian.com
Editor, Katharine Viner
THE HERALD
200 Renfield Street, Glasgow G2 3QB T 0141-302 7000
W www.heraldscotland.com
Editor, Magnus Llewellin
THE INDEPENDENT *AND* i
Northcliffe House, 2 Derry Street, London W8 5HF
T 020-7005 2000 W www.independent.co.uk
Editor, Amol Rajan and Oliver Duff
THE SCOTSMAN
152 Morrison Street, Edinburgh EH3 8EB T 0131-620 8620
W www.scotsman.com
Editor, Ian Stewart
THE SUN
3 Thomas More Square, London E98 1XY T 020-7782 4000
W www.thesun.co.uk
Editor, Tony Gallagher
THE TIMES
1 Pennington Street, London E98 1TT T 020-7782 5000
W www.thetimes.co.uk
Editor, John Witherow

WEEKLY NEWSPAPERS
DAILY STAR SUNDAY
Northern and Shell Building, 10 Lower Thames Street, London EC3R 6EN T 020-8612 7000
W www.dailystar.co.uk/sunday
Editor, Stuart James
INDEPENDENT ON SUNDAY
Northcliffe House, 2 Derry Street, London W8 5TT
T 020-7005 2000 W www.independent.co.uk
Editor, Lisa Markwell
MAIL ON SUNDAY
2 Derry Street, London W8 HFT T 020-7938 6000
W www.mailonsunday.co.uk
Editor, Geordie Greig
THE OBSERVER
Kings Place, 90 York Way, London N1 9GU T 020-3353 2000
W www.observer.theguardian.com
Editor, John Mulholland
THE SUNDAY PEOPLE
1 Canada Square, Canary Wharf, London E14 5AP
T 020-7293 3000 W www.people.co.uk
Editor, James Scott
SCOTLAND ON SUNDAY
Barclay House, 108 Holyrood Road, Edinburgh EH8 8AS
T 0131-620 8620 W www.scotlandonsunday.com
Editor, Ian Stewart
THE SUN ON SUNDAY
3 Thomas More Square, London E98 1XY T 020-7782 4000
W www.thesun.co.uk
Editor, Victoria Newton
SUNDAY EXPRESS
Northern & Shell Building, 10 Lower Thames Street, London EC4R 6EN T 020-8612 7000
W www.sundayexpress.co.uk
Editor, Martin Townsend
SUNDAY HERALD
200 Renfield Street, Glasgow G2 3QB T 0141-302 7000
W www.sundayherald.com
Editor, Richard Walker
SUNDAY MAIL
1 Central Quay, Glasgow G3 8DA T 0141-309 3000
W www.sundaymail.com
Editor, Jim Wilson

SUNDAY MIRROR
1 Canada Square, Canary Wharf, London E14 5AP
T 020-7293 3000 W www.sundaymirror.co.uk
Editor, Lloyd Embley
SUNDAY POST
144 Port Dundas Road, Glasgow G4 0HZ T 0141-332 9933
W www.sundaypost.com
Editor, Donald Martin
SUNDAY TELEGRAPH
111 Buckingham Palace Road, London SW1W 0DT
T 020-7931 2000 W www.telegraph.co.uk
Editor, Ian MacGregor
THE SUNDAY TIMES
3 Thomas More Square, London E98 1XY T 020-7782 5000
W www.thesundaytimes.co.uk
Editor, Martin Ivens

REGIONAL DAILY NEWSPAPERS
EAST ANGLIA
CAMBRIDGE NEWS
Winship Road, Milton, Cambs. CB24 6PP T 01223-434434
W www.cambridge-news.co.uk
Editor, Paul Brackley
EAST ANGLIAN DAILY TIMES
Lower Brook Street, Ipswich IP4 1AN T 01473-230023
W www.eadt.co.uk
Editor, Terry Hunt
EASTERN DAILY PRESS
Prospect House, Rouen Road, Norwich NR1 1RE T 01603-628311
W www.edp24.co.uk
Editor, Nigel Pickover
IPSWICH STAR
Lower Brook Street, Ipswich, Suffolk IP4 1AN T 01473-230023
W www.ipswichstar.co.uk
Editor, Terry Hunt
NORWICH EVENING NEWS
Prospect House, Rouen Road, Norwich NR1 1RE T 01603-628311
W www.eveningnews24.co.uk
Editor, Nigel Pickover

EAST MIDLANDS
BURTON MAIL
65–68 High Street, Burton upon Trent DE14 1LE T 01283-512345
W www.burtonmail.co.uk
Editor, Emma Turton
DERBY TELEGRAPH
Northcliffe House, Meadow Road, Derby DE1 2BH
T 01332-291111 W www.derbytelegraph.co.uk
Editor, Neil White
THE LEICESTER MERCURY
St George Street, Leicester LE1 9FQ T 0116-251 2512
W www.leicestermercury.co.uk
Editor, Kevin Booth
LINCOLNSHIRE ECHO
Witham Wharf, Brayford Wharf East, Lincoln LN5 7HY
T 01522-820000 W www.lincolnshireecho.co.uk
Editor, Mel West
NORTHAMPTON CHRONICLE & ECHO
Albert House, Victoria Street, Northants NN1 3NR
T 01604-467000 W www.northamptonchron.co.uk
Editor, David Summers
NOTTINGHAM POST
City Gate, Tollhouse Hill, Notts NG1 5FS T 0115-948 2000
W www.nottinghampost.com
Editor, Mike Sassi

LONDON
EVENING STANDARD
Northcliffe House, 2 Derry Street, London W8 5TT
T 020-3367 7000 W www.standard.co.uk
Editor, Sarah Sands

METRO
Northcliffe House, 2 Derry Street, London W8 5TT
T 020-3615 3480 W www.metro.co.uk
Editor, Ted Young

NORTH EAST
EVENING CHRONICLE
Groat Market, Newcastle upon Tyne NE1 1ED T 0191-232 7500
W www.chroniclelive.co.uk
Editor, Darren Thwaites
HARTLEPOOL MAIL
New Clarence House, Wesley Square, Hartlepool TS24 8BX
T 01429-239333 W www.hartlepoolmail.co.uk
Editor, Joy Yates
THE JOURNAL
Groat Market, Newcastle upon Tyne NE1 1ED T 0191-201 6491
W www.thejournal.co.uk
Editor, Brian Aitken
THE NORTHERN ECHO
PO Box 14, Priestgate, Darlington, Co. Durham DL1 1NF
T 01325-381313 W www.thenorthernecho.co.uk
Editor, Peter Barron
THE SHIELDS GAZETTE
Chapter Row, South Shields, Tyne & Wear NE33 1BL
T 0191-427 4800 W www.shieldsgazette.com
Editor, Joy Yates
THE SUNDAY SUN
Groat Market, Newcastle upon Tyne NE1 1ED T 0191-232 7500
W www.sundaysun.co.uk
Editor, Matt McKenzie
SUNDERLAND ECHO
Echo House, Pennywell, Sunderland SR4 9ER T 0191-501 5800
W www.sunderlandecho.com
Editor, John Szymanski
TEESIDE GAZETTE
Borough Road, Middlesbrough TS1 3AZ T 01642-345401
W www.gazettelive.co.uk
Editor, Chris Styles

NORTH WEST
THE BLACKPOOL GAZETTE
Avroe House, Avroe Crescent, Blackpool FY4 2DP T 01253-400888
W www.blackpoolgazette.co.uk
Editor, Jon Rhodes
THE BOLTON NEWS
The Wellsprings, Victoria Square, Bolton BL1 1AR T 01204-522345
W www.theboltonnews.co.uk
Editor, Ian Savage
CARLISLE NEWS AND STAR
Newspaper House, Dalston Road, Carlisle CA2 5UA
T 01228-612600 W www.newsandstar.co.uk
Editor, David Helliwell
LANCASHIRE EVENING POST
Oliver's Place, Preston PR2 9ZA T 01772-254841 W www.lep.co.uk
Editor, Gillian Gray
LANCASHIRE TELEGRAPH
1 High Street, Newspaper House, Blackburn, Lancs. BB1 1HT
T 01254 678678 W www.lancashiretelegraph.co.uk
Editor, Kevin Young
LIVERPOOL ECHO
PO Box 48, Old Hall Street, Liverpool L69 3EB T 0151-227 2000
W www.liverpoolecho.co.uk
Editor, Alastair Machray
MANCHESTER EVENING NEWS
Mitchell Henry House, Hollinwood Avenue, Chadderton OL9 8EF
T 0161-832 7200 W www.manchestereveningnews.co.uk
Editor, Rob Irvine
NORTH-WEST EVENING MAIL
Abbey Road, Barrow-in-Furness, Cumbria LA14 5QS
T 01229-840100 W www.nwemail.co.uk
Editor, Jonathan Lee

OLDHAM EVENING CHRONICLE
PO Box 47, 172 Union Street, Oldham, Lancs. OL1 1EQ
   T 0161-633 2121 W www.oldham-chronicle.co.uk
   Editor, Dave Whaley

SOUTH EAST
THE ARGUS
Argus House, Crowhurst Road, Hollingbury, Brighton BN1 8AR
   T 01273-544544 W www.theargus.co.uk
   Editor, Mike Gilson
ECHO
Newspaper House, Chester Hall Lane, Basildon, Essex SS14 3BL
   T 01268-522792 W www.echo-news.co.uk
   Editor, Chris Hatton
MEDWAY MESSENGER
Medway House, Ginsbury Close, Sir Thomas Longley Road, Strood,
   Kent ME2 4DU T 01634-227800
   W www.kentonline.co.uk/medway
   Editor, Bob Bounds
THE NEWS, PORTSMOUTH
1000 Lakeside, North Harbour, Portsmouth PO6 3EN
   T 023-9266 4488 W www.portsmouth.co.uk
   Editor, Mark Waldron
OXFORD MAIL
Osney Mead, Oxford OX2 0EJ T 01865-425262
   W www.oxfordmail.co.uk
   Editor, Simon O'Neill
READING EVENING POST
8 Tessa Road, Reading, Berks. RG1 8NS T 0118-918 3000
   W www.getreading.co.uk
   Editor, Andy Murrill
THE SOUTHERN DAILY ECHO
Newspaper House, Test Lane, Redbridge, Southampton SO16 9JX
   T 023-8042 4777 W www.dailyecho.co.uk
   Editor, Ian Murray

SOUTH WEST
BRISTOL POST
Temple Way, Bristol BS2 0BY T 0117-934 3000
   W www.bristolpost.co.uk
   Editor, Mike Norton
DAILY ECHO
Richmond Hill, Bournemouth BH2 6HH T 01202-554601
   W www.bournemouthecho.co.uk
   Editor, Toby Granville
DORSET ECHO
Fleet House, Hampshire Road, Weymouth, Dorset DT4 9XD
   T 01305-830930 W www.dorsetecho.co.uk
   Editor, Toby Granville
EXETER EXPRESS & ECHO
Heron Road, Sowton, Exeter EX2 7NF T 01392-442220
   W www.exeterexpressandecho.co.uk
   Editor, Jon-Paul Hedge
GLOUCESTER CITIZEN
6–8 The Oxebode, Gloucester GL1 2RZ T 01242-278000
   W www.gloucestercitizen.co.uk
   Editor, Jenny Eastwood
GLOUCESTERSHIRE ECHO
St James's Square, Cheltenham GL50 3PR T 01242-278000
   W www.gloucestershireecho.co.uk
   Editor, Matt Holmes
THE HERALD
3rd Floor, Millbay Road, Plymouth PL1 3LF T 01752-293000
   W www.plymouthherald.co.uk
   Editor, Paul Burton
SUNDAY INDEPENDENT
Sunday Independent Ltd, Tindle Suite, Webbs House, Cornwall
   PL14 6AH T 01579-342174 W www.sundayindependent.co.uk
   Editor, John Collings

SWINDON ADVERTISER
100 Victoria Road, Old Town, Swindon SN1 3BE T 01793-528144
   W www.swindonadvertiser.co.uk
   Editor, Gary Lawrence
TORQUAY HERALD EXPRESS
Barton Hill Road, Torquay, Devon TQ2 8JN T 01803-676000
   W www.torquayheraldexpress.co.uk
   Editor, Jim Parker
WESTERN DAILY PRESS
Temple Way, Bristol BS99 7HD T 0117-934 3000
   W www.westerndailypress.co.uk
   Editor, Rob Stokes
THE WESTERN MORNING NEWS
3rd Floor, Millbay Road, Plymouth PL1 3LF T 01752-293000
   W www.westernmorningnews.co.uk
   Editor, Bill Martin

WEST MIDLANDS
BIRMINGHAM MAIL
6th Floor, Fort Dunlop, Fort Parkway, Birmingham B24 9FF
   T 0121-234 5536 W www.birminghammail.co.uk
   Editor, David Brookes
THE BIRMINGHAM POST
6th Floor, Fort Dunlop, Fort Parkway, Birmingham B24 9FF
   T 0121-236 3366 W www.birminghampost.co.uk
   Editor, Stacey Barnfield
COVENTRY TELEGRAPH
Corporation Street, Coventry CV1 1FP T 024-7663 3633
   W www.coventrytelegraph.net
   Editor, Keith Perry
EXPRESS & STAR
51–53 Queen Street, Wolverhampton WV1 1ES T 01902-313131
   W www.expressandstar.com
   Editor, Keith Harrison
THE SENTINEL
Sentinel House, Bethesda Street, Stoke-on-Trent ST1 3GN
   T 01782-864100 W www.stokesentinel.co.uk
   Editor, Martin Tideswell
SHROPSHIRE STAR
Waterloo Road, Ketley, Telford TF1 5HU T 01952-242424
   W www.shropshirestar.com
   Editor, Martin Wright
WORCESTER NEWS
Berrows House, Hylton Road, Worcester WR2 5JX
   T 01905-748200 W www.worcesternews.co.uk
   Editor, Peter John

YORKSHIRE AND HUMBERSIDE
GRIMSBY TELEGRAPH
80 Cleethorpe Road, Grimsby, Lincs DN31 3EH T 01472-360360
   W www.grimsbytelegraph.co.uk
   Editor, Michelle Lalor
HALIFAX COURIER
PO Box 19, King Cross Street, Halifax HX1 2SF T 01422-260200
   W www.halifaxcourier.co.uk
   Editor, John Kenealy
THE HUDDERSFIELD DAILY EXAMINER
Pennine Business Park, Longbow Close, Bradley Road, Huddersfield
   HD2 1GQ T 01484-430000 W www.examiner.co.uk
   Editor, Roy Wright
HULL DAILY MAIL
Blundell's Corner, Beverley Road, Hull HU3 1XS T 01482-327111
   W www.hulldailymail.co.uk
   Editor, Neil Hodgkinson
THE PRESS
PO Box 29, 76–86 Walmgate, York YO1 9YN T 01904-567131
   W www.yorkpress.co.uk
   Editor, Perry Austin-Clarke

SCARBOROUGH NEWS
17–23 Aberdeen Walk, Scarborough, N. Yorks YO11 1BB
T 01723-363636 W www.thescarboroughnews.co.uk
Editor, Ed Asquith
SHEFFIELD STAR
York Street, Sheffield S1 1PU T 0114-276 7676
W www.thestar.co.uk
Editor, James Mitchinson
TELEGRAPH & ARGUS
Hall Ings, Bradford BD1 1JR T 01274-729511
W www.telegraphandargus.co.uk
Editor, Perry Austin-Clarke
YORKSHIRE EVENING POST
26 Whitehall Road, Leeds LS12 1BE T 0113-243 2701
W www.yorkshireeveningpost.co.uk
Editor, Jeremy Clifford
YORKSHIRE POST
26 Whitehall Road, Leeds LS12 1BE T 0113-243 2701
W www.yorkshirepost.co.uk
Editor, Jeremy Clifford

SCOTLAND
THE COURIER
80 Kingsway East, Dundee DD4 8SL T 01382-223131
W www.thecourier.co.uk
Editor, Richard Neville
DUNDEE EVENING TELEGRAPH
80 Kingsway East, Dundee DD4 8SL T 01382-575331
W www.eveningtelegraph.co.uk
Editor, Richard Prest
EDINBURGH EVENING NEWS
Barclay House, 108 Holyrood Road, Edinburgh EH8 8AS
T 0131-620 8620 W www.edinburghnews.scotsman.com
Editor, Frank O'Donnell
EVENING EXPRESS
Aberdeen Journals Ltd, Lang Stracht, Mastrick, Aberdeen
AB15 6DF T 01224-691212 W www.eveningexpress.co.uk
Editor, Alan McCabe
GLASGOW EVENING TIMES
200 Renfield Street, Glasgow G2 3QB T 0141-302 7000
W www.eveningtimes.co.uk
Editor, Tony Carlin
INVERNESS COURIER
New Century House, Stadium Road, Inverness IV1 1FF
T 01463-233059 W www.inverness-courier.co.uk
Editor, Robert Taylor
PAISLEY DAILY EXPRESS
1 Central Quay, Glasgow G3 8DA T 0141-887 7911
W www.paisleydailyexpress.co.uk
Editor, John Hutcheson
THE PRESS AND JOURNAL
Lang Stracht, Aberdeen AB15 6DF T 01224-690222
W www.pressandjournal.co.uk
Editor, Damian Bates

WALES
THE LEADER
Mold Business Park, Mold, Flintshire CH7 1XY T 01352-707707
W www.leaderlive.co.uk
Editor, Barrie Jones
SOUTH WALES ARGUS
Cardiff Road, Maesglas, Newport NP20 3QN T 01633-810000
W www.southwalesargus.co.uk
Editor, Kevin Ward
SOUTH WALES ECHO
6 Park Street, Cardiff CF10 1XR T 029-2024 3630
W www.walesonline.co.uk
Editor, Catrin Pascoe

SOUTH WALES EVENING POST
Urban Village, High Street, Swansea SA1 1NW T 01792-545500
W www.southwales-eveningpost.co.uk
Editor, Jonathan Roberts
WESTERN MAIL
6 Park Street, Cardiff CF10 1XR T 029-2024 3630
W www.walesonline.co.uk
Editor, Alan Edmunds

NORTHERN IRELAND
BELFAST TELEGRAPH
124–144 Royal Avenue, Belfast BT1 1DN T 028-9026 4000
W www.belfasttelegraph.co.uk
Editor, Mike Gilson
IRISH NEWS
113–117 Donegall Street, Belfast BT1 2GE T 028-9032 2226
W www.irishnews.com
Editor, Noel Doran
NEWS LETTER
Ground Floor, Metro Building, 6–9 Donegall Sq. South,
Belfast BT1 5JA T 028-9089 7700 W www.newsletter.co.uk
Editor, Rankin Armstrong
SUNDAY LIFE
124–144 Royal Avenue, Belfast BT1 1EB T 028-9026 4000
W www.sundaylife.co.uk
Editor, Martin Breen

CHANNEL ISLANDS
GUERNSEY PRESS
PO Box 57, Braye Road, Vale, Guernsey GY1 3BW
T 01481-240240 W www.guernseypress.com
Editor, Shaun Green
JERSEY EVENING POST
Guiton House, Five Oaks, St Saviour, Jersey JE4 8XQ
T 01534-611611 W www.jerseyeveningpost.com
Editor, Andy Sibcy

PERIODICALS

ART
AESTHETICA
PO Box 371, York YO23 1WL T 01904-629137
W www.aestheticamagazine.com
Editor, Cherie Federico
APOLLO
22 Old Queen Street, London SW1H 9HP T 020-7961 0150
W www.apollo-magazine.com
Editor, Thomas Marks
ART MONTHLY
28 Charing Cross Road, London WC2H 0DB T 020-7240 0389
W www.artmonthly.co.uk
Editor, Patricia Bickers
ARTREVIEW
1 Honduras Street, London EC1Y 0TH T 020-7490 8138
W www.artreview.com
Editor, Mark Rappolt
TATE ETC.
Tate, Millbank, London SW1P 4RG T 020-7887 8724
W www.tate.org.uk
Editor, Simon Grant

BUSINESS AND FINANCE
THE ECONOMIST
25 St James's Street, London SW1A 1HG T 020-7830 7000
W www.economist.com
Editor, Zanny Minton Beddoes
MANAGEMENT TODAY
Haymarket, Teddington Studios, Broom Road, Teddington
TW11 9BE T 01604-828702 W www.managementtoday.co.uk
Editor, Matthew Gwyther

MARKETING WEEK
79 Wells Street, London W1T 3QN **T** 020-7292 3711
    W www.marketingweek.co.uk
    Editor, Russell Parsons
MONEYWEEK
8th Floor, Friars Bridge Court, 41-45 Blackfriars Road, London
    SE1 8NZ **T** 020-7633 3780 **W** www.moneyweek.com
    Editor, Merryn Somerset Webb
PUBLIC FINANCE
17 Britton Street, London EC1M 5TP **T** 020-8950 9117
    W www.publicfinance.co.uk
    Editor, Vivienne Russell

CELEBRITY
CLOSER
Endeavour House, 189 Shaftesbury Avenue, London WC2H 8JG
    T 020-7859 8463 **W** www.closeronline.co.uk
    Editor, Lisa Burrow
HEAT
Endeavour House, 189 Shaftesbury Avenue, London WC2H 8JG
    T 020-7437 9011 **W** www.heatworld.com
    Editor, Lucie Cave
HELLO!
Wellington House, 69–71 Upper Ground, London SE1 9PQ
    T 020-7667 8901 **W** www.hellomagazine.com
    Editor, Rosie Nixon
OK!
10 Lower Thames Street, London EC3R 6EN **T** 020-8612 7000
    W www.ok.co.uk
    Editor, Kirsty Tyler

CHILDREN'S AND FAMILY
THE BEANO
185 Fleet Street, London EC4A 2HS **W** www.beano.com
    Editor, Craig Graham
MOTHER & BABY
Endeavour House, 189 Shaftesbury Avenue, London WC2H 8JG
    T 020-7437 9011 **W** www.motherandbaby.co.uk
    Editor, Claire Irvin
YOUR CAT
BPG Stamford Ltd, 1-6 Buckminster Yard, Main Street,
    Buckminster, Grantham, Lincs NG33 5SA **T** 0844-848-8257
    W www.yourcat.co.uk
    Editor, Chloë Hukin
YOUR DOG
BPG Stamford Ltd, 1-6 Buckminster Yard, Main Street,
    Buckminster, Grantham, Lincs NG33 5SA **T** 0844-848 8257
    W www.yourdog.co.uk
    Editor, Sarah Wright
YOUR HORSE
Media House, Peterborough Business Park, Lynch Wood,
    Peterborough PE2 6EA **T** 01733-468000
    W www.yourhorse.co.uk
    Editor, Imogen Johnson

CLASSICAL AND OPERA MUSIC
BBC MUSIC
Immediate Media Company Bristol Ltd, Tower House,
    Fairfax Street, Bristol BS1 3BN **T** 0117-927 9009
    W www.classical-music.com
    Editor, Oliver Condy
CLASSICAL MUSIC
Rhinegold House, 20 Rugby Street, London WC1N 3QZ
    T 020-7333 1729 **W** www.classicalmusicmagazine.org
    Editor, Kimon Daltas
GRAMOPHONE
Haymarket, Teddington Studios, Broom Road, Teddington,
    Middlesex TW11 9BE **T** 020-8267 5000
    W www.gramophone.co.uk
    Editor, Martin Cullingford

OPERA
36 Black Lion Lane, London W6 9BE **T** 020-8563 8893
    W www.opera.co.uk
    Editor, John Allison

COMPUTERS AND TECHNOLOGY
ANDROID
Imagine Publishing, Richmond House, 33 Richmond Hill,
    Bournemouth BH2 6EZ **T** 01202-586200
    W www.littlegreenrobot.co.uk
    Deputy Editor, Jack Parsons
EDGE
Future Publishing Ltd, 2 Balcombe Street, London NW1 6NW
    T 01225-442244 **W** www.edge-online.com
    Editor, Tony Mott
PC PRO
Dennis Technology, 30 Cleveland Street, London W1T 4JD
    T 020-7907 6000 **W** www.alphr.com
    Editor, Tim Danton
STUFF
Haymarket, Teddington Studios, Broom Road, Teddington,
    Middlesex TW11 9BE **T** 020-8267 5036 **W** www.stuff.tv
    Editor, Will Findlater
T3
Future Publishing, 2 Balcombe Street, London NW1 6NW
    T 020-7042 4000 **W** www.t3.com
    Editor, Dan Grabham
WEB USER
Dennis Publishing, 30 Cleveland Street, London W1T 4JD
    T 020-7907 6000 **W** www.webuser.co.uk
    Editor, Daniel Booth
WIRED
Condé Nast, Vogue House, Hanover Square, London W1S 1JU
    T 0844-848 5202 **W** www.wired.co.uk
    Editor, Scott Dadich

CRAFT
CARDMAKING & PAPERCRAFT
Immediate Media, Tower House, Fairfax Street, Bristol BS1 3BN
    T 0117-933 8081 **W** www.cardmakingandpapercraft.com
    Editor, Kirstie Sleight
SIMPLY KNITTING
Future Publishing Ltd, 30 Monmouth Street, Bath BA1 2BW
    T 01225-442244 **W** www.simplyknitting.co.uk
    Editor, Kirstie McLeod
THE WORLD OF CROSS STITCHING
Immediate Media, Tower House, Fairfax Street, Bristol BS1 3BN
    T 0117-314 8351 **W** www.cross-stitching.com
    Editor, Ruth Southorn

ENTERTAINMENT
EMPIRE
Endeavour House, 189 Shaftesbury Avenue, London WC2H 8JG
    T 020-7437 9011 **W** www.empireonline.com
    Editor (acting), Ian Nathan
RADIO TIMES
Vineyard House, 44 Brook Green, London W6 7BT
    T 020-7150 5800 **W** www.radiotimes.com
    Editor, Ben Preston
SIGHT & SOUND
3rd Floor Chancery Exchange, 10 Furnival Street, London
    EC4A 1AB **T** 020-8955 7070 **W** www.bfi.org.uk/sightandsound
    Editor, Nick James
TIME OUT
4th Floor, 125 Shaftesbury Avenue, London WC2H 8AD
    T 020-7813 3000 **W** www.timeout.com
    Editor, Caroline McGinn

TOTAL FILM
2 Balcombe Street, London NW1 6NW **T** 020-7042 4000
W www.gamesradar.com/totalfilm
Editor, Jane Crowther

FASHION AND BEAUTY
COSMOPOLITAN
Hearst Magazines, 33 Broadwick Street, London W1F 0DQ
T 020-7439 5000 **W** www.cosmopolitan.co.uk
Editor, Louise Court
ELLE
Hearst Magazines, 72 Broadwick Street, London W1F 9EP
T 020-7150 7000 **W** www.elleuk.com
Editor, Lorraine Candy
GLAMOUR
Condé Nast, Vogue House, Hanover Square, London W1S 1JU
T 020-7499 9080 **W** www.glamourmagazine.co.uk
Editor, Cindi Leive
GRAZIA
Endeavour House, 189 Shaftesbury Avenue, London WC2H 8JG
T 0845-601 1356 **W** www.graziadaily.co.uk
Editor, Angela Buttolph
HARPER'S BAZAAR
Hearst Magazines, 72 Broadwick Street, London W1F 9EP
T 0844-848 5203 **W** www.harpersbazaar.co.uk
Editor, Justine Picardie
MARIE CLAIRE
Blue Fin Building, 110 Southwark Street, London SE1 4SU
T 020-3148 5000 **W** www.marieclaire.co.uk
Editor, Trish Halpin
VOGUE
Condé Nast, Vogue House, Hanover Square, London W1S 1JU
T 0844-848 5202 **W** www.vogue.co.uk
Editor, Alexandra Shulman

FOOD AND DRINK
FOOD AND TRAVEL
Suite 51, The Business Centre, Ingate Place, London SW8 3NS
T 020-7501 0511 **W** www.foodandtravel.com
Editor, Renate Ruge
GOOD FOOD
44 Vineyard House, Brook Green, London W6 7BT
T 020-7150 5022 **W** www.bbcgoodfood.com
Editor, Gillian Carter
JAMIE
800 Guillat Avenue, Kent Science Park, Sittingbourne ME9 8GU
T 0844-249 0478 **W** www.jamieoliver.com/magazine
Editor, Andy Harris
OLIVE
Vineyard House, 44 Brook Green, London W6 7BT
T 020-7150 5024 **W** www.olivemagazine.com
Editor, Christine Hayes
WHISKY
St Faiths House, Mountergate, Norwich NR1 1PY
T 01603-633 808 **W** www.whiskymag.com
Editor, Rupert Wheeler

GENERAL INTEREST
BBC HISTORY
Tower House, Fairfax Street, Bristol BS1 3BN **T** 0117-927 9009
W www.historyextra.com
Editor, Rob Attar
BOOKSELLER
Crowne House, 56-58 Southwark Street, London SE1 1UN
T 01604-251040 **W** www.thebookseller.com
Editor, Philip Jones
HISTORY TODAY
25 Bedford Avenue, London WC1B 3AT **T** 020-3219 7810
W www.historytoday.com
Editor, Paul Lay

LITERARY REVIEW
44 Lexington Street, London W1F OLW **T** 020-7437 9392
W www.literaryreview.co.uk
Editor, Nancy Sladek
NEW STATESMAN
John Carpenter House, 7 Carmelite Street, Blackfriars, London
EC4Y 0AN **T** 020-7936 6400 **W** www.newstatesman.com
Editor, Jason Cowley
PRIVATE EYE
6 Carlisle Street, London W1D 3BN **T** 020-7437 4017
W www.private-eye.co.uk
Editor, Ian Hislop
PROSPECT
25 Sackville Street, London W1S 3HQ **T** 020-7255 1281
W www.prospectmagazine.co.uk
Editor, Bronwen Maddox
RAILWAY
Mortons Media Ltd, Horncastle, Lincs LN9 6JR **T** 01507-529529
W www.railwaymagazine.co.uk
Editor, Nick Pigott
READER'S DIGEST
PO Box 7853, Ringwood BH24 9FH **T** 0844-332 4994
W www.readersdigest.co.uk
Editor, Liz Vaccariello
SAGA
Saga Publishing Ltd, Enbrook Park, Folkestone, Kent CT20 3SE
T 01303-771111 **W** www.saga.co.uk
Editor, Katy Bravery
THE SPECTATOR
22 Old Queen Street, London SW1H 9HP **T** 020-7961 0200
W www.spectator.co.uk
Editor, Fraser Nelson
TLS (THE TIMES LITERARY SUPPLEMENT)
1 London Bridge Street, London SE1 9GF **T** 020-7782 5000
W www.the-tls.co.uk
Editor, Peter Stothard
THE WEEK
30 Cleveland Street, London W1T 4JD **T** 020-7907 6000
W www.theweek.co.uk
Editor, Holden Frith
WHO DO YOU THINK YOU ARE?
Tower House, Fairfax Street, Bristol BS1 3BN **T** 0117-314 7400
W www.whodoyouthinkyouaremagazine.com
Editor, Sarah Williams

HEALTH AND FITNESS
HEALTH & FITNESS
30 Cleveland Street, London W1T 4JD **T** 020-7907 6000
W www.womensfitness.co.uk
Editor, Mary Comber
MEN'S FITNESS
Dennis Publishing, 30 Cleveland Street, London W1T 4JD
T 020-7907 6000 **W** www.mensfitness.co.uk
Editor, Max Anderton
MEN'S HEALTH
Hearst Magazines, 72 Broadwick Street, London W1F 9EP
T 01858-438851 **W** www.menshealth.co.uk
Editor, Toby Wiseman
RUNNER'S WORLD
33 Broadwick Street, London W1F 9EP **T** 020-7339 4409
W www.runnersworld.co.uk
Editor, David Wiley
WEIGHT WATCHERS
Millennium House, Ludlow Road, Maidenhead, Berkshire SL6 2SL
T 07900-494 736 **W** www.weightwatchers.co.uk
Editor, Julie Lee
WOMEN'S FITNESS
30 Cleveland Street, London W1T 4JD **T** 020-7907 6000
W www.womensfitness.co.uk
Editor, Joanna Knight

HOBBIES AND GAMES
AIRFIX MODEL WORLD
Key Publishing Ltd, PO Box 100, Stamford PE9 1XQ
T 01780-755131 W www.airfixmodelworld.com
Editor, Chris Clifford
ANGLING TIMES
Bauer Consumer Media Ltd, 1 Lincoln Court, Lincoln Road,
Peterborough PE1 2RF T 01733-395097
W www.gofishing.co.uk
Editor, Steve Fitzpatrick
BRITISH RAILWAY MODELLING
Warners Group Publications, The Maltings, West Street,
Bourne, Lincs PE10 9PH T 01778-391000
W www.model-railways-live.co.uk
Editor, Ben Jones
CHESS
Chess & Bridge Ltd, 44 Baker Street, London W1U 7RT
T 020-7486 7015 W www.chess.co.uk
Editor, John Saunders
COIN NEWS
Token Publishing Ltd, Orchard House, Duchy Road, Heathpark,
Honiton, Devon EX14 1YD T 01404-46972
W www.tokenpublishing.com
Editor, John Mussell
HORNBY
Key Publishing Ltd, PO Box 100, Stamford PE9 1XQ
T 01780-755131 W www.hornbymagazine.com
Editor, Mike Wild

HOME AND GARDEN
GARDENERS' WORLD
Immediate Media, 5th Floor, Vineyard House, 44 Brook Green,
London W6 7BT T 020-7150 5700
W www.gardenersworld.com
Editor, Lucy Hall
GOOD HOUSEKEEPING
Hearst Magazines, 72 Broadwick Street, London W1F 9EP
T 020-7439 5000 W www.goodhousekeeping.co.uk
Editor, Jane Francisco
HOUSE & GARDEN
Condé Nast Publications, Vogue House, Hanover Square,
London W1S 1JU T 020-7499 9080
W www.houseandgarden.co.uk
Editor, Susan Crew
LIVING ETC
IPC Media, Blue Fin Building, 110 Southwark Street, London
SE1 0SU T 020-3148 7443
W www.housetohome.co.uk/livingetc
Editor, Sarah Baldwin

MEN'S LIFESTYLE
ATTITUDE
Vitality Publishing Ltd, 3rd Floor, 207 Old Street, London EC1V 9NR
T 020-7608 6300 W www.attitude.co.uk
Editor, Matthew Todd
ESQUIRE
Hearst Magazines, 72 Broadwick Street, London W1F 9EP
T 020-7439 5000 W www.esquire.co.uk
Editor, Alex Bilmes
FHM
Endeavour House, 189 Shaftesbury Avenue, London WC2H 8JG
T 020-7295 8534 W www.fhm.com
Editor, Joe Barnes
GAY TIMES
Millivres Prowler Group, Spectrum House, 32-34 Gordon House
Road, London NW5 1LP T 020-7424 7400
W www.gaytimes.co.uk
Editor, Darren Scott

GQ
Vogue House, 1 Hanover Square, London W1S 1JU
T 020-7499 9080 W www.gq-magazine.co.uk
Editor, Dylan Jones
LOADED
Clarenden House, Shenley Road, Borehamwood, Herts WD6 1AG
T 020-7580 6419 W www.loaded.co.uk
Editor, Aaron Tinney

MOTORING
BIKE
Bauer Media, Media House, Lynchwood, Peterborough PE2 6EA
T 01733-468000 W www.bikemagazine.co.uk
Editor, Brice Minnigh
CARAVAN
Warners Group Publications, The Maltings, West Street,
Bourne, Lincs PE10 9PH T 01778-392450
W www.outandaboutlive.co.uk
Editor, John Sootheran
F1 RACING
Haymarket, Teddington Studios, Broom Road, Teddington
TW11 9BE T 020-8267 5806 W www.f1racing.co.uk
Editor, Anthony Rowlinson
OCTANE
Dennis Publishing Ltd, 30 Cleveland Street, London W1T 4JD
T 020-7907 6000 W www.classicandperformancecar.com
Editor, David Lillywhite
PRACTICAL CARAVAN
Haymarket, Teddington Studios, Teddington Lock, Broom Road,
Teddington TW11 9BE T 020-8267 5629
W www.practicalcaravan.com
Editor, Nigel Donnelly
TOP GEAR
Energy Centre, Media Centre, 201 Wood Lane, London W12 7TQ
T 020-8433 3598 W www.topgear.com
Editor, Charlie Turner

PHOTOGRAPHY
AMATEUR PHOTOGRAPHER
Blue Fin Building, 110 Southwark Street, London SE1 0SU
T 020-3148 4138 W www.amateurphotographer.co.uk
Editor, Nigel Atherton
DIGITAL PHOTOGRAPHER
Imagine Publishing, Richmond House, 33 Richmond Hill,
Bournemouth BH2 6EZ T 01202-586200
W www.dphotographer.co.uk
Editor, Amy Squibb
PHOTOGRAPHY MONTHLY
Archant House, Oriel Road, Cheltenham GL50 1BB
T 01242-211080 W www.photographymonthly.com
Editor, Jeff Meyer
PROFESSIONAL PHOTOGRAPHER
Archant House, Oriel Road, Cheltenham GL50 1BB
T 0844-848 5232 W www.professionalphotographer.co.uk
Editor, Adam Scorey

POPULAR MUSIC
CLASH
194 Hercules Road, London SE1 7LD T 020-7628 2312
W www.clashmusic.com
Editor, Simon Harper
CLASSIC ROCK
Prospect Business Centre, 3 Stanley Boulevard, Blantyre G72 0BN
T 01604-251040 W www.classicrock.teamrock.com
Editor, Scott Rowley
DIY
Arch 462, Kingsland Viaduct, 83 Rivington Street, London
EC2A 3AY W www.diymag.com
Editor, Stephen Ackroyd

GUITARIST
Future Publishing Ltd, Beauford Court, 30 Monmouth Street,
Bath BA1 2BW **T** 01225-442244
W www.musicradar.com/guitarist
Editor, Mick Taylor
KERRANG!
Bauer Media, Media House, Lynchwood, Peterborough PE2 6EA
T 01733-468000 **W** www.kerrang.com
Editor, James McMahon
MOJO
Endeavour House, 189 Shaftesbury Avenue, London WC2H 8JG
T 020-7208 3443 **W** www.mojo4music.com
Editor, Phil Alexander
NME
9th Floor, Blue Fin Building, 110 Southwark Street, London
SE1 0SU **T** 0845-676 7778 **W** www.nme.com
Editor, Mike Williams
Q
Endeavour House, 189 Shaftesbury Avenue, London WC2H 8JG
T 020-7295 5000 **W** www.qthemusic.com
Editor, Phil Alexander
UNCUT
Blue Fin Building, 110 Southwark Street, London SE1 0SU
T 020-3148 5000 **W** www.uncut.co.uk
Editor, John Mulvey

SCIENCE AND NATURE
BBC WILDLIFE
4th Floor, Tower House, Fairfax Street, Bristol BS1 3BN
T 0117-314 7366 **W** www.discoverwildlife.com
Editor, Matt Swaine
BIRD WATCHING
Bauer Media, Media House, Lynch Wood, Peterborough PE2 6EA
T 01733-468000 **W** www.birdwatching.co.uk
Editor, Matthew Merritt
COUNTRYFILE
9th Floor, Tower House, Fairfax Street, Bristol BS1 3BN
T 0117-927 9009 **W** www.countryfile.com
Editor, Fergus Collins
FOCUS
Bristol Magazines Ltd, Tower House, Fairfax Street, Bristol BS1 3BN
T 0117-314 7388 **W** www.sciencefocus.com
Editor, Graham Southorn
HOW IT WORKS
Imagine Publishing Ltd, Richmond House, 33 Richmond Hill,
Bournemouth BH2 6EZ **T** 01202-586200
W www.howitworksdaily.com
Editor, Dave Farfield
NEW SCIENTIST
Lacon House, 84 Theobalds Road, London WC1X 8NS
T 020-7611 1206 **W** www.newscientist.com
Editor, Sumit Paul-Choudhury
SKY AT NIGHT
Immediate Media Company Bristol Ltd, Tower House, Fairfax
Street, Bristol BS1 3BN **T** 0844 844 0254
W www.skyatnightmagazine.com
Editor, Chris Bramley

SPORT
ALL OUT CRICKET
TriNorth Ltd, Unit 3.40 Canterbury Court, 1–3 Brixton Road,
London SW9 6DE **T** 020-3176 0187 **W** www.alloutcricket.com
Editor, Phil Walker
BOXING MONTHLY
Topwave Ltd, 40 Morpeth Road, London E9 7LD **T** 020-8986 4141
W www.boxing-monthly.co.uk
Editor, Graham Houston

COUNTRY WALKING
Bauer Media, 1 Lincoln Court, Lincoln Road, Peterborough,
PE1 2RF **T** 01733-468205 **W** www.livefortheoutdoors.com
Editor, Mark Sutcliffe
THE CRICKETER
The Cricketer Publishing Ltd, 70 Great Portland Street,
London W1W 7UW **T** 020-7460 5200
W www.thecricketer-magazine.com
Editor, Simon Hughes
FOURFOURTWO
Haymarket, Teddington Studios, Broom Road, Teddington,
Middlesex TW11 9BE **T** 020-8267 5661
W www.fourfourtwo.com
Editor, Hitesh Ratna
GOLF MONTHLY
9th Floor, Blue Fin Building, 110 Southwark Street,
London SE1 0SU **T** 020-3148 4527
W www.golf-monthly.co.uk
Editor, Michael Harris
HORSE & HOUND
Blue Fin Building, 110 Southwark Street, London SE1 0SU
T 020-3148 4562 **W** www.horseandhound.co.uk
Editor, Sarah Jenkins
MATCH
Media House, Lynchwood, Peterborough PE2 6EA
T 01733-468008 **W** www.matchmag.co.uk
Editor, James Bandy
RUGBY WORLD
Blue Fin Building, 110 Southwark Street, London SE1 0SU
T 0844-848 0848 **W** www.rugbyworld.com
Editor, Owain Jones
SPORT
Third Floor, Courtyard Building, 11 Curtain Road, London
EC2A 3LT **T** 020-7959 7942 **W** www.sport-magazine.co.uk
Editor, Simon Caney
SUPERBIKE
Blaze Publishing, Lawrence House, Morrell Street,
Leamington Spa CV37 5SZ **T** 020-8873 4454
W www.superbike.co.uk
Editor, John Hogan
TENNISHEAD
PO Box 70948, London SW19 9GL **T** 020-8408 7148
W www.tennishead.net
Editor, Lee Goodall
WORLD SOCCER
Blue Fin Building, 110 Southwark Street, London SE1 0SU
T 020-3148 4817 **W** www.worldsoccer.com
Editor, Gavin Hamilton

TRAVEL
CONDÉ NAST TRAVELLER
Vogue House, Hanover Square, London W1S 1JU
T 0844-848 2851 **W** www.cntraveller.com
Editor, Melinda Stevens
FRANCE
Archant House, 3 Oriel Road, Cheltenham GL50 1BB
T 01242-216050 **W** www.completefrance.com
Editor, Carolyn Boyd
LONELY PLANET
Media Centre (GH0S), 201 Wood Lane, London W12 7TQ
T 020-8433 1333 **W** www.lonelyplanet.com
Editor, Peter Grunert
NATIONAL GEOGRAPHIC TRAVELLER
Absolute Publishing Ltd, 197-199 City Road,
London EC1V 1JN **T** 020-7253 9906
W www.natgeotraveller.co.uk
Editor, Pat Riddell

TRADE AND PROFESSIONAL BODIES

The following is a list of employers' and trade associations and other professional bodies in the UK. It does not represent a comprehensive list. For further professional bodies *see* Professional Education.

ASSOCIATIONS

ABTA – THE TRAVEL ASSOCIATION, 30 Park Street, London SE1 9EQ T 020-3117 0500 E abta@abta.co.uk
W www.abta.com
Chief Executive, Mark Tanzer
ADVERTISING ASSOCIATION, 7th Floor North, Artillery House, 11–19 Artillery Row, London SW1P 1RT T 020-7340 1100
E aa@adassoc.org.uk W www.adassoc.org.uk
Chief Executive, Tim Lefroy
AEROSPACE DEFENCE SECURITY, Salamanca Square, 9 Albert Embankment, London SE1 7SP T 020-7091 4500
E enquiries@adsgroup.org.uk W www.adsgroup.org.uk
Chief Executive, Paul Everitt
AGRICULTURAL ENGINEERS ASSOCIATION, Samuelson House, 62 Forder Way, Hampton, Peterborough PE7 8JB T 0845-644 8748 E ab@aea.uk.com
W www.aea.uk.com
Chief Executive, Ruth Bailey
ASBESTOS REMOVAL CONTRACTORS ASSOCIATION, Unit 1, Stretton Business Park 2, Brunel Drive, Stretton DE13 0BY T 01283-566467 E info@arca.org.uk
W www.arca.org.uk
Chief Executive, Steve Sadley
ASSOCIATION FOR CONSULTANCY AND ENGINEERING, Alliance House, 12 Caxton Street, London SW1H 0QL T 020-7222 6557 E consult@acenet.co.uk
W www.acenet.co.uk
Chief Executive, Dr Nelson Ogunshakin, OBE
ASSOCIATION OF ACCOUNTING TECHNICIANS, 140 Aldersgate Street, London EC1A 4HY T 020-7397 3000
E aat@aat.org.uk W www.aat.org.uk
Chief Executive, Mark Farrar
ASSOCIATION OF ANAESTHETISTS OF GREAT BRITAIN AND IRELAND, 21 Portland Place, London W1B 1PY T 020-7631 1650 E info@aagbi.org
W www.aagbi.org
President, Dr Andrew Hartle
ASSOCIATION OF BRITISH INSURERS, 51 Gresham Street, London EC2V 7HQ T 020-7600 3333 E info@abi.org.uk
W www.abi.org.uk
Director-General, Huw Evans
ASSOCIATION OF BUSINESS RECOVERY PROFESSIONALS, 8th Floor, 120 Aldersgate Street, London EC1A 4JQ T 020-7566 4200 E association@r3.org.uk
W www.r3.org.uk
Chief Executive, Graham Rumney
ASSOCIATION OF CONSULTING SCIENTISTS, 5 Willow Heights, Cradley Heath B64 7PL T 0121-602 3515
E secretary@consultingscientists.co.uk
Secretary, Dr Stuart Guy
ASSOCIATION OF CONVENIENCE STORES LTD, Federation House, 17 Farnborough Street, Farnborough GU14 8AG T 01252-515001 E acs@acs.org.uk
W www.acs.org.uk
Chief Executive, James Lowman
ASSOCIATION OF CORPORATE TREASURERS, 51 Moorgate, London EC2R 6BH T 020-7847 2540
E enquiries@treasurers.org W www.treasurers.org
Chief Executive, Colin Tyler

ASSOCIATION OF DRAINAGE AUTHORITIES, 6 Electric Parade, Surbiton KT6 5NT T 020-8399 7350
E admin@ada.org.uk W www.ada.org.uk
Chief Executive, Jean Venables, CBE, FRENG
BOOKSELLERS ASSOCIATION, 6 Bell Yard, London WC2A 2JR T 020-7421 4640 E mail@booksellers.org.uk
W www.booksellers.org.uk
Chief Executive, T. E. Godfray
BPI (BRITISH PHONOGRAPHIC INDUSTRY), Riverside Building, County Hall, Westminster Bridge Road, London SE1 7JA T 020-7803 1300 E general@bpi.co.uk
W www.bpi.co.uk
Chief Executive, Geoff Taylor
BRITISH ANTIQUE DEALERS' ASSOCIATION, 20 Rutland Gate, London SW7 1BD T 020-7589 4128
E info@bada.org W www.bada.org
Secretary-General, Mark Dodgson
BRITISH ASSOCIATION OF SOCIAL WORKERS, 16 Kent Street, Birmingham B5 6RD T 0121-622 3911
E online@basw.co.uk W www.basw.co.uk
Chief Executive, Bridget Robb
BRITISH BANKERS' ASSOCIATION, Pinners Hall, 105–108 Old Broad Street, London EC2N 1EX
T 020-7216 8800 E info@bba.org.uk W www.bba.org.uk
Chief Executive, Anthony Browne
BRITISH BEER & PUB ASSOCIATION, Ground Floor, Brewers' Hall, Aldermanbury Square, London EC2V 7HR
T 020-7627 9191 E contact@beerandpub.com
W www.beerandpub.com
Chief Executive, Brigid Simmonds, OBE
BRITISH CHAMBERS OF COMMERCE, 65 Petty France, London SW1H 9EU T 020-7654 5800
W www.britishchambers.org.uk
Director-General, John Longworth
BRITISH ELECTROTECHNICAL AND ALLIED MANUFACTURERS ASSOCIATION (BEAMA), Westminster Tower, 3 Albert Embankment, London SE1 7SL
T 020-7793 3000 E info@beama.org.uk W www.beama.org.uk
Chief Executive, Dr Howard Porter
BRITISH HOROLOGICAL INSTITUTE, Upton Hall, Upton, Newark NG23 5TE T 01636-813795
E clocks@bhi.co.uk W www.bhi.co.uk
Chief Executive, Dudley Giles
BRITISH HOSPITALITY ASSOCIATION, Queens House, 55–56 Lincoln's Inn Fields, London WC2A 3BH
T 020-7404 7744 E bha@bha.org.uk W www.bha.org.uk
Chief Executive, Ufi Ibrahim
BRITISH INSTITUTE OF PROFESSIONAL PHOTOGRAPHY, The Coach House, The Firs, High Street, Whitchurch, Aylesbury HP22 4SJ T 01296-642020
E info@bipp.com W www.bipp.com
Chief Executive, Chris Harper
BRITISH INSURANCE BROKERS' ASSOCIATION, 8th Floor, John Stow House, 18 Bevis Marks, London EC3A 7JB T 0870-950 1790 E enquiries@biba.org.uk
W www.biba.org.uk
Chief Executive, Steve White
BRITISH MARINE FEDERATION, Marine House, Thorpe Lea Road, Egham TW20 8BF T 01784-473377
E info@britishmarine.co.uk W www.britishmarine.co.uk
Chief Executive, Howard Pridding
BRITISH MEDICAL ASSOCIATION, BMA House, Tavistock Square, London WC1H 9JP T 020-7387 4499
W www.bma.org.uk
Chief Executive, Keith Ward

BRITISH OFFICE SUPPLIES AND SERVICES (BOSS) FEDERATION, c/o British Printing Industries Federation, 2 Villiers Court, Meriden Business Park, Copse Drive, Coventry CV5 9RN T 01676-526030
E info@bossfederation.co.uk W www.bossfederation.co.uk
Chief Executive, Michael Gardner

BRITISH PLASTICS FEDERATION, 6 Bath Place, Rivington Street, London EC2A 3JE T 020-7457 5000
E reception@bpf.co.uk W www.bpf.co.uk
Director-General, Philip Law

BRITISH PORTS ASSOCIATION, 1st Floor, 30 Park Street, London SE1 9EQ T 020-7260 1780
E info@britishports.org.uk W www.britishports.org.uk
Director, David Whitehead

BRITISH PRINTING INDUSTRIES FEDERATION, 2 Villiers Court, Meriden Business Park, Copse Drive, Coventry CV5 9RN T 0845-250 7050 W www.britishprint.com
Chief Executive, Charles Jarrold

BRITISH PROPERTY FEDERATION, 5th Floor, St Albans House, 57–59 Haymarket, London SW1Y 4QX T 020-7828 0111 E info@bpf.org.uk W www.bpf.org.uk
Chief Executive, Melanie Leech

BRITISH RETAIL CONSORTIUM, 21 Dartmouth Street, London SW1H 9BP T 020-7854 8900 E info@brc.org.uk W www.brc.org.uk
Director-General, Helen Dickinson

BRITISH TYRE MANUFACTURERS' ASSOCIATION LTD, 5 Berewyk Hall Court, White Colne, Colchester CO6 2QB T 01787-226995 E mail@btmauk.com W www.btmauk.com
Chief Executive, Graham Willson

BUILDING SOCIETIES ASSOCIATION, York House, 23 Kingsway, London WC2B 6UJ T 020-7520 5900
E simon.rex@bsa.org.uk W www.bsa.org.uk
Chief Executive, Robin Fieth

CHARTERED ASSOCIATION OF BUILDING ENGINEERS, Lutyens House, Billing Brook Road, Weston Favell, Northampton NN3 8NW T 01604-404121
W www.cbuilde.com
Chief Executive, Dr John Hooper

CHARTERED INSTITUTE FOR ARCHAEOLOGISTS, Miller Building, University of Reading RG6 6AB
T 0118-378 6446 E admin@archaeologists.net
W www.archaeologists.net
Chief Executive, Peter Hinton

CHARTERED INSTITUTE OF ENVIRONMENTAL HEALTH, Chadwick Court, 15 Hatfields, London SE1 8DJ
T 020-7928 6006 E information@cieh.org W www.cieh.org
Chief Executive, Graham Jukes

CHARTERED INSTITUTE OF JOURNALISTS, 2 Dock Offices, Surrey Quays Road, London SE16 2XU
T 020-7252 1187 E memberservices@cioj.co.uk
W www.cioj.co.uk
General Secretary, Dominic Cooper

CHARTERED INSTITUTE OF PURCHASING AND SUPPLY, Easton House, Church Street, Easton on the Hill, Stamford PE9 3NZ T 01780-756777 W www.cips.org
Chief Executive, David Noble

CHARTERED INSTITUTE OF TAXATION, 1st Floor Artillery House, 11–19 Artillery Row, London SW1P 1RT
T 020-7340 0550 W www.tax.org.uk
Chief Executive, Peter Fanning

CHARTERED INSURANCE INSTITUTE, 42–48 High Road, South Woodford, London E18 2JP T 020-8989 8464
E customer.serv@cii.co.uk W www.cii.co.uk
Chief Executive, Dr Sandy Scott

CHARTERED MANAGEMENT INSTITUTE, Management House, Cottingham Road, Corby NN17 1TT
T 01536-204222 E enquiries@managers.org.uk
W www.managers.org.uk
Chief Executive, Anne Francke

CHARTERED QUALITY INSTITUTE, 2nd Floor North, Chancery Exchange, 10 Furnival Street, London EC4A 1AB
T 020-7245 6722 E membership@thecqi.org
W www.thecqi.org
Chief Executive, Simon Feary

CHEMICAL INDUSTRIES ASSOCIATION, Kings Buildings, Smith Square, London SW1P 3JJ T 020-7834 3399
E enquiries@cia.org.uk W www.cia.org.uk
Chief Executive, Steve Elliott

CONFEDERATION OF PAPER INDUSTRIES, 1 Rivenhall Road, Swindon SN5 7BD T 01793-889600 E cpi@paper.org.uk
W www.paper.org.uk
Director-General, David Workman

CONFEDERATION OF PASSENGER TRANSPORT UK, Drury House, 34–43 Russell Street, London WC2B 5HA
T 020-7240 3131 E admin@cpt-uk.org W www.cpt-uk.org
Chief Executive, Simon Posner

CONSTRUCTION PRODUCTS ASSOCIATION, 26 Store Street, London WC1E 7BT T 020-7323 3770
W www.constructionproducts.org.uk
Chief Executive, Diana Montgomery

DAIRY UK, 6th floor, 210 High Holborn, London WC1V 7EP
T 020-7405 1484 E info@dairyuk.org W www.dairyuk.org
Chief Executive, Dr Judith Bryans

EEF, THE MANUFACTURERS' ORGANISATION, Broadway House, Tothill Street, London SW1H 9NQ
T 020-7222 7777 E enquiries@eef.org.uk W www.eef.org.uk
Chief Executive, Terry Scuoler

ENERGY UK, Charles House, 5–11 Regent Street, London SW1Y 4LR T 020-7930 9390 W www.energy-uk.org.uk
Chief Executive (interim), Lawrence Slade

FEDERATION OF BAKERS, 6 Catherine Street, London WC2B 5JW T 020-7420 7190 E info@bakersfederation.org.uk
W www.bakersfederation.org.uk
Director, Gordon Polson

FEDERATION OF MASTER BUILDERS, David Croft House, 25 Ely Place, London EC1N 6TD T 020-7025 2900
W www.fmb.org.uk
Chief Executive, Brian Berry

FEDERATION OF SPORTS AND PLAY ASSOCIATIONS, Office 8, Rural Innovation Centre, Unit 169 – Avenue H, Stoneleigh Park, Kenilworth CV8 2LG
T 024-7641 4999 E info@sportsandplay.com
W www.sportsandplay.com
Managing Director, Jane Montgomery

FINANCE AND LEASING ASSOCIATION, 2nd Floor, Imperial House, 15–19 Kingsway, London WC2B 6UN
T 020-7836 6511 E info@fla.org.uk W www.fla.org.uk
Director-General, Stephen Sklaroff

FOOD AND DRINK FEDERATION, 6 Catherine Street, London WC2B 5JJ T 020-7836 2460 W www.fdf.org.uk
Director-General, Ian Wright

FREIGHT TRANSPORT ASSOCIATION LTD, Hermes House, St John's Road, Tunbridge Wells TN4 9UZ
T 01892-526171 E enquiry@fta.co.uk W www.fta.co.uk
Chief Executive, David Wells

GLASGOW CHAMBER OF COMMERCE, 30 George Square, Glasgow G2 1EQ T 0141-204 2121
E chamber@glasgowchamberofcommerce.com
W www.glasgowchamberofcommerce.com
Chief Executive, Stuart Patrick

INSTITUTE OF BREWING & DISTILLING, 44A Curlew Street, Butler's Wharf, London SE1 2ND
T 020-7499 8144 E enquiries@ibd.org.uk W www.ibd.org.uk
Executive Director, Simon Jackson

INSTITUTE OF BRITISH ORGAN BUILDING, 13 Ryefields, Thurston, Bury St Edmunds IP31 3TD
T 01359-233433 E administrator@ibo.co.uk W www.ibo.co.uk
President, Dr Christopher Batchelor

INSTITUTE OF CHARTERED FORESTERS,
59 George Street, Edinburgh EH2 2JG **T** 0131-240 1425
E icf@charteredforesters.org **W** www.charteredforesters.org
Executive Director, Shireen Chambers

INSTITUTE OF CHARTERED SECRETARIES AND
ADMINISTRATORS, Saffron House, 6–10 Kirby Street,
London EC1N 8TS **T** 020-7580 4741 **E** info@icsa.org.uk
W www.icsa.org.uk
Chief Executive, Simon Osborne

INSTITUTE OF CHARTERED SHIPBROKERS,
85 Gracechurch Street, London EC3V 0AA **T** 020-7623 1111
E enquiries@ics.org.uk **W** www.ics.org.uk
Director, Julie Lithgow

INSTITUTE OF DIRECTORS, 116 Pall Mall, London
SW1Y 5ED **T** 020-7766 8888 **E** enquiries@iod.com
W www.iod.com
Director-General, Simon Walker

INSTITUTE OF EXPORT, Export House, Minerva Business
Park, Lynch Wood, Peterborough PE2 6FT **T** 01733-404400
W www.export.org.uk
Director-General, Lesley Batchelor, OBE

INSTITUTE OF FINANCIAL ACCOUNTANTS,
The Podium, 1 Eversholt Street, London NW1 2DN
T 020-7554 0730 **E** mail@ifa.org.uk **W** www.ifa.org.uk
Chief Executive, David Woodgate

INSTITUTE OF HEALTHCARE MANAGEMENT,
John Snow House, 59 Mansell Street, London E1 8AN
T 020-7265 7321 **E** enquiries@ihm.org.uk **W** www.ihm.org.uk
Chief Executive, Shirley Cramer, CBE

INSTITUTE OF HOSPITALITY, Trinity Court, 34 West Street,
Sutton, Surrey SM1 1SH **T** 020-8661 4900
W www.instituteofhospitality.org
Chief Executive, Peter Ducker

INSTITUTE OF INTERNAL COMMUNICATION,
Suite G10, Gemini House, Sunrise Parkway, Linford Wood,
MK14 6PW **T** 01908-232168 **E** enquiries@ioic.org.uk
W www.ioic.org.uk
Chief Executive, Steve Doswell

INSTITUTE OF MANAGEMENT SERVICES,
Brooke House, 24 Dam Street, Lichfield WS13 6AA
T 01543-266909 **E** admin@ims-stowe.fsnet.co.uk
W www.ims-productivity.com
Chair, Dr Andrew Muir

INSTITUTE OF QUARRYING, McPherson House,
8A Regan Way, Chetwynd Business Park, Chilwell, Nottingham
NG9 6RZ **T** 0115-972 9995 **E** mail@quarrying.org
W www.quarrying.org
Executive Director, Phil James

INSTITUTE OF THE MOTOR INDUSTRY, Fanshaws,
Brickendon, Hertford SG13 8PQ **T** 01992-511521
E comms@theimi.org.uk **W** www.theimi.org.uk
Chief Executive, Steve Nash

INSTITUTION OF OCCUPATIONAL SAFETY AND
HEALTH, The Grange, Highfield Drive, Wigston LE18 1NN
T 0116-257 3100 **E** reception@iosh.co.uk **W** www.iosh.co.uk
Chief Executive, Jan Chmiel

IP FEDERATION, 5th Floor, 63–66 Hatton Garden,
London EC1N 8LE **T** 020-7242 3923 **E** admin@ipfederation.com
W www.ipfederation.com
President, Carol Arnold

MAGISTRATES' ASSOCIATION, 28 Fitzroy Square,
London W1T 6DD **T** 020-7387 2353
E information@magistrates-association.org.uk
W www.magistrates-association.org.uk
Chief Executive, Chris Brace

MANAGEMENT CONSULTANCIES ASSOCIATION,
5th Floor, 36–38 Cornhill, London EC3V 3NG **T** 020-7645 7950
E info@mca.org.uk **W** www.mca.org.uk
Chief Executive, Alan Leaman, OBE

MASTER LOCKSMITHS ASSOCIATION, 5D Great
Central Way, Woodford Halse, Daventry NN11 3PZ
T 01327-262 255 **E** enquiries@locksmiths.co.uk
W www.locksmiths.co.uk
Director of Development, Dr Steffan George

NATIONAL ASSOCIATION OF BRITISH MARKET
AUTHORITIES, The Guildhall, Oswestry,
Shrops SY11 1PZ **T** 01691-680713
E nabma@nabma.com **W** www.nabma.com
Chief Executive, Graham Wilson, OBE

NATIONAL ASSOCIATION OF ESTATE AGENTS,
Arbon House, 6 Tournament Court, Edgehill Drive, Warwick
CV34 6LG **T** 0845-250 6001 **W** www.naea.co.uk
President, Simon Gerrard

NATIONAL CATTLE ASSOCIATION (DAIRY), Brick House,
Risbury, Leominster HR6 0NQ **T** 01568-760632
E timbrigstocke@hotmail.com
Executive Secretary, Tim Brigstocke, MBE

NATIONAL FARMERS' UNION (NFU), Agriculture
House, Stoneleigh Park, Stoneleigh CV8 2LZ **T** 024-7685 8500
W www.nfuonline.com
Director-General, Andy Robertson

NATIONAL FEDERATION OF RETAIL NEWSAGENTS,
Yeoman House, Sekforde Street, London EC1R 0HF
T 020-7253 4225 **E** service@nfrnonline.com
W www.nfrnonline.com
Chief Executive, Paul Baxter

NATIONAL LANDLORDS ASSOCIATION, 2nd Floor,
200 Union Street, London SE1 0LX **T** 020-7840 8900
E info@landlords.org.uk **W** www.landlords.org.uk
Chief Executive, Richard Lambert

NATIONAL MARKET TRADERS FEDERATION,
Hampton House, Hawshaw Lane, Hoyland, Barnsley S74 0HA
T 01226-749021 **E** genoffice@nmtf.co.uk **W** www.nmtf.co.uk
Chief Executive, Joe Harrison

NATIONAL PHARMACY ASSOCIATION, Mallinson House,
38–42 St Peter's Street, St Albans, Herts AL1 3NP
T 01727-858687 **E** npa@npa.co.uk **W** www.npa.co.uk
Chief Executive, vacant

NEWS MEDIA ASSOCIATION, 292 Vauxhall Bridge Road,
London SW1V 1AE **T** 020-7963 7480 **E** nma@newsmediauk.org
W www.newsmediauk.org
Chief Executive, David Newell

OIL AND GAS UK, 6th Floor East, Portland House,
Bressenden Place, London SW1E 5BH **T** 020-7802 2400
E info@oilandgasuk.co.uk **W** www.oilandgasuk.co.uk
Chief Executive, Malcolm Webb

PROPERTY CARE ASSOCIATION, 11 Ramsay Court,
Kingfisher Way, Hinchingbrooke Business Park, Huntingdon
PE29 6FY **T** 0844-375 4301 **E** pca@property-care.org
W www.property-care.org
Chief Executive, Stephen Hodgson

PUBLISHERS ASSOCIATION, 29B Montague Street,
London WC1B 5BW **T** 020-7691 9191
E mail@publishers.org.uk **W** www.publishers.org.uk
Chief Executive, Richard Mollet

RADIOCENTRE, 6th Floor, 55 New Oxford Street,
London WC1A 1BS **T** 020-7010 0600 **E** info@radiocentre.org
W www.radiocentre.org
Chief Executive, Siobhan Kenny

ROAD HAULAGE ASSOCIATION LTD, Roadway House,
Bretton PE3 8DD **T** 01274-863100 **W** www.rha.uk.net
Chief Executive, Richard Burnett

ROYAL ASSOCIATION OF BRITISH DAIRY FARMERS,
Dairy House, Unit 31, Abbey Park, Stareton, Kenilworth
CV8 2LY **T** 0845-458 2711 **E** office@rabdf.co.uk
W www.rabdf.co.uk
Chief Executive, Nick Everington

ROYAL FACULTY OF PROCURATORS IN GLASGOW,
12 Nelson Mandela Place, Glasgow G2 1BT T 0141-332 3593
E library@rfpg.org W www.rfpg.org
Chief Executive, John McKenzie

SHELLFISH ASSOCIATION OF GREAT BRITAIN,
Fishmongers' Hall, London Bridge, London EC4R 9EL
T 020-7283 8305 W www.shellfish.org.uk
Director, David Jarrad

SOCIETY OF LOCAL AUTHORITY CHIEF EXECUTIVES
AND SENIOR MANAGERS (SOLACE), Suite 1.3A,
1st Floor, 21–24 Millbank Tower, Millbank, London SW1P 4QP
T 0845-652 4010 E debbie.wood@solace.org.uk
W www.solace.org.uk
Directors, Graeme McDonald; Terry McDougal;
Debbie Wood

SOCIETY OF MOTOR MANUFACTURERS AND
TRADERS LTD, 71 Great Peter Street, London SW1P 2BN
T 020-7235 7000 E communications@smmt.co.uk
W www.smmt.co.uk
Chief Executive, Mike Hawes

TIMBER TRADE FEDERATION, The Building Centre,
26 Store Street, London WC1E 7BT T 020-3205 0067
E ttf@ttf.co.uk W www.ttf.co.uk
Chief Executive, vacant

TRADING STANDARDS INSTITUTE, 1 Sylvan Court,
Sylvan Way, Southfields Business Park, Basildon SS15 6TH
T 01268-582200 E institute@tsi.org.uk
W www.tradingstandards.gov.uk
Chief Executive, Leon Livermore

UK CHAMBER OF SHIPPING, 30 Park Street, London SE1 9EQ
T 020-7417 2800 E query@ukchamberofshipping.com
W www.ukchamberofshipping.com
Chief Executive, Guy Platten

UK FASHION AND TEXTILE ASSOCIATION, 3 Queen
Square, London WC1N 3AR T 020-7843 9460 E info@ukft.org
W www.ukft.org
Chief Executive, John Miln

UK LEATHER FEDERATION, Leather Trade House,
Kings Park Road, Moulton Park, Northampton NN3 6JD
T 01604-679999 E info@uklf.org W www.ukleather.org
Director, Dr Kerry Senior

UK PETROLEUM INDUSTRY ASSOCIATION LTD,
Quality House, Quality Court, Chancery Lane,
London WC2A 1HP T 020-7269 7600 E info@ukpia.com
W www.ukpia.com
Director-General, Chris Hunt

ULSTER FARMERS' UNION, 475 Antrim Road,
Belfast BT15 3DA T 028-9037 0222 E info@ufuhq.com
W www.ufuni.org
Chief Executive, Wesley Aston

WINE AND SPIRIT TRADE ASSOCIATION,
International Wine and Spirit Centre, 39–45 Bermondsey Street,
London SE1 3XF T 020-7089 3877 E info@wsta.co.uk
W www.wsta.co.uk
Chief Executive, Miles Beale

CBI

Cannon Place, 78 Cannon Street, London EC4N 6HN
T 020-7379 7400 E enquiries@coi.org.uk W www.cbi.org.uk

The CBI was founded in 1965 and is an independent non-party political body financed by industry and commerce. It works with the UK government, international legislators and policymakers to help UK businesses compete effectively. It is the recognised spokesman for the business viewpoint and is consulted as such by the government.

The CBI speaks for some 190,000 businesses that together employ approximately one-third of the private sector workforce. Member companies, which decide all policy positions, include FTSE 100 index listed companies, small- and medium-size firms, micro businesses, private and family owned businesses, start-ups and trade associations.

The CBI board is chaired by the president and meets four times a year. It is assisted by 14 expert standing committees which advise on the main aspects of policy. There are 13 regional councils and offices, covering the administrative regions of England, Wales, Scotland and Northern Ireland. There are also offices in Beijing, Brussels, New Delhi and Washington DC.

Director-General, John Cridland, CBE

WALES, 2 Caspian Point, Caspian Way, Cardiff Bay, Cardiff
CF10 4DQ T 029-2097 7600 E wales.mail@cbi.org.uk
Regional Director, Emma Watkins

SCOTLAND, 160 West George Street, Glasgow G2 2HQ
T 0141-222 2184 E scot.mail@cbi.org.uk
Regional Director, Hugh Aitken

NORTHERN IRELAND, Hamilton House, 3 Joy Street,
Belfast BT2 8LE T 028-9010 1100 E ni.mail@cbi.org.uk
Regional Director, Nigel Smyth

TRADE UNIONS

A trade union is an organisation of workers formed for the purpose of collective bargaining over pay and working conditions. Trade unions may also provide legal and financial advice, sickness benefits and education facilities to their members. Legally any employee has the right to join a trade union, but not all employers recognise all or any trade unions. Conversely an employee also has the right not to join a trade union, in particular since the practice of a 'closed shop' system, where all employees have to join the employer's preferred union, is no longer permitted. Below is a list of key dates in the development of the British trade unionist movement.

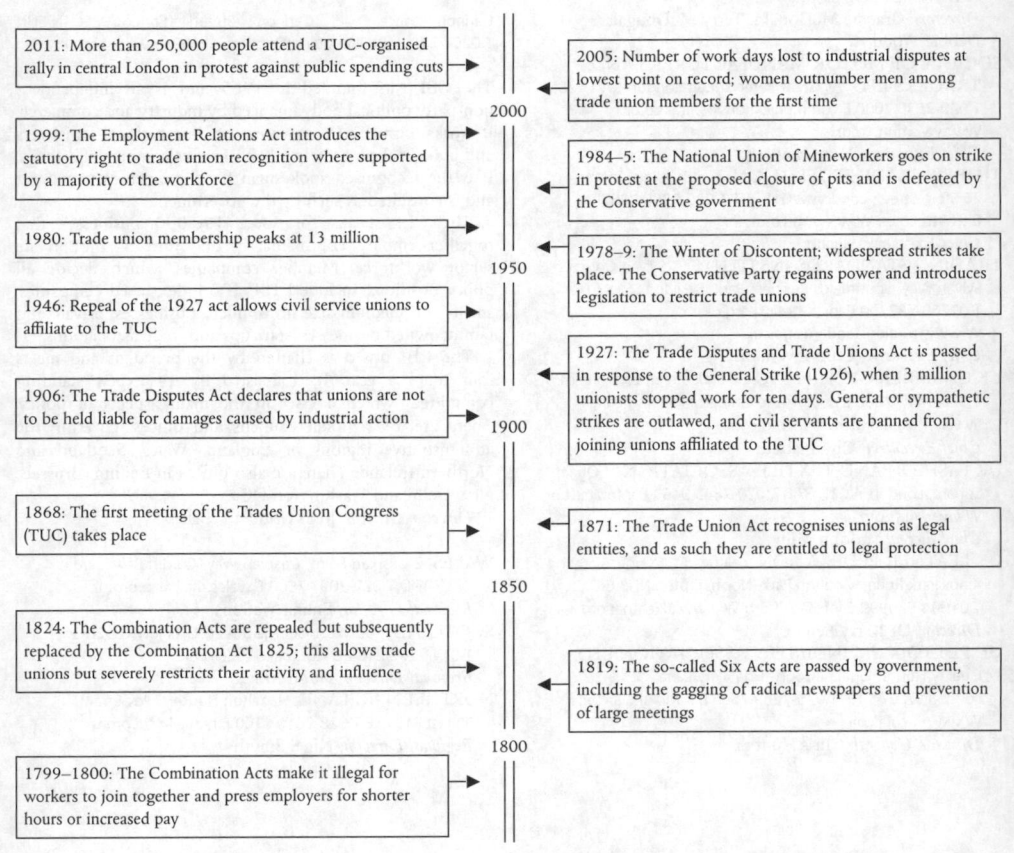

2011: More than 250,000 people attend a TUC-organised rally in central London in protest against public spending cuts

2005: Number of work days lost to industrial disputes at lowest point on record; women outnumber men among trade union members for the first time

2000

1999: The Employment Relations Act introduces the statutory right to trade union recognition where supported by a majority of the workforce

1984–5: The National Union of Mineworkers goes on strike in protest at the proposed closure of pits and is defeated by the Conservative government

1980: Trade union membership peaks at 13 million

1950

1978–9: The Winter of Discontent; widespread strikes take place. The Conservative Party regains power and introduces legislation to restrict trade unions

1946: Repeal of the 1927 act allows civil service unions to affiliate to the TUC

1927: The Trade Disputes and Trade Unions Act is passed in response to the General Strike (1926), when 3 million unionists stopped work for ten days. General or sympathetic strikes are outlawed, and civil servants are banned from joining unions affiliated to the TUC

1906: The Trade Disputes Act declares that unions are not to be held liable for damages caused by industrial action

1900

1868: The first meeting of the Trades Union Congress (TUC) takes place

1871: The Trade Union Act recognises unions as legal entities, and as such they are entitled to legal protection

1850

1824: The Combination Acts are repealed but subsequently replaced by the Combination Act 1825; this allows trade unions but severely restricts their activity and influence

1819: The so-called Six Acts are passed by government, including the gagging of radical newspapers and prevention of large meetings

1800

1799–1800: The Combination Acts make it illegal for workers to join together and press employers for shorter hours or increased pay

THE CENTRAL ARBITRATION COMMITTEE

22nd Floor, Euston Tower, 286 Euston Road, London NW1 3JJ
T 020-7904 2300 E enquiries@cac.gov.uk
W www.gov.uk/government/organisations/central-arbitration-committee

The Central Arbitration Committee's main role is concerned with requests for trade union recognition and de-recognition under the statutory procedures of Schedule A1 of the Employment Rights Act 1999. It also determines disclosure of information complaints under the Trade Union and Labour Relations (Consolidation) Act 1992, considers applications and complaints under the Information and Consultation Regulations 2004, and performs a similar role in relation to European works councils, companies, cooperative societies and cross-border mergers.
Chair, Sir Michael Burton
Chief Executive, Simon Gouldstone

TRADES UNION CONGRESS (TUC)

Congress House, 23–28 Great Russell Street, London WC1B 3LS
T 020-7636 4030
E info@tuc.org.uk W www.tuc.org.uk

The Trades Union Congress (TUC), founded in 1868, is an independent association of trade unions. The TUC promotes the rights and welfare of those in work and helps the unemployed. The TUC brings Britain's unions together to draw up common polices; lobbies the government to implement policies that will benefit people at work; campaigns on economic and social issues; represents working people on public bodies, in the European Union and at the UN employment body – the International Labour Organisation; carries out research on employment-related issues; runs training and education programmes for union representatives; helps unions to develop new services for their members and negotiate with each other; and builds links with other trade union bodies worldwide.

The governing body of the TUC is the annual congress which sets policy. Between congresses, business is conducted by a 56-member general council, which meets every two months to oversee the TUC's work programme and sanction new policy initiatives. Each year, at its first post-congress meeting, the general council appoints an executive committee and the TUC president for that congress year. The executive committee meets monthly to implement and develop policy, manage TUC financial affairs and deal with any urgent business. The president chairs general council and executive meetings and is consulted by the General Secretary on all major issues.

There are 51 affiliated unions, with a total membership of 5.8 million.

President (2015–16), Liz Snape
General Secretary, Frances O'Grady

SCOTTISH TRADES UNION CONGRESS (STUC)

333 Woodlands Road, Glasgow G3 6NG **T** 0141-337 8100
E info@stuc.org.uk **W** www.stuc.org.uk

The congress was formed in 1897 and acts as a national centre for the trade union movement in Scotland. The STUC promotes the rights to welfare of those in work and helps the unemployed. It helps its member unions to promote membership in new areas and industries, and campaigns for rights at work for all employees, including part-time and temporary workers, whether union members or not. It also makes representations to government and employers. In April 2015 the STUC had around 620,000 members from 39 affiliated unions and 20 trade union councils.

The annual congress in April elects a 36-member general council on the basis of six sections.

President (2015–16), Lawrence Wason
General Secretary, Grahame Smith

WALES TUC

Transport House, 1 Cathedral Road, Cardiff CF11 9SD
T 029-2034 7010
E wtuc@tuc.org.uk **W** www.tuc.org.uk/wales

The Wales TUC was established in 1974 to ensure that the role of the TUC was effectively undertaken in Wales. Its structure reflects the four economic regions of Wales and matches the regional committee areas of the National Assembly of Wales. The regional committees oversee the implementation of Wales TUC policy and campaigns in the relevant regions, and liaise with local government, training organisations and regional economic development bodies. The Wales TUC seeks to reduce unemployment, increase the levels of skill and pay, and eliminate discrimination.

The governing body of Wales TUC is the conference, which meets annually in May and elects a general council (usually of around 50 people) that oversees the work of the TUC throughout the year.

There are around 50 affiliated unions representing around 500,000 workers.

President (2015–16), Margaret Thomas
General Secretary, Martin Mansfield

TUC-AFFILIATED UNIONS

As at April 2015

ACCORD, Simmons House, 46 Old Bath Road, Charvil RG10 9QR
  T 0118-934 1808 **E** info@accordhq.org
  W www.accord-myunion.org
  General Secretary, Ged Nichols *Membership:* 24,177

ADVANCE, 2nd Floor, 16–17 High Street, Tring HP23 5AH
  T 01442-891122 **E** info@advance-union.org
  W www.advance-union.org
  General Secretary, Linda Rolph *Membership:* 6,784

AEGIS THE UNION, 1–3 Lochside Crescent, Edinburgh Park,
  Edinburgh EH12 9SE **T** 0131-549 5474
  E members@aegistheunion.co.uk **W** www.aegistheunion.co.uk
  General Secretary, Brian Linn *Membership:* 4,602

AEP (ASSOCIATION OF EDUCATIONAL
  PSYCHOLOGISTS), 4 The Riverside Centre, Frankland Lane,
  Durham DH1 5TA **T** 0191-384 9512 **E** enquiries@aep.org.uk
  W www.aep.org.uk
  General Secretary, Kate Fallon *Membership:* 3,297

AFA (ASSOCIATION OF FLIGHT ATTENDANTS),
  c/o 32 Wingfield Road, London SW2 4DS
  T 0208-276 6723 **E** afalhr@unitedafa.org
  W www.afacwa.org
  President, Anthony King *Membership:* 500

ASLEF (ASSOCIATED SOCIETY OF LOCOMOTIVE
  ENGINEERS AND FIREMEN), 75–77 St John Street,
  Clerkenwell, London EC1M 4NN **T** 020-7324 2400
  E info@aslef.org.uk **W** www.aslef.org.uk
  General Secretary, Mick Whelan *Membership:* 20,054

ATL (ASSOCIATION OF TEACHERS AND
  LECTURERS), 7 Northumberland Street, London WC2N 5RD
  T 020-7930 6441 **E** info@atl.org.uk **W** www.atl.org.uk
  General Secretary, Dr Mary Bousted
  Membership: 127,899

BALPA (BRITISH AIRLINE PILOTS ASSOCIATION),
  BALPA House, 5 Heathrow Boulevard, 278 Bath Road,
  West Drayton UB7 0DQ **T** 020-8476 4000
  E balpa@balpa.org **W** www.balpa.org
  General Secretary, Jim McAuslan *Membership:* 7,900

BDA (BRITISH DIETETIC ASSOCIATION), 5th Floor,
  Charles House, 148–149 Great Charles Street, Queensway,
  Birmingham B3 3HT **T** 0121-200 8080 **E** info@bda.uk.com
  W www.bda.uk.com
  Chief Executive, Andy Burman *Membership:* 7,609

BECTU (BROADCASTING, ENTERTAINMENT,
  CINEMATOGRAPH AND THEATRE UNION),
  373–377 Clapham Road, London SW9 9BT **T** 020-7346 0900
  E info@bectu.org.uk **W** www.bectu.org.uk
  General Secretary, Gerry Morrissey *Membership:* 24,753

BFAWU (BAKERS, FOOD AND ALLIED WORKERS'
  UNION), Stanborough House, Great North Road,
  Stanborough, Welwyn Garden City AL8 7TA **T** 01707-260150
  E info@bfawu.org **W** www.bfawu.org
  General Secretary, Ronnie Draper *Membership:* 20,216

BOS TU (BRITISH ORTHOPTIC SOCIETY TRADE
  UNION), Salisbury House, Station Road, Ely,
  Cambridge CB1 2LA **T** 01353-665541 **E** bios@orthoptics.org.uk
  W www.orthoptics.org.uk
  Chair, Lesley-Anne Baxter *Membership:* 1,019

BSU (BRITANNIA STAFF UNION), Court Lodge,
  Leonard Street, Leek ST13 5JP **T** 01538-399627
  E bsu@themail.co.uk **W** www.britanniasu.org.uk
  General Secretary, John Stoddard *Membership:* 2,373

COMMUNITY, 465C Caledonian Road, London N7 9GX
  T 020-7420 4000 **E** info@community-tu.org
  W www.community-tu.org
  General Secretary, Roy Rickhuss *Membership:* 31,886

CSP (CHARTERED SOCIETY OF PHYSIOTHERAPY),
  14 Bedford Row, London WC1R 4ED **T** 020-7306 6666
  E enquiries@csp.org.uk **W** www.csp.org.uk
  Chief Executive, Karen Middleton, CBE
  Membership: 39,750

CWU (COMMUNICATION WORKERS UNION),
  150 The Broadway, Wimbledon, London SW19 1RX
  T 020-8971 7200 **E** info@cwu.org **W** www.cwu.org
  General Secretary, Billy Hayes *Membership:* 201,729

EIS (EDUCATIONAL INSTITUTE OF SCOTLAND),
  46 Moray Place, Edinburgh EH3 6BH **T** 0131-225 6244
  E enquiries@eis.org.uk **W** www.eis.org.uk
  General Secretary, Larry Flanagan *Membership:* 54,780

EQUITY, Guild House, Upper St Martin's Lane, London WC2H 9EG T 020-7379 6000 E info@equity.org.uk W www.equity.org.uk
General Secretary, Christine Payne *Membership*: 40,160

FBU (FIRE BRIGADES UNION), Bradley House, 68 Coombe Road, Kingston upon Thames KT2 7AE T 020-8541 1765 E office@fbu.org.uk W www.fbu.org.uk
General Secretary, Matt Wrack *Membership*: 39,983

FDA, 8 Leake Street, London SE1 7NN T 020-7401 5555 E info@fda.org.uk W www.fda.org.uk
General Secretary, Dave Penman *Membership*: 16,966

GMB, 22 Stephenson Way, London NW1 2HD T 020-7391 6700 E info@gmb.org.uk W www.gmb.org.uk
General Secretary, Sir Paul Kenny *Membership*: 620,970

HCSA (HOSPITAL CONSULTANTS' AND SPECIALISTS' ASSOCIATION), 1 Kingsclere Road, Overton, Basingstoke RG25 3JA T 01256-771777 E conspec@hcsa.com W www.hcsa.com
Chief Executive, Eddie Saville *Membership*: 3,228

MU (MUSICIANS' UNION), 60–62 Clapham Road, London SW9 0JJ T 020-7582 5566 E info@theMU.org W www.theMU.org
General Secretary, John F. Smith *Membership*: 30,710

NACO (NATIONAL ASSOCIATION OF COOPERATIVE OFFICIALS), 6A Clarendon Place, Hyde SK14 2QZ T 0161-351 7900 E info@naco.coop W www.naco.coop
General Secretary, Neil Buist *Membership*: 1,819

NACODS (NATIONAL ASSOCIATION OF COLLIERY OVERMEN, DEPUTIES AND SHOTFIRERS), Wadsworth House, 130–132 Doncaster Road, Barnsley S70 1TP T 01226-203743 E natnacods@googlemail.com W www.nacods.org.uk
General Secretary, Rowland Soar *Membership*: 233

NAHT (NATIONAL ASSOCIATION OF HEAD TEACHERS), 1 Heath Square, Boltro Road, Haywards Heath RH16 1BL T 01444-472472 E info@naht.org.uk W www.naht.org.uk
General Secretary, Russell Hobby *Membership*: 28,102

NAPO (TRADE UNION AND PROFESSIONAL ASSOCIATION FOR FAMILY COURT AND PROBATION STAFF), 4 Chivalry Road, London SW11 1HT T 020-7223 4887 E info@napo.org.uk W www.napo.org.uk
General Secretary, Ian Lawrence *Membership*: 8,123

NASS (NATIONAL ASSOCIATION OF STABLE STAFF), The New Astley Club, Fred Archer Way, Newmarket CB8 8NT T 01638-663411 E admin@naoss.co.uk W www.naoss.co.uk
Chief Executive, George McGrath *Membership*: 1,782

NASUWT (NATIONAL ASSOCIATION OF SCHOOLMASTERS/UNION OF WOMEN TEACHERS), Hillscourt Education Centre, Rose Hill, Rednal, Birmingham B45 8RS T 0121-453 6150 E nasuwt@mail.nasuwt.org.uk W www.nasuwt.org.uk
General Secretary, Ms Chris Keates
Membership: 295,565

NAUTILUS INTERNATIONAL, 1–2 The Shrubberies, George Lane, South Woodford, London E18 1BD T 020-8989 6677 E enquiries@nautilusint.org W www.nautilusint.org
General Secretary, Mark Dickinson *Membership*: 15,800

NGSU (NATIONWIDE GROUP STAFF UNION), Middleton Farmhouse, 37 Main Road, Middleton Cheney OX17 2QT T 01295-710767 E ngsu@ngsu.org.uk W www.ngsu.co.uk
General Secretary, Tim Poil *Membership*: 11,852

NUJ (NATIONAL UNION OF JOURNALISTS), Headland House, 308–312 Gray's Inn Road, London WC1X 8DP T 020-7843 3700 E info@nuj.org.uk W www.nuj.org.uk
General Secretary, Michelle Stanistreet
Membership: 30,434

NUM (NATIONAL UNION OF MINEWORKERS), Miners' Offices, 2 Huddersfield Road, Barnsley S70 2LS T 01226-215555 E chris.kitchen@num.org.uk W www.num.org.uk
National Secretary, Chris Kitchen *Membership*: 1,283

NUT (NATIONAL UNION OF TEACHERS), Hamilton House, Mabledon Place, London WC1H 9BD T 020-7388 6191 E enquiries@nut.org.uk W www.teachers.org.uk
General Secretary, Christine Blower
Membership: 330,719

PCS (PUBLIC AND COMMERCIAL SERVICES UNION), 160 Falcon Road, London SW11 2LN T 020-7924 2727 W www.pcs.org.uk
General Secretary, Mark Serwotka *Membership*: 247,345

PFA (PROFESSIONAL FOOTBALLERS' ASSOCIATION), 20 Oxford Court, Bishopsgate, Manchester M2 3WQ T 0161-236 0575 E info@thepfa.co.uk W www.thepfa.com
Chief Executive, Gordon Taylor, OBE
Membership: 2,942

POA (PROFESSIONAL TRADE UNION FOR PRISON, CORRECTIONAL AND SECURE PSYCHIATRIC WORKERS), Cronin House, 245 Church Street, London N9 9HW T 020-8803 0255 E general@poauk.org.uk W www.poauk.org.uk
General Secretary, Steve Gillan *Membership*: 31,130

PROSPECT, New Prospect House, 8 Leake Street, London SE1 7NN T 020-7902 6600 E enquiries@prospect.org.uk W www.prospect.org.uk
General Secretary, Mike Clancy *Membership*: 118,761

RMT (NATIONAL UNION OF RAIL, MARITIME AND TRANSPORT WORKERS), Unity House, 39 Chalton Street, London NW1 1JD T 020-7387 4771 E info@rmt.org.uk W www.rmt.org.uk
General Secretary, Mick Cash *Membership*: 80,105

SCP (SOCIETY OF CHIROPODISTS AND PODIATRISTS), 1 Fellmonger's Path, Tower Bridge Road, London SE1 3LY T 020-7234 8620 E reception@scpod.org W www.scpod.org
General Secretary, Joanna Brown *Membership*: 9,298

SOR (SOCIETY OF RADIOGRAPHERS), 207 Providence Square, Mill Street, London SE1 2EW T 020-7740 7200 W www.sor.org
Chief Executive, Richard Evans *Membership*: 26,485

STAFF UNION WEST BROMWICH BUILDING SOCIETY, 374 High Street, West Bromwich B70 8LR T 0870-220 7720 E staffunion@westbrom.co.uk
General Secretary, Julie Holton *Membership*: 523

TSSA (TRANSPORT SALARIED STAFFS' ASSOCIATION), Walkden House, 10 Melton Street, London NW1 2EJ T 020-7387 2101 E enquiries@tssa.org.uk W www.tssa.org.uk
General Secretary, Manuel Cortes *Membership*: 21,726

UCAC (UNDEB CENEDLAETHOL ATHRAWON CYMRU) (NATIONAL UNION OF THE TEACHERS OF WALES), Prif Swyddfa UCAC, Ffordd Penglais, Aberystwyth SY23 2EU T 01970-639950 E ucac@athrawon.com W www.athrawon.com
General Secretary, Elaine Edwards *Membership*: 4,222

UCATT (UNION OF CONSTRUCTION, ALLIED TRADES AND TECHNICIANS), UCATT House, 177 Abbeville Road, London SW4 9RL T 020-7622 2442 E info@ucatt.org.uk W www.ucatt.org.uk
General Secretary, Steve Murphy *Membership*: 86,983

UCU (UNIVERSITY AND COLLEGE UNION), Carlow Street, London NW1 7LH T 020-7756 2500 E hq@ucu.org.uk W www.ucu.org.uk
General Secretary, Sally Hunt *Membership*: 113,227

UNISON, 130 Euston Road, London NW1 2AY
  T 0800-085 7857 W www.unison.org.uk
  General Secretary, Dave Prentis *Membership:* 1,266,711
UNITE, 128 Theobald's Road, London WC1X 8TN
  T 020-7611 2500 W www.unitetheunion.org
  General Secretary, Len McCluskey
  Membership: 1,310,649
URTU (UNITED ROAD TRANSPORT UNION),
  Almond House, Oak Green, Stanley Green Business Park,
  Cheadle Hulme SK8 6QL T 0800-526639 E info@urtu.com
  W www.urtu.com
  General Secretary, Robert Monks *Membership:* 12,200
USDAW (UNION OF SHOP, DISTRIBUTIVE AND
  ALLIED WORKERS), 188 Wilmslow Road,
  Manchester M14 6LJ T 0161-224 2804
  E enquiries@usdaw.org.uk W www.usdaw.org.uk
  General Secretary, John Hannett *Membership:* 433,402
WGGB (WRITERS' GUILD OF GREAT BRITAIN),
  134 Tooley Street, London SE1 2TU T 020-7833 0777
  E admin@writersguild.org.uk W www.writersguild.org.uk
  General Secretary, Bernie Corbett *Membership:* 1,126

NON-AFFILIATED UNIONS

As at April 2015
ASCL (ASSOCIATION OF SCHOOL AND COLLEGE
  LEADERS), 130 Regent Road, Leicester LE1 7PG
  T 0116-299 1122 E info@ascl org.uk W www.ascl.org.uk
  General Secretary, Brian Lightman
  Membership: around 18,000

BDA (BRITISH DENTAL ASSOCIATION),
  64 Wimpole Street, London W1G 8YS T 020-7935 0875
  E enquiries@bda.org W www.bda.org
  Chief Executive, Peter Ward *Membership:* 19,201
CIOJ (CHARTERED INSTITUTE OF JOURNALISTS),
  2 Dock Offices, Surrey Quays Road, London SE16 2XU
  T 020-7252 1187 E memberservices@cioj.co.uk
  W www.cioj.co.uk
  General Secretary, Dominic Cooper
  Membership: around 2,000
NSEAD (NATIONAL SOCIETY FOR EDUCATION IN
  ART AND DESIGN), 3 Mason's Wharf, Potley Lane,
  Corsham SN13 9FY T 01225-810134 E info@nsead.org
  W www.nsead.org
  General Secretary, Mrs Lesley Butterworth
  Membership: 2,000
RCM (ROYAL COLLEGE OF MIDWIVES), 15 Mansfield
  Street, London W1G 9NH T 030-0303 0444 E info@rcm.org.uk
  W www.rcm.org.uk
  General Secretary, Prof. Cathy Warwick, CBE
  Membership: around 42,000
SOCIETY OF AUTHORS, 84 Drayton Gardens, London
  SW10 9SB T 020-7373 6642 E info@societyofauthors.org
  W www.societyofauthors.org
  Chief Executive, Nicola Solomon *Membership:* 9,350
SSTA (SCOTTISH SECONDARY TEACHERS'
  ASSOCIATION), West End House, 14 West End Place,
  Edinburgh EH11 2ED T 0131-313 7300 E info@ssta.org.uk
  W www.ssta.org.uk
  General Secretary, Seamus Searson
  Membership: around 8,500

SPORTS BODIES

SPORTS COUNCILS

SPORT AND RECREATION ALLIANCE,
Burwood House, 14 Caxton Street, London SW1H 0QT
T 020-7976 3900 E info@sportandrecreation.org.uk
W www.sportandrecreation.org.uk
Chief Executive, Emma Borgis

SPORT ENGLAND, 1st Floor, 21 Bloomsbury Street,
London WC1B 3HF T 0845-850 8508
E info@sportengland.org W www.sportengland.org
Chief Executive, Jennie Price

SPORT NORTHERN IRELAND, House of Sport,
2A Upper Malone Road, Belfast BT9 5LA T 028-9038 1222
E info@sportni.net W www.sportni.net
Chief Executive, Antoinette McKeown

SPORTSCOTLAND, Doges, Templeton on the Green,
62 Templeton Street, Glasgow G40 1DA T 0141-534 6500
E website@sportscotland.org.uk W www.sportscotland.org.uk
Chief Executive, Stewart Harris

SPORT WALES, Sophia Gardens, Cardiff CF11 9SW
T 0300-300 3111 E info@sportwales.org.uk
W www.sportwales.org.uk
Chief Executive, Sarah Powell

UK SPORT, Ground Floor, 21 Bloomsbury Street,
London WC1B 3HF T 020-7211 5100 E info@uksport.gov.uk
W www.uksport.gov.uk
Chief Executive, Liz Nicholl, OBE

AMERICAN FOOTBALL

BRITISH AMERICAN FOOTBALL ASSOCIATION,
West House, Hedley on the Hill, Stocksfield NE43 7SW
T 01661-843179 E bafachairman@gmail.com
W www.britishamericanfootball.org
Chair, Charles Macnamara

ANGLING

ANGLING TRUST, Eastwood House, 6 Rainbow Street,
Leominster, Herefordshire HR6 8DQ T 0844-770 0616
E admin@anglingtrust.net W www.anglingtrust.net
Chief Executive, Mark Lloyd

ARCHERY

ARCHERY GB, Lilleshall National Sports Centre,
Newport TF10 9AT T 01952-677888
E enquiries@archerygb.org W www.archerygb.org
Chief Executive, David Sherratt

ASSOCIATION FOOTBALL

FOOTBALL ASSOCIATION, Wembley Stadium,
PO Box 1966, SW1P 9EQ T 0844-980 8200 E info@thefa.com
W www.thefa.com
Chair, Greg Dyke

FOOTBALL ASSOCIATION OF WALES, 11–12 Neptune
Court, Vanguard Way, Cardiff CF24 5PJ T 029-2043 5830
E info@faw.co.uk W www.faw.org.uk
Chief Executive, Jonathan Ford

FOOTBALL LEAGUE, Edward VII Quay, Navigation Way,
Preston PR2 2YF T 0844-463 1888
E enquiries@football-league.co.uk
W www.football-league.co.uk
Chief Executive, Shaun Harvey

IRISH FOOTBALL ASSOCIATION, 20 Windsor Avenue,
Belfast BT9 6EG T 028-9066 9458 E info@irishfa.com
W www.irishfa.com
Chief Executive, Patrick Nelson

PREMIER LEAGUE, 30 Gloucester Place, London W1U 8PL
T 020-7864 9000 E info@premierleague.com
W www.premierleague.com
Chief Executive, Richard Scudamore

SCOTTISH FOOTBALL ASSOCIATION, Hampden Park,
Glasgow G42 9AY T 0141-616 6000 E info@scottishfa.co.uk
W www.scottishfa.co.uk
Chief Executive, Stewart Regan

SCOTTISH PROFESSIONAL FOOTBALL LEAGUE,
The National Stadium, Hampden Park, Glasgow G42 9DE
T 0141-620 4160 E info@spfl.co.uk W www.spfl.co.uk
Chief Executive, Neil Doncaster

ATHLETICS

ATHLETICS NORTHERN IRELAND, Athletics House,
Old Coach Road, Belfast BT9 5PR T 028-9060 2707
E info@athleticsni.org W www.athleticsni.org
General Secretary, John Allen

SCOTTISH ATHLETICS, Caledonia House, South Gyle,
Edinburgh EH12 9DQ T 0131-539 7320
E admin@scottishathletics.org.uk
W www.scottishathletics.org.uk
Chief Executive, Nigel Holl

UK ATHLETICS, Athletics House, Alexander Stadium,
Walsall Road, Birmingham B42 2BE T 0121-713 8400
E enquiries@englandathletics.org
W www.britishathletics.org.uk
Chief Executive, Niels de Vos

WELSH ATHLETICS, Cardiff International Sports Stadium,
Leckwith Road, Cardiff CF11 8AZ T 029-2064 4870
E office@welshathletics.org W www.welshathletics.org
Chief Executive, Matt Newman

BADMINTON

BADMINTON ENGLAND, National Badminton Centre,
Bradwell Road, Milton Keynes MK8 9LA T 01908-268400
E enquiries@badmintonengland.co.uk
W www.badmintonengland.co.uk
Chief Executive, Adrian Christy

BADMINTON SCOTLAND, Cockburn Centre,
40 Bogmoor Place, Glasgow G51 4TQ T 0141-445 1218
E enquiries@badmintonscotland.org.uk
W www.badmintonscotland.org.uk
Chief Executive, Anne Smillie

BADMINTON WALES, Sport Wales National Centre,
Sophia Gardens, Cardiff CF11 9SW T 0300-300 3124
E wbu@badmintonwales.net W www.badmintonwales.net
Chief Executive, Eddie O'Neill

BASEBALL

BASEBALLSOFTBALL UK, Ariel House,
74A Charlotte Street, London W1T 4QJ T 020-7453 7055
W www.baseballsoftballuk.com
Chief Executive, Jenny Fromer

BASKETBALL

BASKETBALL ENGLAND, English Institute of Sport, Sheffield
S9 5DA T 0114-284 1060 E info@basketballengland.co.uk
W www.basketballengland.co.uk
Chief Executive, Mark Clark

BASKETBALL SCOTLAND, Caledonia House, South Gyle,
Edinburgh EH12 9DQ T 0131-317 7260
E enquiries@basketball-scotland.com
W www.basketballscotland.co.uk
Chief Executive, Kevin Pringle

BILLIARDS AND SNOOKER

WORLD SNOOKER, 75 Whiteladies Road, Clifton,
Bristol BS8 2NT T 0117-317 8200 E info@worldsnooker.com
W www.worldsnooker.com
Chair, Jason Ferguson

BOBSLEIGH

BRITISH BOBSLEIGH AND SKELETON ASSOCIATION,
Sports Training Village, University of Bath, Bath BA2 7AY
T 01225-383696 E office@britishskeleton.co.uk
W www.britishskeleton.co.uk
Chair, Lord Clifton Wrottesley

BOWLS

BOWLS ENGLAND, Riverside House, Milverton Hill,·
Royal Leamington Spa CV32 5HZ T 01926-334609
E enquiries@bowlsengland.com W www.bowlsengland.com
Chief Executive, Tony Allcock, MBE
BRITISH ISLES BOWLS COUNCIL, 12/1 Oxgangs Avenue,
Edinburgh EH13 9JB T 01314-455838
E bibcsecretary@aol.co.uk W www.britishislesbowls.com
Hon. Secretary, Duncan McLaren
ENGLISH INDOOR BOWLING ASSOCIATION,
David Cornwell House, Bowling Green, Melton Mowbray
LE13 0FA T 01664-481900 E enquiries@eiba.co.uk
W www.eiba.co.uk
Chief Executive, Peter Thompson

BOXING

AMATEUR BOXING ASSOCIATION OF ENGLAND,
English Institute of Sport, Coleridge Road, Sheffield S9 5DA
T 0114-223 5654 W www.abae.co.uk
Chief Executive, Mark Abberley
BRITISH BOXING BOARD OF CONTROL, 14 North Road,
Cardiff CF10 3DY T 029-2036 7000 E admin@bbbofc.com
W www.bbbofc.com
General Secretary, Robert Smith

CANOEING

BRITISH CANOE UNION, National Water Sport Centre,
Adbolton Lane, Nottingham NG12 2LU T 0845-370 9500
E info@britishcanoeing.org.uk
W www.britishcanoeunion.org.uk
Chief Executive, Paul Owen

CHESS

ENGLISH CHESS FEDERATION, The Watch Oak,
Chain Lane, Battle TN33 0YD T 01424-775222
E office@englishchess.org.uk W www.englishchess.org.uk
Chief Executive, Phil Ehr

CRICKET

ENGLAND AND WALES CRICKET BOARD,
Lord's Cricket Ground, London NW8 8QZ T 020-7432 1200
E feedback@ecb.co.uk W www.ecb.co.uk
Chief Executive, Tom Harrison
MCC, Lord's Cricket Ground, St John's Wood, London NW8 8QN
T 020-7616 8500 E reception@mcc.org.uk W www.lords.org
Chief Executive and Secretary, Derek Brewer

CROQUET

CROQUET ASSOCIATION, Old Bath Road, Cheltenham
GL53 7DF T 01242-242318 E caoffice@croquet.org.uk
W www.croquet.org.uk
Manager, Elizabeth Larsson

CURLING

BRITISH CURLING, Cairnie House, Ingleston EH28 8NB
T 0131-333 3003 E info@britishcurling.com
W www.britishcurling.org.uk
Chief Operating Officer, Bruce Crawford

ROYAL CALEDONIAN CURLING CLUB, Cairnie House,
Ingliston, Newbridge EH28 8NB T 0131-333 3003
E office@royalcaledoniancurlingclub.org
W www.royalcaledoniancurlingclub.org
Chief Executive, Bruce Crawford

CYCLING

BRITISH CYCLING FEDERATION, Stuart Street,
Manchester M11 4DQ T 0161-274 2000
E info@britishcycling.org.uk W www.britishcycling.org.uk
Chief Executive, Ian Drake

DARTS

BRITISH DARTS ORGANISATION, Unit 4,
Glan-y-Llyn Industrial Estate, Taffs Well, Cardiff CF15 7JD
T 02920-811815 E britishdartsorg@btconnect.com
W www.bdodarts.com
Director, Wayne Williams

EQUESTRIANISM

BRITISH EQUESTRIAN FEDERATION, Abbey Park,
Kenilworth CV8 2RH T 02476-698871 E info@bef.co.uk
W www.bef.co.uk
Chief Executive, Andrew Finding, OBE
BRITISH EVENTING, Abbey Park, Kenilworth CV8 2RN
T 024-7669 8856 E info@britisheventing.com
W www.britisheventing.com
Chief Executive, Mike Etherington-Smith

ETON FIVES

ETON FIVES ASSOCIATION, 45 Sandhills Crescent,
Hillfield, Solihull B91 3UE T 07833-600230
E efa@etonfives.co.uk W www.fivesonline.net
Chair, Richard Black

FENCING

BRITISH FENCING, 1 Baron's Gate, 33 Rothschild Road,
London W4 5HT T 020-8742 3032
E headoffice@britishfencing.com W www.britishfencing.com
Chief Executive, Georgina Usher

GLIDING

BRITISH GLIDING ASSOCIATION, 8 Merus Court,
Meridian Business Park, Leicester LE19 1RJ
T 0116-289 2956 E office@gliding.co.uk
W www.gliding.co.uk
Chief Executive, Pete Stratten

GOLF

ENGLAND GOLF, The National Golf Centre, Woodhall Spa
LN10 6PU T 01526-354500 E info@englandgolf.org
W www.englandgolf.org
Chief Executive, David Joy
LADIES' GOLF UNION, The Scores, St Andrews KY16 9AT
T 01334-475811 E info@lgu.org W www.lgu.org
Chief Executive, vacant
THE ROYAL AND ANCIENT GOLF CLUB, Golf Place,
St Andrews KY16 9JD T 01334-460000
E thesecretary@randagc.org W www.randa.org
Secretary, Martin Slumbers

GYMNASTICS

BRITISH GYMNASTICS, Ford Hall, Lilleshall National Sports
Centre, Newport TF10 9NB T 0845-129 7129
E information@british-gymnastics.org
W www.british-gymnastics.org
Chief Executive, Jane Allen

HANDBALL

ENGLAND HANDBALL, The Halliwell Jones Stadium,
Winwick Road, Warrington WA2 7NE T 01925 246482
E handball@englandhandball.com
W www.englandhandball.com
Chief Executive, David Meli

HOCKEY

ENGLAND HOCKEY, Bisham Abbey National Sports Centre,
Marlow SL7 1RR T 01628-897500 E info@englandhockey.co.uk
W www.englandhockey.co.uk
Chief Executive, Sally Munday
HOCKEY WALES, Sport Wales National Centre, Sophie
Gardens, Cardiff CF11 9SW T 0300-300 3126
E info@hockeywales.org.uk W www.hockeywales.org.uk
Chief Executive, Helen Bushell
SCOTTISH HOCKEY UNION, Glasgow National Hockey
Centre, 8 King's Drive, Glasgow G40 1HB T 0141-550 5999
W www.scottish-hockey.org.uk
Chief Executive, David Sweetman

HORSERACING

BRITISH HORSERACING AUTHORITY,
75 High Holborn, London WC1V 6LS T 020-7152 0000
E info@britishhorseracing.com W www.britishhorseracing.com
Chief Executive, Nick Rust
THE JOCKEY CLUB, 75 High Holborn, London WC1V 6LS
T 020-7611 1800 E info@thejockeyclub.co.uk
W www.thejockeyclub.co.uk
Chief Executive, Simon Bazalgette

ICE SKATING

NATIONAL ICE SKATING ASSOCIATION, Grains Building,
High Cross Street, Hockley, Nottingham NG1 3AX T 0115-988
8060 E info@iceskating.org.uk W www.iceskating.org.uk
Chief Executive, Nick Sellwood

LACROSSE

ENGLISH LACROSSE ASSOCIATION, Wenlock Way
Offices, Wenlock Way, Manchester M12 5DH T 0843-658 5006
E info@englishlacrosse.co.uk W www.englishlacrosse.co.uk
Chief Executive, Mark Coups

LAWN TENNIS

LAWN TENNIS ASSOCIATION, National Tennis Centre,
100 Priory Lane, London SW15 5JQ T 020-8487 7000
E info@lta.org.uk W www.lta.org.uk
Chief Executive, Michael Downey

MARTIAL ARTS

BRITISH JUDO ASSOCIATION, Suite B, Loughborough
Technology Centre, Epinal Way, Loughborough LE11 3GE
T 01509-631670 E bja@britishjudo.org.uk
W www.britishjudo.org.uk
Chief Executive, Andrew Scoular
BRITISH JU JITSU ASSOCIATION, 5 Avenue Parade,
Accrington BB5 6PN T 03333-202039 E bjjagb@icloud.com
W www.bjjagb.org.uk
Chair, Prof. Martin Dixon
BRITISH TAEKWONDO, 4 Tinshill Lane, Leeds Ls16 7AP
E admin@britishtaekwondo.org
W www.britishtaekwondo.org.uk
Chair, Adrian Tranter

MODERN PENTATHLON

PENTATHLON GB, 22/23 Eastwood, University of Bath,
Claverton Down, Bath BA2 7AY T 01225-386808
E admin@pentathlongb.org W www.pentathlongb.org
Chief Executive, Nigel Laughton

MOTOR SPORTS

AUTO-CYCLE UNION, ACU House, Wood Street,
Rugby CV21 2YX T 01788-566400 E admin@acu.org.uk
W www.acu.org.uk
General Secretary, Gary Thompson, MBE
MOTOR SPORTS ASSOCIATION, Motor Sports House,
Riverside Park, Colnbrook, SL3 0HG T 01753-765000
W www.msauk.org
Chief Executive, Rob Jones
SCOTTISH AUTO CYCLE UNION, 28 West Main Street,
Uphall EH52 5DW T 01506-858354 E office@sacu.co.uk
W www.sacu.co.uk
President, Ian Barnes

MOUNTAINEERING

BRITISH MOUNTAINEERING COUNCIL,
The Old Church, 177–179 Burton Road, Manchester M20 2BB
T 0161-445 6111 E office@thebmc.co.uk
W www.thebmc.co.uk
Chief Executive, Dave Turnbull

MULTI-SPORTS BODIES

BRITISH OLYMPIC ASSOCIATION, 60 Charlotte Street,
London W1T 2NU T 020-7842 5700 E boa@boa.org.uk
W www.teamgb.com
Chief Executive, Bill Sweeney
BRITISH PARALYMPIC ASSOCIATION,
60 Charlotte Street, London W1T 2NU T 020-7842 5789
E info@paralympics.org.uk W www.paralympics.org.uk
Chief Executive, Tim Hollingsworth
BRITISH UNIVERSITIES AND COLLEGES SPORT,
20–24 Kings Bench Street, London SE1 0QX
T 020-7633 5080 W www.bucs.org.uk
Chief Executive, Karen Rothery
COMMONWEALTH GAMES ENGLAND,
307–308 High Holborn, National Sports Centre,
London WC1V 7LL T 020-7831 3444 E info@weareengland.org
W www.weareengland.org
Chief Executive, Paul Blanchard
COMMONWEALTH GAMES FEDERATION,
CAN Mezzanine, 49–51 East Road, London N1 6AH
T 020-7250 8118 E info@thecgf.com W www.thecgf.com
Chief Executive, David Grevemberg
ENGLISH FEDERATION OF DISABILITY SPORT,
Loughborough University, 3 Oakwood Drive,
Loughborough LE11 3QF T 01509-227750 W www.efds.co.uk
Chief Executive, Barry Horne

NETBALL

ENGLAND NETBALL, Netball House, 1–12 Old Park Road,
Hitchin SG5 2JR T 01462-442344 E info@englandnetball.co.uk
W www.englandnetball.co.uk
Chief Executive, Joanna Adams
NETBALL NI, Unit F, Curley Pavilion, Portside Business Park,
189 Airport Road West, Belfast BT3 9ED T 028-9073 6320
W www.netballni.org
Hon. President, Lorraine Lindsay
NETBALL SCOTLAND, Emirates Arena, 1000 London Road,
Glasgow G40 3HY T 0141-428 3460
E membership@netballscotland.com
W www.netballscotland.com
Chief Executive, Maggie Murray
WELSH NETBALL ASSOCIATION, Sport Wales National
Centre, Sophia Gardens, Cardiff CF11 9SW
T 0845-045 4302 E welshnetball@welshnetball.com
W www.welshnetball.co.uk
Chief Executive, Alun Davies

ORIENTEERING
BRITISH ORIENTEERING, Scholes Mill, Old Coach Road,
Darley Dale, Matlock DE4 5FY T 01629-583037
E info@britishorienteering.org.uk
W www.britishorienteering.org.uk
Chief Executive, Mike Hamilton

POLO
THE HURLINGHAM POLO ASSOCIATION,
Manor Farm, Little Coxwell, Faringdon SN7 7LW
T 01367-242828 E enquiries@hpa-polo.co.uk
W www.hpa-polo.co.uk
Chief Executive, David Woodd

RACKETS AND REAL TENNIS
TENNIS AND RACKETS ASSOCIATION,
c/o The Queen's Club, Palliser Road, London W14 9EQ
T 020-7835 6937 E office@tennisandrackets.com
W www.tennisandrackets.com
Chief Executive, C. S. Davies

ROWING
BRITISH ROWING, 6 Lower Mall, Hammersmith,
London W6 9DJ T 020-8237 6700
E info@gbrowningteam.org.uk W www.britishrowing.org
Chief Executive, Andy Parkinson
HENLEY ROYAL REGATTA, Regatta Headquarters,
Henley-on-Thames RG9 2LY T 01491-572153
W www.hrr.co.uk
Secretary, D. G. M. Grist

RUGBY LEAGUE
BRITISH AMATEUR RUGBY LEAGUE ASSOCIATION,
West Yorkshire House, 4 New North Parade,
Huddersfield HD1 5JP T 01484-599113
E secretary@barla.org.uk W www.barla.org.uk
Chair, Sue Taylor
RUGBY FOOTBALL LEAGUE, Red Hall, Red Hall Lane,
Leeds LS17 8NB T 0844-477 7113 E enquiries@rfl.uk.com
W www.therfl.co.uk
Chief Executive, Nigel Wood

RUGBY UNION
IRISH RUGBY FOOTBALL UNION, 10–12 Lansdowne Road,
Ballsbridge, Dublin 4 T (+353) 1647 3800 E info@irishrugby.ie
W www.irishrugby.ie
Chief Executive, Philip Browne
RUGBY FOOTBALL UNION, Rugby House, Twickenham
Stadium, 200 Whitton Road, Twickenham TW2 7BA
T 0871-222 2120 E enquiries@therfu.com W www.rfu.com
Chief Executive, Ian Ritchie
RUGBY FOOTBALL UNION FOR WOMEN, Rugby House,
Twickenham Stadium, 200 Whitton Road, Twickenham,
TW2 7BA T 0871-222 2120 E enquiries@therfu.com
W www.rfu.com
Managing Director, Rosie Williams
SCOTTISH RUGBY UNION, Murrayfield, Edinburgh EH12 5PJ
T 0131-346 5000 E feedback@sru.org.uk
W www.scottishrugby.org
Chief Executive, Mark Dodson
SCOTTISH WOMEN'S RUGBY UNION, Scottish Rugby
Union, Murrayfield, Edinburgh EH12 5PJ T 0131-346 5000
E feedback@sru.org.uk W www.scottishrugby.org
Chief Executive, Mark Dodson
WELSH RUGBY UNION, Millennium Stadium, Westgate
Street, Cardiff CF10 1NS T 0844-249 1999 E info@wru.co.uk
W www.wru.co.uk
Chief Executive, Roger Lewis

SHOOTING
BRITISH SHOOTING, Bisham Abbey National Sports Centre,
Marlow Road, Bisham, Marlow SL7 1RR T 01628-488800
E admin@britishshooting.org.uk W www.britishshooting.org.uk
Chief Executive, Hamish McInnes
CLAY PIGEON SHOOTING ASSOCIATION,
Edmonton House, National Shooting Centre, Brookwood,
Woking GU24 0NP T 01483-485400 E info@cpsa.co.uk
W www.cpsa.co.uk
Chief Executive, Nick Fellows
NATIONAL RIFLE ASSOCIATION, Bisley, Brookwood,
GU24 0PB T 01483-797777 E info@nra.org.uk
W www.nra.org.uk
Chief Executive, Andrew Mercer
NATIONAL SMALL-BORE RIFLE ASSOCIATION,
Lord Roberts Centre, Bisley Camp, Brookwood,
Woking GU24 0NP T 01483-485505 W www.nsra.co.uk
Chair, Robert Newman

SNOWBOARDING
BRITISH SKI AND SNOWBOARD, 60 Charlotte Street,
London W1T 2NU T 020-7842 5764 E bss@teambss.org.uk
W www.teambss.org.uk
Chief Executive, Dave Edwards

SPEEDWAY
BRITISH SPEEDWAY, ACU Headquarters, Wood Street,
Rugby CV21 2YX T 01788-560648 E office@speedwaygb.co
W www.speedwaygb.co
Chair, Alex Harkess

SQUASH
ENGLAND SQUASH AND RACKETBALL,
National Squash Centre, Sportcity, Manchester M11 3FF
T 0161-231 4499
E enquiries@englandsquashandracketball.com
W www.englandsquashandracketball.com
Chief Executive, Keir Worth
SCOTTISH SQUASH AND RACKETBALL LIMITED,
Caledonia House, 1 Redheughs Rigg, South Gyle,
Edinburgh EH12 9DQ T 0131-625 4425
E info@scottishsquash.org W www.scottishsquash.org
Chief Executive, Shonagh MacVicar
WALES SQUASH AND RACKETBALL, Sport Wales
National Centre, Sophia Close, Cardiff CF11 9SW
T 0845-045 0902 W www.walessquashandracketball.co.uk
Chair, Phil Brailey

SUB-AQUA
BRITISH SUB-AQUA CLUB, Telford's Quay, South Pier Road,
Ellesmere Port CH65 4FL T 0151-350 6200 E info@bsac.com
W www.bsac.com
Chief Executive, Mary Tetley

SWIMMING
AMATEUR SWIMMING ASSOCIATION, Pavilion 3,
Sport Park, 3 Oakwood Drive, Loughborough LE11 3QF
T 01509-618700 E customerservices@swimming.org
W www.swimming.org
Chief Executive, A. Paker
SCOTTISH SWIMMING, National Swimming Academy,
University of Stirling, Stirling, FK9 4LA T 01786-466520
E info@scottishswimming.com W www.scottishswimming.com
Chief Executive, Forbes Dunlop
SWIM WALES, WNPS, Sketty Lane, Swansea SA2 8QG
T 01792-513636 W www.swimwales.org
Chief Executive, Robert James

TABLE TENNIS

ENGLISH TABLE TENNIS ASSOCIATION, Norfolk House,
88 Saxon Gate West, Milton Keynes MK9 2DL
T 01908-208860 E help@tabletennisengland.co.uk
W www.tabletennisengland.co.uk
Chief Executive, Sara Sutcliffe

TABLE TENNIS SCOTLAND, Caledonia House, South Gyle,
Edinburgh EH12 9DQ T 0131-317 8077
E ttsadmin@btconnect.com W www.tabletennisscotland.com
Chair, Terry McLernon

TABLE TENNIS WALES, Glanrhyd, Ebbw View, Beaufort,
Ebbw Vale NP23 5NU T 01244-571335 W www.ttaw.co.uk
Chair, Bernard Carter

TRIATHLON

BRITISH TRIATHLON, PO Box 25, Loughborough LE11 3WX
T 01509-226161 E info@britishtriathlon.org
W www.britishtriathlon.org
Chief Executive, Jack Buckner

VOLLEYBALL

NORTHERN IRELAND VOLLEYBALL ASSOCIATION,
21 Broughton Park, Belfast BT6 0BD W www.nivolleyball.com
General Secretary, Johnny McClenaghan

SCOTTISH VOLLEYBALL ASSOCIATION,
48 The Pleasance, Edinburgh EH8 9TJ T 0131-556 4633
W www.scottishvolleyball.org
Chief Executive, Margaret Ann Fleming

VOLLEYBALL ENGLAND, SportPark,
Loughborough University, 3 Oakwood Drive,
Loughborough LE11 3QF T 01509-227722
E info@volleyballengland.org W www.volleyballengland.org
Chief Executive, Lisa Wainwright

VOLLEYBALL WALES, 13 Beckgrove Close, Pengam Green,
Cardiff CF24 2SE T 029-2041 6537
E ysaker@volleyballwales.org W www.volleyballwales.org
Chair, Yvonne Saker

WALKING

RACE WALKING ASSOCIATION, Hufflers, Heard's Lane,
Shenfield, Brentwood CM15 0SF T 01277-220687
E racewalkingassociation@btinternet.com
W www.racewalkingassociation.org.uk
Hon. General Secretary, Peter Cassidy

WATER SKIING

BRITISH WATER SKI AND WAKEBOARD, The Forum,
Hanworth Lane, Chertsey, KT16 9JX T 01932-560007
E info@bwsf.co.uk W www.bwsw.org.uk
Chief Executive, Patrick Donovan

WEIGHTLIFTING

BRITISH WEIGHT LIFTING, Belmont House, 20 Wood Lane,
Leeds LS6 2AE T 0113-224 9402
E enquiries@britishweightlifting.org
W www.britishweightlifting.org
Chief Executive, Ashley Metcalfe

WRESTLING

BRITISH WRESTLING ASSOCIATION, 12 Westwood Lane,
Chesterfield S43 1PA T 01246-236443
E admin@britishwrestling.org W www.britishwrestling.org
Chief Executive, Colin Nicholson

YACHTING

ROYAL YACHTING ASSOCIATION, RYA House,
Ensign Way, Hamble, Southampton SO31 4YA
T 023-8060 4100 W www.rya.org.uk
Chief Executive, Sarah Treseder

CLUBS

Originally called gentlemen's clubs, these organisations are permanent institutions with a fixed clubhouse, which usually includes restaurants, bars, a library and overnight accommodation. Members are fee-paying and typically vetted for their suitability.

Gentlemen's clubs were created for males of the English upper class and grew out of the 17th-century fashion for coffee houses which enjoyed enormous popularity, despite opposition from Charles II, who believed they encouraged the spreading of royal disaffection. The first of the London clubs – White's – was founded in 1693 by Francesco Bianco in St James's Street, in the area that quickly became known as 'clubland'. Membership to the first of the clubs was a matter of hereditary privilege or special favour, a deliberately exclusionary measure which prompted an enormous growth in the number of clubs throughout the 19th century, fed by a burgeoning and aspirational middle class.

At the turn of the 20th century, there were more than 200 gentlemen's clubs in London alone, half of which had been founded since 1870. Inevitably, this level of competition could not be sustained, particularly given the number of men killed in two world wars. Financial restrictions necessitated greater provision for women and the relaxation of the social qualifications needed for membership. Nevertheless, waiting lists still exist for the leading clubs and a recommendation from at least one current member is almost always required to join.

ARMY AND NAVY CLUB (1837), 36 Pall Mall, London SW1Y 5JN T 020-7930 9721 E secretary@therag.co.uk
W www.armynavyclub.co.uk
Chief Executive and Secretary, Ayres de Souza
Former member: The Duke of Wellington
ARTS CLUB (1863), 40 Dover Street, London W1S 4NP
T 020-7499 8581 E reservations@theartsclub.co.uk
W www.theartsclub.co.uk
Secretary, Rémy Lysé
Former members: Charles Dickens, Algernon Charles Swinburne, Ivan Turgenev
ATHENAEUM (1824), 107 Pall Mall, London SW1Y 5ER
T 020-7930 4843 E library@hellenist.org.uk
W www.athenaeumclub.co.uk
Secretary, J. H. Ford
Former members: Matthew Arnold, Michael Faraday, Anthony Trollope
ATHENAEUM (1797), Church Alley, Liverpool L1 3DD
T 0151-709 7770 E reception@theathenaeum.org.uk
W www.theathenaeum.org.uk
Hon. Secretary, David Honour
Former members: William H. Duncan, William Roscoe
AUTHORS' CLUB (1891), c/o National Liberal Club, Whitehall Place, London SW1A 2HE T 020-7287 3381
E info@authorsclub.co.uk
Honorary Secretary, Victoria Carew Hunt
Former members: Arthur Conan Doyle, Graham Greene, Thomas Hardy, H. G. Wells, Oscar Wilde
BEEFSTEAK CLUB* (1876), 9 Irving Street, London WC2H 7AH T 020-7930 5722 E office@thebeefsteakclub.co.uk
Secretary, Maria Hibbert
Former members: John Betjeman, Rudyard Kipling, Harold Macmillan
BOODLE'S* (1762), 28 St James's Street, London SW1A 1HJ
T 020-7930 7166 E secretary@boodles.org
Secretary, Andrew Phillips
Former members: Winston Churchill, Ian Fleming

BROOKS'S* (1764), St James's Street, London SW1A 1LN
T 020-7493 4411 E secretary@brooksclub.org
Secretary, Ian Faul
Former members: Edward Gibbon, Roy Jenkins, William Pitt
BUCK'S CLUB* (1919), 18 Clifford Street, London W1S 3RF
T 020-7734 2337 E secretary@bucksclub.co.uk
Secretary, Maj. Rupert Lendrum
CALEDONIAN CLUB (1891), 9 Halkin Street, London SW1X 7DR T 020-7235 5162 E admin@caledonianclub.com
W www.caledonianclub.com
Secretary, Ian Campbell
CANNING CLUB (1910), 4 St James's Square, London SW1Y 4JU T 020-7827 5768
E canningclub@theinandout.co.uk W www.theinandout.co.uk
Secretary, Sarah Sinclair
CARLTON CLUB (1832), 69 St James's Street, London SW1A 1PJ T 020-7493 1164 E info@carltonclub.co.uk
W www.carltonclub.co.uk
Secretary, Sandra Boffa
Former members: Stanley Baldwin, Benjamin Disraeli, Harold Macmillan, John Major, Margaret Thatcher
CAVALRY AND GUARDS CLUB (1890), 127 Piccadilly, London W1J 7PX T 020-7499 1261 E secretary@cavgds.co.uk
W www.cavgds.co.uk
Secretary, David Cowdery
Former member: Lawrence Oates
CHELSEA ARTS CLUB (1891), 143 Old Church Street, London SW3 6EB T 020-7376 3311
E office@chelseaartsclub.com W www.chelseaartsclub.com
Secretary, David Cowdery
Former members: Laurie Lee, John Singer Sargent, Walter Sickert, James McNeill Whistler
CITY LIVERY CLUB (1914), Bell Wharf Lane, Upper Thames Street, London EC4R 3TB T 020-7248 0620
E clerk@cityliveryclub.com W www.cityliveryclub.com
Hon. Secretary, Dr Trevor Brignall
CITY OF LONDON CLUB (1832), 19 Old Broad Street, London EC2N 1DS T 020-7588 7991
E secretary@cityoflondonc ub.com
W www.cityoflondonclub.com
Secretary, Edward James
Former members: Robert Peel, Duke of Wellington
CITY UNIVERSITY CLUB (1895), 50 Cornhill, London EC3V 3PD T 020-7626 8571
E secretary@cityuniversityclub.co.uk
W www.cityuniversityclub.co.uk
Secretary, Mary Anne Salisbury
EAST INDIA CLUB* (1849), 16 St James's Square, London SW1Y 4LH T 020-7930 1000
E secretary@eastindiaclub.co.uk W www.eastindiaclub.co.uk
Secretary, Alex Bray
FARMERS CLUB (1842), 3 Whitehall Court, London SW1A 2EL
T 020-7930 3557 E reception@thefarmersclub.com
W www.thefarmersclub.com
Secretary, Air Cdre Stephen Skinner
FOX CLUB (2003), 46 Clarges Street, London W1J 7ER
T 020-7495 3656 E essi@foxclublondon.com
W www.foxclublondon.com
General Manager, Bethan Seaton
GARRICK CLUB* (1831), 15 Garrick Street, London WC2E 9AY T 020-7379 6478
E hallporters@garrickclub.co.uk W www.garrickclub.co.uk
Secretary, Ann Robbie
Former members: Charles Dickens, William Thackeray

GROUCHO CLUB (1985), 45 Dean Street, London W1D 4QB
T 020-7439 4685 E reception@thegrouchoclub.com
W www.thegrouchoclub.com
Manager, Bernie Katz

HURLINGHAM CLUB (1869), Ranelagh Gardens,
London SW6 3PR T 020-7610 7400
E main.reception@hurlinghamclub.org.uk
W www.hurlinghamclub.org.uk
Chief Executive, Rear-Adm. Niall Kilgour, CB

IN & OUT (NAVAL AND MILITARY CLUB) (1862),
4 St James's Square, London SW1Y 4JU T 020-7827 5757
E club@theinandout.co.uk W www.theinandout.co.uk
Secretary, Lt. Col. Christopher Hogan
Former member: Robert Falcon Scott

LANSDOWNE CLUB (1935), 9 Fitzmaurice Place,
London W1J 5JD T 020-7629 7200
E secretary@LansdowneClub.com W www.lansdowneclub.com
Secretary, Tim Cagney

LONDON PRESS CLUB (1882), 7–10 Adam Street,
The Strand, London WC2N 6AA T 020-7520 9082
E info@londonpressclub.co.uk W www.londonpressclub.co.uk
Secretary, Brooke Jacobs
Former members: Lord Astor, Lord Rothermere

NATIONAL LIBERAL CLUB (1882), Whitehall Place,
London SW1A 2HE T 020-7930 9871 E secretary@nlc.org.uk
W www.nlc.org.uk
Secretary, Simon Roberts
Former members: Winston Churchill, William Gladstone,
Ramsay MacDonald, George Bernard Shaw, H. G. Wells

NEW CAVENDISH CLUB (1920), 44 Great Cumberland Place,
London W1H 7BS T 075-0350 4639
E info@newcavendishclub.co.uk
W www.newcavendishclub.co.uk
Club Manager, Alex Maitland
Former member: Lady Bonham-Carter

NEW CLUB (1787), 86 Princes Street, Edinburgh EH2 2BB
T 0131-226 4881 E info@newclub.co.uk
W www.newclub.co.uk
Secretary, Col. A. P. W. Campbell
Former members: Alec Douglas-Home, Walter Scott

NEW CLUB (1874), 2 Montpellier Parade, Cheltenham
GL50 1UD T 01242-541121 E secretary@thenewclub.co.uk
W www.thenewclub.co.uk
Hon. Secretary, Peter Walsh

NORFOLK CLUB (1770), 17 Upper King Street,
Norwich NR3 1RB T 01603-626767
E generalmanager@thenorfolkclub.co.uk
W www.thenorfolkclub.co.uk
General Manager, Lukasz Stachowicz

NORTHERN COUNTIES CLUB (1829), 11 Hood Street,
Newcastle upon Tyne NE1 6LH T 0191-232 2744
E secretary@northerncountiesclub.co.uk
W www.northerncountiesclub.co.uk

ORIENTAL CLUB (1824), Stratford House, Stratford Place,
London W1C 1ES T 020-7629 5126 E sec@orientalclub.org.uk
W www.orientalclub.org.uk
Secretary, M. Rivett

OXFORD AND CAMBRIDGE CLUB (1830), 71 Pall Mall,
London SW1Y 5HD T 020-7930 5151 E club@oandc.uk.com
W www.oxfordandcambridgeclub.co.uk
Secretary, Alistair Telfer
Former members: Clement Attlee, William Gladstone

PORTLAND CLUB (1816), 36 Pall Mall, London SW1Y 4ER
T 020-7930 0444
Secretary, John Burns, CBE

PRATT'S CLUB* (1841), 14 Park Place, London SW1A 1LP
T 020-7493 0397 E secretary@prattsclub.org
Secretary, Lt. Col. O. R. StJ. Breakwell, MBE
Former member: Winston Churchill

REFORM CLUB (1836), 104–105 Pall Mall, London SW1Y 5EW
T 020-7930 9374 E generaloffice@reformclub.com
W www.reformclub.com
Secretary, Crispin Morton
Former members: Isambard Kingdom Brunel, Guy Burgess,
Arthur Conan Doyle, Henry James, David Lloyd George

ROYAL AIR FORCE CLUB (1918), 128 Piccadilly,
London W1J 7PY T 020-7399 1000 E admin@rafclub.org.uk
W www.rafclub.org.uk
Secretary, Miles Pooley

ROYAL AUTOMOBILE CLUB (1897), 89 Pall Mall,
London SW1Y 5HS T 020-7930 2345
E secretary@royalautomobileclub.co.uk
W www.royalautomobileclub.co.uk
Secretary, Miles Wade, CBE
Former members: Winston Churchill, Rudyard Kipling,
Charles Rolls

ROYAL NORTHERN & UNIVERSITY CLUB* (1854),
9 Albyn Place, Aberdeen AB10 1YE T 01224-583292
E secretary@rnuc.org.uk W www.rnuc.org.uk
Manager, Ron Esslemont

ROYAL OVER-SEAS LEAGUE (1910), Over-Seas House,
Park Place, St James's Street, London SW1A 1LR
T 020-7408 0214 E info@rosl.org.uk W www.rosl.org.uk
Director-General, Maj.-Gen. Roddy Porter, MBE

SAVILE CLUB* (1868), 69 Brook Street, London W1K 4ER
T 020-7629 5462 W www.savileclub.co.uk
Secretary, Julian Malone-Lee
Former members: Max Beerbohm, Thomas Hardy,
Robert Louis Stevenson

SCOTTISH ARTS CLUB (1872), 24 Rutland Square,
Edinburgh EH1 2BW T 0131-229 8157
E office@scottishartsclub.co.uk W www.scottishartsclub.co.uk
President, Diana Allen

SLOANE CLUB (1976), Lower Sloane Street, London
SW1W 8BS T 020-7730 9131 E reservations@sloaneclub.co.uk
W www.sloaneclub.co.uk
Membership Secretary, Fran Bremner

TRAVELLERS CLUB* (1819), 106 Pall Mall, London SW1Y 5EP
T 020-7930 8688 E secretary@thetravellersclub.org.uk
W www.thetravellersclub.org.uk
Secretary, David Broadhead
Former members: Arthur Balfour, Alec Douglas-Home,
Anthony Powell, Sir Patrick Leigh-Fermor

TURF CLUB (1868), 5 Carlton House Terrace,
London SW1Y 5AQ T 020-7930 8555 E mail@turfclub.co.uk
Secretary, Col. A. J. E. Malcolm, OBE

ULSTER REFORM CLUB (1885), 4 Royal Avenue,
Belfast BT1 1DA T 028-9032 3411
E info@ulsterreformclub.com W www.ulsterreformclub.com
Chief Executive, A. W. Graham

UNIVERSITY WOMEN'S CLUB† (1886), 2 Audley Square,
London W1K 1DB T 020-7499 2268
E reservations@uwc-london.com
W www.universitywomensclub.com
Chief Executive, Cdr Rod Craig, RN

VINCENT'S* (1863), 1A King Edward Street, Oxford OX1 4HS
T 01865-722984 E bursar@vincents.org W www.vincents.org
Bursar, Stephen Eeley
Former members: Roger Bannister, King Edward VIII

WESTERN CLUB (1825), 32 Royal Exchange Square,
Glasgow G1 3AB T 0141-221 2016
E secretary@westernclub.co.uk W www.westernclub.co.uk
Secretary, Douglas Gifford

WHITE'S* (1693), 37–38 St James's Street, London SW1A 1JG
T 020-7493 6671
Secretary, D. A. Anderson
Former members: David Cameron, Evelyn Waugh

* Men only   † Women only

TIME AND SPACE

ASTRONOMY

The following pages give astronomical data for each month of the year 2016. There are four pages of data for each month. All data are given for 0h Greenwich Mean Time (GMT), ie at the midnight at the beginning of the day named. This applies also to data for the months when British Summer Time is in operation (for dates, *see* below).

The astronomical data are given in a form suitable for observation with the naked eye or with a small telescope. These data do not attempt to replace the *Astronomical Almanac* for professional astronomers.

A fuller explanation of how to use the astronomical data is given on pages 627–629.

CALENDAR FOR EACH MONTH
The calendar for each month comprises dates of general interest plus the dates of birth or death of well-known people. The theme for this edition is 'politics and elections' to tie-in with the 2015 General Election. For key religious, civil and legal dates *see* page 7. For details of flag-flying days *see* page 19. For royal birthdays *see* pages 19 and 20–1. For public holidays *see also* pages 8 and 9.

Fuller explanations of the various calendars can be found under Time Measurement and Calendars.

The zodiacal signs through which the Sun is passing during each month are illustrated. The date of transition from one sign to the next, to the nearest hour, is given under Astronomical Phenomena.

JULIAN DATE
The Julian date on 2016 January 0.0 is 2457387.5. To find the Julian date for any other date in 2016 (at 0h GMT), add the day-of-the-year number on the extreme right of the calendar for each month to the Julian date for January 0.0.

BRITISH SUMMER TIME

British Summer Time is the legal time for general purposes during the period in which it is in operation (*see also* page 632). During this period, clocks are kept one hour ahead of Greenwich Mean Time. The hour of changeover is 01h Greenwich Mean Time. The duration of Summer Time in 2016 is from March 27 01h GMT to October 30 01h GMT.

SEASONS

The seasons are defined astronomically as follows:

Spring from the vernal equinox to the summer solstice
Summer from the summer solstice to the autumnal equinox
Autumn from the autumnal equinox to the winter solstice
Winter from the winter solstice to the vernal equinox

The time when seasons start in 2016 are:

Northern Hemisphere

Vernal Equinox	March 20d 04h 30m GMT
Summer Solstice	June 20d 22h 34m GMT
Autumnal Equinox	September 22d 14h 21m GMT
Winter Solstice	December 21d 10h 44m GMT

Southern Hemisphere

Autumnal Equinox	March 20d 04h 30m GMT
Winter Solstice	June 20d 22h 34m GMT
Vernal Equinox	September 22d 14h 21m GMT
Summer Solstice	December 21d 10h 44m GMT

The longest day of the year, measured from sunrise to sunset, is at the summer solstice. The longest day in the UK will fall on 20 June in 2016.

The shortest day of the year is at the winter solstice. The shortest day in the UK will fall on 21 December in 2016.

The equinox is the point at which day and night are of equal length all over the world.

In popular parlance, the seasons in the northern hemisphere comprise the following months:

Spring	March, April, May
Summer	June, July, August
Autumn	September, October, November
Winter	December, January, February

The March equinox can fall as early as 19 March but this has not happened since 1796 and it will not happen again until 2044. This equinox in 2007 was on 21 March, however in 2008 it occurred on 20 March and will not revert to 21 March again until 2102.

In 2008 the June solstice occurred on 20 June, the first time since 1897. The June solstice in 1975 was on 22 June, but it will not occur on this date again until 2203.

 # JANUARY 2016

FIRST MONTH, 31 DAYS. *Janus*, god of the portal, facing two ways, past and future

1	Friday	Great Britain and Ireland unite as the United Kingdom of Great Britain and Ireland 1801	day 1
2	Saturday	José Antonio Remón Cantera, the president of Panama, is killed at a race track 1955	2
3	Sunday	Joseph Jenkins Roberts is sworn in as the first president of Liberia 1848	3
4	Monday	The Fabian Society, Britain's oldest political think tank, is founded 1884	week 1 day 4
5	Tuesday	The German Worker's Party, predecessor of the Nazi party, is founded in Munich 1919	5
6	Wednesday	Theodore Roosevelt, the 26th US president and the first to win a Nobel Peace Prize *d.* 1919	6
7	Thursday	Robert Devereux, 2nd Earl of Essex, leads a failed rebellion against Queen Elizabeth I 1601	7
8	Friday	François Mitterrand, France's 21st and longest-serving president *d.* 1996	8
9	Saturday	Anthoney Eden resigns as prime minister following the Suez Crisis 1957	9
10	Sunday	Thomas Paine anonymously publishes *Common Sense* in support of American independence 1776	10
11	Monday	Arthur Scargill, trade unionist, president National Union of Mineworkers (1982–2002) *b.* 1938	week 2 day 11
12	Tuesday	Edmund Burke, Irish philosopher and Whig politician who opposed the French Revolution *b.* 1729	12
13	Wednesday	The Independent Labour party is founded in Bradford by James Keir Hardie 1893	13
14	Thursday	Marshal Josip Broz Tito was elected as the first president of Yugoslavia 1953	14
15	Friday	Rosa Luxemburg, revolutionary Marxist of Polish-Jewish descent, is assassinated in Berlin 1919	15
16	Saturday	Ivan the Terrible is crowned Tsar of All the Russias 1547	16
17	Sunday	Benjamin Franklin, Founding Father of the USA, who invented bifocals *b.* 1706	17
18	Monday	Sir Edmund Barton, the first prime minister of Australia *b.* 1849	week 3 day 18
19	Tuesday	The US senate votes against participation in the League of Nations 1920	19
20	Wednesday	Christian II is deposed from the thrones of Denmark and Norway 1523	20
21	Thursday	On his first day in office, US president Jimmy Carter pardons Vietnam War draft evaders 1977	21
22	Friday	Ramsay MacDonald becomes the first Labour prime minister of the UK 1924	22
23	Saturday	William Pitt the Younger, the youngest British prime minister aged 24 *d.* 1806	23
24	Sunday	Frederick II (Frederick the Great), who introduced the potato to the Kingdom of Prussia *b.* 1712	24
25	Monday	The League of Nations is established at the Paris Peace Conference 1919	week 4 day 25
26	Tuesday	India officially becomes an independent republic and its first president is sworn in 1950	26
27	Wednesday	The body of Vladimir Lenin is placed in a mausoleum in Red Square 1924	27
28	Thursday	Sir Thomas Warner establishes Saint Kitts as the first British colony in the Caribbean 1624	28
29	Friday	George III, whose life was longer than any monarch who preceded him *d.* 1820	29
30	Saturday	Charles I is executed for treason outside the Banqueting House, Whitehall, London 1649	30
31	Sunday	Guy Fawkes leaps to his death from the gallows before he could be hung for treason 1606	31

ASTRONOMICAL PHENOMENA

d	*h*	
2	23	Earth at perihelion
3	19	Mars 1° South of the Moon
6	24	Venus 3° South of the Moon
7	05	Saturn 3° South of the Moon
9	04	Saturn 0.1° South of Venus
10	18	Mercury 2° South of the Moon
16	06	Uranus 1° North of the Moon
28	01	Jupiter 1° North of the Moon

MINIMA OF ALGOL

d	*h*	*d*	*h*	*d*	*h*
1	11.9	12	23.2	24	10.5
4	08.8	15	20.0	27	07.3
7	05.6	18	16.9	30	04.2
10	02.4	21	13.7		

CONSTELLATIONS

The following constellations are near the meridian at

	d	*h*		*d*	*h*
December	1	24	January	16	21
December	16	23	February	1	20
January	1	22	February	15	19

Draco (below the Pole), Ursa Minor (below the Pole), Camelopardalis, Perseus, Auriga, Taurus, Orion, Eridanus and Lepus

THE MOON

Phases, Apsides and Node	*d*	*h*	*m*
◑ Last Quarter	2	05	30
● New Moon	10	01	31
◐ First Quarter	16	23	26
○ Full Moon	24	01	46
Apogee (404,277km)	2	11	53
Perigee (369,619km)	15	02	14
Apogee (404,553km)	30	09	10

Mean longitude of ascending node on 1st, 176°

THE SUN

Diam. 32.5″

Day	Right Ascension			Dec.	Equation of time		Rise				Transit		Set				Sidereal time			Transit of first point of Aries		
				−			52°		56°				52°		56°							
	h	m	s	°	m	s	h	m	h	m	h	m	h	m	h	m	h	m	s	h	m	s
1	18	43	28	23.1	−3	06	8	08	8	30	12	03	15	59	15	36	6	40	22	17	19	38
2	18	47	53	23.0	−3	34	8	08	8	30	12	04	16	00	15	38	6	44	18	17	15	42
3	18	52	17	22.9	−4	02	8	07	8	30	12	04	16	01	15	39	6	48	15	17	11	45
4	18	56	42	22.8	−4	30	8	07	8	30	12	05	16	02	15	40	6	52	12	17	07	48
5	19	01	05	22.7	−4	57	8	07	8	29	12	05	16	04	15	41	6	56	08	17	03	52
6	19	05	29	22.6	−5	24	8	07	8	29	12	06	16	05	15	43	7	00	05	16	59	55
7	19	09	52	22.5	−5	51	8	06	8	28	12	06	16	06	15	44	7	04	01	16	55	59
8	19	14	15	22.3	−6	17	8	06	8	28	12	07	16	07	15	46	7	07	58	16	52	02
9	19	18	37	22.2	−6	43	8	05	8	27	12	07	16	09	15	47	7	11	54	16	48	06
10	19	22	59	22.1	−7	08	8	05	8	26	12	07	16	10	15	49	7	15	51	16	44	09
11	19	27	20	21.9	−7	32	8	04	8	25	12	08	16	12	15	51	7	19	47	16	40	13
12	19	31	40	21.8	−7	56	8	04	8	24	12	08	16	13	15	52	7	23	44	16	36	16
13	19	36	00	21.6	−8	20	8	03	8	23	12	09	16	14	15	54	7	27	41	16	32	19
14	19	40	19	21.4	−8	42	8	02	8	23	12	09	16	16	15	56	7	31	37	16	28	23
15	19	44	38	21.3	−9	05	8	01	8	21	12	09	16	18	15	58	7	35	34	16	24	26
16	19	48	56	21.1	−9	26	8	01	8	20	12	10	16	19	15	59	7	39	30	16	20	30
17	19	53	13	20.9	−9	47	8	00	8	19	12	10	16	21	16	01	7	43	27	16	16	33
18	19	57	30	20.7	−10	07	7	59	8	18	12	10	16	22	16	03	7	47	23	16	12	37
19	20	01	46	20.5	−10	26	7	58	8	17	12	11	16	24	16	05	7	51	20	16	08	40
20	20	06	01	20.3	−10	44	7	57	8	15	12	11	16	26	16	07	7	55	16	16	04	44
21	20	10	15	20.1	−11	02	7	56	8	14	12	11	16	27	16	09	7	59	13	16	00	47
22	20	14	29	19.8	−11	19	7	54	8	13	12	11	16	29	16	11	8	03	10	15	56	50
23	20	18	42	19.6	−11	36	7	53	8	11	12	12	16	31	16	13	8	07	06	15	52	54
24	20	22	54	19.4	−11	51	7	52	8	10	12	12	16	32	16	15	8	11	03	15	48	57
25	20	27	05	19.2	−12	06	7	51	8	08	12	12	16	34	16	17	8	14	59	15	45	01
26	20	31	15	18.9	−12	20	7	49	8	06	12	12	16	36	16	19	8	18	56	15	41	04
27	20	35	25	18.7	−12	33	7	48	8	05	12	13	16	38	16	21	8	22	52	15	37	08
28	20	39	34	18.4	−12	45	7	47	8	03	12	13	16	40	16	23	8	26	49	15	33	11
29	20	43	42	18.1	−12	57	7	45	8	01	12	13	16	41	16	25	8	30	45	15	29	15
30	20	47	49	17.9	−13	07	7	44	8	00	12	13	16	43	16	28	8	34	42	15	25	18
31	20	51	56	17.6	−13	17	7	42	7	58	12	13	16	45	16	30	8	38	39	15	21	21

DURATION OF TWILIGHT (in minutes)

Latitude	52°	56°	52°	56°	52°	56°	52°	56°
	1 January		11 January		21 January		31 January	
Civil	41	47	40	45	38	43	37	41
Nautical	84	96	82	93	80	90	78	87
Astronomical	125	141	123	138	120	134	117	130

THE NIGHT SKY

Mercury is an evening object low in the south-west for the first week of January. It moves into the morning sky after inferior conjunction on the 14th and may be spotted in the last week of the month. Mercury's emergence now allows us take in all five classical planets in one sweep before sunrise until about mid-February. Such an opportunity last occurred in December 2004 when the five were in the right order of their increasing distance from the Sun.

Venus starts the year in Scorpius but quickly crosses into Ophiuchus before ending the month in Sagittarius. It rises about three hours before the Sun at the beginning of January but only about 90 minutes beforehand on the 31st. The Moon, Venus, and Saturn form an impressive trio on the 7th with the two planets only a Moon's width apart on the 9th.

Mars rises during the early hours and crosses from Virgo into Libra on the 17th. The planet's deep orange tint now becomes quite pronounced as it brightens from magnitude +1.3 to +0.8. The Moon is near Mars on the 3rd.

Jupiter, magnitude −2.2, rises during the late evening and can be found in Leo. It is stationary on the 8th and then begins to retrograde. The Moon is near Jupiter on the morning of January 1st but much closer on the 28th.

Saturn, magnitude +0.5, is in Ophiuchus and rises more than two hours before the Sun.

THE MOON

Day	R.A. h	R.A. m	Dec. °	Hor. Par. '	Diam. '	Sun's Co-Long. °	PA of Br. Limb °	Ph. %	Age d	Rise 52° h	Rise 52° m	Rise 56° h	Rise 56° m	Transit h	Transit m	Set 52° h	Set 52° m	Set 56° h	Set 56° m
1	11	48	+1.5	54.4	29.7	164	113	62	20.7	—		—		5	17	11	26	11	25
2	12	33	−2.3	54.3	29.6	177	113	52	21.7	0	01	0	03	5	59	11	48	11	45
3	13	18	−5.9	54.3	29.6	189	112	43	22.7	1	03	1	09	6	42	12	11	12	05
4	14	04	−9.3	54.4	29.7	201	111	34	23.7	2	06	2	15	7	25	12	37	12	27
5	14	52	−12.4	54.8	29.8	213	109	25	24.7	3	09	3	21	8	11	13	06	12	53
6	15	41	−15.0	55.2	30.1	225	107	17	25.7	4	12	4	27	8	58	13	39	13	24
7	16	32	−17.0	55.8	30.4	237	105	10	26.7	5	13	5	30	9	48	14	20	14	03
8	17	25	−18.1	56.5	30.8	250	104	5	27.7	6	11	6	30	10	40	15	08	14	50
9	18	21	−18.4	57.1	31.1	262	108	1	28.7	7	04	7	23	11	34	16	05	15	47
10	19	17	−17.6	57.8	31.5	274	162	0	0.1	7	52	8	08	12	28	17	10	16	54
11	20	14	−15.8	58.3	31.8	286	239	1	1.1	8	33	8	47	13	23	18	20	18	08
12	21	10	−13.1	58.8	32.0	298	246	5	2.1	9	08	9	19	14	17	19	35	19	25
13	22	06	−9.5	59.1	32.2	311	247	10	3.1	9	40	9	47	15	10	20	51	20	46
14	23	00	−5.5	59.3	32.3	323	247	18	4.1	10	09	10	12	16	02	22	08	22	07
15	23	55	−1.1	59.3	32.3	335	247	28	5.1	10	36	10	36	16	54	23	25	23	28
16	0	49	+3.4	59.3	32.3	347	247	39	6.1	11	04	11	00	17	46	—		—	
17	1	43	+7.6	59.2	32.2	359	249	50	7.1	11	34	11	25	18	39	0	41	0	48
18	2	38	+11.4	59.0	32.1	11	251	62	8.1	12	07	11	55	19	32	1	56	2	07
19	3	34	+14.6	58.7	32.0	24	254	72	9.1	12	44	12	29	20	27	3	09	3	24
20	4	30	+16.8	58.4	31.8	36	257	82	10.1	13	28	13	11	21	23	4	19	4	35
21	5	28	+18.1	58.0	31.6	48	260	89	11.1	14	19	14	02	22	18	5	21	5	39
22	6	25	+18.3	57.6	31.4	60	262	95	12.1	15	17	15	00	23	12	6	16	6	34
23	7	21	+17.5	57.1	31.1	72	259	99	13.1	16	19	16	04	—		7	02	7	19
24	8	15	+15.8	56.6	30.8	84	206	100	14.1	17	25	17	12	0	05	7	41	7	54
25	9	08	+13.2	56.0	30.5	96	123	99	15.1	18	31	18	21	0	54	8	14	8	25
26	9	58	+10.1	55.5	30.3	108	115	96	16.1	19	37	19	31	1	42	8	42	8	49
27	10	46	+6.7	55.0	30.0	121	114	92	17.1	20	42	20	39	2	28	9	07	9	11
28	11	33	+3.0	54.6	29.8	133	113	85	18.1	21	46	21	46	3	11	9	30	9	31
29	12	18	−0.8	54.4	29.6	145	113	78	19.1	22	49	22	52	3	54	9	52	9	50
30	13	03	−4.5	54.2	29.5	157	112	70	20.1	23	51	23	58	4	37	10	15	10	10
31	13	49	−8.0	54.2	29.6	169	110	61	21.1	—		—		5	19	10	39	10	31

MERCURY

Day	R.A. h	R.A. m	Dec °	Mag.	Diam. "	Phase %	Rise h m	Transit h m	Set h m
1	20	05.5	−21.1	−0.3	7	49	9 26	13 22	17 19
3	20	10.0	−20.4	−0.1	8	40	9 17	13 18	17 19
5	20	11.8	−19.7	+0.3	8	30	9 06	13 11	17 16
7	20	10.5	−19.2	+0.9	9	21	8 52	13 01	17 09
9	20	06.0	−18.7	+1.7	9	12	8 37	12 47	16 58
11	19	58.4	−18.5	+2.8	10	6	8 19	12 31	16 43
13	19	48.5	−18.4	+4.1	10	2	8 01	12 13	16 25
15	19	37.4	−18.4	+4.6	10	1	7 42	11 54	16 06
17	19	26.5	−18.5	+3.6	10	3	7 24	11 36	15 46
19	19	16.9	−18.8	+2.5	10	8	7 09	11 19	15 28
21	19	09.6	−19.0	+1.7	10	14	6 56	11 05	15 12
23	19	04.8	−19.3	+1.1	9	21	6 46	10 53	14 59
25	19	02.7	−19.7	+0.7	9	28	6 39	10 43	14 48
27	19	02.9	−20.0	+0.4	8	34	6 34	10 36	14 39
29	19	05.2	−20.3	+0.3	8	41	6 30	10 31	14 32
31	19	09.4	−20.5	+0.1	8	46	6 29	10 28	14 27

Rising and setting times are for latitude 54°

VENUS

Day	R.A. h	R.A. m	Dec °	Mag.	Diam. "	Phase %	Rise h m	Transit h m	Set h m
1	16	00.6	−18.6	−5.4	15	77	6 00	9 20	13 33
6	16	25.8	−19.8	−5.3	15	79	5 20	9 25	13 30
11	16	51.5	−20.8	−5.2	15	80	5 33	9 31	13 29
16	17	17.6	−21.6	−5.1	14	81	5 45	9 37	13 30
21	17	43.9	−22.2	−5.0	14	83	5 55	9 44	13 33
26	18	10.5	−22.4	−4.9	14	84	6 04	9 51	13 38
31	18	37.1	−22.4	−4.9	13	85	6 11	9 58	13 45

MARS

Day	R.A. h	R.A. m	Dec °	Mag.	Diam. "	Phase %	Rise h m	Transit h m	Set h m
1	13	47.5	−9.5	+1.3	6	91	1 56	7 06	12 16
6	13	58.0	−10.4	+1.2	6	91	1 53	6 57	12 01
11	14	08.4	−11.4	+1.1	6	91	1 49	6 48	11 47
16	14	18.7	−12.3	+1.1	6	91	1 45	6 39	11 32
21	14	28.9	−13.1	+1.0	6	90	1 40	6 29	11 17
26	14	39.0	−13.9	+0.9	7	90	1 36	6 19	11 03
31	14	48.9	−14.7	+0.8	7	90	1 31	6 10	10 48

SUNRISE AND SUNSET

d	London 0° 05' 51° 30' h m	h m	Bristol 2° 35' 51° 28' h m	h m	Birmingham 1° 55' 52° 28' h m	h m	Manchester 2° 15' 53° 28' h m	h m	Newcastle 1° 37' 54° 59' h m	h m	Glasgow 4° 14' 55° 52' h m	h m	Belfast 5° 56' 54° 35' h m	h m
1	8 06	16 02	8 16	16 12	8 18	16 04	8 25	16 00	8 31	15 49	8 47	15 53	8 46	16 08
2	8 06	16 03	8 16	16 13	8 18	16 05	8 25	16 01	8 31	15 50	8 47	15 55	8 46	16 09
3	8 06	16 04	8 16	16 14	8 18	16 06	8 25	16 02	8 31	15 51	8 47	15 56	8 46	16 11
4	8 06	16 05	8 15	16 15	8 18	16 07	8 24	16 03	8 30	15 52	8 46	15 57	8 45	16 12
5	8 05	16 06	8 15	16 16	8 17	16 09	8 24	16 05	8 30	15 54	8 46	15 59	8 45	16 13
6	8 05	16 07	8 15	16 17	8 17	16 10	8 24	16 06	8 30	15 55	8 45	16 00	8 45	16 14
7	8 05	16 08	8 14	16 19	8 17	16 11	8 23	16 07	8 29	15 56	8 45	16 01	8 44	16 16
8	8 04	16 10	8 14	16 20	8 16	16 12	8 23	16 09	8 28	15 58	8 44	16 03	8 43	16 17
9	8 04	16 11	8 13	16 21	8 16	16 14	8 22	16 10	8 28	15 59	8 44	16 05	8 43	16 19
10	8 03	16 12	8 13	16 23	8 15	16 15	8 21	16 12	8 27	16 01	8 43	16 06	8 42	16 20
11	8 03	16 14	8 12	16 24	8 14	16 17	8 21	16 13	8 26	16 02	8 42	16 08	8 41	16 22
12	8 02	16 15	8 12	16 26	8 14	16 18	8 20	16 15	8 25	16 04	8 41	16 09	8 41	16 24
13	8 01	16 17	8 11	16 27	8 13	16 20	8 19	16 16	8 25	16 06	8 40	16 11	8 40	16 25
14	8 00	16 18	8 10	16 28	8 12	16 21	8 18	16 18	8 24	16 07	8 39	16 13	8 39	16 27
15	8 00	16 20	8 10	16 30	8 11	16 23	8 17	16 19	8 23	16 09	8 38	16 15	8 38	16 29
16	7 59	16 21	8 09	16 32	8 10	16 24	8 16	16 21	8 22	16 11	8 37	16 17	8 37	16 30
17	7 58	16 23	8 08	16 33	8 10	16 26	8 15	16 23	8 20	16 13	8 36	16 19	8 36	16 32
18	7 57	16 25	8 07	16 35	8 09	16 28	8 14	16 25	8 19	16 15	8 34	16 20	8 35	16 34
19	7 56	16 26	8 06	16 36	8 07	16 29	8 13	16 26	8 18	16 16	8 33	16 22	8 33	16 36
20	7 55	16 28	8 05	16 38	8 06	16 31	8 12	16 28	8 17	16 18	8 32	16 24	8 32	16 38
21	7 54	16 30	8 04	16 40	8 05	16 33	8 11	16 30	8 16	16 20	8 30	16 26	8 31	16 40
22	7 53	16 31	8 03	16 41	8 04	16 35	8 10	16 32	8 14	16 22	8 29	16 28	8 30	16 41
23	7 52	16 33	8 02	16 43	8 03	16 36	8 08	16 34	8 13	16 24	8 28	16 30	8 28	16 43
24	7 51	16 35	8 00	16 45	8 02	16 38	8 07	16 35	8 11	16 26	8 26	16 32	8 27	16 45
25	7 49	16 36	7 59	16 47	8 00	16 40	8 06	16 37	8 10	16 28	8 24	16 34	8 25	16 47
26	7 48	16 38	7 58	16 48	7 59	16 42	8 04	16 39	8 08	16 30	8 23	16 37	8 24	16 49
27	7 47	16 40	7 57	16 50	7 58	16 44	8 03	16 41	8 07	16 32	8 21	16 39	8 22	16 51
28	7 45	16 42	7 55	16 52	7 56	16 45	8 01	16 43	8 05	16 34	8 19	16 41	8 21	16 53
29	7 44	16 43	7 54	16 54	7 55	16 47	8 00	16 45	8 03	16 36	8 18	16 43	8 19	16 55
30	7 43	16 45	7 52	16 55	7 53	16 49	7 58	16 47	8 02	16 38	8 16	16 45	8 17	16 57
31	7 41	16 47	7 51	16 57	7 52	16 51	7 57	16 49	8 00	16 40	8 14	16 47	8 16	16 59

JUPITER

Day	R.A. h m	Dec °	Mag.	Diam. "	Rise h m	Transit h m	Set h m
1	11 36.0	+3.9	−2.2	39	22 27	4 55	11 19
11	11 36.3	+4.0	−2.2	40	21 48	4 16	10 41
21	11 35.5	+4.1	−2.3	41	21 07	3 36	10 01
31	11 33.5	+4.4	−2.4	42	20 24	2 54	9 21

Equatorial Diam. 41″, Polar Diam. 38″

SATURN

Day	R.A. h m	Dec °	Mag.	Diam. "	Rise h m	Transit h m	Set h m
1	16 38.4	−20.5	+0.5	15	5 56	9 56	13 57
11	16 42.8	−20.6	+0.5	15	5 22	9 22	13 21
21	16 47.0	−20.7	+0.6	16	4 47	8 46	12 45
31	16 50.7	−20.8	+0.6	16	4 13	8 11	12 09

Equatorial Diam. 15″, Polar Diam. 14″
Rings – major axis 35″ minor axis 15″, Tilt 26°

URANUS

Day	R.A. h m	Dec °	Mag.	Diam. "	Rise h m	Transit h m	Set h m
1	1 01.2	+5.8	+6.1	4	11 43	18 18	0 57
11	1 01.6	+5.9	+6.1	4	11 03	17 39	0 18
21	1 02.2	+6.0	+6.2	3	10 24	17 00	23 36
31	1 03.2	+6.1	+6.2	3	9 45	16 22	22 58

NEPTUNE

Day	R.A. h m	Dec °	Mag.	Diam. "	Rise h m	Transit h m	Set h m
1	22 37.3	−9.6	+7.9	2	10 45	15 54	21 04
11	22 38.3	−9.5	+7.9	2	10 06	15 16	20 26
21	22 39.4	−9.3	+8.0	2	9 27	14 38	19 49
31	22 40.6	−9.2	+8.0	2	8 48	14 00	19 11

FEBRUARY 2016

SECOND MONTH, 28 or 29 DAYS. *Februa*, Roman festival of Purification

1	*Monday*	Boris Yeltsin, who in 1991 became the first democratically elected Russian president *b*. 1931	week 5 day 32
2	*Tuesday*	Mehmed VI, the 36th and last Sultan of the Ottoman Empire *b*. 1861	33
3	*Wednesday*	Prime Minister Harold Macmillan delivers his 'winds of change' speech in Cape Town 1960	34
4	*Thursday*	George Washington is elected as the first president of the USA 1789	35
5	*Friday*	Leopold II of Belgium establishes himself as Sovereign of the Congo Free State 1885	36
6	*Saturday*	Tony Blair becomes Labour's longest-serving prime minister after 2,838 days in office 2005	37
7	*Sunday*	The European Union is established with the signing of the Maastricht Treaty 1992	38
8	*Monday*	Mary, Queen of Scots is executed for treason for her part in the Babington Plot 1587	week 6 day 39
9	*Tuesday*	Jefferson Davis is elected president of the Confederate States of America 1861	40
10	*Wednesday*	North Korea publicly announces that it has developed nuclear weapons 2005	41
11	*Thursday*	Traditional date of the foundation of Japan by Jimmu, on his accession as emperor in 660 BC	42
12	*Friday*	Abraham Lincoln, 16th US president who led the country through its civil war *b*. 1809	43
13	*Saturday*	Australian prime minister Kevin Rudd apologises to the country's 'Stolen Generations' 2008	44
14	*Sunday*	Rafik Hariri, former prime minister of Lebanon, is assassinated 2005	45
15	*Monday*	Canada inaugurates a new national flag with a red maple leaf design 1965	week 7 day 46
16	*Tuesday*	Fidel Castro is sworn in as prime minister of Cuba after leading the Cuban Revolution 1959	47
17	*Wednesday*	The Blaine Act ends 13 years of prohibition in the USA 1933	48
18	*Thursday*	Victor Emmanuel II becomes the first king of a united Italy since the 6th century 1861	49
19	*Friday*	The institution of serfdom is abolished in Russia by Tsar Alexander II 1861	50
20	*Saturday*	Gordon Brown, prime minister and leader of the Labour Party (2007–10) *b*. 1951	51
21	*Sunday*	John Rawls, American political philosopher and author of *A Theory of Justice b*. 1971	52
22	*Monday*	A union between Syria and Egypt creates the United Arab Republic 1958	week 8 day 53
23	*Tuesday*	The 1950 General Election takes place with a record 83.9 per cent turnout and victory for Labour	54
24	*Wednesday*	Mexico declares independence from Spain during the Mexican War of Independence 1821	55
25	*Thursday*	Nikita Khrushchev, leader of the Soviet Union, denounces Stalin and the cult of personality 1956	56
26	*Friday*	Golda Meir is elected as the Alignment party leader ahead of becoming prime minister of Israel 1969	57
27	*Saturday*	Benjamin Disraeli becomes prime minister of the UK for the first time 1868	58
28	*Sunday*	Olof Palme, prime minister of Sweden (1969–76), is assassinated 1986	59
29	*Monday*	Morarji Desai, fifth prime minister of India and independence activist *b*. 1896	week 9 day 60

ASTRONOMICAL PHENOMENA

d h
1 09 Mars 3° South of the Moon
3 19 Saturn 3° South of the Moon
6 08 Venus 4° South of the Moon
6 17 Mercury 4° South of the Moon
7 01 Mercury Greatest elongation West
12 14 Uranus 2° North of the Moon
24 04 Jupiter 2° North of the Moon
29 18 Mars 4° South of the Moon

MINIMA OF ALGOL

d	h	d	h	d	h
2	01.0	13	12.3	24	23.6
4	21.8	16	09.1	27	20.4
7	18.6	19	05.9		
10	15.4	22	02.7		

CONSTELLATIONS

The following constellations are near the meridian at

	d	h		d	h
January	1	24	February	15	21
January	16	23	March	1	20
February	1	22	March	16	19

Draco (below the Pole), Camelopardalis, Auriga, Taurus, Gemini, Orion, Canis Minor, Monoceros, Lepus, Canis Major and Puppis

THE MOON

Phases, Apsides and Node	d	h	m
◑ Last Quarter	1	03	28
● New Moon	8	14	39
◐ First Quarter	15	07	46
○ Full Moon	22	18	20
Perigee (364,360km)	11	02	41
Apogee (405,383km)	27	03	28

Mean longitude of ascending node on 1st, 174°

THE SUN

Diam. 32.4″

Day	Right Ascension			Dec. −	Equation of time	Rise 52°		56°		Transit		Set 52°		56°		Sidereal time			Transit of first point of Aries		
	h	m	s	°	m s	h	m	h	m	h	m	h	m	h	m	h	m	s	h	m	s
1	20	56	01	17.3	−13 26	7	41	7	56	12	14	16	47	16	32	8	42	35	15	17	25
2	21	00	06	17.0	−13 35	7	39	7	54	12	14	16	49	16	34	8	46	32	15	13	28
3	21	04	10	16.7	−13 42	7	38	7	52	12	14	16	51	16	36	8	50	28	15	09	32
4	21	08	14	16.5	−13 49	7	36	7	50	12	14	16	52	16	38	8	54	25	15	05	35
5	21	12	16	16.2	−13 55	7	34	7	48	12	14	16	54	16	41	8	58	21	15	01	39
6	21	16	18	15.9	−14 00	7	33	7	46	12	14	16	56	16	43	9	02	18	14	57	42
7	21	20	19	15.5	−14 04	7	31	7	44	12	14	16	58	16	45	9	06	14	14	53	46
8	21	24	19	15.2	−14 08	7	29	7	42	12	14	17	00	16	47	9	10	11	14	49	49
9	21	28	18	14.9	−14 11	7	27	7	40	12	14	17	02	16	49	9	14	08	14	45	52
10	21	32	17	14.6	−14 13	7	26	7	38	12	14	17	04	16	52	9	18	04	14	41	56
11	21	36	15	14.3	−14 14	7	24	7	36	12	14	17	05	16	54	9	22	01	14	37	59
12	21	40	12	13.9	−14 14	7	22	7	33	12	14	17	07	16	56	9	25	57	14	34	03
13	21	44	08	13.6	−14 14	7	20	7	31	12	14	17	09	16	58	9	29	54	14	30	06
14	21	48	03	13.3	−14 13	7	18	7	29	12	14	17	11	17	00	9	33	50	14	26	10
15	21	51	58	12.9	−14 11	7	16	7	27	12	14	17	13	17	03	9	37	47	14	22	13
16	21	55	52	12.6	−14 08	7	14	7	24	12	14	17	15	17	05	9	41	43	14	18	17
17	21	59	45	12.3	−14 05	7	12	7	22	12	14	17	17	17	07	9	45	40	14	14	20
18	22	03	37	11.9	−14 01	7	10	7	20	12	14	17	18	17	09	9	49	37	14	10	23
19	22	07	29	11.6	−13 56	7	08	7	17	12	14	17	20	17	11	9	53	33	14	06	27
20	22	11	20	11.2	−13 50	7	06	7	15	12	14	17	22	17	13	9	57	30	14	02	30
21	22	15	10	10.8	−13 44	7	04	7	13	12	14	17	24	17	16	10	01	26	13	58	34
22	22	19	00	10.5	−13 37	7	02	7	10	12	14	17	26	17	18	10	05	23	13	54	37
23	22	22	49	10.1	−13 30	7	00	7	08	12	13	17	28	17	20	10	09	19	13	50	41
24	22	26	37	9.7	−13 22	6	58	7	05	12	13	17	30	17	22	10	13	16	13	46	44
25	22	30	25	9.4	−13 13	6	56	7	03	12	13	17	31	17	24	10	17	12	13	42	48
26	22	34	13	9.0	−13 04	6	54	7	01	12	13	17	33	17	26	10	21	09	13	38	51
27	22	37	59	8.6	−12 54	6	52	6	58	12	13	17	35	17	29	10	25	05	13	34	55
28	22	41	45	8.3	−12 43	6	49	6	56	12	13	17	37	17	31	10	29	02	13	30	58
29	22	45	31	7.9	−12 32	6	47	6	53	12	12	17	39	17	33	10	32	59	13	27	01

DURATION OF TWILIGHT (in minutes)

Latitude	52°	56°	52°	56°	52°	56°	52°	56°
	1 February		11 February		21 February		31 February	
Civil	37	41	35	39	34	38	34	37
Nautical	77	86	75	83	74	81	73	80
Astronomical	117	130	114	126	113	124	112	124

THE NIGHT SKY

Mercury is a morning object and reaches greatest elongation west (26°) on the 7th. However, it is quite low and will be lost to view after the first ten days or so of February. A slender Moon joins Mercury and Venus on the 6th.

Venus remains a striking herald of the approaching sunrise but is now getting rather low. A clear south-eastern horizon is a prerequisite to seeing Venus easily by the end of February, when its altitude is only 2° at the beginning of civil twilight. Venus crosses from Sagittarius into Capricornus on the 17th.

Mars rises not long after the witching hour at the end of February and will have brightened to magnitude +0.3 by then.

The Red Planet is at western quadrature on the 7th when telescope users will note its gibbous phase. The Last Quarter Moon is nearby on February 1st.

Jupiter rises during the early evening and climbs above the eastern horizon not long after sunset by the end of the month. The Moon is near Jupiter on the 23rd, making for a dramatic sight. Jupiter brightens a little this month from magnitude −2.4 to −2.5.

Saturn rises 3.5 hours before the Sun at the beginning of February and an hour earlier by the end of the month. The waning Moon is near Saturn on the 3rd and 4th.

THE MOON

Day	R.A.		Dec.	Hor. Par.	Diam.	Sun's Co-Long.	PA of Br. Limb	Ph.	Age	Rise				Transit		Set			
										52°		56°				52°		56°	
	h	m	°	'	'	°	°	%	d	h	m	h	m	h	m	h	m	h	m
1	14	35	−11.2	54.4	29.7	181	108	51	22.1	0	53	1	04	6	03	11	06	10	55
2	15	23	−13.9	54.8	29.9	194	105	42	23.1	1	55	2	09	6	49	11	37	11	23
3	16	13	−16.1	55.3	30.1	206	102	33	24.1	2	56	3	12	7	37	12	14	11	58
4	17	04	−17.6	56.0	30.5	218	99	24	25.1	3	55	4	13	8	27	12	58	12	39
5	17	58	−18.3	56.8	30.9	230	95	15	26.1	4	51	5	09	9	20	13	49	13	31
6	18	54	−18.0	57.6	31.4	242	92	8	27.1	5	42	5	58	10	14	14	50	14	33
7	19	51	−16.6	58.4	31.8	254	90	3	28.1	6	26	6	41	11	09	15	59	15	44
8	20	48	−14.3	59.1	32.2	267	97	1	29.1	7	05	7	17	12	05	17	13	17	02
9	21	45	−11.0	59.7	32.5	279	226	0	0.6	7	39	7	48	13	00	18	30	18	23
10	22	42	−7.0	60.0	32.7	291	245	3	1.6	8	10	8	15	13	54	19	50	19	47
11	23	38	−2.6	60.2	32.8	303	247	8	2.6	8	39	8	40	14	48	21	09	21	11
12	0	34	+2.0	60.1	32.8	315	248	15	3.6	9	08	9	05	15	41	22	28	22	34
13	1	29	+6.4	59.8	32.6	328	250	25	4.6	9	38	9	31	16	35	23	45	23	54
14	2	25	+10.4	59.4	32.4	340	252	35	5.6	10	10	10	00	17	29	—		—	
15	3	21	+13.8	58.9	32.1	352	256	46	6.6	10	46	10	32	18	24	0	59	1	13
16	4	18	+16.3	58.4	31.8	4	259	58	7.6	11	28	11	12	19	19	2	10	2	26
17	5	14	+17.8	57.9	31.5	16	263	68	8.6	12	16	11	59	20	13	3	14	3	32
18	6	11	+18.3	57.3	31.2	28	268	78	9.6	13	10	12	52	21	07	4	10	4	29
19	7	06	+17.7	56.8	31.0	41	272	86	10.6	14	10	13	53	21	58	4	58	5	16
20	8	00	+16.3	56.3	30.7	53	275	92	11.6	15	13	14	59	22	48	5	40	5	54
21	8	52	+14.0	55.9	30.4	65	277	97	12.6	16	18	16	07	23	36	6	14	6	26
22	9	42	+11.2	55.4	30.2	77	274	99	13.6	17	23	17	16	—		6	44	6	52
23	10	31	+7.8	55.0	30.0	89	139	100	14.6	18	28	18	24	0	22	7	10	7	15
24	11	18	+4.2	54.7	29.8	101	114	99	15.6	19	33	19	32	1	06	7	34	7	36
25	12	04	+0.5	54.4	29.6	113	112	95	16.6	20	36	20	38	1	50	7	56	7	56
26	12	49	−3.2	54.2	29.5	126	110	91	17.6	21	39	21	44	2	32	8	19	8	15
27	13	34	−6.8	54.1	29.5	138	109	84	18.6	22	41	22	50	3	15	8	43	8	36
28	14	20	−10.1	54.1	29.5	150	107	77	19.6	23	43	23	54	3	58	9	08	8	59
29	15	07	−13.0	54.3	29.6	162	104	69	20.6	—		—		4	43	9	37	9	24

MERCURY

Day	R.A.		Dec	Mag.	Diam.	Phase	Rise		Transit		Set	
	h	m	°		"	%	h	m	h	m	h	m
1	19	12.0	−20.6	+0.1	8	49	6	28	10	27	14	26
3	19	18.3	−20.8	0.0	7	53	6	28	10	26	14	23
5	19	25.7	−20.9	0.0	7	58	6	28	10	26	14	22
7	19	34.0	−21.0	0.0	7	62	6	29	10	26	14	23
9	19	43.1	−20.9	0.0	7	65	6	31	10	28	14	25
11	19	52.9	−20.9	−0.1	6	68	6	32	10	30	14	28
13	20	03.1	−20.7	−0.1	6	71	6	33	10	32	14	32
15	20	13.8	−20.4	−0.1	6	73	6	34	10	35	14	37
17	20	24.9	−20.1	−0.1	6	75	6	35	10	39	14	42
19	20	36.3	−19.7	−0.1	6	78	6	35	10	42	14	49
21	20	47.9	−19.2	−0.1	6	79	6	36	10	46	14	57
23	20	59.8	−18.6	−0.2	6	81	6	35	10	50	15	05
25	21	11.8	−17.9	−0.2	5	83	6	35	10	54	15	14
27	21	24.0	−17.1	−0.2	5	85	6	34	10	59	15	23
29	21	36.4	−16.3	−0.3	5	86	6	33	11	03	15	33

Rising and setting times are for latitude 54°

VENUS

Day	R.A.		Dec	Mag.	Diam.	Phase	Rise		Transit		Set	
	h	m	°		"	%	h	m	h	m	h	m
1	18	42.5	−22.4	−4.8	13	85	6	12	9	59	13	46
6	19	09.1	−22.0	−4.8	13	86	6	16	10	06	13	56
11	19	35.6	−21.4	−4.7	13	87	6	19	10	13	14	07
16	20	01.8	−20.5	−4.6	13	88	6	19	10	19	14	20
21	20	27.6	−19.4	−4.6	12	89	6	17	10	26	14	35
26	20	53.1	−18.0	−4.5	12	90	6	13	10	31	14	50

MARS

Day	R.A.		Dec	Mag.	Diam.	Phase	Rise		Transit		Set	
	h	m	°		"	%	h	m	h	m	h	m
1	14	50.9	−14.9	+0.8	7	90	1	30	6	08	10	46
6	15	00.6	−15.6	+0.7	7	90	1	24	5	58	10	31
11	15	10.1	−16.2	+0.7	7	90	1	18	5	48	10	17
16	15	19.3	−16.9	+0.6	8	90	1	12	5	37	10	02
21	15	28.3	−17.5	+0.5	8	90	1	05	5	26	9	48
26	15	36.9	−18.0	+0.4	8	90	0	57	5	15	9	33

SUNRISE AND SUNSET

d	London 0° 05' 51° 30' h m	h m	Bristol 2° 35' 51° 28' h m	h m	Birmingham 1° 55' 52° 28' h m	h m	Manchester 2° 15' 53° 28' h m	h m	Newcastle 1° 37' 54° 59' h m	h m	Glasgow 4° 14' 55° 52' h m	h m	Belfast 5° 56' 54° 35' h m	h m
1	7 40	16 49	7 49	16 59	7 50	16 53	7 55	16 51	7 58	16 42	8 12	16 49	8 14	17 01
2	7 38	16 51	7 48	17 01	7 49	16 55	7 53	16 53	7 56	16 45	8 10	16 51	8 12	17 03
3	7 36	16 52	7 46	17 03	7 47	16 57	7 52	16 55	7 55	16 47	8 08	16 54	8 10	17 05
4	7 35	16 54	7 45	17 04	7 45	16 59	7 50	16 57	7 53	16 49	8 07	16 56	8 08	17 07
5	7 33	16 56	7 43	17 06	7 44	17 00	7 48	16 59	7 51	16 51	8 05	16 58	8 07	17 09
6	7 32	16 58	7 41	17 08	7 42	17 02	7 46	17 01	7 49	16 53	8 03	17 00	8 05	17 12
7	7 30	17 00	7 40	17 10	7 40	17 04	7 44	17 02	7 47	16 55	8 00	17 02	8 03	17 14
8	7 28	17 02	7 38	17 12	7 38	17 06	7 43	17 04	7 45	16 57	7 58	17 05	8 01	17 16
9	7 26	17 03	7 36	17 13	7 36	17 08	7 41	17 06	7 43	16 59	7 56	17 07	7 59	17 18
10	7 25	17 05	7 35	17 15	7 35	17 10	7 39	17 08	7 41	17 01	7 54	17 09	7 57	17 20
11	7 23	17 07	7 33	17 17	7 33	17 12	7 37	17 10	7 39	17 03	7 52	17 11	7 55	17 22
12	7 21	17 09	7 31	17 19	7 31	17 14	7 35	17 12	7 37	17 06	7 50	17 13	7 53	17 24
13	7 19	17 11	7 29	17 21	7 29	17 16	7 33	17 14	7 35	17 08	7 48	17 15	7 51	17 26
14	7 17	17 13	7 27	17 23	7 27	17 18	7 31	17 16	7 32	17 10	7 45	17 18	7 49	17 28
15	7 15	17 14	7 25	17 24	7 25	17 19	7 29	17 18	7 30	17 12	7 43	17 20	7 46	17 30
16	7 13	17 16	7 23	17 26	7 23	17 21	7 27	17 20	7 28	17 14	7 41	17 22	7 44	17 32
17	7 11	17 18	7 21	17 28	7 21	17 23	7 25	17 22	7 26	17 16	7 39	17 24	7 42	17 34
18	7 10	17 20	7 19	17 30	7 19	17 25	7 23	17 24	7 24	17 18	7 36	17 26	7 40	17 36
19	7 08	17 22	7 17	17 32	7 17	17 27	7 20	17 26	7 21	17 20	7 34	17 29	7 38	17 38
20	7 06	17 23	7 15	17 34	7 15	17 29	7 18	17 28	7 19	17 22	7 32	17 31	7 35	17 41
21	7 04	17 25	7 13	17 35	7 13	17 31	7 16	17 30	7 17	17 24	7 29	17 33	7 33	17 43
22	7 02	17 27	7 11	17 37	7 11	17 33	7 14	17 32	7 14	17 26	7 27	17 35	7 31	17 45
23	6 59	17 29	7 09	17 39	7 08	17 35	7 12	17 34	7 12	17 29	7 24	17 37	7 29	17 47
24	6 57	17 31	7 07	17 41	7 06	17 36	7 09	17 36	7 10	17 31	7 22	17 39	7 26	17 49
25	6 55	17 32	7 05	17 43	7 04	17 38	7 07	17 38	7 07	17 33	7 20	17 42	7 24	17 51
26	6 53	17 34	7 03	17 44	7 02	17 40	7 05	17 40	7 05	17 35	7 17	17 44	7 22	17 53
27	6 51	17 36	7 01	17 46	7 00	17 42	7 03	17 42	7 03	17 37	7 15	17 46	7 19	17 55
28	6 49	17 38	6 59	17 48	6 58	17 44	7 00	17 44	7 00	17 39	7 12	17 48	7 17	17 57
29	6 47	17 40	6 57	17 50	6 55	17 46	6 58	17 46	6 58	17 41	7 10	17 50	7 15	17 59

JUPITER

Day	R.A. h m	Dec °	Mag.	Diam. "	Rise h m	Transit h m	Set h m
1	11 33.2	+4.4	−2.4	43	20 20	2 50	9 17
11	11 30.1	+4.8	−2.4	43	19 35	2 08	8 37
21	11 26.1	+5.2	−2.5	44	18 49	1 24	7 56

Equatorial Diam. 44″, Polar Diam. 41″

SATURN

Day	R.A. h m	Dec °	Mag.	Diam. "	Rise h m	Transit h m	Set h m
1	16 51.0	−20.8	+0.6	16	4 09	8 07	12 05
11	16 54.2	−20.9	+0.5	16	3 33	7 31	11 29
21	16 56.8	−20.9	+0.5	16	2 57	6 54	10 52

Equatorial Diam. 16″, Polar Diam. 15″
Rings – major axis 36″ minor axis 16″, Tilt 26°

URANUS

Day	R.A. h m	Dec °	Mag.	Diam. "	Rise h m	Transit h m	Set h m
1	1 03.3	+6.1	+6.2	3	9 42	16 18	22 55
11	1 04.6	+6.2	+6.2	3	9 03	15 40	22 17
21	2 06.1	+6.4	+6.2	3	8 24	15 02	21 40

NEPTUNE

Day	R.A. h m	Dec °	Mag.	Diam. "	Rise h m	Transit h m	Set h m
1	22 40.8	−9.2	+8.0	2	8 44	13 56	19 07
11	22 42.1	−9.1	+8.0	2	8 06	13 18	18 30
21	22 43.5	−8.9	+8.0	2	7 27	12 40	17 53

MARCH 2016

THIRD MONTH, 31 DAYS. *Mars*, Roman god of battle

1	Tuesday	The Syrian regional Ba'ath party takes power in Syria following a coup d'état 1966	day 61
2	Wednesday	Ho Chi Minh is elected as the first president of Vietnam 1945	62
3	Thursday	The Statute of Rhuddlan introduces the English common law system to Wales 1234	63
4	Friday	In Frankfurt, Frederick Barbarossa (Frederick I) is elected King of Germany 1152	64
5	Saturday	Winston Churchill gives his 'Iron Curtain' speech, condemning the Soviet Union's policy 1946	65
6	Sunday	Ghana became the first black African country to gain independence from Britain 1957	66
7	Monday	In a referendum 98 per cent of Moldovans voted to remain an independent nation 1994	week 10 day 67
8	Tuesday	William Taft, the 27th president, and later, tenth chief justice of the USA d. 1930	68
9	Wednesday	Northern Ireland votes to remain part of the UK in the sovereignty referendum 1973	69
10	Thursday	The 1959 11-day Tibetan uprising against Chinese occupation, begins	70
11	Friday	Sho Tai, the last king of the Ryukyu Kingdom, abdicates the throne 1879	71
12	Saturday	The *Anschluss* begins when Nazi troops march into Austria 1938	72
13	Sunday	Charles Grey, prime minister, whose government abolished slavery in the British Empire b. 1764	73
14	Monday	Gerry Adams, president of Sinn Fein, is injured in an assassination attempt 1984	week 11 day 74
15	Tuesday	Julius Caesar, dictator of the Roman Republic, is assassinated on the Ides of March 44 BC	75
16	Wednesday	Harold Wilson resigns as prime minister and leader of the Labour Party 1976	76
17	Thursday	Parliament abolishes the monarchy in England after the execution of Charles I 1649	77
18	Friday	The Paris Commune is established after the end of Franco–Prussian War 1871	78
19	Saturday	Egon Krenz, the last Communist leader of East Germany b. 1937	79
20	Sunday	Namibia becomes independent of South Africa after 75 years of occupation 1990	80
21	Monday	Otto von Bismarck is appointed as the first chancellor of the German Empire 1871	week 12 day 81
22	Tuesday	The Arab League is founded in Cairo with six members 1945	82
23	Wednesday	The Labour government of James Callaghan survives a vote of no confidence 1977	83
24	Thursday	Death of Harun al-Rashid, caliph of the Abbasid empire AD 809	84
25	Friday	The Slave Trade Act, abolishing the slave trade in the British Empire, receives royal assent 1807	85
26	Saturday	The Social Democrat Party (SDP), which later merged with the Liberal Party, is founded 1981	86
27	Sunday	Jiang Zemin is appointed as the fifth president of the People's Republic of China 1993	87
28	Monday	James Callaghan's Labour government loses a parliamentary vote of no confidence 1979	week 13 day 88
29	Tuesday	The 14th Earl of Derby, prime minister and longest-serving Conservative Party leader b. 1799	89
30	Wednesday	Airey Neave, the shadow Northern Ireland secretary, is killed by a car bomb 1979	90
31	Thursday	A snap general election in 1966 returns Harold Wilson's Labour government with a majority of 96	91

ASTRONOMICAL PHENOMENA

d h
2 07 Saturn 4° South of the Moon
7 11 Venus 4° South of the Moon
8 05 Mercury 4° South of the Moon
8 11 Jupiter at opposition
9 02 Total eclipse of the Sun
11 01 Uranus 2° North of the Moon
20 04 Equinox
22 04 Jupiter 2° North of the Moon
23 12 Penumbral eclipse of the Moon
28 19 Mars 4° South of the Moon
29 15 Saturn 4° South of the Moon

MINIMA OF ALGOL

d	h	d	h	d	h
1	17.2	13	04.5	24	15.8
4	14.0	16	01.3	27	12.6
7	10.8	18	22.1	30	09.4
10	07.7	21	19.0		

CONSTELLATIONS

The following constellations are near the meridian at

	d	h		d	h
February	1	24	March	16	21
February	15	23	April	1	20
March	1	22	April	15	19

Cepheus (below the Pole), Camelopardalis, Lynx, Gemini, Cancer, Leo, Canis Minor, Hydra, Monoceros, Canis Major and Puppis

THE MOON

Phases, Apsides and Node		d	h	m
◗	Last Quarter	1	23	11
●	New Moon	9	01	54
◐	First Quarter	15	17	03
○	Full Moon	23	12	01
◗	Last Quarter	31	15	17

	d	h	m
Perigee (359,510km)	10	07	04
Apogee (406,125km)	25	14	17

Mean longitude of ascending node on 1st, 172°

THE SUN

Diam. 32.2″

Day	Right Ascension			Dec.	Equation of time		Rise		Transit	Set				Sidereal time			Transit of first point of Aries		
							52°	56°		52°		56°							
	h	m	s	°	m	s	h m	h m	h m	h	m	h	m	h	m	s	h	m	s
1	22	49	16	−7.5	−12	21	6 45	6 51	12 12	17	40	17	35	10	36	55	13	23	05
2	22	53	01	−7.1	−12	09	6 43	6 48	12 12	17	42	17	37	10	40	52	13	19	08
3	22	56	45	−6.7	−11	57	6 41	6 45	12 12	17	44	17	39	10	44	48	13	15	12
4	23	00	28	−6.4	−11	44	6 38	6 43	12 12	17	46	17	41	10	48	45	13	11	15
5	23	04	12	−6.0	−11	30	6 36	6 40	12 11	17	48	17	43	10	52	41	13	07	19
6	23	07	55	−5.6	−11	17	6 34	6 38	12 11	17	49	17	46	10	56	38	13	03	22
7	23	11	37	−5.2	−11	03	6 32	6 35	12 11	17	51	17	48	11	00	34	12	59	26
8	23	15	19	−4.8	−10	48	6 29	6 33	12 11	17	53	17	50	11	04	31	12	55	29
9	23	19	01	−4.4	−10	33	6 27	6 30	12 10	17	55	17	52	11	08	28	12	51	32
10	23	22	42	−4.0	−10	18	6 25	6 28	12 10	17	56	17	54	11	12	24	12	47	36
11	23	26	23	−3.6	−10	03	6 23	6 25	12 10	17	58	17	56	11	16	21	12	43	39
12	23	30	04	−3.2	−9	47	6 20	6 22	12 10	18	00	17	58	11	20	17	12	39	43
13	23	33	44	−2.8	−9	31	6 18	6 20	12 09	18	02	18	00	11	24	14	12	35	46
14	23	37	24	−2.4	−9	14	6 16	6 17	12 09	18	03	18	02	11	28	10	12	31	50
15	23	41	04	−2.0	−8	57	6 13	6 14	12 09	18	05	18	04	11	32	07	12	27	53
16	23	44	44	−1.7	−8	40	6 11	6 12	12 09	18	07	18	06	11	36	03	12	23	57
17	23	48	23	−1.3	−8	23	6 09	6 09	12 08	18	09	18	08	11	40	00	12	20	00
18	23	52	02	−0.9	−8	06	6 07	6 07	12 08	18	10	18	10	11	43	57	12	16	03
19	23	55	41	−0.5	−7	48	6 04	6 04	12 08	18	12	18	13	11	47	53	12	12	07
20	23	59	20	−0.1	−7	31	6 02	6 01	12 07	18	14	18	15	11	51	50	12	08	10
21	0	02	59	+0.3	−7	13	6 00	5 59	12 07	18	16	18	17	11	55	46	12	04	14
22	0	06	37	+0.7	−6	55	5 57	5 56	12 07	18	18	18	19	11	59	43	12	00	17
23	0	10	16	+1.1	−6	37	5 55	5 53	12 06	18	19	18	21	12	03	39	11	56	21
24	0	13	54	+1.5	−6	19	5 53	5 51	12 06	18	21	18	23	12	07	36	11	52	24
25	0	17	33	+1.9	−6	00	5 50	5 48	12 06	18	22	18	25	12	11	32	11	48	28
26	0	21	11	+2.3	−5	42	5 48	5 45	12 06	18	24	18	27	12	15	29	11	44	31
27	0	24	49	+2.7	−5	24	5 46	5 43	12 05	18	26	18	29	12	19	26	11	40	34
28	0	28	28	+3.1	−5	06	5 43	5 40	12 05	18	28	18	31	12	23	22	11	36	38
29	0	32	06	+3.5	−4	48	5 41	5 38	12 05	18	29	18	33	12	27	19	11	32	41
30	0	35	45	+3.9	−4	30	5 39	5 35	12 04	18	31	18	35	12	31	15	11	28	45
31	0	39	23	+4.2	−4	12	5 36	5 32	12 04	18	33	18	37	12	35	12	11	24	48

DURATION OF TWILIGHT (in minutes)

Latitude	52°	56°	52°	56°	52°	56°	52°	56°
	1 March		11 March		21 March		31 March	
Civil	34	37	34	37	34	37	34	38
Nautical	73	80	73	80	74	81	75	84
Astronomical	112	124	113	125	115	128	120	135

THE NIGHT SKY

Mercury is not visible this month.

Venus is now a very difficult object and can be considered lost to view for the casual observer. It remains poorly placed to be seen easily until mid-August when it returns to the evening sky.

Mars crosses from Libra into Scorpius on March 13th and rises not long after midnight. It surges in brightness during February to magnitude −0.5. The Moon is close by on the 1st but a little more distant when in the area again on the 29th.

Jupiter, magnitude −2.5, reaches opposition on March 8th in eastern Leo and is visible all night. The Moon is just one day from full when near Jupiter on March 22nd.

Saturn is a morning object in Ophiuchus where it reaches its first stationary point on the 25th and then begins to retrograde. Saturn is 3° from the Moon on the 2nd and forms a wide group with it and Mars on the 29th.

A total solar eclipse on March 9th passes over Sumatra, Borneo, Sulawesi, and a narrow span of the Pacific Ocean. Australia, eastern Asia, and Pacific regions, including Hawaii, will experience a partial eclipse.

A penumbral lunar eclipse on March 23rd is visible from the Americas, Asia, and Australia. The Moon clips the northern edge of the Earth's penumbral shadow so some subtle shading of the Moon's southern hemisphere may be noticed.

THE MOON

Day	R.A. h	R.A. m	Dec. °	Hor. Par. ′	Diam. ′	Sun's Co-Long. °	PA of Br. Limb °	Ph. %	Age d	Rise 52° h	Rise 52° m	Rise 56° h	Rise 56° m	Transit h	Transit m	Set 52° h	Set 52° m	Set 56° h	Set 56° m
1	15	56	−15.3	54.7	29.8	174	101	60	21.6	0	43	0	57	5	29	10	11	9	56
2	16	46	−17.1	55.2	30.1	186	97	50	22.6	1	42	1	58	6	17	10	50	10	33
3	17	38	−18.0	55.9	30.5	199	93	40	23.6	2	38	2	55	7	08	11	36	11	19
4	18	31	−18.1	56.7	30.9	211	89	30	24.6	3	30	3	47	8	00	12	31	12	14
5	19	27	−17.3	57.6	31.4	223	85	21	25.6	4	16	4	32	8	53	13	35	13	19
6	20	23	−15.4	58.6	31.9	235	81	13	26.6	4	57	5	11	9	48	14	46	14	33
7	21	20	−12.5	59.5	32.4	247	78	6	27.6	5	34	5	44	10	43	16	02	15	53
8	22	17	−8.8	60.2	32.8	260	75	2	28.6	6	07	6	13	11	38	17	21	17	16
9	23	14	−4.5	60.7	33.1	272	86	0	0.1	6	37	6	40	12	34	18	43	18	42
10	0	12	+0.1	61.0	33.2	284	251	1	1.1	7	07	7	06	13	29	20	05	20	08
11	1	09	+4.8	60.9	33.2	296	252	5	2.1	7	37	7	32	14	25	21	26	21	34
12	2	07	+9.1	60.6	33.0	308	254	12	3.1	8	10	8	01	15	21	22	45	22	56
13	3	05	+12.8	60.0	32.7	321	257	21	4.1	8	45	8	33	16	17	23	58	—	
14	4	03	+15.6	59.3	32.3	333	261	31	5.1	9	26	9	11	17	13	—		0	14
15	5	01	+17.4	58.6	31.9	345	265	42	6.1	10	13	9	56	18	09	1	06	1	24
16	5	58	+18.2	57.8	31.5	357	269	53	7.1	11	06	10	48	19	03	2	06	2	25
17	6	54	+17.9	57.0	31.1	9	274	64	8.1	12	04	11	47	19	55	2	57	3	15
18	7	48	+16.7	56.4	30.7	21	278	73	9.1	13	06	12	51	20	45	3	40	3	55
19	8	40	+14.6	55.8	30.4	34	282	82	10.1	14	10	13	58	21	33	4	16	4	29
20	9	30	+11.9	55.3	30.1	46	285	89	11.1	15	14	15	05	22	19	4	47	4	56
21	10	18	+8.7	54.9	29.9	58	288	94	12.1	16	19	16	13	23	04	5	14	5	20
22	11	05	+5.2	54.6	29.7	70	291	98	13.1	17	23	17	20	23	47	5	38	5	41
23	11	51	+1.5	54.3	29.6	82	299	100	14.1	18	26	18	27	—		6	01	6	01
24	12	36	−2.2	54.1	29.5	94	97	100	15.1	19	29	19	34	0	30	6	23	6	21
25	13	22	−5.8	54.0	29.4	107	103	98	16.1	20	32	20	39	1	12	6	47	6	41
26	14	07	−9.2	54.0	29.4	119	103	95	17.1	21	34	21	44	1	55	7	11	7	03
27	14	54	−12.2	54.1	29.5	131	101	89	18.1	22	34	22	48	2	39	7	39	7	27
28	15	42	−14.8	54.3	29.6	143	99	83	19.1	23	34	23	49	3	25	8	10	7	56
29	16	31	−16.7	54.7	29.8	155	96	75	20.1	—		—		4	12	8	47	8	30
30	17	22	−17.9	55.2	30.1	167	92	66	21.1	0	30	0	47	5	00	9	29	9	12
31	18	14	−18.2	55.8	30.4	180	88	57	22.1	1	22	1	40	5	50	10	20	10	03

MERCURY

Day	R.A. h	R.A. m	Dec °	Mag.	Diam. ″	Phase %	Rise h m	Transit h m	Set h m
1	21	42.6	−15.8	−0.3	5	87	6 33	11 05	15 39
3	21	55.2	−14.9	−0.4	5	88	6 31	11 10	15 50
5	22	07.8	−13.8	−0.5	5	90	6 29	11 15	16 01
7	22	20.7	−12.7	−0.5	5	91	6 27	11 20	16 13
9	22	33.6	−11.4	−0.6	5	93	6 25	11 25	16 26
11	22	46.7	−10.1	−0.8	5	94	6 22	11 30	16 39
13	22	59.9	−8.7	−0.9	5	95	6 20	11 36	16 53
15	23	13.3	−7.2	−1.0	5	97	6 17	11 41	17 07
17	23	26.8	−5.7	−1.2	5	98	6 14	11 47	17 21
19	23	40.6	−4.1	−1.4	5	99	6 10	11 53	17 37
21	23	54.5	−2.4	−1.6	5	99	6 07	11 59	17 52
23	0	08.6	−0.6	−1.8	5	100	6 04	12 05	18 08
25	0	22.8	+1.2	−1.9	5	100	6 00	12 12	18 25
27	0	37.3	+3.1	−1.8	5	99	5 56	12 18	18 42
29	0	51.9	+5.0	−1.7	5	98	5 52	12 25	18 59
31	1	06.5	+6.9	−1.6	5	96	5 48	12 32	19 17

Rising and setting times are for latitude 54°

VENUS

Day	R.A. h	R.A. m	Dec °	Mag.	Diam. ″	Phase %	Rise h m	Transit h m	Set h m
1	21	13.2	−16.8	−4.5	12	91	6 09	10 36	15 02
6	21	37.9	−15.0	−4.4	12	92	6 03	10 41	15 19
11	22	02.2	−13.1	−4.3	12	93	5 56	10 45	15 35
16	22	26.0	−11.1	−4.3	12	93	5 48	10 49	15 51
21	22	49.5	−8.9	−4.3	11	94	5 39	10 53	16 08
26	23	12.7	−6.6	−4.2	11	95	5 29	10 57	16 24
31	23	35.6	−4.2	−4.2	11	95	5 19	11 00	16 41

MARS

Day	R.A. h	R.A. m	Dec °	Mag.	Diam. ″	Phase %	Rise h m	Transit h m	Set h m
1	15	43.5	−18.4	+0.3	9	90	0 51	5 06	9 21
6	15	51.3	−18.8	+0.2	9	90	0 42	4 54	9 06
11	15	58.6	−19.3	0.0	10	91	0 33	4 42	8 51
16	16	05.3	−19.6	−0.1	10	91	0 22	4 29	8 36
21	16	11.4	−20.0	−0.2	11	91	0 11	4 15	8 20
26	16	16.6	−20.3	−0.4	11	92	23 59	4 01	8 03
31	16	21.0	−20.6	−0.5	12	93	23 46	3 46	7 46

SUNRISE AND SUNSET

	London 0° 05'	51° 30'	Bristol 2° 35'	51° 28'	Birmingham 1° 55'	52° 28'	Manchester 2° 15'	53° 28'	Newcastle 1° 37'	54° 59'	Glasgow 4° 14'	55° 52'	Belfast 5° 56'	54° 35'
d	h m	h m	h m	h m	h m	h m	h m	h m	h m	h m	h m	h m	h m	h m
1	6 45	17 41	6 55	17 51	6 53	17 47	6 56	17 48	6 55	17 43	7 07	17 52	7 12	18 01
2	6 43	17 43	6 53	17 53	6 51	17 49	6 54	17 49	6 53	17 45	7 05	17 54	7 10	18 03
3	6 40	17 45	6 50	17 55	6 49	17 51	6 51	17 51	6 51	17 47	7 02	17 56	7 07	18 05
4	6 38	17 47	6 48	17 57	6 47	17 53	6 49	17 53	6 48	17 49	7 00	17 58	7 05	18 07
5	6 36	17 48	6 46	17 58	6 44	17 55	6 47	17 55	6 46	17 51	6 57	18 01	7 02	18 09
6	6 34	17 50	6 44	18 00	6 42	17 57	6 44	17 57	6 43	17 53	6 55	18 03	7 00	18 11
7	6 32	17 52	6 42	18 02	6 40	17 58	6 42	17 59	6 41	17 55	6 52	18 05	6 58	18 13
8	6 29	17 54	6 39	18 04	6 37	18 00	6 40	18 01	6 38	17 57	6 49	18 07	6 55	18 15
9	6 27	17 55	6 37	18 05	6 35	18 02	6 37	18 03	6 36	17 59	6 47	18 09	6 53	18 17
10	6 25	17 57	6 35	18 07	6 33	18 04	6 35	18 05	6 33	18 01	6 44	18 11	6 50	18 19
11	6 23	17 59	6 33	18 09	6 31	18 06	6 32	18 06	6 31	18 03	6 42	18 13	6 48	18 21
12	6 20	18 00	6 30	18 10	6 28	18 07	6 30	18 08	6 28	18 05	6 39	18 15	6 45	18 23
13	6 18	18 02	6 28	18 12	6 26	18 09	6 28	18 10	6 26	18 07	6 37	18 17	6 43	18 24
14	6 16	18 04	6 26	18 14	6 24	18 11	6 25	18 12	6 23	18 09	6 34	18 19	6 40	18 26
15	6 14	18 06	6 24	18 16	6 21	18 13	6 23	18 14	6 21	18 11	6 31	18 21	6 38	18 28
16	6 11	18 07	6 21	18 17	6 19	18 15	6 20	18 16	6 18	18 13	6 29	18 23	6 35	18 30
17	6 09	18 09	6 19	18 19	6 17	18 16	6 18	18 18	6 16	18 15	6 26	18 25	6 33	18 32
18	6 07	18 11	6 17	18 21	6 14	18 18	6 16	18 19	6 13	18 17	6 23	18 27	6 30	18 34
19	6 05	18 12	6 15	18 22	6 12	18 20	6 13	18 21	6 10	18 19	6 21	18 29	6 28	18 36
20	6 02	18 14	6 12	18 24	6 09	18 22	6 11	18 23	6 08	18 21	6 18	18 32	6 25	18 38
21	6 00	18 16	6 10	18 26	6 07	18 23	6 08	18 25	6 05	18 23	6 16	18 34	6 23	13 40
22	5 58	18 17	6 08	18 27	6 05	18 25	6 06	18 27	6 03	18 25	6 13	18 36	6 20	18 42
23	5 55	18 19	6 05	18 29	6 02	18 27	6 03	18 29	6 00	18 27	6 10	18 38	6 18	18 44
24	5 53	18 21	6 03	18 31	6 00	18 29	6 01	18 30	5 58	18 29	6 08	18 40	6 15	18 46
25	5 51	18 22	6 01	18 33	5 58	18 30	5 59	18 32	5 55	18 31	6 05	18 42	6 13	18 48
26	5 49	18 24	5 59	18 34	5 55	18 32	5 56	18 34	5 53	18 33	6 02	18 44	6 10	18 50
27	5 46	18 26	5 56	18 36	5 53	18 34	5 54	18 36	5 50	18 35	6 00	18 46	6 08	18 52
28	5 44	18 28	5 54	18 38	5 51	18 36	5 51	18 38	5 48	18 36	5 57	18 48	6 05	18 53
29	5 42	18 29	5 52	18 39	5 48	18 37	5 49	18 40	5 45	18 38	5 55	18 50	6 03	18 55
30	5 40	18 31	5 50	18 41	5 46	18 39	5 46	18 41	5 42	18 40	5 52	18 52	6 00	18 57
31	5 37	18 33	5 47	18 43	5 44	18 41	5 44	18 43	5 40	18 42	5 49	18 54	5 58	18 59

JUPITER

Day	R.A. h m	Dec °	Mag.	Diam. "	Rise h m	Transit h m	Set h m
1	11 22.0	+5.7	−2.5	44	18 07	0 45	7 19
11	11 17.2	+6.2	−2.5	44	17 20	0 01	6 38
21	11 12.5	+6.7	−2.5	44	16 33	23 13	5 57
31	11 08.2	+7.1	−2.4	44	15 47	22 30	5 16

Equatorial Diam. 44″, Polar Diam. 41″

SATURN

Day	R.A. h m	Dec °	Mag.	Diam. "	Rise h m	Transit h m	Set h m
1	16 58.6	−21.0	+0.5	17	2 24	6 21	10 18
11	17 00.0	−21.0	+0.5	17	1 46	5 43	9 40
21	17 00.7	−21.0	+0.4	17	1 07	5 04	9 01
31	17 00.6	−21.0	+0.4	17	0 28	4 25	8 22

Equatorial Diam. 17″, Polar Diam. 15″
Rings – major axis 38″ minor axis 17″, Tilt 26°

URANUS

Day	R.A. h m	Dec °	Mag.	Diam. "	Rise h m	Transit h m	Set h m
1	1 07.6	+6.5	+6.2	3	7 49	14 28	21 07
11	1 09.4	+6.7	+6.2	3	7 11	13 51	20 31
21	1 11.4	+6.9	+6.2	3	6 32	13 14	19 55
31	1 13.5	+7.1	+6.2	3	5 54	12 36	19 19

NEPTUNE

Day	R.A. h m	Dec °	Mag.	Diam. "	Rise h m	Transit h m	Set h m
1	22 44.8	−8.8	+8.0	2	6 52	12 06	17 20
11	22 46.2	−8.7	+8.0	2	6 13	11 23	16 43
21	22 47.6	−8.5	+8.0	2	5 35	10 50	16 05
31	22 48.9	−8.4	+8.0	2	4 56	10 12	15 28

 ♈  ♉

APRIL 2016

FOURTH MONTH, 30 DAYS. *Aperire*, to open; Earth opens to receive seed.

1	*Friday*	Slobodan Milosevic, former president of Yugoslavia, is arrested for war crimes 2001	day 92
2	*Saturday*	Georges Pompidou, prime minister and later president of France *d.* 1974	93
3	*Sunday*	Edward II (the Confessor), is crowned at Winchester Cathedral 1043	94
4	*Monday*	Martin Luther King, Jr, American civil rights activist, is assassinated in Memphis 1968	week 14 day 95
5	*Tuesday*	Winston Churchill resigns as prime minister citing poor health 1955	96
6	*Wednesday*	The presidents of Burundi and Rwanda die when their plane is shot down 1994	97
7	*Thursday*	John Stonehouse, MP, resigns the Labour whip, leaving the government in a minority 1976	98
8	*Friday*	Jomo Kenyatta is sentenced to hard labour after the Mau Mau rebellion in Kenya 1953	99
9	*Saturday*	The Conservatives win the 1992 general election despite Labour being ahead in the polls	100
10	*Sunday*	Bobby Sands was elected as the MP for Fermanagh and South Tyrone 1981	101
11	*Monday*	William III and Mary II are crowned joint sovereigns of Britain at Westminster Abbey 1689	week 15 day 102
12	*Tuesday*	Seneca the Younger, Roman stoic philosopher and statesman, commits suicide AD 65	103
13	*Wednesday*	The Roman Catholic Relief Act, allowing catholics to sit in parliament, receives royal assent 1829	104
14	*Thursday*	US president Abraham Lincoln, is fatally shot at Ford's Theatre, Washington 1865	105
15	*Friday*	Pol Pot, Cambodian communist dictator who led the Khmer Rouge *d.* 1998	106
16	*Saturday*	Conservative MP Harvey Proctor is accused of committing four acts of gross indecency 1987	107
17	*Sunday*	Bernadette Devlin, aged 21, becomes Britain's youngest ever female MP 1969	108
18	*Monday*	Michael D. Higgins, president of Ireland who made the first state visit to the UK *b.* 1941	week 16 day 109
19	*Tuesday*	William Wilberforce's first bill to abolish the slave trade is defeated by 163 votes to 88 1791	110
20	*Wednesday*	Conservative minister Enoch Powell delivers his controversial 'Rivers of Blood' speech 1968	111
21	*Thursday*	The Haitian Revolution against slavery, which establishes the Republic of Haiti, begins 1791	112
22	*Friday*	François 'Papa Doc' Duvalier, president of Haiti, dies after 14 years in office 1971	113
23	*Saturday*	Charles II, son of the executed Charles I, is crowned at Westminster Abbey 1661	114
24	*Sunday*	Philippe Pétain, Chief of State of Vichy France (1940–4) who was convicted of treason *b.* 1856	115
25	*Monday*	Oliver Cromwell, MP, military leader and Lord Protector of the Commonwealth *b.* 1599	week 17 day 116
26	*Tuesday*	Paul von Hindenburg becomes the first directly elected president of the Weimar Republic 1925	117
27	*Wednesday*	Betty Boothroyd becomes the first female Speaker of the House of Commons 1992	118
28	*Thursday*	António Salazar, prime minister of Portugal (1932–68) *b.* 1889	119
29	*Friday*	The Easter Rising in Dublin by Irish Republicans against British rule, is suppressed 1916	120
30	*Saturday*	Adolf Hitler and his wife Eva Braun commit suicide in the Führerbunker, Berlin 1945	121

ASTRONOMICAL PHENOMENA

d h
7 14 Uranus 2° North of the Moon
8 08 Moon occults Venus (Sun nearby, so view with great care)
18 14 Mercury Greatest elongation East
18 05 Jupiter 2° North of the Moon
25 04 Mars 5° South of the Moon
25 19 Saturn 3° South of the Moon

MINIMA OF ALGOL

d	*h*	*d*	*h*	*d*	*h*
2	06.2	13	17.5	25	04.8
5	03.1	16	14.3	28	01.6
7	23.9	19	11.2	30	22.4
10	20.7	22	08.0		

CONSTELLATIONS

The following constellations are near the meridian at

	d	*h*		*d*	*h*
March	1	24	April	15	21
March	16	23	May	1	20
April	1	22	May	16	19

Cepheus (below the Pole), Cassiopeia (below the Pole), Ursa Major, Leo Minor, Leo., Sextans, Hydra and Crater

THE MOON

Phases, Apsides and Node	*d*	*h*	*m*
● New Moon	7	11	24
◑ First Quarter	14	03	59
○ Full Moon	22	05	24
◐ Last Quarter	30	03	29

Perigee (357,163km)	7	17	36
Apogee (406,351km)	21	16	05

Mean longitude of ascending node on 1st, 171°

THE SUN

Diam. 31.9″

Day	Right Ascension			Dec. +	Equation of time		Rise 52°		Rise 56°		Transit		Set 52°		Set 56°		Sidereal time			Transit of first point of Aries		
	h	m	s	°	m	s	h	m	h	m	h	m	h	m	h	m	h	m	s	h	m	s
1	0	42	53	4.6	−3	54	5	36	5	32	12	04	18	33	18	37	11	38	59	11	20	52
2	0	46	32	5.0	−3	37	5	34	5	30	12	04	18	34	18	39	11	42	55	11	16	55
3	0	50	11	5.4	−3	19	5	32	5	27	12	03	18	36	18	41	11	46	52	11	12	59
4	0	53	50	5.8	−3	02	5	30	5	24	12	03	18	38	18	43	11	50	48	11	09	02
5	0	57	29	6.1	−2	44	5	27	5	22	12	03	18	40	18	45	11	54	45	11	05	05
6	1	01	09	6.5	−2	27	5	25	5	19	12	03	18	41	18	47	11	58	41	11	01	09
7	1	04	48	6.9	−2	11	5	23	5	17	12	02	18	43	18	49	12	02	38	10	57	12
8	1	08	28	7.3	−1	54	5	20	5	14	12	02	18	45	18	51	12	06	34	10	53	16
9	1	12	08	7.6	−1	38	5	18	5	11	12	02	18	46	18	53	12	10	31	10	49	19
10	1	15	49	8.0	−1	22	5	16	5	09	12	01	18	48	18	55	12	14	28	10	45	23
11	1	19	30	8.4	−1	06	5	14	5	06	12	01	18	50	18	57	12	18	24	10	41	26
12	1	23	11	8.7	−0	50	5	11	5	04	12	01	18	52	18	59	12	22	21	10	37	30
13	1	26	52	9.1	−0	35	5	09	5	01	12	01	18	53	19	01	12	26	17	10	33	33
14	1	30	33	9.5	−0	20	5	07	4	59	12	00	18	55	19	04	12	30	14	10	29	36
15	1	34	15	9.8	−0	05	5	05	4	56	12	00	18	57	19	06	12	34	10	10	25	40
16	1	37	57	10.2	+0	09	5	03	4	54	12	00	18	58	19	08	12	38	07	10	21	43
17	1	41	40	10.5	+0	23	5	00	4	51	12	00	19	00	19	10	12	42	03	10	17	47
18	1	45	23	10.9	+0	37	4	58	4	49	11	59	19	02	19	12	12	46	00	10	13	50
19	1	49	06	11.2	+0	50	4	56	4	46	11	59	19	04	19	14	12	49	57	10	09	54
20	1	52	50	11.6	+1	03	4	54	4	44	11	59	19	05	19	16	12	53	53	10	05	57
21	1	56	34	11.9	+1	15	4	52	4	41	11	59	19	07	19	18	12	57	50	10	02	01
22	2	00	19	12.3	+1	27	4	50	4	39	11	59	19	09	19	20	13	01	46	9	58	04
23	2	04	04	12.6	+1	39	4	48	4	36	11	58	19	10	19	22	13	05	43	9	54	07
24	2	07	49	12.9	+1	50	4	46	4	34	11	58	19	12	19	24	13	09	39	9	50	11
25	2	11	35	13.2	+2	00	4	44	4	32	11	58	19	14	19	26	13	13	36	9	46	14
26	2	15	22	13.6	+2	10	4	41	4	29	11	58	19	15	19	28	13	17	32	9	42	18
27	2	19	09	13.9	+2	20	4	39	4	27	11	58	19	17	19	30	13	21	29	9	38	21
28	2	22	56	14.2	+2	29	4	37	4	24	11	58	19	19	19	32	13	25	26	9	34	25
29	2	26	44	14.5	+2	38	4	35	4	22	11	57	19	20	19	34	13	29	22	9	30	28
30	2	30	33	14.8	+2	45	4	34	4	20	11	57	19	22	19	36	13	33	19	9	26	32

DURATION OF TWILIGHT (in minutes)

Latitude	52°	56°	52°	56°	52°	56°	52°	56°
	1 April		11 April		21 April		31 April	
Civil	34	38	35	39	37	42	39	44
Nautical	76	84	79	89	83	96	89	106
Astronomical	120	136	127	147	137	165	152	204

THE NIGHT SKY

Mercury leaps out of the evening twilight and reaches greatest elongation east (19.9°) on the 18th. The planet is visible right throughout April in the western sky after sunset but is brightest at the beginning of this apparition. The 32.5-hour-old Moon lies 6° to the left of Mercury on the 8th.

A chance sighting of *Venus* in the dawn sky can be discounted this month as the planet is now rising less than 20 minutes before the Sun.

Mars brightens from magnitude −0.5 to −1.4 and appears above the south-eastern horizon during the late evening by the end of April. It moves into Ophiuchus on the 3rd where it is stationary on the 17th and then starts to retrograde, before returning to Scorpius on the 30th. The bright ember is unmistakable 4° below the Moon when both rise on the evening of April 25th.

Jupiter is high in the south-east after nightfall and currently shines at magnitude −2.4 under the body of Leo.

Saturn is rising only half an hour after Mars all month and lies in the southern part of Ophiuchus. The northern aspect of the rings is currently tipped more than 26° earthward. Saturn is 4° to the lower right of the Moon on April 26th.

THE MOON

Day	R.A. h	R.A. m	Dec. °	Hor. Par. '	Diam. '	Sun's Co-Long. °	PA of Br. Limb °	Ph. %	Age d	Rise 52° h	Rise 52° m	Rise 56° h	Rise 56° m	Transit h	Transit m	Set 52° h	Set 52° m	Set 56° h	Set 56° m
1	19	05	−17.8	56.5	30.8	191	84	47	23.0	1	22	1	40	5	50	10	20	10	03
2	19	59	−16.3	57.4	31.3	204	80	37	24.0	2	09	2	26	6	42	11	18	11	02
3	20	54	−14.0	58.4	31.8	216	76	26	25.0	2	51	3	06	7	34	12	23	12	09
4	21	50	−10.7	59.3	32.3	228	72	17	26.0	3	29	3	40	8	28	13	35	13	24
5	22	46	−6.7	60.2	32.8	240	69	9	27.0	4	02	4	10	9	21	14	51	14	44
6	23	43	−2.2	60.9	33.2	252	66	3	28.0	4	33	4	38	10	16	16	11	16	08
7	0	40	+2.5	61.3	33.4	265	54	0	29.0	5	03	5	04	11	11	17	33	17	34
8	1	39	+7.1	61.4	33.5	277	272	0	0.5	5	33	5	30	12	07	18	56	19	01
9	2	38	+11.3	61.1	33.3	289	262	3	1.5	6	05	5	57	13	04	20	18	20	28
10	3	38	+14.6	60.6	33.0	301	263	9	2.5	6	39	6	28	14	03	21	38	21	51
11	4	38	+16.9	59.8	32.6	313	266	17	3.5	7	19	7	05	15	01	22	51	23	08
12	5	38	+18.1	59.0	32.1	326	271	27	4.5	8	05	7	48	15	59	23	57	—	
13	6	36	+18.2	58.0	31.6	338	275	37	5.5	8	58	8	39	16	56	—		0	15
14	7	32	+17.2	57.1	31.1	350	279	48	6.5	9	56	9	38	17	50	0	53	1	11
15	8	25	+15.4	56.3	30.7	2	283	58	7.5	10	58	10	41	18	42	1	40	1	56
16	9	16	+12.8	55.6	30.3	15	286	68	8.5	12	02	11	48	19	31	2	19	2	33
17	10	05	+9.7	55.1	30.0	27	289	77	9.5	13	06	12	57	20	18	2	51	3	01
18	10	52	+6.3	54.6	29.8	39	292	84	10.5	14	11	14	04	21	02	3	19	3	26
19	11	38	+2.6	54.3	29.6	51	294	91	11.5	15	15	15	11	21	46	3	43	3	48
20	12	23	−1.1	54.1	29.5	63	296	95	12.5	16	18	16	18	22	28	4	06	4	08
21	13	08	−4.8	54.0	29.4	75	302	99	13.5	17	21	17	24	23	11	4	29	4	27
22	13	54	−8.3	54.0	29.4	88	338	100	14.5	18	24	18	30	23	53	4	51	4	46
23	14	40	−11.4	54.0	29.4	100	82	100	15.5	19	26	19	36	—		5	15	5	08
24	15	28	−14.1	54.2	29.5	112	91	97	16.5	20	28	20	40	0	37	5	41	5	31
25	16	16	−16.3	54.4	29.7	124	92	93	17.5	21	28	21	43	1	22	6	12	5	58
26	17	07	−17.7	54.8	29.9	136	89	88	18.5	22	25	22	42	2	09	6	46	6	30
27	17	58	−18.4	55.2	30.1	148	86	81	19.5	23	18	23	37	2	57	7	26	7	09
28	18	50	−18.1	55.8	30.4	161	83	72	20.5	—		—		3	46	8	14	7	56
29	19	43	−17.0	56.5	30.8	173	79	63	21.5	0	06	0	25	4	36	9	08	8	51
30	20	37	−15.0	57.2	31.2	185	75	52	22.5	0	50	1	05	5	27	10	10	9	54

MERCURY

Day	R.A. h	R.A. m	Dec °	Mag.	Diam. "	Phase %	Rise h m	Transit h m	Set h m
1	1	13.5	+7.8	−1.5	5	94	5 46	12 35	19 25
3	1	28.1	+9.6	−1.4	5	90	5 42	12 41	19 42
5	1	42.4	+11.4	−1.3	6	86	5 38	12 48	19 59
7	1	56.3	+13.1	−1.1	6	80	5 34	12 53	20 15
9	2	09.7	+14.7	−0.9	6	73	5 29	12 59	20 30
11	2	22.3	+16.1	−0.8	6	66	5 25	13 03	20 43
13	2	34.0	+17.4	−0.5	7	59	5 20	13 06	20 54
15	2	44.7	+18.5	−0.3	7	51	5 15	13 09	21 03
17	2	54.1	+19.4	0.0	7	44	5 11	13 10	21 09
19	3	02.3	+20.1	+0.3	8	38	5 06	13 09	21 13
21	3	09.1	+20.6	+0.6	8	31	5 01	13 08	21 15
23	3	14.4	+21.0	+0.9	9	25	4 55	13 05	21 13
25	3	18.2	+21.2	+1.3	9	20	4 50	13 00	21 09
27	3	20.5	+21.1	+1.8	10	15	4 45	12 54	21 01
29	3	21.4	+20.9	+2.3	10	11	4 39	12 46	20 51

Rising and setting times are for latitude 54°

VENUS

Day	R.A. h	R.A. m	Dec °	Mag.	Diam. "	Phase %	Rise h m	Transit h m	Set h m
1	23	40.0	−3.8	−4.2	11	96	5 17	11 00	16 44
6	0	02.7	−1.3	−4.1	11	96	5 07	11 03	17 00
11	0	25.4	+1.1	−4.1	11	97	4 56	11 06	17 17
16	0	48.1	+3.6	−4.1	11	97	4 46	11 09	17 33
21	1	10.8	+6.0	−4.0	11	98	4 35	11 12	17 50
26	1	33.8	+8.3	−4.0	11	98	4 25	11 15	18 07

MARS

Day	R.A. h	R.A. m	Dec °	Mag.	Diam. "	Phase %	Rise h m	Transit h m	Set h m
1	16	21.8	−20.6	−0.5	12	93	23 43	3 43	7 42
6	16	25.0	−20.9	−0.7	12	93	23 29	3 26	7 24
11	16	27.1	−21.1	−0.8	13	94	23 13	3 09	7 05
16	16	28.0	−21.3	−1.0	14	95	22 56	2 50	6 45
21	16	27.7	−21.4	−1.2	15	96	22 38	2 30	6 24
26	16	26.0	−21.6	−1.3	15	97	22 18	2 09	6 02

SUNRISE AND SUNSET

	London 0° 05' 51° 30'		Bristol 2° 35' 51° 28'		Birmingham 1° 55' 52° 28'		Manchester 2° 15' 53° 28'		Newcastle 1° 37' 54° 59'		Glasgow 4° 14' 55° 52'		Belfast 5° 56' 54° 35'	
d	h m	h m	h m	h m	h m	h m	h m	h m	h m	h m	h m	h m	h m	h m
1	5 35	18 34	5 45	18 44	5 41	18 43	5 42	18 45	5 37	18 44	5 47	18 56	5 55	19 01
2	5 33	18 36	5 43	18 46	5 39	18 44	5 39	18 47	5 35	18 46	5 44	18 58	5 53	19 03
3	5 30	18 38	5 40	18 48	5 37	18 46	5 37	18 49	5 32	18 48	5 42	19 00	5 50	19 05
4	5 28	18 39	5 38	18 49	5 34	18 48	5 34	18 51	5 30	18 50	5 39	19 02	5 48	19 07
5	5 26	18 41	5 36	18 51	5 32	18 50	5 32	18 52	5 27	18 52	5 36	19 04	5 45	19 09
6	5 24	18 43	5 34	18 53	5 30	18 51	5 30	18 54	5 25	18 54	5 34	19 06	5 43	19 11
7	5 21	18 44	5 32	18 54	5 27	18 53	5 27	18 56	5 22	18 56	5 31	19 08	5 40	19 13
8	5 19	18 46	5 29	18 56	5 25	18 55	5 25	18 58	5 20	18 58	5 29	19 10	5 38	19 14
9	5 17	18 48	5 27	18 58	5 23	18 57	5 23	19 00	5 17	19 00	5 26	19 12	5 35	19 16
10	5 15	18 49	5 25	18 59	5 21	18 58	5 20	19 01	5 15	19 02	5 24	19 14	5 33	19 18
11	5 13	18 51	5 23	19 01	5 18	19 00	5 18	19 03	5 12	19 04	5 21	19 16	5 30	19 20
12	5 10	18 53	5 21	19 03	5 16	19 02	5 15	19 05	5 10	19 06	5 18	19 18	5 28	19 22
13	5 08	18 54	5 18	19 04	5 14	19 04	5 13	19 07	5 07	19 08	5 16	19 20	5 26	19 24
14	5 06	18 56	5 16	19 06	5 12	19 05	5 11	19 09	5 05	19 10	5 13	19 22	5 23	19 26
15	5 04	18 58	5 14	19 08	5 09	19 07	5 09	19 11	5 03	19 11	5 11	19 24	5 21	19 28
16	5 02	18 59	5 12	19 09	5 07	19 09	5 06	19 12	5 00	19 13	5 08	19 26	5 18	19 30
17	5 00	19 01	5 10	19 11	5 05	19 10	5 04	19 14	4 58	19 15	5 06	19 28	5 16	19 32
18	4 58	19 03	5 08	19 13	5 03	19 12	5 02	19 16	4 55	19 17	5 03	19 30	5 14	19 34
19	4 56	19 04	5 06	19 14	5 01	19 14	4 59	19 18	4 53	19 19	5 01	19 32	5 11	19 36
20	4 53	19 06	5 03	19 16	4 58	19 16	4 57	19 20	4 51	19 21	4 59	19 34	5 09	19 37
21	4 51	19 08	5 01	19 18	4 56	19 17	4 55	19 23	4 48	19 23	4 56	19 36	5 07	19 39
22	4 49	19 09	4 59	19 19	4 54	19 19	4 53	19 23	4 46	19 25	4 54	19 38	5 04	19 41
23	4 47	19 11	4 57	19 21	4 52	19 21	4 51	19 25	4 44	19 27	4 51	19 40	5 02	19 43
24	4 45	19 13	4 55	19 23	4 50	19 23	4 48	19 27	4 41	19 29	4 49	19 42	5 00	19 45
25	4 43	19 14	4 53	19 24	4 48	19 24	4 46	19 29	4 39	19 31	4 47	19 44	4 58	19 47
26	4 41	19 16	4 51	19 26	4 46	19 26	4 44	19 31	4 37	19 33	4 44	19 46	4 55	19 49
27	4 39	19 18	4 49	19 28	4 44	19 28	4 42	19 32	4 35	19 35	4 42	19 48	4 53	19 51
28	4 37	19 19	4 47	19 29	4 42	19 30	4 40	19 34	4 32	19 37	4 40	19 50	4 51	19 53
29	4 35	19 21	4 46	19 31	4 40	19 31	4 38	19 36	4 30	19 39	4 37	19 53	4 49	19 55
30	4 34	19 23	4 44	19 32	4 38	19 33	4 36	19 38	4 28	19 41	4 35	19 55	4 47	19 56

JUPITER

Day	R.A. h m	Dec °	Mag.	Diam. "	Rise h m	Transit h m	Set h m
1	11 07.8	+7.2	−2.4	44	15 43	22 25	5 12
11	11 04.2	+7.5	−2.4	43	14 58	21 42	4 31
21	11 01.6	+7.8	−2.3	42	14 14	21 00	3 50

Equatorial Diam. 42″, Polar Diam. 40″

SATURN

Day	R.A. h m	Dec °	Mag.	Diam. "	Rise h m	Transit h m	Set h m
1	17 00.6	−21.0	+0.4	17	0 24	4 21	8 18
11	16 59.8	−20.9	+0.3	18	23 40	3 41	7 38
21	16 58.3	−20.9	+0.3	18	22 58	3 00	6 58

Equatorial Diam. 18″, Polar Diam. 16″
Rings – major axis 40″ minor axis 18″, Tilt 26°

URANUS

Day	R.A. h m	Dec °	Mag.	Diam. "	Rise h m	Transit h m	Set h m
1	1 13.7	+7.2	+6.2	3	5 50	12 33	19 15
11	1 15.9	+7.4	+6.2	3	5 11	11 55	18 39
21	1 18.0	+7.6	+6.2	3	4 33	11 18	18 03

NEPTUNE

Day	R.A. h m	Dec °	Mag.	Diam. "	Rise h m	Transit h m	Set h m
1	22 49.0	−8.4	+8.0	2	4 52	10 08	15 24
11	22 50.2	−8.3	+7.9	2	4 13	9 30	14 47
21	22 51.3	−8.2	+7.9	2	3 34	8 52	14 09

MAY 2016 ♊

FIFTH MONTH, 31 DAYS. *Maia*, goddess of growth and increase

1	Sunday	The kingdoms of England and Scotland unite, forming the Kingdom of Great Britain 1707	day 122
2	Monday	In the 1997 general election, the Conservative party suffers its worst defeat since 1906	week 18 day 123
3	Tuesday	Joseph McCarthy, US Senator who raised fears of Communist subversion in the Cold War d. 1957	124
4	Wednesday	Ken Livingstone, an Independent candidate, is appointed as London's first elected mayor 2000	125
5	Thursday	Napoleon Bonaparte dies having spent six years of his life in exile on the island of St Helena 1821	126
6	Friday	Maximilien Robespierre, French revolutionary prominent during the Reign of Terror b. 1758	127
7	Saturday	The Equal Franchise Act ensures women over the age of 21 receive the vote 1928	128
8	Sunday	The publication of the Peoples Charter begins the Chartist movement 1838	129
9	Monday	German philosopher Karl Marx is exiled from Prussia 1849	week 19 day 130
10	Tuesday	Winston Churchill becomes prime minister after the resignation of Neville Chamberlain 1940	131
11	Wednesday	Spencer Perceval becomes the first and only British prime minister to be assassinated 1812	132
12	Thursday	Leader of the Labour Party John Smith suffers a fatal heart attack and dies in office 1994	133
13	Friday	The 2nd Marquess of Rockingham, Whig politician who twice served as prime minister b. 1730	134
14	Saturday	The Soviet Union establishes the Warsaw Pact with its Eastern Bloc allies 1955	135
15	Sunday	Édith Cresson becomes the first woman to be appointed Prime Minister of France 1991	136
16	Monday	Deputy Prime Minister John Prescott punches an egg-throwing protestor in Rhyl, Wales 2001	week 20 day 137
17	Tuesday	Vidkun Quisling founds *Nasjonal Samling* [National Unity], the Norwegian fascist party 1933	138
18	Wednesday	Napoleon Bonaparte is declared Napoleon I, Emperor of the French 1804	139
19	Thursday	Pol Pot, Cambodian communist dictator who led the Khmer Rouge b. 1925	140
20	Friday	Moshe Dayan, Israeli military leader who was defence minister during the Six-Day War b. 1915	141
21	Saturday	President Suharto of Indonesia resigns after 31 years in office 1998	142
22	Sunday	US President Lyndon Johnson formally presents his 'Great Society' reform package 1964	143
23	Monday	Northern Ireland and the Republic of Ireland vote in favour of the Good Friday Agreement 1998	week 21 day 144
24	Tuesday	Harold Wilson, Labour Party leader and prime minister who won four general elections d. 1995	145
25	Wednesday	Britain's last all-Liberal government forms a wartime coalition with the Conservatives 1915	146
26	Thursday	John Stuart, 3rd Earl of Bute becomes the first Scottish and first Tory prime minister 1762	147
27	Friday	Jawaharlal Nehru, first prime minister of an independent India d. 1964	148
28	Saturday	Lord John Russell, British prime minister who proposed the 1832 Reform Act d. 1878	149
29	Sunday	The Fall of Constantinople, bringing an end to the Byzantine Empire 1453	150
30	Monday	Women over the age of 21 vote for the first time in a general election 1929	week 22 day 151
31	Tuesday	Four separate British colonies form the Union of South Africa 1910	152

ASTRONOMICAL PHENOMENA

d h
5   03   Uranus 2° North of the Moon
6   04   Venus 3° North of the Moon
9   15   Transit of Mercury *see* page 626
13 21   Venus 0.4° North of Mercury
15 10   Jupiter 2° North of the Moon
22 22   Saturn 3° South of the Moon
22 11   Mars at opposition

MINIMA OF ALGOL

d	h	d	h	d	h
3	19.3	15	06.5	26	17.8
6	16.1	18	03.3	29	14.6
9	12.9	21	00.2		
12	09.7	23	21.0		

CONSTELLATIONS

The following constellations are near the meridian at

	d	h		d	h
April	1	24	May	16	21
April	15	23	June	1	20
May	1	22	June	15	19

Cepheus (below the Pole), Cassiopeia (below the Pole), Ursa Minor, Ursa Major, Canes Venatici, Coma Berenices, Bootes, Leo, Virgo, Crater, Corvus and Hydra

THE MOON

Phases, Apsides and Node	d	h	m
● New Moon	6	19	30
◐ First Quarter	13	17	02
○ Full Moon	21	21	14
◑ Last Quarter	29	12	12
Perigee (357,827km)	6	04	13
Apogee (405,933km)	18	22	06

Mean longitude of ascending node on 1st, 169°

THE SUN

Diam. 31.7″

Day	Right Ascension			Dec. +	Equation of time		Rise 52°		Rise 56°		Transit		Set 52°		Set 56°		Sidereal time			Transit of first point of Aries		
	h	m	s	°	m	s	h	m	h	m	h	m	h	m	h	m	h	m	s	h	m	s
1	2	34	22	15.1	+2	53	4	32	4	18	11	57	19	24	19	38	13	37	15	9	22	35
2	2	38	12	15.4	+3	00	4	30	4	15	11	57	19	25	19	40	13	41	12	9	18	38
3	2	42	02	15.7	+3	06	4	28	4	13	11	57	19	27	19	42	13	45	08	9	14	42
4	2	45	53	16.0	+3	12	4	26	4	11	11	57	19	29	19	44	13	49	05	9	10	45
5	2	49	44	16.3	+3	17	4	24	4	09	11	57	19	30	19	46	13	53	01	9	06	49
6	2	53	36	16.6	+3	22	4	22	4	07	11	57	19	32	19	48	13	56	58	9	02	52
7	2	57	29	16.9	+3	26	4	20	4	04	11	57	19	34	19	50	14	00	55	8	58	56
8	3	01	22	17.1	+3	29	4	19	4	02	11	57	19	35	19	52	14	04	51	8	54	59
9	3	05	15	17.4	+3	32	4	17	4	00	11	56	19	37	19	54	14	08	48	8	51	03
10	3	09	10	17.7	+3	34	4	15	3	58	11	56	19	39	19	56	14	12	44	8	47	06
11	3	13	04	17.9	+3	36	4	14	3	56	11	56	19	40	19	58	14	16	41	8	43	09
12	3	17	00	18.2	+3	37	4	12	3	54	11	56	19	42	20	00	14	20	37	8	39	13
13	3	20	56	18.4	+3	38	4	10	3	52	11	56	19	43	20	02	14	24	34	8	35	16
14	3	24	52	18.7	+3	38	4	09	3	50	11	56	19	45	20	03	14	28	30	8	31	20
15	3	28	49	18.9	+3	38	4	07	3	49	11	56	19	46	20	05	14	32	27	8	27	23
16	3	32	46	19.1	+3	37	4	06	3	47	11	56	19	48	20	07	14	36	24	8	23	27
17	3	36	45	19.4	+3	35	4	04	3	45	11	56	19	49	20	09	14	40	20	8	19	30
18	3	40	43	19.6	+3	33	4	03	3	43	11	56	19	51	20	11	14	44	17	8	15	34
19	3	44	42	19.8	+3	31	4	01	3	42	11	56	19	52	20	13	14	48	13	8	11	37
20	3	48	42	20.0	+3	27	4	00	3	40	11	57	19	54	20	14	14	52	10	8	07	40
21	3	52	42	20.2	+3	24	3	59	3	38	11	57	19	55	20	16	14	56	06	8	03	44
22	3	56	43	20.4	+3	20	3	57	3	37	11	57	19	57	20	18	15	00	03	7	59	47
23	4	00	44	20.6	+3	15	3	56	3	35	11	57	19	58	20	19	15	03	59	7	55	51
24	4	04	46	20.8	+3	10	3	55	3	34	11	57	19	59	20	21	15	07	56	7	51	54
25	4	08	48	21.0	+3	04	3	54	3	32	11	57	20	01	20	23	15	11	53	7	47	58
26	4	12	51	21.2	+2	58	3	53	3	31	11	57	20	02	20	24	15	15	49	7	44	01
27	4	16	54	21.3	+2	51	3	52	3	29	11	57	20	03	20	26	15	19	46	7	40	05
28	4	20	58	21.5	+2	44	3	51	3	28	11	57	20	05	20	27	15	23	42	7	36	08
29	4	25	02	21.6	+2	36	3	50	3	27	11	57	20	06	20	29	15	27	39	7	32	11
30	4	29	07	21.8	+2	28	3	49	3	26	11	57	20	07	20	30	15	31	35	7	28	15
31	4	33	12	21.9	+2	19	3	48	3	25	11	58	20	08	20	31	15	35	32	7	24	18

DURATION OF TWILIGHT (in minutes)

Latitude	52°	56°	52°	56°	52°	56°	52°	56°
	1 May		11 May		21 May		31 May	
Civil	39	44	41	48	44	53	46	57
Nautical	89	106	97	120	106	141	115	187
Astronomical	152	204	176	TAN	TAN	TAN	TAN	TAN

THE NIGHT SKY

Mercury passes through inferior conjunction on May 9th when it will be seen to transit the Sun. The entire event is visible from Western Europe, Africa, South America and the eastern states of North America. Bordering these regions will see some of the transit, but not Australasia. *See page 626 for more details and timings.* Mercury will not be visible for the rest of May.

Venus is not visible this month as it is rising at roughly the same time as the Sun.

Mars reaches opposition in Scorpius on May 22nd where it burns at magnitude −2.1 and shows an 18 arc-second disk in a telescope. The Full Moon is 5° from Mars on the 21st. Mars crosses into Libra on May 28th.

Jupiter is high in the southern sky in Leo as dusk falls and remains visible for the first half of the night. The giant planet is stationary on the 10th after which its direct motion resumes. The Moon is just past First Quarter when near Jupiter on May 14th and 15th.

Saturn in Ophiuchus rises less than 30 minutes after Mars. The planet will brighten a little from magnitude +0.2 to 0.0 during the month. The Moon is just a day past full when near Saturn on May 22nd.

THE MOON

Day	R.A. h	R.A. m	Dec. °	Hor. Par.	Diam. ′	Sun's Co-Long. °	PA of Br. Limb °	Ph. %	Age d	Rise 52° h	Rise 52° m	Rise 56° h	Rise 56° m	Transit h	Transit m	Set 52° h	Set 52° m	Set 56° h	Set 56° m
1	21	31	−12.1	58.1	31.7	197	72	41	23.5	1	28	1	41	6	19	11	17	11	04
2	22	25	−8.4	59.0	32.1	209	69	31	24.5	2	01	2	11	7	11	12	28	12	19
3	23	20	−4.2	59.8	32.6	222	67	21	25.5	2	32	2	39	8	03	13	44	13	39
4	0	15	+0.4	60.5	33.0	234	65	12	26.5	3	01	3	04	8	56	15	03	15	02
5	1	12	+5.0	61.0	33.3	246	63	5	27.5	3	29	3	28	9	50	16	24	16	27
6	2	11	+9.4	61.3	33.4	258	55	1	28.5	3	59	3	54	10	45	17	46	17	53
7	3	11	+13.3	61.2	33.3	271	319	0	29.5	4	32	4	23	11	43	19	08	19	20
8	4	12	+16.1	60.8	33.1	283	276	2	1.0	5	09	4	56	12	42	20	27	20	42
9	5	13	+17.9	60.1	32.8	295	274	7	2.0	5	52	5	36	13	42	21	39	21	56
10	6	14	+18.4	59.2	32.3	307	277	14	3.0	6	43	6	25	14	42	22	42	23	00
11	7	13	+17.8	58.3	31.8	320	280	23	4.0	7	40	7	22	15	39	23	35	23	52
12	8	09	+16.2	57.3	31.3	332	284	32	5.0	8	43	8	26	16	34	—			
13	9	02	+13.8	56.5	30.8	344	287	42	6.0	9	48	9	34	17	26	0	18	0	33
14	9	52	+10.8	55.7	30.4	356	290	53	7.0	10	55	10	43	18	15	0	53	1	05
15	10	40	+7.4	55.1	30.0	8	292	62	8.0	12	01	11	53	19	00	1	23	1	32
16	11	26	+3.7	54.6	29.7	21	293	71	9.0	13	05	13	01	19	44	1	49	1	55
17	12	12	+0.0	54.3	29.6	33	294	80	10.0	14	09	14	08	20	27	2	12	2	15
18	12	57	−3.7	54.1	29.5	45	295	87	11.0	15	12	15	14	21	09	2	35	2	34
19	13	42	−7.3	54.0	29.4	57	296	92	12.0	16	15	16	21	21	52	2	57	2	53
20	14	28	−10.6	54.1	29.5	69	298	97	13.0	17	18	17	27	22	35	3	20	3	13
21	15	15	−13.5	54.2	29.6	82	308	99	14.0	18	20	18	32	23	20	3	45	3	35
22	16	04	−15.9	54.5	29.7	94	21	100	15.0	19	21	19	36	—		4	14	4	01
23	16	54	−17.5	54.8	29.9	106	74	99	16.0	20	20	20	37	0	06	4	46	4	31
24	17	46	−18.4	55.2	30.1	118	80	96	17.0	21	16	21	34	0	54	5	25	5	08
25	18	38	−18.4	55.6	30.3	130	80	91	18.0	22	06	22	25	1	43	6	10	5	52
26	19	31	−17.5	56.1	30.6	143	77	85	19.0	22	51	23	08	2	34	7	03	6	44
27	20	24	−15.7	56.7	30.9	155	74	76	20.0	23	31	23	45	3	24	8	02	7	45
28	21	17	−13.1	57.3	31.2	167	72	67	21.0	—		—		4	15	9	06	8	53
29	22	10	−9.7	58.0	31.6	179	69	56	22.0	0	05	0	16	5	06	10	15	10	05
30	23	03	−5.7	58.7	32.0	191	67	45	23.0	0	36	0	44	5	57	11	28	11	21
31	23	57	−1.4	59.4	32.4	204	66	34	24.0	1	04	1	08	6	48	12	43	12	40

MERCURY

Day	R.A. h m	Dec °	Mag.	Diam. ″	Phase %	Rise h m	Transit h m	Set h m
1	3 20.8	+20.6	+2.9	11	7	4 33	12 37	20 39
3	3 19.0	+20.0	+3.5	11	4	4 27	12 27	20 24
5	3 16.2	+19.4	+4.2	12	2	4 21	12 16	20 07
7	3 12.6	+18.6	+5.0	12	1	4 15	12 05	19 50
9	3 08.5	+17.7	+5.9	12	0	4 09	11 53	19 32
11	3 04.3	+16.8	+5.6	12	0	4 03	11 41	19 14
13	3 00.2	+16.0	+4.8	12	1	3 57	11 29	18 57
15	2 56.6	+15.1	+4.1	12	3	3 51	11 18	18 41
17	2 53.7	+14.4	+3.5	12	5	3 45	11 07	18 27
19	2 51.6	+13.8	+3.0	12	7	3 39	10 58	18 14
21	2 50.6	+13.3	+2.5	11	10	3 33	10 49	18 03
23	2 50.6	+13.0	+2.1	11	13	3 27	10 42	17 55
25	2 51.7	+12.8	+1.8	10	17	3 22	10 36	17 48
27	2 53.9	+12.8	+1.5	10	20	3 16	10 30	17 44
29	2 57.2	+12.9	+1.3	10	24	3 11	10 26	17 41
31	3 01.5	+13.2	+1.1	9	27	3 05	10 23	17 40

Rising and setting times are for latitude 54°

VENUS

Day	R.A. h m	Dec °	Mag.	Diam. ″	Phase %	Rise h m	Transit h m	Set h m
1	1 57.0	+10.6	−4.0	11	99	4 15	11 19	18 24
6	2 20.5	+12.8	−4.0	11	99	4 06	11 23	18 41
11	2 44.4	+14.9	−3.9	10	99	3 57	11 27	18 58
16	3 08.7	+16.8	−3.9	10	99	3 49	11 32	19 15
21	3 33.5	+18.5	−3.9	10	99	3 43	11 37	19 32
26	3 58.7	+20.0	−3.9	10	100	3 37	11 42	19 48
31	4 24.4	+21.3	−3.9	10	100	3 34	11 48	20 03

MARS

Day	R.A. h m	Dec °	Mag.	Diam. ″	Phase %	Rise h m	Transit h m	Set h m
1	16 22.9	−21.7	−1.5	16	98	21 56	1 46	5 38
6	16 18.5	−21.7	−1.6	17	99	21 33	1 22	5 14
11	16 12.9	−21.7	−1.8	17	99	21 08	0 56	4 48
16	16 06.3	−21.7	−1.9	18	100	20 42	0 30	4 22
21	15 59.0	−21.6	−2.0	18	100	20 14	0 03	3 56
26	15 51.5	−21.5	−2.0	19	100	19 46	23 38	3 29
31	15 44.0	−21.4	−2.0	19	100	19 18	23 11	3 03

SUNRISE AND SUNSET

	London 0° 05'	51° 30'	Bristol 2° 35'	51° 28'	Birmingham 1° 55'	52° 28'	Manchester 2° 15'	53° 28'	Newcastle 1° 37'	54° 59'	Glasgow 4° 14'	55° 52'	Belfast 5° 56'	54° 35'
d	h m	h m	h m	h m	h m	h m	h m	h m	h m	h m	h m	h m	h m	h m
1	4 32	19 24	4 42	19 34	4 36	19 35	4 34	19 39	4 26	19 43	4 33	19 57	4 45	19 58
2	4 30	19 26	4 40	19 36	4 34	19 36	4 32	19 41	4 24	19 44	4 31	19 59	4 42	20 00
3	4 28	19 27	4 38	19 37	4 32	19 38	4 30	19 43	4 22	19 46	4 28	20 01	4 40	20 02
4	4 26	19 29	4 36	19 39	4 30	19 40	4 28	19 45	4 19	19 48	4 26	20 02	4 38	20 04
5	4 24	19 31	4 34	19 41	4 28	19 42	4 26	19 47	4 17	19 50	4 24	20 04	4 36	20 06
6	4 23	19 32	4 33	19 42	4 26	19 43	4 24	19 49	4 15	19 52	4 22	20 06	4 34	20 08
7	4 21	19 34	4 31	19 44	4 25	19 45	4 22	19 50	4 13	19 54	4 20	20 08	4 32	20 09
8	4 19	19 35	4 29	19 45	4 23	19 46	4 20	19 52	4 11	19 56	4 18	20 10	4 30	20 11
9	4 17	19 37	4 28	19 47	4 21	19 48	4 18	19 54	4 09	19 58	4 16	20 12	4 28	20 13
10	4 16	19 39	4 26	19 49	4 19	19 50	4 17	19 55	4 07	19 59	4 14	20 14	4 27	20 15
11	4 14	19 40	4 24	19 50	4 18	19 51	4 15	19 57	4 06	20 01	4 12	20 16	4 25	20 17
12	4 13	19 42	4 23	19 52	4 16	19 53	4 13	19 59	4 04	20 03	4 10	20 18	4 23	20 19
13	4 11	19 43	4 21	19 53	4 14	19 55	4 11	20 00	4 02	20 05	4 08	20 20	4 21	20 20
14	4 10	19 45	4 20	19 55	4 13	19 56	4 10	20 02	4 00	20 07	4 06	20 22	4 19	20 22
15	4 08	19 46	4 18	19 56	4 11	19 58	4 08	20 04	3 58	20 08	4 04	20 24	4 18	20 24
16	4 07	19 48	4 17	19 58	4 10	19 59	4 07	20 05	3 57	20 10	4 02	20 25	4 16	20 25
17	4 05	19 49	4 15	19 59	4 08	20 01	4 05	20 07	3 55	20 12	4 01	20 27	4 14	20 27
18	4 04	19 51	4 14	20 01	4 07	20 02	4 04	20 08	3 53	20 14	3 59	20 29	4 13	20 29
19	4 02	19 52	4 13	20 02	4 05	20 04	4 02	20 10	3 52	20 15	3 57	20 31	4 11	20 30
20	4 01	19 54	4 11	20 03	4 04	20 05	4 01	20 12	3 50	20 17	3 56	20 33	4 10	20 32
21	4 00	19 55	4 10	20 05	4 03	20 07	3 59	20 13	3 49	20 19	3 54	20 34	4 08	20 34
22	3 59	19 56	4 09	20 06	4 01	20 08	3 58	20 15	3 47	20 20	3 52	20 36	4 07	20 35
23	3 57	19 58	4 08	20 07	4 00	20 10	3 56	20 16	3 46	20 22	3 51	20 38	4 05	20 37
24	3 56	19 59	4 06	20 09	3 59	20 11	3 55	20 17	3 44	20 23	3 49	20 39	4 04	20 38
25	3 55	20 00	4 05	20 10	3 58	20 12	3 54	20 19	3 43	20 25	3 48	20 41	4 03	20 40
26	3 54	20 01	4 04	20 11	3 57	20 14	3 53	20 20	3 42	20 26	3 47	20 42	4 01	20 41
27	3 53	20 03	4 03	20 13	3 56	20 15	3 52	20 22	3 40	20 28	3 45	20 44	4 00	20 43
28	3 52	20 04	4 02	20 14	3 55	20 16	3 51	20 23	3 39	20 29	3 44	20 45	3 59	20 44
29	3 51	20 05	4 01	20 15	3 54	20 17	3 49	20 24	3 38	20 31	3 43	20 47	3 58	20 45
30	3 50	20 06	4 00	20 16	3 53	20 19	3 48	20 25	3 37	20 32	3 42	20 48	3 57	20 47
31	3 49	20 07	4 00	20 17	3 52	20 20	3 48	20 27	3 36	20 33	3 41	20 50	3 56	20 48

JUPITER

Day	R.A. h m	Dec °	Mag.	Diam. "	Rise h m	Transit h m	Set h m
1	11 00.0	+7.9	−2.3	41	13 33	20 20	3 10
11	10 59.5	+7.9	−2.2	40	12 53	19 40	2 30
21	11 00.2	+7.8	−2.1	39	12 15	19 01	1 51
31	11 02.0	+7.6	−2.1	37	11 38	18 23	1 12

Equatorial Diam. 39″, Polar Diam. 37″

SATURN

Day	R.A. h m	Dec °	Mag.	Diam. "	Rise h m	Transit h m	Set h m
1	16 56.3	−20.8	+0.2	18	22 17	2 19	6 17
11	16 53.8	−20.7	+0.1	18	21 34	1 37	5 35
21	16 50.9	−20.7	+0.1	18	20 51	0 54	4 54
31	16 47.8	−20.6	0.0	18	20 08	0 12	4 12

Equatorial Diam. 18″, Polar Diam. 17″
Rings – major axis 41″ minor axis 18″, Tilt 26°

URANUS

Day	R.A. h m	Dec °	Mag.	Diam. "	Rise h m	Transit h m	Set h m
1	1 20.1	+7.8	+6.2	3	3 55	10 41	17 27
11	1 22.1	+8.0	+6.2	3	3 16	10 04	16 51
21	1 23.9	+8.2	+6.2	3	2 38	9 26	16 15
31	1 25.7	+8.4	+6.2	3	1 59	8 49	15 38

NEPTUNE

Day	R.A. h m	Dec °	Mag.	Diam. "	Rise h m	Transit h m	Set h m
1	22 52.2	−8.1	+7.9	2	2 55	8 13	13 32
11	22 53.0	−8.0	+7.9	2	2 16	7 35	12 53
21	22 53.6	−8.0	+7.9	2	1 37	6 56	12 15
31	22 54.0	−7.9	+7.9	2	0 58	6 17	11 36

JUNE 2016

SIXTH MONTH, 30 DAYS. *Junius*, Roman *gens* (family)

1	Wednesday	End of the 'Cod War' between Britain and Iceland over fishing rights in the Atlantic 1976	day 153
2	Thursday	As a display of resistance to German nationalism the first Prague Slavic Congress begins 1848	154
3	Friday	Ayatollah Khomeini, first leader of Iran after the 1979 revolution which ousted the Shah *d.* 1989	155
4	Saturday	Suffragette Emily Davidson steps in front of King George V's horse and is killed 1913	156
5	Sunday	Ronald Reagan, 40th US president who was an actor before moving into politics *d.* 2004	157

6	Monday	The UK votes to stay in the European Economic Community in the 1975 referendum	week 23 day 158
7	Tuesday	The Norwegian parliament dissolves the union between Norway and Sweden 1905	159
8	Wednesday	Conservative MP Jonathan Aitken is sentenced to 18 months in prison for perjury 1999	160
9	Thursday	Roman Emperor Nero commits suicide, ending the Julio-Claudian dynasty AD 68	161
10	Friday	Alexander the Great, creator of one of the largest empires in the ancient world *d.* 323 BC	162
11	Saturday	Margaret Thatcher wins her third consecutive term as prime minister 1987	163
12	Sunday	Nelson Mandela is sentenced to life imprisonment 1964	164

13	Monday	Charles the Fat, great-grandson of Charlemagne and the last Carolingian Emperor *b.* AD 839	week 24 day 165
14	Tuesday	Che Guevara, Argentine Marxist revolutionary, key figure in the Cuban Revolution *b.* 1928	166
15	Wednesday	The Magna Carta is signed by King John (Lackland) at Runnymede 1215	167
16	Thursday	Enoch Powell, Conservative MP known for his 'Rivers of Blood' speech *b.* 1912	168
17	Friday	An IRA bomb explodes at the Houses of Parliament, injuring 11 people 1974	169
18	Saturday	The 1970 general election allows people to vote from the age of 18 for the first time	170
19	Sunday	King James I of England and VI of Scotland, who united the two crowns in one person *b.* 1566	171

20	Monday	The 1st Duke of Monmouth leads the Monmouth Rebellion against James II 1685	week 25 day 172
21	Tuesday	Niccolò Machiavelli, author of *The Prince*, from who the word 'Machiavellanism' originates *d.* 1527	173
22	Wednesday	Former Liberal Party leader Jeremy Thorpe is cleared of attempted murder 1979	174
23	Thursday	Two British spies, Guy Burgess and Donald Maclean, defect to the USSR 1951	175
24	Friday	Grover Cleveland, the only US president to serve two non-consecutive terms *d.* 1908	176
25	Saturday	The House of Lords, persuaded by the Duke of Wellington, abolishes the Corn Laws 1846	177
26	Sunday	John F. Kennedy delivers his 'Ich bin ein Berliner' speech to West German citizens 1963	178

27	Monday	The UN court of justice rules that US support of the Contras in Nicaragua is unlawful 1986	week 26 day 179
28	Tuesday	Archduke Franz Ferdinand of Austria is assassinated by Gavrilo Princip in Sarajevo 1914	180
29	Wednesday	Isabel Peron, third wife of Juan Peron, is sworn in as interim president of Argentina 1964	181
30	Thursday	Montezuma II, the last emperor of the Aztecs *d.* 1520	182

ASTRONOMICAL PHENOMENA

d	h	
1	14	Uranus 2° North of the Moon
3	10	Mercury 1° North of the Moon
3	07	Saturn at opposition
5	09	Mercury Greatest elongation West
5	01	Venus 5° North of the Moon
11	20	Jupiter 1° North of the Moon
19	00	Saturn 3° South of the Moon
20	23	Solstice
28	23	Uranus 3° North of the Moon

MINIMA OF ALGOL

d	h	d	h	d	h
1	11.4	12	22.7	24	09.9
4	08.2	15	19.5	27	06.8
7	05.1	18	16.3	30	03.6
10	01.9	21	13.1		

CONSTELLATIONS

The following constellations are near the meridian at

	d	h		d	h
May	1	24	June	15	21
May	16	23	July	1	20
June	1	22	July	16	19

Cassiopeia (below the Pole), Ursa Minor, Draco, Ursa Major, Canes Venatici, Bootes, Corona, Serpens, Virgo and Libra

THE MOON

Phases, Apsides and Node	d	h	m
● New Moon	5	03	00
◐ First Quarter	12	08	10
○ Full Moon	20	11	02
◑ Last Quarter	27	18	19
Perigee (361,140km)	3	10	55
Apogee (405,024km)	15	12	01

Mean longitude of ascending node on 1st, 168°

THE SUN

Diam. 31.5″

Day	Right Ascension			Dec. +	Equation of time		Rise 52°		Rise 56°		Transit		Set 52°		Set 56°		Sidereal time			Transit of first point of Aries		
	h	m	s	°	m	s	h	m	h	m	h	m	h	m	h	m	h	m	s	h	m	s
1	4	37	18	22.1	+2	10	3	47	3	24	11	58	20	09	20	33	15	39	28	7	20	22
2	4	41	24	22.2	+2	01	3	46	3	23	11	58	20	10	20	34	15	43	25	7	16	25
3	4	45	30	22.3	+1	51	3	45	3	22	11	58	20	11	20	35	15	47	22	7	12	29
4	4	49	37	22.5	+1	41	3	45	3	21	11	58	20	12	20	36	15	51	18	7	08	32
5	4	53	44	22.6	−1	30	3	44	3	20	11	58	20	13	20	38	15	55	15	7	04	36
6	4	57	52	22.7	+1	19	3	43	3	19	11	59	20	14	20	39	15	59	11	7	00	39
7	5	01	59	22.8	+1	08	3	43	3	18	11	59	20	15	20	40	16	03	08	6	56	42
8	5	06	07	22.9	+0	57	3	42	3	18	11	59	20	16	20	41	16	07	04	6	52	46
9	5	10	16	22.9	+0	45	3	42	3	17	11	59	20	17	20	42	16	11	01	6	48	49
10	5	14	24	23.0	+0	33	3	42	3	16	11	59	20	18	20	43	16	14	57	6	44	53
11	5	18	33	23.1	+0	21	3	41	3	16	12	00	20	18	20	44	16	18	54	6	40	56
12	5	22	42	23.2	+0	09	3	41	3	16	12	00	20	19	20	44	16	22	51	6	37	00
13	5	26	51	23.2	−0	04	3	41	3	15	12	00	20	20	20	45	16	26	47	6	33	03
14	5	31	00	23.3	−0	17	3	40	3	15	12	00	20	20	20	46	16	30	44	6	29	07
15	5	35	09	23.3	−0	29	3	40	3	15	12	00	20	21	20	46	16	34	40	6	25	10
16	5	39	19	23.4	−0	42	3	40	3	14	12	01	20	21	20	47	16	38	37	6	21	13
17	5	43	28	23.4	−0	55	3	40	3	14	12	01	20	22	20	47	16	42	33	6	17	17
18	5	47	37	23.4	−1	08	3	40	3	14	12	01	20	22	20	48	16	46	30	6	13	20
19	5	51	47	23.4	−1	21	3	40	3	14	12	01	20	22	20	48	16	50	26	6	09	24
20	5	55	57	23.4	−1	34	3	40	3	14	12	01	20	23	20	49	16	54	23	6	05	27
21	6	00	06	23.4	−1	47	3	40	3	15	12	02	20	23	20	49	16	58	20	6	01	31
22	6	04	16	23.4	−2	00	3	41	3	15	12	02	20	23	20	49	17	02	16	5	57	34
23	6	08	25	23.4	−2	13	3	41	3	15	12	02	20	23	20	49	17	06	13	5	53	38
24	6	12	34	23.4	−2	25	3	41	3	15	12	02	20	23	20	49	17	10	09	5	49	41
25	6	16	44	23.4	−2	38	3	42	3	16	12	03	20	23	20	49	17	14	06	5	45	44
26	6	20	53	23.4	−2	51	3	42	3	16	12	03	20	23	20	49	17	18	02	5	41	48
27	6	25	02	23.3	−3	03	3	42	3	17	12	03	20	23	20	49	17	21	59	5	37	51
28	6	29	11	23.3	−3	16	3	43	3	17	12	03	20	23	20	49	17	25	55	5	33	55
29	6	33	19	23.2	−3	28	3	43	3	18	12	03	20	23	20	49	17	29	52	5	29	58
30	6	37	28	23.2	−3	40	3	44	3	19	12	04	20	23	20	48	17	33	49	5	26	02

DURATION OF TWILIGHT (in minutes)

Latitude	52°	56°	52°	56°	52°	56°	52°	56°
	1 June		11 June		21 June		31 June	
Civil	46	58	48	61	49	63	48	61
Nautical	116	TAN	124	TAN	127	TAN	124	TAN
Astronomical	TAN	TAN	TAN	TAN	TAN	TAN	TAN	TAN

THE NIGHT SKY

Mercury is a morning sky object but is not well placed for observation this month. It reaches greatest elongation west (24°) on June 5th.

Venus is at superior conjunction on June 6th and then moves into the evening sky. However, it is still that bit too close to the solar glare to be seen at any stage this month.

Mars is low in the south-east in Libra these evenings. The planet is stationary on the 30th after which its direct motion resumes. Mars very slowly fades from magnitude −2.0 to −1.4 during June but still far outshines the stars in this region of sky.

Jupiter is in the south-west after sunset and now starts its slow slide towards the Sun over the next few months. It sets before midnight by the end of June and also fades a little to magnitude −1.9 in this time. The Moon is close to Jupiter on the 11th.

Saturn reaches opposition on June 3rd in Ophiuchus when at magnitude 0.0. Telescope users will see the planet's disk just over 18 arc-seconds in diameter and the rings tipped more than 26° earthward. Saturn can be found just below the Full Moon during the brief hours of darkness on June 18th.

THE MOON

Day	R.A.		Dec.	Hor. Par.	Diam.	Sun's Co-Long.	PA of Br. Limb	Ph.	Age	Rise 52°		Rise 56°		Transit		Set 52°		Set 56°	
	h	m	°	'	'	°	°	%	d	h	m	h	m	h	m	h	m	h	m
1	0	51	+3.2	60.0	32.7	216	66	23	25.0	1	31	1	32	7	39	14	00	14	02
2	1	47	+7.6	60.4	32.9	228	66	14	26.0	1	59	1	56	8	32	15	20	15	25
3	2	45	+11.7	60.7	33.1	240	66	7	27.0	2	29	2	22	9	27	16	40	16	49
4	3	45	+15.0	60.7	33.1	253	62	2	28.0	3	02	2	51	10	24	17	59	18	13
5	4	46	+17.3	60.4	32.9	265	18	0	29.0	3	41	3	26	11	23	19	15	19	32
6	5	48	+18.5	59.9	32.6	277	292	1	0.5	4	27	4	10	12	23	20	24	20	42
7	6	49	+18.4	59.2	32.2	289	285	5	1.5	5	21	5	04	13	23	21	24	21	42
8	7	47	+17.2	58.3	31.8	302	285	11	2.5	6	23	6	05	14	21	22	12	22	29
9	8	43	+15.0	57.4	31.3	314	288	18	3.5	7	29	7	13	15	15	22	52	23	06
10	9	35	+12.1	56.6	30.8	326	290	27	4.5	8	37	8	24	16	07	23	25	23	36
11	10	25	+8.8	55.8	30.4	338	292	37	5.5	9	45	9	35	16	55	23	53	0	00
12	11	13	+5.1	55.1	30.0	351	293	46	6.5	10	52	10	46	17	40	—		—	
13	11	59	+1.3	54.6	29.8	3	294	56	7.5	11	57	11	54	18	24	0	18	0	22
14	12	44	−2.5	54.3	29.6	15	294	65	8.5	13	01	13	02	19	07	0	40	0	41
15	13	29	−6.2	54.2	29.5	27	293	74	9.5	14	04	14	08	19	49	1	03	1	00
16	14	15	−9.6	54.2	29.5	39	292	82	10.5	15	07	15	14	20	32	1	25	1	20
17	15	02	−12.6	54.3	29.6	52	292	89	11.5	16	09	16	20	21	16	1	49	1	41
18	15	50	−15.2	54.5	29.7	64	291	94	12.5	17	11	17	25	22	02	2	16	2	05
19	16	40	−17.1	54.9	29.9	76	294	98	13.5	18	12	18	28	22	49	2	47	2	32
20	17	32	−18.3	55.3	30.1	88	313	100	14.5	19	09	19	28	23	39	3	23	3	07
21	18	24	−18.6	55.7	30.4	100	49	100	15.5	20	02	20	22	—		4	06	3	48
22	19	18	−18.0	56.2	30.6	113	69	98	16.5	20	50	21	08	0	29	4	57	4	37
23	20	12	−16.4	56.7	30.9	125	71	94	17.5	21	33	21	48	1	21	5	54	5	36
24	21	06	−14.0	57.2	31.2	137	70	87	18.5	22	09	22	22	2	12	6	58	6	42
25	21	59	−10.7	57.7	31.5	149	69	79	19.5	22	41	22	50	3	04	8	06	7	54
26	22	51	−6.9	58.2	31.7	161	68	70	20.5	23	10	23	15	3	55	9	18	9	10
27	23	44	−2.7	58.7	32.0	174	67	59	21.5	23	37	23	39	4	45	10	31	10	27
28	0	37	+1.8	59.1	32.2	186	67	48	22.5	—		—		5	36	11	46	11	46
29	1	31	+6.2	59.5	32.4	198	68	36	23.5	0	03	0	02	6	27	13	03	13	07
30	2	27	+10.3	59.8	32.6	210	69	26	24.5	0	31	0	26	7	19	14	21	14	29

MERCURY

Day	R.A.		Dec.	Mag.	Diam.	Phase	Rise		Transit		Set	
	h	m	°		"	%	h	m	h	m	h	m
1	3	04.0	+13.4	+1.0	9	29	3	03	10	22	17	40
3	3	09.8	+13.9	+0.8	9	33	2	58	10	20	17	42
5	3	16.5	+14.4	+0.6	8	37	2	53	10	19	17	45
7	3	24.2	+15.1	+0.4	8	41	2	49	10	19	17	50
9	3	32.8	+15.8	+0.3	8	45	2	45	10	20	17	56
11	3	42.3	+16.6	+0.1	7	49	2	42	10	22	18	04
13	3	52.7	+17.4	0.0	7	53	2	39	10	25	18	12
15	4	04.0	+18.3	−0.2	7	58	2	36	10	29	18	22
17	4	16.3	+19.2	−0.3	6	63	2	34	10	33	18	33
19	4	29.5	+20.1	−0.5	6	68	2	34	10	39	18	46
21	4	43.7	+20.9	−0.7	6	73	2	34	10	45	18	59
23	4	58.9	+21.7	−0.8	6	78	2	35	10	53	19	12
25	5	15.0	+22.4	−1.0	6	83	2	38	11	01	19	26
27	5	32.0	+23.1	−1.2	5	87	2	42	11	11	19	41
29	5	49.7	+23.6	−1.4	5	92	2	48	11	21	19	55

Rising and setting times are for latitude 54°

VENUS

Day	R.A.		Dec.	Mag.	Diam.	Phase	Rise		Transit		Set	
	h	m	°		"	%	h	m	h	m	h	m
1	4	29.6	+21.6	−3.9	10	100	3	33	11	50	20	06
6	4	55.8	+22.6	−3.9	10	100	3	32	11	56	20	19
11	5	22.3	+23.3	−3.9	10	100	3	33	12	03	20	33
16	5	49.0	+23.8	−3.9	10	100	3	37	12	10	20	43
21	6	15.9	+23.9	−3.9	10	100	3	43	12	17	20	52
26	6	42.8	+23.8	−3.9	10	100	3	51	12	24	20	57

MARS

Day	R.A.		Dec.	Mag.	Diam.	Phase	Rise		Transit		Set	
	h	m	°		"	%	h	m	h	m	h	m
1	15	42.5	−21.4	−2.0	19	99	19	12	23	06	2	58
6	15	35.6	−21.2	−1.9	18	99	18	45	22	39	2	32
11	15	29.6	−21.1	−1.8	18	98	18	18	22	13	2	08
16	15	24.9	−21.0	−1.7	18	97	17	52	21	48	1	44
21	15	21.4	−20.9	−1.6	17	96	17	28	21	25	1	21
26	15	19.4	−20.9	−1.5	17	94	17	06	21	03	0	59

SUNRISE AND SUNSET

d	London 0° 05' / 51° 30' Rise	Set	Bristol 2° 35' / 51° 28' Rise	Set	Birmingham 1° 55' / 52° 28' Rise	Set	Manchester 2° 15' / 53° 28' Rise	Set	Newcastle 1° 37' / 54° 59' Rise	Set	Glasgow 4° 14' / 55° 52' Rise	Set	Belfast 5° 56' / 54° 35' Rise	Set
1	3 49	20 08	3 59	20 18	3 51	20 21	3 47	20 28	3 35	20 35	3 40	20 51	3 55	20 49
2	3 48	20 09	3 58	20 19	3 50	20 22	3 46	20 29	3 34	20 36	3 39	20 52	3 54	20 51
3	3 47	20 10	3 57	20 20	3 49	20 23	3 45	20 30	3 33	20 37	3 38	20 53	3 53	20 52
4	3 47	20 11	3 57	20 21	3 49	20 24	3 44	20 31	3 32	20 38	3 37	20 55	3 52	20 53
5	3 46	20 12	3 56	20 22	3 48	20 25	3 44	20 32	3 31	20 39	3 36	20 56	3 51	20 54
6	3 45	20 13	3 56	20 23	3 47	20 26	3 43	20 33	3 31	20 40	3 35	20 57	3 51	20 55
7	3 45	20 14	3 55	20 24	3 47	20 27	3 42	20 34	3 30	20 41	3 34	20 58	3 50	20 56
8	3 44	20 15	3 55	20 25	3 46	20 28	3 42	20 35	3 30	20 42	3 34	20 59	3 49	20 57
9	3 44	20 16	3 54	20 26	3 46	20 28	3 41	20 36	3 29	20 43	3 33	21 00	3 49	20 58
10	3 44	20 16	3 54	20 26	3 46	20 29	3 41	20 37	3 28	20 44	3 33	21 01	3 48	20 59
11	3 43	20 17	3 54	20 27	3 45	20 30	3 41	20 37	3 28	20 45	3 32	21 02	3 48	20 59
12	3 43	20 18	3 53	20 28	3 45	20 31	3 40	20 38	3 28	20 45	3 32	21 02	3 48	21 00
13	3 43	20 18	3 53	20 28	3 45	20 31	3 40	20 39	3 27	20 46	3 32	21 03	3 47	21 01
14	3 43	20 19	3 53	20 29	3 45	20 32	3 40	20 39	3 27	20 47	3 31	21 04	3 47	21 01
15	3 43	20 19	3 53	20 29	3 44	20 32	3 40	20 40	3 27	20 47	3 31	21 04	3 47	21 02
16	3 43	20 20	3 53	20 30	3 44	20 33	3 40	20 40	3 27	20 48	3 31	21 05	3 47	21 02
17	3 43	20 20	3 53	20 30	3 44	20 33	3 40	20 41	3 27	20 48	3 31	21 05	3 47	21 03
18	3 43	20 21	3 53	20 30	3 44	20 33	3 40	20 41	3 27	20 49	3 31	21 06	3 47	21 03
19	3 43	20 21	3 53	20 31	3 44	20 34	3 40	20 41	3 27	20 49	3 31	21 06	3 47	21 03
20	3 43	20 21	3 53	20 31	3 45	20 34	3 40	20 42	3 27	20 49	3 31	21 06	3 47	21 04
21	3 43	20 21	3 53	20 31	3 45	20 34	3 40	20 42	3 27	20 49	3 31	21 06	3 47	21 04
22	3 43	20 21	3 54	20 31	3 45	20 34	3 40	20 42	3 28	20 50	3 32	21 06	3 48	21 04
23	3 44	20 22	3 54	20 31	3 45	20 34	3 41	20 42	3 28	20 50	3 32	21 07	3 48	21 04
24	3 44	20 22	3 54	20 31	3 46	20 34	3 41	20 42	3 28	20 50	3 32	21 07	3 48	21 04
25	3 44	20 22	3 54	20 31	3 46	20 34	3 41	20 42	3 29	20 50	3 33	21 06	3 49	21 04
26	3 45	20 22	3 55	20 31	3 47	20 34	3 42	20 42	3 29	20 49	3 33	21 06	3 49	21 04
27	3 45	20 21	3 56	20 31	3 47	20 34	3 42	20 42	3 30	20 49	3 34	21 06	3 50	21 04
28	3 46	20 21	3 56	20 31	3 48	20 34	3 43	20 41	3 30	20 49	3 34	21 06	3 50	21 03
29	3 46	20 21	3 57	20 31	3 48	20 34	3 44	20 41	3 31	20 49	3 35	21 05	3 51	21 03
30	3 47	20 21	3 57	20 31	3 49	20 34	3 44	20 41	3 32	20 48	3 36	21 05	3 52	21 03

JUPITER

Day	R.A. h m	Dec °	Mag.	Diam. "	Rise h m	Transit h m	Set h m
1	11 02.2	+7.6	-2.1	37	11 35	18 20	1 09
11	11 05.1	+7.2	-2.0	36	11 00	17 43	0 30
21	11 08.9	+6.8	-1.9	35	10 27	17 08	23 48

Equatorial Diam. 36", Polar Diam. 33"

SATURN

Day	R.A. h m	Dec °	Mag.	Diam. "	Rise h m	Transit h m	Set h m
1	16 47.5	-20.6	0.0	18	20 04	0 08	4 08
11	16 44.3	-20.5	0.0	18	19 21	23 22	3 26
21	16 41.3	-20.4	+0.1	18	18 38	22 39	2 44

Equatorial Diam. 18", Polar Diam. 17"
Rings – major axis 42" minor axis 18", Tilt 26°

URANUS

Day	R.A. h m	Dec °	Mag.	Diam. "	Rise h m	Transit h m	Set h m
1	1 25.8	+8.4	+6.2	3	1 55	8 45	15 34
11	1 27.3	+8.5	+6.2	3	1 16	8 07	14 57
21	1 28.6	+8.6	+6.2	3	0 38	7 29	14 20

NEPTUNE

Day	R.A. h m	Dec °	Mag.	Diam. "	Rise h m	Transit h m	Set h m
1	22 54.0	-7.9	+7.9	2	0 54	6 13	11 32
11	22 54.2	-7.9	+7.9	2	0 15	5 34	10 53
21	22 54.1	-7.9	+7.9	2	23 32	4 55	10 14

JULY 2016

SEVENTH MONTH, 31 DAYS. *Julius* Caesar, formerly *Quintilis*, fifth month of Roman pre-Julian calendar

1	Friday	Hong Kong is returned to China, ending 156 years of British colonial governance 1997	day 183
2	Saturday	President Johnson signs the Civil Rights Act in a televised ceremony at the White House 1964	184
3	Sunday	Louis XI (the Prudent) who was King of France (1461–83) b. 1423	185
4	Monday	William Petty becomes the first Irish-born prime minister of the UK 1782	week 27 day 186
5	Tuesday	Clement Attlee's Labour Party wins the general election two months after VE Day 1945	187
6	Wednesday	George W. Bush, 43rd US president, who launched the War on Terror b. 1946	188
7	Thursday	Israel begins Operation Protective Edge in the Hamas-controlled Gaza Strip 2014	189
8	Friday	Kim Jong-il becomes the first 'Supreme Leader' of North Korea 1994	190
9	Saturday	South Sudan becomes independent of Sudan following a referendum 2011	191
10	Sunday	The Bahamas gains independence after 325 years of British rule 1973	192
11	Monday	Robert the Bruce, King of Scots who fought for Scotland's independence b. 1274	week 28 day 193
12	Tuesday	Ranjit Singh founds the Sikh Empire, based in the Punjab region 1799	194
13	Wednesday	The Congress of Berlin, to determine the territories of the Balkan peninsula states, ends 1878	195
14	Thursday	Gerald Ford, appointed vice-president and later US president (38th) without election b. 1913	196
15	Friday	Emmeline Pankhurst, suffragette who helped women win the right to vote b. 1858	197
16	Saturday	Richard of Bordeaux is crowned Richard II of England 1377	198
17	Sunday	The Russian Imperial family of Tsar Nicholas II are executed 1918	199
18	Monday	The Ballot Act 1872, requiring that elections are held by secret ballot, receives royal assent	week 29 day 200
19	Tuesday	Syngman Rhee, first president of South Korea, in office during the Korean War d. 1965	201
20	Wednesday	Otto John, the head of West Germany's intelligence service, defects to East Germany 1954	202
21	Thursday	Sirimavo Bandaranaike becomes the first female head of government, in Ceylon 1960	203
22	Friday	A military coup in Gambia deposes president Dawda Jawara, who is exiled 1994	204
23	Saturday	The government of Abkhazia declares its independence from Georgia 1992	205
24	Sunday	French president Charles de Gaulle declares 'Long live free Quebec!' on a visit to Canada 1967	206
25	Monday	Arthur Balfour, prime minister who succeeded his uncle, Lord Salisbury b. 1848	week 30 day 207
26	Tuesday	The Labour Party wins the 1945 general election, less than two months after VE Day	208
27	Wednesday	The first article of impeachment charging President Nixon with obstruction of justice is approved 1974	209
28	Thursday	Gen. José de San Martín proclaims Peru independent from Spain after occupying Lima 1821	210
29	Friday	A constitutional referendum in Greece votes in favour of abolishing the monarchy 1973	211
30	Saturday	William Penn, Quaker and founder of the Province of Pennsylvania d. 1718	212
31	Sunday	The IRA declares a complete ceasefire after 25 years of armed operations 1994	213

ASTRONOMICAL PHENOMENA

d h
4 16 Earth at aphelion
9 10 Jupiter 1° North of the Moon
16 18 Venus 0.5° South of Mercury
16 05 Saturn 3° South of the Moon
26 04 Uranus 3° North of the Moon

MINIMA OF ALGOL

d	h	d	h	d	h
3	00.4	14	11.6	25	22.9
5	21.2	17	08.4	28	19.7
8	18.0	20	05.2	31	16.5
11	14.8	23	02.1		

CONSTELLATIONS

The following constellations are near their meridian at

	d	h		d	h
June	1	24	July	16	21
June	15	23	August	1	20
July	1	22	August	16	19

Ursa Minor, Draco, Corona, Hercules, Lyra, Serpens, Ophiuchus, Libra, Scorpius and Sagittarius

THE MOON

Phases, Apsides and Node	d	h	m
● New Moon	4	11	01
◐ First Quarter	12	00	52
○ Full Moon	19	22	57
◑ Last Quarter	26	23	00

Perigee (365,983km)	1	06	40
Apogee (404,269km)	13	05	24
Perigee (369,662km)	27	11	37

Mean longitude of ascending node on 1st, 166°

THE SUN

Diam. 31.5″

Day	Right Ascension			Dec. +	Equation of time		Rise 52°		Rise 56°		Transit		Set 52°		Set 56°		Sidereal time			Transit of first point of Aries		
	h	m	s	°	m	s	h	m	h	m	h	m	h	m	h	m	h	m	s	h	m	s
1	6	41	36	23.1	−3	51	3	45	3	19	12	04	20	23	20	48	17	37	45	5	22	05
2	6	45	44	23.0	−4	03	3	45	3	20	12	04	20	22	20	47	17	41	42	5	18	09
3	6	49	52	22.9	−4	14	3	46	3	21	12	04	20	22	20	47	17	45	38	5	14	12
4	6	54	00	22.9	−4	25	3	47	3	22	12	04	20	21	20	46	17	49	35	5	10	15
5	6	58	07	22.8	−4	36	3	48	3	23	12	05	20	21	20	46	17	53	31	5	06	19
6	7	02	14	22.7	−4	46	3	48	3	24	12	05	20	20	20	45	17	57	28	5	02	22
7	7	06	20	22.6	−4	56	3	49	3	25	12	05	20	20	20	44	18	01	24	4	58	26
8	7	10	26	22.5	−5	05	3	50	3	26	12	05	20	19	20	43	18	05	21	4	54	29
9	7	14	32	22.3	−5	14	3	51	3	27	12	05	20	19	20	43	18	09	18	4	50	33
10	7	18	37	22.2	−5	23	3	52	3	28	12	05	20	18	20	42	18	13	14	4	46	36
11	7	22	42	22.1	−5	31	3	53	3	29	12	05	20	17	20	41	18	17	11	4	42	40
12	7	26	46	21.9	−5	39	3	54	3	31	12	06	20	16	20	40	18	21	07	4	38	43
13	7	30	50	21.8	−5	46	3	55	3	32	12	06	20	15	20	39	18	25	04	4	34	46
14	7	34	53	21.6	−5	53	3	56	3	33	12	06	20	14	20	37	18	29	00	4	30	50
15	7	38	56	21.5	−5	59	3	58	3	35	12	06	20	14	20	36	18	32	57	4	26	53
16	7	42	58	21.3	−6	05	3	59	3	36	12	06	20	13	20	35	18	36	53	4	22	57
17	7	47	00	21.2	−6	10	4	00	3	38	12	06	20	11	20	34	18	40	50	4	19	00
18	7	51	01	21.0	−6	15	4	01	3	39	12	06	20	10	20	32	18	44	47	4	15	04
19	7	55	02	20.8	−6	19	4	03	3	41	12	06	20	09	20	31	18	48	43	4	11	07
20	7	59	02	20.6	−6	22	4	04	3	42	12	06	20	08	20	29	18	52	40	4	07	11
21	8	03	01	20.4	−6	25	4	05	3	44	12	06	20	07	20	28	18	56	36	4	03	14
22	8	07	00	20.2	−6	28	4	06	3	45	12	06	20	06	20	26	19	00	33	3	59	17
23	8	10	59	20.0	−6	30	4	08	3	47	12	06	20	04	20	25	19	04	29	3	55	21
24	8	14	57	19.8	−6	31	4	09	3	49	12	07	20	03	20	23	19	08	26	3	51	24
25	8	18	54	19.6	−6	32	4	11	3	50	12	07	20	02	20	21	19	12	22	3	47	28
26	8	22	51	19.4	−6	32	4	12	3	52	12	07	20	00	20	20	19	16	19	3	43	31
27	8	26	47	19.2	−6	32	4	13	3	54	12	07	19	59	20	18	19	20	16	3	39	35
28	8	30	42	18.9	−6	30	4	15	3	56	12	07	19	57	20	16	19	24	12	3	35	38
29	8	34	37	18.7	−6	29	4	16	3	58	12	06	19	56	20	14	19	28	09	3	31	42
30	8	38	32	18.5	−6	27	4	18	3	59	12	06	19	54	20	12	19	32	05	3	27	45
31	8	42	25	18.2	−6	24	4	19	4	01	12	06	19	52	20	10	19	36	02	3	23	48

DURATION OF TWILIGHT (in minutes)

Latitude	52°	56°	52°	56°	52°	56°	52°	56°
	1 July		11 July		21 July		31 July	
Civil	48	61	47	58	44	53	42	49
Nautical	124	TAN	117	TAN	107	146	98	123
Astronomical	TAN	TAN	TAN	TAN	TAN	TAN	182	TAN

THE NIGHT SKY

Mercury is at superior conjunction on the 7th and then moves into the evening sky. It will be too deep in the twilight to be seen this month though.

Venus might be spotted barely above the north-west horizon just before the end of civil twilight the last few days of July. The observation calls for an exceptional horizon though and may first require sweeping with binoculars to tease out the planet's elusive spark.

Mars sets before midnight at the end of July but is still quite prominent among the stars of Libra. The planet's slow fade from magnitude −1.4 to −0.8 during the month is due to Earth's faster motion round the Sun as we leave Mars behind in its orbit. The Moon lies 7° above Mars on the evening of the 14th.

Jupiter, magnitude −1.7, sinks lower towards the west these evenings and will set only 90 minutes after the Sun by the end of July. The planet is 5° to the Moon's right after sunset on the 9th.

Saturn, magnitude +0.2, is in the southern sky in Ophiuchus after dark. It sets during the early hours at the beginning of July but just after midnight by the end of the month. The Moon is just under 5° from Saturn on July 15th.

THE MOON

Day	R.A. h	R.A. m	Dec. °	Hor. Par. '	Diam. '	Sun's Co-Long. °	PA of Br. Limb °	Ph. %	Age d	Rise 52° h	Rise 52° m	Rise 56° h	Rise 56° m	Transit h	Transit m	Set 52° h	Set 52° m	Set 56° h	Set 56° m
1	3	24	+13.8	59.9	32.6	222	71	16	25.5	1	02	0	53	8	14	15	38	15	50
2	4	23	+16.5	59.9	32.6	235	73	8	26.5	1	37	1	24	9	10	16	53	17	09
3	5	24	+18.1	59.6	32.5	247	73	3	27.5	2	18	2	03	10	08	18	04	18	23
4	6	24	+18.6	59.2	32.3	259	57	0	28.5	3	07	2	49	11	07	19	08	19	27
5	7	24	+17.9	58.7	32.0	271	310	0	29.5	4	05	3	46	12	05	20	02	20	20
6	8	21	+16.1	58.0	31.6	284	293	3	0.9	5	08	4	51	13	02	20	47	21	02
7	9	15	+13.5	57.2	31.2	296	291	8	1.9	6	16	6	02	13	55	21	24	21	36
8	10	07	+10.2	56.4	30.8	308	292	14	2.9	7	25	7	14	14	46	21	54	22	03
9	10	56	+6.6	55.7	30.4	320	293	22	3.9	8	34	8	26	15	33	22	21	22	27
10	11	44	+2.8	55.1	30.0	333	293	31	4.9	9	41	9	37	16	19	22	45	22	47
11	12	30	−1.0	54.7	29.8	345	293	40	5.9	10	47	10	46	17	02	23	07	23	07
12	13	15	−4.8	54.4	29.6	357	292	49	6.9	11	51	11	53	17	45	23	30	23	26
13	14	01	−8.3	54.2	29.6	9	291	59	7.9	12	54	13	00	18	28	23	53	23	46
14	14	47	−11.5	54.3	29.6	22	289	68	8.9	13	56	14	06	19	11	—		—	
15	15	35	−14.3	54.5	29.7	34	287	77	9.9	14	58	15	11	19	56	0	19	0	09
16	16	24	−16.5	54.8	29.9	46	284	84	10.9	15	59	16	15	20	43	0	48	0	34
17	17	15	−17.9	55.3	30.1	58	282	91	11.9	16	58	17	16	21	31	1	21	1	06
18	18	08	−18.6	55.8	30.4	70	280	96	12.9	17	54	18	13	22	22	2	02	1	43
19	19	01	−18.3	56.4	30.7	83	284	99	13.9	18	45	19	03	23	13	2	48	2	29
20	19	56	−17.0	57.0	31.1	95	349	100	14.9	19	30	19	47	—		3	43	3	25
21	20	51	−14.8	57.5	31.4	107	62	99	15.9	20	09	20	24	0	06	4	45	4	29
22	21	45	−11.8	58.0	31.6	119	67	95	16.9	20	44	20	54	0	58	5	54	5	40
23	22	39	−8.1	58.5	31.9	131	67	90	17.9	21	14	21	21	1	50	7	06	6	56
24	23	32	−3.9	58.8	32.0	144	67	82	18.9	21	42	21	46	2	42	8	20	8	14
25	0	26	+0.6	59.1	32.2	156	68	72	19.9	22	09	22	09	3	33	9	36	9	34
26	1	19	+5.0	59.2	32.3	168	69	61	20.9	22	37	22	32	4	24	10	52	10	54
27	2	14	+9.2	59.3	32.3	180	71	50	21.9	23	06	22	58	5	16	12	09	12	15
28	3	10	+12.8	59.3	32.3	192	73	39	22.9	23	38	23	27	6	09	13	25	13	36
29	4	07	+15.7	59.2	32.3	205	77	28	23.9	—		—		7	03	14	40	14	53
30	5	06	+17.7	59.0	32.2	217	80	18	24.9	0	16	0	02	7	59	15	51	16	07
31	6	05	+18.5	58.7	32.0	229	84	10	25.9	1	01	0	43	8	56	16	56	17	14

MERCURY

Day	R.A. h	R.A. m	Dec °	Mag.	Diam. "	Phase %	Rise h m	Transit h m	Set h m
1	6	08.1	+23.9	−1.6	5	95	2 56	11 31	20 08
3	6	27.0	+24.1	−1.8	5	98	3 05	11 43	20 20
5	6	46.0	+24.1	−2.0	5	99	3 16	11 54	20 31
7	7	05.0	+24.0	−2.2	5	100	3 29	12 05	20 40
9	7	23.8	+23.6	−2.0	5	99	3 43	12 16	20 48
11	7	42.2	+23.1	−1.7	5	98	3 58	12 26	20 53
13	8	00.1	+22.4	−1.5	5	96	4 13	12 36	20 57
15	8	17.3	+21.6	−1.2	5	94	4 29	12 45	21 00
17	8	33.8	+20.6	−1.0	5	92	4 45	12 54	21 01
19	8	49.6	+19.6	−0.9	5	89	5 00	13 01	21 01
21	9	04.7	+18.5	−0.7	5	87	5 15	13 08	21 00
23	9	19.0	+17.3	−0.6	5	84	5 29	13 15	20 58
25	9	32.6	+16.0	−0.5	5	81	5 43	13 20	20 55
27	9	45.6	+14.8	−0.3	6	79	5 57	13 25	20 52
29	9	58.0	+13.5	−0.2	6	76	6 09	13 29	20 48
31	10	09.7	+12.1	−0.2	6	73	6 21	13 33	20 43

Rising and setting times are for latitude 54°

VENUS

Day	R.A. h	R.A. m	Dec °	Mag.	Diam. "	Phase %	Rise h m	Transit h m	Set h m
1	7	09.5	+23.4	−4.0	10	99	4 01	12 31	21 01
6	7	36.1	+22.7	−4.0	10	99	4 14	12 38	21 02
11	8	02.3	+21.7	−4.0	11	99	4 28	12 44	21 00
16	8	28.0	+20.4	−4.0	11	98	4 43	12 50	20 57
21	8	53.4	+18.9	−4.0	11	98	5 00	12 56	20 52
26	9	18.2	+17.2	−4.1	11	97	5 16	13 01	20 45
31	9	42.5	+15.3	−4.1	11	97	5 34	13 06	20 37

MARS

Day	R.A. h	R.A. m	Dec °	Mag.	Diam. "	Phase %	Rise h m	Transit h m	Set h m
1	15	18.9	−21.0	−1.4	16	93	16 46	20 42	0 38
6	15	19.8	−21.2	−1.3	16	92	16 28	20 23	0 19
11	15	22.1	−21.4	−1.2	15	91	16 12	20 05	0 00
16	15	25.7	−21.6	−1.1	15	90	15 57	19 49	23 42
21	15	30.5	−21.9	−1.0	14	89	15 44	19 34	23 24
26	15	36.4	−22.3	−0.9	14	88	15 33	19 20	23 06
31	15	43.4	−22.7	−0.8	13	88	15 23	19 07	22 50

SUNRISE AND SUNSET

	London 0° 05' 51° 30'		Bristol 2° 35' 51° 28'		Birmingham 1° 55' 52° 28'		Manchester 2° 15' 53° 28'		Newcastle 1° 37' 54° 59'		Glasgow 4° 14' 55° 52'		Belfast 5° 56' 54° 35'	
d	h m	h m	h m	h m	h m	h m	h m	h m	h m	h m	h m	h m	h m	h m
1	3 48	20 20	3 58	20 30	3 50	20 33	3 45	20 40	3 33	20 48	3 37	21 05	3 53	21 02
2	3 48	20 20	3 59	20 30	3 50	20 33	3 46	20 40	3 33	20 47	3 38	21 04	3 53	21 02
3	3 49	20 20	3 59	20 29	3 51	20 32	3 47	20 40	3 34	20 47	3 38	21 03	3 54	21 01
4	3 50	20 19	4 00	20 29	3 52	20 32	3 47	20 39	3 35	20 46	3 39	21 03	3 55	21 01
5	3 51	20 19	4 01	20 28	3 53	20 31	3 48	20 38	3 36	20 45	3 40	21 02	3 56	21 00
6	3 52	20 18	4 02	20 28	3 54	20 31	3 49	20 38	3 37	20 45	3 42	21 01	3 57	20 59
7	3 53	20 17	4 03	20 27	3 55	20 30	3 50	20 37	3 38	20 44	3 43	21 00	3 58	20 59
8	3 54	20 17	4 04	20 27	3 56	20 29	3 51	20 36	3 39	20 43	3 44	21 00	3 59	20 58
9	3 55	20 16	4 05	20 26	3 57	20 28	3 52	20 35	3 41	20 42	3 45	20 59	4 00	20 57
10	3 56	20 15	4 06	20 25	3 58	20 28	3 54	20 35	3 42	20 41	3 46	20 58	4 02	20 56
11	3 57	20 14	4 07	20 24	3 59	20 27	3 55	20 34	3 43	20 40	3 48	20 56	4 03	20 55
12	3 58	20 14	4 08	20 23	4 00	20 26	3 56	20 33	3 44	20 39	3 49	20 55	4 04	20 54
13	3 59	20 13	4 09	20 23	4 01	20 25	3 57	20 32	3 46	20 38	3 50	20 54	4 05	20 53
14	4 00	20 12	4 10	20 22	4 02	20 24	3 58	20 31	3 47	20 37	3 52	20 53	4 07	20 52
15	4 01	20 11	4 11	20 21	4 04	20 23	4 00	20 29	3 48	20 36	3 53	20 52	4 08	20 51
16	4 02	20 10	4 13	20 20	4 05	20 22	4 01	20 28	3 50	20 34	3 55	20 50	4 09	20 49
17	4 04	20 09	4 14	20 18	4 06	20 21	4 02	20 27	3 51	20 33	3 56	20 49	4 11	20 48
18	4 05	20 07	4 15	20 17	4 08	20 19	4 04	20 26	3 53	20 32	3 58	20 47	4 12	20 47
19	4 06	20 06	4 16	20 16	4 09	20 18	4 05	20 25	3 54	20 30	3 59	20 46	4 14	20 45
20	4 08	20 05	4 18	20 15	4 10	20 17	4 07	20 23	3 56	20 29	4 01	20 44	4 15	20 44
21	4 09	20 04	4 19	20 14	4 12	20 16	4 08	20 22	3 57	20 27	4 03	20 43	4 17	20 42
22	4 10	20 03	4 20	20 12	4 13	20 14	4 10	20 19	3 59	20 26	4 04	20 41	4 18	20 41
23	4 12	20 01	4 22	20 11	4 15	20 13	4 11	20 19	4 01	20 24	4 06	20 40	4 20	20 39
24	4 13	20 00	4 23	20 10	4 16	20 11	4 13	20 17	4 02	20 23	4 08	20 38	4 22	20 38
25	4 14	19 58	4 25	20 08	4 17	20 10	4 14	20 16	4 04	20 21	4 10	20 36	4 23	20 36
26	4 16	19 57	4 26	20 07	4 19	20 08	4 16	20 14	4 06	20 19	4 11	20 34	4 25	20 34
27	4 17	19 55	4 27	20 05	4 20	20 07	4 17	20 13	4 07	20 17	4 13	20 33	4 27	20 33
28	4 19	19 54	4 29	20 04	4 22	20 05	4 19	20 11	4 09	20 16	4 15	20 31	4 28	20 31
29	4 20	19 52	4 30	20 02	4 23	20 04	4 20	20 09	4 11	20 14	4 17	20 29	4 30	20 29
30	4 22	19 51	4 32	20 01	4 25	20 02	4 22	20 08	4 12	20 12	4 19	20 27	4 32	20 27
31	4 23	19 49	4 33	19 59	4 27	20 00	4 24	20 06	4 14	20 10	4 20	20 25	4 33	20 26

JUPITER

Day	R.A. h m	Dec °	Mag.	Diam. "	Rise h m	Transit h m	Set h m
1	11 13.4	+6.3	−1.9	34	9 55	16 33	23 11
11	11 18.8	+5.7	−1.8	33	9 24	15 59	22 33
21	11 24.7	+5.1	−1.8	33	8 55	15 26	21 56
31	11 31.1	+4.4	−1.7	32	8 26	14 53	21 19

Equatorial Diam. 33", Polar Diam. 31"

SATURN

Day	R.A. h m	Dec °	Mag.	Diam. "	Rise h m	Transit h m	Set h m
1	16 38.6	−20.4	+0.2	18	17 56	21 57	2 03
11	16 36.3	−20.3	+0.2	18	17 14	21 16	1 21
21	16 34.4	−20.3	+0.3	18	16 32	20 34	0 40
31	16 33.2	−20.3	+0.3	18	15 52	19 54	0 00

Equatorial Diam. 18", Polar Diam. 16"
Rings – major axis 41" minor axis 18", Tilt 26°

URANUS

Day	R.A. h m	Dec °	Mag.	Diam. "	Rise h m	Transit h m	Set h m
1	1 29.6	+8.7	+6.2	3	23 59	6 51	13 42
11	1 30.3	+8.8	+6.1	4	23 20	6 12	13 04
21	1 30.7	+8.8	+6.1	4	22 41	5 33	12 25
31	1 30.8	+8.8	+6.1	4	22 02	4 54	11 46

NEPTUNE

Day	R.A. h m	Dec °	Mag.	Diam. "	Rise h m	Transit h m	Set h m
1	22 53.9	−8.0	−7.9	2	22 53	4 15	9 34
11	22 53.5	−8.0	−7.8	2	22 13	3 36	8 54
21	22 52.9	−8.1	+7.8	2	21 34	2 56	8 14
31	22 52.1	−8.1	+7.8	2	20 54	2 16	7 33

AUGUST 2016

EIGHTH MONTH, 31 DAYS. *Augustus*, formerly *Sextilis*, sixth month of Roman pre-Julian calendar

1	*Monday*	Hutton Inquiry into the death of former UN weapons inspector Dr David Kelly begins 2003	week 31 day 214
2	*Tuesday*	William II (Rufus) dies after being shot by an arrow while hunting 1100	215
3	*Wednesday*	Stanley Baldwin, Conservative prime minister three times between the World Wars *b*. 1867	216
4	*Thursday*	Idi Amin orders the expulsion of Uganda's 60,000 Asian population 1972	217
5	*Friday*	Plaid Genedlaethol Cymru (National Party of Wales), now Plaid Cymru, is formed 1925	218
6	*Saturday*	Jamaica becomes independent of the UK 1962	219
7	*Sunday*	An Act is passed to make it illegal to employ anyone aged under 21 to sweep chimneys 1840	220

8	*Monday*	George Canning, foreign secretary who had a duel with Lord Castlereagh *d*. 1827	week 32 day 221
9	*Tuesday*	Richard Nixon becomes the first US president to resign, after the Watergate scandal 1974	222
10	*Wednesday*	Herbert Hoover, US president who presided over the Wall Street Crash *b*. 1874	223
11	*Thursday*	MPs in the House of Commons vote for receiving an annual salary, initially set at £400 1911	224
12	*Friday*	The East German army begins to close the border with West Berlin 1961	225
13	*Saturday*	Fidel Castro, Cuban politician and revolutionary, President of Cuba (1976–2008) *b*. 1927	226
14	*Sunday*	Guangxu Emperor of China (1875–1908) and 11th emperor of the Qing dynasty *b*. 1871	227

15	*Monday*	Napoleon Bonaparte, Emperor of the French, who led the Napoleonic Wars *b*. 1769	week 33 day 228
16	*Tuesday*	The Peterloo Massacre takes place in Manchester, when cavalry charge a crowd 1819	229
17	*Wednesday*	US president Bill Clinton admits he had an 'improper' relationship with Monica Lewinsky 1998	230
18	*Thursday*	Genghis Khan, founder of the Mongol Empire, the largest contiguous empire in history *d*. 1227	231
19	*Friday*	Bill Clinton, 42nd US president and aged 46 the third-youngest to take office *b*. 1946	232
20	*Saturday*	Slobodan Milosevic, Yugoslavian president (1997–2000) who died while on trial for war crimes *b*. 1941	233
21	*Sunday*	A coup d'état by Gustav III ends the Age of Liberty and parliamentary rule in Sweden 1772	234

22	*Monday*	Ida Siekmann becomes the first person to die while attempting to cross the Berlin wall 1961	week 34 day 235
23	*Tuesday*	The Baltic Way, a 2 million-strong human chain demonstration against Soviet occupation occurs 1989	236
24	*Wednesday*	Brazilian president Getulio Vargas commits suicide hours after resigning 1954	237
25	*Thursday*	George Rockwell, founder of the American Nazi Party, is shot dead in Virginia 1967	238
26	*Friday*	Sir Robert Walpole, the first and longest-serving prime minister of Great Britain *b*. 1676	239
27	*Saturday*	The Treaty of Montevideo is signed in which Brazil and Argentina recognise the independence of Uruguay 1828	240
28	*Sunday*	Martin Luther King, Jr. delivers his 'I Have a Dream' speech, calling for an end to racism 1963	241

29	*Monday*	The New Jersey legislature establishes the first Native American reservation 1758	week 35 day 242
30	*Tuesday*	East Timor votes for independence from Indonesia in a referendum 1999	243
31	*Wednesday*	The Federation of Malaya becomes an independent sovereign country within the Commonwealth 1957	244

ASTRONOMICAL PHENOMENA

d h

4	06	Venus 3° North of the Moon
4	22	Mercury 0.6° North of the Moon
6	04	Jupiter 0.2° North of the Moon
12	–	Perseid meteor peak
12	12	Saturn 4° South of the Moon
16	21	Mercury Greatest elongation East
20	12	Pallas at opposition
22	10	Uranus 3° North of the Moon
25	18	Saturn 4° North of Mars
27	05	Venus 5° North of Mercury
27	22	Jupiter 0.1° South of Venus

MINIMA OF ALGOL

d	h	d	h	d	h
3	13.3	15	00.5	26	11.8
6	10.1	17	21.4	29	08.6
9	06.9	20	18.2		
12	03.7	23	15.0		

CONSTELLATIONS

The following constellations are near their meridian at

	d	h		d	h
July	1	24	August	16	21
July	16	23	September	1	20
August	1	22	September	15	19

Draco, Hercules, Lyra, Cygnus, Sagitta, Ophiuchus, Serpens, Aquila and Sagittarius

THE MOON

Phases, Apsides and Node	d	h	m
● New Moon	2	20	45
◑ First Quarter	10	18	21
○ Full Moon	18	09	27
◐ Last Quarter	25	03	41
Apogee (404,262km)	10	00	05
Perigee (367,050km)	22	01	19

Mean longitude of ascending node on 1st, 164°

THE SUN

Diam. 31.6″

Day	Right Ascension			Dec. +	Equation of time		Rise 52°		Rise 56°		Transit		Set 52°		Set 56°		Sidereal time			Transit of first point of Aries		
	h	m	s	°	m	s	h	m	h	m	h	m	h	m	h	m	h	m	s	h	m	s
1	8	46	19	18.0	−6	21	4	21	4	03	12	06	19	51	20	09	19	39	58	3	19	52
2	8	50	11	17.7	−6	17	4	22	4	05	12	06	19	49	20	07	19	43	55	3	15	55
3	8	54	03	17.5	−6	12	4	24	4	07	12	06	19	47	20	05	19	47	51	3	11	59
4	8	57	55	17.2	−6	07	4	26	4	09	12	06	19	46	20	03	19	51	48	3	08	02
5	9	01	45	16.9	−6	01	4	27	4	10	12	06	19	44	20	00	19	55	45	3	04	06
6	9	05	36	16.6	−5	55	4	29	4	12	12	06	19	42	19	58	19	59	41	3	00	09
7	9	09	25	16.4	−5	48	4	30	4	14	12	06	19	40	19	56	20	03	38	2	56	13
8	9	13	14	16.1	−5	40	4	32	4	16	12	06	19	39	19	54	20	07	34	2	52	16
9	9	17	02	15.8	−5	32	4	33	4	18	12	06	19	37	19	52	20	11	31	2	48	19
10	9	20	50	15.5	−5	23	4	35	4	20	12	05	19	35	19	50	20	15	27	2	44	23
11	9	24	37	15.2	−5	14	4	37	4	22	12	05	19	33	19	47	20	19	24	2	40	26
12	9	28	24	14.9	−5	04	4	38	4	24	12	05	19	31	19	45	20	23	20	2	36	30
13	9	32	10	14.6	−4	53	4	40	4	26	12	05	19	29	19	43	20	27	17	2	32	33
14	9	35	55	14.3	−4	42	4	41	4	28	12	05	19	27	19	41	20	31	14	2	28	37
15	9	39	40	14.0	−4	31	4	43	4	30	12	05	19	25	19	38	20	35	10	2	24	40
16	9	43	25	13.7	−4	18	4	45	4	32	12	04	19	23	19	36	20	39	07	2	20	44
17	9	47	09	13.4	−4	06	4	46	4	34	12	04	19	21	19	33	20	43	03	2	16	47
18	9	50	52	13.0	−3	52	4	48	4	36	12	04	19	19	19	31	20	47	00	2	12	50
19	9	54	35	12.7	−3	39	4	49	4	38	12	04	19	17	19	29	20	50	56	2	08	54
20	9	58	17	12.4	−3	24	4	51	4	39	12	04	19	15	19	26	20	54	53	2	04	57
21	10	01	59	12.1	−3	10	4	53	4	41	12	03	19	13	19	24	20	58	49	2	01	01
22	10	05	40	11.7	−2	55	4	54	4	43	12	03	19	11	19	21	21	02	46	1	57	04
23	10	09	21	11.4	−2	39	4	56	4	45	12	03	19	08	19	19	21	06	42	1	53	08
24	10	13	02	11.0	−2	23	4	58	4	47	12	03	19	06	19	16	21	10	39	1	49	11
25	10	16	42	10.7	−2	07	4	59	4	49	12	02	19	04	19	14	21	14	36	1	45	15
26	10	20	22	10.3	−1	50	5	01	4	51	12	02	19	02	19	11	21	18	32	1	41	18
27	10	24	01	10.0	−1	33	5	03	4	53	12	02	19	00	19	09	21	22	29	1	37	21
28	10	27	40	9.6	−1	15	5	04	4	55	12	01	18	58	19	06	21	26	25	1	33	25
29	10	31	19	9.3	−0	57	5	06	4	57	12	01	18	55	19	04	21	30	22	1	29	28
30	10	34	57	8.9	−0	39	5	07	4	59	12	01	18	53	19	01	21	34	18	1	25	32
31	10	38	35	8.6	−0	21	5	09	5	01	12	00	18	51	18	59	21	38	15	1	21	35

DURATION OF TWILIGHT (in minutes)

Latitude	52°	56°	52°	56°	52°	56°	52°	56°
	1 August		11 August		21 August		31 August	
Civil	41	49	39	45	37	42	35	40
Nautical	97	121	90	107	84	97	79	90
Astronomical	179	TAN	154	210	139	168	128	148

THE NIGHT SKY

Mercury is in the evening sky and reaches greatest elongation east (27°) on the 16th but is still hopelessly low after sunset to be seen from the UK.

Venus should put in an appearance in the evening sky from mid-August but it will be a very difficult sighting as Venus lies almost on the horizon at the end of civil twilight. This is disappointing as Venus is less than 5 arc-minutes from Jupiter on the 27th.

Mars moves from Libra into Scorpius on August 2nd, through Ophiuchus between the 21st and 27th, and then back to Scorpius. The Red Planet, magnitude −1.7, passes within 2° of Antares, magnitude +1.1, on August 24th. Mars sets around three hours after the Sun during the month.

Jupiter, magnitude −1.7, sets 1.5 hours after the Sun at the beginning of August but only 30 minutes after by the 31st. The three-day old Moon is nearby on the 5th. Jupiter moves from Leo into Virgo on August 9th.

Saturn, magnitude +0.4, is stationary in Ophiuchus on August 13th after which its direct motion resumes. The planet sets late-evening by the end of August. The Moon lies 4.5° to the upper left of Saturn on the 12th and Mars passes about 4.5° from Saturn on the 25th.

The *Perseid meteor* shower peaks on August 11th/12th this year. Moonset is before local midnight so the second half of the night will offer a good dark sky period to catch this annual display.

THE MOON

Day	R.A.		Dec.	Hor. Par.	Diam.	Sun's Co-Long.	PA of Br. Limb	Ph.	Age	Rise 52°		Rise 56°		Transit		Set 52°		Set 56°	
	h	m	°	′	′	°	°	%	d	h	m	h	m	h	m	h	m	h	m
1	07	03	+18.2	58.4	31.8	241	86	4	26.9	1	53	1	34	9	53	17	52	18	11
2	08	00	+16.9	57.9	31.5	254	84	1	27.9	2	53	2	34	10	50	18	41	18	57
3	08	56	+14.6	57.3	31.2	266	353	0	28.9	3	58	3	42	11	44	19	21	19	35
4	09	48	+11.6	56.7	30.9	278	296	1	0.4	5	06	4	54	12	36	19	54	20	04
5	10	39	+8.1	56.1	30.6	290	293	5	1.4	6	15	6	06	13	25	20	23	20	30
6	11	27	+4.3	55.5	30.2	303	292	10	2.4	7	24	7	18	14	12	20	48	20	51
7	12	14	+0.4	55.0	30.0	315	292	17	3.4	8	30	8	28	14	56	21	11	21	12
8	13	00	−3.4	54.6	29.7	327	291	25	4.4	9	36	9	37	15	40	21	34	21	31
9	13	46	−7.0	54.3	29.6	339	290	33	5.4	10	40	10	44	16	23	21	57	21	51
10	14	32	−10.4	54.2	29.6	352	288	43	6.4	11	43	11	50	17	06	22	21	22	13
11	15	19	−13.3	54.3	29.6	4	285	52	7.4	12	45	12	56	17	50	22	49	22	37
12	16	07	−15.6	54.6	29.7	16	282	61	8.4	13	46	13	59	18	36	23	20	23	06
13	16	57	−17.4	55.0	30.0	28	279	71	9.4	14	46	15	01	19	23	23	57	23	39
14	17	49	−18.3	55.5	30.3	40	275	79	10.4	15	42	16	00	20	12	—		—	
15	18	42	−18.4	56.2	30.6	53	271	87	11.4	16	35	16	53	21	03	0	39	0	21
16	19	36	−17.5	56.9	31.0	65	267	93	12.4	17	23	17	40	21	55	1	30	1	13
17	20	31	−15.7	57.7	31.4	77	265	97	13.4	18	05	18	20	22	48	2	29	2	13
18	21	26	−12.9	58.3	31.8	89	272	100	14.4	18	42	18	54	23	41	3	36	3	21
19	22	21	−9.4	58.9	32.1	101	62	100	15.4	19	15	19	24	—		4	47	4	36
20	23	16	−5.2	59.4	32.4	114	68	97	16.4	19	45	19	49	0	34	6	03	5	56
21	0	11	−0.7	59.6	32.5	126	69	92	17.4	20	13	20	14	1	26	7	20	7	17
22	1	06	+3.8	59.7	32.6	138	70	84	18.4	20	41	20	38	2	19	8	38	8	39
23	2	01	+8.1	59.7	32.5	150	72	74	19.4	21	10	21	03	3	12	9	56	10	01
24	2	57	+11.9	59.5	32.4	162	75	64	20.4	21	41	21	31	4	05	11	14	11	23
25	3	54	+15.0	59.2	32.3	174	78	52	21.4	22	17	22	04	5	00	12	30	12	43
26	4	52	+17.2	58.8	32.1	187	82	41	22.4	23	00	22	43	5	55	13	42	13	57
27	5	50	+18.3	58.4	31.8	199	87	30	23.4	23	48	23	30	6	51	14	48	15	06
28	6	48	+18.3	58.0	31.6	211	91	21	24.4	—		—		7	47	15	47	16	05
29	7	44	+17.3	57.5	31.3	223	96	13	25.4	0	44	0	26	8	43	16	37	16	54
30	8	39	+15.3	57.0	31.1	236	99	6	26.4	1	46	1	30	9	37	17	19	17	34
31	9	32	+12.6	56.5	30.8	248	102	2	27.4	2	53	2	38	10	28	17	54	18	05

MERCURY

Day	R.A.		Dec °	Mag.	Diam. ″	Phase %	Rise		Transit		Set	
	h	m					h	m	h	m	h	m
1	10	15.4	+11.5	−0.1	6	72	6	27	13	35	20	41
3	10	26.2	+10.2	0.0	6	70	6	37	13	37	20	36
5	10	36.5	+8.8	0.0	6	67	6	47	13	39	20	30
7	10	46.2	+7.5	+0.1	6	65	6	57	13	41	20	25
9	10	55.4	+6.3	+0.1	7	62	7	05	13	42	20	18
11	11	04.0	+5.0	+0.2	7	59	7	12	13	43	20	12
13	11	12.0	+3.8	+0.2	7	57	7	19	13	43	20	05
15	11	19.4	+2.6	+0.3	7	54	7	25	13	42	19	58
17	11	26.2	+1.5	+0.3	7	51	7	30	13	40	19	51
19	11	32.2	+0.5	+0.4	8	48	7	33	13	38	19	43
21	11	37.5	−0.4	+0.5	8	44	7	35	13	35	19	35
23	11	41.9	−1.3	+0.6	8	41	7	36	13	32	19	27
25	11	45.4	−2.0	+0.7	9	37	7	36	13	27	19	18
27	11	47.9	−2.6	+0.8	9	33	7	33	13	21	19	09
29	11	49.2	−3.1	+1.0	9	28	7	28	13	14	19	00
31	11	49.2	−3.3	+1.2	9	24	7	21	13	06	18	51

Rising and setting times are for latitude 54°

VENUS

Day	R.A.		Dec °	Mag.	Diam. ″	Phase %	Rise		Transit		Set	
	h	m					h	m	h	m	h	m
1	9	47.3	+14.9	−4.1	11	96	5	37	13	07	20	35
6	10	11.1	+12.8	−4.2	11	96	5	54	13	11	20	26
11	10	34.5	+10.6	−4.2	11	95	6	12	13	14	20	16
16	10	57.4	+8.2	−4.2	11	94	6	29	13	17	20	05
21	11	20.1	+5.7	−4.3	11	94	6	46	13	20	19	54
26	11	42.5	+3.2	−4.3	12	93	7	02	13	23	19	43
31	12	04.8	+0.7	−4.4	12	92	7	19	13	26	19	31

MARS

Day	R.A.		Dec °	Mag.	Diam. ″	Phase %	Rise		Transit		Set	
	h	m					h	m	h	m	h	m
1	15	44.9	+22.8	−0.8	13	87	15	21	19	04	22	47
6	15	53.0	−23.2	−0.7	13	87	15	12	18	53	22	33
11	16	02.0	−23.6	−0.6	12	86	15	05	18	42	22	19
16	16	11.8	−24.0	−0.5	12	86	14	58	18	32	22	06
21	16	22.3	−24.4	−0.4	11	85	14	52	18	23	21	53
26	16	33.5	−24.8	−0.4	11	85	14	46	18	14	21	42
31	16	45.3	−25.1	−0.3	11	85	14	41	18	06	21	31

SUNRISE AND SUNSET

	London 0° 05'	51° 30'	Bristol 2° 35'	51° 28'	Birmingham 1° 55'	52° 28'	Manchester 2° 15'	53° 28'	Newcastle 1° 37'	54° 59'	Glasgow 4° 14'	55° 52'	Belfast 5° 56'	54° 35'
d	h m	h m	h m	h m	h m	h m	h m	h m	h m	h m	h m	h m	h m	h m
1	4 25	19 48	4 35	19 58	4 28	19 59	4 25	20 04	4 16	20 08	4 22	20 23	4 35	20 24
2	4 26	19 46	4 36	19 56	4 30	19 57	4 27	20 02	4 18	20 06	4 24	20 21	4 37	20 22
3	4 28	19 44	4 38	19 54	4 31	19 55	4 29	20 00	4 20	20 04	4 26	20 19	4 39	20 20
4	4 29	19 43	4 39	19 52	4 33	19 53	4 30	19 59	4 21	20 02	4 28	20 17	4 40	20 18
5	4 31	19 41	4 41	19 51	4 35	19 52	4 32	19 57	4 23	20 00	4 30	20 15	4 42	20 16
6	4 32	19 39	4 42	19 49	4 36	19 50	4 34	19 55	4 25	19 58	4 32	20 13	4 44	20 14
7	4 34	19 37	4 44	19 47	4 38	19 48	4 35	19 53	4 27	19 56	4 34	20 10	4 46	20 12
8	4 35	19 35	4 46	19 45	4 39	19 46	4 37	19 51	4 29	19 54	4 36	20 08	4 48	20 10
9	4 37	19 34	4 47	19 43	4 41	19 44	4 39	19 49	4 31	19 52	4 37	20 06	4 49	20 08
10	4 39	19 32	4 49	19 42	4 43	19 42	4 41	19 47	4 32	19 50	4 39	20 04	4 51	20 06
11	4 40	19 30	4 50	19 40	4 44	19 40	4 42	19 45	4 34	19 48	4 41	20 01	4 53	20 03
12	4 42	19 28	4 52	19 38	4 46	19 38	4 44	19 43	4 36	19 45	4 43	19 59	4 55	20 01
13	4 43	19 26	4 53	19 36	4 48	19 36	4 46	19 41	4 38	19 43	4 45	19 57	4 57	19 59
14	4 45	19 24	4 55	19 34	4 49	19 34	4 47	19 39	4 40	19 41	4 47	19 55	4 58	19 57
15	4 46	19 22	4 57	19 32	4 51	19 32	4 49	19 36	4 42	19 39	4 49	19 52	5 00	19 55
16	4 48	19 20	4 58	19 30	4 53	19 30	4 51	19 34	4 44	19 36	4 51	19 50	5 02	19 52
17	4 50	19 18	5 00	19 28	4 54	19 28	4 53	19 32	4 45	19 34	4 53	19 48	5 04	19 50
18	4 51	19 16	5 01	19 26	4 56	19 26	4 54	19 30	4 47	19 32	4 55	19 45	5 06	19 48
19	4 53	19 14	5 03	19 24	4 58	19 24	4 56	19 28	4 49	19 30	4 57	19 43	5 08	19 46
20	4 54	19 12	5 04	19 22	4 59	19 21	4 58	19 25	4 51	19 27	4 59	19 40	5 09	19 43
21	4 56	19 10	5 06	19 20	5 01	19 19	5 00	19 23	4 53	19 25	5 01	19 38	5 11	19 41
22	4 58	19 08	5 08	19 17	5 03	19 17	5 01	19 21	4 55	19 22	5 03	19 35	5 13	19 39
23	4 59	19 05	5 09	19 15	5 04	19 15	5 03	19 19	4 57	19 20	5 05	19 33	5 15	19 36
24	5 01	19 03	5 11	19 13	5 06	19 13	5 05	19 16	4 58	19 18	5 07	19 30	5 17	19 34
25	5 02	19 01	5 12	19 11	5 08	19 11	5 07	19 14	5 00	19 15	5 09	19 28	5 19	19 31
26	5 04	18 59	5 14	19 09	5 09	19 08	5 08	19 12	5 02	19 13	5 10	19 25	5 20	19 29
27	5 05	18 57	5 16	19 07	5 11	19 06	5 10	19 09	5 04	19 10	5 12	19 23	5 22	19 27
28	5 07	18 55	5 17	19 05	5 13	19 04	5 12	19 07	5 06	19 08	5 14	19 20	5 24	19 24
29	5 09	18 52	5 19	19 02	5 14	19 02	5 14	19 05	5 08	19 05	5 16	19 18	5 26	19 22
30	5 10	18 50	5 20	19 00	5 16	18 59	5 15	19 02	5 10	19 03	5 18	19 15	5 28	19 19
31	5 12	18 48	5 22	18 58	5 18	18 57	5 17	19 00	5 12	19 00	5 20	19 13	5 30	19 17

JUPITER

Day	R.A. h m	Dec °	Mag.	Diam. "	Rise h m	Transit h m	Set h m
1	11 31.8	+4.3	−1.7	32	8 23	14 49	21 16
11	11 38.7	+3.5	−1.7	32	7 55	14 17	20 39
21	11 46.0	+2.7	−1.7	31	7 27	13 45	20 03
31	11 53.5	+1.9	−1.7	31	7 00	13 13	19 26

Equatorial Diam. 31″, Polar Diam. 29″

SATURN

Day	R.A. h m	Dec °	Mag.	Diam. "	Rise h m	Transit h m	Set h m
1	16 33.1	−20.3	+0.4	18	15 48	19 50	23 56
11	16 32.6	−20.3	+0.4	17	15 08	19 10	23 12
21	16 32.7	−20.3	+0.5	17	14 29	18 31	22 33
31	16 33.5	−20.4	+0.5	17	13 51	17 52	21 54

Equatorial Diam. 17″, Polar Diam. 16″
Rings – major axis 39″ minor axis 17″, Tilt 26°

URANUS

Day	R.A. h m	Dec °	Mag.	Diam. "	Rise h m	Transit h m	Set h m
1	1 30.8	+8.8	+6.1	4	21 58	4 50	11 42
11	1 30.6	+8.8	+6.1	4	21 18	4 10	11 03
21	1 30.1	+8.8	+6.1	4	20 39	3 31	10 22
31	1 29.3	+8.7	+6.1	4	19 59	2 50	9 42

NEPTUNE

Day	R.A. h m	Dec °	Mag.	Diam. "	Rise h m	Transit h m	Set h m
1	22 52.1	−8.2	−7.8	2	20 50	2 12	7 29
11	22 51.2	−8.2	−7.8	2	20 10	1 31	6 48
21	22 50.2	−8.3	+7.8	2	19 31	0 51	6 08
31	22 49.2	−8.5	+7.8	2	18 51	0 11	5 27

SEPTEMBER 2016

NINTH MONTH, 30 DAYS. *Septem* (seven), seventh month of Roman pre-Julian calendar

1	*Thursday*	A bloodless military coup in Libya deposes King Idris 1969	day 245
2	*Friday*	The Treaty of Jaffa, between Saladin and Richard I, ends the hostilities of the 3rd Crusade 1192	246
3	*Saturday*	Richard I (Coeur de Lion) is crowned at Westminster Abbey 1189	247
4	*Sunday*	The French Third Republic is proclaimed following the overthrow of Napoleon III 1870	248
5	*Monday*	Sam Houston is elected as the first president of the Republic of Texas 1836	week 36 day 249
6	*Tuesday*	Lithuania's independence is officially recognised by the Soviet Union 1991	250
7	*Wednesday*	Henry Campbell-Bannerman, Liberal Prime Minister (1905–8) *b.* 1836	251
8	*Thursday*	President of Chile Augusto Pinochet survives an assassination attempt 1986	252
9	*Friday*	UK Ambassador Geoffrey Jackson is freed after being held for 8 months by rebels in Uruguay 1971	253
10	*Saturday*	Mary Wollstonecraft, political theorist and advocate of women's rights *d.* 1797	254
11	*Sunday*	Chilean president Salvador Allende commits suicide after his government is toppled in a military coup 1973	255
12	*Monday*	Herbert Asquith, prime minister at the outbreak of the First World War *b.* 1852	week 37 day 256
13	*Tuesday*	Albania withdraws from the Warsaw Pact due to differences with the Soviet Union 1968	257
14	*Wednesday*	Duke of Wellington (1st), leading military and political figure of the 19th century *d.* 1852	258
15	*Thursday*	The Nuremberg Race Laws are unanimously passed by the Reichstag in Nazi Germany 1935	259
16	*Friday*	Owain Glyndwr proclaims himself Prince of Wales and instigates a Welsh revolt against Henry IV 1400	260
17	*Saturday*	The British National Party wins its first council seat in Millwall, London 1993	261
18	*Sunday*	In a referendum the Welsh people vote in favour of a devolved National Assembly for Wales 1997	262
19	*Monday*	New Zealand becomes the first country to grant all women aged 21 and over the right to vote 1893	week 38 day 263
20	*Tuesday*	The South Africa Act 1909 gains royal assent, creating the Union of South Africa	264
21	*Wednesday*	Britain formally annexes the islet of Rockall to prevent Soviet spying 1955	265
22	*Thursday*	Sir Robert Walpole takes up residence at 10 Downing Street, the first prime minister to do so 1735	266
23	*Friday*	Negotiations on the Karlstad Treaty end with an agreement to disunite Sweden and Norway 1905	267
24	*Saturday*	The Rhodesian government agrees to introduce black majority rule 1974	268
25	*Sunday*	Henry Pelham, Whig prime minister during the reign of George II *b.* 1694	269
26	*Monday*	The first televised debate between US presidential candidates (Kennedy and Nixon) occurs 1960	week 39 day 270
27	*Tuesday*	For one day Lancaster, Pennsylvania becomes the capital of the American colonies 1777	271
28	*Wednesday*	The Israeli-Palestinian Interim Agreement on the West Bank and the Gaza Strip is officially signed 1995	272
29	*Thursday*	Lech Walesa, president of Poland and Nobel Peace Prize laureate *b.* 1943	273
30	*Friday*	Neville Chamberlain makes his 'peace for our time' speech on the Munich Agreement 1938	274

ASTRONOMICAL PHENOMENA

d	h	
1	09	Annular eclipse of the Sun
2	22	Jupiter 0.4° South of the Moon
2	17	Neptune at opposition
3	11	Venus 1° South of the Moon
8	21	Saturn 4° South of the Moon
16	19	Penumbral eclipse of the Moon
18	17	Uranus 3° North of the Moon
22	14	Equinox
28	19	Mercury Greatest elongation West
29	11	Mercury 1° North of the Moon
30	16	Jupiter 1° South of the Moon

MINIMA OF ALGOL

d	h	d	h	d	h
1	05.4	12	16.6	24	03.9
4	02.2	15	13.5	27	00.7
6	23.0	18	10.3	29	21.5
9	19.8	21	07.1		

CONSTELLATIONS

The following constellations are near their meridian at

	d	h		d	h
August	1	24	September	15	21
August	16	23	October	1	20
September	1	22	October	16	19

Draco, Cepheus, Lyra, Cygnus, Vulpecula, Sagitta, Delphinus, Equuleus, Aquila, Aquarius and Capricornus

THE MOON

Phases, Apsides and Node	d	h	m
● New Moon	1	09	03
◐ First Quarter	9	11	49
○ Full Moon	16	19	05
◑ Last Quarter	23	09	56
Apogee (405,055km)	6	18	45
Perigee (361,896km)	18	17	00

Mean longitude of ascending node on 1st, 163°

THE SUN

Diam. 31.8″

Day	Right Ascension h	m	s	Dec. °	Equation of time m	s	Rise 52° h	m	Rise 56° h	m	Transit h	m	Set 52° h	m	Set 56° h	m	Sidereal time h	m	s	Transit of first point of Aries h	m	s
1	10	42	13	+8.2	−0	02	5	11	5	03	12	00	18	49	18	56	21	42	11	1	17	39
2	10	45	51	+6.8	+0	17	5	12	5	05	12	00	18	46	18	53	21	46	08	1	13	42
3	10	49	28	+6.5	+0	37	5	14	5	07	12	00	18	44	18	51	21	50	05	1	09	46
4	10	53	05	+6.1	+0	56	5	16	5	09	11	59	18	42	18	48	21	54	01	1	05	49
5	10	56	41	+6.7	+1	16	5	17	5	11	11	59	18	39	18	46	21	57	58	1	01	52
6	11	00	18	+6.4	+1	36	5	19	5	13	11	59	18	37	18	43	22	01	54	0	57	56
7	11	03	54	+6.0	+1	57	5	20	5	15	11	58	18	35	18	40	22	05	51	0	53	59
8	11	07	30	+5.6	+2	17	5	22	5	17	11	58	18	33	18	38	22	09	47	0	50	03
9	11	11	06	+5.2	+2	38	5	24	5	19	11	58	18	30	18	35	22	13	44	0	46	06
10	11	14	41	+4.9	+2	59	5	25	5	21	11	57	18	28	18	33	22	17	40	0	42	10
11	11	18	17	+4.5	+3	20	5	27	5	22	11	57	18	26	18	30	22	21	37	0	38	13
12	11	21	52	+4.1	+3	41	5	29	5	24	11	56	18	23	18	27	22	25	34	0	34	17
13	11	25	27	+3.7	+4	02	5	30	5	26	11	56	18	21	18	25	22	29	30	0	30	20
14	11	29	03	+3.3	+4	24	5	32	5	28	11	56	18	19	18	22	22	33	27	0	26	23
15	11	32	38	+3.0	+4	45	5	33	5	30	11	55	18	16	18	19	22	37	23	0	22	27
16	11	36	13	+2.6	+5	07	5	35	5	32	11	55	18	14	18	17	22	41	20	0	18	30
17	11	39	48	+2.2	+5	28	5	37	5	34	11	55	18	12	18	14	22	45	16	0	14	34
18	11	43	23	+1.8	+5	50	5	38	5	36	11	54	18	09	18	11	22	49	13	0	10	37
19	11	46	58	+1.4	+6	11	5	40	5	38	11	54	18	07	18	09	22	53	09	0	06	41
20	11	50	33	+1.0	+6	33	5	42	5	40	11	54	18	05	18	06	22	57	06	0	02	44
21	11	54	08	+0.6	+6	54	5	43	5	42	11	53	18	02	18	03	23	01	03	23	58	48
22	11	57	44	+0.2	+7	15	5	45	5	44	11	53	18	00	18	01	23	04	59	23	54	51
23	12	01	19	−0.1	+7	36	5	47	5	46	11	53	17	58	17	58	23	08	56	23	50	54
24	12	04	55	−0.5	+7	57	5	48	5	48	11	52	17	55	17	55	23	12	52	23	46	58
25	12	08	30	−0.9	+8	18	5	50	5	50	11	52	17	53	17	53	23	16	49	23	43	01
26	12	12	06	−1.3	+8	39	5	51	5	52	11	52	17	51	17	50	23	20	45	23	39	05
27	12	15	43	−1.7	+8	59	5	53	5	54	11	51	17	48	17	47	23	24	42	23	35	08
28	12	19	19	−2.1	+9	19	5	55	5	56	11	51	17	46	17	45	23	28	38	23	31	12
29	12	22	56	−2.5	+9	39	5	56	5	58	11	50	17	44	17	42	23	32	35	23	27	15
30	12	26	32	−2.9	+9	59	5	58	6	00	11	50	17	41	17	40	23	36	32	23	23	19

DURATION OF TWILIGHT (in minutes)

Latitude	52°	56°	52°	56°	52°	56°	52°	56°
	1 September		11 September		21 September		31 September	
Civil	35	39	34	38	34	37	34	37
Nautical	79	89	76	85	74	82	73	80
Astronomical	127	147	120	136	116	129	113	125

THE NIGHT SKY

Mercury moves into the morning sky after inferior conjunction on the 13th. It is at greatest elongation west (18°) on the 28th and rises two hours before the Sun by the end of September. The Moon is nearby on the 29th.

Things improve a little for *Venus* but it will still be quite low all month. The Moon is nearby on the 3rd.

Mars, magnitude −0.3 to +0.1, now sets three hours after the Sun. It lies 7° below the Moon on the 9th. Mars crosses into Ophiuchus on the 3rd then Sagittarius on the 22nd.

Jupiter might be seen the first few days of September very low in the west after sunset but it is soon swamped by the twilight glow. The planet reaches conjunction on the 26th.

Saturn, magnitude +0.5, sets 3.25 hours after the Sun at the beginning of September but by an hour earlier on the 30th.

Neptune is at opposition on September 2nd when the magnitude 7.8 planet can be found in Aquarius.

An annular solar eclipse on September 1st sweeps across Central Africa and the northern part of Madagascar. Bordering countries will experience a partial solar eclipse.

A penumbral lunar eclipse on September 16th is visible from Eurasia, Africa, and Australia. The eclipse is in progress at moonrise from the UK. The Moon dips 90 per cent of the way into the southern part of the Earth's penumbral shadow so observers should notice a distinct dimming of the northern limb of the Moon.

THE MOON

Day	R.A. h	R.A. m	Dec. °	Hor. Par. '	Diam. '	Sun's Co-Long. °	PA of Br. Limb °	Ph. %	Age d	Rise 52° h	Rise 52° m	Rise 56° h	Rise 56° m	Transit h	Transit m	Set 52° h	Set 52° m	Set 56° h	Set 56° m
1	10	23	+9.3	56.0	30.5	260	102	0	28.4	4	01	3	50	11	18	18	24	18	32
2	11	11	+5.6	55.5	30.3	272	290	0	29.4	5	08	5	01	12	05	18	50	18	55
3	11	59	+1.8	55.1	30.0	285	289	2	0.9	6	15	6	12	12	50	19	14	19	16
4	12	45	−2.1	54.7	29.8	297	288	6	1.9	7	21	7	21	13	35	19	37	19	36
5	13	31	−5.8	54.4	29.6	309	288	12	2.9	8	26	8	29	14	18	20	00	19	56
6	14	17	−9.3	54.2	29.5	321	286	19	3.9	9	30	9	36	15	01	20	24	20	16
7	15	04	−12.3	54.1	29.5	333	284	27	4.9	10	32	10	42	15	45	20	50	20	39
8	15	51	−14.9	54.2	29.6	346	281	36	5.9	11	34	11	46	16	29	21	19	21	06
9	16	40	−16.8	54.5	29.7	358	277	45	6.9	12	34	12	49	17	15	21	53	21	37
10	17	30	−18.0	55.0	30.0	10	273	55	7.9	13	31	13	48	18	03	22	32	22	15
11	18	22	−18.5	55.6	30.3	22	269	64	8.9	14	25	14	43	18	52	23	19	23	02
12	19	15	−18.0	56.3	30.7	35	265	74	9.9	15	14	15	32	19	43	—		23	56
13	20	09	−16.5	57.2	31.1	47	261	82	10.9	15	57	16	14	20	34	0	14	—	
14	21	04	−14.1	58.0	31.6	59	257	90	11.9	16	37	16	50	21	27	1	16	1	01
15	21	59	−10.9	58.9	32.1	71	253	95	12.9	17	11	17	22	22	20	2	24	2	12
16	22	54	−6.9	59.6	32.5	83	248	99	13.9	17	43	17	49	23	13	3	38	3	29
17	23	50	−2.5	60.2	32.8	95	97	100	14.9	18	12	18	15	—		4	55	4	50
18	0	46	+2.2	60.5	33.0	108	76	98	15.9	18	40	18	39	0	07	6	15	6	14
19	1	43	+6.8	60.6	33.0	120	75	93	16.9	19	10	19	05	1	01	7	36	7	39
20	2	40	+10.9	60.4	32.9	132	77	86	17.9	19	41	19	32	1	56	8	56	9	04
21	3	39	+14.3	60.0	32.7	144	80	77	18.9	20	17	20	05	2	52	10	16	10	28
22	4	38	+16.8	59.5	32.4	156	84	67	19.9	20	58	20	42	3	49	11	32	11	47
23	5	37	+18.2	58.8	32.1	168	88	55	20.9	21	45	21	27	4	46	12	41	12	58
24	6	35	+18.4	58.2	31.7	181	93	44	21.9	22	39	22	21	5	43	13	43	14	01
25	7	32	+17.6	57.5	31.4	193	97	33	22.9	23	40	23	22	6	39	14	36	14	53
26	8	26	+15.9	56.9	31.0	205	102	24	23.9	—		—		7	33	15	20	15	35
27	9	19	+13.3	56.4	30.7	217	106	16	24.9	0	44	0	29	8	25	15	56	16	09
28	10	09	+10.2	55.8	30.4	229	109	9	25.9	1	51	1	38	9	14	16	27	16	37
29	10	58	+6.7	55.4	30.2	242	113	4	26.9	2	58	2	49	10	01	16	54	17	00
30	11	45	+2.9	55.0	30.0	254	119	1	27.9	4	04	3	59	10	47	17	18	17	21

MERCURY

Day	R.A. h	R.A. m	Dec °	Mag.	Diam. "	Phase %	Rise h	Rise m	Transit h	Transit m	Set h	Set m
1	11	48.7	−3.4	+1.4	10	21	7	17	13	01	18	46
3	11	46.7	−3.3	+1.7	10	17	7	06	12	51	18	37
5	11	43.4	−3.0	+2.2	10	12	6	53	12	39	18	27
7	11	38.6	−2.4	+2.8	10	8	6	37	12	26	18	18
9	11	32.8	−1.6	+3.5	11	4	6	18	12	12	18	09
11	11	26.3	−0.5	+4.3	11	2	5	58	11	58	18	00
13	11	19.5	+0.7	+4.9	10	1	5	37	11	43	17	53
15	11	13.1	+1.9	+4.4	10	1	5	16	11	29	17	46
17	11	07.7	+3.2	+3.4	10	4	4	57	11	17	17	40
19	11	04.0	+4.3	+2.4	9	9	4	40	11	06	17	35
21	11	02.3	+5.2	+1.5	9	15	4	26	10	57	17	31
23	11	03.0	+5.8	+0.8	8	23	4	16	10	50	17	27
25	11	05.9	+6.1	+0.3	8	32	4	10	10	46	17	24
27	11	11.1	+6.1	−0.1	7	42	4	08	10	44	17	22
29	11	18.3	+5.7	−0.4	7	51	4	09	10	44	17	19

Rising and setting times are for latitude 54°

VENUS

Day	R.A. h	R.A. m	Dec °	Mag.	Diam. "	Phase %	Rise h	Rise m	Transit h	Transit m	Set h	Set m
1	12	09.3	+0.1	−4.4	12	92	7	22	13	26	19	29
6	12	31.5	−2.4	−4.5	12	91	7	39	13	29	19	17
11	12	53.8	−5.0	−4.5	12	90	7	56	13	31	19	06
16	13	16.2	−7.5	−4.6	12	89	8	13	13	34	18	54
21	13	38.8	−10.0	−4.6	13	88	8	30	13	37	18	43
26	14	01.8	−12.4	−4.7	13	87	8	47	13	40	18	32

MARS

Day	R.A. h	R.A. m	Dec °	Mag.	Diam. "	Phase %	Rise h	Rise m	Transit h	Transit m	Set h	Set m
1	16	47.8	−25.2	−0.3	10	85	14	40	18	05	21	30
6	17	00.3	−25.4	−0.2	10	85	14	35	17	57	21	20
11	17	13.3	−25.7	−0.2	10	85	14	30	17	51	21	12
16	17	26.8	−25.8	−0.1	10	85	14	25	17	44	21	04
21	17	40.7	−25.9	0.0	9	85	14	19	17	39	20	58
26	17	55.0	−25.9	0.0	9	85	14	14	17	33	20	52

SUNRISE AND SUNSET

d	London 0° 05' 51° 30'		Bristol 2° 35' 51° 28'		Birmingham 1° 55' 52° 28'		Manchester 2° 15' 53° 28'		Newcastle 1° 37' 54° 59'		Glasgow 4° 14' 55° 52'		Belfast 5° 56' 54° 35'	
	h m	h m	h m	h m	h m	h m	h m	h m	h m	h m	h m	h m	h m	h m
1	5 13	18 46	5 24	18 56	5 19	18 55	5 19	18 58	5 13	18 58	5 22	19 10	5 31	19 14
2	5 15	18 44	5 25	18 54	5 21	18 52	5 21	18 55	5 15	18 55	5 24	19 07	5 33	19 12
3	5 17	18 41	5 27	18 51	5 23	18 50	5 22	18 53	5 17	18 53	5 26	19 05	5 35	19 09
4	5 18	18 39	5 28	18 49	5 24	18 48	5 24	18 51	5 19	18 50	5 28	19 02	5 37	19 07
5	5 20	18 37	5 30	18 47	5 26	18 45	5 26	18 48	5 21	18 48	5 30	19 00	5 39	19 04
6	5 21	18 35	5 31	18 45	5 28	18 43	5 27	18 46	5 23	18 45	5 32	18 57	5 41	19 02
7	5 23	18 32	5 33	18 42	5 29	18 41	5 29	18 43	5 25	18 43	5 34	18 55	5 42	19 00
8	5 25	18 30	5 35	18 40	5 31	18 38	5 31	18 41	5 26	18 40	5 36	18 52	5 44	18 57
9	5 26	18 28	5 36	18 38	5 32	18 36	5 33	18 39	5 28	18 38	5 38	18 49	5 46	18 55
10	5 28	18 25	5 38	18 35	5 34	18 34	5 34	18 36	5 30	18 35	5 40	18 47	5 48	18 52
11	5 29	18 23	5 39	18 33	5 36	18 31	5 36	18 34	5 32	18 33	5 42	18 44	5 50	18 49
12	5 31	18 21	5 41	18 31	5 37	18 29	5 38	18 31	5 34	18 30	5 43	18 41	5 52	18 47
13	5 33	18 19	5 43	18 29	5 39	18 27	5 40	18 29	5 36	18 27	5 45	18 39	5 53	18 44
14	5 34	18 16	5 44	18 26	5 41	18 24	5 41	18 26	5 38	18 25	5 47	18 36	5 55	18 42
15	5 36	18 14	5 46	18 24	5 42	18 22	5 43	18 24	5 39	18 22	5 49	18 33	5 57	18 39
16	5 37	18 12	5 47	18 22	5 44	18 19	5 45	18 21	5 41	18 20	5 51	18 31	5 59	18 37
17	5 39	18 09	5 49	18 19	5 46	18 17	5 47	18 19	5 43	18 17	5 53	18 28	6 01	18 34
18	5 41	18 07	5 51	18 17	5 47	18 15	5 48	18 16	5 45	18 15	5 55	18 26	6 03	18 32
19	5 42	18 05	5 52	18 15	5 49	18 12	5 50	18 14	5 47	18 12	5 57	18 23	6 04	18 29
20	5 44	18 02	5 54	18 12	5 51	18 10	5 52	18 12	5 49	18 09	5 59	18 20	6 06	18 27
21	5 45	18 00	5 55	18 10	5 52	18 08	5 54	18 09	5 51	18 07	6 01	18 18	6 08	18 24
22	5 47	17 58	5 57	18 08	5 54	18 05	5 55	18 07	5 53	18 04	6 03	18 15	6 10	18 22
23	5 49	17 56	5 59	18 05	5 56	18 03	5 57	18 04	5 54	18 02	6 05	18 12	6 12	18 19
24	5 50	17 53	6 00	18 03	5 57	18 01	5 59	18 02	5 56	17 59	6 07	18 10	6 14	18 16
25	5 52	17 51	6 02	18 01	5 59	17 58	6 01	17 59	5 58	17 57	6 09	18 07	6 15	18 14
26	5 53	17 49	6 03	17 59	6 01	17 56	6 02	17 57	6 00	17 54	6 11	18 04	6 17	18 11
27	5 55	17 46	6 05	17 56	6 03	17 53	6 04	17 55	6 02	17 52	6 13	18 02	6 19	18 09
28	5 57	17 44	6 07	17 54	6 04	17 51	6 06	17 52	6 04	17 49	6 15	17 59	6 21	18 06
29	5 58	17 42	6 08	17 52	6 06	17 49	6 08	17 50	6 06	17 46	6 17	17 57	6 23	18 04
30	6 00	17 40	6 10	17 50	6 08	17 46	6 09	17 47	6 08	17 44	6 19	17 54	6 25	18 01

JUPITER

Day	R.A. h m	Dec °	Mag.	Diam. "	Rise h m	Transit h m	Set h m
1	11 54.3	+1.8	−1.7	31	6 57	13 10	19 23
11	12 02.1	+1.0	−1.7	31	6 30	12 38	18 46
21	12 10.0	+0.1	−1.7	31	6 03	12 07	18 10

Equatorial Diam. 31", Polar Diam. 29"

SATURN

Day	R.A. h m	Dec °	Mag.	Diam. "	Rise h m	Transit h m	Set h m
1	16 33.7	−20.4	+0.5	17	13 47	17 48	21 50
11	16 35.2	−20.5	+0.5	16	13 10	17 11	21 11
21	16 37.4	−20.6	+0.6	16	12 34	16 34	20 33

Equatorial Diam. 16", Polar Diam. 15"
Rings – major axis 37" minor axis 16", Tilt 26°

URANUS

Day	R.A. h m	Dec °	Mag.	Diam. "	Rise h m	Transit h m	Set h m
1	1 29.2	+8.7	+6.0	4	19 55	2 46	9 38
11	1 28.2	+8.6	+6.0	4	19 15	2 06	8 57
21	1 26.9	+8.4	+6.0	4	18 32	1 25	8 15

NEPTUNE

Day	R.A. h m	Dec °	Mag.	Diam. "	Rise h m	Transit h m	Set h m
1	22 49.1	−8.5	+7.8	2	18 47	0 07	5 23
11	22 48.1	−8.6	+7.8	2	18 07	23 22	4 42
21	22 47.1	−8.7	+7.8	2	17 28	22 42	4 01

  # OCTOBER 2016

TENTH MONTH, 31 DAYS. *Octo* (eighth), eighth month of Roman pre-Julian calendar

1	*Saturday*	Oswald Mosley founds the British Union of Fascists 1932	day 275
2	*Sunday*	Mohandas Gandhi, leader of the Indian independence movement *b.* 1869	276
3	*Monday*	The reunification of East and West Germany is formerly completed and celebrated 1990	week 40 day 277
4	*Tuesday*	Richard Cromwell, son of Oliver, and 2nd Lord Protector of the Commonwealth *b.* 1626	278
5	*Wednesday*	200 marchers set-out from Jarrow to walk to Westminster in protest at poverty and unemployment 1936	279
6	*Thursday*	Anwar Sadat, president of Egypt, is assassinated during an annual victory parade in Cairo 1981	280
7	*Friday*	Vladimir Putin, president of Russia who was formerly the country's prime minister *b.* 1952	281
8	*Saturday*	Harold Macmillan leads the Conservatives to their third successive general election victory 1959	282
9	*Sunday*	Marxist revolutionary Che Guevara is executed in Bolivia 1967	283
10	*Monday*	Paul Kruger, 5th president of the South African Republic *b.* 1825	week 41 day 284
11	*Tuesday*	The Labour Party wins the second general election of the year with a three-seat majority 1974	285
12	*Wednesday*	The USSR and USA fail to agree on disarmament at a summit in Reykjavik 1986	286
13	*Thursday*	The British government loses its battle to prevent the publication of the book *Spycatcher* in the UK 1988	287
14	*Friday*	George Grenville, Whig prime minister who was dismissed by King George III *b.* 1712	288
15	*Saturday*	The Black Panther Party, a black nationalist organisation, is formed in California 1966	289
16	*Sunday*	Much of the Palace of Westminster is destroyed by fire 1834	290
17	*Monday*	Emperor Jacques I of Haiti is assassinated 1806	week 42 day 291
18	*Tuesday*	Henry John Temple, 3rd Viscount Palmerston, twice prime minister (1855–8 and 1859–65) *d.* 1865	292
19	*Wednesday*	Conservative MPs vote at the Carlton Club to disband the coalition government 1922	293
20	*Thursday*	The Dalai Lama arrives in the UK for the first time at the start of a 10-day tour 1973	294
21	*Friday*	The Royal Navy defeats the combined fleets of the French and Spanish at the Battle of Trafalgar 1805	295
22	*Saturday*	Hu Jintao is re-elected as General Secretary of the Communist Party of China 2007	296
23	*Sunday*	Thousands attend a rally in Budapest, Hungary to demand an end to Soviet rule 1956	297
24	*Monday*	The United Nations is officially established to promote international cooperation 1945	week 43 day 298
25	*Tuesday*	The general election is won by the Conservative Party led by Winston Churchill 1951	299
26	*Wednesday*	The leaders of Israel and Jordon sign a peace treaty, ending 46 years of war 1994	300
27	*Thursday*	Labour suffer its greatest defeat in the 1931 general election, losing 80 per cent of its seats	301
28	*Friday*	The USSR confirms the removal of missiles from Cuba, ending the Cuban Missile Crisis 1962	302
29	*Saturday*	Sir Walter Raleigh was beheaded for conspiring against James I in 1618	303
30	*Sunday*	In a referendum citizens in Quebec narrowly vote for the province to remain part of Canada 1995	304
31	*Monday*	Indira Gandhi, prime minister of India, is assassinated by two of her bodyguards 1984	week 44 day 305

ASTRONOMICAL PHENOMENA

d h

6 08 Saturn 4° South of the Moon
11 04 Jupiter 1° South of Mercury
15 11 Uranus at opposition
16 02 Uranus 3° North of the Moon
21 05 Ceres at opposition
28 10 Jupiter 1° South of the Moon
30 08 Saturn 3° North of Venus
30 19 Mercury 4° South of the Moon

MINIMA OF ALGOL

d	h	d	h	d	h
2	18.3	14	05.6	25	16.8
5	15.1	17	02.4	28	13.6
8	12.0	19	23.2	31	10.5
11	08.8	22	20.0		

CONSTELLATIONS

The following constellations are near their meridian at

	d	h		d	h
September	1	24	October	16	21
September	15	23	November	1	20
October	1	22	November	15	19

Ursa Major (below the Pole), Cepheus, Cassiopeia, Cygnus, Lacerta, Andromeda, Pegasus, Capricornus, Aquarius and Piscis Austrinus

THE MOON

Phases, Apsides and Node	d	h	m
● New Moon	1	00	11
◐ First Quarter	9	04	33
○ Full Moon	16	04	23
◑ Last Quarter	22	19	14
● New Moon	30	17	38

Apogee (406,096km)	4	11	03
Perigee (357,861km)	16	23	34
Apogee (406,662km)	31	19	29

Mean longitude of ascending node on 1st, 161°

THE SUN

Diam. 32.1″

Day	Right Ascension			Dec. −	Equation of time	Rise 52°		Rise 56°		Transit		Set 52°		Set 56°		Sidereal time			Transit of first point of Aries		
	h	m	s	°	m s	h	m	h	m	h	m	h	m	h	m	h	m	s	h	m	s
1	12	30	10	3.3	+10 18	6	00	6	02	11	50	17	39	17	37	23	40	28	23	19	22
2	12	33	47	3.6	+10 37	6	01	6	04	11	50	17	37	17	34	23	44	25	23	15	25
3	12	37	25	4.0	+10 56	6	03	6	06	11	49	17	34	17	32	23	48	21	23	11	29
4	12	41	03	4.4	+11 15	6	05	6	08	11	49	17	32	17	29	23	52	18	23	07	32
5	12	44	41	4.8	+11 33	6	06	6	10	11	49	17	30	17	26	23	56	14	23	03	36
6	12	48	20	5.2	+11 51	6	08	6	12	11	48	17	27	17	24	0	00	11	22	59	39
7	12	51	59	5.6	+12 08	6	10	6	14	11	48	17	25	17	21	0	04	07	22	55	43
8	12	55	39	5.9	+12 25	6	12	6	16	11	48	17	23	17	19	0	08	04	22	51	46
9	12	59	19	6.3	+12 42	6	13	6	18	11	47	17	21	17	16	0	12	01	22	47	50
10	13	02	59	6.7	+12 58	6	15	6	20	11	47	17	18	17	14	0	15	57	22	43	53
11	13	06	40	7.1	+13 13	6	17	6	22	11	47	17	16	17	11	0	19	54	22	39	56
12	13	10	21	7.5	+13 29	6	18	6	24	11	47	17	14	17	08	0	23	50	22	36	00
13	13	14	03	7.8	+13 43	6	20	6	26	11	46	17	12	17	06	0	27	47	22	32	03
14	13	17	45	8.2	+13 58	6	22	6	28	11	46	17	10	17	03	0	31	43	22	28	07
15	13	21	28	8.6	+14 11	6	24	6	30	11	46	17	07	17	01	0	35	40	22	24	10
16	13	25	12	8.9	+14 24	6	25	6	32	11	46	17	05	16	58	0	39	36	22	20	14
17	13	28	56	9.3	+14 37	6	27	6	34	11	45	17	03	16	56	0	43	33	22	16	17
18	13	32	40	9.7	+14 49	6	29	6	36	11	45	17	01	16	53	0	47	30	22	12	21
19	13	36	26	10.0	+15 00	6	31	6	38	11	45	16	59	16	51	0	51	26	22	08	24
20	13	40	11	10.4	+15 11	6	32	6	40	11	45	16	57	16	49	0	55	23	22	04	27
21	13	43	58	10.8	+15 21	6	34	6	42	11	45	16	55	16	46	0	59	19	22	00	31
22	13	47	45	11.1	+15 30	6	36	6	44	11	45	16	52	16	44	1	03	16	21	56	34
23	13	51	33	11.5	+15 39	6	38	6	47	11	44	16	50	16	41	1	07	12	21	52	38
24	13	55	22	11.8	+15 47	6	39	6	49	11	44	16	48	16	39	1	11	09	21	48	41
25	13	59	11	12.2	+15 54	6	41	6	51	11	44	16	46	16	37	1	15	05	21	44	45
26	14	03	01	12.5	+16 01	6	43	6	53	11	44	16	44	16	34	1	19	02	21	40	48
27	14	06	52	12.8	+16 06	6	45	6	55	11	44	16	42	16	32	1	22	59	21	36	52
28	14	10	43	13.2	+16 11	6	47	6	57	11	44	16	40	16	30	1	26	55	21	32	55
29	14	14	36	13.5	+16 16	6	48	6	59	11	44	16	38	16	27	1	30	52	21	28	58
30	14	18	29	13.8	+16 19	6	50	7	01	11	44	16	37	16	25	1	34	48	21	25	02
31	14	22	23	14.2	+16 22	6	52	7	03	11	44	16	35	16	23	1	38	45	21	21	05

DURATION OF TWILIGHT (in minutes)

Latitude	52°	56°	52°	56°	52°	56°	52°	56°
	1 October		11 October		21 October		31 October	
Civil	34	37	34	37	34	38	35	39
Nautical	73	80	73	80	74	81	75	83
Astronomical	113	125	112	124	113	124	114	126

THE NIGHT SKY

Mercury rises 1.5 hours before the Sun and is favourably placed the first half of the month. It meets Jupiter on the 11th when both are less than 1° apart. Mercury passes through superior conjunction on the 27th.

Venus, magnitude −3.9, is still rather low in the west after sunset but should now be more easily seen given a clear horizon. The young Moon is 4° from Venus on the 3rd and the planet passes 3° from Saturn on the 30th.

Mars, magnitude +0.1 to +0.4, spends the month in the distinctive Teapot asterism of Sagittarius and on the 8th is close to the 2.8 magnitude star lambda Sagitarii marking the knob on the pot's lid. The Moon passes through the area on the nights of October 7th and 8th.

Jupiter should be picked up the second week of October after it muscles back into the morning sky. The magnitude −1.7 giant is rising a little more than 2.5 hours before the Sun by the 31st. Catch it close to Mercury on the 11th and 1.5° from the crescent Moon on the 28th.

Saturn, magnitude +0.5, is solely an evening sky object and sets about two hours after the Sun at the end of the month. The Moon is nearby on October 5th and 6th.

Uranus is at opposition in Pisces on the 15th when the magnitude 5.7 planet may be found in steadily held binoculars by referencing a good chart of its position.

THE MOON

Day	R.A. h m	Dec. °	Hor. Par. '	Diam. '	Sun's Co-Long. °	PA of Br. Limb °	Ph. %	Age d	Rise 52° h m	Rise 56° h m	Transit h m	Set 52° h m	Set 56° h m
1	12 32	−1.0	54.6	29.8	266	189	0	28.9	5 10	5 09	11 31	17 41	17 41
2	13 17	−4.8	54.3	29.6	278	276	1	0.3	6 15	6 17	12 14	18 04	18 00
3	14 03	−8.3	54.1	29.5	291	280	4	1.3	7 19	7 24	12 57	18 27	18 20
4	14 50	−11.5	54.0	29.4	303	280	8	2.3	8 22	8 31	13 41	18 52	18 42
5	15 37	−14.3	54.0	29.4	315	278	14	3.3	9 24	9 36	14 25	19 20	19 08
6	16 25	−16.4	54.1	29.5	327	276	21	4.3	10 25	10 39	15 10	19 52	19 36
7	17 14	−17.8	54.4	29.7	339	272	29	5.3	11 23	11 39	15 57	20 28	20 11
8	18 05	−18.5	54.9	29.9	352	268	38	6.3	12 17	12 35	16 45	21 11	20 53
9	18 56	−18.3	55.5	30.2	4	264	48	7.3	13 07	13 25	17 34	22 02	21 43
10	19 49	−17.3	56.2	30.6	16	260	58	8.3	13 52	14 09	18 24	22 59	22 42
11	20 42	−15.3	57.1	31.1	28	256	68	9.3	14 32	14 47	19 14	—	23 48
12	21 36	−12.4	58.0	31.6	40	252	77	10.3	15 07	15 20	20 06	0 03	—
13	22 30	−8.8	59.0	32.1	53	249	86	11.3	15 39	15 48	20 58	1 12	1 02
14	23 25	−4.6	59.9	32.6	65	246	93	12.3	16 09	16 14	21 51	2 27	2 19
15	0 21	+0.1	60.6	33.0	77	240	98	13.3	16 37	16 38	22 45	3 45	3 41
16	1 18	+4.8	61.1	33.3	89	203	100	14.3	17 06	17 03	23 40	5 05	5 06
17	2 17	+9.3	61.3	33.4	101	91	99	15.3	17 37	17 30	—	6 28	6 33
18	3 16	+13.2	61.1	33.3	113	85	95	16.3	18 12	18 01	0 37	7 50	8 00
19	4 17	+16.2	60.7	33.1	125	86	89	17.3	18 51	18 36	1 35	9 11	9 25
20	5 18	+18.0	60.0	32.7	138	90	80	18.3	19 37	19 20	2 34	10 27	10 44
21	6 19	+18.6	59.2	32.3	150	94	70	19.3	20 31	20 13	3 34	11 35	11 53
22	7 17	+18.1	58.3	31.8	162	98	59	20.3	21 31	21 13	4 32	12 33	12 50
23	8 14	+16.5	57.5	31.3	174	103	49	21.3	22 35	22 19	5 28	13 20	13 37
24	9 07	+14.1	56.7	30.9	186	106	38	22.3	23 42	23 29	6 22	13 59	14 13
25	9 58	+11.1	56.0	30.5	198	109	28	23.3	—	—	7 12	14 31	14 42
26	10 47	+7.6	55.4	30.2	211	112	20	24.3	0 49	0 39	8 00	14 59	15 06
27	11 34	+3.9	54.9	29.9	223	114	13	25.3	1 56	1 50	8 45	15 24	15 28
28	12 20	+0.0	54.6	29.7	235	117	7	26.3	3 02	2 59	9 30	15 47	15 47
29	13 06	−3.8	54.3	29.6	247	121	3	27.3	4 06	4 07	10 13	16 09	16 07
30	13 51	−7.5	54.1	29.5	259	134	1	28.3	5 10	5 14	10 55	16 31	16 26
31	14 37	−10.8	53.9	29.4	272	227	0	29.3	6 13	6 21	11 39	16 56	16 47

MERCURY

Day	R.A. h m	Dec °	Mag.	Diam. "	Phase %	Rise h m	Transit h m	Set h m
1	11 27.1	+5.1	−0.7	7	60	4 14	10 45	17 17
3	11 37.2	+4.3	−0.8	6	68	4 21	10 48	17 15
5	11 48.3	+3.3	−0.9	6	75	4 30	10 51	17 12
7	12 00.0	+2.1	−1.0	6	81	4 41	10 55	17 09
9	12 12.2	+0.8	−1.0	6	86	4 52	11 00	17 06
11	12 24.6	−0.6	−1.1	5	90	5 05	11 04	17 03
13	12 37.2	−2.0	−1.1	5	93	5 17	11 09	17 00
15	12 49.8	−3.5	−1.2	5	95	5 30	11 14	16 57
17	13 02.4	−5.0	−1.2	5	97	5 43	11 19	16 53
19	13 15.0	−6.4	−1.2	5	98	5 56	11 23	16 50
21	13 27.6	−7.9	−1.3	5	99	6 09	11 28	16 46
23	13 40.1	−9.3	−1.3	5	100	6 22	11 33	16 43
25	13 52.5	−10.7	−1.4	5	100	6 34	11 37	16 39
27	14 05.0	−12.0	−1.4	5	100	6 47	11 42	16 36
29	14 17.4	−13.4	−1.3	5	100	6 59	11 46	16 32
31	14 29.8	−14.6	−1.2	5	100	7 12	11 51	16 29

Rising and setting times are for latitude 54°

VENUS

Day	R.A. h m	Dec °	Mag.	Diam. "	Phase %	Rise h m	Transit h m	Set h m
1	14 25.1	−14.6	−4.8	13	85	9 04	13 44	18 22
6	14 48.8	−16.7	−4.9	13	84	9 22	13 48	18 13
11	15 13.0	−18.7	−4.9	14	83	9 39	13 52	18 05
16	15 37.6	−20.4	−5.0	14	82	9 56	13 57	17 57
21	16 02.8	−22.0	−5.1	14	81	10 13	14 02	17 52
26	16 28.4	−23.2	−5.2	15	79	10 28	14 08	17 48
31	16 54.4	−24.3	−5.3	15	78	10 42	14 15	17 47

MARS

Day	R.A. h m	Dec °	Mag.	Diam. "	Phase %	Rise h m	Transit h m	Set h m
1	18 09.6	−25.8	+0.1	9	85	14 08	17 28	20 48
6	18 24.4	−25.7	+0.1	9	85	14 02	17 23	20 45
11	18 39.4	−25.4	+0.2	8	85	13 55	17 18	20 42
16	18 54.7	−25.0	+0.2	8	85	13 47	17 14	20 41
21	19 10.0	−24.6	+0.3	8	85	13 39	17 09	20 40
26	19 25.4	−24.0	+0.3	8	86	13 30	17 05	20 40
31	19 40.8	−23.4	+0.4	8	86	13 21	17 01	20 41

SUNRISE AND SUNSET

	London 0° 05'	51° 30'	Bristol 2° 35'	51° 28'	Birmingham 1° 55'	52° 28'	Manchester 2° 15'	53° 28'	Newcastle 1° 37'	54° 59'	Glasgow 4° 14'	55° 52'	Belfast 5° 56'	54° 35'
d	h m	h m	h m	h m	h m	h m	h m	h m	h m	h m	h m	h m	h m	h m
1	6 02	17 37	6 11	17 47	6 09	17 44	6 11	17 45	6 09	17 41	6 20	17 51	6 27	17 59
2	6 03	17 35	6 13	17 45	6 11	17 42	6 13	17 42	6 11	17 39	6 22	17 49	6 28	17 56
3	6 05	17 33	6 15	17 43	6 13	17 39	6 15	17 40	6 13	17 36	6 24	17 46	6 30	17 54
4	6 06	17 30	6 16	17 40	6 14	17 37	6 17	17 38	6 15	17 34	6 26	17 43	6 32	17 51
5	6 08	17 28	6 18	17 38	6 16	17 35	6 18	17 35	6 17	17 31	6 28	17 41	6 34	17 49
6	6 10	17 26	6 20	17 36	6 18	17 32	6 20	17 33	6 19	17 29	6 30	17 38	6 36	17 46
7	6 11	17 24	6 21	17 34	6 20	17 30	6 22	17 30	6 21	17 26	6 32	17 36	6 38	17 44
8	6 13	17 22	6 23	17 32	6 21	17 28	6 24	17 28	6 23	17 24	6 34	17 33	6 40	17 42
9	6 15	17 19	6 25	17 29	6 23	17 26	6 26	17 26	6 25	17 21	6 36	17 31	6 42	17 39
10	6 16	17 17	6 26	17 27	6 25	17 23	6 27	17 23	6 27	17 19	6 39	17 28	6 44	17 37
11	6 18	17 15	6 28	17 25	6 27	17 21	6 29	17 21	6 29	17 16	6 41	17 26	6 46	17 34
12	6 20	17 13	6 30	17 23	6 28	17 19	6 31	17 19	6 31	17 14	6 43	17 23	6 47	17 32
13	6 21	17 11	6 31	17 21	6 30	17 17	6 33	17 16	6 33	17 12	6 45	17 21	6 49	17 29
14	6 23	17 08	6 33	17 18	6 32	17 14	6 35	17 14	6 35	17 09	6 47	17 18	6 51	17 27
15	6 25	17 06	6 35	17 16	6 34	17 12	6 37	17 12	6 37	17 07	6 49	17 16	6 53	17 25
16	6 27	17 04	6 37	17 14	6 35	17 10	6 38	17 10	6 39	17 04	6 51	17 13	6 55	17 22
17	6 28	17 02	6 38	17 12	6 37	17 08	6 40	17 07	6 41	17 02	6 53	17 11	6 57	17 20
18	6 30	17 00	6 40	17 10	6 39	17 06	6 42	17 05	6 43	17 00	6 55	17 08	6 59	17 18
19	6 32	16 58	6 42	17 08	6 41	17 03	6 44	17 03	6 45	16 57	6 57	17 06	7 01	17 15
20	6 33	16 56	6 43	17 06	6 43	17 01	6 46	17 01	6 47	16 55	6 59	17 03	7 03	17 13
21	6 35	16 54	6 45	17 04	6 44	16 59	6 48	16 58	6 49	16 53	7 01	17 01	7 05	17 11
22	6 37	16 52	6 47	17 02	6 46	16 57	6 50	16 56	6 51	16 50	7 03	16 59	7 07	17 08
23	6 39	16 50	6 49	17 00	6 48	16 55	6 52	16 54	6 53	16 48	7 05	16 56	7 09	17 06
24	6 40	16 48	6 50	16 58	6 50	16 53	6 53	16 52	6 55	16 46	7 07	16 54	7 11	17 04
25	6 42	16 46	6 52	16 56	6 52	16 51	6 55	16 50	6 57	16 44	7 09	16 52	7 13	17 02
26	6 44	16 44	6 54	16 54	6 53	16 49	6 57	16 48	6 59	16 41	7 12	16 49	7 15	17 00
27	6 46	16 42	6 56	16 52	6 55	16 47	6 59	16 46	7 01	16 39	7 14	16 47	7 17	16 57
28	6 47	16 40	6 57	16 50	6 57	16 45	7 01	16 44	7 03	16 37	7 16	16 45	7 19	16 55
29	6 49	16 38	6 59	16 48	6 59	16 43	7 03	16 42	7 05	16 35	7 18	16 43	7 21	16 53
30	6 51	16 36	7 01	16 46	7 01	16 41	7 05	16 40	7 07	16 33	7 20	16 40	7 23	16 51
31	6 53	16 34	7 03	16 45	7 03	16 39	7 07	16 38	7 09	16 31	7 22	16 38	7 25	16 49

JUPITER

Day	R.A. h m	Dec °	Mag.	Diam. "	Rise h m	Transit h m	Set h m
1	12 17.9	−0.7	−1.7	31	5 37	11 35	17 34
11	12 25.8	−1.6	−1.7	31	5 10	11 04	16 58
21	12 33.6	−2.4	−1.7	31	4 43	10 33	16 22
31	12 41.3	−3.2	−1.7	31	4 16	10 01	15 46

Equatorial Diam. 31″, Polar Diam. 29″

SATURN

Day	R.A. h m	Dec °	Mag.	Diam. "	Rise h m	Transit h m	Set h m
1	16 40.2	−20.7	+0.6	16	11 58	15 57	19 56
11	16 43.5	−20.9	+0.6	16	11 23	15 21	19 19
21	16 47.3	−21.0	+0.6	16	10 49	14 45	18 43
31	16 51.5	−21.1	+0.6	15	10 14	14 10	18 06

Equatorial Diam. 16″, Polar Diam. 14″
Rings – major axis 35″ minor axis 16″, Tilt 26°

URANUS

Day	R.A. h m	Dec °	Mag.	Diam. "	Rise h m	Transit h m	Set h m
1	1 25.5	+8.3	+6.0	4	17 52	0 45	7 34
11	1 24.0	+8.1	+6.0	4	17 12	0 04	6 52
21	1 22.5	+8.0	+6.0	4	16 32	23 19	6 11
31	1 21.0	+7.8	+6.0	4	15 52	22 38	5 29

NEPTUNE

Day	R.A. h m	Dec °	Mag.	Diam. "	Rise h m	Transit h m	Set h m
1	22 46.2	−8.8	+7.8	2	16 48	22 02	3 20
11	22 45.4	−8.8	+7.8	2	16 08	21 22	2 39
21	22 44.7	−8.9	+7.8	2	15 29	20 42	1 59
31	22 44.2	−9.0	+7.9	2	14 49	20 02	1 19

NOVEMBER 2016

ELEVENTH MONTH, 30 DAYS. *Novem* (nine), ninth month of Roman pre-Julian calendar

1	*Tuesday*	Geoffrey Howe resigns as deputy prime minister over the single currency 1990	day 306
2	*Wednesday*	The Balfour Declaration gives British support for a Jewish state in Palestine 1917	307
3	*Thursday*	Lyndon B. Johnson defeats Barry Goldwater in the US presidential election 1964	308
4	*Friday*	Former actor Ronald Reagan wins the US presidential election 1980	309
5	*Saturday*	Woodrow Wilson wins the US presidential election in a rare four-way contest 1912	310
6	*Sunday*	In a referendum Australia vote to retain the monarchy 1999	311
7	*Monday*	Franklin D. Roosevelt is elected as the US president for a record fourth term 1944	week 45 day 312
8	*Tuesday*	Grover Cleveland wins his 2nd non-consecutive US presidential election 1892	313
9	*Wednesday*	The dismantling of the Berlin Wall begins and border crossings are opened 1989	314
10	*Thursday*	Mustafa Kemal Ataturk, founder and 1st president of the Republic of Turkey d. 1938	315
11	*Friday*	Yasser Arafat, Palestinian leader and chair of the Palestine Liberation Organisation d. 2004	316
12	*Saturday*	Akihito is enthroned as the 125th Emperor of Japan 1990	317
13	*Sunday*	George Grenville, prime minister of Great Britain (1763–5) d. 1770	318
14	*Monday*	The Scottish Nationalist Party contests its first general election 1935	week 46 day 319
15	*Tuesday*	William Pitt the Elder, prime minister during the Seven Years' War b. 1708	320
16	*Wednesday*	Benazir Bhutto is elected prime minister of Pakistan, the first female head of an Islamic state 1988	321
17	*Thursday*	1st Duke of Newcastle, succeeded his younger brother Henry Pelham as prime minister d. 1768	322
18	*Friday*	Chester A. Arthur, US president who succeeded the assassinated James Garfield d. 1886	323
19	*Saturday*	Egyptian president Anwar Sadat becomes the first Arab leader to officially visit Israel 1977	324
20	*Sunday*	Liberal MP Jeremy Thorpe is accused of conspiracy to kill his former lover Norman Scott 1978	325
21	*Monday*	Voltaire, French Enlightenment writer, political philosopher and playwright b. 1694	week 47 day 326
22	*Tuesday*	US president John F. Kennedy is assassinated in Dallas, Texas by Lee Harvey Oswald 1963	327
23	*Wednesday*	Eduard Shevardnadze, president of Georgia, retires from office following the Rose Revolution 2003	328
24	*Thursday*	Zachary Taylor, US President who died sixteen months into his term b. 1784	329
25	*Friday*	Augusto Pinochet, Chilean leader who came to power in 1973 in a violent coup b. 1915	330
26	*Saturday*	Tony Blair becomes the first UK prime minister to address the Irish parliament 1998	331
27	*Sunday*	Helen Clark is elected prime minister of New Zealand 1999	332
28	*Monday*	In a referendum voters in Norway reject joining the European Union 1994	week 48 day 333
29	*Tuesday*	Jacques Chirac, former president and prime minister of France b. 1932	334
30	*Wednesday*	Barbados becomes independent from the UK as granted under the Barbados Independence Act 1966	335

ASTRONOMICAL PHENOMENA

d h
2 19 Saturn 4° South of the Moon
12 11 Uranus 3° North of the Moon
24 01 Saturn 3° North of Mercury
25 02 Jupiter 2° South of the Moon
30 08 Saturn 4° South of the Moon

MINIMA OF ALGOL

d	h	d	h	d	h
3	07.3	14	18.5	26	05.8
6	04.1	17	15.4	29	02.6
9	00.9	20	12.2		
11	21.7	23	09.0		

CONSTELLATIONS

The following constellations are near their meridian at

	d	h		d	h
October	1	24	November	15	21
October	16	23	December	1	20
November	1	22	December	16	19

Ursa Major (below the Pole), Cepheus, Cassiopeia, Andromeda, Pegasus, Pisces, Aquarius and Cetus

THE MOON

Phases, Apsides and Node	d	h	m
◐ First Quarter	7	19	51
○ Full Moon	14	13	52
◑ Last Quarter	21	08	33
● New Moon	29	12	18
Perigee (356,509km)	14	11	21
Apogee (406,554km)	27	20	08

Mean longitude of ascending node on 1st, 159°

THE SUN

Diam. 32.4″

Day	Right Ascension			Dec. −	Equation of time	Rise 52°		Rise 56°		Transit		Set 52°		Set 56°		Sidereal time			Transit of first point of Aries		
	h	m	s	°	m s	h	m	h	m	h	m	h	m	h	m	h	m	s	h	m	s
1	14	26	27	14.5	+16 24	6	55	7	08	11	44	16	31	16	19	2	42	51	21	17	09
2	14	30	23	14.8	+16 25	6	57	7	10	11	44	16	29	16	16	2	46	48	21	13	12
3	14	34	19	15.1	+16 25	6	59	7	12	11	44	16	27	16	14	2	50	44	21	09	16
4	14	38	16	15.4	+16 24	7	01	7	14	11	44	16	26	16	12	2	54	41	21	05	19
5	14	42	14	15.7	+16 23	7	03	7	16	11	44	16	24	16	10	2	58	37	21	01	23
6	14	46	13	16.0	+16 21	7	04	7	18	11	44	16	22	16	08	3	02	34	20	57	26
7	14	50	12	16.3	+16 18	7	06	7	20	11	44	16	20	16	06	3	06	31	20	53	29
8	14	54	13	16.6	+16 14	7	08	7	23	11	44	16	19	16	04	3	10	27	20	49	33
9	14	58	14	16.9	+16 09	7	10	7	25	11	44	16	17	16	02	3	14	24	20	45	36
10	15	02	16	17.2	+16 04	7	12	7	27	11	44	16	16	16	00	3	18	20	20	41	40
11	15	06	19	17.5	+15 57	7	13	7	29	11	44	16	14	15	59	3	22	17	20	37	43
12	15	10	23	17.7	+15 50	7	15	7	31	11	44	16	13	15	57	3	26	13	20	33	47
13	15	14	27	18.0	+15 42	7	17	7	33	11	44	16	11	15	55	3	30	10	20	29	50
14	15	18	33	18.3	+15 33	7	19	7	35	11	45	16	10	15	53	3	34	06	20	25	54
15	15	22	39	18.5	+15 24	7	20	7	37	11	45	16	08	15	52	3	38	03	20	21	57
16	15	26	46	18.8	+15 13	7	22	7	39	11	45	16	07	15	50	3	42	00	20	18	00
17	15	30	54	19.0	+15 02	7	24	7	41	11	45	16	06	15	48	3	45	56	20	14	04
18	15	35	03	19.3	+14 50	7	26	7	43	11	45	16	04	15	47	3	49	53	20	10	07
19	15	39	12	19.5	+14 37	7	27	7	45	11	45	16	03	15	45	3	53	49	20	06	11
20	15	43	23	19.7	+14 23	7	29	7	47	11	46	16	02	15	44	3	57	46	20	02	14
21	15	47	34	20.0	+14 08	7	31	7	49	11	46	16	01	15	42	4	01	42	19	58	18
22	15	51	46	20.2	+13 52	7	32	7	51	11	46	16	00	15	41	4	05	39	19	54	21
23	15	55	59	20.4	+13 36	7	34	7	53	11	47	15	59	15	40	4	09	35	19	50	25
24	16	00	13	20.6	+13 19	7	35	7	55	11	47	15	58	15	38	4	13	32	19	46	28
25	16	04	27	20.8	+13 01	7	37	7	57	11	47	15	57	15	37	4	17	29	19	42	31
26	16	08	42	21.0	+12 42	7	38	7	58	11	47	15	56	15	36	4	21	25	19	38	35
27	16	12	58	21.2	+12 23	7	40	8	00	11	48	15	55	15	35	4	25	22	19	34	38
28	16	17	15	21.3	+12 03	7	41	8	02	11	48	15	54	15	34	4	29	18	19	30	42
29	16	21	33	21.5	+11 42	7	43	8	04	11	48	15	54	15	33	4	33	15	19	26	45
30	16	25	51	21.7	+11 20	7	44	8	05	11	49	15	53	15	32	4	37	11	19	22	49

DURATION OF TWILIGHT (in minutes)

Latitude	52°	56°	52°	56°	52°	56°	52°	56°
	1 November		11 November		21 November		31 November	
Civil	35	40	37	41	38	43	40	45
Nautical	75	84	78	87	80	90	82	93
Astronomical	115	127	117	130	120	134	123	138

THE NIGHT SKY

Mercury sets before the end of civil twilight all month and so will not be seen.

Venus, magnitude −4.1, starts the month near Saturn in the evening sky but pulls away soon after and will slowly gain in altitude as the weeks pass. The slender crescent Moon nearby on the 2nd makes for an attractive sight when both Venus and Saturn ply the evening stage. Venus is setting nearly three hours after the Sun by the 30th.

Mars moves into Capricornus on the 8th where it spends the rest of the month crossing this bright-star poor group. The planet's magnitude declines a little more during November from magnitude +0.4 to +0.6 and it will set mid-evening. The Moon is nearby on the 6th.

Jupiter, magnitude −1.7, greets the early riser all month as it threads its way through Virgo. The Moon is quite close on the morning of the 25th when Jupiter is the sole planet on view during the small hours.

Saturn is now getting quite low in the southwest and will probably be lost to view during the last week of November by which time it is setting only about half an hour after the Sun.

THE MOON

Day	R.A. h	R.A. m	Dec. °	Hor. Par. '	Diam. '	Sun's Co-Long. °	PA of Br. Limb °	Ph. %	Age d	Rise 52° h	Rise 52° m	Rise 56° h	Rise 56° m	Transit h	Transit m	Set 52° h	Set 52° m	Set 56° h	Set 56° m
1	15	26	−13.8	53.9	29.4	284	265	1	0.8	8	17	8	31	13	07	17	52	17	37
2	16	14	−16.1	54.0	29.4	297	269	5	1.8	9	17	9	33	13	53	18	27	18	10
3	17	03	−17.7	54.2	29.5	309	269	9	2.8	10	12	10	31	14	41	19	08	18	49
4	17	53	−18.6	54.4	29.7	321	266	16	3.8	11	03	11	23	15	29	19	55	19	35
5	18	44	−18.7	54.8	29.9	333	263	23	4.8	11	50	12	08	16	18	20	48	20	30
6	19	36	−17.8	55.4	30.2	345	259	32	5.8	12	31	12	47	17	07	21	48	21	32
7	20	28	−16.1	56.1	30.6	358	256	42	6.8	13	07	13	21	17	57	22	54	22	41
8	21	20	−13.6	56.9	31.0	10	252	52	7.8	13	39	13	49	18	47	—		23	55
9	22	12	−10.3	57.8	31.5	22	249	62	8.8	14	08	14	15	19	37	0	04	—	
10	23	05	−6.3	58.7	32.0	34	247	73	9.8	14	36	14	39	20	29	1	17	1	12
11	23	59	−1.9	59.7	32.5	46	245	82	10.8	15	03	15	02	21	22	2	35	2	33
12	0	54	+2.8	60.5	33.0	58	243	90	11.8	15	32	15	27	22	17	3	55	3	58
13	1	51	+7.4	61.1	33.3	71	240	96	12.8	16	04	15	55	23	15	5	17	5	24
14	2	51	+11.6	61.5	33.5	83	225	99	13.8	16	40	16	27	—		6	40	6	51
15	3	52	+15.1	61.5	33.5	95	117	100	14.8	17	24	17	08	0	15	8	00	8	16
16	4	55	+17.6	61.1	33.3	107	97	97	15.8	18	15	17	57	1	16	9	15	9	34
17	5	57	+18.7	60.5	33.0	119	97	91	16.8	19	15	18	56	2	17	10	21	10	40
18	6	59	+18.6	59.6	32.5	131	100	84	17.8	20	20	20	03	3	17	11	15	11	33
19	7	58	+17.3	58.7	32.0	143	103	74	18.8	21	28	21	14	4	14	11	58	12	14
20	8	54	+15.0	57.7	31.4	155	107	64	19.8	22	37	22	26	5	07	12	35	12	47
21	9	47	+12.1	56.8	30.9	168	110	54	20.8	23	46	23	38	5	57	13	04	13	13
22	10	37	+8.6	56.0	30.5	180	112	44	21.8	—		—		6	44	13	30	13	36
23	11	25	+4.8	55.3	30.1	192	113	34	22.8	0	52	0	48	7	29	13	53	13	55
24	12	11	+1.0	54.8	29.8	204	115	25	23.8	1	58	1	57	8	12	14	15	14	14
25	12	57	−2.9	54.4	29.6	216	115	17	24.8	3	02	3	05	8	54	14	37	14	33
26	13	42	−6.6	54.1	29.5	229	116	11	25.8	4	05	4	11	9	37	15	01	14	53
27	14	28	−10.1	54.0	29.4	241	117	6	26.8	5	08	5	18	10	21	15	26	15	15
28	15	14	−13.1	53.9	29.4	253	121	2	27.8	6	10	6	23	11	05	15	54	15	40
29	16	02	−15.6	54.0	29.4	265	143	0	28.8	7	10	7	26	11	51	16	27	16	11
30	16	51	−17.5	54.1	29.5	277	234	0	0.3	8	08	8	26	12	38	17	06	16	47

MERCURY

Day	R.A. h	R.A. m	Dec °	Mag.	Diam. "	Phase %	Rise h	Rise m	Transit h	Transit m	Set h	Set m
1	14	36.3	−15.3	−1.1	5	100	7	18	11	53	16	28
3	14	48.7	−16.4	−1.0	5	99	7	30	11	58	16	25
5	15	01.2	−17.6	−0.9	5	99	7	42	12	02	16	22
7	15	13.8	−18.6	−0.8	5	99	7	54	12	07	16	19
9	15	26.3	−19.6	−0.8	5	98	8	05	12	12	16	17
11	15	39.0	−20.6	−0.7	5	97	8	17	12	16	16	16
13	15	51.7	−21.5	−0.6	5	97	8	28	12	21	16	14
15	16	04.5	−22.3	−0.6	5	96	8	38	12	26	16	13
17	16	17.3	−23.0	−0.6	5	95	8	49	12	31	16	13
19	16	30.2	−23.6	−0.5	5	94	8	59	12	36	16	13
21	16	43.1	−24.2	−0.5	5	93	9	08	12	41	16	13
23	16	56.1	−24.7	−0.5	5	91	9	17	12	46	16	15
25	17	09.0	−25.1	−0.5	5	90	9	26	12	51	16	17
27	17	21.9	−25.4	−0.5	5	88	9	33	12	56	16	19
29	17	34.7	−25.7	−0.5	5	86	9	40	13	01	16	22

Rising and setting times are for latitude 54°

VENUS

Day	R.A. h	R.A. m	Dec °	Mag.	Diam. "	Phase %	Rise h	Rise m	Transit h	Transit m	Set h	Set m
1	16	59.8	−24.4	−5.3	15	78	10	45	14	16	17	47
6	17	26.1	−25.1	−5.4	15	76	10	57	14	23	17	48
11	17	52.6	−25.5	−5.5	16	75	11	07	14	29	17	52
16	18	19.1	−25.6	−5.6	16	73	11	14	14	36	17	58
21	18	45.4	−25.4	−5.7	17	72	11	19	14	43	18	06
26	19	11.4	−24.8	−5.8	17	70	11	21	14	49	18	17

MARS

Day	R.A. h	R.A. m	Dec °	Mag.	Diam. "	Phase %	Rise h	Rise m	Transit h	Transit m	Set h	Set m
1	19	44.0	−23.3	+0.4	7	86	13	19	17	00	20	41
6	19	59.4	−22.5	+0.4	7	86	13	09	16	56	20	43
11	20	14.8	−21.6	+0.5	7	87	12	58	16	51	20	44
16	20	30.1	−20.7	+0.5	7	87	12	47	16	47	20	47
21	20	45.3	−19.7	+0.5	7	87	12	35	16	42	20	49
26	21	00.3	−18.6	+0.6	7	88	12	23	16	38	20	52

SUNRISE AND SUNSET

	London 0° 05'	51° 30'	Bristol 2° 35'	51° 28'	Birmingham 1° 55'	52° 28'	Manchester 2° 15'	53° 28'	Newcastle 1° 37'	54° 59'	Glasgow 4° 14'	55° 52'	Belfast 5° 56'	54° 35'
d	h m	h m	h m	h m	h m	h m	h m	h m	h m	h m	h m	h m	h m	h m
1	6 54	16 33	7 04	16 43	7 04	16 37	7 09	16 36	7 11	16 28	7 24	16 36	7 27	16 47
2	6 56	16 31	7 06	16 41	7 06	16 35	7 11	16 34	7 13	16 26	7 26	16 34	7 29	16 45
3	6 58	16 29	7 08	16 39	7 08	16 34	7 13	16 32	7 15	16 24	7 28	16 32	7 31	16 43
4	7 00	16 27	7 10	16 37	7 10	16 32	7 14	16 30	7 17	16 22	7 31	16 30	7 33	16 41
5	7 02	16 26	7 11	16 36	7 12	16 30	7 16	16 28	7 19	16 20	7 33	16 28	7 35	16 39
6	7 03	16 24	7 13	16 34	7 14	16 28	7 18	16 26	7 21	16 18	7 35	16 26	7 37	16 37
7	7 05	16 22	7 15	16 32	7 15	16 27	7 20	16 25	7 23	16 17	7 37	16 24	7 39	16 35
8	7 07	16 21	7 17	16 31	7 17	16 25	7 22	16 23	7 25	16 15	7 39	16 22	7 41	16 33
9	7 09	16 19	7 18	16 29	7 19	16 23	7 24	16 21	7 27	16 13	7 41	16 20	7 43	16 32
10	7 10	16 18	7 20	16 28	7 21	16 22	7 26	16 19	7 29	16 11	7 43	16 18	7 45	16 30
11	7 12	16 16	7 22	16 26	7 23	16 20	7 28	16 18	7 31	16 09	7 45	16 16	7 47	16 28
12	7 14	16 15	7 24	16 25	7 25	16 19	7 30	16 16	7 33	16 08	7 47	16 14	7 49	16 26
13	7 15	16 13	7 25	16 23	7 26	16 17	7 31	16 15	7 35	16 06	7 50	16 12	7 51	16 25
14	7 17	16 12	7 27	16 22	7 28	16 16	7 33	16 13	7 37	16 04	7 52	16 11	7 53	16 23
15	7 19	16 10	7 29	16 21	7 30	16 14	7 35	16 12	7 39	16 03	7 54	16 09	7 55	16 22
16	7 21	16 09	7 31	16 19	7 32	16 13	7 37	16 10	7 41	16 01	7 56	16 07	7 57	16 20
17	7 22	16 08	7 32	16 18	7 33	16 11	7 39	16 09	7 43	15 59	7 58	16 06	7 58	16 19
18	7 24	16 07	7 34	16 17	7 35	16 10	7 41	16 07	7 45	15 58	8 00	16 04	8 00	16 17
19	7 26	16 05	7 36	16 16	7 37	16 09	7 42	16 06	7 47	15 57	8 02	16 03	8 02	16 16
20	7 27	16 04	7 37	16 14	7 39	16 08	7 44	16 05	7 49	15 55	8 04	16 01	8 04	16 14
21	7 29	16 03	7 39	16 13	7 40	16 06	7 46	16 03	7 51	15 54	8 06	16 00	8 06	16 13
22	7 31	16 02	7 40	16 12	7 42	16 05	7 48	16 02	7 52	15 52	8 07	15 58	8 08	16 12
23	7 32	16 01	7 42	16 11	7 44	16 04	7 49	16 01	7 54	15 51	8 09	15 57	8 10	16 10
24	7 34	16 00	7 44	16 10	7 45	16 03	7 51	16 00	7 56	15 50	8 11	15 56	8 11	16 09
25	7 35	15 59	7 45	16 09	7 47	16 02	7 53	15 59	7 58	15 49	8 13	15 55	8 13	16 08
26	7 37	15 58	7 47	16 08	7 48	16 01	7 55	15 58	8 00	15 48	8 15	15 53	8 15	16 07
27	7 38	15 57	7 48	16 08	7 50	16 00	7 56	15 57	8 01	15 47	8 17	15 52	8 16	16 06
28	7 40	15 57	7 50	16 07	7 52	16 00	7 58	15 56	8 03	15 46	8 18	15 51	8 18	16 05
29	7 41	15 56	7 51	16 06	7 53	15 59	7 59	15 55	8 05	15 45	8 20	15 50	8 20	16 04
30	7 43	15 55	7 53	16 05	7 55	15 58	8 01	15 54	8 06	15 44	8 22	15 49	8 21	16 03

JUPITER

Day	R.A. h m	Dec °	Mag.	Diam. "	Rise h m	Transit h m	Set h m
1	12 42.1	-3.3	-1.7	31	4 13	9 58	15 42
11	12 49.4	-4.1	-1 7	32	3 45	9 26	15 06
21	12 56.4	-4.8	-1.7	32	3 17	8 53	14 30

Equatorial Diam. 32", Polar Diam. 30"

SATURN

Day	R.A. h m	Dec °	Mag.	Diam. "	Rise h m	Transit h m	Set h m
1	16 51.9	-21.1	+0.6	15	10 11	14 07	18 03
11	16 56.5	-21.3	+0.5	15	9 37	13 32	17 27
21	17 01.3	-21.4	+0.5	15	9 04	12 57	16 51

Equatorial Diam. 15", Polar Diam. 14"
Rings – major axis 34" minor axis 15", Tilt 27°

URANUS

Day	R.A. h m	Dec °	Mag.	Diam. "	Rise h m	Transit h m	Set h m
1	1 20.8	+7.8	+6.0	4	15 48	22 34	5 25
11	1 19.5	+7.7	+5.0	4	15 08	21 54	4 43
21	1 18.3	+7.6	+5.0	4	14 28	21 13	4 02

NEPTUNE

Day	R.A. h m	Dec °	Mag.	Diam. "	Rise h m	Transit h m	Set h m
1	22 44.1	-9.0	+7.9	2	14 45	19 58	1 15
11	22 43.8	-9.0	+7.9	2	14 06	19 18	0 35
21	22 43.7	-9.0	+7.9	2	13 26	18 39	23 52

DECEMBER 2016

TWELFTH MONTH, 31 DAYS. *Decem* (ten), tenth month of Roman pre-Julian calendar

1	*Thursday*	Nancy Astor becomes the first woman to sit as an MP in the commons 1919	day 336
2	*Friday*	Fidel Castro takes office as president of Cuba 1976	337
3	*Saturday*	The Eureka Rebellion between miners and UK colonial forces occurs in Australia 1854	338
4	*Sunday*	Francisco Franco, autocratic head of Spain from 1939 until his death in 1975 *b.* 1892	339
5	*Monday*	Herbert Asquith resigns as prime minister during the First World War 1916	week 49 day 340
6	*Tuesday*	David Lloyd George becomes the first Welsh prime minister of the UK 1916	341
7	*Wednesday*	Noam Chomsky, American political commentator and linguist *b.* 1928	342
8	*Thursday*	Russia, Belarus and Ukraine sign the Belavezha Accords dissolving the Soviet Union 1991	343
9	*Friday*	Peter Kropotkin, Russian activist, anarchist and philosopher *b.* 1842	344
10	*Saturday*	King Edward VIII signs his abdication notices in order to marry Wallace Simpson 1936	345
11	*Sunday*	Mussolini declares Italy's withdrawal from the League of Nations 1937	346
12	*Monday*	Delhi replaces Calcutta as the capital of the British Empire in India 1911	week 50 day 347
13	*Tuesday*	Saddam Hussein is captured by US soldiers near Tikrit, Iraq 2003	348
14	*Wednesday*	The 1918 general election takes place with the lowest turnout since records began	349
15	*Thursday*	President Carter announces that the US will formally recognise communist China 1978	350
16	*Friday*	MPs vote in favour for the permanent abolition of the death penalty for murder 1969	351
17	*Saturday*	Simón Bolívar, Venezuelan military leader and politician *d.* 1830	352
18	*Sunday*	Vaclav Havel, the first president of the Czech Republic *d.* 2011	353
19	*Monday*	The 1910 general election sees the Liberal party win the highest number of seats	week 51 day 354
20	*Tuesday*	Luis Carrero Blanco, the prime minister of Spain, is assassinated in Madrid 1973	355
21	*Wednesday*	The 11-member Commonwealth of Independent States is formed 1991	356
22	*Thursday*	The home of former prime minister, Edward Heath, is bombed by the IRA 1974	357
23	*Friday*	Helmut Schmidt, Chancellor of West Germany (1974–82) *b.* 1918	358
24	*Saturday*	MP John Stonehouse is found in Australia after disappearing in Miami, USA 1974	359
25	*Sunday*	Nicolae Ceausescu, president and last Communist leader of Romania *d.* 1989	360
26	*Monday*	Étienne Constantin de Gerlache, first prime minister of Belgium *b.* 1785	week 52 day 361
27	*Tuesday*	Benazir Bhutto, the former prime minister of Pakistan, is assassinated 2007	362
28	*Wednesday*	Woodrow Wilson, 28th President of the USA (1913–21) *b.* 1856	363
29	*Thursday*	William Gladstone, four-time prime minister of the UK *b.* 1809	364
30	*Friday*	Grigori Rasputin, adviser to the Russian royal family, is murdered 1916	365
31	*Saturday*	Queen Victoria names Ottawa as the capital of the Province of Canada 1857	366

ASTRONOMICAL PHENOMENA

d	h	
3	13	Venus 6° South of the Moon
5	11	Mars 3° South of the Moon
9	20	Uranus 3° North of the Moon
11	05	Mercury Greatest elongation East
13	–	Geminid meteor peak
21	11	Solstice
22	17	Jupiter 2° South of the Moon
27	21	Saturn 4° South of the Moon
29	05	Mercury 2° South of the Moon

MINIMA OF ALGOL

d	h	d	h	d	h
1	23.4	13	10.7	24	22.0
4	20.3	16	07.5	27	18.8
7	17.1	19	04.4	30	15.6
10	13.9	22	01.2		

CONSTELLATIONS

The following constellations are near their meridian at

	d	h		d	h
November	1	24	December	16	21
November	15	23	January	1	20
December	1	22	January	16	19

Ursa Major (below the Pole), Ursa Minor (below the Pole), Cassiopeia, Andromeda, Perseus, Triangulum, Aries, Taurus, Cetus and Eridanus

THE MOON

Phases, Apsides and Node	d	h	m
◗ First Quarter	7	09	03
○ Full Moon	14	00	06
◖ Last Quarter	21	01	56
● New Moon	29	06	53
Perigee (358,461km)	12	23	29
Apogee (405,870km)	25	05	55

Mean longitude of ascending node on 1st, 158°

THE SUN

Diam. 32.5"

Day	Right Ascension			Dec. −	Equation of time	Rise 52°		Rise 56°		Transit		Set 52°		Set 56°		Sidereal time			Transit of first point of Aries		
	h	m	s	°	m s	h	m	h	m	h	m	h	m	h	m	h	m	s	h	m	s
1	16	30	09	21.8	+10 58	7	46	8	07	11	49	15	52	15	31	4	41	08	19	18	52
2	16	34	29	22.0	+10 35	7	47	8	08	11	50	15	52	15	30	4	45	04	19	14	56
3	16	38	49	22.1	+10 12	7	49	8	10	11	50	15	51	15	3C	4	49	01	19	10	59
4	16	43	09	22.3	+9 48	7	50	8	11	11	50	15	51	15	29	4	52	58	19	07	02
5	16	47	31	22.4	+9 23	7	51	8	13	11	51	15	50	15	28	4	56	54	19	03	06
6	16	51	52	22.5	+8 58	7	52	8	14	11	51	15	50	15	23	5	00	51	18	59	09
7	16	56	15	22.6	+8 32	7	54	8	16	11	52	15	50	15	27	5	04	47	18	55	13
8	17	00	37	22.7	+8 06	7	55	8	17	11	52	15	49	15	27	5	08	44	18	51	16
9	17	05	00	22.8	+7 40	7	56	8	18	11	53	15	49	15	27	5	12	40	18	47	20
10	17	09	24	22.9	+7 13	7	57	8	19	11	53	15	49	15	26	5	16	37	18	43	23
11	17	13	48	23.0	+6 45	7	58	8	21	11	53	15	49	15	26	5	20	33	18	39	27
12	17	18	12	23.1	+6 17	7	59	8	22	11	54	15	49	15	26	5	24	30	18	35	30
13	17	22	37	23.2	+5 49	8	00	8	23	11	54	15	49	15	26	5	28	27	18	31	33
14	17	27	02	23.2	+5 21	8	01	8	24	11	55	15	49	15	26	5	32	23	18	27	37
15	17	31	27	23.3	+4 52	8	01	8	25	11	55	15	49	15	26	5	36	20	18	23	40
16	17	35	52	23.3	+4 23	8	02	8	25	11	56	15	49	15	26	5	40	16	18	19	44
17	17	40	18	23.4	+3 54	8	03	8	26	11	56	15	50	15	26	5	44	13	18	15	47
18	17	44	44	23.4	+3 25	8	04	8	27	11	57	15	50	15	27	5	48	09	18	11	51
19	17	49	10	23.4	+2 55	8	04	8	28	11	57	15	50	15	27	5	52	06	18	07	54
20	17	53	36	23.4	+2 24	8	05	8	28	11	58	15	51	15	27	5	56	02	18	03	58
21	17	58	03	23.4	+1 56	8	05	8	29	11	58	15	51	15	28	5	59	59	18	00	01
22	18	02	29	23.4	+1 26	8	06	8	29	11	59	15	52	15	28	6	03	56	17	56	04
23	18	06	55	23.4	+0 56	8	06	8	30	11	59	15	52	15	29	6	07	52	17	52	08
24	18	11	22	23.4	+0 26	8	07	8	30	12	00	15	53	15	30	6	11	49	17	48	11
25	18	15	48	23.4	−0 04	8	07	8	30	12	00	15	54	15	30	6	15	45	17	44	15
26	18	20	15	23.4	−0 33	8	07	8	31	12	01	15	54	15	31	6	19	42	17	40	18
27	18	24	41	23.3	−1 03	8	08	8	31	12	01	15	55	15	32	6	23	38	17	36	22
28	18	29	07	23.3	−1 32	8	08	8	31	12	02	15	56	15	33	6	27	35	17	32	25
29	18	33	33	23.2	−2 02	8	08	8	31	12	02	15	57	15	34	6	31	31	17	28	29
30	18	37	58	23.2	−2 31	8	08	8	31	12	03	15	58	15	35	6	35	28	17	24	32
31	18	42	24	23.1	−3 00	8	08	8	31	12	03	15	59	15	36	6	39	25	17	20	35

DURATION OF TWILIGHT (in minutes)

Latitude	52°	56°	52°	56°	52°	56°	52°	56°
	1 December		11 December		21 December		31 December	
Civil	40	45	41	47	41	47	41	47
Nautical	32	93	84	96	85	97	84	96
Astronomical	123	138	125	141	126	142	125	141

THE NIGHT SKY

Mercury is at greatest elongation east (20°) on the 11th and low in the south-western evening sky until the third week of December. The Moon lies 8° above Mercury on the 1st. Mercury passes through inferior conjunction on December 28th and will be lost to view until the New Year.

Venus, magnitude −4.3, is a brilliant seasonal bauble hung above the south-western sky-line these evenings. The crescent Moon nearby on the 3rd makes for a lovely sight.

Mars, magnitude +0.9, is setting nearly 5.5 hours after the Sun by the end of December and moves into Aquarius on the 15th where it ends the year. Mars can be found 3.5° to the Moon's lower right on the 5th.

Jupiter, magnitude −1.8, rises during the early hours. The planet dominates the stars of Virgo where it currently lies, and the Moon in the area on the 22nd and 23rd will add to the scene.

Saturn passes through superior conjunction on the 10th and then surfaces in the morning sky, rising about 1.5 hours before the Sun by the end of 2016. The planet lies 6° to the right of the Moon on December 28th.

The Geminids are now considered the richest of the annual showers but have to contend with an almost Full Moon at their maximum on the night of December 13/14, meaning only the brighter members will be seen. Still, a watch of reasonable length should allow some Geminids to be logged.

THE MOON

Day	R.A.		Dec.	Hor. Par.	Diam.	Sun's Co-Long.	PA of Br. Limb	Ph.	Age	Rise 52°		Rise 56°		Transit		Set 52°		Set 56°	
	h	m	°	'	'	°	°	%	d	h	m	h	m	h	m	h	m	h	m
1	17	41	−18.6	54.4	29.6	289	256	2	1.3	9	01	9	21	13	26	17	50	17	31
2	18	32	−18.9	54.7	29.8	302	259	6	2.3	9	50	10	09	14	15	18	42	18	23
3	19	24	−18.3	55.1	30.0	314	257	11	3.3	10	33	10	50	15	05	19	40	19	23
4	20	15	−16.9	55.5	30.3	326	255	18	4.3	11	10	11	25	15	54	20	43	20	29
5	21	07	−14.6	56.1	30.6	338	252	26	5.3	11	43	11	54	16	43	21	50	21	39
6	21	58	−11.5	56.8	30.9	350	250	36	6.3	12	12	12	21	17	31	23	01	22	54
7	22	49	−7.9	57.5	31.4	3	248	46	7.3	12	39	12	44	18	21	—		—	
8	23	41	−3.7	58.3	31.8	15	246	57	8.3	13	05	13	06	19	11	0	14	0	11
9	0	33	+0.8	59.2	32.2	27	246	68	9.3	13	31	13	29	20	03	1	29	1	30
10	1	28	+5.3	59.9	32.7	39	246	78	10.3	14	00	13	53	20	57	2	48	2	53
11	2	24	+9.7	60.6	33.0	51	246	87	11.3	14	32	14	22	21	54	4	08	4	17
12	3	23	+13.6	61.0	33.3	63	247	94	12.3	15	11	14	57	22	54	5	29	5	42
13	4	25	+16.6	61.2	33.3	75	242	98	13.3	15	58	15	39	23	55	6	47	7	03
14	5	28	+18.4	61.0	33.2	88	178	100	14.3	16	53	16	33	—		7	58	8	18
15	6	31	+18.9	60.5	33.0	100	110	99	15.3	17	57	17	38	0	57	9	00	9	20
16	7	33	+18.2	59.8	32.6	112	106	94	16.3	19	06	18	50	1	57	9	51	10	08
17	8	32	+16.3	58.9	32.1	124	107	88	17.3	20	18	20	05	2	54	10	33	10	47
18	9	28	+13.5	58.0	31.6	136	109	80	18.3	21	29	21	19	3	48	11	06	11	17
19	10	21	+10.1	57.0	31.1	148	111	71	19.3	22	38	22	32	4	38	11	34	11	41
20	11	10	+6.3	56.1	30.6	160	113	61	20.3	23	45	23	43	5	25	11	59	12	02
21	11	58	+2.3	55.4	30.2	172	113	51	21.3	—		—		6	09	12	22	12	22
22	12	44	−1.6	54.8	29.9	185	114	41	22.3	0	51	0	52	6	52	12	44	12	41
23	13	30	−5.4	54.4	29.6	197	113	32	23.3	1	55	2	00	7	35	13	06	13	00
24	14	15	−9.0	54.1	29.5	209	112	23	24.3	2	58	3	06	8	18	13	30	13	21
25	15	02	−12.2	54.0	29.4	221	111	16	25.3	4	00	4	12	9	02	13	57	13	45
26	15	49	−14.9	54.1	29.5	233	109	10	26.3	5	01	5	16	9	47	14	28	14	13
27	16	38	−17.0	54.2	29.5	246	109	5	27.3	6	00	6	18	10	34	15	05	14	47
28	17	28	−18.4	54.5	29.7	258	111	2	28.3	6	56	7	15	11	22	15	47	15	28
29	18	19	−19.0	54.8	29.8	270	142	0	29.3	7	48	8	06	12	12	16	36	16	17
30	19	11	−18.6	55.1	30.1	282	238	0	0.8	8	34	8	51	13	01	17	32	17	15
31	20	03	−17.4	55.6	30.3	294	250	3	1.8	9	13	9	29	13	51	18	35	18	20

MERCURY

Day	R.A.		Dec	Mag.	Diam.	Phase	Rise		Transit		Set	
	h	m	°		"	%	h	m	h	m	h	m
1	17	47.3	−25.8	−0.5	6	83	9	45	13	06	16	26
3	17	59.7	−25.8	−0.5	6	81	9	50	13	10	16	30
5	18	11.6	−25.8	−0.5	6	77	9	53	13	14	16	34
7	18	23.0	−25.6	−0.5	6	73	9	55	13	17	16	39
9	18	33.7	−25.4	−0.5	6	68	9	56	13	19	16	43
11	18	43.4	−25.1	−0.4	7	63	9	55	13	21	16	47
13	18	51.7	−24.7	−0.4	7	56	9	51	13	21	16	51
15	18	58.4	−24.2	−0.2	7	49	9	46	13	19	16	52
17	19	03.0	−23.7	0.0	8	40	9	38	13	15	16	52
19	19	04.9	−23.2	+0.3	8	31	9	28	13	08	16	49
21	19	03.7	−22.6	+0.8	9	22	9	14	12	58	16	43
23	18	59.3	−22.1	+1.6	9	13	8	57	12	44	16	33
25	18	51.6	−21.6	+2.7	10	6	8	37	12	28	16	20
27	18	41.3	−21.2	+4.0	10	2	8	16	12	10	16	04
29	18	29.7	−20.8	+4.8	10	0	7	54	11	50	15	47
31	18	18.2	−20.5	+3.6	10	3	7	33	11	31	15	31

Rising and setting times are for latitude 54°

VENUS

Day	R.A.		Dec	Mag.	Diam.	Phase	Rise		Transit		Set	
	h	m	°		"	%	h	m	h	m	h	m
1	19	37.0	−24.0	−6.0	18	69	11	20	14	55	18	29
6	20	02.0	−22.9	−6.1	19	67	11	17	15	00	18	43
11	20	26.3	−21.6	−6.2	19	65	11	11	15	04	18	58
16	20	49.9	−20.0	−6.4	20	63	11	04	15	08	19	13
21	21	12.7	−18.2	−6.5	21	61	10	55	15	11	19	28
26	21	34.7	−16.3	−6.7	22	59	10	44	15	13	19	42
31	21	55.8	−14.2	−6.8	23	57	10	32	15	14	19	57

MARS

Day	R.A.		Dec	Mag.	Diam.	Phase	Rise		Transit		Set	
	h	m	°		"	%	h	m	h	m	h	m
1	21	15.3	−17.4	+0.6	7	88	12	10	16	33	20	55
6	21	30.1	−16.2	+0.7	6	88	11	57	16	28	20	59
11	21	44.8	−14.9	+0.7	6	89	11	44	16	23	21	02
16	21	59.3	−13.5	+0.8	6	89	11	31	16	18	21	05
21	22	13.7	−12.1	+0.8	6	89	11	17	16	12	21	08
26	22	27.9	−10.7	+0.8	6	90	11	03	16	07	21	11
31	22	42.0	−9.2	+0.9	6	90	10	49	16	01	21	14

SUNRISE AND SUNSET

	London				Bristol				Birmingham				Manchester				Newcastle				Glasgow				Belfast			
	0° 05′		51° 30′		2° 35′		51° 28′		1° 55′		52° 28′		2° 15′		53° 28′		1° 37′		54° 59′		4° 14′		55° 52′		5° 56′		54° 35′	
d	h	m	h	m	h	m	h	m	h	m	h	m	h	m	h	m	h	m	h	m	h	m	h	m	h	m	h	m
1	7	44	15	55	7	54	16	05	7	56	15	57	8	02	15	54	8	08	15	43	8	24	15	48	8	23	16	03
2	7	45	15	54	7	55	16	04	7	57	15	57	8	04	15	53	8	09	15	42	8	25	15	48	8	25	16	02
3	7	47	15	54	7	57	16	04	7	59	15	56	8	05	15	52	8	11	15	42	8	27	15	47	8	26	16	01
4	7	48	15	53	7	58	16	03	8	00	15	56	8	07	15	52	8	12	15	41	8	28	15	46	8	27	16	00
5	7	49	15	53	7	59	16	03	8	01	15	55	8	08	15	51	8	14	15	40	8	30	15	45	8	29	16	00
6	7	51	15	52	8	00	16	02	8	03	15	55	8	09	15	51	8	15	15	40	8	31	15	45	8	30	15	59
7	7	52	15	52	8	02	16	02	8	04	15	54	8	10	15	51	8	17	15	39	8	33	15	44	8	32	15	59
8	7	53	15	52	8	03	16	02	8	05	15	54	8	12	15	50	8	18	15	39	8	34	15	44	8	33	15	59
9	7	54	15	52	8	04	16	02	8	06	15	54	8	13	15	50	8	19	15	39	8	35	15	44	8	34	15	58
10	7	55	15	51	8	05	16	02	8	07	15	54	8	14	15	50	8	20	15	38	8	36	15	43	8	35	15	58
11	7	56	15	51	8	06	16	01	8	08	15	54	8	15	15	50	8	21	15	38	8	38	15	43	8	36	15	58
12	7	57	15	51	8	07	16	01	8	09	15	54	8	16	15	50	8	23	15	38	8	39	15	43	8	37	15	58
13	7	58	15	51	8	08	16	01	8	10	15	54	8	17	15	50	8	24	15	38	8	40	15	43	8	38	15	58
14	7	59	15	51	8	09	16	02	8	11	15	54	8	18	15	50	8	25	15	38	8	41	15	43	8	39	15	58
15	8	00	15	52	8	10	16	02	8	12	15	54	8	19	15	50	8	25	15	38	8	42	15	43	8	40	15	58
16	8	01	15	52	8	10	16	02	8	13	15	54	8	20	15	50	8	26	15	38	8	43	15	43	8	41	15	58
17	8	01	15	52	8	11	16	02	8	14	15	54	8	20	15	50	8	27	15	38	8	43	15	43	8	42	15	58
18	8	02	15	52	8	12	16	02	8	14	15	55	8	21	15	50	8	28	15	39	8	44	15	43	8	43	15	58
19	8	03	15	53	8	12	16	03	8	15	15	55	8	22	15	51	8	29	15	39	8	45	15	44	8	43	15	59
20	8	03	15	53	8	13	16	03	8	16	15	55	8	22	15	51	8	29	15	39	8	45	15	44	8	44	15	59
21	8	04	15	54	8	14	16	04	8	16	15	56	8	23	15	52	8	30	15	40	8	46	15	45	8	44	16	00
22	8	04	15	54	8	14	16	04	8	17	15	56	8	23	15	52	8	30	15	41	8	46	15	45	8	45	16	00
23	8	05	15	55	8	14	16	05	8	17	15	57	8	24	15	53	8	30	15	41	8	47	15	46	8	45	16	01
24	8	05	15	55	8	15	16	05	8	17	15	58	8	24	15	53	8	31	15	42	8	47	15	47	8	46	16	02
25	8	05	15	56	8	15	16	06	8	18	15	58	8	25	15	54	8	31	15	43	8	47	15	47	8	46	16	02
26	8	06	15	57	8	15	16	07	8	18	15	59	8	25	15	55	8	31	15	43	8	48	15	48	8	46	16	03
27	8	06	15	58	8	16	16	08	8	18	16	00	8	25	15	56	8	31	15	44	8	48	15	49	8	46	16	04
28	8	06	15	58	8	16	16	09	8	18	16	01	8	25	15	57	8	32	15	45	8	48	15	50	8	46	16	05
29	8	06	15	59	8	16	16	09	8	18	16	02	8	25	15	58	8	32	15	46	8	48	15	51	8	46	16	06
30	8	06	16	00	8	16	16	10	8	18	16	03	8	25	15	59	8	31	15	47	8	48	15	52	8	46	16	07
31	8	06	16	01	8	16	16	11	8	18	16	04	8	25	16	00	8	31	15	48	8	47	15	53	8	46	16	08

JUPITER

Day	R.A. h m	Dec °	Mag.	Diam. ″	Rise h m	Transit h m	Set h m
1	13 03.0	−5.4	−1.8	33	2 48	8 21	13 53
11	13 09.0	−6.0	−1.8	34	2 18	7 47	13 17
21	13 14.3	−6.5	−1.9	34	1 46	7 13	12 40
31	13 18.8	−6.9	−1.9	35	1 14	6 38	12 03

Equatorial Diam. 34″, Polar Diam. 32″

SATURN

Day	R.A. h m	Dec °	Mag.	Diam. ″	Rise h m	Transit h m	Set h m
1	17 06.2	−21.5	+0.5	15	8 30	12 23	16 16
11	17 11.3	−21.7	+0.4	15	7 57	11 49	15 41
21	17 16.3	−21.8	+0.5	15	7 23	11 15	15 06
31	17 21.3	−21.9	+0.5	15	6 50	10 40	14 31

Equatorial Diam. 15″, Polar Diam. 14″
Rings – major axis 34″ minor axis 15″, Tilt 27°

URANUS

Day	R.A. h m	Dec °	Mag.	Diam. ″	Rise h m	Transit h m	Set h m
1	1 17.3	+7.5	+6.1	4	13 48	20 33	3 21
11	1 16.5	+7.4	+6.1	4	13 09	19 53	2 41
21	1 16.1	+7.4	+6.1	4	12 29	19 13	2 01
31	1 16.0	+7.4	+6.1	4	11 50	18 34	1 21

NEPTUNE

Day	R.A. h m	Dec °	Mag.	Diam. ″	Rise h m	Transit h m	Set h m
1	22 43.9	−9.0	+7.9	2	12 47	18 00	23 13
11	22 44.2	−8.9	+7.9	2	12 08	17 21	22 34
21	22 44.7	−8.9	+7.9	2	11 29	16 42	21 55
31	22 45.5	−8.8	+7.9	2	10 50	16 03	21 17

TRANSIT OF MERCURY 9 MAY 2016

In the present epoch, transits of Mercury occur in May or November. May transits are roughly half as frequent as November transits and this is the last May transit until 2049. The dates of transits are gradually moving later in the year; in the early 1500s they were in April and October.

The interval between May transits is 13 or 33 years, and November transit intervals are 7, 13 or 33 years. For May transits, Mercury has a diameter of 12″ and occur at the descending node of Mercury's orbit. For November transits, Mercury has a diameter of 10″ and occur at the ascending node.

May transits are less frequent than November transits because during a May transit, Mercury is near aphelion whereas during a November transit, it is near perihelion.

Perihelion transits occur more frequently because Mercury moves faster in its orbit at perihelion and can reach the transit node more quickly, and at perihelion Mercury has less parallax as it is closer to the Sun.

Previous Mercury transits were in May 2003 and November 2006, the next are November 2019 and November 2032. For reference, the next Venus transit is not until 11 December 2117.

The transit is visible in its entirety from the UK, western Europe, eastern North America, most of South America and western Africa. No part is visible from Australasia, Japan, and Indonesia.

Times differ little throughout the world and even less from within the UK:

Location	I	II	Greatest Transit (G)	III	IV	Duration
Geocentric	11:12:18	11:15:30	14:57:25	18:39:12	18:42:24	7h 30m 06s
London	11:12:23	11:15:35	14:56:17	18:37:21	18:40:33	7h 28m 10s
Glasgow	11:12:26	11:15:37	14:56:22	18:37:23	18:40:35	7h 28m 09s
Belfast	11:12:28	11:15:40	14:56:24	18:37:23	18:40:35	7h 28m 07s
Capetown	11:12:16	11:15:26	14:56:43	15:58*	—	4h 45m 30s
New York	11:13:31	11:16:44	14:57:53	18:38:11	18:41:23	7h 27m 51s
Rio de Janeiro	11:13:48	11:16:59	14:58:06	18:38:53	18:42:03	7h 28m 15s
Delhi	11:10:42	11:13:53	13:28*	—	—	2h 17m 17s

* Transit ends at sunset

All times are given in Universal Time (GMT)
See diagram above and map below for positions of I, II, G, III and IV

Solar Semi-diameter: 15′ 50.4″
Mercury Semi-diameter: 0′ 06.0″

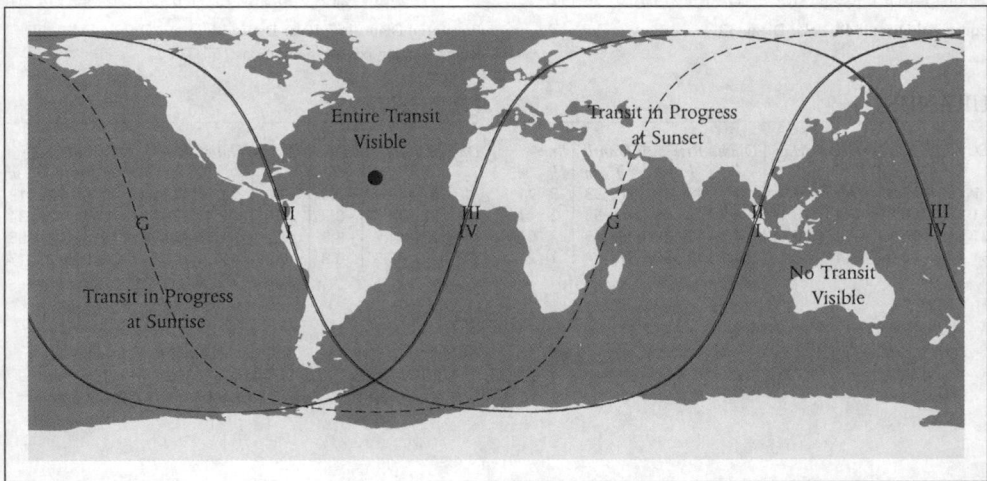

ECLIPSES 2016

ECLIPSES

During 2016 there will be four eclipses, two of the Sun and two of the Moon and a transit of Mercury.

1. A penumbral eclipse of the Moon on March 23 is visible from North and South America at moonset and eastern Asia at moonrise. Eastern Australia, New Zealand and the Pacific will see the whole eclipse. It should be noted that penumbral eclipses are not easy to observe.

2. A total eclipse of the Sun on March 9 is visible from Sumatra, Bangka Island, Palau Belitung, Central Kalimantan, Central Sulawesi, North Maluku and Woleai atoll, ending in the north Pacific Ocean. Partial phases are visable from northern Australia, Papua, Papua New Guinea, China and Alaska.

3. On 9 May a transit of Mercury will be visible in its entirety from the UK, western Europe, eastern North America and most of South America. No part of the transit is visible from Australasia and Japan (see page 626).

4. An annular eclipse of the Sun on September 1 starts in the Gulf of Guinea and is visible from land on Annobon Island, central southern Africa (Gabon, Rep. of the Congo, Democratic Rep. of Congo, Tanzania and Mozambique) and into Madagascar, ending in the southern Indian Ocean.

5. A penumbral eclipse of the Moon on September 16 is visible from the UK and Europe at moonrise and visible in its entirety from eastern Africa and the whole of Asia. Australasia will see it at moonset.

MEAN AND SIDEREAL TIME

The length of a sidereal day in mean time is 23h 56m 04s.09. Hence 1h MT = 1h+9s.86 ST and 1h ST = 1h − 9s.83 MT.

Acceleration						Retardation					
h	m	s	m	s	s	h	m	s	m	s	s
1	0	10	0	00	0	1	0	10	0	00	0
2	0	20	3	02	0	2	0	20	3	03	0
3	0	30	9	07	1	3	0	29	9	09	1
4	0	39	15	13	2	4	0	39	15	15	2
5	0	49	21	18	3	5	0	49	21	21	3
6	0	59	27	23	4	6	0	59	27	28	4
7	1	09	33	28	5	7	1	09	33	34	5
8	1	19	39	34	6	8	1	19	39	40	6
9	1	29	45	39	7	9	1	28	45	46	7
10	1	39	51	44	8	10	1	38	51	53	8
11	1	48	57	49	9	11	1	48	57	59	9
12	1	58	60	00	10	12	1	58	60	00	10
13	2	08				13	2	08			
14	2	18				14	2	18			
15	2	28				15	2	27			
16	2	38				16	2	37			
17	2	48				17	2	47			
18	2	57				18	2	57			
19	3	07				19	3	07			
20	3	17				20	3	17			
21	3	27				21	3	26			
22	3	37				22	3	36			
23	3	47				23	3	46			
24	3	57				24	3	56			

To convert an interval of mean time to the corresponding interval of sidereal time, enter the acceleration table with the given mean time (taking the hours and the minutes and seconds separately) and add the acceleration obtained to the given mean time. To convert an interval of sidereal time to the corresponding interval of mean time, take out the retardation for the given sidereal time and subtract.

The columns for the minutes and seconds of the argument

are in the form known as critical tables. To use these tables, find in the appropriate left-hand column the two entries between which the given number of minutes and seconds lies; the quantity in the right-hand column between these two entries is the required acceleration or retardation. Thus the acceleration for 11m 26s (which lies between the entries 9m 07s and 15m 13s) is 2s. If the given number of minutes and seconds is a tabular entry, the required acceleration or retardation is the entry in the right-hand column above the given tabular entry, eg the retardation for 45m 46s is 7s.

Example – Convert 14h 27m 35s from ST to MT

	h	m	s
Given ST	14	27	35
Retardation for 14h		2	18
Retardation for 27m 35s			5
Corresponding MT	14	25	12

For further explanation see pages 630 and 632

EXPLANATION OF ASTRONOMICAL DATA

Positions of the heavenly bodies are given only to the degree of accuracy required by amateur astronomers for setting telescopes, or for plotting on celestial globes or star atlases. Where intermediate positions are required, linear interpolation may be employed.

Detailed definitions of the terms used cannot be given here. They must be sought in astronomical literature and textbooks.

A special feature has been made of the times when the Sun and Moon are visible in the British Isles. Since two columns, calculated for latitudes 52° and 56°, are devoted to risings and settings, the range 50° to 58° can be covered by interpolation and extrapolation. The times given in these columns are Greenwich Mean Times for the meridian of Greenwich. An observer west of this meridian must add his/her longitude (in time) and vice versa.

In accordance with the usual convention in astronomy, + and − indicate respectively north and south latitudes or declinations.

All data are, unless otherwise stated, for 0h Greenwich Mean Time (GMT), ie at the midnight at the beginning of the day named. Allowance must be made for British Summer Time during the period that this is in operation.

PAGE ONE OF EACH MONTH
The calendar for each month is explained on page 577.

Under the heading Astronomical Phenomena will be found particulars of the more important conjunctions of the Sun, Moon and planets with each other, and also the dates of other astronomical phenomena of special interest.

Times of Minima of Algol are approximate times of the middle of the period of diminished light.

The Constellations listed each month are those that are near the meridian at the beginning of the month at 22h local mean time. Allowance must be made for British Summer Time if necessary. The fact that any star crosses the meridian 4m earlier each night or 2h earlier each month may be used, in conjunction with the lists given each month, to find what constellations are favourably placed at any moment.

The principal phases of the Moon are the GMTs when the difference between the longitude of the Moon and that of the Sun is 0°, 90°, 180° or 270°. The times of perigee and apogee are those when the Moon is nearest to, and farthest from, the Earth, respectively. The nodes or points of intersection of the Moon's orbit and the ecliptic make a complete retrograde circuit of the ecliptic in about 19 years.

From a knowledge of the longitude of the ascending node and the inclination, whose value does not vary much from 5°, the path of the Moon among the stars may be plotted on a celestial globe or star atlas.

PAGE TWO OF EACH MONTH

The Sun's diameter, in arc seconds, is given once a month.

The right ascension and declination (Dec.) is that of the true Sun. The right ascension of the mean Sun is obtained by applying the equation of time, with the sign given, to the right ascension of the true Sun, or, more easily, by applying 12h to the Sidereal Time. The direction in which the equation of time has to be applied in different problems is a frequent source of confusion and error. Apparent Solar Time is equal to the Mean Solar Time plus the Equation of Time. For example, at 12h GMT on August 8 the Equation of Time is −5m 44s and thus at 12h Mean Time on that day the Apparent Time is 12h − 5m 44s = 11h 54m 16s.

The Greenwich Sidereal Time at 0h and the Transit of the First Point of Aries (which is really the mean time when the sidereal time is 0h) are used for converting mean time to sidereal time and vice versa.

The GMT of transit of the Sun at Greenwich may also be taken as the local mean time (LMT) of transit in any longitude. It is independent of latitude. The GMT of transit in any longitude is obtained by adding the longitude to the time given if west, and vice versa.

DECLINATION

The distance in degrees from the ecliptic (the Sun's apparent path through the sky and the path that the planets closely follow) is termed its *declination (Dec.)*. For northern latitudes, higher positive declination means the object is higher in the sky.

LIGHTING-UP TIME

The legal importance of sunrise and sunset is that the Road Vehicles Lighting Regulations 1989 (SI 1989 No. 1796) as amended, make the use of front and rear position lamps on vehicles compulsory during the period between sunset and sunrise. Headlamps on vehicles are required to be used during the hours of darkness on unlit roads, on lit roads with a speed limit exceeding 30mph, or whenever visibility is seriously reduced. The hours of darkness are defined in these regulations as the period between half an hour after sunset and half an hour before sunrise.

In all laws and regulations 'sunset' refers to the local sunset, ie the time at which the Sun sets at the place in question. This common-sense interpretation has been upheld by legal tribunals.

MAGNITUDE

Magnitudes of astronomical objects are measured in what may be considered the reverse to the obvious. Magnitude +3 is brighter than +4, magnitude −2 is brighter than magnitude −1. So from brighter to dimmer: −4, −3, −2, −1, 0, +1, +2, +3 etc, with +6 being the dimmest considered visible with the naked eye in very dark skies. Each magnitude is roughly 2.5 times brighter than the next, so a magnitude +1 object is 100 times brighter than a magnitude +6 object.

SUNRISE AND SUNSET

The times of sunrise and sunset are those when the Sun's upper limb, as affected by refraction, is on the true horizon of an observer at sea-level. Assuming the mean refraction to be 34′, and the Sun's semi-diameter to be 16′, the time given is that when the true zenith distance of the Sun's centre is 90°+34′+16′ or 90° 50′, or, in other words, when the depression of the Sun's centre below the true horizon is 50′. The upper limb is then 34′ below the true horizon, but is brought there by refraction. An observer on a ship might see the Sun for a minute or so longer, because of the dip of the horizon, while another viewing the sunset over hills or mountains would record an earlier time. Nevertheless, the moment when the true zenith distance of the Sun's centre is 90° 50′ is a precise time dependent only on the latitude and longitude of the place, and independent of its altitude above sea-level, the contour of its horizon, the vagaries of refraction or the small seasonal change in the Sun's diameter; this moment is suitable in every way as a definition of sunset (or sunrise) for all statutory purposes.

(For further information, *see* footnote on page 629.)

TWILIGHT

Light reaches us before sunrise and continues to reach us for some time after sunset. The interval between darkness and sunrise or sunset and darkness is called twilight. Astronomically speaking, twilight is considered to begin or end when the Sun's centre is 18° below the horizon, as no light from the Sun can then reach the observer. As thus defined twilight may last several hours; in high latitudes at the summer solstice the depression of 18° is not reached, and twilight lasts from sunset to sunrise.

The need for some sub-division of twilight is met by dividing the gathering darkness into four stages.

(1) *Sunrise or Sunset,* defined as above
(2) *Civil twilight,* which begins or ends when the Sun's centre is 6° below the horizon. This marks the time when operations requiring daylight may commence or must cease. In England it varies from about 30 to 60 minutes after sunset and the same interval before sunrise
(3) *Nautical twilight,* which begins or ends when the Sun's centre is 12° below the horizon. This marks the time when it is, to all intents and purposes, completely dark
(4) *Astronomical twilight,* which begins or ends when the Sun's centre is 18° below the horizon. This marks theoretical perfect darkness. It is of little practical importance, especially if nautical twilight is tabulated

To assist observers the durations of civil, nautical and astronomical twilights are given at intervals of ten days. The beginning of a particular twilight is found by subtracting the duration from the time of sunrise, while the end is found by adding the duration to the time of sunset. Thus the beginning of astronomical twilight in latitude 52°, on the Greenwich meridian, on March 11 is found as 06h 24m − 113m = 04h 31m and similarly the end of civil twilight as 17h 57m +34m = 18h 31m. The letters TAN (twilight all night) are printed when twilight lasts all night.

Under the heading The Night Sky will be found notes describing the position and visibility of the planets and other phenomena.

PAGE THREE OF EACH MONTH

The Moon moves so rapidly among the stars that its position is given only to the degree of accuracy that permits linear interpolation. The right ascension (RA) and declination (Dec.) are geocentric, ie for an imaginary observer at the centre of the Earth. To an observer on the surface of the Earth the position is always different, as the altitude is always less on account of parallax, which may reach 1°.

The lunar terminator is the line separating the bright from the dark part of the Moon's disk. Apart from irregularities of the lunar surface, the terminator is elliptical, because it is a circle seen in projection. It becomes the full circle forming the limb, or edge, of the Moon at New and Full Moon. The selenographic longitude of the terminator is measured from the mean centre of the visible disk, which may differ from the visible centre by as much as 8°, because of libration.

Instead of the longitude of the terminator the Sun's selenographic co-longitude (Sun's co-long.) is tabulated. It is numerically equal to the selenographic longitude of the morning terminator, measured eastwards from the mean centre of the disk. Thus its value is approximately 270° at New Moon, 360° at First Quarter, 90° at Full Moon and 180° at Last Quarter.

The Position Angle (PA) of the Bright Limb is the position angle of the midpoint of the illuminated limb, measured eastwards from the north point on the disk. The Phase column shows the percentage of the area of the Moon's disk illuminated; this is also the illuminated percentage of the diameter at right angles to the line of cusps. The terminator is a semi-ellipse whose major axis is the line of cusps, and whose semi-minor axis is determined by the tabulated percentage; from New Moon to Full Moon the east limb is dark, and vice versa.

The times given as moonrise and moonset are those when the upper limb of the Moon is on the horizon of an observer at sea-level. The Sun's horizontal parallax (Hor. par.) is about 9", and is negligible when considering sunrise and sunset, but that of the Moon averages about 57'. Hence the computed time represents the moment when the true zenith distance of the Moon is 90° 50' (as for the Sun) minus the horizontal parallax. The time required for the Sun or Moon to rise or set is about four minutes (except in high latitudes). *See also* the footnote below.

The GMT of transit of the Moon over the meridian of Greenwich is given; these times are independent of latitude but must be corrected for longitude. For places in the British Isles it suffices to add the longitude if west, and vice versa. For other places a further correction is necessary because of the rapid movement of the Moon relative to the stars. The entire correction is conveniently determined by first finding the west longitude λ of the place. If the place is in west longitude, λ is the ordinary west longitude; if the place is in east longitude λ is the complement to 24h (or 360°) of the longitude and will be greater than 12h (or 180°). The correction then consists of two positive portions, namely λ and the fraction $\lambda/24$ (or $\lambda°/360$) multiplied by the difference between consecutive transits. Thus for Christchurch, New Zealand, the longitude is 11h 31m east, so λ = 12h 29m and the fraction $\lambda/24$ is 0.52. The transit on the local date 26 January 2016 is found as follows:

		d	h	m
GMT of transit at Greenwich	January	25	0	54
λ			12	29
0.52 × (01h 42m – 00h 54m)				25
GMT of transit at Christchurch		25	13	48
Corr. to NZ Standard Time			12	00
Local standard time of transit	January	26	01	48

SUNRISE, SUNSET, MOONRISE AND MOONSET
The tables have been constructed for the meridian of Greenwich and for latitudes 52° and 56°. They give Greenwich Mean Time (GMT) throughout the year. To obtain the GMT of the phenomenon as seen from any other latitude and longitude in the British Isles, first interpolate or extrapolate for latitude by the usual rules of proportion. To the time thus found, the longitude (expressed in time) is to be added (as it usually is in Great Britain) or subtracted if east. If the longitude is expressed in degrees and minutes of arc, it must be converted to time at the rate of 1° = 4m and 15' = 1m.

The GMT at which the planet transits the Greenwich meridian is also given. The times of transit are to be corrected to local meridians in the usual way, as already described.

As is evident, for any given place the quantities λ and the correction to local standard time may be combined permanently, being here 24h 29m.

Positions of Mercury are given for every second day, and those of Venus and Mars for every fifth day; they may be interpolated linearly. The diameter (Diam.) is given in seconds of arc. The phase is the illuminated percentage of the disk. In the case of the inner planets this approaches 100 at superior conjunction and 0 at inferior conjunction. When the phase is less than 50 the planet is crescent-shaped or horned; for greater phases it is gibbous. In the case of the exterior planet Mars, the phase approaches 100 at conjunction and opposition, and is a minimum at the quadratures.

To determine if a planet is visible or not, the transit time should be examined. If the transit time coincides with hours of darkness the planet should be easy to find, provided it is bright enough. If the time of transit is between 00h and 12h the planet should be visible above the eastern horizon; if between 12h and 24h, above the western horizon. The closer the transit time to midnight (0h) the longer it will be visible.

The inner planets – Mercury and Venus can never transit at midnight because they are too close to the Sun. If they transit close to noon (12h) then they will be too close to the Sun to be visible except during a large solar eclipse. The rise or set times should be examined to see if either is near sunrise or sunset. If this also coincides with a large positive declination (Dec.) then conditions are favourable for viewing.

Consulting The Night Sky paragraphs will also help determine observability.

PAGE FOUR OF EACH MONTH
The GMTs of sunrise and sunset for seven cities, whose adopted positions in longitude (W.) and latitude (N.) are given immediately below the name, may be used not only for these phenomena, but also for lighting-up times (*see* page 628 for a fuller explanation).

The particulars for the four outer planets resemble those for the planets on Page Three of each month, except that, because of the inferior brightness of Uranus and Neptune, these two planets require optical aids such as binoculars or a small telescope. The diameters given for the rings of Saturn are those of the major axis (in the plane of the planet's equator) and the minor axis respectively. The former has a small seasonal change due to the slightly varying distance of the Earth from Saturn, but the latter varies from zero when the Earth passes through the ring plane every 15 years to its maximum opening half-way between these periods. The rings were last open at their widest extent (and Saturn at its brightest) in 2002; this will occur again in 2017. The Earth passed through the ring plane in 2009.

TIME

From the earliest ages, the natural division of time into recurring periods of day and night has provided the practical time-scale for the everyday activities of the human race. Indeed, if any alternative means of time measurement is adopted, it must be capable of adjustment so as to remain in general agreement with the natural time-scale defined by the diurnal rotation of the Earth on its axis. Ideally the rotation should be measured against a fixed frame of reference; in practice it must be measured against the background provided by the celestial bodies. If the Sun is chosen as the reference point, we obtain Apparent Solar Time, which is the time indicated by a sundial. It is not a uniform time but is subject to variations which amount to as much as a quarter of an hour in each direction. Such wide variations cannot be tolerated in a practical time-scale, and this has led to the concept of Mean Solar Time in which all the days are exactly the same length and equal to the average length of the Apparent Solar Day.

The positions of the stars in the sky are specified in relation to a fictitious reference point in the sky known as the First Point of Aries (or the Vernal Equinox). It is therefore convenient to adopt this same reference point when considering the rotation of the Earth against the background of the stars. The time-scale so obtained is known as Apparent Sidereal Time.

GREENWICH MEAN TIME

The daily rotation of the Earth on its axis causes the Sun and the other heavenly bodies to appear to cross the sky from east to west. It is convenient to represent this relative motion as if the Sun really performed a daily circuit around a fixed Earth. Noon in Apparent Solar Time may then be defined as the time at which the Sun transits across the observer's meridian. In Mean Solar Time, noon is similarly defined by the meridian transit of a fictitious Mean Sun moving uniformly in the sky with the same average speed as the true Sun. Mean Solar Time observed on the meridian of the transit circle telescope of the Royal Observatory at Greenwich is called Greenwich Mean Time (GMT). The mean solar day is divided into 24 hours and, for astronomical and other scientific purposes, these are numbered 0 to 23, commencing at midnight. Civil time is usually reckoned in two periods of 12 hours, designated am (*ante meridiem,* ie before noon) and pm (*post meridiem,* ie after noon), although the 24 hour clock is increasingly being used.

UNIVERSAL TIME

Before 1925 January 1, GMT was reckoned in 24 hours commencing at noon; since that date it has been reckoned from midnight. To avoid confusion in the use of the designation GMT before and after 1925, since 1928 astronomers have tended to use the term Universal Time (UT) or Weltzeit (WZ) to denote GMT measured from Greenwich Mean Midnight.

In precision work it is necessary to take account of small variations in Universal Time. These arise from small irregularities in the rotation of the Earth. Observed astronomical time is designated UT0. Observed time corrected for the effects of the motion of the poles (giving rise to a 'wandering' in longitude) is designated UT1. There is also a seasonal fluctuation in the rate of rotation of the Earth arising from meteorological causes, often called the annual fluctuation. UT1 corrected for this effect is designated UT2 and provides a time-scale free from short-period fluctuations. It is still subject to small secular and irregular changes.

APPARENT SOLAR TIME

As mentioned above, the time shown by a sundial is called Apparent Solar Time. It differs from Mean Solar Time by an amount known as the Equation of Time, which is the total effect of two causes which make the length of the apparent solar day non-uniform. One cause of variation is that the orbit of the Earth is not a circle but an ellipse, having the Sun at one focus. As a consequence, the angular speed of the Earth in its orbit is not constant; it is greatest at the beginning of January when the Earth is nearest the Sun.

The other cause is due to the obliquity of the ecliptic; the plane of the equator (which is at right angles to the axis of rotation of the Earth) does not coincide with the ecliptic (the plane defined by the apparent annual motion of the Sun around the celestial sphere) but is inclined to it at an angle of $23° 26'$. As a result, the apparent solar day is shorter than

average at the equinoxes and longer at the solstices. From the combined effects of the components due to obliquity and eccentricity, the equation of time reaches its maximum values in February (-14 minutes) and early November ($+16$ minutes). It has a zero value on four dates during the year, and it is only on these dates (approximately April 15, June 14, September 1 and December 25) that a sundial shows Mean Solar Time.

SIDEREAL TIME

A sidereal day is the duration of a complete rotation of the Earth with reference to the First Point of Aries. The term sidereal (or 'star') time is a little misleading since the time-scale so defined is not exactly the same as that which would be defined by successive transits of a selected star, as there is a small progressive motion between the stars and the First Point of Aries due to the precession of the Earth's axis. This makes the length of the sidereal day shorter than the true period of rotation by 0.008 seconds. Superimposed on this steady precessional motion are small oscillations (nutation), giving rise to fluctuations in apparent sidereal time amounting to as much as 1.2 seconds. It is therefore customary to employ Mean Sidereal Time, from which these fluctuations have been removed. The conversion of GMT to Greenwich sidereal time (GST) may be performed by adding the value of the GST at 0h on the day in question (page two of each month) to the GMT converted to sidereal time using the table on page 627.

Example – To find the GST at August 8d 02h 41m 11s GMT

	h	m	s
GST at 0h	20	07	34
GMT	2	41	11
Acceleration for 2h			20
Acceleration for 41m 11s			7
Sum = GST =	22	49	12

If the observer is not on the Greenwich meridian then his/her longitude, measured positively westwards from Greenwich, must be subtracted from the GST to obtain Local Sidereal Time (LST). Thus, in the above example, an observer 5h east of Greenwich, or 19h west, would find the LST as 4h 49m 16s.

EPHEMERIS TIME

An analysis of observations of the positions of the Sun, Moon and planets taken over an extended period is used in preparing ephemerides. (An ephemeris is a table giving the apparent position of a heavenly body at regular intervals of time, eg one day or ten days, and may be used to compare current observations with tabulated positions.) Discrepancies between the positions of heavenly bodies observed over a 300-year period and their predicted positions arose because the time-scale to which the observations were related was based on the assumption that the rate of rotation of the Earth is uniform. It is now known that this rate of rotation is variable. A revised time-scale, Ephemeris Time (ET), was devised to bring the ephemerides into agreement with the observations.

The second of ET is defined in terms of the annual motion of the Earth in its orbit around the Sun (1/31556925.9747 of the tropical year for 1900 January 0d 12h ET). The precise determination of ET from astronomical observations is a lengthy process as the requisite standard of accuracy can only be achieved by averaging over a number of years.

In 1976 the International Astronomical Union adopted Terrestrial Dynamical Time (TDT), a new dynamical time-scale for general use whose scale unit is the SI second (*see* Atomic Time, below). TDT was renamed Terrestrial Time (TT) in 1991. ET is now of little more than historical interest.

TERRESTRIAL TIME
The uniform time system used in computing the ephemerides of the solar system is Terrestrial Time (TT), which has replaced ET for this purpose. Except for the most rigorous astronomical calculations, it may be assumed to be the same as ET. During 2016 the estimated difference TT − UT is about 68 seconds.

ATOMIC TIME
The fundamental standards of time and frequency must be defined in terms of a periodic motion adequately uniform, enduring and measurable. Progress has made it possible to use natural standards, such as atomic or molecular oscillations. Continuous oscillations are generated in an electrical circuit, the frequency of which is then compared or brought into coincidence with the frequency characteristic of the absorption or emission by the atoms or molecules when they change between two selected energy levels. Since the 13th General Conference on Weights and Measures in October 1967, the unit of time, the second, has been defined in the International System of units (SI) as 'the duration of 9 192 631 770 periods of the radiation corresponding to the transition between the two hyperfine levels of the ground state of the caesium-133 atom'.

In the UK, the national time scale is maintained by the National Physical Laboratory (NPL), using an ensemble of atomic clocks based on either caesium or hydrogen atoms. In addition the NPL (along with several other national laboratories) has constructed and operates caesium fountain primary frequency standards, which utilise the cooling of caesium atoms by laser light to determine the duration of the SI second at the highest attainable level of accuracy. Caesium fountain primary standards typically achieve an accuracy of around 2 parts in 10 000 000 000 000 000, which is equivalent to one second in 158 million years.

Timekeeping worldwide is based on two closely related atomic time scales that are established through international collaboration. International Atomic Time (TAI) is formed by combining the readings of more than 400 atomic clocks located in more than 70 institutes and was set close to the astronomically based Universal Time (UT) near the beginning of 1958. It was formally recognised in 1971 and since 1988 January 1 has been maintained by the International Bureau of Weights and Measures (BIPM). Civil time in almost all countries is now based on Coordinated Universal Time (UTC), which differs from TAI by an integer number of seconds and was designed to make both atomic time and UT available with accuracy appropriate for most users. On 1 January 1972 UTC was set to be exactly 10 seconds behind TAI, and since then the UTC time-scale has been adjusted by the insertion (or, in principle, omission) of leap seconds in order to keep it within ±0.9 s of UT. These leap seconds are introduced, when necessary, at the same instant throughout the world, either at the end of December or at the end of June. The last leap second occurred immediately prior to 0h UTC on 2015 July 1, and was the 26th leap second. All leap seconds so far have been positive, with 61 seconds in the final minute of the UTC month. The time 23h 59m 60s UTC is followed one second later by 0h 0m 00s of the first day of the following month. Notices concerning the insertion of leap seconds are issued by the International Earth Rotation and Reference Systems Service (IERS).

The computation of UTC is carried out monthly by the BIPM and takes place in three stages. First, a weighted average known as Echelle Atomique Libre (EAL) is calculated from all of the contributing atomic clocks. In the second stage, TAI is generated by applying small corrections, derived from the results contributed by primary frequency standards, to the scale interval of EAL to maintain its value close to that of the SI second. Finally, UTC is formed from TAI by the addition of an integer number of seconds. The results are published monthly in the BIPM Circular T in the form of offsets at 5-day intervals between UTC and the time scales of contributing organisations.

RADIO TIME-SIGNALS
UTC is made generally available through time-signals and standard frequency broadcasts such as MSF in the UK, CHU in Canada and WWV and WWVH in the USA. These are based on national time-scales that are maintained in close agreement with UTC and provide traceability to the national time-scale and to UTC. The markers of seconds in the UTC scale coincide with those of TAI.

To disseminate the national time-scale in the UK, special signals (call-sign MSF) are broadcast by the National Physical Laboratory. From April 1, 2007 the MSF service, previously broadcast from British Telecom's radio station at Rugby, has been transmitted from Anthorn radio station in Cumbria. The signals are controlled from a caesium beam atomic frequency standard and consist of a precise frequency carrier of 60 kHz which is switched off, after being on for at least half a second, to mark every second. The first second of the minute begins with a period of 500 ms with the carrier switched off, to serve as a minute marker. In the other seconds the carrier is always off for at least one tenth of a second at the start and then it carries an on-off code giving the British clock time and date, together with information identifying the start of the next minute. Changes to and from summer time are made following government announcements. Leap seconds are inserted as announced by the IERS and information provided by them on the difference between UTC and UT is also signalled. Other broadcast signals in the UK include the BBC six pips signal, the BT Timeline ('speaking clock'), the NPL telephone and internet time services for computers, and a coded time-signal on the BBC 198 kHz transmitters which is used for timing in the electricity supply industry. From 1972 January 1 the six pips on the BBC have consisted of five short pips from second 55 to second 59 (six pips in the case of a leap second) followed by one lengthened pip, the start of which indicates the exact minute. From 1990 February 5 these signals have been controlled by the BBC with seconds markers referenced to the satellite-based US navigation system GPS (Global Positioning System) and time and day referenced to the MSF transmitter. Formerly they were generated by the Royal Greenwich Observatory. The NPL telephone and internet time services are directly connected to the national time scale.

Accurate timing may also be obtained from the signals of international navigation systems such as the ground-based eLORAN, or the satellite-based American GPS or Russian GLONASS systems.

STANDARD TIME
Since 1880 the standard time in Britain has been Greenwich Mean Time (GMT); a statute that year enacted that the word 'time' when used in any legal document relating to Britain meant, unless otherwise specifically stated, the mean time of the Greenwich meridian. Greenwich was adopted as the universal meridian on 13 October 1884. A system of standard time by zones is used worldwide, standard time in each zone differing from that of the Greenwich meridian by an integral number of hours or, exceptionally, half-hours or quarter-hours, either fast or slow. The large territories of

the USA and Canada are divided into zones approximately 7.5° on either side of central meridians.

Variations from the standard time of some countries occur during part of the year; they are decided annually and are usually referred to as Summer Time or Daylight Saving Time.

At the 180th meridian the time can be either 12 hours fast on Greenwich Mean Time or 12 hours slow, and a change of date occurs. The internationally recognised date or calendar line is a modification of the 180th meridian, drawn so as to include islands of any one group on the same side of the line, or for political reasons. The line is indicated by joining up the following coordinates:

Lat.	Long.	Lat.	Long.
90° S.	180°	48° N.	180°
51° S.	180°	53° N.	170° E.
45° S.	172.5° W.	65.5° N.	169° W.
15° S.	172.5° W.	68° N.	169° W.
5° S.	180°	90° N.	180°

Changes to the date line would require an international conference.

BRITISH SUMMER TIME

In 1916 an Act ordained that during a defined period of that year the legal time for general purposes in Great Britain should be one hour in advance of Greenwich Mean Time. The Summer Time Acts 1922 and 1925 defined the period during which Summer Time was to be in force, stabilising practice until the Second World War.

During the Second World War (1941–5) and in 1947 Double Summer Time (two hours in advance of Greenwich Mean Time) was used for the period in which ordinary Summer Time would have been in force. During these years clocks were also kept one hour in advance of Greenwich Mean Time in the winter. After the war, ordinary Summer Time was invoked each year from 1948–68.

Between 1968 October 27 and 1971 October 31 clocks were kept one hour ahead of Greenwich Mean Time throughout the year. This was known as British Standard Time.

The most recent legislation is the Summer Time Act 1972, which enacted that 'the period of summer time for the purposes of this Act is the period beginning at two o'clock, Greenwich Mean Time, in the morning of the day after the third Saturday in March or, if that day is Easter Day, the day after the second Saturday in March, and ending at two o'clock, Greenwich Mean Time, in the morning of the day after the fourth Saturday in October.'

The duration of Summer Time can be varied by Order in Council and in recent years alterations have been made to synchronise the period of Summer Time in Britain with that used in Europe. The rule for 1981–94 defined the period of Summer Time in the UK as from the last Sunday in March to the day following the fourth Saturday in October and the hour of changeover was altered to 01h Greenwich Mean Time.

There was no rule for the dates of Summer Time between 1995–7. Since 1998 the 9th European Parliament and Council Directive on Summer Time has harmonised the dates on which Summer Time begins and ends across member states as the last Sundays in March and October respectively. Under the directive Summer Time begins and ends at 01hr Greenwich Mean Time in each member state. Amendments to the Summer Time Act to implement the directive came into force on 11 March 2002.

The duration of Summer Time in 2016 is:
March 27 01h GMT to October 30 01h GMT

MEAN REFRACTION

Alt.		Ref.	Alt.		Ref.	Alt.		Ref.
°	′	′	°	′	′	°	′	′
1	20	21	3	12	13	7	54	6
1	30	20	3	34	12	9	27	5
1	41	19	4	00	11	11	39	4
1	52	18	4	30	10	15	00	3
2	05	17	5	06	9	20	42	2
2	19	16	5	50	8	32	20	1
2	35	15	6	44	7	62	17	0
2	52	14	7	54		90	00	
3	12							

The refraction table is in the form of a critical table (see page 627).

ASTRONOMICAL CONSTANTS

Solar parallax	8″.794
Astronomical unit	149597870 km
Precession for the year 2016	50″.257
Precession in right ascension	3ˢ.075
Precession in declination	20″.043
Constant of nutation	9″.202
Constant of aberration	20″.496
Mean obliquity of ecliptic (2009)	23° 26′ 17″
Moon's equatorial hor. parallax	57′ 02″.70
Velocity of light in vacuo per second	299792.5 km
Solar motion per second	20.0 km
Equatorial radius of the Earth	6378.137 km
Polar radius of the Earth	6356.752 km

North galactic pole (IAU standard)
RA 12h 51m (2000.0). Dec. +27°.1 N.
Solar apex   RA 18h 04m Dec. + 30°

Length of year (in mean solar days)

Tropical	365.24219
Sidereal	365.25636
Anomalistic (perihelion to perihelion)	365.25964
Eclipse	346.62003

Length of month (mean values)	d	h	m	s
Synodic (new Moon to new Moon)	29	12	44	02.0
Sidereal	27	07	43	43.2
Anomalistic (perigee to perigee)	27	13	18	51.8

THE EARTH

The shape of the Earth is that of an oblate spheroid or solid of revolution whose meridian sections are ellipses not differing much from circles, while the sections at right angles are circles. The length of the equatorial axis is about 12,756 km, and that of the polar axis is 12,714 km. The mean density of the Earth is 5.5 times that of water, although that of the surface layer is less. The Earth and Moon revolve about their common centre of gravity in a lunar month; this centre in turn revolves round the Sun in a plane known as the ecliptic, that passes through the Sun's centre. The Earth's equator is inclined to this plane at an angle of 23.4°. This tilt is the cause of the seasons. In mid-latitudes, and when the Sun is high above the Equator, not only does the high noon altitude make the days longer, but the Sun's rays fall more directly on the Earth's surface; these effects combine to produce summer. In equatorial regions the noon altitude is large throughout the year, and there is little variation in the length of the day. In higher latitudes the noon altitude is lower, and the days in summer are appreciably longer than those in winter.

The average velocity of the Earth in its orbit is 30km a second. It makes a complete rotation on its axis in about 23h 56m of mean time, which is the sidereal day. Because of its annual revolution round the Sun, the rotation with respect to the Sun, or the solar day, is more than this by about four minutes. The extremity of the axis of rotation, or the North Pole of the Earth, is not rigidly fixed, but wanders over an area roughly 20 metres in diameter.

Perihelion is when the Earth is closest to the Sun, and *aphelion* when the Earth is furthest from the Sun:

Perihelion	January	2d 22h 49m
		(147,100,176km, 0.983303941au)
Aphelion	July	4d 16h 24m
		(152,103,776km, 1.016750939au)

TERRESTRIAL MAGNETISM

The Earth's main magnetic field corresponds approximately to that of a very strong small bar magnet near the centre of the Earth, but with appreciable smooth spatial departures. The origin of the main field is generally ascribed to electric currents associated with fluid motions in the Earth's core. As a result not only does the main field vary in strength and direction from place to place, but also with time. Superimposed on the main field are local and regional anomalies whose magnitudes may in places approach that of the main field; these are due to the influence of mineral deposits in the Earth's crust. A small proportion of the field is of external origin, mostly associated with electric currents in the ionosphere and magnetosphere. The configuration of the external field and the ionisation of the atmosphere depend on the incident particle and radiation flux from the Sun. There are, therefore, short-term and non-periodic as well as diurnal, 27-day, seasonal and approximate 11-year periodic changes in the magnetic field, dependent upon the position of the Sun, the degree of solar activity and the magnetic field embedded in the solar wind.

A magnetic compass points along the horizontal component of a magnetic line of force. These lines of force converge on the 'magnetic dip-poles', the places where the Earth's magnetic field is vertical. These poles move with time, and their present approximate adopted mean positions are 86.4° N., 166.4° W. and 64.2° S., 136.4° E. Compasses do not point directly, ie via great circle routes, to the dip-poles.

There is also a 'magnetic equator', at all points of which the vertical component of the Earth's magnetic field is zero and a magnetised needle remains horizontal. This line runs between 2° and 12° north of the geographical equator in Asia and Africa, turns sharply south in the Atlantic Ocean and crosses South America south of the geographical equator; it re-crosses the geographical equator in mid-Pacific.

Reference has already been made to secular changes in the Earth's field. The following table indicates the changes in magnetic declination (or variation of the compass relative to true north). Declination is the angle in the horizontal plane between the direction of true north and that in which a magnetic compass points. Similar, though much smaller, changes have occurred in 'dip' or magnetic inclination. Secular changes differ throughout the world.

London (Greenwich)

1580	11°	15′	E.	1900	16° 29′	W.
1622	5°	56′	E.	1925	13° 10′	W.
1665	1°	22′	W.	1950	9° 07′	W.
1730	13°	00′	W.	1975	6° 39′	W.
1773	21°	09′	W.	1998	3° 32′	W.
1850	22°	24′	W.			

In the British Isles, lines of equal declination (isogonics) now run approximately north–northeast to south–southwest. Though there are considerable local deviations due to geological causes, a rough value of magnetic declination may be obtained by assuming that at 50° N. on the meridian of Greenwich, the value in 2016 is 0° 10′ west and allowing an increase of 11′ for each degree of latitude northwards and one of 26′ for each degree of longitude westwards. For example, at 53° N., 5° W., declination will be about 0° 10′ + 33′ + 130′, ie 2° 53′ west. The average annual change at the present time is about 11′ decrease. For navigation by compass using maps with the north lines from the British National Grid (as opposed to lines of equal longitude), account has to be taken of the difference between true north and grid north. This angle can be several degrees. In 2014 the variation of the compass relative to grid north become easterly for the first time in 350 years.

The number of magnetic observatories is about 180, irregularly distributed over the globe. There are three in the UK, run by the British Geological Survey: at Hartland, north Devon; at Eskdalemuir, Dumfries and Galloway; and at Lerwick, Shetland Islands. Some recent annual mean values of the magnetic elements for Hartland:

Year	Declination West ° ′	Dip or inclination ° ′	Horizontal intensity nT	Vertical intensity nT
1960	9 58.8	65 43.9	18707	43504
1970	9 06.5	66 26.1	19033	43636
1980	7 43.8	66 10.3	19330	43768
1990	6 15.0	66 09.7	19539	43896
2000	4 43.6	66 06.9	19508	44051
2014	2 28.1	66 00.0	19728	44310

$nT = nanoTesla$

The magnetic field is also observed by a series of specialised satellites, the latest being a mission called Swarm. Three satellites were successfully launched by the European Space Agency in November 2013, each equipped with magnetometers and star cameras for accurate orientation. With the data from these satellites the Earth's magnetic field and its changes in time can be mapped to unprecedented accuracy.

Reliance on the Earth's magnetic field for navigation by compass is not restricted to land, maritime or aeronautical navigation (in the latter two usually as a fail-safe back-up system). It also extends underground with the oil industry using magnetic survey tools when drilling well-bores. Very accurate estimates of the local magnetic field are required for this, taking into account the crustal and external fields.

MAGNETIC STORMS

Occasionally, sometimes with great suddenness, the Earth's magnetic field is subject for several hours to marked disturbance. During a severe storm in October 2003 the declination at Eskdalemuir changed by over 5° in six minutes. In many instances such disturbances are accompanied by widespread displays of auroras, marked changes in the incidence of cosmic rays, an increase in the reception of 'noise' from the Sun at radio frequencies, and rapid changes in the ionosphere and induced electric currents within the Earth. These can adversely affect satellite operations, telecommunications and electric power transmission systems. The disturbances are caused by changes in the stream of ionised particles which emanates from the Sun and through which the Earth is continuously passing. Some of these changes are associated with visible eruptions on the Sun, usually in the region of sun-spots. There is some tendency for disturbances to recur after intervals of about 27 days, the period of rotation of the Sun on its axis as seen from the Earth. But the sources of many disturbances are shorter lived than this. Predicting such disturbances with any useful accuracy remains challenging. The year 2016 is expected to be about two years after the most recent maximum of the approximate 11-year solar activity cycle. The peak in magnetic activity usually lags that in solar activity by at least two years.

ELEMENTS OF THE SOLAR SYSTEM

Orb	Mean distance from Sun (Earth = 1)	km 10⁶	Sidereal period days	Synodic period days	Incl. of orbit to ecliptic °	'	Diameter km	Mass (Earth = 1)	Period of rotation on axis days
Sun	—	—	—	—	—		1,392,000	332,981	25–35*
Mercury	0.39	58	88.0	116	7	00	4,879	0.0553	58.646
Venus	0.72	108	224.7	584	3	24	12,104	0.8150	243.019r
Earth	1.00	150	365.3	—	—		12,756e	1.0000	0.997
Mars	1.52	228	687.0	780	1	51	6,794e	0.1074	1.026
Jupiter	5.20	778	4,334.4	399	1	18	142,984e 133,708p	317.83	0.410e
Saturn	9.55	1429	10,787.9	378	2	29	120,536e 108,728p	95.16	0.426e
Uranus	19.22	2875	30,773.3	370	0	46	51,118e	14.54	0.718r
Neptune	30.11	4504	60,349.2	367	1	46	49,528e	17.15	0.671
Pluto †	39.80	5954	91,708.2	367	17	09	2,390	0.002	6.387

e equatorial, p polar, r retrograde, * depending on latitude, † reclassified as a dwarf planet since August 2006

THE SATELLITES

Name		Star mag.	Mean distance from primary km	Sidereal period of revolution d
EARTH				
I	Moon	—	384,400	27.322
MARS				
I	Phobos	11	9,378	0.319
II	Deimos	12	23,459	1.262
JUPITER				
XVI	Metis	17	127,960	0.295
XV	Adrastea	19	128,980	0.298
V	Amalthea	14	181,300	0.498
XIV	Thebe	16	221,900	0.675
I	Io	5	421,600	1.769
II	Europa	5	670,900	3.551
III	Ganymede	5	1,070,000	7.155
IV	Callisto	6	1,883,000	16.689
XIII	Leda	20	11,165,000	240.92
VI	Himalia	15	11,460,000	250.57
X	Lysithea	18	11,717,000	259.22
VII	Elara	17	11,741,000	259.65
XII	Ananke	19	21,276,000	629.77r
XI	Carme	18	23,404,000	734.17r
VIII	Pasiphae	17	23,624,000	743.68r
IX	Sinope	18	23,939,000	758.90r
SATURN				
XVIII	Pan	20	133,583	0.575
XV	Atlas	18	137,640	0.602
XVI	Prometheus	16	139,353	0.613
XVII	Pandora	16	141,700	0.629
XI	Epimetheus	15	151,422	0.694
X	Janus	14	151,472	0.695
I	Mimas	13	185,520	0.942
II	Enceladus	12	238,020	1.370
III	Tethys	10	294,660	1.888
XIII	Telesto	19	294,660	1.888
XIV	Calypso	19	294,660	1.888
IV	Dione	10	377,400	2.737
XII	Helene	18	377,400	2.737
V	Rhea	10	527,040	4.518
VI	Titan	8	1,221,850	15.945

Name		Star mag.	Mean distance from primary km	Sidereal period of revolution d
SATURN				
VII	Hyperion	14	1,481,000	21.277
VIII	Iapetus	11	3,561,300	79.330
IX	Phoebe	16	12,952,000	550.48r
URANUS				
VI	Cordelia	24	49,770	0.335
VII	Ophelia	24	53,790	0.376
VIII	Bianca	23	59,170	0.435
IX	Cressida	22	61,780	0.464
X	Desdemona	22	62,680	0.474
XI	Juliet	21	64,350	0.493
XII	Portia	21	66,090	0.513
XIII	Rosalind	22	66,940	0.558
XIV	Belinda	22	75,260	0.624
XV	Puck	20	86,010	0.762
V	Miranda	16	129,390	1.413
I	Ariel	14	191,020	2.520
II	Umbriel	15	266,300	4.144
III	Titania	14	435,910	8.706
IV	Oberon	14	583,520	13.463
XVI	Caliban	22	7,230,000	579.5r
XX	Stephano	24	8,002,000	676.5r
XVII	Sycorax	21	12,179,000	1,283.4r
XVIII	Prospero	23	16,418,000	1,992.8r
XIX	Setebos	23	17,459,000	2,202.2r
NEPTUNE				
III	Naiad	25	48,230	0.294
IV	Thalassa	24	50,080	0.311
V	Despina	23	52,530	0.335
VI	Galatea	22	61,950	0.429
VII	Larissa	22	73,550	0.555
VIII	Proteus	20	117,650	1.122
I	Triton	13	354,760	5.877
II	Nereid	19	5,513,400	360.136
PLUTO				
I	Charon	17	19,600	6.387

The total number of satellites of the outer planets are: Jupiter 67, Saturn 62, Uranus 27, Neptune 14, Pluto 5.

TIME MEASUREMENT AND CALENDARS

MEASUREMENTS OF TIME

Measurements of time are based on the time taken by the Earth to rotate on its axis (day); by the Moon to revolve around the Earth (month); and by the Earth to revolve around the Sun (year). From these, which are not commensurable, certain average or mean intervals have been adopted for ordinary use.

THE DAY
The day begins at midnight and is divided into 24 hours of 60 minutes, each of 60 seconds. The hours are counted from midnight up to 12 noon (when the Sun crosses the meridian), and these hours are designated am *(ante meridiem);* and again from noon up to 12 midnight, which hours are designated pm *(post meridiem),* except when the 24-hour reckoning is employed. The 24-hour reckoning ignores am and pm, numbering the hours 0 to 23 from midnight.

Colloquially the 24 hours are divided into day and night, day being the time while the Sun is above the horizon (including the four stages of twilight defined in the Astronomy section). Day is subdivided into morning, ending at noon; afternoon, from noon to about 6pm; and evening, which may be said to extend from 6pm until midnight. Night begins at the close of astronomical twilight (*see* the Astronomy section) and extends beyond midnight to sunrise the next day.

The names of the days are derived from Old English translations or adaptations of the Roman titles.

Sunday	Sol	Sun
Monday	Luna	Moon
Tuesday	Tiw/Tyr (god of war)	Mars
Wednesday	Woden/Odin	Mercury
Thursday	Thor	Jupiter
Friday	Frigga/Freyja (goddess of love)	Venus
Saturday	Saeterne	Saturn

THE MONTH
The month in the ordinary calendar is approximately the twelfth part of a year, but the lengths of the different months vary from 28 (or 29) days to 31.

THE YEAR
The equinoctial or tropical year is the time that the Earth takes to revolve around the Sun from equinox to equinox, ie 365.24219 mean solar days, or 365 days 5 hours 48 minutes and 45 seconds.

The calendar year usually consists of 365 days but a year containing 366 days is called a bissextile (*see* Roman calendar) or leap year, one day being added to the month of February so that a date 'leaps over' a day of the week. In the Roman calendar the day that was repeated was the sixth day before the beginning of March, the equivalent of 24 February.

A year is a leap year if the date of the year is divisible by four without remainder, unless it is the last year of the century. The last year of a century is a leap year only if its number is divisible by 400 without remainder, eg the years 1800 and 1900 had only 365 days but the year 2000 had 366 days.

THE SOLSTICE
A solstice is the point in the tropical year at which the Sun attains its greatest distance, north or south, from the Equator. In the northern hemisphere the furthest point north of the Equator marks the summer solstice and the furthest point south marks the winter solstice.

The date of the solstice varies according to locality. For example, if the summer solstice falls on 21 June late in the day by Greenwich time, that day will be the longest of the year at Greenwich, but it will fall on 22 June, local date, in Japan, and so 22 June will be the longest day there. The date of the solstice is also affected by the length of the tropical year, which is 365 days 6 hours less about 11 minutes 15 seconds. If a solstice happens late on 21 June in one year, it will be nearly 6 hours later in the next (unless the next year is a leap year), ie early on 22 June, and that will be the longest day.

This delay of the solstice does not continue because the extra day in a leap year brings it back a day in the calendar. However, because of the 11 minutes 15 seconds mentioned above, the additional day in a leap year brings the solstice back too far by 45 minutes, and the time of the solstice in the calendar is earlier, in a four-year pattern, as the century progresses. The last year of a century is in most cases not a leap year, and the omission of the extra day puts the date of the solstice later by about 6 hours. Compensation for this is made by the fourth centennial year being a leap year. The solstice became earlier in date throughout the last century and, because the year 2000 was a leap year, the solstice will get earlier still throughout the 21st century. The date of the winter solstice, the shortest day of the year, is affected by the same factors as the longest day.

At Greenwich the Sun sets at its earliest by the clock about ten days before the shortest day. The daily change in the time of sunset is due in the first place to the Sun's movement southwards at this time of the year, which diminishes the interval between the Sun's transit and its setting. However, the daily decrease of the Equation of Time causes the time of apparent noon to be continuously later day by day, which to some extent counteracts the first effect. The rates of the change of these two quantities are not equal or uniform; their combination causes the date of earliest sunset to be 12 or 13 December at Greenwich. In more southerly latitudes the effect of the movement of the Sun is less, and the change in the time of sunset depends on that of the Equation of Time to a greater degree, and the date of earliest sunset is earlier than it is at Greenwich, eg on the Equator it is about 1 November.

THE EQUINOX
The equinox is the point at which the Sun crosses the Equator and day and night are of equal length all over the world. This occurs in March and September.

DOG DAYS
The days about the heliacal rising of the Dog Star, noted from ancient times as the hottest period of the year in the northern hemisphere, are called the Dog Days. Their incidence has been variously calculated as depending on the Greater or Lesser Dog Star (Sirius or Procyon) and their duration has been reckoned as from 30 to 54 days. A generally accepted period is from 3 July to 15 August.

CHRISTIAN CALENDAR

In the Christian chronological system the years are distinguished by cardinal numbers before or after the birth of Christ, the period being denoted by the letters BC (Before Christ) or, more rarely, AC *(Ante Christum),* and AD *(Anno Domini* – In the Year of Our Lord); BCE (Before the Christian Era) and CE (Christian Era) are now sometimes used instead of BC and AD. The correlative dates of the epoch are the fourth year of the 194th Olympiad, the 753rd year from the foundation of Rome, AM 3761 in Jewish chronology, and the 4,714th year of the Julian period.

The system was introduced into Italy in the sixth century. Though first used in France in the seventh century, it was not universally established there until about the eighth century. It has been said that the system was introduced into England by St Augustine (AD 596), but it was probably not generally used until some centuries later. It was ordered to be used by the bishops at the Council of Chelsea (AD 816).

THE JULIAN CALENDAR

In the Julian calendar (adopted by the Roman Empire in 45 BC) all the centennial years were leap years, and for this reason towards the close of the 16th century there was a difference of ten days between the tropical and calendar years; the equinox fell on 11 March of the calendar, whereas at the time of the Council of Nicaea (AD 325), it had fallen on 21 March. In 1582 Pope Gregory ordained that 5 October should be called 15 October and that of the end-century years only the fourth should be a leap year.

THE GREGORIAN CALENDAR

The Gregorian calendar was adopted by Italy, France, Spain and Portugal in 1582, by Prussia, the Roman Catholic German states, Switzerland, Holland and Flanders on 1 January 1583, by Poland in 1586, Hungary in 1587, the Protestant German and Netherland states and Denmark in 1700, and by Great Britain and its Dominions (including the North American colonies) in 1752, by the omission of 11 days (3 September being reckoned as 14 September). Sweden omitted the leap day in 1700 but observed leap days in 1704 and 1708, and reverted to the Julian calendar by having two leap days in 1712; the Gregorian calendar was adopted in 1753 by the omission of 11 days (18 February being reckoned as 1 March). Japan adopted the calendar in 1872, China in 1912, Bulgaria in 1916, Turkey and Soviet Russia in 1918, Yugoslavia and Romania in 1919, and Greece in 1923.

In the same year that the change was made in England from the Julian to the Gregorian calendar, the start of the new year was also changed from 25 March to 1 January.

THE ORTHODOX CHURCHES

Some Orthodox churches still use the Julian reckoning but the majority of Greek Orthodox churches and the Romanian Orthodox Church have adopted a modified 'New Calendar', observing the Gregorian calendar for fixed feasts and the Julian for movable feasts.

The Orthodox Church year begins on 1 September. There are four fast periods and, in addition to Pascha (Easter), twelve great feasts, as well as numerous commemorations of the saints of the Old and New Testaments throughout the year.

EASTER DAYS AND DOMINICAL LETTERS 1500 TO 2040

Dates up to and including 1752 are according to the Julian calendar. For dominical letters in leap years, *see* note below

		1500–1599	1600–1699	1700–1799	1800–1899	1900–1999	2000–2040
March							
d	22	1573	1668	1761	1818		
e	23	1505/16	1600	1788	1845/56	1913	2008
f	24		1611/95	1706/99		1940	
g	25	1543/54	1627/38/49	1722/33/44	1883/94	1951	2035
A	26	1559/70/81/92	1654/65/76	1749/58/69/80	1815/26/37	1967/78/89	
b	27	1502/13/24/97	1608/87/92	1785/96	1842/53/64	1910/21/32	2005/16
c	28	1529/35/40	1619/24/30	1703/14/25	1869/75/80	1937/48	2027/32
d	29	1551/62	1635/46/57	1719/30/41/52	1807/12/91	1959/64/70	
e	30	1567/78/89	1651/62/73/84	1746/55/66/77	1823/34	1902/75/86/97	
f	31	1510/21/32/83/94	1605/16/78/89	1700/71/82/93	1839/50/61/72	1907/18/29/91	2002/13/24
April							
g	1	1526/37/48	1621/32	1711/16	1804/66/77/88	1923/34/45/56	2018/29/40
A	2	1553/64	1643/48	1727/38	1809/20/93/99	1961/72	
b	3	1575/80/86	1659/70/81	1743/63/68/74	1825/31/36	1904/83/88/94	
c	4	1507/18/91	1602/13/75/86/97	1708/79/90	1847/58	1915/20/26/99	2010/21
d	5	1523/34/45/56	1607/18/29/40	1702/13/24/95	1801/63/74/85/96	1931/42/53	2015/26/37
e	6	1539/50/61/72	1634/45/56	1729/35/40/60	1806/17/28/90	1947/58/69/80	
f	7	1504/77/88	1667/72	1751/65/76	1822/33/44	1901/12/85/96	
g	8	1509/15/20/99	1604/10/83/94	1705/87/92/98	1849/55/60	1917/28	2007/12
A	9	1531/42	1615/26/37/99	1710/21/32	1871/82	1939/44/50	2023/34
b	10	1547/58/69	1631/42/53/64	1726/37/48/57	1803/14/87/98	1955/66/77	2039
c	11	1501/12/63/74/85/96	1658/69/80	1762/73/84	1819/30/41/52	1909/71/82/93	2004
d	12	1506/17/28	1601/12/91/96	1789	1846/57/68	1903/14/25/36/98	2009/20
e	13	1533/44	1623/28	1707/18	1800/73/79/84	1941/52	2031/36
f	14	1555/60/66	1639/50/61	1723/34/45/54	1805/11/16/95	1963/68/74	
g	15	1571/82/93	1655/66/77/88	1750/59/70/81	1827/38	1900/06/79/90	2001
A	16	1503/14/25/36/87/98	1609/20/82/93	1704/75/86/97	1843/54/65/76	1911/22/33/95	2006/17/28
b	17	1530/41/52	1625/36	1715/20	1808/70/81/92	1927/38/49/60	2022/33
c	18	1557/68	1647/52	1731/42/56	1802/13/24/97	1954/65/76	
d	19	1500/79/84/90	1663/74/85	1747/67/72/78	1829/35/40	1908/81/87/92	
e	20	1511/22/95	1606/17/79/90	1701/12/83/94	1851/62	1919/24/30	2003/14/25
f	21	1527/38/49	1622/33/44	1717/28	1867/78/89	1935/46/57	2019/30
g	22	1565/76	1660	1739/53/64	1810/21/32	1962/73/84	
A	23	1508	1671		1848	1905/16	2000
b	24	1519	1603/14/98	1709/91	1859		2011
c	25	1546	1641	1736	1886	1943	2038

No dominical letter is placed against the intercalary day 29 February, but since it is still counted as a weekday and given a name, the series of letters moves back one day every leap year after intercalation. Thus, a leap year beginning with the dominical letter C will change to a year with the dominical letter B on 1 March

MOVEABLE FEASTS TO THE YEAR 2040

Year	Ash Wednesday	Easter	Ascension	Pentecost (Whit Sunday)	Advent Sunday
2016	10 February	27 March	5 May	15 May	27 November
2017	1 March	16 April	25 May	4 June	3 December
2018	14 February	1 April	10 May	20 May	2 December
2019	6 March	21 April	30 May	9 June	1 December
2020	26 February	12 April	21 May	31 May	29 November
2021	17 February	4 April	13 May	23 May	28 November
2022	2 March	17 April	26 May	5 June	27 November
2023	22 February	9 April	18 May	28 May	3 December
2024	14 February	31 March	9 May	19 May	1 December
2025	5 March	20 April	29 May	8 June	30 November
2026	18 February	5 April	14 May	24 May	29 November
2027	10 February	28 March	6 May	16 May	28 November
2028	1 March	16 April	25 May	4 June	3 December
2029	14 February	1 April	10 May	20 May	2 December
2030	6 March	21 April	30 May	9 June	1 December
2031	26 February	13 April	22 May	1 June	30 November
2032	11 February	28 March	6 May	16 May	28 November
2033	2 March	17 April	26 May	5 June	27 November
2034	22 February	9 April	18 May	28 May	3 December
2035	7 February	25 March	3 May	13 May	2 December
2036	27 February	13 April	22 May	1 June	30 November
2037	18 February	5 April	14 May	24 May	29 November
2038	10 March	25 April	3 June	13 June	28 November
2039	23 February	10 April	19 May	29 May	27 November
2040	15 February	1 April	10 May	20 May	2 December

NOTES

Ash Wednesday (first day in Lent) can fall at earliest on 4 February and at latest on 10 March

Mothering Sunday (fourth Sunday in Lent) can fall at earliest on 1 March and at latest on 4 April

Easter Day can fall at earliest on 22 March and at latest on 25 April

Ascension Day is forty days after Easter Day and can fall at earliest on 30 April and at latest on 3 June

Pentecost (Whit Sunday) is seven weeks after Easter and can fall at earliest on 10 May and at latest on 13 June

Trinity Sunday is the Sunday after Whit Sunday

Corpus Christi falls on the Thursday after Trinity Sunday

Sundays after Pentecost – there are not less than 18 and not more than 23

Advent Sunday is the Sunday nearest to 30 November

THE DOMINICAL LETTER

The dominical letter is one of the letters A–G which are used to denote the Sundays in successive years. If the first day of the year is a Sunday the letter is A; if the second, B; the third, C; and so on. A leap year requires two letters, the first for 1 January to 29 February, the second for 1 March to 31 December. For the leap year 2016 the letter given in the table opposite is for the second part of the year (B) and the letter for the first part of the year will be the one given below (C); therefore the dominical letter for 2016 is CB (*see also* page 7).

EPIPHANY

The feast of the Epiphany, commemorating the manifestation of Christ, later became associated with the offering of gifts by the Magi. The day was of great importance from the time of the Council of Nicaea (AD 325), as the primate of Alexandria was charged at every Epiphany feast with the announcement in a letter to the churches of the date of the forthcoming Easter. The day was also of importance in Britain as it influenced dates, ecclesiastical and lay, eg Plough Monday, when work was resumed in the fields, fell on the Monday in the first full week after Epiphany.

LENT

The Teutonic word *Lent,* which denotes the fast preceding Easter, originally meant no more than the spring season; but from Anglo-Saxon times, at least, it has been used as the equivalent of the more significant Latin term *Quadragesima,* meaning the 'forty days' or, more literally, the fortieth day. Ash Wednesday is the first day of Lent, which ends at midnight before Easter Day.

PALM SUNDAY

Palm Sunday, the Sunday before Easter and the beginning of Holy Week, commemorates the triumphal entry of Christ into Jerusalem.

MAUNDY THURSDAY

Maundy Thursday is the day before Good Friday, the name itself being a corruption of *dies mandati* (day of the mandate) when Christ washed the feet of the disciples and gave them the mandate to love one another.

EASTER DAY

Easter Day is the first Sunday after the full moon which happens on, or next after, the 21st day of March; if the full moon happens on a Sunday, Easter Day is the Sunday after.

This definition is contained in an Act of Parliament (24 Geo. II ch. 23) and explanation is given in the preamble to the Act that the day of full moon depends on certain tables that have been prepared. These tables are summarised in the early pages of the Book of Common Prayer. The moon referred to is not the real Moon of the heavens, but a hypothetical moon on whose 'full' the date of Easter depends, and the lunations of this 'calendar' moon consist of 29 and 30 days alternately, with certain necessary modifications to make the date of its full agree as nearly as possible with that of the real Moon, which is known as the Paschal Full Moon.

A FIXED EASTER

In 1928 the House of Commons agreed to a motion for the third reading of a bill proposing that Easter Day shall, in the calendar year next but one after the commencement of the Act and in all subsequent years, be the first Sunday after the second Saturday in April. Easter would thus fall on the second or third Sunday in April, ie between 9 and 15 April (inclusive). A clause in the bill provided that before it shall come into operation, regard shall be had to any opinion expressed officially by the various Christian churches. Efforts by the World Council of Churches to secure a unanimous choice of date for Easter by its member churches have so far been unsuccessful.

ROGATION DAYS

Rogation Days are the Monday, Tuesday and Wednesday preceding Ascension Day and from the fifth century were observed as public fasts with solemn processions and supplications. The processions were discontinued as religious observances at the Reformation, but survive in the ceremony known as 'beating the parish bounds'. Rogation Sunday is the Sunday before Ascension Day.

EMBER DAYS

The Ember days occur on the Wednesday, Friday and Saturday of the same week, four times a year. Used for the ordination of clergy, these days are set aside for fasting and prayer. The weeks in which they fall are: (a) after the third Sunday in Advent, (b) before the second Sunday in Lent, (c) before Trinity Sunday and (d) after Holy Cross day.

TRINITY SUNDAY

Trinity Sunday is eight weeks after Easter Day, on the Sunday following Pentecost (Whit Sunday). Subsequent Sundays are reckoned in the Book of Common Prayer calendar of the Church of England as 'after Trinity'.

Thomas Becket (1118–70) was consecrated Archbishop of Canterbury on the Sunday after Whit Sunday and his first act was to ordain that the day of his consecration should be held as a new festival in honour of the Holy Trinity.

HINDU CALENDAR

The Hindu calendar is a luni-solar calendar of 12 months, each containing 29 days, 12 hours. Each month is divided into a light fortnight (Shukla or Shuddha) and a dark fortnight (Krishna or Vadya) based on the waxing and waning of the Moon. In most parts of India the month starts with the light fortnight, ie the day after the new moon, although in some regions it begins with the dark fortnight, ie the day after the full moon.

The new year according to the civil calendar begins on the first day of the month of Chaitra (March/April) and ends in the month of Phalgun (March). The financial new year begins on the first day of Kartik (Diwali day). For most Hindus, the first day of Chaitra and the first day of Kartik are equally important.

The 12 months – Chaitra, Vaishakh, Jyeshtha, Ashadh, Shravan, Bhadrapad, Ashvin, Kartik, Margashirsh, Paush, Magh and Phalgun – have Sanskrit names derived from 12 asterisms (constellations). There are regional variations to the names of the months but the Sanskrit names are understood throughout India.

Every lunar month that has a solar transit is termed pure *(shuddha)*. The lunar month without a solar transit is impure *(mala)* and called an intercalary month. An intercalary month occurs approximately every 32 lunar months, whenever the difference between the Hindu year of 360 lunar days (354 days 8 hours solar time) and the 365 days 6 hours of the solar year reaches the length of one Hindu lunar month (29 days 12 hours).

The leap month, often referred to as Adhik Maas (extra month), may be added at any point in the Hindu year. The name given to the month varies according to when it occurs but is taken from the month immediately following it. There is no leap month in 2016; the next one will occur in 2018.

The days of the week are called Raviwar (Sunday), Somawar (Monday), Mangalwar (Tuesday), Budhawar (Wednesday), Guruwar (Thursday), Shukrawar (Friday) and Shaniwar (Saturday). The names are derived from the Sanskrit names of the Sun, the Moon and five planets, Mars, Mercury, Jupiter, Venus and Saturn.

Most fasts and festivals are based on the lunar calendar but a few are determined by the apparent movement of the Sun, eg Makar Sankranti and Pongal (in southern India), which are celebrated on 14/15 January to mark the start of the Sun's apparent journey northwards and a change of season.

Festivals celebrated throughout India are Chaitra (the New Year), Raksha-bandhan (the renewal of the kinship bond between brothers and sisters), Navaratri (a nine-night festival dedicated to the goddess Parvati), Dussehra (the victory of Rama over the demon army), Diwali (a festival of lights), Makar Sankranti, Shivaratri (dedicated to Shiva), and Holi (a spring festival). British Hindus commonly celebrate the festival of Diwali as the start of the financial new year.

Regional festivals are Durga-puja (dedicated to the goddess Durga (Parvati)), Sarasvati Puja (dedicated to the goddess Sarasvati), Ganesh Chaturthi (worship of Ganesh on the fourth day (Chaturthi) of the light half of Bhadrapad), Ram Navami (the birth festival of the god Rama) and Krishna Janmashtami (the birth festival of the god Krishna).

The main festivals celebrated in Britain are Navaratri, Dussehra, Durga-puja, Diwali, Holi, Sarasvati Puja, Ganesh Chaturthi, Raksha-bandhan, Ram Navami and Krishna Janmashtami. For dates of the main festivals in 2016, *see* page 7.

JEWISH CALENDAR

The story of the Flood in the Book of Genesis indicates the use of a calendar of some kind and that the writers recognised 30 days as the length of a lunation. However, after the diaspora, Jewish communities were left in considerable doubt as to the times of fasts and festivals. This led to the formation of the Jewish calendar as used today. It is said that this was done in AD 358 by Rabbi Hillel II, though some assert that it did not happen until much later.

The calendar is luni-solar, and is based on the lengths of the lunation and of the tropical year as found by Hipparchus (*c*.120 BC), which differ little from those adopted at the present day. The year AM 5776 (2015–16) is the 19th year of the 304th Metonic (Minor or Lunar) cycle of 19 years and the 8th year of the 207th Solar (or Major) cycle of 28 years since the Era of the Creation. Jews hold that the Creation occurred at the time of the autumnal equinox in the year known in the Christian calendar as 3760 BC (954 of the Julian period). The epoch or starting point of Jewish chronology corresponds to 7 October 3761 BC. At the beginning of each solar cycle, the Tekufah of Nisan (the vernal equinox) returns to the same day and hour.

The hour is divided into 1,080 minims, and the month between one new moon and the next is reckoned as 29 days 12 hours 793 minims. The normal calendar year, called a regular common year, consists of 12 months of 30 days and 29 days alternately. Since 12 months such as these comprise only 354 days, in order that each of them shall not diverge greatly from an average place in the solar year, a 13th month is occasionally added after the fifth month of the civil year (which commences on the first day of the month Tishri), or as the penultimate month of the ecclesiastical year (which commences on the first day of the month Nisan). The years when this happens are called Embolismic or leap years.

Of the 19 years that form a Metonic cycle, seven are leap years; they occur at places in the cycle indicated by the numbers 3, 6, 8, 11, 14, 17 and 19, these places being chosen so that the accumulated excesses of the solar years should be as small as possible.

A Jewish year is of one of the following six types:

minimal common	353 days
regular common	354 days
full common	355 days
minimal leap	383 days
regular leap	384 days
full leap	385 days

The regular year has alternate months of 30 and 29 days. In a full year, Marcheshvan, the second month of the civil year, has 30 days instead of 29; in minimal years Kislev, the third month, has 29 instead of 30. The additional month in leap years is called Adar Sheni (Adar II) and follows the month called Adar Rishon; the usual Adar festivals are observed in Adar Sheni. In a leap year Adar I has 30 days, in all other years it has 29. None of the variations mentioned are allowed to change the number of days in the other months, which still follow the alternation of the normal 12.

These are the main features of the Jewish calendar, which must be considered permanent because as a Jewish law it cannot be altered except by a Great Sanhedrin.

The Jewish day begins between sunset and nightfall. The time used is that of the meridian of Jerusalem, which is 2h 21m in advance of Greenwich Mean Time. Rules for the beginning of sabbaths and festivals were laid down for the latitude of London in the 18th century and hours for nightfall are fixed annually by the Chief Rabbi.

JEWISH CALENDAR 5776–77

AM 5776 is a full leap year of 13 months, 55 sabbaths and 385 days. AM 5777 is a minimal common year of 12 months, 50 sabbaths and 353 days.

Month (length)	AM 5776	AM 5777
Tishri 1 (30)	14 September 2015	3 October 2016
Marcheshvan 1		
(30/29)	14 October	2 November
Kislev 1 (30/29)	13 November	1 November
Tebet 1 (29)	13 December	30 December
Shebat 1 (30)	11 January 2016	28 January 2017
Adar Rishon 1 (30)	10 February	
Adar Sheni 1	11 March	
Nisan 1 (30)	9 April	
Iyar 1 (29)	9 May	
Sivan 1 (30)	7 June	
Tammuz 1 (29)	7 July	
Ab 1 (30)	5 August	
Elul 1 (29)	4 September	

JEWISH FASTS AND FESTIVALS

For dates of principal festivals in 2016, see page 7.

Tishri 1–2	Rosh Hashanah (New Year)
Tishri 3	*Fast of Gedaliah
Tishri 10	Yom Kippur (Day of Atonement)
Tishri 15–22	Succot (Feast of Tabernacles)
Tishri 21	Hoshana Rabba
Tishri 22	Shemini Atseret (Solemn Assembly)
Tishri 23	Simchat Torah (Rejoicing of the Law)
Kislev 25	Hanukkah (Dedication of the Temple) begins
Tebet 10	Fast of Tebet
†Adar 13	§Fast of Esther

†Adar 14	Purim
†Adar 15	Shushan Purim
Nisan 15–22	Pesach (Passover)
Sivan 6–7	Shavuot (Feast of Weeks)
Tammuz 17	*Fast of Tammuz
Ab 9	*Fast of Ab

* If these dates fall on the sabbath the fast is kept on the following day

† Adar Sheni in leap years

§ This fast is observed on Adar 11 (or Adar Sheni 11 in leap years) if Adar 13 falls on a sabbath

MUSLIM CALENDAR

The Muslim era is dated from the Hijrah, or flight of the Prophet Muhammad from Mecca to Medina, the corresponding date of which in the Julian calendar is 16 July AD 622. The lunar hijri calendar is used principally in Iran, Egypt, Malaysia, Pakistan, Mauritania, various Arab states and certain parts of India. Iran uses the solar hijri calendar as well as the lunar hijri calendar. The dating system was adopted about AD 639, commencing with the first day of the month Muharram.

The lunar calendar consists of 12 months of either 30 or 29 days, with the intercalation of one day at the end of the 12th month at stated intervals in each cycle of 30 years. The object of the intercalation is to reconcile the date of the first day of the month with the date of the actual new moon.

Some adherents still take the date of the evening of the first physical sighting of the crescent of the new moon as that of the first of the month. If cloud obscures the Moon the present month may be extended to 30 days, after which the new month will begin automatically regardless of whether the Moon has been seen. (Under religious law a month must have less than 31 days.) This means that the beginning of a new month and the date of religious festivals can vary from the published calendars.

In each cycle of 30 years, 19 years are common and contain 354 days, and 11 years are intercalary (leap years) of 355 days, the latter being called kabisah. The mean length of the Hijrah years is 354 days 8 hours 48 minutes and the period of mean lunation is 29 days 12 hours 44 minutes.

To ascertain if a year is common or kabisah, divide it by 30: the quotient gives the number of completed cycles and the remainder shows the place of the year in the current cycle. If the remainder is 2, 5, 7, 10, 13, 16, 18, 21, 24, 26 or 29, the year is kabisah and consists of 355 days.

MUSLIM CALENDAR 1437–38

Hijrah 1437 (remainder 27) and Hijrah 1438 (remainder 28) are both common years. Calendar dates below are estimates based on calculations of moon phases.

Month (length)	1437 AH	1438 AH
Muharram 1		
(30/30)	14 October 2015	2 October 2016
Safar 1 (29/29)	13 November	1 November
Rabi' I 1 (30/30)	12 December	30 November
Rabi' II 1 (30/30)	11 January 2016	30 December
Jumada I 1 (29/30)	10 February	29 January 2017
Jumada II 1 (29)	10 March	
Rajab 1 (30)	8 April	
Sha'ban 1 (29)	8 May	
Ramadan 1 (30)	6 June	
Shawwal 1 (29)	6 July	
Dhu'l Qa'da 1 (29)	4 August	
Dhu'l Hijjah 1 (30)	2 September	

MUSLIM FESTIVALS

Ramadan is a month of fasting for all Muslims because it is the month in which the revelation of the *Qur'an* (Koran) began. During Ramadan, Muslims abstain from food, drink and sexual pleasure from dawn until after sunset.

The two major festivals are *Eid-ul-Fitr* and *Eid-ul-Adha*. Eid-ul-Fitr marks the end of the Ramadan fast and is celebrated on the day after the sighting of the new moon of the following month. Eid-ul-Adha, the festival of sacrifice (also known as the great festival), celebrates the submission of the Prophet Ibrahim (Abraham) to God. Eid-ul-Adha falls on the tenth day of Dhu'l-Hijjah, coinciding with the day when those on *hajj* (pilgrimage to Mecca) sacrifice animals.

Other days accorded special recognition are:

Muharram 1	New Year's Day
Muharram 10	Ashura (the day Prophet Noah left the Ark and Prophet Moses was saved from Pharaoh (Sunni), the death of the Prophet's grandson Husain (Shi'ite))
Rabi'u-l-Awwal (*Rabi' I*) 12	Mawlid ul-Nabi (birthday of the Prophet Muhammad)
Rajab 27	Laylat ul-Isra' wa'l-Mi'raj (The Night of Journey and Ascension)
Ramadan*	Laylat ul-Qadr (Night of Power)

* Moveable feast

For dates of the major celebrations in 2015–16, *see* page 7.

SIKH CALENDAR

The Sikh calendar is a lunar calendar of 365 days divided into 12 months. The length of the months varies between 29 and 32 days.

There are no prescribed feast days and no fasting periods. The main celebrations are Baisakhi (the new year and the anniversary of the founding of the Khalsa), Diwali Mela (festival of light), Hola Mohalla Mela (a spring festival held in the Punjab), and the Gurpurbs (anniversaries associated with the ten Gurus).

For dates of the major celebrations in 2016, *see* page 7.

THAI CALENDAR

Thailand adopted the Suriyakati calendar, a modified version of the Gregorian calendar, during the reign of King Rama V in 1888, using 1 April as the first day of the year. In 1940 the date of the new year was changed to 1 January. The years are counted from the beginning of the Buddhist era (BE), which is calculated to have commenced upon the death of the Lord Buddha, taken to have occurred in 543 BC, so AD 2016 is BE 2559. The Chinese system of associating years with one of twelve animals is also in use in Thailand. The Chantarakati lunar calendar is used to determine religious holidays; the new year begins on the first day of the waxing moon in November or, if there is a leap month, in December.

CIVIL AND LEGAL CALENDAR

THE HISTORICAL YEAR

Before 1752, two calendar systems were used in England. The civil or legal year began on 25 March and the historical year on 1 January. Thus the civil or legal date 24 March 1658 was the same day as the historical date 24 March 1659; a date in that portion of the year is written as 24 March 1658/9, the earlier date showing the civil or legal year.

THE NEW YEAR

In England in the seventh century, and as late as the 13th, the year was reckoned from Christmas Day, but in the 12th century the Church in England began the year with the feast of the Annunciation of the Blessed Virgin ('Lady Day') on 25 March, and this practice was adopted generally in the 14th century. The civil or legal year in the British dominions (exclusive of Scotland) began with Lady Day until 1751. But in and since 1752 the civil year has begun with 1 January. New Year's Day in Scotland was changed from 25 March to 1 January in 1600.

Elsewhere in Europe, 1 January was adopted as the first day of the year by Venice in 1522, German states in 1544, Spain, Portugal and the Roman Catholic Netherlands in 1556, Prussia, Denmark and Sweden in 1559, France in 1564, Lorraine in 1579, the Protestant Netherlands in 1583, Russia in 1725, and Tuscany in 1751.

REGNAL YEARS

Regnal years are the years of a sovereign's reign and each begins on the anniversary of his or her accession, eg regnal year 65 of the present queen begins on 6 February 2016.

The system was used for dating Acts of Parliament until 1962. The Summer Time Act 1925, for example, is quoted as 15 and 16 Geo. V ch. 64, because it became law in the parliamentary session which extended over part of both of these regnal years. Acts of a parliamentary session during which a sovereign died were usually given two year numbers, the regnal year of the deceased sovereign and the regnal year of his or her successor, eg those passed in 1952 were dated 16 Geo. VI and 1 Elizabeth II. Since 1962 Acts of Parliament have been dated by the calendar year.

QUARTER AND TERM DAYS

Holy days and saints days were the usual means in early times for setting the dates of future and recurrent appointments. The quarter days in England and Wales are the feast of the Nativity (25 December), the feast of the Annunciation (25 March), the feast of St John the Baptist (24 June) and the feast of St Michael and All Angels (29 September).

The term days in Scotland are Candlemas (the feast of the Purification), Whitsunday, Lammas (Loaf Mass) and Martinmas (St Martin's Day). These fell on 2 February, 15 May, 1 August and 11 November respectively. However, by the Term and Quarter Days (Scotland) Act 1990, the dates of the term days were changed to 28 February (Candlemas), 28 May (Whitsunday), 28 August (Lammas) and 28 November (Martinmas).

RED-LETTER DAYS

Red-letter days were originally the holy days and saints days indicated in early ecclesiastical calendars by letters printed in red ink. The days to be distinguished in this way were approved at the Council of Nicaea in AD 325.

These days still have a legal significance, as judges of the Queen's Bench Division wear scarlet robes on red-letter days falling during the law sittings. The days designated as red-letter days for this purpose are:

Holy and saints days
The Conversion of St Paul, the Purification, Ash Wednesday, the Annunciation, the Ascension, the feasts of St Mark, SS Philip and James, St Matthias, St Barnabas, St John the Baptist, St Peter, St Thomas, St James, St Luke, SS Simon and Jude, All Saints, St Andrew.

Civil calendar (for dates, *see* page 7)
Includes the anniversaries of the Queen's accession, the Queen's birthday and the Queen's coronation, the Queen's official birthday, the birthday of the Duke of Edinburgh, the birthday of the Prince of Wales, St David's Day and Lord Mayor's Day.

PUBLIC HOLIDAYS

Public holidays are divided into two categories, common law and statutory. Common law holidays are holidays 'by habit and custom'; in England, Wales and Northern Ireland these are Good Friday and Christmas Day.

Statutory public holidays, known as bank holidays, were first established by the Bank Holidays Act 1871. They were, literally, days on which the banks (and other public institutions) were closed and financial obligations due on that day were payable the following day. The legislation currently governing public holidays in the UK, which is the Banking and Financial Dealings Act 1971, stipulates the days that are to be public holidays in England, Wales, Scotland and Northern Ireland.

If a public holiday falls on a Saturday or a Sunday then another day will be given in lieu, usually the following Monday. For dates of public holidays in 2016 and 2017, *see* pages 8–9

CHRONOLOGICAL CYCLES AND ERAS

SOLAR (OR MAJOR) CYCLE

The solar cycle is a period of 28 years; in any corresponding year of each cycle the days of the week recur on the same day of the month.

METONIC (LUNAR, OR MINOR) CYCLE

In 432 BC, Meton, an Athenian astronomer, found that 235 lunations are very nearly, though not exactly, equal in duration to 19 solar years and so after 19 years the phases of the Moon recur approximately on the same days of the month. The dates of full moon in a cycle of 19 years were inscribed in figures of gold on public monuments in Athens, and the number showing the position of a year in the cycle is called the golden number of that year.

JULIAN PERIOD

The Julian period was proposed by Joseph Scaliger in 1582. The period is 7,980 Julian years, and its first year coincides with the year 4713 BC. The figure of 7,980 is the product of the number of years in the solar cycle, the Metonic cycle and the cycle of the Roman indiction ($28 \times 19 \times 15$).

ROMAN INDICTION

The Roman indiction is a period of 15 years, instituted for fiscal purposes about AD 300.

EPACT

The epact is the age of the calendar Moon, diminished by one day, on 1 January, in the ecclesiastical lunar calendar.

CHINESE CALENDAR

A lunar calendar was the sole calendar in use in China until 1911, when the government adopted the new (Gregorian) calendar for official and most business activities. The Chinese tend to follow both calendars, the lunar calendar playing an important part in personal life, eg birth celebrations, festivals, marriages; and in rural villages the lunar calendar dictates the cycle of activities, denoting the change of weather and farming activities.

The lunar calendar is used in Hong Kong, Singapore, Malaysia, Tibet and elsewhere in south-east Asia. The calendar has a cycle of 60 years. The new year begins at the first new moon after the sun enters the sign of Aquarius, ie the new year falls between 21 January and 19 February in the Gregorian calendar.

Each year in the Chinese calendar is associated with one of 12 animals: the rat, the ox, the tiger, the rabbit, the dragon, the snake, the horse, the sheep, the monkey, the chicken or rooster, the dog, and the pig.

The date of the Chinese new year and the astrological sign for the years 2016–19 are:

2016	8 February	Monkey
2017	28 January	Rooster
2018	16 February	Dog
2019	5 February	Pig

COPTIC CALENDAR

In the Coptic calendar, which is used in parts of Egypt and Ethiopia, the year is made up of 12 months of 30 days each, followed, in general, by five complementary days. Every fourth year is an intercalary or leap year and in these years there are six complementary days. The intercalary year of the Coptic calendar immediately precedes the leap year of the Julian calendar. The era is that of Diocletian or the Martyrs, the origin of which is fixed at 29 August AD 284 (Julian date).

INDIAN ERAS

In addition to the Muslim reckoning, other eras are used in India. The Saka era of southern India, dating from 3 March AD 78, was declared the national calendar of the Republic of India with effect from 22 March 1957, to be used concurrently with the Gregorian calendar. As revised, the year of the new Saka era begins at the spring equinox, with five successive months of 31 days and seven of 30 days in ordinary years, and six months of each length in leap years. The year AD 2016 is 1938 of the revised Saka era.

The year AD 2016 corresponds to the following years in other eras:

Year 2073 of the Vikram Samvat era
Year 1423 of the Bengali San era
Year 1192 of the Kollam era
Year 5117 of the Kaliyuga era
Year 2559 of the Buddha Nirvana era

JAPANESE CALENDAR

The Japanese calendar is essentially the same as the Gregorian calendar, the years, months and weeks being of the same length and beginning on the same days as those of the Gregorian calendar. The numeration of the years is different, based on a system of epochs or periods, each of which begins at the accession of an emperor or other important occurrence. The method is not unlike the British system of regnal years, except that each year of a period closes on 31 December. The Japanese chronology begins about AD 650 and the three latest epochs are defined by the reigns of emperors, whose actual names are not necessarily used:

Epoch
Taisho – 1 August 1912 to 25 December 1926
Showa – 26 December 1926 to 7 January 1989
Heisei – 8 January 1989

The year Heisei 28 begins on 1 January 2016.

The months are known as First Month, Second Month, etc, First Month being equivalent to January. The days of the week are Nichiyobi (Sun-day), Getsuyobi (Moon-day), Kayobi (Fire-day), Suiyobi (Water-day), Mokuyobi (Wood-day), Kinyobi (Metal-day) and Doyobi (Earth-day).

THE MASONIC YEAR

Two dates are quoted in warrants, dispensations, etc, issued by the United Grand Lodge of England, those for the current year being expressed as *Anno Domini* 2016 – *Anno Lucis* 6016. This *Anno Lucis* (year of light) is based on the Book of Genesis 1:3, the 4,000-year difference being derived, in modified form, from *Ussher's Notation*, published in 1654, which places the Creation of the World in 4004 BC.

OLYMPIADS

Ancient Greek chronology was reckoned in Olympiads, cycles of four years corresponding with the Olympic Games held on the plain of Olympia, in Elis. The intervening years were the first, second, etc, of the Olympiad, which received the name of the victor at the Games. The first recorded Olympiad is that of Choroebus, 776 BC.

ZOROASTRIAN CALENDAR

Zoroastrians, followers of the Iranian prophet Zarathushtra (known to the Greeks as Zoroaster) are mostly to be found in Iran and in India, where they are known as Parsees.

The Zoroastrian era dates from the coronation of the last Zoroastrian Sasanian king in AD 631. The Zoroastrian calendar is divided into 12 months, each comprising 30 days, followed by five holy days of the Gathas at the end of each year to make the year consist of 365 days.

In order to synchronise the calendar with the solar year of 365 days, an extra month was intercalated once every 120 years. However, this intercalation ceased in the 12th century and the new year, which had fallen in the spring, slipped back to August. Because intercalation ceased at different times in Iran and India, there was one month's difference between the calendar followed in Iran (Kadmi calendar) and that followed by the Parsees (Shenshai calendar). In 1906 a group of Zoroastrians decided to bring the calendar back in line with the seasons again and restore the new year to 21 March each year (Fasli calendar).

The Shenshai calendar (new year in August) is mainly used by Parsees. The Fasli calendar (new year, 21 March) is mainly used by Zoroastrians living in Iran, in the Indian subcontinent, or elsewhere.

ROMAN CALENDAR

Roman historians adopted as an epoch the foundation of Rome, which is believed to have happened in the year 753 BC. The ordinal number of the years in Roman reckoning is followed by the letters AUC *(ab urbe condita),* so that the year 2016 is 2769 AUC (MMDCCLXIX). The calendar that we know has developed from one said to have been established by Romulus using a year of 304 days divided into ten months, beginning with March. To this Numa added January and February, making the year consist of 12 months of 30 and 29 days alternately, with an additional day so that the total was 355. It is also said that Numa ordered an intercalary month of 22 or 23 days in alternate years, making 90 days in eight years, to be inserted after 23 February.

However, there is some doubt as to the origination and the details of the intercalation in the Roman calendar. In the year 46 BC Julius Caesar found that the calendar had been allowed to fall into some confusion. He sought the help of Egyptian astronomer Sosigenes, which led to the construction and adoption (45 BC) of the Julian calendar, and, by a slight alteration, to the Gregorian calendar now in use. The year 46 BC was made to consist of 445 days and is called the Year of Confusion.

In the Roman (Julian) calendar the days of the month were counted backwards from three fixed points, or days, and an intervening day was said to be so many days before the next coming point, the first and last being counted. These three points were the Kalends, the Nones and the Ides. Their positions in the months and the method of counting from them will be seen in the table below. The year containing 366 days was called *bissextilis annus,* as it had a doubled sixth day *(bissextus dies)* before the March Kalends on 24 February – *ante diem sextum Kalendas Martias,* or a.d. VI Kal. Mart.

Present days of the month	March, May, July, October have thirty-one days	January, August, December have thirty-one days	April, June, September, November have thirty days	February has twenty-eight days, and in leap year twenty-nine
1	Kalendis	Kalendis	Kalendis	Kalendis
2	VI	IV ⎤ ante	IV ⎤ ante	IV ⎤ ante
3	V ⎤ ante	III ⎦ Nonas	III ⎦ Nonas	III ⎦ Nonas
4	IV ⎥ Nonas	pridie Nonas	pridie Nonas	pridie Nonas
5	III ⎦	Nonis	Nonis	Nonis
6	pridie Nonas	VIII	VIII	VIII
7	Nonis	VII	VII	VII
8	VIII	VI ⎤ ante	VI ⎤ ante	VI ⎤ ante
9	VII	V ⎦ Idus	V ⎦ Idus	V ⎦ Idus
10	VI ⎤ ante	IV	IV	IV
11	V ⎦ Idus	III	III	III
12	IV	pridie Idus	pridie Idus	pridie Idus
13	III	Idibus	Idibus	Idibus
14	pridie Idus	XIX	XVIII	XVI
15	Idibus	XVIII	XVII	XV
16	XVII	XVII	XVI	XIV
17	XVI	XVI	XV	XIII
18	XV	XV	XIV	XII
19	XIV	XIV	XIII	XI
20	XIII	XIII	XII	X ⎤ ante Kalendas
21	XII	XII	XI ⎤ ante Kalendas	IX ⎥ Martias
22	XI ⎤ ante Kalendas	XI ⎤ ante Kalendas	X ⎥ (of the month	VIII
23	X ⎥ (of the month	X ⎥ (of the month	IX ⎦ following)	VII
24	IX ⎥ following)	IX ⎦ following)	VIII	*VI
25	VIII	VIII	VII	V
26	VII	VII	VI	IV
27	VI	VI	V	III
28	V	V	IV	pridie Kalendas
29	IV	IV	III	Martias
30	III	III	pridie Kalendas (Maias, Quinctilis, Octobris, Decembris)	
31	pridie Kalendas (Aprilis, Iunias, Sextilis, Novembris)	pridie Kalendas (Februarias, Septembris, Ianuarias)		

* Repeated in leap year

CALENDAR FOR ANY YEAR 1780–2040

To select the correct calendar for any year between 1780 and 2040, consult the index below

* leap year

1780 N*	1813 K	1846 I	1879 G	1912 D*	1945 C	1978 A	2011 M
1781 C	1814 M	1847 K	1880 J*	1913 G	1946 E	1979 C	2012 B*
1782 E	1815 A	1848 N*	1881 M	1914 I	1947 G	1980 F*	2013 E
1783 G	1816 D*	1849 C	1882 A	1915 K	1948 J*	1981 I	2014 G
1784 J*	1817 G	1850 E	1883 C	1916 N*	1949 M	1982 K	2015 I
1785 M	1818 I	1851 G	1884 F*	1917 C	1950 A	1983 M	2016 L*
1786 A	1819 K	1852 J*	1885 I	1918 E	1951 C	1984 B*	2017 A
1787 C	1820 N*	1853 M	1886 K	1919 G	1952 F*	1985 E	2018 C
1788 F*	1821 C	1854 A	1887 M	1920 J*	1953 I	1986 G	2019 E
1789 I	1822 E	1855 C	1888 B*	1921 M	1954 K	1987 I	2020 H*
1790 K	1823 G	1856 F*	1889 E	1922 A	1955 M	1988 L*	2021 K
1791 M	1824 J*	1857 I	1890 G	1923 C	1956 B*	1989 A	2022 M
1792 B*	1825 M	1858 K	1891 I	1924 F*	1957 E	1990 C	2023 A
1793 E	1826 A	1859 M	1892 L*	1925 I	1958 G	1991 E	2024 D*
1794 G	1827 C	1860 B*	1893 A	1926 K	1959 I	1992 H*	2025 G
1795 I	1828 F*	1861 E	1894 C	1927 M	1960 L*	1993 K	2026 I
1796 L*	1829 I	1862 G	1895 E	1928 B*	1961 A	1994 M	2027 K
1797 A	1830 K	1863 I	1896 H*	1929 E	1962 C	1995 A	2028 N*
1798 C	1831 M	1864 L*	1897 K	1930 G	1963 E	1996 D*	2029 C
1799 E	1832 B*	1865 A	1898 M	1931 I	1964 H*	1997 G	2030 E
1800 G	1833 E	1866 C	1899 A	1932 L*	1965 K	1998 I	2031 G
1801 I	1834 G	1867 E	1900 C	1933 A	1966 M	1999 K	2032 J*
1802 K	1835 I	1868 H*	1901 E	1934 C	1967 A	2000 N*	2033 M
1803 M	1836 L*	1869 K	1902 G	1935 E	1968 D*	2001 C	2034 A
1804 B*	1837 A	1870 M	1903 I	1936 H*	1969 G	2002 E	2035 C
1805 E	1838 C	1871 A	1904 L*	1937 K	1970 I	2003 G	2036 F*
1806 G	1839 E	1872 D*	1905 A	1938 M	1971 K	2004 J*	2037 I
1807 I	1840 H*	1873 G	1906 C	1939 A	1972 N*	2005 M	2038 K
1808 L*	1841 K	1874 I	1907 E	1940 D*	1973 C	2006 A	2039 M
1809 A	1842 M	1875 K	1908 H*	1941 G	1974 E	2007 C	2040 B*
1810 C	1843 A	1876 N*	1909 K	1942 I	1975 G	2008 F*	
1811 E	1844 D*	1877 C	1910 M	1943 K	1976 J*	2009 I	
1812 H*	1845 G	1878 E	1911 A	1944 N*	1977 M	2010 K	

A

	January	February	March
Sun.	1 8 15 22 29	5 12 19 26	5 12 19 26
Mon.	2 9 16 23 30	6 13 20 27	6 13 20 27
Tue.	3 10 17 24 31	7 14 21 28	7 14 21 28
Wed.	4 11 18 25	1 8 15 22	1 8 15 22 29
Thur.	5 12 19 26	2 9 16 23	2 9 16 23 30
Fri.	6 13 20 27	3 10 17 24	3 10 17 24 31
Sat.	7 14 21 28	4 11 18 25	4 11 18 25

	April	May	June
Sun.	2 9 16 23 30	7 14 21 28	4 11 18 25
Mon.	3 10 17 24	1 8 15 22 29	5 12 19 26
Tue.	4 11 18 25	2 9 16 23 30	6 13 20 27
Wed.	5 12 19 26	3 10 17 24 31	7 14 21 28
Thur.	6 13 20 27	4 11 18 25	1 8 15 22 29
Fri.	7 14 21 28	5 12 19 26	2 9 16 23 30
Sat.	1 8 15 22 29	6 13 20 27	3 10 17 24

	July	August	September
Sun.	2 9 16 23 30	6 13 20 27	3 10 17 24
Mon.	3 10 17 24 31	7 14 21 28	4 11 18 25
Tue.	4 11 18 25	1 8 15 22 29	5 12 19 26
Wed.	5 12 19 26	2 9 16 23 30	6 13 20 27
Thur.	6 13 20 27	3 10 17 24 31	7 14 21 28
Fri.	7 14 21 28	4 11 18 25	1 8 15 22 29
Sat.	1 8 15 22 29	5 12 19 26	2 9 16 23 30

	October	November	December
Sun.	1 8 15 22 29	5 12 19 26	3 10 17 24 31
Mon.	2 9 16 23 30	6 13 20 27	4 11 18 25
Tue.	3 10 17 24 31	7 14 21 28	5 12 19 26
Wed.	4 11 18 25	1 8 15 22 29	6 13 20 27
Thur.	5 12 19 26	2 9 16 23 30	7 14 21 28
Fri.	6 13 20 27	3 10 17 24	1 8 15 22 29
Sat.	7 14 21 28	4 11 18 25	2 9 16 23 30

EASTER DAYS

March 26	1815, 1826, 1837, 1967, 1978, 1989
April 2	1809, 1893, 1899, 1961
April 9	1871, 1882, 1939, 1950, 2023, 2034
April 16	1786, 1797, 1843, 1854, 1865, 1911, 1922, 1933, 1995, 2006, 2017
April 23	1905

B (LEAP YEAR)

	January	February	March
Sun.	1 8 15 22 29	5 12 19 26	4 11 18 25
Mon.	2 9 16 23 30	6 13 20 27	5 12 19 26
Tue.	3 10 17 24 31	7 14 21 28	6 13 20 27
Wed.	4 11 18 25	1 8 15 22 29	7 14 21 28
Thur.	5 12 19 26	2 9 16 23	1 8 15 22 29
Fri.	6 13 20 27	3 10 17 24	2 9 16 23 30
Sat.	7 14 21 28	4 11 18 25	3 10 17 24 31

	April	May	June
Sun.	1 8 15 22 29	6 13 20 27	3 10 17 24
Mon.	2 9 16 23 30	7 14 21 28	4 11 18 25
Tue.	3 10 17 24	1 8 15 22 29	5 12 19 26
Wed.	4 11 18 25	2 9 16 23 30	6 13 20 27
Thur.	5 12 19 26	3 10 17 24 31	7 14 21 28
Fri.	6 13 20 27	4 11 18 25	1 8 15 22 29
Sat.	7 14 21 28	5 12 19 26	2 9 16 23 30

	July	August	September
Sun.	1 8 15 22 29	5 12 19 26	2 9 16 23 30
Mon.	2 9 16 23 30	6 13 20 27	3 10 17 24
Tue.	3 10 17 24 31	7 14 21 28	4 11 18 25
Wed.	4 11 18 25	1 8 15 22 29	5 12 19 26
Thur.	5 12 19 26	2 9 16 23 30	6 13 20 27
Fri.	6 13 20 27	3 10 17 24 31	7 14 21 28
Sat.	7 14 21 28	4 11 18 25	1 8 15 22 29

	October	November	December
Sun.	7 14 21 28	4 11 18 25	2 9 16 23 30
Mon.	1 8 15 22 29	5 12 19 26	3 10 17 24 31
Tue.	2 9 16 23 30	6 13 20 27	4 11 18 25
Wed.	3 10 17 24 31	7 14 21 28	5 12 19 26
Thur.	4 11 18 25	1 8 15 22 29	6 13 20 27
Fri.	5 12 19 26	2 9 16 23 30	7 14 21 28
Sat.	6 13 20 27	3 10 17 24	1 3 15 22 29

EASTER DAYS

April 1	1804, 1888, 1956, 2040
April 8	1792, 1860, 1928, 2012
April 22	1832, 1984

C

	January	February	March
Sun.	7 14 21 28	4 11 18 25	4 11 18 25
Mon.	1 8 15 22 29	5 12 19 26	5 12 19 26
Tue.	2 9 16 23 30	6 13 20 27	6 13 20 27
Wed.	3 10 17 24 31	7 14 21 28	7 14 21 28
Thur.	4 11 18 25	1 8 15 22	1 8 15 22 29
Fri.	5 12 19 26	2 9 16 23	2 9 16 23 30
Sat.	6 13 20 27	3 10 17 24	3 10 17 24 31

	April	May	June
Sun.	1 8 15 22 29	6 13 20 27	3 10 17 24
Mon.	2 9 16 23 30	7 14 21 28	4 11 18 25
Tue.	3 10 17 24	1 8 15 22 29	5 12 19 26
Wed.	4 11 18 25	2 9 16 23 30	6 13 20 27
Thur.	5 12 19 26	3 10 17 24 31	7 14 21 28
Fri.	6 13 20 27	4 11 18 25	1 8 15 22 29
Sat.	7 14 21 28	5 12 19 26	2 9 16 23 30

	July	August	September
Sun.	1 8 15 22 29	5 12 19 26	2 9 16 23 30
Mon.	2 9 16 23 30	6 13 20 27	3 10 17 24
Tue.	3 10 17 24 31	7 14 21 28	4 11 18 25
Wed.	4 11 18 25	1 8 15 22 29	5 12 19 26
Thur.	5 12 19 26	2 9 16 23 30	6 13 20 27
Fri.	6 13 20 27	3 10 17 24 31	7 14 21 28
Sat.	7 14 21 28	4 11 18 25	1 8 15 22 29

	October	November	December
Sun.	7 14 21 28	4 11 18 25	2 9 16 23 30
Mon.	1 8 15 22 29	5 12 19 26	3 10 17 24 31
Tue.	2 9 16 23 30	6 13 20 27	4 11 18 25
Wed.	3 10 17 24 31	7 14 21 28	5 12 19 26
Thur.	4 11 18 25	1 8 15 22 29	6 13 20 27
Fri.	5 12 19 26	2 9 16 23 30	7 14 21 28
Sat.	6 13 20 27	3 10 17 24	1 8 15 22 29

EASTER DAYS

March 25	1883, 1894, 1951, 2035
April 1	1866, 1877, 1923, 1934, 1945, 2018, 2029
April 8	1787, 1798, 1849, 1855, 1917, 2007
April 15	1781, 1827, 1838, 1900, 1906, 1979, 1990, 2001
April 22	1810, 1821, 1962, 1973

D (LEAP YEAR)

	January	February	March
Sun.	7 14 21 28	4 11 18 25	3 10 17 24 31
Mon.	1 8 15 22 29	5 12 19 26	4 11 18 25
Tue.	2 9 16 23 30	6 13 20 27	5 12 19 26
Wed.	3 10 17 24 31	7 14 21 28	6 13 20 27
Thur.	4 11 18 25	1 8 15 22 29	7 14 21 28
Fri.	5 12 19 26	2 9 16 23	1 8 15 22 29
Sat.	6 13 20 27	3 10 17 24	2 9 16 23 30

	April	May	June
Sun.	7 14 21 28	5 12 19 26	2 9 16 23 30
Mon.	1 8 15 22 29	6 13 20 27	3 10 17 24
Tue.	2 9 16 23 30	7 14 21 28	4 11 18 25
Wed.	3 10 17 24	1 8 15 22 29	5 12 19 26
Thur.	4 11 18 25	2 9 16 23 30	6 13 20 27
Fri.	5 12 19 26	3 10 17 24 31	7 14 21 28
Sat.	6 13 20 27	4 11 18 25	1 8 15 22 29

	July	August	September
Sun.	7 14 21 28	4 11 18 25	1 8 15 22 29
Mon.	1 8 15 22 29	5 12 19 26	2 9 16 23 30
Tue.	2 9 16 23 30	6 13 20 27	3 10 17 24
Wed.	3 10 17 24 31	7 14 21 28	4 11 18 25
Thur.	4 11 18 25	1 8 15 22 29	5 12 19 26
Fri.	5 12 19 26	2 9 16 23 30	6 13 20 27
Sat.	6 13 20 27	3 10 17 24 31	7 14 21 28

	October	November	December
Sun.	6 13 20 27	3 10 17 24	1 8 15 22 29
Mon.	7 14 21 28	4 11 18 25	2 9 16 23 30
Tue.	1 8 15 22 29	5 12 19 26	3 10 17 24 31
Wed.	2 9 16 23 30	6 13 20 27	4 11 18 25
Thur.	3 10 17 24 31	7 14 21 28	5 12 19 26
Fri.	4 11 18 25	1 8 15 22 29	6 13 20 27
Sat.	5 12 19 26	2 9 16 23 30	7 14 21 28

EASTER DAYS

March 24	1940
March 31	1872, 2024
April 7	1844, 1912, 1996
April 14	1816, 1968

E

	January	February	March
Sun.	6 13 20 27	3 10 17 24	3 10 17 24 31
Mon.	7 14 21 28	4 11 18 25	4 11 18 25
Tue.	1 8 15 22 29	5 12 19 26	5 12 19 26
Wed.	2 9 16 23 30	6 13 20 27	6 13 20 27
Thur.	3 10 17 24 31	7 14 21 28	7 14 21 28
Fri.	4 11 18 25	1 8 15 22	1 8 15 22 29
Sat.	5 12 19 26	2 9 16 23	2 9 16 23 30

	April	May	June
Sun.	7 14 21 28	5 12 19 26	2 9 16 23 30
Mon.	1 8 15 22 29	6 13 20 27	3 10 17 24
Tue.	2 9 16 23 30	7 14 21 28	4 11 18 25
Wed.	3 10 17 24	1 8 15 22 29	5 12 19 26
Thur.	4 11 18 25	2 9 16 23 30	6 13 20 27
Fri.	5 12 19 26	3 10 17 24 31	7 14 21 28
Sat.	6 13 20 27	4 11 18 25	1 8 15 22 29

	July	August	September
Sun.	7 14 21 28	4 11 18 25	1 8 15 22 29
Mon.	1 8 15 22 29	5 12 19 26	2 9 16 23 30
Tue.	2 9 16 23 30	6 13 20 27	3 10 17 24
Wed.	3 10 17 24 31	7 14 21 28	4 11 18 25
Thur.	4 11 18 25	1 8 15 22 29	5 12 19 26
Fri.	5 12 19 26	2 9 16 23 30	6 13 20 27
Sat.	6 13 20 27	3 10 17 24 31	7 14 21 28

	October	November	December
Sun.	6 13 20 27	3 10 17 24	1 8 15 22 29
Mon.	7 14 21 28	4 11 18 25	2 9 16 23 30
Tue.	1 8 15 22 29	5 12 19 26	3 10 17 24 31
Wed.	2 9 16 23 30	6 13 20 27	4 11 18 25
Thur.	3 10 17 24 31	7 14 21 28	5 12 19 26
Fri.	4 11 18 25	1 8 15 22 29	6 13 20 27
Sat.	5 12 19 26	2 9 16 23 30	7 14 21 28

EASTER DAYS

March 24	1799
March 31	1782, 1793, 1839, 1850, 1861, 1907, 1918, 1929, 1991, 2002, 2013
April 7	1822, 1833, 1901, 1985
April 14	1805, 1811, 1895, 1963, 1974
April 21	1867, 1878, 1889, 1935, 1946, 1957, 2019, 2030

F (LEAP YEAR)

	January	February	March
Sun.	6 13 20 27	3 10 17 24	2 9 16 23 30
Mon.	7 14 21 28	4 11 18 25	3 10 17 24 31
Tue.	1 8 15 22 29	5 12 19 26	4 11 18 25
Wed.	2 9 16 23 30	6 13 20 27	5 12 19 26
Thur.	3 10 17 24 31	7 14 21 28	6 13 20 27
Fri.	4 11 18 25	1 8 15 22 29	7 14 21 28
Sat.	5 12 19 26	2 9 16 23	1 8 15 22 29

	April	May	June
Sun.	6 13 20 27	4 11 18 25	1 8 15 22 29
Mon.	7 14 21 28	5 12 19 26	2 9 16 23 30
Tue.	1 8 15 22 29	6 13 20 27	3 10 17 24
Wed.	2 9 16 23 30	7 14 21 28	4 11 18 25
Thur.	3 10 17 24	1 8 15 22 29	5 12 19 26
Fri.	4 11 18 25	2 9 16 23 30	6 13 20 27
Sat.	5 12 19 26	3 10 17 24 31	7 14 21 28

	July	August	September
Sun.	6 13 20 27	3 10 17 24 31	7 14 21 28
Mon.	7 14 21 28	4 11 18 25	1 8 15 22 29
Tue.	1 8 15 22 29	5 12 19 26	2 9 16 23 30
Wed.	2 9 16 23 30	6 13 20 27	3 10 17 24
Thur.	3 10 17 24 31	7 14 21 28	4 11 18 25
Fri.	4 11 18 25	1 8 15 22 29	5 12 19 26
Sat.	5 12 19 26	2 9 16 23 30	6 13 20 27

	October	November	December
Sun.	5 12 19 26	2 9 16 23 30	7 14 21 28
Mon.	6 13 20 27	3 10 17 24	1 8 15 22 29
Tue.	7 14 21 28	4 11 18 25	2 9 16 23 30
Wed.	1 8 15 22 29	5 12 19 26	3 10 17 24 31
Thur.	2 9 16 23 30	6 13 20 27	4 11 18 25
Fri.	3 10 17 24 31	7 14 21 28	5 12 19 26
Sat.	4 11 18 25	1 8 15 22 29	6 13 20 27

EASTER DAYS

March 23	1788, 1856, 2008
April 6	1828, 1980
April 13	1884, 1952, 2036
April 20	1924

G

	January	February	March
Sun.	5 12 19 26	2 9 16 23	2 9 16 23 30
Mon.	6 13 20 27	3 10 17 24	3 10 17 24 31
Tue.	7 14 21 28	4 11 18 25	4 11 18 25
Wed.	1 8 15 22 29	5 12 19 26	5 12 19 26
Thur.	2 9 16 23 30	6 13 20 27	6 13 20 27
Fri.	3 10 17 24 31	7 14 21 28	7 14 21 28
Sat.	4 11 18 25	1 8 15 22	1 8 15 22 29

	April	May	June
Sun.	6 13 20 27	4 11 18 25	1 8 15 22 29
Mon.	7 14 21 28	5 12 19 26	2 9 16 23 30
Tue.	1 8 15 22 29	6 13 20 27	3 10 17 24
Wed.	2 9 16 23 30	7 14 21 28	4 11 18 25
Thur.	3 10 17 24	1 8 15 22 29	5 12 19 26
Fri.	4 11 18 25	2 9 16 23 30	6 13 20 27
Sat.	5 12 19 26	3 10 17 24 31	7 14 21 28

	July	August	September
Sun.	6 13 20 27	3 10 17 24 31	7 14 21 28
Mon.	7 14 21 28	4 11 18 25	1 8 15 22 29
Tue.	1 8 15 22 29	5 12 19 26	2 9 16 23 30
Wed.	2 9 16 23 30	6 13 20 27	3 10 17 24
Thur.	3 10 17 24 31	7 14 21 28	4 11 18 25
Fri.	4 11 18 25	1 8 15 22 29	5 12 19 26
Sat.	5 12 19 26	2 9 16 23 30	6 13 20 27

	October	November	December
Sun.	5 12 19 26	2 9 16 23 30	7 14 21 28
Mon.	6 13 20 27	3 10 17 24	1 8 15 22 29
Tue.	7 14 21 28	4 11 18 25	2 9 16 23 30
Wed.	1 8 15 22 29	5 12 19 26	3 10 17 24 31
Thur.	2 9 16 23 30	6 13 20 27	4 11 18 25
Fri.	3 10 17 24 31	7 14 21 28	5 12 19 26
Sat.	4 11 18 25	1 8 15 22 29	6 13 20 27

EASTER DAYS

March 23	1845, 1913
March 30	1823, 1834, 1902, 1975, 1986, 1997
April 6	1806, 1817, 1890, 1947, 1958, 1969
April 13	1800, 1873, 1879, 1941, 2031
April 20	1783, 1794, 1851, 1862, 1919, 1930, 2003, 2014, 2025

I

	January	February	March
Sun.	4 11 18 25	1 8 15 22	1 8 15 22 29
Mon.	5 12 19 26	2 9 16 23	2 9 16 23 30
Tue.	6 13 20 27	3 10 17 24	3 10 17 24 31
Wed.	7 14 21 28	4 11 18 25	4 11 18 25
Thur.	1 8 15 22 29	5 12 19 26	5 12 19 26
Fri.	2 9 16 23 30	6 13 20 27	6 13 20 27
Sat.	3 10 17 24 31	7 14 21 28	7 14 21 28

	April	May	June
Sun.	5 12 19 26	3 10 17 24 31	7 14 21 28
Mon.	6 13 20 27	4 11 18 25	1 8 15 22 29
Tue.	7 14 21 28	5 12 19 26	2 9 16 23 30
Wed.	1 8 15 22 29	6 13 20 27	3 10 17 24
Thur.	2 9 16 23 30	7 14 21 28	4 11 18 25
Fri.	3 10 17 24	1 8 15 22 29	5 12 19 26
Sat.	4 11 18 25	2 9 16 23 30	6 13 20 27

	July	August	September
Sun.	5 12 19 26	2 9 16 23 30	6 13 20 27
Mon.	6 13 20 27	3 10 17 24 31	7 14 21 28
Tue.	7 14 21 28	4 11 18 25	1 8 15 22 29
Wed.	1 8 15 22 29	5 12 19 26	2 9 16 23 30
Thur.	2 9 16 23 30	6 13 20 27	3 10 17 24
Fri.	3 10 17 24 31	7 14 21 28	4 11 18 25
Sat.	4 11 18 25	1 8 15 22 29	5 12 19 26

	October	November	December
Sun.	4 11 18 25	1 8 15 22 29	6 13 20 27
Mon.	5 12 19 26	2 9 16 23 30	7 14 21 28
Tue.	6 13 20 27	3 10 17 24	1 8 15 22 29
Wed.	7 14 21 28	4 11 18 25	2 9 16 23 30
Thur.	1 8 15 22 29	5 12 19 26	3 10 17 24 31
Fri.	2 9 16 23 30	6 13 20 27	4 11 18 25
Sat.	3 10 17 24 31	7 14 21 28	5 12 19 26

EASTER DAYS

March 22	1818
March 29	1807, 1891, 1959, 1970
April 5	1795, 1801, 1863, 1874, 1885, 1931, 1942, 1953, 2015, 2026, 2037
April 12	1789, 1846, 1857, 1903, 1914, 1925, 1998, 2009
April 19	1829, 1835, 1981, 1987

H (LEAP YEAR)

	January	February	March
Sun.	5 12 19 26	2 9 16 23	1 8 15 22 29
Mon.	6 13 20 27	3 10 17 24	2 9 16 23 30
Tue.	7 14 21 28	4 11 18 25	3 10 17 24 31
Wed.	1 8 15 22 29	5 12 19 26	4 11 18 25
Thur.	2 9 16 23 30	6 13 20 27	5 12 19 26
Fri.	3 10 17 24 31	7 14 21 28	6 13 20 27
Sat.	4 11 18 25	1 8 15 22 29	7 14 21 28

	April	May	June
Sun.	5 12 19 26	3 10 17 24 31	7 14 21 28
Mon.	6 13 20 27	4 11 18 25	1 8 15 22 29
Tue.	7 14 21 28	5 12 19 26	2 9 16 23 30
Wed.	1 8 15 22 29	6 13 20 27	3 10 17 24
Thur.	2 9 16 23 30	7 14 21 28	4 11 18 25
Fri.	3 10 17 24	1 8 15 22 29	5 12 19 26
Sat.	4 11 18 25	2 9 16 23 30	6 13 20 27

	July	August	September
Sun.	5 12 19 26	2 9 16 23 30	6 13 20 27
Mon.	6 13 20 27	3 10 17 24 31	7 14 21 28
Tue.	7 14 21 28	4 11 18 25	1 8 15 22 29
Wed.	1 8 15 22 29	5 12 19 26	2 9 16 23 30
Thur.	2 9 16 23 30	6 13 20 27	3 10 17 24
Fri.	3 10 17 24 31	7 14 21 28	4 11 18 25
Sat.	4 11 18 25	1 8 15 22 29	5 12 19 26

	October	November	December
Sun.	4 11 18 25	1 8 15 22 29	6 13 20 27
Mon.	5 12 19 26	2 9 16 23 30	7 14 21 28
Tue.	6 13 20 27	3 10 17 24	1 8 15 22 29
Wed.	7 14 21 28	4 11 18 25	2 9 16 23 30
Thur.	1 8 15 22 29	5 12 19 26	3 10 17 24 31
Fri.	2 9 16 23 30	6 13 20 27	4 11 18 25
Sat.	3 10 17 24 31	7 14 21 28	5 12 19 26

EASTER DAYS

March 29	1812, 1964
April 5	1896
April 12	1868, 1936, 2020
April 19	1840, 1908, 1992

J (LEAP YEAR)

	January	February	March
Sun.	4 11 18 25	1 8 15 22 29	7 14 21 28
Mon.	5 12 19 26	2 9 16 23	1 8 15 22 29
Tue.	6 13 20 27	3 10 17 24	2 9 16 23 30
Wed.	7 14 21 28	4 11 18 25	3 10 17 24 31
Thur.	1 8 15 22 29	5 12 19 26	4 11 18 25
Fri.	2 9 16 23 30	6 13 20 27	5 12 19 26
Sat.	3 10 17 24 31	7 14 21 28	6 13 20 27

	April	May	June
Sun.	4 11 18 25	2 9 16 23 30	6 13 20 27
Mon.	5 12 19 26	3 10 17 24 31	7 14 21 28
Tue.	6 13 20 27	4 11 18 25	1 8 15 22 29
Wed.	7 14 21 28	5 12 19 26	2 9 16 23 30
Thur.	1 8 15 22 29	6 13 20 27	3 10 17 24
Fri.	2 9 16 23 30	7 14 21 28	4 11 18 25
Sat.	3 10 17 24	1 8 15 22 29	5 12 19 26

	July	August	September
Sun.	4 11 18 25	1 8 15 22 29	5 12 19 26
Mon.	5 12 19 26	2 9 16 23 30	6 13 20 27
Tue.	6 13 20 27	3 10 17 24 31	7 14 21 28
Wed.	7 14 21 28	4 11 18 25	1 8 15 22 29
Thur.	1 8 15 22 29	5 12 19 26	2 9 16 23 30
Fri.	2 9 16 23 30	6 13 20 27	3 10 17 24
Sat.	3 10 17 24 31	7 14 21 28	4 11 18 25

	October	November	December
Sun.	3 10 17 24 31	7 14 21 28	5 12 19 26
Mon.	4 11 18 25	1 8 15 22 29	6 13 20 27
Tue.	5 12 19 26	2 9 16 23 30	7 14 21 28
Wed.	6 13 20 27	3 10 17 24	1 8 15 22 29
Thur.	7 14 21 28	4 11 18 25	2 9 16 23 30
Fri.	1 8 15 22 29	5 12 19 26	3 10 17 24 31
Sat.	2 9 16 23 30	6 13 20 27	4 11 18 25

EASTER DAYS

March 28	1880, 1943, 2032
April 4	1920
April 11	1784, 1852, 2004
April 18	1824, 1976

K

	January	February	March
Sun.	3 10 17 24 31	7 14 21 28	7 14 21 28
Mon.	4 11 18 25	1 8 15 22	1 8 15 22 29
Tue.	5 12 19 26	2 9 16 23	2 9 16 23 30
Wed.	6 13 20 27	3 10 17 24	3 10 17 24 31
Thur.	7 14 21 28	4 11 18 25	4 11 18 25
Fri.	1 8 15 22 29	5 12 19 26	5 12 19 26
Sat.	2 9 16 23 30	6 13 20 27	6 13 20 27

	April	May	June
Sun.	4 11 18 25	2 9 16 23 30	6 13 20 27
Mon.	5 12 19 26	3 10 17 24 31	7 14 21 28
Tue.	6 13 20 27	4 11 18 25	1 8 15 22 29
Wed.	7 14 21 28	5 12 19 26	2 9 16 23 30
Thur.	1 8 15 22 29	6 13 20 27	3 10 17 24
Fri.	2 9 16 23 30	7 14 21 28	4 11 18 25
Sat.	3 10 17 24	1 8 15 22 29	5 12 19 26

	July	August	September
Sun.	4 11 18 25	1 8 15 22 29	5 12 19 26
Mon.	5 12 19 26	2 9 16 23 30	6 13 20 27
Tue.	6 13 20 27	3 10 17 24 31	7 14 21 28
Wed.	7 14 21 28	4 11 18 25	1 8 15 22 29
Thur.	1 8 15 22 29	5 12 19 26	2 9 16 23 30
Fri.	2 9 16 23 30	6 13 20 27	3 10 17 24
Sat.	3 10 17 24 31	7 14 21 28	4 11 18 25

	October	November	December
Sun.	3 10 17 24 31	7 14 21 28	5 12 19 26
Mon.	4 11 18 25	1 8 15 22 29	6 13 20 27
Tue.	5 12 19 26	2 9 16 23 30	7 14 21 28
Wed.	6 13 20 27	3 10 17 24	1 8 15 22 29
Thur.	7 14 21 28	4 11 18 25	2 9 16 23 30
Fri.	1 8 15 22 29	5 12 19 26	3 10 17 24 31
Sat.	2 9 16 23 30	6 13 20 27	4 11 18 25

EASTER DAYS
March 28 1869, 1875, 1937, 2027
April 4 1790, 1847, 1858, 1915, 1926, 1999, 2010, 2021
April 11 1819, 1830, 1841, 1909, 1971, 1982, 1993
April 18 1802, 1813, 1897, 1954, 1965
April 25 1886, 1943, 2038

M

	January	February	March
Sun.	2 9 16 23 30	6 13 20 27	6 13 20 27
Mon.	3 10 17 24 31	7 14 21 28	7 14 21 28
Tue.	4 11 18 25	1 8 15 22	1 8 15 22 29
Wed.	5 12 19 26	2 9 16 23	2 9 16 23 30
Thur.	6 13 20 27	3 10 17 24	3 10 17 24 31
Fri.	7 14 21 28	4 11 18 25	4 11 18 25
Sat.	1 8 15 22 29	5 12 19 26	5 12 19 26

	April	May	June
Sun.	3 10 17 24	1 8 15 22 29	5 12 19 26
Mon.	4 11 18 25	2 9 16 23 30	6 13 20 27
Tue.	5 12 19 26	3 10 17 24 31	7 14 21 28
Wed.	6 13 20 27	4 11 18 25	1 8 15 22 29
Thur.	7 14 21 28	5 12 19 26	2 9 16 23 30
Fri.	1 8 15 22 29	6 13 20 27	3 10 17 24
Sat.	2 9 16 23 30	7 14 21 28	4 11 18 25

	July	August	September
Sun.	3 10 17 24 31	7 14 21 28	4 11 18 25
Mon.	4 11 18 25	1 8 15 22 29	5 12 19 26
Tue.	5 12 19 26	2 9 16 23 30	6 13 20 27
Wed.	6 13 20 27	3 10 17 24 31	7 14 21 28
Thur.	7 14 21 28	4 11 18 25	1 8 15 22 29
Fri.	1 8 15 22 29	5 12 19 26	2 9 16 23 30
Sat.	2 9 16 23 30	6 13 20 27	3 10 17 24

	October	November	December
Sun.	2 9 16 23 30	6 13 20 27	4 11 18 25
Mon.	3 10 17 24 31	7 14 21 28	5 12 19 26
Tue.	4 11 18 25	1 8 15 22 29	6 13 20 27
Wed.	5 12 19 26	2 9 16 23 30	7 14 21 28
Thur.	6 13 20 27	3 10 17 24	1 8 15 22 29
Fri.	7 14 21 28	4 11 18 25	2 9 16 23 30
Sat.	1 8 15 22 29	5 12 19 26	3 10 17 24 31

EASTER DAYS
March 27 1785, 1842, 1853, 1910, 1921, 2005
April 3 1825, 1831, 1983, 1994
April 10 1803, 1814, 1887, 1898, 1955, 1966, 1977, 2039
April 17 1870, 1881, 1927, 1938, 1949, 2022, 2033
April 24 1791, 1859, 2011

L (LEAP YEAR)

	January	February	March
Sun.	3 10 17 24 31	7 14 21 28	6 13 20 27
Mon.	4 11 18 25	1 8 15 22 29	7 14 21 28
Tue.	5 12 19 26	2 9 16 23	1 8 15 22 29
Wed.	6 13 20 27	3 10 17 24	2 9 16 23 30
Thur.	7 14 21 28	4 11 18 25	3 10 17 24 31
Fri.	1 8 15 22 29	5 12 19 26	4 11 18 25
Sat.	2 9 16 23 30	6 13 20 27	5 12 19 26

	April	May	June
Sun.	3 10 17 24	1 8 15 22 29	5 12 19 26
Mon.	4 11 18 25	2 9 16 23 30	6 13 20 27
Tue.	5 12 19 26	3 10 17 24 31	7 14 21 28
Wed.	6 13 20 27	4 11 18 25	1 8 15 22 29
Thur.	7 14 21 28	5 12 19 26	2 9 16 23 30
Fri.	1 8 15 22 29	6 13 20 27	3 10 17 24
Sat.	2 9 16 23 30	7 14 21 28	4 11 18 25

	July	August	September
Sun.	3 10 17 24 31	7 14 21 28	4 11 18 25
Mon.	4 11 18 25	1 8 15 22 29	5 12 19 26
Tue.	5 12 19 26	2 9 16 23 30	6 13 20 27
Wed.	6 13 20 27	3 10 17 24 31	7 14 21 28
Thur.	7 14 21 28	4 11 18 25	1 8 15 22 29
Fri.	1 8 15 22 29	5 12 19 26	2 9 16 23 30
Sat.	2 9 16 23 30	6 13 20 27	3 10 17 24

	October	November	December
Sun.	2 9 16 23 30	6 13 20 27	4 11 18 25
Mon.	3 10 17 24 31	7 14 21 28	5 12 19 26
Tue.	4 11 18 25	1 8 15 22 29	6 13 20 27
Wed.	5 12 19 26	2 9 16 23 30	7 14 21 28
Thur.	6 13 20 27	3 10 17 24	1 8 15 22 29
Fri.	7 14 21 28	4 11 18 25	2 9 16 23 30
Sat.	1 8 15 22 29	5 12 19 26	3 10 17 24 31

EASTER DAYS
March 27 1796, 1864, 1932, 2016
April 3 1836, 1904, 1988
April 17 1808, 1892, 1960

N (LEAP YEAR)

	January	February	March
Sun.	2 9 16 23 30	6 13 20 27	5 12 19 26
Mon.	3 10 17 24 31	7 14 21 28	6 13 20 27
Tue.	4 11 18 25	1 8 15 22 29	7 14 21 28
Wed.	5 12 19 26	2 9 16 23	1 8 15 22 29
Thur.	6 13 20 27	3 10 17 24	2 9 16 23 30
Fri.	7 14 21 28	4 11 18 25	3 10 17 24 31
Sat.	1 8 15 22 29	5 12 19 26	4 11 18 25

	April	May	June
Sun.	2 9 16 23 30	7 14 21 28	4 11 18 25
Mon.	3 10 17 24	1 8 15 22 29	5 12 19 26
Tue.	4 11 18 25	2 9 16 23 30	6 13 20 27
Wed.	5 12 19 26	3 10 17 24 31	7 14 21 28
Thur.	6 13 20 27	4 11 18 25	1 8 15 22 29
Fri.	7 14 21 28	5 12 19 26	2 9 16 23 30
Sat.	1 8 15 22 29	6 13 20 27	3 10 17 24

	July	August	September
Sun.	2 9 16 23 30	6 13 20 27	3 10 17 24
Mon.	3 10 17 24 31	7 14 21 28	4 11 18 25
Tue.	4 11 18 25	1 8 15 22 29	5 12 19 26
Wed.	5 12 19 26	2 9 16 23 30	6 13 20 27
Thur.	6 13 20 27	3 10 17 24 31	7 14 21 28
Fri.	7 14 21 28	4 11 18 25	1 8 15 22 29
Sat.	1 8 15 22 29	5 12 19 26	2 9 16 23 30

	October	November	December
Sun.	1 8 15 22 29	5 12 19 26	3 10 17 24 31
Mon.	2 9 16 23 30	6 13 20 27	4 11 18 25
Tue.	3 10 17 24 31	7 14 21 28	5 12 19 26
Wed.	4 11 18 25	1 8 15 22 29	6 13 20 27
Thur.	5 12 19 26	2 9 16 23 30	7 14 21 28
Fri.	6 13 20 27	3 10 17 24	1 8 15 22 29
Sat.	7 14 21 28	4 11 18 25	2 9 16 23 30

EASTER DAYS
March 26 1780
April 2 1820, 1972
April 9 1944
April 16 1876, 2028
April 23 1848, 1916, 2000

GEOLOGICAL TIME

Era	Period	Epoch	Dates*	Evolutionary Stages
Cenozoic	Quaternary	Holocene	11,700 BP†–present	First humans
		Pleistocene	2,588,000–11,700 BP	
	Neogene	Pliocene	5.332–2.588 Mya ‡	} Majority of still existing species
		Miocene	23.03–5.332 Mya	
	Palaeogene	Oligocene	33.9–23.03 Mya	} First modern mammals
		Eocene	55.8–33.9 Mya	
		Palaeocene	65.5–55.8 Mya	
Mesozoic	Cretaceous		145.5–65.5 Mya	
	Jurassic		199.6–145.5 Mya	First birds
	Triassic		251–199.6 Mya	First mammals
Palaeozoic	Permian		299–251 Mya	First reptiles
	Carboniferous		359.2–299 Mya	} First traces of land-living creatures
	Devonian		416–359.2 Mya	
	Silurian		443.7–416 Mya	
	Ordovician		488.3–443.7 Mya	First fish
	Cambrian		542–488.3 Mya	First invertebrates
Precambrian	Proterozoic		2,500–542 Mya	First primitive life forms, eg algae and bacteria
	Archaean		3,800–2,500 Mya	} Earth uninhabited
	Hadean		4,600–3,800 Mya	

* approximate † BP = Before Present ‡ Mya = million years ago

PALAEOZOIC ('ANCIENT LIFE')

Cambrian – Mainly sandstones, slate and shales; limestones in Scotland. Shelled fossils and invertebrates, eg trilobites and brachiopods, and the earliest known vertebrates (jawless fish) appear

Ordovician – Mainly shales and mudstones, eg in north Wales; limestones in Scotland. First fish

Silurian – Shales, mudstones and some limestones, found mostly in Wales and southern Scotland

Devonian – Old red sandstone, shale, limestone and slate, eg in south Wales and the West Country

Carboniferous – Coal-bearing rocks, millstone grit, limestone and shale. First traces of land-living creatures

Permian – Marls, sandstones and clays. First reptile fossils

There were two great phases of mountain building in the Palaeozoic era: the Caledonian, characterised in Britain by NE–SW lines of hills and valleys; and the later Hercynian, widespread in west Germany and adjacent areas, and in Britain exemplified in E–W lines of hills and valleys.

The end of the Palaeozoic era was marked by the extensive glaciations of the Permian period in the southern continents and the decline of amphibians. It was succeeded by an era of warm conditions.

MESOZOIC ('MIDDLE FORMS OF LIFE')

Triassic – Mostly sandstone, eg in the W. Midlands; primitive mammals appear

Jurassic – Mainly limestones and clays, typically displayed in the Jura mountains, and in England in a NE–SW belt from Lincolnshire and the Wash to the Severn and the Dorset coast

Cretaceous – Mainly chalk, clay and sands, eg in Kent and Sussex

Giant reptiles were dominant during the Mesozoic era; marsupial mammals first appeared, as well as *Archaeopteryx lithographica,* the earliest known species of bird. Coniferous trees and flowering plants also developed during the era and, with the birds and the mammals, were the main species to survive into the Cenozoic era. The giant reptiles became extinct.

CENOZOIC ('RECENT LIFE')

Palaeocene } The emergence of new forms of life, including
Eocene } existing species; primates appear

Oligocene – Fossils of a few still existing species

Miocene – Fossil remains show a balance of existing and extinct species

Pliocene } Fossil remains show a majority of still existing
Pleistocene } species

Holocene – The present, post-glacial period. Existing species only, except for a few exterminated by humans

In the last 25 million years, from the Miocene through the Pliocene periods, the Alpine-Himalayan and the circum-Pacific phases of mountain building reached their climax. During the Pleistocene period ice-sheets locked up masses of water as land ice, lowering the sea level by 100–200m. The glaciations and interglacials of the Ice Age are difficult to date and classify, but recent scientific opinion considers the Pleistocene period to have begun *c*.1.64 Mya. The last glacial retreat, merging into the Holocene period, was *c*.10,000 years ago.

HUMAN DEVELOPMENT

All members of the human race belong to one species of animal, *Homo sapiens,* the definition of a species being in biological terms that all its members can interbreed. As a species of mammal it is possible to group humans with other similar types, known as the primates. Amongst these is found a sub-group, the apes, which includes, in addition to humans, the chimpanzees, gorillas, orangutans and gibbons. All lack a tail, have shoulder blades at the back, and a Y-shaped chewing pattern on the surface of their molars, as well as showing the more general primate characteristics of four incisors, a thumb which is able to touch the fingers of the same hand, and finger and toe nails instead of claws. However, there once lived creatures, now extinct, which were closer to modern man than the chimpanzees and gorillas, and which shared with modern man the characteristics of having flat faces (ie the absence of a pronounced muzzle), being bipedal, and possessing large brains.

The debate surrounding evidence for the oldest human ancestors is ongoing. The earliest putative hominin for which there is significant fossil evidence is *Ardipithecus ramidus,* for which an almost complete skeleton, dating to at least 4.4 million years ago (Mya), was discovered in the Afar Rift, Ethiopia in 1992. Analysis of the *Ardipithecus ramidus* skeleton suggests the creature had characteristics of both humans and apes; able to climb trees and walk on two feet.

The subsequent Australopithecines have left more numerous remains in south and east Africa, among which sub-groups may be detected. Living between 4.2 and 1.5 Mya, they were relatives of modern humans in the respect that they walked upright, did not have an extensive muzzle and had similar types of pre-molars. The first australopithecine remains were recognised at Taung in South Africa in 1924 and named *Australopithecus africanus,* dating between 3.3 and 2.3 Mya. The most impressive discovery was made at Hadar, Ethiopia, in 1974 when about half a skeleton of *Australopithecus afarensis,* known as 'Lucy', was found. Some 3.2 Mya, 'Lucy' (who is now considered to be male) certainly walked upright.

Also in east Africa, especially at Olduvai Gorge in Tanzania, between 2.5 and 1.8 Mya, lived a hominid group which not only walked upright, had a flat face, and a large brain case, but also made simple pebble and flake stone tools. Due to their distinctive characteristics, they have been grouped as a separate sub-species, now extinct, of the genus *Homo* and are known as *Homo habilis* or 'handy man'.

The use of fire, again a human characteristic, is associated with another group of extinct hominids whose remains, about a million years old, are found in south and east Africa, China, Indonesia, north Africa and Europe. The ability to make fire probably helped the colonisation of the colder northern areas and in this respect the site of Vertesszollos in Hungary is of particular importance. *Homo ergaster* in Africa and *Homo erectus* in Asia are the names given to this group of fossils and they relate to a number of famous individual discoveries, eg Solo Man, Heidelberg Man, and especially Peking Man who lived at the cave site at Choukoutien which has yielded evidence of fire and burnt bone.

The well-known group the Neanderthals, or *Homo neanderthalensis,* is an extinct form of human that lived between *c.*350,000 and *c.*24,000 years ago, spanning the last Ice Age and living alongside modern humans. The Neanderthals' ability to adapt to the cold climate on the edge of the ice-sheets is one of their characteristic features, with remains being found only in Europe, Asia and the Middle East. Complete Neanderthal skeletons were found during excavations at Tabun in Israel, together with evidence of tool-making and the use of fire. Distinguished by very large brains, it seems that Neanderthals were the first to develop recognisable social customs, especially deliberate burial rites. Why the Neanderthals became extinct is not clear but it may be connected with the climatic changes at the end of the Ice Ages, which would have seriously affected their food supplies; possibly they became too specialised for their own good.

The shin bone of Boxgrove Man found in 1993 – *Homo heidelbergensis* – and the Swanscombe skull are the best known early human fossil remains found in England. Some specialists prefer to group Swanscombe Man (or, more probably, woman) together with the Steinheim skull from Germany, seeing both as a separate sub-species. There is too little evidence as yet on which to form a final judgement.

Anatomically modern humans – *Homo sapiens sapiens* ('doubly wise man') – had evolved to our present physical condition and had colonised much of the world by about 40,000 years ago. There are many previously distinguished individual specimens, eg Cromagnon Man, the first early *Homo sapiens sapiens* of the European Upper Palaeolithic.

The discovery of the structure of DNA in 1953 has come to have a profound effect upon the study of human evolution. For example, it was claimed in 1987 that a common ancestor of all human beings was a person who lived in Africa some 200,000 years ago, thus encouraging the 'out of Africa' theory of hominid migration from east Africa to the Middle East and then throughout the world.

CULTURAL DEVELOPMENT

The Three Age system, whereby prehistory was divided into a Stone Age, a Bronze Age and an Iron Age, was devised by Christian Thomsen, curator of the National Museum of Denmark in the early 19th century, to facilitate the classification of the museum's collections. The adjectives referred to the materials from which the implements and weapons were made and came to be regarded as the dominant features of the societies to which they related. The Three Age system remains a generally accepted concept in the popular mind. However, it is now seen by archaeologists as an inadequate model for human development. Common sense suggests that there were no complete breaks between one so-called Age and another. Nor can the Three Age system be applied universally. In some areas it is necessary to insert a Copper Age, while in South Africa there would seem to be no Bronze Age at all; in Australia, Old Stone Age societies survived, while in South America, New Stone Age communities exist into modern times.

The concept of the 'Neolithic revolution', associated with the domestication of plants and animals, was a development of particular importance in the human cultural pattern. It reflected a gradual change from the hunter-gatherer economies to a more settled agricultural way of life and therefore, so the argument goes, made possible the development of urban civilisation. Though it appears that the cultivation of wheat and barley was first undertaken, together with the domestication of cattle and goats/sheep, around 10,000 years ago in the Fertile Crescent (the area bounded by the rivers Tigris and Euphrates), there is evidence that sorghum was first domesticated in Africa, rice was first deliberately planted and pigs domesticated in South East Asia, maize first cultivated in Central America and llamas first domesticated in South America. Cultural change took place independently in different parts of the world at different rates and different times.

The Neolithic period of cultural development has been difficult to date reliably because it took place long before writing was invented. With the development and refinement of radio-carbon dating and other scientific methods of producing absolute chronologies, it may eventually be possible to obtain a reliable chronological framework, in terms of years, against which the cultural development of any particular area may be set.

TIDES AND TIDAL PREDICTIONS

Tides are the periodic rise and fall of the sea-level caused mainly by the gravitational pull of the Moon and the Sun. This generates the tide raising force (TRF), of which the Moon accounts for approximately 70 per cent and the Sun 30 per cent. There is an 18-year interval between alignments generating the maximum TRF. Routinely when the Moon and the Sun are in line with the Earth they are said to be 'in conjunction' (or syzygy) and their TRFs combine. This produces the largest rise and fall of the tide, known as spring tides; they occur each month just after a full or new Moon. This is amplified when the Moon is at perigee, its closest point to the Earth. When coincident with spring tides (about once every 18 months) this gives rise to very high proxigean tides. The opposite effect, just after the Moon's first and last quarters, when the Sun and Moon are at an angle of 90°, produces neap tides, with a relatively small tidal range between high and low water.

A lunar day is about 24 hours and 50 minutes, giving two complete tidal cycles, with about 12 hours and 25 minutes between successive high waters. These are known as semi-diurnal tides and are applicable in the Atlantic Ocean and around the coasts of north-west Europe. Other parts of the world have diurnal tides, with only one high water and one low water each (lunar) day, or mixed tides which are partly diurnal and partly semi-diurnal.

Land and seabed conditions influence the tides locally. On the south coast of England, for example, double high waters occur between Swanage and Selsey Bill, and low water is much more sharply defined than high water. Tides can also be greatly affected by the Coriolis force, which is induced by the Earth's rotation and, in the northern hemisphere, tends to deflect any moving object to the right. Thus the easterly flood tidal stream in the English Channel is deflected towards the French coast causing higher high waters; on the ebb the opposite happens causing lower low waters. This, coupled with local geography, means that the mean spring range of the tide at St Malo is nearly 11m while the range on the English coast at Portland, 120 miles to the north, is a mere 2m.

Meteorological conditions also affect the tides. Prolonged strong winds and unusually high (or low) atmospheric pressure can significantly lower (or raise) the height of the tide; the drag of the wind alone (wind stress) can affect the predicted times of high and low water by as much as an hour. Variation of pressure by 34 millibars from the norm can cause a height difference of 0.3m.

STORM SURGES AND SEICHES
On the east and west coasts of the UK there are about 20 events each year when surge levels exceed 0.6m. The semi-centennial surge is 1m in the Hebrides and at Land's End but up to 3m in the Thames estuary. Infrequently, surge peaks coincide with high water. The North Sea and the Thames estuary experience the most profound effects, often when a deep depression tracks south-easterly across the UK. Negative surges occur when strong southerly winds in the North Sea may lower tidal levels by 2m below prediction in these areas and the Dover Strait. Intense minor depressions, line squalls, or other abrupt changes in the weather can cause wave oscillations known as seiches. The wave period of a seiche can vary from a few minutes to about 2 hours, with heights of up to a metre. Wick on the north-east coast of Scotland and Fishguard in south-west Wales are particularly prone to seiches.

TIDAL STREAMS
Tidal streams are the horizontal movements of water caused by the rise and fall of the tide. They normally change direction about every 6 hours. Tidal streams should not be confused with ocean currents, such as the Gulf Stream, which run indefinitely in the same direction. The rate, or set, of the stream at any particular place is proportional to the range of the tide. Thus, the rate during spring tides is greater than that at neaps. In the central English Channel the maximum spring rate is nearly 5 knots while the neap rate at the same position is just 3 knots. As with tidal heights, local geography plays a significant role in the rate of the tidal stream. In the narrow waters of the Pentland Firth between mainland Scotland and the Orkney Islands, rates of 16 knots have been recorded.

The tidal stream does not necessarily turn at the same time as high or low water. In the English Channel the stream turns at approximately high and low water at Dover. However, high water at Dover is at about the same time as low water at Plymouth, and vice versa.

Around the UK, the main flood tidal stream sets eastward up the English Channel, north-east into the Bristol Channel, and north up the west coasts of Ireland and Scotland. However, the flood sets south-east through the North Channel and south into the Irish Sea, where it meets the northerly flood through St George's Channel at the Isle of Man. Off the east coasts of Scotland and England the stream sets south as far as the Thames estuary before meeting the north-going stream from the eastern part of the Dover Strait.

DEFINITIONS
Highest Astronomical Tide (HAT) and **Lowest Astronomical Tide (LAT)** are the highest and lowest tide levels predicted to occur under average meteorological, and any combination of astronomical, conditions. For a given area, **Chart Datum (CD)** is the level, as close as possible to LAT, below which charted depths are given. It is also the reference for tidal predictions: the total depth at a given time being equal to the charted depth plus the height of the tide. **Ordnance Datum (OD)** at Newlyn is the datum level of land survey on mainland England, Scotland and Wales, from which heights on UK land maps are measured. OD depends on the tidal range and varies around the UK from about 5m above OD to about 6.5m below. The differences are noted in tide tables, allowing comparison of the tide levels along the coast and reference to Ordnance Survey data. **Duration** of the tide is the interval between low water and the next high water. It can be used to calculate the approximate time of low water when only the time of high water is known. **Mean Sea Level (MSL or ML)** is the average level of the sea's surface over a long period, normally observed over 18.6 years. The **Range** of the tide is the difference in height between successive high and low waters. It is greatest at spring tides, least at neaps. The range may be indicated by **Tidal Coefficients** which are proportional to, but not the same as, the range on a particular day. A coefficient of 95 indicates an average spring tide, while 45 is an average neap tide.

PREDICTIONS
The data which follows gives the daily predictions of the time (Greenwich Mean Time) and height of high water at four ports. For the months when British Summer Time is in operation the hour's time difference should be added. The datum of predictions is the difference of height, in metres, of CD from Ordnance datum (Newlyn).

Tidal predictions for London Bridge, Liverpool, Greenock and Leith © Crown Copyright and/or database rights. Reproduced by permission of the Controller of Her Majesty's Stationery Office and the UK Hydrographic Office (W www.ukho.gov.uk). The section was compiled with the assistance of Chris Stevens and Perrin Towler.

JANUARY 2016   *High Water*   GMT

	LONDON BRIDGE Datum of Predictions 3.20m below				LIVERPOOL (Gladstone Dock) Datum of Predictions 4.93m below				GREENOCK Datum of Predictions 1.62m below				LEITH Datum of Predictions 2.90m below			
	hr m	ht m	hr m	ht m	hr m	ht m	hr m	ht m	hr m	ht m	hr m	ht m	hr m	ht m	hr m	ht m
F 1	05 47	6.3	18 16	6.2	03 14	8.0	15 34	8.1	04 51	3.1	16 45	3.4	07 08	4.7	19 30	4.8
SA 2	06 24	6.0	19 00	6.0	04 04	7.6	16 29	7.7	05 38	3.0	17 30	3.3	07 57	4.6	20 23	4.6
SU 3	07 12	5.8	19 58	5.8	05 04	7.3	17 34	7.4	06 30	2.9	18 22	3.1	08 50	4.4	21 21	4.5
M 4	08 29	5.6	21 08	5.8	06 12	7.3	18 43	7.4	07 32	2.9	19 22	3.0	09 48	4.4	22 22	4.4
TU 5	09 46	5.7	22 14	5.9	07 20	7.4	19 48	7.6	08 42	3.0	20 31	3.0	10 49	4.5	23 25	4.6
W 6	10 49	6.0	23 16	6.2	08 19	7.8	20 44	7.9	09 48	3.1	21 39	3.1	11 50	4.7	—	
TH 7	11 46	6.3	—		09 08	8.2	21 31	8.3	10 41	3.3	22 36	3.2	00 24	4.7	12 45	4.9
F 8	00 11	6.5	12 36	6.6	09 51	8.6	22 12	8.6	11 25	3.4	23 24	3.3	01 15	5.0	13 31	5.2
SA 9	01 00	6.7	13 21	6.8	10 31	9.0	22 52	8.9	12 04	3.5	—		01 58	5.2	14 12	5.4
SU 10	01 45	6.8	14 04	7.0	11 10	9.3	23 32	9.1	00 08	3.4	12 40	3.6	02 38	5.4	14 50	5.5
M 11	02 27	6.9	14 46	7.2	11 49	9.5	—		00 52	3.4	13 16	3.7	03 17	5.5	15 28	5.6
TU 12	03 08	7.0	15 28	7.3	00 12	9.3	12 31	9.6	01 35	3.5	13 54	3.8	03 56	5.6	16 06	5.7
W 13	03 48	7.0	16 10	7.3	00 55	9.3	13 14	9.6	02 18	3.5	14 34	3.8	04 37	5.6	16 47	5.7
TH 14	04 27	7.0	16 52	7.1	01 38	9.2	13 58	9.5	03 01	3.5	15 17	3.8	05 20	5.6	17 31	5.6
F 15	05 08	6.9	17 37	6.9	02 24	9.0	14 46	9.2	03 44	3.5	16 01	3.7	06 07	5.4	18 18	5.5
SA 16	05 51	6.8	18 26	6.7	03 14	8.7	15 39	8.9	04 29	3.4	16 48	3.6	06 58	5.2	19 12	5.3
SU 17	06 41	6.6	19 24	6.5	04 11	8.3	16 40	8.5	05 16	3.3	17 42	3.4	07 58	5.0	20 17	5.0
M 18	07 43	6.4	20 32	6.3	05 18	8.0	17 51	8.3	06 11	3.2	18 50	3.2	09 07	4.8	21 33	4.9
TU 19	08 59	6.3	21 42	6.3	06 34	7.9	19 06	8.2	07 24	3.0	20 19	3.1	10 18	4.8	22 47	4.9
W 20	10 13	6.3	22 55	6.3	07 48	8.1	20 18	8.4	08 57	3.1	21 44	3.1	11 27	4.9	23 56	5.0
TH 21	11 25	6.5	—		08 53	8.5	21 20	8.6	10 09	3.2	22 49	3.3	12 29	5.1	—	
F 22	00 05	6.5	12 29	6.7	09 48	8.8	22 13	8.9	11 05	3.4	23 43	3.4	00 57	5.2	13 24	5.3
SA 23	01 02	6.7	13 23	6.9	10 36	9.1	22 59	9.1	11 52	3.5	—		01 49	5.3	14 11	5.5
SU 24	01 50	6.8	14 09	7.0	11 18	9.3	23 40	9.2	00 32	3.4	12 35	3.6	02 35	5.5	14 54	5.6
M 25	02 33	6.9	14 51	7.1	11 56	9.4	—		01 16	3.4	13 14	3.7	03 16	5.5	15 35	5.6
TU 26	03 11	7.0	15 29	7.1	00 17	9.2	12 33	9.4	01 55	3.3	13 51	3.7	03 56	5.5	16 14	5.5
W 27	03 45	6.9	16 04	7.0	00 52	9.1	13 06	9.2	02 31	3.3	14 26	3.7	04 34	5.4	16 51	5.4
TH 28	04 17	6.9	16 36	6.8	01 25	8.9	13 39	9.0	03 04	3.3	15 01	3.7	05 10	5.2	17 27	5.3
F 29	04 47	6.7	17 07	6.6	01 59	8.6	14 13	8.7	03 40	3.3	15 37	3.6	05 47	5.0	18 04	5.1
SA 30	05 17	6.5	17 38	6.4	02 35	8.3	14 50	8.3	04 17	3.2	16 14	3.5	06 25	4.9	18 44	4.9
SU 31	05 49	6.3	18 13	6.2	03 14	7.9	15 32	7.9	04 57	3.1	16 54	3.3	07 08	4.7	19 29	4.6

FEBRUARY 2016   *High Water*   GMT

	LONDON BRIDGE				LIVERPOOL (Gladstone Dock)				GREENOCK				LEITH			
M 1	06 26	6.1	18 54	6.0	04 02	7.5	16 24	7.5	05 40	3.0	17 39	3.1	07 56	4.5	20 24	4.4
TU 2	07 13	5.8	19 50	5.7	05 03	7.2	17 34	7.2	06 31	2.9	18 33	3.0	08 53	4.4	21 27	4.3
W 3	08 21	5.6	21 15	5.7	06 18	7.2	18 54	7.2	07 36	2.8	19 37	2.9	09 57	4.4	22 36	4.4
TH 4	09 57	5.7	22 31	5.9	07 32	7.4	20 06	7.5	08 58	2.9	20 53	2.9	11 04	4.5	23 45	4.5
F 5	11 07	6.1	23 38	6.3	08 34	7.9	21 03	8.0	10 08	3.0	22 07	3.0	12 10	4.7	—	
SA 6	12 06	6.5	—		09 24	8.4	21 51	8.5	10 59	3.2	23 05	3.1	00 46	4.8	13 05	5.0
SU 7	00 35	6.6	12 58	6.8	10 09	8.9	22 34	8.9	11 41	3.4	23 53	3.3	01 35	5.1	13 50	5.3
M 8	01 25	6.9	13 46	7.1	10 51	9.4	23 15	9.3	12 20	3.5	—		02 18	5.4	14 30	5.6
TU 9	02 10	7.0	14 30	7.3	11 32	9.7	23 57	9.6	00 37	3.3	13 00	3.6	02 57	5.6	15 09	5.8
W 10	02 53	7.2	15 14	7.4	12 14	9.9	—		01 21	3.4	13 40	3.7	03 37	5.8	15 48	5.9
TH 11	03 34	7.3	15 56	7.4	00 39	9.7	12 58	10.0	02 04	3.5	14 22	3.8	04 18	5.8	16 29	5.9
F 12	04 14	7.3	16 38	7.3	01 22	9.6	13 41	9.9	02 45	3.5	15 04	3.8	05 01	5.7	17 13	5.9
SA 13	04 54	7.2	17 21	7.0	02 06	9.3	14 27	9.5	03 27	3.5	15 47	3.7	05 46	5.6	18 00	5.7
SU 14	05 35	7.0	18 06	6.7	02 52	8.9	15 16	9.1	04 08	3.5	16 32	3.6	06 35	5.3	18 52	5.4
M 15	06 22	6.8	18 58	6.4	03 45	8.5	16 14	8.5	04 51	3.3	17 21	3.4	07 32	5.0	19 56	5.0
TU 16	07 19	6.5	20 02	6.2	04 49	8.0	17 26	8.0	05 39	3.2	18 19	3.1	08 40	4.7	21 13	4.8
W 17	08 31	6.3	21 15	6.0	06 08	7.7	18 47	7.8	06 38	3.0	19 55	2.9	09 55	4.6	22 31	4.7
TH 18	09 50	6.2	22 35	6.1	07 30	7.8	20 07	7.9	08 25	2.9	21 40	2.9	11 10	4.7	23 48	4.8
F 19	11 10	6.3	23 51	6.3	08 41	8.2	21 12	8.3	09 54	3.0	22 44	3.1	12 20	4.9	—	
SA 20	12 18	6.6	—		09 37	8.6	22 04	8.6	10 51	3.2	23 35	3.2	00 53	5.0	13 16	5.1
SU 21	00 49	6.6	13 12	6.8	10 23	8.9	22 46	8.9	11 38	3.4	—		01 43	5.2	14 01	5.3
M 22	01 36	6.8	13 56	7.0	11 02	9.2	23 23	9.1	00 20	3.3	12 21	3.5	02 24	5.3	14 41	5.5
TU 23	02 16	6.9	14 35	7.0	11 37	9.3	23 56	9.1	01 00	3.3	12 58	3.6	03 00	5.4	15 17	5.5
W 24	02 51	7.0	15 09	7.0	12 10	9.3	—		01 36	3.3	13 32	3.6	03 34	5.4	15 52	5.5
TH 25	03 23	7.0	15 39	7.0	00 27	9.1	12 41	9.2	02 07	3.3	14 04	3.6	04 07	5.3	16 25	5.4
F 26	03 52	7.0	16 07	6.9	00 58	9.0	13 12	9.1	02 37	3.3	14 36	3.6	04 40	5.2	16 58	5.3
SA 27	04 20	6.9	16 35	6.8	01 28	8.8	13 42	8.8	03 09	3.3	15 10	3.5	05 13	5.1	17 31	5.2
SU 28	04 50	6.8	17 05	6.6	02 00	8.6	14 13	8.5	03 43	3.3	15 45	3.5	05 49	5.0	18 07	5.0
M 29	05 20	6.6	17 38	6.4	02 34	8.2	14 48	8.1	04 18	3.2	16 23	3.3	06 27	4.8	18 48	4.7

MARCH 2016 *High Water* GMT

		LONDON BRIDGE Datum of Predictions 3.20m below				LIVERPOOL (Gladstone Dock) Datum of Predictions 4.93m below				GREENOCK Datum of Predictions 1.62m below				LEITH Datum of Predictions 2.90m below			
		hr	ht m	hr	ht m	hr	ht m	hr	ht m	hr	ht m	hr	ht m	hr	ht m	hr	ht m
TU	1	05 55	6.3	18 15	6.1	03 13	7.8	15 30	7.6	04 56	3.1	17 05	3.1	07 10	4.6	19 36	4.5
W	2	06 37	6.1	19 02	5.9	04 04	7.4	16 30	7.2	05 39	2.9	17 55	2.9	08 03	4.4	20 37	4.3
TH	3	07 31	5.8	20 09	5.7	05 17	7.1	17 56	7.0	06 37	2.7	18 56	2.8	09 08	4.3	21 51	4.3
F	4	08 56	5.7	21 45	5.7	06 42	7.2	19 24	7.3	07 56	2.7	20 12	2.8	10 21	4.3	23 06	4.4
SA	5	10 26	6.0	23 03	6.1	07 56	7.7	20 32	7.8	09 27	2.8	21 40	2.9	11 34	4.6	—	—
SU	6	11 35	6.5	—	—	08 54	8.3	21 25	8.4	10 28	3.1	22 45	3.1	00 15	4.7	12 36	4.9
M	7	00 06	6.6	12 33	6.9	09 43	8.9	22 11	9.0	11 15	3.3	23 34	3.2	01 09	5.1	13 24	5.3
TU	8	01 00	6.9	13 23	7.2	10 28	9.5	22 54	9.5	11 57	3.5	—	—	01 53	5.5	14 06	5.6
W	9	01 47	7.2	14 10	7.4	11 11	9.9	23 37	9.8	00 19	3.3	12 41	3.6	02 34	5.7	14 46	5.9
TH	10	02 31	7.4	14 54	7.5	11 54	10.1	—	—	01 03	3.4	13 24	3.7	03 15	5.9	15 27	6.1
F	11	03 13	7.5	15 37	7.5	00 19	9.9	12 38	10.2	01 45	3.5	14 07	3.8	03 56	5.9	16 10	6.1
SA	12	03 55	7.5	16 19	7.4	01 02	9.8	13 22	10.0	02 26	3.5	14 50	3.8	04 40	5.8	16 55	6.0
SU	13	04 35	7.5	17 01	7.1	01 45	9.5	14 07	9.6	03 06	3.6	15 33	3.7	05 25	5.6	17 44	5.7
M	14	05 18	7.2	17 45	6.7	02 31	9.1	14 56	9.1	03 46	3.5	16 17	3.5	06 14	5.3	18 37	5.4
TU	15	06 04	6.9	18 34	6.4	03 21	8.5	15 53	8.4	04 27	3.4	17 04	3.3	07 09	5.0	19 41	5.0
W	16	06 58	6.6	19 33	6.1	04 24	8.0	17 05	7.8	05 13	3.2	18 00	2.9	08 17	4.7	20 56	4.7
TH	17	08 08	6.3	20 48	5.9	05 44	7.6	18 30	7.5	06 07	2.9	19 41	2.7	09 33	4.5	22 14	4.6
F	18	09 27	6.1	22 11	5.9	07 09	7.6	19 52	7.7	07 47	2.8	21 30	2.8	10 50	4.6	23 34	4.7
SA	19	10 50	6.3	23 29	6.2	08 22	8.0	20 57	8.1	09 32	2.9	22 29	3.0	12 02	4.8	—	—
SU	20	11 59	6.6	—	—	09 18	8.4	21 46	8.5	10 30	3.1	23 16	3.1	00 40	4.9	13 00	5.0
M	21	00 28	6.6	12 52	6.8	10 02	8.7	22 25	8.8	11 17	3.3	23 58	3.2	01 28	5.1	13 44	5.2
TU	22	01 14	6.8	13 35	6.9	10 40	9.0	22 59	9.0	11 58	3.4	—	—	02 06	5.2	14 21	5.3
W	23	01 52	6.9	14 11	6.9	11 13	9.1	23 30	9.1	00 36	3.3	12 36	3.4	02 39	5.3	14 56	5.4
TH	24	02 26	7.0	14 43	7.0	11 44	9.2	—	—	01 09	3.3	13 08	3.4	03 10	5.3	15 28	5.4
F	25	02 56	7.0	15 11	7.0	00 00	9.1	12 15	9.1	01 39	3.3	13 39	3.4	03 40	5.3	15 59	5.4
SA	26	03 24	7.1	15 37	7.0	00 30	9.1	12 45	9.0	02 08	3.3	14 10	3.4	04 11	5.3	16 31	5.3
SU	27	03 53	7.0	16 06	6.9	01 00	8.9	13 14	8.8	02 39	3.4	14 43	3.4	04 43	5.2	17 04	5.2
M	28	04 23	6.9	16 37	6.7	01 30	8.7	13 44	8.5	03 10	3.3	15 18	3.4	05 17	5.0	17 39	5.0
TU	29	04 55	6.7	17 10	6.5	02 02	8.4	14 17	8.2	03 42	3.3	15 55	3.3	05 54	4.9	18 18	4.8
W	30	05 30	6.5	17 46	6.2	02 39	8.1	14 58	7.8	04 17	3.1	16 37	3.1	06 35	4.7	19 03	4.6
TH	31	06 11	6.3	18 31	6.0	03 26	7.7	15 53	7.4	04 56	3.0	17 25	2.9	07 22	4.5	20 00	4.4

APRIL 2016 *High Water* GMT

		LONDON BRIDGE				LIVERPOOL (Gladstone Dock)				GREENOCK				LEITH			
F	1	07 03	6.0	19 31	5.8	04 33	7.4	17 12	7.1	05 47	2.8	18 24	2.8	08 24	4.4	21 11	4.3
SA	2	08 16	5.9	21 01	5.8	05 57	7.3	18 42	7.3	07 01	2.7	19 38	2.7	09 40	4.4	22 29	4.5
SU	3	09 49	6.1	22 26	6.1	07 16	7.7	19 57	7.8	08 38	2.8	21 08	2.8	10 56	4.5	23 40	4.8
M	4	11 02	6.5	23 34	6.6	08 21	8.3	20 56	8.5	09 52	3.0	22 18	3.0	12 01	4.9	—	—
TU	5	12 03	6.9	—	—	09 14	9.0	21 45	9.1	10 44	3.2	23 10	3.2	00 38	5.1	12 53	5.3
W	6	00 31	7.0	12 57	7.2	10 02	9.5	22 30	9.5	11 31	3.4	23 56	3.3	01 26	5.5	13 39	5.6
TH	7	01 21	7.2	13 46	7.4	10 47	9.9	23 14	9.9	12 17	3.6	—	—	02 09	5.8	14 22	5.9
F	8	02 07	7.5	14 32	7.5	11 32	10.2	23 57	10.0	00 40	3.4	13 04	3.6	02 51	5.9	15 06	6.1
SA	9	02 50	7.6	15 16	7.5	12 17	10.2	—	—	01 23	3.5	13 50	3.7	03 34	6.0	15 51	6.1
SU	10	03 34	7.7	15 59	7.3	00 41	9.9	13 03	9.9	02 05	3.6	14 35	3.7	04 18	5.9	16 39	6.0
M	11	04 17	7.6	16 42	7.1	01 25	9.6	13 50	9.5	02 45	3.6	15 20	3.6	05 05	5.6	17 29	5.7
TU	12	05 01	7.3	17 26	6.7	02 11	9.1	14 39	8.9	03 25	3.6	16 04	3.4	05 55	5.3	18 24	5.3
W	13	05 48	7.0	18 13	6.4	03 02	8.6	15 35	8.3	04 06	3.4	16 53	3.2	06 51	5.0	19 27	5.0
TH	14	06 41	6.6	19 08	6.1	04 03	8.0	16 44	7.7	04 51	3.2	17 50	2.9	07 57	4.7	20 37	4.7
F	15	07 46	6.3	20 19	5.9	05 18	7.7	18 03	7.5	05 45	3.0	19 22	2.7	09 09	4.6	21 49	4.5
SA	16	09 00	6.1	21 38	5.9	06 37	7.6	19 23	7.6	07 08	2.8	21 02	2.7	10 21	4.5	23 05	4.6
SU	17	10 18	6.2	22 55	6.1	07 50	7.8	20 29	7.9	08 56	2.9	22 01	2.9	11 32	4.7	—	—
M	18	11 29	6.5	23 56	6.4	08 48	8.2	21 17	8.3	09 58	3.1	22 47	3.1	00 11	4.7	12 31	4.9
TU	19	12 23	6.7	—	—	09 33	8.5	21 56	8.6	10 47	3.2	23 28	3.2	01 01	4.9	13 17	5.0
W	20	00 43	6.7	13 06	6.8	10 11	8.7	22 30	8.8	11 28	3.3	—	—	01 39	5.1	13 55	5.2
TH	21	01 23	6.8	13 42	6.8	10 44	8.9	23 01	8.9	00 05	3.2	12 06	3.3	02 12	5.2	14 30	5.3
F	22	01 57	6.9	14 14	6.9	11 17	8.9	23 32	9.0	00 39	3.3	12 39	3.3	02 43	5.2	15 02	5.3
SA	23	02 28	7.0	14 42	6.9	11 48	9.0	—	—	01 10	3.3	13 10	3.3	03 13	5.3	15 34	5.3
SU	24	02 58	7.1	15 10	6.9	00 03	9.0	12 19	8.9	01 40	3.4	13 42	3.3	03 44	5.3	16 06	5.2
M	25	03 28	7.1	15 41	6.9	00 34	8.9	12 50	8.7	02 09	3.4	14 16	3.4	04 17	5.2	16 40	5.2
TU	26	04 00	7.0	16 14	6.7	01 05	8.8	13 22	8.5	02 40	3.4	14 53	3.3	04 51	5.1	17 16	5.0
W	27	04 34	6.8	16 48	6.5	01 39	8.6	13 57	8.3	03 12	3.4	15 32	3.3	05 27	5.0	17 56	4.9
TH	28	05 11	6.6	17 26	6.3	02 17	8.3	14 39	8.0	03 46	3.3	16 14	3.2	06 07	4.8	18 41	4.7
F	29	05 54	6.4	18 11	6.1	03 04	8.0	15 33	7.6	04 25	3.1	17 02	3.0	06 54	4.7	19 35	4.6
SA	30	06 45	6.2	19 08	5.9	04 06	7.7	16 44	7.4	05 12	3.0	17 58	2.9	07 51	4.5	20 40	4.5

MAY 2016   *High Water*   GMT

		LONDON BRIDGE — Datum of Predictions 3.20m below				LIVERPOOL (Gladstone Dock) — Datum of Predictions 4.93m below				GREENOCK — Datum of Predictions 1.62m below				LEITH — Datum of Predictions 2.90m below			
		hr m	ht m	hr m	ht m	hr m	ht m	hr m	ht m	hr m	ht m	hr m	ht m	hr m	ht m	hr m	ht m
SU	1	07 53	6.1	20 27	5.9	05 23	7.7	18 06	7.5	06 20	2.8	19 08	2.8	09 02	4.5	21 55	4.6
M	2	09 18	6.2	21 52	6.2	06 39	7.9	19 21	8.0	07 52	2.8	20 31	2.9	10 19	4.6	23 06	4.8
TU	3	10 30	6.6	23 01	6.6	07 46	8.4	20 24	8.5	09 13	3.0	21 45	3.1	11 25	4.9	—	
W	4	11 34	6.9	—		08 43	9.0	21 17	9.0	10 13	3.2	22 41	3.2	00 06	5.2	12 22	5.3
TH	5	00 01	6.9	12 31	7.2	09 35	9.4	22 05	9.5	11 05	3.4	23 30	3.4	00 57	5.5	13 12	5.6
F	6	00 54	7.2	13 22	7.3	10 24	9.8	22 51	9.7	11 54	3.5	—		01 43	5.7	13 59	5.9
SA	7	01 42	7.4	14 10	7.3	11 12	10.0	23 37	9.9	00 16	3.5	12 44	3.6	02 28	5.9	14 46	6.0
SU	8	02 29	7.6	14 55	7.3	11 59	9.9	—		01 01	3.6	13 33	3.6	03 13	5.9	15 34	6.0
M	9	03 14	7.6	15 40	7.2	00 22	9.8	12 47	9.7	01 44	3.6	14 20	3.6	03 59	5.8	16 24	5.9
TU	10	03 59	7.5	16 24	7.0	01 08	9.5	13 34	9.3	02 25	3.6	15 07	3.5	04 48	5.6	17 16	5.6
W	11	04 45	7.3	17 08	6.7	01 54	9.1	14 23	8.8	03 06	3.6	15 53	3.5	05 38	5.4	18 10	5.3
TH	12	05 32	7.0	17 54	6.4	02 43	8.7	15 16	8.3	03 48	3.5	16 42	3.1	06 34	5.1	19 09	5.0
F	13	06 23	6.6	18 44	6.1	03 40	8.2	16 17	7.8	04 33	3.3	17 38	2.9	07 35	4.8	20 10	4.7
SA	14	07 21	6.3	19 46	5.9	04 45	7.8	17 26	7.5	05 24	3.1	18 47	2.7	08 39	4.7	21 14	4.5
SU	15	08 27	6.1	20 57	5.9	05 55	7.6	18 38	7.5	06 30	2.9	20 09	2.7	09 44	4.6	22 21	4.5
M	16	09 35	6.1	22 07	6.0	07 05	7.7	19 45	7.7	07 58	2.9	21 16	2.8	10 50	4.6	23 26	4.6
TU	17	10 43	6.2	23 11	6.2	08 06	7.9	20 38	8.0	09 13	3.0	22 07	3.0	11 50	4.7	—	
W	18	11 42	6.4	—		08 55	8.1	21 21	8.3	10 07	3.1	22 51	3.1	00 21	4.7	12 42	4.8
TH	19	00 04	6.5	12 30	6.6	09 37	8.4	21 58	8.6	10 52	3.2	23 30	3.2	01 04	4.9	13 24	5.0
F	20	00 48	6.7	13 09	6.7	10 14	8.6	22 32	8.8	11 31	3.2	—		01 41	5.0	14 01	5.1
SA	21	01 26	6.8	13 44	6.8	10 49	8.7	23 05	8.9	00 07	3.3	12 07	3.2	02 14	5.2	14 36	5.2
SU	22	02 01	6.9	14 16	6.8	11 23	8.8	23 38	9.0	00 41	3.4	12 40	3.2	02 46	5.2	15 10	5.2
M	23	02 34	7.0	14 48	6.9	11 56	8.8	—		01 13	3.4	13 14	3.3	03 20	5.3	15 45	5.2
TU	24	03 06	7.0	15 22	6.8	00 11	9.0	12 30	8.7	01 43	3.5	13 51	3.3	03 54	5.3	16 20	5.2
W	25	03 41	7.0	15 57	6.7	00 46	8.9	13 05	8.6	02 14	3.5	14 30	3.3	04 29	5.2	16 57	5.1
TH	26	04 18	6.9	16 34	6.6	01 22	8.8	13 44	8.4	02 48	3.5	15 12	3.3	05 06	5.1	17 37	5.0
F	27	04 58	6.7	17 13	6.4	02 03	8.6	14 27	8.2	03 25	3.4	15 55	3.2	05 47	5.0	18 23	4.9
SA	28	05 42	6.6	17 58	6.3	02 50	8.3	15 19	8.0	04 03	3.3	16 43	3.1	06 33	4.9	19 14	4.8
SU	29	06 32	6.4	18 52	6.2	03 48	8.1	16 23	7.8	04 51	3.2	17 36	3.0	07 26	4.8	20 15	4.7
M	30	07 35	6.3	20 01	6.1	04 55	8.1	17 35	7.8	05 51	3.0	18 39	3.0	08 31	4.7	21 24	4.8
TU	31	08 51	6.4	21 20	6.3	06 06	8.2	18 47	8.1	07 13	3.0	19 53	3.0	09 44	4.8	22 33	4.9

JUNE 2016   *High Water*   GMT

		LONDON BRIDGE				LIVERPOOL (Gladstone Dock)				GREENOCK				LEITH			
W	1	10 01	6.6	22 30	6.6	07 14	8.5	19 53	8.5	08 36	3.1	21 09	3.1	10 53	5.0	23 35	5.1
TH	2	11 06	6.8	23 33	6.9	08 15	8.9	20 51	8.9	09 44	3.2	22 12	3.2	11 54	5.3	—	
F	3	12 06	7.0	—		09 12	9.2	21 43	9.2	10 41	3.4	23 06	3.3	00 30	5.4	12 49	5.5
SA	4	00 30	7.1	13 01	7.1	10 05	9.5	22 32	9.5	11 35	3.4	23 55	3.5	01 21	5.6	13 41	5.7
SU	5	01 22	7.3	13 51	7.1	10 55	9.6	23 20	9.6	12 26	3.5	—		02 08	5.7	14 31	5.8
M	6	02 11	7.4	14 39	7.2	11 44	9.6	—		00 41	3.5	13 18	3.5	02 56	5.8	15 21	5.8
TU	7	02 59	7.5	15 25	7.1	00 06	9.6	12 32	9.5	01 25	3.6	14 07	3.4	03 43	5.7	16 11	5.7
W	8	03 45	7.4	16 09	7.0	00 52	9.5	13 19	9.2	02 08	3.6	14 54	3.3	04 32	5.6	17 01	5.5
TH	9	04 31	7.2	16 52	6.8	01 37	9.2	14 05	8.8	02 49	3.6	15 40	3.2	05 22	5.4	17 52	5.3
F	10	05 16	6.9	17 34	6.5	02 23	8.8	14 52	8.4	03 30	3.5	16 27	3.1	06 13	5.2	18 44	5.0
SA	11	06 02	6.6	18 18	6.3	03 11	8.4	15 42	8.0	04 13	3.4	17 15	3.0	07 06	5.0	19 36	4.8
SU	12	06 51	6.3	19 09	6.0	04 05	8.0	16 39	7.6	04 59	3.2	18 06	2.9	08 03	4.8	20 31	4.6
M	13	07 47	6.1	20 10	5.9	05 06	7.7	17 42	7.4	05 51	3.0	19 04	2.8	09 00	4.6	21 27	4.5
TU	14	08 47	6.0	21 16	5.9	06 10	7.6	18 48	7.4	06 53	2.9	20 07	2.8	09 58	4.5	22 26	4.5
W	15	09 48	6.0	22 19	6.0	07 14	7.6	19 49	7.7	08 04	2.9	21 11	2.9	10 58	4.5	23 25	4.6
TH	16	10 49	6.1	23 18	6.3	08 12	7.8	20 41	8.0	09 12	2.9	22 06	3.0	11 56	4.6	—	
F	17	11 45	6.4	—		09 01	8.0	21 24	8.3	10 08	3.0	22 54	3.2	00 19	4.7	12 48	4.8
SA	18	00 10	6.5	12 34	6.6	09 44	8.3	22 03	8.6	10 53	3.1	23 36	3.3	01 05	4.9	13 31	4.9
SU	19	00 56	6.7	13 16	6.7	10 23	8.5	22 40	8.8	11 33	3.1	—		01 45	5.1	14 11	5.1
M	20	01 36	6.8	13 55	6.8	11 00	8.6	23 15	8.9	00 14	3.4	12 11	3.2	02 22	5.2	14 48	5.2
TU	21	02 13	6.9	14 32	6.8	11 36	8.7	23 52	9.1	00 48	3.4	12 49	3.2	02 58	5.3	15 24	5.3
W	22	02 50	7.0	15 09	6.8	12 12	8.8	—		01 20	3.5	13 29	3.2	03 34	5.4	16 01	5.3
TH	23	03 27	7.0	15 46	6.8	00 29	9.1	12 51	8.8	01 53	3.5	14 11	3.3	04 10	5.4	16 39	5.3
F	24	04 06	7.0	16 24	6.7	01 09	9.0	13 32	8.7	02 29	3.5	14 54	3.3	04 48	5.3	17 20	5.3
SA	25	04 47	6.9	17 03	6.6	01 51	8.9	14 16	8.6	03 08	3.5	15 38	3.3	05 29	5.3	18 05	5.2
SU	26	05 30	6.8	17 46	6.5	02 37	8.8	15 05	8.4	03 49	3.5	16 24	3.2	06 14	5.2	18 54	5.1
M	27	06 18	6.6	18 35	6.4	03 29	8.6	16 01	8.2	04 34	3.4	17 14	3.2	07 05	5.1	19 50	4.9
TU	28	07 15	6.5	19 35	6.3	04 29	8.4	17 06	8.1	05 28	3.2	18 10	3.1	08 04	5.0	20 55	4.9
W	29	08 24	6.4	20 50	6.3	05 36	8.3	18 17	8.1	06 37	3.1	19 15	3.0	09 15	4.9	22 04	4.9
TH	30	09 33	6.4	22 02	6.5	06 46	8.4	19 26	8.3	08 01	3.1	20 33	3.0	10 26	5.0	23 09	5.0

JULY 2016 *High Water* GMT

		LONDON BRIDGE (3.20m below)				LIVERPOOL (Gladstone Dock) (4.93m below)				GREENOCK (1.62m below)				LEITH (2.90m below)			
		hr	m	ht	hr	m	ht	hr	m	ht	hr	m	ht	hr	m	ht
F	1	10 40	6.5	23 08	6.7	07 53	8.6	20 30	8.6	09 19	3.1	21 46	3.1	11 33	5.1	—	—
SA	2	11 46	6.7	—	—	08 55	8.9	21 27	8.9	10 25	3.2	22 46	3.3	00 09	5.2	12 34	5.3
SU	3	00 11	6.9	12 46	6.8	09 52	9.1	22 19	9.2	11 22	3.3	23 39	3.4	01 04	5.4	13 29	5.5
M	4	01 08	7.1	13 39	6.9	10 44	9.3	23 07	9.4	12 16	3.4	—	—	01 55	5.6	14 20	5.6
TU	5	01 59	7.2	14 27	7.0	11 33	9.3	23 53	9.5	00 26	3.5	13 07	3.3	02 43	5.7	15 09	5.7
W	6	02 47	7.3	15 12	7.1	12 18	9.3	—	—	01 11	3.6	13 55	3.3	03 30	5.7	15 56	5.6
TH	7	03 32	7.3	15 54	7.0	00 36	9.4	13 01	9.1	01 52	3.6	14 40	3.2	04 16	5.6	16 42	5.5
F	8	04 15	7.2	16 33	6.9	01 18	9.2	13 42	8.8	02 31	3.6	15 22	3.2	05 01	5.5	17 27	5.3
SA	9	04 56	7.0	17 11	6.7	01 57	8.9	14 21	8.5	03 10	3.6	16 01	3.1	05 47	5.3	18 12	5.1
SU	10	05 35	6.7	17 48	6.4	02 38	8.6	15 03	8.2	03 49	3.5	16 42	3.0	06 32	5.1	18 57	4.9
M	11	06 14	6.4	18 26	6.2	03 22	8.2	15 49	7.8	04 29	3.3	17 25	3.0	07 19	4.9	19 43	4.7
TU	12	06 58	6.1	19 14	6.0	04 12	7.8	16 44	7.5	05 12	3.2	18 11	2.9	08 10	4.7	20 34	4.5
W	13	07 51	5.9	20 18	5.8	05 11	7.5	17 47	7.3	06 01	3.0	19 04	2.8	09 04	4.5	21 28	4.4
TH	14	08 52	5.8	21 27	5.8	06 18	7.3	18 55	7.4	06 57	2.9	20 06	2.8	10 02	4.4	22 26	4.5
F	15	09 56	5.9	22 31	6.0	07 26	7.4	19 58	7.6	08 04	2.8	21 15	2.9	11 04	4.5	23 27	4.6
SA	16	10 59	6.1	23 32	6.3	08 26	7.7	20 51	8.0	09 15	2.9	22 17	3.1	12 06	4.6	—	—
SU	17	11 58	6.4	—	—	09 16	8.0	21 36	8.4	10 16	3.0	23 07	3.2	00 26	4.8	13 01	4.8
M	18	00 25	6.6	12 49	6.6	09 59	8.3	22 16	8.7	11 05	3.1	23 48	3.3	01 16	5.0	13 46	5.0
TU	19	01 11	6.8	13 34	6.8	10 39	8.6	22 55	9.0	11 47	3.1	—	—	01 59	5.2	14 26	5.2
W	20	01 54	6.9	14 15	6.9	11 17	8.8	23 33	9.2	00 25	3.4	12 29	3.2	02 38	5.4	15 04	5.4
TH	21	02 34	7.1	14 55	7.0	11 56	9.0	—	—	00 59	3.5	13 10	3.2	03 15	5.5	15 42	5.5
F	22	03 14	7.2	15 34	7.0	00 12	9.4	12 36	9.1	01 35	3.6	13 53	3.3	03 52	5.6	16 20	5.5
SA	23	03 54	7.2	16 12	7.0	00 53	9.4	13 17	9.1	02 13	3.6	14 36	3.3	04 30	5.6	17 01	5.5
SU	24	04 34	7.1	16 50	6.9	01 35	9.4	14 00	9.0	02 53	3.6	15 20	3.3	05 11	5.6	17 45	5.4
M	25	05 16	7.0	17 31	6.8	02 20	9.2	14 46	8.7	03 34	3.6	16 04	3.3	05 55	5.5	18 33	5.3
TU	26	06 00	6.7	18 15	6.7	03 08	9.0	15 38	8.5	04 18	3.5	16 50	3.3	06 44	5.3	19 25	5.1
W	27	06 52	6.5	19 10	6.5	04 04	8.6	16 38	8.2	05 07	3.3	17 39	3.2	07 41	5.1	20 28	4.9
TH	28	07 56	6.3	20 20	6.4	05 10	8.3	17 51	8.0	06 06	3.1	18 38	3.1	08 51	5.0	21 39	4.8
F	29	09 07	6.2	21 36	6.4	06 24	8.2	19 06	8.0	07 28	3.0	19 57	3.0	10 07	4.9	22 49	4.9
SA	30	10 18	6.3	22 49	6.5	07 39	8.2	20 17	8.3	09 04	3.0	21 26	3.0	11 19	5.0	23 55	5.1
SU	31	11 31	6.4	23 59	6.7	08 47	8.5	21 18	8.7	10 19	3.1	22 34	3.2	12 26	5.1	—	—

AUGUST 2016 *High Water* GMT

		LONDON BRIDGE				LIVERPOOL (Gladstone Dock)				GREENOCK				LEITH			
M	1	12 36	6.7	—	—	09 46	8.8	22 10	9.1	11 17	3.2	23 27	3.4	00 54	5.3	13 23	5.3
TU	2	00 59	7.0	13 29	6.9	10 36	9.0	22 56	9.3	12 09	3.3	—	—	01 46	5.5	14 12	5.5
W	3	01 50	7.1	14 15	7.0	11 21	9.2	23 38	9.4	00 14	3.5	12 57	3.3	02 31	5.6	14 56	5.6
TH	4	02 35	7.2	14 57	7.1	12 01	9.2	—	—	00 57	3.6	13 41	3.2	03 15	5.7	15 39	5.5
F	5	03 17	7.2	15 35	7.1	00 17	9.4	12 39	9.1	01 35	3.6	14 20	3.2	03 56	5.6	16 19	5.5
SA	6	03 55	7.2	16 10	7.0	00 53	9.3	13 14	8.9	02 11	3.6	14 54	3.2	04 37	5.5	16 58	5.3
SU	7	04 30	7.0	16 43	6.9	01 28	9.1	13 48	8.7	02 46	3.6	15 28	3.1	05 16	5.4	17 36	5.1
M	8	05 03	6.8	17 14	6.7	02 02	8.8	14 23	8.4	03 21	3.5	16 04	3.1	05 55	5.2	18 15	5.0
TU	9	05 34	6.5	17 46	6.4	02 39	8.4	15 03	8.1	03 58	3.4	16 43	3.1	06 35	5.0	18 57	4.8
W	10	06 07	6.2	18 21	6.2	03 20	8.0	15 49	7.7	04 36	3.3	17 25	3.0	07 20	4.7	19 44	4.6
TH	11	06 46	6.0	19 06	5.9	04 11	7.5	16 46	7.3	05 19	3.1	18 13	2.9	08 12	4.5	20 37	4.4
F	12	07 40	5.7	20 15	5.7	05 17	7.2	17 58	7.2	06 11	2.9	19 10	2.8	09 12	4.4	21 37	4.4
SA	13	08 59	5.6	21 42	5.7	06 35	7.1	19 13	7.4	07 13	2.8	20 21	2.8	10 16	4.3	22 42	4.5
SU	14	10 14	5.8	22 52	6.0	07 49	7.3	20 17	7.8	08 26	2.8	21 38	3.0	11 24	4.5	23 48	4.7
M	15	11 23	6.2	23 53	6.4	08 48	7.8	21 08	8.3	09 44	2.9	22 37	3.1	12 28	4.7	—	—
TU	16	12 21	6.5	—	—	09 36	8.2	21 52	8.8	10 43	3.0	23 22	3.3	00 46	4.9	13 20	5.0
W	17	00 44	6.8	13 10	6.8	10 17	8.7	22 32	9.2	11 29	3.1	—	—	01 34	5.2	14 02	5.3
TH	18	01 31	7.0	13 54	7.0	10 57	9.1	23 12	9.5	00 01	3.4	12 11	3.2	02 14	5.5	14 41	5.5
F	19	02 14	7.2	14 35	7.1	11 36	9.3	23 52	9.7	00 38	3.5	12 53	3.3	02 52	5.7	15 20	5.7
SA	20	02 55	7.3	15 15	7.2	12 16	9.5	—	—	01 17	3.6	13 35	3.3	03 29	5.8	15 59	5.8
SU	21	03 36	7.4	15 54	7.3	00 33	9.8	12 58	9.5	01 57	3.7	14 17	3.4	04 09	5.9	16 40	5.8
M	22	04 16	7.3	16 32	7.2	01 16	9.8	13 40	9.3	02 38	3.7	14 59	3.4	04 51	5.9	17 23	5.6
TU	23	04 57	7.1	17 12	7.1	02 00	9.5	14 25	9.0	03 19	3.7	15 41	3.4	05 36	5.7	18 10	5.4
W	24	05 40	6.8	17 56	6.9	02 47	9.2	15 15	8.6	04 02	3.6	16 24	3.4	06 24	5.5	19 01	5.2
TH	25	06 27	6.5	18 47	6.6	03 42	8.7	16 14	8.2	04 48	3.4	17 11	3.3	07 22	5.2	20 04	4.9
F	26	07 27	6.2	19 54	6.4	04 49	8.2	17 30	7.8	05 42	3.1	18 06	3.1	08 34	4.9	21 18	4.8
SA	27	08 41	6.0	21 15	6.3	06 09	7.9	18 52	7.8	07 02	2.9	19 23	3.0	09 54	4.8	22 33	4.8
SU	28	09 59	6.1	22 34	6.4	07 31	7.9	20 08	8.2	09 04	2.9	21 13	3.0	11 12	4.8	23 45	5.0
M	29	11 18	6.3	23 48	6.7	08 42	8.3	21 09	8.6	10 17	3.0	22 22	3.2	12 22	5.0	—	—
TU	30	12 24	6.6	—	—	09 39	8.6	21 59	9.0	11 11	3.2	23 14	3.4	00 46	5.2	13 17	5.2
W	31	00 48	7.0	13 16	6.9	10 25	8.9	22 41	9.2	11 58	3.3	23 58	3.5	01 36	5.4	14 02	5.4

SEPTEMBER 2016 *High Water* GMT

	LONDON BRIDGE Datum 3.20m below				LIVERPOOL (Gladstone Dock) Datum 4.93m below				GREENOCK Datum 1.62m below				LEITH Datum 2.90m below			
	hr m	ht m	hr m	ht m	hr m	ht m	hr m	ht m	hr m	ht m	hr m	ht m	hr m	ht m	hr m	ht m
TH 1	01 37	7.1	13 59	7.0	11 04	9.1	23 19	9.4	12 40	3.3	—	—	02 18	5.6	14 41	5.5
F 2	02 18	7.2	14 37	7.1	11 40	9.2	23 53	9.4	00 38	3.6	13 19	3.3	02 57	5.6	15 17	5.5
SA 3	02 56	7.2	15 11	7.1	12 12	9.2	—	—	01 15	3.6	13 52	3.2	03 34	5.6	15 52	5.4
SU 4	03 29	7.1	15 42	7.1	00 26	9.3	12 44	9.1	01 48	3.6	14 22	3.2	04 09	5.5	16 26	5.4
M 5	03 59	7.0	16 12	7.0	00 57	9.1	13 15	8.9	02 20	3.6	14 53	3.3	04 44	5.4	17 01	5.2
TU 6	04 27	6.8	16 41	6.8	01 28	8.9	13 47	8.6	02 53	3.6	15 27	3.3	05 19	5.2	17 37	5.1
W 7	04 56	6.6	17 11	6.6	02 01	8.5	14 22	8.3	03 27	3.5	16 03	3.2	05 56	5.0	18 15	4.9
TH 8	05 26	6.4	17 44	6.3	02 36	8.1	15 01	7.9	04 04	3.4	16 42	3.1	06 38	4.8	18 59	4.7
F 9	06 01	6.1	18 23	6.1	03 18	7.6	15 50	7.5	04 45	3.2	17 27	3.0	07 26	4.6	19 50	4.5
SA 10	06 44	5.8	19 13	5.8	04 16	7.2	17 01	7.2	05 35	3.0	18 21	2.9	08 25	4.4	20 52	4.4
SU 11	07 45	5.6	20 32	5.6	05 40	6.9	18 25	7.2	06 35	2.8	19 29	2.8	09 33	4.3	22 00	4.4
M 12	09 23	5.6	22 07	5.9	07 08	7.1	19 39	7.6	07 49	2.8	20 54	2.9	10 45	4.4	23 10	4.6
TU 13	10 43	6.0	23 16	6.3	08 17	7.7	20 37	8.2	09 16	2.9	22 03	3.1	11 54	4.7	—	—
W 14	11 47	6.5	—	—	09 09	8.3	21 24	8.8	10 22	3.1	22 51	3.3	00 13	4.9	12 50	5.1
TH 15	00 13	6.8	12 40	6.8	09 52	8.8	22 07	9.4	11 10	3.2	23 33	3.5	01 04	5.3	13 35	5.4
F 16	01 03	7.1	13 26	7.1	10 33	9.3	22 48	9.8	11 52	3.3	—	—	01 47	5.6	14 15	5.7
SA 17	01 48	7.3	14 10	7.3	11 13	9.6	23 29	10.0	00 14	3.6	12 33	3.4	02 26	5.8	14 54	5.9
SU 18	02 32	7.5	14 51	7.4	11 54	9.8	—	—	00 56	3.7	13 14	3.5	03 05	6.0	15 34	6.0
M 19	03 14	7.5	15 31	7.5	00 11	10.1	12 36	9.8	01 39	3.8	13 56	3.5	03 46	6.1	16 16	5.9
TU 20	03 55	7.4	16 11	7.5	00 55	10.0	13 19	9.6	02 22	3.8	14 37	3.6	04 30	6.0	17 00	5.8
W 21	04 36	7.1	16 52	7.3	01 40	9.7	14 04	9.2	03 05	3.8	15 19	3.6	05 17	5.8	17 47	5.5
TH 22	05 18	6.8	17 37	7.0	02 28	9.2	14 54	8.7	03 48	3.6	16 01	3.5	06 08	5.5	18 40	5.2
F 23	06 05	6.4	18 28	6.7	03 23	8.6	15 54	8.2	04 34	3.4	16 47	3.4	07 08	5.2	19 44	4.9
SA 24	07 02	6.1	19 35	6.4	04 33	8.0	17 12	7.8	05 27	3.1	17 41	3.2	08 22	4.9	21 01	4.7
SU 25	08 16	5.9	20 55	6.2	05 56	7.7	18 36	7.8	06 53	2.8	18 57	3.0	09 42	4.7	22 17	4.7
M 26	09 39	6.0	22 16	6.3	07 21	7.8	19 53	8.1	09 01	2.9	20 55	3.0	11 01	4.8	23 30	4.9
TU 27	10 59	6.2	23 31	6.7	08 31	8.2	20 54	8.5	10 06	3.1	22 02	3.2	12 11	5.0	—	—
W 28	12 04	6.6	—	—	09 24	8.6	21 41	8.9	10 55	3.3	22 53	3.4	00 31	5.2	13 04	5.2
TH 29	00 30	7.0	12 54	6.9	10 06	8.9	22 21	9.1	11 38	3.4	23 36	3.5	01 19	5.4	13 45	5.3
F 30	01 16	7.1	13 36	7.0	10 42	9.1	22 55	9.3	12 16	3.4	—	—	01 59	5.5	14 20	5.4

OCTOBER 2016 *High Water* GMT

	LONDON BRIDGE				LIVERPOOL (Gladstone Dock)				GREENOCK				LEITH			
	hr m	ht m	hr m	ht m	hr m	ht m	hr m	ht m	hr m	ht m	hr m	ht m	hr m	ht m	hr m	ht m
SA 1	01 55	7.1	14 11	7.0	11 14	9.2	23 27	9.3	00 15	3.6	12 51	3.4	02 35	5.5	14 53	5.5
SU 2	02 29	7.1	14 43	7.1	11 45	9.2	23 58	9.2	00 50	3.6	13 21	3.4	03 09	5.5	15 24	5.4
M 3	02 59	7.1	15 12	7.1	12 14	9.2	—	—	01 21	3.6	13 49	3.4	03 42	5.5	15 56	5.4
TU 4	03 26	7.0	15 41	7.1	00 28	9.1	12 45	9.0	01 53	3.6	14 20	3.4	04 15	5.4	16 28	5.3
W 5	03 54	6.9	16 11	6.9	00 59	8.9	13 16	8.8	02 25	3.6	14 53	3.5	04 49	5.2	17 02	5.2
TH 6	04 23	6.7	16 42	6.7	01 30	8.6	13 48	8.5	03 00	3.5	15 27	3.4	05 25	5.1	17 39	5.0
F 7	04 54	6.5	17 15	6.5	02 03	8.2	14 24	8.1	03 37	3.4	16 04	3.3	06 05	4.9	18 20	4.8
SA 8	05 27	6.2	17 53	6.2	02 42	7.8	15 09	7.7	04 18	3.3	16 45	3.2	06 50	4.6	19 08	4.7
SU 9	06 08	6.0	18 40	6.0	03 34	7.4	16 12	7.4	05 05	3.1	17 36	3.0	07 45	4.5	20 07	4.5
M 10	07 02	5.7	19 44	5.8	04 50	7.1	17 36	7.3	06 03	2.9	18 43	2.9	08 52	4.4	21 18	4.5
TU 11	08 22	5.6	21 19	5.9	06 21	7.2	18 56	7.7	07 16	2.8	20 05	2.9	10 06	4.5	22 31	4.6
W 12	09 58	5.9	22 36	6.3	07 38	7.7	20 00	8.2	08 44	2.9	21 22	3.1	11 17	4.8	23 37	4.9
TH 13	11 08	6.4	23 38	6.8	08 36	8.3	20 52	8.9	09 55	3.1	22 17	3.4	12 16	5.1	—	—
F 14	12 05	6.8	—	—	09 23	9.0	21 38	9.5	10 45	3.3	23 04	3.5	00 31	5.3	13 05	5.5
SA 15	00 32	7.2	12 56	7.2	10 07	9.5	22 22	9.9	11 28	3.5	23 49	3.7	01 17	5.6	13 48	5.8
SU 16	01 21	7.4	13 42	7.4	10 49	9.8	23 06	10.2	12 10	3.6	—	—	01 59	5.9	14 28	6.0
M 17	02 06	7.5	14 26	7.6	11 32	10.0	23 50	10.2	00 35	3.8	12 53	3.6	02 41	6.1	15 10	6.1
TU 18	02 51	7.5	15 09	7.6	12 15	10.0	—	—	01 21	3.8	13 35	3.7	03 25	6.2	15 53	6.0
W 19	03 34	7.4	15 51	7.6	00 35	10.1	12 59	9.7	02 06	3.8	14 17	3.7	04 12	6.1	16 39	5.8
TH 20	04 17	7.1	16 35	7.4	01 23	9.7	13 45	9.4	02 51	3.8	14 59	3.7	05 01	5.9	17 28	5.6
F 21	05 00	6.8	17 22	7.1	02 12	9.2	14 36	8.8	03 36	3.6	15 42	3.6	05 55	5.5	18 22	5.3
SA 22	05 46	6.4	18 14	6.7	03 08	8.5	15 37	8.3	04 24	3.4	16 28	3.5	06 56	5.2	19 27	5.0
SU 23	06 41	6.1	19 18	6.4	04 16	8.0	16 51	7.9	05 21	3.1	17 21	3.3	08 08	4.9	20 41	4.8
M 24	07 51	5.9	20 32	6.2	05 36	7.6	18 11	7.8	06 48	2.9	18 34	3.1	09 23	4.7	21 54	4.8
TU 25	09 10	5.9	21 48	6.3	06 57	7.7	19 26	8.0	08 37	2.9	20 19	3.1	10 37	4.7	23 04	4.9
W 26	10 27	6.1	23 02	6.5	08 07	8.0	20 27	8.4	09 40	3.1	21 31	3.2	11 46	4.9	—	—
TH 27	11 33	6.4	—	—	08 59	8.4	21 15	8.7	10 28	3.3	22 23	3.4	00 05	5.1	12 40	5.1
F 28	00 02	6.8	12 25	6.7	09 41	8.7	21 54	8.9	11 10	3.4	23 07	3.5	00 55	5.2	13 21	5.2
SA 29	00 49	6.9	13 06	6.8	10 16	8.9	22 29	9.1	11 47	3.5	23 46	3.5	01 35	5.3	13 55	5.3
SU 30	01 27	6.9	13 42	6.9	10 47	9.1	23 01	9.1	12 20	3.5	—	—	02 11	5.4	14 27	5.4
M 31	02 00	7.0	14 14	7.0	11 18	9.2	23 32	9.1	00 21	3.5	12 51	3.5	02 45	5.4	14 57	5.4

NOVEMBER 2016   *High Water*   GMT

LONDON BRIDGE — Datum of Predictions 3.20m below
LIVERPOOL (Gladstone Dock) — Datum of Predictions 4.93m below
GREENOCK — Datum of Predictions 1.62m below
LEITH — Datum of Predictions 2.90m below

Day	LONDON BRIDGE hr m ht	hr m ht	LIVERPOOL hr m ht	hr m ht	GREENOCK hr m ht	hr m ht	LEITH hr m ht	hr m ht
TU 1	02 29 7.0	14 44 7.1	11 48 9.2	— —	00 54 3.5	13 21 3.6	03 17 5.4	15 28 5.4
W 2	02 57 7.0	15 14 7.1	00 03 9.0	12 19 9.1	01 26 3.5	13 52 3.6	03 50 5.3	16 00 5.4
TH 3	03 26 6.9	15 45 7.0	00 35 8.9	12 50 8.9	02 00 3.5	14 24 3.6	04 24 5.2	16 34 5.3
F 4	03 57 6.8	16 17 6.8	01 07 8.6	13 23 8.7	02 36 3.5	14 58 3.6	05 00 5.1	17 10 5.1
SA 5	04 29 6.6	16 53 6.6	01 40 8.3	13 59 8.4	03 14 3.5	15 33 3.5	05 39 5.0	17 49 5.0
SU 6	05 04 6.4	17 32 6.4	02 20 8.0	14 43 8.1	03 55 3.3	16 12 3.3	06 23 4.8	18 35 4.8
M 7	05 44 6.2	18 19 6.2	03 09 7.7	15 40 7.8	04 41 3.2	16 59 3.2	07 15 4.6	19 29 4.6
TU 8	06 34 5.9	19 17 6.1	04 14 7.4	16 54 7.6	05 35 3.0	18 00 3.1	08 16 4.6	20 35 4.6
W 9	07 41 5.8	20 37 6.1	05 36 7.4	18 12 7.8	06 43 3.0	19 17 3.1	09 28 4.6	21 50 4.7
TH 10	09 12 5.9	21 57 6.4	06 54 7.8	19 20 8.3	08 04 3.0	20 37 3.2	10 39 4.8	22 58 4.9
F 11	10 28 6.3	23 02 6.8	07 59 8.3	20 18 8.9	09 19 3.2	21 42 3.4	11 41 5.1	23 56 5.3
SA 12	11 30 6.8	— —	08 53 8.9	21 10 9.4	10 15 3.4	22 36 3.6	12 33 5.5	— —
SU 13	00 01 7.1	12 25 7.1	09 41 9.4	21 58 9.8	11 03 3.5	23 26 3.7	00 47 5.6	13 20 5.8
M 14	00 54 7.3	13 15 7.4	10 26 9.8	22 45 10.1	11 48 3.7	— —	01 34 5.9	14 04 6.0
TU 15	01 43 7.4	14 02 7.6	11 12 10.0	23 33 10.1	00 15 3.8	12 33 3.7	02 21 6.1	14 48 6.0
W 16	02 30 7.4	14 49 7.6	11 57 10.0	— —	01 04 3.8	13 17 3.8	03 08 6.1	15 34 6.0
TH 17	03 15 7.3	15 35 7.6	00 20 10.0	12 43 9.8	01 53 3.8	14 00 3.9	03 57 6.0	16 21 5.9
F 18	04 00 7.1	16 21 7.4	01 09 9.6	13 30 9.5	02 40 3.7	14 43 3.8	04 48 5.8	17 11 5.6
SA 19	04 45 6.8	17 09 7.1	01 59 9.1	14 21 9.0	03 27 3.5	15 26 3.7	05 42 5.5	18 05 5.3
SU 20	05 31 6.5	18 00 6.8	02 53 8.6	15 17 8.5	04 17 3.4	16 12 3.6	06 41 5.2	19 07 5.1
M 21	06 21 6.2	18 57 6.4	03 53 8.1	16 21 8.1	05 12 3.1	17 04 3.4	07 45 4.9	20 15 4.9
TU 22	07 22 6.0	20 02 6.2	05 01 7.7	17 32 7.9	06 22 3.0	18 06 3.2	08 52 4.7	21 22 4.8
W 23	08 32 5.9	21 10 6.2	06 15 7.6	18 43 7.9	07 46 2.9	19 26 3.1	09 59 4.7	22 27 4.8
TH 24	09 43 6.0	22 18 6.3	07 26 7.8	19 48 8.0	08 57 3.0	20 44 3.2	11 05 4.7	23 29 4.9
F 25	10 50 6.2	23 22 6.4	08 23 8.1	20 40 8.3	09 51 3.2	21 45 3.3	12 03 4.9	— —
SA 26	11 46 6.4	— —	09 09 8.4	21 24 8.5	10 35 3.3	22 33 3.4	00 22 5.0	12 49 5.0
SU 27	00 13 6.6	12 32 6.6	09 46 8.7	22 02 8.7	11 15 3.5	23 15 3.4	01 08 5.1	13 27 5.2
M 28	00 55 6.7	13 12 6.8	10 21 8.9	22 37 8.9	11 51 3.5	23 53 3.4	01 47 5.2	14 01 5.3
TU 29	01 31 6.8	13 47 6.9	10 53 9.0	23 10 8.9	12 25 3.6	— —	02 22 5.3	14 33 5.4
W 30	02 03 6.9	14 20 7.0	11 25 9.1	23 43 8.9	00 27 3.5	12 58 3.6	02 56 5.3	15 05 5.4

DECEMBER 2016   *High Water*   GMT

LONDON BRIDGE
LIVERPOOL (Gladstone Dock)
GREENOCK
LEITH

Day	LONDON BRIDGE hr m ht	hr m ht	LIVERPOOL hr m ht	hr m ht	GREENOCK hr m ht	hr m ht	LEITH hr m ht	hr m ht
TH 1	02 33 6.9	14 51 7.0	11 58 9.1	— —	01 02 3.5	13 29 3.7	03 30 5.3	15 38 5.4
F 2	03 05 6.9	15 24 7.0	00 16 8.8	12 31 9.0	01 38 3.5	14 01 3.7	04 04 5.3	16 12 5.3
SA 3	03 38 6.8	15 59 6.9	00 50 8.7	13 06 8.9	02 15 3.5	14 35 3.7	04 40 5.2	16 48 5.2
SU 4	04 13 6.7	16 36 6.8	01 25 8.5	13 43 8.7	02 55 3.5	15 11 3.6	05 19 5.1	17 26 5.1
M 5	04 49 6.5	17 17 6.6	02 05 8.3	14 25 8.5	03 36 3.4	15 50 3.5	06 02 5.0	18 09 5.0
TU 6	05 29 6.4	18 02 6.5	02 51 8.0	15 16 8.2	04 21 3.3	16 34 3.4	06 50 4.9	18 58 4.9
W 7	06 16 6.2	18 55 6.3	03 48 7.8	16 19 8.1	05 10 3.2	17 26 3.3	07 45 4.8	19 57 4.8
TH 8	07 13 6.1	20 03 6.2	04 57 7.7	17 30 8.1	06 08 3.1	18 33 3.2	08 51 4.7	21 07 4.8
F 9	08 29 6.1	21 21 6.4	06 11 7.9	18 41 8.3	07 19 3.1	19 53 3.2	10 01 4.9	22 20 4.9
SA 10	09 50 6.3	22 29 6.6	07 22 8.3	19 46 8.7	08 37 3.2	21 08 3.3	11 06 5.1	23 25 5.2
SU 11	10 57 6.6	23 32 6.8	08 23 8.7	20 45 9.1	09 44 3.3	22 11 3.5	12 04 5.3	— —
M 12	11 58 7.0	— —	09 18 9.2	21 39 9.5	10 39 3.5	23 07 3.6	00 22 5.5	12 57 5.6
TU 13	00 30 7.0	12 53 7.2	10 08 9.5	22 30 9.7	11 29 3.6	— —	01 15 5.7	13 45 5.8
W 14	01 23 7.1	13 44 7.4	10 56 9.8	23 20 9.8	00 00 3.7	12 17 3.7	02 05 5.9	14 31 5.9
TH 15	02 13 7.2	14 33 7.5	11 44 9.9	— —	00 52 3.7	13 02 3.8	02 55 6.0	15 18 5.9
F 16	03 01 7.2	15 22 7.5	00 09 9.8	12 31 9.8	01 42 3.7	13 46 3.9	03 45 5.9	16 06 5.8
SA 17	03 47 7.1	16 09 7.4	00 57 9.5	13 17 9.5	02 30 3.6	14 29 3.9	04 35 5.8	16 56 5.7
SU 18	04 32 6.9	16 55 7.1	01 44 9.2	14 04 9.2	03 17 3.5	15 12 3.8	05 26 5.5	17 47 5.5
M 19	05 15 6.7	17 42 6.8	02 32 8.7	14 52 8.8	04 04 3.3	15 56 3.7	06 19 5.2	18 42 5.2
TU 20	05 59 6.4	18 31 6.5	03 21 8.3	15 44 8.4	04 52 3.2	16 43 3.5	07 14 5.0	19 40 5.0
W 21	06 47 6.1	19 23 6.2	04 16 7.8	16 43 8.0	05 43 3.1	17 33 3.3	08 11 4.7	20 40 4.8
TH 22	07 45 5.9	20 22 6.0	05 19 7.6	17 48 7.7	06 41 3.0	18 30 3.2	09 09 4.6	21 40 4.7
F 23	08 50 5.8	21 23 6.0	06 27 7.5	18 55 7.7	07 47 2.9	19 36 3.1	10 09 4.5	22 41 4.7
SA 24	09 55 5.9	22 26 6.0	07 34 7.6	19 58 7.8	08 55 3.0	20 48 3.1	11 10 4.6	23 41 4.7
SU 25	10 58 6.1	23 27 6.2	08 30 7.9	20 51 8.1	09 54 3.2	21 52 3.2	12 08 4.7	— —
M 26	11 54 6.3	— —	09 16 8.3	21 36 8.3	10 42 3.3	22 43 3.3	00 35 4.8	12 56 4.9
TU 27	00 19 6.4	12 41 6.6	09 55 8.6	22 15 8.5	11 24 3.5	23 26 3.3	01 21 5.0	13 36 5.1
W 28	01 02 6.6	13 22 6.7	10 32 8.8	22 51 8.7	12 03 3.6	— —	02 01 5.1	14 12 5.3
TH 29	01 41 6.7	13 59 6.8	11 06 9.0	23 26 8.8	00 05 3.3	12 38 3.6	02 37 5.2	14 47 5.4
F 30	02 17 6.8	14 34 6.9	11 41 9.1	— —	00 43 3.4	13 10 3.7	03 12 5.3	15 21 5.4
SA 31	02 51 6.8	15 09 7.0	00 00 8.9	12 16 9.2	01 20 3.4	13 42 3.7	03 46 5.3	15 55 5.4

ABBREVIATIONS AND ACRONYMS

A

AAA — Amateur Athletic Association
ABA — Amateur Boxing Association
abr — abridged
ac — alternating current
AC — *ante Christum* before Christ
Companion, Order of Australia
ADC — Aide-de-Camp
ADC (P) — Personal ADC to the Queen
Adj. — Adjutant
Adj. Gen. — Adjutant General
Adm. — Admiral
AE — Air Efficiency award
AEM — Air Efficiency Medal
aet — after extra time
AFC — Air Force Cross
AFM — Air Force Medal
AG — Attorney-General
AH — *anno Hegirae* in the year of the Hegira
AM — Assembly Member (Wales)
ANC — African National Congress
AO — Air Officer
Officer, Order of Australia
AOC — Air Officer Commanding
apptd — appointed
APR — annual percentage rate
ASBO — antisocial behaviour order
AUC — *ab urbe condita* from the foundation of Rome
anno urbis conditae from the founding of the city

B

b. — born
bowled (cricket)
BAF — British Athletics Federation
BAFTA — British Academy of Film and Television Arts
BAS — Bachelor in Agricultural Science
British Antarctic Survey
BBA — British Bankers' Association
BBFC — British Board of Film Classification
BCH (D) — Bachelor of (Dental) Surgery
BCL — Bachelor of Civil Law
BCOM — Bachelor of Commerce
BD — Bachelor of Divinity
BDA — British Dental Association
BDS — Bachelor of Dental Surgery
BED — Bachelor of Education
BEM — British Empire Medal
BENG — Bachelor of Engineering
BFPO — British Forces Post Office
BLIT — Bachelor of Literature
BLITT — Bachelor of Letters
BM — Bachelor of Medicine
BMA — British Medical Association
BMUS — Bachelor of Music
Bp — Bishop
BPHARM — Bachelor of Pharmacy
BPHIL — Bachelor of Philosophy
BPS — British Psychological Society

Brig. — Brigadier
BSI — British Standards Institution
BST — British Summer Time
Bt. — Baronet
BTEC — Business and Technology Education Council
BVMS — Bachelor of Veterinary Medicine and Surgery

C

c. — *circa* about
C. — Conservative
Cantuar: — of Canterbury (Archbishop)
Capt. — Captain
Carliol — of Carlisle (Bishop)
CB — Companion, Order of the Bath
CBE — Commander, Order of the British Empire
CC — Companion, Order of Canada
CCF — Combined Cadet Force
CCHEM — chartered chemist
CD — Civil Defence
Corps Diplomatique
Cdr — Commander
Cdre — Commodore
CDS — Chief of the Defence Staff
CE — civil engineer
Common (or Christian) Era
CENG — chartered engineer
Cestr: — of Chester (Bishop)
CET — Central European Time
cf — *confer* compare
CGC — Conspicuous Gallantry Cross
CGEOL — chartered geologist
CGM — Conspicuous Gallantry Medal
CGS — Chief of General Staff
CH — Companion of Honour
CHB/M — Bachelor/Master of Surgery
CI — Channel Islands
Cicestr: — of Chichester (Bishop)
CID — Criminal Investigation Department
CIE — Companion, Order of the Indian Empire
C-in-C — Commander-in-Chief
CILIP — Chartered Institute of Library and Information Professionals
CIPFA — Chartered Institute of Public Finance and Accountancy
CIS — Commonwealth of Independent States
CLJ — Commander, Order of St Lazarus of Jerusalem
CM — *Chirurgiae Magister* Master of Surgery
CMG — Companion, Order of St Michael and St George
CO — Commanding Officer
C of E — Church of England
Col. — Colonel
cons. — consecrated
Cpl. — Corporal
CPM — Colonial Police Medal

CPS — Crown Prosecution Service
CSI — Companion, Order of the Star of India
CVO — Commander, Royal Victorian Order

D

d — *denarius* penny
d. — died
DAB — Digital Audio Broadcasting
DBE — Dame Commander, Order of the British Empire
DCB — Dame Commander, Order of the Bath
D CH — *Doctor Chirurgiae* Doctor of Surgery
DCL — Doctor of Civil Law
DCM — Distinguished Conduct Medal
DCMG — Dame Commander, Order of St Michael and St George
DCVO — Dame Commander, Royal Victorian Order
DD — Doctor of Divinity
DDS — Doctor of Dental Surgery
DDT — dichlorodiphenyl trichloroethane
DFC — Distinguished Flying Cross
DFM — Distinguished Flying Medal
DIP ED — Diploma in Education
DIP HE — Diploma in Higher Education
DL — Deputy Lieutenant
DLIT — Doctor of Literature
DLITT — Doctor of Letters
DLR — Docklands Light Railway
DMUS — Doctor of Music
DNA — deoxyribonucleic acid
DPH *or* — Doctor of Philosophy
DPHIL
DPP — Director of Public Prosecutions
DSC — Distinguished Service Cross
DSc — Doctor of Science
DSM — Distinguished Service Medal
DSO — Companion, Distinguished Service Order
Dunelm: — of Durham (Bishop)
DUP — Democratic Unionist Party

E

Ebor: — of York (Archbishop)
EC — Elizabeth Cross
European Community
ECG — electrocardiogram
ED — Efficiency Decoration
EEG — electroencephalogram
EEU — Eurasian Economic Union
EIB — European Investment Bank
ER — *Elizabetha Regina* Queen Elizabeth
ERM — exchange rate mechanism
ESA — European Space Agency
ETA — *Euzkadi ta Askatasuna* Basque separatist organisation

et seq — *et sequentia* and the following

Exon: — of Exeter (Bishop)

F

FANY — First Aid Nursing Yeomanry

FAQ — frequently asked questions

FARC — *Fuerzas Armadas Revolucionarias de Colombia* Revolutionary Armed Forces of Colombia

FBA — Fellow, British Academy

FBAA — Fellow, British Association of Accountants and Auditors

FBS — Fellow, Botanical Society

FBU — Fire Brigades Union

FCA — Fellow, Institute of Chartered Accountants in England and Wales

FCCA — Fellow, Chartered Association of Certified Accountants

FCGI — Fellow, City and Guilds of London Institute

FCIA — Fellow, Corporation of Insurance Agents

FCIARB — Fellow, Chartered Institute of Arbitrators

FCIB — Fellow, Chartered Institute of Bankers
Fellow, Corporation of Insurance Brokers

FCIBSE — Fellow, Chartered Institution of Building Services Engineers

FCII — Fellow, Chartered Insurance Institute

FCIPS — Fellow, Chartered Institute of Purchasing and Supply

FCIS — Fellow, Institute of Chartered Secretaries and Administrators

FCIT — Fellow, Chartered Institute of Transport

FCMA — Fellow, Chartered Institute of Management Accountants

FCP — Fellow, College of Preceptors

FD — *Fidei Defensor* Defender of the Faith

FE — further education

FFA — Fellow, Faculty of Actuaries (Scotland)
Fellow, Institute of Financial Accountants

FFAS — Fellow, Faculty of Architects and Surveyors

FFCM — Fellow, Faculty of Community Medicine

FFPHM — Fellow, Faculty of Public Health Medicine

FGS — Fellow, Geological Society

FHS — Fellow, Heraldry Society

FHSM — Fellow, Institute of Health Service Management

FIA — Fellow, Institute of Actuaries

FIBIOL — Fellow, Institute of Biology

FICE — Fellow, Institution of Civil Engineers

FICS — Fellow, Institution of Chartered Shipbrokers

FIEE — Fellow, Institution of Electrical Engineers

FIERE — Fellow, Institution of Electronic and Radio Engineers

FIM — Fellow, Institute of Metals

FIMGT — Fellow, Institute of Management

FIMM — Fellow, Institution of Mining and Metallurgy

FINSTF — Fellow, Institute of Fuel

FINSTP — Fellow, Institute of Physics

FIQS — Fellow, Institute of Quantity Surveyors

FIS — Fellow, Institute of Statisticians

FJI — Fellow, Institute of Journalists

FLS — Fellow, Linnean Society

FMEDSCI — Fellow, Academy of Medical Sciences

fo — folio

FPHS — Fellow, Philosophical Society

FRAD — Fellow, Royal Academy of Dancing

FRAES — Fellow, Royal Aeronautical Society

FRAGS — Fellow, Royal Agricultural Societies

FRAI — Fellow, Royal Anthropological Institute

FRAM — Fellow, Royal Academy of Music

FRAS — Fellow, Royal Asiatic Society
Fellow, Royal Astronomical Society

FRBS — Fellow, Royal Botanic Society
Fellow, Royal Society of British Sculptors

FRCA — Fellow, Royal College of Anaesthetists

FRCGP — Fellow, Royal College of General Practitioners

FRCM — Fellow, Royal College of Music

FRCO — Fellow, Royal College of Organists

FRCOG — Fellow, Royal College of Obstetricians and Gynaecologists

FRCP — Fellow, Royal College of Physicians, London

FRCPATH — Fellow, Royal College of Pathologists

FRCPE *or* FRCPED — Fellow, Royal College of Physicians, Edinburgh

FRCPI — Fellow, Royal College of Physicians, Ireland

FRCPSYCH — Fellow, Royal College of Psychiatrists

FRCR — Fellow, Royal College of Radiologists

FRCS — Fellow, Royal College of Surgeons of England

FRCSE *or* FRCSED — Fellow, Royal College of Surgeons of Edinburgh

FRCSGLAS — Fellow, Royal College of Physicians and Surgeons of Glasgow

FRCSI — Fellow, Royal College of Surgeons in Ireland

FRCVS — Fellow, Royal College of Veterinary Surgeons

FRECONS — Fellow, Royal Economic Society

FRENG — Fellow, Royal Academy of Engineering

FRGS — Fellow, Royal Geographical Society

FRHISTS — Fellow, Royal Historical Society

FRHS — Fellow, Royal Horticultural Society

FRIBA — Fellow, Royal Institute of British Architects

FRICS — Fellow, Royal Institution of Chartered Surveyors

FRMETS — Fellow, Royal Meteorological Society

FRMS — Fellow, Royal Microscopical Society

FRNS — Fellow, Royal Numismatic Society

FRPHARMS — Fellow, Royal Pharmaceutical Society

FRPS — Fellow, Royal Photographic Society

FRS — Fellow, Royal Society

FRSA — Fellow, Royal Society of Arts

FRSC — Fellow, Royal Society of Chemistry

FRSE — Fellow, Royal Society of Edinburgh

FRSH — Fellow, Royal Society of Health

FRSL — Fellow, Royal Society of Literature

FRTPI — Fellow, Royal Town Planning Institute

FSA — Fellow, Society of Antiquaries

FSS — Fellow, Royal Statistical Society

FSVA — Fellow, Incorporated Society of Valuers and Auctioneers

FTI — Fellow, Textile Institute

FTII — Fellow, Chartered Institute of Taxation

FZS — Fellow, Zoological Society

G

GBE — Dame/Knight Grand Cross, Order of the British Empire

GC — George Cross

GCB — Dame/Knight Grand Cross, Order of the Bath

GCLJ — Knight Grand Cross, Order of St Lazarus of Jerusalem

GCMG — Dame/Knight Grand Cross, Order of St Michael and St George

GCSI — Knight Grand Commander, Order of the Star of India

GCVO — Dame/Knight Grand Cross, Royal Victorian Order

Gen. — General

GHQ — general headquarters

GLA — Greater London Authority

GM — George Medal

GMB   Britain's General Union
GOC   General Officer Commanding
Gp Capt.   Group Captain
GPS   Global Positioning System
H
HB   His Beatitude
HBM   Her/His Britannic Majesty('s)
HCF   Honorary Chaplain to the Forces
HE   Her/His Excellency
   higher education
   His Eminence
HH   Her/His Highness
   Her/His Honour
   His Holiness
HIM   Her/His Imperial Majesty
HJS   *hic jacet sepultus* here lies buried
HM   Her/His Majesty('s)
HMAS   Her/His Majesty's Australian Ship
HMC   Headmasters' and Headmistresses' Conference
HMI   Her/His Majesty's Inspector
HMS   Her/His Majesty's Ship
Hon.   Honorary
   Honourable
HRH   Her/His Royal Highness
HRT   hormone replacement therapy
HSE   *hic sepultus est* here is buried
HSH   Her/His Serene Highness
I
IB   International Baccalaureate
IBF   International Boxing Federation
ICC   International Cricket Council
   International Criminal Court
ICJ   International Court of Justice
id   *idem* the same
IP   intellectual property
   internet protocol
IPSA   Independent Parliamentary Standards Authority
iPSC   induced pluripotent stem cell
IRA   Irish Republican Army
IRB   International Rugby Board
IRC   International Rescue Committee
Is   Islands
IS   Islamic State
ISO   Imperial Service Order
   International Organisation for Standardisation
ISP   internet service provider
ISSN   International Standard Serial Number
ITU   International Telecommunication Union
J
J   Judge
   Justice
JP   Justice of the Peace

K
KBE   Knight Commander, Order of the British Empire
KCB   Knight Commander, Order of the Bath
KCLJ   Knight Commander, Order of St Lazarus of Jerusalem
KCMG   Knight Commander, Order of St Michael and St George
KCSI   Knight Commander, Order of the Star of India
KCVO   Knight Commander, Royal Victorian Order
KG   Knight of the Garter
KGB   *Komitet Gosudarstvennoi Bezopasnosti* Committee of State Security (USSR)
KLJ   Knight, Order of St Lazarus of Jerusalem
KP   Knight, Order of St Patrick
KStJ   Knight, Order of St John of Jerusalem
Kt.   Knight
KT   Knight of the Thistle
L
Lab.   Labour
Lat.   Latitude
lbw   leg before wicket (cricket)
lc   lower case (printing)
LCJ   Lord Chief Justice
LCM   least/lowest common multiple
LD   Liberal Democrat
LDS   Licentiate in Dental Surgery
LHD   *Literarum Humaniorum Doctor* Doctor of Humane Letters/Literature
Lib.   Liberal
LITT D   Doctor of Letters
LJ   Lord Justice
LLB   Bachelor of Laws
LLD   Doctor of Laws
LLM   Master of Laws
loc cit   *loco citato* in the place cited
Londin: of London (Bishop)
Long.   longitude
lsd   *librae, solidi, denarii* pounds, shillings and pence
Lt.   Lieutenant
LTA   Lawn Tennis Association
LVO   Lieutenant, Royal Victorian Order
M
m.   married
M   Monsieur
Maj.   Major
MB   *Medicinae Baccalaureus* Bachelor of Medicine
MBA   Master of Business Administration
MBC   Metropolitan Borough Council
MBE   Member, Order of the British Empire
MBO   management buy-out
MC   Master of Ceremonies
   Military Cross
MCB   Muslim Council of Britain
MCC   Marylebone Cricket Club

MCH(D)   Master of (Dental) Surgery
MDS   Master of Dental Surgery
ME   Middle English
   myalgic encephalomyelitis
MED   Master of Education
Mgr   Monsignor
MIT   Massachusetts Institute of Technology
MLA   Member of Legislative Assembly (NI)
   Museums, Libraries and Archives Council
MLITT   Master of Letters
Mlle   Mademoiselle
MM   Military Medal
Mme   Madame
MMR   measles, mumps and rubella (vaccine)
MN   Merchant Navy
MPHIL   Master of Philosophy
MR   Master of the Rolls
MRI   magnetic resonance imaging
MRSA   methicillin-resistant staphylococcus aureus
MS   manuscript (*pl* MSS)
   Master of Surgery
   multiple sclerosis
MSP   Member of Scottish Parliament
MUSB/D   Bachelor/Doctor of Music
MVO   Member, Royal Victorian Order
N
NAAFI   Navy, Army and Air Force Institutes
NAFTA   North American Free Trade Agreement
NAO   National Audit Office
NCO   non-commissioned officer
NDPB   non-departmental public body
NFU   National Farmers' Union
non seq   *non sequitur* it does not follow
Norvic: of Norwich (Bishop)
NP   Notary Public
NSW   New South Wales (Australia)
NUJ   National Union of Journalists
NUS   National Union of Students
NUT   National Union of Teachers
O
Ob *or* obit   died
OBE   Officer, Order of the British Empire
OBR   Office for Budget Responsibility
OE   Old English
OED   *Oxford English Dictionary*
OHMS   On Her/His Majesty's Service
OM   Order of Merit
ono   or near(est) offer
op   *opus* work
op cit   *opere citato* in the work cited
OS   Ordnance Survey
OStJ   Officer, Order of St John of Jerusalem

P

PC	Plaid Cymru
	Police Constable
	Privy Counsellor
Petriburg:	of Peterborough (Bishop)
PG	parental guidance
	postgraduate
PHD	Doctor of Philosophy
pl	plural
PLO	Palestine Liberation Organisation
PM	post mortem
	Prime Minister
PO	Petty Officer
	Pilot Officer
	post office
	postal order
	per procurationem by proxy
PPS	Parliamentary Private Secretary
PR	proportional representation
PRA	President of the Royal Academy
pro tem	*pro tempore* for the time being
prox	*proximo* next month
PRS	President of the Royal Society
PRSE	President of the Royal Society of Edinburgh
Pte.	Private

Q

QBD	Queen's Bench Division
QC	Queen's Counsel
QE	quantitative easing
QED	*quod erat demonstrandum* which was to be proved
QGM	Queen's Gallantry Medal
QHC	Queen's Honorary Chaplain
QHDS	Queen's Honorary Dental Surgeon
QHNS	Queen's Honorary Nursing Sister
QHP	Queen's Honorary Physician
QHS	Queen's Honorary Surgeon
QMG	Quartermaster-General
QPM	Queen's Police Medal
QSO	quasi-stellar object *(quasar)*
	Queen's Service Order
quango	quasi-autonomous non-governmental organisation
qv	*quod vide* which see

R

r.	*recto* on the right-hand page
R	*Regina* Queen
	Rex King
RA	Royal Academy/Academician
	Royal Artillery
RAC	Royal Armoured Corps
	Royal Automobile Club
RADA	Royal Academy of Dramatic Art
RADC	Royal Army Dental Corps
RAEC	Royal Army Educational Corps
RAES	Royal Aeronautical Society
RAM	Royal Academy of Music

RAMC	Royal Army Medical Corps
RAN	Royal Australian Navy
RAOC	Royal Army Ordnance Corps
RAPC	Royal Army Pay Corps
RAVC	Royal Army Veterinary Corps
RBS	Royal Society of British Sculptors
RC	Red Cross
	Roman Catholic
RCN	Royal College of Nursing
RCT	Royal Corps of Transport
RD	Royal Naval and Royal Marine Forces Reserve Decoration
	Rural Dean
RE	Royal Engineers
REME	Royal Electrical and Mechanical Engineers
Rep	Republican
Rep.	Republic
Revd	Reverend
RGS	Royal Geographical Society
RHS	Royal Horticultural Society
RI	Royal Institute of Painters in Watercolours
	Royal Institution
RIR	Royal Irish Regiment
RM	Royal Marines
RMA	Royal Military Academy
RMT	National Union of Rail, Maritime and Transport Workers
RNIB	Royal National Institute of Blind People
RNID	Royal National Institute for Deaf People
RNR	Royal Naval Reserve
RNVR	Royal Naval Volunteer Reserve
RNXS	Royal Naval Auxiliary Service
Roffen:	of Rochester (Bishop)
RPA	Rural Payments Agency
RSA	Royal Scottish Academician
	Royal Society of Arts
RSC	Royal Shakespeare Company
RSE	Royal Society of Edinburgh
Rt. Hon.	Right Honourable
RUC	Royal Ulster Constabulary

S

s	section (Public Acts)
	solidus shilling
Salop	Shropshire
Sarum:	of Salisbury (Bishop)
SCD	Doctor of Science
SDLP	Social Democratic and Labour Party
SEAQ	Stock Exchange Automated Quotations system
SEN	special educational needs
	State Enrolled Nurse
SF	Sinn Fein
SFO	Serious Fraud Office
SI	statutory instrument
	Système International d'Unités International System of Units

sic	*sic* so written
sig	signature
	Signor
SLD	Social and Liberal Democrats
SOE	Special Operations Executive
sp	*sine prole* without issue
Sr	Senior
	Sister (title)
SS	steamship
SSN	standard serial number
stet	*stet* let it stand (printing)
Sub Lt.	sub-lieutenant

T

TD	Territorial Decoration
TEFL	teaching English as a foreign language
TNT	trinitrotoluene (explosive)
trans.	translated
TRH	Their Royal Highnesses
trs	transpose (printing)

U

U	Unionist
uc	upper case (printing)
UDA	Ulster Defence Association
UG	undergraduate
USB	universal serial bus
UTC	*Temps Universel Coordonné* coordinated universal time
UVF	Ulster Volunteer Force

V

v	*versus* against
v.	*verso* on the left-hand page
	Victoria and Albert Order
VAD	Voluntary Aid Detachment (nursing)
VC	Victoria Cross
VD	Volunteer Officers' Decoration
Ven.	Venerable
VRD	Royal Naval Volunteer Reserve Officers' Decoration
VSO	Voluntary Service Overseas

W

w.	widowed
WBC	World Boxing Council
WBC	World Boxing Organisation
WCC	World Council of Churches
WFTU	World Federation of Trade Unions
Wton:	of Winchester (Bishop)
WO	Warrant Officer
WRAC	Women's Royal Army Corps
WRAF	Women's Royal Air Force
WRNS	Women's Royal Naval Service
WRVS	Women's Royal Voluntary Service
WS	Writer to the Signet

Y

YMCA	Young Men's Christian Association
YWCA	Young Women's Christian Association

Z

ZANU-PF	Zimbabwean African National Union-Patriotic Front

INDEX

G 444
216 calendar 8
2017 calendar 9
Aberavon
  constituencies
    UK parliament 166
    Welsh assembly 218
Aberconwy
  constituencies
    UK parliament 166
    Welsh assembly 218
Aberdeen 279
  airport 406
  bishop (RC) 434
  constituencies
    Scottish parliament 224
    UK parliament 169
  museums and art galleries 472
  unitary authority 253, 281
  universities 344, 352
Aberdeen and Orkney, bishop 431
Aberdeenshire
  Scottish parliament constituencies 224
  unitary authority 253, 281
Aberdeenshire West & Kincardine, UK parliament constituency 169
Abertay Dundee, university 345
Aberystwyth, university 345
ABI (Association of British Insurers) 499
abortion
  legal notes 519
academic staff
  see also teachers
Academies Act 2010 329
academies (England only) 329
academies of scholarship 373
Academy of Medical Sciences 373
ACAS (Advisory, Conciliation and Arbitration Service) 196
accidents
  on railways 408
  road 410
accountancy, professional education 355
Achonry, bishop (RC) 435
Action of Churches Together in Scotland 415
actuarial science, professional education 355
additional adoption leave 529
additional maternity leave 529
additional state pension 386
Adjudicator's Office 196
administration court 290
Administrative Appeals Chamber 306
admirals of the fleet 317
admiralty court 290
Adopted Children Register 519
adoption 519
  local authority service 385
Adoption Contact Register 520
adult and continuing education see lifelong learning
Adur, district council 250, 263
advanced (A) level examinations 334
advanced higher national course 336
'advanced skills teacher' grade 342

Advent Sunday 637
Advisory, Conciliation and Arbitration Service (ACAS) 196
Advisory Council on National Records and Archives 196
Advocate-General for Scotland, Office of 186
AFCS (armed forces compensation scheme) 390
agricultural properties
  and inheritance tax 514
  tenancies 534
Agriculture and Horticulture Development Board 196
AHRC (Arts and Humanities Research Council) 375
AIM (Alternative Investment Market) 494
Airdrie & Shotts
  constituencies
    Scottish parliament 224
    UK parliament 169
air force see Royal Air Force
airlines 406
airmail letter rates see international standard mail rates
air passenger numbers 406
airports 406
AIRTO (Association of Independent Research and Technology Organisations Limited) 377
air transport 406
aldermen 248, 269
Alderney 286
  airport 406
Aldershot, constituency 137
Aldridge-Brownhills, constituency 137
A-levels 334
Alexandra, Princess 21
  military ranks and titles 30
  private secretary 25
Alexandra Palace 477
algol, minima of see months of the year eg January, minima of algol
Allerdale, district council 250, 263
Alliance Party of Northern Ireland 126
  development 126
  representation in the House of Commons 120
Almond Valley, Scottish parliament constituency 224
Alternative Investment Market (AIM) 494
Altrincham & Sale West, constituency 137
Alyn & Deeside
  constituencies
    UK parliament 166
    Welsh assembly 218
Amber Valley
  constituency 137
  district council 250, 263
ambulance service 383
Andrew, Prince 20
  military ranks and titles 29
  private secretary 24
Anglesey
  unitary authority 253, 276
  Welsh assembly constituency 219
Anglia Ruskin University 345

Anglican churches 421
Angus
  constituencies
    Scottish parliament 224
    UK parliament 169
  unitary authority 253, 281
Animal Health and Veterinary Laboratories Agency 190
animals, protected 454
Anjou, house of 31
Anne, Princess 20
  military ranks and titles 29
  private secretary 24
Antrim
  constituencies
    Northern Ireland assembly 234
    UK parliament 172
Antrim and Newtownabbey, district council 254, 283
AONBs (areas of outstanding natural beauty) 449
aphelion 632
apostolic nuncios 433
  to Great Britain 433
  to Ireland 434
apparent sidereal time 630
apparent solar time 630
appeal courts see court of appeal
April 590
  astronomical phenomena 590
  calendar 590
  constellations 590
  duration of twilight 591
  high water 651
  Jupiter in 593
  Mars in 592
  Mercury in 592
  minima of algol 590
  Moon 590
    position 592
  Neptune in 593
  night sky 591
  Saturn in 593
  Sun 591
  sunrise and sunset 593
  Uranus in 593
  Venus in 592
archbishop of Canterbury 422
archbishop of Wales 430
archbishop of York 422
archbishops
  Church of England 422
  Church of Ireland 431
  lords spiritual 75
  overseas 431
  Roman Catholic Church
    England and Wales 433
    Ireland 434
Archbishops' Council 421
archdeacons, listing 422
Architects Registration Board 356
architecture
  professional education 356
  see also listed buildings
Architecture and Design Scotland (A+DS) 196
Ardagh and Clonmacnois, bishop (RC) 435
area
  of the UK 15